INDEX TO ORDNANCE SURVEY
MEMOIRS OF IRELAND SERIES

To the memory of my father

Published 2002
The Institute of Irish Studies
Queen's University Belfast
Belfast
www.qub.ac.uk/iis

This project was supported by the European Union, through Co-Operation Ireland, under the Special Programme for Peace and Reconciliation (Northern Ireland and the Border Counties of Ireland).

This publication of this index was assisted by the Ulster Local History Trust.

British Library Cataloguing-in-Publication Data.
A catalogue record for this book is available from the British Library.

Paperback ISBN 0 85389 812 X
Hardback ISBN 0 85389 813 8

Printed by ColourBooks Ltd, Baldoyle, Dublin 13.

Index to Ordnance Survey Memoirs of Ireland Series

People and Places

by

Patrick McWilliams
Institute of Irish Studies
Queen's University Belfast

Contents

Acknowledgements   v

Introduction   vi

General Abbreviations   vi

List of Drawings   vi

List of Maps   ix

List of Parishes and Volumes   x

List of Memoir Writers   xiv

Editorial Notes   xix

Abbreviations for Denominations   xx

Index   1

Acknowledgements

At the conclusion of this Herculean project, the author is indebted to many people. Primary amongst these is the editorial board: Liam Ronayne, Donegal County Librarian; Dr Bill Crawford, formerly of the Federation for Ulster Local Studies; Professor Brian Walker, Director of the Institute of Irish Studies, Queen's University Belfast; and Miss Angélique Day, my colleague and co-editor of the OS Memoirs of Ireland series.

The staff of the Federation for Ulster Local Studies, in particular Janet Lundy and Roddy Hegarty, were extremely generous with their time with regard to the financial administration of the scheme. At Queen's, Dr Philip Graham and Rosemary Gracey were just as helpful.

I am grateful to my friend Nóirín Dobson for the preparatory work she did on the middle part of the project when I was temporarily absent.

Dr Kieran Devine, a tireless worker on our behalf of the years, assisted with several valuable computer programs at the early stage of the work, while Colin Forde of Information Services at Queen's made an enormous technical contribution to the process of resizing the text.

I must also pay tribute to the staff in the Henry Collection in Queen's Library and to Humanities Librarian, Michael Smallman. Maura Pringle of Cartography at Queen's was ever helpful in checking place-name spellings on the various editions of the 6-inch maps.

For providing the index of drawings, maps and parishes, thanks are due to Margaret McNulty, and to Catherine McColgan who typeset the text initially.

The Institute of Irish Studies would like to acknowledge the sponsors of this project: Federation for Ulster Local Studies; Donegal County Council Library Service; Office of the Taoiseach; Department of Education in Ireland; Department for Employment and Learning; Environment and Heritage Service; Ulster Local History Trust; Esme Mitchell Trust; Belfast Natural History and Philosophical Society; Community Relations Council.

Introduction

This index is a pointer to the forty-volume *Ordnance Survey Memoirs of Ireland* series, published by the Institute of Irish Studies, Queen's University Belfast, in association with the Royal Irish Academy, Dublin, between 1990 and 1998. It lists the following information:

(a) All drawings reproduced from the original OS Memoir manuscripts

(b) All maps of towns etc. reproduced from the original OS maps, 1830s

(c) The parishes and the volumes in which they occur

(d) The Memoir writers and each parish for which they wrote an account

(e) Main Index comprising place-names and personal names

For categories (a) to (d), each entry is accompanied by the name of the county, volume number and page number(s). In addition, the main index of names also includes the parish and county name. The main index was accumulated over several years and stored on a MS Access database prior to the final edit. It contains upwards of 73,000 records.

General Abbreviations

Adm.: Admiral
AH: Armagh (county)
AM: Antrim (county)
Brig.: Brigadier
Capt.: Captain
Cllr: Councillor
CN: Cavan (county)
Col: Colonel
Cpl: Corporal
DL: Donegal (county)
DN: Down (county)
Dr: Doctor
FH: Fermanagh
Gen.: General
Gov.: Governor
LH: Louth
LM: Leitrim (county)
Lt: Lieutenant
LY: Londonderry (county)
Maj.: Major
Misc.: Miscellaneous Papers
MN: Monaghan (county)
ph: parish
Priv.: Private

Rev.: Reverend
Sgt: Sergeant
SO: Sligo (county)
td: townland
TE: Tyrone

List of Drawings

Some drawings from the OS Memoir manuscripts were used to illustrate the published volumes and these are indexed here in relation to their parishes. Each volume also contains a full list of all the drawings from the OS Memoir papers relating to the relevant parishes. These are not indexed here.

Aghadowey: battle-axe from Crevolea td, LY 22, 3; peh pipe and seal, LY 22, 31
Aghanloo: King's Chair in Largantea td, LY 11, 6
Antrim: Massereene bridge, AM 29, 10; chair in Antrim Castle, AM 29, 11; church, AM 29, 34
Ardunshion: see Clogher
Armoy: round tower, AM 24, 7
Artrea: seal of the O'Neills, LY 6, 13; copper brooch from Artrea ph, LY 6, 30
Ashlamaduff: see Dungiven
Aughnamullen: giant's grave in Lisnadara td, MN 40, 73

Ballyaghran: old church, LY 33, 9; view of Portstewart, LY 33, 20; cromlech in Crossreagh West td, LY 33, 25
Ballycloghan: see Duneane
Ballyclug: cove from Crebilly, AM 23, 62
Ballycarry: see Island Magee
Ballygowan: see Raloo
Ballyhenry: see Carnmoney
Ballylough: see Billy
Ballylumford: see Island Magee
Ballymartin: church, AM 2, 10; plan of td, AM 2, 14
Ballymoney: new Bann bridge, AM 16, 11; sword from unknown parish, AM 16, 22
Ballynascreen: market house at Draperstown, LY 31, 2; ancient circle at Strawmore td, LY 31, 10; window and interior of old church, LY 31, 28
Ballynure: brass trumpet, AM 32, 55
Ballypriormore: see Island Magee
Ballyreagh: see Ballywillin
Ballyrickardmore: see Raloo
Ballyscullion: man with crutch, Church Island, LY 6, 50; brass boiler from Mullaghboy td, LY 6, 74
Ballywillin: Ballyreagh Castle, LY 33, 49
Balteagh: old church and ground plan, LY 9, 6; Mave stone and King's fort in Kilhoyle td, LY 9, 8; coins from Cloghan td, LY 9, 11; whinstone

near King's fort, LY 9, 19; old spade, LY 9, 23; Giant's Mill near Donald's hill, LY 9, 34

Banagher: coins from Mr Ross' collection, LY 30, 8; Straid old church, door of Banagher old church, LY 30, 40; standing stone in Templemoyle td, LY 30, 45; standing stones in Clagan td, LY 30, 55; giant's grave at Carnenbane td, LY 30, 82; figure of Mercury from Caugh, LY 30, 93; White well in Magheramorne td, LY 30, 106

Bellahill: see Kilroot

Belleaghan: see Raymoghy

Billy: wooden article from Loughlynch td, AM 16, 57; castle door in Ballylough, AM 16, 70

Bolea: see Drumachose

Bovevagh: Duinn rock, LY 25, 11

Brackfield: see Cumber

Browndod: see Donegore

Burt: see Lough Swilly

Cah: see Errigal

Calmore: see Kilcronaghan

Camlin: old church, AM 21, 61

Camus: see Macosquin

Carnenbane: see Banagher

Carnmoney: mether cup from Ballyhenry, carved stone face from Whiteabbey, AM 2, 74; masonry from abbey of Whiteabbey, AM 2, 80

Carrickabrackey: see Clonmany

Carrickfergus: Castle, AM 37, 15; face and cross in Carrickfergus Castle, AM 37, 25; seal of Carrickfergus, AM 37, 36; plan of 1550, AM 37, 61; wooden methers, AM 37, 89; druidical altar, AM 37, 189; discoveries from Carrickfergus, AM 37, 192

Caugh: see Banagher

Church Island: see Ballyscullion

Clagan: see Banagher

Cloghan: see Balteagh

Clogher: gold ornament in Tulnafoile td, TE 5, 34; earthen vase in Ardunshion td, TE 5, 39; brass ornament in Knockmany, TE 5, 40; manor of Cecil, TE 5, 48

Clondavaddog: Fanad lighthouse, DL 38, 2

Clonmany: Carrickabrackey Castle, DL 38, 15

Coagh: see Tamlaght

Comber: tablet in church, DN 7, 36

Cootehill: see Drumgoon

Craigs: see Finvoy

Crebilly: see Ballyclug

Crevolea: see Aghadowey

Crom Castle: see Galloon

Crossreagh West: see Ballyaghran

Cumber (Upper and Lower): foot-bridges across Glenrandal and Faughan rivers, LY 28, 10; mether from Dungiven ph, LY 28, 29; Catholic chapel in

Mullaboy td, LY 28, 33; plans and views of Brackfield Castle, LY 28, 36; giant's grave in Tamneyreagh td, LY 28, 38; grocer's coat of arms from Ervey schoolhouse, LY 28, 78; bell stones in Tamneyreagh td, LY 28, 82

Derryaghy: ground plan of Castle Robin, AM 8, 93; ancient weapon from White mountain, AM 8, 101; date stone Milltown Lodge, AM 8, 105

Derrygonnelly: see Inishmacsaint

Desertlyn: elevated stone and giant's grave in Ballymully td, LY 31, 43

Donegore: moat, AM 29, 103; altar on Browndod, AM 29, 116

Draperstown: see Ballynascreen

Drumachose (Newtownlimavady): aqueduct for mill in Deer Park, LY 9, 52; section of roads from Newtownlimavady, LY 9, 54; silver cup from Bolea td, LY 9, 59

Drumbo: round tower, DN 7, 55; cromlech and Giant's Ring, DN 7, 57

Drumgoon: view of Cootehill, CN 40, 5

Drummaul: coat of arms, Shane's Castle, LY 19, 67; Edenduffcarrick from Shane's Castle, LY 19, 68

Dunadry: see Nilteen

Dunaghy: Cross-Neanaghan in Legnamanna td AM 13, 20

Dunboe: old church, LY 11, 48

Duncrun: see Magilligan

Dundressan: see Island Magee

Duneane: leather vessel from Ballycloghan td, LY 19, 110

Dungiven: Danish pot, LY 15, 28; O'Cathan's priory, LY 15, 38; Lady Cooke's Castle, LY 15, 43; tomb of Cooey-na-Gall, LY 15, 57; copper ornament, LY 15, 82; brass hatchet from Ovil td, LY 15, 90; standing stone in Ashlamaduff td, LY 15, 110; see also Cumber

Edenduffcarrick: see Drummaul

Emlaghfad: castle in Ballymote, SO 40, 178

Enniskillen: plan of Lough Erne cots, FH 4, 42; Enniskillen Castle, FH 4, 51; standard of the Enniskillen Volunteers, FH 4, 53

Errigal: man cutting tree in Cah td, LY 27, 48

Ervey: see Cumber

Fanad: see Clondavaddog

Faughanvale: window of Muff old church, LY 36, 14; Templemore Agricultural Seminary, LY 36, 40; stone house of cottier, LY 36, 101

Finvoy: Broad stone in Craigs td, AM 23, 77

Galloo: views from Crom Castle, FH 4, 99

Gartree: see Killead

Glack: see Tamlaght Finlagan

Glynn: window of church, AM 26, 36

Inishmacsaint: stone cross on Inishmacsaint Island,
FH 14, 76; coat of arms from Derrygonnelly
chapel of ease, FH 14, 78
Inniskeen: round tower in Ennis, MN 40, 126
Island Magee: window in Ballycarry church, AM
10, 44; plans and masonry from old churches, AM
10, 46; details of Castle Chichester, AM 10, 49;
cromlech in Ballylumford td, AM 10, 55; rocking
stone in Dundressan td, AM 10, 57; urn in
Ballypriormore td, AM 10, 61; pier at Portmuck,
AM 10, 79

Kilbroney: giant's grave in Kilfeaghan td, DN 3, 31;
architecture of Kilbroney old church, DN 3, 41
Kilcronaghan: ancient boat from Calmore td, LY 31,
70
Kildollagh: coins, LY 22, 68
Kilfeaghan: see Kilbroney
Kilhoyle: see Balteagh
Kilkeel: Long Stone in Moneydarragh, DN 3, 51;
White cairn in Balleyveabeg, DN 3, 53
Kille Acrue: see Ramoan
Killead: stone chair in Gartree td, AM 35, 32
Killesher: ruin in graveyard, FH 14, 89
Killinchy: Sketerick Castle DN 7, 89
Killowen: Catholic chapel, LY 33, 160
Killyclochan: see Kinawley
Killyglen: see Carncastle and Killyglen
Kilraghts: clasp from Drumaquern td, AM 16, 131
Kilrea: landscape view, LY 27, 107; window in
church, LY 27, 112; Margaret McGrath aged 115,
LY 27, 118; old church, LY 27, 124; church
belfry, LY 27, 125
Kilroot: bawn in Bellahill demesne, AM 26, 70
Kinawley: St Nawley's well, FH 4, 112; castle in
Killyclochan, FH 4, 118; sweathouse in Sheetrim,
FH 4, 120
Kirkinriola: miscellaneous discoveries, AM 23, 123
Knockmany: see Clogher

Lackagh: see Magherafelt
Largantea: see Aghanloo
Legnamanna: see Dunaghy
Lisanoure: see Loughguile
Lisburn: see Blaris
Lisnevenagh: see Shilvodan
Lissan: Glebe House, LY 31, 97
Lough Derg: see Templecarn
Lough Erne: see Enniskillen
Loughguile: standing stones and arrowheads, AM
13, 73; flagon from Lisanoure Castle AM 13, 75
Loughlynch: see Billy

Macosquin: osiers from Camus td, LY 22, 88; coin,
LY 22, 95; articles from Ringrashmore fort, LY
22, 114
Maghera: standing stone, Swatragh, LY 18, 11; lintel
of old church, LY 18, 38; James II brass money,
LY 18, 60
Magherafelt: silver coins from Megargy td, LY 6,
94; arrowheads from Lackagh td, LY 6, 109
Magheramorne: see Banagher
Magilligan (Tamlaghtard): doorway of old church,
LY 11, 87; Duncrun and neighbourhoood, LY 11,
90; communion cup, LY 11, 104; coins, LY 11,
128
Manorhamilton Union: Manorhamilton Castle, LM
40, 51
Massereene: see Antrim
Megargy: see Magherafelt
Moneydarragh: see Kilkeel
Movilla: see Newtownards
Moyadam: see Nilteen
Muff (LY): see Faughanvale
Mullaboy: see Cumber
Mullagh: see Termoneeny
Mullaghboy: see Ballyscullion
Mullaghtironey: see Tamlaght

Narrow Water: see Warrenpoint
Newtownards: Movilla Abbey and graveyard, DN 7,
108; old church, DN 7, 113
Newtownlimavady: see Drumachose
Nilteen: Grey stanes in Moyadam td, AM 35, 95;
standing stone in Moyadam AM 35, 97; stone urn
from Dunadry, AM 35, 99

Ovil: see Dungiven

Portmuck: see Island Magee
Portstewart: see Ballyaghran

Raloo, masonry of church, AM 32, 107; druidical
altars in Ballygowan td, AM 32, 109; cromlech in
Ballyrickardmore td, AM 32, 111; cove and fort in
Ballyrickardmore td, AM 32, 114
Ramoan: priest's headstone at Kille Acrue, AM 24,
104
Raymoghy: Belleaghan Abbey and Raymoghy old
church, DL 39, 134
Macosquin: osiers from Camus td, LY 22, 88, coin,
LY 22, 95, articles from Ringrashmore fort, LY
22, 114

Shane's Castle: see Drummaul
Sheetrim: see Kinawley
Shilvodan: forts from Lisnevenagh td, LY 19, 136
Skerry: gable of church, AM 13, 116
Sketerick: see Killinchy

Straid: see Banagher
Strawmore: see Ballynascreen
Swatragh: see Maghera

Tamlaght (TE): statistical table for Coagh, TE 20,
    101; statistical table for Mullaghtironey, TE 20,
    123
Tamlaght (LY): see Tamlaght O'Crilly
Tamlaght Finlagan: proposed embankment of the
    Roe, LY 25, 67; Walworth old church, LY 25, 86;
    Walworth's Bawn, LY 25, 88; arms of
    Fishmongers' Company, LY 25, 99; Danish pot
    from Glack td, LY 25, 116
Tamlaght O'Crilly: church, LY 18, 93; giant's chair
    Timaconway td, LY 18, 113; view near Tamlaght,
    LY 18, 127
Tamlaghtard: see Magilligan
Tamneyreagh: see Cumber
Templecarn: Station Island, Lough Derg, DL 39,
    159
Templecorran: ground plan of church, AM 26, 109
Templemoyle: see Banagher and Faughanvale
Termoneeny: Mullagh old church LY 6, 123; brass
    knife or spearhead, Mullagh td, LY 6, 127
Timaconway: see Tamlaght O'Crilly
Tulnafoile: see Clogher

Walworth: see Tamlaght Finlagan
Warrenpoint: doorway of Narrow Water Castle, DN
    3, 119; Narrow Water Castle, DN 3, 124
Whiteabbey: see Carnmoney

List of Maps

Each volume contains a map of the county showing
the location of the relevant parishes and also county
maps by Samuel Lewis, 1837. Maps indexed here
are Ordnance Survey maps from the 1830s.

Aghagallon: AM 21, 2
Aghalee: AM 21, 27
Ahoghill AM 23, 2
Antrim: AM 29, 2
Ardglass: DN 17, 2
Armoy: AM 24, 2
Aughnacloy: TE 20, 22

Ballinamallard: FH 14, 92
Ballinderry Lower: AM 21, 42
Ballintoy: AM 24, 11
Ballybofey and Stranorlar: DL 39, 110
Ballycarry: AM 26, 83
Ballycastle: AM 24, 87
Ballyclare: AM 29, 61
Ballyeaston: AM 32, 2

Ballygalley: AM 10, 2
Ballygawley: TE 20, 47
Ballymacarrett: DN 7, 98
Ballymartin: AM 2, 2
Ballymena: AM 23, 89
Ballymoney: AM 16, ?
Ballynahinch: DN 17, 100
Ballynure: AM 32, 32
Ballyronan: LY 6, 6
Ballyshannon: DL 39, 75
Banbridge: DN 12, 2
Bangor: DN 7, 20
Belleek: FH 14, 2
Bellaghy: LY 6, 43
Brookeborough: FH 4, 18
Broughshane: AM 13, 87
Buncrana: DL 38, 23
Bushmills: AM 16, 44

Carnlough: AM 13, 2
Carrickfergus: AM 37, 2
Carrickmacross: MN 40, 145
Castleblayney: MN 40, 163
Castledawson: LY 6, 88
Castlederg: TE 5, 137
Castlewellan: DN 3, 56
Cavan town: CN 40, 25
Claudy: LY 28, 2
Clogher: TE 5, 25
Coleraine: LY 33, 54
Coalisland: TE 20, 139
Comber: DN 7, 29
Connor: see Kells and Connor
Cookstown: TE 20, 65
Cootehill: CN 40, 2
Crossgar: DN 17, 89
Crumlin: AM 21, 65
Cullybackey: AM 23, 11
Cushendall: AM 13, 38
Cushendun: AM 24, 37

Derry city and district: LY 34, 2
Derrygonnelly: FH 14, 71
Doagh: AM 29, 67
Donaghadee: DN 7, 46
Donegal town: DL 39, 43
Downhill and neighbourhood: LY 11, 45
Downpatrick: DN 17, 39
Draperstown: LY 31, 2
Dromore: DN 12, 71
Dunadry and district: AM 35, 85
Dungannon: TE 20, 41
Dungiven: LY 15, 2
Dunmurry: AM 8, 123

Enniskillen: FH 4, 18

Faughanvale (Muff): LY 36, 51
Feeny: LY 30, 28
Fintona: TE 5, 63
Fivemiletown: TE 5, 31

Galgorm and Gracehill: AM 23, 18
Garvagh: LY 27, 36
Giant's Causeway,: AM 16, 37
Glenarm: AM 13, 123
Glenavy: AM 21, 78
Glenoe: AM 32, 81
Glynn: AM 26, 2
Gracehill: see Galgorm and Gracehill

Hillsborough: DN 12, 86
Holywood: DN 7, 74

Irvinestown: FH 14, 32

Keady: AH 1, 48
Kells and Connor: AM 19, 17
Kesh: FH 14, 104
Kilkeel: DN 3, 47
Killough: DN 17, 34
Killybegs: DL 39, 66
Killyleagh: DN 17, 83
Kilmacrenan: DL 38, 51
Kilrea: LY 27, 105

Larne: AM 10, 124
Letterkenny: DL 39, 25
Limavady: LY 9, 47
Lisburn: AM 8, 2
Lisnaskea: FH 4, 2
Lurgan: AH 1, 112

Maghera: LY 18, 2
Magherafelt: LY 6, 80
Maguiresbridge: FH 4, 7
Mallusk: AM 2, 108
Manorhamilton: LM 40, 48
Markethill: AH 1, 95
Moira: DN 12, 118
Monaghan town: MN 40, 160
Moneymore: LY 6, 3
Moville: DL 38, 69
Muff: see Faughanvale

Newbuildings and district: LY 34, 23
Newcastle: DN 3, 42
Newry: DN 3, 62
Newtownards: DN 7, 104
Newtownbutler: FH 4, 88
Newtownhamilton: AM 1, 99
Newtownstewart: TE 5, 3

Omagh: TE 5, 105

Rathlin Island, Church Bay: AM 24, 128

Portadown: AH 1, 31
Portaferry: DN,7, 8
Portglenone: AM 23, 7
Portrush: LY 33, 30
Portstewart: LY 33, 2

Raphoe: DL 39, 122
Ramelton: DL 38, 85
Randalstown: AM 19, 34
Rathfriland: DN 3, 11
Rathmullan: DL 38, 37
Rostrevor: DN 3, 27

Saintfield: DN 7, 115
Shane's Castle and neighbourhood: AM 19, 49
Stewartstown: TE 20, 38
Strabane: TE 5, 118
Strangford: DN 17, 26
Stranorlar and Ballybofey: DL 39, 110
Swatragh: LY 18, 76

Tanderagee: AH 1, 2
Templepatrick: AM 35, 106
Tempo: FH 4, 65
Tobermore: LY 31, 65
Toome: AM 19, 95
Tory Island: see West Town

Warrenpoint: DN 3, 116
West Town, Tory Island: DL 38, 125
Whitehouse: AM 2, 40
Willsborough House and district: LY 36, 9

List of Parishes and Volumes

Aghaderg: DN 12, 1–12
Aghadowey: LY 22, 1–38
Aghagallon: AM 21, 1–25
Aghalee: AM 21, 26–40
Aghaloo: TE 20, 1–5
Aghalurcher: FH 4, 1–16; TE 5, 1
Aghanloo: LY 11, 1–42
Aghavea: FH 4, 17–25
Agivey: LY 22, 39–45
Ahabog: MN 40, 62–68
Ahoghill: AM 23, 1–51
Annaclone: DN 12, 13–19
Annahilt: DN 12, 20–25
Antrim: AM 29, 1–59
Arboe: LY 6, 1
Ardclinis: AM 13, 1–9
Ardglass: DN 17, 1–14

Ardkeen: DN 7, 1–3
Ardquin: DN 7, 4
Ardstaw: TE 5, 2–14
Armoy: AM 24, 1–9
Artrea: LY 6, 2–40: LY 20, 6–10
Aughnamullen: MN 40, 69–77

Ballee: DN 17, 15–24
Ballinderry: AM 21, 41–59
Ballinderry: LY 6, 41; TE 20, 11–14
Ballintoy: AM 24, 10–35
Ballyaghran: LY 33, 1–28
Ballybay: MN 40, 69–77
Ballyclog: TE 20, 15–19
Ballyclug: AM 23, 52–66
Ballycor: AM 32, 1–10
Ballyculter: DN 17, 25–31
Ballyhalbert: DN 7, 5–6
Ballykinler: DN 17, 32
Ballylinny: AM 32, 11–30
Ballymartin: AM 2, 1–18
Ballymascanlan: LH 40, 55–56
Ballymoney: AM 16, 1–30
Ballymore: AH 1, 1–20
Ballymyre: AH 1, 20
Ballynascreen: LY 31, 1–34
Ballynure: AM 32, 31–73
Ballyphilip: DN 7, 7–14
Ballyrashane: AM 16, 31: LY 22, 46–66
Ballyrobert: AM 2, 19–25
Ballyscullion: LY 6, 42–78: LY 19 1–15
Ballytrustan: DN 7, 15
Ballywalter: DN 7, 16–18
Ballywater: AM 2, 26–33
Ballywillin: AM 16, 32–35: LY 33, 29–52
Balteagh: LY 9, 1–45
Banagher: LY 30, 1–132
Bangor: DN 7, 19–25
Belleek: FH 14, 1–7
Billy: AM 16, 36–77
Blaris (Lisburn): AM 8, 1–89: DN 12, 26–56
Bodony: TE 20, 20
Boho: FH 14, 8–10
Bovevagh: LY 25, 1–61
Bright: DN 17, 33–37
Burt: see Lough Swilly

Camlin: AM 21, 60–76
Cappagh: TE 5, 15–23
Carlingford: LH 40, 57–60
Carmavy: AM 35, 1–6
Carncastle and Killyglen: AM 10, 1–13
Carnmoney: AM 2, 34–105
Carnteel: TE 20, 21–24
Carrickfergus: AM 37, 1–195

Castleboy: DN 7, 26–27
Castletown: LH 40, 61
Cleenish: FH 14, 11–30
Clogher: TE 5, 24–61
Clogherny: TE 20, 25–28
Clonallan: DN 3, 1–2
Clondavaddog: DL 38, 1–11
Clondermot: LY 34, 1–133
Clonduff: DN 3, 3–6
Clones: FH 4, 26–29
Clonfeacle: AH 1, 21–26
Clonleigh: DL 39, 1–17
Clonmany: DL 38, 12–20
Clonoe: TE 20, 29–31
Clontibret: MN 40, 85
Cloonclare: see Manorhamilton Union
Cloonlogher: see Manorhamilton Union
Coleraine: LY 33, 53–157
Comber: DN 7, 28–44
Connor: LY 19, 16–31
Convoy: DL 39, 18–23
Conwal: DL 39, 24–29
Cranfield: LY 19, 32
Creggan: AH 1, 27
Culdaff: DL 38, 21–23
Culfeightrin: AM 24, 36–85
Cumber (Upper and Lower): LY 28, 1–127
Currin: MN 40, 86–97

Derryaghy: AM 8, 90–121
Derrybrusk: FH 4, 30–33
Derrykeighan: AM 16, 78–95
Derryvullan: FH 14, 31–46
Desertcreat: TE 20, 32–36
Desertegney: DL 38, 24–30
Desertlyn: LY 31, 35–51
Desertmartin: LY 31, 52–63
Desertoghill: LY 27, 1–34
Devenish: FH 14, 47–61
Doagh: AM 29, 60–100
Donacavey: TE 5, 62–87
Donagh: DL 38, 31–35
Donagh: MN 40, 98–105
Donaghcloney: DN 12, 57–61
Donaghdee: DN 7, 45–51
Donaghedy: TE 5, 88–92
Donaghenry: TE 20, 37–39
Donaghmore: DL 39, 28–41
Donaghmore: DN 3, 7–9
Donaghmoyne: MN 40, 106–111
Donegal: DL 39, 42–58
Donegore: AM 29, 101–134
Down: DN 17, 38–66
Dromara: DN 12, 62–69
Dromore: DN 12, 70–78

Dromore: TE 5, 93–103
Drumachose (Newtownlimavady): LY 9, 46–134
Drumballyrony: DN 3, 10–18
Drumbeg: DN 7, 52–3: AM 8, 122–34
Drumbo: DN 7, 54–63
Drumcree: AH 1, 28–42
Drumgath: DN 3, 19–21
Drumglass: TE 20, 40–45
Drumgooland: DN 3, 22–25
Drumgoon: CN 40, 1–11
Drumhome: DL 39, 58–63
Drumkeeran: FH 14, 62–69
Drumloman: CN 40, 12–18
Drummaul: LY 19, 33–93
Drummully: FH 4, 34–40
Drumragh: TE 5, 104–112
Drumtullagh: AM 16, 96–103
Drung: CN 19–25
Dunaghy: AM 13, 1–9
Dunboe: LY 11, 43–81
Dundermot: AM 13, 29–35
Dundonald: DN 7, 64–66
Duneane: LY 19, 94–126
Dungiven: LY 15, 1–122
Dunluce: AM 16, 104–23
Dunsfort: DN 17, 67–72

Eglish: AH 1, 43–44
Ematris: MN 40, 112–19
Emlaghfad: SO 40, 176–82
Enniskeen: CN 40, 26–30
Enniskillen: FH 4, 41–86
Errigal Keerogue: TE 20, 46–57
Errigal: LY 27, 35–94
Errigal Truagh: MN 40, 120–23

Faughanvale: LY 36, 1–100
Finvoy: AM 23, 67–78
Forkhill: AH 1, 45

Galloon: FH 4, 87–106
Garvaghy: DN 12, 79–84
Glenavy AM 21, 77–91
Glencolumkille: DL 39, 64–66
Glenwhirry: AM 32, 74–79
Glynn: AM 26, 1–48
Grey Abbey: DN 7, 67–72

Hillsborough: DN 12, 85–108
Holywood: DN 7, 73–83

Inch: see Lough Swilly
Inch: DN 17, 73–77
Inishargy: DN 7, 84–85
Inishkeel: DL 39, 67–73
Inishmacsaint: FH 14, 70–80

Inispollan: see Layd and Inispollan
Inniskeen: MN 40, 124–29
Inver: AM 26, 49–55
Island Magee: AM 10, 14–105

Jonesborough: AH 1, 46

Keady: AH 1, 47–50
Kilbarron: DL 39, 74–78
Kilbride: AM 29, 135–57
Kilbroney: DN 3, 26–40
Kilclief: DN 17, 78–79
Kilclooney: AH 1, 51
Kilcoo: DN 3, 41–45
Kilcronaghan: LY 31, 64–88
Kildollagh: LY 22, 67–75
Kildress: TE 20, 58–61
Kilkeel: DN 3, 46–54
Killagan: AM 23, 79–87
Killanny: MN 40, 130–35
Killasnet: see Manorhamilton Union
Killdrumsherdan: CN 40, 31–38
Killea and Taughboyne: DL 39, 79–93
Killead: AM 35, 7–53
Killelagh: LY 27, 95–103
Killeeshil: TE 20, 62–65
Killesher: FH 14, 81–90
Killevy: AH 1, 52–54
Killinchy: DN 7, 86–93
Killoran and Kilvarnet: SO 40, 183–84
Killowen: LY 33, 158–73
Killygarvan: DL 38, 36–49
Killyglen: see Carncastle and Killyglen
Killyleagh: DN 17, 80–87
Killyman: AH 1, 55–6; TE 20, 66–68
Killymard: DL 39, 94–110
Kilmacrenan: DL 38, 50–53
Kilmacteige: SO 40, 185–97
Kilmegan: DN 3, 55–60
Kilmood: DN 7, 94–96
Kilmore: DN 17, 88–93
Kilmore: AH 1, 57–74
Kilmore: MN 40, 136
Kilraghts: AM 16, 124–36
Kilrea: LY 27, 104–30
Kilroot: AM 26, 56–81
Kilskeery: TE 5, 113–16
Kilteevoge: DL 39, 111–14
Kilvarnet: see Killoran and Kilvarnet
Kilwaughter: AM 10, 106–22
Kinawley: FH 4, 107–24
Kirkinriola: AM 23, 88–126
Knockbreda: DN 7, 97–102

Lambeg: AM 8, 134–43

Laragh: CN 40, 39–46
Larne: AM 10, 123–28
Layd: AM 13, 36–53
Layd and Inispollan: AM 13, 54–57
Leck: DL 39, 115–21
Leckpatrick: TE 5, 117–26
Lisburn. see Blaris
Lissan: TE 20, 69; LY 31, 89–110
Longfield (East): TE 5, 131–33
Longfield (Lower): TE 5, 134–35
Longfield (West): TE 5, 127–30
Lough Neagh: AM 21, 92–97
Loughgall: AH 1, 75–83
Loughgilly: AH 1, 84–88
Loughguile: AM 13, 58–77
Loughinisland: DN 17, 94–98
Lough Swilly (with Burt and Inch): DL 38, 98–150

Magheross: MN 40, 143–58
Macosquin: LY 22, 76–123
Maghera: LY 18, 1–81
Magheracloone: MN 40, 137
Magheracross: FH 14, 91–102
Magheraculmoney: FH 14, 103–114
Magheradrool: DN 17, 99–107
Magherafelt: LY 6, 79–120
Magheralin: DN 12, 109–112
Magheragall AM 21, 98–111
Magherally: DN 12, 112–17
Magheramesk AM 21, 112–30
Magheross: MN 40, 143–58
Magilligan (Tamlaghtard): LY 11, 82–146
Mallusk: AM 2, 106–115
Manorhamilton Union (Cloonclare, Cloonlogher and
    Killasnet): LM 40, 47–54
Mevagh: DL 38, 54–63
Mintiaghs (Bar of Inch): DL 38, 64–67
Moira: DN 12, 117–22
Monaghan: MN 40, 159–61
Montiaghs: AH 1, 89–93
Moville: DL 38, 68–79
Muckamore: AM 35, 54–83
Muckno: MN 40, 162–68
Muff: DL 38, 80–3
Mullaghbrack: AH 1, 94–97

Newry: DN 3, 61–114
Newtownards: DN 7, 103–113
Newtown Crommelin: AM 13, 78–85
Newtownhamilton: AH 1, 98–100
Newtownlimavady: see Drumachose
Nilteen: AM 35, 84–104

Pomeroy: TE 20, 70–2

Racavan: AM 13, 86–104

Raloo: AM 32, 80–134
Ramoan: AM 24, 86–126
Raphoe: DL 39, 121–31
Rasharkin: AM 23, 127–141
Rashee: AM 32, 135–41
Rathlin Island: AM 24, 127–34
Rathmullan: DN 17, 108–110
Raymoghy: DL 39, 132–47
Rossorry: FH 14, 115–17

Saintfield: DN 7, 114–20
Saul: DN 17, 111–15
Seagoe: AH 1, 101–110
Seapatrick: DN 12, 123–37
Shankill: AH 1, 111–16; DN 12, 138–39
Shilvodan: LY 19, 127–138
Skerry: AM 13, 105–121
Skirts of Urney and Ardstraw: TE 5, 136–41
Slanes: DN 7, 121

Tamlaght: TE 20, 73–137
Tamlaght Finlagan: LY 25, 62–125
Tamlaght O'Crilly: LY 18, 82–144
Tamlaghtard: see Magilligan
Tartaraghan: AH 1, 117–23
Taughboyne: DL 39, 132–47 (see also Killea and
    Taughboyne.)
Templecarn: FH 14, 118–21; DL 39, 156–72
Templecorran: AM 26, 82–132
Templepatrick: AM 35, 105–54
Termonamongan: TE 5, 142–45
Termoneeny: LY 6, 121–33
Tickmacrevan: AM 13, 122–34
Tomregan: FH 4, 125–32
Trory: FH 14, 122–35
Tullaghobegley: DL 39, 172–73
Tullyaughnish: DL 38, 84–97
Tullylish: DN 12, 140–47
Tullynakill: DN 7, 122–24
Tullyniskan: TE 20, 138–42
Tullyrusk: AM 21, 131–39
Tydavnet: MN 40, 169–73
Tyholland: MN 40, 174–75
Tynan: AH 1, 124–32

Umgall: AM 35, 155–60
Urney: DL 39, 174–82

Warrenpoint: DN 3, 115–24
Witter: DN 7, 125–27

List of Memoir Writers

Alexander, Lieut R. AM: Finvoy 23, 67–68

Bailey, Lieut C. AH: Clonfeacle 1, 23–26;
Loughgall 1, 78–83; Tartaraghan 1, 119–23;
Tynan 1, 124–31. LY: Desertlyn 31, 35. TE:
Aghaloo 20, 1–2; Artrea 20, 6–9; Ballinderry 20,
11–12; Ballyclog 20, 15–18; Desertcreat 20,
32–33; Donaghenry 20, 37–39; Kildress 20,
58–59; Pomeroy 20, 70–72
Ball, R. DL: Kilbarron 39, 74–78
Barrett, J. DL: Inishkeel 39, 67–73
Beatty, Lieut A. CN: Drumloman 40, 12–18
Bennett, Lieut G.A. AM: Glenavy 21, 77–79. AH:
Ballymore 1, 7–19; Drumcree 1, 34–42; Kilmore
1, 60–74; Montiaghs 1, 90–93; Seagoe 1,
104–110. DN: Aghaderg 12, 1–7; Annaclone 12,
13–16; Donaghcloney 12, 57–59; Donaghmore 3,
7–9; Dromara 12, 62–65; Dromore 12, 70–73;
Drumballyroney 3, 13–18; Drumgath 3, 19–21;
Garvaghy 12, 79–81; Magherally 12, 112–114;
Newry 3, 110–111, 112; Seapatrick 12, 123–27;
Shankill 12, 138–39; Tullylish 12, 140–44
Bleakly, J. AM: Ahoghill 23, 33–48; Ballyclug 23,
64–66; Ballylinny 32, 26–30; Ballymartin 2,
15–18; Ballymoney 16, 23–25; Ballynure 32,
63–72; Ballyrobert 2, 24–25; Ballyscullion 19,
7–15; Ballywalter 2, 26–27; Camlin 21, 73–74;
Carncastle and Killyglen 10, 6–7; Carnmoney 2,
81–94; Carrickfergus 37, 133–59; Cranfield 19,
32; Derrykeighan 16, 90–95; Doagh 29, 86–99;
Donegore 29, 129–31; Drummaul 19, 81–91;
Drumtullagh 16, 100–103; Dunaghy 13, 20–25;
Dundermot 13, 34–35; Duneane 19, 111–24;
Glynn 26, 36–47; Inver 26, 52–55; Island Magee
10, 77–103; Kilbride 29, 149–55; Killead 35,
43–52; Kilraghts 16, 132–46; Kilroot 26, 77–81;
Kilwaughter 10, 111–22; Larne 10, 126–28;
Loughguile 13, 71–76; Muckamore 35, 76–77;
Newtown Crommelin 13, 84–85; Nilteen 35,
102–104; Raloo 32, 119–32; Rasharkin 23,
138–40; Shilvodan 19, 137–38; Skerry 13,
119–21; Templecorran 26, 124–32; Templepatrick
35, 142–54. LY: Aghanloo 11, 12–27, 30–31,
39–40; Agivey 22, 42–45; Ballyaghran 33, 19–28;
Ballyrashane 22, 55; Ballywillin 33, 40–51;
Balteagh 9, 37–43; Banagher 30, 95–100;
Bovevagh 25, 53–58; Clondermot 34, 43;
Coleraine 33, 66–67, 128–146, 149–50; Cumber
28, 55–57; Desertoghill 27, 3–5, 13–27, 32–34;
Drumachose 9, 53, 118–29; Dunboe 11, 55–57,
59–81; Dungiven 15, 94–100; Errigal 27, 52–53;
Kilcronaghan 31, 78–88; Killelagh 27, 100–102;
Killowen 33, 165–66; Kilrea 27, 106–30; Lissan
31, 96–110; Maghera 18, 27–34, 48–81;

Magilligan 11, 82–97, 123–43; Tamlaght Finlagan
25, 120–24; Tamlaght Finlagan 25, 79–80;
Termoneeny 6, 128–33
Bordes, Lieut G. DN: Annahilt 12, 20–24; Blaris 12,
26–27; Comber 7, 31–44; Drumbeg 7, 52;
Drumbo 7, 54–56, 58–63; Dundonald 7, 64–66;
Hillsborough 12, 85–88; Holywood 7, 73–80;
Kilmood 7, 94–95; Knockbreda 7, 97–101;
Magherdrool 17, 99–106; Miscellaneous Papers
17, 116–22; Newtownards 7, 111–13; Saintfield 7,
116–20; Tullynakill 7, 122–23
Boscawen, Lieut G. AM: Aghagallon 21, 1–3;
Aghalee 21, 26–28; Magheramesk 21, 112–14
Boteler, Lieut R. AM: Armoy 24, 1–2; Drumtullagh
16, 96–97; Glenwhirry 32, 74–75; Kilwaughter
10, 106–107; Larne 10, 123–26; Skerry 13,
105–108. FH: Belleek 14, 1–7; Derryvullan 14,
31–39; Drumkeeran 14, 62–69;
Magheraculmoney 14, 103–110; Templecarn 14,
118–21; Trory 14, 132–35. MN: Donaghmoyne
40, 106–111; Inniskeen 40, 124–29; Killanny 40,
130–35; Magheracloone 40, 137–42; Magheross
40, 143–56
Boyle, J. AM: Ahoghill 23, 3–24; Antrim 29, 1–44,
52–58; Ardclinis 13, 5–9; Armoy 24, 2–6;
Ballintoy 24, 12–17; Ballyclug 23, 54–60;
Ballycor 32, 1–8; Ballylinny 32, 11–24;
Ballymartin 2, 1–15, 18; Ballynure 32, 31–54;
Ballyrobert 2, 19–24; Ballyscullion 19, 2–7;
Ballywalter 2, 28–33; Billy 16, 38–50; Camlin 21,
63–71, 74–76; Carmavy 35, 1–6; Carncastle and
Killyglen 10, 1–6, 11–13; Carnmoney 2, 34–81;
Carrickfergus 37, 4–107, 132–33; Connor 19,
18–28; Culfeightrin 24, 41–48; Derrykeighan 16,
80–87; Doagh 29, 61–84, 99–100; Donegore 29,
104–128; Drummaul 19, 35–78; Drumtullagh 16,
97–99; Dunaghy 13, 10–17; Dundermot 13,
29–33; Duneane 19, 96–106; Dunluce 16,
106–13; Finvoy 23, 68–75; Glenavy 21, 82–91;
Glenwhirry 32, 75–78; Glynn 26, 3–36; Inver 26,
50–52; Island Magee 10, 14–75; Kilbride 29,
136–49; Killagan 23, 81–86; Killead 35, 7–40;
Kilraghts 16, 125–30; Kilroot 26, 57–74;
Kilwaughter 10, 107–11; Kirkinriola 23, 92–115;
Layd and Inispollan 13, 55–57; Layd 13, 42–53;
Loughguile 13, 60–68; Mallusk 2, 106–115;
Miscellaneous Papers 10, 130–31; Muckamore
35, 56–74; Newtown Crommelin 13, 79–83;
Nilteen 35, 87–101; Racavan 13, 89–96; Raloo
32, 82–119; Ramoan 24, 91–101; Rasharkin 23,
128–36; Rashee 32, 135–40; Rathlin Island 24,
129–33; Shilvodan 19, 128–37; Skerry 13,
108–15; Templecorran 26, 84–117; Templepatrick
35, 105–37; Tickmacrevan 13, 125–34; Tullyrusk
21, 133–39; Umgall 35, 155–60. LY: Artrea 6,

2–22; Ballyscullion 6, 42–63; Desertlyn 31, 36–42, 44–51; Desertmartin 31, 52–55, 58–62; Magherafelt 6, 79–104; Magilligan 11, 145–46

Bremner, Priv. TE: Errigal Keerogue 20, 56–57

Broughton, Lieut D. DL: Donagh 38, 31; Moville 38, 68–69, 73–74, 79

Buchanan, Dr. DN: Miscellaneous Papers 17, 132–33

Buck, Rev. TE. Desertcreat 20, 34–36

Butler, S. LY: Magilligan 11, 126

Cameron, Capt. A. AM: Miscellaneous Papers 10, 131

Campbell, R. DN: Killyleagh 17, 82; Loughinisland 17, 97–98

Casey, J. AM: Ballinderry 21, 41–43

Chaytor, Lieut J. AM: Ardclinis 13, 1–4; Connor 19, 16–18; Derrykeighan 16, 78–80; Layd 13, 36–42; Rasharkin 23, 127–28. FH: Cleenish 14, 11–30; Derrybrusk 4, 30–33; Derryvullan 14, 39–46; Devenish 14, 51–59; Enniskillen 4, 41–86; Magheracross 14, 91–102; Rossorry 14, 115–17; Trory 14, 122–32. LY: Ballywillin 33, 51–52. MN: Aughnamullen 40, 69–77; Ballybay 40, 78–84; Muckno 40, 162–68

Colby, Col T.F. TE: Aghaloo 20, 2

Conroy, G. LH: Carlingford 40, 57–60

Cuthbertson, S. TE: Cappagh 5, 21–23

Dalton, Lieut G. LY: Kilrea 27, 104–106; Tamlaght O'Crilly 18, 82–83, 144. TE: Clonoe 20, 29–31; Drumglass 20, 40–44; Killeeshil 20, 62–64; Tullyniskan 20, 138–42

Dawson, Lieut R.K. LY: Cumber 28, 78–80; Miscellaneous Papers 36, 116–17

Downes, G. LY: Aghanloo 11, 8–11, 32–38; Banagher 30, 112–14; Clondermot 34, 36–38, 102–105; Cumber 28, 80–81, 90–92; Drumachose 9, 129–30; Dungiven 15, 100–106; Faughanvale 36, 33–34; Magilligan 11, 114–18; Tamlaght Finlagan 25, 125

Durnford, Lieut E.W. AM: Ballyclug 23, 52–54; Doagh 29, 60–61; Kilbride 29, 135–36; Kirkinriola 23, 88–92; Racavan 13, 86–89. FH: Clones 4, 26–29; Drummully 4, 34–40; Galloon 4, 87–106; Killesher 14, 81–90; Kinawley 4, 107–112. SO: Miscellaneous Papers 40, 198–200

Ewing, J. DL: Glencolumbkille 39, 64–65

Fagan, T. AM: Aghagallon 21, 5–25; Aghalee 21, 28–40; Ballinderry 21, 46–59; Ballintoy 24, 17–35; Ballynure 32, 54–63; Ballywillin 16, 32–35; Billy 16, 59–76; Blaris 8, 18–86; Carnmoney 2, 94–105; Carrickfergus 37, 159–95; Culfeightrin 24, 48–85; Derryaghy 8, 90–118;

Derrykeighan 16, 88–90; Drumbeg 8, 122–33; Dunluce 16, 116–22; Kilroot 26, 74–77; Lambeg 8, 134–43; Magheragall 21, 98–110; Magheramesk 21, 116–30; Ramoan 24, 101–125; Templecorran 26, 117–24. DN: Blaris 12, 36–39. LY: Aghadowey 22, 16, 18–22, 33 38; Aghanloo 11, 27–30; Artrea 6, 18–39; Ballyrashane 22, 54–66; Ballynascreen 31, 20–32; Ballyscullion 6, 63–78; Balteagh 9, 24–36, 43–45; Banagher 30, 60–95; Bovevagh 25, 28–53, 58–61; Cumber 28, 48–55; Desertoghill 27, 27–32; Drumachose 9, 108–18, 132–34; Dunboe 11, 80; Dungiven 15, 65–94; Errigal 27, 50–52, 53–78; Kilcronaghan 31, 75–78; Kildollagh 22, 72–75; Killelagh 27, 100–102; Killowen 33, 168–72; Kilrea 27, 106–22; Macosquin 22, 99–123; Maghera 18, 36–56; Magherafelt 6, 102–113; Magilligan 11, 125–26; Tamlaght Finlagan 25, 104–20; Tamlaght O'Crilly 18, 102–144

Fenwick, Lieut R. DL: Leck 39, 120. LY: Magilligan 11, 143–45

Foster, J. DL: Killymard 39, 100–109

Frith, J. FH: Devenish 14, 59–61

Gamble, J. DN: Loughinisland 17, 96–97

Gilmore, J. LH: Castletown 40, 61

Graham, Rev. J. DL: Clonleigh 39, 4–17. LY: Magilligan 11, 118–23

Graves, Lieut T. AM: Lough Neagh 21, 92–97

Greatorex, Lieut J. AM: Ballymoney 16, 1–4; Dunaghy 13, 25–28; Killagan 23, 79–81; Kilraghts 16, 124–25; Loughguile 13, 58–60; Newtown Crommelin 13, 78–79. FH: Aghalurcher 4, 1–16; Aghavea 4, 17–25; Kinawley 4, 112–24

Grier, I. DL: Killea and Taughboyne 39, 79–93

Hackett, W. LY: Faughanvale 36, 47

Hamilton, W. AM: Rathlin Island 24, 133–34

Hammond, A., DL: Donegal 39, 51–57

Hanna, J. TE: Tamlaght 20, 78–137

Hannyngton, T.C. AM: Aghagallon 21, 3–5; Ballylinny 32, 24–26; Camlin 21, 71–73; Cranfield 19, 32; Glenwhirry 32, 78–79; Killead 35, 40–43; Nilteen 35, 101–102; Templepatrick 35, 139–41. LY: Balteagh 9, 20–23

Haslett, James. TE: Donaghedy 5, 89–92

Hastings, Rev. A; DL: Kilmacrenan 38, 50–53

Heather, J. AH: Creggan 1, 27; Keady 1, 47; Killevy 1, 52; Loughgilly 1, 84, 87; Newtownhamilton 1, 98–100. DN: Ardkeen 7, 3; Killinchy 7, 91–92; Knockbreda 7, 101–102; Tullynakill 7, 123–24

Hemans, G.W. AM: Drummaul 19, 79–81. LY: Kildollagh 22, 72. TE: Dromore 5, 100–103

Henderson, Capt. A. FH: Boho 14, 8–10

Hore, Lieut T. AM: Ballintoy 24, 10–12; Billy 16, 36–38; Carncastle and Killyglen 10, 8–11; Rathlin Island 24, 127–29; Tickmacrevan 13, 122–25
Hutchinson, F. AM: Blaris 8, 86–89

Inch, N. LY: Killelagh 27, 102–103
Innes, J.C. AH: Drumcree 1, 28–34; Loughgall 1, 75–78; Shankill 1, 115–16. DN: Hillsborough 12, 88–102; Seapatrick 12, 135–37. MN: Clontibret 40, 85; Donagh 40, 98–102; Errigal Truagh 40, 120–22; Tyholland 40, 174–75

Kertland, M.M. AM: Antrim 29, 49–52; Magheramesk 21, 114–16. AH: Keady 1, 47–50; Killevy 1, 52–53. DN: Ardkeen 7, 1–3; Ardquin 7, 4; Ballee 17, 20–21; Ballywalter 7, 16–17; Bangor 7, 21–25; Castleboy 7, 26–27; Comber 7, 28–31; Donaghadee 7, 46–50; Down 17, 38–57; Dundonald 7, 66; Holywood 7, 81–82; Inch 17, 74–75; Inishargy 7, 85; Kilcoo 3, 41–44; Kilmood 7, 96; Knockbreda 7, 102; Loughinisland 17, 94–95; Magherally 12, 114–16; Moira 12, 120–22; Newtownards 7, 110–11; Slanes 7, 121; Witter 7, 127
Kidde, W. LY: Cumber 28, 57–58
King, G. TE: Longfield 5, 134–35

Laing, Priv. DN: Ballyculter 17, 29–31
Lancey, Lieut W. DL: Clondavaddog 38, 1–10; Clonmany 38, 12–20; Desertegney 38, 24–30; Donegal 39, 42–51; Drumhome 39, 58; Killygarvan 38, 36–48; Killymard 39, 94–99; Mevagh 38, 54–63; Mintiaghs 38, 64–67; Templecarn 39, 156–63; Tullyaughnish 38, 84–97. LM: Manorhamilton Union 40, 47–54. TE: Aghavea 5, 10–14; Cappagh 5, 16–21; Clogherny 20, 25–28; Drumragh 5, 104–111; Longfield 5, 131–33
Larcom, Lieut T.A. AM: Island Magee 10, 103–105; Miscellaneous Papers 10, 131–32. DL: Leck 39, 120. DN: Miscellaneous Papers 17, 129. LY: Artrea 6, 40; Balteagh 9, 45; Banagher 30, 112, 114; Clondermot 34, 107; Macosquin 22, 98; Magilligan 11, 143–45; Miscellaneous Papers 36, 118; Tamlaght O'Crilly 18, 144. TE: Artrea 20, 9
Leach, Capt. G.A. AM: Miscellaneous Papers 10, 131
Leslie, Rev. H.T. DN: Kilclief 17, 79
Ligar, C.W. AM: Miscellaneous Papers 10, 129. LY: Aghadowey 22, 15–16; Aghanloo 11, 1–6, 39; Artrea 6, 22; Ballyrashane 22, 46–54; Ballyscullion 6, 42–63; Ballywillin 33, 29–40; Balteagh 9, 1–16; Bovevagh 25, 1–21; Clondermot 34, 17–23; Coleraine 33, 53–96; Cumber 28, 78–80, 85–87; Desertlyn 31, 42–44,

47–48; Desertmartin 31, 56–58; Drumachose 9, 46–60, 69–74, 119–20, 122–23, 130; Dunboe 11, 43–55; Dungiven 15, 1–11, 121–22; Errigal 27, 35–49, 52–53; Faughanvale 36, 1–11, 21–22; Killelagh 27, 95–100; Killowen 33, 158–67; Macosquin 22, 78–79, 96–97; Maghera 18, 10–11, 22–24; Magherafelt 6, 92–104; Magilligan 11, 82–97; Tamlaght Finlagan 25, 124–25; Termoneeny 6, 121–28

Mallock, Lieut C.H. AM: Ballyscullion 19, 1–2; Carrickfergus 37, 1–4; Drummaul 19, 33–35; Duneane 19, 94–96; Kilroot 26, 56–57; Shilvodan 19, 127–28; Templecorran 26, 82–83
Mansfield, G.D. TE: Leckpatrick 5, 117–26
Marks, Rev. S. DL: Moville 38, 74–79
Martin, R. DN: Newry 3, 105–108, 111–12
Matier, W.J. DN: Ballee 17, 22–24; Bright 17, 34–37; Down 17, 57–61; Inch 17, 76–77; Kilclief 17, 78
Maturin, Rev. Henry. DL: Clondavaddog 38, 10–11
McCloskey, J. LY: Banagher 30, 1–24; Miscellaneous Papers 31, 111–44
McEneney, Cpl. DN: Loughinisland 17, 98
McGann, J.: Ballymoney 16, 4–19, 27–30
McIlroy, T.C. AH: Clonfeacle 1, 22–23; Drumcree 1, 28–34; Eglish 1, 43–44; Killyman 1, 55–56; Kilmore 1, 57–58; Montiaghs 1, 89–90; Seagoe 1, 101–103; Shankill 1, 111–15; Tartaraghan 1, 117–19. DN: Blaris 12, 33–36; Hillsborough 12, 88–102; Magheralin 12, 109–11; Moira 12, 117–20. MN: Errigal Truagh 40, 120–22; Donagh 40, 98–102; Tydavnet 40, 169–73
McLachlan, A. LH: Ballymascanlan 40, 55–56
Montgomery, Mr. DL: Lough Swilly 38, 98–149
Morton, J. DN: Newry 3, 108–10
Mulholland, J. DN: Kilmore 17, 92–93

O'Donovan, J. AM: Glynn 26, 48. LY: Artrea 6, 39–40; Ballynascreen 31, 32–34; Ballywillin 33, 51–52; Balteagh 9, 18–20; Banagher 30, 100–110; Clondermot 34, 56–76; Coleraine 33, 155; Cumber 28, 58–72; Drumachose 9, 89–95; Dunboe 11, 57–59; Dungiven 15, 60–64; Faughanvale 36, 11–13, 47–64; Killowen 33, 172; Macosquin 22, 98–99; Magilligan 11, 97–111, 143; Miscellaneous Papers 36, 104–108; Tamlaght Finlagan 25, 97–104; Tamlaght O'Crilly 18, 144. TE: Miscellaneous Papers 5, 146–47
Ogle, J. DN: Ardglass 17, 14
Oldham, P. LY: Banagher 30, 58

Petrie, G. LY: Aghanloo 11, 7–8; Balteagh 9, 43; Banagher 30, 59–60, 112; Clondermot 34, 44–56, 105–106; Cumber 28, 47–48, 66; Dungiven 15,

49–60; Faughanvale 36, 31–33; Macosquin 22, 96–97; Magilligan 11, 97–113, 118; Miscellaneous Papers 36, 103–104; Tamlaght Finlagan 25, 104

Portlock, Capt. J.E. LY: Banagher 30, 116–32; Clondermot 34, 31, 113–33; Cumber 28, 92–127; Drumachose 9, 130; Errigal 27, 79–94; Faughanvale 36, 67–100, 117–8; Magherafelt 6, 113–20

Reid, J. DN: Ballyculter 17, 29–31
Rimington, Lieut T.H. AM: Island Magee 10, 75–77, 103–105. DN: Ardglass 17, 1–9; Ballee 17, 15–20; Down 17, 64–66; Dunsfort 17, 67–72; Kilclief 17, 78–79
Robe, Lieut T.C. AM: Ahoghill 23, 1–3; Culfeightrin 24, 36–41; Dunluce 16, 104–106; Layd and Inispollan 13, 54–55; Ramoan 24, 86–91. LY: Macosquin 22, 98
Rogers, N. DL: Taughboyne 39, 148–55
Rogers, Rev. P. DL: Donagh 38, 31–35
Russell, T. CN: Enniskeen 40, 26–30

Scott, G. AM: Ballinderry 21, 43–46; Blaris 8, 1–18; Camlin 21, 71–73; Glenavy 21, 79–82; Lambeg 8, 143; Magheragall 21, 110–11. AH: Forkhill 1, 45; Jonesborough 1, 46; Kilclooney 1, 51; Killevy 1, 53–54; Loughgilly 1, 87–88. DN: Ardglass 17, 9–13; Ballyculter 17, 25–29; Ballyhalbert 7, 5–6; Ballykinler 17, 32; Ballyphilip 7, 9–14; Ballytrustan 7, 15; Bangor 7, 25; Bright 17, 33; Comber 7, 31; Donaghadee 7, 50–51; Drumbeg 7, 53; Drumbo 7, 56–57; Grey Abbey 7, 70–72; Holywood 7, 80–81; Inch 17, 73–76; Inishargy 7, 84–85; Kilcoo 3, 41–44; Kilkeel 3, 46–52; Killyleagh 17, 80–81; Kilmegan 3, 55–60; Kilmore 17, 88–91; Knockbreda 7, 102; Magheradrool 17, 107; Newtownards 7, 103–110; Saul 17, 111–14; Witter 7, 126. MN: Killanny 40, 135; Magheracloone 40, 142; Magheross 40, 156–58. TE: Cappagh 5, 15–16; Carnteel 20, 21–23; Errigal Keerogue 20, 46–48; Kildress 20, 59–60; Killyman, 20, 66–68
Smith, W. TE: Ballyclog 20, 18–19
Spiller, J. TE: Miscellaneous Papers 5, 147
Stanay, W. DL: Muff 38, 80–83
Stokes, J. AM: Ahoghill 23, 24–28; Armoy 24, 6–9; Ballyclug 23, 60–64; Ballymoney 16, 19–23; Billy 16, 50–59, 76; Derrykeighan 16, 87–88; Drumtullagh 16, 100; Dunaghy 13, 17–20; Dundermot 13, 33–34; Duneane 19, 106–111; Dunluce 16, 113–16; Finvoy 23, 75–78; Killagan 23, 86–87; Kilraghts 16, 130–32; Kirkinriola 23, 122–26; Loughguile 13, 68–70; Newtown Crommelin 13, 84; Racavan 13, 100–104;

Rasharkin 23, 136–38; Skerry 13, 115–19. LY: Aghadowey 22, 1–14, 22–33; Aghanloo 11, 7–12, 31–38; Agivey 22, 39–41; Artrea 6, 2–22; Ballynascreen 31, 1–19; Balteagh 9, 16–24; Banagher 30, 39–57, 60, 111–14; Bovevagh 25, 21–28; Clondermot 34, 23–30, 32–34, 36 38, 102–105; Coleraine 33, 155–56; Cumber 28, 18–32, 37–45, 78–81, 85–87; Desertmartin 31, 55–56; Desertoghill 27, 1–3, 5–12; Drumachose 9, 60, 66–69, 74–89, 219–30; Dunboe 11, 54–55; Dungiven 15, 11–49, 100–113; Faughanvale 36, 14–21, 34–35; Kilcronaghan 31, 64–75; Kildollagh 22, 67–72; Killowen 33, 161–62, 173; Kilrea 27, 106–22; Lissan 31, 89–96; Macosquin 22, 76–97; Maghera 18, 3–23; Magilligan 11, 114–18; Miscellaneous Papers 36, 109–16; Tamlaght Finlagan 25, 90–104, 125; Tamlaght O'Crilly 18, 83–102
Stokes, W. DL: Lough Swilly 38, 149–50
Stotherd, Lieut R.J. AM: Camlin 21, 60–63; Donegore 29, 101–104; Glynn 26, 1–3, 48; Inver 26, 49–50; Muckamore 35, 54–56; Nilteen 35, 84–87; Raloo 32, 80–82; Tullyrusk 21, 131–33. FH: Miscellaneous Papers 4, 133. LY: Bovevagh 25, 21–24; Maghera 18, 1–3. TE: Clogher 5, 24–43; Donacavey 5, 66–82

Tait, J.F. AM: Antrim 29, 44–49. AH: Kilmore 1, 59–60; Mullaghbrack 1, 97. DN: Clonduff 3, 4–6; Drumbo 7, 57–58; Killinchy 7, 92–93; Kilmood 7, 96; Saintfield 7, 114–16. TE: Aghavea 5, 2–9
Taylor, Lieut P. CN: Drumgoon 40, 1–11; Drung 40, 19–24; Killdrumsherdan 40, 31–38; Laragh 40, 39–46. FH: Devenish 14, 47–51; Inishmacsaint 14, 70–80. MN: Aghabog 40, 62–68; Currin 40, 86–97; Ematris 40, 112–19. SO: Emlaghfad 40, 176–82
Toner, J. DL: Raphoe 39, 129–31
Tozer, Cpl W. AH: Loughgilly 1, 84–87
Trimble, Cpl H. SO: Kilmactigue 40, 185–97. TE: Errigal Keerogue 20, 48–49
Tucker, Lieut H. DN: Ardkeen 7, 3; Ardquin 7, 4; Ballyhalbert 7, 6; Ballyphilip 7, 7–8; Bangor 7, 19–21; Castleboy 7, 26; Donaghadee, 7, 45–46; Grey Abbey 7, 67–70; Killinchy 7, 86–91; Newry 3, 114; Witter 7, 125–26

Vicars, Lieut E. LY: Clondermot 34, 107; Cumber 28, 1–4

Waddell, R. DN: Ballee 17, 21–22; Bright 17, 33–34
Ward, J.R. AM: Ballycor 32, 8–9; Connor 19, 28–31; Doagh 29, 84–86; Donegore 29, 131–33; Glenwhirry 32, 78–79; Kilbride 29, 155–57; Nilteen 35, 101–102; Racavan 13, 96–100;

Templepatrick 35, 137–39. AH: Clonfeacle 1,
21–22; Killyman 1, 55–56; Loughgall 1, 75–78.
DN: Aghaderg 12, 7–12; Annaclone 12, 16–19;
Annahilt 12, 24–25; Blaris 12, 33–36; Clonallan
3, 1; Donaghcloney 12, 59–61; Dromore 12,
73–78; Garvaghy 12, 82–84; Hillsborough 12,
88–102; Magheralin 12, 109–11; Moira 12,
117–20; Newry 3, 61–82; Seapatrick 12, 127–35;
Shankill 12, 139; Tullylish 12, 144–45. MN:
Donagh 40, 101; Errigal Truagh 40, 120–23;
Kilmore 40, 136; Monaghan 40, 159–61;
Tydavnet 40, 169–73; Tyholland 40, 174–75. TE:
Aghalurcher 5, 1; Clogher 5, 46–52; Kilskeery 5,
113–16; Skirts of Urney and Ardstraw 5, 136–41;
Termonamongan 5, 142–45
Wilkinson, Lieut I.I. DL: Clonleigh 39, 1–4;
Convoy 39, 18–23; Conwal 39, 24–27;
Donaghmore 39, 28–41; Kilteevoge 39, 111–14;
Leck 39, 115–20; Raphoe 39, 121–28; Raymoghy
39, 132–40; Urney 39, 174–82

Williams, J.B. LY: Ballyaghran 33, 1–18; Balteagh
9, 1–16; Clondermot 34, 17–23; Clondermot 34,
39–40; Coleraine 33, 53–96, 149; Cumber 28, 32;
Desertoghill 27, 1–2; Drumachose 9, 46–74;
Faughanvale 36, 1–11. 21–22, 39; Maghera 18,
34–36; Tamlaght Finlagan 25, 62–90
Williams, J.H. AH: Ballymore 1, 1–7; Kilclooney 1,
51; Mullaghbrack 1, 94–97. DN: Clonduff 3, 3–4;
Dromara 12, 65–69; Drumballyroney 3, 10–13;
Drumgooland 3, 22–25; Garvaghy 12, 84;
Kilbroney 3, 26–40; Kilclief 17, 78; Kilcoo 3,
44–45; Kilkeel 3, 52–54; Kilmegan 3, 55;
Kilmore 17, 91–92; Loughinisland 17, 95–96;
Magheradrool 17, 106–107; Newry 3, 82–83;
Saintfield 7, 114–16; Warrenpoint 3, 115–24. TE:
Aghavea 5, 2–9
Williamson, E.A. AH: Tynan 1, 131–32
Woodhouse, J.O. LY: Coleraine 33, 96–104

Editorial Notes

The main index is an alphabetical list of all place-names and personal names occurring in the printed *OS Memoirs of Ireland* volumes

While names of the people who wrote the Memoirs are listed separately (see List of Memoir Writers above), some also occur in the text of the Memoirs and are therefore listed in the main index.

For the purposes of this index, a place is defined as a locality, physical feature, ancient remains or building: the only exception to this rule are schools which are considered too important to be omitted in any form. The word "locality" is used where the author is unsure of the nature of a place.

Where no local name exists to identify a place, every effort was made to specify its townland. If not possible, the parish name is used, e.g. Antrim turnpike. This of course means that the correct local name may not always appear in the index.

"House" is normally added to the name of a gentleman's seat.

The author has retained the convention of the OS Memoirs archive in referring to Londonderry county and Derry city.

As with the OS Memoirs series, the author took pains to let the text speak for itself and to avoid unnecessary intervention. Consequently, the reader should be aware of the following conventions and rules:

(i) Personal Names: a first name or initial is always sought. If not available, "Mr" or "Miss" is often used with the townland of reference if possible.

Unless there is evidence that multiple instances of a name clearly refer to more than one person, in which case the entries are suffixed by [I], [II] etc., such occurrences are listed as a single record.

However, due to the nature of the archive it is not possible to guarantee that multiple instances of a name always refer to the same person. Further investigation is advisable.

In addition, the reader will note that it was not possible to group occurrences of a name across more than one volume. However, these are listed in sequence and should be easy to check.

With males, two or more first names are abbreviated, e.g. John Joe McCloskey would become McCloskey, J.J., but up to two first names of females are recorded in full.

(ii) A record may occur more than once on each page but this is not indicated separately.

(iii) The author has endeavoured to compile an uncluttered index, using qualifiers as little as possible. For example, (P) for Presbyterian or (S) for Seceding are only used to distinguish between two or more of the same type of worship-house occurring in the same place.

(iv) One notable feature of the Memoirs is a wide variety of spellings of place-names, three or more forms not being uncommon. For the index, it was decided to settle upon the most authoritative version (as per the 1961 *Census of Population*) or that which appears most often, with the most interesting variant listed in parenthesis. The latter is the decision of the author alone, although all variants are recorded and cross-referenced to the correct form.

Entries cross-referenced without page numbers indicate an editorial intervention made at a late stage.

(v) The only titles listed are those of clergymen, soldiers and nobility, and every effort was made to retain the form of title used in the text, e.g. Lord, Marquis, without further qualification.

When a title is used, please note that the process of sorting the records lists it according to its first letter, e.g. Kennedy, Rev. Anthony appears after Kennedy, Peter.

(vi) It is advisable to check as many variations of a surname as possible, e.g. Cahan, Cathan, Kane, Kain or Mullan, Mullen, Mullin, Mallon, with and without the prefixes Mc, Mac, O. Please note that M' has been changed to Mc. Where more than one spelling of the same person's name occurs, the author has settled on one form and the variant is not indicated.

(vii) Variations of spellings in Irish, or obvious attempts at anglicising Irish names, are not indicated by separate records.

(viii) A number of generic terms are used, for example "graveyard" for burial ground or

churchyard; and given the enormous difficulty in identifying remains of antiquity, the term "giant's grave" often replaces tumulus, carn, cairn, grave.

(ix) Places of worship: both Methodist chapel and Methodist meeting house are found in the original manuscripts. However, as the former predominates it is employed in the Index. "Church" refers to the Established religion only.

The Memoir writers also use a wide range of terms to differentiate between religious sects, for example Presbyterians of the Synod of Ulster are often called Orthodox or Trinitarian. No attempt has been made to standardise these.

Abbreviations for Denominations

(A) Arian
(AP) Associate Presbyterian
(C) Catholic
(Cov.) Covenanting
(I) Independent
(M) Methodist
(Mor.) Moravian
(NM) New Methodist
(O) Orthodox
(P) Presbyterian
(PM) Primitive Methodist
(PW) Primitive Wesleyan
(PWM) Primitive Wesleyan Methodist
(Q) Quaker
(R) Remonstrant
(S) Seceding
(T) Trinitarian
(U) Unitarian
(W) Wesleyan
(WAM) Wesleyan Association Methodist
(WM) Wesleyan Methodist

**Each record in the following index comprises five pieces of information:
name of person or place; parish, county, volume and page no(s) where reference occurs.**

A

Aaltaiinoe bay: Lough Swilly DL 38; 123
Aaltawinnae creek: Lough Swilly DL 38; 123
Aalterrine locality: Lough Swilly DL 38; 111
Aaltnanuagh creek: Lough Swilly DL 38; 110
Aasky bay: Lough Swilly DL 38; 107
Abbacie (see Ardquin): Misc. DN 17; 127
Abbey field: Muckamore AM 35; 60, 71
Abbey House: Carnmoney AM 2; 46, 84, 98
Abbey Land locality: Carrickfergus AM 37; 3
Abbey Lodge: Aghalurcher FH 4; 6
Abbey Lodge: Aghavea FH 4; 21
Abbey orchard: Muckamore AM 35; 60, 71, 80
Abbeyhill House: Carnmoney AM 2; 47, 84
Abbeylands House: Carnmoney AM 2; 46, 84, 87
Abbeyvale House: Carnmoney AM 2; 84
Abbeyville House: Carnmoney AM 2; 46, 84
Abbott, Martha: Carrickfergus AM 37; 131
Abbott, N. (Belfast): Blaris DN 12; 51, 56
Abercorn, Earl James of (Viscount Strabane):
   Taughboyne DL 39; 152
Abercorn, family: Taughboyne DL 39; 153–54
Abercorn, Lord: Ardstraw TE 5; 6–7
Abercorn, Lord: Donaghedy TE 5; 91–92
Abercorn, Lord: Leckpatrick TE 5; 117, 120–22,
   124
Abercorn, Lord: Taughboyne DL 39; 148, 151–55
Abercorn, Marquis of: Ardstraw TE 5; 2–4, 10, 12,
   14
Abercorn, Marquis of: Donaghedy TE 5; 89–90
Abercorn, Marquis of: Faughanvale LY 36; 39
Abercorn, Marquis of: Killea and Taughboyne DL
   39; 79, 89
Abercorn, Marquis of: Misc. DL 39; 184, 186
Abercorn, Marquis of: Raphoe DL 39; 121, 125–26
Abercorn, Marquis of: Raymoghy DL 39; 132–33,
   135–41, 143
Abercorn, Marquis of: Urney DL 39; 176–77,
   179–80, 182
Aberdeen: Aghanloo LY 11; 32
Aberdeen: Glynn AM 26; 34
Abernathey, William: Derryaghy AM 8; 94–95
Abernethy, Rev. John: Antrim AM 29; 24, 27
Abernethy, Rev. John: Killowen LY 33; 160

Abernethy, Rev. John: Templepatrick AM 35; 133,
   144
Abocurragh td: Cleenish FH 14; 29
Abohill td: Cleenish FH 14; 29
Abraham, Henry: Aghanloo LY 11; 14, 17, 21, 32
Abraham, Henry: Magilligan LY 11; 125
Abram, Mr (Dublin): Raphoe DL 39; 126
Achadh-ur (Kilkenny): Faughanvale LY 36; 56
Achadrummin td: Clogher TE 5; 46
Achafoi (see Aghafoy): Templecarn DL 39; 157
Achalach lough: Templecarn DL 39; 157
Acheson, Capt. (Portnorris): Drumcree AH 1; 38–39
Acheson, family: Billy AM 16; 58
Acheson, James: Ballyrashane LY 22; 57–58, 65
Acheson, James: Tamlaght O'Crilly LY 18; 119
Acheson, John: Cumber LY 28; 24, 80
Acheson, John: Errigal LY 27; 66
Acheson, Moses: Hillsborough DN 12; 107
Acheson, Mrs: Cumber LY 28; 34
Acheson, Robert: Ballyrashane LY 22; 58
Acheson, Samual [I]: Ballyrashane LY 22; 59
Acheson, Samual [II]: Ballyrashane LY 22; 60
Acheson, Sgt: Galloon FH 4; 105
Acheson, Viscount: Newry DN 3; 100, 105
Acheson, William: Ballyrashane LY 22; 60
Acheson's lough: Templecarn DL 39; 157
Achinleck, James: Clogher TE 5; 40
Achison, family: Billy AM 16; 68
Achonry ph: Carrickfergus AM 37; 102
Achonry ph: Kilmacteige SO 40; 185–86
Ackin, family: Templecorran AM 26; 117, 119
Aclare: Kilmacteige SO 40; 185–86, 188, 190–92,
   197
Aclare barrack: Kilmacteige SO 40; 185
Aclare ford: Kilmacteige SO 40; 185
Acorn bank (England): Ballyscullion LY 6; 57
Acre McCricket td: Kilclief DN 17; 79
Acres td: Ballybay MN 40; 84
Acton House: Ballymore AH 1; 4, 10, 12
Acton House: Misc. DN 17; 130
Acton old church: Ballymore AH 1; 6, 10–11
Acton school: Ballymore AH 1; 9, 11–12
Acton td (see also Curryotragh): Ballymore AH 1; 4,
   9, 12–13, 15, 18

Acton village: Ballymore AH 1; 1, 4, 6, 9–11
Adair, Charles: Carrickfergus AM 37; 42
Adair, Col.: Island Magee AM 10; 65
Adair, Daniel: Ballintoy AM 24; 27–28
Adair, Ellen: Ahoghill AM 23; 37
Adair, family: Ahoghill AM 23; 28
Adair, family: Antrim AM 29; 24
Adair, family: Blaris AM 8; 22
Adair, family: Dunluce AM 16; 117
Adair, family: Island Magee AM 10; 70
Adair, family: Kirkinriola AM 23; 94, 96, 104–05,
  124
Adair, family: Magheragall AM 21; 99
Adair, family: Nilteen AM 35; 89, 91
Adair, Henry: Carrickfergus AM 37; 102
Adair, Henry: Templepatrick AM 35; 117, 136–37,
  144, 150, 152
Adair, Isaac: Clondermot LY 34; 89
Adair, J.B.: Carrickfergus AM 37; 98
Adair, James: Rasharkin AM 23; 141
Adair, Mary Ann: Ahoghill AM 23; 37
Adair, Mr: Templecorran AM 26; 122
Adair, Rev.: Antrim AM 29; 27
Adair, Rev. Patrick: Island Magee AM 10; 94
Adair, Robert: Kirkinriola AM 23; 88, 90, 94,
  117–18
Adair, T.B.: Ahoghill AM 23; 23, 41
Adair, T.B.: Carrickfergus AM 37; 102
Adair, T.B.: Doagh AM 29; 86
Adair, T.B.: Donegore AM 29; 107, 110, 129, 132
Adair, T.B.: Nilteen AM 35; 84–85, 89, 91, 100,
  102–03
Adair, William: Ahoghill AM 23; 2
Adair, William: Antrim AM 29; 37
Adair, William: Ballynure AM 32; 53, 58–59, 71
Adair, William: Carrickfergus AM 37; 98
Adair, William: Hillsborough DN 12; 107
Adair, William [I]: Kirkinriola AM 23; 90, 101
Adair, William [II]: Kirkinriola AM 23; 88, 91, 95,
  100, 103, 106, 110, 119–21
Adam, T.M.: Kilbride AM 29; 157
Adamnan, Abbot of Iona: Dungiven LY 15; 61
Adamnan, Abbot of Iona: Magilligan LY 11; 102
Adams, Alexander: Ballyrashane LY 22; 58
Adams, Alexander: Kildollagh LY 22; 71
Adams, Alexander: Loughguile AM 13; 74
Adams, Allen: Drumgoon CN 40; 8
Adams, Charles: Drumgoon CN 40; 8–10
Adams, Charles: Hillsborough DN 12; 105
Adams, Charles: Killdrumsherdan CN 40; 34, 37
Adams, Charles: Templecorran AM 26; 130
Adams, Daniel: Dunluce AM 16; 119, 122
Adams, David: Kildollagh LY 22; 71
Adams, Elisabeth: Kilraghts AM 16; 132
Adams, Elizabeth: Aghadowey LY 22; 37

Adams, family: Carnmoney AM 2; 76
Adams, family: Derrykeighan AM 16; 89
Adams, family: Desertlyn LY 31; 42
Adams, family: Island Magee AM 10; 70
Adams, family: Kilmore AH 1; 65
Adams, family: Kilraghts AM 16; 128, 130
Adams, family: Kilwaughter AM 10; 115
Adams, family: Macosquin LY 22; 84, 119
Adams, family: Misc. LY 36; 104
Adams, Henry: Carrickfergus AM 37; 187
Adams, Hugh: Derrykeighan AM 16; 92
Adams, James: Ballyrashane LY 22; 65
Adams, James: Balteagh LY 9; 13, 25
Adams, James: Cappagh TE 5; 22
Adams, James: Clondermot LY 34; 93
Adams, James: Kildollagh LY 22; 67
Adams, James: Newry DN 3; 69
Adams, James: Skirts of Urney and Ardstraw TE 5;
  141
Adams, James [I]: Carrickfergus AM 37; 122
Adams, James [II]: Carrickfergus AM 37; 184–85
Adams, Jane: Ballyscullion LY 6; 77
Adams, Jane: Kildollagh LY 22; 71
Adams, John (Jnr): Kilraghts AM 16; 132
Adams, John: Ahoghill AM 23; 34
Adams, John: Desertoghill LY 27; 2, 15
Adams, John: Kilraghts AM 16; 132
Adams, John [I]: Aghadowey LY 22; 5, 8
Adams, John [II]: Aghadowey LY 22; 36
Adams, Lt: Clondermot LY 34; 27
Adams, Margaret: Larne AM 10; 127
Adams, Margret: Balteagh LY 9; 43
Adams, Martha: Kilraghts AM 16; 132
Adams, Mary: Ahoghill AM 23; 38
Adams, Mary: Carncastle and Killyglen AM 10; 7
Adams, Matthew: Ballymoney AM 16; 25
Adams, Mr (Braccagh): Kilmore AH 1; 68
Adams, Mr (Magherafelt): Maghera LY 18; 43
Adams, Mr (Shercock): Aughnamullen MN 40; 76
Adams, Mr: Ahoghill AM 23; 31
Adams, Mr: Drumballyroney DN 3; 16
Adams, Mrs: Ballymoney AM 16; 17
Adams, Mrs James: Carrickfergus AM 37; 185
Adams, Rev. Charles: Ardstraw TE 5; 8
Adams, Rev. Isaac: Ballylinny AM 32; 23–24, 26,
  28
Adams, Rev. James: Ballylinny AM 32; 17
Adams, Rev. James: Drumgoon CN 40; 6
Adams, Robert: Coleraine LY 33; 105
Adams, Samuel: Ballymoney AM 16; 17
Adams, Samuel: Ballyscullion LY 6; 77
Adams, Thomas: Carrickfergus AM 37; 109
Adams, William: Ballinderry AM 21; 50
Adams, William: Ballymoney AM 16; 17
Adams, William: Balteagh LY 9; 26, 28, 30

Adams, William: Clondermot LY 34; 93
Adams, William: Dungiven LY 15; 116
Adams, William: Faughanvale LY 36; 30
Adamson, Charles: Ballynure AM 32; 67
Adamson, John: Donaghcloney DN 12; 61
Adamson, Robert: Ballynure AM 32; 67
Adcock, William: Kilrea LY 27; 107, 124, 128
Addemill (see Adderville): Clonmany DL 38; 12
Adderly, Mrs: Newry DN 3; 104
Adderly, William: Newry DN 3; 100
Addervill (see Adderville): Clonmany DL 38; 20
Adderville td: Clonmany DL 38; 12, 18–20
Addison, James: Carrickfergus AM 37; 76
Adelaide, Queen: Ahoghill AM 23; 19
Adervil (see Adderville): Clonmany DL 38; 18
Adinn lough: Drumkeeran FH 14; 63
Adrain, family: Templecorran AM 26; 117, 119
Adrian, Michael: Newry DN 3; 98, 103
Adverness House: Coleraine LY 33; 73
Afad lough: Inishmacsaint FH 14; 71
Afee, James: Errigal Truagh MN 40; 122
Aganlean td: Layd AM 13; 44
Agar, Mr: Muckamore AM 35; 62
Agar, Rev. James: Blaris AM 8; 66
Aghabog ph: Clogher TE 5; 40
Aghabog ph: Currin MN 40; 86, 88, 90, 92
Aghabog ph: Drumgoon CN 40; 10
Aghabog ph: Drummully FH 4; 34
Aghabog ph: Ematris MN 40; 112, 116–17
Aghabog ph: Galloon FH 4; 95
Aghabog school: Aghabog MN 40; 65
Aghaboy (Aghanboy) td: Drummaul AM 19; 68, 88–91
Aghaboy bridge: Donagh MN 40; 99
Aghaboy corn mill: Drummaul AM 19; 51, 84
Aghaboy flax mill: Drummaul AM 19; 51
Aghaboy North td: Tydavnet MN 40; 169
Aghabrasill td: Donacavey TE 5; 82
Aghacairnan (see Aghacarnan): Ballinderry AM 21; 41
Aghacarnahan td: Duneane AM 19; 119, 122, 124
Aghacarnan (Aughacarnon) td: Ballinderry AM 21; 41, 49, 56–57
Aghacarnan bog: Magheragall AM 21; 107
Aghacarnan school: Ballinderry AM 21; 56–57
Aghacomman (see Aghacommon): Seagoe AH 1; 103
Aghacommon chapel: Seagoe AH 1; 105–06
Aghacommon school [I]: Seagoe AH 1; 102–03
Aghacommon school [II]: Seagoe AH 1; 102–03
Aghacommon td: Seagoe AH 1; 106
Aghacurragh district: Misc. SO 40; 199
Aghadachor lough: Mevagh DL 38; 55
Aghadachor school: Mevagh DL 38; 59
Aghadachor td: Lough Swilly DL 38; 120

Aghadachor td: Mevagh DL 38; 56, 63
Aghadavy td: Aghalee AM 21; 26
Aghade ph (Carlow): Faughanvale LY 36; 12
Aghaderg Glebe House: Aghaderg DN 12; 7, 10
Aghaderg ph: Annaclone DN 12; 13, 16
Aghaderg ph: Ballymore AH 1; 7, 17–18
Aghaderg ph: Donaghmore DN 3; 7–8
Aghaderg ph: Drumballyroney DN 3; 13–15
Aghaderg ph: Drumgath DN 3; 20
Aghaderg ph: Misc. DN 17; 121
Aghaderg ph: Montiaghs AH 1; 91
Aghaderg ph: Seapatrick DN 12; 124, 126
Aghaderg ph: Tullylish DN 12; 140
Aghadhachor (see Aghadachor)
Aghadolgan school: Glenavy AM 21; 79, 91
Aghadolgan td: Glenavy AM 21; 79
Aghadowey: Coleraine LY 33; 104
Aghadowey: Dungiven LY 15; 41, 108
Aghadowey: Kilrea LY 27; 116
Aghadowey bleach green: Aghadowey LY 22; 7, 10, 16, 29
Aghadowey Castle: Aghadowey LY 22; 26–27
Aghadowey church: Aghadowey LY 22; 5–6, 13, 16, 18, 21, 26
Aghadowey church: Misc. LY 36; 110
Aghadowey dispensary: Aghadowey LY 22; 12, 16–18
Aghadowey dispensary: Agivey LY 22; 41
Aghadowey Glebe House (see Blackheath): Aghadowey LY 22; 1
Aghadowey meeting house: Aghadowey LY 22; 5, 12–13, 15–16, 21
Aghadowey old church: Aghadowey LY 22; 26
Aghadowey ph: Agivey LY 22; 39–41
Aghadowey ph: Ballyclug AM 23; 61
Aghadowey ph: Balteagh LY 9; 20
Aghadowey ph: Coleraine LY 33; 73, 104, 120, 144
Aghadowey ph: Desertoghill LY 27; 3, 10, 13, 17
Aghadowey ph: Drumachose LY 9; 90
Aghadowey ph: Errigal LY 27; 35, 46, 49, 53, 60, 63, 78
Aghadowey ph: Killowen LY 33; 162, 172
Aghadowey ph: Kilrea LY 27; 104, 110, 113
Aghadowey ph: Macosquin LY 22; 77, 83, 86, 89, 98
Aghadowey ph: Misc. LY 36; 111–12
Aghadowey ph: Tamlaght O'Crilly LY 18; 89, 106
Aghadowey ph: Termoneeny LY 6; 127, 132
Aghadowey river: Aghadowey LY 22; 1, 33
Aghadowey river: Agivey LY 22; 42
Aghadowey school: Aghadowey LY 22; 13, 18, 22
Aghadowey schools: Aghadowey LY 22; 12–13
Aghadowey Sunday school: Aghadowey LY 22; 13, 21–22
Aghadowey td: Aghadowey LY 22; 5–7, 10, 35–37

Aghadreenan Glebe td: Galloon FH 4; 95, 97

Aghadreenan td: Donacavey TE 5; 80–81

Aghadreencen (see Aghadreenan): Galloon FH 4; 95

Aghadreeneen (see Aghadreenan): Galloon FH 4; 97

Aghadrena corn mill: Donaghmoyne MN 40; 107

Aghadrimglasney (see Aghadrumglasny):
    Aghagallon AM 21; 3, 28

Aghadrum td: Galloon FH 4; 95

Aghadrumglasney (see Aghadrumglasny):
    Aghagallon AM 21; 2

Aghadrumglasny fort: Aghagallon AM 21; 17

Aghadrumglasny fort: Aghalee AM 21; 36

Aghadrumglasny school: Aghagallon AM 21; 2, 5

Aghadrumglasny td: Aghagallon AM 21; 3, 7

Aghadrumglasny td: Aghalee AM 21; 28, 38

Aghadrummin td: Clogher TE 5; 33

Aghadrumsee td: Galloon FH 4; 105

Aghadulla corn mill: Dromore TE 5; 101

Aghafad church: Killanny MN 40; 135

Aghafad school: Killanny MN 40; 135

Aghafad td: Donacavey TE 5; 72, 77, 80–81

Aghafad td: Killanny MN 40; 131

Aghafattan school: Skerry AM 13; 114

Aghafatten td: Skerry AM 13; 106

Aghafin td: Clones FH 4; 26

Aghafoy lough: Templecarn DL 39; 157

Aghafoy td: Templecarn DL 39; 163

Aghagafarty hill: Magheraculmoney FH 14; 113

Aghagallen (see Aghagallon): Misc. DN 17; 122

Aghagallon: Aghalee AM 21; 34

Aghagallon: Blaris AM 8; 76

Aghagallon cairn: Aghagallon AM 21; 11

Aghagallon chapel: Aghagallon AM 21; 8, 20, 24

Aghagallon chapel: Shankill DN 12; 138

Aghagallon fort: Aghagallon AM 21; 8

Aghagallon graveyard: Aghagallon AM 21; 9–10, 21

Aghagallon old chapel: Aghagallon AM 21; 8–9

Aghagallon old church: Aghagallon AM 21; 9–11

Aghagallon ph: Aghalee AM 21; 26, 28–29, 31,
    37–39

Aghagallon ph: Ballinderry AM 21; 41, 46

Aghagallon ph: Blaris AM 8; 1

Aghagallon ph: Camlin AM 21; 72

Aghagallon ph: Glenavy AM 21; 77–78

Aghagallon ph: Magheramesk AM 21; 112, 116

Aghagallon ph: Misc. AM 10; 129

Aghagallon ph: Misc. DN 17; 122

Aghagallon racecourse: Aghagallon AM 21; 13

Aghagallon Sunday school: Aghagallon AM 21; 24

Aghagallon td: Aghagallon AM 21; 2–3, 9

Aghagallon td: Blaris DN 12; 40, 42–43

Aghagallon well: Aghagallon AM 21; 11

Aghagarr td: Tydavnet MN 40; 169

Aghagashlan cromlechs: Drumgoon CN 40; 7

Aghagashlan hill: Drumgoon CN 40; 1, 8

Aghagashlan td: Drumgoon CN 40; 3

Aghagaskin bog: Magherafelt LY 6; 80, 95

Aghagaskin fort: Magherafelt LY 6; 93, 105–06

Aghagaskin td: Magherafelt LY 6; 80, 93, 95,
    105–07, 112

Aghagavarara locality: Misc. LY 36; 112

Aghagay td: Galloon FH 4; 89, 95

Aghaginduff chapel: Killeeshil TE 20; 64

Aghagolrick school: Laragh CN 40; 43

Aghahooran td: Boho FH 14; 9

Aghahull td: Tullyaughnish DL 38; 96

Aghakillymade bog: Kinawley FH 4; 113

Aghakillymade td: Kinawley FH 4; 113, 121

Aghalaghan manor: Misc. FH 4; 133

Aghalane (Killycloghan) Castle: Kinawley FH 4;
    117–18

Aghalane bridge: Kinawley FH 4; 113, 115, 117

Aghalane mountain: Cappagh TE 5; 20

Aghalatty corn mill: Mevagh DL 38; 57

Aghalatty school: Mevagh DL 38; 59

Aghalatty td: Mevagh DL 38; 55, 58, 63

Aghaleague (Aghaleag) td: Magheraculmoney FH
    14; 110–11

Aghaleague wood: Magheraculmoney FH 14; 104

Aghaleck bog: Ramoan AM 24; 125

Aghaleck cave: Ramoan AM 24; 113

Aghaleck school: Ramoan AM 24; 100

Aghaleck standing stone: Ramoan AM 24; 112–13

Aghaleck td: Ramoan AM 24; 112, 116

Aghalee: Aghagallon AM 21; 1–2, 5–7, 23–24

Aghalee: Aghalee AM 21; 26–27, 29, 31–37, 39

Aghalee: Ballinderry AM 21; 41, 46

Aghalee bleach green: Aghalee AM 21; 32–33

Aghalee bridge: Aghalee AM 21; 32–33

Aghalee church (see also Soldierstown): Aghalee
    AM 21; 29

Aghalee church: Aghagallon AM 21; 7, 21

Aghalee church: Ballinderry AM 21; 50

Aghalee cromlech: Aghalee AM 21; 37

Aghalee druid's altar: Aghalee AM 21; 37

Aghalee flour mill: Aghalee AM 21; 32–33

Aghalee fort [I]: Aghalee AM 21; 36

Aghalee fort [II]: Aghalee AM 21; 36

Aghalee Glebe House: Aghalee AM 21; 26, 31

Aghalee grain store: Aghalee AM 21; 32

Aghalee graveyard: Aghalee AM 21; 31

Aghalee hibernian school: Aghalee AM 21; 28, 40

Aghalee Kildare school: Aghalee AM 21; 28, 38–40

Aghalee kilns: Glenavy AM 21; 87

Aghalee old church: Aghagallon AM 21; 9

Aghalee old church: Aghalee AM 21; 27, 32, 35–37

Aghalee old graveyard: Aghalee AM 21; 35–37

Aghalee ph: Aghagallon AM 21; 22–23

Aghalee ph: Ballinderry AM 21; 41

Aghalee ph: Magheramesk AM 21; 112, 116

Aghalee ph: Misc. AM 10; 129

Aghalee pound: Aghalee AM 21; 33

Aghalee rectory: Misc. DN 17; 121

Aghalee river: Aghalee AM 21; 32

Aghalee td: Aghalee AM 21; 27–28, 32

Aghalee td: Blaris DN 12; 40, 42–43

Aghalee well: Aghalee AM 21; 36

Aghalile td: Magheross MN 40; 148

Aghalisk td: Dromore TE 5; 100

Aghalislane (see Aghalislone): Derryaghy AM 8; 91, 98, 100, 113

Aghalisloan (see Aghalislone): Derryaghy AM 8; 119

Aghalislone altar: Derryaghy AM 8; 98

Aghalislone entrenchments: Derryaghy AM 8; 94

Aghalislone forts: Derryaghy AM 8; 95

Aghalislone old church: Derryaghy AM 8; 91

Aghalislone td: Derryaghy AM 8; 91, 98, 100, 113, 119

Aghaloo ph: Errigal Truagh MN 40; 122

Aghaloo ph: Killeeshil TE 20; 62–63

Aghaloo ph: Tynan AH 1; 124, 128

Aghaloughan forts: Drummaul AM 19; 78

Aghalougher td: Termonamongan TE 5; 143

Aghalun (see also Brookeborough): Aghavea FH 4; 19

Aghalun Castle: Aghavea FH 4; 21

Aghalun td: Aghavea FH 4; 23

Aghalurcher Glebe House: Aghalurcher FH 4; 16

Aghalurcher Glebe td: Aghalurcher FH 4; 14

Aghalurcher old church: Aghalurcher FH 4; 9

Aghalurcher ph: Aghavea FH 4; 17, 19, 22

Aghalurcher ph: Cleenish FH 14; 11

Aghalurcher ph: Clogher TE 5; 24, 26, 40, 53

Aghalurcher ph: Clones FH 4; 26

Aghalurcher ph: Derrybrusk FH 4; 30

Aghalurcher ph: Enniskillen FH 4; 41, 48

Aghalurcher ph: Galloon FH 4; 87, 97

Aghalurcher ph: Misc. TE 5; 147

Aghalurcher td: Aghalurcher FH 4; 1

Aghamackalinn school: Errigal Truagh MN 40; 121–22

Aghamakerlin (see Aghamakerr): Aughnamullen MN 40; 77

Aghamakerr school: Aughnamullen MN 40; 77

Aghamakerr td: Aughnamullen MN 40; 69, 75

Aghamilkin td: Clogher TE 5; 35

Aghamore hill: Boho FH 14; 8

Aghamore td: Boho FH 14; 8–9

Aghamuldoony hill: Inishmacsaint FH 14; 71

Aghananimy lough: Monaghan MN 40; 159

Aghananimy mill: Monaghan MN 40; 161

Aghancrossy td: Derrykeighan AM 16; 95

Aghandizart td: Tomregan FH 4; 126

Aghandunvarran (Aghandunverran) td: Hillsborough DN 12; 95, 99, 105

Aghanish Island: Kinawley FH 4; 113

Aghanloo church: Aghanloo LY 11; 2, 8, 21, 23, 28, 32

Aghanloo church: Tamlaght Finlagan LY 25; 69

Aghanloo Glebe House: Aghanloo LY 11; 2–3, 9, 18, 23, 26, 30, 36

Aghanloo graveyard: Aghanloo LY 11; 3

Aghanloo meeting house: Aghanloo LY 11; 8

Aghanloo old church: Aghanloo LY 11; 3, 8, 28

Aghanloo ph: Balteagh LY 9; 44

Aghanloo ph: Drumachose LY 9; 48, 56, 75, 79, 84, 88, 90, 128–29

Aghanloo ph: Dunboe LY 11; 47

Aghanloo ph: Magilligan LY 11; 82, 86, 96–98, 100, 119, 125

Aghanloo ph: Tamlaght Finlagan LY 25; 62, 97, 106–07

Aghanloo school: Aghanloo LY 11; 2

Aghanloo water mills: Aghanloo LY 11; 8

Aghanloo wooden bridge: Aghanloo LY 11; 1, 10, 14, 22

Aghansillagh bridge: Balteagh LY 9; 5, 42

Aghansillagh fort: Balteagh LY 9; 13, 25

Aghansillagh standing stone: Balteagh LY 9; 35

Aghansillagh td: Balteagh LY 9; 5, 13, 25, 32, 35, 39, 44–45

Aghantamy (see Aghananimy): Monaghan MN 40; 161

Aghanunshin ph: Leck DL 39; 115

Aghanunshin ph: Lough Swilly DL 38; 128

Aghanunshin ph: Tullyaughnish DL 38; 84

Agharainy td: Derryvullan FH 14; 45

Aghareagh hill: Currin MN 40; 86

Aghareagh school: Currin MN 40; 92

Aghareagh td: Currin MN 40; 91

Aghareagh West td: Currin MN 40; 86

Agharonan Lower td: Donacavey TE 5; 80–81

Agharonan Upper td: Donacavey TE 5; 80–81

Agharoosky East td: Galloon FH 4; 95

Agharoosky West td: Galloon FH 4; 95

Aghassey spade foundry: Ardstraw TE 5; 14

Aghassissy fort: Ardstraw TE 5; 12

Aghassissy td: Ardstraw TE 5; 12

Aghavannan school: Killygarvan DL 38; 42, 48

Aghavannan td: Killygarvan DL 38; 46

Aghavary bog: Ballyscullion AM 19; 10

Aghavary td: Ballyscullion AM 19; 9, 12

Aghavass school: Cleenish FH 14; 24

Aghavass td: Cleenish FH 14; 29

Aghavea church: Aghavea FH 4; 19

Aghavea Glebe House: Aghavea FH 4; 20, 25

Aghavea Glebe td: Aghavea FH 4; 23

Aghavea graveyard: Aghavea FH 4; 21

Aghavea hill: Aghavea FH 4; 17

Aghavea old church: Aghavea FH 4; 20–21

Aghavea ph: Aghalurcher FH 4; 1, 5–6, 10, 13–14

Aghavea ph: Clogher TE 5; 40

Aghavea ph: Enniskillen FH 4; 41, 48, 65

Aghavea td: Aghavea FH 4; 20, 23

Aghaveagh td: Tamlaght TE 20; 78–79, 83–91, 95, 124–26

Aghavery (see Aghavary): Ballyscullion AM 19; 9

Aghavoory td: Aghalurcher FH 4; 14

Aghawee (Aghavee) td: Clonleigh DL 39; 12, 196

Aghayalloge corn mill: Killevy AH 1; 53

Aghebrassell td: Donacavey TE 5; 82

Agheeghter td: Aghalurcher FH 4; 9, 14

Agheighter (see Agheeghter): Aghalurcher FH 4; 14

Aghendarragh (see Aghindarragh)

Aghendrummond td: Clogher TE 5; 37

Aghenehogh (see Aghnahough): Derryaghy AM 8; 119

Aghengowly (Aghengowley) td: Clogher TE 5; 37

Aghenlark: (see Aghinlark)

Aghenlork: (see Aghinlark)

Aghentain (see Aghintain)

Aghentra Glebe House: Kinawley FH 4; 115

Aghentra td: Kinawley FH 4; 120

Agheraban (see Augheralane): Ballybay MN 40; 81

Agherboy td: Drumlumman CN 40; 17

Agherton dispensary: Ballyaghran LY 33; 1, 4, 6, 12, 18–19, 25

Agherton district: Ballyaghran LY 33; 1

Aghery lough: Annahilt DN 12; 24

Aghery lough: Dromore DN 12; 70, 73

Aghery Lower Island: Dromore DN 12; 73

Aghery Upper Island: Dromore DN 12; 73

Aghilaur td: Drumkeeran FH 14; 67

Aghindarragh (Aghendara) td: Clogher TE 5; 26, 35, 37, 42, 47

Aghindarragh school: Clogher TE 5; 42–43

Aghindarrah (see Aghindarragh)

Aghindrumman (Aghindrumond) td: Clogher TE 5; 37, 48

Aghindrumman chapel: Clogher TE 5; 48

Aghinlark bog: Clogher TE 5; 26

Aghinlark school: Clogher TE 5; 41, 51

Aghinlark td: Clogher TE 5; 37, 41, 47, 51

Aghinlig td: Loughgall AH 1; 79

Aghintain (Aughintain) td: Clogher TE 5; 37, 48–49

Aghintain and Blessingbourne manor: Clogher TE 5; 34–35

Aghintain Castle: Clogher TE 5; 26, 34

Aghintain chapel: Clogher TE 5; 39, 48

Aghintain mountain: Clogher TE 5; 24–26, 44

Aghintain mountain: Donacavey TE 5; 67

Aghintain td: Donacavey TE 5; 75

Aghintain trigonometrical station: Clogher TE 5; 26

Aghlem Point: Lough Swilly DL 38; 105, 114–15

Aghliard td: Leck DL 39; 116, 118

Aghlish td: Cleenish FH 14; 29

Aghlish td: Dromore TE 5; 98

Aghnacarrow td: Derrybrusk FH 4; 30

Agh-na-cavanagh valley: Culfeightrin AM 24; 79

Aghnaclog flax mill: Annaclone DN 12; 14

Aghnaclough (see Aghnacloy)

Aghnacloy Beg td: Kinawley FH 4; 121

Aghnacloy More td: Kinawley FH 4; 121

Aghnacloy td: Aghavea FH 4; 23

Aghnacloy td: Shankill AH 1; 114

Aghnadarragh (Aghnadaragh) td: Camlin AM 21; 60, 67, 71

Aghnadarragh school: Camlin AM 21; 62

Aghnadarragh school [I]: Camlin AM 21; 75

Aghnadarragh school [II]: Camlin AM 21; 73, 75

Aghnadore td: Racavan AM 13; 86, 88

Aghnagap mill: Donagh MN 40; 101

Aghnaglack mountain: Cleenish FH 14; 14

Aghnaglack stone: Boho FH 14; 10

Aghnaglack td: Boho FH 14; 10

Aghnaglough school: Clogher TE 5; 41–42

Aghnaglough td: Clogher TE 5; 38–39, 41, 53

Aghnagrane td: Aghavea FH 4; 23, 25

Aghnahinch td: Galloon FH 4; 95

Aghnahoe House: Killeeshil TE 20; 62–64

Aghnahoe td: Killeeshil TE 20; 62

Aghnahoo school: Termonamongan TE 5; 144

Aghnahoo td: Errigal Keerogue TE 20; 49

Aghnahoo td: Templecarn DL 39; 159, 163

Aghnahoo td: Termonamongan TE 5; 144

Aghnahough forts: Derryaghy AM 8; 94

Aghnahough ruins: Derryaghy AM 8; 99

Aghnahough school: Derryaghy AM 8; 118

Aghnahough td: Derryaghy AM 8; 94, 105, 109, 119

Aghnakeeragh td: Raphoe DL 39; 125

Aghnaloo td: Aghalurcher FH 4; 3

Aghnamacklinn (see Aghamackalinn): Errigal Truagh MN 40; 122

Aghnamoira td: Warrenpoint DN 3; 115

Aghnamore td: Dromore TE 5; 101

Aghnamullen ph: Clogher TE 5; 40

Aghnascue Glebe td: Drummully FH 4; 34, 39

Aghnasedagh lough: Monaghan MN 40; 159

Aghnaskew glebe: Galloon FH 4; 96

Aghnaskew td: Currin MN 40; 86–87, 90–91

Aghnatrisk td: Hillsborough DN 12; 107

Aghnish (see Aughnish): Tullyaughnish DL 38; 97

Aghnonan td: Donacavey TE 5; 77

Aghoo td: Boho FH 14; 8

Aghore (see Ahory): Kilmore AH 1; 60

Aghrevity, William: Ballyscullion LY 6; 57

Aghrifinnigane [or Aghrisingin] district: Misc. SO 40; 199

Aghrim td: Cleenish FH 14; 29
Aghrim td: Devenish FH 14; 57
Aght td: Lough Swilly DL 38; 138
Aghtem (see Aghlem): Lough Swilly DL 38; 105
Aghuismore lough: Templecarn DL 39; 157
Aghyaran chapel: Termonamongan TE 5; 143
Aghyaran td: Termonamongan TE 5, 143
Aghyarran Lodge: Donaghmore DL 39; 28
Aghydulla corn mill: Drumragh TE 5; 110
Aghydulla td: Drumragh TE 5; 110
Aghygalt td: Misc. DL 39; 188
Agivey bawn: Agivey LY 22; 40
Agivey brickfield: Coleraine LY 33; 148
Agivey brickfields: Agivey LY 22; 42
Agivey church: Aghadowey LY 22; 27
Agivey church: Agivey LY 22; 42
Agivey Diamond: Agivey LY 22; 43–44
Agivey Greater water: Aghadowey LY 22; 1, 4, 9,
    11, 27
Agivey Greater water: Agivey LY 22; 39–40
Agivey House: Agivey LY 22; 41–42
Agivey Lower td: Aghadowey LY 22; 36
Agivey Lower water: Aghadowey LY 22; 1, 9, 11
Agivey Lower water: Agivey LY 22; 39–40
Agivey new wooden bridge: Agivey LY 22; 39,
    42–43
Agivey old church: Aghadowey LY 22; 16
Agivey old church: Agivey LY 22; 40–41, 44
Agivey old church: Banagher LY 30; 37
Agivey old wooden bridge: Agivey LY 22; 40,
    42–43
Agivey ph: Aghadowey LY 22; 16, 18
Agivey ph: Ballymoney AM 16; 1
Agivey ph: Coleraine LY 33; 121, 148
Agivey ph: Dungiven LY 15; 15
Agivey ph: Errigal LY 27; 61
Agivey ph: Macosquin LY 22; 76–78, 82
Agivey ph: Misc. LY 36; 111, 116
Agivey potteries: Agivey LY 22; 42
Agivey river: Errigal LY 27; 35, 40–42, 44–45, 57,
    73, 76
Agivey water: Aghadowey LY 22; 33
Agivey water: Agivey LY 22; 40–43
Agivey water: Desertoghill LY 27; 1–2, 4–5, 8,
    12–14, 16
Agivey wooden bridge: Ballymoney AM 16; 11, 20
Agnew, Daniel: Kilwaughter AM 10; 122
Agnew, Dr: Doagh AM 29; 89–90, 93
Agnew, family: Antrim AM 29; 24
Agnew, family: Ballycor AM 32; 5
Agnew, family: Ballynure AM 32; 69
Agnew, family: Doagh AM 29; 73
Agnew, family: Donegore AM 29; 110
Agnew, family: Kilwaughter AM 10; 115
Agnew, family: Raloo AM 32; 94, 121, 127–28

Agnew, family: Rashee AM 32; 138
Agnew, family: Templepatrick AM 35; 118
Agnew, J.: Donegore AM 29; 133
Agnew, James: Artrea LY 6; 29
Agnew, James: Doagh AM 29; 69, 73, 85, 91–92
Agnew, James: Kilwaughter AM 10; 122
Agnew, James: Raloo AM 32; 122
Agnew, John: Tamlaght O'Crilly LY 18; 135
Agnew, John: Termoneeny LY 6; 133
Agnew, Mary Anne: Carrickfergus AM 37; 153
Agnew, Nancy: Carrickfergus AM 37; 111
Agnew, Patrick: Kilwaughter AM 10; 112–113, 115
Agnew, Robert: Drummaul AM 19; 88
Agnew, Samuel: Ballynure AM 32; 54
Agnew, Sarah: Island Magee AM 10; 93
Agnew, Squire: Kilwaughter AM 10; 114
Agnew, Widow: Kilbroney DN 3; 30
Agnew, William: Kilwaughter AM 10; 122
Agnew's hill: Ballycor AM 32; 1
Agnew's hill: Carncastle and Killyglen AM 10; 1,
    11
Agnew's hill: Doagh AM 29; 86
Agnew's hill: Glenwhirry AM 32; 78
Agnew's hill: Inver AM 26; 49
Agnew's hill: Kilwaughter AM 10; 106, 108–09,
    111
Agnew's hill: Racavan AM 13; 103
Agnew's hill: Raloo AM 32; 86
Agnew's hill: Rashee AM 32; 135
Agnus, St: Desertegney DL 38; 24
Agrippa, Cornelius: Misc. LY 31; 125
Ahadara td: Dromore TE 5; 94
Ahaloughan bog: Duneane AM 19; 98
Ahaloughan island: Duneane AM 19; 98
Ahansillagh (see Aghansillagh): Balteagh LY 9; 35,
    44
Ahoghill: Aghadowey LY 22; 23, 25
Ahoghill: Ahoghill AM 23; 2–3, 6, 9, 11–12, 14–15,
    19, 25, 30, 32–33, 37–38, 40–43, 45
Ahoghill: Ballyscullion AM 19; 10
Ahoghill: Drummaul AM 19; 34, 52, 83, 86
Ahoghill: Dunaghy AM 13; 25
Ahoghill: Kirkinriola AM 23; 99, 108
Ahoghill: Rasharkin AM 23; 130–31
Ahoghill brickfields: Ahoghill AM 23; 31
Ahoghill Catholic Sunday school: Ahoghill AM 23;
    45
Ahoghill chapel: Ahoghill AM 23; 2, 30–31, 45
Ahoghill church: Ahoghill AM 23; 2, 9, 11, 24–25,
    30–31, 33, 36, 47
Ahoghill church: Drummaul AM 19; 70
Ahoghill dispensary: Ahoghill AM 23; 15–16, 20,
    24, 32, 36, 36
Ahoghill first meeting house (S): Ahoghill AM 23;
    9, 33, 37

Ahoghill forts: Ahoghill AM 23; 3
Ahoghill Glebe House: Ahoghill AM 23; 12, 16
Ahoghill graveyard: Ahoghill AM 23; 25
Ahoghill meeting house (Cov.): Ahoghill AM 23; 30
Ahoghill meeting house (P): Ahoghill AM 23; 2, 9, 11, 31, 36, 43
Ahoghill meeting houses (S): Ahoghill AM 23; 2, 11, 31
Ahoghill old church: Ahoghill AM 23; 25
Ahoghill ph: Aghadowey LY 22; 23
Ahoghill ph: Ballyclug AM 23; 52–53, 60
Ahoghill ph: Ballyscullion AM 19; 1, 8
Ahoghill ph: Carrickfergus AM 37; 102
Ahoghill ph: Connor AM 19; 16
Ahoghill ph: Drummaul AM 19; 33, 39, 46, 52, 71
Ahoghill ph: Dunaghy AM 13; 19
Ahoghill ph: Dundermot AM 13; 29
Ahoghill ph: Duneane AM 19; 107
Ahoghill ph: Kirkinriola AM 23; 88, 91–92, 99, 115, 119, 124
Ahoghill ph: Rasharkin AM 23; 127, 129, 132
Ahoghill ph: Tamlaght O'Crilly LY 18; 88, 90
Ahoghill school [I]: Ahoghill AM 23; 42
Ahoghill school [II]: Ahoghill AM 23; 43
Ahoghill school [III]: Ahoghill AM 23; 44
Ahoghill school [IV]: Ahoghill AM 23; 51
Ahoghill second meeting house (S): Ahoghill AM 23; 9, 36
Ahoghill Sunday school: Ahoghill AM 23; 47
Ahoghill weighhouse: Ahoghill AM 23; 42
Ahory corn mill [I]: Kilmore AH 1; 61, 63, 66
Ahory corn mill [II]: Kilmore AH 1; 63
Ahory flax mill [I]: Kilmore AH 1; 60
Ahory flax mill [II]: Kilmore AH 1; 60, 66
Ahory hill: Kilmore AH 1; 61
Ahory Leap: Kilmore AH 1; 61
Ahory meeting house: Kilmore AH 1; 63
Ahory td: Kilmore AH 1; 66–67, 69
Aicken, John: Muckamore AM 35; 78–79
Aicken, Peter: Ahoghill AM 23; 15
Aicken, Peter: Ballyclug AM 23; 55, 57
Aicken, Peter: Kirkinriola AM 23; 97, 105
Aicken, Peter: Racavan AM 13; 88, 93
Aickin, John: Kirkinriola AM 23; 113, 119, 122
Aickin, Peter: Duneane AM 19; 100, 102
Aidan, Bishop: Magilligan LY 11; 88
Aidan, St: Banagher LY 30; 6
Aidan, St: Bovevagh LY 25; 5
Aidan, St: Magilligan LY 11; 88, 103–04, 129, 144
Aidan, St: Magilligan LY 11; 88
Aidan's grave: Magilligan LY 11; 89
Aidan's pulpit: Magilligan LY 11; 88–89
Aidus, King of Ireland: Dungiven LY 15; 64
Aidus, King of Ireland: Magilligan LY 11; 105
Aiken, Anne: Coleraine LY 33; 69, 136

Aiken, Capt.: Templecarn DL 39; 170
Aiken, family: Glynn AM 26; 45
Aiken, Irwin: Clonleigh DL 39; 10
Aikin, family: Kirkinriola AM 23; 124
Aikin, John: Misc. DL 39; 194, 196
Aikin, Mary: Macosquin LY 22; 93
Aileach Castle: Clondermot LY 34; 34
Aileach, Lord of Inishowen: Misc. TE 5; 146
Ailild I, Archbishop: Kilkeel DN 3; 54
Ailild II, Archbishop: Kilkeel DN 3; 54
Ainaghan fort: Devenish FH 14; 55
Ainaghan td: Devenish FH 14; 57
Ainmarech, father of Aidus: Magilligan LY 11; 105
Aird grey stone: Billy AM 16; 58, 62
Aird td: Billy AM 16; 36
Aird's Snout: Billy AM 16; 41
Airs, Mr: Balteagh LY 9; 27
Aitcheson, Mr: Templecarn DL 39; 161
Aken, family: Billy AM 16; 68
Aken, Robert: Donagh MN 40; 101
Akilly, Cormac: Ballinderry AM 21; 52
Akin, D.: Drumbo DN 7; 60
Akin, family: Billy AM 16; 58
Alba Landa abbey: Comber DN 7; 31
Albanagh lough: Clogher TE 5; 26
Alcaltan (see Alkatten): Banagher LY 30; 25
Alcorn, Andrew: Tamlaght Finlagan LY 25; 118
Alcorn, family: Misc. LY 36; 104
Alcorn, George: Drumachose LY 9; 117
Alcorn, Martha: Tamlaght Finlagan LY 25; 118
Alcrossagh cove: Armoy AM 24; 8
Alcrossagh fort [I]: Armoy AM 24; 8
Alcrossagh fort [II]: Armoy AM 24; 8
Alcrossagh hill: Armoy AM 24; 1
Alcrossagh td: Armoy AM 24; 8
Alcrossagh well: Armoy AM 24; 7
Alcrow, Mrs: Drumragh TE 5; 107
Alderdice, C.W.: Blaris AM 8; 68–69
Alderdice, C.W.: Blaris DN 12; 32, 46, 50
Alderdice, Edward: Derryaghy AM 8; 95
Alderdice, family: Derryaghy AM 8; 103
Alderwood td: Aghalurcher FH 4; 16
Aldfreck td: Templecorran AM 26; 84, 89
Aldfreck well: Templecorran AM 26; 84
Aldoo locality: Carrickfergus AM 37; 93
Aldoo school: Carrickfergus AM 37; 155–56
Aldoo singing school: Carrickfergus AM 37; 156
Aldridge, Mr: Templecorran AM 26; 126
Alexander III, King of Scotland: Island Magee AM 10; 62
Alexander III, King of Scotland: Kilbride AM 29; 149
Alexander III, King of Scotland: Templecorran AM 26; 114

Alexander III, King of Scotland: Templepatrick AM 35; 130

Alexander III, King of Scotland: Umgall AM 35; 160

Alexander VII, Pope: Ballynure AM 32; 57

Alexander, Alexander: Coleraine LY 33; 64, 142

Alexander, Alexander: Cumber LY 28; 58

Alexander, Alexander: Drumachose LY 9; 77, 104

Alexander, Alexander: Dunboe LY 11; 43

Alexander, Alexander: Faughanvale LY 36; 10, 39, 45

Alexander, Alexander: Killowen LY 33; 168

Alexander, Alexander: Tamlaght Finlagan LY 25; 79, 120

Alexander, Alick: Dunboe LY 11; 64

Alexander, Andrew: Drumachose LY 9; 66, 72–73

Alexander, Anne Jane: Carrickfergus AM 37; 119

Alexander, Archdeacon: Tamlaght O'Crilly LY 18; 123

Alexander, Bishop: Agivey LY 22; 44

Alexander, Bishop: Ahoghill AM 23; 2, 51

Alexander, Bishop: Raphoe DL 39; 126

Alexander, Councillor: Dungiven LY 15; 118

Alexander, David: Island Magee AM 10; 91

Alexander, E.: Muckno MN 40; 164

Alexander, Elizabeth: Faughanvale LY 36; 67

Alexander, family: Carnmoney AM 2; 102

Alexander, family: Carrickfergus AM 37; 93

Alexander, family: Derryaghy AM 8; 103

Alexander, family: Desertoghill LY 27; 5, 30

Alexander, Henry: Donagh DL 38; 31

Alexander, Henry: Dungiven LY 15; 50

Alexander, James: Blaris DN 12; 40

Alexander, James: Drumachose LY 9; 52, 120

Alexander, James: Faughanvale LY 36; 39

Alexander, James: Misc. DL 39; 186

Alexander, James: Tamlaght TE 20; 76, 103

Alexander, John: Annaclone DN 12; 18

Alexander, John: Antrim AM 29; 58

Alexander, John: Ballywalter AM 2; 27

Alexander, John: Blaris AM 8; 72

Alexander, John: Clondermot LY 34; 6, 20, 37, 78, 87, 103–04

Alexander, John: Cumber LY 28; 58

Alexander, John: Drumachose LY 9; 73, 118

Alexander, John: Dunboe LY 11; 59, 69, 75, 81

Alexander, John: Killea and Taughboyne DL 39; 84, 87

Alexander, John: Killowen LY 33; 162, 168

Alexander, John: Misc. DL 39; 191

Alexander, John: Tamlaght Finlagan LY 25; 79–80, 82, 93, 96, 114, 120, 125

Alexander, John: Tamlaght O'Crilly LY 18; 123

Alexander, John: Taughboyne DL 39; 150

Alexander, Kings of Scotland: Antrim AM 29; 37

Alexander, Kings of Scotland: Carrickfergus AM 37; 90

Alexander, L.J.: Clondermot LY 34; 78, 105, 114

Alexander, Lesley: Coleraine LY 33; 104, 142

Alexander, Lesley: Drumachose LY 9; 73

Alexander, Leslie: Cumber LY 28; 94 96

Alexander, Leslie: Faughanvale LY 36; 10

Alexander, Lesly: Dunboe LY 11; 59–60, 66, 70, 72–77, 79

Alexander, Miss: Ahoghill AM 23; 34

Alexander, Mr (Balteagh): Bovevagh LY 25; 1–2

Alexander, Mr (Carrick): Bovevagh LY 25; 28

Alexander, Mr (Kinnycally): Killea and Taughboyne DL 39; 87

Alexander, Mr (Knockbrack): Clondermot LY 34; 37, 104

Alexander, Mr (Trentagh): Raymoghy DL 39; 135

Alexander, Mr: Aghadowey LY 22; 5

Alexander, Mr: Banagher LY 30; 23

Alexander, Mr: Drumachose LY 9; 97

Alexander, Mr: Dungiven LY 15; 63

Alexander, Mrs Robert: Aghadowey LY 22; 22

Alexander, Nathan: Raymoghy DL 39; 135, 142–43

Alexander, Nathaniel: Ballintoy AM 24; 19

Alexander, Nathaniel: Misc. DL 39; 186, 191

Alexander, Nathaniel: Misc. DN 17; 117

Alexander, Rebecca: Drumachose LY 9; 72

Alexander, Rev.: Clonleigh DL 39; 1

Alexander, Rev.: Donegore AM 29; 126, 130

Alexander, Rev.: Errigal LY 27; 57

Alexander, Rev. Charles: Drumcree AH 1; 33, 36, 38, 40

Alexander, Rev. James: Blaris AM 8; 52

Alexander, Rev. James: Termoneeny LY 6; 125, 132

Alexander, Rev. John: Ballyrashane LY 22; 52, 55

Alexander, Rev. John: Kildollagh LY 22; 70

Alexander, Rev. Nathaniel (Bishop of Meath): Desertoghill LY 27; 10

Alexander, Rev. Nathaniel: Blaris AM 8; 52

Alexander, Rev. Nathaniel: Camlin AM 21; 62–63, 66, 69, 73, 75–76

Alexander, Rev. R.: Cumber LY 28; 5, 81

Alexander, Rev. Robert: Aghadowey LY 22; 5–6, 12–13, 18–19, 22, 30

Alexander, Rev. Robert: Ahoghill AM 23; 2, 12, 26, 28, 31, 34–35, 42, 45

Alexander, Rev. Robert: Coleraine LY 33; 104

Alexander, Rev. Robert: Faughanvale LY 36; 39

Alexander, Rev. Robert: Termoneeny LY 6; 132

Alexander, Rev. Thomas: Carncastle and Killyglen AM 10; 6

Alexander, Robert: Aghadowey LY 22; 6

Alexander, Samuel: Newry DN 3; 98

Alexander, Thomas: Dromore TE 5; 97

Alexander, Thomas: Faughanvale LY 36; 24, 34–36, 67

Alexander, Thomas: Island Magee AM 10; 90

Alexander, Thomas: Skerry AM 13; 119

Alexander, William: Carrickfergus AM 37; 113

Alexander, William: Dunaghy AM 13; 24

Alexander, William: Newtown Crommelin AM 13; 84

Alexander's bridge: Aghanloo LY 11; 19

Alexander's mill (Drummanan): Killea and Taughboyne DL 39; 87

Alexander's mill (Kinnycally): Killea and Taughboyne DL 39; 87

Alexandria (Egypt): Kilbroney DN 3; 34

Alfnabracky (see Ardnabrocky): Clondermot LY 34; 59

Algeo, Capt. (Armagh): Loughgilly AH 1; 85

Algeo, Mr (Hollymount): Manorhamilton Union LM 40; 50

Alixander, family: Aghanloo LY 11; 29

Alkatten bridge: Banagher LY 30; 5

Alkatten glen: Banagher LY 30; 2, 27, 108–09

Alkatten water: Banagher LY 30; 25, 29, 59, 108, 110

Alkatten wood: Banagher LY 30; 71, 73–74

All Saints ph: Convoy DL 39; 18

All Saints ph: Lough Swilly DL 38; 144

All Saints ph: Misc. DL 39; 183–91, 193–95

All Saints ph: Raymoghy DL 39; 132–33, 140

All Saints schools: Misc. DL 39; 194

Alla bog: Cumber LY 28; 18

Alla Glebe House: Cumber LY 28; 1, 4, 7, 9, 86, 88

Alla Lower bog: Cumber LY 28; 23

Alla Lower school: Cumber LY 28; 2, 11, 14, 16, 73–74, 76–77, 84

Alla Lower td: Cumber LY 28; 9, 66–67, 83, 109, 115, 121, 125

Alla Lower wood: Cumber LY 28; 115

Alla Upper bog: Cumber LY 28; 23

Alla Upper lime quarries: Cumber LY 28; 121

Alla Upper school: Cumber LY 28; 74, 76

Alla Upper td: Cumber LY 28; 1, 66–67, 109, 115–16, 121, 125

Allabuin lough: Templecarn DL 39; 157

Allan lough: Templecarn DL 39; 157

Allan, family: Island Magee AM 10; 70

Allan, family: Lambeg AM 8; 135

Allan, family: Templecorran AM 26; 117, 119

Allan, Hugh: Misc. DN 17; 117

Allder, Rev.: Saul, DN 17; 113

Allen and Company, Messrs: Donacavey TE 5; 75

Allen lough: Manorhamilton Union LM 40; 51, 54

Allen, Alexander: Inishargy DN 7; 85

Allen, Archie: Templecorran AM 26; 132

Allen, Bishop: Ballynascreen LY 31; 33

Allen, Dr: Derrykeighan AM 16; 78, 80

Allen, Dr: Tullynakill DN 7; 122

Allen, family: Aghalee AM 21; 31

Allen, family: Ballinderry AM 21; 51

Allen, family: Kilroot AM 26; 74–75

Allen, family: Rashee AM 32; 138

Allen, family: Templecorran AM 26; 117, 119

Allen, George: Carrickfergus AM 37; 188–89

Allen, George: Drumachose LY 9; 134

Allen, Isaac: Garvaghy DN 12; 82

Allen, J.: Comber DN 7; 34

Allen, James: Dunaghy AM 13; 17

Allen, John: Drummaul AM 19; 91

Allen, John: Dunboe LY 11; 56–57, 71

Allen, John: Kilcronaghan LY 31; 74

Allen, John: Rashee AM 32; 136–37

Allen, Miss: Doagh AM 29; 91

Allen, Mr: Ballywalter DN 7; 16

Allen, Mr: Derrykeighan AM 16; 95

Allen, Mr: Kilwaughter AM 10; 112

Allen, O.: Kilmegan DN 3; 57–58, 60

Allen, Patrick: Kilbride AM 29; 150

Allen, Rev.: Garvaghy DN 12; 80

Allen, Rev. Robert: Enniskeen CN 40; 30

Allen, Samuel: Derrykeighan AM 16; 84, 92

Allen, Samuel: Kilwaughter AM 10; 112

Allen, Thomas: Clondermot LY 34; 93

Allen, William: Ballywillin LY 33; 50

Allen, William: Dunboe LY 11; 60

Allen, William: Maghera LY 18; 50

Allenbrook bleach mill: Kilwaughter AM 10; 112

Allensbrook (see Allenbrook)

Alley, William: Doagh AM 29; 97

Allfrackyn (see Altfrackyn): Templecorran AM 26; 82

Allice, family: Newry DN 3; 106

Allison: Magilligan LY 11; 130

Allison Sessagh td: Donaghmore DL 39; 35

Allison, family: Templepatrick AM 35; 118

Allison, James: Donegore AM 29; 130

Allison, James: Drumachose LY 9; 118

Allison, James: Muckamore AM 35; 79

Allison, Rev. James: Cumber LY 28; 33, 57, 75–76, 79–80

Allison, William: Magilligan LY 11; 85

Allison's bay: Lough Swilly DL 38; 102–03

Allister, John: Blaris DN 12; 50

Allshane td: Donaghedy TE 5; 91

Allwood, Thomas: Coleraine LY 33; 72

Almanza (Portugal): Kilbroney DN 3; 32

Alps Mountains: Donegal DL 39; 53

Alt lough: Kilmacrenan DL 38; 52

Alt Lower td: Urney DL 39; 181

Alt Mover (see Altnover): Bovevagh LY 25; 58

Alt Upper giant's grave: Urney DL 39; 180–81

Alt Upper meeting house: Urney DL 39; 176
Alt Upper school [I]: Urney DL 39; 182
Alt Upper school [II]: Urney DL 39; 182
Alt Upper td: Donaghmore DL 39; 33
Alt Upper td: Urney DL 39; 181
Altabrock quarry: Aghalurcher FH 4; 7
Altacladdy (see Altaclady)
Altaclady meeting house: Ardstraw TE 5; 3, 7, 11
Altaeasga (see Altihaskey): Misc. LY 31; 143
Altaeglish (see Altnaheglish): Banagher LY 30; 108
Altafort House: Dromore DN 12; 72
Altaghaderry td: Misc. DL 39; 186, 192, 196
Altaghaney (see Altaghoney): Cumber LY 28; 109
Altaghish td: Killeeshil TE 20; 64
Altaghoney (Altahoney) td: Cumber LY 28; 7, 29,
   66–67, 109–10, 116, 121, 125
Altaghoney graveyard: Cumber LY 28; 31–32
Altaghoney quarry: Cumber LY 28; 121
Altaghoney standing stones: Cumber LY 28; 30
Altaghoney td: Banagher LY 30; 108
Altaghony (see Altaghoney): Cumber LY 28; 66
Altagoaghan mountain: Aghalurcher FH 4; 2–3, 5
Altagoaghan school: Aghalurcher FH 4; 11
Altagoaghan td: Aghalurcher FH 4; 3, 14
Altagore Castle: Culfeightrin AM 24; 40–41
Altagore fort: Culfeightrin AM 24; 46
Altagore td: Culfeightrin AM 24; 40–41
Altahalla hill: Clonmany DL 38; 12–13
Altahalla td: Clonmany DL 38; 12, 18, 20
Altaheglish (see Altnaheglish)
Altahullan td: Banagher LY 30; 24
Altakeeragh river: Dunaghy AM 13; 10, 27
Altakeeragh river: Dundermot AM 13; 29–30
Altakeeragh river: Killagan AM 23; 80–83
Altakeeragh river: Loughguile AM 13; 59, 61
Altalevelly (see Altilevelly): Raloo AM 32; 120
Altamoscan (see Altamoskan): Errigal Keerogue TE
   20; 50
Altamoskan (Altamuskan) td: Errigal Keerogue TE
   20; 50, 56
Altamoskan altar: Errigal Keerogue TE 20; 56
Altamoskan forts: Errigal Keerogue TE 20; 50
Altamullan school: Termonamongan TE 5; 144
Altamullan td: Termonamongan TE 5; 144
Altanarvey (see Altanaveragh)
Altanaveragh bog: Clogher TE 5; 26
Altanaveragh td: Clogher TE 5; 33, 37, 44
Altanure (see Altinure): Banagher LY 30; 5
Altaponer td: Aghalurcher FH 4; 14
Altar Green locality: Ahoghill AM 23; 25
Altar stones: Comber DN 7; 44
Altashane td: Donagh DL 38; 31
Altaskin Glebe td: Taughboyne DL 39; 148, 151
Altaturk school: Loughgall AH 1; 81
Altaturk td: Loughgall AH 1; 82

Altaughaderry (see Altaghaderry): Misc. DL 39; 192
Altaveedan mountain: Aghalurcher FH 4; 2–3
Altaveedan mountain: Aghalurcher TE 5; 1
Altaveedan td: Loughguile AM 13; 74
Altawark (Altnawark) td: Aghalurcher FH 4; 3, 11,
   14
Altawark school: Aghalurcher FH 4; 11
Altayesk (see Altihaskey): Ballynascreen LY 31; 12
Altayesky (see Altihaskey): Ballynascreen LY 31; 6
Altbeag (see Altbeagh): Laragh CN 40; 40
Altbeagh Cottage: Laragh CN 40; 42–43, 45
Altbeagh td: Laragh CN 40; 40, 43
Altcattan (see Alkatten): Banagher LY 30; 108
Altclofin (see Altcloghfin): Errigal Keerogue TE 20;
   56
Altcloghfin (Altclogfin) td: Errigal Keerogue TE 20;
   49–50, 56
Altcloghfin corn mill: Errigal Keerogue TE 20; 50
Altduff bogs: Errigal LY 27; 54
Altduff td: Errigal LY 27; 70, 79, 84, 89
Altertate td: Clones FH 4; 26
Altfrackyn glen: Glynn AM 26; 29–30
Altfrackyn glen: Templecorran AM 26; 82, 88, 94,
   107, 115
Altheayaran locality: Bovevagh LY 25; 35
Althemoover (see Altnover): Bovevagh LY 25; 41
Althenamarlagh river: Dungiven LY 15; 92
Altibrian hill: Dunboe LY 11; 43
Altibrian murder hole: Dunboe LY 11; 76
Altibrian td: Dunboe LY 11; 43, 81
Altihalla (see Altahalla): Clonmany DL 38; 13
Altihallan (see Altahalla): Clonmany DL 38; 12
Altihaskey locality: Ballynascreen LY 31; 12, 23
Altihaskey locality: Misc. LY 31; 143
Altihaskey water: Ballynascreen LY 31; 6
Altihaskey Water bridge: Ballynascreen LY 31; 6
Altikeeragh fort: Dunboe LY 11; 49, 74
Altikeeragh mountain: Dunboe LY 11; 59–60, 74
Altikeeragh school: Dunboe LY 11; 56, 70
Altikeeragh Sunday school: Dunboe LY 11; 57
Altikeeragh td: Dunboe LY 11; 79
Altikeeraght (see Altikeeragh): Dunboe LY 11; 57,
   74
Altikeragh (see Altikeeragh): Dunboe LY 11; 59, 70
Altilevelly meeting house: Raloo AM 32; 91, 94–95,
   97–98, 121, 130
Altilevelly school: Raloo AM 32; 121, 130
Altilevelly td: Raloo AM 32; 80, 90, 108, 112,
   116–17, 122, 129, 132
Altilevelly threshing machine: Raloo AM 32; 120
Altilo (see Altilow): Killymard DL 39; 107
Altilow hamlet: Killymard DL 39; 107
Altilow quarries: Killymard DL 39; 98, 106
Altilow td: Killymard DL 39; 101
Altineerin hill: Conwal DL 39; 24

Altinure bog: Banagher LY 30; 77
Altinure bridge: Banagher LY 30; 5
Altinure chapel: Banagher LY 30; 27, 29
Altinure graveyard: Banagher LY 30; 39, 48, 55
Altinure Lower quarry: Banagher LY 30; 126
Altinure Lower td: Banagher LY 30; 35, 60–61, 72,
    116, 121, 126
Altinure td: Banagher LY 30; 22–23, 48, 62, 102,
    108–09, 113, 131
Altinure Upper fort: Banagher LY 30; 48, 77, 79
Altinure Upper quarry: Banagher LY 30; 126
Altinure Upper school: Banagher LY 30; 33, 111
Altinure Upper td: Banagher LY 30; 29, 33, 35, 48,
    60–62, 72, 116–17, 121, 126, 129
Altinure Upper wood: Banagher LY 30; 121
Altito (see Altilow): Killymard DL 39; 101
Altivaddy locality: Carrickfergus AM 37; 93
Altkaltan (see Alkatten): Banagher LY 30; 2
Altlaghan hill: Kilteevoge DL 39; 111
Altlaghan school: Kilteevoge DL 39; 114
Altlaghan td: Kilteevoge DL 39; 113
Altmore hill: Pomeroy TE 20; 70, 72
Altmore td: Pomeroy TE 20; 70
Altnacarney td: Clogher TE 5; 35
Altnagelvin church: Clondermot LY 34; 4–5, 10, 16,
    22–23, 25, 32, 40, 89, 92, 99, 101–02
Altnagelvin corn mill: Clondermot LY 34; 21, 30,
    34, 104, 129
Altnagelvin dispensary: Clondermot LY 34; 5,
    13–14, 17, 20, 85, 91–92, 94, 96, 100–02
Altnagelvin lough: Clondermot LY 34; 113
Altnagelvin meeting house: Clondermot LY 34; 5,
    9–11, 22, 27–28, 77, 83, 92–93, 98, 103
Altnagelvin old meeting house: Clondermot LY 34;
    5, 9, 19–20, 23, 83, 101, 103
Altnagelvin plantation: Clondermot LY 34; 121
Altnagelvin poor shop: Clondermot LY 34; 9–10,
    16, 20, 25, 27–28, 41–42, 93, 97–98, 100, 102–04
Altnagelvin school: Clondermot LY 34; 16, 42, 86,
    89, 91, 94
Altnagelvin Sunday school: Clondermot LY 34;
    92–93
Altnagelvin td: Banagher LY 30; 102
Altnagelvin td: Clondermot LY 34; 5, 23, 30, 37,
    56–57, 60, 108, 112–13, 121, 129
Altnagelvin td: Cumber LY 28; 67, 71
Altnagelvin td: Faughanvale LY 36; 60
Altnagoghan (see Altagoaghan): Aghalurcher FH 4;
    2
Altnagore (Atnagore) td: Errigal Keerogue TE 20;
    48, 50, 56
Altnaheglish enclosure: Banagher LY 30; 46, 56
Altnaheglish glen: Banagher LY 30; 38, 113
Altnaheglish glen: Dungiven LY 15; 21
Altnaheglish hill: Banagher LY 30; 108, 110

Altnaheglish stream: Banagher LY 30; 46
Altnahuncheon td: Loughguile AM 13; 76
Altnakenny td: Clogher TE 5; 53
Altnamallaght stream: Dungiven LY 15; 51, 63–64
Altnamalough (see Altnamallaght)
Altnamuckan meeting house: Newtownhamilton AH
    1; 100
Altnamuckan school: Newtownhamilton AH 1; 100
Altnamullaghbwee mountain: Aghalurcher FH 4; 2
Altnamuscan (see Altamoskan): Errigal Keerogue
    TE 20; 56
Altnapaste mountain: Kilteevoge DL 39; 111
Altnapaste school: Kilteevoge DL 39; 113
Altnarichard td: Loughguile AM 13; 76
Altnariver td: Clogher TE 5; 53
Altnaveagh td: Clogher TE 5; 35, 53
Altnaveigh td: Newry DN 3; 61
Altnawask (see Altawark): Aghalurcher FH 4; 3
Altnover glen: Bovevagh LY 25; 1–2, 10, 23, 41–42
Altnover glen: Kilrea LY 27; 110, 126
Altnover quarry: Banagher LY 30; 3
Altnover stream: Bovevagh LY 25; 2, 4, 22, 41
Altnover water mill: Bovevagh LY 25; 58
Altoneill hill: Misc. LY 31; 116
Altoneill td: Misc. LY 31; 114
Altrest td: Donaghedy TE 5; 91
Alts heights: Banagher LY 30; 108, 110
America: Aghadowey LY 22; 35
America: Aghagallon AM 21; 19
America: Aghaloo TE 20; 5
America: Aghanloo LY 11; 32
America: Ahoghill AM 23; 17
America: Antrim AM 29; 29, 48
America: Ballee DN 17; 18
America: Ballintoy AM 24; 23
America: Ballyaghran LY 33; 14
America: Ballybay MN 40; 82
America: Ballycor AM 32; 7
America: Ballynascreen LY 31; 13, 21
America: Ballynure AM 32; 37
America: Ballyrashane LY 22; 53, 65
America: Ballyscullion LY 6; 56, 63, 77
America: Banagher LY 30; 35, 61, 71
America: Blaris AM 8; 47, 77
America: Bovevagh LY 25; 27, 29, 48, 59
America: Carrickfergus AM 37; 11, 139, 181
America: Clondavaddog DL 38; 11
America: Clondermot LY 34; 16, 29
America: Clonmany DL 38; 17
America: Coleraine LY 33; 99, 132
America: Cranfield AM 19; 32
America: Cumber LY 28; 27, 50, 80
America: Currin MN 40; 97
America: Desertegney DL 38; 27
America: Desertlyn LY 31; 47

America: Desertmartin LY 31; 62
America: Donacavey TE 5; 66, 72
America: Donegal DL 39; 46–47, 50
America: Dromore TE 5; 103
America: Drumglass TE 20; 42
America: Drumgoon CN 40; 9
America: Drummaul AM 19; 61–62
America: Drung CN 40; 22
America: Dungiven LY 15; 74–75
America: Errigal LY 27; 47–48, 57, 65
America: Faughanvale LY 36; 44
America: Glenavy AM 21; 79
America: Glenwhirry AM 32; 78
America: Glynn AM 26; 29
America: Inishkeel DL 39; 71, 73
America: Island Magee AM 10; 38, 90
America: Kilbroney DN 3; 30, 34
America: Kilcronaghan LY 31; 73
America: Kildollagh LY 22; 71, 75
America: Killagan AM 23; 85
America: Killea and Taughboyne DL 39; 86
America: Killeeshil TE 20; 63
America: Killowen LY 33; 165, 171
America: Killygarvan DL 38; 43
America: Killymard DL 39; 98
America: Kilmacteige SO 40; 192
America: Kilrea LY 27; 118
America: Lissan LY 31; 94, 100
America: Macosquin LY 22; 122
America: Magheragall AM 21; 108–09
America: Magheramesk AM 21; 120, 130
America: Manorhamilton Union LM 40; 53
America: Mevagh DL 38; 60
America: Misc. DL 39; 187
America: Misc. LY 31; 121
America: Newry DN 3; 109
America: Pomeroy TE 20; 71
America: Raloo AM 32; 106
America: Ramoan AM 24; 99, 120
America: Rasharkin AM 23; 133
America: Rathlin Island AM 24; 133
America: Skirts of Urney and Ardstraw TE 5; 141
America: Tamlaght Finlagan LY 25; 69, 112
America: Templecarn DL 39; 160
America: Termonamongan TE 5; 145
America: Tullyaughnish DL 38; 87, 93, 95
America: Tullyniskan TE 20; 140
America: Tynan AH 1; 130
America: Urney DL 39; 177
America, British: Ballybay MN 40; 82
America, British: Ballynure AM 32; 51
America, British: Banagher LY 30; 8
America, British: Carnmoney AM 2; 63
America, British: Cleenish FH 14; 23
America, British: Duneane AM 19; 104

America, British: Dunluce AM 16; 112
America, British: Glynn AM 26; 29
America, British: Raloo AM 32; 85, 106
America, British: Tamlaght Finlagan LY 25; 107
America, British: Templecarn FH 14; 120
America, British: Templecorran AM 26; 87
America, North: Ballyaghran LY 33; 18
America, North: Ballyscullion AM 19; 7
America, North: Blaris DN 12; 30
America, North: Carmavy AM 35; 4
America, North: Clondermot LY 34; 61
America, North: Coleraine LY 33; 86–87
America, North: Desertoghill LY 27; 12
America, North: Doagh AM 29; 78
America, North: Drummully FH 4; 37
America, North: Dungiven LY 15; 22–23
America, North: Warrenpoint DN 3; 119–20
America, United States: Aghalurcher FH 4; 12
America, United States: Aghanloo LY 11; 11
America, United States: Armoy AM 24; 6
America, United States: Artrea LY 6; 18
America, United States: Ballintoy AM 24; 17
America, United States: Ballybay MN 40; 82
America, United States: Ballycor AM 32; 7
America, United States: Ballynure AM 32; 37, 51
America, United States: Ballyrashane LY 22; 53
America, United States: Ballywillin LY 33; 37
America, United States: Banagher LY 30; 9
America, United States: Belleek FH 14; 5
America, United States: Billy AM 16; 48
America, United States: Carnmoney AM 2; 63
America, United States: Carrickfergus AM 37; 104
America, United States: Cleenish FH 14; 23
America, United States: Coleraine LY 33; 74
America, United States: Culfeightrin AM 24; 48
America, United States: Derrykeighan AM 16; 86
America, United States: Derryvullan FH 14; 35, 43
America, United States: Devenish FH 14; 49
America, United States: Doagh AM 29; 78
America, United States: Donegore AM 29; 114
America, United States: Down DN 17; 49
America, United States: Drumachose LY 9; 87, 105
America, United States: Drumkeeran FH 14; 66
America, United States: Drumlumman CN 40; 16
America, United States: Drummaul AM 19; 62
America, United States: Drummully FH 4; 37
America, United States: Drumtullagh AM 16; 99
America, United States: Dunboe LY 11; 54
America, United States: Duneane AM 19; 104
America, United States: Dungiven LY 15; 48, 104
America, United States: Dunluce AM 16; 112
America, United States: Dunsfort DN 17; 69
America, United States: Faughanvale LY 36; 31
America, United States: Galloon FH 4; 93
America, United States: Glynn AM 26; 47

America, United States: Inver AM 26; 52
America, United States: Kilbroney DN 3; 30, 34
America, United States: Killyleagh DN 17; 85
America, United States: Kilraghts AM 16; 129
America, United States: Kilrea LY 27; 118
America, United States: Kilwaughter AM 10; 111
America, United States: Kinawley FH 4; 109, 121
America, United States: Kirkinriola AM 23; 107
America, United States: Maghera LY 18; 19–22, 55
America, United States: Magheracross FH 14; 99
America, United States: Magheraculmoney FH 14; 108
America, United States: Magherafelt LY 6; 101
America, United States: Magilligan LY 11; 115, 140
America, United States: Raloo AM 32; 85, 106
America, United States: Skerry AM 13; 114
America, United States: Tamlaght Finlagan LY 25; 92
America, United States: Tamlaght O'Crilly LY 18; 136–37
America, United States: Templecarn FH 14; 120
America, United States: Templecorran AM 26; 87
America, United States: Tickmacrevan AM 13; 131
America, United States: Tomregan FH 4; 130
America, United States: Trory FH 14; 129, 134
Amhaddi lough: Mevagh DL 38; 55
Amsterdam: Dunboe LY 11; 61
Amurey, Paul: Banagher LY 30; 39
Anacloy td: Hillsborough DN 12; 107
Anadale (Scotland): Glynn AM 26; 41
Anadorn (see Annadorn): Misc. DN 17; 117
Anagarvey (see Annagarvey)
Anagh (see Annagh): Misc. LY 31; 112
Anagh: Dungiven LY 15; 63
Anagh lough: Longfield TE 5; 127
Anagh td: Clogher TE 5; 44
Anaghabogy bog: Desertoghill LY 27; 4–5, 14–15
Anaghabogy bog: Kilrea LY 27; 120
Anaghabogy stream: Desertoghill LY 27; 4–5, 15
Anaghclea old wood: Tamlaght O'Crilly LY 18; 127
Anaghclea wood: Tamlaght O'Crilly LY 18; 87
Anagheena Island: Ballyscullion LY 6; 68
Anaghilla (Anahilla) td: Errigal Keerogue TE 20; 50, 56
Anaghilla forts: Errigal Keerogue TE 20; 50
Anaghilla quarry: Errigal Keerogue TE 20; 50
Anaghmore (see Annaghmore): Drummully FH 4; 39
Analaik day school: Clogher TE 5; 42
Analoist (see Annaloist): Seagoe AH 1; 105
Analoughan td: Ballymascanlan LH 40; 56
Anassin lough: Mevagh DL 38; 55
Anciany Lower td: Clonleigh DL 39; 12
Anciany Upper td: Clonleigh DL 39; 12
Anders, family: Kilmacteige SO 40; 190

Anderson and Greer, Messrs: Newry DN 3; 99, 104
Anderson, Alixander: Bovevagh LY 25; 60
Anderson, Anne: Shankill AH 1; 116
Anderson, Barbara: Maghera LY 18; 79
Anderson, Capt.: Down DN 17; 50
Anderson, Daniel: Ramoan AM 24; 120
Anderson, David: Macosquin LY 22; 122
Anderson, David: Maghera LY 18; 79
Anderson, David [I]: Ballyrashane LY 22; 58
Anderson, David [II]: Ballyrashane LY 22; 61
Anderson, Dr (Draperstown): Ballynascreen LY 31; 1
Anderson, Edward: Coleraine LY 33; 141
Anderson, family: Ballynure AM 32; 56
Anderson, family: Billy AM 16; 58, 68
Anderson, family: Carrickfergus AM 37; 93
Anderson, family: Derrykeighan AM 16; 89
Anderson, family: Drumbeg AM 8; 123
Anderson, family: Dunluce AM 16; 117
Anderson, family: Enniskillen FH 4; 58
Anderson, family: Kirkinriola AM 23; 124
Anderson, family: Macosquin LY 22; 84, 119
Anderson, family: Maghera LY 18; 13, 24, 47
Anderson, George: Carrickfergus AM 37; 185
Anderson, George: Maghera LY 18; 79
Anderson, Hugh: Ballyrashane LY 22; 50, 61
Anderson, Hugh: Billy AM 16; 56, 62–63
Anderson, Hugh: Coleraine LY 33; 127
Anderson, Isabella: Maghera LY 18; 79
Anderson, James (Jnr): Maghera LY 18; 53
Anderson, James (Snr): Maghera LY 18; 53–54, 56, 73
Anderson, James: Aghadowey LY 22; 37
Anderson, James: Balteagh LY 9; 33–34
Anderson, James: Bovevagh LY 25; 9–10, 18, 34
Anderson, James: Derrykeighan AM 16; 94
Anderson, James: Donacavey TE 5; 81
Anderson, James: Dungiven LY 15; 74, 90
Anderson, James: Dunluce AM 16; 118
Anderson, James: Faughanvale LY 36; 42, 45
Anderson, James: Maghera LY 18; 53
Anderson, James: Newry DN 3; 104
Anderson, James: Ramoan AM 24; 113
Anderson, James: Rasharkin AM 23; 139
Anderson, James: Skirts of Urney and Ardstraw TE 5; 139
Anderson, James: Termonamongan TE 5; 143–44
Anderson, James [I]: Carrickfergus AM 37; 33
Anderson, James [II]: Carrickfergus AM 37; 193
Anderson, Jane: Maghera LY 18; 79
Anderson, John: Ballynure AM 32; 55
Anderson, John: Ballyrashane LY 22; 60
Anderson, John: Blaris DN 12; 46, 50
Anderson, John: Carrickfergus AM 37; 171
Anderson, John: Lissan LY 31; 101

Anderson, John: Maghera LY 18; 53
Anderson, John: Magheragall AM 21; 102, 106, 109
Anderson, Joseph: Ballymoney AM 16; 15–16
Anderson, man named: Misc. LY 36; 112
Anderson, Margaret: Kilrea LY 27; 129
Anderson, Margaret Jane: Macosquin LY 22; 122
Anderson, Martha: Maghera LY 18; 79
Anderson, Mathew: Carrickfergus AM 37; 184, 187
Anderson, Matthew: Maghera LY 18; 79
Anderson, Messrs Drummond and Son: Blaris DN
    12; 43
Anderson, Mr (Galladuff): Moville DL 38; 70
Anderson, Mr: Blaris AM 8; 84
Anderson, Nathaniel: Maghera LY 18; 79
Anderson, R.J.: Saul DN 17; 112, 114
Anderson, Rev.: Antrim AM 29; 27
Anderson, Rev.: Kilbroney DN 3; 36
Anderson, Rev. James: Warrenpoint DN 3; 117
Anderson, Richard: Kilrea LY 27; 122
Anderson, Samuel: Carrickfergus AM 37; 193
Anderson, Samuel: Maghera LY 18; 53
Anderson, Sarah: Maghera LY 18; 79
Anderson, Thomas: Ballyscullion LY 6; 61
Anderson, Thomas: Carrickfergus AM 37; 193
Anderson, Thomas: Dromore TE 5; 97
Anderson, Thomas: Lough Swilly DL 38; 144
Anderson, Thomas: Tamlaght TE 20; 96
Anderson, Widow: Ballymoney AM 16; 17
Anderson, Widow: Maghera LY 18; 44
Anderson, William: Ballyrashane LY 22; 58
Anderson, William: Bovevagh LY 25; 14, 34
Anderson, William: Carrickfergus AM 37; 195
Anderson, William: Coleraine LY 33; 72
Anderson, William: Dunboe LY 11; 55, 69, 72
Anderson, William [I]: Maghera LY 18; 53–54, 78
Anderson, William [II]: Maghera LY 18; 79
Andrew, Mr: Holywood DN 7; 83
Andrew, Widow: Ahoghill AM 23; 34
Andrews Grove: Derrykeighan AM 16; 94
Andrews, family: Ballintoy AM 24; 20
Andrews, Francis: Newry DN 3; 98
Andrews, J.: Dundonald DN 7; 65
Andrews, J.: Newtownards DN 7; 109
Andrews, James (Dublin): Misc. DN 17; 122
Andrews, John: Ahoghill AM 23; 22, 42
Andrews, John: Comber DN 7; 33, 35, 37–41, 44
Andrews, John: Drumachose LY 9; 53
Andrews, Marcus: Killowen LY 33; 170
Andrews, Matthew: Drumachose LY 9; 116, 121
Andrews, Messrs James and Sons: Blaris AM 8; 70
Andrews, Michael: Kilroot AM 26; 78
Andrews, Mr: Kilmood DN 7; 95
Andrews, Robert: Tamlaght O'Crilly LY 18; 139,
    143
Andrews, W.F.: Clondermot LY 34; 83

Andrews, William: Ballyaghran LY 33; 28
Andrews, William: Coleraine LY 33; 94, 131
Andrumaghta district: Misc. SO 40; 199
Anearn lough: Devenish FH 14; 47
Anglesea (see Anglesey)
Anglesey, Earl of: Tamlaght Finlagan LY 25; 69
Anglesey, Marquis of: Carlingford LH 40; 57–60
Anglesey, Marquis of: Newry DN 3; 81, 107–08
Angola (see Annagola): Tynan AH 1; 132
Angus, James: Kirkinriola AM 23; 121
Anketell, Matthew: Donagh MN 40; 100
Anketell, Mrs (Snr): Donagh MN 40; 103
Anketell, Mrs: Donagh MN 40; 101
Anketell, Rodger: Tydavnet MN 40; 173
Anketell, Roger: Donagh MN 40; 103, 105
Anketell, Thomas: Donagh MN 40; 103, 105
Anketell, William: Donagh MN 40; 101, 103, 105
Anketell, William: Errigal Truagh MN 40; 122
Anketell's Grove: Donagh MN 40; 100
Ann's hill: Antrim AM 29; 29
Anna hill: Kilmore AH 1; 61
Anna's well (see Crockanna): Lissan LY 31; 90
Annaboe td: Kilmore AH 1; 57, 66, 68, 70–71
Annaclone chapel: Annaclone DN 12; 14
Annaclone church: Annaclone DN 12; 14, 17
Annaclone Glebe House: Annaclone DN 12; 17
Annaclone Glebe school: Annaclone DN 12; 18
Annaclone meeting house (P): Annaclone DN 12;
    14, 17
Annaclone meeting house (S): Annaclone DN 12;
    14, 17
Annaclone meeting house: Newry DN 3; 111
Annaclone ph: Aghaderg DN 12; 1, 8
Annaclone ph: Drumballyroney DN 3; 13–15
Annaclone ph: Garvaghy DN 12; 79
Annaclone ph: Newry DN 3; 82–83, 110
Annaclone ph: Seapatrick DN 12; 124
Annaclone rectory: Annaclone DN 12; 15
Annacloy bog: Inch DN 17; 76
Annacloy bridge: Inch DN 17; 76
Annacloy bridge: Kilmore DN 17; 89
Annacloy meeting house: Blaris DN 12; 35
Annacloy river: Down DN 17; 38
Annacloy river: Inch DN 17; 73
Annacloy river: Kilmore DN 17; 89, 91–93
Annacloy school: Inch DN 17; 74, 76
Annacloy smithy: Inch DN 17; 76
Annacloy td: Blaris DN 12; 35
Annacramph bog: Tyholland MN 40; 174
Annacroff bog: Killanny MN 40; 130
Annadorn bog: Loughinisland DN 17; 98
Annadorn cromlech: Loughinisland DN 17; 98
Annadorn flour mill: Loughinisland DN 17; 95, 98
Annadorn gravel pit: Loughinisland DN 17; 98
Annadorn school: Loughinisland DN 17; 95, 98

Annadorn smithy: Loughinisland DN 17; 98
Annadorn td: Loughinisland DN 17; 98
Annadorn village: Misc. DN 17; 117, 122, 128
Annagariff lough: Killyman AH 1; 55
Annagarriff lough: Tartaraghan AH 1; 117, 119–21
Annagarvey (Annagarvy) td: Clogher TE 5; 32, 36, 46, 49, 53
Annagarvey corn mill: Clogher TE 5; 46, 49
Annagh (see Cranagh): Cumber LY 28; 83
Annagh (see Enagh): Clondermot LY 34; 46
Annagh bog: Misc. LY 31; 112
Annagh chapel: Desertmartin LY 31; 54, 63
Annagh chapel: Misc. LY 31; 128
Annagh corn mill: Desertmartin LY 31; 55
Annagh demesne: Tomregan FH 4; 126
Annagh Demesne td: Clogher TE 5; 47–48
Annagh flax mill: Desertmartin LY 31; 55
Annagh flax mill: Misc. LY 31; 135
Annagh fort: Manorhamilton Union LM 40; 52
Annagh House: Aghaloo TE 20; 1
Annagh lough: Tomregan FH 4; 126–28
Annagh ph: Drummully FH 4; 34
Annagh ph: Drung CN 40; 19
Annagh ph: Galloon FH 4; 92
Annagh river: Drumgoon CN 40; 2, 8
Annagh river: Drung CN 40; 19, 21
Annagh river: Killdrumsherdan CN 40; 31–32, 34
Annagh td: Clogher TE 5; 34–35, 37, 53–54
Annagh td: Clonmany DL 38; 18, 20
Annagh td: Coleraine LY 33; 100
Annagh td: Desertmartin LY 31; 52, 57, 62
Annagh td: Drumcree AH 1; 41
Annagh td: Drumlumman CN 40; 17
Annagh td: Errigal Truagh MN 40; 120
Annagh td: Kilmacteige SO 40; 196
Annagh td: Lough Swilly DL 38; 128, 133, 136
Annagh td: Misc. LY 31; 142
Annagh wood: Tomregan FH 4; 127
Annagha (see Annagh): Killdrumsherdan CN 40; 31
Annaghaghey (see Annahaia): Aughnamullen MN 40; 75
Annaghane lough: Currin MN 40; 86
Annaghane td: Currin MN 40; 86, 91
Annaghanoon bog: Donaghcloney DN 12; 57
Annaghanoon td: Donaghcloney DN 12; 58
Annaghard lough: Drumgoon CN 40; 2
Annaghavoy (Anaghavogy) td: Tamlaght O'Crilly LY 18; 86
Annaghavoy bog: Tamlaght O'Crilly LY 18; 86, 129
Annaghavoy Island: Tamlaght O'Crilly LY 18; 86, 129
Annaghbann td: Donaghmore DN 3; 8
Annaghbo td: Donacavey TE 5; 76–77, 82
Annaghdroghal (Anadhrohall) td: Shankill DN 12; 138

Annaghdroghal bridge: Shankill DN 12; 139
Annaghdroghal hill: Shankill DN 12; 138
Annaghean (see Annahean): Killanny MN 40; 131
Annagher mill: Clonoe TE 20; 31
Annagher td: Clonoe TE 20; 29
Annaghhaghey (see Annahaia): Aughnamullen MN 40; 71
Annaghhullian td: Clones FH 4; 26
Annaghlee corn mills: Drumgoon CN 40; 7
Annaghlee hill: Drung CN 40; 20
Annaghlee House: Killdrumsherdan CN 40; 34
Annaghlee river: Drumgoon CN 40; 7
Annaghlee river: Drung CN 40; 24
Annaghlee river: Killdrumsherdan CN 40; 32
Annaghlin Point: Lough Swilly DL 38; 115
Annaghmakeonan td: Donaghcloney DN 12; 58
Annaghmarrow district: Misc. SO 40; 198
Annaghmore (Anaghmore) td: Magherafelt LY 6; 93, 95, 105, 112
Annaghmore bog: Duneane AM 19; 111
Annaghmore burial garden: Magherafelt LY 6; 93, 105
Annaghmore Castle: Magherafelt LY 6; 93, 107
Annaghmore druid's temple: Drummully FH 4; 40
Annaghmore glebe: Galloon FH 4; 96
Annaghmore Glebe td: Drummully FH 4; 34, 39
Annaghmore school: Drummully FH 4; 39
Annaghmore school: Loughgall AH 1; 81
Annaghmore td: Drummully FH 4; 35, 39–40
Annaghmore td: Duneane AM 19; 111, 124
Annaghmore td: Kilmacteige SO 40; 186
Annaghmore td: Loughgall AH 1; 79
Annaghmore td: Magherafelt LY 6; 105
Annaghmullen td: Drummully FH 4; 39
Annaghmurnin (Annaghmurneen) td: Donacavey TE 5; 76–77, 82, 84
Annaghneboe td: Donacavey TE 5; 85
Annaghoe House: Aghaloo TE 20; 1
Annaghone coal pits: Donaghenry TE 20; 38
Annaghraa td: Drummully FH 4; 39
Annaghreagh (see Annaveagh): Currin MN 40; 86
Annaghs (see Annagh): Clogher TE 5; 54
Annaghveyarig corn mill: Aughnamullen MN 40; 72
Annaghveyarig td: Aughnamullen MN 40; 75
Annaghybawn lough: Ematris MN 40; 112, 116
Annagola bridge: Tynan AH 1; 128
Annagola House: Tynan AH 1; 132
Annagrane (see Aghnagrane): Aghavea FH 4; 25
Annahagh td: Tydavnet MN 40; 169
Annahaia chapel: Aughnamullen MN 40; 71
Annahaia td: Aughnamullen MN 40; 75
Annahaid td: Killevy AH 1; 53
Annahavil river: Arboe LY 6; 1
Annahean bog: Killanny MN 40; 130
Annahean graveyard: Killanny MN 40; 132

Annahean tannery: Killanny MN 40; 131
Annahill House: Kilmore AH 1; 62, 65
Annahilt meeting house: Hillsborough DN 12; 87
Annahilt ph: Dromara DN 12; 62, 65
Annahilt ph: Dromore DN 12; 70, 73
Annahilt ph: Drumballyroney DN 3; 18
Annahilt ph: Drumbo DN 7; 54
Annahilt ph: Garvaghy DN 12; 81
Annahilt ph: Hillsborough DN 12; 88
Annahilt ph: Misc. DN 17; 121
Annahilt school: Hillsborough DN 12; 100
Annahon collieries: Ballyclog TE 20; 18
Annahorish (Anahorish) td: Artrea LY 6; 14
Annahorish national school: Artrea LY 6; 18
Annahorish school: Artrea LY 6; 18
Annahue (see Annahugh): Kilmore AH 1; 66
Annahugh (Anahugh) td: Drumcree AH 1; 37
Annahugh school: Kilmore AH 1; 58, 64, 66
Annahugh Sunday school: Kilmore AH 1; 64
Annahugh td: Ballymore AH 1; 16, 18
Annahugh td: Kilmore AH 1; 61, 65–66, 68, 70–71, 73
Annahunshigo (Annahinchigo) td: Drumballyroney DN 3; 10–11, 13–14
Annairgia lough: Killymard DL 39; 94
Annakeera (Annagouragh) td: Drumcree AH 1; 37–38
Annaloghan (see Annaloughan): Clogher TE 5; 35
Annaloghin (see Annaloughan): Clogher TE 5; 53
Annaloist td: Seagoe AH 1; 105–06
Annalong: Kilkeel DN 3; 47, 49–50
Annalong bridge: Kilkeel DN 3; 49
Annalong harbour: Kilkeel DN 3; 47, 50
Annalong river: Kilkeel DN 3; 46, 49
Annaloughan td: Clogher TE 5; 35, 45, 53
Annamarran bog: Killanny MN 40; 130
Annamoore td: Ballyscullion LY 6; 58
Annamullen (see Aughnamullen): Enniskeen CN 40; 29
Annandale, Earl of: Ballinderry AM 21; 51
Annaneese forts: Ballybay MN 40; 81
Annaneese hill: Ballybay MN 40; 78
Annaneese td: Ballybay MN 40; 84
Annaniese (see Annaneese): Ballybay MN 40; 84
Annarea (see Annareagh): Kilmore AH 1; 66
Annareagh td: Kilmore AH 1; 65–67, 71–72
Annas, priest: Dungiven LY 15; 36
Annasamory school: Loughgall AH 1; 81
Annatiugh (see Annahugh): Kilmore AH 1; 58
Annaveagh hill: Currin MN 40; 86
Annaveagh td: Currin MN 40; 88
Anne, Queen: Blaris AM 8; 7
Anne, Queen: Carnmoney AM 2; 72
Anne, Queen: Carrickfergus AM 37; 24
Anne, Queen: Culfeightrin AM 24; 53

Anne, Queen: Duneane AM 19; 109
Anne, Queen: Kilbride AM 29; 154
Anne, Queen: Kirkinriola AM 23; 90, 94, 117
Anne, Queen: Maghera LY 18; 42–44
Anne, Queen: Magherafelt LY 6; 89
Anne, Queen: Magheramesk AM 21; 126
Anne, Queen: Raloo AM 32; 122
Anne, Queen: Templepatrick AM 35; 145
Annesborough (see Dromara): Dromara DN 12; 68
Annesborough flax mill: Kilmegan DN 3; 58
Annesborough House: Kilmegan DN 3; 58
Annesley, A.: Clonoe TE 20; 29
Annesley, Catherine (see Beresford): Tamlaght Finlagan LY 25; 69
Annesley, Dean: Misc. DN 17; 118
Annesley, Earl: Comber DN 7; 37
Annesley, Earl: Dundonald DN 7; 65
Annesley, Earl: Kilcoo DN 3; 43–45
Annesley, Earl: Misc. DN 17; 116
Annesley, family (see also Valencia): Holywood DN 7; 73
Annesley, Francis: Island Magee AM 10; 77
Annesley, James: Down DN 17; 52
Annesley, Lord: Ballee DN 17; 22
Annesley, Lord: Clonoe TE 20; 29
Annesley, Lord: Comber DN 7; 39–41
Annesley, Lord: Drumballyroney DN 3; 12, 18
Annesley, Lord: Drumgath DN 3; 21
Annesley, Lord: Drumgooland DN 3; 23, 25
Annesley, Lord: Kilmegan DN 3; 58
Annesley, Lord: Newry DN 3; 110
Annesley, Mrs: Clogher TE 5; 41
Annesley, Rev.: Clogher TE 5; 40
Annesley, Rev. William: Down DN 17; 42–44
Annet, James: Newry DN 3; 100, 104
Annett, George: Derryaghy AM 8; 98
Anney (see Annagh): Clonmany DL 38; 18
Anney fort: Clogherny TE 20; 28
Annies bog: Currin MN 40; 87
Annies Castle: Ballymascanlan LH 40; 55
Annies hill: Currin MN 40; 86
Annies td: Ballymascanlan LH 40; 55
Annies td: Currin MN 40; 88
Annigh (see Annagh): Clonmany DL 38; 20
Anny (see Annagh): Lough Swilly DL 38; 128
Anny bridge: Killygarvan DL 38; 46
Anny graveyard: Aughnamullen MN 40; 73
Anny td: Aughnamullen MN 40; 69, 75
Anny td: Killygarvan DL 38; 46
Annyart fort: Muckno MN 40; 166
Annyart school: Muckno MN 40; 168
Annygoas lough: Aghabog MN 40; 62
Annyneese (see Annaneese): Ballybay MN 40; 81
Ansell, family: Carrickfergus AM 37; 93
Anstruther, Col.: Drummaul AM 19; 41

Anthony, Charles: Ballyscullion LY 6; 58
Anthrona ferry: Antrim AM 29; 5
Anticur (Anticor) td: Rasharkin AM 23; 139
Anticur corn mill: Rasharkin AM 23; 131
Anticur cove: Rasharkin AM 23; 137–39
Anticur fort: Rasharkin AM 23; 139
Antidoney school: Rasharkin AM 23; 141
Antigua (West Indies): Newry DN 3; 68
Antiville beetling works: Larne AM 10; 125
Antiville td: Larne AM 10; 125
Antoninus Pius, Emperor: Misc. DN 17; 130–31
Antrim bank: Antrim AM 29; 16
Antrim bank: Donegore AM 29; 130
Antrim barony: Camlin AM 21; 60
Antrim barracks: Antrim AM 29; 14
Antrim bay: Antrim AM 29; 1
Antrim bay: Drummaul AM 19; 36, 67
Antrim bay: Killead AM 35; 25
Antrim bay: Lough Neagh AM 21; 94
Antrim bay: Muckamore AM 35; 57, 74
Antrim bay: Tullyrusk AM 21; 135
Antrim boys classical school: Antrim AM 29; 42,
    45, 58
Antrim brewery: Antrim AM 29; 15–16, 38, 49
Antrim bridewell: Antrim AM 29; 9
Antrim bridge: Antrim AM 29; 2, 5, 7, 22
Antrim bridge: Muckamore AM 35; 58
Antrim Castle: Antrim AM 29; 3, 5–6, 10–12, 14,
    21, 23, 44, 49
Antrim Castle: Drummaul AM 19; 70–71
Antrim Castle: Muckamore AM 35; 55, 59–62, 75
Antrim Castle bridge: Muckamore AM 35; 62, 64
Antrim Castle mound: Antrim AM 29; 36
Antrim chapel (C): Antrim AM 29; 7, 9, 12, 38–39,
    41, 43–45, 48
Antrim chapel (C): Donegore AM 29; 112
Antrim chapel (C): Muckamore AM 35; 66
Antrim chapel (C): Shilvodan AM 19; 133
Antrim chapel (M): Antrim AM 29; 7, 9, 41, 44–45
Antrim chapel (PWM): Antrim AM 29; 7, 9, 27,
    44–45
Antrim chapel Sunday school: Antrim AM 29; 41
Antrim church: Antrim AM 29; 5, 7–8, 12, 22, 26,
    29, 33–35, 37–39, 43–45, 48–49, 51
Antrim church: Drummaul AM 19; 70–72
Antrim church: Island Magee AM 10; 20, 44, 78
Antrim church: Killead AM 35; 41
Antrim church: Muckamore AM 35; 64
Antrim church: Templepatrick AM 35; 115
Antrim coast: Ballintoy AM 24; 34
Antrim coast: Ballynure AM 32; 44
Antrim coast: Carrickfergus AM 37; 37, 45, 51, 55
Antrim coast: Culfeightrin AM 24; 84
Antrim coast: Glynn AM 26; 14–15, 17, 41
Antrim coast: Misc. LY 31; 113

Antrim coast: Moville DL 38; 70
Antrim coast: Raloo AM 32; 85, 93–94
Antrim coast: Ramoan AM 24; 93–94
Antrim coast: Rathlin Island AM 24; 131
Antrim coast: Templecorran AM 26; 96
Antrim corn mill: Antrim AM 29; 15, 47–48, 50
Antrim corn mills: Muckamore AM 35; 58
Antrim county: Ballymoney AM 16; 1
Antrim county: Ballyphilip DN 7; 13
Antrim county: Ballyscullion LY 6; 58, 73
Antrim county: Blaris AM 8; 3, 72
Antrim county: Blaris DN 12; 26, 33
Antrim county: Carrickfergus AM 37; 2, 4, 18, 62
Antrim county: Cumber LY 28; 18
Antrim county: Donacavey TE 5; 72
Antrim county: Drumachose LY 9; 128
Antrim county: Dungiven LY 15; 32, 66–67, 104
Antrim county: Enniskillen FH 4; 60, 80
Antrim county: Faughanvale LY 36; 33, 44–45
Antrim county: Galloon FH 4; 100
Antrim county: Magherafelt LY 6; 106
Antrim county: Magilligan LY 11; 119
Antrim county: Moira DN 12; 117
Antrim county: Termoneeny LY 6; 132
Antrim county: Urney DL 39; 177
Antrim county court house: Carrickfergus AM 37; 2,
    12, 14, 19–22, 30–31, 33, 38, 92, 142, 152, 164
Antrim county gaol: Antrim AM 29; 7
Antrim county gaol: Carrickfergus AM 37; 2, 4, 12,
    14, 19–22, 25, 65–66, 70, 80, 90, 92, 103–32,
    141, 144, 150, 159–60, 164, 171–72, 176,
    178–79, 190, 192–95
Antrim county gaol: Kilwaughter AM 10; 117
Antrim county gaol: Kirkinriola AM 23; 90
Antrim county gaol: Templecorran AM 26; 115
Antrim county old gaol: Carrickfergus AM 37;
    20–21, 31
Antrim court house: Antrim AM 29; 7, 9, 25
Antrim court house: Ballylinny AM 32; 30
Antrim day school [I]: Antrim AM 29; 46
Antrim day school [II]: Antrim AM 29; 46
Antrim Deer Park forts: Muckamore AM 35; 74
Antrim deerpark: Antrim AM 29; 18, 20
Antrim deerpark: Drummaul AM 19; 40, 52
Antrim deerpark: Muckamore AM 35; 54, 57, 59,
    61–62, 71–72, 75, 81, 83
Antrim dispensary: Antrim AM 29; 13, 18, 25,
    38–40, 43–44, 46–47, 51
Antrim dispensary: Muckamore AM 35; 66
Antrim Erasmus Smith female school: Antrim AM
    29; 7, 9, 18, 41, 45, 58
Antrim Erasmus Smith male school: Antrim AM 29;
    7, 9, 18, 41, 45, 58
Antrim female day school: Antrim AM 29; 42, 46
Antrim female school: Antrim AM 29; 46

Antrim fort: Antrim AM 29; 37
Antrim forts: Antrim AM 29; 43
Antrim Glens: Armoy AM 24; 1
Antrim Glens: Ballynure AM 32; 44
Antrim Glens: Carrickfergus AM 37; 80
Antrim Glens: Glynn AM 26; 17
Antrim Glens: Raloo AM 32; 94
Antrim Glens: Templecorran AM 26; 122
Antrim graveyard: Antrim AM 29; 37
Antrim graveyard: Antrim AM 29; 6–8, 35
Antrim infant school: Antrim AM 29; 18, 41, 46
Antrim iron mills: Templepatrick AM 35; 131
Antrim ironworks: Carnmoney AM 2; 72
Antrim ironworks: Nilteen AM 35; 97
Antrim ladies' boarding school: Antrim AM 29; 42
Antrim ladies' day school: Antrim AM 29; 42, 46, 59
Antrim Lower barony: Ahoghill AM 23; 1, 28
Antrim Lower barony: Ballyclug AM 23; 52
Antrim Lower barony: Connor AM 19; 16, 30
Antrim Lower barony: Dunaghy AM 13; 10
Antrim Lower barony: Racavan AM 13; 86, 90, 96
Antrim Lower barony: Skerry AM 13; 105
Antrim market house: Antrim AM 29; 6–7, 9, 17, 44, 47–48
Antrim meeting house (Q): Antrim AM 29; 7
Antrim meeting house (U): Antrim AM 29; 7–8, 38–39, 44–45
Antrim meeting house Sunday school: Antrim AM 29; 8, 41
Antrim Methodist Sunday school: Antrim AM 29; 41
Antrim mill–dam: Nilteen AM 35; 85
Antrim mills: Antrim AM 29; 2
Antrim mountains: Layd and Inispollan AM 13; 55
Antrim mountains: Loughguile AM 13; 60
Antrim mountains: Skerry AM 13; 108
Antrim mountains: Tickmacrevan AM 13; 125
Antrim national school: Antrim AM 29; 42, 45
Antrim new meeting house (P): Antrim AM 29; 7–8, 38–39, 41, 43–45, 49
Antrim old church: Antrim AM 29; 5–6
Antrim old meeting house (P): Antrim AM 29; 7–8, 24, 44–45
Antrim paper mill: Antrim AM 29; 15–16, 25, 27, 48, 50
Antrim paper mills: Muckamore AM 35; 58
Antrim ph: Carnmoney AM 2; 72
Antrim ph: Connor AM 19; 16
Antrim ph: Doagh AM 29; 87
Antrim ph: Donegore AM 29; 101, 105, 112, 115, 129
Antrim ph: Drummaul AM 19; 33, 46, 58, 82
Antrim ph: Killead AM 35; 20, 46
Antrim ph: Misc. AM 10; 129

Antrim ph: Muckamore AM 35; 54, 57–58, 63–64, 66, 74, 76
Antrim ph: Nilteen AM 35; 84, 87, 96, 101
Antrim ph: Shilvodan AM 19; 127, 131, 133
Antrim ph: Templepatrick AM 35; 131, 143, 145
Antrim pier: Antrim AM 29; 20
Antrim pier: Coleraine LY 33; 99
Antrim private school: Antrim AM 29; 42, 45–46, 58–59
Antrim road bridge: Doagh AM 29; 71, 92
Antrim road bridge: Kilbride AM 29; 139
Antrim round tower (see Steeple)
Antrim savings bank: Antrim AM 29; 16, 38, 43–44, 47
Antrim school [I]: Antrim AM 29; 58
Antrim school [II]: Antrim AM 29; 59
Antrim school [III]: Antrim AM 29; 59
Antrim school [IV]: Antrim AM 29; 59
Antrim school [V]: Antrim AM 29; 59
Antrim school [VI]: Antrim AM 29; 59
Antrim school [VII]: Antrim AM 29; 59
Antrim school [VIII]: Antrim AM 29; 59
Antrim sessions house: Antrim AM 29; 44, 47–48
Antrim spa: Antrim AM 29; 3–4, 49
Antrim Sunday schools: Antrim AM 29; 18
Antrim toll–gate: Antrim AM 29; 21
Antrim toll–gate: Nilteen AM 35; 90
Antrim town: Aghagallon AM 21; 1, 7–8, 10, 24
Antrim town: Aghalee AM 21; 27, 32, 34
Antrim town: Aghanloo LY 11; 38
Antrim town: Ahoghill AM 23; 28
Antrim town: Antrim AM 29; 1–9, 12–26, 29–30, 33, 35, 37–51
Antrim town: Ballinderry AM 21; 42, 47–48, 52, 58
Antrim town: Ballycor AM 32; 1
Antrim town: Ballylinny AM 32; 11, 14, 16, 30
Antrim town: Ballymartin AM 2; 1, 4, 6
Antrim town: Ballynure AM 32; 31–32, 34, 38–39, 45, 72
Antrim town: Ballyrobert AM 2; 20
Antrim town: Ballyscullion AM 19; 2–3, 5
Antrim town: Ballywalter AM 2; 29
Antrim town: Banagher LY 30; 60
Antrim town: Camlin AM 21; 62–63, 65, 67, 72
Antrim town: Carmavy AM 35; 2
Antrim town: Carnmoney AM 2; 39, 41, 46, 49–50, 54, 69, 76, 84–85, 98, 105
Antrim town: Carrickfergus AM 37; 58–59, 71, 100, 143, 168
Antrim town: Coleraine LY 33; 97, 99
Antrim town: Connor AM 19; 17, 20, 22, 30
Antrim town: Derryaghy AM 8; 101
Antrim town: Doagh AM 29; 60, 62, 64, 67, 70–73, 86, 88, 90, 96, 98

Antrim town: Donegore AM 29; 102, 106, 108, 110, 113, 115, 131–32, 134

Antrim town: Drummaul AM 19; 34, 45, 47, 50–52, 60, 63–64, 72, 85

Antrim town: Duneane AM 19; 109, 111, 118

Antrim town: Glenavy AM 21; 78, 81, 84

Antrim town: Kilbride AM 29; 135–39, 141, 148, 156

Antrim town: Killead AM 35; 11, 14–16, 23, 26, 42

Antrim town: Kilroot AM 26; 73

Antrim town: Kirkinriola AM 23; 108

Antrim town: Lough Neagh AM 21; 97

Antrim town: Maghera LY 18; 2, 8, 35

Antrim town: Magheragall AM 21; 102

Antrim town: Magheramesk AM 21; 118–19

Antrim town: Magilligan LY 11; 139

Antrim town: Mallusk AM 2; 107

Antrim town: Misc. DN 17; 119

Antrim town: Muckamore AM 35; 54–55, 58–65, 68, 70–71, 73, 75–77, 83

Antrim town: Nilteen AM 35; 84–91, 95, 97, 101–03

Antrim town: Raloo AM 32; 86, 88, 92, 96

Antrim town: Shilvodan AM 19; 127–31

Antrim town: Templepatrick AM 35; 105, 108, 111, 113–15, 117, 123–24, 126, 131, 137–40, 142, 146–47

Antrim town: Tullyrusk AM 21; 132, 134

Antrim town: Umgall AM 35; 156, 158, 160

Antrim town pump: Antrim AM 29; 17

Antrim Townparks td: Antrim AM 29; 43–44

Antrim tumulus: Antrim AM 29; 44

Antrim turnpike: Antrim AM 29; 13

Antrim turnpike: Ballylinny AM 32; 14

Antrim turnpike: Ballymartin AM 2; 4

Antrim turnpike: Carnmoney AM 2; 49

Antrim turnpike: Mallusk AM 2; 107

Antrim turnpike: Templepatrick AM 35; 113

Antrim Upper barony: Antrim AM 29; 3, 5, 14, 22

Antrim Upper barony: Ballycor AM 32; 3

Antrim Upper barony: Camlin AM 21; 63

Antrim Upper barony: Doagh AM 29; 60, 63, 67, 70–71, 86

Antrim Upper barony: Donegore AM 29; 101, 106, 109, 132

Antrim Upper barony: Kilbride AM 29; 135, 139, 156

Antrim Upper barony: Kilwaughter AM 10; 108

Antrim Upper barony: Muckamore AM 35; 59

Antrim Upper barony: Nilteen AM 35; 84

Antrim Upper barony: Templepatrick AM 35; 105

Antrim vicarage: Antrim AM 29; 23

Antrim water: Killead AM 35; 40–41

Antrim, Countess: Tickmacrevan AM 13; 123–124, 130–31

Antrim, Earl Alexander: Tickmacrevan AM 13; 129

Antrim, Earl of: Ballymoney AM 16; 7

Antrim, Earl of: Culfeightrin AM 24; 59

Antrim, Earls of: Dunluce AM 16; 105–06

Antrim, family: Ballintoy AM 24; 11

Antrim, family: Ballyphilip DN 7; 13

Antrim, family: Ballywillin LY 33; 35

Antrim, family: Culfeightrin AM 24; 40, 48, 59–60, 62, 65–66, 69, 72–74, 81

Antrim, family: Dunaghy AM 13; 15, 28

Antrim, family: Dunluce AM 16; 110, 113, 115–16, 120–21

Antrim, family: Inver AM 26; 55

Antrim, family: Loughguile AM 13; 64

Antrim, family: Raloo AM 32; 86

Antrim, family: Ramoan AM 24; 88, 95, 98, 122, 125

Antrim, family: Rasharkin AM 23; 127

Antrim, family: Rathlin Island AM 24; 129

Antrim, family: Tickmacrevan AM 13; 123–24, 129, 132

Antrim, Lady: Ballymoney AM 16; 13

Antrim, Lady Marchioness Rose: Drummaul AM 19; 40–42, 53, 62, 64, 69–70

Antrim, Lady Marchioness Rose: Racavan AM 13; 88, 93

Antrim, Lord: Antrim AM 29; 48

Antrim, Lord: Drumachose LY 9; 95

Antrim, Lord: Dunaghy AM 13; 12

Antrim, Lord: Raloo AM 32; 116

Antrim, Lord: Rathlin Island AM 24; 134

Antrim, Marquis of: Drummaul AM 19; 40, 70, 82, 87

Antyduff td: Donaghmoyne MN 40; 106

Antynanum td: Racavan AM 13; 88

Antynanum td: Tickmacrevan AM 13; 125

Anvaran (see Awaughran): Kilmacteige SO 40; 195

Anveroo (Inveroo) river: Tamlaght O'Crilly LY 18; 83

Anvoran (see Awaughran): Kilmacteige SO 40; 193

Aodh, King of Dalriada: Carrickfergus AM 37; 11

Aodh, King of Dalriada: Island Magee AM 10; 66

Aodha, grandson of Cathbar: Donegal DL 39; 51

Aoi (Scotland): Bovevagh LY 25; 46

Apollo: Misc. LY 31; 138

Applebee (Abalteen) td: Connor AM 19; 26–27

Applebee school: Connor AM 19; 26–27

Apsely, Solomon: Carrickfergus AM 37; 79

Apsley, William: Carrickfergus AM 37; 186

Araboy (Arraboy) td: Ballintoy AM 24; 23–24

Araboy bog: Ballintoy AM 24; 12, 25

Araboy cave: Ballintoy AM 24; 25

Araboy druid's altar: Ballintoy AM 24; 25

Araboy lough: Ballintoy AM 24; 13

Araboy meeting house: Ballintoy AM 24; 15

Araboy pool: Ballintoy AM 24; 12
Araboy standing stones: Ballintoy AM 24; 25
Araboy wood: Ballintoy AM 24; 25
Araheeries locality: Lough Swilly DL 38; 106
Araheery (see also Fanad Point): Lough Swilly DL 38; 98
Araheery village: Lough Swilly DL 38; 99
Arbatt hill: Kilteevoge DL 39; 111
Arbatt school: Kilteevoge DL 39; 114
Arbatt td: Kilteevoge DL 39; 113
Arbo (see Arboe): Tamlaght TE 20; 102
Arboe: Ballinderry TE 20; 11
Arboe: Tamlaght TE 20; 91, 114
Arboe abbey: Artrea LY 6; 2
Arboe church: Arboe LY 6; 1
Arboe ph: Artrea TE 20; 6
Arboe ph: Ballinderry TE 20; 11
Arboe ph: Ballyclog TE 20; 15, 18
Arboe ph: Clonoe TE 20; 29
Arboe ph: Lissan LY 31; 90
Arboe ph: Tamlaght TE 20; 73, 82, 85, 102
Arbothnot, William: Rasharkin AM 23; 139
Arbuckle, J.: Clonleigh DL 39; 9
Arbuckle, James: Donaghadee DN 7; 46
Arbuthnot, James: Newry DN 3; 81
Arbuthnot, John: Maghera LY 18; 81
Arbuthnot, William: Ahoghill AM 23; 50
Archbold, family: Derryaghy AM 8; 103
Archbold, Rev. (Rathmullan): Bright DN 17; 36
Archdale manor: Misc. FH 4; 133
Archdale, Charles: Derryvullan FH 14; 34
Archdale, Edward: Derryvullan FH 14; 36
Archdale, Edward: Magheracross FH 14; 102
Archdale, Edward: Magheraculmoney FH 14; 108
Archdale, Edward: Misc. TE 5; 147
Archdale, Edward: Trory FH 14; 125–27, 130
Archdale, Gen.: Cleenish FH 14; 23, 28–30
Archdale, Gen.: Derryvullan FH 14; 33, 36
Archdale, Gen.: Devenish FH 14; 50, 55–56, 58–59
Archdale, Gen.: Dromore TE 5; 98–99
Archdale, Gen.: Drumkeeran FH 14; 67
Archdale, Gen.: Drumragh TE 5; 107
Archdale, Gen.: Inishmacsaint FH 14; 74, 79
Archdale, Gen.: Magheraculmoney FH 14; 103, 106, 108
Archdale, Gen.: Misc. TE 5; 147
Archdale, Gen.: Rossorry FH 14; 115
Archdale, Mervyn: Kilskeery TE 5; 114
Archdale, Mr: Magheraculmoney FH 14; 113
Archdale, Nicholas: Drumkeeran FH 14; 65
Archdall, Mervyn: Magilligan LY 11; 105
Archer, Henry: Hillsborough DN 12; 106
Archer, Isaac: Hillsborough DN 12; 105
Archer, James (Jnr): Hillsborough DN 12; 106
Archer, James: Hillsborough DN 12; 106

Archer, Jonathan: Hillsborough DN 12; 105
Archer, Josiah: Hillsborough DN 12; 106
Archer, Miss: Derryaghy AM 8; 116
Archer, Rev. Richard: Clonduff DN 3; 4
Archer, Tom: Ahoghill AM 23; 34
Archer, William: Hillsborough DN 12; 97, 103, 106
Archibald, David: Ballyrashane LY 22; 57
Archibald, John: Doagh AM 29; 89
Archibald, Rev. (Rathmullan): Down DN 17; 50
Archill bay: Rathlin Island AM 24; 131
Archill fort: Ardstraw TE 5; 12
Archill td: Ardstraw TE 5; 12
Archy's bushes: Carrickfergus AM 37; 176
Archy's bushes: Templecorran AM 26; 115
Ard Magilligan locality: Magilligan LY 11; 89
Arda td: Derryvullan FH 14; 45
Ardada school: Laragh CN 40; 43
Ardaganny td: Leck DL 39; 118
Ardagh altar: Ramoan AM 24; 114
Ardagh diocese: Drumlumman CN 40; 18
Ardagh district: Lough Swilly DL 38; 133, 135
Ardagh hamlet: Ramoan AM 24; 114
Ardagh Irish td: Misc. DL 39; 195
Ardagh Scotch td: Misc. DL 39; 195
Ardagh td: Ballinderry TE 20; 13
Ardagh td: Clonmany DL 38; 18, 20
Ardagh td: Culfeightrin AM 24; 65
Ardagh td: Ramoan AM 24; 115
Ardagh vineyard: Ramoan AM 24; 114
Ardagh waterfall: Ramoan AM 24; 88
Ardaghy td: Carlingford LH 40; 57
Ardahee td: Leck DL 39; 115, 117–18
Ardanarive (Ardenaver) td: Banagher LY 30; 23–24
Ardanarriv (see Ardinarive): Bovevagh LY 25; 59
Ardaobhin school: Donegal DL 39; 49
Ardara: Inishkeel DL 39; 72–73
Ardaragh (see Ardarragh): Newry DN 3; 110
Ardarragh school: Newry DN 3; 81
Ardarragh td: Newry DN 3; 61, 81, 110
Ardascanlan td: Lough Swilly DL 38; 136
Ardatinny td: Donacavey TE 5; 76–77, 81, 85
Ardaugh quarry: Taughboyne DL 39; 150
Ardaugh td: Killea and Taughboyne DL 39; 80
Ardaugh td: Taughboyne DL 39; 148, 151
Ardbane corn mills: Mevagh DL 38; 57
Ardbane hill: Skirts of Urney and Ardstraw TE 5; 136
Ardbane lough: Mevagh DL 38; 55
Ardbane td: Mevagh DL 38; 63
Ardbawn (see Ardbane): Mevagh DL 38; 55
Ardbo (see Ardboe): Drummaul AM 19; 70
Ardboe: Drummaul AM 19; 70–71
Ardboe church: Drummaul AM 19; 71
Ardboe monastery: Drummaul AM 19; 71
Ardboley td: Carrickfergus AM 37; 93, 171, 173

Ardbraccan House: Enniskeen CN 40; 29

Ardbrin flax mill: Annaclone DN 12; 14

Ardbrin mill [I]: Annaclone DN 12; 18

Ardbrin mill [II]: Annaclone DN 12; 18

Ardbrin td: Annaclone DN 12; 13–14, 16–17

Ardbuckle, John: Maghera LY 18; 61

Ardcame td: Donaghedy TE 5; 91

Ardchinnan (see Ardihannon): Billy AM 16; 77

Ardclare: Kilmacteige SO 40; 193

Ardclinis old church: Ardclinis AM 13; 7

Ardclinis ph: Ahoghill AM 23; 5

Ardclinis ph: Carnmoney AM 2; 34

Ardclinis ph: Dunaghy AM 13; 25

Ardclinis ph: Kirkinriola AM 23; 92

Ardclinis ph: Layd AM 13; 36, 43, 53

Ardclinis ph: Misc. AM 10; 129

Ardclinis ph: Skerry AM 13; 105

Ardclinis ph: Tickmacrevan AM 13; 122

Ardclinis td: Ardclinis AM 13; 4, 7

Ardcree td: Killoran and Kilvarnet SO 40; 183

Ardee: Drumcree AH 1; 39

Ardee: Enniskeen CN 40; 26

Ardee: Killanny MN 40; 131–32

Ardee: Magheracloone MN 40; 139

Ardee: M<Ardee: Magheross MN 40; 146, 152

Ardee barony: Killanny MN 40; 130

Ardee dispensary: Inniskeen MN 40; 127

Ardee td: Misc. DL 39; 185, 194

Ardes (see Ards): Kilbroney DN 3; 32

Ardess (Ardesh) td: Magheraculmoney FH 14; 103, 110

Ardess Glebe House: Magheraculmoney FH 14; 105

Ardess school: Magheraculmoney FH 14; 108

Ardess td: Donacavey TE 5; 76

Ardgaire locality: Clondermot LY 34; 60

Ardgart td: Magheracross FH 14; 102

Ardgarvan (Ardgarvin) td: Drumachose LY 9; 55, 86–87, 96, 132, 134

Ardgarvan school: Drumachose LY 9; 85, 123

Ardgarvan Sunday school: Drumachose LY 9; 85, 132

Ardgarven (see Ardgarvan)

Ardgascin district: Misc. SO 40; 198

Ardgee (see Argery): Clonleigh DL 39; 10

Ardgehan td: Misc. DN 17; 124

Ardglass: Ardglass DN 17; 1–5, 9, 11–14

Ardglass: Ballee DN 17; 21, 23

Ardglass: Ballyculter DN 17; 27–28

Ardglass: Blaris AM 8; 72, 76

Ardglass: Down DN 17; 49

Ardglass: Dunsfort DN 17; 68, 70

Ardglass: Killyleagh DN 17; 86

Ardglass: Misc. DN 17; 122, 128

Ardglass bay: Ardglass DN 17; 3

Ardglass Castle (see King's Castle): Ardglass DN 17; 1

Ardglass chapel: Ardglass DN 17; 3, 9, 122

Ardglass church: Ardglass DN 17; 3, 5, 9, 11, 13, 133

Ardglass coastguard station: Ardglass DN 17; 9

Ardglass dispensary: Ardglass DN 17; 4, 9–10

Ardglass Erasmus Smith school: Ardglass DN 17; 4, 7, 10

Ardglass grand pier: Ardglass DN 17; 3, 6–7, 9–10

Ardglass harbour: Ardglass DN 17; 1, 3, 6–7, 9–10, 12

Ardglass harbour: Dunsfort DN 17; 67

Ardglass infant school: Ardglass DN 17; 4, 7, 10

Ardglass lighthouse: Ardglass DN 17; 3, 6, 10

Ardglass lighthouse: Dunsfort DN 17; 67

Ardglass meeting house: Ardglass DN 17; 9–10

Ardglass national school: Ardglass DN 17; 4

Ardglass old castles: Ardglass DN 17; 7, 9, 12

Ardglass old lighthouse: Ardglass DN 17; 10

Ardglass old pier: Ardglass DN 17; 3, 6, 10

Ardglass ph: Ballee DN 17; 15

Ardglass ph: Dunsfort DN 17; 68, 70

Ardglass ph: Killyleagh DN 17; 86

Ardglass ph: Misc. DN 17; 122, 128, 133

Ardglass pier: Dunsfort DN 17; 67

Ardglass private school [I]: Ardglass DN 17; 4, 7

Ardglass private school [II]: Ardglass DN 17; 4, 7

Ardglass td: Ardglass DN 17; 1, 7

Ardglass, Earl of (see also Cromwell): Misc. DN 17; 119

Ardglass, Earl of: Down DN 17; 42

Ardglass, Viscount: Kilmegan DN 3; 59

Ardgonnell bridge: Tynan AH 1; 124, 128

Ardgonnell old castle: Tynan AH 1; 128

Ardgonnell td: Tynan AH 1; 124

Ardgre (see Argery): Clonleigh DL 39; 5

Ardground bleach green: Cumber LY 28; 80

Ardground giant's grave: Cumber LY 28; 52

Ardground quarry: Cumber LY 28; 104

Ardground tannery: Cumber LY 28; 35, 106–107

Ardground td: Cumber LY 28; 43, 46, 48, 51–53, 60–61, 94, 99, 104

Ardground wood: Cumber LY 28; 99

Ardhane (see Ardbane): Mevagh DL 38; 57

Ardholl (see Ardtole): Ardglass DN 17; 12

Ardiagh td: Magheross MN 40; 148

Ardicoan chapel: Layd and Inispollan AM 13; 55

Ardicoan td: Layd and Inispollan AM 13; 55

Ardihannon cove: Billy AM 16; 55–56, 59, 64

Ardihannon enclosure: Billy AM 16; 72

Ardihannon flax mill: Billy AM 16; 46

Ardihannon school: Billy AM 16; 77

Ardihannon standing stone: Billy AM 16; 58

Ardihannon td: Billy AM 16; 38, 46

Ardihannon tomb: Billy AM 16; 55
Ardina bridge: Dunboe LY 11; 62
Ardina flax mill: Dunboe LY 11; 46, 60
Ardina td: Dunboe LY 11; 81
Ardinarive (Ardinariff) td: Bovevagh LY 25; 4, 26,
  55, 59–61
Ardinarive corn mill: Bovevagh LY 25; 21, 57
Ardinarive fort: Bovevagh LY 25; 19
Ardinarive spring: Bovevagh LY 25; 2, 22
Ardinarrive (see Ardinarive): Bovevagh LY 25; 21
Ardinskine district: Misc. SO 40; 199
Ardiss, Charles: Carnmoney AM 2; 98–99
Ardiss, Sarah: Doagh AM 29; 77, 93
Arditinny td: Donacavey TE 5; 80
Ardkeen church: Ardkeen DN 7; 2
Ardkeen corn mill: Ardkeen DN 7; 2
Ardkeen Glebe House: Ardkeen DN 7; 2
Ardkeen manor: Misc. DN 17; 122
Ardkeen ph: Ballyhalbert DN 7; 6
Ardkeen ph: Ballyphilip DN 7; 10
Ardkeen ph: Castleboy DN 7; 26
Ardkeen ph: Misc. DN 17; 120
Ardkeen ph: Witter DN 7; 125
Ardkeen school: Ardkeen DN 7; 2
Ardkeen td: Ardkeen DN 7; 2
Ardkeen windmill: Ardkeen DN 7; 2
Ardkeene district: Misc. SO 40; 200
Ardkeragh td: Donaghmore DN 3; 8
Ardkill corn mill: Clondermot LY 34; 129
Ardkill House: Clondermot LY 34; 6, 20
Ardkill quarry: Clondermot LY 34; 129
Ardkill spade mill: Clondermot LY 34; 21, 30, 34
Ardkill spinning mill: Clondermot LY 34; 30, 34,
  105
Ardkill td: Clondermot LY 34; 38, 56–58, 62, 108,
  113, 121, 129
Ardlee district: Misc. SO 40; 198
Ardloane district: Misc. SO 40; 198
Ardlough corn mill: Clondermot LY 34; 129
Ardlough flax mill: Clondermot LY 34; 129
Ardlough td: Clondermot LY 34; 3, 18, 32, 38, 56,
  58, 77, 80, 108, 112–13, 121, 129
Ardlough td: Loughguile AM 13; 76
Ardlow, Joseph: Donaghcloney DN 12; 61
Ardlughran district: Misc. SO 40; 199
Ardmach (see Armagh): Dungiven LY 15; 33
Ardmaile district: Misc. SO 40; 200
Ardmalin district: Lough Swilly DL 38; 107–08, 111
Ardmalin tower: Lough Swilly DL 38; 108
Ardmeeghan district: Misc. SO 40; 200
Ardmeen td: Down DN 17; 52, 57
Ardmeenan (see Ardminan): Misc. DN 17; 127
Ardmic-Giollagan locality: Magilligan LY 11; 143
Ardmillan bridge: Killinchy DN 7; 90
Ardmillan corn mill: Ardkeen DN 7; 3

Ardmillan flax mill: Ardkeen DN 7; 3
Ardmillan ph: Misc. DN 17; 118
Ardmillan school: Ardkeen DN 7; 3
Ardmillan village: Ardkeen DN 7; 3
Ardmillan village: Misc. DN 17; 117
Ardmillan, Lord of: Ardkeen DN 7, 3
Ardminan (Ardmenan) td: Ballyphilip DN 7; 8
Ardminan td: Misc. DN 17; 125, 127
Ardmoney td: Aghavea FH 4; 23
Ardmore (Derryadd) church: Montiaghs AH 1;
  89–90, 92–93
Ardmore (Derryadd) Glebe House: Montiaghs AH
  1; 90, 92–93
Ardmore (Derryadd) school: Montiaghs AH 1; 90,
  92–93
Ardmore altar: Bovevagh LY 25; 8, 17
Ardmore altar: Clondermot LY 34; 4–6, 19, 21, 24
Ardmore altar: Dungiven LY 15; 47
Ardmore altar: Faughanvale LY 36; 33
Ardmore bleach green: Balteagh LY 9; 13, 28, 36
Ardmore bleach green: Clondermot LY 34; 6–7,
  21–22, 30, 34, 100, 103–04
Ardmore bridge: Clondermot LY 34; 7, 22
Ardmore Castle: Balteagh LY 9; 7
Ardmore causeway: Balteagh LY 9; 28
Ardmore church: Balteagh LY 9; 30
Ardmore district: Misc. SO 40; 200
Ardmore female school: Balteagh LY 9; 17, 39
Ardmore female school: Clondermot LY 34; 8, 11,
  16, 41–42, 86, 90–91, 94
Ardmore female Sunday school: Clondermot LY 34;
  93
Ardmore flax mill: Balteagh LY 9; 13–14, 41
Ardmore flour mill: Balteagh LY 9; 13, 41
Ardmore fort: Killead AM 35; 26, 31, 33, 50
Ardmore graveyard: Balteagh LY 9; 30
Ardmore House: Balteagh LY 9; 3–4
Ardmore House: Clondermot LY 34; 6, 8, 20–21,
  77, 100–01, 103, 105
Ardmore House: Macosquin LY 22; 81
Ardmore male school: Clondermot LY 34; 8, 16,
  41–42, 86, 90, 94
Ardmore male Sunday school: Clondermot LY 34;
  93
Ardmore old castle: Balteagh LY 9; 7, 26, 28
Ardmore old church: Balteagh LY 9; 28
Ardmore old church: Montiaghs AH 1; 90
Ardmore plantations: Clondermot LY 34; 4, 19
Ardmore Point: Killead AM 35; 8
Ardmore Point: Montiaghs AH 1; 89–90
Ardmore quarries: Clondermot LY 34; 129
Ardmore school: Clondermot LY 34; 9, 41
Ardmore school [I]: Balteagh LY 9; 16–17, 39
Ardmore school [II]: Balteagh LY 9; 18
Ardmore standing stones: Muff DL 38; 82

Ardmore Sunday school: Clondermot LY 34; 9, 41, 92

Ardmore td: Aghavea FH 4; 23

Ardmore td: Balteagh LY 9; 13–14, 16–18, 26, 28, 30, 35–36, 39–41, 43, 45

Ardmore td: Clondermot LY 34; 3, 15, 18, 24–25, 38, 42, 56, 59, 70, 74, 108, 112–13, 121, 129

Ardmore td: Donaghedy TE 5; 91

Ardmore td: Killead AM 35; 35, 40

Ardmore td: Montiaghs AH 1; 93

Ardmore td: Muff DL 38; 80

Ardmore wood: Clondermot LY 34; 24

Ardnabrocky House: Clondermot LY 34; 6, 20

Ardnabrocky td: Clondermot LY 34; 37–38, 56, 59, 71, 80, 108, 112–14, 121, 129

Ardnabrocky td: Cumber LY 28; 61

Ardnadittion (Ardnadishan) td: Raymoghy DL 39; 136, 141, 198

Ardnagannagh td: Donaghmore DL 39; 35

Ardnaglass hill: Ballyscullion AM 19; 9

Ardnaglass td: Ballyscullion AM 19; 9, 12–13

Ardnaglass td: Clonleigh DL 39; 12, 197

Ardnaglass td: Templecarn DL 39; 163

Ardnagle (see Ardnargle): Tamlaght Finlagan LY 25; 100

Ardnagran hill: Banagher LY 30; 108, 110

Ardnaguineag (see Ardnaguniog): Faughanvale LY 36; 53

Ardnaguinnog td: Cumber LY 28; 68

Ardnaguinog (see Ardnaguniog): Faughanvale LY 36; 53

Ardnaguniog school: Faughanvale LY 36; 24–25, 35

Ardnaguniog td: Faughanvale LY 36; 17, 53–54, 67, 70, 80, 92, 98

Ardnamoghal td: Misc. DL 39; 196

Ardnancel Point: Lough Swilly DL 38; 147

Ardnaraf spa well: Dungiven LY 15; 112

Ardnaragh district: Drumachose LY 9; 74

Ardnaree fort: Tullyaughnish DL 38; 91

Ardnaree td: Lough Swilly DL 38; 102

Ardnaree td: Tullyaughnish DL 38; 86, 97

Ardnargle bridge: Tamlaght Finlagan LY 25; 104

Ardnargle House: Tamlaght Finlagan LY 25; 81, 95, 100

Ardnargle td: Aghanloo LY 11; 22

Ardnargle td: Balteagh LY 9; 36

Ardnargle td: Drumachose LY 9; 129

Ardnargle td: Tamlaght Finlagan LY 25; 63, 81, 93, 105, 119

Ardnasool td: Misc. DL 39; 197

Ardneckennagh district: Misc. SO 40; 199

Ardnegher district: Misc. SO 40; 200

Ardnover (see Altnover): Kilrea LY 27; 126

Ardoorgarmon district: Misc. SO 40; 200

Ardoragarragh (see Aghnadarragh): Camlin AM 21; 67

Ardore td: Magheraculmoney FH 14; 103

Ardpatrick lough: Artrea TE 20; 9

Ardpatrick td: Donaghenry TE 20; 39

Ardquin Castle: Killinchy DN 7; 89

Ardquin ph: Ballyphilip DN 7; 7–8, 10, 13–14

Ardquin ph: Misc. DN 17; 118, 126

Ardquin td: Ardquin DN 7; 4

Ardquin td: Misc. DN 17; 126–27

Ardreagh bog: Aghadowey LY 22; 2

Ardreagh td: Aghadowey LY 22; 34

Ardree lough: Emlaghfad SO 40; 178

Ardree school: Emlaghfad SO 40; 179

Ardress East school: Loughgall AH 1; 81

Ardress House: Loughgall AH 1; 78, 80

Ardress td: Loughgall AH 1; 79

Ardress West pottery: Loughgall AH 1; 80

Ardrumndon td: Tullyaughnish DL 38; 97

Ards (Donegal): Aghaderg DN 12; 6

Ards (Donegal): Maghera LY 18; 6, 50, 72

Ards (Donegal): Tullylish DN 12; 141

Ards bar: Ballyphilip DN 7; 9

Ards bar: Grey Abbey DN 7; 70

Ards bar: Lough Swilly DL 38; 119–20

Ards barony: Ballyhalbert DN 7; 6

Ards barony: Ballyphilip DN 7; 7

Ards barony: Ballywalter DN 7; 16

Ards barony: Bangor DN 7; 19

Ards barony: Castleboy DN 7; 26

Ards barony: Donaghadee DN 7; 45–46

Ards barony: Grey Abbey DN 7; 67

Ards barony: Holywood DN 7; 80

Ards barony: Misc. DN 17; 116, 124–25

Ards barony: Witter DN 7; 125

Ards channel: Lough Swilly DL 38; 105

Ards district: Ardglass DN 17; 12

Ards district: Dunaghy AM 13; 12

Ards district: Grey Abbey DN 7; 68–69

Ards district: Kilbroney DN 3; 32

Ards district: Killinchy DN 7; 88

Ards district: Misc. DN 17; 119, 121, 133

Ards district: Muckamore AM 35; 56

Ards district: Newtownards DN 7; 103

Ards harbour: Lough Swilly DL 38; 119

Ards House: Lough Swilly DL 38; 119

Ards House: Mevagh DL 38; 56

Ards lime-kiln: Lough Swilly DL 38; 119

Ards Little district: Ballyphilip DN 7; 12–13

Ards mill: Lough Swilly DL 38; 122

Ards town: Grey Abbey DN 7; 72

Ards, Viscount: Newtownards DN 7; 107

Ardsallagh district: Misc. SO 40; 198, 200

Ardsbeg school: Tullaghobegley DL 39; 172

Ardshankil td: Drumkeeran FH 14; 63

Ardstraw (see also Newtownstewart)
Ardstraw bridge: Ardstraw TE 5; 5, 11, 14
Ardstraw bridge graveyard: Ardstraw TE 5; 12
Ardstraw corn mill: Ardstraw TE 5; 4
Ardstraw old bridge: Ardstraw TE 5; 5, 14
Ardstraw ph: Cappagh TE 5; 16–17, 19
Ardstraw ph: Cumber LY 28; 48
Ardstraw ph: Drumragh TE 5; 104
Ardstraw ph: Longfield TE 5; 131
Ardstraw ph: Maghera LY 18; 57
Ardstraw ph: Urney DL 39; 174, 176
Ardstraw school: Ardstraw TE 5; 6, 13
Ardstraw Sunday school: Ardstraw TE 5; 7
Ardstraw village: Ardstraw TE 5; 2
Ardtannagh (Artanagh) td: Dromara DN 12; 63–66
Ardtannagh meeting house: Dromara DN 12; 63
Ardtannagh school: Dromara DN 12; 64
Ardtole church: Ardglass DN 17; 2–3, 12
Ardtole hill: Ardglass DN 17; 9
Ardtole td: Ardglass DN 17; 7
Ardtonnagh (Artanagh) td: Cleenish FH 14; 14, 29
Ardtonnagh school: Cleenish FH 14; 24
Ardugh (see Ardagh): Clonmany DL 38; 20
Ardunchin (see Ardunsheon): Clogher TE 5; 53
Ardunsheon (Ardunshion) td: Clogher TE 5; 32, 38, 46
Ardunshin (see Ardunsheon): Aghavea FH 4; 23
Ardvarness Cottage: Macosquin LY 22; 80, 101–02
Ardvarness demesne: Macosquin LY 22; 117
Ardvarness fort: Macosquin LY 22; 117
Ardvarness hill: Macosquin LY 22; 76
Ardvarness House: Macosquin LY 22; 80, 93, 101, 117
Ardvarness mound: Macosquin LY 22; 117
Ardvarness td: Macosquin LY 22; 117, 122
Ardvarnock Glebe td: Raphoe DL 39; 125
Ardvernagh (see Ardverney): Magheraculmoney FH 14; 110
Ardverness (see Ardvarness): Macosquin LY 22; 93
Ardverney td: Magheraculmoney FH 14; 110
Ardview House: Killinchy DN 7; 86
Ardville House: Killyleagh DN 17; 81
Argery bog: Clonleigh DL 39; 5
Argery House: Clonleigh DL 39; 6, 10
Argery plantation: Clonleigh DL 39; 5
Argory bog: Misc. DL 39; 187
Argory locality: Misc. DL 39; 186
Argory wood: Misc. DL 39; 189
Argyle, Duke of: Misc. DN 17; 119
Argyllshire (Scotland): Carrickfergus AM 37; 31
Argyllshire: Clondermot LY 34; 63
Argyllshire: Connor AM 19; 23
Argyllshire: Culfeightrin AM 24; 44, 46
Argyllshire: Island Magee AM 10; 74
Arigle school: Killdrumsherdan CN 40; 36

Arigle td: Killdrumsherdan CN 40; 34
Arigna ironworks: Tomregan FH 4; 128
Arklow hill: Currin MN 40; 88
Arkwright, Mr (England): Carrickfergus AM 37; 137
Arlin (Cambridge): Clonleigh DL 39; 13
Arlish td: Aghavea FH 4; 23
Armagh abbey: Island Magee AM 10; 43, 60
Armagh and Rathmoran manor: Misc. FH 4; 133
Armagh barony: Clonfeacle AH 1; 22–23
Armagh barony: Eglish AH 1; 43
Armagh barony: Loughgall AH 1; 75, 78
Armagh barony: Tynan AH 1; 124–25
Armagh Castle: Newry DN 3; 65
Armagh Cathedral: Derryvullan FH 14; 42
Armagh Cathedral: Desertmartin LY 31; 57
Armagh church: Cumber LY 28; 71
Armagh city: Aghaloo TE 20; 1
Armagh city: Agivey LY 22; 42
Armagh city: Ballyclog TE 20; 19
Armagh city: Ballymore AH 1; 1, 3, 5, 8–10, 12–13, 16, 18
Armagh city: Ballynascreen LY 31; 19
Armagh city: Blaris AM 8; 51
Armagh city: Clogher TE 5; 30, 52
Armagh city: Clondermot LY 34; 12, 30, 68
Armagh city: Clonfeacle AH 1; 21–25
Armagh city: Clonleigh DL 39; 13
Armagh city: Clonoe TE 20; 30–31
Armagh city: Coleraine LY 33; 63, 126
Armagh city: Culfeightrin AM 24; 48
Armagh city: Currin MN 40; 88
Armagh city: Down DN 17; 45
Armagh city: Drumcree AH 1; 28, 30, 35–36, 39–40
Armagh city: Drumglass TE 20; 42
Armagh city: Drumhome DL 39; 62
Armagh city: Dungiven LY 15; 109
Armagh city: Eglish AH 1; 43
Armagh city: Enniskillen FH 4; 83
Armagh city: Keady AH 1; 47
Armagh city: Kilkeel DN 3; 54
Armagh city: Killdrumsherdan CN 40; 36
Armagh city: Kilmore AH 1; 57–58, 60, 62–73, 73
Armagh city: Kirkinriola AM 23; 99
Armagh city: Lissan LY 31; 103
Armagh city: Loughgall AH 1; 80–82
Armagh city: Magheross MN 40; 147, 151, 157
Armagh city: Misc. DN 17; 131
Armagh city: Muckno MN 40; 164–66
Armagh city: Mullaghbrack AH 1; 94, 96
Armagh city: Newry DN 3; 78, 87, 114
Armagh city: Newtownhamilton AH 1; 98
Armagh city: Seagoe AH 1; 101, 107
Armagh city: Shankill AH 1; 111, 113
Armagh city: Tartaraghan AH 1; 121–22

Armagh city: Tullyaughnish DL 38; 87
Armagh city: Tyholland MN 40; 174
Armagh city: Tynan AH 1; 125–26, 128, 130–31
Armagh College: Loughgilly AH 1; 85
Armagh county: Aghabog MN 40; 65
Armagh county: Aghaderg DN 12; 1, 6, 8
Armagh county: Blaris AM 8; 3, 5, 75
Armagh county: Clonfeacle AH 1; 23
Armagh county: Currin MN 40; 88
Armagh county: Donaghcloney DN 12; 57, 59
Armagh county: Donaghmore DN 3; 7
Armagh county: Drumgath DN 3; 19
Armagh county: Drumhome DL 39; 63
Armagh county: Enniskeen CN 40; 26
Armagh county: Enniskillen FH 4; 60, 75
Armagh county: Kilbroney DN 3; 34–35
Armagh county: Killyman AH 1; 55
Armagh county: Magheralin DN 12; 109
Armagh county: Misc. LY 31; 103, 132
Armagh county: Montiaghs AH 1; 91–92
Armagh county: Muckno MN 40; 167
Armagh county: Newry DN 3; 61, 72–73, 75, 79, 87
Armagh county: Tynan AH 1; 127
Armagh county: Warrenpoint DN 3; 118
Armagh diocese: Aghagallon AM 21; 1
Armagh diocese: Ballyclog TE 20; 17
Armagh diocese: Ballymyre AH 1; 20
Armagh diocese: Clogherny TE 20; 25
Armagh diocese: Clondermot LY 34; 60
Armagh diocese: Clonfeacle AH 1; 22
Armagh diocese: Clonoe TE 20; 29
Armagh diocese: Donaghenry TE 20; 39
Armagh diocese: Drumcree AH 1; 30
Armagh diocese: Drumglass TE 20; 44
Armagh diocese: Dungiven LY 15; 33
Armagh diocese: Errigal Keerogue TE 20; 52, 57
Armagh diocese: Glenavy AM 21; 77
Armagh diocese: Keady AH 1; 47
Armagh diocese: Kildress TE 20; 58
Armagh diocese: Killeeshil TE 20; 63
Armagh diocese: Killygarvan DL 38; 42
Armagh diocese: Kilmore AH 1; 65–66, 68, 70–71, 73
Armagh diocese: Magherafelt LY 6; 81, 88
Armagh diocese: Magheramesk AM 21; 112
Armagh diocese: Mullaghbrack AH 1; 94
Armagh diocese: Newry DN 3; 66
Armagh diocese: Ramoan AM 24; 102
Armagh diocese: Tullyniskan TE 20; 142
Armagh diocese: Tynan AH 1; 125–26
Armagh hospital: Clonleigh DL 39; 16
Armagh manor: Newry DN 3; 65
Armagh mountains: Kilbroney DN 3; 29
Armagh old cathedral: Maghera LY 18; 55
Armagh ph: Clonfeacle AH 1; 23

Armagh ph: Eglish AH 1; 43
Armagh ph: Loughgall AH 1; 78–80
Armagh ph: Mullaghbrack AH 1; 94
Armagh ph: Tynan AH 1; 124, 131
Armagh, Archbishop of: Derrykeighan AM 16; 90
Armagh, Archbishop of: Drumglass TE 20; 44
Armagh, Archbishop of: Dungiven LY 15; 55
Armagh, Archbishop of: Killeeshil TE 20; 63
Armagh, Archbishop of: Kilmore AH 1; 65
Armagh, Archbishop of: Maghera LY 18; 69
Armagh, Archbishop of: Tullyniskan TE 20; 142
Armar, Margetson: Clogher TE 5; 32
Armer, Edward: Hillsborough DN 12; 105
Armour, family: Maghera LY 18; 13
Armour, John: Maghera LY 18; 53–54
Armour, Samuel: Carrickfergus AM 37; 194
Armour, William: Drummaul AM 19; 90
Armour, William: Kilraghts AM 16; 134
Armour, William: Maghera LY 18; 53
Armour's Hole cave: Kilkeel DN 3; 47
Armoy: Armoy AM 24; 1, 4–5, 8
Armoy: Ballymoney AM 16; 25
Armoy: Dunaghy AM 13; 27
Armoy: Dundermot AM 13; 33
Armoy: Kirkinriola AM 23; 117
Armoy: Loughguile AM 13; 61
Armoy: Ramoan AM 24; 88–90, 97, 107, 117
Armoy bridge: Armoy AM 24; 3, 5
Armoy bridge: Loughguile AM 13; 64
Armoy church: Armoy AM 24; 2, 4, 6–7
Armoy church: Glynn AM 26; 30
Armoy flax mill: Armoy AM 24; 4
Armoy glebe: Armoy AM 24; 2
Armoy Glebe House: Armoy AM 24; 4, 6
Armoy lime-kilns: Kirkinriola AM 23; 101–02
Armoy market place: Armoy AM 24; 4
Armoy old church: Armoy AM 24; 6
Armoy ph: Ballymoney AM 16; 3
Armoy ph: Culfeightrin AM 24; 36, 40
Armoy ph: Derrykeighan AM 16; 78, 80
Armoy ph: Drumtullagh AM 16; 96
Armoy ph: Loughguile AM 13; 58
Armoy ph: Misc. AM 10; 129
Armoy ph: Ramoan AM 24; 86, 91–92
Armoy quarries: Armoy AM 24; 1
Armoy round tower: Antrim AM 29; 30
Armoy round tower: Inniskeen MN 40; 125
Armoy school: Armoy AM 24; 6
Armoy standing stones: Armoy AM 24; 9
Armstrong, Andrew: Mevagh DL 38; 57, 60
Armstrong, Arthur: Derryaghy AM 8; 94
Armstrong, Charles: Camlin AM 21; 67–69, 72–73
Armstrong, Charles: Glenavy AM 21; 87
Armstrong, Col: Carlingford LH 40; 57–59
Armstrong, Ellen: Drumachose LY 9; 85

Armstrong, family: Aghagallon AM 21; 9

Armstrong, family: Currin MN 40; 94

Armstrong, family: Enniskillen FH 4; 58, 75

Armstrong, family: Rossorry FH 14; 117

Armstrong, family: Templepatrick AM 35; 118

Armstrong, George: Blaris DN 12; 46, 50

Armstrong, Gilbraith: Blaris DN 12; 46, 50

Armstrong, H.: Enniskillen FH 4; 82

Armstrong, Hugh: Donagh MN 40; 102

Armstrong, Hugh: Tullyaughnish DL 38; 97

Armstrong, J.T.: Tynan AH 1; 127, 130

Armstrong, J.W.: Finvoy AM 23; 71

Armstrong, James: Derryaghy AM 8; 94, 104

Armstrong, James: Kilbride AM 29; 152

Armstrong, James: Killead AM 35; 48

Armstrong, James: Tamlaght O'Crilly LY 18; 116, 118

Armstrong, John: Aghanloo LY 11; 14

Armstrong, John: Ballinderry AM 21; 54

Armstrong, John: Camlin AM 21; 62

Armstrong, John: Drumachose LY 9; 104

Armstrong, John: Galloon FH 4; 91

Armstrong, John: Killead AM 35; 12, 44

Armstrong, John [I]: Carrickfergus AM 37; 107

Armstrong, John [II]: Carrickfergus AM 37; 130

Armstrong, Joseph: Hillsborough DN 12; 105

Armstrong, Margaret: Carrickfergus AM 37; 109

Armstrong, Mary: Carrickfergus AM 37; 107

Armstrong, Miss (Isle of Wight): Carrickfergus AM 37; 79

Armstrong, Mr (Mowhan): Loughgilly AH 1; 86

Armstrong, Mr: Cleenish FH 14; 30

Armstrong, Mr: Magheracross FH 14; 95

Armstrong, Mr: Manorhamilton Union LM 40; 52

Armstrong, Mrs (Aughnamullan): Killead AM 35; 22, 50

Armstrong, Mrs: Drumachose LY 9; 70, 124

Armstrong, Rev.: Blaris DN 12; 46

Armstrong, Rev. J.: Drumachose LY 9; 85

Armstrong, Rev. William: Blaris AM 8; 10, 24, 31, 83

Armstrong, Rev. William: Magheragall AM 21; 99

Armstrong, Rev. William: Shankill AH 1; 115

Armstrong, Robert: Dungiven LY 15; 24

Armstrong, Robert: Misc. DN 17; 119

Armstrong, Samuel: Ballyclug AM 23; 65

Armstrong, Simon: Magheraculmoney FH 14; 108

Armstrong, Thomas: Boho FH 14; 8

Armstrong, Thomas: Cleenish FH 14; 29

Armstrong, Thomas: Drumragh TE 5; 109

Armstrong, Thomas [I]: Tamlaght O'Crilly LY 18; 118

Armstrong, Thomas [II]: Tamlaght O'Crilly LY 18; 138

Armstrong, William: Artrea LY 6; 19, 21

Armstrong, William: Blaris AM 8; 69

Armstrong, William: Derryvullan FH 14; 44

Armstrong, William: Templecorran AM 26; 132

Armstrong's hill: Templepatrick AM 35; 141

Arney brickworks: Cleenish FH 14; 25

Arney bridge: Killesher FH 14, 82, 84

Arney Lodge: Cleenish FH 14; 22

Arney river: Cleenish FH 14; 11, 13–15, 25, 27–28

Arney river: Enniskillen FH 4; 62

Arney river: Killesher FH 14; 81, 83–84, 88

Arney td: Killesher FH 14; 85

Arney td: Kinawley FH 4; 109

Arno's Vale House: Kilbroney DN 3; 35

Arnold, G.S: Ardstraw TE 5; 5

Arnold, Hugh: Magheradrool DN 17; 102

Arnold, John: Tamlaght TE 20; 83, 91

Arnold, Rev. Samuel: Warrenpoint DN 3; 117

Arnold, Thomas: Ahoghill AM 23; 40

Arrabwee (see Araboy): Ballintoy AM 24; 12

Arran Island: Island Magee AM 10; 74

Arran, Earl of: Donegal DL 39; 45–46, 48, 50–51, 53–55

Arran, Earl of: Killymard DL 39; 98, 100–02, 106

Arroughdale lough: Conwal DL 39; 24

Arstraw td: Ardstraw TE 5; 12

Art Ogue's mill: Duneane AM 19; 117, 119

Art, family: Drumgath DN 3; 20

Artabrackagh (Artebracca) td: Drumcree AH 1; 42

Artabrackagh corn mill: Drumcree AH 1; 32, 42

Artahallian spring: Bovevagh LY 25; 22

Artany hill: Laragh CN 40; 39, 43

Artany td: Laragh CN 40; 40

Artclea td: Aghalurcher FH 4; 16

Artedillon td: Clondermot LY 34; 71

Arthbutnot, Robert: Ahoghill AM 23; 37

Artho, N.B.: Misc. DN 17; 119

Artholobeg td: Carlingford LH 40; 57

Artholomore td: Carlingford LH 40; 57

Arthur, family: Magherafelt LY 6; 95

Arthur, James: Antrim AM 29; 21, 50

Arthur, John: Island Magee AM 10; 64

Arthur, John: Macosquin LY 22; 117

Arthur, King: Devenish FH 14; 61

Arthur, Samuel: Drumachose LY 9; 123

Arthur, Widow: Macosquin LY 22; 110

Arthur, William: Blaris AM 8; 70

Arthurs, William: Island Magee AM 10; 90

Arthurstown ph: Killanny MN 40; 130

Articarney school: Rasharkin AM 23; 136

Articlare (see Articlave)

Articlave bridge: Dunboe LY 11; 62

Articlave burn: Dunboe LY 11; 43, 59

Articlave church: Dunboe LY 11; 57–58, 64, 71

Articlave church Sunday school: Dunboe LY 11; 57, 71

Articlave corn mill: Dunboe LY 11; 46, 59
Articlave flax mill [I]: Dunboe LY 11; 59
Articlave flax mill [II]: Dunboe LY 11; 59
Articlave graveyard: Dunboe LY 11; 64
Articlave meeting house: Dunboe LY 11; 58, 65–66
Articlave meeting house Sunday school: Dunboe LY
    11; 57
Articlave river: Dunboe LY 11; 46, 58, 62
Articlave school: Dunboe LY 11; 46, 53, 80
Articlave springs: Dunboe LY 11; 78
Articlave td: Dunboe LY 11; 59, 69, 71, 80–81
Articlave td: Killowen LY 33; 161
Articlave Upper td: Dunboe LY 11; 66
Articlave village: Dunboe LY 11; 44, 54–55, 58, 62,
    67, 80
Articone Point: Ardkeen DN 7; 3
Articrunaght cave: Ballyrashane LY 22; 50
Articrunaght flax mill: Ballyrashane LY 22; 48, 56
Articrunaght North cave [I]: Ballyrashane LY 22; 62
Articrunaght North cave [II]: Ballyrashane LY 22;
    62
Artidillon (Artidillan) td: Dunboe LY 11; 50
Artidillon cave: Dunboe LY 11; 50, 73–74
Artidillon spring: Dunboe LY 11; 79
Artiferral bog: Kilraghts AM 16; 126
Artiferral lough: Kilraghts AM 16; 125
Artiferral td: Kilraghts AM 16; 124, 126
Artikelly brickfield: Aghanloo LY 11; 2, 32
Artikelly pound: Aghanloo LY 11; 23
Artikelly school: Aghanloo LY 11; 2, 15, 23
Artikelly td: Aghanloo LY 11; 2–3, 12, 14, 17–18,
    21, 23–24, 31, 33, 37, 40–42
Artikelly td: Balteagh LY 9; 30
Artlone fort: Duneane AM 19; 115
Artlone hill: Duneane AM 19; 96
Artlone td: Duneane AM 19; 115
Artnabracky (see Ardnabrocky): Clondermot LY 34;
    20
Artnabrocky (see Ardnabrocky): Clondermot LY 34;
    80
Artnagh td: Galloon FH 4; 95
Artogues td: Muckamore AM 35; 69
Artogues water: Skerry AM 13; 109–10
Artonagh (see Ardtonnagh)
Artougues (see Artogues)
Artrea bridges: Artrea LY 6; 8–9
Artrea chapel: Desertlyn LY 31; 46
Artrea church: Artrea LY 6; 7
Artrea church: Artrea TE 20; 7, 10
Artrea freestone quarries: Artrea TE 20; 8
Artrea Glebe House: Artrea LY 6; 8
Artrea kilns: Artrea TE 20; 6
Artrea lime quarries: Artrea TE 20; 8
Artrea meeting house (P): Desertlyn LY 31; 46
Artrea meeting house (S): Desertlyn LY 31; 46

Artrea old graveyard: Artrea LY 6; 18
Artrea parish school: Artrea LY 6; 20
Artrea ph: Ballyclog TE 20; 15
Artrea ph: Ballyscullion LY 6; 42
Artrea ph: Coleraine LY 33; 97
Artrea ph: Desertcreat TE 20; 32, 35
Artrea ph: Desertlyn LY 31; 35–37, 45, 49
Artrea ph: Donaghenry TE 20; 37
Artrea ph: Duneane AM 19; 94
Artrea ph: Lissan LY 31; 92–93
Artrea ph: Magherafelt LY 6; 79, 98
Artrea ph: Tamlaght TE 20; 73, 120, 126
Artrea rectory: Artrea TE 20; 8, 10
Artrea river: Arboe LY 6; 1, 39
Artrea river: Artrea TE 20; 8–9
Artrea village: Artrea TE 20; 7, 9
Artresnahan forts: Drummaul AM 19; 78, 88
Arts, family: Newry DN 3; 106
Artstraw (see Ardstraw)
Artygarven (see Ardgarvan)
Artykellys td: Convoy DL 39; 19
Arushgaran td: Dungiven LY 15; 75
Ash lough: Donaghedy TE 5; 90
Ash, Bishop: Devenish FH 14; 60
Ash, family: Artrea LY 6; 8
Ash, family: Enniskillen FH 4; 58
Ash, family: Faughanvale LY 36; 13, 15
Ash, family: Magherafelt LY 6; 95
Ash, G.H.: Ballyscullion LY6; 48
Ash, Hugh: Loughinisland DN 17; 96
Ash, John: Artrea LY 6; 8
Ash, Mr: Clondermot LY 34; 38
Ash, Rev. George: Ballyscullion LY 6; 65
Ash, Samuel: Carrickfergus AM 37; 111
Ash, Thomas: Ballyscullion LY 6; 45, 56
Ash, Thomas: Magherafelt LY 6; 81–83, 87, 101,
    104
Ash, W.H.: Banagher LY 30; 22, 120, 131
Ash, W.H.: Clondermot LY 34; 6, 8, 20, 27, 37, 78,
    80, 101–06, 115–17
Ash, W.H.: Coleraine LY 33; 64
Ash, W.H.: Cumber LY 28; 33, 96–98
Ash, W.H.: Faughanvale LY 36; 17, 23, 40, 42, 45
Ashbrook House: Aghalurcher FH 4; 8
Ashbrook House: Ballywillin AM 16; 35
Ashbrook House: Clondermot LY 34; 6, 8, 20–21,
    101–03
Ashbrook House: Coleraine LY 33; 64
Ashbrook td: Aghalurcher FH 4; 4
Ashe, Bishop St George: Clogher TE 5; 28
Ashe, Mr: Aghanloo LY 11; 21
Ashe, Mr: Dungiven LY 15; 34
Ashe, R.H.: Newry DN 3; 98, 100
Ashen Pool: Tamlaght Finlagan LY 25; 105

Ashfield church: Killdrumsherdan CN 40; 31, 33, 36

Ashfield demesne: Killdrumsherdan CN 40; 37

Ashfield Glebe: Killdrumsherdan CN 40; 34

Ashfield House: Dromara DN 12; 68

Ashfield House: Drumgoon CN 40; 8

Ashfield House: Holywood DN 7; 82

Ashfield Lodge: Killdrumsherdan CN 40; 33–35, 37

Ashfield manor: Killdrumsherdan CN 40; 32–33, 37

Ashford House: Tynan AH 1; 124, 128, 132

Ashfort (see Ashford)

Ashgrove House: Misc. DL 39; 185

Ashgrove td: Misc. DL 39; 196

Ashlamaduff standing stones: Dungiven LY 15; 49

Ashlamaduff td: Banagher LY 30; 22

Ashlamaduff td: Dungiven LY 15; 27, 49, 60, 64

Ashmore, family: Eglish AH 1; 44

Ashpark House: Banagher LY 30; 4, 15, 29–30, 59, 96, 100

Ashton, Alexander: Raloo AM 32; 128

Ashton, James: Raloo AM 32; 129

Ashton, Jane: Raloo AM 32; 129

Ashton, Robert: Raloo AM 32; 128

Ashtree Hill House: Kilmore AH 1; 73

Askill td: Galloon FH 4; 95

Askin, James: Carrickfergus AM 37; 162

Asladee lough: Aghalurcher FH 4; 3, 5

Assaroe waterfall: Clondermot LY 34; 69

Assington Hall (Essex): Carnmoney AM 2; 93

Astura lough: Killymard DL 39; 94

Atcheson, family: Magheramesk AM 21; 124

Atcheson, R.: Aghaderg DN 12; 7

Atchison, James: Ballywillin LY 33; 50

Athboy: Drumachose LY 9; 94

Athboy district: Enniskeen CN 40; 29

Atheiarty lough: Templecarn DL 39; 157

Athenish ph: Tullyaughnish DL 38; 84

Athlone: Banagher LY 30; 57

Athlone: Drummaul AM 19; 53

Athol, Duke of: Carrickfergus AM 37; 79

Athol, Duke of: Tickmacrevan AM 13; 124

Atholl Cottage: Ballymore AH 1; 11

Atidirigh td: Killymard DL 39; 100

Atkins, Mrs: Newry DN 3; 98, 103

Atkinson, Capt. (Crow Hill): Kilmore AH 1; 71

Atkinson, Charles: Loughgall AH 1; 78

Atkinson, Dr (Newbliss): Aghabog MN 40; 65

Atkinson, James: Ballylinny AM 32; 27

Atkinson, James: Drumcree AH 1; 33

Atkinson, James: Kilcronaghan LY 31; 77

Atkinson, James: Kilmore AH 1; 72

Atkinson, James: Magherafelt LY 6; 110

Atkinson, John: Tamlaght O'Crilly LY 18; 129

Atkinson, John: Tartaraghan AH 1; 120–22

Atkinson, John: Termoneeny LY 6; 132

Atkinson, Laurence: Tamlaght O'Crilly LY 18; 99

Atkinson, Lt: Donaghcloney DN 12; 60

Atkinson, Miss (Tanderagee): Ballymore AH 1; 9

Atkinson, Mr: Artrea TE 20; 7

Atkinson, Mr: Kilkeel DN 3; 49

Atkinson, Mrs: Drummaul AM 19; 88

Atkinson, Mrs Thomas: Tartaraghan AH 1; 119

Atkinson, Overnan and Pedon, Messrs: Seagoe AH 1; 109

Atkinson, Rev. C.F.: Kilmore AH 1; 68, 71, 73

Atkinson, Rev. Guy: Blaris AM 8; 25

Atkinson, Robert: Tamlaght O'Crilly LY 18; 129

Atkinson, Rodger: Enniskillen FH 4; 57

Atkinson, Sarah: Termoneeny LY 6; 132

Atkinson, T.: Drumcree AH 1; 35–36

Atkinson, T.J.: Kilbarron DL 39; 74, 77

Atkinson, Thomas: Tartaraghan AH 1; 118–19

Atkinson, Thomas: Tullyrusk AM 21; 139

Atkinson, William: Killevy AH 1; 53–54

Atkinson, William: Loughgilly AH 1; 85–87

Atlantic Ocean: Ballintoy AM 24; 10

Atlantic Ocean: Banagher LY 30; 37

Atlantic Ocean: Billy AM 16; 38

Atlantic Ocean: Clondavaddog DL 38; 1–2, 6, 10

Atlantic Ocean: Clondermot LY 34; 15, 29

Atlantic Ocean: Clonmany DL 38; 12–13, 16

Atlantic Ocean: Desertegney DL 38; 26

Atlantic Ocean: Donagh DL 38; 31

Atlantic Ocean: Donegal DL 39; 44

Atlantic Ocean: Dunboe LY 11; 58

Atlantic Ocean: Dungiven LY 15; 12

Atlantic Ocean: Emlaghfad SO 40; 177

Atlantic Ocean: Faughanvale LY 36; 31

Atlantic Ocean: Glencolumbkille DL 39; 64

Atlantic Ocean: Killea and Taughboyne DL 39; 87

Atlantic Ocean: Lough Swilly DL 38; 98, 113, 130

Atlantic Ocean: Magilligan LY 11; 83

Atlantic Ocean: Manorhamilton Union LM 40; 48

Atlantic Ocean: Mevagh DL 38; 54, 56, 58–59

Atlantic Ocean: Mintiaghs DL 38; 64

Atlantic Ocean: Misc. DL 39; 183

Atlantic Ocean: Moville DL 38; 68, 70

Atlantic Ocean: Rathlin Island AM 24; 127

Attaghmore school: Donacavey TE 5; 65, 82

Attaghmore td: Donacavey TE 5; 65, 76–77, 80–82

Atterrive lough: Cappagh TE 5; 17

Atthill, Rev. William: Clogher TE 5; 53

Atthill, Rev. William: Donacavey TE 5; 66, 68, 76, 85

Atthill, Rev. William: Magheraculmoney FH 14; 105, 106, 108

Atthill, Robert: Kilskeery TE 5; 115

Atthill, William (Jnr): Donacavey TE 5; 65

Atthill, William: Clogher TE 5; 41

Attirrive (see Atterrive)

Attlilou (see Altilow): Killymard DL 39; 98
Attybarren td: Aghalurcher FH 4; 13
Attymore td: Donacavey TE 5; 85
Atwell, Miss: Enniskillen FH 4; 85
Auburn Inn (Fermanagh): Banagher LY 30; 57
Auchantaraghan td: Misc. DN 17; 130–31
Auchenleck, Alexander: Donacavey TE 5; 81
Auchey, chieftain: Desertoghill LY 27; 31
Auchinleck, family: Drumbeg AM 8; 123
Auchinleck, James: Down DN 17; 50
Auchinleck, John: Clogher TE 5; 41
Auchinleck, Mr: Clogher TE 5; 41
Auchinleck, Mr: Donacavey TE 5; 77, 81
Auchinleck, William: Ardstraw TE 5; 4
Audley, family: Ballyculter DN 17; 28
Audley, family: Ballyphilip DN 7; 12
Audley's Acre td: Down DN 17; 52, 57
Audley's Castle: Ballyculter DN 17; 25, 28, 28, 30
Audley's Roads locality: Ballyculter DN 17; 25, 28
Audleystown corn mill: Ballyculter DN 17; 25
Audleystown td: Ballyculter DN 17; 25, 28, 30
Aughabog (see Aghabog): Currin MN 40; 86
Aughacarnaghan (see Aghacarnahan): Duneane AM
   19; 119
Aughaclane river: Galloon FH 4; 102
Aughadamph (see Aughnadamph): Muckno MN 40;
   162
Aughadanagh td: Clogher TE 5; 53
Aughadarra td: Dromore TE 5; 98
Aughadehier (see Aghadachor): Mevagh DL 38; 59
Aughadehur (see Aghadachor): Mevagh DL 38; 55
Aughadreenan td: Donacavey TE 5; 76–77, 83, 85
Aughadrenna fort: Clondavaddog DL 38; 6
Aughadrumdoney td: Currin MN 40; 86
Aughadrumkeen meeting house: Aghabog MN 40;
   63
Aughadrumkeen td: Ematris MN 40; 116
Aughadrummin chapel: Clogher TE 5; 39
Aughadulla mountain: Dromore TE 5; 93
Aughadulla td: Dromore TE 5; 98
Aughafad (Tatefada) td: Donacavey TE 5; 67, 76,
   78, 84, 85
Aughafad fort: Donacavey TE 5; 84
Aughafad td: Donaghedy TE 5; 91
Aughafattan (see Aghafattan): Skerry AM 13; 114
Aughafy (see Aghafoy): Templecarn DL 39; 163
Aughagachland (see Aghagashlan): Drumgoon CN
   40; 7
Aughagashland (see Aghagashlan): Drumgoon CN
   40; 1
Aughahull (see Aghahull): Tullyaughnish DL 38; 96
Aughakista td: Aughnamullen MN 40; 75
Aughalatty (see Aghalatty): Mevagh DL 38; 55
Aughaletty (see Aghalatty): Mevagh DL 38; 63
Aughalish school: Drummaul AM 19; 92

Aughaloo (see Aghnahoo): Templecarn DL 39; 163
Aughalough corn mill: Aghabog MN 40; 62
Aughalough td: Aghabog MN 40; 62
Aughalough td: Templecarn DL 39; 163
Aughamakerlin (see Aghamakerr): Aughnamullen
   MN 40; 75
Aughamakirlin (see Aghamakerr): Aughnamullen
   MN 40; 69
Aughameclan school: Inishmacsaint FH 14; 78
Aughameen td: Ballymascanlan LH 40; 55–56
Aughamuldoney td: Inishmacsaint FH 14; 70
Aughanagaddy Glebe td: Tullyaughnish DL 38; 96
Aughandrumman td: Clogher TE 5; 43
Aughanergill td (see also Corglass): Drumcree AH
   1; 37
Aughanhoy (see Aughnahoy): Ahoghill AM 23; 38
Aughansillagh (see Aghansillagh): Balteagh LY 9;
   39
Aughantaraghan (Aghantaraghan) td: Ballymore AH
   1; 8, 11, 15–16
Aughanunchin (see Aghanunshin): Tullyaughnish
   DL 38; 84
Aughanurshin td: Tullyaughnish DL 38; 96
Aughareagh (see Aghareagh): Currin MN 40; 86
Augharonan td: Donacavey TE 5; 76, 78, 83, 85
Aughatotin school: Killdrumsherdan CN 40; 36
Aughavannan (see Aghavannan): Killygarvan DL
   38; 42
Aughavennan (see Aghavannan): Killygarvan DL
   38; 46
Aughavogher mountain: Tomregan FH 4; 126
Aughavturaghan (see Auchantaraghan): Misc. DN
   17; 130
Aughaward td: Enniskillen FH 4; 81
Aughaweal bog: Desertegney DL 38; 24
Aughaweal hill: Desertegney DL 38; 24, 26–27
Aughayallog td: Misc. DN 17; 131
Aughboys td: Ballymascanlan LH 40; 55
Aughdoorish hill: Cumber LY 28; 3, 5
Aughdrimony spade forge: Clonoe TE 20; 31
Aughebrack td: Donaghedy TE 5; 91
Aughee, family: Aghalee AM 21; 31
Aughendara (see Aghindarragh)
Aughendrummon td: Clogher TE 5; 53
Aughentain (see Aghentain)
Augher: Clogher TE 5; 26–27, 30–31, 33, 44, 50,
   52, 60
Augher: Donacavey TE 5; 62
Augher: Errigal Keerogue TE 20; 46, 49–52, 54–55
Augher borough: Clogher TE 5; 30
Augher Castle: Clogher TE 5; 25, 30–32, 49
Augher female school: Clogher TE 5; 42–43
Augher lough: Clogher TE 5; 27
Augher male school: Clogher TE 5; 43
Augher manor: Clogher TE 5; 34–35, 38

Augher old castle: Clogher TE 5; 34
Augher Palace (Meath): Carrickfergus AM 37; 78
Augher school: Clogher TE 5; 42, 51
Augher td: Clogher TE 5; 42, 51
Augher td: Dromore TE 5; 98
Augher tenements corn mill: Clogher TE 5; 49
Augheralane td: Ballybay MN 40; 81, 84
Aughereagh (see Aghareagh): Currin MN 40; 86
Aughermelkin td: Clogher TE 5; 53
Aughersekilla td: Tomregan FH 4; 126
Augheygault Big school: Convoy DL 39; 22
Augheygault Big td: Convoy DL 39; 19
Augheygault Little school: Convoy DL 39; 22
Augheygault td: Convoy DL 39; 19
Aughil chapel: Tamlaght Finlagan LY 25; 106
Aughill (Aughel) td: Magilligan LY 11; 94–95, 126,
    134
Aughill (see Aghaghull): Tullyaughnish DL 38; 96
Aughin manor: Clogher TE 5; 53
Aughinlack td: Clogher TE 5; 53
Aughintain (see Aghintain)
Aughintober bog: Donaghmore DN 3; 7, 9
Aughintober td: Donaghmore DN 3; 7–8
Aughintubber (see Aughintober): Donaghmore DN
    3; 7
Aughintuber (see Aughintober): Donaghmore DN 3;
    8
Aughkelly school: Convoy DL 39; 22
Aughkelly td: Convoy DL 39; 18–19
Aughlerim fort: Manorhamilton Union LM 40; 52
Aughlish bog: Banagher LY 30; 48, 56, 76
Aughlish carn: Banagher LY 30; 89
Aughlish fort: Banagher LY 30; 89
Aughlish glen: Banagher LY 30; 24
Aughlish lough: Dromore TE 5; 95
Aughlish mountain: Banagher LY 30; 92
Aughlish quarry: Banagher LY 30; 3, 126
Aughlish river: Banagher LY 30; 88, 100
Aughlish river: Dromore TE 5; 95
Aughlish stone circles: Banagher LY 30; 7
Aughlish td: Ballymore AH 1; 1, 7, 10, 12, 17–18
Aughlish td: Banagher LY 30; 22, 31, 35–36, 52–54,
    56–58, 61–62, 85–86, 88–89, 95–97, 100, 102,
    109, 117, 121–22, 126, 129, 131
Aughlish td: Bovevagh LY 25; 47
Aughlish td: Dromore TE 5; 93, 97
Aughlish wood: Banagher LY 30; 122
Aughly td: Saintfield DN 7; 120
Aughmore old chapel: Inishmacsaint FH 14; 75
Aughmore td: Inishmacsaint FH 14; 75
Aughnabrae hill: Templepatrick AM 35; 105, 141
Aughnacarnaghan (see Aghacarnahan): Duneane
    AM 19; 124
Aughnacavan (see Aughnacaven): Donaghmore DN
    3; 8

Aughnacaven flax mill: Donaghmore DN 3; 8
Aughnacaven td: Donaghmore DN 3; 8
Aughnacavin (see Aughnacaven): Donaghmore DN
    3; 8
Aughnacleagh flax mill: Ahoghill AM 23; 13
Aughnacleagh school: Ahoghill AM 23; 45, 48, 50
Aughnacleagh Sunday school: Ahoghill AM 23; 48
Aughnaclough td: Galloon FH 4; 95
Aughnacloy: Aghaloo TE 20; 2, 4
Aughnacloy: Carnteel TE 20; 21–22, 24
Aughnacloy: Clogher TE 5; 33, 61
Aughnacloy: Clogherny TE 20; 27
Aughnacloy: Coleraine LY 33; 97
Aughnacloy: Donacavey TE 5; 62
Aughnacloy: Donagh MN 40; 99
Aughnacloy: Drumragh TE 5; 110
Aughnacloy: Errigal Keerogue TE 20; 46, 48, 52, 54
Aughnacloy: Errigal Truagh MN 40; 121, 123
Aughnacloy: Killeeshil TE 20; 63
Aughnacloy: Magheross MN 40; 152
Aughnacloy: Tynan AH 1; 125
Aughnacloy church: Aghaloo TE 20; 3
Aughnacloy church: Carnteel TE 20; 21–22, 24
Aughnacloy inn: Carnteel TE 20; 24
Aughnacloy meeting house: Carnteel TE 20; 21, 24
Aughnacloy mill: Annaclone DN 12; 18
Aughnacloy mills: Carnteel TE 20; 23
Aughnacloy preaching house (PWM): Carnteel TE
    20; 21
Aughnacloy preaching house (WM): Carnteel TE
    20; 21–22
Aughnacloy preaching houses (M): Carnteel TE 20;
    24
Aughnacloy school: Carnteel TE 20; 24
Aughnacloy td: Annaclone DN 12; 16, 18
Aughnacue corn mill: Aghabog MN 40; 62
Aughnacue glebe: Aghabog MN 40; 63
Aughnacue plantation: Aghabog MN 40; 67
Aughnacue Rectory: Aghabog MN 40; 63
Aughnacue school: Aghabog MN 40; 65
Aughnadamph meeting house: Muckno MN 40; 165
Aughnadamph td: Muckno MN 40; 162
Aughnadarragh (see Aghnadarragh): Camlin AM 21;
    75
Aughnadarragh td: Killinchy DN 7; 86
Aughnadrumman td: Moira DN 12; 120
Aughnadunvarren td: Hillsborough DN 12; 85–86
Aughnafosker td: Moira DN 12; 120
Aughnagar school: Clogherny TE 20; 26
Aughnagashland (see Aghagashlan): Drumgoon CN
    40; 3
Aughnaglnugh (see Aghnaglough)
Aughnaglough (see Aghnaglough)
Aughnagon td: Newry DN 3; 61
Aughnagurgan lough: Keady AH 1; 47, 50

Aughnagurgan td: Keady AH 1; 50

Aughnahaglish td: Ballyscullion LY 6; 49, 73

Aughnaheely (see Aughnakeely): Ahoghill AM 23; 22

Aughnaholle td: Culfeightrin AM 24; 38–39

Aughnahough (see Aghnahough): Derryaghy AM 8; 105, 109

Aughnahoy cave: Ahoghill AM 23; 35

Aughnahoy fort: Ahoghill AM 23; 35

Aughnahoy td: Ahoghill AM 23; 37–38

Aughnakeely school (see Craigs): Ahoghill AM 23; 22

Aughnaleck school: Annahilt DN 12; 23

Aughnaleck td: Annahilt DN 12; 20–21, 23

Aughnaleesh school: Ahoghill AM 23; 23

Aughnalough (see Aghnahough) td: Derryaghy AM 8; 118

Aughnamoe hill: Dromore TE 5; 93

Aughnamoe lough: Dromore TE 5; 95

Aughnamoe td: Dromore TE 5; 93, 96, 98

Aughnamullan corn mill: Killead AM 35; 14, 42, 48

Aughnamullan cove: Killead AM 35; 32

Aughnamullan flax mill: Killead AM 35; 15, 42, 49

Aughnamullan school: Killead AM 35; 38

Aughnamullan td: Killead AM 35; 22, 32, 40, 50

Aughnamullen bleach green: Aughnamullen MN 40; 72

Aughnamullen corn mill: Aughnamullen MN 40; 72

Aughnamullen Glebe House: Enniskeen CN 40; 29

Aughnamullen House: Aughnamullen MN 40; 71

Aughnamullen ph: Ballybay MN 40; 78

Aughnamullen ph: Donaghmoyne MN 40; 106

Aughnamullen ph: Drumgoon CN 40; 1, 3

Aughnamullen ph: Ematris MN 40; 112

Aughnamullen ph: Magheross MN 40; 143

Aughnamullen school: Aughnamullen MN 40; 77

Aughnamullen td: Aughnamullen MN 40; 75

Aughnascrieve (see Aghnaskew): Currin MN 40; 91

Aughnaskeagh td: Ballymascanlan LH 40; 55

Aughnaskeigh locality: Carrickfergus AM 37; 93

Aughnaskew graveyard: Aughnamullen MN 40; 73

Aughnaskew td: Aughnamullen MN 40; 75

Aughnaskieve (see Aghnaskew): Currin MN 40; 86

Aughnavallog (Aughnavollog) td: Drumballyroney DN 3; 10, 13–16, 18

Aughnavallog school: Drumballyroney DN 3; 17–18

Aughneskeagh mills: Dromara DN 12; 63

Aughneskeagh td: Dromara DN 12; 63, 65

Aughnish flax mill: Tullyaughnish DL 38; 89

Aughnish fort: Tullyaughnish DL 38; 91

Aughnish graveyard: Tullyaughnish DL 38; 90

Aughnish Island: Lough Swilly DL 38; 102, 104

Aughnish Island: Tullyaughnish DL 38; 84, 86, 90–91, 95, 97

Aughnish old church: Tullyaughnish DL 38; 90–91

Aughnish ph: Tullyaughnish DL 38; 90, 92–93, 96–97

Aughnish td: Lough Swilly DL 38; 103–04

Aughnish td: Tullyaughnish DL 38; 97

Aughrim (Wicklow): Misc. LY 31; 127

Aughrim: Devenish FH 14; 48, 60

Aughrim: Enniskillen FH 4; 51

Aughrim: Galloon FH 4; 102

Aughrim: Inishmacsaint FH 14; 74

Aughrim: Tomregan FH 4; 125

Aughrim flax mill: Artrea LY 6; 37

Aughrim fort: Artrea LY 6; 10, 22

Aughrim fort: Devenish FH 14; 55

Aughrim hill: Derryaghy AM 8; 90

Aughrim rock: Cleenish FH 14; 12

Aughrim spade foundry: Artrea LY 6; 37

Aughrim Sunday school: Artrea LY 6; 21

Aughrim td: Artrea LY 6; 13, 20, 22–23, 38

Aughrim td: Devenish FH 14; 59

Aughrimbeg bog: Donaghmoyne MN 40; 106

Aughrimmore bog: Donaghmoyne MN 40; 106

Aught mountain: Muff DL 38; 80

Aught river: Muff DL 38; 80

Aught td: Muff DL 38; 80

Aughtadrum church: Templecarn FH 14; 120

Aughtawaddy hill: Cumber LY 28; 3, 5

Aughterdrum chapel: Belleek FH 14; 3

Aughterdrum church: Belleek FH 14; 1, 3

Aughtermoy td: Donaghedy TE 5; 91

Aughtery, family: Carnmoney AM 2; 76

Aughtymore (Aughtimore) td: Magilligan LY 11; 88, 134

Augustine, St: Devenish FH 14; 61

Augustine, St: Dungiven LY 15; 55

Augustus, Stanislaus: Newry DN 3; 68

Auhadrumsee and Killygarman church: Clones FH 4; 26

Auhadrumsee td: Clones FH 4; 26, 28

Auhanagh td: Cleenish FH 14; 29

Auhey td: Derryvullan FH 14; 45

Aul, John: Drumachose LY 9; 97

Aull, Agnas: Ballyrashane LY 22; 49

Aull, family: Carnmoney AM 2; 51

Aull, family: Maghera LY 18; 13

Aull, James: Maghera LY 18; 53

Aull, John: Killowen LY 33; 169

Aull, Patt: Carnmoney AM 2; 100

Aull, Samuel: Maghera LY 18; 53

Aull's Hotel: Dunboe LY 11; 60, 63

Aull's Hotel bridge: Dunboe LY 11; 63

Aura glen: Culfeightrin AM 24; 79–80

Aura td: Finvoy AM 23; 68

Austin, Andrew: Leckpatrick TE 5; 125

Austin, Mr: Donaghedy TE 5; 92

Austin, St: Errigal LY 27; 42, 73

Austin, St: Misc. LY 36; 115
Australia: Clondermot LY 34; 16
Australia: Faughanvale LY 36; 44
Australia: Inishmacsaint FH 14; 78
Australia: Killead AM 35; 24, 51
Auterson, Arthur: Kilcronaghan LY 31; 76, 82, 140
Auterson, Rev. Samuel: Desertoghill LY 27; 15
Auterson, Rev. Samuel: Tamlaght O'Crilly LY 18;
    90, 99, 106, 111, 136, 143
Authorson, Samual: Errigal LY 27; 66
Avaghon lough: Aughnamullen MN 40; 69, 72
Avaghon mill-race: Aughnamullen MN 40; 72
Avah, warrior: Errigal LY 27; 77
Avenue giant's grave: Kilbride AM 29; 147
Averill, Capt.: Termoneeny LY 6; 124, 131
Averill, David: Termoneeny LY 6; 133
Averill, John: Termoneeny LY 6; 133
Averill, Sarah: Termoneeny LY 6; 133
Averill, Thomas: Termoneeny LY 6; 133
Averin, William: Maghera LY 18; 62
Avery, John: Clondermot LY 34; 5, 19
Avery's Castle: Ardstraw TE 5; 11
Avigh lough: Drumkeeran FH 14; 63
Aviltygort td: Donaghmore DL 39; 35
Avish (Evish) td: Clondermot LY 34; 56, 67, 72, 75,
    108, 113–14, 121, 129
Avish hill: Clondermot LY 34; 1, 17

Avish hill: Faughanvale LY 36; 2
Avish school: Clondermot LY 34; 89
Avish Sunday school: Clondermot LY 34; 92–93
Avish td: Magilligan LY 11; 95, 126
Avish wood: Clondermot LY 34; 121
Avishacrew td: Dunaghy AM 13; 22
Avondale (Wicklow): Loughgall AH 1; 76
Avoon lough: Culfeightrin AM 24; 42
Awain Ban (see White Water): Misc. LY 31; 114
Awary td: Magheross MN 40; 148
Awaughran lough: Kilmacteige SO 40; 193
Awaughran village: Kilmacteige SO 40; 195
Aynough Castle: Cumber LY 28; 72
Aynsworth, Mr: Ballyculter DN 17; 31
Ayr (Scotland): Carrickfergus AM 37; 10, 60
Ayr: Dungiven LY 15; 27
Ayr: Kirkinriola AM 23; 88, 117
Ayr: Templecorran AM 26; 109
Ayr: Templepatrick AM 35; 132
Ayr, Thomas: Eglish AH 1; 44
Ayrshire: Ballee DN 17; 16
Ayrshire: Ballyaghran LY 33; 6
Ayrshire: Drumglass TE 20; 43
Ayrshire: Dunsfort DN 17; 70
Ayrshire: Glynn AM 26; 29
Ayrshire: Island Magee AM 10; 41

B

Baarnanroan creek: Lough Swilly DL 38; 120
Baawe (see Boa): Derryvullan FH 14; 38
Babbington, Dr: Donaghmore DL 39; 30
Babbington, Matthew: Cumber LY 28; 65
Babbington, Mr: Coleraine LY 33; 122
Babbington, Rev. David: Drumcree AH 1; 33
Babbington, Rev. Thomas: Billy AM 16; 74
Babbington, Thomas: Drumtullagh AM 16; 101
Babbystone Bray hill: Bovevagh LY 25; 49
Babington, Adam: Ballyscullion LY 6; 57
Babington, Anthony: Banagher LY 30; 73
Babington, Anthony: Clondermot LY 34; 27, 104–05
Babington, Capt.: Clondavaddog DL 38; 5, 8
Babington, Capt.: Lough Swilly DL 38; 127
Babington, Capt.: Mevagh DL 38; 60
Babington, David: Duneane AM 19; 114
Babington, David: Faughanvale LY 36; 9, 13–15, 20, 22, 34
Babington, Ellen: Faughanvale LY 36; 22
Babington, Humphrey: Mevagh DL 38; 58
Babington, Humphrey: Tullyaughnish DL 38; 96–97
Babington, Mr: Inishkeel DL 39; 71
Babington, Mr: Tamlaght Finlagan LY 25; 80
Babington, Murray: Killymard DL 39; 98, 100
Babington, Rev. Richard: Clondermot LY 34; 104
Babylon hill: Ballymore AH 1; 7, 17
Baccus Hill cave: Dunboe LY 11; 73
Baccus, Robert: Ahoghill AM 23; 39
Back burn: Ardstraw TE 5; 4
Back burn: Drumachose LY 9; 46, 48
Back burn bridge: Drumachose LY 9; 56
Back Burn water: Termoneeny LY 6; 121
Back Hill td: Misc. DL 39; 197
Back Lower bleach mill: Ballyclog TE 20; 16
Back Shore coast: Killinchy DN 7; 88
Back Strand: Aghanloo LY 11; 14
Back Strand: Drumachose LY 9; 76
Back Strand: Dunboe LY 11; 60, 79–80
Back Strand: Magilligan LY 11; 114, 116, 125, 137–38, 141–42
Back Strand rock: Magilligan LY 11; 99
Back td: Tamlaght Finlagan LY 25; 93
Back Upper school: Ballyclog TE 20; 16
Back Upper td: Ballyclog TE 20; 16

Back, James: Muckamore AM 35; 56, 75
Back, Mr: Ballywillin LY 33; 51
Back, Mr: Nilteen AM 35; 102
Backaderry flax mill: Drumgooland DN 3; 25
Backaderry td: Drumgooland DN 3; 25
Backan Naglisha stone: Ballynascreen LY 31; 26
Backets school: Killeeshil TE 20; 64
Backfence bogs: Leckpatrick TE 5; 120
Backfence td: Leckpatrick TE 5; 120
Backhill td: Clonleigh DL 39; 12
Backnamullagh school: Hillsborough DN 12; 73, 95, 99–100
Backnamullough (see Backnamullagh)
Backsheskin river: Faughanvale LY 36; 2
Bacon, Mr: Kilmore AH 1; 65–67, 69–73
Bacon, Mr: Magilligan LY 11; 142
Bacon, Rev. Benjamin: Magilligan LY 11; 89
Bacon, William: Aghanloo LY 11; 13
Badger fort (see also Dunore fort): Muckamore AM 35; 72
Badger, family: Magherafelt LY 6; 95
Badger, William: Maghera LY 18; 60
Badoney (see Bodoney): Kildress TE 20; 58
Bagbey, Mr (Mandeville Hall): Kilmore AH 1; 72
Baghil ford: Down DN 17; 38, 49
Bagnal, Ann: Newry DN 3; 74
Bagnal, Arthur: Newry DN 3; 64
Bagnal, Blanch: Magilligan LY 11; 93
Bagnal, Dudley: Newry DN 3; 65
Bagnal, family: Newry DN 3; 65
Bagnal, Henry: Newry DN 3; 65, 74
Bagnal, Nicholas: Ardglass DN 17; 12
Bagnal, Nicholas: Newry DN 3; 64–66
Bagnal, Nicholas: Tullyrusk AM 21; 131
Bagnal, William: Newry DN 3; 65
Bagot, Rev. Daniel: Kilcronaghan LY 31; 82
Bagot, Rev. Daniel: Newry DN 3; 93, 95, 100, 105
Bagwell, Dean: Clogher TE 5; 53
Bagwell, Mrs: Clogher TE 5; 41
Bahanbwee td: Donaghmore DL 39; 35
Bahernamahery td: Killinchy DN 7; 86
Bailey, Benjamin: Doagh AM 29; 89
Bailey, David: Ballyscullion AM 19; 12, 14–15
Bailey, G.: Kilmood DN 7; 95

Bailey, John: Carnmoney AM 2; 62, 88, 102
Bailey, John: Kilmacteige SO 40; 193
Bailey, Lt C.: Aghaloo TE 20; 2, 1–2
Bailey, Lt C.: Artrea TE 20; 6–9
Bailey, Lt C.: Desertlyn LY 31; 35
Bailey, Robert: Ballyaghran LY 33; 19, 23–24
Bailey, Robert: Blaris DN 12; 46, 49
Bailey, Thomas: Galloon FH 4; 91–93
Bailey, Thomas: Killowen LY 33; 161, 170
Bailey's corn mill: Drumbo DN 7; 58
Bailie, family: Carnmoney AM 2; 76
Bailie, family: Dunsfort DN 17; 68
Bailie, Maj.: Newry DN 3; 98, 103
Bailie, Robert: Blaris AM 8; 83–84
Bailie, Samuel: Newry DN 3; 99, 103
Bailieborough: Drumgoon CN 40; 7
Bailieborough: Killdrumsherdan CN 40; 34
Bailieborough: Laragh CN 40; 41–42
Baillewbhuil Island: Killymard DL 39; 95–96
Baillewbhuil manor: Killymard DL 39; 96
Baillie, Mary: Ballymoney AM 16; 18
Baillie, Rev. J.K.: Artrea LY 6; 8
Baillie's burn: Carncastle and Killyglen AM 10; 2
Bailly, Margaret: Carrickfergus AM 37; 126
Baily, Avely: Kilwaughter AM 10; 112
Baily, Henry: Coleraine LY 33; 128
Baily, Margaret: Duneane AM 19; 114
Baily, Miss: Killyleagh DN 17; 80
Baily, William: Duneane AM 19; 123
Baily, William: Ramoan AM 24; 117
Bain, John: Clondermot LY 34; 87
Bain, Michael: Carrickfergus AM 37; 195
Bain, Rev. James: Ballynure AM 32; 50, 53, 69–70
Baine, family: Glynn AM 26; 45
Baine, James: Glynn AM 26; 45
Baird, Alexander: Aghadowey LY 22; 9
Baird, Andrew: Carrickfergus AM 37; 158
Baird, Ann: Tamlaght Finlagan LY 25; 118
Baird, Elenor: Tamlaght Finlagan LY 25; 118
Baird, family: Island Magee AM 10; 70
Baird, Hans: Hillsborough DN 12; 105
Baird, James (Jnr): Tamlaght Finlagan LY 25; 118
Baird, James (Snr): Tamlaght Finlagan LY 25; 118
Baird, James: Misc. DL 39; 186, 188
Baird, John: Tamlaght Finlagan LY 25; 118
Baird, Jonathan: Ballyaghran LY 33; 28
Baird, Martha: Tamlaght Finlagan LY 25; 118
Baird, Maryann: Tamlaght Finlagan LY 25; 118
Baird, Mr: Clondermot LY 34; 43
Baird, Robert: Tamlaght Finlagan LY 25; 118
Baird, Samuel: Clondermot LY 34; 78
Baird, Thomas: Clondermot LY 34; 78, 80
Baird, William: Blaris AM 8; 45
Baird, William: Maghera LY 18; 33
Baird, William: Tamlaght Finlagan LY 25; 118

Baird, William [I]: Aghadowey LY 22; 9
Baird, William [II]: Aghadowey LY 22; 24
Bairdiville (see Beardiville): Dunluce AM 16; 120
Baker, John: Clondermot LY 34; 59
Balaghalair bog: Donaghedy TE 5; 89
Balaghalan td: Donaghedy TE 5; 91
Balany (see Baleny): Armoy AM 24; 1
Balbriggan (Dublin): Lough Swilly DL 38; 118
Bald, Mr: Ballymoney AM 16; 11
Bald, Mr: Carrickfergus AM 37; 173
Bald, William: Agivey LY 22; 39
Bald, William: Ballymoney AM 16; 12
Baldearg (see O'Donnell of Tyrconnel): Dungiven
   LY 15; 32
Baldrick, Mr: Desertegney DL 38; 26
Baldrige, family: Ballywillin AM 16; 32
Baldwin, Cusack: Drumachose LY 9; 64
Baleny (Balleny) td: Armoy AM 24; 1
Baleny bog: Armoy AM 24; 1, 3
Baleny quarries: Armoy AM 24; 1
Balfour, family: Aghalurcher FH 4; 6, 9
Balfour, family: Enniskillen FH 4; 58
Balfour, H.: Kirkinriola AM 23; 122
Balfour, Miss: Ballymoney AM 16; 17
Balfour, Miss: Kilbroney DN 3; 34
Balfour, Misses: Kirkinriola AM 23; 114
Balfour, Mr: Killanny MN 40; 134
Balfour, Mrs (Dublin): Kilbroney DN 3; 34
Balfour, Mrs: Kilbroney DN 3; 35
Balfour, Rev. Harrison: Magilligan LY 11; 89
Balie, James: Kilwaughter AM 10; 113
Balintine, family: Misc. LY 36; 104
Baliol, John: Carnmoney AM 2; 72
Baliol, John: Carrickfergus AM 37; 90
Baliol, John: Island Magee AM 10; 62
Baliol, John: Kilbride AM 29; 149
Baliol, John: Rathlin Island AM 24; 129
Ball and Company, Messrs (Dublin): Kilcronaghan
   LY 31; 71
Ball, Andrew: Clonleigh DL 39; 10, 13
Ball, family: Enniskillen FH 4; 58, 75
Ball, James: Clonleigh DL 39; 4, 6, 8, 10, 13–14
Ball, Mr (Enniskillen): Enniskillen FH 4; 48, 78
Ball, Mr: Clogher TE 5; 40
Ball, Mr: Clonleigh DL 39; 16
Ball, Mr: Donaghedy TE 5; 89, 92
Ball, Mr: Raymoghy DL 39; 138
Ball, Mrs: Newry DN 3; 99
Ball, Rev.: Raymoghy DL 39; 136
Ball, Rev. Robert: Drumhome DL 39; 58
Ball, Rev. Robert: Kilbarron DL 39; 74
Ball, William: Devenish FH 14; 60
Ball, William: Hillsborough DN 12; 106
Ball, William: Raymoghy DL 39; 140
Ball's Point: Magilligan LY 11; 84

Ball's Point giant's grave: Magilligan LY 11; 118

Ballackivagan district: Misc. SO 40; 200

Balladian (Ballydian) td: Ballybay MN 40; 81, 84

Balladian bog: Ballybay MN 40; 78

Balladian bridge: Ballybay MN 40; 80

Ballagan school: Carlingford LH 40; 59

Ballagan td: Carlingford LH 40; 57

Ballagh hill: Templecorran AM 26; 84, 88

Ballagh lough: Clogher TE 5; 25, 47, 58

Ballagh school: Clogher TE 5; 41

Ballagh td: Clogher TE 5; 35, 35, 41, 47, 53

Ballagh td: Galloon FH 4; 95

Ballagh, Donald: Coleraine LY 33; 157

Ballaghan, Roly: Drumtullagh AM 16; 102

Ballagharty td: Ballinderry TE 20; 13

Ballaghbeg school [I]: Kilcoo DN 3; 43

Ballaghbeg school [II]: Kilcoo DN 3; 44

Ballaghbeg spa well: Kilcoo DN 3; 41

Ballaghmore cave: Dunluce AM 16; 106, 116, 118

Ballaghmore td: Ballymoney AM 16; 25

Ballaghmore td: Dunluce AM 16; 119

Ballaghmore td: Rossorry FH 14; 116

Ballaghnagearn bog: Magheracloone MN 40; 137

Ballaghneed meeting house: Clogher TE 5; 48

Ballaghneed td: Clogher TE 5; 37, 43, 48

Ballahar td: Moville DL 38; 70

Ballaher (see Ballure): Kilmacteige SO 40; 196

Ballainen (see Balleenan): Loughgilly AH 1; 86

Ballalloly (see Ballyalloly): Comber DN 7; 39

Ballanaman (see Bellanaman): Donagh MN 40; 101

Ballanleen district: Blaris AM 8; 86

Ballanogh day school: Clogher TE 5; 42

Ballanrus (see Ballinrus): Dunboe LY 11; 57

Ballantarson forts: Derryvullan FH 14; 42

Ballantarson td: Derryvullan FH 14; 42, 45

Ballantimpo td: Cleenish FH 14; 29

Ballantine, family: Kilwaughter AM 10; 115

Ballantine, Mr: Kirkinriola AM 23; 94, 116

Ballantine, Thomas: Kilwaughter AM 10; 116, 118

Ballantine, William: Kilwaughter AM 10; 116

Ballatrasna td: Carlingford LH 40; 58

Ballauch-carragh village: Kilmacteige SO 40; 193

Ballavarty td: Carlingford LH 40; 58

Balle Moenestraghe village: Grey Abbey DN 7; 68

Ballea td: Ahoghill AM 23; 34

Balleaghan (see Balleeghan): Raymoghy DL 39; 134

Ballealy td: Drummaul AM 19; 91

Balleblake (Ballinapistragh) td: Grey Abbey DN 7; 68

Ballebrene td: Grey Abbey DN 7; 68

Ballecaflen td: Grey Abbey DN 7; 68

Ballee and Ross ph: Ardglass DN 17; 1

Ballee bridge: Ballee DN 17; 17

Ballee chapel: Ballee DN 17; 17, 21, 24

Ballee church: Ballee DN 17; 17, 21, 23

Ballee corn mill: Ballee DN 17; 15

Ballee demesne: Ballee DN 17; 15

Ballee meeting house: Ardglass DN 17; 5

Ballee meeting house: Ballee DN 17; 17, 21, 23–24

Ballee meeting house: Dunsfort DN 17; 69

Ballee national school: Ballee DN 17; 17, 23

Ballee ph: Ardglass DN 17; 7

Ballee ph: Kilkeel DN 3; 51

Ballee ph: Misc. DN 17; 120, 122, 128

Ballee rectory: Misc. DN 17; 122

Ballee school: Ballee DN 17; 17

Ballee td: Ballee DN 17; 22

Ballee td: Ballyclug AM 23; 65

Ballee td: Connor AM 19; 18, 20

Balleeghan abbey: Raymoghy DL 39; 134–35, 186

Balleeghan graveyard: Raymoghy DL 39; 134, 186

Balleeghan td: Moville DL 38; 68

Balleeghan td: Raymoghy DL 39; 136, 141–43, 186, 191, 198

Balleek church: Loughgilly AH 1; 85–86

Balleek ph (see Loughgilly): Loughgilly AH 1; 84

Balleek school: Loughgilly AH 1; 84, 87

Balleek td: Loughgilly AH 1; 85

Balleek village: Loughgilly AH 1; 84

Balleenan meeting house: Loughgilly AH 1; 86

Balleenan td: Loughgilly AH 1; 85

Balleevy (Balleivy) td: Seapatrick DN 12; 123, 126, 133

Balleevy House: Seapatrick DN 12; 125

Balleevy mill [I]: Seapatrick DN 12; 133

Balleevy mill [II]: Seapatrick DN 12; 133

Balleighan (see Balleeghan): Raymoghy DL 39; 141

Balleivy (see Balleevy): Seapatrick DN 12; 125

Ballemurcock td: Grey Abbey DN 7; 68

Ballenaboyle td: Grey Abbey DN 7; 68

Ballenamallaght: Derryvullan FH 14; 39

Ballenamonybradshaw (see Ballynamony Bradshaw): Carlingford LH 40; 57

Ballenamonymurphy (see Ballynamony Murphy): Carlingford LH 40; 57

Ballenescore td: Grey Abbey DN 7; 68

Ballenlae (see Ballinlea): Ballintoy AM 24; 11

Ballenleskin td: Carlingford LH 40; 58

Ballenregan chapel: Misc. DN 17; 122

Ballentine, family: Magheragall AM 21; 99

Ballentother chapel: Misc. DN 17; 122

Balleny school: Dromore DN 12; 73

Ballerney td: Balteagh LY 9; 40

Ballevranellan (Ballenellan) td: Grey Abbey DN 7; 68

Ballgreen Point: Lough Swilly DL 38; 102–03

Ballgreen td: Tullyaughnish DL 38; 95, 97

Ballibay (see Ballybay)

Ballidivity (see Ballydivity)

Ballie, Adam: Templepatrick AM 35; 153
Ballie, Thomas: Templepatrick AM 35; 153
Balliggan church: Inishargy DN 7; 85
Balliggan flax mill: Ballyhalbert DN 7; 5
Balliggan school: Inishargy DN 7; 85
Balliggan td: Ballyhalbert DN 7; 5
Balliggan td: Inishargy DN 7; 85
Balliggin td: Ballywalter DN 7; 18
Balliggin td: Misc. DN 17; 125
Balliholly (see Ballyholly)
Ballimoney (see Ballymoney): Bovevagh LY 25; 60
Ballimony (see Ballymoney): Bovevagh LY 25; 33
Ballina (Mayo): Clondermot LY 34; 30
Ballina: Emlaghfad SO 40; 182
Ballina: Killoran and Kilvarnet SO 40; 183
Ballina: Killymard DL 39; 109
Ballina: Kilmacteige SO 40; 190, 194–95
Ballinabragget meeting house: Donaghcloney DN
  12; 58
Ballinabragget td: Donaghcloney DN 12; 58
Ballinabrine td: Clonleigh DL 39; 12, 197
Ballinacarra td: Killoran and Kilvarnet SO 40; 183
Ballinacarry (see Ballynacally): Aghadowey LY 22;
  13
Ballinacor chapel: Donaghmore DL 39; 32
Ballinacor school: Donaghmore DL 39; 39
Ballinacor td: Donaghmore DL 39; 36
Ballinacrea Lower cave: Dunluce AM 16; 106
Ballinadroman (see Drummond): Donacavey TE5;
  85
Ballinafern (see Ballynafern): Annaclone DN 12; 13
Ballinafoy hill: Annaclone DN 12; 13
Ballinafoy td: Annaclone DN 12; 14–15
Ballinagarvy (Ballingarvey) td: Finvoy AM 23; 67
Ballinagarvy school [I]: Finvoy AM 23; 74
Ballinagarvy school [II]: Finvoy AM 23; 75
Ballinagross Lower td: Ballee DN 17; 20
Ballinagross Upper td: Ballee DN 17; 20
Ballinahatty (see Ballynahatty): Drumbo DN 7; 59,
  61
Ballinahinch: (see Ballynahinch)
Ballinakillew district: Drumhome DL 39; 62
Ballinakillew quarry: Drumhome DL 39; 61
Ballinalargy (see Ballynalargy): Magheramesk AM
  21; 115
Ballinaleck: Killesher FH 14; 87
Ballinamallard: Enniskillen FH 4; 70
Ballinamallard: Magheracross FH 14; 92–93, 95, 97,
  100
Ballinamallard bridges: Magheracross FH 14; 94
Ballinamallard chapels: Magheracross FH 14; 94
Ballinamallard church: Magheracross FH 14; 94
Ballinamallard corn mills: Magheracross FH 14; 95
Ballinamallard river: Magheracross FH 14; 93,
  95–96, 102

Ballinamallard river: Trory FH 14; 122–26
Ballinamallard school [I]: Magheracross FH 14; 99
Ballinamallard school [II]: Magheracross FH 14; 99
Ballinamallard school [III]: Magheracross FH 14;
  99
Ballinamallard school [IV]: Magheracross FH 14;
  99
Ballinamallard td: Magheracross FH 14; 102
Ballinamallard td: Misc. TE 5; 147
Ballinamard (see Ballinamallard)
Ballinamarry td: Carlingford LH 40; 57
Ballinamean (see Ballynameen): Errigal LY 27; 78
Ballinameen (see Ballynameen): Errigal LY 27; 60
Ballinamoneybradshaw (see Ballynamony
  Bradshaw): Carlingford LH 40; 57
Ballinamoneymurphy (see Ballynamony Murphy):
  Carlingford LH 40; 57
Ballinareagh td: Ballymore AH 1; 9, 12–13, 16
Ballinasaggart (see Ballynasaggart)
Ballinascreen (see Ballynascreen): Maghera LY 18;
  9
Ballinasloe: Drummaul AM 19; 35
Ballinasloe: Killymard DL 39; 104
Ballinatagart (see Ballintaggart)
Ballinatibert mountain: Ardstraw TE 5; 10
Ballinavalley (see Ballynavally): Drumbo DN 7; 60
Ballinavally (see Ballynavally): Drumbo DN 7; 61
Ballincleave td: Ballyculter DN 17; 30
Ballincurry td: Kilbroney DN 3; 31
Ballindarragh bridge: Aghalurcher FH 4; 3, 8
Ballinderry: Blaris AM 8; 54, 73, 76
Ballinderry: Coleraine LY 33; 97
Ballinderry: Derryaghy AM 8; 103
Ballinderry: Magheragall AM 21; 98–104, 109
Ballinderry: Magheramesk AM 21; 114, 116, 118
Ballinderry bog: Misc. LY 31; 112
Ballinderry bogs: Killead AM 35; 22
Ballinderry bridge: Ballinderry LY 6; 41
Ballinderry bridge: Ballinderry TE 20; 11
Ballinderry bridge: Tamlaght TE 20; 102
Ballinderry chapel (Brethern): Ballinderry AM 21;
  57
Ballinderry chapel (C): Ballinderry AM 21; 44, 46
Ballinderry chapel (C): Ballinderry TE 20; 13
Ballinderry chapel (M): Ballinderry AM 21; 47–48
Ballinderry chapel (M): Ballinderry TE 20; 13
Ballinderry chapel graveyard: Ballinderry AM 21;
  41, 47–48
Ballinderry church: Ballinderry AM 21; 44, 46, 49,
  51–52, 57
Ballinderry church: Ballinderry LY 6; 41
Ballinderry church: Ballinderry TE 20; 13
Ballinderry corn mill: Ballinderry AM 21; 47
Ballinderry distillery: Artrea LY 6; 7
Ballinderry forts: Ballinderry AM 21; 43

Ballinderry free school: Ballinderry AM 21; 57

Ballinderry Glebe House: Ballinderry TE 20; 11, 13

Ballinderry graveyard: Ballinderry AM 21; 44, 50–51, 54–55

Ballinderry hill: Ballinderry TE 20; 13

Ballinderry Lower: Aghagallon AM 21; 7

Ballinderry Lower: Aghalee AM 21; 34

Ballinderry Lower: Ballinderry AM 21; 41–51, 54, 57–58

Ballinderry Lower bog: Ballinderry AM 21; 43

Ballinderry Lower chapel: Ballinderry AM 21; 41, 44

Ballinderry Lower corn mill: Ballinderry AM 21; 44–45, 49

Ballinderry Lower corn store: Ballinderry AM 21; 45

Ballinderry Lower female school: Ballinderry AM 21; 57–58

Ballinderry Lower male school: Ballinderry AM 21; 58

Ballinderry Lower mill-dam: Ballinderry AM 21; 49

Ballinderry Lower Moravian school: Ballinderry AM 21; 57

Ballinderry Lower post office: Ballinderry AM 21; 44–45, 49

Ballinderry Lower public house: Ballinderry AM 21; 45

Ballinderry Lower school: Ballinderry AM 21; 41, 47, 49

Ballinderry Lower smithy: Ballinderry AM 21; 45

Ballinderry Lower td: Blaris DN 12; 40–42

Ballinderry meeting house: Ballinderry AM 21; 41, 44, 49–50

Ballinderry new school: Ballinderry AM 21; 56

Ballinderry old chapel: Ballinderry AM 21; 48

Ballinderry old church: Ballinderry AM 21; 42–44, 50–52, 54–55

Ballinderry old meeting house: Ballinderry AM 21; 50

Ballinderry parish school: Ballinderry AM 21; 46, 57, 59

Ballinderry parish Sunday school: Ballinderry AM 21; 59

Ballinderry ph: Aghagallon AM 21; 1, 9, 23

Ballinderry ph: Aghalee AM 21; 26, 28–29, 38

Ballinderry ph: Artrea LY 6; 7, 15

Ballinderry ph: Artrea TE 20; 6

Ballinderry ph: Blaris AM 8; 46

Ballinderry ph: Camlin AM 21; 65

Ballinderry ph: Derryaghy AM 8; 119

Ballinderry ph: Desertcreat TE 20; 35

Ballinderry ph: Glenavy AM 21; 77, 81–83

Ballinderry ph: Kilcronaghan LY 31; 72, 80, 82

Ballinderry ph: Magheramesk AM 21; 112, 116, 123

Ballinderry ph: Misc. AM 10; 129

Ballinderry ph: Tamlaght TE 20; 73, 94

Ballinderry pound: Blaris DN 12; 42

Ballinderry river (see also Kildress): Kildress TE 20; 61

Ballinderry river: Artrea TE 20; 9

Ballinderry river: Ballinderry AM 21; 42–43

Ballinderry river: Ballinderry LY 6; 41

Ballinderry river: Ballinderry TE 20; 11, 13

Ballinderry river: Desertcreat TE 20; 34

Ballinderry river: Desertlyn LY 31; 36

Ballinderry river: Lissan LY 31; 89

Ballinderry river: Lough Neagh AM 21; 93

Ballinderry schools: Ballinderry TE 20; 13

Ballinderry td: Ballinderry AM 21; 41

Ballinderry td: Ballinderry LY 6; 41

Ballinderry td: Ballinderry TE 20; 13

Ballinderry td: Desertmartin LY 31; 54, 142

Ballinderry Upper: Ballinderry AM 21; 43–45

Ballinderry Upper church: Ballinderry AM 21; 45

Ballinderry Upper public houses: Ballinderry AM 21; 45

Ballinderry Upper school: Ballinderry AM 21; 41

Ballinderry Upper smithy: Ballinderry AM 21; 45

Ballinderry Upper td: Blaris DN 12; 40–42

Ballinderry water: Coleraine LY 33; 97

Ballindoalty td: Kilbroney DN 3; 28, 31

Ballindrait bridge: Clonleigh DL 39; 14

Ballindrait Castle: Clonleigh DL 39; 14

Ballindrait chapel: Clonleigh DL 39; 2

Ballindrait corn mill: Clonleigh DL 39; 2

Ballindrait flax mill: Clonleigh DL 39; 2

Ballindrait forges: Clonleigh DL 39; 2

Ballindrait meeting house: Clonleigh DL 39; 2, 15

Ballindrait mill: Clonleigh DL 39; 13–14

Ballindrait orchards: Clonleigh DL 39; 5, 189

Ballindrait school: Clonleigh DL 39; 2, 9

Ballindrait td: Clonleigh DL 39; 12, 185, 197

Ballindrait village: Clonleigh DL 39; 2, 7, 9–10, 13–14

Ballindran corn mill: Culfeightrin AM 24; 45

Ballindreat (see Ballindrait): Misc. DL 39; 197

Ballindreen Irish td: Ballyrashane LY 22; 58

Ballindreen Scotch cave: Ballyrashane LY 22; 50, 57

Ballindreen Scotch fort: Ballyrashane LY 22; 50, 57

Ballindreen Scotch td: Ballyrashane LY 22; 57–58, 65

Ballindrum fort: Artrea LY 6; 31–32

Ballindrum school: Artrea LY 6; 18

Ballindrum td: Artrea LY 6; 31–32, 38

Ballindrum td: Desertlyn LY 31; 35

Ballineskeagh ph: Misc. DN 17; 118

Ballingorragh td: Clogher TE 5; 53

Ballingowen (see Ballygowan): Aghaderg DN 12; 1

Ballinigrange (Tullymuckly) td: Grey Abbey DN 7; 68

Ballinlea Lower chapel: Ballintoy AM 24; 11, 15

Ballinlea Lower flax mill: Ballintoy AM 24; 15–16

Ballinlea quarry: Ballintoy AM 24; 28

Ballinlea school: Ballintoy AM 24; 35

Ballinlea Upper corn mill: Ballintoy AM 24, 16

Ballinlig House: Layd AM 13; 48

Ballinlig td: Layd AM 13; 48

Ballinlis chapel: Killevy AH 1; 53

Ballinlis school: Killevy AH 1; 53

Ballinloo (see Ballinlea): Ballintoy AM 24; 35

Ballinlough bog: Mintiaghs DL 38; 64

Ballinlough td: Mintiaghs DL 38; 64, 66–67

Ballinran td: Kilbroney DN 3; 31

Ballinrees day school: Dunboe LY 11; 71

Ballinrees hill: Dunboe LY 11; 43

Ballinrees meeting house: Dunboe LY 11; 44, 46, 66

Ballinrees school: Aghadowey LY 22; 13, 19, 21

Ballinrees school: Dunboe LY 11; 56

Ballinrees Sunday school: Aghadowey LY 22; 13, 20–21

Ballinrees Sunday school: Dunboe LY 11; 57, 71

Ballinrees td: Aghadowey LY 22; 38

Ballinrees td: Dunboe LY 11; 56–57, 71

Ballinress (see Ballinrees): Dunboe LY 11; 46

Ballinrus (see Ballinrees)

Ballintaggart bog: Macosquin LY 22; 84, 109

Ballintaggart gravel pit: Macosquin LY 22; 88, 109

Ballintaggart House: Kilmore AH 1; 63

Ballintaggart meeting house: Kilmore AH 1; 57, 63, 68

Ballintaggart school: Kilmore AH 1; 64, 68

Ballintaggart td: Aghaderg DN 12; 1, 8

Ballintaggart td: Kilmore AH 1; 61, 68, 70

Ballintaggart td: Macosquin LY 22; 78, 84, 98, 109–10, 122

Ballintagh (see Ballylintagh): Macosquin LY 22; 95

Ballintample ph: Drumlumman CN 40; 12

Ballinteer bog: Coleraine LY 33; 149

Ballinteer bog: Macosquin LY 22; 76, 76–79, 87–88, 90, 111, 116

Ballinteer North bog: Killowen LY 33; 158

Ballinteer North bog: Macosquin LY 22; 77, 111

Ballinteer North cove: Macosquin LY 22; 87

Ballinteer North fort: Macosquin LY 22; 112

Ballinteer North school: Macosquin LY 22; 91

Ballinteer North td: Macosquin LY 22; 79

Ballinteer South bog: Macosquin LY 22; 77, 112

Ballinteer South fort: Macosquin LY 22; 85, 112

Ballinteer South graveyard: Macosquin LY 22; 111–12

Ballinteer South school: Macosquin LY 22; 91, 93

Ballinteer South springs: Macosquin LY 22; 113

Ballinteer South Sunday school: Macosquin LY 22; 93

Ballinteer South td: Macosquin LY 22; 84, 111, 122–23

Ballinteer td: Macosquin LY 22; 89

Ballintemple bogs: Errigal LY 27; 54

Ballintemple cave: Errigal LY 27; 67

Ballintemple church: Errigal LY 27; 37, 41–42, 49, 58, 67, 70, 73

Ballintemple Cottage: Errigal LY 27; 70

Ballintemple demesne: Errigal LY 27; 58

Ballintemple fort [I]: Errigal LY 27; 43, 70

Ballintemple fort [II]: Errigal LY 27; 43, 71

Ballintemple glen: Errigal LY 27; 35, 45

Ballintemple graveyard: Errigal LY 27; 41

Ballintemple hill: Misc. LY 36; 114

Ballintemple House: Errigal LY 27; 40, 58

Ballintemple old church: Cumber LY 28; 69

Ballintemple old church: Misc. LY 36; 114

Ballintemple school: Errigal LY 27; 50–52

Ballintemple Sunday school: Errigal LY 27; 52

Ballintemple td: Clondermot LY 34; 63

Ballintemple td: Cumber LY 28; 69

Ballintemple td: Errigal LY 27; 40, 45, 66, 71, 77, 79, 84, 89, 91

Ballintemple well: Errigal LY 27; 43, 70

Ballintere (see Ballinteer): Macosquin LY 22; 76

Ballintier (see Ballinteer): Macosquin LY 22; 76

Ballintiskin corn mill: Carlingford LH 40; 59

Ballintlieve Cottage: Mintiaghs DL 38; 65

Ballintlieve hill: Mintiaghs DL 38; 64

Ballintlieve td: Mintiaghs DL 38; 66–67

Ballintogher corn mill: Saul DN 17; 111

Ballintogher school: Saul DN 17; 114–15

Ballintogher td: Saul DN 17; 114

Ballintoy: Armoy AM 24; 1

Ballintoy: Ballintoy AM 24; 10–11, 14–16, 19–20, 24, 26, 28–33

Ballintoy: Billy AM 16; 40

Ballintoy: Drummaul AM 19; 70–71

Ballintoy: Island Magee AM 10; 65

Ballintoy: Ramoan AM 24; 89, 97, 104

Ballintoy Castle: Ballintoy AM 24; 15, 19, 30

Ballintoy Castle: Drummaul AM 19; 71

Ballintoy caves: Ballintoy AM 24; 14, 33

Ballintoy church: Ballintoy AM 24; 11, 15, 19–20, 31, 33, 35

Ballintoy church: Billy AM 16; 64

Ballintoy Demesne school: Ballintoy AM 24; 17

Ballintoy Demesne standing stone: Ballintoy AM 24; 21

Ballintoy Demesne td: Ballintoy AM 24; 15

Ballintoy druid's altar: Ballintoy AM 24; 26

Ballintoy estate: Ballintoy AM 24; 30, 35

Ballintoy graveyard: Ballintoy AM 24; 20

Ballintoy old church: Ballintoy AM 24; 15, 19
Ballintoy ph: Billy AM 16; 36, 38
• Ballintoy ph: Culfeightrin AM 24; 48
Ballintoy ph: Drumtullagh AM 16; 96
Ballintoy ph: Misc. AM 10; 129
Ballintoy ph: Ramoan AM 24; 86, 90–91, 100, 106
Ballintoy ph: Rathlin Island AM 24; 132
Ballintoy quarry: Ballintoy AM 24; 26
Ballintoy school: Ballintoy AM 24; 35
Ballintoy td: Ballintoy AM 24; 27
Ballintoy vault: Ballintoy AM 24; 26
Ballintra: Drumhome DL 39; 58–62
Ballintra mill: Ballybay MN 40; 81
Ballintraire (see Ballintlieve): Mintiaghs DL 38; 64
Ballintrave (see Ballintlieve): Mintiaghs DL 38; 64
Ballintreve (see Ballintlieve): Mintiaghs DL 38; 65
Ballintur td: Kilbroney DN 3; 32
Ballinure (see Ballynure): Ballynascreen LY 31; 7
Balliskeagh: (see Ballyskeagh)
Ballitrasna td: Carlingford LH 40; 57
Ballnareagh (see Ballinareagh): Ballymore AH 1; 12
Balloch td: Clogher TE 5; 34
Balloo (Ballow) Lower td: Bangor DN 7; 19, 21
Balloo corn mill: Island Magee AM 10; 23
Balloo corn mill: Killinchy DN 7; 91
Balloo flax mill: Killinchy DN 7; 91
Balloo graveyard: Killinchy DN 7; 91
Balloo House: Bangor DN 7; 23
Balloo meeting house: Killinchy DN 7; 91
Balloo standing stone: Island Magee AM 10; 59
Balloo td: Antrim AM 29; 3
Balloo td: Bangor DN 7; 19
Balloo td: Island Magee AM 10; 15, 23, 40, 59, 73,
    81, 95, 101–03
Balloo td: Killinchy DN 7; 86, 88, 91
Balloo td: Misc. DN 17; 124
Balloo td: Muckamore AM 35; 54, 56, 68, 79–80,
    82–83
Balloo water mill: Island Magee AM 10; 73
Ballooly chapel: Magherally DN 12; 113
Ballooly school: Garvaghy DN 12; 82–83
Ballooly td: Garvaghy DN 12; 82–83
Balloonigan td: Magheralin DN 12; 109
Balloonigan td: Moira DN 12; 120
Ballow (see Balloo): Misc. DN 17; 124
Ballure td: Clondavaddog DL 38; 3, 5
Ballure td: Misc. DN 17; 131
Ballure village: Kilmacteige SO 40; 193, 196
Bally McPherson td: Misc. LY 31; 142
Ballyabrian (see Ballybrian)
Ballyadam td: Witter DN 7; 125
Ballyagan adult school: Desertoghill LY 27; 10,
    29–30
Ballyagan bog: Desertoghill LY 27; 14
Ballyagan bridge: Desertoghill LY 27; 16

Ballyagan cloth mill: Desertoghill LY 27; 5
Ballyagan flax mill [I]: Desertoghill LY 27; 5, 16
Ballyagan flax mill [II]: Desertoghill LY 27; 5, 16
Ballyagan school: Desertoghill LY 27; 4, 10–11, 16,
    18, 29, 32–33
Ballyagan Sunday school: Desertoghill LY 27; 4
Ballyagan td: Desertoghill LY 27; 11, 19–20, 29
Ballyagan wooden bridge: Desertoghill LY 27; 16
Ballyagharty (see Ballyagherty): Saintfield DN 7;
    120
Ballyagherty td: Saintfield DN 7; 117–18, 120
Ballyagholly td: Kilbroney DN 3; 32
Ballyaghran church: Ballyaghran LY 33; 20, 23
Ballyaghran female Sunday school: Ballyaghran LY
    33; 17
Ballyaghran Glebe House: Ballyaghran LY 33; 7
Ballyaghran graveyard: Ballyaghran LY 33; 8
Ballyaghran male Sunday school: Ballyaghran LY
    33; 17
Ballyaghran old church: Ballyaghran LY 33; 8, 10,
    16, 22–23
Ballyaghran ph: Ballywillin LY 33; 29, 36, 46
Ballyaghran ph: Coleraine LY 33; 95, 104, 120, 140,
    143–44
Ballyaghran ph: Dunboe LY 11; 43
Ballyalaght school: Billy AM 16; 77
Ballyalbanagh (Ballyalbona) td: Ballycor AM 32; 2
Ballyalbanagh school [I]: Rashee AM 32; 140
Ballyalbanagh school [II]: Rashee AM 32; 141
Ballyallicock td: Newtownards DN 7; 111
Ballyallnork td: Misc. DN 17; 123
Ballyalloly House: Comber DN 7; 35
Ballyalloly lough: Comber DN 7; 32, 43
Ballyalloly td: Comber DN 7; 32, 37, 39, 41–43
Ballyalloly td: Dundonald DN 7; 65
Ballyaltakilligan (see Ballyaltikilligan)
Ballyaltikiligan (see Ballyaltikilligan): Comber DN
    7; 42
Ballyaltikilligan flax mill: Comber DN 7; 31, 35
Ballyaltikilligan td: Comber DN 7; 31, 35, 37–38,
    42–43
Ballyaltikillyan (see Ballyaltikilligan): Comber DN
    7; 43
Ballyaltimernary td: Ballylinny AM 32; 30
Ballyalton cromlech: Ballee DN 17; 19, 21, 24
Ballyalton flax mill: Newtownards DN 7; 110
Ballyalton td: Ballee DN 17; 19–23
Ballyalton td: Comber DN 7; 37, 39, 42–43
Ballyalton td: Newtownards DN 7; 110
Ballyannon bog: Desertegney DL 38; 24
Ballyannon standing stone: Desertegney DL 38; 26
Ballyannon td: Desertegney DL 38; 24, 28
Ballyantrim td: Ballylinny AM 32; 30
Ballyar (see Ballyarr): Tullyaughnish DL 38; 86
Ballyara abbey: Kilmacteige SO 40; 185–86

Ballyara Castle: Kilmacteige SO 40; 185–86
Ballyara graveyard: Kilmacteige SO 40; 185
Ballyara td: Kilmacteige SO 40; 186
Ballyard school: Kilskeery TE 5; 115
Ballyard td: Kilskeery TE 5; 115
Ballyardbrin (see Ardbrin): Annaclone DN 12; 16
Ballyardmabrigie td: Ballylinny AM 32; 30
Ballyardmoydeigmore td: Ballylinny AM 32; 30
Ballyardmoydoigbegg td: Ballylinny AM 32; 30
Ballyargan (Ballyargin) td: Ballymore AH 1; 1, 8, 13–14
Ballyargan chapel: Ballymore AH 1; 6, 10
Ballyargus td: Moville DL 38; 73
Ballyarnet (see Ballyarnot): Muckamore AM 35; 78
Ballyarnett (see Ballyarnot): Killead AM 35; 51
Ballyarnot td: Cumber LY 28; 66
Ballyarnot td: Killead AM 35; 51
Ballyarnot td: Muckamore AM 35; 54, 78, 83
Ballyarr bleach green: Tullyaughnish DL 38; 89
Ballyarr corn mill: Tullyaughnish DL 38; 89
Ballyarr fort: Tullyaughnish DL 38; 91
Ballyarr House: Tullyaughnish DL 38; 89
Ballyarr td: Tullyaughnish DL 38; 96
Ballyarr wood: Tullyaughnish DL 38; 86
Ballyarrell fort: Donaghmore DL 39; 35
Ballyarrell school: Donaghmore DL 39; 39
Ballyarrell td: Donaghmore DL 39; 36
Ballyartan (Ballyarton) td: Cumber LY 28; 6, 9, 12, 21, 66–67, 83, 110, 116, 121, 125
Ballyartan bog: Cumber LY 28; 23
Ballyartan bridge: Cumber LY 28; 4
Ballyartan corn mill: Cumber LY 28; 86, 121
Ballyartan flax mills: Cumber LY 28; 28, 86, 121
Ballyartan quarry: Cumber LY 28; 121
Ballyartan school: Cumber LY 28; 2, 16, 73, 76–77
Ballyartan wood: Cumber LY 28; 116
Ballyarton td: Banagher LY 30; 63
Ballyattwood (see Ballyatwood) td: Misc. DN 17; 125
Ballyatwood House: Ballywalter DN 7; 16
Ballyatwood td: Ballywalter DN 7; 16, 18
Ballyaughian flax mill [I]: Clonduff DN 3; 4
Ballyaughian flax mill [II]: Clonduff DN 3; 4
Ballyaughian flax mill [III]: Clonduff DN 3; 5
Ballyaughian flax mill [IV]: Clonduff DN 3; 5
Ballyaughian td: Clonduff DN 3; 4–5
Ballyavelin North td: Drumachose LY 9; 87
Ballyavelin td: Balteagh LY 9; 31, 40, 44–45
Ballyavelin td: Drumachose LY 9; 96, 96, 133
Ballyavlin (see Ballyavelin): Balteagh LY 9; 45
Ballybantra (see Bentra): Templecorran AM 26; 82
Ballybarnes td: Ballylinny AM 32; 22, 30
Ballybarnis (see Ballybarnes): Ballylinny AM 32; 22
Ballybay: Aghabog MN 40; 65

Ballybay: Aughnamullen MN 40; 69–71, 73–74, 76
Ballybay: Ballybay MN 40; 79, 81–83
Ballybay: Comber DN 7; 41
Ballybay: Donaghmoyne MN 40; 107
Ballybay: Drumgoon CN 40; 4
Ballybay: Ematris MN 40; 114–15
Ballybay: Enniskeen CN 40; 29
Ballybay: Magheross MN 40; 146, 152, 157
Ballybay: Muckno MN 40; 166
Ballybay: Newry DN 3; 78
Ballybay Castle: Ballybay MN 40; 80
Ballybay chapel: Ballybay MN 40; 79–80
Ballybay church: Ballybay MN 40; 79–81
Ballybay dispensary: Ballybay MN 40; 80, 82, 84
Ballybay ford: Ballybay MN 40; 78
Ballybay graveyard: Ballybay MN 40; 79
Ballybay market house: Ballybay MN 40; 79–80
Ballybay meeting house: Ballybay MN 40; 79–80
Ballybay parish chapel: Ballybay MN 40; 79
Ballybay ph: Aughnamullen MN 40; 69, 74
Ballybay ph: Clogher TE 5; 40
Ballybay ph: Drumgoon CN 40; 7
Ballybay ph: Muckno MN 40; 163
Ballybay river: Aughnamullen MN 40; 69–71, 73
Ballybay river: Drumcree AH 1; 34
Ballybay river: Kilmore AH 1; 61
Ballybay road cave: Magheross MN 40; 146
Ballybay road cromlech: Magheross MN 40; 146
Ballybay td: Dundonald DN 7; 65
Ballybeen House: Comber DN 7; 35
Ballybeen td: Comber DN 7; 37–38, 40, 42–43
Ballybeen td: Dundonald DN 7; 65
Ballybeg cove: Ahoghill AM 23; 35
Ballybeg fort: Ahoghill AM 23; 35
Ballybeg school [I]: Ahoghill AM 23; 23, 41, 46
Ballybeg school [II]: Ahoghill AM 23; 49
Ballybeg Sunday school: Ahoghill AM 23; 46
Ballybeg td: Dunsfort DN 17; 72
Ballybegley (see Ballybegly): Misc. DL 39; 186
Ballybegly td: Misc. DL 39; 184, 186, 194
Ballybentra (see Bentra): Templecorran AM 26; 82
Ballybentragh old church: Nilteen AM 35; 104
Ballybentragh td: Nilteen AM 35; 84, 94
Ballybentreagh (see Ballybentragh): Nilteen AM 35; 84
Ballyberaw td: Ballylinny AM 32; 30
Ballyberidagh South hills: Culfeightrin AM 24; 78
Ballyblack bog: Grey Abbey DN 7; 67
Ballyblack chapel: Newtownards DN 7; 104
Ballyblack Little td: Grey Abbey DN 7; 67, 67
Ballyblack Newtownards td: Misc. DN 17; 123
Ballyblack schools: Grey Abbey DN 7; 70
Ballyblack td: Ballyphilip DN 7; 8
Ballyblack td: Grey Abbey DN 7; 67
Ballyblack td: Misc. DN 17; 123–24, 126

Ballyblack td: Newtownards DN 7; 104, 112–13

Ballyblagh td: Donaghmore DN 3; 9

Ballybo td: Killygarvan DL 38; 46

Ballyboard td: Ballyphilip DN 7; 7

Ballyboe fort: Tullyaughnish DL 38; 91

Ballyboe graveyard: Convoy DL 39; 18

Ballyboe meeting house: Convoy DL 39; 18

Ballyboe Point: Lough Swilly DL 38; 116

Ballyboe school: Convoy DL 39; 18

Ballyboe td: Ballyscullion LY 6; 56

Ballyboe td: Convoy DL 39; 19

Ballyboe td: Leck DL 39; 118

Ballyboe td: Misc. DL 39; 189, 194–195, 198

Ballyboe td: Raymoghy DL 39; 134, 136, 141

Ballyboe td: Tullyaughnish DL 38; 97

Ballybofey: Donaghmore DL 39; 28–30

Ballybofey: Inishkeel DL 39; 73

Ballybofey: Killymard DL 39; 108

Ballybofey: Kilteevoge DL 39; 110, 112

Ballybofey: Misc. DL 39; 188

Ballybogan graveyard: Clonleigh DL 39; 3

Ballybogan old church: Clonleigh DL 39; 3

Ballybogan school: Clonleigh DL 39; 4

Ballybogey Castle: Ballyrashane LY 22; 58

Ballybogey td: Ballyrashane LY 22; 54

Ballyboggan Churchtown td: Misc. DL 39; 197

Ballyboggan Milltown td: Misc. DL 39; 197

Ballyboggy (see Ballybogey): Ballyrashane LY 22; 58

Ballyboghilbo td: Grey Abbey DN 7; 67

Ballyboghilbo td: Misc. DN 17; 123

Ballyboghillbow (see Ballyboghilbo)

Ballyboghilboo (see Ballyboghilbo)

Ballyboght (see Ballybot): Newry DN 3; 87

Ballybogie td: Derrykeighan AM 16; 87

Ballybogy (Balyboggy) td: Dunluce AM 16; 116

Ballybogy cave: Dunaghy AM 13; 23–24

Ballybogy caves: Dunluce AM 16; 116, 119

Ballybogy flax mills: Dunluce AM 16; 110

Ballybogy paper mill: Dunluce AM 16; 110

Ballybogy school: Dunaghy AM 13; 16

Ballybogy td: Dunaghy AM 13; 23–24

Ballybokeel td: Tullyaughnish DL 38; 96

Ballyboley (Ballybole) td: Doagh AM 29; 60, 90–91

Ballyboley bog: Ballycor AM 32; 8

Ballyboley bog: Inver AM 26; 53

Ballyboley bog: Kilbride AM 29; 153

Ballyboley bridge: Ballycor AM 32; 4, 9

Ballyboley flax mill: Ballycor AM 32; 4

Ballyboley hill: Ballycor AM 32; 1, 8–9

Ballyboley hill: Kilbride AM 29; 153

Ballyboley river: Ballynure AM 32; 72

Ballyboley school: Ballycor AM 32; 7

Ballyboley school: Grey Abbey DN 7; 69–70

Ballyboley school: Rashee AM 32; 140–41

Ballyboley td: Ballycor AM 32; 9

Ballyboley td: Grey Abbey DN 7; 67, 69–70

Ballyboley td: Kilbride AM 29; 135

Ballyboley td: Misc. DN 17; 123

Ballybollen (Ballybollan) td: Drummaul AM 19; 78

Ballybollen forts: Drummaul AM 19; 78, 88

Ballybollen House: Ahoghill AM 23; 12, 31

Ballybolley (see Ballyboley): Kilbride AM 29; 153

Ballybolly (see Ballyboley): Doagh AM 29; 91

Ballybot bridewell: Newry DN 3; 78–79

Ballybot bridge: Newry DN 3; 70

Ballybot school: Newry DN 3; 87

Ballybot td: Newry DN 3; 72, 74

Ballybotample church: Kilteevoge DL 39; 111

Ballybotample Glebe House: Kilteevoge DL 39; 111

Ballybotample graveyard: Kilteevoge DL 39; 111

Ballybotample td: Kilteevoge DL 39; 113

Ballybow td: Taughboyne DL 39; 148, 152

Ballybowell td: Ballylinny AM 32; 30

Ballyboylands Lower beetling mill: Ballymoney AM 16; 10

Ballyboylands Lower corn mill: Ballymoney AM 16; 10

Ballyboylands Lower flax mill: Ballymoney AM 16; 10

Ballyboylands Lower td: Ballymoney AM 16; 25

Ballyboylands school: Ballymoney AM 16; 26

Ballyboylands standing stone: Ballymoney AM 16; 21

Ballyboylands Upper standing stone: Ballymoney AM 16; 25

Ballyboys (see Ballybollen): Ahoghill AM 23; 31

Ballyboysbeg td: Castletown LH 40; 61

Ballyboysmore td: Castletown LH 40; 61

Ballybrack House: Moville DL 38; 70

Ballybrack td: Grey Abbey DN 7; 70

Ballybrack td: Moville DL 38; 68, 70

Ballybracken cave [I]: Ballynure AM 32; 60, 67

Ballybracken cave [II]: Ballynure AM 32; 60

Ballybracken cave [III]: Ballynure AM 32; 60

Ballybracken cave [IV]: Ballynure AM 32; 67

Ballybracken fort: Kilbride AM 29; 149, 155

Ballybracken fort [I]: Ballynure AM 32; 60

Ballybracken fort [II]: Ballynure AM 32; 60

Ballybracken school: Kilbride AM 29; 149, 152

Ballybracken Sunday school: Kilbride AM 29; 152

Ballybracken td: Ballynure AM 32; 63, 68, 70

Ballybracken td: Kilbride AM 29; 136, 155

Ballybradden standing stone: Loughguile AM 13; 69, 74

Ballybradden td: Loughguile AM 13; 69, 74

Ballybrain td: Misc. DN 17; 123

Ballybranagh (see Ballybrannagh): Ballee DN 17; 22

Ballybranagh td: Down 17; 47

Ballybranaghs (see Ballybranagh): Down DN 17; 47

Ballybranigan (see Ballybrannigan): Ballyphilip DN 7; 8

Ballybrannagh Lower td: Ballee DN 17; 20–21

Ballybrannagh td: Ballee DN 17; 22–23

Ballybrannagh Upper td: Ballee DN 17; 20–21

Ballybrannigan (Ballybranagan) td: Misc. DN 17; 125–26

Ballybrannigan td: Ballyphilip DN 7; 8

Ballybreagh flax mill: Kilmore AH 1; 63, 67

Ballybreagh hill: Kilmore AH 1; 61

Ballybreagh td: Kilmore AH 1; 64, 66–67, 69–70, 72

Ballybredagh td: Killinchy DN 7; 86

Ballybreen td: Grey Abbey DN 7; 67

Ballybreenan bog: Emlaghfad SO 40; 176

Ballybregagh cashel: Loughguile AM 13; 69

Ballybregagh td: Loughguile AM 13; 68, 70, 75

Ballybrentagh (see Ballybentragh): Nilteen AM 35; 94

Ballybrian td: Ballywalter DN 7; 18

Ballybrian td: Grey Abbey DN 7; 67

Ballybrick: (see Ballymeilbrick)

Ballybrickland district: Aghaderg DN 12; 1

Ballybriest (Ballybreeve) td: Lissan LY 31; 90–94, 96, 98, 102, 106, 108

Ballybriest bleach green: Lissan LY 31; 90, 92, 94, 98

Ballybriest bleach mill: Lissan LY 31; 98

Ballybriest bog: Lissan LY 31; 99

Ballybriest giant's grave: Lissan LY 31; 91

Ballybright bog: Dunboe LY 11; 73

Ballybrissel (Ballybrissell) td: Aghanloo LY 11; 12, 15, 21, 37, 40–41

Ballybrissel mountain: Aghanloo LY 11; 1

Ballybrist (see Ballybriest): Lissan LY 31; 96

Ballybritain (Ballybrittain) td: Aghadowey LY 22; 6, 8, 37

Ballybritain bleach green: Aghadowey LY 22; 8–9, 12

Ballybritain bog: Aghadowey LY 22; 2, 30, 32–33

Ballybritain bridge: Aghadowey LY 22; 10

Ballybulgan river: Drumhome DL 39; 61

Ballybullion (see Ballyclare): Doagh AM 29; 82

Ballybun td: Donaghmore DL 39; 36

Ballybunden td: Kilmood DN 7; 94–96

Ballybuttle td: Donaghadee DN 7; 45

Ballybuttle td: Misc. DN 17; 124

Ballycaghan (Ballycahan) td: Aghadowey LY 22; 1, 10

Ballycaghan hill: Aghadowey LY 22; 1

Ballycaghan standing stone: Aghadowey LY 22; 32

Ballycairn fort [I]: Aghagallon AM 21; 11, 14

Ballycairn fort [II]: Aghagallon AM 21; 11, 14

Ballycairn mount: Kildollagh LY 22; 69

Ballycairn school: Aghagallon AM 21; 23–25

Ballycairn Sunday school: Aghagallon AM 21; 24

Ballycairn td: Aghagallon AM 21; 3, 11, 18–19

Ballycairne (see Ballycairn): Aghagallon AM 21; 25

Ballycallaghan quarry: Cumber LY 28; 121

Ballycallaghan school: Cumber LY 28; 2, 71

Ballycallaghan td: Cumber LY 28; 20, 66–67, 110, 116, 121, 125

Ballycallaghan wood: Cumber LY 28; 116

Ballycallan corn mill: Clondavaddog DL 38; 5

Ballycam (Ballycalm) td: Bright DN 17; 33, 35, 125

Ballycamlin td: Camlin AM 21; 60

Ballycanal td: Moira DN 12; 120

Ballycargnan (see Ballycarrongannon): Drumbo DN 7; 61

Ballycarn (Ballycairn) td: Drumbo DN 7; 56, 59, 61–62

Ballycarn church: Drumbo DN 7; 60

Ballycarn meeting house: Drumbo DN 7; 56, 59

Ballycarn mount: Killowen LY 33; 162, 168

Ballycarn td: Killowen LY 33; 165, 169, 172

Ballycarney mountain: Ardstraw TE 5; 10

Ballycarrickmaddy fort [I]: Magheragall AM 21; 99

Ballycarrickmaddy fort [II]: Magheragall AM 21; 104

Ballycarrickmaddy fort [III]: Magheragall AM 21; 104

Ballycarrickmaddy fort [IV]: Magheragall AM 21; 104

Ballycarrickmaddy fort [V]: Magheragall AM 21; 106

Ballycarrickmaddy fort [VI]: Magheragall AM 21; 106

Ballycarrickmaddy fort [VII]: Magheragall AM 21; 106

Ballycarrickmaddy fort [VIII]: Magheragall AM 21; 106

Ballycarrickmaddy forts: Magheragall AM 21; 104

Ballycarrickmaddy meeting house: Magheragall AM 21; 99, 111

Ballycarrickmaddy old meeting house: Magheragall AM 21; 99

Ballycarrickmaddy school: Magheragall AM 21; 109–11

Ballycarrickmaddy Sunday school: Magheragall AM 21; 110

Ballycarrickmaddy td: Magheragall AM 21; 109

Ballycarrickmady (see Ballycarrickmaddy): Magheragall AM 21; 111

Ballycarrongannon td: Drumbo DN 7; 58, 60–61

Ballycarry (Ballycary) td: Rathlin Island AM 24; 129

Ballycarry: Ballynure AM 32; 32–34, 39, 67, 71

Ballycarry: Carrickfergus AM 37; 24

Ballycarry: Glynn AM 26; 16, 39, 42, 46

Ballycarry: Island Magee AM 10; 40, 45, 91

Ballycarry: Kilroot AM 26; 79

Ballycarry: Raloo AM 32; 130–31

Ballycarry: Templecorran AM 26; 82–86, 89, 91–95, 98, 100, 102, 106, 109, 115, 117, 121, 123–28, 130–32

Ballycarry causeway: Templecorran AM 26; 112, 119

Ballycarry fairgreen: Templecorran AM 26; 124

Ballycarry forges: Templecorran AM 26; 125

Ballycarry fort: Templecorran AM 26; 83

Ballycarry graveyard: Templecorran AM 26; 11, 83, 87, 108, 112, 117–20

Ballycarry meeting house (P): Templecorran AM 26; 85, 92–93, 100–01, 104, 116, 127–29, 132

Ballycarry meeting house (U): Templecorran AM 26; 83, 85, 92–93, 100–01, 112, 116, 125, 127–28, 131

Ballycarry meeting houses: Glynn AM 26; 23

Ballycarry meeting houses: Kilroot AM 26; 56

Ballycarry national school [I]: Templecorran AM 26; 87, 93, 100, 116, 125, 130–31

Ballycarry national school [II]: Templecorran AM 26; 87, 115–16

Ballycarry North West graveyard: Templecorran AM 26; 113, 120

Ballycarry North West td: Templecorran AM 26; 108, 119, 127, 132

Ballycarry old church: Templecorran AM 26; 11, 83, 92, 97, 107–10, 112–13, 117–20

Ballycarry old meeting house: Templecorran AM 26; 85

Ballycarry ph: Carrickfergus AM 37; 134

Ballycarry post office: Templecorran AM 26; 85, 92, 127

Ballycarry South West td: Templecorran AM 26; 87, 108, 113, 115, 119

Ballycarry Sunday school: Templecorran AM 26; 87–88, 93, 100, 116, 129–30, 132

Ballycarry threshing machine: Templecorran AM 26; 125

Ballycarry village graveyard: Templecorran AM 26; 120

Ballycarry weighhouse: Templecorran AM 26; 125

Ballycarry well: Rathlin Island AM 24; 130

Ballycarry, Bard of: Templecorran AM 26; 11, 87, 108, 118

Ballycarten (see Ballycarton)

Ballycartin (see Ballyartan): Cumber LY 28; 86

Ballycarton corn mill: Magilligan LY 11; 86, 132

Ballycarton fort: Magilligan LY 11; 91–92, 127

Ballycarton school: Aghanloo LY 11; 31–32

Ballycarton td: Aghanloo LY 11; 11, 17–18, 21, 31, 33, 37–38, 41–42

Ballycarton td: Drumachose LY 9; 121

Ballycarton td: Magilligan LY 11; 86, 92, 94, 97, 107, 118, 120, 124, 126, 132, 135

Ballycaschoni school: Hillsborough DN 12; 101

Ballycassidy bridge: Trory FH 14; 123

Ballycassidy manor: Trory FH 14; 129

Ballycassidy mill: Trory FH 14; 125

Ballycassidy mills bridge: Trory FH 14; 126

Ballycassidy river: Derryvullan FH 14; 31

Ballycassidy td: Misc. TE 5; 147

Ballycassidy td: Trory FH 14; 127–28

Ballycastle: Aghadowey LY 22; 26

Ballycastle: Aghanloo LY 11; 4, 8

Ballycastle: Armoy AM 24; 1, 4–5

Ballycastle: Ballintoy AM 24; 10–11, 15–16, 32–33

Ballycastle: Ballyaghran LY 33; 2, 27

Ballycastle: Ballyrashane LY 22; 47–49, 54, 56

Ballycastle: Ballywillin LY 33; 38

Ballycastle: Banagher LY 30; 18

Ballycastle: Billy AM 16; 47

Ballycastle: Blaris AM 8; 54

Ballycastle: Coleraine LY 33; 91, 128

Ballycastle: Culfeightrin AM 24; 38, 40, 43–48, 50–52, 54–55, 59, 63, 65, 67, 69, 71–75, 77, 79, 82, 84

Ballycastle: Derrykeighan AM 16; 83

Ballycastle: Dunboe LY 11; 46, 60

Ballycastle: Island Magee AM 10; 76

Ballycastle: Killagan AM 23; 83

Ballycastle: Killowen LY 33; 172

Ballycastle: Kilrea LY 27; 110, 126

Ballycastle: Kirkinriola AM 23; 91, 104, 120

Ballycastle: Layd AM 13; 39–40, 47

Ballycastle: Magilligan LY 11; 92, 125

Ballycastle: Misc. AM 10; 129

Ballycastle: Ramoan AM 24; 87, 90–98, 100, 104–05, 107–10, 112, 115, 117, 120, 123–24

Ballycastle: Rasharkin AM 23; 131

Ballycastle: Rathlin Island AM 24; 127, 129

Ballycastle: Tickmacrevan AM 13; 124

Ballycastle bay: Culfeightrin AM 24; 42–44

Ballycastle bay: Ramoan AM 24; 88, 92–93

Ballycastle bleach green: Ramoan AM 24; 89

Ballycastle brewery: Ramoan AM 24; 93

Ballycastle bridge: Ramoan AM 24; 97

Ballycastle Castle: Ramoan AM 24; 88, 90, 93, 98, 125

Ballycastle chapel (C): Ramoan AM 24; 89, 94

Ballycastle chapel (M): Ramoan AM 24; 89, 94

Ballycastle church: Culfeightrin AM 24; 38

Ballycastle church: Ramoan AM 24; 86, 88–89, 93–94, 96, 99, 101–02

Ballycastle church school: Ramoan AM 24; 126

Ballycastle collieries: Ramoan AM 24; 89, 94, 96–97, 101–03

Ballycastle corn mill: Ramoan AM 24; 96

Ballycastle dispensary: Culfeightrin AM 24; 47
Ballycastle dispensary: Ramoan AM 24; 95, 98, 100
Ballycastle fishery: Ramoan AM 24; 101
Ballycastle forts: Aghanloo LY 11; 5, 25
Ballycastle gaol: Ramoan AM 24; 94
Ballycastle glasshouse: Ramoan AM 24; 89, 93, 96–98, 101–03
Ballycastle glasshouses: Ramoan AM 24; 89
Ballycastle Glebe House: Ramoan AM 24; 89
Ballycastle harbour: Culfeightrin AM 24; 50, 55, 63
Ballycastle harbour: Ramoan AM 24; 88–89, 97–98, 101–03, 120
Ballycastle hibernian school [I]: Ramoan AM 24; 99
Ballycastle hibernian school [II]: Ramoan AM 24; 99
Ballycastle hibernian school [III]: Ramoan AM 24; 99–100
Ballycastle inns: Ramoan AM 24; 89, 94
Ballycastle Lower td: Grey Abbey DN 7; 67
Ballycastle Lower td: Misc. DN 17; 123
Ballycastle manor: Culfeightrin AM 24; 47
Ballycastle manufactories: Ramoan AM 24; 97
Ballycastle market house: Ramoan AM 24; 94–95
Ballycastle meeting house: Ramoan AM 24; 89, 94
Ballycastle old bawn: Aghanloo LY 11; 3–4, 8
Ballycastle old castle: Aghanloo LY 11; 21, 25–28
Ballycastle old graveyard: Ramoan AM 24; 112
Ballycastle orchard: Magilligan LY 11; 84
Ballycastle pay school [I]: Ramoan AM 24; 126
Ballycastle pay school [II]: Ramoan AM 24; 126
Ballycastle pay school [III]: Ramoan AM 24; 126
Ballycastle pay school [IV]: Ramoan AM 24; 126
Ballycastle pay school [V]: Ramoan AM 24; 126
Ballycastle pay school [VI]: Ramoan AM 24; 126
Ballycastle pier: Culfeightrin AM 24; 50
Ballycastle pier: Ramoan AM 24; 88, 90, 93, 97, 101, 120
Ballycastle pottery: Ramoan AM 24; 101
Ballycastle private school: Ramoan AM 24; 99
Ballycastle quarries: Ramoan AM 24; 88, 103
Ballycastle quay: Culfeightrin AM 24; 63
Ballycastle quay: Ramoan AM 24; 89, 94, 103, 120, 124
Ballycastle quay school: Ramoan AM 24; 126
Ballycastle school: Aghanloo LY 11; 31
Ballycastle school: Grey Abbey DN 7; 69–70
Ballycastle tanneries: Ramoan AM 24; 93
Ballycastle td: Aghanloo LY 11; 3, 12–13, 18–19, 21–23, 28, 31–33, 36–42
Ballycastle td: Grey Abbey DN 7; 67, 69–70
Ballycastle Upper td: Grey Abbey DN 7; 67
Ballycastle Upper td: Misc. DN 17; 123
Ballycaw td: Misc. DN 17; 126
Ballychone (see Ballyhowne): Ballylinny AM 32; 22, 30

Ballyclaber evening school: Coleraine LY 33; 66
Ballyclaber fort: Coleraine LY 33; 92, 94, 132
Ballyclaber meeting house: Coleraine LY 33; 91, 95, 141
Ballyclaber school: Coleraine LY 33; 66, 133
Ballyclaber td: Coleraine LY 33; 66, 143, 155
Ballyclaghan (see Ballycaghan): Aghadowey LY 22; 32
Ballyclaghan (see Ballycloghan): Duneane AM 19; 108
Ballyclamper td: Misc. DN 17; 124
Ballyclander (Ballyclanders) td: Ballee DN 17; 22–23
Ballyclander Lower td: Ballee DN 17; 20–21
Ballyclander Upper td: Ballee DN 17; 20–21
Ballyclare: Antrim AM 29; 22, 37
Ballyclare: Ballycor AM 32; 3–4, 8
Ballyclare: Ballylinny AM 32; 13–14, 16, 25, 28–29
Ballyclare: Ballynure AM 32; 32–33, 38, 42, 47, 56, 63, 69–70
Ballyclare: Carnmoney AM 2; 49, 70, 76, 85–86, 88, 93
Ballyclare: Carrickfergus AM 37; 73, 79, 165
Ballyclare: Connor AM 19; 30
Ballyclare: Doagh AM 29; 60, 63–67, 70–71, 73–75, 77, 80–82, 84–87, 89–91, 94, 96, 98–99
Ballyclare: Donegore AM 29; 106, 108, 132
Ballyclare: Glenwhirry AM 32; 75, 77
Ballyclare: Inver AM 26; 51, 55
Ballyclare: Island Magee AM 10; 93
Ballyclare: Kilbride AM 29; 135–36, 138–39, 147–48, 150, 154, 156
Ballyclare: Kilwaughter AM 10; 110
Ballyclare: Nilteen AM 35; 89–90, 95
Ballyclare: Raloo AM 32; 91
Ballyclare: Rashee AM 32; 136–37
Ballyclare: Templepatrick AM 35; 111, 148–49
Ballyclare bleaching mill: Ballynure AM 32; 43, 67–68, 72
Ballyclare bog: Doagh AM 29; 84
Ballyclare Book Club room: Doagh AM 29; 89
Ballyclare bridge: Doagh AM 29; 60, 64–65, 89, 91–92
Ballyclare Catholic Sunday school: Doagh AM 29; 83–84, 97
Ballyclare chapel (C): Ballymartin AM 2; 7
Ballyclare chapel (C): Ballynure AM 32; 69
Ballyclare chapel (C): Ballyrobert AM 2; 21
Ballyclare chapel (C): Ballywalter AM 2; 30
Ballyclare chapel (C): Doagh AM 29; 64–65, 74–75, 83, 85, 88, 90, 97
Ballyclare chapel (C): Kilbride AM 29; 142
Ballyclare chapel (C): Mallusk AM 2; 111
Ballyclare chapel (C): Templepatrick AM 35; 119
Ballyclare chapel (M): Ballycor AM 32; 6

Ballyclare chapel (M): Doagh AM 29; 60, 64–65, 74, 85, 88–90, 97–98

Ballyclare chapel (WM): Doagh AM 29; 75, 88

Ballyclare classical school: Doagh AM 29; 97, 99

Ballyclare corn mill: Doagh AM 29; 70, 86, 88

Ballyclare coves: Doagh AM 29; 79

Ballyclare dispensary: Ballynure AM 32; 42

Ballyclare district: Ballynure AM 32; 64

Ballyclare fairgreen: Doagh AM 29; 90

Ballyclare flour mill: Doagh AM 29; 70, 93

Ballyclare foot-go: Doagh AM 29; 82

Ballyclare fort: Ballynure AM 32; 62

Ballyclare Green Sunday school: Ballynure AM 32; 53, 71

Ballyclare infant school: Doagh AM 29; 88, 95, 97

Ballyclare meeting house (Cov.): Doagh AM 29; 64, 74–75, 85, 87, 90

Ballyclare meeting house (P): Ballylinny AM 32; 17, 26

Ballyclare meeting house (P): Ballynure AM 32; 54

Ballyclare meeting house (U): Doagh AM 29; 60, 64, 74–75, 85–87, 90

Ballyclare Methodist school: Doagh AM 29; 88

Ballyclare Methodist Sunday school: Ballynure AM 32; 53

Ballyclare Methodist Sunday school: Doagh AM 29; 98

Ballyclare muslin factory: Ballynure AM 32; 34, 53

Ballyclare national school: Doagh AM 29; 82–83, 91, 97, 99

Ballyclare old cotton mill: Ballynure AM 32; 43, 68

Ballyclare old flax mill: Ballynure AM 32; 43, 68

Ballyclare paper mill: Ballynure AM 32; 34, 43, 67–68, 72

Ballyclare paper mill: Doagh AM 29; 70, 88, 92–93, 95–96

Ballyclare post office: Doagh AM 29; 90–91

Ballyclare Presbyterian Sunday school: Ballynure AM 32; 54

Ballyclare private school [I]: Doagh AM 29; 83, 91

Ballyclare private school: Rashee AM 32; 141

Ballyclare private school [II]: Doagh AM 29; 83, 98

Ballyclare private school [III]: Doagh AM 29; 97

Ballyclare pumps: Doagh AM 29; 90

Ballyclare reading house: Ballynure AM 32; 53

Ballyclare road bridge: Carnmoney AM 2; 85

Ballyclare road bridge: Rashee AM 32; 137

Ballyclare school [I]: Rashee AM 32; 141

Ballyclare school [II]: Rashee AM 32; 141

Ballyclare school [III]: Rashee AM 32; 141

Ballyclare Sunday school: Doagh AM 29; 83, 98

Ballyclare td: Ballynure AM 32; 63

Ballyclare td: Doagh AM 29; 60–61, 63, 80, 85

Ballyclare Wesleyan Methodist school: Doagh AM 29; 83, 88

Ballyclare Wesleyan Methodist Sunday school: Doagh AM 29; 83

Ballyclaverty cove: Donegore AM 29; 123

Ballyclaverty td: Donegore AM 29; 101, 131

Ballycleward td: Ballylinny AM 32; 30

Ballycloch td: Ahoghill AM 23; 40

Ballyclog church: Ballyclog TE 20; 15, 18

Ballyclog glebe: Ballyclog TE 20; 16, 18

Ballyclog Glebe House: Ballyclog TE 20; 15

Ballyclog hibernian schools: Ballyclog TE 20; 18

Ballyclog independent schools: Ballyclog TE 20; 18

Ballyclog Kildare school: Ballyclog TE 20; 18

Ballyclog meeting house: Ballyclog TE 20; 18

Ballyclog parish school (see Killoon): Ballyclog TE 20; 16

Ballyclog ph: Clonoe TE 20; 29

Ballyclog ph: Donaghenry TE 20; 37

Ballyclog ph: Tamlaght TE 20; 73

Ballyclogh (Ballyclough) td: Dunluce AM 16; 115

Ballyclogh cave: Dunluce AM 16; 116–17, 119

Ballyclogh fort: Dunluce AM 16; 106, 119

Ballyclogh fort: Magheragall AM 21; 103

Ballyclogh giant's grave: Magheragall AM 21; 103

Ballyclogh graveyard: Dunluce AM 16; 113, 119

Ballyclogh graveyard: Magheragall AM 21; 103

Ballyclogh old church: Magheragall AM 21; 102–03

Ballyclogh school: Dunluce AM 16; 112

Ballyclogh South cave: Dunluce AM 16; 119

Ballyclogh standing stones: Magheragall AM 21; 103

Ballyclogh stone column: Dunluce AM 16; 117

Ballyclogh td: Magheragall AM 21; 109

Ballycloghan cave: Duneane AM 19; 120

Ballycloghan corn mill: Killinchy DN 7; 91

Ballycloghan fort: Duneane AM 19; 108, 110, 120

Ballycloghan td: Holywood DN 7; 77

Ballycloghan td: Killinchy DN 7; 86, 88, 91

Ballycloghanduff td: Ballylinny AM 32; 22, 30

Ballycloghtogall td: Misc. DN 17; 121

Ballyclose district: Drumachose LY 9; 48, 75–76, 79, 82, 112–15

Ballyclose rivulet: Drumachose LY 9; 79

Ballyclose school: Drumachose LY 9; 70

Ballyclose stream: Drumachose LY 9; 46, 48

Ballyclough td: Aghadowey LY 22; 28, 35–38

Ballyclough td: Misc. LY 36; 116

Ballycloughan (Ballycloghan) td: Holywood DN 7; 79–80, 82

Ballycloughan td: Skerry AM 13; 105

Ballyclougher td: Ballylinny AM 32; 30

Ballyclug forts: Ballyclug AM 23; 64

Ballyclug graveyard: Ballyclug AM 23; 60

Ballyclug old church: Ballyclug AM 23; 60

Ballyclug ph: Ahoghill AM 23; 1

Ballyclug ph: Artrea TE 20; 6

Ballyclug ph: Connor AM 19; 16, 18, 24
Ballyclug ph: Glenwhirry AM 32; 74
Ballyclug ph: Kirkinriola AM 23; 88, 92, 106, 115, 120
Ballyclug ph: Racavan AM 13; 86
Ballyclug school: Ballyclug AM 23; 59–60
Ballyclug schools: Ballyclug AM 23; 58
Ballycoghill bridge: Aughnamullen MN 40; 73
Ballycogogie td: Ballylinny AM 32; 22, 30
Ballycollin cairns: Derryaghy AM 8; 97
Ballycollin fort: Derryaghy AM 8; 95
Ballycollin td: Derryaghy AM 8; 91–92, 100–101, 108–09, 114–115, 121
Ballycommagh td: Ballylinny AM 32; 30
Ballyconally td: Leck DL 39; 118
Ballyconnel (see Ballyconnell): Kinawley FH 4; 115
Ballyconnell: Tomregan FH 4; 126–27, 131
Ballyconnell bleaching mill: Tomregan FH 4; 128–30
Ballyconnell bridge: Tomregan FH 4; 128
Ballyconnell Castle: Tomregan FH 4; 127–28
Ballyconnell chapel: Tomregan FH 4; 127
Ballyconnell church: Tomregan FH 4; 127
Ballyconnell corn mill: Tomregan FH 4; 128–30
Ballyconnell dispensary: Tomregan FH 4; 129
Ballyconnell market house: Tomregan FH 4; 127
Ballyconnell meeting house: Tomregan FH 4; 127
Ballyconnell old church: Tomregan FH 4; 128
Ballyconnell school [I]: Tomregan FH 4; 129
Ballyconnell school [II]: Tomregan FH 4; 129
Ballyconnelly (Ballyconnolly) td: Ahoghill AM 23; 35, 38–39, 50
Ballyconnelly fort: Ahoghill AM 23; 35
Ballyconnelly school: Ahoghill AM 23; 50
Ballyconnelly td: Tullyaughnish DL 38; 85, 97
Ballycoofin td: Ballylinny AM 32; 22, 30
Ballycoos td: Carncastle and Killyglen AM 10; 2
Ballycopeland corn mill: Donaghadee DN 7; 49
Ballycopeland meeting house: Donaghadee DN 7; 49
Ballycopeland td: Donaghadee DN 7; 45, 49–50
Ballycopeland td: Misc. DN 17; 124
Ballycopeland windmill: Donaghadee DN 7; 49
Ballycor: Ballycor AM 32; 3–4, 9
Ballycor bleach green: Ballycor AM 32; 4
Ballycor bog: Kilbride AM 29; 153
Ballycor corn mill [I]: Ballycor AM 32; 4, 9
Ballycor corn mill [II]: Ballycor AM 32; 4, 9
Ballycor forts: Ballycor AM 32; 8
Ballycor graveyard: Ballycor AM 32; 4
Ballycor linen mill: Ballycor AM 32; 4
Ballycor mountains: Glenwhirry AM 32; 75
Ballycor old church: Ballycor AM 32; 4
Ballycor ph: Connor AM 19; 17, 19
Ballycor ph: Doagh AM 29; 60, 100

Ballycor ph: Glenwhirry AM 32; 74, 79
Ballycor ph: Kilwaughter AM 10; 106
Ballycor ph: Misc. AM 10; 129
Ballycor ph: Rashee AM 32; 138
Ballycor rivulet: Ballycor AM 32; 4
Ballycor school: Ballycor AM 32; 7, 10
Ballycor td: Ballycor AM 32; 4
Ballycor td: Doagh AM 29; 96
Ballycor washing mill [I]: Ballycor AM 32; 4
Ballycor washing mill [II]: Ballycor AM 32; 4
Ballycor washing mill [III]: Ballycor AM 32; 4
Ballycormick td: Misc. DN 17; 124
Ballycorra td: Ballylinny AM 32; 30
Ballycoshine (Ballycoshone) td: Clonduff DN 3; 4
Ballycoshine corn mill: Clonduff DN 3; 3–4
Ballycowan (Ballygowan) td: Connor AM 19; 18, 21
Ballycowan corn mill: Drumbo DN 7; 56, 59
Ballycowan flax mill [I]: Drumbo DN 7; 56
Ballycowan flax mill [II]: Drumbo DN 7; 56
Ballycowan hill: Connor AM 19; 19
Ballycowan school: Drumbo DN 7; 57
Ballycowan td: Drumbo DN 7; 54, 56–57, 59, 61, 63
Ballycraggy (see Ballycraigy)
Ballycraig (see Ballycraigy): Carnmoney AM 2; 34
Ballycraig caves: Dunluce AM 16; 118
Ballycraig giant's grave: Derrykeighan AM 16; 88
Ballycraig giant's grave: Dunluce AM 16; 115, 122
Ballycraig North td: Dunluce AM 16; 122
Ballycraig td: Dunluce AM 16; 116, 121
Ballycraigy (Ballycraiggy) td: Ballyclug AM 23; 53, 66
Ballycraigy bleach greens: Antrim AM 29; 50
Ballycraigy cave: Ballyclug AM 23; 64
Ballycraigy fairy bush: Carnmoney AM 2; 99
Ballycraigy fort: Ballyclug AM 23; 64
Ballycraigy forts: Antrim AM 29; 43
Ballycraigy House: Antrim AM 29; 20, 50
Ballycraigy House: Muckamore AM 35; 56
Ballycraigy meeting house: Carnmoney AM 2; 44–45, 55, 57, 75, 82
Ballycraigy quarries: Larne AM 10; 123
Ballycraigy school: Carnmoney AM 2; 77, 85, 88
Ballycraigy Sunday school: Carnmoney AM 2; 79
Ballycraigy td: Carnmoney AM 2; 34, 62, 73, 88, 92, 99, 102
Ballycraigy td: Larne AM 10; 123, 125–26
Ballycranbeg td: Misc. DN 17; 125
Ballycranmore td: Misc. DN 17; 125
Ballycraskenan td: Ballylinny AM 32; 30
Ballycreeganconley td: Ballylinny AM 32; 30
Ballycreely td: Comber DN 7; 37, 39, 42–43
Ballycreen td: Magheradrool DN 17; 99, 102

Ballycregagh (Ballycreagagh) td: Dunaghy AM 13; 24

Ballycregagh Lower beetling mill: Loughguile AM 13; 63

Ballycregagh Lower flax mill: Loughguile AM 13; 63

Ballycregagh school: Dunaghy AM 13; 16

Ballycregagh school: Loughguile AM 13; 67

Ballycregagh td: Loughguile AM 13; 67, 70, 75–76

Ballycreiglderry td: Ballylinny AM 32; 30

Ballycrevie (see Crewy): Aghaderg DN 12; 1

Ballycriggey (see Ballycraigy): Carnmoney AM 2; 88

Ballycrochan td: Misc. DN 17; 124

Ballycroghan td: Bangor DN 7; 19

Ballycronan td: Island Magee AM 10; 81

Ballycronanbeg Sunday school: Island Magee AM 10; 70

Ballycronanbeg td: Island Magee AM 10; 31

Ballycronanmore td: Island Magee AM 10; 23, 58, 61–62, 71, 102–03

Ballycronnanmore (see Ballycronanmore)

Ballycross school: Dungiven LY 15; 18

Ballycross td: Donaghadee DN 7; 45

Ballycross td: Magherally DN 12; 112–14

Ballycross td: Misc. DN 17; 124

Ballycrum mountain: Drumachose LY 9; 46, 74

Ballycrum private school: Drumachose LY 9; 85

Ballycrum school: Balteagh LY 9; 17

Ballycrum school: Drumachose LY 9; 50, 123

Ballycrum standing stone: Drumachose LY 9; 58, 126

Ballycrum td: Balteagh LY 9; 17

Ballycrum td: Drumachose LY 9; 50, 56, 58, 87, 96–97, 101, 109–10, 123, 126, 133

Ballycrune school: Annahilt DN 12; 21–22

Ballycrune td: Annahilt DN 12; 20–21

Ballycruttle td: Ballee DN 17; 20–22, 24

Ballycuggely td: Ballylinny AM 32; 30

Ballycuggery td: Ballylinny AM 32; 30

Ballyculter chapel: Ballyculter DN 17; 27

Ballyculter church: Ballyculter DN 17; 25, 30

Ballyculter Glebe House: Ballyculter DN 17; 27

Ballyculter Kildare school: Ballyculter DN 17; 29

Ballyculter Lower corn mill: Ballyculter DN 17; 25, 30

Ballyculter Lower flax mill: Ballyculter DN 17; 30

Ballyculter ph: Ballee DN 17; 15

Ballyculter ph: Down DN 17; 44, 51

Ballyculter ph: Killyleagh DN 17; 85

Ballyculter ph: Misc. DN 17; 120, 122, 128

Ballyculter ph: Saul DN 17; 112

Ballyculter Upper almshouses: Ballyculter DN 17; 28

Ballyculter Upper school: Ballyculter DN 17; 28, 30

Ballyculter Upper td: Ballyculter DN 17; 27, 30

Ballycultra school: Holywood DN 7; 76

Ballycultra td: Holywood DN 7; 76–77, 79–80

Ballyculty school: Killead AM 35; 53

Ballycushan corn mill: Templepatrick AM 35; 140, 142

Ballycushan flax mill: Templepatrick AM 35; 142

Ballycushan threshing machine: Templepatrick AM 35; 113, 146

Ballycushion (see Ballycushan): Templepatrick AM 35; 146

Ballycushion td: Ballymartin AM 2; 15

Ballycushion td: Misc. DL 39; 195

Ballydargin (Ballydurgen) td: Bright DN 17; 33, 35, 37

Ballydavey td: Holywood DN 7; 77–78, 80

Ballydawley fort: Artrea LY 6; 11, 31

Ballydawley td: Artrea LY 6; 9, 11, 31

Ballydawley td: Tamlaght TE 20; 103, 120, 125–26

Ballydawly (see Ballydawley): Tamlaght TE 20; 125

Ballyderg corn mill: Tamlaght Finlagan LY 25; 83, 101, 121

Ballyderg flax mill [I]: Tamlaght Finlagan LY 25; 83, 101, 121

Ballyderg flax mill [II]: Tamlaght Finlagan LY 25; 101

Ballyderg new school: Tamlaght Finlagan LY 25; 80

Ballyderg school [I]: Tamlaght Finlagan LY 25; 80

Ballyderg school [II]: Tamlaght Finlagan LY 25; 80

Ballyderg spade mill: Tamlaght Finlagan LY 25; 83, 121

Ballyderg tanyard: Tamlaght Finlagan LY 25; 83–84, 122

Ballydergh (see Ballyderg): Tamlaght Finlagan LY 25; 101

Ballydermot bog: Ballyscullion LY 6; 68–69

Ballydermot forts: Ballyscullion LY 6; 50, 72

Ballydermot td: Ballyscullion LY 6; 50, 63

Ballydevitt Beg td: Killymard DL 39; 100

Ballydevitt bleach green: Aghadowey LY 22; 8–9, 12

Ballydevitt bog: Aghadowey LY 22; 2

Ballydevitt church: Killymard DL 39; 96–97, 103

Ballydevitt creek: Killymard DL 39; 103

Ballydevitt fort: Killymard DL 39; 97

Ballydevitt hamlet: Killymard DL 39; 107

Ballydevitt House: Aghadowey LY 22; 6–7, 12

Ballydevitt House: Macosquin LY 22; 93

Ballydevitt More td: Killymard DL 39; 101

Ballydevitt td: Aghadowey LY 22; 6, 8

Ballydian: Aughnamullen MN 40; 76

Ballydivit (see Ballydevitt): Killymard DL 39; 96

Ballydivitty (see Ballydivity): Derrykeighan AM 16; 95

Ballydivity hill: Derrykeighan AM 16; 80

Ballydivity House: Derrykeighan AM 16; 78, 84
Ballydivity td: Derrykeighan AM 16; 78, 89
Ballydivity td: Dunaghy AM 13; 26
Ballydivity Upper td: Derrykeighan AM 16; 95
Ballydock td (see also Carstown): Misc. DN 17; 125
Ballydogherty flax mill [I]: Loughgilly AH 1; 86
Ballydogherty flax mill [II]: Loughgilly AH 1; 86
Ballydogherty td: Loughgilly AH 1; 84
Ballydolaghan (see Ballydollaghan): Drumbo DN 7; 60, 62
Ballydollaghan corn mill: Drumbo DN 7; 60
Ballydollaghan flax mills: Knockbreda DN 7; 102
Ballydollaghan td: Drumbo DN 7; 60–62
Ballydollaghan td: Knockbreda DN 7; 102
Ballydonagan td: Bovevagh LY 25; 9
Ballydonaghy bog: Leckpatrick TE 5; 120
Ballydonaghy bridge: Glenavy AM 21; 80
Ballydonaghy forts: Camlin AM 21; 71
Ballydonaghy lough: Tamlaght Finlagan LY 25; 120
Ballydonaghy school: Camlin AM 21; 62, 72, 75–76
Ballydonaghy td: Camlin AM 21; 60
Ballydonaghy td: Leckpatrick TE 5; 117, 120
Ballydonaghy td: Seagoe AH 1; 102, 107
Ballydonaghy td: Tamlaght Finlagan LY 25; 93
Ballydonal td: Ballinderry TE 20; 13
Ballydonedrow td: Ballylinny AM 32; 30
Ballydonegan fort: Banagher LY 30; 51, 94
Ballydonegan graveyard: Banagher LY 30; 39, 55
Ballydonegan monument: Banagher LY 30; 44, 56
Ballydonegan quarry: Banagher LY 30; 126
Ballydonegan standing stones: Banagher LY 30; 46
Ballydonegan sweathouse: Banagher LY 30; 34, 112
Ballydonegan td: Banagher LY 30; 22–23, 33, 36, 44, 52, 62, 86–87, 95, 102, 108–09, 113–14, 117, 122, 126, 129, 131–32
Ballydonity td: Down DN 17; 52, 56
Ballydonnell (Ballydonnel) td: Down DN 17; 52, 56–57
Ballydonnell td: Ballinderry LY 6; 41
Ballydonnelly (Ballydonelly) td: Duneane AM 19; 96, 123
Ballydonnelly corn mill: Rasharkin AM 23; 131
Ballydonnelly flax mill: Rasharkin AM 23; 131
Ballydonnelly hill: Duneane AM 19; 96
Ballydonnity (see Ballydonity): Down DN 17; 56
Ballydoo hill: Drumgath DN 3; 19
Ballydoo td: Drumgath DN 3; 21
Ballydoogan (see Ballydoonan): Banagher LY 30; 26
Ballydoolagh giant's grave: Magheracross FH 14; 97
Ballydoolagh hill: Derryvullan FH 14; 40
Ballydoolagh hill: Magheracross FH 14; 91, 102
Ballydoolagh lough: Magheracross FH 14; 91
Ballydoolagh school: Magheracross FH 14; 99

Ballydoolagh td: Magheracross FH 14; 91, 97, 102
Ballydoon td: Drumachose LY 9; 91, 129
Ballydoonan district: Banagher LY 30; 108, 110
Ballydoonan rocks: Banagher LY 30; 26
Ballydorn standing stone: Killinchy DN 7; 90
Ballydorn td: Killinchy DN 7; 86, 86, 90
Ballydoulagh (see Ballydoolagh): Magheracross FH 14; 91
Ballydowan-mivil td: Ballylinny AM 32; 30
Ballydowey td: Misc. DN 17; 127
Ballydown bridge: Seapatrick DN 12; 125
Ballydown meeting house: Seapatrick DN 12; 125, 132
Ballydown mill [I]: Seapatrick DN 12; 134
Ballydown mill [II]: Seapatrick DN 12; 134
Ballydown moat: Island Magee AM 10; 99
Ballydown td: Island Magee AM 10; 58–59, 71, 99, 102
Ballydown td: Seapatrick DN 12; 123, 126, 132, 134
Ballydownan td: Misc. DN 17; 124
Ballydrain House: Drumbeg AM 8; 126
Ballydrain school: Tullynakill DN 7; 122
Ballydrain td: Newtownards DN 7; 105
Ballydrain td: Tullynakill DN 7; 122–23
Ballydrentagh (see Ballynadrentagh): Killead AM 35; 40
Ballydrummaul (see Ballydunmaul): Drummaul AM 19; 89
Ballydrummon td: Drumgooland DN 3; 22
Ballyduff (Ballydhu) td: Carnmoney AM 2; 34, 44–45, 62, 72, 81, 85, 88, 98, 102, 105
Ballyduff Bray hill: Carnmoney AM 2; 98
Ballyduff fort [I]: Carnmoney AM 2; 100
Ballyduff fort [II]: Carnmoney AM 2; 100–01
Ballyduff Manse: Carnmoney AM 2; 81
Ballyduff meeting house (see Carnmoney): Carnmoney AM 2; 72
Ballyduff session house: Carnmoney AM 2; 105
Ballyduff Sunday school: Carnmoney AM 2; 79
Ballyduff td: Clonleigh DL 39; 12
Ballydugan flour mill: Down DN 17; 49
Ballydugan lough: Down DN 17; 38
Ballydugan td: Down DN 17; 50, 52, 54
Ballydugan td: Tullylish DN 12; 140, 143–44
Ballydugan windmill: Down DN 17; 49
Ballydugenan (see Ballydugennan): Duneane AM 19; 124
Ballydugennan td: Duneane AM 19; 122, 124
Ballydulaney school: Clonallan DN 3; 1
Ballydulaney td: Clonallan DN 3; 1
Ballydullaghan bog: Desertoghill LY 27; 5, 25
Ballydullaghan fort [I]: Desertoghill LY 27; 26
Ballydullaghan fort [II]: Desertoghill LY 27; 26
Ballydullaghan stream: Desertoghill LY 27; 5

Ballydullaghan td: Desertoghill LY 27; 8, 17, 19, 26

Ballydunmaul school: Drummaul AM 19; 76, 87, 92

Ballydunmaul td: Drummaul AM 19; 89–91, 91

Ballydurnian church: Ramoan AM 24; 113

Ballydurnian td: Ramoan AM 24; 107

Ballyear mill [I]: Seapatrick DN 12; 134

Ballyear mill [II]: Seapatrick DN 12; 134

Ballyear td: Seapatrick DN 12; 134

Ballyearle td: Ballylinny AM 32; 29

Ballyeastan td: Ballywalter DN 7; 18

Ballyeaston: Ballycor AM 32; 3, 7–8

Ballyeaston: Ballynure AM 32; 72

Ballyeaston bog: Ballycor AM 32; 8

Ballyeaston church: Ballycor AM 32; 3, 8

Ballyeaston church: Doagh AM 29; 75

Ballyeaston district: Ballylinny AM 32; 26

Ballyeaston district: Ballynure AM 32; 65

Ballyeaston district: Doagh AM 29; 91

Ballyeaston district: Rashee AM 32; 138

Ballyeaston meeting house (P): Ballycor AM 32; 3, 7–9

Ballyeaston meeting house (P): Ballylinny AM 32; 17, 26

Ballyeaston meeting house (S): Ballycor AM 32; 3–4, 8–9

Ballyeaston meeting house school [I]: Ballycor AM 32; 7

Ballyeaston meeting house school [II]: Ballycor AM 32; 7

Ballyeaston road bridge: Ballycor AM 32; 4, 9

Ballyeaston school [I]: Rashee AM 32; 140

Ballyeaston school [II]: Rashee AM 32; 140

Ballyeaston school [III]: Rashee AM 32; 141

Ballyeaston schools: Ballycor AM 32; 3, 7

Ballyeaston td: Aghanloo LY 11; 40

Ballyeaston td: Ballycor AM 32; 3

Ballyeaston td: Doagh AM 29; 93

Ballyeaston td: Kilbride AM 29; 150–51, 154

Ballyedmond House: Kilbroney DN 3; 28–29

Ballyedmond td: Kilbroney DN 3; 28, 31

Ballyedock Lower td: Dunsfort DN 17; 72

Ballyedock Upper td: Dunsfort DN 17; 68, 72

Ballyedom td: Misc. DN 17; 125

Ballyedwagh td: Ballylinny AM 32; 30

Ballyedward chapel: Glynn AM 26; 32, 44

Ballyedward fort: Glynn AM 26; 44

Ballyedward fort: Kilwaughter AM 10; 118

Ballyedward graveyard: Glynn AM 26; 30, 32, 44

Ballyedward hill: Glynn AM 26; 3

Ballyedward td: Ballylinny AM 32; 30

Ballyedward td: Glynn AM 26; 1, 41

Ballyedward td: Kilwaughter AM 10; 118

Ballyedwardmore hill: Templecorran AM 26; 88

Ballyeglish fort: Artrea LY 6; 31

Ballyeglish td: Artrea LY 6; 9, 17, 31, 34

Ballyemon glen: Layd AM 13; 42

Ballyemon river: Layd AM 13; 40, 43–44

Ballyesborough school: Ballyhalbert DN 7; 6

Ballyesborough td: Ballyhalbert DN 7; 6

Ballyesborough td: Ballywalter DN 7; 18

Ballyestine td: Muckamore AM 35; 82

Ballyeston (see Ballyeaston): Rashee AM 32; 140

Ballyfad fort: Layd AM 13; 41

Ballyfad td: Layd AM 13; 41

Ballyferis td: Misc. DN 17; 125

Ballyfinaghy House: Drumbeg AM 8; 125, 130

Ballyfinaghy td: Drumbeg AM 8; 133

Ballyfineragh manor: Misc. DN 17; 124–25

Ballyfineragh td: Misc. DN 17; 126

Ballyfinragh lough: Witter DN 7; 125

Ballyfirnis td: Ballywalter DN 7; 18

Ballyflanagan Island: Inishmacsaint FH 14; 76

Ballyfodrin mill: Drumcree AH 1; 32, 41

Ballyfodrin td: Drumcree AH 1; 41

Ballyfoland and Ballyglinn td: Ballylinny AM 32; 30

Ballyfone td: Misc. DN 17; 125

Ballyfoner td: Ballyphilip DN 7; 7

Ballyfore bog: Raloo AM 32; 80, 83, 86, 88

Ballyfore hill: Raloo AM 32; 82, 86

Ballyfore moss: Ballynure AM 32; 68

Ballyfore moss: Glynn AM 26; 42

Ballyfore moss: Raloo AM 32; 120

Ballyfore td: Raloo AM 32; 80, 93, 132

Ballyforiskey (see Ballyroosky)

Ballyforlea bridge: Lissan LY 31; 90, 99

Ballyforlea hill: Lissan LY 31; 99

Ballyforlea school: Lissan LY 31; 95

Ballyforlea td: Lissan LY 31; 108–09

Ballyfotherly td: Bangor DN 7; 19

Ballyfotherly td: Donaghadee DN 7; 45

Ballyfotherly td: Misc. DN 17; 124

Ballyfour lough: Racavan AM 13; 89, 97

Ballyfrench td: Ballywalter DN 7; 17

Ballyfrench td: Misc. DN 17; 125

Ballyfrenis td: Misc. DN 17; 124

Ballygabry td: Ballylinny AM 32; 30

Ballygalagh (see Ballygallagh): Ballyaghran LY 33; 12

Ballygalget chapel: Witter DN 7; 126–27

Ballygalget hill: Witter DN 7; 125

Ballygalget td: Ballyphilip DN 7; 13

Ballygalget td: Misc. DN 17; 125

Ballygalget td: Witter DN 7; 126

Ballygallagh (see Ballygalliagh): Ballylinny AM 32; 14

Ballygallagh East flax mill: Ballyaghran LY 33; 15–16, 26

Ballygallagh East td: Ballyaghran LY 33; 28

Ballygallagh td: Ballyaghran LY 33; 12

Ballygallagh West td: Ballyaghran LY 33; 27–28

Ballygallantrym td: Ballylinny AM 32; 30

Ballygallen (see Ballygallin): Ballyaghran LY 33; 21

Ballygalliagh tanyard: Ballylinny AM 32; 14, 25

Ballygalliagh td: Ballylinny AM 32; 22, 26, 30

Ballygallin fort: Ballyaghran LY 33; 10, 23

Ballygallin spring: Ballyaghran LY 33; 21

Ballygallin td: Ballyaghran LY 33; 16

Ballygallon (see Ballygallin) td: Coleraine LY 33; 62

Ballygallon td: Conwal DL 39; 26

Ballygallum (Ballygallam) td: Bright DN 17; 33, 35

Ballygally (Ballygalley) td: Carncastle and Killyglen AM 10; 3, 6–8, 10

Ballygally (Ballygawley) td: Inch DN 17; 77

Ballygally bay: Carncastle and Killyglen AM 10; 11

Ballygally Castle: Carncastle and Killyglen AM 10; 1, 6, 11

Ballygally church: Carncastle and Killyglen AM 10; 3, 8

Ballygally cotton mill: Carncastle and Killyglen AM 10; 3

Ballygally Head: Carncastle and Killyglen AM 10; 1, 3, 9, 11

Ballygally Head: Glynn AM 26; 4

Ballygally Head: Island Magee AM 10; 26, 58, 74

Ballygally Head: Templecorran AM 26; 96

Ballygally hill: Carncastle and Killyglen AM 10; 1

Ballygally private school: Carncastle and Killyglen AM 10; 7

Ballygally school: Carncastle and Killyglen AM 10; 7

Ballygally school: Inch DN 17; 73

Ballygally village: Carncastle and Killyglen AM 10; 9

Ballygally village: Island Magee AM 10; 19

Ballygargin td: Seagoe AH 1; 104, 107

Ballygarvan td: Ballywalter DN 7; 18

Ballygarvey bleach green: Kirkinriola AM 23; 91, 104, 119

Ballygarvey House: Kirkinriola AM 23; 91

Ballygarvey mills: Kirkinriola AM 23; 119–20

Ballygarvey school: Kirkinriola AM 23; 112

Ballygarvey td: Kirkinriola AM 23; 88, 91, 120–21

Ballygarvigan (Ballygarvagan) td: Misc. DN 17; 124–25, 127

Ballygarvigan school: Misc. DN 17; 128

Ballygarvy (see Ballygarvey): Kirkinriola AM 23; 119

Ballygasey (Ballygawsey) td: Loughgall AH 1; 81

Ballygasey kiln: Clonfeacle AH 1; 26

Ballygasey kilns: Loughgall AH 1; 80, 82

Ballygasey mill: Loughgall AH 1; 78

Ballygaullagait (see Ballygaullagart): Kilmacteige SO 40; 186

Ballygaullagart village: Kilmacteige SO 40; 186, 193

Ballygawley (Ballygowly) td: Aghadowey LY 22; 11, 36

Ballygawley: Aughnamullen MN 40; 75

Ballygawley: Carnteel TE 20, 21

Ballygawley: Clogher TE 5; 30, 60–61

Ballygawley: Clogherny TE 20; 26

Ballygawley: Donacavey TE 5; 62

Ballygawley: Drumragh TE 5; 109

Ballygawley: Errigal Keerogue TE 20; 46–48, 50–56

Ballygawley: Killeeshil TE 20; 62–64

Ballygawley bog: Aghadowey LY 22; 2

Ballygawley brewery: Errigal Keerogue TE 20; 51

Ballygawley corn mill: Errigal Keerogue TE 20; 51

Ballygawley dispensary: Clogher TE 5; 60

Ballygawley hotel: Errigal Keerogue TE 20; 47

Ballygawley House: Errigal Keerogue TE 20; 46, 51, 54

Ballygawley meeting house: Errigal Keerogue TE 20; 51

Ballygawley mountain: Clogher TE 5; 24

Ballygawley school: Errigal Keerogue TE 20; 49

Ballygawley td: Conwal DL 39; 26

Ballygawley td: Errigal Keerogue TE 20; 51, 56

Ballygawley water: Carnteel TE 20; 23

Ballygawley water: Killeeshil TE 20; 64

Ballygawly bog: Saintfield DN 7; 114

Ballygawly td: Saintfield DN 7; 114

Ballygay corn mill: Tullyaughnish DL 38; 89

Ballygay flax mill: Tullyaughnish DL 38; 89

Ballygay meeting house: Tullyaughnish DL 38; 88

Ballygay td: Tullyaughnish DL 38; 96–97

Ballygeesy (see Ballysessy): Camlin AM 21; 76

Ballygelach td: Misc. DN 17; 125

Ballygelagh td: Ardkeen DN 7; 1

Ballygelly td: Racavan AM 13; 88

Ballygelly Upper hill: Racavan AM 13; 89

Ballygeolagh (see Ballygalliagh): Ballylinny AM 32; 22

Ballygigon td: Killinchy DN 7; 86–87

Ballygilbert national school: Carncastle and Killyglen AM 10; 6

Ballygilbert school: Carncastle and Killyglen AM 10; 5

Ballygilbert td: Bangor DN 7; 19

Ballygilbert td: Bright DN 17; 33, 35

Ballygilbert td: Carncastle and Killyglen AM 10; 5

Ballygill North fort: Rathlin Island AM 24; 129

Ballygillen Beg td: Artrea LY 6; 34–35, 38

Ballygillen More cave: Artrea LY 6; 35

Ballygillen More forts: Artrea LY 6; 11, 35

Ballygillen More td: Artrea LY 6; 11, 35, 38

Ballyginiff (see Ballyginniff): Killead AM 35; 47

Ballyginiff td: Coleraine LY 33; 99

Ballyginniff (Ballygenny) td: Killead AM 35; 17, 24, 35, 47

Ballyginniff Castle: Killead AM 35; 50

Ballyginniff corn mill: Killead AM 35; 15, 35, 49

Ballyginniff forts: Ballymartin AM 2; 18

Ballyginniff forts: Killead AM 35; 26

Ballyginniff orchard: Killead AM 35; 35

Ballygirvan td: Killinchy DN 7; 89

Ballyglass fort: Manorhamilton Union LM 40; 52

Ballyglenullar (see Ballylenully)

Ballyglighorn td: Tullynakill DN 7; 122

Ballygoan td: Misc. TE 5; 147

Ballygolan (Ballygolliagh) td: Carnmoney AM 2; 34, 39, 47, 81, 92, 102

Ballygolan fort: Carnmoney AM 2; 101

Ballygoland (see Ballygolan): Carnmoney AM 2; 47

Ballygollan (see Ballygolan): Carnmoney AM 2; 81

Ballygoneybeg (see Ballygonybeg): Tamlaght TE 20; 79

Ballygonnell fort: Devenish FH 14; 55

Ballygonnell td: Devenish FH 14; 57

Ballygonnymore meeting house: Arboe LY 6; 1

Ballygonnymore td: Arboe LY 6; 1

Ballygonybeg td: Tamlaght TE 20; 78–80

Ballygooden td: Banagher LY 30; 22

Ballygooly td: Ballymascanlan LH 40; 56

Ballygoore td: Ballylinny AM 32; 30

Ballygorman td: Lough Swilly DL 38; 108

Ballygorman td: Loughgilly AH 1; 84

Ballygortgarve corn mill: Camlin AM 21; 67, 73

Ballygortgarve flax mill: Camlin AM 21; 67, 73

Ballygortgarve school: Camlin AM 21; 75–76

Ballygortgarve td: Camlin AM 21; 60

Ballygowan altar: Raloo AM 32; 108–11, 116–17, 122

Ballygowan bog: Ballynure AM 32; 61

Ballygowan chapel: Ballynure AM 32; 50, 69

Ballygowan chapel: Kilwaughter AM 10; 116

Ballygowan chapel: Raloo AM 32; 81, 83–84, 91, 94, 98, 107, 121–23, 126–27, 133

Ballygowan corn mill: Kilkeel DN 3; 52

Ballygowan cotton factory: Raloo AM 32; 126

Ballygowan cove: Raloo AM 32; 122

Ballygowan druid's altar: Ballynure AM 32; 61–62

Ballygowan flax mill: Ballynure AM 32; 34, 43–44, 68

Ballygowan flax mill: Killinchy DN 7; 91

Ballygowan fort: Ballynure AM 32; 61–62

Ballygowan fort: Donegore AM 29; 127–28

Ballygowan graveyard: Raloo AM 32; 91, 121

Ballygowan hill: Donegore AM 29; 104

Ballygowan old church: Raloo AM 32; 107–08

Ballygowan school: Raloo AM 32; 131

Ballygowan standing stone [I]: Ballynure AM 32; 61

Ballygowan standing stone [II]: Ballynure AM 32; 62

Ballygowan stone circle: Raloo AM 32; 111, 117

Ballygowan td: Aghaderg DN 12; 1, 3

Ballygowan td: Ballynure AM 32; 44, 61, 63, 68, 70, 72

Ballygowan td: Comber DN 7; 37, 40, 42–43

Ballygowan td: Donegore AM 29; 101

Ballygowan td: Drumragh TE 5; 110

Ballygowan td: Kilkeel DN 3; 52

Ballygowan td: Killinchy DN 7; 86, 91

Ballygowan td: Kilwaughter AM 10; 115

Ballygowan td: Moira DN 12; 117, 121

Ballygowan td: Raloo AM 32; 80, 93–94, 102–03, 106, 115, 117, 119, 122–23, 126–29, 132–33

Ballygowan tuck mill: Killinchy DN 7; 91

Ballygowan washing mill: Killinchy DN 7; 91

Ballygowny river: Arboe LY 6; 1

Ballygraffin td: Ballywalter DN 7; 18

Ballygraffin td: Kilmood DN 7; 94

Ballygraffin td: Misc. DN 17; 125

Ballygrainey flax windmill: Bangor DN 7; 22

Ballygrainey quarry: Bangor DN 7; 22

Ballygrainey school: Holywood DN 7; 76

Ballygrainey td: Bangor DN 7; 19, 22

Ballygrainey td: Holywood DN 7; 76–78, 80

Ballygraney td: Misc. DN 17; 124

Ballygrangee td: Grey Abbey DN 7; 67

Ballygrangey (see Ballygrangee) td: Misc. DN 17; 123

Ballygreenalay td: Glynn AM 26; 30

Ballygreenan td: Clogher TE 5; 35

Ballygrenlawy td: Inver AM 26; 49

Ballygroll bog: Cumber LY 28; 42

Ballygroll giant's grave: Cumber LY 28; 42, 55

Ballygroll td: Cumber LY 28; 40, 43, 54–55, 60–61, 67, 81, 94, 99, 104, 107–09

Ballygrooby corn mill: Drummaul AM 19; 84

Ballygrooby cotton mills: Drummaul AM 19; 84

Ballygrooby flour mills: Drummaul AM 19; 84

Ballygrooby school: Drummaul AM 19; 92

Ballygrooby td: Drummaul AM 19; 88–91

Ballygrooby village: Drummaul AM 19; 33

Ballygrooly (see Ballygrooby): Drummaul AM 19; 33

Ballygrot td: Bangor DN 7; 19

Ballygrubby (see Ballygruby)

Ballygruby church: Island Magee AM 10; 73

Ballygruby fort: Artrea LY 6; 11

Ballygruby Island: Artrea LY 6; 11, 33

Ballygruby school: Artrea LY 6; 19

Ballygruby td: Artrea LY 6; 11, 31, 33, 38–39

Ballygruby td: Artrea TE 20; 8

Ballygrueby (see Ballygruby): Island Magee AM
10; 73

Ballygudden (Ballygoodin) td: Dungiven LY 15; 23,
26, 60, 64, 74, 90, 104

Ballygudden (see Ballyguddin): Bovevagh LY 25;
45

Ballygudden bog. Dungiven LY 15; 95

Ballygudden bridge (see Buttermilk bridge):
Dungiven LY 15; 11

Ballygudden bridge: Dungiven LY 15; 97

Ballygudden td: Faughanvale LY 36; 17, 53–54, 58,
67, 70, 80–81, 92, 98

Ballyguddin (see Ballygudden): Faughanvale LY 36;
58

Ballyguddin bog: Bovevagh LY 25; 22–23, 45

Ballyguddin td: Bovevagh LY 25; 13

Ballygunaghan (Ballynagunikan) td: Donaghcloney
DN 12; 58–59

Ballygunaghan school: Donaghcloney DN 12; 58

Ballygunnigan td: Donaghmore DL 39; 36

Ballygurk corn mill: Artrea LY 6; 37

Ballygurk corn mill: Artrea TE 20; 9

Ballygurk fort: Artrea LY 6; 31

Ballygurk td: Artrea LY 6; 9, 31, 34, 37

Ballyhackamore td: Holywood DN 7; 77, 79–80

Ballyhacket Glenahorry cave: Dunboe LY 11; 50, 75

Ballyhacket Glenahorry fort: Dunboe LY 11; 49, 75

Ballyhacket Glenahorry td: Dunboe LY 11; 51, 81

Ballyhacket Glenahoy (see Ballyhacket
Glenahorry): Dunboe LY 11; 81

Ballyhacket Lisawilig (see Ballyhacket Lisawilling):
Dunboe LY 11; 76

Ballyhacket Lisawilling fort: Dunboe LY 11; 49–50,
75

Ballyhacket Lisawilling td: Dunboe LY 11; 76

Ballyhacket Magilligan cataract: Dunboe LY 11; 75

Ballyhacket Magilligan cove: Dunboe LY 11; 50

Ballyhacket Magilligan forts: Dunboe LY 11; 49, 75

Ballyhacket Magilligan td: Dunboe LY 11; 75

Ballyhacket mountain: Dunboe LY 11; 60

Ballyhacket td: Carncastle and Killyglen AM 10; 10

Ballyhacket td: Dunboe LY 11; 73, 75

Ballyhacket Toberclaw (Toberclare) td: Dunboe LY
11; 76

Ballyhacket Toberclaw forts: Dunboe LY 11; 49, 79

Ballyhacket Toberclaw school: Dunboe LY 11; 70

Ballyhacket Tuberclare (see Ballyhacket
Toberclaw): Dunboe LY 11; 76

Ballyhaft td: Misc. DN 17; 123

Ballyhaft td: Newtownards DN 7; 111, 113

Ballyhagan bog: Kilmore AH 1; 62

Ballyhagan td: Kilmore AH 1; 61, 65–66, 68–69, 71

Ballyhaise corn mills: Tomregan FH 4; 128, 131

Ballyhalbert (St Andrews) ph: Ardkeen DN 7; 1

Ballyhalbert: Ballyhalbert DN 7; 5

Ballyhalbert: Ballywalter DN 7; 18

Ballyhalbert: Inishargy DN 7; 84

Ballyhalbert: Misc. DN 17; 117

Ballyhalbert coastguard station: Ballyhalbert DN 7;
6

Ballyhalbert corn mill: Ballyhalbert DN 7; 5 6

Ballyhalbert manor: Ballywalter DN 7; 17

Ballyhalbert national school: Ballyhalbert DN 7; 5

Ballyhalbert old church: Ballyhalbert DN 7; 5

Ballyhalbert ph: Down DN 17; 43

Ballyhalbert standing stone: Ballyhalbert DN 7; 5

Ballyhalbert td: Ballyhalbert DN 7; 5

Ballyhalbert td: Ballywalter DN 7; 17

Ballyhalbert td: Misc. DN 17; 125

Ballyhallaghan school: Clogherny TE 20; 26

Ballyhamage beetling mill: Kilbride AM 29; 139,
150, 156

Ballyhamage bridge: Kilbride AM 29; 151

Ballyhamage House: Kilbride AM 29; 139

Ballyhamage rectory: Doagh AM 29; 93

Ballyhamage td: Kilbride AM 29; 136, 148, 152

Ballyhampton springs: Kilwaughter AM 10; 112

Ballyhampton td: Kilwaughter AM 10; 107, 112

Ballyhanadin (see Ballyhanedin): Banagher LY 30;
59

Ballyhaneden (see Ballyhanedin): Banagher LY 30;
95

Ballyhanedin (Ballaghanedin) td: Banagher LY 30;
22, 24, 33–34, 36, 62, 95, 102–03, 109, 117, 122,
126, 129, 131

Ballyhanedin meeting house: Banagher LY 30; 14,
27, 29, 33, 59

Ballyhanedin wood: Banagher LY 30; 122

Ballyhanidy td: Aghanloo LY 11; 40

Ballyhanna carn: Aghanloo LY 11; 5

Ballyhanna giant's graves: Aghanloo LY 11; 30

Ballyhanna mound: Aghanloo LY 11; 28

Ballyhanna mountain: Aghanloo LY 11; 1, 7, 30

Ballyhanna td: Aghanloo LY 11; 5, 21, 31, 41

Ballyhannen td: Seagoe AH 1; 107

Ballyhanney td: Misc. DN 17; 124

Ballyhanwood td: Comber DN 7; 37, 40, 42–43

Ballyharagan (see Ballyharigan): Bovevagh LY 25;
55

Ballyhare: Currin MN 40; 89–90, 94

Ballyhargan td: Banagher LY 30; 23–24

Ballyharigan altar: Bovevagh LY 25; 17–18, 41

Ballyharigan cave: Bovevagh LY 25; 53

Ballyharigan corn mill: Bovevagh LY 25; 4, 20–21,
58

Ballyharigan flax mill: Bovevagh LY 25; 4, 20–21,
58

Ballyharigan glen: Bovevagh LY 25; 57

Ballyharigan graveyard: Bovevagh LY 25; 8, 52–53

Ballyharigan House: Bovevagh LY 25; 3–4, 23

Ballyharigan school: Bovevagh LY 25; 55
Ballyharigan td: Bovevagh LY 25; 4, 10, 19, 33, 41–42, 60–61
Ballyharigan wood: Bovevagh LY 25; 2, 22
Ballyharrigan (see Ballyharigan): Bovevagh LY 25; 20
Ballyharrigan quarries: Magilligan LY 11; 85
Ballyharrigan td: Magilligan LY 11; 124
Ballyharry church: Island Magee AM 10; 20, 34, 44, 71, 76, 90
Ballyharry flax mill: Newtownards DN 7; 104
Ballyharry graveyard: Island Magee AM 10; 43, 45, 99–100
Ballyharry old church: Island Magee AM 10; 44
Ballyharry pier: Island Magee AM 10; 80
Ballyharry td: Island Magee AM 10; 16, 20, 34, 44–45, 63, 71, 76, 99–103, 103
Ballyharry td: Misc. DN 17; 123
Ballyharry td: Newtownards DN 7; 104
Ballyhartfield fort [I]: Ballymartin AM 2; 15, 17
Ballyhartfield fort [II]: Ballymartin AM 2; 15, 17
Ballyhartfield fort [III]: Ballymartin AM 2; 15, 17
Ballyhartfield td: Ballymartin AM 2; 15–17
Ballyharvey (Ballyhervey) td: Muckamore AM 35; 78, 83
Ballyharvey Lower cove [I]: Muckamore AM 35; 72
Ballyharvey Lower cove [II]: Muckamore AM 35; 72
Ballyharvey Lower fort: Muckamore AM 35; 71–72, 74
Ballyharvey Lower forts: Muckamore AM 35; 56
Ballyharvey Lower graveyard: Muckamore AM 35; 71
Ballyharvey Lower standing stone: Muckamore AM 35; 71
Ballyharvey Lower td: Muckamore AM 35; 54
Ballyharvey Upper forts: Muckamore AM 35; 56, 72, 74
Ballyharvey Upper td: Muckamore AM 35; 54
Ballyhase td: Devenish FH 14; 57
Ballyhaskin td: Misc. DN 17; 124
Ballyhasky bog: Misc. DL 39; 187–88
Ballyhasky spring: Misc. DL 39; 188
Ballyhasky td: Misc. DL 39; 194
Ballyhay bog: Donaghadee DN 7; 51
Ballyhay td: Donaghadee DN 7; 45, 51
Ballyhay td: Misc. DN 17; 124
Ballyhaze (see Ballyhare): Killdrumsherdan CN 40; 34
Ballyheather td: Donaghedy TE 5; 91
Ballyheelan: Drumlumman CN 40; 17
Ballyheeran corn mill: Clondavaddog DL 38; 5
Ballyheeran quarry: Lough Swilly DL 38; 129
Ballyheifer tannery: Magherafelt LY 6; 92

Ballyheifer td: Magherafelt LY 6; 91–92, 95, 107, 112
Ballyhemlin cairn: Billy AM 16; 67
Ballyhemlin corn mill: Ballyhalbert DN 7; 5–6
Ballyhemlin meeting house: Ballyhalbert DN 7; 5
Ballyhemlin td: Ballyhalbert DN 7; 5
Ballyhemlin td: Misc. DN 17; 125
Ballyhendry Point: Ballyphilip DN 7; 9
Ballyhenny td: Tullyaughnish DL 38; 97
Ballyhenry (Ballyhendry) td: Tamlaght Finlagan LY 25; 93, 119
Ballyhenry church: Island Magee AM 10; 78
Ballyhenry East td: Aghanloo LY 11; 23, 40–41
Ballyhenry fort [I]: Carnmoney AM 2; 101
Ballyhenry fort [II]: Carnmoney AM 2; 101–02
Ballyhenry hill: Ballyphilip DN 7; 9
Ballyhenry Major td: Comber DN 7; 37, 39, 42–43
Ballyhenry Minor td: Comber DN 7; 37, 39, 42–43
Ballyhenry td: Aghanloo LY 11; 13, 18, 21, 33, 37, 39, 42
Ballyhenry td: Carnmoney AM 2; 34, 46–47, 73, 81, 93, 99, 102
Ballyhenry td: Island Magee AM 10; 78
Ballyhenry td: Misc. DN 17; 125–26
Ballyhenry West td: Tamlaght Finlagan LY 25; 93
Ballyheny locality: Lough Swilly DL 38; 104
Ballyherley (Ballyhearly) td: Misc. DN 17; 125–26
Ballyherly corn mills: Ardquin DN 7; 4
Ballyherly lough: Ardquin DN 7; 4
Ballyherly lough: Ballyphilip DN 7; 7
Ballyherly td: Ardquin DN 7; 4
Ballyhernan bay: Lough Swilly DL 38; 106, 117
Ballyhernan Lower church: Clondavaddog DL 38; 5
Ballyhernan standing stones: Clondavaddog DL 38; 6
Ballyhernan td: Clondavaddog DL 38; 4, 9
Ballyhernan td: Lough Swilly DL 38; 129
Ballyherney (see Ballyherly): Ballyphilip DN 7; 8
Ballyhewn hill: Desertoghill LY 27; 1
Ballyhewn hill: Errigal LY 27; 35
Ballyhibistock td: Derrykeighan AM 16; 88, 94–95
Ballyhill (Bellahill) td: Kilroot AM 26; 56, 59, 61, 64, 67, 72–73, 77, 79–80
Ballyhill Bawn: Kilroot AM 26; 59, 61, 70–71, 74
Ballyhill Bawn: Templecorran AM 26; 86
Ballyhill bog: Kilroot AM 26; 72
Ballyhill Castle: Kilroot AM 26; 75–76, 78, 80
Ballyhill cave [I]: Kilroot AM 26; 71, 76
Ballyhill cave [II]: Kilroot AM 26; 76–77
Ballyhill corn kiln: Kilroot AM 26; 57, 60, 77
Ballyhill corn mill: Kilroot AM 26; 60, 77–78
Ballyhill demesne: Kilroot AM 26; 58
Ballyhill fort [I]: Kilroot AM 26; 71
Ballyhill fort [II]: Kilroot AM 26; 71, 77
Ballyhill hill: Killead AM 35; 7

Ballyhill hill: Kilroot AM 26; 57
Ballyhill House: Ballynure AM 32; 52
Ballyhill House: Kilroot AM 26; 57, 59, 63, 70–73, 75–80
Ballyhill House: Templecorran AM 26; 118
Ballyhill lime kiln: Kilroot AM 26; 80
Ballyhill Lower fort [I]: Killead AM 35; 39
Ballyhill Lower fort [II]: Killead AM 35; 39
Ballyhill Lower td: Killead AM 35; 27, 40
Ballyhill quarry: Kilroot AM 26; 80
Ballyhill school: Killead AM 35; 52
Ballyhill td: Killead AM 35; 22, 50
Ballyhimlin td: Ballywalter DN 7; 17
Ballyhoe bridge: Drummully FH 4; 36, 40
Ballyhoe bridge: Loughguile AM 13; 74
Ballyhoe lough: Magheracloone MN 40; 137
Ballyhoe school: Drummully FH 4; 39
Ballyholly bridge: Cumber LY 28; 11
Ballyholly mountain: Doagh AM 29; 94
Ballyholly quarries: Cumber LY 28; 121
Ballyholly quarry: Tamlaght Finlagan LY 25; 71
Ballyholly td: Cumber LY 28; 17, 66–67, 110, 116, 121, 125
Ballyholly td: Drumachose LY 9; 101
Ballyholly td: Tamlaght Finlagan LY 25; 73
Ballyholme bay: Bangor DN 7; 22
Ballyholme corn windmill: Bangor DN 7; 22
Ballyholme flour mill: Bangor DN 7; 22
Ballyholme td: Bangor DN 7; 19, 22
Ballyholme td: Misc. DN 17; 124
Ballyholy bog: Raphoe DL 39; 121
Ballyholy Far td: Raphoe DL 39; 125
Ballyholy Near td: Raphoe DL 39; 125
Ballyholy school: Raphoe DL 39; 128
Ballyhome (Ballyhomes) td: Dunluce AM 16; 106, 120
Ballyhome altar stone: Dunluce AM 16; 118
Ballyhome cave: Dunluce AM 16; 115
Ballyhome fort: Dunluce AM 16; 115, 119
Ballyhome hill: Dunluce AM 16; 106
Ballyhome school: Dunluce AM 16; 112, 122–23
Ballyhome standing stones: Dunluce AM 16; 118
Ballyhomra td: Blaris DN 12; 34
Ballyhomra td: Hillsborough DN 12; 86, 105
Ballyhone bog: Glynn AM 26; 27
Ballyhone cotton factory: Glynn AM 26; 3, 5, 40, 43
Ballyhone footbridge: Glynn AM 26; 43
Ballyhone td: Glynn AM 26; 1, 4, 28, 41–42, 47–48
Ballyhorbarnegas td: Ballylinny AM 32; 30
Ballyhorharnegan td: Ballylinny AM 32; 22
Ballyhork giant's grave: Clondavaddog DL 38; 5–6
Ballyhork lough: Clondavaddog DL 38; 3
Ballyhork standing stone: Clondavaddog DL 38; 6
Ballyhornan coastguard station: Dunsfort DN 17; 71
Ballyhornan td: Dunsfort DN 17; 67, 71–72

Ballyhorney td: Ballylinny AM 32; 22, 30
Ballyhoskin td: Donaghadee DN 7; 45
Ballyhosset (Ballyhossit) td: Ballee DN 17; 15, 18–22
Ballyhosset Milltown td: Ballee DN 17; 20, 22
Ballyhosset td: Ardglass DN 17; 7
Ballyhoura td: Hillsborough DN 12; 85
Ballyhowme (see Ballyhowne): Ballylinny AM 32; 21
Ballyhowne (Ballyhone) td: Ballylinny AM 32; 22, 30
Ballyhowne (Ballyhone) td: Carnmoney AM 2; 34, 81, 102
Ballyhowne corn mill: Carnmoney AM 2; 49, 93
Ballyhowne cotton mill: Carnmoney AM 2; 48, 92
Ballyhowne coves: Ballylinny AM 32; 21
Ballyhowne coves: Carnmoney AM 2; 71
Ballyhowne flax mill [I]: Carnmoney AM 2; 48, 92–93
Ballyhowne flax mill [II]: Carnmoney AM 2; 49, 93
Ballyhowne fort [I]: Carnmoney AM 2; 100
Ballyhowne fort [II]: Carnmoney AM 2; 100
Ballyhowne forts: Ballylinny AM 32; 21, 27
Ballyhowne mill: Carnmoney AM 2; 48, 92
Ballyhowne old town: Ballylinny AM 32; 21, 26
Ballyhowne standing stone: Carnmoney AM 2; 70, 98
Ballyhubert td: Comber DN 7; 42
Ballyhullagh td: Galloon FH 4; 95
Ballyhumully td: Ballylinny AM 32; 22
Ballyhunsley (Ballyhunsly) td: Dunluce AM 16; 106, 113
Ballyhunsley cave: Dunluce AM 16; 116, 120
Ballyhunsley fort: Dunluce AM 16; 120
Ballyhunsley North cave: Dunluce AM 16; 106
Ballyhunsley South flax mill: Dunluce AM 16; 110
Ballyhunsley South paper mill: Dunluce AM 16; 110
Ballyhurk (see Ballyhork): Clondavaddog DL 38; 3
Ballyhutherland cave: Dundermot AM 13; 34
Ballyhutherland fort: Dundermot AM 13; 34
Ballyhutherland td: Dundermot AM 13; 29, 34
Ballyilly chapel: Garvaghy DN 12; 80
Ballyilly corn mill: Garvaghy DN 12; 82
Ballyilly flax mill: Garvaghy DN 12; 82
Ballyilly House: Garvaghy DN 12; 80
Ballyilly td: Garvaghy DN 12; 80, 80–82
Ballyillymore mills: Garvaghy DN 12; 80
Ballyillymore td: Garvaghy DN 12; 81
Ballyily (see Ballyilly) chapel: Newry DN 3; 111
Ballyinahinch (see Ballynahinch): Kilmore DN 17; 91
Ballyindoalty (see Ballindoalty): Kilbroney DN 3; 28
Ballyisbro td: Misc. DN 17; 125

Ballyislin td: Ballylinny AM 32; 30

Ballyjamesduff: Drumlumman CN 40; 14

Ballyjamesduff: Laragh CN 40; 41

Ballyjohn (see Ballyhowne): Ballylinny AM 32; 22

Ballykee cave: Island Magee AM 10; 72

Ballykee td: Island Magee AM 10; 72

Ballykeel Artifinny school: Hillsborough DN 12; 95, 99–100

Ballykeel Artifinny td: Hillsborough DN 12; 86, 88, 95, 99, 106

Ballykeel Artikenny (see Ballykeel Artifinny): Hillsborough DN 12; 88

Ballykeel Castle: Island Magee AM 10; 71

Ballykeel cave [I]: Ballyclug AM 23; 65

Ballykeel cave [II]: Ballyclug AM 23; 65

Ballykeel church: Kilroot AM 26; 73

Ballykeel church: Templecorran AM 26; 107

Ballykeel corn mill: Killevy AH 1; 53

Ballykeel Edenagonnel school: Hillsborough DN 12; 95, 100

Ballykeel Edenagonnel td: Hillsborough DN 12; 86–87, 95, 100, 106–07

Ballykeel Edenagonnell meeting house: Hillsborough DN 12; 95

Ballykeel fort: Ballyclug AM 23; 65

Ballykeel fort: Clogherny TE 20; 28

Ballykeel fort [I]: Aghagallon AM 21; 17

Ballykeel fort [II]: Aghagallon AM 21; 17

Ballykeel fort [III]: Aghagallon AM 21; 17

Ballykeel graveyard: Island Magee AM 10; 29, 43, 70, 99–100

Ballykeel Lougherne school: Annahilt DN 12; 23

Ballykeel Lougherne school: Hillsborough DN 12; 100

Ballykeel Lougherne td: Annahilt DN 12; 21, 23

Ballykeel moat: Ballyclug AM 23; 54, 64–65

Ballykeel old church: Island Magee AM 10; 32, 45, 71

Ballykeel old corn kiln: Island Magee AM 10; 66

Ballykeel old graveyard: Island Magee AM 10; 47

Ballykeel school: Down DN 17; 52, 59

Ballykeel school: Dromore DN 12; 73, 78

Ballykeel school: Holywood DN 7; 76, 82

Ballykeel school: Kilmood DN 7; 95

Ballykeel td: Aghagallon AM 21; 3, 19

Ballykeel td: Ahoghill AM 23; 34

Ballykeel td: Ballyclug AM 23; 53, 65

Ballykeel td: Comber DN 7; 37–38, 42–43

Ballykeel td: Down DN 17; 52, 56–57

Ballykeel td: Dromore DN 12; 70, 73, 78

Ballykeel td: Drumgath DN 3; 21

Ballykeel td: Holywood DN 7; 76–77, 79–80

Ballykeel td: Island Magee AM 10; 19, 47, 87, 99–100

Ballykeel td: Kilmood DN 7; 95

Ballykeel td: Kilwaughter AM 10; 113

Ballykeel td: Magheralin DN 12; 109

Ballykeel td: Seapatrick DN 12; 123, 126–27

Ballykeel td: Tullynakill DN 7; 123

Ballykeel Watch carn: Kilwaughter AM 10; 119

Ballykeel windmill: Holywood DN 7; 76

Ballykeen (Ballyking) td: Tamlaght Finlagan LY 25; 72–74, 93, 119

Ballykeigle td: Kilmood DN 7; 94

Ballykeil td: Dunluce AM 16; 116, 121

Ballykeile td: Ballylinny AM 32; 30

Ballykell (see Ballykeel): Dromore DN 12; 70

Ballykell (see Ballykeel): Drumgath DN 3; 21

Ballykelly: Balteagh LY 9; 3

Ballykelly: Bovevagh LY 25; 29

Ballykelly: Clondermot LY 34; 61, 74

Ballykelly: Drumachose LY 9; 76, 84, 99, 105, 108

Ballykelly: Faughanvale LY 36; 5

Ballykelly: Lough Swilly DL 38; 138, 140, 142

Ballykelly: Tamlaght Finlagan LY 25; 63, 66, 68, 70–72, 74, 82–85, 90, 93–96, 98–99, 102, 104, 107–08, 110, 120, 123–25

Ballykelly bridge: Tamlaght Finlagan LY 25; 84–85, 98, 120, 122

Ballykelly Canal: Tamlaght Finlagan LY 25; 66–67, 71, 84–85, 90, 93, 95, 98, 100, 107

Ballykelly Castle: Tamlaght Finlagan LY 25; 68, 96, 99, 102

Ballykelly chapel: Drumachose LY 9; 107

Ballykelly church: Tamlaght Finlagan LY 25; 68–69, 82, 85, 87, 100, 102

Ballykelly corn mill [I]: Tamlaght Finlagan LY 25; 101

Ballykelly corn mill [II]: Tamlaght Finlagan LY 25; 101

Ballykelly dispensary: Cumber LY 28; 15, 25–26, 83

Ballykelly dispensary: Faughanvale LY 36; 27

Ballykelly dispensary: Magilligan LY 11; 93

Ballykelly dispensary: Tamlaght Finlagan LY 25; 68, 70, 72–74, 90, 93, 96, 100, 120, 125

Ballykelly farmhouse: Tamlaght Finlagan LY 25; 68, 70

Ballykelly female school: Tamlaght Finlagan LY 25; 68, 70, 74–79, 84, 90, 96, 100, 104, 123

Ballykelly female Sunday school: Tamlaght Finlagan LY 25; 124

Ballykelly glen: Tamlaght Finlagan LY 25; 62

Ballykelly male school: Tamlaght Finlagan LY 25; 68, 70, 74–79, 84, 90, 96, 100, 104, 123

Ballykelly male Sunday school: Tamlaght Finlagan LY 25; 124

Ballykelly market house: Tamlaght Finlagan LY 25; 68, 70, 90, 93, 100, 107

Ballykelly meeting house: Drumachose LY 9; 107

Ballykelly meeting house: Magilligan LY 11; 125
Ballykelly meeting house: Tamlaght Finlagan LY 25; 68–70, 90, 92, 100, 125
Ballykelly nursery: Tamlaght Finlagan LY 25; 66, 71
Ballykelly old chapel: Drumachose LY 9; 107
Ballykelly old church: Tamlaght Finlagan LY 25; 99
Ballykelly old meeting house: Tamlaght Finlagan LY 25; 69–70
Ballykelly post office: Tamlaght Finlagan LY 25; 68, 107
Ballykelly river: Tamlaght Finlagan LY 25; 62–63, 66, 70, 79, 83–85, 95, 97–98, 121
Ballykelly schools: Drumachose LY 9; 108
Ballykelly shambles: Tamlaght Finlagan LY 25; 107
Ballykelly Sunday school: Tamlaght Finlagan LY 25; 96
Ballykelly td: Aghanloo LY 11; 24
Ballykelly td: Seapatrick DN 12; 123–24, 126
Ballykelly td: Tamlaght Finlagan LY 25; 72–74, 87, 93, 111, 119
Ballykelly wood: Faughanvale LY 36; 3
Ballykelly wood: Tamlaght Finlagan LY 25; 71, 98
Ballykennedy cave: Ahoghill AM 23; 35
Ballykennedy church: Carmavy AM 35; 2, 4
Ballykennedy church: Killead AM 35; 25
Ballykennedy fort: Killead AM 35; 39
Ballykennedy graveyard: Killead AM 35; 25
Ballykennedy mound: Killead AM 35; 27
Ballykennedy td: Ahoghill AM 23; 1, 3, 9, 16, 18, 32, 49
Ballykennedy td: Killead AM 35; 40–41
Ballykenver td: Armoy AM 24; 1, 4
Ballykiel (see Ballykeel): Templecorran AM 26; 107
Ballykilbeg House: Down DN 17; 49
Ballykilbeg new chapel: Down DN 17; 49
Ballykilbeg old chapel: Down DN 17; 49, 60
Ballykilbeg td: Down DN 17; 49, 52, 56–57
Ballykilbride td: Ballylinny AM 32; 30
Ballykillare td: Bangor DN 7; 19, 25
Ballykillien hill: Lough Swilly DL 38; 108
Ballykilly church: Ballinderry AM 21; 41
Ballykilly td: Ballinderry AM 21; 44
Ballykilmakee td: Ballylinny AM 32; 22, 30
Ballykim Lower school: Magheradrool DN 17; 102
Ballykim Lower td: Magheradrool DN 17; 99, 102
Ballykim Upper td: Magheradrool DN 17; 99, 102
Ballykinard river: Clondavaddog DL 38; 3
Ballykine td: Dromara DN 12; 65
Ballykinlar school: Hillsborough DN 12; 102
Ballykinler: Ardglass DN 17; 12
Ballykinler Upper corn mill: Ballykinler DN 17; 32
Ballykinnegar [or Ballykenegane] district: Misc. SO 40; 199–200

Ballyknock (Ballynock) td: Killelagh LY 27; 98–99, 102
Ballyknock corn mill: Killelagh LY 27; 96
Ballyknock coves: Loughguile AM 13; 72
Ballyknock flax mill: Killelagh LY 27; 96
Ballyknock fort: Killelagh LY 27; 97
Ballyknock Glebe House: Connor AM 19; 21
Ballyknock school: Hillsborough DN 12; 100
Ballyknock td: Kilmore AH 1; 64, 67, 69, 72–73
Ballyknock td: Loughguile AM 13; 59, 69, 72, 75–76
Ballyknockan corn mill: Saintfield DN 7; 114
Ballyknockan flax mill: Saintfield DN 7; 114
Ballyknockan td: Saintfield DN 7; 114, 117–18
Ballyknocken standing stone: Dunluce AM 16; 118
Ballykurk (see Ballyhork): Clondavaddog DL 38; 5
Ballylagan bog: Errigal Keerogue TE 20; 51
Ballylagan cove: Macosquin LY 22; 87, 108
Ballylagan fort: Ballynure AM 32; 62
Ballylagan fort: Errigal Keerogue TE 20; 51
Ballylagan hill: Macosquin LY 22; 76
Ballylagan meeting house: Macosquin LY 22; 80, 90, 100–01
Ballylagan South plantation: Ballywillin LY 33; 29
Ballylagan td: Ballynure AM 32; 61–63, 68, 72
Ballylagan td: Ballywillin LY 33; 51
Ballylagan td: Carrickfergus AM 37; 93, 173
Ballylagan td: Errigal Keerogue TE 20; 48, 51, 56
Ballylagan td: Macosquin LY 22; 102
Ballylaggan (see Ballylagan): Ballynure AM 32; 68
Ballylaghe td: Muckamore AM 35; 82
Ballylame td: Desertoghill LY 27; 19
Ballylane flax mill: Kilclooney AH 1; 51
Ballylast td: Urney DL 39; 181
Ballylaster river: Clogher TE 5; 26–27
Ballylawn school: Moville DL 38; 74
Ballylawn school: Raymoghy DL 39; 140, 198
Ballylawn td: Moville DL 38; 73, 75
Ballylawn td: Raymoghy DL 39; 136, 141
Ballyleagry corn mill: Balteagh LY 9; 13
Ballyleagry fort: Balteagh LY 9; 12
Ballyleagry td: Balteagh LY 9; 12–13, 45
Ballyleany td: Kilmore AH 1; 61, 65–67, 70–72
Ballyleck lough: Monaghan MN 40; 159
Ballyleck td: Monaghan MN 40; 159
Ballyleckan td: Dunluce AM 16; 107
Ballyleese adult school: Ballyaghran LY 33; 17
Ballyleese cave [I]: Ballyaghran LY 33; 24
Ballyleese cave [II]: Ballyaghran LY 33; 24
Ballyleese infant school: Ballyaghran LY 33; 22
Ballyleese North cave [I]: Ballyaghran LY 33; 11, 22
Ballyleese North cave [II]: Ballyaghran LY 33; 11
Ballyleese North cave [III]: Ballyaghran LY 33; 11

Ballyleese North female school: Ballyaghran LY 33;
    7, 16–17
Ballyleese North male school: Ballyaghran LY 33;
    7, 16–17
Ballyleese td: Ballyaghran LY 33; 7, 20–21, 27–28
Ballyleeson (see Ballylesson): Ballyclug AM 23; 64
Ballyleidy House: Bangor DN 7; 23
Ballyleidy td: Bangor DN 7; 19
Ballyleighery (Ballyleighry) Lower td: Magilligan
    LY 11; 82–83, 95, 142
Ballyleighery cave: Magilligan LY 11; 103
Ballyleighery corn mill: Balteagh LY 9; 40
Ballyleighery coves: Magilligan LY 11; 99, 102
Ballyleighery fort: Balteagh LY 9; 24
Ballyleighery rock: Drumachose LY 9; 76
Ballyleighery rock: Magilligan LY 11; 98–99
Ballyleighery school: Magilligan LY 11; 110, 138
Ballyleighery South td: Magilligan LY 11; 134
Ballyleighery td: Aghanloo LY 11; 38
Ballyleighery td: Balteagh LY 9; 21, 23–24, 27, 40,
    44
Ballyleighery td: Magilligan LY 11; 86, 94, 123,
    126, 135
Ballyleighery Upper td: Magilligan LY 11; 95
Ballyleighrey (see Ballyleighery): Balteagh LY 9; 27
Ballyleighrey bridge: Bovevagh LY 25; 58
Ballyleighry (see Ballyleighery): Balteagh LY 9; 24
Ballyleihrey (see Ballyleighery): Magilligan LY 11;
    99
Ballylenagh td: Ballyculter DN 17; 30
Ballylennan corn mill: Skirts of Urney and Ardstraw
    TE 5; 138
Ballylennan meeting house: Skirts of Urney and
    Ardstraw TE 5; 138
Ballylennan td: Skirts of Urney and Ardstraw TE 5;
    138
Ballylennon td: Misc. DL 39; 195
Ballylenully flax mill: Duneane AM 19; 115
Ballylenully meeting house: Duneane AM 19; 96,
    100, 114
Ballylenully td: Duneane AM 19; 123–24
Ballylessan (see Ballylesson): Drumbo DN 7; 62
Ballylessen (see Ballylesson): Drumbo DN 7; 60–61
Ballylesson (Ballylessan) td: Ballyclug AM 23; 53,
    61
Ballylesson (Ballylissan) td: Glynn AM 26; 1, 18,
    41, 48
Ballylesson church: Drumbo DN 7; 59–60
Ballylesson cove: Ballyclug AM 23; 64, 64
Ballylesson fort: Glynn AM 26; 44
Ballylesson fort [I]: Ballyclug AM 23; 62, 64
Ballylesson fort [II]: Ballyclug AM 23; 64
Ballylesson fort [III]: Ballyclug AM 23; 64
Ballylesson fort [IV]: Ballyclug AM 23; 64
Ballylesson graveyard: Ballyclug AM 23; 53, 64

Ballylesson moat: Ballyclug AM 23; 61
Ballylesson td: Drumbo DN 7; 54, 56, 59, 61–62
Ballyleven (see Ballylevin)
Ballylevin td: Raymoghy DL 39; 136, 198
Ballylick (see Ballylisk): Kilmore AH 1; 64
Ballylieghrey (see Ballyleighery): Magilligan LY 11;
    135
Ballyliehery (see Ballyleighery): Balteagh LY 9; 21
Ballyliehery (see Ballyleighery): Magilligan LY 11;
    98
Ballyliffin: Clonmany DL 38; 14, 16, 18, 20
Ballyliffin: Donagh DL 38; 32
Ballyliffin bog: Clonmany DL 38; 13
Ballyliffin school: Clonmany DL 38; 17
Ballyliffin standing stones: Clonmany DL 38; 16
Ballyliffin td: Clonmany DL 38; 20
Ballyliffin td: Lough Swilly DL 38; 136
Ballylifford chapel: Ballinderry LY 6; 41
Ballylifford td: Ballinderry LY 6; 41
Ballylifford td: Ballinderry TE 20; 13
Ballylig (Ballyligg) td: Bright DN 17; 33, 35, 37
Ballylig coastguard station: Glynn AM 26; 40
Ballylig corn mill: Ramoan AM 24; 96
Ballylig cove: Glynn AM 26; 32, 44
Ballylig demesne: Glynn AM 26; 11, 14, 43
Ballylig hill: Glynn AM 26; 3
Ballylig House: Glynn AM 26; 5–6, 8, 10, 13–14,
    21–22, 41, 43–44
Ballylig limeworks: Glynn AM 26; 2, 6–7, 9, 14–15,
    18–19, 23, 26, 33–34, 36, 39–44, 47
Ballylig limeworks: Island Magee AM 10; 29,
    82–83
Ballylig plantation: Glynn AM 26; 3–4, 6
Ballylig quays: Glynn AM 26; 9, 15, 27, 33, 41,
    43–44
Ballylig school: Skerry AM 13; 114
Ballylig standing stone: Ramoan AM 24; 104
Ballylig Sunday school: Glynn AM 26; 36
Ballylig td: Down DN 17; 58
Ballylig td: Glynn AM 26; 1, 14, 17, 21, 40–41,
    47–48
Ballylig td: Raloo AM 32; 125
Ballyligg (see Ballylig)
Ballyligpatrick cove: Racavan AM 13; 102
Ballyligpatrick td: Glynn AM 26; 17
Ballyligpatrick td: Racavan AM 13; 86, 88–89
Ballylimp td: Ballywalter DN 7; 18
Ballylimp td: Misc. DN 17; 125
Ballylin td: Lough Swilly DL 38; 104
Ballylin td: Tullyaughnish DL 38; 97
Ballyliney td: Ramoan AM 24; 101
Ballylinin quarry: Taughboyne DL 39; 150
Ballylinin td: Taughboyne DL 39; 148, 152
Bally-Linney (see Ballylinny)
Ballylinney (see Ballylinny): Ballylinny AM 32; 15

Ballylinney cave: Billy AM 16; 64

Ballylinny (Ballylinney) ph: Ballymartin AM 2; 3, 15

Ballylinny burn: Ballylinny AM 32; 12, 24–25

Ballylinny district: Ballyrobert AM 2; 20

Ballylinny district: Ballywalter AM 2; 29

Ballylinny district. Mallusk AM 2; 109–10

Ballylinny flax mill: Ballylinny AM 32; 25–26

Ballylinny graveyard: Ballylinny AM 32; 14, 21, 26–27

Ballylinny manor: Ballycor AM 32; 3, 5

Ballylinny manor: Ballylinny AM 32; 15, 22

Ballylinny manor: Ballymartin AM 2; 5–6, 15

Ballylinny manor: Ballynure AM 32; 32

Ballylinny manor: Ballyrobert AM 2; 21

Ballylinny manor: Ballywalter AM 2; 26, 30

Ballylinny manor: Carnmoney AM 2; 54

Ballylinny manor: Doagh AM 29; 63

Ballylinny manor: Rashee AM 32; 138

Ballylinny manor: Templepatrick AM 35; 108, 118, 142

Ballylinny manor: Umgall AM 35; 158

Ballylinny meeting house: Ballylinny AM 32; 13, 15, 17, 24, 26, 28

Ballylinny old church: Ballylinny AM 32; 14, 21, 26

Ballylinny old school: Ballylinny AM 32; 26

Ballylinny paper mill: Nilteen AM 35; 86

Ballylinny ph: Ballynure AM 32; 31–32, 64

Ballylinny ph: Ballywalter AM 2; 26–27, 30

Ballylinny ph: Carnmoney AM 2; 36–37, 56–57, 61–62, 64, 81–82, 84

Ballylinny ph: Carrickfergus AM 37; 1

Ballylinny ph: Doagh AM 29; 60, 62–63, 84–87, 92, 100

Ballylinny ph: Mallusk AM 2; 109

Ballylinny ph: Misc. AM 10; 129

Ballylinny ph: Templepatrick AM 35; 145

Ballylinny school: Ballylinny AM 32; 22–23, 25, 29–30

Ballylinny singing school: Ballylinny AM 32; 17

Ballylinny Sunday school: Ballylinny AM 32; 24, 28

Ballylinny td: Ballylinny AM 32; 22, 29–30

Ballylintagh cove: Aghadowey LY 22; 32

Ballylintagh cove: Macosquin LY 22; 95, 117

Ballylintagh meeting house: Aghadowey LY 22; 5, 13

Ballylintagh standing stone: Aghadowey LY 22; 32

Ballylintagh td: Aghadowey LY 22; 32

Ballylintagh td: Macosquin LY 22; 77, 122

Ballylintagh tumulus: Aghadowey LY 22; 28–29

Ballylintough td: Annahilt DN 12; 20–21, 23–24

Ballylisbredin corn mill: Comber DN 7; 40

Ballylisbredin td: Comber DN 7; 40, 43

Ballylisbredin td: Dundonald DN 7; 65

Ballylish (see Ballylisk): Kilmore AH 1; 64

Ballylisk school: Kilmore AH 1; 64, 67

Ballylisk td: Kilmore AH 1; 60, 64–65, 67–68, 72–73

Ballyliss td: Misc. DN 17; 131

Ballylissisladdy td: Ballylinny AM 32; 30

Ballylogan (see Ballybogan): Clonleigh DL 39; 12

Ballyloghan (see Ballyloughan): Comber DN 7; 34

Ballylogpatrick td: Racavan AM 13; 102

Ballylone Big flax mill: Magheradrool DN 17; 103

Ballylone Big td: Magheradrool DN 17; 99, 103

Ballylone Little td: Magheradrool DN 17; 99, 103

Ballylorn corn and flax mill: Larne AM 10; 125

Ballylorn td: Larne AM 10; 123, 125

Ballyloskey quarry: Lough Swilly DL 38; 135

Ballyloskey td: Donagh DL 38; 31

Ballylough Castle: Billy AM 16; 59, 70–71

Ballylough coves: Kilraghts AM 16; 130, 134

Ballylough fort: Kilraghts AM 16; 133

Ballylough graveyard: Kilraghts AM 16; 130

Ballylough hill: Kilraghts AM 16; 125

Ballylough hill: Seapatrick DN 12; 124

Ballylough House: Billy AM 16; 45

Ballylough lake: Kilraghts AM 16; 125–26

Ballylough pigeon house: Billy AM 16; 71

Ballylough school: Seapatrick DN 12; 135

Ballylough td: Billy AM 16; 36, 41

Ballylough td: Donaghmore DN 3; 7–8

Ballylough td: Kilraghts AM 16; 130, 135

Ballylough td: Seapatrick DN 12; 123–24, 126, 135

Ballyloughan flax mill: Kilmore AH 1; 63, 67

Ballyloughan school: Kilmore AH 1; 64, 67

Ballyloughan td: Comber DN 7; 34, 37–38, 42–43

Ballyloughan td: Kilmore AH 1; 61, 66–67, 72

Ballyloughanmore td: Ballylinny AM 32; 30

Ballyloughbeg carn: Billy AM 16; 55

Ballyloughbeg fort: Billy AM 16; 55

Ballyloughbeg standing stones: Billy AM 16; 58, 72

Ballyloughbeg td: Billy AM 16; 56, 61, 69

Ballyloughmore castle: Billy AM 16; 52–53

Ballyloughmore td: Billy AM 16; 45–46

Ballyloughran bridge: Lissan LY 31; 99

Ballylucas mill: Derryvullan FH 14; 41

Ballylucas mill: Enniskillen FH 4; 69

Ballylucas td: Bright DN 17; 35, 37

Ballylucas td: Enniskillen FH 4; 71, 82

Ballyluken standing stone [I]: Culfeightrin AM 24; 52

Ballyluken standing stone [II]: Culfeightrin AM 24; 52

Ballylumford cromlech: Island Magee AM 10; 56, 71, 76, 100–101

Ballylumford hill: Island Magee AM 10; 14

Ballylumford td: Island Magee AM 10; 16, 21, 55–56, 58–59, 71–72, 76, 95, 100

Ballylumford witch stone: Island Magee AM 10; 101

Ballylumford yellow stone: Island Magee AM 10; 59, 100

Ballylummin fort: Ahoghill AM 23; 35

Ballylummin school: Ahoghill AM 23; 46, 48

Ballylummin Sunday school: Ahoghill AM 23; 46

Ballylummin td: Ahoghill AM 23; 40

Ballylune (see Ballyhone): Glynn AM 26; 4

Ballylurgan bog: Drummaul AM 19; 87

Ballylurgan fort: Drummaul AM 19; 88

Ballylurgan td: Drummaul AM 19; 87

Ballylurgan td: Duneane AM 19; 124

Ballymacaffry td: Aghalurcher FH 4; 14

Ballymacaldrack chapel: Finvoy AM 23; 68, 70–71

Ballymacaldrack coves: Finvoy AM 23; 76

Ballymacaldrack giant's grave: Finvoy AM 23; 77–78

Ballymacaldrack graveyard: Finvoy AM 23; 75–76

Ballymacaldrack hill: Finvoy AM 23; 68

Ballymacaldrack lough: Finvoy AM 23; 68

Ballymacaldrack old chapel: Finvoy AM 23; 77

Ballymacallion (Ballymacallian) td: Dungiven LY 15; 22, 26, 46, 60, 63, 70, 75, 89

Ballymacallion bog: Dungiven LY 15; 45

Ballymacallion chapel: Dungiven LY 15; 60

Ballymacallion hill: Dungiven LY 15; 70

Ballymacallion school: Banagher LY 30; 12

Ballymacallion school [I]: Dungiven LY 15; 8, 18–19, 117–118

Ballymacallion school [II]: Dungiven LY 15; 117

Ballymacallion td: Banagher LY 30; 23

Ballymacan lough: Clogher TE 5; 47

Ballymacan td: Clogher TE 5; 35, 47

Ballymacanallen td: Tullylish DN 12; 143

Ballymacaramery td: Saintfield DN 7; 117–19

Ballymacarattybeg corn mill: Donaghmore DN 3; 8

Ballymacarattybeg school: Donaghmore DN 3; 8

Ballymacarattybeg td: Donaghmore DN 3; 8

Ballymacarattymore fort: Donaghmore DN 3; 7

Ballymacarattymore meeting house: Donaghmore DN 3; 8

Ballymacarattymore td: Donaghmore DN 3; 7–8

Ballymacarett (see Ballymacarret)

Ballymacarn flax mill: Magheradrool DN 17; 106

Ballymacarn North td: Magheradrool DN 17; 99, 103

Ballymacarn South spa wells: Magheradrool DN 17; 103

Ballymacarn South td: Magheradrool DN 17; 99, 103, 106

Ballymacarn td: Magheradrool DN 17; 102

Ballymacarattymore (see Ballymacarattymore): Donaghmore DN 3; 8

Ballymacarret brickfields: Knockbreda DN 7; 99

Ballymacarret chapel: Knockbreda DN 7; 99

Ballymacarret church: Knockbreda DN 7; 99

Ballymacarret corn mill: Knockbreda DN 7; 99

Ballymacarret foundry: Knockbreda DN 7; 99

Ballymacarret glass house: Knockbreda DN 7; 99

Ballymacarret meeting house: Knockbreda DN 7; 99

Ballymacarret ph: Misc. DN 17; 118

Ballymacarret rope and canvas manufactory: Knockbreda DN 7; 99

Ballymacarret starch works: Knockbreda DN 7; 99

Ballymacarret td: Knockbreda DN 7; 98–100

Ballymacarret vitriol works: Knockbreda DN 7; 99

Ballymacarter (see Ballymacarthur): Moville DL 38; 68

Ballymacarthur td: Moville DL 38; 68, 70

Ballymacarton (see Ballymacarthur): Moville DL 38; 70

Ballymacarton House: Aghanloo LY 11; 12

Ballymacashan graveyard: Killinchy DN 7; 91

Ballymacashan td: Killinchy DN 7; 86–88, 91

Ballymacavenny td: Templecarn DL 39; 160, 163

Ballymacbrennan school: Hillsborough DN 12; 101

Ballymacbrinean (see Ballymacbrennan): Drumbo DN 7; 61

Ballymacfin fort: Derrykeighan AM 16; 94

Ballymacfin td: Billy AM 16; 76

Ballymacfin td: Derrykeighan AM 16; 90

Ballymacgilhainy td: Faughanvale LY 36; 48

Ballymacgowland td: Magilligan LY 11; 126

Ballymachan td: Clogher TE 5; 53

Ballymachileer (see Ballymacilcur): Maghera LY 18; 42

Ballymachugh dispensary: Drumlumman CN 40; 15

Ballymachugh ph: Drumlumman CN 40; 12, 15, 17–18

Ballymacilcur bog: Maghera LY 18; 56–57

Ballymacilcur flax mill: Maghera LY 18; 27

Ballymacilcur td: Maghera LY 18; 42, 75, 79–80

Ballymacilcur wood: Maghera LY 18; 48, 56

Ballymacilrany (Ballymacilreny) td: Aghagallon AM 21; 3, 14–15, 19, 21

Ballymacilrany corn mill: Aghagallon AM 21; 13

Ballymacilrany flax mill: Aghagallon AM 21; 13

Ballymacilrany fort [I]: Aghagallon AM 21; 14

Ballymacilrany fort [II]: Aghagallon AM 21; 17

Ballymacilrany fort [III]: Aghagallon AM 21; 17

Ballymacilrany tanyard: Aghagallon AM 21; 14

Ballymacilrany wood: Aghagallon AM 21; 5

Ballymacilur fort [I]: Maghera LY 18; 61

Ballymacilur fort [II]: Maghera LY 18; 61

Ballymackataggurth td: Derryvullan FH 14; 33

Ballymackbrennan (Ballymacbrennen) td: Drumbo DN 7; 59–61

Ballymackbrennan school: Drumbo DN 7; 59

Ballymackelroy (Ballymacelroy) td: Errigal
Keerogue TE 20; 51, 56

Ballymackelroy chapel: Errigal Keerogue TE 20; 51

Ballymackelroy gravel pits: Errigal Keerogue TE
20; 51

Ballymackemore td: Muckamore AM 35; 82

Ballymackerammery (see Ballymacaramory):
Saintfield DN 7; 119

Ballymackfinn td: Drumtullagh AM 16; 103

Ballymackilroy td: Drummaul AM 19; 91

Ballymacklehoyle td: Killead AM 35; 35, 40

Ballymackmary (see Ballymacmary): Killead AM
35; 44

Ballymackney: Killanny MN 40; 130–32

Ballymackney: Magheracloone MN 40; 139

Ballymackney: Magheross MN 40; 147

Ballymackney church: Killanny MN 40; 131

Ballymackney forge: Killanny MN 40; 131

Ballymackney graveyard: Killanny MN 40; 131–32

Ballymackney House: Killanny MN 40; 131

Ballymackney river: Killanny MN 40; 130

Ballymackney td: Donaghmoyne MN 40; 108

Ballymackpeake (Ballymacpeake) td: Termoneeny
LY 6; 122, 129

Ballymackward (see Ballymacward): Derryaghy
AM 8; 117

Ballymaclanigan td: Cumber LY 28; 4, 24, 66–68,
110, 116, 125

Ballymaclanigan Top hill: Cumber LY 28; 5–6

Ballymaclanighan (see Ballymaclanigan): Cumber
LY 28; 5

Ballymaclara school (see Ballymaclary): Magilligan
LY 11; 110

Ballymaclary Clagan school: Magilligan LY 11; 110

Ballymaclary school: Magilligan LY 11; 110, 138

Ballymaclary td: Magilligan LY 11; 94–95, 126,
129, 132–33, 138, 142

Ballymaclevennon (Ballymacklevenon) td:
Ballywillin LY 33; 50–51

Ballymaclevennon td: Ballywillin AM 16; 32

Ballymaclevennon West meeting house: Ballywillin
LY 33; 33, 36, 42, 45–47

Ballymacmary td: Killead AM 35; 40, 44

Ballymacmurty td: Clonmany DL 38; 13, 18, 20

Ballymacmurty td: Lough Swilly DL 38; 136

Ballymacnamee td: Misc. DN 17; 125, 127

Ballymacollion (see Ballymacallion)

Ballymacombsbeg bogs: Ballyscullion LY 6; 70

Ballymacombsbeg Island: Ballyscullion LY 6; 51

Ballymacombsbeg td: Ballyscullion LY 6; 51, 70,
75, 78

Ballymacombsmore bogs: Ballyscullion LY 6; 71

Ballymacombsmore fort: Ballyscullion LY 6; 51, 72

Ballymacombsmore td: Ballyscullion LY 6; 43,
51–52, 63, 66, 71, 75, 77–78

Ballymaconnell corn mills: Bangor DN 7; 22

Ballymaconnell corn windmill: Bangor DN 7; 22

Ballymaconnell flax mill: Bangor DN 7; 22

Ballymaconnell school: Bangor DN 7; 22

Ballymaconnell td: Bangor DN 7; 19, 22

Ballymaconnell td: Misc. DN 17; 124

Ballymaconnellan td: Grey Abbey DN 7; 67

Ballymaconnelly school: Rasharkin AM 23; 135–36

Ballymacool locality: Leck DL 39; 115

Ballymacormick coastguard station: Bangor DN 7;
22

Ballymacormick Point: Bangor DN 7; 22

Ballymacormick td: Bangor DN 7; 19, 22

Ballymacoss (Ballymacust) td: Derryaghy AM 8;
94, 99, 103, 112, 118–19

Ballymacoss fort: Derryaghy AM 8; 95

Ballymacoss House: Derryaghy AM 8; 104–05

Ballymacoss House: Magheragall AM 21; 108

Ballymacoss old house: Derryaghy AM 8; 99, 105

Ballymacoss private school: Derryaghy AM 8; 116

Ballymacoss school: Derryaghy AM 8; 103, 116,
118

Ballymacoss Sunday school: Derryaghy AM 8; 117

Ballymacpeak (see Ballymacpeake): Maghera LY
18; 11

Ballymacpeake (Ballymackpeake) td: Maghera LY
18; 11, 44, 57

Ballymacpeake (Ballymcpeake) td: Tamlaght
O'Crilly LY 18; 91, 98, 108, 135, 137–38

Ballymacpeake bog: Maghera LY 18; 43, 56, 59

Ballymacpeake carn: Maghera LY 18; 44

Ballymacpeake fort: Maghera LY 18; 11, 62

Ballymacpeake Glebe House: Tamlaght O'Crilly LY
18; 108

Ballymacpeake Island: Maghera LY 18; 11, 23–24

Ballymacpeake lough: Maghera LY 18; 59, 62

Ballymacpeake lough: Tamlaght O'Crilly LY 18; 83,
95, 124

Ballymacpeake Lower bogs: Tamlaght O'Crilly LY
18; 84, 132–33

Ballymacpeake Lower cave: Tamlaght O'Crilly LY
18; 118

Ballymacpeake Lower fort: Tamlaght O'Crilly LY
18; 117

Ballymacpeake Lower loughs: Tamlaght O'Crilly
LY 18; 115, 124

Ballymacpeake Lower td: Tamlaght O'Crilly LY 18;
83, 117, 123, 138

Ballymacpeake Upper woods: Maghera LY 18; 4, 48

Ballymacpeake wood: Maghera LY 18; 56

Ballymacran td: Aghanloo LY 11; 1, 24

Ballymacran td: Drumachose LY 9; 99, 101

Ballymacran td: Tamlaght Finlagan LY 25; 66, 93,
95, 98, 107, 125

Ballymacran timber yard: Tamlaght Finlagan LY 25; 107

Ballymacrandle td: Seagoe AH 1; 107

Ballymacranemy td: Saintfield DN 7; 120

Ballymacrea fort: Dunluce AM 16; 119

Ballymacrea td: Dunluce AM 16; 120

Ballymacreely td: Killinchy DN 7; 86–87

Ballymacrevan (Ballymacravin) td: Camlin AM 21; 60, 62, 67, 71

Ballymacrevan school: Ballinderry AM 21; 46–47, 58

Ballymacricket chapel: Glenavy AM 21; 77, 81, 85, 88, 90

Ballymacricket chapel: Killead AM 35; 20

Ballymacricket school: Glenavy AM 21; 79–80, 90–91

Ballymacricket Sunday school: Glenavy AM 21; 90

Ballymacricket td: Glenavy AM 21; 79, 85

Ballymacrickett (see Ballymacricket): Glenavy AM 21; 80

Ballymacross bog: Maghera LY 18; 64

Ballymacross flax mill: Maghera LY 18; 63

Ballymacross fort [I]: Maghera LY 18; 47

Ballymacross fort [II]: Maghera LY 18; 60

Ballymacross fort [III]: Maghera LY 18; 60

Ballymacross td: Maghera LY 18; 8, 13, 17, 77

Ballymacruise (Ballymacruse) td: Donaghadee DN 7; 50

Ballymacruise td: Misc. DN 17; 124

Ballymacully td: Kilclooney AH 1; 51

Ballymacward Lower td: Derryaghy AM 8; 120

Ballymacward Lower td: Glenavy AM 21; 80

Ballymacward school: Derryaghy AM 8; 117

Ballymacward Sunday school: Derryaghy AM 8; 118

Ballymacward Upper chapel: Derryaghy AM 8; 120

Ballymacward Upper fort: Derryaghy AM 8; 95

Ballymacward Upper standing stone: Derryaghy AM 8; 98

Ballymacward Upper td: Derryaghy AM 8; 104, 109, 120

Ballymacwilliam school: Kilraghts AM 16; 136

Ballymaddigan (see Ballymadigan): Dunboe LY 11; 79

Ballymadigan cave: Dunboe LY 11; 50, 79

Ballymadigan td: Dunboe LY 11; 63

Ballymagaghran corn mill: Belleek FH 14; 4

Ballymagaghran td: Belleek FH 14; 4

Ballymagahan td: Comber DN 7; 42

Ballymagahy lough: Clondavaddog DL 38; 3

Ballymagahy South corn mill: Clondavaddog DL 38; 5

Ballymaganlis bleach green: Dromore DN 12; 76

Ballymaganlis bleaching mill: Dromore DN 12; 72

Ballymaganlis mill: Dromore DN 12; 78

Ballymaganlis schools: Dromore DN 12; 73

Ballymaganlis td: Dromore DN 12; 78

Ballymagaraghan td: Moira DN 12; 121

Ballymagaraghey td: Moville DL 38; 68, 70

Ballymagarahey (see Ballymagaraghey): Moville DL 38; 70

Ballymagarahy (see Ballymagaraghey): Moville DL 38; 68

Ballymagarrick (see Ballynagarrick): Saul DN 17; 115

Ballymagarrick td: Drumbo DN 7; 59, 61–62

Ballymagarry Castle: Ballywillin LY 33; 35

Ballymagarry Castle: Drummaul AM 19; 70–71

Ballymagarry Castle: Dunluce AM 16; 120

Ballymagarry church: Drummaul AM 19; 70

Ballymagarry House: Dunluce AM 16; 110, 120

Ballymagarry school: Dunluce AM 16; 112

Ballymagarry standing stone: Dunluce AM 16; 118

Ballymagarry td: Dunluce AM 16; 105

Ballymagaughey (see Ballymagaughy)

Ballymagaughey flax mill: Comber DN 7; 31, 35

Ballymagaughy (Ballymegaughy) td: Comber DN 7; 35, 37, 39, 43

Ballymagaughy flax mill: Comber DN 7; 39

Ballymagee td: Bangor DN 7; 19

Ballymagee td: Misc. DN 17; 124

Ballymageeghan district: Lough Swilly DL 38; 134

Ballymagerny (Ballymagerney) td: Loughgall AH 1; 80

Ballymagerny meeting house: Loughgall AH 1; 76, 80

Ballymaghan (Ballymeekan) td: Holywood DN 7; 76–77, 79

Ballymaghan (see Ballymoghan): Magherafelt LY 6; 95

Ballymaghan school: Holywood DN 7; 76

Ballymaghare td: Magherafelt LY 6; 95

Ballymagher (see Ballymather): Killead AM 35; 42

Ballymaghery corn mill: Clonduff DN 3; 5

Ballymaghery td: Clonduff DN 3; 5

Ballymagig td: Conwal DL 39; 26

Ballymaglaff flax mill: Comber DN 7; 35, 40

Ballymaglaff td: Comber DN 7; 35, 37, 40, 42–43

Ballymaglave North: Magheradrool DN 17; 104

Ballymaglave North td: Magheradrool DN 17; 99, 104

Ballymaglave South td: Magheradrool DN 17; 99, 104

Ballymaglave td: Magheradrool DN 17; 102

Ballymaglin td: Aghanloo LY 11; 18–19, 22, 26, 32–33, 35–37, 40–42

Ballymaglin td: Tamlaght Finlagan LY 25; 108

Ballymaglinn (see Ballymaglin): Aghanloo LY 11; 36

Ballymagluire school: Artrea TE 20; 10

Ballymagoan Lower fort: Clondavaddog DL 38; 6

Ballymagoland td: Magilligan LY 11; 94–95, 129

Ballymagorry village: Leckpatrick TE 5; 125

Ballymagowan td: Clogher TE 5; 26, 35, 53

Ballymagowan td: Lough Swilly DL 38; 117, 129

Ballymagraffin td: Kilmood DN 7; 95

Ballymagreevy district. Misc. SO 40; 200

Ballymagrorty district: Drumhome DL 39; 62

Ballymaguigan bog: Artrea LY 6; 4, 12, 24

Ballymaguigan fort: Artrea LY 6; 24

Ballymaguigan school [I]: Artrea LY 6; 20

Ballymaguigan school [II]: Artrea LY 6; 20

Ballymaguigan td: Artrea LY 6; 4, 7–8, 11, 14, 20, 24–25, 39

Ballymaguigan td: Artrea TE 20; 8

Ballymaguiggan (see Ballymaguigan): Artrea LY 6; 7–8

Ballymahatty district: Donacavey TE 5; 71

Ballymakeever fort: Dungiven LY 15; 41, 85

Ballymakeever td: Banagher LY 30; 22

Ballymakeever td: Dungiven LY 15; 23, 26, 60, 74

Ballymakenny td: Aghalurcher FH 4; 13

Ballymakernaghan district: Lough Swilly DL 38; 144

Ballymakernaghan Lower td: Lough Swilly DL 38; 145

Ballymakernaghan quarry: Lough Swilly DL 38; 148

Ballymakernaghan Upper td: Lough Swilly DL 38; 145

Ballymakesh (see Ballymacoss): Blaris AM 8; 50–51

Ballymalady td: Comber DN 7; 37, 39, 42–43

Ballymalidy (see Ballymalady): Comber DN 7; 37

Ballymanone locality: Cleenish FH 14; 28

Ballymarlow (Ballymarlogh) td: Ballyclug AM 23; 53, 65

Ballymarlow cave [I]: Ballyclug AM 23; 65

Ballymarlow cave [II]: Ballyclug AM 23; 65

Ballymarlow giant's grave: Ballyclug AM 23; 61, 65

Ballymarlow school: Ballyclug AM 23; 66

Ballymarrett td: Blaris AM 8; 51

Ballymarrish (see Ballymarter) td: Ballyphilip DN 7; 7

Ballymarter td: Ballyculter DN 17; 28

Ballymarter td: Witter DN 7; 126

Ballymartin burn: Ballyrobert AM 2; 25

Ballymartin corn: Tullynakill DN 7; 122

Ballymartin cove: Ballymartin AM 2; 11, 13, 15, 18

Ballymartin flax mill: Tullynakill DN 7; 122

Ballymartin fort [I]: Ballymartin AM 2; 11, 15–17

Ballymartin fort [II]: Ballymartin AM 2; 18

Ballymartin forts: Ballymartin AM 2; 12–13, 15, 18

Ballymartin graveyard: Ballymartin AM 2; 5, 11, 13, 15, 17

Ballymartin meeting house: Kilkeel DN 3; 49

Ballymartin old chapel: Kilkeel DN 3; 49

Ballymartin old church: Ballymartin AM 2; 11–13, 15, 17–18

Ballymartin old village: Ballymartin AM 2; 17

Ballymartin ph: Antrim AM 29; 50

Ballymartin ph: Ballylinny AM 32; 17, 24, 29

Ballymartin ph: Ballyrobert AM 2; 19, 24

Ballymartin ph: Ballywalter AM 2; 26, 28, 30

Ballymartin ph: Carnmoney AM 2; 56

Ballymartin ph: Kilbride AM 29; 137, 150, 155

Ballymartin ph: Killead AM 35; 20

Ballymartin ph: Mallusk AM 2; 106

Ballymartin ph: Nilteen AM 35; 87

Ballymartin ph: Templepatrick AM 35; 107, 117, 132, 138, 143–45

Ballymartin rectory: Carnmoney AM 2; 64

Ballymartin standing stone [I]: Ballymartin AM 2; 12, 17

Ballymartin standing stone [II]: Ballymartin AM 2; 12, 17

Ballymartin td: Ballylinny AM 32; 22, 30

Ballymartin td: Ballymartin AM 2; 5, 15–18

Ballymartin td: Ballyphilip DN 7; 8

Ballymartin td: Tullynakill DN 7; 122

Ballymartin tuck mill: Ballymartin AM 2; 16–17

Ballymartin water: Ballymartin AM 2; 3–5, 11–13, 15–18

Ballymartin water: Ballyrobert AM 2; 19

Ballymartin water: Mallusk AM 2; 106–07

Ballymartin water: Templepatrick AM 35; 107, 137, 139, 141–42

Ballymartin well: Ballymartin AM 2; 12

Ballymartyr td: Misc. DN 17; 124

Ballymascanlan: Newry DN 3; 85, 105, 109

Ballymascanlan td: Ballymascanlan LH 40; 55

Ballymascanlon (see Ballymascanlan)

Ballymastocker bay: Clondavaddog DL 38; 3, 5, 7

Ballymastocker bay: Lough Swilly DL 38; 98, 100, 129, 133

Ballymastocker strand: Lough Swilly DL 38; 100

Ballymastocker td: Lough Swilly DL 38; 128

Ballymastoker (see Ballymastocker): Lough Swilly DL 38; 128

Ballymastrain (see Ballyneas Strain): Ballyscullion LY 6; 77

Ballymather (Ballymeather) td: Killead AM 35; 35, 51

Ballymather adult school: Killead AM 35; 19, 47

Ballymather meeting house: Carmavy AM 35; 3

Ballymather meeting house: Killead AM 35; 11–12, 20, 42, 46–47

Ballymather meeting house: Umgall AM 35; 159

Ballymather print-works: Killead AM 35; 15, 49

Ballymather Sunday school: Killead AM 35; 52

Ballymatimber (see Ballymultimber)

Ballymatoskerty (Ballymatuskerty) td: Duneane AM 19; 96, 114, 123

Ballymatoskerty chapel: Duneane AM 19; 96, 100

Ballymatoskerty corn mill: Ballyscullion AM 19; 7

Ballymatoskerty corn mill: Duneane AM 19; 101, 113–14

Ballymatoskerty school: Duneane AM 19; 125

Ballymaul woods: Maghera LY 18; 4

Ballymave fort [I]: Magheragall AM 21; 104

Ballymave fort [II]: Magheragall AM 21; 104

Ballymcegan district: Misc. SO 40; 199

BallyMcIllvannan (see Ballymaclevennon)

Ballymclary (see Ballymaclary): Magilligan LY 11; 110

Ballymcpeake (see Ballymacpeake): Maghera LY 18; 44

Ballymearagh td: Ballylinny AM 32; 30

Ballymeavoge td: Ballylinny AM 32; 30

Ballymechan (see Ballymaghan)

Ballymeenaroarty td: Clonmany DL 38; 16

Ballymeglaff (see Ballymaglaff): Comber DN 7; 35, 37, 42–43

Ballymegoughy (see Ballymagaughy)

Ballymeilbrick (Ballymulbrick) td: Drumballyroney DN 3; 10, 16, 18

Ballymeilbrick fort: Drumballyroney DN 3; 16

Ballymeilbrick hill: Drumballyroney DN 3; 14

Ballymeilbrick school: Drumballyroney DN 3; 17–18

Ballymelady (see Ballymalady): Comber DN 7; 42

Ballymena (Ballymenagh) td: Skerry AM 13; 106–07, 110–11, 117

Ballymena: Ahoghill AM 23; 1–3, 8–9, 11–15, 24, 30–31, 33–34, 40–42, 44–45

Ballymena: Antrim AM 29; 7, 9, 19, 22, 24, 27, 37, 39, 48, 50

Ballymena: Ballyclug AM 23; 52–57, 60–62, 64

Ballymena: Ballycor AM 32; 4, 9

Ballymena: Ballylinny AM 32; 25

Ballymena: Ballynure AM 32; 64

Ballymena: Ballyscullion AM 19; 1–4, 8, 10, 14

Ballymena: Banagher LY 30; 60

Ballymena: Carnmoney AM 2; 49, 85

Ballymena: Coleraine LY 33; 89, 97

Ballymena: Connor AM 19; 16–17, 22–24, 29–31

Ballymena: Doagh AM 29; 60–61, 67, 71, 86, 89, 93

Ballymena: Donegore AM 29; 107–08, 110, 115, 119

Ballymena: Drummaul AM 19; 34, 38, 41, 43, 45–47, 51–52, 54, 80, 85–86, 89

Ballymena: Dunaghy AM 13; 11, 13, 25–26

Ballymena: Duneane AM 19; 100, 104, 112–13, 116

Ballymena: Dungiven LY 15; 26, 67

Ballymena: Finvoy AM 23; 70, 77

Ballymena: Glenwhirry AM 32; 75–76, 79

Ballymena: Glynn AM 26; 38

Ballymena: Grey Abbey DN 7; 72

Ballymena: Inver AM 26; 54–55

Ballymena: Island Magee AM 10; 65

Ballymena: Kilbride AM 29; 135–36, 153–54

Ballymena: Killagan AM 23; 83

Ballymena: Killead AM 35; 42

Ballymena: Kilwaughter AM 10; 106–07, 110–11

Ballymena: Kirkinriola AM 23; 88–100, 102–05, 107–13, 115, 119–22, 124–26

Ballymena: Layd AM 13; 39–40

Ballymena: Muckamore AM 35; 63

Ballymena: Nilteen AM 35; 90

Ballymena: Racavan AM 13; 87–88, 91, 103

Ballymena: Ramoan AM 24; 109–10, 112, 115

Ballymena: Rasharkin AM 23; 127, 130–31, 137, 139

Ballymena: Rashee AM 32; 137

Ballymena: Shilvodan AM 19; 127–31

Ballymena: Tamlaght O'Crilly LY 18; 83

Ballymena: Templecorran AM 26; 95, 115, 122

Ballymena: Templepatrick AM 35; 113

Ballymena barrack: Kirkinriola AM 23; 95

Ballymena beetling mill [I]: Kirkinriola AM 23; 104

Ballymena beetling mill [II]: Kirkinriola AM 23; 104

Ballymena Belfast bank: Kirkinriola AM 23; 99, 118

Ballymena bleach green: Kirkinriola AM 23; 91, 104, 119

Ballymena brewery: Ballyclug AM 23; 52

Ballymena bridewell: Kirkinriola AM 23; 90, 95–96, 117

Ballymena Bridge St chandlery: Kirkinriola AM 23; 99

Ballymena burn: Ballylinny AM 32; 12, 24

Ballymena burn: Ballynure AM 32; 31

Ballymena Castle: Kirkinriola AM 23; 104, 119

Ballymena Castle demesne: Kirkinriola AM 23; 116, 121

Ballymena Castle St meeting house (P): Kirkinriola AM 23; 90, 94–95, 103, 106, 116

Ballymena Castle St Sunday school: Kirkinriola AM 23; 114

Ballymena chapel (C): Kirkinriola AM 23; 90, 104, 119

Ballymena chapel (WM): Kirkinriola AM 23; 90, 94, 114, 117

Ballymena church: Kirkinriola AM 23; 90, 94, 103, 116–17, 124

Ballymena Church St chandlery [I]: Kirkinriola AM 23; 99

Ballymena Church St chandlery [II]: Kirkinriola AM 23; 99

Ballymena classical school: Kirkinriola AM 23; 114
Ballymena corn mill: Kirkinriola AM 23; 99, 119
Ballymena court house: Kirkinriola AM 23; 90, 95, 117–18
Ballymena court house Sunday school: Kirkinriola AM 23; 95, 114, 117
Ballymena diocesan school: Kirkinriola AM 23; 91, 96, 102, 111, 113, 118–20
Ballymena distillery: Kirkinriola AM 23; 99
Ballymena estate: Carrickfergus AM 37; 98
Ballymena fairgreen: Kirkinriola AM 23; 100, 118
Ballymena female national school: Kirkinriola AM 23; 96, 102, 113, 119
Ballymena female school: Kirkinriola AM 23; 102–03, 114
Ballymena fort: Skerry AM 13; 110
Ballymena free school: Kirkinriola AM 23; 91, 102, 113–14
Ballymena free Sunday school: Kirkinriola AM 23; 114
Ballymena Galgorm St tannery: Kirkinriola AM 23; 99
Ballymena giant's grave: Skerry AM 13; 117, 119
Ballymena hibernian school: Kirkinriola AM 23; 102–03, 113
Ballymena hotel: Kirkinriola AM 23; 95
Ballymena ladies' school: Kirkinriola AM 23; 114, 122
Ballymena linen hall: Kirkinriola AM 23; 100, 118
Ballymena Little cave [I]: Ballynure AM 32; 58
Ballymena Little cave [II]: Ballynure AM 32; 60
Ballymena Little fort: Ballynure AM 32; 59–60
Ballymena Little school: Skerry AM 13; 114
Ballymena Little td: Ballynure AM 32; 68
Ballymena Little td: Carrickfergus AM 37; 33, 38, 42
Ballymena manor: Kirkinriola AM 23; 88, 97, 120
Ballymena manufactories: Kirkinriola AM 23; 93
Ballymena market house: Ahoghill AM 23; 34
Ballymena market house: Kirkinriola AM 23; 90, 94–95, 100–01, 114, 117, 122
Ballymena market place: Kirkinriola AM 23; 95
Ballymena mathematical school: Kirkinriola AM 23; 114
Ballymena meeting house (S): Kirkinriola AM 23; 90, 94, 106, 117
Ballymena meeting houses (P): Kirkinriola AM 23; 103, 117
Ballymena Methodist Sunday school: Kirkinriola AM 23; 114
Ballymena mill: Kirkinriola AM 23; 119
Ballymena Mill St tannery: Kirkinriola AM 23; 99
Ballymena mountain: Skerry AM 13; 109
Ballymena news room: Kirkinriola AM 23; 98

Ballymena Northern bank: Kirkinriola AM 23; 99, 118
Ballymena old church: Ahoghill AM 23; 25
Ballymena old church: Kirkinriola AM 23; 94, 122
Ballymena Parsonage: Ballyclug AM 23; 58
Ballymena Parsonage: Kirkinriola AM 23; 104–06
Ballymena Provincial bank: Kirkinriola AM 23; 96, 99, 118
Ballymena public crane: Kirkinriola AM 23; 99–100, 117
Ballymena quarries: Ahoghill AM 23; 2
Ballymena quarries: Kirkinriola AM 23; 102
Ballymena river (see Artogues water): Skerry AM 13; 109
Ballymena road bridge: Doagh AM 29; 71, 92
Ballymena road bridge: Kilbride AM 29; 151
Ballymena ropeworks: Kirkinriola AM 23; 99
Ballymena school [I]: Kirkinriola AM 23; 122
Ballymena school [II]: Kirkinriola AM 23; 122
Ballymena school [III]: Kirkinriola AM 23; 122
Ballymena school [IV]: Kirkinriola AM 23; 122
Ballymena school [V]: Kirkinriola AM 23; 122
Ballymena school [VI]: Kirkinriola AM 23; 122
Ballymena school [VII]: Kirkinriola AM 23; 122
Ballymena shambles: Kirkinriola AM 23; 95, 101, 117
Ballymena small market house: Kirkinriola AM 23; 117
Ballymena td: Ballynure AM 32; 63
Ballymena Town Parks td: Kirkinriola AM 23; 88, 90–91
Ballymena weigh–house: Kirkinriola AM 23; 95
Ballymena Wellington St meeting house (P): Kirkinriola AM 23; 90, 94, 106, 116
Ballymenagh (see Ballymena): Ahoghill AM 23; 1
Ballymenagh bog: Aghadowey LY 22; 1
Ballymenagh booley houses: Skerry AM 13; 117, 119
Ballymenagh bridge: Aghadowey LY 22; 10
Ballymenagh church: Carnmoney AM 2; 64
Ballymenagh fort [I]: Artrea LY 6; 11
Ballymenagh fort [II]: Artrea LY 6; 11
Ballymenagh House: Holywood DN 7; 76
Ballymenagh locality: Lough Swilly DL 38; 110
Ballymenagh meeting house: Aghadowey LY 22; 6, 14
Ballymenagh td: Aghadowey LY 22; 16
Ballymenagh td: Artrea LY 6; 11–12
Ballymenagh td: Desertoghill LY 27; 3, 19, 29
Ballymenagh td: Dunsfort DN 17; 72
Ballymenagh td: Holywood DN 7; 73, 76–77
Ballymenagh td: Tullyniskan TE 20; 138
Ballymenagh windmill: Holywood DN 7; 76
Ballymenish td: Misc. DN 17; 125
Ballymenna (see Ballymena): Ballynure AM 32; 68

Ballymenoch td: Holywood DN 7; 79–80
Ballymenock td: Ballywalter AM 2; 26, 29
Ballymilidy (see Ballymalady): Comber DN 7; 39
Ballyminetra td: Bangor DN 7; 19
Ballyminetuagh td: Misc. DN 17; 124
Ballyminister td: Ahoghill AM 23; 33, 36, 38
Ballyminister td: Misc. DL 39; 197
Ballyministra corn mill: Kilmood DN 7; 95
Ballyministra flax mill: Kilmood DN 7; 95
Ballyministra school: Kilmood DN 7; 95
Ballyministra td: Kilmood DN 7; 94–95
Ballyministra windmill: Kilmood DN 7; 95
Ballymiscanlin (see Ballymascanlan): Newry DN 3; 105
Ballymiscaw td: Comber DN 7; 40, 43
Ballymiscaw td: Dundonald DN 7; 65–66
Ballymisert td: Holywood DN 7; 77, 79–80
Ballymoate (Ballymote) td: Glenavy AM 21; 79
Ballymoate school: Glenavy AM 21; 79, 91
Ballymoder td: Ballylinny AM 32; 30
Ballymoghan (Ballymoyhan) td: Magherafelt LY 6; 95
Ballymoghan Beg td: Artrea TE 20; 6
Ballymoghan More bog: Magherafelt LY 6; 80
Ballymoghan More fort: Magherafelt LY 6; 110
Ballymoghan More td: Magherafelt LY 6; 80, 92, 94, 109–111
Ballymonan school: Dungiven LY 15; 117
Ballymonan td: Banagher LY 30; 22
Ballymonan td: Dungiven LY 15; 22, 27, 41, 60, 74, 85–86
Ballymoney: Aghadowey LY 22; 10, 12, 18, 20, 34
Ballymoney: Agivey LY 22; 39–40, 42–43
Ballymoney: Ahoghill AM 23; 3, 9, 12, 14, 31, 40, 43–45
Ballymoney: Armoy AM 24; 1, 4
Ballymoney: Ballintoy AM 24; 11, 16, 27, 31
Ballymoney: Ballymoney AM 16; 1–2, 4, 12–13, 16, 19
Ballymoney: Ballyrashane LY 22; 49, 51, 53, 56–57
Ballymoney: Ballywillin LY 33; 32–34, 42, 47
Ballymoney: Banagher LY 30; 19, 60
Ballymoney: Clondermot LY 34; 30
Ballymoney: Coleraine LY 33; 67, 91, 128, 150
Ballymoney: Culfeightrin AM 24; 39
Ballymoney: Cumber LY 28; 58
Ballymoney: Derrykeighan AM 16; 83, 88
Ballymoney: Desertoghill LY 27; 16
Ballymoney: Dunaghy AM 13; 25–26
Ballymoney: Dungiven LY 15; 26, 67
Ballymoney: Dunluce AM 16; 111
Ballymoney: Errigal LY 27; 79–84
Ballymoney: Finvoy AM 23; 67–68, 70–71, 77
Ballymoney: Inver AM 26; 54
Ballymoney: Island Magee AM 10; 23

Ballymoney: Kildollagh LY 22; 67–68, 70–73
Ballymoney: Killagan AM 23; 79, 83
Ballymoney: Kilraghts AM 16; 124
Ballymoney: Kilrea LY 27; 105
Ballymoney: Kirkinriola AM 23; 96–97, 104–05, 108, 117–18, 126
Ballymoney: Loughguile AM 13; 59, 68
Ballymoney: Macosquin LY 22; 81, 91–92
Ballymoney: Misc. LY 36; 117
Ballymoney: Ramoan AM 24; 88–91, 95, 97, 104–05
Ballymoney: Rasharkin AM 23; 127, 130–31, 137, 139–40
Ballymoney: Tamlaght O'Crilly LY 18; 83
Ballymoney: Templepatrick AM 35; 143
Ballymoney bog: Dunboe LY 11; 73
Ballymoney bridewell: Ballymoney AM 16; 2, 6, 8
Ballymoney castle [I]: Ballymoney AM 16; 20
Ballymoney castle [II]: Ballymoney AM 16; 21
Ballymoney chapel: Ballymoney AM 16; 2, 7
Ballymoney chapel: Bovevagh LY 25; 3, 58
Ballymoney chapel: Island Magee AM 10; 21, 34, 70, 73, 76, 78, 104
Ballymoney chapel: Kilcoo DN 3; 44–45
Ballymoney church: Ballymoney AM 16; 2, 6
Ballymoney Church St school: Ballymoney AM 16; 26
Ballymoney corn mill: Bovevagh LY 25; 4, 21, 57–58
Ballymoney court house: Ballymoney AM 16; 2
Ballymoney cross [I]: Bovevagh LY 25; 33–34
Ballymoney cross [II]: Bovevagh LY 25; 34
Ballymoney dispensary: Ballymoney AM 16; 14–16
Ballymoney dispensary: Finvoy AM 23; 72
Ballymoney district: Bovevagh LY 25; 17
Ballymoney flax mill: Kilcoo DN 3; 45
Ballymoney fort: Dunboe LY 11; 49
Ballymoney giant's grave [I]: Bovevagh LY 25; 8, 10, 18
Ballymoney giant's grave [II]: Bovevagh LY 25; 9, 18, 39
Ballymoney giant's graves: Bovevagh LY 25; 7
Ballymoney Glebe House: Ballymoney AM 16; 1, 18
Ballymoney grain store: Ballymoney AM 16; 8
Ballymoney graveyard: Bovevagh LY 25; 9–10, 14, 19, 35, 38, 40
Ballymoney hotels: Ballymoney AM 16; 8
Ballymoney Main St school [I]: Ballymoney AM 16; 26
Ballymoney Main St school [II]: Ballymoney AM 16; 27
Ballymoney market house: Ballymoney AM 16; 6, 8, 14

Ballymoney meeting house (Cov.): Ballymoney AM 16; 2, 7

Ballymoney meeting house (P): Ballymoney AM 16; 2, 7

Ballymoney meeting house (S): Ballymoney AM 16; 2, 7

Ballymoney meeting house (U): Ballymoney AM 16; 7

Ballymoney meeting house: Kildollagh LY 22; 70

Ballymoney Meeting House Lane school: Ballymoney AM 16; 26

Ballymoney mill: Bovevagh LY 25; 40

Ballymoney new flax mill: Kilcoo DN 3; 45

Ballymoney old chapel: Ballymoney AM 16; 7

Ballymoney old church: Ballymoney AM 16; 2, 6, 19

Ballymoney old gaol: Ballymoney AM 16; 8

Ballymoney ph: Ahoghill AM 23; 3, 17

Ballymoney ph: Coleraine LY 33; 142

Ballymoney ph: Derrykeighan AM 16; 78, 80, 87

Ballymoney ph: Finvoy AM 23; 67–68

Ballymoney ph: Kildollagh LY 22; 67, 72

Ballymoney ph: Loughguile AM 13; 58

Ballymoney ph: Misc. AM 10; 129

Ballymoney ph: Rasharkin AM 23; 128

Ballymoney Piper Row school: Ballymoney AM 16; 26

Ballymoney Point: Lough Swilly DL 38; 104, 143, 147

Ballymoney private school: Island Magee AM 10; 68

Ballymoney public school: Ballymoney AM 16; 8

Ballymoney river: Ballymoney AM 16; 1, 4–5, 9–10

Ballymoney school: Ballymoney AM 16; 6

Ballymoney school: Bovevagh LY 25; 28, 55, 58

Ballymoney school: Island Magee AM 10; 96

Ballymoney school: Kilcoo DN 3; 45

Ballymoney school: Magherally DN 12; 116

Ballymoney standing stones: Bovevagh LY 25; 40

Ballymoney Sunday school: Island Magee AM 10; 70

Ballymoney Sunday school: Magherally DN 12; 116

Ballymoney td: Aghanloo LY 11; 3, 12, 20, 26, 40–42

Ballymoney td: Banagher LY 30; 23–24, 56

Ballymoney td: Bovevagh LY 25; 9, 13–15, 18–19, 33–35, 38, 60–61

Ballymoney td: Dunboe LY 11; 73

Ballymoney td: Island Magee AM 10; 16, 21, 68, 70–71, 73, 76, 78, 96, 104

Ballymoney td: Kilbroney DN 3; 31

Ballymoney td: Kilcoo DN 3; 44–45

Ballymoney td: Lough Swilly DL 38; 142, 145

Ballymoney td: Magherally DN 12; 114

Ballymoney td: Misc. DN 17; 124

Ballymoney td: Seapatrick DN 12; 123, 126

Ballymoney water: Island Magee AM 10; 81

Ballymoney water: Kilraghts AM 16; 124, 126

Ballymoney well: Aghanloo LY 11; 3

Ballymoney well: Bovevagh LY 25; 34

Ballymoney wooden bridge: Ballymoney AM 16; 9

Ballymoneymore (Ballyminimore) td: Glenavy AM 21; 77, 79–80

Ballymoneymore school: Glenavy AM 21; 79, 91

Ballymonimore (see Ballymoneymore): Glenavy AM 21; 77

Ballymonlon td: Blaris AM 8; 86

Ballymontena (see Ballymontenagh): Ahoghill AM 23; 47

Ballymontenagh fort: Ahoghill AM 23; 33

Ballymontenagh school: Ahoghill AM 23; 41, 47, 49

Ballymontenagh Sunday school: Ahoghill AM 23; 47

Ballymontenagh td: Ahoghill AM 23; 37–38

Ballymonymore (see Ballymoneymore): Glenavy AM 21; 79

Ballymoon (Kildare): Clondermot LY 34; 64

Ballymore bleach green: Tamlaght Finlagan LY 25; 115

Ballymore bridge: Tamlaght Finlagan LY 25; 85, 123

Ballymore flax mill: Tamlaght Finlagan LY 25; 83, 101, 121

Ballymore foundry: Tamlaght Finlagan LY 25; 114–15

Ballymore ph: Ballymore AH 1; 15

Ballymore ph: Kilmore AH 1; 57, 60–61, 67, 69, 72

Ballymore ph: Mullaghbrack AH 1; 94

Ballymore springs: Tamlaght Finlagan LY 25; 83

Ballymore td: Ballymore AH 1; 1, 13, 18

Ballymore td: Loughgilly AH 1; 85

Ballymore td: Tamlaght Finlagan LY 25; 89, 93, 114, 114, 118

Ballymorran td: Killinchy DN 7; 86

Ballymorter td: Misc. DN 17; 127

Ballymote: Emlaghfad SO 40; 176–77, 180, 182

Ballymote barrack: Emlaghfad SO 40; 177

Ballymote Castle: Emlaghfad SO 40; 178–79, 182

Ballymote chapel (C): Emlaghfad SO 40; 177

Ballymote chapel (M): Emlaghfad SO 40; 177

Ballymote church: Emlaghfad SO 40; 177, 179–80

Ballymote court house: Emlaghfad SO 40; 177, 179

Ballymote court house school: Emlaghfad SO 40; 179

Ballymote dispensary: Emlaghfad SO 40; 177, 179

Ballymote Lower td: Down DN 17; 55

Ballymote Middle td: Down DN 17; 55

Ballymote school: Emlaghfad SO 40; 179

Ballymote sessions house: Emlaghfad SO 40; 177

Ballymote td: Down DN 17; 52

Ballymote tower: Emlaghfad SO 40; 176

Ballymote trigonometrical station: Emlaghfad SO 40; 176

Ballymote Upper td: Down DN 17; 56

Ballymote Vicarage: Emlaghfad SO 40; 178

Ballymount (see Hollymount): Down DN 17; 55

Ballymoy Castle (see also Burnt House): Billy AM 16; 52, 64–65

Ballymoy Castle: Drummaul AM 19; 71

Ballymoy cave: Billy AM 16; 64

Ballymoy fort: Billy AM 16; 65

Ballymoy td: Ballylinny AM 32; 30

Ballymoyrent chapel: Loughgilly AH 1; 86

Ballymuckamore td: Ballylinny AM 32; 22, 30

Ballymuckleheany bog: Desertlyn LY 31; 44

Ballymuckleheany fort: Desertlyn LY 31; 44

Ballymulbrick (see Ballymeilbrick): Drumballyroney DN 3; 16

Ballymulderg Beg bog: Artrea LY 6; 23

Ballymulderg Beg school: Artrea LY 6; 20

Ballymulderg Beg td: Artrea LY 6; 12, 20, 23, 39

Ballymulderg giant's grave: Artrea LY 6; 10

Ballymulderg More fort: Artrea LY 6; 11, 23, 30

Ballymulderg More national school: Artrea LY 6; 19

Ballymulderg More Sunday school: Artrea LY 6; 21

Ballymulderg More td: Artrea LY 6; 11, 22–23, 30, 38

Ballymulderg td: Artrea LY 6; 10

Ballymuldery (see Ballymulderg)

Ballymuldrogh (Ballymuldrough) td: Island Magee AM 10; 15, 58, 63, 71, 101–02

Ballymuldrogh court knowe: Island Magee AM 10; 63

Ballymuldry (see Ballymulderg)

Ballymulholland td: Magilligan LY 11; 95, 126, 132, 142

Ballymullaghbritt td: Ballylinny AM 32; 22, 30

Ballymullaghferns td: Ballylinny AM 32; 30

Ballymullan corn mill: Bangor DN 7; 25

Ballymullan hill: Blaris DN 12; 27

Ballymullan school [I]: Bangor DN 7; 25

Ballymullan school [II]: Bangor DN 7; 25

Ballymullan td: Ballylinny AM 32; 30

Ballymullan td: Bangor DN 7; 19, 25

Ballymullans (see Ballymullins)

Ballymullany district: Misc. SO 40; 199

Ballymullay (see Ballymully): Balteagh LY 9; 37

Ballymullens (see Ballymullins)

Ballymulligan canopy stone: Artrea LY 6; 10

Ballymulligan forts: Artrea LY 6; 28

Ballymulligan giant's grave: Artrea LY 6; 28

Ballymulligan school: Artrea LY 6; 19

Ballymulligan td: Artrea LY 6; 10, 12, 28–29, 31

Ballymullin mountain: Dungiven LY 15; 19

Ballymullin mountains: Dungiven LY 15; 27, 111

Ballymullin mountains: Misc. LY 36; 110

Ballymullins chapel: Banagher LY 30; 15, 59

Ballymullins district: Banagher LY 30; 5, 31, 34–35, 72, 108, 110, 112–13

Ballymullins district: Clondermot LY 34; 34

Ballymullins district: Cumber LY 28; 11, 18, 87

Ballymullins district: Misc. LY 31; 116

Ballymully bridge: Balteagh LY 9; 5, 42

Ballymully cairns: Balteagh LY 9; 10, 30

Ballymully cloth mill: Balteagh LY 9; 14, 37, 41

Ballymully corn mill: Desertlyn LY 31; 42

Ballymully giant's grave: Desertlyn LY 31; 43–44, 48

Ballymully glen: Lissan LY 31; 101

Ballymully graveyard: Desertlyn LY 31; 42–43

Ballymully old church: Desertlyn LY 31; 42–43

Ballymully standing stones: Balteagh LY 9; 10, 28

Ballymully td: Ballylinny AM 32; 30

Ballymully td: Balteagh LY 9; 10, 14, 21, 28–30, 37, 40–41, 43, 45

Ballymully td: Desertcreat TE 20; 34

Ballymully td: Desertlyn LY 31; 47

Ballymullygan (see Ballymulligan): Artrea LY 6; 10

Ballymulnamossagh td: Ballylinny AM 32; 30

Ballymultimber (Ballymatimber) td: Magilligan LY 11; 94–95, 117, 126

Ballymultinner (see Ballymultimber)

Ballymultrea td: Ballinderry LY 6; 41

Ballymultrea td: Ballinderry TE 20; 13

Ballymurphy manor: Misc. DN 17; 125

Ballymurphy td: Annahilt DN 12; 20–22

Ballymurphy td: Misc. DN 17; 123

Ballymurray td: Ballee DN 17; 20, 22

Ballymurry td: Killoran and Kilvarnet SO 40; 183

Ballymyre chapel: Ballymyre AH 1; 20

Ballymyre church: Ballymyre AH 1; 20

Ballymyre House: Ballymyre AH 1; 20

Ballymyre td: Ballymyre AH 1; 20

Ballynaback (see Ballynaleck): Ballymore AH 1; 10

Ballynabarnish (Ballynabarnice) td: Templepatrick AM 35; 111, 114, 116, 124, 131, 135–36, 141, 144, 149, 152–53

Ballynabragget td: Donaghcloney DN 12; 59

Ballynacaird meeting house: Racavan AM 13; 92, 98

Ballynacaird td: Racavan AM 13; 88, 92, 98

Ballynacally bog: Aghadowey LY 22; 1

Ballynacally bridge: Aghadowey LY 22; 10

Ballynacally flax mill: Aghadowey LY 22; 9

Ballynacally school: Aghadowey LY 22; 13, 18

Ballynacally Sunday school: Aghadowey LY 22; 13

Ballynacallybeg td: Aghadowey LY 22; 9, 30, 32

Ballynacallymore bog: Aghadowey LY 22; 30–31

Ballynacallymore td: Aghadowey LY 22; 32, 35, 37

Ballynacamman (see Ballynacannon): Macosquin LY 22; 78

Ballynacannon (Ballinacannon) td: Macosquin LY 22; 83, 98

Ballynacannon bog: Macosquin LY 22; 78, 120

Ballynacannon flax mill: Macosquin LY 22; 83, 105

Ballynacannon fort: Macosquin LY 22; 120

Ballynacargy: Drung CN 40; 20, 23

Ballynacargy corn mill: Drung CN 40; 21

Ballynaclough Killymorris td: Loughguile AM 13; 74

Ballynaconnon (see Ballynacannon): Macosquin LY 22; 98

Ballynacor td: Seagoe AH 1; 101, 105, 107

Ballynacoy bog: Glenavy AM 21; 78

Ballynacoy bridge: Glenavy AM 21; 80

Ballynacoy forts: Glenavy AM 21; 90

Ballynacoy td: Glenavy AM 21; 79

Ballynacraig church: Inch DN 17; 73

Ballynacraig hill: Inch DN 17; 73

Ballynacraig school: Inch DN 17; 73

Ballynacraig td: Inch DN 17; 77

Ballynacraigy corn mill: Drummaul AM 19; 51

Ballynacraigy forts: Drummaul AM 19; 78

Ballynacreagan (see Ballynaragan): Tamlaght TE 20; 87

Ballynacree (Ballynacrea) td: Ballymoney AM 16; 22

Ballynacree demesne: Ballymoney AM 16; 5

Ballynacree House: Ballymoney AM 16; 1, 9

Ballynacree Skein (Skrin) td: Ballymoney AM 16; 3

Ballynacree Skein factory: Ballymoney AM 16; 3

Ballynacree Skein flax mill: Ballymoney AM 16; 10

Ballynacree-more td: Ballymoney AM 16; 5, 9

Ballynacross td: Maghera LY 18; 53–54

Ballynacross Upper td: Maghera LY 18; 53

Ballynadolly bog: Magheragall AM 21; 103, 107

Ballynadolly td: Magheragall AM 21; 106–07, 109–10

Ballynadrentagh td: Killead AM 35; 40, 53

Ballynadrinta (see Ballynadrentagh): Killead AM 35; 53

Ballynafeigh (Ballinafie) td: Derrykeighan AM 16; 78, 93–94

Ballynafern hill: Annaclone DN 12; 13

Ballynafern school: Annaclone DN 12; 15, 19

Ballynafern td: Annaclone DN 12; 16, 19

Ballynafey td: Duneane AM 19; 123

Ballynafie (see Ballynafey): Duneane AM 19; 123

Ballynafir fort: Ahoghill AM 23; 35

Ballynafoy hill: Annaclone DN 12; 16

Ballynafoy td: Annaclone DN 12; 16

Ballynag Lower cave: Ballyrashane LY 22; 50, 60

Ballynag Lower fort: Ballyrashane LY 22; 49–50, 53, 60

Ballynag Lower td: Ballyrashane LY 22; 47, 58

Ballynag Upper cave [I]: Ballyrashane LY 22; 50, 60

Ballynag Upper cave [II]: Ballyrashane LY 22; 60

Ballynagallagh td: Bright DN 17; 33, 35

Ballynagappag school: Hillsborough DN 12, 101

Ballynagappoge (Ballingossog) td: Clonduff DN 3; 4

Ballynagappoge school: Clonduff DN 3; 4

Ballynagard bog: Rathlin Island AM 24; 129

Ballynagard House: Clondermot LY 34; 100

Ballynagard House: Culfeightrin AM 24; 40, 72

Ballynagard td: Culfeightrin AM 24; 53

Ballynagarrick corn mill: Tullylish DN 12; 142

Ballynagarrick meeting house: Tullylish DN 12; 141

Ballynagarrick school: Tullylish DN 12; 144

Ballynagarrick smithy: Saul DN 17; 115

Ballynagarrick td: Saul DN 17; 114

Ballynagarrick td: Tullylish DN 12; 141–44

Ballynagarve fort: Artrea LY 6; 26

Ballynagarve td: Artrea LY 6; 26

Ballynagashel Castle: Loughguile AM 13; 76

Ballynagashel td: Loughguile AM 13; 69–70, 76

Ballynagashell (see Ballynagashel): Loughguile AM 13; 70, 76

Ballynageeragh fort: Killead AM 35; 29–30, 39

Ballynageeragh td: Killead AM 35; 35, 40

Ballynagelty mountain: Kilbroney DN 3; 26, 28

Ballynagg (see Ballynag): Ballyrashane LY 22; 47

Ballynagh: Drumlumman CN 40; 13–15, 17

Ballynaghten fort: Aghalee AM 21; 36

Ballynaghten hill: Magheramesk AM 21; 114

Ballynaghten school: Aghalee AM 21; 28

Ballynaghten td: Aghalee AM 21; 28

Ballynaghten wood: Aghalee AM 21; 28

Ballynaghy (Ballynaghey) td: Seagoe AH 1; 107

Ballynaghy corn mill: Seagoe AH 1; 107

Ballynaghy mill [I]: Seagoe AH 1; 103

Ballynaghy mill [II]: Seagoe AH 1; 103

Ballynaglogh (Ballynaglough) td: Culfeightrin AM 24; 55

Ballynaglogh Castle: Culfeightrin AM 24; 55–56

Ballynaglogh church: Culfeightrin AM 24; 36, 39–40, 45, 76

Ballynaglogh fort: Culfeightrin AM 24; 55

Ballynaglogh graveyard: Culfeightrin AM 24; 55–56

Ballynaglogh school: Culfeightrin AM 24; 85

Ballynaglogh standing stones: Culfeightrin AM 24; 55, 76

Ballynagone td: Drumcree AH 1; 41

Ballynagor school: Billy AM 16; 49

Ballynagor td: Billy AM 16; 40

Ballynagor td: Derrykeighan AM 16; 92

Ballynagor td: Drumtullagh AM 16; 103

Ballynagoragh (see Ballynagurragh)

Ballynagown (Ballynagowan) td: Desertmartin LY
    31; 62, 132, 142

Ballynagrass (see Ballynagross): Ballee DN 17; 22

Ballynagreagh (see Ballinareagh): Ballymore AH 1;
    9

Ballynagross Lower td: Ballee DN 17; 22

Ballynagross td: Annaclone DN 12; 16

Ballynagross td: Ballee DN 17; 22

Ballynagross Upper td: Ballee DN 17; 22

Ballynagunaghan (see Ballygunaghan)

Ballynagurragh (Ballynagoragh) td: Clogher TE 5;
    35, 42, 51

Ballynagurragh fort: Clogher TE 5; 39

Ballynagurragh school: Clogher TE 5; 42, 51

Ballynahaigha quarry: Drumgoon CN 40; 4

Ballynahany td: Drummaul AM 19; 90

Ballynaharry flax mill: Drumachose LY 9; 53

Ballynaharry td: Drumachose LY 9; 53

Ballynahatty beetling mill: Drumbo DN 7; 60

Ballynahatty corn mill: Drumragh TE 5; 110

Ballynahatty flour mill: Drumbo DN 7; 59

Ballynahatty giant's ring: Drumbo DN 7; 57

Ballynahatty log mill: Drumbo DN 7; 60

Ballynahatty meeting house: Drumragh TE 5;
    107–108

Ballynahatty old castle: Drumragh TE 5; 108

Ballynahatty school: Drumragh TE 5; 109

Ballynahatty td: Drumbo DN 7; 57, 59, 61–62

Ballynahatty td: Drumragh TE 5; 107, 109

Ballynahatty village: Drumragh TE 5; 108, 110–11

Ballynahaye hill: Killeeshil TE 20; 64

Ballynahaye td: Killeeshil TE 20; 62

Ballynahery (Ballynaharry) td: Drumachose LY 9;
    87, 96

Ballynahinch: Annahilt DN 12; 22

Ballynahinch: Blaris AM 8; 73, 76

Ballynahinch: Comber DN 7; 37, 39

Ballynahinch: Holywood DN 7; 77

Ballynahinch: Inch DN 17; 74

Ballynahinch: Kilmore DN 17; 89, 91–92

Ballynahinch: Knockbreda DN 7; 102

Ballynahinch: Loughinisland DN 17; 95–96

Ballynahinch: Magheradrool DN 17; 99–102,
    105–07

Ballynahinch: Misc. DN 17; 116, 120

Ballynahinch bleach mills: Magheradrool DN 17;
    107

Ballynahinch bridge: Magheradrool DN 17; 106

Ballynahinch chapel: Magheradrool DN 17; 106

Ballynahinch charter school: Magheradrool DN 17;
    101

Ballynahinch church: Magheradrool DN 17; 106–07

Ballynahinch corn mill: Magheradrool DN 17; 102,
    106–07

Ballynahinch dispensary [I]: Magheradrool DN 17;
    102

Ballynahinch dispensary [II]: Magheradrool DN 17;
    102

Ballynahinch dispensary [III]: Magheradrool DN
    17; 102

Ballynahinch dispensary [IV]: Magheradrool DN
    17; 102

Ballynahinch Dromore St school [I]: Magheradrool
    DN 17; 101

Ballynahinch Dromore St school [II]: Magheradrool
    DN 17; 101

Ballynahinch flax mill: Magheradrool DN 17; 102,
    107

Ballynahinch Glebe House: Magheradrool DN 17;
    106–07

Ballynahinch hibernian school: Magheradrool DN
    17; 101

Ballynahinch hills: Kilmore AH 1; 61

Ballynahinch market house: Magheradrool DN 17;
    101

Ballynahinch Market St school: Magheradrool DN
    17; 101

Ballynahinch meeting house (P): Magheradrool DN
    17; 101, 106

Ballynahinch meeting house (S): Magheradrool DN
    17; 106

Ballynahinch national school: Kilmore AH 1; 59,
    64, 67

Ballynahinch ph: Ballinderry AM 21; 51

Ballynahinch residentiary house: Magheradrool DN
    17; 101

Ballynahinch river (see Quoile river): Dromara DN
    12; 62

Ballynahinch school: Kilmore AH 1; 64

Ballynahinch Scotch meeting house: Magheradrool
    DN 17; 106

Ballynahinch spa: Magheradrool DN 17; 101

Ballynahinch td: Kilmore AH 1; 61, 66–67, 72

Ballynahinch td: Magheradrool DN 17; 107

Ballynahinch td school: Magheradrool DN 17; 101

Ballynahone Beg td: Termoneeny LY 6; 122, 131

Ballynahone bog: Maghera LY 18; 58

Ballynahone bog: Termoneeny LY 6; 132

Ballynahone bridge: Termoneeny LY 6; 131

Ballynahone More bog: Termoneeny LY 6; 124

Ballynahone More school: Termoneeny LY 6; 124,
    128

Ballynahone More Sunday school: Termoneeny LY
    6; 124, 128

Ballynahone More td: Termoneeny LY 6; 121, 126,
    128, 131–33

Ballynahone td: Loughguile AM 13; 76

Ballynahone td: Maghera LY 18; 5, 14, 52, 54–55,
    58

Ballynahone td: Termoneeny LY 6; 121, 126, 131, 133

Ballynahonebeg bog: Maghera LY 18; 4, 57

Ballynahonebeg school: Maghera LY 18; 28

Ballynahonebeg td: Maghera LY 18; 47, 70, 77

Ballynahowlane td: Ballylinny AM 32; 30

Ballynahuich (see Ballynahinch): Kilmore AH 1; 61

Ballynain (see Ballynian): Tamlaght O'Crilly LY 18; 135

Ballynakill td: Devenish FH 14; 57–58

Ballynakillue td: Lough Swilly DL 38; 144–45

Ballynalargy (Ballynelargy) td: Magheramesk AM 21; 113, 122, 130

Ballynalargy fort [I]: Magheramesk AM 21; 122

Ballynalargy fort [II]: Magheramesk AM 21; 125

Ballynalargy forts: Magheragall AM 21; 105

Ballynalargy meeting house: Magheramesk AM 21; 113, 115, 128

Ballynalargy quarries: Magheragall AM 21; 107

Ballynalargy td: Magheragall AM 21; 107, 109

Ballynalargy well: Magheramesk AM 21; 122

Ballynalargy wood: Magheramesk AM 21; 122

Ballynaleaney (see Ballylenully): Duneane AM 19; 124

Ballynaleck (Ballinaleck) td: Ballymore AH 1; 9, 13–14, 18

Ballynaleck graveyard: Ballymore AH 1; 10, 12

Ballynaleck td: Cleenish FH 14; 29

Ballynaliggy td: Ballylinny AM 32; 30

Ballynally (see Ballynelly): Moville DL 38; 70

Ballynaloch (see Ballynalough): Umgall AM 35; 159

Ballynalosht Sunday school: Clondavaddog DL 38; 7

Ballynalough bog: Templepatrick AM 35; 130, 150

Ballynalough fort: Templepatrick AM 35; 150

Ballynalough school: Templepatrick AM 35; 135, 153

Ballynalough td: Templepatrick AM 35; 131, 144, 147–48

Ballynalough td: Umgall AM 35; 159

Ballynalube fort: Killagan AM 23; 80

Ballynalube school: Killagan AM 23; 85

Ballynalube td: Killagan AM 23; 79

Ballynalurgan locality: Clogher TE 5; 31

Ballynamaddy church: Clondermot LY 34; 63

Ballynamaddy moss: Dunaghy AM 13; 23

Ballynamagna (Ballynemagenagh) td: Drumballyroney DN 3; 12, 18

Ballynamagna mill: Drumballyroney DN 3; 16

Ballynamallard (see Ballinamallard)

Ballynaman td: Donaghmore DL 39; 36

Ballynameen bridge: Desertoghill LY 27; 2, 16

Ballynameen bridge: Drumachose LY 9; 76

Ballynameen bridge: Errigal LY 27; 40–41, 60

Ballynameen corn kiln: Desertoghill LY 27; 4

Ballynameen graveyard: Desertoghill LY 27; 30

Ballynameen hamlet: Desertoghill LY 27; 13

Ballynameen old church: Desertoghill LY 27; 5–6, 15, 18, 22–23, 31

Ballynameen td: Desertoghill LY 27; 1 2, 8, 19–21, 23, 29–30

Ballynameen td: Errigal LY 27; 78

Ballynamony Bradshaw td: Carlingford LH 40; 57

Ballynamony Murphy td: Carlingford LH 40; 57

Ballynamoor (see Ballynamore): Cumber LY 28; 48

Ballynamore (Ballinamore) td: Cumber LY 28; 48, 60–61, 63–64, 92, 94, 99, 104, 107

Ballynamore bog: Cumber LY 28; 46, 46

Ballynamore school [I]: Cumber LY 28; 34, 74–75, 79

Ballynamore school [II]: Cumber LY 28; 74

Ballynamullan td: Duneane AM 19; 119, 123–24

Ballynamullin td: Ballylinny AM 32; 30

Ballynana (Ballnana) td: Errigal Keerogue TE 20; 48, 51

Ballynana quarry: Errigal Keerogue TE 20; 51

Ballynanaghten fort [I]: Aghalee AM 21; 35

Ballynanaghten fort [II]: Aghalee AM 21; 35

Ballynanaghten td: Aghalee AM 21; 28

Ballynanaghten wood: Aghalee AM 21; 35

Ballynanny td: Annaclone DN 12; 14, 16–17

Ballynaragan td: Tamlaght TE 20; 85, 87

Ballynard td: Errigal Keerogue TE 20; 56

Ballynaree quarry: Lough Swilly DL 38; 135

Ballynaris td: Dromore DN 12; 76

Ballynarrag (see Ballynarrig): Tamlaght Finlagan LY 25; 121

Ballynarrig burn: Tamlaght Finlagan LY 25; 121

Ballynarrig school: Tamlaght Finlagan LY 25; 96

Ballynarrig td: Tamlaght Finlagan LY 25; 93, 118

Ballynarry (Ballynary) td: Tartaraghan AH 1; 117

Ballynarry fort: Ballynure AM 32; 61

Ballynarry graveyard: Billy AM 16; 51–52

Ballynarry hill: Ballynure AM 32; 31

Ballynarry Lower cave: Billy AM 16; 73

Ballynarry Lower fort: Billy AM 16; 55, 72–73

Ballynarry Lower old church: Billy AM 16; 51

Ballynarry meeting house: Tartaraghan AH 1; 118

Ballynarry school: Ballynure AM 32; 52–53, 71, 73

Ballynarry standing stone: Ballynure AM 32; 54

Ballynarry Sunday school: Ballynure AM 32; 53, 71

Ballynarry td: Ballynure AM 32; 63, 68, 72

Ballynarry td: Dunluce AM 16; 109

Ballynarry td: Saul DN 17; 114

Ballynarry td: Tartaraghan AH 1; 120

Ballynarry Upper td: Derrykeighan AM 16; 95

Ballynasaggart (Ballynasagart) td: Errigal Keerogue TE 20; 48, 51, 56

Ballynasaggart church: Errigal Keerogue TE 20; 48, 51

Ballynasaggart forts: Errigal Keerogue TE 20; 51

Ballynasaggart old church: Errigal Keerogue TE 20; 51, 53

Ballynasaggart school: Errigal Keerogue TE 20; 48

Ballynascarvy bridge: Aughnamullen MN 40; 73

Ballynascreen bleach green: Misc. LY 31; 134

Ballynascreen chapels: Tamlaght Finlagan LY 25; 103

Ballynascreen church: Maghera LY 18; 9

Ballynascreen church: Magilligan LY 11; 105, 146

Ballynascreen churchlands: Misc. LY 31; 121

Ballynascreen corn mills: Misc. LY 31; 135

Ballynascreen dispensary: Ballynascreen LY 31; 13, 18

Ballynascreen dispensary: Kilcronaghan LY 31; 71

Ballynascreen forge: Kilrea LY 27; 112

Ballynascreen glebe: Ballynascreen LY 31; 19

Ballynascreen Glebe House: Ballynascreen LY 31; 6, 20, 128

Ballynascreen graveyard: Ballynascreen LY 31; 9, 19

Ballynascreen House: Carrickfergus AM 37; 134

Ballynascreen locality: Carrickfergus AM 37; 93, 173

Ballynascreen meeting house: Kilcronaghan LY 31; 82

Ballynascreen mountains: Maghera LY 18; 3

Ballynascreen old chapel: Ballynascreen LY 31; 5

Ballynascreen old church: Ballynascreen LY 31; 5, 7–9, 11, 14, 19, 24–25, 27–29

Ballynascreen old church: Banagher LY 30; 37

Ballynascreen old church: Kilcronaghan LY 31; 77

Ballynascreen old church: Maghera LY 18; 10

Ballynascreen old church: Misc. LY 31; 116–17

Ballynascreen ph: Ballyscullion LY 6; 42

Ballynascreen ph: Banagher LY 30; 1, 5, 10, 15, 31, 36, 95, 99, 112

Ballynascreen ph: Clondermot LY 34; 76

Ballynascreen ph: Cumber LY 28; 61, 66, 71

Ballynascreen ph: Desertmartin LY 31; 55

Ballynascreen ph: Dungiven LY 15; 1, 37, 50

Ballynascreen ph: Kilcronaghan LY 31; 64, 69, 71–73, 80, 82

Ballynascreen ph: Kilrea LY 27; 119

Ballynascreen ph: Lissan LY 31; 91–94, 106

Ballynascreen ph: Maghera LY 18; 13, 17, 39, 64–65, 69

Ballynascreen ph: Magherafelt LY 6; 79

Ballynascreen ph: Misc. LY 31; 111–13, 116–44

Ballynascreen ph: Misc. LY 36; 105

Ballynascreen ph: Tamlaght O'Crilly LY 18; 111

Ballynascreen quarries: Ballynascreen LY 31; 5

Ballynascreen Sunday schools: Misc. LY 31; 126

Ballynascreen tannery: Misc. LY 31; 134

Ballynascreen td: Artrea LY 6; 24, 39

Ballynascreen td: Dungiven LY 15; 12, 65, 96

Ballynascreen td: Magilligan LY 11; 100

Ballynascreen tuck mill: Misc. LY 31; 130, 134

Ballynashanagh lough: Clondavaddog DL 38; 3

Ballynashee corn mill: Rashee AM 32; 136–37

Ballynashee td: Rashee AM 32; 136

Ballynaskeagh td: Aghaderg DN 12; 1

Ballynaskelgie (see Skelgagh)

Ballynasolus hill: Kildress TE 20; 61

Ballynasolus hill: Lissan TE 20; 69

Ballynass td: Clogher TE 5; 25

Ballynastraid altar: Ballintoy AM 24; 21

Ballynastraid battery: Ballintoy AM 24; 21

Ballynastraid cromlech: Ballintoy AM 24; 20

Ballynastraid east fort: Ballintoy AM 24; 21

Ballynastraid enclosure: Ballintoy AM 24; 20–21

Ballynastraid td: Ballintoy AM 24; 20, 22

Ballynastraid west fort: Ballintoy AM 24; 21

Ballynatone td: Kilteevoge DL 39; 113

Ballynavalley (see Ballynavally): Drumbo DN 7; 62

Ballynavally corn mill: Drumbo DN 7; 56, 60

Ballynavally flax mill: Drumbo DN 7; 56

Ballynavally log mill: Drumbo DN 7; 60

Ballynavally td: Drumbo DN 7; 54, 56, 60–62

Ballynaverin House: Carrickfergus AM 37; 135

Ballynavilly (see Ballynacally): Aghadowey LY 22; 18

Ballynavrainy td: Ballylinny AM 32; 30

Ballynealbanagh td: Ballylinny AM 32; 30

Ballynean lough: Aughnamullen MN 40; 70

Ballyneary mountain: Donaghedy TE 5; 89

Ballyneas (see Ballynease)

Ballynease (see Ballyleese): Ballyaghran LY 33; 20

Ballynease bogs: Ballyscullion LY 6; 69

Ballynease grey stone: Ballyscullion LY 6; 50, 73

Ballynease Helton fort: Ballyscullion LY 6; 72

Ballynease Helton td: Ballyscullion LY 6; 50, 72

Ballynease Strain td: Ballyscullion LY 6; 73, 77–78

Ballynease td: Ballyscullion LY 6; 69

Ballynease-McPeake forts: Ballyscullion LY 6; 51, 72

Ballynease-McPeake school: Ballyscullion LY 6; 61

Ballynease-McPeake td: Ballyscullion LY 6; 43, 51, 71, 75

Ballynebentra td: Ballylinny AM 32; 30

Ballyneclogh td: Ballylinny AM 32; 22, 30

Ballynecreigh td: Ballylinny AM 32; 30

Ballyneddan td: Kilbroney DN 3; 28, 31

Ballyneese (see Ballyleese): Ballyaghran LY 33; 7

Ballyneil (Ballyneal) td: Artrea LY 6; 8, 34

Ballyneil House: Artrea LY 6; 8

Ballyneil More forts: Artrea LY 6; 10, 26

Ballyneil More Sunday school: Artrea LY 6; 21

Ballyneil More td: Artrea LY 6; 10, 26

Ballyneill td: Faughanvale LY 36; 57

Ballynelly school [I]: Moville DL 38; 69

Ballynelly school [II]: Moville DL 38; 69

Ballynelly Sunday school: Moville DL 38; 69

Ballynelly td: Moville DL 38; 68, 70

Ballynelossonbeg td: Ballylinny AM 32; 30

Ballynemagheriawly (see Magherally): Magherally DN 12; 112

Ballynemenis td: Ballylinny AM 32; 30

Ballynemony quarry: Seagoe AH 1; 107

Ballynemony td: Seagoe AH 1; 107

Ballynenagh chapel: Artrea LY 6; 7

Ballynenagh chapel: Artrea TE 20; 8

Ballynenagh fort: Artrea LY 6; 29

Ballynenagh td: Artrea LY 6; 7, 20–21, 29–31, 33, 38

Ballynepallady (see Ballypalladay): Ballylinny AM 32; 22

Ballynephellott td: Ballylinny AM 32; 30

Ballynerowlane td: Ballylinny AM 32; 30

Ballynerry (see Ballynarry): Ballynure AM 32; 73

Ballynery td: Montiaghs AH 1; 93

Ballyness bar: Lough Swilly DL 38; 122–24

Ballyness bleaching mill: Macosquin LY 22; 102

Ballyness bog: Balteagh LY 9; 28

Ballyness bridge: Dungiven LY 15; 96

Ballyness caves: Billy AM 16; 63

Ballyness corn mill: Dungiven LY 15; 9, 97

Ballyness cove: Billy AM 16; 56

Ballyness creek: Lough Swilly DL 38; 122

Ballyness fishery: Coleraine LY 33; 149

Ballyness fort: Billy AM 16; 41

Ballyness hill: Dungiven LY 15; 70

Ballyness House: Macosquin LY 22; 80, 102

Ballyness paper mill: Dunluce AM 16; 110

Ballyness school: Macosquin LY 22; 92–94

Ballyness Sunday school: Clondavaddog DL 38; 7

Ballyness Sunday school: Macosquin LY 22; 94

Ballyness td (Donegal): Clondermot LY 34; 69

Ballyness td: Balteagh LY 9; 26, 28

Ballyness td: Banagher LY 30; 23

Ballyness td: Billy AM 16; 39, 41

Ballyness td: Clogher TE 5; 37, 53

Ballyness td: Coleraine LY 33; 149

Ballyness td: Dungiven LY 15; 23, 27, 45, 48–49, 51, 60, 64, 71, 73, 89, 105

Ballyness td: Macosquin LY 22; 83, 105

Ballyness wood: Dungiven LY 15; 3, 96

Ballynester td: Grey Abbey DN 7; 67

Ballynestor (see Ballynester) td: Misc. DN 17; 123

Ballynevally td: Ballylinny AM 32; 30

Ballynewey (Ballynewy) td: Artrea LY 6; 32, 38

Ballynewey evening school: Artrea LY 6; 19

Ballynewoodeage td: Ballylinny AM 32; 30

Ballynewport td: Bright DN 17; 35, 37

Ballynewry lough: Mullaghbrack AH 1; 94

Ballynewry school: Mullaghbrack AH 1; 97

Ballynewry td: Mullaghbrack AH 1; 94

Ballynian bog: Tamlaght O'Crilly LY 18; 84–86, 114, 129

Ballynian flax mill: Tamlaght O'Crilly LY 18; 91, 109

Ballynian fort [I]: Tamlaght O'Crilly LY 18; 95, 113–14

Ballynian fort [II]: Tamlaght O'Crilly LY 18; 102

Ballynian Islands: Tamlaght O'Crilly LY 18; 130

Ballynian old forts: Tamlaght O'Crilly LY 18; 114

Ballynian school: Tamlaght O'Crilly LY 18; 139

Ballynian td: Tamlaght O'Crilly LY 18; 84, 87, 97, 102, 119, 129, 135, 137–38

Ballynichol td: Ballyphilip DN 7; 7–8

Ballynichol td: Misc. DN 17; 125

Ballynickle td: Comber DN 7; 37, 40, 42–44

Ballynicol (see Ballynichol): Ballyphilip DN 7; 8

Ballyno (see Ballynoe): Donegore AM 29; 134

Ballynock (Ballyknock) td: Moira DN 12; 118, 120–21

Ballynock (see Ballyknock): Loughguile AM 13; 76

Ballynock school: Moira DN 12; 118, 120–21

Ballynock td: Maghera LY 18; 68

Ballynocker td: Magherafelt LY 6; 95, 112

Ballynoe cove: Donegore AM 29; 123

Ballynoe cromlech: Bright DN 17; 33

Ballynoe flax mill: Donegore AM 29; 104

Ballynoe forts: Donegore AM 29; 127

Ballynoe school: Bright DN 17; 36

Ballynoe school: Donegore AM 29; 134

Ballynoe stream: Donegore AM 29; 102, 105, 133

Ballynoe stream: Nilteen AM 35; 86, 88, 90

Ballynoe td: Bright DN 17; 33, 35

Ballynoe td: Donegore AM 29; 101–02, 125

Ballynoe td: Misc. DN 17; 124

Ballynow td: Ballylinny AM 32; 30

Ballyntine, Rev. Thomas: Templepatrick AM 35; 144, 147

Ballynully (see Ballylenully): Duneane AM 19; 96

Ballynure: Ballycor AM 32; 8–9

Ballynure: Ballylinny AM 32; 14

Ballynure: Ballymartin AM 2; 4

Ballynure: Ballynure AM 32; 31–35, 37–42, 44, 46–47, 49, 55–57, 59–60, 63–64, 66–72

Ballynure: Ballywalter AM 2; 29

Ballynure: Carnmoney AM 2; 44, 49, 85

Ballynure: Carrickfergus AM 37; 3, 32, 59

Ballynure: Doagh AM 29; 89

Ballynure: Inver AM 26; 53

Ballynure: Kilwaughter AM 10; 107, 111

Ballynure: Raloo AM 32; 84, 119, 122, 126, 130

Ballynure: Templecorran AM 26; 85–86, 95, 108

Ballynure bridge: Ballynascreen LY 31; 7

Ballynure bridge: Ballynure AM 32; 33–34, 39, 70

Ballynure caves: Ballynure AM 32; 60

Ballynure chapel: Ballynure AM 32; 67

Ballynure church (see also Toberdowney): Ballynure AM 32; 33

Ballynure church: Kilroot AM 26; 63–64

Ballynure church: Templecorran AM 26; 101

Ballynure corn mill: Ballynure AM 32; 66, 68

Ballynure dam: Ballynure AM 32; 43

Ballynure Fair hill: Ballynure AM 32; 41

Ballynure graveyard: Ballynascreen LY 31; 31–32

Ballynure graveyard: Desertoghill LY 27; 6–7

Ballynure library: Ballynure AM 32; 65

Ballynure manor: Ballynure AM 32; 34–35, 38, 40

Ballynure meeting house: Ballynure AM 32; 33, 39, 49–50, 64–65, 67, 69, 71–72

Ballynure old chapel: Ballynure AM 32; 56

Ballynure old church: Ballynascreen LY 31; 31

Ballynure ph: Ballylinny AM 32; 12

Ballynure ph: Carnmoney AM 2; 57

Ballynure ph: Carrickfergus AM 37; 1, 142, 151

Ballynure ph: Doagh AM 29; 60, 85, 87, 100

Ballynure ph: Kilroot AM 26; 61, 65, 72, 78–79

Ballynure ph: Kilwaughter AM 10; 106, 114

Ballynure ph: Misc. AM 10; 129

Ballynure ph: Raloo AM 32; 80, 89, 99, 101, 106

Ballynure ph: Templecorran AM 26; 101, 127

Ballynure private school [I]: Ballynure AM 32; 53

Ballynure private school [II]: Ballynure AM 32; 53

Ballynure rectory: Kilroot AM 26; 64, 68

Ballynure rectory: Templecorran AM 26; 101

Ballynure school: Misc. LY 31; 125–26

Ballynure stream: Ballynure AM 32; 31–32, 38–39, 43–44

Ballynure Sunday school: Ballynure AM 32; 49, 65, 71

Ballynure td: Misc. LY 31; 142–43

Ballynure worship house (M): Ballynure AM 32; 69

Ballynure worship house (P): Ballynure AM 32; 69

Ballyoan (Ballyowen) td: Clondermot LY 34; 38, 56, 58–60, 62, 72, 75–76, 80, 108, 112–14, 121, 129

Ballyoan quarry: Clondermot LY 34; 129

Ballyoan school: Clondermot LY 34; 90

Ballyoan wood: Clondermot LY 34; 121

Ballyobegan House: Inishargy DN 7; 85

Ballyobegan td: Inishargy DN 7; 85

Ballyobigan (see Ballyobegan) td: Misc. DN 17; 125

Ballyoglah bog: Billy AM 16; 75

Ballyoglah cave: Billy AM 16; 64

Ballyoglah cromlech: Billy AM 16; 54, 75

Ballyoglah school: Billy AM 16; 77

Ballyoglah standing stone: Billy AM 16; 58–59, 62

Ballyoglah td: Billy AM 16; 74

Ballyoglough (see Ballyoglah): Billy AM 16; 77

Ballyon (see Ballyoan): Clondermot LY 34; 90

Ballyonan td: Carlingford LH 40; 57

Ballyonemagaile td: Ballylinny AM 32; 30

Ballyoran corn mill: Comber DN 7; 40

Ballyoran flour mill: Dundonald DN 7; 66

Ballyoran td: Comber DN 7; 40, 43

Ballyoran td: Drumcree AH 1; 41

Ballyoran td: Dundonald DN 7; 65–66

Ballyore Castle: Clondermot LY 34; 14, 19, 23, 49–50

Ballyore td: Clondermot LY 34; 56, 60, 108, 112, 114, 121–22, 129

Ballyore wood: Clondermot LY 34; 122

Ballyoren (see Straid): Banagher LY 30; 39

Ballyorgan td: Ballee DN 17; 15

Ballyorgan td: Dunsfort DN 17; 67

Ballyorgan windmill: Rathmullan DN 17; 108

Ballyorgus td: Moville DL 38; 75

Ballyoriskey (see Ballyroosky)

Ballyorisky (see Ballyroosky)

Ballyornagh td: Cleenish FH 14; 29

Ballyoughagan td: Mevagh DL 38; 63

Ballypalidy (see Ballypallady): Ballymartin AM 2; 17

Ballypalladay burn: Ballylinny AM 32; 11–12

Ballypallady (Ballypallidy) td: Ballymartin AM 2; 12, 15

Ballypallady burn: Ballymartin AM 2; 3, 12

Ballypallady burn: Ballyrobert AM 2; 19

Ballypallady burn: Ballywalter AM 2; 28

Ballypallady forts: Ballymartin AM 2; 15, 17–18

Ballypallady school: Ballymartin AM 2; 7, 15

Ballypallady singing school: Ballylinny AM 32; 29

Ballypallady td: Ballylinny AM 32; 22, 30

Ballypalliday (see Ballypallady): Ballylinny AM 32; 29

Ballypatrick bog: Culfeightrin AM 24; 82

Ballypatrick cave: Culfeightrin AM 24; 73

Ballypatrick flax mill: Culfeightrin AM 24; 45

Ballypatrick loughs: Culfeightrin AM 24; 73

Ballypatrick td: Ballylinny AM 32; 30

Ballypatrick td: Ballymoney AM 16; 9

Ballypatrick td: Culfeightrin AM 24; 73, 83

Ballyphilip Glebe House: Ballyphilip DN 7; 14

Ballyphilip ph: Ballyhalbert DN 7; 5

Ballyphilip ph: Ballytrustan DN 7; 15

Ballyphilip ph: Grey Abbey DN 7; 70

Ballyphilip ph: Inishargy DN 7; 84

Ballyphilip ph: Misc. DN 17; 126

Ballyphilip ph: Witter DN 7; 126

Ballyphilip td: Ballyphilip DN 7; 7, 14

Ballyphilip union: Witter DN 7; 125

Ballypitmave bog: Glenavy AM 21; 78, 83

Ballypitmave td: Glenavy AM 21; 78–79

Ballyplunt (Ballyplant) td: Bright DN 17; 35–37

Ballypollard td: Glynn AM 26; 1, 28, 41–42

Ballyportery flax mill: Loughguile AM 13; 63

Ballyportery North corn mill: Loughguile AM 13; 63

Ballyportery South beetling mill: Loughguile AM 13; 63

Ballyprior graveyard: Island Magee AM 10; 70, 99

Ballyprior monastery: Island Magee AM 10; 43

Ballyprior td: Island Magee AM 10; 81, 99

Ballypriorbeg td: Island Magee AM 10; 43

Ballypriormore graveyard: Island Magee AM 10; 43

Ballypriormore td: Island Magee AM 10; 23, 43, 60

Ballyquentin (see Ballyquintin): Ballyphilip DN 7; 7

Ballyquiggan td: Ballyscullion LY 6; 58

Ballyquillan chapel: Carmavy AM 35; 3

Ballyquillan chapel: Killead AM 35; 11–12, 20, 41, 45, 47, 52

Ballyquillan corn mill: Killead AM 35; 14, 48

Ballyquillan graveyard: Killead AM 35; 12, 45

Ballyquillan old chapel: Killead AM 35; 45

Ballyquillan school: Killead AM 35; 36, 39, 43, 52

Ballyquillan Sunday school: Killead AM 35; 39, 52

Ballyquillan td: Killead AM 35; 14, 17, 21–22, 35, 40, 50

Ballyquin bridge: Aghadowey LY 22; 10

Ballyquin forts: Balteagh LY 9; 25

Ballyquin td: Aghadowey LY 22; 1, 7

Ballyquin td: Balteagh LY 9; 12–13, 25, 30, 32, 40, 43, 45

Ballyquinn (see Ballyquin): Balteagh LY 9; 13

Ballyquintin manor: Misc. DN 17; 125

Ballyquintin ph: Witter DN 7; 125

Ballyquintin Point: Ballyphilip DN 7; 9

Ballyquintin td: Ballyphilip DN 7; 7–8

Ballyquintin td: Misc. DN 17; 127

Ballyquinun (see Ballyquintin)

Ballyraine bridge: Lough Swilly DL 38; 98, 103–04

Ballyrainey flax mill: Comber DN 7; 41

Ballyrainey flax mill: Newtownards DN 7; 110

Ballyrainey td: Comber DN 7; 41, 43

Ballyrainey td: Dundonald DN 7; 65

Ballyrainey td: Newtownards DN 7; 110

Ballyrally td: Seapatrick DN 12; 134

Ballyranell td: Ballylinny AM 32; 30

Ballyrare td: Misc. DN 17; 124

Ballyrashane Castle: Misc. LY 36; 109

Ballyrashane church: Ballyrashane LY 22; 47, 49, 62

Ballyrashane church: Kildollagh LY 22; 71

Ballyrashane glebe: Ballyrashane LY 22; 55

Ballyrashane Glebe House: Ballyrashane LY 22; 48

Ballyrashane graveyard: Ballyrashane LY 22; 62

Ballyrashane meeting house: Ballyrashane LY 22; 61

Ballyrashane mills: Ballyrashane LY 22; 46

Ballyrashane old church: Ballyrashane LY 22; 49, 55, 58, 62

Ballyrashane ph: Ballymoney AM 16; 1

Ballyrashane ph: Ballywillin LY 33; 33, 37, 43

Ballyrashane ph: Blaris AM 8; 61

Ballyrashane ph: Coleraine LY 33; 55, 73, 95, 104, 130, 142–44

Ballyrashane ph: Misc. AM 10; 129

Ballyrashane stonehenge: Aghadowey LY 22; 32

Ballyrashane stonehenge: Ballyrashane LY 22; 53

Ballyrassell td: Bangor DN 7; 19

Ballyratahan Lower td: Derrykeighan AM 16; 95

Ballyratahan Upper brickfield: Derrykeighan AM 16; 79, 84

Ballyratahan Upper td: Derrykeighan AM 16; 87, 95

Ballyrathbegg td: Ballylinny AM 32; 30

Ballyratten td: Moville DL 38; 73

Ballyrawer (Ballynoe) td: Donaghadee DN 7; 45

Ballyrawer meeting house: Donaghadee DN 7; 49

Ballyrawer td: Donaghadee DN 7; 45, 49

Ballyrea (see Ballyreagh): Derrybrusk FH 4; 31

Ballyrea td: Misc. DN 17; 123–24

Ballyrea td: Newtownards DN 7; 111, 113

Ballyreagh bog: Derrybrusk FH 4; 33

Ballyreagh Castle: Ballyrashane LY 22; 58

Ballyreagh Castle: Ballywillin LY 33; 34–35, 40, 48–49

Ballyreagh forts: Dunaghy AM 13; 18, 21

Ballyreagh giant's graves: Derrybrusk FH 4; 32

Ballyreagh hill: Derrybrusk FH 4; 31

Ballyreagh mill: Carnteel TE 20; 23

Ballyreagh mill: Killeeshil TE 20; 64

Ballyreagh school: Derrybrusk FH 4; 31

Ballyreagh standing stones: Dunaghy AM 13; 21

Ballyreagh td: Aghavea FH 4; 23

Ballyreagh td: Ballymore AH 1; 9, 12–14, 16, 18

Ballyreagh td: Ballywillin LY 33; 45

Ballyreagh td: Culfeightrin AM 24; 50

Ballyreagh td: Derrybrusk FH 4; 30–31

Ballyreagh td: Dunaghy AM 13; 18, 21, 23

Ballyreagh Upper fort: Culfeightrin AM 24; 72

Ballyreagh Upper giant's grave: Culfeightrin AM 24; 72

Ballyreagh water: Carnteel TE 20; 23

Ballyreagh water: Killeeshil TE 20; 64

Ballyreanew (see Ballyrenan): Ballee DN 17; 22

Ballyree td: Bangor DN 7; 19

Ballyreenan (see Ballyrenan) td: Clogher TE 5; 53

Ballyregan church: Comber DN 7; 41

Ballyregan meeting house: Comber DN 7; 41

Ballyregan school: Comber DN 7; 41

Ballyregan school: Dundonald DN 7; 64

Ballyregan td: Comber DN 7; 41, 43

Ballyregan td: Dundonald DN 7; 64–65

Ballyregin (see Ballyargan): Ballymore AH 1; 13

Ballyrenan (Ballyreanan) td: Ardstraw TE 5; 4

Ballyrenan corn mill: Ardstraw TE 5; 4, 14

Ballyrenan flax mill: Ardstraw TE 5; 4, 14

Ballyrenan saw mill: Ardstraw TE 5; 4

Ballyrenan school: Ardstraw TE 5; 13

Ballyrenan td: Ballee DN 17; 20, 22, 22–23

Ballyrenan td: Inch DN 17; 76

Ballyrenan wood: Inch DN 17; 73

Ballyrennan (see Ballyrenan)

Ballyricartbeg (see Ballyrickardbeg): Raloo AM 32; 133

Ballyricartmore (see Ballyrickardmore): Raloo AM 32; 133

Ballyrickard td: Ballylinny AM 32; 30

Ballyrickard td: Comber DN 7; 37, 39, 43

Ballyrickard td: Raloo AM 32; 128–29

Ballyrickardbeg fort: Raloo AM 32; 117, 123

Ballyrickardbeg school: Raloo AM 32; 85, 118–19, 125, 130–31, 133

Ballyrickardbeg Sunday school: Raloo AM 32; 119, 130

Ballyrickardbeg td: Raloo AM 32; 80, 82, 90, 133

Ballyrickardmore cove [I]: Raloo AM 32; 113–14, 117, 123

Ballyrickardmore cove [II]: Raloo AM 32; 123

Ballyrickardmore cromlech: Raloo AM 32; 111, 117

Ballyrickardmore fort [I]: Raloo AM 32; 113–14, 117, 123

Ballyrickardmore fort [II]: Raloo AM 32; 117, 123

Ballyrickardmore stone circle: Raloo AM 32; 111–12, 117

Ballyrickardmore td: Raloo AM 32; 80, 112, 133

Ballyrickartbeg (see Ballyrickardbeg): Raloo AM 32; 80

Ballyrickartmore (see Ballyrickardmore): Raloo AM 32; 80

Ballyridley td: Ardquin DN 7; 4

Ballyridley td: Misc. DN 17; 125

Ballyriff Sunday school: Artrea LY 6; 21

Ballyriff td: Artrea LY 6; 28, 38–39

Ballyrilland (see Ballyryland): Raloo AM 32; 122

Ballyrisk Beg td: Drumachose LY 9; 87, 96

Ballyrisk More stone: Drumachose LY 9; 83

Ballyrisk More td: Drumachose LY 9; 83, 87, 96, 134

Ballyrisk td: Drumachose LY 9; 97

Ballyrobbin (see Ballyrobin): Killead AM 35; 48

Ballyrobert chapel: Mallusk AM 2; 115

Ballyrobert church: Templepatrick AM 35; 133

Ballyrobert fort [I]: Ballyrobert AM 2; 24–25

Ballyrobert fort [II]: Ballyrobert AM 2; 24–25

Ballyrobert fort [III]: Ballyrobert AM 2; 24–25

Ballyrobert grange: Ballymartin AM 2; 5

Ballyrobert graveyard: Ballyrobert AM 2; 20, 24–25

Ballyrobert ph: Ballylinny AM 32; 11

Ballyrobert ph: Kilbride AM 29; 150

Ballyrobert ph: Misc. AM 10; 129

Ballyrobert ph: Muckamore AM 35; 56

Ballyrobert ph: Templepatrick AM 35; 124

Ballyrobert ph: Umgall AM 35; 158

Ballyrobert rectory: Kirkinriola AM 23; 88

Ballyrobert school: Holywood DN 7; 76

Ballyrobert td: Holywood DN 7; 76–78, 80–81

Ballyrobin church: Killead AM 35; 25

Ballyrobin corn mill: Killead AM 35; 14, 42, 48

Ballyrobin cove [I]: Killead AM 35; 32, 40, 49

Ballyrobin cove [II]: Killead AM 35; 50

Ballyrobin flax mill [I]: Killead AM 35; 15, 42, 48

Ballyrobin flax mill [II]: Killead AM 35; 15, 42

Ballyrobin fort [I]: Killead AM 35; 30–31, 39, 50

Ballyrobin fort [II]: Killead AM 35; 31, 39, 50

Ballyrobin graveyard: Killead AM 35; 25

Ballyrobin mills: Killead AM 35; 35

Ballyrobin mound: Killead AM 35; 27

Ballyrobin school: Killead AM 35; 37–38, 52–53

Ballyrobin Sunday school: Killead AM 35; 38, 52

Ballyrobin td: Ballymoney AM 16; 25

Ballyrobin td: Killead AM 35; 19, 21, 35, 40–41, 50–51

Ballyrobin well: Killead AM 35; 32

Ballyrock (Ballyrek) Scotch td: Ballyrashane LY 22; 54

Ballyrock bogs: Ballyrashane LY 22; 57

Ballyrock school: Ballyrashane AM 16; 31

Ballyrock South td: Ballyrashane LY 22; 66

Ballyrogan bogs: Errigal LY 27; 54

Ballyrogan bridge: Errigal LY 27; 59

Ballyrogan cave: Errigal LY 27; 43, 69

Ballyrogan corn mill: Newtownards DN 7; 110

Ballyrogan flax windmill: Newtownards DN 7; 110

Ballyrogan fort [I]: Errigal LY 27; 42, 69

Ballyrogan fort [II]: Errigal LY 27; 42–43, 69

Ballyrogan kiln: Errigal LY 27; 91

Ballyrogan school: Newtownards DN 7; 110

Ballyrogan td: Errigal LY 27; 60, 65–66, 70, 79, 84–85, 89, 91–92

Ballyrogan td: Newtownards DN 7; 110

Ballyrollee td: Ballylinny AM 32; 30

Ballyrolly td: Down DN 17; 52, 55, 57, 124

Ballyronan: Artrea LY 6; 6, 39

Ballyronan: Artrea TE 20; 7–9

Ballyronan: Ballinderry TE 20; 14

Ballyronan: Ballynascreen LY 31; 5, 32

Ballyronan: Ballyscullion LY 6; 47

Ballyronan: Coleraine LY 33; 99

Ballyronan: Desertlyn LY 31; 40

Ballyronan: Duneane AM 19; 112

Ballyronan: Maghera LY 18; 7

Ballyronan: Magherafelt LY 6; 81, 86, 95

Ballyronan brewery: Artrea LY 6; 7, 15

Ballyronan brewery and distillery: Ballinderry LY 6; 41

Ballyronan dispensary: Artrea LY 6; 15

Ballyronan distillery: Artrea LY 6; 15

Ballyronan More forts: Artrea LY 6; 28–29

Ballyronan More td: Artrea LY 6; 8, 28–30

Ballyronan school: Artrea LY 6; 19

Ballyronan Sunday school [I]: Artrea LY 6; 21

Ballyronan Sunday school [II]: Artrea LY 6; 22

Ballyronan td: Artrea LY 6; 6, 10, 14, 17, 26

Ballyronan td: Ballinderry TE 20; 13

Ballyroney bog: Aghaderg DN 12; 5

Ballyroney bridge: Drumballyroney DN 3; 11, 13, 16

Ballyroney church: Drumballyroney DN 3; 10, 13, 15

Ballyroney Glebe House: Drumballyroney DN 3; 10, 15, 17

Ballyroney Glebe House: Drumgooland DN 3; 22

Ballyroney lough: Drumballyroney DN 3; 10, 14, 16–17

Ballyroney meeting house: Drumballyroney DN 3; 10

Ballyroney mound: Drumballyroney DN 3; 16, 18

Ballyroney school: Drumballyroney DN 3; 13

Ballyroney td: Drumballyroney DN 3; 10, 14–16, 18

Ballyroney td: Drumgooland DN 3; 23

Ballyroosky bay: Clondavaddog DL 38; 9

Ballyroosky bay: Lough Swilly DL 38; 106, 114

Ballyroosky lough: Clondavaddog DL 38; 2

Ballyroosky standing stone: Clondavaddog DL 38; 6

Ballyrory td: Cumber LY 28; 1, 66, 68, 110, 116, 121, 125

Ballyrush td: Comber DN 7; 37, 39, 42–43

Ballyrusheall td: Ballylinny AM 32; 30

Ballyrusley (Ballyrussley) td: Misc. DN 17; 124, 126

Ballyrusley td: Ballyphilip DN 7; 7–8

Ballyrussell td: Comber DN 7; 37, 40, 42–43

Ballyrussly (see Ballyrusley): Ballyphilip DN 7; 8

Ballyruther corn mill: Carncastle and Killyglen AM 10; 4

Ballyruther flax mill: Carncastle and Killyglen AM 10; 4

Ballyruther td: Carncastle and Killyglen AM 10; 4

Ballyryland (Ballyvriland) td: Raloo AM 32; 80, 97, 103, 117, 122–23, 126, 128–29, 132

Ballyryland cove: Raloo AM 32; 122

Ballyryland fort: Raloo AM 32; 117

Ballyryland plantation: Raloo AM 32; 81

Ballysadare (Sligo): Clondermot LY 34; 69

Ballysadare: Emlaghfad SO 40; 176, 182

Ballysadare ph: Kilmacteige SO 40; 186

Ballysadare river: Emlaghfad SO 40; 176, 182

Ballysadare waterfall: Emlaghfad SO 40; 177

Ballysallagh (Ballyfallaght) td: Ballee DN 17; 20, 22, 22

Ballysallagh Major flax mill: Bangor DN 7; 25

Ballysallagh Major td: Bangor DN 7; 19, 25

Ballysallagh Minor school: Bangor DN 7; 25

Ballysallagh Minor td: Bangor DN 7; 19, 25

Ballysallagh td: Comber DN 7; 37, 39

Ballysallough td: Dromore DN 12; 71

Ballysally fort: Coleraine LY 33; 92, 132

Ballysally House: Coleraine LY 33; 91

Ballysally td: Coleraine LY 33; 128, 145

Ballysavage cove: Donegore AM 29; 130

Ballysavage fort: Donegore AM 29; 127

Ballysavage td: Donegore AM 29; 101

Ballyscalley (see Ballyscally)

Ballyscally (Ballyshally) td: Clogher TE 5; 35, 42, 47, 51, 53

Ballyscally school: Clogher TE 5; 42–43, 51

Ballyscolly (Ballyscrolly) td: Ballinderry AM 21; 41, 44

Ballyscolly church: Ballinderry AM 21; 41

Ballyscolly school: Ballinderry AM 21; 41, 44, 57

Ballyscullion bog: Ballyscullion AM 19; 7–8

Ballyscullion Castle: Ballyscullion LY 6; 46

Ballyscullion chapel: Ballyscullion AM 19; 12

Ballyscullion church: Ballyscullion LY 6; 45

Ballyscullion church: Coleraine LY 33; 98

Ballyscullion East glebe: Ballyscullion LY 6; 54

Ballyscullion forts: Ballyscullion AM 19; 2

Ballyscullion Glebe House: Ballyscullion LY 6; 48, 54

Ballyscullion House: Ballyscullion LY 6; 62

Ballyscullion House: Coleraine LY 33; 98

Ballyscullion meeting house: Ballyscullion AM 19; 12

Ballyscullion meeting house: Ballyscullion LY 6; 54

Ballyscullion ph: Ahoghill AM 23; 1

Ballyscullion ph: Antrim AM 29; 6

Ballyscullion ph: Artrea LY 6; 4, 39

Ballyscullion ph: Artrea TE 20; 6, 8–9

Ballyscullion ph: Ballyclug AM 23; 63

Ballyscullion ph: Drummaul AM 19; 33

Ballyscullion ph: Duneane AM 19; 94, 107, 111, 113

Ballyscullion ph: Maghera LY 18; 14, 17, 68

Ballyscullion ph: Magherafelt LY 6; 79, 88–89, 91

Ballyscullion ph: Misc. AM 10; 130

Ballyscullion ph: Tamlaght TE 20; 73

Ballyscullion potteries: Ballyscullion LY 6; 48

Ballyscullion school: Ballyscullion LY 6; 62

Ballyscullion td: Ballyscullion AM 19; 12

Ballyscullion td: Ballyscullion LY 6; 48–49, 73–75

Ballyscullion td: Magilligan LY 11; 94–95, 126

Ballyscullion West bogs: Ballyscullion LY 6; 69

Ballyscullion West fort [I]: Ballyscullion LY 6; 50, 72

Ballyscullion West fort [II]: Ballyscullion LY 6; 51, 72

Ballyscullion West fort [III]: Ballyscullion LY 6; 72

Ballyscullion West td: Ballyscullion LY 6; 50–51, 63, 69, 72–73, 77

Ballyscully td: Killead AM 35; 40

Ballysessy (Ballycessy) td: Camlin AM 21; 60, 62

Ballysessy school: Camlin AM 21; 73, 75–76

Ballyshagg td: Glynn AM 26; 30

Ballyshagg td: Inver AM 26; 49

Ballyshanaghill (Ballyshanaghy) td: Camlin AM 21; 60, 62

Ballyshanaghill forts: Camlin AM 21; 71

Ballyshancole (see Shankhill): Aghaderg DN 12; 3

Ballyshane td: Muckamore AM 35; 82

Ballyshaneog td: Muckamore AM 35; 83

Ballyshanholes (see Shankhill): Aghaderg DN 12; 3

Ballyshannon: Aghalurcher FH 4; 2, 16

Ballyshannon: Belleek FH 14; 3

Ballyshannon: Clondermot LY 34; 69

Ballyshannon: Convoy DL 39; 18

Ballyshannon: Derryvullan FH 14; 38–39

Ballyshannon: Devenish FH 14; 51

Ballyshannon: Donegal DL 39; 45–46, 49

Ballyshannon: Drumhome DL 39; 62

Ballyshannon: Drumkeeran FH 14; 68–69

Ballyshannon: Drumlumman CN 40; 12

Ballyshannon: Dungiven LY 15; 34

Ballyshannon: Enniskillen FH 4; 45, 61–62, 67, 83

Ballyshannon: Inishmacsaint FH 14; 72

Ballyshannon: Kilbarron DL 39; 74–78

Ballyshannon: Killesher FH 14; 88

Ballyshannon: Killymard DL 39; 108–09

Ballyshannon: Kinawley FH 4; 123

Ballyshannon: Magheraculmoney FH 14; 109

Ballyshannon: Manorhamilton Union LM 40; 50, 54

Ballyshannon: Raphoe DL 39; 121

Ballyshannon: Templecarn DL 39; 158, 161–63, 170

Ballyshannon: Trory FH 14; 131, 134

Ballyshannon bar: Kilbarron DL 39; 76

Ballyshannon distillery: Enniskillen FH 4; 46

Ballyshannon fishery: Enniskillen FH 4; 80

Ballyshannon fishery: Rossorry FH 14; 115

Ballyshannon harbour: Enniskillen FH 4; 44, 46–47

Ballyshannon harbour: Kilbarron DL 39; 76

Ballyshannon soap manufactory: Kilbarron DL 39; 78

Ballyshaskey (see Ballyshasky): Clondermot LY 34; 91

Ballyshasky chapel: Clondermot LY 34; 24

Ballyshasky flax mill: Clondermot LY 34; 129

Ballyshasky night school: Clondermot LY 34; 42–43

Ballyshasky school: Clondermot LY 34; 16, 20, 42, 86, 91, 94

Ballyshasky td: Clondermot LY 34; 20, 23, 38, 56, 60–61, 65, 67, 72, 108, 112, 114, 122, 129

Ballyshasky wood: Clondermot LY 34; 122

Ballysheil td: Annaclone DN 12; 16

Ballyshesky td: Dungiven LY 15; 33

Ballyshielbeg bleach mill: Ballymore AH 1; 13

Ballyshielbeg flax mill: Ballymore AH 1; 8, 10, 13

Ballyshielbeg td: Ballymore AH 1; 13–14, 16–17

Ballyshielmore flax mill: Ballymore AH 1; 10, 13

Ballyshielmore td: Ballymore AH 1; 7, 13–15

Ballysilly [or Ballygilly] lough: Saintfield DN 7; 117

Ballyskeagh High flax windmill: Newtownards DN 7; 110

Ballyskeagh High td: Newtownards DN 7; 110

Ballyskeagh Low school: Newtownards DN 7; 110

Ballyskeagh Low td: Newtownards DN 7; 110

Ballyskeagh school: Lambeg AM 8; 143

Ballyskeagh td: Blaris AM 8; 86

Ballyskeagh td: Lambeg AM 8; 143

Ballysleweromagh td: Ballylinny AM 32; 30

Ballysnod hill: Inver AM 26; 50

Ballysnod Lower hill: Inver AM 26; 50

Ballysnod plantation: Inver AM 26; 50

Ballysnod school: Inver AM 26; 50–53

Ballysnod Sunday school: Inver AM 26; 53

Ballysnod td: Glynn AM 26; 30

Ballysnod td: Inver AM 26; 49, 52–53

Ballysoanagh td: Cleenish FH 14; 29

Ballyspallan bog: Tamlaght Finlagan LY 25; 110

Ballyspallan td: Tamlaght Finlagan LY 25; 72–74, 93, 110

Ballyspallen (see Ballyspallan): Tamlaght Finlagan LY 25; 72

Ballyspurge td: Ballyphilip DN 7; 8

Ballyspurge td: Misc. DN 17; 125, 127

Ballyspurge td: Slanes DN 7; 121

Ballystockart corn mill: Comber DN 7; 31, 35, 40

Ballystockart flax mill: Comber DN 7; 31, 35, 40

Ballystockart school: Comber DN 7; 30, 34, 40

Ballystockart td: Comber DN 7; 30–31, 35, 37, 40, 42–43

Ballystockert (see Ballystockart): Comber DN 7; 34

Ballystokes bog: Ballee DN 17; 23

Ballystokes td: Ballee DN 17; 20, 22

Ballystraidinnairshe td: Ballylinny AM 32; 22, 30

Ballystrang hill: Conwal DL 39; 24

Ballystrang td: Conwal DL 39; 26

Ballystraw (see Ballystrew): Down DN 17; 55

Ballystrew td: Down DN 17; 52, 55, 57

Ballystrone church: Macosquin LY 22; 116

Ballystrone glen: Macosquin LY 22; 76

Ballystrone hill: Dunboe LY 11; 43

Ballystrone old church: Macosquin LY 22; 84

Ballystrone school: Dunboe LY 11; 56, 71

Ballystrone Sunday school: Dunboe LY 11; 57, 72

Ballystrone td: Dunboe LY 11; 56, 71

Ballystrone td: Macosquin LY 22; 76

Ballystrone Top hill: Macosquin LY 22; 76

Ballysugagh (Ballysugah) td: Saul DN 17; 114

Ballysugagh chapel: Saul DN 17; 115

Ballysugagh school: Saul DN 17; 114–15

Ballysugagh smithy: Saul DN 17; 115

Ballytaggart school: Loughguile AM 13; 77

Ballytaggart td: Loughguile AM 13; 76

Ballytempfin ph: Misc. DN 17; 120

Ballytemple td: Ballylinny AM 32; 22, 30

Ballytibbert school [I]: Dunluce AM 16; 123

Ballytibbert school [II]: Dunluce AM 16; 123

Ballytibert (see Ballytibbert): Dunluce AM 16; 123

Ballytober bog: Dunluce AM 16; 116, 120

Ballytober fort: Dunluce AM 16; 118

Ballytober standing stone: Dunluce AM 16; 118

Ballytober td: Carncastle and Killyglen AM 10; 10

Ballytober td: Dunluce AM 16; 107, 118

Ballytober td: Island Magee AM 10; 15, 71

Ballytober well: Dunluce AM 16; 113

Ballytollynardelly td: Ballylinny AM 32; 30

Ballytraie district: Drumgoon CN 40; 7

Ballytrain: Aughnamullen MN 40; 70, 74–75

Ballytrain: Ematris MN 40; 115

Ballytrain bridge: Aughnamullen MN 40; 73

Ballytrain chapel: Aughnamullen MN 40; 70

Ballytrain school: Aughnamullen MN 40; 70, 77

Ballytrantur td: Ballyphilip DN 7; 8

Ballytreenan td: Emlaghfad SO 40; 180

Ballytresna cove: Drummaul AM 19; 66, 88

Ballytresna forts: Drummaul AM 19; 78

Ballytresna Lower school: Drummaul AM 19; 92

Ballytresna school: Drummaul AM 19; 77

Ballytresna Sunday school: Drummaul AM 19; 77–78

Ballytresna td: Drummaul AM 19; 86, 89–90

Ballytresnaghan (see Ballytresna): Drummaul AM 19; 92

Ballytresnait td: Ballylinny AM 32; 30

Ballytrew td: Kilmore AH 1; 61, 66, 70, 73

Ballytromery flax mill: Camlin AM 21; 67, 73

Ballytromery school: Camlin AM 21; 62, 69, 73, 75

Ballytromery td: Camlin AM 21; 60

Ballytrustain (see Ballytrustan) td: Ballywalter DN 7; 18

Ballytrustan church: Ballytrustan DN 7; 15

Ballytrustan corn mill: Ballytrustan DN 7; 15

Ballytrustan flax mills: Ballytrustan DN 7; 15

Ballytrustan td: Misc. DN 17; 125

Ballytrustin (see Ballytrustan) td: Ballee DN 17; 20, 22–23

Ballytun school: Finvoy AM 23; 75

Ballytweedy fort: Templepatrick AM 35; 150

Ballytweedy fort [I]: Killead AM 35; 30

Ballytweedy fort [II]: Killead AM 35; 30

Ballytweedy House: Carmavy AM 35; 4

Ballytweedy House: Killead AM 35; 14, 42, 47

Ballytweedy td: Killead AM 35; 14, 35, 40, 49

Ballytyrone school: Loughgall AH 1; 81

Ballytyrone td: Loughgall AH 1; 75

Ballyucan td: Culfeightrin AM 24; 74, 84

Ballyumgall td: Ballylinny AM 32; 22, 30

Ballyutoag fort: Templepatrick AM 35; 130, 137, 152

Ballyutoag hill: Templepatrick AM 35; 105, 145

Ballyutoag school: Templepatrick AM 35; 135–36, 153–54

Ballyutoag Sunday school: Templepatrick AM 35; 136, 154

Ballyutoag td: Misc. AM 10; 131

Ballyutoag td: Templepatrick AM 35; 116, 129, 131–32, 137, 145, 152

Ballyutoag td: Umgall AM 35; 157, 159

Ballyutogue (see Ballyutoag): Templepatrick AM 35; 152

Ballyuttoge (see Ballyutoag) td: Ballylinny AM 32; 22, 30

Ballyvadden td: Clogher TE 5; 38, 43, 47, 54

Ballyvadigan locality: Clondermot LY 34; 60

Ballyvallagh (Ballyvallough) td: Raloo AM 32; 80, 93, 127, 132

Ballyvallagh adult school: Raloo AM 32; 97, 129

Ballyvallagh hill: Raloo AM 32; 80, 82, 86

Ballyvallagh school: Raloo AM 32; 118, 130–31

Ballyvallagh spade mill: Raloo AM 32; 92

Ballyvallagh Sunday school: Raloo AM 32; 118, 127, 131

Ballyvalley td: Loughgilly AH 1; 85

Ballyvally mill [I]: Seapatrick DN 12; 134

Ballyvally mill [II]: Seapatrick DN 12; 134

Ballyvally mill [III]: Seapatrick DN 12; 134

Ballyvally td: Clonallan DN 3; 2

Ballyvally td: Seapatrick DN 12; 123, 126

Ballyvally td: Tamlaght TE 20; 100

Ballyvalter (see Ballywalter): Ballylinny AM 32; 30

Ballyvanen (Ballyvannon) td: Glenavy AM 21; 79

Ballyvanen school: Glenavy AM 21; 91

Ballyvange meeting house: Down DN 17; 41

Ballyvange td: Down DN 17; 52, 55

Ballyvannon td: Cumber LY 28; 108–09

Ballyvardagh td: Culfeightrin AM 24; 52–53

Ballyvardon td: Clogher TE 5; 59

Ballyvarley td: Aghaderg DN 12; 1, 5

Ballyvarnet flax mill: Bangor DN 7; 22

Ballyvarnet td: Bangor DN 7; 22

Ballyvastin td: Bright DN 17; 35

Ballyveabeg cairn: Kilkeel DN 3; 51

Ballyveabeg td: Kilkeel DN 3; 51

Ballyvealy altar: Ramoan AM 24; 108

Ballyvealy caves: Ramoan AM 24; 123

Ballyvealy cromlech: Ramoan AM 24; 123–24

Ballyvealy Danes' houses: Ramoan AM 24; 108–09

Ballyvealy druid's altar: Ramoan AM 24; 107

Ballyvealy giant's grave: Ramoan AM 24; 123

Ballyvealy mountain: Ramoan AM 24; 106–07

Ballyvealy standing stones: Ramoan AM 24; 108, 123

Ballyvealy td: Ramoan AM 24; 109, 125

Ballyveasey (see Ballyvesey): Carnmoney AM 2; 99

Ballyveely (Ballyvealy) South td: Loughguile AM 13; 74

Ballyveely Lower corn mill: Loughguile AM 13; 63

Ballyveely school: Loughguile AM 13; 77

Ballyveely td: Culfeightrin AM 24; 79

Ballyveely td: Loughguile AM 13; 77

Ballyvelton House: Ballyrashane LY 22; 47–48

Ballyvelton Lower td: Ballyrashane LY 22; 65

Ballyvelton td: Ballyrashane LY 22; 47

Ballyvelton Upper cave: Ballyrashane LY 22; 50, 61

Ballyvelton Upper fort: Ballyrashane LY 22; 47, 49, 60–61

Ballyvelton Upper school: Ballyrashane LY 22; 53–54

Ballyvelton Upper Sunday school: Ballyrashane LY 22; 54

Ballyvelton Upper td: Ballyrashane LY 22; 65

Ballyvely (see Ballyveely)

Ballyvennaght altar: Culfeightrin AM 24; 75

Ballyvennaght cave: Culfeightrin AM 24; 73

Ballyvennaght fort: Culfeightrin AM 24; 73

Ballyvennaght giant's grave: Culfeightrin AM 24; 84

Ballyvennaght House: Culfeightrin AM 24; 67

Ballyvennaght lough: Culfeightrin AM 24; 84

Ballyvennaght quarry: Culfeightrin AM 24; 82

Ballyvennaght standing stone: Culfeightrin AM 24; 82

Ballyvennaght td: Culfeightrin AM 24; 42, 83

Ballyvennox coves: Macosquin LY 22; 87

Ballyvennox fort [I]: Macosquin LY 22; 115–16

Ballyvennox fort [II]: Macosquin LY 22; 116

Ballyvennox springs: Macosquin LY 22; 116

Ballyvennox td: Macosquin LY 22; 84–85, 116–17, 122

Ballyverdough (see Ballyvardagh): Culfeightrin AM 24; 53

Ballyvernet td: Misc. DN 17; 124

Ballyvernstown (Ballyverstown) td: Glynn AM 26; 1, 41, 47–48

Ballyvernstown fort: Glynn AM 26; 32, 45

Ballyversal school: Ballyrashane AM 16; 31

Ballyversal school: Ballyrashane LY 22; 53

Ballyversal td: Ballyrashane LY 22; 66

Ballyvesey (Ballyvessey) td: Carnmoney AM 2; 34, 58, 62, 72, 92, 99–100, 102

Ballyvesey hill: Carnmoney AM 2; 35, 72

Ballyvester td: Donaghadee DN 7; 45

Ballyvester td: Inishargy DN 7; 84

Ballyvester td: Misc. DN 17; 124

Ballyvesy (see Ballyvesey): Carnmoney AM 2; 34

Ballyvicknacally (Ballyvicknakelly) td: Dromore DN 12; 72, 78

Ballyvicknacally flax mill: Dromore DN 12; 72

Ballyvicknacally school: Dromore DN 12; 73, 78

Ballyviggis corn mill: Bright DN 17; 33

Ballyviggis td: Bright DN 17; 33, 35

Ballyvollen td: Camlin AM 21; 60, 64, 71

Ballyvollen td: Glenavy AM 21; 80, 83

Ballyvorally bleach green: Glenavy AM 21; 81, 85, 88

Ballyvorally bleach mill: Glenavy AM 21; 79

Ballyvorally td: Glenavy AM 21; 79–80, 83

Ballyvoy coves: Kilbride AM 29; 147, 154

Ballyvoy druid's altar: Culfeightrin AM 24; 71

Ballyvoy fort: Culfeightrin AM 24; 72

Ballyvoy House: Donegore AM 29; 107, 110

Ballyvoy House: Kilbride AM 29; 138, 141, 150

Ballyvoy House: Killead AM 35; 46

Ballyvoy td: Culfeightrin AM 24; 39, 71, 77

Ballyvoy td: Doagh AM 29; 95–96, 98

Ballyvoy td: Kilbride AM 29; 150–51, 155

Ballyvoy well: Kilbride AM 29; 147, 154

Ballywaddan (Ballywaddes) td: Ardquin DN 7; 4

Ballywaddan corn mill: Ardquin DN 7; 4

Ballywaddan td: Misc. DN 17; 126

Ballywaddin (see Ballywaddan) td: Misc. DN 17; 126–27

Ballywallon (Ballywallan) td: Ardquin DN 7; 4

Ballywallon flax mill: Ardquin DN 7; 4

Ballywallon Island: Misc. DN 17; 127

Ballywallon td: Misc. DN 17; 126–27

Ballywallon water mill: Misc. DN 17; 126

Ballywalter: Ballywalter DN 7; 17

Ballywalter: Misc. DN 17; 117

Ballywalter bog: Doagh AM 29; 94

Ballywalter bog: Kilbride AM 29; 153

Ballywalter bridge: Doagh AM 29; 92

Ballywalter coastguard station: Ballywalter DN 7; 17

Ballywalter corn mill: Ballywalter DN 7; 17

Ballywalter corn windmill: Ballywalter DN 7; 17

Ballywalter fort: Ballywalter AM 2; 27

Ballywalter graveyard: Ballylinny AM 32; 21

Ballywalter harbour: Ballywalter DN 7; 16

Ballywalter manor: Ballywalter DN 7; 17
Ballywalter manor: Misc. DN 17; 125
Ballywalter meeting house (I): Ballywalter DN 7; 17
Ballywalter meeting house (P): Ballywalter DN 7; 17
Ballywalter mound: Ballywalter AM 2; 33
Ballywalter old church: Ballylinny AM 32; 21
Ballywalter old church: Ballywalter AM 2; 27, 32
Ballywalter ph: Ballylinny AM 32; 11, 24, 26
Ballywalter ph: Carnmoney AM 2; 64
Ballywalter ph: Doagh AM 29; 60, 62, 78
Ballywalter ph: Donaghadee DN 7; 45
Ballywalter ph: Grey Abbey DN 7; 67
Ballywalter ph: Kilbride AM 29; 150
Ballywalter ph: Misc. AM 10; 129
Ballywalter ph: Misc. DN 17; 118, 121
Ballywalter school: Ballywalter DN 7; 17
Ballywalter td: Ballee DN 17; 20, 22–23
Ballywalter td: Ballylinny AM 32; 22, 30
Ballywalter td: Ballywalter DN 7; 17–18
Ballywalter tumulus: Ballylinny AM 32; 21
Ballywalter yarn store: Ballywalter AM 2; 26
Ballyward church: Drumgooland DN 3; 22
Ballyward corn mill: Drumgooland DN 3; 24
Ballyward female school: Drumgooland DN 3; 25
Ballyward flax mill: Drumgooland DN 3; 24
Ballyward Lodge: Drumgooland DN 3; 22, 25
Ballyward lough: Drumgooland DN 3; 22
Ballyward male school: Drumgooland DN 3; 25
Ballyward td: Drumgooland DN 3; 22, 24–25
Ballyward td: Misc. DN 17; 124–25
Ballyware House: Clonduff DN 3; 4
Ballywarren td: Down DN 17; 52, 56, 58
Ballywarren West td: Down DN 17; 48
Ballywatermoy td: Ahoghill AM 23; 37–38
Ballywaticock td: Misc. DN 17; 123
Ballywatt East flax mill: Ballyrashane LY 22; 48
Ballywatt Leggs cave: Ballyrashane LY 22; 50, 64
Ballywatt Leggs corn mill: Ballyrashane LY 22; 48
Ballywatt Leggs meeting house: Ballyrashane LY 22; 47–48, 52, 55–56
Ballywatt Leggs meeting house: Ballywillin LY 33; 33
Ballywatt Leggs td: Ballyrashane LY 22; 66
Ballywatt Legs (see Ballywatt Leggs): Ballyrashane LY 22; 64
Ballywatt West cave [I]: Ballyrashane LY 22; 50, 63
Ballywatt West cave [II]: Ballyrashane LY 22; 50, 63
Ballywatt West cave [III]: Ballyrashane LY 22; 50, 63
Ballywatt West td: Ballyrashane LY 22; 63
Ballywattick school: Ballymoney AM 16; 27
Ballyweaney (see Ballyweany): Loughguile AM 13; 72

Ballyweany coves: Loughguile AM 13; 71–72
Ballyweany fort: Loughguile AM 13; 71
Ballyweany school: Loughguile AM 13; 66, 77
Ballyweany td: Loughguile AM 13; 66, 71–72, 77
Ballywee corn mill: Donegore AM 29; 134
Ballywee corn mill: Kilbride AM 29; 139, 150, 156
Ballywee East school: Kilbride AM 29; 157
Ballywee flax mill: Donegore AM 29; 134
Ballywee flax mill: Kilbride AM 29; 139, 150–51, 156
Ballywee fort: Donegore AM 29; 120–21, 127–28
Ballywee td: Doagh AM 29; 96
Ballywee td: Donegore AM 29; 101, 131
Ballywee td: Kilbride AM 29; 136, 148
Ballyweel hamlet: Killymard DL 39; 107
Ballyweel harbour: Killymard DL 39; 109
Ballyweel quay: Killymard DL 39; 109
Ballyweel td: Killymard DL 39; 100, 104
Ballyweird td: Ballyphilip DN 7; 7
Ballywell (see Ballywee): Kilbride AM 29; 157
Ballywell td: Faughanvale LY 36; 57
Ballywhil district: Clondavaddog DL 38; 4
Ballywhilert td: Misc. DN 17; 125
Ballywhisken td: Misc. DN 17; 124
Ballywhite manor: Misc. DN 17; 125
Ballywhite td: Misc. DN 17; 126
Ballywholan td: Clogher TE 5; 35, 47, 53
Ballywhollan (see Ballywholan)
Ballywhoolan (Balliswhillen) td: Ballyclog TE 20; 16, 18
Ballywhoolan monastery: Ballyclog TE 20; 16
Ballywildrick (Ballywildrake) Lower td: Dunboe LY 11; 47, 49
Ballywildrick coves: Dunboe LY 11; 50, 77
Ballywildrick flax mill: Dunboe LY 11; 47, 60
Ballywildrick standing stone: Dunboe LY 11; 74
Ballywildrick td: Dunboe LY 11; 63, 81
Ballywillan spring: Dunboe LY 11; 79
Ballywillan td: Killyleagh DN 17; 83
Ballywillen td: Galloon FH 4; 95
Ballywilliam cove: Macosquin LY 22; 94, 113
Ballywilliam flax mill: Comber DN 7; 31, 35, 39
Ballywilliam school: Comber DN 7; 34
Ballywilliam school: Donaghadee DN 7; 49
Ballywilliam school: Macosquin LY 22; 92–93
Ballywilliam Sunday school: Macosquin LY 22; 93
Ballywilliam td: Comber DN 7; 31, 35, 37, 39, 42–43
Ballywilliam td: Donaghadee DN 7; 49
Ballywilliam td: Macosquin LY 22; 82, 93, 104
Ballywilliam td: Misc. DN 17; 124
Ballywillin (Ballywillan) td: Aghadowey LY 22; 9, 36
Ballywillin bog: Ballyaghran LY 33; 13, 21
Ballywillin bog: Coleraine LY 33; 130

Ballywillin Bog spring: Ballywillin LY 33; 42
Ballywillin Bog td: Ballywillin LY 33; 29, 45,
    49–50
Ballywillin bridge: Aghadowey LY 22; 10
Ballywillin cave: Ballywillin LY 33; 51
Ballywillin church: Ballywillin AM 16; 32–33
Ballywillin church: Ballywillin LY 33; 31–33, 36,
    40, 42–43, 46–47, 51
Ballywillin corn mill: Aghadowey LY 22; 9
Ballywillin corn mill: Raloo AM 32; 91
Ballywillin flax mill: Aghadowey LY 22; 9
Ballywillin flax mill: Raloo AM 32; 91–92
Ballywillin glebe: Ballywillin LY 33; 47
Ballywillin Glebe cave: Ballywillin LY 33; 35,
    50–51
Ballywillin Glebe House: Ballywillin LY 33; 33, 42,
    50–51
Ballywillin Glebe td: Ballywillin LY 33; 42
Ballywillin graveyard: Ballywillin AM 16; 32
Ballywillin graveyard: Ballywillin LY 33; 43, 47
Ballywillin hill: Raloo AM 32; 133
Ballywillin moss: Ballywillin LY 33; 39, 44
Ballywillin old church: Ballywillin LY 33; 34, 40
Ballywillin old church: Dunluce AM 16; 114
Ballywillin old corn mill: Raloo AM 32; 91
Ballywillin ph: Ballyaghran LY 33; 12–13, 22,
    26–27
Ballywillin ph: Ballyrashane LY 22; 52, 58
Ballywillin ph: Coleraine LY 33; 73, 95, 104,
    142–44
Ballywillin ph: Dunluce AM 16; 114
Ballywillin ph: Misc. AM 10; 129
Ballywillin plantation: Raloo AM 32; 81
Ballywillin school: Ballywillin AM 16; 35
Ballywillin school: Ballywillin LY 33; 40
Ballywillin school: Raloo AM 32; 85
Ballywillin Sunday school: Ballywillin LY 33; 41
Ballywillin td: Ballywillin LY 33; 45, 51
Ballywillin td: Coleraine LY 33; 129
Ballywillin td: Raloo AM 32; 80, 89, 133
Ballywillwill demesne: Kilmegan DN 3; 55
Ballywillwill House: Kilmegan DN 3; 55
Ballywillwill river: Kilmegan DN 3; 55
Ballywillwill td: Kilmegan DN 3; 55
Ballywillwill threshing mill: Kilmegan DN 3; 55
Ballywilly slaughterhouse: Kilmore AH 1; 67
Ballywilly td: Kilmore AH 1; 61, 66–67, 73
Ballywind td: Ballyphilip DN 7; 8
Ballywindilland (Ballywindelan) td: Kildollagh LY
    22; 67, 72
Ballywindilland bog: Kildollagh LY 22; 67, 72
Ballywitticock (Ballywittycock) td: Newtownards
    DN 7; 111, 113
Ballywollen td: Misc. DN 17; 125
Ballywoodan (Ballywooden) td: Saul DN 17; 114

Ballywoodan chapel: Saul DN 17; 114–15
Ballywoodan school: Saul DN 17; 114
Ballywoodan td: Misc. DN 17; 125
Ballywoodock bridge: Dunboe LY 11; 63
Ballywoodock corn mill: Dunboe LY 11; 47, 60
Ballywoodock cove: Dunboe LY 11; 51
Ballywoodock flax mill: Dunboe LY 11; 47, 59
Ballywoodock fort: Donegore AM 29; 104
Ballywoodock pound: Dunboe LY 11; 60
Ballywoodock td: Donegore AM 29; 101–02, 131,
    133
Ballywoodock td: Dunboe LY 11; 63, 73, 81
Ballyworfy (Ballyworfey) td: Hillsborough DN 12;
    85, 105–06
Ballyworfy meeting house: Hillsborough DN 12; 86
Ballyworkan (Ballyworken) td: Drumcree AH 1; 28,
    34–35, 37, 42
Ballyworkan House: Drumcree AH 1; 36
Ballyworkan school: Drumcree AH 1; 30, 33, 36, 42
Ballywry td: Misc. DN 17; 123
Ballyyelly td: Tullyaughnish DL 38; 96
Balmer, John: Blaris DN 12; 42
Balmer, Matthew: Hillsborough DN 12; 106
Balmer, William: Hillsborough DN 12; 106
Balmer's glen: Magheramesk AM 21; 112
Balmoney (see Ballymoney)
Balnacallymore (see Ballynacallymore): Aghadowey
    LY 22; 35
Balnagarnon td: Donacavey TE 5; 81, 85
Baloo (see Balloo): Muckamore AM 35; 79
Balsarach locality: Billy AM 16; 51, 68
Balteagh bleach green: Bovevagh LY 25; 1–2
Balteagh church: Balteagh LY 9; 36
Balteagh cloth mill: Balteagh LY 9; 22
Balteagh corn mills: Balteagh LY 9; 22
Balteagh Cross td: Balteagh LY 9; 35
Balteagh crossroads: Balteagh LY 9; 30
Balteagh flax mill: Balteagh LY 9; 22
Balteagh flour mill: Balteagh LY 9; 22
Balteagh Glebe House: Balteagh LY 9; 3, 7, 15
Balteagh Lower bogs: Macosquin LY 22; 78, 119
Balteagh Lower flax mill: Macosquin LY 22; 82,
    105
Balteagh Lower springs: Macosquin LY 22; 119
Balteagh Lower td: Macosquin LY 22; 119
Balteagh mills: Balteagh LY 9; 22
Balteagh old church: Balteagh LY 9; 5–6, 19, 33, 35
Balteagh ph: Aghadowey LY 22; 1
Balteagh ph: Aghanloo LY 11; 10
Balteagh ph: Banagher LY 30; 1, 39
Balteagh ph: Bovevagh LY 25; 1, 22
Balteagh ph: Drumachose LY 9; 56, 67, 84, 88, 90,
    95, 101, 108
Balteagh ph: Dungiven LY 15; 17, 34, 50, 112
Balteagh ph: Faughanvale LY 36; 1, 60

Balteagh ph: Magilligan LY 11; 98
Balteagh ph: Tamlaght Finlagan LY 25; 62, 106
Balteagh river: Balteagh LY 9; 28
Balteagh school: Balteagh LY 9; 3
Balteagh school: Seagoe AH 1; 102–03, 106–07
Balteagh td: Macosquin LY 22; 89
Balteagh td: Seagoe AH 1; 105, 107
Balteagh Upper bog: Macosquin LY 22; 78, 119
Balteagh Upper springs: Macosquin LY 22; 119
Baltic Sea: Warrenpoint DN 3; 120
Baltimore (America): Ballyrashane LY 22; 53, 66
Baltimore: Carrickfergus AM 37; 157
Baltimore: Derryvullan FH 14; 43
Baltimore: Kilbroney DN 3; 30–31, 33–34
Baltimore: Lissan LY 31; 109
Baltinglass (Wicklow): Newry DN 3; 66
Baltreagh td: Galloon FH 4; 95
Baltylum td: Drumcree AH 1; 41
Balyhaice (see Ballyhaise): Tomregan FH 4; 128
Bamber, G.: Magherafelt LY 6; 91
Bamborough, Jonas: Carrickfergus AM 37; 194
Bamford, family: Drumbeg AM 8; 123
Banachuir lough: Killymard DL 39; 95
Banada: Kilmacteige SO 40; 186, 188, 190–93
Banada Abbey: Kilmacteige SO 40; 187–88, 192, 196
Banada Abbey House: Kilmacteige SO 40; 190, 192
Banada Castle: Kilmacteige SO 40; 188, 192, 196
Banada corn mill: Kilmacteige SO 40; 194
Banada district: Balteagh LY 9; 16
Banada friary: Kilmacteige SO 40; 188
Banada graveyard: Kilmacteige SO 40; 188
Banada school: Kilmacteige SO 40; 195
Banada td: Kilmacteige SO 40; 187–88, 192, 196
Banagh barony: Killymard DL 39; 94, 100, 108
Banaghan fort: Devenish FH 14; 55
Banaghan td: Devenish FH 14; 57
Banagher (Offaly): Banagher LY 30; 110
Banagher church (see Rallagh): Banagher LY 30; 32
Banagher Cottage: Balteagh LY 9; 11
Banagher Cottage: Banagher LY 30; 57
Banagher crab-tree: Banagher LY 30; 58
Banagher glebe: Banagher LY 30; 14, 115
Banagher Glebe House: Banagher LY 30; 5, 7, 15, 27, 29–32, 59, 96, 115, 131
Banagher glen: Dungiven LY 15; 21
Banagher glens: Banagher LY 30; 2, 18, 24, 27, 31, 35, 59, 99, 113
Banagher meeting house: Cumber LY 28; 19
Banagher mountains: Banagher LY 30; 2, 10, 57
Banagher mountains: Cumber LY 28; 11
Banagher mountains: Dungiven LY 15; 11, 51
Banagher mountains: Misc. LY 31; 116, 133
Banagher old church (see also Magheramore): Banagher LY 30; 6

Banagher old church: Ballynascreen LY 31; 15
Banagher old church: Bovevagh LY 25; 51
Banagher old church: Dungiven LY 15; 65
Banagher old church: Faughanvale LY 36; 14
Banagher ph: Aghanloo LY 11; 3
Banagher ph: Ballynascreen LY 31; 2, 15 16
Banagher ph: Bovevagh LY 25; 2, 6, 9–10, 22, 24–27, 29, 45–46, 59
Banagher ph: Clondermot LY 34; 3, 18, 66
Banagher ph: Cumber LY 28; 1, 4–6, 8, 11, 14, 19, 22, 25, 47, 79–80, 83–87, 89–90
Banagher ph: Drumachose LY 9; 84
Banagher ph: Duneane AM 19; 109
Banagher ph: Dungiven LY 15; 1, 7, 14, 18–19, 26, 50, 52, 93
Banagher ph: Faughanvale LY 36; 1, 54
Banagher ph: Killelagh LY 27; 99
Banagher ph: Lissan LY 31; 94
Banagher ph: Maghera LY 18; 54
Banagher ph: Magilligan LY 11; 115
Banagher ph: Misc. LY 31; 111
Banagher ph: Misc. LY 36; 105, 119
Banagher ph: Tamlaght Finlagan LY 25; 72, 103
Banagher pond: Banagher LY 30; 72
Banagher rectory: Banagher LY 30; 14
Banagher river: Banagher LY 30; 59
Banagher rocks (Clare): Banagher LY 30; 101
Banagher schools: Banagher LY 30; 13
Banaghy td: Drumgoon CN 40; 3
Banba's plain: Drumachose LY 9; 93
Banbridge: Aghaderg DN 12; 4–5, 10
Banbridge: Aghadowey LY 22; 26
Banbridge: Annaclone DN 12; 15, 18
Banbridge: Antrim AM 29; 18
Banbridge: Ballinderry AM 21; 49
Banbridge: Ballymore AH 1; 3, 5, 8, 10
Banbridge: Blaris AM 8; 51
Banbridge: Camlin AM 21; 67, 72
Banbridge: Clondermot LY 34; 30
Banbridge: Coleraine LY 33; 53, 96
Banbridge: Donaghcloney DN 12; 57
Banbridge: Donaghmore DN 3; 7–8
Banbridge: Drumballyroney DN 3; 17
Banbridge: Drumcree AH 1; 35
Banbridge: Garvaghy DN 12; 80–81
Banbridge: Glenavy AM 21; 84
Banbridge: Magherally DN 12; 113–14
Banbridge: Misc. DN 17; 116
Banbridge: Montiaghs AH 1; 91
Banbridge: Mullaghbrack AH 1; 96
Banbridge: Seagoe AH 1; 106
Banbridge: Seapatrick DN 12; 124–27, 133
Banbridge: Templepatrick AM 35; 111, 149
Banbridge: Tullynakill DN 7; 122

Banbridge Bridge St school: Seapatrick DN 12; 129, 134–135

Banbridge chapel (PWM): Seapatrick DN 12; 125, 129

Banbridge chapel (WM): Seapatrick DN 12; 125, 129

Banbridge church: Seapatrick DN 12; 128, 132

Banbridge court house: Seapatrick DN 12; 129

Banbridge dispensary: Aghaderg DN 12; 5

Banbridge dispensary: Annaclone DN 12; 15

Banbridge dispensary: Magherally DN 12; 113

Banbridge dispensary: Seapatrick DN 12; 131, 133

Banbridge dispensary: Tullylish DN 12; 142

Banbridge Dromore St school: Seapatrick DN 12; 129, 135

Banbridge Lancasterian school: Hillsborough DN 12; 101

Banbridge Lancasterian school: Seapatrick DN 12; 101, 129, 135

Banbridge Library Lane school: Seapatrick DN 12; 135

Banbridge linen hall: Seapatrick DN 12; 129

Banbridge meeting house (A): Seapatrick DN 12; 125, 128

Banbridge meeting house (P): Seapatrick DN 12; 125, 128–29

Banbridge shambles: Seapatrick DN 12; 129

Banbrook House: Dunboe LY 11; 61, 64

Banbury, James: Clogher TE 5; 49

Banchran (see Bancran): Misc. LY 31; 137

Bancran Glebe school: Ballynascreen LY 31; 16

Bancran Glebe td: Ballynascreen LY 31; 15

Bancran td: Ballynascreen LY 31; 15

Bancran td: Misc. LY 31; 137, 143

Bandore fort: Killead AM 35; 40

Bane, family: Kilwaughter AM 10; 115

Bane, John: Kilwaughter AM 10; 122

Bane, Joseph: Kilwaughter AM 10; 122

Bane, Patrick (see Kane): Banagher LY 30; 96

Bane, Robert: Kilwaughter AM 10; 122

Bane, Sarah: Kilwaughter AM 10; 122

Banef, family: Maghera LY 18; 48

Banes, Mr: Derryaghy AM 8; 99

Banestown ruins: Derryaghy AM 8; 99

Banfield td: Tamlaght O'Crilly LY 18; 116

Bangibbon (see also Clondermot): Clondermot LY 34; 53

Bangibbon river: Cumber LY 28; 72

Bangor (Wales): Coleraine LY 33; 121

Bangor: Banagher LY 30; 1, 36, 101, 110

Bangor: Bangor DN 7; 20, 23

Bangor: Blaris AM 8; 4

Bangor: Carrickfergus AM 37; 40, 46, 170

Bangor: Donegal DL 39; 46

Bangor: Grey Abbey DN 7; 69

Bangor: Holywood DN 7; 75, 77, 82

Bangor: Misc. DN 17; 117, 121, 124, 128

Bangor: Rathmullan DN 17; 108

Bangor: Templecorran AM 26; 96

Bangor abbey: Misc. DN 17; 121–22

Bangor bay: Bangor DN 7; 22

Bangor Bog td: Bangor DN 7; 19

Bangor Castle: Bangor DN 7; 23–24

Bangor Castle St school: Bangor DN 7; 24

Bangor church: Bangor DN 7; 24

Bangor church: Misc. DN 17; 117

Bangor Church Quarter infant school: Bangor DN 7; 25

Bangor Church Quarter school: Bangor DN 7; 24

Bangor coastguard station: Bangor DN 7; 25

Bangor corn mill: Bangor DN 7; 24

Bangor Corporation td: Bangor DN 7; 19

Bangor cotton manufactories: Bangor DN 7; 24

Bangor dispensary: Bangor DN 7; 23, 25

Bangor harbour: Bangor DN 7; 25

Bangor Main St school [I]: Bangor DN 7; 25

Bangor Main St school [II]: Bangor DN 7; 25

Bangor manor: Misc. DN 17; 124

Bangor market house: Bangor DN 7; 24

Bangor meeting house (M): Bangor DN 7; 24

Bangor meeting house (P) [I]: Bangor DN 7; 24

Bangor meeting house (P) [II]: Bangor DN 7; 24

Bangor monastery: Banagher LY 30; 110

Bangor monastery: Misc. DN 17; 122

Bangor ph: Donaghadee DN 7; 45

Bangor ph: Holywood DN 7; 73

Bangor ph: Misc. DN 17; 121

Bangor poor house: Bangor DN 7; 24

Bangor quay: Carrickfergus AM 37; 45

Bangor, Bishop of (Wales): Newry DN 3; 74

Bangor, Lady: Ballyculter DN 17; 30

Bangor, Lord: Ardglass DN 17; 5, 11

Bangor, Lord: Ballee DN 17; 18, 21–23

Bangor, Lord: Ballyculter DN 17; 25, 27–31

Bangor, Lord: Bangor DN 7; 24

Bangor, Lord: Bright DN 17; 33–34, 36–37

Bangor, Lord: Down DN 17; 51–52

Bangor, Lord: Dunsfort DN 17; 69

Bangor, Lord: Holywood DN 7; 77

Bangor, Lord: Killyleagh DN 17; 86

Bangor, Lord: Saul DN 17; 113–14

Bangor, Viscount: Killinchy DN 7; 90

Banis (see Banus): Templecarn DL 39; 163

Bank coal store: Glynn AM 26; 13, 27, 38, 45

Bank coal store: Inver AM 26; 54–55

Bank district: Glynn AM 26; 39, 42–43

Bank inn: Glynn AM 26; 40

Bank quays: Glynn AM 26; 2, 5, 13, 20, 38, 40, 44–45

Bank quays: Inver AM 26; 54–55

Bank td: Clogher TE 5; 36, 45, 53

Bankhead, family: Templecorran AM 26; 117, 119

Bankhead, Rev. John: Templecorran AM 26; 101, 128, 130

Bankish hill: Aghanloo LY 11; 5

Bankish Hill cove: Dunboe LY 11; 50–51

Bankmore td: Ballyphilip DN 7; 8

Banks, Stewart: Carrickfergus AM 37; 43

Bann bridge: Ahoghill AM 23; 17

Bann bridge: Ballymoney AM 16; 3

Bann bridge: Rasharkin AM 23; 130–31

Bann ferry: Ahoghill AM 23; 17

Bann ferry: Ballyscullion AM 19; 2, 4

Bann ferry: Coleraine LY 33; 58

Bann ferry: Kilrea LY 27; 127

Bann fishery: Duneane AM 19; 113, 117

Bann fishery: Kilrea LY 27; 105

Bann fishery: Macosquin LY 22; 96

Bann fishery: Rasharkin AM 23; 128–29

Bann national school: Tullylish DN 12; 147

Bann river: Aghadowey LY 22; 1, 4, 7, 11–12, 15, 33

Bann river: Agivey LY 22; 39, 41–44

Bann river: Ahoghill AM 23; 1–7, 12–16, 26, 28–32

Bann river: Annaclone DN 12; 13, 16

Bann river: Antrim AM 29; 4

Bann river: Artrea LY 6; 2–4, 12, 30, 36

Bann river: Artrea TE 20; 6

Bann river: Ballyaghran LY 33; 1–2, 24, 27

Bann river: Ballymoney AM 16; 1, 4, 6, 9–10

Bann river: Ballynure AM 32; 45

Bann river: Ballyrashane LY 22; 46, 50

Bann river: Ballyscullion AM 19; 1–4, 7–8

Bann river: Ballyscullion LY 6; 42, 45, 71

Bann river: Blaris AM 8; 89

Bann river: Clondermot LY 34; 47–48

Bann river: Clonduff DN 3; 3–6

Bann river: Coleraine LY 33; 53–56, 58, 74–78, 82, 88, 91, 93, 96–103, 118–19, 121–22, 130–31, 146–51, 153, 156

Bann river: Connor AM 19; 20

Bann river: Desertlyn LY 31; 40

Bann river: Desertmartin LY 31; 57

Bann river: Desertoghill LY 27; 1, 21

Bann river: Drumballyroney DN 3; 10–14, 16

Bann river: Drumcree AH 1; 28, 30, 32, 34–36, 39, 41

Bann river: Drummaul AM 19; 33, 40, 46, 52, 79

Bann river: Dunboe LY 11; 43, 58

Bann river: Duneane AM 19; 94–99, 101, 105, 112, 117

Bann river: Dungiven LY 15; 37, 63

Bann river: Errigal Keerogue TE 20; 48

Bann river: Errigal LY 27; 78

Bann river: Finvoy AM 23; 67–74, 76

Bann river: Garvaghy DN 12; 79, 82

Bann river: Glynn AM 26; 17

Bann river: Kilcoo DN 3; 45

Bann river: Kildollagh LY 22; 67–70, 72–74

Bann river: Killelagh LY 27; 95

Bann river: Killowen LY 33; 158–59, 161–62, 167–70

Bann river: Kilmore AH 1; 57–58, 60–63, 68, 72

Bann river: Kilrea LY 27; 104–08, 110, 113–14, 117, 120, 122–23, 126, 128

Bann river: Kirkinriola AM 23; 101–02

Bann river: Layd AM 13; 40

Bann river: Lough Neagh AM 21; 93–96

Bann river: Lough Swilly DL 38; 137

Bann river: Macosquin LY 22; 76–78, 80–83, 85, 90, 96, 101–02, 105–07, 119

Bann river: Maghera LY 18; 3

Bann river: Magherafelt LY 6; 90

Bann river: Magherally DN 12; 115

Bann river: Misc. LY 31; 116

Bann river: Misc. LY 36; 109–12

Bann river: Montiaghs AH 1; 89–93

Bann river: Newry DN 3; 82, 90–91, 111

Bann river: Raloo AM 32; 93–94

Bann river: Ramoan AM 24; 90, 101

Bann river: Rasharkin AM 23; 127–32, 137

Bann river: Seagoe AH 1; 101–02, 104–05, 107, 109–10

Bann river: Seapatrick DN 12; 124–25, 127

Bann river: Skerry AM 13; 105

Bann river: Tamlaght O'Crilly LY 18; 82–84, 88, 90, 92–93, 96, 111, 123, 134

Bann river: Tartaraghan AH 1; 117, 119–21, 123

Bann river: Tickmacrevan AM 13; 132

Bann river: Tullylish DN 12; 140, 144

Bann river bridge: Seapatrick DN 12; 129

Banna, Queen: Dungiven LY 15; 63

Bannagh barony: Inishkeel DL 39; 67

Bannagh bridge: Drumkeeran FH 14; 65

Bannagh river: Drumkeeran FH 14; 63–65

Bannaghan (see Banaghan): Devenish FH 14; 55

Bannbrook (Banbrook) td: Dunboe LY 11; 77

Bannbrook fort: Dunboe LY 11; 49, 77

Bannbrook House: Dunboe LY 11; 46

Bannbrook House: Killowen LY 33; 172

Bannfield bog: Drumballyroney DN 3; 10, 14

Bannfield Steps ford: Drumballyroney DN 3; 16

Bannfoot locality: Coleraine LY 33; 53, 97

Bannin (see Binnion): Clonmany DL 38; 12

Bannin (see Binnion): Mintiaghs DL 38; 64

Bannion (see Binnion): Clonmany DL 38; 16

Bannister, family: Blaris AM 8; 21

Bannon (see Binnion): Clonmany DL 38; 13

Bannon (see Binnion): Mintiaghs DL 38; 65

Bannsfoot ferry: Montiaghs AH 1; 90–92

Bannsfoot ferry: Seagoe AH 1; 106
Bannsfoot ferry: Tartaraghan AH 1; 120
Bannside district: Finvoy AM 23; 68
Bannside district: Macosquin LY 22; 92, 102
Bannside td: Killowen LY 33; 158, 168
Bannville House: Tullylish DN 12; 141
Banny, J.P.: Kilmegan DN 3; 59
Banoge flour and corn mill: Donaghcloney DN 12; 58
Banoge flour mills: Donaghcloney DN 12; 59
Banoge td: Donaghcloney DN 12; 59
Bansley, Mr (Donaghadee): Ballymore AH 1; 17
Banus (see also Banis, Barnas)
Banus fort: Templecarn DL 39; 160
Banus lough: Templecarn DL 39; 157
Banus td: Templecarn DL 39; 163
Banview House: Macosquin LY 22; 80, 101
Bar Chapel hill: Donaghmore DN 3; 7
Bar Chapel hill chapel: Donaghmore DN 3; 7
Bar district: Donacavey TE 5; 73
Bar Hall bay: Witter DN 7; 125
Bar Hall farmhouse: Witter DN 7; 126
Bar mouth: Ballyaghran LY 33; 27
Bar mouth: Coleraine LY 33; 75, 77, 147
Bar mouth: Killowen LY 33; 169
Bar mouth: Lough Swilly DL 38; 137
Bar of Inch (see Mintiaghs): Mevagh DL 38; 57
Bar of Shancurragh fort: Manorhamilton Union LM 40; 52
Bara td: Magheracross FH 14; 95
Baradahissia (see Bardahessia): Desertcreat TE 20; 34
Baraghilly td: Ardclinis AM 13; 7
Baran td: Carlingford LH 40; 58
Baranagh td: Donacavey TE 5; 80
Barbados (West Indies): Carrickfergus AM 37; 21
Barbar, family: Billy AM 16; 58, 68
Barber, family: Tamlaght O'Crilly LY 18; 93
Barber, James: Drumachose LY 9; 118, 123
Barber, James: Templepatrick AM 35; 135, 153–54
Barber, Mr: Drumgath DN 3; 21
Barber, Richard: Carrickfergus AM 37; 193
Barber, Robert: Ballinderry AM 21; 57
Barber, Robert: Desertoghill LY 27; 16, 18
Barber, Robert: Drumachose LY 9; 104, 128
Barbour, family: Blaris AM 8; 22
Barbour, John: Lambeg AM 8; 139
Barbour, William: Blaris AM 8; 55, 66
Barbour, William: Blaris DN 12; 45
Barbour, William: Lambeg AM 8; 138–39, 142
Barcelona (Spain): Carrickfergus AM 37; 24
Barclay, John: Lambeg AM 8; 136
Barclay, John: Tamlaght O'Crilly LY 18; 133
Barclay, man named: Misc. LY 36; 116
Barclay, Miss: Raphoe DL 39; 127

Barclay, Mr: Raphoe DL 39; 127
Barclay, Samuel: Carrickfergus AM 37; 175
Barclie, Alexander: Coleraine LY 33; 127
Bardahessia (Bordahessia) td: Desertcreat TE 20; 33–34
Bardahessia quarry: Desertcreat TE 20; 35
Bardahessia slate quarry: Desertcreat TE 20; 33
Bardonagh td: Magheross MN 40; 148
Barefoot, family: Kilbride AM 29; 140
Bareton, James: Templecorran AM 26; 132
Barginnis Castle: Templepatrick AM 35; 150
Barginnis mount: Templepatrick AM 35; 129–30, 137, 150
Barginnis, Lord: Templepatrick AM 35; 130, 150
Barinleakan td: Magheraculmoney FH 14; 110
Barker, Peter: Carrickfergus AM 37; 110
Barker, Rev. John: Clonleigh DL 39; 4, 12
Barker's mill: Aghaderg DN 12; 4
Barkley, Archibald: Larne AM 10; 126
Barkley, family: Ballyclug AM 23; 60
Barkley, family: Ballynure AM 32; 56
Barkley, family: Maghera LY 18; 48
Barkley, G.: Aughnamullen MN 40; 76
Barklie, Alexander: Aghadowey LY 22; 8–9, 12, 29
Barklie, Archibald: Inver AM 26; 51–55
Barklie, family: Ballynure AM 32; 56
Barklie, family: Maghera LY 18; 24
Barklie, George: Aghadowey LY 22; 8–9, 12
Barklie, Messrs: Inver AM 26; 49, 51
Barklie, Mr: Aghadowey LY 22; 5
Barklimore, family: Ballynure AM 32; 56
Barkly, family: Carrickfergus AM 37; 93
Barkly, Robert: Ahoghill AM 23; 34
Barley hill: Carrickfergus AM 37; 133
Barley Park: Drumachose LY 9; 51
Barley Park House: Drumachose LY 9; 52, 83, 91
Barley, Robert: Hillsborough DN 12; 107
Barley, William: Hillsborough DN 12; 107
Barlow, Rev. Frank: Cumber LY 28; 90
Barn Cottage: Carrickfergus AM 37; 57, 136, 138
Barn hill: Comber DN 7; 43
Barn hill: Drumcree AH 1; 40
Barn hill: Island Magee AM 10; 86
Barn hill school: Comber DN 7; 34, 43
Barn's O'Neally mountain: Donegal DL 39; 53
Barnaduarg Head: Lough Swilly DL 38; 116
Barnagirve (see Barnagrow): Drumgoon CN 40; 3
Barnagrove (see Barnagrow): Drumgoon CN 40; 1
Barnagrow hill: Drumgoon CN 40; 1
Barnagrow lough: Drumgoon CN 40; 1–2
Barnagrow td: Drumgoon CN 40; 2–3
Barnakilly school: Faughanvale LY 36; 35
Barnakilly td: Faughanvale LY 36; 17, 53–54, 67, 70, 81, 92, 98
Barnakilly td: Tamlaght Finlagan LY 25; 72–74

Barnard, Col: Urney DL 39; 179–80

Barnard, family: Aghadowey LY 22; 16

Barnard, Gen.: Aghadowey LY 22; 5, 16

Barnard, Rev.: Muff DL 38; 80–82

Barnard, Rev. Henry: Aghadowey LY 22; 16, 22, 27

Barnard, Rev. Henry: Agivey LY 22; 40, 42

Barnard, Rev. Henry: Maghera LY 18; 24, 58, 66

Barnas (see Barnus): Templecarn DL 39; 160

Barnasroan (see Altamoskan): Errigal Keerogue TE 20; 56

Barnes Gap (see also Barnesmore Gap): Donegal DL 39; 49, 53

Barnes Lower td: Mevagh DL 38; 55

Barnes mountain: Killymard DL 39; 105

Barnes, Arthur: Ahoghill AM 23; 22, 42, 46, 50

Barnes, David: Ahoghill AM 23; 43

Barnesmore Gap: Donaghmore DL 39; 28

Barnesmore Gap: Donegal DL 39; 42, 44, 47

Barnesmore hills: Donaghmore DL 39; 28

Barnesmore hills: Donegal DL 39; 44–45, 52–53, 55

Barnesmore hills: Killea and Taughboyne DL 39; 83

Barnesmore hills: Killymard DL 39; 94

Barnesmore hills: Taughboyne DL 39; 149

Barnesmore Owen Gap: Donaghmore DL 39; 28

Barness hill: Banagher LY 30; 24, 108–10

Barnet, John: Artrea LY 6; 29

Barnet, John: Bovevagh LY 25; 49

Barnet, Robert: Artrea LY 6; 29

Barnett (see Barnard): Maghera LY 18; 58

Barnett, Bishop: Dunboe LY 11; 46, 61

Barnett, family: Dunboe LY 11; 61, 64

Barnett, James: Carrickfergus AM 37; 47, 138, 141, 162, 172

Barnett, Mr: Saintfield DN 7; 117

Barnett, Rev. John: Artrea LY 6; 16

Barnett, Rev. John: Desertlyn LY 31; 39, 51

Barnett, Rev. John: Lissan LY 31; 93, 95, 103–04

Barnett, William: Killead AM 35; 53

Barney's Point: Island Magee AM 10; 77

Barnfarm locality: Carrickfergus AM 37; 174

Barnies school: Connor AM 19; 27

Barnish cave: Culfeightrin AM 24; 77

Barnish chapel: Culfeightrin AM 24; 40, 45, 71, 75

Barnish coves: Drummaul AM 19; 66, 89

Barnish fort [I]: Culfeightrin AM 24; 50

Barnish fort [II]: Culfeightrin AM 24; 76

Barnish forts: Drummaul AM 19; 89

Barnish giant's grave: Drummaul AM 19; 66, 78

Barnish graveyard: Culfeightrin AM 24; 71

Barnish standing stone: Drummaul AM 19; 89

Barnish td: Culfeightrin AM 24; 50

Barnish td: Drummaul AM 19; 64, 78

Barnmeen cave: Drumgath DN 3; 20

Barnmeen chapel: Drumgath DN 3; 20

Barnmeen school: Drumgath DN 3; 21

Barnmeen stone: Drumgath DN 3; 20

Barnmeen td: Drumgath DN 3; 19–21

Barnmeen well: Drumgath DN 3; 20

Barns, family: Ballinderry AM 21; 48

Barns, Henry: Blaris DN 12; 42

Barns, William: Ahoghill AM 23; 43

Barnsley, family: Blaris AM 8; 21

Barnus lough: Donegal DL 39; 42

Baroghy td: Aughnamullen MN 40; 75

Baron td: Donaghedy TE 5; 91

Baron, Robert: Doagh AM 29; 98

Baron, W.W.: Clonduff DN 3; 3, 6

Baronagh fort: Donacavey TE 5; 70, 82

Baronagh td: Donacavey TE 5; 67, 70, 76, 78, 81–82, 85

Baronial House (see Ballymoney market house): Ballymoney AM 16; 8

Baronscourt demesne: Ardstraw TE 5; 2, 10, 12, 14

Baronscourt House: Ardstraw TE 5; 5

Baronscourt House: Urney DL 39; 176

Baronscourt old castle: Ardstraw TE 5; 11

Baronscourt school: Ardstraw TE 5; 13

Baronstown barony: Inniskeen MN 40; 124

Barony bridge: Clogherny TE 20; 27

Barr Cregg cromlech: Cumber LY 28; 29

Barr Cregg giant's grave: Cumber LY 28; 43, 54

Barr Cregg td: Cumber LY 28; 66, 68, 110, 116, 121, 125

Barr td: Kinawley FH 4; 121

Barr, Allan: Hillsborough DN 12; 107

Barr, Catherine: Maghera LY 18; 77

Barr, Dr: Maghera LY 18; 49, 52, 55, 69, 72

Barr, family: Billy AM 16; 58, 68

Barr, family: Island Magee AM 10; 70

Barr, family: Misc. LY 36; 104

Barr, George: Carrickfergus AM 37; 194

Barr, Hickenbottom: Aghadowey LY 22; 33

Barr, James: Coleraine LY 33; 72, 143

Barr, John: Clondermot LY 34; 91, 95

Barr, Samuel: Aghadowey LY 22; 38

Barr, William: Maghera LY 18; 77

Barr's inn: Muff DL 38; 80

Barr's Point: Island Magee AM 10; 17–18, 89, 101–02

Barra school: Magheracross FH 14; 99

Barra td: Magheracross FH 14; 102

Barrack hill td: Donacavey TE 5; 67

Barrack mountain: Pomeroy TE 20; 70, 72

Barrackfield locality: Carrickfergus AM 37; 94

Barracks hamlet: Clondermot LY 34; 23

Barrad td: Layd AM 13; 44

Barragh lough: Killdrumsherdan CN 40; 31

Barraghy lough: Drumgoon CN 40; 3

Barratitoppy td: Tydavnet MN 40; 169

Barratitoppy Upper td: Tydavnet MN 40; 169

Barratoher chapel: Kilmacteige SO 40; 186, 189, 192–94

Barratoher village: Kilmacteige SO 40; 186, 193–194

Barren, Robert: Donaghmoyne MN 40; 111

Barret, Mrs: Newry DN 3; 108

Barret, Thomas: Carrickfergus AM 37; 120

Barrett, John: Drumachose LY 9; 61

Barrett, Rev. John: Inishkeel DL 39; 67

Barrick td: Conwal DL 39; 26

Barrington, family: Ardglass DN 17; 12

Barrington, Jonah: Dungiven LY 15; 60

Barron, Elizabeth: Carnmoney AM 2; 94, 102

Barron, family: Ballylinny AM 32; 15, 27

Barron, family: Templepatrick AM 35; 118

Barron, H.W.: Faughanvale LY 36; 45

Barron, Joseph: Templepatrick AM 35; 146, 148, 152

Barron, Michael: Muckamore AM 35; 81

Barron, Thomas: Ballylinny AM 32; 29

Barronagh (see Baronagh)

Barrotoher (see Barratoher): Kilmacteige SO 40; 186

Barrow lough: Inishkeel DL 39; 70

Barrow, James: Templepatrick AM 35; 150–51

Barry, D.: Newry DN 3; 84

Barry, family: Derrykeighan AM 16; 89

Barry, George: Kilroot AM 26; 77

Barry, Gerald (Cambrensis): Galloon FH 4; 97

Barry, J.: Comber DN 7; 32

Barry, John: Coleraine LY 33; 72

Barry, John: Loughgall AH 1; 78

Barry, Mary Anne: Carrickfergus AM 37; 124

Barry, Michael: Annaclone DN 12; 18

Barry, Rev.: Drummaul AM 19; 69

Barry, Rigby: Duneane AM 19; 116

Barry, Thomas: Carrickfergus AM 37; 76

Barry, William: Magherafelt LY 6; 110

Barrymead, family: Blaris AM 8; 22

Barrysland locality: Carrickfergus AM 37; 94, 174

Bars West chapel: Manorhamilton Union LM 40; 53

Bars West td: Manorhamilton Union LM 40; 54

Bartholomew, John: Ahoghill AM 23; 34

Bartin's bay: Aghagallon AM 21; 2, 4

Bartin's bay: Glenavy AM 21; 82

Bartley, Mary: Aghadowey LY 22; 21

Bartley, Mary: Magheradrool DN 17; 101

Bartley, Mr: Leck DL 39; 118

Bartley, William: Magheradrool DN 17; 101

Barton, B.J.: Donagh MN 40; 102–03

Barton, Capt.: Clondavaddog DL 38; 5

Barton, Col: Drumkeeran FH 14; 67

Barton, Col: Templecarn FH 14; 119–21

Barton, F.W.: Drumkeeran FH 14; 64, 67–68

Barton, James: Drumachose LY 9; 104

Barton, King: Ardstraw TE 5; 4

Barton, Richard: Killead AM 35; 34

Barton, Susanah: Forkhill AH 1; 45

Barton, Thomas: Enniskillen FH 4; 57

Barton, William: Drumachose LY 9; 65

Barton, William: Magheross MN 40; 146

Bashford, family: Carrickfergus AM 37; 93

Bashford, James: Donaghmoyne MN 40; 107

Bashfordsland locality: Carrickfergus AM 37; 94

Basin river: Blaris DN 12; 41

Baskin, John: Ardstraw TE 5; 4

Bason hill: Blaris AM 8; 48

Basset, Arthur: Newry DN 3; 74

Bassill, Mr: Clondermot LY 34; 64

Bastille (Paris): Banagher LY 30; 30

Bat, J.: Comber DN 7; 34

Bates, family: Ballinderry AM 21; 48

Bates, Mrs: Ballinderry AM 21; 48

Bates, Robert: Carrickfergus AM 37; 130

Bateson, Lady: Knockbreda DN 7; 102

Bateson, Lady: Magherafelt LY 6; 103

Bateson, Lady: Moira DN 12; 120

Bateson, Messrs William and Richard: Carnmoney AM 2; 91

Bateson, Mr: Cappagh TE 5; 21–22

Bateson, Robert (Belvoir): Faughanvale LY 36; 40, 45

Bateson, Robert (Milltown): Faughanvale LY 36; 40

Bateson, Robert: Artrea LY 6; 19–20

Bateson, Robert: Artrea TE 20; 6

Bateson, Robert: Ballinderry TE 20; 14

Bateson, Robert: Ballyscullion LY 6; 47

Bateson, Robert: Clondermot LY 34; 78

Bateson, Robert: Coleraine LY 33; 104, 142

Bateson, Robert: Cumber LY 28; 86

Bateson, Robert: Desertlyn LY 31; 50

Bateson, Robert: Drumbo DN 7; 59

Bateson, Robert: Glynn AM 26; 39

Bateson, Robert: Knockbreda DN 7; 97, 101–02

Bateson, Robert: Maghera LY 18; 7, 67

Bateson, Robert: Magherafelt LY 6; 91

Bateson, Robert: Magheramesk AM 21; 116

Bateson, Robert: Moira DN 12; 119–20

Bateson, Robert: Tamlaght Finlagan LY 25; 79, 120

Bateson, Robert: Tamlaght O'Crilly LY 18; 107

Bateson, Thomas: Faughanvale LY 36; 45

Bath (England): Blaris AM 8; 84

Bath Lodge: Culfeightrin AM 24; 45, 63

Bath, Marquis of: Donaghmoyne MN 40; 108, 110

Bath, Marquis of: Inniskeen MN 40; 128

Bath, Marquis of: Killanny MN 40; 132, 134

Bath, Marquis of: Magheracloone MN 40; 139

Bath, Marquis of: Magheross MN 40; 146–49, 151–52, 157

Bathurst, Henry: Ballintoy AM 24; 21

Batt, Messrs: Mallusk AM 2; 107
Batt, Messrs: Templepatrick AM 35; 142
Batt, Mr: Drumbo DN 7; 59
Batt, Mr: Magherally DN 12; 114
Batt, Mr: Tullylish DN 12; 140
Batt, Mrs: Drumbo DN 7; 60
Batt, Narcissus: Drumbo DN 7; 54, 57, 60
Batt, Narcissus: Kilbroney DN 3; 32
Battery bridge: Glenwhirry AM 32; 79
Battery bridge: Rashee AM 32; 135
Battery Hill school: Enniskillen FH 4; 55
Battery port: Tamlaght TE 20; 102, 122
Battle burn: Raphoe DL 39; 125
Battle hill: Magherafelt LY 6; 108
Battlefield village: Kilmacteige SO 40; 196
Battleford bridge: Coleraine LY 33; 97
Battleford bridge: Eglish AH 1; 43
Battleford bridge: Killeeshil TE 20; 64
Batty, Mr: Ballymascanlan LH 40; 55
Baughan lough: Mevagh DL 38; 55
Baullure (see Ballure): Kilmacteige SO 40; 193
Bavan corn mill: Clonallan DN 3; 1
Bavan flax mill: Clonallan DN 3; 1
Bawllahear (see Ballure): Kilmacteige SO 40; 193
Bawn Islands: Aughnamullen MN 40; 70
Bawn Isle: Misc. DN 17; 121
Bawn lough: Aughnamullen MN 40; 70–71
Bawn, family: Drumgath DN 3; 20
Baxter, Anne: Drummaul AM 19; 90
Baxter, Bell: Drummaul AM 19; 90
Baxter, Edward: Drummaul AM 19; 90
Baxter, Elizabeth: Drummaul AM 19; 90
Baxter, Elizabeth Sarah: Blaris AM 8; 21
Baxter, family: Carrickfergus AM 37; 93
Baxter, family: Umgall AM 35; 158
Baxter, Isaac: Carrickfergus AM 37; 40, 175
Baxter, John: Blaris AM 8; 21
Baxter, John: Island Magee AM 10; 91
Baxter, Martha: Drummaul AM 19; 90
Baxter, Samuel [I]: Carrickfergus AM 37; 151
Baxter, Samuel [II]: Carrickfergus AM 37; 195
Baxter, T.: Magilligan LY 11; 93
Baxter, Thomas: Carrickfergus AM 37; 194
Baxter, Warren: Coleraine LY 33; 73
Baxter, William: Coleraine LY 33; 146
Baxter, William: Drummaul AM 19; 90
Bay (see Bays): Raymoghy DL 39; 142
Bay hill cairn: Derryaghy AM 8; 97
Bay Lodge: Ardclinis AM 13; 3, 7
Bay school: Ardclinis AM 13; 9
Bay td: Ardclinis AM 13; 3, 7, 9
Bay tuck mill: Ardclinis AM 13; 3
Bayle, Mr (Baily): Inishargy DN 7; 84
Bayley, Henery: Blaris AM 8; 55
Bayley, Lewis: Newry DN 3; 74

Bayley, Nicholas: Newry DN 3; 74
Bayley, Rev.: Antrim AM 29; 27
Baylie, J. (see Bailey): Carnmoney AM 2; 102
Bayly, Edward: Newry DN 3; 65
Bayne, Thomas: Kilbride AM 29; 151
Bays Lower td: Raymoghy DL 39; 141
Bays Middle td: Raymoghy DL 39; 141
Bays td: Raymoghy DL 39; 142
Bays Upper td: Raymoghy DL 39; 141
Beack, Rev. Benjamin: Ahoghill AM 23; 46
Beacon, family: Ballywillin LY 33; 44
Beacon, Robert: Ballywillin LY 33; 39, 44
Beacon, William: Aghanloo LY 11; 13–14, 17,
    21–22, 26, 31
Beacon, William: Drumachose LY 9; 126
Beag lough: Templecarn DL 39; 157
Beagh and Tullyhern td: Clogher TE 5; 54
Beagh bridge: Clogherny TE 20; 27
Beagh corn mill: Clogherny TE 20; 27
Beagh fort: Clogherny TE 20; 28
Beagh fort: Drumragh TE 5; 109
Beagh hill: Magheracross FH 14; 91
Beagh Spiritual fort [I]: Maghera LY 18; 60
Beagh Spiritual fort [II]: Maghera LY 18; 60
Beagh Spiritual school: Maghera LY 18; 33, 51
Beagh Spiritual Sunday school: Maghera LY 18; 29
Beagh Spiritual td: Killelagh LY 27; 102
Beagh Spiritual td: Maghera LY 18; 8, 12, 40, 42,
    64–65, 74, 79
Beagh td: Aghalurcher FH 4; 16
Beagh td: Aghalurcher TE 5; 1
Beagh td: Aughnamullen MN 40; 75
Beagh td: Clogher TE 5; 26, 39
Beagh td: Drumragh TE 5; 109
Beagh td: Enniskillen FH 4; 82
Beagh td: Maghera LY 18; 25
Beagh td: Magheracross FH 14; 93, 102
Beagh td: Magheross MN 40; 148
Beagh Temporal bridge: Maghera LY 18; 64
Beagh Temporal fort [I]: Maghera LY 18; 61
Beagh Temporal fort [II]: Maghera LY 18; 61
Beagh Temporal fort [III]: Maghera LY 18; 62
Beagh Temporal td: Maghera LY 18; 80
Beagho td: Cleenish FH 14; 28, 28
Bealnafaula valley: Ramoan AM 24; 125
Bear, Edward: Ballyscullion LY 6; 61–62
Bear, Miss: Ballyscullion LY 6; 71
Bear, Rev. Thomas: Aghadowey LY 22; 14
Bear, Thomas: Termoneeny LY 6; 133
Bear's Brae hill: Templepatrick AM 35; 105
Beard, Betty: Kilwaughter AM 10; 116
Beard, David: Ballymoney AM 16; 21, 25
Beard, family: Nilteen AM 35; 103
Beard, Jackson: Kilbride AM 29; 150
Beard, John: Macosquin LY 22; 84, 111–12

Beardiville demesne: Ballywillin AM 16; 34

Beardiville fort: Ballywillin AM 16; 34

Beardiville House: Ballywillin LY 33; 29, 33, 35–36, 45

Beardiville plantation: Ballywillin LY 33; 29, 33

Beardiville td: Ballyrashane LY 22; 54

Beardiville td: Ballywillin LY 33; 51

Bearnach, Con: Misc. TE 5; 147

Bearnach, Niall: Misc. TE 5; 147

Bearns, family: Aghalee AM 21; 36

Bears, Rev. J.A.: Clonduff DN 3; 4

Beatson, Robert: Donaghmore DL 39; 36–37, 39

Beatson, Robert: Killea and Taughboyne DL 39; 79–80, 83, 87, 89

Beatson, Robert: Misc. DL 39; 186, 189, 192

Beattie, Adam: Desertlyn LY 31; 50

Beattie, Anne: Faughanvale LY 36; 30

Beattie, family: Culfeightrin AM 24; 59

Beattie, Mrs: Blaris AM 8; 84

Beatty, Arthur: Carrickfergus AM 37; 126

Beatty, David: Blaris AM 8; 49, 55, 68

Beatty, David: Blaris DN 12; 46, 50

Beatty, Dorothy: Hillsborough DN 12; 106

Beatty, Edward: Clogher TE 5; 35

Beatty, Eliza: Carrickfergus AM 37; 126

Beatty, family: Ballynure AM 32; 56

Beatty, family: Enniskillen FH 4; 75

Beatty, Francis: Moira DN 12; 120

Beatty, George: Hillsborough DN 12; 99, 106

Beatty, Henry: Muckamore AM 35; 77

Beatty, James: Hillsborough DN 12; 105–06

Beatty, James: Muckamore AM 35; 80

Beatty, John: Muckamore AM 35; 80

Beatty, Lt: Enniskillen FH 4; 66

Beatty, Miss: Ballynure AM 32; 66

Beatty, Mr: Blaris DN 12; 32, 41

Beatty, Mr: Donaghmore DL 39; 36

Beatty, Mrs: Blaris AM 8; 85

Beatty, Mrs: Blaris DN 12; 46, 50

Beatty, Mrs Robert: Ballynure AM 32; 65

Beatty, Rev.: Convoy DL 39; 23

Beatty, Rev. John: Donaghcloney DN 12; 61

Beatty, Robert: Ballynure AM 32; 53, 64–66, 71

Beatty, Stewart: Hillsborough DN 12; 106

Beatty, Susan: Carrickfergus AM 37; 126

Beatty, Thomas: Blaris AM 8; 68

Beatty, Thomas: Hillsborough DN 12; 106

Beatty, William: Donegore AM 29; 130

Beatty, William: Hillsborough DN 12; 106

Beatty, William: Tamlaght TE 20; 124

Beatty, Wilson: Hillsborough DN 12; 106

Beatus, Bishop: Magilligan LY 11; 143

Beaty, John: Dunboe LY 11; 81

Beauchamp, Rev. Robert: Carrickfergus AM 37; 71, 145

Beauclerk, Maj.: Ardglass DN 17; 3, 5, 9–10

Beauclerk, Maj.: Ballee DN 17; 22

Beauclerk, Maj.: Bright DN 17; 33–35

Beauclerk, Maj.: Dunsfort DN 17; 69

Beauclerk, Maj.: Killyleagh DN 17; 86

Beaufort fort: Cumber LY 28; 9

Beaufort House: Cumber LY 28; 9, 18, 83

Beaufort td: Cumber LY 28; 7

Beck, family: Donegore AM 29; 110

Beck, family: Kilbride AM 29; 140

Beck, family: Misc. LY 36; 104

Beck, family: Nilteen AM 35; 91

Beck, James: Muckamore AM 35; 80

Beck, Mr: Magilligan LY 11; 106, 111

Beck, William: Donegore AM 29; 129

Beck, William: Muckamore AM 35; 63, 76

Becket, Robert: Hillsborough DN 12; 106

Beckett, Dr: Dundermot AM 13; 35

Beckett, Gilbert: Ballyscullion LY 6; 57

Beckett, Mary: Ballyscullion LY 6; 57

Beckett, Thomas: Blaris AM 8; 62

Beckett, Thomas: Blaris DN 12; 45, 49

Beckett, William: Ballyscullion LY 6; 57

Bective (Dublin): Newry DN 3; 66

Bedell, Bishop: Kinawley FH 4; 116–17

Bedford, Dr: Clondavaddog DL 38; 7

Bedlam hill: Donacavey TE 5; 67

Bedlam school: Tullaghobegley DL 39; 172

Beds stones: Templecarn DL 39; 160

Beech Hill House: Clondermot LY 34; 6, 20–21, 97, 102–04

Beech Hill House: Dungiven LY 15; 33

Beech Hill school (see Ardmore): Clondermot LY 34; 41

Beef Park td: Killymard DL 39; 101

Beehive House: Laragh CN 40; 42

Beer, Elizabeth: Tamlaght Finlagan LY 25; 118

Beer, James: Tamlaght Finlagan LY 25; 118

Beer, Jane: Tamlaght Finlagan LY 25; 118

Beer, Samual: Tamlaght Finlagan LY 25; 118

Beer's mills: Holywood DN 7; 76

Beerhill td: Derrykeighan AM 16; 95

Beerlooms district: Carrickfergus AM 37; 1–2, 35, 37, 40, 45, 65

Beers, F.C.: Drumgooland DN 3; 22, 24–25

Beers, John: Raymoghy DL 39; 134

Beers, Miss: Drumgooland DN 3; 25

Beers, Rev.: Drumgooland DN 3; 25

Beers, Rev. James: Drumballyroney DN 3; 10, 13

Beg lough (Glinsk): Clondavaddog DL 38; 2

Beg lough (Meenagh): Clondavaddog DL 38; 3

Beg lough: Donaghmore DL 39; 29

Beg lough: Errigal Truagh MN 40; 122

Beg lough [I]: Clondavaddog DL 38; 2

Beg lough [II]: Clondavaddog DL 38; 3

Beggs, family: Ballynure AM 32; 56

Beggs, family: Templecorran AM 26; 117, 119

Beggs, John: Doagh AM 29; 98

Beggs, John: Kilwaughter AM 10; 117

Beggs, William: Ahoghill AM 23; 12

Beggs, William: Templecorran AM 26; 130

Begley, Charles: Aghanloo LY 11; 23

Begley, Charles: Magilligan LY 11; 125–26, 135

Begley, Neill: Bovevagh LY 25; 59

Begley, William: Faughanvale LY 36; 24, 35–36, 66

Begley, William: Magilligan LY 11; 131, 133

Begly, Edward: Coleraine LY 33; 72, 143

Begly, Henry: Ballyaghran LY 33; 17

Begly, Thomas: Magheragall AM 21; 110–11

Begney lough: Dromara DN 12; 62, 65–66

Begney mills: Dromara DN 12; 63

Begney td: Dromara DN 12; 63, 65

Behan, James: Enniskillen FH 4; 66

Behnes, Messrs (London): Drumachose LY 9; 77

Behy hamlet: Kilbarron DL 39; 77

Beirs, John: Raphoe DL 39; 124

Belagrey school: Clondermot LY 34; 42

Belags mountain: Donaghedy TE 5; 89

Belags td: Donaghedy TE 5; 91

Belalt (Bealalt) td: Donaghmore DL 39; 36

Belalt South corn mill: Templecarn DL 39; 158, 158

Belbennett td: Donaghedy TE 5; 91

Belclare Castle: Kilmacteige SO 40; 185–86, 193

Belclare td: Kilmacteige SO 40; 193, 196

Belclare village: Kilmacteige SO 40; 185–86, 193

Beleermanon hill: Lissan TE 20; 69

Beleernamore hill: Kildress TE 20; 61

Belfast: Aghadowey LY 22; 7, 22, 24

Belfast: Aghagallon AM 21; 2–3, 5

Belfast: Aghalee AM 21; 29, 32–34

Belfast: Aghaloo TE 20; 1–3

Belfast: Aghalurcher FH 4; 13, 15

Belfast: Aghanloo LY 11; 38

Belfast: Aghavea FH 4; 21

Belfast: Ahoghill AM 23; 3–4, 8, 29, 31

Belfast: Annahilt DN 12; 22

Belfast: Antrim AM 29; 3, 5, 7, 14–15, 17–22, 25, 39, 45, 47–48, 50

Belfast: Ardclinis AM 13; 3

Belfast: Ardglass DN 17; 7

Belfast: Artrea LY 6; 7, 39

Belfast: Artrea TE 20; 7, 9

Belfast: Aughnamullen MN 40; 74, 76

Belfast: Ballee DN 17; 19

Belfast: Ballinderry AM 21; 45

Belfast: Ballinderry TE 20; 12, 14

Belfast: Ballybay MN 40; 80

Belfast: Ballyclug AM 23; 53, 55–56, 64

Belfast: Ballycor AM 32; 3, 8

Belfast: Ballyculter DN 17; 27

Belfast: Ballylinny AM 32; 14–15, 17–19, 25, 27–29

Belfast: Ballymartin AM 2; 4, 6, 9, 15–16

Belfast: Ballymore AH 1; 5, 9, 16

Belfast: Ballynascreen LY 31; 8, 19, 30

Belfast: Ballynure AM 32; 33–34, 38, 41, 46–47, 51, 64, 69–70, 72

Belfast: Ballyphilip DN 7; 12, 14

Belfast: Ballyrashane LY 22; 51

Belfast: Ballyrobert AM 2; 20–21, 23

Belfast: Ballyscullion AM 19; 4, 8, 10

Belfast: Ballyscullion LY 6; 52, 56

Belfast: Ballywalter AM 2; 29–30, 32

Belfast: Ballywillin LY 33; 30, 33, 42

Belfast: Banagher LY 30; 31, 112

Belfast: Blaris AM 8; 16, 50–51, 69–72, 76, 88

Belfast: Bovevagh LY 25; 12, 30

Belfast: Bright DN 17; 35

Belfast: Camlin AM 21; 62–63, 66–68, 72

Belfast: Cappagh TE 5; 19

Belfast: Carmavy AM 35; 2–4

Belfast: Carnmoney AM 2; 35–39, 41–44, 46–50, 52–60, 62, 65, 67, 69, 81–82, 84–86, 88, 91–92, 95, 97, 100–01, 103–05

Belfast: Carrickfergus AM 37; 2–3, 5, 10–11, 32, 38, 44, 49–51, 55–57, 59–60, 63–64, 68, 71–72, 74, 84, 88, 90, 100, 104, 135, 137–38, 143, 150, 154–55, 165, 168–71, 175, 177–79, 182

Belfast: Clondermot LY 34; 3, 6–7, 17–18, 21–22, 30, 34, 87, 95, 116

Belfast: Clones FH 4; 27

Belfast: Clonfeacle AH 1; 24–25

Belfast: Coleraine LY 33; 66, 85–86, 88–89, 91, 95, 99, 119, 126, 130, 142–43, 152

Belfast: Comber DN 7; 29, 33, 36–38, 40–41, 44

Belfast: Connor AM 19; 16, 22, 30–31

Belfast: Culfeightrin AM 24; 68

Belfast: Cumber LY 28; 7–8, 11, 15, 20–21, 50, 86

Belfast: Currin MN 40; 94

Belfast: Derryaghy AM 8; 119–21

Belfast: Desertlyn LY 31; 35, 37, 40–41

Belfast: Desertoghill LY 27; 13

Belfast: Doagh AM 29; 60–61, 63, 66–67, 69–72, 74–76, 80, 86–90, 92–95

Belfast: Donaghenry TE 20; 38

Belfast: Donagore AM 29; 102, 110, 126, 128–29

Belfast: Down DN 17; 47, 49, 58

Belfast: Drumachose LY 9; 117, 134

Belfast: Drumballyroney DN 3; 18

Belfast: Drumbeg AM 8; 122

Belfast: Drumbo DN 7; 59–60

Belfast: Drumcree AH 1; 28, 30, 32, 35, 40–41

Belfast: Drumglass TE 20; 40

Belfast: Drumgoon CN 40; 10

Belfast: Drummaul AM 19; 34, 40, 44–47, 49–51, 54, 62, 69, 73, 80–81

Belfast: Drummully FH 4; 37–38

Belfast: Dunaghy AM 13; 15

Belfast: Dundonald DN 7; 65

Belfast: Duneane AM 19; 95, 99, 101, 104, 112–13

Belfast: Dungiven LY 15; 26, 67–68, 75

Belfast: Enniskillen FH 4; 61, 75, 83

Belfast: Errigal LY 27; 38, 62

Belfast: Faughanvale LY 36; 10, 58, 67

Belfast: Finvoy AM 23; 67, 70–71

Belfast: Galloon FH 4; 90

Belfast: Glenavy AM 21; 78, 85, 87

Belfast: Glenwhirry AM 32; 79

Belfast: Glynn AM 26; 2, 4, 11, 13, 15–16, 20, 22, 27, 37–38, 45

Belfast: Hillsborough DN 12; 93

Belfast: Holywood DN 7; 75, 77

Belfast: Inishargy DN 7; 85

Belfast: Inver AM 26; 50, 53–54

Belfast: Island Magee AM 10; 38, 62, 64, 77, 84, 93, 105

Belfast: Kilbride AM 29; 135, 139–40, 142, 146, 154

Belfast: Kilcronaghan LY 31; 82

Belfast: Kildollagh LY 22; 72

Belfast: Kilkeel DN 3; 48

Belfast: Killagan AM 23; 80

Belfast: Killdrumsherdan CN 40; 36

Belfast: Killead AM 35; 13–16, 18, 22, 41–44, 46, 49–50

Belfast: Killelagh LY 27; 101

Belfast: Killinchy DN 7; 89

Belfast: Killyleagh DN 17; 84–86

Belfast: Killymard DL 39; 109

Belfast: Kilmore AH 1; 58, 60, 62–63, 67, 69, 71

Belfast: Kilrea LY 27; 110

Belfast: Kilroot AM 26; 56–57, 60, 62, 64, 66–67, 73

Belfast: Kirkinriola AM 23; 90–91, 93, 95, 98–99, 101–02, 104–05, 108, 116, 118, 120

Belfast: Knockbreda DN 7; 99–100

Belfast: Larne AM 10; 123, 125

Belfast: Layd AM 13; 39, 47

Belfast: Lissan LY 31; 102

Belfast: Lough Neagh AM 21; 97

Belfast: Lough Swilly DL 38; 119

Belfast: Loughgall AH 1; 77

Belfast: Maghera LY 18; 2, 5, 7–9, 35, 67–68, 71

Belfast: Magheradrool DN 17; 101, 107

Belfast: Magherafelt LY 6; 86–87, 90–91, 96, 107

Belfast: Magherally DN 12; 114

Belfast: Magheramesk AM 21; 113, 115, 119–21

Belfast: Magilligan LY 11; 121, 129, 139

Belfast: Mallusk AM 2; 107, 109, 112, 115

Belfast: Misc. DN 17; 119, 121

Belfast: Misc. LY 31; 135

Belfast: Moville DL 38; 73

Belfast: Muckamore AM 35; 55, 62–65, 70, 75

Belfast: Newry DN 3; 61, 67, 78, 84–85, 87, 114

Belfast: Newtownards DN 7; 108

Belfast: Nilteen AM 35; 84, 86, 89–91, 97, 99, 101–03

Belfast: Racavan AM 13; 103

Belfast: Raloo AM 32; 81, 95, 99, 102, 106–07, 116, 126, 132

Belfast: Ramoan AM 24; 93, 95, 113

Belfast: Rasharkin AM 23; 128, 131, 133

Belfast: Rashee AM 32; 137

Belfast: Saul DN 17; 112

Belfast: Seagoe AH 1; 101, 106–07

Belfast: Seapatrick DN 12; 133

Belfast: Shankill AH 1; 111, 113

Belfast: Shilvodan AM 19; 127, 130, 136

Belfast: Skirts of Urney and Ardstraw TE 5; 141

Belfast: Tamlaght Finlagan LY 25; 71–72, 101, 107

Belfast: Tamlaght O'Crilly LY 18; 108

Belfast: Templecorran AM 26; 83, 85–86, 91, 93–95, 97–99, 105, 107, 125–27

Belfast: Templepatrick AM 35; 108–09, 111, 113–17, 119, 121, 123, 126, 130–31, 133, 137–40, 142–45, 147, 149–52

Belfast: Tomregan FH 4; 132

Belfast: Tullynakill DN 7; 122–23

Belfast: Tullyniskan TE 20; 140

Belfast: Tullyrusk AM 21; 132, 134–36

Belfast: Tyholland MN 40; 174

Belfast: Tynan AH 1; 127

Belfast: Umgall AM 35; 156–58, 160

Belfast: Urney DL 39; 176

Belfast barony: Derryaghy AM 8; 90

Belfast barony: Island Magee AM 10; 75

Belfast barony: Larne AM 10; 123

Belfast Canal (see also Lagan Canal): Aghagallon AM 21; 1

Belfast Canal: Aghalee AM 21; 26–27

Belfast Canal: Ahoghill AM 23; 4, 8

Belfast Canal: Artrea TE 20; 9

Belfast Canal: Blaris DN 12; 26

Belfast Canal: Coleraine LY 33; 99, 101

Belfast Canal: Donaghenry TE 20; 38

Belfast Canal: Drumbo DN 7; 54

Belfast Canal: Lough Neagh AM 21; 92

Belfast Canal: Magheramesk AM 21; 113, 116

Belfast Canal broad water: Aghalee AM 21; 28

Belfast chapel: Mallusk AM 2; 111

Belfast church: Misc. DN 17; 117

Belfast Corn Exchange: Kilcronaghan LY 31; 73

Belfast custom house: Island Magee AM 10; 34

Belfast Gate school: Blaris AM 8; 81–82

Belfast harbour: Carnmoney AM 2; 97
Belfast harbour: Doagh AM 29; 95
Belfast harbour: Magheramesk AM 21; 115
Belfast House of Correction: Carrickfergus AM 37; 103, 105–09, 112–32
Belfast House of Industry (see Belfast Poor House)
Belfast kilns: Ballynure AM 32; 42
Belfast Linen Hall: Drumgoon CN 40; 9
Belfast Linen Hall: Emlaghfad SO 40; 180
Belfast Lough: Ballylinny AM 32; 12
Belfast Lough: Bangor DN 7; 19, 22
Belfast Lough: Carnmoney AM 2; 34–39, 43–44, 46, 50–51, 54, 65–68, 71, 95, 101
Belfast Lough: Carrickfergus AM 37; 1, 3, 5–10, 28, 37, 40, 55–56, 60–61, 79, 81, 83
Belfast Lough: Glynn AM 26; 16
Belfast Lough: Holywood DN 7; 73
Belfast Lough: Island Magee AM 10; 16–19, 26, 48, 74
Belfast Lough: Kilroot AM 26; 56–59, 61, 66, 68–69
Belfast Lough: Knockbreda DN 7; 97
Belfast Lough: Magheramesk AM 21; 114
Belfast Lough: Misc. AM 10; 130–31
Belfast Lough: Misc. LY 31; 113
Belfast Lough: Templecorran AM 26; 82, 84–85, 88–90, 96, 99
Belfast Lower barony: Ballylinny AM 32; 14
Belfast Lower barony: Ballymartin AM 2; 4
Belfast Lower barony: Ballynure AM 32; 32, 34, 38
Belfast Lower barony: Ballyrobert AM 2; 20
Belfast Lower barony: Ballywalter AM 2; 29
Belfast Lower barony: Carrickfergus AM 37; 1
Belfast Lower barony: Doagh AM 29; 63
Belfast Lower barony: Glynn AM 26; 1, 5, 11, 15, 20
Belfast Lower barony: Inver AM 26; 49
Belfast Lower barony: Island Magee AM 10; 30, 86
Belfast Lower barony: Kilroot AM 26; 56, 60
Belfast Lower barony: Kilwaughter AM 10; 108
Belfast Lower barony: Mallusk AM 2; 107
Belfast Lower barony: Raloo AM 32; 80, 86, 92, 95
Belfast Lower barony: Templecorran AM 26; 82
Belfast Lower barony: Templepatrick AM 35; 105
Belfast mail coach road bridge: Carnmoney AM 2; 84
Belfast mountains: Donegore AM 29; 109, 114, 120
Belfast mountains: Hillsborough DN 12; 96
Belfast museum: Ballywalter AM 2; 27
Belfast museum: Desertmartin LY 31; 57
Belfast museum: Donegore AM 29; 104
Belfast museum: Drummaul AM 19; 69
Belfast museum: Killead AM 35; 49
Belfast museum: Magheragall AM 21; 103
Belfast museum: Mallusk AM 2; 115

Belfast museum: Templepatrick AM 35; 130
Belfast new bridge: Connor AM 19; 16
Belfast ph: Carnmoney AM 2; 87, 102
Belfast ph: Misc. DN 17; 117
Belfast Poor House: Killead AM 35; 44
Belfast Poor House: Newry DN 3; 94
Belfast port: Carrickfergus AM 37; 45–46
Belfast quarries: Donegore AM 29; 102
Belfast quay: Carnmoney AM 2; 71
Belfast quay: Carrickfergus AM 37; 45
Belfast road bridge: Doagh AM 29; 71
Belfast Royal Academical Institution: Errigal LY 27; 51
Belfast Royal Academical Institution: Nilteen AM 35; 93
Belfast toll-gate: Antrim AM 29; 22
Belfast toll-gate: Nilteen AM 35; 90
Belfast turnpike: Ballymartin AM 2; 4
Belfast turnpike: Carnmoney AM 2; 49
Belfast turnpike: Carrickfergus AM 37; 59
Belfast turnpike: Mallusk AM 2; 107
Belfast turnpike: Shilvodan AM 19; 130
Belfast turnpike: Templepatrick AM 35; 113
Belfast Upper barony: Ballymartin AM 2; 4
Belfast Upper barony: Killead AM 35; 9
Belfast Upper barony: Templepatrick AM 35; 106, 108, 113–14, 142
Belfast Upper barony: Umgall AM 35; 155–56
Belfast, Earl of: Ballyscullion AM 19; 8
Belfast, Earl of: Carrickfergus AM 37; 102, 145
Belfast, Lord: Kilbride AM 29; 153
Belfast, Lord: Killead AM 35; 46
Belindsley, William: Drumgooland DN 3; 25
Belish td: Derrykeighan AM 16; 93
Bell and Calvert, Messrs: Carnmoney AM 2; 41, 48, 52, 91
Bell and Co., Messrs: Kilwaughter AM 10; 112
Bell Crag rock: Clondermot LY 34; 32
Bell Hole locality: Ballynascreen LY 31; 29
Bell House (see Belt): Clondermot LY 34; 20
Bell Isle (see Belle Isle): Cleenish FH 14; 19
Bell stones: Cumber LY 28; 37–39, 44–45, 81–82
Bell, Alexander: Blaris AM 8; 62
Bell, Alexander: Blaris DN 12; 46, 50
Bell, Alexander: Drummaul AM 19; 87
Bell, Alexander: Kilbride AM 29; 144, 152
Bell, Andrew: Carrickfergus AM 37; 121
Bell, Andrew: Tamlaght TE 20; 116, 121
Bell, Ann: Blaris DN 12; 46, 50
Bell, Arthur: Blaris DN 12; 49
Bell, Arthur: Glenavy AM 21; 89
Bell, Capt.: Ballyclog TE 20; 15
Bell, Cllr (Ballynaleck): Ballymore AH 1; 12
Bell, Custine: Ballyscullion LY 6; 57
Bell, David: Ballynure AM 32; 72

Bell, Edmund: Tamlaght TE 20; 76
Bell, Edward: Blaris DN 12; 40
Bell, Edward: Newry DN 3; 99, 103
Bell, Elizabeth: Carrickfergus AM 37; 76
Bell, family: Aghagallon AM 21; 9
Bell, family: Antrim AM 29; 24
Bell, family: Ballinderry AM 21; 48
Bell, family: Ballycor AM 32; 5
Bell, family: Ballylinny AM 32; 15
Bell, family: Ballynure AM 32; 35, 56
Bell, family: Billy AM 16; 58, 68
Bell, family: Blaris AM 8; 21
Bell, family: Camlin AM 21; 68
Bell, family: Carnmoney AM 2; 76
Bell, family: Enniskillen FH 4; 58, 75
Bell, family: Glenavy AM 21; 86
Bell, family: Kilwaughter AM 10; 115
Bell, family: Kirkinriola AM 23; 124
Bell, family: Lambeg AM 8; 135
Bell, family: Magherafelt LY 6; 95
Bell, family: Templepatrick AM 35; 118, 148
Bell, George: Doagh AM 29; 89
Bell, Harry: Tamlaght TE 20; 82, 136
Bell, Henery: Blaris AM 8; 26, 55
Bell, Henery: Lambeg AM 8; 139
Bell, Henry: Aghagallon AM 21; 13
Bell, Henry: Blaris DN 12; 39, 46, 50
Bell, Henry: Lambeg AM 8; 134, 137–38, 140–43
Bell, Henry [I]: Hillsborough DN 12; 106
Bell, Henry [II]: Hillsborough DN 12; 106
Bell, Isaac: Magheramesk AM 21; 125
Bell, James: Carrickfergus AM 37; 127
Bell, James: Hillsborough DN 12; 107
Bell, James: Kilmore AH 1; 58
Bell, James: Templecorran AM 26; 132
Bell, Jane: Kilrea LY 27; 129
Bell, John: Ballymartin AM 2; 15
Bell, John: Ballymoney AM 16; 16
Bell, John: Ballynure AM 32; 72
Bell, John: Carrickfergus AM 37; 118
Bell, John: Derryaghy AM 8; 111
Bell, John: Drumbeg AM 8; 127
Bell, John: Hillsborough DN 12; 107
Bell, John: Killevy AH 1; 54
Bell, John: Kilwaughter AM 10; 122
Bell, John: Misc. DN 17; 130, 132
Bell, John: Tamlaght TE 20; 108
Bell, John: Templecorran AM 26; 132
Bell, Joseph: Desertoghill LY 27; 20
Bell, Margaret: Ballynure AM 32; 72
Bell, Margaret: Desertoghill LY 27; 20
Bell, Mary: Ballynure AM 32; 72
Bell, Miss: Doagh AM 29; 83, 97
Bell, Mr (Clanmartin): Drumcree AH 1; 38
Bell, Mr (Dungannon): Ballynascreen LY 31; 33

Bell, Mr: Artrea LY 6; 22
Bell, Mr: Enniskillen FH 4; 49
Bell, Mr: Newry DN 3; 107, 109
Bell, Mrs (Templepatrick): Templepatrick AM 35; 147
Bell, Mrs: Ballynure AM 32; 43, 53, 67, 71
Bell, Mrs: Doagh AM 29; 91
Bell, Mrs: Newry DN 3; 104
Bell, person named: Blaris AM 8; 60
Bell, Rev.: Drumtullagh AM 16; 101
Bell, Rev. James: Ballymore AH 1; 3
Bell, Rev. John: Ballymore AH 1; 5
Bell, Richard: Magheramesk AM 21; 124
Bell, Robert (Jnr): Tamlaght TE 20; 116
Bell, Robert (Snr): Tamlaght TE 20; 115
Bell, Robert: Ballynure AM 32; 57
Bell, Robert: Hillsborough DN 12; 106
Bell, Robert: Lissan LY 31; 109
Bell, Robert: Tamlaght TE 20; 81, 121
Bell, Samuel: Magheramesk AM 21; 125–26
Bell, Samuel: Newry DN 3; 99–100, 103
Bell, Samuel [I]: Tamlaght TE 20; 81
Bell, Samuel [II]: Tamlaght TE 20; 107
Bell, Thomas: Ballinderry AM 21; 56
Bell, Thomas: Coleraine LY 33; 146
Bell, Thomas: Tamlaght TE 20; 115, 121
Bell, Warwick: Artrea LY 6; 8
Bell, William: Blaris DN 12; 46, 50
Bell, William: Carrickfergus AM 37; 124
Bell, William: Galloon FH 4; 105
Bell's moss: Skerry AM 13; 120
Bellaclare (see Belclare): Kilmacteige SO 40; 185
Bellagan Point: Warrenpoint DN 3; 120
Bellaghy: Ahoghill AM 23; 17
Bellaghy: Antrim AM 29; 16
Bellaghy: Artrea LY 6; 9
Bellaghy: Ballyscullion AM 19; 4
Bellaghy: Ballyscullion LY 6; 43–45, 47–48, 52–53, 58, 63, 74, 77–78
Bellaghy: Desertlyn LY 31; 40
Bellaghy: Desertoghill LY 27; 29
Bellaghy: Maghera LY 18; 8–9, 29–30, 33, 51, 64–65, 68, 71, 73
Bellaghy: Magherafelt LY 6; 99, 104
Bellaghy: Misc. LY 31; 116
Bellaghy: Tamlaght O'Crilly LY 18; 91–92, 107–09, 138
Bellaghy: Termoneeny LY 6; 131
Bellaghy Castle: Ballyscullion LY 6; 45, 53
Bellaghy chapel (C): Ballyscullion LY 6; 47, 64, 77
Bellaghy chapel (M): Ballyscullion LY 6; 46, 61–62, 76
Bellaghy church: Ballyscullion LY 6; 45–46, 65, 76
Bellaghy classical school: Ballyscullion LY 6; 62
Bellaghy corn kilns: Ballyscullion LY 6; 76

Bellaghy corn mill: Ballyscullion LY 6; 45, 49, 51, 66, 70, 75–76

Bellaghy cove [I]: Rasharkin AM 23; 139

Bellaghy cove [II]: Rasharkin AM 23; 139

Bellaghy dispensary: Ballyscullion LY 6; 47, 54, 60, 76

Bellaghy district: Misc. LY 31; 129 30, 143

Bellaghy estate: Ballyscullion LY 6; 71

Bellaghy female school: Ballyscullion LY 6; 47, 61

Bellaghy fort [I]: Rasharkin AM 23; 139

Bellaghy fort [II]: Rasharkin AM 23; 139

Bellaghy Glebe House: Ballyscullion LY 6; 65

Bellaghy meeting house (P): Ballyscullion LY 6; 47, 63–64, 76–77

Bellaghy meeting house (S): Ballyscullion LY 6; 46, 63–64, 76–77

Bellaghy Methodist school: Ballyscullion LY 6; 61

Bellaghy old malt house: Ballyscullion LY 6; 76

Bellaghy post office: Ballyscullion LY 6; 76

Bellaghy pound: Ballyscullion LY 6; 65

Bellaghy Presbyterian Sunday school: Ballyscullion LY 6; 63

Bellaghy private school: Ballyscullion LY 6; 61–62, 76

Bellaghy private school: Rasharkin AM 23; 135

Bellaghy rent office: Ballyscullion LY 6; 76

Bellaghy school: Ballyscullion LY 6; 46–47, 60–61, 76

Bellaghy school: Rasharkin AM 23; 134, 141

Bellaghy Seceding Sunday school: Ballyscullion LY 6; 63

Bellaghy td: Rasharkin AM 23; 138–39

Bellaghy waste houses: Ballyscullion LY 6; 76

Bellaghy Wesleyan school: Ballyscullion LY 6; 46–47, 61

Bellaghy Wesleyan Sunday school: Ballyscullion LY 6; 62

Bellahill House: Carrickfergus AM 37; 102, 140

Bellamont Forest demesne: Drumgoon CN 40; 7

Bellamont Forest House: Drumgoon CN 40; 2, 6, 8, 10

Bellamont Forest House: Killdrumsherdan CN 40; 37

Bellamont, Earl of: Drumgoon CN 40; 6

Bellanagare (Roscommon): Faughanvale LY 36; 63

Bellanaleck church (see Belnaleck)

Bellanaman school: Donagh MN 40; 100–01

Bellanamean river: Kilmacteige SO 40; 191, 195

Bellanmean (see Bellanamean): Kilmacteige SO 40; 195

Bellanode: Tydavnet MN 40; 171

Bellanode bridge: Tydavnet MN 40; 171

Bellanode church: Tydavnet MN 40; 171

Bellanode school: Tydavnet MN 40; 171–73

Bellany cove: Dunboe LY 11; 50

Bellany td: Dunboe LY 11; 77, 81

Bellarena: Aghanloo LY 11; 1, 10, 14–15

Bellarena: Magilligan LY 11; 94, 98, 125

Bellarena bridge: Magilligan LY 11; 82

Bellarena bridge: Tamlaght Finlagan LY 25; 62

Bellarena corn mill: Magilligan LY 11; 86, 123

Bellarena demesne: Magilligan LY 11; 83, 117, 119, 136, 141

Bellarena House: Magilligan LY 11; 85, 101

Bellarena td: Drumachose LY 9; 101

Bellarena td: Magilligan LY 11; 86, 95, 126, 136

Bellarena wooden bridge: Magilligan LY 11; 82, 86–87, 100, 115–16, 124–25

Bellarena wooden bridge: Tamlaght Finlagan LY 25; 108

Bellas, Hugh: Ballyrashane LY 22; 55, 59

Bellas, Hugh: Coleraine LY 33; 72, 127

Bellas, Hugh: Killowen LY 33; 172

Bellashanny (see Ballyshannon): Derryvullan FH 14; 39

Bellashanone (see Ballyshannon): Derryvullan FH 14; 38

Bellatrain: Magheross MN 40; 157

Bellclare (see Belclare): Kilmacteige SO 40; 186

Bellcoo East td: Cleenish FH 14; 29

Bellcoo West td: Cleenish FH 14; 29

Belle Isle House: Cleenish FH 14; 11–12, 17, 19, 28–29

Belle Isle House: Kinawley FH 4; 117

Belleek: Aghalurcher FH 4; 2, 16

Belleek: Belleek FH 14; 3–6

Belleek: Devenish FH 14; 49, 51

Belleek: Drumkeeran FH 14; 69

Belleek: Enniskillen FH 4; 44–46, 61, 67

Belleek: Inishmacsaint FH 14; 72, 77, 79

Belleek: Kilbarron DL 39; 74, 76, 78

Belleek bridges: Belleek FH 14; 4

Belleek corn and tuck mill: Belleek FH 14; 4

Belleek Glebe House: Belleek FH 14; 4

Belleek ph: Clogher TE 5; 40

Belleek ph: Templecarn DL 39; 156

Belleek ph: Templecarn FH 14; 118

Belleek police station: Belleek FH 14; 5

Belleek school [I]: Belleek FH 14; 6

Belleek school [II]: Belleek FH 14; 7

Belleisle (see Bellisle)

Bellemont More cave [I]: Ballyaghran LY 33; 11, 22

Bellemont More cave [II]: Ballyaghran LY 33; 11, 22

Bellemont More cave [III]: Ballyaghran LY 33; 11, 22

Bellemont North td: Ballyaghran LY 33; 27

Bellemont td: Ballyaghran LY 33; 27

Bellemonte House: Faughanvale LY 36; 46

Bellevue gate: Clondermot LY 34; 92

Bellevue House: Clondermot LY 34; 6, 20–21, 103

Bellevue House: Dungiven LY 15; 9, 99

Bellevue House: Kilbroney DN 3; 28

Bellevue school: Clondermot LY 34; 16, 43, 87, 90–91, 94–95

Bellevue Sunday school [I]: Clondermot LY 34; 92

Bellevue Sunday school [II]: Clondermot LY 34; 93

Bellew, John: Forkhill AH 1; 45

Bellgarrow td: Dunboe LY 11; 77

Belligan school: Ballymoney AM 16; 27

Bellihill, Gilbert: Templepatrick AM 35; 132

Bellinagraugh bridge: Kilmacteige SO 40; 194

Bellinagunaugh day school: Clogher TE 5; 43

Bellingham, A.O.: Ballybay MN 40; 82

Bellingham, A.O.: Magheross MN 40; 149

Bellingham, A.O.: Muckno MN 40; 164–65, 167

Bellingham, Andrew: Tamlaght O'Crilly LY 18; 110

Bellingham, Misses: Ematris MN 40; 119

Bellisle (Belisle) td: Derrykeighan AM 16; 78, 88, 94

Bellisle bog: Derrykeighan AM 16; 81–82

Bellmont House: Carnteel TE 20; 21, 23

Bellmount House: Ballyclog TE 20; 15–16

Bellmount House: Clonleigh DL 39; 13

Bellmount House: Holywood DN 7; 82

Bellmount td: Carlingford LH 40; 58

Bellmount td: Galloon FH 4; 95

Bellsfarm locality: Carrickfergus AM 37; 94

Bellsize House: Derryaghy AM 8; 106

Bellug td: Carlingford LH 40; 57–58

Bellugarry td: Killea and Taughboyne DL 39; 79

Bellurgan td: Castletown LH 40; 61

Bellury (Belury) td: Desertoghill LY 27; 1, 3, 13, 19–21, 29

Bellury bridge: Desertoghill LY 27; 16

Bellury fort: Desertoghill LY 27; 23

Bellury wood: Desertoghill LY 27; 14

Bellview (see Bellevue): Clondermot LY 34; 43

Bellview House: Kilmore AH 1; 65

Bellville wood: Clonoe TE 20; 31

Belly td: Kirkinriola AM 23; 91

Bellybeney td: Donaghedy TE 5; 91

Bellynenac td: Donaghedy TE 5; 91

Belmer, John: Blaris DN 12; 40

Belmont Cottage: Kilroot AM 26; 59, 78

Belmont House: Killead AM 35; 46

Belmore abbey: Cleenish FH 14; 19–20

Belmore hills: Currin MN 40; 91

Belmore mountain: Boho FH 14; 8–9

Belmore mountain: Cleenish FH 14; 12, 15, 19, 24, 26

Belmore mountain: Killesher FH 14; 83–84

Belmore, Earl: Donacavey TE 5; 73, 76–77, 85–87

Belmore, Earl: Dromore TE 5; 98–99

Belmore, Earl: Enniskillen FH 4; 47, 50, 58, 66–67, 69, 71, 77–82

Belmore, Earl: Killymard DL 39; 106

Belmore, family: Derryvullan FH 14; 40

Belmore, Lord: Cappagh TE 5; 21–22

Belmore, Lord: Clogherny TE 20; 26–27

Belmore, Lord: Derrybrusk FH 4; 30, 33

Belmore, Lord: Derryvullan FH 14; 40–41, 43–46

Belmore, Lord: Donacavey TE 5; 73, 81

Belmore, Lord: Donaghedy TE 5; 91

Belmore, Lord: Drumragh TE 5; 109

Belmore, Lord: Misc. TE 5; 147

Belmore, Lord: Rossorry FH 14; 115

Belnaboe td: Donaghedy TE 5; 91

Belnaclogh (Belnaclough) td: Clogher TE 5; 36, 45–46

Belnaclogh meeting house: Clogher TE 5; 45

Belnagarnan (Belnargnon) td: Donacavey TE 5; 62, 64, 76–78, 82

Belnagarnan corn mill: Donacavey TE 5; 64

Belnagarnan hammer mill: Donacavey TE 5; 69

Belnagarnan spade mill: Donacavey TE 5; 82

Belnaleck church: Cleenish FH 14; 16, 19

Belnaleck church: Derryvullan FH 14; 45

Belnaleck House: Cleenish FH 14; 18

Belnaleck school: Cleenish FH 14; 24

Belnaleck td: Cleenish FH 14; 14

Belnamalaght td: Donaghedy TE 5; 91

Belraugh bog: Errigal LY 27; 45, 54, 70

Belraugh fort: Errigal LY 27; 43, 45, 70

Belraugh quarry: Errigal LY 27; 89

Belraugh school: Errigal LY 27; 50

Belraugh td: Errigal LY 27; 80, 85, 89, 92

Belshaw, George: Blaris DN 12; 50

Belshaw, John: Blaris DN 12; 46

Belshaw, Thomas: Magheragall AM 21; 106

Belsher, Joseph: Tamlaght TE 20; 77

Belsom, A.: Desertegney DL 38; 26

Belt House: Clondermot LY 34; 6, 20

Beltany (Beltinny) td: Clogher TE 5; 36, 41, 45, 53

Beltany female school: Clogher TE 5; 41, 43, 45

Beltany graveyard: Raphoe DL 39; 124

Beltany male school: Clogher TE 5; 41–42, 45

Beltany school: Raphoe DL 39; 128

Beltany td: Raphoe DL 39; 125

Belteagh corn mill: Tynan AH 1; 128

Belteagh manor: Tynan AH 1; 125

Belteagh td: Tynan AH 1; 124

Beltiny (see Beltany)

Beltoy (Beltie) td: Glynn AM 26; 1, 41, 48

Beltoy cove: Raloo AM 32; 122

Beltoy flax mill: Raloo AM 32; 84, 122, 127, 134

Beltoy hill: Raloo AM 32; 86

Beltoy school: Raloo AM 32; 85

Beltoy td: Raloo AM 32; 80, 129, 133–34

Belturbet: Cleenish FH 14; 18

Belturbet: Clones FH 4; 27

Belturbet: Drummully FH 4; 36–39

Belturbet: Enniskillen FH 4; 44–45, 53, 80

Belturbet: Galloon FH 4; 92, 101–02, 105

Belturbet: Killdrumsherdan CN 40; 35

Belturbet: Kinawley FH 4; 107–08, 114–15, 119, 121–23

Belturbet: Tomregan FH 4; 131

Belturbet distillery: Aghalurcher FH 4; 15

Belturbet market house: Galloon FH 4; 101

Belud locality: Clondermot LY 34; 60

Belvarley district: Derryaghy AM 8; 114

Belvedere House: Drumbo DN 7; 56

Belview (Drumcoo) td: Enniskillen FH 4; 82

Belview House: Enniskillen FH 4; 66

Belvoir Park (Belfast): Cumber LY 28; 86

Belvoir Park: Knockbreda DN 7; 97, 101

Belvue (see Belview): Enniskillen FH 4; 66

Bembrandagh river: Misc. LY 36; 109

Ben Neagh House: Killead AM 35; 14, 47

Bena td: Carlingford LH 40; 58

Benade, Rev. Samuel: Artrea LY 6; 16

Benagh td: Newry DN 3; 109

Ben-an-Ouran Head: Billy AM 16; 39, 41

Benaughlin hill: Killesher FH 14; 81, 83–84

Benbane Head: Billy AM 16; 41

Benbradach (see Benbradagh): Dungiven LY 15; 110

Benbradagh mountain: Aghadowey LY 22; 27

Benbradagh mountain: Aghanloo LY 11; 3

Benbradagh mountain: Balteagh LY 9; 4–5, 43

Benbradagh mountain: Banagher LY 30; 3–4, 30, 43, 58, 94

Benbradagh mountain: Bovevagh LY 25; 5, 9, 15, 23, 35

Benbradagh mountain: Dungiven LY 15; 1, 3, 11, 13, 16, 20, 33, 41, 46, 50, 54, 63, 83, 90–92, 94–95, 104, 110–11

Benbradagh mountain: Errigal LY 27; 35, 77–78

Benbradagh mountain: Macosquin LY 22; 83

Benbradagh mountain: Misc. LY 31; 111, 113

Benbradagh mountain: Tamlaght Finlagan LY 25; 81–82

Benbradagh quarries: Banagher LY 30; 3

Benbradagh rabbit's rock: Dungiven LY 15; 91

Benbradagh sounding hole: Dungiven LY 15; 91

Benbradden (see Benbradagh): Banagher LY 30; 3

Benbradden (see Benbradagh): Bovevagh LY 25; 35

Benburb: Cumber LY 28; 68

Benburb: Eglish AH 1; 43

Benburb: Tynan AH 1; 124

Benburb bridge: Eglish AH 1; 43

Benchair church: Misc. DN 17; 128

Bendooragh meeting house: Ballymoney AM 16; 9

Bendooragh school: Ballymoney AM 16; 26

Beneda glen: Banagher LY 30; 2

Beneda glen: Bovevagh LY 25; 20

Beneda glen: Dungiven LY 15; 1, 11, 15–16, 18, 20–21, 27–29, 39, 41, 50, 79–80, 84–85, 105, 111

Beneda glen: Misc. LY 36; 113

Benevanagh (see Binevenagh)

Benevena (see Binevenagh)

Benevenagh (see Binevenagh)

Bengal (East Indies): Macosquin LY 22; 79

Bengal: Billy AM 16; 76

Bengore Head: Ballintoy AM 24; 15

Bengore Head: Billy AM 16; 36, 39, 41, 43

Bengorrems (see Bhingorrems): Lough Swilly DL 38; 108

Benhagorms (see Bhingorrems): Lough Swilly DL 38; 120

Benison, Capt.: Tomregan FH 4; 127–28, 130

Benn [or Binn], family: Carrickfergus AM 37; 93

Benn, Esther: Carrickfergus AM 37; 124

Benn, Mr: Dunaghy AM 13; 18–20, 22, 24

Benn, Mr: Dundermot AM 13; 34

Benn, Mr: Kirkinriola AM 23; 126

Benn, Mr: Saul DN 17; 111

Benn, Rev. (Straid): Carnmoney AM 2; 57, 82

Benn, Sally: Kilwaughter AM 10; 122

Benn, W.: Racavan AM 13; 103

Bennarees td: Dunboe LY 11; 81

Bennelly td: Donaghedy TE 5; 91

Bennet, Mr: Misc. LY 36; 109

Bennet, Rev.: Donegore AM 29; 126

Bennett, Adam: Lissan LY 31; 100, 109

Bennett, family: Macosquin LY 22; 83, 119

Bennett, family: Magheramesk AM 21; 124

Bennett, Frances: Coleraine LY 33; 142

Bennett, Francis: Macosquin LY 22; 80, 101, 117, 121

Bennett, James: Lissan LY 31; 109

Bennett, John: Lissan LY 31; 109

Bennett, John [I]: Magheramesk AM 21; 119, 125

Bennett, John [II]: Magheramesk AM 21; 121

Bennett, Lt G.A.: Aghaderg DN 12; 1–7

Bennett, Lt G.A.: Culfeightrin AM 24; 48

Bennett, Lt G.A.: Donaghmore DN 3; 7–9

Bennett, Lt G.A.: Drummaul AM 19; 66

Bennett, Lt G.A.: Muckamore AM 35; 76

Bennett, Lt G.A.: Nilteen AM 35; 103

Bennett, Lt G.A.: Templepatrick AM 35; 142

Bennett, Martha: Lissan LY 31; 109

Bennett, Mrs Stephen: Coleraine LY 33; 71, 142

Bennett, Richard: Ballywillin LY 33; 39

Bennett, Richard: Coleraine LY 33; 63, 73, 104, 127

Bennett, Richard: Macosquin LY 22; 80, 93, 101, 117

Bennett, Samuel: Lissan LY 31; 100, 109

Bennett, Stephen: Ballywillin LY 33; 31, 39, 43

Bennett, Stephen: Coleraine LY 33; 105, 142

Bennett, Stephen: Macosquin LY 22; 80–81, 92–93, 101, 104, 121

Bennett, Thomas: Aghadowey LY 22; 2, 5–6, 8–9, 12

Bennett, Thomas: Coleraine LY 33; 63, 104, 127, 142

Bennett, Thomas: Macosquin LY 22; 92–93

Bennie, John: Newry DN 3; 99, 103

Benone (see Bunowen)

Benson td: Taughboyne DL 39; 148

Benson, Christina: Carrickfergus AM 37; 116

Benson, family: Blaris AM 8; 21

Benson, family: Carrickfergus AM 37; 60

Benson, John: Newry DN 3; 75

Benson, Peter: Dungiven LY 15; 96

Benson, Richard: Enniskeen CN 40; 29

Benson's hill: Blaris AM 8; 20

Benson's hill fort: Blaris AM 8; 20

Bently, Edward: Drumachose LY 9; 66

Bentra Castle: Island Magee AM 10; 66

Bentra district: Templecorran AM 26; 82

Bentra fort: Templecorran AM 26; 114, 117, 121

Bentra standing stone: Templecorran AM 26; 114, 121

Bentra td: Island Magee AM 10; 66

Bentra threshing machine [I]: Templecorran AM 26; 125

Bentra threshing machine [II]: Templecorran AM 26; 125

Benvarden (see Benvardin): Ballyrashane LY 22; 56

Benvardin bogs: Ballyrashane LY 22; 56

Benvardin bridge: Dunluce AM 16; 109–10

Benvardin demesne: Derrykeighan AM 16; 81

Benvardin demesne: Kilraghts AM 16; 128

Benvardin fort: Dunluce AM 16; 106, 119

Benvardin House: Ballyrashane LY 22; 56

Benvardin House: Coleraine LY 33; 64

Benvardin House: Derrykeighan AM 16; 78

Benvardin House: Dunluce AM 16; 104–05, 109, 117

Benvardin school: Dunluce AM 16; 112

Benvenu Cottage: Kilbroney DN 3; 35

Benwilt (Benwith) td: Drumgoon CN 40; 6

Benwilt hill: Drumgoon CN 40; 8

Benyevenagh (see Binevenagh): Magilligan LY 11; 143

Beragh: Clogherny TE 20; 26–27

Beragh bridge: Clogherny TE 20; 27

Beragh chapel: Clogherny TE 20; 25

Beragh fort: Clogherny TE 20; 28

Beragh school: Clogherny TE 20; 26

Berby, John: Rasharkin AM 23; 134, 141

Beresford, Arthur: Tamlaght Finlagan LY 25; 69

Beresford, C.: Clondermot LY 34; 27

Beresford, Catherine (nee Annesley): Tamlaght Finlagan LY 25; 69

Beresford, Col.: Dungiven LY 15; 60

Beresford, family: Aghadowey LY 22; 27

Beresford, family: Aghanloo LY 11; 26

Beresford, family: Billy AM 16; 72

Beresford, family: Drumachose LY 9; 107

Beresford, family: Faughanvale LY 36; 3, 10

Beresford, family: Kilbride AM 29; 140

Beresford, family: Tamlaght Finlagan LY 25; 65, 68–69, 98–100

Beresford, George: Coleraine LY 33; 63

Beresford, H.B.: Aghanloo LY 11; 13, 33

Beresford, H.B.: Banagher LY 30; 39

Beresford, H.B.: Bovevagh LY 25; 19

Beresford, H.B.: Clondermot LY 34; 35, 78

Beresford, H.B.: Coleraine LY 33; 63

Beresford, H.B.: Cumber LY 28; 4–5, 8, 22, 70, 81, 86

Beresford, H.B.: Drumachose LY 9; 104

Beresford, H.B.: Dungiven LY 15; 14, 99, 106

Beresford, H.B.: Faughanvale LY 36; 40, 45

Beresford, H.B.: Maghera LY 18; 7, 67, 75–76

Beresford, H.B.: Tamlaght Finlagan LY 25; 69

Beresford, J.B.: Banagher LY 30; 22, 116, 131

Beresford, J.C.: Banagher LY 30; 22, 113, 118–19, 131

Beresford, J.C.: Clondermot LY 34; 34–35, 42, 106

Beresford, J.C.: Coleraine LY 33; 57, 72, 142

Beresford, J.C.: Cumber LY 28; 9, 77, 115

Beresford, J.D.: Tamlaght Finlagan LY 25; 69

Beresford, J.P.: Errigal LY 27; 81, 83

Beresford, John: Coleraine LY 33; 57, 65, 142, 150, 153

Beresford, John: Cumber LY 28; 110–13

Beresford, John: Drumachose LY 9; 73

Beresford, John: Macosquin LY 22; 118

Beresford, Lord (Bishop of Raphoe): Raphoe DL 39; 123, 127

Beresford, Lord: Aghadowey LY 22; 5

Beresford, Lord: Carnmoney AM 2; 81

Beresford, Lord: Desertoghill LY 27; 10

Beresford, Lord: Errigal LY 27; 81–83

Beresford, Mark: Dungiven LY 15; 59

Beresford, Messrs J.C. and Co.: Donacavey TE 5; 75

Beresford, Michael: Cumber LY 28; 67, 70

Beresford, Miss: Clondermot LY 34; 9, 41–42

Beresford, Miss: Maghera LY 18; 18, 72

Beresford, Randel: Tamlaght Finlagan LY 25; 69

Beresford, Rev. C.C.: Coleraine LY 33; 63

Beresford, Rev. Charles: Killesher FH 14; 81, 86

Beresford, Rev. J.G.: Clogher TE 5; 28

Beresford, Rev. M.G.: Coleraine LY 33; 64

Beresford, Rev. Marcus: Drung CN 40; 21, 24

Beresford, Rev. Marcus: Laragh CN 40; 41, 43, 46

Beresford, Sarah: Dungiven LY 15; 60

Beresford, Tristram: Aghadowey LY 22; 27

Beresford, Tristram: Banagher LY 30; 105, 107

Beresford, Tristram: Clondermot LY 34; 58, 71, 75

Beresford, Tristram: Coleraine LY 33; 56, 59, 129

Beresford, Tristram: Dungiven LY 15; 60

Beresford, Tristram: Faughanvale LY 36; 57, 59–60, 62

Berginnis (see Barginnis) mount: Killead AM 35; 7

Berk hill: Kirkinriola AM 23; 92

Berkenthorpe (Lincolnshire): Clonleigh DL 39; 15

Berkshire (England): Drumglass TE 20; 43

Bermingham, Catherine (see Cullin): Manorhamilton Union LM 40; 51

Bernabeg school: Island Magee AM 10; 69

Bernabeg td: Island Magee AM 10; 69

Bernard, Peter: Comber DN 7; 41

Bernard, St: Clondermot LY 34; 72

Bernard, St: Cumber LY 28; 63

Bernard, St: Newry DN 3; 66

Berney, J.: Clogher TE 5; 53

Berniere, Capt.: Blaris AM 8; 20

Berniere, Mary Madeleine: Blaris AM 8; 20

Berriman, George: Aghanloo LY 11; 11, 31

Berriman, John: Maghera LY 18; 81

Berry, Col: Galloon FH 4; 102–03

Berry, Elisabeth: Duneane AM 19; 123

Berry, George: Kilroot AM 26; 80

Berry, James: Carrickfergus AM 37; 57, 140

Berry, Mark: Blaris AM 8; 69

Berry, Mary: Galloon FH 4; 90

Berry, Mary: Kilroot AM 26; 67, 79

Berry, Mr: Tomregan FH 4; 128

Berry, Richard: Galloon FH 4; 90

Berry, Robert: Duneane AM 19; 111, 113–14

Berry, Sarah: Dromore DN 12; 77

Berry, Theady: Termoneeny LY 6; 133

Berry, Thomas: Duneane AM 19; 106, 125

Berry's Point: Newry DN 3; 88

Berryhill, family: Glynn AM 26; 45

Berryman [or Berrymore], Mary: Ballynascreen LY 31; 14, 21

Berryman, Daniel: Tamlaght TE 20; 102

Berryman, David: Tamlaght TE 20; 80

Berryman, Robert: Tamlaght TE 20; 93

Berrymount district: Tomregan FH 4; 125

Bertfrid, Gen.: Carnmoney AM 2; 51

Bertfrid, Gen.: Carrickfergus AM 37; 61

Bertfrid, Gen.: Templepatrick AM 35; 116

Berwick (Scotland): Clondermot LY 34; 45

Berwick Hall locality: Donaghmore DL 39; 34

Berwick, Duke of: Donaghmore DL 39; 34

Berwick, Duke of: Enniskillen FH 4; 52–53

Berwick, Duke of: Misc. DN 17; 120

Berwick, Duke of: Trory FH 14; 129

Beshaw, family: Magheragall AM 21; 99

Bessbrook bridge: Tamlaght Finlagan LY 25; 85, 123

Bessbrook glen: Drumachose LY 9; 106

Bessbrook glen: Tamlaght Finlagan LY 25; 62

Bessbrook House: Dungiven LY 15; 101, 106

Bessbrook House: Tamlaght Finlagan LY 25; 69, 81–82, 101

Bessbrook river: Tamlaght Finlagan LY 25; 62–64, 69, 83, 86, 97

Bessie Graw's bridge: Doagh AM 29; 96, 98

Bessmont Park House: Tyholland MN 40; 174

Bessmount House: Dundonald DN 7; 65

Bessy Bell cairn: Ardstraw TE 5; 12

Bessy Bell mountain: Ardstraw TE 5; 2, 4, 10–12

Bessy Bell mountain: Cappagh TE 5; 16–17, 20

Bessy Bell mountain: Skirts of Urney and Ardstraw TE 5; 139

Best, family: Aghagallon AM 21; 9

Best, John: Kirkinriola AM 23; 121

Best, John: Newry DN 3; 100, 104

Best, Margaret: Carrickfergus AM 37; 126

Best, Robert: Blaris DN 12; 40

Bestall, W.L.: Urney DL 39; 179

Beteacem td: Kilmacteige SO 40; 188

Betham, William: Drumachose LY 9; 95

Bethesda (Palestine): Banagher LY 30; 12

Betnaglogh td: Clogher TE 5; 53

Bettie, James: Tamlaght TE 20; 93

Betty, C.W.: Magheracross FH 14; 97

Between-the-mosses district: Finvoy AM 23; 68

Beverland, family: Macosquin LY 22; 84, 119

Beverley, John: Ballyscullion LY 6; 57

Bhelsheid lough: Killymard DL 39; 95

Bhinaalt district: Lough Swilly DL 38; 145, 147

Bhinaalt quarry: Lough Swilly DL 38; 148

Bhinagawra creek: Lough Swilly DL 38; 110

Bhinagharrell creek: Lough Swilly DL 38; 109

Bhinbaan rock: Lough Swilly DL 38; 108

Bhingorrems rocks: Lough Swilly DL 38; 108–09, 120

Bhinns cliffs: Lough Swilly DL 38; 109, 132, 134

Bhudacrappan locality: Lough Swilly DL 38; 121–22

Bickelstown td: Donaghmore DL 39; 39

Bickerstaff, family: Glenavy AM 21; 86

Bickerstaff, John: Kilwaughter AM 10; 122

Biddick, Mr: Ardglass DN 17; 9

Biddulph, John: Blaris DN 12; 46, 50

Big bog: Killowen LY 33; 168

Big bog: Macosquin LY 22; 78

Big bog: Magherally DN 12; 113

Big Collin mountain: Ballycor AM 32; 8

Big Collin mountain: Carnmoney AM 2; 34

Big Collin mountain: Rashee AM 32; 135

Big Drain bridge: Magilligan LY 11; 88, 123

Big Drain water: Magilligan LY 11; 83, 99–100, 120, 142

Big Glebe fort: Dunboe LY 11; 49–50

Big hills: Bovevagh LY 25; 1, 33

Big Isle: Leck DL 39; 115

Big Isle: Misc. DN 17; 121

Big Isle td: Raymoghy DL 39; 136

Big moss: Kilroot AM 26; 77

Big Moss Loanen: Aghagallon AM 21; 7

Big Ross td: Aghalurcher FH 4; 14

Big Swilly rock: Lough Swilly DL 38; 99

Big Well spring: Magilligan LY 11; 86

Bigam, family: Dunluce AM 16; 117

Biggam, James: Aghanloo LY 11; 17

Biggam, John: Aghanloo LY 11; 17

Biggam, John: Kilwaughter AM 10; 122

Biggam, Robert: Aghanloo LY 11; 10, 14

Biggam's Brae hill: Ballymartin AM 2; 17

Biggan, John: Aghanloo LY 11; 27–28

Biggar, David: Carnmoney AM 2; 81, 99

Biggar, family: Carnmoney AM 2; 76, 99

Biggar's Bray: Templepatrick AM 35; 148, 150

Biggars, Leonix: Newry DN 3; 106

Biggarts well: Macosquin LY 22; 109

Bigger, family: Carrickfergus AM 37; 93

Bigger, family: Mallusk AM 2; 110

Biggins, John: Aghanloo LY 11; 25

Bigh (see Beagh)

Bighouse cave: Culfeightrin AM 24; 73

Bighouse giant's grave: Culfeightrin AM 24; 57

Bighouse td: Culfeightrin AM 24; 56–58, 74

Bignian lough: Kilkeel DN 3; 46

Bigwood td: Templecarn FH 14; 118

Bilberry Island: Cleenish FH 14; 13, 29

Bilfoar, family: Ballywillin AM 16; 32

Billar well: Drumachose LY 9; 118

Billery td: Clones FH 4; 26

Billory td: Templecarn DL 39; 163

Billy church: Billy AM 16; 37, 45, 60

Billy dispensary: Billy AM 16; 47

Billy Glebe House: Billy AM 16; 46

Billy Glebe well: Billy AM 16; 68

Billy graveyard: Billy AM 16; 51, 68–69

Billy old church: Billy AM 16; 50–51, 68

Billy ph: Ballintoy AM 24; 10, 13, 16

Billy ph: Derrykeighan AM 16; 78, 80, 95

Billy ph: Drummaul AM 19; 71

Billy ph: Drumtullagh AM 16; 101, 103

Billy ph: Island Magee AM 10; 65

Billy ph: Misc. AM 10; 129

Billy ph: Ramoan AM 24; 101

Billy td: Billy AM 16; 57, 69, 74

Billycargan (see Killycoogan) td: Ahoghill AM 23; 38

Bimlogher td: Aghalurcher FH 4; 5

Bin hill: Longfield TE 5; 127

Bin hill: Skirts of Urney and Ardstraw TE 5; 136

Bin rock: Skirts of Urney and Ardstraw TE 5; 139

Binaghlun mountain: Killesher FH 14; 90

Binaghlun standing stone: Killesher FH 14; 90

Binalan hill: Clondavaddog DL 38; 4

Binavilnore Head: Lough Swilly DL 38; 99, 103–04

Binawooda corn mill: Skirts of Urney and Ardstraw TE 5; 138

Binawooda td: Skirts of Urney and Ardstraw TE 5; 136, 138

Binbawn td: Aghalurcher FH 4; 5

Binevenagh mountain: Aghanloo LY 11; 1, 3, 7, 9, 12

Binevenagh mountain: Balteagh LY 9; 4–5, 43

Binevenagh mountain: Banagher LY 30; 4

Binevenagh mountain: Clondermot LY 34; 7, 22

Binevenagh mountain: Drumachose LY 9; 51, 56

Binevenagh mountain: Dunboe LY 11; 58

Binevenagh mountain: Dungiven LY 15; 11–12

Binevenagh mountain: Faughanvale LY 36; 11

Binevenagh mountain: Lough Swilly DL 38; 113

Binevenagh mountain: Macosquin LY 22; 76

Binevenagh mountain: Magilligan LY 11; 82–83, 85, 92–93, 98–100, 102, 116–117, 119, 121–22, 127, 136, 143

Binevenagh mountain: Misc. LY 31; 113

Binevenagh mountain: Tamlaght Finlagan LY 25; 81–82, 97, 101

Bin-garriv hill: Culfeightrin AM 24; 79

Bingham, family (Mayo): Manorhamilton Union LM 40; 51

Bingham, family: Dunsfort DN 17; 68

Bingham, John: Carrickfergus AM 37; 110

Bingham, Lady: Manorhamilton Union LM 40; 51

Bingley, Ralph: Clondermot LY 34; 67–69, 74

Binh Bustea cliffs: Lough Swilly DL 38; 99

Binina lough: Templecarn DL 39; 157

Binion (Binnion) td: Killea and Taughboyne DL 39; 80

Binion hill: Killea and Taughboyne DL 39; 79–80, 89, 92

Binion hill: Misc. DL 39; 187

Binion hill: Taughboyne DL 39; 150–53

Binion td: Misc. DL 39; 195

Binlards village: Donegal DL 39; 56

Binmore church: Inishmacsaint FH 14; 74, 77

Binmore rectory: Inishmacsaint FH 14; 74

Binmore td: Aughnamullen MN 40; 75

Binn lough: Cumber LY 28; 6

Binn quarry: Cumber LY 28; 122

Binn td: Cumber LY 28; 7, 66, 68, 110–11, 116–17, 121–22, 125

Binn td: Killygarvan DL 38; 46

Binn wood: Cumber LY 28; 117

Binn, Mr (Belfast): Carrickfergus AM 37; 188

Binna (see Binn): Cumber LY 28; 6

Binnault Point: Lough Swilly DL 38; 144

Binnian (see Binnion): Lough Swilly DL 38; 132

Binnington district: Clondavaddog DL 38; 3

Binnion coastguard station: Clonmany DL 38; 20

Binnion creek: Lough Swilly DL 38; 132

Binnion fishery: Lough Swilly DL 38; 132

Binnion ford: Lough Swilly DL 38; 133

Binnion graveyard: Clonmany DL 38; 14–15

Binnion Head: Clonmany DL 38; 13, 16, 19–20

Binnion hill: Clonmany DL 38; 12–13, 16

Binnion hill: Desertegney DL 38; 29

Binnion hill: Lough Swilly DL 38; 132, 135

Binnion hill: Mintiaghs DL 38; 64–65

Binnion House: Clonmany DL 38; 14, 17

Binnion river: Lough Swilly DL 38; 132

Binnion td: Clonmany DL 38; 14

Birch Hill House: Antrim AM 29; 14, 20–21, 25, 49–50

Birch Hill lough: Donegal DL 39; 44

Birch Hill td: Antrim AM 29; 20, 50

Birch, H.R.: Duneane AM 19; 114, 118

Birch, Mr: Comber DN 7; 35, 37–38

Birch, T.L.: Misc. DN 17; 120

Birch, T.L.: Saintfield DN 7; 114

Birch, William: Duneane AM 19; 116–17

Birches district: Tartaraghan AH 1; 120

Bircog td: Templecarn DL 39; 163–64

Bird Island: Tullynakill DN 7; 124

Birdiville (see Beardiville)

Birdstown district: Muff DL 38; 80

Birdstown House: Urney DL 39; 176

Birdstown td: Clonleigh DL 39; 1, 12, 197

Birkby, John: Ahoghill AM 23; 44, 47, 50

Birkby, Thomas: Drummaul AM 19; 75, 86

Birkmire, family: Templepatrick AM 35; 148

Birkmire, Mary: Templepatrick AM 35; 122, 148

Birlyclough td: Enniskillen FH 4; 81

Birmingham (England): Cumber LY 28; 58

Birmingham Tower: Kilkeel DN 3; 53

Birnaghs (Birniaghs) td: Ardstraw TE 5; 2–4, 10

Birnaghs school: Ardstraw TE 5; 13

Birnaghs tuck mill: Ardstraw TE 5; 4, 14

Birney, family: Carnmoney AM 2; 102

Birney, J.B.: Clogher TE 5; 40

Birney, John: Blaris AM 8; 54–55, 60

Birney, John: Blaris DN 12; 45, 49

Birney, Mrs: Blaris AM 8; 84–85

Birney, Patrick: Ballyscullion LY 6; 50, 72

Birney, Thomas: Clogher TE 5; 34

Birnie and Cunningham, Messrs: Rasharkin AM 23; 127

Birnie, family: Ballynure AM 32; 56

Birnie, family: Carnmoney AM 2; 76

Birnie, Hugh: Rasharkin AM 23; 141

Birnie, John: Antrim AM 29; 40

Birnie, Miss: Rasharkin AM 23; 135

Birnie, Mr: Bright DN 17; 36

Birnie, Mr: Rasharkin AM 23; 140

Birnie, Rev. Thomas: Aghavea FH 4; 20, 25

Birnie, Thomas: Kirkinriola AM 23; 105

Birnie, Thomas: Rasharkin AM 23; 128, 130–32, 134–35, 137–38, 141

Birnie's Hill school: Loughguile AM 13; 76

Birnie's Hill td: Loughguile AM 13; 76

Birnor (see Binion)

Birr (Offaly): Coleraine LY 33; 126

Birr: Blaris AM 8; 89

Birr: Cumber LY 28; 59

Birre (see Birr)

Birt (see Burt): Clondermot LY 34; 34

Birt, John: Artrea LY 6; 10, 29

Bishop Aidan's Chair: Magilligan LY 11; 128

Bishop Mill hamlet: Misc. DN 17; 127

Bishop's Court bawn: Dunsfort DN 17; 68

Bishop's Court ph: Misc. DN 17; 118

Bishop's Court td: Dunsfort DN 17; 72

Bishop's Demesne td: Clogher TE 5; 53

Bishop's manor: Magheracross FH 14; 102

Bishops Pole station: Belleek FH 14; 1

Bisset, family: Carrickfergus AM 37; 79

Bisset, family: Larne AM 10; 125

Bisset, family: Raloo AM 32; 115

Bisset, Hugh: Clondermot LY 34; 45

Bisset, Hugh: Tickmacrevan AM 13; 124

Bisset, John: Tickmacrevan AM 13; 124, 127

Bisset, Mary: Tickmacrevan AM 13; 127

Bisset, Robert: Tickmacrevan AM 13; 124

Bissett, Bishop: Loughgall AH 1; 79

Bissett, Rev. William: Raphoe DL 39; 121–24, 127

Bittles, Mr (Fairgrove): Ballymore AH 1; 13

Blaberine hill: Templecarn DL 39; 156

Black Abbey (Blackabbey) td: Misc. DN 17; 122, 124

Black abbey: Donaghadee DN 7; 45

Black Abbey td: Grey Abbey DN 7; 67

Black bog: Dromore DN 12; 70, 73

Black bog: Drumkeeran FH 14; 63–64

Black burn: Dungiven LY 15; 93

Black burn: Glenavy AM 21; 78

Black burn: Misc. LY 36; 110

Black bush: Bovevagh LY 25; 14

Black Bush fort: Bovevagh LY 25; 14, 34

Black cave: Larne AM 10; 126

Black Cave North td: Larne AM 10; 125

Black cove: Island Magee AM 10; 101
Black fort: Dungiven LY 15; 44, 101
Black fort: Kilcronaghan LY 31; 86
Black Fort td: Donacavey TE 5; 67, 82
Black Head: Antrim AM 29; 1
Black Head: Carnmoney AM 2; 35, 37
Black Head: Carrickfergus AM 37; 5
Black Head: Island Magee AM 10; 16–19, 72, 76, 89, 94
Black Head: Nilteen AM 35; 87
Black Head: Templecorran AM 26; 88
Black Head coastguard station: Kilroot AM 26; 80
Black hill: Aghadowey LY 22; 1
Black hill: Ahoghill AM 23; 4
Black hill: Ballynascreen LY 31; 8, 17
Black hill: Glynn AM 26; 1, 3–4, 8–9
Black hill: Kilcronaghan LY 31; 88
Black hill: Templecorran AM 26; 93, 124
Black Hill bog: Templecorran AM 26; 84
Black Hill fort: Templecorran AM 26; 120
Black Hill graveyard: Templecorran AM 26; 120
Black Hill school (see also Mutton Burn): Templecorran AM 26; 116
Black hill school: Ballynascreen LY 31; 17
Black Hill school: Glynn AM 26; 46
Black Hill td: Templecorran AM 26; 82–84, 113, 115, 123, 132
Black Hole locality: Kilwaughter AM 10; 107
Black Island: Ematris MN 40; 114
Black Island House: Ematris MN 40; 114
Black Islands td: Ballyculter DN 17; 31
Black Isle: Muckno MN 40; 162
Black lough: Aughnamullen MN 40; 70
Black lough: Culfeightrin AM 24; 81
Black lough: Derryvullan FH 14; 31
Black lough: Drumlumman CN 40; 12
Black lough: Killdrumsherdan CN 40; 31
Black lough: Kilmacteige SO 40; 193
Black lough: Templecarn DL 39; 157
Black lough [I]: Tamlaght O'Crilly LY 18; 83, 95, 102, 120–21, 123
Black lough [II]: Tamlaght O'Crilly LY 18; 83, 95, 125
Black mountain: Dungiven LY 15; 93
Black Nib Point: Witter DN 7; 125
Black Park hill: Ballintoy AM 24; 11
Black Park locality: Carrickfergus AM 37; 174
Black Rack waterfall: Skerry AM 13; 110
Black Repentance td: Raphoe DL 39; 125
Black river: Cleenish FH 14; 14–15, 18, 27–28
Black river: Lough Swilly DL 38; 120
Black rock: Antrim AM 29; 1
Black rock: Billy AM 16; 38, 43
Black rock: Drummaul AM 19; 35, 86
Black rock: Raymoghy DL 39; 144

Black rock: Warrenpoint DN 3; 120
Black Rock House: Ballyscullion AM 19; 10
Black rock quay: Drummaul AM 19; 35
Black rocks: Lough Swilly DL 38; 99, 114–15, 121
Black valley (see Dunglen): Dromara DN 12; 65
Black, Adam: Newry DN 3; 99, 103
Black, Alexander: Ballywillin AM 16; 34
Black, Alexander: Rathlin Island AM 24; 133
Black, Ann: Macosquin LY 22; 123
Black, Archibald: Blaris AM 8; 78
Black, Archie [I]: Ballintoy AM 24; 20
Black, Archie [II]: Ballintoy AM 24; 22
Black, Archie [III]: Ballintoy AM 24; 31
Black, Duncan: Ramoan AM 24; 117
Black, Eliza (Jnr): Macosquin LY 22; 123
Black, Eliza (Snr): Macosquin LY 22; 123
Black, Eliza: Coleraine LY 33; 146
Black, Ellen: Ballywillin LY 33; 51
Black, Ellen: Dunboe LY 11; 81
Black, family: Ballintoy AM 24; 20
Black, family: Culfeightrin AM 24; 59, 71
Black, family: Glynn AM 26; 45
Black, family: Rathlin Island AM 24; 131
Black, family: Templecorran AM 26; 117, 119
Black, George (Belfast): Coleraine LY 33; 143
Black, Henderson: Blaris AM 8; 51
Black, Hugh: Macosquin LY 22; 123
Black, J.M.: Aghanloo LY 11; 16
Black, James (Ballycastle): Ramoan AM 24; 124–25
Black, James: Artrea LY 6; 26
Black, James: Ballintoy AM 24; 25
Black, James: Ballyrashane LY 22; 66
Black, James: Ballywillin AM 16; 34–35
Black, James: Carrickfergus AM 37; 123
Black, James: Drummaul AM 19; 84
Black, James: Kirkinriola AM 23; 121
Black, James: Macosquin LY 22; 123
Black, James: Newry DN 3; 99–100, 104
Black, James [I]: Coleraine LY 33; 105, 142
Black, James [II]: Coleraine LY 33; 146
Black, Jane: Carrickfergus AM 37; 75, 151
Black, John: Ballymascanlan LH 40; 55
Black, John: Carrickfergus AM 37; 39, 149
Black, John: Coleraine LY 33; 105
Black, John: Macosquin LY 22; 92, 121
Black, John: Rasharkin AM 23; 135, 141
Black, John [I]: Ballintoy AM 24; 28
Black, John [I]: Culfeightrin AM 24; 52
Black, John [II]: Ballintoy AM 24; 29
Black, John [II]: Culfeightrin AM 24; 59
Black, Joseph: Coleraine LY 33; 146
Black, Joseph: Lissan LY 31; 106–07
Black, Loughlin: Billy AM 16; 62
Black, Mary: Blaris AM 8; 83
Black, Mary Ann: Blaris AM 8; 78

Black, Maryanne: Coleraine LY 33; 146

Black, Matilda: Ballywillin LY 33; 51

Black, Matty: Coleraine LY 33; 146

Black, Mr (Letterkenny): Mevagh DL 38; 60

Black, Mr (Mullaghglass): Ballymore AH 1; 11, 13, 17

Black, Mr: Annahilt DN 12; 22

Black, Mr: Blaris AM 8; 86

Black, Mr: Comber DN 7; 37, 39

Black, Mr: Derryvullan FH 14; 42

Black, Mr: Dromara DN 12; 69

Black, Mr: Holywood DN 7; 77

Black, Mr: Magheradrool DN 17; 99, 102–03

Black, Mrs: Newry DN 3; 104

Black, Murphy and Kelly, Messrs: Ballymore AH 1; 12

Black, P.A.: Drummaul AM 19; 76, 86

Black, Patrick: Ramoan AM 24; 107

Black, R.M.: Bovevagh LY 25; 30

Black, Rachel: Carrickfergus AM 37; 129

Black, Rev. G.M.: Newtown Crommelin AM 13; 81

Black, Rev. Moses: Kilmore DN 17; 91

Black, Robert: Coleraine LY 33; 146

Black, Robert: Macosquin LY 22; 123

Black, Samuel: Ballywillin LY 33; 51

Black, Samuel: Kilcronaghan LY 31; 86

Black, Samuel: Raloo AM 32; 123

Black, Sarah: Ballywillin LY 33; 51

Black, Sibby: Coleraine LY 33; 146

Black, Stewart: Coleraine LY 33; 146

Black, T.M.: Bovevagh LY 25; 30

Black, Thomas: Coleraine LY 33; 63, 72, 104–05, 142

Black, Widow: Muckamore AM 35; 81

Black, William: Ballyaghran LY 33; 24

Black, William: Coleraine LY 33; 94, 129–30

Black, William: Macosquin LY 22; 123

Black's Hotel: Newry DN 3; 70, 74, 84

Blackall, Rev. Andrew: Kilrea LY 27; 126

Blackall, Rev. Andrew: Misc. LY 31; 136

Blackburn, Adam: Blaris AM 8; 44

Blackburn, Alexander: Derryaghy AM 8; 94, 105

Blackburn, family: Blaris AM 8; 21

Blackburn, Rev. Anthony: Enniskeen CN 40; 28–29

Blackburn, Samuel: Misc. DL 39; 186

Blackburn, Thomas: Blaris AM 8; 45

Blacker (see De Blacquiere): Clondermot LY 34; 27

Blacker, Capt.: Misc. DN 17; 127

Blacker, Col: Banagher LY 30; 38

Blacker, Henry: Coleraine LY 33; 64

Blacker, Mr: Banagher LY 30; 23

Blacker, Mr: Misc. TE 5; 147

Blacker, Mrs William: Seagoe AH 1; 106, 109

Blacker, Rev (Markethill): Kilclooney AH 1; 51

Blacker, Rev. (Markethill): Misc. DN 17; 127

Blacker, Rev. George: Seagoe AH 1; 102

Blacker, Rev. S.: Ballyphilip DN 7; 8

Blacker, William: Ballymore AH 1; 12–14, 16, 18

Blacker, William: Killyleagh DN 17; 86

Blacker, William: Loughgilly AH 1; 84–85

Blacker, William: Seagoe AH 1; 101 03, 101–08

Blackfort forts: Donacavey TE 5; 82

Blackfort mill: Donacavey TE 5; 82

Blackfort school: Donacavey TE 5; 65, 82

Blackfort td: Donacavey TE 5; 65, 76, 78, 85

Blackforth (see Blackfort)

Blackham, George: Newry DN 3; 66, 99, 103

Blackham, Henry: Newry DN 3; 100, 104

Blackham, William: Newry DN 3; 93, 99, 103

Blackheath (England): Drummaul AM 19; 70

Blackheath House: Aghadowey LY 22; 1, 6–7, 12, 18, 22, 27

Blackheath school: Aghadowey LY 22; 18, 22

Blackheath Sunday school: Aghadowey LY 22; 22

Blackhill td: Enniskillen FH 4; 82

Blackhill td: Misc. LY 36; 113, 116

Blackinston, Richard: Glynn AM 26; 39

Blackistone, Richard: Tynan AH 1; 130

Blackland td: Tullyaughnish DL 38; 96

Blacklands bog: Clogher TE 5; 26

Blacklands td: Clogher TE 5; 38

Blackley, James: Ballyclug AM 23; 65–66

Blackley, Robert: Ahoghill AM 23; 33

Blacklion: Killesher FH 14; 86, 88

Blacklion: Manorhamilton Union LM 40; 50

Blackrock Cottage: Billy AM 16; 46

Blackrock House: Billy AM 16; 46

Blackrock school: Clonleigh DL 39; 2

Blackrock td: Clonleigh DL 39; 12

Blackrock td: Coleraine LY 33; 99

Blackrock td: Misc. DL 39; 197

Blacks Glen td: Tullyaughnish DL 38; 97

Blacksessagh corn mill: Drumragh TE 5; 110

Blacksessagh flax mill: Drumragh TE 5; 110

Blacksessagh td: Drumragh TE 5; 110

Blackslee hill: Inishmacsaint FH 14; 70–71

Blackslee school: Inishmacsaint FH 14; 79

Blackslee td: Inishmacsaint FH 14; 70

Blackstaff bridge: Ardkeen DN 7; 3

Blackstock, J.: Newtownards DN 7; 112

Blackwater bog: Killyman TE 20; 68

Blackwater bridge: Ballynascreen LY 31; 20

Blackwater river: Aghaloo TE 20; 1–4

Blackwater river: Antrim AM 29; 6

Blackwater river: Ballintoy AM 24; 13

Blackwater river: Ballynascreen LY 31; 19

Blackwater river: Billy AM 16; 36, 40

Blackwater river: Carnteel TE 20; 21, 23

Blackwater river: Clogher TE 5; 25–27, 47, 58

Blackwater river: Clonfeacle AH 1; 21–24

Blackwater river: Clonoe TE 20; 30–31
Blackwater river: Coleraine LY 33; 97
Blackwater river: Derrykeighan AM 16; 78, 80–82
Blackwater river: Desertmartin LY 31; 57
Blackwater river: Donagh MN 40; 98–99
Blackwater river: Drumtullagh AM 16; 96–97, 101
Blackwater river: Eglish AH 1; 43–44
Blackwater river: Errigal Keerogue TE 20; 46, 52, 54
Blackwater river: Errigal Truagh MN 40; 120–22
Blackwater river: Killeeshil TE 20; 64
Blackwater river: Killinchy DN 7; 87, 91
Blackwater river: Killyman AH 1; 55–56
Blackwater river: Killyman TE 20; 66, 68
Blackwater river: Kilmore AH 1; 58
Blackwater river: Longfield TE 5; 134
Blackwater river: Lough Neagh AM 21; 93–94
Blackwater river: Loughgall AH 1; 75, 79–80
Blackwater river: Loughgilly AH 1; 86
Blackwater river: Misc. LY 31; 111
Blackwater river: Monaghan MN 40; 159
Blackwater river: Pomeroy TE 20; 72
Blackwater river: Tartaraghan AH 1; 117, 119–21
Blackwater river: Tullyniskan TE 20; 138, 140
Blackwater river: Tydavnet MN 40; 169–71
Blackwater river: Tyholland MN 40; 174
Blackwater river: Tynan AH 1; 124, 128, 131
Blackwater stream: Mallusk AM 2; 106
Blackwater stream: Templepatrick AM 35; 141
Blackwatertown: Clonfeacle AH 1; 22–25
Blackwatertown: Clonoe TE 20; 30
Blackwatertown: Coleraine LY 33; 97
Blackwatertown: Loughgall AH 1; 75, 79–82
Blackwatertown: Tynan AH 1; 125–26
Blackwatertown bridge: Clonfeacle AH 1; 23
Blackwatertown dispensary: Clonfeacle AH 1; 25
Blackwood, James: Ballyculter DN 17; 27, 29
Blackwood, Margret: Tamlaght TE 20; 77
Blackwood, Mary: Carrickfergus AM 37; 112
Blackwood, Mr: Comber DN 7; 37, 40
Blackwood, Reilly: Holywood DN 7; 77
Blackwood, Rev. W.S.: Armoy AM 24; 4
Blackwood, Rev. W.S.: Coleraine LY 33; 127
Blackwood, Robert [I]: Tamlaght TE 20; 77, 92, 103
Blackwood, Robert [II]: Tamlaght TE 20; 106
Bladensberg House: Kilbroney DN 3; 29, 31–32, 34, 38
Bladensburgh (USA): Kilbroney DN 3; 34
Blagh fort: Coleraine LY 33; 92, 131
Blagh td: Coleraine LY 33; 145
Blain, David: Tamlaght Finlagan LY 25; 80, 108
Blair, Andrew: Doagh AM 29; 88
Blair, Col (Keely): Agivey LY 22; 42
Blair, Daniel: Carrickfergus AM 37; 102, 172
Blair, family: Aghagallon AM 21; 9

Blair, family: Carrickfergus AM 37; 93
Blair, family: Doagh AM 29; 73, 94
Blair, family: Island Magee AM 10; 70
Blair, family: Kilroot AM 26; 74–75
Blair, family: Kilwaughter AM 10; 115
Blair, family: Raloo AM 32; 94, 108, 123, 126
Blair, family: Rasharkin AM 23; 136
Blair, family: Templepatrick AM 35; 118
Blair, Hugh: Carrickfergus AM 37; 129
Blair, J.H.: Donaghadee DN 7; 46
Blair, J.S.: Raloo AM 32; 118
Blair, James: Aghadowey LY 22; 37
Blair, James: Carnmoney AM 2; 84
Blair, James: Macosquin LY 22; 84, 113
Blair, James: Newry DN 3; 67, 100, 105
Blair, James [I]: Dunboe LY 11; 60, 73
Blair, James [II]: Dunboe LY 11; 81
Blair, James [III]: Dunboe LY 11; 81
Blair, Jane: Glynn AM 26; 47
Blair, John: Carnmoney AM 2; 99
Blair, John: Island Magee AM 10; 94, 102–03
Blair, John: Macosquin LY 22; 122
Blair, John [I]: Aghadowey LY 22; 8
Blair, John [II]: Aghadowey LY 22; 8
Blair, Joseph: Aghadowey LY 22; 37
Blair, Mary: Dunboe LY 11; 81
Blair, Mary: Glynn AM 26; 47
Blair, Miss: Holywood DN 7; 76
Blair, Mrs (Ballycastle): Ramoan AM 24; 125
Blair, Mrs: Rasharkin AM 23; 138
Blair, Mrs James: Carnmoney AM 2; 84
Blair, Richard: Aghagallon AM 21; 15–16
Blair, Robert: Aghadowey LY 22; 37
Blair, Robert: Carnmoney AM 2; 99
Blair, Robert: Carrickfergus AM 37; 126
Blair, Robert [I]: Macosquin LY 22; 106, 112
Blair, Robert [II]: Macosquin LY 22; 122
Blair, Rose: Carrickfergus AM 37; 121
Blair, Rosey: Aghadowey LY 22; 37
Blair, S.: Magilligan LY 11; 100
Blair, Samual: Balteagh LY 9; 34
Blair, Samual: Bovevagh LY 25; 59
Blair, Samuel: Ballylinny AM 32; 26
Blair, Sarah: Glynn AM 26; 47
Blair, Thomas: Magilligan LY 11; 132
Blair, Tom: Ahoghill AM 23; 34
Blair, Widow: Glynn AM 26; 44
Blair, William (Jnr): Glynn AM 26; 47
Blair, William (Snr): Glynn AM 26; 47
Blair, William: Carncastle and Killyglen AM 10; 7
Blair, William: Carrickfergus AM 37; 117
Blair, William: Dunboe LY 11; 60
Blair, William: Island Magee AM 10; 69, 84, 86, 89, 91, 93, 95, 97, 103
Blair, William: Raloo AM 32; 128

Blair, William: Templecorran AM 26; 130

Blairstown td: Donaghmore DL 39; 36

Blake, family: Culfeightrin AM 24; 59

Blake, John: Aghadowey LY 22; 19, 21

Blake, Rev.: Comber DN 7; 32–33, 44

Blake, Rev.: Kilmood DN 7; 96

Blake, Rev. Dr: Newry DN 3; 99, 105

Blakely, Matthew: Donacavey TE 5; 65

Blakely, Rev.: Comber DN 7; 35, 38

Blakely, Rev.: Desertegney DL 38; 26

Blakely, Rev.: Drumbo DN 7; 60

Blakely, Rev. Theophilus: Carrickfergus AM 37; 102

Blakes Lower td: Dunboe LY 11; 46

Blakes spring: Dunboe LY 11; 79

Blakes td: Dunboe LY 11; 61

Blanan lough: Templecarn DL 39; 157

Bland, Miss: Carnmoney AM 2; 90

Bland, Rev. R.W.: Carnmoney AM 2; 46, 84, 90

Blane, John: Ballylinny AM 32; 29

Blaney, family: Ardglass DN 17; 4

Blaney, family: Dunsfort DN 17; 68

Blaney, Henry: Ahoghill AM 23; 39

Blaney, Henry: Dromore TE 5; 97

Blaney, James: Ballyclug AM 23; 64

Blaney, James: Carrickfergus AM 37; 194

Blaney, Rev. Patrick: Killead AM 35; 45

Blaney, Patrick: Skerry AM 13; 120

Blaney, William: Aghanloo LY 11; 27

Blanket Nook locality: Lough Swilly DL 38; 143

Blantyre (Scotland): Drumachose LY 9; 100

Blany's bush: Magheramesk AM 21; 123

Blanye, Arthur: Derryvullan FH 14; 39

Blaris graveyard: Blaris AM 8; 60

Blaris ph: Antrim AM 29; 6–7

Blaris ph: Derryaghy AM 8; 90, 118

Blaris ph: Drumbo DN 7; 54

Blaris ph: Hillsborough DN 12; 87–88, 94, 104, 107

Blaris ph: Lambeg AM 8; 134

Blaris ph: Magheragall AM 21; 108–09

Blaris ph: Magheramesk AM 21; 112, 116, 127

Blaris ph: Misc. AM 10; 129

Blaris ph: Misc. DN 17; 118

Blaris school: Blaris DN 12; 34–38

Blaris school: Hillsborough DN 12; 100

Blaris Sunday school: Blaris DN 12; 38

Blaris td: Blaris AM 8; 47, 77

Blaris td: Blaris DN 12; 28

Blaris tollgate: Blaris AM 8; 34, 37, 44

Blathwayt, Capt.: Magherafelt LY 6; 91, 96

Blayney, family: Muckno MN 40; 164

Blayney, Lady: Muckno MN 40; 165, 168

Blayney, Lord: Ballybay MN 40; 82, 84

Blayney, Lord: Carrickfergus AM 37; 41, 62, 64, 142, 172

Blayney, Lord: Magheramesk AM 21; 123

Blayney, Lord: Muckno MN 40; 164–65, 165, 167–68

Blayney's school: Muckno MN 40; 165, 168

Bleach green field: Magherafelt LY 6; 108

Bleake, William: Carrickfergus AM 37; 107

Bleakly, J.: Ballyaghran LY 33; 16

Bleakly, J.: Ballynascreen LY 31; 16

Bleakly, J.: Ballynure AM 32; 67

Bleakly, J.: Ballyrashane LY 22; 55

Bleakly, J.: Banagher LY 30; 113

Bleakly, J.: Carncastle and Killyglen AM 10; 6–7

Bleakly, J.: Clondermot LY 34; 43, 98

Bleakly, J.: Coleraine LY 33; 67, 72

Bleakly, J.: Cranfield AM 19; 32

Bleakly, J.: Desertoghill LY 27; 3

Bleakly, J.: Dungiven LY 15; 6

Bleakly, J.: Kilcronaghan LY 31; 73

Bleakly, J.: Killelagh LY 27; 102

Bleakly, J.: Kilrea LY 27; 119, 122

Bleakly, J.: Maghera LY 18; 26

Bleakly, J.: Tamlaght Finlagan LY 25; 80

Bleanish Island td: Galloon FH 4; 87, 95

Bleary school: Tullylish DN 12; 144

Bleary td: Tullylish DN 12; 143–44

Bleeks, Constantine: Derryaghy AM 8; 113–14

Bleeks, Thomas: Derryaghy AM 8; 98, 113

Bleerick fort: Antrim AM 29; 44

Blenil (see Blind): Kilmacteige SO 40; 191

Blenish (see Bleanish): Galloon FH 4; 95

Blessingbourne Cottage: Clogher TE 5; 33, 48, 51

Blessingbourne Cottage: Derryvullan FH 14; 38

Blessingbourne Cottage demesne: Clogher TE 5; 38

Blessingbourne manor: Clogher TE 5; 31–32, 37–38, 43–44

Blessingburne (see Blessingbourne)

Blessington manor: Aghalurcher TE 5; 1

Blessington, Earl of: Clogher TE 5; 54

Blessington, Earl of: Faughanvale LY 36; 40

Blessington, family: Tullyaughnish DL 38; 87

Blessington, Lord: Cappagh TE 5; 20–22

Blind Island: Muckno MN 40; 162

Blind lough: Clondavaddog DL 38; 2

Blind lough: Killygarvan DL 38; 37

Blind lough: Kilmacteige SO 40; 191, 194

Blind Pool lough: Templecarn DL 39; 156

Blizard, family: Ballinderry AM 21; 51

Blois, Capt.: Ramoan AM 24; 94

Bloody bridge: Cappagh TE 5; 20

Bloody bridge: Kilkeel DN 3; 49

Bloody bridge river: Kilkeel DN 3; 46

Bloody church: Finvoy AM 23; 76

Bloody Foreland: Lough Swilly DL 38; 122–23

Bloody hill: Racavan AM 13; 89, 101, 103

Bloody hill cairn: Racavan AM 13; 102

Bloody Pass: Galloon FH 4; 101–02, 105
Bloom Hill House: Kilmore AH 1; 73
Bloomfield, Maj.: Belleek FH 14; 3, 5–6
Bloomfield, Maj.: Cleenish FH 14; 30
Bloomfield, Mr: Cleenish FH 14; 29–30
Bloomhill hill: Tullyniskan TE 20; 138
Bloomhill House: Tullyniskan TE 20; 139, 141
Bloomhill quarry: Errigal Keerogue TE 20; 50
Bloomhill td: Errigal Keerogue TE 20; 50–52, 54
Bloomhill td: Tullyniskan TE 20; 138
Blore, Edward: Galloon FH 4; 91
Blore, Edward: Templepatrick AM 35; 112, 145
Blount, Charles (see Mountjoy): Clonoe TE 20; 31
Blow, Edwin: Nilteen AM 35; 86
Blow, family: Nilteen AM 35; 91
Blow, James: Nilteen AM 35; 89, 102–03
Blow, James: Templepatrick AM 35; 110, 144
Bloxham, Rev. Mark: Tamlaght O'Crilly LY 18; 82,
    91, 107–08, 142
Bloxham, Richard: Newry DN 3; 99, 104
Blue Brae waterfall: Cumber LY 28; 44
Blue Coat Hospital (Dublin): Tynan AH 1; 127
Blue hill: Tullaghobegley DL 39; 172
Blue lough: Kilkeel DN 3; 46
Blue Stack mountains: Killymard DL 39; 96
Blue, John: Drumtullagh AM 16; 101
Blue, John: Tickmacrevan AM 13; 133
Blundell, Francis: Kilmegan DN 3; 59
Blundell, George: Clondermot LY 34; 54
Blunick (see Blunnick): Killesher FH 14; 86
Blunnick school: Killesher FH 14; 86
Blunnick td: Killesher FH 14; 87
Blunt, Charles (see Mountjoy): Down DN 17; 42
Blythe, James: Island Magee AM 10; 94
Blythe, Robert: Hillsborough DN 12; 106
Boa Island: Derryvullan FH 14; 38
Boa Island: Drumkeeran FH 14; 62–63
Boa Island: Templecarn FH 14; 118–19, 121
Boadh rock: Ramoan AM 24; 120
Boagh bleachfield [I]: Drumgoon CN 40; 7
Boagh bleachfield [II]: Drumgoon CN 40; 7
Boagh corn mill: Drumgoon CN 40; 7
Boagh td: Drumgoon CN 40; 3
Boal, Adam: Ramoan AM 24; 105–06
Boal, Michael: Loughgilly AH 1; 86
Boal, William: Misc. DL 39; 186, 189–90
Boar, Mr: Clogher TE 5; 43
Board Mill school: Hillsborough DN 12; 101
Boarran quarry: Lough Swilly DL 38; 148
Boarran td: Galloon FH 4; 95
Boarran td: Lough Swilly DL 38; 145
Boat Hole pool: Clondermot LY 34; 107
Boay, Mr: Clogher TE 5; 43
Bobby stones: Tamlaght O'Crilly LY 18; 134
Bochell (see Bouchell): Tullyrusk AM 21; 132

Bochill hill: Templepatrick AM 35; 126, 141, 152
Bochill hill: Umgall AM 35; 155, 160
Bochill stone: Templepatrick AM 35; 126, 152
Bochill stone: Umgall AM 35; 160
Bockan Island: Kinawley FH 4; 113
Bocombra td: Seagoe AH 1; 107
Boconnell td: Seagoe AH 1; 107
Boddin, family: Misc. LY 36; 104
Boden, Sareah: Magherafelt LY 6; 112
Bodkin, Martha: Lissan LY 31; 96, 108
Bodkin, Mr: Lissan LY 31; 108
Bodley, Josias: Coleraine LY 33; 155
Bodoney church: Bodoney TE 20; 20
Bodoney Lower ph: Ardstraw TE 5; 4, 6
Bodoney Lower ph: Cappagh TE 5; 15–16
Bodoney mountains: Ardstraw TE 5; 10
Bodoney old church: Ballynascreen LY 31; 9, 24
Bodoney ph: Ballynascreen LY 31; 2, 11, 25
Bodoney ph: Banagher LY 30; 1
Bodoney ph: Kildress TE 20; 58
Bodoney ph: Misc. LY 31; 111
Bodony td: Dromore TE 5; 98
Boe (see Boa): Drumkeeran FH 14; 62
Boeshall td: Templecarn DL 39; 164
Bogach (see Bogagh): Clondermot LY 34; 56
Bogagh spring: Clondermot LY 34; 3, 103, 105
Bogagh td: Clondermot LY 34; 56, 61, 108, 112,
    114, 122, 129
Bogagh wood: Clondermot LY 34; 122
Bogay plantation: Misc. DL 39; 189
Bogay td: Misc. DL 39; 194
Boggagh Roe marsh: Drumachose LY 9; 118, 127
Boggagh td: Raphoe DL 39; 125
Boggan forts: Manorhamilton Union LM 40; 52
Boggan td: Manorhamilton Union LM 40; 54
Boggs, Mr: Belleek FH 14; 3
Boggs, Rev.: Loughgilly AH 1; 86
Boggy, Laird of (see Elliott, Robert [I]): Maghera
    LY 18; 53
Boghead House: Muckamore AM 35; 62
Boghead mill: Muckamore AM 35; 76
Bogher hill: Ematris MN 40; 115
Bogher td: Ematris MN 40; 113, 116
Boghill bog: Coleraine LY 33; 128
Boghill td: Coleraine LY 33; 128, 145
Bogie, James: Enniskillen FH 4; 65
Bogossin loughs: Tamlaght O'Crilly LY 18; 83, 124
Bogtown of Dooish td: Raymoghy DL 39; 141
Bogtown spring: Dunboe LY 11; 79
Bogtown td: Dunboe LY 11; 81
Bogtown td: Kilwaughter AM 10; 122
Bohard hill: Aghaloo TE 20; 1
Bohasset td: Galloon FH 4; 95
Bohattan td: Aghalurcher FH 4; 14

Bohel Brogha (see Bohilbregha): Dungiven LY 15; 92

Bohevnia td: Cleenish FH 14; 14, 29

Bohilboy (Boughalboy) td: Desertoghill LY 27; 19

Bohilboy corn mill: Desertoghill LY 27; 4

Bohilboy flax mill [I]: Desertoghill LY 27; 4, 13

Bohilboy flax mill [II]: Desertoghill LY 27; 13

Bohilboy spring: Desertoghill LY 27; 4, 13

Bohilboy stream: Desertoghill LY 27; 13

Bohilbregha hill: Dungiven LY 15; 92–93

Bohiviny td: Inishmacsaint FH 14; 70

Boho church: Boho FH 14; 8

Boho corn mills: Boho FH 14; 10

Boho Glebe House: Boho FH 14; 8

Boho mountain: Devenish FH 14; 47

Boho mountain: Inishmacsaint FH 14; 70

Boho ph: Cleenish FH 14; 11

Boho ph: Clogher TE 5; 40

Bohoe (see Boho)

Bohora td: Galloon FH 4; 95

Bohulkin td: Enniskillen FH 4; 74, 82

Bohullian distillery: Lough Swilly DL 38; 143

Bohullian td: Lough Swilly DL 38; 142, 144–45

Boid, John: Banagher LY 30; 74

Boilnecrannagh district: Misc. SO 40; 199

Bolags td: Clogher TE 5; 53

Bole, family: Aghadowey LY 22; 11

Bole, family: Glynn AM 26; 42, 45

Bole, family: Island Magee AM 10; 70

Bole, Jamfry: Island Magee AM 10; 85

Bole, John: Nilteen AM 35; 84

Bole, man named (Dungiven): Misc. LY 36; 110

Bole, Robert: Island Magee AM 10; 32, 94

Bolea bleach green: Drumachose LY 9; 53

Bolea flax mill: Drumachose LY 9; 53

Bolea fort: Drumachose LY 9; 58, 60, 127

Bolea mills: Aghanloo LY 11; 23

Bolea old bleach green: Drumachose LY 9; 121

Bolea old corn mill: Drumachose LY 9; 53

Bolea td: Drumachose LY 9; 49, 53, 58, 60, 75, 83–84, 87, 96, 101, 120, 127, 129, 134

Bolea td: Dunboe LY 11; 76

Bolea vapour bath: Drumachose LY 9; 84

Boleran cave [I]: Errigal LY 27; 44, 69

Boleran cave [II]: Errigal LY 27; 44–45, 69

Boleran cave [III]: Errigal LY 27; 78–79

Boleran chapel: Errigal LY 27; 39, 55–56

Boleran graveyard: Errigal LY 27; 55

Boleran school: Errigal LY 27; 51

Boleran standing stone: Errigal LY 27; 45, 70

Boleran td: Errigal LY 27; 39, 42, 60, 66, 69, 80, 85, 89, 92

Boleyhill td: Aghalurcher FH 4; 13

Bolf, Peter: Carrickfergus AM 37; 181

Bolie Columbkille giant's graves: Ballynascreen LY 31; 10, 26

Bolie Columbkille glen: Ballynascreen LY 31; 9–10, 24, 26, 117

Bolie Columbkille standing stone: Ballynascreen LY 31; 10

Bolie td: Faughanvale LY 36; 17, 53–54, 67, 70, 81, 92, 98

Bolies houses: Bovevagh LY 25; 40

Bolies td: Clogher TE 5; 37

Bolies td: Clondermot LY 34; 56, 61, 72, 108, 112, 114, 122, 129

Bollabracken (see Boltabracken): Cumber LY 28; 5

Bollnagarnan td: Donacavey TE 5; 80

Bollonfortey village: Kilmacteige SO 40; 195

Boltabracken hill: Cumber LY 28; 5, 47, 71

Boltnaconnell cove: Killead AM 35; 32

Boltnaconnell fort: Killead AM 35; 31, 39

Boltnaconnell mound: Killead AM 35; 28, 39

Boltnaconnell td: Killead AM 35; 30, 40

Bolton td: Loughgilly AH 1; 85

Bolton, Edward: Blaris DN 12; 45, 49

Bolton, Eliza: Tamlaght O'Crilly LY 18; 138

Bolton, John (Snr): Tamlaght O'Crilly LY 18; 129

Bolton, Mable: Drumcree AH 1; 29

Bolton, Mr: Ballyphilip DN 7; 8

Bolton, Mr: Blaris AM 8; 10

Bolton, Mr: Blaris DN 12; 41

Bolton, Samuel: Tamlaght O'Crilly LY 18; 95, 114, 119

Bolton, William: Tamlaght O'Crilly LY 18; 119

Bolusky hill: Inishmacsaint FH 14; 71

Bolusky td: Inishmacsaint FH 14; 70

Bomacatall school: Longfield TE 5; 128

Bomacatall td: Longfield TE 5; 128

Bomany school: Conwal DL 39; 27

Bomany td: Conwal DL 39; 26

Bonafoble: Donagh DL 38; 32

Bonamargy abbey: Culfeightrin AM 24; 40, 46, 48, 60–67, 70, 76

Bonamargy abbey: Drumtullagh AM 16; 101

Bonamargy abbey: Ramoan AM 24; 109–10, 120

Bonamargy bridge: Culfeightrin AM 24; 63

Bonamargy Castle: Culfeightrin AM 24; 69

Bonamargy convent: Finvoy AM 23; 73

Bonamargy corn mill: Culfeightrin AM 24; 45

Bonamargy district: Drumtullagh AM 16; 100, 103

Bonamargy district: Ramoan AM 24; 102

Bonamargy graveyard: Culfeightrin AM 24; 59–60, 66

Bonamargy, Black Nun of: Culfeightrin AM 24; 63

Bonanaboigh (see Bonnanaboigh): Bovevagh LY 25; 22

Bonanimma hill: Aughnamullen MN 40; 69

Bonaparte, Napoleon: Kilrea LY 27; 126

Bond and Lynn, Messrs: Clondermot LY 34; 118
Bond, Anne: Dunboe LY 11; 81
Bond, Barbara: Dunboe LY 11; 81
Bond, family: Ballywillin AM 16; 32
Bond, family: Cumber LY 28; 32
Bond, family: Misc. LY 36; 104
Bond, H.C.: Tynan AH 1; 127, 130
Bond, Henry: Clondermot LY 34; 43, 87, 91, 94
Bond, John: Drumachose LY 9; 85
Bond, John: Dunboe LY 11; 81
Bond, John: Maghera LY 18; 81
Bond, Margret: Dunboe LY 11; 81
Bond, Martha: Kilmore AH 1; 59
Bond, Martha: Maghera LY 18; 81
Bond, Mary: Dunboe LY 11; 81
Bond, Rev. William: Ballee DN 17; 17, 20–22
Bond, Robert: Cumber LY 28; 53
Bond, W.J.: Clonfeacle AH 1; 21–22, 24–25
Bond, William: Clondermot LY 34; 27, 37, 93, 104
Bond's glen: Cumber LY 28; 5, 12, 16–17, 32, 35,
    45–48, 51–53, 78–79, 87
Bond's glen burn: Cumber LY 28; 46, 79
Bond's glen school: Cumber LY 28; 75
Bondville House: Tynan AH 1; 127
Bone, family: Misc. LY 36; 104
Bonecastle td: Down DN 17; 52, 56
Bones, family: Connor AM 19; 23
Bones, Martha: Carrickfergus AM 37; 78
Bones, Rev. James: Drumgoon CN 40; 5
Bones, Samuel: Ballyclug AM 23; 66
Bonet river: Manorhamilton Union LM 40; 47–48,
    54
Boney hill: Magilligan LY 11; 129
Boneyclassagh fort: Dunluce AM 16; 119
Boneyclassagh standing stone: Dunluce AM 16; 118
Boneyfoble (see Bonyfoble): Lough Swilly DL 38;
    142
Bonfire hill: Kilcronaghan LY 31; 64, 73
Bonifoble (see Bonyfoble): Moville DL 38; 78
Bonnamargy (see Bonamargy): Drumtullagh AM
    16; 103
Bonnanaboigh (Bonnanabough) td: Bovevagh LY
    25; 54
Bonnanaboigh river: Bovevagh LY 25; 22
Bonnanaboigh school: Bovevagh LY 25; 3, 25, 28
Bonnanaboigh Sunday school: Bovevagh LY 25; 25
Bonnanaboigh td: Banagher LY 30; 23–24
Bonner, family: Racavan AM 13; 100
Bonny fort: Desertoghill LY 27; 8, 27, 34
Bonny Glen td: Killymard DL 39; 98
Bonnybefore school: Carrickfergus AM 37; 153
Bonnybefore village: Carrickfergus AM 37; 164–65,
    174
Bonnybrook td: Derrybrusk FH 4; 30
Bono river: Killdrumsherdan CN 40; 31

Bonone td: Donaghedy TE 5; 91
Bontin, John: Magherafelt LY 6; 98
Bony hills: Magilligan LY 11; 92
Bonybefore (see Bonnybefore): Carrickfergus AM
    37; 164
Bonyfabb (see Moville): Moville DL 38; 70
Bonyfoble (see also Moville): Moville DL 38; 68
Bonyfoble: Lough Swilly DL 38; 135, 140
Bonyfoble river: Moville DL 38; 78
Bonyfoble spring: Lough Swilly DL 38; 142
Bonyhone hill: Inishmacsaint FH 14; 71
Bonyhone lough: Inishmacsaint FH 14; 71
Bonyhone td: Inishmacsaint FH 14; 72
Boolmer, family: Lambeg AM 8; 135
Boomer, family: Blaris AM 8; 21
Boomer, family: Derryaghy AM 8; 103
Boomer, George: Blaris AM 8; 50
Boomer, George: Blaris DN 12; 45–46, 49–50
Boomer, Jane: Derryaghy AM 8; 114
Boomer, John: Blaris AM 8; 74
Boomer, John: Blaris DN 12; 43, 46, 50
Boomer, John: Derryaghy AM 8; 96
Boomer, Mr (Belfast): Ballymore AH 1; 12, 17
Boomer, Mr (Belfast): Drumcree AH 1; 40
Boomer, Mr: Blaris AM 8; 84
Boomer, Renny: Blaris AM 8; 50
Boomer, Renny: Blaris DN 12; 46, 50
Boomer, Renny: Derryaghy AM 8; 91, 96
Boomer, William: Blaris DN 12; 46, 50
Boon, Charles: Ballynascreen LY 31; 32
Boorman, James: Ahoghill AM 23; 39
Boorman, John: Rasharkin AM 23; 139
Booth, family: Carrickfergus AM 37; 93
Booth, John: Tamlaght TE 20; 107
Booth, Reid: Seagoe AH 1; 103
Booth, Thomas: Macosquin LY 22; 122
Bootown corn mill: Grey Abbey DN 7; 67
Bootown corn mill: Inishargy DN 7; 85
Bootown td: Ballymoney AM 16; 20
Bootown td: Grey Abbey DN 7; 67
Bootown td: Inishargy DN 7; 85
Bordes, Lt G.: Drumbeg DN 7; 52
Borland, family: Kilraghts AM 16; 127–28
Borland, John: Ballymoney AM 16; 17
Borland, John [I]: Kilraghts AM 16; 132
Borland, John [II]: Kilraghts AM 16; 132
Borland, Thomas: Kilraghts AM 16; 133
Borland, William: Kilraghts AM 16; 133–35
Borlin, Thomas: Hillsborough DN 12; 106
Bormas (see Banus): Templecarn DL 39; 157
Borthwick and Andrews, Messrs: Kilroot AM 26; 60
Boscawen, Lt G.: Aghagallon AM 21; 1–3
Boshanny td: Cleenish FH 14; 28
Bossing (Cornwall): Antrim AM 29; 23
Boston (America): Duneane AM 19; 123

Boston: Errigal LY 27; 48, 66

Boston, Rev. Nicholas: Clondermot LY 34; 33–34, 47, 63

Boston, Rev. Thomas: Killowen LY 33; 171

Boteler, Lt R.: Armoy AM 24; 1–2, 4

Boteler, Lt R.: Belleek FH 14; 1–7

Boteler, Lt R · Donaghmoyne MN 40, 111

Bothick, family: Macosquin LY 22; 84, 119

Bottier (Bottear) td: Moira DN 12; 120–21

Bottier school: Moira DN 12; 121

Bottle hill: Kilmore AH 1; 61

Bottlehill (Bottle Hill) td: Kilmore AH 1; 58, 68, 70, 72

Bottlehill school: Kilmore AH 1; 58, 64, 68

Bottlehill Sunday school: Kilmore AH 1; 64

Bottom fort: Kirkinriola AM 23; 125

Bottom mound: Kirkinriola AM 23; 124–26

Bottom standing stone: Kirkinriola AM 23; 120, 124, 126

Bottom td: Kirkinriola AM 23; 91, 104

Bouchell hill: Tullyrusk AM 21; 135

Bouchell stone: Tullyrusk AM 21; 132–33, 135

Boughil Braigs standing stones: Desertoghill LY 27; 8, 26

Boughilboy (see Bohilboy): Desertoghill LY 27; 4

Boughill (see Bochill): Templepatrick AM 35; 152

Boulter, Bishop: Rathlin Island AM 24; 132

Boulter, Mr: Clondermot LY 34; 98

Boulter, Mr: Faughanvale LY 36; 65

Boulton, John: Drummaul AM 19; 87

Bourke, Oliver: Clogher TE 5; 32

Bourke, Robert: Enniskeen CN 40; 29

Bourne, Rev.: Ballinderry TE 20; 13

Bousley, Mr: Ballymore AH 1; 12

Bouverie, Capt.: Magherafelt LY 6; 90

Bovagh bridge: Aghadowey LY 22; 11

Bovagh Castle: Aghadowey LY 22; 27

Bovagh Castle: Dungiven LY 15; 35

Bovagh chapel: Aghadowey LY 22; 16

Bovagh corn mill: Aghadowey LY 22; 9

Bovagh forge: Kilrea LY 27; 112

Bovagh House: Aghadowey LY 22; 6, 16, 33

Bovagh House: Coleraine LY 33; 73

Bovagh Lower water: Aghadowey LY 22; 11

Bovagh river (see Agivey): Agivey LY 22; 42

Bovagh Sunday school: Aghadowey LY 22; 16

Bovagh td: Aghadowey LY 22; 4, 6–7, 10, 20, 27, 36–37

Bovally spring: Drumachose LY 9; 118

Bovally td: Drumachose LY 9; 49, 87, 96, 99, 118, 128

Boveady (see Bovedy)

Boveagh mine: Misc. LY 31; 113

Boveagh quarry: Misc. LY 31; 114

Boveagh td: Desertmartin LY 31; 62, 141–42

Bovedy (Boveedy) td: Tamlaght O'Crilly LY 18; 97, 100, 102, 135, 137–38

Bovedy bogs: Tamlaght O'Crilly LY 18; 85, 115, 132

Bovedy day school: Tamlaght O'Crilly LY 18; 143

Bovedy hibernian school: Tamlaght O'Crilly LY 18; 139

Bovedy meeting house: Kilrea LY 27; 118, 126

Bovedy meeting house: Tamlaght O'Crilly LY 18; 89–90, 101–03, 136

Bovedy school: Tamlaght O'Crilly LY 18; 90, 103

Bovedy stream: Kilrea LY 27; 120

Bovedy Sunday school: Tamlaght O'Crilly LY 18; 143

Bovedy td: Desertoghill LY 27; 29

Bovedy village: Tamlaght O'Crilly LY 18; 103

Boveel (see Boviel): Banagher LY 30; 22

Boveil (see Boviel): Dungiven LY 15; 27

Bovel, Thomas: Ballyscullion AM 19; 13

Bovel, William: Ballyscullion AM 19; 13

Bovelly td: Drumachose LY 9; 132

Bovenett td: Aghaderg DN 12; 1

Boveran Valley Head: Billy AM 16; 41

Bovevagh abbey: Banagher LY 30; 6

Bovevagh abbey: Bovevagh LY 25; 21

Bovevagh bog: Dungiven LY 15; 110

Bovevagh bridges: Banagher LY 30; 5

Bovevagh bridges: Bovevagh LY 25; 24

Bovevagh chapel: Banagher LY 30; 33

Bovevagh chapel: Bovevagh LY 25; 23

Bovevagh church: Bovevagh LY 25; 3, 23–24, 38

Bovevagh flax mill: Bovevagh LY 25; 4, 20, 29, 57

Bovevagh Glebe House: Banagher LY 30; 4, 14

Bovevagh Glebe House: Bovevagh LY 25; 3, 22–23, 54

Bovevagh glen: Bovevagh LY 25; 1

Bovevagh graveyard: Bovevagh LY 25; 5–6

Bovevagh graveyards: Ahoghill AM 23; 24

Bovevagh meeting house school: Bovevagh LY 25; 25

Bovevagh mills: Bovevagh LY 25; 23–24

Bovevagh old church: Banagher LY 30; 6, 11, 110

Bovevagh old church: Bovevagh LY 25; 5–6, 18, 26, 29, 38, 46, 51, 53–54

Bovevagh ph: Ballyaghran LY 33; 8

Bovevagh ph: Ballyclug AM 23; 63

Bovevagh ph: Balteagh LY 9; 20, 31

Bovevagh ph: Banagher LY 30; 1–5, 7, 9, 11, 13–15, 17, 23–25, 36, 56, 68, 89, 92, 95

Bovevagh ph: Bovevagh LY 25; 2

Bovevagh ph: Cumber LY 28; 1, 4–6, 14, 45, 84, 86

Bovevagh ph: Drumachose LY 9; 75, 84, 86, 117

Bovevagh ph: Dungiven LY 15; 5, 7, 26–27, 34, 50, 52, 61–62, 93

Bovevagh ph: Faughanvale LY 36; 21

Bovevagh ph: Killowen LY 33; 172

Bovevagh ph: Kirkinriola AM 23; 125

Bovevagh ph: Lissan LY 31; 92

Bovevagh ph: Magilligan LY 11; 85, 124

Bovevagh ph: Misc. LY 31; 114

Bovevagh ph: Tamlaght Finlagan LY 25; 62, 64, 79, 92, 94, 97–98, 106, 109

Bovevagh river: Bovevagh LY 25; 2, 4, 20, 22, 57

Bovevagh school: Bovevagh LY 25; 25, 28, 55

Bovevagh schools: Banagher LY 30; 13

Bovevagh Sunday school: Bovevagh LY 25; 25

Bovevagh td: Banagher LY 30; 23–24, 89

Bovevagh td: Bovevagh LY 25; 18, 23, 38, 41, 57, 60–61

Bovevagh td: Drumachose LY 9; 117

Bovevagh well: Banagher LY 30; 11, 69

Bovevagh well: Bovevagh LY 25; 5, 18, 38, 46, 54

Boviel (Boville) td: Banagher LY 30; 22, 84

Boviel druid's altar: Dungiven LY 15; 41, 80

Boviel mass altar: Dungiven LY 15; 47

Boviel td: Dungiven LY 15; 22, 27, 46, 61, 65, 71, 75–77, 80, 83, 92, 101, 105

Boviel td: Misc. LY 36; 112

Bovil (see Boviel): Dungiven LY 15; 105

Bovil, Elisa: Ballyscullion AM 19; 13

Bovil, John (Jnr): Ballyscullion AM 19; 13

Bovil, John (Snr): Ballyscullion AM 19; 13

Bovil, Rachael (Jnr): Ballyscullion AM 19; 13

Bovil, Thomas: Ballyscullion AM 19; 13

Bovil, William: Ballyscullion AM 19; 13

Bovill (see Boviel): Banagher LY 30; 84

Bovolcan fort: Derryaghy AM 8; 95

Bovolcan standing stone: Derryaghy AM 8; 98

Bovolcan td: Derryaghy AM 8; 91, 101, 109, 115, 121

Bovolgan (see Bovolcan): Derryaghy AM 8; 121

Bow lough: Saintfield DN 7; 117, 119

Bowdell, William: Carrickfergus AM 37; 121

Bowden, family: Carrickfergus AM 37; 93

Bowden, Mr: Misc. DN 17; 122

Bowelk td: Aughnamullen MN 40; 75

Bowen, Rev. Edward: Faughanvale LY 36; 40, 45

Bowen, Rev. Edward: Killea and Taughboyne DL 39; 79, 92

Bowen, Rev. Edward: Misc. DL 39; 184, 189, 194

Bowen, Rev. Edward: Taughboyne DL 39; 148, 150

Bower, Patrick: Coleraine LY 33; 139

Bowes, family: Blaris AM 8; 21

Bowie, John: Carrickfergus AM 37; 135, 141–42

Bowman, Davis: Carrickfergus AM 37; 161

Bowman, family: Carrickfergus AM 37; 93

Bowman, family: Magherafelt LY 6; 95

Bowman, Russel: Carrickfergus AM 37; 161–62

Bowton, Hugh: Desertoghill LY 27; 20

Bowtown td: Misc. DN 17; 123

Bowtown td: Newtownards DN 7; 111

Boxer, Capt.: Killygarvan DL 38; 48

Boyagh bog: Clonleigh DL 39; 1

Boyagh td: Clonleigh DL 39; 12, 197

Boyce, Frederick: Drumachose LY 9; 104

Boyce, John: Coleraine LY 33; 63

Boyce, Samuel: Coleraine LY 33; 61, 63, 72, 94, 127, 131

Boyd, Alexander: Balteagh LY 9; 40

Boyd, Alexander: Carnmoney AM 2; 88

Boyd, Alexander: Ramoan AM 24; 102

Boyd, Andrew (Jnr): Kilraghts AM 16; 132

Boyd, Andrew (Snr): Kilraghts AM 16; 132

Boyd, Andrew: Ballywillin AM 16; 32

Boyd, Andrew: Carnmoney AM 2; 98, 100

Boyd, Andrew: Dundermot AM 13; 31

Boyd, Andrew: Tamlaght Finlagan LY 25; 89, 114

Boyd, Ann: Ballymoney AM 16; 17

Boyd, Archibald: Derrykeighan AM 16; 87

Boyd, Archy: Ramoan AM 24; 119–20

Boyd, Capt.: Blaris AM 8; 4, 88

Boyd, Catherine: Aghadowey LY 22; 37

Boyd, Charles: Coleraine LY 33; 68, 135

Boyd, Charles: Ramoan AM 24; 116, 126

Boyd, Clotworthy: Drummaul AM 19; 92

Boyd, Cornelius: Desertoghill LY 27; 20

Boyd, Cunningham: Blaris AM 8; 54, 85

Boyd, Cunningham: Blaris DN 12; 46

Boyd, David: Comber DN 7; 39

Boyd, E.D.: Ramoan AM 24; 103

Boyd, Edward [I]: Carrickfergus AM 37; 112

Boyd, Edward [II]: Carrickfergus AM 37; 121

Boyd, Eliza: Kilraghts AM 16; 132

Boyd, Eliza: Kilwaughter AM 10; 122

Boyd, Elizabeth: Desertoghill LY 27; 20

Boyd, Ellen: Ballyaghran LY 33; 27

Boyd, Esther: Aghadowey LY 22; 36

Boyd, family: Ballintoy AM 24; 20

Boyd, family: Ballyclug AM 23; 63

Boyd, family: Ballynure AM 32; 56

Boyd, family: Billy AM 16; 58, 68

Boyd, family: Blaris AM 8; 21

Boyd, family: Carnmoney AM 2; 51, 76

Boyd, family: Derrykeighan AM 16; 89

Boyd, family: Desertmartin LY 31; 55

Boyd, family: Desertoghill LY 27; 8

Boyd, family: Donegore AM 29; 110

Boyd, family: Drumbeg AM 8; 123

Boyd, family: Dunluce AM 16; 117

Boyd, family: Glynn AM 26; 45

Boyd, family: Kirkinriola AM 23; 124

Boyd, family: Mallusk AM 2; 110

Boyd, family: Ramoan AM 24; 98, 100, 107–08, 124

Boyd, family: Templepatrick AM 35; 118, 148

Boyd, George: Derrykeighan AM 16; 87

Boyd, Grizle (nee Mongomery): Desertmartin LY 31; 55

Boyd, Henry: Coleraine LY 33; 145

Boyd, Hugh (Jnr): Culfeightrin AM 24; 47

Boyd, Hugh (Jnr): Ramoan AM 24; 100–01

Boyd, Hugh (Snr): Culfeightrin AM 24; 46, 50, 74

Boyd, Hugh (Snr): Ramoan AM 24; 88–89, 93–94, 96–97, 99, 101–03, 120, 124

Boyd, Hugh: Ballymoney AM 16; 15

Boyd, Hugh: Blaris DN 12; 45

Boyd, Hugh: Newry DN 3; 90–91, 103

Boyd, Humphry: Blaris DN 12; 46, 50

Boyd, J.: Blaris AM 8; 54

Boyd, James: Ballynure AM 32; 63

Boyd, James: Banagher LY 30; 110

Boyd, James: Coleraine LY 33; 106

Boyd, James: Desertmartin LY 31; 55

Boyd, James [I]: Carrickfergus AM 37; 111

Boyd, James [II]: Carrickfergus AM 37; 191

Boyd, Jane (Jnr): Desertoghill LY 27; 20

Boyd, Jane (Snr): Desertoghill LY 27; 20

Boyd, Jane: Ballyscullion LY 6; 61

Boyd, Jane: Banagher LY 30; 33, 111

Boyd, Jean: Ballywillin AM 16; 32

Boyd, John (Jnr): Drumgoon CN 40; 9

Boyd, John (Snr): Drumgoon CN 40; 9

Boyd, John: Aghadowey LY 22; 37

Boyd, John: Ballyaghran LY 33; 11–12, 27

Boyd, John: Ballymoney AM 16; 15

Boyd, John: Ballyrashane AM 16; 31

Boyd, John: Ballyrashane LY 22; 66

Boyd, John: Ballywillin LY 33; 31, 39, 43

Boyd, John: Carnmoney AM 2; 83, 88

Boyd, John: Carrickfergus AM 37; 185

Boyd, John: Coleraine LY 33; 59, 62–64, 72, 88, 142, 148

Boyd, John: Conwal DL 39; 27

Boyd, John: Desertmartin LY 31; 55

Boyd, John: Donacavey TE 5; 81

Boyd, John: Drummaul AM 19; 77, 85

Boyd, John: Duneane AM 19; 124

Boyd, John: Hillsborough DN 12; 106

Boyd, John: Kildollagh LY 22; 71–72

Boyd, John: Layd AM 13; 53

Boyd, John: Newry DN 3; 92, 95, 99, 101, 104

Boyd, John [I]: Ramoan AM 24; 102

Boyd, John [II]: Ramoan AM 24; 113–14

Boyd, John [III]: Ramoan AM 24; 115–16, 119, 125

Boyd, Kennedy: Macosquin LY 22; 92

Boyd, Margaret (Jnr): Ballyaghran LY 33; 27

Boyd, Margaret (Jnr): Carnmoney AM 2; 88

Boyd, Margaret (Snr): Carnmoney AM 2; 88

Boyd, Margaret: Desertoghill LY 27; 20

Boyd, Margaret: Kilbride AM 29; 144, 152

Boyd, Margrat: Derrykeighan AM 16; 87

Boyd, Martha: Carrickfergus AM 37; 122

Boyd, Mary: Carrickfergus AM 37; 122

Boyd, Mary: Desertoghill LY 27; 20

Boyd, Messrs: Blaris AM 8; 17, 36

Boyd, Messrs: Blaris DN 12; 32, 50

Boyd, Miss. Ballymoney AM 16; 17

Boyd, Miss: Ramoan AM 24; 99

Boyd, Misses: Ballymoney AM 16; 17

Boyd, Mr (Belfast): Ballinderry AM 21; 52

Boyd, Mr (Killibleught): Bovevagh LY 25; 22

Boyd, Mr (Newry): Loughgilly AH 1; 85

Boyd, Mr: Aghalurcher FH 4; 14

Boyd, Mr: Magherafelt LY 6; 98

Boyd, Mr: Newry DN 3; 107

Boyd, Mrs: Ballymoney AM 16; 15

Boyd, Mrs: Ramoan AM 24; 94

Boyd, Olivia: Desertmartin LY 31; 55

Boyd, Rev. Archibald: Aghadowey LY 22; 22

Boyd, Rev. Charles: Magheradrool DN 17; 106–07

Boyd, Rev. H.E.: Dromara DN 12; 64, 66–69

Boyd, Rev. H.E.: Tullynakill DN 7; 122

Boyd, Rev. William: Leck DL 39; 118

Boyd, Robert: Drumachose LY 9; 132

Boyd, Robert: Kilwaughter AM 10; 122

Boyd, Robert: Misc. DN 17; 130

Boyd, Robert: Mullaghbrack AH 1; 97

Boyd, Robert: Nilteen AM 35; 94, 103

Boyd, Robert [I]: Carrickfergus AM 37; 191

Boyd, Robert [II]: Carrickfergus AM 37; 193

Boyd, Samuel: Ballymoney AM 16; 15, 17

Boyd, Samuel: Carrickfergus AM 37; 132

Boyd, Samuel: Newry DN 3; 98, 103

Boyd, Samuel and Co., Messrs: Carnmoney AM 2; 91

Boyd, Thomas: Aghadowey LY 22; 36

Boyd, Thomas: Ballyaghran LY 33; 27

Boyd, Thomas: Ballyscullion LY 6; 57

Boyd, Thomas: Carrickfergus AM 37; 184

Boyd, Thomas: Macosquin LY 22; 116

Boyd, Thomas: Newry DN 3; 99

Boyd, Valentine: Carrickfergus AM 37; 102, 141

Boyd, W.J.: Carnmoney AM 2; 88

Boyd, William: Carnmoney AM 2; 96, 100

Boyd, William: Conwal DL 39; 26

Boyd, William: Dundermot AM 13; 34

Boyd, William: Errigal LY 27; 55, 60

Boyd, William: Newry DN 3; 98

Boyd, William: Ramoan AM 24; 114

Boyd, William: Tamlaght O'Crilly LY 18; 114

Boyde, Alexander: Carrickfergus AM 37; 151

Boyde, Andrew: Ahoghill AM 23; 39

Boyde, Archabald: Ballymoney AM 16; 24

Boyde, Capt.: Kilcronaghan LY 31; 83

Boyde, James: Faughanvale LY 36; 24, 35–36, 66

Boyde, James: Muckamore AM 35; 81
Boyde, John: Ballynure AM 32; 67
Boyde, Mary Ann: Faughanvale LY 36; 36, 66
Boyde, Mrs: Conwal DL 39; 27
Boyde, Rev.: Maghera LY 18; 67
Boyde, Wilson: Carrickfergus AM 37; 135
Boydes Hole creek: Lough Swilly DL 38; 100
Boydstown rock: Ballyclug AM 23; 65
Boyes, David: Aghadowey LY 22; 37
Boyes, Elizabeth: Carnmoney AM 2; 62, 88
Boyes, Elizabeth: Magheragall AM 21; 99
Boyes, family: Ballinderry AM 21; 48, 53
Boyes, family: Derryaghy AM 8; 111, 113
Boyes, James (Jnr): Aghadowey LY 22; 37
Boyes, James (Snr): Aghadowey LY 22; 37
Boyes, James: Blaris DN 12; 42
Boyes, James: Derryaghy AM 8; 101, 111
Boyes, James: Magheragall AM 21; 99
Boyes, John: Aghadowey LY 22; 37
Boyes, John: Templepatrick AM 35; 150
Boyes, Leslie: Aghadowey LY 22; 37
Boyes, Mr: Derryaghy AM 8; 111
Boyes, Rev. William: Ballyscullion AM 19; 10–11, 13
Boyes, Rev. William: Duneane AM 19; 100, 114, 116–17, 125–26
Boyes, Richard: Magheramesk AM 21; 130
Boyes, Samuel: Ballyrashane LY 22; 47–48, 50, 55–57, 61–62
Boyes, Thomas: Blaris DN 12; 42
Boyes, William: Derryaghy AM 8; 111
Boyhill corn mill: Aghavea FH 4; 20
Boyhill td: Aghavea FH 4; 23
Boylagh barony: Inishkeel DL 39; 67
Boylagh barony: Killymard DL 39; 108
Boylagh barony: Mevagh DL 38; 58
Boylagh barony: Misc. DL 39; 188
Boylagh barony: Raymoghy DL 39; 146
Boylan: Dunluce AM 16; 117
Boylan, family: Derrykeighan AM 16; 89
Boylan, family: Tamlaght O'Crilly LY 18; 93
Boylan, James: Derrykeighan AM 16; 95
Boylan, John: Coleraine LY 33; 72
Boyland, James: Derrykeighan AM 16; 93
Boylane, Rev. B.: Carrickfergus AM 37; 102
Boyle (Roscommon): Muckno MN 40; 167–68
Boyle: Emlaghfad SO 40; 177–78
Boyle: Misc. SO 40; 200
Boyle: Newry DN 3; 66
Boyle abbey: Misc. SO 40; 200
Boyle barony: Misc. SO 40; 199–200
Boyle manor: Misc. SO 40; 200
Boyle, Alexander: Drumachose LY 9; 73
Boyle, Armor: Newry DN 3; 100, 105
Boyle, Bell: Bovevagh LY 25; 60

Boyle, Capt.: Balteagh LY 9; 36
Boyle, Capt.: Magherafelt LY 6; 83
Boyle, Daniel: Agivey LY 22; 44
Boyle, Daniel: Ahoghill AM 23; 40
Boyle, Daniel: Maghera LY 18; 81
Boyle, Dennis: Loughgilly AH 1; 87
Boyle, Edward: Drumachose LY 9; 77, 103–04, 107
Boyle, Edward: Duneane AM 19; 124
Boyle, Edward [I]: Carrickfergus AM 37; 114
Boyle, Edward [II]: Carrickfergus AM 37; 127
Boyle, Elenor: Balteagh LY 9; 43
Boyle, Eliza: Kilraghts AM 16; 132
Boyle, family: Culfeightrin AM 24; 59, 71
Boyle, family: Dunaghy AM 13; 14
Boyle, family: Dunboe LY 11; 61
Boyle, family: Dunluce AM 16; 117
Boyle, family: Glynn AM 26; 42
Boyle, family: Island Magee AM 10; 70
Boyle, family: Kilbride AM 29; 140
Boyle, family: Templecorran AM 26; 117, 119
Boyle, Francis: Aghadowey LY 22; 38
Boyle, Hariot: Drummaul AM 19; 87
Boyle, Harry: Banagher LY 30; 30
Boyle, Henry: Banagher LY 30; 120
Boyle, Hugh: Balteagh LY 9; 4
Boyle, Hugh: Culfeightrin AM 24; 65, 70–71
Boyle, Hugh: Tamlaght Finlagan LY 25; 82, 101
Boyle, Hugh [I]: Duneane AM 19; 124
Boyle, Hugh [II]: Duneane AM 19; 124
Boyle, J.: Aghalee AM 21; 36
Boyle, J.: Ahoghill AM 23; 28
Boyle, J.: Antrim AM 29; 49
Boyle, J.: Ardclinis AM 13; 5–9
Boyle, J.: Armoy AM 24; 2–6
Boyle, J.: Ballycor AM 32; 1–8
Boyle, J.: Ballynure AM 32; 64, 70, 73
Boyle, J.: Ballyscullion AM 19; 2–7
Boyle, J.: Blaris AM 8; 66
Boyle, J.: Carmavy AM 35; 1–6
Boyle, J.: Carrickfergus AM 37; 189
Boyle, J.: Connor AM 19; 29
Boyle, J.: Doagh AM 29; 86
Boyle, J.: Donegore AM 29; 129, 133
Boyle, J.: Drumachose LY 9; 66
Boyle, J.: Dunboe LY 11; 46
Boyle, J.: Duneane AM 19; 109, 119
Boyle, J.: Dungiven LY 15; 96
Boyle, J.: Errigal Truagh MN 40; 122
Boyle, J.: Glynn AM 26; 37–39, 41–47
Boyle, J.: Kilbride AM 29; 154
Boyle, J.: Longfield TE 5; 131
Boyle, J.: Macosquin LY 22; 116
Boyle, J.: Magheragall AM 21; 103
Boyle, J.: Raloo AM 32; 122, 130–31
Boyle, J.: Templecorran AM 26; 124, 129

Boyle, J.: Templepatrick AM 35; 149

Boyle, James: Carrickfergus AM 37; 127

Boyle, James: Desertoghill LY 27; 21, 28, 31

Boyle, James: Dunluce AM 16; 119

Boyle, James: Maghera LY 18; 30

Boyle, Jane: Ahoghill AM 23; 44

Boyle, John: Balteagh LY 9; 14, 40, 43

Boyle, John: Coleraine LY 33; 63

Boyle, John: Desertmartin LY 31; 60

Boyle, John: Desertoghill LY 27; 26, 28–29, 31

Boyle, John: Drumachose LY 9; 104

Boyle, John: Glynn AM 26; 44

Boyle, John: Maghera LY 18; 81

Boyle, John: Misc. DN 17; 117

Boyle, John: Rasharkin AM 23; 139

Boyle, John [I]: Bovevagh LY 25; 56

Boyle, John [II]: Bovevagh LY 25; 59

Boyle, Joseph: Balteagh LY 9; 43

Boyle, Joseph: Killead AM 35; 37

Boyle, man named: Ahoghill AM 23; 34

Boyle, Margaret: Ballymoney AM 16; 17

Boyle, Mary: Aghadowey LY 22; 38

Boyle, Mary: Carrickfergus AM 37; 114, 129

Boyle, Maryann: Balteagh LY 9; 43

Boyle, Maxwell: Drumgoon CN 40; 8

Boyle, Maxwell: Drung CN 40; 23

Boyle, Maxwell: Killdrumsherdan CN 40; 34–35, 37

Boyle, Mr: Clondermot LY 34; 27, 117

Boyle, Mr: Drumachose LY 9; 78, 85, 97

Boyle, Mr: Dungiven LY 15; 42

Boyle, Mrs: Coleraine LY 33; 73

Boyle, Mrs William: Newry DN 3; 104

Boyle, Nathaniel: Maghera LY 18; 81

Boyle, Neal: Leck DL 39; 120

Boyle, Neill: Rasharkin AM 23; 141

Boyle, Pat: Aghadowey LY 22; 36

Boyle, Patrick: Agivey LY 22; 45

Boyle, Patrick: Donaghmore DL 39; 40

Boyle, Patrick: Drummaul AM 19; 83

Boyle, Patrick: Dunaghy AM 13; 22–23

Boyle, Patrick: Newry DN 3; 99, 104

Boyle, Rev. Adam: Tamlaght O'Crilly LY 18; 90, 99–100, 103

Boyle, Rev. Constantine: Carrickfergus AM 37; 103, 174

Boyle, Rev. Constantine: Raloo AM 32; 126

Boyle, Rev. Peter: Drummaul AM 19; 69, 82

Boyle, Rev. Roger: Clogher TE 5; 28

Boyle, Rev. Roger: Magheross MN 40; 146

Boyle, Rev. W.: Clondermot LY 34; 12

Boyle, Roger: Misc. DN 17; 117

Boyle, Sally: Balteagh LY 9; 43

Boyle, Stephen: Maghera LY 18; 81

Boyle, Susanna: Balteagh LY 9; 43

Boyle, Thomas: Coleraine LY 33; 72, 139, 143

Boyle, William: Artrea LY 6; 37

Boyle, William: Island Magee AM 10; 64, 100–01

Boyle, William: Magilligan LY 11; 127, 130

Boyle's bridge: Magheramesk AM 21; 114–15

Boyle's bridge: Moira DN 12; 119

Boyle's flax mill: Bovevagh LY 25; 58

Boyle's hotel: Seapatrick DN 12; 132

Boylease, Dennis: Loughgilly AH 1; 86

Boylen, family: Aghabog MN 40; 66

Boyne river: Ahoghill AM 23; 6, 9, 14

Boyne river: Ballymore AH 1; 5

Boyne river: Ballyscullion LY 6; 46

Boyne river: Drummaul AM 19; 70

Boyne river: Enniskillen FH 4; 51–53, 59, 73

Boyne river: Misc. LY 31; 127

Boyne, Lord: Mevagh DL 38; 58

Boyne, Lord: Tullyaughnish DL 38; 88

Boys grave: Donaghmore DL 39; 34

Bozet, Abbe: Faughanvale LY 36; 67

Brabazon, Earl of Bessborough: Cumber LY 28; 58

Brabazon, H.: Carlingford LH 40; 57–59

Braccagh (Bracchagh) td: Ballymore AH 1; 11, 14–17

Braccagh House: Kilmore AH 1; 68

Braccagh school: Kilmore AH 1; 64, 68

Braccagh Sunday school: Kilmore AH 1; 64

Braccagh td: Kilmore AH 1; 61, 65, 67–68, 73

Bracclee (see Bruslee): Ballylinny AM 32; 30

Bracegirdel, family: Blaris AM 8; 21

Braceland, James: Donaghmore DL 39; 41

Braceland, Patrick: Clonleigh DL 39; 4

Bracey hill: Belleek FH 14; 1

Brachagh (see Braccagh): Kilmore AH 1; 64

Brackagh (Bracca) td: Errigal Keerogue TE 20; 49–51, 56

Brackagh (see Brockagh): Cumber LY 28; 49

Brackagh carn: Ballynascreen LY 31; 30

Brackagh Disert school: Ballynascreen LY 31; 16

Brackagh lough: Ballynascreen LY 31; 11, 26

Brackagh mountain: Ballynascreen LY 31; 30

Brackagh Rowley female school: Kilcronaghan LY 31; 88

Brackagh Rowley fort: Kilcronaghan LY 31; 86

Brackagh Rowley male school: Kilcronaghan LY 31; 87

Brackagh Rowley mountain: Kilcronaghan LY 31; 78

Brackagh Rowley national school: Kilcronaghan LY 31; 87

Brackagh Rowley td: Kilcronaghan LY 31; 71, 73, 78, 84–86, 142

Brackagh Rowley trigonometrical station: Kilcronaghan LY 31; 86

Brackagh Slieve Gallion td: Desertmartin LY 31; 57, 62, 141–42

Brackagh td: Ballynascreen LY 31; 7, 19, 143

Brackagh td: Faughanvale LY 36; 57

Brackagh td: Loughgilly AH 1; 85

Brackagh td: Magheross MN 40; 153

Brackaghgreilly (Bracknagrilly) td: Maghera LY 18; 22, 36–37, 45, 59, 65, 74, 81

Brackaghgreilly cave: Maghera LY 18; 12, 37

Brackaghgreilly fort: Maghera LY 18; 12, 37, 62

Brackaghgreilly mass house: Maghera LY 18; 69

Brackaghgreilly school: Maghera LY 18; 33

Brackaghgrilly (see Brackaghgreilly): Maghera LY 18; 36

Brackaghlislea hill: Kilcronaghan LY 31; 64

Brackaghlislea td: Kilcronaghan LY 31; 64

Brackamore hill: Desertmartin LY 31; 52

Brackaville coal pits: Donaghenry TE 20; 38

Bracken lough: Desertcreat TE 20; 33

Bracken, family: Killesher FH 14; 84

Bracken, St: Cumber LY 28; 71

Bracken's cave: Rathlin Island AM 24; 128–29

Brackenridge, family: Island Magee AM 10; 70

Brackfield Castle: Clondermot LY 34; 34

Brackfield Castle: Cumber LY 28; 36–37, 44, 53, 56

Brackfield meeting house: Banagher LY 30; 31

Brackfield meeting house: Cumber LY 28; 19, 25, 32–33, 35, 53, 79–80

Brackfield moor: Cumber LY 28; 61

Brackfield quarry: Cumber LY 28; 104

Brackfield rectory: Cumber LY 28; 53

Brackfield td: Clondermot LY 34; 57

Brackfield td: Cumber LY 28; 46, 48, 56, 60–61, 67, 94–95, 99, 104, 107, 109

Brackfield well: Cumber LY 28; 37

Brackfield wood: Cumber LY 28; 99

Brackinridge, Thomas: Island Magee AM 10; 90

Brackley hill: Aughnamullen MN 40; 69

Brackley school: Kilclooney AH 1; 51

Brackley Sunday school: Kilclooney AH 1; 51

Brackley td: Aughnamullen MN 40; 75

Bracklow church: Drumlumman CN 40; 14

Bracklow House: Drumlumman CN 40; 14

Bracklow lough: Drumlumman CN 40; 12

Bracklow td: Drumlumman CN 40; 17

Brackly lough: Donaghmoyne MN 40; 106

Brackmoy td: Clondermot LY 34; 57

Brackna hill: Kilbride AM 29; 150

Bracknahill td: Doagh AM 29; 93

Bracknamuckley (Bracknamucklagh) td: Ahoghill AM 23; 13, 38–39

Bracknamuckley corn mill: Ahoghill AM 23; 13

Bracknamuckley fort: Ahoghill AM 23; 34

Brackney Castle: Culfeightrin AM 24; 68–69

Brackney flower garden: Culfeightrin AM 24; 55

Brackney fort: Culfeightrin AM 24; 54–55

Brackney graveyard: Culfeightrin AM 24; 54

Brackney school: Culfeightrin AM 24; 85

Brackney td: Culfeightrin AM 24; 54

Brackrymore td: Manorhamilton Union LM 40; 54

Bracky fort: Derryvullan FH 14; 42

Bracky td: Derryvullan FH 14; 42, 45

Bradach, robber: Dungiven LY 15; 20

Bradach, robber: Misc. LY 36; 113

Bradagh, Brian: Dungiven LY 15; 111

Bradagh, Brian: Kilrea LY 27; 113

Bradan (see Bragan): Errigal Truagh MN 40; 120

Bradan locality: Lough Swilly DL 38; 115

Bradbury, George: Blaris AM 8; 67

Bradbury, George: Hillsborough DN 12; 107

Bradbury, John: Blaris AM 8; 19

Bradbury, Mr: Blaris DN 12; 32

Bradden Point: Lough Swilly DL 38; 116

Braddley, George: Macosquin LY 22; 109

Braddock, General: Kilbroney DN 3; 32

Braden, family: Misc. LY 36; 104

Bradey, Hugh [I]: Maghera LY 18; 8, 68

Bradey, Hugh [II]: Maghera LY 18; 32

Bradford, family: Ematris MN 40; 118

Bradford, family: Island Magee AM 10; 70

Bradford, J.: Island Magee AM 10; 64

Bradford, James: Island Magee AM 10; 99

Bradford, James: Newry DN 3; 100

Bradford, William: Templepatrick AM 35; 151–52

Bradlaw, Mr: Drumbo DN 7; 59

Bradley, Andrew: Tamlaght O'Crilly LY 18; 91, 96, 109, 116, 132

Bradley, Ann: Balteagh LY 9; 44

Bradley, Anne: Ballyaghran LY 33; 27

Bradley, Charles: Killelagh LY 27; 101

Bradley, Daniel: Dungiven LY 15; 75

Bradley, Dominick: Misc. LY 31; 137

Bradley, Dr: Maghera LY 18; 69

Bradley, Elenor: Ballynascreen LY 31; 21

Bradley, Elenor: Magherafelt LY 6; 112

Bradley, Eliza: Ballyscullion LY 6; 78

Bradley, family: Killelagh LY 27; 99

Bradley, family: Macosquin LY 22; 84, 119

Bradley, family: Maghera LY 18; 14, 24, 48, 74

Bradley, family: Magherafelt LY 6; 95

Bradley, family: Misc. LY 31; 137

Bradley, friar: Banagher LY 30; 91

Bradley, friar: Maghera LY 18; 68

Bradley, Henry: Killelagh LY 27; 100

Bradley, Hugh: Ballynascreen LY 31; 20–24, 27

Bradley, Hugh: Desertoghill LY 27; 21

Bradley, Izabela: Ballyscullion LY 6; 78

Bradley, James: Dungiven LY 15; 92

Bradley, James: Killelagh LY 27; 100

Bradley, James [I]: Ballynascreen LY 31; 21

Bradley, James [I]: Ballyscullion LY 6; 61, 75
Bradley, James [I]: Maghera LY 18; 8, 68
Bradley, James [II]: Ballynascreen LY 31; 22
Bradley, James [II]: Ballyscullion LY 6; 77
Bradley, James [II]: Maghera LY 18; 43
Bradley, James [III]: Ballyscullion LY 6; 78
Bradley, James [III]: Maghera LY 18; 78
Bradley, James [IV]: Ballyscullion LY 6; 78
Bradley, James [V]: Ballyscullion LY 6; 78
Bradley, John: Ballynascreen LY 31; 22
Bradley, John: Maghera LY 18; 78
Bradley, John: Tamlaght O'Crilly LY 18; 126
Bradley, John [I]: Carrickfergus AM 37; 116
Bradley, John [II]: Carrickfergus AM 37; 194
Bradley, Joseph: Ballynascreen LY 31; 21
Bradley, Lawrence: Maghera LY 18; 57
Bradley, man named: Misc. LY 36; 110
Bradley, Manus: Maghera LY 18; 46
Bradley, Mary: Balteagh LY 9; 44
Bradley, Mary: Kilrea LY 27; 129
Bradley, Michael: Maghera LY 18; 50
Bradley, Mr: Newry DN 3; 99
Bradley, Neill: Killelagh LY 27; 101
Bradley, Patrick: Banagher LY 30; 111
Bradley, Patrick: Dungiven LY 15; 93
Bradley, Patrick: Killelagh LY 27; 102
Bradley, Patrick: Kilrea LY 27; 129
Bradley, Patrick: Maghera LY 18; 40
Bradley, Patrick: Tamlaght O'Crilly LY 18; 137
Bradley, Paul: Desertlyn LY 31; 50–51
Bradley, Peter: Dungiven LY 15; 92
Bradley, Rev. Andrew: Misc. LY 31; 137
Bradley, Rev. Patrick: Misc. LY 31; 137
Bradley, Rev. Paul: Magilligan LY 11; 93, 125
Bradley, Robert: Maghera LY 18; 77
Bradley, Rosey: Ballynascreen LY 31; 21
Bradley, Thomas: Carrickfergus AM 37; 118
Bradley, Thomas: Tamlaght TE 20; 82
Bradley, Widow: Artrea LY 6; 33
Bradley, William: Maghera LY 18; 80
Bradley's Lock: Aghagallon AM 21; 6
Bradly, family: Culfeightrin AM 24; 59
Bradly, Felix: Maghera LY 18; 62
Bradly, Hugh: Desertoghill LY 27; 15, 25
Bradly, James: Banagher LY 30; 75
Bradly, John: Banagher LY 30; 75
Bradly, John: Desertoghill LY 27; 25
Bradly, John: Errigal LY 27; 44, 69
Bradly, Michael: Coleraine LY 33; 73
Bradly, Patrick: Desertoghill LY 27; 16, 26
Bradly, Rose: Maghera LY 18; 59
Bradock (Bradick) Island: Killinchy DN 7; 86, 92
Bradshaw, Arthur: Hillsborough DN 12; 107
Bradshaw, David: Hillsborough DN 12; 107
Bradshaw, George: Blaris AM 8; 19

Bradshaw, George [I]: Hillsborough DN 12; 107
Bradshaw, George [II]: Hillsborough DN 12; 107
Bradshaw, Harvey: Hillsborough DN 12; 107
Bradshaw, Hercules: Blaris DN 12; 34, 36
Bradshaw, Hercules: Hillsborough DN 12; 97,
    102–03, 105
Bradshaw, J.F.: Hillsborough DN 12; 102, 105
Bradshaw, John: Donegore AM 29; 134
Bradshaw, John [or Samuel]: Rasharkin AM 23; 136
Bradshaw, Mary: Rasharkin AM 23; 135
Bradshaw, R.S.: Carrickfergus AM 37; 102
Bradshaw, Rev. John: Blaris AM 8; 55
Bradshaw, Rev. John: Island Magee AM 10; 97
Bradshaw, Rev. John: Lambeg AM 8; 135, 137,
    142–43
Bradshaw, Richard: Derryaghy AM 8; 102, 117–18
Bradshaw, Robert: Ballyscullion LY 6; 57
Bradshaw, Samuel: Hillsborough DN 12; 107
Bradshaw, Samuel: Tamlaght O'Crilly LY 18; 139
Bradshaw, Samuel [or John]: Rasharkin AM 23;
    136, 141
Bradshaw, William: Derryaghy AM 8; 90, 97, 100
Brady (see Bready): Misc. DL 39; 188
Brady, Andrew: Tamlaght O'Crilly LY 18; 132
Brady, Cathrine (nee Lavery): Aghagallon AM 21;
    21–22
Brady, D.C.: Newry DN 3; 75, 95, 99, 101, 104–05
Brady, family: Currin MN 40; 94
Brady, family: Kilraghts AM 16; 127
Brady, John: Ballyclug AM 23; 60, 66
Brady, John: Hillsborough DN 12; 107
Brady, John: Newry DN 3; 82
Brady, Joseph: Kilraghts AM 16; 132
Brady, Patrick: Duneane AM 19; 106, 125
Brady, Patt: Aghagallon AM 21; 21
Brady, Pillip: Currin MN 40; 90
Brady, Rev. Hugh: Laragh CN 40; 41
Brady, Rev. Thomas: Dromara DN 12; 66
Brady-glen (see Bredagh Glen): Moville DL 38; 70
Brae Head hill: Clondermot LY 34; 4, 19, 89, 101
Brae hill: Glenwhirry AM 32; 75
Brae td: Skerry AM 13; 118, 121
Bragan lough: Errigal Truagh MN 40; 120
Bragan lough: Longfield TE 5; 127
Bragan lough: Tydavnet MN 40; 169
Bragan mountain: Errigal Truagh MN 40; 120
Bragan td: Errigal Truagh MN 40; 120
Bragg, Henry: Doagh AM 29; 70, 93
Bragg, Henry: Kilbride AM 29; 139, 150
Bragg, Henry: Templepatrick AM 35; 112, 142, 146
Brague (see also Dromorebreda): Aghaderg DN 12;
    2
Brague school: Aghaderg DN 12; 10–11
Brague td: Aghaderg DN 12; 4
Braid (see Bready): Misc. DL 39; 197

Braid river: Ahoghill AM 23; 4–5, 13, 29–30
Braid river: Ballyclug AM 23; 52–55, 57, 61
Braid river: Connor AM 19; 17, 19
Braid river: Drummaul AM 19; 36
Braid river: Glenwhirry AM 32; 75
Braid river: Kirkinriola AM 23; 88, 91–93, 95–96, 104, 115–18, 120–21
Braid river: Racavan AM 13; 86–90, 93, 97, 99
Braid river: Skerry AM 13; 106, 109–10, 112
Braid river bridge: Kirkinriola AM 23; 104
Braid river bridges: Skerry AM 13; 112
Braid td: Clonleigh DL 39; 12
Braidisland district: Ballynure AM 32; 51–52
Braidisland district: Kilroot AM 26; 61, 71–72
Braidisland district: Raloo AM 32; 125, 130
Braidisland district: Templecorran AM 26; 82, 86, 96, 131
Braidisland ph: Templecorran AM 26; 82
Braidy (see Bready): Misc. DL 39; 186
Brainy Island (see Braidisland): Templecorran AM 26; 96
Bran lough: Clondavaddog DL 38; 3
Bran lough: Killelagh LY 27; 95, 102
Bran lough: Maghera LY 18; 27, 63
Branagan, William: Carrickfergus AM 37; 114
Branan, Arthur: Termoneeny LY 6; 131
Branan, family: Desertlyn LY 31; 43
Branan, James [I]: Termoneeny LY 6; 133
Branan, James [II]: Termoneeny LY 6; 133
Branan, James [III]: Termoneeny LY 6; 133
Branan, John: Termoneeny LY 6; 133, 133
Branan, Rodger: Termoneeny LY 6; 133
Brander, James: Carrickfergus AM 37; 193
Brandight district: Misc. SO 40; 200
Brandon, Mrs: Clogher TE 5; 41
Brandy hill: Donaghmore DL 39; 28
Brangin's Hotel: Kirkinriola AM 23; 95
Branish td: Galloon FH 4; 95
Branken, John: Aghagallon AM 21; 14
Brankin, family: Ballinderry AM 21; 54
Brann, dog named: Ramoan AM 24; 115
Brannan, James: Duneane AM 19; 122
Brannan, James: Island Magee AM 10; 90
Brannan, Mr (Washington): Maghera LY 18; 21
Brannen, Francis: Desertoghill LY 27; 28
Brannen, William: Kilmacteige SO 40; 186
Brannigan, Denis: Newry DN 3; 98, 103
Brannock chapel: Ballymore AH 1; 10, 13
Brannock corn mill: Ballymore AH 1; 5–6, 10, 13
Brannock flax mill: Ballymore AH 1; 6
Brannock Hall: Ballymore AH 1; 9
Brannock school: Ballymore AH 1; 11, 13
Brannock td: Ballymore AH 1; 8–10, 12–13, 15–16, 18
Bransan, Mr: Misc. TE 5; 147

Branter td: Clogher TE 5; 36
Brassington and Gayle, Messrs: Cumber LY 28; 53
Brattin, family: Misc. LY 36; 104
Bratwell td: Dunboe LY 11; 81
Brawkaugh (see Brockagh): Kilmacteige SO 40; 193
Brawley, James: Bovevagh LY 25; 51
Brawley, John: Drumachose LY 9; 132
Brawley, Michael: Bovevagh LY 25; 51
Brawley, Patrick: Cumber LY 28; 75
Brawley, Patt: Bovevagh LY 25; 60
Brawley, Robert: Tamlaght Finlagan LY 25; 105, 107, 116
Bray Land hill: Carrickfergus AM 37; 174
Brayhead school: Tamlaght Finlagan LY 25; 96
Breac, Breasal: Banagher LY 30; 110
Breachy (see Breaghy): Tullyaughnish DL 38; 93
Breaden, family: Carrickfergus AM 37; 93
Breaden, John: Balteagh LY 9; 33
Breadthwaite, family: Lambeg AM 8; 135
Bready spring: Taughboyne DL 39; 150, 188
Bready td: Taughboyne DL 39; 148, 152, 186–87, 192, 195, 197
Breagh church: Tartaraghan AH 1; 118, 120
Breagh school: Drumcree AH 1; 30, 33, 36, 40
Breagh school: Tartaraghan AH 1; 121
Breagh td: Drumcree AH 1; 40
Breagh td: Seagoe AH 1; 107
Breagho (see Breaghoe)
Breaghoe hill: Derryvullan FH 14; 40
Breaghoe hill: Enniskillen FH 4; 43, 49, 74
Breaghoe hill: Magheracross FH 14; 93
Breaghoe td: Enniskillen FH 4; 73, 81
Breaghy brickfields: Tullyaughnish DL 38; 93
Breaghy Head: Lough Swilly DL 38; 120–21
Breaghy td: Donaghmore DL 39; 36
Breaghy td: Tullyaughnish DL 38; 96
Breahead td: Raphoe DL 39; 125
Breakagh (see Breckagh)
Breakagh chapel: Devenish FH 14; 55
Breakagh fort: Devenish FH 14; 55
Breakagh td: Devenish FH 14; 57–58
Breakback hill: Racavan AM 13; 103, 103
Breakcloonta (see Breaklunt): Magheraculmoney FH 14; 113
Breakley td: Aghalurcher FH 4; 16
Breaklunt Barr locality: Magheraculmoney FH 14; 113
Breaklunt Bunn td: Magheraculmoney FH 14; 113
Breaklunt td: Magheraculmoney FH 14; 111–12
Breaky (see Breaghy): Tullyaughnish DL 38; 96
Breandrum td: Aghavea FH 4; 23
Breandrum td: Enniskillen FH 4; 82
Breannan Barr td: Magheraculmoney FH 14; 113
Breannan Bunn td: Magheraculmoney FH 14; 113

Breason, Bernard: Tamlaght Finlagan LY 25; 109–10

Breathwait, family: Glenavy AM 21; 86

Brecan, St: Clondermot LY 34; 47, 75

Brecan, St: Faughanvale LY 36; 50

Brecart bog: Duneane AM 19; 111

Brecart Cottage: Duneane AM 19; 101, 117

Brecart td: Duneane AM 19; 98, 101, 111, 113, 117, 123

Brecart tower: Duneane AM 19; 116–17

Breccagh Lower mill: Manorhamilton Union LM 40; 50

Breckagh (Breackagh) td: Ballymoney AM 16; 25

Breckagh cove: Ballymoney AM 16; 24

Breckaugh chapel: Skerry AM 13; 107, 111, 113

Breckaugh td: Skerry AM 13; 113

Breckenhill House: Rashee AM 32; 136

Breckfield (see Brickfield): Killea and Taughboyne DL 39; 79

Breda corn mill: Moville DL 38; 68

Breda stream: Moville DL 38; 70, 73

Bredagh Glen td: Moville DL 38; 68, 70

Bredin, family: Lambeg AM 8; 135

Bredin, Rev. John: Lambeg AM 8; 136

Bree fort: Muckno MN 40; 166

Bree td: Muckno MN 40; 162

Bree, Andrew: Tamlaght TE 20; 75

Breedin, family: Ballinderry AM 21; 54

Breen Castle: Culfeightrin AM 24; 69

Breen hill: Armoy AM 24; 1–3

Breen school: Armoy AM 24; 6

Breen td: Convoy DL 39; 19

Breeson, Michael: Banagher LY 30; 50, 90–91

Breeson, William: Artrea LY 6; 35

Breffney (see Breffni): Manorhamilton Union LM 40; 51

Breffni district: Manorhamilton Union LM 40; 51

Bremner, Priv.: Errigal Keerogue TE 20; 53, 56

Brenan, family: Templecorran AM 26; 119

Brennagh, Mrs William: Ballinderry AM 21; 52

Brennagh, William: Ballinderry AM 21; 52

Brennan, Anne: Carrickfergus AM 37; 129

Brennan, family: Island Magee AM 10; 70

Brennan, family: Templecorran AM 26; 117

Brennan, Jane: Carrickfergus AM 37; 123

Brennan, Joseph: Loughguile AM 13; 76

Brennan, Mr (Kinnegalliagh): Glenwhirry AM 32; 74

Brennan, Mrs: Hillsborough DN 12; 106

Brennan, Rev.: Aughnamullen MN 40; 71

Brennan, William: Island Magee AM 10; 94

Brenturk (see Dunturkcy): Ballynure AM 32; 34

Brereton, family: Blaris AM 8; 21

Brereton, Henry: Hillsborough DN 12; 106

Brereton, William: Hillsborough DN 12; 106

Bresagh church: Tullynakill DN 7; 123

Bresagh corn mill: Tullynakill DN 7; 123

Bresagh flax mill: Tullynakill DN 7; 123

Bresagh meeting house: Saintfield DN 7; 114

Bresagh meeting house: Tullynakill DN 7; 123

Bresagh school: Tullynakill DN 7; 123

Bresagh td: Saintfield DN 7; 114, 118

Bresagh td: Tullynakill DN 7; 122

Breslie bay: Lough Swilly DL 38; 107

Bretherton, Peter: Carrickfergus AM 37; 194

Brett, Patrick: Kilmacteige SO 40; 186, 194

Brevolaghan, family: Maghera LY 18; 24, 48

Brewster, J.: Drumachose LY 9; 104

Brewster, John: Macosquin LY 22; 84, 116

Brian Bradagh's Cash locality: Kilrea LY 27; 113

Brian, John: Termonamongan TE 5; 144

Brianlagne (see Bryantang): Carrickfergus AM 37; 93

Briant, John: Blaris AM 8; 25

Briantange (see Bryantang): Carrickfergus AM 37; 174

Brice, Charles: Island Magee AM 10; 42

Brice, Edward (Jnr): Island Magee AM 10; 42

Brice, Edward (Snr): Island Magee AM 10; 42

Brice, family: Carnmoney AM 2; 76

Brice, family: Kilroot AM 26; 73–74

Brice, family: Templecorran AM 26; 11

Brice, Mr: Ballyphilip DN 7; 8

Brice, Randall: Templecorran AM 26; 117–18

Brice, Rev. Edward: Island Magee AM 10; 45

Brice, Rev. Edward: Kilroot AM 26; 68–69, 73, 75

Brice, Rev. Edward: Templecorran AM 26; 11, 85–86, 97, 101, 107–08, 112, 117–19, 128

Brice, Robert: Island Magee AM 10; 42

Brice, Robert: Kilroot AM 26; 73

Brice, Robert: Templecorran AM 26; 108, 117–18

Brick Kiln bridge: Agivey LY 22; 40, 43

Brickfield district: Killea and Taughboyne DL 39; 79, 87

Brickfield school: Blaris AM 8; 79

Brickfield Sunday school: Blaris AM 8; 83

Brickkilns quarry: Clondermot LY 34; 129

Brickkilns td: Clondermot LY 34; 38, 57, 72, 108, 112, 114, 122, 129

Brickkilns wood: Clondermot LY 34; 122

Brickland td: Aghaderg DN 12; 8

Bricks hotel: Clondermot LY 34; 83

Bridge End bleach green: Tullyaughnish DL 38; 84–85, 89–90

Bridge End bridge: Tullyaughnish DL 38; 90

Bridge End flour mill: Tullyaughnish DL 38; 84–85, 89

Bridge End Hill village: Misc. DN 17; 117

Bridge End Lodge: Tullyaughnish DL 38; 89

Bridge End td: Tullyaughnish DL 38; 97

Bridge End wood: Tullyaughnish DL 38; 86

Bridge, Pheenix: Blaris AM 8; 36

Bridge, Rev. Ralph: Blaris AM 8; 9, 23, 32, 60–62, 83

Bridge, Rev. Ralph: Blaris DN 12; 35, 45, 48–49

Bridgend school: Ahoghill AM 23; 41, 46, 48

Bridgend school: Ballymartin AM 2; 18

Bridgend Sunday school: Ahoghill AM 23; 46

Bridges, John: Coleraine LY 33; 64–65

Bridges, John: Templecorran AM 26; 123

Bridget, Andrew: Tamlaght TE 20; 116

Bridget, St: Ballyclug AM 23; 63

Bridget, St: Ballyscullion AM 19; 10

Bridget, St: Carrickfergus AM 37; 80, 171

Bridget, St: Down DN 17; 43, 60–61

Bridget, St: Duneane AM 19; 106, 118

Bridget, St: Faughanvale LY 36; 51, 62

Bridget, St: Finvoy AM 23; 73

Bridget, St: Kilbride AM 29; 140, 146, 153

Bridget, St: Maghera LY 18; 69

Bridget, St: Magheramesk AM 21; 123

Bridget, William: Tamlaght TE 20; 81, 118, 121

Bridget's graveyard (see also Kille Brieda): Artrea LY 6; 25

Bridgetown meeting house: Skirts of Urney and Ardstraw TE 5; 138

Bridgetown td: Skirts of Urney and Ardstraw TE 5; 138

Bridle Fort hill: Drumgath DN 3; 19

Brien, J.: Aughnamullen MN 40; 75

Brien, J.: Ematris MN 40; 115

Brien, John: Inishmacsaint FH 14; 76

Briens, family: Aghalee AM 21; 36

Briens, John: Devenish FH 14; 48–50, 53, 55–56, 58–59

Brigadie House: Kirkinriola AM 23; 91, 104, 119, 121

Briggs rocks: Templecorran AM 26; 91

Briggs, family: Magheramesk AM 21; 124

Briggs, J.: Newry DN 3; 100

Briggs, Thomas: Carrickfergus AM 37; 194

Briggs, Widow: Hillsborough DN 12; 107

Brigh meeting house: Ballyclog TE 20; 15

Bright Castle: Bright DN 17; 33

Bright church: Bright DN 17; 33, 36

Bright graveyard: Bright DN 17; 36

Bright ph: Ballee DN 17; 15

Bright ph: Down DN 17; 51

Bright ph: Inch DN 17; 75

Bright ph: Misc. DN 17; 120, 128

Bright school: Bright DN 17; 33, 36

Bright school: Misc. DN 17; 122

Bright td: Bright DN 17; 33–35

Brigs, family: Blaris AM 8; 21

Brillaghan, Rev. Patrick: Killelagh LY 27; 102

Brin lough: Templecarn DL 39; 157

Briney, Joseph: Clogher TE 5; 29

Brinson, Joseph: Tomregan FH 4; 129

Brioselunagh fort: Manorhamilton Union LM 40; 52

Brishey (Briskey) td: Dungiven LY 15; 22, 27, 46, 51, 61

Brishey td: Banagher LY 30; 22

Brisk lough: Derryvullan FH 14; 31

Brisk lough: Magheraculmoney FH 14; 103

Briskenagh td: Currin MN 40; 92

Brisland, Patrick: Donaghmore DL 39; 40

Brison hill: Taughboyne DL 39; 148

Brison, family: Kilbride AM 29; 152

Brison, Harpur: Drummaul AM 19; 90

Bristol (England): Cumber LY 28; 58

Bristol: Enniskillen FH 4; 61

Bristol, Earl (Bishop of Derry): Tamlaght Finlagan LY 25; 68–69, 100

Bristol, Earl: Ballyscullion LY 6; 45

Bristol, Earl of (Bishop of Derry): Cumber LY 28; 1

Bristol, Earl of (Bishop of Derry): Faughanvale LY 36; 6

Bristol, Earl of: Dunboe LY 11; 58

Bristol, family: Agivey LY 22; 41–42

Bristol, Lord (Bishop of Derry): Banagher LY 30; 28, 72, 115

Bristol, Lord (Bishop of Derry): Coleraine LY 33; 98

Bristol, Lord: Aghanloo LY 11; 1, 3, 8

Bristol, Lord: Ballyscullion LY 6; 48–49, 51, 65, 72

Bristol, Lord: Dunboe LY 11; 44, 46–47, 49, 52–54, 58, 60, 65–66

Bristol, Lord: Magherafelt LY 6; 89

Bristol, Lord: Magilligan LY 11; 86, 103, 121

Bristow, Dr: Blaris AM 8; 52

Bristow, Mr: Antrim AM 29; 20–21

Bristow, Rev. William: Agivey LY 22; 43

Bristow, William: Glynn AM 26; 12, 14

Brit, Michael: Kilmacteige SO 40; 193

Britain, Edward: Killead AM 35; 52

Britain, Neil [I]: Maghera LY 18; 61

Britain, Neil [II]: Maghera LY 18; 81

Britan, John: Maghera LY 18; 60

British (Brittas) td: Killead AM 35; 22, 26, 35, 50–51

British lough: Killead AM 35; 49

British Museum: Templepatrick AM 35; 130, 150

British school: Killead AM 35; 53

British td: Muckamore AM 35; 69

Broad field: Muckamore AM 35; 80

Broad Meadow locality: Enniskillen FH 4; 50

Broad stone: Finvoy AM 23; 68, 73, 76–78

Broad water: Aghalee AM 21; 26

Broadhurst (Sussex): Clondermot LY 34; 41, 45

Broadisland (see Braidisland): Templecorran AM 26; 82

Broadlee td: Misc. DL 39; 198

Broadlee td: Raphoe DL 39; 125

Broadpath td: Convoy DL 39; 19

Broagh bleach green: Termoneeny LY 6; 129

Broagh bleach mill: Termoneeny LY 6; 129

Broagh district: Misc. AM 10; 130

Broagh forts: Termoneeny LY 6; 131

Broagh td: Termoneeny LY 6; 124, 126, 129, 132–33

Broaghanore (see Broughanore): Killagan AM 23; 84

Broaghderagh (see Broughderg): Kildress TE 20; 59

Broaghderrig td: Laragh CN 40; 40

Broaidh, Bishop: Magilligan LY 11; 105

Brobrohan td: Aghalurcher FH 4; 14

Brock burn: Coleraine LY 33; 55

Brockaboy (see Brockaghboy): Errigal LY 27; 44

Brockagh (see Breckaugh): Skerry AM 13; 111

Brockagh bogs: Errigal LY 27; 55

Brockagh chapel: Kilteevoge DL 39; 111

Brockagh hill: Cumber LY 28; 45

Brockagh hill: Errigal LY 27; 73

Brockagh hill: Kilcronaghan LY 31; 69

Brockagh old houses: Cumber LY 28; 41

Brockagh quarry: Errigal LY 27; 89

Brockagh Reily (see Brackaghgreilly): Maghera LY 18; 45

Brockagh school: Cumber LY 28; 75

Brockagh td: Cleenish FH 14; 29

Brockagh td: Cumber LY 28; 47, 49, 60–61, 95, 99–100, 104, 107, 109

Brockagh td: Errigal LY 27; 39, 45, 56, 60, 66, 71, 80, 85, 89, 92

Brockagh td: Kilmacteige SO 40; 189

Brockagh td: Kilteevoge DL 39; 114

Brockagh td: Misc. DL 39; 195

Brockagh village: Kilmacteige SO 40; 193

Brockagh wood: Cumber LY 28; 100

Brockaghboy (Brochaboy) td: Errigal LY 27; 44, 66, 72, 80, 85, 89, 92

Brockaghboy bogs: Errigal LY 27; 55

Brockaghboy fort [I]: Errigal LY 27; 43, 71–72

Brockaghboy fort [II]: Errigal LY 27; 43, 72

Brockaghboy fort [III]: Errigal LY 27; 43, 72

Brockaghboy fort [IV]: Errigal LY 27; 43, 72

Brockaghboy fort [V]: Errigal LY 27; 72

Brockaghboy freestone quarry: Errigal LY 27; 89

Brockaghboy giant's grave: Errigal LY 27; 78

Brockaghboy giant's grave: Macosquin LY 22; 98

Brockaghboy lime quarry: Errigal LY 27; 89

Brockanbane td: Banagher LY 30; 100

Brockaogh (see Brockagh): Cumber LY 28; 60

Brockaugh td: Taughboyne DL 39; 148, 152

Brockish bay: Coleraine LY 33; 101

Brocklamont cave [I]: Ahoghill AM 23; 33

Brocklamont cave [II]: Ahoghill AM 23; 33

Brocklamont td: Ahoghill AM 23; 12, 37

Brodera (East Indies): Newry DN 3; 68

Broderick, Allen: Clondermot LY 34; 90

Brodley, Robert: Longfield TE 5; 128

Brody Glen (see Bredagh Glen): Moville DL 38; 68

Brogher mountain: Enniskillen FH 4; 43, 72

Brogher priory: Enniskillen FH 4; 71

Brogher td: Enniskillen FH 4; 71, 82

Broglasco (Burglasgow) td: Tamlaght Finlagan LY 25; 72–74, 93, 119, 122

Broglasco bog: Tamlaght Finlagan LY 25; 65, 113, 115

Broharris (Breheris) td: Tamlaght Finlagan LY 25; 72–74, 93, 119, 122

Broharris bridge: Tamlaght Finlagan LY 25; 122

Broharris school: Tamlaght Finlagan LY 25; 75, 77

Broighter td: Tamlaght Finlagan LY 25; 72–74, 93

Broken bridge: Killanny MN 40; 132

Brolagh hill: Inishmacsaint FH 14; 71

Brolagh td: Inishmacsaint FH 14; 70

Brolley, Patrick: Bovevagh LY 25; 33–35

Brolley, Rev. Charles: Bovevagh LY 25; 35

Brolly, Robert: Killowen LY 33; 159

Broncar, Henry: Clondermot LY 34; 67–68

Brook bridge: Coleraine LY 33; 91, 129–30

Brook Hall demesne: Ballyrashane LY 22; 61

Brook Hall House: Aghanloo LY 11; 33

Brook Hall House: Ballyrashane LY 22; 47–48, 55–56, 56

Brook Hall House: Coleraine LY 33; 63–64, 131

Brook Hall House: Dungiven LY 15; 99, 106

Brook Hall House: Tullyaughnish DL 38; 89

Brook, Catherine: Coleraine LY 33; 145

Brook, Col.: Kilbroney DN 3; 31

Brook, Hugh: Coleraine LY 33; 145

Brook, James: Clondermot LY 34; 6

Brooke, Arthur: Aghalurcher FH 4; 4, 7, 10, 13–14

Brooke, Arthur: Aghavea FH 4; 18, 20, 22–23

Brooke, Basil: Donegal DL 39; 45, 48

Brooke, Basill: Clondermot LY 34; 54

Brooke, family: Aghalurcher FH 4; 7

Brooke, family: Aghavea FH 4; 19, 21

Brooke, family: Donegal DL 39; 48

Brooke, H.V.: Drumkeeran FH 14; 67

Brooke, H.V.: Tullyaughnish DL 38; 89

Brooke, Henry: Aghalurcher FH 4; 3, 5, 7–8, 10

Brooke, Henry: Aghavea FH 4; 19–20, 22

Brooke, Lady: Aghavea FH 4; 20, 24

Brooke, Mr (Lough Eske): Killymard DL 39; 96–99

Brooke, Mr: Blaris AM 8; 84

Brooke, Mrs: Tullyaughnish DL 38; 97

Brooke, Rev. Butler: Trory FH 14; 125, 128–29

Brooke, Thomas: Tullyaughnish DL 38; 96–97

Brookeborough: Aghalurcher FH 4; 5, 7–8, 10, 13, 13

Brookeborough: Aghavea FH 4; 18–19, 21–23, 25

Brookeborough: Tydavnet MN 40; 170, 172

Brookeborough chapel: Aghavea FH 4; 20

Brookeborough church: Aghavea FH 4; 20

Brookeborough court house: Aghavea FH 4; 19

Brookeborough dispensary: Aghavea FH 4; 22

Brookeborough manor: Misc. FH 4; 133

Brookeborough market house: Aghavea FH 4; 20

Brookeborough meeting house: Aghavea FH 4; 20

Brookeborough pottery: Aghavea FH 4; 23

Brookeborough school: Aghavea FH 4; 19–20, 22

Brookeborough Townparks td: Aghavea FH 4; 23

Brookfield hill: Killesher FH 14; 81, 84

Brookfield House: Kilbride AM 29; 138, 150, 153

Brookfield school: Magheramesk AM 21; 128–30

Brookfield spinning mill: Kilbride AM 29; 139, 151, 153

Brookhall (see Brook Hall)

Brookhill demesne: Magheragall AM 21; 100, 103

Brookhill demesne fort [I]: Magheragall AM 21; 104

Brookhill demesne fort [II]: Magheragall AM 21; 104

Brookhill demesne fort [III]: Magheragall AM 21; 104

Brookhill demesne fort [IV]: Magheragall AM 21; 104

Brookhill demesne fort [V]: Magheragall AM 21; 104

Brookhill demesne fort [VI]: Magheragall AM 21; 104

Brookhill demesne forts: Magheragall AM 21; 100

Brookhill giant's grave: Magheragall AM 21; 100

Brookhill graveyard: Magheragall AM 21; 100

Brookhill House: Ballinderry AM 21; 48–49

Brookhill House: Blaris AM 8; 3–4, 51, 87–88

Brookhill House: Blaris DN 12; 33

Brookhill House: Magheragall AM 21; 99–101, 103, 109

Brookhill old castle: Magheragall AM 21; 100

Brookhill old church: Magheragall AM 21; 100

Brookmire, Betty: Templepatrick AM 35; 152

Brookmire, Isabella: Templepatrick AM 35; 152

Brookmire, Jane: Templepatrick AM 35; 152

Brookmire, John: Templepatrick AM 35; 152

Brookmire, Margaret: Templepatrick AM 35; 152

Brookmire, Martha: Templepatrick AM 35; 152

Brooks, Widow: Ballymoney AM 16; 17

Broom fort: Desertoghill LY 27; 27, 33

Broombeg cross: Ramoan AM 24; 125

Broombeg grave: Ramoan AM 24; 106

Broombeg standing stone [I]: Ramoan AM 24; 119

Broombeg standing stone [II]: Ramoan AM 24; 119

Broombeg td: Ramoan AM 24; 113

Broombeg wood: Ramoan AM 24; 92

Broomfield House: Donaghmoyne MN 40; 107, 111

Broomfield House: Killanny MN 40; 134

Broomfield House: Kilmore AH 1; 65

Broomfield police station: Donaghmoyne MN 40; 108

Broomhedge: Magheramesk AM 21; 118, 126

Broomhedge chapel (see also Broughmore): Blaris AM 8; 10, 29

Broomhedge corn mill: Magheramesk AM 21; 119

Broomhedge school: Blaris AM 8; 54, 78, 82

Broomhedge Sunday school: Blaris AM 8; 83

Broomhidge (see Broomhedge)

Broommore caves: Ramoan AM 24; 116

Broommore fort [I]: Ramoan AM 24; 116

Broommore fort [II]: Ramoan AM 24; 91, 116

Broommore td: Ramoan AM 24; 115–16, 119, 125

Broommount demesne: Aghalee AM 21; 28

Broommount demesne fort: Aghalee AM 21; 35–36

Broommount House: Aghalee AM 21; 26, 29, 31–32, 37

Broomore (see Broommore): Ramoan AM 24; 91

Broomquarter td: Misc. DN 17; 125

Brosney td: Donaghedy TE 5; 91

Broster, Alexander: Dunboe LY 11; 80

Broster, Jane: Dunboe LY 11; 81

Broster, Mary: Dunboe LY 11; 81

Broster, Thomas: Dunboe LY 11; 81

Brostor, Ann: Clondermot LY 34; 81

Brostor, Mary: Clondermot LY 34; 81

Brothwick, John: Kilroot AM 26; 78

Brougham, Mr: Raymoghy DL 39; 144

Broughanlea cave: Culfeightrin AM 24; 76

Broughanlea cross: Culfeightrin AM 24; 55

Broughanlea fort: Culfeightrin AM 24; 52

Broughanlea graveyard: Culfeightrin AM 24; 55

Broughanlea td: Culfeightrin AM 24; 45, 76

Broughanore (Broghanore) td: Killagan AM 23; 79–80, 84

Broughanore cove: Killagan AM 23; 87

Broughanore graveyard: Killagan AM 23; 80, 84, 86

Broughanore hill: Killagan AM 23; 79–81

Broughatten td: Ballymascanlan LH 40; 55

Broughclone standing stone: Ahoghill AM 23; 35

Broughclone td: Ahoghill AM 23; 40

Broughderg hill: Aghavea FH 4; 17

Broughderg river: Kildress TE 20; 59, 61

Broughderg river: Lissan TE 20; 69

Broughderg td: Aghavea FH 4; 23

Broughderg td: Lissan TE 20; 69

Broughdom (see Broughdown): Ahoghill AM 23; 44

Broughdown fort: Ahoghill AM 23; 33

Broughdown school: Ahoghill AM 23; 44

Broughgammon bog: Ballintoy AM 24; 31
Broughgammon cave: Ballintoy AM 24; 31
Broughmore cave: Culfeightrin AM 24; 52
Broughmore chapel: Blaris AM 8; 10, 29
Broughmore fort [I]: Blaris AM 8; 19
Broughmore fort [II]: Blaris AM 8; 19
Broughmore hamlet: Culfeightrin AM 24; 52
Broughmore preaching house: Blaris AM 8; 29
Broughmore school: Blaris AM 8; 18
Broughmore td: Blaris AM 8; 19, 48, 77, 82
Broughmore td: Blaris DN 12; 28
Broughmore td: Culfeightrin AM 24; 78
Broughshane: Ballyclug AM 23; 53, 57, 60, 65–66
Broughshane: Ballycor AM 32; 3–4, 8–9
Broughshane: Connor AM 19; 30
Broughshane: Doagh AM 29; 60–61, 63, 71, 86
Broughshane: Drummaul AM 19; 70–71
Broughshane: Glenwhirry AM 32; 75, 77, 79
Broughshane: Kilwaughter AM 10; 107, 110
Broughshane: Kirkinriola AM 23; 90–91, 104,
    119–21
Broughshane: Racavan AM 13; 87, 90, 95, 97
Broughshane: Rashee AM 32; 137, 137
Broughshane: Skerry AM 13; 107
Broughshane beetling mill: Racavan AM 13; 92, 98
Broughshane bridge: Racavan AM 13; 92
Broughshane Castle: Racavan AM 13; 101
Broughshane church: Racavan AM 13; 87, 91, 97
Broughshane court house: Racavan AM 13; 88,
    97–98
Broughshane dispensary: Racavan AM 13; 88, 93,
    97–99
Broughshane dispensary: Skerry AM 13; 112
Broughshane flax mill: Racavan AM 13; 92, 98
Broughshane Lower linen factory: Racavan AM 13;
    99
Broughshane Lower td: Racavan AM 13; 86, 89
Broughshane market house: Racavan AM 13; 88,
    91, 97–98
Broughshane meeting house: Racavan AM 13; 87,
    91, 94, 97
Broughshane paper mill: Racavan AM 13; 92, 98
Broughshane racecourse: Racavan AM 13; 88, 95
Broughshane road bridge: Glenwhirry AM 32; 77
Broughshane school: Racavan AM 13; 88, 96, 100
Broughshane spinning mill: Racavan AM 13; 92, 98
Broughshane Upper td: Racavan AM 13; 86, 89, 95
Broughten, Mr: Enniskillen FH 4; 84
Broughton (Scotland): Killymard DL 39; 100
Broughton, Lt D.: Donagh DL 38; 31
Brown (ne McAvraghan), man named: Cumber LY
    28; 43, 54, 83
Brown bog: Annaclone DN 12; 14
Brown bog: Seagoe AH 1; 105
Brown George rock: Lough Swilly DL 38; 99

Brown Know (see Brownknowe): Tullyaughnish DL
    38; 86
Brown moss: Tullyrusk AM 21; 132
Brown mountain: Clondermot LY 34; 1, 17, 99
Brown, A.G.: Carnmoney AM 2; 46, 48, 81, 84–85,
    90, 93
Brown, A.W.: Carrickfergus AM 37; 110
Brown, Alexander [I]: Ballyaghran LY 33; 27
Brown, Alexander [II]: Ballyaghran LY 33; 28
Brown, Alixander: Drumachose LY 9; 134
Brown, Andrew: Aghadowey LY 22; 26
Brown, Andrew: Artrea LY 6; 37
Brown, Andrew: Dunluce AM 16; 118
Brown, Ann: Tamlaght TE 20; 76
Brown, Capt.: Bright DN 17; 35–36
Brown, Capt.: Down DN 17; 51
Brown, Capt.: Kilmore DN 17; 88
Brown, David: Ballymoney AM 16; 24–25
Brown, Ellen: Kilwaughter AM 10; 122
Brown, family: Armoy AM 24; 6
Brown, family: Artrea LY 6; 14
Brown, family: Blaris DN 12; 30
Brown, family: Carnmoney AM 2; 76
Brown, family: Carrickfergus AM 37; 93
Brown, family: Culfeightrin AM 24; 59
Brown, family: Cumber LY 28; 54
Brown, family: Derryaghy AM 8; 103
Brown, family: Dunluce AM 16; 117
Brown, family: Dunsfort DN 17; 68
Brown, family: Island Magee AM 10; 29, 43, 70, 86
Brown, family: Killagan AM 23; 84
Brown, family: Kilraghts AM 16; 130
Brown, family: Maghera LY 18; 24, 48
Brown, family: Magherafelt LY 6; 95
Brown, family: Magheragall AM 21; 99
Brown, family: Ramoan AM 24; 107
Brown, family: Templepatrick AM 35; 118, 145
Brown, Francis: Skerry AM 13; 120
Brown, George: Culfeightrin AM 24; 78
Brown, George: Newry DN 3; 81
Brown, Henry: Ballywillin LY 33; 41
Brown, Henry: Faughanvale LY 36; 24, 35, 66
Brown, Hugh: Island Magee AM 10; 95
Brown, Isabella: Kilraghts AM 16; 132
Brown, J.: Newtownards DN 7; 112
Brown, J.G.: Muckamore AM 35; 77–78
Brown, J.H.: Bovevagh LY 25; 4, 21, 57
Brown, James: Ahoghill AM 23; 35
Brown, James: Ballycor AM 32; 7
Brown, James: Ballylinny AM 32; 29
Brown, James: Dunaghy AM 13; 22
Brown, James: Magheradrool DN 17; 106
Brown, James: Tamlaght O'Crilly LY 18; 141
Brown, James: Tamlaght TE 20; 107, 132–33

Brown, Jane (nee Caldwell): Ballyrobert AM 2; 23–24

Brown, Jane: Kilraghts AM 16; 132

Brown, John: Ballyhalbert DN 7; 5

Brown, John: Ballywillin LY 33; 51

Brown, John: Blaris DN 12; 40

Brown, John: Carnmoney AM 2; 84

Brown, John: Clondermot LY 34; 78–79

Brown, John: Culfeightrin AM 24; 80

Brown, John: Donaghcloney DN 12; 58

Brown, John: Drummaul AM 19; 82–83

Brown, John: Faughanvale LY 36; 30

Brown, John: Hillsborough DN 12; 106

Brown, John: Island Magee AM 10; 103

Brown, John: Kilraghts AM 16; 132

Brown, John: Kilrea LY 27; 129

Brown, John: Magherafelt LY 6; 111

Brown, John: Tamlaght Finlagan LY 25; 112

Brown, Jonathon: Drumbeg AM 8; 122, 128

Brown, Joseph: Artrea LY 6; 35

Brown, Joseph: Killead AM 35; 37

Brown, Joseph: Maghera LY 18; 64

Brown, Joseph: Tamlaght Finlagan LY 25; 108

Brown, Margaret: Carnmoney AM 2; 102

Brown, Margaret: Glynn AM 26; 44

Brown, Mary (Jnr): Kilwaughter AM 10; 122

Brown, Mary (Snr): Kilwaughter AM 10; 122

Brown, Mary: Ballywillin LY 33; 51

Brown, Mary: Carrickfergus AM 37; 130

Brown, Miss: Connor AM 19; 21

Brown, Mr (Waterside): Clondermot LY 34; 43, 98

Brown, Mr: Annaclone DN 12; 14

Brown, Mr: Banagher LY 30; 31

Brown, Mr: Carrickfergus AM 37; 157

Brown, Mr: Dungiven LY 15; 10

Brown, Mr: Kilmegan DN 3; 57

Brown, Mr: Kirkinriola AM 23; 106, 115

Brown, Mr [I]: Clondermot LY 34; 48

Brown, Mr [II]: Clondermot LY 34; 120

Brown, Mrs (Waterside): Clondermot LY 34; 8, 43, 98

Brown, Mrs D.: Ballymoney AM 16; 17

Brown, Nancy: Ballywillin LY 33; 51

Brown, Neil: Magherafelt LY 6; 105, 107

Brown, Patt: Culfeightrin AM 24; 49, 52, 78, 81

Brown, R.J.: Newry DN 3; 67

Brown, Rev. (Draperstown): Enniskeen CN 40; 30

Brown, Rev.: Ballinderry AM 21; 50

Brown, Rev.: Cumber LY 28; 19, 84

Brown, Rev. Dr: Drumgoon CN 40; 6, 8

Brown, Rev. J.S.: Magheragall AM 21; 99

Brown, Rev. James: Desertoghill LY 27; 3–4, 10–11, 13, 17

Brown, Rev. James: Errigal LY 27; 46, 52, 63–64

Brown, Rev. John: Aghadowey LY 22; 5, 12–13, 15–16, 22

Brown, Rev. John: Ballinderry AM 21; 46

Brown, Rev. John: Ballyscullion AM 19; 8

Brown, Rev. John: Desertoghill LY 27; 3

Brown, Rev. Solomon: Magherafelt LY 6; 99

Brown, Rev. William: Kilcronaghan LY 31; 72, 79–80, 82, 88

Brown, Rev. William: Misc. LY 31; 128, 136

Brown, Robert: Aghadowey LY 22; 27–28

Brown, Robert: Kilrea LY 27; 129

Brown, Robert: Kilwaughter AM 10; 122

Brown, Robert: Tamlaght O'Crilly LY 18; 124, 131

Brown, Samuel: Carrickfergus AM 37; 111

Brown, Samuel: Coleraine LY 33; 72

Brown, Samuel: Derrykeighan AM 16; 91

Brown, Samuel: Newry DN 3; 67

Brown, Samuel: Raloo AM 32; 117, 129

Brown, Sarah: Ballywillin LY 33; 51

Brown, Thomas: Aghadowey LY 22; 38

Brown, Thomas: Magherafelt LY 6; 108

Brown, Tom: Tamlaght TE 20; 91

Brown, Warnock and Co., Messrs: Carrickfergus AM 37; 57, 139

Brown, William: Artrea LY 6; 27, 34–35

Brown, William: Blaris DN 12; 41

Brown, William: Clondermot LY 34; 78–80

Brown, William: Cumber LY 28; 56

Brown, William: Derryaghy AM 8; 91

Brown, William: Drumachose LY 9; 132

Brown, William: Dungiven LY 15; 69

Brown, William: Magherafelt LY 6; 111

Brown's bay: Island Magee AM 10; 17, 31, 43, 89

Brown's bay: Mevagh DL 38; 62

Brown's Bay Sunday school: Island Magee AM 10; 98

Brown's bleach mills: Magheradrool DN 17; 103

Brown's Bray fort: Tamlaght Finlagan LY 25; 111

Brown's Bray gravel pit: Tamlaght Finlagan LY 25; 111

Brown's Bray hill: Tamlaght Finlagan LY 25; 111

Brown's cairn: Island Magee AM 10; 14

Brown's day school: Island Magee AM 10; 96

Brown's hill: Island Magee AM 10; 71

Brown's hotel.: Drumachose LY 9; 129

Browndod altars: Donegore AM 29; 115–16, 118, 125, 127–28

Browndod enclosures: Donegore AM 29; 116–18, 127–28

Browndod fort: Donegore AM 29; 122, 125, 127–28

Browndod fort: Killead AM 35; 33

Browndod hill: Donegore AM 29; 101, 104, 115–19, 122, 125, 127–28

Browndod hill: Kilbride AM 29; 154

Browndod standing stone [I]: Donegore AM 29; 118–19, 127

Browndod standing stone [II]: Donegore AM 29; 118–19

Browndod standing stone [III]: Donegore AM 29; 119

Browndod standing stones: Donegore AM 29; 128

Browndod td: Donegore AM 29; 101–02, 115, 131, 133

Browndod td: Glynn AM 26; 30

Browndod td: Inver AM 26; 49, 52

Browndod tumuli: Donegore AM 29; 118, 127

Browndod tumuli: Kilbride AM 29; 154

Browne, David: Duneane AM 19; 125

Browne, Elizabeth: Ballyscullion LY 6; 57

Browne, family: Carrickfergus AM 37; 179

Browne, family: Cumber LY 28; 73, 76

Browne, John: Ballyscullion LY 6; 57

Browne, John: Cumber LY 28; 4–5, 7–9, 12, 18, 22, 73, 76, 83, 86–87, 90, 110–11

Browne, John: Killead AM 35; 53

Browne, Miss: Coleraine LY 33; 72

Browne, Mr: Urney DL 39; 181

Browne, Mrs: Newry DN 3; 104

Browne, Rev. Alexander: Donegore AM 29; 129

Browne, Rev. John: Raymoghy DL 39; 133

Browne, Rev. Solomon: Magherafelt LY 6; 98

Browne, Thomas: Banagher LY 30; 32, 112

Browne, Thomas: Killead AM 35; 53

Brownhall estate: Drumhome DL 39; 58

Brownhall estate: Inishkeel DL 39; 70

Brownhall estate: Killymard DL 39; 100

Brownhall river: Drumhome DL 39; 61

Brownhall td: Conwal DL 39; 26

Brownhall wood: Drumhome DL 39; 59

Browning, family: Enniskillen FH 4; 58

Brownknowe school: Tullyaughnish DL 38; 92

Brownknowe td: Tullyaughnish DL 38; 86, 97

Brownlee, Alexander: Blaris AM 8; 69

Brownlee, Alexander: Blaris DN 12; 46, 50

Brownlee, John: Blaris DN 12; 46, 50

Brownlee, Olivia: Moira DN 12; 120

Brownlee, Robert: Carrickfergus AM 37; 125

Brownlees, Elizabeth: Ahoghill AM 23; 49

Brownlees, family: Shilvodan AM 19; 136

Brownlough (see Brownlow): Drumcree AH 1; 36

Brownlow, Archibald: Ballymoney AM 16; 16

Brownlow, Charles: Drumcree AH 1; 32–33, 36–41

Brownlow, Charles: Lough Neagh AM 21; 94

Brownlow, Charles: Montiaghs AH 1; 90–93

Brownlow, Charles: Seagoe AH 1; 103, 105–10

Brownlow, Charles: Shankill AH 1; 113, 115

Brownlow, Charles: Shankill DN 12; 139

Brownlow, family: Shankill AH 1; 111

Brownlow, Lady C.: Cumber LY 28; 76

Brownlow, Mr: Leckpatrick TE 5; 119–22, 124–25

Brownlow, Mrs: Kilbroney DN 3; 35

Brownlow, Rev. Charles: Magheross MN 40; 149

Brownlow, Rev. Francis: Clondermot LY 34; 78

Brownlow, Rev. Francis: Cumber LY 28; 9, 11, 19, 75–77, 83, 85–86, 88, 90, 109, 115

Brownlow, Rev. Francis: Faughanvale LY 36; 40

Brownlow, Rev. Francis: Leckpatrick TE 5; 117

Brownlow, Rev. James: Magheracloone MN 40; 141

Brownlow, Rev. John: Ballynascreen LY 31; 6, 14, 16–17

Brownlow's Derry manor: Seagoe AH 1; 104

Brownoe (see Brownknowe): Tullyaughnish DL 38; 97

Browster, James: Macosquin LY 22; 102

Broxton, family: Desertlyn LY 31; 42

Bruce, Andrew: Carrickfergus AM 37; 156–57

Bruce, Andrew: Island Magee AM 10; 98

Bruce, Capt.: Maghera LY 18; 72

Bruce, David (King of Scotland): Island Magee AM 10; 62

Bruce, David: Carnmoney AM 2; 72

Bruce, David: Carrickfergus AM 37; 90

Bruce, David: Kilbride AM 29; 149

Bruce, David: Umgall AM 35; 160

Bruce, Edward: Ballynure AM 32; 44, 46, 68

Bruce, Edward: Clondermot LY 34; 45

Bruce, Edward: Down DN 17; 42

Bruce, Edward: Kilroot AM 26; 60–61, 63, 69, 73, 78–79, 81

Bruce, Edward: Larne AM 10; 125

Bruce, Edward: Misc. LY 36; 109

Bruce, Edward: Raloo AM 32; 93, 106, 112, 115

Bruce, Edward: Templecorran AM 26; 108

Bruce, Edward [I]: Carrickfergus AM 37; 4, 56, 135, 141–42, 185

Bruce, Edward [II]: Carrickfergus AM 37; 39, 148

Bruce, family: Drumachose LY 9; 108

Bruce, family: Kilroot AM 26; 73

Bruce, family: Lambeg AM 8; 135

Bruce, family: Templecorran AM 26; 108

Bruce, H.H.: Ballyscullion LY 6; 48

Bruce, H.H.: Banagher LY 30; 13, 17, 22

Bruce, H.H.: Donaghedy TE 5; 91–92

Bruce, H.H.: Dunboe LY 11; 46, 49, 58, 65

Bruce, H.H.: Maghera LY 18; 62

Bruce, H.H.: Magilligan LY 11; 85, 125

Bruce, H.H.: Misc. LY 31; 129, 143

Bruce, H.H.: Tamlaght Finlagan LY 25; 81

Bruce, James: Banagher LY 30; 73, 113

Bruce, James: Coleraine LY 33; 104, 110, 127

Bruce, James: Donaghedy TE 5; 88

Bruce, James: Drumachose LY 9; 106

Bruce, James: Drumragh TE 5; 109

Bruce, James: Dunboe LY 11; 44, 46, 52–53, 55, 58–62, 64–66, 69–70, 73–74, 79

Bruce, James: Faughanvale LY 36; 39, 45

Bruce, James: Maghera LY 18; 72

Bruce, James: Magilligan LY 11; 86, 99, 107, 110, 114–16, 120, 131–35, 138–40, 142, 144–45

Bruce, Lady: Dunboe LY 11; 69

Bruce, Michael: Killinchy DN 7; 87

Bruce, Michael: Misc. DN 17; 121

Bruce, Miss: Dunboe LY 11; 57, 72

Bruce, Mrs: Carrickfergus AM 37; 133

Bruce, R.N.: Kilbroney DN 3; 35

Bruce, Rev.: Blaris AM 8; 26

Bruce, Rev. Henry: Aghadowey LY 22; 22

Bruce, Rev. Henry: Drumachose LY 9; 65–66, 73

Bruce, Robert (King of Scotland): Island Magee AM 10; 62

Bruce, Robert: Carnmoney AM 2; 72

Bruce, Robert: Carrickfergus AM 37; 90

Bruce, Robert: Down DN 17; 42

Bruce, Robert: Drummaul AM 19; 69

Bruce, Robert: Kilkeel DN 3; 53

Bruce, Robert: Magheramesk AM 21; 126

Bruce, Robert: Raloo AM 32; 93, 116

Bruce, Robert: Rathlin Island AM 24; 129–30, 132, 134

Bruce, Robert: Templecorran AM 26; 114

Bruce, S.C.: Banagher LY 30; 73, 99–100, 113, 117–20, 131

Bruce, S.C.: Coleraine LY 33; 63, 91

Bruce, S.C.: Faughanvale LY 36; 40, 45

Bruce, William: Blaris AM 8; 10

Bruce's cairn: Raloo AM 32; 93, 112, 115–16

Bruce's Castle: Rathlin Island AM 24; 128–31, 134

Bruce's cave: Rathlin Island AM 24; 130–31

Bruce's hill: Shilvodan AM 19; 128

Bruce's stones: Raloo AM 32; 93, 115

Bruckagh td: Enniskillen FH 4; 82

Brucklass td: Ardstraw TE 5; 12

Bruff (Limerick): Faughanvale LY 36; 53, 62

Bruice, Richard: Carrickfergus AM 37; 134

Brumhall, Mrs: Moville DL 38; 75, 78

Bruncaurragh village: Kilmacteige SO 40; 187, 194

Brunker, W.: Aughnamullen MN 40; 71, 75–76

Brunker, W.: Ematris MN 40; 119

Brunker, William: Clones FH 4; 29

Bruno, St: Kilbroney DN 3; 26

Bruno, St: Misc. DN 17; 120

Brunswick, Mary: Ahoghill AM 23; 49

Brush, Crane: Aghaderg DN 12; 6

Brush, Crane: Drumballyroney DN 3; 15, 17–18

Brush, Crane: Drumgath DN 3; 21

Brush, Crane: Kilmore AH 1; 66–73

Brush, Mr: Ballymascanlan LH 40; 55

Brushy td: Dungiven LY 15; 74

Bruslee bog: Ballylinny AM 32; 13, 25

Bruslee Flush locality: Carrickfergus AM 37; 33

Bruslee log mill: Ballylinny AM 32; 13, 27

Bruslee night school: Ballylinny AM 32; 28

Bruslee private school: Ballylinny AM 32; 23, 28, 30

Bruslee school: Ballylinny AM 32; 23, 25, 29

Bruslee spade mill: Ballylinny AM 32; 13, 25, 27

Bruslee td: Ballylinny AM 32; 22, 26, 30

Bruslee water: Ballynure AM 32; 43

Brussell's well: Maghera LY 18; 39

Brussels (Belgium): Newry DN 3; 74

Bryan, Andrew: Kilcronaghan LY 31; 85

Bryan, family: Desertmartin LY 31; 55

Bryan, family: Glenwhirry AM 32; 77

Bryan, Henry: Kilcronaghan LY 31; 85

Bryan, James: Kilcronaghan LY 31; 85

Bryan, Josiah: Magherafelt LY 6; 84, 92, 96

Bryan, Messrs and Company: Magherafelt LY 6; 92

Bryan, Mr: Ballyclog TE 20; 15, 18

Bryan, Rev. N.: Misc. LY 31; 117

Bryan, Rev. Robert: Misc. LY 31; 136

Bryan, Rev. William: Kilcronaghan LY 31; 66, 80, 83, 136

Bryan, Robert: Kilcronaghan LY 31; 67, 76, 78–79, 83, 86, 112, 140

Bryans, John: Kilcronaghan LY 31; 85

Bryans, Rev.: Kilcronaghan LY 31; 76

Bryans, Robert: Dungiven LY 15; 93

Bryans, Thomas: Kilcronaghan LY 31; 85

Bryansford: Clonduff DN 3; 6

Bryansford: Kilcoo DN 3; 44

Bryansford Hotel: Kilcoo DN 3; 44

Bryanstown stream: Bangor DN 7; 19

Bryantang fort: Ballynure AM 32; 63

Bryantang river: Ballynure AM 32; 59

Bryantang td: Ballynure AM 32; 63, 68

Bryantang td: Carrickfergus AM 37; 93, 174

Bryce, Capt.: Carrickfergus AM 37; 145

Bryce, Mr (Kilroot): Saul DN 17; 114

Bryce, Rev. Edward: Island Magee AM 10; 27

Bryce, Rev. James: Aghadowey LY 22; 14, 22–26, 31

Bryce, S.: Drumbo DN 7; 59

Bryce, Thomas: Ballyscullion LY 6; 57

Bryden, Miss: Newry DN 3; 99, 104

Brydges, John: Coleraine LY 33; 152

Brynan, family: Island Magee AM 10; 70

Brynan, family: Templecorran AM 26; 117, 119

Bryson, E.: Antrim AM 29; 46

Bryson, family: Kilbride AM 29; 153

Bryson, family: Kilroot AM 26; 74–75

Bryson, James: Kilbride AM 29; 154

Bryson, Jane: Antrim AM 29; 59

Bryson, John: Carnmoney AM 2; 99

Bryson, John: Carrickfergus AM 37; 108
Bryson, John: Killowen LY 33; 161, 170
Bryson, Mary: Antrim AM 29; 59
Bryson, Mary [I]: Kilbride AM 29; 144
Bryson, Mary [II]: Kilbride AM 29; 144, 152
Bryson, Miss: Antrim AM 29; 42, 46
Bryson, Mr: Antrim AM 29; 59
Bryson, Rev. James: Blaris AM 8; 26
Bryson, Rev. William: Antrim AM 29; 27
Bryson, Robert: Kilbride AM 29; 155
Bualt td: Templecarn DL 39; 163
Buchanan, Andrew: Banagher LY 30; 42, 44, 54, 72, 80–81, 83–84, 89
Buchanan, Anna: Loughgall AH 1; 78
Buchanan, Archibald: Banagher LY 30; 42, 54, 88–89
Buchanan, family: Banagher LY 30; 42
Buchanan, family: Donacavey TE 5; 71
Buchanan, George: Drumachose LY 9; 72
Buchanan, George: Drumragh TE 5; 107, 109, 111
Buchanan, George: Misc. DN 17; 132–33
Buchanan, John: Ardstraw TE 5; 4
Buchanan, John: Donacavey TE 5; 80–81
Buchanan, John: Drumragh TE 5; 107
Buchanan, John: Hillsborough DN 12; 107
Buchanan, Joseph: Hillsborough DN 12; 107
Buchanan, Matthew: Clonleigh DL 39; 4, 9
Buchanan, Moses: Hillsborough DN 12; 107
Buchanan, Mr: Cappagh TE 5; 18–19
Buchanan, Mrs: Misc. DN 17; 132
Buchanan, Robert: Banagher LY 30; 57, 99–100
Buchanan, Thomas: Donacavey TE 5; 65, 81
Buchanan, William: Banagher LY 30; 89
Buchanan, William: Donacavey TE 5; 81
Buchanan, William: Hillsborough DN 12; 107
Buchanan's hill: Blaris DN 12; 42
Buchannan, William: Newry DN 3; 100
Buchanon, James: Blaris AM 8; 28
Buck Islands (see Garroo Islands): Cleenish FH 14; 13
Buck, Rev. John: Clonoe TE 20; 29
Buck, Rev. John: Desertcreat TE 20; 34
Buckbee, Mr (Kernan): Seagoe AH 1; 109
Buckingham, Duchess of: Drumachose LY 9; 95
Buckingham, Duke of: Clogher TE 5; 24
Bucklawn chapel: Creggan AH 1; 27
Buckley, Rev. Richard: Seagoe AH 1; 102
Buckna (Bucknaw) td: Racavan AM 13; 88, 96, 100
Buckna manor: Glenwhirry AM 32; 78
Buckna manor: Racavan AM 13; 86, 93
Buckna meeting house: Racavan AM 13; 88–89, 96
Buckna school: Racavan AM 13; 96, 100
Budor (see Budore): Tullyrusk AM 21; 139
Budore bog: Tullyrusk AM 21; 134
Budore hill: Tullyrusk AM 21; 132–33

Budore school [I]: Tullyrusk AM 21; 132, 139
Budore school [II]: Tullyrusk AM 21; 132, 139
Budore td: Ballinderry AM 21; 53
Budore td: Tullyrusk AM 21; 131–33
Buenos Aires (Argentina): Coleraine LY 33; 86
Buggan school: Devenish FH 14; 50
Buggan td: Devenish FH 14; 48
Buick, Rev. Frederick: Ahoghill AM 23; 33, 41
Buillig Hoanawaesh rock: Lough Swilly DL 38; 124
Buillig Point: Lough Swilly DL 38; 124
Builligchonnels rocks: Lough Swilly DL 38; 126
Buillig-Skreggagh rock: Lough Swilly DL 38; 124
Buinaraa Point: Lough Swilly DL 38; 143
Bulbin hill: Clonmany DL 38; 12–13, 16, 20
Bulbin hill: Mintiaghs DL 38; 64
Bulbon (see Bulbin): Clonmany DL 38; 12
Bulbuoy mine: Manorhamilton Union LM 40; 49
Bull Head: Rathlin Island AM 24; 130
Bull rocks: Lough Swilly DL 38; 101
Bull, Rev.: Island Magee AM 10; 32
Bullers, William: Carrickfergus AM 37; 193
Bullick, Miss: Clogher TE 5; 43
Bullick's bridge: Aghagallon AM 21; 1
Bullion, John: Derrykeighan AM 16; 90
Bullion, John: Macosquin LY 22; 82, 105
Bullion, John: Magilligan LY 11; 127
Bullion, Robert: Maghera LY 18; 61
Bullmer, family: Lambeg AM 8; 135
Bullock Park hill: Dunboe LY 11; 73
Bullock, family: Aghagallon AM 21; 9
Bullock, family: Aghalee AM 21; 31
Bullock, John: Aghagallon AM 21; 12–13, 17, 21
Bullock, Rev.: Down DN 17; 58
Bullock's Track standing stone: Ahoghill AM 23; 27, 35
Bullock's Track standing stone: Dunaghy AM 13; 19
Bullogfeam creek: Lough Swilly DL 38; 113, 116
Bulloyfeam (see Bullogfeam): Lough Swilly DL 38; 116
Bulteel, family: Enniskillen FH 4; 58
Bun bridge: Galloon FH 4; 105
Bun school: Galloon FH 4; 96
Bun td: Galloon FH 4; 95
Bunagee td: Leck DL 39; 117–18
Bunagee td: Lough Swilly DL 38; 110
Bunagoee (see Bunagee)
Bunbury, Isaac: Saintfield DN 7; 117–18
Bunbury, J.R.: Clogher TE 5; 27, 30–32, 49
Bunbury, Lady: Dromore TE 5; 102
Bunbury, Mrs: Dromore TE 5; 98–99
Bunchanacloney (see Bunshanacloney): Armoy AM 24; 1
Buncrana: Clonmany DL 38; 14, 17–20
Buncrana: Desertegney DL 38; 24–29

Buncrana: Donagh DL 38; 32

Buncrana: Drumragh TE 5; 109

Buncrana: Killygarvan DL 38; 40, 45

Buncrana: Lough Swilly DL 38; 101, 126, 149

Buncrana: Mintiaghs DL 38; 64–66

Buncrana: Misc. DL 39; 187

Buncrana: Muff DL 38; 80

Buncrana: Tullyaughnish DL 38; 95

Buncrana bleach green: Desertegney DL 38; 29

Buncrana Castle: Clondermot LY 34; 34

Buncrana Castle: Lough Swilly DL 38; 98, 101

Buncrana dispensary: Desertegney DL 38; 27

Buncrana dispensary: Mintiaghs DL 38; 65

Buncrana tuck mill: Desertegney DL 38; 28

Bunderg fort: Ardstraw TE 5; 12

Bunderg td: Ardstraw TE 5; 12

Bundoran: Enniskillen FH 4; 83

Bundoran: Misc. FH 4; 133

Bundourragh: Dungiven LY 15; 35

Bundroose district: Enniskillen FH 4; 51

Bundroose river: Galloon FH 4; 102

Buneyfoble (see Bonyfoble): Lough Swilly DL 38; 140

Bunininver creek: Lough Swilly DL 38; 122–23, 126

Buniniver (see Bunininver)

Buninver (see Bunininver)

Bunker, Thomas: Aughnamullen MN 40; 71

Bunkers hill: Holywood DN 7; 81

Bunlin locality: Lough Swilly DL 38; 113

Bunlogher (see Bunlougher): Aghavea FH 4; 19

Bunlougher quarry: Aghavea FH 4; 19

Bunlougher td: Aghavea FH 4; 17, 19

Bunn (see Bun): Galloon FH 4; 95

Bunnafubble (see Bonyfoble): Lough Swilly DL 38; 135

Bunnananey village: Kilmacteige SO 40; 195

Bunnaninver td: Derryvullan FH 14; 33

Bunneal td: Galloon FH 4; 95

Bunnentin village: Lough Swilly DL 38; 100

Bunno chapel: Drung CN 40; 21

Bunno river: Drung CN 40; 19, 21

Bunno school: Drung CN 40; 21

Bunowen corn mill: Donaghedy TE 5; 88

Bunowen flax mill: Donaghedy TE 5; 88

Bunowen river: Magilligan LY 11; 106, 126, 133

Bunowen stream: Donaghedy TE 5; 88

Bunowen td: Donaghedy TE 5; 88

Bunowen td: Magilligan LY 11; 95, 133

Bunseantuinne palace: Clondermot LY 34; 47

Bunshanacloney cove: Armoy AM 24; 9

Bunshanacloney td: Armoy AM 24; 1, 4

Bunshancloney (see Bunshanacloney): Armoy AM 24; 4

Buntin, John: Magherafelt LY 6; 98

Bunting, Mr (Belfast): Kilroot AM 26; 72

Bunting, Thomas: Hillsborough DN 12; 107

Bunting's River school: Blaris AM 8; 81

Bunton, family: Aghagallon AM 21; 9

Bunton, Turtle: Blaris DN 12; 40

Burdantien td: Clones FH 4; 26

Burden, Dr: Newry DN 3; 98

Burdot, John: Coleraine LY 33; 94

Burfield, Ferdinand: Enniskillen FH 4; 57

Burge, Patrick: Templepatrick AM 35; 152

Burges, family: Glynn AM 26; 45

Burges, Mr (Annaloist): Seagoe AH 1; 106

Burgess, Mr (Castlecaulfield): Drumcree AH 1; 39

Burgess, Richard: Donacavey TE 5; 63

Burgess, Robert: Clogherny TE 20; 25

Burgh, Catharine: Kilkeel DN 3; 53

Burgh, family: Kilkeel DN 3; 52

Burgoine, Bridget: Carrickfergus AM 37; 157

Burgoyne, Gen. John: Ardstraw TE 5; 5

Burgoyne, Gen. John: Drumragh TE 5; 109

Burgoyne, Gen. John: Faughanvale LY 36; 40

Burgus, John: Errigal LY 27; 56

Burial Ground well: Macosquin LY 22; 84, 119

Burk, George: Tamlaght O'Crilly LY 18; 124

Burk, John: Blaris AM 8; 73

Burk, Mr: Bovevagh LY 25; 52

Burke, family: Dungiven LY 15; 31

Burke, H.A.: Clogher TE 5; 40

Burke, John: Blaris AM 8; 20

Burke, John: Ramoan AM 24; 104

Burke, Mr: Clogher TE 5; 51

Burke, Samuel: Blaris AM 8; 55

Burke, William: Carrickfergus AM 37; 195

Burkett, Patrick: Artrea LY 6; 32

Burkmills school: Billy AM 16; 77

Burleigh Hill House: Carrickfergus AM 37; 23, 56, 136, 141, 174, 181

Burleigh, family: Aghalurcher FH 4; 6, 9

Burleigh, family: Carrickfergus AM 37; 93, 174

Burleigh, George: Carrickfergus AM 37; 23, 56, 136

Burleigh, Lord: Aghalurcher FH 4; 9

Burleigh, Thomas: Coleraine LY 33; 72

Burleigh, William [I]: Carrickfergus AM 37; 28, 65, 102, 135, 139, 141–42, 144, 149, 162, 172

Burleigh, William [II]: Carrickfergus AM 37; 56, 98, 136

Burleigh's Castle: Aghalurcher FH 4; 9

Burley, Mr (Carrick): Drumcree AH 1; 39

Burly, Capt.: Blaris AM 8; 88

Burn Gushet water: Ballymoney AM 16; 1

Burn, Andrew: Kilroot AM 26; 81

Burn, John: Clonleigh DL 39; 9

Burn, Patrick: Carrickfergus AM 37; 118

Burn's Folly House: Longfield TE 5; 131–33

Burn's Mountain td: Killymard DL 39; 101

Burnaboigh (see Bonnanaboigh): Banagher LY 30; 23

Burnaboight (see Bonnanaboigh): Banagher LY 30; 24

Burnally school: Tamlaght Finlagan LY 25; 80, 95

Burnally Sunday school: Tamlaght Finlagan LY 25; 96

Burnally td: Tamlaght Finlagan LY 25; 93, 110, 115, 119

Burndale district: Raphoe DL 39; 129

Burndale river: Clonleigh DL 39; 1, 3, 7, 14, 16

Burndale river: Convoy DL 39; 18

Burndale river: Conwal DL 39; 24

Burndale river: Donaghmore DL 39; 28–29

Burndale river: Misc. DL 39; 188

Burndale river: Raphoe DL 39; 121, 129

Burndanet river: Leckpatrick TE 5; 123

Burndinnett td: Donaghedy TE 5; 91

Burnett, Rev.: Donegore AM 29; 129

Burnett, Samuel: Coleraine LY 33; 69, 140

Burnett, Sinclair: Ballyrashane LY 22; 66

Burnett, Sinclair: Ballywillin LY 33; 51

Burnett, William: Ahoghill AM 23; 35

Burney, Capt.: Kilmegan DN 3; 59

Burney, James: Down DN 17; 51

Burnfoot bridge: Bovevagh LY 25; 4, 58

Burnfoot church: Muff DL 38; 80

Burnfoot locality: Lough Swilly DL 38; 103, 116, 144

Burnfoot locality: Templecarn DL 39; 158

Burnfoot school: Bovevagh LY 25; 27, 55

Burnfoot td: Bovevagh LY 25; 8, 52–53, 57

Burnfoot td: Muff DL 38; 81

Burnfoot wooden bridge: Bovevagh LY 25; 58

Burnquarter td: Ballymoney AM 16; 6, 21, 23

Burns, Alexander: Glynn AM 26; 47

Burns, Anne: Kilcoo DN 3; 45

Burns, David: Dromore DN 12; 77

Burns, Duncan: Carrickfergus AM 37; 131

Burns, Edward: Newry DN 3; 100

Burns, family: Ballintoy AM 24; 20

Burns, family: Dunluce AM 16; 117

Burns, family: Newry DN 3; 108

Burns, Henry: Carrickfergus AM 37; 90

Burns, Hugh: Dromore DN 12; 78

Burns, James: Ahoghill AM 23; 35

Burns, James: Carrickfergus AM 37; 102, 149

Burns, James: Macosquin LY 22; 87, 111

Burns, Jemmy: Ballynascreen LY 31; 15

Burns, John: Aghanloo LY 11; 31–32

Burns, John: Carrickfergus AM 37; 131

Burns, John: Glynn AM 26; 36, 47

Burns, Laughlin: Carrickfergus AM 37; 131

Burns, Maria Ann: Carnmoney AM 2; 78

Burns, Matilda: Kilcronaghan LY 31; 88

Burns, Patrick: Misc. DN 17; 119

Burns, Phillip: Derryaghy AM 8; 105

Burns, Robbie: Banagher LY 30; 11

Burns, Robert: Carrickfergus AM 37; 116

Burns, Robert: Misc. LY 31; 140

Burns, Rodger: Ballymure AM 32, 72

Burns, William: Clonleigh DL 39; 10

Burnside: Ballyaghran LY 33; 7, 21–22, 24

Burnside cave: Ballywillin LY 33; 50

Burnside Cottage: Ballyaghran LY 33; 22

Burnside flax mill: Kilbride AM 29; 135, 156

Burnside public house: Ballyaghran LY 33; 7

Burnside school: Ballyaghran LY 33; 17

Burnside school: Kilwaughter AM 10; 119

Burnside stream: Ballyaghran LY 33; 1

Burnside td: Donegore AM 29; 129

Burnside td: Kilbride AM 29; 136, 138–39

Burnside td: Kilwaughter AM 10; 119

Burnside td: Raphoe DL 39; 125

Burnside, Dr: Faughanvale LY 36; 18

Burnside, Jane: Carrickfergus AM 37; 115

Burnside, Mathew: Clogher TE 5; 44

Burnside, Mr (Carrakeel): Clondermot LY 34; 37–38, 104

Burnside, Mrs (Ervey): Cumber LY 28; 57

Burnside, Rev. S.: Newry DN 3; 103

Burnside, Rev. William: Clogher TE 5; 33

Burnside, W.S.: Clogher TE 5; 48

Burnside, William: Clondermot LY 34; 93

Burnside, William: Kilcronaghan LY 31; 85

Burnt hill: Carnmoney AM 2; 94

Burnt House (see also Ballymoy Castle): Billy AM 16; 52, 64–65

Burnt Island hill: Loughgall AH 1; 79

Burnthaw td: Taughboyne DL 39; 148, 151, 195

Burntollet bridge: Cumber LY 28; 34–35

Burntollet glen: Bovevagh LY 25; 1

Burntollet glen: Cumber LY 28; 35, 45

Burntollet river: Clondermot LY 34; 69

Burntollet river: Cumber LY 28; 6, 18, 29, 44–47, 53, 66–67, 86, 92–93

Burntollet river: Faughanvale LY 36; 1, 4, 21

Burntollet river: Misc. LY 36; 119

Burny, David: Newry DN 3; 79

Burny, John: Kilcoo DN 3; 45

Burop, Rev.: Cumber LY 28; 75

Burrel, Anne: Seagoe AH 1; 103

Burrell, Richard: Coleraine LY 33; 72

Burren td: Dromara DN 12; 62–63, 65

Burren td: Dunboe LY 11; 57

Burren td: Warrenpoint DN 3; 115

Burrian (see Burren): Dunboe LY 11; 57

Burrowes, Alexander: Hillsborough DN 12; 105

Burrowes, David: Hillsborough DN 12; 106

Burrowes, James: Hillsborough DN 12; 106

Burrowes, Rev, Robert: Drumragh TE 5; 111
Burrowes, Robert: Hillsborough DN 12; 106
Burrowes, Thomas: Drumgoon CN 40; 8
Burrows field: Muckamore AM 35; 80
Burrows, Anne Jane: Carrickfergus AM 37; 119
Burrows, Dean: Enniskillen FH 4; 58
Burrows, family: Lambeg AM 8; 135
Burrows, family: Magherafelt LY 6; 95
Burrows, family: Magheramesk AM 21; 124
Burrows, Maj. (Stradone): Drung CN 40; 23
Burrows, Maj. (Stradone): Killdrumsherdan CN 40; 37
Burrows, Maj.: Laragh CN 40; 41, 43, 45
Burrows, Rev.: Cumber LY 28; 19, 76
Burrows, Rev. Lewis: Desertoghill LY 27; 17
Burrows, William: Blaris DN 12; 46, 50
Burrows, William: Magheragall AM 21; 104
Burt bay: Lough Swilly DL 38; 147
Burt Castle: Clondermot LY 34; 34
Burt district: Lough Swilly DL 38; 109
Burt district: Mintiaghs DL 38; 66–67
Burt district: Raymoghy DL 39; 135
Burt House: Lough Swilly DL 38; 103–04
Burt Island: Lough Swilly DL 38; 103, 127, 142–48
Burt old church: Lough Swilly DL 38; 143
Burt ph: Clondermot LY 34; 98
Burt ph: Lough Swilly DL 38; 103–04, 143
Burt, George: Tamlaght O'Crilly LY 18; 108
Burthall td: Killea and Taughboyne DL 39; 80
Burton, Lt: Drumlumman CN 40; 15
Burton, William: Drumachose LY 9; 65
Busby, Elizabeth: Carncastle and Killyglen AM 10; 6
Busby, James: Errigal Truagh MN 40; 122
Bush Bank demense: Derrykeighan AM 16; 78
Bush Bank demesne: Ballymoney AM 16; 10
Bush fishery: Billy AM 16; 46
Bush fishery: Dunluce AM 16; 104, 110
Bush hill: Macosquin LY 22; 76, 81
Bush House: Antrim AM 29; 21, 50
Bush Island: Killinchy DN 7; 86, 92
Bush river: Armoy AM 24; 1, 3–5
Bush river: Ballymoney AM 16; 1, 3, 5, 9–10
Bush river: Ballyrashane LY 22; 46
Bush river: Billy AM 16; 36–41, 43
Bush river: Derrykeighan AM 16; 78, 80–81, 94
Bush river: Drumtullagh AM 16; 97
Bush river: Dungiven LY 15; 91
Bush river: Dunluce AM 16; 104, 106
Bush river: Lough Neagh AM 21; 96
Bush river: Loughguile AM 13; 59–61
Bush river bridge: Derrykeighan AM 16; 85
Bush river bridge: Loughguile AM 13; 64
Bush school: Antrim AM 29; 41–42, 51
Bush stone bridges: Ballymoney AM 16; 3

Bush td: Drummaul AM 19; 70, 72
Bushbank House: Derrykeighan AM 16; 78, 84, 89–90, 94
Bushbank House: Dunluce AM 16; 107
Bushe, Anne: Ballinderry AM 21; 57
Bushford House: Aughnamullen MN 40; 71, 73, 75–76
Bushmills: Ballintoy AM 24; 11, 15, 17, 20, 24, 26, 28–31, 33
Bushmills: Ballyaghran LY 33; 13
Bushmills: Ballymoney AM 16; 5
Bushmills: Ballyrashane LY 22; 49, 51
Bushmills: Ballywillin LY 33; 29, 32–34, 40–41, 45–48
Bushmills: Billy AM 16; 37, 43–44, 47–48, 50
Bushmills: Coleraine LY 33; 91, 95, 121, 128–29, 132, 143
Bushmills: Drumcree AH 1; 39
Bushmills: Dunluce AM 16; 105, 119
Bushmills: Killowen LY 33; 164, 173
Bushmills: Misc. AM 10; 129
Bushmills: Tamlaght Finlagan LY 25; 124
Bushmills bridge: Billy AM 16; 45
Bushmills bridge: Dunluce AM 16; 109
Bushmills chapel (C): Billy AM 16; 37
Bushmills chapel (C): Coleraine LY 33; 95, 143
Bushmills chapel (C): Dunluce AM 16; 105, 109
Bushmills chapel (M): Billy AM 16; 44
Bushmills church: Dunluce AM 16; 105, 109, 113, 117
Bushmills corn mills: Dunluce AM 16; 110
Bushmills court house: Billy AM 16; 44
Bushmills dispensary: Ballyrashane LY 22; 51
Bushmills dispensary: Dunluce AM 16; 111
Bushmills Glebe House: Dunluce AM 16; 105, 110
Bushmills graveyard: Dunluce AM 16; 117
Bushmills hotel: Billy AM 16; 45
Bushmills House: Billy AM 16; 45, 76
Bushmills House: Tamlaght Finlagan LY 25; 81
Bushmills iron foundry: Billy AM 16; 46
Bushmills market place: Billy AM 16; 45
Bushmills meeting house: Billy AM 16; 44
Bushmills meeting house: Dunluce AM 16; 105, 109
Bushmills school [I]: Billy AM 16; 49
Bushmills school [II]: Billy AM 16; 49
Bushmills spade factory: Billy AM 16; 46
Bushmills td (see Magherabower): Billy AM 16; 37
Bushtown cove [I]: Macosquin LY 22; 87, 112
Bushtown cove [II]: Macosquin LY 22; 95, 97
Bushtown springs: Macosquin LY 22; 113
Bushtown td: Macosquin LY 22; 76, 112
Bushview school: Ballymoney AM 16; 26
Bushy bank: Lough Swilly DL 38; 100
Bushy field: Skerry AM 13; 111
Bushy td: Dungiven LY 15; 83

Buskhill td: Donaghmore DN 3; 7, 9

Butcher hill: Derryaghy AM 8; 115

Bute, Edward: Carrickfergus AM 37; 119

Butler, Anne: Carrickfergus AM 37; 115

Butler, Brinsley: Galloon FH 4; 90

Butler, family: Ballintoy AM 24; 20

Butler, family: Dallyscullion LY 6; 57

Butler, family: Culfeightrin AM 24; 71

Butler, family: Galloon FH 4; 89

Butler, Francis: Galloon FH 4; 90

Butler, Henry: Carrickfergus AM 37; 130

Butler, Henry: Culfeightrin AM 24; 83–84

Butler, Humphrey: Galloon FH 4; 90

Butler, John: Culfeightrin AM 24; 83

Butler, John: Galloon FH 4; 90

Butler, Mr (Dublin): Kilbroney DN 3; 35

Butler, Patrick: Culfeightrin AM 24; 73

Butler, R.H.: Galloon FH 4; 90

Butler, Rev. Samuel: Aghanloo LY 11; 25

Butler, Rev. Samuel: Drumachose LY 9; 104

Butler, Rev. Samuel: Magilligan LY 11; 84, 93, 104,
    106–10, 118, 125–26, 128, 130

Butler, Richard: Misc. SO 40; 200

Butler, Stephen: Galloon FH 4; 90

Butler, Susan: Carrickfergus AM 37; 122

Butler, Theophilus: Galloon FH 4; 90

Butler, Thomas: Drummaul AM 19; 77, 85, 87

Butler, William: Culfeightrin AM 24; 67, 73, 82–83

Butt, family: Drumgath DN 3; 20

Butt, Pat: Kilmacteige SO 40; 194

Butt, Rev.: Kilteevoge DL 39; 111

Butter mountain (see Slieve Muggthan): Clonduff
    DN 3; 5

Buttermilk bridge: Dungiven LY 15; 11

Butters, Mary: Carnmoney AM 2; 75–76

Butterstone standing stone: Dunaghy AM 13; 19, 22

Buttle, family: Blaris AM 8; 21

Buttle, Rev. John: Blaris AM 8; 24, 30, 83

Buttle, Thomas: Duneane AM 19; 109, 119, 122

Buxton, Mr: Kilbroney DN 3; 31

Bwellindhawoa locality: Lough Swilly DL 38; 134

Bwelloore creek: Lough Swilly DL 38; 132–33

Bwellorsky Point: Lough Swilly DL 38; 106–07,
    113

Byers, Alexander: Kilbride AM 29; 152

Byers, John: Blaris AM 8; 51

Byers, Joseph: Banagher LY 30; 66

Byers, Margaret: Kilbride AM 29; 152

Byers, Mary: Kilbride AM 29; 152

Byers, William: Loughgilly AH 1; 86

Bylett's bay: Lough Swilly DL 38; 147

Bylett's district: Lough Swilly DL 38; 144–45

Bylett's spa: Lough Swilly DL 38; 148

Byng, John: Ballyscullion LY 6; 77

Byng, Messrs John and Co.: Ballyscullion LY 6; 66

Bynnadharee Keenan (see Benbradagh): Dungiven
    LY 15; 46

Byrch, J.: Drumballyroney DN 3; 18

Byrn, Charles: Agivey LY 22; 45

Byrn, James: Agivey LY 22; 45

Byrne, family: Killanny MN 40; 132

Byrne, Harden: Ballinderry AM 21; 49

Byrne, Harden: Blaris DN 12; 42–43, 47

Byrne, Henry: Magheross MN 40; 144

Byrne, James: Newry DN 3; 103

Byrne, John: Newry DN 3; 98, 103

Byrne, man named: Donaghmore DL 39; 34

Byrne, Manus: Donaghmore DL 39; 35

Byrne, Miss: Newry DN 3; 99, 104

Byrne, Mr: Newry DN 3; 99

Byrne, P.C.: Newry DN 3; 99, 104

Byrns, Arthur: Killead AM 35; 53

Byrns, family: Aghagallon AM 21; 10

Byrns, Mr: Tullaghobegley DL 39; 172

Byrns, Patrick: Templepatrick AM 35; 113, 142, 146

Byrns, Thomas: Templepatrick AM 35; 153

Byrom, Joshua: Newry DN 3; 100

Byrttsland locality: Carrickfergus AM 37; 94, 174

C

Caan lough: Killygarvan DL 38; 37

Caarnaharwee rocks: Lough Swilly DL 38; 122

Caarreen quarry: Lough Swilly DL 38; 129

Caaslagh creek: Lough Swilly DL 38; 147

Cabhan-an-churadh locality: Clondermot LY 34; 106–07

Cabin Hill House: Coleraine LY 33; 91

Cabin hill quarry: Coleraine LY 33; 121

Cabra Cottage: Donaghmoyne MN 40; 107

Cabra td: Hillsborough DN 12; 85

Cabragh (Cabra) td: Kirkinriola AM 23; 91

Cabragh chapel: Billy AM 16; 45

Cabragh chapel: Clonduff DN 3; 3

Cabragh flax mill [I]: Clonallan DN 3; 1

Cabragh flax mill [II]: Clonallan DN 3; 1

Cabragh fort: Ballybay MN 40; 81

Cabragh hill: Kirkinriola AM 23; 92

Cabragh meeting house: Billy AM 16; 37

Cabragh new bridge school: Hillsborough DN 12; 95, 100

Cabragh quarry: Killdrumsherdan CN 40; 33

Cabragh td: Ballybay MN 40; 84

Cabragh td: Billy AM 16; 45

Cabragh td: Clonduff DN 3; 3

Cabragh td: Drumgoon CN 40; 7

Cabragh td: Hillsborough DN 12; 95, 100

Cabragh td: Termoneeny LY 6; 122, 132

Cabry quarry: Moville DL 38; 74

Cabry school: Moville DL 38; 74

Cabry td: Moville DL 38; 73, 75, 78

Cadan (see Aidan): Magilligan LY 11; 104

Caddy cove: Drummaul AM 19; 66, 88

Caddy school: Drummaul AM 19; 75, 86

Caddy, William: Enniskillen FH 4; 59

Cadman, Sampson: Carrickfergus AM 37; 192

Cady druid's temple: Drumachose LY 9; 112

Cady locality: Aghanloo LY 11; 29

Caen, John: Magilligan LY 11; 89

Caesar, Julius: Magilligan LY 11; 102

Cah bogs: Errigal LY 27; 54, 74

Cah fort [I]: Errigal LY 27; 42, 49, 68

Cah fort [II]: Errigal LY 27; 42, 68

Cah fort [III]: Errigal LY 27; 42, 68

Cah fort [IV]: Errigal LY 27; 68

Cah House: Clondermot LY 34; 6, 20, 103–04

Cah plantation: Clondermot LY 34; 122

Cah quarry: Clondermot LY 34; 129

Cah school (see Salem): Clondermot LY 34; 86

Cah school: Errigal LY 27; 50–51

Cah Sunday school: Errigal LY 27; 51

Cah td: Clondermot LY 34; 38, 56, 61, 76, 86–87, 89, 91, 108, 112, 114, 122, 129

Cah td: Errigal LY 27; 35, 41, 47–48, 60–61, 64–65, 68, 79–80, 85, 89, 92

Cah wood: Clondermot LY 34; 122

Cah wood: Errigal LY 27; 35, 74

Cahan, William: Ramoan AM 24; 123

Caharey (see Cahery): Drumachose LY 9; 127

Cahelnamamore, priest: Bovevagh LY 25; 15, 35

Caheny bridge: Aghadowey LY 22; 11

Caheny td: Aghadowey LY 22; 35–36, 38

Caher Righ fort: Culfeightrin AM 24; 41

Caherty cove [I]: Ballyclug AM 23; 62

Caherty cove [II]: Ballyclug AM 23; 62

Caherty fort [I]: Ballyclug AM 23; 64

Caherty fort [II]: Ballyclug AM 23; 65

Caherty fort [III]: Ballyclug AM 23; 65

Caherty giant's grave: Ballyclug AM 23; 61–62, 64–65

Caherty standing stone: Ballyclug AM 23; 61

Caherty td: Ballyclug AM 23; 53, 64–65

Cahery bridge: Drumachose LY 9; 56

Cahery td: Drumachose LY 9; 56–57, 87, 96, 111, 127

Cahery td: Dungiven LY 15; 29

Cahey, Arthur: Carrickfergus AM 37; 158

Cahill, Patrick: Drumbeg AM 8; 125

Cahoon, Arthur: Blaris DN 12; 40

Cahoon, family: Blaris AM 8; 22

Cahoon, family: Derryaghy AM 8; 103

Cahoon, James: Magheramesk AM 21; 126

Cahore school: Ballynascreen LY 31; 18

Cahore td: Ballynascreen LY 31; 13, 21–22, 143

Cahore td: Magheraculmoney FH 14; 111

Caiaphas, priest: Dungiven LY 15; 36

Caig lough (see Kock lough): Garvaghy DN 12; 79

Cailan, St: Down DN 17; 42

Cain, family: Ramoan AM 24; 107

Cain, Neal: Billy AM 16; 74
Caineach, St: Balteagh LY 9; 19
Caineach, St: Clondermot LY 34; 47
Caineach, St: Faughanvale LY 36; 13, 50
Cairn hill: Glenavy AM 21; 82
Cairn Lock: Aghagallon AM 21; 6
Cairn stone: Muckamore AM 35, 71
Cairnabrock locality: Carrickfergus AM 37; 93
Cairn-a-finn locality: Drumachose LY 9; 57, 111
Cairnalbanagh (Cairnalbina) td: Tickmacrevan AM
    13; 124
Cairnalbanagh mountain: Tickmacrevan AM 13; 124
Cairnalbanagh school: Tickmacrevan AM 13; 133
Cairnamrock locality: Carrickfergus AM 37; 174
Cairnan Glass hill: Ballintoy AM 24; 28
Cairn-an-truagh stones: Armoy AM 24; 2
Cairn-an-truagh stones: Ramoan AM 24; 91
Cairnarosie (see Carnrawsie): Carrickfergus AM 37;
    93
Cairnbane td: Newry DN 3; 74
Cairnconlan locality: Carrickfergus AM 37; 93
Cairndaisy (see Carndaisy): Desertlyn LY 31; 35
Cairne (see Carn): Templecarn DL 39; 156
Cairne House: Tullyaughnish DL 38; 86
Cairnenbane stones: Culfeightrin AM 24; 53
Cairnes, J.E.: Ballyaghran LY 33; 19
Cairnes, J.E.: Coleraine LY 33; 63, 104, 127
Cairnes, Mrs: Clogher TE 5; 53
Cairngaver mountain: Dundonald DN 7; 64
Cairnkeela [or Cairnakecla] locality: Carrickfergus
    AM 37; 93, 174
Cairnkirk forts: Billy AM 16; 61
Cairnmall cairn: Aghagallon AM 21; 11
Cairnmoon (see Carnmoon): Billy AM 16; 71
Cairnrassy (see Carnrawsie): Carrickfergus AM 37;
    174
Cairns td: Lough Swilly DL 38; 128
Cairns, Daniel: Culfeightrin AM 24; 72
Cairns, Edward: Blaris DN 12; 35, 37–38
Cairns, family: Carnmoney AM 2; 76
Cairns, Hugh: Hillsborough DN 12; 105
Cairns, John: Balteagh LY 9; 44
Cairns, John: Macosquin LY 22; 80, 102
Cairns, John: Tamlaght TE 20; 75, 131, 136
Cairns, Rev.: Carrickfergus AM 37; 102
Cairntaggart td: Ballyculter DN 17; 30
Cairntogher (see Carntogher)
Cairr bay: Lough Swilly DL 38; 102
Calbeck, William: Blaris DN 12; 44
Calbraith, John: Carrickfergus AM 37; 32
Caldbeck, family: Blaris AM 8; 21
Caldbeck, James: Blaris AM 8; 54–55
Caldbeck, Mrs: Blaris AM 8; 84–85
Caldbeck, William: Blaris AM 8; 51, 54
Caldbeck, William: Blaris DN 12; 40, 45, 49

Calder, A.: Killygarvan DL 38; 46
Caldernagh graveyard: Finvoy AM 23; 75–76
Caldernagh td: Finvoy AM 23; 76
Calderwood, J.: Coleraine LY 33; 73
Calderwood, W.: Coleraine LY 33; 73
Caldragh graveyard: Donaghmoyne MN 40; 108
Caldrum hill: Inishmacsaint FH 14; 71
Caldrum td: Clogher TE 5; 53
Caldrum td: Inishmacsaint FH 14; 71, 75
Caldwell, Capt.: Derryaghy AM 8; 99
Caldwell, family: Ballyrobert AM 2; 21
Caldwell, family: Ballywillin LY 33; 44
Caldwell, family: Drumbeg AM 8; 123
Caldwell, family: Kilwaughter AM 10; 115
Caldwell, family: Magilligan LY 11; 130
Caldwell, Henry: Cumber LY 28; 56
Caldwell, James: Coleraine LY 33; 72
Caldwell, Jane (see Brown): Ballyrobert AM 2; 23
Caldwell, Jane: Kilwaughter AM 10; 116
Caldwell, John: Belleek FH 14; 3–4
Caldwell, John: Clondermot LY 34; 78
Caldwell, John: Magilligan LY 11; 132
Caldwell, John: Templecarn FH 14; 120
Caldwell, Joseph: Ballymoney AM 16; 17
Caldwell, Mathew: Macosquin LY 22; 101–02, 109,
    123
Caldwell, Mr (Ballyforlea): Lissan LY 31; 99
Caldwell, Mr (Killdrum): Killea and Taughboyne
    DL 39; 87
Caldwell, Mr: Blaris DN 12; 49
Caldwell, Mr: Drumachose LY 9; 128
Caldwell, Mr: Faughanvale LY 36; 16
Caldwell, Mrs: Coleraine LY 33; 73
Caldwell, Neil: Maghera LY 18; 81
Caldwell, Robert: Skirts of Urney and Ardstraw TE
    5; 140
Caldwell, Thomas: Blaris AM 8; 55
Caldwell, Thomas: Rasharkin AM 23; 139
Caldwell, William: Ballyrobert AM 2; 24
Caldwell, William: Blaris AM 8; 54–55
Caldwell, William: Blaris DN 12; 51
Caldwell, William: Dunaghy AM 13; 21
Caldwell, William: Macosquin LY 22; 94
Caldwell's mill: Killea and Taughboyne DL 39; 87
Caledon: Aghaloo TE 20; 1–4
Caledon: Ballymore AH 1; 12
Caledon: Carnteel TE 20; 21
Caledon: Clonfeacle AH 1; 22
Caledon: Coleraine LY 33; 97
Caledon: Donagh MN 40; 100
Caledon: Eglish AH 1; 43
Caledon: Magheross MN 40; 152
Caledon: Tynan AH 1; 124–26, 128–30
Caledon barrack: Aghaloo TE 20; 3
Caledon bridge: Tynan AH 1; 124, 128

Caledon chapel: Aghaloo TE 20; 3–4
Caledon church: Aghaloo TE 20; 1, 3
Caledon court house: Aghaloo TE 20; 3
Caledon demesne: Aghaloo TE 20; 2
Caledon demesne: Tynan AH 1; 124
Caledon Demesne school: Aghaloo TE 20; 1, 5
Caledon dispensary: Aghaloo TE 20; 3, 5
Caledon flour mill [I]: Aghaloo TE 20; 4
Caledon flour mill [II]: Aghaloo TE 20; 4
Caledon flour mills: Aghaloo TE 20; 1–2
Caledon hospital: Aghaloo TE 20; 4
Caledon House: Aghaloo TE 20; 4
Caledon inn: Aghaloo TE 20; 1, 3
Caledon meeting house: Aghaloo TE 20; 1, 3–4
Caledon mills: Clonfeacle AH 1; 24
Caledon mills: Tynan AH 1; 124
Caledon news room: Aghaloo TE 20; 3
Caledon post house: Aghaloo TE 20; 3
Caledon td: Aghaloo TE 20; 3
Caledon, Earl of: Aghaloo TE 20; 1–5
Caledon, Earl of: Faughanvale LY 36; 40, 45
Caledon, Earl of: Moville DL 38; 75, 77
Caledon, Earl of: Tynan AH 1; 129–30
Caledon, Lady: Aghaloo TE 20; 5
Caledonia (Scotland): Carrickfergus AM 37; 18
Calewell, Alexander: Saintfield DN 7; 115
Calf Island: Ardkeen DN 7; 3
Calhame (Callhame) td: Clonleigh DL 39; 12
Calhame td: Convoy DL 39; 20
Calhame td: Donaghmore DL 39; 33, 36
Calhame td: Leck DL 39; 118
Calhame td: Misc. DL 39; 194, 197
Calhame td: Urney DL 39; 181
Calherne td: Ballymoney AM 16; 21, 24
Calhoon, John: Bovevagh LY 25; 33–34, 40
Calkill bridge: Cappagh TE 5; 20
Call, family: Blaris AM 8; 22
Callaghan, James: Drumachose LY 9; 132–33
Callaghan, John: Drumachose LY 9; 130
Callaghan, Joseph: Drumachose LY 9; 133
Callaghbeg district: Misc. SO 40; 198
Callagheen hill: Inishmacsaint FH 14; 71
Callaghill td: Currin MN 40; 86, 88, 91, 95
Callaghmore district: Misc. SO 40; 198
Callan bog: Donaghedy TE 5; 89
Callan bridge: Loughgall AH 1; 76
Callan river: Clonfeacle AH 1; 21, 23
Callan river: Coleraine LY 33; 97
Callan river: Keady AH 1; 50
Callan river: Loughgall AH 1; 75–76, 79
Callan, Michael: Newry DN 3; 98
Callan, Patrick: Newry DN 3; 98, 103
Callanagh Lower td: Drumlumman CN 40; 13, 17
Callanagh Middle td: Drumlumman CN 40; 17
Callawoo ridge: Lough Swilly DL 38; 99

Callawoo rocks: Lough Swilly DL 38; 99
Calleen Braigs standing stones: Desertoghill LY 27;
    8, 26
Callen td: Convoy DL 39; 20
Callenagh (see Callanagh): Drumlumman CN 40; 13
Callenath (see Callanagh): Drumlumman CN 40; 17
Callencor td: Convoy DL 39; 20
Calliagh giant's grave: Aghabog MN 40; 64
Calliagh hill: Aghabog MN 40; 62, 64
Calliagh trigonometrical station: Aghabog MN 40;
    64
Callighan, Frank: Kilcronaghan LY 31; 85
Callintrough (see Cullintrough): Comber DN 7; 40
Calliogh (see Calliagh): Aghabog MN 40; 64
Callisnagh flax mill: Layd AM 13; 48
Callisnagh td: Ardclinis AM 13; 7
Callisnagh td: Layd AM 13; 48
Callowhill church: Kinawley FH 4; 111, 116
Callowhill House: Kinawley FH 4; 115
Callowhill old church: Kinawley FH 4; 116–17
Callowhill td: Kinawley FH 4; 111, 114, 121
Callwell, Jane: Ballymoney AM 16; 17
Callwell, John: Kilwaughter AM 10; 119
Callwell, John: Magherafelt LY 6; 98
Callwell, Mrs: Ballymoney AM 16; 17
Calmore (Culmore) td: Kilcronaghan LY 31; 68, 73,
    75, 78, 85, 87
Calmore bog: Kilcronaghan LY 31; 64
Calmore Castle: Kilcronaghan LY 31; 64, 68–69,
    73, 76–77, 86–87, 117, 142
Calmore corn mill: Kilcronaghan LY 31; 67
Calmore fort: Kilcronaghan LY 31; 87
Calmore hill: Kilcronaghan LY 31; 64
Calmore Island: Kilcronaghan LY 31; 77
Calmore lough: Kilcronaghan LY 31; 69–70, 76–77,
    87
Calms td: Misc. DL 39; 197
Calor td: Donacavey TE 5; 77
Calpey td: Muff DL 38; 80
Calvert, Adam: Blaris DN 12; 50
Calvert, Daniel: Billy AM 16; 75
Calvert, John: Donaghcloney DN 12; 61
Calvert, Rev. Henry: Muckamore AM 35; 60, 65
Calvert, Robert: Billy AM 16; 62, 75
Calvert, Robert: Enniskillen FH 4; 57
Calwell, William: Ballynure AM 32; 73
Cam lough: Killymard DL 39; 94
Camac, family: Derrykeighan AM 16; 89
Camac, family: Drumbeg AM 8; 123
Camac, Jacob: Magheralin DN 12; 109
Camac, Mr (Philadelphia): Misc. DN 17; 126–27
Camagh (see Carnagh): Drumlumman CN 40; 15
Camaghy church: Magheracloone MN 40; 138
Camaghy Glebe House: Magheracloone MN 40;
    138

Camaghy school: Magheracloone MN 40; 142

Caman lough: Kinawley FH 4; 113

Cambell, family: Culfeightrin AM 24; 46, 59

Cambell, family: Rashee AM 32; 138

Camble, family: Enniskillen FH 4; 75

Camble, Mr: Clogher TE 5; 43

Camden, historian: Billy AM 16; 38

Camdry td: Dromore TE 5; 98

Cam-eirge locality: Misc. TE 5; 146

Camerin, Patrick: Killowen LY 33; 171

Cameron, Alexander: Carrickfergus AM 37; 194

Cameron, Alexander: Templepatrick AM 35; 135, 153

Cameron, Angus: Ballywillin LY 33; 33, 42

Cameron, Anthony: Island Magee AM 10; 93, 101

Cameron, Capt. A.: Misc. AM 10; 131

Cameron, Daniel: Ballymoney AM 16; 17

Cameron, family: Shilvodan AM 19; 136

Cameron, family: Templecorran AM 26; 117, 119

Cameron, J.: Kirkinriola AM 23; 113

Cameron, James: Ballymoney AM 16; 17

Cameron, James: Templecorran AM 26; 125

Cameron, Miss: Kirkinriola AM 23; 113

Cameron, Rev. Simon: Macosquin LY 22; 90, 101

Cameron, Robert: Island Magee AM 10; 99

Cameron, Robert: Templecorran AM 26; 121, 125

Cameron, William: Drummaul AM 19; 90

Camla td: Monaghan MN 40; 159

Camlin Glebe House: Glenavy AM 21; 77

Camlin graveyard: Ballinderry AM 21; 54

Camlin old church: Ballinderry AM 21; 53–54

Camlin old church: Camlin AM 21; 60–61, 63, 71

Camlin ph: Aghagallon AM 21; 4–5

Camlin ph: Blaris DN 12; 40

Camlin ph: Glenavy AM 21; 77–78, 84, 87–88

Camlin ph: Killead AM 35; 8, 11–12, 18–19, 43

Camlin ph: Misc. AM 10; 129

Camlin ph: Tullyrusk AM 21; 131, 133, 137–38

Camlin Rectory: Camlin AM 21; 63

Camlin river: Killead AM 35; 34

Camlin td: Blaris DN 12; 42

Camlough: Kildress TE 20; 59, 61

Camlough: Killevy AH 1; 54

Camlough: Misc. DN 17; 131

Camly, Pat: Artrea LY 6; 23

Cammusmore harbour: Lough Swilly DL 38; 124–25

Camna, Mr: Ballyphilip DN 7; 8

Camnish bog: Bovevagh LY 25; 30

Camnish bog: Dungiven LY 15; 90

Camnish meeting house: Banagher LY 30; 14

Camnish meeting house: Bovevagh LY 25; 3, 23, 27, 54

Camnish school: Bovevagh LY 25; 28

Camnish td: Banagher LY 30; 23–24

Camnish td: Bovevagh LY 25; 54, 56, 59

Camnish td: Dungiven LY 15; 85, 95, 97

Camoghy (see Camaghy): Magheracloone MN 40; 138

Camohey (see Camaghy): Magheracloone MN 40; 138

Camowen meeting house: Cappagh TE 5; 18

Camowen river: Cappagh TE 5; 17, 20, 22

Camowen river: Clogherny TE 20; 25

Camowen river: Drumragh TE 5; 104, 107

Camowen river: Pomeroy TE 20; 72

Camowen Sunday school: Cappagh TE 5; 18

Camp hill (see also Castle hill): Balteagh LY 9; 28

Camp hill: Ahoghill AM 23; 34

Camp hill: Balteagh LY 9; 7

Camp hill: Carnmoney AM 2; 51, 64, 69, 98

Camp hill: Galloon FH 4; 98

Camp stone: Island Magee AM 10; 100

Campbel, James: Drumachose LY 9; 104

Campbell, A.: Tamlaght Finlagan LY 25; 77, 92

Campbell, A.J.: Maghera LY 18; 7, 67

Campbell, Alexander: Drumragh TE 5; 107

Campbell, Alexander: Tamlaght O'Crilly LY 18; 129

Campbell, Alexander: Tamlaght TE 20; 122

Campbell, Ann: Tamlaght O'Crilly LY 18; 137

Campbell, Anne: Newry DN 3; 80

Campbell, Anne-Jane: Carrickfergus AM 37; 114

Campbell, Archibald: Newry DN 3; 82

Campbell, Archibald: Tamlaght O'Crilly LY 18; 129

Campbell, Archie: Skerry AM 13; 120

Campbell, Archy: Dunluce AM 16; 118

Campbell, Archy: Kilcronaghan LY 31; 84

Campbell, Bernard: Carrickfergus AM 37; 129

Campbell, Bernard: Magherafelt LY 6; 112

Campbell, Bryan: Aghagallon AM 21; 12

Campbell, Charles: Ballynascreen LY 31; 30

Campbell, Charles: Drummaul AM 19; 71

Campbell, Charles: Kilcronaghan LY 31; 84

Campbell, Charles: Tamlaght TE 20; 131

Campbell, Daniel: Tamlaght TE 20; 76, 103

Campbell, David: Ballywillin AM 16; 33–34

Campbell, David: Hillsborough DN 12; 107

Campbell, David: Tamlaght O'Crilly LY 18; 107, 118, 125

Campbell, Dr: Clogher TE 5; 28

Campbell, Edward: Coleraine LY 33; 73

Campbell, Elizabeth: Rathlin Island AM 24; 133

Campbell, family: Antrim AM 29; 24

Campbell, family: Ballinderry AM 21; 48

Campbell, family: Ballintoy AM 24; 16, 20

Campbell, family: Ballynure AM 32; 56

Campbell, family: Ballywillin AM 16; 32

Campbell, family: Camlin AM 21; 68

Campbell, family: Carnmoney AM 2; 76

Campbell, family: Carrickfergus AM 37; 93

Campbell, family: Connor AM 19; 23
Campbell, family: Culfeightrin AM 24; 59
Campbell, family: Derrykeighan AM 16; 89
Campbell, family: Donegore AM 29; 110
Campbell, family: Dromara DN 12; 67
Campbell, family: Dunaghy AM 13; 17
Campbell, family: Dunluce AM 16; 117
Campbell, family: Enniskillen FH 4; 58, 75
Campbell, family: Island Magee AM 10; 70
Campbell, family: Killead AM 35; 17
Campbell, family: Kilrea LY 27; 114
Campbell, family: Kilroot AM 26; 74–75
Campbell, family: Maghera LY 18; 13, 48, 74
Campbell, family: Maghera LY 18; 24
Campbell, family: Magheragall AM 21; 99
Campbell, family: Muckamore AM 35; 65
Campbell, family: Nilteen AM 35; 91
Campbell, family: Ramoan AM 24; 107
Campbell, family: Rathlin Island AM 24; 134
Campbell, family: Skerry AM 13; 112
Campbell, family: Tartaraghan AH 1; 121
Campbell, family: Templecorran AM 26; 117, 119
Campbell, Francis: Drumbeg AM 8; 125
Campbell, George: Donaghmore DL 39; 41
Campbell, George: Tyholland MN 40; 175
Campbell, Henry: Aghagallon AM 21; 13, 21
Campbell, Henry: Muckamore AM 35; 81
Campbell, Hill: Loughguile AM 13; 75
Campbell, Hugh: Drumachose LY 9; 66
Campbell, Hugh: Macosquin LY 22; 85, 115
Campbell, James: Ballyscullion LY 6; 65
Campbell, James: Ballywillin LY 33; 48
Campbell, James: Banagher LY 30; 61, 76
Campbell, James: Donacavey TE 5; 65
Campbell, James: Kilwaughter AM 10; 115, 121
Campbell, James: Magheragall AM 21; 101, 107
Campbell, James: Magheramesk AM 21; 121
Campbell, James: Tamlaght Finlagan LY 25; 119
Campbell, James: Tamlaght O'Crilly LY 18; 129
Campbell, James: Termoneeny LY 6; 133
Campbell, James [I]: Carrickfergus AM 37; 40, 148
Campbell, James [II]: Carrickfergus AM 37; 40, 148
Campbell, John: Ardstraw TE 5; 5
Campbell, John: Ballintoy AM 24; 22
Campbell, John: Ballyaghran LY 33; 19, 21
Campbell, John: Ballynascreen LY 31; 30
Campbell, John: Balteagh LY 9; 40
Campbell, John: Blaris DN 12; 42
Campbell, John: Coleraine LY 33; 72
Campbell, John: Culfeightrin AM 24; 53
Campbell, John: Derrykeighan AM 16; 91
Campbell, John: Desertoghill LY 27; 17, 25
Campbell, John: Donagh MN 40; 101
Campbell, John: Donegore AM 29; 126
Campbell, John: Faughanvale LY 36; 37

Campbell, John: Kilcronaghan LY 31; 76–78
Campbell, John: Killead AM 35; 37, 39, 53
Campbell, John: Kilrea LY 27; 129
Campbell, John: Macosquin LY 22; 116
Campbell, John: Maghera LY 18; 53
Campbell, John: Magilligan LY 11; 134
Campbell, John: Skerry AM 13; 119
Campbell, John: Tamlaght Finlagan LY 25; 118
Campbell, John: Tamlaght O'Crilly LY 18; 137
Campbell, John [I]: Carrickfergus AM 37; 102
Campbell, John [II]: Carrickfergus AM 37; 113
Campbell, John [III]: Carrickfergus AM 37; 148
Campbell, Maj.: Tynan AH 1; 130
Campbell, Margot: Tamlaght TE 20; 77
Campbell, Mary: Ballymoney AM 16; 17
Campbell, Mary: Carrickfergus AM 37; 76
Campbell, Mary: Tamlaght Finlagan LY 25; 118
Campbell, Mary Anne: Newry DN 3; 82
Campbell, Maryann: Tamlaght Finlagan LY 25; 118
Campbell, minor: Balteagh LY 9; 45
Campbell, Mr (Ballykelly): Tamlaght Finlagan LY
  25; 93, 96, 125
Campbell, Mr (Snr): Newry DN 3; 99
Campbell, Mr: Antrim AM 29; 44, 49
Campbell, Mr: Donaghmoyne MN 40; 111
Campbell, Mr: Drumragh TE 5; 104
Campbell, Mr: Enniskillen FH 4; 84
Campbell, Mr: Kilwaughter AM 10; 118
Campbell, Mr: Muckno MN 40; 168
Campbell, Neil: Termoneeny LY 6; 133
Campbell, Patrick: Lissan LY 31; 110
Campbell, Peter: Lissan LY 31; 109
Campbell, R.: Killyleagh DN 17; 82
Campbell, R.: Saul DN 17; 115
Campbell, Rev.: Antrim AM 29; 27
Campbell, Rev.: Loughgilly AH 1; 84
Campbell, Rev. Charles: Ardglass DN 17; 7
Campbell, Rev. Charles: Dunboe LY 11; 66
Campbell, Rev. Charles: Newry DN 3; 66, 71,
  76–77, 79, 99, 104
Campbell, Rev. Edward: Ballymore AH 1; 6
Campbell, Rev. James: Carnmoney AM 2; 102
Campbell, Rev. John: Newry DN 3; 76
Campbell, Rev. Robert: Templepatrick AM 35; 119,
  133, 139, 143–44, 147–48
Campbell, Rev. William: Carnmoney AM 2; 39, 57,
  75, 78–79, 86–87
Campbell, Rev. William: Island Magee AM 10; 34,
  68, 70, 85, 87–89, 96–98
Campbell, Rev. William: Templecorran AM 26; 128
Campbell, Robert: Carrickfergus AM 37; 114
Campbell, Robert: Drumachose LY 9; 66, 73
Campbell, Robert: Kilcronaghan LY 31; 84
Campbell, Robert: Layd AM 13; 53
Campbell, Robert: Newry DN 3; 99

Campbell, Robert: Tamlaght O'Crilly LY 18; 137

Campbell, Robert [I]: Tamlaght TE 20; 79, 83

Campbell, Robert [II]: Tamlaght TE 20; 122

Campbell, Sam: Ballymoney AM 16; 17

Campbell, Thomas: Bovevagh LY 25; 13–14, 34–35

Campbell, Thomas: Carrickfergus AM 37; 195

Campbell, Thomas: Island Magee AM 10; 90

Campbell, Thomas: Ramoan AM 24; 108

Campbell, Thomas: Tamlaght TE 20; 82

Campbell, Widow: Donagh DL 38; 32

Campbell, William: Aghadowey LY 22; 20, 34

Campbell, William: Aghagallon AM 21; 20

Campbell, William: Ballyaghran LY 33; 15, 26

Campbell, William: Ballywillin AM 16; 34

Campbell, William: Donegore AM 29; 126

Campbell, William: Drumachose LY 9; 134

Campbell, William: Kilcronaghan LY 31; 85

Campbell, William: Maghera LY 18; 78

Campbell, William: Magilligan LY 11; 132–33

Campbell, William: Tamlaght TE 20; 79

Campbell, William [I]: Aghoghill AM 23; 22, 42, 46

Campbell, William [I]: Tamlaght O'Crilly LY 18; 91, 110, 117

Campbell, William [II]: Aghoghill AM 23; 50

Campbell, William [II]: Tamlaght O'Crilly LY 18; 138

Campbell's High St Academy: Newry DN 3; 82

Campbell's locality: Muckamore AM 35; 81

Campbelltown (Scotland): Coleraine LY 33; 89

Campbelltown: Drumachose LY 9; 117

Campbelltown: Tullyaughnish DL 38; 94

Campion, Arthur: Clones FH 4; 29

Campsey brickfield: Faughanvale LY 36; 16

Campsey House: Faughanvale LY 36; 10

Campsey Lower school: Faughanvale LY 36; 8, 24, 27, 34–36, 66

Campsey Lower td: Faughanvale LY 36; 2, 17, 53–54, 67, 70, 81, 92

Campsey Lower wood: Faughanvale LY 36; 81

Campsey td: Faughanvale LY 36; 10, 16, 53

Campsey Upper td: Faughanvale LY 36; 2, 17, 54, 67, 70–71, 81, 92

Campsey Upper wood: Faughanvale LY 36; 81

Campsey, James: Dungiven LY 15; 24

Campsie (see Campsey): Faughanvale LY 36; 2

Campsie bridge: Cappagh TE 5; 20

Camron, family: Dunluce AM 16; 117

Camus bog: Macosquin LY 22; 77–78, 84, 87, 106, 109–10

Camus cave: Macosquin LY 22; 87, 106

Camus church: Clondermot LY 34; 48

Camus church: Macosquin LY 22; 90

Camus Cottage: Macosquin LY 22; 80, 102

Camus graveyard: Macosquin LY 22; 80, 83–84, 87, 105–06, 119

Camus kilns: Killowen LY 33; 172

Camus old church: Macosquin LY 22; 81, 83–84, 89, 102, 105–06, 109–10, 119

Camus ph: Ballyaghran LY 33; 26

Camus ph: Clonleigh DL 39; 1, 7, 13

Camus ph: Urney DL 39, 174

Camus school: Macosquin LY 22; 92–93

Camus spring: Macosquin LY 22; 119–20

Camus Sunday school: Macosquin LY 22; 93

Camus td: Clonleigh DL 39; 3, 12

Camus td: Macosquin LY 22; 76–77, 87, 106, 122

Canada: Aghabog MN 40; 66

Canada: Aghalurcher FH 4; 12

Canada: Ahoghill AM 23; 17

Canada: Ardclinis AM 13; 8

Canada: Artrea LY 6; 18

Canada: Ballyclug AM 23; 59

Canada: Ballycor AM 32; 7

Canada: Ballynure AM 32; 37

Canada: Ballyscullion LY 6; 56

Canada: Ballywillin LY 33; 37

Canada: Balteagh LY 9; 16

Canada: Belleek FH 14; 5

Canada: Bovevagh LY 25; 59

Canada: Camlin AM 21; 71

Canada: Clondermot LY 34; 16, 29

Canada: Connor AM 19; 25, 31

Canada: Cumber LY 28; 28, 80

Canada: Currin MN 40; 94

Canada: Derryvullan FH 14; 35

Canada: Desertmartin LY 31; 60

Canada: Donacavey TE 5; 72

Canada: Donegore AM 29; 114

Canada: Drumachose LY 9; 87

Canada: Drumkeeran FH 14; 66

Canada: Drumlumman CN 40; 16

Canada: Drummully FH 4; 37

Canada: Drung CN 40; 23

Canada: Dunaghy AM 13; 15

Canada: Dundermot AM 13; 33

Canada: Emlaghfad SO 40; 180

Canada: Faughanvale LY 36; 31

Canada: Finvoy AM 23; 73

Canada: Glenavy AM 21; 89

Canada: Inishmacsaint FH 14; 78

Canada: Killagan AM 23; 85

Canada: Killdrumsherdan CN 40; 36

Canada: Killesher FH 14; 85

Canada: Kilraghts AM 16; 129

Canada: Kilrea LY 27; 118

Canada: Kilskeery TE 5; 116

Canada: Kinawley FH 4; 109

Canada: Kirkinriola AM 23; 107

Canada: Laragh CN 40; 44

Canada: Layd AM 13; 50

Canada: Layd and Inispollan AM 13; 57
Canada: Loughguile AM 13; 65
Canada: Magheraculmoney FH 14; 108
Canada: Misc. AM 10; 130
Canada: Newtown Crommelin AM 13; 83
Canada: Ramoan AM 24; 99
Canada: Rasharkin AM 23; 133
Canada: Skerry AM 13; 114
Canada: Tamlaght Finlagan LY 25; 92, 125
Canada: Tartaraghan AH 1; 122
Canada: Tomregan FH 4; 130
Canada: Trory FH 14; 134
Canada: Tullyrusk AM 21; 138
Canada, British: Ballymoney AM 16; 19
Canagolabeg td: Drumcree AH 1; 34, 40
Canal bridge: Aghalee AM 21; 33–34
Canal quay [I]: Aghalee AM 21; 34
Canal quay [II]: Aghalee AM 21; 34
Canan, magician: Errigal LY 27; 45, 77
Cananeale td: Drumcree AH 1; 40
Cananegahill district: Misc. SO 40; 199
Canary school: Clonfeacle AH 1; 25
Canderry corn mill: Dromore TE 5; 101
Canderry td: Dromore TE 5; 101
Canders, John: Desertoghill LY 27; 16, 18, 23
Cane, John: Racavan AM 13; 96, 100
Cane, Maj.: Drumachose LY 9; 95
Cane, Sarah: Clondermot LY 34; 89
Canecowan chapel: Dunaghy AM 13; 26
Caneese fort: Lissan LY 31; 101
Caneese td: Lissan LY 31; 108–09
Canfield giant's grave [I]: Laragh CN 40; 42
Canfield giant's grave [II]: Laragh CN 40; 42
Canice, St: Faughanvale LY 36; 48
Canning and Co., Messrs: Ballyaghran LY 33; 19
Canning and Co., Messrs: Ballywillin LY 33; 39
Canning moss: Desertoghill LY 27; 14
Canning, Alexander: Newry DN 3; 95, 100, 103
Canning, Annjane: Drumachose LY 9; 133
Canning, David: Aghadowey LY 22; 38
Canning, family: Agivey LY 22; 40, 44
Canning, family: Clondermot LY 34; 32
Canning, family: Desertoghill LY 27; 14
Canning, family: Dunboe LY 11; 79
Canning, family: Shilvodan AM 19; 136
Canning, George: Magilligan LY 11; 132
Canning, George: Tamlaght O'Crilly LY 18; 105
Canning, George [I]: Errigal LY 27; 37, 41, 56
Canning, George [II]: Errigal LY 27; 37
Canning, James: Ballymoney AM 16; 15, 17
Canning, James: Clondermot LY 34; 78
Canning, James: Coleraine LY 33; 72
Canning, James: Cumber LY 28; 56–57
Canning, James: Dungiven LY 15; 74
Canning, John: Coleraine LY 33; 66, 134

Canning, John: Maghera LY 18; 76
Canning, John [I]: Drumachose LY 9; 104, 110
Canning, John [II]: Drumachose LY 9; 133
Canning, man named (Glack): Tamlaght Finlagan
    LY 25; 114
Canning, man named: Desertoghill LY 27; 14, 23
Canning, Marcus: Drumachose LY 9; 133
Canning, Mary: Aghadowey LY 22; 36
Canning, Mr: Dungiven LY 15; 34
Canning, Mr: Misc. LY 36; 111
Canning, Patrick: Magilligan LY 11; 88
Canning, Paul: Errigal LY 27; 35, 74
Canning, Rose: Magilligan LY 11; 131
Canning, Thomas: Banagher LY 30; 52, 88
Canning, William: Aghalee AM 21; 36
Canning, William: Clondermot LY 34; 78
Cannon hill: Loughguile AM 13; 74
Cannon stone: Loughguile AM 13; 70, 74
Cannon, John: Blaris DN 12; 40–41
Cannon, John: Doagh AM 29; 88
Cannon, Miss: Ballyscullion AM 19; 14
Cannon, Mrs Philip: Ballyscullion AM 19; 14–15
Cannon, Philip: Ballyscullion AM 19; 3, 9, 14
Cannoreagh td: Misc. DN 17; 124
Cannyreagh td: Donaghadee DN 7; 45
Canon's field: Magilligan LY 11; 143
Canterbury, Archbishop of: Misc. DN 17; 118
Caolin lough: Culfeightrin AM 24; 81
Cape Castle bog: Ramoan AM 24; 117, 124
Cape Castle cave: Ramoan AM 24; 116
Cape Castle meeting house: Ramoan AM 24; 106
Cape Castle td: Ramoan AM 24; 88
Cape Dobbs (Canada): Kilroot AM 26; 73
Cape Feare (New Brunswick): Kilroot AM 26; 73
Cape of Good Hope (Africa): Drumgoon CN 40; 1
Caple, Mr (Prospect House): Kilmore AH 1; 72
Capnagh hill: Kilwaughter AM 10; 119
Cappagh church: Cappagh TE 5; 18
Cappagh corn mill: Annaclone DN 12; 14
Cappagh flax mill: Annaclone DN 12; 14
Cappagh fort: Annaclone DN 12; 13
Cappagh Glebe House: Cappagh TE 5; 18
Cappagh meeting house: Cappagh TE 5; 18
Cappagh mill [I]: Annaclone DN 12; 18
Cappagh mill [II]: Annaclone DN 12; 18
Cappagh More td: Ballyaghran LY 33; 8
Cappagh More wood: Ballyaghran LY 33; 1
Cappagh mountain: Pomeroy TE 20; 70, 72
Cappagh old church: Cappagh TE 5; 18
Cappagh ph: Ardstraw TE 5; 2
Cappagh ph: Clogherny TE 20; 25, 28
Cappagh ph: Drumragh TE 5; 104, 110–11
Cappagh schools: Cappagh TE 5; 18
Cappagh Sunday school: Cappagh TE 5; 18
Cappagh td: Annaclone DN 12; 14, 16, 18

Cappenagh district: Misc. SO 40; 198

Cappog bridge: Tydavnet MN 40; 171

Cappy corn mill: Derrybrusk FH 4; 31

Cappy td: Derrybrusk FH 4; 30–32

Capragh td: Donaghmoyne MN 40; 106

Captain's lough: Kilrea LY 27; 112–13

Car hill: Kilcronaghan LY 31; 69

Car Island: Trory FH 14; 122

Car td: Clogher TE 5; 36

Car well: Desertoghill LY 27; 25

Car, Joseph: Clondermot LY 34; 83

Carabane td: Bright DN 17; 34–35

Carabard district: Rasharkin AM 23; 140

Caraclogher demesne: Clogher TE 5; 26

Caracloughan td: Drumtullagh AM 16; 96

Caradoan (see Carradoan): Killygarvan DL 38; 47

Caradorn td: Saintfield DN 7; 120

Caradowan (see Carradoan): Killygarvan DL 38; 38

Caraher, John: Newry DN 3; 99, 104

Carahran (see Carrowcrin)

Caralaverty school: Armoy AM 24; 9

Caraloan td: Magherafelt LY 6; 111

Carannamaragh corn mill: Kilskeery TE 5; 114

Carannamaragh td: Kilskeery TE 5; 114

Carantall, family: Carnmoney AM 2; 76

Carbalintober (Carballintober) td: Desertoghill LY
    27; 19–20, 25

Carbalintober flax mill: Desertoghill LY 27; 5

Carbalintober school: Desertoghill LY 27; 3, 18, 20,
    25, 32–33

Carbalintober standing stones: Desertoghill LY 27;
    7, 25

Carbalintober stream: Desertoghill LY 27; 5

Carbalintober Sunday school: Desertoghill LY 27; 3

Carbalintober well: Desertoghill LY 27; 5–7

Carbary, John: Muckamore AM 35; 79

Carbary, Mr (Tirgracey): Muckamore AM 35; 68

Carbullion brickfield: Aghanloo LY 11; 2, 32

Carbullion td: Aghanloo LY 11; 1–3, 10, 14, 18–19,
    22, 24–25, 31, 37, 39–41

Carcloughey flax mill: Derrykeighan AM 16; 79

Carcreeghy td: Newry DN 3; 105–06

Carcullion corn mill: Clonduff DN 3; 5

Carcullion td: Clonduff DN 3; 5

Cardie village: Grey Abbey DN 7; 68

Cardie village: Misc. DN 17; 123

Cardonaghy (Carndonaghy) td: Ahoghill AM 23; 12,
    35, 37–38

Cardonaghy corn mill: Ahoghill AM 23; 13

Cardonaghy coves: Ahoghill AM 23; 27, 35

Cardonaghy fort [I]: Ahoghill AM 23; 35

Cardonaghy fort [II]: Ahoghill AM 23; 35

Cardonaghy fort [III]: Ahoghill AM 23; 35

Cardwell, family: Glenavy AM 21; 86

Carentall mill: Clogher TE 5; 34

Carew, James: Rasharkin AM 23; 135, 141

Carey (see also Cary)

Carey and Field, Messrs: Banagher LY 30; 22, 131

Carey glen: Culfeightrin AM 24; 64

Carey Mill corn mill: Culfeightrin AM 24; 45, 63

Carey standing stone: Ramoan AM 24; 120

Carey water: Culfeightrin AM 24; 40–43, 52–53, 55,
    63, 67

Carey, Arthur: Bovevagh LY 25; 17–18, 43

Carey, Col: Aghanloo LY 11; 14

Carey, Edward: Cumber LY 28; 62

Carey, family: Bovevagh LY 25; 7

Carey, George: Agivey LY 22; 43

Carey, Henry: Skerry AM 13; 120

Carey, John: Newry DN 3; 79

Carey, Rev.: Raloo AM 32; 83

Carey, Rev. Anthony: Taughboyne DL 39; 148, 154

Carey, Rev. John: Coleraine LY 33; 95, 142

Carey, Sarah: Banagher LY 30; 120

Carey, Thomas: Ballyscullion LY 6; 57

Carey, William: Duneane AM 19; 116

Cargabane td: Aughnamullen MN 40; 75

Cargacreevy td: Annahilt DN 12; 21–22

Cargaduff td: Aughnamullen MN 40; 75

Cargagh chapel: Ballyculter DN 17; 30

Cargagh td: Clogher TE 5; 36

Cargagh td: Down DN 17; 52, 57

Cargagh td: Inch DN 17; 77

Cargaghmore school: Magheross MN 40; 150

Cargaghmore td: Magheross MN 40; 148

Cargaghnabraig td: Down DN 17; 56

Cargaghogue td: Magheross MN 40; 148

Cargagray td: Annahilt DN 12; 20–21

Cargan (Cargon) td: Dunaghy AM 13; 14, 17, 22, 24

Cargan church: Dunaghy AM 13; 17

Cargan rock giant's bed: Dunaghy AM 13; 24

Cargan standing stone: Dunaghy AM 13; 20, 22

Cargan, James: Hillsborough DN 12; 106

Cargans school: Ballymore AH 1; 11, 15

Cargans td: Ballymore AH 1; 8, 11, 15–18

Cargaragh mountain: Aghalurcher FH 4; 2

Cargavane td: Newry DN 3; 61

Cargin chapel: Duneane AM 19; 95, 100, 115, 119,
    122

Cargin district: Misc. SO 40; 199

Cargin old chapel: Duneane AM 19; 115

Cargin school: Duneane AM 19; 125

Cargin td: Duneane AM 19; 124

Cargragh td: Clogher TE 5; 53

Cargycroy td: Drumbo DN 7; 61

Carhill school (see Carbalintober): Desertoghill LY
    27; 33

Carhookeel td: Enniskillen FH 4; 82

Carhoonagiltiagh school: Enniskillen FH 4; 83

Carhoonagiltiagh td: Enniskillen FH 4; 82

Carhoonaleg td: Cleenish FH 14; 29
Carickatain td: Donaghedy TE 5; 91
Carinaff td: Moville DL 38; 73
Carinamalert td: Misc. DN 17; 124
Carinshanaugh td: Taughboyne DL 39; 152
Carivcashel cashel: Loughguile AM 13; 69
Carivcashel graveyard: Loughguile AM 13; 68, 72
Carivcashel td: Loughguile AM 13; 68–70, 72
Carkoonagilliagh (see Carhoonagiltiagh):
    Enniskillen FH 4; 82
Carlan Upper district: Clondavaddog DL 38; 4
Carland river: Drumglass TE 20; 40, 44
Carland, James: Raymoghy DL 39; 140
Carlane td: Duneane AM 19; 123
Carlaragh td: Tamlaght Finlagan LY 25; 93
Carleton, Christopher: Boho FH 14; 8
Carleton, Dr: Blaris DN 12; 44, 47–48
Carleton, family: Blaris AM 8; 21
Carleton, family: Clondermot LY 34; 53
Carleton, Mary Anne: Seapatrick DN 12; 135
Carleton, Mr (Green Park): Kilbroney DN 3; 35
Carleton, Mr (Portadown): Seagoe AH 1; 108
Carleton, Patrick: Loughguile AM 13; 77
Carleton, Rev. Peter: Aghadowey LY 22; 22
Carleton, Rev. Richard: Killead AM 35; 20, 44
Carleton, Thomas (Jnr): Blaris DN 12; 40
Carleton, Thomas: Blaris AM 8; 35, 37, 45, 55, 67,
    74
Carley, family: Kilroot AM 26; 74–75
Carley, Rev. James: Antrim AM 29; 12, 26–27, 42,
    44–45, 58
Carlile, Rev.: Carnmoney AM 2; 75
Carlile, Richard: Kilcronaghan LY 31; 81
Carlin, family: Clondermot LY 34; 53
Carlin, George: Cumber LY 28; 28
Carlin, Margaret (Jnr): Killead AM 35; 51
Carlin, Margaret (Snr): Killead AM 35; 51
Carlin, Nancy: Killead AM 35; 51
Carlin, William: Cumber LY 28; 28
Carline stone: Faughanvale LY 36; 15
Carlingford: Clonallan DN 3; 2
Carlingford: Drumgath DN 3; 20
Carlingford: Kilbroney DN 3; 32, 35, 37
Carlingford: Killyleagh DN 17; 84, 86
Carlingford: Newry DN 3; 64, 73, 85, 87
Carlingford bar: Newry DN 3; 90
Carlingford bay: Drumgath DN 3; 19
Carlingford bay: Newry DN 3; 73
Carlingford bay: Warrenpoint DN 3; 120
Carlingford Castle: Kilkeel DN 3; 53
Carlingford Castle: Newry DN 3; 65
Carlingford Castle: Warrenpoint DN 3; 120
Carlingford chapel (C): Carlingford LH 40; 60
Carlingford chapel (WM): Carlingford LH 40; 60
Carlingford church: Carlingford LH 40; 60

Carlingford corn mill: Carlingford LH 40; 59
Carlingford dispensary: Carlingford LH 40; 59
Carlingford harbour: Newry DN 3; 86–87
Carlingford lighthouse: Newry DN 3; 86
Carlingford Lough: Kilbroney DN 3; 26, 28, 32
Carlingford Lough: Kilkeel DN 3; 46–48, 52
Carlingford Lough: Newry DN 3; 61, 72, 86
Carlingford Lough: Warrenpoint DN 3; 115–17,
    119–20
Carlingford manor: Newry DN 3; 64–65
Carlingford meeting house: Carlingford LH 40; 60
Carlingford mountains: Kilbroney DN 3; 29
Carlingford mountains: Warrenpoint DN 3; 116
Carlingford quarries: Warrenpoint DN 3; 119
Carlingford school [I]: Carlingford LH 40; 59
Carlingford school [II]: Carlingford LH 40; 60
Carlingford school [III]: Carlingford LH 40; 60
Carlingford, Earl of: Misc. SO 40; 198
Carlisle deanery: Dromore DN 12; 74
Carlisle, Mrs: Hillsborough DN 12; 106
Carlisle, Mrs: Newry DN 3; 98, 103
Carlisle, Rev. Robert: Ballinderry AM 21; 50
Carlisle, Rev. Samuel: Ballyrashane LY 22; 62
Carlisle, Rev. Samuel: Coleraine LY 33; 95, 140–41
Carlisle, Rev. Samuel: Macosquin LY 22; 90, 100
Carlisle, Robert: Newry DN 3; 74
Carlisle, William [I]: Hillsborough DN 12; 107
Carlisle, William [II]: Hillsborough DN 12; 107
Carlongford td: Cumber LY 28; 64
Carloton Blaris district: Blaris AM 8; 86
Carlow county: Faughanvale LY 36; 12
Carlow town: Kilcronaghan LY 31; 81
Carlow, John: Clondermot LY 34; 82
Carlton, John: Drummaul AM 19; 91
Carlton, Margaret: Drummaul AM 19; 91
Carlton, Thomas: Drummaul AM 19; 91
Carlton, William: Artrea LY 6; 21
Carlusk (see Corlust): Ballymore AH 1; 16
Carmagarve td: Moville DL 38; 70
Carmaigraw fort: Ahoghill AM 23; 35
Carmaigraw td: Ahoghill AM 23; 37, 39–40
Carmalt, Thomas: Clondermot LY 34; 6, 37–38, 78,
    104
Carmaquigley (see Carrickmaquigley): Moville DL
    38; 75
Carmarthen, Marquis of: Donacavey TE 5; 74
Carmavy cove: Killead AM 35; 49
Carmavy cove [I]: Carmavy AM 35; 5–6
Carmavy cove [II]: Carmavy AM 35; 6
Carmavy fort: Carmavy AM 35; 5–6
Carmavy graveyard: Carmavy AM 35; 2, 4, 6
Carmavy hill: Carmavy AM 35; 1
Carmavy old church: Carmavy AM 35; 2, 4
Carmavy ph: Killead AM 35; 9, 20
Carmavy ph: Misc. AM 10; 129

Carmavy ph: Templepatrick AM 35; 106, 142
Carmavy rivulet: Carmavy AM 35; 5
Carmavy school: Carmavy AM 35; 3, 6
Carmavy school [I]: Killead AM 35; 43, 51, 53
Carmavy school [II]: Killead AM 35; 53
Carmavy Sunday school: Carmavy AM 35; 3, 6
Carmavy Sunday school: Killead AM 35; 51
Carmean td: Artrea TE 20; 6
Carmichael, Daniel: Ballyscullion LY 6; 58
Carmichael, David: Donaghadee DN 7; 51
Carmichael, family: Ballyclug AM 23; 63
Carmichael, family: Derryaghy AM 8; 103
Carmichael, family: Drumbeg AM 8; 123
Carmichael, Hugh: Ballyscullion AM 19; 11
Carmichael, Margaret: Carrickfergus AM 37; 126
Carmichael, Mrs: Donaghadee DN 7; 51
Carmichael, Rev. James: Carncastle and Killyglen
    AM 10; 7
Carmichael, Samuel: Moville DL 38; 75, 78
Carmichael, William: Donaghadee DN 7; 51
Carmonalea td: Galloon FH 4; 95
Carmoney school: Faughanvale LY 36; 34–35
Carmoney td: Faughanvale LY 36; 17, 53–54, 67,
    71, 81–82, 92, 98
Carmoney td: Mevagh DL 38; 55
Carmony (see Carmoney): Faughanvale LY 36; 53
Carmoon cove: Billy AM 16; 56
Carmoon td: Ramoan AM 24; 120
Carmorn (Carmain) td: Duneane AM 19; 111, 117,
    124
Carn: Clonmany DL 38; 14, 16–18, 20
Carn: Culdaff DL 38; 22
Carn: Desertegney DL 38; 28–28
Carn: Donagh DL 38; 32–34
Carn: Lough Swilly DL 38; 135
Carn: Mintiaghs DL 38; 64–66
Carn: Muff DL 38; 81
Carn Billy hill: Carrickfergus AM 37; 5
Carn bog: Dunboe LY 11; 73
Carn bogs: Macosquin LY 22; 78, 119
Carn burn: Dungiven LY 15; 47, 49, 80
Carn cave: Ballintoy AM 24; 30
Carn cloth mill: Lough Swilly DL 38; 137
Carn dispensary: Mintiaghs DL 38; 65
Carn druid's altar: Dungiven LY 15; 41
Carn fort: Dunboe LY 11; 73
Carn fort: Dungiven LY 15; 45, 87, 89
Carn Gool giant's grave: Aghabog MN 40; 64
Carn graveyard: Templecarn DL 39; 156, 159
Carn Greine church: Templepatrick AM 35; 133
Carn Greine grave: Templepatrick AM 35; 107, 110,
    115, 125–26, 129, 132, 137, 140, 151
Carn hill: Aghabog MN 40; 62
Carn hill: Killelagh LY 27; 100–01
Carn hill: Kinawley FH 4; 113

Carn inns: Donagh DL 38; 32
Carn Little td: Derryvullan FH 14; 46
Carn mountain: Bovevagh LY 25; 42
Carn mountain: Clonduff DN 3; 5
Carn mountain: Dungiven LY 15; 1, 30, 78
Carn Neill (see Carneal): Ardclinis AM 13; 3
Carn old church: Templecarn DL 39; 156, 159
Carn old wood: Donagh DL 38; 32
Carn rock: Duneane AM 19; 112
Carn school: Clondermot LY 34; 87, 95
Carn school: Donagh DL 38; 31, 33
Carn school: Dungiven LY 15; 18, 117–18
Carn springs: Macosquin LY 22; 119
Carn standing stone: Ballintoy AM 24; 30
Carn td: Aghabog MN 40; 64, 67
Carn td: Banagher LY 30; 3, 7, 22, 104
Carn td: Boho FH 14; 9
Carn td: Clondermot LY 34; 38, 56, 61–62, 67, 108,
    112–14, 122, 130
Carn td: Drumachose LY 9; 118
Carn td: Dungiven LY 15; 10, 16, 19, 22, 27, 45–46,
    49, 53, 61, 63, 66, 71, 74, 78, 83, 90, 92, 101, 105
Carn td: Enniskillen FH 4; 82
Carn td: Kinawley FH 4; 113
Carn td: Macosquin LY 22; 122
Carn td: Maghera LY 18; 9, 65
Carn td: Magheraculmoney FH 14; 103, 113
Carn td: Mintiaghs DL 38; 67
Carn td: Templecarn DL 39; 164
Carn trigonometrical station: Aghabog MN 40; 64
Carn wood: Clondermot LY 34; 122
Carnabaartan rock: Lough Swilly DL 38; 121–22
Carnaboy meeting house: Ballywillin LY 33; 33, 43
Carnaboy td: Killead AM 35; 35
Carnacally (see Carnacully): Kilmore DN 17; 88
Carnacally bog: Newry DN 3; 110
Carnacally td: Newry DN 3; 106
Carnacaw cromlech: Ballee DN 17; 19
Carnacaw td: Ballee DN 17; 20, 22–23
Carnachan, family: Finvoy AM 23; 76
Carnaclare trigonometrical station: Desertoghill LY
    27; 16
Carnacullia giant's grave: Cleenish FH 14; 22
Carnacullia stone circle: Cleenish FH 14; 22
Carnacullia td: Cleenish FH 14; 22
Carnacully church: Kilmore DN 17; 88, 92
Carnacully corn mill: Kilmore DN 17; 88, 92
Carnacully flax mill: Kilmore DN 17; 88, 92
Carnacully quarry: Kilmore DN 17; 93
Carnadore td: Donaghmore DL 39; 36
Carnafarn td: Clondermot LY 34; 56, 62, 108, 112,
    114–15, 122, 130
Carnafarn wood: Clondermot LY 34; 122
Carnaff bog: Derrykeighan AM 16; 81
Carnaff fort: Derrykeighan AM 16; 91

Carnaff fort: Dunluce AM 16; 116
Carnaff school: Derrykeighan AM 16; 86
Carnaff td: Derrykeighan AM 16; 94
Carnagariff td: Moville DL 38; 68
Carnagat td: Clogher TE 5; 53
Carnagat td: Enniskillen FH 4; 74, 82
Carnageeragh (Carnageragh) td: Kilraghts AM 16;
  136
Carnageeragh cove: Kilraghts AM 16; 131–32, 134
Carnageeragh hill: Kilraghts AM 16; 128
Carnageeragh meeting house: Kilraghts AM 16;
  124, 127
Carnageeraragh (see Carnageeragh): Kilraghts AM
  16; 128
Carnagh Lower td: Drumlumman CN 40; 15, 17
Carnagh td: Bright DN 17; 35
Carnaghan, family: Carrickfergus AM 37; 93
Carnaghan, Jane: Carrickfergus AM 37; 76
Carnaghan, William (Snr): Hillsborough DN 12; 107
Carnaghan, William: Annahilt DN 12; 23
Carnaghan, William: Tamlaght TE 20; 79, 83–84
Carnaghlis (see Carnaghliss): Killead AM 35; 7
Carnaghliss coal mine: Killead AM 35; 50
Carnaghliss hill: Killead AM 35; 7
Carnaghliss td: Killead AM 35; 30, 40, 52
Carnaghts (Carnaght) td: Connor AM 19; 21, 29
Carnaghts meeting house: Connor AM 19; 21, 29
Carnaghts school: Connor AM 19; 27
Carnagiltagh hill: Aghavea FH 4; 17
Carnagilty (see Cornagilty): Tydavnet MN 40; 172
Carnagore td: Mevagh DL 38; 55, 63
Carnagormeg mountain: Skerry AM 13; 118, 120
Carnagribban td: Donaghedy TE 5; 91
Carnahan, William: Hillsborough DN 12; 107
Carnahenny (see Carnahinny)
Carnahinny (Carnakinny) td: Clogher TE 5; 35, 53
Carnakilly Lower td: Faughanvale LY 36; 17, 55,
  67, 71, 82, 92, 98
Carnakilly Lower wood: Faughanvale LY 36; 82
Carnakilly td: Faughanvale LY 36; 53
Carnakilly Upper td: Faughanvale LY 36; 17, 55,
  67, 71, 82, 92, 98
Carnalbanagh fort: Ballyaghran LY 33; 11, 24
Carnalbina (see Cairnalbanagh): Tickmacrevan AM
  13; 133
Carnalblanagh East td: Moira DN 12; 120
Carnalblanagh West td: Moira DN 12; 120
Carnalea (Carnaleagh) td: Bangor DN 7; 19
Carnalea fort: Donacavey TE 5; 83
Carnalea mountain: Dromore TE 5; 93
Carnalea river: Donacavey TE 5; 62
Carnalea td: Donacavey TE 5; 76–78, 80–81, 83, 85
Carnalea td: Dromore TE 5; 98
Carnalea td: Misc. DN 17; 124
Carnaloe (see Carnalea)

Carnalridge flax mill: Ballywillin LY 33; 39–40, 44,
  48
Carnalridge td: Ballywillin LY 33; 48
Carnamaddy district: Lough Swilly DL 38; 103, 145
Carnamail td: Muff DL 38; 80
Carnamenagh corn mill: Loughguile AM 13; 63
Carnamenagh flax mill: Loughguile AM 13; 63
Carnamenagh fort: Loughguile AM 13; 71
Carnamenagh td: Loughguile AM 13; 71
Carnamoney bridge: Ballynascreen LY 31; 6–7
Carnamoney female school: Ballynascreen LY 31;
  17
Carnamoney graveyard: Ballynascreen LY 31; 31
Carnamoney graveyard: Desertoghill LY 27; 7
Carnamoney male school: Ballynascreen LY 31; 17
Carnamoney td: Ballynascreen LY 31; 31, 141–43
Carnamucklagh (see Cornamucklagh): Carlingford
  LH 40; 58
Carnamuclagh td: Clogher TE 5; 53
Carnamuff td: Faughanvale LY 36; 17, 53, 55, 67,
  71, 82, 93, 98
Carnamuff td: Tamlaght Finlagan LY 25; 72–74
Carnan (see Carran): Errigal Keerogue TE 20; 56
Carnan Rory (see Roly Ballaghan's Grave):
  Drumtullagh AM 16; 101
Carnan Thruir stones: Ramoan AM 24; 118
Carnanbaan (see Carnanbane): Dungiven LY 15; 18
Carnanbalagh (see Carnalbanagh): Ballyaghran LY
  33; 11
Carnanbane (Carnanbaan) td: Banagher LY 30; 3,
  10, 22, 31–32, 35–36, 44, 48, 61–62, 69, 76, 81,
  84, 95, 99, 103, 109, 112, 117, 122, 126, 129, 131
Carnanbane (Carnenbane) td: Dungiven LY 15; 45,
  92
Carnanbane bridge: Banagher LY 30; 49
Carnanbane cairn: Banagher LY 30; 57
Carnanbane cave: Banagher LY 30; 47–48, 78
Carnanbane enclosure: Banagher LY 30; 49, 56
Carnanbane flax mill: Banagher LY 30; 29, 126
Carnanbane giant's grave: Banagher LY 30; 47, 56,
  82–83
Carnanbane graveyard: Banagher LY 30; 78
Carnanbane hill: Banagher LY 30; 24, 43, 81
Carnanbane hill: Bovevagh LY 25; 10
Carnanbane old church: Banagher LY 30; 49
Carnanbane quarry: Banagher LY 30; 126
Carnanbane quarry: Cumber LY 28; 122
Carnanbane school: Dungiven LY 15; 18
Carnanbane standing stone: Banagher LY 30; 100
Carnanbane td: Cumber LY 28; 30–31, 66, 68, 111,
  117, 122, 125
Carnanbane well: Banagher LY 30; 100
Carnanbane wood: Banagher LY 30; 2, 100, 122
Carnanee bridge: Ballyaghran LY 33; 10
Carnanee forts: Ballymartin AM 2; 15, 17

Carnanee paper mill: Ballymartin AM 2; 4

Carnanee school: Ballymartin AM 2; 13

Carnanee Sunday school: Ballymartin AM 2; 13

Carnanee td: Ballyaghran LY 33; 10, 24

Carnanee td: Ballylinny AM 32; 22, 30

Carnanee td: Ballymartin AM 2; 11, 15–16

Carnaneigh cave: Culfeightrin AM 24; 41

Carnaneigh hill: Culfeightrin AM 24; 36, 39, 41

Carnaneigh trigonometrical station: Culfeightrin AM
24; 41

Carnanena carn: Drumtullagh AM 16; 102

Carnanmore cove: Culfeightrin AM 24; 75

Carnanmore stones: Culfeightrin AM 24; 75–76

Carnan-na-cuillic stones: Culfeightrin AM 24; 57

Carnanny td: Drumgath DN 3; 21

Carnanreagh fort: Cumber LY 28; 30

Carnanreagh standing stone: Cumber LY 28; 32

Carnanreagh td: Cumber LY 28; 66, 68, 111, 117,
122, 125

Carn-an-truagh stones: Armoy AM 24; 8

Carnany Lower td: Ballymoney AM 16; 25

Carnany Upper td: Ballymoney AM 16; 25

Carnareagh (see Carnaveagh): Aughnamullen MN
40; 71

Carnaree (see Carnanee): Ballymartin AM 2; 15

Carnarook (see Carnarousk)

Carnaroosk (see Carnarousk)

Carnarousk td: Donacavey TE 5; 76–78, 80–81, 83,
85

Carnarusk (see Carnarousk)

Carnarvonshire church (Wales): Banagher LY 30;
101

Carnashamer creek: Lough Swilly DL 38; 137

Carnately (Carnealty) td: Ramoan AM 24; 116–17,
124

Carnately cave [I]: Ramoan AM 24; 116

Carnately cave [II]: Ramoan AM 24; 116–17

Carnately mill: Ramoan AM 24; 88

Carnately mound: Ramoan AM 24; 117

Carnaught (see Carnaghts): Connor AM 19; 27

Carnaveagh House: Aughnamullen MN 40; 71

Carnaveagh school: Aughnamullen MN 40; 77

Carnaveagh td: Aughnamullen MN 40; 75

Carnavery td: Dungiven LY 15; 88

Carnbaan Island: Lough Swilly DL 38; 111

Carnbane demesne: Blaris DN 12; 32

Carnbane locality: Lissan LY 31; 102

Carnbane td: Blaris DN 12; 34

Carnbane td: Hillsborough DN 12; 107

Carnbeg carn: Dunaghy AM 13; 21

Carnbeg cave: Dunaghy AM 13; 24

Carnbeg corn mill: Loughgilly AH 1; 86

Carnbeg flax mill: Loughgilly AH 1; 86

Carnbeg fort: Dunaghy AM 13; 28

Carnbeg fort: Newtown Crommelin AM 13; 81

Carnbeg graveyard: Dunaghy AM 13; 17

Carnbeg meeting house: Dunaghy AM 13; 13

Carnbeg old graveyard: Dunaghy AM 13; 24

Carnbeg standing stones: Dunaghy AM 13; 19, 22

Carnbeg td: Dunaghy AM 13; 13, 19, 21–22

Carnben td: Clogher TE 5; 53

Carnbore cairn: Billy AM 16; 73

Carnbore cove: Billy AM 16; 56, 74

Carnbore old graveyard: Billy AM 16; 52, 74

Carnbore river: Billy AM 16; 36, 40

Carnbore td: Billy AM 16; 58–59, 73

Carnbrock td: Kilroot AM 26; 72

Carnbrock td: Templecorran AM 26; 114, 121

Carnbrock threshing machine: Templecorran AM
26; 125

Carnbuck mountain: Dunaghy AM 13; 11

Carnbuck mountain: Dundermot AM 13; 30

Carnbuck mountain: Killagan AM 23; 80, 82

Carnbuck mountain: Loughguile AM 13; 59–61

Carncaggy fort: Derrykeighan AM 16; 91

Carncastle: Kilwaughter AM 10; 116

Carncastle Castle: Carncastle and Killyglen AM 10;
11

Carncastle church: Kilwaughter AM 10; 116

Carncastle national school: Carncastle and Killyglen
AM 10; 6

Carncastle ph: Ballycor AM 32; 5

Carncastle ph: Kilwaughter AM 10; 106, 111, 117

Carncastle ph: Misc. AM 10; 129

Carncastle ph: Raloo AM 32; 116

Carncastle ph: Rashee AM 32; 138

Carncastle ph: Templecorran AM 26; 103

Carncastle ph: Tickmacrevan AM 13; 122

Carncastle school: Carncastle and Killyglen AM 10;
6

Carncloghey (see Carncoggy)

Carncoagh (Carncoa) td: Skerry AM 13; 118–20

Carncoagh cave: Skerry AM 13; 119

Carncoagh fort: Skerry AM 13; 120

Carncoagh mountain: Skerry AM 13; 105

Carncoggy (Carncloghey) td: Derrykeighan AM 16;
78–79, 87, 95

Carncoggy flax mills: Derrykeighan AM 16; 84

Carncoghan school: Termonamongan TE 5; 144

Carncoghan td: Termonamongan TE 5; 144

Carncolach (see Carncullagh): Derrykeighan AM
16; 87

Carncormick mountain: Skerry AM 13; 105, 109

Carncorran Glebe chapel: Skirts of Urney and
Ardstraw TE 5; 138

Carncose td: Desertmartin LY 31; 57, 62, 141–42

Carncross, Hugh: Drumachose LY 9; 66

Carncullagh fort: Derrykeighan AM 16; 91

Carncullagh Lower meeting house: Derrykeighan
AM 16; 79

Carncullagh Lower td: Derrykeighan AM 16; 93

Carncullagh meeting house: Derrykeighan AM 16; 84

Carncullagh td: Derrykeighan AM 16; 87–88, 91–93

Carncullagh Upper fort: Derrykeighan AM 16; 80, 91

Carndaisy fort: Desertlyn LY 31; 44

Carndaisy glen: Desertlyn LY 31; 35–36, 42

Carndaisy hill: Desertlyn LY 31; 36

Carndaisy meeting house: Desertlyn LY 31; 42

Carndaisy school: Desertlyn LY 31; 42

Carndaisy td: Lissan LY 31; 98

Carndonagh (see Carn)

Carndonagh ph: Lough Swilly DL 38; 135

Carndonagh td: Donagh DL 38; 31

Carndoogan (see Carndougan): Macosquin LY 22; 122

Carndougan cove: Macosquin LY 22; 87

Carndougan standing stones: Macosquin LY 22; 87, 108

Carndougan td: Macosquin LY 22; 108, 122

Carndreelagh sound: Lough Swilly DL 38; 111

Carnduff cave: Ramoan AM 24; 119

Carnduff hill: Inver AM 26; 50

Carnduff school: Ramoan AM 24; 100, 126

Carnduff td: Glynn AM 26; 30

Carnduff td: Inver AM 26; 49, 52

Carne (see Carn)

Carneal fort: Raloo AM 32; 117, 122, 133

Carneal mountain: Ardclinis AM 13; 1, 3, 5

Carneal mountain: Layd AM 13; 36

Carneal mountain: Raloo AM 32; 82

Carneal school: Raloo AM 32; 117–18, 133

Carneal spade mill: Raloo AM 32; 120

Carneal Sunday school: Raloo AM 32; 118–19

Carneal td: Raloo AM 32; 80, 103, 128, 133

Carneal tumulus: Raloo AM 32; 112–13

Carnean td: Ballee DN 17; 22

Carneany (see Carnearny): Shilvodan AM 19; 129

Carneany (see Carninney): Ahoghill AM 23; 28

Carnearney (see Carninney): Ahoghill AM 23; 38

Carnearny mountain: Antrim AM 29; 1

Carnearny mountain: Connor AM 19; 19, 28

Carnearny mountain: Donegore AM 29; 104–05, 115, 122

Carnearny mountain: Shilvodan AM 19; 128–29

Carnearny quarry: Donegore AM 29; 101

Carnearny quarry: Muckamore AM 35; 70

Carnearny td: Connor AM 19; 16

Carnearny td: Donegore AM 29; 119

Carneckananny (see Carrickananny): Loughgilly AH 1; 86

Carnegarve (Donegal): Cumber LY 28; 80

Carnegat td: Clogher TE 5; 37

Carnegraney (see Carngranny): Ballylinny AM 32; 22

Carnegy, family: Billy AM 16; 58, 68

Carneighaneigh (Carnicaneigh) td: Culfeightrin AM 24; 39

Carneighaneigh hill: Culfeightrin AM 24; 36, 41, 83

Carneighaneigh stones: Culfeightrin AM 24; 83

Carneighaniegh (see Carneighaneigh): Culfeightrin AM 24; 36

Carneihaneigh (see Carneighaneigh): Culfeightrin AM 24; 41

Carnelt, family: Misc. LY 36; 104

Carnen field: Balteagh LY 9; 10

Carnen graveyard: Balteagh LY 9; 30

Carnenbane (see Carnanbane): Banagher LY 30; 61

Carneshrah locality: Clondermot LY 34; 69

Carnesure td: Comber DN 7; 37, 40, 42–43

Carnet fort: Balteagh LY 9; 12, 26

Carnet td: Balteagh LY 9; 12, 26, 40, 43, 45

Carnetowne locality: Clondermot LY 34; 59

Carnew Cottage: Garvaghy DN 12; 80

Carnew hill: Garvaghy DN 12; 79–80

Carnew House: Garvaghy DN 12; 80

Carnew td: Clonallan DN 3; 2

Carnew td: Garvaghy DN 12; 80–81

Carney hill: Cleenish FH 14; 12

Carney Hill td: Misc. DN 17; 124

Carney House: Witter DN 7; 126

Carney lough: Donaghmore DL 39; 28

Carney, Mrs: Clondermot LY 34; 43

Carney, Samual: Balteagh LY 9; 29

Carney's Island td: Clones FH 4; 26

Carneyhill td: Cleenish FH 14; 14, 29

Carnfeogue standing stone: Derrykeighan AM 16; 93

Carnfeogue td: Derrykeighan AM 16; 92, 94

Carnfinton rivulet: Rasharkin AM 23; 133

Carnfinton school: Rasharkin AM 23; 140–41

Carnfinton td: Rasharkin AM 23; 133, 139

Carngaver hill: Holywood DN 7; 73

Carnglass Beg fort: Ballyrashane LY 22; 49, 63

Carnglass bogs: Ballyrashane LY 22; 57

Carnglass carn: Ballyrashane LY 22; 62–63

Carnglass school: Ballyrashane AM 16; 31

Carnglass school: Ballyrashane LY 22; 53–54

Carnglass Sunday school: Ballyrashane LY 22; 54

Carnglass td: Ballyrashane LY 22; 50, 62, 66

Carngranney (see Carngranny)

Carngranny fort: Antrim AM 29; 43

Carngranny fort: Templepatrick AM 35; 152

Carngranny td: Ballylinny AM 32; 22, 30

Carngranny td: Ballymartin AM 2; 16

Carnick House: Moville DL 38; 70

Carninard (see Ballyboley): Ballycor AM 32; 1

Carninney (Carnearny) td: Ahoghill AM 23; 13, 38

Carninney corn mill: Ahoghill AM 23; 13
Carninney flax mill: Ahoghill AM 23; 13
Carninney moat: Ahoghill AM 23; 28
Carninney school: Ahoghill AM 23; 44, 48
Carninney Sunday school: Ahoghill AM 23; 48
Carnisk House: Tullyaughnish DL 38; 89
Carnisk td: Tullyaughnish DL 38; 97
Carnkearn (see Carnkeeran): Skerry AM 13; 107
Carnkeeran fort: Derrykeighan AM 16; 91
Carnkeeran graveyard: Skerry AM 13; 107
Carnkeeran td: Derrykeighan AM 16; 87
Carnkeeran td: Skerry AM 13; 107, 111
Carnkeine (see Carnkeeran): Skerry AM 13; 107
Carnkilly hill: Glenavy AM 21; 77
Carnkilly Lower hill: Glenavy AM 21; 82
Carnkilly Lower td: Glenavy AM 21; 79
Carnkilly Upper td: Glenavy AM 21; 79
Carnkirk bog: Billy AM 16; 59
Carnkirk cashel: Billy AM 16; 55, 59
Carnkirk lough: Billy AM 16; 39
Carnkirk td: Billy AM 16; 39, 56, 66
Carnkirn (Carnkurn) td: Drumtullagh AM 16; 96, 100–02
Carnklinty school: Rasharkin AM 23; 134
Carnlea flax mill: Rashee AM 32; 136–37
Carnlea fort: Kirkinriola AM 23; 125–26
Carnlea school: Rashee AM 32; 141
Carnlea stream: Donacavey TE 5; 64
Carnlea td: Kirkinriola AM 23; 88, 91, 121
Carnleagh (see Carnaneigh): Culfeightrin AM 24; 36
Carnlelis (Cairnlelis) td: Ballintoy AM 24; 12–13, 27–28
Carnlelis cave [I]: Ballintoy AM 24; 27
Carnlelis cave [II]: Ballintoy AM 24; 27
Carnlelis cave [III]: Ballintoy AM 24; 28
Carnlelis giant's graves: Ballintoy AM 24; 27
Carnlelis grey stone: Ballintoy AM 24; 27
Carnlelis hamlet: Ballintoy AM 24; 27
Carnlelis standing stones: Ballintoy AM 24; 27
Carnlough: Ardclinis AM 13; 1–3, 6
Carnlough: Kirkinriola AM 23; 101–02
Carnlough bay: Tickmacrevan AM 13; 122, 125–26
Carnlough corn mill: Ardclinis AM 13; 3, 7
Carnlough flax mill: Ardclinis AM 13; 3
Carnlough pier: Ardclinis AM 13; 6
Carnlough river: Ardclinis AM 13; 3, 3, 5
Carnlough river: Tickmacrevan AM 13; 125
Carnlough school: Ardclinis AM 13; 4, 9
Carnlough td: Ardclinis AM 13; 6–7, 9
Carnlougherin (Carnloughrin) td: Magheramesk AM 21; 113, 117, 121
Carnlougherin graveyard: Magheramesk AM 21; 120
Carnmalin valley: Lough Swilly DL 38; 113

Carnmeen bleach green: Newry DN 3; 78, 106
Carnmeen flax mill [I]: Newry DN 3; 78
Carnmeen flax mill [II]: Newry DN 3; 78
Carnmeen school: Newry DN 3; 106
Carnmeen td: Clonallan DN 3; 2
Carnmeen td: Newry DN 3; 78, 106
Carnmegrum (see Carmaigraw): Ahoghill AM 23; 50
Carnmon (see Carnmore): Aghavea FH 4; 17
Carnmoney (Cairnmoney) td: Carnmoney AM 2; 34, 44, 46, 58, 67, 72, 75, 81, 92, 102
Carnmoney: Carnmoney AM 2; 38–39, 44, 73, 83, 90, 103
Carnmoney bog: Carnmoney AM 2; 36–37
Carnmoney bogs: Ballymartin AM 2; 9
Carnmoney bogs: Ballywalter AM 2; 32
Carnmoney bogs: Mallusk AM 2; 112
Carnmoney cairn: Carnmoney AM 2; 70
Carnmoney Castle: Carnmoney AM 2; 50
Carnmoney church: Ballylinny AM 32; 16–17
Carnmoney church: Ballymartin AM 2; 7
Carnmoney church: Ballywalter AM 2; 30
Carnmoney church: Carnmoney AM 2; 44–45, 55–56, 60, 66–67, 69, 71, 77, 82, 84, 86, 94, 96–98, 101, 105
Carnmoney church: Mallusk AM 2; 111
Carnmoney corn mill (see Carnmoney manor mill)
Carnmoney coves: Carnmoney AM 2; 71
Carnmoney female school: Carnmoney AM 2; 85–86
Carnmoney flax mill: Carnmoney AM 2; 49, 93
Carnmoney forts: Carnmoney AM 2; 50, 70, 81
Carnmoney Glebe House: Carnmoney AM 2; 46, 84, 93–94
Carnmoney graveyard: Carnmoney AM 2; 45, 76, 82, 97, 102
Carnmoney hill: Antrim AM 29; 49
Carnmoney hill: Carnmoney AM 2; 34–37, 70–71
Carnmoney hill: Carrickfergus AM 37; 5
Carnmoney kilns: Ballylinny AM 32; 15
Carnmoney kilns: Carmavy AM 35; 2
Carnmoney kilns: Drummaul AM 19; 45–46
Carnmoney kilns: Killead AM 35; 18
Carnmoney kilns: Mallusk AM 2; 109
Carnmoney kilns: Nilteen AM 35; 91
Carnmoney limeworks: Antrim AM 29; 17, 24
Carnmoney limeworks: Ballynure AM 32; 46
Carnmoney limeworks: Ballyrobert AM 2; 21
Carnmoney limeworks: Ballywalter AM 2; 29
Carnmoney limeworks: Carnmoney AM 2; 60
Carnmoney limeworks: Carrickfergus AM 37; 50
Carnmoney limeworks: Doagh AM 29; 66, 69, 72
Carnmoney limeworks: Donegore AM 29; 110
Carnmoney limeworks: Kilbride AM 29; 140

Carnmoney limeworks: Templepatrick AM 35; 109, 114

Carnmoney limeworks: Umgall AM 35; 157

Carnmoney linenworks: Carnmoney AM 2; 52

Carnmoney manor mill: Carnmoney AM 2; 49, 92–93

Carnmoney meeting house (Cov.): Carnmoney AM 2; 44–46, 55, 57, 75, 82, 105

Carnmoney meeting house (P): Ballylinny AM 32; 17, 26

Carnmoney meeting house (P): Carnmoney AM 2; 44–45, 55–56, 72, 75, 77, 81–82, 85, 99

Carnmoney monastery: Carnmoney AM 2; 94

Carnmoney national school [I]: Carnmoney AM 2; 77, 86

Carnmoney national school [II]: Carnmoney AM 2; 55, 77, 85–86, 88

Carnmoney old church: Carnmoney AM 2; 72, 93

Carnmoney ph: Ballylinny AM 32; 11–12, 14, 16–17, 20, 26

Carnmoney ph: Ballymartin AM 2; 1, 3, 6–7, 15

Carnmoney ph: Ballynure AM 32; 42

Carnmoney ph: Ballyrobert AM 2; 19, 21, 23

Carnmoney ph: Ballywalter AM 2; 26, 28, 30

Carnmoney ph: Carrickfergus AM 37; 1, 18, 62–63, 72, 80, 86, 170

Carnmoney ph: Drummaul AM 19; 33

Carnmoney ph: Duneane AM 19; 94

Carnmoney ph: Mallusk AM 2; 106–07, 110, 113

Carnmoney ph: Misc. AM 10; 129–30

Carnmoney ph: Shilvodan AM 19; 127

Carnmoney ph: Templepatrick AM 35; 107, 139, 142, 144–45

Carnmoney quarries: Carnmoney AM 2; 52

Carnmoney td: Glynn AM 26; 30

Carnmoney vicarage: Carnmoney AM 2; 64

Carnmoney well: Carnmoney AM 2; 99

Carnmoon (Carmoon) td: Billy AM 16; 48, 71, 76

Carnmoon cairn: Billy AM 16; 71

Carnmoon caves: Billy AM 16; 64

Carnmoon stones: Ramoan AM 24; 120

Carnmore mountain: Aghalurcher FH 4; 1–4, 8

Carnmore mountain: Aghavea FH 4; 17–18

Carnmore mountain: Clones FH 4; 26–28

Carnmore mountain: Galloon FH 4; 87, 92

Carnmore td: Dunaghy AM 13; 19, 24

Carn-na-neade hill: Carrickfergus AM 37; 86, 183

Carnone (see Carnowen): Donaghmore DL 39; 32

Carnowen hill: Donaghmore DL 39; 28

Carnowen meeting house: Donaghmore DL 39; 32

Carnowen td: Donaghmore DL 39; 36

Carnowry (Carnouvy) td: Magilligan LY 11; 95, 126

Carnowry rocks: Magilligan LY 11; 135

Carnrawsie church: Carrickfergus AM 37; 81, 181

Carnrawsie graveyard: Carrickfergus AM 37; 81, 181

Carnrawsie locality: Carrickfergus AM 37; 93, 174

Carnrawsie well: Carrickfergus AM 37; 81

Carnreagh school: Blaris DN 12; 37–38

Carnreagh school: Hillsborough DN 12; 101

Carnreagh Sunday school: Blaris DN 12; 38

Carnreagh td: Hillsborough DN 12; 107

Carnrig fort: Derrykeighan AM 16; 91

Carnrig fort: Dunluce AM 16; 116

Carnrig hill: Derrykeighan AM 16; 80

Carnroe (Carnrow) td: Aghadowey LY 22; 13, 28, 36

Carnroe bridge: Aghadowey LY 22; 11

Carnroe cromlech: Aghadowey LY 22; 30

Carnroe hill: Currin MN 40; 86

Carnroe Tamlaght td: Aghadowey LY 22; 12

Carnroe td: Aghabog MN 40; 64

Carnroe td: Currin MN 40; 87–88, 91–92, 95

Carns (Carn) td: Kilmacteige SO 40; 190–91, 195–96

Carns corn mill: Kilmacteige SO 40; 194

Carns pound: Kilmacteige SO 40; 194

Carnsaggart (Carnsegart) td: Ramoan AM 24; 88, 104, 125

Carnsaggart altar: Ramoan AM 24; 104

Carnsaggart bog: Ramoan AM 24; 125

Carnsaggart hill: Ramoan AM 24; 91, 104

Carnsampson bog: Ramoan AM 24; 117

Carnsampson td: Ramoan AM 24; 116–17

Carnshannagh (Carnshennagh) td: Clonleigh DL 39; 2, 185, 195

Carnside carn: Billy AM 16; 55

Carnside fort: Billy AM 16; 55, 62

Carnside td: Ramoan AM 24; 101

Carnspindle bay: Island Magee AM 10; 16–18, 26, 28–29, 31, 39, 73, 82

Carnspindle corn mill: Island Magee AM 10; 22–23, 81

Carnspindle pier: Island Magee AM 10; 22, 76, 81, 85

Carnspindle quay: Island Magee AM 10; 80

Carnspindle td: Island Magee AM 10; 22–23, 31, 41, 72–73, 81, 87, 95, 102

Carnspindle water mill: Island Magee AM 10; 73

Carnstall (see Carntall): Ballylinny AM 32; 30

Carnstroan and Douglass td: Racavan AM 13; 88

Carntall school: Ballylinny AM 32; 30

Carntall td: Ballylinny AM 32; 29

Carntall td: Carrickfergus AM 37; 33

Carntall td: Clogher TE 5; 37, 43, 53

Carntallbeg corn mill: Clogher TE 5; 49

Carntallbeg td: Clogher TE 5; 49

Carntallmore meeting house: Clogher TE 5; 48

Carntallmore td: Clogher TE 5; 33, 48

Carnteal (see Carnteel)

Carnteel hibernian school: Carnteel TE 20; 23

Carnteel pay school: Carnteel TE 20; 23

Carnteel ph: Aghaloo TE 20; 4

Carnteel ph: Misc. TE 5; 146

Carnteel village: Carnteel TE 20; 24

Carntogher mountain: Ballynascreen LY 31; 20

Carntogher mountain: Desertoghill LY 27; 1

Carntogher mountain: Dungiven LY 15; 1, 10, 31, 44–45, 50–51, 78

Carntogher mountain: Dungiven LY 15; 79–80

Carntogher mountain: Killelagh LY 27; 95–96, 99, 102

Carntogher mountain: Kilrea LY 27; 106

Carntogher mountain: Maghera LY 18; 1, 3–4, 8, 10, 27–28, 56, 63

Carntogher mountain: Misc. LY 36; 113

Carntogher mountain: Tamlaght O'Crilly LY 18; 83

Carntogher mountain: Termoneeny LY 6; 121

Carntogher td: Coleraine LY 33; 155

Carntogher td: Dungiven LY 15; 66

Carntoll (see Carntall)

Carntown td: Ballyphilip DN 7; 8

Carntressy td: Templecarn DL 39; 164

Carntrone td: Aghavea FH 4; 19

Carntullmore td: Clogher TE 5; 46

Carnure flax mill: Loughgilly AH 1; 86

Carnwhissock hill: Carrickfergus AM 37; 5

Carny hill: Templepatrick AM 35; 152

Carny, Felix: Kilcronaghan LY 31; 85

Carny, Patrick: Kilcronaghan LY 31; 85

Carolan, bard: Clondermot LY 34; 106

Carolan, harper: Dungiven LY 15; 27

Carolan, Mrs: Clondermot LY 34; 34

Carolina (United States): Kilroot AM 26; 73

Carolina House: Killygarvan DL 38; 40

Caronstown flour mills: Saintfield DN 7; 119

Carother, family: Desertoghill LY 27; 5

Carpendale, Rev. Maxwell: Kilmore AH 1; 59–60, 68

Carpendale, Rev. Maxwell: Tamlaght TE 20; 78

Carpenham House: Kilbroney DN 3; 34–35

Carpenter, Mr (Dublin): Clondavaddog DL 38; 4

Carpinduff (see Coskemduff): Drumgoon CN 40; 7

Carpre, son of Niall: Faughanvale LY 36; 51

Carr moss: Drumbo DN 7; 54

Carr school: Drumbo DN 7; 58

Carr school: Hillsborough DN 12; 101

Carr td: Clogher TE 5; 53

Carr td: Drumbo DN 7; 54, 58, 60–61

Carr, Anne: Ballyscullion LY 6; 59

Carr, Arabella: Ballyscullion LY 6; 58

Carr, Arthur: Tamlaght TE 20; 78

Carr, Charles: Ballyscullion LY 6; 58

Carr, family: Culfeightrin AM 24; 59

Carr, family: Derryaghy AM 8; 103

Carr, family: Derrykeighan AM 16; 89

Carr, family: Magherafelt LY 6; 95

Carr, family: Newry DN 3; 108

Carr, Grizelda (see Dawson): Ballyscullion LY 6; 58

Carr, Hyndman: Balteagh LY 9; 30–31

Carr, Michael: Camlin AM 21; 75

Carr, Mrs Thomas: Newry DN 3; 97, 101

Carr, Robert: Killesher FH 14; 90

Carr, Thomas (Dublin): Ballyscullion LY 6; 58

Carr, Thomas: Newry DN 3; 92, 97, 101–02

Carr's bridge: Kinawley FH 4; 108

Carra House: Drummully FH 4; 35–36

Carra td: Drummully FH 4; 34–35, 39

Carrablagh (see Carrowblagh): Moville DL 38; 68

Carrabligh td: Donagh DL 38; 31

Carrackoghy td: Derrykeighan AM 16; 91

Carrackrovady td: Misc. DN 17; 131

Carraclogher td: Clogher TE 5; 39

Carracut ph: Misc. DN 17; 118

Carradillur td: Aghalurcher FH 4; 13

Carradoan bridge: Killygarvan DL 38; 47

Carradoan glen: Killygarvan DL 38; 42

Carradoan td: Killygarvan DL 38; 38, 47

Carradoan wood: Killygarvan DL 38; 38

Carradressex td: Bright DN 17; 35

Carragh, Rory: Banagher LY 30; 54, 85–86

Carraghalane td: Dungiven LY 15; 71

Carraghbaghran (Carrawbaghern) td: Ballee DN 17; 20, 22

Carraghlane quarry: Clonleigh DL 39; 3

Carraghmore House: Drumkeeran FH 14; 64

Carraghmore td: Drumkeeran FH 14; 64

Carraghowen fort: Dungiven LY 15; 49

Carraghreagh (see Carrowreagh): Clonmany DL 38; 16

Carragin, name of: Clondermot LY 34; 34

Carrah td: Killoran and Kilvarnet SO 40; 183

Carrahue (see Carrowhugh): Moville DL 38; 68

Carrakeel lough: Clondermot LY 34; 115

Carrakeel plantation: Clondermot LY 34; 122

Carrakeel td: Clondermot LY 34; 38, 56, 62, 109, 112–13, 115, 122, 130

Carrakeel td: Faughanvale LY 36; 2, 55

Carral hill: Inishmacsaint FH 14; 71

Carralea rock: Lough Swilly DL 38; 121

Carraloan (Caraloan) td: Artrea LY 6; 10, 12–13, 22, 24–25, 29

Carraloan fort: Artrea LY 6; 24

Carraloan money stones: Artrea LY 6; 29

Carramenagh (see Carrowmenagh): Moville DL 38; 70

Carramore td: Donagh DL 38; 31

Carran fort: Errigal Keerogue TE 20; 51

Carran quarry: Errigal Keerogue TE 20; 51

Carran td: Drumachose LY 9; 87, 96

Carran td: Errigal Keerogue TE 20; 48, 51, 56

Carranbreamaul (see Carrantreemaul): Cleenish FH 14; 29

Carrane (see Carraun): Kilmacteige SO 40; 196

Carrangartin bleach green: Kilbarron DL 39; 78

Carranrallagh bog: Aghadowey LY 22; 2

Carranrallagh td: Aghadowey LY 22; 38

Carrans td: Donaghmore DL 39; 36

Carrans td: Killesher FH 14; 87

Carrantreemaul td: Cleenish FH 14; 25, 29

Carrareagh (see Carrowreagh): Clonmany DL 38; 16

Carratrasna td: Moville DL 38; 68, 70

Carraun td: Kilmacteige SO 40; 195–96

Carravaghan Glebe House: Drung CN 40; 20–21

Carravogy corn mill: Drung CN 40; 21

Carrawreagh (see Carrowreagh): Kilmacteige SO 40; 189

Carre, family: Carnmoney AM 2; 76

Carre, Henry: Clondavaddog DL 38; 10

Carregullan td: Killinchy DN 7; 87

Carren td: Lough Swilly DL 38; 128

Carren td: Tamlaght Finlagan LY 25; 108

Carrey, William: Hillsborough DN 12; 105

Carrick altars: Bovevagh LY 25; 7–8, 52

Carrick bridge: Mevagh DL 38; 58

Carrick chapel: Drumlumman CN 40; 16

Carrick creek: Lough Swilly DL 38; 116, 123

Carrick demesne: Seagoe AH 1; 105–06

Carrick district: Misc. SO 40; 199

Carrick East bleach green: Balteagh LY 9; 36

Carrick East cove stones: Balteagh LY 9; 18–19

Carrick East td: Balteagh LY 9; 1–2, 7, 13, 18, 36, 40, 45

Carrick evening school: Balteagh LY 9; 18

Carrick giant's grave: Bovevagh LY 25; 8, 52

Carrick hill: Drumcree AH 1; 34, 38

Carrick hill: Drumlumman CN 40; 13

Carrick House: Seagoe AH 1; 101, 105, 107

Carrick lough: Inishmacsaint FH 14; 71, 76

Carrick lough: Killygarvan DL 38; 37

Carrick manor: Cleenish FH 14; 28

Carrick manor: Derryvullan FH 14; 45–46

Carrick manor: Enniskillen FH 4; 82

Carrick McDermot district: Misc. SO 40; 198

Carrick Point: Lough Swilly DL 38; 126

Carrick rocks: Balteagh LY 9; 1–2, 4

Carrick rocks: Bovevagh LY 25; 2, 4, 7–9, 52–53

Carrick rocks: Drumachose LY 9; 75

Carrick school: Balteagh LY 9; 16, 18, 39

Carrick school: Bovevagh LY 25; 25, 28, 55

Carrick school: Clogher TE 5; 41

Carrick school: Drumlumman CN 40; 15–16

Carrick school: Seagoe AH 1; 102–03

Carrick td: Balteagh LY 9; 16, 18, 39, 45

Carrick td: Banagher LY 30; 23–24

Carrick td: Bovevagh LY 25; 28, 60

Carrick td: Donagh DL 38; 31

Carrick td: Donaghmore DL 39; 36

Carrick td: Drumlumman CN 40; 13, 17

Carrick td: Inishmacsaint FH 14; 72

Carrick td: Mevagh DL 38; 55, 63

Carrick td: Raymoghy DL 39; 141

Carrick td: Seagoe AH 1; 101, 107

Carrick well: Donaghmore DL 39; 34

Carrick West school: Balteagh LY 9; 17

Carrick West td: Balteagh LY 9; 17, 40, 45

Carrick, Earl of: Killinchy DN 7; 90

Carrick, Mr (Foymount): Drumcree AH 1; 40

Carrickabane fort: Drumlumman CN 40; 14

Carrickabane td: Drumlumman CN 40; 17

Carrickabeaghan td: Cleenish FH 14; 21, 29

Carrickabeaghan well: Cleenish FH 14; 21

Carrickabrackey (see Carrickabrahy): Clonmany DL 38; 13

Carrickabrackly (see Carrickabrahy): Clonmany DL 38; 16

Carrickabracky (see Carrickabrahy): Clonmany DL 38; 18

Carrickabrahy Castle: Clonmany DL 38; 13, 15–16, 19

Carrickabrahy td: Clonmany DL 38; 16–18, 20

Carrickabrick td: Drumlumman CN 40; 17

Carrickacrommen hill: Laragh CN 40; 39

Carrickacrommen school: Laragh CN 40; 43

Carrickacrommen td: Laragh CN 40; 40, 42–43, 46

Carrickacrommenn (see Carrickacrommen): Laragh CN 40; 42

Carrickadawson td: Clonleigh DL 39; 2

Carrickadawson td: Taughboyne DL 39; 152

Carrickadranton td: Cleenish FH 14; 29

Carrickaduff lough: Donaghmore DL 39; 29

Carrickaheenan mountain: Aghavea FH 4; 17

Carrickaheenan td: Aghalurcher FH 4; 3

Carrickaheenan td: Aghavea FH 4; 17

Carrickaheenan td: Cleenish FH 14; 29

Carrickakeilt (see Carricknakielt): Termoneeny LY 6; 131

Carrickakielt (see Carricknakielt): Termoneeny LY 6; 128

Carrickakillne td: Drumlumman CN 40; 17

Carrickalaugan bog: Conwal DL 39; 24

Carrickalaugan td: Conwal DL 39; 24, 26

Carrickalinny td: Killdrumsherdan CN 40; 34

Carrickallen hill: Laragh CN 40; 39

Carrickallen td: Laragh CN 40; 43

Carrickaloughan td: Cleenish FH 14; 29

Carrickananny (Carrickmanny) td: Loughgilly AH 1; 85, 87

Carrickananny chapel: Loughgilly AH 1; 86

Carrickananny corn mill: Loughgilly AH 1; 86

Carrickananny flax mill: Loughgilly AH 1; 86

Carrickanare bog: Ballybay MN 40; 78

Carrickanare fort: Ballybay MN 40; 81

Carrickanare giant's grave: Ballybay MN 40; 81

Carrickanare td: Ballybay MN 40; 84

Carrickaneagle promontory: Banagher LY 30; 69

Carrickanean (see Carrickanare): Ballybay MN 40; 81

Carrickanear (see Carrickanare): Ballybay MN 40; 84

Carrickanee ferry: Lough Swilly DL 38; 144

Carrickanee Point: Lough Swilly DL 38; 144, 147

Carrickanee quarry: Lough Swilly DL 38; 148

Carrickanee td: Lough Swilly DL 38; 144–45

Carrickaness glen: Longfield TE 5; 127

Carrickaness mill [I]: Eglish AH 1; 44

Carrickaness mill [II]: Eglish AH 1; 44

Carrickannaslate td: Misc. DL 39; 197

Carrickapolline (see Carrickpolin): Aghalurcher FH 4; 2

Carrickarede bridge: Ballintoy AM 24; 14, 34–35

Carrickarede cave: Ballintoy AM 24; 14

Carrickarede fisheries: Ballintoy AM 24; 12

Carrickarede Island: Ballintoy AM 24; 14–15

Carrickareilty (see Carrickaveilty): Aughnamullen MN 40; 70

Carrickartagh td: Magheross MN 40; 148

Carrickashane meeting house: Donaghmore DL 39; 32

Carrickashane td: Donaghmore DL 39; 36

Carrickaslean (see Carrickasleane): Muckno MN 40; 163

Carrickasleane bog: Muckno MN 40; 163

Carrickasleane corn mill: Muckno MN 40; 166

Carrickasleane flax mill: Muckno MN 40; 166

Carrickasleane forts: Muckno MN 40; 166

Carrickasleane school: Muckno MN 40; 168

Carrick-a-stoken hill: Longfield TE 5; 127

Carrickatee hill: Aughnamullen MN 40; 69

Carrickatee td: Aughnamullen MN 40; 70, 75

Carrickavallan bog: Killanny MN 40; 130

Carrickaveilly (see Carrickaveilty): Aughnamullen MN 40; 77

Carrickaveilty school: Aughnamullen MN 40; 77

Carrickaveilty td: Aughnamullen MN 40; 70, 75

Carrickavoy lough: Clogher TE 5; 47

Carrickavoy td: Clogher TE 5; 36, 47

Carrickavraghad: Kilbroney DN 3; 32

Carrickawick td: Aghalurcher FH 4; 13

Carrickayeon td: Donaghedy TE 5; 91

Carrickballydooey (Carrickballydowey) td: Raymoghy DL 39; 136, 198

Carrickballydooey Glebe td: Raymoghy DL 39; 136

Carrickbawa (see Carrickabane): Drumlumman CN 40; 14

Carrickbawn (see Carrickabane): Drumlumman CN 40; 17

Carrickbawn House: Kilbroney DN 3; 34–35

Carrickbrack fort: Ballymore AH 1; 7

Carrickbrack td: Ballymore AH 1; 7, 9, 13–14, 16–17

Carrickbrack td: Convoy DL 39; 20

Carrickbrack td: Raphoe DL 39; 125

Carrickbreda House: Newry DN 3; 105

Carrickbrede locality: Clondermot LY 34; 59, 76

Carrickcallan (see Carrickallen): Laragh CN 40; 39

Carrickcallen (see Carrickallen): Laragh CN 40; 43

Carrickcarnon td: Ballymascanlan LH 40; 55

Carrickclionagh rock: Killesher FH 14; 81, 83–84

Carrickcroy school: Drumbo DN 7; 58

Carrickdown td: Manorhamilton Union LM 40; 54

Carrickdrummon td: Aghaderg DN 12; 2

Carrickedny td: Magheross MN 40; 148

Carrickeery forts: Manorhamilton Union LM 40; 52

Carrickfergus: Ahoghill AM 23; 14

Carrickfergus: Antrim AM 29; 7, 17, 37

Carrickfergus: Ardglass DN 17; 12

Carrickfergus: Ballylinny AM 32; 12–14, 25, 27

Carrickfergus: Ballymartin AM 2; 4–5, 12, 16

Carrickfergus: Ballynure AM 32; 31–32, 34–36, 38–39, 42, 45, 47, 51–52, 54–55, 59, 61, 69–70, 72, 72

Carrickfergus: Ballywalter AM 2; 29

Carrickfergus: Banagher LY 30; 20

Carrickfergus: Blaris AM 8; 3, 5, 47–48, 76, 87–88

Carrickfergus: Bovevagh LY 25; 45

Carrickfergus: Carnmoney AM 2; 36, 38–39, 41–43, 47, 50–51, 57, 64–65, 67, 69, 75–76, 82, 85, 88, 94–95, 97–98, 100–03, 105

Carrickfergus: Carrickfergus AM 37; 1–3, 5–7, 9–11, 13–14, 28–30, 32, 36, 38, 43–44, 48–50, 52–54, 57–64, 66, 70–71, 74–75, 78–79, 83, 90–94, 98–99, 101, 103, 105, 107, 132, 135, 137–38, 140–41, 143, 145–47, 150–51

Carrickfergus: Clondermot LY 34; 45–46

Carrickfergus: Culfeightrin AM 24; 74

Carrickfergus: Derryaghy AM 8; 114

Carrickfergus: Derrykeighan AM 16; 78

Carrickfergus: Doagh AM 29; 62–64, 66–67, 70–72, 95–96, 98

Carrickfergus: Donegore AM 29; 101, 106–08, 126, 129

Carrickfergus: Drummaul AM 19; 87

Carrickfergus: Dunaghy AM 13; 12

Carrickfergus: Dungiven LY 15; 31, 56

Carrickfergus: Faughanvale LY 36; 55

Carrickfergus: Glynn AM 26; 4–5, 11, 16–18, 20, 23, 29, 39, 46

Carrickfergus: Holywood DN 7; 78, 82

Carrickfergus: Inver AM 26; 51–53

Carrickfergus: Island Magee AM 10; 24, 26, 30, 36, 38, 40, 42, 60, 64–66, 72, 75, 82, 84, 86, 88, 91–92, 94, 105

Carrickfergus: Kilbride AM 29; 139–40, 146, 148

Carrickfergus: Kilbroney DN 3; 32

Carrickfergus: Killagan AM 23; 84

Carrickfergus: Kilraghts AM 16; 127

Carrickfergus: Kilrea LY 27; 117

Carrickfergus: Kilroot AM 26; 56–57, 59–63, 66–68, 70, 72–75, 78–80

Carrickfergus: Kilwaughter AM 10; 115

Carrickfergus: Kirkinriola AM 23; 90, 101

Carrickfergus: Magherafelt LY 6; 89

Carrickfergus: Misc. AM 10; 129, 131

Carrickfergus: Misc. DN 17; 120–21

Carrickfergus: Newry DN 3; 65

Carrickfergus: Nilteen AM 35; 90, 97, 103

Carrickfergus: Raloo AM 32; 81, 83–84, 89, 92–93, 95, 102, 115–16, 124, 126, 129, 132

Carrickfergus: Templecorran AM 26; 85–86, 89, 91–99, 101, 105, 107–09, 115, 119, 122, 124, 126–27, 129, 131

Carrickfergus: Templepatrick AM 35; 105, 113, 126, 131, 141–42, 145, 148

Carrickfergus: Termoneeny LY 6; 127, 132

Carrickfergus: Tullyrusk AM 21; 131

Carrickfergus: Umgall AM 35; 156

Carrickfergus abbey: Carrickfergus AM 37; 178–79, 190

Carrickfergus adult class: Carrickfergus AM 37; 156

Carrickfergus assembly room: Carrickfergus AM 37; 48, 136, 157

Carrickfergus Back Lane flowering school: Carrickfergus AM 37; 156

Carrickfergus Back Lane school: Carrickfergus AM 37; 153

Carrickfergus bakery: Carrickfergus AM 37; 161

Carrickfergus ballast office: Carrickfergus AM 37; 45–46, 136

Carrickfergus ballast pier: Carrickfergus AM 37; 27–28

Carrickfergus bank: Carrickfergus AM 37; 48, 175

Carrickfergus bay: Ballyrobert AM 2; 24

Carrickfergus bay: Mallusk AM 2; 109, 114

Carrickfergus bay: Misc. DN 17; 121

Carrickfergus bay: Templepatrick AM 35; 116

Carrickfergus bay: Umgall AM 35; 159

Carrickfergus brewery: Carrickfergus AM 37; 51

Carrickfergus brickyard [I]: Carrickfergus AM 37; 45, 47–48, 50, 137

Carrickfergus brickyard [II]: Carrickfergus AM 37; 45, 47, 50, 136–37

Carrickfergus Castle: Ballynure AM 32; 51

Carrickfergus Castle: Carnmoney AM 2; 38, 64, 69, 94, 97

Carrickfergus Castle: Carrickfergus AM 37; 2–3, 9–11, 14–20, 22, 27, 30, 36, 42–43, 60, 77, 80, 83–84, 132, 136, 160–61, 169, 174, 177–78, 191–92

Carrickfergus Castle: Island Magee AM 10; 16, 26, 72

Carrickfergus Castle: Kilroot AM 26; 72

Carrickfergus chapel (C): Carrickfergus AM 37; 3, 14, 27, 48, 71, 88, 100, 133, 136, 144, 160, 169

Carrickfergus chapel (C): Glynn AM 26; 23

Carrickfergus chapel (C): Island Magee AM 10; 35

Carrickfergus chapel (C): Kilroot AM 26; 65

Carrickfergus chapel (C): Raloo AM 32; 98

Carrickfergus chapel (C): Templecorran AM 26; 101

Carrickfergus chapel (PM): Carrickfergus AM 37; 14, 27, 71, 100, 134, 143, 162, 169

Carrickfergus chapel (WAM): Carrickfergus AM 37; 71, 100, 134, 144, 156–57, 169

Carrickfergus chapel (WM): Carrickfergus AM 37; 3, 14, 27, 31, 71, 100, 134, 145, 157, 169

Carrickfergus chapel graveyard: Carrickfergus AM 37; 133, 160

Carrickfergus church: Carnmoney AM 2; 56

Carrickfergus church: Carrickfergus AM 37; 3, 10, 14, 23–26, 30, 34, 60, 68–70, 79–81, 92–93, 99–100, 132, 144, 146–47, 152, 157, 160–61, 169, 179, 190

Carrickfergus church: Drummaul AM 19; 70

Carrickfergus church: Kilroot AM 26; 56, 63–64

Carrickfergus church: Raloo AM 32; 98

Carrickfergus church: Templecorran AM 26; 101, 107

Carrickfergus Church St school: Carrickfergus AM 37; 152

Carrickfergus Church Sunday school: Carrickfergus AM 37; 157

Carrickfergus circulating library: Carrickfergus AM 37; 149

Carrickfergus coal stores: Kilroot AM 26; 61

Carrickfergus coastguard house: Carrickfergus AM 37; 30

Carrickfergus commons: Kilroot AM 26; 67

Carrickfergus congregational library: Carrickfergus AM 37; 149

Carrickfergus corn and threshing mill: Carrickfergus AM 37; 57, 140

Carrickfergus corporation school: Carrickfergus AM 37; 154, 156

Carrickfergus Corporation Sunday school: Carrickfergus AM 37; 156–57

Carrickfergus cotton and print mills: Carrickfergus AM 37; 3, 44, 51, 55, 71

Carrickfergus cotton mill: Carrickfergus AM 37; 6

Carrickfergus county: Ballynure AM 32; 46

Carrickfergus county: Carnmoney AM 2; 37

Carrickfergus county: Carrickfergus AM 37; 1–4, 7,
9–10, 12, 19–23, 32–34, 38, 40, 43, 45, 52–53,
56, 59, 62, 65–66, 68–69, 71, 75, 79, 84, 90–91,
95, 98–99, 103, 134–35, 140–42, 145, 150–51,
155–56, 159, 161, 164, 172–75, 177

Carrickfergus county: Glynn AM 26; 10, 16

Carrickfergus county: Raloo AM 32; 82–83, 130

Carrickfergus county: Templecorran AM 26; 82, 128

Carrickfergus court house (see also Antrim county):
Carrickfergus AM 37; 2, 12, 21–23, 30, 142, 161,
163–64

Carrickfergus court house: Templecorran AM 26;
129

Carrickfergus crane: Carrickfergus AM 37; 22, 167

Carrickfergus custom house: Blaris AM 8; 7

Carrickfergus custom house: Carrickfergus AM 37;
30, 46

Carrickfergus day and boarding school:
Carrickfergus AM 37; 67, 151

Carrickfergus deanery: Mallusk AM 2; 109

Carrickfergus dispensary: Carrickfergus AM 37; 52,
66, 95–96, 99–100, 145

Carrickfergus dispensary: Kilroot AM 26; 63, 79

Carrickfergus distillery: Carrickfergus AM 37; 3,
44–45, 47, 138, 141, 161, 177–78

Carrickfergus distillery: Kilroot AM 26; 62

Carrickfergus district: Island Magee AM 10; 86

Carrickfergus district: Raloo AM 32; 127

Carrickfergus district: Templepatrick AM 35; 139

Carrickfergus Ellis Row flowering school:
Carrickfergus AM 37; 156

Carrickfergus Ellis St school: Carrickfergus AM 37;
153

Carrickfergus fever hospital: Carrickfergus AM 37;
145

Carrickfergus fishing green: Carrickfergus AM 37;
161

Carrickfergus fishing quay: Carrickfergus AM 37;
14, 27–28, 136, 138, 164

Carrickfergus flax mills: Carrickfergus AM 37; 44,
74

Carrickfergus Friends' graveyard: Carrickfergus AM
37; 164

Carrickfergus gallows: Carrickfergus AM 37; 88

Carrickfergus gaol: Carrickfergus AM 37; 2, 12,
20–23, 161, 163

Carrickfergus graveyard: Carrickfergus AM 37; 31,
92–93, 179

Carrickfergus harbour (see also Carrickfergus
shipping quay): Carrickfergus AM 37; 10, 27, 41,
45–47, 55, 136, 164, 172–73

Carrickfergus Harmonic Society room:
Carrickfergus AM 37; 68

Carrickfergus High St school: Carrickfergus AM 37;
152

Carrickfergus Independent Sunday school:
Carrickfergus AM 37; 157

Carrickfergus Irish Quarter school: Carrickfergus
AM 37; 152–53, 155

Carrickfergus ladies' boarding and day school:
Carrickfergus AM 37; 151–52

Carrickfergus Lancasterian female school:
Carrickfergus AM 37; 154

Carrickfergus Lancasterian male school:
Carrickfergus AM 37; 153–54

Carrickfergus Lancasterian school: Carrickfergus
AM 37; 71, 100, 143–44, 157, 160

Carrickfergus Lancasterian Sunday school:
Carrickfergus AM 37; 153

Carrickfergus liberties: Carrickfergus AM 37; 18,
38, 43

Carrickfergus lough: Carnmoney AM 2; 35

Carrickfergus lough: Carrickfergus AM 37; 5

Carrickfergus market house: Carrickfergus AM 37;
14, 22, 30, 45, 68, 147, 157, 162

Carrickfergus market place: Carrickfergus AM 37;
14, 22–23, 31, 41, 49, 163, 168

Carrickfergus maypole: Carrickfergus AM 37; 136

Carrickfergus meeting house (I): Carrickfergus AM
37; 3, 14, 26–27, 30, 70, 100, 133, 143, 157, 169,
178

Carrickfergus meeting house (P): Carrickfergus AM
37; 3, 14, 26, 31, 68, 70, 99–100, 133, 144, 149,
156–57, 169

Carrickfergus meeting house (U): Carrickfergus AM
37; 14, 26, 70, 100, 134, 143–44, 162, 169

Carrickfergus meeting houses: Kilroot AM 26; 56

Carrickfergus mendicity: Carrickfergus AM 37;
145–46, 174

Carrickfergus Methodist adult class: Carrickfergus
AM 37; 156

Carrickfergus Methodist library: Carrickfergus AM
37; 157

Carrickfergus Methodist Sunday school:
Carrickfergus AM 37; 157

Carrickfergus mineral spring: Carrickfergus AM 37;
8

Carrickfergus monastery: Carrickfergus AM 37; 4,
25, 80

Carrickfergus mountains: Glynn AM 26; 4

Carrickfergus mountains: Raloo AM 32; 82

Carrickfergus new flax mill: Carrickfergus AM 37;
138–40

Carrickfergus news room: Carrickfergus AM 37; 45,
68, 136, 149

Carrickfergus North St school: Carrickfergus AM
37; 153

Carrickfergus old bleach mill: Carrickfergus AM 37; 139

Carrickfergus old brewery: Carrickfergus AM 37; 161, 164

Carrickfergus old chapel: Carrickfergus AM 37; 174

Carrickfergus old cotton factory: Carrickfergus AM 37; 162

Carrickfergus old cotton mill: Carrickfergus AM 37; 153

Carrickfergus old customs house: Carrickfergus AM 37; 46, 177

Carrickfergus old distillery: Carrickfergus AM 37; 3, 141, 164

Carrickfergus old market house: Carrickfergus AM 37; 136, 142, 164

Carrickfergus old market place: Carrickfergus AM 37; 30, 49

Carrickfergus old meeting house (P) [I]: Carrickfergus AM 37; 70, 163

Carrickfergus old meeting house (P) [II]: Carrickfergus AM 37; 26, 70

Carrickfergus old tanyard: Carrickfergus AM 37; 23, 163

Carrickfergus old windmill: Carrickfergus AM 37; 178

Carrickfergus parade ground: Carrickfergus AM 37; 3

Carrickfergus pawn-office: Carrickfergus AM 37; 74, 96–97

Carrickfergus ph: Ballynure AM 32; 64

Carrickfergus ph: Carnmoney AM 2; 62, 64, 87

Carrickfergus ph: Doagh AM 29; 87

Carrickfergus ph: Glynn AM 26; 23

Carrickfergus ph: Island Magee AM 10; 34

Carrickfergus ph: Kilroot AM 26; 57–59, 64–65, 69

Carrickfergus ph: Mallusk AM 2; 111, 114

Carrickfergus ph: Misc. AM 10; 129

Carrickfergus ph: Raloo AM 32; 80, 82, 85, 87–89, 98, 132

Carrickfergus ph: Templecorran AM 26; 82, 88–89, 101

Carrickfergus port: Carrickfergus AM 37; 27, 43, 46, 132

Carrickfergus post office: Carrickfergus AM 37; 175

Carrickfergus pound: Carrickfergus AM 37; 161

Carrickfergus Presbyterian adult class: Carrickfergus AM 37; 156

Carrickfergus Presbyterian Sunday school: Carrickfergus AM 37; 149, 156–57

Carrickfergus Presbyterian Sunday school library: Carrickfergus AM 37; 149

Carrickfergus private day school: Carrickfergus AM 37; 152

Carrickfergus reservoir: Carrickfergus AM 37; 3, 171

Carrickfergus river: Carrickfergus AM 37; 41

Carrickfergus road bridge: Carnmoney AM 2; 85

Carrickfergus Scotch Quarter school: Carrickfergus AM 37; 153

Carrickfergus sessions room: Carrickfergus AM 37; 136

Carrickfergus shipping pier: Carrickfergus AM 37; 27

Carrickfergus shipping quay: Carrickfergus AM 37; 2, 14, 27–28, 30, 43, 45, 50, 64, 157, 164, 171, 177

Carrickfergus singing school: Carrickfergus AM 37; 157

Carrickfergus spring: Carrickfergus AM 37; 8

Carrickfergus stamp office: Carrickfergus AM 37; 150

Carrickfergus standing stone: Carrickfergus AM 37; 33

Carrickfergus stone pier: Carrickfergus AM 37; 28

Carrickfergus stoneyard: Carrickfergus AM 37; 50

Carrickfergus Sunday school: Carrickfergus AM 37; 157

Carrickfergus tanyard: Carrickfergus AM 37; 45, 47, 137

Carrickfergus timber and slate–yard [I]: Carrickfergus AM 37; 50, 161, 170

Carrickfergus timber and slate–yard [II]: Carrickfergus AM 37; 50, 162, 170

Carrickfergus toll-gate: Antrim AM 29; 22

Carrickfergus toll-gate: Nilteen AM 35; 90

Carrickfergus town hall: Carrickfergus AM 37; 36, 136, 147, 149

Carrickfergus turnpike: Carnmoney AM 2; 49

Carrickfergus walls: Carrickfergus AM 37; 3, 10, 12–18, 29–30, 44, 89–92, 132, 161, 177–78

Carrickfergus water mills: Carrickfergus AM 37; 43

Carrickfergus weighbridge: Carrickfergus AM 37; 22

Carrickfergus weighhouse: Carrickfergus AM 37; 136

Carrickfergus well: Carrickfergus AM 37; 16, 18

Carrickfergus Wesleyan Methodist Sunday school: Carrickfergus AM 37; 157

Carrickfergus windmill: Carrickfergus AM 37; 88

Carrickfergus worship house (U): Carrickfergus AM 37; 144

Carrickfergus worship room (PWM): Carrickfergus AM 37; 71, 100, 143–44

Carrickfodin td: Donagh DL 38; 31

Carrickgalloghey (Carrickgalloghy) td: Loughgilly AH 1; 85

Carrickgallogley flax mill: Loughgilly AH 1; 86

Carrickgallogley school: Loughgilly AH 1; 87

Carrickglass td: Donacavey TE 5; 85

Carrickgull district: Mevagh DL 38; 56

Carrickhugh quarries: Faughanvale LY 36; 93

Carrickhugh td: Faughanvale LY 36; 53–55, 67, 71, 82, 93

Carrickhugh td: Tamlaght Finlagan LY 25; 72–74

Carrickhugh wood: Faughanvale LY 36; 82

Carrickinara (see Carrickanare): Ballybay MN 40; 78

Carricklane hill: Tynan AH 1; 124

Carricklee hill: Urney DL 39; 174

Carrickleitrim forts: Manorhamilton Union LM 40; 52

Carrickleitrim rock: Manorhamilton Union LM 40; 47

Carricklongfield bog: Aghaloo TE 20; 1

Carricklongfield hill: Aghaloo TE 20; 1

Carrickmaclew td: Saintfield DN 7; 120

Carrickmaclim meeting house: Magheross MN 40; 145

Carrickmaclim school: Magheross MN 40; 145, 150

Carrickmaclim td: Magheross MN 40; 148

Carrickmacmea holy wells: Enniskillen FH 4; 71

Carrickmacmea school: Enniskillen FH 4; 84

Carrickmacmea td: Enniskillen FH 4; 71, 82

Carrickmacosker td: Aghalurcher FH 4; 4, 13

Carrickmacraurk (see Carrickmacrourk): Cleenish FH 14; 13

Carrickmacross: Aughnamullen MN 40; 70, 73–75

Carrickmacross: Ballybay MN 40; 80–81, 83

Carrickmacross: Creggan AH 1; 27

Carrickmacross: Donaghmoyne MN 40; 106–11

Carrickmacross: Inniskeen MN 40; 125, 127–28

Carrickmacross: Killanny MN 40; 131–34

Carrickmacross: Killevy AH 1; 52

Carrickmacross: Loughgilly AH 1; 84

Carrickmacross: Magheracloone MN 40; 137–41

Carrickmacross: Magheross MN 40; 143–44, 146–49, 153–55, 157

Carrickmacross: Misc. DN 17; 131

Carrickmacross: Muckno MN 40; 165, 167

Carrickmacross: Newtownhamilton AH 1; 100

Carrickmacross bishop's house: Magheross MN 40; 145

Carrickmacross bridewell: Magheross MN 40; 151

Carrickmacross bridge: Magheracloone MN 40; 139

Carrickmacross chapel: Magheross MN 40; 144–45, 151, 157

Carrickmacross church: Magheross MN 40; 144, 151, 157

Carrickmacross dispensary: Inniskeen MN 40; 127

Carrickmacross dispensary: Magheross MN 40; 152, 157

Carrickmacross distillery: Magheross MN 40; 145, 149, 152, 157

Carrickmacross endowed school: Magheross MN 40; 151

Carrickmacross graveyard: Magheross MN 40; 144

Carrickmacross hotel: Magheross MN 40; 151

Carrickmacross market house: Donaghmoyne MN 40; 108

Carrickmacross market house: Magheracloone MN 40; 140

Carrickmacross market house: Magheross MN 40; 147, 151, 157

Carrickmacross national school: Magheross MN 40; 145, 150–51, 157

Carrickmacross old castle: Magheross MN 40; 144

Carrickmacross ph: Clogher TE 5; 40

Carrickmacross police barrack: Magheross MN 40; 151

Carrickmacross quarries: Drumgoon CN 40; 10

Carrickmacross quarries: Killdrumsherdan CN 40; 37

Carrickmacross savings bank: Magheross MN 40; 152

Carrickmacross school [I]: Magheross MN 40; 150

Carrickmacross school [II]: Magheross MN 40; 150

Carrickmacross Sunday school: Magheross MN 40; 150

Carrickmacross turnpike: Killanny MN 40; 132

Carrickmacrourk Island: Cleenish FH 14; 13, 29

Carrickmacsparrow giant's grave: Cleenish FH 14; 22

Carrickmacsparrow td: Cleenish FH 14; 22, 29

Carrickmacullow td: Aghalurcher FH 4; 3

Carrickmaderrow corn mill: Tullynakill DN 7; 122

Carrickmaderrow flax mill: Tullynakill DN 7; 122

Carrickmaderrow meeting house: Tullynakill DN 7; 122–23

Carrickmaderrow school: Tullynakill DN 7; 122

Carrickmaderrow td: Tullynakill DN 7; 122–23

Carrickmaflagharty td: Cleenish FH 14; 29

Carrickmagra school: Donaghmore DL 39; 39

Carrickmagra td: Donaghmore DL 39; 35–36

Carrickmannan (Carrickmannon) td: Killinchy DN 7; 86, 91–92

Carrickmannan chapel: Killinchy DN 7; 91–92

Carrickmannan corn mill: Killinchy DN 7; 91–92

Carrickmannan school: Killinchy DN 7; 92

Carrickmaquigley church: Moville DL 38; 78

Carrickmaquigley lough: Moville DL 38; 78

Carrickmaquigley school: Moville DL 38; 74

Carrickmaquigley td: Moville DL 38; 73, 75, 77

Carrickmoiety manor: Manorhamilton Union LM 40; 51

Carrickmore bog: Killea and Taughboyne DL 39; 80, 148, 153

Carrickmore creek: Killea and Taughboyne DL 39; 84

Carrickmore dyke: Culfeightrin AM 24; 39

Carrickmore ferry: Killea and Taughboyne DL 39;
   79, 150, 153
Carrickmore td: Killea and Taughboyne DL 39; 80
Carrickmore td: Taughboyne DL 39; 148, 153, 184,
   186, 188, 195
Carricknabrattoge td: Aghalurcher FH 4; 3, 13
Carricknabrattogue (see Carricknabrattoge):
   Aghalurcher FH 4; 3
Carricknabrock mountain: Errigal Truagh MN 40;
   120
Carricknacessnagh td: Saintfield DN 7; 117
Carricknadarriff td: Annahilt DN 12; 20–22
Carricknahorna hamlet: Kilbarron DL 39; 77
Carricknakielt fort: Termoneeny LY 6; 131
Carricknakielt td: Termoneeny LY 6; 124, 127–28,
   131–33
Carricknamanna td: Donaghmore DL 39; 36
Carricknamart school: Raymoghy DL 39; 140
Carricknamart td: Raymoghy DL 39; 136, 141, 198
Carricknamarts (see Carricknamart): Raymoghy DL
   39; 141
Carricknaquigley: Lough Swilly DL 38; 140
Carricknaseer td: Cleenish FH 14; 29
Carricknaugh td: Saintfield DN 7; 120
Carricknaveagh meeting houses: Tullynakill DN 7;
   123
Carricknaveagh school: Hillsborough DN 12; 101
Carricknaveagh school: Tullynakill DN 7; 123
Carricknaveagh td: Tullynakill DN 7; 123
Carrickneveagh (see Carricknaveagh)
Carrickpolin mountain: Aghalurcher FH 4; 2
Carrickpolin td: Aghalurcher FH 4; 14
Carrickreagh td: Devenish FH 14; 57
Carrickreevagh (see Carrickrevagh): Manorhamilton
   Union LM 40; 52
Carrickrevagh forts: Manorhamilton Union LM 40;
   52
Carrickrevagh graveyard: Manorhamilton Union
   LM 40; 52
Carrickrevagh standing stone: Manorhamilton
   Union LM 40; 52
Carrickrock td: Drumlumman CN 40; 17
Carrickrory td: Templecarn DL 39; 164
Carrickrovaddy td: Donaghmore DN 3; 9
Carrickshandrum td: Donaghmore DL 39; 36
Carrig abbey: Inch DN 17; 75
Carrig O'Donnel rock: Lough Swilly DL 38; 100
Carrigabraghey district: Lough Swilly DL 38;
   133–34
Carrigachaanrooa rock: Lough Swilly DL 38; 106
Carrigachaskim creek: Lough Swilly DL 38; 99
Carrigan td: Devenish FH 14; 58
Carriganagowna (see Carrigeenagowna):
   Kilmacteige SO 40; 196

Carrigans: Killea and Taughboyne DL 39; 79, 81,
   86–89, 92
Carrigans: Misc. DL 39; 185–86, 188
Carrigans: Taughboyne DL 39; 150, 154
Carrigans district: Clonleigh DL 39; 16
Carrigans harbour: Killea and Taughboyne DL 39;
   84
Carrigans mill: Taughboyne DL 39; 150
Carrigans school: Forkhill AH 1; 45
Carrigans td: Donagh MN 40; 98
Carrigans td: Galloon FH 4; 95
Carrigans td: Misc. DL 39; 196
Carrigans Upper hill: Emlaghfad SO 40; 176
Carrigans Upper td: Emlaghfad SO 40; 181
Carrigans wood: Misc. DL 39; 189
Carrigart bay: Mevagh DL 38; 62
Carrigart chapel: Mevagh DL 38; 57
Carrigart church: Mevagh DL 38; 57
Carrigart corn mill: Mevagh DL 38; 57
Carrigart graveyard: Mevagh DL 38; 60
Carrigart mill-pond: Mevagh DL 38; 55
Carrigart school: Mevagh DL 38; 59
Carrigart td: Lough Swilly DL 38; 113, 116–17, 129
Carrigart td: Mevagh DL 38; 54–55, 57, 59, 61, 63
Carrigatee (see Carrickatee): Aughnamullen MN 40;
   69
Carrigatooder hill: Lough Swilly DL 38; 99
Carrigatuimpeal Island: Lough Swilly DL 38;
   131–32
Carrigavel locality: Lough Swilly DL 38; 109
Carrigavuoel Head: Lough Swilly DL 38; 113
Carrigbann td: Donaghmore DN 3; 7, 9
Carrigbaun (see Carrigbann): Donaghmore DN 3; 7
Carrig-Coeen rocks: Lough Swilly DL 38; 108
Carrigeenagowna td: Kilmacteige SO 40; 193, 196
Carrigeennagowan (see Carrigeenagowna):
   Kilmacteige SO 40; 193
Carriggannagh Island: Lough Swilly DL 38; 109
Carriggannagh rock: Lough Swilly DL 38; 113
Carrig-ghonel rocks: Lough Swilly DL 38; 106
Carrighollap rock: Lough Swilly DL 38; 111
Carrigkollegh rock: Lough Swilly DL 38; 111
Carrignahaa creek: Lough Swilly DL 38; 147
Carrignahaa Point: Lough Swilly DL 38; 144
Carrigolagh td: Inishmacsaint FH 14; 76
Carrigullan td: Killinchy DN 7; 86–87
Carrihew (see Carrowhugh): Moville DL 38; 70
Carrinan bog: Killea and Taughboyne DL 39; 80
Carrinmore creek: Killea and Taughboyne DL 39;
   84
Carrintrough nursery: Muckno MN 40; 167
Carrivemurphy mountain: Ardclinis AM 13; 2
Carrlan, family: Clondermot LY 34; 53
Carrobeg (see Carrowbeg): Moville DL 38; 68

Carrodowan (see Carradoan): Killygarvan DL 38; 38

Carroghel (see Carroghill): Mintiaghs DL 38; 65

Carroghill brook: Mintiaghs DL 38; 64

Carroghill school: Mintiaghs DL 38; 65

Carroghill td: Mintiaghs DL 38; 66–67

Carrokeel (see Carrowkeel): Moville DL 38; 74

Carrokiel (see Carrowkeel): Moville DL 38; 73

Carrol, family: Aghalee AM 21; 31

Carrol, Martha: Carrickfergus AM 37; 119

Carroll, John: Ballinderry AM 21; 47, 56

Carroll, Mr (Sligo): Clondermot LY 34; 26

Carroll, Patrick: Donacavey TE 5; 65

Carroll, Patrick: Shankill AH 1; 115

Carroll, Rev. John: Kilmore AH 1; 59

Carroll, Rev. William: Carnmoney AM 2; 75

Carroll's bridge: Glenavy AM 21; 78

Carromenagh (see Carrowmenagh): Moville DL 38; 68

Carromore (see Carrowmore)

Carron td: Loughgilly AH 1; 85

Carron, Rev.: Clondermot LY 34; 27, 103

Carronashon td: Grey Abbey DN 7; 68

Carrontullerrekin (Turnaran) td: Grey Abbey DN 7; 68

Carrouquigley (see Carrickmaquigley): Moville DL 38; 75

Carroreagh (see Carrowreagh): Magilligan LY 11; 137

Carrother, family: Desertoghill LY 27; 30

Carrothers, C.B.: Drummaul AM 19; 44

Carrothers, James [I]: Carrickfergus AM 37; 126

Carrothers, James [II]: Carrickfergus AM 37; 126

Carrothers, John: Hillsborough DN 12; 105

Carrough, Bryan: Billy AM 16; 38

Carrouther, family: Ballymartin AM 2; 15

Carrow lough: Devenish FH 14; 52, 57

Carrow td: Devenish FH 14; 58

Carrowan td: Lough Swilly DL 38; 103, 145

Carrowantavy td: Killoran and Kilvarnet SO 40; 184

Carrowardgullum district: Misc. SO 40; 199

Carrowatroune td: Killoran and Kilvarnet SO 40; 183

Carrowbeg school: Moville DL 38; 69

Carrowbeg Sunday school: Moville DL 38; 69

Carrowbeg td: Moville DL 38; 68, 70

Carrowblagh td: Lough Swilly DL 38; 99

Carrowblagh td: Moville DL 38; 68, 70

Carrowblaw (see Carrowblagh): Moville DL 38; 70

Carrowbofin (see Corrabofin): Ballybay MN 40; 78

Carrowbrack manor: Seagoe AH 1; 104

Carrowbracken district: Misc. SO 40; 198

Carrowcanbeg td: Emlaghfad SO 40; 177

Carrowcarlin bog: Saul DN 17; 115

Carrowcarlin chapel: Saul DN 17; 115

Carrowcarlin school: Saul DN 17; 115

Carrowcarlin td: Saul DN 17; 114

Carrowcastle standing stone: Tullyaughnish DL 38; 91

Carrowcastle td: Tullyaughnish DL 38; 97

Carrowclare (Carraclare) td: Tamlaght Finlagan LY 25; 66, 93, 104, 116, 120

Carrowcloghan (Carrowcloughane) td: Drumtullagh AM 16; 98

Carrowcloghan brickfield: Drumtullagh AM 16; 98

Carrowcloghan hill: Drumtullagh AM 16; 97

Carrowcloghan murder holes: Drumtullagh AM 16; 103

Carrowclooneen td: Killoran and Kilvarnet SO 40; 183

Carrowcreagh quarry: Enniskillen FH 4; 62

Carrowcreagh quarry: Trory FH 14; 130

Carrowcrin school: Loughguile AM 13; 77

Carrowcrin td: Loughguile AM 13; 74

Carrowcroey standing stone: Ballintoy AM 24; 28

Carrowdare (see Carrowclare): Tamlaght Finlagan LY 25; 93

Carrowdore Castle: Donaghadee DN 7; 45, 49–50

Carrowdore Castle: Newtown Crommelin AM 13; 81

Carrowdore meeting house: Donaghadee DN 7; 50

Carrowdore school: Donaghadee DN 7; 50

Carrowdore td: Grey Abbey DN 7; 68

Carrowdore village: Donaghadee DN 7; 50

Carrowgarragh td: Aghalurcher FH 4; 13

Carrowgarrow district: Misc. SO 40; 200

Carrowgavneen td: Killoran and Kilvarnet SO 40; 183

Carrowgeeragh district: Misc. SO 40; 200

Carrowgskill district: Misc. SO 40; 199

Carrowhugh td: Moville DL 38; 68, 70

Carrowkeel bog: Tyholland MN 40; 174

Carrowkeel corn mill: Tullyaughnish DL 38; 89

Carrowkeel druid's altar: Moville DL 38; 74

Carrowkeel fort: Tullyaughnish DL 38; 91

Carrowkeel meeting house: Clondavaddog DL 38; 4

Carrowkeel meeting house: Tullyaughnish DL 38; 88

Carrowkeel school: Emlaghfad SO 40; 179

Carrowkeel school: Tullyaughnish DL 38; 92

Carrowkeel stream: Moville DL 38; 78

Carrowkeel td: Moville DL 38; 73, 75

Carrowkeel td: Tullyaughnish DL 38; 96

Carrowkeele district (Roscommon): Misc. SO 40; 200

Carrowkeele district (Sligo): Misc. SO 40; 198

Carrowkit td: Carlingford LH 40; 58

Carrowleaghery td: Ballee DN 17; 22

Carrowlearn td: Killoran and Kilvarnet SO 40; 183

Carrowloughan td: Killoran and Kilvarnet SO 40;
    183
Carrowmacarrick td: Killoran and Kilvarnet SO 40;
    183
Carrowmacaw windmill: Ballyculter DN 17; 25
Carrowmaculla hill: Galloon FH 4; 87, 92
Carrowmaculla td: Galloon FH 4; 95
Carrowmannon td: Loughgilly AH 1; 85
Carrowmenagh (Caramenagh) td: Killelagh LY 27;
    99, 101–02
Carrowmenagh bog: Killelagh LY 27; 95
Carrowmenagh forts: Killelagh LY 27; 97
Carrowmenagh giant's chair: Killelagh LY 27; 98,
    100
Carrowmenagh old church: Killelagh LY 27; 95
Carrowmenagh school: Tamlaght Finlagan LY 25;
    96, 124
Carrowmenagh Sunday school: Tamlaght Finlagan
    LY 25; 96
Carrowmenagh td: Moville DL 38; 68, 70
Carrowmenagh td: Tamlaght Finlagan LY 25; 93,
    104
Carrowmore district: Misc. SO 40; 199
Carrowmore td: Emlaghfad SO 40; 182
Carrowmore td: Galloon FH 4; 95
Carrowmuddle (Carrymuddle) td: Tamlaght
    Finlagan LY 25; 93–94, 104, 111, 119
Carrowmuddle td: Drumachose LY 9; 101, 106
Carrowmullin td: Killoran and Kilvarnet SO 40; 183
Carrowmully district: Misc. SO 40; 198
Carrowmurlane district: Misc. SO 40; 198
Carrownabarry td: Killoran and Kilvarnet SO 40;
    183
Carrownagapple td: Aughnamullen MN 40; 76
Carrownageragh td: Killoran and Kilvarnet SO 40;
    183
Carrownagoppal td: Kilmacteige SO 40; 196
Carrownanty round tower: Emlaghfad SO 40; 182
Carrownany district: Misc. SO 40; 198
Carrownaskea td: Killoran and Kilvarnet SO 40;
    183
Carrownathan district: Misc. DN 17; 121
Carrowne Coonany district: Misc. SO 40; 198
Carrowneclia td: Killoran and Kilvarnet SO 40; 183
Carrownlobane td: Kilmacteige SO 40; 196
Carrowreagh (Caroreagh) td: Finvoy AM 23; 68, 73
Carrowreagh (Carrareagh) td: Tamlaght Finlagan LY
    25; 93, 104, 120
Carrowreagh (Carryreagh) td: Desertoghill LY 27;
    10–11, 17, 19–20
Carrowreagh altar stones: Clonmany DL 38; 16
Carrowreagh bleach green: Comber DN 7; 41
Carrowreagh corn mill: Kilmacteige SO 40; 194
Carrowreagh district: Misc. SO 40; 199–200
Carrowreagh flax mill: Dundonald DN 7; 66

Carrowreagh fort: Desertoghill LY 27; 27
Carrowreagh forts: Billy AM 16; 61
Carrowreagh hill: Drumtullagh AM 16; 97
Carrowreagh school (see also Crosshan):
    Drumtullagh AM 16; 99
Carrowreagh school: Derrykeighan AM 16; 95
Carrowreagh school: Tamlaght Finlagan LY 25; 124
Carrowreagh td: Clonmany DL 38; 16, 18, 20
Carrowreagh td: Comber DN 7; 41, 43
Carrowreagh td: Cumber LY 28; 68
Carrowreagh td: Drumtullagh AM 16; 101
Carrowreagh td: Dundonald DN 7; 65–66
Carrowreagh td: Kilmacteige SO 40; 189, 193, 196
Carrowreagh td: Magilligan LY 11; 95, 126, 137
Carrowshee manor: Misc. FH 4; 133
Carrowtrasna district: Misc. SO 40; 200
Carrowtrukin district: Misc. SO 40; 199
Carrowvanny (Caravanny) td: Saul DN 17; 114
Carrowvanny corn mill: Saul DN 17; 111, 115
Carrumon district: Killea and Taughboyne DL 39;
    84
Carruth, family: Ballymartin AM 2; 6, 15
Carruth, family: Templepatrick AM 35; 118
Carry bridge: Derryvullan FH 14; 41
Carry td: Derryvullan FH 14; 45
Carryblagh td: Clondavaddog DL 38; 5
Carryclogher Deanery: Clogher TE 5; 49
Carryclogher td: Clogher TE 5; 49
Carrycoagh td: Skerry AM 13; 120
Carrycowan (Carrycavan) td: Dunaghy AM 13; 11,
    13
Carrycowan chapel: Dunaghy AM 13; 13
Carrycowan school: Dunaghy AM 13; 17
Carrycowen (see Carrycowan): Dunaghy AM 13; 11
Carrydarragh evening Sunday school: Desertlyn LY
    31; 51
Carrydarragh fort: Desertlyn LY 31; 44
Carrydarragh glen: Desertlyn LY 31; 35–36
Carrydarragh school: Desertlyn LY 31; 50–51
Carrydarragh Sunday school: Desertlyn LY 31; 51
Carrydarragh water: Desertlyn LY 31; 35–36
Carrydoo forts: Drumachose LY 9; 58–59, 112, 128
Carrydoo td: Drumachose LY 9; 58–59, 87, 96–97,
    101, 112
Carryduff corn mill: Drumbo DN 7; 56, 58
Carryduff flax mill: Drumbo DN 7; 56, 58
Carryduff school: Drumbo DN 7; 57–58
Carryduff school: Hillsborough DN 12; 102
Carryduff td: Drumbo DN 7; 56–58, 60, 63
Carrygally td: Leck DL 39; 118
Carryglass (Carriglass) td: Donacavey TE 5; 65–68,
    76, 78, 80, 84
Carryglass bog: Donacavey TE 5; 67
Carryglass pound: Donacavey TE 5; 84
Carryglass school: Donacavey TE 5; 65–66, 84

Carryhul district: Lough Swilly DL 38; 137

Carrymuddle (see Carrowmuddle): Drumachose LY 9; 101

Carrynaney district: Templepatrick AM 35; 116

Carscadden, William: Coleraine LY 33; 67, 70, 133

Carson: Racavan AM 13; 100

Carson monument: Ematris MN 40; 114–15

Carson td: Drumgoon CN 40; 6

Carson, Alexander: Lissan LY 31; 109

Carson, Andrew: Ahoghill AM 23; 35

Carson, Andrew: Drummaul AM 19; 90

Carson, Andrew: Kilraghts AM 16; 132

Carson, Archibald: Ballymoney AM 16; 15

Carson, Esther: Lissan LY 31; 109

Carson, family: Ahoghill AM 23; 25

Carson, family: Carnmoney AM 2; 51, 76

Carson, family: Kilraghts AM 16; 130

Carson, family: Templepatrick AM 35; 118

Carson, G.L.: Coleraine LY 33; 72, 141–42

Carson, James: Carrickfergus AM 37; 130

Carson, Jane: Kilraghts AM 16; 132

Carson, Janet: Island Magee AM 10; 66, 94

Carson, John: Carrickfergus AM 37; 118

Carson, Mr: Raphoe DL 39; 126

Carson, Powaxe: Ballyclug AM 23; 61, 65

Carson, Rev.: Clondermot LY 34; 22, 24, 27, 37, 88, 92, 95, 103–04

Carson, Rev.: Tomregan FH 4; 129

Carson, Rev. Alexander: Desertlyn LY 31; 42

Carson, Rev. Alexander: Kilcronaghan LY 31; 66–67, 72, 74, 79–82, 128, 136

Carson, Rev. Henry: Faughanvale LY 36; 33

Carson, Rev. John: Ballymartin AM 2; 13

Carson, Rev. John: Templepatrick AM 35; 119, 133, 135, 143–44, 153–54

Carson, Robert: Drummaul AM 19; 91

Carson, Robert: Hillsborough DN 12; 105–06

Carson, Thomas: Drummaul AM 19; 90

Carson, William: Carnmoney AM 2; 100

Carsonstown hamlet: Ballyclug AM 23; 65

Carsonstown td: Saintfield DN 7; 117–19

Carsore td: Magheraculmoney FH 14; 112

Carstown td (see also Ballydock): Misc. DN 17; 125

Carte manor: Ballyclug AM 23; 57

Carter, family: Aghabog MN 40; 66

Carter, family: Aghagallon AM 21; 9

Carter, George: Aghalee AM 21; 32–33

Carter, George: Ahoghill AM 23; 44

Carter, J.T.: Newry DN 3; 98

Carter, John: Newry DN 3; 104

Carter, Mrs Henry: Carrickfergus AM 37; 154

Carter, person named: Blaris AM 8; 60

Carter, Rev. Henry: Carrickfergus AM 37; 28, 144, 146, 150, 157, 178

Carter, Rev. Thomas: Ballymore AH 1; 3, 6, 10–11, 15, 17

Carter's river: Blaris AM 8; 48

Carthage House: Lough Swilly DL 38; 113

Cartin, Maryann: Tamlaght Finlagan LY 25; 118

Cartin, Michael: Tamlaght Finlagan LY 25; 118

Cartob (see Cartron): Kilmacteige SO 40; 194

Carton, family: Blaris AM 8; 22

Cartrain (see Cortreane): Currin MN 40; 92

Cartrasnagh td: Drumlumman CN 40; 17

Cartron corn mill: Kilmacteige SO 40; 194

Cartron mill: Kilmacteige SO 40; 187

Cartron village: Kilmacteige SO 40; 187, 194

Cartronatemple chapel: Manorhamilton Union LM 40; 52

Cartroneighteragh [or Cartroneaghtragh] district: Misc. SO 40; 198

Cartronfree spa: Drumlumman CN 40; 13

Cartwright, Robert: Clondermot LY 34; 54

Caruth, Alexander: Templepatrick AM 35; 132

Carvadoon cove: Finvoy AM 23; 78

Carvadoon fort: Finvoy AM 23; 78

Carvill, Eliza (Jnr): Aghagallon AM 21; 19

Carvill, Eliza (Snr): Aghagallon AM 21; 19

Carvill, Francis: Newry DN 3; 100, 104

Carvill, James (Jnr): Aghagallon AM 21; 19

Carvill, James (Snr): Aghagallon AM 21; 19

Cary barony: Armoy AM 24; 1–2

Cary barony: Ballintoy AM 24; 10

Cary barony: Billy AM 16; 36, 38–39

Cary barony: Culfeightrin AM 24; 36, 56

Cary barony: Drumtullagh AM 16; 96–97

Cary barony: Layd and Inispollan AM 13; 54

Cary barony: Ramoan AM 24; 86, 91

Cary barony: Rathlin Island AM 24; 127

Cary barony: Tickmacrevan AM 13; 124, 127

Cary ph: Culfeightrin AM 24; 36

Cary, Anne: Dungiven LY 15; 60

Cary, Col (Dungiven): Banagher LY 30; 41, 80–81, 98

Cary, Col.: Dungiven LY 15; 28, 42–43, 76, 84, 110

Cary, Edward: Dungiven LY 15; 60

Cary, family: Dungiven LY 15; 42, 58

Cary, Gen.: Dungiven LY 15; 30

Cary, George: Banagher LY 30; 105, 107

Cary, George: Clondermot LY 34; 66–67, 74

Cary, George: Dungiven LY 15; 43, 60

Cary, George: Moville DL 38; 75

Cary, Mr (Greencastle): Tamlaght O'Crilly LY 18; 89, 102

Cary, Mr: Clonmany DL 38; 18

Cary, Rev. A.: Mintiaghs DL 38; 66

Cary, Rev. A.G.: Clondermot LY 34; 6, 11, 20, 27, 37, 40, 77, 83, 86–87, 92, 94–95, 98, 104

Cary, Rev. A.G.: Faughanvale LY 36; 33

Cary, Rev. Lucius: Ballynascreen LY 31; 4, 129, 143
Cary, Rev. Lucius: Moville DL 38; 75, 77–78
Cary, Robert: Donagh DL 38; 32
Cary, Tristram: Moville DL 38; 78
Cary's Castle: Bovevagh LY 25; 45
Cary's Castle: Dungiven LY 15; 24
Cary's creek: Lough Swilly DL 38; 108
Carysduff hill: Aughnamullen MN 40; 69
Casan river: Shilvodan AM 19; 138
Casedy, family: Culfeightrin AM 24; 71
Casement, Edmond: Inver AM 26; 52–54
Casement, Edward: Kilwaughter AM 10; 112
Casement, family: Ballinderry AM 21; 51
Casement, John: Inver AM 26; 51
Casement, Mr: Ahoghill AM 23; 34
Casement, Mr: Blaris AM 8; 34
Casement, Mrs: Ballyclug AM 23; 55
Casement, Mrs: Blaris AM 8; 9, 34, 85
Casement, Mrs: Blaris DN 12; 49
Casement, Rev. Robert: Culfeightrin AM 24; 45
Casement, Thomas: Kirkinriola AM 23; 96
Casey, Duncan: Loughguile AM 13; 72
Casey, family: Loughguile AM 13; 64
Casey, Rev. Bernard: Galloon FH 4; 97
Casey, Widow: Donagh DL 38; 32
Cash bridge: Blaris DN 12; 34
Cash locality: Derryvullan FH 14; 38
Cashel (Tipperary): Coleraine LY 33; 63
Cashel (Tipperary): Newry DN 3; 66
Cashel bleach green: Dungiven LY 15; 9, 98
Cashel bog: Macosquin LY 22; 78, 120
Cashel bridge: Macosquin LY 22; 81, 103
Cashel caves: Ballintoy AM 24; 30–31
Cashel chapel: Dungiven LY 15; 18–19, 117
Cashel chapel: Dungiven LY 15; 8, 99
Cashel corn mill: Tullyaughnish DL 38; 89
Cashel cromlech: Errigal LY 27; 78
Cashel druidical altar: Dungiven LY 15; 41
Cashel fort (Dungiven): Faughanvale LY 36; 15
Cashel fort: Ballintoy AM 24; 30–31
Cashel fort: Dungiven LY 15; 13, 15, 41, 101, 111
Cashel fort: Errigal LY 27; 70
Cashel fort: Faughanvale LY 36; 13, 21, 57
Cashel Glebe fort: Clondavaddog DL 38; 6
Cashel graveyard: Macosquin LY 22; 120
Cashel manor: Ahoghill AM 23; 2, 15
Cashel rock: Macosquin LY 22; 76
Cashel school: Dungiven LY 15; 18–19, 116–18
Cashel school: Macosquin LY 22; 91, 94
Cashel standing stone: Dungiven LY 15; 41, 101
Cashel standing stone: Macosquin LY 22; 86
Cashel Sunday school: Macosquin LY 22; 94
Cashel td: Banagher LY 30; 22
Cashel td: Bovevagh LY 25; 29
Cashel td: Donagh DL 38; 31

Cashel td: Dungiven LY 15; 3, 9, 23, 27, 31, 43, 61,
    64–65, 74, 80, 88, 92, 99, 101
Cashel td: Lough Swilly DL 38; 120, 135
Cashel td: Macosquin LY 22; 76, 123
Cashel td: Magilligan LY 11; 97
Cashel wood: Dungiven LY 15; 3, 96
Cashell (see Cashel): Faughanvale LY 36; 57
Cashell td: Aghadowey LY 22; 10
Cashellin td: Donaghmore DL 39; 36
Cashlinny td: Templecarn DL 39; 164
Caskerable mountain: Misc. SO 40; 198
Caskey, Ann (Jnr): Tamlaght Finlagan LY 25; 119
Caskey, Ann (Snr): Tamlaght Finlagan LY 25; 118
Caskey, Eliza: Tamlaght Finlagan LY 25; 119
Caskey, family: Desertoghill LY 27; 5, 30
Caskey, family: Tamlaght O'Crilly LY 18; 93
Caskey, Francis: Maghera LY 18; 53, 63
Caskey, John: Tamlaght Finlagan LY 25; 119
Caskey, Joseph: Coleraine LY 33; 139
Caskey, Joseph: Dunboe LY 11; 77
Caskey, Margret Jane: Tamlaght Finlagan LY 25;
    119
Caskey, Mary: Tamlaght Finlagan LY 25; 119
Caskey, Milly: Tamlaght Finlagan LY 25; 119
Caskey, Samual: Tamlaght Finlagan LY 25; 118
Caskey, William: Dunboe LY 11; 72
Caskey, William: Tamlaght O'Crilly LY 18; 113
Caskum td: Aghaderg DN 12; 1, 9
Casky, family: Billy AM 16; 58, 68
Casley, Thomas: Ramoan AM 24; 114–15
Caspian Sea: Clondermot LY 34; 61
Caspinduff (see Coskemduff): Drumgoon CN 40; 3
Cass (see Sess): Errigal Keerogue TE 20; 57
Cassels, Mr: Enniskillen FH 4; 68
Cassidy Lodge: Derryvullan FH 14; 34
Cassidy, Charles: Carrickfergus AM 37; 131
Cassidy, Charles: Maghera LY 18; 81
Cassidy, Daniel: Tamlaght O'Crilly LY 18; 112,
    125–26
Cassidy, family: Desertoghill LY 27; 30
Cassidy, family: Kilcronaghan LY 31; 68
Cassidy, Francis: Errigal LY 27; 74
Cassidy, Francis: Tamlaght O'Crilly LY 18; 133
Cassidy, Frank: Kilrea LY 27; 129
Cassidy, Frank: Maghera LY 18; 78
Cassidy, Hugh: Ballyscullion LY 6; 71
Cassidy, Hugh: Tamlaght Finlagan LY 25; 80
Cassidy, Hugh [I]: Maghera LY 18; 37
Cassidy, Hugh [II]: Maghera LY 18; 45
Cassidy, James: Coleraine LY 33; 146
Cassidy, James: Errigal LY 27; 66
Cassidy, James: Maghera LY 18; 30, 59
Cassidy, John: Dungiven LY 15; 75
Cassidy, John: Maghera LY 18; 80
Cassidy, John: Tamlaght O'Crilly LY 18; 133

Cassidy, Joseph: Dungiven LY 15; 70

Cassidy, Lewis: Maghera LY 18; 20

Cassidy, man named: Misc. LY 31; 138

Cassidy, Martha: Carrickfergus AM 37; 123

Cassidy, Mr (Aughantaraghan): Ballymore AH 1; 11

Cassidy, Patrick: Ballynascreen LY 31; 20, 26, 30, 32

Cassidy, Patrick: Devenish FH 14; 54

Cassidy, Patrick: Maghera LY 18; 8, 68

Cassidy, Patt: Errigal LY 27; 55

Cassidy, Rev. Edward: Devenish FH 14; 54

Cassidy, Rev. Mark: Comber DN 7; 37–38

Cassidy, Rev. Mark: Newtownards DN 7; 109

Cassidy, Rev. Thomas: Carrickfergus AM 37; 102, 174

Cassidy, Rev. Thomas: Raloo AM 32; 126

Cassidy, Robert: Artrea LY 6; 38

Cassidy, Samuel: Magherafelt LY 6; 91

Cassidy, Sarah: Carrickfergus AM 37; 118

Cassidy, Thomas: Ballyscullion LY 6; 51, 72

Cassidy, Thomas: Macosquin LY 22; 110

Castellchrack (see Castlecarragh): Kilmacteige SO 40; 193

Castey cloghogle stones: Ardstraw TE 5; 12

Castey td: Ardstraw TE 5; 12

Castle abbey: Donegore AM 29; 114

Castle Archdall: Derryvullan FH 14; 33–34

Castle Archdall: Drumkeeran FH 14; 67

Castle Archdall: Magheraculmoney FH 14; 108

Castle Archdall old church: Derryvullan FH 14; 34

Castle Balfour demesne: Aghalurcher FH 4; 6, 13

Castle Blagh (see Castleblaugh): Raymoghy DL 39; 141

Castle bridge: Drumachose LY 9; 56–57, 109

Castle Brinsley td: Galloon FH 4; 89, 105

Castle Caldwell: Belleek FH 14; 1–5

Castle Caldwell: Templecarn FH 14; 120

Castle Caldwell graveyard: Belleek FH 14; 4

Castle Caldwell old church: Belleek FH 14; 4

Castle Caldwell school: Belleek FH 14; 6

Castle Caragh (see Castlecarragh): Kilmacteige SO 40; 187

Castle Carra: Culfeightrin AM 24; 40, 46

Castle Chichester: Glynn AM 26; 39

Castle Chichester: Island Magee AM 10; 27–29, 31, 42, 47–50, 71, 76, 83, 86–87, 93, 98–99, 102, 104

Castle Chichester: Kilroot AM 26; 73

Castle Chichester: Templecorran AM 26; 108, 120

Castle Chichester and Portmuck manor: Island Magee AM 10; 31

Castle Chichester coastguard station: Templecorran AM 26; 125–26

Castle Chichester manor: Island Magee AM 10; 74, 86

Castle Chichester pier: Island Magee AM 10; 22, 76, 80, 82

Castle Coole: Derryvullan FH 14; 41, 43

Castle Coole: Drumragh TE 5; 109

Castle Coole: Enniskillen FH 4; 66–68, 74, 81

Castle Coole demesne: Derryvullan FH 14; 40

Castle Coole demesne: Enniskillen FH 4; 50

Castle Coole House: Killymard DL 39; 106

Castle Coole lough: Cleenish FH 14; 14

Castle Coole lough: Derryvullan FH 14; 40

Castle Coole manor: Derryvullan FH 14; 45–46

Castle Coole manor: Enniskillen FH 4; 82

Castle Coole manor: Misc. FH 4; 133

Castle Coole td: Derryvullan FH 14; 46

Castle creek: Lough Swilly DL 38; 147

Castle Deffrick: Billy AM 16; 55

Castle Deffrick: Drumtullagh AM 16; 101

Castle Deffrick fort: Billy AM 16; 61

Castle Dermot: Clondermot LY 34; 65

Castle Dillon House: Loughgall AH 1; 80

Castle Dillon lough: Loughgall AH 1; 79

Castle Dillon obelisk: Loughgall AH 1; 78

Castle Dobbs (New Brunswick): Kilroot AM 26; 73

Castle Dobbs: Ballynure AM 32; 46–47, 51–52, 64

Castle Dobbs: Kilroot AM 26; 58–59, 67, 69, 72–79

Castle Dobbs bleach mills: Kilroot AM 26; 56, 76

Castle Dobbs bowling green: Kilroot AM 26; 76

Castle Dobbs bridge: Ballynure AM 32; 64

Castle Dobbs cave: Kilroot AM 26; 76

Castle Dobbs demesne: Kilroot AM 26; 76

Castle Dobbs forts: Kilroot AM 26; 71, 76

Castle Dobbs mills: Kilroot AM 26; 76

Castle Dobbs quarry: Kilroot AM 26; 57

Castle Dobbs school: Kilroot AM 26; 74, 80–81

Castle Dobbs Sunday school: Kilroot AM 26; 74, 81

Castle Enegan: Newry DN 3; 112

Castle Enegan bog: Newry DN 3; 105

Castle Enegan td: Newry DN 3; 112

Castle Espie: Killinchy DN 7; 87

Castle Espie: Killyleagh DN 17; 84

Castle Espie td: Tullynakill DN 7; 122

Castle field: Donegore AM 29; 114

Castle field: Magherafelt LY 6; 88

Castle Flack: Magheraculmoney FH 14; 106

Castle fort: Kirkinriola AM 23; 125–26

Castle Forward demesne: Misc. DL 39; 188

Castle Forward House: Misc. DL 39; 187

Castle Forward plantation: Misc. DL 39; 189

Castle Forward td: Misc. DL 39; 194

Castle Gardens: Blaris AM 8; 1, 8, 13, 22–23, 40

Castle Gardens: Blaris DN 12; 27, 32

Castle Gore: Manorhamilton Union LM 40; 52

Castle Grove: Lough Swilly DL 38; 103

Castle Hasset manor: Misc. FH 4; 133

Castle hill: Ardkeen DN 7; 1

Castle hill: Ballyrashane LY 22; 46
Castle hill: Balteagh LY 9; 7
Castle hill: Clogher TE 5; 29
Castle hill: Drumballyroney DN 3; 12, 14, 16
Castle hill: Drumgath DN 3; 19
Castle hill: Dunluce AM 16; 115, 119
Castle hill: Kilbride AM 29; 154
Castle hill bawn: Donacavey TE 5; 68
Castle Hill fort [I]: Ardclinis AM 13; 4, 7
Castle Hill fort [II]: Ardclinis AM 13; 4, 7
Castle Hill House: Clogher TE 5; 54–55
Castle Hill Peninsula: Ardkeen DN 7; 2
Castle House (see Grave): Urney DL 39; 181
Castle House: Kirkinriola AM 23; 91
Castle House demesne: Kirkinriola AM 23; 91
Castle Hume: Devenish FH 14; 55
Castle Hume: Enniskillen FH 4; 68
Castle Irvine demesne: Derryvullan FH 14; 33
Castle Irvine demesne: Magheracross FH 14; 91
Castle Island (Co. Down): Dungiven LY 15; 26
Castle Island: Saul DN 17; 111, 114
Castle Isle ph: Misc. DN 17; 121
Castle Lecky: Magilligan LY 11; 85–86, 101, 123, 123, 127
Castle Lecky enclosure: Magilligan LY 11; 117
Castle Lecky old castle: Magilligan LY 11; 117
Castle Leslie: Ballybay MN 40; 79–80
Castle Leslie: Donagh MN 40; 98, 101
Castle Mervyn demesne: Kilskeery TE 5; 114
Castle Murray: Magheracross FH 14; 93, 97
Castle Norton (see Upton Castle): Ballyscullion LY 6; 58
Castle of Moneygelvin td: Taughboyne DL 39; 148, 152
Castle Park field: Culfeightrin AM 24; 56
Castle Park td: Culfeightrin AM 24; 38, 45
Castle Park tower: Culfeightrin AM 24; 40
Castle Quarter quarry: Lough Swilly DL 38; 148
Castle Quarter td: Lough Swilly DL 38; 144–45
Castle Quarter village: Lough Swilly DL 38; 147
Castle Reagh: Misc. DN 17; 120
Castle river: Balteagh LY 9; 1–2, 5, 7, 9, 13–14, 20–21, 23
Castle river: Drumachose LY 9; 46, 48, 56–57, 74–75, 89, 101
Castle river: Faughanvale LY 36; 1–2, 4, 21
Castle river bridge: Balteagh LY 9; 5
Castle river bridge: Drumachose LY 9; 83, 91
Castle Robin: Ballinderry AM 21; 52
Castle Robin: Blaris AM 8; 48
Castle Robin: Derryaghy AM 8; 92–94, 101, 107, 120
Castle Robin: Templepatrick AM 35; 114, 145
Castle Robin mount: Derryaghy AM 8; 93
Castle Robin turnpike: Derryaghy AM 8; 108

Castle rock: Dunboe LY 11; 65
Castle Rock td: Kilmacteige SO 40; 185–87, 191, 193–96
Castle Rock trigonometrical station: Kilmacteige SO 40; 187
Castle Roe: Kilmore AH 1; 63, 68
Castle Roe: Misc. LY 36; 109
Castle Rose: Dungiven LY 15; 33
Castle Sanderson: Drummully FH 4; 35–36
Castle Sanderson: Laragh CN 40; 45
Castle Solace: Leck DL 39; 118
Castle Wall locality: Magheragall AM 21; 100
Castle Ward: Ardglass DN 17; 5
Castle Water House manor: Misc. FH 4; 133
Castle Wholme locality: Tullaghobegley DL 39; 172
Castle Worraigh (see Antrim county old gaol): Carrickfergus AM 37; 20
Castle Wray: Lough Swilly DL 38; 103
Castleaverry (Castlenaverry): Comber DN 7; 37, 39, 43
Castlebane Castle: Armoy AM 24; 2, 8
Castlebar: Kilmacteige SO 40; 190
Castlebawn (see Castlebane): Armoy AM 24; 2
Castlebeg td: Comber DN 7; 41, 43
Castlebeg td: Dundonald DN 7; 65
Castlebeg wash mill: Comber DN 7; 41
Castlebellingham (Louth): Newry DN 3; 100
Castlebellingham: Ballybay MN 40; 82
Castlebellingham: Enniskeen CN 40; 29
Castleblaney (see Castleblayney)
Castleblaugh td: Raymoghy DL 39; 136, 141, 198
Castleblayney: Aughnamullen MN 40; 74, 76
Castleblayney: Ballybay MN 40; 80–83
Castleblayney: Donaghmoyne MN 40; 107–08
Castleblayney: Killanny MN 40; 132
Castleblayney: Magheracloone MN 40; 140
Castleblayney: Magheross MN 40; 146–47, 149, 152, 157
Castleblayney: Muckno MN 40; 162, 164, 166–67
Castleblayney: Newry DN 3; 78
Castleblayney: Newtownhamilton AH 1; 98
Castleblayney: Tyholland MN 40; 175
Castleblayney: Tynan AH 1; 128
Castleblayney bridewell: Muckno MN 40; 164
Castleblayney Castle: Muckno MN 40; 164
Castleblayney chapel (C): Muckno MN 40; 164
Castleblayney chapel (M): Muckno MN 40; 164
Castleblayney church: Muckno MN 40; 164
Castleblayney demesne: Muckno MN 40; 164, 166
Castleblayney graveyard: Muckno MN 40; 164
Castleblayney inn: Muckno MN 40; 164
Castleblayney market house: Muckno MN 40; 164
Castleblayney mill: Muckno MN 40; 162
Castleblayney parish school: Muckno MN 40; 167
Castleblayney school [I]: Muckno MN 40; 168

Castleblayney school [II]: Muckno MN 40; 168
Castleblayney school [III]: Muckno MN 40; 168
Castleblayney school [IV]: Muckno MN 40; 168
Castleblayney sessions house: Muckno MN 40; 164
Castleblayney shambles: Muckno MN 40; 165
Castleblayney tanyards: Muckno MN 40; 165
Castleblayney turnpike: Muckno MN 40; 166
Castleboy (Castlebuoy) td: Castleboy DN 7; 27, 125
Castleboy old church: Castleboy DN 7; 27
Castleboy ph: Ballyphilip DN 7; 7
Castleboy ph: Witter DN 7; 125
Castleboy td: Ballywalter DN 7; 18
Castlecarra td: Carlingford LH 40; 58
Castlecarragh village: Kilmacteige SO 40; 187, 193
Castlecary House: Moville DL 38; 78
Castlecary wood: Moville DL 38; 75
Castlecat fort: Billy AM 16; 61
Castlecat td: Derrykeighan AM 16; 95
Castlecaulfield: Drumcree AH 1; 39
Castlecaulfield: Tullyniskan TE 20; 141
Castlecoole manor: Derrybrusk FH 4; 30
Castlecooly td: Lough Swilly DL 38; 145
Castlecunningham: Misc. DL 39; 187
Castlecunningham manor: Misc. DL 39; 184
Castledawson: Artrea LY 6; 9
Castledawson: Ballyscullion AM 19; 10
Castledawson: Ballyscullion LY 6; 43, 45, 47–48,
    53, 57, 59, 75
Castledawson: Banagher LY 30; 30, 60, 74
Castledawson: Desertmartin LY 31; 62
Castledawson: Drumachose LY 9; 117
Castledawson: Drummaul AM 19; 71
Castledawson: Dungiven LY 15; 26, 67
Castledawson: Errigal LY 27; 62
Castledawson: Kilcronaghan LY 31; 65, 79
Castledawson: Killead AM 35; 17
Castledawson: Lough Neagh AM 21; 94
Castledawson: Maghera LY 18; 2, 27–28, 34, 65,
    68, 75
Castledawson: Magherafelt LY 6; 79, 87, 89–90,
    95–96, 100–01, 104
Castledawson: Misc. LY 31; 116
Castledawson: Tamlaght O'Crilly LY 18; 91, 109
Castledawson bleach green: Ballyscullion LY 6; 65
Castledawson bridge: Ballyscullion LY 6; 47
Castledawson calico factory: Artrea TE 20; 7
Castledawson chapel: Ballyscullion LY 6; 47, 59,
    63, 76
Castledawson chapel: Drummaul AM 19; 71
Castledawson chapel: Magherafelt LY 6; 91
Castledawson chapel of ease: Magherafelt LY 6; 89
Castledawson corn kiln: Ballyscullion LY 6; 76
Castledawson corn mill: Ballyscullion LY 6; 66, 76
Castledawson cotton factory: Ballyscullion LY 6;
    48, 66, 76

Castledawson cotton mill: Ballyscullion LY 6; 49
Castledawson cotton mill: Magherafelt LY 6; 90
Castledawson cotton store: Ballyscullion LY 6; 76
Castledawson cotton yarn store: Ballyscullion LY 6;
    76
Castledawson crockery yard: Dungiven LY 15; 68
Castledawson demesne: Ballyscullion LY 6; 44
Castledawson dispensary: Magherafelt LY 6; 91
Castledawson district: Ballyscullion LY 6; 51, 57
Castledawson district: Magherafelt LY 6; 96
Castledawson drying house: Ballyscullion LY 6; 76
Castledawson flour mills: Ballyscullion LY 6;
    48–49, 66, 76
Castledawson flour mills: Maghera LY 18; 51
Castledawson forge: Kilrea LY 27; 112
Castledawson forges: Ballyscullion LY 6; 76
Castledawson grain market: Magherafelt LY 6; 89
Castledawson House: Ballyscullion LY 6; 59
Castledawson ironworks: Misc. LY 31; 113
Castledawson Lodge: Ballyscullion LY 6; 43, 48, 53
Castledawson manor: Artrea TE 20; 6
Castledawson manor: Ballyscullion LY 6; 57
Castledawson mechanics workshop: Ballyscullion
    LY 6; 76
Castledawson meeting house: Ballyscullion LY 6;
    58
Castledawson meeting house: Magherafelt LY 6; 89,
    95, 98
Castledawson mill-dam: Maghera LY 18; 3
Castledawson obelisk: Magherafelt LY 6; 89
Castledawson oil store: Ballyscullion LY 6; 76
Castledawson school: Ballyscullion LY 6; 47, 60, 76
Castledawson school: Magherafelt LY 6; 91
Castledawson Sunday school: Ballyscullion LY 6;
    62
Castledawson weir: Misc. LY 31; 111
Castledawson wheat kiln: Ballyscullion LY 6; 76
Castledawson wheat stores: Ballyscullion LY 6; 76
Castlederg (see also Dergbridge): Skirts of Urney
    and Ardstraw TE 5; 136
Castlederg: Donaghmore DL 39; 29–30, 32
Castlederg: Magheraculmoney FH 14; 109
Castlederg: Templecarn DL 39; 162
Castlederg: Urney DL 39; 180
Castlederg barrack: Skirts of Urney and Ardstraw
    TE 5; 137
Castlederg bridge: Skirts of Urney and Ardstraw TE
    5; 139
Castlederg Castle: Skirts of Urney and Ardstraw TE
    5; 136
Castlederg church: Skirts of Urney and Ardstraw TE
    5; 137, 141
Castlederg court house: Skirts of Urney and
    Ardstraw TE 5; 137

Castlederg dispensary: Skirts of Urney and Ardstraw TE 5; 139–40

Castlederg dispensary: Termonamongan TE 5; 144

Castlederg meeting house: Skirts of Urney and Ardstraw TE 5; 138, 141

Castlederg school: Skirts of Urney and Ardstraw TE 5; 140

Castledirk fort: Billy AM 16; 55, 61

Castledooey td: Raymoghy DL 39; 136, 141

Castlefin school: Skirts of Urney and Ardstraw TE 5; 140

Castlefin td: Skirts of Urney and Ardstraw TE 5; 140

Castlefinn: Clonleigh DL 39; 3, 13, 13

Castlefinn: Donaghmore DL 39; 29–35

Castlefinn: Raphoe DL 39; 130

Castlefinn: Urney DL 39; 174, 176, 180

Castlefinn bridge: Donaghmore DL 39; 30, 33

Castlefinn Castle: Donaghmore DL 39; 30, 33

Castlefinn chapel: Donaghmore DL 39; 31–32

Castlefinn cornstore: Donaghmore DL 39; 30

Castlefinn graveyard: Donaghmore DL 39; 32

Castlefinn mansion house: Donaghmore DL 39; 32

Castlefinn market house: Donaghmore DL 39; 32

Castlefinn post office: Donaghmore DL 39; 32

Castlefinn quay: Donaghmore DL 39; 30

Castlefinn school [I]: Donaghmore DL 39; 32

Castlefinn school [II]: Donaghmore DL 39; 40

Castlefinn school [III]: Donaghmore DL 39; 40

Castlefinn td: Donaghmore DL 39; 36

Castleford (see Castleforward): Lough Swilly DL 38; 134

Castleforward Deerpark td: Lough Swilly DL 38; 145

Castleforward demesne: Lough Swilly DL 38; 142

Castleforward House: Clonleigh DL 39; 16

Castleforward House: Lough Swilly DL 38; 144

Castleforward td: Lough Swilly DL 38; 103, 134

Castlegrove td: Tullyaughnish DL 38; 95

Castlehaven, Earl of: Donacavey TE 5; 70–71

Castlehaven, Lord: Dungiven LY 15; 34

Castlehaven, Lord: Killesher FH 14; 84

Castlehench, Baron: Galloon FH 4; 102

Castlehill Demesne td: Clogher TE 5; 36

Castlehill locality: Lough Swilly DL 38; 145

Castlehill lough: Clogher TE 5; 58

Castlehill Point: Lough Swilly DL 38; 142–43

Castleisland crockery yard: Dungiven LY 15; 68

Castleleigh manor: Donacavey TE 5; 68, 70–71, 76–77, 85, 85–87

Castlemahon hill: Ballyculter DN 17; 25

Castlemahon td: Ballyculter DN 17; 30

Castlemellan td: Donaghedy TE 5; 91

Castlemoyle bridge: Ardstraw TE 5; 14

Castlenagree bog: Billy AM 16; 69

Castlenagree cashel: Billy AM 16; 55, 59

Castlenagree fort: Billy AM 16; 60

Castlenagree td: Billy AM 16; 76

Castleneverry (see Castleaverry)

Castleoffin td: Island Magee AM 10; 82

Castlepollard district: Enniskeen CN 40; 29

Castlequarter caves: Loughguile AM 13; 70–71

Castlequarter td: Loughguile AM 13; 58–62, 71

Castleraw td: Kilmore AH 1; 61, 63, 66, 68, 70

Castlereagh (Roscommon): Banagher LY 30; 108

Castlereagh barony: Blaris DN 12; 27

Castlereagh barony: Kilmood DN 7; 94

Castlereagh barony: Knockbreda DN 7; 97

Castlereagh barony: Misc. DN 17; 116

Castlereagh Lower barony: Bangor DN 7; 19

Castlereagh Lower barony: Comber DN 7; 31

Castlereagh Lower barony: Drumbo DN 7; 54

Castlereagh Lower barony: Dundonald DN 7; 64

Castlereagh Lower barony: Holywood DN 7; 73, 80

Castlereagh Lower barony: Killinchy DN 7; 86–87

Castlereagh school: Hillsborough DN 12; 101

Castlereagh school: Knockbreda DN 7; 102

Castlereagh Upper barony: Blaris DN 12; 26, 33

Castlereagh Upper barony: Comber DN 7; 31

Castlereagh Upper barony: Holywood DN 7; 80

Castlereagh Upper barony: Killinchy DN 7; 86–87

Castlereagh Upper barony: Saintfield DN 7; 116

Castlereagh village: Misc. DN 17; 119–20

Castlereagh, Lord: Ballintoy AM 24; 17

Castlereagh, Lord: Newtownards DN 7; 106

Castlereagh, Viscount: Grey Abbey DN 7; 70

Castlereagh, Viscount: Newry DN 3; 105

Castlerobin hill: Blaris DN 12; 27

Castleroddy fort: Cappagh TE 5; 18

Castleroe Castle: Dungiven LY 15; 35

Castleroe Castle: Macosquin LY 22; 76, 82, 85, 88, 90, 97, 101–03, 106–07, 109

Castleroe corn mill: Macosquin LY 22; 83, 105

Castleroe flour mill: Macosquin LY 22; 105

Castleroe House: Macosquin LY 22; 80, 101

Castleroe old mill: Macosquin LY 22; 80, 83

Castleroe school: Macosquin LY 22; 92–93, 121

Castleroe school: Misc. LY 36; 109

Castleroe Sunday school: Macosquin LY 22; 93

Castleroe td: Coleraine LY 33; 66, 143

Castleroe td: Macosquin LY 22; 102, 122–23

Castleroe wells: Macosquin LY 22; 109

Castles, Robert: Dunboe LY 11; 64

Castlescreen td: Inch DN 17; 75

Castlesessagh chapel: Skirts of Urney and Ardstraw TE 5; 138

Castlesessagh corn mill: Skirts of Urney and Ardstraw TE 5; 138

Castlesessagh td: Skirts of Urney and Ardstraw TE 5; 138

Castleshanaghan corn mill: Tullyaughnish DL 38; 89

Castleshanaghan td: Tullyaughnish DL 38; 97

Castleskreen (Castlescreen) td: Bright DN 17; 34–35, 37

Castleskreen fort: Bright DN 17; 33, 36

Castleskreen tower: Bright DN 17; 33

Castlestuart, Earl of: Ballyclog TE 20; 18

Castlestuart, Earl of: Tullyniskan TE 20; 140–41

Castletarra ph: Drung CN 40; 19, 19, 21

Castlethird fort: Taughboyne DL 39; 152

Castlethird td: Killea and Taughboyne DL 39; 79

Castlethird td: Taughboyne DL 39; 148, 152, 195

Castletoodry (Castle Toothery) td: Killowen LY 33; 165, 170, 172

Castletoodry bog: Killowen LY 33; 158

Castletoodry Castle: Killowen LY 33; 161

Castletoodry cove: Killowen LY 33; 161, 170

Castletorrison td: Convoy DL 39; 20

Castletown (Dernafougher) manor: Misc. FH 4; 133

Castletown bridge: Ballynure AM 32; 59, 68

Castletown Castle: Ballynure AM 32; 33, 41, 59, 63, 67–69

Castletown Castle: Manorhamilton Union LM 40; 51

Castletown cave: Island Magee AM 10; 72

Castletown church: Donacavey TE 5; 83

Castletown druid's altar: Ballynure AM 32; 62

Castletown entrenchment: Island Magee AM 10; 99

Castletown flax mill: Ballynure AM 32; 59

Castletown flax mill: Taughboyne DL 39; 152

Castletown fort: Manorhamilton Union LM 40; 52

Castletown fort [I]: Ahoghill AM 23; 35

Castletown fort [I]: Ballynure AM 32; 58–59

Castletown fort [II]: Ahoghill AM 23; 35

Castletown fort [II]: Ballynure AM 32; 59

Castletown fort [III]: Ahoghill AM 23; 35

Castletown hill: Ballynure AM 32; 72

Castletown House: Devenish FH 14; 48–50

Castletown manor: Devenish FH 14; 53, 55

Castletown Monea school: Devenish FH 14; 55–56

Castletown Monea td: Devenish FH 14; 58

Castletown mountain: Ballynure AM 32; 60

Castletown old castle: Donacavey TE 5; 83

Castletown standing stone [I]: Ballynure AM 32; 59

Castletown standing stone [II]: Ballynure AM 32; 67

Castletown td: Ahoghill AM 23; 35, 38

Castletown td: Ballynure AM 32; 33, 38, 62–63, 68, 72

Castletown td: Donacavey TE 5; 67, 76–78, 80–82, 85

Castletown td: Island Magee AM 10; 19, 22, 31, 47, 72, 82, 99

Castletown td: Killea and Taughboyne DL 39; 80, 87

Castletown td: Killymard DL 39; 106

Castletown td: Loughguile AM 13; 61–62

Castletown td: Misc. DL 39; 195

Castletown td: Taughboyne DL 39; 148, 152

Castletowncooly td: Carlingford LH 40; 58

Castlevenan (see Castlevennon): Garvaghy DN 12; 81

Castlevennan (see Castelvennon): Garvaghy DN 12; 81

Castlevennon school: Garvaghy DN 12; 83

Castlevennon td: Garvaghy DN 12; 81–83

Castleward House: Ballyculter DN 17; 27, 29

Castleward House: Bright DN 17; 35

Castleward House: Down DN 17; 51

Castleward mill: Ballyculter DN 17; 30

Castleward smithy: Ballyculter DN 17; 30

Castleward td: Ballyculter DN 17; 27, 30

Castlewarren td: Donaghedy TE 5; 91

Castlewellan: Blaris AM 8; 72–73

Castlewellan: Clonduff DN 3; 3, 6

Castlewellan: Comber DN 7; 37, 39–41

Castlewellan: Drumgath DN 3; 21

Castlewellan: Dundonald DN 7; 65

Castlewellan: Killyleagh DN 17; 87

Castlewellan: Kilmegan DN 3; 57–60

Castlewellan: Loughinisland DN 17; 95–96

Castlewellan: Magheradrool DN 17; 106–07

Castlewellan chapel [I]: Kilmegan DN 3; 58

Castlewellan chapel [II]: Kilmegan DN 3; 58

Castlewellan corn mill: Kilmegan DN 3; 58

Castlewellan Cottage: Kilmegan DN 3; 55, 58

Castlewellan crane: Kilmegan DN 3; 58

Castlewellan dispensary: Kilmegan DN 3; 59

Castlewellan flax mill [I]: Kilmegan DN 3; 58

Castlewellan flax mill [II]: Kilmegan DN 3; 58

Castlewellan market house: Kilmegan DN 3; 58

Castlewellan meeting house: Kilmegan DN 3; 58

Castlewellan school [I]: Kilmegan DN 3; 59

Castlewellan school [II]: Kilmegan DN 3; 60

Caston, family: Carnmoney AM 2; 76

Castrews td: Misc. DL 39; 194

Cat cairn: Carnmoney AM 2; 98–99

Catanus, St: Magilligan LY 11; 104

Caten, Rev.: Loughgall AH 1; 76

Caters, family: Carrickfergus AM 37; 93

Catharine's Island: Lough Swilly DL 38; 121

Cathcart, Alexander: Aghadowey LY 22; 34

Cathcart, family: Enniskillen FH 4; 58

Cathcart, family: Island Magee AM 10; 70

Cathcart, family: Kirkinriola AM 23; 124

Cathcart, Rev. John: Drummaul AM 19; 53, 69, 82

Cather, David: Banagher LY 30; 23

Cather, David: Drumachose LY 9; 69, 84, 97, 104, 118, 121, 130

Cather, David: Faughanvale LY 36; 21

Cather, David: Magilligan LY 11; 85, 100, 135

Cather, David: Tamlaght Finlagan LY 25; 83, 87, 92, 112, 121–22

Cather, George: Drumachose LY 9; 69

Cather, John: Cumber LY 28; 56

Cather, Mr: Magilligan LY 11; 85

Cather, William: Drumachose LY 9; 69, 120

Cather, William: Tamlaght Finlagan LY 25; 108

Catherine lough: Ardstraw TE 5; 2, 4, 10–11

Catherine's Grove td: Carlingford LH 40; 58

Cathers, William: Clondermot LY 34; 78

Catherwood, Alexander: Rasharkin AM 23; 139

Catherwood, family: Carrickfergus AM 37; 93, 179

Catherwood, family: Rasharkin AM 23; 136, 138

Catherwood, Hugh: Carrickfergus AM 37; 177, 184, 187, 190–91

Catherwood, Samuel: Carrickfergus AM 37; 172

Catherwood, William: Carrickfergus AM 37; 172

Cathewood, James: Killowen LY 33; 159

Catney, John: Hillsborough DN 12; 106

Cator (Cattore) td: Donacavey TE 5; 76, 78, 81, 84–85

Cats bush: Macosquin LY 22; 118

Cats Causeway: Macosquin LY 22; 96

Cats Causeway: Misc. LY 36; 112

Cattens, family: Carrickfergus AM 37; 93

Cattocks (see Cattogs): Comber DN 7; 42

Cattogs td: Comber DN 7; 35, 37, 39, 42–44

Cattogs windmill: Comber DN 7; 35, 39

Cattor td: Donacavey TE 5; 80

Caufield, James: Ballyscullion LY 6; 65

Caufield, Jane: Ballymoney AM 16; 17

Caufield, Widow: Ballyscullion LY 6; 72

Caugh (Cah) td: Banagher LY 30; 76, 84, 88–89, 92

Caugh cairn: Banagher LY 30; 56

Caugh district: Banagher LY 30; 48, 52

Caugh fort [I]: Banagher LY 30; 30

Caugh fort [II]: Banagher LY 30; 71

Caugh hill: Banagher LY 30; 24, 29, 37, 44, 56, 56–58, 108, 110

Caugh hill: Bovevagh LY 25; 47

Caugh hill: Dungiven LY 15; 111

Caugh locality: Bovevagh LY 25; 47

Caugh standing stones: Banagher LY 30; 58

Caugh standing stones: Bovevagh LY 25; 47

Caughran, Mr: Balteagh LY 9; 36

Caul, family: Ahoghill AM 23; 25

Caul, Jack: Drumgath DN 3; 20

Cauldhame locality: Carrickfergus AM 37; 93, 174

Cauldruin td: Clogher TE 5; 36

Caulfield, Archdeacon: Devenish FH 14; 59

Caulfield, E.H.: Ballyclog TE 20; 17

Caulfield, E.H.: Donaghenry TE 20; 39

Caulfield, Henry: Coleraine LY 33; 145

Caulfield, Hugh: Seagoe AH 1; 103

Caulfield, Jane: Ahoghill AM 23; 39

Caulfield, John: Coleraine LY 33; 68, 72, 135

Caulfield, Lord: Loughgall AH 1; 80

Caulfield, Mary: Ahoghill AM 23; 45, 48

Caulfield, Messrs Dennis and Co.: Newry DN 3; 99

Caulfield, Mr: Rasharkin AM 23; 127

Caulfield, Mrs: Clogher TE 5; 41

Caulfield, Rev. H.: Kilmore AH 1; 65, 71

Caulfield, Rev. H.: Loughgall AH 1; 80

Caulfield, Samuel: Ahoghill AM 23; 39

Caulfield, William: Coleraine LY 33; 95, 138

Cauragh glebe: Killesher FH 14; 86

Cauragh td: Kinawley FH 4; 110

Cauran (see Carraun): Kilmacteige SO 40; 195

Causeland, William: Donaghmore DL 39; 37

Causeway water: Kilbroney DN 3; 26, 28

Causeway water: Kilkeel DN 3; 46–47, 52

Causeway Water bridge: Kilkeel DN 3; 52

Cavan chapel: Killyman TE 20; 67–68

Cavan corn mill: Dromore TE 5; 101

Cavan county: Aghabog MN 40; 65

Cavan county: Aughnamullen MN 40; 70, 74

Cavan county: Ballyscullion LY 6; 59

Cavan county: Currin MN 40; 86, 88, 90

Cavan county: Drumhome DL 39; 63

Cavan county: Drummully FH 4; 36

Cavan county: Enniskillen FH 4; 44, 51, 64, 80

Cavan county: Faughanvale LY 36; 56, 62

Cavan county: Galloon FH 4; 92, 100–01

Cavan county: Kilbarron DL 39; 77

Cavan county: Kinawley FH 4; 107–08, 111–13

Cavan county: Magheross MN 40; 143

Cavan county: Manorhamilton Union LM 40; 47

Cavan county: Newry DN 3; 87

Cavan county: Tomregan FH 4; 125–26

Cavan gaol: Drumgoon CN 40; 8

Cavan hill: Donaghedy TE 5; 88

Cavan Lower school: Donaghmore DL 39; 41

Cavan Lower td: Donaghmore DL 39; 36

Cavan meeting house: Donacavey TE 5; 64, 82

Cavan mill: Donacavey TE 5; 82

Cavan Oneil well: Aghaloo TE 20; 1

Cavan td: Clogher TE 5; 36, 47, 53

Cavan td: Clonleigh DL 39; 12, 190, 192, 197

Cavan td: Donacavey TE 5; 64, 67, 74, 76, 78, 80–82, 85

Cavan td: Dromore TE 5; 101

Cavan td: Drumballyroney DN 3; 18

Cavan td: Kilmore AH 1; 61, 68–69, 71–72

Cavan town: Banagher LY 30; 19, 96

Cavan town: Clondermot LY 34; 63

Cavan town: Clones FH 4; 26–27

Cavan town: Drumglass TE 20; 43
Cavan town: Drummully FH 4; 35, 40
Cavan town: Drung CN 40; 20–21, 23
Cavan town: Enniskillen FH 4; 51–53
Cavan town: Killdrumsherdan CN 40; 33–34
Cavan town: Laragh CN 40; 41–43
Cavan Upper school: Donaghmore DL 39; 41
Cavan Upper td: Donaghmore DL 39; 36
Cavan Walk district: Enniskeen CN 40; 29
Cavan, family: Drumlumman CN 40; 15
Cavanacaw (Cavanaca) td: Drumragh TE 5; 108–09
Cavanacaw fort: Drumragh TE 5; 109
Cavanacaw House: Misc. DL 39; 186
Cavanacaw school: Drumragh TE 5; 109
Cavanacaw td: Clonleigh DL 39; 2, 12, 195, 197
Cavanacor (see Cavanacaw): Misc. DL 39; 186
Cavanacross hill: Derryvullan FH 14; 40
Cavanacross td: Derryvullan FH 14; 46
Cavanaff td: Moville DL 38; 75
Cavanagarvan td: Aghavea FH 4; 23
Cavanagarven hill: Tynan AH 1; 124
Cavanageragh td: Magheross MN 40; 148
Cavanagh td: Drummully FH 4; 34, 39
Cavanagh td: Tomregan FH 4; 126
Cavanagh, J.B.: Aghanloo LY 11; 22, 30
Cavanaghlough (see Cavanalough): Magheracross
    FH 14; 92
Cavanakeery td: Devenish FH 14; 58
Cavanakirk td: Clogher TE 5; 37
Cavanaleck meeting house: Aghalurcher FH 4; 6
Cavanaleck mountain: Aghalurcher FH 4; 2
Cavanaleck school: Aghalurcher FH 4; 11
Cavanaleck td: Aghalurcher FH 4; 14
Cavanaleck td: Enniskillen FH 4; 81
Cavanaleek (see Cavanaleck): Aghalurcher FH 4; 2
Cavanalough glebe: Magheracross FH 14; 92, 98
Cavanalough td: Magheracross FH 14; 100, 102
Cavan-an-churaidh hill: Dungiven LY 15; 64
Cavanarainy hill: Drung CN 40; 19–20
Cavanaweery td: Urney DL 39; 181
Cavancarragh (see Cavancurragh): Cleenish FH 14;
    21
Cavancurragh forts: Derryvullan FH 14; 42
Cavancurragh td: Cleenish FH 14; 21, 29
Cavancurragh td: Derryvullan FH 14; 42, 46
Cavancurragh td: Galloon FH 4; 95
Cavandoogan td: Tynan AH 1; 124
Cavankallan td: Laragh CN 40; 46
Cavanmore td: Cleenish FH 14; 29
Cavanreagh bog: Ballynascreen LY 31; 20
Cavanreagh corn mill: Ballynascreen LY 31; 8
Cavanreagh td: Ballynascreen LY 31; 11, 27, 143
Cavanreany (see Cavanarainy): Drung CN 40; 20
Cavanreeny (see Cavanarainy): Drung CN 40; 19
Cavans bog: Aghavea FH 4; 18

Cavans hill: Aghavea FH 4; 17
Cavans td: Aghavea FH 4; 23, 25
Cavantillycormick druid's circle: Magheracross FH
    14; 97
Cavantillycormick td: Magheracross FH 14; 102
Cavantreedraff (see Cavantreeduff): Cleenish FH
    14; 12
Cavantreeduff mountain: Cleenish FH 14; 12
Cavantreeduff td: Cleenish FH 14; 29
Cavany hill: Currin MN 40; 86
Cavany td: Currin MN 40; 86, 91, 95
Cave fort: Tamlaght Finlagan LY 25; 113
Cave hill (see Cove hill): Coleraine LY 33; 132
Cave Hill mountain: Ballylinny AM 32; 20
Cave Hill mountain: Ballymartin AM 2; 1, 3, 9
Cave Hill mountain: Ballyrobert AM 2; 23
Cave Hill mountain: Carnmoney AM 2; 34–37, 50,
    63, 67, 70
Cave Hill mountain: Mallusk AM 2; 106, 112
Cave Hill mountain: Templepatrick AM 35; 105,
    107, 139
Cave Hill mountain: Umgall AM 35; 155
Cave stones: Banagher LY 30; 83
Cavencork td: Clogher TE 5; 54
Cavey fort: Errigal Keerogue TE 20; 51
Cavey quarry: Errigal Keerogue TE 20; 51
Cavey td: Errigal Keerogue TE 20; 51, 57
Cavin (see Cavan): Misc. DL 39; 190
Cavin High td: Tullyaughnish DL 38; 97
Cavin Low td: Tullyaughnish DL 38; 97
Cavin, family: Maghera LY 18; 13, 54
Cavin, Richard: Maghera LY 18; 29, 54
Cavin, Samuel: Maghera LY 18; 54
Cavin, William: Coleraine LY 33; 72
Cavinaca td: Taughboyne DL 39; 148, 152
Cavinshanagh Glebe td: Taughboyne DL 39; 148
Cavner, Rev.: Carrickfergus AM 37; 174
Caws (see Cah): Clondermot LY 34; 86
Cealey, Daniel: Balteagh LY 9; 26, 28, 34, 36
Cealey, James: Balteagh LY 9; 43
Ceanorth, chieftain: Raloo AM 32; 110
Ceanorth's Wa's altar: Raloo AM 32; 108–11,
    116–17, 122–23
Cearc lough: Templecarn DL 39; 157
Cecil Demesne td: Clogher TE 5; 36
Cecil House: Clogher TE 5; 27, 32, 38, 46, 49
Cecil manor: Clogher TE 5; 25, 32–34, 36, 38, 53
Cedithathach, Con: Misc. LY 36; 112
Ceide Upper plantation: Donegal DL 39; 51
Ceide Upper school: Donegal DL 39; 49
Celbridge (Kildare): Drummaul AM 19; 71
Cellach, Bishop: Magilligan LY 11; 88
Cenick, Rev. John: Ballinderry AM 21; 48
Cerny, family: Kilcronaghan LY 31; 68
Cess td: Clogher TE 5; 53

Chaine, family: Ahoghill AM 23; 25

Chaine, Messrs: Muckamore AM 35; 58, 63, 65

Chaine, Rev. John: Carrickfergus AM 37; 56, 68, 70, 102, 135–36, 146, 154, 172

Chaine, Rev. John: Glynn AM 26; 39

Chaine, Rev. John: Kilwaughter AM 10; 120

Chaine, Rev. John: Raloo AM 32; 95, 98, 121, 124, 131–32

Chaine, William (Jnr): Antrim AM 29; 21, 50

Chaine, William (Snr): Antrim AM 29; 20, 50

Chaine, William (Snr): Muckamore AM 35; 56, 64–66, 75–80

Chair hill: Ballynascreen LY 31; 11

Chalmer, Mr: Misc. LY 36; 118

Chaloner, Rev. Charles: Desertoghill LY 27; 17

Chambers, David: Magherafelt LY 6; 83

Chambers, Dr: Magheradrool DN 17; 102

Chambers, Elizabeth: Magherafelt LY 6; 112

Chambers, F.: Newtownards DN 7; 112

Chambers, family: Dunsfort DN 17; 68

Chambers, family: Leck DL 39; 118

Chambers, family: Templecorran AM 26; 117, 119

Chambers, James: Aghanloo LY 11; 14, 17, 22

Chambers, James: Hillsborough DN 12; 106

Chambers, James: Maghera LY 18; 57–58

Chambers, John: Ardstraw TE 5; 4

Chambers, John: Blaris AM 8; 35

Chambers, John: Cappagh TE 5; 22

Chambers, John: Clonleigh DL 39; 10

Chambers, John: Derryaghy AM 8; 107

Chambers, John: Duneane AM 19; 114

Chambers, John: Misc. DL 39; 186, 194

Chambers, John: Urney DL 39; 179

Chambers, Joseph: Hillsborough DN 12; 106

Chambers, Mr: Donaghmore DL 39; 38

Chambers, Rev.: Leck DL 39; 117

Chambers, Rev. John: Ballinderry AM 21; 48

Chambers, Robert: Blaris AM 8; 35

Chambers, Thomas: Hillsborough DN 12; 106

Chambers, William: Desertoghill LY 27; 24

Chambrey, H.W.: Killevy AH 1; 53

Chancellor, Joseph: Drumbo DN 7; 58

Chanter Hill House: Enniskillen FH 4; 65

Chantinee td: Aughnamullen MN 40; 75

Chapel day school: Clogher TE 5; 41, 43

Chapel field: Glynn AM 26; 44

Chapel field: Island Magee AM 10; 47

Chapel fort: Aghagallon AM 21; 2

Chapel Green td: Clonleigh DL 39; 12

Chapel hill: Blaris AM 8; 20

Chapel Hill chapel: Blaris AM 8; 24

Chapel Island: Grey Abbey DN 7; 68

Chapel Island td: Ballyculter DN 17; 31

Chapel locality: Carrickfergus AM 37; 174

Chapel Lock: Aghagallon AM 21; 6

Chapel Park field: Enniskillen FH 4; 71

Chapel td: Clogher TE 5; 41

Chapel well: Enniskillen FH 4; 71

Chapel Yard locality: Enniskillen FH 4; 71

Chapelfield House: Coleraine LY 33; 73

Chaplin, family: Carrickfergus AM 37; 93

Chaplin, John: Carrickfergus AM 37; 98

Chapman, Edward: Aghalee AM 21; 29

Chapman, Eliza: Blaris AM 8; 77

Chapman, family: Blaris AM 8; 22

Chapman, family: Lambeg AM 8; 135

Chapman, G.C.: Aghalee AM 21; 38

Chapman, Isabella: Carrickfergus AM 37; 114

Chapman, Jane: Blaris AM 8; 77

Chapman, John: Aghalee AM 21; 36

Chapman, John: Blaris AM 8; 55

Chapman, John: Blaris DN 12; 45, 49

Chapman, John: Derryaghy AM 8; 95–96, 98, 100, 113

Chapman, John: Hillsborough DN 12; 107

Chapman, John: Lambeg AM 8; 134, 136, 140

Chapman, Mr: Blaris AM 8; 14, 84

Chapman, Thomas: Ballyscullion AM 19; 9–11

Chapman, William: Blaris AM 8; 77

Chapman, William: Blaris DN 12; 40–41

Chapman, William: Hillsborough DN 12; 106–07

Charden, John: Misc. DN 17; 117

Charlemont: Clonfeacle AH 1; 21–24

Charlemont: Devenish FH 14; 60

Charlemont: Dungiven LY 15; 60

Charlemont: Kilmore AH 1; 73

Charlemont: Loughgall AH 1; 76, 80–81

Charlemont bridge: Clonfeacle AH 1; 23

Charlemont bridge: Loughgall AH 1; 79–80

Charlemont Castle: Loughgall AH 1; 80

Charlemont church: Loughgall AH 1; 76–77, 80

Charlemont fort: Carrickfergus AM 37; 19, 174

Charlemont fort: Loughgall AH 1; 80–81

Charlemont school: Loughgall AH 1; 80–81

Charlemont, Earl of: Loughgall AH 1; 80, 82

Charlemont, Earl of: Tartaraghan AH 1; 119

Charlemont, Lord: Kilclooney AH 1; 51

Charlemont, Lord: Killeeshil TE 20; 63

Charlemont, Lord: Loughgilly AH 1; 85

Charles I, King: Antrim AM 29; 10–11, 37

Charles I, King: Ardglass DN 17; 12

Charles I, King: Ballinderry AM 21; 44, 51

Charles I, King: Ballynure AM 32; 35

Charles I, King: Ballywillin LY 33; 50

Charles I, King: Banagher LY 30; 57

Charles I, King: Blaris AM 8; 8

Charles I, King: Carmavy AM 35; 6

Charles I, King: Carnmoney AM 2; 72

Charles I, King: Coleraine LY 33; 121–22, 129, 156

Charles I, King: Drumachose LY 9; 95

Charles I, King: Glenavy AM 21; 84

Charles I, King: Inishmacsaint FH 14; 74

Charles I, King: Killead AM 35; 32

Charles I, King: Kilrea LY 27; 128

Charles I, King: Kirkinriola AM 23; 90, 94, 101, 105, 118

Charles I, King: Lough Neagh AM 21; 95

Charles I, King: Magheragall AM 21; 103

Charles I, King: Misc. DN 17; 123

Charles II, King: Aghalee AM 21; 29

Charles II, King: Ahoghill AM 23; 28

Charles II, King: Antrim AM 29; 37

Charles II, King: Ardglass DN 17; 12

Charles II, King: Ballylinny AM 32; 16, 29

Charles II, King: Ballywalter DN 7; 17

Charles II, King: Banagher LY 30; 7, 57, 102–06, 108

Charles II, King: Blaris AM 8; 7, 23, 52

Charles II, King: Carnmoney AM 2; 72

Charles II, King: Carrickfergus AM 37; 38, 147

Charles II, King: Clondermot LY 34; 57, 60, 62–73, 75

Charles II, King: Coleraine LY 33; 122

Charles II, King: Connor AM 19; 18

Charles II, King: Culfeightrin AM 24; 69

Charles II, King: Cumber LY 28; 61–62, 65–67, 69–71

Charles II, King: Desertlyn LY 31; 37, 45

Charles II, King: Donacavey TE 5; 82

Charles II, King: Dromara DN 12; 68

Charles II, King: Drummaul AM 19; 69

Charles II, King: Enniskillen FH 4; 57, 63

Charles II, King: Faughanvale LY 36; 54–64

Charles II, King: Glenwhirry AM 32; 78

Charles II, King: Glynn AM 26; 1, 18

Charles II, King: Hillsborough DN 12; 89, 91–92

Charles II, King: Killead AM 35; 34

Charles II, King: Kilrea LY 27; 111

Charles II, King: Lough Neagh AM 21; 92

Charles II, King: Maghera LY 18; 14

Charles II, King: Magherafelt LY 6; 95

Charles II, King: Mallusk AM 2; 110

Charles II, King: Manorhamilton Union LM 40; 50

Charles II, King: Misc. DN 17; 133

Charles II, King: Misc. LY 31; 118

Charles II, King: Misc. LY 36; 103

Charles II, King: Muckamore AM 35; 61

Charles II, King: Newry DN 3; 74

Charles II, King: Shilvodan AM 19; 136

Charles II, King: Templecorran AM 26; 93

Charles II, King: Templepatrick AM 35; 117, 130

Charles II, King: Umgall AM 35; 158, 160

Charles, John: Lissan LY 31; 102

Charles, King of Spain: Carrickfergus AM 37; 24

Charles, W.: Derryvullan FH 14; 43

Charleston (America): Carrickfergus AM 37; 158

Charlestown: Drummaul AM 19; 90–91

Charlestown: Glynn AM 26; 47

Charlestown: Kildress TE 20; 58, 61

Charlestown: Kilwaughter AM 10; 122

Charlestown: Macosquin LY 22; 122

Charlestown: Montiaghs AH 1; 90, 92

Charlestown: Raloo AM 32; 128–29

Charleton, family: Aghalee AM 21; 31

Charleton, George: Ballyscullion AM 19; 9

Charleton, man named: Galloon FH 4; 101

Charleton, Mr: Clonmany DL 38; 14

Charley and Roberts, Messrs: Blaris AM 8; 70

Charley, John: Blaris AM 8; 55, 70, 85

Charley, John: Drumbeg AM 8; 125, 130

Charley, John: Drumbeg DN 7; 53

Charley, William: Blaris AM 8; 66, 70

Charley, William: Derryaghy AM 8; 96, 106, 110

Charley's Ghost stump: Lissan LY 31; 93, 101

Charley's well: Macosquin LY 22; 107

Charlton, Edward: Galloon FH 4; 100

Charlton, George: Ballyclug AM 23; 63

Charlton, John: Dromore TE 5; 97

Charlton, John: Tamlaght TE 20; 80, 92, 101

Charlton, Rev. I.: Blaris AM 8; 12

Charlton, Robert: Tamlaght TE 20; 80, 92, 101

Charlton, William [I]: Tamlaght TE 20; 80, 101

Charlton, William [II]: Tamlaght TE 20; 80, 101

Charters, John: Carrickfergus AM 37; 117

Charters, John: Muckamore AM 35; 79

Charters, Mr: Camlin AM 21; 67

Charters, William: Aghalurcher FH 4; 8, 10

Charters, William: Cleenish FH 14; 22, 29

Charters, William: Derrybrusk FH 4; 32

Charters, William: Muckamore AM 35; 79

Chase, family: Magilligan LY 11; 130

Chasnut, family: Derrykeighan AM 16; 89

Chasse, Benjamin: Camlin AM 21; 75

Chasse, Joshua: Templepatrick AM 35; 134, 154

Chassey, Mary: Killead AM 35; 38

Chassey, Thomas: Killead AM 35; 38

Chatham Hall corn mill: Derrykeighan AM 16; 79, 84

Chatham Hall td: Derrykeighan AM 16; 95

Chatham House (see St Columb's): Clondermot LY 34; 6

Chatham locality: Clondermot LY 34; 38

Chaytor, Lt J.: Ardclinis AM 13; 1–4

Chaytor, Lt J.: Ballywillin LY 33; 51–52

Checker Hall: Loughguile AM 13; 64

Cheltenham (England): Newry DN 3; 105

Chermside, Robert: Kilbroney DN 3; 30, 37

Chermside, Robert: Warrenpoint DN 3; 124

Cherry Valley House: Camlin AM 21; 62, 65, 67–68, 72

Cherry Valley House: Glenavy AM 21; 87
Cherry Valley House: Killead AM 35; 12
Cherry, James: Carrickfergus AM 37; 108
Cherry, John: Drumachose LY 9; 104
Cherry, John: Hillsborough DN 12; 107
Cherry, Miss: Ballymore AH 1; 12, 15
Cherry, Susana: Dromore DN 12; 77
Cherryvalley House: Tullynakill DN 7; 122
Cherryvalley td: Comber DN 7; 37, 39, 42–43
Cheshire (England): Misc. LY 31; 132
Chesney, Robert: Duneane AM 19; 115
Chesnutt, Moses: Dunluce AM 16; 116, 119
Chesnutt, Robert: Ballyrashane LY 22; 63, 66
Chester (England): Ballynure AM 32; 52
Chester: Blaris AM 8; 8
Chester monastery: Banagher LY 30; 101
Chestney, John: Kilraghts AM 16; 133
Chetwood, Mr: Tynan AH 1; 127
Chichester lough (see Lough Neagh): Lough Neagh
    AM 21; 95
Chichester, Arthur: Antrim AM 29; 23
Chichester, Arthur: Ballylinny AM 32; 15
Chichester, Arthur: Ballymartin AM 2; 5
Chichester, Arthur: Ballyphilip DN 7; 13
Chichester, Arthur: Ballyrobert AM 2; 20
Chichester, Arthur: Ballywalter AM 2; 29
Chichester, Arthur: Carnmoney AM 2; 51
Chichester, Arthur: Carrickfergus AM 37; 14, 24,
    31, 42, 45, 80, 102, 143, 162
Chichester, Arthur: Clonmany DL 38; 18
Chichester, Arthur: Coleraine LY 33; 122, 155
Chichester, Arthur: Doagh AM 29; 80
Chichester, Arthur: Donaghadee DN 7; 46
Chichester, Arthur: Donegore AM 29; 101
Chichester, Arthur: Drumachose LY 9; 60, 93
Chichester, Arthur: Enniskillen FH 4; 57
Chichester, Arthur: Glynn AM 26; 1, 17
Chichester, Arthur: Inver AM 26; 49, 52
Chichester, Arthur: Island Magee AM 10; 31, 77
Chichester, Arthur: Kilbride AM 29; 148, 155
Chichester, Arthur: Lough Neagh AM 21; 95
Chichester, Arthur: Lough Swilly DL 38; 136
Chichester, Arthur: Magilligan LY 11; 88, 124
Chichester, Arthur: Mallusk AM 2; 109
Chichester, Arthur: Moville DL 38; 76, 78
Chichester, Arthur: Muckamore AM 35; 56
Chichester, Arthur: Templepatrick AM 35; 108, 116
Chichester, Arthur: Tullyrusk AM 21; 131
Chichester, Edward: Carrickfergus AM 37; 102
Chichester, Edward: Coleraine LY 33; 122
Chichester, Edward: Glynn AM 26; 1
Chichester, Edward: Glynn AM 26; 1
Chichester, Edward: Island Magee AM 10; 77
Chichester, family (see also Donegall): Raloo AM
    32; 86

Chichester, family: Ballycor AM 32; 5
Chichester, family: Ballymartin AM 2; 5
Chichester, family: Ballynure AM 32; 35
Chichester, family: Carnmoney AM 2; 94
Chichester, family: Carrickfergus AM 37; 93
Chichester, family: Coleraine LY 33; 101
Chichester, family: Doagh AM 29; 71
Chichester, family: Donegore AM 29; 109
Chichester, family: Dunaghy AM 13; 12
Chichester, family: Glynn AM 26; 17, 30
Chichester, family: Island Magee AM 10; 27, 42,
    74, 86, 99
Chichester, family: Kilbride AM 29; 140
Chichester, family: Muckamore AM 35; 65
Chichester, family: Nilteen AM 35; 91
Chichester, family: Umgall AM 35; 157
Chichester, John: Carrickfergus AM 37; 24
Chichester, John: Glynn AM 26; 29–30
Chichester, John: Templecorran AM 26; 94, 107,
    122
Chichester, Lady: Carrickfergus AM 37; 24
Chichester, Rev.: Clonmany DL 38; 14
Chichester, Rev. Edward: Antrim AM 29; 26
Chichester, Rev. Edward: Kilmore AH 1; 57–60, 63,
    65–66, 68, 73
Chichester, S.S.: Carrickfergus AM 37; 42
Chickel, John: Carrickfergus AM 37; 193
Chief's chair rock: Dunboe LY 11; 50, 76
Chimney Tops pillars: Billy AM 16; 41–42
Chimney Tops pillars: Dunluce AM 16; 108
Chimneys House: Tartaraghan AH 1; 121
Chisholm, David: Antrim AM 29; 41
Chisholm, Hugh: Newry DN 3; 99
Chism, family: Carnmoney AM 2; 76
Chism, James: Carnmoney AM 2; 88
Chisom, family: Carnmoney AM 2; 76
Chittick, Mr: Raymoghy DL 39; 138–39
Chlome (see Chloone): Magheraculmoney FH 14;
    111
Chlonee (see Chloone): Magheraculmoney FH 14;
    112
Chloone td: Magheraculmoney FH 14; 111–12
Chreheenan (see Creehennan): Moville DL 38; 75
Christ's Church (Dublin): Bovevagh LY 25; 54
Christ's Church: Drummaul AM 19; 71
Christ's hospital (London): Coleraine LY 33; 156
Christian, family: Derryaghy AM 8; 103
Christie, Alexander: Tamlaght O'Crilly LY 18; 100,
    104
Christie, Andrew: Killead AM 35; 51
Christie, John: Ahoghill AM 23; 33
Christie, Rev. David: Magilligan LY 11; 89
Christie, Rev. James: Faughanvale LY 36; 7, 19, 29,
    36–37, 42, 64, 66
Christie, Samuel: Killead AM 35; 51

Christy, Abigail: Carrickfergus AM 37; 114
Christy, Alex: Derrykeighan AM 16; 92, 94
Christy, Denis: Loughguile AM 13; 76
Christy, J.: Kilmore AH 1; 72
Christy, James: Kilcronaghan LY 31; 83
Christy, John: Drummaul AM 19; 88
Christy, John: Tullylish DN 12; 141, 146
Christy, Mrs: Hillsborough DN 12; 96
Christy, Thomas: Muckamore AM 35; 79
Christy, William: Bovevagh LY 25; 43
Christy, William: Muckamore AM 35; 79
Christystown school: Killead AM 35; 53
Chrohonagh lough: Donegal DL 39; 43
Chroughnagour village: Kilmacteige SO 40; 195
Church Ballee school: Ballee DN 17; 20
Church Ballee td: Ballee DN 17; 21–23, 23
Church bay: Rathlin Island AM 24; 127, 129–31
Church bog: Annaclone DN 12; 14, 16
Church bog: Magherally DN 12; 113, 115
Church burn: Drumachose LY 9; 46, 48
Church field: Lissan LY 31; 91, 101
Church field: Nilteen AM 35; 86
Church Fields locality: Ballinderry AM 21; 52
Church hill: Tamlaght O'Crilly LY 18; 94, 116
Church hill: Tartaraghan AH 1; 119
Church Hill graveyard: Muckno MN 40; 162, 166
Church Hill House (Fermanagh): Lissan LY 31; 106
Church Hill House: Coleraine LY 33; 104
Church Hill House: Muckno MN 40; 165
Church Hill North td: Muckno MN 40; 162
Church Island: Artrea LY 6; 3, 3
Church Island: Ballyscullion LY 6; 42, 53–54, 56
Church Island: Coleraine LY 33; 98
Church Island: Duneane AM 19; 97, 109, 122
Church Island church: Ballyscullion LY 6; 49, 60, 65
Church Island church: Killead AM 35; 25
Church Minister school: Clonleigh DL 39; 9
Church Minister td: Clonleigh DL 39; 10
Church Pool creek: Inishkeel DL 39; 70
Church Quarter meeting house: Comber DN 7; 41
Church Quarter meeting house: Dundonald DN 7; 66
Church Quarter school: Comber DN 7; 41
Church Quarter school: Dundonald DN 7; 64, 66
Church Quarter school: Rathlin Island AM 24; 133
Church Quarter td: Comber DN 7; 41, 43
Church Quarter td: Dundonald DN 7; 64–66
Church Quarter td: Rathlin Island AM 24; 128–29, 131
Church Tamlaght school: Rasharkin AM 23; 134
Church Tamlaght td: Rasharkin AM 23; 127, 130
Church Town village (see also Tamlaght): Tamlaght O'Crilly LY 18; 88, 102
Church well: Magherafelt LY 6; 93, 111

Church, Arthur: Coleraine LY 33; 61
Church, Arthur: Termoneeny LY 6; 127, 132
Church, family: Desertoghill LY 27; 3, 14–15, 30
Church, family: Magilligan LY 11; 130, 142
Church, George: Drumachose LY 9; 104
Church, Jane: Aghanloo LY 11; 15
Church, John: Desertoghill LY 27; 3, 13, 15
Church, John: Drumachose LY 9; 73
Church, John: Misc. TE 5; 147
Church, John: Tamlaght Finlagan LY 25; 93, 100
Church, John: Tamlaght O'Crilly LY 18; 105
Church, Margaret: Termoneeny LY 6; 127, 132
Church, Mary: Kilrea LY 27; 113, 128
Church, Mary: Termoneeny LY 6; 127, 132
Church, Mr: Magilligan LY 11; 120
Church, Mrs R.H.: Aghanloo LY 11; 12, 15
Church, Paul: Aghanloo LY 11; 15
Church, R.H.: Aghanloo LY 11; 9, 12–13, 15–18, 22, 31, 33–34, 37, 42
Church, Robert: Coleraine LY 33; 94, 131
Church, Thomas: Kilrea LY 27; 111, 113, 128
Church, Thomas: Magilligan LY 11; 129, 132–33
Churchchill td: Donaghedy TE 5; 91
Churchfield House: Culfeightrin AM 24; 45
Churchfield td: Culfeightrin AM 24; 45–46, 69
Churchill: Devenish FH 14; 49
Churchill: Inishmacsaint FH 14; 73–74
Churchill dispensary: Inishmacsaint FH 14; 77
Churchill House: Killyman AH 1; 55–56
Churchland manor: Derryvullan FH 14; 43, 45–46
Churchlands district: Moville DL 38; 75, 78
Churchlands school: Donagh DL 38; 31
Churchminister td: Misc. DL 39; 186
Churchtown (see Church Town): Tamlaght O'Crilly LY 18; 88
Churchtown Ballybogan td: Clonleigh DL 39; 12
Churchtown chapel: Skirts of Urney and Ardstraw TE 5; 141
Churchtown church: Lough Swilly DL 38; 144
Churchtown quarry: Lough Swilly DL 38; 135
Churchtown td: Killea and Taughboyne DL 39; 79
Churchtown td: Lough Swilly DL 38; 143–44
Churchtown td: Misc. DL 39; 186, 192, 195
Churchyard field: Macosquin LY 22; 84, 116
Cil Sillach monastery: Clondermot LY 34; 106
Cillytober beetling mill: Carrickfergus AM 37; 58
Cillytober cotton factory: Carrickfergus AM 37; 58
Cillytober spring: Carrickfergus AM 37; 138
Cillytober stream: Carrickfergus AM 37; 7, 47, 58, 93, 139, 174
Cinnamon, Alexander: Templecorran AM 26; 130
Cinnamon's inn: Templecorran AM 26; 130
Cinnamond, Dr: Muckamore AM 35; 78
Cinnamond, family: Aghalee AM 21; 36
Cinnamond, family: Ballinderry AM 21; 51

Cinnamond, family: Killead AM 35; 17

Cinnamond, Joseph: Muckamore AM 35; 78

Cintullogh village: Kilmacteige SO 40; 193

Cip lough: Templecarn DL 39; 157

Cirarooy river: Lough Swilly DL 38; 122

Clabay td: Clogher TE 5; 59

Clabby: Donacavey TE 5; 70, 73–74

Clabby: Enniskillen FH 4; 50, 65, 77

Clabby manor: Enniskillen FH 4; 65, 75, 82

Clabby td: Derryvullan FH 14; 45

Claboy (see Clabby): Enniskillen FH 4; 65

Claby manor: Misc. FH 4; 133

Clachar (see Clogher): Donegal DL 39; 43

Cladagh river (see also Swanlinbar): Kinawley FH 4; 107–08, 110

Cladagh river: Killesher FH 14; 82–83, 88–89

Claddagh td: Kilmacteige SO 40; 195–96

Claddaghluaghan bay: Lough Swilly DL 38; 119

Claddy hill: Ardstraw TE 5; 10

Cladebuoys (see Clandeboys): Ballymartin AM 2; 5

Clady (see Claudy): Bovevagh LY 25; 24

Clady Blair td: Ardstraw TE 5; 3

Clady bleach green [I]: Tamlaght O'Crilly LY 18; 109

Clady bleach green [II]: Tamlaght O'Crilly LY 18; 91, 109

Clady bridge: Clonleigh DL 39; 1

Clady bridge: Umgall AM 35; 156

Clady bridge: Urney DL 39; 177

Clady burn: Nilteen AM 35; 101

Clady chapel: Tickmacrevan AM 13; 123

Clady corn mills: Tamlaght O'Crilly LY 18; 92, 108–09

Clady glen: Tamlaght O'Crilly LY 18; 108

Clady grinding corn mill: Tamlaght O'Crilly LY 18; 109

Clady meeting house: Urney DL 39; 175–76

Clady mountain: Layd and Inispollan AM 13; 55

Clady river: Killelagh LY 27; 95–96

Clady river: Maghera LY 18; 2–3

Clady river: Tamlaght O'Crilly LY 18; 83–84, 90, 92, 108, 120–21

Clady td: Ballymore AH 1; 13, 16, 18

Clady td: Layd and Inispollan AM 13; 55

Clady td: Tickmacrevan AM 13; 123

Clady village: Cumber LY 28; 68

Clady village: Dungiven LY 15; 24, 67

Clady village: Maghera LY 18; 64

Clady village: Misc. DL 39; 188

Clady village: Tamlaght O'Crilly LY 18; 88, 108, 110–11, 111–12, 141

Clady village: Urney DL 39; 174, 176, 181

Clady water: Ballymartin AM 2; 1

Clady water: Carmavy AM 35; 1

Clady water: Killead AM 35; 7, 9, 15–16, 40–42, 50

Clady water: Loughgilly AH 1; 86

Clady water: Muckamore AM 35; 57–59, 83

Clady water: Templepatrick AM 35; 106–07, 111, 115, 126–27, 129, 131, 139, 141, 146

Clady water: Umgall AM 35; 155–56

Clady water bridges: Templepatrick AM 35; 111

Cladyblair forts: Ardstraw TE 5; 12

Cladyblair td: Ardstraw TE 5; 12

Cladyhallyday fort: Ardstraw TE 5; 12

Cladyhallyday td: Ardstraw TE 5; 12

Cladymore corn mill: Kilclooney AH 1; 51

Cladymore flax mill: Kilclooney AH 1; 51

Cladymore meeting house: Kilclooney AH 1; 51

Clagan (Claggan) td: Magilligan LY 11; 94–95, 125–26, 136–137

Clagan (Cleggan) td: Banagher LY 30; 22–23, 34–36, 46, 53, 56, 60–65, 95, 103, 109, 117, 122, 126, 129, 131

Clagan bleach mill: Lissan LY 31; 90, 98

Clagan cairn: Banagher LY 30; 46–47, 56

Clagan corn mill: Lissan LY 31; 90, 98

Clagan flax mill: Banagher LY 30; 126

Clagan fort: Banagher LY 30; 64

Clagan giant's graves: Banagher LY 30; 55

Clagan hill: Banagher LY 30; 64

Clagan old church: Lissan LY 31; 90–91, 101

Clagan school: Magilligan LY 11; 110

Clagan spade mill: Lissan LY 31; 101

Clagan standing stones: Banagher LY 30; 46, 54–55, 62–63

Clagan Sunday school: Lissan LY 31; 96, 108

Clagan tannery: Banagher LY 30; 29, 113, 129

Clagan tannery: Cumber LY 28; 84

Clagan td: Aghadowey LY 22; 1

Clagan td: Lissan LY 31; 93, 99–100, 103, 108–09

Clagan td: Tamlaght Finlagan LY 25; 88, 93, 98, 113, 119

Claggan (see Clagan): Banagher LY 30; 22

Claggan (see Clagan): Lissan LY 31; 96

Claggan fort: Tullyaughnish DL 38; 91

Claggan giant's grave: Tullyaughnish DL 38; 91

Claggan Point: Lough Swilly DL 38; 122

Claggan td: Bovevagh LY 25; 45

Claggan td: Lough Swilly DL 38; 110, 136

Claggan td: Tullyaughnish DL 38; 96

Claggen (see Clagan): Banagher LY 30; 61

Claggin (see Claggan): Lough Swilly DL 38; 122

Claghey school [I]: Ballymoney AM 16; 26

Claghey school [II]: Ballymoney AM 16; 26

Clainon, family: Maghera LY 18; 48

Claira water: Muckamore AM 35; 83

Clairbawn bridge: Donaghmoyne MN 40; 108

Clairy, Donald: Dungiven LY 15; 33

Clamparnowe (see Clampernow): Clondermot LY 34; 56

Clamperlane td: Clonleigh DL 39; 12, 197

Clampernoe (see Clampernow): Clondermot LY 34; 62

Clampernow quarry: Clondermot LY 34; 130

Clampernow td: Clondermot LY 34; 56, 62, 109, 112, 115, 122, 130

Clampernow wood: Clondermot LY 34; 122

Clan Connel (see Waringstown): Donaghcloney DN 12; 59

Clan Connor, family: Clondermot LY 34; 50–51

Clan Dermot deanery: Ballyrobert AM 2; 24

Clan Dermot deanery: Mallusk AM 2; 109, 114

Clan Dermot district: Umgall AM 35; 159

Clan Dermott, family: Clondermot LY 34; 50–53

Clanaboy (see Clandeboy): Culfeightrin AM 24; 80

Clanawley barony: Killesher FH 14; 85

Clanawley barony: Kinawley FH 4; 107, 109, 111

Clancarish hill: Tartaraghan AH 1; 119

Clancarty, Lady: Ballyscullion LY 6; 54

Clancarty, Lady: Tamlaght O'Crilly LY 18; 138

Clancarty, Lord: Ballyscullion LY 6; 54

Clandeboy district: Ahoghill AM 23; 1

Clandeboy district: Ardglass DN 17; 12

Clandeboy district: Ballynure AM 32; 51

Clandeboy district: Carrickfergus AM 37; 43

Clandeboy district: Donegore AM 29; 101

Clandeboy district: Drummaul AM 19; 63, 78

Clandeboy district: Glynn AM 26; 17

Clandeboy district: Kirkinriola AM 23; 88

Clandeboy district: Misc. DN 17; 120–21

Clandeboy district: Skerry AM 13; 105

Clandeboy Lower barony: Ballymartin AM 2; 5

Clandeboy Lower district: Ballyclug AM 23; 52

Clandeboy Lower district: Ballylinny AM 32; 15

Clandeboy Lower district: Ballynure AM 32; 45, 47

Clandeboy Lower district: Connor AM 19; 18

Clandeboy Lower district: Glynn AM 26; 17–18, 30

Clandeboy Lower district: Inver AM 26; 49

Clandeboy Lower district: Kilroot AM 26; 61, 71–72

Clandeboy Lower district: Mallusk AM 2; 109

Clandeboy Lower district: Muckamore AM 35; 56

Clandeboy Lower district: Raloo AM 32; 93

Clandeboy Lower district: Templecorran AM 26; 96–97

Clandeboy North district: Glynn AM 26; 1

Clandeboy North district: Raloo AM 32; 80

Clandeboy Upper barony: Glenavy AM 21; 77

Clandeboy, Lord: Ballynure AM 32; 45, 47, 51–52

Clandeboy, Lord: Raloo AM 32; 93

Clandeboye (see Clandeboy)

Clandeboys (see Clandeboy)

Clandonnell district: Misc. LY 31; 111

Claneboy Upper barony: Tullyrusk AM 21; 131

Claneboy Upper district: Camlin AM 21; 60

Claneboy, Viscount: Killyleagh DN 17; 81

Claneboy, Viscount: Newtownards DN 7; 107

Clanloughlangrillie, family: Faughanvale LY 36; 48

Clanmartin td: Drumcree AH 1; 38

Clanmola td: Drumcree AH 1; 38

Clanmore td: Clogher TE 5; 53

Clannaboy (see Clandeboy): Ardglass DN 17; 12

Clanricarde district: Dungiven LY 15; 31

Clanricarde, family: Kilkeel DN 3; 53

Clanrickard, Earl of: Misc. SO 40; 200

Clanrola (Clanrole) td: Shankill DN 12; 138

Clanrola td: Seagoe AH 1; 107

Clanroot (see Clonroot): Kilmore AH 1; 68

Clanrye river: Newry DN 3; 65

Clantefinnan (see Clontyfinnan): Loughguile AM 13; 76–77

Clanterkee td: Faughanvale LY 36; 17, 25, 53, 55, 66, 68, 71–72, 82–83, 93

Clantilew hill: Tartaraghan AH 1; 119

Clantilew House: Tartaraghan AH 1; 120, 122

Clanwilliam, Earl: Aghaderg DN 12; 11

Clanwilliam, Earl: Donaghcloney DN 12; 59

Clanwilliam, Lord: Aghaderg DN 12; 9

Clanwilliam, Lord: Dromore DN 12; 71–72, 76, 78

Clanwilliam, Lord: Magheralin DN 12; 110

Clanwilliam, Lord: Tullylish DN 12; 143

Clar Lough Eske bleach green: Donegal DL 39; 47

Clar Lough Eske corn mill: Donegal DL 39; 47

Clar Lough Eske village: Donegal DL 39; 56

Clara (see Claragh): Tullyaughnish DL 38; 84

Clara Cairn hill: Currin MN 40; 88

Claragh brickfields: Kilrea LY 27; 110

Claragh bridge: Tullyaughnish DL 38; 84, 90

Claragh corn mill: Kilrea LY 27; 127

Claragh flax mill: Loughinisland DN 17; 96

Claragh hill: Drumgoon CN 40; 1

Claragh House: Tullyaughnish DL 38; 89

Claragh river: Loughinisland DN 17; 96

Claragh school: Loughinisland DN 17; 96

Claragh standing stone: Tullyaughnish DL 38; 91

Claragh td: Killoran and Kilvarnet SO 40; 184

Claragh td: Kilrea LY 27; 115

Claragh td: Loughinisland DN 17; 96

Claragh td: Tullyaughnish DL 38; 94–95, 97

Claraghmore quarries: Longfield TE 5; 132

Claraghmore td: Longfield TE 5; 131–33

Claraghy td: Aghalurcher FH 4; 14

Claraghy td: Ematris MN 40; 116

Clarai mill: Templepatrick AM 35; 133

Clare bog: Tullylish DN 12; 140

Clare bridge: Skirts of Urney and Ardstraw TE 5; 139

Clare Castle: Ballymore AH 1; 14

Clare Castle: Ramoan AM 24; 123

Clare cave [I]: Ramoan AM 24; 90, 93

Clare cave [II]: Ramoan AM 24; 116
Clare cave [III]: Ramoan AM 24; 122
Clare caves: Ramoan AM 24; 119
Clare chapel: Donaghcloney DN 12; 58
Clare chapel: Tullylish DN 12; 141, 145
Clare church: Kildress TE 20; 59, 61
Clare corn mill: Ballymore AH 1; 5, 8, 10, 14
Clare county: Clogher TE 5; 39
Clare flax mill: Ballymore AH 1; 8, 10, 14
Clare meeting house (P): Ballymore AH 1; 5, 10, 14
Clare meeting house (S): Ballymore AH 1; 5, 10, 14
Clare meeting house: Moville DL 38; 78
Clare moss: Donaghcloney DN 12; 57
Clare Park demesne: Ramoan AM 24; 123
Clare Park House: Ramoan AM 24; 90, 96, 122–23
Clare river: Moville DL 38; 78
Clare school: Ardstraw TE 5; 13
Clare school: Ballymore AH 1; 11, 14
Clare school: Ramoan AM 24; 126
Clare school: Skirts of Urney and Ardstraw TE 5;
　140
Clare school: Tullylish DN 12; 144
Clare Street (see Clare)
Clare td: Ballymore AH 1; 4–5, 8, 10, 13–15, 17
Clare td: Drummaul AM 19; 91
Clare td: Moira DN 12; 120
Clare td: Moville DL 38; 73, 75
Clare td: Tullylish DN 12; 141, 143–44
Clare Upper td: Skirts of Urney and Ardstraw TE 5;
　140
Clare village: Loughgilly AH 1; 85
Clare village: Tullylish DN 12; 141
Clarehill (Clarhill) td: Aghadowey LY 22; 16, 36
Clarehill bog: Aghadowey LY 22; 32
Clarehill bridge: Aghadowey LY 22; 10
Claremont House: Carnmoney AM 2; 46
Claremont, Lord: Ballymascanlan LH 40; 55
Claremont, Lord: Carlingford LH 40; 58
Claremore td: Clogher TE 5; 33
Claremount: Ballymore AH 1; 8
Claremount House: Moville DL 38; 78
Clarence, Duke of: Killymard DL 39; 100
Clarendon, Lord: Misc. DN 17; 118
Clareview school: Magheraculmoney FH 14; 108
Clark, Adam: Ballintoy AM 24; 17
Clark, Alexander (Jnr): Maghera LY 18; 16
Clark, Alexander (Maghera): Killelagh LY 27; 96
Clark, Alexander (Snr): Maghera LY 18; 2, 4–5,
　7–8, 16, 27–28, 31–32, 34–35, 49, 51–52, 62–63,
　65, 67–68, 71–73
Clark, Angus: Culfeightrin AM 24; 63, 65, 69, 71
Clark, Capt.: Derryaghy AM 8; 105
Clark, David: Maghera LY 18; 56
Clark, Edward: Newry DN 3; 99
Clark, family: Aghalee AM 21; 36

Clark, family: Ahoghill AM 23; 25
Clark, family: Ballinderry AM 21; 55
Clark, family: Billy AM 16; 58, 68
Clark, family: Blaris DN 12; 30
Clark, family: Culfeightrin AM 24; 59, 71
Clark, family: Derryaghy AM 8; 103
Clark, family: Derrykeighan AM 16; 89
Clark, family: Island Magee AM 10; 70
Clark, family: Kilcronaghan LY 31; 68
Clark, family: Maghera LY 18; 24, 48
Clark, family: Magheragall AM 21; 99
Clark, family: Racavan AM 13; 100
Clark, family: Templecorran AM 26; 117, 119
Clark, James: Clonleigh DL 39; 5, 10, 13
Clark, James: Coleraine LY 33; 72
Clark, James: Derryaghy AM 8; 115
Clark, James: Maghera LY 18; 15, 49
Clark, James: Magheragall AM 21; 103
Clark, James: Newry DN 3; 103
Clark, Jane: Carrickfergus AM 37; 114, 129
Clark, Jeane (nee Echline): Derrykeighan AM 16;
　87
Clark, John: Island Magee AM 10; 64
Clark, John [I]: Carrickfergus AM 37; 115
Clark, John [II]: Carrickfergus AM 37; 124
Clark, Lt: Blaris DN 12; 32, 36
Clark, Lt: Hillsborough DN 12; 102, 107
Clark, Mark: Derryaghy AM 8; 115
Clark, Mary: Drummaul AM 19; 76, 85, 92
Clark, Miss (see Stevenson): Maghera LY 18; 18
Clark, Mr: Clonmany DL 38; 14
Clark, Mr: Tullyaughnish DL 38; 87
Clark, Mrs: Muckamore AM 35; 81
Clark, Mrs Alexander: Maghera LY 18; 18, 50, 63,
　67, 72
Clark, Rev. Alexander: Templepatrick AM 35; 133,
　144
Clark, Samuel: Drumachose LY 9; 104
Clark, Thomas: Newry DN 3; 99
Clark, W.: Comber DN 7; 34
Clark, W.E.: Derrykeighan AM 16; 90
Clark, W.F.: Derrykeighan AM 16; 87
Clark, W.W.: Maghera LY 18; 71
Clark, William: Antrim AM 29; 32
Clark, William: Blaris DN 12; 40
Clark, William: Clonleigh DL 39; 10
Clark, William: Killelagh LY 27; 95–96, 102
Clark, William: Magheragall AM 21; 103, 105
Clark, William: Magheramesk AM 21; 125
Clark, William [I]: Maghera LY 18; 53
Clark, William [II]: Maghera LY 18; 74
Clarke, A.J.: Blaris DN 12; 46, 50
Clarke, Abel: Loughguile AM 13; 77
Clarke, Adam: Ballyaghran LY 33; 14
Clarke, Adam: Ballywillin LY 33; 31, 43

Clarke, Adam: Maghera LY 18; 22, 73
Clarke, Alexander: Artrea LY 6; 26
Clarke, Angus: Doagh AM 29; 88
Clarke, Ann: Carnmoney AM 2; 88
Clarke, Archy: Loughguile AM 13; 71
Clarke, Arthur: Artrea LY 6; 26
Clarke, Bell: Carnmoney AM 2; 88
Clarke, Betsy: Carnmoney AM 2; 88
Clarke, Catherine: Carnmoney AM 2; 88
Clarke, Colan: Drumballyroney DN 3; 12
Clarke, Daniel: Aghadowey LY 22; 19–20
Clarke, Dearby (Dublin): Clondermot LY 34; 81
Clarke, Dick: Kilrea LY 27; 113
Clarke, Dr (Curraghlane): Clonleigh DL 39; 3, 10, 13
Clarke, Dr: Currin MN 40; 96
Clarke, Edmond: Carnmoney AM 2; 88
Clarke, Edward: Newry DN 3; 105
Clarke, Eneas: Culfeightrin AM 24; 55
Clarke, family: Aghalee AM 21; 31
Clarke, family: Ardglass DN 17; 4
Clarke, family: Ballinderry AM 21; 51
Clarke, family: Ballyscullion AM 19; 9
Clarke, family: Ballywillin AM 16; 32
Clarke, family: Blaris AM 8; 21–22
Clarke, family: Carrickfergus AM 37; 93
Clarke, family: Dunboe LY 11; 79
Clarke, family: Ematris MN 40; 118
Clarke, family: Enniskillen FH 4; 58
Clarke, family: Macosquin LY 22; 84, 119
Clarke, family: Magilligan LY 11; 130
Clarke, G.J.: Antrim AM 29; 14, 21, 25, 32, 47, 50
Clarke, Gabriel: Ballyscullion AM 19; 9
Clarke, Gabriel: Billy AM 16; 77
Clarke, Gabriel: Kilraghts AM 16; 136
Clarke, Hugh: Ahoghill AM 23; 39
Clarke, Hugh: Ballyrashane LY 22; 66
Clarke, Hugh: Clondermot LY 34; 79
Clarke, Hugh: Drumachose LY 9; 73
Clarke, Isaac: Ballyscullion AM 19; 9
Clarke, J.K.: Hillsborough DN 12; 97
Clarke, J.S.: Ballyaghran LY 33; 14
Clarke, Jackson: Blaris AM 8; 70
Clarke, James: Artrea LY 6; 38
Clarke, James: Ballywillin AM 16; 34
Clarke, James: Coleraine LY 33; 105
Clarke, James: Dunboe LY 11; 59, 78
Clarke, James: Tamlaght O'Crilly LY 18; 102, 104, 118, 128, 131
Clarke, James [I]: Maghera LY 18; 61
Clarke, James [II]: Maghera LY 18; 80
Clarke, Jane: Dunboe LY 11; 81
Clarke, John (Jnr): Blaris DN 12; 40
Clarke, John: Blaris DN 12; 46, 49
Clarke, John: Culfeightrin AM 24; 58

Clarke, John: Shankill DN 12; 139
Clarke, John [I]: Ballyaghran LY 33; 14
Clarke, John [I]: Ballyscullion AM 19; 13
Clarke, John [I]: Dunboe LY 11; 81
Clarke, John [II]: Ballyaghran LY 33; 26
Clarke, John [II]: Ballyscullion AM 19; 13
Clarke, John [II]: Dunboe LY 11; 81
Clarke, John [III]: Ballyscullion AM 19; 13
Clarke, Joseph: Ballymoney AM 16; 17
Clarke, Joseph: Kilrea LY 27; 120, 128
Clarke, Margaret (Jnr): Carnmoney AM 2; 88
Clarke, Margaret (Snr): Carnmoney AM 2; 88
Clarke, Mary: Carnmoney AM 2; 88
Clarke, Matthew: Kilcronaghan LY 31; 84
Clarke, Miss: Ballyaghran LY 33; 14
Clarke, Miss: Blaris AM 8; 84
Clarke, Mr: Aghalurcher FH 4; 13
Clarke, Mr: Clogher TE 5; 40
Clarke, Mr: Connor AM 19; 16
Clarke, Mr: Drumballyroney DN 3; 12
Clarke, Mr: Tomregan FH 4; 129
Clarke, Nancy: Dunboe LY 11; 81
Clarke, Nathaniel: Maghera LY 18; 80
Clarke, Rev.: Kilrea LY 27; 119, 126
Clarke, Rev. Mathew: Ardstraw TE 5; 3
Clarke, Rev. Samuel: Coleraine LY 33; 154
Clarke, Rev. Thomas: Dromara DN 12; 66
Clarke, Samual: Ballyaghran LY 33; 21
Clarke, Samual: Macosquin LY 22; 104
Clarke, Samuel: Ballyscullion AM 19; 9–10
Clarke, Samuel: Clondermot LY 34; 40, 78, 80
Clarke, Samuel: Hillsborough DN 12; 107
Clarke, Samuel: Tamlaght O'Crilly LY 18; 127–28, 141, 144
Clarke, Sarah: Kilcronaghan LY 31; 84
Clarke, Saywell: Blaris DN 12; 46, 50
Clarke, Teressa: Carnmoney AM 2; 88
Clarke, Thomas: Aghagallon AM 21; 8
Clarke, Thomas: Ballywillin AM 16; 34
Clarke, Thomas: Carnmoney AM 2; 88
Clarke, Thomas: Newry DN 3; 99
Clarke, W.E.: Kilbroney DN 3; 33
Clarke, Walter: Ballyscullion AM 19; 3, 9
Clarke, Widow (Shanreagh): Tamlaght Finlagan LY 25; 109, 112–13
Clarke, William: Artrea LY 6; 33
Clarke, William: Dunboe LY 11; 56–57, 70
Clarke's hotel: Clondermot LY 34; 7, 78, 81
Clarke's lough: Kilrea LY 27; 106–07, 112–13
Clarkill td: Kilmegan DN 3; 57
Clarkill wood: Kilmegan DN 3; 57
Clarkin, Edward: Currin MN 40; 91
Clarkin, family: Aghabog MN 40; 66
Clarmore td: Clogher TE 5; 32, 36, 46
Clarn spring: Down DN 17; 61

Clarnagh td: Enniskillen FH 4; 74, 82

Clarnon, family: Maghera LY 18; 24

Clarnon, Hugh: Magherafelt LY 6; 108

Clarr village: Donegal DL 39; 56

Clarret Rock td: Ballymascanlan LH 40; 55

Clashagarvan (see Clashygowan)

Clashigowan (see Clashygowan)

Clashygawan (see Clashygowan)

Clashygowan corn mill: Taughboyne DL 39; 152

Clashygowan flax mill: Taughboyne DL 39; 152

Clashygowan orchard: Taughboyne DL 39; 152, 189

Clashygowan td: Killea and Taughboyne DL 39; 79

Clashygowan td: Misc. DL 39; 186, 195

Clashygowan td: Taughboyne DL 39; 148, 150, 152

Clashygowan wood: Taughboyne DL 39; 148

Clasygowan (see Clashygowan): Misc. DL 39; 186

Clattering ford: Desertoghill LY 27; 11, 24

Clatterknowes (see Clatteryknowes): Glenwhirry AM 32; 79

Clatteryknowes bog: Glenwhirry AM 32; 79

Clatteryknowes corn mill: Glenwhirry AM 32; 76, 79

Claudy: Banagher LY 30; 5, 29, 31, 54, 90

Claudy: Bovevagh LY 25; 24, 53

Claudy: Clondermot LY 34; 8, 97, 102, 113, 117

Claudy: Cumber LY 28; 1, 4, 6–9, 12, 15–16, 18, 20–21, 23–24, 28, 32, 79, 84–86, 112, 114, 126–27

Claudy: Drumachose LY 9; 76

Claudy: Dungiven LY 15; 10–11, 37

Claudy: Faughanvale LY 36; 10, 77

Claudy: Tamlaght Finlagan LY 25; 62, 84, 123

Claudy barracks: Cumber LY 28; 1, 7, 84, 86

Claudy bog: Cumber LY 28; 23

Claudy chapel: Cumber LY 28; 1, 7, 14, 85

Claudy post office: Cumber LY 28; 7

Claudy quarry: Cumber LY 28; 122

Claudy school: Cumber LY 28; 16, 73–74, 76, 84, 90

Claudy sessions house: Cumber LY 28; 1, 7, 84, 86

Claudy td: Cumber LY 28; 7, 66, 68, 111, 117, 122, 125

Claudy Top hill: Cumber LY 28; 5–6

Claudy water (see Cladagh river): Killesher FH 14; 82

Claudy wood: Cumber LY 28; 117

Claughey water: Ballymoney AM 16; 1, 5–6, 10

Claverhouse, John: Bovevagh LY 25; 17, 43

Clawson, Mary: Ballyrobert AM 2; 25

Clawson, Thomas: Ballyrobert AM 2; 25

Clay lough: Keady AH 1; 50

Clay river: Keady AH 1; 50

Clay school: Keady AH 1; 50

Clay td: Annaclone DN 12; 14, 16

Clay, John: Ballyscullion LY 6; 56–57

Clayhoghill hill: Desertoghill LY 27; 1

Clayton, Rev. Robert: Clogher TE 5; 28

Clea td: Killinchy DN 7; 86

Cleagh chapel: Clonmany DL 38; 12, 14, 17, 20

Cleagh corn mill: Clonmany DL 38; 14

Cleagh td: Clonmany DL 38; 12, 18

Clealand, Surgeon: Hillsborough DN 12; 105

Cleanally (Clananelly) td: Errigal Keerogue TE 20; 50–51, 57

Cleanally corn mill: Errigal Keerogue TE 20; 51

Cleanally quarry: Errigal Keerogue TE 20; 50

Clear Holes springs: Aghanloo LY 11; 12

Clear Holes springs: Dunboe LY 11; 59–60, 68, 79

Clearken, Andrew: Ballynascreen LY 31; 22

Cleary td: Donagh MN 40; 98

Cleary, Niece: Ballynascreen LY 31; 29

Cleary, Rev.: Enniskillen FH 4; 41, 70, 82

Cleaver, family: Ahoghill AM 23; 25

Clee, James: Leck DL 39; 120

Cleen td: Aghalurcher FH 4; 14

Cleenagh td: Drummully FH 4; 39

Cleenaghan td: Magheracross FH 14; 102

Cleenish bridges: Cleenish FH 14; 18

Cleenish Glebe House: Cleenish FH 14; 17, 19

Cleenish Island: Cleenish FH 14; 13, 30

Cleenish Island abbey: Cleenish FH 14; 19

Cleenish Island graveyard: Cleenish FH 14; 20

Cleenish ph: Aghalurcher FH 4; 1

Cleenish ph: Boho FH 14; 8

Cleenish ph: Clogher TE 5; 40

Cleenish ph: Derrybrusk FH 4; 30, 32–33

Cleenish ph: Enniskillen FH 4; 41, 43, 48

Cleenish ph: Killesher FH 14; 81, 85

Cleenish ph: Kinawley FH 4; 107, 109

Cleenish ph: Rossorry FH 14; 115

Cleenish school: Cleenish FH 14; 24

Cleenriss td: Aghalurcher FH 4; 13

Cleens New td: Devenish FH 14; 58

Cleens Old td: Devenish FH 14; 58

Cleery, Andrew: Ballyscullion LY 6; 57

Clegan Altnacree td: Donaghedy TE 5; 91

Clegan td: Moville DL 38; 73

Clegg lough: Aughnamullen MN 40; 70

Clegg, family: Enniskillen FH 4; 75

Cleggan flax mill: Armoy AM 24; 4

Cleggan hibernian school: Rathlin Island AM 24; 133

Cleggan hunting lodge: Skerry AM 13; 106, 110–11

Cleggan private school: Rathlin Island AM 24; 133

Cleggan river: Skerry AM 13; 110

Cleggan td: Donaghedy TE 5; 91

Cleggan td: Skerry AM 13; 106, 111

Cleggin school: Cleenish FH 14; 24

Cleggin td: Cleenish FH 14; 29

Cleghogue td: Enniskillen FH 4; 82

Clegnagh cave: Ballintoy AM 24; 25

Clegnagh druid's altar [I]: Ballintoy AM 24; 25

Clegnagh druid's altar [II]: Ballintoy AM 24; 25

Clegnagh standing stones: Ballintoy AM 24; 26, 31

Clegnagh td: Ballintoy AM 24; 10, 17, 26–27

Clegnagh td: Drumtullagh AM 16; 103

Cleland, J.R.: Bangor DN 7; 23

Cleland, Rev. J.: Comber DN 7; 37, 40–41

Cleland, Rev. J.: Dundonald DN 7; 65

Cleland, Rev. J.: Holywood DN 7; 77

Cleland, Samuel: Dundonald DN 7; 66

Cleland, William: Ballymore AH 1; 5

Clement, family: Ahoghill AM 23; 25

Clement's bridge: Killdrumsherdan CN 40; 35

Clements hill: Ballynure AM 32; 62–63

Clements Hill House: Ballynure AM 32; 72

Clements Hill school: Ballynure AM 32; 73

Clements Hill td: Ballynure AM 32; 63, 71

Clements, Col (Ashfield): Drumgoon CN 40; 8

Clements, Col (Ashfield): Killdrumsherdan CN 40; 33, 35, 37

Clements, family: Ballynure AM 32; 56, 62–63

Clements, family: Carrickfergus AM 37; 93, 179

Clements, Henry: Coleraine LY 33; 63

Clements, John: Kilwaughter AM 10; 122

Clements, Lucas: Drumgoon CN 40; 8

Clements, Lucas: Drung CN 40; 21–23

Clements, Robert: Carrickfergus AM 37; 33, 39, 148

Clements, Robert: Newry DN 3; 74

Clements, T.E.: Drumgoon CN 40; 8

Clements, William: Tamlaght O'Crilly LY 18; 93, 123

Clementstown: Currin MN 40; 90

Clementstown: Killdrumsherdan CN 40; 33–35

Clenally (see Cleanally): Errigal Keerogue TE 20; 57

Clenborin td: Killymard DL 39; 101

Clendinning, Mr (Wheatfield): Kilmore AH 1; 67

Clendinning, Thomas: Tamlaght TE 20; 75, 128, 136

Clerk's well: Magilligan LY 11; 99

Clerkan, family: Ballynascreen LY 31; 9

Clermont, Lord: Newry DN 3; 86

Clevaghy (see Roosky): Galloon FH 4; 91

Clewlow (see Clulow): Carnmoney AM 2; 89

Clewls, Rev.: Killyleagh DN 17; 80

Clibborn, Edward: Seapatrick DN 12; 127

Clibborn, Thomas: Seapatrick DN 12; 134

Cliffany td: Aghavea FH 4; 19, 23, 25

Cliffernagh chapel: Laragh CN 40; 41

Cliffernagh corn mill: Laragh CN 40; 39

Cliffernagh lough: Laragh CN 40; 39

Cliffernagh school: Laragh CN 40; 43

Clifford, John: Ballymoney AM 16; 17

Clifford, Mr: Clogher TE 5; 41

Clignagh (see Clegnagh): Ballintoy AM 24; 10

Clinagore td: Drummully FH 4; 39

Clincallick td: Drummully FH 4; 35–36, 39

Clincarn td: Galloon FH 4; 95

Clincloughey td: Drummully FH 4; 39

Clincorrick td: Drummully FH 4; 39

Clinelty td: Galloon FH 4; 95

Clinestin td: Drummully FH 4; 39

Clinfad fort: Currin MN 40; 90

Clinfad hill: Currin MN 40; 86

Clinfad monastery: Currin MN 40; 90

Clinfad td: Currin MN 40; 88, 90

Clinfad well: Currin MN 40; 90

Clinfadd (see Clonfard): Drummully FH 4; 39

Clinfard (see Clonfard): Drummully FH 4; 34

Clingowney td: Drummully FH 4; 39

Clinkee td: Drummully FH 4; 34, 39

Clinkeelan td: Drummully FH 4; 39

Clinlura td: Drummully FH 4; 39

Clinmoalin Glebe td: Galloon FH 4; 95–97

Clinnagun td: Clones FH 4; 27

Clinnurson glebe: Killesher FH 14; 86–87

Clinooney td: Drummully FH 4; 35–36, 39

Clinowley td: Drummully FH 4; 39

Clinrigh td: Drummully FH 4; 39

Clinshanway (see Clonshanvo)

Clintacoora td: Cleenish FH 14; 28

Clintagh bog: Aghadowey LY 22; 1–2

Clintagh school: Annahilt DN 12; 22

Clintagh td: Aghadowey LY 22; 36

Clintagh td: Annahilt DN 12; 20–22

Clintanagullion td: Dromara DN 12; 65

Clintask (see Clontask): Drummully FH 4; 39

Clintellaghan td: Kinawley FH 4; 110

Clinticarty hill: Tynan AH 1; 124

Clintincally td: Comber DN 7; 37, 40, 42

Clinton, family: Ardglass DN 17; 4

Clinton, family: Dunsfort DN 17; 68

Clinton, man named: Kilrea LY 27; 112

Clinton, Paul: Errigal LY 27; 37, 63

Clinton, William: Desertoghill LY 27; 23

Clintonecally (see Clintincally): Comber DN 7; 40

Clintough (see Clintagh): Annahilt DN 12; 20

Clinty (Clentagh) td: Kirkinriola AM 23; 91

Clinty bog: Kirkinriola AM 23; 93

Clinty school: Kirkinriola AM 23; 112–13, 121–22

Clintymullen brickfield: Killesher FH 14; 84

Clinumphra td: Galloon FH 4; 95

Clinurson (see Clinnurson): Killesher FH 14; 87

Clipburn, Mr: Seapatrick DN 12; 125

Clipper, man named: Carrickfergus AM 37; 93

Clipperstown td: Carrickfergus AM 37; 93, 145

Cliumin (see Clonmin): Galloon FH 4; 95

Clloyd, James: Drumachose LY 9; 66

Cloak hill: Coleraine LY 33; 131

Cloanaveel td: Cleenish FH 14; 29

Cloane bog: Ballynascreen LY 31; 1

Cloane bridge: Ballynascreen LY 31; 6–7

Cloane cromlech: Ballynascreen LY 31; 12

Cloane giant's grave: Ballynascreen LY 31; 12, 19, 22

Cloane td: Ballynascreen LY 31; 1, 7, 141–43

Cloch-a-phoill stone (Carlow): Faughanvale LY 36; 12, 55

Clocher (see Clogher): Donegal DL 39; 53

Clochore (see Cloghore): Clondermot LY 34; 56

Clogh (Cloghs) td: Layd AM 13; 41, 49

Clogh Castle: Dunaghy AM 13; 12, 17, 20, 28

Clogh church: Dunaghy AM 13; 26

Clogh court house: Dunaghy AM 13; 26

Clogh court house: Finvoy AM 23; 70

Clogh Hotel: Dunaghy AM 13; 12

Clogh manor court house: Dunaghy AM 13; 12

Clogh meeting house: Dunaghy AM 13; 26

Clogh Point: Dunaghy AM 13; 10

Clogh river: Ahoghill AM 23; 4–5, 12, 14

Clogh river: Dunaghy AM 13; 10–11, 14, 17, 26–27

Clogh river: Dundermot AM 13; 29–31

Clogh river: Kirkinriola AM 23; 92–93, 104, 116, 121

Clogh river: Newtown Crommelin AM 13; 79

Clogh river: Skerry AM 13; 109–10, 112

Clogh river bridge: Ahoghill AM 23; 14

Clogh river bridges: Dunaghy AM 13; 14

Clogh river bridges: Skerry AM 13; 112

Clogh schools: Dunaghy AM 13; 15, 17, 26

Clogh village: Armoy AM 24; 5

Clogh village: Dunaghy AM 13; 11–12, 14, 25

Clogh village: Dundermot AM 13; 32

Clogh village: Finvoy AM 23; 72

Clogh village: Killagan AM 23; 79–80, 84

Clogh village: Killead AM 35; 43

Clogh village: Kirkinriola AM 23; 90–91, 94, 104, 120, 122

Clogh village: Newtown Crommelin AM 13; 83

Clogh village: Rasharkin AM 23; 132, 136

Cloghagal td: Donaghedy TE 5; 91

Cloghan (see Clagan): Banagher LY 30; 36

Cloghan bridge: Devenish FH 14; 53

Cloghan church: Kinawley FH 4; 111, 115

Cloghan druid's altar: Balteagh LY 9; 31

Cloghan school [I]: Balteagh LY 9; 17, 39

Cloghan school [II]: Balteagh LY 9; 17, 39

Cloghan td: Balteagh LY 9; 11, 17, 31, 39, 44–45

Cloghan td: Kilmore AH 1; 61, 65, 69, 71, 73

Cloghan td: Kinawley FH 4; 111, 115, 121

Cloghandooh creek: Lough Swilly DL 38; 107

Cloghanduff corn mill: Templepatrick AM 35; 113, 146

Cloghanduff cove: Templepatrick AM 35; 130

Cloghanduff fort: Templepatrick AM 35; 137, 150

Cloghanduff school: Templepatrick AM 35; 134–35, 153–54

Cloghanduff Sunday school: Templepatrick AM 35; 135, 154

Cloghanduff td: Templepatrick AM 35; 130, 132, 143, 150

Cloghanduff waterfall: Templepatrick AM 35; 149

Cloghaneely district: Mevagh DL 38; 58

Cloghaneely district: Raymoghy DL 39; 146

Cloghanmurray (see Cloghanmurry): Ramoan AM 24; 96

Cloghanmurry Castle: Ramoan AM 24; 105–06

Cloghanmurry cave: Ramoan AM 24; 118

Cloghanmurry flax mill: Ramoan AM 24; 96–97

Cloghanmurry fort: Ramoan AM 24; 91

Cloghanmurry school: Ramoan AM 24; 100

Cloghanmurry standing stones: Ramoan AM 24; 106

Cloghanmurry td: Ramoan AM 24; 117

Cloghanmurry tower: Ramoan AM 24; 91

Cloghanmurry trigonometrical station: Ramoan AM 24; 91

Cloghanramer cave [I]: Newry DN 3; 107

Cloghanramer cave [II]: Newry DN 3; 107

Cloghanramer school: Newry DN 3; 106

Cloghanramer td: Newry DN 3; 81, 106–07

Clogharevan td: Killevy AH 1; 53

Clogharevan thread mill: Killevy AH 1; 54

Cloghbeg td: Donaghedy TE 5; 91

Cloghberragh stone: Ramoan AM 24; 115

Cloghboys village: Inishkeel DL 39; 71

Cloghcor cairn: Derryvullan FH 14; 42

Cloghcor chapel: Derryvullan FH 14; 41

Cloghcor forts: Derryvullan FH 14; 42

Cloghcor td: Derryvullan FH 14; 41–43, 46

Cloghcor td: Leckpatrick TE 5; 120

Cloghcur (see Cloghcor): Derryvullan FH 14; 42, 46

Clogher (Clougher) td: Kirkinriola AM 23; 91

Clogher: Billy AM 16; 51

Clogher: Clogher TE 5; 27, 29–30, 44, 50–51, 60

Clogher: Clogherny TE 20; 27

Clogher: Clondermot LY 34; 62

Clogher: Donacavey TE 5; 62

Clogher: Drumachose LY 9; 95

Clogher: Errigal Truagh MN 40; 122

Clogher: Killeeshil TE 20; 63

Clogher Anderson cave: Billy AM 16; 63

Clogher Anderson meeting house: Billy AM 16; 63

Clogher Anderson td: Billy AM 16; 56

Clogher barony: Aghalurcher FH 4; 1

Clogher barony: Clogher TE 5; 24, 52–53

Clogher barony: Donacavey TE 5; 70, 76–77, 83, 85–87

Clogher barony: Misc. LY 36; 105

Clogher Bishop's Palace: Clogher TE 5; 28, 32, 49, 52
Clogher bog: Ballybay MN 40; 78
Clogher bog: Donegal DL 39; 53
Clogher bridewell: Clogher TE 5; 29
Clogher Camp hill: Hillsborough DN 12; 88, 96
Clogher cathedral: Clogher TE 5; 27, 29, 39, 52
Clogher cathedral: Derryvullan FH 14; 42
Clogher cathedral: Donacavey TE 5; 66
Clogher cave: Billy AM 16; 56, 62
Clogher corn mill: Drummully FH 4; 36
Clogher court house: Clogher TE 5; 29
Clogher day school: Clogher TE 5; 28, 43
Clogher deanery: Carrickfergus AM 37; 78
Clogher Deanery: Clogher TE 5; 33
Clogher demesne: Clogher TE 5; 28
Clogher Demesne td: Clogher TE 5; 35, 49
Clogher diocese: Aghabog MN 40; 67
Clogher diocese: Aghalurcher FH 4; 6, 14, 16
Clogher diocese: Aghavea FH 4; 19, 23, 25
Clogher diocese: Aughnamullen MN 40; 77
Clogher diocese: Ballybay MN 40; 79, 84
Clogher diocese: Belleek FH 14; 6
Clogher diocese: Boho FH 14; 8
Clogher diocese: Carrickfergus AM 37; 78
Clogher diocese: Cleenish FH 14; 11
Clogher diocese: Clogher TE 5; 39
Clogher diocese: Clondermot LY 34; 62
Clogher diocese: Clones FH 4; 26
Clogher diocese: Currin MN 40; 89, 97
Clogher diocese: Derrybrusk FH 4; 30, 33
Clogher diocese: Derryvullan FH 14; 39
Clogher diocese: Donacavey TE 5; 73, 76–77
Clogher diocese: Donagh MN 40; 99, 101
Clogher diocese: Dromore TE 5; 93
Clogher diocese: Drumkeeran FH 14; 67
Clogher diocese: Drummully FH 4; 37, 39
Clogher diocese: Ematris MN 40; 114, 119
Clogher diocese: Enniskillen FH 4; 41, 82
Clogher diocese: Galloon FH 4; 89, 92, 96
Clogher diocese: Inishmacsaint FH 14; 79
Clogher diocese: Inniskeen MN 40; 126, 129
Clogher diocese: Killanny MN 40; 135
Clogher diocese: Kilskeery TE 5; 113
Clogher diocese: Magheracross FH 14; 100
Clogher diocese: Magheraculmoney FH 14; 108
Clogher diocese: Magheross MN 40; 146, 150–51
Clogher diocese: Muckno MN 40; 168
Clogher diocese: Rossorry FH 14; 115
Clogher diocese: Templecarn DL 39; 156, 159, 163
Clogher diocese: Trory FH 14; 127, 129–30
Clogher diocese: Tydavnet MN 40; 170–71
Clogher diocese: Tynan AH 1; 127
Clogher dispensary: Clogher TE 5; 29, 32, 50, 52, 60

Clogher district: Misc. SO 40; 199
Clogher female school: Clogher TE 5; 42–43
Clogher fort: Billy AM 16; 69
Clogher graveyard: Donacavey TE 5; 75
Clogher male school: Clogher TE 5; 41
Clogher manor: Clogher TE 5; 29, 34–35, 38, 53
Clogher market house: Clogher TE 5; 52
Clogher monastery: Clogher TE 5; 27
Clogher North td: Billy AM 16; 46
Clogher ph: Aghaloo TE 20; 2
Clogher ph: Aghalurcher FH 4; 1, 16
Clogher ph: Aghalurcher TE 5; 1
Clogher ph: Aghavea FH 4; 17
Clogher ph: Clogher TE 5; 40
Clogher ph: Clogherny TE 20; 25, 27
Clogher ph: Donacavey TE 5; 62, 66–67, 84
Clogher ph: Enniskillen FH 4; 41, 48
Clogher ph: Errigal Keerogue TE 20; 49
Clogher ph: Errigal Truagh MN 40; 123
Clogher river (see also Launy river): Clogher TE 5; 25
Clogher school: Billy AM 16; 49
Clogher school: Clogher TE 5; 30, 51
Clogher school: Kirkinriola AM 23; 121
Clogher session house: Clogher TE 5; 52
Clogher standing stone: Billy AM 16; 58, 69
Clogher td: Ballybay MN 40; 84
Clogher td: Billy AM 16; 36, 41
Clogher td: Clogher TE 5; 35, 41, 51
Clogher td: Derryaghy AM 8; 105, 119
Clogher td: Donacavey TE 5; 86
Clogher td: Donegal DL 39; 43–44
Clogher td: Down DN 17; 52–53, 56
Clogher td: Drumbo DN 7; 58, 60, 62
Clogher td: Drummully FH 4; 35–36, 38–39
Clogher td: Hillsborough DN 12; 85, 88–89, 106
Clogher, Bishop of: Cleenish FH 14; 29–30
Clogher, Bishop of: Clogher TE 5; 39–40, 49–50, 53, 55, 59
Clogher, Bishop of: Derrybrusk FH 4; 33
Clogher, Bishop of: Derryvullan FH 14; 43, 45
Clogher, Bishop of: Dungiven LY 15; 59
Clogher, Bishop of: Enniskillen FH 4; 51, 77, 82
Clogher, Bishop of: Galloon FH 4; 94
Clogher, Bishop of: Lough Neagh AM 21; 92
Clogher, Bishop of: Rossorry FH 14; 115
Clogher, Bishop of: Trory FH 14; 129
Clogher, Deans of: Clogher TE 5; 24, 53–54
Cloghernagh td: Lough Swilly DL 38; 134, 136
Clogher-na-glen stream: Banagher LY 30; 24–25, 29
Cloghernagly td: Donagh MN 40; 98
Clogherneagh standing stone: Dungiven LY 15; 49
Clogherney (see Clogherny)
Clogherny abbey: Clogherny TE 20; 28
Clogherny church: Clogherny TE 20; 25

Clogherny glebe: Clogherny TE 20; 25
Clogherny leap mill: Clogherny TE 20; 28
Clogherny Lower school: Clogherny TE 20; 26
Clogherny mill: Cappagh TE 5; 19
Clogherny ph: Cappagh TE 5; 16, 19
Clogherny ph: Clogher TE 5; 24
Clogherny ph: Donacavey TE 5; 66, 82–83
Clogherny ph: Drumragh TE 5; 104
Clogherny ph: Pomeroy TE 20; 71
Clogherny td: Donaghedy TE 5; 91
Clogherny Upper fort: Clogherny TE 20; 28
Clogherny Upper Glebe flax mill: Clogherny TE 20; 27
Cloghferns (see Croghfern): Carnmoney AM 2; 87
Cloghfin camp stone: Island Magee AM 10; 47, 59
Cloghfin graveyard: Island Magee AM 10; 47
Cloghfin river: Cappagh TE 5; 17
Cloghfin river: Clogherny TE 20; 25
Cloghfin river: Pomeroy TE 20; 72
Cloghfin school: Clonleigh DL 39; 4
Cloghfin td: Clonleigh DL 39; 12, 185, 195, 197
Cloghfin td: Island Magee AM 10; 47, 59, 71, 76
Cloghfin td: Urney DL 39; 181
Cloghfinn locality: Bovevagh LY 25; 35
Cloghglass td: Lough Swilly DL 38; 144–45, 148
Cloghinarney td: Racavan AM 13; 88
Cloghlin td: Clogher TE 5; 35
Cloghmaghera Dunaghy standing stone: Dunaghy AM 13; 19
Cloghmills: Ballymoney AM 16; 25
Cloghmills: Dunaghy AM 13; 14
Cloghmills: Dundermot AM 13; 31
Cloghmills: Killagan AM 23; 79–85
Cloghmills: Killead AM 35; 43
Cloghmills: Killyman TE 20; 66
Cloghmills: Kirkinriola AM 23; 104, 108
Cloghmills bridge: Killagan AM 23; 80, 83
Cloghmills corn mill: Killagan AM 23; 83
Cloghmills meeting house: Dunaghy AM 13; 26
Cloghmills school: Dunaghy AM 13; 17
Cloghmills standing stone: Killagan AM 23; 86
Cloghmills stream: Killagan AM 23; 79
Cloghmills td: Killagan AM 23; 79, 86
Cloghmore church: Clones FH 4; 26
Cloghmore lough: Clondavaddog DL 38; 3
Cloghmore standing stone: Clonallan DN 3; 1
Cloghmore standing stone: Kilbroney DN 3; 39
Cloghmore td: Clones FH 4; 28
Cloghogal td: Donaghedy TE 5; 89
Cloghoge river: Cumber LY 28; 72
Cloghoge td: Ballymore AH 1; 13–5, 18
Cloghogle chapel: Ardstraw TE 5; 8
Cloghogue school: Drummaul AM 19; 75–76, 86
Cloghole corn mill: Faughanvale LY 36; 16, 22, 97

Cloghole plough manufactory: Faughanvale LY 36; 16
Cloghole standing stone: Faughanvale LY 36; 11, 15
Cloghole td: Faughanvale LY 36; 17, 53, 55–56, 68, 72, 83, 93
Cloghore caves: Ballywillin AM 16; 32
Cloghore golden stone: Ballywillin AM 16; 32
Cloghore quarry: Clondermot LY 34; 130
Cloghore standing stone: Ballywillin AM 16; 32
Cloghore td: Ballywillin AM 16; 32, 35
Cloghore td: Clondermot LY 34; 56, 62, 76, 109, 112, 115, 123, 130
Cloghore wood: Clondermot LY 34; 123
Cloghreagh flax mill: Killevy AH 1; 54
Cloghreagh thread mill: Killevy AH 1; 53
Cloghskelt meeting house: Drumgooland DN 3; 22, 25
Cloghskelt school: Drumgooland DN 3; 25
Cloghskelt td: Drumgooland DN 3; 22, 25
Cloghtogal stones: Enniskillen FH 4; 73
Cloghtogal td: Enniskillen FH 4; 73–74, 82
Cloghwelly lough: Kilmacteige SO 40; 193
Cloghwolly Lower td: Magheross MN 40; 148
Cloghwolly Upper td: Magheross MN 40; 148
Cloghy (Cloughy) td: Castleboy DN 7; 26–27
Cloghy bay: Ardkeen DN 7; 1
Cloghy bay: Ballyphilip DN 7; 7
Cloghy bay: Castleboy DN 7; 26
Cloghy corn mill: Castleboy DN 7; 26
Cloghy corn windmill: Castleboy DN 7; 26
Cloghy court house: Misc. DN 17; 122
Cloghy manor: Ballywalter DN 7; 17–18
Cloghy manor: Misc. DN 17; 122
Cloghy school: Castleboy DN 7; 27
Cloghy td: Ballywalter DN 7; 18
Cloghy td: Misc. DN 17; 125
Clogkerny school: Bodoney TE 20; 20
Clonalan (see Clonallan): Drumgath DN 3; 19
Clonallan House: Warrenpoint DN 3; 122
Clonallan ph: Ballynascreen LY 31; 33
Clonallan ph: Drumgath DN 3; 19–20
Clonallan ph: Kilbroney DN 3; 26
Clonallan ph: Loughgall AH 1; 75
Clonallan ph: Newry DN 3; 61, 109, 114
Clonallan ph: Warrenpoint DN 3; 115
Clonard (Meath): Clondermot LY 34; 63
Clonatrig ferry: Derryvullan FH 14; 41
Clonawilliam td: Aughnamullen MN 40; 75
Clonbarry (see Cloonbarry): Kilmacteige SO 40; 189
Clonboy fort [I]: Drummaul AM 19; 78, 88
Clonboy fort [II]: Drummaul AM 19; 88
Clonboy hill: Drummaul AM 19; 36
Clonboy td: Drummaul AM 19; 91
Clonca ph: Faughanvale LY 36; 48

Clonca ph: Lough Swilly DL 38; 135, 142
Cloncash td: Misc. DL 39; 197
Cloncaw chapel: Donagh MN 40; 99
Cloncknaverly (see Scarva): Aghaderg DN 12; 3
Cloncoohy lough: Tomregan FH 4; 126
Clondallon bridge: Killygarvan DL 38; 47
Clondallon fort: Mevagh DL 38; 58
Clondallon lough: Killygarvan DL 38; 47
Clondallon td: Killygarvan DL 38; 37, 41, 47
Clondallon wood: Killygarvan DL 38; 38
Clondavaddog ph: Killygarvan DL 38; 36, 42
Clondavaddog ph: Mevagh DL 38; 59
Clondavaddog ph: Tullyaughnish DL 38; 84
Clondermont deanery: Carnmoney AM 2; 64
Clondermot Castle: Dungiven LY 15; 33
Clondermot chapel: Cumber LY 28; 25
Clondermot church: Cumber LY 28; 58
Clondermot glebe: Clondermot LY 34; 109
Clondermot Glebe House: Clondermot LY 34; 26,
   98–99
Clondermot glueworks: Clondermot LY 34; 19
Clondermot graveyard: Clondermot LY 34; 5, 12,
   40–41, 106
Clondermot hill: Clondermot LY 34; 1, 5, 7, 17, 22,
   100–01, 105
Clondermot hill: Cumber LY 28; 35
Clondermot liberties: Clondermot LY 34; 113
Clondermot meeting house: Tamlaght Finlagan LY
   25; 69
Clondermot old church: Clondermot LY 34; 27, 40,
   45, 63, 74, 89
Clondermot ph: Balteagh LY 9; 16
Clondermot ph: Banagher LY 30; 25, 27, 56, 84, 95,
   102, 104–07
Clondermot ph: Cumber LY 28; 6, 14, 19, 22, 24,
   40, 45, 61, 65, 67–68, 71
Clondermot ph: Dungiven LY 15; 47, 103
Clondermot ph: Faughanvale LY 36; 1–4, 10, 23,
   27–28, 48–49, 54–55, 57, 60
Clondermot ph: Magilligan LY 11; 82
Clondermot ph: Misc. LY 36; 119
Clondermot ph: Tamlaght Finlagan LY 25; 125
Clondermot quarry: Clondermot LY 34; 130
Clondermot river: Clondermot LY 34; 1, 3, 17–18,
   21, 31, 34, 53–54
Clondermot school: Cumber LY 28; 34, 79
Clondermot Sunday school: Clondermot LY 34;
   92–93
Clondermot td: Banagher LY 30; 103
Clondermot td: Clondermot LY 34; 38, 56, 63, 109,
   112, 115, 123, 130
Clondermot wood: Clondermot LY 34; 123
Clondermott (see Clondermot)
Clonderrigan td: Laragh CN 40; 39
Clonduff church (see Hilltown): Clonduff DN 3; 4

Clonduff ph: Drumballyroney DN 3; 11, 13–14
Clonduff ph: Drumcree AH 1; 28
Clonduff ph: Drumgath DN 3; 19
Clonduff ph: Kilbroney DN 3; 26
Clonduff ph: Kilcoo DN 3; 45
Clonduff td: Drumballyroney DN 3; 14
Clone (see Cloane): Ballynascreen LY 31; 22
Clone, Patt: Killelagh LY 27; 101
Cloneblaugh (Cloneblough) td: Clogher TE 5; 32,
   46, 53
Clonekey [or Clonskey] district: Clondermot LY 34;
   59–61
Clonelly (Devonshire): Dungiven LY 15; 60
Clonelly House: Drumkeeran FH 14; 67
Clonervie House: Coleraine LY 33; 64
Clones: Aghabog MN 40; 64–65
Clones: Aghalurcher FH 4; 1, 8
Clones: Aughnamullen MN 40; 73, 75, 77
Clones: Ballybay MN 40; 80–83
Clones: Clogher TE 5; 29
Clones: Clones FH 4; 26–29
Clones: Currin MN 40; 89–92, 94
Clones: Drumgoon CN 40; 4, 7
Clones: Drummully FH 4; 34, 36–38
Clones: Ematris MN 40; 115
Clones: Enniskillen FH 4; 61
Clones: Galloon FH 4; 90–94
Clones abbey: Clones FH 4; 26, 29
Clones chapel: Clones FH 4; 27
Clones church: Clogher TE 5; 29
Clones church: Clones FH 4; 27, 29
Clones cross: Clones FH 4; 29
Clones dispensary: Clones FH 4; 27
Clones dispensary: Currin MN 40; 92
Clones dispensary: Drummully FH 4; 37
Clones district: Aghavea FH 4; 25
Clones district: Enniskeen CN 40; 29
Clones Glebe House: Clones FH 4; 27, 29
Clones market house: Clones FH 4; 27
Clones meeting houses: Clones FH 4; 27
Clones national school: Clones FH 4; 28
Clones parish school: Clones FH 4; 28
Clones ph: Aghalurcher FH 4; 1
Clones ph: Clogher TE 5; 40
Clones ph: Currin MN 40; 86
Clones ph: Drummully FH 4; 35
Clones ph: Galloon FH 4; 87–88, 94
Clones ph: Tydavnet MN 40; 169
Clones rectory: Clones FH 4; 29
Clones round tower: Clones FH 4; 29
Clonetrace (Clanatrace) td: Skerry AM 13; 107, 114,
   116
Clonetrace fort: Skerry AM 13; 116, 119
Clonetrace school: Skerry AM 13; 114
Cloney (see Clooney): Clondermot LY 34; 46

Cloneyblagh (see Cloneblaugh)
Clonfad (see Glenfad): Clonleigh DL 39; 10
Clonfard td: Drummully FH 4; 34, 39
Clonfeacle ph: Drumglass TE 20; 40
Clonfeacle ph: Eglish AH 1; 43
Clonfeacle ph: Killeeshil TE 20; 63
Clonfeacle ph: Killyman AH 1; 55
Clonfeacle ph: Loughgall AH 1; 78–79
Clonfert (Galway): Clondermot LY 34; 63
Clongill Glebe House: Enniskeen CN 40; 29
Clonie (see Clooney): Clondermot LY 34; 38
Clonish abbey: Inniskeen MN 40; 126
Clonkee barony: Magheross MN 40; 143
Clonkeen (Louth): Clondermot LY 34; 68
Clonkelly barony: Clones FH 4; 26, 29
Clonkelly barony: Galloon FH 4; 87, 89, 92
Clonkilly (see Clonkelly): Galloon FH 4; 87
Clonknaverly (see Scarva): Aghaderg DN 12; 7
Clonlee House: Clonleigh DL 39; 13–14
Clonlee springs: Clonleigh DL 39; 13
Clonleigh bog: Misc. DL 39; 187
Clonleigh old church: Clonleigh DL 39; 14
Clonleigh ph: Clondermot LY 34; 53
Clonleigh ph: Donaghmore DL 39; 28, 32
Clonleigh ph: Misc. DL 39; 183–89, 191, 193,
    196–97
Clonleigh ph: Raphoe DL 39; 121
Clonleigh ph: Urney DL 39; 174
Clonleigh schools: Misc. DL 39; 194
Clonleigh td: Misc. DL 39; 198
Clonloghan td: Drumlumman CN 40; 17
Clonlogher (see Cloonlogher): Manorhamilton
    Union LM 40; 50
Clonlum td: Killevy AH 1; 53
Clonmacane td: Clondermot LY 34; 80
Clonmacnoise (Offaly): Clondermot LY 34; 63
Clonmahon barony: Drumlumman CN 40; 12
Clonmain bleach green: Loughgall AH 1; 80
Clonmain meeting house: Loughgall AH 1; 76, 80
Clonmain school: Loughgall AH 1; 76–77
Clonmain windmill: Loughgall AH 1; 78, 81
Clonmakane td: Cumber LY 28; 60–61, 95, 100,
    104, 107
Clonmany bridge: Clonmany DL 38; 14
Clonmany bridge: Lough Swilly DL 38; 132–33,
    136
Clonmany church: Clonmany DL 38; 12, 14, 16, 20
Clonmany graveyard: Clonmany DL 38; 14
Clonmany monastery: Clonmany DL 38; 14
Clonmany ph: Clondavaddog DL 38; 9
Clonmany ph: Desertegney DL 38; 24, 26, 29
Clonmany ph: Donagh DL 38; 32
Clonmany ph: Killygarvan DL 38; 39
Clonmany ph: Lough Swilly DL 38; 133–37, 142
Clonmany ph: Mevagh DL 38; 57, 59, 62

Clonmany ph: Mintiaghs DL 38; 64–65, 67
Clonmany river: Clonmany DL 38; 12, 20
Clonmany river: Lough Swilly DL 38; 132–33
Clonmany river: Mintiaghs DL 38; 64
Clonmany school: Clonmany DL 38; 17
Clonmel (Tipperary): Clondermot LY 34; 63
Clonmess Islands: Lough Swilly DL 38; 120
Clonmess Point: Lough Swilly DL 38; 120
Clonmin Glebe td: Galloon FH 4; 95, 97
Clonmore chapel: Killyman AH 1; 55
Clonnelly House: Drumkeeran FH 14; 64, 68
Clonnelly stream: Drumkeeran FH 14; 64
Clonoe chapel: Clonoe TE 20; 31
Clonoe church: Clonoe TE 20; 31
Clonoe mass yard: Clonoe TE 20; 31
Clonoe ph: Ballyclog TE 20; 15, 18
Clonoe ph: Donaghenry TE 20; 37
Clonoe ph: Drumglass TE 20; 41
Clonoe ph: Killyman TE 20; 67
Clonoe ph: Tullyniskan TE 20; 140
Clonoe schools: Clonoe TE 20; 31
Clonookill district: Misc. SO 40; 199
Clonroanny td: Lough Swilly DL 38; 141
Clonroot td: Kilmore AH 1; 66, 68–70
Clonsedy bog: Magheracloone MN 40; 137
Clonshanvo (Clinshanaugh) td: Drummully FH 4;
    39
Clonshranchan (see Colenacran): Aghaderg DN 12;
    2
Clontacalley (see Clontinacally): Drumbo DN 7; 63
Clontagh (see Cloontagh): Clonmany DL 38; 20
Clontagher school: Dungiven LY 15; 19
Clontall td: Ballymoney AM 16; 9
Clontallagh locality: Lough Swilly DL 38; 115
Clontarf (Dublin): Clondermot LY 34; 63
Clontask td: Drummully FH 4; 37, 39
Clontibret: Ballybay MN 40; 82
Clontibret ph: Aughnamullen MN 40; 69
Clontibret ph: Ballybay MN 40; 78
Clontibret ph: Donaghmoyne MN 40; 106
Clontibret ph: Monaghan MN 40; 159
Clontibret ph: Muckno MN 40; 162, 165
Clontibret ph: Tyholland MN 40; 174
Clontibret ph: Tynan AH 1; 124
Clontibret rectory: Clones FH 4; 29
Clontibret td: Clogher TE 5; 40
Clontinacally school: Hillsborough DN 12; 101
Clontinacally td: Drumbo DN 7; 60–61, 63
Clontinically school: Drumbo DN 7; 60
Clontonacally (see Clontinacally)
Clontonically (see Clontinacally): Drumbo DN 7; 60
Clontrain corn mill: Magheracloone MN 40; 142
Clontrain school: Magheracloone MN 40; 142
Clontyfinnan East td: Loughguile AM 13; 70, 76
Clontyfinnan school [I]: Loughguile AM 13; 76

Clontyfinnan school [II]: Loughguile AM 13; 77

Clontyfinnan td: Loughguile AM 13; 75–76

Clontyfinnan West td: Loughguile AM 13; 76

Clonvaraghan chapel: Kilmegan DN 3; 55

Clonyblagh td: Clogher TE 5; 36

Cloon district: Killea and Taughboyne DL 39; 87

Cloon district: Misc. SO 40; 200

Cloon House: Killea and Taughboyne DL 39; 80, 87

Cloon td: Cleenish FH 14; 28, 28

Cloon td: Killea and Taughboyne DL 39; 79, 194

Cloonacloghan lough: Emlaghfad SO 40; 176

Cloonagurn forts: Manorhamilton Union LM 40; 52

Cloonan trigonometrical station: Emlaghfad SO 40; 176

Cloonaneenagh district: Misc. SO 40; 200

Cloonaree village: Kilmacteige SO 40; 193

Cloonaroo td: Drummully FH 4; 39

Cloonarrell td: Donaghmore DL 39; 36

Cloonatrig ferry: Cleenish FH 14; 18

Cloonatrig hill: Cleenish FH 14; 12

Cloonatrig td: Cleenish FH 14; 29

Cloonatumper td: Killesher FH 14; 87

Cloonaveel td: Cleenish FH 14; 28

Cloonavoan td: Enniskillen FH 4; 74, 82

Cloonbarn (see Cloonbarry): Kilmacteige SO 40; 195

Cloonbarry House: Kilmacteige SO 40; 189, 195

Cloonbarry td: Kilmacteige SO 40; 189–90, 192, 195–96

Cloonbunniagh td: Rossorry FH 14; 116

Cloonca Middle td: Kilmacteige SO 40; 196

Cloonca td: Kilmacteige SO 40; 196

Clooncabeg village: Kilmacteige SO 40; 196

Clooncabeg village: Kilmacteige SO 40; 196

Cloonclare old church: Manorhamilton Union LM 40; 51

Cloonclare ph: Boho FH 14; 8

Cloonclare ph: Cleenish FH 14; 11

Cloonclare ph: Manorhamilton Union LM 40; 47–48, 51–53

Cloondeveon (see Cloonydiveen): Kilmacteige SO 40; 196

Cloone district: Lough Swilly DL 38; 120

Cloonemiege district: Misc. SO 40; 200

Cloonesallagh district: Misc. SO 40; 198

Clooney bog: Kilcronaghan LY 31; 64, 78

Clooney church: Clondermot LY 34; 46, 63

Clooney fort [I]: Kilcronaghan LY 31; 86

Clooney fort [II]: Kilcronaghan LY 31; 86

Clooney House: Clondermot LY 34; 6, 20, 104

Clooney plantation: Clondermot LY 34; 123

Clooney quarries: Clondermot LY 34; 130

Clooney reservoir: Clondermot LY 34; 4, 19, 23

Clooney saltworks: Clondermot LY 34; 106

Clooney school [I]: Clondermot LY 34; 90

Clooney school [II]: Clondermot LY 34; 90

Clooney school [III]: Clondermot LY 34; 90

Clooney td: Aghanloo LY 11; 13, 18, 21, 23, 25, 37, 40–42

Clooney td: Clondermot LY 34; 7, 12, 22, 26, 30, 33, 38, 56, 59–60, 63, 68, 82–83, 87, 102, 105–06, 109, 112, 115, 123, 130

Clooney td: Cumber LY 28; 61

Clooney td: Kilcronaghan LY 31; 83

Clooney td: Magilligan LY 11; 94–95, 126, 130–31, 133, 142

Clooney td: Tullyaughnish DL 38; 96

Clooneymore td: Tullyaughnish DL 38; 96

Cloonfreese district: Misc. SO 40; 200

Cloongoonagh td: Kilmacteige SO 40; 186, 193, 196

Cloongooney (see Cloongoonagh): Kilmacteige SO 40; 186

Cloonhagless district: Misc. SO 40; 198

Cloonkeen Cole td: Clones FH 4; 26

Cloonlogher church: Manorhamilton Union LM 40; 51

Cloonlogher forts: Manorhamilton Union LM 40; 52

Cloonlogher glen: Manorhamilton Union LM 40; 47

Cloonlogher ph: Manorhamilton Union LM 40; 47–50, 52, 54

Cloonmeenagh district: Misc. SO 40; 200

Cloonohill ph: Emlaghfad SO 40; 176

Cloonriggen (see Cloonbarry): Kilmacteige SO 40; 189

Cloontagh td: Clonmany DL 38; 12–13, 19–20

Cloontagh, Miss: Clonmany DL 38; 18

Cloontaghs (see Cloontagh): Clonmany DL 38; 13

Cloontubbret td: Clones FH 4; 26

Cloontullagh td: Mevagh DL 38; 63

Cloonty bog: Billy AM 16; 56, 67

Cloonty fort: Billy AM 16; 61

Cloony (see Clooney): Clondermot LY 34; 56

Cloonyandaugh (see Banada): Kilmacteige SO 40; 196

Cloonycappogue (Cloonacappogue) td: Clogher TE 5; 36

Cloonydiveen td: Kilmacteige SO 40; 196

Cloonyhamey village: Kilmacteige SO 40; 196

Clootagh (see Cloontagh): Clonmany DL 38; 19

Clornacherat lough: Devenish FH 14; 47

Closaghmore school: Aughnamullen MN 40; 77

Close burn: Carncastle and Killyglen AM 10; 2

Close graveyard: Raphoe DL 39; 125

Close hamlet: Ballymore AH 1; 17

Close House: Raphoe DL 39; 125

Close river: Montiaghs AH 1; 89

Close, family: Ballinderry AM 21; 51, 53

Close, family: Raloo AM 32; 94, 128

Close, Hugh: Derryaghy AM 8; 95

Close, James: Carrickfergus AM 37; 148, 158

Close, Maxwell: Aghanloo LY 11; 31
Close, Mrs W.J.: Ballymore AH 1; 7
Close, Neill: Carncastle and Killyglen AM 10; 7
Close, Rev.: Kilkeel DN 3; 48, 50
Close, W.J.: Ballymore AH 1; 4, 7, 9–18
Close, W.J.: Killevy AH 1; 52
Close, W.J.: Loughgilly AH 1; 85
Close, W.J.: Misc. DN 17; 131
Close, W.J.: Tynan AH 1; 130
Close, William: Blaris AM 8; 43–44, 46, 59
Close, William: Blaris DN 12; 40–41, 43, 51
Close, William: Derryaghy AM 8; 104
Closet river: Seagoe AH 1; 104
Closhaghbeg td: Aughnamullen MN 40; 71, 75
Closhaghmore td: Aughnamullen MN 40; 75
Closnaharron td: Cleenish FH 14; 29
Closse, family: Ballinderry AM 21; 55
Clotworthy, A.J.: Coleraine LY 33; 122
Clotworthy, David: Hillsborough DN 12; 106
Clotworthy, family (see also Massereene): Killead
    AM 35; 25
Clotworthy, family: Antrim AM 29; 6, 14, 23, 35, 47
Clotworthy, family: Carmavy AM 35; 2
Clotworthy, family: Muckamore AM 35; 65
Clotworthy, George: Muckamore AM 35; 74, 79
Clotworthy, Hugh: Antrim AM 29; 6, 10, 23
Clotworthy, John: Antrim AM 29; 6, 23
Clotworthy, Mary: Ballyscullion LY 6; 58
Clotworthy, Rose: Muckamore AM 35; 73
Clough: Aghoghill AM 23; 44
Clough: Ballykinler DN 17; 32
Clough: Down DN 17; 61
Clough: Island Magee AM 10; 65
Clough: Killyleagh DN 17; 87
Clough: Loughinisland DN 17; 94, 96
Clough barrack: Loughinisland DN 17; 94
Clough Berragh stone [I]: Armoy AM 24; 8
Clough Berragh stone [II]: Armoy AM 24; 8
Clough Castle: Loughguile AM 13; 68, 76
Clough Castle: Loughinisland DN 17; 94
Clough fort: Loughinisland DN 17; 94, 97
Clough meeting house: Loughinisland DN 17; 96
Clough new meeting house: Loughinisland DN 17;
    94
Clough old castle: Loughinisland DN 17; 97
Clough old meeting house: Loughinisland DN 17;
    94
Clough Patrick stone: Banagher LY 30; 11–12
Clough Patrick stone: Dungiven LY 15; 42, 48, 102
Clough post office: Loughinisland DN 17; 94
Clough river: Drummaul AM 19; 36
Clough river: Skerry AM 13; 106, 108
Clough smithy: Loughinisland DN 17; 97
Clough td: Ballynascreen LY 31; 7
Clough, R.: Derrybrusk FH 4; 32

Cloughacarha standing stone: Culfeightrin AM 24;
    82
Cloughadrandan standing stones: Culfeightrin AM
    24; 83
Cloughagaddy standing stone: Galloon FH 4; 105
Cloughagaddy td: Galloon FH 4; 95, 105
Clough-a-kinney rock: Maghera LY 18; 60
Cloughan (see Cloghan): Kilmore AH 1; 73
Cloughan fort: Balteagh LY 9; 12, 24
Cloughan Lodge: Kilteevoge DL 39; 112
Cloughan td: Balteagh LY 9; 12
Clougha-nanca stones: Culfeightrin AM 24; 82–83
Cloughanbeg td: Kilteevoge DL 39; 112, 114
Cloughanduff (see Cloghanduff): Templepatrick AM
    35; 143
Cloughanmore bridge: Kilteevoge DL 39; 112
Cloughanmore td: Kilteevoge DL 39; 114
Cloughanmurry (see Cloghanmurry): Ramoan AM
    24; 91
Cloughard td: Donaghmore DL 39; 36
Cloughbally Lower cave: Magheross MN 40; 158
Cloughballyrobert td: Ballylinny AM 32; 22, 30
Cloughcon td: Layd AM 13; 44
Cloughcurragh hill: Ahoghill AM 23; 34
Clougher (see Clogher): Drumbo DN 7; 60, 62
Cloughernagh sweathouse: Banagher LY 30; 52, 87
Clougheroe td: Convoy DL 39; 19
Cloughey (see Cloghy): Misc. DN 17; 125
Cloughey Land locality: Carrickfergus AM 37; 93
Cloughfin (see Cloghfin): Misc. DL 39; 185
Cloughfin private school: Island Magee AM 10; 69
Cloughfin spring: Killea and Taughboyne DL 39;
    84, 150
Cloughfin td: Ballynascreen LY 31; 21–22
Cloughfin td: Island Magee AM 10; 69, 95, 100
Cloughfin td: Kilcronaghan LY 31; 67, 84
Cloughfin td: Killea and Taughboyne DL 39; 79, 87,
    143
Cloughgaldanagh td: Dunaghy AM 13; 20
Cloughgore td: Convoy DL 39; 19
Clough-hogle (see Cloughole): Balteagh LY 9; 7
Cloughin Tullybroom td: Clogher TE 5; 53
Cloughmaconnel rock: Dungiven LY 15; 92
Cloughmills (see Cloghmills)
Cloughmore standing stone: Drumballyroney DN 3;
    16
Cloughnabogaty stone: Mevagh DL 38; 58, 62
Cloughneingobban caves: Ramoan AM 24; 111–12
Cloughneingobban church: Ramoan AM 24; 110–11
Cloughneingobban fort: Ramoan AM 24; 111
Cloughogal monument: Banagher LY 30; 39
Cloughogals cromlech: Errigal LY 27; 78
Cloughogle giant's grave: Desertoghill LY 27; 8, 23,
    26

Cloughogle standing stone: Desertoghill LY 27; 8, 23

Cloughole cove stones: Balteagh LY 9; 7, 24

Cloughole cove well: Balteagh LY 9; 24

Cloughole td: Balteagh LY 9; 24, 40, 45

Cloughorr (Cloughore) td: Ballywillin LY 33; 35

Cloughorr standing stone: Ballywillin LY 33; 35, 50–51

Cloughoughe village: Kilmacteige SO 40; 196

Cloughram corn mill: Kilmegan DN 3; 60

Cloughram school: Kilmegan DN 3; 60

Cloughram td: Kilmegan DN 3; 60

Cloughthinnhagh stone: Dungiven LY 15; 91

Cloughtin (see Cloughfin)

Cloughtucka td: Drumgoon CN 40; 4

Cloughtyfinnan (see Clontyfinnan): Loughguile AM 13; 76

Cloughurnagh stone: Dungiven LY 15; 41

Cloughwann stone: Banagher LY 30; 77

Cloveneden (Clonneden) td: Loughgall AH 1; 76, 80

Cloveneden meeting house: Loughgall AH 1; 80

Clover Hill fort: Termoneeny LY 6; 122

Clover Hill House: Errigal LY 27; 55

Clover Hill House: Killead AM 35; 12, 14, 45–47

Clover Hill House: Termoneeny LY 6; 122, 127, 130–32

Clowey, Robert: Ramoan AM 24; 116

Clownagh tanyard: Drumcree AH 1; 36, 41

Cloyfin (Clayfin) South td: Ballyrashane LY 22; 62, 66

Cloyfin (see Cloughfin): Kilcronaghan LY 31; 84

Cloyfin North school: Ballywillin LY 33; 33, 41, 45–47

Cloyfin school: Ballywillin AM 16; 35

Cloyfin South cave: Ballyrashane LY 22; 50, 62

Cloyfin Sunday school: Ballywillin LY 33; 41

Cloyfin td: Ballywillin LY 33; 51

Cloyfinn (see Cloyfin): Ballywillin LY 33; 51

Cloyn Lynn chapel: Finvoy AM 23; 74

Cluain-I church: Faughanvale LY 36; 50

Clubbs ford: Carrickfergus AM 37; 32

Clugstone, Hugh: Ballylinny AM 32; 27

Clulow, Mrs (Claremont): Carnmoney AM 2; 46, 84, 89

Cluney (see Clooney): Clondermot LY 34; 106

Cluntageera (see Cluntygeeragh): Dungiven LY 15; 3

Cluntageeragh (see Cluntygeeragh): Dungiven LY 15; 1

Cluntagh td: Dromore DN 12; 73

Cluntybacker mill: Clonoe TE 20; 31

Cluntygeeragh (Cluntygeera) td: Dungiven LY 15; 3, 23, 27, 45, 47, 49, 61, 63, 65, 74, 81–82, 85, 87, 91–93

Cluntygeeragh bog: Dungiven LY 15; 81

Cluntygeeragh fort: Dungiven LY 15; 44

Cluntygeeragh schools: Dungiven LY 15; 18

Cluntygeeragh td: Banagher LY 30; 22

Cluntygeeragh td: Bovevagh LY 25; 29

Cluntygeerah (see Cluntygeeragh): Dungiven LY 15; 3

Cluny (see Clooney): Clondermot LY 34; 12

Clutterbuck, Rev. Richard: Kilrea LY 27; 108, 111, 125–26

Clyde river (Scotland): Glynn AM 26; 2, 33

Clyde river: Carnmoney AM 2; 38

Clyde river: Lough Swilly DL 38; 119

Clyde, John: Balteagh LY 9; 44

Clyde, John: Desertoghill LY 27; 23

Clyde, Mr: Drumachose LY 9; 109

Clyde, Robert: Bovevagh LY 25; 57

Clyde, Robert: Magilligan LY 11; 137

Clyde, Samuel: Errigal LY 27; 44, 75–76

Clyde, Samuel: Killead AM 35; 49

Clydesdale (Scotland): Kilroot AM 26; 73

Clydesdale: Templecorran AM 26; 97, 107

Cnoc Glass (see Crockglass): Clondavaddog DL 38; 5

Coa chapel: Magheracross FH 14; 95

Coa school: Magheracross FH 14; 99

Coa td: Magheracross FH 14; 102

Coachmill chapel: Leck DL 39; 116

Coachmill td: Leck DL 39; 118

Coagh: Arboe LY 6; 1

Coagh: Artrea LY 6; 7

Coagh: Artrea TE 20; 6, 8–10

Coagh: Ballinderry TE 20; 11–13

Coagh: Desertlyn LY 31; 39

Coagh: Lissan LY 31; 95, 99

Coagh: Tamlaght TE 20; 73–79, 81–82, 90–91, 114, 121–22, 127–28, 131–35, 137

Coagh brickfields: Tamlaght TE 20; 102

Coagh corn mill: Tamlaght TE 20; 74, 102

Coagh flax mill: Tamlaght TE 20; 74, 102

Coagh Gardens td: Tamlaght TE 20; 93–94, 103–07

Coagh inn [I]: Tamlaght TE 20; 74

Coagh inn [II]: Tamlaght TE 20; 74

Coagh quarries: Tamlaght TE 20; 102

Coagh river: Coleraine LY 33; 97

Coagh river: Tamlaght TE 20; 127, 137

Coagh td: Banagher LY 30; 3

Coagh td: Devenish FH 14; 58

Coagh td: Tamlaght TE 20; 80, 91–100, 102–03, 117, 119, 130–31

Coahen td: Killesher FH 14; 82

Coalhill td: Aghalurcher FH 4; 5

Coalisland: Aghaderg DN 12; 5

Coalisland: Antrim AM 29; 3, 20, 35

Coalisland: Artrea TE 20; 8

Coalisland: Ballyclog TE 20; 17

Coalisland: Blaris AM 8; 70–71, 73

Coalisland: Clonoe TE 20; 30–31

Coalisland: Desertcreat TE 20; 33

Coalisland: Donaghenry TE 20; 37–39

Coalisland: Drumachose LY 9; 116

Coalisland: Drumcree AH 1; 32

Coalisland: Drumglass TE 20; 42–43

Coalisland: Killyman TE 20; 68

Coalisland: Muckamore AM 35; 55

Coalisland: Tullyniskan TE 20; 140

Coalisland coalmines: Coleraine LY 33; 99

Coalisland flour mill: Ballyclog TE 20; 19

Coalisland flour mill: Donaghenry TE 20; 37

Coalisland pottery: Donaghenry TE 20; 37

Coalisland spade mill: Donaghenry TE 20; 37

Coallane school: Aghalee AM 21; 39

Coan lough: Ballyphilip DN 7; 9

Coan lough: Down DN 17; 60

Coane, Mr: Kilbarron DL 39; 74

Coanestack (see Cornastauk): Manorhamilton Union
   LM 40; 48

Coar, family: Kilcronaghan LY 31; 68

Coassan td: Cleenish FH 14; 28–29

Coates and Young, Messrs: Ballinderry AM 21; 51

Coates and Young, Messrs: Carnmoney AM 2; 82

Coates and Young, Messrs: Nilteen AM 35; 86

Coates, Ann: Blaris AM 8; 47

Coates, George: Blaris AM 8; 83

Coates, Jeorge: Blaris AM 8; 48

Coates, John: Carrickfergus AM 37; 133, 145–46,
   149, 172, 178

Coates, Miss: Ballyscullion AM 19; 14

Coates, Symon: Macosquin LY 22; 104

Coats, Mr: Blaris DN 12; 50

Coats, William: Drumbeg AM 8; 133

Cobane, Thomas: Kilwaughter AM 10; 116

Cobham, Rev. James: Carrickfergus AM 37; 26

Cobham, Rev. James: Island Magee AM 10; 94

Cobham, Rev. John: Templecorran AM 26; 101, 128

Cobham, woman named: Carnmoney AM 2; 93

Cobhran, St: Clondermot LY 34; 47

Cobley, Thomas: Clondermot LY 34; 78

Cobourn, John: Drumhome DL 39; 62

Coburn, David: Hillsborough DN 12; 106–07

Cochran, Alexander: Desertoghill LY 27; 4–5, 16

Cochran, Andrew: Aghadowey LY 22; 38

Cochran, Capt.: Lough Swilly DL 38; 118

Cochran, David: Ballymoney AM 16; 15, 17

Cochran, Edward (Jnr): Clondermot LY 34; 78

Cochran, family: Ballywillin AM 16; 32

Cochran, family: Culfeightrin AM 24; 59

Cochran, family: Derrykeighan AM 16; 89

Cochran, family: Templepatrick AM 35; 118

Cochran, Henry: Kilrea LY 27; 129

Cochran, Hugh: Coleraine LY 33; 61

Cochran, Hugh [I]: Ballyaghran LY 33; 17

Cochran, Hugh [II]: Ballyaghran LY 33; 27

Cochran, J.G.: Bovevagh LY 25; 28, 55

Cochran, James: Billy AM 16; 64

Cochran, James: Clondermot LY 34; 37, 78, 104

Cochran, James: Newtown Crommelin AM 13; 84

Cochran, Jane: Kilrea LY 27; 129

Cochran, John: Ballywillin LY 33; 44, 49

Cochran, John: Billy AM 16; 60

Cochran, John: Coleraine LY 33; 72, 104–07, 144

Cochran, John: Desertoghill LY 27; 4

Cochran, John: Killygarvan DL 38; 43, 47

Cochran, Margaret (Jnr): Kilrea LY 27; 129

Cochran, Margaret (Snr): Kilrea LY 27; 129

Cochran, Mary: Kilrea LY 27; 129

Cochran, Mr (Clones): Currin MN 40; 92, 96

Cochran, Robert: Kilrea LY 27; 129

Cochran, Samuel: Carrickfergus AM 37; 121

Cochran, Samuel: Drumachose LY 9; 104

Cochran, Sgt: Blaris AM 8; 69

Cochran, William: Aghadowey LY 22; 9, 21, 34–35

Cochran, William: Artrea LY 6; 24

Cochran, William: Coleraine LY 33; 104

Cochran, William: Donagh MN 40; 103

Cochran, William: Dunboe LY 11; 59, 78

Cochrane and Brown, Messrs (Glasgow): Newry
   DN 3; 85

Cochrane, Mr (Letterkenny): Mevagh DL 38; 60

Cochrane, Mr: Enniskillen FH 4; 75

Cochrane, Mrs: Clogher TE 5; 41

Cochrane, William: Hillsborough DN 12; 107

Cock Hall House: Clondermot LY 34; 6, 20, 97, 102

Cock hill: Tartaraghan AH 1; 117, 119

Cock Hill chapel: Mintiaghs DL 38; 65

Cock hill windmill: Tartaraghan AH 1; 120

Cock mountain: Clonduff DN 3; 5

Cock, J.: Saul DN 17; 115

Cockburn, General: Bright DN 17; 34–35

Cockhill td: Tynan AH 1; 131

Cockran, Mr: Donaghmore DL 39; 37

Cockrien td: Magheross MN 40; 148

Cocks, Ellis: Ballyscullion LY 6; 57

Cocktown td: Killea and Taughboyne DL 39; 79

Cocktry, family: Templecorran AM 26; 117, 119

Coe, Miss: Clogher TE 5; 43

Coen lough: Killinchy DN 7; 89

Coey, family: Kilwaughter AM 10; 115

Coffey's ford: Kinawley FH 4; 108

Coffin stone: Rasharkin AM 23; 140

Coggrey (Cogree) td: Doagh AM 29; 61

Coggrey bridge: Doagh AM 29; 92–93

Coggrey corn mill: Doagh AM 29; 70, 85, 92–93,
   96

Coggrey td: Kilbride AM 29; 150

Coggry (see Coggrey): Doagh AM 29; 92

Coghlan, John: Drumachose LY 9; 119, 123
Coghlan, Michael: Drumachose LY 9; 85
Coghran, Mr (Ballymagrorty): Drumhome DL 39;
  62
Cogry (see Coggrey): Kilbride AM 29; 150
Cogwell, J.M.: Misc. DN 17; 117
Cohair td: Drumcree AH 1; 37
Cohen, Rev.: Kilbroney DN 3; 34
Cohey, Agnes: Island Magee AM 10; 95
Cohey, Jane: Island Magee AM 10; 95
Cohey, Samuel: Island Magee AM 10; 95
Coille lough: Donegal DL 39; 44
Colby, Col T.F.: Aghaloo TE 20; 2
Colby, Col T.F.: Artrea TE 20; 9
Colby, Col T.F.: Clondermot LY 34; 91
Colby, Col T.F.: Culdaff DL 38; 22
Colby, Col T.F.: Cumber LY 28; 5
Colby, Col T.F.: Faughanvale LY 36; 67
Colby, Col T.F.: Mevagh DL 38; 63
Colby, Col T.F.: Misc. LY 36; 117–18
Colby, Col T.F.: Moville DL 38; 73
Colby, Laurence: Ballyscullion LY 6; 56
Coldagh bridge: Ballymoney AM 16; 5
Coldagh flax mill: Ballymoney AM 16; 10
Coldroy, Francis: Carrickfergus AM 37; 193
Coldrum (see Culdrum): Misc. LY 36; 112
Coldwell, John: Magilligan LY 11; 134
Cole bay: Lough Swilly DL 38; 103, 134, 142–43
Cole td: Clogher TE 5; 26, 37, 53
Cole, A.H.: Enniskillen FH 4; 58–59
Cole, A.H.: Killesher FH 14; 88
Cole, Ellen: Kilrea LY 27; 130
Cole, family (see also Enniskillen): Enniskillen FH
  4; 50, 64, 71, 75
Cole, G.L.: Enniskillen FH 4; 58
Cole, James (Jnr): Kilrea LY 27; 130
Cole, James (Snr): Kilrea LY 27; 130
Cole, Lord: Cleenish FH 14; 22
Cole, Lord: Enniskillen FH 4; 41, 59
Cole, Lord: Killesher FH 14; 83–86
Cole, Maria: Carrickfergus AM 37; 125
Cole, Michael [I]: Enniskillen FH 4; 57
Cole, Michael [II]: Enniskillen FH 4; 58
Cole, Mrs: Aughnamullen MN 40; 76
Cole, W.W.: Enniskillen FH 4; 58
Cole, W.W.: Rossorry FH 14; 117
Cole, William: Derryvullan FH 14; 38–39
Cole, William: Enniskillen FH 4; 50–51, 57
Colebourne and Richards, Messrs: Aghalurcher FH
  4; 7
Colebrook (see Colebrooke): Aghalurcher FH 4; 3
Colebrooke demesne: Aghalurcher FH 4; 5–8, 10,
  14, 16
Colebrooke district: Aghavea FH 4; 22–23
Colebrooke House: Aghalurcher FH 4; 3–4, 7–8, 14

Colebrooke mountain: Aghalurcher FH 4; 2
Colebrooke river: Aghalurcher FH 4; 3, 5, 8
Colebrooke river: Aghavea FH 4; 17
Colehill creek: Lough Swilly DL 38; 103, 142
Colehill td: Misc. DL 39; 194
Coleman Island: Drummully FH 4; 35
Coleman td: Drummully FH 4; 39
Coleman, Bernard: Newry DN 3; 98, 103
Coleman, Cochran: Dunboe LY 11; 80
Coleman, Mary: Dunboe LY 11; 80
Colenacran td: Aghaderg DN 12; 2
Colenane td: Aghalurcher TE 5; 1
Colepepper, Elizabeth (see Hamilton): Taughboyne
  DL 39; 152
Colepepper, John: Taughboyne DL 39; 152
Coleraine: Aghadowey LY 22; 6–7, 10–12, 19,
  27–28, 33
Coleraine: Aghanloo LY 11; 7, 17–19, 23–24, 35,
  37–38
Coleraine: Agivey LY 22; 39–40, 42–44
Coleraine: Ahoghill AM 23; 3–5, 31
Coleraine: Antrim AM 29; 13, 17, 22, 39, 48
Coleraine: Ballintoy AM 24; 11, 15–16
Coleraine: Ballyaghran LY 33; 1, 4–8, 11, 13, 15,
  17, 20–24, 26
Coleraine: Ballyclug AM 23; 63
Coleraine: Ballymartin AM 2; 4
Coleraine: Ballymoney AM 16; 1
Coleraine: Ballynascreen LY 31; 21
Coleraine: Ballynure AM 32; 64
Coleraine: Ballyrashane LY 22; 47–49, 51–54,
  56–57
Coleraine: Ballyscullion LY 6; 46
Coleraine: Ballywillin LY 33; 29, 31–34, 36, 39–47,
  50
Coleraine: Banagher LY 30; 3, 5, 18–19, 30, 32, 39,
  60–61, 106, 113
Coleraine: Billy AM 16; 47, 50
Coleraine: Bovevagh LY 25; 2, 13, 24, 31, 57
Coleraine: Carnmoney AM 2; 49
Coleraine: Clondermot LY 34; 30
Coleraine: Coleraine LY 33; 53, 55–66, 69, 71–75,
  77, 81, 85–86, 88–93, 95–96, 98–100, 102–07,
  110, 119–20, 123, 125, 128–32, 134, 137–39,
  139–44, 146–47, 149, 151
Coleraine: Connor AM 19; 22
Coleraine: Culfeightrin AM 24; 39, 63
Coleraine: Cumber LY 28; 21, 23, 52, 58
Coleraine: Derrykeighan AM 16; 83
Coleraine: Desertcreat TE 20; 33
Coleraine: Desertlyn LY 31; 35, 37, 40–41
Coleraine: Desertoghill LY 27; 3, 13–14
Coleraine: Donaghenry TE 20; 37–38
Coleraine: Drumachose LY 9; 61, 76, 117, 121
Coleraine: Drumglass TE 20; 40, 42, 45

Coleraine: Drummaul AM 19; 46, 79
Coleraine: Dunboe LY 11; 44, 46–47, 52, 59, 62
Coleraine: Dungiven LY 15; 14, 26, 33, 53, 56,
    66–68, 105
Coleraine: Errigal LY 27; 36–41, 50, 57, 59–62, 64,
    79–84
Coleraine: Faughanvale LY 36; 39, 47
Coleraine: Finvoy AM 23; 67, 70, 73
Coleraine: Inver AM 26; 54
Coleraine: Kilcronaghan LY 31; 66, 69, 75, 83
Coleraine: Kildollagh LY 22; 68–73
Coleraine: Killagan AM 23; 80
Coleraine: Killelagh LY 27; 96
Coleraine: Killowen LY 33; 158, 160–65, 168–72
Coleraine: Killymard DL 39; 108
Coleraine: Kilraghts AM 16; 125
Coleraine: Kilrea LY 27; 105, 110–11, 122, 127
Coleraine: Kirkinriola AM 23; 91, 95, 102, 108, 118
Coleraine: Layd AM 13; 38
Coleraine: Lough Neagh AM 21; 93, 95
Coleraine: Lough Swilly DL 38; 106, 149
Coleraine: Macosquin LY 22; 78, 80–83, 85, 87–89,
    91–93, 96, 98–99, 101–03, 106, 109–12, 117, 121
Coleraine: Maghera LY 18; 2, 4–5, 8–9, 35, 52–53,
    71
Coleraine: Magherafelt LY 6; 86–87
Coleraine: Magilligan LY 11; 84, 111, 113, 116–17,
    132, 136, 139, 141
Coleraine: Mallusk AM 2; 107
Coleraine: Misc. LY 36; 109–10, 116
Coleraine: Moville DL 38; 71, 73
Coleraine: Muckamore AM 35; 63
Coleraine: Nilteen AM 35; 90
Coleraine: Raloo AM 32; 94
Coleraine: Ramoan AM 24; 90, 93, 96–97
Coleraine: Rasharkin AM 23; 128–29, 132–33
Coleraine: Shilvodan AM 19; 130
Coleraine: Tamlaght Finlagan LY 25; 72, 82, 84,
    112–13
Coleraine: Templepatrick AM 35; 113
Coleraine: Termoneeny LY 6; 132
Coleraine abbey: Coleraine LY 33; 91, 94, 133
Coleraine academy: Coleraine LY 33; 67–68, 95,
    137–38
Coleraine ballast office: Coleraine LY 33; 58, 85,
    95, 138
Coleraine Baptist female school: Coleraine LY 33;
    57, 67, 73, 135, 141
Coleraine Baptist male school: Coleraine LY 33; 57,
    67, 73, 135, 141
Coleraine Baptist Sunday school: Coleraine LY 33;
    70, 139
Coleraine barony: Banagher LY 30; 43
Coleraine barony: Faughanvale LY 36; 60
Coleraine barony: Kilrea LY 27; 104, 112

Coleraine barony: Misc. LY 36; 105
Coleraine barony: Tamlaght O'Crilly LY 18; 82
Coleraine boarding school: Coleraine LY 33; 68,
    137
Coleraine bowling green: Coleraine LY 33; 59
Coleraine brewery: Coleraine LY 33; 86
Coleraine bridewell: Coleraine LY 33; 58
Coleraine bridge: Coleraine LY 33; 54, 56, 58, 75,
    91, 147
Coleraine bridge: Killowen LY 33; 158, 160–62,
    167–68
Coleraine bridge: Macosquin LY 22; 81, 102, 102
Coleraine Bridge St female school: Coleraine LY
    33; 68, 135–36
Coleraine Bridge St school: Coleraine LY 33; 68,
    135
Coleraine Brook St school: Coleraine LY 33; 69,
    135–36
Coleraine Castle: Coleraine LY 33; 157
Coleraine cattle market: Killowen LY 33; 159
Coleraine chandlery: Coleraine LY 33; 86
Coleraine chapel: Coleraine LY 33; 56–57, 70, 95,
    140, 142, 147, 153
Coleraine chapel: Kildollagh LY 22; 71
Coleraine chapel: Macosquin LY 22; 90, 97
Coleraine church: Coleraine LY 33; 56–57, 69, 94,
    118, 129, 140, 147, 153–54
Coleraine church: Lissan LY 31; 89
Coleraine Church Sunday school: Coleraine LY 33;
    69, 140
Coleraine citadel: Coleraine LY 33; 56
Coleraine corn mill: Coleraine LY 33; 91, 94, 130,
    150
Coleraine cornstore: Coleraine LY 33; 57, 141
Coleraine cotton manufactory: Coleraine LY 33; 144
Coleraine court house: Coleraine LY 33; 62
Coleraine custom house: Coleraine LY 33; 55, 58,
    77, 82, 85, 87–88
Coleraine dispensary: Ballyrashane LY 22; 51
Coleraine dispensary: Coleraine LY 33; 73–74,
    120–21, 148
Coleraine dispensary: Dunboe LY 11; 52, 69
Coleraine dispensary: Kildollagh LY 22; 70
Coleraine dispensary: Killowen LY 33; 163
Coleraine dispensary: Macosquin LY 22; 89
Coleraine district: Clondermot LY 34; 69
Coleraine district: Killowen LY 33; 173
Coleraine evening school: Coleraine LY 33; 137
Coleraine female evening school: Coleraine LY 33;
    69
Coleraine female school: Coleraine LY 33; 57, 67,
    69–70, 73, 133–34, 140, 146, 154
Coleraine female Sunday school: Coleraine LY 33;
    69, 140

Coleraine Ferry Quay St school: Coleraine LY 33; 67, 69, 136
Coleraine fishery: Coleraine LY 33; 101
Coleraine fishery: Desertoghill LY 27; 12
Coleraine fishery: Kilrea LY 27; 105
Coleraine flax mill: Coleraine LY 33; 91, 94, 130
Coleraine gaol: Coleraine LY 33; 58, 62, 151
Coleraine grain store: Coleraine LY 33; 119
Coleraine graveyard: Coleraine LY 33; 55–56
Coleraine harbour: Coleraine LY 33; 74–75
Coleraine Horned Stag hotel: Dungiven LY 15; 109
Coleraine hotel: Coleraine LY 33; 104, 106
Coleraine icehouses: Coleraine LY 33; 55
Coleraine infirmary: Coleraine LY 33; 71
Coleraine inn: Coleraine LY 33; 58
Coleraine liberties: Ballymoney AM 16; 1
Coleraine library: Coleraine LY 33; 58, 65, 110–11
Coleraine Lodge: Coleraine LY 33; 91
Coleraine male school: Coleraine LY 33; 57, 66–67, 70, 73, 133–34, 143, 146, 154
Coleraine male Sunday School: Coleraine LY 33; 70, 139
Coleraine market house: Coleraine LY 33; 56, 85, 147, 150
Coleraine market place: Coleraine LY 33; 58–59, 61, 119, 129
Coleraine mass–house: Coleraine LY 33; 95
Coleraine meeting house (B): Coleraine LY 33; 56–57, 67, 70, 95, 135, 141
Coleraine meeting house (P): Coleraine LY 33; 56–57, 95, 140, 142, 149, 153
Coleraine meeting house (P): Kildollagh LY 22; 70
Coleraine meeting house (S): Coleraine LY 33; 56–57, 70, 95, 139–40, 142, 153
Coleraine meeting house (S): Killowen LY 33; 159
Coleraine Methodist Sunday school: Coleraine LY 33; 70, 140
Coleraine New Row meeting house (P): Coleraine LY 33; 56–57, 70, 95, 140, 142, 153
Coleraine New Row school: Coleraine LY 33; 68, 134
Coleraine New Row Sunday school: Coleraine LY 33; 140
Coleraine news room: Coleraine LY 33; 58, 65, 104, 106, 144
Coleraine old bridge: Coleraine LY 33; 58
Coleraine old corn mill: Coleraine LY 33; 118, 150
Coleraine old court house: Coleraine LY 33; 129
Coleraine old market place: Coleraine LY 33; 56–57
Coleraine old poor house: Coleraine LY 33; 144
Coleraine paper mills: Coleraine LY 33; 151
Coleraine ph: Ballyaghran LY 33; 13, 15, 26–27
Coleraine ph: Ballywillin LY 33; 31–32, 37–38
Coleraine ph: Kildollagh LY 22; 67
Coleraine ph: Killowen LY 33; 158, 166

Coleraine ph: Macosquin LY 22; 76
Coleraine ph: Misc. LY 36; 111
Coleraine poor house: Coleraine LY 33; 57, 71–72, 118, 129, 144, 154
Coleraine poor house: Killowen LY 33; 164
Coleraine port: Coleraine LY 33; 82–83, 87–88
Coleraine post office: Coleraine LY 33; 88, 150
Coleraine post office: Misc. LY 36; 116
Coleraine Presbyterian Sunday school: Coleraine LY 33; 70
Coleraine public house: Coleraine LY 33; 133
Coleraine quay: Coleraine LY 33; 74–77
Coleraine quay: Killowen LY 33; 172
Coleraine ramparts: Coleraine LY 33; 55–56, 59, 75
Coleraine Rectory: Coleraine LY 33; 73
Coleraine sandpit: Coleraine LY 33; 149
Coleraine savings bank: Ballyaghran LY 33; 6
Coleraine savings bank: Coleraine LY 33; 58, 107–10, 119, 126–27, 139
Coleraine Seceding Sunday school: Coleraine LY 33; 70, 139–40
Coleraine select school: Coleraine LY 33; 68, 136
Coleraine sessions house: Coleraine LY 33; 58
Coleraine Shamble St school: Coleraine LY 33; 68, 135
Coleraine shambles: Coleraine LY 33; 59, 61, 119, 151
Coleraine soapery: Coleraine LY 33; 86
Coleraine Society St school: Coleraine LY 33; 69, 136
Coleraine storehouse: Coleraine LY 33; 95, 143
Coleraine tanneries: Coleraine LY 33; 86
Coleraine temperance hotel: Coleraine LY 33; 118
Coleraine timber and coal yard: Coleraine LY 33; 77
Coleraine timber yards: Coleraine LY 33; 77
Coleraine town hall: Coleraine LY 33; 56–58, 65, 95, 106, 129, 143, 150–51
Coleraine townparks: Coleraine LY 33; 149
Coleraine warehouse: Coleraine LY 33; 77–78
Coleraine watchtower: Misc. LY 36; 110
Coleraine weighhouse: Coleraine LY 33; 59, 61
Coles, William: Misc. FH 4; 133
Coleston, Thomas: Blaris AM 8; 60
Coletor, Francis: Donacavey TE 5; 65
Colgagh bog: Donaghmoyne MN 40; 106
Colgan, Bartholemy: Billy AM 16; 56, 65–66
Colgan, Bishop: Killelagh LY 27; 102
Colgan, Catherine: Carrickfergus AM 37; 120
Colgan, Charles: Kilcronaghan LY 31; 85
Colgan, historian: Dungiven LY 15; 63–64
Colgan, historian: Magilligan LY 11; 97, 101, 105–06, 143, 146
Colgan, Rev.: Inishmacsaint FH 14; 75
Colgin, John: Cumber LY 28; 55
Colhom, St: Killygarvan DL 38; 47

Colhoon, Charles: Raymoghy DL 39; 140–41
Colhoon, Thomas: Raymoghy DL 39; 142, 186
Colhoon, William: Raymoghy DL 39; 135–36, 142, 186
Colkittagh, chieftain: Kilrea LY 27; 118
Coll, James: Dungiven LY 15; 24
Colleen village: Kilmacteige SO 40; 193
College Lands district: Clones FH 4; 26
College manor: Donegal DL 39; 51, 54
Collier, Samuel: Magheragall AM 21; 109–10
Collin adult school: Derryaghy AM 8; 117
Collin bleach green: Derryaghy AM 8; 107, 111
Collin glen: Blaris AM 8; 70
Collin House: Derryaghy AM 8; 107
Collin mountain: Blaris DN 12; 27
Collin mountain: Carnmoney AM 2; 34
Collin mountain: Derryaghy AM 8; 90–92, 97, 107
Collin mountain: Dunaghy AM 13; 10
Collin mountain: Kilbride AM 29; 135–36, 155
Collin mountain: Rashee AM 32; 137
Collin mountain: Skerry AM 13; 108, 113
Collin Sunday school: Derryaghy AM 8; 118
Collin Top hill: Ardclinis AM 13; 1, 4–5
Collin Top hill: Derryaghy AM 8; 97
Collin well: Derryaghy AM 8; 92
Collin, Arthur: Derryaghy AM 8; 97
Collins bleach green: Aghadowey LY 22; 8–9, 12
Collins corn mill: Aghadowey LY 22; 9
Collins district: Misc. LY 36; 111
Collins hill: Aghadowey LY 22; 1
Collins mill: Macosquin LY 22; 96
Collins school: Aghadowey LY 22; 13, 19–20
Collins Sunday school: Aghadowey LY 22; 13, 20
Collins td: Aghadowey LY 22; 8, 29, 38
Collins, Arthur: Newry DN 3; 100
Collins, Cornelius: Ballymoney AM 16; 16
Collins, Daniel: Newry DN 3; 99–00, 103
Collins, Dr: Tomregan FH 4; 131
Collins, family: Drumbeg AM 8; 123
Collins, family: Maghera LY 18; 24, 48
Collins, Henry: Newry DN 3; 98, 103
Collins, Hugh: Misc. DL 39; 192
Collins, James: Aghaloo TE 20; 4
Collins, James: Dromore DN 12; 75
Collins, John: Artrea LY 6; 26
Collins, John: Donagh MN 40; 101
Collins, John: Drumbeg AM 8; 133
Collins, John: Muckamore AM 35; 81
Collins, John: Newry DN 3; 100, 104
Collins, Joseph: Newry DN 3; 100
Collins, Mr: Blaris AM 8; 84
Collins, Mr: Clogher TE 5; 40
Collins, Patrick: Artrea LY 6; 26
Collins, Rev.: Kilbroney DN 3; 34
Collins, Rev. J.C.: Currin MN 40; 89

Collins, Robert: Blaris AM 8; 83
Collins, Thomas: Blaris DN 12; 40
Collins, Thomas: Clondermot LY 34; 81
Collins, Widow: Magheragall AM 21; 105
Collins, William: Ahoghill AM 23; 39
Collins, William: Blaris AM 8; 52, 62
Collins, William: Blaris DN 12; 46, 50, 50
Collinward (Callanardh) td: Carnmoney AM 2; 34, 46, 58, 90, 102
Collinward cairn: Carnmoney AM 2; 70
Collinward hill: Carnmoney AM 2; 35, 98
Collis, M.: Coleraine LY 33; 56
Collooney: Emlaghfad SO 40; 177–78, 180
Collooney waterfall: Emlaghfad SO 40; 177
Colltemannow district: Misc. SO 40; 198
Collum, Mr: Enniskillen FH 4; 69
Collumbine, family: Misc. LY 36; 104
Colman, family: Ballywillin AM 16; 32
Colman, family: Carmavy AM 35; 2
Colman, family: Kilbride AM 29; 140
Colman, Owen: Banagher LY 30; 91
Colman, P.: Banagher LY 30; 90
Colman, Richard: Clondermot LY 34; 55
Colman, St: Aghagallon AM 21; 10
Colman, St: Magilligan LY 11; 88
Colqhoun, A.W.: Ardstraw TE 5; 3, 5, 11, 13
Colquhoun, Mr: Bovevagh LY 25; 18
Colquoun, Maj.: Ardstraw TE 5; 3
Colrane (see Coleraine)
Colter, Daniel: Dromore TE 5; 97
Colthurst, Rev.: Donaghmore DL 39; 37
Colthurst, Rev. Charles: Desertoghill LY 27; 17
Colthurst, Rev. Charles: Kilrea LY 27; 126
Colthurst, Rev. Charles: Misc. LY 31; 127, 136
Colthurst, Rev. John: Bovevagh LY 25; 3
Colthurst, Rev. John: Dungiven LY 15; 5
Coltrim bog: Lissan LY 31; 89, 96, 103
Coltrim school: Lissan LY 31; 95
Coltrim spade mill: Lissan LY 31; 102
Coltrim td: Desertlyn LY 31; 35
Coltrim td: Lissan LY 31; 103, 107–09
Colum, Jane: Ahoghill AM 23; 37
Colum, Margaret: Ahoghill AM 23; 37
Colum, Robert: Ahoghill AM 23; 37
Columb kiln: Tartaraghan AH 1; 120
Columba, St (see Columbkille)
Columbkille, St (see also Columb): Aghagallon AM 21; 17
Columbkille, St: Aghanloo LY 11; 7
Columbkille, St: Ahoghill AM 23; 14, 25, 28
Columbkille, St: Ballynascreen LY 31; 9–10, 23–24, 26–27, 29, 33–34
Columbkille, St: Banagher LY 30; 109
Columbkille, St: Bovevagh LY 25; 5, 46

Columbkille, St: Clondermot LY 34; 33–34, 45, 47, 52, 56, 63, 102, 106–07

Columbkille, St: Clonmany DL 38; 14

Columbkille, St: Culfeightrin AM 24; 67–68

Columbkille, St: Desertoghill LY 27; 6, 22, 31

Columbkille, St: Down DN 17; 43, 60–61

Columbkille, St: Drumragh TE 5; 108

Columbkille, St: Drumtullagh AM 16; 103

Columbkille, St: Dunboe LY 11; 61

Columbkille, St: Dungiven LY 15; 18, 64

Columbkille, St: Faughanvale LY 36; 13, 50

Columbkille, St: Kilmacrenan DL 38; 50

Columbkille, St: Maghera LY 18; 9, 39

Columbkille, St: Magilligan LY 11; 90, 103, 105–06, 143, 146

Columbkille, St: Mevagh DL 38; 58

Columbkille, St: Misc. AM 10; 130

Columbkille, St: Misc. LY 31; 117, 124

Columbkille, St: Misc. LY 36; 114

Columbkille, St: Misc. TE 5; 146–47

Columbkille, St: Muckamore AM 35; 56, 69, 81–83

Columbkille, St: Nilteen AM 35; 94

Columbkille, St: Raphoe DL 39; 124

Columbkille, St: Rathlin Island AM 24; 132, 134

Columbkille, St: Tamlaght Finlagan LY 25; 102–03

Columbkille, St: Tullyaughnish DL 38; 90–91

Colvill, family: Glenwhirry AM 32; 77

Colvill, William: Drumachose LY 9; 65

Colville, Dr: Ahoghill AM 23; 2, 12, 17–18, 31, 35

Colville, family: Newtownards DN 7; 107

Colville, Robert: Island Magee AM 10; 20, 27, 39, 78, 85, 94

Colville, Robert: Kilroot AM 26; 79

Colville, Robert: Newtownards DN 7; 107

Colvin, Eliza: Blaris AM 8; 81

Colvin, family: Island Magee AM 10; 70

Colvin, William: Derrykeighan AM 16; 87, 95

Colwell, Eliza: Balteagh LY 9; 44

Colwell, J.: Kilmore AH 1; 73

Colwell, Mr: Drumbo DN 7; 59

Colwell, Thomas: Balteagh LY 9; 44

Comaghy td: Aghalurcher FH 4; 14

Comber: Blaris AM 8; 70

Comber: Comber DN 7; 28–29, 33, 39, 41, 44

Comber: Dundonald DN 7; 65

Comber: Killyleagh DN 17; 84

Comber: Kilmood DN 7; 95–96

Comber: Misc. DN 17; 116, 120–21

Comber: Newtownards DN 7; 109

Comber: Tullynakill DN 7; 122

Comber abbey: Comber DN 7; 44

Comber abbey: Misc. DN 17; 121–22

Comber bleach green: Comber DN 7; 44

Comber bleach mill: Comber DN 7; 33, 39, 44

Comber chapel: Comber DN 7; 28, 32, 44

Comber church: Comber DN 7; 28, 32, 35–36, 44

Comber church: Misc. DN 17; 117

Comber corn mills: Comber DN 7; 33, 39, 44

Comber distilleries: Comber DN 7; 33, 39, 44

Comber distillery: Killinchy DN 7; 89

Comber flax mill: Comber DN 7; 33

Comber flax mill: Holywood DN 7; 83

Comber Glebe House: Comber DN 7; 33

Comber meeting house (P): Comber DN 7; 28, 32, 44

Comber meeting house (U): Comber DN 7; 28

Comber ph: Drumbo DN 7; 54

Comber ph: Dundonald DN 7; 64

Comber ph: Holywood DN 7; 82

Comber ph: Killinchy DN 7; 86

Comber ph: Knockbreda DN 7; 97

Comber ph: Saintfield DN 7; 116

Comber poor house: Comber DN 7; 33

Comber poor house: Holywood DN 7; 83

Comber river: Comber DN 7; 28, 30, 32, 42–43

Comber saw and wash mill: Comber DN 7; 33, 39, 44

Comber Square school: Comber DN 7; 34, 44

Comber suburbs: Comber DN 7; 37

Comber td: Comber DN 7; 39, 42–43

Comber town school [I]: Comber DN 7; 28–29, 34

Comber town school [II]: Comber DN 7; 29, 34

Comber town school [III]: Comber DN 7; 29, 34

Comber wash mill: Comber DN 7; 33, 39

Comecannaman (see Cornecanmon): Killea and Taughboyne DL 39; 80

Comer td: Cumber LY 28; 28

Comgall, abbot: Banagher LY 30; 110

Comgall, St: Aghagallon AM 21; 10

Comgall, St: Balteagh LY 9; 20

Common td: Raphoe DL 39; 125, 127

Common wood: Tamlaght Finlagan LY 25; 65

Common, Widow: Faughanvale LY 36; 16

Commons district: Ballynure AM 32; 72

Commons district: Kilroot AM 26; 80

Commons locality: Ardglass DN 17; 1

Commons Middle td: Carlingford LH 40; 58

Commons North td: Carlingford LH 40; 58

Commons quarries: Carrickfergus AM 37; 171

Commons school: Belleek FH 14; 6

Commons South td: Carlingford LH 40; 58

Commons standing stones: Carrickfergus AM 37; 86, 187

Commons td: Carrickfergus AM 37; 1, 3, 6, 8, 33, 41, 50, 77, 88, 140, 142, 171, 175–77, 186

Commons td: Killyleagh DN 17; 82

Commons well: Carrickfergus AM 37; 186

Commons, Samuel: Templecorran AM 26; 124

Compton, Rev. John: Raloo AM 32; 97–98, 118, 120, 129–30

Conagher td: Ballymoney AM 16; 25

Conagher, John: Ballee DN 17; 18
Conaghey Home well: Drumachose LY 9; 126
Conaghrud td: Tullyaughnish DL 38; 97
Conaghy, Alexander: Ahoghill AM 23; 40
Conaghy, family: Ballynure AM 32; 56
Conaghy, James: Ahoghill AM 23; 40
Conaghy, John: Billy AM 16; 64
Conall, son of Aidus: Dungiven LY 15; 64
Conaway, James: Aghanloo LY 11; 39
Conaye, Thomas: Drumachose LY 9; 66
Concra hill: Muckno MN 40; 162
Condle, Mary: Aghanloo LY 11; 39
Condon, Stephen: Coleraine LY 33; 73
Condon, Stephen: Macosquin LY 22; 101
Coneglan, Rev. James: Ballyscullion LY 6; 76–77
Conelly, family: Lissan LY 31; 91, 106
Conery, Hugh: Maghera LY 18; 42
Conery, Michael: Maghera LY 18; 45–46
Conery, Roger: Maghera LY 18; 43
Coney (Cunnea) Island: Kinawley FH 4; 113–14
Coney Burrow locality: Kilrea LY 27; 113
Coney Island: Ballyscullion LY 6; 50, 58
Coney Island: Lough Neagh AM 21; 95
Coney Island: Lough Swilly DL 38; 103, 142–43
Coney Island: Misc. DN 17; 122
Coney Island: Tartaraghan AH 1; 117, 119, 121
Coney Island fort: Ballyscullion LY 6; 60
Coney Island pier: Ardglass DN 17; 3
Coney Island td: Ardglass DN 17; 1, 5, 7
Coneyberry (Cunnyberry) td: Clonleigh DL 39; 10, 12–13, 16, 197
Congo hill: Drumglass TE 20; 44
Conic, St: Drumachose LY 9; 91
Conilogue, Rev. Bernard: Cumber LY 28; 84
Conkera td: Galloon FH 4; 95
Conkerroe fort: Devenish FH 14; 55
Conkerroe td: Devenish FH 14; 58
Conky, family: Ballynure AM 32; 56
Conla the Artificer: Magilligan LY 11; 105–06
Conlan, family: Carrickfergus AM 37; 93
Conlan, John: Desertmartin LY 31; 61
Conlan, Mathew: Newry DN 3; 99, 104
Conlan, Mrs: Newry DN 3; 98
Conlan, William: Hillsborough DN 12; 107
Conlay's Island: Killinchy DN 7; 86
Conlig (Conig) td: Misc. DN 17; 124, 126
Conlig lead mine: Rathmullan DN 17; 108
Conlig manor: Misc. DN 17; 124
Conlig school: Bangor DN 7; 22
Conlig td: Bangor DN 7; 19
Conlig td: Grey Abbey DN 7; 67
Conlin, Mathew: Tamlaght TE 20; 77, 103
Conloch, warrior: Banagher LY 30; 12
Conlon, family: Lissan LY 31; 91, 106, 106
Conlon, Matthew: Lissan LY 31; 90

Conlon, Peter: Lissan LY 31; 98, 101–02, 106
Conly, Rev.: Loughgilly AH 1; 86
Conn, family: Magilligan LY 11; 130
Conn, James: Artrea LY 6; 29, 38
Conn, James: Magherafelt LY 6; 112
Conn, James: Magilligan LY 11; 129
Conn, John: Drumachose LY 9; 133
Conn, John: Magherafelt LY 6; 112
Conn, Joseph: Magilligan LY 11; 127
Conn, King: Kirkinriola AM 23; 88
Conn, Robert: Ballyscullion LY 6; 57
Conn, Robert: Drumachose LY 9; 79, 83, 97, 104, 129–30
Conn, Samuel: Aghadowey LY 22; 5, 8, 11–12
Conn, Thomas: Ballyscullion LY 6; 57
Conn, W.: Ardglass DN 17; 9
Conn's water: Holywood DN 7; 73, 76
Conn's water bridge: Holywood DN 7; 76
Connaghan river: Raymoghy DL 39; 140, 144
Connaghan's bridge: Raymoghy DL 39; 132, 135
Connaghligar (see Connaught): Ahoghill AM 23; 22
Connal, giant: Dungiven LY 15; 92
Connaught: Aghagallon AM 21; 21
Connaught: Aghalurcher FH 4; 12
Connaught: Banagher LY 30; 71, 96
Connaught: Blaris AM 8; 88
Connaught: Cappagh TE 5; 22
Connaught: Clondermot LY 34; 71, 75
Connaught: Cumber LY 28; 23
Connaught: Drumhome DL 39; 61
Connaught: Dunaghy AM 13; 12
Connaught: Dungiven LY 15; 34
Connaught: Emlaghfad SO 40; 180
Connaught: Errigal LY 27; 47
Connaught: Faughanvale LY 36; 54
Connaught: Inishkeel DL 39; 69
Connaught: Killymard DL 39; 104–05
Connaught: Kilmacteige SO 40; 186, 192
Connaught: Misc. FH 4; 133
Connaught: Misc. LY 31; 134
Connaught: Tullaghobegley DL 39; 172
Connaught coalfield: Killesher FH 14; 83
Connaught Ligar school: Ahoghill AM 23; 22, 49
Connaught Ligar Sunday school: Ahoghill AM 23; 46
Connaul, giant: Balteagh LY 9; 35
Connell, David: Magilligan LY 11; 128, 135–36
Connell, family: Errigal LY 27; 41
Connell, John: Ballymoney AM 16; 25
Connell, John: Magilligan LY 11; 129
Connell, Rose: Carrickfergus AM 37; 129
Connell, son of Niall: Faughanvale LY 36; 47
Connell, William: Aghanloo LY 11; 21
Connelly, Patt: Ballynascreen LY 31; 22
Conner, family: Culfeightrin AM 24; 59

Connery, Andrew: Carrickfergus AM 37; 128

Connery, Charles: Ballynascreen LY 31; 21

Connery, John: Ballynascreen LY 31; 21

Conningham, John: Drummaul AM 19; 92

Connoll, John: Kilmacteige SO 40; 193

Connolly, Charles: Newry DN 3; 99–100, 104

Connolly, Col: Enniskillen FH 4; 80

Connolly, Col: Rossorry FH 14; 115

Connolly, Col.: Belleek FH 14; 6

Connolly, Col.: Killesher FH 14; 88

Connolly, Col.: Trory FH 14; 131

Connolly, family: Carnmoney AM 2; 102

Connolly, family: Currin MN 40; 94

Connolly, family: Drumhome DL 39; 58

Connolly, George: Duneane AM 19; 123

Connolly, J.: Faughanvale LY 36; 22–23

Connolly, Jane: Carrickfergus AM 37; 111

Connolly, John: Ballycor AM 32; 10

Connolly, Matthew: Maghera LY 18; 80

Connolly, Mr (Killygordon): Donaghmore DL 39; 29

Connolly, Mrs C.: Newry DN 3; 104

Connolly, Owen: Nilteen AM 35; 89, 103

Connolly, Rev. Luke: Ramoan AM 24; 86, 90, 93

Connolly, Richard: Carrickfergus AM 37; 115

Connolly, Thomas: Maghera LY 18; 52–53

Connolly, Thomas: Tamlaght Finlagan LY 25; 105

Connolly, Widow: Ballymoney AM 16; 17

Connolly, William: Drummaul AM 19; 71

Connor: Antrim AM 29; 4, 21–22, 50

Connor: Ballyclug AM 23; 61

Connor: Ballylinny AM 32; 14

Connor: Ballyrobert AM 2; 20

Connor: Ballywalter AM 2; 29

Connor: Connor AM 19; 16–17, 19–23, 26, 29–30

Connor: Donegore AM 29; 102, 107–09, 115, 119, 128, 132, 134

Connor: Drummaul AM 19; 52

Connor: Kilbride AM 29; 139, 146, 154

Connor: Kirkinriola AM 23; 122

Connor: Magherafelt LY 6; 95

Connor: Nilteen AM 35; 85, 90

Connor: Rashee AM 32; 136

Connor: Shilvodan AM 19; 127, 130, 135

Connor: Templepatrick AM 35; 111, 114

Connor [or Connory], Patrick: Ballynascreen LY 31; 10, 24

Connor abbey: Connor AM 19; 21, 29

Connor abbey: Doagh AM 29; 68, 78

Connor abbey: Donegore AM 29; 114, 122

Connor abbey: Shilvodan AM 19; 135

Connor bogs: Kilbride AM 29; 143–44

Connor Castle: Connor AM 19; 21

Connor cathedral: Connor AM 19; 21

Connor cathedral: Ramoan AM 24; 102

Connor cathedral: Shilvodan AM 19; 135

Connor church: Connor AM 19; 16, 18, 21, 29

Connor church: Kirkinriola AM 23; 94

Connor city: Shilvodan AM 19; 135

Connor corn mill: Connor AM 19; 17, 22

Connor deanery: Carrickfergus AM 37; 10, 69, 79, 100

Connor deanery: Mallusk AM 2; 111, 114

Connor deanery: Raloo AM 32; 80, 98, 107

Connor diocese: Aghagallon AM 21; 1

Connor diocese: Aghalee AM 21; 26

Connor diocese: Ahoghill AM 23; 1

Connor diocese: Ardclinis AM 13; 1

Connor diocese: Ballintoy AM 24; 10

Connor diocese: Ballycor AM 32; 3

Connor diocese: Ballynure AM 32; 32, 38

Connor diocese: Ballyrashane LY 22; 55

Connor diocese: Camlin AM 21; 60, 65

Connor diocese: Carnmoney AM 2; 56, 89

Connor diocese: Carrickfergus AM 37; 56, 68–69, 79, 135, 146, 172

Connor diocese: Coleraine LY 33; 153

Connor diocese: Derrykeighan AM 16; 82

Connor diocese: Doagh AM 29; 63

Connor diocese: Donegore AM 29; 101, 106

Connor diocese: Dunaghy AM 13; 12

Connor diocese: Duneane AM 19; 94

Connor diocese: Finvoy AM 23; 67

Connor diocese: Glenavy AM 21; 77, 84

Connor diocese: Glynn AM 26; 1, 11

Connor diocese: Island Magee AM 10; 86

Connor diocese: Killagan AM 23; 79

Connor diocese: Kirkinriola AM 23; 88, 93

Connor diocese: Layd AM 13; 36

Connor diocese: Magheramesk AM 21; 112

Connor diocese: Nilteen AM 35; 84

Connor diocese: Rathlin Island AM 24; 127, 132

Connor diocese: Templecorran AM 26; 101

Connor diocese: Templepatrick AM 35; 108

Connor diocese: Tullyrusk AM 21; 131

Connor dispensary: Connor AM 19; 24–26, 30

Connor dispensary: Shilvodan AM 19; 132

Connor district: Muckamore AM 35; 81

Connor forts: Connor AM 19; 18, 21

Connor Glebe House: Connor AM 19; 18, 29–30

Connor Glebe House: Kilmore AH 1; 64

Connor meeting house: Connor AM 19; 16, 18, 21, 24, 26, 29

Connor meeting house: Shilvodan AM 19; 127

Connor meeting house school: Connor AM 19; 26

Connor monastery: Connor AM 19; 21

Connor old church: Ahoghill AM 23; 25

Connor old church: Culfeightrin AM 24; 70

Connor ph: Ahoghill AM 23; 1, 18

Connor ph: Antrim AM 29; 1, 27
Connor ph: Ballyclug AM 23; 52–55, 60–61, 65
Connor ph: Ballywalter AM 2; 27
Connor ph: Doagh AM 29; 79
Connor ph: Donegore AM 29; 101–02, 104–05, 115, 119, 122, 133
Connor ph: Drummaul AM 19; 33, 36
Connor ph: Glenwhirry AM 32; 74–75
Connor ph: Kilbride AM 29; 135, 137–38
Connor ph: Killead AM 35; 25
Connor ph: Kirkinriola AM 23; 102
Connor ph: Misc. AM 10; 129
Connor ph: Muckamore AM 35; 70
Connor ph: Nilteen AM 35; 84, 88
Connor ph: Rashee AM 32; 135
Connor ph: Shilvodan AM 19; 127–28, 133, 135
Connor ph: Templepatrick AM 35; 145
Connor quarries: Antrim AM 29; 17
Connor schools: Connor AM 19; 24–25, 27, 30
Connor spring: Connor AM 19; 19–20
Connor standing stone: Connor AM 19; 29
Connor td: Connor AM 19; 21, 29
Connor vicarage: Killagan AM 23; 79
Connor, Archibald: Carrickfergus AM 37; 158
Connor, Bernard: Balteagh LY 9; 12, 24
Connor, Charles: Ahoghill AM 23; 49
Connor, Charles [I]: Carrickfergus AM 37; 111, 195
Connor, Charles [II]: Carrickfergus AM 37; 124
Connor, David: Blaris DN 12; 42
Connor, Dr: Newry DN 3; 99, 103
Connor, Edward: Kilmacteige SO 40; 194, 194
Connor, Eliza: Bovevagh LY 25; 60
Connor, family: Ahoghill AM 23; 25
Connor, family: Kilcronaghan LY 31; 68
Connor, family: Killelagh LY 27; 99
Connor, family: Magheramesk AM 21; 124
Connor, Hamilton: Bovevagh LY 25; 7, 36, 38
Connor, Henry: Carrickfergus AM 37; 123
Connor, Hugh: Donegore AM 29; 130
Connor, James: Dunaghy AM 13; 24
Connor, James: Loughguile AM 13; 67
Connor, James: Tamlaght Finlagan LY 25; 115
Connor, John: Banagher LY 30; 89
Connor, John: Maghera LY 18; 81
Connor, John [I]: Carrickfergus AM 37; 76
Connor, John [II]: Carrickfergus AM 37; 122, 125
Connor, John [III]: Carrickfergus AM 37; 193
Connor, Margret: Bovevagh LY 25; 60
Connor, Matilda: Tamlaght Finlagan LY 25; 119
Connor, Michael: Balteagh LY 9; 29, 34, 36
Connor, Mrs (Derryard): Bovevagh LY 25; 45
Connor, Robert: Carrickfergus AM 37; 158
Connor, Robert: Tamlaght Finlagan LY 25; 114
Connor, Susana [I]: Carrickfergus AM 37; 158
Connor, Susana [II]: Carrickfergus AM 37; 158

Connor, William (Jnr): Carrickfergus AM 37; 158
Connor, William (Snr): Carrickfergus AM 37; 158
Connor, William: Drumachose LY 9; 132
Connor, William: Hillsborough DN 12; 107
Connor, William [I]: Carrickfergus AM 37; 158
Conolan, Michael: Lissan LY 31; 99
Conolly, family: Carnmoney AM 2; 76
Conolly, family: Drumachose LY 9; 74, 82
Conolly, family: Magilligan LY 11; 83
Conolly, family: Tamlaght Finlagan LY 25; 105
Conolly, George: Duneane AM 19; 123
Conolly, Mr: Drumachose LY 9; 90
Conolly, Mr: Misc. LY 31; 129
Conolly, Pakenham: Kilbarron DL 39; 74
Conolly, Thomas: Drumachose LY 9; 73
Conolly, Thomas: Magilligan LY 11; 83
Conor, son of Fergal: Clondermot LY 34; 50–51
Conroy, Andrew: Maghera LY 18; 8, 68
Conroy, Mary: Maghera LY 18; 78
Conroy, Patrick: Ballymore AH 1; 7
Conroy, Thomas: Maghera LY 18; 8, 68
Constance lough: Drummaul AM 19; 79
Contham Head: Billy AM 16; 41
Convent locality: Kilmacteige SO 40; 188
Convery, Ambrose: Kilcronaghan LY 31; 85
Convery, Bernard: Maghera LY 18; 81
Convery, Bridget: Maghera LY 18; 69
Convery, Edward: Maghera LY 18; 81
Convery, family: Maghera LY 18; 14, 24, 48, 74
Convery, Frank: Maghera LY 18; 81
Convery, Henry [I]: Maghera LY 18; 81
Convery, Henry [II]: Maghera LY 18; 81
Convery, Hugh: Maghera LY 18; 81
Convery, James [I]: Maghera LY 18; 81
Convery, James [II]: Maghera LY 18; 81
Convery, John (Jnr): Maghera LY 18; 81
Convery, John (Snr): Maghera LY 18; 81
Convery, John [I]: Maghera LY 18; 81
Convery, Michael: Maghera LY 18; 81
Convery, Nicholas: Maghera LY 18; 81
Convery, Patrick [I]: Maghera LY 18; 59
Convery, Patrick [II]: Maghera LY 18; 81
Convery, Peter: Maghera LY 18; 54, 80
Convery, Rose: Ballynascreen LY 31; 14, 21
Convery, William [I]: Maghera LY 18; 81
Convery, William [II]: Maghera LY 18; 81
Convey, family: Drumachose LY 9; 92
Convill, Anthony: Artrea LY 6; 33
Convoy: Convoy DL 39; 18
Convoy: Leck DL 39; 116
Convoy: Raphoe DL 39; 130
Convoy chapel: Convoy DL 39; 18
Convoy chapel: Raphoe DL 39; 130
Convoy chapel graveyard: Raphoe DL 39; 130
Convoy church: Convoy DL 39; 18

Convoy church: Raphoe DL 39; 130
Convoy corn mill: Convoy DL 39; 18–19
Convoy Demesne td: Convoy DL 39; 20
Convoy flax mill: Convoy DL 39; 18–19
Convoy forges: Convoy DL 39; 18
Convoy graveyard: Raphoe DL 39; 130
Convoy meeting house: Convoy DL 39; 18
Convoy meeting house: Raphoe DL 39; 130
Convoy meeting house graveyard: Raphoe DL 39; 130
Convoy old meeting house: Raphoe DL 39; 130
Convoy ph: Clonleigh DL 39; 1, 14
Convoy ph: Conwal DL 39; 24
Convoy ph: Donaghmore DL 39; 28, 32
Convoy ph: Kilteevoge DL 39; 111
Convoy ph: Leck DL 39; 115
Convoy ph: Raphoe DL 39; 121
Convoy post office: Convoy DL 39; 18
Convoy school: Convoy DL 39; 23
Convoy Townparks td: Convoy DL 39; 20
Conwal Brae: Leck DL 39; 118
Conwal ph: Clonleigh DL 39; 1
Conwal ph: Convoy DL 39; 18
Conwal ph: Kilteevoge DL 39; 111
Conwal ph: Leck DL 39; 115–16
Conwal ph: Raphoe DL 39; 129
Conwal ph: Tullaghobegley DL 39; 172
Conwal ph: Tullyaughnish DL 38; 84
Conway water: Bovevagh LY 25; 22
Conway, Bishop: Killelagh LY 27; 102
Conway, Bishop: Maghera LY 18; 69
Conway, Bishop: Misc. LY 31; 137–38
Conway, David: Errigal LY 27; 54, 66
Conway, Earl: Ballinderry AM 21; 56
Conway, Earl: Blaris AM 8; 22
Conway, Edward: Tullyrusk AM 21; 131
Conway, family: Ballinderry AM 21; 43
Conway, family: Ballintoy AM 24; 20
Conway, family: Ballynascreen LY 31; 12
Conway, family: Camlin AM 21; 62, 68
Conway, family: Glenavy AM 21; 80, 84, 86
Conway, family: Magheramesk AM 21; 117
Conway, family: Tullyrusk AM 21; 131, 135
Conway, Fulk: Blaris AM 8; 3–4, 7–8
Conway, Fulk: Blaris DN 12; 32
Conway, Fulk: Tullyrusk AM 21; 131
Conway, Henry: Ballyscullion LY 6; 58
Conway, Hugh: Errigal LY 27; 60, 68
Conway, James: Bovevagh LY 25; 27
Conway, James: Carrickfergus AM 37; 148
Conway, Lord: Blaris AM 8; 25, 87–88
Conway, Lord: Blaris DN 12; 33
Conway, Lord: Camlin AM 21; 60
Conway, Lord: Lambeg AM 8; 138
Conway, Lord: Newry DN 3; 65

Conway, Mrs: Saul DN 17; 113
Conway, Patt: Banagher LY 30; 72, 81, 100
Conway, poet: Misc. LY 31; 136
Conway, Rev. Christopher: Misc. LY 31; 138
Conway, Rev. Thomas: Lissan LY 31; 104
Conway, T.J.: Banagher LY 30; 22, 119, 131
Conway, William: Drumachose LY 9; 132
Conway, William. Errigal LY 27; 65
Conway's fort: Errigal LY 27; 68
Conway's House: Magheramesk AM 21; 117
Conwell, Eliza: Ahoghill AM 23; 37
Conwell, Mr: Artrea LY 6; 34
Conygam, family: Newry DN 3; 108
Conyngham, Col: Inishkeel DL 39; 70
Conyngham, family: Lissan LY 31; 91, 106
Conyngham, George: Artrea LY 6; 32
Conyngham, Marquis of: Donaghmore DL 39; 33, 37–39
Conyngham, Marquis of: Inishkeel DL 39; 67
Conyngham, Marquis of: Killymard DL 39; 98, 100–01
Conyngham, Mr: Artrea LY 6; 33
Conyngham, Mrs: Kilmegan DN 3; 59
Conyngham, W.L.: Artrea LY 6; 8, 15, 31–32
Conyngham, W.L.: Faughanvale LY 36; 40
Conyngham, W.L.: Lissan LY 31; 92, 103
Conyngham, W.L.: Tamlaght TE 20; 93, 96–100, 105–07, 118–20, 123, 125, 131–35
Cooas corn mill: Aughnamullen MN 40; 72
Cooas td: Aughnamullen MN 40; 75
Cooben lough: Aghalurcher FH 4; 3
Cooby bog: Donaghedy TE 5; 89
Cooch, family: Racavan AM 13; 100
Cooey Baughlagh's Castle: Bovevagh LY 25; 7, 10, 35–36
Cooey Baughlagh's well: Bovevagh LY 25; 10
Cooey-na-Gall: Banagher LY 30; 5, 93
Cooey-na-Gall: Dungiven LY 15; 28, 30, 39–40, 46, 54, 56, 84, 104
Cooey-na-Gall monument: Dungiven LY 15; 101
Cooey-na-Gall tomb: Dungiven LY 15; 56–58, 110
Cook, Andrew: Kilwaughter AM 10; 122
Cook, Ann: Drumachose LY 9; 132
Cook, Archibald: Tamlaght TE 20; 78
Cook, Bell: Drumachose LY 9; 132
Cook, Daniel: Drumachose LY 9; 132
Cook, Edward: Banagher LY 30; 79
Cook, Hugh: Ballynure AM 32; 72
Cook, James (Jnr): Drumachose LY 9; 132
Cook, James (Snr): Drumachose LY 9; 132
Cook, James: Carrickfergus AM 37; 194
Cook, James: Dungiven LY 15; 46
Cook, James: Kilwaughter AM 10; 122
Cook, Jane (Jnr): Drumachose LY 9; 132
Cook, Jane (Snr): Drumachose LY 9; 132

Cook, Jes: Banagher LY 30; 78
Cook, John: Drumachose LY 9; 61
Cook, John: Kilwaughter AM 10; 122
Cook, Kittyann: Drumachose LY 9; 132
Cook, Lawrence: Kilmacteige SO 40; 193
Cook, William: Ballynure AM 32; 72
Cook, William: Ballyscullion LY 6; 57
Cook, William: Kilwaughter AM 10; 122
Cooke, Anne: Banagher LY 30; 102–03, 105, 107
Cooke, E.: Enniskillen FH 4; 82
Cooke, Esther: Duneane AM 19; 123
Cooke, George: Dungiven LY 15; 42
Cooke, Henry: Maghera LY 18; 22, 68
Cooke, John: Drummaul AM 19; 87
Cooke, Lady: Dungiven LY 15; 30, 42–43, 46, 48,
    60, 104
Cooke, Rev. Henry: Donegore AM 29; 126, 129
Cooke, Rev. Henry: Duneane AM 19; 114
Cooke, Rev. Henry: Templepatrick AM 35; 110
Cooke, Sally (Jnr): Duneane AM 19; 123
Cooke, Sally (Snr): Duneane AM 19; 123
Cooke, W.J. (Jnr): Duneane AM 19; 123
Cooke, W.J. (Snr): Duneane AM 19; 123
Cooke, William: Ballyscullion LY 6; 57
Cookstown: Aghadowey LY 22; 22, 24
Cookstown: Antrim AM 29; 39, 48
Cookstown: Arboe LY 6; 1
Cookstown: Artrea TE 20; 10
Cookstown: Ballinderry TE 20; 12–13
Cookstown: Ballyclog TE 20; 17
Cookstown: Ballynascreen LY 31; 2, 6–7, 16, 20
Cookstown: Banagher LY 30; 5, 14, 27, 31, 118,
    120, 131
Cookstown: Bovevagh LY 25; 24
Cookstown: Cumber LY 28; 23, 109, 111, 113–15
Cookstown: Desertcreat TE 20; 32, 34, 36, 36
Cookstown: Desertlyn LY 31; 35, 37, 41
Cookstown: Donaghenry TE 20; 37
Cookstown: Drummaul AM 19; 34, 73, 81
Cookstown: Duneane AM 19; 95, 99
Cookstown: Dungiven LY 15; 26, 53, 67
Cookstown: Kilcronaghan LY 31; 64, 69, 86–87
Cookstown: Kildress TE 20; 58–61
Cookstown: Lissan LY 31; 90, 92, 94–96, 99, 103
Cookstown: Lissan TE 20; 69
Cookstown: Magherafelt LY 6; 86, 90–91
Cookstown: Misc. LY 31; 116–17, 130–31, 134
Cookstown: Pomeroy TE 20; 70, 72
Cookstown: Tamlaght TE 20; 73, 78–82, 91, 95, 99,
    102, 114, 122, 127, 137
Cookstown: Templecorran AM 26; 128
Cookstown: Tullyniskan TE 20; 139–41
Cookstown bog: Killea and Taughboyne DL 39; 80
Cookstown dispensary: Lissan LY 31; 106
Cookstown locality: Taughboyne DL 39; 155

Cookstown meeting house: Lissan LY 31; 89
Cookstown quarries: Artrea TE 20; 6
Cookstown td: Misc. DN 17; 125
Cool (see Coole)
Cooladawson td: Donaghmore DL 39; 36
Cooladerry td: Raphoe DL 39; 125
Coolafinny Lower td: Faughanvale LY 36; 17
Coolafinny td: Faughanvale LY 36; 53, 56, 60, 68,
    72, 83, 93, 98
Coolafinny Upper td: Faughanvale LY 36; 17
Coolafinny wood: Faughanvale LY 36; 83
Coolagery (Coolgeary) td: Errigal Keerogue TE 20;
    51, 57
Coolagh district: Kinawley FH 4; 123
Coolagh quarry: Faughanvale LY 36; 93
Coolagh td: Faughanvale LY 36; 17, 53, 56, 68, 72,
    83, 93, 98
Coolaghy corn mill: Drumragh TE 5; 110
Coolaghy flax mill: Drumragh TE 5; 110
Coolaghy Glebe td: Raphoe DL 39; 125
Coolaghy school: Ardstraw TE 5; 13
Coolaghy td: Drumragh TE 5; 110
Coolaghy td: Raphoe DL 39; 125
Coolaha school: Killanny MN 40; 135
Coolaness (Knockrow) school: Derryvullan FH 14;
    35
Coolany td: Killoran and Kilvarnet SO 40; 183
Coolaran td: Aghalurcher FH 4; 13
Coolatee td: Clonleigh DL 39; 12, 16, 197
Coolaughty td: Magheraculmoney FH 14; 112–13
Coolavannagh mill: Longfield TE 5; 128
Coolavannagh td: Longfield TE 5; 128
Coolavin barony: Misc. SO 40; 198–99
Coolaward harbour: Lough Swilly DL 38; 115–16
Coolbanagher (Laois): Banagher LY 30; 110
Coolbeg creek: Kilbarron DL 39; 78
Coolbrick (see Coolbuck): Derryvullan FH 14; 46
Coolbuck cairn: Derryvullan FH 14; 42
Coolbuck giant's grave: Derryvullan FH 14; 42
Coolbuck td: Derryvullan FH 14; 42, 46
Coolcoghill td: Aghavea FH 4; 23
Coolcollict school: Donagh MN 40; 100–01
Coolcorraugh village: Kilmacteige SO 40; 193
Coolcoscreaghan bogs: Errigal LY 27; 54
Coolcoscreaghan bridge: Errigal LY 27; 41, 59
Coolcoscreaghan cairn: Errigal LY 27; 44
Coolcoscreaghan fort: Errigal LY 27; 43, 72–73
Coolcoscreaghan giant's grave: Errigal LY 27; 43
Coolcoscreaghan quarry: Errigal LY 27; 90
Coolcoscreaghan td: Errigal LY 27; 44, 66, 73, 80,
    85–86, 89–90, 92
Coolcoscreaghan td: Misc. LY 36; 111–12
Coolcoscreaghan well: Errigal LY 27; 54
Coolcran td: Enniskillen FH 4; 74, 82
Coolcrannel school: Aghalurcher FH 4; 11

Coolderry chapel of ease: Magheracloone MN 40; 138

Coolderry House: Magheracloone MN 40; 138

Coolderry spring: Magheross MN 40; 143

Coolderry td: Donaghmoyne MN 40; 108

Coolderry td: Killanny MN 40; 132

Coolderry td: Magheracloone MN 40; 139

Coolderry td: Magheross MN 40; 147–48, 153

Coole barony: Drummully FH 4; 34, 36–37, 39

Coole barony: Galloon FH 4; 87, 89, 92

Coole church: Carnmoney AM 2; 69

Coole city: Carnmoney AM 2; 50–51, 66, 68–70, 73, 93–94, 96, 98–99, 102

Coole graveyard: Carnmoney AM 2; 67–68

Coole hill: Derrykeighan AM 16; 80

Coole hill: Ramoan AM 24; 89

Coole lough: Enniskillen FH 4; 68

Coole lough: Mevagh DL 38; 55

Coole manor: Derryvullan FH 14; 40

Coole old church: Carnmoney AM 2; 44–45, 56, 64, 66–68

Coole td: Derrykeighan AM 16; 95

Coole td: Macosquin LY 22; 99

Coolecoscreaghan (see Coolcoscreaghan): Misc. LY 36; 112

Coolecranagh district: Clondermot LY 34; 59–60

Coolecronagh (see Coolecranagh): Clondermot LY 34; 60

Coolenbiudh (see Cullion Boy): Donegal DL 39; 43

Coolenbuidh (see Cullion Boy): Donegal DL 39; 43

Coolesker bridge: Clogherny TE 20; 27

Coolesker corn mill: Clogherny TE 20; 27

Coolesker forts: Clogherny TE 20; 28

Coolessan (Coollessan) td: Drumachose LY 9; 52, 87, 96, 134

Coolessan ford: Drumachose LY 9; 83

Coolessan td: Tamlaght Finlagan LY 25; 80

Cooley district: Newry DN 3; 64

Cooley Glebe House: Moville DL 38; 74

Cooley old church: Moville DL 38; 74

Cooley school: Moville DL 38; 74, 77

Cooley td: Moville DL 38; 73, 73, 75

Cooleyhill House: Ballymore AH 1; 11

Cooleyhill td: Ballymore AH 1; 14–15

Coolfore td: Magheross MN 40; 148

Coolgarron td: Magheracross FH 14; 102

Coolhill Beg td: Kinawley FH 4; 121

Coolhill More td: Kinawley FH 4; 121

Coolhill td: Aghadowey LY 22; 11

Coolinfin (Coolinfinn) td: Kinawley FH 4; 86, 110

Coolinfin glebe: Killesher FH 14; 86

Coolistrane locality: Clondermot LY 34; 58

Coolkeenaght td: Faughanvale LY 36; 17, 53, 56, 68, 72, 83, 93

Coolkeenaght td: Tamlaght Finlagan LY 25; 72–73

Coolkeeragh td: Longfield TE 5; 132

Coolkeeragh td: Tamlaght Finlagan LY 25; 105

Coolkenny (Coolykenny) td: Ramoan AM 24; 96

Coolkenny hill: Ramoan AM 24; 91

Coolkenny meeting house: Ramoan AM 24; 89, 96

Coolkernan td: Loughguile AM 13; 76

Coolkill (see Cockhill): Tynan AH 1; 131

Coolkill East school: Ematris MN 40; 117

Coolkill hill: Ematris MN 40; 112

Coolkill lough: Ematris MN 40; 112, 116

Coolkill Point: Lough Swilly DL 38; 110

Coolmaghery td: Donaghedy TE 5; 91

Coolmaghra pool: Ballintoy AM 24; 12

Coolmaghra standing stone [I]: Ballintoy AM 24; 32

Coolmaghra standing stone [II]: Ballintoy AM 24; 32

Coolmaghra td: Ballintoy AM 24; 32

Coolmillish td: Mullaghbrack AH 1; 94

Coolmore (Co. Cork): Ballyscullion LY 6; 59

Coolnacolpach (see Coolnacolpagh): Cumber LY 28; 66

Coolnacolpagh bridge: Cumber LY 28; 11

Coolnacolpagh flax mill: Cumber LY 28; 122

Coolnacolpagh td: Cumber LY 28; 66, 68–69, 111, 117, 122, 125

Coolnacran td: Aghaderg DN 12; 10

Coolnacrunaght (Coolnacranaght) td: Skirts of Urney and Ardstraw TE 5; 138, 140

Coolnacrunaght corn mill: Skirts of Urney and Ardstraw TE 5; 138

Coolnady (see Culnady): Maghera LY 18; 2

Coolnafree locality: Clondermot LY 34; 64

Coolnagappoge hamlet: Culfeightrin AM 24; 39, 45

Coolnagoppag (see Coolnagappoge): Culfeightrin AM 24; 39

Coolnagrans td: Aghavea FH 4; 17

Coolnamonan (Culnamurran) td: Banagher LY 30; 22–23, 35–36, 61–62, 67, 95–96, 100, 103, 109, 113, 117, 122, 126–27, 129, 131

Coolnamonan (see Coolymann): Desertoghill LY 27; 8

Coolnamonan Castle: Dungiven LY 15; 33

Coolnamonan fort: Banagher LY 30; 75–77

Coolnamonan quarry: Banagher LY 30; 127

Coolnamonan standing stone: Banagher LY 30; 46, 75, 77

Coolnamuneen (see Coolnamonan)

Coolnamunnen (see Coolnamonan)

Coolnashanton td: Derrybrusk FH 4; 30

Coolnasillagh corn mill: Errigal LY 27; 58

Coolnasillagh cromlech: Ballynascreen LY 31; 31

Coolnasillagh graveyard: Ballynascreen LY 31; 31

Coolnasillagh kiln: Errigal LY 27; 92

Coolnasillagh mountain: Ballynascreen LY 31; 1–2

Coolnasillagh quarry: Errigal LY 27; 90

Coolnasillagh river: Errigal LY 27; 60
Coolnasillagh school: Errigal LY 27; 50
Coolnasillagh td: Errigal LY 27; 60, 65, 80–81, 86, 90, 92
Coolnasillagh td: Galloon FH 4; 95
Coolnasillagh td: Misc. LY 31; 142–43
Coolnegratten td: Donaghmoyne MN 40; 107
Coolnemony hill: Killanny MN 40; 130
Coolrakelly td: Aghavea FH 4; 23, 25
Coolrecuill td: Kilmacteige SO 40; 186, 188, 193, 196
Coolrecuill wood: Kilmacteige SO 40; 186, 194
Coolrecull (see Coolrecuill): Kilmacteige SO 40; 196
Coolsallagh mill [I]: Dromore DN 12; 72, 78
Coolsallagh mill [II]: Dromore DN 12; 72, 78
Coolsallagh td: Dromore DN 12; 72–73, 76, 78
Coolsara (see Coolsaragh)
Coolsaragh (Coolsarragh) td: Kilcronaghan LY 31; 67, 75, 82, 84, 118, 141–42
Coolsaragh fort: Misc. LY 31; 119
Coolsaragh moss: Misc. LY 31; 118
Coolsarragh bog: Kilcronaghan LY 31; 64, 69
Coolsarragh fort: Kilcronaghan LY 31; 86
Coolshinny (Coolshinney) td: Magherafelt LY 6; 94–95, 101, 110, 112
Coolshinny school: Magherafelt LY 6; 102
Coolshinny Sunday school: Magherafelt LY 6; 102
Coolsythe td: Drummaul AM 19; 89–91
Cooltrain church: Aghalurcher FH 4; 6
Cooltrain td: Aghalurcher FH 4; 6
Cooltrain td: Magheracross FH 14; 102
Cooltrim td: Aughnamullen MN 40; 75
Cooltrimeagish td: Aughnamullen MN 40; 75
Coolymann td: Desertoghill LY 27; 8, 17–18, 20
Coolyramer td: Desertoghill LY 27; 19
Coolyround td: Cleenish FH 14; 29
Coolyslinn td: Urney DL 39; 181
Coolyveally td: Culfeightrin AM 24; 38
Coolyvenny (Coolyvenney) td: Aghadowey LY 22; 30, 32
Coolyvenny bog: Macosquin LY 22; 78
Coolyvenny cave: Macosquin LY 22; 110
Coolyvenny cove: Aghadowey LY 22; 30, 32
Coolyvenny gravel pit: Macosquin LY 22; 98
Coolyvenny school: Macosquin LY 22; 92–93, 98
Coolyvenny Sunday school: Macosquin LY 22; 93
Coolyvenny td: Macosquin LY 22; 77, 96, 98
Coolyvenny td: Misc. LY 36; 111
Cooneen corn mill: Aghalurcher FH 4; 3, 8
Cooneen school: Aghalurcher FH 4; 11
Cooneen td: Aghalurcher FH 4; 11, 13–14
Coonien (see Cooneen): Aghalurcher FH 4; 3
Cooper, Archibald: Muckamore AM 35; 78
Cooper, Capt.: Galloon FH 4; 104

Cooper, Daniel: Ballymoney AM 16; 17
Cooper, David: Hillsborough DN 12; 107
Cooper, Ellen: Carrickfergus AM 37; 117
Cooper, family: Drumbeg AM 8; 123
Cooper, family: Ramoan AM 24; 107
Cooper, family: Templepatrick AM 35; 145
Cooper, George: Killowen LY 33; 159
Cooper, James: Killead AM 35; 50
Cooper, James: Muckamore AM 35; 78
Cooper, John: Carnmoney AM 2; 48, 89
Cooper, John: Newtownards DN 7; 104
Cooper, John: Templepatrick AM 35; 147
Cooper, John [I]: Drummaul AM 19; 82, 84
Cooper, John [II]: Drummaul AM 19; 89–90
Cooper, Messrs John and W.H.: Carnmoney AM 2; 52, 85, 92
Cooper, Mr: Boho FH 14; 8
Cooper, Samuel: Dunboe LY 11; 73
Cooper, Thomas: Hillsborough DN 12; 107
Cooper, W.H.: Carnmoney AM 2; 48
Cooper's Island: Kilmacteige SO 40; 187, 195
Cooper's mills (see Monkstown print–works): Carnmoney AM 2; 85
Coopershill House: Boho FH 14; 8
Coose school: Tullylish DN 12; 144
Coose td: Tullylish DN 12; 143
Coot, Richard: Misc. FH 4; 133
Coote, Charles: Coleraine LY 33; 100
Coote, Charles: Derryvullan FH 14; 38
Coote, Charles: Drumgoon CN 40; 6, 8, 10
Coote, Charles: Dungiven LY 15; 59
Coote, Charles: Killdrumsherdan CN 40; 37
Coote, Charles: Laragh CN 40; 42
Coote, Charles: Leck DL 39; 118
Coote, Charles: Tomregan FH 4; 128–29
Coote, Thomas: Aghabog MN 40; 67
Coote, Thomas: Drumgoon CN 40; 8
Cootehill: Aughnamullen MN 40; 70–71, 73, 75–76
Cootehill: Ballybay MN 40; 81, 83
Cootehill: Clondermot LY 34; 30
Cootehill: Currin MN 40; 86, 89–90, 92, 94
Cootehill: Drumgoon CN 40; 3–4, 7–11
Cootehill: Drummully FH 4; 37
Cootehill: Drung CN 40; 20–21, 23
Cootehill: Ematris MN 40; 112, 114–16
Cootehill: Killdrumsherdan CN 40; 31, 33–35, 37
Cootehill: Laragh CN 40; 41–43
Cootehill: Muckno MN 40; 166
Cootehill bank: Drumgoon CN 40; 4–5
Cootehill barrack: Drumgoon CN 40; 5, 8
Cootehill chapel (C): Drumgoon CN 40; 4, 6, 11
Cootehill chapel (M): Drumgoon CN 40; 4–5
Cootehill church: Drumgoon CN 40; 4, 6, 9, 11
Cootehill court house: Drumgoon CN 40; 4–5, 8
Cootehill court house: Drung CN 40; 22

Cootehill dispensary: Currin MN 40; 92
Cootehill dispensary: Drumgoon CN 40; 8–9
Cootehill dispensary: Drung CN 40; 22
Cootehill dispensary: Killdrumsherdan CN 40; 35
Cootehill graveyard: Drumgoon CN 40; 1, 4
Cootehill infants school: Drumgoon CN 40; 11
Cootehill market house: Drumgoon CN 40; 4–5, 8
Cootehill mecting house (Mor.): Drumgoon CN 40;
  4, 6
Cootehill meeting house (P): Drumgoon CN 40; 4–5
Cootehill meeting house (Q): Drumgoon CN 40; 4
Cootehill meeting house (S): Drumgoon CN 40; 4–5
Cootehill old church: Drumgoon CN 40; 1, 4, 6
Cootehill reading room: Drumgoon CN 40; 5
Cootehill savings bank: Drumgoon CN 40; 5
Cootehill school [I]: Drumgoon CN 40; 11
Cootehill school [II]: Drumgoon CN 40; 11
Cootehill school [III]: Drumgoon CN 40; 11
Cootehill school [IV]: Drumgoon CN 40; 11
Cootehill school [IX]: Drumgoon CN 40; 11
Cootehill school [V]: Drumgoon CN 40; 11
Cootehill school [VI]: Drumgoon CN 40; 11
Cootehill school [VII]: Drumgoon CN 40; 11
Cootehill school [VIII]: Drumgoon CN 40; 11
Cootehill school [X]: Drumgoon CN 40; 11
Cootehill school [XI]: Drumgoon CN 40; 11
Cootehill shambles: Drumgoon CN 40; 4
Cootehill slaughterhouse: Drumgoon CN 40; 5
Cootehill Town Parks: Drumgoon CN 40; 5
Cootinaglugg district: Ballyaghran LY 33; 14
Copagh td: Killoran and Kilvarnet SO 40; 183
Copany hill: Drumhome DL 39; 59
Cope manor: Clogher TE 5; 34–35, 37–38, 53
Cope manor: Donacavey TE 5; 71, 76–77, 85–87
Cope, Anthony: Donacavey TE 5; 69–70
Cope, Arthur: Loughgall AH 1; 78, 82
Cope, Arthur: Loughgilly AH 1; 84–85
Cope, James: Carrickfergus AM 37; 162
Cope, Mrs (Drumilly): Drumcree AH 1; 41–42
Cope, Mrs (Drumilly): Loughgall AH 1; 80–82
Cope, Mrs (Drumilly): Seagoe AH 1; 107–08
Cope, Mrs: Kilmore AH 1; 65, 68–71
Cope, Richard: Clogher TE 5; 38
Cope, William: Donacavey TE 5; 69, 71
Copeland bridge: Carrickfergus AM 37; 32
Copeland Islands: Bangor DN 7; 19, 21–22
Copeland Islands: Island Magee AM 10; 26, 74
Copeland Islands: Misc. AM 10; 130–31
Copeland Islands: Misc. DN 17; 121
Copeland Islands graveyard: Bangor DN 7; 21
Copeland Islands lighthouse: Carrickfergus AM 37;
  10
Copeland water: Carrickfergus AM 37; 7, 32
Copeland water: Kilroot AM 26; 58, 60
Copeland water: Misc. AM 10; 130–31

Copeland, family: Carrickfergus AM 37; 60
Copeland, family: Newry DN 3; 107
Copeland, James: Cleenish FH 14; 18
Copeland, Mr (Enniskillen): Mevagh DL 38; 60
Copeland, Thomas: Killead AM 35; 50
Copeland, W.T.: Coleraine LY 33; 65, 73, 104, 127,
  139, 142
Copenagh corn mill: Drung CN 40; 21
Copenagh flax mill: Drung CN 40; 21
Copenagh hill: Killdrumsherdan CN 40; 31
Copenhagen (Denmark): Donacavey TE 5; 74
Coppogue td: Rossorry FH 14; 117
Cor lough: Currin MN 40; 86
Cor river: Monaghan MN 40; 159
Cor river: Tydavnet MN 40; 170
Cor Tynan bog: Tynan AH 1; 125
Cor Tynan td: Tynan AH 1; 124
Coracarlan td: Kinawley FH 4; 121
Coraclare td: Kinawley FH 4; 121
Coradooey td: Donaghmore DL 39; 34, 36
Coragany (see Corragarry): Ematris MN 40; 112
Coragarr (see Corragore): Ematris MN 40; 112
Coragh lough: Drumgoon CN 40; 2, 6–8
Coraghan td: Currin MN 40; 95
Coraghy td: Magheross MN 40; 143, 148
Coragore (see Corragore): Ematris MN 40; 117
Coranny hill: Aghabog MN 40; 62
Coranny td: Currin MN 40; 91
Coratrasna (see Cortrasna): Kinawley FH 4; 121
Coravacan chapel of ease: Ematris MN 40; 114
Coravacan hill: Ematris MN 40; 112, 115
Coravackan (see Coravacan): Ematris MN 40; 115
Coravoghy hill: Killdrumsherdan CN 40; 31
Corbally (Corbilly) td: Ahoghill AM 23; 41, 48
Corbally (Corbolly) td: Donacavey TE 5; 76, 78, 80,
  84–85
Corbally (Corbully) td: Dromore TE 5; 95, 97
Corbally bog: Garvaghy DN 12; 80
Corbally cave: Ballywillin AM 16; 33
Corbally fort: Ballywillin AM 16; 34
Corbally mill: Dromore TE 5; 95
Corbally orchard: Killead AM 35; 35
Corbally standing stone: Ahoghill AM 23; 27
Corbally td: Down DN 17; 53, 56–57
Corbally td: Dunsfort DN 17; 67, 72
Corbally td: Garvaghy DN 12; 80–81
Corbally td: Killead AM 35; 22, 35, 40
Corbally td: Killyleagh DN 17; 82
Corballyquill hill: Killdrumsherdan CN 40; 31
Corballyquill school: Killdrumsherdan CN 40; 35
Corbane td: Magheross MN 40; 148
Corbaud td: Clogher TE 5; 43
Corbeagh corn mill: Killdrumsherdan CN 40; 34
Corbeagh school: Killdrumsherdan CN 40; 35
Corbeagh td: Killdrumsherdan CN 40; 33

Corbelagh td: Donacavey TE 5; 77, 81

Corberryquill (see Corballyquill): Killdrumsherdan CN 40; 35

Corbet bridge: Seapatrick DN 12; 125–26

Corbet flow bog: Magherally DN 12; 115

Corbet lough: Garvaghy DN 12; 79–80, 82

Corbet lough: Magherally DN 12; 112, 115

Corbet td: Garvaghy DN 12; 82

Corbet td: Magherally DN 12; 114–15

Corbet, Samuel: Drumgooland DN 3; 23, 25

Corbet, William: Coleraine LY 33; 96

Corbett, family: Dromara DN 12; 67

Corbett, Hugh: Newry DN 3; 93

Corbett, John: Drumgooland DN 3; 24

Corbett, John: Newry DN 3; 99

Corboe bog: Clogher TE 5; 26

Corboe td: Clogher TE 5; 33, 37

Corbofin (see Corrabofin): Ballybay MN 40; 84

Corbolly Hamilton td: Dromore TE 5; 98

Corbolly McCaron td: Dromore TE 5; 98

Corbrack td: Ballybay MN 40; 84

Corbracky td: Drumcree AH 1; 39

Corby lough: Galloon FH 4; 105

Corby Mill school: Dunaghy AM 13; 17

Corcan Island td: Misc. DL 39; 197

Corcashey td: Convoy DL 39; 20

Corcaum td: Donaghmore DL 39; 36

Corcen (see Correen)

Corcloghan hill: Drumgoon CN 40; 1

Corcloghan school: Drumgoon CN 40; 11

Corcloghan td: Drumgoon CN 40; 2

Corcloghy (Corcloghey) td: Clogher TE 5; 35

Corcoran, family: Kilroot AM 26; 74–75

Corcoran, John: Donaghmore DL 39; 30–31

Corcrain (Corcraine) td: Drumcree AH 1; 29–30, 36, 41

Corcreagh chapel: Magheross MN 40; 145

Corcreagh locality: Magheross MN 40; 146, 152

Corcreagh td: Killanny MN 40; 132

Corcreany (see Corcreeny)

Corcreem (see Corcrum): Ballymore AH 1; 13

Corcreen (see Corcrum): Ballymore AH 1; 9

Corcreeny (see Corcreevy): Kilmore AH 1; 68

Corcreeny td: Donaghcloney DN 12; 59

Corcreeny td: Hillsborough DN 12; 85, 95, 99, 105–06

Corcreevy Barnside td: Clogher TE 5; 38

Corcreevy corn mill: Clogher TE 5; 49

Corcreevy House: Clogher TE 5; 33, 48

Corcreevy td: Clogher TE 5; 44, 48–49, 54

Corcreevy td: Kilmore AH 1; 68–69, 71–73

Corcriaghan td: Drumgoon CN 40; 6

Corcrievy (see Corcreevy)

Corcrigah td: Magheross MN 40; 148

Corcrum td: Ballymore AH 1; 9, 12–17

Corcullentrabeg td: Drumcree AH 1; 41

Corcullentramore mill: Drumcree AH 1; 41

Corcullentramore td: Drumcree AH 1; 41

Corcullogue td: Magheross MN 40; 148

Cordanaghy (see Cardonaghy): Ahoghill AM 23; 35

Cordby, Pat: Blaris AM 8; 77

Cordeggan td: Laragh CN 40; 39

Cordevlish school: Aughnamullen MN 40; 77

Cordevlish td: Aughnamullen MN 40; 72, 75

Cordiessigo (see Cordressigo): Ematris MN 40; 112

Cordner, Alexander: Hillsborough DN 12; 106

Cordner, Mrs: Blaris AM 8; 84–85

Cordner, Rev. E.J.: Blaris AM 8; 49

Cordner, Rev. E.J.: Blaris DN 12; 45, 49

Cordner, Rev. E.J.: Drumbo DN 7; 58–59

Cordner, Robert: Blaris DN 12; 46, 50

Cordoagh Vicarage: Killdrumsherdan CN 40; 34

Cordonaghy (see Cardonaghy): Ahoghill AM 23; 37

Cordra (see Cordrain): Kilmore AH 1; 59

Cordrain check factory: Kilmore AH 1; 63, 69

Cordrain school: Kilmore AH 1; 59

Cordrain steam engine: Kilmore AH 1; 63

Cordrain td: Kilmore AH 1; 63, 67, 69, 73

Cordressigo hill: Ematris MN 40; 112

Cordressigo td: Ematris MN 40; 113, 116

Cordromedy corn mill: Kilskeery TE 5; 114

Cordromedy td: Kilskeery TE 5; 114

Corduff hill: Aghabog MN 40; 62

Corduff hill: Magheross MN 40; 143

Corduff Kelly bog: Magheross MN 40; 146

Corduff Kelly td: Magheross MN 40; 143, 148

Corduff Mountain chapel: Magheross MN 40; 145

Corduff Mountain td: Magheross MN 40; 148

Corduff school: Magheross MN 40; 150

Corduff td: Magheross MN 40; 156

Coreek td: Clogher TE 5; 53

Coreenan td: Aghaderg DN 12; 8

Corenenty td: Magheross MN 40; 148

Coreniar td: Loughgilly AH 1; 84–85

Corenmar (see Corernagh): Ballymore AH 1; 11

Corensigagh td: Magheross MN 40; 148

Corenure (see Coreniar): Loughgilly AH 1; 84

Corernagh school: Ballymore AH 1; 11, 14

Corernagh td: Ballymore AH 1; 13–14, 17–18

Corethers, James: Tullylish DN 12; 147

Corethers, Mary Anne: Tullylish DN 12; 147

Corethers, Sarah: Drummaul AM 19; 87

Corfad (Corfadd) td: Aughnamullen MN 40; 71, 75

Corfad corn mill: Aughnamullen MN 40; 72

Corfad flax mill: Aughnamullen MN 40; 72

Corfad school: Killdrumsherdan CN 40; 35–36

Corfad td: Ballybay MN 40; 84

Corfaghone (see Corfeehone): Laragh CN 40; 39

Corfand lough: Laragh CN 40; 40

Corfeehone hill: Laragh CN 40; 40

Corfeehone lough: Laragh CN 40; 40

Corfeehone td: Laragh CN 40; 39

Corfewhone (see Corfeehone): Laragh CN 40; 40

Corgah td: Dromore TE 5; 98

Corgan (see Cargin): Duneane AM 19; 119

Corgannive creek: Lough Swilly DL 38; 122

Corgary td: Donaghmore DL 39; 35, 37

Corglass td (see also Aughanergill): Drumcree AH 1; 37

Corgorin td: Tullyniskan TE 20; 138

Corgreagh td: Aughnamullen MN 40; 75

Corgrey td: Donaghmore DN 3; 7, 9

Corick bog: Dungiven LY 15; 3, 51

Corick bridge: Ballynascreen LY 31; 7

Corick bridge: Dungiven LY 15; 11, 52

Corick cave: Ballynascreen LY 31; 11, 27

Corick enclosure: Ballynascreen LY 31; 29

Corick giant's chair: Ballynascreen LY 31; 11, 26–27

Corick giant's grave: Ballynascreen LY 31; 22

Corick House: Clogher TE 5; 33, 49, 61

Corick mountain: Ballynascreen LY 31; 26, 29

Corick mountain: Dungiven LY 15; 1, 10

Corick td: Ballynascreen LY 31; 11, 19, 21–22, 143

Corick td: Banagher LY 30; 22, 26

Corick td: Clogher TE 5; 35

Corick td: Dungiven LY 15; 27, 47, 61, 63, 82, 93

Corivin, George: Clondermot LY 34; 55

Cork: Ballyscullion LY 6; 53

Cork: Clondermot LY 34; 67

Cork: Cumber LY 28; 50

Cork: Donegal DL 39; 47

Cork county: Ardstraw TE 5; 8

Cork county: Clondermot LY 34; 46

Cork county: Dungiven LY 15; 12

Cork county: Faughanvale LY 36; 44

Cork hill: Racavan AM 13; 103

Cork Hill House: Clogher TE 5; 33

Cork, Bishop of: Dungiven LY 15; 104

Cork, Dean of: Drumragh TE 5; 112

Cork, Lord: Drummaul AM 19; 87

Corkadile, Hugh: Dunluce AM 16; 118

Corkdell, family: Billy AM 16; 68

Corke, George: Cumber LY 28; 67–69

Corkeeran hill: Ematris MN 40; 115

Corkeeran lough: Aughnamullen MN 40; 69

Corkeeran td: Aughnamullen MN 40; 76

Corkeeran td: Ballybay MN 40; 84

Corkeerin (see Corkeeran): Aughnamullen MN 40; 76

Corkelly bog: Kinawley FH 4; 114

Corkelshina td: Aughnamullen MN 40; 75

Corken, James: Blaris DN 12; 40

Corken, Miss: Blaris AM 8; 84

Corken, Mrs: Blaris DN 12; 45, 49

Corken, Rev. John: Aghagallon AM 21; 1

Corken, Rev. John: Aghalee AM 21; 26

Corken, Rev. John: Derryaghy AM 8; 106

Corken, Rev. John: Magherally DN 12; 114

Corken, Rev. John: Magheramesk AM 21; 112

Corkermain (Corker Maine) td: Carncastle and Killyglen AM 10; 3, 5, 7–8, 10

Corkermain meeting house (P): Carncastle and Killyglen AM 10; 3

Corkermain meeting house (U): Carncastle and Killyglen AM 10; 3

Corkermain school [I]: Carncastle and Killyglen AM 10; 5, 7

Corkermain school [II]: Carncastle and Killyglen AM 10; 7

Corkey (Corky) td: Loughguile AM 13; 59, 69, 72, 77

Corkey corn mill: Raymoghy DL 39; 133

Corkey graveyard: Loughguile AM 13; 72

Corkey Lower td: Raymoghy DL 39; 141

Corkey Middle corn mill: Loughguile AM 13; 63

Corkey Middle flax mill: Loughguile AM 13; 63

Corkey Middle school: Loughguile AM 13; 66

Corkey Middle td: Loughguile AM 13; 66

Corkey North school: Loughguile AM 13; 67

Corkey North td: Loughguile AM 13; 67

Corkey school: Loughguile AM 13; 77

Corkey standing stones: Loughguile AM 13; 69–70, 72

Corkey td: Killagan AM 23; 79

Corkey td: Raymoghy DL 39; 134, 136, 198

Corkey Upper td: Raymoghy DL 39; 141

Corkeys (see Corkey): Raymoghy DL 39; 141

Corkfreeth district: Misc. SO 40; 199

Corkhill Demesne td: Clogher TE 5; 44

Corkhill mills: Kildress TE 20; 60

Corkhill td: Clogher TE 5; 37, 53

Corkin Island td: Clonleigh DL 39; 12

Corkragh corn mill: Kilskeery TE 5; 114

Corkragh td: Kilskeery TE 5; 114

Corky (see Corkey)

Corkydall, family: Billy AM 16; 58, 68

Corlackey (see Corlacky): Killelagh LY 27; 102

Corlacky (Curalackey) td: Killelagh LY 27; 99, 102

Corlacky giant's grave: Killelagh LY 27; 101

Corlacky td: Aghalurcher FH 4; 14

Corlacky td: Maghera LY 18; 1

Corlaghard td: Aughnamullen MN 40; 76

Corlaghdergan bog: Dromore TE 5; 93

Corlaghdergan hill: Dromore TE 5; 93

Corlaghdergan td: Dromore TE 5; 93, 98

Corlamlall meeting house: Newtownhamilton AH 1; 100

Corlatt Island: Galloon FH 4; 88, 91

Corlatt td: Aughnamullen MN 40; 76

Corlatt td: Galloon FH 4; 95

Corlatt td: Kinawley FH 4; 114

Corlattallan td: Errigal Truagh MN 40; 120

Corlea bog: Magheracloone MN 40; 137

Corlea corn mill: Kilskeery TE 5; 114

Corlea meeting house: Aughnamullen MN 40; 71

Corlea school: Aughnamullen MN 40; 77

Corlea school: Drumragh TE 5; 109

Corlea td: Aughnamullen MN 40; 76

Corlea td: Donaghmore DL 39; 36

Corlea td: Drumragh TE 5; 109, 111

Corlea td: Kilskeery TE 5; 113–14

Corlea td: Magheracloone MN 40; 137

Corlea td: Magheross MN 40; 148

Corleaghan td: Clogher TE 5; 35, 47

Corleaght td: Magheraculmoney FH 14; 112

Corlecky td: Kilteevoge DL 39; 114

Corlerryquinil (see Corballyquill): Killdrumsherdan CN 40; 31

Corley td: Templecarn DL 39; 164

Corlough (see Cooneen): Aghalurcher FH 4; 14

Corlough school: Aghaloo TE 20; 5

Corloughy td: Clogher TE 5; 47

Corlust (Corlusk) td: Ballymore AH 1; 1, 7–8, 13–14, 16

Corlust school: Ballymore AH 1; 7, 11, 14

Cormac's Temple (see Templecormac): Ballinderry AM 21; 43

Cormakelly td: Urney DL 39; 181

Cormean (see Cormeen)

Cormeen corn mill: Laragh CN 40; 42

Cormeen lough: Currin MN 40; 86

Cormeen td: Aughnamullen MN 40; 76

Cormeen td: Currin MN 40; 91

Cormeen td: Ematris MN 40; 115

Cormeen td: Laragh CN 40; 40, 43

Cormic, family: Ballinderry AM 21; 54

Cormore forts: Clogher TE 5; 45

Cormore td: Clogher TE 5; 36, 45, 53

Cornabaste cromlech: Drung CN 40; 21

Cornabaste school: Drung CN 40; 22

Cornabeagher hill: Killdrumsherdan CN 40; 31

Cornabeast (see Cornabaste): Drung CN 40; 22

Cornabracken giant's grave: Drumragh TE 5; 109

Cornabracken well: Drumragh TE 5; 108

Cornabrass td: Galloon FH 4; 95

Cornabroag td: Donaghmore DL 39; 36

Cornacaghan td: Drummully FH 4; 39

Cornacaple moss: Misc. DN 17; 131

Cornacarrow beetling mill: Aughnamullen MN 40; 72

Cornacarrow spinning factory: Aughnamullen MN 40; 72

Cornacarrow td: Aughnamullen MN 40; 76

Cornacreeve td: Donagh MN 40; 98

Cornacrew td: Mullaghbrack AH 1; 94

Cornadalum td: Inishmacsaint FH 14; 70

Cornafannoge hill: Aghavea FH 4; 17

Cornafannoge td: Aghavea FH 4; 17

Cornafanogue (see Cornafannoge): Aghavea FH 4; 17

Cornagall hill: Drung CN 40; 19

Cornagall lough: Drung CN 40; 19

Cornagall lough: Killdrumsherdan CN 40; 34

Cornagall stream: Killdrumsherdan CN 40; 34

Cornagarren hill: Drung CN 40; 19

Cornaghgarrew hill: Killdrumsherdan CN 40; 31

Cornagillagh td: Convoy DL 39; 20

Cornagiltagh (see Cornagilty): Tydavnet MN 40; 169

Cornagilty school: Tydavnet MN 40; 172

Cornagilty td: Tydavnet MN 40; 169

Cornagrade Castle: Enniskillen FH 4; 47, 52

Cornagrade manor: Derryvullan FH 14; 45–46

Cornagrade manor: Enniskillen FH 4; 81

Cornagrade manor: Misc. FH 4; 133

Cornagrade quarry: Enniskillen FH 4; 78

Cornagrade quarry: Magheracross FH 14; 94, 101

Cornagrade quarry: Trory FH 14; 123

Cornagrade td: Enniskillen FH 4; 48, 78, 81

Cornagradie (see Cornagrade)

Cornagrally td: Loughgilly AH 1; 85

Cornahoe Lower td: Clontibret MN 40; 85

Cornahoe td: Donagh MN 40; 99

Cornahole td: Kinawley FH 4; 121

Cornakessagh td: Aghalurcher FH 4; 14

Cornalack td: Drumcree AH 1; 36, 38

Cornalaragh bog: Magheracloone MN 40; 137

Cornaleast (see Cornabaste): Drung CN 40; 21

Cornaleck td: Kinawley FH 4; 121

Cornamuck td: Dromore TE 5; 98

Cornamucka (see Cornamucklagh): Carlingford LH 40; 60

Cornamuckla chapel: Aghavea FH 4; 20

Cornamuckla td: Aghavea FH 4; 23

Cornamuckla td: Clogher TE 5; 36

Cornamuckla td: Drumglass TE 20; 40

Cornamucklagh hill: Drumcree AH 1; 34, 38

Cornamucklagh school: Carlingford LH 40; 60

Cornamucklagh td: Carlingford LH 40; 58

Cornamucklagh td: Dromore TE 5; 98

Cornamucklagh td: Drumcree AH 1; 34–35, 38

Cornamuckleglash td: Ballybay MN 40; 84

Cornamuclagh (Cornamucklagh) td: Aghadowey LY 22; 4, 38

Cornamuclagh bog: Aghadowey LY 22; 4

Cornamuclagh bog: Agivey LY 22; 39

Cornanure mill: Tydavnet MN 40; 173

Cornanurny td: Killdrumsherdan CN 40; 33

Cornaparte (see Cornapaste): Currin MN 40; 86

Cornapaste corn mill: Currin MN 40; 90

Cornapaste td: Currin MN 40; 86, 88, 91

Cornarnel standing stone: Tullyaughnish DL 38; 91

Cornarooslan td: Aghalurcher FH 4; 14

Cornasassonagh school: Magheross MN 40; 150

Cornasassonagh td: Magheross MN 40; 148

Cornashanell mountain: Aghalurcher FH 4; 2

Cornashee (Cornaskee) td: Aghalurcher FH 4; 9, 13

Cornashee manor: Aghalurcher FH 4; 13, 16

Cornashee school: Aghalurcher FH 4; 11

Cornaskea (see Cornashee)

Cornassanagh (see Cornasassonagh): Magheross
MN 40; 150

Cornastack (see Cornastauk): Manorhamilton Union
LM 40; 52

Cornastauk fort: Manorhamilton Union LM 40; 52

Cornastauk td: Manorhamilton Union LM 40; 48

Cornavray td: Galloon FH 4; 95

Cornawall hill: Ematris MN 40; 112

Cornawall td: Ematris MN 40; 116

Cornbracken td: Drumragh TE 5; 108–09

Corncammon td: Misc. DL 39; 194

Corncarrow (see Cornacarrow): Aughnamullen MN
40; 72

Corncivall school: Ematris MN 40; 117

Corndale school: Tamlaght Finlagan LY 25; 96

Corndale td: Tamlaght Finlagan LY 25; 93, 105,
111, 119

Corndale Upper td: Tamlaght Finlagan LY 25; 63

Cornealty lough: Killdrumsherdan CN 40; 34

Cornecanmon bog: Killea and Taughboyne DL 39;
80

Cornecanmon locality: Killea and Taughboyne DL
39; 79

Cornecar (see Carnacaw): Ballee DN 17; 19

Cornecarkaw (see Cornacarrow): Aughnamullen
MN 40; 76

Cornelius, King of Ulster: Culfeightrin AM 24;
55–56

Cornelough td: Newry DN 3; 65

Corneparte (see Cornapaste): Currin MN 40; 90

Corner of Killead hill: Killead AM 35; 7

Corner, person named (Tamnamore): Kilmore AH 1;
73

Corner, Rev.: Annahilt DN 12; 23

Corner, Rev.: Comber DN 7; 37–39

Corner, Rev.: Hillsborough DN 12; 85

Corner, Samuel: Killead AM 35; 49

Corner's Grave locality: Kilmore AH 1; 73

Cornerscube House: Kilmore AH 1; 69

Cornerscube td: Kilmore AH 1; 66–67, 69–71, 73

Cornesasonagh (see Cornasassonagh): Magheross
MN 40; 148

Cornihoe fort: Ballybay MN 40; 81

Cornihoe td: Ballybay MN 40; 84

Cornihore (see Cornihoe): Ballybay MN 40; 81

Cornreany hill: Donaghcloney DN 12; 57

Cornreany school: Donaghcloney DN 12; 58

Cornreany td: Donaghcloney DN 12; 58–59

Cornroe school: Currin MN 40; 92–93

Cornwall (England): Misc. LY 36; 104

Cornwall, Edward: Carrickfergus AM 37; 130

Cornwall, Ellen: Carrickfergus AM 37; 130

Cornwallis, Lord: Drumachose LY 9; 65

Corothers, Thomas: Seapatrick DN 12; 134

Corper district: Misc. SO 40; 199

Corporation Arms Hotel: Carrickfergus AM 37; 28,
30, 161, 171

Corporation chapel: Killyleagh DN 17; 82

Corporation female school: Killyleagh DN 17; 82

Corporation forts: Killyleagh DN 17; 82

Corporation Land td: Misc. DL 39; 195

Corporation male school: Killyleagh DN 17; 82

Corporation meeting house: Killyleagh DN 17; 82

Corr lough: Longfield TE 5; 127

Corr pottery: Loughgall AH 1; 80

Corr river: Coleraine LY 33; 97

Corr river: Tyholland MN 40; 174

Corr td: Ballyscullion LY 6; 57

Corr td: Loughgall AH 1; 76, 80

Corr, Anna: Lissan LY 31; 93, 100

Corr, Eliza: Drumbeg AM 8; 133

Corr, family: Lissan LY 31; 106

Corr, Mary: Drumbeg AM 8; 133

Corr, Michael: Newry DN 3; 100

Corr, Patt: Banagher LY 30; 61

Corrabofin td: Ballybay MN 40; 78, 84

Corracharra school: Aughnamullen MN 40; 77

Corracharra td: Aughnamullen MN 40; 76

Corrachrow td: Aghalurcher FH 4; 13

Corrack House: Clogher TE 5; 55

Corrackcroppan chapel: Killevy AH 1; 54

Corracrin chapel: Donagh MN 40; 99

Corradillar td: Kinawley FH 4; 115

Corradooey td: Convoy DL 39; 20

Corradreen td: Kinawley FH 4; 110

Corrag td: Misc. DN 17; 125

Corragaldra td: Aughnamullen MN 40; 76

Corragarry bog: Donaghmoyne MN 40; 106

Corragarry hill: Ematris MN 40; 112

Corragarry lough: Donaghmoyne MN 40; 106

Corragarry school: Currin MN 40; 92

Corragarry td: Currin MN 40; 92

Corragarry td: Ematris MN 40; 112

Corragary (see Corragarry): Currin MN 40; 92

Corragh district: Killinchy DN 7; 86

Corraghariff td: Drung CN 40; 19

Corraghveetragh td: Clones FH 4; 28

Corraghveetragh windmill: Clones FH 4; 28

Corragore school: Ematris MN 40; 117

Corrahara (see Corracharra): Aughnamullen MN 40; 77

Corrahin td: Kinawley FH 4; 110

Corrakarra (see Corracharra): Aughnamullen MN 40; 76

Corral (see Correll): Inishmacsaint FH 14; 71

Corralongford td: Aghalurcher FH 4; 14

Corramahon td: Kinawley FH 4; 110

Corrame td: Kinawley FH 4; 110

Corrameen school: Kinawley FH 4; 111

Corran barony: Misc. SO 40; 198

Corran school: Keady AH 1; 47

Corran td: Drumkeeran FH 14; 65

Corran, family: Misc. LY 36; 101

Corranagh td: Leck DL 39; 117–18

Corrant, family: Blaris AM 8; 21

Corrard House: Cleenish FH 14; 17

Corrard td: Cleenish FH 14; 19, 29

Corraskea td: Aughnamullen MN 40; 71

Corratandy forts: Muckno MN 40; 166

Corrateebeg rock: Lough Swilly DL 38; 110

Corrateemore rock: Lough Swilly DL 38; 110

Corratistine ferry: Kinawley FH 4; 115

Corratrasna Point: Lough Swilly DL 38; 137

Corratrasna td: Lough Swilly DL 38; 137

Corravally bog: Magheross MN 40; 144

Corravally td: Magheross MN 40; 148

Corravoghy (see Corravogy)

Corravogy hill: Drumgoon CN 40; 1

Corravogy school: Killdrumsherdan CN 40; 36

Corrcen (see Correen)

Correan (see Correen): Skerry AM 13; 114

Correen bleach green: Racavan AM 13; 99

Correen bleach green: Skerry AM 13; 106, 111

Correen school: Skerry AM 13; 114

Correen td: Skerry AM 13; 106–07, 111

Correfrin school: Donaghmore DL 39; 40

Correfrin td: Donaghmore DL 39; 36

Correll td: Inishmacsaint FH 14; 71–72

Correlly td: Newry DN 3; 110

Correvan school: Aghabog MN 40; 65

Corrick bridge: Killdrumsherdan CN 40; 35

Corrick chapel: Killdrumsherdan CN 40; 33

Corrick demesne: Clogher TE 5; 49

Corrick td: Clogher TE 5; 50

Corrickvrack rock: Banagher LY 30; 56

Corridinna mountain: Drumragh TE 5; 104, 111

Corridinna mountain: Longfield TE 5; 131–32

Corridinna td: Drumragh TE 5; 104

Corridinna td: Longfield TE 5; 133

Corrigan, Ellen: Carrickfergus AM 37; 111

Corrinshigo corn mill: Currin MN 40; 90

Corrinshigo hill: Currin MN 40; 86

Corrinshigo mill–race: Currin MN 40; 88

Corrinshigo school: Killevy AH 1; 53

Corrinshigo td: Currin MN 40; 91–92

Corrintrough bog: Muckno MN 40; 163

Corrintrough school: Muckno MN 40; 168

Corrisesk (Coveysesk) td: Donacavey TE 5; 76, 78, 80–81, 84–85

Corriston, Catherine: Kilrea LY 27; 129

Corriston, Jane: Kilrea LY 27; 129

Corriston, William: Kilrea LY 27; 129

Corroda (see Currudda)

Corroddy (see Corrody): Clondermot LY 34; 56

Corrody reservoir: Clondermot LY 34; 4, 19, 23

Corrody td: Clondermot LY 34; 56, 63–64, 72, 109, 112, 115, 123, 130

Corrody wood: Clondermot LY 34; 123

Corroughel (see Carroghill): Mintiaghs DL 38; 64

Corrowlissan district: Misc. SO 40; 198

Corrstown standing stones: Ballywillin LY 33; 35

Corrstown td: Ballywillin LY 33; 48, 50

Corry (see Belmore, Earl): Enniskillen FH 4; 58, 68, 75

Corry wood: Kilmegan DN 3; 57

Corry, Caezarea: Newry DN 3; 68

Corry, Col.: Blaris DN 12; 34

Corry, David: Island Magee AM 10; 90

Corry, E.L.: Drumachose LY 9; 65

Corry, Edward: Newry DN 3; 75

Corry, family (see Belmore): Derryvullan FH 14; 40

Corry, family: Clondermot LY 34; 51

Corry, Felix: Aghagallon AM 21; 12

Corry, H.P.: Newry DN 3; 68

Corry, Hugh: Kilwaughter AM 10; 116

Corry, Isaac: Newry DN 3; 67–68, 75

Corry, James: Aghagallon AM 21; 13

Corry, James: Enniskillen FH 4; 52, 68

Corry, John: Dromore TE 5; 97

Corry, John: Skerry AM 13; 119

Corry, Mary (nee Pollock): Newry DN 3; 67

Corry, Miss: Newry DN 3; 81, 103, 110

Corry, Miss C.: Newry DN 3; 103

Corry, Misses: Newry DN 3; 98

Corry, Mr: Newry DN 3; 107

Corry, Mrs: Hillsborough DN 12; 105

Corry, Mrs William: Newry DN 3; 99, 103

Corry, Robert: Enniskillen FH 4; 53

Corry, Robert: Galloon FH 4; 105

Corry, Smithson: Garvaghy DN 12; 81, 84

Corry, Smithson: Kilbroney DN 3; 29, 33

Corry, Smithson: Newry DN 3; 100, 105

Corry, Somerset: Ballymoney AM 16; 15

Corry, T.: Donaghmore DN 3; 7–9

Corry, T.C.: Aghabog MN 40; 65

Corry, T.C.: Ematris MN 40; 114–16, 119

Corry, Thomas: Dunluce AM 16; 123

Corry, Trevor: Garvaghy DN 12; 81

Corry, Trevor: Kilbroney DN 3; 35

Corry, Trevor: Newry DN 3; 68, 71, 80, 84, 98, 103

Corry, William: Enniskillen FH 4; 58–59

Corrybrannon td: Ballybay MN 40; 84

Corrygarry (see Corragarry): Currin MN 40; 92

Corryglass school: Cleenish FH 14; 25

Corryglass td: Donacavey TE 5; 77, 81

Corryglass td [I]: Cleenish FH 14; 29

Corryglass td [II]: Cleenish FH 14; 29

Corryhagan td: Aughnamullen MN 40; 76

Corryheskum td: Dromore TE 5; 98

Corryhole locality: Lough Swilly DL 38; 106

Corrylagh hill: Drung CN 40; 19

Corrylea Island: Cleenish FH 14; 13, 30

Corrylea td: Cleenish FH 14; 29

Corrysesk td: Donacavey TE 5; 77

Corsail td: Galloon FH 4; 95

Corscreenagh td: Galloon FH 4; 95

Corsension td: Galloon FH 4; 95

Corsilliga (see Corsilloga): Aughnamullen MN 40; 76

Corsilligo (see Corsilloga): Aughnamullen MN 40; 69

Corsilloga lough: Aughnamullen MN 40; 69

Corsilloga lough: Drumgoon CN 40; 3

Corsilloga td: Aughnamullen MN 40; 76

Corslea td: Galloon FH 4; 95

Cortannel td: Aughnamullen MN 40; 76

Cortia hamlet: Kilbarron DL 39; 77

Cortigarn (see Cortgarn)

Cortinel (see Cortannel): Aughnamullen MN 40; 76

Cortivel (see Cortannel): Aughnamullen MN 40; 76

Cortnacarrow (see Gortnacarrow): Drummully FH 4; 38

Cortrasna giant's grave: Kinawley FH 4; 116

Cortrasna quarry: Kinawley FH 4; 116

Cortrasna td: Kinawley FH 4; 117, 121

Cortreane school: Currin MN 40; 92

Cortreane td: Currin MN 40; 92

Cortubber hill: Ematris MN 40; 112

Cortubber hill: Killdrumsherdan CN 40; 31

Cortubber plantation: Currin MN 40; 97

Cortubber school: Currin MN 40; 92

Cortubber school: Killdrumsherdan CN 40; 35

Cortubber td: Aughnamullen MN 40; 76

Cortubber td: Currin MN 40; 91

Cortubbert (see Cortubber)

Cortynan (see Cor Tynan): Tynan AH 1; 124

Corudda (see Currudda)

Corunna (Spain): Kilbroney DN 3; 34

Corvacken td: Aughnamullen MN 40; 76

Corvaghan corn mill: Drummully FH 4; 36

Corvaghan td: Drummully FH 4; 36

Corvalle td: Grey Abbey DN 7; 68

Corvally (Corvelly) td: Ramoan AM 24; 89, 114

Corvally caves: Ramoan AM 24; 114

Corvally chapel: Ramoan AM 24; 89, 96

Corvally Danes' houses: Ramoan AM 24; 113–14

Corvally standing stones: Ramoan AM 24; 113

Corvillen (see Corwillin): Aughnamullen MN 40; 76

Corvin bridge: Donegal DL 39; 44, 47

Corvin td: Donegal DL 39; 44

Corvoo td: Ematris MN 40; 113

Corweana td: Aughnamullen MN 40; 73

Corwilliam (see Corwillin): Aughnamullen MN 40; 72

Corwillin td: Aughnamullen MN 40; 72, 76

Corwillis hill: Killdrumsherdan CN 40; 31

Cory, Henry: Aghagallon AM 21; 13

Cory, Jane: Ballinderry AM 21; 53

Cory, Patrick: Aghagallon AM 21; 13, 19

Coryfeagh td: Killygarvan DL 38; 47

Cosby, Mr: Garvaghy DN 12; 80

Cosbystown school: Inishmacsaint FH 14; 78

Cosey hill: Tynan AH 1; 124

Cosgrave, Anne: Carrickfergus AM 37; 120

Cosgrave, Elinor: Antrim AM 29; 59

Cosgrave, family: Coleraine LY 33; 72

Cosgrave, J.: Comber DN 7; 34

Cosgrave, Jane: Coleraine LY 33; 68, 137

Cosgrave, Larkin, Burrell and Boyd, Messrs: Blaris AM 8; 37

Cosgrave, Louisa: Coleraine LY 33; 68, 137

Cosgrave, Mary: Coleraine LY 33; 68, 137

Cosgrave, Mrs: Blaris DN 12; 50

Cosgrove, Patrick: Ballyscullion LY 6; 69

Cosgrove, Redmond: Newry DN 3; 99

Coshkib fort: Layd AM 13; 41

Coshkib td: Layd AM 13; 41

Coshly, family: Aghalee AM 21; 31

Coskchran, family: Desertmartin LY 31; 55

Coskemduff bog: Drumgoon CN 40; 7

Coskemduff lough: Drumgoon CN 40; 3

Coskemduff td: Drumgoon CN 40; 8

Cosker, Charles: Maghera LY 18; 46

Cosmutty lough: Drung CN 40; 19

Cossigan, John: Newry DN 3; 99

Cossley, John: Magheramesk AM 21; 121

Cossley, William: Magheramesk AM 21; 121, 125

Cossycon td: Devenish FH 14; 58

Costello, Elizabeth: Magherafelt LY 6; 112

Costello, Henry: Duneane AM 19; 123

Costello, Hugh: Ballyscullion LY 6; 52, 73–74

Costello, James: Termoneeny LY 6; 133

Costello, John [I]: Duneane AM 19; 119

Costello, John [II]: Duneane AM 19; 123

Costello, Michael: Termoneeny LY 6; 133

Costello, Mr: Kilcronaghan LY 31; 73

Costello, Patrick: Termoneeny LY 6; 133

Costello, William: Artrea LY 6; 38

Costerton, family: Aghadowey LY 22; 11

Costerton, man named: Misc. LY 36; 111
Costley, Henry: Killead AM 35; 52
Cottage Grove House: Kilrea LY 27; 122
Cottage td: Raymoghy DL 39; 136
Cottenham, Thomas: Currin MN 40; 89, 91–92, 96
Cottenham, Thomas: Drumgoon CN 40; 9
Cotter, William: Clonduff DN 3; 6
Cotton Bank House: Duneane AM 19; 114
Cotton, A.: Kilkeel DN 3; 51
Cottonmount muslin factory: Templepatrick AM 35; 112, 146
Cottonmount print–works: Templepatrick AM 35; 112–13, 146
Cottown manor: Misc. DN 17; 124
Cottown school: Bangor DN 7; 22
Cottown td: Bangor DN 7; 19
Cottown td: Misc. DN 17; 124
Cottown td: Raphoe DL 39; 125
Coubery, Dr: Saul DN 17; 113
Coughlan, John: Balteagh LY 9; 18
Coughlan, John: Drumachose LY 9; 85, 132
Coughlin, Ann: Bovevagh LY 25; 60
Coulkenny (see Coolkenny): Ramoan AM 24; 89
Coulmaghra td: Ballintoy AM 24; 11
Coulson, family: Blaris AM 8; 21
Coulson, Foster: Carrickfergus AM 37; 102
Coulson, James: Blaris AM 8; 66, 84
Coulson, John: Galloon FH 4; 97
Coulson, Messrs: Blaris AM 8; 17, 23
Coulson, Messrs: Blaris DN 12; 46, 49
Coulson, Miss: Blaris AM 8; 84
Coulson, Mr: Blaris DN 12; 33
Coulson, Mrs: Blaris AM 8; 85
Coulson, Mrs William: Blaris AM 8; 84
Coulson, Walter: Blaris AM 8; 84
Coulson, William: Blaris AM 8; 60, 66
Coulson, William: Blaris DN 12; 36
Coulter, George: Carrickfergus AM 37; 127
Coulter, John: Derryaghy AM 8; 107
Coulter, Mary: Tamlaght TE 20; 129
Coulter, Misses: Newry DN 3; 106
Coulter, Mr: Ballymascanlan LH 40; 55
Coulter, Mr: Carlingford LH 40; 58
Coulter, Mr: Newry DN 3; 106
Coulter, Robert: Tamlaght TE 20; 78, 82, 125, 127
Coulter, Susanna: Carrickfergus AM 37; 125
Coultson, family: Blaris DN 12; 30
Counaght td: Loughgilly AH 1; 85
Countenan hill: Laragh CN 40; 40
Countenan lough: Laragh CN 40; 39–40
Countenan Parsonage: Laragh CN 40; 42
Countenan td: Laragh CN 40; 40–41
County Cairn stones: Donaghmore DL 39; 34
County moss: Donaghcloney DN 12; 57
County water: Muckno MN 40; 162

Couper, family: Carrickfergus AM 37; 93, 179
Couples, Rev. Snowden: Blaris AM 8; 9
Coursehill House: Kilmore AH 1; 65
Court and Portleen manor: Tullyaughnish DL 38; 96–97
Court hill: Killead AM 35; 19, 31
Court McMartin fort: Layd AM 13; 41
Court Now locality: Island Magee AM 10; 102
Court wall: Killead AM 35; 50
Courthill school: Killead AM 35; 53
Courtnay, James: Tamlaght O'Crilly LY 18; 84, 88, 90–92, 96, 105, 108–10, 112
Courtnay, Joseph: Tamlaght O'Crilly LY 18; 108
Courtnay, Robert: Maghera LY 18; 39, 41
Courtney, Capt.: Kilmacteige SO 40; 185
Courtney, E.H.: Newry DN 3; 100, 104
Courtney, family: Ballyclug AM 23; 63
Courtney, James: Doagh AM 29; 88, 90
Courtney, James: Duneane AM 19; 113
Courtney, James: Maghera LY 18; 53
Courtney, Joseph: Ballyscullion AM 19; 9, 11
Courtney, Maria: Warrenpoint DN 3; 122
Courtney, Miss: Kirkinriola AM 23; 95
Courtney, Mr: Magherafelt LY 6; 91
Courtney, Rev. D.C.: Ballycor AM 32; 4, 6
Courtney, Samuel: Drummaul AM 19; 90
Courtney, Thomas: Ahoghill AM 23; 49
Courtney, Thomas: Ballyscullion AM 19; 9
Courtney, Thomas: Drummaul AM 19; 83
Courtney's Island: Aghagallon AM 21; 16
Cousins, family: Aghalee AM 21; 36
Cove Briar mound: Tamlaght Finlagan LY 25; 88–89
Cove cairn: Banagher LY 30; 43
Cove carn grave: Banagher LY 30; 58
Cove fort: Tamlaght Finlagan LY 25; 88
Cove hill: Ahoghill AM 23; 33
Cove hill: Coleraine LY 33; 92, 132
Cove hill: Desertoghill LY 27; 7
Cove hill cave: Ahoghill AM 23; 33
Cove hill cave: Desertoghill LY 27; 7
Cove rock: Killesher FH 14; 83
Cove stones: Balteagh LY 9; 7
Cove stones: Banagher LY 30; 44
Cove well: Balteagh LY 9; 7
Coveall school: Inishmacsaint FH 14; 78
Coveysesk (see Corrisesk)
Cow glen: Maghera LY 18; 62
Cow Park falls: Ahoghill AM 23; 29
Cow Park mills: Ahoghill AM 23; 29
Cowaghan td: Drummully FH 4; 39
Cowan, A.: Drumballyroney DN 3; 18
Cowan, A.: Garvaghy DN 12; 81
Cowan, Alexander: Clondermot LY 34; 78, 80
Cowan, Andrew: Hillsborough DN 12; 97

Cowan, Arthur: Templecorran AM 26; 132

Cowan, Capt.: Comber DN 7; 37, 40

Cowan, Eliza: Carrickfergus AM 37; 123–24

Cowan, family: Ahoghill AM 23; 25

Cowan, family: Newry DN 3; 108

Cowan, family: Racavan AM 13; 100

Cowan, J.: Comber DN 7; 34

Cowan, J.C.: Newry DN 3; 108

Cowan, James: Carrickfergus AM 37; 40, 47, 57–58, 102, 136, 138–40, 154

Cowan, James: Convoy DL 39; 22

Cowan, John: Clondermot LY 34; 78, 80

Cowan, John: Faughanvale LY 36; 8, 16, 18, 22

Cowan, John: Tamlaght TE 20; 129, 133

Cowan, John: Templepatrick AM 35; 133

Cowan, Lt: Hillsborough DN 12; 106

Cowan, Mr: Drumballyroney DN 3; 18

Cowan, Mr: Drumbo DN 7; 60

Cowan, Mr: Faughanvale LY 36; 16

Cowan, Oliver: Clondermot LY 34; 78, 80

Cowan, Rev. T.C.: Misc. DL 39; 186

Cowan, Rev. Thomas: Antrim AM 29; 27

Cowan, Richard: Clonleigh DL 39; 12

Cowan, Robert: Tamlaght TE 20; 76, 92, 103, 129

Cowan, Thomas: Lissan LY 31; 109

Cowan, W. and Reid, Messrs: Carnmoney AM 2; 43, 47, 61, 78–79, 83, 86, 89, 91–92

Cowan, W.J.: Tamlaght TE 20; 75

Cowan, William: Newry DN 3; 100

Cowd Castle: Ardglass DN 17; 3, 12

Cowdan, Alexander: Tamlaght TE 20; 77, 104, 129

Cowdan, John: Tamlaght TE 20; 75, 128, 136

Cowdan, William: Tamlaght TE 20; 76, 103

Cowden, Thomas: Tamlaght TE 20; 131

Cowen, family: Misc. LY 36; 104

Cowen, Maj.: Faughanvale LY 36; 20

Cowey lough: Ardquin DN 7; 4

Cox, Alexander: Annahilt DN 12; 22

Cox, family: Carrickfergus AM 37; 93

Cox, family: Misc. LY 36; 104

Cox, Isaac: Hillsborough DN 12; 106

Cox, Mr: Kilmore AH 1; 70

Cox, William: Dunluce AM 16; 119

Coxtown House: Drumhome DL 39; 58–60, 62

Coyah td: Dromore TE 5; 96

Coyl, family: Billy AM 16; 68

Coyle, Bernard: Carrickfergus AM 37; 193

Coyle, family: Billy AM 16; 58

Coyle, family: Culfeightrin AM 24; 59

Coyle, family: Errigal LY 27; 41

Coyle, James: Drumtullagh AM 16; 101–02

Coyle, John: Drumtullagh AM 16; 101–02

Coyle, John: Magilligan LY 11; 134

Coyle, Patt: Ballintoy AM 24; 35

Coyle, Patt: Killowen LY 33; 171

Coyle, Patt: Ramoan AM 24; 104

Coyle, Sally: Killowen LY 33; 171

Coyls, family: Ramoan AM 24; 107

Coyn lough: Inch DN 17; 75

Coyne, Rev. John: Drumcree AH 1; 29

Coyne, Rev. Michael: Drumcree AH 1; 29

Coyne, Samuel: Kilmore AH 1; 59

Crab lough: Kilrea LY 27; 106, 112–13

Craharkey (Crabarky) td: Dungiven LY 15; 3, 20, 22, 27, 31, 45, 50, 61, 64–65, 74, 79, 88, 92–93

Crabarkey bog: Dungiven LY 15; 94–95

Crabarkey flax mill: Dungiven LY 15; 9, 97

Crabarkey school: Dungiven LY 15; 18

Crabarkey td: Banagher LY 30; 22

Crackadoos (see Creaghadoos): Killea and Taughboyne DL 39; 84

Crackdoos (see Creaghadoos): Killea and Taughboyne DL 39; 80

Cracken, John: Banagher LY 30; 86

Cracking cove: Island Magee AM 10; 101

Cradian [or Cradya] chapel: Derryvullan FH 14; 40

Cradya [or Cradian] district: Derryvullan FH 14; 45

Craford, James: Artrea LY 6; 25

Craford, James: Bovevagh LY 25; 60

Craford, Joseph: Tamlaght Finlagan LY 25; 119

Craford, Rev. Andrew: Carnmoney AM 2; 75

Craford, Robert: Drumachose LY 9; 110

Craford, William: Antrim AM 29; 37

Cragadick (see Craigadick): Maghera LY 18; 37

Cragadooes (see Creaghadoos): Misc. DL 39; 195

Cragagh hill: Ramoan AM 24; 108

Crage (see Cregg): Cumber LY 28; 72

Craghadooes (see Creaghadoos): Misc. DL 39; 189

Craghan school: Magheracross FH 14; 99

Craghan td: Magheracross FH 14; 93, 102

Cragmore (see Craigmore): Maghera LY 18; 37

Cragnaherna td: Donagh DL 38; 31

Crahan (see Craghan): Magheracross FH 14; 93

Craidfadd (see Craigfadd): Culfeightrin AM 24; 59

Craig carn: Billy AM 16; 54, 68–69

Craig cave: Ballintoy AM 24; 21

Craig cave: Dunluce AM 16; 116, 118

Craig corn mill: Magilligan LY 11; 86, 123

Craig cove: Billy AM 16; 56, 63

Craig cromlech: Billy AM 16; 54

Craig enclosure: Ballintoy AM 24; 21

Craig fort: Billy AM 16; 54, 60

Craig hill: Ballintoy AM 24; 33

Craig hill: Billy AM 16; 39

Craig hill: Blaris AM 8; 13

Craig hill: Doagh AM 29; 62, 84

Craig lough: Donegal DL 39; 43

Craig Mananan rock: Ballintoy AM 24; 34

Craig McLoughlin school (see Gortachork): Donaghmore DL 39; 39

Craig mill: Magilligan LY 11; 128
Craig of Vengeance locality: Derrykeighan AM 16; 87, 95
Craig old castle: Magilligan LY 11; 144
Craig precipices: Magilligan LY 11; 106
Craig td: Billy AM 16; 69
Craig td: Magilligan LY 11; 86, 89, 95, 116, 120, 122, 126, 128, 134, 146
Craig, Agnes: Kilrea LY 27; 129
Craig, Alexander: Donaghmore DL 39; 39
Craig, Alexander: Drumbeg AM 8; 133
Craig, Alexander: Tamlaght O'Crilly LY 18; 91, 110
Craig, Alexander [I]: Kilrea LY 27; 120
Craig, Alexander [II]: Kilrea LY 27; 129
Craig, Anne: Carrickfergus AM 37; 121
Craig, Biddy: Carrickfergus AM 37; 121, 124
Craig, Catherine [I]: Drummaul AM 19; 91
Craig, Catherine [II]: Drummaul AM 19; 91
Craig, Clara [I]: Drummaul AM 19; 91
Craig, Clara [II]: Drummaul AM 19; 91
Craig, Cllr: Comber DN 7; 40
Craig, Cllr: Dundonald DN 7; 65
Craig, David: Carrickfergus AM 37; 55, 164
Craig, Edward: Drumbeg AM 8; 126, 133
Craig, Eliza (Jnr): Drumbeg AM 8; 133
Craig, Eliza (Snr): Drumbeg AM 8; 133
Craig, family: Ballycor AM 32; 5
Craig, family: Blaris AM 8; 22
Craig, family: Dromara DN 12; 67
Craig, family: Drumbeg AM 8; 123
Craig, family: Raloo AM 32; 108, 123
Craig, family: Templecorran AM 26; 117, 119
Craig, Hugh: Derrykeighan AM 16; 94
Craig, J.: Magilligan LY 11; 136
Craig, James (Jnr): Hillsborough DN 12; 106
Craig, James: Ballylinny AM 32; 29
Craig, James: Ballymartin AM 2; 13, 15
Craig, James: Clondermot LY 34; 78–80
Craig, James: Drumbeg AM 8; 126
Craig, James: Errigal LY 27; 66
Craig, James: Glynn AM 26; 44
Craig, James: Hillsborough DN 12; 106
Craig, James: Kilrea LY 27; 129
Craig, James: Tamlaght Finlagan LY 25; 121
Craig, James: Templepatrick AM 35; 150
Craig, James [I]: Carrickfergus AM 37; 26
Craig, James [II]: Carrickfergus AM 37; 42, 57, 98, 134–35, 142, 183
Craig, James [III]: Carrickfergus AM 37; 107
Craig, John: Clondermot LY 34; 78–80
Craig, John: Donaghmore DL 39; 36
Craig, John: Drumbeg AM 8; 126, 133
Craig, John: Drummaul AM 19; 84
Craig, John: Dundermot AM 13; 33
Craig, John: Hillsborough DN 12; 106

Craig, John: Kilbride AM 29; 149, 152
Craig, John: Killowen LY 33; 172
Craig, John: Kilrea LY 27; 129
Craig, John: Kirkinriola AM 23; 112
Craig, John: Misc. DN 17; 122
Craig, John: Tamlaght Finlagan LY 25; 119
Craig, Magy: Tamlaght Finlagan LY 25; 119
Craig, man named: Ahoghill AM 23; 34
Craig, Maryanne: Kilrea LY 27; 129
Craig, Messrs: Faughanvale LY 36; 18
Craig, Mr (Kilnappy): Faughanvale LY 36; 19
Craig, Mr: Cumber LY 28; 76
Craig, Mr: Drumcree AH 1; 39
Craig, Mr: Layd AM 13; 36
Craig, Mrs (North Lodge): Carrickfergus AM 37; 135–36
Craig, Mrs Edward: Drumbeg AM 8; 133
Craig, Rev. Andrew: Blaris AM 8; 26, 61
Craig, Rev. George: Coleraine LY 33; 127
Craig, Rev. George: Macosquin LY 22; 81, 93, 121
Craig, Rev. William: Carnmoney AM 2; 75
Craig, Rev. William: Dromara DN 12; 67
Craig, Richard: Clondermot LY 34; 78
Craig, Robert: Derrykeighan AM 16; 93
Craig, Robert: Dungiven LY 15; 116
Craig, Robert: Errigal LY 27; 66
Craig, Robert: Raloo AM 32; 129
Craig, Sam: Lough Swilly DL 38; 103–04
Craig, Sarah: Kilrea LY 27; 129
Craig, Stewart: Seapatrick DN 12; 125, 131
Craig, Thomas: Aghadowey LY 22; 35
Craig, Thomas: Clondermot LY 34; 89
Craig, William: Carrickfergus AM 37; 148
Craig, William: Dromara DN 12; 66
Craig, William: Drumbeg AM 8; 133
Craig, William: Drummaul AM 19; 88
Craig, William: Kilrea LY 27; 129
Craig, William: Raphoe DL 39; 128
Craig's Isles: Tullyaughnish DL 38; 86
Craigaboney td: Dunluce AM 16; 106
Craigacroy school: Drumbo DN 7; 58
Craigacroy td: Drumbo DN 7; 58, 60
Craigadick bridge: Maghera LY 18; 9, 52
Craigadick corn mill: Maghera LY 18; 27, 35
Craigadick grave: Maghera LY 18; 12
Craigadick td: Maghera LY 18; 9, 31, 37, 45, 52, 63–64, 78
Craigafad (see Craigavad)
Craigahorne td: Kilwaughter AM 10; 111
Craigahullar (Craigacullier) td: Ballywillin LY 33; 51
Craigahullar cave: Ballywillin AM 16; 33
Craigahullar caves: Ballywillin LY 33; 50
Craigahullar fort: Ballywillin AM 16; 34
Craigahullar td: Ballywillin AM 16; 34

Craigakeeran hill: Misc. LY 31; 113

Craiganariff fort: Ballyaghran LY 33; 10, 24

Craiganee bog: Glynn AM 26; 4

Craiganee bogs: Ballintoy AM 24; 12–13

Craiganee td: Glynn AM 26; 1, 41, 48

Craiganorne cotton factory: Kilwaughter AM 10; 110, 113

Craiganorne national school: Kilwaughter AM 10; 120

Craiganorne school: Kilwaughter AM 10; 111, 119

Craiganorne td: Kilwaughter AM 10; 110, 113, 115, 119, 122

Craiganure rock: Banagher LY 30; 112

Craigarodden (Craigrodin) td: Misc. DN 17; 124, 126–27

Craigarodden td: Ballyphilip DN 7; 7–8

Craigaroddin (see Craigarodden): Ballyphilip DN 7; 7

Craigarogan (Craignarogan) td: Templepatrick AM 35; 107, 110, 112, 115–16, 122, 124–25, 129, 132, 137, 146, 148–50, 152–53

Craigarogan bleach works: Templepatrick AM 35; 142

Craigarogan cove: Templepatrick AM 35; 130

Craigarogan cromlech: Templepatrick AM 35; 125, 137

Craigarogan forest: Templepatrick AM 35; 107

Craigarogan plantation: Templepatrick AM 35; 139

Craigarogan print-works: Templepatrick AM 35; 138

Craigarogan school: Templepatrick AM 35; 134–36, 138–40

Craigarogan Sunday school: Templepatrick AM 35; 135–36

Craigarogan td: Misc. AM 10; 131

Craigartake (see Craigastuke): Cumber LY 28; 67

Craigaruskey (see Craigarusky): Killinchy DN 7; 91

Craigarusky flax mills: Killinchy DN 7; 91

Craigarusky td: Killinchy DN 7; 86, 91

Craigastuke hill: Cumber LY 28; 44, 60, 66–67

Craigatempin td: Ballymoney AM 16; 23–24

Craigavad district: Misc. DN 17; 117

Craigavad House: Holywood DN 7; 76

Craigavad td: Holywood DN 7; 77, 79–80

Craigavole bog: Desertoghill LY 27; 25

Craigavole chapel: Desertoghill LY 27; 2, 5, 13, 15, 28

Craigavole chapel: Kilrea LY 27; 128

Craigavole flax mill: Desertoghill LY 27; 5, 13

Craigavole fort [I]: Desertoghill LY 27; 2, 15

Craigavole fort [II]: Desertoghill LY 27; 25

Craigavole school: Desertoghill LY 27; 34

Craigavole td: Desertoghill LY 27; 8, 19, 26, 32

Craigbane graveyard: Culfeightrin AM 24; 68

Craigbane td: Culfeightrin AM 24; 79

Craigbolie Castle: Magilligan LY 11; 91–92, 102

Craigbolie fort (see Craigbolie Castle): Magilligan LY 11; 92, 102

Craigboy locality: Carrickfergus AM 37; 32, 93

Craigboy td: Misc. DN 17; 124

Craigbrack td: Faughanvale LY 36; 53, 56–57, 68, 72, 83, 93, 98

Craigbuy (see Craigboy): Carrickfergus AM 37; 32

Craigdhu td: Convoy DL 39; 20

Craigdoo mountain: Clonduff DN 3; 5

Craigdoo mountain: Kilcoo DN 3; 45

Craigdooish (see Cruckdooish)

Craigdouish (see Cruckdooish)

Craigdunloof school: Dunaghy AM 13; 16

Craigdunloof td: Dunaghy AM 13; 14

Craige td: Billy AM 16; 36

Craigfadd fort [I]: Culfeightrin AM 24; 59

Craigfadd fort [II]: Culfeightrin AM 24; 59

Craigfadd standing stones: Culfeightrin AM 24; 59

Craiggy Hall cave: Antrim AM 29; 36

Craighbrack (see Craigbrack): Faughanvale LY 36; 68

Craigmacagan lough: Rathlin Island AM 24; 130

Craigmacagan stream: Rathlin Island AM 24; 130

Craigmadden td: Killygarvan DL 38; 47

Craigmelord altar: Ballintoy AM 24; 20

Craigmore cove: Aghadowey LY 22; 29, 32

Craigmore cove: Drummaul AM 19; 66

Craigmore cove: Macosquin LY 22; 94, 97

Craigmore Danes' mill: Maghera LY 18; 47

Craigmore fort: Maghera LY 18; 62

Craigmore giant's chair: Drummaul AM 19; 66, 89

Craigmore hill: Aghadowey LY 22; 33

Craigmore hill: Drummaul AM 19; 35–36

Craigmore meeting house: Ballyscullion AM 19; 13

Craigmore meeting house: Drummaul AM 19; 35, 47, 57–58, 77, 83, 85, 89

Craigmore school: Maghera LY 18; 35

Craigmore Sunday school: Drummaul AM 19; 77, 85

Craigmore td: Aghadowey LY 22; 1, 10, 16, 25–26, 32

Craigmore td: Ballyscullion AM 19; 11

Craigmore td: Drummaul AM 19; 35, 69, 79, 88–89

Craigmore td: Macosquin LY 22; 86

Craigmore td: Maghera LY 18; 12, 37, 39, 41, 47, 60

Craignaboy cove: Glynn AM 26; 32, 44

Craignaboy fort [I]: Glynn AM 26; 44

Craignaboy fort [II]: Glynn AM 26; 44

Craignaboy fort [III]: Glynn AM 26; 44

Craignaboy hill: Glynn AM 26; 9

Craignaboy td: Glynn AM 26; 1, 18, 41, 47–48

Craignabrahir (see Friar's rock): Carrickfergus AM 37; 81

Craignachoke (see Craignashoke)

Craignadarriff (see Carricknadarriff): Annahilt DN 12; 22

Craig–na–gath rock: Culfeightrin AM 24; 85

Craignageeraght fort [I]: Ahoghill AM 23; 35

Craignageeraght fort [II]: Ahoghill AM 23; 35

Craignagopple hill: Donaghedy TE 5; 88

Craignagrawe rock: Bovevagh LY 25; 14

Craignaguiroe mountain: Desertcreat TE 20; 33

Craignahorn td: Ballywillin LY 33; 51

Craignahorn td: Coleraine LY 33; 61–62

Craignarive (see Craiganariff): Ballyaghran LY 33; 24

Craignashoke mountain: Ballynascreen LY 31; 12, 16, 25

Craignashoke mountain: Bovevagh LY 25; 23

Craignashoke mountain: Dungiven LY 15; 12

Craignashoke mountain: Dunluce AM 16; 117

Craignashoke mountain: Magilligan LY 11; 100

Craignashoke mountain: Misc. LY 31; 111, 113–14

Craignashoke td: Cumber LY 28; 66

Craignasiguart rock: Leck DL 39; 115, 118

Craignasiguart trigonometrical station: Leck DL 39; 115

Craignatogue mountain: Ardstraw TE 5; 10

Craigs beetling mill: Ahoghill AM 23; 13, 29, 31

Craigs Castle mills: Ahoghill AM 23; 29

Craigs cove [I]: Finvoy AM 23; 77

Craigs cove [II]: Finvoy AM 23; 78

Craigs fort [I]: Finvoy AM 23; 68, 72, 77

Craigs fort [II]: Finvoy AM 23; 78

Craigs fort [III]: Finvoy AM 23; 78

Craigs graveyard: Ahoghill AM 23; 24, 34

Craigs hill: Finvoy AM 23; 67–68

Craigs locality: Taughboyne DL 39; 153

Craigs lough: Carnteel TE 20; 23

Craigs Lower bleach mill: Ahoghill AM 23; 13, 31

Craigs mill falls: Ahoghill AM 23; 29

Craigs of Lisbuoy rocks: Kilraghts AM 16; 131, 135

Craigs old church: Ahoghill AM 23; 25

Craigs school: Ahoghill AM 23; 34

Craigs school: Finvoy AM 23; 75

Craigs school: Rasharkin AM 23; 135

Craigs school [I]: Ahoghill AM 23; 22, 50

Craigs school [II]: Ahoghill AM 23; 40, 45

Craigs standing stone: Ahoghill AM 23; 24

Craigs Sunday school: Ahoghill AM 23; 45

Craigs td: Ahoghill AM 23; 12, 38–40

Craigs td: Finvoy AM 23; 68, 73, 76, 78

Craigs td: Raphoe DL 39; 125

Craig-sapperg td: Muff DL 38; 80

Craigtown td: Clondermot LY 34; 56, 64, 76, 109, 112, 115, 123, 130

Craigtown wood: Ballyaghran LY 33; 1

Craigtown wood: Clondermot LY 34; 123

Craigtownbeg fort: Ballyaghran LY 33; 24

Craigtownbeg td: Ballyaghran LY 33; 27

Craigtownbeg td: Ballywillin LY 33; 50

Craigtownmore cave: Ballyaghran LY 33; 11, 24

Craigtownmore fort: Ballyaghran LY 33; 10–11, 24

Craigtownmore fort: Ballywillin LY 33; 50

Craigtownmore td: Ballyaghran LY 33; 27

Craigywarren (Craigawarren) td: Kirkinriola AM 23; 88, 91

Craigywarren hill: Kirkinriola AM 23; 92

Craigywarren school: Kirkinriola AM 23; 112, 121

Craigywarren wood: Kirkinriola AM 23; 91, 121

Cralindoes (see Creaghadoos): Killea and Taughboyne DL 39; 79

Cramerhill rectory: Racavan AM 13; 86

Crampsie, James: Magilligan LY 11; 134

Crampsie, William: Magilligan LY 11; 134

Crampton, John: Newry DN 3; 99, 103

Crampton, Robert: Clondermot LY 34; 90

Cramsey, Hugh: Dungiven LY 15; 74

Cramsey, James (alias Breeson): Dungiven LY 15; 91

Cramsie, Alexander: Ballymoney AM 16; 15

Cramsie, James: Ballymoney AM 16; 8, 15–17

Cramsie, John: Ballymoney AM 16; 15–16

Cramsie, Miss: Ballymoney AM 16; 15, 17

Cramsie, Mr: Ballymoney AM 16; 4, 20

Cran td: Aghalurcher FH 4; 4, 14

Cranagh bridge: Aghagallon AM 21; 7, 18

Cranagh chapel: Bodoney TE 20; 20

Cranagh fishery: Coleraine LY 33; 53, 93, 122, 147, 149

Cranagh fishery: Killowen LY 33; 170

Cranagh fort: Cumber LY 28; 43, 45, 52–53, 83

Cranagh hill: Killowen LY 33; 158, 169

Cranagh hill national school: Dunboe LY 11; 56

Cranagh House: Coleraine LY 33; 91

Cranagh school: Dunboe LY 11; 72

Cranagh school: Killowen LY 33; 172

Cranagh td: Killowen LY 33; 172

Cranaghan Glebe House: Tomregan FH 4; 127, 131

Cranaghan lough: Tomregan FH 4; 126

Cranaghan plantation: Tomregan FH 4; 126

Cranaghan school: Tomregan FH 4; 129

Cranbrook district: Aghavea FH 4; 23

Cranbrook House: Aghalurcher FH 4; 8, 10

Cranbrooke (see Cranbrook): Aghalurcher FH 4; 10

Crane Island: Muckno MN 40; 162

Cranegill hill: Tartaraghan AH 1; 119

Cranegill House: Tartaraghan AH 1; 120

Cranegill td: Tartaraghan AH 1; 121

Craney, William: Glenavy AM 21; 91

Cranfield chapel: Ahoghill AM 23; 26

Cranfield chapel: Cranfield AM 19; 32

Cranfield chapel: Duneane AM 19; 96

Cranfield church: Ballyscullion LY 6; 56
Cranfield church: Drummaul AM 19; 71
Cranfield church: Duneane AM 19; 99
Cranfield cross: Cranfield AM 19; 32
Cranfield graveyard: Duneane AM 19; 96
Cranfield lighthouse: Kilkeel DN 3; 52
Cranfield lighthouse: Newry DN 3; 72
Cranfield lighthouse: Warrenpoint DN 3; 119–20
Cranfield old church: Antrim AM 29; 31
Cranfield old church: Killead AM 35; 25
Cranfield ph: Drummaul AM 19; 56, 70–71
Cranfield ph: Duneane AM 19; 94–96
Cranfield ph: Misc. AM 10; 129
Cranfield Point: Kilkeel DN 3; 52
Cranfield Point: Newry DN 3; 72
Cranfield Point: Warrenpoint DN 3; 119
Cranfield Point coastguard station: Kilbroney DN 3; 30
Cranfield Point coastguard station: Kilkeel DN 3; 52
Cranfield school: Duneane AM 19; 126
Cranfield td: Cranfield AM 19; 32
Cranfield well: Cranfield AM 19; 32
Cranfield well: Drummaul AM 19; 71
Cranfield well: Duneane AM 19; 96, 104
Cranfield, name of: Faughanvale LY 36; 60
Cranford td: Mevagh DL 38; 55
Cranford td: Tullyaughnish DL 38; 86–87, 94
Cranfwer locality: Lough Swilly DL 38; 128–29
Cranfwer Park Point: Lough Swilly DL 38; 117
Crangill, Henry: Magheramesk AM 21; 121
Crangill, John: Magheramesk AM 21; 116, 124
Crangill, Sareah: Magheramesk AM 21; 124
Crangle, family: Ardglass DN 17; 4
Crangle, Rev. William: Killead AM 35; 45
Crangle, Samuel: Hillsborough DN 12; 106
Crankey td: Loughgilly AH 1; 84
Crankhill hill: Ahoghill AM 23; 4
Crankhill td: Ahoghill AM 23; 38
Crankill (see Cranegill): Tartaraghan AH 1; 121
Cranlome td: Killeeshil TE 20; 62
Cranmer, family: Carrickfergus AM 37; 93
Crann (see Cran): Aghalurcher FH 4; 14
Crann td: Drumgoon CN 40; 6
Crannagh graveyard: Ballywillin AM 16; 34
Crannagh hill: Ballywillin AM 16; 34
Crannagh river: Lough Swilly DL 38; 101
Crannogue (Cranogue) td: Pomeroy TE 20; 70, 72
Crannogue hill: Pomeroy TE 20; 70
Cranny bridge: Cappagh TE 5; 20
Cranny English td: Dromore TE 5; 98
Cranny fort: Donacavey TE 5; 82
Cranny school: Desertmartin LY 31; 54, 61
Cranny school: Misc. LY 31; 125–26
Cranny Scott td: Dromore TE 5; 98
Cranny Slevin td: Dromore TE 5; 98

Cranny td: Desertmartin LY 31; 62, 141–42
Cranny td: Donacavey TE 5; 76, 78, 80–82, 85
Cranny wood: Misc. LY 31; 112
Cranoge chapel: Misc. DN 17; 122
Crans lough: Carnteel TE 20; 23
Crany, Mr: Hillsborough DN 12; 87
Cranygill (see Cranegill): Tartaraghan AH 1; 120
Crasly, family: Aghagallon AM 21; 9
Cratlagc chapel: Tullyaughnish DL 38; 89
Cratlage flax mill: Tullyaughnish DL 38; 89
Cratlage td: Mevagh DL 38; 55, 57
Cratlage td: Tullyaughnish DL 38; 96
Cratlage wood: Tullyaughnish DL 38; 86
Cratlagh locality: Clondavaddog DL 38; 2
Crauford, family: Donacavey TE 5; 71
Cravenny Irish hill: Carnteel TE 20; 23
Crawford, A.: Cleenish FH 14; 29–30
Crawford, A.: Magheracross FH 14; 100, 102
Crawford, Alexander: Coleraine LY 33; 73
Crawford, Andrew: Donacavey TE 5; 85
Crawford, Andrew: Killesher FH 14; 87
Crawford, Andrew: Kinawley FH 4; 110
Crawford, Andrew: Misc. TE 5; 147
Crawford, Benjamin: Maghera LY 18; 60
Crawford, Brice: Tamlaght Finlagan LY 25; 80
Crawford, Capt.: Blaris AM 8; 9, 33–34
Crawford, Capt.: Blaris DN 12; 43
Crawford, Charles: Clonleigh DL 39; 1, 4, 12
Crawford, Daniel: Derrykeighan AM 16; 90
Crawford, David: Donegal DL 39; 50–51
Crawford, David: Raloo AM 32; 128
Crawford, Dr (London): Billy AM 16; 67
Crawford, Dr: Blaris AM 8; 36
Crawford, F.: Donacavey TE 5; 76, 81
Crawford, family: Carnmoney AM 2; 76
Crawford, family: Doagh AM 29; 73, 94
Crawford, family: Donegore AM 29; 110
Crawford, family: Enniskillen FH 4; 58, 75
Crawford, family: Maghera LY 18; 13
Crawford, family: Raloo AM 32; 108, 123
Crawford, George: Seapatrick DN 12; 127, 133–34
Crawford, Hugh: Lissan LY 31; 99–100
Crawford, J.: Blaris AM 8; 85
Crawford, James (Jnr): Raloo AM 32; 128
Crawford, James (Snr): Raloo AM 32; 128
Crawford, James: Blaris DN 12; 46, 50
Crawford, James: Donegal DL 39; 56
Crawford, James: Duneane AM 19; 117
Crawford, James: Errigal LY 27; 38–39, 63
Crawford, James: Maghera LY 18; 51
Crawford, James: Newry DN 3; 98, 103
Crawford, Janea: Carncastle and Killyglen AM 10; 7
Crawford, John: Ahoghill AM 23; 34
Crawford, John: Duneane AM 19; 112–14, 119, 121
Crawford, John: Finvoy AM 23; 75

Crawford, John: Kilwaughter AM 10; 113
Crawford, John: Muckamore AM 35; 78
Crawford, John: Templepatrick AM 35; 148
Crawford, Jones: Ardstraw TE 5; 5
Crawford, Jones: Donacavey TE 5; 85
Crawford, Joseph: Raloo AM 32; 128
Crawford, Maj.: Ardstraw TE 5; 5, 11
Crawford, Maj.: Donacavey TE 5; 76, 81
Crawford, Maj.: Misc. TE 5; 147
Crawford, Mary: Raloo AM 32; 128
Crawford, Messrs: Seapatrick DN 12; 125
Crawford, Miss (Moneyhaw): Lissan LY 31; 101
Crawford, Miss: Blaris AM 8; 85
Crawford, Miss: Blaris DN 12; 45, 49
Crawford, Mr (Dublin): Ballee DN 17; 22
Crawford, Mr: Holywood DN 7; 77
Crawford, R.: Blaris AM 8; 60
Crawford, Rev. Alexander: Drummaul AM 19; 69,
    82, 86
Crawford, Rev. Thomas: Donegore AM 29; 129
Crawford, Rev. William: Racavan AM 13; 86
Crawford, Rev. William: Skerry AM 13; 107, 111
Crawford, Robert: Aghalee AM 21; 36
Crawford, Robert: Dromore TE 5; 97
Crawford, Robert: Killead AM 35; 37, 53
Crawford, Robert: Lissan LY 31; 109
Crawford, Robert: Maghera LY 18; 53, 60
Crawford, Robert: Newtownards DN 7; 104
Crawford, Samuel: Ballyscullion LY 6; 48
Crawford, Samuel David: Magherafelt LY 6; 96
Crawford, Sharman: Ballyscullion AM 19; 8
Crawford, Sharman: Bangor DN 7; 23, 25
Crawford, Sharman: Drumballyroney DN 3; 18
Crawford, Sharman: Killyleagh DN 17; 83
Crawford, Sharman: Kilmore DN 17; 91
Crawford, Thomas: Blaris AM 8; 25
Crawford, Thomas: Carnmoney AM 2; 76
Crawford, Thomas: Carrickfergus AM 37; 125
Crawford, Thomas: Seapatrick DN 12; 127, 132–34
Crawford, W.: Cleenish FH 14; 29
Crawford, W.S.: Annaclone DN 12; 16
Crawford, Widow: Muckamore AM 35; 80
Crawford, William: Antrim AM 29; 16
Crawford, William: Clondermot LY 34; 78, 80
Crawford, William: Maghera LY 18; 29, 51
Crawford, William: Muckamore AM 35; 81
Crawford, William: Raloo AM 32; 128
Crawford, William: Templepatrick AM 35; 152
Crawford's Croaghan td: Clonleigh DL 39; 12
Crawford's Hill td: Devenish FH 14; 58
Crawford's Table stone: Killygarvan DL 38; 41
Crawfordsburn: Misc. DN 17; 117
Crawfordsburn House: Bangor DN 7; 23, 25
Crawfordshill fort: Devenish FH 14; 55
Crawfordsland td: Kilbride AM 29; 136, 140, 155

Crawfordstown school: Skirts of Urney and
    Ardstraw TE 5; 140
Crawley's Quarter td: Bright DN 17; 34–35
Crayton, Mr: Cleenish FH 14; 29–30
Creagh bog: Coleraine LY 33; 97–98, 101
Creagh bog: Duneane AM 19; 94–95, 98
Creagh district: Artrea LY 6; 2–5, 14–17, 39–40
Creagh district: Artrea TE 20; 6
Creagh district: Lough Neagh AM 21; 94
Creagh td: Aghavea FH 4; 17, 23, 25
Creagh, Michael: Newry DN 3; 68
Creaghadoos Lower td: Misc. DL 39; 195
Creaghadoos Lower td: Taughboyne DL 39; 148,
    152
Creaghadoos Lower well: Taughboyne DL 39; 152
Creaghadoos orchard: Misc. DL 39; 189
Creaghadoos quarry: Taughboyne DL 39; 150
Creaghadoos td: Killea and Taughboyne DL 39;
    79–80, 84
Creaghadoos td: Taughboyne DL 39; 151, 154–55,
    190
Creaghadoos Upper bog: Taughboyne DL 39; 152
Creaghadoos Upper td: Taughboyne DL 39; 148,
    152, 195
Creaghadoos wood: Taughboyne DL 39; 148
Creaghamanone Island: Aghalurcher FH 4; 3, 14
Creaghanacorick Island: Aghalurcher FH 4; 3, 14
Creaghanaddy Island: Aghalurcher FH 4; 14
Creaghanameelta Island: Aghalurcher FH 4; 3, 14
Creaghanarourke Island: Aghalurcher FH 4; 3, 14
Creaghanchreesty Island: Aghalurcher FH 4; 3, 14
Creaghawaddy Island: Aghalurcher FH 4; 3
Creagheer td: Donaghedy TE 5; 91
Creaghmacwallen Island: Cleenish FH 14; 13, 29
Creaghnarourk Island: Cleenish FH 14; 13, 29
Creaghroe lough: Donegal DL 39; 44
Creainey, family: Aghagallon AM 21; 10
Crean, Samuel: Carrickfergus AM 37; 111
Creaner, Edward: Aghagallon AM 21; 6–7
Creaney, James: Ballinderry AM 21; 49
Creanmore lough: Mevagh DL 38; 55
Creany, John: Ballylinny AM 32; 30
Creary, family: Ballynure AM 32; 56
Creath, Robert: Ballintoy AM 24; 28
Creatland td: Taughboyne DL 39; 148, 152
Creavamoy (see Creevamoy)
Creavary td: Killygarvan DL 38; 47
Creavary Upper giant's grave: Killygarvan DL 38;
    41
Creavary Upper td: Killygarvan DL 38; 37
Creavery school: Shilvodan AM 19; 132
Crebarkey (see Crabarkey)
Crebilly (Craigbilly) td: Ballyclug AM 23; 53,
    55–56, 59, 64, 66
Crebilly beetling mill: Ballyclug AM 23; 56

Crebilly Castle: Ballyclug AM 23; 56–57, 60–61, 65
Crebilly chapel: Ballyclug AM 23; 53, 55, 65
Crebilly chapel: Connor AM 19; 18
Crebilly chapel: Kirkinriola AM 23; 90
Crebilly corn mill: Ballyclug AM 23; 56
Crebilly cove: Ballyclug AM 23; 62, 65
Crebilly flax mill: Ballyclug AM 23; 56
Crebilly hamlet: Ballyclug AM 23; 55–58, 65–66
Crebilly hill: Ballyclug AM 23; 52–53
Crebilly House: Ballyclug AM 23; 52–53, 55–57, 60
Crebilly school: Ballyclug AM 23; 59, 66
Crebilly td: Loughguile AM 13; 60, 63
Creden, family: Enniskillen FH 4; 75
Cree, James: Blaris DN 12; 46, 50–51
Creecussane (see Creeghassaun): Kilmacteige SO 40; 196
Creeghassaun td: Kilmacteige SO 40; 196
Creeghduff (Craigduff) td: Loughinisland DN 17; 95
Creeghduff flax mill: Loughinisland DN 17; 95, 97
Creehennan school: Moville DL 38; 74
Creehennan td: Moville DL 38; 73–75
Creek, James: Newry DN 3; 100, 104–05
Creek, William: Newry DN 3; 100, 104
Creely, family: Kilroot AM 26; 75
Creely, Patrick: Newry DN 3; 65
Creen, family: Ardglass DN 17; 4
Creenagh district: Misc. SO 40; 199
Creenagh fort: Magheramesk AM 21; 119
Creenagh graveyard: Magheramesk AM 21; 120
Creenagh school: Tullyniskan TE 20; 140–41
Creenagh td: Kilmore AH 1; 65–66, 69, 71, 73
Creenagh td: Magheramesk AM 21; 113, 120, 126
Creenahhiv td: Cleenish FH 14; 29
Creenard td: Ematris MN 40; 113
Creeramoy (see Creevamoy)
Creery td: Ardstraw TE 5; 2
Creery, C.A.: Kilmore AH 1; 67–69, 71–73
Creery, family: Kilroot AM 26; 74
Creery, John: Ballymore AH 1; 3
Creery, Rev.: Billy AM 16; 46
Creery, Rev.: Dromore TE 5; 98–99
Creery, Rev.: Kilmore DN 17; 88
Creery, Rev. L.: Ballymore AH 1; 3
Creery, Widow: Donacavey TE 5; 81
Creevaghlea td: Clones FH 4; 26
Creevamoy beetling and wash mill: Racavan AM 13; 92, 98
Creevamoy beetling mill [I]: Racavan AM 13; 92, 99
Creevamoy beetling mill [II]: Racavan AM 13; 92, 99
Creevamoy bleach green: Racavan AM 13; 92, 98
Creevamoy meeting house: Racavan AM 13; 88
Creevamoy td: Racavan AM 13; 86, 88, 98–99
Creeve (Creve) td: Aghaloo TE 20; 1

Creeve bleach green: Aughnamullen MN 40; 71–72
Creeve bleach greens: Ballybay MN 40; 79, 81
Creeve bleach mill: Lissan LY 31; 91, 101
Creeve bleaching mills: Aughnamullen MN 40; 69, 72
Creeve bog: Misc. DL 39; 187
Creeve bridge: Lough Swilly DL 38; 101
Creeve creek: Lough Swilly DL 38; 98, 101
Creeve district: Misc. SO 40; 199–200
Creeve House: Aughnamullen MN 40; 71, 74
Creeve lough: Aghaloo TE 20; 1–2
Creeve loughs: Aughnamullen MN 40; 69, 71–72
Creeve meeting house: Aughnamullen MN 40; 71
Creeve river: Aghalurcher FH 4; 3–4
Creeve school: Aughnamullen MN 40; 77
Creeve school: Duneane AM 19; 105
Creeve td: Aughnamullen MN 40; 76
Creeve td: Lissan LY 31; 91, 101
Creeve td: Misc. DL 39; 194
Creevedonnel (see Creevedonnell): Clondermot LY 34; 109
Creevedonnell td: Clondermot LY 34; 56, 64, 109, 112, 115, 123, 130
Creevehill mill: Enniskillen FH 4; 69
Creevehill school: Enniskillen FH 4; 84
Creevehill td: Enniskillen FH 4; 82
Creeveoughter bog: Killygarvan DL 38; 38, 44
Creeveoughter bridge: Killygarvan DL 38; 47
Creeveoughter giant's grave: Killygarvan DL 38; 41
Creeveoughter lough: Killygarvan DL 38; 47
Creeveoughter td: Killygarvan DL 38; 46–47
Creevey, Eliza: Dunboe LY 11; 69–70
Creevy fort: Mevagh DL 38; 58
Creevy lough: Saintfield DN 7; 117, 119
Creevy rocks: Misc. DN 17; 120
Creevy td: Drumbo DN 7; 58, 60–61
Creevy td: Mevagh DL 38; 63
Creevy, Eliza: Dunboe LY 11; 55
Creevy–Beg td: Killinchy DN 7; 86
Creevyloughgar (see Creevyloughgare): Saintfield DN 7; 117, 120
Creevyloughgare td: Saintfield DN 7; 117–20
Creevytennent td: Magheradrool DN 17; 99, 103
Cregaghduargs rock: Lough Swilly DL 38; 108
Cregalnacky rock: Lough Swilly DL 38; 108
Cregamullin Point: Lough Swilly DL 38; 134–35
Cregan chapel: Faughanvale LY 36; 6–7, 29, 33
Cregan mountain: Ardclinis AM 13; 2
Cregan quarry: Faughanvale LY 36; 53, 93
Cregan td: Cumber LY 28; 28
Cregan td: Faughanvale LY 36; 17, 30, 53, 57, 68, 72–73, 83–84, 93
Cregan wood: Faughanvale LY 36; 3, 84
Cregan, George: Hillsborough DN 12; 106
Cregan, James: Hillsborough DN 12; 105

Cregbwee locality: Lough Swilly DL 38; 140
Cregg (Craig) td: Cumber LY 28; 6–7, 28, 66, 68–69, 84, 111, 117, 122, 125
Cregg bridge: Cumber LY 28; 9
Cregg corn mill: Cumber LY 28; 86, 122
Cregg flax mill: Cumber LY 28; 86, 86, 122
Cregg graveyard: Cumber LY 28; 28–29
Cregg meeting house: Cumber LY 28; 1, 8, 14, 19, 86
Cregg old church: Cumber LY 28; 29
Cregg school: Cumber LY 28; 2, 16, 72–73, 76–77
Cregg standing stone: Cumber LY 28; 28–29
Cregg tannery: Cumber LY 28; 125
Cregg well: Cumber LY 28; 29
Cregg wood: Cumber LY 28; 117
Creggan (see Cregan): Faughanvale LY 36; 53
Creggan corn mill: Loughgilly AH 1; 86
Creggan flag quarry: Drumachose LY 9; 117
Creggan flax mill: Duneane AM 19; 101
Creggan flax mill: Loughgilly AH 1; 86
Creggan ph: Donaghmoyne MN 40; 106
Creggan ph: Inniskeen MN 40; 124
Creggan ph: Muckno MN 40; 162
Creggan river: Loughgilly AH 1; 86
Creggan school: Raphoe DL 39; 127–28
Creggan td: Raphoe DL 39; 125
Creggan, Martha: Carrickfergus AM 37; 118
Cregganboy cave: Ramoan AM 24; 93
Cregganboy td: Ramoan AM 24; 120
Creggans (see Creggan)
Creghadoos (see Creaghadoos): Misc. DL 39; 190
Cregkannans stones: Banagher LY 30; 43–44, 81
Cregmacconnack rock: Lough Swilly DL 38; 147
Cregnadutchagh rock: Lough Swilly DL 38; 107
Cregnashoke (see Craignashoke)
Crehan Island td: Galloon FH 4; 87, 95
Crehennan (see Creehennan): Moville DL 38; 74
Creight, family: Carrickfergus AM 37; 93
Creighton, Col (see Crichton): Clonleigh DL 39; 1
Creighton, David: Templecorran AM 26; 132
Creighton, Elizabeth: Coleraine LY 33; 146
Creighton, family: Errigal LY 27; 41
Creighton, George: Carrickfergus AM 37; 158
Creighton, Jane: Templecorran AM 26; 132
Creighton, John: Banagher LY 30; 46, 75
Creighton, Mary: Templecorran AM 26; 132
Creighton, Patrick: Island Magee AM 10; 95
Creighton, Rev.: Dromore TE 5; 98
Creighton, William: Coleraine LY 33; 146
Creighton's Green locality: Holywood DN 7; 76
Creiton, Ann: Aghadowey LY 22; 37
Creiton, Fanny: Aghadowey LY 22; 37
Cremorne barony: Aughnamullen MN 40; 69
Cremorne barony: Ballybay MN 40; 78
Cremorne barony: Donaghmoyne MN 40; 106

Cremorne barony: Drumgoon CN 40; 3
Cremorne barony: Ematris MN 40; 112
Cremorne barony: Magheross MN 40; 143
Cremorne barony: Misc. LY 36; 106
Cremorne barony: Muckno MN 40; 162, 164
Cremorne barony: Tyholland MN 40; 174
Cremorne bleach green: Aughnamullen MN 40; 72
Cremorne Green House: Aughnamullen MN 40; 71
Cremorne lough: Ematris MN 40; 113
Cremorne scutching mill: Aughnamullen MN 40; 72
Cremorne, family: Ematris MN 40; 114–15
Cremorne, Lady: Donagh MN 40; 103
Cremorne, Lady: Drumgoon CN 40; 8
Cremorne, Lady: Ematris MN 40; 117
Cremorne, Lady: Errigal Truagh MN 40; 122
Cremorne, Lord: Aghabog MN 40; 67
Cremorne, Lord: Aughnamullen MN 40; 76, 76
Cremorne, Lord: Clonfeacle AH 1; 25
Cremorne, Lord: Currin MN 40; 92, 96
Cremorne, Lord: Drummully FH 4; 37
Cremorne, Lord: Ematris MN 40; 113–15, 119
Cremourne (see Cremorne)
Crenenagh td: Cappagh TE 5; 22
Cresslagh: Mevagh DL 38; 60
Cressycrib stream: Tamlaght Finlagan LY 25; 97
Cressycrib td: Aghanloo LY 11; 13, 20, 40–42
Cresteel (see Gresteel): Tamlaght Finlagan LY 25; 96
Cretland orchard: Misc. DL 39; 189
Cretland td: Misc. DL 39; 195
Crevane td: Killoran and Kilvarnet SO 40; 183
Creve school: Cranfield AM 19; 32
Creveoughtar (see Creeveoughter): Killygarvan DL 38; 46
Crevery forts: Antrim AM 29; 43
Crevery school: Antrim AM 29; 41
Crevillyvalley beetling and wash mill: Connor AM 19; 22
Crevillyvalley beetling mill: Connor AM 19; 22
Crevillyvalley bleach green: Connor AM 19; 22
Crevnish old castle: Magheraculmoney FH 14; 106
Crevolea bleach green: Aghadowey LY 22; 10
Crevolea bog: Aghadowey LY 22; 2, 32
Crevolea Glebe td: Aghadowey LY 22; 6
Crevolea td: Aghadowey LY 22; 3, 8, 32, 38
Crew adult school: Maghera LY 18; 34
Crew bog: Maghera LY 18; 27, 56–57
Crew bridge: Maghera LY 18; 63
Crew burn: Glenavy AM 21; 78
Crew flax mill: Maghera LY 18; 27, 35
Crew fort: Errigal Keerogue TE 20; 51
Crew hill: Ballinderry AM 21; 43, 45
Crew hill: Donaghenry TE 20; 39
Crew hill: Glenavy AM 21; 77–79, 82
Crew Lower bridge: Ardstraw TE 5; 14

Crew Lower fort: Ardstraw TE 5; 12
Crew Lower standing stones: Ardstraw TE 5; 12
Crew Lower td: Ardstraw TE 5; 12
Crew mill: Ardstraw TE 5; 13
Crew quarry: Errigal Keerogue TE 20; 51
Crew school: Maghera LY 18; 32, 34, 66
Crew school [I]: Glenavy AM 21; 79–80, 90
Crew school [II]: Glenavy AM 21; 91
Crew td: Ardglass DN 17; 7
Crew td: Errigal Keerogue TE 20; 48, 51, 57
Crew td: Glenavy AM 21; 79
Crew td: Maghera LY 18; 18, 22, 58, 80–81
Crew Upper corn mill: Ardstraw TE 5; 5, 14
Crewbeg (Crubeg) td: Ballymore AH 1; 1, 8, 13–14, 16, 18
Crewcat td: Kilmore AH 1; 69, 72
Crewhill (see Creevehill): Enniskillen FH 4; 84
Crewmore td: Ballymore AH 1; 9, 14, 17–18
Crews td: Ballee DN 17; 22
Crewy td: Aghaderg DN 12; 1
Cribbrit lough: Killymard DL 39; 94
Crichton, Brig.: Kinawley FH 4; 117
Crichton, Col (see Creighton): Galloon FH 4; 100–02, 105
Crichton, David: Galloon FH 4; 91
Crichton, family: Enniskillen FH 4; 52
Crichton, J.: Rossorry FH 14; 115
Crichton, John: Aghalurcher FH 4; 10–11, 14
Crichton, John: Galloon FH 4; 92, 96
Crichton, John: Killesher FH 14; 87
Crichton, John: Kinawley FH 4; 113, 115–16, 119–22
Crick, William: Carrickfergus AM 37; 194
Crickard, George: Hillsborough DN 12; 97, 105
Crieve Glebe td: Leck DL 39; 118
Crieve Smith td: Leck DL 39; 118
Crievekeeran hill: Tynan AH 1; 124
Crievekeeran old castle: Tynan AH 1; 128
Crievekieran (see Crievekeeran): Tynan AH 1; 124
Crig, family: Carrickfergus AM 37; 93
Criggan, Mr: Cappagh TE 5; 18
Criggan, Rev.: Cappagh TE 5; 17
Criggan, Rev.: Dromore TE 5; 99
Crilley, family: Maghera LY 18; 48
Crilly Hill td: Termonamongan TE 5; 143
Crilly House: Aghaloo TE 20; 1
Crilly td: Templecarn DL 39; 164
Crilly, Ann: Errigal LY 27; 66
Crilly, Arthur: Maghera LY 18; 81
Crilly, Bernard: Errigal LY 27; 66
Crilly, Bridget: Errigal LY 27; 66
Crilly, Catherine: Carrickfergus AM 37; 120
Crilly, Catherine: Tamlaght O'Crilly LY 18; 137
Crilly, family: Maghera LY 18; 24
Crilly, Francis: Tamlaght O'Crilly LY 18; 93

Crilly, Hugh: Maghera LY 18; 80
Crilly, James: Desertoghill LY 27; 17, 26
Crilly, James: Kilcronaghan LY 31; 85
Crilly, James: Newry DN 3; 99
Crilly, James [I]: Maghera LY 18; 62
Crilly, James [II]: Maghera LY 18; 80
Crilly, James [III]: Maghera LY 18; 80
Crilly, John: Errigal LY 27; 66
Crilly, John: Maghera LY 18; 81
Crilly, John: Tamlaght O'Crilly LY 18; 91, 109, 114, 129–30, 135
Crilly, Mary: Tamlaght O'Crilly LY 18; 137
Crilly, Michael: Errigal LY 27; 65
Crilly, Mr: Maghera LY 18; 19
Crilly, Mrs: Maghera LY 18; 19
Crilly, Patrick: Ballynascreen LY 31; 20, 22–23, 30
Crimlin td: Magheraculmoney FH 14; 112
Crindle (Crendle) td: Tamlaght Finlagan LY 25; 65, 93, 116
Crindle school: Tamlaght Finlagan LY 25; 80, 96
Crindle Sunday school: Tamlaght Finlagan LY 25; 124
Cristie, George: Ballintoy AM 24; 31
Cristy, family: Dunluce AM 16; 117
Croagan chapel: Aghalurcher FH 4; 11
Croagh Beg Castle: Misc. LY 36; 109–10
Croagh Connalagh mountain: Donegal DL 39; 53–54
Croagh Garrow mountain: Donegal DL 39; 53–54
Croagh Meen mountain: Donegal DL 39; 53
Croagh meeting house: Ballintoy AM 24; 23
Croagh Onagh mountain: Donegal DL 39; 53–54
Croagh td: Templecarn DL 39; 164
Croaghan (Croghan) td: Magilligan LY 11; 95, 126
Croaghan bogs: Macosquin LY 22; 119
Croaghan chapel: Aghalurcher FH 4; 6
Croaghan Chapel td: Misc. DL 39; 185, 197
Croaghan Crawford's td: Misc. DL 39; 197
Croaghan fort: Clondavaddog DL 38; 6
Croaghan graveyard: Macosquin LY 22; 85
Croaghan hill: Armoy AM 24; 2
Croaghan hill: Ballintoy AM 24; 12
Croaghan hill: Clondavaddog DL 38; 9
Croaghan hill: Clonleigh DL 39; 1, 3, 5, 13, 15
Croaghan hill: Killygarvan DL 38; 36–37, 42
Croaghan hill: Loughguile AM 13; 58–60
Croaghan hill: Misc. DL 39; 187
Croaghan hill: Urney DL 39; 176
Croaghan Island: Clondavaddog DL 38; 4, 6
Croaghan New Rowin td: Misc. DL 39; 197
Croaghan old church: Macosquin LY 22; 118
Croaghan Pounds rocks: Macosquin LY 22; 79, 118
Croaghan quarries: Clonleigh DL 39; 8
Croaghan river: Killygarvan DL 38; 37
Croaghan school: Aghalurcher FH 4; 11

Croaghan springs: Macosquin LY 22; 119

Croaghan td: Aghalurcher FH 4; 13

Croaghan td: Killygarvan DL 38; 38

Croaghan td: Lough Swilly DL 38; 129

Croaghan td: Macosquin LY 22; 79, 84, 118

Croaghan td: Magilligan LY 11; 135

Croaghan td: Tullyaughnish DL 38; 97

Croaghan trigonometrical station: Clonleigh DL 39; 1

Croaghan well: Clonleigh DL 39; 5

Croaghan wood: Clonleigh DL 39; 5

Croaghbeg (see Cross): Ballymoney AM 16; 20

Croaghbeg bog: Ballintoy AM 24; 24–25

Croaghbeg td: Ballintoy AM 24; 24

Croaghbrack hill: Templecarn DL 39; 158, 164

Croaghbrack td: Templecarn DL 39; 161–62, 164

Croaghdooh Head: Lough Swilly DL 38; 113

Croagheen td: Devenish FH 14; 58

Croaghmore cave [I]: Ballintoy AM 24; 23

Croaghmore cave [II]: Ballintoy AM 24; 23

Croaghmore cave [III]: Ballintoy AM 24; 23–24

Croaghmore druid's altar: Ballintoy AM 24; 23

Croaghmore druid's stone: Ballintoy AM 24; 24

Croaghmore fort [I]: Ballintoy AM 24; 23

Croaghmore fort [II]: Ballintoy AM 24; 23

Croaghmore fort [III]: Ballintoy AM 24; 23

Croaghmore hill: Ballintoy AM 24; 10, 17, 24

Croaghmore hills: Drumtullagh AM 16; 103

Croaghmore quarry: Ballintoy AM 24; 23

Croaghmore standing stones [I]: Ballintoy AM 24; 24

Croaghmore standing stones [II]: Ballintoy AM 24; 24

Croaghmore td: Ballintoy AM 24; 22

Croaghpatrick Mountain: Faughanvale LY 36; 52

Croaghrin td: Rossorry FH 14; 116

Croaghross (Crawris) td: Clondavaddog DL 38; 6, 8

Croaghross coastguard station: Clondavaddog DL 38; 6, 8

Croaghross coastguard station: Tullyaughnish DL 38; 92

Croan flax mill [I]: Clonallan DN 3; 1

Croan flax mill [II]: Clonallan DN 3; 1

Crobane flour mills: Newry DN 3; 108

Crobane school: Newry DN 3; 81, 108

Crobane td: Newry DN 3; 81, 108

Crocandoo mountain: Tickmacrevan AM 13; 125

Crock Rusky hill: Donagh DL 38; 31

Crockacleaven (Crocknacleaven) td: Aghalurcher FH 4; 16

Crockacleaven lough: Aghalurcher TE 5; 1

Crockaleven (see Crockacleaven)

Crockaness td: Aghalurcher FH 4; 13

Crockanin td: Dungiven LY 15; 61

Crockanna hill: Lissan LY 31; 93, 100

Crockanna well: Lissan LY 31; 90, 93, 100

Crockan–naboghal hill: Culfeightrin AM 24; 83

Crockavar (see Crockravar): Ardclinis AM 13; 1

Crockbrack (see Croaghbrack): Templecarn DL 39; 158

Crockduff td: Loughguile AM 13; 70

Crockeningo hill: Templecarn DL 39; 156, 158

Crockeningo td: Templecarn DL 39; 162

Crocket, Archibald: Tamlaght O'Crilly LY 18; 131

Crocket, Isaac: Tamlaght O'Crilly LY 18; 115, 131

Crocket, John: Tamlaght O'Crilly LY 18; 128

Crocket, Mr: Clonleigh DL 39; 10

Crocket's hill: Drumcree AH 1; 34, 38

Crockett, family: Maghera LY 18; 13

Crockett, George: Misc. DL 39; 186

Crockett, Mrs: Maghera LY 18; 53

Crockglass district: Clondavaddog DL 38; 4

Crockglass hill: Clondavaddog DL 38; 5

Crockindollagh bogs: Errigal LY 27; 54

Crockindollagh flax mill [I]: Errigal LY 27; 40

Crockindollagh flax mill [II]: Errigal LY 27; 59, 92

Crockindollagh fort [I]: Errigal LY 27; 42, 67

Crockindollagh fort [II]: Errigal LY 27; 42

Crockindollagh quarry: Errigal LY 27; 90

Crockindollagh stream: Errigal LY 27; 67

Crockindollagh td: Errigal LY 27; 68–69, 81, 86, 90, 92

Crockmore mountain: Ballynascreen LY 31; 1, 11

Crocknacrieve demesne: Magheracross FH 14; 93

Crocknacrieve House: Magheracross FH 14; 95–96

Crocknacunny hill: Templecarn DL 39; 164

Crocknaferbrague (Knocknefarbreagea) td: Donacavey TE 5; 76, 78, 80–81, 84, 86

Crocknagowan td: Aghalurcher FH 4; 13

Crocknagrally td: Aghalurcher FH 4; 14

Crocknahoish td: Galloon FH 4; 87, 95

Crocknahull td: Aghalurcher FH 4; 16

Crocknakeera td: Killesher FH 14; 87

Crocknanane td: Aghalurcher FH 4; 13

Crockravar mountain: Ardclinis AM 13; 1, 5

Crofton, Capt.: Kilbroney DN 3; 31

Crofton, E.: Misc. SO 40; 200

Crofton, H.: Aughnamullen MN 40; 75–76

Crofton, Rev. James: Blaris AM 8; 23, 62, 83

Crofton, Rev. James: Blaris DN 12; 35

Croghan (see Croaghan): Misc. DL 39; 187

Croghan hill: Drumachose LY 9; 93

Croghan hill: Misc. LY 36; 120

Croghan td: Cumber LY 28; 63

Croghanwood td: Clonleigh DL 39; 12

Croghenerragate (see Crooghanarget): Killymard DL 39; 100

Croghfern (Croughfern) td: Carnmoney AM 2; 34, 58, 71, 81, 87–88, 93, 95, 102

Croghfern cave [I]: Carnmoney AM 2; 95

Croghfern cave [II]: Carnmoney AM 2; 71, 95

Croghfern cave [III]: Carnmoney AM 2; 95

Croghfern caves: Carnmoney AM 2; 71

Croghfern fort: Carnmoney AM 2; 101

Croghfern school: Carnmoney AM 2; 78, 86

Crohadoes (see Creaghadoos): Taughboyne DL 39; 148

Crohan (see Croaghan)

Crohane (see Croaghan)

Crohonagh giant's bed: Donaghmore DL 39; 35

Crohonagh td: Donaghmore DL 39; 28, 35, 37

Croish (Cross) td: Ardstraw TE 5; 12

Croish cloghogle stones: Ardstraw TE 5; 12

Croish fort: Ardstraw TE 5; 12

Croish House: Ardstraw TE 5; 3, 5, 11

Croken, family: Derryaghy AM 8; 103

Crolly, Rev. William: Carrickfergus AM 37; 133

Crolly, Rev. William: Doagh AM 29; 88

Crolly, Rev. William: Misc. DN 17; 119

Crom Castle: Enniskillen FH 4; 52, 59

Crom Castle: Galloon FH 4; 87–89, 91–93, 95–96, 98–103, 105

Crom Castle: Killesher FH 14; 87

Crom Castle: Kinawley FH 4; 115–17, 119–23

Crom school: Galloon FH 4; 96

Crom td: Galloon FH 4; 95

Crom woods: Kinawley FH 4; 114

Crom, family: Ballynure AM 32; 56

Cromaghs bog: Armoy AM 24; 1, 3

Cromaghs chapel: Armoy AM 24; 2, 4

Cromie, Anne: Carrickfergus AM 37; 125

Cromie, family: Ballyaghran LY 33; 8

Cromie, Fanny: Ballyaghran LY 33; 5

Cromie, John (Jnr): Ballyaghran LY 33; 3–7, 11–12, 14–22, 24, 26–27

Cromie, John (Snr): Ballyaghran LY 33; 3

Cromie, John: Annahilt DN 12; 21–23

Cromie, John: Ballymoney AM 16; 27

Cromie, John: Coleraine LY 33; 63–64, 104, 127

Cromie, John: Drumachose LY 9; 104

Cromie, John: Drumballyroney DN 3; 13

Cromie, John: Faughanvale LY 36; 45

Cromie, John: Hillsborough DN 12; 106

Cromie, John: Killead AM 35; 49

Cromie, John: Loughinisland DN 17; 97

Cromie, John: Magheradrool DN 17; 104–06

Cromie, John: Tamlaght Finlagan LY 25; 80–81, 108

Cromie, Mr: Aghadowey LY 22; 5

Cromie, Mrs John: Ballyaghran LY 33; 12–13, 16–17

Cromie, Widow: Shilvodan AM 19; 138

Cromkill (Crumpkill) td: Clondermot LY 34; 38, 45, 56, 64, 76, 109, 112, 115, 123, 130

Cromlin river: Misc. DN 17; 117

Crommelin, Ann [I]: Blaris AM 8; 20

Crommelin, Ann [II]: Blaris AM 8; 21

Crommelin, Easther: Blaris AM 8; 21

Crommelin, family: Blaris AM 8; 21, 45

Crommelin, family: Down DN 17; 59

Crommelin, Gilliot: Blaris AM 8; 21

Crommelin, Henriett: Blaris AM 8; 21

Crommelin, Henrietta: Blaris AM 8; 21

Crommelin, James: Blaris AM 8; 21

Crommelin, Jane: Blaris AM 8; 21

Crommelin, Lewis: Blaris AM 8; 7, 20

Crommelin, Louis: Blaris AM 8; 20

Crommelin, Louis: Derryaghy AM 8; 105

Crommelin, Magdalen: Blaris AM 8; 21

Crommelin, Mr: Killead AM 35; 17

Crommelin, N.D.: Blaris DN 12; 47

Crommelin, N.D.: Comber DN 7; 37, 39–40

Crommelin, N.D.: Donaghadee DN 7; 46, 49–50

Crommelin, N.D.: Dunaghy AM 13; 17

Crommelin, N.D.: Layd AM 13; 39, 42, 45

Crommelin, N.D.: Newtown Crommelin AM 13; 78–83

Crommelin, Nicholas: Derryaghy AM 8; 110

Crommelin, S.L.: Blaris AM 8; 21

Crommey, Edward: Dungiven LY 15; 93

Crommey, James: Dungiven LY 15; 93

Crommey, John: Dungiven LY 15; 74, 93

Crommey, Mr: Dungiven LY 15; 88

Crommey's fort: Dungiven LY 15; 88

Cromore House: Ballyaghran LY 33; 3, 7, 16, 20–22

Cromore House: Coleraine LY 33; 63

Cromore plantation: Ballyaghran LY 33; 20

Crompt, John: Drumachose LY 9; 61

Cromwell, Edward (see Oakham): Down DN 17; 42

Cromwell, Elizabeth (see Southwell): Misc. DN 17; 119

Cromwell, family: Ardglass DN 17; 12

Cromwell, Lord: Kilmegan DN 3; 59

Cromwell, Oliver: Aghagallon AM 21; 9–10

Cromwell, Oliver: Aghalurcher FH 4; 9

Cromwell, Oliver: Aghanloo LY 11; 26

Cromwell, Oliver: Ahoghill AM 23; 34

Cromwell, Oliver: Ballinderry AM 21; 52–53, 55–56

Cromwell, Oliver: Ballintoy AM 24; 18

Cromwell, Oliver: Ballymartin AM 2; 17

Cromwell, Oliver: Ballynure AM 32; 64, 68

Cromwell, Oliver: Ballyscullion LY 6; 53

Cromwell, Oliver: Ballywillin AM 16; 33

Cromwell, Oliver: Banagher LY 30; 81, 102–06, 108

Cromwell, Oliver: Blaris AM 8; 8

Cromwell, Oliver: Clondermot LY 34; 34, 57, 60, 62–63, 65, 67–68, 70–73, 75

Cromwell, Oliver: Coleraine LY 33; 121–22

Cromwell, Oliver: Connor AM 19; 18

Cromwell, Oliver: Cumber LY 28; 20, 61–62, 65–67, 69–71

Cromwell, Oliver: Derryaghy AM 8; 102

Cromwell, Oliver: Donegal DL 39; 51

Cromwell, Oliver: Drumballyroney DN 3; 16

Cromwell, Oliver: Drumbeg AM 8; 129

Cromwell, Oliver: Drumragh TE 5; 108

Cromwell, Oliver: Ematris MN 40; 114–15

Cromwell, Oliver: Faughanvale LY 36; 50, 54–64

Cromwell, Oliver: Kilmacteige SO 40; 189

Cromwell, Oliver: Kilmegan DN 3; 59

Cromwell, Oliver: Lambeg AM 8; 136

Cromwell, Oliver: Leck DL 39; 118

Cromwell, Oliver: Lough Neagh AM 21; 95

Cromwell, Oliver: Macosquin LY 22; 95

Cromwell, Oliver: Magheramesk AM 21; 113, 124–26

Cromwell, Oliver: Misc. LY 36; 107, 110

Cromwell, Oliver: Templecarn DL 39; 159

Cromwell, Thomas (see Ardglass): Down DN 17; 42

Cromwell, Tommy: Galloon FH 4; 97

Cromwell, V.E.: Down DN 17; 42

Cromwell, William (see also Ardglass): Misc. DN 17; 119

Cromwell, woman named: Leck DL 39; 118

Cromy and Taggartsland td: Donegore AM 29; 101, 131

Cronaglacken hill: Conwal DL 39; 24

Cronamuck hill: Conwal DL 39; 24

Cronaugh, St: Kilcronaghan LY 31; 68, 76

Cronbannagh library: Coleraine LY 33; 136–37

Cronbannagh school: Coleraine LY 33; 69, 71, 134, 136–37, 153

Cronbannagh Sunday school: Coleraine LY 33; 69, 71, 134, 136

Crone, Ellen: Carrickfergus AM 37; 127

Crone, family: Derryaghy AM 8; 103

Crone, John: Carrickfergus AM 37; 119

Crone, John: Derryaghy AM 8; 91–92, 100, 105, 107

Crone, John: Drumbeg AM 8; 129

Crone, Mr (Derryene): Tartaraghan AH 1; 122

Crone, Richard: Blaris AM 8; 64

Crone, Richard: Derryaghy AM 8; 93, 103

Crone, Widow: Derryaghy AM 8; 91

Cronghill bog: Aghaloo TE 20; 1

Cronien td: Magheraculmoney FH 14; 111

Cronkeeran td: Killymard DL 39; 100

Cronkurris hill: Lough Swilly DL 38; 101, 131, 133

Cronstown td: Misc. DN 17; 124

Cronyscairne hill: Templecarn DL 39; 156

Croocks, family: Desertlyn LY 31; 42

Croocks, Rev. Henry: Desertlyn LY 31; 42

Crooghanarget td: Killymard DL 39; 99–100

Crook, Mr: Enniskillen FH 4; 84

Crook, Rev.: Tamlaght Finlagan LY 25; 69

Crookdooish (see Cruckdooish): Cumber LY 28; 3

Crookdouish (see Cruckdooish): Cumber LY 28; 5

Crooke, E.: Enniskillen FH 4; 69

Crooke, family: Enniskillen FH 4; 58, 75

Crooke, Margaret (see Moor): Enniskillen FH 4; 72

Crooked bridge: Tullyaughnish DL 38; 90

Crooked burn: Banagher LY 30; 100

Crooked Rig (see Friar's glen): Carrickfergus AM 37; 82

Crooked river: Tomregan FH 4; 125–26, 128

Crooked stone: Killead AM 35; 49

Crookedstone bridge: Killead AM 35; 49

Crookedstone corn mill [I]: Killead AM 35; 14–15, 42, 48

Crookedstone corn mill [II]: Killead AM 35; 15, 42, 48

Crookedstone td: Killead AM 35; 22, 35, 49–51

Crookenaboughelly rock: Kilmacteige SO 40; 187, 193

Crookenalaughilly (see Crookenaboughelly): Kilmacteige SO 40; 193

Crooknabaya fort: Skerry AM 13; 120

Crookondoela village: Kilmacteige SO 40; 193

Crookoneaurrough village: Kilmacteige SO 40; 196

Crooks, family: Carrickfergus AM 37; 93

Crooks, George: Magheramesk AM 21; 120, 126

Crooks, John: Magheramesk AM 21; 127

Crooks, Robert: Tamlaght TE 20; 75, 131, 136

Crooks, Samuel: Tamlaght TE 20; 92–93, 103

Crookshank, H.C: Clogher TE 5; 41

Crookshank, Rev. C.H.: Drummaul AM 19; 69

Crookshanks, Mary: Tamlaght TE 20; 106

Crooky's locality: Mintiaghs DL 38; 65

Croonalaghy hill: Donaghmore DL 39; 28

Croonalaghy td: Donaghmore DL 39; 37

Croppy hill: Macosquin LY 22; 116

Croreagh (Crowreagh) td: Newry DN 3; 81, 108

Crorey, Rev. Samuel: Dromore DN 12; 76

Crosach, Shane (see O'Mullan)

Crosby, family: Derryaghy AM 8; 103

Crosdong House: Laragh CN 40; 45

Croset, John: Magherafelt LY 6; 109–11

Crosh school: Ardstraw TE 5; 13

Crosh td: Ardstraw TE 5; 3

Crosier, Mrs: Ballymoney AM 16; 15

Crosier, William: Ballymoney AM 16; 16

Croslamuck td: Misc. DN 17; 123

Cross (see Draperstown): Ballynascreen LY 31; 3

Cross bleach green: Ballyclug AM 23; 53, 55–56

Cross bleach green: Connor AM 19; 22

Cross bog: Ballyclug AM 23; 55

Cross bridge: Ballymoney AM 16; 1

Cross burn: Desertlyn LY 31; 42

Cross Castle: Ballymoney AM 16; 4, 20, 23
Cross Castle: Dungiven LY 15; 35
Cross cave: Culfeightrin AM 24; 67, 81
Cross church: Killevy AH 1; 54
Cross district: Killea and Taughboyne DL 39; 87
Cross druid's temple: Culfeightrin AM 24; 81
Cross flax mill: Killevy AH 1; 54
Cross flax mill: Taughboyne DL 39; 152
Cross Glebe cove: Coleraine LY 33; 92, 132
Cross Glebe fort: Coleraine LY 33; 92, 132
Cross Glebe td: Coleraine LY 33; 145
Cross hill: Aghavea FH 4; 17
Cross hill: Ballyclug AM 23; 52, 54
Cross hill: Derrykeighan AM 16; 87, 95
Cross hill: Donaghmore DL 39; 28
Cross hill: Faughanvale LY 36; 10, 14–15, 31
Cross hill: Raloo AM 32; 80, 82, 86, 121
Cross Hill meeting house: Raloo AM 32; 130
Cross Island: Tullynakill DN 7; 124
Cross mountain: Aghalurcher FH 4; 2
Cross O'Donel locality: Misc. LY 36; 109
Cross quarry: Taughboyne DL 39; 152
Cross Slieve mountain: Layd AM 13; 37
Cross stone: Ballywillin LY 33; 48
Cross td: Ballyclug AM 23; 52–53
Cross td: Ballymoney AM 16; 4, 20
Cross td: Culfeightrin AM 24; 42, 59, 67, 72, 81
Cross td: Drumgath DN 3; 19, 21
Cross td: Enniskillen FH 4; 81
Cross td: Maghera LY 18; 65
Cross td: Moville DL 38; 73
Cross td: Taughboyne DL 39; 148, 152, 195
Cross, John: Tynan AH 1; 130
Cross, M.: Tynan AH 1; 125, 127
Cross, Richard: Eglish AH 1; 44
Crossa (see Cross): Ballyclug AM 23; 55
Crossalaney td: Carlingford LH 40; 58
Crossalone lough: Donaghmoyne MN 40; 106
Crossan school: Kilskeery TE 5; 115
Crossan td: Drumbo DN 7; 59–61
Crossan td: Kilskeery TE 5; 115
Crossan, family: Faughanvale LY 36; 49–50
Crossan, family: Misc. LY 36; 106–07
Crossan, John: Carrickfergus AM 37; 120
Crossballycormick td: Cumber LY 28; 35, 46, 48, 55, 60–62, 95, 100, 104, 107
Crossballycormick wood: Cumber LY 28; 100
Crossbuy bog: Errigal Keerogue TE 20; 52
Crossbuy td: Errigal Keerogue TE 20; 48, 52, 57
Crosscanley (Crosscally) Glebe td: Aghadowey LY 22; 38
Crosscanley td: Aghadowey LY 22; 10
Crosscanley tumulus: Aghadowey LY 22; 29
Crossconnell district: Lough Swilly DL 38; 133, 136
Crossconnell strand: Lough Swilly DL 38; 132

Crossconnell td: Clonmany DL 38; 20
Crossdall lough: Clontibret MN 40; 85
Crossdall school: Tynan AH 1; 129
Crossdall td: Tynan AH 1; 124
Crossdernot corn mill: Pomeroy TE 20; 70
Crossduff chapel of ease: Aughnamullen MN 40; 71
Crossduff school: Aughnamullen MN 40; 77
Crossduff td: Aughnamullen MN 40; 76
Crossen, Catherine: Derryaghy AM 8; 115
Crossen, Elizabeth: Derryaghy AM 8; 115
Crosset, Elizabeth: Ahoghill AM 23; 37
Crosset, James: Ahoghill AM 23; 37
Crosset, Jane: Ahoghill AM 23; 37
Crosset, Martha: Ahoghill AM 23; 37
Crossey, family: Ballinderry AM 21; 54
Crossey, family: Magheragall AM 21; 99
Crossgar: Inch DN 17; 74
Crossgar: Killyleagh DN 17; 87
Crossgar: Kilmore DN 17; 88, 90–91, 93
Crossgar: Misc. DN 17; 128
Crossgar bog: Kilmore DN 17; 92
Crossgar chapel: Kilmore DN 17; 90, 92
Crossgar flax mill: Kilmore DN 17; 88, 92
Crossgar House: Kilmore DN 17; 88
Crossgar market house: Kilmore DN 17; 90
Crossgar meeting house: Kilmore DN 17; 90
Crossgar mills: Dromara DN 12; 63
Crossgar national school: Kilmore DN 17; 90, 92
Crossgar pay school [I]: Kilmore DN 17; 92
Crossgar pay school [II]: Kilmore DN 17; 92
Crossgar post office: Kilmore DN 17; 90
Crossgar quarry: Kilmore DN 17; 93
Crossgar school: Dromara DN 12; 64
Crossgar td: Coleraine LY 33; 66, 143
Crossgar td: Dromara DN 12; 62–64
Crossgar td: Kilmore DN 17; 88
Crossgare bridge: Macosquin LY 22; 81, 103
Crossgare cave: Macosquin LY 22; 113
Crossgare meeting house: Macosquin LY 22; 80, 90, 100
Crossgare standing stone: Aghadowey LY 22; 32
Crossgare standing stones: Macosquin LY 22; 86, 98, 113
Crossgare td: Aghadowey LY 22; 33
Crossgare td: Macosquin LY 22; 99, 122
Crossgreen locality: Carrickfergus AM 37; 93, 174
Crossgrove, Daniel: Muckamore AM 35; 81
Crosshan school: Drumtullagh AM 16; 99
Crosshill corn mill: Killead AM 35; 42
Crosshill flour mills: Killead AM 35; 42
Crosshill fort: Killead AM 35; 27, 39
Crosshill school: Killead AM 35; 36–37, 43, 53
Crosshill td: Killead AM 35; 13–14, 19, 44, 47–48, 50–51
Crosshill windmill: Killead AM 35; 42

Crosskennan fort: Antrim AM 29; 30, 43

Crosskennan Lower hill: Antrim AM 29; 1

Crosskennan mound: Antrim AM 29; 36

Crosskennan tumulus: Antrim AM 29; 44

Crosskeys school: Aughnamullen MN 40; 77

Crosskeys td: Ahoghill AM 23; 40

Crosskeys td: Aughnamullen MN 40; 76

Crosskeys td: Ballyscullion AM 19; 9–10, 12

Crossland bog: Desertoghill LY 27; 25

Crossland td: Desertoghill LY 27; 3, 11, 14, 18–21, 24, 29, 32

Crosslea grey stone: Aghadowey LY 22; 27–28, 32, 34

Crosslea grey stone: Macosquin LY 22; 94, 119

Crosslea td: Aghadowey LY 22; 27

Crosslea td: Macosquin LY 22; 94

Crossley (see Crossbuy): Errigal Keerogue TE 20; 57

Crossley, Capt.: Errigal Keerogue TE 20; 48–49

Crossley, Capt.: Killeeshil TE 20; 62–64

Crossley, family: Blaris AM 8; 21

Crossley, Francis: Blaris AM 8; 32, 61

Crossley, John (Jnr): Blaris AM 8; 32, 58

Crossley, John (Snr): Blaris AM 8; 13, 16, 31, 50–51, 61, 71, 84

Crossley, John: Blaris DN 12; 45, 49

Crossley, John [I]: Blaris AM 8; 61

Crossley, Maj.: Blaris AM 8; 84–85

Crossley, Maj.: Drumbeg AM 8; 124, 130

Crossley, Miss: Maghera LY 18; 18, 72

Crossley, Mr (Ballygawley): Aughnamullen MN 40; 75–76

Crossley, Mr (Newtownbutler): Aughnamullen MN 40; 76

Crossley, William: Errigal LY 27; 46, 64

Crossmacahilly td: Seagoe AH 1; 105, 108

Crossmaglen: Creggan AH 1; 27

Crossmaglen chapel (see also Bucklawn): Creggan AH 1; 27

Crossmaglen school [I]: Creggan AH 1; 27

Crossmaglen school [II]: Creggan AH 1; 27

Crossmahilly (see Crossmacahilly): Seagoe AH 1; 105

Crossmakeever (Crossmakever) td: Aghadowey LY 22; 1, 10, 36

Crossmary hill: Carrickfergus AM 37; 32

Crossmary hill: Raloo AM 32; 108

Crossmary nunnery: Kilroot AM 26; 68–69, 77

Crossmary td: Carrickfergus AM 37; 93

Crossmary td: Kilroot AM 26; 56, 61, 69, 77, 79

Crossnacreevy school: Comber DN 7; 30

Crossnacreevy td: Comber DN 7; 30, 42

Crossnacreevy td: Holywood DN 7; 82

Crossnadonnald locality: Drumachose LY 9; 128

Crossnamucklagh (see Knocknamuckly): Seagoe AH 1; 104

Crossnamuckly td: Newtownards DN 7; 112–13

Cross-neanaghan cross: Dunaghy AM 13; 19–20

Crossowen td: Clogher TE 5; 35, 53

Crosspatrick td (see also Ballydawley): Artrea LY 6; 32

Crosspatrick well: Artrea LY 6; 9, 32

Crossreagh cromlech: Ballywillin LY 33; 35, 50

Crossreagh East well: Ballyaghran LY 33; 21

Crossreagh gravel pit: Ballywillin LY 33; 50

Crossreagh rocking stone: Ballyaghran LY 33; 23–24

Crossreagh standing stone: Ballywillin AM 16; 34

Crossreagh standing stone: Ballywillin LY 33; 35

Crossreagh td: Ballywillin LY 33; 45, 48, 51

Crossreagh tumulus: Ballywillin LY 33; 35, 40

Crossreagh West altar: Ballyaghran LY 33; 23

Crossreagh West cave: Ballyaghran LY 33; 10, 16, 23

Crossreagh West cromlech: Ballyaghran LY 33; 10, 16, 24–25

Crossreagh West fort: Ballyaghran LY 33; 11, 24

Crossreagh West td: Ballyaghran LY 33; 22

Crosstagherty (Crosstagerty) td: Kilraghts AM 16; 133

Crosstagherty cove: Kilraghts AM 16; 133

Crosstagherty hill: Kilraghts AM 16; 125

Crossvale House: Ballymore AH 1; 11

Crot forts: Devenish FH 14; 55

Crot hill: Devenish FH 14; 52

Crot td: Devenish FH 14; 58

Crothers, Alexander: Ballymore AH 1; 5–6

Crothers, Eliza: Tamlaght Finlagan LY 25; 119

Crothers, Jane: Tamlaght Finlagan LY 25; 119

Crothers, John: Hillsborough DN 12; 106, 106

Crothers, Margret: Tamlaght Finlagan LY 25; 119

Crothers, Maryann: Tamlaght Finlagan LY 25; 119

Crothers, Samual: Tamlaght Finlagan LY 25; 119

Crotland lough: Mevagh DL 38; 55

Crotlieve mountain: Clonduff DN 3; 5

Crotten td: Cleenish FH 14; 29

Crouching bush: Drumachose LY 9; 127

Croughanara lough: Killymard DL 39; 95

Croughross bay: Lough Swilly DL 38; 98, 100

Croukagapple hill: Drumhome DL 39; 59

Crow Island: Kilmacteige SO 40; 195

Crow, Daniel: Macosquin LY 22; 113

Crow, David: Macosquin LY 22; 84

Crow, James: Killowen LY 33; 161, 168–69

Crow, Jane: Clondermot LY 34; 81

Crow, John: Carrickfergus AM 37; 116

Crow, John: Macosquin LY 22; 113

Crow, William (Dublin): Clondermot LY 34; 81

Crow, William: Macosquin LY 22; 113

Crowe, Charles: Drummully FH 4; 36
Crowe, Charles: Galloon FH 4; 92
Crowe, family: Muckamore AM 35; 65
Crowe, John: Derryaghy AM 8; 100
Crowe, John: Urney DL 39; 179, 182
Crowehill (see Crowhill)
Crowhill House: Kilmore AH 1; 71
Crowhill House: Tartaraghan AH 1; 118–22
Crown bridge: Newry DN 3; 107–08
Crown fort: Newry DN 3; 108
Crown mound: Newry DN 3; 108
Crownegallagh district: Misc. SO 40; 200
Crowris (see Croaghross)
Croyer Whins locality: Billy AM 16; 57, 60
Crozier, family: Enniskillen FH 4; 58
Crozier, James: Hillsborough DN 12; 105
Crozier, John: Galloon FH 4; 91
Crozier, Miss: Newry DN 3; 103
Crozier, Misses: Newry DN 3; 99
Crozier, Mr: Magheracross FH 14; 95, 102
Crozier, Rev. William: Kilmore DN 17; 91
Crozier, Richard: Kilmore AH 1; 60
Crozier, T.: Drumbo DN 7; 58
Cruachanargoid (see Crooghanarget): Killymard DL
  39; 99
Cruck Nephraim hill: Banagher LY 30; 46
Cruckahenny td: Moville DL 38; 73
Cruckaleen td: Derryvullan FH 14; 46
Cruckanim (Cruckanima) td: Dungiven LY 15; 27,
  63, 75
Cruckanim td: Banagher LY 30; 22
Cruckanin (see Cruckanim)
Cruckareddy td: Cleenish FH 14; 14, 29
Cruckawody td: Clones FH 4; 26
Cruckdooish hill: Cumber LY 28; 3, 5, 7, 31, 71,
  84–85
Cruckdooish hill: Magilligan LY 11; 145
Cruckdooish standing stone: Cumber LY 28; 30
Cruckglass td: Moville DL 38; 73
Crucknagralery locality: Lough Swilly DL 38; 115
Crucknahulla Point: Lough Swilly DL 38; 111
Crucknakelly td: Clones FH 4; 26
Crucknamurlog standing stone: Mevagh DL 38; 58
Crucknamurlog td: Mevagh DL 38; 57, 63
Crucknasleiga mountain: Lough Swilly DL 38; 118
Crugans Lower td: Loughgilly AH 1; 84
Crugans Upper td: Loughgilly AH 1; 84
Cruhennan (see Creehennan): Moville DL 38; 74
Cruic Earceil (see Donald's hill): Dungiven LY 15;
  111
Cruiheen, giant: Tamlaght O'Crilly LY 18; 112
Crum, M.: Derrykeighan AM 16; 95
Crumkill (see Cromkill): Clondermot LY 34; 45
Crumkill school: Connor AM 19; 27
Crumkill td: Connor AM 19; 18

Crumlin: Aghagallon AM 21; 4, 7, 20
Crumlin: Aghalee AM 21; 37
Crumlin: Antrim AM 29; 48
Crumlin: Ballinderry AM 21; 42, 45, 49, 53
Crumlin: Camlin AM 21; 62–68, 70–75
Crumlin: Carmavy AM 35; 2
Crumlin: Carrickfergus AM 37; 165
Crumlin: Drummaul AM 19; 45
Crumlin: Glenavy AM 21; 77–78, 81, 86–87
Crumlin: Killead AM 35; 7–9, 11, 13, 15–16, 18,
  42, 50
Crumlin: Magheramesk AM 21; 115
Crumlin: Muckamore AM 35; 55, 60, 62–64, 75
Crumlin: Templepatrick AM 35; 113, 142
Crumlin: Tullyrusk AM 21; 132–36
Crumlin: Umgall AM 35; 156
Crumlin academy: Camlin AM 21; 62, 66, 73–76
Crumlin bay: Lough Neagh AM 21; 95
Crumlin bridge: Camlin AM 21; 66–67, 72
Crumlin bridge: Killead AM 35; 9, 16, 47–48
Crumlin corn mill: Killead AM 35; 14, 48
Crumlin court house: Camlin AM 21; 66, 72–74
Crumlin dispensary: Camlin AM 21; 66, 69, 72–74
Crumlin dispensary: Carmavy AM 35; 3
Crumlin dispensary: Glenavy AM 21; 87
Crumlin dispensary: Killead AM 35; 19
Crumlin dispensary: Tullyrusk AM 21; 136
Crumlin flax mill: Killead AM 35; 48
Crumlin flour mills: Camlin AM 21; 65–66, 68–70
Crumlin flour mills: Carmavy AM 35; 2
Crumlin flour mills: Glenavy AM 21; 87
Crumlin flour mills: Killead AM 35; 11, 14, 18–19,
  45, 47–48
Crumlin flour mills: Muckamore AM 35; 65
Crumlin forts: Camlin AM 21; 71
Crumlin Glebe House: Camlin AM 21; 67
Crumlin inn: Camlin AM 21; 66, 72
Crumlin meeting house: Camlin AM 21; 63, 66, 72
Crumlin old church (see Camlin): Ballinderry AM
  21; 53
Crumlin old meeting house: Camlin AM 21; 66
Crumlin public house: Camlin AM 21; 62, 65
Crumlin river: Ballinderry AM 21; 53
Crumlin river: Ballymartin AM 2; 18
Crumlin river: Camlin AM 21; 60, 62–67
Crumlin river: Coleraine LY 33; 97
Crumlin river: Drummaul AM 19; 67
Crumlin river: Killead AM 35; 7–11, 13–14, 16–17,
  26–27, 41–43
Crumlin river: Lough Neagh AM 21; 93–94
Crumlin river: Misc. AM 10; 130
Crumlin river: Muckamore AM 35; 55
Crumlin river: Tullyrusk AM 21; 131–35
Crumlin school [I]: Camlin AM 21; 76
Crumlin school [II]: Camlin AM 21; 76

Crumlin smithy: Camlin AM 21; 62, 65
Crumlin toll–gate: Killead AM 35; 49
Crumlin turnpike: Killead AM 35; 15
Crumlin turnpike: Templepatrick AM 35; 114
Crumlin waterfoot: Coleraine LY 33; 99
Crumlin waterfoot: Killead AM 35; 26
Crumlin windmill: Killead AM 35; 14, 48
Crumlin, name of: Hillsborough DN 12; 88
Crummer, Andrew: Killymard DL 39; 107–08
Crummisbeg village: Kilmacteige SO 40; 196
Crummy's bay: Lough Swilly DL 38; 131
Crummy's Head: Lough Swilly DL 38; 101
Crumore (see Crewmore): Ballymore AH 1; 17
Crun lough: Clonmany DL 38; 12
Cruncheys (see Corrinshigo): Currin MN 40; 88
Crunchigo (see Corrinshigo): Currin MN 40; 86
Crushybracken (Croshnabrackin) td: Rasharkin AM
   23; 137–38, 140
Crymble, Capt.: Carrickfergus AM 37; 33
Crymble, family: Carrickfergus AM 37; 85
Crymble, Miss: Ballylinny AM 32; 26
Crymble, Miss: Carrickfergus AM 37; 142
Cuailgne district (Louth): Faughanvale LY 36; 60
Cuan lough: Carrickfergus AM 37; 11
Cubbindale (see Cubbindall): Ballymoney AM 16;
   25
Cubbindall td: Ballymoney AM 16; 23, 25
Cubit, John: Blaris AM 8; 77
Cuchullan: Ballintoy AM 24; 34
Cuchullan: Ballynascreen LY 31; 10, 24
Cuchullan: Banagher LY 30; 12
Cuckoo Bray hill: Tamlaght Finlagan LY 25; 109
Cudden, Andrew: Artrea LY 6; 22
Cudden, Frank: Duneane AM 19; 124
Cudden, William: Artrea LY 6; 13, 22
Cuddy, Alexander: Annaclone DN 12; 17, 19
Cuddy, Alexander: Lissan LY 31; 101
Cuddy, family: Maghera LY 18; 24
Cuddy, Henry: Muckamore AM 35; 80
Cudy, family: Maghera LY 18; 48
Cue, family: Enniskillen FH 4; 58
Cue, John: Enniskillen FH 4; 75
Cuff, Col.: Dromore TE 5; 99
Cuff, Mr: Devenish FH 14; 55
Cuff, William: Carrickfergus AM 37; 125
Cuilbane bog: Desertoghill LY 27; 27
Cuilbane cave: Desertoghill LY 27; 7
Cuilbane fort: Desertoghill LY 27; 27
Cuilbane standing stones: Desertoghill LY 27; 27
Cuilbane td: Desertoghill LY 27; 19–20
Cuilcagh mountain: Enniskillen FH 4; 67
Cuilcagh mountain: Killesher FH 14; 81–83
Cuilcagh mountain: Kinawley FH 4; 107–08, 113,
   123–24
Cuilceagh (see Cuilcagh)

Cuilkeeragh (see Culkeeragh): Clondermot LY 34;
   56
Cuingnary td: Cappagh TE 5; 21
Cuisla giant's grave: Culfeightrin AM 24; 72
Culbane bog: Ballyscullion LY 6; 43
Culbane corn mill: Loughguile AM 13; 63
Culbane graveyard: Loughguile AM 13; 68, 72
Culbane td: Loughguile AM 13; 68, 72
Culbert Castle: Culfeightrin AM 24; 54–55
Culbert, family: Ballinderry AM 21; 51
Culbert, Jacob: Carrickfergus AM 37; 165
Culbert, James: Blaris DN 12; 42
Culbert, Martha: Ballywalter AM 2; 26, 32
Culbert, Mr (Killdrum): Killea and Taughboyne DL
   39; 87
Culbert, Thomas: Misc. DL 39; 186
Culbert's mill: Killea and Taughboyne DL 39; 87
Culbidagh school: Layd AM 13; 51
Culbrim Lower plantation: Ballymoney AM 16; 1
Culcavy (Culcavey) td: Blaris DN 12; 34, 36
Culcavy Cottage: Blaris DN 12; 34
Culcavy distillery: Blaris DN 12; 34
Culcavy mill: Blaris DN 12; 36
Culcavy td: Hillsborough DN 12; 107
Culcrow bridge [I]: Agivey LY 22; 40, 43
Culcrow bridge [II]: Agivey LY 22; 40, 43
Culcrow corn mill: Agivey LY 22; 39, 44
Culcrow td: Agivey LY 22; 41–43
Culcrum wood: Killagan AM 23; 82
Culdaff: Donagh DL 38; 32
Culdaff: Lough Swilly DL 38; 110, 135
Culdaff bay: Culdaff DL 38; 21
Culdaff bay: Lough Swilly DL 38; 110
Culdaff ph: Lough Swilly DL 38; 111, 113, 141–42
Culdaff ph: Misc. LY 31; 138
Culdaff ph: Moville DL 38; 68, 70, 73, 78
Culdaff Point: Lough Swilly DL 38; 110
Culdaff river: Lough Swilly DL 38; 108, 110, 112
Culdalee (see Culdaly): Kilmacteige SO 40; 196
Culdaly td: Kilmacteige SO 40; 193, 196
Culderry school: Kildollagh LY 22; 71–72
Culderry South fort: Kildollagh LY 22; 69, 74
Culderry South td: Kildollagh LY 22; 67, 75
Culdoo bog: Ballymoney AM 16; 6
Culdoo td: Ballymoney AM 16; 6
Culdrum bogs: Macosquin LY 22; 78, 118
Culdrum bridge: Aghadowey LY 22; 10
Culdrum springs: Macosquin LY 22; 117
Culdrum td: Macosquin LY 22; 77, 90, 118, 121
Culdrum tumulus: Aghadowey LY 22; 28, 32
Culdrum tumulus: Misc. LY 36; 112
Culduff school: Ballymoney AM 16; 26
Culfeightrin collieries: Culfeightrin AM 24; 38–40,
   45–47, 63

Culfeightrin old church: Culfeightrin AM 24; 40, 46, 54, 69–71
Culfeightrin ph: Armoy AM 24; 1–2
Culfeightrin ph: Layd AM 13; 36
Culfeightrin ph: Layd and Inispollan AM 13; 54
Culfeightrin ph: Loughguile AM 13; 58
Culfeightrin ph: Misc. AM 10; 129
Culfeightrin ph: Ramoan AM 24; 86, 90, 92, 96, 100, 106, 108
Culfore td: Ballymascanlan LH 40; 55
Culhame (see Cuilbane): Desertoghill LY 27; 7
Culhame bog: Desertegney DL 38; 24
Culin, St: Aghagallon AM 21; 10
Culine, Capt.: Tomregan FH 4; 127
Culkeeragh House: Clondermot LY 34; 6, 20, 100
Culkeeragh quarries: Clondermot LY 34; 130
Culkeeragh school: Clondermot LY 34; 41, 89
Culkeeragh td: Clondermot LY 34; 7, 35, 38, 56, 64, 103, 109, 112–13, 115–16, 123, 130
Culkeeran school: Loughguile AM 13; 77
Culkeeran td: Loughguile AM 13; 77
Culkeevan (see Culkeeran)
Culky td: Rossorry FH 14; 115, 117
Cull, James: Kilbroney DN 3; 38
Cullagh td: Kilteevoge DL 39; 114
Cullaghmore chapel: Derryvullan FH 14; 33
Cullamore td: Clogher TE 5; 47
Cullamore td: Errigal Truagh MN 40; 122
Cullan td: Devenish FH 14; 58
Cullaneen td: Moville DL 38; 73, 75
Cullantragh hill: Killesher FH 14; 81
Cullaville: Donaghmoyne MN 40; 107–08
Cullaville bridge: Donaghmoyne MN 40; 108
Culldalee (see Culdaly): Kilmacteige SO 40; 193
Cullean td: Drumglass TE 20; 40
Cullen fort: Devenish FH 14; 55
Cullen, Anne: Carrickfergus AM 37; 127
Cullen, Arthur: Derryaghy AM 8; 114
Cullen, Darby: Derryaghy AM 8; 113–14
Cullen, Edward: Carrickfergus AM 37; 121
Cullen, Frances: Derryaghy AM 8; 114
Cullen, Hugh: Derryaghy AM 8; 90
Cullen, James: Carrickfergus AM 37; 127
Cullen, Jane: Carrickfergus AM 37; 118, 121
Cullen, Mr (Armagh city): Drumcree AH 1; 39
Cullen, Sarah: Carrickfergus AM 37; 127
Cullenbrone bog: Errigal Keerogue TE 20; 52
Cullenbrone brickfields: Errigal Keerogue TE 20; 52
Cullenbrone plantation: Errigal Keerogue TE 20; 52
Cullenbrone td: Errigal Keerogue TE 20; 49, 52, 57
Cullentra (see Cullintraw): Comber DN 7; 42
Cullentra lough: Aghalurcher TE 5; 1
Cullentra td: Agalurcher FH 4; 16
Cullentra td: Aghalurcher TE 5; 1

Cullentrough (Cullintrough) td: Ballymore AH 1; 7, 13, 16
Cullentrough Lodge: Ballymore AH 1; 11, 13
Culliagh (Cullia) td: Cleenish FH 14; 28–29
Culliagh td: Derryvullan FH 14; 46
Cullian chapel: Tullyniskan TE 20; 138
Cullian lough: Tullyniskan TE 20; 138
Cullian school: Tullyniskan TE 20; 140–41
Cullian td: Leck DL 39; 118
Cullian td: Tullyniskan TE 20; 138
Culliandoo td: Galloon FH 4; 95
Cullien hill: Devenish FH 14; 52
Cullien td: Enniskillen FH 4; 74, 82
Cullien td: Galloon FH 4; 95
Cullileenan td: Tomregan FH 4; 125
Cullin hill: Killdrumsherdan CN 40; 31
Cullin td: Donaghedy TE 5; 91
Cullin, Andrew: Ballyscullion LY 6; 66
Cullin, Bernard: Drummaul AM 19; 88
Cullin, Catherine (nee Bermingham): Manorhamilton Union LM 40; 51
Cullin, Col (Screeny): Manorhamilton Union LM 40; 50–51, 53
Cullin, family: Manorhamilton Union LM 40; 49, 53
Cullin, John: Manorhamilton Union LM 40; 51
Cullin, Mr (Glenade): Manorhamilton Union LM 40; 52–54
Cullin, Mr (Snr): Manorhamilton Union LM 40; 49–50
Cullin, Richard: Derryaghy AM 8; 104
Cullinkil ph: Drumlumman CN 40; 18
Cullintra (see Cullentra): Aghalurcher FH 4; 16
Cullintragh Duff lough: Donaghmoyne MN 40; 106
Cullintraw (Cullintrough) td: Comber DN 7; 35, 37, 40, 42–43
Cullintraw corn mill: Comber DN 7; 40
Cullintraw windmill: Comber DN 7; 35, 40
Cullion Boy lough: Donegal DL 39; 43
Cullion Boy td: Donegal DL 39; 43
Cullion chapel: Desertmartin LY 31; 54, 128
Cullion hill: Templecarn DL 39; 162
Cullion td: Desertmartin LY 31; 62, 141–42
Cullion td: Templecarn DL 39; 164
Cullion, Jane: Ballyscullion LY 6; 78
Cullmore (see Calmore): Kilcronaghan LY 31; 68
Culloden (Scotland): Clogher TE 5; 26
Culloden: Kilrea LY 27; 119
Culloden: Misc. LY 31; 138
Culloville (see Cullaville)
Cully, Richard: Newry DN 3; 98, 103
Cullybackey: Aghadowey LY 22; 25
Cullybackey: Ahoghill AM 23; 2, 6, 10, 12, 19, 25, 30, 42, 44
Cullybackey: Kirkinriola AM 23; 94, 122

Cullybackey bleach green: Ahoghill AM 23; 13,
  30–31
Cullybackey bridge: Ahoghill AM 23; 2, 11, 27, 30,
  35
Cullybackey corn mills: Ahoghill AM 23; 13, 30–31
Cullybackey Creggan school: Ahoghill AM 23; 51
Cullybackey meeting house (Cov.): Ahoghill AM
  23; 2, 11, 30–31
Cullybackey meeting house (P): Ahoghill AM 23; 2,
  11, 30–31
Cullybackey new school: Ahoghill AM 23; 49
Cullybackey school: Ahoghill AM 23; 21, 42
Cullybackey standing stone: Ahoghill AM 23; 27,
  35
Cullybackey td: Ahoghill AM 23; 37
Cullycapple (Cullycaple) td: Aghadowey LY 22; 2,
  36
Cullycapple bog: Aghadowey LY 22; 2
Cullycapple bridge: Errigal LY 27; 60
Cullycapple preaching house: Aghadowey LY 22; 26
Cullynane corn mill: Aghalurcher FH 4; 8
Cullynane corn mill: Aghalurcher TE 5; 1
Cullynane mountain: Aghalurcher FH 4; 2
Cullynane school: Aghalurcher TE 5; 1
Cullynane td: Aghalurcher FH 4; 16
Cullynane td: Aghalurcher TE 5; 1
Cullyramer (Coolyramer) td: Desertoghill LY 27; 1,
  18
Cullyramer cave: Desertoghill LY 27; 7
Cullyramer fort [I]: Desertoghill LY 27; 7, 23
Cullyramer fort [II]: Desertoghill LY 27; 23
Cullyramer hill: Desertoghill LY 27; 23
Cullyramer td: Aghadowey LY 22; 38
Cullys td: Drumgoon CN 40; 2
Cullytrummin House: Finvoy AM 23; 71
Cullyvenny (see Coolyvenny): Macosquin LY 22;
  93
Culmore ferry: Clondermot LY 34; 22, 35
Culmore House: Finvoy AM 23; 71
Culmore House: Tamlaght Finlagan LY 25; 82, 101,
  125
Culmore Lower td: Tamlaght Finlagan LY 25; 93
Culmore Point: Aghanloo LY 11; 24
Culmore Point: Balteagh LY 9; 40
Culmore Point: Clondermot LY 34; 106
Culmore Point: Drumachose LY 9; 106
Culmore school: Clondermot LY 34; 43
Culmore school: Rasharkin AM 23; 141
Culmore td: Clondermot LY 34; 64
Culmore td: Tamlaght Finlagan LY 25; 113, 119,
  119
Culmore Upper td: Tamlaght Finlagan LY 25; 93
Culnaddy (see Culnady): Maghera LY 18; 63
Culnady bog: Maghera LY 18; 64
Culnady bridge: Maghera LY 18; 9, 28, 63

Culnady corn mill: Maghera LY 18; 28, 35, 64
Culnady flax mill [I]: Maghera LY 18; 28, 35, 56
Culnady flax mill [II]: Maghera LY 18; 28, 35
Culnady fort [I]: Maghera LY 18; 61
Culnady fort [II]: Maghera LY 18; 61
Culnady meeting house: Maghera LY 18; 2, 7,
  28–29, 34–35, 64, 66, 75–76
Culnady meeting house: Termoneeny LY 6; 130
Culnady td: Maghera LY 18; 9, 22, 28, 32, 41–42,
  64–65, 81
Culnady wood [I]: Maghera LY 18; 4, 48, 56
Culnady wood [II]: Maghera LY 18; 56
Culnafay brickyard: Ballyscullion AM 19; 1, 3
Culnafay td: Ballyscullion AM 19; 9, 13
Culnafoy (see Culnafay): Ballyscullion AM 19; 9
Culnagrew bog: Maghera LY 18; 59
Culnagrew bridge: Maghera LY 18; 64
Culnagrew flax mill: Maghera LY 18; 27
Culnagrew grave: Maghera LY 18; 11–12
Culnagrew hill: Maghera LY 18; 58
Culnagrew standing stone: Maghera LY 18; 11, 22,
  24, 41, 58–59
Culnagrew td: Maghera LY 18; 11, 22, 25, 39–41,
  81
Culnaha bog: Errigal Keerogue TE 20; 52
Culnaha td: Errigal Keerogue TE 20; 52, 57
Culnaha tuck mill: Errigal Keerogue TE 20; 52
Culnaver hill: Carnteel TE 20; 23
Culnavey Island: Finvoy AM 23; 78
Culramoney Island: Ballymoney AM 16; 21–22
Culramoney td: Ballymoney AM 16; 21, 23–25
Culramony (see Culramoney): Ballymoney AM 16;
  24–25
Culrathain (see Coleraine): Dungiven LY 15; 33
Culteagh mountains: Aghalurcher FH 4; 4
Cultra House: Holywood DN 7; 76
Cultra quay: Holywood DN 7; 73
Cumber bleach greens: Cumber LY 28; 3, 20–21, 24
Cumber cairn: Cumber LY 28; 4
Cumber church: Cumber LY 28; 1, 4, 8, 84, 88–89
Cumber demesne: Cumber LY 28; 6, 8–9
Cumber Faughan bridge: Cumber LY 28; 4, 9
Cumber Glenrandal bridge: Cumber LY 28; 4, 9
Cumber House: Cumber LY 28; 4–8, 12, 18, 83, 86
Cumber Lower chapel: Clondermot LY 34; 9
Cumber Lower old church: Cumber LY 28; 58, 66,
  69
Cumber ph: Banagher LY 30; 1, 24–25, 31–33, 36,
  39, 44, 51, 59–60, 84, 95, 103, 105, 108–09, 112,
  131
Cumber ph: Bovevagh LY 25; 1, 17, 22
Cumber ph: Clondermot LY 34; 1, 8, 15, 25, 36,
  38–39, 53, 69, 78, 96–97, 104–05
Cumber ph: Donacavey TE 5; 85
Cumber ph: Drumachose LY 9; 84

Cumber ph: Dungiven LY 15; 7, 15, 17, 37, 107
Cumber ph: Faughanvale LY 36; 2–3, 27–28, 60
Cumber ph: Finvoy AM 23; 76
Cumber ph: Macosquin LY 22; 81, 98
Cumber ph: Magilligan LY 11; 145
Cumber ph: Misc. LY 36; 112, 119
Cumber ph: Tamlaght Finlagan LY 25; 101, 103
Cumber poor shop: Cumber LY 28; 25
Cumber school (see Claudy): Cumber LY 28; 90
Cumber school: Donacavey TE 5; 65, 83
Cumber sessions house: Cumber LY 28; 87
Cumber td: Clondermot LY 34; 58
Cumber td: Cumber LY 28; 8, 63, 66–67, 69, 111,
    117, 122, 125
Cumber td: Donacavey TE 5; 65, 76–78, 80–81, 83
Cumber td: Magheradrool DN 17; 99, 104
Cumber Upper dispensary: Faughanvale LY 36; 27
Cumber wood: Cumber LY 28; 117
Cumber wooden bridge: Clondermot LY 34; 7, 22
Cumberland (England): Ballyscullion LY 6; 57
Cumberland: Glynn AM 26; 38
Cumberland: Inver AM 26; 54
Cumberland: Killyleagh DN 17; 84
Cumberland: Misc. AM 10; 130
Cumberland: Misc. LY 31; 123
Cumberland, Duke of: Kilbroney DN 3; 32
Cuming, family: Carnmoney AM 2; 102
Cummin, family: Dunluce AM 16; 117
Cummin, John (Jnr): Newry DN 3; 104
Cummin, John (Snr): Newry DN 3; 99
Cumming, family: Ahoghill AM 23; 25
Cumming, family: Carnmoney AM 2; 76
Cumming, family: Kilraghts AM 16; 127
Cumming, Mr: Kilbroney DN 3; 30
Cumming, Patrick: Clogher TE 5; 41
Cumming, Rev.: Kilrea LY 27; 126
Cumming, Rev. H.S.: Ahoghill AM 23; 44
Cumming, Rev. H.S.: Ballyclug AM 23; 52, 58
Cumming, Rev. H.S.: Kirkinriola AM 23; 104–06,
    115
Cummings, John: Carrickfergus AM 37; 110
Cummings, John: Coleraine LY 33; 133
Cummings, Miss: Down DN 17; 53, 57
Cummings, Mr: Comber DN 7; 40
Cummings, Mr: Dundonald DN 7; 65
Cummings, Mr: Kilraghts AM 16; 128
Cummins, John: Drumcree AH 1; 32
Cummins, Thomas: Ballylinny AM 32; 23, 28
Cumnish (see Camnish): Bovevagh LY 25; 23
Cumrey (see Cumry): Aughnamullen MN 40; 76
Cumry beetling mill: Aughnamullen MN 40; 72
Cumry school: Aughnamullen MN 40; 77
Cumry td: Aughnamullen MN 40; 76
Cunifar sandbank: Holywood DN 7; 73
Cunliffe, William: Glynn AM 26; 14, 38

Cunnea (Coney) Island: Kinawley FH 4; 113–14
Cunning Burn manor: Misc. DN 17; 123
Cunning Burn td: Misc. DN 17; 123
Cunning, James: Blaris AM 8; 81
Cunning, John: Duneane AM 19; 123
Cunningburn corn mill: Newtownards DN 7; 104,
    112
Cunningburn flax mills: Newtownards DN 7; 104,
    112
Cunningburn td: Newtownards DN 7; 104, 111–13
Cunningburn windmill: Newtownards DN 7; 112
Cunningham, Adam: Carrickfergus AM 37; 179
Cunningham, Archibald: Enniskillen FH 4; 77
Cunningham, Catherine Anna: Carrickfergus AM
    37; 152
Cunningham, David: Maghera LY 18; 28
Cunningham, David: Tamlaght O'Crilly LY 18; 91,
    109
Cunningham, David: Termoneeny LY 6; 129
Cunningham, family: Agivey LY 22; 41
Cunningham, family: Ballintoy AM 24; 20
Cunningham, family: Billy AM 16; 58, 68
Cunningham, family: Carnmoney AM 2; 102
Cunningham, family: Carrickfergus AM 37; 93
Cunningham, family: Drumbeg AM 8; 123
Cunningham, family: Island Magee AM 10; 70
Cunningham, family: Killead AM 35; 17, 34
Cunningham, family: Maghera LY 18; 24, 48
Cunningham, family: Raymoghy DL 39; 135
Cunningham, Felix: Kilcoo DN 3; 45
Cunningham, George: Killead AM 35; 48–49
Cunningham, Hugh: Ballymoney AM 16; 17
Cunningham, James: Aughnamullen MN 40; 71
Cunningham, James: Balteagh LY 9; 43
Cunningham, James: Carnmoney AM 2; 76
Cunningham, James: Errigal LY 27; 68
Cunningham, James: Killead AM 35; 46
Cunningham, James: Templepatrick AM 35; 145
Cunningham, John: Aughnamullen MN 40; 71–72,
    75
Cunningham, John: Carnmoney AM 2; 46, 81, 84,
    89
Cunningham, John: Carrickfergus AM 37; 131
Cunningham, John: Coleraine LY 33; 67, 135
Cunningham, John: Drumgooland DN 3; 25
Cunningham, John: Errigal LY 27; 50–51
Cunningham, John: Rasharkin AM 23; 128, 130
Cunningham, Margaret: Macosquin LY 22; 93
Cunningham, Margaret Jane: Carrickfergus AM 37;
    152
Cunningham, Matthew: Magilligan LY 11; 92,
    127–28
Cunningham, Messrs: Aughnamullen MN 40; 71
Cunningham, Michael: Newry DN 3; 100, 104
Cunningham, Miss: Raphoe DL 39; 127

Cunningham, Mr (Creeve): Aughnamullen MN 40; 71

Cunningham, Mr: Agivey LY 22; 39

Cunningham, Mr: Lough Neagh AM 21; 92

Cunningham, Rev.: Killea and Taughboyne DL 39; 87

Cunningham, Rev.: Templecorran AM 26; 101, 128

Cunningham, Rev. Felix: Duneane AM 19; 115

Cunningham, Rev. James: Antrim AM 29; 27

Cunningham, Robert: Misc. DN 17; 117

Cunningham, Samuel: Killead AM 35; 12, 20, 39, 44, 46

Cunningham, Samuel: Misc. DL 39; 186, 190

Cunningham, Sarah: Coleraine LY 33; 67, 135

Cunningham, Thomas: Macosquin LY 22; 113

Cunningham, Thomas: Newry DN 3; 99, 103

Cunningham, Thomas: Raymoghy DL 39; 135

Cunningham, Waddell: Blaris AM 8; 36

Cunningham, William: Ahoghill AM 23; 13, 33

Cunningham, William: Enniskillen FH 4; 56

Cunningham, William: Killowen LY 33; 170

Cunningham, William: Macosquin LY 22; 122

Cunningham, William [I]: Carrickfergus AM 37; 111

Cunningham, William [II]: Carrickfergus AM 37; 112

Cunningham's mill: Killea and Taughboyne DL 39; 87

Cunninghams Town td: Clonleigh DL 39; 12, 197

Cunyngham, family: Carnmoney AM 2; 102

Cuppage, family: Culfeightrin AM 24; 61

Cuppage, Fulton and Turner, Messrs: Seagoe AH 1; 109

Cuppage, Gen.: Layd AM 13; 36, 40, 48

Cuppage, John: Ramoan AM 24; 90

Cuppage, Messrs: Shankill AH 1; 111

Cuppage, Mr (Silverwood): Seagoe AH 1; 105

Cuppage, Mrs John: Culfeightrin AM 24; 49

Cuppage, Mrs John: Ramoan AM 24; 90, 96

Cuppidge, Anne: Ballyscullion LY 6; 59

Cupples, Charles: Blaris AM 8; 55, 60

Cupples, Charles: Blaris DN 12; 45, 49

Cupples, Dr: Blaris AM 8; 20

Cupples, Edward: Blaris DN 12; 49

Cupples, family: Blaris AM 8; 21

Cupples, James: Dunaghy AM 13; 21

Cupples, Miss: Blaris AM 8; 85

Cupples, Miss: Blaris DN 12; 45, 49

Cupples, Mrs (Lisburn): Carrickfergus AM 37; 142

Cupples, Mrs Charles: Blaris AM 8; 84–85

Cupples, Rev. Edward: Blaris AM 8; 33, 52, 66, 84

Cupples, Rev. Edward: Blaris DN 12; 45

Cupples, Rev. Edward: Camlin AM 21; 62–63, 69, 76

Cupples, Rev. Edward: Glenavy AM 21; 77, 88

Cupples, Rev. Edward: Tullyrusk AM 21; 131, 137

Cupples, Rev. Snowden: Blaris AM 8; 52, 60–61, 84

Cupples, Rev. Snowden: Blaris DN 12; 36

Cupples, Rev. Snowden: Carrickfergus AM 37; 135

Cupples, Rev. Thomas: Ballyrashane LY 22; 48, 52–55

Cupples, Rev. Thomas: Blaris AM 8; 32, 58, 61

Cupples, Rev. Thomas: Coleraine LY 33; 127

Cups and Saucers fort: Dunluce AM 16; 116

Cur bridge: Devenish FH 14; 53

Cur bridge: Tynan AH 1; 131

Cur fort: Clogherny TE 20; 28

Cur river: Tynan AH 1; 124, 126, 128

Cur td: Clogherny TE 20; 27

Cur td: Devenish FH 14; 57–58

Cur td: Tynan AH 1; 131

Curcloughin Freighmore td: Clogher TE 5; 53

Curcloughin Lismore td: Clogher TE 5; 53

Curcullian td: Donaghmore DL 39; 37

Curdy, family: Ballynure AM 32; 56

Cure (see Cur): Tynan AH 1; 131

Curell, Randal: Carnmoney AM 2; 100

Curikfinn td: Dungiven LY 15; 51

Curkisbane td: Magheross MN 40; 148

Curkisduff td: Magheross MN 40; 148

Curlan, family: Clondermot LY 34; 53

Curland, family: Clondermot LY 34; 53

Curlets hill: Kilmegan DN 3; 55

Curley (see Curly)

Curling, family: Clondermot LY 34; 53

Curlough lough: Aghalurcher TE 5; 1

Curlusk (see Corlust): Ballymore AH 1; 8

Curly river: Aghanloo LY 11; 1–2, 21, 37

Curly river: Balteagh LY 9; 1

Curly river: Drumachose LY 9; 46, 48, 53, 60, 75–76, 83–84, 89, 101, 110, 119, 128–29

Curly river bridge: Drumachose LY 9; 56, 91

Curmere, family: Blaris DN 12; 30

Curmoy hill: Aghabog MN 40; 62

Curnacray td: Kinawley FH 4; 110

Curnacullia td: Cleenish FH 14; 29

Curnaghea td: Cleenish FH 14; 29

Curnagun td: Kinawley FH 4; 110

Curnahaul (see Curnahoul): Cleenish FH 14; 24

Curnahoul school: Cleenish FH 14; 24

Curnahoul td: Cleenish FH 14; 29

Curoe, Rev. Daniel: Antrim AM 29; 27, 45

Curoe, Rev. Daniel: Drummaul AM 19; 44, 57–58, 69, 74, 77, 82, 84–85

Curoe, Rev. Daniel: Shilvodan AM 19; 131, 133, 137–38

Curr td: Desertmartin LY 31; 62, 142

Currabla river: Donegal DL 39; 44

Curraderrabrock td: Cleenish FH 14; 29

Currafad tuck mill: Aghalurcher FH 4; 8

Curragboy td: Kilmacteige SO 40; 196

Curragh (Kildare): Clondermot LY 34; 64

Curragh bog: Macosquin LY 22; 77–78, 87, 107–08

Curragh bridge: Macosquin LY 22; 102

Curragh Camon forest: Clondermot LY 34; 7, 35, 103

Curragh corn mill: Maghera LY 18; 28, 35

Curragh flax mill: Maghera LY 18; 28

Curragh Hole locality: Desertegney DL 38; 24

Curragh lough: Donegal DL 39; 42

Curragh school: Leck DL 39; 119–20

Curragh td: Leck DL 39; 117–18

Curragh td: Macosquin LY 22; 102, 108, 122

Curragh td: Maghera LY 18; 13, 17, 28, 42, 53–54, 64, 73, 78–79

Curragh wood: Maghera LY 18; 56

Curraghalane (see Curraghlane): Dungiven LY 15; 76, 86

Curraghalane House: Clonleigh DL 39; 13

Curraghalane school: Clonleigh DL 39; 9

Curraghalane td: Clonleigh DL 39; 6, 12

Curraghanall td: Aghavea FH 4; 23

Curraghlane td: Banagher LY 30; 22

Curraghlane td: Dungiven LY 15; 27, 49, 61, 76, 86, 105

Curraghlaur td: Derryvullan FH 14; 46

Curraghmore td: Drumkeeran FH 14; 65

Curraghmore td: Magheraculmoney FH 14; 107

Curraghoore fort: Manorhamilton Union LM 40; 52

Curraghs church: Manorhamilton Union LM 40; 51

Curraghs td: Manorhamilton Union LM 40; 51

Curralongford corn mill: Aghalurcher FH 4; 3

Curralongford mill: Aghalurcher FH 4; 8

Curralongford td: Aghalurcher FH 4; 3

Curramoney cromlech: Ballintoy AM 24; 27–28

Curramoney graveyard: Ballintoy AM 24; 27

Curramoney standing stone: Billy AM 16; 58, 68

Curramoney standing stones: Ballintoy AM 24; 28

Curran (see Currin): Clones FH 4; 26

Curran (see Currin): Drung CN 40; 19

Curran: Kilcronaghan LY 31; 79

Curran and Drumaliss locality: Larne AM 10; 125

Curran bog: Maghera LY 18; 56

Curran bridge [I]: Maghera LY 18; 9, 64

Curran bridge [II]: Maghera LY 18; 9, 64

Curran corn mill: Maghera LY 18; 27, 64

Curran district: Raloo AM 32; 94

Curran hibernian school: Maghera LY 18; 30–31, 35

Curran meeting house (P): Maghera LY 18; 75

Curran meeting house (S): Maghera LY 18; 75

Curran mill-dam: Desertmartin LY 31; 52

Curran national school: Maghera LY 18; 7, 17, 31, 33, 35, 75

Curran night school: Maghera LY 18; 33

Curran Point: Island Magee AM 10; 21, 25, 31, 76, 79

Curran Point: Larne AM 10; 123

Curran Point coastguard station: Glynn AM 26; 21, 40

Curran Point salt pans: Larne AM 10; 125

Curran quarry: Tullyniskan TE 20; 141

Curran school: Maghera LY 18; 74

Curran smithy: Maghera LY 18; 6, 49

Curran Sunday school: Maghera LY 18; 29

Curran td: Enniskillen FH 4; 81

Curran td: Larne AM 10; 123

Curran td: Maghera LY 18; 6, 13, 54, 78

Curran village: Maghera LY 18; 6, 17, 22, 27, 30, 49–50, 65, 74–75

Curran village: Termoneeny LY 6; 122, 124

Curran, family: Dunsfort DN 17; 68

Curran, Henry: Raloo AM 32; 126

Curran, J.P.: Newry DN 3; 75

Curran, John: Conwal DL 39; 27

Curran, Mary: Doagh AM 29; 83, 95

Curran, William: Ballynure AM 32; 61

Currandale lough: Templecarn DL 39; 157

Curratheskin td: Cleenish FH 14; 29

Curraughean locality: Clondermot LY 34; 111

Curreen Point: Lough Swilly DL 38; 106

Currel, Andrew: Carnmoney AM 2; 47, 84

Currel, Daniel: Kirkinriola AM 23; 104

Currell, D.: Blaris AM 8; 70

Currell, John: Blaris AM 8; 70

Curren school: Magheracross FH 14; 99

Curren td: Magheracross FH 14; 102

Curren, Mr: Misc. AM 10; 129

Currin Lower district: Clondavaddog DL 38; 4

Currin ph: Aghabog MN 40; 62, 64, 66–67

Currin ph: Clogher TE 5; 40

Currin ph: Clones FH 4; 26

Currin ph: Currin MN 40; 91

Currin ph: Drummully FH 4; 34, 37, 39

Currin ph: Drung CN 40; 19

Currin ph: Ematris MN 40; 112–13, 115, 118

Currin ph: Galloon FH 4; 95–96

Currin ph: Killdrumsherdan CN 40; 34

Currin Upper district: Clondavaddog DL 38; 4

Curroghbinee (see Curraghboy): Kilmacteige SO 40; 196

Currogs td: Aghalurcher FH 4; 13

Currowaddy td: Conwal DL 39; 24, 26

Curroy school: Kilmacteige SO 40; 194–95

Curroy td: Kilmacteige SO 40; 188, 190, 196

Curroy, John: Kilmacteige SO 40; 188

Currudda (Curradda) td: Dungiven LY 15; 23, 27, 30, 53, 61, 63–64, 74, 92

Currudda td: Banagher LY 30; 23

Currudda td: Bovevagh LY 25; 29

Currudda td: Clondermot LY 34; 63

Curry, Daniel: Billy AM 16; 58, 72

Curry, David: Ballyrashane LY 22; 62
Curry, Edward: Ballyscullion LY 6; 58
Curry, Eugene: Ballynascreen LY 31; 33
Curry, family: Ballintoy AM 24; 20
Curry, family: Billy AM 16; 58, 68
Curry, family: Blaris AM 8; 22
Curry, family: Derryaghy AM 8; 103
Curry, family: Faughanvale LY 36; 33
Curry, family: Kilwaughter AM 10; 115
Curry, family: Misc. LY 36; 101
Curry, family: Ramoan AM 24; 107
Curry, Hanson: Macosquin LY 22; 112
Curry, Henery: Blaris AM 8; 70
Curry, Hugh: Dunluce AM 16; 117
Curry, Isabella: Larne AM 10; 128
Curry, James: Billy AM 16; 77
Curry, John: Clondermot LY 34; 90
Curry, John: Coleraine LY 33; 63
Curry, John: Macosquin LY 22; 111
Curry, Mr (Ballybrack): Moville DL 38; 70
Curry, Mr: Clonmany DL 38; 18
Curry, Nancy: Ballymoney AM 16; 18
Curry, Neill: Tamlaght Finlagan LY 25; 117
Curry, Richard: Billy AM 16; 72
Curry, Robert: Carrickfergus AM 37; 115
Curry, Samuel: Doagh AM 29; 89
Curry, William: Macosquin LY 22; 111
Curryfree quarry: Clondermot LY 34; 130
Curryfree school: Clondermot LY 34; 87, 91, 95
Curryfree td: Clondermot LY 34; 56, 64, 109, 112,
   116, 123, 130
Currynierin chapel: Clondermot LY 34; 5, 9, 19–20,
   23, 42, 92, 96
Currynierin female school: Clondermot LY 34; 42,
   96
Currynierin female Sunday school: Clondermot LY
   34; 93
Currynierin male Sunday school: Clondermot LY
   34; 93
Currynierin Sunday school: Clondermot LY 34; 92
Currynierin td: Clondermot LY 34; 20, 56, 60,
   64–65, 76, 109, 112, 116, 123–24, 130
Curryotragh td (see also Acton): Ballymore AH 1; 9,
   12
Currysheskin corn mill: Ballintoy AM 24; 16
Curtis, Edward: Blaris AM 8; 64, 66
Curtis, Edward: Drumbeg AM 8; 124, 128, 133
Curtis, Griffin: Coleraine LY 33; 73, 154
Curtrain (see Cortreane): Currin MN 40; 92
Curudda (see Currudda)
Curwen, Mr (Cumberland): Misc. LY 31; 123
Cushcapal (see Cushcapple): Banagher LY 30; 24
Cushcapple hill: Banagher LY 30; 24–25, 108–10
Cushcapple water: Banagher LY 30; 26, 31, 59, 99
Cushely, Henry: Killead AM 35; 36

Cushenagh td: Drumcree AH 1; 37
Cushendall: Ahoghill AM 23; 14
Cushendall: Armoy AM 24; 1
Cushendall: Ballywillin LY 33; 51
Cushendall: Carrickfergus AM 37; 55
Cushendall: Culfeightrin AM 24; 39–40, 45–46,
   50–52, 55, 63, 73, 75, 82–83
Cushendall: Kirkinriola AM 23; 104
Cushendall: Layd AM 13; 37–39, 45–47
Cushendall: Misc. AM 10; 129
Cushendall: Ramoan AM 24; 95
Cushendall: Rasharkin AM 23; 131
Cushendall bay: Layd AM 13; 39–40, 45
Cushendall chapel: Layd AM 13; 47
Cushendall church: Layd AM 13; 46
Cushendall corn mills: Layd AM 13; 39, 48
Cushendall dispensary: Layd AM 13; 47, 49
Cushendall dispensary: Layd and Inispollan AM 13;
   56
Cushendall flax mills: Layd AM 13; 39
Cushendall inn: Layd AM 13; 46
Cushendall old church: Layd AM 13; 39
Cushendall old mill: Layd AM 13; 46
Cushendall school [I]: Layd AM 13; 40, 47, 51
Cushendall school [II]: Layd AM 13; 47, 51
Cushendall school [III]: Layd AM 13; 53
Cushendall td: Layd AM 13; 47
Cushendall tower: Layd AM 13; 46
Cushendall tuck mill: Layd AM 13; 39
Cushendun: Ballyclug AM 23; 56
Cushendun: Culfeightrin AM 24; 36, 38–40, 44–45,
   50, 79–80, 84
Cushendun: Island Magee AM 10; 19, 26, 79
Cushendun bay: Culfeightrin AM 24; 43–45
Cushendun bay: Layd AM 13; 39–40, 45
Cushendun Head: Island Magee AM 10; 58
Cushendun Head: Templecorran AM 26; 96
Cushendun House: Armoy AM 24; 4
Cushendun House: Culfeightrin AM 24; 45
Cushendun school: Culfeightrin AM 24; 85
Cushendun td: Culfeightrin AM 24; 45
Cusher river: Ballymore AH 1; 5–6, 8, 10, 16–19
Cusher river: Coleraine LY 33; 96
Cusher river: Drumcree AH 1; 34
Cusher river: Kilmore AH 1; 61
Cusher river: Loughgilly AH 1; 86
Cusher river: Seagoe AH 1; 104
Cushleake Mountain South td: Culfeightrin AM 24;
   85
Cushleake td: Culfeightrin AM 24; 39
Cushnahan, Hugh: Ballyclug AM 23; 65
Cushrush Island: Killesher FH 14; 81
Cushsown old castle: Devenish FH 14; 55
Cushwash mill: Aghalurcher FH 4; 8
Cushwash td: Aghalurcher FH 4; 13

Cushy Glen, James: Magilligan LY 11; 138
Cushy Glen, Paddy: Magilligan LY 11; 138
Cusick, family: Ramoan AM 24; 107
Cust, family: Magilligan LY 11; 142
Cust, Johannus: Magilligan LY 11; 89
Custre, family: Lissan LY 31; 91, 106
Cut of the Hill school: Ballyscullion LY 6; 61
Cut of the Hill Sunday school: Ballyscullion LY 6;
  62
Cuthbert and McCarter [or McArthur], Messrs:
  Coleraine LY 33; 73, 143
Cuthbert, George: Faughanvale LY 36; 7, 18, 20
Cuthbert, James: Clondermot LY 34; 89
Cuthbert, Mr: Cumber LY 28; 79

Cuthbertson, Mr: Cappagh TE 5; 21
Cutleagh mountains: Aghavea FH 4; 18
Cuts fishery: Coleraine LY 33; 94, 147
Cuts fishery: Faughanvale LY 36; 50
Cuts fishery: Lough Neagh AM 21; 95
Cuts rocks: Misc. LY 36; 109
Cuts waterfall: Coleraine LY 33; 53–55, 93, 121,
  146, 149
Cuts waterfall: Killowen LY 33; 162
Cuts waterfall: Macosquin LY 22; 76, 80, 98, 102
Cuttamon Hill td: Taughboyne DL 39; 148, 152, 195
Cuttimonhill (see Cuttamon)
Cutts (see Cuts): Faughanvale LY 36; 50
Cuyll district: Clondermot LY 34; 70

D

D'Arcy, William: Derryvullan FH 14; 33–34, 36–37
D'Arcy, William: Magheraculmoney FH 14; 110
Dabin, James: Derrykeighan AM 16; 92
Dacre, family: Aghavea FH 4; 25
Dacre, Lord: Clones FH 4; 29
Daff cave: Desertoghill LY 27; 21
Daff fort: Desertoghill LY 27; 7–8, 21
Daff graveyard: Desertoghill LY 27; 8, 22
Daff graveyard: Dungiven LY 15; 41
Daff, John: Island Magee AM 10; 90
Daft (see Daff): Desertoghill LY 27; 21
Dails, William: Hillsborough DN 12; 106
Daily, Rev.: Ballymore AH 1; 6, 12
Daire (see Dart): Banagher LY 30; 59
Daire Calgae locality: Dungiven LY 15; 32
Dairt (see Dart)
Daisy Hill demesne: Clogher TE 5; 26, 46
Daisy Hill House (see also Roe Park): Tamlaght
    Finlagan LY 25; 80
Daisy Hill House: Ballymoney AM 16; 27
Daisy Hill House: Clogher TE 5; 33
Daisy Hill House: Rasharkin AM 23; 128
Daisy hill trigonometrical station: Tamlaght
    Finlagan LY 25; 103
Dal Dichu district: Down DN 17; 41–42
Dal mBuinne locality: Misc. TE 5; 146
Dalaradia (see Dalriada): Carrickfergus AM 37; 18
Dale lough: Convoy DL 39; 18
Dale lough: Conwal DL 39; 24
Dale, Eliza: Bovevagh LY 25; 59
Dale, James: Balteagh LY 9; 40
Dale, John: Bovevagh LY 25; 59
Dale, John: Errigal Keerogue TE 20; 48–49
Dale, Margaret: Ballymoney AM 16; 17
Dale, William: Bovevagh LY 25; 59
Dale, William: Errigal LY 27; 75
Dales fort: Kildollagh LY 22; 69, 74
Daley, Margrett: Artrea LY 6; 38
Daley, Michael: Artrea LY 6; 19
Dalfiatacian, family: Kilkeel DN 3; 54
Dalhouse, John: Finvoy AM 23; 75
Dalhouse, Thomas: Errigal LY 27; 65, 69
Dalhouse, William: Errigal LY 27; 50
Dall river: Layd AM 13; 38, 40, 43, 45

Dall river bridge: Layd AM 13; 46, 48
Dallas, family: Derrykeighan AM 16; 89
Dallas, George: Drumtullagh AM 16; 101
Dallas, Lettitia: Dunboe LY 11; 56, 69
Dallas, Robert: Coleraine LY 33; 65, 73
Dallis, John: Ahoghill AM 23; 33
Dalriada district: Ballymartin AM 2; 5
Dalriada district: Ballynure AM 32; 45
Dalriada district: Carrickfergus AM 37; 18
Dalriada district: Clondermot LY 34; 51
Dalriada district: Glynn AM 26; 17
Dalriada district: Misc. TE 5; 146
Dalriada district: Racavan AM 13; 86
Dalriada district: Raloo AM 32; 93
Dalrymple, Capt.: Macosquin LY 22; 107
Dalrymple, Elizabeth: Carnmoney AM 2; 77
Dalton, Isaac: Hillsborough DN 12; 107
Dalton, Lt: Ballyscullion AM 19; 1
Dalton, William: Hillsborough DN 12; 107
Dalua, St: Cumber LY 28; 63
Dalway manor: Ballynure AM 32; 41, 45, 47, 51
Dalway manor: Kilroot AM 26; 61, 72
Dalway manor: Templecorran AM 26; 96, 99
Dalway, Dr: Blaris DN 12; 50
Dalway, family: Ballynure AM 32; 51
Dalway, family: Kilroot AM 26; 71–73, 79
Dalway, family: Templecorran AM 26; 11, 82,
    85–86, 99, 117–19
Dalway, Foulk: Ballynure AM 32; 52
Dalway, Giles: Ballynure AM 32; 51–52
Dalway, Helen (nee Edmonstone): Ballynure AM
    32; 52
Dalway, Jane (nee Ewen): Ballynure AM 32; 47, 51
Dalway, Jane (nee O'Byrne): Ballynure AM 32; 51
Dalway, Jane (nee O'Byrne): Kilroot AM 26; 61,
    71–73
Dalway, Jane (nee O'Byrne): Templecorran AM 26;
    96
Dalway, John: Carrickfergus AM 37; 80, 178
Dalway, John: Kilroot AM 26; 59, 61, 71–73
Dalway, John: Templecorran AM 26; 96–97, 108,
    119
Dalway, John [I]: Ballynure AM 32; 33, 38, 41, 45,
    47, 51–52, 64, 68

Dalway, John [II]: Ballynure AM 32; 47, 52

Dalway, John [III]: Ballynure AM 32; 52

Dalway, Margaret (see Dobbs)

Dalway, Marriott (Jnr): Kilroot AM 26; 56, 59–61, 63, 70–73, 75–80

Dalway, Marriott (Jnr): Templecorran AM 26; 86, 118

Dalway, Marriott (Snr): Carrickfergus AM 37; 25, 32, 102, 172

Dalway, Marriott (Snr): Kilroot AM 26; 59, 78

Dalway, Noah: Carrickfergus AM 37; 33, 141, 148

Dalway, Noah: Kilroot AM 26; 78

Dalway, Noah: Templecorran AM 26; 118

Dalway, Robert: Kilroot AM 26; 60, 77–78

Daly, Charles: Coleraine LY 33; 72, 104

Daly, Daniel: Tamlaght O'Crilly LY 18; 90, 111

Daly, Dominick: Newry DN 3; 99, 104

Daly, James: Coleraine LY 33; 72

Daly, James: Magherafelt LY 6; 103

Daly, James: Tamlaght O'Crilly LY 18; 90, 111

Daly, John (Jnr): Tamlaght O'Crilly LY 18; 90, 111

Daly, John (Snr): Tamlaght O'Crilly LY 18; 90, 111

Daly, Joseph: Maghera LY 18; 33

Daly, Mary: Carrickfergus AM 37; 115

Daly, Rev.: Newry DN 3; 99

Daly, Rev. Robert: Enniskeen CN 40; 28

Daly, Thomas: Artrea LY 6; 21

Daly, William: Dungiven LY 15; 69

Dalzel, Widow: Newtownards DN 7; 112

Dalzell, Hugh: Newry DN 3; 100, 104

Dalzell, J.M.: Newtownards DN 7; 112

Dalzell, J.M.: Tullynakill DN 7; 122

Dalzell, Jane: Carrickfergus AM 37; 116

Dalzell, John: Coleraine LY 33; 104–05

Damhead school: Kildollagh LY 22; 71–72

Damhead Sunday school: Kildollagh LY 22; 72

Damhead td: Coleraine LY 33; 66, 128, 143

Damhead td: Kildollagh LY 22; 68, 71, 73, 75

Damland td: Killymard DL 39; 100

Damolly corn mill: Newry DN 3; 78, 107

Damolly flour mill: Newry DN 3; 78

Damolly spade mill: Newry DN 3; 107

Damolly td: Newry DN 3; 78, 107

Dampon, Edward: Ballyscullion LY 6; 57

Danagh, William: Tamlaght TE 20; 83

Dancey, John: Aughnamullen MN 40; 73

Dane, family: Enniskillen FH 4; 58, 75

Dane, Richard: Enniskillen FH 4; 58, 66, 79–80

Danes Hill td: Coleraine LY 33; 145

Danes Mill enclosure: Ballyscullion LY 6; 73

Danes Mill stream: Ballyscullion LY 6; 74

Danes' bridge: Dungiven LY 15; 81

Danes' Cast: Aghaderg DN 12; 7

Danes' Cast: Aghagallon AM 21; 11

Danes' Cast: Ballynascreen LY 31; 33

Danes' Cast: Donaghmore DN 3; 8

Danes' Cast: Misc. DN 17; 128, 130–32

Danes' Causey road: Aghagallon AM 21; 16

Danes' mill: Aghagallon AM 21; 11, 16

Dangan House (Meath): Carrickfergus AM 37; 23

Daniel, James: Ballyrashane LY 22; 49

Daniel, Rev. Averell: Clonleigh DL 39; 15, 185

Daniel, St: Banagher LY 30; 101

Daniel, William [I]: Killanny MN 40; 131

Daniel, William [II]: Killanny MN 40; 133

Danzig (Prussia): Newry DN 3; 68

Danzig: Warrenpoint DN 3; 119

Darachrean hill: Glenavy AM 21; 77, 82

Daragh, family: Ballinderry AM 21; 55

Daragh, family: Culfeightrin AM 24; 59

Daragh, Sarah: Kilrea LY 27; 118, 129

Darby, Dr: Donaghmore DL 39; 37

Darby, Mr: Drumbeg AM 8; 124

Darby, Rev.: Ballymore AH 1; 6–7

Darby, Rev. Arthur: Drumcree AH 1; 29

Darby's Bed stones: Clonmany DL 38; 16

Darcus, John: Clondermot LY 34; 82

Darcus, Mr: Lough Swilly DL 38; 144

Darcus, Solomon: Tullyaughnish DL 38; 85, 96–97

Darey, Mathew: Newry DN 3; 104

Darkley beetling mill: Keady AH 1; 49

Darkley spinning mill: Keady AH 1; 49

Darley, Capt.: Killygarvan DL 38; 48

Darragh Island: Killinchy DN 7; 92

Darragh Moore Island: Killinchy DN 7; 86

Darragh, Alexander: Billy AM 16; 64

Darragh, Anne: Donagh MN 40; 101

Darragh, Archy: Culfeightrin AM 24; 56, 66

Darragh, Eliza: Ahoghill AM 23; 38

Darragh, Eliza: Carrickfergus AM 37; 124

Darragh, family: Billy AM 16; 58, 68

Darragh, family: Culfeightrin AM 24; 59, 71

Darragh, James: Ahoghill AM 23; 38

Darragh, James: Carrickfergus AM 37; 110

Darragh, James: Connor AM 19; 27

Darragh, Patrick: Ahoghill AM 23; 38

Darragh, Robert: Carrickfergus AM 37; 111, 195

Darragh, William: Ahoghill AM 23; 38

Darraghrean (see Darachrean): Glenavy AM 21; 82

Darry coalfield: Tullyniskan TE 20; 140

Darry quarry: Tullyniskan TE 20; 141

Darry spade manufactory: Tullyniskan TE 20; 139

Darry tile manufactory: Tullyniskan TE 20; 139

Dart hill: Banagher LY 30; 24, 59, 108, 110

Dart hill: Donaghedy TE 5; 88

Dart hill: Faughanvale LY 36; 4, 119

Darton House: Tynan AH 1; 127

Dartree (see Dartry)

Dartress bridge: Dunboe LY 11; 63

Dartress spring: Dunboe LY 11; 79

Dartress td: Dunboe LY 11; 63
Dartrey (see Dartry)
Dartry barony: Aghabog MN 40; 62
Dartry barony: Clones FH 4; 26, 29
Dartry barony: Currin MN 40; 86, 89
Dartry barony: Drumgoon CN 40; 7
Dartry barony: Drummully FH 4; 34, 36–37, 39
Dartry barony: Drung CN 40; 19
Dartry barony: Ematris MN 40; 112, 115
Dartry district: Inishmacsaint FH 14; 76
Dartry Lodge: Clonfeacle AH 1; 23–24, 26
Daugherty, family: Culfeightrin AM 24; 71
Daughglass (see Dughglass): Lough Swilly DL 38; 111
Davadys, John: Carrickfergus AM 37; 90
Davagh td: Ballynascreen LY 31; 9, 23
Davenport, Charles: Clondermot LY 34; 60, 68, 71
Davenport, George: Lough Swilly DL 38; 110
Davers, Gov.: Dungiven LY 15; 32
Davey, family: Ballinderry AM 21; 55
Davey, family: Carrickfergus AM 37; 93
Davey, family: Kilroot AM 26; 75
David I, King: Templepatrick AM 35; 130
David, James: Carrickfergus AM 37; 116
David, King of Scotland: Templecorran AM 26; 114
Davids, Archabald: Kilraghts AM 16; 132
Davidson, Andrew: Kilcronaghan LY 31; 73, 79
Davidson, Catherine: Kilrea LY 27; 129
Davidson, Isaac: Newry DN 3; 100, 104
Davidson, John: Magheradrool DN 17; 104, 107
Davidson, Mr (Laragh): Aughnamullen MN 40; 71–74, 76
Davidson, Mr: Donaghmore DL 39; 36
Davidson, Mr: Drumballyroney DN 3; 16
Davidson, Mr: Drumgath DN 3; 21
Davidson, Mr: Dunaghy AM 13; 26
Davidson, Mrs (Laragh): Aughnamullen MN 40; 71
Davidson, W.J.: Newry DN 3; 99, 103
Davidson's corn mills: Magheradrool DN 17; 104
Davies, John: Tomregan FH 4; 129
Davin lough: Drumlumman CN 40; 12
Davis, Alexander: Hillsborough DN 12; 107
Davis, Alexander: Killymard DL 39; 107–08
Davis, Barbara [I]: Carrickfergus AM 37; 115, 125
Davis, Barbara [II]: Carrickfergus AM 37; 120
Davis, Dr (Stranorlar): Kilteevoge DL 39; 112
Davis, Edward: Artrea LY 6; 23
Davis, Edward: Enniskillen FH 4; 41
Davis, Edward: Magheragall AM 21; 106
Davis, family: Billy AM 16; 58, 68
Davis, family: Blaris AM 8; 21
Davis, family: Carrickfergus AM 37; 93
Davis, family: Island Magee AM 10; 70
Davis, family: Magheramesk AM 21; 124
Davis, family: Raymoghy DL 39; 135

Davis, Francis: Magheramesk AM 21; 122
Davis, Henry: Hillsborough DN 12; 97
Davis, Henry: Newry DN 3; 67–68
Davis, J.I.: Carrickfergus AM 37; 111
Davis, James: Hillsborough DN 12; 107
Davis, John: Dungiven LY 15; 35
Davis, John: Hillsborough DN 12; 107
Davis, John: Island Magee AM 10; 91, 100
Davis, Mary: Carrickfergus AM 37; 122
Davis, Mr: Blaris DN 12; 50
Davis, Mr: Longfield TE 5; 132
Davis, Rev. James: Drumglass TE 20; 43
Davis, Rev. James: Seapatrick DN 12; 128
Davis, Rev. John: Newry DN 3; 68
Davis, Rev. John: Warrenpoint DN 3; 117, 122
Davis, Rev. Moses: Raymoghy DL 39; 135
Davis, Robert: Cumber LY 28; 74, 76
Davis, Robert: Drumachose LY 9; 104
Davis, Surgeon: Newry DN 3; 100, 104
Davis, Thomas: Hillsborough DN 12; 107
Davis, Thomas: Newry DN 3; 99, 103
Davis, William: Ahoghill AM 23; 35
Davis, William: Carrickfergus AM 37; 122, 124
Davis' Hotel: Blaris AM 8; 51
Davis' Hotel: Newry DN 3; 70, 74, 84
Davison, Adam [I]: Drummaul AM 19; 68, 88
Davison, Adam [II]: Drummaul AM 19; 81, 84
Davison, Alexander: Carrickfergus AM 37; 193
Davison, Alexander: Skerry AM 13; 106, 111
Davison, Andrew: Donegore AM 29; 130
Davison, Archibald: Ballyscullion LY 6; 52, 73
Davison, David: Derrykeighan AM 16; 94
Davison, Edward: Carrickfergus AM 37; 120
Davison, Ellen: Ahoghill AM 23; 38
Davison, family: Racavan AM 13; 100
Davison, family: Templecorran AM 26; 117, 119
Davison, James: Carrickfergus AM 37; 148
Davison, James: Drummaul AM 19; 89
Davison, John: Ahoghill AM 23; 50
Davison, John: Ballyaghran LY 33; 27
Davison, Lt: Ballyaghran LY 33; 27
Davison, Matthew: Carrickfergus AM 37; 155
Davison, Messrs: Skerry AM 13; 113
Davison, Richard: Kilwaughter AM 10; 116
Davison, Robert: Ahoghill AM 23; 49
Davison, Robert: Carrickfergus AM 37; 194
Davison, Robert: Duneane AM 19; 114
Davison, Samuel: Carrickfergus AM 37; 75–76
Davison, Smith: Lissan LY 31; 99, 107
Davison, Thomas: Drummaul AM 19; 88
Davison, Thomas: Dunaghy AM 13; 15
Davison, Thomas: Tickmacrevan AM 13; 128, 131
Davison, Widow: Tamlaght TE 20; 83
Davison, William: Carrickfergus AM 37; 131
Davison, William: Drummaul AM 19; 89

Davisson, Nancy: Raloo AM 32; 129

Davock, Thomas: Coleraine LY 33; 73

Davy, Edward: Kilroot AM 26; 77

Davy, family: Kilroot AM 26; 74

Davy's Castle: Carrickfergus AM 37; 162

Davy's Island: Magheraculmoney FH 14; 103, 106

Davys, Edmond: Carrickfergus AM 37; 179

Davys, family: Carrickfergus AM 37; 30, 93, 162, 179

Davys, James: Carrickfergus AM 37; 186

Davys, John: Carrickfergus AM 37; 41, 43, 46

Davys, Samuel: Carrickfergus AM 37; 147, 186

Dawgan, family: Culfeightrin AM 24; 59

Dawlis, Thomas: Tamlaght TE 20; 86

Dawris harbour: Inishkeel DL 39; 70

Dawris spring: Inishkeel DL 39; 70

Dawson Grove demesne: Ematris MN 40; 113, 119

Dawson Grove House: Ematris MN 40; 113–114, 116

Dawson, Alexander: Carrickfergus AM 37; 141

Dawson, Baron: Magherafelt LY 6; 88

Dawson, Charles: Drumgoon CN 40; 9

Dawson, Charles: Ematris MN 40; 115–16

Dawson, Eliza: Blaris DN 12; 46, 50

Dawson, family (Castledawson): Ballyscullion LY 6; 47–48, 57–60 (passim, genealogy)

Dawson, family: Carnmoney AM 2; 51, 76

Dawson, family: Derryaghy AM 8; 103

Dawson, family: Drumachose LY 9; 107

Dawson, family: Ematris MN 40; 118

Dawson, family: Magherafelt LY 6; 88, 95

Dawson, family: Magheragall AM 21; 99

Dawson, family: Misc. LY 31; 138

Dawson, G.R.: Ballyscullion LY 6; 47–48, 60, 67

Dawson, G.R.: Ballywillin LY 33; 33, 42

Dawson, G.R.: Faughanvale LY 36; 40, 45

Dawson, G.R.: Magherafelt LY 6; 89, 91

Dawson, George: Cumber LY 28; 33

Dawson, George: Magheragall AM 21; 104

Dawson, George: Misc. LY 31; 138

Dawson, John: Hillsborough DN 12; 107

Dawson, Joshua: Drummaul AM 19; 71

Dawson, Joshua: Magherafelt LY 6; 96

Dawson, Lt R.K.: Aghaloo TE 20; 2–3

Dawson, Lt R.K.: Ahoghill AM 23; 29–30, 32

Dawson, Lt R.K.: Antrim AM 29; 44, 49

Dawson, Lt R.K.: Ballintoy AM 24; 14

Dawson, Lt R.K.: Ballyclug AM 23; 55

Dawson, Lt R.K.: Ballylinny AM 32; 24

Dawson, Lt R.K.: Banagher LY 30; 30, 46, 55–57, 112

Dawson, Lt R.K.: Bovevagh LY 25; 18–19, 57–58

Dawson, Lt R.K.: Clondermot LY 34; 4, 10, 15, 17, 96–97, 100–01, 105

Dawson, Lt R.K.: Coleraine LY 33; 66

Dawson, Lt R.K.: Culfeightrin AM 24; 41, 44

Dawson, Lt R.K.: Cumber LY 28; 34, 37–40, 42, 44–45, 80–81, 85–86

Dawson, Lt R.K.: Doagh AM 29; 84

Dawson, Lt R.K.: Drummaul AM 19; 79–81

Dawson, Lt R.K.: Dungiven LY 15; 114

Dawson, Lt R.K.: Errigal Truagh MN 40; 122

Dawson, Lt R.K.: Kilbride AM 29; 155

Dawson, Lt R.K.: Misc. LY 36; 117

Dawson, Lt R.K.: Ramoan AM 24; 94–95

Dawson, Lt R.K.: Rashee AM 32; 135

Dawson, Lt R.K.: Rathlin Island AM 24; 131

Dawson, Lt R.K.: Tamlaght Finlagan LY 25; 85, 91, 98, 103, 124

Dawson, Lt R.K.: Templecorran AM 26; 84–85

Dawson, Lt R.K.: Templepatrick AM 35; 137, 141

Dawson, Mrs: Carrickfergus AM 37; 28

Dawson, Mrs Vesey: Kilbroney DN 3; 34–35

Dawson, Rev. Hammond: Templepatrick AM 35; 112, 136, 138–39, 143, 151, 153–54

Dawson, Rev. Vesey: Kilbroney DN 3; 35

Dawson, Rev. William: Aghagallon AM 21; 9–10

Dawson, Rev. William: Ballinderry AM 21; 55

Dawson, Rev. William: Ematris MN 40; 117

Dawson, Richard: Carnmoney AM 2; 95, 101

Dawson, Richard: Drumgoon CN 40; 6

Dawson, Richard: Ematris MN 40; 114–15

Dawson, Richard: Magheragall AM 21; 104

Dawson, Robert: Carnmoney AM 2; 81

Dawson, Thomas: Artrea LY 6; 9

Dawson, W.: Ematris MN 40; 115

Dawson, William: Blaris DN 12; 46, 50

Dawson, William: Drumgoon CN 40; 9

Dawson's Bridge (see also Castledawson): Ballyscullion LY 6; 57–58

Dawson's Bridge: Magherafelt LY 6; 88, 96

Dawson's chapel: Drumachose LY 9; 107

Dayly, Michael: Magherafelt LY 6; 112

De Beaumont, Elie: Currin MN 40; 89

De Berkway, John: Clondermot LY 34; 45

De Blacquiere, Lord: Clondermot LY 34; 27, 38, 104, 118, 120

De Blacquiere, Lord: Cumber LY 28; 96

De Burgo, Elizabeth: Dungiven LY 15; 31

De Burgo, family: Dungiven LY 15; 31–32

De Burgo, Odo: Dungiven LY 15; 31

De Burgo, Richard: Carrickfergus AM 37; 80

De Burgo, Robert: Dungiven LY 15; 31

De Burgo, William: Ballynure AM 32; 45

De Burgo, William: Clondermot LY 34; 45–46

De Burgo, William: Dungiven LY 15; 31

De Burgo, William: Glynn AM 26; 17

De Burgo, William: Raloo AM 32; 93

De Carrig, Duncan: Carrickfergus AM 37; 79

De Clifford hospital: Down DN 17; 45, 48, 51–52

De Clifford, family: Down DN 17; 42, 66
De Clifford, family: Saul DN 17; 113
De Clifford, Lord: Ballee DN 17; 21–22
De Clifford, Lord: Ballyculter DN 17; 30
De Clifford, Lord: Bright DN 17; 33–35
De Clifford, Lord: Down DN 17; 45, 50, 52–53, 57, 59, 65
De Clifford, Lord: Dunsfort DN 17; 67
De Clifford, Lord: Inch DN 17; 74
De Clifford, Lord: Saul DN 17; 114–15
De Courcy, Affrica: Down DN 17; 41, 60
De Courcy, Affrica: Grey Abbey DN 7; 68, 71
De Courcy, Affrica: Inch DN 17; 75
De Courcy, family: Carrickfergus AM 37; 18
De Courcy, family: Inch DN 17; 75
De Courcy, family: Raloo AM 32; 93
De Courcy, Grania: Kilmacteige SO 40; 187
De Courcy, John: Ballybay MN 40; 81
De Courcy, John: Ballyculter DN 17; 28
De Courcy, John: Ballyphilip DN 7; 12
De Courcy, John: Clondermot LY 34; 51–52
De Courcy, John: Down DN 17; 41–42, 60
De Courcy, John: Dunaghy AM 13; 20
De Courcy, John: Faughanvale LY 36; 50
De Courcy, John: Grey Abbey DN 7; 68, 71
De Courcy, John: Inch DN 17; 75
De Courcy, John: Kilmacteige SO 40; 187, 192–93
De Courcy, John: Kilmegan DN 3; 59–60
De Courcy, John: Misc. DN 17; 119
De Courcy, John: Muckamore AM 35; 82
De Croft, Gilbert: Muckamore AM 35; 56, 82
De Fellenberg, M. (Switzerland): Faughanvale LY 36; 39, 67
De Golvia, Allan: Carrickfergus AM 37; 79
De Hunt, John: Faughanvale LY 36; 48
De Jordan, Simon: Down DN 17; 53
De Lacherois, family: Blaris AM 8; 7, 21, 45
De Lacherois, family: Blaris DN 12; 30
De Lacherois, Lewis: Blaris AM 8; 21
De Lacherois, Mary: Blaris AM 8; 21
De Lacherois, Nicolas: Blaris AM 8; 21
De Lacherois, Samuel: Lambeg AM 8; 138
De Lacy, Eleanor: Kilkeel DN 3; 53
De Lacy, Eliza: Kilkeel DN 3; 53
De Lacy, Hugh: Carrickfergus AM 37; 80
De Lacy, Hugh: Clones FH 4; 29
De Lacy, Hugh: Kilmegan DN 3; 60
De Lacy, Hugh: Magilligan LY 11; 104
De Lacy, Hugh: Newry DN 3; 63
De Lacy, Jane: Kilkeel DN 3; 53
De Lacy, Katharine: Kilkeel DN 3; 53
De Lacy, Margaret: Kilkeel DN 3; 53
De Lacy, Mary: Kilkeel DN 3; 53
De Lacy, Richard: Kilkeel DN 3; 53
De Lacy, Walter: Kilkeel DN 3; 53

De Lacy, Walter: Kilmegan DN 3; 60
De Le–Glen, Richard: Clondermot LY 34; 45
De Ramorgny, John: Clondermot LY 34; 46
De Ros, Lord: Ballee DN 17; 22
De Ros, Lord: Ballyculter DN 17; 27, 29–31
De Ros, Lord: Bright DN 17; 34–35
De Ros, Lord: Down DN 17; 52
De Ros, Lord: Dunsfort DN 17; 69
De Ros, Lord: Killyleagh DN 17; 85
De Salis, Count: Kilmore AH 1; 60, 65, 67–69, 71–73
De Sandall, Stephen: Muckamore AM 35; 56
De Verdon, Richard: Carlingford LH 40; 59
Deacon, Mr: Aghadowey LY 22; 5
Dead Island: Tamlaght O'Crilly LY 18; 124
Dead wife's grave: Carrickfergus AM 37; 32
Deal Island: Cleenish FH 14; 13, 29
Dean, Mr (Dublin): Kilmacteige SO 40; 195
Dean, Stephen: Ballynascreen LY 31; 24
Dean, Thomas: Ballynascreen LY 31; 23
Dean, William: Templepatrick AM 35; 152
Dean's Road locality: Tullyaughnish DL 38; 86
Deane, family: Finvoy AM 23; 76
Deane, Rev. Robert: Carnmoney AM 2; 75
Deane, Thomas: Ballynascreen LY 31; 27
Deans lough: Devenish FH 14; 47
Deans, William: Kirkinriola AM 23; 104, 116, 119
Deany, Harry: Lough Swilly DL 38; 99
Deargbruach church: Clondermot LY 34; 47
Dearg-chruac church: Faughanvale LY 36; 50
Dearmott, Andrew: Tamlaght Finlagan LY 25; 119
Dearmott, Ann: Tamlaght Finlagan LY 25; 119
Dearmott, Eliza: Tamlaght Finlagan LY 25; 119
Dearmott, Fanney: Tamlaght Finlagan LY 25; 119
Dearmott, girl: Tamlaght Finlagan LY 25; 119
Dearmott, Sallyann: Tamlaght Finlagan LY 25; 119
Dease, Gerald: Drumlumman CN 40; 15, 17
Dease, James: Drumlumman CN 40; 15
Deathye, John: Carrickfergus AM 37; 34, 43
Deavy, Jane [I]: Carrickfergus AM 37; 75
Deavy, Jane [II]: Carrickfergus AM 37; 76
Debhimore (see Devlinmore): Mevagh DL 38; 55
Deboys, family: Templepatrick AM 35; 118
Declan, St: Faughanvale LY 36; 62
Deehan, John: Banagher LY 30; 95
Deehan, Mary: Bovevagh LY 25; 60
Deehan, Michael: Bovevagh LY 25; 60
Deehan, Neill: Bovevagh LY 25; 60
Deehommed chapel: Drumgooland DN 3; 23
Deehommed mountain: Drumgooland DN 3; 23–24
Deehommed td: Drumgooland DN 3; 22–23
Deehommed td: Newry DN 3; 83
Deehommod (see Deehommed): Drumgooland DN 3; 22
Deen, family: Billy AM 16; 58, 68

Deen, family: Dunluce AM 16; 117

Deen, Hugh: Billy AM 16; 67

Deen, Robert: Billy AM 16; 66

Deen, William: Billy AM 16; 67

Deenish (see Coney Island): Ballyscullion LY 6; 50, 58

Deens, James: Dungiven LY 15; 71, 85

Deeny, Harry: Lough Swilly DL 38; 127

Deeny, John: Banagher LY 30; 61, 75

Deepstow td: Derrykeighan AM 16; 95

Deer Park bleach mill: Drumachose LY 9; 52

Deer Park demesne: Aghavea FH 4; 18

Deer Park fort: Drumachose LY 9; 91

Deer Park hill: Dromara DN 12; 62–63

Deer Park locality: Bangor DN 7; 19

Deer Park quarry: Drumachose LY 9; 79

Deer Park school: Glenavy AM 21; 79

Deer Park td: Aghavea FH 4; 17, 21, 23

Deer Park td: Balteagh LY 9; 2

Deer Park td: Drumachose LY 9; 52, 91

Deer Park td: Glenavy AM 21; 77–80, 84

Deer Park td: Tamlaght Finlagan LY 25; 114

Deer Park wood: Balteagh LY 9; 5

Deer Park woods: Drumachose LY 9; 46, 49, 52, 57, 74–76, 89, 97, 101

Deer's Hole locality: Banagher LY 30; 46, 64

Deer's meadow (see also King's meadow): Clonduff DN 3; 3

Deer's Meadow locality: Seapatrick DN 12; 124

Deerfin bog: Ballyclug AM 23; 55

Deerfin fort: Ballyclug AM 23; 61–65

Deerfin moss: Ballyclug AM 23; 66

Deerfin school: Ballyclug AM 23; 66

Deerfin td: Ballyclug AM 23; 53

Deering, Cllr: Derrybrusk FH 4; 31–33

Deering, Cllr: Devenish FH 14; 58–59

Deering, family: Enniskillen FH 4; 58

Deering, John: Enniskillen FH 4; 58

Deerpark fort: Ardstraw TE 5; 12

Deerpark House: Ardstraw TE 5; 11

Deerpark locality: Kilwaughter AM 10; 112

Deerpark td: Ardstraw TE 5; 12

Deerpark td: Drumragh TE 5; 109

Deerpark td: Killesher FH 14; 87

Deerpark td: Kinawley FH 4; 121

Deerpark td: Manorhamilton Union LM 40; 50

Deerpark td: Raphoe DL 39; 125

Deertin (see Deerfin): Ballyclug AM 23; 66

Deery, James: Dungiven LY 15; 24

Deery, Mr: Magherafelt LY 6; 110

Deesart (see Disert): Misc. LY 31; 143

Deescort hill: Aghabog MN 40; 62

Deffrick (Defrick) td: Billy AM 16; 55, 61

Deffrick td: Drumtullagh AM 16; 101

Degnavanty (see Dinginavanty): Killdrumsherdan CN 40; 32

Degney, John: Tamlaght TE 20; 78

Delacherois, Daniel: Donaghadee DN 7; 46

Delacherois, Samuel: Donaghadee DN 7; 46

Delagross, Redmond: Ballyscullion LY 6; 57

Delamont House: Killyleagh DN 17; 81

Delany, Charles: Carrickfergus AM 37; 129

Delany, Henry: Ballywillin LY 33; 44

Delany, Rev. Patrick: Derryvullan FH 14; 34

Delap, A.B.: Tullyaughnish DL 38; 97, 143

Delap, Col: Donaghmore DL 39; 35–38

Delap, John: Drumachose LY 9; 104

Delap, John: Drummaul AM 19; 92

Delap, Misses: Donaghmore DL 39; 39

Delap, Mr: Kilmore AH 1; 73

Delap, Rev. Robert: Donaghmore DL 39; 31, 39

Delap, Samuel: Donaghmore DL 39; 30–31, 38

Delap, W.: Coleraine LY 33; 73

Delargy, John: Culfeightrin AM 24; 68, 78

Delaware (America): Maghera LY 18; 21

Delaware river: Maghera LY 18; 21

Delayan, Bernard: Termoneeny LY 6; 133

Dellagan, man named: Maghera LY 18; 71

Dellit, John: Newtown Crommelin AM 13; 84

Dellit, Mrs John: Newtown Crommelin AM 13; 84

Delves Broughton, Lieut D.: Donagh 38; 31

Delvinmore (see Devlinmore) td: Mevagh DL 38; 56

Demarara (Guyana): Magherafelt LY 6; 100

Demerara: Raloo AM 32; 129

Demesne fort: Ballintoy AM 24; 30

Demesne hibernian school: Down DN 17; 48, 52

Demesne Lands locality: Carrickfergus AM 37; 94

Demesne national school: Down DN 17; 48

Demesne rock: Ballintoy AM 24; 33

Demesne school: Rathlin Island AM 24; 128, 133

Demesne school [I]: Down DN 17; 48, 52

Demesne school [II]: Down DN 17; 48, 52

Demesne school [III]: Down DN 17; 48, 52

Demesne td: Ballintoy AM 24; 31, 33

Demesne td: Donaghmore DL 39; 37

Demesne td: Down DN 17; 53, 59

Demesne td: Enniskillen FH 4; 74, 82

Demesne td: Kilwaughter AM 10; 106–09

Demesne td: Rathlin Island AM 24; 131

Demolly (see Damolly): Newry DN 3; 107

Demone corn mill: Ballymore AH 1; 10, 15

Demone td: Ballymore AH 1; 8, 12, 14–17

Dempsey, James: Billy AM 16; 77

Dempsey, John: Agivey LY 22; 40, 44

Dempsey, John: Newry DN 3; 100

Dempsey, man named: Finvoy AM 23; 74

Dempsey, Robert: Raloo AM 32; 122

Dempsey, William: Ahoghill AM 23; 38

Dempsy, John: Kilrea LY 27; 128
Dempsy, John: Rasharkin AM 23; 141
Dempsy, Rev. Edward: Blaris AM 8; 27
Dempsy, William: Desertoghill LY 27; 23
Deneight school: Blaris DN 12; 37–38
Deneight Sunday school: Blaris DN 12; 38
Denelow district: Misc. SO 40; 199
Denergan fort: Maghera LY 18; 60
Denergan hill: Maghera LY 18; 58, 60
Dengene (see Derryene): Tartaraghan AH 1; 119
Denham, family: Enniskillen FH 4; 58
Denham, James: Cleenish FH 14; 17, 22
Denham, Rev. James: Enniskillen FH 4; 58
Denide river: Clondermot LY 34; 70
Denin, Michael: Maghera LY 18; 44
Denit river: Donaghedy TE 5; 89–90
Denmark, King of: Errigal LY 27; 77
Dennamona Upper td: Donacavey TE 5; 81
Dennis, Charles: Lambeg AM 8; 134, 137, 139, 141
Dennis, George: Carrickfergus AM 37; 111, 195
Dennis, John: Lambeg AM 8; 134, 140
Dennis, William: Carrickfergus AM 37; 127
Dennison, Adam: Carrickfergus AM 37; 39
Dennison, John: Mevagh DL 38; 58
Denniston's rock: Lough Swilly DL 38; 116
Denny, Mr: Devenish FH 14; 59
Dent, William: Clondermot LY 34; 83
Denvir, Cornelius: Bright DN 17; 37
Denvir, family: Ballee DN 17; 16
Denvir, James: Bright DN 17; 37
Denvir, Michael: Newry DN 3; 99, 102–03
Denvir, Rev. Dr: Carnmoney AM 2; 57, 102
Denvir, Rev. James: Aghagallon AM 21; 8, 20, 24
Denvir, Rev. James: Ballinderry AM 21; 46
Dequavanty (see Dinginavanty): Killdrumsherdan CN 40; 36
Deralleglish td: Loughgall AH 1; 78
Derart td: Tomregan FH 4; 125
Derby, giant: Donaghmore DL 39; 34
Derby, John: Artrea LY 6; 21
Derby, Messrs: Donaghmore DL 39; 38
Derby, Samuel: Artrea LY 6; 21
Dercassan (see Doocassan): Drung CN 40; 20
Deregnalore td: Kilteevoge DL 39; 114
Derg (see Castlederg)
Derg Lodge: Termonamongan TE 5; 143
Derg river: Ardstraw TE 5; 4–5, 10, 12–14
Derg river: Donaghmore DL 39; 29
Derg river: Kildress TE 20; 61
Derg river: Skirts of Urney and Ardstraw TE 5; 136, 139
Derg river: Templecarn DL 39; 162, 170
Derg river: Termonamongan TE 5; 142
Derg river bridge: Ardstraw TE 5; 14
Derganagh bog: Termoneeny LY 6; 124

Derganagh forts: Termoneeny LY 6; 131
Derganagh td: Termoneeny LY 6; 121–22, 124, 126, 130, 133
Dergany McGuire td: Dromore TE 5; 98
Dergany Neville td: Dromore TE 5; 98
Dergbridge (see also Castlederg): Skirts of Urney and Ardstraw TE 5; 136
Dergbridge: Drumkeeran FH 14; 68
Dergbrough standing stone: Cumber LY 28; 28
Dergh (Donegal): Tamlaght Finlagan LY 25; 122
Dergonagh (see Derganagh): Termoneeny LY 6; 124
Derikeenan district: Kinawley FH 4; 116
Derintinny td: Tomregan FH 4; 126
Derlitt td: Loughgilly AH 1; 85, 87
Derllough (see Drollagh): Muckno MN 40; 162
Derminey, man named: Banagher LY 30; 66
Dermot and Grania's Bed: Kilmacteige SO 40; 187, 193
Dermott and Grania's Bed: Banagher LY 30; 44, 50, 75, 91
Dermott and Grania's Bed: Bovevagh LY 25; 9, 53
Dermott and Grania's Bed: Culfeightrin AM 24; 78
Dermott, James: Magilligan LY 11; 134
Dernacally (Durnakally) td: Taughboyne DL 39; 148, 153, 195
Dernafougher (Castletown) manor: Misc. FH 4; 133
Dernagross td: Aghadowey LY 22; 35
Dernakish chapel of ease: Drumgoon CN 40; 6, 9
Dernakish hill: Drumgoon CN 40; 1
Dernamoyle old church: Ematris MN 40; 114
Dernamoyle td: Ematris MN 40; 113, 116
Dernan school: Lissan LY 31; 94–95
Dernan td: Lissan LY 31; 108–10
Dernascobe td: Clogher TE 5; 36
Dernascoby and Banter td: Clogher TE 5; 53
Dernaseer bog: Dromore TE 5; 93
Dernaseer td: Dromore TE 5; 93, 95, 97
Dernion fort: Muckno MN 40; 166
Dernish Island td: Galloon FH 4; 87, 95
Derniveagh (Durneveagh) td: Kirkinriola AM 23; 91
Derniveagh school: Kirkinriola AM 23; 122
Deroon plantation: Emlaghfad SO 40; 179
Derrachrier (see Derrychrier): Banagher LY 30; 38
Derracorby td: Galloon FH 4; 95, 105
Derracormick td: Cleenish FH 14; 28–29
Derraghelvin glebe: Killesher FH 14; 86
Derraghelvin td: Kinawley FH 4; 110
Derragharra (see Derrychara)
Derraghhurra (see Derrychara)
Derraghlegna td: Kinawley FH 4; 110
Derraghurra (see Derrychara)
Derraginnady td: Galloon FH 4; 95
Derragooney (see Derrygoony): Aughnamullen MN 40; 77

Derrahullion (see Derrycullion): Aghalurcher FH 4; 11

Derralea (see Derrylea): Kinawley FH 4; 110

Derramacrow td: Galloon FH 4; 95

Derraraghan td: Magheracross FH 14; 102

Derravarry (see Derryvary)

Derre (see Derry)

Derreens East td: Cleenish FH 14; 29

Derreens West td: Cleenish FH 14; 29

Derrgal (see Derryall): Drumcree AH 1; 34

Derriaghy (see Derryaghy)

Derries Big td: Devenish FH 14; 58

Derries hill: Devenish FH 14; 52

Derries Little td: Devenish FH 14; 58

Derries td: Clogher TE 5; 36

Derrin mountain: Enniskillen FH 4; 43

Derrin mountain: Templecarn FH 14; 119

Derrin td: Enniskillen FH 4; 82

Derrinleagh district: Misc. SO 40; 200

Derrinmonagh district: Misc. SO 40; 200

Derrinraw td: Tartaraghan AH 1; 120, 123

Derrintoney td: Aghalurcher FH 4; 14

Derrivolgie (see Derryvolgie): Lambeg AM 8; 137, 142

Derry abbey: Clondermot LY 34; 47, 67, 70, 106

Derry Artillery Lane school: Clondermot LY 34; 43

Derry asylum: Banagher LY 30; 34

Derry asylum: Clondermot LY 34; 13, 85

Derry asylum: Cumber LY 28; 14, 25

Derry asylum: Faughanvale LY 36; 27

Derry bog: Magheracloone MN 40; 137

Derry bridge: Clondermot LY 34; 4–5, 7, 13, 19–20, 22–23, 28, 35, 38–39, 98, 100–02

Derry bridge: Faughanvale LY 36; 19

Derry Cathedral: Clondermot LY 34; 12, 40, 81

Derry Cathedral: Cumber LY 28; 69, 89

Derry Cathedral: Island Magee AM 10; 60

Derry Cathedral: Tullyaughnish DL 38; 88

Derry city: Aghadowey LY 22; 7, 22

Derry city: Aghanloo LY 11; 4, 17–18, 33, 37–38

Derry city: Ahoghill AM 23; 6, 26

Derry city: Antrim AM 29; 5, 18, 22, 39, 48

Derry city: Ardstraw TE 5; 9, 13

Derry city: Ballintoy AM 24; 35

Derry city: Ballyaghran LY 33; 6

Derry city: Ballybay MN 40; 80

Derry city: Ballyclug AM 23; 53

Derry city: Ballymartin AM 2; 5, 12, 16

Derry city: Ballynascreen LY 31; 6, 8, 16, 19

Derry city: Ballyscullion LY 6; 46

Derry city: Ballywillin LY 33; 30

Derry city: Balteagh LY 9; 38, 44

Derry city: Banagher LY 30; 3–5, 14, 18–19, 25, 27, 29–31, 35, 38, 44, 59–61, 66, 73, 99–100, 108, 112, 116–21, 131

Derry city: Bovevagh LY 25; 4, 9, 24, 56–57

Derry city: Camlin AM 21; 72

Derry city: Carnmoney AM 2; 49

Derry city: Carnteel TE 20; 23–24

Derry city: Carrickfergus AM 37; 76

Derry city: Clogher TE 5; 31, 33

Derry city: Clogherny TE 20; 27

Derry city: Clondermot LY 34; 1–2, 4–9, 12–15, 17, 19–26, 28, 30–31, 34–36, 38–41, 43–46, 48–50, 53–55, 59, 60, 67, 71, 74, 77–78, 81–82, 87–88, 97, 100–03, 106, 113–17

Derry city: Clonleigh DL 39; 3, 10, 13–14, 16

Derry city: Clonmany DL 38; 17–19

Derry city: Coleraine LY 33; 63, 78, 85–86, 88–89, 94, 121, 126, 147, 149, 155

Derry city: Convoy DL 39; 18

Derry city: Culdaff DL 38; 21

Derry city: Culfeightrin AM 24; 44

Derry city: Cumber LY 28; 1, 3–4, 7–9, 11, 20–24, 32–35, 49, 52–54, 58, 79–80, 84–86, 94–99, 109–15

Derry city: Desertegney DL 38; 28–29

Derry city: Desertlyn LY 31; 37

Derry city: Donagh DL 38; 32

Derry city: Donaghedy TE 5; 91

Derry city: Donaghmore DL 39; 28–30, 32

Derry city: Donaghmoyne MN 40; 107

Derry city: Donegal DL 39; 45–47, 53–54, 57

Derry city: Drumachose LY 9; 76, 117

Derry city: Drumhome DL 39; 62

Derry city: Drumkeeran FH 14; 68

Derry city: Drummaul AM 19; 33, 40, 46, 51, 67, 71, 73, 81

Derry city: Drumragh TE 5; 107

Derry city: Dunboe LY 11; 59, 61

Derry city: Duneane AM 19; 99, 106–07

Derry city: Dungiven LY 15; 7, 26, 51, 53, 65–68, 75, 99, 106, 109

Derry city: Enniskillen FH 4; 51–52, 61

Derry city: Errigal Keerogue TE 20; 47, 51–55

Derry city: Errigal LY 27; 61–62

Derry city: Faughanvale LY 36; 1, 3–4, 6, 8, 10, 13, 16, 19, 21, 29, 33, 39, 70, 72–80

Derry city: Finvoy AM 23; 70–71

Derry city: Galloon FH 4; 100–02, 105

Derry city: Inver AM 26; 54

Derry city: Killea and Taughboyne DL 39; 79, 84, 86, 88, 90

Derry city: Killead AM 35; 17

Derry city: Killelagh LY 27; 99

Derry city: Killesher FH 14; 87

Derry city: Killowen LY 33; 160, 168, 173

Derry city: Killygarvan DL 38; 43, 45

Derry city: Killymard DL 39; 99, 108–09

Derry city: Kilmacrenan DL 38; 50

Derry city: Kilrea LY 27; 110–12, 119
Derry city: Kirkinriola AM 23; 91, 93, 95, 102, 104,
    108, 118, 120
Derry city: Leck DL 39; 116–17
Derry city: Leckpatrick TE 5; 125–26
Derry city: Lissan LY 31; 90, 94, 97, 99, 101, 103
Derry city: Lissan TE 20; 69
Derry city: Lough Swilly DL 38; 106, 140, 146, 148
Derry city: Maghera LY 18; 2, 5, 8–9, 35, 41, 55,
    68, 71, 74
Derry city: Magheracross FH 14; 94, 101
Derry city: Magherafelt LY 6; 87, 91
Derry city: Magheross MN 40; 151–52, 157
Derry city: Magilligan LY 11; 89, 92–93, 111, 117,
    121, 130, 135, 139, 141, 146
Derry city: Mallusk AM 2; 107, 115
Derry city: Mevagh DL 38; 61
Derry city: Misc. DL 39; 184, 187, 193
Derry city: Misc. LY 31; 116–17, 137
Derry city: Misc. LY 36; 105, 116
Derry city: Misc. TE 5; 146
Derry city: Moville DL 38; 68, 72–74, 76–79
Derry city: Muckamore AM 35; 63
Derry city: Muff DL 38; 80, 82
Derry city: Newry DN 3; 93
Derry city: Nilteen AM 35; 90
Derry city: Ramoan AM 24; 95
Derry city: Raphoe DL 39; 121, 123, 130
Derry city: Rasharkin AM 23; 131
Derry city: Raymoghy DL 39; 133, 135, 144–47
Derry city: Shilvodan AM 19; 130
Derry city: Skirts of Urney and Ardstraw TE 5; 137
Derry city: Tamlaght Finlagan LY 25; 65, 68–69,
    71–72, 80, 82, 84, 89, 98, 101, 107, 109, 112–13,
    122–23, 125
Derry city: Tamlaght O'Crilly LY 18; 105, 108
Derry city: Taughboyne DL 39; 150–51, 153–54
Derry city: Templecorran AM 26; 115
Derry city: Templepatrick AM 35; 109, 113, 131
Derry city: Termoneeny LY 6; 127, 132
Derry city: Trory FH 14; 129
Derry city: Tullyaughnish DL 38; 87, 93, 95
Derry city: Umgall AM 35; 160
Derry city: Urney DL 39; 174–77, 180
Derry deanery: Clondermot LY 34; 98
Derry deanery: Lough Swilly DL 38; 144
Derry diocesan school: Misc. LY 31; 136
Derry diocese: Ardstraw TE 5; 7, 10
Derry diocese: Ballyscullion LY 6; 45
Derry diocese: Bovevagh LY 25; 19
Derry diocese: Cappagh TE 5; 16
Derry diocese: Clondermot LY 34; 63
Derry diocese: Clonleigh DL 39; 1–2, 4–5, 12, 15
Derry diocese: Clonmany DL 38; 12
Derry diocese: Coleraine LY 33; 122, 153

Derry diocese: Cumber LY 28; 1
Derry diocese: Donaghmore DL 39; 28, 33
Derry diocese: Donegal DL 39; 45
Derry diocese: Drumachose LY 9; 96
Derry diocese: Drumragh TE 5; 104
Derry diocese: Faughanvale LY 36; 64
Derry diocese: Killelagh LY 27; 102
Derry diocese: Longfield TE 5; 131
Derry diocese: Lough Swilly DL 38; 144
Derry diocese: Magherafelt LY 6; 88
Derry diocese: Magilligan LY 11; 145
Derry diocese: Misc. DL 39; 185–86
Derry diocese: Misc. LY 31; 127, 137, 143
Derry diocese: Moville DL 38; 70, 74
Derry diocese: Raphoe DL 39; 121
Derry diocese: Raymoghy DL 39; 132, 137–38
Derry diocese: Tamlaght Finlagan LY 25; 68
Derry diocese: Tullyaughnish DL 38; 89
Derry diocese: Urney DL 39; 174, 180
Derry gaol: Clondermot LY 34; 101
Derry gaol: Coleraine LY 33; 153
Derry gaol: Faughanvale LY 36; 18
Derry harbour: Clondermot LY 34; 47
Derry harbour: Faughanvale LY 36; 50
Derry harbour: Taughboyne DL 39; 149
Derry infirmary: Clondermot LY 34; 13, 17
Derry Island: Clondermot LY 34; 48
Derry Kiltullagh (see Derrykillultagh): Ballinderry
    AM 21; 56
Derry liberties: Clondermot LY 34; 1, 8, 40, 42, 82
Derry liberties: Mintiaghs DL 38; 67
Derry liberties: Misc. DL 39; 185
Derry Little bridge: Balteagh LY 9; 18, 42
Derry Little carn: Balteagh LY 9; 32
Derry Little td: Balteagh LY 9; 18, 32, 40, 43–45
Derry mendicity asylum: Newry DN 3; 94
Derry monastery: Dungiven LY 15; 61
Derry nunnery: Clondermot LY 34; 73–74
Derry playhouse: Clondermot LY 34; 43
Derry port: Dungiven LY 15; 105
Derry port: Tamlaght Finlagan LY 25; 93, 95
Derry post office: Clondermot LY 34; 39–40
Derry Presbyterian school: Clondermot LY 34; 42
Derry rocks: Dromara DN 12; 62, 65
Derry saltworks: Taughboyne DL 39; 150, 154
Derry Streetstown school: Clondermot LY 34; 43
Derry td: Aughnamullen MN 40; 76
Derry td: Ballyphilip DN 7; 8
Derry td: Dromara DN 12; 63, 65
Derry td: Misc. DN 17; 124, 126
Derry td: Shankill AH 1; 114
Derry toll-gate: Clondermot LY 34; 38
Derry William St distillery: Clondermot LY 34; 30,
    104
Derry, Archdeacon of: Dunboe LY 11; 55, 67

Derry, Bishop of: Aghadowey LY 22; 5
Derry, Bishop of: Ballyscullion LY 6; 45
Derry, Bishop of: Banagher LY 30; 14
Derry, Bishop of: Clondermot LY 34; 11, 77–78, 116, 118, 120
Derry, Bishop of: Coleraine LY 33; 153
Derry, Bishop of: Cumber LY 28; 8, 33
Derry, Bishop of: Desertoghill LY 27; 5
Derry, Bishop of: Drumragh TE 5; 111
Derry, Bishop of: Dungiven LY 15; 8, 98, 116
Derry, Bishop of: Faughanvale LY 36; 42
Derry, Bishop of: Killowen LY 33; 159
Derry, Bishop of: Leckpatrick TE 5; 117
Derry, Bishop of: Maghera LY 18; 15, 72
Derry, Bishop of: Misc. LY 31; 128
Derry, Bishop of: Newry DN 3; 107
Derry, Dean of: Clondermot LY 34; 9, 11, 26, 41, 59, 77–78, 86–87, 89, 91, 94–95, 99–100, 103, 105, 113, 118
Derry, Dean of: Faughanvale LY 36; 7, 29, 33–34, 64–66, 73–74, 77
Derryad td: Galloon FH 4; 87, 95
Derryadd (see Derryad): Galloon FH 4; 87
Derryadd bay: Coleraine LY 33; 98, 101–02
Derryadd bay: Montiaghs AH 1; 92
Derryadd church (see Ardmore): Montiaghs AH 1; 89
Derryadd Glebe House (see Ardmore): Montiaghs AH 1; 90
Derryadd school (see Ardmore): Montiaghs AH 1; 92
Derryadd school: Tartaraghan AH 1; 121
Derryadd td: Montiaghs AH 1; 89–90, 92–93
Derryadd windmill: Montiaghs AH 1; 92
Derryadde (see Derryadd): Montiaghs AH 1; 92
Derryaghey (see Derryaghy): Derryaghy AM 8; 120
Derryaghna td: Cleenish FH 14; 28–29
Derryaghnan (see Draughton)
Derryaghy bleach green: Derryaghy AM 8; 110
Derryaghy chapel: Derryaghy AM 8; 104
Derryaghy chapel: Drumbeg AM 8; 131
Derryaghy chapel: Tullyrusk AM 21; 137
Derryaghy church: Derryaghy AM 8; 92, 99–100, 102–03, 107, 117
Derryaghy church: Drumbeg AM 8; 129
Derryaghy corn mills: Derryaghy AM 8; 112
Derryaghy Cottage: Derryaghy AM 8; 105
Derryaghy flax mill: Derryaghy AM 8; 111
Derryaghy forges: Blaris DN 12; 30
Derryaghy forts: Derryaghy AM 8; 95–96
Derryaghy glen: Derryaghy AM 8; 100
Derryaghy graveyard: Derryaghy AM 8; 103
Derryaghy old house: Derryaghy AM 8; 100
Derryaghy old vault: Derryaghy AM 8; 98
Derryaghy ph: Ballinderry AM 21; 41

Derryaghy ph: Blaris AM 8; 3, 22, 51, 85
Derryaghy ph: Blaris DN 12; 26–27
Derryaghy ph: Camlin AM 21; 64
Derryaghy ph: Carnmoney AM 2; 34
Derryaghy ph: Down DN 17; 58
Derryaghy ph: Drumbeg AM 8; 122
Derryaghy ph: Drumbeg DN 7; 52
Derryaghy ph: Glenavy AM 21; 77-78, 80, 83
Derryaghy ph: Lambeg AM 8; 134
Derryaghy ph: Magheragall AM 21; 108
Derryaghy ph: Magheramesk AM 21; 119
Derryaghy ph: Misc. AM 10; 129
Derryaghy ph: Misc. DN 17; 122
Derryaghy ph: Templepatrick AM 35; 114
Derryaghy ph: Tullyrusk AM 21; 131–33
Derryaghy river: Derryaghy AM 8; 106
Derryaghy Rock House: Derryaghy AM 8; 99
Derryaghy school: Derryaghy AM 8; 115, 118
Derryaghy spade factory: Derryaghy AM 8; 109
Derryaghy spring: Derryaghy AM 8; 90
Derryaghy Sunday school: Derryaghy AM 8; 117
Derryaghy td: Derryaghy AM 8; 91–92, 110, 113–14, 120
Derryall td: Drumcree AH 1; 34, 39
Derryallen flax mill: Ballymore AH 1; 8, 10, 16
Derryallen meeting house: Ballymore AH 1; 10, 16
Derryallen school: Ballymore AH 1; 16
Derryallen td: Ballymore AH 1; 7–8, 13, 15, 17–18
Derryan (see Derryallen): Ballymore AH 1; 15
Derryanny manor: Galloon FH 4; 94–95
Derryanny td: Galloon FH 4; 93, 95
Derryanvil chapel: Drumcree AH 1; 39
Derryanvil meeting house: Drumcree AH 1; 30, 36
Derryanvil td: Drumcree AH 1; 39
Derryanvill (see Derryanvil): Drumcree AH 1; 39
Derryard bog: Bovevagh LY 25; 23, 45
Derryard Castle: Balteagh LY 9; 26
Derryard Castle: Bovevagh LY 25; 15–18, 36, 43, 46
Derryard Castle: Dungiven LY 15; 94
Derryard graveyard: Bovevagh LY 25; 18
Derryard old castle: Bovevagh LY 25; 17
Derryard plantation: Bovevagh LY 25; 20, 23
Derryard spring: Bovevagh LY 25; 22
Derryard td: Banagher LY 30; 23–24
Derryard td: Bovevagh LY 25; 7, 13, 22, 29, 35–36, 38, 43–46, 54, 60
Derryard Turret locality: Bovevagh LY 25; 7
Derryarkan (see Derryarkin): Faughanvale LY 36; 22
Derryarkin flax mill: Faughanvale LY 36; 16
Derryarkin glen: Faughanvale LY 36; 7
Derryarkin Lower flax mill: Faughanvale LY 36; 97–98

Derryarkin Lower td: Faughanvale LY 36; 17, 53, 68, 73, 84, 93, 98

Derryarkin Lower wood: Faughanvale LY 36; 84

Derryarkin school: Faughanvale LY 36; 34, 66

Derryarkin td: Clondermot LY 34; 80

Derryarkin td: Faughanvale LY 36; 53, 57–58

Derryarkin Upper flax mill: Faughanvale LY 36; 22

Derryarkin Upper td: Faughanvale LY 36; 17, 68, 73, 84, 93, 98

Derryarkin Upper wood: Faughanvale LY 36; 84

Derryasgin hill: Trory FH 14; 122

Derryasna td: Aghalurcher FH 4; 13

Derryaugh Point: Tartaraghan AH 1; 119

Derrybard (Derribard) td: Donacavey TE 5; 70, 80

Derrybard demesne: Donacavey TE 5; 70

Derrybard House: Donacavey TE 5; 64, 69–71, 73–74

Derrybard Lower td: Donacavey TE 5; 81

Derrybard td: Donacavey TE 5; 63, 67, 69, 71, 76–78, 80, 83, 85

Derrybard Upper td: Donacavey TE 5; 81

Derrybeg bridge: Drumachose LY 9; 119

Derrybeg district: Misc. SO 40; 198

Derrybeg East td: Galloon FH 4; 87, 95

Derrybeg td: Drumachose LY 9; 87, 96–97, 101, 109–11, 126–27, 134

Derrybeg West td: Galloon FH 4; 95

Derryboy td: Newry DN 3; 106

Derrybrack td: Drummully FH 4; 39

Derrybroghus td: Drumcree AH 1; 39

Derrybrusk demesne: Derrybrusk FH 4; 32

Derrybrusk Glebe House: Derrybrusk FH 4; 31

Derrybrusk House: Derrybrusk FH 4; 31

Derrybrusk ph: Aghalurcher FH 4; 1

Derrybrusk ph: Cleenish FH 14; 11, 29

Derrybrusk ph: Clogher TE 5; 40

Derrybrusk ph: Enniskillen FH 4; 41, 43, 65, 68, 80

Derrybrusk ph: Magheracross FH 14; 91

Derrybrusk td: Derrybrusk FH 4; 30–31, 33

Derrycallaghan td: Cleenish FH 14; 29

Derrycannon td: Galloon FH 4; 95

Derrycarran td: Drumcree AH 1; 39

Derrycaw House: Clonfeacle AH 1; 21, 24

Derrycaw pottery: Clonfeacle AH 1; 24

Derrycaw school: Clonfeacle AH 1; 21–22, 25

Derrycaw td: Clonfeacle AH 1; 21–22

Derrycaw td: Drumcree AH 1; 34, 39

Derrychara td: Cleenish FH 14; 22, 29

Derrychara td: Enniskillen FH 4; 82

Derrychrear (see Derrychrier): Banagher LY 30; 17

Derrychrier altar: Banagher LY 30; 38, 70

Derrychrier corn mill: Banagher LY 30; 17, 29, 127

Derrychrier flax mill: Banagher LY 30; 29, 127

Derrychrier fulling mill: Banagher LY 30; 129

Derrychrier mount: Banagher LY 30; 83

Derrychrier school: Dungiven LY 15; 18

Derrychrier school [I]: Banagher LY 30; 33, 111

Derrychrier school [II]: Banagher LY 30; 111

Derrychrier standing stones: Banagher LY 30; 46, 49–50, 56, 70, 83–84

Derrychrier standing stones: Dungiven LY 15; 94

Derrychrier td: Banagher LY 30; 21, 35, 38–39, 56, 61, 70, 84, 95, 99, 103, 109, 117–18, 122, 127, 129, 131

Derrychrier td: Dungiven LY 15; 94

Derrychrier tuck mill: Banagher LY 30; 29

Derrychrier well: Banagher LY 30; 44

Derrychrier wood: Banagher LY 30; 122

Derrychrin td: Ballinderry TE 20; 13

Derrycleawannon (see Derrycleawaun): Derryvullan FH 14; 42

Derrycleawaun fort: Derryvullan FH 14; 42

Derrycleawaun school: Derryvullan FH 14; 44

Derrycleawaun td: Derryvullan FH 14; 42, 46

Derryclone bog: Aghagallon AM 21; 3, 14

Derryclone forts: Aghagallon AM 21; 17

Derryclone Peninsula: Aghagallon AM 21; 3–4

Derryclone school: Aghagallon AM 21; 25

Derryclone td: Aghagallon AM 21; 2–3, 13, 18–19

Derryconey (see Derrycory): Drumcree AH 1; 36

Derrycoosh td: Loughgall AH 1; 79

Derrycormuck (see Derrydrummuck): Aghaderg DN 12; 2

Derrycorr hill: Tartaraghan AH 1; 119

Derrycorr school: Tartaraghan AH 1; 122

Derrycorr td: Montiaghs AH 1; 93

Derrycorr td: Tartaraghan AH 1; 121

Derrycorry td: Killyman AH 1; 55

Derrycory (Derrycorey) td: Drumcree AH 1; 39

Derrycory school: Drumcree AH 1; 29–30, 33, 36, 39

Derrycraw school: Donaghmore DN 3; 8

Derrycraw td: Donaghmore DN 3; 9

Derrycree (see Derrycrew): Loughgall AH 1; 79

Derrycrew pottery: Loughgall AH 1; 80

Derrycrew wood: Loughgall AH 1; 79

Derrycrin Eglish td: Tamlaght TE 20; 94, 97

Derrycrin-Cunningham altar: Ballinderry TE 20; 12

Derrycrin-Eglish corn mill: Ballinderry TE 20; 11

Derrycrum mountain: Aghalurcher FH 4; 2

Derrycrum td: Aghalurcher FH 4; 14

Derrycullion (Derryhullia) td: Aghalurcher FH 4; 9, 11, 13–14

Derrycullion school: Aghalurcher FH 4; 11

Derrydoon td: Galloon FH 4; 87, 95

Derrydorragh bog: Macosquin LY 22; 87

Derrydorragh bridge: Macosquin LY 22; 82, 103

Derrydorragh mound: Macosquin LY 22; 117

Derrydorragh springs: Macosquin LY 22; 117

Derrydorragh td: Macosquin LY 22; 82

Derrydorraphy td: Tydavnet MN 40; 169

Derrydrummond td: Clogher TE 5; 36, 53

Derrydrummuck (Derrydromuck) td: Aghaderg DN 12; 2, 8, 12

Derrydrummuck hill: Aghaderg DN 12; 8

Derrydrummuck mill: Aghaderg DN 12; 12

Derrydrumult td: Moira DN 12; 120

Derryduff school: Dungiven LY 15; 101, 117–18

Derryduff td: Banagher LY 30; 22

Derryduff td: Dungiven LY 15; 26, 61, 74

Derryelvin td: Drummully FH 4; 39

Derryene td: Tartaraghan AH 1; 119, 122

Derryetta td: Montiaghs AH 1; 91, 93

Derrygally demesne: Killyman TE 20; 68

Derryganard evening Sunday school: Lissan LY 31; 108

Derryganard Sunday school: Lissan LY 31; 92, 96, 107–08

Derryganard td: Lissan LY 31; 103, 108, 110

Derrygarran td: Ballyscullion LY 6; 58

Derrygarve bog: Artrea LY 6; 4, 23

Derrygarve chapel: Artrea LY 6; 7

Derrygarve fort: Artrea LY 6; 27

Derrygarve school: Artrea LY 6; 18

Derrygarve Sunday school: Artrea LY 6; 21

Derrygarve td: Artrea LY 6; 4, 7, 22, 27–28, 38–39

Derrygassan Lower td: Donagh MN 40; 98

Derrygerderry td: Kinawley FH 4; 120–21

Derrygerriff chapel: Artrea TE 20; 8

Derrygiff td: Cleenish FH 14; 28–29

Derrygoinnill (see Derrygonnelly): Inishmacsaint FH 14; 74

Derrygonigan bleach mill: Artrea TE 20; 7

Derrygonnelly: Devenish FH 14; 47, 49, 53, 55

Derrygonnelly: Inishmacsaint FH 14; 71, 73–74, 77, 79

Derrygonnelly chapel: Devenish FH 14; 48

Derrygonnelly chapel: Inishmacsaint FH 14; 74

Derrygonnelly old chapel: Inishmacsaint FH 14; 75

Derrygonnelly session house: Devenish FH 14; 49

Derrygonnelly td: Inishmacsaint FH 14; 72

Derrygooly (Derrygooley) td: Aghaloo TE 20; 1

Derrygooly chapel: Aghaloo TE 20; 1, 4

Derrygoon giant's grave: Ardstraw TE 5; 12

Derrygoon td: Ardstraw TE 5; 12

Derrygooney (see Derrygoony): Aughnamullen MN 40; 70

Derrygoony bleach green: Aughnamullen MN 40; 72

Derrygoony corn mills: Aughnamullen MN 40; 72

Derrygoony lough: Aughnamullen MN 40; 70

Derrygoony school: Aughnamullen MN 40; 77

Derrygoony td: Aughnamullen MN 40; 73, 76

Derrygoony td: Laragh CN 40; 39

Derrygoose td: Drummully FH 4; 39

Derrygowan cave [I]: Duneane AM 19; 108, 120

Derrygowan cave [II]: Duneane AM 19; 120

Derrygowan fort: Duneane AM 19; 108, 120

Derrygowan td: Duneane AM 19; 123

Derryhale (Derryhead) td: Kilmore AH 1; 57, 61, 65, 67, 69–72

Derryhale bog: Kilmore AH 1; 61

Derryhale school: Kilmore AH 1; 59, 64, 70

Derryhallagh school: Donagh MN 40; 100–02

Derryhallagh td: Donagh MN 40; 98–99

Derryharney td: Cleenish FH 14; 29

Derryhassan lough: Mevagh DL 38; 55

Derryhassan school: Mevagh DL 38; 59

Derryhassan td: Mevagh DL 38; 63

Derryhaw flax mill: Tynan AH 1; 128

Derryhaw hill: Tynan AH 1; 124

Derryhay (see Derryhaw): Tynan AH 1; 124

Derryheely quarry: Aghavea FH 4; 19

Derryheely td: Aghalurcher FH 4; 7

Derryheely td: Aghavea FH 4; 23

Derryhillagh td: Derryvullan FH 14; 46

Derryhirk school: Aghagallon AM 21; 24

Derryhirk td: Aghagallon AM 21; 1, 3, 12, 18–19

Derryhoany td: Cleenish FH 14; 24, 28

Derryholaght td: Cleenish FH 14; 29

Derryhollagh bog: Duneane AM 19; 109–11, 120–21

Derryhollagh corn mill: Duneane AM 19; 101

Derryhollagh Island: Muckamore AM 35; 69

Derryhollagh td: Duneane AM 19; 109–11, 116–17, 122–23

Derryhowlaght brickfield: Killesher FH 14; 84

Derryhowlaght school: Killesher FH 14; 86

Derryhowlaght td: Killesher FH 14; 87

Derryhubbert td: Killyman AH 1; 55

Derryhullia school: Belleek FH 14; 6

Derryhurdin (Derrahorbin) td: Aghalurcher FH 4; 14

Derryhurdin school: Aghalurcher FH 4; 11

Derryinch td: Cleenish FH 14; 29

Derryinch td: Trory FH 14; 130

Derryinver td: Coleraine LY 33; 53, 97

Derryinver td: Montiaghs AH 1; 90–93

Derrykeeghan corn mill: Enniskillen FH 4; 69

Derrykeeghan corn mill: Magheracross FH 14; 92

Derrykeeghan school: Enniskillen FH 4; 84

Derrykeeghan td: Enniskillen FH 4; 81

Derrykeehan (see Derrykeeghan): Enniskillen FH 4; 81

Derrykeeran td: Tartaraghan AH 1; 122–23

Derrykeevan td: Tartaraghan AH 1; 122–23

Derrykeighan bridges: Derrykeighan AM 16; 85

Derrykeighan church: Derrykeighan AM 16; 87

Derrykeighan Glebe House: Derrykeighan AM 16; 79, 84, 87, 89

Derrykeighan graveyard: Derrykeighan AM 16; 88

Derrykeighan old church: Derrykeighan AM 16; 79, 89–90

Derrykeighan old church: Kilraghts AM 16; 130, 132

Derrykeighan ph: Armoy AM 24; 1–2

Derrykeighan ph: Ballymoney AM 16; 1

Derrykeighan ph: Billy AM 16; 36, 38–40

Derrykeighan ph: Drummaul AM 19; 71

Derrykeighan ph: Drumtullagh AM 16; 96, 99

Derrykeighan ph: Loughguile AM 13; 58

Derrykeighan ph: Misc. AM 10; 129

Derrykeighan school: Derrykeighan AM 16; 86, 95

Derrykeighan td: Derrykeighan AM 16; 84, 88, 90, 92, 94

Derrykeighan village: Derrykeighan AM 16; 79, 84

Derrykenny td: Galloon FH 4; 87, 95

Derrykerrib td: Drummully FH 4; 39

Derrykillultagh school [I]: Ballinderry AM 21; 41, 44, 56

Derrykillultagh school [II]: Ballinderry AM 21; 57

Derrykilultagh (see Derrykillultagh): Ballinderry AM 21; 44

Derrykinnard td: Ematris MN 40; 113

Derrylackagh (see Derryleckagh): Newry DN 3; 107

Derrylane bog: Bovevagh LY 25; 45

Derrylane burn: Bovevagh LY 25; 57

Derrylane Canal: Bovevagh LY 25; 37

Derrylane corn mill: Bovevagh LY 25; 4, 18, 20–21, 57

Derrylane old mill: Bovevagh LY 25; 14

Derrylane td: Banagher LY 30; 23–24

Derrylane td: Bovevagh LY 25; 13, 30–31, 37, 58, 60–61

Derrylard hill: Tartaraghan AH 1; 119

Derrylard school: Tartaraghan AH 1; 118–19, 122

Derrylard td: Tartaraghan AH 1; 120

Derrylavan bridge: Magheross MN 40; 146

Derrylavan school: Magheross MN 40; 156

Derrylavan td: Magheross MN 40; 148, 156

Derrylavin (see Derrylavan): Magheross MN 40; 156

Derrylawn td: Dromore TE 5; 98

Derrylea td: Galloon FH 4; 95

Derrylea td: Kinawley FH 4; 110, 121

Derryleck td: Cleenish FH 14; 28–29

Derryleckagh corn mill: Newry DN 3; 78

Derryleckagh flour mill [I]: Newry DN 3; 78

Derryleckagh flour mill [II]: Newry DN 3; 78

Derryleckagh lough: Newry DN 3; 61, 108

Derryleckagh td: Newry DN 3; 61, 78, 107–08

Derrylee corn mill: Tartaraghan AH 1; 120

Derrylee meeting house: Tartaraghan AH 1; 118, 120

Derrylee school: Tartaraghan AH 1; 122

Derrylee td: Killyman AH 1; 55

Derrylee td: Tartaraghan AH 1; 117, 119

Derryleg td: Drummully FH 4; 39

Derrylester chapel: Killesher FH 14; 83

Derrylester chapel: Kinawley FH 4; 107

Derrylester school: Killesher FH 14; 86

Derrylester td: Killesher FH 14; 82, 87

Derrylettiffe td: Drumcree AH 1; 40

Derrylevick bridge: Errigal Truagh MN 40; 121

Derrylileagh Island: Tartaraghan AH 1; 120

Derrylileagh td: Tartaraghan AH 1; 121

Derrylin: Kinawley FH 4; 108–09, 111, 115, 119, 121

Derrylin chapel: Kinawley FH 4; 115, 119

Derrylin school: Kinawley FH 4; 119

Derrylin td: Kinawley FH 4; 121

Derrylinn (see Derrylin): Kinawley FH 4; 121

Derrylister (see Derrylester): Killesher FH 14; 86

Derryloagher td: Templecarn FH 14; 118

Derryloman mountain: Aghalurcher FH 4; 2

Derryloman td: Aghalurcher FH 4; 14

Derryloran ph: Artrea TE 20; 6

Derryloran ph: Desertcreat TE 20; 32, 35

Derryloran ph: Kildress TE 20; 58

Derryloran ph: Tamlaght TE 20; 73

Derrylosset school: Ematris MN 40; 117

Derrylosset td: Ematris MN 40; 116

Derrylost td: Montiaghs AH 1; 93

Derrylough corn mill: Annaclone DN 12; 14, 18

Derrylough td: Annaclone DN 12; 16, 18

Derryloughan td: Kilmore AH 1; 60–61, 68, 70, 73

Derrylumman (see Derryloman): Aghalurcher FH 4; 2

Derrymacash (Derryvicasse) td: Montiaghs AH 1; 93

Derrymacash chapel: Montiaghs AH 1; 92

Derrymacash chapel: Seagoe AH 1; 102

Derrymacfall td: Drumcree AH 1; 34, 39

Derrymakeen td: Enniskillen FH 4; 82

Derrymarfal (see Derrymacfall): Drumcree AH 1; 34

Derrymattry td: Drumcree AH 1; 39

Derrymeen (Derrymene) td: Errigal Keerogue TE 20; 52, 57

Derrymeen bog: Errigal Keerogue TE 20; 52

Derrymeen quarries: Errigal Keerogue TE 20; 52

Derrymeen wood: Errigal Keerogue TE 20; 52

Derrymore corn mill: Killevy AH 1; 54

Derrymore fort: Drumachose LY 9; 58, 60, 128

Derrymore House: Killevy AH 1; 54

Derrymore meeting house: Drumachose LY 9; 49, 120

Derrymore old church: Aghagallon AM 21; 1

Derrymore school: Aghagallon AM 21; 2, 24

Derrymore td: Aghagallon AM 21; 3, 7, 13, 15–16, 18–19, 21

Derrymore td: Drumachose LY 9; 49, 58, 60, 87, 96, 128, 134

Derrymore td: Killea and Taughboyne DL 39; 79

Derrymore td: Taughboyne DL 39; 148, 153, 195

Derrynaflaw (Dernaflaw) td: Banagher LY 30; 2, 23–24

Derrynaflaw fort: Bovevagh LY 25; 33

Derrynaflaw hills: Bovevagh LY 25; 1

Derrynaflaw stream: Bovevagh LY 25; 14

Derrynaflaw td: Bovevagh LY 25; 1, 9, 18, 31–32, 53, 59, 61

Derrynaflaw td: Drumachose LY 9; 117

Derrynaflaw wartstone: Bovevagh LY 25; 19

Derrynaflaw wood: Banagher LY 30; 2

Derrynaflaw wood: Bovevagh LY 25; 2, 22

Derrynagrew td: Tydavnet MN 40; 169

Derrynaloobinagh Glebe House: Ballybay MN 40; 81

Derrynaloobinagh td: Ballybay MN 40; 84

Derrynanamph bog: Tydavnet MN 40; 170

Derrynanny wood: Derryvullan FH 14; 32

Derrynascobe bog: Magheracloone MN 40; 137

Derrynaseer (Dernaseer) td: Aghagallon AM 21; 2–3, 8, 19

Derrynaseer chapel: Aghagallon AM 21; 2, 4, 13

Derrynaseer chapel: Aghalee AM 21; 28

Derrynaseer fort: Aghagallon AM 21; 13

Derrynaseer school: Aghagallon AM 21; 2, 24–25

Derrynasell td: Tydavnet MN 40; 170

Derrynashandra td: Cleenish FH 14; 28–29

Derrynashesk school: Drumkeeran FH 14; 67

Derrynavogy td: Aghalurcher FH 4; 14

Derryneill corn mill: Drumgooland DN 3; 24

Derryneill td: Drumgooland DN 3; 24

Derrynim td: Cleenish FH 14; 28–29

Derryniquirke district: Misc. SO 40; 200

Derrynisk (Derrynish) td: Magheramesk AM 21; 113, 120

Derrynisk (see Derryroosk): Aughnamullen MN 40; 76

Derrynisk bog: Magheramesk AM 21; 116

Derrynisk fort [I]: Magheramesk AM 21; 120

Derrynisk fort [II]: Magheramesk AM 21; 125

Derrynisk grey stone: Magheramesk AM 21; 120, 122

Derrynisk wood: Magheramesk AM 21; 122

Derryniskin td: Drumcree AH 1; 34, 39

Derrynoid (see Derrynoyd): Misc. LY 31; 114

Derrynoose ph: Eglish AH 1; 43

Derrynoose ph: Muckno MN 40; 162

Derrynoose ph: Tynan AH 1; 124, 131

Derrynoyd bog: Ballynascreen LY 31; 26

Derrynoyd bridge: Misc. LY 31; 116

Derrynoyd hill: Misc. LY 31; 114

Derrynoyd Lodge: Ballynascreen LY 31; 1, 5–6, 20, 115

Derrynoyd school: Ballynascreen LY 31; 16

Derrynoyd td: Ballynascreen LY 31; 1, 6, 11, 15, 22–23, 30, 143

Derrynure td: Drummully FH 4; 39

Derryolam Glebe House: Magheross MN 40; 145

Derryolam Glebe td: Magheross MN 40; 145

Derryolam td: Magheross MN 40, 149

Derryolan (see Derryolam): Magheross MN 40; 149

Derryolin (see Derryolam): Magheross MN 40; 145

Derryork bog: Bovevagh LY 25; 30

Derryork bog: Dungiven LY 15; 90

Derryork flax mill: Dungiven LY 15; 9, 97

Derryork hills: Dungiven LY 15; 70, 105

Derryork school: Dungiven LY 15; 18, 116

Derryork td: Banagher LY 30; 23

Derryork td: Bovevagh LY 25; 47

Derryork td: Drumachose LY 9; 126

Derryork td: Dungiven LY 15; 9, 22, 26–27, 47–48, 61, 70, 74, 85, 95, 104–05

Derrypark (see Derryhirk): Aghagallon AM 21; 19

Derryree td: Aghalurcher FH 4; 14

Derryrome Glebe td: Belleek FH 14; 1

Derryroosk flax mill: Aughnamullen MN 40; 72

Derryroosk td: Aughnamullen MN 40; 69, 76

Derryrough district: Misc. SO 40; 200

Derryrusk (see Derryroosk): Aughnamullen MN 40; 69

Derrys and Lisgoran td: Clogher TE 5; 53

Derryscallop (see Derryscollop)

Derryscobe (Derrascobe) td: Cleenish FH 14; 28–29

Derryscobe school: Cleenish FH 14; 24

Derryscollop school: Clonfeacle AH 1; 25

Derryscollop td: Clonfeacle AH 1; 21

Derryscollop village: Clonfeacle AH 1; 21

Derryseele mill: Kildress TE 20; 60

Derrysolough (see Derryhollagh): Duneane AM 19; 101

Derrysteaton td: Galloon FH 4; 87, 95

Derrytrasna td: Montiaghs AH 1; 89–91, 93

Derrytresk bog: Killyman TE 20; 66

Derryvalley meeting house (P): Ballybay MN 40; 80

Derryvalley meeting house (S): Ballybay MN 40; 80

Derryvalley td: Ballybay MN 40; 83–84

Derryvane school: Drumcree AH 1; 36, 39

Derryvane td: Drumcree AH 1; 39

Derryvary (Derryvaragh) td: Devenish FH 14; 47, 55

Derryvary Beg forts: Devenish FH 14; 55

Derryvary hill: Devenish FH 14; 47

Derryveen td: Donagh MN 40; 98

Derryveg td: Magheraculmoney FH 14; 112

Derryvicafoe td: Montiaghs AH 1; 90–91

Derryvoag td: Cleenish FH 14; 28–29

Derryvolan ph: Clogher TE 5; 40

Derryvolgie House: Lambeg AM 8; 137, 142

Derryvolgie manor: Blaris AM 8; 53

Derryvolgie manor: Blaris DN 12; 32

Derryvolgie manor: Derryaghy AM 8; 90

Derryvolgie manor: Lambeg AM 8; 137, 139, 142

Derryvolgie manor court house: Lambeg AM 8; 139

Derryvolley (see Derryvalley): Ballybay MN 40; 80

Derryvore td: Enniskillen FH 4; 74, 82

Derryvore td: Seagoe AH 1; 105, 108

Derryvrane td: Kinawley FH 4; 115

Derryvree td: Aghavea FH 4; 23

Derryvullan bridges: Derryvullan FH 14; 34

Derryvullan chapel: Derryvullan FH 14; 40

Derryvullan church: Derryvullan FH 14; 40

Derryvullan North ph: Magheracross FH 14; 91

Derryvullan North ph: Trory FH 14; 122, 132

Derryvullan ph: Cleenish FH 14; 11, 16, 22

Derryvullan ph: Derrybrusk FH 4; 30

Derryvullan ph: Drumkeeran FH 14; 65

Derryvullan ph: Enniskillen FH 4; 41, 43, 48, 66, 68, 80

Derryvullan ph: Magheracross FH 14; 91

Derryvullan ph: Magheraculmoney FH 14; 103, 107

Derryvullan td: Derryvullan FH 14; 39–40, 46

Derryware td: Banagher LY 30; 22

Derryware td: Dungiven LY 15; 26, 61

Derrywarragh Island: Tartaraghan AH 1; 121

Derrywarragh td: Tartaraghan AH 1; 120

Dervaghcrog (see Dervaghcroy): Clogherny TE 20; 26

Dervaghcroy meeting house: Clogherny TE 20; 25

Dervaghcroy school: Clogherny TE 20; 26

Dervock: Aghadowey LY 22; 25

Dervock: Ballintoy AM 24; 16

Dervock: Ballyrashane LY 22; 49, 51, 53–54

Dervock: Billy AM 16; 40, 76

Dervock: Coleraine LY 33; 66, 129, 141

Dervock: Derrykeighan AM 16; 78–79, 82

Dervock: Killagan AM 23; 80, 83

Dervock: Loughguile AM 13; 75–76

Dervock: Ramoan AM 24; 95

Dervock bridge: Derrykeighan AM 16; 82

Dervock church: Derrykeighan AM 16; 79, 82, 89

Dervock corn mill: Derrykeighan AM 16; 79, 84

Dervock river (see also Blackwater river): Billy AM 16; 36, 40

Dervock school [I]: Derrykeighan AM 16; 83, 86, 95

Dervock school [II]: Derrykeighan AM 16; 86, 95

Dervock tannery: Derrykeighan AM 16; 79, 84

Dervock wash mill: Derrykeighan AM 16; 84

Desborough (Northampton): Dromore DN 12; 74

Deseart td: Magheross MN 40; 157

Desert (Desarts) td: Newry DN 3; 78, 108–09

Desert bog: Newry DN 3; 109

Desert bridges: Newry DN 3; 109

Desert church: Desertoghill LY 27; 31

Desert corn mill: Newry DN 3; 109

Desert flax mill [I]: Newry DN 3; 78, 109

Desert flax mill [II]: Newry DN 3; 78, 109

Desertcreat altar: Desertcreat TE 20; 33

Desertcreat bleach green: Desertcreat TE 20; 32, 34, 36

Desertcreat church: Desertcreat TE 20; 32

Desertcreat national school: Desertcreat TE 20; 32

Desertcreat old church: Ballynascreen LY 31; 9, 24

Desertcreat ph: Artrea TE 20; 6

Desertcreat ph: Ballyclog TE 20; 18

Desertcreat ph: Donaghenry TE 20; 37, 39

Desertcreat ph: Kildress TE 20; 58, 61

Desertcreat ph: Pomeroy TE 20; 70–71

Desertcreat ph: Tullyniskan TE 20; 138

Desertcreat river: Ballinderry TE 20; 11

Desertcreat river: Desertcreat TE 20; 33–34

Desertcreat schools: Desertcreat TE 20; 32, 36

Desertcreat slate quarry: Desertcreat TE 20; 32–33

Desertegney Glebe House: Desertegney DL 38; 26

Desertegney ph: Clondavaddog DL 38; 5

Desertegney ph: Clonmany DL 38; 12–13, 20

Desertegney ph: Desertegney DL 38; 26

Desertegney ph: Killygarvan DL 38; 36, 39, 45

Desertegney ph: Mevagh DL 38; 57

Desertegney ph: Mintiaghs DL 38; 64–66

Desertegney ph: Tullyaughnish DL 38; 95

Desertlyn House: Desertlyn LY 31; 42

Desertlyn old church: Ballynascreen LY 31; 9, 24

Desertlyn ph: Artrea LY 6; 5, 16, 22, 39

Desertlyn ph: Artrea TE 20; 6–7

Desertlyn ph: Faughanvale LY 36; 48

Desertlyn ph: Lissan LY 31; 89, 93

Desertlyn ph: Magherafelt LY 6; 79

Desertmartin: Ballynascreen LY 31; 5–7, 20

Desertmartin: Desertlyn LY 31; 50

Desertmartin: Desertmartin LY 31; 52–56, 58, 60–63

Desertmartin: Kilcronaghan LY 31; 66–67, 74, 77–78, 88

Desertmartin: Kilrea LY 27; 104, 110

Desertmartin: Lissan LY 31; 94

Desertmartin: Maghera LY 18; 5

Desertmartin: Misc. LY 31; 112, 115, 121, 128, 134

Desertmartin bleach greens: Misc. LY 31; 134

Desertmartin bog: Misc. LY 31; 121

Desertmartin church: Ballyscullion LY 6; 45

Desertmartin church: Desertmartin LY 31; 63

Desertmartin classical school: Misc. LY 31; 138

Desertmartin corn mills: Misc. LY 31; 135

Desertmartin court house: Desertmartin LY 31; 53, 56

Desertmartin female school: Desertmartin LY 31; 60

Desertmartin forts: Desertmartin LY 31; 56

Desertmartin gaol: Desertmartin LY 31; 53, 56, 62, 115

Desertmartin Glebe House: Desertmartin LY 31; 59, 116

Desertmartin graveyard: Desertmartin LY 31; 55

Desertmartin meeting house: Desertlyn LY 31; 46

Desertmartin meeting house: Desertmartin LY 31; 54

Desertmartin old church: Desertmartin LY 31; 53, 55–56, 117–127

Desertmartin old graveyard: Kilcronaghan LY 31; 76

Desertmartin ph: Ballynascreen LY 31; 11, 32

Desertmartin ph: Desertlyn LY 31; 35

Desertmartin ph: Desertoghill LY 27; 14, 18

Desertmartin ph: Kilcronaghan LY 31; 64, 71–72, 76, 80, 82

Desertmartin ph: Lissan LY 31; 91, 102

Desertmartin ph: Maghera LY 18; 17, 27, 52, 64, 68

Desertmartin ph: Magheramesk AM 21; 121

Desertmartin ph: Misc. LY 31; 111–12, 114, 116–42, 144

Desertmartin ph: Tamlaght O'Crilly LY 18; 82

Desertmartin plantation: Misc. LY 31; 115

Desertmartin quarries: Maghera LY 18; 1

Desertmartin river (see Grange): Desertmartin LY 31; 52

Desertmartin school: Desertmartin LY 31; 54, 60

Desertmartin Sunday school: Misc. LY 31; 126

Desertoghill bridges: Desertoghill LY 27; 16

Desertoghill fort: Misc. LY 36; 117

Desertoghill old church (see also Ballynameen): Desertoghill LY 27; 5

Desertoghill old church: Banagher LY 30; 37

Desertoghill old church: Misc. LY 36; 114

Desertoghill ph: Aghadowey LY 22; 32

Desertoghill ph: Errigal LY 27; 39, 46, 49, 60, 63

Desertoghill ph: Kilrea LY 27; 104, 114

Desertoghill ph: Maghera LY 18; 17, 27, 34

Desertoghill ph: Misc. LY 36; 116–17

Desertoghill ph: Tamlaght O'Crilly LY 18; 99, 106, 136

Desertowen td: Clondermot LY 34; 76

Desmond, Earl of: Kilkeel DN 3; 53

Devanny, Francis: Ballynure AM 32; 60

Devanny, John: Ballynure AM 32; 62

Devanny, John: Blaris DN 12; 49

Devanny, William: Derryaghy AM 8; 92, 97

Devanny, William: Killowen LY 33; 172

Devenagh stream: Ballyclug AM 23; 54

Devenagh stream: Racavan AM 13; 88, 90, 97

Devenish Abbey: Devenish FH 14; 59–61

Devenish Island: Devenish FH 14; 52, 56, 59–60

Devenish Island: Enniskillen FH 4; 72

Devenish old church: Devenish FH 14; 52, 59

Devenish ph: Boho FH 14; 8

Devenish ph: Cleenish FH 14; 11, 14

Devenish ph: Clogher TE 5; 40

Devenish ph: Enniskillen FH 4; 62, 68

Devenish ph: Inishmacsaint FH 14; 70–71, 77

Devenish ph: Rossorry FH 14; 115

Devenish ph: Trory FH 14; 122, 129

Devenish priory: Devenish FH 14; 52, 54

Devenish priory: Trory FH 14; 127

Devenish Rectory: Devenish FH 14; 53

Devenish tower: Devenish FH 14; 52, 54, 59, 61

Devenish tower church: Devenish FH 14; 60

Deveny, William: Dunboe LY 11; 81

Devereux, Letice (nee Knolles): Carrickfergus AM 37; 84

Devereux, Mr: Clogher TE 5; 40

Devereux, Mrs Nicholas: Ematris MN 40; 117

Devereux, Rev. Nicholas: Ematris MN 40; 114, 117, 119

Devereux, Walter: Ballynure AM 32; 33

Devereux, Walter: Carrickfergus AM 37; 84

Deverny bridge: Pomeroy TE 20; 72

Devick, Charles: Down DN 17; 59

Devil's Hole pit: Tamlaght Finlagan LY 25; 110

Devilin, family: Desertlyn LY 31; 42

Devilinmore (see Devlinmore): Mevagh DL 38; 63

Devine, Anne: Carrickfergus AM 37; 121

Devine, Edward: Banagher LY 30; 93, 95

Devine, John: Banagher LY 30; 90

Devine, John: Bovevagh LY 25; 6, 50–51

Devine, John: Drumachose LY 9; 117

Devine, John: Kilcronaghan LY 31; 85

Devine, John: Tamlaght Finlagan LY 25; 119

Devine, man named: Cumber LY 28; 32

Devine, Margaret: Ballynascreen LY 31; 14, 21

Devine, Michael: Ballymoney AM 16; 18

Deviney, Martin: Kilwaughter AM 10; 115

Devit, Ferdinand: Convoy DL 39; 23

Devitt, John: Banagher LY 30; 53, 89

Devitt, William: Ballyscullion LY 6; 57

Devlin creek: Lough Swilly DL 38; 105, 116–17

Devlin, Ann: Bovevagh LY 25; 60

Devlin, Ann: Magherafelt LY 6; 112

Devlin, Anne: Kilcronaghan LY 31; 84

Devlin, Arthur: Ballyscullion AM 19; 13

Devlin, Bernard: Artrea LY 6; 28

Devlin, Cathrine: Artrea LY 6; 38

Devlin, Charley: Lissan LY 31; 93, 101

Devlin, Connor: Balteagh LY 9; 33

Devlin, Daniel: Duneane AM 19; 124

Devlin, David: Carrickfergus AM 37; 118

Devlin, Dennis [I]: Bovevagh LY 25; 60

Devlin, Dennis [II]: Bovevagh LY 25; 60

Devlin, Edward: Balteagh LY 9; 33
Devlin, family: Aghalee AM 21; 36
Devlin, family: Artrea LY 6; 14
Devlin, Henry: Artrea LY 6; 21
Devlin, Hugh: Tamlaght TE 20; 81, 109
Devlin, James: Balteagh LY 9; 35
Devlin, James: Bovevagh LY 25; 60
Devlin, Jane: Carrickfergus AM 37; 122
Devlin, Jane [I]: Lissan LY 31; 109
Devlin, Jane [II]: Lissan LY 31; 109
Devlin, John: Artrea LY 6; 19, 21
Devlin, John: Ballyscullion AM 19; 13
Devlin, John: Lissan LY 31; 108
Devlin, John: Magherafelt LY 6; 103
Devlin, John: Tamlaght TE 20; 81, 109
Devlin, Joseph: Artrea LY 6; 20, 38
Devlin, Lily: Tamlaght TE 20; 92
Devlin, man named: Misc. LY 31; 118
Devlin, Margret: Bovevagh LY 25; 60
Devlin, Martha: Lissan LY 31; 109
Devlin, Mary: Bovevagh LY 25; 60
Devlin, Mary: Lissan LY 31; 109
Devlin, Messrs Edward and Co.: Balteagh LY 9; 35
Devlin, Michael: Maghera LY 18; 80
Devlin, Miss: Aghanloo LY 11; 10
Devlin, Molly: Bovevagh LY 25; 60
Devlin, Molly: Lissan LY 31; 104
Devlin, Patrick: Artrea LY 6; 28
Devlin, Patrick: Balteagh LY 9; 17, 39
Devlin, Patrick: Carrickfergus AM 37; 115
Devlin, Patrick: Duneane AM 19; 123
Devlin, Patrick: Lissan LY 31; 109
Devlin, Patrick: Maghera LY 18; 36
Devlin, Patrick: Misc. LY 31; 124
Devlin, Patrick: Tamlaght TE 20; 121
Devlin, Patt: Ballyscullion AM 19; 9
Devlin, Paul: Maghera LY 18; 80
Devlin, Peter: Bovevagh LY 25; 60
Devlin, Peter: Kilcronaghan LY 31; 85
Devlin, Peter: Tamlaght TE 20; 81
Devlin, Rev.: Kilbroney DN 3; 34
Devlin, Rev. Hugh: Duneane AM 19; 115
Devlin, Rev. Peter: Magheralin DN 12; 110
Devlin, Robert [I]: Tamlaght TE 20; 81, 109
Devlin, Robert [II]: Tamlaght TE 20; 125
Devlin, Rose: Maghera LY 18; 52
Devlin, Sarah: Artrea LY 6; 38
Devlin, Sareah: Artrea LY 6; 38
Devlin, Thomas: Carrickfergus AM 37; 118
Devlin, William: Carrickfergus AM 37; 193
Devlin, William: Drumachose LY 9; 85, 123
Devlinmore corn mill: Mevagh DL 38; 57
Devlinmore fort: Mevagh DL 38; 58
Devlinmore td: Mevagh DL 38; 55, 63
Devonport borough: Ballyscullion LY 6; 60

Devonshire (England): Ballyscullion LY 6; 46
Devonshire: Down DN 17; 42
Devonshire: Misc. LY 36; 104
Devoul, Mr: Donegal DL 39; 46
Devyre, family: Blaris DN 12; 30
Dhaidd td: Banagher LY 30; 63
Dhoorish Croagh td: Clonleigh DL 39; 12
Dhu lough: Mintiaghs DL 38; 64
Dhuan (see Doon): Kilmacrenan DL 38; 50
Dhuross Point: Derryvullan FH 14; 31
Diamond Cross locality: Kilmore AH 1; 70
Diamond hill: Kilmore AH 1; 61, 70
Diamond rocks: Kilkeel DN 3; 46, 48
Diamond, Ann: Ballynascreen LY 31; 14, 21
Diamond, Anne: Kilrea LY 27; 129
Diamond, D.: Tamlaght Finlagan LY 25; 122
Diamond, Daniel: Agivey LY 22; 45
Diamond, Daniel: Tamlaght Finlagan LY 25; 119
Diamond, Edward: Magilligan LY 11; 133
Diamond, Ellen: Kilrea LY 27; 129
Diamond, family: Artrea LY 6; 14
Diamond, family: Ballyscullion LY 6; 53
Diamond, family: Billy AM 16; 58, 68
Diamond, family: Dunluce AM 16; 117
Diamond, family: Maghera LY 18; 24, 48
Diamond, Francis: Killelagh LY 27; 102
Diamond, Francis: Maghera LY 18; 55
Diamond, Hugh: Kilrea LY 27; 129
Diamond, James: Agivey LY 22; 45
Diamond, James [I]: Kilrea LY 27; 129
Diamond, James [II]: Kilrea LY 27; 129
Diamond, Jane: Kilrea LY 27; 129
Diamond, John: Balteagh LY 9; 43
Diamond, John: Carrickfergus AM 37; 110
Diamond, John: Kilrea LY 27; 129
Diamond, John: Tamlaght Finlagan LY 25; 119
Diamond, Lawrence: Desertoghill LY 27; 26
Diamond, man named: Maghera LY 18; 22
Diamond, Margaret: Kilrea LY 27; 129
Diamond, Maryann: Balteagh LY 9; 43
Diamond, Neill: Maghera LY 18; 8, 68
Diamond, Patrick: Kilrea LY 27; 129
Diamond, Patt: Errigal LY 27; 66
Diamond, priest: Kilrea LY 27; 111, 125
Diamond, Rose (Jnr): Kilrea LY 27; 129
Diamond, Rose (Snr): Kilrea LY 27; 129
Diamond, William: Kilrea LY 27; 129
Dichu, prior: Down DN 17; 50
Dichu, prior: Saul DN 17; 113
Dick, family: Enniskillen FH 4; 58
Dick, family: Templecorran AM 26; 117, 119
Dick, James: Island Magee AM 10; 70, 98
Dick, Jane: Drumachose LY 9; 70, 85, 125
Dick, Mary: Drumachose LY 9; 70, 125
Dick, Rebecca: Enniskillen FH 4; 56

Dick, Rev.: Kilcronaghan LY 31; 82
Dick, Robert: Island Magee AM 10; 90
Dicken, family: Culfeightrin AM 24; 59
Dickenson, Mr: Newry DN 3; 109–10
Dickey, Bernard: Magheramesk AM 21; 130
Dickey, Debby: Magheramesk AM 21; 130
Dickey, Elizabeth (Jnr): Magheramesk AM 21; 130
Dickey, Elizabeth (Snr): Magheramesk AM 21; 130
Dickey, English: Magheramesk AM 21; 130
Dickey, family: Ballyclug AM 23; 63
Dickey, family: Billy AM 16; 58, 68
Dickey, family: Blaris AM 8; 22
Dickey, family: Racavan AM 13; 100
Dickey, James: Kilbroney DN 3; 32
Dickey, James: Magheramesk AM 21; 130
Dickey, James: Templepatrick AM 35; 112, 142, 146
Dickey, John: Ahoghill AM 23; 34
Dickey, John: Doagh AM 29; 93
Dickey, John [I]: Ahoghill AM 23; 12
Dickey, John [II]: Ahoghill AM 23; 12
Dickey, Mary: Magheramesk AM 21; 130
Dickey, Miss: Antrim AM 29; 46
Dickey, Mr: Drummaul AM 19; 84
Dickey, Nathaniel: Blaris DN 12; 42
Dickey, Nathaniel: Magheramesk AM 21; 130
Dickey, Norris: Magheramesk AM 21; 130
Dickey, Robert: Drummaul AM 19; 68, 87
Dickey, Robert: Magheramesk AM 21; 130
Dickey, Robert: Rasharkin AM 23; 140
Dickey, Thomas: Ballyscullion LY 6; 64
Dickey, William: Magheramesk AM 21; 130
Dickeystown: Tickmacrevan AM 13; 124
Dickie, family: Carnmoney AM 2; 76
Dickinson, Rev. Daniel: Seapatrick DN 12; 132, 135
Dickson, Anne: Hillsborough DN 12; 90
Dickson, Cllr: Kilbarron DL 39; 74
Dickson, family: Ballintoy AM 24; 20
Dickson, family: Carnmoney AM 2; 76
Dickson, family: Enniskillen FH 4; 58
Dickson, family: Lambeg AM 8; 135
Dickson, Hugh: Ballintoy AM 24; 31
Dickson, James: Hillsborough DN 12; 105
Dickson, John: Banagher LY 30; 74
Dickson, John: Derryaghy AM 8; 111
Dickson, John: Dungiven LY 15; 113
Dickson, John: Hillsborough DN 12; 107
Dickson, John: Misc. LY 31; 130, 140
Dickson, Messrs: Magilligan LY 11; 117
Dickson, Mr: Donacavey TE 5; 82
Dickson, R.: Dromore DN 12; 72
Dickson, Rev. John: Finvoy AM 23; 73
Dickson, Rev. John: Hillsborough DN 12; 89
Dickson, Rev. John: Rasharkin AM 23; 128, 130, 141
Dickson, Richard: Carnmoney AM 2; 101

Dickson, Robert: Carnmoney AM 2; 62, 102
Dickson, Samuel: Hillsborough DN 12; 107
Dickson, William: Hillsborough DN 12; 90
Dickson, William: Misc. DN 17; 117
Dickson, William: Newry DN 3; 98, 103
Dicky, Rev. William: Donaghmore DL 39; 32
Dicky's fort: Desertoghill LY 27; 21
Diernamen td: Inishmacsaint FH 14; 70
Diet, Robert: Dunluce AM 16; 121–22
Difflin td: Raphoe DL 39; 125
Digh lough: Aghalurcher FH 4; 3–4
Dileey Hall night school: Clondermot LY 34; 42
Dileey Hall school: Clondermot LY 34; 42
Dilergy, family: Culfeightrin AM 24; 71
Dill, family: Ballyclug AM 23; 60
Dill, Marcus: Aghanloo LY 11; 22, 30
Dill, Marcus: Drumachose LY 9; 80, 104, 108, 129
Dill, Marcus: Tamlaght Finlagan LY 25; 72
Dill, Mr: Tullyaughnish DL 38; 94
Dill, Mrs John: Carnmoney AM 2; 87
Dill, Rev. John: Carnmoney AM 2; 56, 75, 77–78, 81, 85, 87, 90, 94, 99
Dill, Rev. Richard: Donaghmore DL 39; 32
Dill, Rev. Richard: Drumachose LY 9; 107–108
Dill, Rev. Richard: Tamlaght Finlagan LY 25; 69–70, 82
Dill, Rev. S.M.: Magherally DN 12; 115
Dilling, Rev.: Comber DN 7; 41
Dillon td: Ballee DN 17; 20, 22–23
Dillon, Charles: Donegal DL 39; 56
Dillon, family: Blaris AM 8; 21
Dillon, family: Clondermot LY 34; 71, 76
Dillon, family: Culfeightrin AM 24; 59
Dillon, Hugh: Carrickfergus AM 37; 131
Dillon, James: Carrickfergus AM 37; 108
Dillon, Mr: Blaris AM 8; 84
Dillon, Mrs: Donegal DL 39; 46
Dillon, William (Jnr): Blaris AM 8; 55
Dillon, William (Snr): Blaris AM 8; 52, 55
Dillon, William (Snr): Blaris DN 12; 45, 49
Dillon's Hotel: Donegal DL 39; 46
Dima, Bishop: Magilligan LY 11; 88
Dimond, Andrew: Desertoghill LY 27; 29, 32
Dimond, Ann: Ballyscullion LY 6; 77
Dimond, Bernard: Tamlaght O'Crilly LY 18; 126
Dimond, Charles: Aghadowey LY 22; 20
Dimond, Charles: Ballyscullion LY 6; 68
Dimond, Daniel: Artrea LY 6; 28
Dimond, James: Artrea LY 6; 28
Dimond, James: Ballyscullion LY 6; 69
Dimond, James: Tamlaght O'Crilly LY 18; 137
Dimond, John: Artrea LY 6; 38
Dimond, John: Drumbeg AM 8; 128
Dimond, John: Lambeg AM 8; 139

Dimond, John: Tamlaght O'Crilly LY 18; 95, 114–15, 125, 131

Dimond, John: Tamlaght TE 20; 86

Dimond, Michael: Desertoghill LY 27; 31

Dimond, Michael: Drumbeg AM 8; 129, 131

Dimond, Patrick: Ballynascreen LY 31; 22, 24

Dimond, Patrick: Ballyscullion LY 6; 72

Dimond, Paul: Artrea LY 6; 38

Dimond, Susana: Artrea LY 6; 38

Dimond, William: Artrea LY 6; 29

Dimond, William: Ballyscullion LY 6; 76

Dineady td: Aghanloo LY 11; 12

Dinginavanty school: Killdrumsherdan CN 40; 36

Dinginavanty td: Killdrumsherdan CN 40; 32

Dinnen, Rev. John: Ballyaghran LY 33; 3

Dinnen, Rev. John: Coleraine LY 33; 72

Dinnydoon td: Rossorry FH 14; 116

Dinsmoor, family: Billy AM 16; 58, 68

Dinsmoor, James: Billy AM 16; 74

Dinsmore, family: Misc. LY 36; 104

Dinsmore, Hugh: Finvoy AM 23; 75

Dinsmore, Robert: Clondermot LY 34; 42, 87, 90–91, 93, 95

Dinsmore, William: Finvoy AM 23; 74

Diora lough: Clondavaddog DL 38; 3

Dirnagh td: Clonoe TE 20; 29

Dirran (see Dirraw): Finvoy AM 23; 69

Dirraw bog: Finvoy AM 23; 69

Dirraw td: Finvoy AM 23; 73

Dirren mountain: Templecarn FH 14; 118

Dirtagh bridge: Aghanloo LY 11; 23

Dirtagh burn: Aghanloo LY 11; 27

Dirtagh fort: Aghanloo LY 11; 5, 27

Dirtagh school: Aghanloo LY 11; 31

Dirtagh td: Aghanloo LY 11; 11, 20, 23, 31, 40–41

Dirty lough: Mintiaghs DL 38; 64

Disart, Andrew: Rasharkin AM 23; 140

Discart graveyard: Dunaghy AM 13; 17, 24

Discart standing stone: Dunaghy AM 13; 19

Discart td: Dunaghy AM 13; 17, 19, 24

Diseart (see Discart)

Disert (Desert) td: Ballynascreen LY 31; 7, 11, 13, 21–22, 33, 143

Disert abbey: Glynn AM 26; 1

Disert hill: Ballynascreen LY 31; 2

Disert Patrick church: Faughanvale LY 36; 51

Disert wood: Ballynascreen LY 31; 2

Disertowen school: Clondermot LY 34; 89

Disertowen td: Clondermot LY 34; 37, 56, 65, 67, 105, 109, 112, 116, 124, 130

Dishalier [or Dishlier] locality: Muff DL 38; 81

Disney, Messrs: Donaghmore DL 39; 38

Disney, Rev. James: Loughgall AH 1; 77–78

Ditton, Ralph: Mevagh DL 38; 58

Diver, Mr: Clonleigh DL 39; 4

Diver, William: Ballynascreen LY 31; 17

Divert, family: Misc. LY 36; 104

Divinagh (Diviniagh) td: Clogher TE 5; 36, 46

Divine, Mr: Enniskillen FH 4; 85

Diviney, family: Ballynure AM 32; 69

Diviny td: Drumcree AH 1; 37

Divis Little hill: Templepatrick AM 35; 141

Divis Mountain: Ballymartin AM 2; 1, 3

Divis Mountain: Blaris AM 8; 13

Divis Mountain: Blaris DN 12; 27

Divis Mountain: Camlin AM 21; 63–64

Divis Mountain: Carmavy AM 35; 1

Divis Mountain: Carnmoney AM 2; 98

Divis Mountain: Carrickfergus AM 37; 5

Divis Mountain: Derryaghy AM 8; 91

Divis Mountain: Doagh AM 29; 86

Divis Mountain: Glenavy AM 21; 80

Divis Mountain: Killead AM 35; 7–9, 42

Divis Mountain: Misc. AM 10; 131

Divis Mountain: Muckamore AM 35; 58

Divis Mountain: Templepatrick AM 35; 105, 116, 132, 139, 141–42

Divis Mountain: Tullyrusk AM 21; 132–33, 135, 138

Divis Mountain: Umgall AM 35; 155–57

Divlinmore (see Devlinmore): Mevagh DL 38; 55

Divlinreagh td: Mevagh DL 38; 55, 63

Dixon, Anne: Magheradrool DN 17; 101

Dixon, Charity (see O'Neill)

Dixon, Col.: Clogher TE 5; 48

Dixon, Colvin: Dromore DN 12; 78

Dixon, David: Annaclone DN 12; 18

Dixon, family: Blaris DN 12; 30

Dixon, family: Culfeightrin AM 24; 59

Dixon, Francis: Ballyscullion LY 6; 78

Dixon, John: Ballynascreen LY 31; 8

Dixon, John: Ballyscullion LY 6; 52, 71, 75, 78

Dixon, Margret: Ballyscullion LY 6; 78

Dixon, Moore: Dunaghy AM 13; 21

Dixon, Rev.: Templecarn DL 39; 161

Dixon, Rev. Stephen: Ballycor AM 32; 5

Dixon, Rev. Stephen: Carncastle and Killyglen AM 10; 7

Dixon, Rev. Stephen: Kilwaughter AM 10; 116–17

Dixon, Rev. Stephen: Rashee AM 32; 138

Dixon, Robert: Blaris DN 12; 46, 50

Dixon, Robert: Drummaul AM 19; 70

Dixon, S.: Antrim AM 29; 46

Dixon, William: Ballyscullion LY 6; 78

Dixy, Rev.: Galloon FH 4; 100

Dixy, Woolston: Galloon FH 4; 100–01

Doagh: Antrim AM 29; 25

Doagh: Ballyclug AM 23; 53

Doagh: Ballycor AM 32; 5

Doagh: Ballylinny AM 32; 14, 16, 25, 30

Doagh: Ballymartin AM 2; 17
Doagh: Ballynure AM 32; 66
Doagh: Ballyrobert AM 2; 20
Doagh: Ballywalter AM 2; 26–27, 29–30
Doagh: Carnmoney AM 2; 49, 70, 85, 93
Doagh: Connor AM 19; 16–17, 22, 29–30
Doagh: Doagh AM 29; 60–61, 63–64, 67–71, 73–75, 80–82, 85–86, 88–89, 91–92, 94, 96, 98–99
Doagh: Donegore AM 29; 102–03, 106, 108, 110–11, 131–32, 134
Doagh: Faughanvale LY 36; 55
Doagh: Glynn AM 26; 21
Doagh: Kilbride AM 29; 135–41, 144, 148, 151, 154–56
Doagh: Mevagh DL 38; 61
Doagh: Nilteen AM 35; 90, 101–02
Doagh: Raloo AM 32; 96
Doagh: Rashee AM 32; 137–38
Doagh abbey: Doagh AM 29; 67–68, 71, 78, 92
Doagh bay: Mevagh DL 38; 63
Doagh beetling mill: Doagh AM 29; 68, 70, 85, 93
Doagh bleach mill: Doagh AM 29; 60, 68, 70, 93
Doagh bog: Magheracloone MN 40; 137
Doagh Book Club room: Doagh AM 29; 68–69, 72, 74, 77, 89, 94–95, 97, 99
Doagh Castle: Lough Swilly DL 38; 133
Doagh chapel (C): Ballylinny AM 32; 17
Doagh chapel (C): Ballynure AM 32; 36, 50
Doagh chapel (M): Doagh AM 29; 60, 75, 85, 92, 99
Doagh corn mill: Doagh AM 29; 85, 93
Doagh coves: Doagh AM 29; 68, 79, 84
Doagh dispensary: Ballycor AM 32; 5
Doagh dispensary: Ballynure AM 32; 36
Doagh dispensary: Ballywalter AM 2; 26, 30
Doagh dispensary: Doagh AM 29; 66, 69, 73–74, 81, 84, 86, 90, 92, 94–97, 100
Doagh dispensary: Donegore AM 29; 111
Doagh dispensary: Kilbride AM 29; 141, 151
Doagh dispensary: Nilteen AM 35; 91
Doagh dispensary: Rashee AM 32; 138
Doagh dispensary bridge: Doagh AM 29; 92
Doagh evening school: Doagh AM 29; 97
Doagh flax mill: Doagh AM 29; 68, 70, 85, 93
Doagh flour mill (see Ballyclare): Doagh AM 29; 93
Doagh forge: Doagh AM 29; 68, 70, 72
Doagh fort [I]: Doagh AM 29; 61
Doagh fort [II]: Doagh AM 29; 68, 79–80, 84, 98
Doagh graveyard: Doagh AM 29; 61, 67–68, 78–80, 92–93, 98
Doagh graveyard coves: Doagh AM 29; 79–80
Doagh hill: Devenish FH 14; 47–48
Doagh hotel: Doagh AM 29; 68–69, 92, 95
Doagh ironworks: Doagh AM 29; 85

Doagh Island: Clonmany DL 38; 13, 15–16, 19–20
Doagh Island: Lough Swilly DL 38; 133–35
Doagh lough: Devenish FH 14; 47
Doagh Masonic lodge room: Doagh AM 29; 74, 95
Doagh Methodist Sunday school: Doagh AM 29; 99–00
Doagh Methodist worship house: Doagh AM 29; 68
Doagh national school: Doagh AM 29; 68–69, 74, 82–83, 86, 89, 91–92, 94, 97, 99
Doagh night school: Doagh AM 29; 69, 74
Doagh old church: Doagh AM 29; 78–80, 84
Doagh old corn mill: Doagh AM 29; 70, 93
Doagh old road bridge: Doagh AM 29; 92
Doagh paper mill (see Ballyclare): Doagh AM 29; 93
Doagh ph: Ballycor AM 32; 6
Doagh ph: Ballylinny AM 32; 11, 13, 20
Doagh ph: Ballymartin AM 2; 7
Doagh ph: Ballynure AM 32; 38
Doagh ph: Ballyrobert AM 2; 21
Doagh ph: Ballywalter AM 2; 30–31
Doagh ph: Carrickfergus AM 37; 73
Doagh ph: Doagh AM 29; 87
Doagh ph: Donegore AM 29; 111–12, 129, 133
Doagh ph: Kilbride AM 29; 135, 137, 141–42, 147–48, 150–51
Doagh ph: Misc. AM 10; 129
Doagh ph: Nilteen AM 35; 92
Doagh ph: Raloo AM 32; 132
Doagh ph: Rashee AM 32; 135, 138
Doagh ph: Templepatrick AM 35; 119
Doagh private school: Doagh AM 29; 83
Doagh rectory: Doagh AM 29; 93
Doagh river: Doagh AM 29; 61–63, 67, 70–71, 79–80, 82, 84, 93
Doagh river: Kilbride AM 29; 136–37, 139, 155
Doagh river: Rashee AM 32; 135–36
Doagh river bridge: Kilbride AM 29; 151
Doagh river bridge [I]: Doagh AM 29; 71
Doagh river bridge [II]: Doagh AM 29; 71
Doagh river bridge [III]: Doagh AM 29; 71
Doagh river foot–go: Doagh AM 29; 93
Doagh schools: Kilbride AM 29; 142
Doagh td: Doagh AM 29; 60–61, 67, 70
Doagh td: Mevagh DL 38; 63
Doagh Upper td: Magilligan LY 11; 95
Doaghbeg: Clondavaddog DL 38; 4, 9
Doaghbeg caves: Clondavaddog DL 38; 4
Doaghbeg harbour: Lough Swilly DL 38; 98–99
Doaghbeg Point: Lough Swilly DL 38; 99–100
Doaghcrabeen (see Doagherabeen): Lough Swilly DL 38; 100
Doagherabeen Point: Lough Swilly DL 38; 98–100
Doaghmore Point: Lough Swilly DL 38; 114–15, 134

Doaghmore td: Clondavaddog DL 38; 3, 5, 9

Doaghrahin Castle: Clondavaddog DL 38; 6

Doaghs isthmus: Clonmany DL 38; 13

Doaghs Lower td: Magilligan LY 11; 92, 95, 124, 127

Doaghs Middle td: Magilligan LY 11; 95

Doaghs school: Clonmany DL 38; 17

Doaghs td: Magilligan LY 11; 126

Doaghs Upper td: Magilligan LY 11; 142

Doak, John: Dromore DN 12; 78

Doalt glen: Cumber LY 28; 67, 71

Dobbin, family: Carrickfergus AM 37; 29–30, 93, 161–62, 179

Dobbin, family: Lambeg AM 8; 135

Dobbin, James: Ballyscullion AM 19; 9–10

Dobbin, Leonard: Eglish AH 1; 44

Dobbin, Maj.: Duneane AM 19; 107

Dobbin, Miss: Termoneeny LY 6; 127, 132

Dobbin, Mr (Armagh city): Drumcree AH 1; 39

Dobbin, Mr: Blaris DN 12; 46

Dobbin, Mr: Termoneeny LY 6; 127, 132

Dobbin, Mrs: Tynan AH 1; 129

Dobbin, Rev. H.J.: Hillsborough DN 12; 87, 97, 99, 102, 105

Dobbin, Rev. Hamilton: Shankill AH 1; 115

Dobbin, Thomas: Magheramesk AM 21; 126

Dobbin, William: Duneane AM 19; 113

Dobbin's Castle: Carrickfergus AM 37; 161

Dobbings, Ezekil: Ballyscullion LY 6; 78

Dobbings, Henery: Ballyscullion LY 6; 78

Dobbings, Isias: Ballyscullion LY 6; 78

Dobbings, James: Ballyscullion LY 6; 78

Dobbings, Robert: Ballyscullion LY 6; 78

Dobbings, William (Jnr): Ballyscullion LY 6; 78

Dobbings, William (Snr): Ballyscullion LY 6; 78

Dobbs, Arthur: Kilroot AM 26; 59, 73, 76, 78

Dobbs, C.E.: Carrickfergus AM 37; 98, 102

Dobbs, C.P.: Carrickfergus AM 37; 25

Dobbs, C.P.: Kilroot AM 26; 78

Dobbs, C.R.: Ballymore AH 1; 4, 6, 10–12

Dobbs, C.R.: Ballynure AM 32; 40, 46–47, 68

Dobbs, C.R.: Carrickfergus AM 37; 32–33, 42, 98, 102, 135, 139, 143

Dobbs, C.R.: Kilroot AM 26; 56, 59, 67, 73–74, 77–79

Dobbs, Cllr: Ardclinis AM 13; 1

Dobbs, Cllr: Clonmany DL 38; 18

Dobbs, Dean: Island Magee AM 10; 16, 26, 72

Dobbs, family: Ballynure AM 32; 47, 56, 59, 63, 69

Dobbs, family: Blaris AM 8; 21

Dobbs, family: Carrickfergus AM 37; 77, 93, 176, 179, 186

Dobbs, family: Kilroot AM 26; 76

Dobbs, family: Templecorran AM 26; 86

Dobbs, Helen: Glynn AM 26; 39

Dobbs, Hercules: Ballynure AM 32; 47, 52

Dobbs, Jane: Carrickfergus AM 37; 145

Dobbs, John: Ballynure AM 32; 45, 51–52, 64, 69

Dobbs, John: Kilroot AM 26; 61, 73

Dobbs, Lt: Blaris AM 8; 8

Dobbs, Margaret (nee Dalway): Ballynure AM 32; 45, 47, 51–52, 64, 69

Dobbs, Margaret: Kilroot AM 26; 61, 73

Dobbs, Mary: Blaris AM 8; 21

Dobbs, Miss: Kilroot AM 26; 74, 81

Dobbs, Mr: Glenavy AM 21; 83

Dobbs, Mrs John: Carrickfergus AM 37; 28, 142, 162

Dobbs, Mrs Richard: Kilroot AM 26; 74, 80

Dobbs, Rev.: Clonmany DL 38; 14

Dobbs, Rev. Francis: Coleraine LY 33; 127

Dobbs, Rev. Francis: Derrykeighan AM 16; 84

Dobbs, Rev. John: Carrickfergus AM 37; 135–36

Dobbs, Rev. R.: Carrickfergus AM 37; 23, 25

Dobbs, Rev. Richard: Blaris AM 8; 21

Dobbs, Rev. Stewart: Ardclinis AM 13; 7

Dobbs, Rev. Stewart: Layd AM 13; 45

Dobbs, Richard (Jnr): Ballynure AM 32; 59, 67

Dobbs, Richard (Snr): Ballynure AM 32; 59

Dobbs, William: Blaris AM 8; 25

Dobbs, William: Carrickfergus AM 37; 57, 136

Dobbsland cave [I]: Kilroot AM 26; 57

Dobbsland cave [II]: Kilroot AM 26; 71

Dobbsland td: Kilroot AM 26; 56, 59, 61, 73–74, 79

Dobson, Capt.: Leck DL 39; 115, 118–19

Dobson, George: Aghagallon AM 21; 15

Dobson, Mrs: Drumachose LY 9; 70, 122

Dobson, Thomas: Tamlaght TE 20; 92

Dobyn, Peter: Carrickfergus AM 37; 43

Docwra, Henry: Ballynure AM 32; 52

Docwra, Henry: Clogher TE 5; 31

Docwra, Henry: Clondermot LY 34; 53–55, 66

Docwra, Henry: Kilroot AM 26; 73

Doddington, family: Coleraine LY 33; 57

Dodington, Edward: Coleraine LY 33; 94

Dodington, Edward: Drumachose LY 9; 61

Dodington, Edward: Dungiven LY 15; 52

Dodington, Elizabeth: Coleraine LY 33; 94

Dodington, family: Dungiven LY 15; 42

Dodwell, George: Emlaghfad SO 40; 177, 181

Doe Castle: Lough Swilly DL 38; 120

Doe Castle: Mevagh DL 38; 56–57

Doe Castle ford: Lough Swilly DL 38; 120

Doe channel: Lough Swilly DL 38; 118, 120

Doe district: Lough Swilly DL 38; 128–29

Doe district: Mevagh DL 38; 58

Doe's hill: Taughboyne DL 39; 148, 151, 153–54

Doel, family: Ballyclug AM 23; 60

Doey, Robert: Ahoghill AM 23; 39

Doff, James: Island Magee AM 10; 95

Doff, William: Island Magee AM 10; 95

Dofin, Mary: Tamlaght TE 20; 77

Dog Leap (see also Roe Green): Drumachose LY 9; 52

Dog Leap bleach green: Drumachose LY 9; 83

Dog Leap bridge: Drumachose LY 9; 83, 91

Dog Leap Castle: Drumachose LY 9; 92

Dog Leap td: Drumachose LY 9; 120

Doggan, Hamilton: Leck DL 39; 119

Dogherty, Ann: Bovevagh LY 25; 60

Dogherty, Ann: Tamlaght Finlagan LY 25; 120

Dogherty, Anthony: Banagher LY 30; 33, 111

Dogherty, Bernard: Drumachose LY 9; 112

Dogherty, Bridget: Dungiven LY 15; 56

Dogherty, Bunton, Gorman and Co., Messrs: Ballinderry AM 21; 47

Dogherty, Conoley: Drumachose LY 9; 133

Dogherty, Edward: Balteagh LY 9; 33

Dogherty, Edward: Macosquin LY 22; 90, 121

Dogherty, family: Clonmany DL 38; 16, 18

Dogherty, Hannah: Agivey LY 22; 45

Dogherty, Hugh: Bovevagh LY 25; 42

Dogherty, James: Ardstraw TE 5; 7

Dogherty, James: Drumachose LY 9; 132

Dogherty, James: Tamlaght TE 20; 129

Dogherty, John: Ballymoney AM 16; 16

Dogherty, John: Ballywillin AM 16; 35

Dogherty, John: Hillsborough DN 12; 107

Dogherty, John: Killowen LY 33; 170

Dogherty, John: Macosquin LY 22; 120

Dogherty, John: Tamlaght Finlagan LY 25; 120

Dogherty, M.: Clonmany DL 38; 14, 18

Dogherty, Marcus: Bovevagh LY 25; 59

Dogherty, Margret: Tamlaght Finlagan LY 25; 120

Dogherty, Michael: Bovevagh LY 25; 42

Dogherty, Micky: Desertegney DL 38; 28

Dogherty, Mr: Donaghmore DL 39; 40

Dogherty, Patrick: Camlin AM 21; 76

Dogherty, poet: Clonmany DL 38; 17

Dogherty, Rebecca: Macosquin LY 22; 90, 121

Dogherty, Rev. Anthony: Templecarn DL 39; 160

Dogherty, Rev. John: Blaris AM 8; 31

Dogherty, Robert: Desertoghill LY 27; 20

Dogherty, Robert: Tamlaght Finlagan LY 25; 120

Dogherty, Sally: Tamlaght Finlagan LY 25; 120

Dogherty, Shane (see MacAvergy): Clonmany DL 38; 17

Dogherty, Thomas: Faughanvale LY 36; 24, 35–36, 66

Dogherty, William: Macosquin LY 22; 118, 121

Dogherty, William: Tamlaght Finlagan LY 25; 120

Dogherty, William: Termonamongan TE 5; 144

Dogs Big hill: Devenish FH 14; 47

Dogs Little hill: Devenish FH 14; 47

Doharrick school: Killdrumsherdan CN 40; 35

Dohatel (see Doohallat): Drumgoon CN 40; 11

Doherty, Anne: Carrickfergus AM 37; 122

Doherty, Charles: Carrickfergus AM 37; 111, 195

Doherty, Connor: Coleraine LY 33; 72

Doherty, Daniel: Dungiven LY 15; 95–96

Doherty, Daniel: Macosquin LY 22; 91

Doherty, Edward: Carrickfergus AM 37; 128

Doherty, Edward: Magilligan LY 11; 94, 129

Doherty, Ellen: Magilligan LY 11; 94

Doherty, family: Macosquin LY 22; 84, 119

Doherty, family: Magilligan LY 11; 114, 130

Doherty, Frank [I]: Maghera LY 18; 80

Doherty, Frank [II]: Maghera LY 18; 80

Doherty, George: Coleraine LY 33; 73

Doherty, George: Magilligan LY 11; 94, 131, 133, 137

Doherty, Hanah: Aghadowey LY 22; 37

Doherty, Henry: Maghera LY 18; 81

Doherty, Hugh: Maghera LY 18; 80

Doherty, James: Coleraine LY 33; 73

Doherty, James: Desertoghill LY 27; 21

Doherty, James: Magilligan LY 11; 134

Doherty, Jane: Magilligan LY 11; 94

Doherty, John: Ballymoney AM 16; 17

Doherty, John: Ballyrashane LY 22; 57

Doherty, John: Ballyscullion LY 6; 72

Doherty, John: Carrickfergus AM 37; 110

Doherty, John: Coleraine LY 33; 72

Doherty, John: Desertoghill LY 27; 15–16

Doherty, John: Dunboe LY 11; 56–57, 61, 70

Doherty, John: Loughguile AM 13; 67

Doherty, John: Maghera LY 18; 46–47

Doherty, John: Magilligan LY 11; 94, 123–24, 131, 133

Doherty, Joseph: Ballyaghran LY 33; 28

Doherty, Margaret: Carrickfergus AM 37; 132

Doherty, Mary: Carrickfergus AM 37; 114

Doherty, Mary: Maghera LY 18; 78

Doherty, Michael: Magilligan LY 11; 94

Doherty, Mr: Donaghmore DL 39; 37

Doherty, Mrs Patrick: Ballyaghran LY 33; 21

Doherty, Nancy: Magilligan LY 11; 94

Doherty, P.: Nilteen AM 35; 102

Doherty, Patrick: Ballyaghran LY 33; 21, 23–24, 26

Doherty, Patrick: Maghera LY 18; 81

Doherty, Patrick: Magilligan LY 11; 131

Doherty, Peter: Ballyscullion LY 6; 69, 72

Doherty, Rebecca: Carrickfergus AM 37; 124

Doherty, Rev. John: Bovevagh LY 25; 58–59

Doherty, Rev. John: Donegore AM 29; 126, 129, 133

Doherty, Rev. John: Dungiven LY 15; 76

Doherty, Robert: Desertoghill LY 27; 21

Doherty, Robert: Dunboe LY 11; 75–76

Doherty, Robert: Errigal LY 27; 61–62

Doherty, Sarah: Ballyaghran LY 33; 28
Doherty, Widow: Ballymoney AM 16; 17
Doherty, William: Ballyscullion LY 6; 51–52, 72
Doherty, William: Maghera LY 18; 81
Doherty, William [I]: Magilligan LY 11; 94
Doherty, William [II]: Magilligan LY 11; 94
Doherty, William [III]: Magilligan LY 11; 131–33, 138
Doin Erin bridge: Mevagh DL 38; 58
Doinan's public house: Glenavy AM 21; 78
Dolan, family: Killesher FH 14; 84
Dolan, John: Killesher FH 14; 88
Dolan, Mrs: Enniskillen FH 4; 85
Dolling, Rev. Boghey: Magheralin DN 12; 110
Doluskey fort: Artrea LY 6; 33
Doluskey td: Artrea LY 6; 23, 33, 39
Doluskey td: Artrea TE 20; 8
Domain td: Misc. DN 17; 125–27
Domangard, St: Kilkeel DN 3; 54
Dommey's bridge: Tamlaght Finlagan LY 25; 108
Donacavey mills: Donacavey TE 5; 69
Donacavey old church: Donacavey TE 5; 70, 82
Donacavey ph: Clogher TE 5; 24, 44
Donacavey ph: Clogherny TE 20; 25
Donacavey ph: Longfield TE 5; 133
Donacavey td: Donacavey TE 5; 70, 76, 78, 82, 85
Donacavy ph: Drumragh TE 5; 104
Donacavy ph: Enniskillen FH 4; 41, 48
Donachy's bridge: Glenwhirry AM 32; 79
Donagh bogs: Lough Swilly DL 38; 134
Donagh chapel: Donagh DL 38; 33
Donagh chapel: Galloon FH 4; 90–91
Donagh church: Donagh DL 38; 32–33
Donagh church: Galloon FH 4; 91
Donagh corn mill: Galloon FH 4; 91
Donagh court house: Galloon FH 4; 91
Donagh graveyard: Galloon FH 4; 91–92, 97
Donagh House: Galloon FH 4; 91
Donagh manor: Drummully FH 4; 34, 36–37, 39
Donagh manor: Galloon FH 4; 94–95
Donagh manor: Misc. FH 4; 133
Donagh ph: Clogher TE 5; 40
Donagh ph: Clonmany DL 38; 12–13, 16, 20
Donagh ph: Errigal Truagh MN 40; 120
Donagh ph: Lough Swilly DL 38; 133–35, 142
Donagh ph: Mintiaghs DL 38; 64
Donagh ph: Monaghan MN 40; 159
Donagh ph: Moville DL 38; 73, 78
Donagh ph: Tydavnet MN 40; 169
Donagh ph: Tyholland MN 40; 174
Donagh ph: Tynan AH 1; 124, 127
Donagh Ramor, King of Ossory: Faughanvale LY 36; 50
Donagh rock: Clonmany DL 38; 12
Donagh school: Donagh DL 38; 33

Donagh school: Donagh MN 40; 100–01
Donagh school: Galloon FH 4; 90
Donagh td: Donagh MN 40; 98
Donagh td: Galloon FH 4; 91, 93, 95
Donagh village: Galloon FH 4; 90, 102–03
Donaghadee: Ballymore AH 1; 17
Donaghadee: Bangor DN 7; 21
Donaghadee: Carrickfergus AM 37; 46
Donaghadee: Donaghadee DN 7; 45–47
Donaghadee: Loughgilly AH 1; 84
Donaghadee: Misc. DN 17; 117, 119, 124
Donaghadee: Newry DN 3; 106
Donaghadee: Saintfield DN 7; 118
Donaghadee: Templecorran AM 26; 96
Donaghadee barracks: Donaghadee DN 7; 49
Donaghadee Castle: Donaghadee DN 7; 47
Donaghadee chapel: Donaghadee DN 7; 47
Donaghadee church: Donaghadee DN 7; 47
Donaghadee church: Misc. DN 17; 117
Donaghadee harbour: Donaghadee DN 7; 46–47, 49
Donaghadee lighthouse: Donaghadee DN 7; 47
Donaghadee magazine: Donaghadee DN 7; 48
Donaghadee manor: Misc. DN 17; 124
Donaghadee Masonic hall: Donaghadee DN 7; 48
Donaghadee meeting house [I]: Donaghadee DN 7; 47
Donaghadee meeting house [II]: Donaghadee DN 7; 47
Donaghadee ph: Ballyhalbert DN 7; 6
Donaghadee ph: Bangor DN 7; 19
Donaghadee ph: Grey Abbey DN 7; 67
Donaghadee ph: Holywood DN 7; 82
Donaghadee ph: Misc. DN 17; 118, 121
Donaghadee schools: Donaghadee DN 7; 48
Donaghanie forts: Clogherny TE 20; 28
Donaghanie graveyard: Clogherny TE 20; 27
Donaghanie old church: Clogherny TE 20; 25, 27
Donaghanie td: Clogherny TE 20; 25, 28
Donaghcloney bleach green: Donaghcloney DN 12; 58, 61
Donaghcloney bridge: Donaghcloney DN 12; 58, 60
Donaghcloney fort: Donaghcloney DN 12; 59
Donaghcloney mill: Donaghcloney DN 12; 58
Donaghcloney parish school: Donaghcloney DN 12; 61
Donaghcloney ph: Dromore DN 12; 70, 73
Donaghcloney ph: Magheralin DN 12; 109
Donaghcloney ph: Magherally DN 12; 112, 114
Donaghcloney ph: Misc. DN 17; 121
Donaghcloney ph: Seagoe AH 1; 104
Donaghcloney ph: Seapatrick DN 12; 124
Donaghcloney ph: Tullylish DN 12; 140
Donaghcloney school: Donaghcloney DN 12; 58, 61
Donaghcloney td: Donaghcloney DN 12; 58–59

Donaghclony (see Donaghcloney): Seagoe AH 1; 104

Donaghedy ph: Clondermot LY 34; 1, 15, 25, 97, 104–05

Donaghedy ph: Cumber LY 28; 1, 48

Donaghedy ph: Leckpatrick TE 5; 119

Donaghenry ph: Artrea TE 20; 6, 9

Donaghenry ph: Ballyclog TE 20; 15, 18

Donaghenry ph: Clonoe TE 20; 29

Donaghenry ph: Desertcreat TE 20; 32

Donaghenry ph: Tamlaght TE 20; 73, 89, 113, 135

Donaghenry ph: Tullyniskan TE 20; 138

Donaghenry quarries: Tullyniskan TE 20; 141

Donaghey td: Donaghenry TE 20; 39

Donaghey village: Ballyclog TE 20; 16

Donaghey village: Donaghenry TE 20; 39

Donaghey, John: Artrea LY 6; 34

Donaghey, John: Bovevagh LY 25; 13, 39–40

Donaghey, Mr: Clondermot LY 34; 103

Donaghey, Roger: Artrea LY 6; 33–34

Donaghmore church: Donaghmore DL 39; 31, 34

Donaghmore church: Donaghmore DN 3; 7–8

Donaghmore corn mill: Donaghmore DL 39; 33

Donaghmore Glebe House: Donaghmore DL 39; 31

Donaghmore Glebe House: Donaghmore DN 3; 7–8

Donaghmore Glebe td: Donaghmore DL 39; 37

Donaghmore graveyard: Donaghmore DL 39; 34

Donaghmore meeting house: Newry DN 3; 77, 106, 109

Donaghmore old church: Donaghmore DL 39; 34

Donaghmore ph: Aghaderg DN 12; 1, 7–8

Donaghmore ph: Ballymore AH 1; 7

Donaghmore ph: Clonleigh DL 39; 1

Donaghmore ph: Convoy DL 39; 18

Donaghmore ph: Donegal DL 39; 42–43

Donaghmore ph: Drumgath DN 3; 19

Donaghmore ph: Drumglass TE 20; 40, 43–44

Donaghmore ph: Killeeshil TE 20; 62–64

Donaghmore ph: Misc. DL 39; 185

Donaghmore ph: Newry DN 3; 61, 77, 81, 106

Donaghmore ph: Pomeroy TE 20; 70

Donaghmore ph: Raphoe DL 39; 121, 129

Donaghmore ph: Tullyniskan TE 20; 138, 141

Donaghmore ph: Urney DL 39; 174, 179

Donaghmoyne (Donaghmoyn) td: Clogher TE 5; 37

Donaghmoyne church: Donaghmoyne MN 40; 107–08

Donaghmoyne church: Killanny MN 40; 132

Donaghmoyne church: Magheracloone MN 40; 139

Donaghmoyne church: Magheross MN 40; 147

Donaghmoyne Glebe House (see Vicarsdale): Donaghmoyne MN 40; 107

Donaghmoyne graveyard: Donaghmoyne MN 40; 107

Donaghmoyne House: Donaghmoyne MN 40; 107

Donaghmoyne old church: Donaghmoyne MN 40; 107–08

Donaghmoyne ph: Aughnamullen MN 40; 69–70

Donaghmoyne ph: Clogher TE 5; 40

Donaghmoyne ph: Inniskeen MN 40; 124, 126

Donaghmoyne ph: Killanny MN 40; 130

Donaghmoyne ph: Magheross MN 40; 143, 153

Donaghmoyne ph: Muckno MN 40; 162–63

Donaghmoyne school: Donaghmoyne MN 40; 107

Donaghmoyne td: Clogher TE 5; 46

Donaghmoyne td: Donaghmoyne MN 40; 111

Donaghoe, James: Maghera LY 18; 78

Donaghoe, Mrs (Cheltenham): Newry DN 3; 105

Donaghrisk bleach green: Desertcreat TE 20; 32

Donaghrisk quarries: Desertcreat TE 20; 33

Donaghue, family: Ballee DN 17; 16

Donaghy, Charles: Carrickfergus AM 37; 123

Donaghy, Edward: Carrickfergus AM 37; 121

Donaghy, Elidia: Tamlaght TE 20; 78

Donaghy, John: Antrim AM 29; 41

Donaghy, John: Ballyrashane AM 16; 31

Donaghy, John: Ballyrashane LY 22; 54

Donaghy, John: Larne AM 10; 126

Donaghy, Peter: Culfeightrin AM 24; 76

Donahey, Roger: Artrea LY 6; 38

Donahoe, Edward: Maghera LY 18; 81

Donahoe, Mr (Drumnagoon): Seagoe AH 1; 108

Donahoe, Mrs (Warrenpoint): Newry DN 3; 100

Donahoe, Patrick: Termoneeny LY 6; 133

Donahy, Nancy: Dunboe LY 11; 80

Donald, family: Donegore AM 29; 110

Donald, family: Glynn AM 26; 45

Donald, John: Aghanloo LY 11; 15–16

Donald, John: Magilligan LY 11; 135, 137–38, 140

Donald, Loughlin: Dunaghy AM 13; 21

Donald, man named: Carnmoney AM 2; 72

Donald, man named: Island Magee AM 10; 58

Donald, Robert: Carrickfergus AM 37; 148

Donald, Roddy: Cappagh TE 5; 19

Donald, Samuel: Cumber LY 28; 56

Donald, Thomas: Clondermot LY 34; 88, 91, 96

Donald, William: Island Magee AM 10; 90

Donald's carn: Island Magee AM 10; 14, 58–59, 71, 101

Donald's hill: Aghadowey LY 22; 1

Donald's hill: Aghanloo LY 11; 3

Donald's hill: Balteagh LY 9; 1–2, 4–5, 7, 16, 18, 20–21, 23–24, 34, 43

Donald's hill: Drumachose LY 9; 74, 91

Donald's hill: Dungiven LY 15; 11, 17, 111

Donald's hill: Errigal LY 27; 35

Donald's hill: Tamlaght Finlagan LY 25; 81

Donald's hill quarries: Balteagh LY 9; 22

Donald's Island: Carnmoney AM 2; 72

Donald's mound: Camlin AM 21; 60, 62–63

Donald's Pot chasm: Balteagh LY 9; 1, 11, 34

Donaldson, family: Carnmoney AM 2; 76

Donaldson, family: Errigal LY 27; 41

Donaldson, family: Island Magee AM 10; 43, 70

Donaldson, Henry: Carrickfergus AM 37; 126

Donaldson, Hugh: Island Magee AM 10; 94

Donaldson, James: Carrickfergus AM 37; 119

Donaldson, John: Ballynure AM 32; 60, 62

Donaldson, John: Island Magee AM 10; 90

Donaldson, Mr (Coleraine): Macosquin LY 22; 113

Donaldson, Mr: Belleek FH 14; 6

Donaldson, person named: Blaris AM 8; 60

Donaldson, Rev. David: Tartaraghan AH 1; 119

Donaldson, Samuel: Misc. DN 17; 127

Donaldson, Widow: Muckamore AM 35; 81

Donaldson, William: Bovevagh LY 25; 60

Donaldson, William: Coleraine LY 33; 72, 89, 127, 143

Donaldson, William: Kilrea LY 27; 120

Donamine (see Donaghmoyne)

Donamonagh (see Dunnamona)

Donamonay (see Dunnamona)

Donard cove: Kilcoo DN 3; 41

Donard Lodge: Kilcoo DN 3; 41, 43

Donaughy, family: Armoy AM 24; 6

Dondonnell, Lord: Killea and Taughboyne DL 39; 84

Donegal abbey: Donegal DL 39; 48–49

Donegal barrack: Donegal DL 39; 46

Donegal Bay: Donegal DL 39; 42, 44, 49, 54–55, 57

Donegal Bay: Drumhome DL 39; 62

Donegal Bay: Enniskillen FH 4; 44

Donegal Bay: Inishmacsaint FH 14; 72

Donegal Bay: Kilbarron DL 39; 78

Donegal Bay: Killymard DL 39; 94–97, 99, 103

Donegal bridewell: Donegal DL 39; 45

Donegal bridge: Donegal DL 39; 42, 44, 47, 49

Donegal Castle: Aghavea FH 4; 20

Donegal Castle: Donegal DL 39; 45, 47–49, 51

Donegal Castle: Drumhome DL 39; 58

Donegal Castle bridge: Donegal DL 39; 48

Donegal chapel: Donegal DL 39; 45

Donegal church: Donegal DL 39; 45, 49

Donegal convent: Templecarn DL 39; 160

Donegal cornstores: Donegal DL 39; 46

Donegal county: Banagher LY 30; 60, 71

Donegal county: Carrickfergus AM 37; 168

Donegal county: Clondermot LY 34; 35, 62, 67, 75, 106–07

Donegal county: Clonleigh DL 39; 14, 16

Donegal county: Coleraine LY 33; 98

Donegal county: Donegal DL 39; 53

Donegal county: Drumachose LY 9; 128

Donegal county: Drumkeeran FH 14; 62

Donegal county: Drumlumman CN 40; 12

Donegal county: Dungiven LY 15; 32–33, 35, 66–67, 104

Donegal county: Dunluce AM 16; 108

Donegal county: Enniskillen FH 4; 44

Donegal county: Errigal LY 27; 62–63

Donegal county: Faughanvale LY 36; 3, 21, 31, 44

Donegal county: Inishmacsaint FH 14; 70–71

Donegal county: Kilbride AM 29; 142, 151

Donegal county: Killowen LY 33; 164

Donegal county: Killygarvan DL 38; 48

Donegal county: Magilligan LY 11; 97, 107, 118–19

Donegal county: Misc. LY 31; 138

Donegal county: Raymoghy DL 39; 141–42, 146–47

Donegal county: Tamlaght O'Crilly LY 18; 95, 120

Donegal county: Templecarn DL 39; 163

Donegal county: Templecarn FH 14; 118

Donegal county: Termoneeny LY 6; 127, 132

Donegal county court house: Clonleigh DL 39; 1

Donegal court house: Donegal DL 39; 45, 49

Donegal dispensary: Donegal DL 39; 46

Donegal dispensary: Killymard DL 39; 97

Donegal fish market: Donegal DL 39; 46

Donegal graveyard: Donegal DL 39; 49

Donegal harbour: Donegal DL 39; 46–47, 49, 51

Donegal harbour: Killymard DL 39; 95, 99

Donegal ladies' school: Donegal DL 39; 46, 56

Donegal market house: Donegal DL 39; 45–46

Donegal mass-room: Donegal DL 39; 45

Donegal meeting house: Donegal DL 39; 45

Donegal meeting room: Donegal DL 39; 45

Donegal mountains: Balteagh LY 9; 5

Donegal mountains: Faughanvale LY 36; 4, 11

Donegal mountains: Longfield TE 5; 127

Donegal new pier: Donegal DL 39; 46

Donegal old bridge: Donegal DL 39; 45

Donegal old pier: Donegal DL 39; 46

Donegal parish school: Donegal DL 39; 49

Donegal ph: Donaghmore DL 39; 28

Donegal ph: Drumhome DL 39; 59

Donegal ph: Killymard DL 39; 94–96, 99, 106

Donegal ph: Kilteevoge DL 39; 111

Donegal port: Donegal DL 39; 47

Donegal quay: Killymard DL 39; 106

Donegal Royal School: Raphoe DL 39; 123

Donegal salmon-weir: Donegal DL 39; 51

Donegal schools: Donegal DL 39; 46, 49, 56

Donegal shambles: Donegal DL 39; 46

Donegal spa: Drumhome DL 39; 61

Donegal town: Donegal DL 39; 43–45, 47, 49–51, 53, 55

Donegal town: Drumhome DL 39; 62

Donegal town: Inishkeel DL 39; 71

Donegal town: Killymard DL 39; 94–96, 98–99, 102–03, 105–09

Donegal town: Mevagh DL 38; 62

Donegal town: Raphoe DL 39; 130
Donegal town: Raymoghy DL 39; 145
Donegal town: Templecarn DL 39; 158, 162, 170
Donegal town: Tullyaughnish DL 38; 89
Donegal townparks: Donegal DL 39; 46
Donegal wharf: Donegal DL 39; 46
Donegall Arms Hotel: Carnmoney AM 2; 69
Donegall fort: Devenish FH 14; 55
Donegall td: Devenish FH 14; 57–58
Donegall, Earl of: Blaris AM 8, 4–5, 88
Donegall, Earl of: Carrickfergus AM 37; 25
Donegall, family (see also Chichester): Island
  Magee AM 10; 86
Donegall, family: Ballylinny AM 32; 15, 17, 30
Donegall, family: Carnmoney AM 2; 82
Donegall, family: Carrickfergus AM 37; 1–2, 23–24,
  26, 160, 174, 179
Donegall, family: Coleraine LY 33; 93, 122, 149
Donegall, family: Derryaghy AM 8; 91
Donegall, family: Doagh AM 29; 65–66
Donegall, family: Duneane AM 19; 95, 105
Donegall, family: Glynn AM 26; 1, 21–22, 39, 41
Donegall, family: Inver AM 26; 49, 52, 55
Donegall, family: Killead AM 35; 9
Donegall, family: Kilroot AM 26; 61, 64, 79
Donegall, family: Mallusk AM 2; 109
Donegall, family: Nilteen AM 35; 84
Donegall, family: Raloo AM 32; 86, 93–94
Donegall, family: Rashee AM 32; 137–38
Donegall, family: Templepatrick AM 35; 106
Donegall, Lord: Artrea TE 20; 8
Donegall, Lord: Ballylinny AM 32; 16, 27
Donegall, Lord: Blaris AM 8; 69
Donegall, Lord: Blaris DN 12; 28
Donegall, Lord: Carrickfergus AM 37; 148
Donegall, Lord: Coleraine LY 33; 149
Donegall, Lord: Drumbeg AM 8; 123, 126, 130
Donegall, Lord: Island Magee AM 10; 29, 31, 75,
  77, 82, 85–86, 103
Donegall, Lord: Mintiaghs DL 38; 64
Donegall, Lord: Racavan AM 13; 86, 94
Donegall, Lord: Raloo AM 32; 96, 128
Donegall, Lord: Rasharkin AM 23; 128
Donegall, Lord: Rashee AM 32; 141
Donegall, Marquis of: Aghagallon AM 21; 2, 5
Donegall, Marquis of: Antrim AM 29; 25–26, 47
Donegall, Marquis of: Ballycor AM 32; 5
Donegall, Marquis of: Ballymartin AM 2; 5–6,
  15–16
Donegall, Marquis of: Ballyrobert AM 2; 20–21, 24
Donegall, Marquis of: Ballyscullion AM 19; 8
Donegall, Marquis of: Ballywalter AM 2; 26, 29
Donegall, Marquis of: Carnmoney AM 2; 49, 51,
  54, 56, 58, 81, 83, 93, 102

Donegall, Marquis of: Carrickfergus AM 37; 24, 41,
  62, 64, 102, 142, 153, 172
Donegall, Marquis of: Clondermot LY 34; 104
Donegall, Marquis of: Clonmany DL 38; 18
Donegall, Marquis of: Desertegney DL 38; 25, 28
Donegall, Marquis of: Doagh AM 29; 60–61, 68–69,
  71, 73, 84–86, 90–92, 94–95
Donegall, Marquis of: Donegore AM 29; 101–02,
  110–11
Donegall, Marquis of: Drummaul AM 19; 58
Donegall, Marquis of: Duneane AM 19; 113
Donegall, Marquis of: Glynn AM 26; 39
Donegall, Marquis of: Kilbride AM 29; 135,
  140–41, 152–53
Donegall, Marquis of: Lough Neagh AM 21; 94
Donegall, Marquis of: Lough Swilly DL 38; 144
Donegall, Marquis of: Mallusk AM 2; 110
Donegall, Marquis of: Moville DL 38; 75–76, 78
Donegall, Marquis of: Muckamore AM 35; 54, 65
Donegall, Marquis of: Nilteen AM 35; 91, 102
Donegall, Marquis of: Templepatrick AM 35; 116,
  118–19
Donegall's mountain (see My Lord's): Carrickfergus
  AM 37; 184
Donegore altar: Donegore AM 29; 124
Donegore beetling engine: Donegore AM 29; 129
Donegore beetling mill: Nilteen AM 35; 102
Donegore church: Doagh AM 29; 74–75
Donegore church: Donegore AM 29; 104, 108–09,
  111–12, 114, 129–30, 132–33
Donegore church: Kilbride AM 29; 142
Donegore church: Nilteen AM 35; 92, 94
Donegore corn mill: Donegore AM 29; 104, 129
Donegore corn mill: Nilteen AM 35; 86, 90, 102
Donegore coves: Donegore AM 29; 123
Donegore enclosure: Kilbride AM 29; 148
Donegore flax mill: Donegore AM 29; 129, 133
Donegore flax mill: Nilteen AM 35; 102
Donegore forts: Donegore AM 29; 120, 123
Donegore giant's grave: Kilbride AM 29; 147
Donegore graveyard: Donegore AM 29; 114
Donegore hamlet: Donegore AM 29; 102, 107–08,
  132
Donegore hill: Doagh AM 29; 80
Donegore hill: Donegore AM 29; 101, 104, 106–09,
  113–15, 119–21, 124–25, 127, 131, 134
Donegore hill: Kilbride AM 29; 150
Donegore hill: Nilteen AM 35; 101–02
Donegore hill standing stones: Donegore AM 29;
  119–20
Donegore Moat cove: Donegore AM 29; 123
Donegore Moat hill: Donegore AM 29; 101,
  103–04, 107, 114, 120, 124–25, 127–28, 131, 134
Donegore old church: Donegore AM 29; 108
Donegore old meeting house: Donegore AM 29; 129

Donegore old school: Donegore AM 29; 111
Donegore ph: Antrim AM 29; 6
Donegore ph: Carrickfergus AM 37; 100
Donegore ph: Connor AM 19; 16
Donegore ph: Doagh AM 29; 80, 96
Donegore ph: Drummaul AM 19; 58
Donegore ph: Island Magee AM 10; 60
Donegore ph: Kilbride AM 29; 135–37, 141–42,
    147–48, 150–51, 156
Donegore ph: Killead AM 35; 33
Donegore ph: Misc. AM 10; 129
Donegore ph: Nilteen AM 35; 84–88, 91–94, 96,
    101–03
Donegore ph: Shilvodan AM 19; 133
Donegore school: Nilteen AM 35; 86, 100, 102
Donegore school [I]: Donegore AM 29; 104, 134
Donegore school [II]: Donegore AM 29; 126,
    133–34
Donegore standing stones: Donegore AM 29; 127
Donegore stone circle: Donegore AM 29; 119
Donegore stream: Donegore AM 29; 107, 121
Donegore Sunday school: Nilteen AM 35; 92, 100
Donegore td: Donegore AM 29; 101, 107, 111, 114,
    120, 124, 129–30
Donegore td: Kilbride AM 29; 155
Donegore td: Nilteen AM 35; 84
Donelly, Bernard: Lissan LY 31; 109
Donelly, family: Lissan LY 31; 91
Donelly, robber: Dungiven LY 15; 30
Donelly's hill: Kilcronaghan LY 31; 64
Donelong river: Donaghedy TE 5; 90
Donelong td: Donaghedy TE 5; 92
Dongon (see Dungonnell): Killead AM 35; 42
Dongonell (see Dungonnell): Killead AM 35; 48
Donlevy, Mr (Donegal): Killymard DL 39; 100–02
Donnaldson, James: Ballynure AM 32; 60
Donnan, Archibald: Island Magee AM 10; 22, 82,
    100
Donnan, Rev.: Aghadowey LY 22; 24, 26
Donnan's pier: Island Magee AM 10; 29
Donne, Richard: Ballyscullion LY 6; 57
Donnedy, Bernard: Glenavy AM 21; 91
Donnel, family: Kilbride AM 29; 140
Donnel, John: Drumachose LY 9; 104
Donnel, John: Kildollagh LY 22; 74
Donnell, James: Island Magee AM 10; 22, 79
Donnell, James: Misc. DN 17; 116
Donnell, John: Artrea LY 6; 24
Donnell, Thomas: Carrickfergus AM 37; 40, 175
Donnell, Thomas: Clondermot LY 34; 89
Donnelly, Bridget: Artrea LY 6; 38
Donnelly, Charles: Lissan LY 31; 101
Donnelly, Daniel: Glenavy AM 21; 90
Donnelly, David: Lissan LY 31; 94, 107
Donnelly, family: Lissan LY 31; 106

Donnelly, family: Magherafelt LY 6; 95
Donnelly, Francis: Maghera LY 18; 37
Donnelly, Henry: Maghera LY 18; 81
Donnelly, Hugh: Glenavy AM 21; 91
Donnelly, Hugh: Lissan LY 31; 109
Donnelly, James: Ballynascreen LY 31; 21
Donnelly, James: Macosquin LY 22; 92
Donnelly, James: Maghera LY 18; 41
Donnelly, James [I]: Donacavey TE 5; 65
Donnelly, James [II]: Donacavey TE 5; 65
Donnelly, John: Ballintoy AM 24; 32–33
Donnelly, John: Ballynascreen LY 31; 32
Donnelly, John: Maghera LY 18; 43
Donnelly, John: Newry DN 3; 98, 103
Donnelly, John: Tamlaght TE 20; 118
Donnelly, Michael: Tamlaght TE 20; 75, 128, 136
Donnelly, Patt: Ballynascreen LY 31; 21
Donnelly, Phillip: Lissan LY 31; 95
Donnelly, Rev. James: Errigal LY 27; 46, 63
Donnelly, Rev. Thomas: Lissan LY 31; 104
Donnelly, William: Artrea LY 6; 20
Donnelly, William: Carrickfergus AM 37; 153
Donnelly, William: Dunboe LY 11; 55, 69
Donnelly's stone: Dungiven LY 15; 93
Donnen, John: Templecorran AM 26; 120–21
Donnigan, Widow: Ballymoney AM 16; 18
Donnybrewer bog: Faughanvale LY 36; 2
Donnybrewer Canal: Faughanvale LY 36; 8, 10
Donnybrewer flax mill: Faughanvale LY 36; 98
Donnybrewer Lock: Faughanvale LY 36; 10
Donnybrewer school: Faughanvale LY 36; 34
Donnybrewer td: Clondermot LY 34; 47
Donnybrewer td: Faughanvale LY 36; 13, 17, 30,
    53, 57, 60, 68, 73, 84, 93–94, 98
Donnybrewer wood: Faughanvale LY 36; 84
Donnybrook (Dublin): Newry DN 3; 67
Donoghmore (Navan): Carrickfergus AM 37; 78
Donogue td: Magheross MN 40; 148
Donohey, Bernard: Ballyscullion LY 6; 73
Donohey, Bryan: Bovevagh LY 25; 53
Donohey, family: Banagher LY 30; 74
Donohey, H.: Banagher LY 30; 63
Donohey, Hugh: Banagher LY 30; 90
Donohey, James: Banagher LY 30; 71, 73–74
Donohey, John: Artrea LY 6; 24
Donohey, John: Bovevagh LY 25; 42
Donohoe, John: Drumachose LY 9; 121
Donohoe, Michael: Cumber LY 28; 20
Donohy, John: Magherafelt LY 6; 110–11
Donovar (see Dunover): Ballywalter DN 7; 18
Doo cove: Island Magee AM 10; 101
Doo Holes waterfall: Kilwaughter AM 10; 119
Doo lough: Castleboy DN 7; 26
Doo lough: Culfeightrin AM 24; 37–38, 42
Doo lough: Kilmacteige SO 40; 193

Doo td: Culfeightrin AM 24; 42

Dooalt (see Doalt): Cumber LY 28; 71

Dooballagh bog: Leck DL 39; 115

Dooballagh bog: Raymoghy DL 39; 133

Dooballagh hills: Leck DL 39; 115

Dooballagh td: Leck DL 39; 118

Doocarrick fort: Clondavaddog DL 38; 6

Doocassan church: Drung CN 40; 21

Doocassan td: Drung CN 40; 20

Dooederny td: Aghalurcher FH 4; 14

Dooey chalk quarry: Billy AM 16; 37

Dooey creek: Lough Swilly DL 38; 118

Dooey td: Billy AM 16; 36–37

Doogal, family: Culfeightrin AM 24; 59

Doogan, James: Killowen LY 33; 170

Doogan, John: Clonleigh DL 39; 9

Doogan, Mr: Ballynascreen LY 31; 31

Doogan, William: Ballynascreen LY 31; 31–32

Doogary corn mill: Tynan AH 1; 128

Dooghan school: Donaghmore DL 39; 41

Dooghan td: Donaghmore DL 39; 37

Dooh lough: Aghalurcher FH 4; 3

Doohallat school: Drumgoon CN 40; 11

Doohallat td: Drumgoon CN 40; 2

Doohard (see Dooharn): Aghalurcher FH 4; 5

Dooharn rock: Aghalurcher FH 4; 1–2, 5

Dooharn rock: Aghavea FH 4; 17, 19

Dooharn td: Aghalurcher FH 4; 5

Doohat Castle: Galloon FH 4; 105

Doohat td: Galloon FH 4; 95, 105

Doohatil (see Doohallat): Drumgoon CN 40; 2

Doohatt school: Aghabog MN 40; 65

Doohatta (see Doohatty)

Doohatty Glebe td: Killesher FH 14; 86–87

Doohatty td: Magheross MN 40; 143, 156

Doohragh lough: Dromore TE 5; 95

Doohrah (see Dooragh)

Dooish chapel: Longfield TE 5; 129

Dooish hill: Dromore TE 5; 100

Dooish hill: Longfield TE 5; 127, 133

Dooish hill: Misc. DL 39; 186–87

Dooish hill: Raymoghy DL 39; 135, 140, 142

Dooish hill: Tullyaughnish DL 38; 87

Dooish school: Raymoghy DL 39; 140

Dooish td: Longfield TE 5; 129

Dooish td: Raymoghy DL 39; 136, 141

Dooish Upper td: Raymoghy DL 39; 132

Dool, Samuel: Tamlaght TE 20; 83

Dool, William: Tamlaght O'Crilly LY 18; 142

Doole, Archibald: Templepatrick AM 35; 135, 153

Doolertown td: Donaghedy TE 5; 92

Dooley, Samuel: Carrickfergus AM 37; 109

Doon bay: Lough Swilly DL 38; 148

Doon bridge: Ballynascreen LY 31; 7

Doon bridge: Misc. LY 31; 116

Doon fort: Lough Swilly DL 38; 148

Doon Gorberry fort: Kilraghts AM 16; 133

Doon hill: Banagher LY 30; 108, 110

Doon lough: Drumkeeran FH 14; 63

Doon Lower bay: Lough Swilly DL 38; 147

Doon mill: Enniskillen FH 4; 69

Doon Point: Rathlin Island AM 24; 130–31

Doon rock: Killymard DL 39; 94, 97

Doon rock: Kilmacrenan DL 38; 50, 52

Doon td: Ballynascreen LY 31; 7, 14, 29–31

Doon td: Enniskillen FH 4; 48, 74, 82

Doon td: Misc. LY 31; 143

Doon tower: Lough Swilly DL 38; 148

Doon Upper bay: Lough Swilly DL 38; 147–48

Doon well: Kilmacrenan DL 38; 52

Doon well: Tullyaughnish DL 38; 93

Doon wells: Clondavaddog DL 38; 7

Doon wood: Ballynascreen LY 31; 15

Doon, Robert: Billy AM 16; 53

Doonagh, Matthew: Kilmacteige SO 40; 196

Doonaldragh Island: Lough Swilly DL 38; 108

Doonaldragh Point: Lough Swilly DL 38; 108

Doonan (Doonans) td: Armoy AM 24; 4

Doonan corn mill: Armoy AM 24; 4

Doonan East waterfall: Killymard DL 39; 95

Doonan hamlet: Killymard DL 39; 107

Doonan rock (see Doon): Killymard DL 39; 97

Doonan school: Armoy AM 24; 6

Doonan td: Killymard DL 39; 100

Doonan, woman named: Cumber LY 28; 30, 32

Doonans district: Lough Swilly DL 38; 129

Doonans fishery: Lough Swilly DL 38; 118

Doonans harbour: Lough Swilly DL 38; 119–20

Doonasarn fort: Donegal DL 39; 51

Doonavernon fort: Loughguile AM 13; 69–70

Doonbought flax mill: Dunaghy AM 13; 13

Doonbought fort: Dunaghy AM 13; 17–18, 23, 28

Doonbought Point: Dunaghy AM 13; 10

Doonbought standing stone: Dunaghy AM 13; 23

Doonbought td: Dunaghy AM 13; 13, 23

Doonbwee Head: Lough Swilly DL 38; 121–22

Doone, Margaret: Aghagallon AM 21; 19

Dooneen td: Enniskillen FH 4; 82

Dooneven Castle: Dungiven LY 15; 33

Dooneven district: Dungiven LY 15; 33

Doonfin (Duinfinn) td: Ramoan AM 24; 114

Doonfin bog: Ramoan AM 24; 90

Doonfin fort: Ramoan AM 24; 114–15

Doonfin standing stone: Ramoan AM 24; 116

Doonfinn (see Doonfin): Ramoan AM 24; 90

Doongaup locality: Lough Swilly DL 38; 121–22

Doongillen td: Cumber LY 28; 62

Doonmore locality: Lough Swilly DL 38; 134

Doons td: Kinawley FH 4; 121

Doontinny Point: Lough Swilly DL 38; 100

Doonyougherty Point: Lough Swilly DL 38; 131

Doorable td: Raphoe DL 39; 126

Dooragh hill: Drumkeeran FH 14; 64

Dooragh td: Aughnamullen MN 40; 76

Doorah (see Dooragh)

Dooran Point: Killymard DL 39; 109

Dooran rock: Donegal DL 39; 46, 51

Doorat mountain: Donaghedy TE 5; 89

Doorat td: Donaghedy TE 5; 92

Dooris, James: Errigal LY 27; 66

Dooris, Mary: Errigal LY 27; 66

Doorish Balliboe td: Misc. DL 39; 198

Doorish Bogtown td: Misc. DL 39; 198

Doorish Castle td: Misc. DL 39; 198

Doorish Gentle td: Misc. DL 39; 198

Doorish Larggy td: Misc. DL 39; 198

Doorish td: Misc. DL 39; 197

Doorish, James: Carrickfergus AM 37; 120

Dooross td: Aghalurcher FH 4; 4, 14

Doran, Bernard: Misc. DN 17; 119

Doran, Daniel: Newry DN 3; 103

Doran, family: Desertoghill LY 27; 5

Doran, family: Misc. LY 36; 104

Doran, John: Ballyphilip DN 7; 8

Doran, Peter: Culfeightrin AM 24; 52

Doran, Rev: Newry DN 3; 104

Doran, Rev.: Killead AM 35; 44

Doran's Rock school: Saintfield DN 7; 116

Doran's Rock td: Saintfield DN 7; 116

Dorane, Cornelius: Misc. DN 17; 119

Dorans, Alexander: Ballymoney AM 16; 17

Doras (see Dooross): Aghalurcher FH 4; 4

Doras church: Tullyniskan TE 20; 138

Doraville House: Derryvullan FH 14; 32–33

Dorchraan Island: Kinawley FH 4; 113

Doris, family: Lissan LY 31; 91, 106

Dorisland locality: Carrickfergus AM 37; 94

Dorman, family: Ballynure AM 32; 56

Dorn, Rev. John: Kilbroney DN 3; 33, 38

Dornagaugh td: Cleenish FH 14; 29

Dornahan, family: Magherafelt LY 6; 95

Dornan, family: Culfeightrin AM 24; 59

Dornan, James: Blaris DN 12; 46

Dornan, James: Carrickfergus AM 37; 130

Dornan, John: Derryaghy AM 8; 98

Dornan, John: Skerry AM 13; 120

Dornan, Thomas: Dunluce AM 16; 118

Dorning, William: Tamlaght TE 20; 91

Dornon, James: Blaris DN 12; 50

Dorothy, Mrs (Drumcree): Drumcree AH 1; 29

Dorran, family: Desertoghill LY 27; 30

Dorrety, William: Maghera LY 18; 28

Dorrian, Patrick: Down DN 17; 58

Dorrins, James: Blaris AM 8; 35

Dorrins, John: Macosquin LY 22; 84, 118

Dorsay, Hugh: Ballyclug AM 23; 59

Dorsy corn mill: Creggan AH 1; 27

Dougall, family: Carnmoney AM 2; 76

Dougall, family: Maghera LY 18; 24, 48

Dougall, John: Carrickfergus AM 37; 127

Dougan, George: Blaris DN 12; 50

Dough's hill: Killea and Taughboyne DL 39; 79–80, 84

Doughan fort: Drumachose LY 9; 127–28

Dougherdey's inn: Muff DL 38; 80

Dougherty, family: Ballynascreen LY 31; 9

Dougherty, family: Culfeightrin AM 24; 59

Dougherty, family: Errigal LY 27; 41

Dougherty, Mr (Carn): Donagh DL 38; 33

Dougherty, Mr: Clogher TE 5; 43

Dougherty, Mr: Lough Swilly DL 38; 136

Dougherty, Patrick: Magheradrool DN 17; 105

Dougherty, Rev.: Donaghmore DL 39; 35

Dougherty, Robert: Tamlaght TE 20; 96, 102

Dougherty, William: Cumber LY 28; 74

Dougherty's rocks: Lough Swilly DL 38; 111

Doughglass (see Dughglass): Lough Swilly DL 38; 111

Doughill, Patt: Kilmacteige SO 40; 195

Doughro lough: Killymard DL 39; 105

Doughro mountain: Killymard DL 39; 102

Doughro td: Killymard DL 39; 101

Doughrock td: Dromore TE 5; 98

Douglas bridge: Ardstraw TE 5; 14

Douglas burn: Ardstraw TE 5; 10

Douglas hill: Glenwhirry AM 32; 75, 79

Douglas meeting house: Ardstraw TE 5; 11

Douglas mountain: Ardstraw TE 5; 10

Douglas school: Ardstraw TE 5; 13

Douglas water: Ballynascreen LY 31; 1, 6–7, 19

Douglas Water bridge: Ballynascreen LY 31; 6

Douglas, Charles: Coleraine LY 33; 127

Douglas, family: Billy AM 16; 38

Douglas, James: Banagher LY 30; 4, 15, 23

Douglas, James: Bovevagh LY 25; 3–4, 20, 29, 57

Douglas, John: Balteagh LY 9; 2, 25, 28–30

Douglas, Margret: Tamlaght O'Crilly LY 18; 138

Douglas, Miss: Blaris AM 8; 85

Douglas, Mrs: Blaris AM 8; 84

Douglas, Rev. Charles: Faughanvale LY 36; 40

Douglas, Thomas: Errigal LY 27; 92

Douglas, William: Tamlaght O'Crilly LY 18; 138

Douglass, Alexander: Dunluce AM 16; 113, 119

Douglass, Alice (nee Devlin): Aghanloo LY 11; 14

Douglass, Andrew: Coleraine LY 33; 146

Douglass, Charles: Annaclone DN 12; 16

Douglass, Charles: Billy AM 16; 58, 76

Douglass, Charles: Carrickfergus AM 37; 110

Douglass, Charles: Derrykeighan AM 16; 83

Douglass, David: Loughgilly AH 1; 86

Douglass, family: Ballymartin AM 2; 6, 15
Douglass, family: Billy AM 16; 58, 68
Douglass, family: Derrykeighan AM 16; 89
Douglass, family: Kilbride AM 29; 140
Douglass, family: Nilteen AM 35; 91
Douglass, George: Aghanloo LY 11; 25
Douglass, George: Drumachose LY 9; 133
Douglass, Jacob: Blaris DN 12; 42
Douglass, Jacob: Magheramesk AM 21; 125
Douglass, James: Ballywillin AM 16; 32
Douglass, James: Dungiven LY 15; 85
Douglass, John: Ballymartin AM 2; 15–16
Douglass, John: Ballywillin AM 16; 32–33, 35
Douglass, John: Carncastle and Killyglen AM 10; 8
Douglass, John: Dunluce AM 16; 121–22
Douglass, Margret: Drumachose LY 9; 133
Douglass, Miss: Dunluce AM 16; 110
Douglass, Mr: Loughguile AM 13; 75–76
Douglass, Mrs: Derryaghy AM 8; 100
Douglass, Murray: Derryaghy AM 8; 100, 106, 110
Douglass, Rev.: Derrykeighan AM 16; 79
Douglass, Samuel: Blaris AM 8; 50
Douglass, T.: Dromore DN 12; 71–72
Douglass, Thomas: Drumachose LY 9; 126
Douglass, William: Billy AM 16; 51
Douglass, William: Bovevagh LY 25; 27–28, 55
Douglass, William: Loughgilly AH 1; 86
Douglassland coves: Kilbride AM 29; 149
Douglassland td: Kilbride AM 29; 136, 140, 148
Dougles well: Macosquin LY 22; 99
Douglis, James: Bovevagh LY 25; 60
Doul, Mrs: Clondermot LY 34; 81
Doune (see Doon): Kilmacrenan DL 38; 50
Dover, Mr: Derryvullan FH 14; 44
Dowagh (see also Danes' Cast): Misc. DN 17; 128, 130
Dowd, Denis: Dunaghy AM 13; 23
Dowd, family: Drummaul AM 19; 53
Dowd, Patrick: Dundermot AM 13; 35
Dowdal, Patrick: Newry DN 3; 104
Dowdall, Ferdinand: Blaris AM 8; 79
Dowdall, John: Blaris AM 8; 80
Dowdall, John: Blaris DN 12; 40–41
Dowdall, Rev. John: Dromore DN 12; 77
Dowdall, Rev. Launcelot: Artrea LY 6; 5, 8, 22
Dowdle, Robert: Newry DN 3; 103
Dowell, family: Lambeg AM 8; 135
Dowell, Mrs (nee Hogset): Kilroot AM 26; 79
Dowey td: Misc. DN 17; 125, 127
Dowey, Hugh: Ballyclug AM 23; 66
Doweybeg td: Coleraine LY 33; 61–62
Dowlaghmore lough: Drumhome DL 39; 61
Dowlan, family: Culfeightrin AM 24; 59
Dowlan, Rev. William: Seagoe AH 1; 102
Dowland bridge: Aghanloo LY 11; 23

Dowland hill: Magilligan LY 11; 127
Dowland spa: Aghanloo LY 11; 7
Dowland td: Aghanloo LY 11; 24, 31, 40–41
Dowling, Daniel: Antrim AM 29; 59
Dowling, John: Newry DN 3; 100
Down and Connor diocese: Aghalee AM 21; 31
Down and Connor diocese: Antrim AM 29; 26
Down and Connor diocese: Ballinderry AM 21; 44
Down and Connor diocese: Ballyclug AM 23; 52
Down and Connor diocese: Ballymoney AM 16; 1
Down and Connor diocese: Ballyphilip DN 7; 12
Down and Connor diocese: Ballyrobert AM 2; 24
Down and Connor diocese: Bangor DN 7; 19
Down and Connor diocese: Blaris AM 8; 3, 5, 52
Down and Connor diocese: Blaris DN 12; 26–27
Down and Connor diocese: Carnmoney AM 2; 64, 93
Down and Connor diocese: Carrickfergus AM 37; 32, 69, 71, 79
Down and Connor diocese: Comber DN 7; 32
Down and Connor diocese: Connor AM 19; 16, 18
Down and Connor diocese: Donaghadee DN 7; 46
Down and Connor diocese: Holywood DN 7; 74
Down and Connor diocese: Island Magee AM 10; 34, 75
Down and Connor diocese: Killead AM 35; 20
Down and Connor diocese: Knockbreda DN 7; 97
Down and Connor diocese: Loughguile AM 13; 58
Down and Connor diocese: Magheragall AM 21; 108
Down and Connor diocese: Mallusk AM 2; 115
Down and Connor diocese: Racavan AM 13; 86
Down and Connor diocese: Ramoan AM 24; 86, 102
Down and Connor diocese: Skerry AM 13; 105
Down and Connor diocese: Templepatrick AM 35; 142
Down and Connor diocese: Tickmacrevan AM 13; 127
Down and Connor, Bishop of: Ahoghill AM 23; 15
Down and Connor, Bishop of: Blaris AM 8; 26, 52
Down and Connor, Bishop of: Derryaghy AM 8; 106
Down and Connor, Bishop of: Holywood DN 7; 82
Down and Connor, Bishop of: Island Magee AM 10; 77
Down and Connor, Bishop of: Killead AM 35; 12, 44
Down and Connor, Bishop of: Misc. DN 17; 133
Down county: Blaris AM 8; 3, 47, 72–73, 75
Down county: Carrickfergus AM 37; 55, 168
Down county: Dungiven LY 15; 66–67
Down county: Enniskillen FH 4; 80
Down county: Faughanvale LY 36; 44–45
Down county: Galloon FH 4; 100
Down county: Island Magee AM 10; 29, 82–83

Down county: Montiaghs AH 1; 91–92

Down county: Urney DL 39; 177

Down diocese: Ballyphilip DN 7; 8

Down manor: Newry DN 3; 65

Down old cathedral: Inch DN 17; 75

Down ph: Ballee DN 17; 15

Down ph: Misc. DN 17; 120, 122, 128

Down, Archdeacon of: Hillsborough DN 12; 91, 97, 102–03, 105

Down, Bishop of: Ahoghill AM 23; 3

Down, Bishop of: Banagher LY 30; 22

Down, Bishop of: Dunsfort DN 17; 69–70

Down, Bishop of: Kilclief DN 17; 78–79

Down, Chancellor of: Ardglass DN 17; 5, 7

Down, Chancellor of: Misc. DN 17; 133

Down, Dean of: Ballee DN 17; 17, 20

Down, Dean of: Down DN 17; 43–45

Downerreruin district: Misc. SO 40; 198

Downes (see Dowris): Kilmacteige SO 40; 188

Downes, George: Banagher LY 30; 29, 37, 57, 112

Downes, George: Clondermot LY 34; 17, 26, 32, 103, 105

Downes, George: Cumber LY 28; 81

Downes, George: Desertoghill LY 27; 25

Downes, George: Faughanvale LY 36; 23, 40

Downes, George: Kilmacrenan DL 38; 50

Downes, George: Tamlaght Finlagan LY 25; 91, 98, 125

Downes, John: Saintfield DN 7; 114

Downes, Lt: Cumber LY 28; 25

Downes, Rev. (Co. Down): Aghadowey LY 22; 26

Downes, Robert: Faughanvale LY 36; 56

Downes, Robert: Misc. DN 17; 117

Downey, A.: Newry DN 3; 98, 103

Downey, Alexander: Maghera LY 18; 43, 58

Downey, Bernard: Ballynascreen LY 31; 25

Downey, Charles: Carrickfergus AM 37; 132

Downey, Edward [I]: Maghera LY 18; 80

Downey, Edward [II]: Maghera LY 18; 81

Downey, Elizabeth: Garvaghy DN 12; 83

Downey, family: Ballyscullion LY 6; 53

Downey, family: Kilroot AM 26; 75

Downey, Francis: Ballynascreen LY 31; 25

Downey, Fullerton: Ballintoy AM 24; 19

Downey, John [I]: Maghera LY 18; 60

Downey, John [II]: Maghera LY 18; 80

Downey, Michael: Newry DN 3; 98, 103

Downey, Mrs: Newry DN 3; 98, 103

Downey, Nesbit: Banagher LY 30; 119

Downey, Robert: Kilroot AM 26; 67, 79

Downey, Samuel: Kilroot AM 26; 67, 79

Downey, Thomas: Ballyscullion LY 6; 56–57

Downey, women named: Maghera LY 18; 59

Downham [or Townham], William: Magilligan LY 11; 93

Downham, James: Clondermot LY 34; 63

Downhill demesne: Magilligan LY 11; 117, 141

Downhill female school: Dunboe LY 11; 55, 69

Downhill fort: Dunboe LY 11; 49

Downhill glen spring: Dunboe LY 11; 79

Downhill House: Aghanloo LY 11; 1

Downhill House: Ballyaghran LY 33; 3

Downhill House: Banagher LY 30; 3

Downhill House: Drumragh TE 5; 109

Downhill House: Dunboe LY 11; 43–47, 49, 51–52, 54, 58, 60, 62, 74, 79

Downhill House: Killowen LY 33; 161, 169

Downhill House: Magilligan LY 11; 129, 135

Downhill House: Misc. LY 31; 114

Downhill House: Misc. LY 36; 110

Downhill mausoleum: Dunboe LY 11; 51

Downhill monument: Dunboe LY 11; 61

Downhill old church: Dunboe LY 11; 61, 73

Downhill palace: Aghanloo LY 11; 8

Downhill school: Dunboe LY 11; 55, 69

Downhill Sunday school: Dunboe LY 11; 57, 72

Downhill td: Dunboe LY 11; 58, 73

Downhill td: Magilligan LY 11; 124

Downhill temple: Dunboe LY 11; 51, 53, 60–61

Downing, Adam: Ballyscullion LY 6; 46

Downing, Bernard: Ballyscullion LY 6; 65

Downing, family: Ballyscullion LY 6; 46

Downing, family: Desertlyn LY 31; 42

Downing, family: Maghera LY 18; 13

Downing, Hartfoot: Maghera LY 18; 61

Downing, J.N.: Ballyscullion AM 19; 10

Downing, J.N. [I]: Maghera LY 18; 16, 49

Downing, J.N. [II]: Maghera LY 18; 53–54

Downing, James: Ballyscullion LY 6; 66

Downing, John: Ballyscullion LY 6; 46

Downing, John: Termoneeny LY 6; 129, 131

Downing, John [I]: Maghera LY 18; 66, 73

Downing, John [II]: Maghera LY 18; 51–52, 64, 74

Downing, John [III]: Maghera LY 18; 54, 73–75

Downing, Patrick: Killead AM 35; 37, 53

Downing, Samuel: Termoneeny LY 6; 130

Downing, Walter: Ballyscullion LY 6; 57

Downing, William: Tamlaght TE 20; 75, 79, 103

Downing's bar: Mevagh DL 38; 55

Downings Bar td: Mevagh DL 38; 63

Downings coastguard station: Mevagh DL 38; 59

Downings fort: Mevagh DL 38; 58

Downings td: Mevagh DL 38; 63

Downings village: Mevagh DL 38; 56, 61

Downkillybegs forts: Drummaul AM 19; 78, 88

Downland hill: Magilligan LY 11; 92

Downpatrick: Ardglass DN 17; 1, 4–6, 9, 12

Downpatrick: Ballee DN 17; 15–18, 21–23

Downpatrick: Ballyculter DN 17; 27–28

Downpatrick: Ballyphilip DN 7; 12

Downpatrick: Bright DN 17; 33, 35–36
Downpatrick: Clondermot LY 34; 51–52
Downpatrick: Clonduff DN 3; 3
Downpatrick: Comber DN 7; 29
Downpatrick: Derryaghy AM 8; 114
Downpatrick: Down DN 17; 38–39, 41–42, 46–47, 49, 51, 58–59, 61, 66
Downpatrick: Drumbo DN 7; 60
Downpatrick: Drumgath DN 3; 21
Downpatrick: Dunsfort DN 17, 67–69
Downpatrick: Inch DN 17; 73–74
Downpatrick: Kilkeel DN 3; 49
Downpatrick: Killinchy DN 7; 89
Downpatrick: Killyleagh DN 17; 81, 85–86
Downpatrick: Kilmegan DN 3; 59–60
Downpatrick: Kilmore DN 17; 88–92
Downpatrick: Loughinisland DN 17; 94
Downpatrick: Magheradrool DN 17; 103, 105, 107
Downpatrick: Misc. DN 17; 116, 118–19, 122, 128
Downpatrick: Newry DN 3; 78
Downpatrick: Saul DN 17; 112–13
Downpatrick: Templecorran AM 26; 85
Downpatrick abbey: Misc. DN 17; 118
Downpatrick abbey: Muckamore AM 35; 82
Downpatrick almshouses: Down DN 17; 65
Downpatrick barracks: Down DN 17; 45
Downpatrick Blue School: Down DN 17; 59
Downpatrick Cathedral: Ballee DN 17; 17, 20
Downpatrick Cathedral: Blaris DN 12; 27
Downpatrick Cathedral: Down DN 17; 40–45, 48, 51, 59–61, 117–19, 133
Downpatrick Cathedral: Killyleagh DN 17; 85
Downpatrick Cathedral: Saul DN 17; 113
Downpatrick Cathedral graveyard: Killyleagh DN 17; 85
Downpatrick chapel (C): Down DN 17; 41, 58–60
Downpatrick chapel (M): Down DN 17; 58, 60
Downpatrick chapel (PWM): Down DN 17; 40, 60
Downpatrick chapel (WM): Down DN 17; 60
Downpatrick chapel school: Down DN 17; 58
Downpatrick church: Blaris AM 8; 52
Downpatrick church: Down DN 17; 41, 59
Downpatrick church: Killyleagh DN 17; 85
Downpatrick church graveyard: Killyleagh DN 17; 85
Downpatrick classical school [I]: Down DN 17; 58
Downpatrick classical school [II]: Down DN 17; 58
Downpatrick classical school [III]: Down DN 17; 59
Downpatrick classical school [IV]: Down DN 17; 59
Downpatrick clock tower: Down DN 17; 41–42
Downpatrick county rooms: Down DN 17; 40
Downpatrick court house: Down DN 17; 40, 60
Downpatrick dispensary: Down DN 17; 46, 65, 132
Downpatrick fort: Down DN 17; 52
Downpatrick fort: Magilligan LY 11; 128

Downpatrick gaol: Ardkeen DN 7; 1
Downpatrick gaol: Down DN 17; 40, 47, 53, 60–64
Downpatrick gaol: Killyleagh DN 17; 83
Downpatrick gaol: Newry DN 3; 84
Downpatrick hospital: Ballee DN 17; 16
Downpatrick hospital: Down DN 17; 46, 60, 65, 132
Downpatrick hospital: Dunsfort DN 17; 68
Downpatrick hotel: Down DN 17; 41
Downpatrick infant school: Down DN 17; 58
Downpatrick infirmary: Down DN 17; 40, 45–46, 51, 60, 65, 132
Downpatrick infirmary: Dunsfort DN 17; 68
Downpatrick Irish St school: Down DN 17; 58
Downpatrick Kildare school: Down DN 17; 58
Downpatrick ladies' school [I]: Down DN 17; 59
Downpatrick ladies' school [II]: Down DN 17; 59
Downpatrick ladies' school [III]: Down DN 17; 59
Downpatrick library: Down DN 17; 46–47
Downpatrick linen factory: Killyleagh DN 17; 85
Downpatrick market house: Down DN 17; 40, 60
Downpatrick meeting house (P): Down DN 17; 41, 47, 58, 60
Downpatrick meeting house (R): Down DN 17; 41, 60
Downpatrick meeting house graveyard [I]: Killyleagh DN 17; 86
Downpatrick meeting house graveyard [II]: Killyleagh DN 17; 86
Downpatrick news room: Down DN 17; 47
Downpatrick old church: Culfeightrin AM 24; 70
Downpatrick old graveyard: Down DN 17; 59
Downpatrick old linen hall: Down DN 17; 40
Downpatrick police barrack: Down DN 17; 45
Downpatrick Presbyterian school: Down DN 17; 58
Downpatrick round tower: Down DN 17; 43, 61
Downpatrick Saul St school: Down DN 17; 59
Downpatrick Scotch St school: Down DN 17; 59
Downpatrick widows' houses: Down DN 17; 47–48
Downs glen: Leckpatrick TE 5; 121
Downs, James: Enniskillen FH 4; 55
Downs, Margaret: Kilbride AM 29; 152
Downshire Arms Hotel: Newry DN 3; 70
Downshire estate: Derryaghy AM 8; 114
Downshire, Arthur: Donaghadee DN 7; 46
Downshire, family: Hillsborough DN 12; 89
Downshire, Lady: Blaris DN 12; 34, 36
Downshire, Lady: Hillsborough DN 12; 99–100
Downshire, Lord: Aghaderg DN 12; 6, 9
Downshire, Lord: Annaclone DN 12; 15–18
Downshire, Lord: Annahilt DN 12; 21–23, 25
Downshire, Lord: Blaris AM 8; 66
Downshire, Lord: Blaris DN 12; 26, 32, 34, 36–37
Downshire, Lord: Comber DN 7; 40
Downshire, Lord: Donaghcloney DN 12; 58–59
Downshire, Lord: Dromara DN 12; 64–65, 69

Downshire, Lord: Drumbo DN 7; 58–59

Downshire, Lord: Hillsborough DN 12; 85–88, 90–91, 93–95, 97, 99–100, 102–05

Downshire, Lord: Magherally DN 12; 114

Downshire, Lord: Moira DN 12; 118–19, 121

Downshire, Lord: Seapatrick DN 12; 125–26, 128, 130–31, 135

Downshire, Lord: Tullylish DN 12; 140, 144

Downshire, Lord: Tullynakill DN 7; 122–23

Downshire, Marquis of: Carrickfergus AM 37; 2, 26, 41, 62, 64, 137, 140, 142, 145, 172, 174

Downshire, Marquis of: Clonallan DN 3; 2

Downshire, Marquis of: Clonduff DN 3; 4–5

Downshire, Marquis of: Comber DN 7; 37

Downshire, Marquis of: Down DN 17; 42, 52–53, 57

Downshire, Marquis of: Drumballyroney DN 3; 13, 18

Downshire, Marquis of: Drumgath DN 3; 21

Downshire, Marquis of: Kilcoo DN 3; 45

Downshire, Marquis of: Kilmegan DN 3; 57, 59–60

Downshire, Marquis of: Knockbreda DN 7; 102

Downshire, Marquis of: Misc. DN 17; 118

Downshire, Marquis of: Newry DN 3; 65, 71, 75, 100, 105

Downshire, Marquis of: Saintfield DN 7; 118

Downshireland locality: Carrickfergus AM 37; 94, 174

Downy, family: Kilroot AM 26; 74

Downy, family: Misc. LY 36; 104

Dowris td: Kilmacteige SO 40; 188, 192, 196

Doyle, Alexander: Ballynascreen LY 31; 25

Doyle, family: Aghagallon AM 21; 9

Doyle, family: Carrickfergus AM 37; 93

Doyle, John (Jnr): Lissan LY 31; 109

Doyle, John (Snr): Lissan LY 31; 109

Doyle, Margaret: Lissan LY 31; 109

Doyle, Martin: Ballynure AM 32; 49

Doyle, Mary: Lissan LY 31; 109

Doyle, Patrick: Newry DN 3; 99, 103

Doyle, Philip: Lissan LY 31; 109

Doyle, Rev. (Bishop of Raphoe): Clondavaddog DL 38; 1

Doyle, Rev.: Kilcronaghan LY 31; 81

Doyle, Rev. Michael: Lissan LY 31; 100

Doyle, Rev. Patrick: Lissan LY 31; 104

Doyle, William: Newry DN 3; 99, 104

Doyle's Hole locality: Newry DN 3; 88

Drain td: Raymoghy DL 39; 136–37, 186, 198

Drain, Catherine: Ballymoney AM 16; 17

Drake, Francis: Blaris AM 8; 8, 77

Drake, Hugh: Hillsborough DN 12; 106

Drake, John: Hillsborough DN 12; 106

Drake, William: Blaris AM 8; 77

Dramaween (see Drumaweer): Moville DL 38; 70

Dramnamalragh td: Cleenish FH 14; 28

Drane, Mary: Derryaghy AM 8; 114

Drane, Richard: Derryaghy AM 8; 98, 114

Draper, John: Ballyscullion LY 6; 57

Drapers' Lodge House: Ballynascreen LY 31; 6

Drapers' manor: Kilcronaghan LY 31; 68

Draperstown: Ballynascreen LY 31; 1–3, 6–8, 13, 16–17, 19, 21, 32

Draperstown: Banagher LY 30; 31, 118

Draperstown: Faughanvale LY 36; 49

Draperstown: Kilcronaghan LY 31; 65–67, 71, 79, 82

Draperstown: Tamlaght TE 20; 73

Draperstown building ground: Ballynascreen LY 31; 5, 32

Draperstown court room: Ballynascreen LY 31; 3

Draperstown Cross: Ballynascreen LY 31; 3, 16–19, 23, 32

Draperstown Cross: Banagher LY 30; 100

Draperstown Cross: Kilcronaghan LY 31; 74, 78, 87

Draperstown Cross: Lissan LY 31; 99

Draperstown Cross: Misc. LY 31; 144

Draperstown dispensary: Ballynascreen LY 31; 3–4, 13, 18, 121

Draperstown district: Enniskeen CN 40; 30

Draperstown estate: Misc. LY 31; 122

Draperstown fairground: Ballynascreen LY 31; 3

Draperstown graveyard: Ballynascreen LY 31; 5

Draperstown inn: Ballynascreen LY 31; 3, 5

Draperstown market house: Ballynascreen LY 31; 3–4

Draperstown meeting house: Ballynascreen LY 31; 5

Draperstown meeting room: Ballynascreen LY 31; 5

Draperstown new market house: Ballynascreen LY 31; 5, 19

Draperstown police house: Ballynascreen LY 31; 3

Draperstown revenue police house: Ballynascreen LY 31; 3

Draperstown road bridge: Kilcronaghan LY 31; 67

Draperstown school: Ballynascreen LY 31; 16–17

Draperstown well: Ballynascreen LY 31; 1

Draughton (Drafton) td: Donacavey TE 5; 65–67, 76–78, 80–83, 85

Draughton bridge: Donacavey TE 5; 64

Draughton fort: Donacavey TE 5; 83

Draughton school: Donacavey TE 5; 65–66, 83

Drayton Manor (Staffordshire): Ballyscullion LY 6; 60

Drean td: Donaghedy TE 5; 92

Dreanare td: Raymoghy DL 39; 141

Dree school: Dromara DN 12; 64

Dree td: Dromara DN 12; 64–66

Dreen cave: Ahoghill AM 23; 27, 35, 35

Dreen evening school: Ahoghill AM 23; 43

Dreen flax mill: Rasharkin AM 23; 131

Dreen fort: Ahoghill AM 23; 27, 35
Dreen fort: Rasharkin AM 23; 140
Dreen new school: Ahoghill AM 23; 49
Dreen school: Ahoghill AM 23; 42, 46, 49
Dreen Sunday school: Ahoghill AM 23; 46
Dreen td: Ahoghill AM 23; 39
Dreen td: Banagher LY 30; 22–23, 35, 50, 60–62, 72, 79, 91, 103, 107–09, 118, 122–23, 127, 129, 131–32
Dreen td: Bovevagh LY 25; 9
Dreenan bleach greens: Donaghmore DL 39; 32–33
Dreenan bog: Maghera LY 18; 58
Dreenan bridge: Maghera LY 18; 9, 63–64
Dreenan fort [I]: Maghera LY 18; 61
Dreenan fort [II]: Maghera LY 18; 61
Dreenan moss: Maghera LY 18; 48
Dreenan school: Donaghmore DL 39; 40
Dreenan school: Maghera LY 18; 30, 35
Dreenan stream: Maghera LY 18; 61
Dreenan td: Donaghmore DL 39; 37
Dreenan td: Maghera LY 18; 12–13, 16, 22, 44, 48–49, 58–59, 65–66, 73–74, 81
Dreenan wood: Maghera LY 18; 56
Dreenan, Joseph: Killead AM 35; 51
Drenan td: Ballyscullion LY 6; 56
Drene, Hugh: Carrickfergus AM 37; 131
Drennagh (see Fruithill): Drumachose LY 9; 118
Drennan meeting house: Drumbo DN 7; 57–58
Drennan td: Drumbo DN 7; 57, 60–61
Drennan, James: Carrickfergus AM 37; 124
Drenning, family: Carrickfergus AM 37; 93
Dresden House: Clonmany DL 38; 13–14, 19
Dresdernan td: Inishmacsaint FH 14; 75
Dresnagh td: Urney DL 39; 181
Dressog (see Dressoge)
Dressoge bog: Dromore TE 5; 93
Dressoge corn mill: Drumragh TE 5; 110
Dressoge school: Drumragh TE 5; 109
Dressoge school: Longfield TE 5; 132
Dressoge td: Aghavea FH 4; 23
Dressoge td: Dromore TE 5; 93, 97–98
Dressoge td: Drumragh TE 5; 109–110
Dressoge td: Longfield TE 5; 132
Dressogue (see Dressoge)
Dresternan Castle: Kinawley FH 4; 115
Dresternan td: Kinawley FH 4; 114
Drew, Rev. Thomas: Racavan AM 13; 94, 98
Driddan school: Loughguile AM 13; 77
Driddan td: Loughguile AM 13; 77
Drim lough: Mevagh DL 38; 55
Drimacarry td: Killymard DL 39; 101
Drimadirig hill: Ballynascreen LY 31; 10
Drimadone (see Drumaduin): Culfeightrin AM 24; 85
Drimahan fort: Manorhamilton Union LM 40; 52

Drimbane td: Magheraculmoney FH 14; 113
Drimbane td: Urney DL 39; 181
Drimbaran td: Magheraculmoney FH 14; 112
Drimbarren village: Donegal DL 39; 56
Drimboarty td: Magheraculmoney FH 14; 111, 113
Drimbwee Point: Lough Swilly DL 38; 104, 142–44
Drimcahey td: Magheraculmoney FH 14; 111
Drimclamp school: Ardstraw TE 5; 11, 13
Drimcliff td: Killymard DL 39, 101
Drimcoes td: Magheraculmoney FH 14; 111
Drimconlon td [I]: Cleenish FH 14; 28
Drimconlon td [II]: Cleenish FH 14; 29
Drimconlon td [III]: Cleenish FH 14; 29
Drimcurrin td: Magheraculmoney FH 14; 110
Drimditton (see Drumdutton): Mevagh DL 38; 55
Drimdoit fort: Urney DL 39; 181
Drimdoit school: Urney DL 39; 182
Drimdoit td: Urney DL 39; 181
Drimelly td: Cleenish FH 14; 29
Drimern td: Magheraculmoney FH 14; 112
Drimfergus td: Donaghmore DL 39; 37
Drimgiveny (see Drumgivery)
Drimgoman td: Killymard DL 39; 100
Drimgunna bay: Killymard DL 39; 95
Drimina corn mill: Kilmacteige SO 40; 194
Drimina td: Kilmacteige SO 40; 196
Drimkeen graveyard: Convoy DL 39; 19
Drimkeen old church: Convoy DL 39; 19
Drimkeen school [I]: Convoy DL 39; 23
Drimkeen school [II]: Convoy DL 39; 23
Drimkeen td: Convoy DL 39; 20
Drimkeen td: Magheraculmoney FH 14; 110
Drimkennian td: Donaghmore DL 39; 37
Drimlaught village: Donegal DL 39; 56
Drimleagh bleach mill: Kildress TE 20; 61
Drimleagh td: Kildress TE 20; 58
Drimleaghan meeting house: Ardstraw TE 5; 11
Drimlecks corn mill: Donegal DL 39; 47
Drimlegagh corn mills: Ardstraw TE 5; 14
Drimlegagh flax mill: Ardstraw TE 5; 14
Drimlegagh school: Ardstraw TE 5; 13
Drimlene (see Drumleene): Clonleigh DL 39; 1
Drimluackagh (see Drumluackagh): Lough Swilly DL 38; 120
Drimmark td: Killymard DL 39; 100
Drimmeenenagh td: Killymard DL 39; 101
Drimmenaugh td: Tullaghobegley DL 39; 173
Drimminny river: Donegal DL 39; 44, 54
Drimminy (see Drimminny): Donegal DL 39; 44
Drimnacraig district: Lough Swilly DL 38; 100
Drimnacrow td: Convoy DL 39; 20
Drimnacrush bog: Cumber LY 28; 29–30
Drimnacrush td: Magheraculmoney FH 14; 110
Drimnaght hill: Conwal DL 39; 24
Drimnaght td: Conwal DL 39; 27

Drimnagreagh mountain: Carncastle and Killyglen AM 10; 10

Drimnaha (see Drumnaha): Clonleigh DL 39; 3

Drimnahoagh Mountain td: Conwal DL 39; 27

Drimnahoagh school: Conwal DL 39; 27

Drimnahoagh td: Conwal DL 39; 27

Drimnahoagh td: Leck DL 39; 118

Drimnahoo td: Killymard DL 39; 100

Drimnasrene school: Inishmacsaint FH 14; 79

Drimoneny td: Raphoe DL 39; 126

Drimrain td: Magheraculmoney FH 14; 113

Drimroosk td: Killymard DL 39; 100, 107–08

Drimsavney Little district: Magheraculmoney FH 14; 111

Drimsavney td: Magheraculmoney FH 14; 110–11

Drimslavlin td: Killymard DL 39; 101

Drin td: Dromara DN 12; 64

Driniaray td: Inishmacsaint FH 14; 75

Drinn school: Dromara DN 12; 64

Drinulla village: Kilmacteige SO 40; 193

Drips, family: Maghera LY 18; 24, 48

Drips, George: Maghera LY 18; 56

Drips, James: Maghera LY 18; 51

Drips, John: Maghera LY 18; 58, 70

Drips, Matthew: Errigal LY 27; 54, 69

Drips, Robert: Maghera LY 18; 42

Drips, Thomas: Maghera LY 18; 41

Driver, Col.: Clogher TE 5; 33

Droan hills: Ballyscullion LY 6; 71

Droghed bog: Aghadowey LY 22; 4

Droghed bog: Agivey LY 22; 39

Droghed school: Aghadowey LY 22; 13, 19, 21

Droghed Sunday school: Aghadowey LY 22; 13

Drogheda: Antrim AM 29; 37

Drogheda: Ballyscullion LY 6; 57

Drogheda: Carrickfergus AM 37; 43

Drogheda: Cumber LY 28; 50

Drogheda: Derryaghy AM 8; 114

Drogheda: Derryvullan FH 14; 39

Drogheda: Drumlumman CN 40; 17

Drogheda: Killyleagh DN 17; 84, 86

Drogheda: Magheross MN 40; 149, 152

Droghert mountain: Donaghmore DL 39; 28

Drohmsavish (see Drimsavney): Magheraculmoney FH 14; 111

Drokabawn td: Drumgoon CN 40; 2

Drollagh school: Muckno MN 40; 168

Drollagh td: Muckno MN 40; 162

Drollough (see Drollagh): Muckno MN 40; 168

Dromachose (see Drumachose)

Dromacorn (see Drumacon): Muckno MN 40; 163

Dromagore (see Drumagore): Clondermot LY 34; 57

Dromahair barony: Manorhamilton Union LM 40; 47

Dromaird locality: Kilmacteige SO 40; 187

Dromalis td: Drumcree AH 1; 40

Dromally rectory: Clones FH 4; 29

Dromantine demesne: Donaghmore DN 3; 8

Dromantine demesne loughs: Donaghmore DN 3; 7

Dromantine hills: Misc. DN 17; 131

Dromantine House: Donaghmore DN 3; 8

Dromantine td: Donaghmore DN 3; 7–9

Dromantine td: Misc. DN 17; 130–31

Dromara: Dromara DN 12; 62–65, 68

Dromara: Drumballyroney DN 3; 10

Dromara: Garvaghy DN 12; 81

Dromara: Loughinisland DN 17; 96

Dromara: Magheradrool DN 17; 107

Dromara: Tullynakill DN 7; 122

Dromara bridge: Dromara DN 12; 69

Dromara chapel (C): Dromara DN 12; 66

Dromara chapel (W): Dromara DN 12; 68

Dromara church: Dromara DN 12; 63, 68

Dromara corn mill: Dromara DN 12; 63, 69

Dromara Glebe House: Dromara DN 12; 63, 69

Dromara hill: Dromara DN 12; 68

Dromara meeting house (P): Dromara DN 12; 66

Dromara meeting house (S): Dromara DN 12; 63

Dromara old church: Dromara DN 12; 63

Dromara old corn mill: Dromara DN 12; 69

Dromara ph: Donaghcloney DN 12; 57

Dromara ph: Dromore DN 12; 70, 73

Dromara ph: Drumgooland DN 3; 24

Dromara ph: Garvaghy DN 12; 79

Dromara ph: Holywood DN 7; 80

Dromara ph: Misc. DN 17; 121

Dromara ph: Moira DN 12; 117

Dromara td: Dromara DN 12; 63, 65

Dromaragh (see Dromara)

Dromard td: Ballymascanlan LH 40; 55

Dromatihue td: Hillsborough DN 12; 85, 88, 105–06

Drombragh td: Magheross MN 40; 148

Dromeril deerpark: Inniskeen MN 40; 128–29

Dromerloghmore hill: Magheracloone MN 40; 137

Dromganney td: Magheross MN 40; 148

Dromgoan td: Magheross MN 40; 148

Dromherick td: Donacavey TE 5; 82

Drominear (see Drumnashane): Aghaderg DN 12; 2

Drommond (see Drummond)

Dromoare (see Dromore)

Dromona House: Ahoghill AM 23; 13

Dromore: Aghaderg DN 12; 6

Dromore: Ballyclog TE 20; 17

Dromore: Blaris AM 8; 3, 71

Dromore: Clogherny TE 20; 27

Dromore: Comber DN 7; 40

Dromore: Dromara DN 12; 65

Dromore: Dromore DN 12; 71, 74, 76

Dromore: Dromore TE 5; 94, 96, 100

Dromore: Garvaghy DN 12; 81

Dromore: Magheradrool DN 17; 101, 107
Dromore: Magherally DN 12; 113
Dromore: Magheramesk AM 21; 122
Dromore: Misc. DN 17; 116
Dromore: Newry DN 3; 65, 109
Dromore Bishop's Palace: Dromore DN 12; 72, 76
Dromore bog: Macosquin LY 22; 78, 118
Dromore bridge: Kildollagh LY 22; 68
Dromore Castle: Ballyrashane LY 22; 58
Dromore Castle: Dromore DN 12; 72
Dromore Castle: Kildollagh LY 22; 69, 73
Dromore chapel (C): Dromore DN 12; 71, 74
Dromore chapel (M): Dromore DN 12; 71, 74
Dromore chapel: Dromore TE 5; 101
Dromore church: Desertmartin LY 31; 54
Dromore church: Dromore DN 12; 72, 74, 102
Dromore church: Dromore TE 5; 100, 102
Dromore church: Misc. LY 31; 117, 127
Dromore Church St school: Dromore DN 12; 77
Dromore corn mill: Tamlaght Finlagan LY 25; 83
Dromore court house: Dromore DN 12; 75–76
Dromore cove: Rasharkin AM 23; 137, 139
Dromore diocese: Aghaderg DN 12; 8
Dromore diocese: Aghalee AM 21; 26
Dromore diocese: Annaclone DN 12; 13
Dromore diocese: Ballinderry AM 21; 44
Dromore diocese: Dromore DN 12; 70
Dromore diocese: Drumballyroney DN 3; 13
Dromore diocese: Drumgath DN 3; 19, 21
Dromore diocese: Kilbroney DN 3; 32
Dromore diocese: Magherally DN 12; 112
Dromore diocese: Seagoe AH 1; 104
Dromore diocese: Seapatrick DN 12; 123
Dromore diocese: Shankill AH 1; 111
Dromore diocese: Shankill DN 12; 138
Dromore diocese: Tullylish DN 12; 144
Dromore diocese: Warrenpoint DN 3; 117
Dromore dispensary: Dromara DN 12; 67
Dromore dispensary: Dromore DN 12; 77
Dromore flax mill: Tamlaght Finlagan LY 25; 83
Dromore flax mills: Taughboyne DL 39; 153
Dromore fort: Dromore DN 12; 72
Dromore fort [I]: Rasharkin AM 23; 137, 139
Dromore fort [II]: Rasharkin AM 23; 138
Dromore giant's grave: Dromore TE 5; 102
Dromore Glebe House: Desertmartin LY 31; 54
Dromore Glebe House: Dromore TE 5; 100–02
Dromore Glebe House: Misc. LY 31; 127
Dromore lough: Drumgoon CN 40; 3, 7–8
Dromore Lower school: Layd AM 13; 51
Dromore Lower td: Clogher TE 5; 44
Dromore Lower td: Killymard DL 39; 101
Dromore meeting house (A): Dromore DN 12; 71, 74

Dromore meeting house (P): Dromore DN 12; 71, 75
Dromore meeting house: Dromore TE 5; 101
Dromore meeting house: Rasharkin AM 23; 128, 130
Dromore mill: Tyholland MN 40; 175
Dromore national school [I]: Dromore DN 12; 75, 77
Dromore national school [II]: Dromore DN 12; 75, 77
Dromore old abbey: Dromore TE 5; 100
Dromore old castle: Dromore DN 12; 72
Dromore old church: Dromore DN 12; 72
Dromore old church: Misc. DN 17; 117
Dromore old church: Muckamore AM 35; 82
Dromore ph: Clogher TE 5; 40
Dromore ph: Derryvullan FH 14; 31
Dromore ph: Donacavey TE 5; 66, 82–84
Dromore ph: Donaghcloney DN 12; 57, 59
Dromore ph: Dromara DN 12; 62, 65
Dromore ph: Drumragh TE 5; 104
Dromore ph: Garvaghy DN 12; 79
Dromore ph: Hillsborough DN 12; 87–89, 95
Dromore ph: Kilskeery TE 5; 113
Dromore ph: Longfield TE 5; 131
Dromore ph: Magheraculmoney FH 14; 103
Dromore ph: Magheralin DN 12; 109
Dromore ph: Magherally DN 12; 112, 114
Dromore ph: Misc. TE 5; 147
Dromore ph: Moira DN 12; 117
Dromore ph: Tullylish DN 12; 140
Dromore school: Dromore TE 5; 101–02
Dromore school: Rasharkin AM 23; 134–35, 141
Dromore school: Tamlaght Finlagan LY 25; 95
Dromore spa: Taughboyne DL 39; 150, 153
Dromore springs: Macosquin LY 22; 117
Dromore stream: Donacavey TE 5; 67
Dromore Sunday school: Tamlaght Finlagan LY 25; 95
Dromore td: Clogher TE 5; 26, 37, 53
Dromore td: Clonleigh DL 39; 12
Dromore td: Desertmartin LY 31; 62, 118, 142
Dromore td: Donaghmore DL 39; 37
Dromore td: Dromore TE 5; 95, 97–98
Dromore td: Kildollagh LY 22; 67
Dromore td: Leck DL 39; 118
Dromore td: Macosquin LY 22; 77, 93, 118
Dromore td: Tamlaght Finlagan LY 25; 92–93, 104
Dromore td: Taughboyne DL 39; 148, 153, 195, 197
Dromore Upper td: Killymard DL 39; 101
Dromore, Bishop of: Aghagallon AM 21; 14
Dromore, Bishop of: Annaclone DN 12; 16
Dromore, Bishop of: Dromore DN 12; 70–71
Dromore, Bishop of: Kilbroney DN 3; 33–34
Dromore, Bishop of: Magherally DN 12; 114

Dromorebrague fort: Aghaderg DN 12; 8
Dromorebrague td: Aghaderg DN 12; 2, 11
Dromorebreda (see Dromorebrague)
Dromores (see Dromore)
Drought, Rev. Adolphos: Enniskeen CN 40; 29
Drout, Mr: Devenish FH 14; 58–59
Druamadoon (see Drumadoon): Killagan AM 23; 85
Drue, Richard: Ballyaghran LY 33; 19
Drue, Richard: Coleraine LY 33; 127
Druim Conan (see Drumconan): Clondermot LY 34;
   56
Druim Loughraman rock: Banagher LY 30; 91
Druimcruach corn mill: Donegal DL 39; 47
Druimghornan corn mill: Killymard DL 39; 96
Druimros East fort: Killymard DL 39; 97
Druimros spa: Killymard DL 39; 95, 106
Druimstibhlin fort: Killymard DL 39; 97
Drum (see Drumhallagh): Killygarvan DL 38; 40
Drum: Aghabog MN 40; 64
Drum: Currin MN 40; 86, 89–90, 92, 94
Drum: Ematris MN 40; 115
Drum bridge: Drumbeg AM 8; 125
Drum bridge: Drumbeg DN 7; 52
Drum Ceat hill: Ballynascreen LY 31; 34
Drum Ceat hill: Bovevagh LY 25; 46
Drum Ceat hill: Clondermot LY 34; 106–07
Drum Ceat hill: Culfeightin AM 24; 67–68
Drum Ceat hill: Dungiven LY 15; 33, 64
Drum Ceat hill: Tamlaght Finlagan LY 25; 101–03
Drum chapel of ease: Currin MN 40; 89, 93
Drum church: Drumbeg AM 8; 129
Drum fort [I]: Bovevagh LY 25; 10, 17–18, 31–32
Drum fort [II]: Bovevagh LY 25; 32
Drum grey stone: Bovevagh LY 25; 51
Drum hill: Bovevagh LY 25; 1
Drum hill: Currin MN 40; 86
Drum House: Drumbeg DN 7; 53
Drum Locks: Drumbeg AM 8; 127
Drum Lodge: Leck DL 39; 116
Drum lough: Currin MN 40; 86, 91
Drum meeting house (P): Currin MN 40; 89
Drum meeting house (S): Currin MN 40; 89
Drum of Inch locality: Lough Swilly DL 38; 147
Drum Point: Lough Swilly DL 38; 147
Drum quarry: Bovevagh LY 25; 53
Drum school: Bovevagh LY 25; 25, 27–28
Drum school: Currin MN 40; 92
Drum Sunday school: Bovevagh LY 25; 25
Drum td: Banagher LY 30; 23–24, 92
Drum td: Bovevagh LY 25; 13–14, 17, 19, 26,
   31–32, 37, 51, 60–61
Drum td: Currin MN 40; 91–92
Drum td: Lough Swilly DL 38; 145
Drum wood: Bovevagh LY 25; 2, 22
Drum, Patrick: Magherafelt LY 6; 105, 107

Drumabeest lough: Kilraghts AM 16; 125
Drumaboichan (see Drumalorchan): Finvoy AM 23;
   68
Drumacanny (see Drumcanon): Aughnamullen MN
   40; 76
Drumacarney old church: Tamlaght Finlagan LY 25;
   86–87, 93, 100, 111–12
Drumacarney td: Tamlaght Finlagan LY 25; 71–72,
   93, 118, 123
Drumacarny (see Drumacarney)
Drumachon td: Drung CN 40; 19
Drumachose bleach greens: Drumachose LY 9; 83
Drumachose cemetery: Dungiven LY 15; 32
Drumachose church: Drumachose LY 9; 50, 122
Drumachose flax mills: Drumachose LY 9; 83, 91
Drumachose Glebe House: Drumachose LY 9; 51,
   83, 89, 91
Drumachose Methodist school: Drumachose LY 9;
   122
Drumachose old church: Bovevagh LY 25; 13, 45
Drumachose old church: Drumachose LY 9; 19, 48,
   50, 55–56, 91, 126, 128
Drumachose ph: Aghadowey LY 22; 1
Drumachose ph: Aghanloo LY 11; 7, 9–10
Drumachose ph: Balteagh LY 9; 1, 14, 20, 37, 44
Drumachose ph: Dungiven LY 15; 29, 33, 112
Drumachose ph: Faughanvale LY 36; 13, 29
Drumachose ph: Kilcronaghan LY 31; 77
Drumachose ph: Macosquin LY 22; 76
Drumachose ph: Magilligan LY 11; 96, 98
Drumachose ph: Tamlaght Finlagan LY 25; 62, 69,
   85, 97, 106–08
Drumack fort: Rasharkin AM 23; 140
Drumack td: Rasharkin AM 23; 128, 137, 140
Drumackin (see Drummackin): Enniskillen FH 4; 74
Drumacloughan td: Tullyaughnish DL 38; 97
Drumacon bog: Muckno MN 40; 163
Drumacon North td: Muckno MN 40; 162
Drumacon school: Muckno MN 40; 168
Drumaconnal (see Drumaconnell): Saintfield DN 7;
   119
Drumaconnell East td: Saintfield DN 7; 118, 120
Drumaconnell td: Saintfield DN 7; 119–20
Drumaconnell West td: Saintfield DN 7; 118, 120
Drumacony corn mill: Tamlaght Finlagan LY 25; 83,
   121
Drumacony td: Tamlaght Finlagan LY 25; 93
Drumacribb flax mill: Muckno MN 40; 166
Drumacrieve td: Ematris MN 40; 116
Drumacrow td: Aghadowey LY 22; 10, 35, 38
Drumacullin cave: Culfeightrin AM 24; 49
Drumacullin fort: Culfeightrin AM 24; 49
Drumacullin standing stones: Culfeightrin AM 24;
   79
Drumacullin td: Culfeightrin AM 24; 49

Drumadaragh (Drumaduragh) td: Killagan AM 23; 79

Drumadaragh bleach green: Killagan AM 23; 80, 83

Drumadaragh bridge: Killagan AM 23; 80

Drumadaragh corn mill: Killagan AM 23; 83

Drumadarragh bleach mills: Kilbride AM 29; 150

Drumadarragh bridge: Kilbride AM 29; 151

Drumadarragh cromlech: Kilbride AM 29; 154

Drumadarragh enclosure: Kilbride AM 29; 148–49

Drumadarragh forts: Kilbride AM 29; 149, 155

Drumadarragh giant's grave: Kilbride AM 29; 146–47, 149, 154–55

Drumadarragh hill: Kilbride AM 29; 135, 137, 148, 154–55

Drumadarragh House: Kilbride AM 29; 138–39

Drumadarragh plantation: Kilbride AM 29; 155

Drumadarragh print mill: Kilbride AM 29; 135, 156

Drumadarragh standing stone: Kilbride AM 29; 147

Drumadarragh td: Kilbride AM 29; 135–36, 139, 150

Drumadarragh trench: Kilbride AM 29; 146

Drumadarragh tumuli: Kilbride AM 29; 154

Drumaderry td: Aghanloo LY 11; 19, 40–42

Drumadonaghy fort: Kilwaughter AM 10; 119

Drumadonaghy td: Kilwaughter AM 10; 116, 122

Drumadoney td: Dromara DN 12; 64–65

Drumadonnell bog: Drumgooland DN 3; 23

Drumadonnell td: Drumgooland DN 3; 23

Drumadoon (Drumadoan) td: Killagan AM 23; 81, 83, 85

Drumadoon hill: Killagan AM 23; 81

Drumadoon school: Killagan AM 23; 85–86

Drumadooney (see Drumadoney): Dromara DN 12; 64

Drumadown fort: Devenish FH 14; 55

Drumadown td: Cleenish FH 14; 23

Drumadown td: Devenish FH 14; 58

Drumadragh td: Coleraine LY 33; 155

Drumadreen bog: Bovevagh LY 25; 30, 49

Drumadreen fort: Balteagh LY 9; 19

Drumadreen fort: Bovevagh LY 25; 47, 49

Drumadreen td: Balteagh LY 9; 19

Drumadreen td: Banagher LY 30; 24

Drumadreen td: Bovevagh LY 25; 12, 59

Drumaduan causeway: Kildollagh LY 22; 74

Drumaduan cave: Kildollagh LY 22; 69, 74

Drumaduan fort [I]: Kildollagh LY 22; 69, 73

Drumaduan fort [II]: Kildollagh LY 22; 69, 73–74

Drumaduan td: Kildollagh LY 22; 68, 70, 73

Drumaduff td: Banagher LY 30; 23–24, 89

Drumaduff td: Bovevagh LY 25; 50, 59

Drumaduin cave [I]: Culfeightrin AM 24; 51

Drumaduin cave [II]: Culfeightrin AM 24; 52

Drumaduin fort [I]: Culfeightrin AM 24; 51

Drumaduin fort [II]: Culfeightrin AM 24; 51–52

Drumaduin school: Culfeightrin AM 24; 85

Drumaduin standing stone: Culfeightrin AM 24; 51

Drumaduin td: Culfeightrin AM 24; 50

Drumadune (see Drumadoon): Killagan AM 23; 81

Drumafievy (see Drumnafivey)

Drumafife locality: Clondermot LY 34; 111

Drumagarner bogs: Tamlaght O'Crilly LY 18; 85, 112, 125

Drumagarner chapel: Tamlaght O'Crilly LY 18; 89–90, 105–06, 109, 136, 143

Drumagarner hibernian school: Tamlaght O'Crilly LY 18; 139–40

Drumagarner private school: Tamlaght O'Crilly LY 18; 140

Drumagarner Sunday school: Tamlaght O'Crilly LY 18; 143

Drumagarner td: Tamlaght O'Crilly LY 18; 92, 94, 97, 106, 109–10, 116, 136–37, 144

Drumagavenny td: Balteagh LY 9; 14

Drumagelvin fort: Muckno MN 40; 166

Drumagelvin td: Tyholland MN 40; 174

Drumaghlis (Drumaghlish) td: Kilmore DN 17; 89

Drumaghlis flax mill: Kilmore DN 17; 91

Drumaghlis meeting house: Kilmore DN 17; 91

Drumaghlis ruin: Kilmore DN 17; 89

Drumaghlis td: Inch DN 17; 75

Drumaglea td: Dundermot AM 13; 34

Drumagore td: Clondermot LY 34; 57, 76, 109, 112, 116, 124, 130

Drumagorgan cairn: Donegore AM 29; 124

Drumagorgan giant's grave: Donegore AM 29; 104, 124

Drumagorgan td: Donegore AM 29; 101–02, 130

Drumagosker bleach green: Balteagh LY 9; 4, 13, 28, 36

Drumagosker bridge: Balteagh LY 9; 5, 42

Drumagosker flax mill: Balteagh LY 9; 14, 40

Drumagosker House: Balteagh LY 9; 3–4

Drumagosker standing stones: Balteagh LY 9; 10, 29

Drumagosker td: Balteagh LY 9; 4, 10, 13–14, 27–28, 36, 40, 43, 45

Drumaguill (see Drumaquill) td: Killowen LY 33; 172

Drumagully td: Dunboe LY 11; 58, 81

Drumagully td: Macosquin LY 22; 97

Drumagurland (see Drumgurland)

Drumagusker (see Drumagosker): Balteagh LY 9; 27

Drumahammond school: Culfeightrin AM 24; 48

Drumahare fort: Templecarn DL 39; 160

Drumahare standing stone: Templecarn DL 39; 160

Drumahare well: Templecarn DL 39; 160

Drumahay hill: Killinchy DN 7; 86

Drumaheglis (Drumahaigles) td: Ballymoney AM 16; 3, 10

Drumaheglis distillery: Ballymoney AM 16; 3, 10

Drumahitt td: Culfeightrin AM 24; 67–68

Drumahoe: Clondermot LY 34; 114, 117

Drumahoe academy: Clondermot LY 34; 9, 86–88, 95

Drumahoe bridge: Clondermot LY 34; 7

Drumahoe corn mill: Clondermot LY 34; 130–31

Drumahoe evening school: Clondermot LY 34; 86

Drumahoe flax mill: Clondermot LY 34; 21, 34, 131

Drumahoe lime quarry: Clondermot LY 34; 130

Drumahoe road quarry: Clondermot LY 34; 6, 101, 130

Drumahoe school: Clondermot LY 34; 88–90, 95

Drumahoe Sunday school: Clondermot LY 34; 92–93

Drumahoe td: Banagher LY 30; 103

Drumahoe td: Clondermot LY 34; 3, 14, 18, 56, 65, 67, 88, 102–03, 109–10, 112, 116, 124, 130–31

Drumahoe td: Faughanvale LY 36; 57

Drumahoe td: Kilwaughter AM 10; 111, 113

Drumahorgan td: Magilligan LY 11; 95, 134, 142

Drumahorragan (see Drumahorgan): Magilligan LY 11; 142

Drumaile kilns: Killowen LY 33; 172

Drumain school: Loughgall AH 1; 81

Drumainy td: Cleenish FH 14; 29

Drumainy td: Derrybrusk FH 4; 30

Drumakearny (see Drumacarney): Tamlaght Finlagan LY 25; 123

Drumakill school: Muckno MN 40; 168

Drumakill td: Muckno MN 40; 166

Drumaleet bog: Aghagallon AM 21; 12

Drumaleet fort [I]: Aghagallon AM 21; 12

Drumaleet fort [II]: Aghagallon AM 21; 17

Drumaleet td: Aghagallon AM 21; 1, 3, 16, 19, 21–22

Drumalief cave: Aghanloo LY 11; 5, 27

Drumalief td: Aghanloo LY 11; 5, 21, 31, 40–41

Drumalief td: Drumachose LY 9; 128

Drumalig td: Saintfield DN 7; 118, 120

Drumalisk forts: Muckno MN 40; 166

Drumalisk meeting house: Muckno MN 40; 165

Drumalisk school: Muckno MN 40; 168

Drumaliss td: Larne AM 10; 123

Drumalla (see Drumhallagh): Lough Swilly DL 38; 101

Drumalorchan fort: Finvoy AM 23; 68, 72

Drumanacannon (see Drumnacanon): Tamlaght O'Crilly LY 18; 99

Drumanagh td: Killyman TE 20; 68

Drumanan (see Drumany): Ematris MN 40; 112

Drumanasarragh td: Desertmartin LY 31; 56–57

Drumanaway td: Drummaul AM 19; 90

Drumane (Drimane) td: Tamlaght O'Crilly LY 18; 97–98, 109, 116, 125, 136, 138, 144

Drumane bogs: Tamlaght O'Crilly LY 18; 126, 144

Drumane school: Tamlaght O'Crilly LY 18; 142

Drumanee td: Ballyscullion LY 6; 67

Drumaness school: Magheradrool DN 17; 104

Drumaness td: Magheradrool DN 17; 99, 104

Drumanny (see Drumany): Kinawley FH 4; 121

Drumanocken td: Dromore DN 12; 70

Drumanphy (Drumanfy) td: Tartaraghan AH 1; 117, 120

Drumans (see Drummans)

Drumantine (see Dromantine): Donaghmore DN 3; 9

Drumanure hill: Devenish FH 14; 47

Drumanure td: Devenish FH 14; 47

Drumany Beg td: Kinawley FH 4; 121

Drumany hill: Ematris MN 40; 112

Drumany lough: Ematris MN 40; 112

Drumany More td: Kinawley FH 4; 121

Drumany school: Kinawley FH 4; 111

Drumany td: Aghalurcher FH 4; 3, 14

Drumany td: Clondavaddog DL 38; 7

Drumany td: Ematris MN 40; 115–16

Drumaqueran (see Drumaquern): Kilraghts AM 16; 130

Drumaquern td: Kilraghts AM 16; 130–32, 135

Drumaquill (Drumaguil) td: Killowen LY 33; 165, 172

Drumaquill bog: Killowen LY 33; 158

Drumara (see Dromara): Dromara DN 12; 62

Drumaran (Drummarron) td: Tullylish DN 12; 143–44

Drumaran lough: Tullylish DN 12; 140, 143–44

Drumaraw school: Devenish FH 14; 55–56

Drumard bog: Maghera LY 18; 43, 56, 58

Drumard bogs: Tamlaght O'Crilly LY 18; 85, 118, 131–32

Drumard brickfield: Tamlaght TE 20; 114

Drumard cave: Maghera LY 18; 12, 59–60

Drumard fort: Lissan LY 31; 89, 101

Drumard fort: Tamlaght O'Crilly LY 18; 118

Drumard fort [I]: Maghera LY 18; 60

Drumard fort [II]: Maghera LY 18; 60

Drumard fort [III]: Maghera LY 18; 61

Drumard Jones td: Kilmore AH 1; 64, 66, 69

Drumard lough: Maghera LY 18; 46

Drumard lough: Maghera LY 18; 59

Drumard Primate td: Kilmore AH 1; 68, 70–71

Drumard school: Ballynascreen LY 31; 18

Drumard school: Killyman TE 20; 67

Drumard school: Maghera LY 18; 30, 35

Drumard td: Ballynascreen LY 31; 13, 21–22, 32

Drumard td: Lissan LY 31; 99–100, 107–09

Drumard td: Maghera LY 18; 3, 12, 17, 22, 24, 43–44, 46, 54, 58, 60, 64, 71, 80–81

Drumard td: Misc. LY 31; 143

Drumard td: Tamlaght O'Crilly LY 18; 97–98, 136, 138

Drumard td: Tamlaght TE 20; 81, 107–15

Drumard well: Maghera LY 18; 43

Drumard wood: Ballynascreen LY 31; 2

Drumard wood: Lissan LY 31; 89

Drumardagh td: Leck DL 39; 119

Drumardin td: Ballywalter DN 7; 18

Drumardin td: Misc. DN 17; 125

Drumardinquarter td: Misc. DN 17; 125

Drumark td: Clonfeacle AH 1; 24

Drumarkin td: Drumballyroney DN 3; 14, 18

Drumaroad chapel: Loughinisland DN 17; 96

Drumaroad corn mill: Loughinisland DN 17; 95–96

Drumaroad flax mill: Loughinisland DN 17; 95–96

Drumaroad td: Loughinisland DN 17; 95

Drumart td: Ballymoney AM 16; 25

Drumary school: Devenish FH 14; 50

Drumash td: Kilskeery TE 5; 113

Drumason (see Drumacon): Muckno MN 40; 168

Drumaspil corn mill: Killyman TE 20; 67

Drumastickle (see Springmount): Dundermot AM 13; 31

Drumatoland school: Raymoghy DL 39; 140

Drumatoland td: Raymoghy DL 39; 137, 141, 198

Drumatrummon graveyard: Tullyaughnish DL 38; 91

Drumatrummon td: Tullyaughnish DL 38; 96

Drumavail lough: Currin MN 40; 86

Drumavally td: Magilligan LY 11; 95, 126

Drumavan td: Currin MN 40; 91

Drumaville bogs: Lough Swilly DL 38; 135

Drumavoley cave: Ramoan AM 24; 109

Drumavoley druid's altar: Ramoan AM 24; 108

Drumavoley hamlet: Ramoan AM 24; 109

Drumavoley td: Ramoan AM 24; 109

Drumawark td: Templecarn DL 39; 164

Drumaweer church: Moville DL 38; 68

Drumaweer school: Moville DL 38; 69

Drumaweer Sunday school: Moville DL 38; 69

Drumaweer td: Moville DL 38; 68, 70

Drumawhy school: Newtownards DN 7; 105

Drumawhy td: Misc. DN 17; 123

Drumawhy td: Newtownards DN 7; 105, 112–13

Drumawier (see Drumaweer): Moville DL 38; 68

Drumawillin cave: Ramoan AM 24; 107

Drumawillin flax mill: Ramoan AM 24; 97

Drumawillin school: Ramoan AM 24; 100

Drumawillin spring: Ramoan AM 24; 92

Drumawillin tuck mill: Ramoan AM 24; 97

Drumay td: Misc. DL 39; 194

Drumbaarly td: Magheraculmoney FH 14; 112

Drumbacagh hill: Ematris MN 40; 112

Drumbad hill: Inishmacsaint FH 14; 71

Drumbad td: Inishmacsaint FH 14; 70–71

Drumbadbeg td: Aghalurcher FH 4; 14

Drumbadmeen school: Inishmacsaint FH 14; 79

Drumbadmore td: Aghalurcher FH 4; 14

Drumbag (see Drumbad)

Drumbally hill: Misc. LY 31; 119

Drumballydonaghy td: Tamlaght Finlagan LY 25; 93, 119

Drumballydonohey (see Drumballydonaghy)

Drumballyhagan Clarke td: Kilcronaghan LY 31; 84

Drumballyhagan td: Kilcronaghan LY 31; 71, 142

Drumballyroney chapel: Drumballyroney DN 3; 15

Drumballyroney fort: Annaclone DN 12; 15

Drumballyroney ph: Aghaderg DN 12; 1, 8

Drumballyroney ph: Annaclone DN 12; 13, 15–16

Drumballyroney ph: Drumgath DN 3; 19–20

Drumballyroney ph: Drumgooland DN 3; 22–24

Drumballyroney ph: Misc. DN 17; 121

Drumballyroney ph: Newry DN 3; 82, 110–11

Drumballyroney school: Drumballyroney DN 3; 15

Drumballyrony (see Drumballyroney): Newry DN 3; 110

Drumban (see Drumbane): Aghanloo LY 11; 12

Drumban corn mill: Magheraculmoney FH 14; 105

Drumbanada convent: Kilmacteige SO 40; 196

Drumbanada friary: Kilmacteige SO 40; 196

Drumbanada locality: Kilmacteige SO 40; 188

Drumbanagher Castle: Ballymore AH 1; 4

Drumbanagher House: Ballymore AH 1; 7, 9, 15

Drumbanagher House: Killevy AH 1; 52

Drumbanagher House: Loughgilly AH 1; 85

Drumbanagher td: Ballymore AH 1; 12, 16

Drumbanaway chapel: Ballyclog TE 20; 15

Drumbane (see Drumlane): Tamlaght O'Crilly LY 18; 97

Drumbane bog: Dungiven LY 15; 95

Drumbane bogs: Errigal LY 27; 55

Drumbane fort: Bovevagh LY 25; 13, 19, 47–48

Drumbane fort: Dungiven LY 15; 47–48

Drumbane hill: Aghanloo LY 11; 25

Drumbane old church: Aghanloo LY 11; 26

Drumbane school: Aghanloo LY 11; 32

Drumbane td: Aghanloo LY 11; 9, 12, 15, 18–19, 22, 26, 32–33, 36–37, 39–42

Drumbane td: Ballybay MN 40; 84

Drumbane td: Dungiven LY 15; 95

Drumbane td: Errigal LY 27; 44, 74, 81, 86, 90

Drumbane td: Moira DN 12; 120

Drumbane td: Skerry AM 13; 120

Drumbannadi (see Drumbanada): Kilmacteige SO 40; 188

Drumbannew corn mill: Drumlumman CN 40; 14

Drumbare cairn: Dundermot AM 13; 34

Drumbare cave: Dundermot AM 13; 35

Drumbare fort: Dundermot AM 13; 34

Drumbare mass stone: Dundermot AM 13; 35

Drumbare meeting house: Dundermot AM 13; 31
Drumbare td: Dundermot AM 13; 31, 34–35
Drumbargy td: Cleenish FH 14; 14, 29
Drumbarley td: Longfield TE 5; 132
Drumbarnet Lower td: Raymoghy DL 39; 137, 141
Drumbarnet Middle td: Raymoghy DL 39; 137
Drumbarnet spring: Misc. DL 39; 188
Drumbarnet td: Misc. DL 39; 187, 194, 198
Drumbarnet Upper td: Raymoghy DL 39; 137, 141
Drumbarnett (see Drumbarnet): Misc. DL 39; 194
Drumbarry td: Galloon FH 4; 95
Drumbear td: Lough Swilly DL 38; 117
Drumbeast (see Drumbest): Kilraghts AM 16; 134
Drumbeg bleach green: Drumbeg DN 7; 52
Drumbeg bridge: Drumbeg AM 8; 127
Drumbeg church: Drumbeg AM 8; 131
Drumbeg church: Drumbeg DN 7; 53
Drumbeg church: Misc. DN 17; 117
Drumbeg corn mill: Drumbeg DN 7; 53
Drumbeg flax mills: Taughboyne DL 39; 153
Drumbeg ph: Derryaghy AM 8; 90, 118
Drumbeg ph: Drumbo DN 7; 54
Drumbeg ph: Holywood DN 7; 83
Drumbeg ph: Misc. AM 10; 129
Drumbeg ph: Misc. DN 17; 120–21
Drumbeg td: Drumbeg DN 7; 53
Drumbeg td: Misc. DL 39; 195
Drumbeg td: Taughboyne DL 39; 148, 153
Drumbeggan bog: Devenish FH 14; 52
Drumbeggan fort: Devenish FH 14; 55
Drumbeggan school: Devenish FH 14; 55–56
Drumbeggan td: Devenish FH 14; 58
Drumbern bay: Tullyaughnish DL 38; 86
Drumbern td: Tullyaughnish DL 38; 94, 96
Drumberne (see Drumbern): Tullyaughnish DL 38; 86
Drumberney td: Devenish FH 14; 58
Drumbest coves: Kilraghts AM 16; 134
Drumbest flax mill: Kilraghts AM 16; 127
Drumbest fort: Kilraghts AM 16; 134
Drumbest td: Kilraghts AM 16; 131–32, 136
Drumbinis (see Drumbinnis): Kinawley FH 4; 111
Drumbinnis school: Killesher FH 14; 85
Drumbinnis school: Kinawley FH 4; 111
Drumbinnis td: Kinawley FH 4; 110
Drumbo: Blaris AM 8; 76
Drumbo: Blaris DN 12; 33
Drumbo: Drumbo DN 7; 54, 59
Drumbo bleach green: Drumbo DN 7; 55
Drumbo church: Drumbo DN 7; 56, 60
Drumbo corn mill: Drumbo DN 7; 56, 59
Drumbo dispensary: Drumbo DN 7; 60
Drumbo House: Drumbo DN 7; 56
Drumbo meeting house: Drumbo DN 7; 54, 56, 59
Drumbo ph: Blaris DN 12; 26–27

Drumbo ph: Comber DN 7; 31
Drumbo ph: Drumbeg DN 7; 52
Drumbo ph: Knockbreda DN 7; 97
Drumbo ph: Misc. DN 17; 120–21
Drumbo ph: Saintfield DN 7; 116
Drumbo school: Drumbo DN 7; 57
Drumbo td: Drumbo DN 7; 54, 56–57, 59, 61–62
Drumbo tower: Drumbo DN 7; 55–56, 59
Drumbo tower: Misc. DN 17; 121
Drumboary td: Devenish FH 14; 57–58
Drumboe td: Duneane AM 19; 123
Drumbog glebe: Galloon FH 4; 96
Drumboghanagh Glebe td: Drummully FH 4; 34, 39
Drumboghil td: Dungiven LY 15; 64
Drumbolg meeting house: Tamlaght O'Crilly LY 18; 89, 99–100, 103–04, 106–07, 110, 136, 142
Drumbolg sessions house: Tamlaght O'Crilly LY 18; 89
Drumbolg Sunday school: Tamlaght O'Crilly LY 18; 142
Drumbolg td: Tamlaght O'Crilly LY 18; 99, 103, 140
Drumbollog td: Galloon FH 4; 95
Drumboory school: Magheracloone MN 40; 142
Drumborisk td: Currin MN 40; 91
Drumboy td: Clonleigh DL 39; 16
Drumbrain plantation: Aghabog MN 40; 63, 67
Drumbrain td: Aghabog MN 40; 63
Drumbrecas (see Drumbrughas): Killesher FH 14; 85
Drumbridge House: Drumbo DN 7; 59
Drumbristan chapel: Errigal Truagh MN 40; 121
Drumbrohas (see Drumbrughas): Galloon FH 4; 95
Drumbrugghus (see Drumbrughas): Killesher FH 14; 84
Drumbrughas (Drumbrocas) td: Aghalurcher FH 4; 14
Drumbrughas brickfield: Killesher FH 14; 84
Drumbrughas Castle: Galloon FH 4; 92
Drumbrughas East Castle: Galloon FH 4; 105
Drumbrughas East corn mill: Galloon FH 4; 92
Drumbrughas East td: Galloon FH 4; 92, 95, 105
Drumbrughas school: Aghalurcher FH 4; 11
Drumbrughas school: Killesher FH 14; 85
Drumbrughas td: Aghavea FH 4; 23
Drumbrughas td: Killesher FH 14; 87
Drumbrughas West td: Galloon FH 4; 95, 95
Drumbuckin td: Magheracross FH 14; 102
Drumbuckless td: Drumlumman CN 40; 13
Drumbulgan bog: Ballyclog TE 20; 15
Drumbulkin hill: Rasharkin AM 23; 133, 136, 138–40
Drumbulkin well: Rasharkin AM 23; 137
Drumbwee lough: Inniskeen MN 40; 124
Drumbwee Point: Lough Swilly DL 38; 103

Drumbwee td: Misc. DL 39; 186, 194, 197

Drumcairn td: Raymoghy DL 39; 137, 141, 198

Drumcall hill: Ematris MN 40; 112

Drumcalpin loughs: Laragh CN 40; 40

Drumcalpin td: Laragh CN 40; 39

Drumcannea (see Drumcanon): Aughnamullen MN 40; 76

Drumcannon (see Drumcanon)

Drumcanon td: Aughnamullen MN 40; 76

Drumcanon td: Killesher FH 14; 84, 87

Drumcar House: Enniskeen CN 40; 29

Drumcarbin td: Devenish FH 14; 58

Drumcard school: Killesher FH 14; 85

Drumcard td: Killesher FH 14; 87

Drumcashelbone td: Newry DN 3; 107

Drumcattan chapel: Donaghmoyne MN 40; 107

Drumcaw bog: Derryvullan FH 14; 32

Drumcaw corn mill: Loughinisland DN 17; 97

Drumcaw td: Galloon FH 4; 95

Drumceiribe fort: Templecarn DL 39; 160

Drumchrin (see Drummackin): Enniskillen FH 4; 82

Drumclanf Sunday school [I]: Ardstraw TE 5; 7

Drumclanf Sunday school [II]: Ardstraw TE 5; 7

Drumclay td: Enniskillen FH 4; 81

Drumcliff church: Faughanvale LY 36; 51

Drumcloy (Drumclay) td: Galloon FH 4; 95, 98

Drumco td: Cleenish FH 14; 29

Drumco td: Magheralin DN 12; 110

Drumcoe td: Drumglass TE 20; 40

Drumcollick hill: Drung CN 40; 19

Drumcon school: Rasharkin AM 23; 134–35

Drumconan flax mill: Clondermot LY 34; 131

Drumconan quarry: Clondermot LY 34; 131

Drumconan td: Clondermot LY 34; 56, 62, 65, 109, 112, 116, 124, 131

Drumcondra: Magheracloone MN 40; 138–39

Drumcondra: Magheross MN 40; 144, 146, 151–52, 157

Drumcondra bridge: Magheracloone MN 40; 139

Drumconien (see Drumcunnion): Aughnamullen MN 40; 76

Drumconis td: Dromore TE 5; 97

Drumconnelly fort: Drumragh TE 5; 109

Drumconnelly td: Drumragh TE 5; 109

Drumconnen (see Drumcunnion): Aughnamullen MN 40; 73

Drumconnis td: Dromore TE 5; 93, 98

Drumconnor bog: Cleenish FH 14; 15

Drumconnor td: Cleenish FH 14; 29

Drumconready forge: Maghera LY 18; 74

Drumconready fort: Maghera LY 18; 62

Drumconready td: Kilcronaghan LY 31; 79

Drumconready td: Maghera LY 18; 11, 22, 36, 46, 59, 62, 65, 74, 79–81

Drumconway quarry: Tamlaght TE 20; 121

Drumconway td: Tamlaght TE 20; 75, 80–81, 95, 98, 103, 115–20, 120–22, 126, 131, 134

Drumcoo (Belview) td: Enniskillen FH 4; 82

Drumcoonien (see Drumcunnion): Aughnamullen MN 40; 71

Drumcor td: Drumlumman CN 40; 13

Drumcork td: Errigal Keerogue TE 20; 48, 52, 57

Drumcormick district: Misc. SO 40; 200

Drumoormick hill. Desertlyn LY 31; 36

Drumcose td: Devenish FH 14; 58–59

Drumcovid (see Drumcovit)

Drumcovit cave: Banagher LY 30; 2, 48, 76

Drumcovit flax mill: Banagher LY 30; 72–73

Drumcovit fort [I]: Banagher LY 30; 71

Drumcovit fort [II]: Banagher LY 30; 71–72

Drumcovit fort [III]: Banagher LY 30; 72

Drumcovit House: Banagher LY 30; 4, 16–18, 27, 29–30, 71, 74, 96, 99

Drumcovit quarry: Banagher LY 30; 127

Drumcovit soup kitchen: Banagher LY 30; 20, 98

Drumcovit standing stone: Banagher LY 30; 46, 74

Drumcovit td: Banagher LY 30; 3, 22–23, 34–36, 43, 46, 48, 61–62, 95, 100, 103, 109, 118, 123, 127, 131

Drumcovit td: Dungiven LY 15; 65, 100

Drumcovit wood: Banagher LY 30; 123

Drumcovitt (see Drumcovit): Banagher LY 30; 2

Drumcree chapel: Drumcree AH 1; 29

Drumcree church: Drumcree AH 1; 29, 35

Drumcree Glebe House: Drumcree AH 1; 36, 38

Drumcree ph: Ballymore AH 1; 17–18

Drumcree ph: Kilmore AH 1; 57, 60–61, 65, 67–68, 70–73

Drumcree ph: Montiaghs AH 1; 89, 92

Drumcree ph: Seagoe AH 1; 101, 104–05

Drumcree ph: Tartaraghan AH 1; 117, 119–20

Drumcree td: Drumcree AH 1; 29, 35, 38

Drumcreen td: Magheracross FH 14; 102

Drumcrin church: Drummully FH 4; 34–35

Drumcrin church: Galloon FH 4; 96

Drumcrin ph: Currin MN 40; 91

Drumcrin ph: Drummully FH 4; 34, 39–40

Drumcrin ph: Galloon FH 4; 95–96

Drumcrin td: Drummully FH 4; 34–35, 39

Drumcrin td: Templecarn DL 39; 164

Drumcroo td: Aghalurcher FH 4; 4

Drumcroo td: Galloon FH 4; 95

Drumcroon bleach green: Macosquin LY 22; 82, 104

Drumcroon cove: Macosquin LY 22; 94–95

Drumcroon hill: Macosquin LY 22; 76

Drumcroon House: Aghadowey LY 22; 30

Drumcroon House: Macosquin LY 22; 80

Drumcroon standing stones: Macosquin LY 22; 94

Drumcroon td: Macosquin LY 22; 79

Drumcrottagh td: Derrykeighan AM 16; 93

Drumcroumf td: Cleenish FH 14; 28

Drumcrovil td: Derryvullan FH 14; 46

Drumcrow bog: Taughboyne DL 39; 148, 152

Drumcrow bridge: Kilcronaghan LY 31; 67, 75, 79

Drumcrow fort: Kilcronaghan LY 31; 85

Drumcrow school: Tickmacrevan AM 13; 133

Drumcrow td: Derrybrusk FH 4; 30

Drumcrow td: Laragh CN 40; 40

Drumcrow td: Misc. LY 31; 143

Drumcrow td: Taughboyne DL 39; 148, 152, 195

Drumcrughil hill: Drumgoon CN 40; 8

Drumcruian td: Drumgoon CN 40; 3

Drumculla chapel: Galloon FH 4; 89

Drumculla school: Galloon FH 4; 96

Drumculla td: Galloon FH 4; 89–90, 95, 98

Drumcullia td: Cleenish FH 14; 29

Drumcullien (see Drumcullion)

Drumcullion bog: Errigal Keerogue TE 20; 52

Drumcullion fort: Errigal Keerogue TE 20; 52

Drumcullion school: Magheracross FH 14; 99

Drumcullion td: Derrybrusk FH 4; 30

Drumcullion td: Errigal Keerogue TE 20; 52, 57

Drumcullion td: Kinawley FH 4; 110

Drumcullion td: Magheracross FH 14; 93, 95, 102

Drumcunna td: Magheracross FH 14; 102

Drumcunnion chapel: Aughnamullen MN 40; 71

Drumcunnion graveyard: Aughnamullen MN 40; 73

Drumcunnion td: Aughnamullen MN 40; 69, 76

Drumcunny td: Aghalurcher FH 4; 14

Drumcur mill: Enniskillen FH 4; 69

Drumcur td: Enniskillen FH 4; 82

Drumcurrian (see Drumcunnion): Aughnamullen
    MN 40; 69

Drumdallagh (Drumdollagh) td: Loughguile AM 13;
    74, 76

Drumdallagh flax mill: Loughguile AM 13; 63

Drumderg bridge: Ballynascreen LY 31; 6

Drumderg carn: Ballynascreen LY 31; 10

Drumderg cave: Misc. LY 31; 118

Drumderg cromlech: Ballynascreen LY 31; 22, 118

Drumderg fort: Ballynascreen LY 31; 11, 24

Drumderg locality: Misc. TE 5; 146

Drumderg td: Ballynascreen LY 31; 24, 33, 143

Drumderg td: Dromore TE 5; 98

Drumderg td: Duneane AM 19; 114

Drumderrig bog: Cleenish FH 14; 15

Drumderrig lough: Tomregan FH 4; 126

Drumderrig school: Cleenish FH 14; 24

Drumderrig td: Cleenish FH 14; 14, 29

Drumdesco chapel: Tydavnet MN 40; 170–72

Drumdesco school: Tydavnet MN 40; 172

Drumditton (see Drumdutton): Mevagh DL 38; 58

Drumdonaugh td: Taughboyne DL 39; 148, 153

Drumdoney sweathouse: Kinawley FH 4; 120

Drumdoney td: Kinawley FH 4; 121

Drumdony (see Drumdoney): Kinawley FH 4; 120

Drumdoo td: Misc. LY 31; 143

Drumdoonagh td: Misc. DL 39; 195

Drumdoony district: Misc. SO 40; 198

Drumdreenagh (Drumdrinagh) td: Drumballyroney
    DN 3; 13, 16

Drumdreenagh school: Drumballyroney DN 3; 13,
    17–18

Drumdreenagh school: Hillsborough DN 12; 101

Drumdron td: Cleenish FH 14; 28

Drumduff chapel: Killesher FH 14; 83

Drumduff td: Killesher FH 14; 85

Drumdutton Castle: Mevagh DL 38; 58

Drumdutton td: Mevagh DL 38; 55, 63

Drumean (see Drumane): Tamlaght O'Crilly LY 18;
    97

Drumear House (Louth): Drummully FH 4; 37

Drumeavish td: Donaghmore DL 39; 37

Drumee td: Aghavea FH 4; 23

Drumeechey (see Drumneechy): Banagher LY 30;
    95

Drumeen td: Misc. DL 39; 195

Drumeeny (Drimeeny) td: Ramoan AM 24; 88–89,
    109, 112

Drumeeny cave: Ramoan AM 24; 109

Drumeeny cromlech: Ramoan AM 24; 112

Drumeeny old church: Ramoan AM 24; 110

Drumeil bog: Aghadowey LY 22; 4

Drumeil bog: Agivey LY 22; 39

Drumeil td: Aghadowey LY 22; 1, 13

Drumemric (Drumimeric) td: Tamlaght O'Crilly LY
    18; 86–87, 125, 128

Drumemric bog: Tamlaght O'Crilly LY 18; 86, 128

Drumemric wood: Tamlaght O'Crilly LY 18; 87,
    125

Drumenagh hill: Drumcree AH 1; 34

Drumenagh td: Artrea LY 6; 14

Drumenagh td: Drumcree AH 1; 39

Drumenalig (see Drumnaleg): Ballymore AH 1; 15

Drumenenaghbeg school: Inishmacsaint FH 14; 78

Drumenequin hill: Devenish FH 14; 47

Drumenighan school: Devenish FH 14; 50

Drumennan td: Misc. DL 39; 191, 195

Drumero td: Loughgilly AH 1; 84

Drumess hill: Aghaloo TE 20; 1

Drumett hill: Aghabog MN 40; 62

Drumett lough: Aghabog MN 40; 62

Drumfad fort: Taughboyne DL 39; 153

Drumfad Lower lough: Clondavaddog DL 38; 3

Drumfad Lower standing stone: Clondavaddog DL
    38; 6

Drumfad Lower td: Lough Swilly DL 38; 128

Drumfad school: Clondavaddog DL 38; 7

Drumfad td: Donaghadee DN 7; 45

Drumfad td: Misc. DN 17; 124
Drumfad td: Taughboyne DL 39; 148, 153, 195
Drumfad Upper lough: Clondavaddog DL 38; 3
Drumfane cove [I]: Kirkinriola AM 23; 124
Drumfane cove [II]: Kirkinriola AM 23; 125
Drumfane moat: Ballyclug AM 23; 61
Drumfane moat: Dundermot AM 13; 33
Drumfane moat: Kirkinriola AM 23; 124, 126
Drumfane school: Kirkinriola AM 23; 113
Drumfane td: Kirkinriola AM 23; 91
Drumfin td: Kirkinriola AM 23; 91
Drumfin td: Mevagh DL 38; 63
Drumfinwell bridge: Balteagh LY 9; 5, 42
Drumfoldra beetling mill: Aughnamullen MN 40; 72
Drumfoldra corn mill: Aughnamullen MN 40;
    71–72, 75
Drumfoldra flour mill: Aughnamullen MN 40; 72
Drumfoldra House: Aughnamullen MN 40; 71
Drumfoldra td: Aughnamullen MN 40; 76
Drumfolmas (see Drumfoldra): Aughnamullen MN
    40; 71
Drumfreehan td: Aughnamullen MN 40; 76
Drumfresky td: Layd and Inispollan AM 13; 54
Drumgaig td: Killesher FH 14; 87
Drumgain td: Loughgilly AH 1; 85
Drumgale (see Drumgole): Ematris MN 40; 112
Drumgallen td: Galloon FH 4; 95
Drumgally td: Donaghedy TE 5; 92
Drumgara td: Ballybay MN 40; 84
Drumgarkin hill: Ematris MN 40; 112
Drumgarly school: Aghabog MN 40; 65
Drumgarr td: Aughnamullen MN 40; 76
Drumgarrog (see Drumgarrow): Enniskillen FH 4;
    74
Drumgarrow bog: Trory FH 14; 124
Drumgarrow river: Trory FH 14; 123–24
Drumgarrow school: Trory FH 14; 128–29
Drumgarrow td: Enniskillen FH 4; 74, 81
Drumgarrow td: Trory FH 14; 122, 124
Drumgask td: Seagoe AH 1; 101, 104, 108
Drumgath chapel (C): Drumballyroney DN 3; 15
Drumgath chapel (M): Drumballyroney DN 3; 15
Drumgath church: Drumballyroney DN 3; 15
Drumgath corn mills: Drumgath DN 3; 20
Drumgath flax mills: Drumgath DN 3; 20
Drumgath graveyard: Drumgath DN 3; 20
Drumgath meeting house (Cov.): Drumballyroney
    DN 3; 15
Drumgath meeting house (P): Drumballyroney DN
    3; 15
Drumgath meeting house (Q): Drumballyroney DN
    3; 15
Drumgath meeting house (S): Drumballyroney DN
    3; 15
Drumgath ph: Drumballyroney DN 3; 13, 15

Drumgath ph: Newry DN 3; 108
Drumgath ph: Warrenpoint DN 3; 115
Drumgath td: Drumballyroney DN 3; 14
Drumgath td: Drumgath DN 3; 20–21
Drumgavenny (Drumgaveny) Lower td: Balteagh
    LY 9; 4, 36, 39, 45
Drumgavenny bleach greens: Balteagh LY 9; 28, 36
Drumgavenny bog: Balteagh LY 9; 43
Drumgavenny bridges: Balteagh LY 9; 5, 42
Drumgavenny flax mill: Balteagh LY 9; 14, 40
Drumgavenny Lower bleach green: Balteagh LY 9;
    4, 13, 36
Drumgavenny rolling mill: Balteagh LY 9; 40
Drumgavenny td: Balteagh LY 9; 27–28, 40
Drumgavenny Upper td: Balteagh LY 9; 39, 45
Drumgavenny water: Balteagh LY 9; 40–41
Drumgavlin (Drumgavelin) td: Dromara DN 12;
    65–66
Drumgavlin meeting house: Dromara DN 12; 65
Drumgay lough: Enniskillen FH 4; 47
Drumgay lough: Magheracross FH 14; 91
Drumgay lough: Trory FH 14; 123
Drumgay td: Enniskillen FH 4; 74, 81
Drumgeries td: Magheross MN 40; 148
Drumgerna bog: Magheross MN 40; 146
Drumgesh (Drumgash) td: Balteagh LY 9; 33–34,
    38, 44–45
Drumgesh holy well: Balteagh LY 9; 33
Drumgim (see Drumgun): Templecarn DL 39; 164
Drumgish (see Drumgesh): Balteagh LY 9; 38, 40,
    45
Drumgivery (Drimgivery) td: Magheraculmoney FH
    14; 103, 110, 113
Drumgivry (see Drumgivery)
Drumglady td: Ballyscullion LY 6; 56
Drumglass collieries: Clonoe TE 20; 30–31
Drumglass collieries: Drumglass TE 20; 42–44
Drumglass collieries: Kildress TE 20; 59
Drumglass collieries: Tullyniskan TE 20; 140
Drumglass ph: Artrea TE 20; 8
Drumglass ph: Clonoe TE 20; 30
Drumglass ph: Desertcreat TE 20; 33
Drumglass ph: Donaghenry TE 20; 39
Drumglass ph: Tullyniskan TE 20; 138, 141–42
Drumglass quarries: Drumglass TE 20; 43
Drumglass ship canal: Drumglass TE 20; 43
Drumglassagh hill: Maghera LY 18; 61
Drumgoal (see Drumgole)
Drumgoland school: Galloon FH 4; 96
Drumgoland td: Galloon FH 4; 95
Drumgole hill: Ematris MN 40; 112
Drumgole td: Ematris MN 40; 113, 116
Drumgole td: Galloon FH 4; 95
Drumgoolagh fort: Ballybay MN 40; 81
Drumgoolagh Lower td: Ballybay MN 40; 84

Drumgoolagh Upper td: Ballybay MN 40; 84

Drumgooland bog: Loughinisland DN 17; 98

Drumgooland corn mill: Loughinisland DN 17; 95, 98

Drumgooland flax mill: Loughinisland DN 17; 95, 98

Drumgooland forts: Loughinisland DN 17; 98

Drumgooland old church: Drumgooland DN 3; 22

Drumgooland ph: Ballinderry AM 21; 51

Drumgooland ph: Dromara DN 12; 62, 65

Drumgooland ph: Drumballyroney DN 3; 13

Drumgooland ph: Faughanvale LY 36; 60

Drumgooland ph: Garvaghy DN 12; 79

Drumgooland ph: Misc. DN 17; 121

Drumgooland ph: Newry DN 3; 82, 110–11

Drumgooland smithy: Loughinisland DN 17; 98

Drumgooland stone cross: Drumgooland DN 3; 22

Drumgooland td: Loughinisland DN 17; 98

Drumgoon fort: Drumgoon CN 40; 1

Drumgoon glebe: Drumgoon CN 40; 4

Drumgoon hill: Drumgoon CN 40; 1

Drumgoon House: Aghalurcher FH 4; 8

Drumgoon mill: Aghalurcher FH 4; 8

Drumgoon ph: Aughnamullen MN 40; 69–70

Drumgoon ph: Killdrumsherdan CN 40; 31–32, 35

Drumgoon ph: Laragh CN 40; 44–45

Drumgoon td: Aghalurcher FH 4; 4

Drumgoose bog: Donaghmoyne MN 40; 106

Drumgoose Cottage: Drumcree AH 1; 38

Drumgoose school: Drumcree AH 1; 30, 33, 36, 38

Drumgoose td: Drumcree AH 1; 38

Drumgor td: Seagoe AH 1; 108

Drumgormly hill: Devenish FH 14; 47

Drumgorran td: Aghavea FH 4; 23

Drumgowan td: Lough Swilly DL 38; 145

Drumgramph hill: Currin MN 40; 86, 89

Drumgramph td: Currin MN 40; 92

Drumgramph td: Drummully FH 4; 39

Drumgrass td: Lissan LY 31; 99, 104

Drumgreen hill: Drumgoon CN 40; 1

Drumgreen school: Drumgoon CN 40; 11

Drumgreena td: Drumgath DN 3; 21

Drumgregan td: Leck DL 39; 118

Drumgriston Upper td: Donaghmoyne MN 40; 108

Drumgrole td: Ballybay MN 40; 84

Drumgrove td: Currin MN 40; 91

Drumguff (see Drumguiff): Aghalurcher FH 4; 3

Drumguiff bog: Aghalurcher FH 4; 4

Drumguiff td: Aghalurcher FH 4; 3, 14

Drumgullagh td: Galloon FH 4; 95

Drumgumberland demesne: Raphoe DL 39; 131

Drumgumberland td: Convoy DL 39; 20

Drumgumerland (see Drumgumberland)

Drumgun td: Killymard DL 39; 100

Drumgun td: Templecarn DL 39; 164

Drumgunland (see Drumgurland)

Drumgunna lough: Templecarn DL 39; 157

Drumgurland (Drumgorland) td: Island Magee AM 10; 23, 81, 95

Drumgurland windmill: Island Magee AM 10; 23, 81

Drumhack school: Killesher FH 14; 85

Drumhack td: Killesher FH 14; 87

Drumhalla (see Drumhallagh): Killygarvan DL 38; 37

Drumhallagh bay: Killygarvan DL 38; 46, 98, 101

Drumhallagh bridge: Killygarvan DL 38; 37, 47

Drumhallagh district: Lough Swilly DL 38; 101

Drumhallagh House: Killygarvan DL 38; 39–40

Drumhallagh Lower td: Killygarvan DL 38; 38

Drumhallagh td: Killygarvan DL 38; 47

Drumhallagh Upper bog: Killygarvan DL 38; 38, 44

Drumhallagh Upper giant's grave: Killygarvan DL 38; 41

Drumharif (Drumherriff) td: Loughgilly AH 1; 85

Drumharif corn mill: Loughgilly AH 1; 87

Drumharif flax mill: Loughgilly AH 1; 87

Drumhart chapel: Killdrumsherdan CN 40; 33

Drumhart church: Killdrumsherdan CN 40; 33, 36

Drumhart cromlech: Killdrumsherdan CN 40; 35

Drumhart hill: Killdrumsherdan CN 40; 31

Drumhart school: Killdrumsherdan CN 40; 36

Drumhaw td: Aghalurcher FH 4; 14

Drumhawan hill: Ballybay MN 40; 78

Drumhawan td: Ballybay MN 40; 84

Drumhawens (see Drumhawan): Ballybay MN 40; 78

Drumhergall (see Druminargall): Ballymore AH 1; 12

Drumherick td: Donacavey TE 5; 82

Drumheriff td: Cleenish FH 14; 29

Drumherk Alcan td: Clogher TE 5; 53

Drumherk td: Derryvullan FH 14; 46

Drumherk td: Enniskillen FH 4; 82

Drumherk Walker td: Clogher TE 5; 53

Drumherriff hill: Drung CN 40; 19

Drumherriff lough: Drung CN 40; 19

Drumherriff school: Drumcree AH 1; 36, 40

Drumherriff td: Drumcree AH 1; 40

Drumherriff td: Templecarn DL 39; 164

Drumherve corn mill: Tullyaughnish DL 38; 85, 89

Drumherve flax mill: Tullyaughnish DL 38; 85, 89

Drumherve td: Tullyaughnish DL 38; 97

Drumhilla (see Drumhillagh)

Drumhillagh hill: Aghabog MN 40; 62

Drumhillagh school: Currin MN 40; 93

Drumhillagh td: Aughnamullen MN 40; 76

Drumhillagh td: Ballybay MN 40; 84

Drumhillery meeting house: Tynan AH 1; 127

Drumhirk manor: Misc. DN 17; 123

Drumhirk school: Kilmood DN 7; 96

Drumhirk school: Newtownards DN 7; 105

Drumhirk td: Clogher TE 5; 35, 39

Drumhirk td: Kilmood DN 7; 94–95

Drumhirk td: Misc. DN 17; 124

Drumhirk td: Newtownards DN 7; 105

Drumhoas td: Galloon FH 4; 95

Drumholgony td: Cleenish FH 14; 28–29

Drumhome dispensary: Drumhome DL 39; 61

Drumhome glebe: Drumhome DL 39; 58–59

Drumhome meeting house: Donegal DL 39; 45, 47

Drumhome ph: Donegal DL 39; 42, 44

Drumhome ph: Kilbarron DL 39; 76

Drumhome ph: Killymard DL 39; 94, 96–97, 99

Drumhome ph: Templecarn DL 39; 156–57

Drumhome scutch mills: Drumhome DL 39; 62

Drumhome warren: Drumhome DL 39; 58

Drumhonish td: Longfield TE 5; 132

Drumhork td: Tullylish DN 12; 143

Drumhose hill: Killdrumsherdan CN 40; 31

Drumhourag td: Drumlumman CN 40; 12

Drumhowna chapel: Drumlumman CN 40; 14–15

Drumhowna druid's altar: Drumlumman CN 40; 14

Drumhowna school: Drumlumman CN 40; 15–16

Drumhoy td: Aghavea FH 4; 23

Drumiagh td: Magheraculmoney FH 14; 103

Drumigarner (see Drumagarner): Tamlaght O'Crilly
    LY 18; 136

Drumillard td: Aughnamullen MN 40; 69, 76

Drumiller hill: Misc. DN 17; 131

Drumiller td: Misc. DN 17; 131

Drumilly demesne: Loughgall AH 1; 79

Drumilly House: Loughgall AH 1; 80

Drumilly manor: Loughgall AH 1; 81

Drumilly td: Loughgall AH 1; 75

Drumimeric bog: Kilrea LY 27; 106

Drumin (see Druminure): Ballymore AH 1; 5

Drumin district: Misc. SO 40; 200

Drumin td: Drumgoon CN 40; 2

Drumina (see Drumnaha): Clonleigh DL 39; 12

Druminalduff td: Drumcree AH 1; 38

Druminargall House: Ballymore AH 1; 12, 17

Druminargall td: Ballymore AH 1; 12, 15, 17

Druminkelly td: Derryaghy AM 8; 121

Druminnegall (see Druminargall): Ballymore AH 1;
    12

Druminny female school: Leck DL 39; 119

Druminny male school: Leck DL 39; 116, 119

Druminny td: Leck DL 39; 116–17, 119

Drumintin school: Ematris MN 40; 117

Drumintin td: Ematris MN 40; 112, 116

Druminure corn mill: Ballymore AH 1; 5, 8, 10, 15

Druminure td: Ballymore AH 1; 8, 13–15, 17–18

Druminvaghan td: Devenish FH 14; 58

Drumitt td: Loughgilly AH 1; 84

Drumkeanagh td: Cleenish FH 14; 29

Drumkee td: Killyman TE 20; 66

Drumkeen House: Laragh CN 40; 45

Drumkeen locality: Raphoe DL 39; 129

Drumkeen td: Magheracross FH 14; 102

Drumkeen td: Magheraculmoney FH 14; 105–06

Drumkeenan td: Killymard DL 39; 100

Drumkeenragh td: Enniskillen FH 4; 74, 82

Drumkeeran bog: Shilvodan AM 19; 128

Drumkeeran chapel: Drumkeeran FH 14; 64

Drumkeeran dispensary: Drumkeeran FH 14; 67

Drumkeeran meeting house: Templecarn DL 39; 158

Drumkeeran mills: Drumkeeran FH 14; 65

Drumkeeran ph: Clogher TE 5; 40

Drumkeeran ph: Magheraculmoney FH 14; 103, 107

Drumkeeran ph: Templecarn DL 39; 156, 167

Drumkeith lough: Inniskeen MN 40; 124

Drumkellen td: Kinawley FH 4; 121

Drumkera td: Dromara DN 12; 65

Drumkerriffe (see Drumherriff): Drumcree AH 1; 40

Drumkillagh hill: Laragh CN 40; 39

Drumkirk td: Cleenish FH 14; 29

Drumkrin (see Drumcrin)

Drumlack chapel: Mullaghbrack AH 1; 96

Drumlackagh fort: Mevagh DL 38; 58

Drumlackagh td: Mevagh DL 38; 58, 62–63

Drumlaghan td: Donacavey TE 5; 77, 80–81, 85

Drumlaghar (see Drumlagher)

Drumlagher (see also Drumlaghan) td: Donacavey
    TE 5; 76, 78, 84

Drumlaghy chapel: Killesher FH 14; 83

Drumlaghy td: Cleenish FH 14; 14, 29

Drumlain (see Drumlane): Tamlaght O'Crilly LY
    18; 135

Drumlamph bog: Maghera LY 18; 56–57

Drumlamph cave: Maghera LY 18; 62

Drumlamph flax mill: Maghera LY 18; 28

Drumlamph forts: Maghera LY 18; 62

Drumlamph hibernian school [I]: Maghera LY 18;
    35

Drumlamph hibernian school [II]: Maghera LY 18;
    35

Drumlamph td: Maghera LY 18; 11–14, 24, 42–43,
    54, 57, 72

Drumlamph td: Magherafelt LY 6; 94

Drumlamph wood: Maghera LY 18; 4, 48, 56

Drumlane abbey: Tomregan FH 4; 128

Drumlane bogs: Tamlaght O'Crilly LY 18; 85, 118,
    123, 133–35

Drumlane corn mill: Ballybay MN 40; 81

Drumlane fort: Tamlaght O'Crilly LY 18; 116, 118

Drumlane forts: Ballybay MN 40; 81

Drumlane hill: Ballybay MN 40; 78

Drumlane holy well: Tamlaght O'Crilly LY 18; 135

Drumlane Island: Tamlaght O'Crilly LY 18; 133

Drumlane ph: Kinawley FH 4; 112–13

Drumlane ph: Tomregan FH 4; 125–26, 128

Drumlane td: Laragh CN 40; 39

Drumlane td: Tamlaght O'Crilly LY 18; 97, 118, 128, 144

Drumlane well: Tamlaght O'Crilly LY 18; 93

Drumlarkey hill: Drumgoon CN 40; 1

Drumleage hill: Killdrumsherdan CN 40; 31

Drumleagues bog: Aghalurcher FH 4; 4

Drumlease ph: Manorhamilton Union LM 40; 47, 52

Drumleck corn mill: Muckno MN 40; 165

Drumleckney meeting house: Racavan AM 13; 92, 98

Drumleckney td: Racavan AM 13; 88, 92, 98

Drumlee bog: Finvoy AM 23; 69

Drumlee bowling green: Finvoy AM 23; 69

Drumlee fort: Finvoy AM 23; 69

Drumlee meeting house: Drumgooland DN 3; 22, 25

Drumlee school: Drumgooland DN 3; 25

Drumlee td: Drumgooland DN 3; 22, 25

Drumlee td: Finvoy AM 23; 73

Drumleen (see Drumleene): Clonleigh DL 39; 5

Drumleene bog: Clonleigh DL 39; 1, 5

Drumleene td: Clonleigh DL 39; 12, 197

Drumlegagh corn mill: Ardstraw TE 5; 4

Drumlegagh flax mill: Ardstraw TE 5; 4

Drumlegagh meeting house: Ardstraw TE 5; 3, 6–7

Drumlegagh school: Ardstraw TE 5; 6

Drumlegagh Sunday school: Ardstraw TE 5; 7

Drumlegagh td: Ardstraw TE 5; 3–4

Drumleggagh (see Drumlegagh)

Drumlellum td: Drumcree AH 1; 39

Drumliff td: Aghalurcher FH 4; 4

Drumliffe bridge: Dunboe LY 11; 63

Drumlion td: Rossorry FH 14; 115

Drumlish bog: Dromore TE 5; 93

Drumlish td: Dromore TE 5; 93, 98

Drumlish td: Kinawley FH 4; 110

Drumlisnagrilly td: Seagoe AH 1; 108

Drumload td: Aughnamullen MN 40; 76

Drumloan (see Drumlone): Galloon FH 4; 95

Drumlogan hill: Killdrumsherdan CN 40; 33

Drumlogan td: Killdrumsherdan CN 40; 33

Drumloman (see Drumlumman): Drumlumman CN 40; 12

Drumlona td: Ematris MN 40; 116

Drumlonagh (see Drumlonnagh): Laragh CN 40; 40

Drumlone corn mill: Aghavea FH 4; 20

Drumlone school [I]: Galloon FH 4; 96

Drumlone school [II]: Galloon FH 4; 96

Drumlone td: Aghavea FH 4; 17

Drumlone td: Galloon FH 4; 95

Drumlongfield td: Drumkeeran FH 14; 62

Drumlonnagh hill: Laragh CN 40; 40

Drumlonnagh school: Laragh CN 40; 43

Drumlonnagh td: Laragh CN 40; 41–42

Drumlough bog: Dromore DN 12; 73

Drumlough lough: Drumgath DN 3; 19

Drumlough meeting house: Dromore DN 12; 71, 76

Drumlough school: Dromore DN 12; 73

Drumlough school: Drumgath DN 3; 21

Drumlough td: Dromore DN 12; 70, 76

Drumlough td: Drumgath DN 3; 19, 21

Drumlough td: Newry DN 3; 108

Drumlough td: Warrenpoint DN 3; 115

Drumlougher td: Misc. DL 39; 194

Drumluackagh bridge: Lough Swilly DL 38; 120

Drumluackagh quarry: Lough Swilly DL 38; 120

Drumluackagh td: Lough Swilly DL 38; 129

Drumlught td: Aghalurcher FH 4; 14

Drumlumman chapels: Drumlumman CN 40; 14

Drummaa td: Galloon FH 4; 95

Drummackin td: Enniskillen FH 4; 74, 82

Drummad td: Aughnamullen MN 40; 76

Drummadravy House: Derryvullan FH 14; 34

Drummageever td: Cleenish FH 14; 28–29

Drummain bridge: Cleenish FH 14; 15

Drummain bridge: Killesher FH 14; 84

Drummain td: Cleenish FH 14; 29

Drummanagh (see Drumenagh): Drumcree AH 1; 39

Drummanan House: Killea and Taughboyne DL 39; 87

Drummanan td: Killea and Taughboyne DL 39; 80

Drummaneny td: Faughanvale LY 36; 17, 53, 57, 68, 73, 84, 94

Drummaneny wood: Faughanvale LY 36; 84

Drummanillar fishery: Belleek FH 14; 6

Drummanillar td: Belleek FH 14; 6

Drummannon bog: Tullylish DN 12; 140

Drummannon td: Tartaraghan AH 1; 120

Drummanny (see Drumany)

Drummans (Drummons) Lower td: Magilligan LY 11; 95, 127

Drummans cave: Ramoan AM 24; 115

Drummans Middle td: Magilligan LY 11; 95

Drummans standing stone: Ramoan AM 24; 115

Drummans td: Magilligan LY 11; 126, 128, 142, 144–45

Drummans td: Ramoan AM 24; 123

Drummans Upper td: Magilligan LY 11; 94–95

Drummar fort: Ballybay MN 40; 81

Drummar hill: Ballybay MN 40; 78

Drummar td: Ballybay MN 40; 84

Drummaran td: Cleenish FH 14; 29

Drummaraw fort: Devenish FH 14; 55

Drummard td: Clones FH 4; 26

Drummard td: Derryvullan FH 14; 46

Drummard td: Enniskillen FH 4; 82

Drummarit td: Dromore TE 5; 98

Drummarrow (see Drumaran)

Drummartin td: Kilmacteige SO 40; 196

Drummass flax and tuck mill: Inniskeen MN 40; 125

Drummaul bog: Antrim AM 29; 3

Drummaul bog: Muckamore AM 35; 68

Drummaul bog: Shilvodan AM 19; 128

Drummaul bogs: Killead AM 35; 22

Drummaul church (see Randalstown): Drummaul AM 19; 34

Drummaul forts: Drummaul AM 19; 35, 65–66, 69

Drummaul giant's grave: Kilbride AM 29; 147

Drummaul graveyard: Drummaul AM 19; 35, 62

Drummaul linen manufactory: Drummaul AM 19; 34

Drummaul old church: Drummaul AM 19; 35, 62, 68, 71, 87

Drummaul old graveyard: Drummaul AM 19; 87

Drummaul ph: Ahoghill AM 23; 1

Drummaul ph: Antrim AM 29; 1, 3, 6–7, 17, 19, 27, 29

Drummaul ph: Ballymartin AM 2; 9

Drummaul ph: Ballyscullion AM 19; 1, 3, 5, 8

Drummaul ph: Connor AM 19; 16

Drummaul ph: Donegore AM 29; 112

Drummaul ph: Duneane AM 19; 94, 98, 101–03, 122

Drummaul ph: Kirkinriola AM 23; 101

Drummaul ph: Misc. AM 10; 129–30

Drummaul ph: Muckamore AM 35; 57

Drummaul ph: Shilvodan AM 19; 127, 133

Drummaul schools: Drummaul AM 19; 78

Drummaul td: Drummaul AM 19; 42

Drummavaddy td: Seapatrick DN 12; 124

Drummawillen td: Cleenish FH 14; 29

Drummee td: Derryvullan FH 14; 44, 46

Drummeen (see Drumane): Tamlaght O'Crilly LY 18; 136

Drummeen district: Errigal LY 27; 75

Drummeen Glebe House: Lissan LY 31; 103

Drummeen td: Lissan LY 31; 108–09

Drummeen td: Taughboyne DL 39; 148, 153

Drummenagh fort: Artrea LY 6; 10, 24, 27

Drummenagh private school: Artrea LY 6; 19

Drummenagh td: Artrea LY 6; 9–10, 12, 22, 24, 27, 36, 38

Drummenan flax mill: Taughboyne DL 39; 153

Drummenan orchard: Taughboyne DL 39; 153

Drummenan td: Taughboyne DL 39; 148, 150, 153

Drummenan wood: Taughboyne DL 39; 148

Drummenny td: Donaghedy TE 5; 92

Drummiarran school: Billy AM 16; 77

Drummiller (Drummillar) td: Aghaderg DN 12; 1–2, 4, 7–8

Drummiller bleaching mill: Dromore DN 12; 72

Drummiller cairn: Aghaderg DN 12; 7

Drummiller corn mill: Donaghmore DN 3; 8

Drummiller corn mill: Dromore DN 12; 72

Drummiller fort: Donaghmore DN 3; 8

Drummiller meeting house: Aghaderg DN 12; 4

Drummiller td: Donaghmore DN 3; 8–9

Drummiller td: Dromore DN 12; 70, 72–73

Drummiller td: Tullylish DN 12; 143

Drummineagh hill: Clonmany DL 38; 12

Drummod td: Cleenish FH 14; 25, 29

Drummoey Glebe House: Killanny MN 40; 131

Drummoghill (Drimochill) td: Raymoghy DL 39; 135, 137, 141

Drummoghill chapel: Raymoghy DL 39; 133

Drummole school: Laragh CN 40; 43

Drummon (see Drummond): Tullyaughnish DL 38; 96

Drummon td: Cleenish FH 14; 29

Drummon td: Donaghedy TE 5; 92

Drummona (see Drummond)

Drummonaghan td: Lough Swilly DL 38; 128

Drummond (Drummon) td: Donacavey TE 5; 76–78, 80–81, 83, 85

Drummond bog: Magheracloone MN 40; 137

Drummond bog: Tamlaght Finlagan LY 25; 65

Drummond bridge: Balteagh LY 9; 36

Drummond bridge: Drumachose LY 9; 56, 109, 118

Drummond bridge: Tullyaughnish DL 38; 90

Drummond corn mill: Aghaloo TE 20; 1, 4

Drummond corn mill: Drumachose LY 9; 53

Drummond flax mill: Balteagh LY 9; 36

Drummond flax mill [I]: Tynan AH 1; 128

Drummond flax mill [II]: Drumachose LY 9; 53

Drummond flax mill [II]: Drumachose LY 9; 53

Drummond hill: Inniskeen MN 40; 124

Drummond hill: Tynan AH 1; 124

Drummond House: Tamlaght Finlagan LY 25; 82

Drummond Itra td: Magheross MN 40; 148

Drummond Otra td: Magheross MN 40; 143, 148

Drummond school: Drumachose LY 9; 50, 85, 122

Drummond td: Balteagh LY 9; 36

Drummond td: Drumachose LY 9; 50, 53, 56, 87, 87, 96, 101, 108, 122, 126, 132, 134

Drummond td: Loughgilly AH 1; 84

Drummond td: Magheracloone MN 40; 137

Drummond td: Tamlaght Finlagan LY 25; 72–74, 93, 119

Drummond td: Tullyaughnish DL 38; 96

Drummond water: Drumachose LY 9; 53

Drummond, Dr: Kilcronaghan LY 31; 82

Drummond, family: Raloo AM 32; 94, 108, 123

Drummond, James: Ahoghill AM 23; 21, 41

Drummond, James: Kilbride AM 29; 144, 152

Drummond, James: Kilwaughter AM 10; 115

Drummond, John: Donegore AM 29; 113, 130

Drummond, man named: Nilteen AM 35; 93

Drummond, Margaret: Carrickfergus AM 37; 108

Drummond, Samuel: Kilwaughter AM 10; 113, 119

Drummond, Samuel: Raloo AM 32; 123

Drummond, William: Raloo AM 32; 128

Drummonds (see Drummans): Magilligan LY 11; 144

Drummonds chapel: Manorhamilton Union LM 40; 53

Drummone (see Dromore): Taughboyne DL 39; 148

Drummons (see Drummond): Donacavey TE 5; 77

Drummons td: Clones FH 4; 26

Drummore (Drumore) td: Tamlaght Finlagan LY 25; 118–19

Drummore (see Dromore): Taughboyne DL 39; 150

Drummore burn: Tamlaght Finlagan LY 25; 121

Drummore corn mill: Tamlaght Finlagan LY 25; 121

Drummore flax mill: Tamlaght Finlagan LY 25; 121

Drummore hill: Ematris MN 40; 112, 114

Drummore lough: Drumgoon CN 40; 2

Drummore lough: Killdrumsherdan CN 40; 32

Drummore river: Killdrumsherdan CN 40; 31–34

Drummore school: Tamlaght Finlagan LY 25; 123

Drummore td: Devenish FH 14; 58

Drummuck bleach green: Killyman TE 20; 68

Drummuck bog: Maghera LY 18; 41

Drummuck bridge: Maghera LY 18; 63

Drummuck carn: Maghera LY 18; 44

Drummuck fort [I]: Maghera LY 18; 61

Drummuck fort [II]: Maghera LY 18; 61

Drummuck giant's grave: Maghera LY 18; 44

Drummuck hill: Ballybay MN 40; 78

Drummuck school: Maghera LY 18; 30, 35

Drummuck td: Ballybay MN 40; 84

Drummuck td: Killesher FH 14; 87

Drummuck td: Maghera LY 18; 22, 44, 64, 78, 80–81

Drummuck td: Racavan AM 13; 86, 88

Drummucklough lime-kiln: Taughboyne DL 39; 153

Drummucklough quarry: Taughboyne DL 39; 150

Drummucklough td: Taughboyne DL 39; 148, 153

Drummulla hill: Ematris MN 40; 115

Drummulla windmill: Ematris MN 40; 112

Drummullan corn mill: Arboe LY 6; 1

Drummullan kiln: Arboe LY 6; 1

Drummullan td: Arboe LY 6; 1

Drummullard Big fort: Muckno MN 40; 166

Drummullard td: Muckno MN 40; 162

Drummulligan school: Carlingford LH 40; 60

Drummullin corn mill: Aghabog MN 40; 62

Drummullough td: Carlingford LH 40; 58

Drummully graveyard: Drummully FH 4; 40

Drummully mill [I]: Donagh MN 40; 101

Drummully mill [II]: Donagh MN 40; 101

Drummully old church: Drummully FH 4; 36

Drummully ph: Clogher TE 5; 40

Drummully ph: Galloon FH 4; 87, 92, 95–97, 105

Drummully td: Drummully FH 4; 39–40

Drummurphy school: Donaghmore DL 39; 40

Drummurphy td: Donaghmore DL 39; 37

Drummurril Glebe td: Galloon FH 4; 95, 97

Drummurrish (see Dunmaurice): Ballybay MN 40; 81

Drummurry td: Killdrumsherdan CN 40; 33

Drummurry td: Magheracross FH 14; 97, 102

Drummusky td: Galloon FH 4; 95

Drumnabony school: Ardstraw TE 5; 13

Drumnabratty td: Raphoe DL 39; 126

Drumnacannan (see Drumnacanon)

Drumnacannon (see Drumnacanon)

Drumnacanon (Drumnacanan) td: Tamlaght O'Crilly LY 18; 86, 91, 95, 97, 99, 110, 115, 128, 132, 135, 137, 144

Drumnacanon bogs: Tamlaght O'Crilly LY 18; 86, 131

Drumnacanon bridge: Tamlaght O'Crilly LY 18; 92, 109

Drumnacanon corn mill: Tamlaght O'Crilly LY 18; 91, 110

Drumnacanon flax mill: Tamlaght O'Crilly LY 18; 110

Drumnacanveny td: Seagoe AH 1; 108

Drumnacarn td: Shankill DN 12; 138

Drumnacarne td: Ballymascanlan LH 40; 55

Drumnacavanagh school: Killesher FH 14; 85

Drumnaconagher bridge: Kilmore DN 17; 89

Drumnaconagher corn mill: Kilmore DN 17; 88

Drumnaconagher flax mill [I]: Kilmore DN 17; 88

Drumnaconagher flax mill [II]: Kilmore DN 17; 88

Drumnaconagher td: Kilmore DN 17; 89

Drumnaconnel (see Drumaconnell): Saintfield DN 7; 120

Drumnacur fort: Ardclinis AM 13; 4, 7

Drumnacur graveyard: Ardclinis AM 13; 7

Drumnacur school: Ardclinis AM 13; 9

Drumnacur td: Ardclinis AM 13; 4, 7

Drumnadonaghy fort: Kilwaughter AM 10; 118

Drumnadonaghy td: Kilwaughter AM 10; 116, 118–19

Drumnadreagh (Drumnadrough) td: Glynn AM 26; 1, 41, 48

Drumnadreagh school: Glynn AM 26; 35, 47

Drumnadreen td: Drumgath DN 3; 21

Drumnadrogh (see Drumnadrough): Carnmoney AM 2; 54

Drumnadrough flax mill: Carnmoney AM 2; 48

Drumnadrough td: Carnmoney AM 2; 34, 54, 84, 91, 93, 102

Drumnafivey (Drumafivey) td: Loughguile AM 13; 70, 75–76

Drumnafivey flax mill: Loughguile AM 13; 63

Drumnafivey meeting house: Kilraghts AM 16; 127

Drumnaforke school: Longfield TE 5; 132

Drumnaforke td: Longfield TE 5; 132

Drumnagally td: Seapatrick DN 12; 123, 126

Drumnagee fort [I]: Ballintoy AM 24; 22

Drumnagee fort [II]: Ballintoy AM 24; 22

Drumnagee giant's chair: Ballintoy AM 24; 23

Drumnagee school: Ballintoy AM 24; 35

Drumnagee td: Ballintoy AM 24; 23

Drumnagee td: Billy AM 16; 46

Drumnagluntagh (Druminagluntagh) td: Ballymore AH 1; 14–17

Drumnaglunter (see Drumnagluntagh)

Drumnagoon td: Seagoe AH 1; 108

Drumnagress hill: Killdrumsherdan CN 40; 31

Drumnaha giant's grave: Clonleigh DL 39; 3

Drumnaha td: Clonleigh DL 39; 12, 197

Drumnaha td: Urney DL 39; 181

Drumnahan (see Drumnaha): Clonleigh DL 39; 12

Drumnahare hill: Aghaderg DN 12; 8

Drumnahare td: Aghaderg DN 12; 8

Drumnahay (Drumnahy) td: Magilligan LY 11; 95, 126, 128, 137

Drumnahay school: Magilligan LY 11; 110, 138

Drumnaheigh td: Drumtullagh AM 16; 103

Drumnahoe cotton factories: Kilwaughter AM 10; 109

Drumnahoe cotton works: Kilwaughter AM 10; 111

Drumnahoe school: Kilwaughter AM 10; 119

Drumnahoe td: Kilwaughter AM 10; 107, 109, 119

Drumnahoney td: Loughgilly AH 1; 85

Drumnahorgan td: Magilligan LY 11; 126

Drumnahunshin (Drumnahuncheon) td: Kilmore AH 1; 67–70

Drumnahunshin chapel: Kilmore AH 1; 58, 63, 69

Drumnahunshin td: Loughgilly AH 1; 85

Drumnakelly (Drumnakilly) td: Drumcree AH 1; 35, 42

Drumnakelly chapel: Drumcree AH 1; 30, 42

Drumnakelly meeting house: Drumcree AH 1; 36

Drumnakelly mill: Drumcree AH 1; 32, 42

Drumnakelly td: Seagoe AH 1; 108

Drumnakill caves: Culfeightrin AM 24; 52, 57

Drumnakill church: Culfeightrin AM 24; 57–58

Drumnakill fort [I]: Culfeightrin AM 24; 52, 74

Drumnakill fort [II]: Culfeightrin AM 24; 52

Drumnakill graveyard: Culfeightrin AM 24; 57–58

Drumnakill old church: Culfeightrin AM 24; 73

Drumnakill standing stone: Culfeightrin AM 24; 52

Drumnakill td: Culfeightrin AM 24; 51, 77

Drumnaleg (Druminaleg) td: Ballymore AH 1; 8, 15–18

Drumnaleg school: Ballymore AH 1; 11, 15

Drumnally td: Ballymore AH 1; 7

Drumnamalragh td: Cleenish FH 14; 29

Drumnameeal td: Enniskillen FH 4; 82

Drumnamitta td: Errigal Keerogue TE 20; 52

Drumnaoil school: Donegal DL 39; 49

Drumnaquean corn and flour mill: Killdrumsherdan CN 40; 34

Drumnascamph (Drumnascamp) td: Tullylish DN 12; 141–43, 145–46

Drumnascamph flax mill: Tullylish DN 12; 142

Drumnascamph meeting house: Tullylish DN 12; 141, 145

Drumnascamph mill [I]: Tullylish DN 12; 146

Drumnascamph mill [II]: Tullylish DN 12; 146

Drumnascamph school: Hillsborough DN 12; 101

Drumnascreagh graveyard: Ballintoy AM 24; 31

Drumnashane td: Aghaderg DN 12; 2

Drumnasheer td: Misc. DL 39; 186, 196

Drumnaskeie bank: Lough Swilly DL 38; 117

Drumnasole (Drimnasole) td: Ardclinis AM 13; 3, 7

Drumnasole female school: Ardclinis AM 13; 9

Drumnasole House: Ardclinis AM 13; 3, 6

Drumnasole school: Ardclinis AM 13; 4, 7, 9

Drumnasole td: Ardclinis AM 13; 9

Drumnasoo td: Drumcree AH 1; 41

Drumnasylla td: Ballymascanlan LH 40; 55

Drumnatraid hill: Killdrumsherdan CN 40; 31

Drumnavaddy lough: Magherally DN 12; 112, 115

Drumnavaddy lough: Seapatrick DN 12; 124, 127

Drumnavaddy td: Seapatrick DN 12; 123, 126–27

Drumnawhillian cromlech: Killdrumsherdan CN 40; 35

Drumnechy (see Drumneechy)

Drumneechy fort: Bovevagh LY 25; 16, 50

Drumneechy school: Bovevagh LY 25; 3, 25, 27–28, 55

Drumneechy school: Dungiven LY 15; 66

Drumneechy td: Banagher LY 30; 23–24, 95

Drumneechy td: Bovevagh LY 25; 56, 59

Drumneechy td: Dungiven LY 15; 66, 96

Drumneesha (see Drumneechy): Banagher LY 30; 23

Drumneguille (see Drumagully): Dunboe LY 11; 58

Drumnegully (see Drumagully): Dunboe LY 11; 58

Drumneill lough: Clontibret MN 40; 85

Drumneill td: Clontibret MN 40; 85

Drumnescue td: Templecarn DL 39; 164

Drumneth td: Magherally DN 12; 114

Drumnevin td: Drumcree AH 1; 40

Drumnicannon (see Drumnacanon): Tamlaght O'Crilly LY 18; 135

Drumnisin td: Dungiven LY 15; 90

Drumnoheskea td: Donacavey TE 5; 77

Drumo and Drumco mill [I]: Magheralin DN 12; 110

Drumo and Drumco mill [II]: Magheralin DN 12; 110

Drumo and Drumco mill [III]: Magheralin DN 12; 111

Drumo and Drumco mill [IV]: Magheralin DN 12; 111

Drumo and Drumco mill [V]: Magheralin DN 12; 111

Drumo td: Magheralin DN 12; 110

Drumod td: Drumgoon CN 40; 3

Drumoghal td: Misc. DL 39; 198

Drumond (see Drummond): Magheracloone MN 40; 137

Drumond td: Magheraculmoney FH 14; 105

Drumoo td: Tydavnet MN 40; 169

Drumoolish bogs: Tamlaght O'Crilly LY 18; 85–86, 118, 123–24, 131

Drumoolish school: Tamlaght O'Crilly LY 18; 140, 144

Drumoolish Sunday school: Tamlaght O'Crilly LY 18; 144

Drumoolish td: Tamlaght O'Crilly LY 18; 97–98, 128, 135, 137–38, 144

Drumore (see Dromore)

Drumoris td: Aghavea FH 4; 23

Drumough (see Drumsough): Drummaul AM 19; 85

Drumowen mill: Longfield TE 5; 128

Drumowen td: Longfield TE 5; 128

Drumownay chapel: Drung CN 40; 21

Drumquin: Ardstraw TE 5; 4, 14

Drumquin: Longfield TE 5; 127–28, 131, 134

Drumquin dispensary: Longfield TE 5; 132

Drumquin meeting house: Longfield TE 5; 131

Drumquin post office: Longfield TE 5; 130

Drumquin school: Longfield TE 5; 128

Drumquin water: Longfield TE 5; 127

Drumra manor: Inishmacsaint FH 14; 79

Drumra td: Drumbo DN 7; 58, 60–61

Drumragh bridge: Cappagh TE 5; 20

Drumragh chapel: Drumragh TE 5; 107–08

Drumragh old castle: Drumragh TE 5; 111

Drumragh old church: Drumragh TE 5; 108

Drumragh old churches: Drumragh TE 5; 111

Drumragh ph: Ardstraw TE 5; 10

Drumragh ph: Cappagh TE 5; 16, 19–20

Drumragh ph: Clogherny TE 20; 25–26

Drumragh ph: Donacavey TE 5; 71, 82

Drumragh ph: Dromore TE 5; 100

Drumragh ph: Longfield TE 5; 131, 133

Drumragh ph: Misc. TE 5; 147

Drumragh river: Cappagh TE 5; 17

Drumragh river: Clogherny TE 20; 25

Drumragh river: Donacavey TE 5; 67

Drumragh river: Dromore TE 5; 100

Drumragh river: Drumragh TE 5; 104

Drumragh school: Drumragh TE 5; 109

Drumragh td: Drumragh TE 5; 111

Drumraighland (Drumreaghlin) td: Tamlaght Finlagan LY 25; 93, 118

Drumraighland bridge: Tamlaght Finlagan LY 25; 122

Drumraighland fort [I]: Tamlaght Finlagan LY 25; 90, 108

Drumraighland fort [II]: Tamlaght Finlagan LY 25; 90

Drumraighland school: Tamlaght Finlagan LY 25; 96, 124

Drumraighland turning mill: Tamlaght Finlagan LY 25; 83, 122

Drumrain td: Galloon FH 4; 95

Drumrainbawn td: Galloon FH 4; 95

Drumrainey moat: Magherafelt LY 6; 107

Drumrainey school: Magherafelt LY 6; 102

Drumrainey td: Magherafelt LY 6; 102, 112

Drumrainy td: Magheracross FH 14; 102

Drumramer td: Drumachose LY 9; 58, 87, 96–97, 101, 110, 118, 133

Drumrammer locality: Carrickfergus AM 37; 93

Drumrane td: Tamlaght Finlagan LY 25; 65, 93, 110

Drumrankin (Drumranklin) td: Ahoghill AM 23; 13, 39

Drumrankin cave: Ahoghill AM 23; 35

Drumrankin corn mill: Ahoghill AM 23; 13

Drumrankin cove: Loughguile AM 13; 70–71

Drumrankin td: Loughguile AM 13; 71, 74

Drumrat House: Donegal DL 39; 56

Drumrath ph: Donacavey TE 5; 66

Drumraw (see Drumra): Drumbo DN 7; 61

Drumraw bog: Ahoghill AM 23; 28

Drumraw fort [I]: Ahoghill AM 23; 34–35

Drumraw fort [II]: Ahoghill AM 23; 34–35

Drumraw fort [III]: Ahoghill AM 23; 34

Drumraw moss: Ahoghill AM 23; 34

Drumraw school: Tartaraghan AH 1; 122

Drumraw td: Devenish FH 14; 58

Drumrawn Lodge: Longfield TE 5; 131, 133

Drumraymond (Dunraymond) td: Duneane AM 19; 95, 100, 117–18

Drumraymond bog: Duneane AM 19; 111

Drumraymond Cottage (see Raymond)

Drumreagh (see Drumragh): Ardstraw TE 5; 10

Drumreagh Etra quarries: Tullyniskan TE 20; 141

Drumreagh Etra td: Tullyniskan TE 20; 141

Drumreagh graveyard: Killinchy DN 7; 91

Drumreagh Otra spade manufactory: Tullyniskan TE 20; 139

Drumreagh td: Errigal LY 27; 53

Drumreagh td: Kilbroney DN 3; 32

Drumreagh td: Killinchy DN 7; 86, 91

Drumrearty td: Galloon FH 4; 95

Drumreaver House: Killanny MN 40; 133

Drumreaver school [I]: Killanny MN 40; 135

Drumreaver school [II]: Killanny MN 40; 135
Drumrollagh td: Galloon FH 4; 95
Drumroosk td: Aghalurcher FH 4; 3
Drumrot fort [I]: Lissan LY 31; 100
Drumrot fort [II]: Lissan LY 31; 100
Drumrot td: Lissan LY 31; 108
Drumrughill school: Ematris MN 40; 117
Drumrughill td: Ematris MN 40; 113, 116
Drumsallagh monastery: Aghaderg DN 12; 7
Drumsallagh td: Aghaderg DN 12; 2, 7
Drumsallagh td: Cleenish FH 14; 29
Drumsallin river: Muff DL 38; 80
Drumsamney fort: Kilcronaghan LY 31; 86
Drumsamney td: Kilcronaghan LY 31; 84, 112, 142
Drumsara (see Drumsaragh)
Drumsaragh (Drumsarragh) td: Tamlaght O'Crilly
  LY 18; 97, 119, 136, 138, 144
Drumsaragh bogs: Tamlaght O'Crilly LY 18; 86,
  116, 126
Drumsaragh school: Tamlaght O'Crilly LY 18; 140
Drumsaragh Sunday school: Tamlaght O'Crilly LY
  18; 143
Drumsarrah (see Drumsaragh)
Drumsastry td: Galloon FH 4; 95
Drumsaul lough: Ematris MN 40; 112
Drumsaul td: Ematris MN 40; 116, 116
Drumscillen td: Muff DL 38; 80
Drumscollop fort: Devenish FH 14; 55
Drumscollop td: Devenish FH 14; 58
Drumscor mill: Tydavnet MN 40; 173
Drumsesk House: Kilbroney DN 3; 35
Drumsesk td: Kilbroney DN 3; 32
Drumshaghs school: Ballymoney AM 16; 26
Drumshanbo bridge: Ardstraw TE 5; 14
Drumshanbo td: Kildress TE 20; 59
Drumshanbow (see Drumshanbo)
Drumshanely corn mill: Drumragh TE 5; 110
Drumshanely td: Drumragh TE 5; 110
Drumshanes td: Derryvullan FH 14; 38
Drumsheal td: Dromore TE 5; 98
Drumsheare td: Tydavnet MN 40; 169
Drumsheel lough: Killdrumsherdan CN 40; 31
Drumshellan (see Drumskellan): Muff DL 38; 80
Drumshill (see Drumsill): Blaris DN 12; 42
Drumshreve hill: Drung CN 40; 19
Drumshroel brickfield: Killesher FH 14; 84
Drumshroel td: Killesher FH 14; 87
Drumsill fort [I]: Magheragall AM 21; 106
Drumsill fort [II]: Magheragall AM 21; 106
Drumsill td: Blaris DN 12; 42
Drumsill td: Magheragall AM 21; 109
Drumsillagh corn mill: Killdrumsherdan CN 40; 34
Drumsillagh td: Cleenish FH 14; 28
Drumskea td: Ballymoney AM 16; 21
Drumskee corn mill: Dromore DN 12; 72

Drumskee td: Dromore DN 12; 70, 72–73, 78
Drumskellan td: Lough Swilly DL 38; 138
Drumskellan td: Muff DL 38; 80
Drumskellen (see Drumskellan)
Drumskelt td: Aughnamullen MN 40; 76
Drumskimbly td: Inishmacsaint FH 14; 75
Drumskiny hill: Dromore TE 5; 93
Drumskiny lough: Dromore TE 5; 95
Drumskiny td: Dromore TE 5; 98
Drumslade fort: Ballyaghran LY 33; 11, 24
Drumslade td: Ballyaghran LY 33; 27–28
Drumsladhe park: Errigal LY 27; 44, 74
Drumslieve (Drumslave) td: Banagher LY 30; 22,
  53, 57, 62, 86–87, 91, 98, 100, 113
Drumslieve bog: Banagher LY 30; 87
Drumslieve hamlet: Banagher LY 30; 27, 31,
  108–10
Drumslieve rock: Banagher LY 30; 88
Drumsloe chapel: Drummully FH 4; 35
Drumsloe lough: Magheracross FH 14; 92
Drumsloe school: Drummully FH 4; 39
Drumsloe td: Drummully FH 4; 35, 39
Drumsna td: Rossorry FH 14; 115
Drumsnade td: Magheradrool DN 17; 99, 104
Drumsnat ph: Clogher TE 5; 40
Drumsnat ph: Clones FH 4; 26
Drumsnat ph: Drummully FH 4; 34
Drumsnat ph: Emlaghfad SO 40; 177, 181
Drumsnat ph: Galloon FH 4; 95
Drumsnat ph: Tydavnet MN 40; 169
Drumsnatt (see Drumsnat)
Drumsoards chapel: Clones FH 4; 28
Drumsoards td: Clones FH 4; 28
Drumsonnis hill: Magheracross FH 14; 91
Drumsonus corn mill: Kilskeery TE 5; 114
Drumsonus td: Kilskeery TE 5; 114
Drumsough cove: Drummaul AM 19; 66
Drumsough forts: Drummaul AM 19; 78, 88
Drumsough school: Drummaul AM 19; 75, 77
Drumsough Sunday school: Drummaul AM 19; 77
Drumsough td: Drummaul AM 19; 40, 85, 90
Drumsruhil td: Cleenish FH 14; 28–29
Drumsteeple quarry: Agivey LY 22; 43
Drumsteeple stonehenge: Aghadowey LY 22; 28, 32
Drumsteeple td: Aghadowey LY 22; 31, 33–35
Drumstor td: Magheracross FH 14; 102
Drumsurn bridge: Balteagh LY 9; 42
Drumsurn fort: Balteagh LY 9; 29
Drumsurn hamlet: Bovevagh LY 25; 21
Drumsurn hill: Balteagh LY 9; 35
Drumsurn Lower bridge: Balteagh LY 9; 5
Drumsurn Lower chapel: Balteagh LY 9; 3, 41
Drumsurn Lower school: Balteagh LY 9; 17
Drumsurn Lower td: Balteagh LY 9; 3, 10–11, 17,
  39, 45

Drumsurn school: Balteagh LY 9; 16, 18, 38

Drumsurn td: Balteagh LY 9; 18, 29, 35–36, 38, 41, 44

Drumsurn td: Dungiven LY 15; 96

Drumsurn Upper giant's grave: Balteagh LY 9; 7, 35

Drumsurn Upper giant's mill: Balteagh LY 9; 11, 35

Drumsurn Upper td: Balteagh LY 9; 7, 9, 11, 30, 36, 39, 45

Drumtullagh carn: Drumtullagh AM 16; 102

Drumtullagh ph: Armoy AM 24; 1–2

Drumtullagh ph: Ballintoy AM 24; 10, 12–13

Drumtullagh ph: Billy AM 16; 36, 38

Drumtullagh ph: Derrykeighan AM 16; 80

Drumtullagh ph: Misc. AM 10; 129

Drumtullagh ph: Ramoan AM 24; 86, 91

Drumtullagh ph: Templepatrick AM 35; 150

Drumuck (see Drummuck): Maghera LY 18; 35

Drumucklagh td: Misc. DL 39; 195

Drumulla (see Drummulla): Ematris MN 40; 115

Drumurcher clothier's mill: Currin MN 40; 90

Drumurcher hill: Currin MN 40; 86

Drumurcher td: Currin MN 40; 91

Drumurchur (see Drumurcher): Currin MN 40; 86

Drumwardin td: Misc. DN 17; 122

Drumwhinny brickworks: Magheraculmoney FH 14; 108

Drumwhisker td: Donacavey TE 5; 76, 78, 80–82, 85

Drumyale (see Drumgole): Ematris MN 40; 113

Drung church: Drung CN 40; 21

Drung druid's altar: Moville DL 38; 74

Drung ph: Killdrumsherdan CN 40; 31

Drung ph: Laragh CN 40; 39–40

Drung school: Drung CN 40; 22

Drung school: Moville DL 38; 74

Drung stream: Moville DL 38; 78

Drung td: Moville DL 38; 73, 75

Drung waterfall: Moville DL 38; 78–79

Drungesh td: Balteagh LY 9; 40

Drunkendult td: Ballymoney AM 16; 5

Drunnick school: Racavan AM 13; 100

Drunnick td: Racavan AM 13; 100

Drury, John: Misc. SO 40; 199

Drutainy school: Drumgoon CN 40; 11

Dryburgh (Scotland): Carrickfergus AM 37; 79

Dryburgh abbey: Carnmoney AM 2; 64

Drymen (Scotland): Kilroot AM 26; 73

Drymen: Templecorran AM 26; 97, 107

Duaderney td: Rossorry FH 14; 116

Duanan (see Doonan): Killymard DL 39; 95

Duanrach Loch Beag: Templecarn DL 39; 156

Duanrach lough: Templecarn DL 39; 156

Duanrach Lough Minagh: Templecarn DL 39; 156

Duanrack (see Duanrach): Templecarn DL 39; 156

Dubhbeag lough: Templecarn DL 39; 157

Dubhleach lough: Clondavaddog DL 38; 3

Dubhmor lough: Templecarn DL 39; 157

Dublin: Aghabog MN 40; 64

Dublin: Aghadowey LY 22; 12, 23, 33

Dublin: Aghaloo TE 20; 3

Dublin: Aghalurcher FH 4; 5–6, 8, 13, 15

Dublin: Aghanloo LY 11; 38

Dublin: Antrim AM 29; 5, 9, 18, 27

Dublin: Ardglass DN 17; 6–7, 10–11

Dublin: Ardstraw TE 5; 9

Dublin: Aughnamullen MN 40; 76

Dublin: Ballee DN 17; 19

Dublin: Ballinderry AM 21; 44

Dublin: Ballinderry TE 20; 13

Dublin: Ballyaghran LY 33; 5, 27

Dublin: Ballybay MN 40; 80

Dublin: Ballymore AH 1; 8

Dublin: Ballynure AM 32; 39, 56, 64

Dublin: Ballyscullion AM 19; 8

Dublin: Ballywillin LY 33; 29, 33, 42

Dublin: Banagher LY 30; 19

Dublin: Blaris AM 8; 8, 16, 50, 84, 89

Dublin: Carnmoney AM 2; 39

Dublin: Carnteel TE 20; 22–24

Dublin: Carrickfergus AM 37; 10, 36, 38, 45, 68, 137, 155, 160, 178

Dublin: Clogher TE 5; 33

Dublin: Clogherny TE 20; 27

Dublin: Clondermot LY 34; 6–8, 12, 22, 27, 34, 52–53, 119–20

Dublin: Clones FH 4; 27

Dublin: Clonfeacle AH 1; 22, 24

Dublin: Clonleigh DL 39; 16

Dublin: Clonoe TE 20; 30

Dublin: Coleraine LY 33; 64, 80, 84, 86, 119, 143

Dublin: Comber DN 7; 37

Dublin: Convoy DL 39; 18

Dublin: Cumber LY 28; 15, 49–50, 58

Dublin: Derryaghy AM 8; 114

Dublin: Desertlyn LY 31; 41

Dublin: Doagh AM 29; 67, 82, 94, 96

Dublin: Donaghenry TE 20; 37–38

Dublin: Donaghmore DL 39; 33

Dublin: Donaghmoyne MN 40; 107

Dublin: Donegore AM 29; 129

Dublin: Down DN 17; 47, 58

Dublin: Drumachose LY 9; 93

Dublin: Drumballyroney DN 3; 18

Dublin: Drumbeg AM 8; 127

Dublin: Drumcree AH 1; 30, 35, 38–39

Dublin: Drumglass TE 20; 40, 43

Dublin: Drumgooland DN 3; 22

Dublin: Drumgoon CN 40; 4, 7, 10

Dublin: Drumhome DL 39; 60

Dublin: Drummaul AM 19; 46, 70, 81

Dublin: Drumragh TE 5; 109
Dublin: Duneane AM 19; 99
Dublin: Dungiven LY 15; 109
Dublin: Ematris MN 40; 115
Dublin: Emlaghfad SO 40; 178
Dublin: Enniskeen CN 40; 26
Dublin: Enniskillen FH 4; 46, 83
Dublin: Errigal Keerogue TE 20; 47, 53, 55
Dublin: Glenavy AM 21; 81, 85
Dublin: Inishargy DN 7; 85
Dublin: Keady AH 1; 47
Dublin: Kilbroney DN 3; 31, 34–35
Dublin: Kilcronaghan LY 31; 83
Dublin: Kilkeel DN 3; 48
Dublin: Killead AM 35; 17, 35, 42
Dublin: Killowen LY 33; 160, 168
Dublin: Killyleagh DN 17; 85
Dublin: Killymard DL 39; 99, 109
Dublin: Kilmegan DN 3; 59–60
Dublin: Kilmore AH 1; 62
Dublin: Kilmore DN 17; 90
Dublin: Kirkinriola AM 23; 102
Dublin: Lambeg AM 8; 136
Dublin: Lissan LY 31; 100
Dublin: Lough Swilly DL 38; 118
Dublin: Loughgilly AH 1; 84
Dublin: Maghera LY 18; 2, 4, 8–9, 35, 69, 71
Dublin: Magheramesk AM 21; 119–20
Dublin: Magheross MN 40; 146, 151–52, 157
Dublin: Magilligan LY 11; 121
Dublin: Manorhamilton Union LM 40; 50
Dublin: Mevagh DL 38; 61, 63
Dublin: Misc. LY 36; 103
Dublin: Muckno MN 40; 164
Dublin: Mullaghbrack AH 1; 94, 96
Dublin: Newry DN 3; 61, 67, 74, 78, 84–85, 87,
    93–94
Dublin: Ramoan AM 24; 95, 123
Dublin: Raymoghy DL 39; 140
Dublin: Seapatrick DN 12; 133
Dublin: Shankill AH 1; 111
Dublin: Tamlaght Finlagan LY 25; 105
Dublin: Templecorran AM 26; 93, 101, 117–18, 128
Dublin: Templepatrick AM 35; 109
Dublin: Tickmacrevan AM 13; 129
Dublin: Tomregan FH 4; 132
Dublin: Tullyniskan TE 20; 140
Dublin: Tynan AH 1; 125–27
Dublin: Urney DL 39; 177
Dublin: Warrenpoint DN 3; 119
Dublin bay: Drummaul AM 19; 70
Dublin bay: Newry DN 3; 86
Dublin bridge: Newry DN 3; 70, 86, 90
Dublin Capel St meeting house: Donegore AM 29;
    129

Dublin Castle: Blaris AM 8; 71, 76
Dublin Castle: Clondermot LY 34; 45
Dublin Castle: Clonleigh DL 39; 15
Dublin Castle: Kilraghts AM 16; 128
Dublin county: Ballynascreen LY 31; 33
Dublin county: Cumber LY 28; 18
Dublin county: Drumlumman CN 40; 16
Dublin county: Faughanvale LY 36; 44
Dublin linen hall: Drumgoon CN 40; 9
Dublin linen hall: Emlaghfad SO 40; 180
Dublin museum: Ballyaghran LY 33; 23
Dublin museum: Culfeightrin AM 24; 53
Dublin museum: Kilcronaghan LY 31; 69, 86
Dublin museum: Misc. LY 31; 117
Dublin North Hall: Clondavaddog DL 38; 4
Dublin school: Kilrea LY 27; 116
Dubourdieu, family: Blaris DN 12; 30
Dubourdieu, family: Magheragall AM 21; 107
Dubourdieu, Mr: Misc. AM 10; 130
Dubourdieu, Rev. John: Camlin AM 21; 62
Dubourdieu, Rev. John: Coleraine LY 33; 100
Dubourdieu, Rev. John: Drumballyroney DN 3; 10,
    13, 15, 18
Dubourdieu, Rev. John: Drumgooland DN 3; 22
Dubourdieu, Rev. Saumarez: Blaris AM 8; 8, 25, 39
Dubourdieu, Rev. Saumarez: Lambeg AM 8; 135
Dubourdieu, Shem (Jnr): Magheragall AM 21; 107
Dubourdieu, Shem (Snr): Magheragall AM 21; 107
Ducart, engineer: Clonoe TE 20; 30
Ducart, engineer: Drumglass TE 20; 43
Ducassan (see Doocassan): Drung CN 40; 21
Duchall, Rev.: Antrim AM 29; 27
Duck Island: Glenavy AM 21; 83
Ducking Pool locality: Drumachose LY 9; 83
Duddly, family: Misc. LY 36; 104
Duddy, Peter: Clondermot LY 34; 78
Duddy's hill: Banagher LY 30; 24–25
Duff lough: Carncastle and Killyglen AM 10; 1
Duff, D.: Drumglass TE 20; 42
Duff, Eliza Maria: Newry DN 3; 80
Duff, family: Carrickfergus AM 37; 174
Duff, family: Dunluce AM 16; 117
Duff, James: Tamlaght TE 20; 129
Duff, Robert: Tamlaght TE 20; 115
Duff, Samuel: Comber DN 7; 40–41
Duff, Samuel: Dundonald DN 7; 65
Duff, Samuel: Island Magee AM 10; 103
Duff, Samuel: Kilmood DN 7; 95
Duff, Thomas: Shilvodan AM 19; 137
Duff, Thomas: Tamlaght TE 20; 74, 106, 115, 123
Duff, Thomas: Warrenpoint DN 3; 115
Duff, Walter: Tamlaght TE 20; 74–75, 103, 128
Duff's hill: Carrickfergus AM 37; 93, 174
Duff's hill quarry: Carrickfergus AM 37; 50, 170
Duffclughathawla district: Kilmacteige SO 40; 189

Duffen, William: Muckamore AM 35; 81
Dufferin barony: Holywood DN 7; 80
Dufferin barony: Killinchy DN 7; 86–87
Dufferin barony: Misc. DN 17; 116
Dufferin, family: Killinchy DN 7; 90
Dufferin, Lady: Killyleagh DN 17; 82
Dufferin, Lord: Bangor DN 7; 22–23, 25
Dufferin, Lord: Comber DN 7; 37, 40
Dufferin, Lord: Connor AM 19; 18
Dufferin, Lord: Grey Abbey DN 7; 70–71
Dufferin, Lord: Killinchy DN 7; 92
Dufferin, Lord: Killyleagh DN 17; 80, 82–83
Dufferin, Lord: Newtownards DN 7; 106
Duffield, W.: Magheradrool DN 17; 102
Duffin, Catherine: Ahoghill AM 23; 38
Duffin, Cormick: Skerry AM 13; 121
Duffin, Edward: Ballyscullion AM 19; 9
Duffin, Edward: Skerry AM 13; 118, 121
Duffin, Ellen: Carrickfergus AM 37; 118
Duffin, family: Skerry AM 13; 115
Duffin, John: Artrea LY 6; 31
Duffin, John: Ballyclug AM 23; 64
Duffin, John: Skerry AM 13; 121
Duffin, Margaret: Ahoghill AM 23; 38
Duffin, Margaret: Ballyscullion AM 19; 13, 15
Duffin, Neil: Skerry AM 13; 120–21
Duffin, Richard: Skerry AM 13; 121
Duffin, William: Ballyclug AM 23; 64
Duffy, Bernard: Tamlaght Finlagan LY 25; 111
Duffy, E.: Enniskillen FH 4; 59
Duffy, family: Ballynascreen LY 31; 12
Duffy, family: Killesher FH 14; 84
Duffy, John: Tydavnet MN 40; 173
Duffy, Malchia: Killead AM 35; 53
Duffy, man named: Kilbroney DN 3; 37
Duffy, Patrick: Ballynascreen LY 31; 13, 21
Duffy, Peter: Misc. LY 31; 140
Duffy, Rev. James: Muckno MN 40; 165
Duffy, Rev. Peter: Tydavnet MN 40; 172
Duffy, Thomas: Coleraine LY 33; 146
Dugall, family: Culfeightrin AM 24; 59
Dugan, family: Killelagh LY 27; 99
Dugan, family: Macosquin LY 22; 90
Dugan, George: Blaris DN 12; 46
Dugan, Hugh: Killinchy DN 7; 92
Dugan, Isaac: Dunboe LY 11; 79
Dugan, James: Dunboe LY 11; 62–65, 67, 69, 71,
   79–80
Dugan, John: Hillsborough DN 12; 106
Dugan, John: Lissan LY 31; 110
Dugan, Mr: Kirkinriola AM 23; 119
Dugan, Patrick: Maghera LY 18; 59–60
Dugan, Thomas: Blaris DN 12; 46
Dugan, William: Down DN 17; 59
Dugan, William: Magherally DN 12; 116

Dugan's library: Kirkinriola AM 23; 98
Duggan, Charles: Tamlaght O'Crilly LY 18; 127
Duggan, William: Macosquin LY 22; 107
Dugh lough: Clondavaddog DL 38; 2–3
Dugh lough: Garvaghy DN 12; 79–80
Dughan, James: Magilligan LY 11; 132
Dughery td: Seapatrick DN 12; 123–24, 126
Dughglass Island: Lough Swilly DL 38; 111
Dughglass rock: Lough Swilly DL 38; 111, 113
Duglas, Mrs A.: Drumgoon CN 40; 11
Duglas, Rev. A.: Drumgoon CN 40; 3–4, 6, 8–9, 11
Duglen td: Dromara DN 12; 65
Duhatty (see Doohatty): Magheross MN 40; 143
Duin fort: Ballintoy AM 24; 33
Duin fort: Drumachose LY 9; 58
Duin Meve well: Artrea LY 6; 9, 34
Duinaneeny bridge: Ramoan AM 24; 122
Duinaneeny Castle: Culfeightrin AM 24; 54, 69
Duinaneeny Castle: Ramoan AM 24; 90, 106,
   119–20, 122–23
Duinas (see Hass): Dungiven LY 15; 47
Duin-aworry caves: Culfeightrin AM 24; 84
Duin-aworry fort: Culfeightrin AM 24; 84
Duinbuy battery: Ballintoy AM 24; 20
Duinbuy caves: Ballintoy AM 24; 20
Duinbuy fort: Ballintoy AM 24; 20
Duineeny (see Duinaneeny): Ramoan AM 24; 106
Duinknowe (see Dunmore fort): Drumachose LY 9;
   83
Duinmore fort: Culfeightrin AM 24; 72
Duinn rock: Bovevagh LY 25; 8, 17, 19, 41
Duinn rock fort: Bovevagh LY 25; 10–11
Duinnagregor Castle: Ramoan AM 24; 119–20
Duinnagregor Head: Ramoan AM 24; 119–20
Duinnamallaght fort: Culfeightrin AM 24; 76
Duinnamallaght fort: Ramoan AM 24; 91, 124
Duinnamallaght hill: Culfeightrin AM 24; 64
Duinnas (see Carn td): Dungiven LY 15; 83
Duke, family: Blaris AM 8; 21
Duke, Henry: Clones FH 4; 29
Duke, Mary: Clones FH 4; 29
Dukey, John: Hillsborough DN 12; 106
Dullaghan bog: Dromore TE 5; 93
Dullaghan mountain: Dromore TE 5; 93
Dullaghan td: Dromore TE 5; 93, 95, 98
Dullaghy bog: Desertoghill LY 27; 17, 24
Dullaghy bridge: Desertoghill LY 27; 3, 16, 28
Dullaghy fort [I]: Desertoghill LY 27; 24
Dullaghy fort [II]: Desertoghill LY 27; 24
Dullaghy giant's stone: Desertoghill LY 27; 31
Dullaghy stream: Desertoghill LY 27; 16
Dullaghy td: Desertoghill LY 27; 1, 14, 16, 19–21,
   29, 31–32
Dullahan (see Dullaghan)
Dullerton hill: Donaghedy TE 5; 88

Dullyaghy (see Dullaghy): Desertoghill LY 27; 1

Dulrush fort: Belleek FH 14; 4

Dulrush td: Belleek FH 14; 4

Dulse cove: Island Magee AM 10; 101

Dulybeg (see Drummard): Derryvullan FH 14; 46

Dumbarton (Scotland): Antrim AM 29; 8

Dumbo td: Duneane AM 19; 94

Dumbrack (see Dunbrock): Tamlaght Finlagan LY 25; 115

Dun Cruithen (see Duncrun): Magilligan LY 11; 105, 117

Dun Patrick fort: Magilligan LY 11; 92

Dun river: Layd AM 13; 38

Dun, Thomas: Kilmacteige SO 40; 193

Dunaan graveyard: Desertoghill LY 27; 25

Dunaan hill: Desertoghill LY 27; 7

Dunabane chapel: Carnteel TE 20; 23

Dunadry: Nilteen AM 35; 85, 88–89, 94, 100, 102–03

Dunadry: Templepatrick AM 35; 110, 131, 144

Dunadry: Umgall AM 35; 160

Dunadry bawn: Nilteen AM 35; 85–86

Dunadry bridge: Nilteen AM 35; 85, 89–90, 101, 103

Dunadry bridge: Templepatrick AM 35; 111, 115

Dunadry church: Nilteen AM 35; 86, 89, 94

Dunadry flax mill: Nilteen AM 35; 86, 90, 102–03

Dunadry fort: Nilteen AM 35; 89, 94, 97–98, 100

Dunadry graveyard: Nilteen AM 35; 89, 94

Dunadry paper mill: Nilteen AM 35; 85–86, 89, 92, 100, 102–03

Dunadry td: Nilteen AM 35; 84, 88, 97, 99, 101

Dunady td: Cumber LY 28; 30, 66, 69, 111–12, 117–18, 122, 125

Dunady wood: Cumber LY 28; 117–18

Dunaff bay: Lough Swilly DL 38; 98, 100, 131, 142

Dunaff fort: Clonmany DL 38; 16

Dunaff Head: Clonmany DL 38; 13, 16, 19

Dunaff Head: Lough Swilly DL 38; 98, 131, 136

Dunaff td: Clonmany DL 38; 18, 20

Dunaff td: Lough Swilly DL 38; 133

Dunaghy church: Dunaghy AM 13; 13

Dunaghy fort: Dunaghy AM 13; 18–19, 24, 28

Dunaghy Glebe House: Dunaghy AM 13; 13

Dunaghy ph: Ardclinis AM 13; 1

Dunaghy ph: Dundermot AM 13; 29

Dunaghy ph: Finvoy AM 23; 72

Dunaghy ph: Killagan AM 23; 79–81

Dunaghy ph: Killead AM 35; 27

Dunaghy ph: Kirkinriola AM 23; 88, 93, 115, 126

Dunaghy ph: Layd AM 13; 36

Dunaghy ph: Loughguile AM 13; 58, 60

Dunaghy ph: Newtown Crommelin AM 13; 78

Dunaghy ph: Rasharkin AM 23; 132, 138

Dunaghy ph: Skerry AM 13; 105

Dunaghy standing stones: Dunaghy AM 13; 19

Dunaghy Sunday school: Dunaghy AM 13; 16

Dunaghy td: Ballymoney AM 16; 21, 25

Dunaird (Dunnaird) td: Racavan AM 13; 86, 88, 99

Dunaird flax mills: Racavan AM 13; 92, 99

Dunaird td: Racavan AM 13; 99

Dunalis coves: Dunboe LY 11; 50–51, 75, 79

Dunalis fort: Dunboe LY 11; 50, 76

Dunalis standing stone: Dunboe LY 11; 76

Dunalis td: Dunboe LY 11; 75

Dunalis Upper forts: Dunboe LY 11; 49–50

Dunalis Upper td: Dunboe LY 11; 49

Dunallis (see Dunalis):

Dunally td: Clonmany DL 38; 18

Dunalong creek: Killea and Taughboyne DL 39; 84

Dunalong ferry: Misc. DL 39; 189

Dunamoney fort: Magherafelt LY 6; 93, 111

Dunamoney old windmill: Magherafelt LY 6; 111

Dunamoney td: Magherafelt LY 6; 79, 93, 95, 111

Dunamoy corn mill: Rashee AM 32; 136–37

Dunamoy moat: Kilbride AM 29; 148

Dunamuggy cove: Donegore AM 29; 127–28

Dunamuggy fort: Donegore AM 29; 121, 123, 127–28

Dunamuggy meeting house: Donegore AM 29; 104, 108, 111, 129–30, 132–33

Dunamuggy school: Donegore AM 29; 104, 126, 133–34

Dunamuggy td: Donegore AM 29; 101

Dunamuggy tumulus: Donegore AM 29; 123, 127

Dunan, John: Templecorran AM 26; 125

Dunanelly (see Dunnanelly): Inch DN 17; 76

Dunanney (Duneaney) td: Carnmoney AM 2; 34, 71, 81, 92, 102

Dunanney corn mill: Carnmoney AM 2; 49

Dunanney coves: Carnmoney AM 2; 71

Dunanney fort [I] (see Nancey's fort): Carnmoney AM 2; 35

Dunanney fort [II]: Carnmoney AM 2; 101

Dunanney fort [III]: Carnmoney AM 2; 101

Dunaree lough: Donaghmoyne MN 40; 106

Dunargus Head: Lough Swilly DL 38; 107, 134

Dunarnon fort: Magherafelt LY 6; 93, 108

Dunarnon td: Magherafelt LY 6; 81, 93, 95, 108

Dunavally pottery: Loughgall AH 1; 80

Dunavally td: Loughgall AH 1; 76, 80

Dunavenny (see Dunnavenny): Errigal LY 27; 41

Dunaverny bog: Ballymoney AM 16; 25

Dunaverny td: Ballymoney AM 16; 21, 25

Dunawley td: Donaghadee DN 7; 45

Dunbane fort: Banagher LY 30; 92

Dunbar and Drumraw manor: Misc. FH 4; 133

Dunbar and Stewart, Messrs: Seapatrick DN 12; 126–27

Dunbar and Stewart, Messrs: Tullylish DN 12; 147

Dunbar manor: Inishmacsaint FH 14; 79

Dunbar, Alexander: Enniskillen FH 4; 57

Dunbar, family: Inishmacsaint FH 14; 75

Dunbar, George (ne Orr): Kilrea LY 27; 110

Dunbar, George: Aghadowey LY 22; 7

Dunbar, J.G.: Carnmoney AM 2; 89

Dunbar, J.G.: Donaghadee DN 7; 46

Dunbar, J.G.: Loughgilly AH 1; 84

Dunbar, Jane: Kilrea LY 27; 129

Dunbar, Margaret: Kilrea LY 27; 129

Dunbar, Mary (Jnr): Kilrea LY 27; 129

Dunbar, Mary (Snr): Kilrea LY 27; 129

Dunbar, Mary: Island Magee AM 10; 66, 94–95

Dunbar, Mary [I]: Kilrea LY 27; 129

Dunbar, Mr (Belfast): Ballymore AH 1; 16

Dunbar, Mr: Clogher TE 5; 41

Dunbar, Mr: Seapatrick DN 12; 125

Dunbar, Mrs: Island Magee AM 10; 34, 87

Dunbar, Rev.: Island Magee AM 10; 34, 87

Dunbar, Rev. John: Rasharkin AM 23; 136, 140

Dunbar, Thomas: Donacavey TE 5; 65

Dunbarron locality: Faughanvale LY 36; 54

Dunbeg (Duinn Beg) td: Drumachose LY 9; 87, 96–97, 111, 134

Dunbeg giant's houses: Drumachose LY 9; 111–12

Dunbeg hill: Drumachose LY 9; 111

Dunbeg lough: Dromara DN 12; 66

Dunbeg Lower td: Dromara DN 12; 62–63, 65

Dunbeg Upper td: Dromara DN 12; 65

Dunbiggan church: Clogher TE 5; 45

Dunbiggan Glebe House: Clogher TE 5; 45

Dunbiggan td: Clogher TE 5; 32, 36, 45, 53

Dunbiggen (see Dunbiggan)

Dunbiggin (see Dunbiggan)

Dunblesque (Munster): Tamlaght Finlagan LY 25; 102

Dunbo (see Downhill td): Dunboe LY 11; 58

Dunboe church: Dunboe LY 11; 44

Dunboe cove: Misc. LY 36; 117

Dunboe female school: Dunboe LY 11; 55, 69

Dunboe flax mill: Dunboe LY 11; 58

Dunboe Glebe House: Dunboe LY 11; 46, 53, 58, 61, 80

Dunboe meeting house: Dunboe LY 11; 44

Dunboe meeting house: Magilligan LY 11; 125

Dunboe old church: Dunboe LY 11; 47–49, 80

Dunboe ph: Aghadowey LY 22; 18

Dunboe ph: Aghanloo LY 11; 5, 7

Dunboe ph: Ballyrashane LY 22; 50

Dunboe ph: Coleraine LY 33; 73, 104, 120, 142, 144

Dunboe ph: Drumachose LY 9; 90

Dunboe ph: Killowen LY 33; 161, 164, 170

Dunboe ph: Lough Swilly DL 38; 137

Dunboe ph: Macosquin LY 22; 76, 82, 84, 90, 116

Dunboe ph: Magilligan LY 11; 97, 100, 105, 107, 143, 146

Dunboe ph: Misc. LY 36; 110

Dunboe ph: Misc. TE 5; 146

Dunboe school: Dunboe LY 11; 55, 69

Dunboe strand cave: Dunboe LY 11; 77

Dunboe td: Clondermot LY 34; 71

Dunbought fort: Dunaghy AM 13; 20

Dunbrock bog: Tamlaght Finlagan LY 25; 115

Dunbrock hill: Tamlaght Finlagan LY 25; 62

Dunbrock school: Tamlaght Finlagan LY 25; 96, 124

Dunbrock Sunday school: Tamlaght Finlagan LY 25; 96

Dunbrock td: Tamlaght Finlagan LY 25; 72–74, 93

Dunbulkin (see Drumbulkin): Rasharkin AM 23; 133

Dunbunrawer td: Ardstraw TE 5; 4

Duncan, Andrew: Loughguile AM 13; 72, 74

Duncan, Dr: Carrickfergus AM 37; 136

Duncan, family: Artrea LY 6; 14

Duncan, family: Culfeightrin AM 24; 59

Duncan, family: Derryaghy AM 8; 103

Duncan, family: Kilwaughter AM 10; 115

Duncan, family: Magherafelt LY 6; 95

Duncan, family: Ramoan AM 24; 107

Duncan, George: Blaris AM 8; 55, 84

Duncan, George: Blaris DN 12; 46, 50

Duncan, Isabella: Magherafelt LY 6; 112

Duncan, James: Ballywillin LY 33; 51

Duncan, James: Duneane AM 19; 124

Duncan, John: Cranfield AM 19; 32

Duncan, John: Culfeightrin AM 24; 57–58, 74–75

Duncan, John: Drumachose LY 9; 66

Duncan, John: Raloo AM 32; 129

Duncan, Mary: Artrea LY 6; 24

Duncan, Mary: Tamlaght O'Crilly LY 18; 138

Duncan, Mr: Magherafelt LY 6; 84

Duncan, Mrs: Drumragh TE 5; 107

Duncan, Patrick: Cranfield AM 19; 32

Duncan, Rev.: Ardclinis AM 13; 4

Duncan, Rev. David: Ballyaghran LY 33; 10, 13, 23

Duncan, Rev. David: Misc. LY 36; 109

Duncan, Rev. William: Donaghcloney DN 12; 59

Duncan, Robert: Tamlaght O'Crilly LY 18; 138

Duncan, William: Carrickfergus AM 37; 102

Duncan, William: Newry DN 3; 100, 104

Duncan's bog: Ballycor AM 32; 2

Duncansland td: Kilbride AM 29; 136, 140

Duncarbit Burnt House: Culfeightrin AM 24; 68

Duncarbit Castle: Culfeightrin AM 24; 54, 68–69

Duncarbit fort [I]: Culfeightrin AM 24; 68

Duncarbit fort [II]: Culfeightrin AM 24; 82

Duncarbit td: Culfeightrin AM 24; 48, 79

Duncey Island: Killinchy DN 7; 86, 92

Duncey rock: Killinchy DN 7; 86

Dun-Chouchobhair fort: Balteagh LY 9; 19
Dunclug td: Kirkinriola AM 23; 88, 91
Duncrew (see Duncrue): Carrickfergus AM 37; 174
Duncrotagh locality: Lough Swilly DL 38; 147
Duncrue bridge: Carrickfergus AM 37; 140
Duncrue Castle: Carrickfergus AM 37; 182
Duncrue church: Carrickfergus AM 37; 4, 81, 132, 181–82
Duncrue cotton mill: Carrickfergus AM 37; 58, 139–40, 154
Duncrue fort: Carrickfergus AM 37; 4, 81, 84, 87, 93, 173–74, 182
Duncrue graveyard: Carrickfergus AM 37; 81, 181
Duncrue school: Carrickfergus AM 37; 155–56
Duncrue Sunday school: Carrickfergus AM 37; 156
Duncrue td: Carrickfergus AM 37; 93, 173–74
Duncruin (see Duncrun)
Duncrum (see Duncrun): Magilligan LY 11; 83
Duncrun (Duncreen) td: Magilligan LY 11; 83, 86, 90–92, 94–95, 101–02, 116–17, 126, 128–29, 134–37, 142–43
Duncrun abbey: Magilligan LY 11; 88–90, 117, 126, 129, 143, 145–46
Duncrun bleach green: Magilligan LY 11; 123
Duncrun bridge: Magilligan LY 11; 88, 124
Duncrun Castle: Magilligan LY 11; 90–91, 144
Duncrun caves: Magilligan LY 11; 92
Duncrun church: Magilligan LY 11; 105, 124, 129
Duncrun flax mill: Magilligan LY 11; 86, 123
Duncrun fort: Dungiven LY 15; 113
Duncrun forts: Magilligan LY 11; 91, 102, 127
Duncrun old church: Magilligan LY 11; 102, 129
Duncrun td: Aghanloo LY 11; 38
Duncruthen (see Duncrun): Magilligan LY 11; 143
Duncullian (see Dungullion): Faughanvale LY 36; 13
Duncy (see Duncey)
Dunda's weir: Enniskillen FH 4; 45, 80
Dundalk: Aughnamullen MN 40; 70–71, 75
Dundalk: Ballybay MN 40; 80, 83
Dundalk: Ballymascanlan LH 40; 55
Dundalk: Castletown LH 40; 61
Dundalk: Currin MN 40; 87, 90
Dundalk: Drumgath DN 3; 21
Dundalk: Drumgoon CN 40; 9–10
Dundalk: Ematris MN 40; 112
Dundalk: Inniskeen MN 40; 128
Dundalk: Killanny MN 40; 132, 134–35
Dundalk: Killyleagh DN 17; 85
Dundalk: Magheracloone MN 40; 141
Dundalk: Magheross MN 40; 144, 149, 152, 157
Dundalk: Misc. DN 17; 130
Dundalk: Muckno MN 40; 165–67
Dundalk: Newry DN 3; 63, 87, 106
Dundalk: Raloo AM 32; 93

Dundalk td: Ballymascanlan LH 40; 55
Dundalk turnpike: Magheross MN 40; 145–46
Dundalk Upper barony: Inniskeen MN 40; 124
Dundass, James: Misc. DN 17; 117
Dundee (Scotland): Lissan LY 31; 109
Dundee: Magherafelt LY 6; 86
Dundee td: Taughboyne DL 39; 148, 152, 195
Dundee, John: Ballylinny AM 32; 23, 29
Dunderg bleach green: Macosquin LY 22; 82, 103
Dunderg bog: Macosquin LY 22; 111
Dunderg bridge: Macosquin LY 22; 82, 103
Dunderg td: Macosquin LY 22; 85, 88, 108
Dundermot bridge: Dunaghy AM 13; 14
Dundermot bridge: Dundermot AM 13; 31
Dundermot bridge: Rasharkin AM 23; 131
Dundermot fort: Dunaghy AM 13; 28
Dundermot fort: Dundermot AM 13; 33–34
Dundermot ph: Ahoghill AM 23; 1, 4
Dundermot ph: Dunaghy AM 13; 20, 25
Dundermot ph: Finvoy AM 23; 68
Dundermot ph: Killagan AM 23; 79–81, 83
Dundermot ph: Kirkinriola AM 23; 88, 93, 115
Dundermot ph: Rasharkin AM 23; 127, 129
Dundermot td: Dundermot AM 13; 29, 33, 35
Dunderrin td: Donacavey TE 5; 77
Dundesert burn: Killead AM 35; 24, 27
Dundesert church: Carmavy AM 35; 2, 4
Dundesert church: Killead AM 35; 24–25, 27, 32, 35, 49
Dundesert fort [I]: Killead AM 35; 24, 32, 35
Dundesert fort [II]: Killead AM 35; 27, 39
Dundesert graveyard: Killead AM 35; 25, 49
Dundesert td: Killead AM 35; 40, 51
Dundevan td: Drumlumman CN 40; 17
Dundivin (Dundiven) td: Donacavey TE 5; 67–68, 72, 74, 76, 80–81
Dundivin forts: Donacavey TE 5; 84
Dundivin glebe: Donacavey TE 5; 76, 78
Dundivin Glebe House: Donacavey TE 5; 72
Dundivin Glebe td: Donacavey TE 5; 84–85
Dundoan (see Dundooan): Mevagh DL 38; 54
Dundonagh Glebe House: Donagh MN 40; 100
Dundonald: Comber DN 7; 41
Dundonald: Dundonald DN 7; 64
Dundonald: Holywood DN 7; 77
Dundonald: Misc. DN 17; 119, 121
Dundonald bleach green: Dundonald DN 7; 65
Dundonald church: Dundonald DN 7; 64, 66
Dundonald Glebe House: Dundonald DN 7; 65
Dundonald meeting house: Dundonald DN 7; 64
Dundonald mound: Dundonald DN 7; 65
Dundonald ph: Comber DN 7; 31
Dundonald ph: Holywood DN 7; 73, 80
Dundonald ph: Knockbreda DN 7; 97
Dundooan cave [I]: Coleraine LY 33; 92, 131

Dundooan cave [II]: Coleraine LY 33; 92, 131–32

Dundooan cave [III]: Coleraine LY 33; 92, 132–33

Dundooan corn mill: Coleraine LY 33; 91, 94, 128–29

Dundooan district: Lough Swilly DL 38; 128

Dundooan flax mill: Coleraine LY 33; 91, 94, 128–30

Dundooan fort [I]: Coleraine LY 33; 92, 94, 131

Dundooan fort [II]: Coleraine LY 33; 92, 131

Dundooan harbour: Lough Swilly DL 38; 115

Dundooan kiln: Coleraine LY 33; 92

Dundooan Lower td: Mevagh DL 38; 54, 63

Dundooan Point: Lough Swilly DL 38; 115

Dundooan rocks: Lough Swilly DL 38; 115–16

Dundooan td: Coleraine LY 33; 135, 145

Dundooan td: Mevagh DL 38; 56

Dundooan Upper td: Mevagh DL 38; 63

Dundressan td: Island Magee AM 10; 57–58, 76

Dundrod bridge: Tullyrusk AM 21; 133–35

Dundrod Castle: Ballinderry AM 21; 53

Dundrod corn mill: Tullyrusk AM 21; 134

Dundrod flax mill: Tullyrusk AM 21; 133–34

Dundrod forts: Tullyrusk AM 21; 139

Dundrod hamlet: Camlin AM 21; 67

Dundrod hamlet: Tullyrusk AM 21; 134–35

Dundrod meeting house: Tullyrusk AM 21; 132, 134, 136–37

Dundrod school [I]: Tullyrusk AM 21; 132, 138–39

Dundrod school [II]: Tullyrusk AM 21; 139

Dundrod td: Ballinderry AM 21; 53

Dundrod td: Tullyrusk AM 21; 131–32, 134

Dundrum: Ballywalter DN 7; 16

Dundrum: Bright DN 17; 33

Dundrum: Kilkeel DN 3; 54

Dundrum: Killyleagh DN 17; 87

Dundrum: Kilmegan DN 3; 57, 59–60

Dundrum bay: Drumgooland DN 3; 24

Dundrum bay: Kilcoo DN 3; 41

Dundrum bay: Kilmegan DN 3; 57

Dundrum bay: Saul DN 17; 113

Dundrum bleach mill: Keady AH 1; 47

Dundrum Castle: Kilmegan DN 3; 58–60

Dundrum corn mill: Keady AH 1; 50

Dundrum harbour: Down DN 17; 38, 41, 50

Dundrum harbour: Kilmegan DN 3; 55, 57, 59

Dundrum hotel: Kilmegan DN 3; 57

Dundrum pier: Kilmegan DN 3; 60

Dundrum school: Hillsborough DN 12; 101

Dundrum school: Kilmegan DN 3; 57

Dunduff's Fort td: Raymoghy DL 39; 137

Dunean Cloughog school: Duneane AM 19; 124–25

Duneane chapel: Duneane AM 19; 104, 111

Duneane chapels: Ballyscullion AM 19; 1, 6

Duneane church: Ballyscullion AM 19; 6

Duneane church: Duneane AM 19; 106–07, 113–16, 118, 125

Duneane corn mills: Duneane AM 19; 97, 113

Duneane forts: Duneane AM 19; 96, 108

Duneane graveyard: Duneane AM 19; 107

Duneane old graveyard: Duneane AM 19; 107

Duneane parish school: Duneane AM 19; 125

Duneane ph: Antrim AM 29; 7

Duneane ph: Ballynure AM 32; 67

Duneane ph: Ballyscullion AM 19; 1, 8, 10–11

Duneane ph: Drummaul AM 19; 33, 53, 56

Duneane ph: Duneane AM 19; 94

Duneane ph: Lough Neagh AM 21; 95

Duneane schools: Duneane AM 19; 102

Duneane td: Muckamore AM 35; 69

Duneany (Duneaney) td: Rasharkin AM 23; 138

Duneany (see Dunanney): Carnmoney AM 2; 49

Duneany cove: Rasharkin AM 23; 138

Duneany fort [I]: Rasharkin AM 23; 138

Duneany fort [II]: Rasharkin AM 23; 138

Duneany graveyard: Rasharkin AM 23; 136, 138

Duneany old church: Rasharkin AM 23; 136–37

Duneany standing stone: Rasharkin AM 23; 137, 139

Duneboe td: Donaghedy TE 5; 92

Dunegrannon td: Ballyscullion LY 6; 56

Duneight mill: Blaris DN 12; 36

Duneight school: Blaris DN 12; 34–35

Duneight td: Blaris DN 12; 34–36

Dunelty bog: Killanny MN 40; 130

Dunemana (see Dunnamanagh)

Dunemanna (see Dunnamanagh)

Dunfadden (see Dunnyvaden): Ballyclug AM 23; 55

Dunfanaghy: Lough Swilly DL 38; 119, 121

Dunfanaghy: Mevagh DL 38; 57, 62

Dunfanaghy bawn: Lough Swilly DL 38; 121

Dunfanaghy bay: Lough Swilly DL 38; 121

Dunfanaghy bridge: Lough Swilly DL 38; 121

Dunfanaghy harbour: Lough Swilly DL 38; 119

Dunfanaghy quarry: Lough Swilly DL 38; 121

Dung lough: Drumgoon CN 40; 3

Dung quarry: Drumgoon CN 40; 4

Dungall cove: Kirkinriola AM 23; 125

Dungall fort: Kirkinriola AM 23; 125

Dungall td: Kirkinriola AM 23; 91, 125

Dungallon fort: Ardclinis AM 13; 4, 7

Dungannon: Aghadowey LY 22; 33

Dungannon: Aghaloo TE 20; 1, 3–4

Dungannon: Agivey LY 22; 40

Dungannon: Ahoghill AM 23; 6

Dungannon: Artrea LY 6; 22

Dungannon: Ballynascreen LY 31; 33

Dungannon: Ballywillin LY 33; 30

Dungannon: Banagher LY 30; 19

Dungannon: Blaris AM 8; 16, 51

Dungannon: Carnteel TE 20; 21, 24
Dungannon: Clogherny TE 20; 27
Dungannon: Clondermot LY 34; 70
Dungannon: Clonfeacle AH 1; 24–25
Dungannon: Clonoe TE 20; 30–31
Dungannon: Coleraine LY 33; 89
Dungannon: Desertcreat TE 20; 32–34, 36
Dungannon: Desertlyn LY 31; 35, 37, 40–41
Dungannon: Doortoghill LY 27; 13
Dungannon: Donaghenry TE 20; 37–38
Dungannon: Drumcree AH 1; 28, 36
Dungannon: Drumglass TE 20; 40, 42–44
Dungannon: Drumragh TE 5; 111
Dungannon: Dungiven LY 15; 99
Dungannon: Errigal Keerogue TE 20; 49, 53
Dungannon: Errigal LY 27; 36, 39, 64
Dungannon: Kilcronaghan LY 31; 66, 83
Dungannon: Killeeshil TE 20; 62–64
Dungannon: Killelagh LY 27; 96
Dungannon: Killowen LY 33; 160, 168
Dungannon: Killyman AH 1; 55
Dungannon: Killyman TE 20; 68
Dungannon: Kilmore AH 1; 63
Dungannon: Kirkinriola AM 23; 99
Dungannon: Loughgall AH 1; 77, 81–82
Dungannon: Maghera LY 18; 5–6, 9
Dungannon: Magherafelt LY 6; 86–87
Dungannon: Newry DN 3; 78
Dungannon: Pomeroy TE 20; 70–72
Dungannon: Tamlaght TE 20; 73
Dungannon: Tartaraghan AH 1; 117–18, 122
Dungannon: Tullyniskan TE 20; 138–41
Dungannon barony: Artrea TE 20; 6
Dungannon barony: Ballinderry TE 20; 11
Dungannon barony: Ballyclog TE 20; 15
Dungannon barony: Clogher TE 5; 59
Dungannon barony: Clonoe TE 20; 29
Dungannon barony: Desertcreat TE 20; 32, 34
Dungannon barony: Donaghenry TE 20; 37
Dungannon barony: Drumglass TE 20; 40
Dungannon barony: Kildress TE 20; 58
Dungannon barony: Killeeshil TE 20; 62
Dungannon barony: Pomeroy TE 20; 70
Dungannon barony: Tullyniskan TE 20; 138
Dungannon barrack: Drumglass TE 20; 44
Dungannon brewery: Drumglass TE 20; 44
Dungannon chapel (C): Drumglass TE 20; 40, 44
Dungannon chapel school: Drumglass TE 20; 40, 42
Dungannon chapels (M): Drumglass TE 20; 40, 44
Dungannon church: Drumglass TE 20; 40, 42, 44
Dungannon court house: Drumglass TE 20; 40, 42
Dungannon dispensary: Drumglass TE 20; 42
Dungannon distillery: Cappagh TE 5; 20
Dungannon distillery: Drumglass TE 20; 40–41, 44

Dungannon Erasmus Smith school: Drumglass TE 20; 42
Dungannon fort: Drumglass TE 20; 44
Dungannon fort: Dunboe LY 11; 73
Dungannon infants school: Drumglass TE 20; 42
Dungannon kiln (see Kilcoan): Island Magee AM 10; 81
Dungannon mansion house: Drumglass TE 20; 44
Dungannon market house: Drumglass TE 20; 44
Dungannon meeting house: Drumglass TE 20; 40, 44
Dungannon old church: Drumglass TE 20; 40
Dungannon pay school: Drumglass TE 20; 42
Dungannon port house: Drumglass TE 20; 44
Dungannon private school: Drumglass TE 20; 42
Dungannon quarries: Drumglass TE 20; 43
Dungannon Royal College: Drumglass TE 20; 41, 44
Dungannon Royal School: Ahoghill AM 23; 19–20
Dungannon Royal School: Ballynascreen LY 31; 33
Dungannon Royal School: Lough Neagh AM 21; 92
Dungannon Sunday schools: Drumglass TE 20; 42
Dungannon townparks: Drumglass TE 20; 43
Dungannon, family: Carrickfergus AM 37; 32
Dungannon, Lord: Comber DN 7; 37, 37–38
Dungannon, Lord: Dromara DN 12; 64–65
Dungannon, Lord: Drumbo DN 7; 56, 59–60
Dungannon, Lord: Drumcree AH 1; 37, 39
Dungannon, Lord: Drumgooland DN 3; 22
Dungannon, Lord: Island Magee AM 10; 27–29, 31, 33, 36–37, 74–75, 77, 81, 84, 91, 101, 103
Dungannon, Lord: Kilmore AH 1; 65, 68
Dungannon, Lord: Kilroot AM 26; 68
Dungannon, Lord: Saintfield DN 7; 118
Dungannon, Lord: Seagoe AH 1; 108–09
Dungannon, Lord: Seapatrick DN 12; 126, 133
Dungannon, Lord [I]: Raloo AM 32; 94, 128
Dungannon, Lord [II]: Raloo AM 32; 128
Dungannon, Viscount: Glynn AM 26; 1, 39
Dungannon, Viscount: Island Magee AM 10; 85–88
Dungannon, Viscount: Kilbroney DN 3; 32
Dungannon, Viscount: Raloo AM 32; 80, 90–91, 93, 95–96, 98, 118, 120–21, 123–25, 128, 131–33
Dungarven (Waterford): Carncastle and Killyglen AM 10; 7
Dungiven: Aghadowey LY 22; 10, 20
Dungiven: Aghanloo LY 11; 18
Dungiven: Ballyaghran LY 33; 15, 26
Dungiven: Ballynascreen LY 31; 2, 6, 8, 16, 18, 20, 22, 25
Dungiven: Ballywillin LY 33; 38
Dungiven: Banagher LY 30; 2–6, 10, 13–16, 18–19, 25, 27, 29–31, 38–39, 44, 48, 53–54, 56, 58–59, 61, 80, 85, 87, 99–100, 105, 112, 116–21, 131

Dungiven: Bovevagh LY 25; 4, 7, 9, 16–17, 19,
    23–24, 27, 31, 35–36, 48, 50, 53, 56
Dungiven: Clondermot LY 34; 4–7, 14, 19–22, 96,
    103, 106, 113–14, 116–20
Dungiven: Coleraine LY 33; 94
Dungiven: Cumber LY 28; 1, 4, 7, 9, 11, 21, 23–24,
    32–35, 45, 49, 78–79, 84–85, 94–99, 110–15
Dungiven: Desertmartin LY 31; 54, 62
Dungiven: Desertoghill LY 27; 17, 33
Dungiven: Drumachose LY 9; 55, 74, 76, 79, 84, 90,
    117
Dungiven: Dunboe LY 11; 46, 58, 60
Dungiven: Dungiven LY 15; 1, 4–6, 9, 14, 17–18,
    20–21, 23–26, 29, 51–53, 62, 65, 67–71, 75–76,
    86, 99, 105, 121
Dungiven: Errigal LY 27; 39–41, 45, 50–51, 56–57,
    59–60, 79–84
Dungiven: Kilcronaghan LY 31; 67, 75, 78
Dungiven: Killelagh LY 27; 96, 99
Dungiven: Killowen LY 33; 172
Dungiven: Kilrea LY 27; 126
Dungiven: Lissan LY 31; 90
Dungiven: Lissan TE 20; 69
Dungiven: Maghera LY 18; 2, 8–9, 32–33, 35, 65
Dungiven: Magilligan LY 11; 111
Dungiven: Misc. LY 31; 115–16, 118, 130
Dungiven: Misc. LY 36; 111
Dungiven: Tamlaght Finlagan LY 25; 70, 79–80,
    83–85, 93, 104, 106, 120–23
Dungiven abbey: Dungiven LY 15; 38–40, 54–55,
    101–02
Dungiven abbey cell: Dungiven LY 15; 41
Dungiven abbey standing stone: Dungiven LY 15;
    41
Dungiven bawn: Aghadowey LY 22; 27
Dungiven bawn: Banagher LY 30; 5
Dungiven bleach green: Banagher LY 30; 19
Dungiven bleach green: Dungiven LY 15; 9, 66, 98
Dungiven bridge: Banagher LY 30; 4–5, 26
Dungiven bridge: Dungiven LY 15; 3–4, 10–11, 53,
    63, 97
Dungiven bridge: Tamlaght Finlagan LY 25; 104
Dungiven Castle: Banagher LY 30; 80
Dungiven Castle: Dungiven LY 15; 35, 42, 46, 48
Dungiven cemetery: Dungiven LY 15; 58
Dungiven chapel: Banagher LY 30; 14
Dungiven chapel: Dungiven LY 15; 8, 20, 62,
    98–99, 102, 117
Dungiven cholera hospital: Dungiven LY 15; 98
Dungiven church: Banagher LY 30; 4, 14, 49, 62,
    115–16
Dungiven church: Dungiven LY 15; 3–4, 20, 24, 55,
    58–59, 102
Dungiven classical school: Dungiven LY 15; 18, 118
Dungiven classical school [I]: Banagher LY 30; 12

Dungiven classical school [II]: Banagher LY 30; 12
Dungiven corn mill: Dungiven LY 15; 9, 83, 97
Dungiven crane: Banagher LY 30; 4
Dungiven dispensary: Banagher LY 30; 10, 34, 60,
    112
Dungiven dispensary: Bovevagh LY 25; 25, 59
Dungiven dispensary: Cumber LY 28; 14–16
Dungiven dispensary: Dungiven LY 15; 7, 21–22,
    24, 52, 75, 99, 101, 119–21
Dungiven district: Enniskeen CN 40; 30
Dungiven female school: Banagher LY 30; 13
Dungiven female school [I]: Dungiven LY 15;
    116–17, 119
Dungiven female school [II]: Dungiven LY 15; 116
Dungiven female school [III]: Dungiven LY 15; 117,
    119
Dungiven fort: Dungiven LY 15; 100, 102
Dungiven freestone quarries: Banagher LY 30; 3
Dungiven graveyard: Dungiven LY 15; 48
Dungiven hill: Banagher LY 30; 2
Dungiven hill: Dungiven LY 15; 105
Dungiven Hotel: Dungiven LY 15; 5
Dungiven inn: Dungiven LY 15; 12
Dungiven Lancasterian school: Banagher LY 30;
    12–13
Dungiven Lancasterian school: Dungiven LY 15; 4,
    8, 18, 117, 119
Dungiven market house: Dungiven LY 15; 4, 52,
    102
Dungiven meeting house: Bovevagh LY 25; 54
Dungiven meeting house: Dungiven LY 15; 20, 102
Dungiven New St school: Dungiven LY 15; 119
Dungiven old castle: Bovevagh LY 25; 45
Dungiven old castle: Dungiven LY 15; 3
Dungiven old chapel: Banagher LY 30; 13
Dungiven old church: Ballynascreen LY 31; 9, 24
Dungiven old church: Banagher LY 30; 5–7, 11, 39,
    49–50, 57, 62
Dungiven old church: Bovevagh LY 25; 23
Dungiven old church: Dungiven LY 15; 54, 62
Dungiven old church: Faughanvale LY 36; 14
Dungiven old church: Tamlaght Finlagan LY 25;
    102
Dungiven ph: Ballynascreen LY 31; 2, 16
Dungiven ph: Balteagh LY 9; 2, 20
Dungiven ph: Banagher LY 30; 1–2, 5, 7, 9, 11,
    14–15, 22, 32, 34, 36, 50, 60, 68, 84, 95, 113–16
Dungiven ph: Bovevagh LY 25; 1–2, 9, 22–23,
    26–27, 46, 59
Dungiven ph: Clondermot LY 34; 60, 62–63, 66
Dungiven ph: Cumber LY 28; 32
Dungiven ph: Drumachose LY 9; 129
Dungiven ph: Errigal LY 27; 35, 77–78
Dungiven ph: Kirkinriola AM 23; 125
Dungiven ph: Lissan LY 31; 92–93

Dungiven ph: Misc. LY 31; 111
Dungiven ph: Misc. LY 36; 105, 110, 112
Dungiven ph: Tamlaght Finlagan LY 25; 101, 106
Dungiven priory: Banagher LY 30; 5
Dungiven priory: Dungiven LY 15; 30
Dungiven school [I]: Dungiven LY 15; 116
Dungiven school [II]: Dungiven LY 15; 116
Dungiven school [III]: Dungiven LY 15; 116
Dungiven school [IV]: Dungiven LY 15; 116
Dungiven school [V]: Dungiven LY 15; 117
Dungiven school [VI]: Dungiven LY 15; 117–19
Dungiven school [VII]: Dungiven LY 15; 118
Dungiven schools: Dungiven LY 15; 18–19
Dungiven shambles: Dungiven LY 15; 66
Dungiven soup kitchen: Banagher LY 30; 20
Dungiven Sunday school: Dungiven LY 15; 18
Dungiven td: Banagher LY 30; 22
Dungiven td: Bovevagh LY 25; 45
Dungiven td: Dungiven LY 15; 2, 8–9, 22, 26, 46,
    49, 62, 74, 84, 104
Dungiven tumulus: Banagher LY 30; 7
Dungiven well: Bovevagh LY 25; 45
Dunglady (Dungleady) td: Maghera LY 18; 22, 25,
    65, 78, 81
Dunglady bog: Maghera LY 18; 41
Dunglady bridge: Maghera LY 18; 9, 63
Dunglady flax mill: Maghera LY 18; 74
Dunglady fort: Maghera LY 18; 4, 11, 22–23, 42,
    48, 58, 61, 70, 73–74
Dunglady fort: Misc. LY 36; 116–17
Dunglady fort: Tamlaght O'Crilly LY 18; 102
Dunglady woods: Maghera LY 18; 4
Dunglass, Lord: Killyleagh DN 17; 86
Dungloe: Blaris AM 8; 73
Dungloe: Conwal DL 39; 25
Dungloe: Leck DL 39; 116
Dunglow (see Dungloe)
Dungoghy td: Aghavea FH 4; 25
Dungonnell (Dungonnel) td: Dunaghy AM 13; 11,
    14
Dungonnell Castle: Killead AM 35; 25–26
Dungonnell corn mill: Killead AM 35; 15, 35, 42,
    48
Dungonnell dancing school: Killead AM 35; 23
Dungonnell fort: Dunaghy AM 13; 17, 20, 22
Dungonnell fort: Killead AM 35; 26–27, 39
Dungonnell fort: Rasharkin AM 23; 138–39
Dungonnell hill: Dunaghy AM 13; 10
Dungonnell moat: Killead AM 35; 27, 32
Dungonnell orchard: Killead AM 35; 35
Dungonnell school [I]: Killead AM 35; 36, 38
Dungonnell school [II]: Killead AM 35; 36, 52–53
Dungonnell singing school: Killead AM 35; 23
Dungonnell Sunday school: Killead AM 35; 38, 52
Dungonnell td: Killead AM 35; 40, 51

Dungonnell well: Killead AM 35; 26
Dungoran fort: Donacavey TE 5; 84
Dungoran td: Donacavey TE 5; 76–78, 80–81,
    84–85
Dungorbery (Dungorberry) td: Kilraghts AM 16;
    125, 133
Dungorbery flax mill: Kilraghts AM 16; 127
Dungorbery hill: Kilraghts AM 16; 128
Dungorkin (Dungorcan) td: Cumber LY 28; 4, 47,
    66, 69, 112, 118, 122, 125–26
Dungorkin bog: Cumber LY 28; 23, 32
Dungorkin flax mill: Cumber LY 28; 86, 122
Dungorkin fort: Cumber LY 28; 30, 32, 43, 47, 84
Dungorkin wood: Cumber LY 28; 118
Dungorman beetling engine: Killyman TE 20; 68
Dungorman td: Donaghmore DL 39; 37
Dungorran (see Dungoran)
Dunguillian td (Cumber): Faughanvale LY 36; 61
Dungullion td: Faughanvale LY 36; 13, 17, 53, 57,
    68, 73, 84–85, 94
Dungullion td: Tamlaght Finlagan LY 25; 73–74
Dunhugh quarries: Clondermot LY 34; 131
Dunhugh td: Clondermot LY 34; 56, 65–66, 109,
    112, 116, 124, 131
Dunhugh td: Faughanvale LY 36; 54–55
Dunigan, family: Aghalee AM 21; 36
Duninneeny (see Duinaneeny): Ramoan AM 24; 90
Dunisland fort: Raloo AM 32; 117, 122
Dunisland moat: Raloo AM 32; 112, 116
Dunisland water: Glynn AM 26; 3–4, 10
Dunisland water: Raloo AM 32; 81–84, 86, 88,
    133–34
Dunkin, family: Culfeightrin AM 24; 59
Dunkin, family: Dunluce AM 16; 117
Dunkin, John: Coleraine LY 33; 142
Dunkin, Rev. David: Coleraine LY 33; 105, 127
Dunlade Glebe td: Faughanvale LY 36; 13, 17, 53,
    57–58, 68, 73–74, 85, 94
Dunlady House: Dundonald DN 7; 65
Dunlady td: Comber DN 7; 41, 43
Dunlady td: Dundonald DN 7; 65
Dunlap, Archibald: Desertoghill LY 27; 6, 18
Dunlap, family: Carnmoney AM 2; 76
Dunlap, family: Derryaghy AM 8; 103
Dunlap, family: Derrykeighan AM 16; 89
Dunlap, family: Desertoghill LY 27; 5
Dunlap, John [I]: Coleraine LY 33; 96
Dunlap, John [II]: Coleraine LY 33; 146
Dunlap, Miss: Coleraine LY 33; 137
Dunlap, Mr: Derryaghy AM 8; 105
Dunlap, Mr: Tullyaughnish DL 38; 87
Dunlap, Mrs Archabald: Coleraine LY 33; 143
Dunlap, Rev. Robert: Coleraine LY 33; 95, 141
Dunlap, Rev. Samuel: Derryaghy AM 8; 95, 111

Dunlap, Robert: Magheramesk AM 21; 117, 119, 124

Dunlap, Simon: Agivey LY 22; 44

Dunlap, Thomas: Desertoghill LY 27; 18

Dunleavy, Mr: Enniskillen FH 4; 84

Dunleeny fort: Lough Swilly DL 38; 147

Dunleeny Point: Lough Swilly DL 38; 147

Dunleer Glebe House: Enniskeen CN 40; 29

Dunlen, King of Ulster: Kilmegan DN 3; 60

Dunleve (see Dunlua): Misc. DN 17; 119

Dunlewy school: Tullaghobegley DL 39; 172

Dunlogan hill: Misc. LY 31; 114–15

Dunlogan plantation: Ballynascreen LY 31; 2

Dunlogan td: Misc. LY 31; 141, 143

Dunlogan wood: Misc. LY 31; 112

Dunlop, Alexander: Ahoghill AM 23; 49

Dunlop, Alexander: Ballymoney AM 16; 17

Dunlop, Alexander: Coleraine LY 33; 145

Dunlop, Allen: Ballywillin LY 33; 51

Dunlop, C.: Drumbo DN 7; 59

Dunlop, David: Coleraine LY 33; 72, 144

Dunlop, David: Dunluce AM 16; 120

Dunlop, David: Killowen LY 33; 159

Dunlop, Eliza: Carrickfergus AM 37; 117

Dunlop, Ellen Jane: Kilrea LY 27; 129

Dunlop, family: Armoy AM 24; 6

Dunlop, family: Ballintoy AM 24; 20

Dunlop, family: Ballywillin AM 16; 32

Dunlop, family: Culfeightrin AM 24; 59

Dunlop, family: Desertoghill LY 27; 30

Dunlop, family: Maghera LY 18; 24, 48

Dunlop, George: Aghanloo LY 11; 19

Dunlop, James: Clondermot LY 34; 78, 80

Dunlop, James: Coleraine LY 33; 145

Dunlop, Jane: Dunboe LY 11; 81

Dunlop, John: Aghanloo LY 11; 3–4, 12–16, 18–19, 21–28, 33, 37

Dunlop, John: Ballywillin LY 33; 50

Dunlop, John: Derrykeighan AM 16; 88

Dunlop, John: Drummaul AM 19; 77, 85

Dunlop, John: Dunaghy AM 13; 17

Dunlop, John: Dunluce AM 16; 122

Dunlop, John: Killowen LY 33; 158

Dunlop, John: Magilligan LY 11; 125

Dunlop, Matilda: Kilrea LY 27; 129

Dunlop, Mr: Mallusk AM 2; 114

Dunlop, P.: Drumbo DN 7; 60

Dunlop, Robert: Blaris AM 8; 69

Dunlop, Robert: Carrickfergus AM 37; 111, 195

Dunlop, Robert: Tamlaght O'Crilly LY 18; 112

Dunlop, Thomas: Coleraine LY 33; 65, 73, 142–43

Dunlop, Thomas: Desertoghill LY 27; 22

Dunlop, Widow: Dunluce AM 16; 120

Dunlop, William: Ahoghill AM 23; 35

Dunlop, William: Tamlaght TE 20; 79, 83

Dunlope, Bryce: Ramoan AM 24; 108

Dunlope, family: Derrykeighan AM 16; 89

Dunlope, George: Ramoan AM 24; 102

Dunloughan bank: Castleboy DN 7; 26

Dunloughey td: Lough Swilly DL 38; 150

Dunloy: Dunaghy AM 13; 26

Dunloy: Finvoy AM 23; 67–68, 70, 72, 77

Dunloy: Killagan AM 23; 80

Dunloy giant's grave: Finvoy AM 23; 77

Dunloy hill: Finvoy AM 23; 75

Dunloy inn: Finvoy AM 23; 70

Dunloy school: Finvoy AM 23; 75

Dunloy td: Finvoy AM 23; 67, 70, 78

Dunlua, prince: Misc. DN 17; 119

Dunluce barony: Tickmacrevan AM 13; 127

Dunluce Castle: Ahoghill AM 23; 26

Dunluce Castle: Ballyclug AM 23; 63

Dunluce Castle: Ballymoney AM 16; 20

Dunluce Castle: Ballywillin AM 16; 33

Dunluce Castle: Ballywillin LY 33; 31, 34–35, 44–45

Dunluce Castle: Billy AM 16; 42, 59, 71

Dunluce Castle: Culfeightrin AM 24; 54, 79–80

Dunluce Castle: Derrykeighan AM 16; 88

Dunluce Castle: Drumachose LY 9; 57

Dunluce Castle: Drummaul AM 19; 71

Dunluce Castle: Dungiven LY 15; 29, 32–33

Dunluce Castle: Dunluce AM 16; 105, 108, 112–16, 121

Dunluce Castle: Lambeg AM 8; 141

Dunluce Castle: Misc. LY 36; 109

Dunluce Castle: Ramoan AM 24; 122–23

Dunluce cave: Dunluce AM 16; 116, 122

Dunluce chapel: Misc. LY 36; 109

Dunluce church: Billy AM 16; 37, 45

Dunluce district: Ballywillin LY 33; 36

Dunluce fort: Dunluce AM 16; 121

Dunluce gaol: Dunluce AM 16; 121

Dunluce hill: Dunluce AM 16; 106

Dunluce Lower barony: Billy AM 16; 36, 39

Dunluce Lower barony: Derrykeighan AM 16; 78, 80

Dunluce Lower barony: Dunluce AM 16; 104

Dunluce Lower barony: Layd and Inispollan AM 13; 54

Dunluce Lower barony: Loughguile AM 13; 60

Dunluce old church: Dunluce AM 16; 106, 116–17

Dunluce ph: Ballyaghran LY 33; 15, 26

Dunluce ph: Ballymoney AM 16; 1

Dunluce ph: Ballyrashane LY 22; 46, 58

Dunluce ph: Ballywillin LY 33; 38

Dunluce ph: Billy AM 16; 37–38, 43, 51

Dunluce ph: Coleraine LY 33; 95, 143

Dunluce ph: Derrykeighan AM 16; 78

Dunluce ph: Drummaul AM 19; 71

Dunluce ph: Misc. AM 10; 129

Dunluce td: Banagher LY 30; 3

Dunluce td: Dunluce AM 16; 116

Dunluce town: Dunluce AM 16; 115, 121

Dunluce Upper barony: Armoy AM 24; 2

Dunluce Upper barony: Ballymoney AM 16; 1–2

Dunluce Upper barony: Billy AM 16; 38

Dunluce Upper barony: Killagan AM 23; 79, 81

Dunluce Upper barony: Kilraghts AM 16, 124

Dunluce Upper barony: Loughguile AM 13; 58

Dunluce, Lord: Ballymoney AM 16; 13

Dunluce, Viscount: Ramoan AM 24; 125

Dunluhy (see Dunlewy): Tullaghobegley DL 39;
    172

Dunmacalter td: Culfeightrin AM 24; 66

Dunmall fort: Ardclinis AM 13; 4, 7

Dunmaul td: Culfeightrin AM 24; 63

Dunmaurice fort: Ballybay MN 40; 81

Dunmaurice td: Ballybay MN 40; 84

Dunminning beetling mill [I]: Rasharkin AM 23;
    131

Dunminning beetling mill [II]: Rasharkin AM 23;
    131

Dunminning beetling mill [III]: Rasharkin AM 23;
    131

Dunminning beetling mill [IV]: Rasharkin AM 23;
    131

Dunminning beetling mill [V]: Rasharkin AM 23;
    131

Dunminning bridge: Ahoghill AM 23; 12

Dunminning bridge: Rasharkin AM 23; 131

Dunminning female school: Rasharkin AM 23; 135

Dunminning House: Rasharkin AM 23; 129–30,
    132, 137

Dunminning mills: Ahoghill AM 23; 29

Dunminning rock: Ahoghill AM 23; 4

Dunminning school: Rasharkin AM 23; 134, 141

Dunminning td: Ahoghill AM 23; 29–30

Dunminning td: Rasharkin AM 23; 130

Dunminning wood: Rasharkin AM 23; 128

Dunmore (Duinn More) td: Drumachose LY 9; 58,
    75, 83, 87, 91, 96–97, 110–11, 127

Dunmore bank: Lough Swilly DL 38; 113

Dunmore bank: Moville DL 38; 72

Dunmore Castle: Drummaul AM 19; 64, 70

Dunmore chapel: Dromara DN 12; 63, 66

Dunmore chapel: Kilkeel DN 3; 49

Dunmore church: Drummaul AM 19; 34

Dunmore fort: Drummaul AM 19; 65, 78

Dunmore forts: Drumachose LY 9; 58, 83–84, 91,
    127

Dunmore Head: Clonmany DL 38; 13, 110, 113

Dunmore hill: Dromara DN 12; 62–63, 65

Dunmore hill: Drumachose LY 9; 111

Dunmore House: Killea and Taughboyne DL 39; 81,
    88, 186, 189

Dunmore House: Magheradrool DN 17; 106

Dunmore Lodge: Killea and Taughboyne DL 39; 90

Dunmore lough: Mevagh DL 38; 55

Dunmore school: Dromara DN 12; 64

Dunmore standing stone: Tullyaughnish DL 38; 91

Dunmore td: Annahilt DN 12; 21–22

Dunmore td: Dromara DN 12; 63–65, 69

Dunmore td: Drummaul AM 19; 92

Dunmore td: Killea and Taughboyne DL 39; 79,
    184, 196

Dunmore td: Mevagh DL 38; 55, 63

Dunmore td: Tullyaughnish DL 38; 96

Dunmoyle (Dunmoile) td: Errigal Keerogue TE 20;
    50, 52, 57

Dunmull hill: Ballywillin AM 16; 34

Dunmull hill: Ballywillin LY 33; 29, 33

Dunmull hill: Dungiven LY 15; 37

Dunmull td: Ballywillin AM 16; 33

Dunmurrish (see Dunmaurice): Ballybay MN 40; 84

Dunmurry: Blaris AM 8; 70

Dunmurry: Drumbeg AM 8; 122, 133

Dunmurry: Drumbeg DN 7; 52

Dunmurry bleach green: Drumbeg AM 8; 126

Dunmurry bleach green: Drumbeg DN 7; 52

Dunmurry bridge: Ballynascreen LY 31; 7

Dunmurry bridge [I]: Drumbeg AM 8; 127

Dunmurry bridge [II]: Drumbeg AM 8; 127

Dunmurry Canal bridge: Drumbeg AM 8; 128

Dunmurry corn mills: Drumbeg AM 8; 125, 127

Dunmurry demesne: Drumbeg AM 8; 124

Dunmurry flour mill: Drumbeg AM 8; 127

Dunmurry fort: Derryaghy AM 8; 102

Dunmurry forts: Drumbeg AM 8; 124, 129

Dunmurry graveyard: Drumbeg AM 8; 123

Dunmurry House [I]: Drumbeg AM 8; 124–25,
    129–30

Dunmurry House [II]: Drumbeg AM 8; 126, 130

Dunmurry Lodge: Drumbeg AM 8; 126, 130

Dunmurry Lower demesne: Drumbeg AM 8; 130

Dunmurry Lower House: Drumbeg AM 8; 125, 130

Dunmurry meeting house: Drumbeg AM 8; 122–23,
    130

Dunmurry mountain: Dungiven LY 15; 1

Dunmurry school: Drumbeg AM 8; 132–33

Dunmurry stream: Misc. LY 31; 113

Dunmurry td: Misc. LY 31; 141, 143

Dunn, Adam: Derryaghy AM 8; 115

Dunn, Alexander: Derryaghy AM 8; 115

Dunn, Bessy: Carrickfergus AM 37; 131

Dunn, Dolly: Derryaghy AM 8; 115

Dunn, family: Ballee DN 17; 16

Dunn, family: Ballinderry AM 21; 53

Dunn, family: Blaris AM 8; 22

Dunn, family: Kilroot AM 26; 74–75

Dunn, J.: Newry DN 3; 99

Dunn, James: Ballyscullion LY 6; 69

Dunn, James: Drumachose LY 9; 104

Dunn, James: Dunboe LY 11; 78

Dunn, James: Tamlaght Finlagan LY 25; 84, 122

Dunn, Joseph: Killesher FH 14; 87

Dunn, man named: Ahoghill AM 23; 34

Dunn, Miss: Banagher LY 30; 57

Dunn, Mr: Conwal DL 39; 24

Dunn, Richard: Killead AM 35; 46

Dunn, Robert: Aghanloo LY 11; 29

Dunn, Robert: Banagher LY 30; 100

Dunn, Robert: Billy AM 16; 77

Dunn, Robert: Bovevagh LY 25; 56

Dunn, Robert: Carrickfergus AM 37; 187

Dunn, Robert: Macosquin LY 22; 87, 117

Dunn, Robert: Tamlaght Finlagan LY 25; 110

Dunn, Samuel: Dunboe LY 11; 62, 73

Dunn, Stewart: Carrickfergus AM 37; 57, 102,
   135–36, 139, 159, 183, 185

Dunn, William: Cumber LY 28; 80

Dunn, William: Derryaghy AM 8; 115

Dunnabraggy bog: Lissan LY 31; 89, 96

Dunnabraggy fort [I]: Lissan LY 31; 91, 99–100

Dunnabraggy fort [II]: Lissan LY 31; 100

Dunnabraggy td: Lissan LY 31; 106–08

Dunnaff (see Dunaff): Lough Swilly DL 38; 98

Dun-na-Gall (see Donegal): Dungiven LY 15; 35

Dunnaluck hill: Currin MN 40; 92

Dunnaluck Pole locality: Currin MN 40; 91

Dunnaluck td: Currin MN 40; 91

Dunnamanagh: Banagher LY 30; 71

Dunnamanagh: Clondermot LY 34; 105, 115

Dunnamanagh: Cumber LY 28; 31

Dunnamanagh: Donaghedy TE 5; 88–89, 91

Dunnamanagh: Dungiven LY 15; 11

Dunnamanagh district: Clondermot LY 34; 35

Dunnamanagh td: Donaghedy TE 5, 92

Dunnamena (see Dunnamona)

Dunnamona (Donamona) td: Donacavey TE 5; 67,
   71–73, 76–78, 80–82, 85, 92, 147

Dunnamona fort: Donacavey TE 5; 82

Dunnamona glebe: Donacavey TE 5; 72, 76, 78, 83

Dunnamona Glebe td: Donacavey TE 5; 85

Dunnamona school: Donacavey TE 5; 71, 82

Dunnamore (Dunamore) td: Kildress TE 20; 59

Dunnamore chapel: Kildress TE 20; 59–61

Dunnamuggy (see Dunamuggy): Donegore AM 29;
   130

Dunnan td: Drumbo DN 7; 58

Dunnan td: Lissan LY 31; 99

Dunnanelly gravel pit: Inch DN 17; 76

Dunnanelly school: Inch DN 17; 73

Dunnavenny bogs: Errigal LY 27; 55

Dunnavenny bridge: Errigal LY 27; 41, 59

Dunnavenny carn [I]: Errigal LY 27; 43, 71

Dunnavenny carn [II]: Errigal LY 27; 43, 71

Dunnavenny carn [III]: Errigal LY 27; 75

Dunnavenny carn [IV]: Errigal LY 27; 75

Dunnavenny carn [V]: Errigal LY 27; 75

Dunnavenny fort: Errigal LY 27; 43, 71

Dunnavenny giant's grave [I]: Errigal LY 27; 43, 71

Dunnavenny giant's grave [II]: Errigal LY 27; 71

Dunnavenny td: Errigal LY 27; 74, 81, 86, 90

Dunne, soldier: Antrim AM 29; 6

Dunnelong (see Dunalong)

Dunnigan, James: Ballinderry AM 21; 52

Dunnihoo, family: Ramoan AM 24; 107

Dunnivaddin (see Dunnyvaden): Ballyclug AM 23;
   53

Dunnycally td: Killea and Taughboyne DL 39; 79

Dunnygarron td: Ahoghill AM 23; 40

Dunnyloop chapel: Urney DL 39; 175–76

Dunnyloop td: Urney DL 39; 181

Dunnymuggy (see Dunamuggy): Donegore AM 29;
   134

Dunnyvaden (Dunnavaddin) td: Ballyclug AM 23;
   53, 65

Dunnyvaden bog: Ballyclug AM 23; 55

Dunnyvaden fort [I]: Ballyclug AM 23; 65

Dunnyvaden fort [II]: Ballyclug AM 23; 65

Dunnyvaden hill: Ballyclug AM 23; 54

Dunnyvaden old chapel: Ballyclug AM 23; 65

Dunodis td: Killoran and Kilvarnet SO 40; 183

Dunoraver td: Misc. DN 17; 125

Dunore fort (see also Badger fort): Muckamore AM
   35; 72, 74

Dunore river: Killead AM 35; 7, 9–10

Dunore river: Muckamore AM 35; 57, 59, 72, 74

Dunore wood: Muckamore AM 35; 56

Dunover House: Ballywalter DN 7; 16

Dunover td: Ballywalter DN 7; 16, 18

Dunover windmill: Ballywalter DN 7; 17

DuNoyer, George: Ballynascreen LY 31; 33

Dunoyne House: Rasharkin AM 23; 130

Dunpatrick fort: Magilligan LY 11; 102

Dunravely td: Misc. DN 17; 125

Dunree bay: Lough Swilly DL 38; 101

Dunree bridge: Desertegney DL 38; 26

Dunree fort: Clondavaddog DL 38; 4–5

Dunree fort: Desertegney DL 38; 24–27

Dunree fort: Killygarvan DL 38; 36

Dunree fort: Lough Swilly DL 38; 101, 133

Dunree Head: Desertegney DL 38; 24–25

Dunree spring: Desertegney DL 38; 25

Dunriny fort: Culfeightrin AM 24; 76

Dunronan bog: Desertlyn LY 31; 35–36, 44

Dunronan fort: Desertlyn LY 31; 44

Dunronan td: Desertlyn LY 31; 48

Dunseath, Rev. James: Ballymoney AM 16; 15–17

Dunseith, James: Tamlaght TE 20; 77

Dunseverick cashel: Billy AM 16; 54, 59

Dunseverick Castle: Ballintoy AM 24; 12, 33

Dunseverick Castle: Billy AM 16; 38, 53–54, 59–60, 66

Dunseverick church: Billy AM 16; 48

Dunseverick forts: Billy AM 16; 60

Dunseverick rock: Billy AM 16; 59

Dunseverick stream: Ballintoy AM 24; 11–13

Dunsfort chapel: Dunsfort DN 17; 68–69

Dunsfort church: Dunsfort DN 17; 68–69

Dunsfort church: Misc. DN 17; 133

Dunsfort old school: Dunsfort DN 17; 68

Dunsfort ph: Ardglass DN 17; 1, 5

Dunsfort ph: Ballee DN 17; 15

Dunsfort ph: Down DN 17; 43

Dunsfort ph: Misc. DN 17; 121–22, 128, 133

Dunsfort school [I]: Dunsfort DN 17; 68

Dunsfort school [II]: Dunsfort DN 17; 68

Dunsfort td: Dunsfort DN 17; 68, 72

Dunsilly burn: Antrim AM 29; 3–4

Dunsilly forts: Antrim AM 29; 36, 43

Dunsilly td: Antrim AM 29; 4

Dunsport (see Dunsfort): Misc. DN 17; 133

Dunsrim lough: Currin MN 40; 86, 90

Dunsrim td: Currin MN 40; 86

Dunstall, John: Carrickfergus AM 37; 132

Dunstan, Anne: Carrickfergus AM 37; 123

Duntibryan (see Duntybrian): Ballynascreen LY 31; 30

Dunturk district: Derryaghy AM 8; 114

Dunturkey and Toberdowney Sunday school: Ballynure AM 32; 71

Dunturkey bog: Ballynure AM 32; 57

Dunturkey caves [I]: Ballynure AM 32; 57

Dunturkey caves [II]: Ballynure AM 32; 58

Dunturkey caves [III]: Ballynure AM 32; 62

Dunturkey corn mill: Ballynure AM 32; 34, 41, 43–44

Dunturkey fort [I]: Ballynure AM 32; 57

Dunturkey fort [II]: Ballynure AM 32; 58

Dunturkey fort [III]: Ballynure AM 32; 60–61

Dunturkey school: Ballynure AM 32; 73

Dunturkey td: Ballynure AM 32; 38, 58, 63, 68

Duntybrian cave: Ballynascreen LY 31; 30

Duntybrian fort: Ballynascreen LY 31; 8, 30

Duntybrian school: Misc. LY 31; 125–26

Duntybrian td: Ballynascreen LY 31; 8, 33, 141, 143

Duntybrian td: Kilcronaghan LY 31; 80

Duntybryan (see Duntybrian): Ballynascreen LY 31; 33

Dunurgan school: Layd AM 13; 53

Dunverin (see Dunvern): Faughanvale LY 36; 54

Dunvern fort: Faughanvale LY 36; 13, 15, 54

Duprey, family: Blaris DN 12; 30

Duras, John: Maghera LY 18; 81

Durham, Andrew: Drumbo DN 7; 56

Durham, Robert: Ballinderry AM 21; 54

Durhamsland td: Doagh AM 29; 96

Durhamsland td: Donegore AM 29; 101, 106, 125, 127, 130–31

Durkan, Patt: Kilmacteige SO 40; 187, 194

Durkan, Philip: Kilmacteige SO 40; 187–88, 192

Durkan, Thomas: Kilmacteige SO 40; 193–95

Durnacally (see Dernacally)

Durnan, Joseph: Magherafelt LY 6; 110

Durnascallon (Dernascallon) td: Desertmartin LY 31; 57, 62, 141–42

Durnford, Lt E.W.: Drummully FH 4; 40

Durrow (Offaly): Faughanvale LY 36; 62

Dutchman's rock: Lough Swilly DL 38; 134

Dyan corn mill: Aghaloo TE 20; 1, 4

Dyan public house: Aghaloo TE 20; 4

Dyan village: Aghaloo TE 20; 3–4

Dyan village: Coleraine LY 33; 97

Dyanmore (see Freame): Ematris MN 40; 115

Dyatt, John: Dunluce AM 16; 118

Dyatt, Robert: Dunluce AM 16; 118

Dyer, Eliza: Carrickfergus AM 37; 130

Dyer, family: Glynn AM 26; 45

Dyer, John: Carrickfergus AM 37; 194

Dyer, Michael: Carrickfergus AM 37; 126–27

Dyes, Robert: Carrickfergus AM 37; 193

Dykes, Rev.: Maghera LY 18; 67

Dynes hill: Seagoe AH 1; 105

Dysart, John: Aghanloo LY 11; 27

Dysart, John: Drumachose LY 9; 128

Dysart, John: Faughanvale LY 36; 40

Dysart, John: Mintiaghs DL 38; 66

Dysart, Rachel: Aghanloo LY 11; 39

Dysart, Rev. William: Desertmartin LY 31; 54

Dysart, Robert: Maghera LY 18; 78

Dysert, Archie: Ahoghill AM 23; 34

Dysertstown school: Ahoghill AM 23; 49

E

Eachiheen mountains: Moville DL 38; 78

Eachy, son of Enna: Faughanvale LY 36; 12, 55

Eadan mountain: Dungiven LY 15; 49

Eadenacligh (Edanaclygh) td: Magheraculmoney FH 14; 105, 113

Eadenacligh school: Magheraculmoney FH 14; 108

Eadenacligh wood: Magheraculmoney FH 14; 105

Eadenclaw (see Eadenacligh): Magheraculmoney FH 14; 108

Eadengranna locality: Carrickfergus AM 37; 93

Eager, family: Derryaghy AM 8; 103

Eagish lough: Aughnamullen MN 40; 69, 72–73

Eagle hill: Billy AM 16; 39

Eagle hill: Layd AM 13; 42

Eagle hill: Loughguile AM 13; 61

Eagle hill td: Layd AM 13; 44

Eagle Island: Belleek FH 14; 2

Eagle mountain: Kilkeel DN 3; 46

Eagle rock: Magilligan LY 11; 82, 100, 146

Eagle Rock mountain: Clonduff DN 3; 5

Eagleson, man named: Ahoghill AM 23; 34

Eagleson, William: Ahoghill AM 23; 38

Eagluis td: Killymard DL 39; 99

Eagralougher (Eganalurghan) td: Loughgall AH 1; 75, 80

Eagralougher chapel: Loughgall AH 1; 80

Eagry cove: Billy AM 16; 56, 63

Eagry distillery: Billy AM 16; 46

Eagry flax mill: Billy AM 16; 46

Eagry fort: Billy AM 16; 60

Eagry school: Billy AM 16; 49, 77

Eagry td: Billy AM 16; 53, 58, 66–67

Eaken's glen: Carrickfergus AM 37; 185

Eakin, Alexander: Balteagh LY 9; 43

Eakin, Dr: Carrickfergus AM 37; 145

Eakin, James: Banagher LY 30; 99, 113

Eakin, William: Coleraine LY 33; 61

Eakin, William: Magherafelt LY 6; 105

Eanach church: Faughanvale LY 36; 50

Eanagh (see Enagh): Clondermot LY 34; 56

Eany water: Killymard DL 39; 105

Earan (see Avaghon): Aughnamullen MN 40; 69

Earcul, giant: Drumachose LY 9; 91

Earl rock: Warrenpoint DN 3; 120

Earlfield House: Emlaghfad SO 40; 177–78

Earlfield plantation: Emlaghfad SO 40; 179

Earls Quarter td: Carlingford LH 40; 58

Early, family: Faughanvale LY 36; 48

Earnagh (see Erinagh): Bright DN 17; 37

Eary House: Ballyclog TE 20; 15

Eary Lower school: Ballyclog TE 20; 16

Eas Feenan waterfall: Clondermot LY 34; 69

Eas MacEirce church: Faughanvale LY 36; 51

Eason, Samuel: Magilligan LY 11; 138

Easruaidh church: Faughanvale LY 36; 51

East Division cotton manufactories: Carrickfergus AM 37; 3

East Division td: Carrickfergus AM 37; 4, 174

East Indies: Coleraine LY 33; 86

East Indies: Killygarvan DL 38; 42

East Town (Tory Island): Lough Swilly DL 38; 124

East Town bog: Lough Swilly DL 38; 124

Easter meadow: Ballymoney AM 16; 18

Eaton, Cristy: Magilligan LY 11; 127

Eaton, family: Kilwaughter AM 10; 115

Eaton, Mary: Drumachose LY 9; 134

Eaton, Thomas: Magilligan LY 11; 134

Eavens, George: Tamlaght O'Crilly LY 18; 109

Ebbitt, John: Galloon FH 4; 105

Ebenezer chapel (see Newry chapel (I)): Newry DN 3; 79

Eccles, Adam: Lissan LY 31; 104–05, 107

Eccles, Charles: Donacavey TE 5; 62, 64, 66, 68–69, 71, 73, 76–77, 81, 83

Eccles, Daniel: Donacavey TE 5; 69

Eccles, Daniel: Galloon FH 4; 94

Eccles, Edward: Muckamore AM 35; 81

Eccles, J.D.: Clogher TE 5; 55, 57

Eccles, J.D.: Donacavey TE 5; 69, 77, 85–87

Eccles, James: Coleraine LY 33; 94, 131

Eccles, John: Carrickfergus AM 37; 162

Eccles, John: Lissan LY 31; 101, 104

Eccles, Patrick: Coleraine LY 33; 94, 131

Eccles, William: Lissan LY 31; 101, 107

Eccleston, family: Carrickfergus AM 37; 93

Eccleston, J.M.: Carrickfergus AM 37; 154

Ecclesville chapel: Donacavey TE 5; 64, 83

Ecclesville demesne: Donacavey TE 5; 69–70

Ecclesville Demesne td: Donacavey TE 5; 76, 78, 83, 85

Ecclesville estate: Donacavey TE 5; 71, 73

Ecclesville forts: Donacavey TE 5; 83

Ecclesville House: Donacavey TE 5; 64, 69

Ecclesville td: Donacavey TE 5; 64, 80

Ecclesville, family: Donacavey TE 5; 72

Echlin, John: Ballyhalbert DN 7; 6

Echlin, John: Ballyphilip DN 7; 8

Echlin, John: Ballywalter DN 7; 18

Echlin, John: Inishargy DN 7; 84

Echlin, John: Misc. DN 17; 125–26

Echlin, Rev. Robert: Kilroot AM 26; 73

Echlin, Rev. Robert: Misc. DN 17; 117

Echlin, Rev. Robert: Newry DN 3; 74

Echlin, Rev. Robert: Templecorran AM 26; 97, 107

Echline, Agnes: Derrykeighan AM 16; 87

Echline, Eupham: Derrykeighan AM 16; 87

Echline, Isobel: Derrykeighan AM 16; 87

Echline, John: Derrykeighan AM 16; 87

Echline, Margaret: Derrykeighan AM 16; 87

Echline, Mary: Derrykeighan AM 16; 87

Echline, Rev. Robert: Derrykeighan AM 16; 87

Echline, William: Derrykeighan AM 16; 87

Echlinville House: Inishargy DN 7; 84

Echlinville school: Ballyhalbert DN 7; 6

Echlinville td: Ballyhalbert DN 7; 6

Echlinville td: Ballywalter DN 7; 18

Echlinville td: Misc. DN 17; 122

Eckland, Rev.: Carnmoney AM 2; 86

Edanaveygh Bunn td: Magheraculmoney FH 14; 112

Edanaveygh td: Magheraculmoney FH 14; 111–12

Edantlahy td: Magheraculmoney FH 14; 111

Edbrooke, George: Seagoe AH 1; 103

Eddarowen td: Derrykeighan AM 16; 92

Edderagole (see Edergole): Aghalurcher FH 4; 14

Edderdauglash td: Cleenish FH 14; 28–29

Edderdauglash td: Derryvullan FH 14; 46

Eddergole (see Edergool)

Eddergool td: Drummully FH 4; 36, 39

Eddie, John: Newtownards DN 7; 112

Eden (Eaden) td: Dungiven LY 15; 27, 53, 62, 92

Eden bogs: Tamlaght O'Crilly LY 18; 86, 117, 126–27

Eden Castle: Tamlaght O'Crilly LY 18; 93–94, 122

Eden cave: Tamlaght O'Crilly LY 18; 127

Eden Cottage: Carrickfergus AM 37; 135

Eden day school: Tamlaght O'Crilly LY 18; 144

Eden forge: Tamlaght O'Crilly LY 18; 95

Eden fort [I]: Tamlaght O'Crilly LY 18; 95, 117

Eden fort [II]: Tamlaght O'Crilly LY 18; 117

Eden glen: Banagher LY 30; 25

Eden hibernian school: Tamlaght O'Crilly LY 18; 140–41

Eden House: Carrickfergus AM 37; 135

Eden mountain: Dungiven LY 15; 1, 92

Eden old castle: Tamlaght O'Crilly LY 18; 128

Eden school: Finvoy AM 23; 75

Eden standing stone: Banagher LY 30; 46

Eden Sunday school: Dungiven LY 15; 14, 118–19

Eden Sunday school: Tamlaght O'Crilly LY 18; 144

Eden td: Banagher LY 30; 35, 61–62, 72, 104, 109, 118, 123, 127, 129, 131

Eden td: Donaghedy TE 5; 92

Eden td: Misc. AM 10; 130

Eden td: Tamlaght O'Crilly LY 18; 87, 93–94, 96–98, 127, 132, 136, 138

Eden village: Carrickfergus AM 37; 3, 55–56, 93, 164

Eden village: Kilroot AM 26; 80–81

Eden village: Tamlaght O'Crilly LY 18; 92, 109

Eden village: Templecorran AM 26; 127

Eden wood: Tamlaght O'Crilly LY 18; 127

Eden, family: Ballinderry AM 21; 51

Edenacullo (see Edenticullo): Hillsborough DN 12; 86

Edenafogry (Ednafogry) td: Donacavey TE 5; 74, 76, 78, 80–82, 85

Edenagilhorn td: Aghavea FH 4; 23, 25

Edenamagh flax and tuck mill: Inniskeen MN 40; 125

Edenanean (see Edenaneane): Ballybay MN 40; 80

Edenaneane td: Ballybay MN 40; 80, 84

Edenaneane wood: Ballybay MN 40; 79

Edenappa td: Jonesborough AH 1; 46

Edenaslate (see Edenslate): Comber DN 7; 42

Edenasop (Edinsop) West td: Donacavey TE 5; 64, 76

Edenasop td: Donacavey TE 5; 81, 85

Edenasop West corn mill: Donacavey TE 5; 64

Edenballymore td: Banagher LY 30; 103–04

Edenballymore td: Faughanvale LY 36; 56, 59

Edenbane (see Edenbrone): Aughnamullen MN 40; 76

Edenbane td: Desertoghill LY 27; 1, 14, 19

Edenbrone td: Aughnamullen MN 40; 76

Edenbrone tuck mill: Aughnamullen MN 40; 72

Edendarragh hill: Kilrea LY 27; 106

Edendarriff (Edendariff) td: Dromara DN 12; 63, 65, 67

Edendarriff corn mill: Dromara DN 12; 67

Edendarriff mill: Dromara DN 12; 63

Edenderry female school: Seagoe AH 1; 106

Edenderry House: Drumbo DN 7; 56, 59

Edenderry male school: Seagoe AH 1; 106

Edenderry meeting house: Seagoe AH 1; 102

Edenderry mill [I]: Seapatrick DN 12; 134

Edenderry mill [II]: Seapatrick DN 12; 134

Edenderry mill [III]: Seapatrick DN 12; 134

Edenderry mill [IV]: Seapatrick DN 12; 134
Edenderry mills: Drumbo DN 7; 56
Edenderry td: Aghaderg DN 12; 2
Edenderry td: Drumbo DN 7; 55–56, 60–62
Edenderry td: Misc. DN 17; 130
Edenderry td: Seagoe AH 1; 108
Edenderry td: Seapatrick DN 12; 123, 126–27, 134
Edendoit (Edendoita) td: Desertcreat TE 20; 32, 34
Edendoit bleach green: Desertcreat TE 20; 32
Edendoit bleach mill: Desertcreat TE 20; 34
Edendork hill: Tullyniskan TE 20; 138
Edendork quarry: Tullyniskan TE 20; 141
Edenduffcarrick Castle: Drummaul AM 19; 63, 68, 70
Edenduffcarrick manor: Drummaul AM 19; 40–41, 47, 56, 71, 83
Edenduffcarrick manor: Shilvodan AM 19; 132
Edenduffcarrick stone: Drummaul AM 19; 67–68, 71, 78
Edenfaran (see Edenforan): Aughnamullen MN 40; 76
Edenfogry (see Edenafogry)
Edenforan td: Aughnamullen MN 40; 72, 76
Edenfore hill: Killeeshil TE 20; 64
Edenforgery (see Edenafogry)
Edenmore graveyard: Misc. DL 39; 185
Edenmore House: Donaghmore DL 39; 30–31
Edenmore House: Killygarvan DL 38; 47
Edenmore old church: Clonleigh DL 39; 3, 185
Edenmore school: Magheralin DN 12; 110, 110
Edenmore td: Balteagh LY 9; 40, 43, 45
Edenmore td: Clonleigh DL 39; 10, 12, 197
Edenmore td: Donaghmore DL 39; 37
Edenmore td: Enniskillen FH 4; 64, 74, 82
Edenmore td: Magheralin DN 12; 110
Edenmore td: Newry DN 3; 109
Edenohill td: Donaghmore DL 39; 37
Edenordinary corn mill: Dromore DN 12; 72
Edenordinary mill: Dromore DN 12; 78
Edenordinary td: Dromore DN 12; 72, 78
Edenreagh Beg giant's grave: Clondermot LY 34; 44
Edenreagh Beg td: Clondermot LY 34; 66, 110, 113, 116, 124, 131
Edenreagh More td: Clondermot LY 34; 66, 110, 113, 116, 124, 131
Edenreagh spade foundry: Ballyscullion LY 6; 49, 65
Edenreagh Sunday school: Ballyscullion LY 6; 63
Edenreagh td: Ballyscullion LY 6; 49, 78
Edenreagh td: Clondermot LY 34; 56, 72
Edenreagh td: Cumber LY 28; 65
Edenslate corn mill: Comber DN 7; 39
Edenslate flax mill: Comber DN 7; 39
Edenslate td: Comber DN 7; 35, 37, 39, 42–43

Edenticall (Edenticaul) td: Dungiven LY 15; 14, 23, 31, 66, 72, 74, 79, 88–89
Edenticall td: Banagher LY 30; 23
Edenticall td: Bovevagh LY 25; 29
Edenticullo (Ednacullo) td: Hillsborough DN 12; 86, 95, 99, 106
Edenticullo school: Hillsborough DN 12; 95, 99, 101
Edentober td: Ballymascanlan LH 40; 55
Edentrillick school: Dromore DN 12; 73, 78
Edentrillick school: Hillsborough DN 12; 100
Edentrillick td: Dromore DN 12; 70, 78
Edentrumley td: Clonallan DN 3; 1–2
Edenturcher td: Glenavy AM 21; 79
Ederadacurragh (see Ederdacurragh)
Ederdacurragh House: Aghalurcher FH 4; 8
Ederdacurragh td: Aghalurcher FH 4; 4, 10
Edergacal td: Clogher TE 5; 53
Edergill (see Edergole): Killymard DL 39; 101
Edergole chapel: Ematris MN 40; 114, 116
Edergole giant's grave: Ematris MN 40; 116
Edergole graveyard: Ematris MN 40; 114, 116
Edergole Island: Aghalurcher FH 4; 3, 14
Edergole mountains: Killymard DL 39; 102, 105
Edergole td: Clogher TE 5; 26, 37
Edergole td: Ematris MN 40; 116
Edergole td: Killymard DL 39; 95, 101
Edergoole corn mill: Drumragh TE 5; 110
Edergoole td: Drumragh TE 5; 110
Edernagh td: Artrea TE 20; 9–10
Ederny: Drumkeeran FH 14; 63, 65
Ederny: Magheraculmoney FH 14; 105, 107–08
Ederny bridge: Drumkeeran FH 14; 65
Ederny td: Magheraculmoney FH 14; 105
Ederwella locality: Banagher LY 30; 46, 48, 72, 76
Edgar, family: Blaris AM 8; 22
Edgar, family: Dunluce AM 16; 117
Edgar, G.: Newtownards DN 7; 112
Edgar, John: Clonduff DN 3; 4
Edgar, John: Duneane AM 19; 108, 120
Edgar, John: Newtownards DN 7; 112
Edgar, Joseph: Newry DN 3; 99
Edgar, Mr (Buncrana): Desertegney DL 38; 25
Edgar, Rev.: Magheradrool DN 17; 106
Edgar, Widow: Newtownards DN 7; 112
Edgar, William: Blaris DN 12; 46, 50
Edger, family: Dunluce AM 16; 117
Edgeworth, Edward: Misc. DN 17; 117
Edgeworth, Maj.: Tynan AH 1; 130
Edgeworth, Mr: Antrim AM 29; 21
Edgeworth, Mr: Muckamore AM 35; 63
Edgeworth, Mr: Nilteen AM 35; 90
Edinagilhorn (see Edenagilhorn): Aghavea FH 4; 25
Edinanay td: Ballybay MN 40; 84
Edinaneane (see Edenaneane): Ballybay MN 40; 79

Edinasop East td: Donacavey TE 5; 76, 78, 83

Edinasop West meeting house: Donacavey TE 5; 83

Edinasop West mill: Donacavey TE 5; 83

Edinasop West td: Donacavey TE 5; 78, 83

Edinatoodry (Ednatoodry) td: Donacavey TE 5; 67, 76–78, 80–81, 84–85

Edinburgh: Aghadowey LY 22; 14, 24–25

Edinburgh: Blaris AM 8; 8

Edinburgh: Donacavey TE 5; 75

Edinburgh: Galloon FH 4; 91

Edinburgh: Newry DN 3; 68

Edinburgh House of Refuge: Newry DN 3; 93

Edinmore (see Edenmore)

Edirowens td: Drumtullagh AM 16; 102

Edmondstone, Maj.: Carrickfergus AM 37; 136

Edmonson, Widow: Tamlaght TE 20; 84

Edmonson, William: Tamlaght TE 20; 78, 84, 90

Edmonston, Archibald: Misc. DN 17; 119

Edmonston, Elizabeth (see Montgomery): Misc. DN 17; 119

Edmonston, James: Island Magee AM 10; 94

Edmonston, Rev. James: Moira DN 12; 118

Edmonstone, Archibald: Templecorran AM 26; 100, 130

Edmonstone, family: Templecorran AM 26; 11, 85–86, 93, 97, 117–18, 127, 131

Edmonstone, Helen (see Dalway)

Edmonstone, John: Templecorran AM 26; 115

Edmonstone, Mrs Archibald: Templecorran AM 26; 100, 130

Edmonstone, Robert: Loughguile AM 13; 71

Edmonstone, William (Laird of Duntreath): Kilroot AM 26; 61, 72

Edmonstone, William: Ballynure AM 32; 51–52

Edmonstone, William: Templecorran AM 26; 94, 97, 99, 108, 119

Edmundson, William: Blaris AM 8; 7

Ednaculla (see Edenticullo): Hillsborough DN 12; 101

Ednagarry td: Drumballyroney DN 3; 14, 16, 18

Ednagone td: Dromore TE 5; 98

Ednasop (see Edenasop)

Ednasor td: Donacavey TE 5; 77

Ednavigh school: Drumkeeran FH 14; 67

Ednego td: Dromore DN 12; 72

Ednigal (see Edergole): Killymard DL 39; 95

Edrim glebe: Killymard DL 39; 96

Edrim old church: Killymard DL 39; 97

Edus, son of Anmerich: Muckamore AM 35; 82

Edward I, King: Clondermot LY 34; 45

Edward I, King: Drummaul AM 19; 69

Edward I, King: Island Magee AM 10; 62

Edward I, King: Kilbride AM 29; 149

Edward I, King: Killead AM 35; 32

Edward I, King: Misc. LY 31; 117–18

Edward I, King: Templepatrick AM 35; 130

Edward I, King: Umgall AM 35; 160

Edward II, King: Ballyclug AM 23; 65

Edward II, King: Carrickfergus AM 37; 34, 42

Edward II, King: Drummaul AM 19; 69

Edward II, King: Island Magee AM 10; 62

Edward II, King: Kilbride AM 29; 149

Edward II, King: Killead AM 35; 32

Edward II, King: Maghera LY 18; 57

Edward II, King: Templepatrick AM 35; 130

Edward III, King: Drummaul AM 19; 69

Edward III, King: Island Magee AM 10; 62

Edward III, King: Kilbride AM 29; 149

Edward III, King: Killead AM 35; 32

Edward III, King: Misc. LY 31; 118

Edward III, King: Shilvodan AM 19; 136

Edward IV, King: Carrickfergus AM 37; 18, 43

Edward IV, King: Clogher TE 5; 28

Edward IV, King: Magheramesk AM 21; 126

Edward VI, King: Clones FH 4; 29

Edward VI, King: Drummaul AM 19; 69

Edward VI, King: Newry DN 3; 64

Edward VI, King: Umgall AM 35; 160

Edward, Kings named: Carrickfergus AM 37; 83

Edward, Kings named: Kilroot AM 26; 69, 75

Edwards, Anne Jane: Donaghmore DL 39; 39

Edwards, B.: Drumbo DN 7; 59

Edwards, Charles: Carrickfergus AM 37; 194

Edwards, E.A.: Banagher LY 30; 4, 15, 23

Edwards, E.A.: Bovevagh LY 25; 3

Edwards, family: Culfeightrin AM 24; 59

Edwards, H.G.: Clogher TE 5; 30, 33, 44–45, 53

Edwards, H.G.: Donacavey TE 5; 73, 76–77, 81, 85–86

Edwards, Rev. Jonathon: Magilligan LY 11; 89

Edwards, Sarah: Bovevagh LY 25; 2–4, 20, 22–23, 57

Eessnabrockey altar: Errigal LY 27; 74

Eessnabrockey waterfall: Errigal LY 27; 74

Egan, Rev. Bernard: Emlaghfad SO 40; 177

Egan, Thomas: Drumbo DN 7; 56

Egerley, family: Ramoan AM 24; 107

Egerton, Francis: Newry DN 3; 89

Egfrid, King: Carnmoney AM 2; 51

Egfrid, King: Carrickfergus AM 37; 61

Egfrid, King: Misc. AM 10; 131

Egfrid, King: Templepatrick AM 35; 116

Egfrid, King: Umgall AM 35; 156–57

Eggleson, Samuel: Connor AM 19; 29

Egglybaan td: Donaghmore DL 39; 37

Eglantine demesne: Blaris DN 12; 26, 34

Eglinton, Alexander: Clonleigh DL 39; 9

Eglinton, Alexander: Skirts of Urney and Ardstraw TE 5; 140

Eglish (Iglish) td: Killymard DL 39; 101

Eglish chapel: Tartaraghan AH 1; 120
Eglish cromlech: Culfeightrin AM 24; 53
Eglish giant's grave: Artrea LY 6; 10, 27
Eglish graveyard: Artrea LY 6; 9, 17, 34
Eglish graveyard: Ballinderry TE 20; 11
Eglish graveyard: Tartaraghan AH 1; 121
Eglish Lower graveyard: Artrea LY 6; 10, 27
Eglish mountain: Culfeightrin AM 24; 53–54, 72
Eglish mountain: Killymard DL 39; 102
Eglish old graveyard: Artrea LY 6; 25
Eglish ph: Clonfeacle AH 1; 22
Eglish school: Dunaghy AM 13; 16
Eglish school: Skerry AM 13; 114
Eglish standing stones: Culfeightrin AM 24; 54, 72
Eglish td: Culfeightrin AM 24; 53
Eglish td: Dunaghy AM 13; 21–22
Eglish td: Skerry AM 13; 114, 118, 120
Eglish td: Tartaraghan AH 1; 118, 121
Egypt: Kilbroney DN 3; 31, 34
Eilagh district: Misc. SO 40; 199
Eimbin (see Evin)
Eisc (see Eise)
Eise lough (see Castle Coole lough): Derryvullan
    FH 14; 40
Eise lough: Enniskillen FH 4; 48
Eivers, John: Culdaff DL 38; 22
Eken, family: Ballinderry AM 21; 51
Ekin, Elin: Magherafelt LY 6; 98
Ekin, James [I]: Tamlaght TE 20; 76, 91, 103
Ekin, James [II]: Tamlaght TE 20; 116
Ekin, James [III]: Tamlaght TE 20; 128
Ekin, John: Tamlaght TE 20; 76, 91, 103
Ekin, Mary: Tamlaght TE 20; 133–34
Elagh (see Aileach): Clondermot LY 34; 34
Elagh bog: Killygarvan DL 38; 38, 44
Elagh td: Killygarvan DL 38; 46
Elanaghlughtoo Island: Kilmacteige SO 40; 194
Elbe river (Germany): Blaris AM 8; 89
Elder, Ellen: Agivey LY 22; 45
Elder, Henry: Desertoghill LY 27; 20
Elder, John: Balteagh LY 9; 27
Elder, John: Desertoghill LY 27; 31
Elder, Joseph: Balteagh LY 9; 27
Elder, Rev.: Duneane AM 19; 114
Elder, Rev. John: Aghadowey LY 22; 22
Elder, Rev. Matthew: Kilraghts AM 16; 132
Elder, Rev. Robert: Desertoghill LY 27; 10
Elder, Robert: Rasharkin AM 23; 134, 139–40
Elder, William: Loughguile AM 13; 67
Elder's spring: Desertoghill LY 27; 13
Eldertin, Joseph: Tamlaght TE 20; 82, 130, 136
Eldertin, Saly: Tamlaght TE 20; 77, 104
Eldertin, William: Tamlaght TE 20; 77, 80
Eldon, Mary: Ballyaghran LY 33; 17
Eldon, Mary: Coleraine LY 33; 67

Eleven Balliboes td: Moville DL 38; 70
Eleven Ballyboes td: Moville DL 38; 68
Elgin (Scotland): Aghadowey LY 22; 31
Elginny school: Skerry AM 13; 114
Elginny td: Skerry AM 13; 107
Elizabeth I, Queen: Aghadowey LY 22; 28
Elizabeth I, Queen: Ahoghill AM 23; 6, 14, 17, 26
Elizabeth I, Queen: Antrim AM 29; 23, 37
Elizabeth I, Queen: Armoy AM 24; 9
Elizabeth I, Queen: Artrea LY 6; 8
Elizabeth I, Queen: Ballylinny AM 32; 27
Elizabeth I, Queen: Ballymartin AM 2; 12, 16–17
Elizabeth I, Queen: Ballynascreen LY 31; 22
Elizabeth I, Queen: Ballynure AM 32; 35, 55, 61
Elizabeth I, Queen: Ballyrashane LY 22; 49, 58
Elizabeth I, Queen: Banagher LY 30; 7, 84, 100
Elizabeth I, Queen: Blaris AM 8; 3, 8, 89
Elizabeth I, Queen: Blaris DN 12; 32
Elizabeth I, Queen: Bovevagh LY 25; 21
Elizabeth I, Queen: Camlin AM 21; 60, 68
Elizabeth I, Queen: Carmavy AM 35; 6
Elizabeth I, Queen: Carnmoney AM 2; 51, 72, 93,
    96
Elizabeth I, Queen: Carrickfergus AM 37; 1, 13–14,
    18, 32, 34, 38, 42–43, 62, 148, 178
Elizabeth I, Queen: Clondavaddog DL 38; 6
Elizabeth I, Queen: Clondermot LY 34; 54–55, 61
Elizabeth I, Queen: Clones FH 4; 29
Elizabeth I, Queen: Clonoe TE 20; 31
Elizabeth I, Queen: Culfeightrin AM 24; 68
Elizabeth I, Queen: Cumber LY 28; 67, 72
Elizabeth I, Queen: Currin MN 40; 90
Elizabeth I, Queen: Derryaghy AM 8; 93
Elizabeth I, Queen: Dromara DN 12; 68
Elizabeth I, Queen: Drumlumman CN 40; 14
Elizabeth I, Queen: Drummaul AM 19; 69, 72
Elizabeth I, Queen: Dungiven LY 15; 35, 59
Elizabeth I, Queen: Dunsfort DN 17; 68
Elizabeth I, Queen: Faughanvale LY 36; 49, 63
Elizabeth I, Queen: Glenavy AM 21; 86
Elizabeth I, Queen: Hillsborough DN 12; 88
Elizabeth I, Queen: Island Magee AM 10; 62
Elizabeth I, Queen: Kilbride AM 29; 149
Elizabeth I, Queen: Kilbroney DN 3; 32
Elizabeth I, Queen: Kilkeel DN 3; 54
Elizabeth I, Queen: Killead AM 35; 17, 32, 49
Elizabeth I, Queen: Killygarvan DL 38; 41
Elizabeth I, Queen: Killyleagh DN 17; 81
Elizabeth I, Queen: Kilmacteige SO 40; 188–89
Elizabeth I, Queen: Kilroot AM 26; 69, 71, 75
Elizabeth I, Queen: Maghera LY 18; 24, 57
Elizabeth I, Queen: Magheragall AM 21; 103
Elizabeth I, Queen: Magheramesk AM 21; 126
Elizabeth I, Queen: Misc. LY 31; 118, 137
Elizabeth I, Queen: Misc. LY 36; 115

Elizabeth I, Queen: Muckamore AM 35; 56, 82
Elizabeth I, Queen: Newry DN 3; 65, 108
Elizabeth I, Queen: Nilteen AM 35; 99
Elizabeth I, Queen: Raloo AM 32; 81, 116
Elizabeth I, Queen: Rasharkin AM 23; 128, 130
Elizabeth I, Queen: Shilvodan AM 19; 136
Elizabeth I, Queen: Templecarn DL 39; 163
Elizabeth I, Queen: Templepatrick AM 35; 130
Elizabeth I, Queen: Tullyaughnish DL 38; 91
Elizabeth I, Queen: Tullyrusk AM 21; 131, 135
Elizabeth I, Queen: Umgall AM 35; 160
Ellagh district: Misc. SO 40; 199
Ellanbough chapel: Layd AM 13; 47
Ellanbough td: Layd AM 13; 47
Ellen's Brae hill: Faughanvale LY 36; 22
Elliot, family: Aghagallon AM 21; 9
Elliot, family: Maghera LY 18; 13
Elliot, family: Misc. LY 36; 104
Elliot, James: Coleraine LY 33; 72
Elliot, Mr (see Minto)
Elliot, Thomas: Aghagallon AM 21; 10
Elliot, Thomas: Aghalee AM 21; 32
Elliot, William: Blaris DN 12; 46, 50
Elliot, William: Kilrea LY 27; 129
Elliott, Agness: Maghera LY 18; 31
Elliott, family: Killesher FH 14; 84
Elliott, George (see Saunders): Carrickfergus AM
    37; 111
Elliott, George: Enniskillen FH 4; 77
Elliott, John: Urney DL 39; 182
Elliott, Mary: Carrickfergus AM 37; 130
Elliott, Patrick: Newry DN 3; 99
Elliott, Robert [I]: Maghera LY 18; 53
Elliott, Robert [II]: Maghera LY 18; 16, 49, 53
Elliott, Robert [III]: Maghera LY 18; 54
Elliott, S.M.: Island Magee AM 10; 31, 86
Elliott, Samuel: Maghera LY 18; 53
Elliott, Thomas: Skerry AM 13; 119
Elliott, William: Enniskillen FH 4; 69
Elliott, William: Killea and Taughboyne DL 39; 87
Elliott, William [I]: Maghera LY 18; 31
Elliott, William [II]: Maghera LY 18; 53
Ellis, Capt.: Carrickfergus AM 37; 183
Ellis, Edmund: Templepatrick AM 35; 132
Ellis, F.: Aughnamullen MN 40; 76
Ellis, family: Ballynure AM 32; 56
Ellis, family: Ballyscullion LY 6; 53
Ellis, family: Dunluce AM 16; 117
Ellis, family: Misc. LY 36; 104
Ellis, H.: Aughnamullen MN 40; 76
Ellis, H.C.: Ballynure AM 32; 50, 55, 69
Ellis, H.C.: Carrickfergus AM 37; 27, 33, 56,
    135–36, 183
Ellis, Harkness: Duneane AM 19; 116
Ellis, Henry: Ballybay MN 40; 84

Ellis, Henry: Tamlaght O'Crilly LY 18; 105, 108
Ellis, Hercules: Carrickfergus AM 37; 99
Ellis, Hercules: Tamlaght O'Crilly LY 18; 87, 90,
    98, 105, 108
Ellis, John: Newry DN 3; 99, 103
Ellis, Miss: Carrickfergus AM 37; 136
Ellis, Mr: Carrickfergus AM 37; 161
Ellis, Mr: Kirkinriola AM 23; 106
Ellis, Nicholas: Clones FH 4; 27, 29
Ellis, Valentine: Hillsborough DN 12; 105
Ellis, William: Clondermot LY 34; 83
Ellis, William: Hillsborough DN 12; 105–06
Ellisholding chapel: Killevy AH 1; 52
Ellisholding school: Killevy AH 1; 53
Ellison, James: Muckamore AM 35; 78
Ellison, Rev. Thomas: Banagher LY 30; 73
Elo, Colman (see Columbkille): Muckamore AM
    35; 56
Elram, family: Misc. LY 36; 104
Elspiaiden's well: Magilligan LY 11; 129
Elton, John: Ballynure AM 32; 73
Elwin, John: Clondermot LY 34; 72–73
Elwood, Rev. E.L.: Ballymore AH 1; 3
Ely Island: Devenish FH 14; 52, 57, 59
Ely Island bridge: Devenish FH 14; 53
Ely Lodge: Devenish FH 14; 52–53, 55, 57
Ely Lodge: Inishmacsaint FH 14; 74
Ely, Lady: Devenish FH 14; 56
Ely, Marchioness of: Inishmacsaint FH 14; 78
Ely, Marquis of: Devenish FH 14; 50, 52–53, 55–59
Ely, Marquis of: Enniskillen FH 4; 62
Ely, Marquis of: Inishmacsaint FH 14; 76, 79
Ely, Marquis of: Rossorry FH 14; 115
Ely. Marquis of: Enniskillen FH 4; 64
Emania palace: Misc. LY 36; 105
Ematris corn mill: Aghabog MN 40; 62
Ematris ph: Aghabog MN 40; 62, 64, 66–67
Ematris ph: Aughnamullen MN 40; 69–70
Ematris ph: Clogher TE 5; 40
Ematris ph: Currin MN 40; 86, 88, 91–92
Ematris ph: Drumgoon CN 40; 1, 10
Emdeal td: Drumballyroney DN 3; 14, 16, 18
Emerson, John: Hillsborough DN 12; 107
Emerson, Miss: Comber DN 7; 34
Emerson, Robert: Hillsborough DN 12; 106–07
Emgaill (see Umgall): Mallusk AM 2; 115
Emlagation trigonometrical station: Emlaghfad SO
    40; 176
Emlagh district: Misc. SO 40; 199
Emlaghfad abbey: Emlaghfad SO 40; 182
Emlaghfad glebe: Emlaghfad SO 40; 180
Emlaghfad old church: Emlaghfad SO 40; 177, 179,
    182
Emlaghfad td: Emlaghfad SO 40; 177
Emlaghnaghten district: Misc. SO 40; 198

Emmcroo [or Emmerroo] school: Enniskillen FH 4; 83

Emmcroo [or Emmerroo] td: Enniskillen FH 4; 82

Emmerroo [or Emmcroo] school: Enniskillen FH 4; 83

Emmerroo [or Emmcroo] td: Enniskillen FH 4; 82

Emvagh lough: Ardstraw TE 5; 2

Emy lough: Donagh MN 40; 98

Emy td: Donagh MN 40; 98

Emyvale: Donagh MN 40; 99, 101, 105

Emyvale: Errigal Truagh MN 40; 121

Emyvale bridge: Donagh MN 40; 99

Emyvale chapel: Donagh MN 40; 99

Emyvale lough: Donagh MN 40; 98

Enach (see Enagh): Clondermot LY 34; 34

Enagh (Enaught) td: Drumachose LY 9; 87, 96, 108

Enagh (Enoch) td: Garvaghy DN 12; 80–82

Enagh barony: Clondermot LY 34; 46

Enagh bog: Clondermot LY 34; 34

Enagh Brack fort: Balteagh LY 9; 12, 25

Enagh Castle: Banagher LY 30; 95

Enagh Castle: Clondermot LY 34; 3, 18, 34, 48–49, 53–55, 60, 106

Enagh Castle: Dungiven LY 15; 33

Enagh Castle: Misc. LY 36; 105

Enagh church: Clondermot LY 34; 3, 12, 18, 27, 33, 46, 66–67, 69, 74–75, 81

Enagh corn mill: Clondermot LY 34; 3, 18

Enagh district: Clondermot LY 34; 60–61, 74, 76

Enagh female school: Drumachose LY 9; 50, 125

Enagh graveyard: Clondermot LY 34; 34, 46, 106

Enagh lough: Aghaloo TE 20; 2

Enagh lough: Banagher LY 30; 95

Enagh lough: Clondermot LY 34; 1, 3–4, 17–18, 31, 33–34, 36, 46, 48, 57, 66, 106, 116, 120

Enagh lough: Misc. LY 36; 105

Enagh Lough bridge [I]: Clondermot LY 34; 7

Enagh Lough bridge [II]: Clondermot LY 34; 7

Enagh Lough district: Clondermot LY 34; 14

Enagh Lough hamlet: Clondermot LY 34; 4, 24, 26, 48

Enagh Lower td: Ballymoney AM 16; 9

Enagh meeting house: Garvaghy DN 12; 80, 82

Enagh school: Drumachose LY 9; 86

Enagh spring: Clondermot LY 34; 18

Enagh Sunday school: Drumachose LY 9; 85, 132

Enagh td: Clondermot LY 34; 38, 56, 64, 66–67, 76, 110, 112, 116, 124, 131

Enagh td: Drumachose LY 9; 125

Enagh Upper td: Ballymoney AM 16; 1

Enan, man named: Clondermot LY 34; 47

Enda, St: Faughanvale LY 36; 58

Endeus, father of Mochaimoc: Enniskillen FH 4; 70

Enenbawn td: Enniskillen FH 4; 82

Enerrigate lough: Killymard DL 39; 105

Enery, Col: Donaghedy TE 5; 89

Enery, Col: Tomregan FH 4; 127, 131

Enery, Frances (nee Nixon): Kinawley FH 4; 116

Enever river: Desertoghill LY 27; 4

England: Aghabog MN 40; 66–67

England: Aghadowey LY 22; 16, 38

England: Aghalurcher FH 4; 12

England: Aghanloo LY 11; 11, 32, 34–35

England: Ahoghill AM 23; 10, 19

England: Antrim AM 29; 6, 17, 23, 48

England: Ardglass DN 17; 5

England: Artrea LY 6; 39

England: Aughnamullen MN 40; 74–75

England: Ballee DN 17; 18–19

England: Ballintoy AM 24; 17

England: Ballyaghran LY 33; 14

England: Ballybay MN 40; 82

England: Ballyclug AM 23; 59

England: Ballycor AM 32; 7

England: Ballymoney AM 16; 19

England: Ballynascreen LY 31; 13, 22–23

England: Ballynure AM 32; 35

England: Ballyrashane LY 22; 51, 53, 66

England: Ballyscullion AM 19; 9

England: Ballyscullion LY 6; 57, 63

England: Ballywillin LY 33; 36–37

England: Balteagh LY 9; 16

England: Banagher LY 30; 5, 18, 35–36, 60–61, 99

England: Belleek FH 14; 5

England: Billy AM 16; 46

England: Blaris AM 8; 70–71, 77

England: Blaris DN 12; 31

England: Bovevagh LY 25; 27, 54–55, 60–61

England: Camlin AM 21; 68, 70

England: Carnmoney AM 2; 51–53, 60, 71, 92

England: Carrickfergus AM 37; 13, 62–63, 75, 89, 137, 171

England: Clondavaddog DL 38; 7, 11

England: Clondermot LY 34; 5, 16, 24, 28

England: Clonmany DL 38; 17

England: Coleraine LY 33; 98, 102–03, 119, 126, 143, 152

England: Comber DN 7; 37

England: Connor AM 19; 25

England: Cumber LY 28; 18, 28, 50, 52, 58

England: Currin MN 40; 94, 96–97

England: Derryaghy AM 8; 114

England: Derrybrusk FH 4; 33

England: Desertegney DL 38; 27

England: Desertlyn LY 31; 40, 47

England: Desertmartin LY 31; 60, 62

England: Desertoghill LY 27; 8, 12

England: Doagh AM 29; 66, 95

England: Donaghmoyne MN 40; 109

England: Donegal DL 39; 50
England: Down DN 17; 52
England: Drumachose LY 9; 87, 134
England: Drumcree AH 1; 35, 37
England: Drumglass TE 20; 42
England: Drumgoon CN 40; 10
England: Drumkeeran FH 14; 66
England: Drumlumman CN 40; 16–17
England: Drummaul AM 19; 62
England: Drummully FH 4; 37
England: Drumragh TE 5; 109
England: Dungiven LY 15; 32, 74–75, 100
England: Dunluce AM 16; 112
England: Dunsfort DN 17; 70
England: Ematris MN 40; 118
England: Enniskeen CN 40; 28
England: Enniskillen FH 4; 49, 61
England: Errigal LY 27; 47–48, 62, 66
England: Faughanvale LY 36; 18, 20, 31, 34
England: Finvoy AM 23; 73
England: Glenavy AM 21; 87, 89
England: Glynn AM 26; 7
England: Grey Abbey DN 7; 70
England: Inishargy DN 7; 85
England: Inishkeel DL 39; 68–69, 71
England: Inishmacsaint FH 14; 78
England: Inniskeen MN 40; 128
England: Inver AM 26; 52
England: Kilcronaghan LY 31; 73, 85
England: Kilkeel DN 3; 47
England: Killagan AM 23; 80, 84–85
England: Killanny MN 40; 133
England: Killdrumsherdan CN 40; 37
England: Killead AM 35; 14, 17, 48
England: Killeeshil TE 20; 63
England: Killelagh LY 27; 99
England: Killesher FH 14; 85
England: Killowen LY 33; 165, 172
England: Killymard DL 39; 96
England: Kilmacteige SO 40; 192
England: Kilmegan DN 3; 58, 60
England: Kilmore AH 1; 65
England: Kilrea LY 27; 110
England: Kilskeery TE 5; 116
England: Kilteevoge DL 39; 113
England: Kinawley FH 4; 109, 119, 121, 123
England: Kirkinriola AM 23; 91, 108
England: Lambeg AM 8; 139
England: Laragh CN 40; 45
England: Layd AM 13; 50
England: Layd and Inispollan AM 13; 57
England: Leck DL 39; 117
England: Lough Swilly DL 38; 130
England: Macosquin LY 22; 123
England: Maghera LY 18; 68

England: Magheracloone MN 40; 140
England: Magheraculmoney FH 14; 108
England: Magherafelt LY 6; 104
England: Magheross MN 40; 148
England: Magilligan LY 11; 140
England: Manorhamilton Union LM 40; 53
England: Misc. LY 31; 118, 134
England: Montiaghs AH 1; 92
England: Moville DL 38; 72
England: Muckamore AM 35; 61
England: Newry DN 3; 68, 72
England: Nilteen AM 35; 94
England: Pomeroy TE 20; 71
England: Raloo AM 32; 85, 128
England: Ramoan AM 24; 99, 101
England: Raphoe DL 39; 131
England: Rasharkin AM 23; 133
England: Rashee AM 32; 140
England: Tamlaght O'Crilly LY 18; 97, 101, 111, 138
England: Tartaraghan AH 1; 122
England: Taughboyne DL 39; 152
England: Templecorran AM 26; 87–88, 126
England: Templepatrick AM 35; 121, 123, 145
England: Termoneeny LY 6; 126
England: Tickmacrevan AM 13; 131
England: Trory FH 14; 129, 134
England: Tullyaughnish DL 38; 91, 93–94
England: Tullyniskan TE 20; 140
England: Tullyrusk AM 21; 135
England: Umgall AM 35; 156
English, family: Templecorran AM 26; 117, 119
English, John: Ballinderry AM 21; 52
English, John: Glynn AM 26; 44
English, Nathaniel: Killead AM 35; 53
English, Thomas: Island Magee AM 10; 95
English, Thomas: Magheramesk AM 21; 120
English, William: Ballinderry AM 21; 56
English, William: Camlin AM 21; 74
Englishman's cove: Ballintoy AM 24; 29–30
Englishman's Mountain locality: Carrickfergus AM 37; 33, 94
Englishtown: Blaris AM 8; 38, 47
Englishtown bleach green: Macosquin LY 22; 82, 104
Englishtown bog: Macosquin LY 22; 78
Englishtown bridge: Blaris AM 8; 35
Englishtown cave: Macosquin LY 22; 95
Englishtown House: Macosquin LY 22; 80–81, 101
Englishtown meeting house: Macosquin LY 22; 79–81, 94, 99–100
Englishtown Sunday school: Macosquin LY 22; 94
Englishtown td: Coleraine LY 33; 104, 106
Englishtown td: Macosquin LY 22; 77, 94, 99
Eniskeane (see Enniskillen): Enniskillen FH 4; 41

Enler river: Comber DN 7; 30
Ennaught pound: Drumachose LY 9; 121
Ennaught school: Drumachose LY 9; 121–22
Ennaught td: Drumachose LY 9; 122
Ennerwore lough: Mevagh DL 38; 55
Ennis O'Donnell Island: Donegal DL 39; 47
Ennis round tower: Inniskeen MN 40; 125–26
Ennish corn mill: Killeeshil TE 20; 62, 64
Enniskeen (Monaghan): (see Inniskeen)
Enniskerry district: Ballynascreen LY 31; 33
Enniskillen: Aghaloo TE 20; 1
Enniskillen: Aghalurcher FH 4; 2, 5–6, 8, 15–16
Enniskillen: Aghavea FH 4; 19, 21, 24
Enniskillen: Belleek FH 14; 2–3
Enniskillen: Blaris AM 8; 51
Enniskillen: Boho FH 14; 9
Enniskillen: Cleenish FH 14; 15–16, 18, 25, 27
Enniskillen: Clogher TE 5; 30, 52
Enniskillen: Clones FH 4; 26–27
Enniskillen: Derrybrusk FH 4; 30, 32–33
Enniskillen: Derryvullan FH 14; 38–39, 43–45
Enniskillen: Devenish FH 14; 51, 56–57, 59
Enniskillen: Donaghmore DL 39; 29, 32
Enniskillen: Donegal DL 39; 57
Enniskillen: Dromore TE 5; 96
Enniskillen: Drumkeeran FH 14; 69
Enniskillen: Drummully FH 4; 35–36
Enniskillen: Drumragh TE 5; 107, 110
Enniskillen: Dungiven LY 15; 84
Enniskillen: Enniskillen FH 4; 41, 43–45, 47,
    50–52, 56, 59, 61–62, 65, 67, 69–71, 75, 77,
    82–83
Enniskillen: Errigal Truagh MN 40; 123
Enniskillen: Galloon FH 4; 90, 98, 100–01
Enniskillen: Inishmacsaint FH 14; 72
Enniskillen: Killeeshil TE 20; 64
Enniskillen: Killesher FH 14; 86, 88
Enniskillen: Kilskeery TE 5; 114
Enniskillen: Kinawley FH 4; 108–10, 114–15,
    121–23
Enniskillen: Longfield TE 5; 132
Enniskillen: Magheracross FH 14; 94–95, 97,
    100–01
Enniskillen: Manorhamilton Union LM 40; 47, 50
Enniskillen: Rossorry FH 14; 116
Enniskillen: Templecarn DL 39; 158, 161, 170
Enniskillen: Trory FH 14; 128–31, 134
Enniskillen: Tyholland MN 40; 174
Enniskillen: Tynan AH 1; 127
Enniskillen Abbey St school [I]: Enniskillen FH 4;
    85
Enniskillen Abbey St school [II]: Enniskillen FH 4;
    85
Enniskillen barracks: Enniskillen FH 4; 54
Enniskillen brewery: Enniskillen FH 4; 54

Enniskillen carding and spinning factory:
    Enniskillen FH 4; 75
Enniskillen Castle: Enniskillen FH 4; 50, 57
Enniskillen Castle barracks: Enniskillen FH 4; 54
Enniskillen chapel (C): Enniskillen FH 4; 54
Enniskillen chapels (M): Enniskillen FH 4; 54
Enniskillen church: Enniskillen FH 4; 52–53,
    71–73, 76
Enniskillen Coles Row school [I]: Enniskillen FH 4;
    85
Enniskillen Coles Row school [II]: Enniskillen FH
    4; 85
Enniskillen corn market: Enniskillen FH 4; 54
Enniskillen county gaol: Enniskillen FH 4; 54
Enniskillen court house: Enniskillen FH 4; 54, 75
Enniskillen Dame St school [I]: Enniskillen FH 4;
    85
Enniskillen Dame St school [II]: Enniskillen FH 4;
    85
Enniskillen Darling St school: Enniskillen FH 4;
    84–85
Enniskillen dispensary: Magheracross FH 14; 98
Enniskillen distillery: Enniskillen FH 4; 54
Enniskillen east bridge: Enniskillen FH 4; 55
Enniskillen graveyard: Enniskillen FH 4; 72
Enniskillen hospital: Rossorry FH 14; 117
Enniskillen infirmary: Derrybrusk FH 4; 32
Enniskillen infirmary: Derryvullan FH 14; 43
Enniskillen Island: Enniskillen FH 4; 41, 44
Enniskillen Main St school: Enniskillen FH 4; 84
Enniskillen market house: Enniskillen FH 4; 54, 60
Enniskillen Mary St school: Enniskillen FH 4; 84
Enniskillen meeting house: Enniskillen FH 4; 54
Enniskillen mountain: Cappagh TE 5; 21
Enniskillen New Market school: Enniskillen FH 4;
    84
Enniskillen old castle: Enniskillen FH 4; 72
Enniskillen old racecourse: Enniskillen FH 4; 63
Enniskillen old school: Enniskillen FH 4; 63
Enniskillen ph: Aghalurcher FH 4; 1, 3
Enniskillen ph: Aghavea FH 4; 17
Enniskillen ph: Cleenish FH 14; 11
Enniskillen ph: Clogher TE 5; 24, 40
Enniskillen ph: Derrybrusk FH 4; 30, 33
Enniskillen ph: Donacavey TE 5; 66, 84
Enniskillen ph: Magheracross FH 14; 91
Enniskillen ph: Rossorry FH 14; 115
Enniskillen ph: Trory FH 14; 122
Enniskillen Pudding Lane school: Enniskillen FH 4;
    84
Enniskillen Royal School: Cleenish FH 14; 29–30
Enniskillen royal school: Enniskillen FH 4; 63
Enniskillen Royal School: Killesher FH 14; 87
Enniskillen Royal School: Kinawley FH 4; 110

Enniskillen School House Lane school: Enniskillen FH 4; 85

Enniskillen shambles: Enniskillen FH 4; 54

Enniskillen Wellington St school [I]: Enniskillen FH 4; 84

Enniskillen Wellington St school [II]: Enniskillen FH 4; 84

Enniskillen west battery: Rossorry FH 14; 117

Enniskillen west bridge: Enniskillen FH 4; 55

Enniskillen, Earl (late 1700s): Enniskillen FH 4; 58, 61, 74–75

Enniskillen, Earl: Enniskillen FH 4; 63, 77, 81–82, 84

Enniskillen, Earl: Kinawley FH 4; 109, 111, 119, 121

Enniskillen, family: Enniskillen FH 4; 60

Enniskillen, family: Kinawley FH 4; 117

Enniskillen, Lord (1690s): Enniskillen FH 4; 52

Enniskillen, Lord: Cleenish FH 14; 22, 29–30

Enniskillen, Lord: Derryvullan FH 14; 46

Enniskillen, Lord: Killesher FH 14; 81–88

Enniskillen, Lord: Magheracross FH 14; 102

Enniskillen, Lord: Magheross MN 40; 151

Enniskillen, Lord: Rossorry FH 14; 115

Ennislargie td: Ballyphilip DN 7; 8

Enniss, John: Drummaul AM 19; 90

Enniss, Widow: Muckamore AM 35; 81

Enogh school: Ballymoney AM 16; 27

Enos, St: Clondermot LY 34; 65

Enraght, Rev. Matthew: Desertlyn LY 31; 39

Entrenchment hill: Raloo AM 32; 115–17, 122–23

Entrican, family: Misc. LY 36; 104

Entrumnia (see Antrim): Antrim AM 29; 5

Entwistle, Thomas: Carrickfergus AM 37; 132

Entwistle, William: Ballinderry AM 21; 56, 58

Envagh chapel: Ardstraw TE 5; 11

Envagh fort: Ardstraw TE 5; 12

Envagh lough: Ardstraw TE 5; 10

Envagh td: Ardstraw TE 5; 12

Erck, Mr: Clonleigh DL 39; 15

Erdinagh td: Aghalurcher FH 4; 14

Erdith, Rev.: Ballynure AM 32; 65

Erean (see Avaghon): Aughnamullen MN 40; 72

Erenagh (see Erynagh): Inch DN 17; 75

Ergal district: Clogher TE 5; 24, 27

Ergana bog: Kilrea LY 27; 107

Erganagh (Erginagh) td: Ardstraw TE 5; 12

Erganagh fort: Ardstraw TE 5; 12

Erganagh school: Ardstraw TE 5; 6, 13

Erinagh quarry: Bright DN 17; 37

Erinagh td: Bright DN 17; 34, 37

Ernagh (see Erinagh): Bright DN 17; 34

Ernagh school: Killevy AH 1; 54

Erne Canal: Templecarn DL 39; 170

Erne river: Belleek FH 14; 1, 6

Erne river: Clondermot LY 34; 69

Erne river: Drumlumman CN 40; 12–13

Erne river: Drummully FH 4; 34

Erne river: Drung CN 40; 19

Erne river: Enniskillen FH 4; 44

Erne river: Kilbarron DL 39; 74, 76–78

Erne river: Templecarn DL 39; 158

Erne td: Magheraculmoney FH 14; 110

Erne, Earl of: Aghalurcher FH 4; 6, 8–11, 13, 16

Erne, Earl of: Clonleigh DL 39; 1, 4–5, 12

Erne, Earl of: Galloon FH 4; 91, 94, 98

Erne, Earl of: Kinawley FH 4; 119, 121

Erne, Earl of: Misc. DL 39; 186, 189

Erne, family: Kinawley FH 4; 117

Erne, Lord: Boho FH 14; 8

Erne, Lord: Clonleigh DL 39; 4

Erne, Lord: Taughboyne DL 39; 151

Errarooey locality: Lough Swilly DL 38; 122

Errigal Bank district: Errigal LY 27; 77

Errigal bog: Errigal Keerogue TE 20; 52

Errigal bridge: Errigal LY 27; 45, 59–60, 71

Errigal chapel: Errigal Keerogue TE 20; 46

Errigal church: Ballyscullion LY 6; 49

Errigal church: Errigal Keerogue TE 20; 46

Errigal forts: Errigal Keerogue TE 20; 52

Errigal giant's footsteps: Errigal LY 27; 42

Errigal Glebe House: Errigal LY 27; 40, 51

Errigal Glebe td: Errigal Keerogue TE 20; 57

Errigal graveyard: Clondermot LY 34; 34

Errigal Keerogue (Ballynasaggart) ph: Clogher TE 5; 24, 53–55, 57–59

Errigal Keerogue ph: Carnteel TE 20; 23

Errigal Keerogue ph: Clogherny TE 20; 25

Errigal Keerogue ph: Donacavey TE 5; 62

Errigal meeting house: Errigal Keerogue TE 20; 46

Errigal mountain: Clondavaddog DL 38; 6

Errigal national school [I]: Errigal Keerogue TE 20; 48

Errigal national school [II]: Errigal Keerogue TE 20; 48

Errigal old church (see Ballintemple): Errigal LY 27; 37

Errigal old glebe house: Errigal LY 27; 57–58

Errigal ph: Aghadowey LY 22; 4, 15–16, 32

Errigal ph: Aghanloo LY 11; 3, 28

Errigal ph: Balteagh LY 9; 20

Errigal ph: Banagher LY 30; 1, 36, 53

Errigal ph: Bovevagh LY 25; 44

Errigal ph: Clogher TE 5; 40

Errigal ph: Cumber LY 28; 65, 69

Errigal ph: Desertoghill LY 27; 1, 9–10, 12–13, 16–17

Errigal ph: Dungiven LY 15; 50

Errigal ph: Macosquin LY 22; 98

Errigal ph: Misc. LY 36; 113

Errigal ph: Skerry AM 13; 108
Errigal ph: Tamlaght Finlagan LY 25; 69
Errigal school: Errigal Truagh MN 40; 121–22
Errigal td: Errigal Keerogue TE 20; 52, 57
Errigal Truagh ph: Clogher TE 5; 24–25, 53
Errigal Truagh ph: Donagh MN 40; 98
Errigal Truagh ph: Errigal Keerogue TE 20; 49
Errigal Truagh ph: Killeeshil TE 20; 64
Errigal Truagh ph: Tydavnet MN 40; 169
Errigle (see Errigal)
Erritty td: Misc. DL 39; 198
Errity Churchland td: Raymoghy DL 39; 137
Errity meeting house: Raymoghy DL 39; 133
Errity td: Raymoghy DL 39; 137, 141
Errol, James: Carrickfergus AM 37; 194
Erskine, Anne (Jnr): Carrickfergus AM 37; 158
Erskine, Anne (Snr): Carrickfergus AM 37; 158
Erskine, Arthur: Killead AM 35; 37
Erskine, Betty: Carrickfergus AM 37; 158
Erskine, Henry: Carrickfergus AM 37; 158
Erskine, Isabella: Carrickfergus AM 37; 158
Erskine, James: Carrickfergus AM 37; 150
Erskine, Jane: Carrickfergus AM 37; 158
Erskine, Margaret: Carrickfergus AM 37; 158
Erskine, Rev.: Laragh CN 40; 41–42
Erskine, Richard (Jnr): Carrickfergus AM 37; 158
Erskine, Richard (Snr): Carrickfergus AM 37; 158
Erskine, Robert: Carrickfergus AM 37; 158
Erskine, William: Carrickfergus AM 37; 158
Erskine's public house: Muckamore AM 35; 76
Ervey (Irvey) td: Cumber LY 28; 56–57, 60, 62, 64, 95, 100, 104, 107, 109
Ervey bog: Cumber LY 28; 46, 48
Ervey meeting house: Enniskeen CN 40; 28
Ervey school: Cumber LY 28; 26, 34, 74–76, 79
Ervey standing stone: Cumber LY 28; 42–43, 45
Ervey Sunday school: Cumber LY 28; 24
Ervey td: Aghavea FH 4; 23
Ervey wood: Cumber LY 28; 100
Ervin, Eleanor: Hillsborough DN 12; 107
Erwin, David: Hillsborough DN 12; 106
Erwin, James: Hillsborough DN 12; 107
Erwin, John: Clogher TE 5; 41
Erwine, person named: Kilbroney DN 3; 30
Erynach (see Erynagh): Inch DN 17; 75
Erynagh monastery: Down DN 17; 61
Erynagh monastery: Inch DN 17; 75
Erynagh well: Inch DN 17; 75
Esbrick lough: Clogher TE 5; 47
Escalane school: Connor AM 19; 28
Escort hamlet: Culfeightrin AM 24; 45
Esera td: Clogher TE 5; 37
Eshacorran td: Aghavea FH 4; 23
Eshanummer td: Aghalurcher FH 4; 14
Eshbane td: Aghalurcher FH 4; 4, 14

Eshbralley td: Aghalurcher FH 4; 14
Eshcarcage td: Aghalurcher FH 4; 14
Eshclofin hill: Tydavnet MN 40; 169
Eshery hill: Layd AM 13; 37, 42
Eshery td: Layd AM 13; 37, 44
Eshka (see Ess): Ballynascreen LY 31; 12
Eshlanaduff td: Dungiven LY 15; 75
Eshmeen mountain: Aghalurcher FH 4; 2
Eshmeen td: Aghalurcher FH 4; 14
Eshnadarragh td: Aghavea FH 4; 23
Eshnaglough hill: Tydavnet MN 40; 169
Eshnaglough td: Tydavnet MN 40; 169
Eshnagorr td: Aghalurcher FH 4; 14
Eshnanumera td: Aghavea FH 4; 23
Eshnascreen td: Aghalurcher FH 4; 14
Eshnasillogmore td: Aghalurcher FH 4; 14
Eshthomas td: Aghalurcher FH 4; 14
Eskaheen hill: Muff DL 38; 80
Eskaheen mass-house: Muff DL 38; 81–82
Eskaheen old church: Muff DL 38; 81
Eskaheen td: Muff DL 38; 80, 82
Eskard school: Clogher TE 5; 42
Eske lough: Donegal DL 39; 42, 44, 47, 49, 54–55
Eske lough: Killymard DL 39; 94–96, 99, 102, 105
Eske river: Donegal DL 39; 42, 44–45, 47–49, 51, 54
Eske river: Killymard DL 39; 94–97, 105, 108
Esker bog: Dromore TE 5; 93
Esker td: Dromore TE 5; 93, 97–98
Eskeragh (see Eskragh): Kilmacteige SO 40; 190
Eskeragh td: Aghalurcher FH 4; 14
Eskeratrool (Eskerschool) td: Clogher TE 5; 42
Eskeratrool day school: Clogher TE 5; 43
Eskeratrool school: Clogher TE 5; 42
Eskermore school: Clogher TE 5; 46
Eskermore td: Clogher TE 5; 32, 36, 46, 53
Eskermore td: Clogherny TE 20; 27
Eskernabrogue td: Clogher TE 5; 32, 36, 53
Eskin, Samuel: Carrickfergus AM 37; 163
Eskragh (Eskeragh) td: Clogher TE 5; 26, 41, 45, 53
Eskragh chapel: Clogher TE 5; 38–39
Eskragh school: Clogher TE 5; 41
Eskragh td: Kilmacteige SO 40; 190, 193, 196
Eskregh (see Eskragh)
Eskylane cove [I]: Shilvodan AM 19; 136, 138
Eskylane cove [II]: Shilvodan AM 19; 136, 138
Eskylane forts: Shilvodan AM 19; 137
Eskylane mound: Shilvodan AM 19; 136
Eskylane well: Shilvodan AM 19; 138
Esler, family: Racavan AM 13; 100
Esler, Nancy: Carrickfergus AM 37; 126
Esler, William: Island Magee AM 10; 101
Espie, Daniel: Newry DN 3; 99, 104
Espy, David: Kilcronaghan LY 31; 84
Espy, Jane: Kilcronaghan LY 31; 84

Espy, Sarah: Kilcronaghan LY 31; 84
Ess waterfall: Ballynascreen LY 31; 12, 114
Essabuck stream: Lough Swilly DL 38; 137
Essex, Earl of: Ballynure AM 32; 33, 47, 51
Essex, Earl of: Carrickfergus AM 37; 13–14, 62, 78, 160
Essex, Earl of: Island Magee AM 10; 26–27, 72
Essex, Earl of: Kilroot AM 26; 59, 61, 72
Essex, Earl of: Magheracloone MN 40; 141, 142
Essex, Earl of: Magheross MN 40; 146, 148, 151
Essex, Earl of: Templecorran AM 26; 86, 96–97
Essex, family: Donaghmoyne MN 40; 109
Essex, Lord: Killanny MN 40; 134
Essex, Rev. William: Ahoghill AM 23; 49
Essex's Castle: Magheross MN 40; 146, 151
Essexford bog: Killanny MN 40; 130
Essexford school [I]: Killanny MN 40; 135
Essexford school [II]: Killanny MN 40; 135
Essexford td: Killanny MN 40; 131
Estler, Betty: Kilwaughter AM 10; 116
Estler, Eliza: Island Magee AM 10; 95
Estler, family: Kilwaughter AM 10; 115
Estler, Margaret: Island Magee AM 10; 95
Estler, Robert: Island Magee AM 10; 87
Estrabane td: Donacavey TE 5; 81
Etherton, John: Carrickfergus AM 37; 108
Etre bog: Artrea LY 6; 12, 29
Etre td: Artrea LY 6; 12, 28, 36, 39–40
Ettle, family: Ramoan AM 24; 107
Eugenius, St: Cumber LY 28; 48
Eunan, St: Raphoe DL 39; 124
Eust, William: Magilligan LY 11; 114
Eustace, Christy: Carrickfergus AM 37; 128
Eustace, May: Carrickfergus AM 37; 127
Eustace, Thomas: Carrickfergus AM 37; 128
Evalt's wood: Magheross MN 40; 156
Evans, family: Kilmacteige SO 40; 189
Evans, Francis: Tyholland MN 40; 175
Evans, George: Carrickfergus AM 37; 193
Evans, Hugh: Dunboe LY 11; 81
Evans, Jane: Killead AM 35; 51
Evans, John: Mevagh DL 38; 60
Evans, Mr (Armagh city): Kilmore AH 1; 69
Evans, Mr (Armagh city): Loughgilly AH 1; 85
Evans, Mr (Baltylum): Drumcree AH 1; 41
Evans, Mrs (Lislea): Kilmacteige SO 40; 196
Evans, R.: Drumglass TE 20; 42
Evans, Rebecca: Mevagh DL 38; 60
Evans, Rev. E.J.: Kilbroney DN 3; 33, 35, 38

Evans, Robert: Magherafelt LY 6; 83, 87
Evans, Robert: Mevagh DL 38; 60
Evans, Samuel: Artrea LY 6; 19
Evans, Samuel: Donacavey TE 5; 73, 76–77, 85–87
Evans, Stewart: Killead AM 35; 51
Evans, Thomas: Kilmacteige SO 40; 196
Evans, William: Artrea LY 6; 21
Evatt, Charles: Clogher TE 5; 41
Evatt, James: Killanny MN 40; 134
Evatt, James: Magheross MN 40; 149
Evens, John: Magherafelt LY 6; 105
Ever's hill: Island Magee AM 10; 102
Evin, St: Clondermot LY 34; 68
Evin, St: Dungiven LY 15; 55
Evin, St: Magilligan LY 11; 97, 101
Evishacrow (Evishachraw) td: Dunaghy AM 13; 14, 19, 24
Evishacrow booley houses: Dunaghy AM 13; 19
Evishagaran td: Dungiven LY 15; 22, 27, 62, 64
Evishageran (see Evishagaran)
Evishagore (see Evishgore): Ballynascreen LY 31; 19
Evishanoran td: Kildress TE 20; 59
Evishegeran td: Banagher LY 30; 22
Evishgore glen: Ballynascreen LY 31; 19
Evishgore hill: Misc. LY 31; 111, 113
Evishnablay td: Skerry AM 13; 120
Eward, Samuel: Artrea LY 6; 38
Ewart, Davis: Hillsborough DN 12; 107
Ewart, family: Magheragall AM 21; 99
Ewart, James: Blaris DN 12; 37
Ewart, James: Hillsborough DN 12; 107
Ewart, Robert: Ahoghill AM 23; 38
Ewe bridge: Boho FH 14; 10
Ewen, Jane (see Dobbs)
Ewing, family: Doagh AM 29; 73, 94
Ewing, family: Kilraghts AM 16; 130
Ewing, James: Carrickfergus AM 37; 116
Ewing, John: Doagh AM 29; 93
Ewing, Rev.: Kilcronaghan LY 31; 81–82
Ewing, Rev.: Misc. DL 39; 194
Ewing, Rev. Robert: Kilraghts AM 16; 130, 132
Ewing, Samuel: Clondermot LY 34; 6, 20, 37, 78, 80, 97, 102, 104
Ewingtown fort: Doagh AM 29; 98
Exorna (Exorner) td: Dunboe LY 11; 50, 74, 79
Exorna cove [I]: Dunboe LY 11; 50, 74
Exorna cove [II]: Dunboe LY 11; 50, 74
Exorna spring: Dunboe LY 11; 79

F

Faccary corn mill: Cappagh TE 5; 15
Faccary demesne: Cappagh TE 5; 20
Faccary Lodge: Cappagh TE 5; 15–17
Faccary mills: Cappagh TE 5; 19
Faccary td: Cappagh TE 5; 15
Fad lough: Clonmany DL 38; 12–13
Fadd lough: Ardclinis AM 13; 5
Fadda Lough: Clogher TE 5; 33, 47
Fadda lough: Templecarn DL 39; 157
Faddan lough: Clogher TE 5; 25
Fadden lough: Culfeightrin AM 24; 38, 42
Fadian, family: Lough Swilly DL 38; 116
Fads td: Magheross MN 40; 148
Fagan, Owen: Clonallan DN 3; 1
Fagan, T.: Aghadowey LY 22; 16, 18, 20
Fagan, T.: Ballynascreen LY 31; 16, 18
Fagan, T.: Banagher LY 30; 112, 114
Fagan, T.: Blaris AM 8; 56, 58, 66
Fagan, T.: Bovevagh LY 25; 59
Fagan, T.: Clondermot LY 34; 104
Fagan, T.: Cumber LY 28; 83
Fagan, T.: Drumbeg AM 8; 133
Fagan, T.: Dunboe LY 11; 80
Fagan, T.: Errigal LY 27; 50
Fagan, T.: Kilrea LY 27; 122
Fagan, T.: Tamlaght Finlagan LY 25; 90, 109
Fagher (Louth): Raloo AM 32; 93
Fahan channel: Lough Swilly DL 38; 103–04, 144, 147–48
Fahan district: Killygarvan DL 38; 40–41, 48
Fahan district: Lough Swilly DL 38; 103, 127, 139, 143–44, 147–48
Fahan district: Muff DL 38; 80
Fahan Lower ph: Desertegney DL 38; 24
Fahan Lower ph: Mintiaghs DL 38; 64–65
Fahan Lower ph: Moville DL 38; 78
Fahan ph: Aghadowey LY 22; 16
Fahan Point: Lough Swilly DL 38; 104
Fahar hill: Newry DN 3; 105, 107
Fair Field hill: Lambeg AM 8; 138
Fair Head: Ballintoy AM 24; 15
Fair Head: Carrickfergus AM 37; 1–2, 35, 37, 40, 45, 65

Fair Head: Culfeightrin AM 24; 36–37, 39, 41–44, 81–82
Fair Head: Ramoan AM 24; 90, 93, 96, 122
Fair Head trigonometrical station: Culfeightrin AM 24; 36
Fair hill: Ballynure AM 32; 62–63, 70, 72
Fair hill: Coleraine LY 33; 106
Fair hill: Kilcronaghan LY 31; 75
Fair hill: Raloo AM 32; 96, 123, 126
Fair View House: Aughnamullen MN 40; 71
Fair View House: Ballyscullion LY 6; 47
Fair, family: Derryaghy AM 8; 103
Fair, family: Drumbeg AM 8; 123
Fairfield demesne: Ematris MN 40; 116
Fairfield House: Ematris MN 40; 114
Fairfoot, family: Carrickfergus AM 37; 93
Fairgrove House: Ballymore AH 1; 11, 13
Fairies Castle rock: Maghera LY 18; 60
Fairies' cave: Bovevagh LY 25; 52
Fairis, Bernard: Maghera LY 18; 8, 68
Fairis, Bryan: Drumachose LY 9; 123
Fairis, Catherine: Maghera LY 18; 80
Fairlawn bridge: Clonfeacle AH 1; 23
Fairlawn bridge: Loughgall AH 1; 79
Fairly, Robert: Clondermot LY 34; 78–80
Fairly, Robert: Faughanvale LY 36; 5, 18–19
Fairview House: Donagh DL 38; 32
Fairview House: Seagoe AH 1; 109
Fairwood Park: Cleenish FH 14; 17, 19, 22
Fairy bushes: Carrickfergus AM 37; 185
Fairy hill: Derrykeighan AM 16; 87, 95
Fairy hill: Muckamore AM 35; 80
Fairy Hill House: Kilbroney DN 3; 35
Fairy Mount fort: Blaris AM 8; 20
Fairy Mount fort: Carrickfergus AM 37; 87, 175, 186
Fairy Now hill: Drumachose LY 9; 110
Fairy water: Ardstraw TE 5; 2, 10, 14
Fairy water: Cappagh TE 5; 17, 20
Fairy water: Drumragh TE 5; 104
Fairy water: Longfield TE 5; 127, 131, 133–34
Fairy water: Skirts of Urney and Ardstraw TE 5; 136, 139
Fairy, robber: Kilrea LY 27; 113

Faith, Mary: Banagher LY 30; 110
Faith, Mary: Desertoghill LY 27; 20
Faith, Solomon: Carrickfergus AM 37; 35
Falachartha forts: Manorhamilton Union LM 40; 52
Falakeran td: Kilcronaghan LY 31; 75
Falgortreevy (Falgortrevy) td: Maghera LY 18; 14, 45, 65, 74, 78
Falgortreevy mill: Maghera LY 18; 50
Falkland (see Farkland): Bovevagh LY 25; 22
Falkland, Lord: Ballyscullion LY 6; 58
Fallaghearan (see Fallagheran)
Fallaghearn (Fallagherin) td: Errigal Keerogue TE 20; 50, 52–53, 56–57
Fallaghearn school: Errigal Keerogue TE 20; 53, 56
Fallaghearn td: Donacavey TE 5; 67, 76, 78, 80–82, 85
Fallagheran (see Fallaghearn)
Fallagloon bog: Maghera LY 18; 57
Fallagloon bridge: Maghera LY 18; 64
Fallagloon chapel: Maghera LY 18; 35, 69
Fallagloon fort: Maghera LY 18; 62
Fallagloon graveyard: Maghera LY 18; 10
Fallagloon iron mine: Maghera LY 18; 74
Fallagloon mountain: Maghera LY 18; 42
Fallagloon school: Ballynascreen LY 31; 18
Fallagloon school: Maghera LY 18; 32, 35
Fallagloon springs: Killelagh LY 27; 96
Fallagloon standing stones: Maghera LY 18; 42
Fallagloon td: Maghera LY 18; 8, 22, 37, 44–46, 52, 65, 68, 78–81
Fallahogy (Fallaghogy) td: Kilrea LY 27; 115, 129
Fallahogy flax mill: Kilrea LY 27; 120
Fallalay (Fallowlea) td: Killelagh LY 27; 99, 102
Fallalay quarry: Killelagh LY 27; 102
Fallalay river: Killelagh LY 27; 95
Fallanees district: Clondavaddog DL 38; 4
Fallanees standing stone: Clondavaddog DL 38; 6
Fallgherin (see Fallaghearn)
Fallinerlea fort: Layd AM 13; 41
Fallinerlea td: Layd AM 13; 41
Fallon, family: Aghagallon AM 21; 9
Falloon, Edward: Blaris DN 12; 40
Falloon, Rev. Marcus: Layd AM 13; 40, 46
Falloon, Samuel: Carrickfergus AM 37; 112
Falloward (Fallaward) td: Faughanvale LY 36; 17, 53, 57–58, 68, 74, 85, 94, 98
Falloward school: Faughanvale LY 36; 35
Falloward wood: Faughanvale LY 36; 85
Fallowlea (Fallylea) td: Maghera LY 18; 68
Fallowlea House: Faughanvale LY 36; 9, 13, 20, 22–23, 28, 34
Fallowlea literary school: Faughanvale LY 36; 10, 23
Fallowlea mass-house: Maghera LY 18; 69
Fallowlea private school: Faughanvale LY 36; 10

Fallowlea quarry: Faughanvale LY 36; 94
Fallowlea river: Maghera LY 18; 1
Fallowlea river: Termoneeny LY 6; 121
Fallowlea school: Faughanvale LY 36; 9
Fallowlea td: Cumber LY 28; 69, 69
Fallowlea td: Drumachose LY 9; 104
Fallowlea td: Faughanvale LY 36; 17, 41, 53, 58, 68, 74, 85, 94
Fallowlea wood: Faughanvale LY 36; 85
Fallowlee (see Fallowlea)
Falls district (Belfast): Misc. DN 17; 122
Falls district: Faughanvale LY 36; 58
Falls, Alexander: Maghera LY 18; 8, 50–52, 57, 63, 68
Falls, James: Maghera LY 18; 54
Falls, Maj.: Newry DN 3; 105
Falls, Peebles and Co., Messrs: Cappagh TE 5; 20
Falls' Hotel: Maghera LY 18; 5, 62–63
Fallylea (see Fallowlea)
Fallyloon (see Fallagloon): Maghera LY 18; 78
Falnasugane td: Killoran and Kilvarnet SO 40; 184
Faloon, Eliza: Aghagallon AM 21; 19
Faloon, family: Aghagallon AM 21; 9
Faloon, Rev.: Annahilt DN 12; 22–23
Faloon, Stewart: Aghalee AM 21; 36
Faloon, Susana: Aghagallon AM 21; 19
Faloon, Thomas: Aghalee AM 21; 35
Faloon, William: Aghagallon AM 21; 19
Fanad district: Clondavaddog DL 38; 1–10
Fanad district: Clonmany DL 38; 16
Fanad district: Drumachose LY 9; 93
Fanad district: Faughanvale LY 36; 63
Fanad district: Killymard DL 39; 96
Fanad district: Lough Swilly DL 38; 105–06, 113–14, 116–19, 127–29, 132, 137
Fanad district: Mevagh DL 38; 57, 59, 61–63
Fanad district: Misc. TE 5; 146
Fanad district: Raymoghy DL 39; 144
Fanad district: Tullyaughnish DL 38; 86, 88–89, 91, 93
Fanad Glebe House: Clondavaddog DL 38; 5, 11
Fanad lighthouse: Clondavaddog DL 38; 2–5, 9
Fanad lighthouse: Killygarvan DL 38; 45
Fanad lighthouse: Lough Swilly DL 38; 98–99, 106
Fanad lighthouse: Tullyaughnish DL 38; 95
Fanad lough: Lough Swilly DL 38; 113–14, 117
Fanad manor: Tullyaughnish DL 38; 92, 96
Fanad Point: Lough Swilly DL 38; 98, 106
Fanaghy (see Fenaghy): Ahoghill AM 23; 13
Fanavuntly district: Clondavaddog DL 38; 4
Fane district: Misc. SO 40; 200
Fane eel-weirs: Inniskeen MN 40; 124
Fane river: Donaghmoyne MN 40; 106–08
Fane river: Inniskeen MN 40; 124, 127
Fane, family: Dungiven LY 15; 111

Fane, Henry: Tickmacrevan AM 13; 132

Fanet (see Fanad): Clondavaddog DL 38; 10

Fannahendron td: Clogher TE 5; 53

Fannanoughan td: Tullyaughnish DL 38; 97

Fannet (see Fanad): Clondavaddog DL 38; 11

Fanning, Joanna: Maghera LY 18; 30

Fanning, Rev. Audley: Tamlaght O'Crilly LY 18; 108

Fanning, Rev. Audley: Termoneeny LY 6; 125, 129, 132

Fanning, William [I]: Desertoghill LY 27; 15, 24

Fanning, William [II]: Desertoghill LY 27; 16–17, 19, 34

Fannon, William: Desertoghill LY 27; 31

Fanny lough: Ardstraw TE 5; 2, 10

Fanny lough: Clondavaddog DL 38; 3

Fanny's fort: Desertoghill LY 27; 27

Fanny's Hole creek: Lough Swilly DL 38; 115–16, 119

Fannybrack (see Tawnybrack): Connor AM 19; 28

Fanssive (see Faussive): Inishmacsaint FH 14; 79

Far Paddock locality: Muckamore AM 35; 80

Faraghy td: Magheross MN 40; 148

Faran spring: Derryvullan FH 14; 42

Faranlessary cave: Ballymoney AM 16; 21, 23

Faranlessary td: Ballymoney AM 16; 23, 25

Farantemple (see Farrantemple)

Farbagh hill: Devenish FH 14; 52

Fardross Demesne school: Clogher TE 5; 41, 51

Fardross Demesne td: Clogher TE 5; 51

Fardross House: Clogher TE 5; 33, 49

Fardross mountain: Clogher TE 5; 26

Fardross school: Clogher TE 5; 41

Fardross td: Clogher TE 5; 26, 34, 38–39, 41, 53

Fardsum td: Devenish FH 14; 58

Farganlack Point: Rathlin Island AM 24; 130

Fargans td: Convoy DL 39; 20

Fargey, John: Macosquin LY 22; 122

Fargrim (Fargreen) td: Galloon FH 4; 91, 95

Faries, family: Island Magee AM 10; 70

Faris, John: Hillsborough DN 12; 106, 106

Farkland (Farclone) td: Bovevagh LY 25; 13, 39, 60

Farkland bog: Bovevagh LY 25; 12, 40

Farkland fort: Bovevagh LY 25; 40

Farkland mountain: Bovevagh LY 25; 57

Farkland spring: Bovevagh LY 25; 22

Farkland td: Banagher LY 30; 23–24

Farlagh td: Aughnamullen MN 40; 76

Farlan (see Farlow)

Farland channel: Lough Swilly DL 38; 102, 104, 147–48

Farland ferry: Lough Swilly DL 38; 104, 143, 147

Farland Point: Lough Swilly DL 38; 123, 143, 147

Farlough bleach greens: Tullyniskan TE 20; 139

Farlough bog: Drummaul AM 19; 87

Farlough river: Drumglass TE 20; 44

Farlough river: Tullyniskan TE 20; 138

Farlough school: Drummaul AM 19; 85

Farlough td: Drummaul AM 19; 87, 90–91

Farlough td: Tullyniskan TE 20; 138–39, 141

Farlow bog: Tamlaght Finlagan LY 25; 65, 120

Farlow brickyard: Tamlaght Finlagan LY 25; 120

Farlow House: Aghanloo LY 11; 33

Farlow House: Drumachose LY 9; 84

Farlow House: Tamlaght Finlagan LY 25; 82

Farlow school: Tamlaght Finlagan LY 25; 96

Farlow Sunday school [I]: Tamlaght Finlagan LY 25; 96

Farlow Sunday school [II]: Tamlaght Finlagan LY 25; 96

Farlow Sunday school [III]: Tamlaght Finlagan LY 25; 96

Farlow Sunday school [IV]: Tamlaght Finlagan LY 25; 96

Farlow td: Tamlaght Finlagan LY 25; 72–74, 93, 120, 122

Farm Hill House: Carrickfergus AM 37; 57, 134, 136

Farm Hill House: Coleraine LY 33; 91

Farm Hill House: Magherafelt LY 6; 91, 96

Farm Lodge: Kirkinriola AM 23; 104

Farm td: Galloon FH 4; 95

Farmagh td: Tullyaughnish DL 38; 97

Farmhill (see Formill): Aughnamullen MN 40; 71

Farmhill House: Drummully FH 4; 35–36

Farmhill House: Galloon FH 4; 92

Farmhill House: Leckpatrick TE 5; 125

Farmill (see Formill): Aughnamullen MN 40; 76

Farms chapel: Tickmacrevan AM 13; 129

Farms td: Tickmacrevan AM 13; 129

Farn td: Ballyphilip DN 7; 8

Farnaconnell td: Boho FH 14; 8

Farnaght td: Derryvullan FH 14; 46

Farnamullen td: Cleenish FH 14; 29

Farnascullogue (see Farransculloge): Aghalurcher FH 4; 2

Farneetra td: Clogher TE 5; 35

Farney barony: Donaghmoyne MN 40; 106

Farney barony: Inniskeen MN 40; 124

Farney barony: Killanny MN 40; 130

Farney barony: Magheracloone MN 40; 137

Farney barony: Magheross MN 40; 143, 148, 151–52

Farney dispensary: Donaghmoyne MN 40; 109

Farney dispensary: Killanny MN 40; 133

Farney dispensary: Magheracloone MN 40; 140

Farney dispensary: Magheross MN 40; 147, 150

Farney district: Donaghmoyne MN 40; 109

Farnflough (see Farlough): Drummaul AM 19; 85

Farnham, Lord: Drumglass TE 20; 43

Farnham, Lord: Drumlumman CN 40; 15–18

Farnlagh td: Blaris AM 8; 81

Farnlester (see Farranlester): Dunboe LY 11; 77, 81

Farnlough Sunday school: Drummaul AM 19; 85–86

Farnortragh td: Clogher TE 5; 53

Farnsaggart park: Drumachose LY 9; 126

Farquagh td: Kinawley FH 4; 117, 121

Farquar td: Tullyaughnish DL 38; 96

Farquhar, family: Carnmoney AM 2; 76, 102

Farr, family: Glenavy AM 21; 86

Farra hill: Drumcree AH 1; 34, 40

Farra td: Drumcree AH 1; 40

Farrah, Francis: Hillsborough DN 12; 105

Farran, John: Aghanloo LY 11; 26

Farranaconahy td: Aghalurcher FH 4; 14

Farranacurky td: Aghalurcher FH 4; 14

Farranacushog td: Dunaghy AM 13; 21, 24

Farranalissary (see Faranlessary): Ballymoney AM 16; 25

Farranalossay (see Faranlessary): Ballymoney AM 16; 23

Farranasculloge (see Farransculloge): Aghalurcher FH 4; 14

Farranlester cove: Dunboe LY 11; 50, 77

Farranlester day school (see Cranagh school): Dunboe LY 11; 72

Farranlester td: Dunboe LY 11; 72, 77, 81

Farransculloge mountain: Aghalurcher FH 4; 2

Farransculloge td: Aghalurcher FH 4; 14

Farranseer (Farrenseer) td: Macosquin LY 22; 87, 111

Farranseer cove: Macosquin LY 22; 87, 111

Farrantemple fort: Misc. LY 36; 117

Farrantemple fort [I]: Errigal LY 27; 42, 66, 76, 79

Farrantemple fort [II]: Errigal LY 27; 42, 66

Farrantemple Glebe House: Errigal LY 27; 57–58, 76

Farrantemple Glebe td: Errigal LY 27; 40, 81, 86, 90, 92

Farrantemple high fort: Errigal LY 27; 42, 66

Farrantemple hill: Misc. LY 36; 114

Farrantemple low fort: Errigal LY 27; 42, 66

Farrantemple Sunday school: Errigal LY 27; 51

Farrantemple td: Errigal LY 27; 42, 45, 65–66, 71, 76

Farrantemple td: Misc. LY 36; 111

Farre's Point: Island Magee AM 10; 17–18, 24–25, 79, 87

Farre's Point lighthouse: Island Magee AM 10; 21

Farre's Point lighthouse: Templecorran AM 26; 89

Farrel, family: Magherafelt LY 6; 95

Farrel, John: Carrickfergus AM 37; 123

Farrel, John: Maghera LY 18; 46

Farrel, Mary: Carrickfergus AM 37; 117

Farrell, David: Newry DN 3; 99

Farrell, Edward: Blaris DN 12; 46

Farrell, Eliza: Drummaul AM 19; 91

Farrell, Francis: Blaris DN 12; 45, 49

Farrell, Henry: Maghera LY 18; 81

Farrell, J.A.: Glynn AM 26; 1, 5, 14, 16, 18, 33, 41, 43

Farrell, J.A.: Island Magee AM 10; 29, 82

Farrell, J.A.: Raloo AM 32; 125

Farrell, James: Lissan LY 31; 109

Farrell, John: Drummaul AM 19; 91

Farrell, John: Kilmacteige SO 40; 188–89

Farrell, Mr: Derryvullan FH 14; 37

Farrell, William: Aghalurcher FH 4; 7

Farrell's Hotel: Doagh AM 29; 86

Farren, James: Magilligan LY 11; 94

Farrenlester fort: Macosquin LY 22; 111

Farrenlester td: Macosquin LY 22; 122–23

Farrenmacallen cave [I]: Culfeightrin AM 24; 84

Farrenmacallen cave [II]: Culfeightrin AM 24; 84

Farrentemple (see Farrantemple): Errigal LY 27; 40

Farres locality: Island Magee AM 10; 83

Farres, family: Island Magee AM 10; 70

Farries, family: Island Magee AM 10; 70

Farril, Patt: Bovevagh LY 25; 60

Farriter corn mill: Killeeshil TE 20; 62, 64

Farron, Edward: Blaris AM 8; 53

Farsagh td: Devenish FH 14; 58

Farsetmore td: Leck DL 39; 119

Fartagh td: Dromore TE 5; 98

Farterun td: Tomregan FH 4; 126

Farthagorman td: Magheross MN 40; 148

Fathom Castle: Newry DN 3; 64

Fathom Castle: Warrenpoint DN 3; 115

Fathom Lock: Newry DN 3; 86, 88–90

Fathom Park House: Enniskeen CN 40; 29

Faucett, Andrew: Killymard DL 39; 107

Faugh old church: Derrybrusk FH 4; 32

Faugh td: Derrybrusk FH 4; 30, 32

Faughamy village: Kilmacteige SO 40; 193

Faughan bridge: Clondermot LY 34; 3, 5, 14, 18, 20–22, 34, 89, 92–93, 102–03, 117, 119

Faughan bridge: Faughanvale LY 36; 1, 4, 10

Faughan fishery: Clondermot LY 34; 103

Faughan old bridge: Faughanvale LY 36; 10

Faughan river: Banagher LY 30; 24–25, 29, 48, 50–51, 59, 79, 91, 105, 108, 131

Faughan river: Clondermot LY 34; 1, 3–4, 6–7, 17–19, 21–22, 24, 28, 36–37, 53–54, 56, 59–60, 64, 75, 100–01, 107, 113–20

Faughan river: Cumber LY 28; 4–9, 11, 24, 30, 34–35, 37, 44–47, 53, 60, 66–68, 72, 78–80, 84–86, 93

Faughan river: Drumachose LY 9; 99

Faughan river: Dungiven LY 15; 55, 97–98

Faughan river: Faughanvale LY 36; 1–4, 10–11, 50, 54, 72, 78

Faughan river: Misc. LY 36; 119

Faughan river: Tamlaght Finlagan LY 25; 64, 66, 93

Faughan wood: Dungiven LY 15; 26, 68, 101

Faughan wooden bridge: Cumber LY 28; 35

Faughander, family: Aghadowey LY 22; 11

Faughanvale church: Balteagh LY 9; 19

Faughanvale corn mill: Faughanvale LY 36; 16, 21

Faughanvale dispensary: Clondermot LY 34; 17

Faughanvale flax mill: Faughanvale LY 36; 21

Faughanvale forge: Faughanvale LY 36; 6

Faughanvale Glebe House: Faughanvale LY 36; 12, 15, 33

Faughanvale glen: Faughanvale LY 36; 1

Faughanvale graveyard: Faughanvale LY 36; 13–14

Faughanvale hamlet: Faughanvale LY 36; 6, 21, 29

Faughanvale meeting house: Faughanvale LY 36; 6, 29

Faughanvale old church: Faughanvale LY 36; 58

Faughanvale orchard: Faughanvale LY 36; 85

Faughanvale ph: Banagher LY 30; 27, 107

Faughanvale ph: Clondermot LY 34; 1, 3, 6–8, 25, 35–36, 38–39, 47, 55, 67, 72, 83, 94, 96, 98

Faughanvale ph: Cumber LY 28; 1, 14–15, 17, 27–28, 45, 49, 62, 66, 68–69

Faughanvale ph: Drumachose LY 9; 84, 117

Faughanvale ph: Lough Swilly DL 38; 138, 142

Faughanvale ph: Magilligan LY 11; 82

Faughanvale ph: Tamlaght Finlagan LY 25; 72, 74, 77–78, 97, 106

Faughanvale quarries: Faughanvale LY 36; 10, 19

Faughanvale river: Faughanvale LY 36; 1–3, 6

Faughanvale school: Faughanvale LY 36; 24, 35, 67

Faughanvale td: Faughanvale LY 36; 6, 17, 53, 58, 68, 74, 85, 94, 98

Faughanvale waterfall: Faughanvale LY 36; 15

Faughard td: Cleenish FH 14; 28–29

Faughart Lower td: Ballymascanlan LH 40; 55

Faughart Upper td: Ballymascanlan LH 40; 55

Faulkner, Elen: Tamlaght TE 20; 77

Faulkner, James: Tamlaght TE 20; 77, 104

Faulkner, John: Hillsborough DN 12; 107

Faulkner, Robert: Tamlaght O'Crilly LY 18; 116

Faulkner, William: Tamlaght O'Crilly LY 18; 114

Faulls, John: Dunluce AM 16; 120

Fauls td: Enniskillen FH 4; 82

Fausetermore village: Kilmacteige SO 40; 195

Faussett, Capt.: Cleenish FH 14; 17, 22

Faussive school: Inishmacsaint FH 14; 79

Faussive td: Inishmacsaint FH 14; 75

Favor Royal demesne: Clogher TE 5; 25, 30, 61

Favor Royal demesne: Errigal Truagh MN 40; 123

Favor Royal House: Errigal Truagh MN 40; 123

Fawcett, C.: Kinawley FH 4; 115

Fawcett, Mr: Cleenish FH 14; 29

Fawcett, Mr: Devenish FH 14; 59

Fawcett, Rev. H.: Devenish FH 14; 59–60

Fawcett, Rev. William: Cleenish FH 14; 29

Fawney cove: Cumber LY 28; 43–44

Fawney Cross school: Cumber LY 28; 92

Fawney Cross td: Cumber LY 28; 92

Fawney td: Cumber LY 28; 46, 48, 56, 60, 62, 95, 100, 104–05, 107

Fawney well: Cumber LY 28; 43

Fayduff school: Tynan AH 1; 129

Fea lough: Inishkeel DL 39; 70

Fea lough: Lissan LY 31; 89–93, 96, 101–02

Fea lough: Lissan TE 20; 69

Fea lough: Magheracloone MN 40; 137–38

Fea lough: Magheross MN 40; 143, 156–57

Fea stream: Lissan LY 31; 89–90

Fea, Christopher: Connor AM 19; 26

Feagh hill: Aghabog MN 40; 62

Feagh lough: Aghabog MN 40; 62

Feagh school: Aghabog MN 40; 65

Feaghroy district: Misc. SO 40; 200

Feahoe bog: Magheracloone MN 40; 137

Feale river: Dungiven LY 15; 63

Fearis, family: Ballinderry AM 21; 48

Fearn hill: Urney DL 39; 174

Fearn td: Urney DL 39; 181

Fearon, family: Newry DN 3; 112

Fearon, John: Newry DN 3; 98, 103

Feary, Cathrine: Magheramesk AM 21; 130

Feary, Edward: Magheramesk AM 21; 130

Feary, Mary: Magheramesk AM 21; 130

Feary, Thomas: Magheramesk AM 21; 130

Feary, William: Magheramesk AM 21; 130

Feather Beds bog: Glenwhirry AM 32; 74

Fechin, St: Faughanvale LY 36; 52

Feckland, Rev.: Carnmoney AM 2; 75

Fedany bog: Garvaghy DN 12; 80

Fedany td: Garvaghy DN 12; 80–82

Feddan bog: Errigal Keerogue TE 20; 52

Feddan forts: Errigal Keerogue TE 20; 52

Feddan quarry: Errigal Keerogue TE 20; 52

Feddan td: Ematris MN 40; 115

Feddan td: Errigal Keerogue TE 20; 52, 57

Fedden (see Feddan): Errigal Keerogue TE 20; 57

Fedden td: Derryvullan FH 14; 46

Feddens school: Drumkeeran FH 14; 67

Feddhill td: Ematris MN 40; 112

Feddin (see Feddan): Errigal Keerogue TE 20; 52

Feddyglass td: Taughboyne DL 39; 148, 153, 196

Feddyglass wood: Taughboyne DL 39; 148, 153, 155, 189

Federcan td: Killoran and Kilvarnet SO 40; 184

Federnagh td: Ballymore AH 1; 8–9, 12, 14–16, 18

Fedian fort: Devenish FH 14; 55

Fee, family: Carnmoney AM 2; 76
Fee, John: Carnmoney AM 2; 99
Fee, John: Templepatrick AM 35; 152
Feed td: Ballymascanlan LH 40; 55
Feegavla lough: Donaghmoyne MN 40; 106
Feehogue cove: Drummaul AM 19; 66
Feehogue td: Drummaul AM 19; 61, 71–72
Feenagh district: Misc. SO 40; 199
Feenan td: Donacavey TE 5; 76–78, 80–81, 83, 86
Feenanmore td: Desertlyn LY 31; 47
Feeney, Bernard: Balteagh LY 9; 26
Feeney, Cormac: Cumber LY 28; 73, 77
Feeney, James: Dungiven LY 15; 73
Feeney, Michael: Ballyscullion AM 19; 12
Feeney, William: Dungiven LY 15; 73, 89
Feeney's fort: Balteagh LY 9; 26
Feeny: Ballynascreen LY 31; 2, 8, 15, 19
Feeny: Banagher LY 30; 2–6, 10, 13–14, 19, 27,
    29–31, 44, 57, 59–61, 74, 96, 99–100, 104,
    112–113, 130
Feeny: Bovevagh LY 25; 9, 24
Feeny: Cumber LY 28; 21
Feeny: Dungiven LY 15; 10, 67, 106
Feeny: Misc. LY 31; 116
Feeny: Tamlaght Finlagan LY 25; 62
Feeny carn: Banagher LY 30; 75
Feeny chapel: Banagher LY 30; 15, 33, 39
Feeny crane: Banagher LY 30; 27
Feeny cromlech: Banagher LY 30; 75
Feeny dispensary: Banagher LY 30; 10
Feeny enclosure: Banagher LY 30; 47
Feeny fort [I]: Banagher LY 30; 75
Feeny fort [II]: Banagher LY 30; 75
Feeny fort [III]: Banagher LY 30; 75
Feeny glen: Banagher LY 30; 35
Feeny school: Dungiven LY 15; 19
Feeny standing stones: Banagher LY 30; 46, 75
Feeny td: Banagher LY 30; 22, 24, 35–36, 45, 56,
    61–62, 93, 95, 104, 109, 118, 123, 127, 129,
    131–32
Feeny wood: Banagher LY 30; 123
Feeny, Bernard: Balteagh LY 9; 12
Feeny, Hugh: Banagher LY 30; 61
Feeny, John: Banagher LY 30; 61
Feeny, Laurence: Banagher LY 30; 61
Feeny, Samuel: Island Magee AM 10; 95
Feeny's fort: Balteagh LY 9; 12
Fegan, Bernard: Kilbroney DN 3; 38
Fegan, Mathew: Newry DN 3; 99, 103
Fegan, Mrs: Newry DN 3; 99
Fegan, Owen: Newry DN 3; 99, 103
Fegan, Rev. Marcus: Kilbroney DN 3; 34
Fegan, Samuel: Newry DN 3; 98, 103
Fehary Island: Killinchy DN 7; 86, 92
Fehogue (see Feehogue): Drummaul AM 19; 71

Fehorney cromlech: Rasharkin AM 23; 137
Fehorney giant's chair: Rasharkin AM 23; 137
Feigh (see Feagh): Aghabog MN 40; 62
Feigh mountain: Billy AM 16; 57, 59
Feine, Thomas: Killanny MN 40; 132
Fellous, family: Racavan AM 13; 100
Fellow's Hall: Drumragh TE 5; 109
Fellow's Hall: Tynan AH 1; 127, 130
Felloward (see Falloward): Faughanvale LY 36; 53
Fenagh forts: Manorhamilton Union LM 40; 52
Fenagh Hillhead hill: Ahoghill AM 23; 4
Fenagh monastery: Banagher LY 30; 104
Fenaghy (Finaghy) td: Ahoghill AM 23; 38
Fenaghy bleach mill: Ahoghill AM 23; 31
Fenaghy House: Ahoghill AM 23; 12
Fenaghy mills: Ahoghill AM 23; 13
Fencashel td: Templecarn DL 39; 164
Fence bleach mill: Kilbride AM 29; 135
Fendermore td: Clogher TE 5; 53
Fenmore hill: Drumhome DL 39; 59
Fenmore td: Glenavy AM 21; 79
Fenton, family: Drummaul AM 19; 53
Fenton, family: Duneane AM 19; 101
Fenton, John: Faughanvale LY 36; 40, 42, 45
Fenton, John: Urney DL 39; 179
Fenton, Joseph: Connor AM 19; 27
Fenton, William: Island Magee AM 10; 94
Fenwick, Lt R.: Culdaff DL 38; 22
Fenwick, Lt R.: Leck DL 39; 120
Fenwick, Rev.: Leck DL 39; 119
Fenwick, William: Faughanvale LY 36; 45
Fenwick, William: Raphoe DL 39; 123–27
Feran, George: Kilbroney DN 3; 33
Feran, James: Kilbroney DN 3; 33
Feranalessary (see Faranlessary): Ballymoney AM
    16; 21
Ferara, Andre: Lissan LY 31; 101
Ferara, Andrea: Coleraine LY 33; 94
Ferdachrioch (see Tigernach): Clogher TE 5; 29
Fergal, King of Ireland: Dungiven LY 15; 56
Fergans td: Lough Swilly DL 38; 144
Fergus, King: Carnmoney AM 2; 64, 67, 94
Fergus, King: Carrickfergus AM 37; 18
Ferguson and Fowke, Messrs: Antrim AM 29; 16,
    48
Ferguson, Alexander: Tamlaght TE 20; 96–97
Ferguson, Andrew: Artrea LY 6; 10, 27
Ferguson, Andrew: Clondermot LY 34; 104
Ferguson, Andrew: Donagh DL 38; 34
Ferguson, Andrew: Faughanvale LY 36; 40, 45
Ferguson, Andrew: Lough Swilly DL 38; 103–04,
    145
Ferguson, Andrew: Mintiaghs DL 38; 66
Ferguson, Andrew: Misc. DL 39; 194
Ferguson, Andrew: Raymoghy DL 39; 135

Ferguson, Andrew: Tamlaght TE 20; 122
Ferguson, Archibald: Muckamore AM 35; 77
Ferguson, David: Hillsborough DN 12; 105
Ferguson, Eliza: Carrickfergus AM 37; 127
Ferguson, family: Artrea LY 6; 14
Ferguson, family: Billy AM 16; 58, 68
Ferguson, family: Derrykeighan AM 16; 89
Ferguson, family: Donegore AM 29; 110
Ferguson, family: Island Magee AM 10; 70
Ferguson, family: Kilbride AM 29; 140, 153
Ferguson, family: Kilcronaghan LY 31; 68
Ferguson, family: Nilteen AM 35; 91
Ferguson, Grace: Newtownards DN 7; 112, 112
Ferguson, H.: Newtownards DN 7; 112
Ferguson, H.J.: Kilcronaghan LY 31; 86
Ferguson, Harvey: Misc. DL 39; 186
Ferguson, J.: Newtownards DN 7; 112
Ferguson, J.S.: Nilteen AM 35; 86, 102–03
Ferguson, James: Bovevagh LY 25; 61
Ferguson, James: Dungiven LY 15; 70
Ferguson, James: Kilwaughter AM 10; 117
Ferguson, James: Loughguile AM 13; 70, 75
Ferguson, James: Newry DN 3; 99, 104
Ferguson, James: Tamlaght TE 20; 79–80
Ferguson, Jane: Duneane AM 19; 123
Ferguson, John: Carnmoney AM 2; 99
Ferguson, John: Island Magee AM 10; 90
Ferguson, John: Tamlaght TE 20; 122
Ferguson, M.: Bovevagh LY 25; 16, 50
Ferguson, Margaret: Duneane AM 19; 123
Ferguson, Margaret: Raloo AM 32; 129
Ferguson, Mathew: Tamlaght Finlagan LY 25; 80, 108
Ferguson, Messrs J.S. and Co.: Nilteen AM 35; 103
Ferguson, Mr: Antrim AM 29; 48–49
Ferguson, Mr: Drumbo DN 7; 60
Ferguson, Mr: Tullynakill DN 7; 122
Ferguson, Mrs (Tildarg): Rashee AM 32; 136
Ferguson, Mrs: Doagh AM 29; 91
Ferguson, P.: Newtownards DN 7; 112
Ferguson, Patrick: Island Magee AM 10; 94
Ferguson, R.A.: Clondermot LY 34; 12, 27, 78–80, 101, 104–05
Ferguson, R.A.: Donaghmore DL 39; 33, 36–40
Ferguson, R.A.: Faughanvale LY 36; 40, 42, 45
Ferguson, R.A.: Longfield TE 5; 133
Ferguson, R.A.: Skirts of Urney and Ardstraw TE 5; 137, 139
Ferguson, R.A.: Templecarn DL 39; 162
Ferguson, R.A.: Termonamongan TE 5; 142–44
Ferguson, Robert [I]: Tamlaght TE 20; 80, 96, 101
Ferguson, Robert [II]: Tamlaght TE 20; 108
Ferguson, Samuel: Aghanloo LY 11; 39
Ferguson, Samuel: Carrickfergus AM 37; 148
Ferguson, Samuel: Clondermot LY 34; 79–80

Ferguson, Samuel: Tamlaght TE 20; 82, 130, 136
Ferguson, Sarah Ann: Tamlaght TE 20; 118
Ferguson, Thomas [I]: Tamlaght TE 20; 82, 136
Ferguson, Thomas [II]: Tamlaght TE 20; 104
Ferguson, Thomas [III]: Tamlaght TE 20; 122
Ferguson, Thomas [IV]: Tamlaght TE 20; 129
Ferguson, W.: Newtownards DN 7; 112
Ferguson, William: Ballymoney AM 16; 18
Ferguson, William: Ballynascreen LY 31; 16
Ferguson, William: Carrickfergus AM 37; 109, 125, 193
Ferguson, William: Doagh AM 29; 98
Ferguson, William: Donegore AM 29; 102, 106, 129–30, 132–33
Ferguson, William: Duneane AM 19; 123
Ferguson, William: Nilteen AM 35; 84, 99, 102–03
Ferguson, William [I]: Tamlaght TE 20; 77, 103
Ferguson, William [II]: Tamlaght TE 20; 129
Fergusonsland corn mill: Donegore AM 29; 104, 108, 129, 132, 134
Fergusonsland flax mill: Donegore AM 29; 104, 108, 129, 132
Fergusonsland quarries: Donegore AM 29; 102
Fergusonsland td: Donegore AM 29; 101, 131
Fergusson, Elenor: Ballyrashane LY 22; 65
Fergusson, Elizabeth: Ballyrashane LY 22; 65
Fergusson, family: Blaris AM 8; 21
Fergusson, family: Culfeightrin AM 24; 59
Fergusson, J.W.: Ballyscullion LY 6; 65
Fergusson, James: Blaris AM 8; 19, 44, 48
Fergusson, Jane: Ballyrashane LY 22; 65
Fergusson, John: Ballyrashane LY 22; 56
Fergusson, John: Bovevagh LY 25; 59
Fergusson, John: Drumachose LY 9; 115
Fergusson, Joseph: Artrea LY 6; 27
Fergusson, Margret: Ballyrashane LY 22; 65
Fergusson, Martha: Ballyrashane LY 22; 65
Fergusson, Mary: Ballyrashane LY 22; 65
Fergusson, Robert: Magheragall AM 21; 104
Fergusson, Rosey: Ballyrashane LY 22; 65
Fergusson, Windofer: Drumachose LY 9; 116, 118
Feris, Charles: Blaris DN 12; 40
Fermanagh: Aghabog MN 40; 65
Fermanagh: Banagher LY 30; 18, 71
Fermanagh: Cappagh TE 5; 19, 22
Fermanagh: Clondermot LY 34; 51, 57, 63, 69, 106
Fermanagh: Clonleigh DL 39; 7
Fermanagh: Currin MN 40; 86, 88, 90, 97
Fermanagh: Donaghmore DL 39; 32
Fermanagh: Drumhome DL 39; 63
Fermanagh: Drumlumman CN 40; 12
Fermanagh: Drumragh TE 5; 110
Fermanagh: Dungiven LY 15; 84
Fermanagh: Enniskillen FH 4; 64
Fermanagh: Faughanvale LY 36; 44, 56

Fermanagh: Kilbarron DL 39; 77–78
Fermanagh: Kirkinriola AM 23; 101
Fermanagh: Loughgall AH 1; 82
Fermanagh: Misc. LY 31; 133
Fermanagh: Misc. TE 5; 147
Fermanagh: Taughboyne DL 39; 149
Fermanagh: Templecarn DL 39; 157–58, 163
Fermanagh: Urney DL 39; 180
Fermanagh county infirmary: Enniskillen FH 4, 33, 62, 81, 83
Fermoyle td: Dunboe LY 11; 81
Fermullen cave: Dunboe LY 11; 76–77
Fern lough: Kilmacrenan DL 38; 50
Fern lough: Mevagh DL 38; 57
Fern lough: Tullyaughnish DL 38; 84, 95
Fern tree locality: Kilmacteige SO 40; 187, 193
Fernamenagh (Fernamerna) td: Errigal Keerogue TE 20; 50, 52, 57
Fernandrum td: Clogher TE 5; 36, 44
Ferny Island: Trory FH 14; 122–23
Ferny td: Magheracross FH 14; 102
Ferran, family: Carnmoney AM 2; 102
Ferran, family: Templecorran AM 26; 119
Ferran, William: Killowen LY 33; 171
Ferrard, Lord: Antrim AM 29; 3, 9–10, 14, 18, 25, 47, 58
Ferrard, Lord: Ballyscullion AM 19; 2, 4, 8, 10
Ferrard, Lord: Ballyscullion LY 6; 66
Ferrard, Lord: Clogher TE 5; 32
Ferrard, Lord: Connor AM 19; 16, 18, 26–27, 30
Ferrard, Lord: Killead AM 35; 33, 41
Ferrard, Lord: Muckamore AM 35; 54–55, 57, 60–61, 75, 78, 80–81
Ferrard, Viscount: Blaris AM 8; 66
Ferrell, family: Carrickfergus AM 37; 93
Ferrier: Dunluce AM 16; 117
Ferrier, family: Finvoy AM 23; 76
Ferrier, Thomas: Dunluce AM 16; 119
Ferrier, William: Maghera LY 18; 45
Ferrigan, James: Newry DN 3; 99, 104
Ferrinmontercassidy school: Inishmacsaint FH 14; 79
Ferris: Magherafelt LY 6; 95
Ferris, family: Camlin AM 21; 68
Ferris, family: Glenavy AM 21; 86
Ferris, James: Carrickfergus AM 37; 108
Ferris, John: Island Magee AM 10; 91
Ferris, Patrick: Ballyscullion LY 6; 57
Ferris, William (Jnr): Aghagallon AM 21; 6–7, 21, 23
Ferris, William (Jnr): Aghalee AM 21; 29, 31–37, 39
Ferris, William (Snr): Aghalee AM 21; 33
Ferris, William: Blaris DN 12; 42
Ferriss, family: Ballinderry AM 21; 48
Ferriss, John: Carrickfergus AM 37; 185

Ferry house: Tullyaughnish DL 38; 95
Ferry td: Clondermot LY 34; 82
Ferryer, family: Dunluce AM 16; 117
Ferryquarter school: Ballyculter DN 17; 29–30
Ferryquarter td: Ballyculter DN 17; 30
Ferson, William: Magilligan LY 11; 94
Fesian td: Devenish FH 14; 58
Fetters, John: Hillsborough DN 12; 106
Fettis, John: Dromore DN 12; 77
Feugh school: Galloon FH 4; 96
Feugh td: Galloon FH 4; 95
Fews barony: Inniskeen MN 40; 124
Fews Lower barony: Mullaghbrack AH 1; 94
Fews mountains: Coleraine LY 33; 96
Fews Upper barony: Donaghmoyne MN 40; 106
Ffolliott, H.: Magheracross FH 14; 93
Fial, woman named: Dungiven LY 15; 63
Fichpattrik, Eillip: Enniskillen FH 4; 70
Fiddawn river: Kilmacteige SO 40; 191, 195
Fidelawn (see Fiddawn): Kilmacteige SO 40; 191
Fidge, Mr: Faughanvale LY 36; 22
Fidli Elo forest: Muckamore AM 35; 82
Field, Anne: Banagher LY 30; 120
Fieldmount House: Kilmore AH 1; 64, 70
Fields, Andrew: Artrea LY 6; 31
Fields, Jackson: Tamlaght TE 20; 78
Fields, John: Tamlaght TE 20; 76
Fien Dooh bog: Donegal DL 39; 53
Fife, family: Kilroot AM 26; 74–75
Fifty Acres td: Kilbride AM 29; 136, 148
Figanny td: Errigal Truagh MN 40; 120
Figgert locality: Lough Swilly DL 38; 134
Figgivey district: Drumachose LY 9; 116
Figuart td: Raphoe DL 39; 126
Filgate, Rev. William: Magherally DN 12; 115
Filgate, William: Inniskeen MN 40; 128–29
Fillan, warrior: Banagher LY 30; 12
Fin McCool's chair: Magheracloone MN 40; 139
Fin McCool's chair: Magheross MN 40; 157
Fin McCool's stone: Aghanloo LY 11; 6, 29
Fin McCool's stone: Ballynascreen LY 31; 15
Fin McCool's stone: Banagher LY 30; 75, 94
Fin McCool's stone: Loughguile AM 13; 72
Fin McCool's stone: Maghera LY 18; 22
Fin McCoole's Castle: Drumballyroney DN 3; 16
Finaghwe [or Finagaie] district: Misc. SO 40; 198
Finaghy td: Blaris AM 8; 70
Finahan lough: Clondavaddog DL 38; 3
Finally, John: Dundermot AM 13; 34–35
Finaly, Archibald: Ballymartin AM 2; 9
Finaly, William: Ballymartin AM 2; 16
Fincaran (see Fincarn)l: Dungiven LY 15; 18
Fincarn (Fincairn) td: Clondermot LY 34; 56, 67, 71, 76, 80, 110, 112, 116–17, 124, 131
Fincarn altar: Clondermot LY 34; 5, 24

Fincarn altar: Faughanvale LY 36; 34
Fincarn chapel: Banagher LY 30; 27, 29, 59
Fincarn cove: Clondermot LY 34; 44
Fincarn flax mill: Banagher LY 30; 29, 127
Fincarn forts: Banagher LY 30; 76
Fincarn giant's grave: Donaghmoyne MN 40; 108
Fincarn glen: Clondermot LY 34; 5, 23–24, 32, 35, 44
Fincarn glen: Faughanvale LY 36; 4, 33
Fincarn hamlet: Banagher LY 30; 27
Fincarn hill: Donaghmoyne MN 40; 106
Fincarn meeting house: Clondermot LY 34; 5, 9, 20, 89, 103
Fincarn quarry: Banagher LY 30; 127
Fincarn river: Banagher LY 30; 76
Fincarn school: Dungiven LY 15; 18
Fincarn school [I]: Banagher LY 30; 27, 29, 32–34, 59, 73, 111
Fincarn school [II]: Banagher LY 30; 33–34, 73, 111
Fincarn standing stones: Banagher LY 30; 46
Fincarn Sunday school: Clondermot LY 34; 93
Fincarn td: Banagher LY 30; 7, 9, 22, 36, 61–62, 86, 95, 100, 104, 109, 113, 118, 123, 127, 129–31
Fincarn wood: Banagher LY 30; 123
Fincarne (see Fincarn): Donaghmoyne MN 40; 106
Fincharn (see Fincarn): Clondermot LY 34; 56
Findermore td: Clogher TE 5; 33, 38–39, 46
Findrum (Fendrum) td: Errigal Keerogue TE 20; 52–53, 57
Findrum td: Convoy DL 39; 20
Fines, Widow: Ballymoney AM 16; 17
Fines, William: Ballymoney AM 16; 17
Finey, William: Ballintoy AM 24; 19
Finford of Glinsk locality: Lough Swilly DL 38; 115
Fingain lough: Cappagh TE 5; 22
Fingal (see McCool)
Fingal's fort: Misc. LY 36; 117
Fingarvil corn mill: Maghera LY 18; 35
Finghrian lough: Templecarn DL 39; 157
Finglass bridge: Magheradrool DN 17; 101
Finglen burn: Banagher LY 30; 99
Finglen hill: Banagher LY 30; 24
Finglen td: Banagher LY 30; 61–62, 99, 104, 109, 118, 123, 127, 131
Finglen valley: Banagher LY 30; 24
Finglen valley: Clondermot LY 34; 67
Finian, St: Misc. DN 17; 121
Finian, St: Newtownards DN 7; 107
Finigan, Claud: Donacavey TE 5; 81
Finisk river (Waterford): Clondermot LY 34; 67
Finiston, Rev.: Templepatrick AM 35; 132
Finiston, Samuel (Jnr): Duneane AM 19; 111, 117–18
Finiston, Samuel (Snr): Duneane AM 19; 117
Finkiltagh flax mill: Ahoghill AM 23; 34

Finkiltagh graveyard: Ahoghill AM 23; 26, 34
Finkiltagh standing stone: Ahoghill AM 23; 26–27
Finkiltagh stone circle: Ahoghill AM 23; 26, 34
Finkiltagh td: Ahoghill AM 23; 27–28, 38, 40
Finlagan church: Tamlaght Finlagan LY 25; 97
Finlagan Glebe bridge: Tamlaght Finlagan LY 25; 122–23
Finlagan Glebe House: Tamlaght Finlagan LY 25; 81, 85, 101, 122, 125
Finlagan grey stone: Tamlaght Finlagan LY 25; 89, 110, 112
Finlagan old church: Drumachose LY 9; 107
Finlagan old church: Tamlaght Finlagan LY 25; 102
Finlagan ph: Magilligan LY 11; 82, 119
Finlagan schools: Drumachose LY 9; 108
Finlagan td: Tamlaght Finlagan LY 25; 89, 112, 119
Finlagan, disciple: Tamlaght Finlagan LY 25; 102
Finlane hill: Killesher FH 14; 81
Finlane td: Killesher FH 14; 82
Finlay, Agnes: Drummaul AM 19; 92
Finlay, Ann (Jnr): Drumbeg AM 8; 133
Finlay, Ann (Snr): Drumbeg AM 8; 133
Finlay, Archibald: Carrickfergus AM 37; 123
Finlay, David: Blaris DN 12; 46, 50
Finlay, Edward: Ballyscullion LY 6; 61
Finlay, family: Raloo AM 32; 108, 123
Finlay, James: Drumbeg AM 8; 124, 126, 128, 133
Finlay, James: Macosquin LY 22; 84, 118–19
Finlay, John: Blaris DN 12; 50–51
Finlay, Mary: Macosquin LY 22; 122
Finlay, Matthew: Hillsborough DN 12; 107
Finlay, Messrs: Down DN 17; 59
Finlay, Rev.: Comber DN 7; 41
Finlay, Rev. Moses: Donaghmore DN 3; 8
Finlay, Rev. Moses: Newry DN 3; 81
Finlay, Robert (Jnr): Drumbeg AM 8; 133
Finlay, Robert (Snr): Drumbeg AM 8; 133
Finlay, Robert: Macosquin LY 22; 122
Finlay, William: Carrickfergus AM 37; 135
Finlay, William: Hillsborough DN 12; 107
Finlay's glen: Raloo AM 32; 122
Finley, Jacob: Dunboe LY 11; 75
Finley, James: Killowen LY 33; 169
Finley, James: Muckamore AM 35; 79
Finley, Mr: Manorhamilton Union LM 40; 52
Finley, Thomas: Newry DN 3; 99
Finley, William: Dunboe LY 11; 74
Finlough td: Killoran and Kilvarnet SO 40; 184
Finn Cottage: Urney DL 39; 176
Finn lough: Inishkeel DL 39; 70
Finn lough: Misc. DL 39; 188
Finn river: Clones FH 4; 28
Finn river: Clonleigh DL 39; 1, 3, 5, 7, 13–14, 16
Finn river: Cumber LY 28; 68
Finn river: Donaghmore DL 39; 28–31, 33–35

Finn river: Donegal DL 39; 49
Finn river: Drummully FH 4; 35, 39
Finn river: Galloon FH 4; 88, 97
Finn river: Killymard DL 39; 105
Finn river: Kilteevoge DL 39; 111–13
Finn river: Misc. DL 39; 185, 188
Finn river: Taughboyne DL 39; 149–50
Finn river: Urney DL 39; 174–77, 180
Finn, family: Ballinderry AM 21; 55
Finn, Gen.: Kilmacteige SO 40; 187
Finn, John: Aghagallon AM 21; 16
Finnabrogue (Finnebrogue) td: Inch DN 17; 74, 76–77
Finnabrogue corn mill: Inch DN 17; 73, 77
Finnabrogue demesne: Inch DN 17; 73
Finnabrogue House: Ballee DN 17; 23
Finnabrogue House: Bangor DN 7; 22
Finnabrogue House: Down DN 17; 51, 57
Finnabrogue House: Inch DN 17; 73–74
Finnabrogue House: Killyleagh DN 17; 85
Finnagan, Rev.: Carlingford LH 40; 60
Finnard (Finers) td: Newry DN 3; 109–10
Finnard Point: Newry DN 3; 109
Finnen church: Inishmacsaint FH 14; 74
Finney, family: Carnmoney AM 2; 76
Finney, Rev. T.H.: Enniskeen CN 40; 29
Finneydurk Glebe td: Convoy DL 39; 20
Finnigan, Eliza: Ballyscullion LY 6; 78
Finnigan, John: Aghagallon AM 21; 24
Finnigan, Michael: Ballyscullion LY 6; 78
Finnighan, Miss: Clogher TE 5; 43
Finnighan, Widow: Clogher TE 5; 43
Finnis cave: Dromara DN 12; 63, 67
Finnis chapel: Dromara DN 12; 63
Finnis mill: Dromara DN 12; 63
Finnis td: Dromara DN 12; 63, 65, 67
Finnra td: Drumlumman CN 40; 12, 14
Finny, William: Balteagh LY 9; 28
Finors (see Finnard): Newry DN 3; 109
Finton, Dr: Urney DL 39; 181
Finton, family: Camlin AM 21; 68
Finton, John: Donaghmore DL 39; 37–38
Finton, Mr: Raphoe DL 39; 126
Finton, St: Clondermot LY 34; 63
Finton, St: Magilligan LY 11; 88
Finton, St: Tamlaght Finlagan LY 25; 102
Fintona: Banagher LY 30; 19
Fintona: Clogher TE 5; 44, 60
Fintona: Clogherny TE 20; 27
Fintona: Clondermot LY 34; 30
Fintona: Cumber LY 28; 58
Fintona: Donacavey TE 5; 62–63, 66, 68, 70–75, 82
Fintona: Dromore TE 5; 97
Fintona: Enniskillen FH 4; 44, 48, 61, 70
Fintona bridge: Donacavey TE 5; 64

Fintona bridge: Dromore TE 5; 102
Fintona chapel (C): Donacavey TE 5; 62, 69
Fintona chapel (M): Donacavey TE 5; 62, 69
Fintona church: Donacavey TE 5; 62, 64, 67–69
Fintona dispensary: Clogher TE 5; 60
Fintona dispensary: Donacavey TE 5; 64, 71
Fintona glebe: Donacavey TE 5; 77
Fintona Glebe House: Clogher TE 5; 55
Fintona Glebe House: Donacavey TE 5; 74
Fintona meeting house: Donacavey TE 5; 62, 69
Fintona ph: Clogher TE 5; 41, 53–55, 57, 59–60
Fintona ph: Donacavey TE 5; 84, 86–87
Fintona ph: Dromore TE 5; 95–96
Fintona river: Donacavey TE 5; 69
Fintona school [I]: Donacavey TE 5; 65
Fintona school [II]: Donacavey TE 5; 65
Fintona school [III]: Donacavey TE 5; 65
Fintona school [IV]: Donacavey TE 5; 65
Fintona school [V]: Donacavey TE 5; 65
Fintona school [VI]: Donacavey TE 5; 65
Fintona stream: Donacavey TE 5; 67
Fintona td: Donacavey TE 5; 76, 78, 81, 83, 86
Fintonagh td: Devenish FH 14; 58
Fintown: Conwal DL 39; 25
Fintown: Killymard DL 39; 105
Fintown: Kilteevoge DL 39; 112–13
Fintown: Leck DL 39; 116
Finvey td: Desertcreat TE 20; 33
Finvola, woman named: Dungiven LY 15; 33
Finvor td: Mevagh DL 38; 63
Finvoy brickfields: Finvoy AM 23; 71
Finvoy causeway: Finvoy AM 23; 69
Finvoy church school: Finvoy AM 23; 75
Finvoy coves: Finvoy AM 23; 78
Finvoy Glebe House: Finvoy AM 23; 68, 71–72
Finvoy graveyard: Finvoy AM 23; 76
Finvoy hills: Ballymoney AM 16; 4
Finvoy ph: Ballymoney AM 16; 1, 5, 21
Finvoy ph: Ballyscullion AM 19; 2
Finvoy ph: Drummaul AM 19; 35
Finvoy ph: Dunaghy AM 13; 26
Finvoy ph: Duneane AM 19; 96
Finvoy ph: Killagan AM 23; 79, 81
Finvoy ph: Kirkinriola AM 23; 126
Finvoy ph: Misc. AM 10; 129
Finvoy ph: Rasharkin AM 23; 127–29, 133
Finvoy standing stones: Finvoy AM 23; 78
Fior glen (see Fore): Faughanvale LY 36; 21
Fir field: Antrim AM 29; 18–19, 29
Fir field: Muckamore AM 35; 62, 68, 80
Fir fort: Desertoghill LY 27; 27
Fir lough: Belleek FH 14; 1
Fir mountain: Lissan TE 20; 69
Firenson, Alex: Tamlaght TE 20; 105
Firreagh lough: Drumragh TE 5; 104

Firreagh td: Drumragh TE 5; 107–08

Fish Loughan cave: Kildollagh LY 22; 73

Fish Loughan hamlet: Kildollagh LY 22; 67

Fish Loughan td: Kildollagh LY 22; 67–73

Fish Quarter td: Ballywalter DN 7; 18

Fish Quarter td: Misc. DN 17; 125

Fishbourne, Jane: Aghalee AM 21; 40

Fishbourne, John: Aghalee AM 21; 40

Fishbourne, John: Dromara DN 12; 69

Fisher, Archibald: Drumachose LY 9; 104

Fisher, Archibald: Errigal LY 27; 37–38, 61–62

Fisher, family: Magheragall AM 21; 99

Fisher, Hugh: Drummaul AM 19; 87

Fisher, James: Aghadowey LY 22; 38

Fisher, James: Blaris DN 12; 41

Fisher, James: Hillsborough DN 12; 106

Fisher, John: Ballyaghran LY 33; 22

Fisher, John: Drumachose LY 9; 127

Fisher, John: Larne AM 10; 127

Fisher, John: Muckamore AM 35; 81

Fisher, Mr: Killyleagh DN 17; 82

Fisher, Mrs: Blaris DN 12; 50

Fisher, Patrick: Muckamore AM 35; 81

Fisher, Robert: Muckamore AM 35; 80

Fisher, Samuel: Aghadowey LY 22; 38

Fisher, Samuel: Carrickfergus AM 37; 120

Fisher, Samuel: Misc. DL 39; 186

Fisher, Thomas: Carrickfergus AM 37; 193

Fisher, William: Aghanloo LY 11; 27

Fishers Quarter (see Fish Quarter)

Fisherwick demesne: Doagh AM 29; 60, 67, 69

Fisherwick House: Doagh AM 29; 68–69, 71, 73,
   84–86, 92, 96

Fisherwick plantation: Doagh AM 29; 61

Fishery Lodge: Dunluce AM 16; 110

Fishing bay: Lough Neagh AM 21; 92

Fishing Rod tree: Kilcronaghan LY 31; 64

Fithuston, Rev.: Drung CN 40; 21

Fitsimmons, Rev.: Ballyclug AM 23; 59

FitzAlan, Brian: Clondermot LY 34; 45

Fitzgerald, Clements: Ballinderry AM 21; 57

Fitzgerald, Dr: Ardstraw TE 5; 12

Fitzgerald, E.: Ballybay MN 40; 84

Fitzgerald, Elizabeth: Ardstraw TE 5; 7

Fitzgerald, Frederick: Ardstraw TE 5; 7

Fitzgerald, Gerald: Ardglass DN 17; 12

Fitzgerald, John: Ardstraw TE 5; 7

Fitzgerald, Lord: Dungiven LY 15; 34

Fitzgerald, Mr: Cumber LY 28; 75

Fitzgerald, Rev. Gerald: Ardstraw TE 5; 7, 9

Fitzgerald, Robert: Ballyscullion LY 6; 58

Fitzgerald, William: Carnmoney AM 2; 104

Fitzgerrald, P.: Newtownards DN 7; 112

Fitzimond, family: Ballyphilip DN 7; 12

Fitzjames (Duke of Berwick): Enniskillen FH 4; 52

FitzJohn, Thomas: Kilkeel DN 3; 53

Fitzmairs, Capt.: Devenish FH 14; 59–60

Fitzmaurice, Gerald: Carrickfergus AM 37; 80

Fitzmaurice, Lt: Ardstraw TE 5; 5

Fitzpatrick, family: Dunsfort DN 17; 68

Fitzpatrick, family: Ramoan AM 24; 107

Fitzpatrick, Margaret: Carrickfergus AM 37; 76

Fitzpatrick, Rev.: Carrickfergus AM 37; 174

Fitzpatrick, Rev. John: Newry DN 3; 71, 95, 99,
   101, 104

Fitzroy, Henry: Ardglass DN 17; 9

Fitzroy, Jane: Ardglass DN 17; 9

Fitzsimmons, Mr: Tullynakill DN 7; 122

Fitzsimmons, Rev. John: Saintfield DN 7; 114

Fitzsimmons, Samuel: Clonduff DN 3; 3

Fitzsimonds, family: Ballyculter DN 17; 28

Fitzsimons, Nicholas: Kilclief DN 17; 79

Fitzsimons, Patrick: Newry DN 3; 114

Fitzsimons, Rev. John: Saul DN 17; 114

Fitzsimons, Rev. Patrick: Drung CN 40; 21

Fitz-Stephen, Robert: Ballyscullion LY 6; 57

FitzThomas, Maurice: Kilkeel DN 3; 53

FitzWarrin, William: Clondermot LY 34; 45

Five Finger Point: Lough Swilly DL 38; 107

Five Islands lough: Loughguile AM 13; 61

Fiveacres td: Drumtullagh AM 16; 103

Fivemile hill: Donaghmore DN 3; 7

Fivemiletown: Aghalurcher FH 4; 1, 7–8

Fivemiletown: Aghavea FH 4; 21

Fivemiletown: Clogher TE 5; 25, 27, 31–32, 34–35,
   38, 50–51, 60–61

Fivemiletown: Derryvullan FH 14; 38

Fivemiletown: Donacavey TE 5; 62

Fivemiletown: Enniskillen FH 4; 48, 70

Fivemiletown chapel (M): Clogher TE 5; 51

Fivemiletown chapel of ease: Clogher TE 5; 32

Fivemiletown church: Clogher TE 5; 39, 51

Fivemiletown day school: Clogher TE 5; 42

Fivemiletown dispensary: Clogher TE 5; 60

Fivemiletown female school: Clogher TE 5; 32,
   41–42, 50–51

Fivemiletown male school: Clogher TE 5; 32,
   41–43, 50–51

Fivemiletown meeting house: Clogher TE 5; 32

Fivemiletown police barracks: Clogher TE 5; 32

Fivemiletown sessions house: Clogher TE 5; 32, 51

Fivemiletown shambles: Clogher TE 5; 32

Fivemiletown td: Clogher TE 5; 44, 47, 50

Fivey, William: Seagoe AH 1; 108

Fivey, William [I]: Aghaderg DN 12; 3

Fivey, William [I]: Misc. DN 17; 131

Fivey, William [II]: Aghaderg DN 12; 6, 10, 12

Fivey, William [II]: Misc. DN 17; 131

Flack, James: Island Magee AM 10; 68, 97, 102

Flack, Matthew: Tamlaght TE 20; 129

Flagherty, Owen: Termonamongan TE 5; 144
Flagstaff hill: Rathlin Island AM 24; 129
Flan of Bute, poet: Magilligan LY 11; 104
Flanagan, Mr: Enniskillen FH 4; 85
Flanders (Belgium): Dunboe LY 11; 61
Flanders bog: Bovevagh LY 25; 2
Flanders Castle: Bovevagh LY 25; 15
Flanders Castle: Dungiven LY 15; 33
Flanders Derryard td: Balteagh LY 9; 26
Flanders fort: Bovevagh LY 25; 8, 14–15, 18–19, 36–37
Flanders lime-kiln: Bovevagh LY 25; 44
Flanders round house: Bovevagh LY 25; 38
Flanders td: Banagher LY 30; 23–24
Flanders td: Bovevagh LY 25; 7, 10, 13, 17, 19, 23, 29, 35–36, 38, 43–45, 60–61
Flanderstown (see Flanders): Bovevagh LY 25; 19
Flanigan, Allice: Drumachose LY 9; 133
Flanigan, Eliza: Drumachose LY 9; 133
Flanigan, James: Drumachose LY 9; 133
Flanigan, John: Drumachose LY 9; 133
Flanigan, Maryann: Drumachose LY 9; 133
Flannagan: Dunluce AM 16; 117
Flannigan, Edward: Newry DN 3; 98, 103
Flannigan, Patrick: Ballynascreen LY 31; 24
Flannigan, Robert: Magherafelt LY 6; 107
Fleeting, person named: Blaris AM 8; 60
Fleming and McClaverty, Messrs: Glynn AM 26; 38
Fleming, Alexander: Aughnamullen MN 40; 75
Fleming, Alexander: Drummully FH 4; 37
Fleming, Andrew: Ahoghill AM 23; 35
Fleming, Andrew: Maghera LY 18; 77
Fleming, Edward: Aghadowey LY 22; 18
Fleming, family: Antrim AM 29; 24
Fleming, family: Blaris AM 8; 22
Fleming, family: Maghera LY 18; 13
Fleming, Isaac: Maghera LY 18; 22, 53, 68, 73
Fleming, James: Ballymoney AM 16; 17, 26
Fleming, James: Banagher LY 30; 61
Fleming, James: Carrickfergus AM 37; 113
Fleming, John: Aghadowey LY 22; 35
Fleming, John: Ballinderry AM 21; 47
Fleming, John: Blaris DN 12; 40
Fleming, John: Carrickfergus AM 37; 115
Fleming, John: Magilligan LY 11; 132
Fleming, Joseph: Bovevagh LY 25; 16, 50
Fleming, Makey: Muckamore AM 35; 80
Fleming, Mrs Robert: Bovevagh LY 25; 12, 30
Fleming, Patt: Kilmacteige SO 40; 194
Fleming, Rev. Robert: Ballyscullion LY 6; 63–64, 77
Fleming, Richard: Carrickfergus AM 37; 110
Fleming, Robert: Bovevagh LY 25; 12, 30, 49
Fleming, Robert: Dungiven LY 15; 74, 90
Fleming, Samual: Tamlaght Finlagan LY 25; 114

Fleming, Samuel: Balteagh LY 9; 13, 25
Fleming, William: Aghanloo LY 11; 31–32
Fleming, William: Bovevagh LY 25; 27, 55
Fleming, William: Carrickfergus AM 37; 118
Fleming, William: Dungiven LY 15; 66, 73
Fleming, William: Magilligan LY 11; 128, 130
Fleming, Willim: Maghera LY 18; 42
Flemingstown td: Raphoe DL 39; 126
Flemming, family: Magilligan LY 11; 130
Flemming, James: Donacavey TE 5; 81
Flemming, James: Maghera LY 18; 77
Flemming, Mrs: Comber DN 7; 34
Flemming, Mrs: Muckamore AM 35; 79
Flemming, Nancy: Muckamore AM 35; 81
Flemming, Sarah: Maghera LY 18; 77
Flemming, Widow: Muckamore AM 35; 81
Fletcher, Capt.: Kilroot AM 26; 77
Fletcher, Edward: Aghagallon AM 21; 6–7
Fletcher, Edward: Aghalee AM 21; 34
Fletcher, family: Blaris AM 8; 21
Fletcher, family: Blaris DN 12; 30
Fletcher, family: Derryaghy AM 8; 103
Fletcher, family: Templecorran AM 26; 117–19
Fletcher, Matthew: Newry DN 3; 104
Fletcher, Miss: Blaris AM 8; 19, 84–85
Fletcher, Miss: Blaris DN 12; 45, 49
Fletcher, Philip: Kilroot AM 26; 59, 67, 78–79
Fletcher, Rev. Phillip: Aghalee AM 21; 31
Fletcher, Richard: Carrickfergus AM 37; 25
Fletcher, William: Newry DN 3; 100
Flin, Edward: Hillsborough DN 12; 107
Flinter, Alicia: Donacavey TE 5; 65
Flinter, family: Carrickfergus AM 37; 93
Flinter, Rev. William: Ballynure AM 32; 69
Flinter, Rev. William: Carrickfergus AM 37; 102, 144
Flixton (Lancashire): Aghalee AM 21; 31
Florence (Italy): Carrickfergus AM 37; 160
Florencecourt House: Enniskillen FH 4; 50, 61, 67
Florencecourt House: Killesher FH 14; 82–85, 87–88
Florencecourt House: Kinawley FH 4; 107–09
Florencecourt House: Manorhamilton Union LM 40; 50
Florida (America): Comber DN 7; 40–41
Florida: Dundonald DN 7; 65
Florida: Saintfield DN 7; 118
Florida bridge: Killinchy DN 7; 86
Florida House: Kilmood DN 7; 95
Florida school: Kilmood DN 7; 96
Flow moss bog: Misc. DL 39; 188
Flower hill: Dunluce AM 16; 116–17, 120
Flower Hill House: Dunluce AM 16; 120
Flowerfield House: Aghadowey LY 22; 6
Flowerfield House: Ballyaghran LY 33; 7–9, 12

Flowerfield plough manufactory: Faughanvale LY 36; 16

Floyd, Ellis: Clondermot LY 34; 49

Floyd, Thomas: Kilmood DN 7; 95

Floyer, Mrs: Blaris AM 8; 84–85

Floyer, Mrs: Blaris DN 12; 45

Flughland td: Moville DL 38; 73

Flush hill quarry: Enniskillen FH 4; 62

Flush school: Connor AM 19; 27

Fofannybane td: Kilcoo DN 3; 45

Fogart td: Clogher TE 5; 37, 43, 53

Fogarty, Philip: Antrim AM 29; 14, 25

Fogher td: Devenish FH 14; 58

Foglish mountain: Aghalurcher FH 4; 2

Foglish td: Aghalurcher FH 4; 14

Folan, Rev.: Carrickfergus AM 37; 161

Foley, Samuel: Misc. DN 17; 117

Folliot, John: Derryvullan FH 14; 38–39

Folsidde, Thomas: Donacavey TE 5; 81

Fomullen (Fermullen) td: Dunboe LY 11; 76, 81

Fool Jock (see Lafferty): Island Magee AM 10; 94

Fooranemoor spring: Galloon FH 4; 88

Foot, Capt.: Carrickfergus AM 37; 141

Foot, J.: Annaclone DN 12; 15

Foot, J.: Seapatrick DN 12; 125

Foot, J.: Tullylish DN 12; 141–42

Foot, Richard: Blaris AM 8; 31

Foote, Rev. Simon: Seagoe AH 1; 103

Foote, Richard: Blaris DN 12; 46, 50

Forbes, Alexander: Artrea LY 6; 24

Forbes, Capt.: Termoneeny LY 6; 122, 130

Forbes, family: Maghera LY 18; 13, 24, 48

Forbes, family: Shilvodan AM 19; 136

Forbes, George: Artrea LY 6; 36

Forbes, John: Ardstraw TE 5; 7

Forbes, Mr (Tooay): Aughnamullen MN 40; 72–74

Forbes, Mr: Holywood DN 7; 77

Forbes, Mrs: Aughnamullen MN 40; 71

Forbes, Mrs: Muckamore AM 35; 80

Forbes, Robert: Carrickfergus AM 37; 150

Ford, Adam: Ardstraw TE 5; 8

Ford, family: Killagan AM 23; 84

Ford, Francis: Hillsborough DN 12; 99

Ford, James: Tamlaght TE 20; 80, 121

Ford, Mary: Blaris AM 8; 80

Ford, Robert: Hillsborough DN 12; 106

Ford, T.: Hillsborough DN 12; 87

Ford, Thomas: Tamlaght TE 20; 115

Ford, William (Jnr): Dunboe LY 11; 46, 64

Ford, William (Snr): Dunboe LY 11; 46, 61

Ford, William: Coleraine LY 33; 56

Forde, Col: Loughinisland DN 17; 94–96

Forde, Col.: Ardkeen DN 7; 2

Forde, Col.: Ballyphilip DN 7; 8

Forde, Col.: Down DN 17; 49, 57, 61

Forde, Col.: Dromara DN 12; 65, 67, 69

Forde, Col.: Killyleagh DN 17; 85

Forde, Col.: Magheradrool DN 17; 104

Forde, Col.: Misc. DN 17; 126–27

Forde, Harriet (nee Savage): Down DN 17; 52, 57–59

Forde, Harriet: Dromara DN 12; 69

Forde, Harriet: Killyleagh DN 17; 85

Forde, Harriet: Loughinisland DN 17; 94, 97

Forde, Harriet: Saul DN 17; 114

Forde, Matthew: Ballee DN 17; 15

Forde, Matthew: Down DN 17; 53

Forde, Mr (Raughlin): Montiaghs AH 1; 92–93

Forde, Mr: Coleraine LY 33; 99

Forde, Rev.: Carlingford LH 40; 60

Forde, Rev. Robert: Drumgooland DN 3; 22, 25

Forde, Thomas: Carrickfergus AM 37; 195

Forde, William: Magheramesk AM 21; 130

Fordross day school: Clogher TE 5; 42

Fore Glen corn mill: Bovevagh LY 25; 4

Fore Glen flax mill: Bovevagh LY 25; 4

Fore Glen river: Bovevagh LY 25; 1, 4, 7, 21, 57

Fore Glen river: Cumber LY 28; 4, 6, 11, 29, 45, 85–86

Fore Glen river: Faughanvale LY 36; 21

Fore Glen stone bridge: Cumber LY 28; 11, 85

Fore Glen valley: Banagher LY 30; 24, 31

Fore Glen valley: Bovevagh LY 25; 9, 17, 24

Fore Glen valley: Cumber LY 28; 112, 114

Fore strand: Magilligan LY 11; 120, 141–42

Foreign mountain: Rasharkin AM 23; 139

Forein Fin spring: Balteagh LY 9; 42

Foreman, Samuel: Dunboe LY 11; 79

Foremass (Foremas) td: Errigal Keerogue TE 20; 57

Foremass corn mill: Errigal Keerogue TE 20; 53

Foremass Lower corn mill: Errigal Keerogue TE 20; 56

Foremass Lower td: Errigal Keerogue TE 20; 48, 50, 53, 56

Foremass quarry: Errigal Keerogue TE 20; 53

Foremass td: Galloon FH 4; 95

Foremass Upper td: Errigal Keerogue TE 20; 48, 50, 53, 56

Forest View House: Ematris MN 40; 115

Forest, David: Drumachose LY 9; 104

Forester, Michael: Banagher LY 30; 90

Forester, Mr (Cloverhill): Misc. LY 31; 113

Forfey House: Aghalurcher FH 4; 8

Forfey td: Aghalurcher FH 4; 3–4, 14

Forfey, Edward: Carrickfergus AM 37; 107

Forge bridge: Ballynascreen LY 31; 8

Forge bridge: Maghera LY 18; 46

Forge bridge: Magheralin DN 12; 110

Forge Lodge foundry: Derryaghy AM 8; 110

Forge lough: Kilrea LY 27; 112

Forge lough: Tamlaght O'Crilly LY 18; 95

Forgetown: Misc. LY 31; 113

Forgetown bridge: Misc. LY 31; 116

Forguill, St Dallan: Ballynascreen LY 31; 33–34

Forgy, family: Billy AM 16; 58, 68

Forked bridge: Racavan AM 13; 93

Forket bridge: Ballinderry AM 21; 42

Forkhill (Forkil): Misc. DN 17; 130–31

Fork-hill (see Forkhill): Misc. DN 17; 131

Forkhill: Forkhill AH 1; 45

Forkhill chapel: Forkhill AH 1; 45

Forkhill church: Forkhill AH 1; 45

Forkhill market house: Forkhill AH 1; 45

Forkhill mill: Forkhill AH 1; 45

Forkhill ph: Loughgilly AH 1; 84

Forkland (see Farkland): Bovevagh LY 25; 57

Forley, Rev. Thomas: Kilbroney DN 3; 34

Formil hill: Drumkeeran FH 14; 64

Formil td: Bovevagh LY 25; 60

Formil td: Dungiven LY 15; 62, 64

Formill House: Aughnamullen MN 40; 71

Formill td: Aughnamullen MN 40; 76

Formill td: Muckno MN 40; 165

Formoyle td: Tydavnet MN 40; 169

Formullen (Fermullen) td: Dunboe LY 11; 50

Formullen cove: Dunboe LY 11; 50

Forrast, family: Blaris AM 8; 21

Forres Abbey: Aghadowey LY 22; 31

Forrest, John: Bovevagh LY 25; 60

Forrest, Thomas: Bovevagh LY 25; 60

Forrest, William: Newry DN 3; 99, 103

Forrester, Alexander: Maghera LY 18; 72

Forrester, Anthony: Termoneeny LY 6; 122, 127, 130, 132

Forrester, Arthur [I]: Termoneeny LY 6; 127, 132

Forrester, Arthur [II]: Termoneeny LY 6; 127, 132

Forrester, Catherine: Termoneeny LY 6; 127, 132

Forrester, James: Carrickfergus AM 37; 113

Forrester, Rev. Alexander: Termoneeny LY 6; 127, 132

Forrester, Rev. William: Termoneeny LY 6; 127, 132

Forrester, Robert: Errigal LY 27; 55

Forrester, Robert: Maghera LY 18; 57, 59

Forrester, Robert [I]: Termoneeny LY 6; 122, 127, 130–32

Forrester, Robert [II]: Termoneeny LY 6; 127, 132

Forrester, Thomas: Carrickfergus AM 37; 193

Forrester, William: Artrea LY 6; 22

Forrester, William [II]: Termoneeny LY 6; 127, 132

Forrester, William [II]: Termoneeny LY 6; 127, 132

Forrester, William [III]: Termoneeny LY 6; 127, 132

Forsey (see Forfey): Aghalurcher FH 4; 3

Forshilly td: Ballyphilip DN 7; 8

Forster, A.J.: Killanny MN 40; 134

Forster, Francis: Killygarvan DL 38; 48

Forster, George: Magheracloone MN 40; 138, 141

Forster, R.A.: Newry DN 3; 84–85, 93, 95, 100–01, 101–02, 104

Forster, Rev. A.: Drumgoon CN 40; 8

Forster, Rev. Nicholas: Raphoe DL 39; 123–24

Forster, Rev. Thomas: Magheracloone MN 40; 138

Forster's school: Raphoe DL 39; 123–24

Forsyth, family: Aghagallon AM 21; 9

Forsyth, family: Ballynure AM 32; 35, 56

Forsyth, George: Carrickfergus AM 37; 102, 135, 141, 145, 150, 172

Forsyth, James: Seagoe AH 1; 103

Forsyth, John: Ballynure AM 32; 34, 40, 57, 64

Forsyth, John: Carrickfergus AM 37; 98

Forsyth, Rose: Carrickfergus AM 37; 115

Forsyth, William: Carrickfergus AM 37; 122

Forsyth's hill: Desertlyn LY 31; 36

Forsythe, Andrew: Macosquin LY 22; 99

Forsythe, Andrew: Magherafelt LY 6; 110

Forsythe, Jacob: Aghanloo LY 11; 4

Forsythe, James: Aghanloo LY 11; 31–32

Forsythe, James: Carrickfergus AM 37; 141

Forsythe, John: Magilligan LY 11; 130–31, 133, 138, 141–42

Forsythe, Matthew: Balteagh LY 9; 17–18, 39

Forsythe, Mrs: Magilligan LY 11; 131

Forsythe, Rev. James: Ballynure AM 32; 64

Forsythe, Robert: Balteagh LY 9; 17, 39

Forsythe, William: Aghalee AM 21; 36

Forsythe, William: Lissan LY 31; 107

Fort Breda House: Comber DN 7; 40

Fort Garden locality: Tamlaght O'Crilly LY 18; 112–13

Fort hill: Ahoghill AM 23; 27–28

Fort hill: Templecorran AM 26; 84

Fort Hill House: Connor AM 19; 21

Fort Nelson locality: Tamlaght O'Crilly LY 18; 119–20

Fort Royal House: Killygarvan DL 38; 40, 42

Fort Singleton House (Monaghan): Termoneeny LY 6; 132

Fort Stewart (old) td: Tullyaughnish DL 38; 97

Fort Stewart ferry: Misc. DL 39; 189

Fort Stewart ferry: Tullyaughnish DL 38; 90–91

Fort Stewart fort: Tullyaughnish DL 38; 91

Fort Stewart House: Killea and Taughboyne DL 39; 79

Fort Stewart House: Leck DL 39; 117

Fort Stewart House: Lough Swilly DL 38; 102, 105

Fort Stewart House: Tullyaughnish DL 38; 86–91, 94

Fort Stewart manor: Tullyaughnish DL 38; 92, 95–97

Fort Stewart quay: Lough Swilly DL 38; 103–04

Fort Stewart standing stone: Tullyaughnish DL 38; 91

Fort Stewart td: Killygarvan DL 38; 41

Fort stone: Banagher LY 30; 56

Fort Town: Ballymoney AM 16; 21

Fort Town school: Ballymoney AM 16; 27

Fort well: Errigal LY 27; 69

Fort William bridge: Misc. LY 31; 116

Fort William demesne: Misc. LY 31; 115

Fort William House: Ballynascreen LY 31; 13, 23, 32

Fort William House: Kilcronaghan LY 31; 66–67, 71, 75, 83, 87

Fort William House: Killdrumsherdan CN 40; 34

Fort William House: Misc. LY 31; 115, 118, 129

Fortescue manor: Ahoghill AM 23; 2, 11, 15

Fortescue school: Hillsborough DN 12; 101

Fortescue, Col.: Magherally DN 12; 113

Fortescue, Faithful: Carrickfergus AM 37; 43

Fortescue, James: Newry DN 3; 86

Fortescue, Thomas: Carrickfergus AM 37; 43

Fortesque school: Donaghcloney DN 12; 61

Forth House: Misc. DL 39; 189

Forth river (Scotland): Templepatrick AM 35; 116

Forth td: Raymoghy DL 39; 141–42, 186, 199

Forthill cave: Templecorran AM 26; 114, 121

Forthill fort: Templecorran AM 26; 120

Forthill plantation: Templecorran AM 26; 121

Forthill td: Ballyclug AM 23; 60

Forthill td: Templecorran AM 26; 82–83, 109, 119

Fortiscue, Mr: Ballymascanlan LH 40; 55–56

Fortry td: Currin MN 40; 86, 91

Fortsyth, John: Bovevagh LY 25; 49

Forttown td: Ballymoney AM 16; 20

Fortwilliam bridge: Maghera LY 18; 63

Fortwilliam House: Maghera LY 18; 14, 35, 55

Fosbury, Mrs: Kilbroney DN 3; 33, 35

Fossey hill: Aughnamullen MN 40; 69

Foster and Greer, Messrs: Blaris AM 8; 51

Foster, Andrew: Tydavnet MN 40; 173

Foster, Arthur: Ardstraw TE 5; 6

Foster, E.J.: Killanny MN 40; 134

Foster, F.: Aughnamullen MN 40; 75

Foster, family: Blaris AM 8; 21–22

Foster, family: Magherafelt LY 6; 95

Foster, James: Drummaul AM 19; 91

Foster, James: Tamlaght TE 20; 125

Foster, James: Tullyaughnish DL 38; 96

Foster, Joshua: Lough Swilly DL 38; 128

Foster, Mr (Fosters Court): Killymard DL 39; 102

Foster, Mr: Aghabog MN 40; 65

Foster, Mrs: Clogher TE 5; 41

Foster, Mrs: Killdrumsherdan CN 40; 36

Foster, Rev. Andrew: Clogher TE 5; 40

Foster, Rev. Andrew: Currin MN 40; 89

Foster, Rev. Andrew: Killdrumsherdan CN 40; 34

Foster, Rev. C.S.: Tamlaght O'Crilly LY 18; 91, 108, 124

Foster, Rev. C.S.: Termoneeny LY 6; 125, 132

Foster, Rev. William: Clogher TE 5; 28

Foster, Thomas: Tydavnet MN 40; 173

Foster, William: Magherafelt LY 6; 104–05

Fosters Court creek: Killymard DL 39; 103

Fosters Court House: Killymard DL 39; 102–03

Fosters Court td: Killymard DL 39; 100

Foughill Otra td: Jonesborough AH 1; 46

Foul ford: Ballynure AM 32; 55

Foul ford bridge: Ballynure AM 32; 55

Four Courts (Dublin): Bovevagh LY 25; 59

Four Mile burn: Donegore AM 29; 101–02, 105, 129, 131, 133–34

Four Mile burn: Kilbride AM 29; 136–37, 139, 155

Four Mile burn: Nilteen AM 35; 88, 101

Four Mile Burn bleach mill: Donegore AM 29; 104

Four Mile Burn hamlet: Donegore AM 29; 85–86, 102–03, 107, 126, 132

Four Mile Burn public house: Donegore AM 29; 132

Four Roads school: Kilmegan DN 3; 59

Four Towns hill: Duneane AM 19; 96

Fourscoreacres locality: Carrickfergus AM 37; 94

Fourscoreacres school: Carncastle and Killyglen AM 10; 7

Fowke, John: Antrim AM 29; 12, 44

Fowkes, Hugh: Antrim AM 29; 37

Fowler, Archibald: Balteagh LY 9; 35

Fowler, David: Hillsborough DN 12; 107

Fowler, Eliza: Carrickfergus AM 37; 116

Fowler, James: Hillsborough DN 12; 107

Fowler, James: Kilcronaghan LY 31; 85

Fowler, R.J.: Blaris DN 12; 36

Fowler, R.J.: Hillsborough DN 12; 103

Fowler, Rev. Robert: Urney DL 39; 175

Fowler, William: Hillsborough DN 12; 107

Fox Island: Tamlaght O'Crilly LY 18; 85, 125, 133

Fox, A.K.: Maghera LY 18; 53

Fox, Capt.: Donaghmore DL 39; 36

Fox, George: Blaris AM 8; 7

Fox, John: Newry DN 3; 99

Fox, Miss: Blaris AM 8; 85

Fox, Miss: Blaris DN 12; 45

Fox, Mr: Manorhamilton Union LM 40; 53

Fox, Mrs (Castlefinn): Donaghmore DL 39; 32

Fox, Rev. J.J.: Enniskillen FH 4; 58–59

Fox, Rev. J.J.: Kinawley FH 4; 111, 115, 119–20

Foxall, John: Killevy AH 1; 53

Foxes rock: Clonmany DL 38; 12

Foy, John: Drumgoon CN 40; 9

Foy, Miss: Enniskillen FH 4; 85

Foybeg td: Drumcree AH 1; 34, 40

Foydragh td: Aghavea FH 4; 23, 25
Foyfin school: Ardstraw TE 5; 13
Foyfin td: Urney DL 39; 181
Foyle brewery: Clondermot LY 34; 4, 14, 21, 34, 102–03
Foyle ferry: Clondermot LY 34; 7
Foyle fishery: Misc. DL 39; 188
Foyle ice-house: Misc. DL 39; 188
Foyle Park House (see Fallowlea): Faughanvale LY 36; 10
Foyle river: Clogher TE 5; 58
Foyle river: Clondermot LY 34; 1, 3–5, 7–8, 17–23, 37, 39, 43–44, 47–50, 53, 60, 64, 70, 101, 105, 114–20
Foyle river: Clonleigh DL 39; 1, 3, 7, 13–14
Foyle river: Convoy DL 39; 18
Foyle river: Donacavey TE 5; 67
Foyle river: Donaghedy TE 5; 88, 90–91
Foyle river: Killea and Taughboyne DL 39; 79, 83–84, 88
Foyle river: Killymard DL 39; 105
Foyle river: Leckpatrick TE 5; 117, 120, 123
Foyle river: Macosquin LY 22; 96
Foyle river: Misc. DL 39; 184–85, 188–89
Foyle river: Tamlaght Finlagan LY 25; 95, 104
Foyle river: Taughboyne DL 39; 149–50
Foyle View House: Clondermot LY 34; 6, 20
Foyle View House: Faughanvale LY 36; 9
Foylish (see Foglish): Aghalurcher FH 4; 14
Foymore td: Drumcree AH 1; 40
Foymount farm: Drumcree AH 1; 40
Foyrun ph: Drumlumman CN 40; 12
Frame, J.: Comber DN 7; 34
Frame, William: Carrickfergus AM 37; 121
France: Coleraine LY 33; 98–99
France: Drummaul AM 19; 71
France: Dungiven LY 15; 34
France: Galloon FH 4; 105
France: Kilbroney DN 3; 34
France: Kilmegan DN 3; 58
France: Kilrea LY 27; 119
France: Misc. LY 31; 118
France: Muff DL 38; 83
France: Tamlaght O'Crilly LY 18; 96
France: Templepatrick AM 35; 132, 141
Francis, J.: Newtownards DN 7; 112
Francis, St: Aghaderg DN 12; 7
Francis, St: Banagher LY 30; 97, 114
Francis, St: Culfeightrin AM 24; 66
Francis, St: Holywood DN 7; 73–74
Frank's Hole creek: Lough Swilly DL 38; 121
Frankfort farm: Donaghmore DN 3; 7, 9
Frankfort House: Donaghmore DN 3; 8
Frankfort meeting house: Muckno MN 40; 165
Franklin, William: Carnmoney AM 2; 69

Frazer, family: Armoy AM 24; 6
Frazer, family: Ramoan AM 24; 107
Frazer, Margaret: Carrickfergus AM 37; 122, 127
Frazer, Mr: Newry DN 3; 104
Frazer, Mrs: Newry DN 3; 99
Frazer, William: Blaris DN 12; 46, 50
Frazier, A.: Drumbo DN 7; 58
Frazier, James: Ballintoy AM 24; 33
Frazier, Mr: Kilkeel DN 3; 49
Frazier, Samuel: Killevy AH 1; 53
Freaghadoone rocks: Lough Swilly DL 38; 114
Freaghencarrow district: Misc. SO 40; 200
Fream, Maryjane: Aghadowey LY 22; 37
Freame Mount fort: Ematris MN 40; 115
Freame Mount House: Currin MN 40; 91–92
Freame Mount House: Ematris MN 40; 115
Freazer, family: Ramoan AM 24; 107
Frederickstown (Canada): Cumber LY 28; 28
Freeduff meeting house: Creggan AH 1; 27
Freeduff td: Drumlumman CN 40; 17
Freehall (Moneyvennon) td: Aghanloo LY 11; 11, 20, 33, 40–41
Freehall fishery: Dunboe LY 11; 61, 79
Freehall fort: Aghanloo LY 11; 5, 24
Freehall spring: Dunboe LY 11; 79
Freehall td: Dunboe LY 11; 65, 77–78
Freeland, Rev.: Killead AM 35; 46
Freeman [or Truman], Mr: Clogher TE 5; 43
Freeman, Edward: Clondermot LY 34; 70
Freeman, Hugh: Ballyrashane LY 22; 56
Freeman, James: Kildollagh LY 22; 75
Freeman, John: Clondermot LY 34; 14, 55
Freeman, Samuel: Carrickfergus AM 37; 194
Freemanstown (Freemansland) td: Donegore AM 29; 101, 131
Freemanstown flax mill: Donegore AM 29; 108, 132, 134
Freemore manor: Aghanloo LY 11; 23, 26, 42
Freemore manor: Dungiven LY 15; 50, 60–62
Freighmore (see Freughmore)
French hill: Clondermot LY 34; 49–50
French, Alderman (Dublin): Clondermot LY 34; 81
French, George: Misc. SO 40; 200
French, John: Drummaul AM 19; 84, 89
French, Martha: Drummaul AM 19; 90
French, Mary: Drummaul AM 19; 90
French, Mr: Dungiven LY 15; 99
French, Rev. Edward: Dungiven LY 15; 3, 103
French, Rose: Duneane AM 19; 120
French, Sarah: Drummaul AM 19; 91
French, William: Duneane AM 19; 120
Frenchman's rock: Mevagh DL 38; 56
Freugh (Frugh) td: Errigal LY 27; 44, 65–66, 70, 81, 86, 90, 92
Freugh bogs: Errigal LY 27; 54

Freugh fort: Errigal LY 27; 43
Freugh mountain: Balteagh LY 9; 1, 20
Freugh quarry: Errigal LY 27; 90
Freugh td: Dungiven LY 15; 35
Freugh td: Macosquin LY 22; 98
Freughlough school: Skirts of Urney and Ardstraw TE 5; 140
Freughmore (Freeghmore) td: Donacavey TE 5; 68, 76–78, 80–81, 83, 86
Freughmore forts: Donacavey TE 5; 83
Freughmore td: Clogher TE 5; 35, 53
Frew, family: Antrim AM 29; 24
Frew, R.: Kilmood DN 7; 95
Frew, William (see Lorimore): Muckamore AM 35; 80
Friar Island: Aghalurcher FH 4; 3
Friar, Robert: Aghalee AM 21; 28–29, 38
Friar, Robert: Carrickfergus AM 37; 110
Friar's bush: Carrickfergus AM 37; 185
Friar's Bush enclosure [I]: Carrickfergus AM 37; 185
Friar's Bush enclosure [II]: Carrickfergus AM 37; 185
Friar's garden: Carrickfergus AM 37; 80
Friar's glen: Aghalee AM 21; 26, 28
Friar's glen: Carrickfergus AM 37; 82–83, 184
Friar's Glen enclosures: Carrickfergus AM 37; 133, 185
Friar's Glen priory: Carrickfergus AM 37; 90
Friar's Glen tumulus: Carrickfergus AM 37; 87–88, 185
Friar's Glen well: Carrickfergus AM 37; 83, 185
Friar's rock: Carrickfergus AM 37; 81, 186
Friar's well: Ballynascreen LY 31; 9, 22
Friar's well: Banagher LY 30; 70
Friar's wells: Ramoan AM 24; 114
Friars Walk pass: Belleek FH 14; 4
Friars' House: Ramoan AM 24; 114
Friars' Island: Maghera LY 18; 58
Friary and Island td: Killymard DL 39; 101
Friary bog: Loughguile AM 13; 59
Friary td: Loughguile AM 13; 76
Friel, Rev. J.: Clondavaddog DL 38; 4
Friell, James: Macosquin LY 22; 88
Friell, John: Macosquin LY 22; 112–13
Frith, B.G.: Enniskillen FH 4; 58–59
Frith, family: Enniskillen FH 4; 58, 75
Frith, J.N.: Enniskillen FH 4; 54
Frith, John: Devenish FH 14; 59–61
Frith, Miss: Enniskillen FH 4; 85
Frith, S.: Magheracross FH 14; 102
Frith, William: Enniskillen FH 4; 59
Frizell, Peggy: Ballyscullion AM 19; 10
Frizzel, Jane: Ballymoney AM 16; 17
Frizzle, Daniel: Carrickfergus AM 37; 131

Frood, James: Drumgath DN 3; 21
Frosses caves: Dundermot AM 13; 34–35
Frosses school: Dundermot AM 13; 33
Frosses td: Dundermot AM 13; 29, 33, 35
Froud, Robert: Ballyscullion LY 6; 56
Frough (see Freugh)
Frughmor (see Freughmore)
Frughmore (see Freughmore)
Fruitfield House: Kilmore AH 1; 65
Fruithill demesne: Aghanloo LY 11; 3
Fruithill demesne: Drumachose LY 9; 56–57, 74, 76, 88–89, 96, 111, 118
Fruithill gate locality: Drumachose LY 9; 55
Fruithill House: Balteagh LY 9; 41
Fruithill House: Drumachose LY 9; 50–51, 82, 84, 91, 98, 118, 122, 128, 130
Fruithill House: Errigal LY 27; 53
Fruithill House: Tamlaght Finlagan LY 25; 109, 122
Fruithill school: Drumachose LY 9; 122–23
Fruithill td: Drumachose LY 9; 48, 51, 57, 83, 87, 97, 108, 111, 118
Fry, Christopher: Connor AM 19; 27
Fugart standing stones: Clonmany DL 38; 16
Fugart td: Clonmany DL 38; 18, 20
Fulgrave, Robert: Dunboe LY 11; 81
Fullaghboy district: Misc. SO 40; 199
Fullaghearn (see Fallaghearn): Errigal Keerogue TE 20; 53
Fullaghraghan district: Misc. SO 40; 199
Fullar, James: Carrickfergus AM 37; 109
Fullarton lough: Killygarvan DL 38; 37–38
Fullarton, Archabald: Desertoghill LY 27; 14, 24
Fullarton, family: Raloo AM 32; 94, 126
Fullarton, John: Desertoghill LY 27; 17
Fullarton, William: Desertoghill LY 27; 15–16, 18, 24, 26
Fullen, Mr: Cappagh TE 5; 22
Fullerton, Dugan: Ramoan AM 24; 107
Fullerton, family: Ahoghill AM 23; 25
Fullerton, family: Ballynure AM 32; 56
Fullerton, family: Billy AM 16; 58, 68
Fullerton, family: Derrykeighan AM 16; 89
Fullerton, family: Desertoghill LY 27; 5, 30
Fullerton, family: Ramoan AM 24; 107
Fullerton, George: Billy AM 16; 56, 63
Fullerton, Hugh: Ballynure AM 32; 59, 62–63
Fullerton, James: Ballynure AM 32; 56
Fullerton, James: Ballyscullion LY 6; 71
Fullerton, James: Billy AM 16; 58, 62
Fullerton, James: Clondermot LY 34; 67
Fullerton, John: Ballynure AM 32; 56–57, 62
Fullerton, man named: Carrickfergus AM 37; 176
Fullerton, Mr (Glencairn): Tullyaughnish DL 38; 94
Fullerton, Mr: Drumachose LY 9; 76–77, 129
Fullerton, Rev. Archibald: Aghadowey LY 22; 22

Fullerton, Rev. Arthur: Aghanloo LY 11; 14
Fullerton, Rev. Arthur: Drumachose LY 9; 67, 120
Fullerton, Robert: Carrickfergus AM 37; 113
Fullerton, Robert: Island Magee AM 10; 89
Fullerton, Samuel: Island Magee AM 10; 89–90
Fullerton's Island: Ballyscullion LY 6; 71
Fulton, A.: Blaris DN 12; 46, 50
Fulton, Abraham: Coleraine LY 33; 72
Fulton, Andrew: Carrickfergus AM 37; 131
Fulton, Capt. (Lisburn): Loughgilly AH 1; 84
Fulton, Daniel: Ahoghill AM 23; 34
Fulton, Daniel: Coleraine LY 33; 73
Fulton, Daniel: Macosquin LY 22; 112
Fulton, David: Carnmoney AM 2; 88
Fulton, David: Carrickfergus AM 37; 184
Fulton, David: Macosquin LY 22; 113
Fulton, Ellen: Carrickfergus AM 37; 135
Fulton, family: Ballynure AM 32; 56
Fulton, family: Blaris AM 8; 21
Fulton, family: Blaris DN 12; 30
Fulton, family: Carnmoney AM 2; 51, 76
Fulton, family: Enniskillen FH 4; 58
Fulton, family: Lambeg AM 8; 135
Fulton, family: Maghera LY 18; 13
Fulton, family: Ramoan AM 24; 107
Fulton, James: Aghadowey LY 22; 38
Fulton, James: Kilraghts AM 16; 134
Fulton, James: Misc. DL 39; 186, 192
Fulton, John: Blaris AM 8; 69, 83
Fulton, John: Kilwaughter AM 10; 116
Fulton, John: Macosquin LY 22; 91
Fulton, Joseph: Blaris AM 8; 60–61

Fulton, man named: Aghadowey LY 22; 28
Fulton, Margret: Aghadowey LY 22; 38
Fulton, Maryann (Jnr): Aghadowey LY 22; 38
Fulton, Maryann (Snr): Aghadowey LY 22; 37
Fulton, Miss: Blaris AM 8; 85
Fulton, Rev. D.: Ardstraw TE 5; 6
Fulton, Robert: Aghadowey LY 22; 38
Fulton, Samual: Drumachose LY 9; 111
Fulton, Samuel (Jnr): Aghadowey LY 22; 38
Fulton, Samuel (Snr): Aghadowey LY 22; 37
Fulton, Thomas: Aghadowey LY 22; 38
Fulton, Thomas: Maghera LY 18; 53–54
Fulton, William: Blaris AM 8; 55
Fulton, William: Kilbride AM 29; 154
Fulton, William: Maghera LY 18; 53
Fulton, Wrightman and Co., Messrs: Blaris AM 8; 37
Furgrave, James: Errigal LY 27; 68
Furgrave, Thomas: Errigal LY 27; 65
Furness (Lancashire): Inch DN 17; 75
Furnish td: Enniskillen FH 4; 82
Fury, Rodger: Duneane AM 19; 124
Furze glen: Banagher LY 30; 5
Futt, Rev.: Doagh AM 29; 81, 87
Fweealt district: Inishmacsaint FH 14; 75–76
Fycorranagh school: Leck DL 39; 120
Fycorranagh td: Leck DL 39; 119
Fye, Kate: Faughanvale LY 36; 30
Fye, Sarah: Faughanvale LY 36; 30
Fymore Moutray school: Errigal Truagh MN 40; 123

G

Galloway: Island Magee AM 10; 19, 26

Gabbett, William: Enniskillen FH 4; 58–59, 59, 75

Gad Island: Kinawley FH 4; 113

Gaddagh Island: Aghalurcher FH 4; 3

Gaddis hill: Killinchy DN 7; 86

Gaddyduff fort: Clonmany DL 38; 16

Gaddyduff td: Clonmany DL 38; 18, 20

Gadfrey, Thomas: Carrickfergus AM 37; 76

Gage, Conolly: Aghanloo LY 11; 1–2, 7, 12, 14–15, 23, 38, 42

Gage, Conolly: Donaghmore DL 39; 37–38

Gage, Conolly: Drumachose LY 9; 78, 84, 100, 104, 106, 119, 130

Gage, Conolly: Faughanvale LY 36; 40, 45

Gage, Conolly: Magilligan LY 11; 82–83, 85–86, 99, 101, 103, 107, 110, 113–17, 119–20, 125, 128, 135–37, 140, 142

Gage, Conolly: Tamlaght Finlagan LY 25; 93

Gage, Conolly: Urney DL 39; 176–77, 179–82

Gage, family: Agivey LY 22; 41–42

Gage, family: Magilligan LY 11; 109, 130

Gage, Gilbert: Tamlaght O'Crilly LY 18; 134

Gage, Hudson: Magilligan LY 11; 110, 115

Gage, James: Dunboe LY 11; 73, 75

Gage, James: Killowen LY 33; 172

Gage, Marcus: Drumachose LY 9; 51, 73, 82, 84, 91, 97, 104

Gage, Marcus: Errigal LY 27; 82

Gage, Marcus: Magilligan LY 11; 85, 87, 125

Gage, Mathew: Killowen LY 33; 171

Gage, Miss: Coleraine LY 33; 72

Gage, Mr: Agivey LY 22; 41

Gage, Rev. Robert: Drumachose LY 9; 67–68, 72

Gage, Rev. Robert: Ramoan AM 24; 94

Gage, Rev. Robert: Rathlin Island AM 24; 128–29, 131

Gage, William: Coleraine LY 33; 56

Gage, William: Magilligan LY 11; 88, 103

Gagin mountain: Kilteevoge DL 39; 111

Gahan, Daniel: Dungiven LY 15; 33

Gaillich, woman named: Dungiven LY 15; 63

Galagher, Mrs Alexander: Cumber LY 28; 80

Galaugher, family: Culfeightrin AM 24; 59

Galaway, John: Derryaghy AM 8; 95, 109

Galbally (Galbolly) td: Dromore TE 5; 99, 147

Galbally corn mill: Pomeroy TE 20; 70

Galbally lough: Dromore TE 5; 95

Galbally lough: Magheracross FH 14; 92, 96

Galboly (see Galbally): Magheracross FH 14; 92

Galboly mountain: Ardclinis AM 13; 2–3

Galbraeat, family: Kilwaughter AM 10; 115

Galbraith, family: Clogherny TE 20; 25

Galbraith, James: Clogherny TE 20; 25–26

Galbraith, James: Clonleigh DL 39; 10

Galbraith, James: Faughanvale LY 36; 18, 40

Galbraith, James: Killymard DL 39; 106

Galbraith, James: Raphoe DL 39; 127

Galbraith, James: Urney DL 39; 176, 180

Galbraith, John: Carrickfergus AM 37; 108

Galbraith, John: Clogherny TE 20; 25–26

Galbraith, John: Drumragh TE 5; 107, 109

Galbraith, John: Enniskillen FH 4; 75

Galbraith, Lady: Donaghmore DL 39; 37–39

Galbraith, Lady: Raphoe DL 39; 126

Galbraith, Lady: Urney DL 39; 176, 180–82

Galbraith, Mary: Aghanloo LY 11; 26

Galbraith, Mr: Kilmore DN 17; 88

Galbraith, Rev. Matthew: Desertoghill LY 27; 17

Galbraith, Samuel: Dromore TE 5; 99

Galbraith, Samuel: Drumragh TE 5; 107–09, 111

Galdanagh (Galdinagh) td: Tickmacrevan AM 13; 122

Galdanagh (see Galdonagh): Raymoghy DL 39; 141

Galdanagh school: Finvoy AM 23; 74–75

Galdonagh (Galdannagh) td: Raymoghy DL 39; 137, 141, 199

Galdonagh bog: Raymoghy DL 39; 144

Galdonagh Glebe td: Raymoghy DL 39; 137, 199

Galdonagh Lower td: Raymoghy DL 39; 141

Galdonagh school: Raymoghy DL 39; 140

Galdonagh Upper td: Raymoghy DL 39; 141

Galen school: Ardstraw TE 5; 13

Galgorm Castle: Ahoghill AM 23; 2–3, 12, 15, 17–18, 24, 28, 31, 35

Galgorm cave: Ahoghill AM 23; 26

Galgorm chapel: Ahoghill AM 23; 28

Galgorm court house: Ahoghill AM 23; 11, 21, 41, 47

Galgorm fort: Ahoghill AM 23; 26, 35

Galgorm old church: Ahoghill AM 23; 24–25, 35

Galgorm Parks standing stone: Ahoghill AM 23; 28

Galgorm Parks td: Ahoghill AM 23; 24

Galgorm school: Ahoghill AM 23; 21, 41–42, 47

Galgorm Sunday school: Ahoghill AM 23; 47

Galgorm td: Ahoghill AM 23; 26, 37

Galgorm village: Ahoghill AM 23; 2, 6, 11, 15, 20, 30, 41

Gall bog: Dromore DN 12; 71, 73

Gall bog: Garvaghy DN 12; 80

Gall bog: Hillsborough DN 12; 89

Gall Island: Devenish FH 14; 52, 59

Gallagh bog: Duneane AM 19; 109, 111, 122, 126

Gallagh Kildare school: Duneane AM 19; 125

Gallagh national school: Duneane AM 19; 105, 116, 126

Gallagh night school: Duneane AM 19; 116

Gallagh Sunday school: Duneane AM 19; 116

Gallagh td: Duneane AM 19; 124, 124

Gallagh td: Killesher FH 14; 87

Gallagher, Anne: Carrickfergus AM 37; 117

Gallagher, Bishop: Killelagh LY 27; 102

Gallagher, Daniel: Tullaghobegley DL 39; 173

Gallagher, family: Aghagallon AM 21; 9

Gallagher, family: Ballynascreen LY 31; 9

Gallagher, family: Culfeightrin AM 24; 59

Gallagher, Henry: Raloo AM 32; 129

Gallagher, Hugh: Clonleigh DL 39; 9

Gallagher, John: Aghanloo LY 11; 39

Gallagher, John: Carrickfergus AM 37; 115

Gallagher, John: Tullaghobegley DL 39; 172

Gallagher, Laurence: Enniskillen FH 4; 73

Gallagher, man named: Dungiven LY 15; 34

Gallagher, Mr (Carrigans): Killea and Taughboyne DL 39; 87, 90

Gallagher, Mr (Letterkenny): Leck DL 39; 116

Gallagher, Mr (Port lough): Killea and Taughboyne DL 39; 87

Gallagher, Mr (Toberslane): Misc. DL 39; 192

Gallagher, Mr: Clogher TE 5; 43

Gallagher, Pat: Drumachose LY 9; 132

Gallagher, Richard: Aghanloo LY 11; 39

Gallagher, Susan: Duneane AM 19; 106

Gallagher, William: Donaghmore DL 39; 40

Gallagher, William: Misc. DL 39; 186

Gallagher, woman named: Duneane AM 19; 111

Gallagher's mill [I]: Killea and Taughboyne DL 39; 87

Gallagher's mill [II]: Killea and Taughboyne DL 39; 87

Gallanagh chapel: Ardclinis AM 13; 6

Gallanagh td: Ardclinis AM 13; 6–7

Gallanagh tuck mill: Ardclinis AM 13; 7

Gallaney (see Gallany): Banagher LY 30; 61

Gallany bleach green: Banagher LY 30; 29

Gallany bleach mill: Banagher LY 30; 29

Gallany bog: Banagher LY 30; 89

Gallany corn mill: Banagher LY 30; 17, 29, 127

Gallany flax mill: Banagher LY 30; 29, 127

Gallany fort: Banagher LY 30; 90

Gallany quarry: Banagher LY 30; 3, 127

Gallany standing stone: Banagher LY 30; 76

Gallany td: Banagher LY 30; 3, 9–10, 22, 35–36, 53, 61–62, 90, 95, 100, 104, 109, 118–19, 123, 127, 130–31

Gallany water: Banagher LY 30; 25, 59

Gallaway, James: Derryaghy AM 8; 117–18

Gallaway, John: Derryaghy AM 8; 115

Gallaway, Thomas: Derryaghy AM 8; 115

Gallaway, William: Drummaul AM 19; 88

Gallay, Richard: Aghalee AM 21; 36

Gallen, John: Ballintoy AM 24; 27

Gallenreagh quarry: Drumgoon CN 40; 4

Galley, family: Aghalee AM 21; 36

Galley, John: Blaris AM 8; 50

Galley, John: Hillsborough DN 12; 107

Galley, Robert (Jnr): Hillsborough DN 12; 107

Galley, Robert: Hillsborough DN 12; 107

Galley, Thomas: Hillsborough DN 12; 105, 107

Galliagh (see Gallagh): Duneane AM 19; 111

Galliagh lough: Rossorry FH 14; 116

Galliagh td: Clondermot LY 34; 79

Galligher, John: Bovevagh LY 25; 58

Galligher, Michael: Kilcronaghan LY 31; 85

Gallnane (see Galluane)

Gallon mountain: Ardstraw TE 5; 10

Gallony House: Urney DL 39; 176

Galloon friary: Drummully FH 4; 40

Galloon friary: Galloon FH 4; 97

Galloon graveyard: Galloon FH 4; 92, 97

Galloon ph: Aghalurcher FH 4; 1, 5, 13

Galloon ph: Clogher TE 5; 41

Galloon ph: Clones FH 4; 26

Galloon ph: Drummully FH 4; 34, 36, 39–40

Galloon ph: Killesher FH 14; 84

Galloon td: Galloon FH 4; 87, 95

Galloway (Scotland): Carnmoney AM 2; 50

Galloway: Aghanloo LY 11; 11

Galloway: Ballee DN 17; 16

Galloway: Carrickfergus AM 37; 10, 60

Galloway: Culfeightrin AM 24; 44, 46

Galloway: Dunsfort DN 17; 70

Galloway: Glynn AM 26; 6

Galloway: Island Magee AM 10; 19, 26

Galloway: Kilroot AM 26; 61

Galloway: Nilteen AM 35; 89, 91

Galloway: Templecorran AM 26; 85, 109

Galloway, James: Ahoghill AM 23; 38

Galloway, Neal: Ballymoney AM 16; 17

Galloway, Robert: Ahoghill AM 23; 38
Gallows Corner locality: Duneane AM 19; 113–14
Gallows Green locality: Carrickfergus AM 37; 175, 191
Gallows Green locality: Enniskillen FH 4; 74
Gallows hill: Drumachose LY 9; 108–09, 127
Gallows hill: Drumglass TE 20; 40, 44
Gallows hill: Dunluce AM 16; 115, 121
Gallows hill: Killowen LY 33; 161, 168–69
Gallows hill: Loughguile AM 13; 61
Gallows hill: Ramoan AM 24; 106–08
Gallows hill: Tamlaght O'Crilly LY 18; 94, 121–22
Gallows stone: Clonleigh DL 39; 3
Galluane lough: Clogher TE 5; 25, 47
Galluane lough: Tydavnet MN 40; 169
Gallway, Michael: Derryaghy AM 8; 115
Gallwooly td: Kilteevoge DL 39; 114
Gally Hill cove: Antrim AM 29; 36–37
Gally, John: Ballinderry AM 21; 57
Galmoy, Lord: Enniskillen FH 4; 52
Galmoy, Lord: Galloon FH 4; 91, 100–01, 105
Galston, family: Blaris AM 8; 21
Galt, C.A.: Coleraine LY 33; 72
Galt, family: Doagh AM 29; 73
Galt, family: Templepatrick AM 35; 118
Galt, John: Ballyaghran LY 33; 19
Galt, John: Misc. DN 17; 118
Galt, Peter: Rashee AM 32; 141
Galt, Robert: Ballymoney AM 16; 17
Galtrim's Land td: Carlingford LH 40; 58
Galvally cave [I]: Ballyaghran LY 33; 11, 24
Galvally cave [II]: Ballyaghran LY 33; 11, 24
Galvally corn mill: Ballyaghran LY 33; 15, 26
Galvally flax mill: Ballyaghran LY 33; 15, 26
Galvally old flax mill: Ballyaghran LY 33; 15, 26
Galvally spring: Ballyaghran LY 33; 24
Galvin, family: Glynn AM 26; 45
Galway: Cumber LY 28; 50
Galway: Currin MN 40; 90
Galway: Misc. DL 39; 187
Galway county: Emlaghfad SO 40; 180
Galway county: Errigal LY 27; 62
Galway county: Faughanvale LY 36; 44
Galway county: Island Magee AM 10; 66
Galway river: Dungiven LY 15; 63
Galway, family: Magheragall AM 21; 99
Galway, James: Skerry AM 13; 114
Galway, James: Tamlaght TE 20; 76, 103
Gamble, A.A.: Antrim AM 29; 14, 25
Gamble, A.A.: Ballycor AM 32; 5
Gamble, A.A.: Ballylinny AM 32; 16, 30
Gamble, A.A.: Ballymartin AM 2; 6
Gamble, A.A.: Ballyrobert AM 2; 21
Gamble, A.A.: Ballywalter AM 2; 30
Gamble, A.A.: Carnmoney AM 2; 54

Gamble, A.A.: Doagh AM 29; 73
Gamble, A.A.: Donegore AM 29; 111
Gamble, A.A.: Kilbride AM 29; 141
Gamble, A.A.: Mallusk AM 2; 110
Gamble, A.A.: Muckamore AM 35; 65
Gamble, A.A.: Rashee AM 32; 138
Gamble, A.A.: Templepatrick AM 35; 108, 118
Gamble, A.A.: Umgall AM 35; 158
Gamble, Alexander: Ballymoney AM 16; 16
Gamble, family: Blaris AM 8; 21
Gamble, family: Derrykeighan AM 16; 89
Gamble, family: Enniskillen FH 4; 75
Gamble, J.: Saul DN 17; 115
Gamble, James: Ballymoney AM 16; 17
Gamble, James: Coleraine LY 33; 63
Gamble, James: Macosquin LY 22; 93
Gamble, John: Macosquin LY 22; 84, 110
Gamble, Joseph: Ballymoney AM 16; 15
Gamble, Margaret (nee Tomkins): Clondermot LY 34; 82
Gamble, Miss: Blaris AM 8; 85
Gamble, Mr: Comber DN 7; 39
Gamble, Mr: Devenish FH 14; 53
Gamble, Mrs: Ballymoney AM 16; 15, 17
Gamble, Nancy: Derrykeighan AM 16; 92
Gamble, Rev. Henry: Cumber LY 28; 97
Gamble, Rich: Cumber LY 28; 28
Gamble, Robert: Billy AM 16; 67
Gamble, Robert: Carrickfergus AM 37; 140
Gamble, Robert: Clondermot LY 34; 82
Gamble, Robert: Dungiven LY 15; 101, 117, 119
Gamble, Samuel: Blaris AM 8; 37, 43
Gamble, Samuel: Blaris DN 12; 41, 45, 49
Gamble, William: Ballintoy AM 24; 24
Gamble, William: Ballymoney AM 16; 16
Gamble, William: Clondermot LY 34; 82
Gamble, William [I]: Carrickfergus AM 37; 119, 125
Gamble, William [II]: Carrickfergus AM 37; 121
Ganaby school [I]: Kilraghts AM 16; 130, 136
Ganaby school [II]: Kilraghts AM 16; 130
Ganaby td: Kilraghts AM 16; 134–36
Ganaway (Ganway) td: Ballywalter DN 7; 17–18
Ganaway corn mill: Ballywalter DN 7; 17
Ganaway corn windmill: Ballywalter DN 7; 17
Ganaway td: Misc. DN 17; 124–25
Gann Cottage: Kilbroney DN 3; 35
Gannon, family: Billy AM 16; 58
Gannon, Patrick: Coleraine LY 33; 146
Gannon, Ritchard: Killowen LY 33; 171
Ganohan, Patrick: Derryaghy AM 8; 94
Gap locality: Kilmacteige SO 40; 190, 192, 194–95
Garagh Highland Shawn locality: Skerry AM 13; 121
Garahaynalaniv graveyard: Errigal LY 27; 42, 73

Garamore td: Tullyaughnish DL 38; 96

Garbally cave [I]: Ballywillin LY 33; 51

Garbally cave [II]: Ballywillin LY 33; 51

Garbally cave [III]: Ballywillin LY 33; 51

Garborgle druid's temple: Ballyaghran LY 33; 24

Garborgle td: Ballyaghran LY 33; 27

Garden fort: Macosquin LY 22; 107

Garden fort: Tamlaght Finlagan LY 25; 89, 114–15

Garden Hill House: Cleenish FH 14; 17

Garden House: Macosquin LY 22; 106

Gardener, Andrew: Carrickfergus AM 37; 160

Gardener, family: Ballylinny AM 32; 15

Gardenhill district: Clogher TE 5; 38

Gardenhill td: Cleenish FH 14; 17, 29

Gardenina district: Lough Swilly DL 38; 128

Gardin, Mr: Newry DN 3; 106

Gardiner, Charles: Ardstraw TE 5; 6

Gardiner, Charles: Cappagh TE 5; 17–19

Gardiner, Charles: Clonoe TE 20; 29

Gardiner, family: Carrickfergus AM 37; 179

Gardiner, William: Ardstraw TE 5; 11

Gardle, family: Billy AM 16; 68

Gardner, family: Ballylinny AM 32; 27

Gardner, family: Carrickfergus AM 37; 93

Gardner, Henry: Donaghadee DN 7; 46

Gardner, Henry: Killyleagh DN 17; 85

Gardner, Mr: Convoy DL 39; 19–21

Gardner, Mrs: Hillsborough DN 12; 105

Gardner, Robert: Ballylinny AM 32; 26–27

Gardner, Robert: Carrickfergus AM 37; 34

Gardner, William: Ballylinny AM 32; 29

Gardner, William: Ballyscullion LY 6; 56

Gardner, William: Carnmoney AM 2; 88

Gardner, William: Hillsborough DN 12; 105, 107

Gardner, William: Muckamore AM 35; 78

Gardrum meeting house: Dromore TE 5; 101

Gardrum school: Cleenish FH 14; 24

Gardrum td: Cleenish FH 14; 28–29

Gardrum td: Dromore TE 5; 93, 99, 101

Gargarry chapel: Drumgooland DN 3; 22

Gargarry corn mill: Drumgooland DN 3; 24

Gargarry td: Drumgooland DN 3; 22, 24

Gargiam and Chlimlifinnaches locality:
   Magheraculmoney FH 14; 111

Gargrim td: Donacavey TE 5; 67, 76–77, 79–81, 83,
   86

Garmany Island: Muckno MN 40; 162

Garmlan lough: Cumber LY 28; 72

Garmon, family: Billy AM 16; 68

Garmoyle district: Carnmoney AM 2; 36, 38

Garmoyle district: Carrickfergus AM 37; 37, 40

Garner, Mr: Derryaghy AM 8; 107

Garnet, family: Tamlaght O'Crilly LY 18; 93

Garnett, Rev.: Carnmoney AM 2; 75

Garnett, Rev. John: Clogher TE 5; 28

Garole, family: Billy AM 16; 58

Garraghan school: Skirts of Urney and Ardstraw TE
   5; 140

Garraghan td: Skirts of Urney and Ardstraw TE 5;
   140

Garran (Gerran) td: Aghabog MN 40; 62

Garran giant's graves: Aghabog MN 40; 64

Garran hill: Aghabog MN 40; 62

Garranbaans locality: Lough Swilly DL 38; 114

Garran-Otra bog: Tyholland MN 40; 174

Garraroosky td: Galloon FH 4; 95

Garraway, Rev. James: Drumachose LY 9; 73

Garrett, family: Magheragall AM 21; 99

Garrett, H.J.: Blaris AM 8; 63

Garrett, H.J.: Blaris DN 12; 46

Garrett, H.J.: Magheragall AM 21; 101

Garrett, Henery (Snr): Magheragall AM 21; 101

Garrett, John: Blaris AM 8; 67

Garrett, Miss: Blaris DN 12; 50

Garrett, Mr: Kilmacteige SO 40; 189

Garrett, Mrs: Blaris AM 8; 85

Garrett, Robert: Blaris AM 8; 33

Garrett, William: Hillsborough DN 12; 106

Garretts Burn House: Magheragall AM 21; 101

Garrick, John: Derryaghy AM 8; 98

Garrin, James: Magherafelt LY 6; 98

Garrison: Devenish FH 14; 47–49, 51

Garrison: Inishmacsaint FH 14; 72–74, 77, 79

Garrison barrack: Devenish FH 14; 48

Garrison chapel: Inishmacsaint FH 14; 74

Garrison church: Inishmacsaint FH 14; 74

Garrison Hill td: Donaghmore DL 39; 37

Garrit, Rev. John: Emlaghfad SO 40; 177–78

Garrive Islands: Lough Swilly DL 38; 107–08, 111,
   113, 138

Garriwerry td: Tomregan FH 4; 126

Garron Point: Ardclinis AM 13; 1–6

Garron Point: Culfeightrin AM 24; 46

Garron Point: Island Magee AM 10; 19, 26, 58, 74

Garron Point: Templecorran AM 26; 96

Garronory (Gawory) td: Donacavey TE 5; 82

Garroo Islands: Cleenish FH 14; 13, 30

Garry and Drumart school: Ballymoney AM 16; 26

Garry bog: Ballymoney AM 16; 1–2, 4–5

Garry bog: Dunluce AM 16; 104, 107

Garry Lower td: Ballymoney AM 16; 6, 25

Garry Upper td: Ballymoney AM 16; 6, 25

Garry's Craig rock: Dunaghy AM 13; 22

Garrybane td: Aughnamullen MN 40; 76

Garrydoo bog: Ballymoney AM 16; 2, 6

Garrydoo td: Aughnamullen MN 40; 76

Garrygart td: Tullyaughnish DL 38; 96

Garrymore (Gerrymore) td: Inver AM 26; 49

Garrymore td: Glynn AM 26; 30

Garryross td: Inishmacsaint FH 14; 70

Garrysbish bridge: Kildollagh LY 22; 68–69, 73

Garshooey (Garshiney) td: Killea and Taughboyne DL 39; 79, 87, 194

Garshuey (see Garshooey): Misc. DL 39; 194

Gartan loughs: Tullyaughnish DL 38; 84

Gartlan, James: Magheracloone MN 40; 139

Gartlan, T.M.: Killanny MN 40; 131

Gartlan, T.M.: Magheross MN 40; 152, 156–57

Gartlana td: Aughnamullen MN 40; 76

Gartland, family: Clondermot LY 34; 53

Gartree church: Killead AM 35; 11–12, 20, 24, 38, 42, 44–45, 47, 52

Gartree graveyard: Killead AM 35; 12, 24, 44

Gartree school: Killead AM 35; 37–39, 52

Gartree Sunday school: Killead AM 35; 38–39, 52

Gartree td: Killead AM 35; 23–24, 32, 40

Garty, James: Tamlaght TE 20; 102

Garvagh: Aghadowey LY 22; 5–7, 10, 12, 18–20, 26

Garvagh: Aghanloo LY 11; 24

Garvagh: Agivey LY 22; 42

Garvagh: Banagher LY 30; 5, 14, 36, 60

Garvagh: Bovevagh LY 25; 2, 24, 48

Garvagh: Clondermot LY 34; 34

Garvagh: Cumber LY 28; 21, 23

Garvagh: Desertoghill LY 27; 2–3, 5, 9, 11, 13–17, 21–25, 28–30, 32–34

Garvagh: Drumachose LY 9; 55, 76, 117

Garvagh: Dungiven LY 15; 33–35, 53, 67, 109, 111

Garvagh: Errigal LY 27; 36–37, 39–41, 45–46, 48–51, 53, 55–56, 58–63, 66, 71, 78–84, 93–94

Garvagh: Kilcronaghan LY 31; 69

Garvagh: Killelagh LY 27; 96, 102

Garvagh: Killowen LY 33; 160, 165, 168

Garvagh: Kilrea LY 27; 105, 111, 115, 127

Garvagh: Macosquin LY 22; 80, 82–83, 89–92, 98, 101–03

Garvagh: Maghera LY 18; 6, 8, 73, 76

Garvagh: Misc. LY 36; 111–13, 116

Garvagh: Misc. TE 5; 147

Garvagh: Tamlaght Finlagan LY 25; 103, 121–22

Garvagh: Tamlaght O'Crilly LY 18; 83–84, 87–88, 90, 92, 102, 104, 106, 108–09, 111–12, 120–21, 123, 139–42

Garvagh Associate Presbyterian Sunday school: Errigal LY 27; 52

Garvagh bogs: Errigal LY 27; 55, 75

Garvagh bridge: Desertoghill LY 27; 3–4, 16–17, 21, 29

Garvagh bridge: Errigal LY 27; 41, 60

Garvagh chapel (WM): Errigal LY 27; 37

Garvagh chapel of ease: Errigal LY 27; 37, 56

Garvagh church: Errigal LY 27; 37, 41, 52, 56

Garvagh classic school: Errigal LY 27; 51

Garvagh cloughogal monument: Aghadowey LY 22; 32

Garvagh cloughogal monument: Banagher LY 30; 39

Garvagh corn mill: Desertoghill LY 27; 16

Garvagh corn mill: Errigal LY 27; 60

Garvagh demesne: Errigal LY 27; 35, 57, 61

Garvagh dispensary: Desertoghill LY 27; 9, 18

Garvagh dispensary: Errigal LY 27; 38, 46, 49, 53

Garvagh estate: Errigal LY 27; 74

Garvagh flax mill: Errigal LY 27; 38

Garvagh fort: Errigal LY 27; 43, 45, 75

Garvagh giant's grave: Errigal LY 27; 78

Garvagh graveyard: Errigal LY 27; 56

Garvagh hibernian school: Errigal LY 27; 50

Garvagh House: Errigal LY 27; 39

Garvagh inn: Errigal LY 27; 38

Garvagh Kildare female school: Errigal LY 27; 38, 50

Garvagh Kildare male school: Errigal LY 27; 38, 50

Garvagh market place: Errigal LY 27; 37

Garvagh meeting house (AP): Desertoghill LY 27; 13

Garvagh meeting house (AP): Errigal LY 27; 37, 52, 57, 64

Garvagh meeting house (P): Desertoghill LY 27; 10, 13, 17

Garvagh meeting house (P): Errigal LY 27; 37, 52, 56–57

Garvagh meeting house (S): Desertoghill LY 27; 13

Garvagh meeting house (S): Errigal LY 27; 37, 52, 57, 65

Garvagh mission school: Errigal LY 27; 51–52

Garvagh mission Sunday school: Errigal LY 27; 52

Garvagh Presbyterian Sunday school: Errigal LY 27; 52

Garvagh quarry: Errigal LY 27; 90

Garvagh Seceding Sunday school: Errigal LY 27; 52

Garvagh shambles: Errigal LY 27; 62

Garvagh standing stone: Errigal LY 27; 78

Garvagh Sunday school: Errigal LY 27; 52

Garvagh td: Donaghmore DL 39; 34

Garvagh td: Dungiven LY 15; 84

Garvagh td: Errigal LY 27; 39, 81–82, 87, 90, 92

Garvagh water (see Agivey water): Desertoghill LY 27; 12

Garvagh, family: Agivey LY 22; 44

Garvagh, Lady: Desertmartin LY 31; 60

Garvagh, Lady: Errigal LY 27; 50

Garvagh, Lord: Aghadowey LY 22; 5

Garvagh, Lord: Comber DN 7; 37–38

Garvagh, Lord: Desertmartin LY 31; 62

Garvagh, Lord: Desertoghill LY 27; 10, 14

Garvagh, Lord: Dromore DN 12; 78

Garvagh, Lord: Drumgoon CN 40; 8, 10

Garvagh, Lord: Errigal LY 27; 37–39, 44–46, 49–50, 57, 61, 63, 72, 76, 80, 83

Garvagh, Lord: Misc. LY 31; 129

Garvagh, Lord: Newry DN 3; 110

Garvaghey (see Garvaghy): Ahoghill AM 23; 34

Garvaghullion school: Longfield TE 5; 132

Garvaghullion td: Longfield TE 5; 132

Garvaghy (Garvaghey) td: Errigal Keerogue TE 20; 48–49, 53, 57

Garvaghy chapel: Errigal Keerogue TE 20; 53

Garvaghy church: Garvaghy DN 12; 80, 82, 82

Garvaghy corn mill: Errigal Keerogue TE 20; 53

Garvaghy East fort: Ahoghill AM 23; 35

Garvaghy East school: Ahoghill AM 23; 22, 42, 46

Garvaghy East Sunday school: Ahoghill AM 23; 46–47

Garvaghy fort [I]: Ahoghill AM 23; 34

Garvaghy fort [II]: Ahoghill AM 23; 34

Garvaghy fort [III]: Ahoghill AM 23; 34

Garvaghy fort [IV]: Ahoghill AM 23; 34

Garvaghy Glebe House: Garvaghy DN 12; 80, 82–83

Garvaghy hill: Garvaghy DN 12; 79

Garvaghy meeting house: Ahoghill AM 23; 11, 30

Garvaghy meeting house: Newry DN 3; 111

Garvaghy ph: Annaclone DN 12; 13, 13, 16

Garvaghy ph: Dromara DN 12; 62, 65

Garvaghy ph: Dromore DN 12; 70, 73

Garvaghy ph: Drumgooland DN 3; 24

Garvaghy ph: Magherally DN 12; 112, 114

Garvaghy ph: Misc. DN 17; 121

Garvaghy ph: Newry DN 3; 82, 110

Garvaghy ph: Seapatrick DN 12; 124

Garvaghy river: Errigal Keerogue TE 20; 53

Garvaghy school: Garvaghy DN 12; 83

Garvaghy td: Ahoghill AM 23; 37, 49–50

Garvaghy td: Drumcree AH 1; 35, 41

Garvaghy td: Garvaghy DN 12; 80–81

Garvaghy West school: Ahoghill AM 23; 21–22

Garvahey (see Garvaghy): Ahoghill AM 23; 42

Garvahy (see Garvaghy): Ahoghill AM 23; 34

Garvallagh (Garvola) td: Donacavey TE 5; 64–65, 68–69, 76–77, 79–80, 82–83, 86

Garvallagh corn mill: Donacavey TE 5; 64, 83

Garvallagh Lower td: Donacavey TE 5; 80–81

Garvallagh school: Donacavey TE 5; 65

Garvallagh Upper td: Donacavey TE 5; 81

Garvan, family: Killygarvan DL 38; 36

Garvan, St: Killygarvan DL 38; 36

Garveghey (see Garvaghy): Errigal Keerogue TE 20; 48

Garven, Eliza: Aghanloo LY 11; 39

Garven, Mary: Aghanloo LY 11; 39

Garven, Patt: Drumachose LY 9; 133

Garvery nursery: Enniskillen FH 4; 80

Garvery school: Enniskillen FH 4; 84

Garvery td: Belleek FH 14; 2

Garvery td: Enniskillen FH 4; 80, 82

Garvery td: Rossorry FH 14; 116

Garvetagh hill: Skirts of Urney and Ardstraw TE 5; 136

Garvetagh meeting house: Ardstraw TE 5; 11

Garvetagh meeting house: Skirts of Urney and Ardstraw TE 5; 138

Garvetagh td: Skirts of Urney and Ardstraw TE 5; 138

Garvey td: Clogher TE 5; 59

Garvin, James: Desertoghill LY 27; 5

Garvolagh (see Garvallagh)

Garvy, Henry: Ballyscullion LY 6; 57

Garwallagh (see Garvallagh)

Garwory (Gasonory) td: Donacavey TE 5; 82

Gary (see Garry)

Gas, William: Kilclooney AH 1; 51

Gasonory (Garwory) td: Donacavey TE 5; 82

Gasten, James: Rasharkin AM 23; 138

Gaston, family: Ballywillin AM 16; 32

Gaston, Hugh: Ballywillin LY 33; 51

Gaston, James: Dunluce AM 16; 118

Gaston, Robert: Ballywillin LY 33; 51

Gate district: Culfeightrin AM 24; 52

Gate spring: Culfeightrin AM 24; 52

Gateside district: Drumachose LY 9; 106

Gateside school: Coleraine LY 33; 66–67, 69, 128, 134–35, 140

Gateside Sunday school: Coleraine LY 33; 69, 140

Gattney, family: Magheramesk AM 21; 124

Gauge, James: Carrickfergus AM 37; 193

Gaul, son of Morni: Banagher LY 30; 12

Gauley, Saunders: Carrickfergus AM 37; 193

Gault, Ellen: Killowen LY 33; 166

Gault, family: Ahoghill AM 23; 25

Gault, family: Doagh AM 29; 94

Gault, James: Doagh AM 29; 87, 93

Gault, James: Macosquin LY 22; 109

Gault, John: Raloo AM 32; 129

Gault, Joseph: Glynn AM 26; 37

Gault, Marcus: Balteagh LY 9; 41

Gault, Patrick: Doagh AM 29; 83, 91

Gault, Robert: Ahoghill AM 23; 46

Gault, Thomas: Balteagh LY 9; 28, 30, 36–38, 42

Gault, Thomas: Drumachose LY 9; 104, 109

Gault, William: Coleraine LY 33; 91, 105, 132, 142

Gault, William: Doagh AM 29; 94

Gault, William: Tamlaght Finlagan LY 25; 119

Gaunt, John of: Drummaul AM 19; 89

Gaussen, David: Artrea LY 6; 8

Gaussen, James: Ballinderry TE 20; 13

Gaussen, Messrs: Artrea LY 6; 7, 14, 39

Gaussen, Messrs: Artrea TE 20; 7

Gaussen, Messrs: Ballinderry LY 6; 41

Gaussen, Messrs: Maghera LY 18; 7

Gaussen, Messrs: Magherafelt LY 6; 84

Gaussen, William: Magherafelt LY 6; 83

Gavagh Highland Shawn locality: Skerry AM 13; 118

Gaw, Alexander: Hillsborough DN 12; 105

Gaw, family: Ballintoy AM 24; 20

Gaw, Thomas: Coleraine LY 33; 72

Gawan, family: Magherafelt LY 6; 95

Gawdy, R.A.: Aghanloo LY 11; 24

Gawdy's well: Aghanloo LY 11; 24

Gawin, James: Kilbride AM 29; 149

Gawlagher, family: Kilmacteige SO 40; 186

Gawlagher, John: Kilmacteige SO 40; 187

Gawley school: Aghagallon AM 21; 24

Gawley, James: Ballymartin AM 2; 15

Gawley, James [I]: Ballylinny AM 32; 28

Gawley, James [II]: Ballylinny AM 32; 29

Gawley, John: Blaris DN 12; 40

Gawley, Josias: Templepatrick AM 35; 142, 144, 150

Gawley, William: Ballymartin AM 2; 17

Gawley's Gate: Aghagallon AM 21; 7

Gawn, J.H.: Larne AM 10; 128

Gawn, J.H.: Rashee AM 32; 140

Gay, Catherine: Coleraine LY 33; 68, 135–36

Gay, Thomas: Drumcree AH 1; 30

Gayer, Charles: Clogher TE 5; 41

Gayer, Edward: Blaris AM 8; 10

Gayer, Elizabeth: Derryaghy AM 8; 114

Gayer, family: Derryaghy AM 8; 103

Gayer, Rev. Philip: Derryaghy AM 8; 99

Gazeboe House: Ballyaghran LY 33; 20

Geary, John: Coleraine LY 33; 72

Geary, Miss: Clogher TE 5; 43

Geary, Robert: Loughgilly AH 1; 86

Geaton, family: Maghera LY 18; 24, 48

Gedis, family: Killesher FH 14; 85

Gee, Col: Duneane AM 19; 119, 121

Geearach lough: Templecarn DL 39; 157

Geisecke, Charles: Tullylish DN 12; 141

Geisly (Lincolnshire): Clonleigh DL 39; 15

Gelasius, Archbishop of Armagh: Island Magee AM 10; 60

Gelespie, Edward: Artrea LY 6; 33

Gelgay rock: Newry DN 3; 88

Gelston, Thomas: Ballyphilip DN 7; 11

Gelstone, John: Bangor DN 7; 25

Gelvin bridge: Bovevagh LY 25; 4, 16–17

Gelvin bridge: Dungiven LY 15; 66

Gelvin bridge: Tamlaght Finlagan LY 25; 104

Gelvin td: Banagher LY 30; 95

Gelvin td: Bovevagh LY 25; 43

Gelvin td: Dungiven LY 15; 64

Gelvin water: Bovevagh LY 25; 2, 4, 16, 22, 50

Gelvin water: Dungiven LY 15; 9, 63, 65–66, 95, 97

Gembell, family: Templecorran AM 26; 117, 119

Genegan school: Clogher TE 5; 42–43

Genegan td: Clogher TE 5; 42

General's bridge: Banagher LY 30; 5

Geneva (Switzerland): Templepatrick AM 35; 132

Geneva lough: Lough Neagh AM 21; 92

Gennings, Richard: Ballyscullion LY 6; 56

Gentle Bush fort: Banagher LY 30; 56

Gentle Dooish td: Raymoghy DL 39; 141

Gentle Owen's lough: Keady AH 1; 50

Geoffrey, family: Misc. LY 36; 104

Geoghegan, William: Aghaderg DN 12; 11

George I, King: Duneane AM 19; 108

George I, King: Templepatrick AM 35; 148

George II, King: Aghadowey LY 22; 14

George II, King: Kilrea LY 27; 119

George II, King: Misc. LY 31; 119

George II, King: Saul DN 17; 113

George II, King: Templepatrick AM 35; 148

George III, King: Ahoghill AM 23; 1, 16

George III, King: Banagher LY 30; 10

George III, King: Blaris AM 8; 27

George III, King: Bovevagh LY 25; 46

George III, King: Carrickfergus AM 37; 148

George III, King: Coleraine LY 33; 71

George III, King: Down DN 17; 42–44

George III, King: Faughanvale LY 36; 22

George III, King: Kilbride AM 29; 153

George III, King: Templepatrick AM 35; 148

George IV, King: Antrim AM 29; 40

George IV, King: Carrickfergus AM 37; 104

George IV, King: Coleraine LY 33; 59, 76, 79, 84, 107, 109–10, 125, 127, 147, 151

George IV, King: Drumcree AH 1; 32

George IV, King: Kilbride AM 29; 153

George IV, King: Newry DN 3; 71

George IV, King: Rathmullan DN 17; 109

George, Alexander: Balteagh LY 9; 43

George, Alexander: Killead AM 35; 49

George, family: Aghalee AM 21; 31

George, family: Macosquin LY 22; 107

George, James: Balteagh LY 9; 36

George, John: Tamlaght TE 20; 93

George, John: Templecorran AM 26; 116, 131

George, Kings named: Magheramesk AM 21; 126

George, Lord: Moira DN 12; 117

George, Mathew [I]: Tamlaght TE 20; 91, 106

George, Mathew [II]: Tamlaght TE 20; 122

George, Mr: Muckamore AM 35; 81

George, Prince of Denmark: Aghaderg DN 12; 6, 11

George, Rev.: Emlaghfad SO 40; 177

George, Robert: Dungiven LY 15; 70–71, 73–74

George, Squire: Macosquin LY 22; 107

George, Widow: Artrea LY 6; 32

George, William: Balteagh LY 9; 13, 27, 36, 41

George, William: Tamlaght TE 20; 75, 103
George's Island: Ballinderry AM 21; 43
George's locality: Muckamore AM 35; 80
George's Point: Bangor DN 7; 22
Geragaonn lough: Templecarn DL 39; 157
Geraghty, Mr: Tullyniskan TE 20; 139
Germany: Blaris AM 8; 89
Gerneby, family: Ballinderry AM 21; 55
Gernon, John: Carlingford LH 40; 57
Gernon, Peter: Carlingford LH 40; 57
Gernon, Stephen: Kilkeel DN 3; 53
Gerty, Thomas: Tamlaght TE 20; 93
Gervais mill: Clogherny TE 20; 27
Gervais, Rev. Francis: Clogher TE 5; 24, 27, 30,
    32–34, 38–39, 46, 49, 53, 55, 57, 61
Gervais, Rev. Francis: Drummully FH 4; 37, 39
Gervais' female school: Clogher TE 5; 42–43
Gervais' male school: Clogher TE 5; 42–43
Getty, Catherine: Kilraghts AM 16; 132
Getty, E.: Island Magee AM 10; 102
Getty, family: Billy AM 16; 58, 68
Getty, family: Carnmoney AM 2; 76
Getty, family: Maghera LY 18; 24, 48
Getty, James: Ahoghill AM 23; 40, 45
Getty, James: Ballyrashane LY 22; 63
Getty, James: Billy AM 16; 55 ,62
Getty, James: Kilraghts AM 16; 135
Getty, James: Rasharkin AM 23; 135
Getty, John: Ballymoney AM 16; 15
Getty, John: Drummaul AM 19; 92
Getty, John: Kilraghts AM 16; 132
Getty, John: Kirkinriola AM 23; 114
Getty, Joseph: Tamlaght Finlagan LY 25; 118
Getty, Mr: Drumbo DN 7; 59
Getty, Mr: Misc. LY 31; 130
Getty, William: Carnmoney AM 2; 46, 84, 98
Getty, William: Dunaghy AM 13; 24
Getty, William: Kilraghts AM 16; 134, 136
Ghann river: Kilbroney DN 3; 26, 29
Ghosthall bridge: Holywood DN 7; 83
Giant's Bed stones: Finvoy AM 23; 68
Giant's Causeway: Antrim AM 29; 19
Giant's Causeway: Armoy AM 24; 1
Giant's Causeway: Ballintoy AM 24; 34
Giant's Causeway: Ballyrashane LY 22; 50
Giant's Causeway: Ballywillin LY 33; 43, 45
Giant's Causeway: Billy AM 16; 36–37, 41–43, 47,
    49–50
Giant's Causeway: Coleraine LY 33; 147,150
Giant's Causeway: Culfeightrin AM 24; 36–37
Giant's Causeway: Derrykeighan AM 16; 80
Giant's Causeway: Drummaul AM 19; 79,81
Giant's Causeway: Dunboe LY 11; 51
Giant's Causeway: Dungiven LY 15; 37
Giant's Causeway: Dunluce AM 16; 108

Giant's Causeway: Misc. LY 31; 125
Giant's Causeway: Misc. LY 36; 110
Giant's Causeway: Rathlin Island AM 24; 131–32
Giant's Causeway: Termoneeny LY 6; 129
Giant's chair: Dunboe LY 11; 49
Giant's Cut inlet: Ballintoy AM 24; 34
Giant's finger stone: Ahoghill AM 23; 26–28
Giant's finger stone: Dunaghy AM 13; 19
Giant's foot track stone: Ballywillin AM 16; 33
Giant's Head Track stone: Ballywillin AM 16; 33
Giant's Leg stone: Drumachose LY 9; 112
Giant's Loom pillars: Billy AM 16; 42
Giant's Mill standing stones: Balteagh LY 9; 23
Giant's Ring: Drumbo DN 7; 55
Giant's Ring: Misc. DN 17; 121
Giant's Sconce: Dunboe LY 11; 49, 58
Giant's Theatre (see Port Reostan): Billy AM 16; 41
Giants stones: Donegal DL 39; 45
Gibb, family: Enniskillen FH 4; 58
Gibb, Mr: Comber DN 7; 37
Gibbin, Anne: Donegore AM 29; 130
Gibbin, James: Donegore AM 29; 130
Gibbins, James: Tamlaght TE 20; 93
Gibbons lough: Killygarvan DL 38; 37
Giberaltar locality: Bovevagh LY 25; 34–35
Gibraltar: Ballyscullion LY 6; 58
Gibraltar: Misc. AM 10; 130
Gibraltar bog: Tyholland MN 40; 174
Gibsey, family: Magherafelt LY 6; 107
Gibson, Adam: Magheross MN 40; 145
Gibson, Alexander: Tamlaght TE 20; 79
Gibson, David: Hillsborough DN 12; 106
Gibson, Edward: Blaris AM 8; 84
Gibson, Edward: Blaris DN 12; 46, 50
Gibson, Edward: Macosquin LY 22; 107
Gibson, Esther: Newry DN 3; 68
Gibson, family: Blaris AM 8; 21
Gibson, family: Glynn AM 26; 45
Gibson, family: Misc. LY 36; 104
Gibson, family: Racavan AM 13; 100
Gibson, family: Templepatrick AM 35; 118
Gibson, Francis: Dromore TE 5; 97
Gibson, George: Artrea LY 6; 32
Gibson, George: Ballynascreen LY 31; 21
Gibson, Isaac (Jnr): Hillsborough DN 12; 106
Gibson, Isaac: Hillsborough DN 12; 106
Gibson, James: Ballinderry AM 21; 52
Gibson, James: Killead AM 35; 46
Gibson, James: Tamlaght O'Crilly LY 18; 123
Gibson, James: Templepatrick AM 35; 122, 145,
    148
Gibson, James [I]: Tamlaght TE 20; 75, 103
Gibson, James [II]: Tamlaght TE 20; 81
Gibson, James [III]: Tamlaght TE 20; 92
Gibson, John: Hillsborough DN 12; 106

Gibson, John: Misc. DN 17; 117
Gibson, John: Newry DN 3; 68
Gibson, John: Tamlaght TE 20; 92
Gibson, Joseph: Drumachose LY 9; 104
Gibson, Joseph: Hillsborough DN 12; 106
Gibson, Josiah: Hillsborough DN 12; 106
Gibson, Maj.: Antrim AM 29; 8
Gibson, Margaret: Carrickfergus AM 37; 119
Gibson, Matthew: Kilkeel DN 3; 48
Gibson, Mrs: Coleraine LY 33; 73
Gibson, Nancy: Ahoghill AM 23; 39
Gibson, Peter: Tartaraghan AH 1; 123
Gibson, Peter: Tynan AH 1; 131
Gibson, Rev.: Cappagh TE 5; 18
Gibson, Rev. Joseph: Dungiven LY 15; 100, 103
Gibson, Samuel: Hillsborough DN 12; 106
Gibson, Samuel: Tamlaght TE 20; 79
Gibson, Thomas: Ballynascreen LY 31; 21
Gibson, Thomas: Coleraine LY 33; 143
Gibson, Widow: Hillsborough DN 12; 106
Gibson, Widow: Tamlaght TE 20; 107
Gibson, William: Hillsborough DN 12; 105
Gibson, William: Kilcronaghan LY 31; 85
Gibson, William: Killead AM 35; 46
Gibson, William: Tamlaght TE 20; 84
Gibson, William: Termoneeny LY 6; 133
Giffen, Robertson and Co., Messrs: Kilwaughter
    AM 10; 112
Giffen, Samuel: Carnmoney AM 2; 85, 105
Giffin, family: Ramoan AM 24; 107
Gifford, Giles: Clondermot LY 34; 81
Gifford, John: Cumber LY 28; 64
Gifford, Mary: Clondermot LY 34; 81
Giggan bank: Lough Swilly DL 38; 113
Gigmagaw's grave: Ballyrashane LY 22; 64
Gihon, Andrew: Kirkinriola AM 23; 96, 104
Gihon, William: Ahoghill AM 23; 12, 15
Gihon, William: Kirkinriola AM 23; 95, 103, 105,
    110, 119
Gilbert, Ann: Aghagallon AM 21; 21
Gilbert, Capt.: Ramoan AM 24; 94
Gilbert, Ellen: Island Magee AM 10; 95
Gilbert, family: Aghagallon AM 21; 9
Gilbert, family: Ballinderry AM 21; 51
Gilbert, Jane: Island Magee AM 10; 95
Gilbert, John: Island Magee AM 10; 103
Gilbert, Mr: Cumber LY 28; 28
Gilbert, Nancy: Island Magee AM 10; 95
Gilbert, Stephen: Aghagallon AM 21; 17
Gilbert, Thomas (Jnr): Island Magee AM 10; 95
Gilbert, Thomas (Snr): Island Magee AM 10; 95
Gilbert, William: Island Magee AM 10; 103
Gilbert's bridge: Aghagallon AM 21; 1
Gilbreath, Hugh: Tamlaght TE 20; 78, 86, 90
Gilchist, Rev.: Kilrea LY 27; 126

Gilchrest, Thomas: Muckamore AM 35; 78–79
Gilchrest's locality: Muckamore AM 35; 80
Gilchrist, Catherine: Magilligan LY 11; 94
Gilchrist, family: Ardglass DN 17; 4
Gilchrist, family: Dunsfort DN 17; 68
Gilchrist, John: Magilligan LY 11; 94
Gilchrist, Rev. H.R.: Killead AM 35; 51
Gilchrist, Sarah: Magilligan LY 11; 94
Gilchrist, William (Jnr): Magilligan LY 11; 94
Gilchrist, William (Snr): Magilligan LY 11; 94
Gilderson, Ann: Tamlaght Finlagan LY 25; 118
Gilderson, John: Tamlaght Finlagan LY 25; 118
Gilderson, Mary: Tamlaght Finlagan LY 25; 118
Gilderson, Thomas: Tamlaght Finlagan LY 25; 118
Gilderson, William (Jnr): Tamlaght Finlagan LY 25;
    118
Gilderson, William (Snr): Tamlaght Finlagan LY 25;
    118
Giles, family: Templecorran AM 26; 117, 119
Giles, Lt: Mevagh DL 38; 58
Giles, Mr: Carlingford LH 40; 58
Giles, Rev. Henery: Blaris AM 8; 24, 31
Giles, Rev. Henery: Magheragall AM 21; 99
Gilespie, W.J.: Killead AM 35; 51
Gilfillan, person named: Faughanvale LY 36; 30
Gilford: Drumcree AH 1; 41
Gilford: Montiaghs AH 1; 91
Gilford: Seagoe AH 1; 110
Gilford bridge: Tullylish DN 12; 142, 145
Gilford school: Tullylish DN 12; 144
Gilford td: Tydavnet MN 40; 169
Gilford village: Tullylish DN 12; 141, 145
Gilky Hill td: Banagher LY 30; 112
Gilky Hill td: Cumber LY 28; 47, 83
Gill lough: Manorhamilton Union LM 40; 47, 54
Gill, Alfred: Blaris DN 12; 40
Gill, family: Carrickfergus AM 37; 93, 179
Gill, G.: Drumachose LY 9; 107
Gill, George: Blaris DN 12; 40
Gill, Henry: Carrickfergus AM 37; 98, 142
Gill, Jeremiah: Urney DL 39; 179
Gill, John: Clondermot LY 34; 42, 86, 91, 93–94
Gill, John: Faughanvale LY 36; 34
Gill, Silas: Carrickfergus AM 37; 111
Gill, Thomas: Hillsborough DN 12; 107
Gill's lough: Saintfield DN 7; 117, 119
Gillan, family: Ballynascreen LY 31; 27, 29
Gillan, family: Culfeightrin AM 24; 59
Gillan, family: Derrykeighan AM 16; 89
Gillan, family: Dunaghy AM 13; 17
Gillan, John: Blaris DN 12; 50
Gilland, family: Kilwaughter AM 10; 115
Gilland, James: Magilligan LY 11; 131, 133
Gilland, Thomas: Carrickfergus AM 37; 114
Gilland, William: Carrickfergus AM 37; 158

Gillas, Hannah: Kilwaughter AM 10; 122
Gillas, Mary: Kilwaughter AM 10; 122
Gillas, Robert: Kilwaughter AM 10; 122
Gillas, Samuel: Kilwaughter AM 10; 122
Gillas, William: Kilwaughter AM 10; 122
Gillaw, James: Armoy AM 24; 9
Gilleland, Samual: Tamlaght Finlagan LY 25; 115
Gillen, John: Ballintoy AM 24, 27
Gillen, John: Blaris DN 12; 46, 50
Gillespie, Charles: Carrickfergus AM 37; 132
Gillespie, Dr: Clonleigh DL 39; 10
Gillespie, Dr: Donaghmore DL 39; 35
Gillespie, Dr: Magilligan LY 11; 83
Gillespie, Dr: Tamlaght Finlagan LY 25; 105
Gillespie, Edward: Magilligan LY 11; 131, 133
Gillespie, Esther: Ahoghill AM 23; 38
Gillespie, family: Dunluce AM 16; 117
Gillespie, family: Finvoy AM 23; 74
Gillespie, Henery: Ballynascreen LY 31; 21–22, 27
Gillespie, John: Doagh AM 29; 90
Gillespie, man named: Finvoy AM 23; 74
Gillespie, Mr (Jnr): Clogher TE 5; 43
Gillespie, Mr (Snr): Clogher TE 5; 43
Gillespie, Mr: Banagher LY 30; 112
Gillespie, Richard: Ballyscullion LY 6; 57
Gillespie, Thomas: Blaris AM 8; 62, 84
Gillespie, Thomas: Blaris DN 12; 46, 49–50
Gillespie, William: Ballintoy AM 24; 35
Gillespie, Wilson: Carrickfergus AM 37; 132
Gillhall demense: Dromore DN 12; 71, 73
Gillhall district: Blaris AM 8; 70
Gillhall House: Dromore DN 12; 72, 76
Gilliestown td: Misc. DL 39; 195
Gilligan, Catherine: Carrickfergus AM 37; 127
Gilligan, James: Hillsborough DN 12; 106
Gilligan, William: Hillsborough DN 12; 106
Gilliland, David: Carrickfergus AM 37; 107
Gilliland, Edward: Carrickfergus AM 37; 124
Gilliland, family: Carrickfergus AM 37; 93
Gilliland, family: Drumbeg AM 8; 123
Gilliland, family: Lambeg AM 8; 135
Gilliland, family: Templepatrick AM 35; 118
Gilliland, Francis: Carrickfergus AM 37; 107
Gilliland, James: Drummaul AM 19; 90
Gilliland, James: Island Magee AM 10; 90
Gillis, Messrs David and Co.: Newry DN 3; 99, 103
Gillistown hill: Ballyscullion AM 19; 2
Gillistown td: Ballyscullion AM 19; 9, 13
Gillon, Domnick: Ballynascreen LY 31; 21
Gillon, John: Blaris AM 8; 55
Gillon, Mary: Aghadowey LY 22; 36
Gilloovier Point: Lough Swilly DL 38; 110
Gillott, Abraham: Blaris AM 8; 21
Gillott, family: Blaris AM 8; 21
Gills bridge: Macosquin LY 22; 82, 103

Gills ferry: Macosquin LY 22; 77, 81
Gills fort [I]: Macosquin LY 22; 107
Gills fort [II]: Macosquin LY 22; 107
Gills fort [III]: Macosquin LY 22; 107
Gills td: Macosquin LY 22; 122
Gills Tower (see Gillstown): Taughboyne DL 39; 148
Gills' Tow (see Gillistown): Ballyscullion AM 19; 2
Gillstown td: Taughboyne DL 39; 148, 153
Gillygooley chapel: Drumragh TE 5; 107
Gillygooley corn mill: Drumragh TE 5; 110
Gillygooley flax mill: Drumragh TE 5; 110
Gillygooley fort: Drumragh TE 5; 109
Gillygooley school: Drumragh TE 5; 109
Gillygooley td: Drumragh TE 5; 107, 109–11
Gillygordan td: Clogher TE 5; 53
Gillygraney (see Glengillagrana): Mevagh DL 38; 55
Gillygranny (see Glengillagrana): Mevagh DL 38; 63
Gillyholm Ely td: Devenish FH 14; 58
Gillyholm L'Estrange td: Devenish FH 14; 58
Gilmer, David: Seapatrick DN 12; 135
Gilmer, James: Coleraine LY 33; 72
Gilmer, Rev. James: Kilbroney DN 3; 34
Gilmor, family: Ballintoy AM 24; 20
Gilmor, family: Ballyclug AM 23; 60
Gilmor, family: Kirkinriola AM 23; 124
Gilmore, Alexander: Tamlaght O'Crilly LY 18; 137
Gilmore, Andrew: Drumachose LY 9; 131
Gilmore, Ann: Artrea LY 6; 38
Gilmore, Ann: Newtownards DN 7; 112
Gilmore, David: Artrea LY 6; 38
Gilmore, Elizabeth: Saintfield DN 7; 116
Gilmore, family: Carnmoney AM 2; 76
Gilmore, family: Desertoghill LY 27; 5, 30
Gilmore, family: Magheramesk AM 21; 124
Gilmore, Henry: Muckamore AM 35; 81
Gilmore, Hugh: Carrickfergus AM 37; 115, 129, 194
Gilmore, Hugh: Duneane AM 19; 120
Gilmore, J.: Castletown LH 40; 61
Gilmore, James (Jnr): Artrea LY 6; 38
Gilmore, James (Snr): Artrea LY 6; 38
Gilmore, James: Errigal LY 27; 55, 58–60, 75
Gilmore, Jane: Artrea LY 6; 38
Gilmore, John: Muckamore AM 35; 78
Gilmore, John: Tamlaght O'Crilly LY 18; 91, 109
Gilmore, man named: Clonleigh DL 39; 12
Gilmore, Margaret: Tamlaght O'Crilly LY 18; 137
Gilmore, Mary: Hillsborough DN 12; 106
Gilmore, Mary [I]: Artrea LY 6; 38
Gilmore, Mary [II]: Artrea LY 6; 38
Gilmore, Nail: Muckamore AM 35; 81
Gilmore, Rev. A.T.: Killead AM 35; 20, 38, 44, 47, 52

Gilmore, Richard: Billy AM 16; 61
Gilmore, Robert: Kirkinriola AM 23; 121
Gilmore, Robert: Tamlaght O'Crilly LY 18; 103
Gilmore, Widow: Tamlaght TE 20; 83, 123
Gilmore, William: Blaris AM 8; 50
Gilmore, William: Muckamore AM 35; 81
Gilmour, Edward: Ballyrobert AM 2; 24–25
Gilmour, family: Ballyrobert AM 2; 21
Gilmour, family: Magherafelt LY 6; 95
Gilmour, Henry: Drummaul AM 19; 90
Gilmour, J.B.: Carrickfergus AM 37; 135, 141
Gilmour, James: Coleraine LY 33; 145
Gilmour, Jane: Kilcronaghan LY 31; 84
Gilmour, John [I]: Carrickfergus AM 37; 108
Gilmour, John [II]: Carrickfergus AM 37; 117
Gilmour, Maria: Ballyscullion AM 19; 14
Gilmour, Mr: Moville DL 38; 75
Gilmour, Nancy: Kilcronaghan LY 31; 84
Gilmour, Patrick: Faughanvale LY 36; 45
Gilnahirk flax mill: Knockbreda DN 7; 102
Gilnahirk td: Knockbreda DN 7; 102
Gilpin, Richard: Ahoghill AM 23; 48
Gilpin, Surgeon: Hillsborough DN 12; 105
Ginachan, Mabhe: Misc. DN 17; 131
Gingling hole: Rasharkin AM 23; 138
Ginsurry (see Garshooey): Killea and Taughboyne
	DL 39; 87
Ginty, Bryan: Kilmacteige SO 40; 196
Ginty, Dennis: Kilmacteige SO 40; 193
Ginty, John: Kilmacteige SO 40; 186
Ginty, Patt: Kilmacteige SO 40; 188
Girlan, Patt: Kilmacteige SO 40; 193
Girlaw td: Clogher TE 5; 54
Girvan, family: Glynn AM 26; 45
Girvan, James: Tamlaght TE 20; 130
Girvan, John: Kilwaughter AM 10; 116
Girvan, John: Raloo AM 32; 103, 126
Girvel, Mr: Drumgoon CN 40; 10
Girven, family: Carnmoney AM 2; 76
Girvin, Mary: Carrickfergus AM 37; 154
Girvin, Mr: Glynn AM 26; 45
Gittrick, Eliza: Ramoan AM 24; 126
Giveen, Mr: Blaris AM 8; 71
Given glen: Balteagh LY 9; 19
Given, Anne: Kirkinriola AM 23; 122
Given, Ben: Dunluce AM 16; 116, 119
Given, Benjamin: Coleraine LY 33; 63, 72, 141–42
Given, D.: Coleraine LY 33; 72
Given, family: Derrykeighan AM 16; 89
Given, family: Maghera LY 18; 13
Given, Henry: Muckamore AM 35; 81
Given, J.: Coleraine LY 33; 72
Given, J.S.: Coleraine LY 33; 63–64, 91
Given, James: Ballymoney AM 16; 17
Given, Jane: Drumachose LY 9; 70, 85, 124

Given, John: Aghanloo LY 11; 33
Given, John: Ballymoney AM 16; 16
Given, John: Carnmoney AM 2; 99
Given, John: Drumachose LY 9; 69, 73, 84, 104,
	130
Given, John: Tamlaght Finlagan LY 25; 82, 124
Given, Lilly: Maghera LY 18; 53
Given, Martha: Drumachose LY 9; 71, 86, 125, 130
Given, Mr (Ballymena): Kirkinriola AM 23; 122
Given, Mr (Magherabuoy): Ballywillin LY 33; 45
Given, Mrs: Coleraine LY 33; 72
Given, Robert: Billy AM 16; 56, 62
Given, Robert [I]: Coleraine LY 33; 65, 72
Given, Robert [II]: Coleraine LY 33; 145
Given, Thomas: Dunluce AM 16; 119
Given, William: Drumachose LY 9; 117, 133
Givin, Henry: Dungiven LY 15; 117
Glaak td: Lough Swilly DL 38; 145
Glaanry river: Lough Swilly DL 38; 120
Glaar locality: Lough Swilly DL 38; 142
Glack bog: Tamlaght Finlagan LY 25; 123
Glack fort: Tamlaght Finlagan LY 25; 113–14
Glack hill: Tamlaght Finlagan LY 25; 62
Glack kiln: Tamlaght Finlagan LY 25; 84
Glack td: Tamlaght Finlagan LY 25; 72–74, 89, 93,
	106–07, 110–11, 115, 119
Gladowen td: Clones FH 4; 26
Glamorganshire (Wales): Cumber LY 28; 59
Glanastranchermore (see Strangemore): Dungiven
	LY 15; 46, 84
Glanawoo (see Glennawoo): Kilmacteige SO 40;
	194
Glandstown td: Donaghedy TE 5; 92
Glanesmol (Leinster): Ballynascreen LY 31; 33
Glangory district: Kinawley FH 4; 111
Glann Marah (see Mary's Holme): Dungiven LY 15;
	79
Glannafurragh glen: Dungiven LY 15; 82
Glannan mill: Donagh MN 40; 101
Glanree lough: Mevagh DL 38; 55
Glanree td: Mevagh DL 38; 63
Glaraford (see Glaryford): Ahoghill AM 23; 12
Glarryford bridge: Kirkinriola AM 23; 104
Glaryford bridge: Ahoghill AM 23; 12
Glaryford bridge: Dunaghy AM 13; 25
Glaryford bridge: Dundermot AM 13; 31
Glasakeeran giant's grave: Faughanvale LY 36; 11,
	15, 21
Glasakeeran hill: Faughanvale LY 36; 1, 3
Glasakeeran td: Faughanvale LY 36; 17, 21, 53, 58,
	68, 74, 85, 94, 98
Glasakeeran td: Tamlaght Finlagan LY 25; 72
Glasco, Daniel: Kilrea LY 27; 129
Glasco, James: Duneane AM 19; 124
Glasco, James: Lissan LY 31; 108

Glasco, Robert: Lissan LY 31; 102

Glasco, William: Lissan LY 31; 109

Glascock, William: Kilbroney DN 3; 31

Glascorn hill: Donegal DL 39; 42

Glascorn hill: Killymard DL 39; 94, 96

Glasdrumman (Glasdrummon) td: Saintfield DN 7;
114, 117, 120

Glasdrumman (Glasdrummond) td: Magheradrool
DN 17; 99, 104–05

Glasdrumman (Glassdruimmon) td: Derrybrusk FH
4; 30

Glasdrumman (Glassdrummon) td: Aghalurcher FH
4; 4, 14

Glasdrumman (Glassdrummond) td: Kinawley FH
4; 115

Glasdrumman (Glassdrumond) td: Misc. DN 17;
131

Glasdrumman corn mill: Kinawley FH 4; 115

Glasdrumman corn mill: Saintfield DN 7; 114

Glasdrumman flax mill: Saintfield DN 7; 114

Glasdrumman school: Magheradrool DN 17; 105

Glasdrummond (Glassdrumman) td: Kilclooney AH
1; 51

Glasdrummond (Glassdrummond) td: Killevy AH 1;
53

Glasdrummond bleach mill: Killevy AH 1; 53

Glasdrummond church: Kilclooney AH 1; 51

Glasgo, Robert: Lissan LY 31; 100

Glasgow: Aghadowey LY 22; 14

Glasgow: Agivey LY 22; 45

Glasgow: Ahoghill AM 23; 37–40

Glasgow: Antrim AM 29; 8

Glasgow: Ardglass DN 17; 6

Glasgow: Ballee DN 17; 19

Glasgow: Ballylinny AM 32; 29

Glasgow: Ballyscullion AM 19; 12–13

Glasgow: Ballywillin LY 33; 30

Glasgow: Bright DN 17; 35

Glasgow: Carnmoney AM 2; 64, 82, 88–89

Glasgow: Carrickfergus AM 37; 63, 158–59

Glasgow: Clondermot LY 34; 14, 30, 87, 95, 100

Glasgow: Coleraine LY 33; 73, 86, 89, 123–24, 148,
151

Glasgow: Comber DN 7; 37

Glasgow: Cranfield AM 19; 32

Glasgow: Culdaff DL 38; 21

Glasgow: Desertoghill LY 27; 20–21

Glasgow: Doagh AM 29; 78, 98

Glasgow: Donegal DL 39; 47

Glasgow: Donegore AM 29; 130

Glasgow: Down DN 17; 47, 58

Glasgow: Drumachose LY 9; 69, 117

Glasgow: Drumgoon CN 40; 9

Glasgow: Drummaul AM 19; 62, 89–91

Glasgow: Duneane AM 19; 123–24

Glasgow: Dungiven LY 15; 6, 69

Glasgow: Dunluce AM 16; 112

Glasgow: Enniskillen FH 4; 61

Glasgow: Glynn AM 26; 47

Glasgow: Island Magee AM 10; 28, 64, 95

Glasgow: Kilbride AM 29; 152

Glasgow: Kilcronaghan LY 31; 84–85

Glasgow: Killyleagh DN 17; 85

Glasgow: Kilroot AM 26; 73

Glasgow: Kilwaughter AM 10; 122

Glasgow: Lissan LY 31; 94, 109–10

Glasgow: Maghera LY 18; 7, 22, 67, 80

Glasgow: Mallusk AM 2; 110, 114

Glasgow: Misc. DL 39; 188

Glasgow: Muckamore AM 35; 77

Glasgow: Muff DL 38; 80

Glasgow: Newry DN 3; 85

Glasgow: Nilteen AM 35; 93

Glasgow: Raloo AM 32; 106, 129

Glasgow: Ramoan AM 24; 95

Glasgow: Shilvodan AM 19; 135, 137

Glasgow: Templecorran AM 26; 97, 107, 132

Glasgow: Templepatrick AM 35; 123, 146, 152–53

Glasgow: Tickmacrevan AM 13; 122

Glasgow: Tullyaughnish DL 38; 94

Glasgow University: Templepatrick AM 35; 132

Glasgow, Rev. James: Magherafelt LY 6; 98–99

Glasgow, Rev. John: Coleraine LY 33; 141

Glashagh bay: Lough Swilly DL 38; 106, 123, 126

Glashmere mountain: Muff DL 38; 80

Glashmere quarry: Muff DL 38; 80

Glashock bridge: Tullyaughnish DL 38; 90

Glaskeeran (see Glasakeeran): Faughanvale LY 36;
11

Glasker chapel: Aghaderg DN 12; 4

Glasker hill: Aghaderg DN 12; 8

Glasker school: Aghaderg DN 12; 5

Glasker td: Aghaderg DN 12; 4–5

Glaskerbeg East ph: Aghaderg DN 12; 8

Glaskerbeg Large td: Aghaderg DN 12; 2

Glaskerbeg Little td: Aghaderg DN 12; 2

Glaskermore td: Aghaderg DN 12; 2

Glaslough: Aghaloo TE 20; 4

Glaslough: Aughnamullen MN 40; 76

Glaslough: Donagh MN 40; 98–01, 105

Glaslough: Down DN 17; 57

Glaslough: Muckno MN 40; 167

Glaslough: Tyholland MN 40; 175

Glaslough and Emyvale dispensary: Donagh MN
40; 102–05

Glaslough bog: Donagh MN 40; 98

Glaslough chapel: Donagh MN 40; 100

Glaslough church: Donagh MN 40; 100

Glaslough female school: Donagh MN 40; 100–01

Glaslough lough: Donagh MN 40; 98

Glaslough td: Donagh MN 40; 99

Glasmullin school: Ardstraw TE 5; 13

Glass Island: Ramoan AM 24; 89

Glass Moss td: Holywood DN 7; 82

Glass, Daniel: Ballintoy AM 24; 22–24, 28

Glass, Eneas: Ballintoy AM 24; 29

Glass, family: Ballintoy AM 24; 20

Glass, family: Carrickfergus AM 37; 93

Glass, family: Culfeightrin AM 24; 59

Glass, family: Ramoan AM 24; 107

Glass, Hesther Anne: Seapatrick DN 12; 135

Glass, John: Ballintoy AM 24; 22

Glass, Mr: Aghadowey LY 22; 28

Glass, Neal: Ballintoy AM 24; 28

Glass, Robert: Ballymoney AM 16; 15, 17

Glass, William: Ballymoney AM 16; 17

Glassagh spring: Magilligan LY 11; 127

Glassakeeran (see Glasakeeran): Faughanvale LY 36; 58

Glassaneeran fort: Billy AM 16; 55, 74

Glassaneeran td: Billy AM 16; 57, 59, 75–76

Glassaneeran Upper td: Billy AM 16; 39

Glasscarrick td: Drumlumman CN 40; 17

Glassdrummon (see Glasdrumman)

Glassdrummond td: Ballymore AH 1; 9, 12–13, 16, 18

Glasseasach lough: Templecarn DL 39; 157

Glassen rocks: Lough Swilly DL 38; 116

Glassgort old church: Agivey LY 22; 43

Glassgort td: Aghadowey LY 22; 36

Glassgort td: Agivey LY 22; 43, 45

Glassheady Island: Clonmany DL 38; 13, 15–16, 18–19

Glasskeeragh td: Templecarn DL 39; 164

Glassley td: Convoy DL 39; 21

Glasslough (see Glaslough)

Glassmullagh chapel: Kinawley FH 4; 119

Glassmullagh school: Kinawley FH 4; 119

Glassmullagh td: Cleenish FH 14; 28–29

Glassmullagh td: Derrybrusk FH 4; 30

Glassmullagh td: Magheraculmoney FH 14; 112

Glassmullan hill: Mintiaghs DL 38; 64–65

Glassmullan td: Mintiaghs DL 38; 64, 66–67

Glassmullen td: Misc. DL 39; 196

Glastry hedge school: Inishargy DN 7; 85

Glastry manor: Misc. DN 17; 125

Glastry meeting house: Inishargy DN 7; 85

Glastry td: Ballywalter DN 7; 18

Glastry td: Inishargy DN 7; 84–85

Glasveagh (see Glasvey): Tamlaght Finlagan LY 25; 119

Glasvey flax mill: Tamlaght Finlagan LY 25; 83, 120–21

Glasvey td: Tamlaght Finlagan LY 25; 72–74, 93, 119

Gleannconchadhain (see Glenconkeen): Dungiven LY 15; 11

Glebe bog: Annaclone DN 12; 14

Glebe bog: Devenish FH 14; 52

Glebe bridge: Dunboe LY 11; 62

Glebe bridge: Macosquin LY 22; 82, 103

Glebe Carnmoney td: Carnmoney AM 2; 34

Glebe Castle: Ballyaghran LY 33; 10, 16, 23

Glebe church: Ballyaghran LY 33; 7

Glebe church: Killelagh LY 27; 96–97, 102–03

Glebe East bog: Ballyscullion LY 6; 70

Glebe East td: Ballyscullion LY 6; 70

Glebe farm: Finvoy AM 23; 72

Glebe flax mill: Faughanvale LY 36; 98

Glebe fort: Dunboe LY 11; 73

Glebe forts: Killelagh LY 27; 97

Glebe hill: Ballymore AH 1; 7

Glebe hill: Desertoghill LY 27; 15

Glebe Hill giant's grave: Errigal LY 27; 78

Glebe Hill House: Errigal LY 27; 39–40, 46, 78

Glebe Hill td: Errigal LY 27; 41

Glebe Lower td: Killymard DL 39; 101

Glebe river: Moville DL 38; 78

Glebe round tower: Armoy AM 24; 2, 4, 6–7, 9

Glebe school: Aghaderg DN 12; 5

Glebe school: Annaclone DN 12; 17

Glebe school: Clondermot LY 34; 11, 41, 77, 87, 89, 91, 95, 99

Glebe school: Donegal DL 39; 46, 56

Glebe school: Drumachose LY 9; 51

Glebe school: Dunboe LY 11; 56, 70

Glebe school: Faughanvale LY 36; 24–25, 27, 35

Glebe school: Killelagh LY 27; 100

Glebe school: Kilteevoge DL 39; 114

Glebe standing stone: Desertegney DL 38; 26

Glebe Sunday school: Clondermot LY 34; 92–93

Glebe Sunday school: Dunboe LY 11; 57, 72

Glebe td: Aghanloo LY 11; 18, 40–41

Glebe td: Ahoghill AM 23; 12

Glebe td: Annahilt DN 12; 20–21, 23

Glebe td: Armoy AM 24; 4

Glebe td: Aughnamullen MN 40; 69

Glebe td: Ballyaghran LY 33; 8

Glebe td: Ballynascreen LY 31; 7, 11, 21–22

Glebe td: Ballywillin AM 16; 32

Glebe td: Balteagh LY 9; 40, 45

Glebe td: Banagher LY 30; 23–24

Glebe td: Billy AM 16; 45

Glebe td: Clogher TE 5; 53

Glebe td: Derrykeighan AM 16; 95

Glebe td: Donaghmore DN 3; 7, 9

Glebe td: Drumachose LY 9; 95

Glebe td: Dunaghy AM 13; 13

Glebe td: Dunboe LY 11; 73, 81

Glebe td: Faughanvale LY 36; 17, 53, 58, 61, 68, 74, 85–86, 94, 99
Glebe td: Finvoy AM 23; 71
Glebe td: Killelagh LY 27; 99
Glebe td: Kilmacteige SO 40; 196
Glebe td: Kilteevoge DL 39; 114
Glebe td: Kinawley FH 4; 114
Glebe td: Macosquin LY 22; 107
Glebe td: Magherafelt LY 6; 110, 112
Glebe td: Mevagh DL 38; 63
Glebe td: Misc. DL 39; 197
Glebe td: Moville DL 38; 73
Glebe td: Rasharkin AM 23; 130
Glebe td: Tullyaughnish DL 38; 96
Glebe td: Tullyniskan TE 20; 141
Glebe Upper td: Killymard DL 39; 101
Glebe well: Ballyaghran LY 33; 23
Glebe well: Billy AM 16; 51
Glebe West bog: Ballyscullion LY 6; 70
Glebe West td: Ballyscullion LY 6; 70
Glebes (see Glebe): Clondermot LY 34; 91
Gleck (see Glack): Tamlaght Finlagan LY 25; 123
Gledstane, Mr: Clogher TE 5; 51
Gledstanes, family: Clogher TE 5; 33
Gledstone, A.U.: Clogher TE 5; 49
Gledstone, Aylmer: Clogher TE 5; 53
Gleeneask Cottage: Kilmacteige SO 40; 195
Gleer td: Clones FH 4; 26
Glen Ballyemon glen: Layd AM 13; 49
Glen bay: Glencolumbkille DL 39; 64–65
Glen bridge: Ballinderry AM 21; 41
Glen bridge: Dunboe LY 11; 63
Glen chapel: Donaghmore DN 3; 7
Glen chapel: Errigal LY 27; 39, 56
Glen district: Carrickfergus AM 37; 160
Glen East school: Inishmacsaint FH 14; 79
Glen Flusk locality: Aghaderg DN 12; 4
Glen hill: Inishmacsaint FH 14; 71
Glen hill: Mevagh DL 38; 54
Glen House: Clonmany DL 38; 14
Glen House: Misc. DN 17; 131
Glen locality: Magheramesk AM 21; 118
Glen lough: Mevagh DL 38; 54–56
Glen Lough mountain: Glencolumbkille DL 39; 64
Glen Lower standing stone: Tullyaughnish DL 38; 91
Glen Lower td: Tullyaughnish DL 38; 97
Glen mill: Lough Swilly DL 38; 129
Glen Randle (see Glenrandal): Misc. LY 36; 119
Glen river [I]: Glencolumbkille DL 39; 64
Glen river [II]: Glencolumbkille DL 39; 64
Glen school: Enniskillen FH 4; 84
Glen stone: Bovevagh LY 25; 9, 51
Glen stream: Blaris DN 12; 28
Glen stream: Drumbeg DN 7; 52

Glen td: Ematris MN 40; 115–16
Glen td: Enniskillen FH 4; 72, 74, 82
Glen td: Inishmacsaint FH 14; 71
Glen td: Killymard DL 39; 101
Glen td: Misc. DN 17; 130
Glen Upper td: Tullyaughnish DL 38; 97
Glen village: Drumlumman CN 40; 13–14
Glen village: Lough Swilly DL 38; 128–29
Glen village: Mevagh DL 38; 57–58, 61
Glen wood: Misc. LY 31; 112
Glen, David: Errigal LY 27; 53
Glen, John: Coleraine LY 33; 72
Glen, William: Coleraine LY 33; 72
Glenaan glen: Layd AM 13; 37–38, 49
Glenaan river: Layd AM 13; 37, 40, 43–44
Glenaan school: Layd AM 13; 51
Glenaan valley: Layd AM 13; 42
Glenade hill: Manorhamilton Union LM 40; 52
Glenade House: Manorhamilton Union LM 40; 50, 54
Glenade plantation: Manorhamilton Union LM 40; 50
Glenade td: Manorhamilton Union LM 40; 49
Glenade valley: Manorhamilton Union LM 40; 47–48
Glenagaad Head: Lough Swilly DL 38; 108–11
Glenagaad valley: Lough Swilly DL 38; 113
Glenageera td: Clogher TE 5; 36
Glenagivney (see Glennagiveny): Moville DL 38; 70
Glenaguivna creek: Lough Swilly DL 38; 113, 141
Glenalla altar: Tullyaughnish DL 38; 91
Glenalla church: Tullyaughnish DL 38; 90
Glenalla hill: Killygarvan DL 38; 36
Glenalla hill: Tullyaughnish DL 38; 84–85, 90–92, 95
Glenalla House: Tullyaughnish DL 38; 89, 95
Glenalla school: Tullyaughnish DL 38; 92
Glenalla standing stone: Tullyaughnish DL 38; 91
Glenalla td: Lough Swilly DL 38; 128–29, 146
Glenalla td: Tullyaughnish DL 38; 97
Glenalla wood: Tullyaughnish DL 38; 85
Glenalong hill: Inishmacsaint FH 14; 71
Glenalong td: Inishmacsaint FH 14; 70–71
Glenamohill silver mine: Inishkeel DL 39; 70
Glenamullick td: Rossorry FH 14; 116
Glenan td: Donacavey TE 5; 80
Glenane (see Glenaan): Layd AM 13; 51
Glenarb td: Tynan AH 1; 128
Glenarewan lough: Inishmacsaint FH 14; 71
Glenarewen (see Glenarewan)
Glenariff bridge: Ardclinis AM 13; 7
Glenariff glen: Ardclinis AM 13; 1–2, 5–6, 8
Glenariff glen: Layd AM 13; 36, 43–44, 50–52, 49
Glenariff glen: Layd and Inispollan AM 13; 56

Glenariff graveyard: Layd AM 13; 41
Glenariff mountains: Ardclinis AM 13; 2
Glenariff river: Ardclinis AM 13; 3, 5
Glenariff river: Layd AM 13; 36, 38–40, 45
Glenarm: Ardclinis AM 13; 2–4, 6
Glenarm: Ballynure AM 32; 34
Glenarm: Carrickfergus AM 37; 13, 51, 55–57, 59
Glenarm: Culfeightrin AM 24; 63
Glenarm: Dunaghy AM 13; 15
Glenarm: Glenwhirry AM 32; 77
Glenarm: Glynn AM 26; 15
Glenarm: Island Magee AM 10; 19, 26, 74, 94
Glenarm: Kilwaughter AM 10; 116, 121
Glenarm: Kirkinriola AM 23; 101–02
Glenarm: Layd AM 13; 39
Glenarm: Misc. AM 10; 129
Glenarm: Racavan AM 13; 91
Glenarm: Raloo AM 32; 107, 116
Glenarm: Ramoan AM 24; 122–23
Glenarm: Tickmacrevan AM 13; 122–23, 127–29, 131, 133
Glenarm barony: Kilwaughter AM 10; 106
Glenarm barony: Larne AM 10; 123
Glenarm barony: Tickmacrevan AM 13; 124, 127
Glenarm bay: Kilwaughter AM 10; 108
Glenarm bay: Tickmacrevan AM 13; 126, 131
Glenarm bridges: Tickmacrevan AM 13; 128
Glenarm Castle: Carncastle and Killyglen AM 10; 6
Glenarm Castle: Killead AM 35; 46
Glenarm Castle: Tickmacrevan AM 13; 124, 126, 129–30
Glenarm chapel: Tickmacrevan AM 13; 127
Glenarm church: Tickmacrevan AM 13; 123, 129
Glenarm deerpark: Carncastle and Killyglen AM 10; 10
Glenarm deerpark: Templecorran AM 26; 96
Glenarm deerpark: Tickmacrevan AM 13; 122–24, 126, 129
Glenarm fishery: Tickmacrevan AM 13; 124
Glenarm fort: Killead AM 35; 33
Glenarm Head: Island Magee AM 10; 58
Glenarm Lower barony: Ardclinis AM 13; 1
Glenarm Lower barony: Carncastle and Killyglen AM 10; 8
Glenarm Lower barony: Dunaghy AM 13; 10
Glenarm Lower barony: Layd AM 13; 36, 45
Glenarm Lower barony: Layd and Inispollan AM 13; 54
Glenarm Lower barony: Tickmacrevan AM 13; 122, 125
Glenarm manor: Kilwaughter AM 10; 116
Glenarm market house: Tickmacrevan AM 13; 127
Glenarm meeting house (P): Tickmacrevan AM 13; 127

Glenarm meeting house (U): Tickmacrevan AM 13; 129
Glenarm monastery: Tickmacrevan AM 13; 124, 127
Glenarm old castle: Tickmacrevan AM 13; 130
Glenarm river: Carncastle and Killyglen AM 10; 10, 12
Glenarm river: Kilwaughter AM 10; 108
Glenarm river: Racavan AM 13; 90, 97
Glenarm river: Tickmacrevan AM 13; 124–25, 127
Glenarm school [I]: Tickmacrevan AM 13; 127, 129, 132
Glenarm school [II]: Tickmacrevan AM 13; 129, 132–33
Glenarm school [III]: Tickmacrevan AM 13; 129, 132–33
Glenarm Upper barony: Carncastle and Killyglen AM 10; 8
Glenarm Upper barony: Raloo AM 32; 86
Glenarm Upper barony: Templecorran AM 26; 91, 95
Glenarm Upper barony: Tickmacrevan AM 13; 127
Glenarm valley: Carncastle and Killyglen AM 10; 9
Glenarm valley: Tickmacrevan AM 13; 125–26
Glenarn hill: Drumkeeran FH 14; 62
Glenarn hill: Magheraculmoney FH 14; 103–05
Glenavney (see Glengomna): Ballynascreen LY 31; 19
Glenavy: Aghagallon AM 21; 21
Glenavy: Ballinderry AM 21; 41–42, 45–47, 49, 58
Glenavy: Blaris AM 8; 48, 73
Glenavy: Blaris DN 12; 41
Glenavy: Camlin AM 21; 67, 70
Glenavy: Garvaghy DN 12; 81
Glenavy: Glenavy AM 21; 77–81, 83–87, 90
Glenavy: Killead AM 35; 15
Glenavy: Magheragall AM 21; 99, 102, 109
Glenavy: Magheramesk AM 21; 112–13, 115
Glenavy: Tullyrusk AM 21; 132, 134
Glenavy bogs: Killead AM 35; 22
Glenavy bridge: Camlin AM 21; 67
Glenavy bridge: Glenavy AM 21; 78, 81, 84–86
Glenavy chapel: Glenavy AM 21; 77, 81, 85, 88
Glenavy chapel: Killead AM 35; 45
Glenavy church: Camlin AM 21; 63, 72
Glenavy church: Glenavy AM 21; 77, 80–81, 84–85, 88, 90
Glenavy church: Tullyrusk AM 21; 137
Glenavy corn mill: Glenavy AM 21; 79, 85
Glenavy cotton factory: Glenavy AM 21; 79–81, 85, 88
Glenavy district: Carmavy AM 35; 3
Glenavy district: Killead AM 35; 20
Glenavy flax mill: Glenavy AM 21; 80
Glenavy forts: Glenavy AM 21; 90

Glenavy little bridge: Blaris DN 12; 42

Glenavy Lower td: Blaris DN 12; 40, 42

Glenavy meeting house (see Glenavy chapel):
  Glenavy AM 21; 81

Glenavy mill: Blaris DN 12; 42

Glenavy ph: Aghagallon AM 21; 1, 4

Glenavy ph: Ballinderry AM 21; 41

Glenavy ph: Camlin AM 21; 60, 62–65, 69

Glenavy ph: Derryaghy AM 8; 90, 119

Glenavy ph: Killead AM 35; 46

Glenavy ph: Misc. AM 10; 129

Glenavy ph: Templepatrick AM 35; 115

Glenavy ph: Tullyrusk AM 21; 131, 133, 135, 137

Glenavy post office: Glenavy AM 21; 84

Glenavy public house: Glenavy AM 21; 84

Glenavy rectory: Misc. DN 17; 121

Glenavy river: Camlin AM 21; 60, 62–64

Glenavy river: Glenavy AM 21; 77–86

Glenavy river: Lough Neagh AM 21; 93

Glenavy river: Tullyrusk AM 21; 131–35

Glenavy school: Glenavy AM 21; 79, 91

Glenavy td: Blaris DN 12; 43

Glenavy td: Glenavy AM 21; 79

Glenavy Upper td: Blaris DN 12; 40, 42

Glenavy waterfall: Camlin AM 21; 63

Glenavy waterfall: Glenavy AM 21; 80, 83

Glenavy waterfoot: Glenavy AM 21; 77

Glenawley (see Glenalla): Lough Swilly DL 38; 146

Glenawley barony: Boho FH 14; 8

Glenawley barony: Cleenish FH 14; 11–12, 29

Glenawley barony: Enniskillen FH 4; 63

Glenawley barony: Killesher FH 14; 81

Glenawley barony: Kinawley FH 4; 111–12

Glenawley barony: Rossorry FH 14; 115, 117

Glenawly (see Glenawley)

Glenawoo (see Glennawoo): Kilmacteige SO 40;
  189

Glenbank House: Culfeightrin AM 24; 49, 61

Glenbank House: Ramoan AM 24; 90, 96, 115

Glenboar lough: Clogher TE 5; 47

Glenboy bleach green: Manorhamilton Union LM
  40; 50, 53

Glenboy td: Manorhamilton Union LM 40; 54

Glenboy valley: Manorhamilton Union LM 40; 47

Glenbrook House: Magherafelt LY 6; 91

Glenbuck (Glenbrook) td: Rasharkin AM 23; 127,
  137–38, 141

Glenbuck bog: Rasharkin AM 23; 137–38

Glenbuck carn: Rasharkin AM 23; 139

Glenbuck rock: Loughguile AM 13; 74

Glenbuck school [I]: Rasharkin AM 23; 135, 141

Glenbuck school [II]: Rasharkin AM 23; 141

Glenbuide (see Glenboy): Manorhamilton Union
  LM 40; 50

Glenbuidhe (see Glenboy): Manorhamilton Union
  LM 40; 54

Glenbuoy (see Glenboy): Manorhamilton Union LM
  40; 47

Glenburn bleach green: Drumbeg AM 8; 124, 126

Glenburn demesne: Drumbeg AM 8; 124, 126

Glenburn House: Blaris AM 8; 61, 85

Glenburn House: Drumbeg AM 8; 124, 128, 130

Glenburn House: Drumbeg DN 7; 52

Glenburn House: Maghera LY 18; 53

Glenburn House: Tamlaght O'Crilly LY 18; 88, 90,
  96, 108

Glenburn old forge: Drumbeg AM 8; 127

Glenburn river: Drumbeg AM 8; 124, 128

Glenburne (see Glenburn)

Glenburnie Cottage: Ematris MN 40; 115

Glenbush valley: Loughguile AM 13; 60

Glencairn House: Skerry AM 13; 111

Glencairn House: Tullyaughnish DL 38; 94

Glencankeine valley: Cumber LY 28; 61

Glencar hill: Manorhamilton Union LM 40; 52

Glencar lough: Manorhamilton Union LM 40; 47

Glencar valley: Manorhamilton Union LM 40;
  47–48

Glencarrick House: Holywood DN 7; 81

Glencash school: Clonleigh DL 39; 9

Glencash td: Clonleigh DL 39; 12

Glencaw td: Moville DL 38; 73

Glenchiel school: Bodoney TE 20; 20

Glenchuil (Glenchull) td: Errigal Keerogue TE 20;
  53, 57

Glenchuil forts: Errigal Keerogue TE 20; 53

Glenchuil school: Errigal Keerogue TE 20; 53

Glencloy mountain: Tickmacrevan AM 13; 122, 125

Glencloy river: Tickmacrevan AM 13; 124

Glencloy valley: Skerry AM 13; 109

Glencloy valley: Tickmacrevan AM 13; 125

Glencoagh td: Killymard DL 39; 101

Glencock (see Glencash): Clonleigh DL 39; 9

Glencolumbkille church: Glencolumbkille DL 39;
  65

Glencolumbkille old church: Glencolumbkille DL
  39; 64–65

Glencolumbkille ph: Killymard DL 39; 104

Glencolumbkille school: Glencolumbkille DL 39; 65

Glencon hill: Tullyniskan TE 20; 138

Glenconkeen (see Glenshane): Dungiven LY 15; 11

Glenconkein (see Glenshane): Dungiven LY 15; 51

Glenconkyne (see Glenshane)

Glenconway fort: Bovevagh LY 25; 51–52

Glenconway freestone quarry: Bovevagh LY 25; 52

Glenconway freestone quarry: Drumachose LY 9;
  117

Glenconway glen: Glenavy AM 21; 82

Glenconway hill: Bovevagh LY 25; 1, 28–29

Glenconway hill: Tamlaght Finlagan LY 25; 62
Glenconway limestone quarry: Bovevagh LY 25; 52
Glenconway lough: Bovevagh LY 25; 28
Glenconway school: Bovevagh LY 25; 28, 55
Glenconway td: Banagher LY 30; 23–24
Glenconway td: Bovevagh LY 25; 29, 60
Glenconway td: Killowen LY 33; 172
Glenconway village: Glenavy AM 21; 83
Glencooma td: Magheracross FH 14; 102
Glencosh (see Glencash): Clonleigh DL 39; 12
Glencovet Glebe td: Enniskillen FH 4; 82
Glencovit td: Donaghmore DL 39; 37
Glencross hill: Killygarvan DL 38; 36–38
Glencross td: Killygarvan DL 38; 47
Glencross wood: Killygarvan DL 38; 38
Glencrow td: Moville DL 38; 73, 75
Glencull td: Killeeshil TE 20; 63
Glencullen (Leinster): Ballynascreen LY 31; 33
Glencunny td: Rossorry FH 14; 115
Glencurb bog: Aghadowey LY 22; 1, 30, 32
Glencurb hill: Aghadowey LY 22; 1
Glencush td: Donaghedy TE 5; 89, 92
Glendallan (Sligo): Ballynascreen LY 31; 33
Glendalough: Dungiven LY 15; 55
Glendalough Cathedral: Shilvodan AM 19; 138
Glendarragh Cottage: Killead AM 35; 13–14,
    41–42, 47
Glendarragh glen: Camlin AM 21; 64
Glendarragh glen: Killead AM 35; 7, 9, 13
Glendarragh glen: Lough Neagh AM 21; 94
Glendarragh hill: Aghaloo TE 20; 1
Glendarragh House: Camlin AM 21; 70
Glendarragh old mill: Camlin AM 21; 71
Glendarragh td: Killead AM 35; 41
Glendarragh waterfall: Camlin AM 21; 63
Glendarrah (see Glendarragh): Lough Neagh AM
    21; 94
Glendarvagh (see Glendarragh): Camlin AM 21; 70
Glendergan river: Skirts of Urney and Ardstraw TE
    5; 139
Glendergan river: Termonamongan TE 5; 142
Glendermagh monastery: Clondermot LY 34; 106
Glendermot (see Clondermot): Clondermot LY 34; 1
Glenderoe district: Misc. LY 36; 111
Glenderowen giant's grave: Clondermot LY 34; 44
Glenderowen glen: Clondermot LY 34; 121
Glenderowen quarry: Clondermot LY 34; 131
Glenderowen td: Clondermot LY 34; 32, 44, 56, 60,
    63, 67, 72, 110, 112, 117, 124–25, 131
Glendinnen, Rev. James: Carnmoney AM 2; 75
Glendoire Owen (see Glenderowen): Clondermot
    LY 34; 56
Glendun bridges: Layd AM 13; 48
Glendun glen: Layd AM 13; 37, 42, 45, 49
Glendun glen: Layd and Inispollan AM 13; 54, 56

Glendun river: Culfeightrin AM 24; 36, 41, 45–46
Glendun river: Layd AM 13; 37, 39, 43
Glendun river: Layd and Inispollan AM 13; 54–55
Glendun school: Layd and Inispollan AM 13; 57
Glendun td: Layd and Inispollan AM 13; 57
Glendun valley: Layd and Inispollan AM 13; 55
Glendy, Rev.: Maghera LY 18; 67–68
Glendy, Rev. William: Carrickfergus AM 37; 134
Glendy, Rev. William: Kilroot AM 26; 79–80
Glendy, Rev. William: Raloo AM 32; 118, 130
Glendy, Rev. William: Templecorran AM 26;
    100–01, 128–31
Glendy, S.K.: Maghera LY 18; 68
Glenedra cromlech: Banagher LY 30; 46
Glenedra rock: Banagher LY 30; 56
Glenedra td: Ballynascreen LY 31; 19
Glenedra td: Banagher LY 30; 46, 48, 61–62, 81,
    100, 104–05, 109, 119, 123–24, 127, 131
Glenedra valley: Banagher LY 30; 24, 26–27,
    31–32, 72
Glenedra water: Banagher LY 30; 26, 46, 56, 59
Gleneely school: Donaghmore DL 39; 39
Gleneely td: Donaghmore DL 39; 37
Gleneeragh td: Mevagh DL 38; 63
Glenegeeragh (see Glennageeragh)
Glenerin valley: Banagher LY 30; 108–10
Glenern (see Glenerin): Banagher LY 30; 109
Glenfad bog: Clonleigh DL 39; 5
Glenfad House: Clonleigh DL 39; 10, 13
Glenfad orchard: Misc. DL 39; 189
Glenfad td: Clonleigh DL 39; 4, 12, 16, 186, 197
Glenfanet school: Clondavaddog DL 38; 7
Glenfarn chapel: Manorhamilton Union LM 40;
    52–53
Glenfarn House: Manorhamilton Union LM 40; 48,
    50, 54
Glenfarn valley: Manorhamilton Union LM 40; 47
Glenfield Cottage: Carrickfergus AM 37; 135, 141
Glenfield printworks: Carrickfergus AM 37; 58, 139
Glenfin ph: Misc. LY 31; 137
Glenfin ph: Raphoe DL 39; 129
Glenfin valley: Kilteevoge DL 39; 111
Glenfinn (see Glenfin)
Glengad Head: Moville DL 38; 70
Glengamna (see Glengomna): Ballynascreen LY 31;
    26
Glengannow td: Donaghedy TE 5; 92
Glengavna (see Glengomna): Misc. LY 31; 116
Glengeen mountain: Dromore TE 5; 93
Glengeen td: Dromore TE 5; 95, 99
Glengeera fort: Clogher TE 5; 45
Glengesh td: Enniskillen FH 4; 82
Glengillagrana td: Mevagh DL 38; 55, 63
Glengiven district: Drumachose LY 9; 91

Glengomna (Glengavney) td: Ballynascreen LY 31;
11, 22, 33, 116, 143

Glengomna fort: Ballynascreen LY 31; 22, 26

Glengomna standing stones: Ballynascreen LY 31;
10–11, 19, 23

Glengormley coves: Carnmoney AM 2; 71

Glengormley fort [I]: Carnmoney AM 2; 101

Glengormley fort [II]: Carnmoney AM 2; 101

Glengormley House: Carnmoney AM 2; 46, 84

Glengormley moss: Carnmoney AM 2; 93

Glengormley td: Carnmoney AM 2; 34, 81, 90

Glengormley threshing machine: Carnmoney AM 2;
48, 93

Glengormly (see Glengormley): Carnmoney AM 2;
71

Glenhall school: Macosquin LY 22; 91

Glenhall td: Macosquin LY 22; 108

Glenhall well: Macosquin LY 22; 108

Glenhead district: Killymard DL 39; 108

Glenhead hill: Glenwhirry AM 32; 74–75, 79

Glenherdel mountain: Cappagh TE 5; 19, 21

Glenholme, Mr: Misc. LY 31; 130, 135

Glenhordial (see Glenherdel)

Glenhorrick standing stones: Ematris MN 40; 116

Glenhow hill: Mevagh DL 38; 54

Glenhow td: Mevagh DL 38; 55, 63

Glenhoy (Glenhoyse) td: Clogher TE 5; 32, 36,
45–46, 53

Glenhugh (Glenhue) td: Ahoghill AM 23; 21

Glenhugh school [I]: Ahoghill AM 23; 21

Glenhugh school [II]: Ahoghill AM 23; 43, 47, 49

Glenhugh Sunday school: Ahoghill AM 23; 47

Glenigiviny (see Glennagiveny): Moville DL 38; 68

Glenkeel valley: Manorhamilton Union LM 40; 47

Glenkeen altar: Errigal LY 27; 42

Glenkeen bog: Aghadowey LY 22; 2

Glenkeen bogs: Errigal LY 27; 54

Glenkeen bridge: Errigal LY 27; 41, 60

Glenkeen Castle: Dungiven LY 15; 33

Glenkeen corn mill: Errigal LY 27; 40, 58, 92–93

Glenkeen flax mill: Errigal LY 27; 93

Glenkeen fort: Errigal LY 27; 42, 66–67, 79

Glenkeen fort: Maghera LY 18; 23

Glenkeen fort: Misc. LY 36; 116

Glenkeen House: Clondermot LY 34; 6, 20

Glenkeen quarry: Clondermot LY 34; 131

Glenkeen quarry: Errigal LY 27; 90

Glenkeen spring: Errigal LY 27; 54

Glenkeen td: Clondermot LY 34; 38, 56, 67–68, 70,
74, 76, 107, 110, 112–13, 117, 125, 131

Glenkeen td: Drumachose LY 9; 75, 87–88, 96, 133

Glenkeen td: Errigal LY 27; 41, 66, 82, 87, 90,
92–93

Glenkeen td: Tullyaughnish DL 38; 96

Glenkeeran (Glenkeerin) td: Raphoe DL 39; 126

Glenkeeran bog: Leck DL 39; 115

Glenkeeran bog: Raphoe DL 39; 121

Glenknock chapel: Ardstraw TE 5; 8

Glenlary school: Tullyaughnish DL 38; 92

Glenlary td: Tullyaughnish DL 38; 96

Glenleary bog: Macosquin LY 22; 77–78, 88, 97,
110–11

Glenleary Castle: Macosquin LY 22; 97

Glenleary Castle: Misc. LY 36; 109–11

Glenleary cave: Macosquin LY 22; 87, 110

Glenleary South td: Macosquin LY 22; 122

Glenleary td: Aghadowey LY 22; 11

Glenleary td: Coleraine LY 33; 106

Glenleary td: Dungiven LY 15; 34

Glenleary td: Macosquin LY 22; 99, 119

Glenleary td: Misc. LY 36; 111

Glenlee (see Clonlee): Clonleigh DL 39; 14

Glenlesly td: Dunaghy AM 13; 22

Glenlevan (Glenlivin) td: Inishmacsaint FH 14;
71–72

Glenlough quarry: Cumber LY 28; 123

Glenlough td: Ballymoney AM 16; 24–25

Glenlough td: Cumber LY 28; 66, 69, 112, 118, 123,
126

Glenlough wood: Cumber LY 28; 118

Glenloughan stone: Aghaderg DN 12; 7

Glenloughan td: Aghaderg DN 12; 2–3

Glenluce (see Glenhugh): Ahoghill AM 23; 43

Glenmacuil (see Glenmaquill): Magherafelt LY 6;
112

Glenmakeen td: Donagh DL 38; 31

Glenmakeeran bog: Culfeightrin AM 24; 43

Glenmakeeran cromlech: Layd and Inispollan AM
13; 57

Glenmakeeran graveyard: Culfeightrin AM 24; 73

Glenmakeeran mountain: Culfeightrin AM 24; 39,
42, 83

Glenmakeeran ridge: Culfeightrin AM 24; 36

Glenmakeeran river: Culfeightrin AM 24; 41–43,
73, 83

Glenmakeeran td: Culfeightrin AM 24; 72–73

Glenmakeeran Top hill: Layd and Inispollan AM 13;
55

Glenmanus corn mill: Ballywillin LY 33; 35–36,
39–40, 44, 48

Glenmanus old corn mill: Ballywillin LY 33; 40, 44

Glenmanus school: Ballywillin LY 33; 44

Glenmanus td: Ballywillin LY 33; 51

Glenmaquill old grave: Magherafelt LY 6; 108

Glenmaquill td: Magherafelt LY 6; 107–08, 112

Glenmaquin Lower td: Raphoe DL 39; 126

Glenmaquin td: Raphoe DL 39; 125

Glenmaquin Upper td: Raphoe DL 39; 126

Glenmeena (see Glenmenagh): Mevagh DL 38; 58

Glenmeenagh (see Glenmenagh): Mevagh DL 38; 55

Glenmeenan (see Glenmenagh)

Glenmeinagh (see Glenmenagh): Mevagh DL 38; 57

Glenmenagh corn mill: Mevagh DL 38; 57

Glenmenagh fort: Mevagh DL 38; 58

Glenmenagh hill: Mevagh DL 38; 54

Glenmenagh td: Mevagh DL 38; 55, 58, 63

Glenmona House: Culfeightrin AM 24; 45

Glenmona td: Culfeightrin AM 24; 45

Glenmore chapel: Carlingford LH 40; 60

Glenmore House: Blaris AM 8; 85

Glenmore House: Lambeg AM 8; 139

Glenmore td: Carlingford LH 40; 58

Glenmorning quarry: Leckpatrick TE 5; 123

Glenmorning river: Leckpatrick TE 5; 121, 123

Glenmunagh (see Glenmenagh): Mevagh DL 38; 55

Glenn chapel: Kilcronaghan LY 31; 80

Glenn chapel: Maghera LY 18; 8, 17, 29, 46, 65, 68–69

Glenn district: Maghera LY 18; 74

Glenn female school: Maghera LY 18; 29

Glenn graveyard: Maghera LY 18; 8

Glenn male school: Maghera LY 18; 29

Glenn, Billy: Drumtullagh AM 16; 102–03

Glenn, Cushey: Dunboe LY 11; 44, 76, 78

Glenn, Cushey: Magilligan LY 11; 115

Glenn, family: Ballywillin AM 16; 32

Glenn, Hugh: Ballywillin LY 33; 39, 44, 48–49

Glenn, Hugh: Coleraine LY 33; 92, 132–33

Glenn, James: Carrickfergus AM 37; 121

Glenn, John: Skerry AM 13; 120

Glenn, Joy: Blaris DN 12; 46, 50–51

Glenn, Samuel: Coleraine LY 33; 133

Glenn, Samuel: Dunboe LY 11; 66

Glenn, William: Ballywillin LY 33; 51

Glenn, William: Coleraine LY 33; 94, 130

Glennagannon river: Donagh DL 38; 31

Glennageeragh (Glenegeera) td: Clogher TE 5; 32, 45–46

Glennagiveny fort: Moville DL 38; 68

Glennagiveny school: Moville DL 38; 69

Glennagiveny td: Moville DL 38; 68, 70

Glennan fort: Donacavey TE 5; 67, 82

Glennan td: Donacavey TE 5; 76, 79, 81–82, 86

Glennawoo Island: Kilmacteige SO 40; 194

Glennawoo mine: Kilmacteige SO 40; 189, 195

Glennawoo td: Kilmacteige SO 40; 194, 196

Glennawoo wells: Kilmacteige SO 40; 196

Glenneely td: Lough Swilly DL 38; 135

Glennelly corn mill: Ardstraw TE 5; 14

Glennelly river: Ardstraw TE 5; 2, 5, 9–10

Glennigivinny (see Glennagiveny): Moville DL 38; 69

Glennoo td: Clogher TE 5; 34–35, 38–39

Glenny, David: Newry DN 3; 104

Glenny, George: Newry DN 3; 112

Glenny, I.O.: Newry DN 3; 99, 103

Glenny, I.W.: Newry DN 3; 98, 103, 112

Glenny, Isaac: Newry DN 3; 98, 100, 103, 111–12

Glenny, Joseph: Newry DN 3; 99, 104

Glenny, Melling: Newry DN 3; 103

Glenny, Messrs I.W. and Sons: Warrenpoint DN 3; 118

Glenny, Mr: Newry DN 3; 107, 110

Glenny, Robert: Newry DN 3; 100

Glenny, Samuel: Newry DN 3; 99, 103

Glenny, William: Newry DN 3; 92

Glennygannon quarry: Lough Swilly DL 38; 135

Glenoa (see Glenoe)

Glenoak House: Camlin AM 21; 70

Glenoak House: Killead AM 35; 11, 14, 46–48

Glenoe: Raloo AM 32; 80–84, 87, 89–92, 107, 115–17, 123–26, 128–29, 132–33

Glenoe adult school: Raloo AM 32; 97, 129

Glenoe bleaching mill: Raloo AM 32; 89–90, 124–25

Glenoe bridge: Raloo AM 32; 119

Glenoe chapel: Raloo AM 32; 121

Glenoe church: Raloo AM 32; 90, 95, 97–98, 105

Glenoe corn mill [I]: Raloo AM 32; 84, 89, 119–20, 125

Glenoe corn mill [II]: Raloo AM 32; 84

Glenoe cotton factory: Raloo AM 32; 81, 96, 120, 133

Glenoe district: Misc. AM 10; 129

Glenoe flax mill: Raloo AM 32; 84, 89, 120, 125

Glenoe forge: Raloo AM 32; 125

Glenoe fort: Raloo AM 32; 89

Glenoe meeting house: Raloo AM 32; 130

Glenoe national school: Raloo AM 32; 129

Glenoe ph: Tamlaght TE 20; 73

Glenoe plantation: Raloo AM 32; 132

Glenoe quarry: Raloo AM 32; 133

Glenoe school: Raloo AM 32; 90, 97, 117, 125, 129, 133

Glenoe Sunday school: Raloo AM 32; 130–32

Glenoe valley: Carrickfergus AM 37; 5

Glenoe valley: Glynn AM 26; 3–4, 6, 8–10, 16–17

Glenoe valley: Inver AM 26; 53

Glenoe valley: Kilroot AM 26; 60

Glenoe valley: Raloo AM 32; 80–82, 84–89, 92–93

Glenoe valley: Templecorran AM 26; 95

Glenoe water: Glynn AM 26; 4, 10

Glenoe water: Raloo AM 32; 80, 82–83, 86–89, 91–93, 124, 132

Glenoe waterfall: Raloo AM 32; 80–83, 87, 89–90, 121, 124, 132–33

Glenogira td: Clogher TE 5; 53

Glenone bog: Tamlaght O'Crilly LY 18; 122

Glenone bogs: Tamlaght O'Crilly LY 18; 86, 134

Glenone bridge: Tamlaght O'Crilly LY 18; 90, 111

Glenone fort: Tamlaght O'Crilly LY 18; 123, 134

Glenone Glebe House: Tamlaght O'Crilly LY 18; 91, 107

Glenone Kildare school: Tamlaght O'Crilly LY 18; 138, 142

Glenone national school: Tamlaght O'Crilly LY 18; 90, 111

Glenone Sunday school: Tamlaght O'Crilly LY 18; 142

Glenone td: Tamlaght O'Crilly LY 18; 90, 93, 98, 123, 136–38

Glenone village: Tamlaght O'Crilly LY 18; 82, 111

Glenoo lough: Clogher TE 5; 47

Glenoo mountain: Aghalurcher FH 4; 2

Glenoo td: Clogher TE 5; 47, 53

Glenoory (Glenorry) td: Mevagh DL 38; 56, 63

Glenoughty td: Leck DL 39; 119

Glenrandal bridges: Cumber LY 28; 9

Glenrandal footbridge: Cumber LY 28; 9–11, 85

Glenrandal glen: Cumber LY 28; 72, 78

Glenrandal river: Banagher LY 30; 108

Glenrandal river: Cumber LY 28; 4–9, 11, 18, 21, 24, 30–31, 67, 71–72, 84

Glenrandal river: Misc. LY 36; 119

Glenrandall (see Glenrandal): Cumber LY 28; 67

Glenravel glen: Dunaghy AM 13; 14

Glenravel glen: Skerry AM 13; 109

Glenravel river: Island Magee AM 10; 65

Glenravel river: Skerry AM 13; 120

Glenravel valley: Dunaghy AM 13; 10

Glenravelin cottage: Dunaghy AM 13; 19–20

Glenroan corn mill: Bodoney TE 20; 20

Glenroan school: Bodoney TE 20; 20

Glenrock chapel: Ardstraw TE 5; 11

Glenrock cloghogle stones: Ardstraw TE 5; 12

Glenrock td: Ardstraw TE 5; 12

Glens Cottage: Culfeightrin AM 24; 45

Glens td: Culfeightrin AM 24; 45

Glenshane altar: Dungiven LY 15; 93

Glenshane bridge: Dungiven LY 15; 10–11, 50, 52

Glenshane church: Ballynascreen LY 31; 9

Glenshane district: Misc. LY 31; 111

Glenshane mountain: Banagher LY 30; 74

Glenshane mountain: Drumachose LY 9; 129

Glenshane mountain: Killelagh LY 27; 99, 102

Glenshane mountain: Maghera LY 18; 74

Glenshane td: Banagher LY 30; 23

Glenshane td: Drumachose LY 9; 74, 101, 129

Glenshane td: Dungiven LY 15; 27, 51, 62–63, 103

Glenshane valley: Dungiven LY 15; 1, 3, 10–11, 51, 65, 80, 92, 106, 113

Glenshesk bridge: Culfeightrin AM 24; 39–40

Glenshesk bridge: Ramoan AM 24; 97

Glenshesk chapel: Ramoan AM 24; 113

Glenshesk glen: Culfeightrin AM 24; 42–43, 45–46, 48, 65, 79–80, 82

Glenshesk glen: Ramoan AM 24; 93, 98, 109

Glenshesk hills: Culfeightrin AM 24; 64

Glenshesk hills: Ramoan AM 24; 110

Glenshesk river: Armoy AM 24; 3

Glenshesk river: Culfeightrin AM 24; 36, 38–40, 42, 46, 49, 53–54, 64–65, 67–68, 78

Glenshesk river: Layd and Inispollan AM 13; 55

Glenshesk river: Ramoan AM 24; 86, 88–92, 96–97, 109, 114–15, 125

Glenshesk wood: Ramoan AM 24; 93

Glenside locality: Carrickfergus AM 37; 93

Glensiggan (see Glenviggan): Misc. LY 31; 143

Glensmill corn mill: Raymoghy DL 39; 133

Glensmoil (Glensmoyle) td: Clonleigh DL 39; 12, 197

Glenstaghy (Glenstahy) td: Ballintoy AM 24; 11, 32, 34

Glenstaghy Danish houses: Ballintoy AM 24; 32, 34

Glenstaghy enclosures: Ballintoy AM 24; 34

Glenstaghy grey stones: Ballintoy AM 24; 32

Glenstaghy hamlet: Ballintoy AM 24; 32

Glenstaghy rock: Ballintoy AM 24; 34

Glenstall flour mill: Ballymoney AM 16; 10

Glenstall td: Coleraine LY 33; 104

Glenswilly chapel: Conwal DL 39; 24

Glenswilly district: Conwal DL 39; 26

Glenswilly monastery: Faughanvale LY 36; 52

Glentaker (see Glentogher)

Glentaugher (see Glentogher): Donagh DL 38; 31

Glentidally fort: Tullyaughnish DL 38; 91

Glentidally Glebe td: Tullyaughnish DL 38; 97

Glentidally school: Tullyaughnish DL 38; 92

Glentidally standing stone: Tullyaughnish DL 38; 91

Glentidally td: Tullyaughnish DL 38; 97

Glenties: Blaris AM 8; 73

Glenties: Inishkeel DL 39; 71–72

Glentillade td: Leck DL 39; 119

Glentogher mine: Donagh DL 38; 31

Glentogher plantation: Donagh DL 38; 31

Glentogher river: Donagh DL 38; 31

Glentogher school: Donagh DL 38; 31

Glentogher td: Donagh DL 38; 31–32

Glentogher td: Muff DL 38; 81

Glentoosker hill: Lough Swilly DL 38; 109

Glentop mountain: Layd and Inispollan AM 13; 55

Glentown quarry: Misc. DL 39; 186

Glentown td: Misc. DL 39; 195

Glenullae (see Glenuller)

Glenullan (see Glenullin)

Glenuller grave: Dungiven LY 15; 111

Glenuller mountain: Desertoghill LY 27; 4, 17

Glenuller mountain: Dungiven LY 15; 63, 78, 80

Glenuller valley: Aghadowey LY 22; 4
Glenuller valley: Errigal LY 27; 35, 39, 41, 43, 59, 72, 76–77
Glenulleragh (see Glenullin)
Glenullin valley: Dungiven LY 15; 34, 103, 109
Glenullin valley: Misc. LY 36; 112, 114
Glenvagh (see Glenvar): Clondavaddog DL 38; 3
Glenvale House: Ballywillin LY 33; 48
Glenvale House: Newry DN 3; 111–12
Glenvannon hill: Drumkeeran FH 14; 62, 64
Glenvar bay: Lough Swilly DL 38; 100–01
Glenvar district: Clondavaddog DL 38; 9–10
Glenvar mass-house: Clondavaddog DL 38; 4
Glenvar river: Clondavaddog DL 38; 3
Glenvar river: Lough Swilly DL 38; 117
Glenvar valley: Clondavaddog DL 38; 6
Glenveagh lough: Mevagh DL 38; 54, 57
Glenviggan bogs: Ballynascreen LY 31; 2
Glenviggan td: Ballynascreen LY 31; 19, 143
Glenville cotton factory: Glynn AM 26; 40
Glenville House: Layd AM 13; 40, 47
Glenwar Burnfoot (see Glenvar): Lough Swilly DL 38; 100
Glenwhirry bridge: Glenwhirry AM 32; 77
Glenwhirry bridge: Rashee AM 32; 137
Glenwhirry meeting house: Glenwhirry AM 32; 75–76, 78–79
Glenwhirry mountains: Glenwhirry AM 32; 74–75
Glenwhirry ph: Ballyclug AM 23; 52, 54
Glenwhirry ph: Ballycor AM 32; 4, 9
Glenwhirry ph: Connor AM 19; 16–17, 19, 28
Glenwhirry ph: Doagh AM 29; 66, 90
Glenwhirry ph: Kilbride AM 29; 135
Glenwhirry ph: Kilwaughter AM 10; 106
Glenwhirry ph: Misc. AM 10; 129
Glenwhirry ph: Racavan AM 13; 86, 86, 93
Glenwhirry ph: Tickmacrevan AM 13; 122
Glenwhirry river: Ballyclug AM 23; 53–55
Glenwhirry river: Ballycor AM 32; 1–2, 8
Glenwhirry river: Connor AM 19; 17, 19, 28
Glenwhirry river: Donegore AM 29; 115
Glenwhirry river: Glenwhirry AM 32; 74–77, 79
Glenwhirry river: Kilwaughter AM 10; 108
Glenwhirry river: Rashee AM 32; 135–37
Glenwhirry school [I]: Connor AM 19; 28
Glenwhirry school [II]: Connor AM 19; 28
Glenwhirry valley: Ballycor AM 32; 1, 5
Glenwhirry valley: Glenwhirry AM 32; 75, 77
Glenwhirry valley: Rashee AM 32; 135–37
Glenwinny hill: Inishmacsaint FH 14; 71
Glenwoo (see Glenawoo): Kilmacteige SO 40; 196
Glenwood district: Clondermot LY 34; 49–50
Glenwood glen: Dungiven LY 15; 96
Glesly bridge: Raphoe DL 39; 131
Glinlougher (see Glentogher): Donagh DL 38; 31

Glinsk fort: Clondavaddog DL 38; 6
Glinsk village: Lough Swilly DL 38; 4, 115–16
Glinskin locality: Lough Swilly DL 38; 115
Gloona (see Gloonan): Ahoghill AM 23; 35
Gloonan Cottage: Ahoghill AM 23; 12, 15
Gloonan fort: Ahoghill AM 23; 35
Gloucester (England): Donaghcloney DN 12; 60
Gloucester: Donegal DL 39; 47
Gloucester, Earl of: Kilkeel DN 3; 53
Glover, family: Ballyscullion AM 19; 4
Glover, James: Ahoghill AM 23; 49, 51
Glover, James: Duneane AM 19; 106, 116, 120, 126
Glover, Jane: Drummaul AM 19; 90
Glover, John: Ballyscullion AM 19; 12
Glover, Joseph: Ballyscullion AM 19; 12
Glover, Martha: Drummaul AM 19; 91
Glover, Rodger: Drummaul AM 19; 83
Glover, Sally: Duneane AM 19; 123
Glover, StJohn: Duneane AM 19; 119
Glover, William: Aghagallon AM 21; 14, 17
Gloverstown td: Duneane AM 19; 123–24
Glower river: Banagher LY 30; 69
Gluaire church: Glynn AM 26; 17, 30
Glynfield (see Glenfield): Carrickfergus AM 37; 141
Glynford mills: Raloo AM 32; 133
Glynn: Glynn AM 26; 3–6, 9–14, 16, 20–22, 28, 30, 37, 39–44, 46
Glynn: Raloo AM 32; 83, 88, 119–20, 124
Glynn: Templecorran AM 26; 94, 107
Glynn bank: Raloo AM 32; 128
Glynn bleach green: Glynn AM 26; 5, 12, 14
Glynn bridge: Glynn AM 26; 6, 39
Glynn church: Glynn AM 26; 20, 22–23, 38–39, 44
Glynn church room: Glynn AM 26; 22, 35, 38, 47
Glynn corn mill: Glynn AM 26; 3, 5, 14, 37–38, 44
Glynn cotton factory: Glynn AM 26; 5, 12, 14, 38
Glynn estate: Glynn AM 26; 16, 18, 20, 28, 30, 43
Glynn female school: Glynn AM 26; 46–47
Glynn flax mill: Glynn AM 26; 3, 5, 12, 14, 37–38, 44
Glynn flax store: Glynn AM 26; 38
Glynn graveyard: Glynn AM 26; 30, 32, 45
Glynn hibernian school: Glynn AM 26; 35
Glynn hill: Glynn AM 26; 3–4, 9
Glynn House: Glynn AM 26; 5, 41
Glynn lime-kilns: Templecorran AM 26; 99
Glynn manor: Glynn AM 26; 30, 42
Glynn national school: Glynn AM 26; 5, 8, 12, 34–35, 44, 46
Glynn old church: Glynn AM 26; 3, 5, 12, 17, 30–32, 36, 38, 44–45
Glynn Park House: Carrickfergus AM 37; 57, 135, 141
Glynn ph: Carrickfergus AM 37; 71, 100
Glynn ph: Inver AM 26; 49, 55

Glynn ph: Island Magee AM 10; 15, 25, 27, 29, 35, 42, 48

Glynn ph: Kilroot AM 26; 62, 65

Glynn ph: Misc. AM 10; 129

Glynn ph: Raloo AM 32; 80, 82–83, 85, 88, 93, 98–99, 101, 125, 128

Glynn ph: Templecorran AM 26; 82, 84, 89, 99, 101–03, 128

Glynn public houses: Glynn AM 26; 37

Glynn saltworks: Glynn AM 26; 38

Glynn scutch mill: Glynn AM 26; 14, 38

Glynn spinning mill: Glynn AM 26; 3, 5, 12, 14, 37–38, 44

Glynn Sunday school: Glynn AM 26; 13, 35–36, 47

Glynn td: Glynn AM 26; 1, 11, 18, 41

Glynn water: Glynn AM 26; 3–6, 10–11, 14, 30, 37–39, 41

Glynn water: Raloo AM 32; 83, 87–88, 132

Glynnes (see Glynns)

Glynns district: Glynn AM 26; 1

Glynns district: Inver AM 26; 49

Glynns district: Raloo AM 32; 80

Goalstown (Westmeath): Ballyphilip DN 7; 13

Goat Island: Inishmacsaint FH 14; 70, 72

Goats, family: Muckamore AM 35; 65

Gob-an-Gharoan locality: Ardclinis AM 13; 3

Gobbin chapel field: Island Magee AM 10; 100

Gobbin corn mill: Island Magee AM 10; 81

Gobbin's Heir Castle: Ramoan AM 24; 90–91

Gobbins cliffs: Island Magee AM 10; 17–18, 64–65, 72, 75–77, 85, 90, 102, 104

Gobbins fort: Raloo AM 32; 123, 132

Gobbins Head: Racavan AM 13; 103

Gobbins Head: Templecorran AM 26; 122–23

Gobnascale Castle: Clondermot LY 34; 49

Gobnascale school [I]: Clondermot LY 34; 89

Gobnascale school [II]: Clondermot LY 34; 90

Gobnascale td: Clondermot LY 34; 8, 12, 38, 43, 56, 68, 76, 83, 107, 110, 112, 117, 125, 131

Gobnascale td: Convoy DL 39; 21

Gobnascale td: Donaghedy TE 5; 92

Gobnaskeal (see Gobnascale): Clondermot LY 34; 38

Gobnescale (see Gobnascale): Clondermot LY 34; 83

Gobrana hill: Camlin AM 21; 63

Gobrana House: Camlin AM 21; 62–63

Gobrana td: Camlin AM 21; 60

Goddart, Mr: Carrickfergus AM 37; 135

Godfred, King: Grey Abbey DN 7; 71

Godfrey, Ann: Ballyscullion LY 6; 77

Godfrey, Arthur: Ballyscullion LY 6; 49, 73

Godfrey, Capt.: Ballyscullion LY 6; 67

Godfrey, Edward: Ballyscullion LY 6; 73

Godfrey, family: Carnmoney AM 2; 76

Godfrey, John: Ballyscullion LY 6; 77

Godfrey, Rowland: Ballyscullion LY 6; 77

Godfrey, Thomas: Carrickfergus AM 37; 39, 148

Godred, King: Inch DN 17; 75

Goeenkoeggal creek: Lough Swilly DL 38; 123, 126

Goff, James: Killeeshil TE 20; 63

Gola abbey: Derrybrusk FH 4; 32

Gola House; Aghavea FH 4, 20

Gola Island: Lough Swilly DL 38; 123, 126

Gola lough: Ballyscullion LY 6; 44

Gola td: Aghavea FH 4; 23

Gola td: Derrybrusk FH 4; 30, 32

Goladuff td: Drummully FH 4; 39

Golagh lough: Donegal DL 39; 43

Golagh lough: Templecarn DL 39; 156–57

Golan hill: Donagh MN 40; 98

Golan school: Ardstraw TE 5; 13

Golan Sproul corn mill: Skirts of Urney and Ardstraw TE 5; 138

Golan Sproul td: Skirts of Urney and Ardstraw TE 5; 138

Golan td: Mevagh DL 38; 55

Goland Lower td: Dromore TE 5; 99

Goland river: Dromore TE 5; 95

Goland school: Donaghmore DL 39; 39

Goland td: Donaghmore DL 39; 37

Goland td: Dromore TE 5; 93

Goland Upper td: Dromore TE 5; 99

Golands td: Killymard DL 39; 101

Golden field: Island Magee AM 10; 58, 61, 103

Golden hill: Culfeightrin AM 24; 56, 58

Golden, James: Kilmacteige SO 40; 186

Golden, Rev.: Dunboe LY 11; 62

Golden, William: Kilmacteige SO 40; 194

Goldsmiths' Hall: Cumber LY 28; 58

Gole td: Kinawley FH 4; 114

Goles locality: Banagher LY 30; 100

Golladough td: Donacavey TE 5; 80

Golley, family: Aghalee AM 21; 36

Gondy, Dr: Comber DN 7; 34

Gonghree, family: Drumgath DN 3; 20

Goodall, William: Carrickfergus AM 37; 108

Goodland td: Culfeightrin AM 24; 74

Goodlatte's ferry: Clonfeacle AH 1; 24

Goodman, family: Lambeg AM 8; 135

Goodriche, Barton: Dromore DN 12; 74

Goodricke, Widow: Carlingford LH 40; 58

Goodwin, Lawrence: Ballynascreen LY 31; 24

Goodwin, Margaret: Carrickfergus AM 37; 122

Goodwin, Rev. J.: Currin MN 40; 89

Goodwin, Thomas: Carrickfergus AM 37; 131

Goodwine, Sarah: Banagher LY 30; 107

Goodwine, Sarah: Cumber LY 28; 65

Goold, family (Limerick): Clondermot LY 34; 60

Gooldy, W.R.: Carrickfergus AM 37; 112

Gooley, John: Hillsborough DN 12; 106
Goorteen (see Gorteen): Aghavea FH 4; 25
Goragh lough: Clondavaddog DL 38; 3
Gorden, Mr: Newry DN 3; 106
Gorden, Mrs: Newry DN 3; 108
Gordon, Alexander: Island Magee AM 10; 102–03
Gordon, David: Carrickfergus AM 37; 102
Gordon, David: Comber DN 7; 37, 39–41
Gordon, David: Drumbo DN 7; 60
Gordon, David: Dundonald DN 7; 65
Gordon, David: Island Magee AM 10; 95
Gordon, David: Killyleagh DN 17; 81, 85
Gordon, David: Kilmood DN 7; 95
Gordon, David: Magheradrool DN 17; 104
Gordon, David: Saintfield DN 7; 118
Gordon, E.: Blaris AM 8; 84
Gordon, Edward: Ahoghill AM 23; 39
Gordon, family: Ballynure AM 32; 56
Gordon, family: Bovevagh LY 25; 8, 52
Gordon, family: Carnmoney AM 2; 76
Gordon, family: Derryaghy AM 8; 103
Gordon, family: Derrykeighan AM 16; 89
Gordon, family: Island Magee AM 10; 85
Gordon, family: Kirkinriola AM 23; 124
Gordon, family: Racavan AM 13; 100
Gordon, family: Raloo AM 32; 123
Gordon, George: Down DN 17; 50
Gordon, George: Tamlaght Finlagan LY 25; 119
Gordon, J.T.: Island Magee AM 10; 69, 96
Gordon, James: Ballymoney AM 16; 17
Gordon, James: Blaris DN 12; 46
Gordon, James: Kilrea LY 27; 120
Gordon, James: Macosquin LY 22; 122
Gordon, Jean: Derrykeighan AM 16; 87
Gordon, John: Aghanloo LY 11; 31
Gordon, John: Carnmoney AM 2; 100
Gordon, John: Carrickfergus AM 37; 158
Gordon, John: Island Magee AM 10; 102
Gordon, John: Newry DN 3; 74
Gordon, Mr (Ballymoney): Ballyrashane LY 22; 63
Gordon, Mr (Ballymoney): Kirkinriola AM 23; 126
Gordon, Rev. J.F.: Down DN 17; 48
Gordon, Rev. J.F.: Loughinisland DN 17; 95–96
Gordon, Robert: Ballyscullion AM 19; 12
Gordon, Robert: Bovevagh LY 25; 53
Gordon, Robert: Carrickfergus AM 37; 186
Gordon, Samuel: Bovevagh LY 25; 8, 52–53
Gordon, Sarah: Ahoghill AM 23; 33
Gordon, Stewart: Clondermot LY 34; 41
Gordon, William: Ballymoney AM 16; 16
Gordonaghy td: Cleenish FH 14; 29
Gordonall td: Grey Abbey DN 7; 68
Gordonall td: Misc. DN 17; 123
Gore, F.: Faughanvale LY 36; 72
Gore, family: Manorhamilton Union LM 40; 52

Gore, Mr: Clondermot LY 34; 34
Gore, Mr: Garvaghy DN 12; 81
Gore, Mrs: Glenavy AM 21; 81, 85
Gore, R.B.: Emlaghfad SO 40; 181
Gore, Rev. Francis: Donaghenry TE 20; 39
Gore's bridge: Derryaghy AM 8; 109
Goremount House: Glenavy AM 21; 81, 85
Gores Island: Saul DN 17; 111, 114
Gorey Point: Lough Swilly DL 38; 134
Gorlachbeag lough: Templecarn DL 39; 157
Gormalsland locality: Carrickfergus AM 37; 94
Gorman, family: Aghalee AM 21; 31
Gorman, family: Ballynure AM 32; 56
Gorman, family: Shilvodan AM 19; 136
Gorman, Isaac: Hillsborough DN 12; 107
Gorman, John: Hillsborough DN 12; 106
Gorman, Philip: Hillsborough DN 12; 107
Gorman, Thomas: Templecorran AM 26; 106, 120,
    124
Gorman, William: Aghalee AM 21; 26, 29, 31, 37
Gormish Island: Inishmacsaint FH 14; 70
Gormley, Ann: Banagher LY 30; 91
Gormley, family: Carnmoney AM 2; 34
Gormley, Farril: Banagher LY 30; 91
Gormley, John: Banagher LY 30; 91
Gormley, Mary: Duneane AM 19; 115
Gormley, Patrick: Maghera LY 18; 47, 55
Gormly, Rev. Roger: Misc. LY 31; 122, 136
Gormon, family: Ballymartin AM 2; 15
Gormon's mountain: Derryaghy AM 8; 98
Gorn church: Aghabog MN 40; 63
Gorran school: Aghadowey LY 22; 20–21
Gorran Sunday school: Aghadowey LY 22; 21–22
Gorran td: Aghadowey LY 22; 20, 35
Gorring, S.: Kildress TE 20; 60
Gorry Grum's well: Macosquin LY 22; 107
Gorry's Castle: Ballyrashane LY 22; 57–58
Gort farm: Desertoghill LY 27; 22
Gort Glebe House: Clonmany DL 38; 12, 14
Gort Glebe td: Raphoe DL 39; 126
Gort graveyard: Ballinderry TE 20; 11
Gort graveyard: Errigal Keerogue TE 20; 53
Gort of Cooladerry td: Raphoe DL 39; 126
Gort old church: Errigal Keerogue TE 20; 50, 53
Gort school: Errigal Keerogue TE 20; 53
Gort td: Clonmany DL 38; 12
Gort td: Errigal Keerogue TE 20; 50, 53, 57
Gort td: Magilligan LY 11; 95, 126, 136–37
Gort td: Misc. DL 39; 197
Gort td [I]: Moville DL 38; 73
Gort td [II]: Moville DL 38; 73
Gortacharn td: Aghalurcher FH 4; 14
Gortachork school: Donaghmore DL 39; 39
Gortachork td: Donaghmore DL 39; 29, 37
Gortaclare flax mill: Clogherny TE 20; 27

Gortaclare fort: Bovevagh LY 25; 30

Gortaclare td: Banagher LY 30; 23–24

Gortaclare td: Bovevagh LY 25; 13, 16, 19, 29, 31, 47, 50, 59

Gortaclare td: Donaghedy TE 5; 92

Gortadee school: Layd AM 13; 53

Gortadrehid Big td: Rossorry FH 14; 117

Gortadrehid td: Cleenish FH 14; 29

Gortagharn td: Drummaul AM 19, 33

Gortagherty cave: Faughanvale LY 36; 15

Gortagherty Lower td: Faughanvale LY 36; 17, 23, 58, 68, 74–75, 86, 94, 99

Gortagherty td: Faughanvale LY 36; 11, 15, 53

Gortagherty Upper td: Faughanvale LY 36; 17, 58, 68, 75, 86, 94

Gortagilly bog: Desertlyn LY 31; 44

Gortagilly hill: Desertlyn LY 31; 36

Gortagilly school: Desertlyn LY 31; 50–51

Gortagilly Sunday school: Desertlyn LY 31; 51

Gortagriffen td: Killesher FH 14; 87

Gortahar (Gortahare) td: Rasharkin AM 23; 139

Gortahar fort: Rasharkin AM 23; 139

Gortahar school: Rasharkin AM 23; 141

Gortaherron fort: Ahoghill AM 23; 34

Gortaherty (see Gortagherty): Faughanvale LY 36; 86

Gortahork: Lough Swilly DL 38; 122–23

Gortahurk (small) td: Cleenish FH 14; 29

Gortahurk bog: Kilcronaghan LY 31; 64

Gortahurk coal mines: Misc. LY 31; 113

Gortahurk corn mill: Kilcronaghan LY 31; 67, 82–83

Gortahurk fort: Kilcronaghan LY 31; 86

Gortahurk hill: Kilcronaghan LY 31; 75

Gortahurk House: Kilcronaghan LY 31; 67

Gortahurk quarry: Tomregan FH 4; 130

Gortahurk td: Cleenish FH 14; 20, 29

Gortahurk td: Kilcronaghan LY 31; 64, 76, 78–79, 83, 85, 141–42

Gortahurk td: Lissan LY 31; 102

Gortahurk td: Tomregan FH 4; 130

Gortahurk wood: Kilcronaghan LY 31; 64, 86

Gortakeerin td: Killoran and Kilvarnet SO 40; 183

Gortaloughan school: Magheracross FH 14; 99

Gortaloughan td: Magheracross FH 14; 102

Gortalughany (Gortalackney) td: Killesher FH 14; 87

Gortalughany (Gortaluckny) td: Kinawley FH 4; 110

Gortamney bog: Kilcronaghan LY 31; 78

Gortamney fort: Kilcronaghan LY 31; 86

Gort-an-Anama village: Drumachose LY 9; 90

Gortanewry glen: Desertmartin LY 31; 52

Gortanewry td: Desertmartin LY 31; 62, 112, 141–42

Gortanny td: Moville DL 38; 73

Gortanury (see Gortanewry): Misc. LY 31; 112

Gortaquigley td: Raphoe DL 39; 126

Gortareddin school: Tomregan FH 4; 129

Gortaree school: Tomregan FH 4; 129

Gortatoal (see Gortatole): Killesher FH 14; 82–83

Gortatole (Gortatoal) td: Killesher FH 14; 82–83, 87

Gortatole td: Cleenish FH 14; 29

Gortaway td: Tullyaughnish DL 38; 97

Gortbrannan td: Galloon FH 4; 95

Gortcally td: Tullyaughnish DL 38; 96

Gortconny bog: Ramoan AM 24; 120

Gortconny cave: Ramoan AM 24; 122

Gortconny standing stone: Ramoan AM 24; 120

Gortconny td: Ramoan AM 24; 103, 120, 125

Gortcorbies (Gortcorbus) td: Drumachose LY 9; 58, 84, 87, 96–97, 101, 110

Gortcorbries (see Gortcorbies)

Gortcross td: Killygarvan DL 38; 47

Gorteade bleach green: Maghera LY 18; 32

Gorteade bleach mill: Maghera LY 18; 32

Gorteade fort: Maghera LY 18; 61

Gorteade hibernian school: Ballynascreen LY 31; 18

Gorteade hibernian school: Maghera LY 18; 32, 35

Gorteade school [I]: Maghera LY 18; 32

Gorteade school [II]: Maghera LY 18; 32

Gorteade td: Maghera LY 18; 22, 25, 65, 73, 79–81

Gorteally meeting house: Lough Swilly DL 38; 117

Gorteclar (see Gortalare)

Gorteen td: Aghavea FH 4; 23, 25

Gorteen td: Cleenish FH 14; 29

Gorteen td: Enniskillen FH 4; 65

Gortemore (see Gortermone): Kilmacteige SO 40; 193

Gortenlearm (see Gortinlieve): Misc. DL 39; 186

Gortenleave (see Gortinlieve): Misc. DL 39; 192

Gortenny (Gorthinny) td: Faughanvale LY 36; 17, 53, 58, 68, 75, 86, 94

Gortenny wood: Faughanvale LY 36; 86

Gortereghy flax mill: Rasharkin AM 23; 131

Gortermone td: Kilmacteige SO 40; 193, 196

Gortersluin (Quarterslane) td: Kilmacteige SO 40; 194–96

Gortersluin pound: Kilmacteige SO 40; 194

Gortfad bleach green: Errigal LY 27; 40, 58–59

Gortfad bridge: Errigal LY 27; 41, 59

Gortfad carn: Errigal LY 27; 44, 75–76

Gortfad flax mill [I]: Errigal LY 27; 40, 59, 93

Gortfad flax mill [II]: Errigal LY 27; 93

Gortfad giant's grave: Errigal LY 27; 44, 76

Gortfad old church: Ahoghill AM 23; 14, 25

Gortfad preaching house: Ahoghill AM 23; 25

Gortfad saw mill: Errigal LY 27; 40, 59

Gortfad td: Ahoghill AM 23; 50

Gortfad td: Donaghmore DL 39; 37

Gortfad td: Errigal LY 27; 41, 65, 82, 87, 90, 92

Gortflugh td: Killygarvan DL 38; 47

Gortflugh wood: Killygarvan DL 38; 38

Gortfree (see Gortree): Clondermot LY 34; 56

Gortfugh (see Gortflugh)

Gortgare td: Faughanvale LY 36; 17, 53, 58, 68, 75, 86, 94–95, 99

Gortgare td: Tamlaght Finlagan LY 25; 72–74

Gortgargon fort: Manorhamilton Union LM 40; 52

Gortgarn (Gortigarn) td: Drumachose LY 9; 87, 96, 101–02, 128, 131, 133

Gortgarn bridge: Drumachose LY 9; 119

Gortgarn chapel: Banagher LY 30; 13–14

Gortgarn chapel: Dungiven LY 15; 8, 20, 102

Gortgarn glebe: Drumachose LY 9; 96

Gortgarn hills: Dungiven LY 15; 70, 105

Gortgarn nunnery: Dungiven LY 15; 94

Gortgarn old chapel: Dungiven LY 15; 94

Gortgarn school: Banagher LY 30; 13

Gortgarn school: Drumachose LY 9; 85, 131

Gortgarn school: Dungiven LY 15; 116

Gortgarn td: Banagher LY 30; 23

Gortgarn td: Dungiven LY 15; 8, 22, 26, 46, 48, 62, 64, 70, 74–75, 83, 86, 89, 94, 105

Gortgarren (see Gortgarn): Drumachose LY 15; 128, 131

Gortgarren td: Galloon FH 4; 95

Gortgarron (see Gortgarn)

Gortgarron moss: Duneane AM 19; 119

Gortgarron td: Duneane AM 19; 119

Gortgill td: Duneane AM 19; 94, 123–24

Gortgleck td: Galloon FH 4; 95

Gortgole corn mill: Ahoghill AM 23; 13

Gortgole flax mill: Ahoghill AM 23; 13

Gortgole school: Ahoghill AM 23; 21, 45, 48

Gortgole Sunday school: Ahoghill AM 23; 48

Gortgole td: Ahoghill AM 23; 39

Gortgommon corn mill [I]: Galloon FH 4; 92

Gortgommon corn mill [II]: Galloon FH 4; 92

Gortgommon td: Galloon FH 4; 95

Gortgonis potteries: Tullyniskan TE 20; 139–40

Gortgonnel td: Enniskillen FH 4; 82

Gortgorgan school: Kinawley FH 4; 119

Gortgrana (see Gortgranagh): Clonleigh DL 39; 12

Gortgranagh demesne: Clonleigh DL 39; 4

Gortgranagh House: Clonleigh DL 39; 2

Gortgranagh plantation: Clonleigh DL 39; 5

Gortgranagh school: Galloon FH 4; 96

Gortgranagh td: Clondermot LY 34; 38, 56, 68, 110, 112, 117, 125, 131

Gortgranagh td: Clonleigh DL 39; 6, 12, 16, 192, 197

Gortgranagh td: Galloon FH 4; 95

Gortgranna (see Gortgranagh)

Gortgrannagh (see Gortgranagh): Galloon FH 4; 95

Gortgurran td: Aghalurcher FH 4; 9

Gorthagerty (see Gortagherty): Faughanvale LY 36; 94

Gorthmore locality: Drumachose LY 9; 111

Gorthraw td: Galloon FH 4; 91, 95

Gortica Sunday school: Clondermot LY 34; 93

Gortica td: Clondermot LY 34; 56, 68, 110, 112–13, 117, 125, 131

Gortica Upper school (see Racecourse): Clondermot LY 34; 89

Gorticah (see Gortica): Clondermot LY 34; 56

Gortican (see Gortica): Clondermot LY 34; 89

Gorticlar (see Gortaclare): Banagher LY 30; 24

Gorticlare (see Gortaclare)

Gorticloghan cave: Ballyrashane LY 22; 50, 62

Gorticloghan chapel: Ballyrashane LY 22; 62

Gorticloghan old church: Ballyrashane LY 22; 61

Gorticloghan td: Ballyrashane LY 22; 61–62, 66

Gorticloughan (see Gorticloghan): Ballyrashane LY 22; 66

Gorticloughan (see Gortycloghan): Desertoghill LY 27; 29

Gorticross (Gortycross) td: Clondermot LY 34; 56, 68–69, 72, 74, 110, 112–13, 117, 125, 131

Gorticross hill: Cumber LY 28; 27, 49–50, 80

Gorticross quarry: Clondermot LY 34; 36, 131

Gorticross quarry: Faughanvale LY 36; 4

Gorticross Sunday school: Clondermot LY 34; 92

Gorticross Upper school: Clondermot LY 34; 89

Gortigarn (see Gortgarn)

Gortigran td: Dunboe LY 11; 58

Gortilea school [I]: Cumber LY 28; 2, 16, 72–74, 76–78

Gortilea school [II]: Cumber LY 28; 72

Gortilea school [III]: Cumber LY 28; 73

Gortilea td: Cumber LY 28; 20, 66, 69, 112, 118, 123, 126

Gortileck td: Donaghedy TE 5; 92

Gortin: Ardstraw TE 5; 5

Gortin: Bodoney TE 20; 20

Gortin: Cumber LY 28; 21

Gortin: Drumragh TE 5; 107

Gortin: Kildress TE 20; 58, 60

Gortin flour mill: Tullyniskan TE 20; 140

Gortin gap: Cappagh TE 5; 17

Gortin hill: Kinawley FH 4; 113

Gortin Mayoghill bleach green: Aghadowey LY 22; 8–9, 12

Gortin Mayoghill bog: Aghadowey LY 22; 4

Gortin Mayoghill bridge: Aghadowey LY 22; 11

Gortin Mayoghill td: Aghadowey LY 22; 4, 11

Gortin school: Clondermot LY 34; 87, 91, 95

Gortin Sunday school: Clondermot LY 34; 92

Gortin td: Aghadowey LY 22; 8, 38

Gortin td: Clondermot LY 34; 38, 56, 68, 76, 110, 112, 117, 125, 131

Gortin td: Clonleigh DL 39; 10, 12, 197
Gortin td: Kinawley FH 4; 121
Gortinanima td: Drumachose LY 9; 96
Gortinare (see Gortinure): Killelagh LY 27; 97
Gortinbeg td: Misc. DL 39; 197
Gortindarragh tuck mill: Desertcreat TE 20; 32–34
Gorting (see Gortin): Kinawley FH 4; 113
Gortinlieve (Gortinleave) td: Misc. DL 39; 186, 189, 192, 194
Gortinmore td: Clonleigh DL 39; 12, 186, 189, 192, 194, 197
Gortinnagh (see Gortinreagh)
Gortinreagh td: Clonleigh DL 39; 12, 197
Gortinrede (see Gortinreid): Cumber LY 28; 47
Gortinreid (Gortnarede) td: Cumber LY 28; 47, 49, 60, 62, 95–96, 100, 105, 107–09
Gortinreid bog: Cumber LY 28; 47
Gortinreid wood: Cumber LY 28; 100
Gortinure (Gortanure) td: Killelagh LY 27; 99, 102
Gortinure forts: Killelagh LY 27; 97
Gortinure school: Killelagh LY 27; 100
Gortinure td: Banagher LY 30; 102
Gortinure td: Clondermot LY 34; 38, 56, 68–69, 110, 112, 117, 125, 131
Gortjonis (see Gortgonis): Tullyniskan TE 20; 139
Gortkelly td: Urney DL 39; 181
Gortlack chapel: Desertegney DL 38; 25–26
Gortlack old church: Desertegney DL 38; 25–26
Gortlack td: Desertegney DL 38; 27–28
Gortlaugh locality: Clondermot LY 34; 69
Gortlosky td: Killymard DL 39; 100
Gortlough: Killygarvan DL 38; 37
Gortlough td: Killygarvan DL 38; 37, 47
Gortmacrane bogs: Tamlaght O'Crilly LY 18; 86, 112, 126
Gortmacrane caves: Tamlaght O'Crilly LY 18; 112, 115
Gortmacrane fort: Tamlaght O'Crilly LY 18; 112
Gortmacrane giant's chair: Tamlaght O'Crilly LY 18; 112
Gortmacrane school: Tamlaght O'Crilly LY 18; 140, 143
Gortmacrane Sunday school: Tamlaght O'Crilly LY 18; 143
Gortmacrane td: Tamlaght O'Crilly LY 18; 97, 101, 125, 136, 138, 144
Gortmagole (see Gortnagole): Clonleigh DL 39; 12
Gortmessan td: Derryvullan FH 14; 46
Gortmessan td: Donaghedy TE 5; 92
Gortmessen (see Gortmessan)
Gortmesson (see Gortmessan)
Gortmillian (see Gortmillish): Armoy AM 24; 8
Gortmillish stones: Armoy AM 24; 8–9
Gortmonley td: Donaghedy TE 5; 92
Gortmore barracks: Drumragh TE 5; 106

Gortmore Birney td: Clogher TE 5; 38
Gortmore cave: Magilligan LY 11; 92, 127
Gortmore House: Magilligan LY 11; 131
Gortmore precipice: Magilligan LY 11; 98
Gortmore rocks: Magilligan LY 11; 99
Gortmore school: Magilligan LY 11; 110, 138
Gortmore td: Clogher TE 5; 44, 47, 51, 54
Gortmore td: Magilligan LY 11; 90–92, 95, 99–100, 126–28
Gortnabeade (see Gortnabrade): Mevagh DL 38; 63
Gortnabrade td: Mevagh DL 38; 55, 63
Gortnacapple standing stone: Dunluce AM 16; 118
Gortnacarrow bridge: Drummully FH 4; 35, 38, 40
Gortnacarrow td: Drummully FH 4; 39
Gortnachor Sunday school: Clondavaddog DL 38; 7
Gortnacor (Gortnacory) td: Magheramesk AM 21; 119
Gortnacor fort: Magheramesk AM 21; 125
Gortnacor Lower td: Magheramesk AM 21; 113
Gortnacor td: Blaris DN 12; 28
Gortnacor Upper corn mill: Magheramesk AM 21; 115
Gortnacor Upper td: Magheramesk AM 21; 114
Gortnacross (see Gortnagross)
Gortnacully school: Killesher FH 14; 86
Gortnaderrig td: Cleenish FH 14; 29
Gortnafry (see Gortnessy): Clondermot LY 34; 113
Gortnagallen (see Gortnagallon): Killead AM 35; 53
Gortnagallon school: Killead AM 35; 39, 51, 53
Gortnagallon Sunday school: Killead AM 35; 39, 51
Gortnagallon td: Killead AM 35; 40
Gortnagarn hill: Pomeroy TE 20; 70, 72
Gortnaghey (see Gortnahey): Bovevagh LY 25; 58
Gortnaghy (see Gortnahey)
Gortnaglin lough: Clondavaddog DL 38; 2
Gortnaglush meeting house: Tullyniskan TE 20; 138
Gortnagole giant's grave: Clonleigh DL 39; 3
Gortnagole td: Clonleigh DL 39; 12, 197
Gortnagorn td: Manorhamilton Union LM 40; 54
Gortnagrace td: Urney DL 39; 181
Gortnagranagh (see Gortgranagh): Clonleigh DL 39; 4
Gortnagrass (see Gortnagross)
Gortnagross (Gorticross) td: Dungiven LY 15; 26, 62, 70, 74, 85, 96, 105, 22
Gortnagross hill: Dungiven LY 15; 70, 105
Gortnagross quarries: Kildress TE 20; 59
Gortnagross td: Banagher LY 30; 23
Gortnagross wood: Dungiven LY 15; 3, 96
Gortnagullan (see Gortnagallon): Killead AM 35; 51
Gortnagullen td: Dromore TE 5; 93
Gortnahey Beg bog: Bovevagh LY 25; 51
Gortnahey Beg td: Bovevagh LY 25; 60
Gortnahey Canal: Bovevagh LY 25; 15, 31
Gortnahey fort: Bovevagh LY 25; 15, 31

Gortnahey More chapel: Bovevagh LY 25; 3, 58
Gortnahey td: Banagher LY 30; 23–24
Gortnahey td: Bovevagh LY 25; 9, 13, 19, 31, 45,
    51, 61
Gortnahy (see Gortnahey): Bovevagh LY 25; 15
Gortnaliblut fort: Manorhamilton Union LM 40; 52
Gortnaloghog td: Mevagh DL 38; 55, 63
Gortnalughog bank: Lough Swilly DL 38; 115
Gortnamoney td: Aghanloo LY 11; 17–19, 23, 37,
    40, 42
Gortnamoy td: Bovevagh LY 25; 44
Gortnamoyagh bog: Errigal LY 27; 49, 54
Gortnamoyagh fort: Errigal LY 27; 43, 71
Gortnamoyagh giant's footsteps: Errigal LY 27; 67
Gortnamoyagh giant's grave: Aghadowey LY 22; 32
Gortnamoyagh giant's grave: Errigal LY 27; 44, 71,
    78
Gortnamoyagh House: Errigal LY 27; 40, 58
Gortnamoyagh quarries: Errigal LY 27; 91
Gortnamoyagh standing stone: Errigal LY 27; 49, 78
Gortnamoyagh standing stone: Misc. LY 36; 116
Gortnamoyagh td: Banagher LY 30; 53
Gortnamoyagh td: Errigal LY 27; 42, 45, 66, 71, 73,
    82, 87, 90–92
Gortnamoyagh td: Misc. LY 36; 113–14, 116
Gortnamoyah (see Gortnamoyagh)
Gortnamuck school: Donaghmore DL 39; 39–40
Gortnamuck td: Donaghmore DL 39; 37
Gortnannyah td: Skerry AM 13; 108
Gortnaran td: Cumber LY 28; 6, 9, 67, 69, 83, 112,
    118, 123, 126
Gortnaran wood: Cumber LY 28; 118
Gortnare td: Cumber LY 28; 62
Gortnaread (see Gortinreid): Cumber LY 28; 49
Gortnarney td: Balteagh LY 9; 34, 39, 44–45
Gortnaskea (see Gortnaskey): Ballynascreen LY 31;
    33
Gortnaskea (see Gortnaskey): Cumber LY 28; 123
Gortnaskea House: Ballyclog TE 20; 15
Gortnaskea td: Ballyclog TE 20; 17
Gortnaskeay (see Gortnaskey): Misc. LY 31; 119
Gortnaskey (Gortnassey) td: Cumber LY 28; 30, 32,
    66, 112, 118, 123, 126
Gortnaskey bridge: Ballynascreen LY 31; 7
Gortnaskey quarry: Cumber LY 28; 123
Gortnaskey school: Cumber LY 28; 73
Gortnaskey td: Ballynascreen LY 31; 33, 119, 141,
    143
Gortnaskey wood: Cumber LY 28; 118
Gortnataragh (see Gortnatraw): Clondavaddog DL
    38; 6
Gortnatra (see Gortnatraw): Clondavaddog DL 38; 2
Gortnatrade (see Gortnabrade): Mevagh DL 38; 55
Gortnatraw district: Clondavaddog DL 38; 4
Gortnatraw forts: Clondavaddog DL 38; 6

Gortnatraw lough: Clondavaddog DL 38; 2
Gortnavein locality: Lough Swilly DL 38; 129
Gortnaverne cromlech: Tullyaughnish DL 38; 91
Gortnaverne forts: Tullyaughnish DL 38; 91
Gortnaverne td: Tullyaughnish DL 38; 91, 96
Gortnavernnear locality: Lough Swilly DL 38; 128
Gortnavernon (see Gortnaverne): Tullyaughnish DL
    38; 91
Gortnavilly td: Clonleigh DL 39; 12, 197
Gortnecrannaght district: Misc. SO 40; 200
Gortnee cave: Dunluce AM 16; 116, 118
Gortnefry (see Gortnessy): Clondermot LY 34; 72
Gortnegrane (see Gortigran): Dunboe LY 11; 58
Gortneskea (see Gortnaskey): Cumber LY 28; 73
Gortnessey (see Gortnessy): Clondermot LY 34; 42
Gortnessey (see Gortnessy): Templecarn DL 39; 160
Gortnessy fort: Templecarn DL 39; 160
Gortnessy school [I]: Clondermot LY 34; 42, 88
Gortnessy school [II]: Clondermot LY 34; 88
Gortnessy Sunday school: Clondermot LY 34;
    92–93
Gortnessy td: Clondermot LY 34; 56, 69, 72, 80,
    110, 113, 117, 125, 131
Gortnessy td: Templecarn DL 39; 164
Gortnest td: Raphoe DL 39; 126
Gortnomony td: Moira DN 12; 120
Gortonelan lough: Tomregan FH 4; 126
Gortree td: Clondermot LY 34; 56, 62, 69, 110,
    112–13, 117, 125, 131
Gortree td: Misc. DL 39; 194
Gortscreagan (Gortscreaghan) td: Cumber LY 28; 1,
    67, 69–70, 112, 118, 123, 126
Gortscreagan chapel: Banagher LY 30; 33
Gortscreagan chapel: Cumber LY 28; 1, 8, 14, 25
Gortscreagan school: Cumber LY 28; 72–73
Gortscreagan wood: Cumber LY 28; 118
Gortscregan (see Gortscreagan): Cumber LY 28; 1
Gortscreighan (see Gortscreagan): Cumber LY 28; 8
Gortsgreachan (see Gortscreagan): Cumber LY 28;
    67
Gortshalgan td: Drumglass TE 20; 40
Gorttyarran quarry: Lough Swilly DL 38; 135
Gortwey td: Donaghedy TE 5; 92
Gortycavan (Gorticavan) td: Dunboe LY 11; 43, 73
Gortycavan fort: Dunboe LY 11; 73
Gortycaw (see Gortica): Clondermot LY 34; 93
Gortycloghan fort [I]: Desertoghill LY 27; 26
Gortycloghan fort [II]: Desertoghill LY 27; 27
Gortycloghan td: Desertoghill LY 27; 19–21, 26, 29
Gortygrana (see Gortgranna): Misc. DL 39; 192
Gosford demesne: Mullaghbrack AH 1; 96
Gosford school: Mullaghbrack AH 1; 96
Gosford, Earl of: Tynan AH 1; 130
Gosford, Lady: Mullaghbrack AH 1; 96
Gosford, Lord: Ballymore AH 1; 12–14

Gosford, Lord: Kilclooney AH 1; 51
Gosford, Lord: Killyleagh DN 17; 86
Gosford, Lord: Loughgilly AH 1; 84–85
Gosheden fort: Cumber LY 28; 43–44
Gosheden td: Cumber LY 28; 40, 42, 46, 48, 60, 62, 67, 96, 100–01, 105, 107–09
Gosheden wood: Cumber LY 28; 101
Goshendon td: Clondermot LY 34; 38
Goss, Thomas: Carrickfergus AM 37; 193
Gosten, William: Rasharkin AM 23; 139
Goston, David: Artrea LY 6; 29
Goudy, Alexander: Newry DN 3; 104
Goudy, W.: Comber DN 7; 34, 43
Gough, John: Blaris AM 8; 18
Gough, Rev. T.B.: Clondermot LY 34; 99
Gould, family: Clondermot LY 34; 56
Gouldsberry, Rev. Francis: Cumber LY 28; 9, 70, 86
Gouldsberry, Rev. Francis: Longfield TE 5; 131
Gouna lough: Enniskillen FH 4; 44
Gourlay, Robert: Carnmoney AM 2; 78
Gourley, John: Saintfield DN 7; 116
Gourly, Thomas: Donegore AM 29; 130
Gow's lough: Kilmacteige SO 40; 193
Goward td: Clonduff DN 3; 5
Gowdy, family: Templepatrick AM 35; 118
Gowdy, Gilbert: Derryaghy AM 8; 96
Gowdy's bridge: Aghagallon AM 21; 6
Gowdy's Lock: Aghagallon AM 21; 6
Gowlagher, Capt.: Kilmacteige SO 40; 190
Gowlan village: Kilmacteige SO 40; 196
Gowna lough: Drumlumman CN 40; 12, 15
Gowragh (Gourach) td: Misc. DN 17; 130–31
Goyer, family: Blaris AM 8; 7
Goyer, William: Ballynure AM 32; 53
Goyer, William: Rashee AM 32; 141
Graan hill: Devenish FH 14; 52
Graan td: Devenish FH 14; 52–53, 58
Grace, Eliza: Drummaul AM 19; 91
Grace, John: Drummaul AM 19; 91
Gracefield: Artrea LY 6; 7, 14, 16
Gracefield: Artrea TE 20; 8
Gracefield Academy: Artrea TE 20; 9
Gracefield Academy: Ballinderry AM 21; 48
Gracefield chapel: Artrea TE 20; 9
Gracefield Cottage: Maghera LY 18; 8
Gracefield female Sunday school: Artrea LY 6; 21
Gracefield House: Maghera LY 18; 8, 73
Gracefield male Sunday school: Artrea LY 6; 21
Gracefield Moravian church: Artrea LY 6; 7–8
Gracehill Academy: Ahoghill AM 23; 3, 10–11, 18–20, 32, 40, 46
Gracehill Academy: Ballinderry AM 21; 48
Gracehill church: Ahoghill AM 23; 3, 10–11, 18–19
Gracehill cove: Ahoghill AM 23; 28
Gracehill day school: Ahoghill AM 23; 40

Gracehill female Sunday school: Ahoghill AM 23; 46
Gracehill fort: Derrykeighan AM 16; 91
Gracehill forts: Ahoghill AM 23; 28
Gracehill graveyard: Ahoghill AM 23; 19
Gracehill hotel: Ahoghill AM 23; 10
Gracehill House: Ballinderry AM 21; 48
Gracehill House: Derrykeighan AM 16; 84, 87
Gracehill House: Kirkinriola AM 23; 117
Gracehill inn: Ahoghill AM 23; 3, 10
Gracehill Ladies' Academy: Ahoghill AM 23; 3, 10, 19–20, 32
Gracehill male Sunday school: Ahoghill AM 23; 46
Gracehill post office: Ahoghill AM 23; 10
Gracehill pound: Ahoghill AM 23; 10
Gracehill savings bank: Ahoghill AM 23; 3, 10, 19–20, 24, 30
Gracehill savings bank: Kirkinriola AM 23; 99
Gracehill school [I]: Ahoghill AM 23; 49
Gracehill school [II]: Ahoghill AM 23; 49
Gracehill td: Coleraine LY 33; 126
Gracehill td: Derrykeighan AM 16; 78, 89, 91
Gracehill td: Killead AM 35; 42
Gracehill village: Ahoghill AM 23; 2–3, 6, 9–12, 18–20, 29–32, 35, 40
Gracehill village: Artrea TE 20; 8
Gracehill village: Ballyclug AM 23; 60
Gracehill village: Derrykeighan AM 16; 78
Gracehill village: Kirkinriola AM 23; 99, 120
Gracey, family: Ballee DN 17; 16
Gracey, Mr: Ballee DN 17; 15, 18–19
Gracey, Mr: Down DN 17; 58
Gracey's flax mill: Comber DN 7; 39
Graffan, Rev. James: Magilligan LY 11; 89
Graffog, giantess: Errigal LY 27; 44, 70
Graffog's grave: Errigal LY 27; 44, 70
Graffy td: Kinawley FH 4; 110
Graffy td: Urney DL 39; 181
Gragarnagh corn mill: Aughnamullen MN 40; 72
Gragarnagh td: Aughnamullen MN 40; 76
Graham, Alexander: Drumtullagh AM 16; 101
Graham, Alexander: Muckamore AM 35; 62
Graham, Andrew: Tamlaght O'Crilly LY 18; 138
Graham, Anne: Kilrea LY 27; 129
Graham, C.: Mevagh DL 38; 60
Graham, Christopher: Kinawley FH 4; 116
Graham, David: Aghanloo LY 11; 25–26
Graham, David: Tamlaght TE 20; 92
Graham, Eliza: Tamlaght O'Crilly LY 18; 138
Graham, Elizabeth: Larne AM 10; 128
Graham, family: Carnmoney AM 2; 76
Graham, family: Derryaghy AM 8; 103
Graham, family: Glenwhirry AM 32; 77
Graham, family: Island Magee AM 10; 70
Graham, family: Maghera LY 18; 13, 24, 48

Graham, family: Magherally DN 12; 114
Graham, family: Racavan AM 13; 100
Graham, family: Templecorran AM 26; 117, 119
Graham, Francis: Magheramesk AM 21; 130
Graham, H.: Down DN 17; 60
Graham, Jacob: Desertoghill LY 27; 21, 29
Graham, James (Jnr): Kilrea LY 27; 129
Graham, James (Snr): Kilrea LY 27; 129
Graham, James: Ballyscullion AM 19; 13
Graham, James: Dunboe LY 11; 60
Graham, James: Garvaghy DN 12; 83
Graham, James: Glenwhirry AM 32; 77
Graham, James: Magheramesk AM 21; 122,
    124–25, 130
Graham, James: Tamlaght TE 20; 76, 103
Graham, James [I]: Maghera LY 18; 29
Graham, James [II]: Maghera LY 18; 51
Graham, Jane: Carrickfergus AM 37; 21
Graham, John: Blaris AM 8; 45
Graham, John: Blaris DN 12; 40
Graham, John: Down DN 17; 59
Graham, John: Drumbo DN 7; 58
Graham, John: Kilrea LY 27; 129
Graham, Jonathan: Maghera LY 18; 51
Graham, Margaret: Drumbeg AM 8; 133
Graham, Mr (Ballyplunt): Bright DN 17; 36
Graham, Mr (Devlinreagh): Lough Swilly DL 38;
    117
Graham, Mr: Donegal DL 39; 47
Graham, Mr: Enniskillen FH 4; 85
Graham, Mr: Killymard DL 39; 96
Graham, Mr: Misc. AM 10; 129
Graham, Mrs: Blaris AM 8; 84
Graham, Mrs: Muckamore AM 35; 79
Graham, Nancy: Kilrea LY 27; 129
Graham, Rea: Tamlaght O'Crilly LY 18; 116
Graham, Rebecca: Magheramesk AM 21; 130
Graham, Rev. Charles: Lissan LY 31; 104
Graham, Rev. Jackson: Loughguile AM 13; 77
Graham, Rev. James: Clogher TE 5; 53
Graham, Rev. James: Errigal Keerogue TE 20; 49
Graham, Rev. James: Errigal LY 27; 44, 76
Graham, Rev. John: Aghanloo LY 11; 14
Graham, Rev. John: Clonleigh DL 39; 9, 17, 186
Graham, Rev. John: Coleraine LY 33; 155
Graham, Rev. John: Lissan LY 31; 104
Graham, Rev. John: Magilligan LY 11; 85, 89, 93,
    115, 118, 124–25, 144, 146
Graham, Rev. Robert: Kilrea LY 27; 126
Graham, Rev. Robert: Magilligan LY 11; 89
Graham, Robert (Jnr): Maghera LY 18; 53
Graham, Robert (Snr): Maghera LY 18; 53
Graham, Robert: Aghalurcher FH 4; 8, 14
Graham, Robert: Blaris DN 12; 45, 49
Graham, Robert: Kilrea LY 27; 129

Graham, Sally: Kilrea LY 27; 129
Graham, Samuel: Kilrea LY 27; 129
Graham, Watty: Maghera LY 18; 74
Graham, William: Aghalee AM 21; 38, 40
Graham, William: Blaris AM 8; 37, 49, 55, 60,
    67–68, 77
Graham, William: Blaris DN 12; 32, 45, 49
Graham, William: Carrickfergus AM 37; 195
Graham, William: Derryaghy AM 8; 97
Graham, William: Dunboe LY 11; 59–60, 73
Graham, William: Kilrea LY 27; 129
Graham, William: Kinawley FH 4; 116
Graham's bridge: Dundonald DN 7; 65
Grahame, Lt: Derryvullan FH 14; 39
Grahamsland school: Donaghmore DL 39; 40
Grahamsland td: Donaghmore DL 39; 37
Grainger, family: Carnmoney AM 2; 76
Grainger, family: Derryaghy AM 8; 103
Grainia Castle: Island Magee AM 10; 48
Grakey (see Grawkey): Raymoghy DL 39; 141
Grakeys (see Grawkey): Raymoghy DL 39; 141
Grallaghgreenan meeting house: Drumballyroney
    DN 3; 15
Grallaghgreenan td: Drumballyroney DN 3; 14, 18
Grallon, Rev.: Magheraculmoney FH 14; 113
Grampian (Scotland): Misc. LY 31; 140
Granagh (Grannagh) td: Aghanloo LY 11; 10,
    18–19, 22–23, 25, 37, 39–42
Granagh school: Rasharkin AM 23; 134
Granagh school [I]: Aghanloo LY 11; 15
Granagh school [II]: Aghanloo LY 11; 15
Granagh td: Ballyphilip DN 7; 8
Granagh td: Misc. DN 17; 125
Granaghan (Granahan) td: Killelagh LY 27; 95, 99,
    101–02
Granaghan carn: Killelagh LY 27; 101
Granaghan Castle: Killelagh LY 27; 97, 100
Granaghan chapel: Killelagh LY 27; 96, 98, 100,
    102–03
Granaghan flax mill: Killelagh LY 27; 96
Granaghan fort: Killelagh LY 27; 97
Granaghan hill: Killelagh LY 27; 102
Granaghan Irish school: Killelagh LY 27; 100
Granaghan school: Killelagh LY 27; 100
Granaghan stone chamber: Killelagh LY 27; 100
Granaghan td: Maghera LY 18; 25, 64
Granaghan, William: Magilligan LY 11; 89
Granan, family: Ballyclug AM 23; 63
Granard (Longford): Drumlumman CN 40; 13–5,
    17–18
Granard barrack: Clonleigh DL 39; 12
Grand causeway: Billy AM 16; 42
Grand cave: Billy AM 16; 42
Grandison, Lord: Blaris AM 8; 5, 88
Grandison, Lord: Blaris DN 12; 33

Grandshaw (see Gransha)

Grandy, Joseph: Newry DN 3; 99, 104

Grange bog: Desertmartin LY 31; 53, 62, 112

Grange chapel: Carlingford LH 40; 60

Grange chapel: Misc. DN 17; 122

Grange district: Misc. SO 40; 200

Grange East mountain: Aghanloo LY 11; 1

Grange fort: Errigal Keerogue TE 20; 53

Grange hamlet: Desertcreat TE 20; 32, 34, 36

Grange House: Ballyscullion AM 19; 9

Grange House: Killyman TE 20; 67

Grange Irish td: Carlingford LH 40; 58

Grange Lower school: Kilmore AH 1; 64, 70

Grange Lower td: Kilmore AH 1; 60–61, 70, 73

Grange meeting house: Ballyscullion AM 19; 10

Grange meeting house: Desertcreat TE 20; 32

Grange meeting house: Killyman TE 20; 67

Grange meeting house: Lissan LY 31; 103–104

Grange mill: Ballyscullion AM 19; 13, 15

Grange Mill Quarter school: Ballyscullion AM 19; 13

Grange Mill Quarter Sunday school: Ballyscullion AM 19; 13

Grange Mill Quarter td: Ballyscullion AM 19; 11

Grange Mill school: Ballyscullion AM 19; 13, 15

Grange Mountain Bar td: Clogher TE 5; 47

Grange North mountain: Aghanloo LY 11; 1

Grange old meeting house: Ballyscullion AM 19; 8

Grange Park corn mill: Ballyscullion AM 19; 3, 10–11

Grange Park House: Ballyscullion AM 19; 11

Grange Park House: Killyman TE 20; 67

Grange Park td: Aghanloo LY 11; 20, 40, 42

Grange Park td: Ballyscullion AM 19; 13

Grange ph: Clonfeacle AH 1; 22

Grange ph: Drumcree AH 1; 34

Grange ph: Eglish AH 1; 43

Grange ph: Loughgall AH 1; 75

Grange quarry: Lough Swilly DL 38; 148

Grange river: Desertmartin LY 31; 52–55

Grange river: Donaghedy TE 5; 90

Grange school: Desertmartin LY 31; 61

Grange school: Killyman TE 20; 67

Grange td: Ballyscullion AM 19; 11

Grange td: Clogher TE 5; 35

Grange td: Clondermot LY 34; 47

Grange td: Desertmartin LY 31; 54, 62, 142, 144

Grange td: Donaghedy TE 5; 92

Grange td: Errigal Keerogue TE 20; 49, 53, 57

Grange td: Kilmore AH 1; 66, 70–71

Grange td: Lough Swilly DL 38; 142, 144–45, 148

Grange Upper td: Drumcree AH 1; 34

Grange Upper td: Kilmore AH 1; 60, 66, 68, 70, 73

Grangebawn (see Grangicam): Down DN 17; 48

Grangee td: Donaghadee DN 7; 45

Grangee td: Misc. DN 17; 124

Granger, family: Carnmoney AM 2; 102

Grangewalls (Grange Walls) td: Bright DN 17; 34–35

Grangicam (Grangeicam) td: Down DN 17; 48, 53, 55, 57

Grania's Bed: Banagher LY 30; 94

Grania's Bed: Bovevagh LY 25; 8–9, 53

Grania's Bed: Dungiven LY 15; 16, 20, 46, 90–91

Grania's Parlour: Bovevagh LY 25; 52

Graniagh glen: Cumber LY 28; 5

Grann, family: Magheramesk AM 21; 124

Granna hill: Mevagh DL 38; 54

Grannagh district: Misc. SO 40; 199

Granny school: Kilcronaghan LY 31; 74

Granny Sunday school: Kilcronaghan LY 31; 74–75

Granny td: Kilcronaghan LY 31; 73, 84–85, 143

Granny, family: Drummaul AM 19; 53

Granny, Neil: Ballyclug AM 23; 65

Granny, William: Lough Swilly DL 38; 136

Granny's bed: Clonmany DL 38; 16

Granny's bed: Tullyaughnish DL 38; 91

Granny's grave (see Carn Greine): Templepatrick AM 35; 110

Granra hill: Clondavaddog DL 38; 6

Gransha (Granshaw) td: Misc. DN 17; 124–25

Gransha cave: Newry DN 3; 110

Gransha corn mill: Comber DN 7; 31, 35, 38

Gransha flax mill: Newry DN 3; 78, 110

Gransha flax mill [I]: Comber DN 7; 30, 35, 38

Gransha flax mill [II]: Comber DN 7; 31, 35, 38

Gransha flax mill [III]: Comber DN 7; 31, 35, 38

Gransha fort: Dromara DN 12; 62

Gransha fort: Garvaghy DN 12; 79

Gransha forts: Newry DN 3; 110

Gransha graveyard: Island Magee AM 10; 99–100

Gransha lough: Clondermot LY 34; 118

Gransha manor: Misc. DN 17; 124

Gransha meeting house: Comber DN 7; 31, 35, 38

Gransha mill: Dromara DN 12; 63

Gransha old church: Island Magee AM 10; 100

Gransha old church: Island Magee AM 10; 47

Gransha paper mill: Newry DN 3; 110

Gransha private school [I]: Island Magee AM 10; 69

Gransha private school [II]: Island Magee AM 10; 69

Gransha river: Comber DN 7; 30

Gransha salt spring: Island Magee AM 10; 76

Gransha school: Bangor DN 7; 22

Gransha school: Clondermot LY 34; 41

Gransha school: Comber DN 7; 34, 38

Gransha school: Dromara DN 12; 64

Gransha school: Island Magee AM 10; 97

Gransha school: Newry DN 3; 82, 110

Gransha standing stone: Island Magee AM 10; 59

Gransha td: Ballywalter DN 7; 18

Gransha td: Bangor DN 7; 19

Gransha td: Clondermot LY 34; 38, 47, 56, 60–61, 67, 69, 76, 80, 110, 112, 117–18, 125, 132

Gransha td: Comber DN 7; 30–31, 35, 37–38, 42–43

Gransha td: Donaghadee DN 7; 45

Gransha td: Dromara DN 12; 63–65

Gransha td: Drumachose LY 9; 107

Gransha td: Island Magee AM 10; 14, 16, 33, 47, 58–59, 63, 69, 71, 76, 90, 95, 97, 99–100, 102

Gransha td: Newry DN 3; 78, 82, 110

Gransha td: Templecorran AM 26; 130

Gransha Upper school: Island Magee AM 10; 97

Gransha Upper td: Island Magee AM 10; 97, 101

Granshagh (see Gransha): Comber DN 7; 42

Granshagh Big quarry: Rossorry FH 14; 116

Granshagh Big td: Rossorry FH 14; 116

Granshaghmore meeting house: Clones FH 4; 28

Granshaghmore td: Clones FH 4; 28

Granshaw (see Gransha)

Grant, E.: Newry DN 3; 104

Grant, Edward: Carrickfergus AM 37; 112

Grant, family: Carrickfergus AM 37; 93

Grant, family: Kirkinriola AM 23; 124

Grant, Francis: Duneane AM 19; 105, 125

Grant, Henry: Newry DN 3; 99, 104

Grant, Hugh: Duneane AM 19; 122

Grant, Hugh: Newry DN 3; 81

Grant, James: Newry DN 3; 99

Grant, John: Carrickfergus AM 37; 195

Grant, Neil: Duneane AM 19; 123

Grant, Patrick: Newry DN 3; 99, 104

Grant, Rev.: Carrickfergus AM 37; 174

Grant, Rev. Joseph: Saintfield DN 7; 114

Grant, Thomas: Carrickfergus AM 37; 124

Grant, Widow: Hillsborough DN 12; 106

Grantshaw (see Gransha)

Grattan, H.: Aughnamullen MN 40; 75–76

Graughan, family: Island Magee AM 10; 70

Grave House: Urney DL 39; 181

Graves, Capt. (Castledawson): Magherafelt LY 6; 90, 96

Graves, Lt. T.: Lough Neagh AM 21; 92–93

Graves, Mrs (Castledawson): Ballyaghran LY 33; 21

Graves, Mrs Thomas: Magherafelt LY 6; 90

Graves, Rev. Thomas: Carrickfergus AM 37; 102

Graves, William: Artrea LY 6; 10, 26

Graveyard enclosure: Ballyrashane LY 22; 64

Graveyard field: Ballyrashane LY 22; 64

Grawkey (see Grawky)

Grawky Glebe td: Raymoghy DL 39; 137

Grawky Lower td: Raymoghy DL 39; 141

Grawky td: Raymoghy DL 39; 135, 137, 141, 199

Grawky Upper td: Raymoghy DL 39; 141

Gray stane: Templepatrick AM 35; 126, 151

Gray, Alexander: Tamlaght TE 20; 83

Gray, family: Drumbeg AM 8; 123

Gray, family: Dunsfort DN 17; 68

Gray, family: Kilroot AM 26; 74–75

Gray, family: Kirkinriola AM 23; 124

Gray, family: Racavan AM 13; 100

Gray, family: Ramoan AM 24; 107

Gray, family: Templecorran AM 26; 117, 119

Gray, Henry: Muckamore AM 35; 81

Gray, Hugh: Drumachose LY 9; 104

Gray, James: Muckamore AM 35; 80–81

Gray, John: Kirkinriola AM 23; 122

Gray, John: Magheramesk AM 21; 130

Gray, Leonard: Ardglass DN 17; 12

Gray, Leonard: Down DN 17; 42–43, 60

Gray, Lord Deputy: Kilmegan DN 3; 59

Gray, Matthew: Derrykeighan AM 16; 87

Gray, Rev.: Banagher LY 30; 14

Gray, Rev.: Bovevagh LY 25; 24

Gray, Rev.: Dungiven LY 15; 103

Gray, Robert: Ballyaghran LY 33; 22

Gray, Robert: Muckamore AM 35; 78

Gray, Samuel: Kilmore DN 17; 90

Gray, Widow: Ballymoney AM 16; 18

Gray, William: Derrykeighan AM 16; 87

Gray's locality: Muckamore AM 35; 80

Graycoil td: Clogher TE 5; 53

Graydon, J.M.: Clogher TE 5; 41

Graystone td: Donaghedy TE 5; 92

Grayton, Mr: Clogher TE 5; 54

Greagh bog: Ballybay MN 40; 78

Greagh hill: Ballybay MN 40; 78

Greagh hill: Errigal Truagh MN 40; 120

Greagh Island: Inishmacsaint FH 14; 73

Greagh td: Aghavea FH 4; 23

Greagh td: Ballybay MN 40; 84

Greagh td: Errigal Truagh MN 40; 120

Greagh td: Kinawley FH 4; 121

Greaghafeart td: Cleenish FH 14; 29

Greaghawoghan td: Kinawley FH 4; 110

Greaghcashel td: Galloon FH 4; 95

Greaghcrottagh school: Drung CN 40; 22

Greaghdromitt td: Magheross MN 40; 148

Greaghdromwisk td: Magheross MN 40; 148

Greaghgibney hill: Laragh CN 40; 39

Greaghlane td: Magheross MN 40; 148

Greaghlaticapil td: Magheross MN 40; 148

Greaghnaglearagh td: Cleenish FH 14; 25, 29

Greaghnaroogue td: Magheross MN 40; 148

Greaghrawer (Greagharower) td: Enniskillen FH 4; 48, 82

Greame Dyke (Scotland): Misc. DN 17; 130

Great Ards district: Grey Abbey DN 7; 68–69

Great Ballyhenry (see Ballyhenry Major): Comber DN 7; 42

Great Britain: Ardglass DN 17; 13–14

Great Britain: Banagher LY 30; 71

Great Britain: Blaris DN 12; 53

Great Britain: Clondermot LY 34; 85

Great Britain: Magilligan LY 11; 119

Great Britain: Misc. DL 39; 187

Great Britain: Misc. DN 17; 128

Great Britain: Misc. LY 31; 121

Great Deer Park Cottage: Tickmacrevan AM 13; 130

Great Deer Park fort: Tickmacrevan AM 13; 124

Great Deer Park td: Tickmacrevan AM 13; 124, 126

Great Mound fort: Glenavy AM 21; 79

Great Patrick cross: Carrickfergus AM 37; 30, 83, 91, 133, 180, 191

Great standing stone (see Culnagrew)

Great Steucan promontory: Billy AM 16; 41–42

Greatorex, Lt J.: Ballymoney AM 16; 1–4

Greatorix, engineer: Drumglass TE 20; 43

Greddy td: Lough Swilly DL 38; 144

Gree, David: Drumragh TE 5; 111

Greece: Misc. LY 31; 140

Green bog: Magherally DN 12; 113, 115

Green district: Carrickfergus AM 37; 92

Green field: Ahoghill AM 23; 17

Green Graves (see Ballycloghtogall): Misc. DN 17; 121

Green Hills House: Raphoe DL 39; 123

Green Island: Ardkeen DN 7; 1

Green Island: Ballyhalbert DN 7; 6

Green Island: Clondermot LY 34; 3, 18

Green Island: Killinchy DN 7; 86

Green Island: Killymard DL 39; 95

Green Island: Lough Swilly DL 38; 99

Green Island: Newry DN 3; 61, 87

Green Island: Saul DN 17; 111, 114

Green Island: Tartaraghan AH 1; 120

Green Island: Warrenpoint DN 3; 120

Green Island harbour: Killymard DL 39; 106

Green Island House: Carrickfergus AM 37; 135, 137

Green Island printing establishment: Carrickfergus AM 37; 137

Green lough: Tamlaght O'Crilly LY 18; 84, 94, 106, 121–22

Green Lough Castle: Tamlaght O'Crilly LY 18; 121–22

Green Lough chapel: Tamlaght O'Crilly LY 18; 90, 94, 106, 121, 136, 143

Green Lough Island: Tamlaght O'Crilly LY 18; 121–22

Green Lough school: Tamlaght O'Crilly LY 18; 141

Green Lough Sunday school: Tamlaght O'Crilly LY 18; 143

Green mill: Kirkinriola AM 23; 119

Green Mound hill: Glenavy AM 21; 82

Green Park House: Kilbroney DN 3; 35

Green Vale bleach green: Kilmegan DN 3; 58

Green Vale flax mill: Kilmegan DN 3; 58

Green Vale House: Kilmegan DN 3; 58

Green, Jacob: Magheramesk AM 21; 117, 119–20, 130

Green, James: Carrickfergus AM 37; 128

Green, John (Blaris): Hillsborough DN 12; 107

Green, John [I]: Hillsborough DN 12; 97, 106

Green, John [II]: Hillsborough DN 12; 106

Green, Patrick: Ballinderry AM 21; 46, 55

Green, Patt: Aghalee AM 21; 35

Green, Rev.: Ballymoney AM 16; 1, 15, 17

Green, Rev. William: Carrickfergus AM 37; 102

Green, Sarah: Carrickfergus AM 37; 120

Green, Thomas: Magheramesk AM 21; 120

Green, William: Hillsborough DN 12; 106

Greenagh potteries: Tullyniskan TE 20; 139

Greenan bog: Culfeightrin AM 24; 49

Greenan Ely: Faughanvale LY 36; 58

Greenan mill [I]: Aghaderg DN 12; 12

Greenan mill [II]: Aghaderg DN 12; 12

Greenan mill [III]: Aghaderg DN 12; 12

Greenan mountain: Kinawley FH 4; 107–08, 111

Greenan school: Faughanvale LY 36; 8, 24–25, 35–36, 66

Greenan td: Aghaderg DN 12; 2

Greenan td: Clondermot LY 34; 80

Greenan td: Culfeightrin AM 24; 49–50

Greenan td: Duneane AM 19; 120

Greenan td: Faughanvale LY 36; 17–18, 30, 53, 58, 68, 75, 86–87, 95, 99

Greenan td: Killymard DL 39; 101

Greenan td: Kinawley FH 4; 110

Greenan Top hill: Culfeightrin AM 24; 41

Greenan wood: Faughanvale LY 36; 87

Greenan woods: Killymard DL 39; 96

Greenan, Jeremiah: Lissan LY 31; 109

Greenan, John: Lissan LY 31; 109

Greenan, William: Lissan LY 31; 109

Greenanmore hill: Culfeightrin AM 24; 77–78

Greenaway, R.: Ballymore AH 1; 3

Greencastle (see Killycloghan): Kinawley FH 4; 117

Greencastle: Donagh DL 38; 32

Greencastle: Kilbroney DN 3; 30, 37

Greencastle: Lough Swilly DL 38; 137, 140, 142

Greencastle: Magilligan LY 11; 84, 88, 106, 123–24

Greencastle: Mevagh DL 38; 57

Greencastle: Moville DL 38; 69–71

Greencastle: Muff DL 38; 80–81

Greencastle: Newry DN 3; 65

Greencastle: Warrenpoint DN 3; 120

Greencastle Castle: Kilkeel DN 3; 52–54

Greencastle Castle: Moville DL 38; 70

Greencastle Castle: Newry DN 3; 64

Greencastle church: Moville DL 38; 71
Greencastle cotton factory: Carnmoney AM 2; 104
Greencastle district: Misc. LY 31; 116
Greencastle ferry: Moville DL 38; 76
Greencastle fort: Moville DL 38; 70
Greencastle Island: Lough Swilly DL 38; 117
Greencastle mountains: Moville DL 38; 78
Greencastle pier: Moville DL 38; 69
Greencastle Point: Kilkeel DN 3; 52
Greencastle td: Kilkeel DN 3; 52
Greene, Rev. John: Ballyaghran LY 33; 13, 22
Greene, Rev. John: Ballywillin LY 33; 37
Greene, Rev. John: Coleraine LY 33; 95, 143
Greene, Rev. William: Antrim AM 29; 26, 45
Greene, W.F.: Ballymoney AM 16; 17
Greenfield House: Connor AM 19; 21
Greenfield House: Convoy DL 39; 19
Greenfield House: Macosquin LY 22; 80–81, 83,
    92–93, 101, 104, 121
Greenfield House: Misc. DN 17; 130
Greenfield House: Raphoe DL 39; 130–31
Greenfield House: Templecorran AM 26; 128
Greenfield mill: Aghadowey LY 22; 8
Greenfield school: Connor AM 19; 27
Greenfield td: Convoy DL 39; 20
Greenfield, Robert: Ballynure AM 32; 43, 67–68
Greenfield, Robert: Doagh AM 29; 70, 87–88,
    92–93, 95–96
Greenfort House: Clondavaddog DL 38; 5
Greenfort Isle: Lough Swilly DL 38; 99–100
Greenhall House: Kilmore AH 1; 68, 71, 73
Greenhill bleach green: Aghadowey LY 22; 9
Greenhill corn mill: Aghavea FH 4; 20
Greenhill demesne: Aghavea FH 4; 18, 22
Greenhill Demesne chapel: Errigal Keerogue TE 20;
    54
Greenhill Demesne td: Errigal Keerogue TE 20;
    53–54
Greenhill farm: Aghadowey LY 22; 15
Greenhill House: Aghadowey LY 22; 6
Greenhill House: Aghavea FH 4; 20
Greenhill House: Killesher FH 14; 87
Greenhill locality: Taughboyne DL 39; 155
Greenhill quarry: Glenwhirry AM 32; 74
Greenhill td: Aghavea FH 4; 20, 25
Greenlaw bog: Leckpatrick TE 5; 120
Greenlaw td: Leckpatrick TE 5; 120
Greenlees, James: Carrickfergus AM 37; 118
Greenlough td: Banagher LY 30; 74
Greenlough td: Dungiven LY 15; 113
Greenlough td: Tamlaght O'Crilly LY 18; 90, 100
Greenmount bleach mills: Muckamore AM 35; 76
Greenmount fort: Banagher LY 30; 38, 48, 67–68
Greenmount House: Ahoghill AM 23; 17
Greenmount House: Clogherny TE 20; 25

Greenmount House: Drumragh TE 5; 109
Greenmount House: Muckamore AM 35; 55, 62, 75
Greenmount mill: Clontibret MN 40; 85
Greenmount td: Clogherny TE 20; 26
Greenmount td: Clontibret MN 40; 85
Greenoch (see Greenock): Tullyaughnish DL 38; 94
Greenock (Scotland): Drumachose LY 9; 117
Greenock: Clondermot LY 34; 30
Greenock: Coleraine LY 33; 89
Greenock: Dunboe LY 11; 64
Greenock: Lough Swilly DL 38; 119
Greenock: Tullyaughnish DL 38; 94
Greenore lighthouse: Newry DN 3; 72, 86
Greenore lighthouse: Warrenpoint DN 3; 119
Greenore Point: Warrenpoint DN 3; 119–20
Greenore td: Carlingford LH 40; 57–58
Greenshields Upper flax mill: Ballymoney AM 16;
    10
Greentown school: Killesher FH 14; 86
Greenville plantation: Ballymoney AM 16; 1
Greenville td: Ballymoney AM 16; 25
Greenwell, Andrew: Carrickfergus AM 37; 121
Greenwich (England): Island Magee AM 10; 79
Greenwoodhill td: Cleenish FH 14; 29
Greeny, James: Carrickfergus AM 37; 193
Greer and Boyd, Messrs: Blaris AM 8; 69
Greer, Archibald: Rasharkin AM 23; 141
Greer, Arthur: Ballymartin AM 2; 17
Greer, Arthur: Templepatrick AM 35; 150
Greer, Capt. (Randalstown): Drummaul AM 19; 72
Greer, Colin: Carrickfergus AM 37; 110
Greer, Ellen: Templepatrick AM 35; 148
Greer, family: Ballymartin AM 2; 6, 15
Greer, family: Blaris DN 12; 30
Greer, family: Magheragall AM 21; 99
Greer, George: Blaris AM 8; 81
Greer, George: Dromore DN 12; 78
Greer, J.: Kilmore AH 1; 72
Greer, Jacob: Templepatrick AM 35; 123, 145
Greer, James: Ballywillin LY 33; 40
Greer, James: Camlin AM 21; 73
Greer, James: Carrickfergus AM 37; 116
Greer, James: Coleraine LY 33; 131, 145
Greer, James: Drumragh TE 5; 107
Greer, James: Hillsborough DN 12; 105–06
Greer, James: Templecorran AM 26; 132
Greer, Jane: Blaris DN 12; 46
Greer, Jane: Templepatrick AM 35; 148
Greer, John: Hillsborough DN 12; 107
Greer, John: Island Magee AM 10; 95
Greer, John: Tamlaght O'Crilly LY 18; 113
Greer, Joseph: Derryaghy AM 8; 95
Greer, Joseph: Magherafelt LY 6; 107
Greer, Messrs Anderson and Co.: Blaris AM 8; 50
Greer, Miss: Blaris DN 12; 50

Greer, Moses: Kilmore AH 1; 60
Greer, Mr: Blaris DN 12; 32
Greer, Mr: Newry DN 3; 107
Greer, P.: Drumcree AH 1; 38
Greer, R.W.: Newry DN 3; 72, 98–99, 104
Greer, Robert: Artrea LY 6; 35
Greer, Robert: Blaris AM 8; 81
Greer, Robert: Tamlaght O'Crilly LY 18; 91, 109, 113
Greer, Samuel: Donaghcloney DN 12; 59
Greer, Samuel: Dunboe LY 11; 57
Greer, William: Artrea LY 6; 12, 31
Greer, William: Drumachose LY 9; 132
Greer, William: Hillsborough DN 12; 107
Greer, Willliam: Blaris DN 12; 46
Greer's lough: Saintfield DN 7; 117, 119
Greeves, John: Blaris DN 12; 45, 49
Greeves, Miss: Blaris AM 8; 85
Greeves, Misses: Blaris AM 8; 84
Gregarna (see Gragarnagh): Aughnamullen MN 40; 76
Gregg and Campbell, Messrs: Misc. LY 31; 143
Gregg, Anne Jane: Termoneeny LY 6; 133
Gregg, Cunningham: Holywood DN 7; 77
Gregg, David: Dundermot AM 13; 34
Gregg, David: Termoneeny LY 6; 133, 133
Gregg, Eliza: Termoneeny LY 6; 133
Gregg, Ellen: Termoneeny LY 6; 133
Gregg, family: Blaris AM 8; 21
Gregg, family: Carnmoney AM 2; 76
Gregg, family: Enniskillen FH 4; 58
Gregg, George: Termoneeny LY 6; 124
Gregg, Hugh: Termoneeny LY 6; 133, 133
Gregg, James: Ahoghill AM 23; 38
Gregg, James: Ballylinny AM 32; 26
Gregg, James: Coleraine LY 33; 110
Gregg, James: Dundermot AM 13; 35
Gregg, Jane: Carrickfergus AM 37; 135
Gregg, John: Carnmoney AM 2; 76
Gregg, John: Carrickfergus AM 37; 134–35
Gregg, John: Termoneeny LY 6; 133
Gregg, Joseph: Termoneeny LY 6; 133
Gregg, Mary: Ballymoney AM 16; 18
Gregg, Mary Anne: Termoneeny LY 6; 133
Gregg, Mr: Blaris AM 8; 85
Gregg, Mrs: Blaris AM 8; 24, 85
Gregg, Mrs: Blaris DN 12; 45, 49
Gregg, Rev. John: Carrickfergus AM 37; 70
Gregg, Thomas: Ballylinny AM 32; 15, 23, 25, 29
Gregg, Thomas: Ballywalter AM 2; 26, 29
Gregg, Thomas: Blaris AM 8; 36
Gregg, W.F.: Aghagallon AM 21; 20
Gregg, W.F.: Aghalee AM 21; 37
Gregg, W.F.: Blaris AM 8; 30, 51–55, 60, 66, 84

Gregg, W.F.: Blaris DN 12; 39–41, 43–45, 48–49, 51
Gregg, W.F.: Glenavy AM 21; 80, 87
Gregg, W.F.: Lambeg AM 8; 137, 139, 142
Gregg, W.F.: Magheramesk AM 21; 128
Gregg, W.F.: Tullyrusk AM 21; 133–34, 136
Gregg's mill: Loughgall AH 1; 81
Gregorlough hill: Magheralin DN 12; 109
Gregorlough td: Magheralin DN 12; 109
Gregory, family: Ballinderry AM 21; 55
Gregory, family: Macosquin LY 22; 84, 119
Gregory, John: Carrickfergus AM 37; 121
Gregory, Mrs: Coleraine LY 33; 72
Gregory, Widow: Muckamore AM 35; 78
Gregstown floodgate: Newtownards DN 7; 104
Gregstown td: Misc. DN 17; 124
Gregstown td: Newtownards DN 7; 104, 111
Grenally chapel: Agivey LY 22; 41–42
Grennan bog: Dromore TE 5; 93
Grennan mountain: Dromore TE 5; 93
Grennan td: Aghaderg DN 12; 12
Grennan td: Dromore TE 5; 93, 95, 99
Grennans (see Greenan): Killymard DL 39; 101
Grensha (see Gransha)
Gresham, David: Tamlaght Finlagan LY 25; 83, 122
Gresham, William: Carrickfergus AM 37; 111
Gresson, Henry: Aghalurcher FH 4; 14
Gresson, R.G.: Clogher TE 5; 53
Gresteel Beg school: Faughanvale LY 36; 8, 24, 27, 34–36, 66–67
Gresteel Beg td: Faughanvale LY 36; 17, 59, 68, 75, 87, 95, 99
Gresteel Beg td: Tamlaght Finlagan LY 25; 72–74
Gresteel More school (see Gresteel Beg): Faughanvale LY 36; 66
Gresteel More td: Faughanvale LY 36; 17, 59, 68, 75–76, 87, 95, 99
Gresteel More td: Tamlaght Finlagan LY 25; 72–74
Gresteel school: Tamlaght Finlagan LY 25; 78, 96
Gresteel td: Faughanvale LY 36; 53
Gresviske district: Misc. SO 40; 200
Greville, W.F.: Drumgoon CN 40; 8
Greville, W.F.: Drumlumman CN 40; 18
Grey Abbey abbey: Carnmoney AM 2; 64
Grey Abbey abbey: Muckamore AM 35; 69
Grey Abbey church: Grey Abbey DN 7; 68, 71
Grey Abbey corn mills: Grey Abbey DN 7; 69
Grey Abbey Danish mills: Grey Abbey DN 7; 72
Grey Abbey infant school: Grey Abbey DN 7; 69
Grey Abbey Island: Grey Abbey DN 7; 71
Grey Abbey meeting house: Grey Abbey DN 7; 68, 71
Grey Abbey monastery: Grey Abbey DN 7; 68–69, 71

Grey Abbey new meeting house: Grey Abbey DN 7; 68, 71

Grey Abbey ph: Ballyhalbert DN 7; 6

Grey Abbey ph: Donaghadee DN 7; 45

Grey Abbey school: Grey Abbey DN 7; 68, 70–71

Grey Abbey td: Misc. DN 17; 123

Grey Abbey village: Ardkeen DN 7; 2

Grey Abbey village: Grey Abbey DN 7; 67–68, 70

Grey fort: Kilmacteige SO 40; 196

Grey lough: Dunboe LY 11; 68

Grey Man's Path: Culfeightrin AM 24; 37–38, 44, 81

Grey Mare's Tail waterfall: Killymard DL 39; 95, 97, 105

Grey Point: Bangor DN 7; 22

Grey Stane Brae: Antrim AM 29; 37

Grey Stane Brae: Muckamore AM 35; 68

Grey Stane Brae: Nilteen AM 35; 96

Grey Stone farm: Magheramesk AM 21; 122

Grey Stone Park: Drumachose LY 9; 57, 111

Grey, A.: Carrickfergus AM 37; 43

Grey, David: Macosquin LY 22; 87, 106

Grey, Dr: Maghera LY 18; 53–54, 60

Grey, Edward: Aghalee AM 21; 34

Grey, Elenor: Drumachose LY 9; 132

Grey, family: Billy AM 16; 58, 68

Grey, family: Maghera LY 18; 13

Grey, James: Maghera LY 18; 53

Grey, Jane: Kilrea LY 27; 121

Grey, John: Billy AM 16; 60

Grey, John: Maghera LY 18; 50

Grey, Joseph: Carrickfergus AM 37; 118

Grey, Mrs Robert: Aghadowey LY 22; 33

Grey, Robert: Aghadowey LY 22; 34

Grey, Robert: Blaris AM 8; 23, 74

Grey, Robert: Magheragall AM 21; 105

Grey, Samual: Macosquin LY 22; 106

Grey, Surgeon: Newry DN 3; 99, 103

Grey, Thomas: Errigal LY 27; 61

Grey, Wesley: Magheramesk AM 21; 125

Grey, William: Ahoghill AM 23; 43

Grey, William: Blaris AM 8; 73

Greyabbey (see Grey Abbey)

Greyatirrive td: Galloon FH 4; 95

Greyhillan td: Loughgilly AH 1; 85

Greyhound lough: Lissan LY 31; 91, 102

Greysteel (see Gresteel): Faughanvale LY 36; 34

Greystone Hall: Drumachose LY 9; 51–52

Grianan of Aileach: Dunboe LY 11; 49

Grianan of Aileach: Faughanvale LY 36; 50

Grianan of Aileach: Misc. LY 36; 106, 108

Grianan of Aileach: Kirkinriola AM 23; 125

Grianans (see Greenan): Killymard DL 39; 96

Gribben, Edward: Carrickfergus AM 37; 109

Gribben, Edward: Coleraine LY 33; 73, 139

Gribben, Edward: Killowen LY 33; 159

Gribben, Henry: Carrickfergus AM 37; 121

Gribben, James: Coleraine LY 33; 73

Gribben, James: Drummaul AM 19; 75, 84

Gribben, Margaret: Killowen LY 33; 159

Gribben, Robert: Carrickfergus AM 37; 109

Gribben, Thomas: Carrickfergus AM 37; 109

Gribbin, Cornelius: Dunaghy AM 13; 24

Gribbin, Elenor: Aghagallon AM 21; 19

Gribbin, family: Dunaghy AM 13; 17

Gribbin, James: Desertoghill LY 27; 20

Gribbin, James: Tickmacrevan AM 13; 134

Gribbin, John: Errigal LY 27; 55, 74

Gribbin, John: Killelagh LY 27; 101

Gribbin, Neil: Ahoghill AM 23; 39

Gribbin, Owen: Aghagallon AM 21; 17

Gribbin, Patrick (Jnr): Aghagallon AM 21; 19

Gribbin, Patrick (Snr): Aghagallon AM 21; 19

Gribbin, Patt: Errigal LY 27; 44, 74

Gribbin, Thomas: Killelagh LY 27; 101

Grien mount (see Greenmount): Banagher LY 30; 38

Grien stones: Banagher LY 30; 38

Grier, James: Tullynakill DN 7; 123

Grier, Mr: Tullyaughnish DL 38; 87

Grier, Thomas: Desertcreat TE 20; 34, 36

Grier, Thomas: Magheragall AM 21; 111

Grier, William: Desertcreat TE 20; 36

Grierson, Messrs: Rathmullan DN 17; 109

Grierson, Mr (Moville): Moville DL 38; 70

Griffin, Denis: Carrickfergus AM 37; 118

Griffin, George: Newry DN 3; 100, 104

Griffin, James: Carrickfergus AM 37; 110

Griffin, Rev. G.: Clogher TE 5; 53

Griffin, Richard: Newry DN 3; 100, 104

Griffith, Benjamin: Ballymoney AM 16; 17

Griffith, Francis: Cumber LY 28; 73, 76, 84

Griffith, Hugh: Drumachose LY 9; 61

Griffith, Mr: Killesher FH 14; 83

Griffith, Patrick: Carrickfergus AM 37; 111

Griffith, Rev. Richard: Magilligan LY 11; 89

Griffith, Rev. Valentine: Rathlin Island AM 24; 131

Grifford, Rev. John: Kilrea LY 27; 126

Grig, Mr: Clondermot LY 34; 93

Grigorna (see Gragarnagh): Aughnamullen MN 40; 72

Grillagh abbey: Maghera LY 18; 10, 38, 41

Grillagh bridge: Maghera LY 18; 33, 64, 73

Grillagh corn mill: Maghera LY 18; 48

Grillagh evening school: Maghera LY 18; 33

Grillagh House (see also Gracefield): Maghera LY 18; 8

Grillagh monastery: Maghera LY 18; 73

Grillagh river: Killelagh LY 27; 95–97

Grillagh river: Maghera LY 18; 3, 48, 64

Grillagh Sunday school: Maghera LY 18; 29

Grillagh td: Maghera LY 18; 17, 22, 38, 41, 52, 68, 73

Grimes, Alexander: Billy AM 16; 64, 72

Grimes, Rev. Roger: Kilcronaghan LY 31; 65, 76

Grimes, Walter: Maghera LY 18; 42

Grimshaw, Edmund: Carnmoney AM 2; 46–47, 81, 83–84, 89, 103–04

Grimshaw, family: Carnmoney AM 2; 51, 76, 83

Grimshaw, James: Carnmoney AM 2; 42–43, 45–47, 54–55, 77, 79, 83–84, 93, 103, 105

Grimshaw, Messrs James and Thomas: Carnmoney AM 2; 41–42, 47–48, 51–53, 58, 61, 83, 89, 92, 103–05

Grimshaw, Mrs Edmund: Carnmoney AM 2; 87

Grimshaw, Mrs James: Carnmoney AM 2; 77, 79

Grimshaw, Nicholas: Carnmoney AM 2; 41, 51, 83, 104

Grimshaw, Nicholas: Carrickfergus AM 37; 62–63

Grimshaw, Robert: Carnmoney AM 2; 47–48, 53, 84, 89, 92

Grimshaw, Thomas: Carnmoney AM 2; 47, 83–84, 88–89, 105

Grimshaw, Weston: Carnmoney AM 2; 104

Grindle (see Crindle): Tamlaght Finlagan LY 25; 124

Groagy (see Grogey): Aghalurcher FH 4; 2

Grocers' Castle: Faughanvale LY 36; 2, 7, 12, 15, 31

Grocers' Hall (see Fallowlea): Faughanvale LY 36; 9

Grocers' mill: Faughanvale LY 36; 16, 28

Grogan, Elenor: Derryaghy AM 8; 98, 103, 114

Grogan, Joseph: Derryaghy AM 8; 92, 99–101, 103, 112–13

Grogan, Joseph: Drumbeg AM 8; 129

Grogan, William: Derryaghy AM 8; 95, 114

Grogey mountain: Aghalurcher FH 4; 2

Grogey td: Aghalurcher FH 4; 14

Groggan (Grogan) td: Drummaul AM 19; 39, 71–72, 90–91

Groggan bog: Drummaul AM 19; 39

Groggan bog: Duneane AM 19; 122

Groggan forts: Drummaul AM 19; 78, 88

Groggan Island bog: Ballyscullion AM 19; 3

Groman, Mr: Racavan AM 13; 102

Groman's tomb: Racavan AM 13; 101

Gronell chapel: Misc. DN 17; 122

Groog mountain stone: Loughguile AM 13; 69

Groog td: Loughguile AM 13; 70

Grooma, Neal: Bovevagh LY 25; 17, 43–44

Groomsport: Misc. DN 17; 117

Groomsport td: Bangor DN 7; 19, 21

Groomsport td: Misc. DN 17; 124

Groove Hill farm: Drumcree AH 1; 39

Grouse Hall: Templecarn DL 39; 158, 162

Grouse Hall mansion house: Drumlumman CN 40; 13–14

Grouse Hall td: Templecarn DL 39; 164

Grouse Lodge: Lissan LY 31; 90–91, 93–96, 98–100, 106

Grouse Lodge school: Lissan LY 31; 93–95, 100

Grouse Lodge Sunday school: Lissan LY 31; 95–96

Grove bridge: Desertoghill LY 27; 14, 16, 28

Grove Green Cottage: Blaris AM 8; 34

Grove House: Desertoghill LY 27; 3, 15–16, 24

Grove House: Errigal LY 27; 58

Grove meeting house: Muckno MN 40; 165

Grove td: Desertoghill LY 27; 29

Groves, family: Enniskillen FH 4; 58

Groves, William: Drumgoon CN 40; 11

Groves, William: Emlaghfad SO 40; 182

Growell (Growel) td: Dromore DN 12; 70, 73

Gruba bleach mill: Ahoghill AM 23; 13, 30–31

Gruba mills: Ahoghill AM 23; 29

Gruce lough: Devenish FH 14; 47

Gruig mountain: Layd AM 13; 37

Grumley, James: Aghanloo LY 11; 29

Grumley, Joseph: Aghanloo LY 11; 29

Gruy mountain: Loughguile AM 13; 58

Gub (see Gubb): Galloon FH 4; 87

Gubb school: Galloon FH 4; 96

Gubb td: Galloon FH 4; 87, 95

Gubbinagunnia td: Templecarn FH 14; 119–20

Gubbreesdinna td: Cleenish FH 14; 29

Gubdoo td: Drummully FH 4; 39

Gubnacruck corn mill: Killesher FH 14; 84

Gubrawella meeting house: Drummully FH 4; 35

Gubrawella td: Drummully FH 4; 35

Guckin, family: Magheramesk AM 21; 124

Gucking, family: Maghera LY 18; 48

Gucking, Peter: Maghera LY 18; 55

Guick, Mr: Kildress TE 20; 60

Guiey, family: Misc. LY 36; 104

Guile lough: Loughguile AM 13; 60, 62–63

Guiler, William: Dungiven LY 15; 116

Guiness td: Dromara DN 12; 65

Guinness, James: Carrickfergus AM 37; 130

Gulban, Conall: Donegal DL 39; 48, 51

Guldonaghy td: Cleenish FH 14; 14

Gull cove: Dunboe LY 11; 78

Gullado (see Gulladoo)

Gulladoo (Galladuff) td: Moville DL 38; 68, 70

Gulladoo (Gulladhue) td: Donacavey TE 5; 67, 76, 79, 81–83, 86

Gulladoo House: Moville DL 38; 70

Gulladoo school: Moville DL 38; 69

Gulladuff (Cullyduff) td: Maghera LY 18; 6, 22, 43, 45, 60

Gulladuff bog: Maghera LY 18; 56

Gulladuff female school: Maghera LY 18; 33

Gulladuff fort: Maghera LY 18; 61

Gulladuff male school: Maghera LY 18; 33, 51

Gulladuff td: Tamlaght O'Crilly LY 18; 110

Gulladuff td: Termoneeny LY 6; 129

Gulladuff village: Maghera LY 18; 6–7, 14, 51–52, 64, 74, 77, 81

Gulldalee (see Culdaly): Kilmacteige SO 40; 193

Gullen (see Gullion)

Gullion lough: Montiaghs AH 1; 89–93

Gully (see Ely Island): Devenish FH 14; 52

Gumersall, Hanna: Blaris AM 8; 81

Gumoge church: Ballintoy AM 24; 23

Gunick lough: Donaghmore DL 39; 29

Gunnalouge, Rev.: Cumber LY 28; 19

Gunnel td: Clogher TE 5; 34–35

Gunnell, John: Drumachose LY 9; 85, 122

Gunner, Thomas [I]: Ballyscullion AM 19; 12

Gunner, Thomas [II]: Ballyscullion AM 19; 13

Gunning, Alexander [I]: Carrickfergus AM 37; 33

Gunning, Alexander [II]: Carrickfergus AM 37; 142

Gunning, Daniel: Carrickfergus AM 37; 102

Gunning, family: Carrickfergus AM 37; 93

Gunning, Mrs: Carrickfergus AM 37; 162

Guns Island: Dunsfort DN 17; 71–72

Gurk, family: Blaris AM 8; 21

Gurlaw td: Clogher TE 5; 37

Gurley, William: Carrickfergus AM 37; 169

Gurney, Elizabeth: Balteagh LY 9; 18

Gurrtermore (see Gortermone): Kilmacteige SO 40; 196

Gurtadragon td: Convoy DL 39; 21

Gurtaskalee village: Kilmacteige SO 40; 193

Gurteen td: Tullyaughnish DL 38; 97

Gurteenagunnel fort: Manorhamilton Union LM 40; 52

Gurterslane (see Gortersluin): Kilmacteige SO 40; 194

Gusson, Mr (Sheebeg): Aghalurcher FH 4; 8

Gustavus III, King: Templepatrick AM 35; 150

Gustry, Rev. R.: Saul DN 17; 111

Guthrie, James: Coleraine LY 33; 72, 105, 148

Guthrie, Mrs: Coleraine LY 33; 72

Gutrie, James: Dunboe LY 11; 74

Gutrie, Mrs: Dunboe LY 11; 74

Guy, Adam: Newry DN 3; 100, 102, 104

Guy, George: Newry DN 3; 99, 104

Guy, John: Kirkinriola AM 23; 90, 96, 102, 113, 118–19, 122

Guy, John: Newry DN 3; 99, 104

Guy, Letitia: Bovevagh LY 25; 60

Guy, Maryann: Bovevagh LY 25; 60

Guy, Mrs: Newry DN 3; 100, 104

Guy's school: Kirkinriola AM 23; 90–91, 96, 102, 113, 118–20, 122

Guystown td: Clonleigh DL 39; 12, 197

Gweebarra bar: Inishkeel DL 39; 70

Gweebarra river: Inishkeel DL 39; 70

Gweedore district: Lough Swilly DL 38; 122, 126

Gwyllan, family: Glenavy AM 21; 86

Gwyn, Mr: Antrim AM 29; 44, 47

Gwynn, John: Clonleigh DL 39; 13

Gwynn, Rev. John: Ballynure AM 32; 50

Gwynn, Rev. John: Carrickfergus AM 37; 136

Gwynn, Rev. John: Kilroot AM 26; 59, 64, 78–79

Gwynn, Rev. John: Templecorran AM 26; 101, 127, 129

Gwynne, Jane: Urney DL 39; 182

Gyle, family: Carrickfergus AM 37; 179

Gynn, William: Carrickfergus AM 37; 185

H

Hillsborough Castle: Newry DN 3; 65
Hacker [or Harke], Rev. C.F.: Ahoghill AM 23; 40
Hacket, Dr: Newry DN 3; 100, 104
Hacket, Mr: Clogher TE 5; 41
Hackett, J.B.: Faughanvale LY 36; 66–67
Hackett, Rev. J.C.: Muckno MN 40; 167
Hackett, Rev. T.: Muckno MN 40; 167–68
Hackett, Thomas: Misc. DN 17; 117
Hackett, W.: Faughanvale LY 36; 47
Hacknahay school: Seagoe AH 1; 102–03, 106, 108
Hacknahay td: Seagoe AH 1; 102, 108
Hacknahey (see Hacknahay): Seagoe AH 1; 103
Haddick, Ben: Ballinderry AM 21; 48
Haddock, J.: Drumballyroney DN 3; 18
Haddock, James: Killead AM 35; 51
Haddock, John: Hillsborough DN 12; 107
Haddock, Mary: Island Magee AM 10; 41
Haddock, Molly: Island Magee AM 10; 95
Haddock, Mr (Mount Pleasant): Kilmore AH 1; 72
Haddock, Rev. Isaac: Carrickfergus AM 37; 25
Haddock, Thomas (Jnr): Killead AM 35; 51
Haddock, Thomas (Snr): Killead AM 35; 51
Haddock's town: Blaris DN 12; 42
Haddon, Woolsley: Drumcree AH 1; 30, 33
Hadron, Richard: Ballyscullion LY 6; 57
Hadson, family: Magheracloone MN 40; 142
Hadson's Fee Farm district: Magheracloone MN 40;
    142
Haffner, Dr: Kilcronaghan LY 31; 81
Hagan, Arthur: Artrea LY 6; 10, 26
Hagan, Arthur: Drummaul AM 19; 70–71
Hagan, Bridget: Ballynascreen LY 31; 14, 21
Hagan, Eliza: Lissan LY 31; 109
Hagan, family: Ballynure AM 32; 56
Hagan, family: Ballyscullion LY 6; 58
Hagan, family: Maghera LY 18; 19, 24, 48
Hagan, Hugh: Ballynascreen LY 31; 21
Hagan, James: Blaris DN 12; 46, 49
Hagan, James: Carrickfergus AM 37; 117
Hagan, James: Kilcronaghan LY 31; 85
Hagan, John: Carrickfergus AM 37; 115–16, 121
Hagan, John: Kirkinriola AM 23; 122
Hagan, John: Lough Swilly DL 38; 148
Hagan, Lawrence: Clonduff DN 3; 5

Hagan, man named: Duneane AM 19; 121
Hagan, man named: Misc. LY 31; 117
Hagan, Margaret: Kilrea LY 27; 130
Hagan, Martha (see O'Neill)
Hagan, Michael: Ahoghill AM 23; 33, 36
Hagan, Michael: Kilcronaghan LY 31; 85
Hagan, Nancy: Lissan LY 31; 109
Hagan, O.: Carlingford LH 40; 59
Hagan, Patrick: Carrickfergus AM 37; 128
Hagan, Patrick: Clonduff DN 3; 5
Hagan, Patrick: Drumachose LY 9; 131
Hagan, Patrick: Kilcronaghan LY 31; 85
Hagan, Peter: Banagher LY 30; 111
Hagan, Peter [I]: Lissan LY 31; 109
Hagan, Peter [II]: Lissan LY 31; 109
Hagan, Rev. Edward: Balteagh LY 9; 15, 44
Hagan, Sarah: Carrickfergus AM 37; 126
Hagan, Thomas: Carrickfergus AM 37; 155
Hagan, W.H.: Maghera LY 18; 51
Hagansland locality: Carrickfergus AM 37; 94
Hagerty, George: Errigal LY 27; 72
Hagerty, John: Errigal LY 27; 72
Hagerty, William: Errigal LY 27; 56, 58–60, 76
Haggan, family: Carrickfergus AM 37; 93
Haggan, Robert: Muckamore AM 35; 81
Haggan, William: Ballynure AM 32; 57
Haggen, Edward: Templecorran AM 26; 121
Haggins, man named: Kilmacteige SO 40; 188
Haghan, family: Skerry AM 13; 115
Hagherty, Charles: Drumachose LY 9; 109
Hagherty, George: Skirts of Urney and Ardstraw TE
    5; 137
Hagherty, Joseph: Drumachose LY 9; 132
Hagherty, Pat: Bovevagh LY 25; 19, 40, 42
Haghey, Dennis: Lissan LY 31; 101
Haghey, John: Ballynascreen LY 31; 13, 21
Hagin, Capt.: Clondermot LY 34; 113
Hagin, Henery: Tamlaght TE 20; 92
Haginin, family: Carnmoney AM 2; 76
Hairs, Rev. William: Clondermot LY 34; 5, 19, 23,
    97, 101
Haistings, Mr: Ballyphilip DN 7; 8
Haizly, Mr: Blaris DN 12; 44
Hale, Mr: Ballymascanlan LH 40; 55

Hales, Rev. Edward: Killdrumsherdan CN 40; 33
Hales, Rev. William: Drumgoon CN 40; 8
Half Town bog: Errigal Keerogue TE 20; 54
Half Town school: Errigal Keerogue TE 20; 54
Half Town td: Errigal Keerogue TE 20; 54
Halferty, family: Magherafelt LY 6; 95
Halferty, John: Magherafelt LY 6; 107
Halfgayne (Halfgain) td: Killelagh LY 27; 99, 102
Halfgayne school: Killelagh LY 27; 100
Halfpenny gate: Magheramesk AM 21; 118
Halfpenny Gate bridge: Blaris AM 8; 35
Halftate school: Magheracloone MN 40; 142
Halftown td: Donegore AM 29; 101, 131
Halftown td: Urney DL 39; 181
Halifax (Canada): Kilbroney DN 3; 31, 34
Halifax: Kilroot AM 26; 59, 78
Hall bridge: Kilbroney DN 3; 29
Hall Craig House: Devenish FH 14; 53
Hall House: Killea and Taughboyne DL 39; 87
Hall td: Taughboyne DL 39; 148, 153, 197
Hall, Alexander: Magheragall AM 21; 105
Hall, Anthony: Antrim AM 29; 37
Hall, Anthony: Carrickfergus AM 37; 90
Hall, Cathrine: Blaris AM 8; 60
Hall, Collins: Hillsborough DN 12; 107
Hall, Dr: Raphoe DL 39; 123
Hall, Edward: Carrickfergus AM 37; 158
Hall, Edward: Kilcronaghan LY 31; 69
Hall, family: Aghalee AM 21; 31
Hall, family: Drumbeg AM 8; 123
Hall, family: Enniskillen FH 4; 58
Hall, family: Misc. LY 36; 104
Hall, family: Racavan AM 13; 100
Hall, J.: Blaris AM 8; 60
Hall, James: Derryaghy AM 8; 105
Hall, John: Aghadowey LY 22; 34
Hall, John: Aghalee AM 21; 35
Hall, John: Ballyscullion LY 6; 57
Hall, John: Blaris AM 8; 20, 77
Hall, Margaret: Bovevagh LY 25; 28
Hall, Mary Ann: Blaris AM 8; 60
Hall, Miss: Enniskillen FH 4; 44
Hall, Mr: Cleenish FH 14; 28–30
Hall, Mrs: Blaris AM 8; 85
Hall, Mrs: Blaris DN 12; 50
Hall, Mrs Roger: Killevy AH 1; 54
Hall, Mrs Roger: Warrenpoint DN 3; 122
Hall, Nathaniel: Magheragall AM 21; 105
Hall, R.: Dunsfort DN 17; 67, 69
Hall, R.F.: Blaris AM 8; 8, 18, 25, 31–32
Hall, R.F.: Blaris DN 12; 44, 47–48
Hall, Rev. George: Ardstraw TE 5; 8–9
Hall, Rev. John: Ardstraw TE 5; 7–11
Hall, Rev. Lindsay: Donegore AM 29; 126, 129
Hall, Rev. Savage: Ballinderry AM 21; 46, 57, 59

Hall, Robert: Carrickfergus AM 37; 75, 151
Hall, Rodger: Newry DN 3; 74
Hall, Roger: Kilbroney DN 3; 32
Hall, Roger: Killevy AH 1; 54
Hall, Roger: Misc. DN 17; 130–31
Hall, Roger: Warrenpoint DN 3; 115–18, 120–22
Hall, S.: Derryaghy AM 8; 103
Hall, Savage: Warrenpoint DN 3; 120
Hall, Susanna: Ardstraw TE 5; 8
Hall, T.: Drumcree AH 1; 40
Hall, William: Ardstraw TE 5; 8
Hall, William: Enniskillen FH 4; 57
Hall, William: Killowen LY 33; 159
Hall, William: Templepatrick AM 35; 132
Hall's mill (see Laurencetown): Tullylish DN 12; 141
Halladay, man named: Ahoghill AM 23; 34
Halliday, A.H.: Carnmoney AM 2; 83, 90
Halliday, Dr: Carnmoney AM 2; 81
Halliday, family: Ballintoy AM 24; 18
Halliday, John: Hillsborough DN 12; 106
Halliday, Messrs: Carnmoney AM 2; 58, 102
Halliday, Mr (Derry): Clonmany DL 38; 20
Halliday, Mr: Desertegney DL 38; 29
Halliday, Mr: Killygarvan DL 38; 45
Halliday, Mr: Trory FH 14; 125
Halliday, Mrs A.H.: Carnmoney AM 2; 79, 85
Halliday, William: Blaris AM 8; 55
Halliday's bridge: Blaris DN 12; 28
Halpin, Dr: Drung CN 40; 22
Halpin, Dr: Killdrumsherdan CN 40; 34
Halpin, Dr: Laragh CN 40; 43
Halpin, George: Island Magee AM 10; 79
Haltridge, Robert: Derrykeighan AM 16; 88, 91, 93
Halyday, Arbuckle: Newry DN 3; 92, 99, 103
Halyday, J.T.: Newry DN 3; 99
Ham, Patt: Kilmacteige SO 40; 195–96
Hamal, Michael: Muckamore AM 35; 81
Hamburg (Germany): Carrickfergus AM 37; 137
Hametion, family: Tamlaght O'Crilly LY 18; 93
Hamil, Charles: Ballymoney AM 16; 17
Hamil, Mary: Carrickfergus AM 37; 116
Hamil, Patrick: Dunaghy AM 13; 22
Hamil, Thomas: Carrickfergus AM 37; 121
Hamill, Andrew: Donacavey TE 5; 81
Hamill, Eliza: Carrickfergus AM 37; 119
Hamill, family: Ballymartin AM 2; 6, 15
Hamill, family: Ballyrobert AM 2; 21, 24
Hamill, family: Ballywillin AM 16; 32
Hamill, family: Carnmoney AM 2; 76
Hamill, family: Derrykeighan AM 16; 89
Hamill, family: Lambeg AM 8; 135
Hamill, family: Skerry AM 13; 115
Hamill, Hugh: Kilroot AM 26; 78
Hamill, James: Ballymartin AM 2; 16

Hamill, James: Billy AM 16; 56

Hamill, James: Kilroot AM 26; 79

Hamill, James: Macosquin LY 22; 80, 101

Hamill, James: Newry DN 3; 100, 104

Hamill, John: Ballyrobert AM 2; 24

Hamill, John: Drumtullagh AM 16; 101

Hamill, John: Dunaghy AM 13; 23

Hamill, John: Magheramesk AM 21; 121, 123–24, 126

Hamill, John: Tamlaght O'Crilly LY 18; 90, 111

Hamill, Mrs (nee Hogset): Kilroot AM 26; 79

Hamill, Mrs: Ballyrobert AM 2; 25

Hamill, Mrs: Coleraine LY 33; 72

Hamill, Patrick: Carnmoney AM 2; 90

Hamill, Robert: Carrickfergus AM 37; 113

Hamill, Samuel: Ballymartin AM 2; 16–17

Hamill, William: Billy AM 16; 58

Hamilton and Young, Messrs: Coleraine LY 33; 143

Hamilton manor: Manorhamilton Union LM 40; 50

Hamilton, A.W: Ardstraw TE 5; 2

Hamilton, Alexander: Carrickfergus AM 37; 40, 148

Hamilton, Alexander: Maghera LY 18; 80

Hamilton, Alexander: Tamlaght TE 20; 84

Hamilton, Andrew: Killea and Taughboyne DL 39; 84

Hamilton, Andrew: Taughboyne DL 39; 150

Hamilton, Ann: Bovevagh LY 25; 59

Hamilton, Anthony: Down DN 17; 59

Hamilton, Anthony: Galloon FH 4; 103

Hamilton, Betty: Tamlaght TE 20; 77, 104

Hamilton, Capt. (Killyleagh Castle): Killyleagh DN 17; 83

Hamilton, Capt. (Wexford): Newry DN 3; 105

Hamilton, Capt. [II]: Killyleagh DN 17; 83

Hamilton, Charles: Tamlaght TE 20; 77

Hamilton, Charles: Tullyaughnish DL 38; 96–97

Hamilton, Cllr: Newtownhamilton AH 1; 98

Hamilton, Col: Glenwhirry AM 32; 77

Hamilton, Col.: Newry DN 3; 98, 103

Hamilton, Colin: Dromore TE 5; 101

Hamilton, D.A.: Aughnamullen MN 40; 75–77

Hamilton, D.A.: Tydavnet MN 40; 171–72

Hamilton, Dawe: Ematris MN 40; 115

Hamilton, Eccles: Tamlaght TE 20; 122

Hamilton, Edward: Ballyscullion LY 6; 59

Hamilton, Eliza: Tamlaght TE 20; 76, 91, 103

Hamilton, Elizabeth (nee Colepepper): Taughboyne DL 39; 152

Hamilton, family: Ballynascreen LY 31; 12

Hamilton, family: Ballywillin AM 16; 32

Hamilton, family: Bright DN 17; 33

Hamilton, family: Carrickfergus AM 37; 93

Hamilton, family: Drumhome DL 39; 59

Hamilton, family: Drumragh TE 5; 107

Hamilton, family: Dunluce AM 16; 117

Hamilton, family: Enniskillen FH 4; 58, 75

Hamilton, family: Glynn AM 26; 45

Hamilton, family: Island Magee AM 10; 70

Hamilton, family: Killagan AM 23; 82

Hamilton, family: Killyleagh DN 17; 81

Hamilton, family: Layd AM 13; 49

Hamilton, family: Manorhamilton Union LM 40; 50

Hamilton, family: Misc. DL 39; 185

Hamilton, family: Tamlaght Finlagan LY 25; 68

Hamilton, family: Taughboyne DL 39; 152

Hamilton, family: Urney DL 39; 181

Hamilton, Francis: Misc. FH 4; 133

Hamilton, Frederick: Manorhamilton Union LM 40; 49–51

Hamilton, Frederick: Tamlaght Finlagan LY 25; 68–69, 87

Hamilton, Gen.: Drumragh TE 5; 109–11

Hamilton, Gen.: Galloon FH 4; 100

Hamilton, George: Ballymore AH 1; 6

Hamilton, George: Hillsborough DN 12; 106

Hamilton, Givan: Tamlaght TE 20; 78

Hamilton, Gustavus: Enniskillen FH 4; 51–52

Hamilton, H.M.: Ballymoney AM 16; 17

Hamilton, Hans: Newry DN 3; 74

Hamilton, Henery: Macosquin LY 22; 102

Hamilton, Henry: Aghaderg DN 12; 6

Hamilton, Henry: Ballyscullion LY 6; 59

Hamilton, Henry: Drumachose LY 9; 65

Hamilton, Henry: Kilbroney DN 3; 34–35, 38

Hamilton, Henry: Lough Swilly DL 38; 142

Hamilton, Henry: Tamlaght TE 20; 81

Hamilton, Henry: Tullylish DN 12; 141–44

Hamilton, Hugh: Tamlaght O'Crilly LY 18; 114

Hamilton, Hugh: Tamlaght TE 20; 82

Hamilton, J.: Aughnamullen MN 40; 77

Hamilton, J.: Donaghedy TE 5; 91–92

Hamilton, J.P.: Galloon FH 4; 91–92, 94

Hamilton, J.W.: Ardstraw TE 5; 9, 13

Hamilton, J.W.: Drumglass TE 20; 42

Hamilton, James (Jnr): Taughboyne DL 39; 152

Hamilton, James (see also Clandeboy): Ballynure AM 32; 45

Hamilton, James (Snr): Taughboyne DL 39; 152

Hamilton, James: Ballylinny AM 32; 15

Hamilton, James: Ballymartin AM 2; 5

Hamilton, James: Ballyrobert AM 2; 20

Hamilton, James: Ballywalter AM 2; 29

Hamilton, James: Cleenish FH 14; 29

Hamilton, James: Derrykeighan AM 16; 90

Hamilton, James: Glynn AM 26; 17–18

Hamilton, James: Killinchy DN 7; 90

Hamilton, James: Killyleagh DN 17; 81

Hamilton, James: Killymard DL 39; 100–01, 106

Hamilton, James: Kilroot AM 26; 61, 72

Hamilton, James: Loughguile AM 13; 76

Hamilton, James: Mallusk AM 2; 109

Hamilton, James: Misc. DN 17; 117, 130

Hamilton, James: Newry DN 3; 74

Hamilton, James: Rasharkin AM 23; 141

Hamilton, James: Tullyrusk AM 21; 131

Hamilton, James: Tydavnet MN 40; 173

Hamilton, James: Urney DL 39; 179

Hamilton, James [I]: Tamlaght TE 20; 81, 108, 111

Hamilton, James [II]: Tamlaght TE 20; 129

Hamilton, Jane: Tamlaght Finlagan LY 25; 68–69, 87

Hamilton, John (Garvagh): Desertoghill LY 27; 3

Hamilton, John (Swatragh): Desertoghill LY 27; 17, 29

Hamilton, John: Ballywillin LY 33; 32, 38, 46

Hamilton, John: Bovevagh LY 25; 28, 55

Hamilton, John: Carrickfergus AM 37; 132

Hamilton, John: Coleraine LY 33; 72

Hamilton, John: Donegal DL 39; 44, 47, 49–51

Hamilton, John: Drumachose LY 9; 104

Hamilton, John: Drumhome DL 39; 58–62

Hamilton, John: Dungiven LY 15; 116, 118–19

Hamilton, John: Hillsborough DN 12; 105

Hamilton, John: Killymard DL 39; 97–98

Hamilton, John: Templecorran AM 26; 121

Hamilton, John [I]: Tamlaght TE 20; 74, 76–78, 80, 96, 101–02, 107–08, 110, 112, 114–15

Hamilton, John [II]: Tamlaght TE 20; 108

Hamilton, Jones: Cleenish FH 14; 18, 29–30

Hamilton, Joseph: Bovevagh LY 25; 59

Hamilton, Joseph: Drumachose LY 9; 115

Hamilton, July: Tamlaght TE 20; 76

Hamilton, M.A.: Clondermot LY 34; 86, 90, 94

Hamilton, man named: Muckamore AM 35; 81

Hamilton, Mary: Rasharkin AM 23; 135

Hamilton, Mary Anne: Carrickfergus AM 37; 116, 130

Hamilton, Michael: Newry DN 3; 99, 104

Hamilton, minor: Drumhome DL 39; 58–59

Hamilton, minor: Inishkeel DL 39; 67, 70

Hamilton, Miss (Killough): Bright DN 17; 36

Hamilton, Mr (Ballymoney): Kirkinriola AM 23; 126

Hamilton, Mr: Ballymoney AM 16; 23

Hamilton, Mr: Bright DN 17; 35

Hamilton, Mr: Clogher TE 5; 43

Hamilton, Mr: Layd AM 13; 38

Hamilton, Mr: Mevagh DL 38; 60

Hamilton, Mr: Saintfield DN 7; 118

Hamilton, Mr: Tullylish DN 12; 141

Hamilton, Mrs: Ballymoney AM 16; 16

Hamilton, Mrs: Killyleagh DN 17; 83

Hamilton, Mrs: Kilmore DN 17; 88

Hamilton, Mrs: Templecarn DL 39; 158

Hamilton, Mrs: Termoneeny LY 6; 124

Hamilton, Mrs Henry: Kilbroney DN 3; 38

Hamilton, Oliver: Blaris AM 8; 82

Hamilton, Oliver: Blaris DN 12; 40

Hamilton, Pierce: Dromore TE 5; 99

Hamilton, Rev. H.: Inishmacsaint FH 14; 74

Hamilton, Rev.: Ballynure AM 32; 69

Hamilton, Rev.: Clondavaddog DL 38; 7

Hamilton, Rev.: Connor AM 19; 18

Hamilton, Rev.: Donaghmore DL 39; 35–37

Hamilton, Rev. A.T.: Donaghedy TE 5; 89

Hamilton, Rev. A.T.: Dromore TE 5; 99

Hamilton, Rev. Abraham: Enniskillen FH 4; 58

Hamilton, Rev. Abraham: Manorhamilton Union LM 40; 52

Hamilton, Rev. Archibald: Skirts of Urney and Ardstraw TE 5; 138–40

Hamilton, Rev. George: Carrickfergus AM 37; 102, 144

Hamilton, Rev. H.: Clogher TE 5; 40–41

Hamilton, Rev. H.: Inishmacsaint FH 14; 76, 78–79

Hamilton, Rev. Hugh: Garvaghy DN 12; 80–81, 83

Hamilton, Rev. Hugh: Lissan LY 31; 93, 106

Hamilton, Rev. James: Ardglass DN 17; 11

Hamilton, Rev. James: Bright DN 17; 36

Hamilton, Rev. James: Down DN 17; 47

Hamilton, Rev. James: Drumgoon CN 40; 11

Hamilton, Rev. Samuel: Aghadowey LY 22; 22

Hamilton, Rev. W.: Rathlin Island AM 24; 133–34

Hamilton, Rev. William: Coleraine LY 33; 72, 95, 141–42

Hamilton, Rev. William: Donegal DL 39; 51

Hamilton, Rev. William: Drumachose LY 9; 73

Hamilton, Richard: Ballymoney AM 16; 15, 17

Hamilton, Richard: Tamlaght TE 20; 77, 129

Hamilton, Robert: Derryaghy AM 8; 98, 104

Hamilton, Robert: Dromore TE 5; 97–98

Hamilton, Robert: Dunluce AM 16; 117

Hamilton, Robert: Kilwaughter AM 10; 122

Hamilton, Robert: Newry DN 3; 100

Hamilton, Robert: Rasharkin AM 23; 135

Hamilton, Sackville: Ballyscullion LY 6; 59

Hamilton, Samuel: Ballee DN 17; 21–22

Hamilton, Samuel [I]: Bovevagh LY 25; 50, 54

Hamilton, Samuel [II]: Bovevagh LY 25; 60

Hamilton, Sarah: Tamlaght TE 20; 129

Hamilton, soldier: Killyleagh DN 17; 85

Hamilton, son of James (Snr): Taughboyne DL 39; 152

Hamilton, Thomas: Maghera LY 18; 50

Hamilton, Viscount: Ballyphilip DN 7; 13

Hamilton, W.: Aughnamullen MN 40; 75–76

Hamilton, W.J.: Clonleigh DL 39; 4

Hamilton, Walter: Glynn AM 26; 47

Hamilton, Widow [I]: Tamlaght TE 20; 108

Hamilton, Widow [II]: Tamlaght TE 20; 109

Hamilton, William: Ballyclug AM 23; 66
Hamilton, William: Carnmoney AM 2; 103
Hamilton, William: Dromore TE 5; 97
Hamilton, William: Hillsborough DN 12; 106
Hamilton, William: Muckno MN 40; 164–65
Hamilton, William: Templepatrick AM 35; 152
Hamilton's Hill manor: Bright DN 17; 33
Hamiltonsbawn: Mullaghbrack AH 1; 97
Hamish, family: Newry DN 3; 106
Hammand, family: Aghalee AM 21, 31
Hammel, James: Ahoghill AM 23; 38
Hammel, John: Maghera LY 18; 81
Hammel, John: Templepatrick AM 35; 152
Hammel, Patrick: Maghera LY 18; 81
Hammel, Robert: Derryaghy AM 8; 104
Hammel, Rose: Ahoghill AM 23; 38
Hammel, Samuel: Ahoghill AM 23; 38
Hammil, Culbert: Kilroot AM 26; 67, 79
Hammil, John: Derryaghy AM 8; 92
Hammil, Mrs: Derryaghy AM 8; 116
Hammil, Rev.: Derryaghy AM 8; 102
Hammill, Charles: Kilroot AM 26; 75
Hammill, Daniel: Billy AM 16; 75
Hammill, family: Ballinderry AM 21; 53
Hammill, J.: Comber DN 7; 37, 40
Hammill, James: Billy AM 16; 73
Hammill, Rev. Hugh: Billy AM 16; 67
Hammill, William: Billy AM 16; 62, 75
Hammond, Andrew: Donegal DL 39; 56–57
Hammond, David: Blaris AM 8; 55
Hammond, David: Blaris DN 12; 45, 49
Hammond, family: Aghalee AM 21; 31
Hammond, family: Tamlaght O'Crilly LY 18; 92
Hammond, Henry: Magheramesk AM 21; 119
Hammond, Mr: Garvaghy DN 12; 80
Hammond, Thomas: Magheramesk AM 21; 121
Hammond's bridge: Aghalee AM 21; 26–27
Hammond's bridge: Blaris DN 12; 28
Hampsey, Elizabeth: Desertoghill LY 27; 20
Hampsey, Jane: Desertoghill LY 27; 20
Hampsey, Patrick: Desertoghill LY 27; 20
Hampson, Darby: Banagher LY 30; 71
Hampson, James (Jnr): Banagher LY 30; 69–70
Hampson, James (Snr): Banagher LY 30; 69–70
Hampson, James: Banagher LY 30; 71
Hampson, John: Errigal LY 27; 66
Hampson, Joseph: Banagher LY 30; 89
Hampson, Joseph: Bovevagh LY 25; 47
Hampton Court House: Enniskillen FH 4; 57
Hampton Court Palace: Drumachose LY 9; 60
Hanagan, Mr: Donaghmore DL 39; 40
Hanan, family: Ballinderry AM 21; 55
Hanan, William: Drummaul AM 19; 90
Hancock, Dr: Blaris DN 12; 46, 50
Hancock, John: Blaris AM 8; 18

Hancock, John: Lambeg AM 8; 139
Hancock, Robert: Newry DN 3; 99
Hancock, W.J.: Blaris AM 8; 36, 50, 62
Hancock, W.J.: Drumcree AH 1; 36–40
Hancock, W.J.: Montiaghs AH 1; 93
Hancock, W.J.: Shankill AH 1; 115
Hancock, W.J.: Shankill DN 12; 139
Hancock, William: Newry DN 3; 92, 100, 104
Handcock, Fulton and McCance, Messrs: Blaris AM 8; 36
Handcock, George: Drummaul AM 19; 44, 54–56
Handcock, H.: Killyman TE 20; 67
Handcock, Hugh: Cumber LY 28; 29
Handcock, John: Blaris DN 12; 33
Handcock, John: Carrickfergus AM 37; 132
Handcock, Mr: Clogher TE 5; 41
Handcock, Thomas: Cumber LY 28; 28, 84
Haney, Hugh: Connor AM 19; 28
Haney's bridge (see Heaney's): Aghagallon AM 21; 1
Hanger, family: Coleraine LY 33; 154
Hanging fort: Errigal Keerogue TE 20; 51
Hanging rock (see Carrickclionagh): Killesher FH 14; 81
Hanging stone: Clondermot LY 34; 44
Hanging thorn: Templepatrick AM 35; 131, 145
Hangman's cave: Carrickfergus AM 37; 86
Hanley, John: Carrickfergus AM 37; 184, 188–90
Hanley, P.: Clondermot LY 34; 82
Hanley, Thomas: Glynn AM 26; 35, 46
Hanley, William: Carrickfergus AM 37; 153, 184–85, 188, 190
Hanlon, family: Magheramesk AM 21; 124
Hanlon, Mrs: Newry DN 3; 98, 103
Hanly, family: Carrickfergus AM 37; 93
Hanly, Robert: Carrickfergus AM 37; 62
Hanna, A.: Misc. LY 31; 130, 135, 140
Hanna, Dr (Belfast): Carrickfergus AM 37; 58, 137
Hanna, family: Antrim AM 29; 24
Hanna, family: Ardglass DN 17; 4
Hanna, family: Carrickfergus AM 37; 93
Hanna, family: Dromara DN 12; 67
Hanna, family: Duneane AM 19; 101
Hanna, family: Misc. LY 36; 104
Hanna, Felix: Carrickfergus AM 37; 76
Hanna, Hugh: Carrickfergus AM 37; 76
Hanna, James: Blaris DN 12; 46, 50
Hanna, James: Clondermot LY 34; 86, 90, 93–94
Hanna, James: Hillsborough DN 12; 106
Hanna, James: Kilcronaghan LY 31; 77
Hanna, James: Monaghan MN 40; 161
Hanna, John (Jnr): Hillsborough DN 12; 107
Hanna, John: Hillsborough DN 12; 106
Hanna, John: Loughgilly AH 1; 86

Hanna, John: Tamlaght TE 20; 74–75, 78–79, 81–82, 84, 86, 88, 90–91, 109–11, 113–14, 124–28

Hanna, Susan: Holywood DN 7; 76

Hanna, W.J.: Kirkinriola AM 23; 113

Hanna, William: Annaclone DN 12; 16, 18

Hanna, William: Carrickfergus AM 37; 40, 175

Hanna, William: Saintfield DN 7; 116, 118–19

Hannae lough: Clondavaddog DL 38; 3

Hannah, Anne: Drummaul AM 19; 91

Hannah, Bernard: Drummaul AM 19; 88

Hannah, Eliza: Coleraine LY 33; 145

Hannah, Eliza: Drummaul AM 19; 91

Hannah, family: Ballee DN 17; 16

Hannah, family: Finvoy AM 23; 76

Hannah, Henry: Coleraine LY 33; 145

Hannah, Hugh: Drummaul AM 19; 91

Hannah, James: Desertoghill LY 27; 22

Hannah, James: Drummaul AM 19; 91

Hannah, James: Kilcronaghan LY 31; 85

Hannah, Jane: Ballywillin LY 33; 40

Hannah, John (Jnr): Drummaul AM 19; 91

Hannah, John (Snr): Drummaul AM 19; 88, 91

Hannah, John: Coleraine LY 33; 145

Hannah, Lydia: Coleraine LY 33; 145

Hannah, Margaret: Drummaul AM 19; 91

Hannah, Martha (Jnr): Coleraine LY 33; 145

Hannah, Martha (Snr): Coleraine LY 33; 145

Hannah, Martha: Drummaul AM 19; 91

Hannah, Mary: Coleraine LY 33; 145

Hannah, Mr (Brickkilns): Clondermot LY 34; 37–38, 104

Hannah, Rev.: Doagh AM 29; 84, 97

Hannah, Robert: Coleraine LY 33; 145

Hannah, Robert: Dundermot AM 13; 35

Hannah, Sarah (Jnr): Drummaul AM 19; 91

Hannah, Sarah (Snr): Drummaul AM 19; 91

Hannah, Thomas: Drummaul AM 19; 91

Hannah, William: Drummaul AM 19; 90

Hannah, William: Loughguile AM 13; 72

Hannahstown chapel: Lambeg AM 8; 136

Hannahstown graveyard: Lambeg AM 8; 136

Hannahstown td: Derryaghy AM 8; 91, 108

Hannan, family: Shilvodan AM 19; 136

Hannan, Peter: Muckamore AM 35; 81

Hannan, Widow: Muckamore AM 35; 81

Hannastown (see Hannahstown): Lambeg AM 8; 136

Hannay, James: Ballywillin LY 33; 39

Hannay, James: Coleraine LY 33; 63, 105

Hannay, James: Macosquin LY 22; 80, 101

Hannigan, Patt: Kilmacteige SO 40; 194

Hannington, Mr: Balteagh LY 9; 13

Hannon, Thomas: Aghalee AM 21; 29, 31–32

Hannyngton, Mr: Drumglass TE 20; 41

Hannyngton, T.C.: Aghagallon AM 21; 3–5

Hannyngton, T.C.: Aghalee AM 21; 27

Hannyngton, T.C.: Ballyclug AM 23; 55

Hannyngton, T.C.: Connor AM 19; 28

Hannyngton, T.C.: Cranfield AM 19; 32

Hannyngton, T.C.: Kirkinriola AM 23; 94

Hanover's hill: Island Magee AM 10; 102

Hansard, Lady (nee Marbury): Clonleigh DL 39; 15

Hansard, Richard: Clonleigh DL 39; 2, 7, 12–15

Hansard, Richard: Misc. DL 39; 185

Hansard, William: Clonleigh DL 39; 15

Hansard, William: Tullyaughnish DL 38; 87

Hanson, family: Aghadowey LY 22; 11

Hanson, family: Misc. LY 36; 111

Hanson, John: Coleraine LY 33; 105

Hanson, man named: Misc. LY 36; 111

Hanson, Rev.: Ballynure AM 32; 69

Hanson, Robert: Killowen LY 33; 158

Hant, family: Ballinderry AM 21; 55

Hanvey, Edward: Artrea LY 6; 38

Hanvey, Mary: Artrea LY 6; 38

Hanvey, Sareah: Artrea LY 6; 38

Hanway, family: Ballee DN 17; 16

Happer, James: Tamlaght TE 20; 108

Happer, John: Tamlaght TE 20; 81

Hara, Kate: Faughanvale LY 36; 30

Hara, Owen: Kilcronaghan LY 31; 85

Haran, Daniel: Bovevagh LY 25; 59

Harbeson, Adam: Ahoghill AM 23; 33

Harbeson, family: Maghera LY 18; 13

Harbeson, Henry: Maghera LY 18; 54

Harbeson, John: Ballyscullion AM 19; 14

Harbeson, Peter: Ahoghill AM 23; 35

Harbeson, Robert: Ahoghill AM 23; 39

Harbison, family: Dunluce AM 16; 117

Harbison, family: Kirkinriola AM 23; 124

Harbison, James: Artrea LY 6; 36

Harbison, James: Carrickfergus AM 37; 111

Harbison, John: Artrea LY 6; 36

Harbison, John: Muckamore AM 35; 81

Harbison, William: Artrea LY 6; 36

Harbison, William: Derryaghy AM 8; 91

Harcourt, Richard: Newry DN 3; 99

Harden, Henry: Newry DN 3; 99, 104

Harden, Robert: Ballymore AH 1; 4–5, 10–15

Harden, Thomas: Carrickfergus AM 37; 192

Harding, Richard: Carrickfergus AM 37; 80

Harding, Richard: Kinawley FH 4; 117

Hardy, Abraham: Ballymore AH 1; 15

Hardy, Hugh: Ballyscullion AM 19; 12

Hardy, J.: Ballymore AH 1; 14

Hardy, John: Carrickfergus AM 37; 114, 120

Hardy, John: Drumcree AH 1; 41

Hardy, John: Kilmore AH 1; 68–71

Hardy, John: Loughgall AH 1; 77, 79

Hardy, John: Loughgilly AH 1; 84
Hardy, Mr (Mourne): Newry DN 3; 110
Hardy, Mrs: Loughgall AH 1; 78
Hardy, Robert: Ballymore AH 1; 14
Hardy, Robert: Loughgilly AH 1; 85
Hardy, Thomas: Tamlaght TE 20; 76
Hardys and Allison, Messrs: Coleraine LY 33; 72
Hare Island: Saul DN 17; 114
Hare, James: Aghaloo AM 21, 39
Hare, James: Aghalurcher FH 4; 6, 9, 12
Hare, James: Hillsborough DN 12; 107
Hare, Joseph: Drumachose LY 9; 134
Hare, Mr: Clogher TE 5; 40
Hare, Mrs: Aghalurcher FH 4; 6, 9
Hare, Patrick: Carrickfergus AM 37; 117
Hare, Rev.: Faughanvale LY 36; 33
Hare, Rev. Hamilton: Aghabog MN 40; 63
Hare, Trevor: Hillsborough DN 12; 107
Hargan, Robert: Banagher LY 30; 65
Hargrave, Robert: Ballintoy AM 24; 35
Hargraves, Mr (England): Carrickfergus AM 37; 137
Harke [or Hacker], Rev. C.F.: Ahoghill AM 23;
    19–20
Harken, Edward: Banagher LY 30; 84
Harken, Thomas: Aghanloo LY 11; 28
Harken, Thomas: Drumachose LY 9; 111
Harkin, Andrew: Aghadowey LY 22; 36
Harkin, Charles: Maghera LY 18; 50–51, 63, 71, 74
Harkin, family: Kilmacteige SO 40; 186
Harkin, family: Templecorran AM 26; 119
Harkin, John: Ardstraw TE 5; 9
Harkin, John: Drumragh TE 5; 111
Harkness, James: Carrickfergus AM 37; 119
Harkness, James: Lissan LY 31; 105
Harkness, Jane: Muckamore AM 35; 81
Harkness, John [I]: Lissan LY 31; 95
Harkness, John [II]: Lissan LY 31; 108
Harkness, Mary: Carrickfergus AM 37; 129
Harkness, Samuel [I]: Tamlaght TE 20; 92
Harkness, Samuel [II]: Tamlaght TE 20; 115
Harkness, Thomas: Lissan LY 31; 104
Harkness, William: Rasharkin AM 23; 139–40
Harley, Robert: Carnmoney AM 2; 79
Harley, William: Carrickfergus AM 37; 194
Harlin, John: Blaris AM 8; 33, 55
Harlin, John: Blaris DN 12; 39, 46
Harlin, Miss: Blaris DN 12; 50
Harman, H.J.: Donacavey TE 5; 77, 86
Harman, John: Blaris AM 8; 23
Harman, Thomas: Desertlyn LY 31; 51
Harmon, Robert: Carrickfergus AM 37; 193
Harold, William: Drumachose LY 9; 131
Harper, Arthur: Muckamore AM 35; 79
Harper, Edward: Newry DN 3; 79
Harper, family: Carnmoney AM 2; 51, 76

Harper, family: Killead AM 35; 17
Harper, family: Templepatrick AM 35; 118
Harper, family: Umgall AM 35; 158
Harper, George: Aughnamullen MN 40; 74
Harper, James: Carrickfergus AM 37; 128
Harper, James: Doagh AM 29; 92, 98
Harper, James [I]: Macosquin LY 22; 110–11
Harper, James [II]: Macosquin LY 22; 122
Harper, man named: Muckamore AM 35; 78
Harper, Rev. James: Maghera LY 18; 75
Harper, Rev. James: Termoneeny LY 6; 130
Harper, Samuel: Hillsborough DN 12; 106
Harper, Samuel: Templepatrick AM 35; 153
Harper, Thomas: Muckamore AM 35; 79
Harper, Widow: Hillsborough DN 12; 106
Harper, William: Hillsborough DN 12; 106
Harper's Island: Muckno MN 40; 162
Harphall chapel: Tickmacrevan AM 13; 123, 129
Harphall school: Tickmacrevan AM 13; 132–33
Harphall td: Tickmacrevan AM 13; 123, 125, 129,
    132
Harpin [or Harpur], David: Clondermot LY 34; 87,
    95
Harpur [or Harpin], David: Clondermot LY 34; 87,
    95
Harpur, Adam: Drummaul AM 19; 89
Harpur, Daniel: Dunaghy AM 13; 21
Harpur, family: Carmavy AM 35; 2
Harpur, Henry: Killead AM 35; 47
Harpur, Jane: Muckamore AM 35; 77
Harpur, John: Dunaghy AM 13; 21
Harpur, Margaret: Muckamore AM 35; 77
Harpur, Samuel: Dunaghy AM 13; 21, 23
Harras, Mr: Aghanloo LY 11; 31
Harrell, family: Maghera LY 18; 24
Harren, M.: Misc. LY 31; 129
Harrigan, William: Warrenpoint DN 3; 118
Harringtown district: Templecorran AM 26; 82
Harris, Brace: Drumgooland DN 3; 25
Harris, family: Derryaghy AM 8; 103
Harris, George: Clogher TE 5; 40
Harris, George: Derryaghy AM 8; 94
Harris, George: Lissan LY 31; 101
Harris, Hugh: Tynan AH 1; 124, 128, 130, 132
Harris, J.: Derryaghy AM 8; 99
Harris, John: Ballyscullion AM 19; 7, 9
Harris, Joseph: Ballyscullion AM 19; 10
Harris, Mr: Kilmore DN 17; 88
Harris, Rev.: Derrybrusk FH 4; 30–31, 33
Harris, Rev. John: Drumgoon CN 40; 8
Harris, Rev. John: Killdrumsherdan CN 40; 33–34
Harris, Rev. William: Aghabog MN 40; 63
Harris, Richard: Ballyscullion LY 6; 57
Harris, William: Ballyscullion AM 19; 7
Harris, William: Drumballyroney DN 3; 13

Harrison, Capt.: Carrickfergus AM 37; 135
Harrison, Charles: Clondermot LY 34; 55
Harrison, George: Carrickfergus AM 37; 162
Harrison, Henry: Ballyscullion LY 6; 57
Harrison, Hugh: Culfeightrin AM 24; 70
Harrison, Hugh: Kirkinriola AM 23; 104, 119
Harrison, Jacob: Hillsborough DN 12; 100
Harrison, James: Banagher LY 30; 61
Harrison, John: Hillsborough DN 12; 107
Harrison, Joseph: Hillsborough DN 12; 105
Harrison, Joshua: Hillsborough DN 12; 105
Harrison, Martha: Ballyscullion LY 6; 57
Harrison, Michael: Ballyclug AM 23; 57, 65
Harrison, Michael: Connor AM 19; 18
Harrison, Michael: Culfeightrin AM 24; 45
Harrison, Michael: Kirkinriola AM 23; 95–96, 114
Harrison, Mr: Kilmegan DN 3; 60
Harrison, Mr: Muckno MN 40; 165
Harrison, Mrs Michael: Kirkinriola AM 23; 103, 114
Harrison, Rev. Michael: Ramoan AM 24; 108
Harrisson, James: Tickmacrevan AM 13; 133
Harrisson, Mary: Tickmacrevan AM 13; 133
Harron, Michael: Ballynascreen LY 31; 22
Harrowgate (Yorkshire): Drumachose LY 9; 75
Harrowgate: Carrickfergus AM 37; 8
Harrowgate spa: Inishkeel DL 39; 70
Harrybrook House: Ballymore AH 1; 10–11, 13–15
Harryville bridge: Ballyclug AM 23; 52, 55, 57
Harryville bridge: Kirkinriola AM 23; 88, 93–96, 118
Harryville hamlet: Ballyclug AM 23; 52–53, 55, 57
Harryville hamlet: Kirkinriola AM 23; 88, 95, 118
Harshaw, James: Annaclone DN 12; 15
Hart, Adm.: Muff DL 38; 82
Hart, Capt. (Doe): Mevagh DL 38; 56
Hart, family: Carnmoney AM 2; 76
Hart, family: Muff DL 38; 82
Hart, Gen.: Desertegney DL 38; 25
Hart, Gen.: Faughanvale LY 36; 40
Hart, Gen.: Lough Swilly DL 38; 120
Hart, Gen.: Muff DL 38; 80, 82
Hart, George: Clondermot LY 34; 58–59, 62, 70, 72
Hart, Henry: Muff DL 38; 82–83
Hart, John: Faughanvale LY 36; 40
Hart, Mary: Kilcronaghan LY 31; 84
Hart, Mr: Conwal DL 39; 26
Hart, Mr: Saintfield DN 7; 118
Hart, Rev.: Cappagh TE 5; 18
Hart, Rev. Edward: Desertegney DL 38; 25–26
Hart, Rev. Edward: Muff DL 38; 82
Hart, Rev. G.V.: Muff DL 38; 82
Hart, Rev. G.V.: Tullyaughnish DL 38; 85, 89, 92, 95, 97
Hart, Samuel: Coleraine LY 33; 66, 72, 110

Hart, Thomas: Kilbroney DN 3; 33
Hart, Thomas: Kilcronaghan LY 31; 84
Harte, Henry: Clondermot LY 34; 55
Harte, P.H.: Tamlaght Finlagan LY 25; 74, 77–78, 123–24
Hartford, Robert: Ballymoney AM 16; 26
Hartin, family: Dunluce AM 16; 117
Harton, Andrew: Magherally DN 12; 116
Harton, James: Ballywillin AM 16; 35
Hartwell, Francis: Hillsborough DN 12; 90
Hartwell, Henrietta: Hillsborough DN 12; 90
Harvey, family: Ardclinis AM 13; 8
Harvey, family: Layd AM 13; 49, 52
Harvey, family: Mintiaghs DL 38; 65
Harvey, family: Misc. LY 36; 104
Harvey, family: Templecorran AM 26; 117, 119
Harvey, Harriet: Magherafelt LY 6; 103
Harvey, Hugh: Layd AM 13; 53
Harvey, Jeremiah: Blaris AM 8; 69
Harvey, Jeremiah: Blaris DN 12; 49
Harvey, Jeremiah: Hillsborough DN 12; 97
Harvey, John (Jnr): Clonmany DL 38; 18
Harvey, John (Jnr): Donagh DL 38; 32
Harvey, John (Jnr): Lough Swilly DL 38; 109
Harvey, John: Island Magee AM 10; 95
Harvey, Lt F.: Coleraine LY 33; 73
Harvey, M.: Newry DN 3; 105
Harvey, Miss: Coleraine LY 33; 67, 70, 139
Harvey, Miss: Donaghmore DL 39; 36, 38–39
Harvey, Miss: Newry DN 3; 105
Harvey, Mr: Cappagh TE 5; 22
Harvey, Mr: Faughanvale LY 36; 18
Harvey, Mr: Rasharkin AM 23; 127
Harvey, Patrick: Carrickfergus AM 37; 130
Harvey, Rev. Edward: Coleraine LY 33; 69, 73, 140
Harvey, Rev. John: Banagher LY 30; 14–15, 23
Harvey, Rev. John: Bovevagh LY 25; 24, 26, 54
Harvey, Rev. John: Dungiven LY 15; 58
Harvey, Rev. W.H.: Clonmany DL 38; 18, 20
Harvey, Rev. W.H.: Desertegney DL 38; 24–25, 27–30
Harvey, Richard: Ardstraw TE 5; 8
Harvey, S.: Macosquin LY 22; 108
Harvey, William: Blaris DN 12; 46
Harvey, William: Lough Swilly DL 38; 136
Harvey, William: Mintiaghs DL 38; 65–67
Harwich (Essex): Ballyscullion LY 6; 60
Hasard, Jason: Drummully FH 4; 35
Haslet, family: Ballyclug AM 23; 60
Haslet, Henry: Drumachose LY 9; 104
Haslett, William: Faughanvale LY 36; 45
Haslitt, Samuel: Clondermot LY 34; 6, 20, 37, 97, 102, 104
Hass quarry: Dungiven LY 15; 51
Hass td: Banagher LY 30; 22

Hass td: Dungiven LY 15; 22, 27, 46–47, 62, 64, 74, 83

Hass, Mr: Misc. LY 31; 130

Hassan, family: Banagher LY 30; 31, 112–13

Hassan, Hugh: Banagher LY 30; 33, 73, 111

Hassan, James: Cumber LY 28; 28

Hassan, John: Bovevagh LY 25; 43

Hassan, Patrick: Bovevagh LY 25; 58

Hassan, Patrick: Desertmartin LY 31; 56

Hassan, Peter: Ramoan AM 24; 124–25

Hassans channel: Clondavaddog DL 38; 1–3, 9

Hassans channel: Mevagh DL 38; 56

Hassans channel: Tullyaughnish DL 38; 86

Hassans rocks: Lough Swilly DL 38; 105, 113, 116–17

Hassard, family: Enniskillen FH 4; 58

Hassard, George: Cleenish FH 14; 17, 22, 27, 30

Hassard, George: Enniskillen FH 4; 58

Hassard, Jason: Cleenish FH 14; 29, 30

Hassard, Jason: Derryvullan FH 14; 44

Hassard, Jason: Enniskillen FH 4; 58

Hassard, T.: Cleenish FH 14; 29

Hassard, William: Cleenish FH 14; 17, 29–30

Hassen, George: Banagher LY 30; 53, 87, 92

Hassen, James: Banagher LY 30; 74

Hassen, John: Banagher LY 30; 61, 66–67, 73–74, 79, 86, 96

Hassen, Michael: Banagher LY 30; 53, 87, 91–92

Hassen, Nelly: Banagher LY 30; 96–97, 112–13

Hassen, Owen: Banagher LY 30; 61, 75

Hassen, Patrick: Banagher LY 30; 53, 61, 80, 87

Hassen, Rev. Patrick: Banagher LY 30; 73

Hassen, William: Dungiven LY 15; 76

Hassin, family: Maghera LY 18; 24

Hassin, Pat: Ballynascreen LY 31; 31

Hasson, Ann: Bovevagh LY 25; 60

Hasson, family: Maghera LY 18; 48

Hasson, Henery: Bovevagh LY 25; 60

Hasson, Hugh: Dungiven LY 15; 91

Hasson, Lawrence: Ballynascreen LY 31; 24

Hasson, man named: Cumber LY 28; 30

Hasson, Patt: Errigal LY 27; 45, 73

Hastie, Mr (Downpatrick): Misc. DN 17; 127

Hastings, Rev.: Drummully FH 4; 40

Hastings, Rev.: Galloon FH 4; 95–96

Hastings, Rev.: Kilskeery TE 5; 114

Hastings, Rev. Anthony: Kilmacrenan DL 38; 53

Hastings, Rev. Anthony: Mevagh DL 38; 60

Hatley, William: Island Magee AM 10; 94

Hatrick, Ezekiel: Clondermot LY 34; 79

Hatrick, William: Clondermot LY 34; 20

Hatte, family: Billy AM 16; 58, 68

Hatton, Hugh: Ballynure AM 32; 72

Hatton, John: Hillsborough DN 12; 105

Hatton, Patrick: Ahoghill AM 23; 33

Hattrick, Mr: Clondermot LY 34; 37, 104

Hattridge, family: Island Magee AM 10; 87, 95

Hattridge, James: Island Magee AM 10; 66–67, 94

Hattridge, Mrs: Island Magee AM 10; 94

Hattridge, Rev. James: Island Magee AM 10; 87

Haugh chapel: Killymard DL 39; 96

Haugh td: Killymard DL 39; 101, 186, 195

Haughey, family: Dunluce AM 16; 117

Haughey, James: Convoy DL 39; 22

Haughey, John: Carrickfergus AM 37; 194

Haughey, Michael: Carrickfergus AM 37; 119

Haughey, Patrick: Newry DN 3; 100

Haughton, Benjamin: Tullylish DN 12; 141, 147

Haughton, R.R.: Blaris DN 12; 40, 51

Haulbowling lighthouse: Kilkeel DN 3; 52

Haulbowling lighthouse: Warrenpoint DN 3; 119–20

Haussons channel: Killymard DL 39; 106

Hauxton, William: Drumachose LY 9; 117

Havis, family: Misc. LY 36; 104

Havlen, James: Banagher LY 30; 51, 94

Havlow, Rev. Francis: Misc. LY 31; 136

Haw td: Clonleigh DL 39; 12

Haw, Archibald: Termoneeny LY 6; 130

Hawes, Mr: Clogher TE 5; 43

Hawkins bridge: Newry DN 3; 108

Hawkins, Bishop: Raphoe DL 39; 122

Hawkins, family: Templecorran AM 26; 117

Hawkins, Mr: Drumballyroney DN 3; 12, 16

Hawkshaw, family: Blaris AM 8; 21

Hawkshaw, J.S.: Blaris DN 12; 32, 36, 38

Hawkshaw, J.S.: Hillsborough DN 12; 97, 102–03, 107

Hawkshaw, John: Tydavnet MN 40; 170

Hawkshaw, Miss: Blaris AM 8; 18, 32, 77, 84–85

Hawksnest locality: Lough Swilly DL 38; 102, 104, 144

Hawksworth, Mr: Raphoe DL 39; 121, 126

Hawney, John: Drummaul AM 19; 92

Hawthorn Hill House: Killevy AH 1; 53

Hawthorn, Archibald: Doagh AM 29; 96

Hawthorn, family: Magherafelt LY 6; 95

Hawthorn, Rev. Robert: Ballymore AH 1; 5, 9

Hawthorn, Thomas: Banagher LY 30; 73

Hawthorne, Charles (Dublin): Down DN 17; 53, 57

Hawthorne, John: Hillsborough DN 12; 106

Hawthorne, Samuel: Carrickfergus AM 37; 119

Hawton, Robert: Carrickfergus AM 37; 120

Hay, family: Ballynure AM 32; 56

Hay, family: Carrickfergus AM 37; 93

Hay, family: Templecorran AM 26; 117, 119

Hay, John: Templecorran AM 26; 131

Hay, Mr (Milford): Mevagh DL 38; 60

Hay, Mr (Milford): Tullyaughnish DL 38; 86, 88, 94

Hay, Mrs: Donacavey TE 5; 76, 86

Hay, Rev. George: Faughanvale LY 36; 40, 42, 45

Hay, Robert: Clondermot LY 34; 79–80

Hay, Samuel: Carrickfergus AM 37; 58, 134, 140, 143, 157, 164

Hay, Thomas: Kilroot AM 26; 77

Hay, William: Carrickfergus AM 37; 40, 175

Hay's store: Lough Swilly DL 38; 117

Hayden, Rev. John: Clondermot LY 34; 79

Hayden, Rev. John: Cumber LY 28; 34, 57, 75–76, 80, 83, 91–92, 96

Hayes House: Enniskeen CN 40; 29

Hayes, Edmund: Convoy DL 39; 18–22

Hayes, Edmund: Donaghmore DL 39; 30

Hayes, Edmund: Faughanvale LY 36; 45

Hayes, Edmund: Leck DL 39; 115–19

Hayes, Edmund: Raphoe DL 39; 126

Hayes, F.W.: Seapatrick DN 12; 125–26, 134

Hayes, Richard: Seapatrick DN 12; 125, 134

Hayes, Samuel: Faughanvale LY 36; 40

Hayes, William: Seapatrick DN 12; 132

Haynes, Michael: Magilligan LY 11; 89

Hays, Anne Jane: Carrickfergus AM 37; 152

Hays, family: Lough Swilly DL 38; 116

Hays, James: Lough Swilly DL 38; 116

Hays, Messrs William and Sons: Seapatrick DN 12; 126–27

Hays' quay: Lough Swilly DL 38; 116

Hayshanks, G.: Comber DN 7; 41

Hayshanks, G.: Dundonald DN 7; 64

Hazelbank House: Carnmoney AM 2; 46, 84

Hazlebrook House: Rasharkin AM 23; 128, 130, 138, 140

Hazleton, Rev. Edward: Ardstraw TE 5; 8

Hazleton, T.: Drumcree AH 1; 40

Hazlett, Capt.: Killygarvan DL 38; 46–47

Hazlett, Capt.: Tullyaughnish DL 38; 87, 92, 96

Hazlett, Charles: Dunboe LY 11; 81

Hazlett, Charles: Tullyaughnish DL 38; 96

Hazlett, Henry: Bovevagh LY 25; 54, 56

Hazlett, Henry: Dungiven LY 15; 96

Hazlett, Isaac: Coleraine LY 33; 105

Hazlett, Isaac: Dunboe LY 11; 62, 70, 73–74, 79–80

Hazlett, Rev. James: Donaghedy TE 5; 89

Hazlett, Rev. Robert: Coleraine LY 33; 64

Hazlett, Robert: Aghadowey LY 22; 6, 27

Hazlett, Robert: Coleraine LY 33; 63–64, 73, 138

Hazlett, Robert: Killowen LY 33; 159

Hazlewood (see Hazlebrook): Rasharkin AM 23; 130

Hazley, Samuel: Hillsborough DN 12; 107

Hazlit, Rev.: Tamlaght Finlagan LY 25; 69

Hazzard, Lady: Tynan AH 1; 129–30

Head lough: Aghalurcher FH 4; 3–4, 9, 16

Head lough: Aghavea FH 4; 18

Head, Mrs: Kilbroney DN 3; 35

Headford House: Coleraine LY 33; 63

Headley, Lord: Faughanvale LY 36; 45

Headly bridge: Tullyaughnish DL 38; 90

Headly, Mary: Carrickfergus AM 37; 120

Headwood school: Kilwaughter AM 10; 119

Headwood td: Kilwaughter AM 10; 119, 122

Healey, Eliza: Tamlaght Finlagan LY 25; 119

Healey, John: Tamlaght Finlagan LY 25; 119

Healey, Margret: Tamlaght Finlagan LY 25; 119

Healey, Maryann: Tamlaght Finlagan LY 25; 119

Healey, Neil: Tamlaght Finlagan LY 25; 119

Heaney, Ann: Bovevagh LY 25; 60

Heaney, Bernard: Banagher LY 30; 37

Heaney, Edward: Bovevagh LY 25; 47

Heaney, family: Banagher LY 30; 97

Heaney, Frederick: Banagher LY 30; 37, 71, 89

Heaney, Hugh: Bovevagh LY 25; 31

Heaney, Hugh: Drummaul AM 19; 90

Heaney, James: Ballyscullion LY 6; 66

Heaney, James: Banagher LY 30; 88

Heaney, James: Bovevagh LY 25; 47

Heaney, James: Dungiven LY 15; 71, 83, 85–86, 91

Heaney, Margaret: Island Magee AM 10; 39, 94

Heaney, Martha: Lissan LY 31; 105

Heaney, Michael: Banagher LY 30; 95

Heaney, Michael: Bovevagh LY 25; 47

Heaney, Michael: Dungiven LY 15; 118

Heaney, Michael: Lissan LY 31; 101

Heaney, Thomas: Banagher LY 30; 97

Heaney, Widow: Banagher LY 30; 95

Heaney's bridge: Aghagallon AM 21; 1, 6–7

Heany, Bryan: Banagher LY 30; 71

Heany, Dr: Tamlaght O'Crilly LY 18; 90, 111

Heany, family: Banagher LY 30; 71

Heany, Grace: Banagher LY 30; 48, 76, 81

Heany, Hugh: Aghagallon AM 21; 21

Heany, man named: Banagher LY 30; 38

Heany, Michael: Dungiven LY 15; 117

Heany, Pat: Banagher LY 30; 48, 76, 95

Heany, Patrick: Lissan LY 31; 109

Heard, family (Cork): Clondermot LY 34; 46

Heard, Stephen [I]: Clondermot LY 34; 46

Heard, Stephen [II]: Clondermot LY 34; 46

Heaslett, Alexander: Maghera LY 18; 41

Heaslett, Henery: Balteagh LY 9; 24, 36, 41

Heaslett, James: Balteagh LY 9; 24

Heastie, John: Aghalee AM 21; 33

Heastie, Rev. John: Ballinderry AM 21; 50

Heather House: Drumachose LY 9; 118

Heather, J.: Ardkeen DN 7; 3

Heather, J.: Creggan AH 1; 27

Heather, J.: Keady AH 1; 47

Heather, J.: Killevy AH 1; 52

Heather, J.: Knockbreda DN 7; 101

Heather, J.: Tullynakill DN 7; 124

Heathwood, James: Newry DN 3; 100

Heatley, Rev. S.S.: Ballyscullion AM 19; 9, 11

Heatley, Rev. S.S.: Drummaul AM 19; 42, 44, 58, 69, 84, 86

Heats, Nicholas: Ballyscullion LY 6; 57

Heaveron, family: Magheragall AM 21; 99

Hebrides (Scotland): Island Magee AM 10; 19

Hebrides: Glynn AM 26; 33

Hebrides: Racavan AM 13; 103

Heddles cove: Island Magee AM 10; 101

Heffron, James: Donegore AM 29; 134

Hegarty, Bernard: Maghera LY 18; 80

Hegarty, Patt: Kilmacteige SO 40; 194

Hegerty, Thomas: Coleraine LY 33; 145

Hegerty, William: Maghera LY 18; 81

Heggarty, Henry: Agivey LY 22; 44

Heggarty, John: Kilrea LY 27; 129

Heggarty, Susan: Kilrea LY 27; 122

Heiny, family: Culfeightrin AM 24; 59

Heirs, family: Misc. LY 36; 104

Helder (Holland): Kilbroney DN 3; 34

Helferty, Samuel: Maghera LY 18; 81

Hell Hole locality: Aghalee AM 21; 26

Hell Hole locality: Magilligan LY 11; 99

Hemans, Alexander: Tamlaght TE 20; 77

Hemans, G.W.: Duneane AM 19; 97, 105

Hemans, G.W.: Kildollagh LY 22; 72

Hemerston, Joseph: Ballyscullion AM 19; 10

Hemings, Rev. John: Newry DN 3; 103

Hemphill, Curtis: Ballyaghran LY 33; 19

Hemphill, family: Macosquin LY 22; 83, 119

Hemphill, Hugh: Aghadowey LY 22; 37

Hemphill, James: Aghadowey LY 22; 26, 34

Hemphill, James: Coleraine LY 33; 104–05

Hemphill, James: Macosquin LY 22; 80, 102

Hemphill, John: Aghadowey LY 22; 32

Hemphill, John: Macosquin LY 22; 84, 87–88, 108–09

Hemphill, Martha: Kildollagh LY 22; 75

Hemphill, Mrs: Aghadowey LY 22; 5–6

Hemphill, William: Ballywillin AM 16; 35

Hempson, Denis: Magilligan LY 11; 103, 115, 129, 138

Hempton and Co., Messrs: Clondermot LY 34; 77–78, 81

Hempton and Co., Messrs: Faughanvale LY 36; 39

Hempton, Capt.: Lough Swilly DL 38; 113

Hempton's bank: Culdaff DL 38; 21

Hempton's bank: Lough Swilly DL 38; 113, 137–38

Hen Island: Killinchy DN 7; 86, 92

Hen mountain: Clonduff DN 3; 5

Henan, Mr: Newry DN 3; 106–07

Hendern, family: Carrickfergus AM 37; 179

Henderson, Alexander: Blaris DN 12; 49

Henderson, Andrea: Kilcronaghan LY 31; 66

Henderson, Anne: Coleraine LY 33; 146

Henderson, Capt.: Ballyscullion AM 19; 10

Henderson, David: Maghera LY 18; 12, 24, 54, 56–57, 72

Henderson, David: Magherafelt LY 6; 94, 105

Henderson, Edward (Jnr): Tamlaght TE 20; 136

Henderson, Edward (Snr): Tamlaght TE 20; 128

Henderson, Edward: Carnmoney AM 2; 49, 93

Henderson, family: Clondermot LY 34; 104

Henderson, family: Desertoghill LY 27; 5, 30

Henderson, family: Enniskillen FH 4; 58

Henderson, family: Kilcronaghan LY 31; 66, 80

Henderson, family: Racavan AM 13; 100

Henderson, family: Templepatrick AM 35; 133

Henderson, Frederick: Kilcronaghan LY 31; 66

Henderson, Hugh: Dungiven LY 15; 98

Henderson, James (Jnr): Coleraine LY 33; 146

Henderson, James (Snr): Coleraine LY 33; 146

Henderson, James: Ballymoney AM 16; 24

Henderson, James: Carnmoney AM 2; 49, 93

Henderson, James: Clondermot LY 34; 37, 78–79, 104

Henderson, James: Hillsborough DN 12; 87, 97, 99, 105

Henderson, James: Newry DN 3; 100, 104–05

Henderson, James [I]: Coleraine LY 33; 73

Henderson, John: Drummaul AM 19; 90

Henderson, John: Hillsborough DN 12; 97, 102–03

Henderson, John: Maghera LY 18; 56

Henderson, John: Tamlaght TE 20; 75, 136

Henderson, Joseph: Tamlaght TE 20; 136

Henderson, Kennedy: Maghera LY 18; 68

Henderson, Kennedy: Termoneeny LY 6; 129

Henderson, Martha: Doagh AM 29; 83, 98

Henderson, Mr (Strangford): Bright DN 17; 35

Henderson, Mr: Carrickfergus AM 37; 39

Henderson, Rev. Alexander: Blaris AM 8; 24, 26, 54–55, 57–58, 60, 62

Henderson, Rev. Alexander: Blaris DN 12; 35, 46, 50

Henderson, Rev. Andrew: Kilcronaghan LY 31; 66, 136

Henderson, Rev. James: Balteagh LY 9; 4

Henderson, Rev. M.W.: Drummaul AM 19; 92

Henderson, Rev. Robert: Drumachose LY 9; 67

Henderson, Rev. W.: Blaris AM 8; 10

Henderson, Rev. William: Drummaul AM 19; 69, 82

Henderson, Robert: Carrickfergus AM 37; 108

Henderson, Robert: Lissan LY 31; 102–04

Henderson, Robert: Maghera LY 18; 79

Henderson, Robert: Tamlaght TE 20; 81, 118, 121

Henderson, Samuel: Templepatrick AM 35; 147

Henderson, Thomas: Ballyculter DN 17; 27

Henderson, Thomas: Killyleagh DN 17; 85

Hendren, family: Carrickfergus AM 37; 93

Hendren, family: Derryaghy AM 8; 103

Hendren, J.R.: Ballinderry AM 21; 46, 58–59
Hendron, James: Carrickfergus AM 37; 129
Hendron, William: Carrickfergus AM 37; 96–97
Hendy, family: Maghera LY 18; 24, 48
Henery, Charles: Artrea LY 6; 35
Henery, Daniel: Ballynascreen LY 31; 31
Henery, family: Lambeg AM 8; 135
Henery, Henery: Tamlaght O'Crilly LY 18; 137
Henery, Hugh: Errigal LY 27; 69–70
Henery, Hugh: Maghera LY 18; 44
Henery, James: Ballyscullion LY 6; 47
Henery, James: Magherafelt LY 6; 98
Henery, Jane: Ballyscullion LY 6; 60
Henery, John: Ballynascreen LY 31; 21
Henery, Miss: Ballyscullion LY 6; 47
Henery, Molly: Drumachose LY 9; 133
Henery, Pady: Desertlyn LY 31; 42
Henery, Patrick: Ballyscullion LY 6; 50, 72
Henery, Patt: Ballynascreen LY 31; 21
Henery, Rev, Robert: Magherafelt LY 6; 98–99
Henery, Robert: Aghadowey LY 22; 37
Henery, Samual: Macosquin LY 22; 119
Henery, Widow: Ballynascreen LY 31; 21
Heney td: Killymard DL 39; 101
Heney, Bernard: Carrickfergus AM 37; 125
Heney, family: Killagan AM 23; 84
Henry and Mullins, Messrs: Magilligan LY 11; 124
Henry II, King: Antrim AM 29; 37
Henry II, King: Ardglass DN 17; 3
Henry II, King: Ballyclug AM 23; 57
Henry II, King: Carrickfergus AM 37; 18, 34, 42,
    62, 90
Henry II, King: Connor AM 19; 18
Henry II, King: Drummaul AM 19; 53, 69
Henry II, King: Kilbride AM 29; 149
Henry II, King: Manorhamilton Union LM 40; 51
Henry II, King: Muckamore AM 35; 82
Henry II, King: Raloo AM 32; 116
Henry II, King: Templepatrick AM 35; 130
Henry II, King: Umgall AM 35; 160
Henry III, King: Carrickfergus AM 37; 79
Henry III, King: Culfeightrin AM 24; 68
Henry III, King: Drummaul AM 19; 69
Henry III, King: Island Magee AM 10; 62
Henry III, King: Kilbride AM 29; 149
Henry III, King: Larne AM 10; 125
Henry III, King: Templepatrick AM 35; 130
Henry III, King: Tickmacrevan AM 13; 124
Henry III, King: Umgall AM 35; 160
Henry IV, King: Aghadowey LY 22; 31
Henry IV, King: Drummaul AM 19; 69
Henry IV, King: Island Magee AM 10; 62
Henry IV, King: Kilkeel DN 3; 53
Henry VI, King: Ardglass DN 17; 3, 12
Henry VI, King: Connor AM 19; 18

Henry VI, King: Killead AM 35; 32
Henry VII, King: Drummaul AM 19; 69
Henry VII, King: Island Magee AM 10; 62
Henry VII, King: Kilbride AM 29; 149
Henry VIII, King: Ardglass DN 17; 12
Henry VIII, King: Camlin AM 21; 60
Henry VIII, King: Carrickfergus AM 37; 137
Henry VIII, King: Clogher TE 5; 28
Henry VIII, King: Clondermot LY 34; 53
Henry VIII, King: Clones FH 4; 29
Henry VIII, King: Coleraine LY 33; 156–57
Henry VIII, King: Currin MN 40; 90
Henry VIII, King: Drummaul AM 19; 69
Henry VIII, King: Galloon FH 4; 97
Henry VIII, King: Island Magee AM 10; 62
Henry VIII, King: Kilbride AM 29; 149
Henry VIII, King: Kildollagh LY 22; 72
Henry VIII, King: Killead AM 35; 32
Henry VIII, King: Magheramesk AM 21; 126
Henry VIII, King: Muckamore AM 35; 54, 56,
    82–83
Henry VIII, King: Newry DN 3; 63–64
Henry VIII, King: Newtownards DN 7; 107
Henry VIII, King: Rasharkin AM 23; 138
Henry, A.: Clondermot LY 34; 93
Henry, Aaron: Faughanvale LY 36; 16
Henry, Alexander: Kilcronaghan LY 31; 86
Henry, Ann: Aghanloo LY 11; 39
Henry, Arthur: Killead AM 35; 46
Henry, Arthur: Termoneeny LY 6; 132
Henry, Bernard: Maghera LY 18; 81
Henry, Catherine: Ahoghill AM 23; 38
Henry, David: Newry DN 3; 106
Henry, Denis: Ballynascreen LY 31; 11, 22
Henry, Dominick: Maghera LY 18; 81
Henry, Dr: Banagher LY 30; 23
Henry, Dr: Newtownards DN 7; 108
Henry, Elizabeth: Kilrea LY 27; 129
Henry, family: Ballee DN 17; 16
Henry, family: Blaris AM 8; 22
Henry, family: Carnmoney AM 2; 34
Henry, family: Kilraghts AM 16; 130
Henry, family: Maghera LY 18; 13
Henry, family: Misc. LY 31; 122
Henry, family: Newry DN 3; 108
Henry, Frances: Kilrea LY 27; 129
Henry, Frank: Maghera LY 18; 81
Henry, George: Down DN 17; 59
Henry, George: Kilraghts AM 16; 132
Henry, Henry: Maghera LY 18; 81
Henry, Hugh: Kilraghts AM 16; 132
Henry, J.: Magheradrool DN 17; 102
Henry, James: Faughanvale LY 36; 40
Henry, James: Kilbroney DN 3; 38
Henry, James: Kilcronaghan LY 31; 85

Henry, James: Maghera LY 18; 6, 50
Henry, James: Magherafelt LY 6; 103
Henry, James: Tamlaght O'Crilly LY 18; 110, 119, 132
Henry, John: Connor AM 19; 27
Henry, John: Dunluce AM 16; 122
Henry, John: Galloon FH 4; 91
Henry, John: Macosquin LY 22; 85, 108, 113
Henry, John: Maghera LY 18; 28, 54, 76
Henry, John: Tamlaght O'Crilly LY 18; 94, 106, 118, 122, 132
Henry, John [I]: Ahoghill AM 23; 39
Henry, John [II]: Ahoghill AM 23; 39
Henry, Joseph: Ahoghill AM 23; 39
Henry, Joseph: Macosquin LY 22; 92, 120
Henry, kings named: Shilvodan AM 19; 136
Henry, Messrs: Faughanvale LY 36; 4
Henry, Miss: Billy AM 16; 56, 64
Henry, Miss: Coleraine LY 33; 72, 104, 106
Henry, Miss: Magherafelt LY 6; 90
Henry, Mr (Ballynagown): Misc. LY 31; 132
Henry, Mr: Drumballyroney DN 3; 16
Henry, Mr: Kilkeel DN 3; 49
Henry, Mr: Tomregan FH 4; 129
Henry, Mrs: Ballymoney AM 16; 17
Henry, Patrick: Kilcronaghan LY 31; 84
Henry, Patrick [I]: Maghera LY 18; 8, 68
Henry, Patrick [II]: Maghera LY 18; 81
Henry, Peter: Maghera LY 18; 8, 68
Henry, Rev.: Connor AM 19; 18, 21
Henry, Rev.: Loughgilly AH 1; 86
Henry, Rev. Henry: Desertoghill LY 27; 10
Henry, Rev. Michael: Banagher LY 30; 14
Henry, Rev. Michael: Cumber LY 28; 19, 77, 84
Henry, Rev. Thomas: Drummaul AM 19; 69, 82–83
Henry, Rev. William: Loughgall AH 1; 76
Henry, Robert: Killead AM 35; 18, 50
Henry, Robert: Kilraghts AM 16; 136
Henry, Robert: Loughguile AM 13; 66
Henry, Robert: Maghera LY 18; 54
Henry, Rodger: Maghera LY 18; 61
Henry, T.G.: Newry DN 3; 71, 93, 99, 104, 106, 108
Henry, Thomas (Snr): Newry DN 3; 99
Henry, Thomas: Aghanloo LY 11; 39
Henry, Thomas: Kilcronaghan LY 31; 78, 86
Henry, Thomas: Kilrea LY 27; 129
Henry, Thomas: Maghera LY 18; 81
Henry, Thomas: Newry DN 3; 99, 104, 107
Henry, Widow: Ballynascreen LY 31; 14
Henry, William (Jnr): Aghanloo LY 11; 39
Henry, William (Snr): Aghanloo LY 11; 39
Henry, William: Carrickfergus AM 37; 114
Henry, William: Donaghmoyne MN 40; 111
Henry, William: Killanny MN 40; 134
Henry, William: Maghera LY 18; 75

Henry, William: Newry DN 3; 104
Henryfield House: Doagh AM 29; 87
Hepburn, John: Carrickfergus AM 37; 128
Hepburn, Sarah: Carrickfergus AM 37; 131
Hepson, John [I]: Termoneeny LY 6; 133
Hepson, John [II]: Termoneeny LY 6; 133
Herbert, Rev. Nicholas: Coleraine LY 33; 63
Herbeson, G.: Templepatrick AM 35; 132
Herd, family: Drumbeg AM 8; 123
Herd's Seat rock: Leck DL 39; 115
Herd's Seat trigonometrical station: Leck DL 39; 115
Herdman, Billy: Templecorran AM 26; 130
Herdman, John [I]: Carrickfergus AM 37; 75, 151, 176
Herdman, John [II]: Carrickfergus AM 37; 151
Herdman, Messrs Lyons and Co.: Urney DL 39; 177
Herdman, Thomas: Carrickfergus AM 37; 75, 176, 183
Herdman's inn: Templecorran AM 26; 130
Herdstown td: Donaghadee DN 7; 45
Herdstown td: Misc. DN 17; 124
Herman, family: Lambeg AM 8; 135
Hermitage House: Errigal LY 27; 39
Hermitage td: Clonleigh DL 39; 12, 197
Hermitage td: Drummully FH 4; 34, 39
Hero's Road fort: Kilmacteige SO 40; 187
Heroe's rock: Kilmacteige SO 40; 193
Heron Island: Inishmacsaint FH 14; 73
Heron Island: Killinchy DN 7; 87
Heron lough: Killinchy DN 7; 87
Heron, Alexander: Drumballyroney DN 3; 10
Heron, David: Newry DN 3; 98, 103
Heron, Edward: Carrickfergus AM 37; 110
Heron, family: Blaris AM 8; 21
Heron, family: Carnmoney AM 2; 76
Heron, family: Muckamore AM 35; 65
Heron, John: Garvaghy DN 12; 83
Heron, John: Shilvodan AM 19; 138
Heron, M.: Clondermot LY 34; 86
Heron, man named: Muckamore AM 35; 68
Heron, Rev. M.: Desertcreat TE 20; 36
Heron, Rev. Matthew: Killea and Taughboyne DL 39; 87, 92, 186
Heron, Rev. William: Carrickfergus AM 37; 155
Heron, Rev. William: Doagh AM 29; 75, 81–83, 87, 97
Heron, Robert: Killyleagh DN 17; 81, 83
Heron, Samuel: Carrickfergus AM 37; 130
Heron, T.: Garvaghy DN 12; 81
Herrill, Eliza: Drummaul AM 19; 91
Herrill, John: Drummaul AM 19; 91
Herrill, Stewart: Drummaul AM 19; 91
Herron, Cowan: Dromara DN 12; 64
Herron, Cowan: Dromore DN 12; 72

Herron, John: Blaris AM 8; 55, 62
Herron, John: Blaris DN 12; 39, 46, 48, 50
Herron, Master: Blaris AM 8; 84
Herron, Miss: Blaris AM 8; 84
Herron, Mrs: Blaris AM 8; 84–85
Herron, Rev. J.: Drumballyroney DN 3; 15
Herron, Robert: Kilmore DN 17; 90
Herron, Samuel: Blaris DN 12; 44–45, 47–49
Herron, Samuel: Muckamore AM 35; 78
Hertford Arms Hotel: Blaris AM 8; 14–15, 50–51, 54
Hertford Arms Hotel: Derryaghy AM 8; 103
Hertford bridge: Blaris DN 12; 28, 34
Hertford bridge: Magheramesk AM 21; 118
Hertford estate: Blaris AM 8; 14
Hertford estate: Derryaghy AM 8; 91, 102
Hertford, family: Glenavy AM 21; 87
Hertford, family: Magheragall AM 21; 101
Hertford, family: Magheramesk AM 21; 126
Hertford, Lord: Ballinderry AM 21; 56
Hertford, Lord: Blaris AM 8; 3, 5, 8–9, 11–14, 16–18, 22, 25–26, 30–34, 37, 39–44, 48, 54, 59–61, 64–66, 70, 75, 82, 84, 86
Hertford, Lord: Blaris DN 12; 26, 32, 34, 36, 42–44, 47
Hertford, Lord: Carrickfergus AM 37; 38
Hertford, Lord: Derryaghy AM 8; 99, 104, 111, 116, 118
Hertford, Lord: Lambeg AM 8; 137, 139
Hertford, Lord Francis: Blaris AM 8; 25, 27
Hertford, Marquis of: Aghagallon AM 21; 1, 3, 11, 17–19, 21
Hertford, Marquis of: Aghalee AM 21; 26, 28, 31
Hertford, Marquis of: Ballinderry AM 21; 41, 44–50, 52
Hertford, Marquis of: Camlin AM 21; 60, 68–69, 75–76
Hertford, Marquis of: Glenavy AM 21; 77, 79, 85–87, 91
Hertford, Marquis of: Killead AM 35; 8
Hertford, Marquis of: Magheragall AM 21; 99–100, 107
Hertford, Marquis of: Magheramesk AM 21; 112, 114, 117, 119, 130
Hertford, Marquis of: Tullyrusk AM 21; 131, 135, 137, 139
Hervey Hill bridge: Tamlaght O'Crilly LY 18; 92, 108
Hervey Hill female Sunday school: Tamlaght O'Crilly LY 18; 142
Hervey Hill House: Tamlaght O'Crilly LY 18; 87, 91, 98–99, 107, 119, 142
Hervey Hill school: Tamlaght O'Crilly LY 18; 99, 104, 139, 143

Hervey Hill Sunday school: Tamlaght O'Crilly LY 18; 143
Hervey, Bishop: Aghanloo LY 11; 23
Hervey, Bishop: Dunboe LY 11; 60–61, 63
Hervey, Bishop: Magilligan LY 11; 100
Hervey, Bishop: Tamlaght Finlagan LY 25; 108
Hervey, Frederick: Dunboe LY 11; 46
Hervey, George: Dunboe LY 11; 46
Hervey, James: Annaclone DN 12; 18
Heslip, Robert: Antrim AM 29; 42
Hessan, Arthur: Maghera LY 18; 8, 68
Hessan, Edward: Maghera LY 18; 78
Hessan, family: Errigal LY 27; 41
Hessan, Frank: Maghera LY 18; 78
Hessan, Jackson: Kilcronaghan LY 31; 78–79
Hessan, John: Maghera LY 18; 78
Hessan, Margret: Maghera LY 18; 78
Hessan, Mary: Maghera LY 18; 78
Hessan, Nancy: Maghera LY 18; 78
Hessan, Patrick: Maghera LY 18; 8, 68
Hessan, William: Maghera LY 18; 78
Hesson, Jackson: Kilcronaghan LY 31; 82
Hetherington, family: Ballynure AM 32; 56
Hetherington, J.A.: Kilwaughter AM 10; 120
Heuston, Samuel: Kilwaughter AM 10; 120
Hewitt, Absolam: Kilmore AH 1; 58
Hewitt, Alexander: Dromore DN 12; 78
Hewitt, Joseph: Shankill AH 1; 116
Hewitt, Mr: Clogher TE 5; 40
Hewitt, Mr: Kilmore AH 1; 66, 72
Hewitt, Rev. J.P.: Desertlyn LY 31; 41, 49–50
Hewitt, Rev. J.P.: Enniskeen CN 40; 30
Hewney, James: Blaris AM 8; 35
Hewney, John: Blaris AM 8; 78
Hexam, Henry: Dunboe LY 11; 61
Heyland, A.R.: Errigal LY 27; 40, 58
Heyland, Col (Garvagh): Banagher LY 30; 46
Heyland, Col: Killead AM 35; 14
Heyland, Dominic: Tamlaght O'Crilly LY 18; 142
Heyland, family: Aghadowey LY 22; 11
Heyland, family: Derryaghy AM 8; 103
Heyland, H.J.: Errigal LY 27; 40, 46, 58, 63–64, 82
Heyland, H.J.: Kilrea LY 27; 114
Heyland, H.J.: Tamlaght O'Crilly LY 18; 115, 117
Heyland, John: Macosquin LY 22; 102, 105–07, 119
Heyland, L.R.: Aghadowey LY 22; 27
Heyland, L.R.: Errigal LY 27; 79
Heyland, L.R.: Tamlaght O'Crilly LY 18; 82, 89, 102, 107, 140
Heyland, Maj.: Killead AM 35; 11
Heyland, Miss (Ballyness): Macosquin LY 22; 92, 102
Heyland, Mr: Macosquin LY 22; 85
Heyland, Mrs A.R.: Errigal LY 27; 40, 50, 63, 70, 79–80

Heyland, Richard: Coleraine LY 33; 64

Heyland, Richard: Macosquin LY 22; 102

Heyland, Rowley (Crumlin): Macosquin LY 22; 85, 106

Heyland, Rowley (Dublin): Macosquin LY 22; 83, 105

Heyland, Rowley (Glenoak): Errigal LY 27; 40, 58

Heyland, Rowley (Langford Lodge): Killead AM 35; 15, 43

Heyland, Rowley: Tamlaght O'Crilly LY 18; 105, 132

Hibbots, Thomas: Carrickfergus AM 37; 42

Hickeson, Robert: Macosquin LY 22; 92

Hickey, Rev. Thomas: Coleraine LY 33; 95, 142

Hicks, John: Blaris AM 8; 55

Hicks, John: Blaris DN 12; 46, 50

Hicks, Mr: Blaris DN 12; 46

Hickson, Richard: Carrickfergus AM 37; 195

Hide, Joseph: Magheragall AM 21; 104

Hierman, Patt: Kilmacteige SO 40; 195

Higans, Catherin: Tamlaght TE 20; 77

Higans, Duncan: Tamlaght TE 20; 77, 104

Higans, Rachel: Tamlaght TE 20; 77

Higerty, family: Ballynascreen LY 31; 12

Higgan, Patrick: Maghera LY 18; 60

Higginbotham, family: Enniskillen FH 4; 58

Higginbotham, Rev. Robert: Killowen LY 33; 160

Higgins, Bernard [I]: Errigal LY 27; 55

Higgins, Bernard [II]: Errigal LY 27; 65

Higgins, Daniel: Carrickfergus AM 37; 121

Higgins, family: Desertmartin LY 31; 55

Higgins, family: Errigal LY 27; 41

Higgins, family: Maghera LY 18; 24

Higgins, family: Magheragall AM 21; 99

Higgins, Francis: Kilcronaghan LY 31; 76–78

Higgins, Henry: Kilcronaghan LY 31; 77

Higgins, James: Kilcronaghan LY 31; 84

Higgins, James: Lissan LY 31; 102

Higgins, James: Magheragall AM 21; 101, 105

Higgins, John: Ahoghill AM 23; 35

Higgins, John: Dunaghy AM 13; 23

Higgins, John: Lissan LY 31; 102

Higgins, man named (Gortahurk): Kilcronaghan LY 31; 77

Higgins, Michael: Kilmacteige SO 40; 193

Higgins, Rev.: Misc. LY 31; 137

Higgins, Sarah: Kilcronaghan LY 31; 84

Higginson, Agnus Eliza: Blaris AM 8; 56–57, 85

Higginson, Charles: Blaris AM 8; 58, 61

Higginson, family: Ballinderry AM 21; 51

Higginson, family: Carrickfergus AM 37; 93

Higginson, family: Derryaghy AM 8; 103

Higginson, family: Magheragall AM 21; 99

Higginson, George: Blaris DN 12; 30, 41

Higginson, H.T.: Blaris AM 8; 50, 52–55, 60, 84–85

Higginson, H.T.: Blaris DN 12; 40, 43, 46, 50

Higginson, Howe: Blaris DN 12; 40

Higginson, James: Culfeightrin AM 24; 45

Higginson, James: Drummaul AM 19; 56

Higginson, Jane Frances: Blaris AM 8; 57–58

Higginson, John: Ardclinis AM 13; 1, 7

Higginson, John: Dundermot AM 13; 31, 34

Higginson, John: Glenwhirry AM 32; 78

Higginson, Margaret: Derryaghy AM 8; 103

Higginson, Maria: Blaris AM 8; 85

Higginson, Miss (Snr): Blaris AM 8; 85

Higginson, Miss: Blaris AM 8; 58–59, 84–85

Higginson, Mrs: Blaris AM 8; 58, 85

Higginson, Rev. Edward: Derryaghy AM 8; 103

Higginson, Rev. J.: Blaris AM 8; 12

Higginson, Rev. T.E.: Blaris AM 8; 52, 58–59, 61

Higginson, T.: Blaris DN 12; 41

Higgison, Maj.: Duneane AM 19; 116

High bank: Moville DL 38; 77

High Buckna (Bucknaw) td: Racavan AM 13; 96, 100

High Buckna school: Racavan AM 13; 96, 100

High Cairne td: Tullyaughnish DL 38; 86

High Cross td: Donaghenry TE 20; 38

High Gate manor: Misc. FH 4; 133

High Glen td: Mevagh DL 38; 55, 63

High Top (see Top Upper): Ballymoney AM 16; 24

High Trench village: Raphoe DL 39; 125

Highbanks td: Raymoghy DL 39; 132, 137

Highgate Lodge: Galloon FH 4; 91

Highgate manor: Clones FH 4; 26

Highgate manor: Galloon FH 4; 94–95

Highgate td: Galloon FH 4; 93

Highland hill: Ballyscullion AM 19; 2

Highlands (Scotland): Grey Abbey DN 7; 72

Highlands: Ballyaghran LY 33; 6

Highlands: Ballyclug AM 23; 56

Highlands: Ballyrashane LY 22; 49

Highlands: Banagher LY 30; 108

Highlands: Clondermot LY 34; 62–64, 69

Highlands: Enniskeen CN 40; 26

Highlands: Faughanvale LY 36; 60

Highlands: Ramoan AM 24; 103

Highlandtown (Highlandstown) td: Ardclinis AM 13; 4, 7

Highmoor standing stone: Cumber LY 28; 43

Highmoor td: Cumber LY 28; 40–41, 44, 47, 49, 51, 60, 62, 81, 83, 96, 101, 105, 107

Highmoor wood: Cumber LY 28; 101

Hightown fort: Kilwaughter AM 10; 118

Higins, family: Maghera LY 18; 48

Hiland's hill: Desertoghill LY 27; 22

Hilcreboly td: Ballylinny AM 32; 30

Hilden bleach greens: Lambeg AM 8; 138–39

Hilden House: Lambeg AM 8; 138, 142

Hilden thread factory: Lambeg AM 8; 139, 142
Hilden wooden bridge: Lambeg AM 8; 141
Hilditch, family: Carrickfergus AM 37; 179
Hilditch, Leany: Island Magee AM 10; 94
Hilditch, Mr: Carrickfergus AM 37; 145
Hill and Hollow bank: Lough Swilly DL 38; 113
Hill fort: Macosquin LY 22; 110
Hill Head district: Taughboyne DL 39; 148, 151, 153
Hill Head House: Kirkinriola AM 23; 119
Hill Sead (see Hill Head): Taughboyne DL 39; 148
Hill Sunday school: Termoneeny LY 6; 124, 128
Hill, Alexander: Ballintoy AM 24; 25
Hill, Archabald: Coleraine LY 33; 146
Hill, Arthur: Donaghadee DN 7; 46
Hill, Arthur: Hillsborough DN 12; 89, 91–92
Hill, Arthur: Moira DN 12; 117–18
Hill, Charles: Dromara DN 12; 68
Hill, Col.: Island Magee AM 10; 65
Hill, Daniel: Ballintoy AM 24; 25
Hill, David: Ballintoy AM 24; 19
Hill, Ephraim: Island Magee AM 10; 102
Hill, family: Armoy AM 24; 6
Hill, family: Ballynure AM 32; 56
Hill, family: Billy AM 16; 58, 68
Hill, family: Blaris AM 8; 21
Hill, family: Carnmoney AM 2; 76
Hill, family: Carrickfergus AM 37; 93, 179
Hill, family: Hillsborough DN 12; 88
Hill, family: Island Magee AM 10; 70, 86
Hill, family: Magheramesk AM 21; 124
Hill, family: Misc. LY 36; 104
Hill, family: Ramoan AM 24; 107
Hill, G.A.: Carrickfergus AM 37; 42
Hill, G.A.: Hillsborough DN 12; 104
Hill, G.F.: Ballywillin LY 33; 33, 42
Hill, G.F.: Coleraine LY 33; 61–63, 93
Hill, G.F.: Desertoghill LY 27; 4–5
Hill, G.F.: Donaghedy TE 5; 92
Hill, G.F.: Faughanvale LY 36; 42
Hill, G.F.: Kilcronaghan LY 31; 71
Hill, G.F.: Killea and Taughboyne DL 39; 79
Hill, G.F.: Macosquin LY 22; 105
Hill, G.F.: Misc. LY 31; 129, 143
Hill, George: Clondermot LY 34; 6, 20, 27, 37, 47, 104
Hill, George: Coleraine LY 33; 64
Hill, Hugh: Ballymoney AM 16; 25
Hill, Hugh: Connor AM 19; 27
Hill, Hugh: Moira DN 12; 117–18
Hill, J.: Island Magee AM 10; 64
Hill, J.C.: Blaris AM 8; 55, 62, 66
Hill, J.C.: Blaris DN 12; 40–41, 43–44, 46–48, 50
Hill, James: Ahoghill AM 23; 34
Hill, James: Ballintoy AM 24; 23

Hill, James: Glynn AM 26; 44
Hill, James: Island Magee AM 10; 94, 100
Hill, John: Ballintoy AM 24; 23
Hill, John: Ballyscullion LY 6; 46, 52–53, 74
Hill, John: Duneane AM 19; 116
Hill, John: Hillsborough DN 12; 107
Hill, John: Ramoan AM 24; 116–17
Hill, John: Tamlaght O'Crilly LY 18; 83, 95, 115, 124
Hill, Joseph: Drummaul AM 19; 88
Hill, Lady: Hillsborough DN 12; 104
Hill, Lord: Carnmoney AM 2; 81
Hill, M.S.: Coleraine LY 33; 63–64
Hill, M.T.: Coleraine LY 33; 88
Hill, man named: Duneane AM 19; 108
Hill, man named: Island Magee AM 10; 65–66
Hill, Marcus: Carrickfergus AM 37; 42
Hill, Marcus: Newry DN 3; 75, 100, 105
Hill, Margaret: Coleraine LY 33; 146
Hill, Michael: Newry DN 3; 74
Hill, Miss: Blaris AM 8; 84–85
Hill, Misses: Island Magee AM 10; 102
Hill, Moses: Duneane AM 19; 107–08
Hill, Moses: Hillsborough DN 12; 88
Hill, Moses: Muckamore AM 35; 56
Hill, Mr (Co. Antrim): Ballymore AH 1; 18
Hill, Mr: Muckno MN 40; 165
Hill, Rev. (Ernagh): Killevy AH 1; 54
Hill, Rev.: Newtownards DN 7; 108
Hill, Rev. Adam: Ballynure AM 32; 64
Hill, Rev. C.: Culfeightrin AM 24; 40, 45
Hill, Rev. George: Killead AM 35; 39, 51
Hill, Rev. Robert: Aghalee AM 21; 31, 37
Hill, Rev. Robert: Blaris AM 8; 66
Hill, Rev. Robert: Magheramesk AM 21; 116, 127
Hill, Richard: Carrickfergus AM 37; 164
Hill, Robert: Drumachose LY 9; 117
Hill, Robert: Island Magee AM 10; 84, 86, 95
Hill, Robert: Magheross MN 40; 146
Hill, Robert: Ramoan AM 24; 116–17
Hill, Robert: Tamlaght Finlagan LY 25; 105
Hill, S.: Island Magee AM 10; 64
Hill, Samuel: Billy AM 16; 61, 70
Hill, Samuel: Carrickfergus AM 37; 163
Hill, Samuel: Ramoan AM 24; 104–06
Hill, Teron: Derrykeighan AM 16; 95
Hill, Thomas: Magheragall AM 21; 109–10
Hill, Thomas: Templecorran AM 26; 123
Hill, Timothy: Island Magee AM 10; 81
Hill, Trevor: Newry DN 3; 74
Hill, William: Aghadowey LY 22; 37
Hill, William: Ballintoy AM 24; 23
Hill, William: Blaris DN 12; 42
Hill, William: Carrickfergus AM 37; 35
Hill, William: Drumachose LY 9; 109

Hill, William: Island Magee AM 10; 64, 90
Hill, William: Newry DN 3; 65
Hill, William: Ramoan AM 24; 116–17
Hilland, John: Tullyniskan TE 20; 141
Hilland, Neal: Carrickfergus AM 37; 108
Hillditch, family: Carrickfergus AM 37; 93
Hillhall school: Drumbo DN 7; 59
Hillhall school: Hillsborough DN 12; 101
Hillhall td: Drumbo DN 7; 59–60, 63
Hillhall village: Drumbo DN 7; 60
Hillhall village: Misc. DN 17; 120
Hillhead district: Maghera LY 18; 54
Hillhead House: Ahoghill AM 23; 12, 15
Hillhead meeting house: Donagh DL 38; 33
Hillhead school: Ballyscullion LY 6; 61
Hillhead school: Donagh DL 38; 33, 35
Hillhead Sunday school: Ballyscullion LY 6; 62
Hillhead Sunday school: Donagh DL 38; 33
Hillis, family: Aghagallon AM 21; 9
Hillis, Joseph: Faughanvale LY 36; 35
Hillis, Stephen: Faughanvale LY 36; 35
Hillis, William: Annaclone DN 12; 14
Hillis' fort: Annaclone DN 12; 15
Hillman, Catherine: Artrea LY 6; 38
Hillman, Elenor: Artrea LY 6; 38
Hillman, family: Magherafelt LY 6; 95
Hillman, Henery: Artrea LY 6; 38
Hillman, Herculus: Artrea LY 6; 38
Hillman, John: Magherafelt LY 6; 100
Hillman, Thomas: Ballyscullion LY 6; 55
Hillman, Thomas: Magherafelt LY 6; 100
Hillmount bleach green: Ahoghill AM 23; 13, 31, 43
Hillmount House: Ahoghill AM 23; 12, 31
Hillsboro (see Hillsborough): Blaris AM 8; 73
Hillsborough: Aghaderg DN 12; 6
Hillsborough: Annaclone DN 12; 16
Hillsborough: Annahilt DN 12; 20–22
Hillsborough: Antrim AM 29; 5
Hillsborough: Blaris AM 8; 54, 73
Hillsborough: Blaris DN 12; 33–34
Hillsborough: Comber DN 7; 40
Hillsborough: Donaghcloney DN 12; 59
Hillsborough: Drumballyroney DN 3; 18
Hillsborough: Drumbo DN 7; 58–59
Hillsborough: Drumgath DN 3; 21
Hillsborough: Hillsborough DN 12; 87, 89, 93, 96,
  104–05
Hillsborough: Magheradrool DN 17; 107
Hillsborough: Magherally DN 12; 114
Hillsborough: Magheramesk AM 21; 118
Hillsborough: Misc. DN 17; 116
Hillsborough: Newry DN 3; 74
Hillsborough: Tullylish DN 12; 144
Hillsborough: Tullynakill DN 7; 122–23
Hillsborough black hole: Hillsborough DN 12; 102

Hillsborough Castle: Hillsborough DN 12; 88, 91,
  95–96, 105
Hillsborough Castle: Newry DN 3; 65
Hillsborough chapel: Magheramesk AM 21; 128
Hillsborough church: Blaris AM 8; 13
Hillsborough church: Hillsborough DN 12; 88–89
Hillsborough church school [I]: Hillsborough DN
  12; 87, 90, 99
Hillsborough church school [II]: Hillsborough DN
  12; 87, 90, 99
Hillsborough court house: Hillsborough DN 12; 87,
  90–91
Hillsborough demesne: Hillsborough DN 12; 89
Hillsborough dispensary: Blaris DN 12; 34
Hillsborough dispensary: Hillsborough DN 12;
  87–88, 90–91, 96–98
Hillsborough female school [I]: Hillsborough DN
  12; 87
Hillsborough female school [II]: Hillsborough DN
  12; 87
Hillsborough fever hospital: Hillsborough DN 12;
  93
Hillsborough Glebe House: Hillsborough DN 12; 91
Hillsborough hotel: Hillsborough DN 12; 102
Hillsborough male school [I]: Hillsborough DN 12;
  87
Hillsborough male school [II]: Hillsborough DN 12;
  87
Hillsborough market house: Hillsborough DN 12;
  88
Hillsborough meeting house (P): Hillsborough DN
  12; 90
Hillsborough meeting house (Q): Hillsborough DN
  12; 102
Hillsborough mill [I]: Hillsborough DN 12; 87, 99
Hillsborough mill [II]: Hillsborough DN 12; 87, 99
Hillsborough old fort: Hillsborough DN 12; 98
Hillsborough ph: Blaris DN 12; 26–27, 34
Hillsborough ph: Dromore DN 12; 70, 73
Hillsborough ph: Drumbo DN 7; 54
Hillsborough ph: Magheramesk AM 21; 112
Hillsborough ph: Moira DN 12; 117
Hillsborough poor house: Hillsborough DN 12;
  93–94, 98, 102–05
Hillsborough road bridge: Magheramesk AM 21;
  115
Hillsborough school: Hillsborough DN 12; 88, 100
Hillsborough shambles: Hillsborough DN 12; 102
Hillsborough td: Hillsborough DN 12; 85–86, 88, 98
Hillsborough, Earl of: Down DN 17; 42
Hillsborough, Lord: Hillsborough DN 12; 93, 102,
  104–05
Hillsborough, Viscount: Newry DN 3; 74
Hilltown: Clonallan DN 3; 1–2
Hilltown: Clonduff DN 3; 3–5

Hilltown: Kilbroney DN 3; 28, 37
Hilltown church: Clonduff DN 3; 4–6
Hilltown market house: Clonduff DN 3; 6
Hilltown meeting house: Clonduff DN 3; 4, 6
Hilltown school: Hillsborough DN 12; 101
Hilton demesne: Currin MN 40; 87–88, 96–97
Hilton House: Currin MN 40; 89
Hilton House: Galloon FH 4; 94, 105
Hilton, John: Tamlaght O'Crilly LY 18; 137
Hilton, Robert: Ahoghill AM 23; 34
Hilton, Robert: Tamlaght O'Crilly LY 18; 137
Hilton, William: Tamlaght O'Crilly LY 18; 137
Hinchigo (see Hunshigo): Drumballyroney DN 3;
   14
Hinde [or Hindman], Robert: Clondermot LY 34;
   87, 89, 91, 93, 95
Hindeman, John: Drummaul AM 19; 89
Hindes, family: Enniskillen FH 4; 75
Hindman [or Hinde], Robert: Clondermot LY 34;
   87, 89, 91, 93, 95
Hindman, Anne: Coleraine LY 33; 68, 134
Hindman, Margret: Dunboe LY 11; 81
Hindman, Robert: Rasharkin AM 23; 140
Hindman, Samuel: Dunboe LY 11; 75
Hinds, Arthur: Coleraine LY 33; 146
Hinds, Charles: Coleraine LY 33; 146
Hinds, Eliza: Ahoghill AM 23; 38
Hinds, family: Enniskillen FH 4; 75
Hinds, Fredrick: Coleraine LY 33; 146
Hinds, Hariot (Jnr): Coleraine LY 33; 146
Hinds, Hariot (Snr): Coleraine LY 33; 146, 154
Hinds, Hesther: Ahoghill AM 23; 38
Hinds, James: Coleraine LY 33; 146
Hinds, John (Jnr): Coleraine LY 33; 146
Hinds, John (Snr): Coleraine LY 33; 139, 146, 154
Hinds, John: Hillsborough DN 12; 107
Hinds, Mary: Coleraine LY 33; 146
Hinds, Thomas: Ahoghill AM 23; 38
Hinds, William: Coleraine LY 33; 146
Hintry, William: Tyholland MN 40; 175
Hitchcock, John: Antrim AM 29; 12
Hives, Samuel: Duneane AM 19; 120
Hoare, William: Kilmore AH 1; 60
Hobart, B.: Clogher TE 5; 40
Hobson, Rev. John: Connor AM 19; 18, 21, 30
Hobson, Rev. R.J.: Shilvodan AM 19; 133
Hockley Lodge: Loughgall AH 1; 80
Hockley school: Loughgall AH 1; 81
Hodge, John: Balteagh LY 9; 29
Hodgen, family: Derrykeighan AM 16; 89
Hodgen, William: Blaris DN 12; 40
Hodges and Smyth, Messrs: Ballynascreen LY 31;
   34
Hodges, family: Derrykeighan AM 16; 89
Hodges, Mr: Aghadowey LY 22; 27

Hodgins, smith: Kilrea LY 27; 112
Hodgkinson, Rodger: Blaris AM 8; 25
Hodgson, Capt.: Hillsborough DN 12; 105
Hoe lough: Kilmacteige SO 40; 191
Hoey, G.: Clondermot LY 34; 117
Hofferman: Killesher FH 14; 84
Hoffwyl (Switzerland): Faughanvale LY 36; 39
Hog Park Point: Glenavy AM 21; 82
Hogan, Catherine: Carrickfergus AM 37; 118
Hogan, James: Aghalee AM 21; 32
Hogan, John: Lissan LY 31; 109
Hogan, Mary: Lissan LY 31; 109
Hogart, family: Billy AM 16; 58, 68
Hogg deer park: Camlin AM 21; 62
Hogg, family: Lambeg AM 8; 135
Hogg, Henry: Tamlaght TE 20; 81, 108
Hogg, James: Ahoghill AM 23; 47
Hogg, James: Blaris AM 8; 23
Hogg, James: Blaris DN 12; 45, 49
Hogg, James: Lissan LY 31; 107
Hogg, James: Tamlaght TE 20; 97, 105
Hogg, Mary: Tamlaght TE 20; 98, 106
Hogg, Mr: Blaris AM 8; 84
Hogg, Mr: Drumbeg AM 8; 124
Hogg, Mrs: Blaris AM 8; 84–85
Hogg, Mrs: Blaris DN 12; 45, 49
Hogg, Robert: Tamlaght TE 20; 93, 103
Hogg, Thomas: Clondermot LY 34; 5, 19–20
Hogg, William: Blaris AM 8; 39
Hogg's lough: Saintfield DN 7; 117, 119
Hogg's park locality: Carrickfergus AM 37; 93
Hogset, family: Kilroot AM 26; 74–75
Hogset, William: Carrickfergus AM 37; 147
Hogset, William: Kilroot AM 26; 79
Hogsham, Col.: Loughgilly AH 1; 85
Hogshaw, Miss (Lisburn): Seagoe AH 1; 108–09
Hogshaw, Mr: Aughnamullen MN 40; 75–77
Hogstown td: Donaghadee DN 7; 45
Hogstown td: Misc. DN 17; 124
Holden, Robert (Edinburgh): Kilcronaghan LY 31;
   81
Holden, Sarah: Carrickfergus AM 37; 128
Holestone caves: Kilbride AM 29; 136
Holestone House: Doagh AM 29; 86
Holestone House: Donegore AM 29; 132
Holestone House: Kilbride AM 29; 138, 141, 150,
   154, 156
Holestone House: Nilteen AM 35; 102
Holestone House: Rashee AM 32; 138
Holestone plantation: Kilbride AM 29; 136, 155
Holestone standing stone: Kilbride AM 29; 135,
   138, 147, 149, 154, 156–57
Holestone td: Ballylinny AM 32; 26
Holestone td: Doagh AM 29; 96

Holestone td: Kilbride AM 29; 135–36, 138, 147–48, 151

Holland: Coleraine LY 33; 86

Holland: Kilbroney DN 3; 34

Holland: Killea and Taughboyne DL 39; 84

Holland: Magheracloone MN 40; 138

Holland: Newry DN 3; 87

Holland: Raymoghy DL 39; 132

Holland, Charles: Carrickfergus AM 37; 126

Holland, Elizabeth: Cumber LY 28; 68–69

Holland, family: Enniskillen FH 4; 58

Holland, Rev.: Carlingford LH 40; 60

Holland, Rev.: Magilligan LY 11; 89

Hollands (Holland) td: Clonleigh DL 39; 12, 197

Hollings, Joseph: Hillsborough DN 12; 105

Hollings. Thomas: Hillsborough DN 12; 105

Holliwood, family: Ballintoy AM 24; 18

Hollow school: Enniskillen FH 4; 84

Holly Bush enclosure: Bovevagh LY 25; 42–43

Holly Island: Enniskillen FH 4; 43

Holly, Hugh: Tamlaght TE 20; 92

Hollybank (see Edderdauglash): Cleenish FH 14; 28

Hollybrook House: Aghalurcher FH 4; 8

Hollybrook river: Aghalurcher FH 4; 4

Hollybrook td: Aghalurcher FH 4; 3–4, 14

Hollyhill House: Misc. TE 5; 147

Hollymount demesne: Aghavea FH 4; 18

Hollymount farm: Manorhamilton Union LM 40; 53

Hollymount female school: Down DN 17; 52, 59

Hollymount House: Clondermot LY 34; 6, 20, 37–38, 102

Hollymount House: Down DN 17; 49

Hollymount House: Kilkeel DN 3; 54

Hollymount House: Killygarvan DL 38; 40

Hollymount House: Manorhamilton Union LM 40; 50

Hollymount male school: Down DN 17; 52, 59

Hollymount school: Clondermot LY 34; 88

Hollymount td: Down DN 17; 49, 53, 55

Hollyoak, F.: Carlingford LH 40; 57–59

Hollyrood, J.: Carlingford LH 40; 60

Hollywood (see Holywood): Misc. DN 17; 117

Holmes, Dr: Coleraine LY 33; 143

Holmes, family: Aghalee AM 21; 36

Holmes, family: Island Magee AM 10; 70

Holmes, family: Raloo AM 32; 123

Holmes, George: Ahoghill AM 23; 34

Holmes, Henery: Magheragall AM 21; 103

Holmes, Hugh: Ahoghill AM 23; 39

Holmes, Jane: Ballymoney AM 16; 17

Holmes, John: Blaris DN 12; 40

Holmes, John: Derryaghy AM 8; 98

Holmes, John: Magheragall AM 21; 103–04

Holmes, Joseph: Desertoghill LY 27; 20

Holmes, Miss: Kilcronaghan LY 31; 88

Holmes, Mrs: Coleraine LY 33; 72

Holmes, Mrs W.H.: Kilrea LY 27; 122, 126

Holmes, Rev. John: Clondermot LY 34; 5, 22, 24

Holmes, Rev. John: Faughanvale LY 36; 33

Holmes, Rev. William: Antrim AM 29; 27

Holmes, Robert: Misc. SO 40; 200

Holmes, Thomas: Killead AM 35; 46

Holmes, W.H.: Ballyscullion AM 19, 10

Holmes, W.H.: Kilrea LY 27; 108–09, 114, 116, 120–21, 123, 127–29

Holmes, W.H.: Tamlaght O'Crilly LY 18; 90, 106, 111, 139–40

Holmes, William: Carrickfergus AM 37; 116

Holmes, William: Coleraine LY 33; 72, 127, 142

Holmes, William: Island Magee AM 10; 23, 81

Holmes, William: Kilroot AM 26; 77

Holmonstown district: Templecorran AM 26; 82

Holms, family: Carrickfergus AM 37; 93

Holms, George: Desertoghill LY 27; 16

Holy Knowe graveyard: Dunluce AM 16; 113, 120

Holy Now (see Holy Knowe)

Holy river: Lough Neagh AM 21; 93

Holy Well spring: Antrim AM 29; 4, 35

Holy Well td: Antrim AM 29; 4, 35

Holybrook House: Drummaul AM 19; 35, 79, 81

Holyhead (Wales): Blaris AM 8; 8

Holyhill bog: Leckpatrick TE 5; 120

Holyhill demesne: Leckpatrick TE 5; 120

Holyhill House: Lough Swilly DL 38; 150

Holyhill mountain: Leckpatrick TE 5; 121

Holyhill quarry: Leckpatrick TE 5; 123

Holyhill td: Leckpatrick TE 5; 120–21

Holyhill woods: Leckpatrick TE 5; 119

Holywell (Wales): Drummaul AM 19; 70

Holywell corn mill: Cleenish FH 14; 18

Holywell dispensary: Cleenish FH 14; 16, 23

Holywell dispensary: Killesher FH 14; 85

Holywell dispensary: Kinawley FH 4; 109

Holywell hill: Misc. DL 39; 185

Holywell House: Misc. DL 39; 186

Holywell old church: Cleenish FH 14; 19–20

Holywell tanyards: Cleenish FH 14; 25

Holywell tuck mill: Cleenish FH 14; 18

Holywell village: Cleenish FH 14; 15–16, 27

Holywell village: Killesher FH 14; 88

Holywell well: Cleenish FH 14; 21

Holywood: Banagher LY 30; 14

Holywood: Carrickfergus AM 37; 55

Holywood: Holywood DN 7; 79, 81

Holywood: Kilrea LY 27; 119, 126

Holywood Bank Lane school [I]: Holywood DN 7; 75

Holywood Bank Lane school [II]: Holywood DN 7; 75–76

Holywood Bishop's Palace: Holywood DN 7; 76

Holywood chapel: Holywood DN 7; 74–75
Holywood chapel: Misc. DN 17; 122
Holywood church: Holywood DN 7; 74, 78, 81
Holywood church: Misc. DN 17; 117
Holywood dispensary: Holywood DN 7; 81
Holywood friary: Holywood DN 7; 73–74
Holywood hospital: Holywood DN 7; 75
Holywood House: Holywood DN 7; 76
Holywood Main St school: Holywood DN 7; 76
Holywood meeting house (P): Holywood DN 7; 74, 81
Holywood meeting house (U): Holywood DN 7; 74, 81
Holywood Mill St school: Holywood DN 7; 76
Holywood old monastery: Holywood DN 7; 78, 82
Holywood ph: Bangor DN 7; 19
Holywood ph: Comber DN 7; 40
Holywood ph: Dundonald DN 7; 64–65
Holywood ph: Knockbreda DN 7; 97
Holywood ph: Misc. DN 17; 117–18, 121
Holywood poor house: Holywood DN 7; 83
Holywood Presbyterian school: Holywood DN 7; 76, 81
Holywood td: Holywood DN 7; 77, 79–80
Holywood td: Misc. DN 17; 117
Holywood water mills: Holywood DN 7; 76
Holywood, John: Newry DN 3; 99
Home, William: Newry DN 3; 98, 103
Homra demesne: Blaris DN 12; 34
Hondius, Henry: Dunboe LY 11; 61
Hone, Mr: Convoy DL 39; 21
Hone, Mr: Donaghmore DL 39; 36
Hood, James: Termoneeny LY 6; 133
Hood, John: Carrickfergus AM 37; 153
Hood, Mallow: Misc. DL 39; 186
Hood, Mr: Dunaghy AM 13; 27
Hood, Mr: Dundermot AM 13; 34
Hood, Rev. Hood: Clogher TE 5; 40
Hood, Rev. Richard: Aghabog MN 40; 63, 68
Hood, Richard: Tullyrusk AM 21; 139
Hood, Robert: Derryaghy AM 8; 98, 117
Hood, Widow: Muckamore AM 35; 81
Hoods Isle: Lough Swilly DL 38; 103
Hool, James (Jnr): Drumbeg AM 8; 133
Hool, James (Snr): Drumbeg AM 8; 133
Hool, Jonas: Drumbeg AM 8; 133
Hool, Mary: Drumbeg AM 8; 133
Hool, Robert: Drumbeg AM 8; 133
Hope, Elizabeth: Ballinderry AM 21; 59
Hope, family: Culfeightrin AM 24; 59
Hopes, A.: Blaris AM 8; 60
Hopes, family: Ballinderry AM 21; 48
Hopkin, Abraham: Drumachose LY 9; 104
Hopkin, Alexander: Aghanloo LY 11; 5, 27
Hopkin, family: Ramoan AM 24; 107

Hopkin, James: Drumachose LY 9; 53, 60, 120–21, 127
Hopkin, Mrs: Ballymoney AM 16; 17
Hopkin, William: Ballintoy AM 24; 27
Hopkins, Alexander: Aghanloo LY 11; 17, 19–20, 27, 35
Hopkins, Alexander: Errigal LY 27; 53
Hopkins, Bishop: Dunboe LY 11; 64
Hopkins, Eliza (Jnr): Aghanloo LY 11; 39
Hopkins, Eliza (Snr): Aghanloo LY 11; 39
Hopkins, James: Aghanloo LY 11; 19, 35, 39
Hopkins, James: Dunboe LY 11; 76
Hopkins, James: Magilligan LY 11; 138
Hopkins, John (Jnr): Aghanloo LY 11; 39
Hopkins, John (Snr): Aghanloo LY 11; 39
Hopkins, John: Tamlaght TE 20; 93
Hopkins, Mark: Aghanloo LY 11; 19, 35
Hopkins, Matilda: Aghanloo LY 11; 39
Hopkins, Messrs Alixander and Co.: Aghanloo LY 11; 29
Hopkins, Sarah: Ardstraw TE 5; 6
Hopkins, William: Aghanloo LY 11; 39
Hopkins, William: Ballywillin AM 16; 32
Hopkins, William: Ballywillin LY 33; 51
Hopkins, William: Drumtullagh AM 16; 102
Horbison, family: Ballinderry AM 21; 55
Hore, family: Ramoan AM 24; 107
Horn Castle: Ardglass DN 17; 3, 12
Horn Head: Clondavaddog DL 38; 6
Horn Head: Lough Swilly DL 38; 119, 121–22
Horn Head: Mevagh DL 38; 56, 59, 61–62
Horn Head bridge: Lough Swilly DL 38; 129
Horn Head House: Lough Swilly DL 38; 121
Horner, A.: Ballybay MN 40; 81, 84
Horner, family: Magheragall AM 21; 99
Horner, Francis: Clondermot LY 34; 103
Horner, Henry: Balteagh LY 9; 35–36, 38
Horner, Henry: Drumachose LY 9; 104
Horner, Isabella: Templepatrick AM 35; 152
Horner, James: Bovevagh LY 25; 23
Horner, James: Dunboe LY 11; 74, 79
Horner, John: Kilraghts AM 16; 132
Horner, Margaret Jane: Carrickfergus AM 37; 124
Horner, Rev. R.N.: Drumglass TE 20; 42, 44
Hornhead House: Raymoghy DL 39; 140–41
Horoley [or Howley], James: Kilmacteige SO 40; 196
Horsborough, family: Templecorran AM 26; 11, 117–19
Horse Island: Tamlaght O'Crilly LY 18; 84, 133
Horse lough: Bovevagh LY 25; 1, 33
Horse Loup locality: Billy AM 16; 52, 65
Horse Park field: Magheragall AM 21; 100
Horse's Back promontory: Billy AM 16; 41–42
Horseborough, John: Templecorran AM 26; 126

Horsman, Anthony: Carrickfergus AM 37; 39

Horsmansland locality: Carrickfergus AM 37; 94

Hort td: Cleenish FH 14; 29–30

Hottram, Rev. John: Clogher TE 5; 28

Hottram, Rev. John: Donacavey TE 5; 74

Houard, family: Carrickfergus AM 37; 179

Houghton, Maj.: Ballinderry AM 21; 48

Houghton, Maj.: Magheragall AM 21; 100

Houghton, R.: Blaris AM 8; 60

Houghton, Rev. John: Kilrea LY 27; 126

Houghton, Richard: Magheragall AM 21; 98–100, 104, 109

Houghton, Robert: Clondermot LY 34; 81

Houghton, William: Layd AM 13; 47

Hougomont (see Hugomont): Kirkinriola AM 23; 104

Houstan, William: Ahoghill AM 23; 31

Houston, family: Ballynure AM 32; 56

Houston, family: Carnmoney AM 2; 76

Houston, James: Carrickfergus AM 37; 113

Houston, James: Clondermot LY 34; 79

Houston, John: Ahoghill AM 23; 48

Houston, John: Island Magee AM 10; 68, 96, 98

Houston, Mr (Belfast): Comber DN 7; 41

Houston, Mr: Dundonald DN 7; 65

Houston, Rev. (Gortin): Clonleigh DL 39; 10, 15

Houston, Rev. Alexander: Ahoghill AM 23; 12

Houston, Rev. Alexander: Kirkinriola AM 23; 119

Houston, Rev. Clark: Ahoghill AM 23; 42

Houston, Rev. Clark: Kirkinriola AM 23; 122

Houston, Rev. Clark: Macosquin LY 22; 90, 100

Houston, Robert: Carrickfergus AM 37; 129

Houton's rock: Lough Swilly DL 38; 107

Hovel field: Muckamore AM 35; 80

Hovron, family: Ballinderry AM 21; 53

Howard, Col: Misc. LY 31; 143

Howard, Col.: Donaghmore DN 3; 9

Howard, David: Drummaul AM 19; 89–90

Howard, E.G.: Newry DN 3; 103

Howard, family: Carrickfergus AM 37; 93

Howard, family: Enniskillen FH 4; 58, 58

Howard, Griffin: Coleraine LY 33; 62

Howard, Randall: Ballymoney AM 16; 26

Howard, Samuel: Drummaul AM 19; 91

Howard, W.: Newry DN 3; 99

Howard, W.J.: Tamlaght TE 20; 75, 103, 129

Howe, John: Carrickfergus AM 37; 195

Howe, John: Cleenish FH 14; 20

Howe, Robert: Ballynure AM 32; 44, 66–68

Howe, Thomas: Ballynure AM 32; 43, 64–65, 67, 72–73

Howe, Thomas: Carrickfergus AM 37; 58

Howe, Thomas: Glenavy AM 21; 80–81

Howel, Edward: Carrickfergus AM 37; 110

Howes meeting place: Donegore AM 29; 130

Howles, family: Island Magee AM 10; 70

Howley [or Horoley], James: Kilmacteige SO 40; 196

Hown, family: Carnmoney AM 2; 34

Howth (Dublin): Lough Swilly DL 38; 118–19

Hoy, Bernard: Carrickfergus AM 37; 194

Hoy, James: Templecorran AM 26; 123, 127

Hoy, John: Island Magee AM 10; 90

Hoy, Thomas: Kilroot AM 26; 80

Hoy, William: Templecorran AM 26; 127

Hubbard, Rev.: Carrickfergus AM 37; 70

Huchsoun, William: Derrykeighan AM 16; 87, 90

Hudson, Alexander: Drumragh TE 5; 109

Hudson, Alexander: Enniskillen FH 4; 75

Hudson, Charles: Island Magee AM 10; 42, 93

Hudson, family: Blaris AM 8; 21

Hudson, family: Carrickfergus AM 37; 93

Hudson, family: Enniskillen FH 4; 58

Hudson, Mr: Derryaghy AM 8; 106

Hudson, Mr: Donaghedy TE 5; 92

Hudson, Rev.: Drummaul AM 19; 69

Hudson, William: Newry DN 3; 100, 105

Hudson's Bay (Canada): Kilroot AM 26; 73

Huey, Betty: Ballynure AM 32; 72

Huey, Christiana: Ballynure AM 32; 72

Huey, family: Billy AM 16; 58, 68

Huey, family: Culfeightrin AM 24; 59

Huey, family: Derrykeighan AM 16; 89

Huey, family: Dunluce AM 16; 117

Huey, family: Killagan AM 23; 84

Huey, family: Kilraghts AM 16; 130

Huey, Henry: Drumachose LY 9; 73

Huey, James: Kilraghts AM 16; 132

Huey, Margaret: Ballynure AM 32; 72

Huey, Rev. James: Ballywillin LY 33; 33, 37, 39, 41–42, 45–47, 49

Huey, Robert: Ballynure AM 32; 71

Huey, Robert: Billy AM 16; 58–59, 71

Huey, Sarah: Kilraghts AM 16; 132

Huey, William: Ballynure AM 32; 72

Huey, William: Loughguile AM 13; 71

Hugh Boyle's lough: Donegal DL 39; 42

Hugh, son of Ainmireach: Tamlaght Finlagan LY 25; 101

Hughan td: Tullyniskan TE 20; 139

Hughes, Arthur: Dungiven LY 15; 116

Hughes, Daniel: Carrickfergus AM 37; 129

Hughes, Edward: Carrickfergus AM 37; 109

Hughes, Edward: Maghera LY 18; 46

Hughes, family: Carnmoney AM 2; 51, 102

Hughes, family: Desertmartin LY 31; 55

Hughes, family: Maghera LY 18; 24, 48

Hughes, Francis: Aghadowey LY 22; 19, 21

Hughes, John: Artrea LY 6; 28

Hughes, John: Carrickfergus AM 37; 122

Hughes, John: Killowen LY 33; 171
Hughes, John: Maghera LY 18; 43, 47
Hughes, John [I]: Coleraine LY 33; 90
Hughes, John [II]: Coleraine LY 33; 146
Hughes, John [III]: Coleraine LY 33; 146
Hughes, Michael: Carrickfergus AM 37; 125, 132
Hughes, Mrs: Newry DN 3; 100
Hughes, Rev. Ansley: Magheralin DN 12; 110
Hughes, Rev. John: Tynan AH 1; 131–32
Hughes, Rev. Michael: Errigal LY 27; 46, 63, 71
Hughes, Richard: Killowen LY 33; 159
Hughes, Thomas: Loughgall AH 1; 78
Hughes, Thomas: Newry DN 3; 99, 103
Hughes, William: Magherafelt LY 6; 108
Hughs, Edward: Maghera LY 18; 80
Hughs, Henry: Island Magee AM 10; 95
Hughs, John: Kilcronaghan LY 31; 84
Hughs, Mrs (Croghfern): Carnmoney AM 2; 87
Hughs, Thomas: Carnmoney AM 2; 81
Hughy, James: Aghanloo LY 11; 20
Hughy, John: Aghanloo LY 11; 21
Hughy, Mr: Magilligan LY 11; 138
Hughy, William: Faughanvale LY 36; 23
Hugomont House: Kirkinriola AM 23; 91, 104, 119, 121
Hulchell, Mr: Tyholland MN 40; 175
Hulin rocks: Carncastle and Killyglen AM 10; 3
Hull, Adam: Magheramesk AM 21; 118, 122, 130
Hull, Anthony: Magheramesk AM 21; 122
Hull, E.L.: Donaghadee DN 7; 46
Hull, Edward: Aghalee AM 21; 29, 38
Hull, Edward: Donaghadee DN 7; 46
Hull, Edward: Magheramesk AM 21; 122
Hull, family: Aghalee AM 21; 31
Hull, family: Derryaghy AM 8; 103
Hull, family: Maghera LY 18; 24, 48
Hull, family: Ramoan AM 24; 107
Hull, Henrietta: Blaris AM 8; 80
Hull, John: Balteagh LY 9; 29–30
Hull, John: Dungiven LY 15; 74
Hull, John: Magheramesk AM 21; 122
Hull, Joseph: Magheramesk AM 21; 119, 122, 125–26
Hull, Margret: Magheramesk AM 21; 130
Hull, Matilda: Magheramesk AM 21; 130
Hull, Mr: Artrea TE 20; 7
Hull, Mr: Dungiven LY 15; 85
Hull, Mr: Magheragall AM 21; 101
Hull, Richard [I]: Magheramesk AM 21; 130
Hull, Richard [II]: Magheramesk AM 21; 130
Hull, Robert: Derryaghy AM 8; 91, 107, 112
Hull, Robert: Island Magee AM 10; 92
Hull, Welsley: Magheramesk AM 21; 130
Hull, William: Carrickfergus AM 37; 127
Hull, William: Derryaghy AM 8; 107

Hullen, Rev. Bryan: Magheross MN 40; 146
Hultaghan, family: Killesher FH 14; 85
Hum, Andrew: Duneane AM 19; 119
Hum, Iohn: Duneane AM 19; 119
Humber river (England): Templepatrick AM 35; 116
Humberstow, Mrs: Clondermot LY 34; 61
Humbert, Gen.: Newry DN 3; 109
Hume lough: Kilmacteige SO 40; 193
Hume, Andrew: Cranfield AM 19; 32
Hume, Charles: Kilteevoge DL 39; 114
Hume, family: Billy AM 16; 58
Hume, family: Enniskillen FH 4; 58
Hume, family: Inishmacsaint FH 14; 75
Hume, family: Kirkinriola AM 23; 124
Hume, George (see Macartney): Loughguile AM 13; 63
Hume, Gustavus: Devenish FH 14; 55
Hume, John: Inishmacsaint FH 14; 75
Hume, Misses: Blaris AM 8; 15
Hume, Mr: Raloo AM 32; 128
Hume, Mrs: Raloo AM 32; 127
Hume, Mrs Robert: Urney DL 39; 182
Hume, Oliver: Tamlaght Finlagan LY 25; 105
Hume, Rev.: Kilcoo DN 3; 44
Hume, Rev.: Kilmegan DN 3; 58
Hume, Rev.: Tullyaughnish DL 38; 89
Hume, Rev. Andrew: Killead AM 35; 12, 46
Hume, Rev. Robert: Aghadowey LY 22; 22
Hume, Rev. Robert: Urney DL 39; 179–80, 182
Hume, Thomas: Glynn AM 26; 28, 42
Hume, Thomas: Hillsborough DN 12; 106
Hume, William: Raloo AM 32; 123
Humes, family: Billy AM 16; 68
Humfrey, Benjamin: Clonleigh DL 39; 2
Humfrey, Benjamin: Conwal DL 39; 26
Humfrey, Benjamin: Raphoe DL 39; 124
Hummings, Henry: Enniskillen FH 4; 57
Humphrey, family: Templepatrick AM 35; 118
Humphrey, Maj.: Bodoney TE 20; 20
Humphrey, Widow: Leck DL 39; 118
Humphreys, John: Ardstraw TE 5; 5
Humphries, Capt.: Clonleigh DL 39; 10, 13
Humpston, Robert: Island Magee AM 10; 77
Humston, Robert: Misc. DN 17; 117
Hunger's Mother td: Raymoghy DL 39; 137, 199
Hungerford, Rachel (see Massereene): Drummaul AM 19; 71
Hunningstown manor: Misc. FH 4; 133
Hunshigo bog: Drumballyroney DN 3; 11, 14
Hunshigo lough: Drumballyroney DN 3; 10
Hunt, Capt.: Ramoan AM 24; 123
Hunt, Charles: Ballymore AH 1; 4, 9, 13–17
Hunt, Charles: Drumcree AH 1; 35, 38, 41
Hunt, Charles: Kilmore AH 1; 72
Hunt, Charles: Seagoe AH 1; 107, 110

Hunt, Lt: Termonamongan TE 5; 144
Hunt, Rev. A.: Aghalurcher FH 4; 16
Hunt's Hole pool: Ramoan AM 24; 123
Hunter and Algee, Messrs: Killead AM 35; 15, 49
Hunter and Co., Messrs: Kilwaughter AM 10; 112
Hunter Point: Island Magee AM 10; 79
Hunter, Adam: Dunluce AM 16; 120
Hunter, Agnes: Kildollagh LY 22; 75
Hunter, Alexander: Culfeightrin AM 24; 50
Hunter, Alexander: Drumbeg AM 8; 126, 130, 133
Hunter, Andrew: Ballywillin LY 33; 45, 48, 50
Hunter, Andrew: Coleraine LY 33; 105
Hunter, Andrew: Island Magee AM 10; 95
Hunter, Andrew: Tamlaght Finlagan LY 25; 113
Hunter, Anne: Kilrea LY 27; 112
Hunter, Bella: Carrickfergus AM 37; 119
Hunter, Betty: Carrickfergus AM 37; 119
Hunter, Daniel: Culfeightrin AM 24; 72
Hunter, Daniel: Kildollagh LY 22; 75
Hunter, David: Macosquin LY 22; 122
Hunter, Dr (Rathmelton): Tullyaughnish DL 38; 91, 93
Hunter, Eliza: Derryaghy AM 8; 115
Hunter, Elizabeth: Lissan LY 31; 109
Hunter, Elizabeth: Tamlaght Finlagan LY 25; 113
Hunter, family: Ballee DN 17; 16
Hunter, family: Ballynure AM 32; 56
Hunter, family: Ballywillin AM 16; 32
Hunter, family: Billy AM 16; 58, 68
Hunter, family: Culfeightrin AM 24; 59, 71
Hunter, family: Derrykeighan AM 16; 89
Hunter, family: Drumbeg AM 8; 123
Hunter, family: Drummaul AM 19; 53
Hunter, family: Island Magee AM 10; 70
Hunter, family: Killead AM 35; 17
Hunter, family: Kilroot AM 26; 74–75
Hunter, family: Racavan AM 13; 100
Hunter, family: Templecorran AM 26; 117, 119
Hunter, Francis: Derryaghy AM 8; 90, 109
Hunter, George: Agivey LY 22; 42–44
Hunter, H.B.: Ballynascreen LY 31; 8
Hunter, H.B.: Ballyscullion LY 6; 46, 53, 77
Hunter, H.B.: Banagher LY 30; 17, 22, 30, 131
Hunter, H.B.: Dungiven LY 15; 10
Hunter, H.B.: Faughanvale LY 36; 40
Hunter, Hanah: Macosquin LY 22; 122
Hunter, Harris: Ballynure AM 32; 66
Hunter, Hemphill and McFarland, Messrs: Aghadowey LY 22; 7, 12
Hunter, Hugh: Kilraghts AM 16; 136
Hunter, Isaac [I]: Ballywillin LY 33; 42, 45–47
Hunter, Isaac [II]: Ballywillin LY 33; 50
Hunter, Jacob: Macosquin LY 22; 119
Hunter, James (Jnr): Derryaghy AM 8; 115
Hunter, James (Jnr): Kildollagh LY 22; 75

Hunter, James (Snr): Kildollagh LY 22; 75
Hunter, James: Ballintoy AM 24; 35
Hunter, James: Ballymoney AM 16; 15
Hunter, James: Ballyrashane LY 22; 65
Hunter, James: Carnmoney AM 2; 100
Hunter, James: Derryaghy AM 8; 115
Hunter, James: Drumbeg AM 8; 125–26, 130
Hunter, James: Drummaul AM 19; 82
Hunter, James: Hillsborough DN 12; 105
Hunter, James: Kilwaughter AM 10; 119
Hunter, Jane: Ahoghill AM 23; 38
Hunter, Jane: Drumachose LY 9; 86, 125
Hunter, Jane: Kildollagh LY 22; 75
Hunter, Janet: Carnmoney AM 2; 102
Hunter, John (Jnr): Macosquin LY 22; 84, 119
Hunter, John (Snr): Macosquin LY 22; 84, 119
Hunter, John: Aghadowey LY 22; 5–6, 15–16
Hunter, John: Ballyaghran LY 33; 22
Hunter, John: Ballynascreen LY 31; 14, 21
Hunter, John: Ballynure AM 32; 71
Hunter, John: Blaris AM 8; 66
Hunter, John: Coleraine LY 33; 127
Hunter, John: Derryaghy AM 8; 95–96, 114
Hunter, John: Drumachose LY 9; 116–17
Hunter, John: Drumbo DN 7; 56, 58–60
Hunter, John: Dunboe LY 11; 79
Hunter, Joseph: Ahoghill AM 23; 45
Hunter, Kennedy: Muckamore AM 35; 78
Hunter, Margaret: Kildollagh LY 22; 75
Hunter, Mary: Kildollagh LY 22; 75
Hunter, Matthew: Derryaghy AM 8; 115
Hunter, Messrs: Banagher LY 30; 23
Hunter, Michael: Culfeightrin AM 24; 57
Hunter, Moses: Hillsborough DN 12; 105
Hunter, Mr (Tullyowen): Killea and Taughboyne DL 39; 87
Hunter, Mr: Bovevagh LY 25; 22
Hunter, Mr: Clondermot LY 34; 35
Hunter, N.: Cumber LY 28; 77
Hunter, Nancy: Kilrea LY 27; 109, 127
Hunter, Nathaniel: Banagher LY 30; 29–30
Hunter, Nickey: Kildollagh LY 22; 75
Hunter, Rev.: Aghadowey LY 22; 24
Hunter, Rev. J.S.: Banagher LY 30; 30, 54, 59, 96, 112
Hunter, Rev. J.S.: Cumber LY 28; 19, 77, 83, 86–87, 89
Hunter, Rev. James: Ballyaghran LY 33; 13, 24, 27
Hunter, Rev. James: Coleraine LY 33; 95, 139–41, 143
Hunter, Rev. Stevenson: Armoy AM 24; 4
Hunter, Richard: Banagher LY 30; 4, 13, 15, 17, 22, 27, 31, 59, 118, 121, 131
Hunter, Richard: Bovevagh LY 25; 21, 57
Hunter, Richard: Coleraine LY 33; 63–64, 73, 127

Hunter, Richard: Cumber LY 28; 96, 98
Hunter, Richard: Faughanvale LY 36; 40
Hunter, Richard: Killowen LY 33; 162
Hunter, Robert: Kildollagh LY 22; 75
Hunter, Rodger: Drumbo DN 7; 60
Hunter, Samuel: Ballywillin LY 33; 45, 49
Hunter, Samuel: Derryaghy AM 8; 115
Hunter, Sarah: Carrickfergus AM 37; 122
Hunter, Scott: Tamlaght Finlagan LY 25; 118
Hunter, Stephen: Billy AM 16; 77
Hunter, Susan: Derryaghy AM 8; 115
Hunter, Thomas: Carrickfergus AM 37; 118, 120
Hunter, Thomas: Dunboe LY 11; 73–74, 76
Hunter, Thomas: Tamlaght TE 20; 129
Hunter, Widow: Ballymoney AM 16; 17
Hunter, William (Jnr): Derryaghy AM 8; 115
Hunter, William (Jnr): Drumbeg AM 8; 124–27, 130
Hunter, William (Jnr): Hillsborough DN 12; 105
Hunter, William (Jnr): Tamlaght TE 20; 81, 121
Hunter, William (Jnr) [I]: Blaris AM 8; 55, 66
Hunter, William (Jnr) [I]: Blaris DN 12; 36
Hunter, William (Jnr) [II]: Blaris AM 8; 70
Hunter, William (Snr): Derryaghy AM 8; 115
Hunter, William (Snr): Drumbeg AM 8; 126
Hunter, William: Ballynure AM 32; 71
Hunter, William: Ballywillin LY 33; 50
Hunter, William: Carrickfergus AM 37; 119
Hunter, William: Coleraine LY 33; 91
Hunter, William: Culfeightrin AM 24; 57
Hunter, William: Drumachose LY 9; 133–34
Hunter, William: Kildollagh LY 22; 75
Hunter, William: Magherafelt LY 6; 112
Hunter, William: Tamlaght Finlagan LY 25; 113
Hunter, William: Tamlaght TE 20; 116
Huntingdon (England): Galloon FH 4; 90
Huntington, Kent: Ballyscullion LY 6; 57
Hurds hill: Holywood DN 7; 73
Hurl, James: Artrea LY 6; 28
Hurl, Patrick: Artrea LY 6; 27
Hurl, Rev. Patt: Kilmacteige SO 40; 186
Hurley, Alexander: Coleraine LY 33; 72
Hurley, Capt.: Blaris AM 8; 5
Hurley, Francis: Coleraine LY 33; 72
Hurley, Mary: Coleraine LY 33; 146
Hurley, Richard: Coleraine LY 33; 72
Hurst, family: Blaris AM 8; 21
Hurst, Francis: Clogher TE 5; 40
Hurst, John: Ardstraw TE 5; 8
Hurst, Mrs: Clogher TE 5; 41
Hurst, Rev. A.: Clogher TE 5; 40
Hurst, Rev. Francis: Errigal Truagh MN 40; 121–22
Hurst, Rev. William: Donagh MN 40; 103, 105
Hurst, William: Carrickfergus AM 37; 129
Hustin, family: Misc. LY 36; 101
Huston, Ann: Maghera LY 18; 79

Huston, Betty: Maghera LY 18; 79
Huston, Catherine: Kilraghts AM 16; 132
Huston, Charles: Maghera LY 18; 79
Huston, David: Banagher LY 30; 61, 73
Huston, David: Magherafelt LY 6; 102
Huston, Elizabeth: Macosquin LY 22; 122
Huston, family: Ballynure AM 32; 56
Huston, family: Derrykeighan AM 16; 89
Huston, Francis: Tamlaght O'Crilly LY 18; 107,
    119, 126
Huston, Gabriel: Macosquin LY 22; 112
Huston, George: Aghadowey LY 22; 20–21
Huston, Henry: Hillsborough DN 12; 106
Huston, Henry: Maghera LY 18; 79
Huston, Jacob: Tamlaght Finlagan LY 25; 108
Huston, James: Tamlaght O'Crilly LY 18; 130–31
Huston, Jane: Larne AM 10; 127
Huston, John (Jnr): Maghera LY 18; 79
Huston, John (Snr): Maghera LY 18; 79
Huston, John: Dundermot AM 13; 34
Huston, John: Errigal LY 27; 65
Huston, John: Termoneeny LY 6; 131
Huston, John [I]: Maghera LY 18; 79
Huston, Martha: Coleraine LY 33; 140
Huston, Rev. George: Dunboe LY 11; 65
Huston, Robert (Jnr): Coleraine LY 33; 72, 143
Huston, Robert (Snr): Coleraine LY 33; 72, 142
Huston, Robert: Maghera LY 18; 79
Huston, Sally: Maghera LY 18; 79
Huston, Samuel: Aghanloo LY 11; 17, 30
Huston, Samuel: Drumachose LY 9; 104
Huston, Stewart: Tamlaght O'Crilly LY 18; 130
Huston, Thomas: Dunaghy AM 13; 24
Huston, Thomas: Dundermot AM 13; 34
Huston, W.: Tynan AH 1; 131
Huston, William: Ballywillin LY 33; 50
Huston, William: Maghera LY 18; 27
Huston, William: Tamlaght O'Crilly LY 18; 143
Hutchenson, Creighton: Maghera LY 18; 39–40
Hutchenson, James: Artrea LY 6; 31, 34
Hutchenson, James: Tamlaght Finlagan LY 25; 118
Hutchenson, John: Tamlaght Finlagan LY 25; 118
Hutchenson, Ritchard (Jnr): Balteagh LY 9; 25
Hutchenson, Ritchard (Snr): Balteagh LY 9; 25
Hutchenson, Thomas: Artrea LY 6; 34
Hutchenson, Thomas: Drumbo DN 7; 56
Hutchenson, William: Balteagh LY 9; 32
Hutcheson, Miss (Drumagarner): Tamlaght O'Crilly
    LY 18; 94, 116
Hutcheson, Thomas: Tamlaght O'Crilly LY 18; 94,
    116
Hutchins, Francis: Ballyscullion LY 6; 57
Hutchins, Thomas (Jnr): Ballyscullion LY 6; 57
Hutchins, Thomas (Snr): Ballyscullion LY 6; 57
Hutchinson, Anne: Kilraghts AM 16; 132

Hutchinson, Archibald: Ballymoney AM 16; 15

Hutchinson, Bishop: Ahoghill AM 23; 12

Hutchinson, Bishop: Ballyclug AM 23; 56

Hutchinson, Charlotte: Carrickfergus AM 37; 115

Hutchinson, Edward: Misc. DN 17; 133

Hutchinson, Ellen: Carrickfergus AM 37; 126

Hutchinson, Ellen: Kilraghts AM 16; 134

Hutchinson, family: Ahoghill AM 23; 17

Hutchinson, family: Ballymoney AM 16; 1

Hutchinson, family: Derryaghy AM 8; 103

Hutchinson, family: Kilraghts AM 16; 130

Hutchinson, family: Lissan LY 31; 106

Hutchinson, Francis: Blaris AM 8; 21, 86, 88

Hutchinson, Francis: Misc. DN 17; 117, 133

Hutchinson, George: Ballymoney AM 16; 13, 15, 17

Hutchinson, George: Coleraine LY 33; 127

Hutchinson, George: Dunaghy AM 13; 26

Hutchinson, George: Dunluce AM 16; 110

Hutchinson, George: Finvoy AM 23; 68, 70

Hutchinson, James: Ballymoney AM 16; 15

Hutchinson, James: Derrykeighan AM 16; 94

Hutchinson, James: Tickmacrevan AM 13; 133

Hutchinson, John: Carrickfergus AM 37; 115, 124

Hutchinson, John: Misc. LY 31; 122

Hutchinson, Miss (see O'Hara): Ballyclug AM 23; 56

Hutchinson, Miss: Ballymoney AM 16; 24

Hutchinson, Miss: Coleraine LY 33; 73

Hutchinson, Mr: Killea and Taughboyne DL 39; 82

Hutchinson, Mrs: Ballynure AM 32; 34, 44, 68

Hutchinson, Rev. Archy: Duneane AM 19; 114, 116

Hutchinson, Rev. Francis: Blaris AM 8; 85

Hutchinson, Robert: Balteagh LY 9; 43

Hutchinson, Samuel: Misc. DN 17; 133

Hutchinson, William: Carrickfergus AM 37; 43

Hutchison, Andrew: Dunboe LY 11; 73

Hutchison, family: Kilmore AH 1; 65

Hutchison, Hugh: Lissan LY 31; 109

Hutchison, J.: Kilmore AH 1; 73

Hutchison, James: Derryaghy AM 8; 109–10

Hutchison, Mary: Lissan LY 31; 109

Hutchison, name of: Kilmore AH 1; 69

Hutchison, Nancy: Lissan LY 31; 109

Hutchison, Sarah: Lissan LY 31; 109

Hutchison, William: Tamlaght Finlagan LY 25; 112

Hutton, James: Bovevagh LY 25; 60

Hutton, James: Newry DN 3; 99

Hutton, Mr: Convoy DL 39; 21

Hutton, Mr: Donaghedy TE 5; 89

Hutton, W.: Kilmore DN 17; 88

Hy MacCarthen, family: Clondermot LY 34; 50

Hy MacCarthen, family: Misc. LY 36; 105

Hy Neal, family: Faughanvale LY 36; 33, 49–50

Hy Niall, family: Clondermot LY 34; 47

Hy Tuirtre district: Skerry AM 13; 105

Hyde Park bleachworks: Templepatrick AM 35; 141–42

Hyde Park district: Ballynure AM 32; 66

Hyde Park printworks: Mallusk AM 2; 106–07, 111, 114

Hyde, Francis: Blaris DN 12; 42

Hyde, John: Drumcree AH 1; 32

Hyde, John: Mallusk AM 2; 107

Hyde, Robert: Drumcree AH 1; 32

Hyde, T.: Drumcree AH 1; 41

Hyndman, family: Culfeightrin AM 24; 59

Hyndman, family: Misc. LY 36; 101, 104

Hyndman, Mr: Lough Neagh AM 21; 97

Hyndman, Samuel: Donegore AM 29; 134

Hynds, family: Ballee DN 17; 16

Hynds, James: Macosquin LY 22; 106

Hynds, Margret: Ballyrashane LY 22; 66

Hynds, Martha: Ballyrashane LY 22; 66

I

Iarian td: Ballyscullion LY 6; 58
Identicall (see Edenticall)
Ilan, Edus: Muckamore AM 35; 82
Illananoon Island: Lough Swilly DL 38; 101–02, 114
Illanatawee Island: Lough Swilly DL 38; 122
Illanaviaie Island: Lough Swilly DL 38; 113, 116
Illanaweelog Point: Lough Swilly DL 38; 111, 113
Illanceannog locality: Lough Swilly DL 38; 119
Illancranny Point: Lough Swilly DL 38; 118
Illaneeyafta Island: Lough Swilly DL 38; 106
Illanmacaredy Island: Lough Swilly DL 38; 114
Illannacrieve Island: Tamlaght O'Crilly LY 18; 84–85, 133
Illinge, William: Clondermot LY 34; 55
Ilwaine, family: Ballynure AM 32; 56
Imlick td: Misc. DL 39; 196
Inch Abbey: Inch DN 17; 74–76
Inch Abbey: Saul DN 17; 113
Inch Abbey: Templecorran AM 26; 108, 119
Inch battery: Killygarvan DL 38; 39
Inch bay: Lough Swilly DL 38; 147
Inch Castle: Lough Swilly DL 38; 104, 144, 147
Inch corn mill: Lough Swilly DL 38; 148
Inch hill: Lough Swilly DL 38; 145
Inch Island: Inch DN 17; 75
Inch Island: Killygarvan DL 38; 39–40, 42, 45
Inch Island: Lough Swilly DL 38; 102–04, 127, 139, 143–49
Inch Island: Mintiaghs DL 38; 64
Inch Island: Tullyaughnish DL 38; 90, 95
Inch old church: Inch DN 17; 75
Inch old graveyard: Inch DN 17; 75–76
Inch ph: Clondermot LY 34; 98
Inch ph: Down DN 17; 40, 49, 51, 58, 61, 120, 122, 128
Inch priory: Dundonald DN 7; 65
Inch priory: Misc. DN 17; 121
Inch td: Inch DN 17; 74
Inch, George: Clondermot LY 34; 88
Inch, Jane: Drummaul AM 19; 89
Inch, Miss: Maghera LY 18; 18, 72
Inch, Rev. Nathaniel: Killelagh LY 27; 98, 100, 102–03

Inch, William (Snr): Urney DL 39; 179
Inchenny (Tyrone): Faughanvale LY 36; 56
Inchloughgease (see Inchloughjease)
Inchloughjease manor: Enniskillen FH 4; 82
Inchloughjease manor: Magheracross FH 14; 102
Inchloughjease manor: Misc. FH 4; 133
Inchmearing td: Ballywillin LY 33; 51
Inchmearing td: Coleraine LY 33; 61–62, 129
Inchvickeeny monastery: Misc. SO 40; 200
India: Aghanloo LY 11; 18, 34
India: Currin MN 40; 91
India: Faughanvale LY 36; 11, 56
India: Kilroot AM 26; 73
India: Newry DN 3; 68
India: Raloo AM 32; 126
Infant Lodge: Ballymore AH 1; 11, 17
Ingleton, Mr: Faughanvale LY 36; 70
Inglis, Andrew: Kilwaughter AM 10; 118
Inglis, John: Templepatrick AM 35; 132
Ingman, John: Coleraine LY 33; 72
Ingram House: Derryaghy AM 8; 106
Ingram, Mr (Mountnorris): Loughgilly AH 1; 87
Ingram, Mr: Clogher TE 5; 41
Ingram, Mrs: Newry DN 3; 99
Ingram, Percival: Carrickfergus AM 37; 40, 149, 162, 175
Ingram, Samuel: Carrickfergus AM 37; 40
Ingram's public house: Carrickfergus AM 37; 149
Ininfidda Head: Rathlin Island AM 24; 130
Inis Eagan palace: Dungiven LY 15; 33
Iniscarn (Iniscarron) td: Desertmartin LY 31; 57, 62, 119, 141–42
Iniscarn cove: Desertmartin LY 31; 57
Iniscarn female school: Desertmartin LY 31; 54, 60–61, 125–26
Iniscarn giant's chair: Desertmartin LY 31; 57
Iniscarn giant's grave: Desertmartin LY 31; 57–58
Iniscarn hill: Misc. LY 31; 113–14
Iniscarn male school: Desertmartin LY 31; 54, 60–61, 125–26
Iniscarn tummock: Desertmartin LY 31; 57
Inisconaghan td: Bovevagh LY 25; 59
Inis-Courcey abbey: Inch DN 17; 75
Inisfandra (see Inishfendra): Galloon FH 4; 95

Inish Cardigh lough: Clondavaddog DL 38; 3
Inishargy ph: Ballyhalbert DN 7; 5
Inishargy ph: Grey Abbey DN 7; 67
Inishargy td: Ballywalter DN 7; 18
Inishargy td: Misc. DN 17; 125
Inishbaan Island: Lough Swilly DL 38; 111
Inishbeg Island: Lough Swilly DL 38; 122–24
Inishbofin harbour: Lough Swilly DL 38; 123–24
Inishbofin Island: Lough Swilly DL 38; 122–23
Inishbulskin Island: Lough Swilly DL 38; 111
Inishcollan Island: Aghalurcher FH 4; 1
Inishcollan stone: Aghalurcher FH 4; 9
Inishcollan td: Aghalurcher FH 4; 14
Inishcorkish Island: Aghalurcher FH 4; 3, 14
Inishcreagh Island: Cleenish FH 14; 29
Inishdooh Island: Lough Swilly DL 38; 122–24
Inishdooh rocks: Lough Swilly DL 38; 123–24
Inisherk Island: Galloon FH 4; 88, 91
Inishfar Island: Lough Swilly DL 38; 115–16
Inishfendra Island: Galloon FH 4; 87–88, 91–92, 95, 105
Inishfendra Island Castle: Galloon FH 4; 105
Inishfree bay: Lough Swilly DL 38; 126
Inishglass Island: Lough Swilly DL 38; 111, 113
Inish-hirrer Island: Lough Swilly DL 38; 126
Inishhunny Island: Lough Swilly DL 38; 126
Inishkeel ph: Killymard DL 39; 94
Inishkeel ph: Kilteevoge DL 39; 111
Inishkeel quarries: Inishkeel DL 39; 70
Inishkeel schools: Inishkeel DL 39; 71
Inishkeel tuck mill: Inishkeel DL 39; 72
Inishkeen bawn: Inniskeen MN 40; 125
Inishkeen bridge: Inniskeen MN 40; 125
Inishkeen chapel: Inniskeen MN 40; 125
Inishkeen church: Inniskeen MN 40; 125
Inishkeen Glebe House: Inniskeen MN 40; 125
Inishkeen graveyard: Inniskeen MN 40; 126, 128
Inishkeen Island: Cleenish FH 14; 13, 30
Inishkeen mound: Inniskeen MN 40; 125–27
Inishkeen mound: Killanny MN 40; 132
Inishkeen old bridge: Inniskeen MN 40; 124, 127
Inishkeen police station: Inniskeen MN 40; 127
Inishkeen school: Inniskeen MN 40; 125, 129
Inishkeen village: Inniskeen MN 40; 124–25
Inishleag Island: Aghalurcher FH 4; 3
Inishlirrew td: Kinawley FH 4; 121
Inishlougher Island: Devenish FH 14; 59
Inishlught Island: Kinawley FH 4; 113
Inishlught td: Kinawley FH 4; 121
Inishmaan Island: Lough Swilly DL 38; 126
Inishmaan rock: Lough Swilly DL 38; 126
Inishmacgrath ph: Manorhamilton Union LM 40; 51
Inishmacsaint chapel: Inishmacsaint FH 14; 74
Inishmacsaint Island: Inishmacsaint FH 14; 70, 73
Inishmacsaint mills: Inishmacsaint FH 14; 74

Inishmacsaint monastery: Inishmacsaint FH 14; 75
Inishmacsaint old chapel: Inishmacsaint FH 14; 70
Inishmacsaint ph: Cleenish FH 14; 14
Inishmacsaint ph: Clogher TE 5; 41
Inishmacsaint ph: Devenish FH 14; 50
Inishmacsaint ph: Rossorry FH 14; 115
Inishmacsaint school: Inishmacsaint FH 14; 77
Inishmore Island: Cleenish FH 14; 11, 13–14, 19, 28
Inishmore Island: Derryvullan FH 14; 39, 41
Inishonaer Island: Lough Swilly DL 38; 126
Inishora Island: Aghalurcher FH 4; 3
Inishowen barony: Clonmany DL 38; 12
Inishowen barony: Desertegney DL 38; 24
Inishowen barony: Desertoghill LY 27; 8
Inishowen barony: Donagh DL 38; 31
Inishowen barony: Killea and Taughboyne DL 39; 88
Inishowen barony: Lough Swilly DL 38; 138, 141, 144
Inishowen barony: Magilligan LY 11; 90
Inishowen barony: Mintiaghs DL 38; 64
Inishowen barony: Misc. DL 39; 184
Inishowen barony: Moville DL 38; 68, 70, 73–74, 78
Inishowen Head: Lough Swilly DL 38; 109, 113
Inishowen mountains: Balteagh LY 9; 4
Inishowen mountains: Clondermot LY 34; 7, 22
Inishowen mountains: Dunboe LY 11; 51
Inishowen mountains: Magilligan LY 11; 85, 93
Inishowen mountains: Tamlaght Finlagan LY 25; 81–82
Inishowen Peninsula: Ballyaghran LY 33; 3, 6–7, 12, 24
Inishowen Peninsula: Clondavaddog DL 38; 6
Inishowen Peninsula: Clondermot LY 34; 22, 34
Inishowen Peninsula: Clonmany DL 38; 14, 19
Inishowen Peninsula: Desertegney DL 38; 27, 29
Inishowen Peninsula: Dunaghy AM 13; 12
Inishowen Peninsula: Errigal LY 27; 62
Inishowen Peninsula: Faughanvale LY 36; 8–10, 21, 39, 48, 64
Inishowen Peninsula: Inch DN 17; 75
Inishowen Peninsula: Killowen LY 33; 164
Inishowen Peninsula: Killygarvan DL 38; 42
Inishowen Peninsula: Killymard DL 39; 96
Inishowen Peninsula: Lough Swilly DL 38; 107, 109, 112, 128, 131, 136–38, 140–42, 146
Inishowen Peninsula: Magilligan LY 11; 83, 103, 107, 114, 118, 130, 142–43
Inishowen Peninsula: Mevagh DL 38; 57, 63
Inishowen Peninsula: Mintiaghs DL 38; 65, 67
Inishowen Peninsula: Misc. DL 39; 185, 192
Inishowen Peninsula: Misc. LY 36; 105, 137
Inishowen Peninsula: Moville DL 38; 76
Inishowen Peninsula: Tamlaght Finlagan LY 25; 93

Inishowen Peninsula: Tullyaughnish DL 38; 84, 90

Inishroosk td: Aghalurcher FH 4; 14

Inishrush (Inisrush) td: Tamlaght O'Crilly LY 18; 94–95, 97–98, 118, 120–22, 137

Inishrush bogs: Tamlaght O'Crilly LY 18; 87, 119, 132

Inishrush bridge: Tamlaght O'Crilly LY 18; 92

Inishrush Canal: Tamlaght O'Crilly LY 18; 84, 95

Inishrush Castle: Tamlaght O'Crilly LY 18; 94

Inishrush chapel: Tamlaght O'Crilly LY 18; 82

Inishrush corn kilns: Tamlaght O'Crilly LY 18; 88

Inishrush corn mills: Tamlaght O'Crilly LY 18; 84, 88, 91–92, 110, 112

Inishrush demesne: Tamlaght O'Crilly LY 18; 96

Inishrush flax mill: Tamlaght O'Crilly LY 18; 84, 88, 91, 110, 112

Inishrush forge: Kilrea LY 27; 112

Inishrush fort: Tamlaght O'Crilly LY 18; 118–19

Inishrush glen: Tamlaght O'Crilly LY 18; 96

Inishrush grey stone: Tamlaght O'Crilly LY 18; 118–19

Inishrush House: Tamlaght O'Crilly LY 18; 87–88, 90–91, 98, 105, 108

Inishrush Island: Tamlaght O'Crilly LY 18; 84, 94, 121

Inishrush old corn mill: Tamlaght O'Crilly LY 18; 95, 120

Inishrush old house: Tamlaght O'Crilly LY 18; 108

Inishrush school: Tamlaght O'Crilly LY 18; 88, 112, 141, 143

Inishrush sessions house: Tamlaght O'Crilly LY 18; 88, 112

Inishrush storehouse: Tamlaght O'Crilly LY 18; 88

Inishrush Sunday school: Tamlaght O'Crilly LY 18; 143

Inishrush td: Carnteel TE 20; 23

Inishrush td: Tamlaght O'Crilly LY 18; 83–84, 136

Inishrush village: Maghera LY 18; 18

Inishrush village: Tamlaght O'Crilly LY 18; 82, 88, 90, 94, 97, 99, 108, 110–12, 121, 134, 141

Inishrush wood: Tamlaght O'Crilly LY 18; 87, 108

Inishteag Island: Cleenish FH 14; 30

Inishtrahull (see Inishtuahull)

Inishtuahull bank: Lough Swilly DL 38; 113

Inishtuahull Island: Lough Swilly DL 38; 111–13, 137–38

Inishtuahull Island: Moville DL 38; 70

Inishtuahull lighthouse: Ballyaghran LY 33; 5

Inishtuahull lighthouse: Lough Swilly DL 38; 112

Inishtuahull lighthouse: Mevagh DL 38; 61

Inishtuahull sound: Lough Swilly DL 38; 124

Inishturk Island: Aghalurcher FH 4; 3, 14

Inishweal Island: Lough Swilly DL 38; 117

Iniskeen Island: Enniskillen FH 4; 72

Iniskillin (see Enniskillen): Derryvullan FH 14; 39

Iniskilline (see Enniskillen): Derryvullan FH 14; 38

Inisloughlin bog: Magheramesk AM 21; 116

Inisloughlin Castle: Magheramesk AM 21; 125

Inisloughlin corn mill: Magheramesk AM 21; 120

Inisloughlin fort [I]: Magheramesk AM 21; 113, 120, 125–26

Inisloughlin fort [II]: Magheramesk AM 21; 120

Inisloughlin fort [III]: Magheramesk AM 21; 125–26

Inisloughlin fort [IV]: Magheramesk AM 21; 126

Inisloughlin fort [V]: Magheramesk AM 21; 126

Inisloughlin td: Magheramesk AM 21; 114, 118, 120, 126, 129–30

Inispollan ph: Culfeightrin AM 24; 41

Inispollan ph: Layd AM 13; 36

Inispollan ph: Misc. AM 10; 129

Inistrahul (see Inishtuahull): Moville DL 38; 70

Inisusk Island: Templecarn DL 39; 156

Inless rocks: Ballintoy AM 24; 23

Innaghachole lough: Donaghmore DL 39; 28–29

Inner lough: Ematris MN 40; 113

Innes, family: Blaris AM 8; 22

Innes, J.C.: Clontibret MN 40; 85

Innes, J.C.: Hillsborough DN 12; 95

Innes, J.C.: Tyholland MN 40; 175

Innes, Rev. Robert: Magilligan LY 11; 84, 89, 121

Innis, A.: Donaghmore DN 3; 7–9

Innis, Arthur: Misc. DN 17; 131

Innis, Mrs: Donaghmore DN 3; 8

Inniscarron (see Iniscarn): Desertmartin LY 31; 54

Innisconahar td: Banagher LY 30; 23–24

Innish McKill td: Magheraculmoney FH 14; 113–14

Innishargie (see Inishargy)

Innishark Island: Kinawley FH 4; 113–15, 119

Innishcollen (see Inishcollan): Aghalurcher FH 4; 1

Innishcorkish (see Inishcorkish): Aghalurcher FH 4; 3

Innishcreagh Island: Cleenish FH 14; 13

Innishcreenry Island: Aghalurcher FH 4; 3

Innishcullen (see Inishcollan): Aghalurcher FH 4; 9

Innishee Island: Killesher FH 14; 81

Innisherk (see Inisherk): Galloon FH 4; 91

Innishfasey Island: Aghalurcher FH 4; 3

Innishfendra (see Inishfendra): Galloon FH 4; 91

Innishfoger (Inishfougher) Island: Devenish FH 14; 52, 59

Innishgriffin Island: Kinawley FH 4; 113

Innishkeen (see Inniskeen): Enniskillen FH 4; 84

Innishleag Island: Cleenish FH 14; 13

Innishlught (see Inishlught): Kinawley FH 4; 113

Innishrush (see Inishrush): Tamlaght O'Crilly LY 18; 82

Inniskeen church: Enniskillen FH 4; 41

Inniskeen Island: Enniskillen FH 4; 43–44, 70

Inniskeen Island: Inniskeen MN 40; 124

Inniskeen Island school: Enniskillen FH 4; 84

Inniskeen Island td: Enniskillen FH 4; 74, 82

Inniskeen ph: Clogher TE 5; 24, 41

Inniskeen ph: Donaghmoyne MN 40; 106

Inniskeen ph: Killanny MN 40; 133

Inniskeen ph: Magheross MN 40; 153

Inniskeen td: Magheross MN 40; 153

Inniskeen, name of: Inniskeen MN 40; 124

Inniskil td: Killygarvan DL 38; 47

Innis-mic-Nessain church: Dungiven LY 15; 55

Innispollan (see Inispollan)

Innisteedy (see Church Island): Ballyscullion LY 6; 56

Innuran creek: Lough Swilly DL 38; 107

Insh Grange (see Grange Irish): Carlingford LH 40; 58

Inshaleen bleach green: Errigal LY 27; 40, 58

Inshaleen bogs: Errigal LY 27; 55

Inshaleen bridge: Errigal LY 27; 41, 59–60

Inshaleen fort: Errigal LY 27; 75

Inshaleen td: Errigal LY 27; 35, 41, 49, 66, 82, 87, 91–92

Inshamph fort: Dunaghy AM 13; 24

Inshamph td: Dunaghy AM 13; 24

Inshany Lower td: Misc. DL 39; 197

Inshany Upper td: Misc. DL 39; 197

Insterhul (see Inishtuahull): Mevagh DL 38; 61

Inver bleach green: Inver AM 26; 49, 51, 53–55

Inver bridge: Cumber LY 28; 31

Inver flour mills: Inver AM 26; 49, 51, 53–54

Inver Lodge: Inver AM 26; 53

Inver old church: Inver AM 26; 49

Inver old church: Killymard DL 39; 105

Inver ph (Donegal): Inishkeel DL 39; 69

Inver ph: Carrickfergus AM 37; 69, 71, 100

Inver ph: Glynn AM 26; 1, 3, 20, 22–23, 30, 42

Inver ph: Island Magee AM 10; 15, 35

Inver ph: Killymard DL 39; 94, 98, 106, 109

Inver ph: Kilroot AM 26; 65

Inver ph: Kilwaughter AM 10; 106

Inver ph: Larne AM 10; 123, 125

Inver ph: Mallusk AM 2; 111, 114

Inver ph: Misc. AM 10; 129

Inver ph: Raloo AM 32; 80, 82, 93, 98, 101

Inver ph: Templecorran AM 26; 89, 101

Inver plantation: Inver AM 26; 50

Inver priory: Glynn AM 26; 30

Inver quay: Glynn AM 26; 5

Inver quay: Inver AM 26; 51

Inver river: Cumber LY 28; 72

Inver td: Glynn AM 26; 30

Inver td: Inver AM 26; 49, 51–52

Inver threshing machine: Inver AM 26; 54

Inver water: Killymard DL 39; 105

Inver, George: Loughgall AH 1; 80

Inverbeg district: Inver AM 26; 49

Inverhill House: Cleenish FH 14; 19

Invermore district: Inver AM 26; 49

Inveroe stream: Kilrea LY 27; 105

Inveroo (see Inverroe)

Inverroe bridge: Tamlaght O'Crilly LY 18; 92, 108

Inverrue (see Inverroe)

Iona (Scotland): Magilligan LY 11; 88

Iona: Clondermot LY 34; 58, 63

Iona: Clonmany DL 38; 14

Iona: Muckamore AM 35; 82

Iona: Tamlaght Finlagan LY 25; 102

Iredall, Rev. Francis: Donegore AM 29; 129

Ireland, family: Drumbeg AM 8; 123

Ireland, Thomas: Glynn AM 26; 17

Ireland, Wallace: Tullyrusk AM 21; 139

Irelitan, St: Drumachose LY 9; 95

Ireton, Gen.: Drumballyroney DN 3; 16

Irish Channel: Ardclinis AM 13; 1

Irish Channel: Ardglass DN 17; 1, 3

Irish Channel: Ardkeen DN 7; 1, 3

Irish Channel: Ballyhalbert DN 7; 6

Irish Channel: Ballyphilip DN 7; 7

Irish Channel: Bangor DN 7; 19, 22

Irish Channel: Castleboy DN 7; 26

Irish Channel: Donaghadee DN 7; 45

Irish Channel: Dunsfort DN 17; 67

Irish Channel: Inishargy DN 7; 84

Irish Channel: Kilbroney DN 3; 28

Irish Channel: Kilcoo DN 3; 41

Irish Channel: Kilkeel DN 3; 47

Irish Channel: Layd AM 13; 36

Irish Channel: Lough Neagh AM 21; 93

Irish Channel: Tickmacrevan AM 13; 122

Irish Channel: Witter DN 7; 125

Irish Highway: Carnmoney AM 2; 69, 98

Irish Highway: Mallusk AM 2; 115

Irish Highway: Templepatrick AM 35; 130–31, 145

Irish Highway: Umgall AM 35; 160

Irish hill: Ahoghill AM 23; 34

Irish hill: Ballynure AM 32; 54, 70

Irish Houses locality: Banagher LY 30; 39

Irish Houses locality: Killowen LY 33; 162

Irish Houses Sunday school: Killowen LY 33; 166

Irish Kirkyard church: Ballintoy AM 24; 17–18

Irish Lonan road: Doagh AM 29; 98

Irish Quarter corn mill: Carrickfergus AM 37; 45, 47, 138

Irish Quarter td: Carrickfergus AM 37; 8, 29–30, 32, 44, 47, 70, 76, 79, 91–92, 136, 138, 151–52, 161–62, 170, 177–78, 180, 191

Irish Sea: Lough Swilly DL 38; 119

Irishtown school: Antrim AM 29; 59

Irons, John: Dungiven LY 15; 44, 87

Irons, Robert: Dungiven LY 15; 87–88
Irvin [or Irwin], Henry: Tullyaughnish DL 38; 93, 97
Irvin, John: Magheraculmoney FH 14; 110
Irvin, Robert: Ballee DN 17; 23
Irvin, Robert: Blaris DN 12; 46, 50
Irvin, Robert: Tamlaght Finlagan LY 25; 119
Irvin, Samuel: Annaclone DN 12; 18
Irvine, Ann: Tamlaght Finlagan LY 25; 119
Irvine, Arthur: Clogher TE 5; 41
Irvine, Dr: Moville DL 38; 70
Irvine, family: Enniskillen FH 4; 58, 75
Irvine, G.D.: Magheracross FH 14; 100
Irvine, G.D.: Magheraculmoney FH 14; 108
Irvine, George: Enniskillen FH 4; 58
Irvine, George: Tamlaght TE 20; 82
Irvine, Hamilton: Aghavea FH 4; 20, 22
Irvine, Hamilton: Enniskillen FH 4; 58–59
Irvine, Henry: Derryvullan FH 14; 33–34
Irvine, Henry: Macosquin LY 22; 81, 101
Irvine, Hill: Newry DN 3; 99, 104
Irvine, James: Dungiven LY 15; 70, 72, 75
Irvine, James: Tamlaght Finlagan LY 25; 119
Irvine, John: Derryvullan FH 14; 34, 36
Irvine, John: Tamlaght Finlagan LY 25; 112
Irvine, John: Trory FH 14; 133–34
Irvine, Margret: Tamlaght Finlagan LY 25; 120
Irvine, Mary Ann: Tamlaght Finlagan LY 25; 120
Irvine, Mr: Clogher TE 5; 43
Irvine, Mr: Clondermot LY 34; 120
Irvine, Rev. Arthur: Derryvullan FH 14; 34
Irvine, Rev. J.F.: Tamlaght Finlagan LY 25; 120
Irvine, Rev. James: Cleenish FH 14; 22
Irvine, Rev. W.J.: Lissan LY 31; 94–95, 103, 105, 107–08
Irvine, William: Enniskillen FH 4; 66
Irvine, William [I]: Drummaul AM 19; 91
Irvine, William [II]: Drummaul AM 19; 91
Irvinestown: Derryvullan FH 14; 33, 36–38
Irvinestown: Magheracross FH 14; 94, 97, 100
Irvinestown: Trory FH 14; 130
Irvinestown chapel (M): Derryvullan FH 14; 37
Irvinestown chapel (W): Derryvullan FH 14; 37
Irvinestown church: Derryvullan FH 14; 37
Irvinestown school: Derryvullan FH 14; 35
Irving and Farrell, Messrs: Glynn AM 26; 2
Irving, family: Blaris AM 8; 21
Irving, John: Donaghmore DL 39; 33
Irving, John: Glynn AM 26; 1–2, 5–6, 10, 13, 15–16, 18–28, 30, 33–36, 39–41, 43–44, 46
Irving, John: Island Magee AM 10; 29
Irving, John: Kilroot AM 26; 62
Irving, John: Templecorran AM 26; 130
Irving, Rev. Charles: Donaghmore DL 39; 31, 33, 37

Irving, Rev. Charles: Urney DL 39; 179, 181
Irwan, J.: Aughnamullen MN 40; 76
Irwin [or Irvin], Henry: Tullyaughnish DL 38; 93, 97
Irwin, Alexander: Carrickfergus AM 37; 113
Irwin, Andrew: Carrickfergus AM 37; 125
Irwin, Benjamin: Drumachose LY 9; 126
Irwin, David: Duneane AM 19; 123
Irwin, Edward: Cranfield AM 19; 32
Irwin, Esther: Carrickfergus AM 37; 112
Irwin, family: Carrickfergus AM 37; 93
Irwin, family: Enniskillen FH 4; 58, 75
Irwin, family: Templepatrick AM 35; 118
Irwin, family: Umgall AM 35; 158
Irwin, Francis: Newry DN 3; 83
Irwin, Henry: Killygarvan DL 38; 46–47
Irwin, Henry: Lough Swilly DL 38; 101, 128
Irwin, J.: Enniskillen FH 4; 82
Irwin, James: Balteagh LY 9; 13, 41
Irwin, James: Clogher TE 5; 40
Irwin, James: Drumglass TE 20; 43
Irwin, James: Tamlaght TE 20; 96
Irwin, John: Cumber LY 28; 86
Irwin, John: Island Magee AM 10; 82
Irwin, John: Magheraculmoney FH 14; 108
Irwin, Joseph: Drumachose LY 9; 53
Irwin, Maj.: Dromore TE 5; 98–99
Irwin, Matthew: Aghanloo LY 11; 26
Irwin, Matthew: Drumachose LY 9; 126, 128
Irwin, Mr: Clones FH 4; 29
Irwin, Mr: Kildress TE 20; 58, 61
Irwin, Mr: Killesher FH 14; 87
Irwin, Mrs (Dublin): Kilmacteige SO 40; 194
Irwin, Mrs: Drumachose LY 9; 126
Irwin, Nancy: Banagher LY 30; 96
Irwin, Rev.: Killdrumsherdan CN 40; 33, 38
Irwin, Rev. Arthur: Derrybrusk FH 4; 32
Irwin, Rev. Arthur: Kilskeery TE 5; 115
Irwin, Rev. Charles: Drumcree AH 1; 33
Irwin, Rev. I.: Derryvullan FH 14; 43–44
Irwin, Rev. J.: Magheracross FH 14; 95, 100
Irwin, Robert: Annahilt DN 12; 23
Irwin, Samuel: Carrickfergus AM 37; 155
Irwin, Samuel: Dungiven LY 15; 97
Irwin, Sarah: Carrickfergus AM 37; 125
Irwin, Stewart: Lissan LY 31; 109
Irwin, W.: Seagoe AH 1; 109
Irwin, W.: Tynan AH 1; 129, 132
Irwin, W.D.: Magheracross FH 14; 102
Irwin, William: Enniskillen FH 4; 59
Irwin, William: Kilrea LY 27; 129
Irwin, William: Tamlaght Finlagan LY 25; 83, 121
Isaac, Mr: Saintfield DN 7; 119
Iseapa lough: Templecarn DL 39; 157
Iskaheen (see Eskaheen): Muff DL 38; 80

Iskahien (see Eskaheen): Muff DL 38; 80

Iskeheehen (see Eskaheen): Muff DL 38; 80

Iskeheen (see Eskaheen): Muff DL 38; 81

Island bank: Lough Swilly DL 38; 113

Island bog: Drumballyroney DN 3; 14

Island Effrick bogs: Ballyrashane LY 22; 57

Island Effrick North cave: Ballyrashane LY 22; 50, 58

Island Effrick North fort: Ballyrashane LY 22, 49, 58

Island Effrick paper mill: Ballyrashane LY 22; 48

Island Effrick South cave: Ballyrashane LY 22; 58

Island Effrick South fort: Ballyrashane LY 22; 49, 58

Island Flacky td: Ballywillin LY 33; 43

Island Henry td: Bright DN 17; 34

Island Hill td: Donaghadee DN 7; 45

Island Kelly td: Derryaghy AM 8; 91, 120

Island Macallan corn mill: Ballintoy AM 24; 16

Island Macallan school: Ballintoy AM 24; 17

Island Magee druid's altar: Raloo AM 32; 122

Island Magee Masonic house: Island Magee AM 10; 90, 93

Island Magee old church: Island Magee AM 10; 16, 26, 72

Island Magee Peninsula: Ardclinis AM 13; 6

Island Magee Peninsula: Ballynure AM 32; 67

Island Magee Peninsula: Carrickfergus AM 37; 165, 168, 170

Island Magee Peninsula: Glynn AM 26; 9, 41

Island Magee Peninsula: Killyleagh DN 17; 84

Island Magee Peninsula: Kilroot AM 26; 56, 60, 78, 80

Island Magee Peninsula: Larne AM 10; 123

Island Magee Peninsula: Racavan AM 13; 103

Island Magee Peninsula: Templecorran AM 26; 85–86, 88–89, 91–92, 95–96, 109, 114, 120–23, 127

Island Magee ph: Carrickfergus AM 37; 71, 142, 151, 160

Island Magee ph: Down DN 17; 58

Island Magee ph: Glynn AM 26; 17, 23, 29–30, 34, 40, 42

Island Magee ph: Kilroot AM 26; 65, 73

Island Magee ph: Mallusk AM 2; 111, 114

Island Magee ph: Mevagh DL 38; 62

Island Magee ph: Misc. AM 10; 129

Island Magee ph: Misc. DN 17; 121

Island Magee ph: Muckamore AM 35; 56

Island Magee ph: Raloo AM 32; 98, 127–28

Island Magee ph: Templecorran AM 26; 82, 99, 101, 103, 106–08, 124, 128–30

Island Magee public houses: Kilroot AM 26; 68

Island Magee Sunday school: Island Magee AM 10; 98

Island McCallan bog: Ballintoy AM 24; 26

Island McCallan cave [I]: Ballintoy AM 24; 28

Island McCallan cave [II]: Ballintoy AM 24; 28

Island McCallan td: Ballintoy AM 24; 27

Island Moore: Killinchy DN 7; 86

Island Reavey (see Island Reavy): Kilcoo DN 3; 41

Island Reavy lough: Kilcoo DN 3; 41, 45

Island Roy bar (see also Drumfin): Mevagh DL 38; 63

Island Roy locality: Tullyaughnish DL 38; 86

Island Roy td: Mevagh DL 38; 63

Islandagee (see Isleagree): Templecorran AM 26; 82

Islandaho td: Derrykeighan AM 16; 90, 95

Islandban (see Islandbane): Muckamore AM 35; 82

Islandbane (Islandbawn) td: Muckamore AM 35; 54, 63, 80, 82–83

Islandbane beetling and wash mill: Muckamore AM 35; 63

Islandbane beetling mill: Muckamore AM 35; 56, 63, 75–76

Islandbane bleach green: Muckamore AM 35; 75

Islandbane td: Bright DN 17; 35

Islandbane td: Killinchy DN 7; 86

Islandbann (see Islandbane): Muckamore AM 35; 56

Islandboy td: Drumtullagh AM 16; 103

Islandderry lough: Magheralin DN 12; 109

Islandderry school: Dromore DN 12; 73

Islandderry td: Dromore DN 12; 70–72

Islandderry td: Magheralin DN 12; 109

Islandhill td: Misc. DN 17; 124

Islandhoe (see Islandaho): Derrykeighan AM 16; 95

Islandkelly school: Derryaghy AM 8; 117

Islandkelly Sunday school: Derryaghy AM 8; 118

Islandkelly td: Derryaghy AM 8; 115

Islandmore cove: Kilraghts AM 16; 133

Islandmore Sunday school: Ballywillin LY 33; 41

Islandmore td: Ballywillin LY 33; 35, 46

Islandmore td: Clonleigh DL 39; 7, 12, 188, 197

Islandmore td: Coleraine LY 33; 66, 143

Islandmore td: Kilraghts AM 16; 133

Islandmore Upper fort: Ballywillin LY 33; 35, 50

Islandmore Upper td: Ballywillin LY 33; 51

Islandnabracky cove: Skerry AM 13; 121

Islandorisky Island: Lough Swilly DL 38; 114

Islandreagh beetling mill: Nilteen AM 35; 86, 89, 92, 102–03

Islandreagh district: Lough Swilly DL 38; 115–16

Islandreagh school: Nilteen AM 35; 86, 102

Islandreagh standing stone: Nilteen AM 35; 96

Islandreagh td: Donegore AM 29; 102

Islandreagh td: Nilteen AM 35; 84

Islandree (see Islandreagh): Nilteen AM 35; 103

Islands td: Misc. DN 17; 123

Islandtasserty td: Ballyaghran LY 33; 27

Islandvardin cave [I]: Ballyaghran LY 33; 11, 16, 22

Islandvardin cave [II]: Ballyaghran LY 33; 11, 22
Islandvardin cave [III]: Ballyaghran LY 33; 22
Islane lough: Drumlumman CN 40; 12
Islay (Scotland): Island Magee AM 10; 19
Islay: Ardclinis AM 13; 6
Islay: Coleraine LY 33; 155
Islay: Culfeightrin AM 24; 44
Islay: Racavan AM 13; 102–03
Islay: Ramoan AM 24; 93
Isle bank: Moville DL 38; 72
Isle McCricket td: Kilclief DN 17; 79
Isle of Glass locality: Carrickfergus AM 37; 93
Isle of Man: Ardglass DN 17; 7, 13–14
Isle of Man: Ballee DN 17; 18
Isle of Man: Grey Abbey DN 7; 72
Isle of Man: Island Magee AM 10; 19, 26
Isle of Man: Killygarvan DL 38; 45
Isle of Man: Killyleagh DN 17; 84, 86
Isle of Man: Lough Neagh AM 21; 93
Isle of Man: Lough Swilly DL 38; 118, 130
Isle of Man: Templecorran AM 26; 96, 96
Isle of Muck: Island Magee AM 10; 18, 26, 47,
    50–51, 53, 60, 71, 75, 90, 99, 129
Isle of Valley td: Ballyculter DN 17; 31
Isle of Wight: Carrickfergus AM 37; 79
Isleagree district: Templecorran AM 26; 82
Isleagree moss: Templecorran AM 26; 125–26
Isled, Barbara: Dromore DN 12; 74
Isles, Mary Jane: Carrickfergus AM 37; 115, 124
Isles, Mr (Ahory): Kilmore AH 1; 66
Isner, Robert: Island Magee AM 10; 90
Issataughan stream: Dunaghy AM 13; 10–11
Italy: Kilbroney DN 3; 34
Iveach (see Iveagh): Drumballyroney DN 3; 12
Iveagh barony: Seapatrick DN 12; 124
Iveagh district: Ardglass DN 17; 3, 12
Iveagh district: Misc. DN 17; 122
Iveagh hill: Drumballyroney DN 3; 14

Iveagh Lower barony: Aghaderg DN 12; 1, 8
Iveagh Lower barony: Blaris DN 12; 26–27, 33
Iveagh Lower barony: Donaghcloney DN 12; 57, 59
Iveagh Lower barony: Dromara DN 12; 62, 64–65
Iveagh Lower barony: Dromore DN 12; 70, 73
Iveagh Lower barony: Garvaghy DN 12; 79
Iveagh Lower barony: Hillsborough DN 12; 88
Iveagh Lower barony: Holywood DN 7; 80
Iveagh Lower barony: Magheralin DN 12; 109
Iveagh Lower barony: Magherally DN 12; 114
Iveagh Lower barony: Misc. DN 17; 116
Iveagh Lower barony: Moira DN 12; 117
Iveagh Lower barony: Seapatrick DN 12; 123, 126
Iveagh Lower barony: Shankill DN 12; 138–39
Iveagh Lower barony: Tullylish DN 12; 140
Iveagh Lower td: Garvaghy DN 12; 81
Iveagh Upper barony: Aghaderg DN 12; 1, 8
Iveagh Upper barony: Annaclone DN 12; 13, 16
Iveagh Upper barony: Donaghmore DN 3; 7
Iveagh Upper barony: Dromara DN 12; 62, 64
Iveagh Upper barony: Drumballyroney DN 3; 13, 16
Iveagh Upper barony: Drumgath DN 3; 19
Iveagh Upper barony: Drumgooland DN 3; 24
Iveagh Upper barony: Holywood DN 7; 80
Iveagh Upper barony: Kilbroney DN 3; 26
Iveagh Upper barony: Magherally DN 12; 112
Iveagh Upper barony: Misc. DN 17; 116
Iveagh Upper barony: Newry DN 3; 110
Iveagh Upper barony: Seapatrick DN 12; 123, 126
Iveagh Upper barony: Warrenpoint DN 3; 115
Iveagh Upper td: Garvaghy DN 12; 81
Iveagh, family: Drumballyroney DN 3; 12
Ivers, John: Kilteevoge DL 39; 114
Ivers, Michael: Kilteevoge DL 39; 114
Ivy bridge: Drumbeg AM 8; 128
Ivy church: Clondermot LY 34; 46
Ivy Hill old house: Derryaghy AM 8; 98

J

Jack, family: Carrickfergus AM 37; 93

Jack, James: Muckamore AM 35; 78

Jack, William: Carrickfergus AM 37; 40, 149

Jack's Hotel: Kirkinriola AM 23; 95

Jackdaw Island td: Ballyculter DN 17; 31

Jackson Hall: Ballyrashane LY 22; 50

Jackson Hall: Banagher LY 30; 30

Jackson Hall: Coleraine LY 33; 54, 63, 73, 129, 144, 147, 154

Jackson Hall: Killowen LY 33; 158–60, 168, 171

Jackson Hall demesne: Coleraine LY 33; 77

Jackson Hall demesne: Killowen LY 33; 162

Jackson Hall spring: Coleraine LY 33; 77

Jackson, Ann: Ballyscullion LY 6; 46

Jackson, Ann: Killowen LY 33; 159

Jackson, Capt.: Kilmacteige SO 40; 188, 192

Jackson, Charles: Aghanloo LY 11; 22

Jackson, family: Killowen LY 33; 171

Jackson, George: Drummaul AM 19; 77, 86

Jackson, John: Aghanloo LY 11; 12–13, 16–17, 19, 21–22, 27, 31

Jackson, John: Aughnamullen MN 40; 71, 76

Jackson, John: Ballyscullion LY 6; 46

Jackson, John: Muckamore AM 35; 78–79

Jackson, Luke: Island Magee AM 10; 91

Jackson, man named: Muckamore AM 35; 78

Jackson, Margret: Tamlaght Finlagan LY 25; 118

Jackson, Mr (Ballybay): Comber DN 7; 41

Jackson, Mr (Ballybay): Dundonald DN 7; 65

Jackson, Mr (Ballybay): Holywood DN 7; 77

Jackson, Mr (Creeve): Aughnamullen MN 40; 71

Jackson, Mr (Fort William): Kilcronaghan LY 31; 67

Jackson, Mr (Reduff): Aughnamullen MN 40; 69, 71–72

Jackson, Mr: Ballybay MN 40; 79

Jackson, Mr: Coleraine LY 33; 152

Jackson, Mr [I]: Killowen LY 33; 171

Jackson, Mr [II]: Killowen LY 33; 173

Jackson, Mrs: Aghanloo LY 11; 21

Jackson, Rev.: Tynan AH 1; 125

Jackson, Rev. Henry: Seapatrick DN 12; 128

Jackson, Richard: Clones FH 4; 28

Jackson, Richard: Coleraine LY 33; 129, 144

Jackson, Richard: Forkhill AH 1; 45

Jackson, Richard: Killowen LY 33; 159–60

Jackson, Richard: Ramoan AM 24; 102

Jackson, Robert: Balteagh LY 9; 32

Jackson, Thomas: Carnmoney AM 2; 84

Jackson, Thomas: Eglish AH 1; 44

Jackson, Thomas: Kilcronaghan LY 31; 66, 80

Jackson, Thomas: Loughgall AH 1; 77

Jackson, Widow: Muckamore AM 35; 78

Jackson, William: Coleraine LY 33; 62

Jackson, William: Loughgall AH 1; 78

Jacob, Rev. Benjamin: Kilbroney DN 3; 33, 38

Jacob, Rev. R.S.: Clogher TE 5; 41

Jacob, Rev. R.S.: Templecarn DL 39; 163

Jacob, St: Carrickfergus AM 37; 41, 49

Jacob's well: Dunboe LY 11; 49

Jacob's well: Macosquin LY 22; 99

Jacques, Mrs: Carrickfergus AM 37; 176

Jaffrey, family: Carrickfergus AM 37; 93

Jaffrey, family: Raloo AM 32; 94, 108, 123

Jafrey, family: Carrickfergus AM 37; 179

Jamaica: Agivey LY 22; 45

Jamaica: Ballyaghran LY 33; 18

Jamaica: Ballyrashane LY 22; 53, 65

Jamaica: Faughanvale LY 36; 44

James a-Hood, seer: Misc. LY 31; 124

James I, King: Aghadowey LY 22; 11

James I, King: Ahoghill AM 23; 14

James I, King: Antrim AM 29; 37

James I, King: Ardglass DN 17; 3

James I, King: Ardstraw TE 5; 8

James I, King: Ballee DN 17; 16

James I, King: Ballyclug AM 23; 53

James I, King: Ballylinny AM 32; 15–16, 29

James I, King: Ballymartin AM 2; 5, 15

James I, King: Ballymoney AM 16; 21

James I, King: Ballymore AH 1; 8

James I, King: Ballynure AM 32; 35, 41

James I, King: Ballyrashane LY 22; 49, 55

James I, King: Ballyrobert AM 2; 20, 25

James I, King: Ballyscullion LY 6; 52

James I, King: Ballywalter AM 2; 26, 29

James I, King: Banagher LY 30; 30, 102–05, 107

James I, King: Blaris AM 8; 3

James I, King: Blaris DN 12; 32

James I, King: Bovevagh LY 25; 5

James I, King: Camlin AM 21; 62
James I, King: Carnmoney AM 2; 51
James I, King: Carrickfergus AM 37; 1, 18, 32–34, 38, 43, 45, 49, 62, 65, 69, 80, 142, 148, 178
James I, King: Clogher TE 5; 30–31
James I, King: Clondermot LY 34; 57, 60–75
James I, King: Clones FH 4; 29
James I, King: Clonleigh DL 39; 9, 13–15
James I, King: Coleraine LY 33; 59, 93, 121, 147, 149, 151–52, 155
James I, King: Connor AM 19; 18
James I, King: Culfeightrin AM 24; 69
James I, King: Cumber LY 28; 61–62, 65–67, 69–71
James I, King: Desertlyn LY 31; 37, 45
James I, King: Desertmartin LY 31; 58
James I, King: Doagh AM 29; 71, 80
James I, King: Donaghmore DL 39; 29, 33–34
James I, King: Donegal DL 39; 48
James I, King: Donegore AM 29; 101, 109
James I, King: Dromara DN 12; 69
James I, King: Dromore DN 12; 77
James I, King: Drummaul AM 19; 69
James I, King: Enniskillen FH 4; 51
James I, King: Faughanvale LY 36; 13, 48, 50, 54–64
James I, King: Galloon FH 4; 90
James I, King: Glynn AM 26; 1
James I, King: Hillsborough DN 12; 88
James I, King: Inver AM 26; 49
James I, King: Island Magee AM 10; 77, 86
James I, King: Kilbride AM 29; 140, 148–49, 154
James I, King: Killead AM 35; 17
James I, King: Killinchy DN 7; 90
James I, King: Kilroot AM 26; 61, 64, 68, 72
James I, King: Lough Neagh AM 21; 95
James I, King: Maghera LY 18; 24
James I, King: Magherafelt LY 6; 95
James I, King: Magheramesk AM 21; 126
James I, King: Magilligan LY 11; 130
James I, King: Mallusk AM 2; 109–10
James I, King: Misc. DL 39; 183, 185
James I, King: Misc. DN 17; 118
James I, King: Misc. LY 31; 118
James I, King: Misc. LY 36; 103
James I, King: Muckamore AM 35; 54, 56, 82–83
James I, King: Newry DN 3; 64, 114
James I, King: Raloo AM 32; 90
James I, King: Ramoan AM 24; 90, 95, 98
James I, King: Tamlaght Finlagan LY 25; 90
James I, King: Tamlaght O'Crilly LY 18; 96
James I, King: Templecorran AM 26; 96, 101, 108
James I, King: Templepatrick AM 35; 108, 111, 116, 118, 132
James I, King: Tullyrusk AM 21; 135
James I, King: Umgall AM 35; 157–58

James II, King: Ahoghill AM 23; 6, 12
James II, King: Ardstraw TE 5; 11
James II, King: Ballyclug AM 23; 56
James II, King: Ballywillin AM 16; 32
James II, King: Ballywillin LY 33; 43
James II, King: Carnmoney AM 2; 69, 72
James II, King: Carrickfergus AM 37; 76
James II, King: Clondermot LY 34; 4, 23, 46, 48, 55, 72
James II, King: Desertlyn LY 31; 37
James II, King: Devenish FH 14; 48, 60
James II, King: Donaghmore DL 39; 32
James II, King: Drummaul AM 19; 69, 71
James II, King: Drumragh TE 5; 108
James II, King: Enniskillen FH 4; 47, 51–52, 73
James II, King: Faughanvale LY 36; 31
James II, King: Galloon FH 4; 89, 91, 98, 101–02, 105
James II, King: Island Magee AM 10; 62
James II, King: Kilbride AM 29; 149
James II, King: Killead AM 35; 32
James II, King: Kilrea LY 27; 113, 128
James II, King: Kinawley FH 4; 117
James II, King: Loughgall AH 1; 80
James II, King: Maghera LY 18; 13, 24, 50
James II, King: Magheramesk AM 21; 123, 126
James II, King: Misc. DN 17; 122
James II, King: Misc. LY 31; 136, 136–37
James II, King: Muckamore AM 35; 71
James II, King: Newry DN 3; 65, 74
James II, King: Tamlaght O'Crilly LY 18; 96
James II, King: Templecorran AM 26; 114
James II, King: Templepatrick AM 35; 150
James II, King: Trory FH 14; 129
James II, King: Urney DL 39; 177
James VI, King: Tullyaughnish DL 38; 91
James, Edward: Dungiven LY 15; 73
James, J.C.: Clondermot LY 34; 45
James, Margaret: Faughanvale LY 36; 30
James, Robert: Maghera LY 18; 54
James, St: Kilkeel DN 3; 54
James, T.M.: Seapatrick DN 12; 126
James, William: Carnmoney AM 2; 88
Jameson, Ann: Kilraghts AM 16; 132
Jameson, family: Ballintoy AM 24; 20
Jameson, family: Carnmoney AM 2; 76
Jameson, family: Culfeightrin AM 24; 59
Jameson, family: Kilraghts AM 16; 130
Jameson, Hugh: Carrickfergus AM 37; 195
Jameson, Humphrey: Killead AM 35; 50
Jameson, Humphrey: Templepatrick AM 35; 122, 147, 150
Jameson, James: Agivey LY 22; 45
Jameson, James: Culfeightrin AM 24; 59
Jameson, James: Desertoghill LY 27; 2, 15, 17

Jameson, Jane: Agivey LY 22; 45
Jameson, John (Jnr): Coleraine LY 33; 105
Jameson, John (Jnr): Kilraghts AM 16; 132
Jameson, John (Snr): Coleraine LY 33; 61, 105
Jameson, John (Snr): Kilraghts AM 16; 132
Jameson, John: Culfeightrin AM 24; 67
Jameson, John: Derrykeighan AM 16; 93
Jameson, John: Dunboe LY 11; 64
Jameson, John: Ramoan AM 24; 117
Jameson, Jonathan: Kilrea LY 27; 128
Jameson, Margaret: Kilraghts AM 16; 132
Jameson, Mr: Island Magee AM 10; 94
Jameson, Mr: Tullynakill DN 7; 122
Jameson, Patrick: Culfeightrin AM 24; 67
Jameson, Patrick: Kilraghts AM 16; 132
Jameson, Rev. Archibald: Desertoghill LY 27; 2, 15
Jameson, Rev. Archibald: Drummaul AM 19; 69, 82
Jameson, Rev. Archibald: Errigal LY 27; 57
Jameson, Robert: Coleraine LY 33; 105
Jameson, Robert: Desertoghill LY 27; 4, 13, 18
Jameson, Samuel: Ballynure AM 32; 67
Jameson, T.: Annahilt DN 12; 22
Jameson, William: Faughanvale LY 36; 34
Jameson, William: Killead AM 35; 22, 50
Jameson, William: Ramoan AM 24; 119, 122
Jameson, William: Templepatrick AM 35; 152
Jamestown bridge: Magheracross FH 14; 96
Jamestown demesne: Magheracross FH 14; 91, 93
Jamestown House: Magheracross FH 14; 92, 95–97
Jamfrey, Margaret: Carrickfergus AM 37; 75
Jamfrey, William: Carrickfergus AM 37; 39, 148
Jamieson, family: Templepatrick AM 35; 118
Jamieson, William: Cumber LY 28; 74–75
Jamison, Anne: Carrickfergus AM 37; 158
Jamison, family: Carrickfergus AM 37; 93
Jamison, family: Ramoan AM 24; 107
Jamison, James: Aghadowey LY 22; 37
Jamison, James: Carrickfergus AM 37; 193
Jamison, James: Doagh AM 29; 98
Jamison, Jane: Carrickfergus AM 37; 158
Jamison, Jane [I]: Aghadowey LY 22; 35
Jamison, Jane [II]: Aghadowey LY 22; 37
Jamison, Janet: Carrickfergus AM 37; 158
Jamison, Samuel: Tamlaght TE 20; 84
Jamison, Thomas: Carrickfergus AM 37; 158
Jamison's coves: Doagh AM 29; 98
Janet lough spring: Clondermot LY 34; 32
Jebb, Rev. John: Ardstraw TE 5; 8
Jebb, Richard: Carrickfergus AM 37; 57
Jebb, Richard: Comber DN 7; 38
Jebb, Richard: Island Magee AM 10; 77
Jebb, Richard: Kilbroney DN 3; 33
Jebb, Richard: Kilmore AH 1; 68
Jebb, Richard: Raloo AM 32; 80, 132–33
Jebb, Thomas: Kilbroney DN 3; 33

Jebb, William: Donacavey TE 5; 66
Jeffers, family: Misc. LY 36; 104
Jefferson, family: Blaris AM 8; 21
Jefferson, George: Derryaghy AM 8; 94
Jefferson, James: Hillsborough DN 12; 106
Jefferson, John: Blaris DN 12; 50
Jefferson, John: Carrickfergus AM 37; 123
Jefferson, John: Derryaghy AM 8; 94, 99
Jefferson, John: Hillsborough DN 12; 97, 105
Jefferson, Messrs: Blaris DN 12; 45, 49
Jefferson, Mr: Blaris AM 8; 84
Jefferson, Mrs: Newry DN 3; 98, 103
Jefferson, Ralph: Blaris DN 12; 41, 50
Jefferson, Ralph: Derryaghy AM 8; 91, 99, 107
Jefferson, Ralph: Hillsborough DN 12; 107
Jefferson, Ralph: Magheragall AM 21; 102
Jefferson, William: Blaris DN 12; 41
Jellett, Mr: Clogher TE 5; 41
Jemison, Mrs: Tamlaght Finlagan LY 25; 113
Jenkin lough: Aghalurcher FH 4; 3, 5
Jenkins, Capt.: Hillsborough DN 12; 91
Jenkins, Oliver: Clonleigh DL 39; 10
Jenkinstown td: Ballymascanlan LH 40; 56
Jennings, Andrew: Newry DN 3; 100, 104
Jennings, Charles: Newry DN 3; 95, 99, 104
Jennings, Col: Templepatrick AM 35; 148
Jennings, Edward: Ballyscullion LY 6; 70
Jennings, Edward: Clonduff DN 3; 4
Jennings, Francis: Newry DN 3; 99, 104
Jennings, James: Newry DN 3; 104
Jennings, Jane: Clonduff DN 3; 4
Jennings, Richard: Ballyscullion LY 6; 57
Jennings, Robert: Ballyscullion LY 6; 70
Jenny, Henry: Donaghcloney DN 12; 60
Jennymount House: Carnmoney AM 2; 92
Jermane House: Clonmany DL 38; 14
Jernon Glebe House: Coleraine LY 33; 63
Jerrett's Pass: Ballymore AH 1; 9
Jerusalem: Mallusk AM 2; 109
Jervis, Thomas: Ballyscullion LY 6; 57
Jingles, Andrew: Kilwaughter AM 10; 118
Jingles, family: Kilwaughter AM 10; 115
Job, William: Donacavey TE 5; 65
Jocelyn, Lady: Newry DN 3; 106
Jocelyn, Robert: Coleraine LY 33; 74
Jockey's Quarter bog: Glenwhirry AM 32; 79
Joclyn, Rev. Percy: Clogher TE 5; 28
John, King: Ballymartin AM 2; 17
John, King: Carrickfergus AM 37; 33–34, 62
John, King: Dunaghy AM 13; 14
John, King: Kildollagh LY 22; 72
John, King: Killagan AM 23; 84
John, King: Killead AM 35; 32
John, King: Kilmacteige SO 40; 187, 193
John, King: Umgall AM 35; 160

John, St: Banagher LY 30; 11, 96–97, 114
John, St: Bright DN 17; 36
John, St: Carrickfergus AM 37; 23
John, St: Culfeightrin AM 24; 67
John, St: Down DN 17; 60
John, St: Drumachose LY 9; 61
John, St: Killowen LY 33; 170
John, St: Mallusk AM 2; 109, 114
John, St: Misc. LY 31; 124
Johnes, Eustase: Drumachose LY 9; 61
Johnfeer, family: Templecorran AM 26; 117, 119
Johns, Alexander: Ballynure AM 32; 61
Johns, Alexander: Carrickfergus AM 37; 28, 133,
    141, 145–46, 157, 164, 172, 175, 190, 192
Johns, Rev. Bennett: Carrickfergus AM 37; 144
Johns, W.: Saintfield DN 7; 120
Johnson, Alexander: Muckamore AM 35; 73
Johnson, Arthur: Blaris DN 12; 40
Johnson, Ben: Dunaghy AM 13; 17
Johnson, Ben: Kirkinriola AM 23; 112
Johnson, Capt.: Tartaraghan AH 1; 120
Johnson, David: Ahoghill AM 23; 41
Johnson, Dorothea: Lambeg AM 8; 136
Johnson, Edward: Blaris AM 8; 50–51, 60, 66
Johnson, Edward: Derryaghy AM 8; 94, 103–05,
    112, 116, 118
Johnson, Edward: Magheragall AM 21; 108
Johnson, family: Antrim AM 29; 24
Johnson, family: Ballinderry AM 21; 51
Johnson, family: Blaris AM 8; 21
Johnson, family: Carnmoney AM 2; 76
Johnson, family: Carrickfergus AM 37; 93
Johnson, family: Derryaghy AM 8; 103
Johnson, family: Derrykeighan AM 16; 89
Johnson, family: Lambeg AM 8; 135
Johnson, family: Magherafelt LY 6; 95
Johnson, family: Muckamore AM 35; 65
Johnson, family: Nilteen AM 35; 91
Johnson, Henry: Hillsborough DN 12; 106
Johnson, Hugh: Ballymoney AM 16; 16
Johnson, Hugh: Hillsborough DN 12; 106
Johnson, J.M.: Blaris DN 12; 44, 47–48
Johnson, J.M.: Magheradrool DN 17; 101
Johnson, James: Ballymoney AM 16; 17
Johnson, James: Blaris DN 12; 40, 42–43
Johnson, James: Carrickfergus AM 37; 126
Johnson, James: Hillsborough DN 12; 106
Johnson, James: Skerry AM 13; 114
Johnson, James: Tamlaght TE 20; 76
Johnson, John: Ballyscullion LY 6; 66
Johnson, John: Carrickfergus AM 37; 115
Johnson, John: Donagh MN 40; 103
Johnson, John: Drumcree AH 1; 29
Johnson, John: Hillsborough DN 12; 106
Johnson, John: Lambeg AM 8; 136

Johnson, Mary: Doagh AM 29; 99
Johnson, Mary: Tamlaght TE 20; 92
Johnson, Mary Anne: Blaris AM 8; 82
Johnson, Mary Anne [I]: Carrickfergus AM 37; 117
Johnson, Mary Anne [II]: Carrickfergus AM 37; 126
Johnson, Matthew: Tynan AH 1; 126, 132
Johnson, Moore: Blaris DN 12; 44
Johnson, Mr (Cavan): Drumgoon CN 40; 9
Johnson, Mr: Aughnamullen MN 40; 75–76
Johnson, Mr: Blaris DN 12; 39
Johnson, Mr: Drumgath DN 3; 21
Johnson, Mrs: Blaris AM 8; 84–85
Johnson, Rev. G.H.: Kilmegan DN 3; 55
Johnson, Rev. Hunt: Drumgath DN 3; 21
Johnson, Rev. John: Blaris AM 8; 10
Johnson, Rev. P.: Killead AM 35; 52
Johnson, Rev. Phillip: Derryaghy AM 8; 102, 105
Johnson, Rev. Phillip: Magheragall AM 21; 108
Johnson, Robert: Ballymoney AM 16; 17
Johnson, Robert: Carrickfergus AM 37; 108
Johnson, Robert: Hillsborough DN 12; 106
Johnson, Stella (see Swift)
Johnson, Thomas: Blaris AM 8; 45
Johnson, Thomas: Blaris DN 12; 45
Johnson, Thomas: Carrickfergus AM 37; 117
Johnson, W.L.: Nilteen AM 35; 100, 102
Johnson, Whaley: Tamlaght TE 20; 93
Johnson, Widow: Hillsborough DN 12; 106
Johnson, William: Carrickfergus AM 37; 13
Johnson, William: Doagh AM 29; 82–83, 97, 99
Johnson, William: Drumachose LY 9; 61
Johnson, William: Hillsborough DN 12; 106
Johnson, William: Skerry AM 13; 114
Johnson's ford: Carrickfergus AM 37; 32
Johnston, Alexander: Glynn AM 26; 42
Johnston, Arthur: Newry DN 3; 105
Johnston, Bridget: Aghanloo LY 11; 39
Johnston, Capt.: Cleenish FH 14; 28
Johnston, Cllr: Convoy DL 39; 19
Johnston, Cllr: Kilbarron DL 39; 74
Johnston, David: Ahoghill AM 23; 49
Johnston, David: Carnmoney AM 2; 88
Johnston, Dr: Trory FH 14; 125
Johnston, Eliza: Blaris AM 8; 78
Johnston, Eliza: Cumber LY 28; 75
Johnston, family: Aghalee AM 21; 31, 36
Johnston, family: Ballinderry AM 21; 48, 51, 55
Johnston, family: Ballyclug AM 23; 60
Johnston, family: Belleek FH 14; 4
Johnston, family: Billy AM 16; 68
Johnston, family: Blaris AM 8; 21
Johnston, family: Donacavey TE 5; 71
Johnston, family: Drumbeg AM 8; 123
Johnston, family: Dunluce AM 16; 117
Johnston, family: Enniskillen FH 4; 58, 75

Johnston, family: Errigal LY 27; 41
Johnston, family: Glynn AM 26; 12, 14, 42
Johnston, family: Killesher FH 14; 84
Johnston, family: Lambeg AM 8; 135
Johnston, family: Maghera LY 18; 24, 48
Johnston, family: Magheragall AM 21; 99
Johnston, family: Racavan AM 13; 100
Johnston, family: Ramoan AM 24; 107
Johnston, family: Templepatrick AM 35; 118
Johnston, family: Tullylish DN 12; 142–43
Johnston, Frank: Templepatrick AM 35; 152
Johnston, George: Ballynure AM 32; 61
Johnston, George: Hillsborough DN 12; 98
Johnston, Graham: Carlingford LH 40; 58
Johnston, Henry: Hillsborough DN 12; 105
Johnston, Henry: Muckamore AM 35; 80
Johnston, Hugh: Donacavey TE 5; 76, 85–86
Johnston, Hugh: Hillsborough DN 12; 106
Johnston, Hugh: Misc. TE 5; 147
Johnston, Humphrey: Carrickfergus AM 37; 42
Johnston, Isabella: Carnmoney AM 2; 88
Johnston, J.: Holywood DN 7; 76
Johnston, J.B.: Killyleagh DN 17; 85
Johnston, James: Ballinderry AM 21; 47–48, 55–56
Johnston, James: Billy AM 16; 63
Johnston, James: Carnmoney AM 2; 105
Johnston, James: Carrickfergus AM 37; 195
Johnston, James: Conwal DL 39; 26–27
Johnston, James: Donaghmore DL 39; 30–33, 36–38
Johnston, James: Errigal LY 27; 45, 67
Johnston, James: Magherafelt LY 6; 107
Johnston, James: Muckamore AM 35; 79
Johnston, James [I]: Hillsborough DN 12; 106
Johnston, James [II]: Hillsborough DN 12; 106
Johnston, Jane: Aghanloo LY 11; 32, 40
Johnston, Jervis: Termoneeny LY 6; 130
Johnston, John: Artrea LY 6; 25–26, 29
Johnston, John: Ballinderry AM 21; 51–52
Johnston, John: Billy AM 16; 62
Johnston, John: Carnmoney AM 2; 98, 100, 102
Johnston, John: Carrickfergus AM 37; 40, 148
Johnston, John: Desertoghill LY 27; 21
Johnston, John: Donaghmoyne MN 40; 107
Johnston, John: Donegal DL 39; 51
Johnston, John: Down DN 17; 49
Johnston, John: Drumachose LY 9; 133
Johnston, John: Dunboe LY 11; 61
Johnston, John: Faughanvale LY 36; 40
Johnston, John: Inishargy DN 7; 85
Johnston, John: Longfield TE 5; 128
Johnston, John: Muckamore AM 35; 78
Johnston, John: Newry DN 3; 105–06
Johnston, John: Tamlaght Finlagan LY 25; 120
Johnston, John [I]: Aghanloo LY 11; 39
Johnston, John [II]: Aghanloo LY 11; 39

Johnston, Joseph: Donegal DL 39; 51
Johnston, Joseph: Drumhome DL 39; 58–59
Johnston, Joseph: Hillsborough DN 12; 105
Johnston, Margaret: Carnmoney AM 2; 88
Johnston, Mary [I]: Carrickfergus AM 37; 121
Johnston, Mary [II]: Carrickfergus AM 37; 126
Johnston, Mathew: Ballynure AM 32; 62
Johnston, Mathew: Magherafelt LY 6; 110
Johnston, Matthew: Ahoghill AM 23; 22, 41, 46
Johnston, Misses: Glynn AM 26; 47
Johnston, Mr (Fort Breda): Comber DN 7; 33, 37, 40
Johnston, Mr (Hollypark): Killyleagh DN 17; 81
Johnston, Mr (London): Ballee DN 17; 21, 23
Johnston, Mr (Stranorlar): Donegal DL 39; 50
Johnston, Mr: Blaris AM 8; 60
Johnston, Mr: Convoy DL 39; 21
Johnston, Mrs: Magheracross FH 14; 95
Johnston, Mrs John: Tamlaght Finlagan LY 25; 120
Johnston, Mrs R.W.: Glynn AM 26; 12–14, 20, 22, 24–26, 37–39, 41, 43, 45
Johnston, R.W.: Glynn AM 26; 1–2, 5, 12, 18, 34, 40, 46
Johnston, Rev.: Clondavaddog DL 38; 5, 7
Johnston, Rev. G.H.: Tullylish DN 12; 143
Johnston, Rev. G.M.: Aghaderg DN 12; 6
Johnston, Rev. J.A.: Banagher LY 30; 14
Johnston, Rev. James: Donacavey TE 5; 72, 74–76
Johnston, Rev. John: Donaghcloney DN 12; 61
Johnston, Rev. John: Seapatrick DN 12; 135
Johnston, Rev. John: Tullylish DN 12; 145
Johnston, Rev. Thomas: Ballinderry AM 21; 51
Johnston, Richard: Newry DN 3; 75
Johnston, Richard: Tullylish DN 12; 145
Johnston, Robert: Artrea LY 6; 38
Johnston, Robert: Derryaghy AM 8; 106, 110
Johnston, Robert: Derrykeighan AM 16; 89
Johnston, Robert: Drumachose LY 9; 65–66
Johnston, Robert: Killyleagh DN 17; 83
Johnston, S.D.: Cleenish FH 14; 19
Johnston, Samuel: Derryaghy AM 8; 108, 110
Johnston, Samuel: Magheragall AM 21; 106
Johnston, Samuel: Muckamore AM 35; 80–81
Johnston, Samuel: Templepatrick AM 35; 122, 148
Johnston, Thomas: Aghanloo LY 11; 24
Johnston, Thomas: Ballinderry AM 21; 51
Johnston, Thomas: Blaris DN 12; 49
Johnston, Thomas: Clogher TE 5; 40
Johnston, Thomas: Donagh MN 40; 103, 105
Johnston, Thomas: Dunboe LY 11; 81
Johnston, Thomas: Magherafelt LY 6; 110
Johnston, Thomas: Muckamore AM 35; 79
Johnston, Thomas: Tamlaght Finlagan LY 25; 107, 111
Johnston, W.J.: Belleek FH 14; 4–6

Johnston, Widow: Tamlaght TE 20; 108
Johnston, William: Aghanloo LY 11; 5, 24, 39
Johnston, William: Ballinderry AM 21; 56
Johnston, William: Ballymoney AM 16; 15, 17
Johnston, William: Billy AM 16; 77
Johnston, William: Blaris AM 8; 72
Johnston, William: Carnmoney AM 2; 88
Johnston, William: Carrickfergus AM 37; 194
Johnston, William: Donaghmore DL 39; 39
Johnston, William: Down DN 17; 52, 57–58
Johnston, William: Hillsborough DN 12; 106
Johnston, William: Magheradrool DN 17; 101
Johnston, William: Newry DN 3; 74
Johnston, William: Rashee AM 32; 140
Johnston, William: Tullylish DN 12; 143
Johnston's bridge: Derryaghy AM 8; 108
Johnston's flax mill: Magheradrool DN 17; 104
Johnston's inn: Muff DL 38; 80
Johnstone wood: Maghera LY 18; 48
Johnstone, Archy: Carnmoney AM 2; 89
Johnstone, Eliza: Faughanvale LY 36; 24, 35
Johnstone, Eliza: Tamlaght O'Crilly LY 18; 138
Johnstone, family: Billy AM 16; 58
Johnstone, family: Desertlyn LY 31; 42
Johnstone, family: Doagh AM 29; 73, 94
Johnstone, family: Kirkinriola AM 23; 124
Johnstone, family: Maghera LY 18; 13
Johnstone, Frank: Templepatrick AM 35; 153
Johnstone, Henry: Maghera LY 18; 81
Johnstone, Henry: Tamlaght O'Crilly LY 18; 138
Johnstone, Hugh: Dromore TE 5; 97
Johnstone, Jacob: Maghera LY 18; 17, 53
Johnstone, James: Carnmoney AM 2; 89
Johnstone, James: Kilbride AM 29; 150
Johnstone, James: Skerry AM 13; 119
Johnstone, James [I]: Tamlaght O'Crilly LY 18; 116, 126, 135
Johnstone, James [II]: Tamlaght O'Crilly LY 18; 138
Johnstone, Jane: Tamlaght O'Crilly LY 18; 138
Johnstone, John: Artrea LY 6; 12
Johnstone, John: Cappagh TE 5; 22
Johnstone, John: Dunaghy AM 13; 23–24
Johnstone, John: Island Magee AM 10; 69, 97
Johnstone, John: Kilcronaghan LY 31; 74, 84, 86
Johnstone, John: Templepatrick AM 35; 153
Johnstone, Joseph: Carnmoney AM 2; 89
Johnstone, Martha: Muckamore AM 35; 77
Johnstone, Mary Anne: Ahoghill AM 23; 38
Johnstone, Matthew: Ahoghill AM 23; 39
Johnstone, Mr (Ballyutoag): Templepatrick AM 35; 152
Johnstone, Mrs John: Maghera LY 18; 53
Johnstone, Mrs Robert: Maghera LY 18; 52–53
Johnstone, Rev. Beresford: Tynan AH 1; 130

Johnstone, Rev. G.H.: Donegore AM 29; 126, 130, 133
Johnstone, Rev. S.M.: Kilbride AM 29; 139, 142, 151
Johnstone, Rev. S.M.: Nilteen AM 35; 92
Johnstone, Richard: Maghera LY 18; 53
Johnstone, Ritchard (Jnr): Tamlaght O'Crilly LY 18; 138
Johnstone, Ritchard (Snr): Tamlaght O'Crilly LY 18; 138
Johnstone, Robert: Ballyclug AM 23; 65
Johnstone, Robert: Ballyscullion AM 19; 13
Johnstone, Robert: Carnmoney AM 2; 89
Johnstone, Robert: Maghera LY 18; 53, 73
Johnstone, Robert: Magheragall AM 21; 109
Johnstone, Siles: Billy AM 16; 56, 63, 69
Johnstone, Thomas: Carnmoney AM 2; 89
Johnstone, Widow: Blaris AM 8; 60
Johnstone, William: Carnmoney AM 2; 89
Johnstone, William: Dunaghy AM 13; 21
Johnstone, William: Maghera LY 18; 54
Johnstons of the chapel locality: Clogher TE 5; 34
Johnstown House: Clones FH 4; 29
Joice, family: Blaris AM 8; 22
Jolley, family: Ramoan AM 24; 107
Jolly, Archibald: Culfeightrin AM 24; 73–74, 77
Jolly, Hugh: Ramoan AM 24; 112
Jones Agnew, Edward: Carncastle and Killyglen AM 10; 9–11
Jones Agnew, Edward: Doagh AM 29; 68–69, 82, 84, 92, 97
Jones Agnew, Edward: Kilwaughter AM 10; 107–109, 111–12, 115–17, 119–21
Jones Agnew, Edward: Raloo AM 32; 125
Jones Agnew, Margaret: Doagh AM 29; 99
Jones Agnew, Margaret: Glynn AM 26; 39
Jones Agnew, Margaret: Kilwaughter AM 10; 109, 112–13, 115–17
Jones Agnew, Margaret: Raloo AM 32; 125, 128
Jones Agnew, Margaret: Urney DL 39; 179–80
Jones, Bablest: Ballyscullion LY 6; 46, 56–57
Jones, Bumper Squire: Duneane AM 19; 100
Jones, Capt.: Cleenish FH 14; 18, 22
Jones, Daniel: Kilmacteige SO 40; 188, 190, 192
Jones, Edward: Carrickfergus AM 37; 148
Jones, family: Duneane AM 19; 94, 96, 100
Jones, family: Kilmacteige SO 40; 188, 192
Jones, family: Kilmore AH 1; 70
Jones, family: Kilwaughter AM 10; 112
Jones, family: Lambeg AM 8; 135
Jones, Inigo: Carrickfergus AM 37; 80
Jones, J.G.: Ahoghill AM 23; 15
Jones, John: Derryaghy AM 8; 95
Jones, John: Hillsborough DN 12; 107
Jones, M.: Annaclone DN 12; 16

Jones, M.: Rossorry FH 14; 115
Jones, Messrs (London): Carrickfergus AM 37; 139
Jones, Michael: Donacavey TE 5; 81
Jones, Miss: Blaris AM 8; 84–85
Jones, Miss: Blaris DN 12; 45, 49
Jones, Morgan: Ballyscullion LY 6; 57
Jones, Mr (Ballycarton): Aghanloo LY 11; 21
Jones, Mr (Mullantinc): Drumcree AH 1; 41
Jones, Mr: Aughnamullen MN 40; 76
Jones, Mr: Cleenish FH 14; 29
Jones, Mr: Rossorry FH 14; 116
Jones, Mrs (Moneyglass): Duneane AM 19; 100,
 111, 114
Jones, Mrs (Tamlaght O'Crilly): Racavan AM 13;
 103
Jones, Mrs: Cleenish FH 14; 29–30
Jones, Mrs: Kirkinriola AM 23; 104
Jones, Mrs James: Tamlaght O'Crilly LY 18; 119
Jones, N.: Rossorry FH 14; 117
Jones, Paul: Blaris AM 8; 8
Jones, Rev. Henry: Clogher TE 5; 28
Jones, Rev. James (Jnr): Coleraine LY 33; 63
Jones, Rev. James: Misc. LY 31; 136
Jones, Rev. James: Tamlaght O'Crilly LY 18; 91,
 101, 107, 135
Jones, Rev. Thomas: Ballyscullion LY 6; 57
Jones, Richard: Drumachose LY 9; 65
Jones, Six Bottle: Duneane AM 19; 100
Jones, T.M.: Duneane AM 19; 117
Jones, Theobold: Ballyscullion LY 6; 47
Jones, Theobold: Clondermot LY 34; 78–79
Jones, Theobold: Clonleigh DL 39; 3
Jones, Theobold: Coleraine LY 33; 104, 142
Jones, Theobold: Faughanvale LY 36; 20, 45
Jones, Theobold: Maghera LY 18; 7, 67
Jones, Theobold: Tamlaght Finlagan LY 25; 79, 120
Jones, Theobold: Tamlaght O'Crilly LY 18; 89, 107
Jones, Thophilus: Coleraine LY 33; 64
Jones, Valentine: Ballyscullion LY 6; 58
Jones, W.: Cleenish FH 14; 29
Jones, William: Carrickfergus AM 37; 111, 193
Jonesborough: Jonesborough AH 1; 46
Jonesborough: Misc. DN 17; 131
Jonesborough chapel: Jonesborough AH 1; 46
Jonesborough water: Newry DN 3; 107
Jordan river (Palestine): Banagher LY 30; 37
Jordan, Abraham (Jnr): Hillsborough DN 12; 105
Jordan, Abraham: Hillsborough DN 12; 105
Jordan, Andrew: Hillsborough DN 12; 105
Jordan, Andrew: Newry DN 3; 81
Jordan, family: Ballyculter DN 17; 28
Jordan, family: Ballyphilip DN 7; 13
Jordan, family: Carnmoney AM 2; 34
Jordan, family: Carrickfergus AM 37; 60, 93
Jordan, Henry: Newry DN 3; 81

Jordan, John: Carrickfergus AM 37; 116
Jordan, man named: Ardglass DN 17; 3
Jordan, Robert: Ballymoney AM 16; 17
Jordan, Samuel: Carrickfergus AM 37; 123
Jordan, Sarah: Carrickfergus AM 37; 121
Jordan, Simon: Ardglass DN 17; 11
Jordan, William: Hillsborough DN 12; 105
Jordan's Acre td. Down DN 17; 33, 57
Jordan's Castle: Ardglass DN 17; 3, 11
Jordan's Castle: Ballyculter DN 17; 28
Jordan's Crew td: Ballee DN 17; 20, 22–23
Jordansland locality: Carrickfergus AM 37; 94
Jordanstown caves: Carrickfergus AM 37; 184
Jordanstown fort [I]: Carnmoney AM 2; 70, 100
Jordanstown fort [II]: Carnmoney AM 2; 100
Jordanstown fort [III]: Carnmoney AM 2; 100
Jordanstown fort [IV]: Carnmoney AM 2; 100
Jordanstown td: Carnmoney AM 2; 34, 45, 62,
 81–82, 84, 88, 92, 102, 105
Joseph's mountain: Saul DN 17; 111
Josephus I, King: Templepatrick AM 35; 150
Joy, George: Ahoghill AM 23; 12, 15, 31, 33, 47
Joy, George: Carrickfergus AM 37; 102
Joy, Mr: Carnmoney AM 2; 58, 102
Joyce and Atkinson, Messrs: Kilmore AH 1; 70
Joyce, Elenor: Blaris AM 8; 79
Joyce, Hack: Ballyscullion LY 6; 57
Joyce, J.: Cleenish FH 14; 22
Joyce, Maryann: Blaris AM 8; 79
Joyce, Miss: Kilmore AH 1; 73
Joyce, Thomas: Seagoe AH 1; 103
Joyce's bridge: Seagoe AH 1; 102
Joymount Bank ball alley: Carrickfergus AM 37;
 149, 175
Joymount Bank district: Carrickfergus AM 37; 92,
 134, 152, 162, 178
Joymount Bank flax mill: Carrickfergus AM 37;
 44–45, 47, 138
Joymount Castle: Carrickfergus AM 37; 31, 80, 162
Joymount House: Carrickfergus AM 37; 28
Joymount manor: Carrickfergus AM 37; 41, 173
Joytown, Mr (Belfast): Desertegney DL 38; 28
Junk, family: Raloo AM 32; 94, 108
Junk, William: Tamlaght TE 20; 123
Junkin, Betty: Carrickfergus AM 37; 158
Junkin, family: Ballynure AM 32; 56
Junkin, family: Carrickfergus AM 37; 93
Junkin, family: Raloo AM 32; 123
Junkin, Jane: Carrickfergus AM 37; 158
Junkin, Robert: Carrickfergus AM 37; 187
Junkin, Samuel: Raloo AM 32; 129
Jura (Scotland): Glynn AM 26; 34
Juthrin, J.B.: Belleek FH 14; 6
Juxton, Bernard: Ballyscullion LY 6; 56–57

K

Kabbitstown td: Raphoe DL 39; 126

Kailagh td: Magheracross FH 14; 102

Kaimes, Lord: Drumachose LY 9; 100

Kain, family: Carrickfergus AM 37; 174

Kain, John: Blaris DN 12; 35–37

Kain, John: Hillsborough DN 12; 107

Kain, W.H.: Hillsborough DN 12; 106

Kain., family: Island Magee AM 10; 70

Kaine, Ellen: Ballynure AM 32; 71

Kaine, James: Carrickfergus AM 37; 194

Kair, family: Carrickfergus AM 37; 93

Kairnameddy (see Carnamaddy): Lough Swilly DL 38; 103

Kairnamuaddy (see Carnamaddy): Lough Swilly DL 38; 145

Kairns, Robert: Hillsborough DN 12; 106

Kallaghan, Charles: Billy AM 16; 63

Kallanmore, chieftain: Lissan LY 31; 91, 102

Kallowly, teacher: Carlingford LH 40; 60

Kam, William: Tickmacrevan AM 13; 133

Kanally, James: Drumgooland DN 3; 24

Kananelly td: Aghalurcher TE 5; 1

Kane, Archibald: Layd AM 13; 53

Kane, Art: Banagher LY 30; 46

Kane, Bernard: Drummaul AM 19; 91

Kane, Charles: Banagher LY 30; 67–68

Kane, Charles: Carrickfergus AM 37; 113

Kane, Charles: Desertmartin LY 31; 60

Kane, Con: Banagher LY 30; 76

Kane, Edward: Faughanvale LY 36; 12

Kane, Edward: Maghera LY 18; 80

Kane, Elizabeth: Magilligan LY 11; 131

Kane, Ellen: Carrickfergus AM 37; 128

Kane, family: Banagher LY 30; 31, 112–13

Kane, family: Culfeightrin AM 24; 59

Kane, family: Dungiven LY 15; 24

Kane, family: Magherafelt LY 6; 95

Kane, family: Tamlaght Finlagan LY 25; 103

Kane, harper: Dungiven LY 15; 27

Kane, Henry [I]: Tamlaght TE 20; 76

Kane, Henry [II]: Tamlaght TE 20; 123

Kane, Hugh: Maghera LY 18; 59

Kane, Hugh: Magilligan LY 11; 94

Kane, James: Banagher LY 30; 45–46

Kane, James: Desertoghill LY 27; 20

Kane, James: Tamlaght O'Crilly LY 18; 137

Kane, James [I]: Tamlaght TE 20; 77, 104

Kane, James [II]: Tamlaght TE 20; 82

Kane, John: Ballinderry AM 21; 57

Kane, John: Ballyaghran LY 33; 27

Kane, John: Carrickfergus AM 37; 129

Kane, John: Coleraine LY 33; 145

Kane, John: Drumachose LY 9; 104

Kane, John: Dungiven LY 15; 71–72

Kane, John: Magilligan LY 11; 131, 134

Kane, John: Termoneeny LY 6; 133

Kane, John [I]: Banagher LY 30; 44

Kane, John [II]: Banagher LY 30; 111

Kane, Joseph: Carrickfergus AM 37; 124

Kane, man named: Cumber LY 28; 31

Kane, man named: Macosquin LY 22; 85

Kane, Manus: Derrykeighan AM 16; 95

Kane, Margaret: Carrickfergus AM 37; 128

Kane, Maryann: Killowen LY 33; 171

Kane, Michael: Ballynascreen LY 31; 21

Kane, Michael: Dungiven LY 15; 74

Kane, Michael: Lissan LY 31; 101

Kane, Miss: Coleraine LY 33; 92

Kane, Miss: Magilligan LY 11; 131, 133

Kane, Mr (Dublin): Kirkinriola AM 23; 95

Kane, Mr: Convoy DL 39; 21

Kane, Mrs: Coleraine LY 33; 133

Kane, Mrs Charles: Banagher LY 30; 68

Kane, Owen: Dungiven LY 15; 75, 77

Kane, Patrick: Banagher LY 30; 96, 99

Kane, Patrick: Desertoghill LY 27; 26

Kane, Richard: Drummaul AM 19; 71

Kane, Richard: Island Magee AM 10; 90

Kane, Richard: Misc. AM 10; 130

Kane, Robert: Ahoghill AM 23; 50

Kane, Roseanne: Carrickfergus AM 37; 127

Kane, Sarah: Carrickfergus AM 37; 119

Kane, Thomas: Carrickfergus AM 37; 120

Kane, Thomas: Maghera LY 18; 77

Kane, Widow (Loughtilube): Banagher LY 30; 65

Kane, Widow: Loughguile AM 13; 71

Kane, William: Island Magee AM 10; 90

Kane, William: Kilwaughter AM 10; 112

Kane's Hill (see Campsey): Faughanvale LY 36; 34

Kane's hill: Faughanvale LY 36; 3

Kane's hill: Tickmacrevan AM 13; 125

Kane's hill locality: Carrickfergus AM 37; 94, 174

Kane's Quarter locality: Dungiven LY 15; 81

Kanesbrook school: Dungiven LY 15; 118

Kapaneirvor standing stone: Ramoan AM 24; 112–13

Kar, Robart: Derrykeighan AM 16; 87

Karaghaven fort: Dungiven LY 15; 47

Kark burn: Raphoe DL 39; 129

Kark mountain: Raphoe DL 39; 129

Kark td: Convoy DL 39; 21

Karn td: Seagoe AH 1; 109

Karnamony locality: Bovevagh LY 25; 35

Karnkenny forts: Ardstraw TE 5; 12

Karnkenny td: Ardstraw TE 5; 12

Karte manor: Ballyclug AM 23; 52

Karte manor: Connor AM 19; 18

Karteen, St: Clogher TE 5; 29

Kate McCalmont's stone: Island Magee AM 10; 101

Kate McKay's bridge (see Katesbridge)

Katerson, William: Urney DL 39; 182

Katesbridge: Drumballyroney DN 3; 11–12, 14, 16

Katesbridge: Garvaghy DN 12; 80, 84

Katesbridge: Newry DN 3; 82

Kathleen's lough: Kilrea LY 27; 106–07, 112–13

Kavanagh, J.B: Drumachose LY 9; 104

Kavanagh, John: Faughanvale LY 36; 34

Keady (Cady) td: Drumachose LY 9; 110

Keady: Keady AH 1; 47

Keady: Kilclooney AH 1; 51

Keady: Mullaghbrack AH 1; 94, 96

Keady black bush: Drumachose LY 9; 110

Keady bleach mill [I]: Keady AH 1; 47

Keady bleach mill [II]: Keady AH 1; 47

Keady bleach mill [III]: Keady AH 1; 47

Keady bleach mill [IV]: Keady AH 1; 47

Keady bleach mill [V]: Keady AH 1; 47

Keady bleach mill [VI]: Keady AH 1; 47

Keady bleach mill [VII]: Keady AH 1; 47

Keady bleach mill [VIII]: Keady AH 1; 47

Keady bog: Drumachose LY 9; 89

Keady bog: Errigal Keerogue TE 20; 54

Keady bog: Macosquin LY 22; 77

Keady chapel: Keady AH 1; 47, 49

Keady church: Keady AH 1; 49

Keady corn mill [I]: Keady AH 1; 47

Keady corn mill [II]: Keady AH 1; 49

Keady corn mill [III]: Keady AH 1; 49

Keady creek: Lough Swilly DL 38; 117, 147

Keady dispensary: Keady AH 1; 49

Keady flax mill: Keady AH 1; 49

Keady flour mill: Keady AH 1; 49

Keady fort: Drumachose LY 9; 110, 128

Keady fort: Maghera LY 18; 62

Keady giant's leg: Drumachose LY 9; 127

Keady ladies' chair: Drumachose LY 9; 128

Keady market house: Keady AH 1; 49

Keady market house: Kilmore AH 1; 59

Keady meeting house: Keady AH 1; 49

Keady mountain: Aghanloo LY 11; 6, 9, 29

Kcady mountain: Balteagh LY 9; 1, 5

Keady mountain: Clondermot LY 34; 107

Keady mountain: Drumachose LY 9; 46, 48–49, 56–57, 74, 76, 87–88, 91, 108–09, 112, 118, 129

Keady mountain: Dungiven LY 15; 11

Keady mountain: Macosquin LY 22; 76

Keady mountain: Magilligan LY 11; 136

Keady ph: Clondermot LY 34; 107

Keady ph: Loughgall AH 1; 75

Keady ph: Muckno MN 40; 162

Keady police office: Kilmore AH 1; 59

Keady quarry: Tamlaght Finlagan LY 25; 71

Keady school: Drumachose LY 9; 122

Keady school [I]: Keady AH 1; 49

Keady school [II]: Keady AH 1; 49

Keady school [III]: Keady AH 1; 49

Keady school [IV]: Keady AH 1; 49

Keady school [V]: Keady AH 1; 49

Keady spinning mill: Keady AH 1; 49

Keady td: Aghadowey LY 22; 1

Keady td: Drumachose LY 9; 87, 96–97, 101–02, 122, 127

Keady td: Errigal Keerogue TE 20; 48, 54, 57

Keady td: Galloon FH 4; 95

Keady td: Maghera LY 18; 22, 25, 41, 80–81

Keady temple: Drumachose LY 9; 57, 109, 127

Keadybeg flax mill [I]: Loughgilly AH 1; 86

Keadybeg flax mill [II]: Loughgilly AH 1; 86

Keadybeg flax mill [III]: Loughgilly AH 1; 86

Keadybeg td: Loughgilly AH 1; 85, 87

Keadymore td: Loughgilly AH 1; 85

Kealy school: Dungiven LY 15; 19

Kean, family: Dunluce AM 16; 117

Kean, Mr: Dungiven LY 15; 34

Kean's hill (see Kane's): Faughanvale LY 36; 3

Keane, James: Newry DN 3; 99

Keaney, John: Blaris AM 8; 82

Kearn, Robert: Termoneeny LY 6; 130

Kearney bay: Ballytrustan DN 7; 15

Kearney manor: Misc. DN 17; 124

Kearney school: Ballytrustan DN 7; 15

Kearney school: Misc. DN 17; 128

Kearney td: Ballyphilip DN 7; 8

Kearney td: Ballytrustan DN 7; 15

Kearney td: Misc. DN 17; 127, 127

Kearney, Anthony: Aghagallon AM 21; 15, 17

Kearney, Bridget: Kilcronaghan LY 31; 84

Kearney, family: Killelagh LY 27; 99

Kearney, Francis: Banagher LY 30; 74
Kearney, Francis: Dungiven LY 15; 113
Kearney, James [I]: Maghera LY 18; 65
Kearney, James [II]: Maghera LY 18; 81
Kearney, John (Jnr): Newry DN 3; 104
Kearney, John: Kilcronaghan LY 31; 84
Kearney, John: Maghera LY 18; 81
Kearney, John: Newry DN 3; 99, 103
Kearney, Pat: Ballyscullion LY 6; 77
Kearney, Rev. P.: Carlingford LH 40; 60
Kearney, William: Ballyaghran LY 33; 28
Kearns, Anne: Carrickfergus AM 37; 121, 127
Kearns, Bernard: Carrickfergus AM 37; 124
Kearns, family: Aghagallon AM 21; 9
Kearns, J.: Comber DN 7; 33, 39
Kearns, James: Carrickfergus AM 37; 122
Kearns, William: Carrickfergus AM 37; 130
Kearny, William: Ballintoy AM 24; 20
Keating, Hugh: Tamlaght O'Crilly LY 18; 103
Keatings, John: Carrickfergus AM 37; 126
Keatly, William: Termonamongan TE 5; 144
Kebble district: Rathlin Island AM 24; 128, 131
Kee, John: Artrea LY 6; 26
Keeble hill: Rathlin Island AM 24; 129
Keel, Robert: Errigal LY 27; 62, 66
Keelaghan bog: Devenish FH 14; 52
Keelaghan td: Devenish FH 14; 58
Keelagho td: Cleenish FH 14; 29
Keelaghy td: Drummully FH 4; 34, 39
Keelaughey (see Keelaghy): Drummully FH 4; 34
Keelaughy (see Keelaghy): Drummully FH 4; 39
Keelfaurk glebe: Killesher FH 14; 86
Keelfaurk td: Kinawley FH 4; 110
Keeling, Robert: Ballyscullion LY 6; 57
Keeloges (Keelogue) td: Clonleigh DL 39; 12, 197
Keeloges school: Clonleigh DL 39; 9
Keelogs (see Keeloges)
Keelt, family: Maghera LY 18; 24, 48
Keely bleach green: Aghadowey LY 22; 8–9
Keely bog: Aghadowey LY 22; 2
Keely bridge: Aghadowey LY 22; 10
Keely House: Aghadowey LY 22; 6, 12, 19
Keely House: Tamlaght O'Crilly LY 18; 89–90, 103
Keely td: Aghadowey LY 22; 6, 10, 35
Keely, Joseph: Bovevagh LY 25; 57
Keenabawn td: Aughnamullen MN 40; 76
Keenaduff td: Aughnamullen MN 40; 76
Keenaghan corn mill: Emlaghfad SO 40; 178
Keenaghan lough: Belleek FH 14; 4
Keenaghan school: Killesher FH 14; 85
Keenaghan school: Kinawley FH 4; 111
Keenaghan td: Kinawley FH 4; 110
Keenaght (Keenaugh) td: Kilcronaghan LY 31; 73,
    84–85, 141–42
Keenaght (see Kinnea): Clonmany DL 38; 20

Keenaght and Firnacreeva district: Drumachose LY
    9; 92
Keenaght barony: Balteagh LY 9; 19
Keenaght barony: Banagher LY 30; 1, 7, 22, 36
Keenaght barony: Bovevagh LY 25; 5
Keenaght barony: Cumber LY 28; 69
Keenaght barony: Drumachose LY 9; 90, 96, 103
Keenaght barony: Dungiven LY 15; 10, 49–50, 65,
    80
Keenaght barony: Faughanvale LY 36; 3
Keenaght barony: Magilligan LY 11; 97, 144
Keenaght barony: Misc. LY 31; 133
Keenaght barony: Misc. LY 36; 120
Keenaght barony: Tamlaght Finlagan LY 25; 97
Keenaght chapel: Kilcronaghan LY 31; 87
Keenaght district: Faughanvale LY 36; 56
Keenaght district: Misc. LY 31; 114, 123
Keenaght district: Misc. LY 36; 105
Keenaght rivulet: Misc. LY 31; 113
Keenaghy td: Aghalurcher FH 4; 5, 14
Keenan, Bryan: Ramoan AM 24; 113
Keenan, D.: Ballybay MN 40; 81
Keenan, Ellen: Ahoghill AM 23; 37
Keenan, family: Aghalee AM 21; 31
Keenan, family: Carnmoney AM 2; 76
Keenan, family: Dungiven LY 15; 83
Keenan, family: Magherafelt LY 6; 95
Keenan, family: Tamlaght O'Crilly LY 18; 93
Keenan, Felix: Magherafelt LY 6; 105–06
Keenan, James: Ballyscullion LY 6; 68
Keenan, James: Maghera LY 18; 44
Keenan, Jane: Ahoghill AM 23; 37
Keenan, John: Ballyscullion LY 6; 68–69, 71, 77
Keenan, John: Maghera LY 18; 44
Keenan, Joseph: Carrickfergus AM 37; 158
Keenan, Mary: Ahoghill AM 23; 37
Keenan, Messrs Francis and Co.: Dungiven LY 15;
    6
Keenan, Michael: Ballyscullion LY 6; 76
Keenan, Michael: Maghera LY 18; 64
Keenan, Michael: Termoneeny LY 6; 131
Keenan, Michael [I]: Ahoghill AM 23; 37
Keenan, Michael [II]: Ahoghill AM 23; 37
Keenan, Murtha: Termoneeny LY 6; 133
Keenan, Patrick: Maghera LY 18; 44
Keenan, Rev.: Newry DN 3; 99
Keenan, Rose: Ahoghill AM 23; 37
Keenan, Sarah: Ahoghill AM 23; 37
Keenan, Thomas: Maghera LY 18; 44
Keenan, William: Carrickfergus AM 37; 158
Keenaught (see Keenaght): Misc. LY 31; 114
Keenogue school: Kilskeery TE 5; 115
Keenogue td: Kilskeery TE 5; 115
Keeper mountain: Killesher FH 14; 81
Keer, Edward: Derryaghy AM 8; 91

Keer, family: Finvoy AM 23; 76
Keer, John: Tamlaght Finlagan LY 25; 118
Keerachrun school: Loughguile AM 13; 67
Keerachrun td: Loughguile AM 13; 67
Keeran fort: Derryvullan FH 14; 31, 37
Keeran Shemis grave: Culfeightrin AM 24; 79
Keeran td: Derryvullan FH 14; 31
Keeran, John: Ballyclug AM 23; 64
Keeran, St: Errigal Keerogue TE 20; 50
Keeranbaan td: Moville DL 38; 73
Keernageeragh (see Carnageeragh): Kilraghts AM
    16; 136
Keernageragh (see Carnageeragh): Kilraghts AM
    16; 136
Keery, John: Hillsborough DN 12; 107
Keesie, Henery: Magherafelt LY 6; 112
Keesie, Joseph: Magherafelt LY 6; 112
Keeth, Isaac: Ballyaghran LY 33; 27
Keidue Lower td: Donegal DL 39; 43
Keidue Upper td: Donegal DL 39; 42–43
Keighan, Dorothea: Derrykeighan AM 16; 89–90
Keightly, family: Magherafelt LY 6; 95
Keightly, John: Tamlaght TE 20; 75
Keiley, James: Dungiven LY 15; 77
Keiley, Michael: Dungiven LY 15; 77
Keiley, Owen: Dungiven LY 15; 74
Keiley, Roger: Ballyscullion LY 6; 73
Keilt, James: Ballynascreen LY 31; 23, 31
Keilt, James: Maghera LY 18; 80
Keilty, Bernard (Jnr): Drummaul AM 19; 89
Keilty, Bernard (Snr): Drummaul AM 19; 89
Keilty, family: Carrickfergus AM 37; 93
Keilty, Hugh: Drummaul AM 19; 91
Keilty, John: Drummaul AM 19; 89
Keirr, John: Macosquin LY 22; 105
Keith, James: Coleraine LY 33; 72
Keith, Samuel: Coleraine LY 33; 92, 105, 131
Kell, family: Glynn AM 26; 45
Kell, Samuel: Carrickfergus AM 37; 158
Kelley, Roger: Ballyscullion LY 6; 75
Kelling hill: Drumgoon CN 40; 1
Kellmoy, family: Maghera LY 18; 48
Kells: Antrim AM 29; 22, 50
Kells: Ballyclug AM 23; 53, 57, 60
Kells: Ballylinny AM 32; 14
Kells: Ballynure AM 32; 34
Kells: Ballyrobert AM 2; 20
Kells: Ballywalter AM 2; 29
Kells: Connor AM 19; 16–25, 28–31
Kells: Doagh AM 29; 63, 67, 70–71
Kells: Donegore AM 29; 102, 107–09, 115, 131,
    134
Kells: Drummaul AM 19; 52
Kells: Glenwhirry AM 32; 75, 79
Kells: Kilbride AM 29; 139

Kells: Nilteen AM 35; 85, 90
Kells: Rashee AM 32; 137
Kells: Shilvodan AM 19; 130
Kells: Templepatrick AM 35; 111, 114
Kells abbey: Connor AM 19; 20, 29
Kells beetling and washing mill [I]: Connor AM 19;
    22
Kells beetling and washing mill [II]: Connor AM
    19; 22
Kells beetling and washing mill [III]: Connor AM
    19; 22
Kells beetling mills: Connor AM 19; 22
Kells bleach greens: Connor AM 19; 16, 21
Kells bridge [I]: Connor AM 19; 19, 23, 25
Kells bridge [II]: Connor AM 19; 22
Kells corn mill: Connor AM 19; 17, 22
Kells flax mills: Connor AM 19; 17
Kells monastery: Duneane AM 19; 106
Kells road bridge: Kilbride AM 29; 139
Kells school: Connor AM 19; 26–27
Kells td: Connor AM 19; 16–17, 20, 29
Kells tuck mill: Connor AM 19; 22
Kells water (see also Glenwhirry water):
    Kilwaughter AM 10; 108
Kells water: Ballyclug AM 23; 54–55
Kells water: Connor AM 19; 17–23, 28
Kells water: Donegore AM 29; 115
Kells water: Drummaul AM 19; 36
Kells water bridge: Connor AM 19; 31
Kellstack, Kerman: Clogher TE 5; 24
Kellswater meeting house: Carrickfergus AM 37;
    70, 144
Kellucan church: Ballyphilip DN 7; 13
Kelly lough: Kilrea LY 27; 106
Kelly, A.J.: Kilmore AH 1; 70, 73
Kelly, Andrew [I]: Kilcronaghan LY 31; 85–86
Kelly, Andrew [II]: Kilcronaghan LY 31; 85
Kelly, Anne: Ballynascreen LY 31; 22
Kelly, Anne: Carrickfergus AM 37; 124
Kelly, Bernard: Maghera LY 18; 30
Kelly, Betty: Carrickfergus AM 37; 119
Kelly, Betty: Muckamore AM 35; 81
Kelly, Bridget: Magilligan LY 11; 129
Kelly, Charles: Banagher LY 30; 86
Kelly, Charles: Dungiven LY 15; 69
Kelly, Charles: Shilvodan AM 19; 137
Kelly, Cormick: Magilligan LY 11; 129
Kelly, Daniel: Ballynascreen LY 31; 21
Kelly, Dominic: Ballynascreen LY 31; 14
Kelly, Edward: Balteagh LY 9; 24, 32
Kelly, Edward: Banagher LY 30; 67–68
Kelly, Edward: Carrickfergus AM 37; 120
Kelly, family: Aghagallon AM 21; 9
Kelly, family: Ardglass DN 17; 4
Kelly, family: Ballynascreen LY 31; 12

Kelly, family: Banagher LY 30; 67
Kelly, family: Billy AM 16; 58, 68
Kelly, family: Carnmoney AM 2; 76
Kelly, family: Culfeightrin AM 24; 59
Kelly, family: Maghera LY 18; 24, 48
Kelly, family: Magherafelt LY 6; 95
Kelly, Henry: Ballintoy AM 24; 33
Kelly, Henry: Blaris DN 12; 46, 50
Kelly, Henry: Maghera LY 18; 40
Kelly, Hugh: Errigal LY 27; 61, 74
Kelly, Hugh: Kilbride AM 29; 157
Kelly, Hugh: Macosquin LY 22; 102–03
Kelly, I.: Killanny MN 40; 131
Kelly, James: Aghagallon AM 21; 19
Kelly, James: Banagher LY 30; 96
Kelly, James: Cumber LY 28; 28
Kelly, James [I]: Ballynascreen LY 31; 22
Kelly, James [II]: Ballynascreen LY 31; 30
Kelly, John: Errigal LY 27; 51–52
Kelly, John: Kilmacteige SO 40; 188, 194
Kelly, John: Maghera LY 18; 8, 68
Kelly, John: Newry DN 3; 99, 104
Kelly, John [I]: Carrickfergus AM 37; 115
Kelly, John [II]: Carrickfergus AM 37; 162
Kelly, Joseph: Hillsborough DN 12; 105
Kelly, Joseph: Killevy AH 1; 54
Kelly, man named: Banagher LY 30; 67–68
Kelly, man named: Misc. LY 36; 112
Kelly, Martha: Ballynascreen LY 31; 22
Kelly, Martha: Drummaul AM 19; 91
Kelly, Mary: Aghagallon AM 21; 19
Kelly, Mary: Ballynascreen LY 31; 21
Kelly, Mary: Carrickfergus AM 37; 116
Kelly, Mary: Cumber LY 28; 28
Kelly, Messrs David and Co.: Ballyscullion LY 6;
  66
Kelly, Michael: Banagher LY 30; 67–68
Kelly, Michael: Carrickfergus AM 37; 111
Kelly, Michael: Kilcronaghan LY 31; 77
Kelly, Mr (Carrickmacross): Killanny MN 40; 131
Kelly, Mr (Dundalk): Down DN 17; 57
Kelly, Mr (Jnr): Clogher TE 5; 43
Kelly, Mr (Snr): Clogher TE 5; 43
Kelly, Mrs (Armagh city): Drumcree AH 1; 32, 42
Kelly, Mrs: Banagher LY 30; 67–68
Kelly, Ned: Lough Swilly DL 38; 99, 127
Kelly, Patrick [I]: Kilcronaghan LY 31; 78, 85–86
Kelly, Patrick [II]: Kilcronaghan LY 31; 85
Kelly, Paul: Ballynascreen LY 31; 31
Kelly, Paul: Errigal LY 27; 74
Kelly, Peter: Ballynascreen LY 31; 7, 26
Kelly, Peter: Maghera LY 18; 81
Kelly, Philip: Ballynascreen LY 31; 13, 21
Kelly, Philip: Kilcronaghan LY 31; 78
Kelly, Rev. John: Drumgooland DN 3; 22–23

Kelly, Ritchard: Magherafelt LY 6; 112
Kelly, Roger: Ballyscullion LY 6; 51
Kelly, Samuel: Doagh AM 29; 98
Kelly, Sophia: Ballynascreen LY 31; 21
Kelly, T.F.: Misc. LY 36; 103
Kelly, teacher: Desertlyn LY 31; 49
Kelly, Thomas: Ahoghill AM 23; 39
Kelly, Thomas: Doagh AM 29; 83, 97, 99
Kelly, Thomas: Rashee AM 32; 141
Kelly, Timothy: Aghagallon AM 21; 7, 13
Kelly, Widow: Aghadowey LY 22; 35
Kelly, William: Banagher LY 30; 61
Kelly, William: Coleraine LY 33; 145
Kelly, William: Island Magee AM 10; 80
Kelly, William: Magilligan LY 11; 94
Kellysmeadow td: Urney DL 39; 181
Kelmurry (see Kilmurry): Donaghmoyne MN 40;
  106
Kelsey, John: Billy AM 16; 62, 65
Kelsey, William: Billy AM 16; 56, 62, 64–65
Kelsey, William: Blaris DN 12; 40
Kelso, Dr: Blaris DN 12; 46
Kelso, Eleanor: Antrim AM 29; 59
Kelso, family: Magheragall AM 21; 99
Kelso, family: Mallusk AM 2; 110
Kelso, family: Templepatrick AM 35; 148
Kelso, family: Umgall AM 35; 158
Kelso, James: Tamlaght O'Crilly LY 18; 118, 138
Kelso, Jane: Antrim AM 29; 58
Kelso, Messrs: Blaris DN 12; 49
Kelso, Mr: Hillsborough DN 12; 94
Kelso, Paul: Hillsborough DN 12; 102
Kelso, Rev. Joseph: Magheragall AM 21; 105
Kelso, William: Tamlaght O'Crilly LY 18; 118,
  137–38
Kemp stones: Misc. DN 17; 121
Kempston, Esther: Antrim AM 29; 41, 45
Ken, family: Aghalee AM 21; 31
Kenaght (see Keenaght)
Kenaght (see Kinnea): Clonmany DL 38; 18
Kenaught (see Keenaght)
Kenedy, family: Ballyscullion AM 19; 4
Kenedy, family: Lambeg AM 8; 135
Kenedy, Fullerton: Drumachose LY 9; 133
Kenedy, George: Drumachose LY 9; 133
Kenedy, Hugh: Aghadowey LY 22; 36
Kenedy, Hugh: Maghera LY 18; 39
Kenedy, infant: Drumachose LY 9; 133
Kenedy, James: Ballyscullion LY 6; 61, 63
Kenedy, James: Magilligan LY 11; 94
Kenedy, Jane: Drumachose LY 9; 133
Kenedy, Joseph: Balteagh LY 9; 44
Kenedy, Joseph: Drumachose LY 9; 133
Kenedy, Margot: Tamlaght TE 20; 77, 104
Kenedy, Martha: Drumachose LY 9; 133

Kenedy, Mary: Drumachose LY 9; 133
Kenedy, Mathew: Macosquin LY 22; 122
Kenedy, Rachael: Drumachose LY 9; 133
Kenedy, Thomas: Aghadowey LY 22; 21
Kenedy, Thomas: Macosquin LY 22; 110
Kenedy, William: Aghadowey LY 22; 36
Kenedy, William: Macosquin LY 22; 107, 123
Kennaght (see Kinnea): Clonmany DL 38; 12
Kennedy, Alexander: Ballynure AM 32; 57–58
Kennedy, Alexander: Desertoghill LY 27; 17
Kennedy, Alexander: Kilraghts AM 16; 132
Kennedy, Andrew: Loughguile AM 13; 75
Kennedy, Ann: Ahoghill AM 23; 37
Kennedy, Ann: Blaris AM 8; 48
Kennedy, Anne: Ahoghill AM 23; 37
Kennedy, Annie: Kilraghts AM 16; 132
Kennedy, Anthony: Billy AM 16; 51, 59, 68
Kennedy, Bernard: Ahoghill AM 23; 34
Kennedy, Bernard: Duneane AM 19; 121
Kennedy, David: Ballynure AM 32; 58
Kennedy, David: Dunboe LY 11; 74
Kennedy, David: Maghera LY 18; 71
Kennedy, David: Newry DN 3; 99, 104
Kennedy, Denis: Aghagallon AM 21; 17
Kennedy, Denis: Blaris AM 8; 48–49
Kennedy, Denis: Blaris DN 12; 39, 41–42
Kennedy, family: Aghadowey LY 22; 11
Kennedy, family: Aghalee AM 21; 31
Kennedy, family: Ballinderry AM 21; 53
Kennedy, family: Ballyclug AM 23; 60
Kennedy, family: Blaris AM 8; 22
Kennedy, family: Carrickfergus AM 37; 93
Kennedy, family: Desertoghill LY 27; 5, 30
Kennedy, family: Duneane AM 19; 101
Kennedy, family: Faughanvale LY 36; 33
Kennedy, family: Finvoy AM 23; 76
Kennedy, family: Magheragall AM 21; 99
Kennedy, family: Misc. LY 36; 101
Kennedy, H.: Holywood DN 7; 77
Kennedy, Henry [I]: Duneane AM 19; 122
Kennedy, Henry [II]: Duneane AM 19; 124
Kennedy, Henry [III]: Duneane AM 19; 124
Kennedy, Hugh: Carrickfergus AM 37; 102
Kennedy, Hugh: Templepatrick AM 35; 132
Kennedy, J.: Newtownards DN 7; 113
Kennedy, J.B.: Blaris AM 8; 55
Kennedy, James: Ahoghill AM 23; 38
Kennedy, James: Ballymoney AM 16; 17
Kennedy, James: Desertoghill LY 27; 23
Kennedy, James: Kilraghts AM 16; 132
Kennedy, James: Macosquin LY 22; 120
Kennedy, James: Newry DN 3; 100, 104
Kennedy, James [I]: Carrickfergus AM 37; 108
Kennedy, James [II]: Carrickfergus AM 37; 108
Kennedy, Jane: Kilraghts AM 16; 132

Kennedy, John: Ballynure AM 32; 58, 62
Kennedy, John: Carrickfergus AM 37; 109, 194
Kennedy, John: Cumber LY 28; 28
Kennedy, John: Dunaghy AM 13; 23
Kennedy, John: Dunboe LY 11; 74
Kennedy, John: Holywood DN 7; 77, 82
Kennedy, John: Kilraghts AM 16; 132
Kennedy, John: Macosquin LY 22; 94
Kennedy, John: Newry DN 3; 99, 103
Kennedy, John [I]: Ahoghill AM 23; 37
Kennedy, John [II]: Ahoghill AM 23; 37
Kennedy, man named: Kilrea LY 27; 113
Kennedy, man named: Misc. LY 36; 112
Kennedy, Mary: Carnmoney AM 2; 78, 86
Kennedy, Mr (Derry): Mintiaghs DL 38; 66
Kennedy, Mr: Blaris AM 8; 13, 84
Kennedy, Mrs: Carrickfergus AM 37; 152
Kennedy, Mrs: Coleraine LY 33; 73
Kennedy, Neal: Ballymoney AM 16; 16, 18
Kennedy, Neal: Kilraghts AM 16; 132
Kennedy, Neill: Loughguile AM 13; 76
Kennedy, Owen: Drummaul AM 19; 90
Kennedy, Patrick: Drummaul AM 19; 90
Kennedy, Peter: Kilraghts AM 16; 132
Kennedy, Rev.: Seapatrick DN 12; 128
Kennedy, Rev. Anthony: Templepatrick AM 35; 116,
    124, 132–33, 143
Kennedy, Rev. Charles: Maghera LY 18; 7, 17, 52,
    67–68, 72–73
Kennedy, Rev. George: Blaris AM 8; 26
Kennedy, Rev. J.: Artrea TE 20; 8, 10
Kennedy, Rev. John: Carnmoney AM 2; 75
Kennedy, Rev. William: Kilroot AM 26; 74
Kennedy, Robert: Ballymoney AM 16; 24
Kennedy, Robert: Blaris AM 8; 55
Kennedy, Robert: Coleraine LY 33; 72
Kennedy, Robert: Desertoghill LY 27; 21
Kennedy, Robert: Kilraghts AM 16; 132
Kennedy, Samuel: Ballynure AM 32; 62
Kennedy, Samuel: Blaris AM 8; 34, 37
Kennedy, Samuel: Blaris DN 12; 45
Kennedy, Samuel: Derrykeighan AM 16; 91, 94
Kennedy, Samuel: Kilraghts AM 16; 132
Kennedy, Thomas: Coleraine LY 33; 92, 132
Kennedy, Thomas: Desertlyn LY 31; 51
Kennedy, Thomas: Desertoghill LY 27; 19, 23
Kennedy, William: Ballynure AM 32; 58
Kennedy, William: Coleraine LY 33; 145
Kennedy, William: Comber DN 7; 40
Kennedy, William: Maghera LY 18; 81
Kennedy's quay: Holywood DN 7; 83
Kenney, John: Ahoghill AM 23; 49
Kenny, Daniel: Drummaul AM 19; 84
Kenny, family: Ahoghill AM 23; 25
Kenny, Henry: Donaghmoyne MN 40; 107

Kenny, James: Culfeightrin AM 24; 51–52
Kenny, Jane (Jnr): Magherafelt LY 6; 112
Kenny, Jane (Snr): Magherafelt LY 6; 112
Kenny, John: Billy AM 16; 67
Kenny, John: Maghera LY 18; 40–41
Kenny, John: Magheracloone MN 40; 142
Kenny, John: Magherafelt LY 6; 103, 112
Kenny, Mary: Magherafelt LY 6; 112
Kenny, Mr (Rocksavage): Donaghmoyne MN 40; 107
Kenny, Mr (Rocksavage): Inniskeen MN 40; 128
Kenny, Rachael: Coleraine LY 33; 69, 135
Kenny, Sallyann: Magherafelt LY 6; 112
Kenny, William: Island Magee AM 10; 90
Kenny, William: Maghera LY 18; 78
Kenramer (Kenramore) td: Rathlin Island AM 24; 127, 133–34
Kenramer North hill: Rathlin Island AM 24; 129
Kenramer school: Rathlin Island AM 24; 133
Kent, Duke of: Kilbroney DN 3; 34
Kent, family: Maghera LY 18; 6, 50
Kent, Rev. Edward: Shankill AH 1; 114–16
Kent, Thomas: Maghera LY 18; 49–50
Kentagher Killydressy td: Misc. DN 17; 125
Keone, William: Boho FH 14; 8
Keown, family: Dunsfort DN 17; 68
Keown, Richard: Bright DN 17; 33
Keown, Richard: Down DN 17; 52–53, 57
Ker, Col: Drumgoon CN 40; 8
Ker, David: Annahilt DN 12; 22
Ker, David: Bangor DN 7; 21–23
Ker, David: Carrickfergus AM 37; 132
Ker, David: Comber DN 7; 37, 39
Ker, David: Glynn AM 26; 16
Ker, David: Holywood DN 7; 77
Ker, David: Loughinisland DN 17; 96
Ker, David: Magheradrool DN 17; 99, 101–04, 106
Ker, David: Saintfield DN 7; 118
Ker, David: Templecorran AM 26; 85–86, 92–94, 97–102, 124–27, 129–30
Ker, family: Ballyclug AM 23; 60
Ker, family: Carrickfergus AM 37; 179
Ker, family: Templecorran AM 26; 11, 97, 117–19, 127
Ker, R.G.: Carrickfergus AM 37; 32
Ker, R.J.: Templecorran AM 26; 82–83, 94, 97, 100, 125, 127, 129, 131
Ker, Sera: Derrykeighan AM 16; 87
Keranstown td: Killygarvan DL 38; 37
Keranstown wood: Killygarvan DL 38; 38
Kerdnan (see Kernan): Seagoe AH 1; 104
Kerinbeg corn mill: Galloon FH 4; 88, 91
Kerinbeg school: Galloon FH 4; 96
Kerinbeg td: Galloon FH 4; 88, 91, 95
Kerinmore td: Galloon FH 4; 95

Kern Hill td: Tullyaughnish DL 38; 97
Kernaghan, Hugh [I]: Ahoghill AM 23; 35
Kernaghan, Hugh [II]: Ahoghill AM 23; 35
Kernaghan, Rev. Andrew: Clonleigh DL 39; 10
Kernaghan, Rev. Thomas: Ardstraw TE 5; 3, 6
Kernahan, Hugh: Ahoghill AM 23; 37
Kernahan, Jane: Ahoghill AM 23; 37
Kernahan, Nancy: Ahoghill AM 23; 37
Kernan lough: Tullylish DN 12; 140, 144
Kernan manor: Seagoe AH 1; 104
Kernan mill [I]: Tullylish DN 12; 142, 146
Kernan mill [II]: Tullylish DN 12; 146
Kernan mill [III]: Tullylish DN 12; 146
Kernan td: Seagoe AH 1; 109
Kernan td: Tullylish DN 12; 140, 142–44, 146
Kernan, Daniel: Ahoghill AM 23; 35
Kernan, J.B.: Donaghmoyne MN 40; 107
Kernan, J.B.: Magheross MN 40; 151
Kerne, W.: Annahilt DN 12; 22
Kernes, family: Blaris AM 8; 21
Kerney (see Kearney): Misc. DN 17; 124
Kerokeel (see Carrowkeel): Tullyaughnish DL 38; 96
Kerr, A.: Ballybay MN 40; 84
Kerr, A.J.: Coleraine LY 33; 105
Kerr, Alexander: Ballymoney AM 16; 24
Kerr, Alexander: Billy AM 16; 67
Kerr, Alexander: Loughguile AM 13; 72
Kerr, Anne: Kilraghts AM 16; 132
Kerr, Bernard: Errigal LY 27; 40, 54, 58, 63
Kerr, Capt. (Bracklow): Drumlumman CN 40; 14, 17
Kerr, Col (Mountain Lodge): Aughnamullen MN 40; 71, 74–75
Kerr, Col (Mountain Lodge): Ballybay MN 40; 84
Kerr, David: Ballyaghran LY 33; 9
Kerr, David: Carnmoney AM 2; 101
Kerr, Dr: Aghabog MN 40; 67
Kerr, Dr: Aughnamullen MN 40; 76
Kerr, Eliza: Carrickfergus AM 37; 121
Kerr, Eneas: Killead AM 35; 45
Kerr, family: Antrim AM 29; 24
Kerr, family: Billy AM 16; 58, 68
Kerr, family: Blaris AM 8; 22
Kerr, family: Carrickfergus AM 37; 93
Kerr, family: Kilraghts AM 16; 130
Kerr, family: Raloo AM 32; 94, 128
Kerr, George: Carrickfergus AM 37; 107
Kerr, Henery: Tamlaght O'Crilly LY 18; 129
Kerr, Henry: Carrickfergus AM 37; 114
Kerr, Hercules: Hillsborough DN 12; 106
Kerr, Hugh: Muckamore AM 35; 78
Kerr, J.W.: Ballyaghran LY 33; 9
Kerr, Jackson: Killowen LY 33; 161, 170, 172
Kerr, James: Ballyaghran LY 33; 28

Kerr, James: Ballyscullion LY 6; 73
Kerr, James: Termoneeny LY 6; 132–33
Kerr, Jane: Ballyaghran LY 33; 28
Kerr, Jane: Derryaghy AM 8; 114
Kerr, Jane: Kilraghts AM 16; 132
Kerr, John: Ballyaghran LY 33; 22
Kerr, John: Ballyclug AM 23; 64
Kerr, John: Ballyscullion LY 6; 65, 78
Kerr, John: Bright DN 17; 36
Kerr, John: Culfeightrin AM 24; 71
Kerr, John: Drumachose LY 9; 104
Kerr, John: Hillsborough DN 12; 106–07
Kerr, John: Kilraghts AM 16; 132
Kerr, John: Loughguile AM 13; 77
Kerr, John: Maghera LY 18; 64
Kerr, Marcus: Coleraine LY 33; 105
Kerr, Margaret: Ballyaghran LY 33; 9
Kerr, Mark: Ardclinis AM 13; 1
Kerr, Mark: Ballyaghran LY 33; 9, 26
Kerr, Mark: Ballymoney AM 16; 7–8, 13, 15–16
Kerr, Mark: Ballywillin LY 33; 31, 43, 45
Kerr, Mark: Layd AM 13; 36
Kerr, Martha: Ballyaghran LY 33; 28
Kerr, Mary: Ballyaghran LY 33; 28
Kerr, Michael: Camlin AM 21; 76
Kerr, Miss: Ballyaghran LY 33; 9
Kerr, Mr: Dromara DN 12; 65
Kerr, Mrs: Derryaghy AM 8; 95, 114
Kerr, N.R.: Ballyaghran LY 33; 9
Kerr, Nancy: Ballyaghran LY 33; 28
Kerr, Patrick: Maghera LY 18; 36
Kerr, Patt: Carrickfergus AM 37; 188
Kerr, Rachael: Ballyaghran LY 33; 28
Kerr, Robert: Ballyaghran LY 33; 9
Kerr, Robert: Hillsborough DN 12; 107
Kerr, Thomas: Hillsborough DN 12; 106
Kerr, William: Dromore DN 12; 78
Kerr, William: Island Magee AM 10; 23, 81
Kerr, William: Kilraghts AM 16; 132
Kerr, William: Muckamore AM 35; 78
Kerr's bay: Killygarvan DL 38; 38
Kerr's bay: Lough Swilly DL 38; 98, 102
Kerr's bay ferry: Killygarvan DL 38; 40–41
Kerrin, family: Culfeightrin AM 24; 59
Kerrlan, family: Clondermot LY 34; 53
Kerrokeel (see Carrowkeel): Tullyaughnish DL 38; 92
Kerrowkeel (see Carrowkeel): Tullyaughnish DL 38; 91
Kerrsland td: Kilbride AM 29; 140
Kerry: Ballyscullion LY 6; 53
Kerry Castle: Lough Swilly DL 38; 104
Kerrygalt td: Tullyaughnish DL 38; 97
Kerrykeel: Killygarvan DL 38; 40

Kerrykeel: Lough Swilly DL 38; 100–01, 117, 128–29
Kertland, M.M.: Ardkeen DN 7; 1–3
Kertland, M.M.: Ardquin DN 7; 4
Kertland, M.M.: Dundonald DN 7; 66
Kertland, M.M.: Inishargy DN 7; 85
Kertland, M.M.: Kilmood DN 7; 96
Kertland, M.M.: Knockbreda DN 7; 102
Kertland, M.M.: Slanes DN 7; 121
Kertland, M.M.: Witter DN 7; 127
Kesh: Donacavey TE 5; 76
Kesh: Drumkeeran FH 14; 65
Kesh: Magheraculmoney FH 14; 105, 107–09
Kesh: Templecarn FH 14; 120
Kesh bridge: Drumkeeran FH 14; 63, 65
Kesh bridge: Magheraculmoney FH 14; 103
Kesh locality: Termoneeny LY 6; 122, 130
Kesh market house: Magheraculmoney FH 14; 105
Kesh river: Drumkeeran FH 14; 62–63, 67, 69
Kesh river: Magheraculmoney FH 14; 105, 109
Keshends td: Misc. DL 39; 194
Kevan, George: Ballywillin LY 33; 40–41
Kevanagh td: Galloon FH 4; 87, 95
Kevin, George: Artrea LY 6; 12, 24
Kevin, Thomas: Dunluce AM 16; 115
Kew, Patrick: Magherafelt LY 6; 108
Key lough: Misc. SO 40; 200
Key stone: Saul DN 17; 112–13
Key, John: Misc. DL 39; 192
Keys, Miss: Misc. DL 39; 186
Keys, Mr: Enniskillen FH 4; 66
Keys, Rev. William: Ballyscullion LY 6; 62
Keys, Tasker: Clonleigh DL 39; 10, 186
Keys, Thomas: Clonleigh DL 39; 4, 10, 13, 186
Kian, son of Olioll Olum: Dungiven LY 15; 50
Kianachta district: Balteagh LY 9; 19
Kianachta district: Drumachose LY 9; 93
Kianachta district: Dungiven LY 15; 55
Kianachta district: Magilligan LY 11; 103, 105
Kianachta Glen Given district: Balteagh LY 9; 14
Kianachta Glen Given district: Tamlaght Finlagan LY 25; 102
Kianaghts, family: Bovevagh LY 25; 5
Kibberreddug td: Clones FH 4; 26
Kibbins, family: Blaris AM 8; 21
Kidd, family: Desertlyn LY 31; 42
Kidd, family: Macosquin LY 22; 84, 119
Kidd, Jane: Carrickfergus AM 37; 127
Kidd, Jane: Kirkinriola AM 23; 114
Kidd, John: Derryaghy AM 8; 108
Kidd, John: Newry DN 3; 100, 104
Kidd, Rev. Henry: Banagher LY 30; 14, 113
Kidd, Rev. Henry: Bovevagh LY 25; 23, 26, 54
Kidd, Rev. Henry: Enniskeen CN 40; 30
Kidd, William: Carrickfergus AM 37; 114

Kidde, William: Cumber LY 28; 58
Kieganuirk hill: Drumachose LY 9; 58
Kielt, Daniel: Ahoghill AM 23; 40
Kielt, family: Magherafelt LY 6; 95
Kielt, Michael: Maghera LY 18; 60
Kiernan, family: Enniskillen FH 4; 75
Kiernan, woman named: Kilmacteige SO 40; 188
Kiesan, family: Derrykeighan AM 16; 89
Kightley, John: Tamlaght TE 20; 103
Kilawilly lough: Tomregan FH 4; 125–26
Kilbarron flax mills: Kilbarron DL 39; 77
Kilbarron ph: Belleek FH 14; 1
Kilbarron ph: Drumhome DL 39; 58
Kilbarron schools: Kilbarron DL 39; 77
Kilbegs fort: Antrim AM 29; 44
Kilbegs td: Antrim AM 29; 19
Kilbreath, A.: Comber DN 7; 39
Kilbride (Carlow): Faughanvale LY 36; 12, 55
Kilbride bridge: Kilbride AM 29; 151
Kilbride church room: Kilbride AM 29; 135
Kilbride cove [I]: Kilbride AM 29; 154
Kilbride cove [II]: Kilbride AM 29; 154–55
Kilbride graveyard: Kilbride AM 29; 135–36, 140,
    146, 151–54, 156
Kilbride mill-dam: Kilbride AM 29; 155
Kilbride new school: Kilbride AM 29; 151
Kilbride old church: Kilbride AM 29; 140, 146, 153
Kilbride old village: Kilbride AM 29; 146, 154
Kilbride park: Kilbride AM 29; 148
Kilbride ph: Ballycor AM 32; 5–6
Kilbride ph: Ballylinny AM 32; 16
Kilbride ph: Connor AM 19; 16
Kilbride ph: Doagh AM 29; 60, 62, 80, 96
Kilbride ph: Donegore AM 29; 101, 105, 109–12,
    128–29, 133–34
Kilbride ph: Misc. AM 10; 129
Kilbride ph: Nilteen AM 35; 84, 87, 92, 101
Kilbride ph: Rashee AM 32; 138
Kilbride river: Kilbride AM 29; 150
Kilbride sandpit: Kilbride AM 29; 135
Kilbride school [I]: Kilbride AM 29; 135, 149, 152,
    157
Kilbride school [II]: Kilbride AM 29; 149, 156
Kilbride Sunday school: Kilbride AM 29; 152
Kilbride td: Bright DN 17; 34–35
Kilbride td: Doagh AM 29; 70, 82, 96
Kilbride td: Kilbride AM 29; 136, 148, 150, 152,
    154–55
Kilbride tuck and corn mill: Kilmacteige SO 40; 195
Kilbride vault: Kilbride AM 29; 153
Kilbride village: Kilmacteige SO 40; 195
Kilbridge bridge: Kilbride AM 29; 139
Kilbright td: Misc. DN 17; 124
Kilbroaskagh chapel: Cleenish FH 14; 17
Kilbroney bleach green: Kilbroney DN 3; 28

Kilbroney church: Misc. DN 17; 120
Kilbroney cross: Kilbroney DN 3; 29
Kilbroney old church: Kilbroney DN 3; 26, 28–29,
    37–40
Kilbroney ph: Kilkeel DN 3; 52
Kilbroney river (see also Rostrevor river):
    Kilbroney DN 3; 26, 28–29, 33, 36
Kilbroney school: Kilbroney DN 3; 34, 38
Kilbroney td: Kilbroney DN 3; 28, 32
Kilbroney Upper td: Kilbroney DN 3; 26
Kilcadden td: Donaghmore DL 39; 37
Kilcaltan (Kilcalten) td: Dungiven LY 15; 49, 54,
    107, 112
Kilcaltan bridge: Cumber LY 28; 6, 18, 83–84
Kilcaltan House: Banagher LY 30; 7, 47, 56, 64
Kilcaltan House: Cumber LY 28; 9, 31, 84–86
Kilcaltan school: Cumber LY 28; 2–3, 16, 72–74,
    77–78
Kilcaltan td: Cumber LY 28; 4, 6–7, 9, 67, 70, 85,
    85, 112–13, 118, 123, 126
Kilcaltan wood: Cumber LY 28; 6, 118
Kilcalten (see Kilcaltan): Cumber LY 28; 85
Kilcaltin (see Kilcaltan): Cumber LY 28; 2
Kilcar ph: Killymard DL 39; 104
Kilclay td: Clogher TE 5; 36
Kilclean school: Skirts of Urney and Ardstraw TE 5;
    140
Kilclean td: Skirts of Urney and Ardstraw TE 5; 140
Kilclief Castle: Kilclief DN 17; 78
Kilclief church: Kilclief DN 17; 78
Kilclief corn mill: Kilclief DN 17; 78
Kilclief flax mill: Kilclief DN 17; 78
Kilclief Glebe House: Kilclief DN 17; 79
Kilclief old chapel: Kilclief DN 17; 78
Kilclief ph: Ardglass DN 17; 1, 7
Kilclief ph: Ballee DN 17; 15
Kilclief ph: Down DN 17; 61, 118, 122, 128
Kilclief school: Kilclief DN 17; 78
Kilclief village: Misc. DN 17; 122, 128
Kilcloghan td: Drumgoon CN 40; 2
Kilclooney Glebe: Kilclooney AH 1; 51
Kilclooney ph: Mullaghbrack AH 1; 94, 96
Kilcluggah graveyard: Cumber LY 28; 31–32
Kilcluggah old church: Cumber LY 28; 31–32, 48
Kilcluggah standing stone: Cumber LY 28; 30–31
Kilcluggan (see Kilcluggah)
Kilcoan barracks: Island Magee AM 10; 99
Kilcoan graveyard: Island Magee AM 10; 99–100
Kilcoan lime-kiln: Island Magee AM 10; 81
Kilcoan meeting house: Island Magee AM 10; 77,
    97
Kilcoan private school: Island Magee AM 10; 97
Kilcoan public school: Island Magee AM 10; 95
Kilcoan singing school: Island Magee AM 10; 98
Kilcoan Sunday school: Island Magee AM 10; 97

Kilcoan td: Island Magee AM 10; 77, 81, 87, 94, 97–100, 102–03

Kilcoan white house: Island Magee AM 10; 102–03

Kilcoanmore meeting house: Island Magee AM 10; 20, 27, 34, 41, 70, 73, 76, 104

Kilcoanmore old church: Island Magee AM 10; 47

Kilcoanmore private school: Island Magee AM 10; 69

Kilcoanmore school: Island Magee AM 10; 68

Kilcoanmore singing school: Island Magee AM 10; 33

Kilcoanmore Sunday school: Island Magee AM 10; 70

Kilcoanmore td: Island Magee AM 10; 15–16, 33, 40, 47, 67, 69–71, 73, 76, 104

Kilcogy: Drumlumman CN 40; 13, 15

Kilcogy barracks: Drumlumman CN 40; 13

Kilcogy school: Drumlumman CN 40; 13, 15–16

Kilcolman td: Killygarvan DL 38; 47

Kilcon td: Loughgilly AH 1; 85

Kilconway barony: Ahoghill AM 23; 1, 28

Kilconway barony: Ballymoney AM 16; 1

Kilconway barony: Dunaghy AM 13; 12, 25–26

Kilconway barony: Dundermot AM 13; 29

Kilconway barony: Finvoy AM 23; 67–68

Kilconway barony: Killagan AM 23; 79, 81

Kilconway barony: Loughguile AM 13; 58, 60

Kilconway barony: Newtown Crommelin AM 13; 78

Kilconway barony: Rasharkin AM 23; 127

Kilconway fort: Finvoy AM 23; 68, 72

Kilcoo manor: Misc. FH 4; 133

Kilcoo old church: Kilcoo DN 3; 44–45

Kilcoo ph: Ardglass DN 17; 9

Kilcoo ph: Drumgooland DN 3; 24

Kilcoo ph: Misc. DN 17; 121

Kilcoobin cave: Billy AM 16; 56, 64, 66

Kilcoobin old chapel: Billy AM 16; 52, 65–66

Kilcootry fort: Donacavey TE 5; 82

Kilcootry td: Donacavey TE 5; 76–77, 79, 81–82, 86

Kilcoquin estate: Ballyscullion LY 6; 47

Kilcorrig fort [I]: Magheragall AM 21; 105

Kilcorrig fort [II]: Magheragall AM 21; 105

Kilcran mill [I]: Donagh MN 40; 101

Kilcran mill [II]: Donagh MN 40; 101

Kilcran td: Donagh MN 40; 99

Kilcreel (see Kilgreel): Templepatrick AM 35; 138

Kilcreen td: Banagher LY 30; 22–23, 61–62, 72, 105, 109, 113, 119, 124, 127–28, 131

Kilcreen wood: Banagher LY 30; 124

Kilcreg fort: Ramoan AM 24; 91, 110

Kilcreg graveyard: Ramoan AM 24; 113

Kilcreg td: Ramoan AM 24; 113

Kilcroagh cave: Armoy AM 24; 2

Kilcroagh fort: Armoy AM 24; 2

Kilcroagh graveyard: Armoy AM 24; 2, 5, 7

Kilcroanmore td: Island Magee AM 10; 63

Kilcronaghan bog: Desertmartin LY 31; 53

Kilcronaghan church: Kilcronaghan LY 31; 64–69, 71–72, 75, 78–81, 86, 88

Kilcronaghan church: Misc. LY 31; 128

Kilcronaghan corn mills: Misc. LY 31; 135

Kilcronaghan Glebe House: Kilcronaghan LY 31; 67, 128

Kilcronaghan gort: Kilcronaghan LY 31; 65

Kilcronaghan graveyard: Kilcronaghan LY 31; 68

Kilcronaghan nunnery: Kilcronaghan LY 31; 68, 76

Kilcronaghan old church: Kilcronaghan LY 31; 67–68, 76–78, 80, 128

Kilcronaghan ph: Ballyaghran LY 33; 14

Kilcronaghan ph: Ballynascreen LY 31; 6, 8

Kilcronaghan ph: Clondermot LY 34; 63

Kilcronaghan ph: Desertmartin LY 31; 55, 59

Kilcronaghan ph: Lissan LY 31; 91

Kilcronaghan ph: Maghera LY 18; 14–15, 17, 34, 54, 56, 72

Kilcronaghan ph: Misc. LY 31; 111–12, 116, 119–37, 139–44

Kilcronaghan ph: Tamlaght O'Crilly LY 18; 100

Kilcronaghan ph: Termoneeny LY 6; 121

Kilcronaghan school: Kilcronaghan LY 31; 74, 88

Kilcronaghan Sunday school: Kilcronaghan LY 31; 74

Kilcrone td: Laragh CN 40; 39

Kilcross cove: Killead AM 35; 32

Kilcross graveyard: Killead AM 35; 25

Kilcross school [I]: Killead AM 35; 37, 43, 53

Kilcross school [II]: Killead AM 35; 37

Kilcross td: Killead AM 35; 35, 51

Kilcrow church: Ematris MN 40; 114, 117

Kilcrow Rectory: Ematris MN 40; 115

Kilcrow school: Ematris MN 40; 117

Kilcullen church: Drummaul AM 19; 70

Kilculmagrandal td: Cumber LY 28; 67, 70, 113, 118–19, 123, 126

Kilculmagrandall (see Kilculmagrandal): Cumber LY 28; 67

Kilcurren and Gunnel td: Clogher TE 5; 53

Kilcurry (Killycurry) td: Ahoghill AM 23; 27, 35, 39

Kilcurry Long stone: Ahoghill AM 23; 27, 35

Kilcurry school: Ahoghill AM 23; 22, 35, 49

Kildallan (Cavan): Ballynascreen LY 31; 33

Kildare, Earl of: Ardglass DN 17; 12

Kildare, Earl of: Kilkeel DN 3; 53

Kildare, Gerald (9th Earl): Kilmegan DN 3; 59

Kildergh (see Kildarg): Rashee AM 32; 140

Kilderry House: Muff DL 38; 80

Kilderry plantation: Muff DL 38; 80

Kilderry td: Lough Swilly DL 38; 138

Kilderry td: Muff DL 38; 81

Kildoag (Killdogues) td: Cumber LY 28; 27, 48, 53, 60, 63, 96, 101, 105, 107

Kildoag building quarry: Cumber LY 28; 105

Kildoag lime quarry: Cumber LY 28; 105

Kildoag school: Cumber LY 28; 74

Kildoag wood: Cumber LY 28; 101

Kildollagh graveyard: Kildollagh LY 22; 72

Kildollagh mills: Kildollagh LY 22; 72

Kildollagh old church: Ahoghill AM 23; 25

Kildollagh ph: Ballymoney AM 16; 1

Kildollagh ph: Ballyrashane LY 22; 58

Kildollagh ph: Coleraine LY 33; 95, 142–43

Kildollagh ph: Rasharkin AM 23; 133

Kildonan district: Cumber LY 28; 62

Kildoney creek: Kilbarron DL 39; 78

Kildoney village: Kilbarron DL 39; 77

Kildowney cave [I]: Ahoghill AM 23; 35

Kildowney cave [II]: Ahoghill AM 23; 36

Kildowney school: Ahoghill AM 23; 40

Kildress church: Kildress TE 20; 60

Kildress Lower quarries: Kildress TE 20; 59

Kildress Lower td: Kildress TE 20; 59

Kildress ph: Ballinderry TE 20; 11

Kildress ph: Desertcreat TE 20; 32

Kildress ph: Lissan LY 31; 104

Kildress ph: Lissan TE 20; 69

Kildress Rectory: Kildress TE 20; 61

Kildress river: Artrea LY 6; 39

Kildress river: Artrea TE 20; 8

Kildress river: Ballinderry TE 20; 11

Kildress river: Desertcreat TE 20; 33

Kildress river: Kildress TE 20; 59, 61

Kildrum beetling and wash mill: Connor AM 19; 22

Kildrum beetling mill: Connor AM 19; 22

Kildrum bleach green: Connor AM 19; 22

Kildrum bog: Dromore TE 5; 93

Kildrum flax mill: Connor AM 19; 22

Kildrum hill: Dromore TE 5; 93

Kildrum House: Connor AM 19; 21

Kildrum spring: Dromore TE 5; 96

Kildrum td: Connor AM 19; 17, 29

Kildrum td: Dromore TE 5; 93, 96–97, 99

Kildrum td: Killea and Taughboyne DL 39; 79, 87

Kildrum td: Misc. DL 39; 194

Kilecreig (see Kilcreg): Ramoan AM 24; 113

Kileranny (see Killcranny): Killowen LY 33; 161

Kilfaddy demesne: Clogher TE 5; 48

Kilfaddy House: Clogher TE 5; 48

Kilfaddy stream: Magherafelt LY 6; 79

Kilfeaghan giant's grave: Kilbroney DN 3; 29, 39

Kilfeaghan td: Kilbroney DN 3; 32

Kilfennan (see Kilfinnan): Clondermot LY 34; 80

Kilfinan (see Kilfinnan): Clondermot LY 34; 56

Kilfinnan td: Clondermot LY 34; 38, 56, 70, 80, 110, 112, 118, 125, 132

Kilfree district: Misc. SO 40; 198

Kilfury locality: Clondermot LY 34; 59

Kilgad beetling and washing mill: Connor AM 19; 22

Kilgad beetling mill: Connor AM 19; 22

Kilgad bog: Connor AM 19; 20, 28

Kilgad district: Connor AM 19; 18

Kilgad hill: Connor AM 19; 28

Kilgad stream: Ballyclug AM 23; 54

Kilgad td: Connor AM 19; 18, 21

Kilgarrett td: Galloon FH 4; 95, 98

Kilgarrow glebe: Killesher FH 14; 86

Kilgarrow td: Drummully FH 4; 39

Kilgarrow td: Kinawley FH 4; 110

Kilgartnaleag bridge: Magheracross FH 14; 92, 96

Kilgartnaleagh td: Magheracross FH 14; 102

Kilgolagh: Drumlumman CN 40; 13, 16

Kilgolagh barrack: Drumlumman CN 40; 13

Kilgolagh school: Drumlumman CN 40; 15–16

Kilgolah (see Kilgolagh): Drumlumman CN 40; 13

Kilgore, James: Donaghedy TE 5; 88

Kilgore, James: Termoneeny LY 6; 133

Kilgore, Martha: Termoneeny LY 6; 133

Kilgort bog: Killea and Taughboyne DL 39; 80

Kilgort fort: Donacavey TE 5; 82

Kilgort hill: Cumber LY 28; 11, 87

Kilgort td: Cumber LY 28; 24, 30, 67, 70, 113, 119, 123, 126

Kilgort td: Donacavey TE 5; 76–77, 79–82, 86

Kilgort td: Taughboyne DL 39; 80, 148, 153, 195

Kilgort wood: Cumber LY 28; 119

Kilgrange town: Dungiven LY 15; 37

Kilgreel church: Templepatrick AM 35; 124

Kilgreel corn mill: Templepatrick AM 35; 113, 138, 142, 146

Kilgreel coves: Templepatrick AM 35; 130, 152

Kilgreel cromlech: Templepatrick AM 35; 124–25, 151–52

Kilgreel fort: Templepatrick AM 35; 124–25

Kilgreel giant's grave: Templepatrick AM 35; 126

Kilgreel graveyard: Misc. AM 10; 131

Kilgreel graveyard: Templepatrick AM 35; 124, 130, 137

Kilgreel print–works: Templepatrick AM 35; 113, 138, 142, 146

Kilgreel td: Templepatrick AM 35; 116, 124, 132, 145, 152

Kilgreely td: Ballylinny AM 32; 22, 30

Kilgreen Lower td: Errigal Keerogue TE 20; 50, 54

Kilgreen td: Errigal Keeroogue TE 20; 57

Kilgreen Upper td: Errigal Keerogue TE 20; 50, 54

Kilhans (see Killins): Finvoy AM 23; 75

Kilheath, S.: Comber DN 7; 35
Kilhill bridge: Macosquin LY 22; 82, 103
Kilhilt, Laird of: Kirkinriola AM 23; 88, 94, 117
Kilhiltstown (Scotland): Kirkinriola AM 23; 94, 117
Kilhiltstown manor: Kirkinriola AM 23; 88
Kilhoyle giant's grave: Balteagh LY 9; 10, 35
Kilhoyle graveyard: Balteagh LY 9; 20
Kilhoyle hill: Balteagh LY 9; 1, 42
Kilhoyle old church: Balteagh LY 9; 19
Kilhoyle school: Balteagh LY 9; 16
Kilhoyle school: Dungiven LY 15; 19
Kilhoyle standing stone: Balteagh LY 9; 34
Kilhoyle td: Balteagh LY 9; 8–10, 14, 16, 19, 27,
    30, 32–35, 39, 42, 44–45
Kililagh (see Killelagh): Killelagh LY 27; 102
Kilioanmore td: Island Magee AM 10; 68
Kiliwell, Robert: Loughgilly AH 1; 86
Kilkaltan (see Kilcaltan): Cumber LY 28; 78
Kilkeel: Kilkeel DN 3; 48, 50
Kilkeel: Misc. DN 17; 116
Kilkeel church: Kilkeel DN 3; 48
Kilkeel druidical altar: Kilkeel DN 3; 49
Kilkeel meeting house [I]: Kilkeel DN 3; 48
Kilkeel meeting house [II]: Kilkeel DN 3; 49
Kilkeel ph: Down DN 17; 47
Kilkeel ph: Kilbroney DN 3; 26
Kilkeel ph: Misc. DN 17; 121
Kilkeel river: Kilkeel DN 3; 46
Kilkeel school [I]: Kilkeel DN 3; 50
Kilkeel school [II]: Kilkeel DN 3; 50
Kilkeel union: Misc. DN 17; 118
Kilkenny: Blaris AM 8; 89
Kilkenny: Faughanvale LY 36; 48
Kilkenny Castle: Island Magee AM 10; 48
Kilkenny county: Carrickfergus AM 37; 84
Kilkenny West (Westmeath): Banagher LY 30; 57
Kilkinamurry meeting house: Garvaghy DN 12; 80,
    84
Kilkinamurry td: Garvaghy DN 12; 79–81
Kilkit bog: Aughnamullen MN 40; 70
Kilkit td: Aughnamullen MN 40; 76
Kilknock forts: Drummaul AM 19; 78
Kilknock td: Drummaul AM 19; 90
Kill (see Killdrumsherdan): Drumgoon CN 40; 3
Kill Conic (see Temple Conic): Drumachose LY 9;
    91
Kill school: Mevagh DL 38; 59
Kill td: Aghalurcher FH 4; 16
Kill td: Aghalurcher TE 5; 1
Kill td: Clogher TE 5; 53
Kill td: Mevagh DL 38; 55, 63
Killaberry (see Killyberry)
Killack td: Currin MN 40; 91
Killaclowney td: Galloon FH 4; 95
Killaculla td: Enniskillen FH 4; 49, 72–74, 82

Killacully (see Killaculla): Enniskillen FH 4; 49
Killafurt td: Cleenish FH 14; 29
Killagan bridge: Killagan AM 23; 83
Killagan ph: Ahoghill AM 23; 4
Killagan ph: Connor AM 19; 19, 24
Killagan ph: Drummaul AM 19; 36
Killagan ph: Dunaghy AM 13; 20, 25
Killagan ph: Dundermot AM 13; 29
Killagan ph: Finvoy AM 23; 67
Killagan ph: Killagan AM 23; 80, 82–83
Killagan ph: Kilraghts AM 16; 131
Killagan ph: Loughguile AM 13; 58
Killagan ph: Rasharkin AM 23; 127
Killagan ph: Shilvodan AM 19; 133, 135
Killagan standing stone: Killagan AM 23; 87
Killagan water: Killagan AM 23; 80–83
Killaghan village: Misc. DN 17; 117
Killaghey (Killaghy) td: Donaghadee DN 7; 45, 50
Killaghey school: Donaghadee DN 7; 50
Killaghtee ph: Killymard DL 39; 109
Killaghy td: Galloon FH 4; 95
Killaghy td: Shankill DN 12; 138
Killala: Killoran and Kilvarnet SO 40; 183
Killala: Kilmacteige SO 40; 187
Killala and Achonry diocese: Carrickfergus AM 37;
    78
Killalahard school: Galloon FH 4; 96
Killalahard td: Galloon FH 4; 95, 105
Killalavin village: Kilmacteige SO 40; 196
Killalenan graveyard: Culfeightrin AM 24; 59
Killaless (see Killyliss)
Killalifferbann td: Clones FH 4; 26
Killaliss (see Killyliss)
Killallard (see Killalahard): Galloon FH 4; 95
Killally, J.: Enniskillen FH 4; 45–46
Killally, Mr: Coleraine LY 33; 101
Killaloe (Munster): Cumber LY 28; 63
Killaloo bog: Cumber LY 28; 46, 48, 80
Killaloo carn: Cumber LY 28; 29, 44
Killaloo church: Cumber LY 28; 24–25, 32–34, 44,
    57, 60, 79, 91–92
Killaloo district: Cumber LY 28; 43
Killaloo Glebe House: Cumber LY 28; 34–35, 47,
    54, 80, 91
Killaloo quarry: Cumber LY 28; 105
Killaloo school: Cumber LY 28; 24
Killaloo td: Cumber LY 28; 54, 57, 60, 62–63, 69,
    96, 101, 105, 107
Killaloo wood: Cumber LY 28; 101
Killaly district: Misc. SO 40; 200
Killamittan (see Killymittan)
Killamoonan (see Killymoonan)
Killan ph: Aughnamullen MN 40; 69
Killan, Mr: Kirkinriola AM 23; 119
Killan, Rev. James: Blaris AM 8; 24

Killan, Rev. Richard: Blaris AM 8; 27
Killan, Rev. W.D.: Raphoe DL 39; 128
Killandarrogh wood: Misc. DL 39; 189
Killane (Killeen) td: Ahoghill AM 23; 12, 38
Killane Sunday school: Ardstraw TE 5; 7
Killane td: Drumachose LY 9; 48, 56–57, 87, 96,
   109
Killaney (Killeny) td: Clogher TE 5; 37, 53
Killaney church: Tullynakill DN 7; 123
Killaney Lower td: Clogher TE 5; 33, 46
Killaney ph: Drumbo DN 7; 54
Killaney ph: Saintfield DN 7; 116, 120
Killaney td: Garvaghy DN 12; 81
Killaney td: Saintfield DN 7; 120
Killaney td: Tullynakill DN 7; 123
Killaney Upper td: Clogher TE 5; 33, 46
Killanlug Island: Kilmacteige SO 40; 194
Killanny abbey: Killanny MN 40; 131–32
Killanny abbey graveyard: Killanny MN 40; 132
Killanny chapel: Killanny MN 40; 131
Killanny corn mill: Killanny MN 40; 131
Killanny graveyard: Killanny MN 40; 131
Killanny monument: Killanny MN 40; 131
Killanny mound: Killanny MN 40; 132
Killanny ph: Clogher TE 5; 41
Killanny ph: Donaghmoyne MN 40; 106
Killanny ph: Inniskeen MN 40; 128
Killanny ph: Magheracloone MN 40; 137
Killanny ph: Magheross MN 40; 143
Killanny village: Killanny MN 40; 130–31
Killanumery ph: Manorhamilton Union LM 40; 47
Killanure td: Saintfield DN 7; 118
Killarbran td: Aghalurcher FH 4; 14
Killard Lower td: Ballyculter DN 17; 30
Killard td: Galloon FH 4; 95
Killard Upper td: Ballyculter DN 17; 31
Killargy ph: Manorhamilton Union LM 40; 47
Killarn bleach mill: Newtownards DN 7; 110
Killarn flax mill: Newtownards DN 7; 110
Killarn td: Newtownards DN 7; 110
Killarney: Coleraine LY 33; 126
Killarney: Dungiven LY 15; 63
Killarover school: Aghalurcher FH 4; 11
Killartry td: Aghavea FH 4; 23
Killary Glebe td: Clonoe TE 20; 31
Killashandra: Drumlumman CN 40; 14
Killashandra: Drummully FH 4; 40
Killashandra district: Enniskeen CN 40; 29
Killashandra ph: Drumlumman CN 40; 12
Killasnet old church: Manorhamilton Union LM 40;
   52
Killasnet ph: Manorhamilton Union LM 40; 47,
   50–53
Killaspeenan manor: Galloon FH 4; 95
Killaspeenan td: Galloon FH 4; 93, 95

Killaspienan (see Killaspeenan): Galloon FH 4; 95
Killasser td: Kilmacteige SO 40; 193
Killaughey td: Misc. DN 17; 124
Killauxille (Kildare): Dungiven LY 15; 55
Killavees td: Down DN 17; 53, 57
Killavorgan (see Kilmorgan): Emlaghfad SO 40;
   181
Killawell district: Misc. SO 40; 198
Killawillen (see Killywillin)
Killawillin (see Killywillin)
Killawnmore Island: Kilmacteige SO 40; 194
Killboggan (see Killyboggin): Misc. LY 31; 142
Killcaltan (see Kilcaltan): Cumber LY 28; 67
Killcalten (see Kilcaltan): Banagher LY 30; 64
Killcalton (see Kilcaltan): Cumber LY 28; 72
Killclay td: Clogher TE 5; 53
Killcootry td: Donacavey TE 5; 80
Killcranny td: Killowen LY 33; 161, 165, 169, 172
Killcreeny corn mill: Killdrumsherdan CN 40; 34
Killcreeny flax mill: Killdrumsherdan CN 40; 34
Killcrow (see Kilcrow): Ematris MN 40; 115
Killdallen ph: Tomregan FH 4; 125
Killdoag (see Kildoag): Cumber LY 28; 105
Killdonough td: Donaghedy TE 5; 92
Killdowney (see Kildowney): Ahoghill AM 23; 35
Killdrum (see Kildrum)
Killdrumsherdan ph: Drumgoon CN 40; 1, 3, 8, 10
Killdrumsherdan ph: Drung CN 40; 19, 21, 23
Killdrumsherdan ph: Laragh CN 40; 39, 44–45
Kille Acrue graveyard: Ramoan AM 24; 104–05
Kille Alonan graveyard: Ramoan AM 24; 109
Kille Brieda (see also Bridget's graveyard): Artrea
   LY 6; 9, 25
Kille Enan bridge: Ramoan AM 24; 110
Kille Enan church: Ramoan AM 24; 109–12
Kille Enan graveyard: Ramoan AM 24; 109–12
Kille graveyard: Culfeightrin AM 24; 51
Kille graveyard: Ramoan AM 24; 107
Kille Owen graveyard: Culfeightrin AM 24; 67, 75
Kille Owen graveyard: Magherafelt LY 6; 92, 109
Kille Owen hill: Magherafelt LY 6; 93, 110
Kille Phaul graveyard: Ramoan AM 24; 114
Kille standing stone: Culfeightrin AM 24; 51
Kille well: Billy AM 16; 51, 73
Kille well: Ramoan AM 24; 105
Killea and Taughboyne corn mill: Killea and
   Taughboyne DL 39; 88
Killea and Taughboyne flax mills: Killea and
   Taughboyne DL 39; 88
Killea and Taughboyne flour mill: Killea and
   Taughboyne DL 39; 88
Killea and Taughboyne schools: Killea and
   Taughboyne DL 39; 85
Killea bridge: Misc. DL 39; 184, 186
Killea ph: Misc. DL 39; 183–87, 189–93, 196

Killea ph: Taughboyne DL 39; 150
Killea school: Misc. DL 39; 194
Killead church: Camlin AM 21; 72
Killead ph: Aghagallon AM 21; 4–5
Killead ph: Antrim AM 29; 23
Killead ph: Ballinderry AM 21; 55
Killead ph: Camlin AM 21; 60, 63–65, 68–70
Killead ph: Carmavy AM 35; 1–4
Killead ph: Doagh AM 29; 100
Killead ph: Drummaul AM 19; 52, 67
Killead ph: Duneane AM 19; 113
Killead ph: Kirkinriola AM 23; 101
Killead ph: Misc. AM 10; 129–30
Killead ph: Muckamore AM 35; 54, 58–59, 69
Killead ph: Templepatrick AM 35; 106, 115, 120, 129, 142, 144, 150
Killead ph: Tullyrusk AM 21; 131, 133, 137–38
Killead ph: Umgall AM 35; 155–56, 159
Killeagan graveyard: Killagan AM 23; 86
Killeague (Killeage) td: Aghadowey LY 22; 6, 10, 13
Killeague district: Aghadowey LY 22; 24, 26
Killeague graveyard: Aghadowey LY 22; 26
Killeague House: Aghadowey LY 22; 6–7
Killeague meeting house: Aghadowey LY 22; 6, 14, 22, 31
Killeague school: Aghadowey LY 22; 13, 18–19
Killeague Sunday school: Aghadowey LY 22; 13, 22
Killeahouma standing stones: Ballynascreen LY 31; 10, 24
Killeally (see Killealy): Killead AM 35; 18
Killealy fort: Killead AM 35; 18, 29, 39, 46
Killealy meeting house: Killead AM 35; 18, 46
Killealy mill: Killead AM 35; 35
Killealy orchard: Killead AM 35; 35
Killealy td: Killead AM 35; 34, 40, 49–50
Killeany (see Killaney)
Killeany (see Killaney)
Kille-asturrick graveyard: Culfeightrin AM 24; 78
Killeaton forts: Derryaghy AM 8; 96
Killeaton td: Derryaghy AM 8; 96, 115, 119
Killeavy (see Killevy)
Killebreeda cairn: Billy AM 16; 73
Killebreeda church: Billy AM 16; 51
Killebreeda graveyard: Billy AM 16; 73
Killecoan ph: Galloon FH 4; 95
Killee glebe: Magheracross FH 14; 92
Killee graveyard: Magheracross FH 14; 97
Killee lough: Magheracross FH 14; 92
Killee school: Enniskillen FH 4; 84
Killee td: Enniskillen FH 4; 82
Killee td: Magheracross FH 14; 93, 102
Killee well: Magheracross FH 14; 97
Killeef bog: Tyholland MN 40; 174
Killeen td: Comber DN 7; 40

Killeen td: Dundonald DN 7; 65
Killeen td: Holywood DN 7; 77, 79–80
Killeen, Mrs: Carnmoney AM 2; 87
Killeenan (Killernan) td: Kildress TE 20; 59
Killeenan chapel: Kildress TE 20; 59–61
Killeenan school: Kildress TE 20; 60
Killeeshil church: Killeeshil TE 20; 64
Killeeshil Glebe House: Killeeshil TE 20; 62, 64
Killeeshil ph: Carnteel TE 20; 23–24
Killeeshil school: Killeeshil TE 20; 63
Killeeshil td: Killeeshil TE 20; 62–63
Killeevan ph: Clogher TE 5; 41
Killeevan ph: Clones FH 4; 26
Killeevan ph: Drummully FH 4; 34–35
Killeevan ph: Galloon FH 4; 95
Killeharnagh graveyard: Ballintoy AM 24; 22
Killelagh Glebe House: Killelagh LY 27; 95–96, 102
Killelagh lough: Killelagh LY 27; 95, 102
Killelagh old church: Ballynascreen LY 31; 9, 24
Killelagh ph: Banagher LY 30; 1
Killelagh ph: Desertoghill LY 27; 8
Killelagh ph: Faughanvale LY 36; 58
Killelagh ph: Kilcronaghan LY 31; 72, 82
Killelagh ph: Maghera LY 18; 1, 3, 10, 15, 17, 27, 34, 36–37, 40, 57, 63–64, 67–69, 71–72
Killelagh ph: Misc. LY 31; 134
Killelagh ph: Termoneeny LY 6; 121
Killelagh waterfall: Killelagh LY 27; 102
Killeluke caves: Culfeightrin AM 24; 48–49
Killeluke graveyard: Culfeightrin AM 24; 48–49
Killemacromy graveyard: Ballintoy AM 24; 23
Kille-mayangee graveyard: Culfeightrin AM 24; 49–50
Killen and Brucklass fort: Ardstraw TE 5; 12
Killen flax mill: Ardstraw TE 5; 14
Killen td: Ardstraw TE 5; 12
Killen td: Ballymascanlan LH 40; 56
Killen, family: Carnmoney AM 2; 76
Killenaken td: Killinchy DN 7; 86
Killenalurchey day school: Clogher TE 5; 43
Killenan (see Killennan): Cumber LY 28; 96
Killenaterny td: Misc. DN 17; 123
Killencuagh (see Killynenagh): Currin MN 40; 92
Killenenagh (see Killynenagh): Currin MN 40; 87
Killeney (see Killaney)
Killeniner td: Saintfield DN 7; 120
Killennan bog: Cumber LY 28; 47
Killennan cove: Cumber LY 28; 43
Killennan fort: Cumber LY 28; 39–40
Killennan quarry: Cumber LY 28; 105
Killennan standing stones: Cumber LY 28; 43
Killennan td: Cumber LY 28; 37, 49, 60, 62, 96, 101, 105, 107, 109
Killenvale House: Armoy AM 24; 4

Killeny (see Killaney)

Killephadrick graveyard: Culfeightrin AM 24;
    50–51

Killescue (see Killeague): Aghadowey LY 22; 22

Killesher forts: Killesher FH 14; 90

Killesher old church: Killesher FH 14; 81, 84, 88

Killesher ph: Cleenish FH 14; 11

Killesher ph: Kinawley FH 4; 107, 110–11

Killesher td: Killesher FH 14; 81, 87

Killesher well: Killesher FH 14; 81

Killeter bridge: Donaghmore DL 39; 29

Killeter dispensary: Skirts of Urney and Ardstraw
    TE 5; 140

Killeter district: Donegal DL 39; 53

Killeter school: Termonamongan TE 5; 144

Killeter td: Termonamongan TE 5; 144

Killeter village: Donaghmore DL 39; 28–30

Killeter village: Termonamongan TE 5; 143

Killeug (see Killeague): Aghadowey LY 22; 24

Killevalgin td: Misc. DN 17; 124

Killevan ph: Aghabog MN 40; 62

Killevan ph: Currin MN 40; 86

Killevy chapel: Killevy AH 1; 52

Killevy chapel: Misc. DN 17; 131

Killevy church: Killevy AH 1; 52

Killevy corn mill: Killevy AH 1; 52

Killevy Lodge: Killevy AH 1; 53

Killevy Lower school: Killevy AH 1; 52

Killevy meeting house [I]: Killevy AH 1; 52

Killevy meeting house [II]: Killevy AH 1; 52

Killevy ph: Ballymore AH 1; 1, 4, 7, 12, 15–17

Killevy quarry: Kilbroney DN 3; 35

Killevy school: Killevy AH 1; 52

Killewee graveyard: Loughguile AM 13; 68

Killewry, family: Glenavy AM 21; 86

Killey corn mill: Pomeroy TE 20; 70

Killfinan (see Kilfinnan): Clondermot LY 34; 38

Killgad (see Kilgad): Connor AM 19; 18

Killgort (see Kilgort)

Killgreel (see Kilgreel)

Killgreen (see Kilgreen): Errigal Keerogue TE 20;
    57

Killhill (see Kilhill): Macosquin LY 22; 103

Killibleught (Killybleught) td: Bovevagh LY 25; 16,
    19, 31, 46, 60–61

Killibleught bridge: Bovevagh LY 25; 4

Killibleught fort: Balteagh LY 9; 31

Killibleught fort: Bovevagh LY 25; 19

Killibleught school: Bovevagh LY 25; 28, 55

Killibleught spring: Bovevagh LY 25; 22

Killibleught Sunday school: Bovevagh LY 25; 25

Killibleught td: Banagher LY 30; 23–24

Killibleught woods: Bovevagh LY 25; 16

Killicard td: Muckno MN 40; 166

Killicreen (see Killycreen): Tullyaughnish DL 38;
    96

Killigan, William: Carrickfergus AM 37; 158

Killikeen td: Drumlumman CN 40; 17

Killimore (see Killymore)

Killinagh ph: Cleenish FH 14; 11

Killinagh ph: Killesher FH 14; 81

Killinchy: Killinchy DN 7; 91

Killinchy: Tullynakill DN 7; 122

Killinchy boy's school: Killinchy DN 7; 92

Killinchy church: Killinchy DN 7; 91

Killinchy female school: Killinchy DN 7; 92

Killinchy Glebe House: Killinchy DN 7; 91

Killinchy in the Woods td: Killinchy DN 7; 87

Killinchy meeting house: Killinchy DN 7; 92

Killinchy meeting house: Misc. DN 17; 121

Killinchy old church: Killinchy DN 7; 91

Killinchy ph: Comber DN 7; 31

Killinchy ph: Down DN 17; 57

Killinchy ph: Misc. DN 17; 121

Killinchy ph: Saintfield DN 7; 114, 116

Killinchy schools: Killinchy DN 7; 90

Killinchy td: Killinchy DN 7; 86

Killinchy windmill: Killinchy DN 7; 86, 91

Killinclannahy td: Cleenish FH 14; 29

Killiney td: Donaghedy TE 5; 92

Killinnen (see Killennan): Cumber LY 28; 49

Killinorgan (see Kilmorgan): Emlaghfad SO 40; 177

Killins school: Finvoy AM 23; 74–75

Killitra woods: Artrea LY 6; 5

Killive (see Killea): Killea and Taughboyne DL 39;
    80

Killiveny td: Tullyaughnish DL 38; 96

Killmacormick (see Kilmacormick)

Killmactigue (see Kilmacteige): Kilmacteige SO 40;
    196

Killmacuret rectory: Misc. DN 17; 121

Killmakee (see Kilmakee): Derryaghy AM 8; 96

Killmary td: Misc. LY 36; 104

Killmaster, John: Kilmacteige SO 40; 196

Killmore (see Kilmore)

Killmullin td: Drung CN 40; 19

Killmurray (see Kilmurry): Donaghmoyne MN 40;
    108

Killnahough hill: Misc. LY 31; 118

Killnahough standing stones: Misc. LY 31; 118

Killnahushog (see Kilnahusogue)

Killnappy (see Kilnappy)

Killnenagh lough: Laragh CN 40; 39–42

Killoges [or Killavoges] district: Misc. SO 40; 198

Killoon school: Ballyclog TE 20; 16, 18

Killoort bay: Lough Swilly DL 38; 107

Killoran ph: Killoran and Kilvarnet SO 40; 183

Killoran ph: Kilmacteige SO 40; 186

Killoran td: Killoran and Kilvarnet SO 40; 183

Killoran, Matthew: Kilmacteige SO 40; 196
Killough: Ardglass DN 17; 5, 10, 13–14
Killough: Ballee DN 17; 23
Killough: Ballyculter DN 17; 27–28
Killough: Ballykinler DN 17; 32
Killough: Bright DN 17; 33, 35–37
Killough: Down DN 17; 49, 58
Killough: Kilmegan DN 3; 57
Killough: Misc. DN 17; 116, 122, 128
Killough: Rathmullan DN 17; 110
Killough bay: Ardglass DN 17; 1, 3
Killough chapel: Ardglass DN 17; 11
Killough chapel: Bright DN 17; 36
Killough church: Ardglass DN 17; 11
Killough church: Bright DN 17; 36
Killough classical school: Bright DN 17; 36
Killough day school: Bright DN 17; 36
Killough dispensary: Ardglass DN 17; 10
Killough fort [I]: Aghalee AM 21; 36
Killough fort [II]: Aghalee AM 21; 36
Killough harbour: Ardglass DN 17; 1, 9, 11
Killough meeting house: Ardglass DN 17; 11
Killough pier: Ardglass DN 17; 9
Killough pier: Bright DN 17; 37
Killough pier: Rathmullan DN 17; 108
Killough preaching house: Bright DN 17; 36
Killough school: Aghalee AM 21; 40
Killough school: Ardglass DN 17; 11
Killough school: Bright DN 17; 36
Killough td: Aghalee AM 21; 26, 28, 32
Killough td: Bright DN 17; 35
Killough td: Rathmullan DN 17; 108
Killough windmill: Ardglass DN 17; 11
Killoughag corn mill: Layd AM 13; 48
Killoughag td: Layd AM 13; 48
Killowen: Coleraine LY 33; 54–55, 58, 89, 147
Killowen: Killowen LY 33; 158, 160, 162–63,
    166–68, 171
Killowen building ground: Killowen LY 33; 172
Killowen Catholic Sunday school: Killowen LY 33;
    166
Killowen chapel: Coleraine LY 33; 92, 95, 133, 153
Killowen chapel: Kilbroney DN 3; 28, 34
Killowen chapel: Killowen LY 33; 159, 162,
    166–68, 171
Killowen chapel: Warrenpoint DN 3; 120
Killowen church: Coleraine LY 33; 153–54
Killowen church: Killowen LY 33; 159, 161, 164,
    168, 170–71
Killowen Churchlands td: Killowen LY 33; 165
Killowen female school: Killowen LY 33; 165
Killowen female Sunday school: Killowen LY 33;
    166
Killowen Glebe House: Coleraine LY 33; 73, 73
Killowen Glebe House: Killowen LY 33; 160, 164

Killowen graveyard: Killowen LY 33; 161, 170
Killowen inn: Coleraine LY 33; 58
Killowen male school: Killowen LY 33; 165–66
Killowen male Sunday school: Killowen LY 33; 166
Killowen meeting house: Coleraine LY 33; 57, 147
Killowen meeting house: Killowen LY 33; 159, 168
Killowen monastery: Killowen LY 33; 170
Killowen old chapel: Killowen LY 33; 159
Killowen old church: Coleraine LY 33; 153
Killowen old church: Killowen LY 33; 159, 165–66,
    168, 170–71
Killowen ph: Ballyaghran LY 33; 13
Killowen ph: Coleraine LY 33; 71, 73, 104, 120,
    142, 144, 153
Killowen ph: Dunboe LY 11; 53, 66
Killowen ph: Kildollagh LY 22; 69
Killowen ph: Macosquin LY 22; 89, 102
Killowen Point: Kilbroney DN 3; 28, 30
Killowen Point coastguard station: Kilbroney DN 3;
    30
Killowen school (see also Mourne school):
    Kilbroney DN 3; 38
Killowen school: Coleraine LY 33; 147, 153
Killowen school: Killowen LY 33; 161, 166
Killowen storehouse: Coleraine LY 33; 57
Killowen storehouse: Killowen LY 33; 159
Killowen Sunday school: Killowen LY 33; 159
Killowen td: Killowen LY 33; 170, 172
Killowen td: Newry DN 3; 64
Killprocliss district: Misc. SO 40; 198
Killreath, S.: Comber DN 7; 38
Killrooskagh (see Kilrooskagh)
Killsantail Castle: Faughanvale LY 36; 50
Killsill locality: Clondermot LY 34; 33, 102
Killskeery (see Kilskeery)
Killsmallan td: Magheraculmoney FH 14; 111
Killsmullan (see Killsmallan): Magheraculmoney
    FH 14; 111
Killtariff (see Kiltariff): Drumgath DN 3; 21
Kill-Teca (see Aghanloo old church): Aghanloo LY
    11; 8
Killtierney (Kiltierny) td: Magheraculmoney FH 14;
    103, 113
Killtown td: Donaghmore DL 39; 37
Killtown well: Donaghmore DL 39; 34
Killturra ph: Emlaghfad SO 40; 177, 181
Killtyfergal chapel: Kilteevoge DL 39; 111
Killtyfergal td: Kilteevoge DL 39; 114
Killucan td: Kildress TE 20; 59
Killucan water: Kildress TE 20; 59
Killuden district: Misc. SO 40; 200
Killult school: Tullaghobegley DL 39; 172
Killultagh district: Ahoghill AM 23; 1
Killultagh district: Carrickfergus AM 37; 38
Killultagh district: Glenavy AM 21; 77, 80

Killultagh district: Kirkinriola AM 23; 88
Killultagh district: Magheramesk AM 21; 117, 125
Killultagh district: Racavan AM 13; 86
Killultagh district: Tullyrusk AM 21; 131
Killultagh kennel: Blaris AM 8; 34
Killultagh manor: Aghagallon AM 21; 20
Killultagh manor: Aghalee AM 21; 37
Killultagh manor: Ballinderry AM 21; 45, 58
Killultagh manor: Blaris AM 8; 3, 6–7, 11, 13, 23, 43, 49, 52–53, 61, 86
Killultagh manor: Blaris DN 12; 32, 39–41
Killultagh manor: Camlin AM 21; 60, 62, 65
Killultagh manor: Derryaghy AM 8; 90
Killultagh manor: Glenavy AM 21; 84, 87
Killultagh manor: Lambeg AM 8; 137, 139, 142
Killultagh manor: Magheramesk AM 21; 119, 128
Killultagh manor: Tullyrusk AM 21; 131, 136
Killultagh moss: Blaris DN 12; 42
Killultagh rectory: Misc. DN 17; 121
Killultagh school: Ballinderry AM 21; 46, 58–59
Killultagh Sunday school: Ballinderry AM 21; 46, 59
Killunaght (Killinaught) td: Banagher LY 30; 21, 31, 35, 47–48, 56, 61–62, 77–78, 83–84, 95, 105, 109, 119, 124, 128, 130–31
Killunaght bog: Banagher LY 30; 79
Killunaght fort: Banagher LY 30; 77
Killunaght standing stone [I]: Banagher LY 30; 56
Killunaght standing stone [II]: Banagher LY 30; 77
Killunaght td: Bovevagh LY 25; 42
Killuort (see Killoort): Lough Swilly DL 38; 107
Killure bleach green: Macosquin LY 22; 82, 104–05, 113
Killure bridge: Macosquin LY 22; 82, 103
Killure cave: Macosquin LY 22; 113
Killure flax mill: Macosquin LY 22; 82, 105
Killure forts: Macosquin LY 22; 95–96
Killure graveyard: Kilmacteige SO 40; 196
Killure graveyard: Macosquin LY 22; 84, 113
Killure school: Macosquin LY 22; 91–92
Killure td: Kilmacteige SO 40; 196
Killure td: Macosquin LY 22; 78, 82, 84, 96, 103, 113, 122
Killvern (see Killeenan): Kildress TE 20; 61
Killwary (see Kilwary)
Killwoodcraig wood: Muckamore AM 35; 56
Killy Brack td: Cappagh TE 5; 22
Killy lough: Donagh MN 40; 98
Killyann church (see Duncrue): Carrickfergus AM 37; 81
Killyann fort: Carrickfergus AM 37; 182
Killyanne church (see Duncrue): Carrickfergus AM 37; 4
Killybanaway graveyard: Racavan AM 13; 89
Killybanaway td: Racavan AM 13; 101

Killybane (see Kittybane): Clondermot LY 34; 56
Killybane td: Aghalurcher FH 4; 14
Killybaskey bridges: Lissan LY 31; 99
Killybaskey plantation: Lissan LY 31; 103
Killybaskey td: Lissan LY 31; 102, 104, 106–09
Killybeg fort: Ahoghill AM 23; 33
Killybeg hill: Inishmacsaint FH 14; 71
Killybeg school: Inishmacsaint FH 14; 78
Killybegs: Donegal DL 39; 46
Killybegs: Inishkeel DL 39; 66
Killybegs: Killymard DL 39; 99, 106
Killybegs bay: Killymard DL 39; 96
Killybegs iron mine: Inishkeel DL 39; 70
Killybegs ph: Inishkeel DL 39; 68
Killyberry bog: Ballyscullion LY 6; 68
Killyberry Boyd bog: Ballyscullion LY 6; 68
Killyberry Boyd cave: Ballyscullion LY 6; 51, 73
Killyberry Boyd flax mill: Ballyscullion LY 6; 66
Killyberry Boyd fort: Ballyscullion LY 6; 50
Killyberry Boyd td: Ballyscullion LY 6; 50, 69, 71
Killyberry fort: Ballyscullion LY 6; 42, 72
Killyberry td: Ballyscullion LY 6; 52, 69
Killyberry td: Donacavey TE 5; 76–77, 79–81, 84, 86
Killyberry wood: Ballyscullion LY 6; 44
Killyberrydowning bog: Ballyscullion LY 6; 68
Killyberrydowning fort: Ballyscullion LY 6; 72
Killyberrydowning td: Ballyscullion LY 6; 68
Killyblane school: Killesher FH 14; 86
Killyblught (see Killibleught)
Killybluight (see Killibleught): Bovevagh LY 25; 55
Killyblunick Glebe school: Kilskeery TE 5; 115
Killyboggan (see Killyboggin): Desertmartin LY 31; 61
Killyboggin corn mill: Desertmartin LY 31; 55
Killyboggin school: Desertmartin LY 31; 61, 142
Killybrady (see Killybready)
Killybready fort: Aghanloo LY 11; 5, 25
Killybready school: Drumachose LY 9; 50, 86, 123, 131–32
Killybready td: Aghanloo LY 11; 8, 10, 14, 20, 28, 41–42
Killybreagy td: Aghavea FH 4; 23
Killybreda (see Killybready): Drumachose LY 9; 86
Killybrockey bog: Drumglass TE 20; 40
Killybrockey coal pits: Drumglass TE 20; 43
Killybrockey td: Drumglass TE 20; 40
Killycairn (Killeyhern) Lower td: Loughgilly AH 1; 84
Killycairn flax mill: Loughgilly AH 1; 86
Killycairn Upper td: Loughgilly AH 1; 84
Killycargen td: Errigal LY 27; 60
Killycarn (Killycarne) td: Skerry AM 13; 107–08, 118, 121
Killycarn cave: Skerry AM 13; 118–19, 121

Killycarn graveyard: Skerry AM 13; 108
Killycarnan td: Galloon FH 4; 95
Killycarry (see Kilcurry): Aghoghill AM 23; 22
Killyclare school: Drumgoon CN 40; 11
Killyclochan (see Killycloghan): Kinawley FH 4; 117
Killycloghan (Aghalane) Castle: Kinawley FH 4; 117–18
Killycloghan school: Kinawley FH 4; 119
Killycloghan td: Kinawley FH 4; 117, 119
Killyclogher chapel: Cappagh TE 5; 18
Killyclogher td: Cappagh TE 5; 18, 20
Killycloney td: Donaghedy TE 5; 92
Killycloughan (see Killycloghan): Kinawley FH 4; 119
Killycomain td: Seagoe AH 1; 104, 108
Killyconaway td: Rasharkin AM 23; 138
Killyconigan td: Donagh MN 40; 98
Killycoogan (Killycargan) td: Aghoghill AM 23; 37
Killycoogan church: Aghoghill AM 23; 26
Killycoogan graveyard: Aghoghill AM 23; 26
Killycoogan monastery: Aghoghill AM 23; 14
Killycoolan (see Killycoogan): Aghoghill AM 23; 14
Killycoole locality: Lough Swilly DL 38; 120
Killycooly td: Donagh MN 40; 98
Killycor (Killicor) td: Cumber LY 28; 6, 9, 67, 70, 85, 113, 119, 123, 126
Killycor bog: Cumber LY 28; 84
Killycor corn mill: Cumber LY 28; 86, 123
Killycor flax mill: Cumber LY 28; 86, 123
Killycor quarries: Cumber LY 28; 123
Killycor school: Cumber LY 28; 3, 16, 72–74, 77–78, 85
Killycor spring: Cumber LY 28; 4
Killycor standing stone [I]: Cumber LY 28; 30
Killycor standing stone [II]: Cumber LY 28; 31
Killycor wood: Cumber LY 28; 119
Killycore (see Killycor): Cumber LY 28; 72
Killycorr (see Killycor): Cumber LY 28; 67
Killycorran td: Clogher TE 5; 34–35
Killycowan td: Rasharkin AM 23; 140
Killycracken bog: Muckno MN 40; 163
Killycracken North td: Muckno MN 40; 162
Killycramp Rectory: Drumgoon CN 40; 6–7
Killycramph td: Aghavea FH 4; 23
Killycrankie (Scotland): Ballyclug AM 23; 60
Killycreen chapel: Tullyaughnish DL 38; 88
Killycreen corn mill: Rasharkin AM 23; 131
Killycreen East td: Cleenish FH 14; 29
Killycreen fort: Rasharkin AM 23; 139
Killycreen graveyard: Rasharkin AM 23; 137, 140
Killycreen td: Tullyaughnish DL 38; 96
Killycreen West td: Cleenish FH 14; 14, 29
Killycroft [or Killycrott] graveyard: Carrickfergus AM 37; 93

Killycroft [or Killycrott] locality: Carrickfergus AM 37; 174
Killycrutteen td: Aghalurcher FH 4; 14
Killycuiragh bog: Cappagh TE 5; 21
Killycurry td: Donaghedy TE 5; 92
Killydonly (see Killydonnelly): Rasharkin AM 23; 136
Killydonnell Abbey: Tullyaughnish DL 38; 86, 90
Killydonnell fort: Tullyaughnish DL 38; 91
Killydonnell graveyard: Tullyaughnish DL 38; 90
Killydonnell td: Tullyaughnish DL 38; 97
Killydonnelly fort: Rasharkin AM 23; 140
Killydonnelly school: Rasharkin AM 23; 136, 141
Killydonnelly td: Rasharkin AM 23; 132
Killydoon td: Drumlumman CN 40; 17
Killydream lough: Drumlumman CN 40; 12
Killydream td: Drumlumman CN 40; 17
Killydrean (see Killydream): Drumlumman CN 40; 17
Killydressey td: Ballyphilip DN 7; 7–8
Killydressy td: Witter DN 7; 125–26
Killydroy fort: Clogherny TE 20; 28
Killyen, John: Clondermot LY 34; 54
Killyfad corn mill: Drummaul AM 19; 51, 84
Killyfad forts: Drummaul AM 19; 78
Killyfaddy bog: Magherafelt LY 6; 111
Killyfaddy dam: Magherafelt LY 6; 79
Killyfaddy demesne: Clogher TE 5; 26, 37, 46
Killyfaddy fort: Magherafelt LY 6; 93, 110
Killyfaddy House: Clogher TE 5; 33
Killyfaddy manor (see Cope)
Killyfaddy meeting house: Clogher TE 5; 39
Killyfaddy td: Clogher TE 5; 33, 37, 43, 46, 61
Killyfaddy td: Magherafelt LY 6; 93–95, 101, 109–12
Killyfannon (see Killyvannon): Derryvullan FH 14; 42
Killyfargy corn mill: Currin MN 40; 90
Killyfargy lough: Currin MN 40; 86, 90
Killyfargy school: Currin MN 40; 93
Killyfargy td: Currin MN 40; 86–87
Killyfast (Killyfad) td: Duneane AM 19; 96, 123
Killyfast flax mill: Duneane AM 19; 101
Killyfast hill: Duneane AM 19; 96
Killyfast school: Duneane AM 19; 106, 126
Killyflugh cove [I]: Kirkinriola AM 23; 125
Killyflugh cove [II]: Kirkinriola AM 23; 125
Killyflugh cove [III]: Kirkinriola AM 23; 125
Killyflugh foundations: Kirkinriola AM 23; 125
Killyflugh td: Kirkinriola AM 23; 92, 125–26
Killygarbit td: Laragh CN 40; 39
Killygarman td: Clones FH 4; 26, 28
Killygarn (Killygarron) td: Aghoghill AM 23; 13
Killygarn brickfield: Aghoghill AM 23; 13
Killygarn fort: Aghoghill AM 23; 35

Killygarvan bay: Killygarvan DL 38; 38, 40

Killygarvan bay: Lough Swilly DL 38; 102

Killygarvan bay: Tullyaughnish DL 38; 90

Killygarvan bridge: Killygarvan DL 38; 37

Killygarvan bridge: Lough Swilly DL 38; 98, 102, 128–29

Killygarvan church: Clondermot LY 34; 8, 97

Killygarvan Glebe House: Killygarvan DL 38; 40

Killygarvan graveyard: Killygarvan DL 38; 46

Killygarvan harbour: Lough Swilly DL 38; 98

Killygarvan hill: Killygarvan DL 38; 38

Killygarvan Isles: Lough Swilly DL 38; 102

Killygarvan lough: Killygarvan DL 38; 47

Killygarvan Lower td: Killygarvan DL 38; 37

Killygarvan old church: Killygarvan DL 38; 40–41, 46

Killygarvan ph: Clondermot LY 34; 97

Killygarvan ph: Lough Swilly DL 38; 126–28

Killygarvan ph: Mevagh DL 38; 57, 59, 63

Killygarvan ph: Tullyaughnish DL 38; 84–86, 88, 93, 95

Killygarvan river: Lough Swilly DL 38; 102

Killygarvan td: Killygarvan DL 38; 47

Killygarvan Upper hill: Killygarvan DL 38; 36

Killygarvan woods: Killygarvan DL 38; 36, 44

Killygearie td: Magheraculmoney FH 14; 112

Killyglen hill: Carncastle and Killyglen AM 10; 1, 11

Killyglen hill: Kilwaughter AM 10; 108

Killyglen ph: Carncastle and Killyglen AM 10; 8

Killyglen ph: Connor AM 19; 24

Killyglen ph: Finvoy AM 23; 68

Killyglen ph: Kilwaughter AM 10; 106

Killyglen ph: Larne AM 10; 123

Killyglen ph: Misc. AM 10; 129

Killyglen ph: Shilvodan AM 19; 133, 135

Killyglen school: Carncastle and Killyglen AM 10; 8, 13

Killyglen td: Carncastle and Killyglen AM 10; 8

Killyglin (see Killyglen): Carncastle and Killyglen AM 10; 8

Killygoan Island: Cleenish FH 14; 12, 29

Killygolagh Glebe House: Muckno MN 40; 165, 167

Killygollib (see Killygullib): Tamlaght O'Crilly LY 18; 136

Killygordon: Donaghmore DL 39; 29–32, 34–35

Killygordon: Raphoe DL 39; 130

Killygordon bridge: Donaghmore DL 39; 30

Killygordon Castle: Donaghmore DL 39; 34

Killygordon chapel: Donaghmore DL 39; 31, 33

Killygordon Demesne House: Donaghmore DL 39; 31–32

Killygordon dispensary: Donaghmore DL 39; 30, 32, 35

Killygordon fishery: Donaghmore DL 39; 29

Killygordon post office: Donaghmore DL 39; 32, 35

Killygordon school: Donaghmore DL 39; 40

Killygordon tanyard: Donaghmore DL 39; 32

Killygordon td: Clogher TE 5; 37

Killygordon td: Donaghmore DL 39; 37

Killygore (Kellygore) td: Skerry AM 13; 118–19

Killygore fort: Skerry AM 13; 119

Killygore school: Skerry AM 13; 114–15

Killygowan td: Monaghan MN 40; 159

Killygraghy td: Aghabog MN 40; 63

Killygraunia td: Derrybrusk FH 4; 30

Killygreen cave [I]: Ballywillin LY 33; 50

Killygreen cave [II]: Ballywillin LY 33; 50

Killygreen Lower td: Ballywillin LY 33; 35

Killygreen td: Ballywillin LY 33; 46

Killygreen Top cave: Ballywillin LY 33; 35, 50

Killygreen Top hill: Ballywillin LY 33; 50

Killygreen Upper cave [I]: Ballywillin LY 33; 35

Killygreen Upper cave [II]: Ballywillin LY 33; 35

Killygreen Upper fort: Ballywillin LY 33; 35, 50

Killygreen Upper td: Ballywillin LY 33; 35

Killygullan td: Aghalurcher FH 4; 14

Killygullib Glebe bogs: Tamlaght O'Crilly LY 18; 87, 131

Killygullib Glebe bridge: Tamlaght O'Crilly LY 18; 92, 110

Killygullib Glebe fort: Tamlaght O'Crilly LY 18; 116

Killygullib Glebe td: Tamlaght O'Crilly LY 18; 130, 135, 138

Killygullib school: Tamlaght O'Crilly LY 18; 139, 143

Killygullib Sunday school: Tamlaght O'Crilly LY 18; 143

Killygullib td: Tamlaght O'Crilly LY 18; 92, 97, 119, 136–37

Killyhevlin demesne: Enniskillen FH 4; 80

Killyhevlin House: Enniskillen FH 4; 66, 79

Killyhevlin td: Enniskillen FH 4; 82

Killyhoey creek: Lough Swilly DL 38; 121

Killykeeran td: Aghavea FH 4; 23

Killykelly school: Drumgoon CN 40; 11

Killykergan bleach green: Aghadowey LY 22; 8–9

Killykergan bog: Aghadowey LY 22; 4

Killykergan td: Aghadowey LY 22; 8, 10

Killyknock fort: Drummaul AM 19; 88

Killylahard (see Killalahard): Galloon FH 4; 96

Killylane td: Faughanvale LY 36; 17, 53, 59, 68–69, 76, 87, 95, 99

Killylane td: Tamlaght Finlagan LY 25; 72–74

Killylea (see Killyleagh): Kilmore DN 17; 90

Killylea bog: Tynan AH 1; 125

Killylea church: Tynan AH 1; 125, 127

Killylea school: Tynan AH 1; 125, 129

Killylea td: Tynan AH 1; 125
Killylea village: Tynan AH 1; 125, 127, 129–30
Killyleagh: Comber DN 7; 33, 40
Killyleagh: Inch DN 17; 74
Killyleagh: Killyleagh DN 17; 80–81, 83, 85, 87
Killyleagh: Kilmore DN 17; 90, 92
Killyleagh: Misc. DN 17; 117, 120, 122, 128
Killyleagh: Saintfield DN 7; 118
Killyleagh baths: Killyleagh DN 17; 81
Killyleagh Castle: Killyleagh DN 17; 81, 83
Killyleagh chapel (C): Killyleagh DN 17; 80–81
Killyleagh chapel (M): Killyleagh DN 17; 80–81
Killyleagh church: Killyleagh DN 17; 80–81
Killyleagh Corporation td: Misc. DN 17; 122
Killyleagh cotton factory: Killyleagh DN 17; 84
Killyleagh harbour: Killyleagh DN 17; 81, 83
Killyleagh meeting house: Killyleagh DN 17; 80–81
Killyleagh ph: Killinchy DN 7; 86–87, 90
Killyleagh ph: Misc. DN 17; 121–22, 128
Killyleagh pier: Killyleagh DN 17; 83
Killyleagh pier: Misc. DN 17; 120
Killyleagh private school: Killyleagh DN 17; 80
Killyleagh school: Killyleagh DN 17; 80
Killyleagh smithies: Killyleagh DN 17; 82
Killyleagh td: Kilmood DN 7; 95
Killyleg td: Aghabog MN 40; 63
Killyless (Killyleese) td: Ahoghill AM 23; 35,
    38–39
Killyless fort: Ahoghill AM 23; 34–35
Killyless fort: Errigal LY 27; 68
Killyleught (see Killibleught): Bovevagh LY 25; 22
Killylish (see Killyless): Ahoghill AM 23; 34
Killyliss forts: Donacavey TE 5; 67, 83
Killyliss td: Aughnamullen MN 40; 76
Killyliss td: Donacavey TE 5; 67, 76–77, 79–81, 83,
    86
Killyliss td: Enniskillen FH 4; 82
Killyloss td: Ballyscullion AM 19; 13
Killymacken corn mill: Kinawley FH 4; 115
Killymacken td: Kinawley FH 4; 115
Killymaddy bowling green: Finvoy AM 23; 73
Killymaddy forts: Finvoy AM 23; 69
Killymaddy racecourse: Finvoy AM 23; 69
Killymallaght (Kilmalagh) td: Clondermot LY 34;
    38, 42, 56, 70, 110–12, 118, 125–26, 132
Killymallaght night school: Clondermot LY 34; 42
Killymallaght quarry: Clondermot LY 34; 132
Killymallaght school: Clondermot LY 34; 42, 88,
    91, 95, 132
Killymallaght Sunday school: Clondermot LY 34;
    92–93
Killyman bleach mill: Killyman TE 20; 67
Killyman church: Killyman TE 20; 67–68
Killyman meeting house: Killyman TE 20; 67–68
Killyman ph: Carnteel TE 20; 21

Killyman ph: Clonfeacle AH 1; 21, 23
Killyman ph: Clonoe TE 20; 29
Killyman ph: Drumglass TE 20; 40, 43
Killyman ph: Loughgall AH 1; 75
Killyman ph: Tamlaght TE 20; 73
Killyman ph: Tartaraghan AH 1; 117, 119
Killyman ph: Tullyniskan TE 20; 138
Killymaran mill [I]: Tydavnet MN 40; 173
Killymaran mill [II]: Tydavnet MN 40; 173
Killymard chapel: Donegal DL 39; 45
Killymard chapel: Killymard DL 39; 96
Killymard coal mine: Killymard DL 39; 106
Killymard Cottage: Killymard DL 39; 96
Killymard flax mill: Killymard DL 39; 108
Killymard Glebe House: Killymard DL 39; 96–97
Killymard meeting house: Donegal DL 39; 45
Killymard meeting house: Killymard DL 39; 96
Killymard ph: Donegal DL 39; 42, 46–47, 54
Killymard ph: Kilteevoge DL 39; 111
Killymard ph: Templecarn DL 39; 161
Killymard schools: Killymard DL 39; 107
Killymasney hill: Conwal DL 39; 24
Killymasney td: Conwal DL 39; 27
Killymeehan lough: Laragh CN 40; 40
Killymittan school: Magheracross FH 14; 99
Killymittan spade mill: Magheracross FH 14; 95,
    100
Killymittan td: Magheracross FH 14; 92–93, 102
Killymitten (see Killymittan)
Killymoon demesne: Artrea LY 6; 39
Killymoon demesne: Artrea TE 20; 8, 10
Killymoon demesne: Ballinderry TE 20; 13
Killymoon demesne: Desertcreat TE 20; 34
Killymoon House: Desertcreat TE 20; 34
Killymoon House: Kilcronaghan LY 31; 64, 69,
    86–87
Killymoonan td: Donacavey TE 5; 76, 79–82, 86
Killymore corn mill: Ardstraw TE 5; 4
Killymore flax mill: Ardstraw TE 5; 14
Killymore fort: Ardstraw TE 5; 12
Killymore school: Inishmacsaint FH 14; 78
Killymore td: Ardstraw TE 5; 4, 12
Killymore td: Inishmacsaint FH 14; 70
Killymorgan (see Woodtown): Magilligan LY 11;
    126
Killymorgan td: Errigal Keerogue TE 20; 54, 57
Killymorris (see Killymurrys)
Killymuck bogs: Tamlaght O'Crilly LY 18; 86–87,
    115, 130–31
Killymuck fort [I]: Tamlaght O'Crilly LY 18; 95,
    114
Killymuck fort [II]: Tamlaght O'Crilly LY 18; 114
Killymuck fort [III]: Tamlaght O'Crilly LY 18; 114
Killymuck fort [IV]: Tamlaght O'Crilly LY 18; 115

Killymuck Glebe fort: Tamlaght O'Crilly LY 18; 115

Killymuck Glebe td: Tamlaght O'Crilly LY 18; 138

Killymuck school: Tamlaght O'Crilly LY 18; 142, 144

Killymuck Sunday school: Tamlaght O'Crilly LY 18; 143–44

Killymuck td: Ballinderry TE 20; 13

Killymuck td: Tamlaght O'Crilly LY 18; 97, 115, 136–38

Killymurris (see Killymurrys): Finvoy AM 23; 67

Killymurrys coal mines: Killead AM 35; 50

Killymurrys hills: Ahoghill AM 23; 3–4, 9, 13

Killymurrys hills: Drummaul AM 19; 35

Killymurrys hills: Duneane AM 19; 96

Killymurrys hills: Finvoy AM 23; 67–68, 70

Killymurrys hills: Killagan AM 23; 84

Killymurrys hills: Kirkinriola AM 23; 93

Killymurrys hills: Rasharkin AM 23; 127–28, 132

Killymurrys Irish district: Rasharkin AM 23; 128, 132

Killymurrys Scotch district: Rasharkin AM 23; 128, 132

Killynacran td: Galloon FH 4; 95

Killynahawagh House: Kilmore AH 1; 72

Killynamph td: Aghalurcher FH 4; 14

Killynaught bog: Leckpatrick TE 5; 120

Killynaught mountain: Leckpatrick TE 5; 120

Killynaught td: Leckpatrick TE 5; 120

Killyneary hill: Carnteel TE 20; 23

Killyneese fort: Magherafelt LY 6; 93, 104

Killyneese td: Artrea LY 6; 22

Killyneese td: Enniskillen FH 4; 82

Killyneese td: Magherafelt LY 6; 91, 93, 95, 104, 112

Killyneill bog: Tyholland MN 40; 174

Killynenagh hill: Currin MN 40; 87

Killynenagh td: Currin MN 40; 92

Killynether td: Comber DN 7; 37, 39, 42–43

Killynorry td: Raymoghy DL 39; 141

Killynubber td: Galloon FH 4; 87, 95

Killynumber fort [I]: Kilcronaghan LY 31; 86

Killynumber fort [II]: Kilcronaghan LY 31; 86

Killynumber td: Kilcronaghan LY 31; 84, 142

Killynummer (see Killynumber)

Killynure td: Convoy DL 39; 21

Killyoole (see Killywool): Faughanvale LY 36; 53

Killypaddy td: Aghalurcher FH 4; 3

Killyramer corn mill: Ballymoney AM 16; 10

Killyramer cove: Ballymoney AM 16; 24

Killyramer graveyard: Ballymoney AM 16; 24

Killyraw td: Galloon FH 4; 87, 95

Killyreagh td: Derrybrusk FH 4; 30

Killyrean Upper td: Donagh MN 40; 99

Killyroo td: Galloon FH 4; 95

Killyrue forest: Drumgoon CN 40; 3

Killyrue hill: Drumgoon CN 40; 1

Killyrue lough: Drumgoon CN 40; 2–3

Killyrue td: Drumgoon CN 40; 2

Killysavan (Killysavin) td: Donaghmore DN 3; 8–9

Killysavan moss: Misc. DN 17; 130

Killysavan td: Misc. DN 17; 130–31

Killyslaven Moneyglass school: Duneane AM 19; 125

Killytaggart td: Boho FH 14; 8

Killytee bog: Drumgoon CN 40; 4

Killytee hill: Drumgoon CN 40; 1

Killytee td: Drumgoon CN 40; 2, 6

Killytoney bog: Kilcronaghan LY 31; 78

Killytoney fort: Kilcronaghan LY 31; 86

Killytoney school: Kilcronaghan LY 31; 74

Killytoney Sunday school: Misc. LY 31; 126

Killytoney td: Kilcronaghan LY 31; 67, 79, 141–42

Killyvally (Killavalley) td: Desertoghill LY 27; 14, 19–22, 28–29

Killyvally bog: Desertoghill LY 27; 14

Killyvally corn mill: Desertoghill LY 27; 4, 13

Killyvannon fort: Derryvullan FH 14; 42

Killyvannon td: Derryvullan FH 14; 42, 46

Killyvaughan hill: Drumgoon CN 40; 1

Killyvea bog: Devenish FH 14; 52

Killyvea Glebe fort: Devenish FH 14; 55

Killyvea Glebe td: Devenish FH 14; 58

Killyveety bridge: Dunboe LY 11; 62

Killyveety cove: Dunboe LY 11; 50, 73

Killyveety fort: Dunboe LY 11; 49, 73

Killyveety school: Dunboe LY 11; 56, 70

Killyveety Sunday school: Dunboe LY 11; 57

Killyveety td: Dunboe LY 11; 81

Killyverry td: Raymoghy DL 39; 138, 199

Killyvilly td: Enniskillen FH 4; 82

Killywill (see Killywool)

Killywillin corn mills: Cleenish FH 14; 14, 18

Killywillin Mill lough: Cleenish FH 14; 14

Killywillin td: Cleenish FH 14; 14, 17, 25, 29

Killywool quarry: Faughanvale LY 36; 95

Killywool quarry: Tamlaght Finlagan LY 25; 71

Killywool school: Faughanvale LY 36; 25

Killywool school [I]: Faughanvale LY 36; 24, 27, 35

Killywool school [II]: Faughanvale LY 36; 24, 27, 35

Killywool td: Faughanvale LY 36; 17, 53, 59, 69, 76, 87, 95, 99

Kilmacanty corn mill: Kilmore AH 1; 71

Kilmacanty td: Kilmore AH 1; 66, 71, 73

Kilmacauly (see Kilmacanty): Kilmore AH 1; 66

Kilmacavert district: Drummaul AM 19; 67

Kilmacavert district: Killead AM 35; 17, 24

Kilmacavert manor: Killead AM 35; 18

Kilmacavert manor: Misc. AM 10; 130

Kilmacbrack td: Galloon FH 4; 95

Kilmacdoe deanery: Aghabog MN 40; 63

Kilmacduagh (Galway): Faughanvale LY 36; 56

Kilmaconnell (Kilmaconnel) td: Macosquin LY 22; 113, 123

Kilmaconnell graveyard: Macosquin LY 22; 84

Kilmaconnell spring: Macosquin LY 22; 113

Kilmacormick hill: Trory FH 14; 122

Kilmacormick td: Trory FH 14; 129

Kilmacrenan: Killymard DL 39; 94

Kilmacrenan: Kilmacrenan DL 38; 50, 52

Kilmacrenan: Mevagh DL 38; 57

Kilmacrenan: Tullyaughnish DL 38; 89

Kilmacrenan abbey: Kilmacrenan DL 38; 51

Kilmacrenan barony: Conwal DL 39; 24

Kilmacrenan barony: Killygarvan DL 38; 36

Kilmacrenan barony: Lough Swilly DL 38; 128–29

Kilmacrenan barony: Mevagh DL 38; 54

Kilmacrenan barony: Raymoghy DL 39; 144

Kilmacrenan barony: Tullyaughnish DL 38; 96

Kilmacrenan chapel [I]: Kilmacrenan DL 38; 52

Kilmacrenan chapel [II]: Kilmacrenan DL 38; 52

Kilmacrenan church: Kilmacrenan DL 38; 51–52

Kilmacrenan dispensary: Kilmacrenan DL 38; 50

Kilmacrenan giant's grave: Kilmacrenan DL 38; 53

Kilmacrenan graveyard: Kilmacrenan DL 38; 51

Kilmacrenan meeting house: Kilmacrenan DL 38; 52

Kilmacrenan ph: Clondavaddog DL 38; 1

Kilmacrenan ph: Conwal DL 39; 24

Kilmacrenan ph: Killymard DL 39; 97

Kilmacrenan ph: Lough Swilly DL 38; 128

Kilmacrenan ph: Mevagh DL 38; 54–55, 57

Kilmacrenan ph: Tullyaughnish DL 38; 84, 86–87, 93–94

Kilmacrenan post office: Kilmacrenan DL 38; 50

Kilmacrew bog: Magherally DN 12; 115

Kilmacrew td: Magherally DN 12; 112, 114–15

Kilmacteige barrack: Kilmacteige SO 40; 189

Kilmacteige church: Kilmacteige SO 40; 189, 192, 196

Kilmacteige corn mill: Kilmacteige SO 40; 194

Kilmacteige hibernian school: Kilmacteige SO 40; 195

Kilmacteige national school: Kilmacteige SO 40; 195

Kilmacteige old barracks: Kilmacteige SO 40; 192, 196

Kilmacteige pound: Kilmacteige SO 40; 194

Kilmacteige td: Kilmacteige SO 40; 188–89, 193, 195–96

Kilmacteige tuck mill: Kilmacteige SO 40; 194

Kilmactrasna td: Magheross MN 40; 149

Kilmagarnish td: Drumcree AH 1; 39

Kilmahamogue cave: Ballintoy AM 24; 28

Kilmahamogue graveyard: Ballintoy AM 24; 28

Kilmahamogue td: Ballintoy AM 24; 28

Kilmahawey (see Kilnaharvey): Ematris MN 40; 116

Kilmainham (Dublin): Carrickfergus AM 37; 80

Kilmakee cove: Templepatrick AM 35; 127, 130, 137, 149

Kilmakee druid's temple: Templepatrick AM 35; 149

Kilmakee druidical circle: Templepatrick AM 35; 130

Kilmakee fort: Templepatrick AM 35; 127

Kilmakee fort [I]: Derryaghy AM 8; 96

Kilmakee fort [I]: Templepatrick AM 35; 137, 151

Kilmakee fort [II]: Derryaghy AM 8; 96

Kilmakee fort [II]: Templepatrick AM 35; 137, 151

Kilmakee fort [III]: Derryaghy AM 8; 96

Kilmakee fort [III]: Templepatrick AM 35; 151

Kilmakee graveyard: Derryaghy AM 8; 92

Kilmakee td: Derryaghy AM 8; 92, 96, 120

Kilmakee td: Templepatrick AM 35; 126, 130, 132

Kilmakee tumulus: Templepatrick AM 35; 126–27, 132, 137

Kilmakernel fort: Manorhamilton Union LM 40; 52

Kilmakernel graveyard: Manorhamilton Union LM 40; 52

Kilmandil cove: Killagan AM 23; 86–87

Kilmandil fort: Killagan AM 23; 86

Kilmandil graveyard: Killagan AM 23; 86

Kilmandil stream: Killagan AM 23; 86

Kilmandil td: Killagan AM 23; 87

Kilmarerty td: Drumcree AH 1; 34, 41

Kilmarnock: Island Magee AM 10; 92

Kilmary, Abraham: Magilligan LY 11; 94

Kilmary, William: Magilligan LY 11; 125–26

Kilmay, family: Maghera LY 18; 24

Kilmegan ph: Dromara DN 12; 62

Kilmegan ph: Drumgooland DN 3; 24

Kilmegan ph: Misc. DN 17; 121

Kilmegan school: Hillsborough DN 12; 101

Kilminoge td: Moira DN 12; 120

Kilmood church: Kilmood DN 7; 95

Kilmood ph: Comber DN 7; 31–32, 34, 40–41, 44

Kilmood ph: Dundonald DN 7; 65

Kilmood ph: Killinchy DN 7; 86–87

Kilmood school: Kilmood DN 7; 95

Kilmood td: Kilmood DN 7; 94–96

Kilmore bog: Devenish FH 14; 52, 57

Kilmore chapel: Kilmore DN 17; 91, 93

Kilmore church: Kilmore AH 1; 57, 62, 70–71

Kilmore church: Kilmore DN 17; 93

Kilmore corn mill: Pomeroy TE 20; 70

Kilmore corn mill [I]: Shankill DN 12; 138–39

Kilmore corn mill [II]: Shankill DN 12; 138–39

Kilmore diocese: Drumgoon CN 40; 11
Kilmore diocese: Drung CN 40; 23–24
Kilmore diocese: Galloon FH 4; 92
Kilmore diocese: Killdrumsherdan CN 40; 37–38
Kilmore diocese: Killesher FH 14; 86
Kilmore diocese: Kinawley FH 4; 110–11, 120
Kilmore diocese: Laragh CN 40; 41, 45–46
Kilmore diocese: Misc. LY 31; 137
Kilmore East td: Ematris MN 40; 116
Kilmore female school: Kilmore DN 17; 88–89, 93
Kilmore flax mill: Shankill DN 12; 138–39
Kilmore fort: Devenish FH 14; 55
Kilmore Glebe House: Kilmore AH 1; 57, 63, 67
Kilmore Glebe House: Kilmore DN 17; 88
Kilmore graveyard: Kilmore DN 17; 93
Kilmore hill: Kilmore AH 1; 61
Kilmore hill: Shankill DN 12; 138
Kilmore lough: Aghalurcher FH 4; 3, 3
Kilmore lough: Tydavnet MN 40; 169
Kilmore male school: Kilmore DN 17; 88, 93
Kilmore meeting house: Drumkeeran FH 14; 64
Kilmore old school: Kilmore MN 40; 136
Kilmore pay school: Kilmore DN 17; 93
Kilmore ph: Aghabog MN 40; 62
Kilmore ph: Aghaderg DN 12; 6
Kilmore ph: Ballymore AH 1; 1, 7, 11, 13–8
Kilmore ph: Clogher TE 5; 41
Kilmore ph: Drumcree AH 1; 28, 34, 37
Kilmore ph: Killinchy DN 7; 86
Kilmore ph: Loughgall AH 1; 75, 78
Kilmore ph: Misc. DN 17; 118, 122, 128
Kilmore ph: Monaghan MN 40; 159
Kilmore ph: Mullaghbrack AH 1; 94
Kilmore ph: Saintfield DN 7; 116
Kilmore ph: Seagoe AH 1; 101, 104
Kilmore ph: Tartaraghan AH 1; 117
Kilmore ph: Tydavnet MN 40; 169
Kilmore quarry: Cappagh TE 5; 19
Kilmore quarry: Drumragh TE 5; 110
Kilmore school: Kilmore AH 1; 58, 62, 64, 71
Kilmore school: Kilmore MN 40; 136
Kilmore school: Layd AM 13; 53
Kilmore smithy: Kilmore DN 17; 93
Kilmore Sunday school: Kilmore AH 1; 64
Kilmore td: Aghalurcher FH 4; 14
Kilmore td: Clonfeacle AH 1; 22
Kilmore td: Devenish FH 14; 58
Kilmore td: Drumkeeran FH 14; 64
Kilmore td: Galloon FH 4; 95
Kilmore td: Kilmore AH 1; 57, 62, 65–66, 68,
  70–72
Kilmore td: Kilmore DN 17; 88
Kilmore td: Layd AM 13; 41
Kilmore td: Lough Swilly DL 38; 138
Kilmore td: Shankill DN 12; 138–39

Kilmore village: Kilmore AH 1; 62
Kilmore village: Kilmore DN 17; 91, 93
Kilmore village: Misc. DN 17; 117
Kilmore West td: Ematris MN 40; 113, 116
Kilmore West td: Tydavnet MN 40; 169
Kilmore, Bishop of: Drumgoon CN 40; 8
Kilmore, Bishop of: Drung CN 40; 22–23
Kilmore, Bishop of: Killesher FH 14; 86
Kilmorey, F.J., 12th Viscount: Newry DN 3; 66–67,
  69, 71, 75–77, 79, 85, 100, 105–06, 108–10, 112,
  114
Kilmorey, Lord: Kilbroney DN 3; 32
Kilmorey, Lord: Kilkeel DN 3; 48, 50, 52
Kilmorey, Robert, 11th Viscount: Newry DN 3; 65,
  82, 114
Kilmorgan ph: Emlaghfad SO 40; 177, 181
Kilmory, John: Bovevagh LY 25; 10, 41–42
Kilmoyangey hill: Kilraghts AM 16; 125
Kilmoyangey td: Kilraghts AM 16; 125
Kilmoyle bogs: Ballyrashane LY 22; 57
Kilmoyle graveyard: Ballymoney AM 16; 19, 23
Kilmoyle graveyard: Ballyrashane LY 22; 63
Kilmoyle graveyard: Drumtullagh AM 16; 97–98,
  100
Kilmoyle Lower td: Ballymoney AM 16; 20
Kilmoyle old church: Dunluce AM 16; 113
Kilmoyle old graveyard: Dunluce AM 16; 113, 122
Kilmoyle school: Dunluce AM 16; 112, 122
Kilmoyle td: Ballyrashane LY 22; 63
Kilmoyle td: Drumtullagh AM 16; 100
Kilmoyle td: Dunluce AM 16; 115
Kilmoyle Upper td: Ballymoney AM 16; 20
Kilmurry bog: Donaghmoyne MN 40; 106
Kilmurry chapel: Donaghmoyne MN 40; 108
Kiln Pot hollow: Tamlaght O'Crilly LY 18; 93, 123
Kiln Pot locality: Aghanloo LY 11; 5–6, 29
Kilnaclieve district: Desertmartin LY 31; 56
Kilnacran td: Galloon FH 4; 95
Kilnadore flax mill: Layd AM 13; 48
Kilnadore graveyard: Layd AM 13; 41
Kilnadore td: Layd AM 13; 41, 48
Kilnahaltar church: Kilmore MN 40; 136
Kilnaharvey lough: Ematris MN 40; 112, 116
Kilnaheery td: Clogher TE 5; 44, 53
Kilnaheny (see Kilnaheery)
Kilnahushog (see Kilnahusogue)
Kilnahushogue (see Kilnahusogue)
Kilnahusogue (Kilnahushog) td: Clogher TE 5; 26,
  33, 37, 42, 53
Kilnahusogue bog: Clogher TE 5; 26
Kilnahusogue Island: Clogher TE 5; 44
Kilnahusogue school: Clogher TE 5; 42
Kilnakeery td: Clogher TE 5; 36
Kilnakirk td: Galloon FH 4; 95
Kilnakulpagh td: Racavan AM 13; 86, 88

Kilnakushogue (see Kilnahusogue)

Kilnamaddy td: Derrybrusk FH 4; 30

Kilnamraher td: Enniskillen FH 4; 82

Kilnappy td: Clondermot LY 34; 83

Kilnappy td: Faughanvale LY 36; 17–19, 53, 59, 68, 76, 87, 95, 99

Kilnashanbally meeting house: Aghalurcher FH 4; 6

Kilnemannagh district: Misc. SO 40; 200

Kilpatrick, Alexander: Ballintoy AM 24; 28

Kilpatrick, Alexander: Rasharkin AM 23; 139

Kilpatrick, D. (Jnr): Annahilt DN 12; 22

Kilpatrick, Daniel: Dunluce AM 16; 118

Kilpatrick, family: Derrykeighan AM 16; 89

Kilpatrick, John: Ballyrashane LY 22; 66

Kilpatrick, Joseph: Ballintoy AM 24; 28

Kilpatrick, Rev. James: Templepatrick AM 35; 133, 143

Kilpatrick, William: Ballymoney AM 16; 24

Kilpatrick, William [I]: Tamlaght TE 20; 75, 128, 136

Kilpatrick, William [II]: Tamlaght TE 20; 86

Kilpike mill: Seapatrick DN 12; 134

Kilpike td: Seapatrick DN 12; 124, 126, 132, 134

Kilraghts bog: Kilraghts AM 16; 126

Kilraghts Castle: Kilraghts AM 16; 130, 132

Kilraghts corn mill: Kilraghts AM 16; 127

Kilraghts coves: Kilraghts AM 16; 133

Kilraghts forts: Kilraghts AM 16; 133

Kilraghts graveyard: Kilraghts AM 16; 127, 130

Kilraghts meeting house: Kilraghts AM 16; 124, 127

Kilraghts old church: Kilraghts AM 16; 125, 130, 132, 135

Kilraghts ph: Ballymoney AM 16; 1, 5

Kilraghts ph: Dundermot AM 13; 29

Kilraghts ph: Duneane AM 19; 102

Kilraghts ph: Finvoy AM 23; 67

Kilraghts ph: Killagan AM 23; 79–81

Kilraghts ph: Loughguile AM 13; 58

Kilraghts ph: Misc. AM 10; 129

Kilraghts ph: Rasharkin AM 23; 129, 133

Kilraghts school: Kilraghts AM 16; 129–30, 136

Kilraghts standing stones: Kilraghts AM 16; 132

Kilraghts stone circle [I]: Kilraghts AM 16; 134

Kilraghts stone circle [II]: Kilraghts AM 16; 134–35

Kilraghts Sunday school: Kilraghts AM 16; 130

Kilraghts td: Kilraghts AM 16; 136

Kilrea: Aghadowey LY 22; 6–7, 10–12, 19, 27, 32–33

Kilrea: Aghanloo LY 11; 24

Kilrea: Agivey LY 22; 39–40, 42

Kilrea: Ahoghill AM 23; 8, 14, 44

Kilrea: Ballyscullion AM 19; 10

Kilrea: Ballyscullion LY 6; 53

Kilrea: Clondermot LY 34; 29, 32

Kilrea: Coleraine LY 33; 86

Kilrea: Cumber LY 28; 21

Kilrea: Desertoghill LY 27; 2–3, 5, 8–9, 11, 13–16, 21–24, 28–29, 32–33

Kilrea: Drumachose LY 9; 116–17

Kilrea: Dungiven LY 15; 67

Kilrea: Errigal LY 27; 41, 60, 81–84

Kilrea: Finvoy AM 23; 67, 71

Kilrea: Killowen LY 33; 169

Kilrea: Kilrea LY 27; 104, 108–09, 111–16, 118, 120–23, 127–28

Kilrea: Macosquin LY 22; 80–82, 85, 89, 92, 101–02, 106

Kilrea: Maghera LY 18; 8, 11, 23–25, 27, 29, 32, 48–50, 59, 64–65, 71

Kilrea: Misc. LY 31; 134

Kilrea: Rasharkin AM 23; 130–31

Kilrea: Tamlaght O'Crilly LY 18; 82–83, 90–92, 94–97, 102, 105, 107–10, 116, 125, 134–35, 138–42

Kilrea academy: Kilrea LY 27; 122

Kilrea barracks: Kilrea LY 27; 109, 114, 123–25, 127

Kilrea bog [I]: Kilrea LY 27; 107

Kilrea bog [II]: Kilrea LY 27; 107, 128

Kilrea bridge: Aghadowey LY 22; 11

Kilrea bridge: Finvoy AM 23; 73

Kilrea bridge: Kilrea LY 27; 105–06, 108, 123, 127

Kilrea bridge: Rasharkin AM 23; 128

Kilrea Bridge St school: Kilrea LY 27; 121

Kilrea cave: Kilrea LY 27; 130

Kilrea chapel: Kilrea LY 27; 104

Kilrea church: Kilrea LY 27; 104, 108–11, 116, 122–23, 125

Kilrea Coleraine St school: Kilrea LY 27; 121

Kilrea corn and flour mill: Kilrea LY 27; 120

Kilrea deaf and dumb school: Kilrea LY 27; 116, 121

Kilrea dispensary: Desertoghill LY 27; 18

Kilrea dispensary: Finvoy AM 23; 72

Kilrea dispensary: Kilrea LY 27; 108, 110, 119–20, 124, 128

Kilrea dispensary: Maghera LY 18; 6, 77

Kilrea female school: Kilrea LY 27; 120–22

Kilrea fortifications: Kilrea LY 27; 113

Kilrea glebe: Tamlaght O'Crilly LY 18; 82

Kilrea Glebe House: Kilrea LY 27; 104, 109, 117

Kilrea graveyard: Kilrea LY 27; 108

Kilrea hill: Kilrea LY 27; 114, 123

Kilrea hotel: Kilrea LY 27; 108–10, 123–24

Kilrea inn: Kilrea LY 27; 109

Kilrea library: Kilrea LY 27; 109

Kilrea male school: Kilrea LY 27; 120

Kilrea market house: Kilrea LY 27; 108

Kilrea market place: Kilrea LY 27; 105, 124

Kilrea meeting house: Kilrea LY 27; 104, 108, 116–17, 122, 126
Kilrea meeting house: Tamlaght O'Crilly LY 18; 101, 136
Kilrea meeting room: Kilrea LY 27; 108, 117, 126
Kilrea new inn: Kilrea LY 27; 127
Kilrea new meeting house: Kilrea LY 27; 108
Kilrea old barrack: Kilrea LY 27; 123
Kilrea old church: Kilrea LY 27; 112, 114, 122
Kilrea old mill: Kilrea LY 27; 120
Kilrea petty sessions room: Kilrea LY 27; 115
Kilrea ph: Desertoghill LY 27; 6, 10, 15
Kilrea ph: Killelagh LY 27; 102
Kilrea ph: Macosquin LY 22; 96
Kilrea ph: Rasharkin AM 23; 137
Kilrea ph: Tamlaght O'Crilly LY 18; 83, 99, 105–06, 108, 116, 125, 136
Kilrea Presbyterian Sunday school: Kilrea LY 27; 122
Kilrea private school: Kilrea LY 27; 121
Kilrea road bridge: Kilrea LY 27; 111, 127–28
Kilrea Seceding Sunday school: Kilrea LY 27; 122
Kilrea Sunday school: Kilrea LY 27; 122
Kilrea td: Kilrea LY 27; 111, 115, 118, 129–30
Kilready school: Galloon FH 4; 96
Kilready td: Galloon FH 4; 95
Kilrobert cave [I]: Ramoan AM 24; 113
Kilrobert cave [II]: Ramoan AM 24; 113
Kilrobert graveyard: Ramoan AM 24; 116
Kilrobert standing stone: Ramoan AM 24; 115
Kilrobert td: Ramoan AM 24; 113, 113
Kilronan district: Faughanvale LY 36; 50
Kilronan td: Aghalurcher FH 4; 14
Kilroosk fort: Manorhamilton Union LM 40; 52
Kilrooskagh Island: Cleenish FH 14; 13, 29–30
Kilroot bleach green: Kilroot AM 26; 59–60, 78–80
Kilroot bleach green: Raloo AM 32; 127
Kilroot bridge: Kilroot AM 26; 80
Kilroot Castle: Kilroot AM 26; 69–70, 72, 74–76
Kilroot caves: Kilroot AM 26; 71–72
Kilroot coastguard station: Kilroot AM 26; 63, 79–80
Kilroot corn mill: Kilroot AM 26; 60, 77–78
Kilroot demesne: Kilroot AM 26; 69
Kilroot district: Templecorran AM 26; 96–97
Kilroot glen: Kilroot AM 26; 57
Kilroot glen: Templecorran AM 26; 84, 89
Kilroot graveyard: Kilroot AM 26; 57, 69, 74, 79
Kilroot House: Kilroot AM 26; 61, 69, 74
Kilroot House: Templecorran AM 26; 108
Kilroot old church: Kilroot AM 26; 56–57, 61, 68–69, 74–75, 79
Kilroot ph: Ballynure AM 32; 36, 45, 47–48, 50–51
Kilroot ph: Carrickfergus AM 37; 1, 71, 100, 134, 142, 147, 160

Kilroot ph: Glynn AM 26; 23
Kilroot ph: Island Magee AM 10; 32, 34, 42, 45, 66
Kilroot ph: Misc. AM 10; 129
Kilroot ph: Raloo AM 32; 98
Kilroot ph: Templecorran AM 26; 82, 84, 88–89, 99, 101–03, 108, 112, 119, 126–28
Kilroot Point: Kilroot AM 26; 57, 68, 77
Kilroot public house: Kilroot AM 26; 79
Kilroot quarry: Kilroot AM 26; 77
Kilroot salt spring: Kilroot AM 26; 58, 79
Kilroot school: Kilroot AM 26; 63–64, 73, 80–81
Kilroot td: Galloon FH 4; 95
Kilroot td: Kilroot AM 26; 56, 61, 63–64, 69, 73, 79–80
Kilrudden td: Clogher TE 5; 36, 53
Kilrush (Clare): Banagher LY 30; 101
Kilrush church: Blaris DN 12; 27
Kilrush graveyard: Blaris AM 8; 21, 45, 60
Kilrush graveyard: Blaris DN 12; 27
Kilsallagh td: Derrybrusk FH 4; 30
Kilsally td: Ballyclog TE 20; 15
Kilsaran td: Drumlumman CN 40; 12, 17
Kilscornagh district: Misc. SO 40; 198
Kilsea: Ballyscullion AM 19; 13
Kilskeery bridge: Kilskeery TE 5; 114–15
Kilskeery bridge: Magheracross FH 14; 92
Kilskeery glebe: Kilskeery TE 5; 114–15
Kilskeery Glebe House: Donacavey TE 5; 73
Kilskeery Glebe House: Kilskeery TE 5; 114–15
Kilskeery Glebe school: Kilskeery TE 5; 115
Kilskeery ph: Cleenish FH 14; 22
Kilskeery ph: Clogher TE 5; 41
Kilskeery ph: Derrybrusk FH 4; 30
Kilskeery ph: Derryvullan FH 14; 31
Kilskeery ph: Donacavey TE 5; 66
Kilskeery ph: Enniskillen FH 4; 41, 41
Kilskeery ph: Magheracross FH 14; 91–92
Kilskeery river: Kilskeery TE 5; 113, 115
Kilskerry (see Kilskeery)
Kilsorrel school: Dromore DN 12; 73
Kilstrol (see Kilstrule)
Kilstrool (see Kilstrule)
Kilstrule (Kilstrawl) td: Ardstraw TE 5; 7, 12–13
Kilstrule fort: Ardstraw TE 5; 12
Kilstrule school: Ardstraw TE 5; 13
Kilstrule Sunday school: Ardstraw TE 5; 7
Kiltariff td: Drumgath DN 3; 21
Kiltarman td: Aghalurcher FH 4; 16
Kiltarrnan td: Clogher TE 5; 53
Kilteen glebe: Killesher FH 14; 86–87
Kilteevoge and Stranorlar dispensary: Kilteevoge DL 39; 112
Kilteevoge ph: Convoy DL 39; 18
Kilteevoge ph: Conwal DL 39; 24
Kilteevoge ph: Donegal DL 39; 42

Kilteevoge ph: Killymard DL 39; 94–95
Kilteevoge Sunday school: Kilteevoge DL 39; 113
Kilternan ph (Dublin): Ballynascreen LY 31; 33
Kiltest (Kiltess) td: Aghadowey LY 22; 1, 16, 38
Kiltest graveyard: Aghadowey LY 22; 26
Kiltierny abbey: Magheraculmoney FH 14; 106
Kiltinny Lower bogs: Macosquin LY 22; 119
Kiltinny Lower burial garden: Macosquin LY 22;
84, 118
Kiltinny Lower flax mill: Macosquin LY 22; 83, 105
Kiltinny Lower school: Macosquin LY 22; 91, 94
Kiltinny Lower springs: Macosquin LY 22; 119
Kiltinny Lower td: Macosquin LY 22; 84, 118,
122–23
Kiltinny school: Ballyaghran LY 33; 17
Kiltinny Sunday school: Ballyaghran LY 33; 17–18
Kiltinny Sunday school: Macosquin LY 22; 94
Kiltinny td: Ballyaghran LY 33; 21
Kiltinny td: Coleraine LY 33; 61, 66, 143
Kiltinny td: Macosquin LY 22; 94
Kiltinny Upper bogs: Macosquin LY 22; 119
Kiltinnybeg td: Ballyaghran LY 33; 27
Kiltinnymore cave: Ballyaghran LY 33; 11, 22
Kiltinnymore fort: Ballyaghran LY 33; 10, 22
Kiltinnymore td: Ballyaghran LY 33; 27
Kiltoal td: Raphoe DL 39; 126
Kiltober td: Drummully FH 4; 39
Kilturk North td: Galloon FH 4; 95
Kilturk school: Galloon FH 4; 96
Kilturk South td: Galloon FH 4; 95
Kilturk West td: Galloon FH 4; 95
Kiltyfailin td: Cleenish FH 14; 29
Kilultagh (see Killultagh)
Kilunaght (see Killunaght): Banagher LY 30; 124
Kilvarnet ph: Emlaghfad SO 40; 176, 178, 181
Kilvarnet ph: Killoran and Kilvarnet SO 40; 183–84
Kilvarnet ph: Kilmacteige SO 40; 186
Kilvarnet td: Killoran and Kilvarnet SO 40; 184
Kilvergan td: Seagoe AH 1; 104–05, 108
Kilvey lough: Donagh MN 40; 98
Kilvillis old church: Ballyclug AM 23; 63
Kilvillis td: Ballyclug AM 23; 63
Kilvillis td: Ballyscullion AM 19; 10, 12–13
Kilwarlin: Blaris AM 8; 47, 73
Kilwarlin chapel: Aghalee AM 21; 38
Kilwarlin chapel: Hillsborough DN 12; 95
Kilwarlin hills: Magheramesk AM 21; 113
Kilwarlin manor: Dromara DN 12; 68
Kilwarlin school: Hillsborough DN 12; 95, 99–100
Kilwary graveyard: Tullyaughnish DL 38; 91
Kilwary Rae fort: Tullyaughnish DL 38; 91
Kilwary td: Tullyaughnish DL 38; 91
Kilwaughter Castle: Doagh AM 29; 69, 82, 84
Kilwaughter Castle: Kilwaughter AM 10; 106–07,
109, 112–13, 115, 117

Kilwaughter Castle demesne: Kilwaughter AM 10;
106
Kilwaughter Castle graveyard: Kilwaughter AM 10;
116
Kilwaughter Castle Sunday school: Kilwaughter
AM 10; 121
Kilwaughter cotton factory: Raloo AM 32; 126
Kilwaughter demesne: Kilwaughter AM 10, 108–10
Kilwaughter Glebe: Kilwaughter AM 10; 116
Kilwaughter mills: Kilwaughter AM 10; 112
Kilwaughter old graveyard: Kilwaughter AM 10;
117
Kilwaughter ph: Antrim AM 29; 1
Kilwaughter ph: Ballycor AM 32; 1
Kilwaughter ph: Ballylinny AM 32; 11, 27
Kilwaughter ph: Ballymartin AM 2; 1
Kilwaughter ph: Ballynure AM 32; 31, 42, 46, 70
Kilwaughter ph: Carncastle and Killyglen AM 10;
8–9, 11
Kilwaughter ph: Carrickfergus AM 37; 71, 100, 160
Kilwaughter ph: Doagh AM 29; 62
Kilwaughter ph: Glenwhirry AM 32; 74–75, 79
Kilwaughter ph: Inver AM 26; 49–50, 53
Kilwaughter ph: Kilbride AM 29; 137
Kilwaughter ph: Kilroot AM 26; 65
Kilwaughter ph: Larne AM 10; 123
Kilwaughter ph: Misc. AM 10; 129
Kilwaughter ph: Muckamore AM 35; 57, 74
Kilwaughter ph: Nilteen AM 35; 87
Kilwaughter ph: Raloo AM 32; 80, 83, 86, 89, 106
Kilwaughter ph: Rashee AM 32; 135
Kilwaughter ph: Templecorran AM 26; 101
Kilwaughter ph: Templepatrick AM 35; 105
Kilwaughter ph: Tickmacrevan AM 13; 122
Kilwaughter school: Kilwaughter AM 10; 111, 116,
120
Kilwaughter td: Kilwaughter AM 10; 119
Kilwaughter Upper Sunday school: Kilwaughter
AM 10; 120
Kimbolton, Lord: Ballymore AH 1; 3
Kimmitt td: Templecarn DL 39; 164
Kinagar hill: Killygarvan DL 38; 42
Kinaghan school: Killesher FH 14; 86
Kinahan, Mrs: Knockbreda DN 7; 102
Kinalargy fort: Mevagh DL 38; 58
Kinalargy school: Mevagh DL 38; 59
Kinalargy td: Mevagh DL 38; 57, 63
Kinalarty (see Kinelarty)
Kinallen corn mill: Dromore DN 12; 72
Kinallen hill: Dromore DN 12; 70
Kinallen td: Dromore DN 12; 72–73
Kinawley barony: Killesher FH 14; 86
Kinawley chapel: Kinawley FH 4; 108
Kinawley graveyard: Kinawley FH 4; 111
Kinawley old church: Kinawley FH 4; 111

Kinawley old graveyard: Kinawley FH 4; 108–09
Kinawley ph (Cavan): Kinawley FH 4; 112–13
Kinawley ph: Galloon FH 4; 88, 91, 95
Kinawley ph: Killesher FH 14; 81, 85
Kinawley ph: Tomregan FH 4; 125–26
Kinawley td: Kinawley FH 4; 110
Kinawley village: Kinawley FH 4; 107–09, 112
Kinbally td: Skerry AM 13; 105
Kinbane Castle: Ballintoy AM 24; 32, 34
Kinbane Castle: Culfeightrin AM 24; 69
Kinbane Castle: Ramoan AM 24; 90, 106, 119–22
Kinbane caves: Ramoan AM 24; 90, 121
Kinbane Head: Ballintoy AM 24; 14–15
Kinbane Head: Ramoan AM 24; 86, 88, 90–91, 93,
    101, 121–22
Kinbane old castles: Ballintoy AM 24; 33
Kincade, John: Drummaul AM 19; 90
Kincaid, John: Kilmore DN 17; 91
Kincart, James: Templecorran AM 26; 132
Kincart, John: Loughguile AM 13; 71
Kincon td: Kilmore AH 1; 68, 70, 73
Kincraigey (see Kincraigy): Raymoghy DL 39; 132
Kincraigy (Kincraiggy) td: Raymoghy DL 39; 132,
    138, 141, 199
Kincraigy wood: Raymoghy DL 39; 133, 142, 189
Kincuillew td: Kilmacteige SO 40; 193, 196
Kincuillew village: Kilmacteige SO 40; 193
Kinculbrack bridge: Cumber LY 28; 11
Kinculbrack quarry: Cumber LY 28; 124
Kinculbrack td: Cumber LY 28; 67, 70, 113, 119,
    123–24, 126
Kincullea (see Kincuillew): Kilmacteige SO 40; 193
Kincullia (see Kincuillew): Kilmacteige SO 40; 196
Kindrum corn mill: Clondavaddog DL 38; 5
Kindrum Head: Lough Swilly DL 38; 114, 117
Kindrum hill: Clondavaddog DL 38; 1, 9
Kindrum lough: Clondavaddog DL 38; 1–2, 5
Kindrum Sunday school: Clondavaddog DL 38; 7
Kindrum tuck mill: Clondavaddog DL 38; 5
Kindrum tuck mill: Lough Swilly DL 38; 129
Kinego (see Kinnegoe): Loughgall AH 1; 81
Kinekally flax mills: Taughboyne DL 39; 153
Kinekally orchards: Taughboyne DL 39; 153
Kinekally td: Taughboyne DL 39; 148, 153
Kinekally wood: Taughboyne DL 39; 148, 153
Kinelarty barony: Annahilt DN 12; 22
Kinelarty barony: Dromara DN 12; 62, 64–65
Kinelarty barony: Holywood DN 7; 80
Kinelarty barony: Magheradrool DN 17; 101
Kinelarty barony: Misc. DN 17; 116
Kinelarty district: Ardglass DN 17; 3
Kinelarty district: Cumber LY 28; 67
Kinel-Connell, family: Clondermot LY 34; 52, 106
Kinel-Connell, family: Faughanvale LY 36; 33,
    47–48, 63, 101–02, 107

Kinel-Moen, family: Clondermot LY 34; 51
Kinel-Moen, family: Misc. TE 5; 146–47
Kinel-Owen, family: Banagher LY 30; 107–08
Kinel-Owen, family: Clondermot LY 34; 44, 50, 52
Kinel-Owen, family: Faughanvale LY 36; 33, 48,
    54, 57, 60, 63, 105, 107
Kinel-Owen, family: Magilligan LY 11; 118, 145
Kinel-Owen, family: Misc. TE 5; 146
Kinerlow lough: Devenish FH 14; 52
Kinfleogan (see Inishowen barony): Magilligan LY
    11; 90
King James' chair: Derryaghy AM 8; 115
King, A.B.: Enniskillen FH 4; 59
King, Alexander: Kilraghts AM 16; 132, 136
King, Anne: Carrickfergus AM 37; 76
King, Bishop: Magilligan LY 11; 89, 146
King, Capt.: Carrickfergus AM 37; 145
King, Ellen: Carrickfergus AM 37; 117, 119
King, Francis: Carrickfergus AM 37; 119
King, Gilbert: Longfield TE 5; 135
King, Hannah: Duneane AM 19; 123
King, Henry: Misc. SO 40; 200
King, James: Galloon FH 4; 91
King, James: Macosquin LY 22; 87, 116–17
King, James: Tamlaght Finlagan LY 25; 119
King, Jane: Drummaul AM 19; 87
King, Jane: Tamlaght Finlagan LY 25; 119
King, John: Bovevagh LY 25; 47, 49
King, John: Tamlaght Finlagan LY 25; 119
King, Joseph: Drumachose LY 9; 112
King, man named: Drummaul AM 19; 62
King, Margaret: Duneane AM 19; 123
King, Michael: Banagher LY 30; 4, 15
King, Michael: Bovevagh LY 25; 31
King, Michael: Drumachose LY 9; 73, 99, 104
King, Michael: Drummaul AM 19; 82
King, Michael: Dungiven LY 15; 3–5, 9, 11, 53, 98,
    105–06
King, Rev. Gilbert: Longfield TE 5; 128–29, 134
King, Rev. W.: Cleenish FH 14; 17, 29
King, Ritchard: Balteagh LY 9; 36
King, Robert: Ballyscullion LY 6; 57
King, Robert: Misc. SO 40; 198–99
King, S.A.: Derrybrusk FH 4; 30, 33
King, Samual: Ballyrashane LY 22; 53
King, Samuel: Drumachose LY 9; 66
King, Sir Robert: Misc. SO 40; 199
King, Susan: Ballywillin LY 33; 51
King, Thomas: Drumachose LY 9; 111
King, Thomas: Macosquin LY 22; 115
King, Thomas: Newry DN 3; 100, 104
King, Thomas: Tamlaght Finlagan LY 25; 113
King, W.J.: Duneane AM 19; 123
King, W.M.: Drumachose LY 9; 104
King, William (Jnr): Tamlaght Finlagan LY 25; 119

King, William (Snr): Tamlaght Finlagan LY 25; 119
King, William: Carrickfergus AM 37; 130
King, William: Macosquin LY 22; 122
King, William: Newry DN 3; 81
King's Arms Hotel: Antrim AM 29; 10
King's Arms Hotel: Blaris AM 8; 16, 50
King's Arms Hotel: Newry DN 3; 70
King's bog: Ballylinny AM 32; 11–13, 20, 25, 27
King's bog: Ballymartin AM 2; 3
King's bog: Ballyrobert AM 2; 19
King's bog: Ballywalter AM 2; 28
King's bog: Carnmoney AM 2; 36–37, 60–61
King's Castle: Ardglass DN 17; 2–3, 11
King's County (see Offaly): Banagher LY 30; 36
King's Cross hills: Ballywillin LY 33; 48
King's fort: Balteagh LY 8–9; 15–16, 19, 24, 35
King's fort: Banagher LY 30; 39
King's Gap fishery: Coleraine LY 33; 93, 149
King's grave: Dunaghy AM 13; 21
King's Highway: Carnmoney AM 2; 85
King's meadow (see also Deer's meadow): Clonduff
    DN 3; 3
King's mills: Artrea TE 20; 9–10
King's moss: Ballyrobert AM 2; 25
King's moss: Carrickfergus AM 37; 165
King's Palace: Carrickfergus AM 37; 80, 162, 178
King's td: Ballylinny AM 32; 12
Kingare school: Loughguile AM 13; 67
Kingare td: Loughguile AM 13; 67
Kingariff flax mill: Loughguile AM 13; 63
Kingariff td: Loughguile AM 13; 76
Kingarrive td: Kinawley FH 4; 121
Kingarve td: Drumcree AH 1; 37
Kingarve td: Drumglass TE 20; 40
Kinghill corn mill: Clonduff DN 3; 3
Kinghill House: Clonduff DN 3; 3
Kinghill school: Clonduff DN 3; 6
Kinghill td: Clonduff DN 3; 3, 6
Kinghill water: Clonduff DN 3; 4
Kingscourt: Donaghmoyne MN 40; 111
Kingscourt: Enniskeen CN 40; 28–30
Kingscourt: Magheracloone MN 40; 137–39, 141
Kingscourt: Mcgheross MN 40; 146, 151–52, 157
Kingscourt district: Enniskeen CN 40; 26–27
Kingsland locality: Carrickfergus AM 37; 94
Kingsmill, E.B.: Island Magee AM 10; 33, 81, 87,
    89, 99, 102
Kingsmill, family: Donaghmore DL 39; 34
Kingsmill, Gen.: Donaghmore DL 39; 33–34
Kingsmill, Robert (ne Brice): Island Magee AM 10;
    42, 93
Kingsmills corn mill: Loughgilly AH 1; 86
Kingsmills flax mill: Loughgilly AH 1; 86
Kingsmills meeting house: Loughgilly AH 1; 86

Kingsmore, Rev. Robert: Tullyniskan TE 20;
    141–42
Kingston (England): Coleraine LY 33; 124
Kingston, Lord John: Misc. SO 40; 198–200
Kingstown td: Aghalurcher FH 4; 14
Kinkaid, family: Carrickfergus AM 37; 93
Kinkaid, family: Island Magee AM 10; 70
Kinkeel (Kintccl) td: Rathlin Island AM 24; 130
Kinkeel corn mill: Rathlin Island AM 24; 130–31
Kinkeel school: Rathlin Island AM 24; 133
Kinlargy (see Kinalargy): Mevagh DL 38; 63
Kinleater td: Donaghmore DL 39; 29, 37
Kinleatragh td: Killygarvan DL 38; 37
Kinletter td: Faughanvale LY 36; 54
Kinley, family: Aghalee AM 21; 31
Kinlinty school: Rasharkin AM 23; 141
Kinmore td: Aghalurcher FH 4; 3
Kinnacallie (see Dunaff Head): Lough Swilly DL
    38; 98
Kinnaderry corn mill: Kilteevoge DL 39; 112
Kinnaderry flax mill: Kilteevoge DL 39; 112
Kinnaderry td: Kilteevoge DL 39; 114
Kinnaglug td: Donagh DL 38; 31
Kinnagoe bay: Lough Swilly DL 38; 102
Kinnahalla hill: Clonduff DN 3; 5
Kinnahalla plantation: Clonduff DN 3; 5
Kinnalough: Clondavaddog DL 38; 1–3, 6
Kinnalough fort: Clondavaddog DL 38; 6
Kinnard td: Tynan AH 1; 131
Kinnard, family: Ahoghill AM 23; 25
Kinnarlow td: Rossorry FH 14; 116
Kinnea bay: Lough Swilly DL 38; 132
Kinnea district: Lough Swilly DL 38; 136
Kinnea td: Clonmany DL 38; 12, 18, 20
Kinneady td: Cumber LY 28; 31
Kinnegalliagh (Kennegalliagh) td: Glenwhirry AM
    32; 79
Kinnegoe (Kinnego) td: Loughgall AH 1; 79
Kinnegoe Gut inlet: Seagoe AH 1; 105, 110
Kinnegoe school: Loughgall AH 1; 76, 78, 81
Kinnegoe td: Seagoe AH 1; 105, 109
Kinney, family: Ramoan AM 24; 107
Kinney, John: Carrickfergus AM 37; 109
Kinnycally spring: Killea and Taughboyne DL 39;
    85
Kinnycally td: Killea and Taughboyne DL 39; 80
Kinnycally td: Misc. DL 39; 195
Kinnyglass cove [I]: Macosquin LY 22; 95
Kinnyglass cove [II]: Macosquin LY 22; 120
Kinnyglass fort: Macosquin LY 22; 120
Kinnyglass graveyard: Macosquin LY 22; 120
Kinnylough (see Kinnalough): Clondavaddog DL
    38; 1
Kinotragh school: Kinawley FH 4; 119

Kinrammar (see Kenramer): Rathlin Island AM 24; 127

Kinsale (Cork): Donegal DL 39; 48

Kinsellagh, Enna (King): Faughanvale LY 36; 12

Kinsey, Henry: Newry DN 3; 99, 103

Kinsley, Cllr.: Devenish FH 14; 58

Kinstrey, Mr: Drumbo DN 7; 58

Kintagh td: Ballyphilip DN 7; 7

Kinteal bridge: Killygarvan DL 38; 47

Kinteal td: Killygarvan DL 38; 46–47

Kintrae bridge: Lough Swilly DL 38; 135

Kintyre (Scotland): Island Magee AM 10; 19, 26

Kintyre: Ballintoy AM 24; 15

Kintyre: Glynn AM 26; 6, 33

Kintyre: Ramoan AM 24; 93, 120

Kintyre: Rathlin Island AM 24; 131

Kintyre: Templecorran AM 26; 96, 109

Kipley, George: Drumcree AH 1; 32

Kippeen Island: Cleenish FH 14; 13, 29

Kippure mountain: Killesher FH 14; 81

Kiran td: Magheraculmoney FH 14; 113

Kirby, family: Muckamore AM 35; 65

Kirckland, James: Hillsborough DN 12; 107

Kircubbin: Ballyphilip DN 7; 14

Kircubbin: Grey Abbey DN 7; 70

Kircubbin: Inishargy DN 7; 84

Kircubbin: Misc. DN 17; 117

Kircubbin corn mill: Inishargy DN 7; 85

Kircubbin court house: Inishargy DN 7; 84

Kircubbin meeting house: Inishargy DN 7; 85

Kircubbin quay: Inishargy DN 7; 85

Kircubbin school: Inishargy DN 7; 85

Kircubbin td: Ballywalter DN 7; 18

Kircubbin td: Inishargy DN 7; 85

Kircubbin td: Misc. DN 17; 125

Kirgan, family: Lissan LY 31; 91, 106

Kirinbeg (see Kerinbeg): Galloon FH 4; 96

Kirk church: Killowen LY 33; 161, 169

Kirk graveyard: Killowen LY 33; 169

Kirk hill: Convoy DL 39; 18

Kirk hill: Macosquin LY 22; 84, 113

Kirk land (see also Kilcoanmore old church): Island Magee AM 10; 47, 101

Kirk Land field: Killowen LY 33; 161, 169

Kirk Land field: Nilteen AM 35; 94–95, 104

Kirk Park field: Templecorran AM 26; 108, 113, 120

Kirk, Andrew: Ballynure AM 32; 64–66

Kirk, C.E.: Carrickfergus AM 37; 102

Kirk, family: Ballylinny AM 32; 15

Kirk, family: Ballynure AM 32; 35, 56

Kirk, family: Carnmoney AM 2; 76

Kirk, James: Hillsborough DN 12; 107

Kirk, John: Ballynure AM 32; 58

Kirk, Mr: Lough Swilly DL 38; 150

Kirk, Mrs: Carrickfergus AM 37; 163

Kirk, Peter: Carrickfergus AM 37; 42, 56, 102, 135, 141–43, 145–46, 163, 168, 174

Kirk, Thomas: Carrickfergus AM 37; 33, 36, 148

Kirk, William: Carrickfergus AM 37; 32–33, 56, 135

Kirk's Fall locality: Carrickfergus AM 37; 77

Kirkcubbin (see Kircubbin)

Kirkcudbright, Laird of: Killowen LY 33; 161, 170

Kirkdonnel (see Dundonald): Dundonald DN 7; 64

Kirkeel (see Kinkeel): Rathlin Island AM 24; 133

Kirkhill (Kirkhills) td: Ballymoney AM 16; 20

Kirkhill graveyard: Ballymoney AM 16; 20, 25

Kirkhill school: Ballymoney AM 16; 27

Kirkinriola bleach greens: Kirkinriola AM 23; 120

Kirkinriola graveyard: Kirkinriola AM 23; 92, 120, 124

Kirkinriola old church: Kirkinriola AM 23; 120, 122, 124–26

Kirkinriola ph: Ahoghill AM 23; 1, 29

Kirkinriola ph: Ballyclug AM 23; 52–54, 58–59, 61

Kirkinriola ph: Connor AM 19; 20, 24–25

Kirkinriola ph: Dunaghy AM 13; 25

Kirkinriola ph: Dundermot AM 13; 29

Kirkinriola ph: Racavan AM 13; 86

Kirkinriola ph: Skerry AM 13; 105

Kirkinriola standing stone: Kirkinriola AM 23; 88

Kirkinriola td: Kirkinriola AM 23; 92

Kirkistown barley mill: Ballyrashane LY 22; 48–49

Kirkistown broth mill: Ballyrashane LY 22; 56

Kirkistown Castle: Ardkeen DN 7; 1–2

Kirkistown cave: Ballyrashane LY 22; 50, 61

Kirkistown corn mill: Ballyrashane LY 22; 48, 56

Kirkistown fort: Ballyrashane LY 22; 49–50, 61

Kirkistown manor: Misc. DN 17; 125

Kirkistown meeting house: Ballyrashane LY 22; 47, 52, 54–55, 61

Kirkistown moss: Misc. DN 17; 126

Kirkistown old meeting house: Ballyrashane LY 22; 50

Kirkistown td: Ardkeen DN 7; 1–2

Kirkistown td: Ballyrashane LY 22; 47, 54, 66

Kirkistown td: Ballywalter DN 7; 18

Kirkminister hill: Clonleigh DL 39; 3

Kirkminister Lower td: Clonleigh DL 39; 3, 197

Kirkminister Middle standing stones: Clonleigh DL 39; 3

Kirkminister td: Clonleigh DL 39; 2

Kirkminister Upper td: Misc. DL 39; 197

Kirkmoyle old church: Ballymoney AM 16; 19–20

Kirkmoyle Upper td: Ballymoney AM 16; 20

Kirkneedy td: Conwal DL 39; 27

Kirkpatrick, Andrew: Kilraghts AM 16; 132

Kirkpatrick, Andrew: Ramoan AM 24; 115–16

Kirkpatrick, Charles (Ballycastle): Culfeightrin AM 24; 49

Kirkpatrick, Dr: Larne AM 10; 126

Kirkpatrick, family: Ballintoy AM 24; 16, 20

Kirkpatrick, family: Carmavy AM 35; 2

Kirkpatrick, family: Carrickfergus AM 37; 93

Kirkpatrick, family: Faughanvale LY 36; 48

Kirkpatrick, family: Ramoan AM 24; 107

Kirkpatrick, James: Ballymoney AM 16; 26

Kirkpatrick, James: Ramoan AM 24; 103

Kirkpatrick, Jane: Kilraghts AM 16; 132

Kirkpatrick, John: Carrickfergus AM 37; 132

Kirkpatrick, John: Kilraghts AM 16; 132

Kirkpatrick, John: Loughguile AM 13; 76

Kirkpatrick, Mr: Clondermot LY 34; 35, 37, 104

Kirkpatrick, Rev. George: Ahoghill AM 23; 12, 46–47

Kirkpatrick, Samuel: Ahoghill AM 23; 21

Kirkpatrick, Samuel: Loughguile AM 13; 76

Kirkpatrick, Samuel: Ramoan AM 24; 126

Kirkpatrick, Walter: Misc. LY 31; 136

Kirkshall locality: Carrickfergus AM 37; 175

Kirkwood and McCune, Messrs: Newry DN 3; 99, 103

Kirkwood, family: Magherafelt LY 6; 95

Kirkwood, Hugh: Drumbeg AM 8; 129–31

Kirkwood, John: Tamlaght O'Crilly LY 18; 138

Kirkwood, Robert: Tamlaght O'Crilly LY 18; 116

Kirley bog: Maghera LY 18; 65

Kirley td: Maghera LY 18; 22, 37, 46, 81

Kirlish old castle: Longfield TE 5; 134

Kirlish td: Longfield TE 5; 134

Kirnaghan, James: Newry DN 3; 99

Kirnahan, James: Ballinderry AM 21; 56

Kirwan, Mrs (Galway): Faughanvale LY 36; 40

Kirwin, Patrick: Doagh AM 29; 97

Kirwood, John: Kilraghts AM 16; 134

Kissick, William: Maghera LY 18; 27

Kissock, family: Ballyclug AM 23; 60

Kitty's Toppin hill: Raloo AM 32; 123

Kittybane bog: Clondermot LY 34; 44–45

Kittybane quarry: Clondermot LY 34; 132

Kittybane td: Clondermot LY 34; 56, 70, 107, 111–12, 118, 126, 132

Kittylane (see Kittybane): Clondermot LY 34; 44

Kivlin lough: Drumragh TE 5; 104

Knairs, family: Glenavy AM 21; 86

Knappagh hill: Drumgoon CN 40; 1

Knappagh school: Drumgoon CN 40; 11

Knappagh td: Ballybay MN 40; 81, 84

Knappagh water: Drumgoon CN 40; 2, 7

Knather hamlet: Kilbarron DL 39; 77

Kneestone (see St Patrick's footmark): Skerry AM 13; 116

Kneller, Godfrey: Killesher FH 14; 84

Knight, Hugh: Balteagh LY 9; 3

Knight, man named: Dungiven LY 15; 82

Knight, Mrs: Dungiven LY 15; 47, 82

Knight's cairn locality: Dungiven LY 15; 47, 83

Knocbaragh (see Knockbaragh): Kilbroney DN 3; 38

Knock and Breda (see Knockbreda): Down DN 17; 47

Knock bridge: Coleraine LY 33; 96

Knock bridge: Kilmore AH 1; 61, 63, 72

Knock bridges: Seagoe AH 1; 104

Knock church: Comber DN 7; 31

Knock church: Misc. DN 17; 118

Knock Island: Derryvullan FH 14; 39, 46

Knock Iveagh (see also Iveagh hill): Drumballyroney DN 3; 14

Knock Iveagh hill: Aghaderg DN 12; 8

Knock Iveagh hill: Annaclone DN 12; 16

Knock Loghran (see Knockcloghrim)

Knock logwood mill: Knockbreda DN 7; 102

Knock old bridge: Seagoe AH 1; 104

Knock Phelim Roe hill: Tamlaght O'Crilly LY 18; 94–95, 127

Knock school: Comber DN 7; 31

Knock td: Comber DN 7; 31

Knock td: Donaghmore DL 39; 37

Knock td: Knockbreda DN 7; 102

Knock td: Seagoe AH 1; 109

Knock, family: Drumgath DN 3; 20

Knockachraughra hill: Dungiven LY 15; 93

Knockadoe td: Killoran and Kilvarnet SO 40; 183

Knockadoo district: Misc. SO 40; 200

Knockadoo school: Lissan LY 31; 95

Knockadoo td: Lissan LY 31; 108–09

Knockadooney hill: Shankill DN 12; 138

Knockadow (see Knockadoo): Misc. SO 40; 200

Knockaduff bleach green: Misc. LY 36; 111

Knockaduff ovens: Aghadowey LY 22; 29, 32

Knockaduff tappatourzee: Aghadowey LY 22; 27, 32

Knockaduff td: Misc. LY 36; 109, 111–12

Knockaduff warrens: Macosquin LY 22; 77

Knockagarron hill: Raphoe DL 39; 129

Knockageehan chapel: Killesher FH 14; 83

Knockageehan cotton manufactory: Killesher FH 14; 84

Knockageehan school: Killesher FH 14; 86

Knockagh caves: Carrickfergus AM 37; 86, 176–77

Knockagh district: Carrickfergus AM 37; 151, 154, 158

Knockagh enclosures: Carrickfergus AM 37; 87–88, 187–88

Knockagh fort [I]: Carrickfergus AM 37; 185

Knockagh fort [II]: Carrickfergus AM 37; 185–86

Knockagh fort [III]: Carrickfergus AM 37; 186

Knockagh friary: Carrickfergus AM 37; 83

Knockagh hills: Ballylinny AM 32; 24

Knockagh hills: Carrickfergus AM 37; 1, 5, 83, 85–86, 93, 136, 140–41, 159, 173–74, 176–77, 187, 189–91

Knockagh hills: Templecorran AM 26; 115

Knockagh Little locality: Carrickfergus AM 37; 174

Knockagh standing stone: Carrickfergus AM 37; 86, 185

Knockagin (see Knocknagin): Desertmartin LY 31; 62

Knockaginny bridge: Donagh MN 40; 99

Knockaginy hill: Aghaloo TE 20; 1

Knockaholate (see Knockahollet): Loughguile AM 13; 76

Knockahollat (see Knockahollet): Loughguile AM 13; 71

Knockahollet (Knockahullaght) td: Loughguile AM 13; 67, 71, 76

Knockahollet cave: Loughguile AM 13; 71

Knockahollet fort: Loughguile AM 13; 71

Knockahollet school: Loughguile AM 13; 67

Knockahoney td: Kilmacteige SO 40; 195–96

Knockahullen hill: Drumtullagh AM 16; 97

Knockakirwan bog: Errigal Truagh MN 40; 120

Knockalla battery: Clondavaddog DL 38; 4–5

Knockalla battery: Desertegney DL 38; 25

Knockalla battery: Killygarvan DL 38; 36

Knockalla caves: Clondavaddog DL 38; 4

Knockalla coastguard station: Clondavaddog DL 38; 6

Knockalla fort: Killygarvan DL 38; 40

Knockalla fort: Lough Swilly DL 38; 100–01

Knockalla hill: Clondavaddog DL 38; 1, 3–4, 6, 9–10

Knockalla hill: Killygarvan DL 38; 36, 38

Knockalla hill: Lough Swilly DL 38; 100

Knockalla hill: Tullyaughnish DL 38; 84

Knockalla police station: Clondavaddog DL 38; 6

Knockalla revenue station: Clondavaddog DL 38; 6

Knockalla tower: Clondavaddog DL 38; 6

Knockalough td: Enniskillen FH 4; 81

Knockamenny (see Knocknameny): Lough Swilly DL 38; 107

Knockan bleach green: Banagher LY 30; 19, 130

Knockan bog: Banagher LY 30; 92

Knockan bridge: Banagher LY 30; 25

Knockan bridge: Skerry AM 13; 110

Knockan cave: Banagher LY 30; 70

Knockan fort [I]: Banagher LY 30; 46, 70

Knockan fort [II]: Banagher LY 30; 47

Knockan glen: Banagher LY 30; 35

Knockan hill: Banagher LY 30; 65–66

Knockan hill: Bovevagh LY 25; 13, 39

Knockan Holmes hill: Banagher LY 30; 110

Knockan House: Banagher LY 30; 3–5, 15, 27, 29–30, 32, 59, 81, 96, 98–99

Knockan mounts: Banagher LY 30; 76

Knockan td: Banagher LY 30; 3, 22, 25, 29, 34–36, 61–62, 70, 85, 93, 95, 105, 110, 119, 124, 128, 130–31

Knockan td: Dungiven LY 15; 106

Knockan td: Maghera LY 18; 54

Knockan tumuli: Banagher LY 30; 47

Knockan wood: Banagher LY 30; 124

Knockanaffrin fort: Skerry AM 13; 107

Knockanally td: Skerry AM 13; 107

Knockanarny (see Knocknanarny): Donaghmore DN 3; 9

Knockanavrey (see Knocknanarny): Misc. DN 17; 130

Knockanban (see Knockanbane): Drumachose LY 9; 91

Knockanbane (Knockanbaan) td: Banagher LY 30; 31, 62

Knockanbane druidical temple: Dungiven LY 15; 32

Knockanbane hill: Banagher LY 30; 31, 108, 110, 112

Knockanbane hill: Drumachose LY 9; 74

Knockanbane hill: Faughanvale LY 36; 4

Knockanbane stone circle: Drumachose LY 9; 91

Knockanboy bog: Derrykeighan AM 16; 81

Knockanboy flax mill: Derrykeighan AM 16; 79, 84

Knockanboy td: Derrykeighan AM 16; 78, 81

Knockandun bog: Tamlaght Finlagan LY 25; 123

Knockandun hills: Tamlaght Finlagan LY 25; 62

Knockandun td: Tamlaght Finlagan LY 25; 122

Knockanduns (see Knockandun): Tamlaght Finlagan LY 25; 62

Knockanearla hill: Tydavnet MN 40; 169

Knockanearla td: Tydavnet MN 40; 169

Knockaneeney hill: Drumachose LY 9; 108

Knockaniller flax mill: Ardstraw TE 5; 14

Knockanroe hill: Artrea TE 20; 9

Knockanroe Island: Aghagallon AM 21; 16

Knockans bog: Finvoy AM 23; 69

Knockans Castle [I]: Armoy AM 24; 8–9

Knockans Castle [II]: Armoy AM 24; 8

Knockans church: Finvoy AM 23; 68, 70, 75–76

Knockans cove: Armoy AM 24; 8

Knockans cove [I]: Finvoy AM 23; 78

Knockans cove [II]: Finvoy AM 23; 78

Knockans graveyard: Armoy AM 24; 5, 7–8

Knockans graveyard: Finvoy AM 23; 76

Knockans North fort: Layd AM 13; 41

Knockans td: Armoy AM 24; 8–9

Knockantern adult school: Coleraine LY 33; 70, 143

Knockantern female Sunday school [I]: Coleraine LY 33; 70, 140

Knockantern female Sunday school [II]: Coleraine LY 33; 70

Knockantern House: Ballyrashane LY 22; 53, 60

Knockantern House: Ballywillin LY 33; 33

Knockantern House: Coleraine LY 33; 64, 73, 91, 142

Knockantern House: Kildollagh LY 22; 70

Knockantern school: Coleraine LY 33; 67, 69, 135, 140, 143–44

Knockantern Sunday school: Coleraine LY 33; 69–70

Knockantern td: Coleraine LY 33; 66, 128, 144–45, 155

Knockantirn (see Knockantern): Kildollagh LY 22; 70

Knockaraven (Knockaravin) td: Dromore TE 5; 97, 99

Knockarevan school: Inishmacsaint FH 14; 79

Knockarevan td: Inishmacsaint FH 14; 70

Knockarig hill: Tamlaght O'Crilly LY 18; 94, 127

Knockarrinnion td: Dungiven LY 15; 91

Knockashee: Kilmacteige SO 40; 186

Knockataggart corn mill: Laragh CN 40; 39, 42

Knockataggart tuck mill: Laragh CN 40; 42

Knockatallan school: Tydavnet MN 40; 172

Knockathotan fort: Ballywillin AM 16; 34

Knockathotan td: Ballywillin AM 16; 34

Knockatooder (see Knockatudor): Laragh CN 40; 42

Knockatoodor (see Knockatudor): Laragh CN 40; 40

Knockatotem (see Knockertotan): Ballywillin LY 33; 52

Knockatothane td: Killoran and Kilvarnet SO 40; 183

Knockatudor corn mill: Laragh CN 40; 42

Knockatudor mill-race: Drung CN 40; 20

Knockatudor ravine: Laragh CN 40; 40

Knockatudor td: Laragh CN 40; 42

Knockaun bridge: Glenavy AM 21; 77

Knockavallan (Knockavallen) td: Derrykeighan AM 16; 79, 95

Knockavallan meeting house: Derrykeighan AM 16; 79, 84

Knockavannon chapel: Ballymyre AH 1; 20

Knockavernan td: Loughguile AM 13; 76

Knockballymore demesne: Galloon FH 4; 92

Knockballymore House: Galloon FH 4; 88, 91

Knockballymore manor: Galloon FH 4; 94–95

Knockballymore td: Galloon FH 4; 93

Knockballyroney hill: Tydavnet MN 40; 169

Knockballyroney td: Errigal Truagh MN 40; 120

Knockban bog: Tynan AH 1; 125

Knockban corn mill: Tynan AH 1; 128

Knockbane hill: Tamlaght O'Crilly LY 18; 93–94, 128

Knockbaragh school: Kilbroney DN 3; 38

Knockbaragh td: Kilbroney DN 3; 32, 38

Knockbellamore manor: Clones FH 4; 26

Knockbodarra td: Kinawley FH 4; 110

Knockboy bleach green: Racavan AM 13; 99

Knockboy bleach green: Skerry AM 13; 106

Knockboy bleaching mill: Skerry AM 13; 106

Knockboy corn mill: Skerry AM 13; 111

Knockboy House: Skerry AM 13; 106, 111

Knockboy mountain: Skerry AM 13; 105

Knockboy school: Skerry AM 13; 115

Knockboy spinning factory: Skerry AM 13; 106, 111

Knockboy td: Galloon FH 4; 95

Knockboy td: Racavan AM 13; 99

Knockboy td: Skerry AM 13; 106–07, 111

Knockbrack district: Misc. SO 40; 199

Knockbrack ford: Clondermot LY 34; 7, 22

Knockbrack glen: Clondermot LY 34; 1, 17

Knockbrack glen: Cumber LY 28; 43

Knockbrack nursery: Clondermot LY 34; 35

Knockbrack nursery: Cumber LY 28; 23

Knockbrack quarry: Clondermot LY 34; 132

Knockbrack river: Clondermot LY 34; 3, 18

Knockbrack school: Kilmacteige SO 40; 196

Knockbrack td: Clondermot LY 34; 38, 56, 58, 71, 111, 118, 126, 132

Knockbrack td: Culfeightrin AM 24; 42

Knockbrack td: Errigal Keerogue TE 20; 54

Knockbrack td: Kilmacteige SO 40; 196

Knockbrack td: Leck DL 39; 119

Knockbrack wood: Clondermot LY 34; 4, 18

Knockbracken (see Knockbrack): Clondermot LY 34; 18

Knockbrackin (see Knockbreckan): Drumbo DN 7; 61

Knockbreckan (Knockbracken) td: Knockbreda DN 7; 102

Knockbreckan flax mill: Drumbo DN 7; 60

Knockbreckan flax mill: Knockbreda DN 7; 102

Knockbreckan meeting house: Knockbreda DN 7; 102

Knockbreckan school: Knockbreda DN 7; 102

Knockbreckan td: Drumbo DN 7; 60–61, 63

Knockbreda ph: Comber DN 7; 31

Knockbreda ph: Down DN 17; 47

Knockbreda ph: Drumbo DN 7; 54

Knockbreda ph: Dundonald DN 7; 64

Knockbreda ph: Holywood DN 7; 73

Knockbreda ph: Knockbreda DN 7; 99

Knockbreda private school: Knockbreda DN 7; 102

Knockbreda union: Misc. DN 17; 118

Knockbride ph: Aughnamullen MN 40; 69

Knockbride ph: Drumgoon CN 40; 1–2

Knockbride ph: Killdrumsherdan CN 40; 31

Knockcairn (Knockairn) td: Tullyrusk AM 21; 131, 134

Knockcairn bridge: Tullyrusk AM 21; 132–33, 135

Knockcairn Cottage: Blaris AM 8; 51
Knockcairn Cottage: Tullyrusk AM 21; 134, 136
Knockcairn forts: Tullyrusk AM 21; 139
Knockcairn td: Ballinderry AM 21; 53
Knockcloghrim: Aghadowey LY 22; 25
Knockcloghrim: Ballynascreen LY 31; 18
Knockcloghrim: Maghera LY 18; 28, 32, 49, 65, 75
Knockcloghrim: Magherafelt LY 6; 95, 98
Knockcloghrim: Termoneeny LY 6; 129
Knockcloghrim church: Maghera LY 18; 72
Knockcloghrim church: Termoneeny LY 6; 128, 130
Knockcloghrim hill: Dungiven LY 15; 20
Knockcloghrim hill: Magherafelt LY 6; 98
Knockcloghrim hill: Termoneeny LY 6; 121–22,
    129–30
Knockcloghrim meeting house: Maghera LY 18; 48
Knockcruinn hill: Errigal LY 27; 44, 72
Knockdhu Head: Carncastle and Killyglen AM 10; 9
Knockdhu hill: Carncastle and Killyglen AM 10; 1
Knockduff (see Knockaduff): Aghadowey LY 22; 32
Knockeannane district: Misc. SO 40; 200
Knockenhead hill: Tamlaght O'Crilly LY 18; 93,
    123
Knockenkeragh (see Knocknakeeragh):
    Ballyrashane LY 22; 49
Knockennis mountain: Enniskillen FH 4; 43–44
Knockennis td: Enniskillen FH 4; 82
Knockeny fort: Layd AM 13; 41
Knockeny hill: Layd AM 13; 41
Knocker (see Knockagh): Carrickfergus AM 37; 1
Knockertotan td: Ballywillin LY 33; 52
Knocketotem (see Knockertotan): Ballywillin LY
    33; 52
Knockfergus (see Carrickfergus)
Knockfreeth district: Misc. SO 40; 200
Knockglass village: Kilmacteige SO 40; 196
Knockgorm hill: Garvaghy DN 12; 79
Knockgorm lough: Garvaghy DN 12; 79, 81–82
Knockgorm td: Garvaghy DN 12; 79, 81–82
Knockinarney (see Knocknanarny): Donaghmore
    DN 3; 7
Knockinelder (Knockanelda) td: Misc. DN 17; 124,
    127
Knockinelder bay: Ballyphilip DN 7; 7
Knockinelder td: Ballyphilip DN 7; 8
Knockinlough district: Misc. SO 40; 200
Knockintennon hill: Carncastle and Killyglen AM
    10; 11
Knockinteorn (see Knockantern): Coleraine LY 33;
    155
Knockintern (see Knockantern): Coleraine LY 33;
    155
Knockivoe mountain: Leckpatrick TE 5; 120
Knocklade (see Knocklayd)
Knocklaid (see Knocklayd)

Knocklamuckly (see Knocknamuckly): Seagoe AH
    1; 108
Knocklayd cairn: Ramoan AM 24; 116, 118
Knocklayd hill: Aghadowey LY 22; 27
Knocklayd hill: Drumtullagh AM 16; 103
Knocklayd hill: Misc. LY 31; 116
Knocklayd mountain: Armoy AM 24; 1–3, 8
Knocklayd mountain: Culfeightrin AM 24; 42, 64
Knocklayd mountain: Layd AM 13; 36
Knocklayd mountain: Ramoan AM 24; 86, 88–93,
    97, 106, 113, 115–16, 118–19
Knocklayd standing stone: Ramoan AM 24; 118–19
Knocklead (see Knocklayd)
Knockmacmanus td: Aghavea FH 4; 23
Knockmacroony td: Clones FH 4; 26
Knockmaderow td: Galloon FH 4; 95
Knockmaine district: Misc. SO 40; 200
Knockmakegan td: Galloon FH 4; 95
Knockmanny and Longford's glen: Clogher TE 5;
    55
Knockmanoul chapel: Magheracross FH 14; 95
Knockmany demesne: Clogher TE 5; 39
Knockmany druidical altar: Clogher TE 5; 34
Knockmany hill: Clogher TE 5; 24–25, 27, 32,
    38–39, 49, 54
Knockmany td: Clogher TE 5; 32, 36, 46, 53
Knockmasham mills: Comber DN 7; 35
Knockmenagh td: Seagoe AH 1; 109
Knockmore (see Mosside): Drumtullagh AM 16;
    101–02
Knockmore corn mill: Devenish FH 14; 48
Knockmore fort: Blaris AM 8; 19
Knockmore hill: Blaris DN 12; 27
Knockmore hill: Devenish FH 14; 47–48
Knockmore House: Blaris AM 8; 33
Knockmore td: Blaris AM 8; 19, 33, 46–47, 79, 81
Knockmore td: Blaris DN 12; 28, 31
Knockmore td: Devenish FH 14; 48
Knockmoyle chapel: Cappagh TE 5; 18
Knockmoyle td: Cappagh TE 5; 18
Knockmult school: Dunboe LY 11; 56, 72
Knockmult Sunday school: Dunboe LY 11; 57, 72
Knockmult td: Dunboe LY 11; 72, 77, 81
Knocknabrass td: Galloon FH 4; 95
Knocknabrock hill: Tamlaght O'Crilly LY 18; 93,
    123
Knocknacarney td: Clogher TE 5; 37
Knocknacarthe standing stone: Macosquin LY 22;
    86, 113
Knocknaclapagh fort: Manorhamilton Union LM
    40; 52
Knocknacran East chapel: Magheracloone MN 40;
    138
Knocknacran West bog: Magheracloone MN 40;
    137

Knocknacranfy (see Knocknacran): Magheracloone MN 40; 138

Knocknacruigha hill: Drumachose LY 9; 108

Knocknadona (Knocknadowney) td: Magheragall AM 21; 104, 107

Knocknadona fort [I]: Magheragall AM 21; 103

Knocknadona fort [II]: Magheragall AM 21; 105

Knocknadona grey stone: Magheragall AM 21; 104

Knocknadona kilns: Magheragall AM 21; 107

Knocknadona preaching house: Magheragall AM 21; 99, 109–11

Knocknadona school: Magheragall AM 21; 99, 109, 111

Knocknadona Sunday school: Magheragall AM 21; 99, 110

Knocknadouly school: Derryaghy AM 8; 118

Knocknadouly td: Derryaghy AM 8; 118

Knocknadruideen hill: Macosquin LY 22; 117

Knocknagalliagh hill: Ballintoy AM 24; 29

Knocknagarven standing stone: Ballintoy AM 24; 30

Knocknagenny (see Knocknagoney): Holywood DN 7; 73, 77

Knocknagin (see Knocknaginn): Dungiven LY 15; 50

Knocknagin fort: Desertmartin LY 31; 56

Knocknagin hill: Desertmartin LY 31; 53, 62, 115

Knocknagin school: Desertmartin LY 31; 61

Knocknagin td: Desertmartin LY 31; 62, 142

Knocknaginn fort: Dungiven LY 15; 30–31, 44–45, 50, 77

Knocknaginn hill: Bovevagh LY 25; 17, 37–38

Knocknaginn hill: Drumachose LY 9; 58, 110

Knocknaginn hill: Dungiven LY 15; 33, 77

Knocknagoney (Knocknagunney) td: Holywood DN 7; 73, 76–77, 79–82

Knocknagoney school: Holywood DN 7; 76, 81

Knocknagoran chapel: Carlingford LH 40; 60

Knocknagoran school: Carlingford LH 40; 60

Knocknagoran td: Carlingford LH 40; 58

Knocknagore (Knocknagor) td: Tullylish DN 12; 141, 143, 147

Knocknagore school: Tullylish DN 12; 144, 147

Knocknagrain hill: Balteagh LY 9; 34

Knocknagrave school: Donagh MN 40; 99, 102

Knocknagullagh (see Knocknagulliagh): Templecorran AM 26; 125

Knocknagulliagh (Knocknagalliagh) td: Templecorran AM 26; 123, 125, 132

Knocknagunny (see Knocknagoney): Holywood DN 7; 76

Knocknahinch graveyard: Loughguile AM 13; 68, 72

Knocknahinch td: Loughguile AM 13; 60, 68, 72

Knocknahollet school: Loughguile AM 13; 76

Knocknahullar mound: Ramoan AM 24; 117

Knocknahurkle (see Donald's hill): Balteagh LY 9; 34

Knocknakeeragh (Knocknageeragh) td: Ballyrashane LY 22; 46, 49–50, 61, 65

Knocknakeeragh hill: Ballyrashane LY 22; 46

Knocknakeilt (see Knocknakielt): Termoneeny LY 6; 133

Knocknakielt td: Termoneeny LY 6; 121, 126, 133

Knocknamaddy bog: Ballybay MN 40; 78

Knocknamaddy hill: Ballybay MN 40; 78

Knocknamaddy td: Ballybay MN 40; 84

Knocknamaddy wood: Ballybay MN 40; 79

Knocknamadue (see Knocknamaddy): Ballybay MN 40; 84

Knocknameny hill: Lough Swilly DL 38; 107, 134

Knocknamoul (Knockmanoul) td: Magheracross FH 14; 102

Knocknamuckly td: Seagoe AH 1; 104, 108

Knocknanarny (Knockanarney) td: Donaghmore DN 3; 7, 9

Knocknanarny hill: Misc. DN 17; 131

Knocknanarny td: Misc. DN 17; 130

Knocknanoul (see Knocknamoul)

Knocknapeeping hill: Macosquin LY 22; 90, 116

Knocknarea bog: Magheragall AM 21; 106

Knocknarea fort: Magheragall AM 21; 106

Knocknarea school: Magheragall AM 21; 111

Knocknascallion td: Armoy AM 24; 5

Knocknasham mills: Comber DN 7; 39

Knocknashane td: Shankill AH 1; 111

Knocknasligane td: Kilmacteige SO 40; 196

Knocknastackeen td: Enniskillen FH 4; 82

Knocknecally district: Misc. SO 40; 200

Knockninny barony: Galloon FH 4; 87

Knockninny barony: Kinawley FH 4; 107, 111–12, 115

Knockninny barony: Tomregan FH 4; 125

Knockninny hill: Kinawley FH 4; 113, 117

Knockninny House: Galloon FH 4; 87

Knockninny td: Kinawley FH 4; 109, 114, 117, 121

Knocknogher td: Dunboe LY 11; 80–81

KnockO'Neill (see Knockoneill): Maghera LY 18; 10

Knockoneil (see Knockoneill)

Knockoneill carn: Maghera LY 18; 39

Knockoneill graveyard: Desertoghill LY 27; 6

Knockoneill graveyard: Maghera LY 18; 40

Knockoneill monument: Maghera LY 18; 10, 23, 45

Knockoneill quarry: Kilrea LY 27; 104

Knockoneill td: Maghera LY 18; 1, 10, 39–40

Knockoney (Knockenny) td: Errigal Keerogue TE 20; 54, 57

Knockoney school: Errigal Keerogue TE 20; 54

Knockramer mill: Seagoe AH 1; 103

Knockramer mountain: Skerry AM 13; 109

Knockramer td: Seagoe AH 1; 105, 108

Knockrawer td: Donaghmore DL 39; 37

Knockroe flax mill: Ardstraw TE 5; 14

Knockroe fort: Ardstraw TE 5; 12

Knockroe school: Ardstraw TE 5; 13

Knockroe td: Ardstraw TE 5; 12

Knockronan chapel: Errigal Truagh MN 40; 121

Knockrow district: Misc. SO 40; 199

Knockrow school: Derryvullan FH 14; 35

Knocks hill: Killesher FH 14; 81

Knocks td: Aghalurcher FH 4; 3, 14

Knockshee mountain: Kilbroney DN 3; 28

Knocksoghey (Knocksohy) td: Ballintoy AM 24; 31–33

Knocksoghey cave: Ballintoy AM 24; 31

Knocksoghey druid's altar: Ballintoy AM 24; 32

Knocksoghey hill: Ballintoy AM 24; 10–12, 16–17

Knocksoghey standing stone: Ballintoy AM 24; 32

Knocksoghy (see Knocksoghey): Ballintoy AM 24; 10

Knocktenant hill: Tamlaght Finlagan LY 25; 116

Knocktogher (see Knocknogher): Dunboe LY 11; 80

Knockygarron td: Convoy DL 39; 21

Knoctickin corn mill: Loughinisland DN 17; 96

Knoctickin td: Loughinisland DN 17; 96

Knolles, Francis: Carrickfergus AM 37; 84

Knolles, Lettice (see Devereux): Carrickfergus AM 37; 84

Knowhead hill: Carncastle and Killyglen AM 10; 11

Knowhead td: Coleraine LY 33; 61–62

Knowles, family: Kirkinriola AM 23; 124

Knowles, Miss: Holywood DN 7; 76

Knowles, Robert: Ahoghill AM 23; 35

Knox and Pollock, Messrs: Tamlaght Finlagan LY 25; 101

Knox West school: Currin MN 40; 92

Knox, Alexander: Coleraine LY 33; 64

Knox, Alexander: Ramoan AM 24; 94

Knox, Andrew: Ballywillin LY 33; 48, 50

Knox, Andrew: Clondermot LY 34; 5, 8, 13, 20, 90, 92, 101, 114–15, 119

Knox, Andrew: Clonleigh DL 39; 12

Knox, Andrew: Drumhome DL 39; 58–59

Knox, Andrew: Killygarvan DL 38; 39–41, 43–47

Knox, Bishop (Scotland): Killygarvan DL 38; 41, 46

Knox, Bishop (Scotland): Tullyaughnish DL 38; 90

Knox, Bishop of Derry: Ardstraw TE 5; 2

Knox, Bishop of Derry: Clondermot LY 34; 12

Knox, Bishop of Derry: Clonleigh DL 39; 12

Knox, Bishop of Derry: Faughanvale LY 36; 40, 45

Knox, C.J.: Coleraine LY 33; 91, 127

Knox, Capt.: Enniskillen FH 4; 66

Knox, Catherine: Killevy AH 1; 53

Knox, Charles: Lissan LY 31; 102

Knox, Daniel: Billy AM 16; 62, 64, 75

Knox, David: Raloo AM 32; 92, 120

Knox, Dr (Lifford): Killygarvan DL 38; 40

Knox, Eagleson: Ballywillin LY 33; 51

Knox, Elizabeth (see Welsh)

Knox, family: Clondermot LY 34; 8, 83, 97

Knox, family: Desertoghill LY 27; 5, 30

Knox, family: Drumhome DL 39; 60

Knox, family: Killygarvan DL 38; 39, 41

Knox, family: Kilraghts AM 16; 130

Knox, family: Raloo AM 32; 108, 123

Knox, George: Clonleigh DL 39; 10

Knox, J.H.: Newry DN 3; 75

Knox, James: Derrykeighan AM 16; 91

Knox, James: Kilraghts AM 16; 132

Knox, John: Billy AM 16; 75

Knox, John: Carnmoney AM 2; 95–96, 101

Knox, John: Coleraine LY 33; 63–64, 105, 127

Knox, John: Desertoghill LY 27; 22, 29

Knox, John: Drummaul AM 19; 90

Knox, John: Errigal LY 27; 81–83

Knox, John: Hillsborough DN 12; 97, 102, 107

Knox, John: Kilcronaghan LY 31; 68–69

Knox, John: Kilraghts AM 16; 132, 135

Knox, John: Mallusk AM 2; 109

Knox, John: Templepatrick AM 35; 116, 124, 132, 141, 143

Knox, John [I]: Aghadowey LY 22; 5, 7, 10, 12, 18

Knox, John [II]: Aghadowey LY 22; 18, 22

Knox, man named: Killymard DL 39; 97

Knox, Mariana: Killygarvan DL 38; 39

Knox, Mary: Macosquin LY 22; 119

Knox, Mary Anne: Clondermot LY 34; 8, 83–84, 97, 104

Knox, Miss (Derry city): Maghera LY 18; 72

Knox, Mr: Donaghedy TE 5; 91

Knox, Mr: Drumachose LY 9; 83, 87

Knox, Mr [I]: Clondermot LY 34; 38

Knox, Mr [II]: Clondermot LY 34; 94

Knox, Mrs: Dunboe LY 11; 55, 67

Knox, Mrs J.S.: Maghera LY 18; 15–16, 18, 31, 49, 67, 72

Knox, N.A.: Agivey LY 22; 39, 42–43

Knox, R.W.: Tullynakill DN 7; 122

Knox, Rev.: Ballyscullion LY 6; 65

Knox, Rev. Edmond: Kilcronaghan LY 31; 87

Knox, Rev. Edmund: Tamlaght O'Crilly LY 18; 101

Knox, Rev. George: Termonamongan TE 5; 143

Knox, Rev. J.S.: Ballynascreen LY 31; 18

Knox, Rev. J.S.: Coleraine LY 33; 63

Knox, Rev. J.S.: Faughanvale LY 36; 40

Knox, Rev. J.S.: Kilcronaghan LY 31; 64, 66, 69–70, 72–75, 77, 80–81, 86–87

Knox, Rev. J.S.: Loughguile AM 13; 70

Knox, Rev. J.S.: Maghera LY 18; 4, 7–8, 14, 17, 24, 28, 31–32, 35–37, 39, 45, 49–52, 55, 58–59, 66–68, 72–73
Knox, Rev. J.S.: Misc. LY 31; 128, 132, 136
Knox, Rev. J.S.: Tamlaght O'Crilly LY 18; 115
Knox, Rev. James: Ahoghill AM 23; 46
Knox, Rev. Joseph: Dunboe LY 11; 62, 65, 69
Knox, Rev. William: Ballynascreen LY 31; 16
Knox, Rev. William: Clonleigh DL 39; 2, 4
Knox, Rev. William: Desertegney DL 38; 28
Knox, Rev. William: Dunboe LY 11; 44, 66
Knox, Rev. William: Faughanvale LY 36; 40
Knox, Rev. William: Magilligan LY 11; 89, 110
Knox, Rev. William: Misc. LY 31; 128, 131–32, 136
Knox, Rev. William: Taughboyne DL 39; 148
Knox, Robert: Coleraine LY 33; 63, 104
Knox, Robert: Macosquin LY 22; 119
Knox, S.W.: Coleraine LY 33; 63, 127
Knox, Samuel: Ballywillin LY 33; 49
Knox, Samuel: Coleraine LY 33; 63–64, 72, 104, 143
Knox, Thomas: Termoneeny LY 6; 132
Knox, W.J.: Drumachose LY 9; 52, 120
Knox, W.J.: Kilraghts AM 16; 135
Knox, William: Ballynure AM 32; 61–62
Knox, William: Magheraculmoney FH 14; 111
Knoxes Hole creek: Lough Swilly DL 38; 115–16
Kock lough: Garvaghy DN 12; 79–80
Koram mountain: Ardstraw TE 5; 10
Kranah (see Cranagh): Killowen LY 33; 169
Krannagh (see Cranagh): Cumber LY 28; 52
Kraw Bush fort: Killowen LY 33; 161, 169
Kreganuirk hill: Drumachose LY 9; 110
Kreganure rock: Banagher LY 30; 69
Kregkanan rocks: Errigal LY 27; 71
Kregnabarn rocks: Banagher LY 30; 90
Kregnagath rocks: Banagher LY 30; 64–65
Kregnagraw rock: Bovevagh LY 25; 35
Krock-a-navirk hill: Culfeightrin AM 24; 76
Krockarig (see Knockarig): Tamlaght O'Crilly LY 18; 127
Krock-a-thievoir hill: Culfeightrin AM 24; 71
Krockavideen rocks: Ballintoy AM 24; 20
Krockcurry lough: Ballyscullion LY 6; 70
Krock-ranill stones: Culfeightrin AM 24; 79
Kruben td: Galloon FH 4; 94

Kulkeagh (see Cuilcagh)
Kulteagh (see Cuilcagh)
Kurin Bray hill: Desertoghill LY 27; 23
Kurin fort [I]: Desertoghill LY 27; 22, 25
Kurin fort [II]: Desertoghill LY 27; 25
Kurin fort [III]: Desertoghill LY 27; 25
Kurin td: Desertoghill LY 27; 14, 19–20, 22, 29
Kuro, Rev.: Loughinisland DN 17, 96
Kushkeery lough: Aghalurcher FH 4; 3, 5
Kyle, Ann: Ahoghill AM 23; 37
Kyle, Anne: Killowen LY 33; 166
Kyle, Elizabeth: Ahoghill AM 23; 37
Kyle, Ellen: Killowen LY 33; 160
Kyle, family: Maghera LY 18; 24, 48
Kyle, Henry: Coleraine LY 33; 104, 142
Kyle, Hugh: Ahoghill AM 23; 38
Kyle, Isaac: Dundermot AM 13; 34–35
Kyle, James [I]: Ahoghill AM 23; 37
Kyle, James [II]: Ahoghill AM 23; 38
Kyle, John: Blaris DN 12; 35, 38
Kyle, John: Bovevagh LY 25; 54
Kyle, John: Hillsborough DN 12; 107
Kyle, John: Maghera LY 18; 61
Kyle, John [I]: Ahoghill AM 23; 35
Kyle, John [II]: Ahoghill AM 23; 37
Kyle, Joseph: Ahoghill AM 23; 37
Kyle, Joseph: Bovevagh LY 25; 10, 17–18, 31–32
Kyle, man named: Tamlaght Finlagan LY 25; 103
Kyle, Mary-Ann: Ahoghill AM 23; 37
Kyle, Matthew: Ahoghill AM 23; 48
Kyle, Mrs Robert: Coleraine LY 33; 73
Kyle, Mrs Robert: Killowen LY 33; 166, 171
Kyle, Rev.: Banagher LY 30; 20
Kyle, Robert: Coleraine LY 33; 72, 127, 141–42
Kyle, Robert: Killowen LY 33; 158, 165–66, 168
Kyle, Robert: Macosquin LY 22; 82, 104
Kyle, Robert [I]: Ahoghill AM 23; 34
Kyle, Robert [II]: Ahoghill AM 23; 37
Kyle, Widow: Ahoghill AM 23; 34
Kyle, William: Ahoghill AM 23; 37
Kyle, William: Tamlaght O'Crilly LY 18; 133
Kyles, Robert: Hillsborough DN 12; 107
Kynego (see Kinnegoe): Seagoe AH 1; 105
Kynigo (see Kinnegoe)
Kyran (see Kiran): Magheraculmoney FH 14; 113
Kyrue-na-gort, St: Kilmore AH 1; 63

L

L'Estrange, Mr: Cleenish FH 14; 29–30

L'Estrange, Mr: Devenish FH 14; 56, 58–59

Laa Lau church (see Ballinderry): Ballinderry AM 21; 54

Laarlagh rocks: Lough Swilly DL 38; 107

Laavenameadh, Prince: Errigal LY 27; 77

Labadish school: Raymoghy DL 39; 140, 144

Labadish td: Raymoghy DL 39; 138, 141–42, 186, 199

Labadoo td: Convoy DL 39; 21

Labby (Leabby) td: Ballynascreen LY 31; 19, 22, 114, 143

Labby school: Ballynascreen LY 31; 17

Lacca (Lackaboy) td: Donacavey TE 5; 76–77, 79, 81, 84, 86

Lacca corn mill: Donacavey TE 5; 64, 84

Lack: Magheraculmoney FH 14; 103, 105, 108

Lack Hall school: Raphoe DL 39; 127

Lack lough: Longfield TE 5; 127

Lack school: Magheraculmoney FH 14; 108

Lackagh (see Lacca): Donacavey TE 5; 86

Lackagh bleach green: Dungiven LY 15; 9, 98

Lackagh bridge: Mevagh DL 38; 56–58

Lackagh eel-weir: Mevagh DL 38; 56

Lackagh quarry: Cumber LY 28; 105

Lackagh river: Mevagh DL 38; 54–56, 61

Lackagh salmon-weir: Mevagh DL 38; 56, 58

Lackagh school: Cumber LY 28; 74

Lackagh standing stones: Cumber LY 28; 43

Lackagh td: Banagher LY 30; 22

Lackagh td: Cumber LY 28; 48, 60, 63, 96, 101, 105, 107

Lackagh td: Dungiven LY 15; 23, 26, 48, 62, 64, 104

Lackagh td: Mevagh DL 38; 57

Lackagh wood: Cumber LY 28; 53

Lackaghboy td: Derryvullan FH 14; 46

Lackan bog: Aghaderg DN 12; 5

Lackan bog: Annaclone DN 12; 15

Lackan bog: Drumballyroney DN 3; 14

Lackan bog: Newry DN 3; 111

Lackan bogs: Drumgath DN 3; 19

Lackan corn mill: Drumballyroney DN 3; 12, 16

Lackan district: Drumhome DL 39; 62

Lackan flax mill: Drumballyroney DN 3; 13, 16

Lackan lough: Drumballyroney DN 3; 14

Lackan meeting house: Drumballyroney DN 3; 15

Lackan td: Drumballyroney DN 3; 10, 12–14, 14

Lackan td: Drumgooland DN 3; 23

Lackaw (see Lackan): Drumballyroney DN 3; 14

Lackcrom td: Killymard DL 39; 99, 101

Lacken (see Lackan): Drumballyroney DN 3; 10

Lacken lough: Aughnamullen MN 40; 70

Lacken td: Aughnamullen MN 40; 76

Lackey, Mr (Coalisland): Tullyniskan TE 20; 139

Lacoon td: Manorhamilton Union LM 40; 54

Lacrum (see Lackcrom)

Ladden, Bernard: Lissan LY 31; 108

Ladden, John: Lissan LY 31; 108

Ladden, Sarah: Lissan LY 31; 108

Laddin district: Clondavaddog DL 38; 4

Ladies causeway: Carrickfergus AM 37; 32

Ladoga lough: Lough Neagh AM 21; 92

Lady bridge: Aghalee AM 21; 34

Lady bridge: Magheramesk AM 21; 115, 118–19, 122, 126

Lady Castlestuart's school: Ballyclog TE 20; 18

Lady Cooke's Castle: Dungiven LY 15; 106

Lady hill: Shilvodan AM 19; 128

Lady hill: Templecorran AM 26; 95

Lady Hill cove: Antrim AM 29; 36, 44

Lady Hill forts: Antrim AM 29; 43

Lady O'Cahan's bridge (see Lady O'Kane's bridge)

Lady O'Cahan's Castle: Drumachose LY 9; 52, 57

Lady O'Kane's bridge: Aghanloo LY 11; 11, 27

Laferty, Hugh: Carrickfergus AM 37; 169

Laferty, John: Carrickfergus AM 37; 169

Lafferty, Bernard: Bovevagh LY 25; 33

Lafferty, Bernard: Dungiven LY 15; 84

Lafferty, Daniel: Ballyrashane LY 22; 60

Lafferty, family: Derryaghy AM 8; 103

Lafferty, family: Island Magee AM 10; 85

Lafferty, Frederick: Dunboe LY 11; 62

Lafferty, Hugh: Ballyscullion AM 19; 12

Lafferty, Hugh: Island Magee AM 10; 95, 103

Lafferty, Hugh: Maghera LY 18; 80

Lafferty, John (Fool Jock): Island Magee AM 10; 94–95

Lafferty, Margaret: Maghera LY 18; 80
Lafferty, Mary: Maghera LY 18; 80
Lafferty, Samuel: Carrickfergus AM 37; 113
Lafferty, Thomas: Balteagh LY 9; 43
Lafferty, William: Banagher LY 30; 73
Lafferty, William: Dungiven LY 15; 85, 117
Lafferty, William: Magherafelt LY 6; 112
Lagan bridge: Magheracloone MN 40; 139
Lagan Canal: Aghagallon AM 21; 1, 3, 5 7, 13
Lagan Canal: Blaris AM 8; 13, 69
Lagan Canal: Blaris DN 12; 28, 31, 33–34
Lagan Canal: Drumcree AH 1; 32
Lagan Canal: Lambeg AM 8; 134
Lagan Canal: Magheramesk AM 21; 115, 118–19,
 122
Lagan Canal: Moira DN 12; 119
Lagan district: Clondavaddog DL 38; 7
Lagan district: Drumhome DL 39; 62
Lagan district: Leck DL 39; 120
Lagan district: Misc. FH 4; 133
Lagan district: Raymoghy DL 39; 135
Lagan district: Tullyaughnish DL 38; 87
Lagan foundry: Ballinderry AM 21; 51
Lagan foundry: Nilteen AM 35; 86
Lagan Lodge: Dromore DN 12; 72
Lagan Lodge: Lambeg AM 8; 137, 142
Lagan Navigation: Aghalee AM 21; 29, 31, 33–34
Lagan Navigation: Drumbeg AM 8; 122
Lagan Navigation: Hillsborough DN 12; 96
Lagan Navigation: Shankill DN 12; 138–39
Lagan river: Blaris AM 8; 1, 3, 13, 17–19
Lagan river: Blaris DN 12; 26–28, 33–34
Lagan river: Carnmoney AM 2; 50, 67
Lagan river: Carrickfergus AM 37; 5
Lagan river: Comber DN 7; 30
Lagan river: Derryaghy AM 8; 106, 120
Lagan river: Donaghcloney DN 12; 57, 59
Lagan river: Dromara DN 12; 62, 66, 68–69
Lagan river: Dromore DN 12; 70–71, 73
Lagan river: Drumbeg AM 8; 122, 129
Lagan river: Drumbeg DN 7; 52
Lagan river: Drumbo DN 7; 54, 57
Lagan river: Galloon FH 4; 100
Lagan river: Hillsborough DN 12; 89
Lagan river: Killanny MN 40; 130
Lagan river: Knockbreda DN 7; 97, 101
Lagan river: Lambeg AM 8; 134, 138, 140
Lagan river: Lough Neagh AM 21; 97
Lagan river: Magheracloone MN 40; 137–39
Lagan river: Magheralin DN 12; 109
Lagan river: Magheramesk AM 21; 112, 114–15,
 118–20, 125–27
Lagan river: Magheross MN 40; 157
Lagan river: Misc. DN 17; 117
Lagan river: Moira DN 12; 117

Lagan well: Raymoghy DL 39; 135
Lagan, David: Ahoghill AM 23; 35
Lagan, family: Maghera LY 18; 24
Lagan, giant: Raymoghy DL 39; 135
Lagan, Hugh: Maghera LY 18; 79
Lagan, John: Maghera LY 18; 45–46, 81
Lagan, John: Tamlaght TE 20; 93
Lagan, Sarah: Maghera LY 18; 79
Lagan, Thomas: Maghera LY 18; 81
Lagananny td: Blaris DN 12; 28
Lagananny td: Donaghcloney DN 12; 57
Laganvale House: Derryaghy AM 8; 106
Lagg chapel: Tullyaughnish DL 38; 88–89
Lagg sandhills: Lough Swilly DL 38; 134
Laggan (see Lagan)
Laghery, John: Tamlaght TE 20; 77
Laghey district: Drumhome DL 39; 62
Laghnalitter church: Templecorran AM 26; 108,
 112, 119
Laghnalitter graveyard: Templecorran AM 26; 117,
 119
Laghnalitter ph: Templecorran AM 26; 82
Laghtmorris td: Termonamongan TE 5; 145
Lagmacaffrey td: Galloon FH 4; 95
Lagmalittan (see Laghnalitter): Templecorran AM
 26; 82
Lagmore glen: Derryaghy AM 8; 90
Lagmore td: Derryaghy AM 8; 100, 114
Lagnaduff td: Misc. DL 39; 196
Lag-na-Feine locality: Layd AM 13; 41
Lagnapeiste hollow: Ballynascreen LY 31; 15
Lagnapeiste valley: Banagher LY 30; 12, 26, 32, 37,
 52, 56–57, 69–70, 88, 113–14
Lagsands Point: Lough Swilly DL 38; 107
Laherdan chapel: Killygarvan DL 38; 40
Laherdan corn mill: Killygarvan DL 38; 38, 40
Laherdan stream: Killygarvan DL 38; 38
Laid, Mr (Cross): Killea and Taughboyne DL 39; 87
Laid's mill: Killea and Taughboyne DL 39; 87
Laidley, Mr: Antrim AM 29; 44
Laig-a-vallia locality: Dungiven LY 15; 20
Laigavallian (see Legavannon): Faughanvale LY 36;
 47
Laigavallian td: Dungiven LY 15; 20, 35
Laignagreive locality: Dungiven LY 15; 20
Laig-na-naan locality: Dungiven LY 15; 20
Laigndarah (see Legnadaragh): Bovevagh LY 25; 16
Laing, Thomas: Newry DN 3; 99, 104
Laird pier: Island Magee AM 10; 29
Laird, Ann: Island Magee AM 10; 95
Laird, Edward: Raymoghy DL 39; 140
Laird, family: Carnmoney AM 2; 76
Laird, Gilbert: Island Magee AM 10; 64, 80, 101
Laird, Hannah: Kilcronaghan LY 31; 84
Laird, Mary: Island Magee AM 10; 95

Laird, Rev.: Clogher TE 5; 40
Laird, Rev.: Enniskillen FH 4; 73, 82
Lakagh td: Donacavey TE 5; 80
Lakefield (Connaught): Tullyaughnish DL 38; 91
Lakemount House: Dromore TE 5; 97, 101
Lakeview evening school: Ballyscullion AM 19; 14
Lakeview female school: Ballyscullion AM 19; 14
Lakeview House: Artrea LY 6; 8
Lakeview House: Ballyscullion AM 19; 3, 9
Lakeview House: Drummully FH 4; 35–36
Lakeview school: Ballyscullion AM 19; 15
Lakeview Sunday school: Ballyscullion AM 19; 14–15
Laman, James: Ballymoney AM 16; 24
Laman, John: Desertoghill LY 27; 24
Lamb, family: Aghalee AM 21; 31
Lamb, family: Ballinderry AM 21; 55
Lamb, John: Drumbeg AM 8; 128
Lamb, Joshua: Blaris AM 8; 19, 83
Lamb, Mr: Carrickfergus AM 37; 139
Lamb, Rev. P.: Laragh CN 40; 41
Lambeg bleach greens: Blaris AM 8; 36
Lambeg bleach greens: Lambeg AM 8; 135, 140
Lambeg bleach mill: Lambeg AM 8; 143
Lambeg bridge: Lambeg AM 8; 134, 140
Lambeg church: Drumbeg AM 8; 129
Lambeg church: Lambeg AM 8; 134, 136, 140–43
Lambeg Cottage: Lambeg AM 8; 137, 142–43
Lambeg fort: Lambeg AM 8; 141
Lambeg Glebe House: Lambeg AM 8; 137, 142
Lambeg graveyard: Lambeg AM 8; 135–36
Lambeg House: Blaris AM 8; 54
Lambeg House: Lambeg AM 8; 138, 142
Lambeg Lower district: Magilligan LY 11; 103
Lambeg nunnery: Lambeg AM 8; 136
Lambeg ph: Blaris AM 8; 20, 36, 60
Lambeg ph: Blaris DN 12; 27, 33
Lambeg ph: Derryaghy AM 8; 90, 118
Lambeg ph: Drumbeg DN 7; 52
Lambeg ph: Drumbo DN 7; 54
Lambeg ph: Holywood DN 7; 83
Lambeg ph: Misc. DN 17; 118
Lambeg railroad: Lambeg AM 8; 135
Lambeg school: Lambeg AM 8; 142
Lambeg Sunday school: Lambeg AM 8; 142
Lambeg td: Lambeg AM 8; 139, 141
Lambeg tuck mill: Lambeg AM 8; 140
Lambeg Upper district: Blaris AM 8; 87
Lambeg village: Blaris AM 8; 53, 73, 86
Lambeg village: Lambeg AM 8; 134, 136–37, 142
Lambeg watchhouse: Lambeg AM 8; 134
Lambert, Miss: Coleraine LY 33; 72
Lambeth library (England): Clondermot LY 34; 49
Lambeth library: Carrickfergus AM 37; 83, 132
Lambeth library: Faughanvale LY 36; 31

Lammay, J.: Clonleigh DL 39; 12
Lammey, James: Artrea LY 6; 32
Lammins, Hanna: Errigal LY 27; 66
Lammins, James: Errigal LY 27; 66
Lammon, Hugh: Maghera LY 18; 53
Lamon, Alexander: Desertoghill LY 27; 27
Lamon, Daniel: Ballintoy AM 24; 19
Lamon, Daniel: Culfeightrin AM 24; 53
Lamon, family: Maghera LY 18; 13
Lamon, John: Ballywillin LY 33; 41
Lamonerry (see Liminary): Ballyclug AM 23; 64
Lamont, Capt.: Maghera LY 18; 8, 68
Lamont, Hugh: Termoneeny LY 6; 130
Lamont, James: Kilmood DN 7; 95–96
Lamont, William: Blaris AM 8; 55
Lampen, man named: Cumber LY 28; 18, 87
Lamrack, family: Cumber LY 28; 43
Lamrock, family: Cumber LY 28; 55
Lamrock, James: Cumber LY 28; 37
Lamrock, William: Clondermot LY 34; 79
Lanaghran td: Cleenish FH 14; 28–29
Lanaghy (Lanaghey) td: Ballinderry TE 20; 11, 13
Lanaghy mill: Ballinderry TE 20; 11
Lanarkshire (Scotland): Killea and Taughboyne DL 39; 79, 81
Lanatt (see Lannat): Killanny MN 40; 135
Lancashire (England): Derryaghy AM 8; 103
Lancashire: Misc. LY 31; 132
Lancey, Lt W.: Aghanloo LY 11; 8
Lancey, Lt W.: Clondermot LY 34; 97
Lancey, Lt W.: Drumhome DL 39; 58
Lancey, Lt W.: Magilligan LY 11; 143
Lancey, Lt W.: Manorhamilton Union LM 40; 52–53
Land lough [I]: Killymard DL 39; 94
Land lough [II]: Killymard DL 39; 94
Landagivey bog: Agivey LY 22; 39–40, 43
Landagivey fort: Agivey LY 22; 44
Landagivey td: Agivey LY 22; 40, 43–45
Landbrock td: Galloon FH 4; 87, 95
Landen, Rev. J.F.: Drumgoon CN 40; 6
Landford, James: Drumachose LY 9; 121
Landhead school: Ballymoney AM 16; 26
Landhead td: Ballymoney AM 16; 25
Landmore House: Aghadowey LY 22; 7, 28, 33
Landmore td: Aghadowey LY 22; 7, 11, 13
Landmore td: Kilrea LY 27; 110
Lane lough: Clondavaddog DL 38; 3
Lane, Benjamin: Aghanloo LY 11; 9, 12–14, 17, 21, 42
Lane, Benjamin: Drumachose LY 9; 104, 121
Lane, Benjamin: Magilligan LY 11; 86, 97, 100, 107, 116, 120, 124–25, 132, 135
Lane, family: Magilligan LY 11; 130, 142
Lane, Michael: Magilligan LY 11; 137–38
Lane, Mrs: Balteagh LY 9; 26

Lane, Nicholas: Drumachose LY 9; 66

Lanesborough, Lord: Drummully FH 4; 37, 39

Lanesborough, Lord: Galloon FH 4; 89–90, 93

Lang, family: Carrickfergus AM 37; 93, 179

Lang, Hugh: Drummaul AM 19; 81

Lang, Rev.: Drummaul AM 19; 69

Lang, Rev. George: Carnmoney AM 2; 75

Lang, Richard: Carrickfergus AM 37; 179

Langford Lodge: Camlin AM 21; 60, 62, 71

Langford Lodge: Killead AM 35; 12–13, 15, 18, 34, 37–39, 41–44, 47, 49, 52

Langford Lodge: Lough Neagh AM 21; 94

Langford Lodge boathouse: Killead AM 35; 47

Langford Lodge demesne: Killead AM 35; 40

Langford Lodge quay: Killead AM 35; 47

Langford Lodge school (see Gartree): Killead AM 35; 37

Langford Point: Killead AM 35; 7–8, 13, 17

Langford Point quay: Killead AM 35; 16

Langford, family: Camlin AM 21; 68

Langford, family: Carmavy AM 35; 2

Langford, family: Killead AM 35; 17

Langford, family: Muckamore AM 35; 56

Langford, Hercules: Camlin AM 21; 60

Langford, Lady: Killead AM 35; 47

Langford, Lady: Templepatrick AM 35; 151, 154

Langford, Roger: Carrickfergus AM 37; 43

Langford, Roger: Muckamore AM 35; 54, 56, 71, 82–83

Langrishe, Mr: Clogher TE 5; 40

Langrishe, Rev. Hercules: Ballybay MN 40; 81, 84

Langton village: Misc. DN 17; 131

Langtree, Joseph: Shankill DN 12; 139

Langtry, Charlotte: Kilmore AH 1; 60

Langtry, G.: Donaghcloney DN 12; 59

Langtry, George: Doagh AM 29; 91, 98

Langtry, George: Kilbride AM 29; 138, 146, 150–52, 154–55

Lanier, R.J.: Glenavy AM 21; 84, 86, 90

Lanigan, William: Ballintoy AM 24; 30

Lankhill td: Rossorry FH 14; 117

Lanktree [or Ranktree], John: Newtownards DN 7; 104

Lann, person named: Blaris AM 8; 60

Lannat bog: Killanny MN 40; 130

Lannat school: Killanny MN 40; 135

Lannely [or Lonnely], C.: Newtownards DN 7; 113

Lannely [or Lonnely], H.: Newtownards DN 7; 112

Lantaigne, Dr (Dublin): Aughnamullen MN 40; 76

Lanygarve (Langarvy) td: Camlin AM 21; 60

Lanygarve school: Camlin AM 21; 76

Laois: Banagher LY 30; 36

Laois: Blaris AM 8; 89

Laois: Clondermot LY 34; 65

Lapenotiere, John: Magherafelt LY 6; 90

Lappenbawn td: Killdrumsherdan CN 40; 33

Lappendoo td: Killdrumsherdan CN 40; 33

Lappenmore hill: Drung CN 40; 19

Lapper, John: Blaris DN 12; 46

Lappin, J.C.: Blaris DN 12; 49

Lappin, William: Carrickfergus AM 37; 76

Lapsley, John: Maghera LY 18; 53

Lapsley, Ralph: Maghera LY 18; 53

Lara (see Laragh): Ballybay MN 40; 81

Lara lough: Mevagh DL 38; 55

Laracor rectory: Carrickfergus AM 37; 78

Laragh bleach green: Aughnamullen MN 40; 71–73

Laragh chapel: Laragh CN 40; 41

Laragh church: Laragh CN 40; 41, 44

Laragh corn mill: Aughnamullen MN 40; 73

Laragh flax mill: Aughnamullen MN 40; 73

Laragh fort: Ballybay MN 40; 81

Laragh fort: Clogherny TE 20; 28

Laragh lough: Cleenish FH 14; 13

Laragh mill-race [I]: Laragh CN 40; 42

Laragh mill-race [II]: Laragh CN 40; 42

Laragh mine: Ballybay MN 40; 82

Laragh ph: Drumgoon CN 40; 10

Laragh ph: Drung CN 40; 19, 21–24

Laragh quarries: Killdrumsherdan CN 40; 37

Laragh river: Drung CN 40; 19

Laragh river: Laragh CN 40; 39–41, 43

Laragh spinning factory: Aughnamullen MN 40; 73–74

Laragh td: Aughnamullen MN 40; 71, 76

Laragh td: Ballybay MN 40; 84

Laragh td: Desertoghill LY 27; 19, 28

Laragh td: Laragh CN 40; 41

Laragh td: Magheracross FH 14; 95, 100

Laragh td: Trory FH 14; 126–27

Laragh wash and beetling mills: Aughnamullen MN 40; 72

Laragh well: Trory FH 14; 127

Laraghaleas td: Faughanvale LY 36; 17–18, 53, 59–60, 69, 76, 87–88, 95

Laraghbrine (Kildare): Faughanvale LY 36; 59

Laraghleas (see Laraghaleas): Faughanvale LY 36; 18

Larch field: Comber DN 7; 40

Larchfield demesne: Annahilt DN 12; 23

Larchfield demesne: Blaris DN 12; 37

Larchfield House: Comber DN 7; 37–38

Larchfield House: Drumbo DN 7; 59

Larchfield, Patt: Kilmacteige SO 40; 196

Larchmount House: Clondermot LY 34; 6, 20–21, 100, 103, 105

Larcom, Lt T.A.: Aghanloo LY 11; 8

Larcom, Lt T.A.: Artrea LY 6; 40

Larcom, Lt T.A.: Artrea TE 20; 9

Larcom, Lt T.A.: Ballywillin LY 33; 52

Larcom, Lt T.A.: Balteagh LY 9; 45
Larcom, Lt T.A.: Banagher LY 30; 39, 58
Larcom, Lt T.A.: Clondavaddog DL 38; 9
Larcom, Lt T.A.: Clondermot LY 34; 33, 76, 88, 96–97, 102, 107
Larcom, Lt T.A.: Cumber LY 28; 11, 45
Larcom, Lt T.A.: Dungiven LY 15; 111–13, 121
Larcom, Lt T.A.: Faughanvale LY 36; 24, 26–27, 29, 47
Larcom, Lt T.A.: Killoran and Kilvarnet SO 40; 183
Larcom, Lt T.A.: Killygarvan DL 38; 36
Larcom, Lt T.A.: Leck DL 39; 120
Larcom, Lt T.A.: Macosquin LY 22; 98
Larcom, Lt T.A.: Magilligan LY 11; 108
Larcom, Lt T.A.: Mevagh DL 38; 54
Larcom, Lt T.A.: Misc. DN 17; 129
Larcom, Lt T.A.: Misc. LY 36; 118
Larcom, Lt T.A.: Raphoe DL 39; 121
Larcom, Lt T.A.: Tamlaght Finlagan LY 25; 93, 100, 103
Larcom, Lt T.A.: Tamlaght O'Crilly LY 18; 144
Larcom, Lt T.A.: Templecarn DL 39; 163
Larcom, Lt T.A.: Tullyaughnish DL 38; 96
Lardsay, George: Carrickfergus AM 37; 194
Larga (see Largy)
Largadoon fort: Manorhamilton Union LM 40; 52
Largalinny hill: Inishmacsaint FH 14; 71
Largalinny td: Inishmacsaint FH 14; 70
Largan school: Kilmacteige SO 40; 195
Largan td: Kilmacteige SO 40; 190, 194–96
Larganacarran td: Killesher FH 14; 87
Larganacarran td: Kinawley FH 4; 110
Largantea (Largentea) td: Aghanloo LY 11; 1–2, 4–6, 11, 13, 17, 19–20, 24, 35, 37, 41–42
Largantea cave [I]: Aghanloo LY 11; 5
Largantea cave [II]: Aghanloo LY 11; 27
Largantea fort [I]: Aghanloo LY 11; 5, 27
Largantea fort [II]: Aghanloo LY 11; 5, 29
Largantea king's chair: Aghanloo LY 11; 6, 29
Largantea old grave: Aghanloo LY 11; 30
Largantea standing stones [II: Aghanloo LY 11; 4
Largantea standing stones [II]: Aghanloo LY 11; 29
Largantea td: Drumachose LY 9; 48
Largantee (see Largantea): Aghanloo LY 11; 29
Largantogher td: Maghera LY 18; 7, 67
Large Park lough: Hillsborough DN 12; 89
Large Park mill: Hillsborough DN 12; 99
Large Park td: Hillsborough DN 12; 96, 99
Largemour district: Blaris AM 8; 87
Largey td: Raymoghy DL 39; 141
Larghy td: Magheraculmoney FH 14; 111
Largle spinning mill: Tullylish DN 12; 145
Largnaglare (Lurgnaglare) td: Clogher TE 5; 37
Largy bleach green: Tamlaght Finlagan LY 25; 82

Largy bog: Tamlaght Finlagan LY 25; 65, 93, 98, 114
Largy bridge: Tamlaght Finlagan LY 25; 106, 122
Largy chapel: Drumachose LY 9; 107
Largy chapel: Tamlaght Finlagan LY 25; 92, 100
Largy fort: Manorhamilton Union LM 40; 52
Largy fort: Tamlaght Finlagan LY 25; 90, 108–09
Largy hill: Magheraculmoney FH 14; 103, 105
Largy hill: Tamlaght Finlagan LY 25; 109
Largy linen manufactory: Tamlaght Finlagan LY 25; 82–83, 120
Largy meeting house: Tamlaght Finlagan LY 25; 79, 105–06, 120
Largy old bleach green: Tamlaght Finlagan LY 25; 120
Largy school: Ahoghill AM 23; 21, 43, 47
Largy school: Tamlaght Finlagan LY 25; 80, 96
Largy spinning works: Tamlaght Finlagan LY 25; 101
Largy Sunday school: Ahoghill AM 23; 47
Largy Sunday school: Tamlaght Finlagan LY 25; 96
Largy td: Aghavea FH 4; 23
Largy td: Ahoghill AM 23; 37
Largy td: Balteagh LY 9; 1–2
Largy td: Derrybrusk FH 4; 30, 32
Largy td: Tamlaght Finlagan LY 25; 93, 118, 122, 125
Largy wood: Bovevagh LY 25; 8, 52
Largy wood: Dungiven LY 15; 68
Largy wood: Tamlaght Finlagan LY 25; 62, 97–98, 109, 114
Largy's Lane Ends hamlet: Ballinderry AM 21; 41–42
Largybeg fort: Ardstraw TE 5; 12
Largybeg td: Ardstraw TE 5; 12
Largymore Lower td: Blaris DN 12; 40
Largymore Upper td: Blaris DN 12; 40
Largyreagh (Largyrea) td: Drumachose LY 9; 57, 87, 96–97, 133
Largyreagh Bar td: Mevagh DL 38; 63
Largyreagh fort: Mevagh DL 38; 58
Largyreagh td: Mevagh DL 38; 63
Largywood district: Drummaul AM 19; 71
Lark, family: Billy AM 16; 58, 68
Larken and Murrell, Messrs: Derryaghy AM 8; 108
Larkfield forts: Manorhamilton Union LM 40; 52
Larkfield House: Blaris AM 8; 51
Larkfield House: Manorhamilton Union LM 40; 50
Larkhill td: Dunluce AM 16; 107
Larkin, Edward: Artrea LY 6; 11, 28, 30
Larkin, James: Artrea LY 6; 23
Larkin, James: Lissan LY 31; 95, 102
Larkin, John: Carrickfergus AM 37; 116
Larkin, John: Lissan LY 31; 95
Larkin, Mr (Dublin): Drumbeg AM 8; 127

Larkin, Philip: Carrickfergus AM 37; 116
Larky, Mr: Kilmacteige SO 40; 187
Larmer, William: Carrickfergus AM 37; 40, 175
Larmor, Alexander: Magheragall AM 21; 99, 106
Larmor, family: Ballinderry AM 21; 52
Larmor, family: Magheragall AM 21; 99
Larmor, John: Blaris DN 12; 42
Larmor, John: Magheragall AM 21; 101–02, 106, 108
Larmor, Samuel: Magheragall AM 21; 104
Larmour, Alexander: Derryaghy AM 8; 94
Larmour, Edward: Derryaghy AM 8; 99
Larmour, family: Carrickfergus AM 37; 93
Larmour, John: Carrickfergus AM 37; 107
Larmour, William: Carrickfergus AM 37; 150, 152
Larmour, William: Derryaghy AM 8; 94
Larn ford: Skerry AM 13; 120
Larnaglan td: Clogher TE 5; 53
Larne: Antrim AM 29; 25
Larne: Ballee DN 17; 18
Larne: Ballyclug AM 23; 53, 57
Larne: Ballycor AM 32; 3–4, 9
Larne: Ballylinny AM 32; 14, 25, 27–28
Larne: Ballynure AM 32; 32–34, 38–39, 42, 46–47, 51, 66–67, 69–70, 72
Larne: Ballywillin LY 33; 30, 44
Larne: Carncastle and Killyglen AM 10; 10
Larne: Carnmoney AM 2; 42, 103
Larne: Carrickfergus AM 37; 3, 10, 51, 55–56, 59, 64, 140, 142, 164, 171, 177, 187
Larne: Coleraine LY 33; 88–89, 97
Larne: Connor AM 19; 17, 22, 30
Larne: Culfeightrin AM 24; 46
Larne: Doagh AM 29; 64, 66, 71–72, 87, 93–94
Larne: Down DN 17; 49
Larne: Glenwhirry AM 32; 75–76, 79
Larne: Glynn AM 26; 2, 4–5, 9, 11, 13–17, 20–21, 23, 28–29, 33, 37, 39, 41–42, 46
Larne: Inver AM 26; 49–51, 53–54
Larne: Island Magee AM 10; 24–25, 30, 36, 40, 62, 64, 75, 83, 87–88, 91, 105
Larne: Killyleagh DN 17; 84, 86
Larne: Kilmegan DN 3; 60
Larne: Kilroot AM 26; 56–57, 59–60, 62, 70, 72–73, 75, 77–78, 80
Larne: Kilwaughter AM 10; 106–07, 111, 114, 116
Larne: Larne AM 10; 123–25
Larne: Raloo AM 32; 81, 83–84, 86, 88–96, 102–03, 105–06, 115, 122, 124–26, 129, 131–32
Larne: Rashee AM 32; 137
Larne: Templecorran AM 26; 83, 85–86, 89, 91–95, 99, 109, 119, 121, 126–27, 131
Larne: Templepatrick AM 35; 143
Larne: Tickmacrevan AM 13; 128–29
Larne bridge: Inver AM 26; 54

Larne chapel (C): Glynn AM 26; 23
Larne chapel (C): Island Magee AM 10; 35
Larne chapel (C): Larne AM 10; 125
Larne chapel (C): Raloo AM 32; 98
Larne chapel (C): Templecorran AM 26; 101
Larne chapel (W): Larne AM 10; 125
Larne church: Glynn AM 26; 3, 23, 38
Larne church: Inver AM 26; 50–51, 53, 55
Larne church: Larne AM 10; 125
Larne church: Raloo AM 32; 98
Larne classical school: Larne AM 10; 128
Larne corn mill: Glynn AM 26; 20
Larne dispensary: Glynn AM 26; 6, 21, 39
Larne dispensary: Inver AM 26; 51–52
Larne dispensary: Kilwaughter AM 10; 110, 117
Larne district: Carrickfergus AM 37; 160
Larne district: Island Magee AM 10; 86
Larne female private school: Larne AM 10; 128
Larne female school: Larne AM 10; 126–27
Larne flour mills: Glynn AM 26; 20, 38
Larne flour mills: Raloo AM 32; 95
Larne flour mills: Templecorran AM 26; 99
Larne free school: Larne AM 10; 125
Larne harbour: Carrickfergus AM 37; 46
Larne harbour: Glynn AM 26; 45
Larne hills: Templepatrick AM 35; 139
Larne infant school: Larne AM 10; 126–27
Larne lighthouse: Glynn AM 26; 9
Larne Lough: Ballynure AM 32; 31, 44
Larne Lough: Carrickfergus AM 37; 5
Larne Lough: Glynn AM 26; 1, 3–11, 13–18, 20–21, 27, 29–30, 33, 37, 39, 41, 44–45
Larne Lough: Inver AM 26; 49–51
Larne Lough: Island Magee AM 10; 14, 17, 19–21, 26–27, 29, 37, 42, 44–45, 47, 58, 60, 65, 72, 74–76, 79, 83, 86
Larne Lough: Kilroot AM 26; 57
Larne Lough: Larne AM 10; 123
Larne Lough: Raloo AM 32; 82–83, 85, 88, 93
Larne Lough: Templecorran AM 26; 82, 84–86, 88–92, 94, 96, 109, 112, 114, 118, 120, 122, 130
Larne male school: Larne AM 10; 126
Larne meeting house (P): Inver AM 26; 50–51
Larne meeting house (P): Larne AM 10; 125
Larne meeting house (U): Larne AM 10; 125, 127
Larne meeting house [III]: Larne AM 10; 125
Larne meeting houses: Glynn AM 26; 3, 23
Larne ph: Ballynure AM 32; 64
Larne ph: Carncastle and Killyglen AM 10; 8, 11
Larne ph: Carrickfergus AM 37; 71, 100
Larne ph: Glynn AM 26; 9, 20–23, 29, 39
Larne ph: Inver AM 26; 49, 52
Larne ph: Island Magee AM 10; 15, 31, 35, 74
Larne ph: Kilroot AM 26; 65
Larne ph: Mallusk AM 2; 111, 114

Larne ph: Misc. AM 10; 129
Larne ph: Raloo AM 32; 98–99, 117–18
Larne ph: Templecorran AM 26; 101, 103
Larne private school [I]: Larne AM 10; 127
Larne private school [II]: Larne AM 10; 127
Larne private school [III]: Larne AM 10; 128
Larne private school [IV]: Larne AM 10; 128
Larne quay: Carrickfergus AM 37; 45
Larne river: Ballycor AM 32; 1
Larne river: Ballynure AM 32; 31
Larne river: Carrickfergus AM 37; 5
Larne river: Doagh AM 29; 71
Larne river: Inver AM 26; 49–51, 54–55
Larne river: Kilwaughter AM 10; 108–10, 113
Larne river: Larne AM 10; 125
Larne river: Raloo AM 32; 82–83, 85–86, 94, 108,
   111, 113, 133
Larne river: Templecorran AM 26; 88
Larne road bridge: Glenwhirry AM 32; 75
Larne schools: Inver AM 26; 51
Larne Sunday school: Larne AM 10; 126
Larne tuck mill: Inver AM 26; 54
Larragh td: Rossorry FH 14; 116–17
Larraweehan td: Drumgoon CN 40; 2
Larrycormick bog: Desertlyn LY 31; 44
Larrycormick school: Desertlyn LY 31; 50
Larrycormick td: Desertlyn LY 31; 47
Lasbellanagroagh (see Lisbellanagroagh): Ballintoy
   AM 24; 35
Lascelles, Rev. F.E.: Bright DN 17; 34–35
Lascelles, Rev. F.E.: Donaghadee DN 7; 46
Laserian, St (see also Molaise): Trory FH 14; 127
Laserian, St: Devenish FH 14; 51, 54
Laserian, St: Killesher FH 14; 81, 90
Latacrossin (see Lattacrossin): Currin MN 40; 91
Latacrussin (see Lattacrossin): Currin MN 40; 86
Latbeg td: Clogher TE 5; 32, 36, 53
Lathaircranny td: Templecarn DL 39; 161
Latham, John: Carrickfergus AM 37; 120
Latham, Mr: Lough Swilly DL 38; 143
Latham, William: Antrim AM 29; 12
Lathemstown (see Leathemstown): Tullyrusk AM
   21; 135
Latimer, James: Tamlaght TE 20; 75, 128, 136
Latimer, Janet: Island Magee AM 10; 66, 94
Latimer, Robert: Kilroot AM 26; 74, 80
Latin lough: Donaghmoyne MN 40; 106
Latlorcan td: Monaghan MN 40; 159
Latnamard chapel: Aghabog MN 40; 62–63
Latnamard giant's grave: Aghabog MN 40; 64
Latnamard school: Aghabog MN 40; 65
Latta, William: Misc. DL 39; 186, 188, 192
Lattacrom td: Aughnamullen MN 40; 69, 76
Lattacrossin hill: Currin MN 40; 86
Lattacrossin td: Currin MN 40; 86, 91

Latten chapel: Aughnamullen MN 40; 71
Latten old chapel: Aughnamullen MN 40; 71
Latten td: Aughnamullen MN 40; 69, 76
Latten, John: Tamlaght Finlagan LY 25; 119
Lattenfaskey td: Aughnamullen MN 40; 76
Latticrum (see Lattacrom): Aughnamullen MN 40;
   76
Lattimor, Thomas: Carrickfergus AM 37; 158
Lattimore, Anne: Carrickfergus AM 37; 76, 151
Lattimore, William: Kilroot AM 26; 79
Lattin td: Enniskillen FH 4; 82
Lattinalbany td: Magheross MN 40; 148
Lattone (Lattoon) td: Cleenish FH 14; 29
Lattone hill: Cleenish FH 14; 12
Lattully school: Drumgoon CN 40; 11
Lattyloo hill: Drumgoon CN 40; 1
Lattyneel td: Clogher TE 5; 53
Lau, St: Ballinderry AM 21; 55
Laughan hill fort: Billy AM 16; 69
Laughermore (see Loghermore): Aghalurcher FH 4;
   16
Laughill td: Aghalurcher FH 4; 14
Laughlin, Andrew: Bovevagh LY 25; 18, 38
Laughlin, family: Ballinderry AM 21; 48
Laughlin, family: Billy AM 16; 58, 68
Laughlin, family: Desertoghill LY 27; 30
Laughlin, Patrick: Tamlaght TE 20; 104
Laughlin, Timothy: Hillsborough DN 12; 105
Laught Ard rock: Donaghmore DL 39; 35
Laughtalube (see Loughtilube): Banagher LY 30; 22
Laugry, Michael: Drumachose LY 9; 134
Launches Little Island: Saul DN 17; 111, 114
Launches Long Island: Saul DN 17; 111, 114
Launy river (see also Clogher river): Clogher TE 5;
   25–27, 30, 33
Laurel Grove House: Magheramesk AM 21; 113
Laurel Hill House: Coleraine LY 33; 73, 141
Laurel Hill House: Killowen LY 33; 160, 162, 168
Laurel Hill House: Kilmore AH 1; 64, 67
Laurel Hill House: Macosquin LY 22; 104
Laurel Hill infant school: Killowen LY 33; 166
Laurel Hill plantation: Currin MN 40; 97
Laurel Hill school: Killowen LY 33; 165–66, 171
Laurel Hill Sunday school: Killowen LY 33; 166
Laurell Hill House: Derryaghy AM 8; 105
Laurence, John: Dunluce AM 16; 118
Laurencetown: Tullylish DN 12; 141
Laurencetown bridge: Tullylish DN 12; 141–42
Laurencetown chapel: Tullylish DN 12; 141
Laurencetown House: Tullylish DN 12; 141
Lavary (see Lavery): Seagoe AH 1; 103
Laverty, Eneas: Ramoan AM 24; 110–12
Laverty, family: Carrickfergus AM 37; 93
Laverty, family: Culfeightrin AM 24; 59
Laverty, family: Dunluce AM 16; 117

Laverty, Hector: Ramoan AM 24; 111–12
Laverty, Henry: Carrickfergus AM 37; 179
Laverty, Hugh: Culfeightrin AM 24; 85
Laverty, Hugh: Island Magee AM 10; 100, 102
Laverty, Hugh: Ramoan AM 24; 109–10
Laverty, Mary: Maghera LY 18; 19
Laverty, Patrick: Loughguile AM 13; 77
Laverty, Thomas: Carrickfergus AM 37; 131
Laverty, William: Carrickfergus AM 37; 160
Lavery, Cathrine (see Brady)
Lavery, Daniel: Hillsborough DN 12; 100
Lavery, family: Aghagallon AM 21; 9–10, 18
Lavery, family: Ballinderry AM 21; 54
Lavery, Hugh: Aghagallon AM 21; 14, 17
Lavery, James: Aghagallon AM 21; 17
Lavery, James: Carrickfergus AM 37; 109
Lavery, Jane: Carrickfergus AM 37; 119
Lavery, John: Aghagallon AM 21; 23
Lavery, John: Artrea LY 6; 29–30
Lavery, John [I]: Aghagallon AM 21; 13
Lavery, John [II]: Aghagallon AM 21; 14–15
Lavery, Patrick: Aghagallon AM 21; 13, 19
Lavery, Patrick: Hillsborough DN 12; 85
Lavery's bridge: Moira DN 12; 119
Lavery's school: Seagoe AH 1; 102–03
Lavey ph: Maghera LY 18; 68
Lavin (Lavan) td: Loughguile AM 13; 71–72, 76
Lavin cove: Loughguile AM 13; 71
Lavin hill: Loughguile AM 13; 60
Lavin Lower td: Loughguile AM 13; 62, 68
Law, Alexander: Ballyaghran LY 33; 24
Law, Edward: Blaris AM 8; 82
Law, family: Culfeightrin AM 24; 59
Law, H.: Tullylish DN 12; 141
Law, J.: Comber DN 7; 37, 39–41
Law, J.: Drumgath DN 3; 21
Law, J.: Dundonald DN 7; 65
Law, James: Leck DL 39; 119
Law, James: Misc. DL 39; 186
Law, Mr (Dublin): Banagher LY 30; 23
Law, Mr (Dublin): Bovevagh LY 25; 22, 24, 26, 29, 58
Law, Mr: Lough Swilly DL 38; 103
Law, Rev. Samuel: Killea and Taughboyne DL 39; 79–80, 89, 92, 185
Law, Samuel: Seapatrick DN 12; 127
Law, Samuel: Tullylish DN 12; 141
Law, William: Hillsborough DN 12; 106
Law, William: Raymoghy DL 39; 140–41
Lawder, Charles: Donegore AM 29; 129
Lawder, Hugh: Clogher TE 5; 40
Lawes, Anne: Carrickfergus AM 37; 128
Lawrence, J.D.: Ballyscullion LY 6; 57
Lawrence, John: Magherafelt LY 6; 83
Lawrence, Miss: Coleraine LY 33; 72

Lawrence, Rev. Thomas: Clogher TE 5; 28
Lawrence, Samuel: Coleraine LY 33; 72, 77, 142
Lawrence, St: Maghera LY 18; 9
Lawriner, Sarah: Tickmacrevan AM 13; 133
Lawson, Alexander: Blaris AM 8; 46, 50
Lawson, Alexander: Blaris DN 12; 49
Lawson, David: Magherafelt LY 6; 107
Lawson, family: Ballintoy AM 24; 20
Lawson, George: Hillsborough DN 12; 105
Lawson, James: Hillsborough DN 12; 105
Lawson, John: Blaris DN 12; 50
Lawson, John: Carrickfergus AM 37; 112
Lawson, John: Drumachose LY 9; 61
Lawson, John: Kilbride AM 29; 154
Lawson, Thomas: Artrea LY 6; 28
Lawther manor: Magheracross FH 14; 102
Lawther, C.: Nilteen AM 35; 102
Lawther, family: Nilteen AM 35; 91
Lawther, John: Donegore AM 29; 129
Lawther, John: Nilteen AM 35; 104
Lawvarty, family: Derryaghy AM 8; 103
Lay td: Aughnamullen MN 40; 76
Layd Castle: Layd AM 13; 40
Layd chapel: Ardclinis AM 13; 4
Layd Cottage: Layd AM 13; 47
Layd ph: Ardclinis AM 13; 1, 5
Layd ph: Culfeightrin AM 24; 36, 41, 46
Layd ph: Dunaghy AM 13; 19, 25
Layd ph: Layd and Inispollan AM 13; 54
Layd ph: Loughguile AM 13; 58
Layd ph: Misc. AM 10; 129
Layd ph: Ramoan AM 24; 118
Layd td: Layd AM 13; 36
Layd, Trevor: Newry DN 3; 74
Laymore school: Ahoghill AM 23; 44, 47–48
Laymore Sunday school: Ahoghill AM 23; 47–48
Lea Ballyclare bleach green: Ballynure AM 32; 71
Lea Ballyclare district: Doagh AM 29; 88–90
Lea Ballyclare td: Ballynure AM 32; 67
Lea lough: Aghalurcher FH 4; 3
Lea lough: Aghavea FH 4; 19
Leac Phadraig stone: Dungiven LY 15; 54
Leach, Capt. G.A.: Misc. AM 10; 131
Leach, Rev.: Newry DN 3; 105
Leacock, James: Magherafelt LY 6; 112
Leacthrom (see Lackcrom): Killymard DL 39; 99
Leaden, Thomas: Ballynascreen LY 31; 26
Leafin school: Desertegney DL 38; 27
Leafin standing stone: Desertegney DL 38; 26
Leagafainne td: Donegal DL 39; 44
Leagh locality: Clondermot LY 34; 67, 71
Leaghan corn mill: Killdrumsherdan CN 40; 34
Leaghan school: Killdrumsherdan CN 40; 36
Leaght hill: Donaghmore DL 39; 28
Leaght td: Donaghmore DL 39; 28, 37–38

Leagueland td: Convoy DL 39; 21

Leahid locality: Lough Swilly DL 38; 116

Leahy, Mr: Clogher TE 5; 40

Leakamy (see Carrowblagh): Moville DL 38; 68

Lealies corn mills: Kilwaughter AM 10; 110

Lealies td: Kilwaughter AM 10; 107, 110, 119, 122

Leam td: Enniskillen FH 4; 74, 82

Leamacrossan td: Moville DL 38; 73

Leambeg td: Cleenish FH 14; 29

Leambrisslan td: Derryvullan FH 14; 46

Leame district: Misc. SO 40; 200

Leamhain river: Dungiven LY 15; 63

Leammorer td: Cleenish FH 14; 29

Leanamore (see Lenamore)

Leanan (see Lenan): Clonmany DL 38; 16

Leaney, Rev. James: Loughguile AM 13; 77

Leannalea village: Kilmacteige SO 40; 193

Leap bridge: Glenavy AM 21; 78

Leapokes flax mill: Dromore DN 12; 72

Leapokes td: Dromore DN 12; 72

Lear hill: Banagher LY 30; 24, 31

Lear hill: Cumber LY 28; 5

Lear quarry: Cumber LY 28; 124

Lear td: Cumber LY 28; 4, 8, 12, 20, 67, 70, 113,
    119, 124

Lear wood: Cumber LY 28; 119

Learden flax mill: Macosquin LY 22; 82, 105

Learden td: Macosquin LY 22; 90, 116

Learey, family: Banagher LY 30; 10

Learmount chapel (see Gortscreagan)

Learmount church: Banagher LY 30; 32–33

Learmount church: Cumber LY 28; 1, 8, 13, 24–25,
    83, 85–86, 88–90

Learmount district: Banagher LY 30; 19, 60, 115–16

Learmount district: Cumber LY 28; 6, 17, 19, 32,
    88–89, 91

Learmount flax mill: Cumber LY 28; 86

Learmount hill: Banagher LY 30; 31, 112

Learmount House: Banagher LY 30; 25, 29–30, 39,
    59

Learmount House: Cumber LY 28; 4–9, 11, 18, 84,
    86

Learmount plantation: Cumber LY 28; 23–24

Learmount police station: Drumachose LY 9; 84

Learmount td: Banagher LY 30; 31

Learmount threshing machine: Cumber LY 28; 22

Leat td: Donaghedy TE 5; 92

Leatbeg school: Clondavaddog DL 38; 7

Leatbeg td: Clondavaddog DL 38; 3–4

Leath, Reynold: Island Magee AM 10; 94

Leathe, Robert: Carnmoney AM 2; 69

Leathem, Edward: Hillsborough DN 12; 107

Leathem, John: Carrickfergus AM 37; 115

Leathemstown: Ballinderry AM 21; 53

Leathemstown bridge: Tullyrusk AM 21; 135

Leathemstown corn kilns: Ballinderry AM 21; 53

Leathemstown mill-race: Ballinderry AM 21; 53

Leather, Rev. John: Magilligan LY 11; 89, 109–10,
    115

Leaths, Rev. John: Hillsborough DN 12; 90

Leatrim td: Donaghedy TE 5; 92

Leban, family: Desertmartin LY 31; 55

Lecahill district: Grey Abbey DN 7; 72

Lecale barony: Ardglass DN 17; 1, 12

Lecale barony: Ballee DN 17; 15, 23

Lecale barony: Ballyphilip DN 7; 9, 13

Lecale barony: Down DN 17; 38, 41–42, 49–50, 66

Lecale barony: Dunsfort DN 17; 67

Lecale barony: Holywood DN 7; 80

Lecale barony: Misc. DN 17; 116–17

Lecale barony: Rathmullan DN 17; 109

Lecale district: Ballee DN 17; 16

Lecale district: Kilkeel DN 3; 53

Lecale district: Kilmegan DN 3; 59

Lecale district: Misc. DN 17; 119

Lecale, Lady: Bright DN 17; 36

Lecale, Lord: Ardglass DN 17; 3

Lecale, Lord: Bright DN 17; 36

Lecarrow district: Misc. SO 40; 200

Lecarrowreagh district: Misc. SO 40; 198

Leck bog: Macosquin LY 22; 78, 120

Leck boiling spring: Drumachose LY 9; 75, 83, 127

Leck corn mill: Ballyclog TE 20; 16

Leck flax mills: Leck DL 39; 116

Leck forts: Drumachose LY 9; 58–59, 91, 127–28

Leck oat mill: Leck DL 39; 116

Leck ph: Convoy DL 39; 18

Leck ph: Conwal DL 39; 24

Leck ph: Misc. DL 39; 185

Leck ph: Raphoe DL 39; 121, 129

Leck ph: Raymoghy DL 39; 132–33, 140

Leck river bridge: Drumachose LY 9; 91

Leck stone: Drumachose LY 9; 58, 110

Leck td: Ballymoney AM 16; 6

Leck td: Banagher LY 30; 23–24

Leck td: Drumachose LY 9; 58–59, 75, 87, 91,
    96–97, 110, 127, 133–34

Leck td: Leckpatrick TE 5; 117, 125

Leck td: Macosquin LY 22; 76, 122

Leckagh (Lackagh) td: Magherafelt LY 6; 93–94,
    101, 108–09, 111–12

Leckey, Hugh: Coleraine LY 33; 105, 127

Leckey, John: Carncastle and Killyglen AM 10; 7

Leckey, Mr: Donaghmore DL 39; 36, 38–39

Leckey, Mr: Urney DL 39; 181

Leckey, Thomas: Tullyaughnish DL 38; 97

Leckpatrick ph: Clonleigh DL 39; 1, 7

Leckpatrick ph: Donaghedy TE 5; 88

Leckpatrick ph: Leck DL 39; 115

Lecky, Andrew: Ballyscullion LY 6; 46

Lecky, Averil: Magilligan LY 11; 101

Lecky, C.F.: Clondermot LY 34; 115

Lecky, Hugh: Billy AM 16; 46

Lecky, Mr: Clondermot LY 34; 38

Lecky, Mrs: Magilligan LY 11; 85

Lecky, William: Clondermot LY 34; 82–83

Lecumpher meeting house: Desertmartin LY 31; 63, 128, 136

Lecumpher td: Misc. LY 31; 116, 141 42

Lederig td: Desertegney DL 38; 29

Lederig wood: Desertegney DL 38; 24

Ledlie, Adam: Newry DN 3; 98, 103

Ledlie, James: Newry DN 3; 99, 103

Ledlie, Maj.: Lough Neagh AM 21; 97

Ledlie, Maj.: Muckamore AM 35; 78

Ledlie, Mrs E.: Newry DN 3; 105

Ledlie, Rev. J.C.: Donegore AM 29; 126, 129

Ledlie, Samuel: Newry DN 3; 98, 103

Ledlie's mills: Lough Neagh AM 21; 97

Ledwich, Rev. Edward: Cumber LY 28; 9, 86

Lee lough: Longfield TE 5; 127

Lee lough: Skirts of Urney and Ardstraw TE 5; 136

Lee Stone Point coastguard station: Kilkeel DN 3; 50

Lee, Edward: Aghalee AM 21; 40

Lee, Edward: Coleraine LY 33; 72

Lee, family: Carrickfergus AM 37; 93

Lee, family: Dunboe LY 11; 79

Lee, Isaac: Hillsborough DN 12; 106

Lee, Isaac: Newry DN 3; 82

Lee, John: Ballyscullion AM 19; 12, 14

Lee, John: Donacavey TE 5; 82

Lee, John: Hillsborough DN 12; 106

Lee, John: Maghera LY 18; 78

Lee, man named: Raloo AM 32; 122

Lee, Margaret: Carnmoney AM 2; 75–76

Lee, Mary: Maghera LY 18; 78

Lee, Mr (Gracehill): Ahoghill AM 23; 19

Lee, Mrs: Magilligan LY 11; 128

Lee, Rev. (Cambridge): Kilcronaghan LY 31; 81

Lee, Thomas: Clondermot LY 34; 82

Lee, William: Hillsborough DN 12; 106

Lee, William: Tamlaght TE 20; 105

Leebody, Rev. Henry: Ballinderry AM 21; 50

Leech, Alexander: Loughguile AM 13; 76

Leech, Andrew: Ballynascreen LY 31; 21

Leech, Frank: Kilraghts AM 16; 134

Leech, James: Tamlaght TE 20; 79, 86

Leech, John: Aghanloo LY 11; 23

Leech, John: Ahoghill AM 23; 40

Leech, William: Tamlaght TE 20; 81, 108

Leeke (Leek) td: Bovevagh LY 25; 19, 27, 60–61

Leeke standing stone: Bovevagh LY 25; 50

Leeke Water glen: Bovevagh LY 25; 1

Leenan (see Lenan): Clonmany DL 38; 13

Lees, family: Magherafelt LY 6; 95

Lees, H.: Clogher TE 5; 41

Lees, James: Carrickfergus AM 37; 110

Lees, John: Magherafelt LY 6; 110

Lees, Rev.: Carrickfergus AM 37; 174

Lees, Rev. Harcourt: Killanny MN 40; 135

Lees, Thomas: Magherafelt LY 6; 111

Leesborough lough: Ematris MN 40; 112–13, 116

Leesborrow (see Leesborough): Ematris MN 40; 112

Leesburrow (see Leesborough): Ematris MN 40; 116

Leeson, J.F.: Newry DN 3; 99

Leeson, John: Ballyscullion LY 6; 59

Leeson, Mr: Ballyscullion LY 6; 59

Leeson, R.: Banagher LY 30; 113

Leetch, family: Ahoghill AM 23; 25

Leetch, Mr: Antrim AM 29; 10

Lefroy, Rev. Anthony: Aghaderg DN 12; 10

Legachurry locality: Lough Swilly DL 38; 134

Legacorry (see also Rich Hill): Kilmore AH 1; 62, 72

Legacorry corn mill: Drumbo DN 7; 59

Legacorry flax mill: Drumbo DN 7; 59

Legacorry td: Drumbo DN 7; 59–60, 62

Legacurry td: Clonmany DL 38; 16, 18, 20

Legaduff td: Kinawley FH 4; 110

Legaghory (Legahory) td: Cumber LY 28; 46, 48, 60, 63, 96–97, 102, 105, 107

Legaghory td: Faughanvale LY 36; 60

Legaghory wood: Cumber LY 28; 102

Legagorn td: Saintfield DN 7; 120

Legagrane td: Dunaghy AM 13; 24

Legaloy caves: Ballynure AM 32; 58

Legaloy fort: Ballynure AM 32; 58

Legaloy quarry: Ballynure AM 32; 57

Legaloy school: Ballynure AM 32; 73

Legaloy td: Ballynure AM 32; 55, 63, 68

Legamaddy (Ligamaddy) td: Bright DN 17; 34–35, 37

Legamaghery td: Donacavey TE 5; 67, 76, 79, 84

Legan manor: Misc. FH 4; 133

Legananny flax mill: Drumgooland DN 3; 25

Legananny mountain: Dromara DN 12; 62

Legananny td: Drumgooland DN 3; 25

Leganany (see Legananny)

Legandoragh td: Clonleigh DL 39; 12

Leganenan td: Dungiven LY 15; 89

Legannagh (see Leganny): Drumcree AH 1; 38

Leganny td: Drumcree AH 1; 34, 38

Legateriff (see Legatirriff): Ballinderry AM 21; 57

Legaterriff (see Legatirriff): Ballinderry AM 21; 41

Legatiggle school: Donacavey TE 5; 66

Legatiggle td: Donacavey TE 5; 66

Legatirriff (Legatarriff) td: Ballinderry AM 21; 47

Legatirriff school [I]: Ballinderry AM 21; 47, 56, 58–59

Legatirriff school [II]: Ballinderry AM 21; 41, 57

Legatirriff Sunday school: Ballinderry AM 21; 47, 59

Legavalan valley: Errigal LY 27; 78

Legavallan (see Legavannon): Faughanvale LY 36; 60

Legavallen (see Legavannon): Faughanvale LY 36; 11

Legavambush locality: Dungiven LY 15; 91

Legavanan (see Legavannon)

Legavannon bridge [I]: Balteagh LY 9; 5, 42

Legavannon bridge [II]: Balteagh LY 9; 5, 42

Legavannon bridge [III]: Balteagh LY 9; 5, 42

Legavannon mountain: Cumber LY 28; 45

Legavannon mountain: Faughanvale LY 36; 1, 3, 11

Legavannon mountain: Tamlaght Finlagan LY 25; 66, 97

Legavannon Pot: Balteagh LY 9; 1, 4, 20, 23, 40, 42

Legavannon Pot: Banagher LY 30; 84, 95

Legavannon Pot: Faughanvale LY 36; 47, 60

Legavannon td: Faughanvale LY 36; 53, 59, 69, 76, 88, 95

Legavannwell locality: Dungiven LY 15; 91

Legavara hill: Ballintoy AM 24; 10, 12, 17

Legavara standing stone: Ballintoy AM 24; 31

Legg hill: Inishmacsaint FH 14; 71

Legg House: Layd AM 13; 47

Legg Island: Inishmacsaint FH 14; 70

Legg, David: Blaris DN 12; 45, 49

Legg, David [I]: Carrickfergus AM 37; 26

Legg, David [II]: Carrickfergus AM 37; 40, 102, 141–42, 149, 175

Legg, John: Carrickfergus AM 37; 40, 47, 57, 102, 135, 137, 141–42, 172, 175

Legg, Thomas: Carrickfergus AM 37; 39, 148

Legg, Wallace: Blaris AM 8; 54

Leggaloy (see Legaloy): Ballynure AM 32; 68

Leggamaghery (Legamaghry) td: Donacavey TE 5; 77, 81, 86

Leggamaghry (see Leggamaghery)

Leggan school: Aughnamullen MN 40; 77

Leggan td: Aughnamullen MN 40; 76

Leggancurry td: Aghaderg DN 12; 2

Leggandarrough td: Misc. DL 39; 197

Leggatiggle (Loggetigill) td: Donacavey TE 5; 65, 76–77, 79, 81, 83, 86

Leggatiggle school: Donacavey TE 5; 65, 83

Legge, family: Carrickfergus AM 37; 84

Legget, John: Kirkinriola AM 23; 116

Leggetiggle (see Leggatiggle)

Leggigowan (see Leggygowan): Saintfield DN 7; 117, 119

Leggycorry (see Legacorry): Drumbo DN 7; 62

Leggygowan td: Saintfield DN 7; 117, 119

Leghinmore bleach green: Ahoghill AM 23; 13, 31

Leghinmore House: Ahoghill AM 23; 12–13

Leghorn (Italy): Newry DN 3; 87

Legin (see Leginn): Kinawley FH 4; 121

Leginn and Dresternan manor: Kinawley FH 4; 121, 124

Leginn corn mill: Kinawley FH 4; 115

Leginn td: Kinawley FH 4; 115

Legland chapel: Killygarvan DL 38; 37, 39

Legland hill: Devenish FH 14; 47

Legland lough: Killygarvan DL 38; 37

Legland td: Killygarvan DL 38; 37

Leglehid td: Inishmacsaint FH 14; 72

Legmore forts: Derryaghy AM 8; 96

Legmore glen: Derryaghy AM 8; 100

Legmore td: Derryaghy AM 8; 90, 96, 104, 119

Legmore td: Moira DN 12; 120

Legmuckaduff td: Tullyaughnish DL 38; 96

Legmurn hill: Ballyclog TE 20; 15

Legmurn td: Ballyclog TE 20; 17

Legnabrocky td: Killesher FH 14; 82

Legnacraave valley: Errigal LY 27; 78

Legnacrieve td: Donacavey TE 5; 81

Legnadaragh valley: Bovevagh LY 25; 16, 36

Legnagappog td: Ballyculter DN 17; 30, 30

Legnahorna td: Killesher FH 14; 87

Legnalaniv plain: Ballintoy AM 24; 34

Legnamanna td: Dunaghy AM 13; 18

Legnaniel td: Misc. DL 39; 197

Legnasasanagh glen: Ramoan AM 24; 121

Legnasilla graveyard: Dungiven LY 15; 89

Legnatraw (Legnathraw) td: Killea and Taughboyne DL 39; 80, 87, 148, 150, 153, 186, 195

Legnatraw House: Killea and Taughboyne DL 39; 82, 87–88

Legnatraw spa: Taughboyne DL 39; 150, 153

Legnetomack locality: Carrickfergus AM 37; 93, 174

Legnoha (see Legnatraw): Taughboyne DL 39; 148

Legolsy (see Legaloy): Ballynure AM 32; 73

Legoneill td: Clonleigh DL 39; 12

Legphressy td: Longfield TE 5; 132

Legwee corn mill: Drumlumman CN 40; 14

Legwee td: Drumlumman CN 40; 13, 17

Leheny lough: Donegal DL 39; 54

Lehinch td: Galloon FH 4; 95

Leicester (England): Ballee DN 17; 19

Leicester, family: Donegal DL 39; 48

Leich, family: Aghalee AM 21; 31

Leiffaa hill: Killesher FH 14; 81

Leigh abbey: Grey Abbey DN 7; 68

Leigh, Edmund: Clondermot LY 34; 69

Leigh, John: Donacavey TE 5; 68, 70–71

Leigh, John: Newry DN 3; 74

Leigh, Mr: Blaris DN 12; 47

Leighanmore (see Leghinmore): Ahoghill AM 23; 31

Leighlin hill: Drung CN 40; 19

Leighton, Jane: Antrim AM 29; 41, 46

Leighton, Richard: Antrim AM 29; 41, 45

Leinster: Banagher LY 30; 71, 110

Leinster: Clondermot LY 34; 75

Leinster: Cumber LY 28; 72

Leinster: Faughanvale LY 36; 54

Leister's fort: Newry DN 3; 106

Leith (Scotland): Coleraine LY 33; 86

Leitrim: Aghabog MN 40; 65

Leitrim: Coleraine LY 33; 63

Leitrim: Enniskillen FH 4; 51, 64

Leitrim: Galloon FH 4; 87, 92, 102

Leitrim: Inishmacsaint FH 14; 70

Leitrim: Kilbarron DL 39; 78

Leitrim: Kinawley FH 4; 123

Leitrim: Tomregan FH 4; 128

Leitrim Arms Hotel: Manorhamilton Union LM 40; 49–50

Leitrim bogs: Ballyscullion LY 6; 68

Leitrim bridge: Drumgooland DN 3; 25

Leitrim chapel: Drumgooland DN 3; 22

Leitrim chapel: Tyholland MN 40; 174

Leitrim corn mill: Drumgooland DN 3; 23

Leitrim flax mill: Drumgooland DN 3; 23

Leitrim hill: Aghavea FH 4; 17

Leitrim Island: Ballyscullion LY 6; 60

Leitrim manor: Drummully FH 4; 34, 37, 39

Leitrim manor: Galloon FH 4; 95

Leitrim old flax mill: Drumgooland DN 3; 23

Leitrim potteries: Ballyscullion LY 6; 65

Leitrim river: Drumgooland DN 3; 23–25

Leitrim school: Duneane AM 19; 126

Leitrim school [I]: Drummaul AM 19; 76, 86

Leitrim school [II]: Drummaul AM 19; 92

Leitrim Sunday school: Drumgooland DN 3; 22

Leitrim Sunday school: Drummaul AM 19; 86

Leitrim td: Ballymoney AM 16; 25

Leitrim td: Ballyscullion LY 6; 44, 55, 58, 60, 63, 65, 67–68, 71, 77–78

Leitrim td: Drumgooland DN 3; 22–23

Leitrim td: Drummaul AM 19; 90

Leitrim td: Galloon FH 4; 93, 95

Leitrim, Earl of: Lough Swilly DL 38; 118

Leitrim, Earl of: Tullyaughnish DL 38; 93, 96

Leitrim, family: Manorhamilton Union LM 40; 47, 49

Leitrim, family: Mevagh DL 38; 58

Leitrim, Lord: Clondavaddog DL 38; 8

Leitrim, Lord: Kilmacrenan DL 38; 53

Leitrim, Lord: Mevagh DL 38; 57, 60

Leixlip (Kildare): Banagher LY 30; 22

Lelam, Charles: Templepatrick AM 35; 145

Leland, Mr: Donaghmore DN 3; 9

Leland, Rev. Thomas: Ardstraw TE 5; 9

Lely, Peter: Killesher FH 14; 84

Lemaghery (see Levaghery): Seagoe AH 1; 103

Leman, family: Ahoghill AM 23; 25

Lement, Widow: Comber DN 7; 35

Lemnalary House: Ardclinis AM 13; 7

Lemnalary mountain: Ardclinis AM 13; 2

Lemnarory (see Lemnaroy): Termoneeny LY 6; 124

Lemnaroy corn mill: Termoneeny LY 6; 129, 131

Lemnaroy fort: Termoneeny LY 6; 131

Lemnaroy meeting house: Termoneeny LY 6; 130

Lemnaroy school: Termoneeny LY 6; 124, 128

Lemnaroy td: Termoneeny LY 6; 124–25, 130–31

Lemnha locality: Carrickfergus AM 37; 11

Lemnha locality: Island Magee AM 10; 66

Lemon, family: Maghera LY 18; 24

Lemon, Mrs (Gortnaskey): Cumber LY 28; 32

Lemon, Rev. Matthew: Kilbroney DN 3; 34

Lemont, Widow: Comber DN 7; 38

Lemullagh td: Artrea LY 6; 40

Lena Garran td: Dunboe LY 11; 49

Lenaderg mill [I]: Tullylish DN 12; 146

Lenaderg mill [II]: Tullylish DN 12; 146

Lenaderg mill [III]: Tullylish DN 12; 146

Lenaderg mill [IV]: Tullylish DN 12; 146

Lenaderg mill [V]: Tullylish DN 12; 146

Lenaderg mill [VI]: Tullylish DN 12; 146

Lenaderg mill [VII]: Tullylish DN 12; 146

Lenaderg td: Tullylish DN 12; 143, 146

Lenagh cove: Drummaul AM 19; 88

Lenagh fort [I]: Drummaul AM 19; 78, 88

Lenagh fort [II]: Drummaul AM 19; 78, 88

Lenagh school: Drummaul AM 19; 77, 85

Lenagh td: Antrim AM 29; 3

Lenagh td: Drummaul AM 19; 90–91

Lenaghan hill: Inishmacsaint FH 14; 71

Lenaghan td: Inishmacsaint FH 14; 70

Lenamore (Lenymore) td: Magilligan LY 11; 95, 126

Lenamore Castle: Bovevagh LY 25; 15–16, 35–36

Lenamore Castle: Dungiven LY 15; 94

Lenamore hill: Dungiven LY 15; 70

Lenamore school: Dungiven LY 15; 18

Lenamore td: Banagher LY 30; 23

Lenamore td: Dungiven LY 15; 22, 26, 46, 62, 65, 70, 75, 83, 86, 94, 103

Lenan bay: Lough Swilly DL 38; 100, 131, 133

Lenan Point: Lough Swilly DL 38; 131

Lenan td: Clonmany DL 38; 13, 16, 18–20

Lenan td: Desertegney DL 38; 26

Lenan td: Lough Swilly DL 38; 136

Lendray, Robert: Carrickfergus AM 37; 194

Lendrum, George: Enniskillen FH 4; 59, 77, 82

Lendrum, George: Faughanvale LY 36; 40

Lendrum, George: Magheracross FH 14; 95, 97, 100–02

Lendrum, James: Dromore TE 5; 102

Lendrum, Mrs George: Magheracross FH 14; 99

Lendrum, Rev. William: Antrim AM 29; 27

Lendy, Antony: Kilmacteige SO 40; 193

Lenelea td: Conwal DL 39; 27

Lenioee (see Linwee): Kilmacteige SO 40; 191

Lenish flax mill: Clonduff DN 3; 3

Lenish td: Clonduff DN 3; 3

Lennan, Rev. Dr: Newry DN 3; 77, 80, 114

Lennard, J.B.: Aghavea FH 4; 25

Lennard, T.B.: Clones FH 4; 26, 29

Lennie, Hugh: Ballyscullion LY 6; 62

Lennon churn mill: Tullyaughnish DL 38; 85

Lennon fishery: Lough Swilly DL 38; 102

Lennon river: Kilmacrenan DL 38; 50

Lennon river: Tullyaughnish DL 38; 84–87, 91–92, 95

Lennon wharfs: Tullyaughnish DL 38; 87

Lennon, Charles: Island Magee AM 10; 94

Lennon, family: Ballynure AM 32; 56

Lennon, Henry: Ballynure AM 32; 61–62

Lennon, Robert: Tamlaght TE 20; 108

Lennox, Charles: Carrickfergus AM 37; 116

Lennox, Margaret: Desertmartin LY 31; 61

Lennox, R.A.: Dunboe LY 11; 56–57, 71

Lennox, Robert: Carrickfergus AM 37; 154, 156

Lennox, Robert: Tamlaght Finlagan LY 25; 80

Lenon, family: Ballynascreen LY 31; 12

Lenox, Andrew: Tamlaght O'Crilly LY 18; 125

Lenox, Henery: Tamlaght O'Crilly LY 18; 125

Lenox, John: Artrea LY 6; 23

Lenox, John: Magherafelt LY 6; 107

Leny, Y.: Kilmacteige SO 40; 194

Leonard, James: Drumkeeran FH 14; 65

Leppanbawn hill: Drung CN 40; 20

Leraw td: Aghalurcher FH 4; 14

Leryan school: Inishmacsaint FH 14; 79

Leslanow district: Templecorran AM 26; 82

Lesley Hill House: Drumtullagh AM 16; 101

Lesley, family: Maghera LY 18; 13

Lesley, Rev. Henry: Misc. DN 17; 117, 133

Leslie and Co., Messrs: Drumgoon CN 40; 9

Leslie Hill Castle: Ballymoney AM 16; 21

Leslie Hill House: Ballymoney AM 16; 1, 6, 9, 13, 23

Leslie Hill House: Drumtullagh AM 16; 96

Leslie Hill House: Raphoe DL 39; 124

Leslie Hill House: Raymoghy DL 39; 134

Leslie td: Clogher TE 5; 43

Leslie, A.: Raymoghy DL 39; 142

Leslie, C.A.: Aughnamullen MN 40; 75

Leslie, C.A.: Ballee DN 17; 22–23

Leslie, C.A.: Ballybay MN 40; 79–82, 84

Leslie, C.A.: Bright DN 17; 35

Leslie, C.A.: Down DN 17; 52, 57

Leslie, C.A.: Saul DN 17; 114

Leslie, C.P.: Templecarn DL 39; 160–61, 163, 167

Leslie, C.W.: Coleraine LY 33; 63

Leslie, Col: Ematris MN 40; 119

Leslie, D.: Aughnamullen MN 40; 76

Leslie, Henry: Aghalurcher FH 4; 8, 14

Leslie, Henry: Coleraine LY 33; 63

Leslie, Henry: Kilroot AM 26; 73

Leslie, J.E.: Coleraine LY 33; 63, 127

Leslie, James (Jnr): Ballywillin LY 33; 29, 33, 36

Leslie, James: Ballymoney AM 16; 1, 9, 15–16, 23

Leslie, James: Derrykeighan AM 16; 88

Leslie, James: Drumtullagh AM 16; 96

Leslie, James: Dunluce AM 16; 105, 110, 115, 121

Leslie, John: Errigal LY 27; 58

Leslie, Maj.: Aghalurcher FH 4; 11

Leslie, Mr (Donaghadee): Saintfield DN 7; 118

Leslie, Mr: Ballymoney AM 16; 13

Leslie, Mrs: Blaris AM 8; 85

Leslie, Mrs C.A.: Donagh MN 40; 98–101, 103

Leslie, Mrs C.P.: Templecarn DL 39; 161

Leslie, Rev.: Carnmoney AM 2; 84

Leslie, Rev.: Glynn AM 26; 39

Leslie, Rev.: Island Magee AM 10; 86

Leslie, Rev. Charles: Misc. DL 39; 186

Leslie, Rev. Edmund: Blaris AM 8; 55

Leslie, Rev. H.T.: Kilclief DN 17; 78–79, 79

Leslie, Rev. Henry: Ahoghill AM 23; 33

Leslie, Rev. Henry: Carrickfergus AM 37; 102

Leslie, Rev. Henry: Down DN 17; 47

Leslie, Rev. Henry: Templecorran AM 26; 97, 107

Leslie, Rev. John: Clogher TE 5; 28

Leslie, Rev. John: Raphoe DL 39; 122

Leslie, Rev. John: Raymoghy DL 39; 132–34, 136–42

Leslie, Rev. Robert: Clogher TE 5; 28

Leslie, Rev. Thomas: Seagoe AH 1; 103

Leslie, Robert: Ballymoney AM 16; 17

Leslie, Widow (Glaslough): Errigal Keerogue TE 20; 48

Lesly, John: Dunboe LY 11; 77

Lesly, Mrs: Carrickfergus AM 37; 28

Lesly, Robert: Carrickfergus AM 37; 112

Lesly, William: Kilcronaghan LY 31; 84

Less (see Sess): Errigal Keerogue TE 20; 48

Lessons td: Saintfield DN 7; 118

Lester, family: Ramoan AM 24; 107

Lester, Jean: Ramoan AM 24; 120

Lester, Patt: Ramoan AM 24; 120

Lester, Thomas: Blaris AM 8; 25

Lestly, George: Dunboe LY 11; 81

Letfern bridge: Clogherny TE 20; 27

Letfern bridge: Donacavey TE 5; 64
Letfern forts: Clogherny TE 20; 28
Letgallen spade manufactory: Clones FH 4; 28
Letgallen td: Clones FH 4; 28
LeTournell, family: Enniskillen FH 4; 58
Letrim bog: Misc. DL 39; 187
Letrim td: Misc. DL 39; 194
Lett flax mill: Killevy AH 1; 54
Lett school: Killevy AH 1; 54
Lett td: Misc. DN 17; 130–31
Lett, Rev. Charles: Hillsborough DN 12; 87, 91, 97,
    100, 102–03
Letter river: Templecarn DL 39; 166
Letter td: Clonmany DL 38; 18, 20
Letterbailey td: Enniskillen FH 4; 82
Letterbreen police station: Cleenish FH 14; 22
Letterbreen td: Cleenish FH 14; 28–29
Letterbrick td: Kilteevoge DL 39; 114
Letterbrone td: Kilmacteige SO 40; 193, 196
Lettercran td: Templecarn DL 39; 164
Lettercrum (see Lattacrom): Aughnamullen MN 40;
    69
Letteree mountain: Dromore TE 5; 93
Letteree td: Dromore TE 5; 99
Letteree td: Magheraculmoney FH 14; 111
Lettergash (Lettergesh) td: Dromore TE 5; 99
Lettergash hill: Dromore TE 5; 93
Lettergash td: Magheraculmoney FH 14; 110
Lettergreen td: Galloon FH 4; 95
Lettergull (Lettergul) td: Taughboyne DL 39; 148,
    153, 196
Lettergull Sunday school: Taughboyne DL 39; 153
Letterkeen glebe: Drumkeeran FH 14; 68
Letterkeen House: Drumkeeran FH 14; 65
Letterkeen school: Drumkeeran FH 14; 67
Letterkenny: Blaris AM 8; 73
Letterkenny: Clonleigh DL 39; 1, 3, 14, 16
Letterkenny: Coleraine LY 33; 95, 142
Letterkenny: Convoy DL 39; 18
Letterkenny: Conwal DL 39; 24–26
Letterkenny: Kilcronaghan LY 31; 81
Letterkenny: Kilmacrenan DL 38; 50–51
Letterkenny: Leck DL 39; 115, 117–18, 120
Letterkenny: Leckpatrick TE 5; 126
Letterkenny: Lough Swilly DL 38; 104, 106, 129
Letterkenny: Mevagh DL 38; 61
Letterkenny: Misc. DL 39; 189, 193
Letterkenny: Raphoe DL 39; 130
Letterkenny: Raymoghy DL 39; 133, 135, 142, 144
Letterkenny: Taughboyne DL 39; 153
Letterkenny: Tullaghobegley DL 39; 172–73
Letterkenny: Tullyaughnish DL 38; 87–89, 93–94
Letterkenny bridge: Leck DL 39; 120
Letterkenny chapel: Leck DL 39; 116
Letterkenny meeting house: Leck DL 39; 117

Letterkenny Old Town (see Old Town): Leck DL
    39; 115
Letterleague school [I]: Conwal DL 39; 27
Letterleague school [II]: Conwal DL 39; 27
Letterleague td: Conwal DL 39; 27
Letterloan bog: Macosquin LY 22; 78, 88, 113, 120
Letterloan school: Macosquin LY 22; 102
Letterloan td: Macosquin LY 22; 79
Letterlogher (see Letterlougher): Cumber LY 28; 5
Letterlougher td: Cumber LY 28; 67, 70, 113–14,
    119, 124, 126
Letterlougher Top hill: Cumber LY 28; 5–6
Lettermacaward district: Inishkeel DL 39; 70
Lettermire cove: Cumber LY 28; 43
Lettermire hill: Cumber LY 28; 45
Lettermire td: Cumber LY 28; 46, 48, 60, 63, 97,
    102, 105, 107
Lettermore td: Convoy DL 39; 21
Lettermore td: Kilmacteige SO 40; 193
Lettermuck bog: Cumber LY 28; 23
Lettermuck fort: Cumber LY 28; 47
Lettermuck paper mill: Cumber LY 28; 3–4, 18, 21,
    86–87, 126
Lettermuck td: Cumber LY 28; 6, 18, 67, 70, 87,
    114, 119, 124, 126
Lettermuck wood: Cumber LY 28; 119
Lettermunny td: Magheracross FH 14; 102
Lettershamboe school: Convoy DL 39; 22
Lettershamboe td: Convoy DL 39; 21
Lettershamboe td: Kilteevoge DL 39; 114
Lettershendony bog: Cumber LY 28; 43, 47, 49
Lettershendony Castle: Cumber LY 28; 27, 37, 49
Lettershendony td: Cumber LY 28; 49, 51, 60, 64,
    70, 97, 102, 105, 107
Lettersowrey village: Kilmacteige SO 40; 193
Lettery (Letterry) td: Errigal Keerogue TE 20; 49,
    54, 57
Lettice Land (see Scoutbush): Carrickfergus AM 37;
    84
Lettoonigan meeting house: Donagh MN 40; 100
Lettoonigan td: Donagh MN 40; 99
Levaghary (see Levaghery): Seagoe AH 1; 102
Levaghery (Levaghry) td: Seagoe AH 1; 102–03,
    109
Levaghery female school: Seagoe AH 1; 109
Levaghery male school: Seagoe AH 1; 109
Levaghy school: Derryvullan FH 14; 44
Levaghy td: Derryvullan FH 14; 39, 46
Levalleglish td: Loughgall AH 1; 75–76
Levallyclanone td: Kilbroney DN 3; 29, 32, 36
Levallyreagh td: Kilbroney DN 3; 32
Levans, Patrick: Carlingford LH 40; 60
Levarogue (see Leveroge): Drumbo DN 7; 63
Levelly Lower td: Devenish FH 14; 58
Levelly Rectory: Devenish FH 14; 55

Levelly school: Devenish FH 14; 55–56
Levelly Upper fort: Devenish FH 14; 55
Levelly Upper td: Devenish FH 14; 53, 58
Levellyreagh td: Dromara DN 12; 65
Lever, C.J.: Ballyaghran LY 33; 4, 6
Leveroge school: Drumbo DN 7; 59
Leveroge school: Hillsborough DN 12; 101
Leveroge td: Drumbo DN 7; 59–60, 63
Leverogue (see Leveroge): Drumbo DN 7; 59
Levillyclenone (see Levallyclanone)
Levingston, Jacob: Faughanvale LY 36; 16, 21
Levins, Mr (Brickfield): Killea and Taughboyne DL 39; 87
Levins' mill: Killea and Taughboyne DL 39; 87
Levistone, Samuel: Tamlaght Finlagan LY 25; 121
Lewens, family: Carnmoney AM 2; 76
Lewers, family: Ballee DN 17; 16
Lewes, family: Templecorran AM 26; 119
Lewis, Archie: Ahoghill AM 23; 34
Lewis, family: Carrickfergus AM 37; 93
Lewis, family: Templecorran AM 26; 117
Lewis, J.: Aughnamullen MN 40; 76
Lewis, James: Magheragall AM 21; 109–10
Lewis, John: Magheragall AM 21; 107
Lewis, Joseph: Magheragall AM 21; 106
Lewis, Mary: Muckamore AM 35; 81
Lewis, Mary Anne: Templecorran AM 26; 100, 129, 131
Lewis, Mr: Cumber LY 28; 27, 37, 49–50, 80
Lewis, Rev. J.E.: Dromore DN 12; 77
Lewis, Robert: Newtown Crommelin AM 13; 84
Lewrs, family: Carnmoney AM 2; 102
Lewson, Andrew: Derryaghy AM 8; 106
Lewson, family: Derryaghy AM 8; 103
Lewson, John: Derryaghy AM 8; 106
Lewson, Samuel: Lambeg AM 8; 140, 142
Lewson, William: Derryaghy AM 8; 106, 111–12
Lewson's flax mill: Derryaghy AM 8; 111
Leyud (Lugaid), St: Clonfeacle AH 1; 23
Lhan Idloes (Wales): Cumber LY 28; 59
Lhan Trisaint (Wales): Cumber LY 28; 59
Lhyn-y-cymmer (Wales): Cumber LY 28; 59
Lianfin school: Donacavey TE 5; 65
Lianfin td: Donacavey TE 5; 65
Libado hill: Raphoe DL 39; 129
Libado quarry: Raphoe DL 39; 129
Libbert (Libert) West td: Tickmacrevan AM 13; 123
Libbert school [I]: Tickmacrevan AM 13; 134
Libbert school [II]: Tickmacrevan AM 13; 134
Liberty of Carlingford td: Carlingford LH 40; 58–59
Liddle, Adam: Newry DN 3; 100, 104
Liddy, family: Lambeg AM 8; 135
Liddy, Mary: Carrickfergus AM 37; 117
Liddy, Richard: Newry DN 3; 95, 100–01, 104
Lienan (see Lenan): Lough Swilly DL 38; 131

Lienankeel locality: Lough Swilly DL 38; 131, 133
Lieutenant's well: Kilmacteige SO 40; 189, 196
Lievadinn lough: Donaghmoyne MN 40; 106
Liffin lough: Templecarn DL 39; 157
Liffock spring: Dunboe LY 11; 79
Liffock td: Dunboe LY 11; 62, 74
Lifford: Clondermot LY 34; 8, 83, 105
Lifford: Clonleigh DL 39; 1–4, 6, 8, 10, 13, 15–17
Lifford: Convoy DL 39; 18
Lifford: Desertegney DL 38; 28
Lifford: Drumachose LY 9; 94
Lifford: Drumragh TE 5; 107
Lifford: Dungiven LY 15; 34
Lifford: Faughanvale LY 36; 48
Lifford: Leck DL 39; 116
Lifford: Leckpatrick TE 5; 117, 121
Lifford: Misc. DL 39; 185–86, 188, 194
Lifford: Taughboyne DL 39; 151, 153
Lifford: Urney DL 39; 174
Lifford asylum: Clonleigh DL 39; 2, 16
Lifford barrack: Clonleigh DL 39; 2
Lifford bog: Misc. DL 39; 187
Lifford bridge: Clonleigh DL 39; 1, 7, 14, 16
Lifford bridge: Taughboyne DL 39; 149
Lifford Castle: Clonleigh DL 39; 14
Lifford church: Clonleigh DL 39; 1, 15
Lifford classical school: Clonleigh DL 39; 2, 5, 9, 15–16
Lifford court house: Clonleigh DL 39; 1
Lifford distillery: Clonleigh DL 39; 2
Lifford district: Clondermot LY 34; 35, 53
Lifford eel fishery: Clonleigh DL 39; 17
Lifford fishery: Clonleigh DL 39; 10, 17
Lifford gaol: Clonleigh DL 39; 1–2, 5, 7–9, 12, 14–16
Lifford hill: Clonleigh DL 39; 1
Lifford hospital: Clonleigh DL 39; 2, 5, 7, 11–12, 14
Lifford old barrack: Clonleigh DL 39; 12
Lifford old gaol: Clonleigh DL 39; 12
Lifford ph: Killea and Taughboyne DL 39; 79
Lifford ph: Raphoe DL 39; 129
Lifford ph: Taughboyne DL 39; 149, 152
Lifford post office: Clonleigh DL 39; 2
Lifford pump: Clonleigh DL 39; 7–8
Lifford school [I]: Clonleigh DL 39; 9
Lifford school [II]: Clonleigh DL 39; 9
Lifford sessions house: Clonleigh DL 39; 12
Lifford Suburbs td: Misc. DL 39; 197
Lifford td: Clonleigh DL 39; 12, 16, 197
Lifford Town Parks td: Clonleigh DL 39; 5
Lifford well: Clonleigh DL 39; 5
Lifford, Lady: Kilbroney DN 3; 33
Lifford, Lord: Blaris AM 8; 21
Lifford, Lord: Donaghmore DL 39; 36–39
Lifford, Viscount: Dromore TE 5; 93

Ligadow district: Misc. SO 40; 200

Ligamady (see Legamaddy): Bright DN 17; 37

Ligamagary td: Donacavey TE 5; 80

Ligar hill: Loughgall AH 1; 78

Ligar, C.W.: Aghadowey LY 22; 4, 15, 26–27

Ligar, C.W.: Aghanloo LY 11; 3–4, 22

Ligar, C.W.: Agivey LY 22; 41

Ligar, C.W.: Ahoghill AM 23; 27

Ligar, C.W.: Antrim AM 29; 5

Ligar, C.W.. Artrea LY 6; 22

Ligar, C.W.: Ballyaghran LY 33; 16

Ligar, C.W.: Ballywillin LY 33; 40

Ligar, C.W.: Banagher LY 30; 43, 54–55, 57, 113

Ligar, C.W.: Bovevagh LY 25; 19–20, 58–59

Ligar, C.W.: Clondermot LY 34; 96

Ligar, C.W.: Coleraine LY 33; 56

Ligar, C.W.: Culfeightrin AM 24; 41

Ligar, C.W.: Cumber LY 28; 44, 79–80, 87

Ligar, C.W.: Desertlyn LY 31; 36, 38, 42, 47

Ligar, C.W.: Errigal LY 27; 49, 68

Ligar, C.W.: Killelagh LY 27; 99

Ligar, C.W.: Killowen LY 33; 161–62

Ligar, C.W.: Kilmacrenan DL 38; 50

Ligar, C.W.: Lissan LY 31; 108

Ligar, C.W.: Macosquin LY 22; 97

Ligar, C.W.: Maghera LY 18; 10

Ligar, C.W.: Magheramesk AM 21; 121

Ligar, C.W.: Misc. AM 10; 129

Ligar, C.W.: Misc. LY 36; 117

Ligar, C.W.: Raloo AM 32; 82

Ligar, C.W.: Ramoan AM 24; 113

Ligar, C.W.: Rathlin Island AM 24; 131

Ligar, C.W.: Tamlaght Finlagan LY 25; 86, 90, 112–15

Ligat, Rev. (co. Down): Aghadowey LY 22; 26

Ligatiggle (see Leggatiggle)

Ligatigle (see Leggatiggle)

Ligawherry fort: Kilraghts AM 16; 133

Ligawherry td: Kilraghts AM 16; 131, 134–35

Ligfordrum mountain: Ardstraw TE 5; 2

Ligg flax mill: Faughanvale LY 36; 16, 22, 98

Ligg standing stones: Faughanvale LY 36; 11, 15

Ligg tappatouzee: Faughanvale LY 36; 15

Ligg td: Faughanvale LY 36; 17, 22, 53, 59–60, 69, 76, 88, 95

Liggat, Abraham: Killead AM 35; 38, 52

Liggat, family: Killead AM 35; 17

Liggat, Mrs Abraham: Killead AM 35; 50

Liggat's quarry: Longfield TE 5; 132

Liggatiggle (see Leggatiggle)

Ligget, Rev. George: Garvaghy DN 12; 84

Light House Island: Bangor DN 7; 21

Light House Island: Misc. DN 17; 121

Light House Island lighthouse: Bangor DN 7; 21

Lighton, James: Dunboe LY 11; 77

Lighton, Rev. John: Donaghmore DL 39; 33

Lighton, Thomas: Drumachose LY 9; 116

Lignaboy Point: Glenavy AM 21; 82

Lignagopag mountain: Donaghedy TE 5; 89

Lignahuller district: Lough Swilly DL 38; 119

Lignakillagh graveyard: Loughguile AM 13; 68, 72

Lignamonag (see Lisnamanny)

Lignatheau (see Legnatraw)· Killea and Taughboyne DL 39; 82

Lignathraw (see Legnatraw): Killea and Taughboyne DL 39; 87

Lignatra (see Legnatraw): Taughboyne DL 39; 150

Liken, Thomas: Coleraine LY 33; 72

Lilley, Mr: Down DN 17; 42

Lilly, family: Magherafelt LY 6; 95

Lilly, George: Hillsborough DN 12; 106

Lilly, John: Hillsborough DN 12; 106

Lilly, Miss: Ahoghill AM 23; 19–20

Lilly, Robert: Hillsborough DN 12; 106

Lilly, Thomas: Magherafelt LY 6; 107, 112

Limavady (see also Newtownlimavady)

Limavady Castle: Aghanloo LY 11; 4

Limavady Castle: Drumachose LY 9; 108–09

Limavady Castle: Magilligan LY 11; 92

Limavady manor: Drumachose LY 9; 84, 97

Limavady td: Clondermot LY 34; 107

Limavallaghan corn mill: Dunaghy AM 13; 13

Limavallaghan flax mill: Dunaghy AM 13; 13

Limavallaghan school: Dunaghy AM 13; 17

Limavallaghan td: Dunaghy AM 13; 13

Lime Park House: Desertcreat TE 20; 34

Limehill td: Desertcreat TE 20; 34

Limeneagh td: Ballintoy AM 24; 10

Limenenagh td: Carlingford LH 40; 58

Limepark Lodge: Aghaloo TE 20; 1

Limerick: Coleraine LY 33; 126

Limerick county: Clondermot LY 34; 60

Limerick county: Cumber LY 28; 60

Limerick county: Faughanvale LY 36; 53

Limerick, Bishop of: Tamlaght O'Crilly LY 18; 101

Limerick, George: Tamlaght Finlagan LY 25; 83, 121

Limerick, John: Coleraine LY 33; 67, 69, 136

Limerick, Samuel: Drumachose LY 9; 104

Limerick, Samuel: Tamlaght Finlagan LY 25; 83, 111, 121

Liminary (Leminary) td: Ballyclug AM 23; 52–53, 59

Liminary cave: Ballyclug AM 23; 64

Liminary school: Ballyclug AM 23; 59–60

Limineaghs (see Limeneagh): Ballintoy AM 24; 10

Lincension td: Clogher TE 5; 53

Lindisfarne (England): Magilligan LY 11; 88

Lindon and Co., Messrs: Carrickfergus AM 37; 57, 140

Lindon, Rev. Bernard: Donegore AM 29; 126, 129
Lindsay, Capt.: Clondermot LY 34; 27
Lindsay, David: Annaclone DN 12; 15
Lindsay, David: Clonallan DN 3; 2
Lindsay, David: Clonduff DN 3; 4
Lindsay, David: Dromara DN 12; 68
Lindsay, David: Dromore DN 12; 77
Lindsay, David: Drumballyroney DN 3; 17
Lindsay, David: Drumgath DN 3; 20
Lindsay, David: Dunboe LY 11; 56, 70
Lindsay, David: Seapatrick DN 12; 125
Lindsay, family: Ballyclug AM 23; 63
Lindsay, family: Magherafelt LY 6; 95
Lindsay, family: Templepatrick AM 35; 118
Lindsay, Francis: Ballyscullion LY 6; 69, 71
Lindsay, Francis: Clonduff DN 3; 5
Lindsay, Gabriel: Ballyscullion LY 6; 57
Lindsay, J.: Magherally DN 12; 113
Lindsay, James: Templepatrick AM 35; 132
Lindsay, John: Artrea TE 20; 6
Lindsay, John: Clondermot LY 34; 30, 79–80
Lindsay, Messrs James and Sons: Clonduff DN 3; 5
Lindsay, Miss: Down DN 17; 59
Lindsay, Robert: Carrickfergus AM 37; 108
Lindsay, Robert: Desertcreat TE 20; 34
Lindsay, Thomas: Clondermot LY 34; 100
Lindsay, Thomas: Faughanvale LY 36; 40
Lindsay's mill [I]: Clonduff DN 3; 5
Lindsay's mill [II]: Clonduff DN 3; 5
Lindsey, family: Ramoan AM 24; 107
Linen Hill corn mill: Newry DN 3; 82, 111
Linen Hill flax mill: Newry DN 3; 83, 111
Linen Hill House: Newry DN 3; 111
Liness, Joseph: Muckamore AM 35; 79
Liness, Thomas: Muckamore AM 35; 79
Ling corn mill: Cumber LY 28; 86, 124
Ling td: Cumber LY 28; 30, 67, 70, 114, 119–20,
    124, 126
Linigam, Dorathea: Coleraine LY 33; 146
Linn locality: Billy AM 16; 67
Linn waterfall: Ballylinny AM 32; 12
Linn, family: Culfeightrin AM 24; 59
Linn, family: Island Magee AM 10; 70
Linn, John: Blaris DN 12; 42
Linn, John: Ramoan AM 24; 107, 109, 113
Linn, Kitty-Anne: Carrickfergus AM 37; 114
Linn, Michael: Blaris DN 12; 46, 50
Linn, Mr: Lambeg AM 8; 142
Linn, Rev.: Misc. LY 36; 112
Linnon, family: Maghera LY 18; 48
Linsay, E.J.: Killyleagh DN 17; 86
Linsay, James: Ballyscullion AM 19; 13
Linsay, John: Ballyscullion AM 19; 13
Linsay, Margaret: Ballyscullion AM 19; 13
Linsay, Robert: Billy AM 16; 75

Linsey, Eliza: Drumachose LY 9; 134
Linsey, James: Drumachose LY 9; 134
Linsey, Sarah: Drumachose LY 9; 134
Linsfort church: Desertegney DL 38; 25–26
Linsfort corn mill: Desertegney DL 38; 26
Linsfort fort: Desertegney DL 38; 26
Linsfort school: Desertegney DL 38; 27
Linsfort td: Desertegney DL 38; 24–26, 29
Linton, Andrew: Dundermot AM 13; 35
Linton, Anne: Desertoghill LY 27; 20
Linton, Archabald: Desertoghill LY 27; 20
Linton, Catherine (Jnr): Desertoghill LY 27; 20
Linton, Catherine (Snr): Desertoghill LY 27; 20
Linton, David: Desertoghill LY 27; 27
Linton, James: Desertoghill LY 27; 20
Linton, John: Magilligan LY 11; 135, 139
Linton, Joseph: Desertoghill LY 27; 20
Linton, Margaret: Desertoghill LY 27; 20
Linton, Martha: Desertoghill LY 27; 20
Linton, Mary: Carrickfergus AM 37; 115
Linton, Robert: Dundermot AM 13; 35
Linton, Robert: Saul DN 17; 113
Linton, Thomas: Desertoghill LY 27; 20
Linton, William: Desertoghill LY 27; 5, 25
Linuthraive (see Legnatraw): Killea and
    Taughboyne DL 39; 80
Linwee river: Kilmacteige SO 40; 191, 195
Lionel, son of Edward III: Dungiven LY 15; 31
Lions, family: Ballintoy AM 24; 20
Lions, family: Culfeightrin AM 24; 59
Lios Bunny (see Lisbunny): Cumber LY 28; 67
Lios Glas (see Lisglass): Clondermot LY 34; 56
Lios Neill (see Lisneal): Clondermot LY 34; 56
Liosahawly (see Lissahawley): Clondermot LY 34;
    57
Liosnagelvin (see Lisnagelvin): Clondermot LY 34;
    56
Liossaghmore (see Lisaghmore): Clondermot LY 34;
    56
Lipsett, John: Ballywillin LY 33; 39
Lipsie, Mr: Macosquin LY 22; 96
Lisaburny forts: Ardstraw TE 5; 12
Lisaburny td: Ardstraw TE 5; 12
Lisachory (see Lissahawley)
Lisachrin (Lissachrin) td: Desertoghill LY 27; 3, 11,
    19, 24, 26, 29
Lisachrin bog: Desertoghill LY 27; 17
Lisachrin cairn: Desertoghill LY 27; 7
Lisachrin fort [I]: Desertoghill LY 27; 24
Lisachrin fort [II]: Desertoghill LY 27; 24
Lisachrin fort [III]: Desertoghill LY 27; 24
Lisachrin fort [IV]: Desertoghill LY 27; 24
Lisachrin well: Desertoghill LY 27; 6, 24
Lisacullion td: Magheross MN 40; 143, 148
Lisadian meeting house: Loughgilly AH 1; 86

Lisadian td: Hillsborough DN 12; 86, 106

Lisadian td: Loughgilly AH 1; 85

Lisaghmore Castle: Clondermot LY 34; 49

Lisaghmore quarry: Clondermot LY 34; 132

Lisaghmore td: Clondermot LY 34; 38, 44, 49–50, 56, 72, 111–12, 115, 118, 126, 132

Lisagorry Glebe td: Galloon FH 4; 97

Lisahawley (see Lissahawley): Clondermot LY 34; 76

Lisahully hamlet: Kilbarron DL 39; 77

Lisamore (see Lisaghmore): Clondermot LY 34; 38

Lisanadin td: Dromore TE 5; 93

Lisananybeg td: Emlaghfad SO 40; 176

Lisaneill (see Lisoneill): Aghalurcher FH 4; 6

Lisanelly demesne: Cappagh TE 5; 19–20

Lisanelly House: Cappagh TE 5; 17

Lisanelly plantation: Cappagh TE 5; 17

Lisaniske House: Magheross MN 40; 145

Lisaniske td: Magheross MN 40; 148

Lisanore (see Lisanoure)

Lisanoure Castle: Coleraine LY 33; 64

Lisanoure Castle: Derrykeighan AM 16; 78

Lisanoure Castle: Loughguile AM 13; 59–62, 64, 68, 75–76

Lisanoure Castle church: Loughguile AM 13; 76

Lisanoure Cottage: Loughguile AM 13; 75

Lisanoure old castle: Loughguile AM 13; 76

Lisardboy (see Lisserboy): Newry DN 3; 105

Lisatoo hill: Laragh CN 40; 40

Lisatunny school: Ardstraw TE 5; 13

Lisavaddy (Lisavody) td: Donacavey TE 5; 76, 79, 83

Lisavady (see Lisavaddy)

Lisavogue corn mill: Kilmore AH 1; 71

Lisavogue fort: Kilmore AH 1; 71

Lisavogue td: Kilmore AH 1; 71

Lisawilling td: Dunboe LY 11; 75

Lisban (see Lisbane)

Lisbane chapel: Ardkeen DN 7; 2

Lisbane flax mill: Ardkeen DN 7; 2

Lisbane school: Tullynakill DN 7; 122

Lisbane td: Ardkeen DN 7; 2

Lisbane td: Ballymore AH 1; 15–18

Lisbane td: Bangor DN 7; 19

Lisbane td: Misc. DN 17; 124–25

Lisbane td: Saintfield DN 7; 120

Lisbane td: Saul DN 17; 114

Lisbane td: Tullynakill DN 7; 122–23

Lisbarnet school: Kilmood DN 7; 95

Lisbarnet td: Kilmood DN 7; 94–95

Lisbawn (Lisbane) td: Clogher TE 5; 36

Lisbeanduff (see Lisleanduff): Drung CN 40; 21

Lisbeg fort: Errigal LY 27; 79

Lisbeg td: Clogher TE 5; 39

Lisbellanagroagh cave [I]: Ballintoy AM 24; 22

Lisbellanagroagh cave [II]: Ballintoy AM 24; 22

Lisbellanagroagh cave [III]: Ballintoy AM 24; 22

Lisbellanagroagh druid's altar: Ballintoy AM 24; 22

Lisbellanagroagh druid's stone: Ballintoy AM 24; 22

Lisbellanagroagh fort [I]: Ballintoy AM 24; 21–22

Lisbellanagroagh fort [II]: Ballintoy AM 24; 22

Lisbellanagroagh fort [III]: Ballintoy AM 24; 22

Lisbellanagroagh giant's chair: Ballintoy AM 24; 21

Lisbellanagroagh school: Ballintoy AM 24; 17, 35

Lisbellanagroagh td: Ballintoy AM 24; 21–22

Lisbellanagroagh well: Ballintoy AM 24; 21–22

Lisbellaw: Cleenish FH 14; 15–16, 23, 27

Lisbellaw: Derrybrusk FH 4; 32

Lisbellaw: Derryvullan FH 14; 43

Lisbellaw: Enniskillen FH 4; 48, 70

Lisbellaw chapel (C): Cleenish FH 14; 16–17

Lisbellaw chapel (C): Derrybrusk FH 4; 31

Lisbellaw chapel (W) [I]: Cleenish FH 14; 16–17

Lisbellaw chapel (W) [II]: Cleenish FH 14; 16–17

Lisbellaw church: Cleenish FH 14; 16, 16

Lisbellaw corn mill: Cleenish FH 14; 18

Lisbellaw corn mill: Enniskillen FH 4; 48

Lisbellaw meeting house (P): Cleenish FH 14; 16

Lisbellaw meeting house (S): Cleenish FH 14; 17

Lisbellaw national school: Cleenish FH 14; 24

Lisbellaw police station: Cleenish FH 14; 22

Lisbellaw school: Cleenish FH 14; 16, 24

Lisblake td: Killesher FH 14; 87

Lisbofin (Lisboffin) td: Cleenish FH 14; 28–29

Lisbofin House: Cleenish FH 14; 17, 22

Lisbon: Enniskillen FH 4; 81

Lisbon: Misc. LY 31; 137

Lisbotweeney td: Donaghedy TE 5; 92

Lisboy (Lisbuie) td: Clogher TE 5; 33, 38–39, 46, 53

Lisboy (Lisbuoy) td: Kilraghts AM 16; 132, 135

Lisboy (Lisbuy) td: Saul DN 17; 114

Lisboy (Lissbuoy) td: Donacavey TE 5; 86

Lisboy cove [I]: Kilraghts AM 16; 131–32, 134

Lisboy cove [II]: Kilraghts AM 16; 131–32

Lisboy hill: Aghavea FH 4; 17

Lisboy standing stone: Kilraghts AM 16; 130, 133

Lisboy td: Aghadowey LY 22; 37

Lisboy td: Aghavea FH 4; 19, 23, 25

Lisboy windmill: Saul DN 17; 111

Lisbrannon fort: Ematris MN 40; 116

Lisbrannon td: Currin MN 40; 86, 91

Lisbreen fort: Skerry AM 13; 120

Lisbreen giant's grave: Skerry AM 13; 117

Lisbreen standing stone: Skerry AM 13; 120

Lisbreen td: Skerry AM 13; 117, 120–21

Lisbrinon (see Lisbrannon): Currin MN 40; 91

Lisbunney (see Lisbunny): Cumber LY 28; 73

Lisbunny quarry: Cumber LY 28; 124

Lisbunny school: Cumber LY 28; 73

Lisbunny td: Cumber LY 28; 67, 70–71, 114, 120, 124, 126

Lisbuoy (see Lisboy): Clogher TE 5; 39

Lisburn: Aghagallon AM 21; 1–2, 6, 10–11, 20, 22–23

Lisburn: Aghalee AM 21; 28–29, 31–34, 37

Lisburn: Annahilt DN 12; 22–23

Lisburn: Antrim AM 29; 6, 19, 22, 50

Lisburn: Ballee DN 17; 22

Lisburn: Ballinderry AM 21; 42, 44–46, 49–51, 58

Lisburn: Blaris AM 8; 1–3, 5–7, 14, 20, 23, 32, 45–47, 54, 56, 73, 77

Lisburn: Blaris DN 12; 26–27, 30, 32–34, 41–43, 45, 52, 54

Lisburn: Camlin AM 21; 62–63, 69

Lisburn: Carnmoney AM 2; 69

Lisburn: Clondermot LY 34; 30

Lisburn: Comber DN 7; 37–39

Lisburn: Derryaghy AM 8; 92, 119–21

Lisburn: Down DN 17; 58

Lisburn: Drumbeg AM 8; 122

Lisburn: Drumbeg DN 7; 52

Lisburn: Drumbo DN 7; 54, 58, 60

Lisburn: Dundonald DN 7; 65

Lisburn: Glenavy AM 21; 78, 81, 86–88

Lisburn: Hillsborough DN 12; 93, 98

Lisburn: Killead AM 35; 15, 17, 43

Lisburn: Killinchy DN 7; 88

Lisburn: Loughgilly AH 1; 84

Lisburn: Magheradrool DN 17; 105, 107

Lisburn: Magheragall AM 21; 98–104, 107, 109

Lisburn: Magheramesk AM 21; 112–20, 123, 128–30

Lisburn: Misc. AM 10; 129

Lisburn: Misc. DN 17; 117

Lisburn: Muckamore AM 35; 55, 60, 63–64, 75, 75

Lisburn: Seagoe AH 1; 107, 109

Lisburn: Templecorran AM 26; 117–18

Lisburn: Templepatrick AM 35; 145

Lisburn: Tullynakill DN 7; 123

Lisburn: Tullyrusk AM 21; 132, 134, 136–37

Lisburn academy: Blaris AM 8; 33, 40, 80, 82

Lisburn Bakery Entry poor house: Blaris AM 8; 63

Lisburn Bow St school: Blaris AM 8; 81

Lisburn brewery: Blaris AM 8; 67

Lisburn bridewell: Blaris AM 8; 49

Lisburn bridge: Blaris DN 12; 34

Lisburn Bridge St school: Blaris AM 8; 79, 82

Lisburn Bridge St school: Down DN 17; 59

Lisburn Bridge St Sunday school: Blaris AM 8; 84

Lisburn Castle: Blaris AM 8; 7, 22

Lisburn Castle St female school: Blaris AM 8; 79

Lisburn Castle St school [I]: Blaris AM 8; 79, 82

Lisburn Castle St school [II]: Blaris AM 8; 80–81

Lisburn Castle St school [III]: Blaris AM 8; 80–82, 85

Lisburn Castle St school [IV]: Blaris AM 8; 82

Lisburn Castle St school [V]: Blaris AM 8; 82

Lisburn cathedral: Blaris AM 8; 6–7, 23–25

Lisburn cathedral graveyard: Blaris AM 8; 20

Lisburn chapel (C): Blaris AM 8; 9–10, 26–27

Lisburn chapel (C): Blaris DN 12; 32, 83

Lisburn chapel (M): Magheramesk AM 21; 116

Lisburn chapel (NM): Blaris AM 8; 9–10, 24, 29, 31, 83–84

Lisburn chapel (PM): Blaris AM 8; 24, 30

Lisburn chapel (PWM): Blaris AM 8; 23–24, 30, 83

Lisburn chapel (WM): Blaris AM 8; 9–10, 24, 30–31, 83

Lisburn chapels (M): Blaris DN 12; 32

Lisburn cholera hospital: Blaris AM 8; 9, 40

Lisburn church: Blaris AM 8; 52

Lisburn church: Blaris DN 12; 27, 31–32

Lisburn church: Lambeg AM 8; 135

Lisburn church: Misc. DN 17; 118

Lisburn classical seminary: Blaris AM 8; 78, 86

Lisburn constabulary barrack: Blaris AM 8; 49

Lisburn corn market: Blaris AM 8; 11, 41–43, 59

Lisburn corn market: Blaris DN 12; 33, 39

Lisburn corn mill: Blaris AM 8; 36

Lisburn cotton manufactory: Blaris DN 12; 33

Lisburn court house: Aghagallon AM 21; 20

Lisburn court house: Blaris AM 8; 9, 11, 39, 49, 52–53, 55

Lisburn court house: Blaris DN 12; 39–41

Lisburn dispensary: Derryaghy AM 8; 112

Lisburn dispensary: Glenavy AM 21; 87

Lisburn dry dock: Blaris AM 8; 38

Lisburn female school: Blaris AM 8; 18, 32, 77, 83–84

Lisburn female Sunday school: Blaris AM 8; 83

Lisburn fever hospital: Blaris AM 8; 12, 39, 60–61, 86

Lisburn fever hospital: Blaris DN 12; 39, 41, 43

Lisburn flour mills: Blaris AM 8; 37

Lisburn flour mills: Blaris DN 12; 30

Lisburn free school: Blaris AM 8; 18, 31–32, 58, 61, 80, 82

Lisburn free school: Blaris DN 12; 32

Lisburn gasworks: Blaris AM 8; 37

Lisburn girls' school: Blaris DN 12; 32

Lisburn Glebe House: Blaris AM 8; 33

Lisburn infant school: Blaris AM 8; 18, 32, 78, 84

Lisburn infirmary: Aghagallon AM 21; 20

Lisburn infirmary: Aghalee AM 21; 37

Lisburn infirmary: Blaris AM 8; 9, 12, 63–65

Lisburn infirmary: Drumbeg AM 8; 130

Lisburn infirmary: Lambeg AM 8; 142

Lisburn infirmary: Magheramesk AM 21; 128

Lisburn ladies' school: Blaris AM 8; 33, 86
Lisburn linen hall: Blaris AM 8; 9, 11, 44
Lisburn linen manufactory: Blaris DN 12; 27
Lisburn long stone: Blaris AM 8; 19
Lisburn manor: Camlin AM 21; 69
Lisburn market house: Blaris AM 8; 9, 11, 42–43, 56
Lisburn market house: Blaris DN 12; 39–41
Lisburn meeting house (P): Blaris AM 8; 9, 24–26, 58, 84
Lisburn meeting house (P): Blaris DN 12; 32
Lisburn meeting house (Q): Blaris AM 8; 9–10, 24, 28–29
Lisburn meeting house (Q): Blaris DN 12; 32
Lisburn new bridge: Blaris AM 8; 13, 34
Lisburn new bridge: Blaris DN 12; 28
Lisburn old bridge: Blaris AM 8; 35
Lisburn old bridge: Blaris DN 12; 28
Lisburn ph: Blaris DN 12; 29, 32
Lisburn ph: Killyman TE 20; 68
Lisburn post office: Blaris AM 8; 12
Lisburn Presbyterian Sunday school: Blaris AM 8; 84
Lisburn private academy: Blaris AM 8; 18
Lisburn private schools: Blaris DN 12; 33
Lisburn public bakery: Blaris AM 8; 11
Lisburn pump: Blaris DN 12; 40–41
Lisburn Quakers school: Blaris AM 8; 81
Lisburn Quakers school: Blaris DN 12; 32
Lisburn quay bridge: Blaris AM 8; 35
Lisburn quays: Blaris AM 8; 39
Lisburn quays: Blaris DN 12; 39–41
Lisburn religious lending library: Blaris AM 8; 56
Lisburn shambles: Blaris AM 8; 33, 43
Lisburn shambles: Blaris DN 12; 11, 40–41
Lisburn sluice bridge: Blaris DN 12; 41
Lisburn Sunday school (C): Blaris AM 8; 83
Lisburn Sunday school (NM): Blaris AM 8; 83–84
Lisburn Sunday school (PWM): Blaris AM 8; 83
Lisburn Sunday school (WM): Blaris AM 8; 83
Lisburn Sunday school: Blaris AM 8; 83
Lisburn tanneries: Blaris DN 12; 32
Lisburn tanyard [I]: Blaris AM 8; 68
Lisburn tanyard [II]: Blaris AM 8; 68
Lisburn toll-gate: Blaris AM 8; 37
Lisburn vitriol works: Blaris AM 8; 17, 36
Lisburn vitriol works: Blaris DN 12; 27, 32
Lisburn widows' free houses: Blaris AM 8; 59
Lisbury (see Lisboy): Clogher TE 5; 53
Lisbwee bridge: Cappagh TE 5; 20
Liscall altar: Aghadowey LY 22; 32
Liscall altar: Errigal LY 27; 78
Liscall bogs: Errigal LY 27; 54
Liscall bridge: Errigal LY 27; 41, 59
Liscall fort: Errigal LY 27; 42, 69

Liscall giant's grave: Aghadowey LY 22; 32
Liscall giant's grave: Errigal LY 27; 78
Liscall mount: Errigal LY 27; 53–54
Liscall quarry: Errigal LY 27; 91
Liscall school: Errigal LY 27; 51–52
Liscall Sunday school: Errigal LY 27; 52
Liscall td: Errigal LY 27; 41, 60, 69, 82, 87–88, 91–92
Liscallaghan, name of: Clogher TE 5; 31
Lisclamerty td: Raymoghy DL 39; 138, 141, 192, 199
Liscleen td: Donaghedy TE 5; 92
Lisclone td: Laragh CN 40; 39
Liscloughan td: Drumgoon CN 40; 2
Liscolman cave: Billy AM 16; 74
Lisconan (see Lisconnan): Derrykeighan AM 16; 95
Lisconnan bog: Derrykeighan AM 16; 81
Lisconnan corn mill: Derrykeighan AM 16; 79, 84
Lisconnan forts: Derrykeighan AM 16; 80
Lisconnan House: Derrykeighan AM 16; 84
Lisconnan school [I]: Derrykeighan AM 16; 95
Lisconnan school [II]: Derrykeighan AM 16; 95
Lisconnan td: Derrykeighan AM 16; 78–80, 94–95
Lisconnan td: Kilwaughter AM 10; 112
Lisconrea td: Donacavey TE 5; 67, 79
Liscooley bridge: Donaghmore DL 39; 30, 34
Liscooley td: Donaghmore DL 39; 30, 38
Liscorgan (see Lisgorgan): Tamlaght O'Crilly LY 18; 136
Liscosker td: Aghavea FH 4; 23
Liscrievan lough: Derryvullan FH 14; 31
Lisdalgan td: Saintfield DN 7; 117, 120
Lisdalgon (see Lisdalgan): Saintfield DN 7; 117
Lisdead school: Devenish FH 14; 50
Lisdergan td: Donacavey TE 5; 79, 81, 83
Lisdhu House: Tullyniskan TE 20; 139–40
Lisdillon bog: Clondermot LY 34; 15, 25, 97, 105
Lisdillon flax mill: Clondermot LY 34; 132
Lisdillon glen: Clondermot LY 34; 1, 17
Lisdillon river: Clondermot LY 34; 3, 18
Lisdillon school: Clondermot LY 34; 42, 88, 90–92, 95–96
Lisdillon Sunday school [I]: Clondermot LY 34; 42, 92
Lisdillon Sunday school [II]: Clondermot LY 34; 92–93
Lisdillon td: Clondermot LY 34; 33, 36, 38, 56, 71, 71, 74, 76, 111–13, 118, 126, 132
Lisdillon wood: Clondermot LY 34; 4, 18–19
Lisdivin td: Donaghedy TE 5; 92
Lisdivrick church: Killesher FH 14; 90
Lisdivrick school: Killesher FH 14; 86
Lisdoagh school: Drumgoon CN 40; 11
Lisdonney fort: Muckno MN 40; 166
Lisdonogh giant's grave: Aughnamullen MN 40; 74

Lisdoo House: Skirts of Urney and Ardstraw TE 5; 141

Lisdooden hill: Devenish FH 14; 47

Lisdooden td: Devenish FH 14; 47

Lisdoonan chapel: Donaghmoyne MN 40; 107

Lisdoonan chapel of ease: Donaghmoyne MN 40; 107

Lisdoonan td: Saintfield DN 7; 118, 120

Lisdreenagh locality: Clondermot LY 34; 63

Lisdromturk bog: Magheross MN 40; 143

Lisdromturk td: Magheross MN 40; 148

Lisdronturk (see Lisdromturk): Magheross MN 40; 143

Lisdrum abbey: Aghalurcher FH 4; 6

Lisdrum abbey: Aghavea FH 4; 21, 25

Lisdrum demesne: Aghavea FH 4; 18

Lisdrum hill: Aghavea FH 4; 17

Lisdrum td: Aghalurcher FH 4; 6

Lisdrum td: Aghavea FH 4; 25

Lisdrumalane (see Lisdrumclave): Aughnamullen MN 40; 69

Lisdrumclave td: Aughnamullen MN 40; 69, 71, 76

Lisdrumcore (Lisdrumwhorr) Upper td: Loughgilly AH 1; 85

Lisdrumcore bleach mill [I]: Loughgilly AH 1; 87

Lisdrumcore bleach mill [II]: Loughgilly AH 1; 87

Lisdrumcore cotton manufactory: Loughgilly AH 1; 87

Lisdrumcore flax mill: Loughgilly AH 1; 86

Lisdrumcore Lower td: Loughgilly AH 1; 85

Lisdrumcore mill [I]: Loughgilly AH 1; 86–87

Lisdrumcore mill [II]: Loughgilly AH 1; 86

Lisdrumcore school: Loughgilly AH 1; 86

Lisdrumgullion flour mill: Killevy AH 1; 54

Lisdrumher (see Lisdrumcore): Loughgilly AH 1; 86

Lisdrumhorr (see Lisdrumcore): Loughgilly AH 1; 86

Lisduff bog: Aughnamullen MN 40; 70

Lisduff td: Aughnamullen MN 40; 76

Lisduff td: Newry DN 3; 106

Lisenadin td: Dromore TE 5; 99

Liserboy (see Lisserboy)

Liserill td: Magheross MN 40; 148

Liseveny fort: Ematris MN 40; 116

Lisfannan bay: Lough Swilly DL 38; 133

Lisfannan bed: Lough Swilly DL 38; 104

Lisfannan td: Lough Swilly DL 38; 103, 139

Lisfannon (see Lisfannan)

Lisfearty meeting house: Killeeshil TE 20; 64

Lisfordrum mountain: Ardstraw TE 5; 10

Lisgarrin day school: Clogher TE 5; 43

Lisgillan td: Aughnamullen MN 40; 76

Lisglas (see Lisglass): Clondermot LY 34; 38

Lisglass fort: Ballynure AM 32; 57

Lisglass fort: Clondermot LY 34; 71

Lisglass td: Clondermot LY 34; 38, 56, 71, 111–12, 118, 126, 132

Lisgoagh td: Donagh MN 40; 98

Lisgonnell td: Errigal Keerogue TE 20; 54, 57

Lisgool abbey: Rossorry FH 14; 117

Lisgool and Shankill manor: Cleenish FH 14; 21, 23, 28

Lisgool priory: Cleenish FH 14; 21

Lisgool priory: Enniskillen FH 4; 70

Lisgool td: Rossorry FH 14; 115, 117

Lisgorgan bogs: Tamlaght O'Crilly LY 18; 86–87, 130–31

Lisgorgan Glebe fort: Tamlaght O'Crilly LY 18; 115

Lisgorgan Glebe td: Tamlaght O'Crilly LY 18; 138

Lisgorgan td: Tamlaght O'Crilly LY 18; 97, 136

Lisgorman forts: Manorhamilton Union LM 40; 52

Lisgorran school: Clogher TE 5; 42

Lisgorran td: Aughnamullen MN 40; 76

Lisgorran td: Clogher TE 5; 36, 42

Lisgould manor: Misc. FH 4; 133

Lishe Upper district: Blaris AM 8; 87

Lisheffield (see Lissheffield): Kilmore AH 1; 69

Lishill district: Killea and Taughboyne DL 39; 87

Lishnagorp fort: Bovevagh LY 25; 14, 34–35

Lisinisky td: Aughnamullen MN 40; 76

Lisivisaladan (Lissavishaludhan) fort: Maghera LY 18; 46, 62

Liskermalane td: Donacavey TE 5; 81

Liskey (Lishy) td: Clonleigh DL 39; 12, 198

Liskey td: Donacavey TE 5; 77, 81, 83

Liskeyborough fort: Kilmore AH 1; 71

Liskeyborough td: Kilmore AH 1; 60–61, 69, 71, 73

Liskmacloskey church: Duneane AM 19; 96

Lisky (see Liskey): Misc. DL 39; 198

Lisky td: Ardstraw TE 5; 2

Lisky td: Donacavey TE 5; 77, 79, 81

Lislabban cove: Loughguile AM 13; 71

Lislabban td: Loughguile AM 13; 71

Lislagan td: Donacavey TE 5; 77

Lislamfield fort: Aghabog MN 40; 64

Lislane (Lislain) td: Clogher TE 5; 37, 46, 53

Lislane bridge: Balteagh LY 9; 5, 42

Lislane fort: Balteagh LY 9; 12, 19, 25

Lislane meeting house: Balteagh LY 9; 3

Lislane school: Balteagh LY 9; 16–18, 39

Lislane td: Balteagh LY 9; 3, 12, 16–19, 21, 25, 39, 44–45

Lislaris td: Galloon FH 4; 95

Lislea (Lislee) td: Clogher TE 5; 26, 37, 42, 44, 53

Lislea bog: Drumgoon CN 40; 7

Lislea bog: Kilmacteige SO 40; 186

Lislea bog: Kilrea LY 27; 107

Lislea fort: Aghabog MN 40; 64

Lislea fort: Ardstraw TE 5; 12

Lislea school: Clogher TE 5; 42–43

Lislea school: Currin MN 40; 93
Lislea school: Kilrea LY 27; 121
Lislea Sunday school: Kilrea LY 27; 122
Lislea td: Carlingford LH 40; 58
Lislea td: Galloon FH 4; 87–88, 91, 95
Lislea td: Kilmacteige SO 40; 188, 196
Lislea td: Kilrea LY 27; 115, 129
Lisleanduff corn mill: Drung CN 40; 21
Lisleanduff school: Drung CN 40; 22
Lisleanduff td: Drung CN 40; 21
Lisleen chapel: Ardstraw TE 5; 11
Lisleen chapel: Skirts of Urney and Ardstraw TE 5; 138
Lisleen flax mill: Comber DN 7; 30, 35, 38
Lisleen td: Aghanloo LY 11; 31
Lisleen td: Comber DN 7; 30, 35, 37–38, 42–43
Lisleen td: Skirts of Urney and Ardstraw TE 5; 138
Lisleglish school: Loughgall AH 1; 81
Lislooney meeting house: Tynan AH 1; 127
Lislooney td: Tynan AH 1; 129
Lislunshion fort: Ematris MN 40; 116
Lislymore fort: Ardstraw TE 5; 12
Lislymore td: Ardstraw TE 5; 12
Lismacarol (Lioscarrole) td: Clondermot LY 34; 56, 70–71, 111–13, 118–19, 126, 132
Lismacarol corn mill: Clondermot LY 34; 132
Lismacarol flax mill: Clondermot LY 34; 132
Lismacarol quarry: Clondermot LY 34; 132
Lismacarrol (see Lismacarol)
Lismacloskey (Lisknalisky) td: Duneane AM 19; 94, 121, 123–24
Lismacloskey church: Duneane AM 19; 100–01
Lismacloskey school: Duneane AM 19; 105
Lismagonaway fort: Aghabog MN 40; 64
Lismagonaway lough: Aghabog MN 40; 62
Lismagonaway school: Aghabog MN 40; 65
Lismalore td: Aghavea FH 4; 23
Lismanary (see Lismenary): Ballynure AM 32; 61
Lismenary cave: Ballynure AM 32; 61–62, 67
Lismenary fort: Ballynure AM 32; 61, 63
Lismenary td: Ballycor AM 32; 9
Lismenary td: Ballynure AM 32; 63, 68
Lismenary well: Ballynure AM 32; 61
Lismiskie district: Misc. SO 40; 198
Lismochry (see Lismoghrey)
Lismodiffy (see Lismority)
Lismoghery (see Lismoghrey)
Lismoghrey td: Raymoghy DL 39; 138, 141, 199
Lismoile (see Lismoyle): Tamlaght O'Crilly LY 18; 136
Lismonaghan school: Kinawley FH 4; 111
Lismonaghan td: Kinawley FH 4; 110
Lismonaghan td: Leck DL 39; 119
Lismoney td: Lissan LY 31; 108
Lismontigley td: Raphoe DL 39; 126

Lismore abbey: Faughanvale LY 36; 60
Lismore Castle: Errigal Keerogue TE 20; 54
Lismore fort: Errigal Keerogue TE 20; 54
Lismore td: Clogher TE 5; 35, 53
Lismore td: Dunsfort DN 17; 72
Lismore td: Errigal Keerogue TE 20; 54, 57
Lismore wood: Errigal Keerogue TE 20; 54
Lismority (Lismoditty) td: Drumtullagh AM 16, 97, 101–03
Lismority cairn: Drumtullagh AM 16; 100, 102
Lismority fort: Drumtullagh AM 16; 100
Lismority hill: Drumtullagh AM 16; 97
Lismoyle bogs: Tamlaght O'Crilly LY 18; 86, 129
Lismoyle flax mill: Tamlaght O'Crilly LY 18; 91, 109
Lismoyle fort: Tamlaght O'Crilly LY 18; 95, 114
Lismoyle school: Tamlaght O'Crilly LY 18; 139, 143
Lismoyle Sunday school: Tamlaght O'Crilly LY 18; 143
Lismoyle td: Tamlaght O'Crilly LY 18; 96–97, 119, 129, 136, 138
Lismoyle well: Tamlaght O'Crilly LY 18; 114
Lismulkieme district: Misc. SO 40; 199
Lismulladown meeting house: Aghaloo TE 20; 4
Lismullyduff hill: Donaghmore DL 39; 28
Lismullyduff td: Donaghmore DL 39; 38
Lismullyduff trigonometrical station: Donaghmore DL 39; 34
Lismurnaghan (Lismornaghan) td: Ahoghill AM 23; 12
Lismurnaghan chapel: Ahoghill AM 23; 12
Lismurnaghan fort: Ahoghill AM 23; 35
Lismurphy (Lissmurphy) td: Macosquin LY 22; 85
Lismurphy fort: Macosquin LY 22; 85, 108
Lisnabane td: Aghavea FH 4; 17, 23, 25
Lisnabawn (see Lisnabane)
Lisnabert td: Donaghmore DL 39; 38
Lisnabilla forts: Magheramesk AM 21; 113, 124–26
Lisnabilla td: Magheramesk AM 21; 114
Lisnablagh td: Coleraine LY 33; 62
Lisnabragh coves: Derrykeighan AM 16; 91
Lisnabrague (Lisnabreig) td: Aghaderg DN 12; 2, 6, 8, 10, 12
Lisnabrague mill: Aghaderg DN 12; 12
Lisnabrague td: Misc. DN 17; 130–31
Lisnabreag (see Lisnabrague)
Lisnabulravey (see Lisnabulrevey)
Lisnabulrevey (Lisnabulravy) td: Donacavey TE 5; 77, 79, 81, 83, 86
Lisnabulrevey fort: Donacavey TE 5; 83
Lisnabunk district: Blaris AM 8; 86
Lisnabunny td: Errigal Keerogue TE 20; 48, 54
Lisnacannon fort: Rasharkin AM 23; 128, 137–38, 140

Lisnacannon hill: Rasharkin AM 23; 129

Lisnacerne hill: Drumgoon CN 40; 8

Lisnachrehog (see Lisnascreghog)

Lisnaclay clothier's mill: Drumgoon CN 40; 7

Lisnacloon flax mill: Termonamongan TE 5; 143

Lisnacloon House: Skirts of Urney and Ardstraw TE 5; 139

Lisnacloon House: Termonamongan TE 5; 143

Lisnacloon school: Termonamongan TE 5; 144

Lisnacloon td: Termonamongan TE 5; 143–45

Lisnaclusk (see Lismacloskey): Duneane AM 19; 105

Lisnacrappen td: Drumballyroney DN 3; 15, 18

Lisnacreaght corn mill: Ardstraw TE 5; 14

Lisnacreaght fort: Ardstraw TE 5; 12

Lisnacreaght td: Ardstraw TE 5; 12

Lisnacreeve (Lisnacrieve) td: Donacavey TE 5; 65–67, 77, 79–80, 83, 86

Lisnacreeve fort: Donacavey TE 5; 83

Lisnacreeve school: Donacavey TE 5; 65–66, 83

Lisnacreevy td: Drumballyroney DN 3; 18

Lisnacreive (see Lisnacreeve)

Lisnacrogher cave: Skerry AM 13; 119

Lisnacrogher fort: Skerry AM 13; 119

Lisnacrogher td: Skerry AM 13; 119

Lisnacullen (see Lisacullion): Magheross MN 40; 148

Lisnadara (see Lisnadaragh): Aughnamullen MN 40; 74

Lisnadaragh giant's grave: Aughnamullen MN 40; 74

Lisnadarragh td: Aughnamullen MN 40; 76

Lisnadarragh td: Drumlumman CN 40; 17

Lisnadil (see Lisnadill)

Lisnadill ph: Eglish AH 1; 43

Lisnadill ph: Loughgall AH 1; 75

Lisnadin td: Dromore TE 5; 97

Lisnaduff House: Dunluce AM 16; 110

Lisnadurk Middle td: Drummully FH 4; 34, 39

Lisnadurk North td: Drummully FH 4; 34, 39

Lisnadurk South td: Drummully FH 4; 34, 39

Lisnaferty fort: Ardstraw TE 5; 12

Lisnaferty td: Ardstraw TE 5; 12

Lisnafidilly td: Magheross MN 40; 148

Lisnafiffey td: Seapatrick DN 12; 124, 126

Lisnafiffey td: Tullylish DN 12; 143

Lisnafillen (see Lisnafillon): Ahoghill AM 23; 49

Lisnafillon (Lisnafallan) td: Ahoghill AM 23; 31

Lisnafillon bleach green: Ahoghill AM 23; 3, 13, 31

Lisnafillon House: Ahoghill AM 23; 12

Lisnafillon school: Ahoghill AM 23; 49

Lisnafin fort: Ardstraw TE 5; 12

Lisnafin td: Ardstraw TE 5; 12

Lisnagad (see Lisnagade): Aghaderg DN 12; 4

Lisnagade barrow: Misc. DN 17; 130

Lisnagade chapel: Aghaderg DN 12; 4, 10

Lisnagade fort: Aghaderg DN 12; 7

Lisnagade fort: Misc. DN 17; 130

Lisnagade House: Aghaderg DN 12; 10

Lisnagade moat: Misc. DN 17; 131

Lisnagade river: Misc. DN 17; 130

Lisnagade td: Aghaderg DN 12; 2, 5, 7, 10

Lisnagalliagh bleaching mills: Aughnamullen MN 40; 69, 72

Lisnagalliagh td: Aughnamullen MN 40; 76

Lisnagalt bogs: Ballyrashane LY 22; 56–57, 59

Lisnagalt fort [I]: Ballyrashane LY 22; 49, 58–59

Lisnagalt fort [II]: Ballyrashane LY 22; 49, 59

Lisnagannel td: Aghaderg DN 12; 2

Lisnagardy school: Donacavey TE 5; 65

Lisnagardy td: Donacavey TE 5; 65, 67, 77, 79, 81

Lisnagarron fort [I]: Ahoghill AM 23; 34

Lisnagarron fort [II]: Ahoghill AM 23; 34

Lisnagarron fort [III]: Ahoghill AM 23; 34

Lisnagarve school: Rasharkin AM 23; 135–36

Lisnagarvey (see Lisnagarvy)

Lisnagarvy (Lisnagarvie) td: Blaris AM 8; 3–4, 12–13, 20, 45, 77, 81–82, 87

Lisnagarvy bleaching mills: Blaris AM 8; 12

Lisnagarvy corn mill: Blaris AM 8; 13

Lisnagarvy flour mills: Blaris AM 8; 13

Lisnagarvy fort: Blaris AM 8; 20

Lisnagarvy td: Blaris DN 12; 28, 32–33

Lisnagarvy td: Magheragall AM 21; 100

Lisnagat fort: Drumtullagh AM 16; 100

Lisnagat td: Drumtullagh AM 16; 100, 103

Lisnagatt (see Lisnagalt): Ballyrashane LY 22; 56

Lisnageer flour and corn mill: Drumgoon CN 40; 7

Lisnageer hill: Drumgoon CN 40; 1

Lisnageer school: Drumgoon CN 40; 11

Lisnageera (see Lisnageer): Drumgoon CN 40; 7

Lisnageeragh (see Lisnageer): Drumgoon CN 40; 1

Lisnagelvin plough manufactory: Clondermot LY 34; 21, 30, 34

Lisnagelvin td: Clondermot LY 34; 56, 60, 67, 71–72, 79–80, 111–12, 119, 126, 132

Lisnagh fort: Derryvullan FH 14; 42

Lisnagh td: Derryvullan FH 14; 42

Lisnagile (see Lisnagannel): Aghaderg DN 12; 2

Lisnagillagan locality: Clondermot LY 34; 59

Lisnaginell (see Lisnagannel): Aghaderg DN 12; 2

Lisnagiseragh td: Magheross MN 40; 148

Lisnagoan bleachfield: Drumgoon CN 40; 7

Lisnagoan hill: Drumgoon CN 40; 1

Lisnagree corn mill: Kilmore AH 1; 60

Lisnagree meeting house: Ballymore AH 1; 10, 16

Lisnagree school: Ballymore AH 1; 11, 16

Lisnagree td: Ballymore AH 1; 10, 13–14, 16

Lisnagreggan forts: Drummaul AM 19; 78, 88

Lisnagrib bridge: Aghanloo LY 11; 23

Lisnagrib cave: Aghanloo LY 11; 5, 24
Lisnagrib forts: Aghanloo LY 11; 5, 25, 27
Lisnagrib school: Aghanloo LY 11; 31
Lisnagrib td: Aghanloo LY 11; 5, 23, 39–42
Lisnagroat (Lisnagrot) td: Kilrea LY 27; 106
Lisnagroat bog: Kilrea LY 27; 106
Lisnagroat bog: Tamlaght O'Crilly LY 18; 117, 128
Lisnagroat bridge [I]: Tamlaght O'Crilly LY 18; 92, 110
Lisnagroat bridge [II]: Tamlaght O'Crilly LY 18; 92, 110
Lisnagroat corn mill: Tamlaght O'Crilly LY 18; 91, 110, 125
Lisnagroat flax mill: Tamlaght O'Crilly LY 18; 91, 110
Lisnagroat forge: Kilrea LY 27; 112
Lisnagroat fort [I]: Tamlaght O'Crilly LY 18; 117
Lisnagroat fort [II]: Tamlaght O'Crilly LY 18; 117
Lisnagroat iron manufactory: Tamlaght O'Crilly LY 18; 95
Lisnagroat school: Tamlaght O'Crilly LY 18; 141–42
Lisnagroat td: Desertoghill LY 27; 15
Lisnagroat td: Tamlaght O'Crilly LY 18; 83, 86–87, 96–97, 125, 129, 136–37
Lisnagroat wood: Tamlaght O'Crilly LY 18; 87, 129
Lisnagunnen (see Lisnagannel): Aghaderg DN 12; 2
Lisnagunoge caves: Billy AM 16; 55–56, 62
Lisnagunoge church: Billy AM 16; 45
Lisnagunoge td: Billy AM 16; 45, 59, 65
Lisnagunoge Upper cave: Billy AM 16; 62
Lisnahay (Lisnahey) td: Carncastle and Killyglen AM 10; 7
Lisnahay North td: Carncastle and Killyglen AM 10; 1
Lisnahay school: Carncastle and Killyglen AM 10; 7–8
Lisnahay South private school: Carncastle and Killyglen AM 10; 7
Lisnahay South td: Carncastle and Killyglen AM 10; 7
Lisnahilt td: Racavan AM 13; 89
Lisnahulcheon (see Lisnahunshin): Ahoghill AM 23; 34
Lisnahunshin (Lisnahuncheon) td: Ahoghill AM 23; 27–28, 34–35, 39
Lisnahunshin bog: Ahoghill AM 23; 27, 35
Lisnahunshin forts: Ahoghill AM 23; 34–35
Lisnahunshin stone circles: Ahoghill AM 23; 27
Lisnakee td: Ballymore AH 1; 15–18
Lisnakilly hill: Tamlaght Finlagan LY 25; 81
Lisnakilly House: Tamlaght Finlagan LY 25; 82
Lisnakilly td: Tamlaght Finlagan LY 25; 72, 93
Lisnaknock td: Galloon FH 4; 95
Lisnalee flax mill: Loughgilly AH 1; 86

Lisnalee td: Loughgilly AH 1; 84
Lisnalinchy burn: Ballylinny AM 32; 12, 25
Lisnalinchy burn: Ballymartin AM 2; 3
Lisnalinchy cove: Ballylinny AM 32; 22
Lisnalinchy fort [I]: Ballylinny AM 32; 21–22, 24, 27
Lisnalinchy fort [II]: Ballylinny AM 32; 22, 24
Lisnalinchy hill: Ballylinny AM 32; 11
Lisnalinchy night school: Ballylinny AM 32; 23, 28
Lisnalinchy private school: Ballylinny AM 32; 23–24
Lisnalinchy school: Ballylinny AM 32; 23–25, 28, 30
Lisnalinchy Sunday school [I]: Ballylinny AM 32; 24, 28
Lisnalinchy Sunday school [II]: Ballylinny AM 32; 24
Lisnalinchy td: Ballylinny AM 32; 22, 30
Lisnally td: Ballymascanlan LH 40; 55
Lisnalong corn mill: Aughnamullen MN 40; 72
Lisnalong Cottage: Aughnamullen MN 40; 71
Lisnalong td: Aughnamullen MN 40; 76
Lisnalony (see Lisnalong): Aughnamullen MN 40; 71
Lisnalrain district: Blaris AM 8; 87
Lisnamallard brewery: Cappagh TE 5; 20
Lisnamallard mill: Galloon FH 4; 88
Lisnamallard td: Cappagh TE 5; 20
Lisnamallard td: Galloon FH 4; 88
Lisnamanny (Legnamanna) td: Dunaghy AM 13; 11, 18–19, 22–23
Lisnamanny cairns: Dunaghy AM 13; 18
Lisnamanny standing stones: Dunaghy AM 13; 18, 22–23
Lisnamaugheral school: Drumballyroney DN 3; 17–18
Lisnamaugheral td: Drumballyroney DN 3; 15, 18
Lisnamaughry td: Clogher TE 5; 53
Lisnamaul (Lisnemaule) td: Down DN 17; 53, 55, 57
Lisnamaul corn mill: Down DN 17; 49
Lisnamintry school: Seagoe AH 1; 102–03, 106, 109
Lisnamintry td: Seagoe AH 1; 109
Lisnamoghery td: Clogher TE 5; 35
Lisnamonag standing stones: Dunaghy AM 13; 23
Lisnamore flour mill: Kilmore DN 17; 88, 93
Lisnamore fort: Kilmore DN 17; 93
Lisnamore td: Kilmore DN 17; 92–93
Lisnamorrow fort: Artrea LY 6; 11, 24
Lisnamorrow House: Artrea LY 6; 9
Lisnamorrow td: Artrea LY 6; 8–9, 14, 24–25
Lisnamorrow td: Artrea TE 20; 7
Lisnamuck bog: Aghadowey LY 22; 2
Lisnamuck bridge: Misc. LY 31; 116
Lisnamuck fort: Maghera LY 18; 62

Lisnamuck td: Aghadowey LY 22; 37

Lisnamuck td: Kilcronaghan LY 31; 67, 79

Lisnamuck td: Maghera LY 18; 22, 45, 80–81

Lisnamulligan corn mill: Clonduff DN 3; 4

Lisnamulligan flax mill: Clonduff DN 3; 4

Lisnamulligan td: Clonduff DN 3; 4

Lisnamulligan td: Donaghmore DL 39; 38

Lisnamulligan td: Newry DN 3; 110

Lisnamurikin (see Lisnamurrikin)

Lisnamurrican (see Lisnamurrikin)

Lisnamurriken (see Lisnamurrikin)

Lisnamurrikin cove: Racavan AM 13; 102

Lisnamurrikin flax mill: Racavan AM 13; 92, 99

Lisnamurrikin fort: Racavan AM 13; 101, 104

Lisnamurrikin td: Racavan AM 13; 86, 89, 99,
    101–02

Lisnamusky fort: Aghabog MN 40; 64

Lisnanduff school: Dunluce AM 16; 122

Lisnaniske (see Lisaniske): Magheross MN 40; 148

Lisnanon td: Donaghedy TE 5; 92

Lisnarable chapel: Clogher TE 5; 44

Lisnarable td: Clogher TE 5; 36, 44, 53

Lisnarbulreavy td: Donacavey TE 5; 81

Lisnarean hill: Drumgath DN 3; 19

Lisnaree fort: Newry DN 3; 110

Lisnaree standing stone: Glenavy AM 21; 90

Lisnaree td: Convoy DL 39; 21

Lisnaree td: Newry DN 3; 110

Lisnaree td: Seapatrick DN 12; 123, 126

Lisnarg (see Lisnarick): Ballyrashane LY 22; 62

Lisnarick: Derryvullan FH 14; 33, 36, 38

Lisnarick: Drumkeeran FH 14; 65

Lisnarick bogs: Ballyrashane LY 22; 57

Lisnarick fort: Ballyrashane LY 22; 49, 62

Lisnarick graveyard: Derryvullan FH 14; 38

Lisnarick school: Derryvullan FH 14; 35

Lisnarick td: Ballyrashane LY 22; 66

Lisnarrick (see Lisnarick)

Lisnasallagh td: Saintfield DN 7; 117–18

Lisnascreaghog (see Lisnascreghog)

Lisnascreehog (see Lisnascreghog)

Lisnascreghog (Lisnascreagh) td: Errigal LY 27; 41,
    51, 66, 72–73, 76, 78–79, 82–83, 88, 91

Lisnascreghog bog: Errigal LY 27; 35, 55

Lisnascreghog foot-go: Errigal LY 27; 41

Lisnascreghog fort: Banagher LY 30; 38

Lisnascreghog fort: Dungiven LY 15; 111

Lisnascreghog fort: Errigal LY 27; 43, 72, 75–76,
    78–79

Lisnascreghog fort: Misc. LY 36; 112

Lisnascreghog grey stone: Errigal LY 27; 45, 73

Lisnascreghog school: Errigal LY 27; 39, 51–52, 72

Lisnascreghog Sunday school: Errigal LY 27; 51–52

Lisnascreghog td: Cumber LY 28; 69

Lisnascrehog (see Lisnascreghog)

Lisnashillady td: Galloon FH 4; 95

Lisnaskea: Aghalurcher FH 4; 3, 5–6, 8–10, 12–16

Lisnaskea: Aghavea FH 4; 18–19, 21, 23–24

Lisnaskea: Derrybrusk FH 4; 32

Lisnaskea: Enniskillen FH 4; 62

Lisnaskea: Galloon FH 4; 101–03

Lisnaskea: Kinawley FH 4; 115, 119

Lisnaskea Castle: Aghalurcher FH 4; 6, 9

Lisnaskea Castle: Galloon FH 4; 102

Lisnaskea church: Aghalurcher FH 4; 6

Lisnaskea dispensary: Aghalurcher FH 4; 10

Lisnaskea Hotel: Aghalurcher FH 4; 6

Lisnaskea market house: Aghalurcher FH 4; 6

Lisnaskea school: Aghalurcher FH 4; 11

Lisnasliggan flax mill: Annaclone DN 12; 14, 18

Lisnasliggan glebe: Annaclone DN 12; 15

Lisnasliggan Glebe House: Annaclone DN 12; 14

Lisnasliggan school: Annaclone DN 12; 15

Lisnasliggan spring: Annaclone DN 12; 16

Lisnasliggan td: Annaclone DN 12; 13–14, 16,
    16–18

Lisnaslliggan (see Lisnasliggan): Annaclone DN 12;
    17

Lisnastrain td: Drumbo DN 7; 59–60, 62

Lisnastrane td: Clonoe TE 20; 29

Lisnataylor forts: Killead AM 35; 30

Lisnataylor td: Killead AM 35; 22, 35, 40, 50

Lisnaterney td: Aghaderg DN 12; 3

Lisnavalagan (see Limavallaghan): Dunaghy AM
    13; 17

Lisnaward corn mill: Dromore DN 12; 72, 78

Lisnaward lough: Dromore DN 12; 70

Lisnaward td: Dromore DN 12; 70, 72, 78

Lisnawerry (see Lisnawery): Errigal Keerogue TE
    20; 57

Lisnawery (Lisnaweery) td: Errigal Keerogue TE
    20; 49, 54–55, 57

Lisnawery bog: Errigal Keerogue TE 20; 54

Lisnawery fort: Errigal Keerogue TE 20; 54

Lisnawery school: Errigal Keerogue TE 20; 49

Lisnawhiggal beetling and washing mill: Connor
    AM 19; 22

Lisnawhiggal beetling mill: Connor AM 19; 22

Lisneal quarry: Clondermot LY 34; 132

Lisneal td: Clondermot LY 34; 38, 56, 59, 72, 80,
    111–12, 119, 127, 132

Lisneale (see Lisneal): Clondermot LY 34; 59

Lisnegarvy (see Lisnagarvy)

Lisnevanagh (Lisnevenagh) td: Shilvodan AM 19;
    137

Lisnevanagh forts: Shilvodan AM 19; 137

Lisnisk beetling mill: Ballyrashane LY 22; 48

Lisnisk flax mill: Ballyrashane LY 22; 48

Lisnisk fort: Ballyrashane LY 22; 49, 62

Lisnisk fort: Loughguile AM 13; 71

Lisnisk school: Drumballyroney DN 3; 13

Lisnisk td: Drumballyroney DN 3; 10, 13–14

Lisnisk td: Loughgilly AH 1; 85

Lisnisk td: Loughguile AM 13; 71, 76

Lisniskey td: Seagoe AH 1; 109

Lisnoble td: Raphoe DL 39; 126

Lisnod (see Lisnode): Drumbo DN 7; 61

Lisnode td: Drumbo DN 7, 59–61

Lisnoore td: Drumgoon CN 40; 6

Lisnorable chapel: Clogher TE 5; 48

Lisnorable td: Clogher TE 5; 48

Lisoid (Lissoid) td: Bright DN 17; 34–35

Lisolvan (Lisoloan) td: Aghavea FH 4; 19–20, 23

Lisolvan pottery: Aghavea FH 4; 19–20

Lisoneill td: Aghalurcher FH 4; 6, 14

Lisowan (see Lisowen): Saintfield DN 7; 117, 120

Lisowen corn mill: Saintfield DN 7; 119

Lisowen Lower td: Saintfield DN 7; 120

Lisowen td: Saintfield DN 7; 117, 119

Lisowen Upper td: Saintfield DN 7; 120

Lisrah (see Lisreagh)

Lisreagh hill: Magheraculmoney FH 14; 113

Lisreagh td: Derryvullan FH 14; 46

Lisrodden (Lisroddin) td: Ahoghill AM 23; 34, 38

Lisrodden brewery: Ahoghill AM 23; 35

Lisrodden fort: Ahoghill AM 23; 34

Lisrodden school: Ahoghill AM 23; 45, 48, 50

Lisrodden Sunday school: Ahoghill AM 23; 48

Lisruddy td: Rossorry FH 14; 117

Lissaghen trigonometrical station: Emlaghfad SO
40; 176

Lissaghmore (see Lisaghmore): Clondermot LY 34;
44

Lissaghmore bog: Agivey LY 22; 43

Lissaghmore fort: Agivey LY 22; 44

Lissaghmore td: Agivey LY 22; 39–41, 45

Lissagorry Glebe td: Galloon FH 4; 95

Lissahawley quarry: Clondermot LY 34; 132

Lissahawley td: Clondermot LY 34; 38, 57, 66, 72,
76, 111–13, 118, 126, 132

Lissan church (see Tullynure): Lissan LY 31; 89

Lissan demesne: Lissan TE 20; 69

Lissan Demesne td: Lissan LY 31; 109

Lissan fort: Kilcronaghan LY 31; 86

Lissan House: Lissan LY 31; 104

Lissan ironworks: Lissan LY 31; 103

Lissan ph: Artrea TE 20; 6

Lissan ph: Banagher LY 30; 103

Lissan ph: Coleraine LY 33; 63

Lissan ph: Desertlyn LY 31; 35–36, 50

Lissan ph: Kildress TE 20; 58–59

Lissan ph: Misc. LY 31; 111, 122

Lissan ph: Tamlaght Finlagan LY 25; 95

Lissan ph: Tamlaght TE 20; 73

Lissan td: Faughanvale LY 36; 62

Lissanduff td: Dunluce AM 16; 116

Lissara corn mill: Kilmore DN 17; 88, 93

Lissara flax mill: Kilmore DN 17; 88, 93

Lissara meeting house: Kilmore DN 17; 93

Lissavogue corn mill: Kilmore AH 1; 63

Lissavogue td: Kilmore AH 1; 61, 69–70, 73

Lissconrea forts: Donacavey TE 5; 84

Lissconrea td: Donacavey TE 5, 76, 84, 86

Lissdergan td: Donacavey TE 5; 77, 86

Lissderra td: Killesher FH 14; 87

Lissdrum td: Clones FH 4; 26

Lissebaddy (Lisavady) td: Donacavey TE 5; 86

Lisseenan corn mill: Muckno MN 40; 165–66

Lisseenan school: Muckno MN 40; 168

Lisseenan td: Muckno MN 40; 162

Lissen druid's circle: Derryvullan FH 14; 42

Lissen hill: Derryvullan FH 14; 40

Lissen td: Derryvullan FH 14; 40, 45–46

Lissenabreag (see Lisnabrague)

Lissenisk td: Convoy DL 39; 21

Lissenore td: Convoy DL 39; 21

Lisseraw fort: Ballymore AH 1; 7

Lisseraw td: Ballymore AH 1; 11, 13, 13–14, 16–17

Lisserboy td: Newry DN 3; 77, 105

Lisserluss fort: Billy AM 16; 51, 65

Lisserluss graveyard: Billy AM 16; 51, 72

Lisserluss grey stone: Billy AM 16; 72

Lisserluss standing stone: Billy AM 16; 58, 72

Lisserluss td: Billy AM 16; 51, 53

Lissgally td: Killesher FH 14; 90

Lissgool (see Lisgool): Rossorry FH 14; 115

Lissharmebrew td: Donacavey TE 5; 80

Lissheffield tanyard: Kilmore AH 1; 71

Lissheffield td: Kilmore AH 1; 69, 71

Lissize td: Drumballyroney DN 3; 14, 18

Lissize td: Drumgath DN 3; 21, 21

Lisskey (Lisky) td: Donacavey TE 5; 86

Lisslane (see Lislane): Balteagh LY 9; 44

Lisslane td: Balteagh LY 9; 43

Lisslannen td: Clones FH 4; 26

Lisslea (see Lislea): Galloon FH 4; 95

Lissmullyduff (see Lismullyduff)

Lissnacreive (see Lisnacreeve)

Lissnacullen (see Lisacullion): Magheross MN 40;
143

Lissnakarvagh (see Lisnagarvy)

Lissnaroe House: Clones FH 4; 29

Lissnegardy (Lissegarduffe) td: Donacavey TE 5;
77, 83, 86

Lissoarty td: Clones FH 4; 26

Lisson Inn (Fermanagh): Banagher LY 30; 57

Lissue brickyard: Blaris AM 8; 67

Lissue fort: Blaris AM 8; 19

Lissue House: Blaris AM 8; 33

Lissue td: Blaris AM 8; 19, 35, 67, 87

Lissue td: Blaris DN 12; 26, 28, 40–42

Listack td: Conwal DL 39; 27

Listannagh (Listonaugh) td: Taughboyne DL 39; 148, 153, 196

Listellian school: Leck DL 39; 120

Listellian td: Leck DL 39; 119

Lister, Henry: Ballyscullion LY 6; 57

Listerue mountain: Aghalurcher FH 4; 2

Listicall (Lustikill) td: Taughboyne DL 39; 148, 153–54, 187, 196

Listicall flax mill: Taughboyne DL 39; 153

Listicall fort: Taughboyne DL 39; 153

Listicall spring: Misc. DL 39; 188

Liston, Janet (nee Sellar): Island Magee AM 10; 66, 94

Listooder corn mill: Kilmore DN 17; 91

Listrely locality: Clondermot LY 34; 59

Listress bog: Cumber LY 28; 47, 49

Listress corn mill: Cumber LY 28; 34, 80, 105–06

Listress flax mill: Cumber LY 28; 34, 80

Listress ph: Ballynascreen LY 31; 9

Listress td: Cumber LY 28; 41, 47, 60, 64, 67, 97, 102, 105–07

Listress wood: Cumber LY 28; 102

Listullicurran (see Listullycurran): Hillsborough DN 12; 102

Listullyard fort: Seapatrick DN 12; 124–25

Listullycurran (Listullycorran) td: Dromore DN 12; 70, 78

Listullycurran school: Dromore DN 12; 73, 78

Listullycurran school: Hillsborough DN 12; 102

Listullycurran td: Hillsborough DN 12; 89

Lisvilough td: Killoran and Kilvarnet SO 40; 183

Liswatty Lower bog: Ballyrashane LY 22; 46

Liswatty Lower cave: Ballyrashane LY 22; 50, 60

Liswatty Lower fort [I]: Ballyrashane LY 22; 49–50, 59

Liswatty Lower fort [II]: Ballyrashane LY 22; 49–50, 59

Liswatty Upper fort [I]: Ballyrashane LY 22; 49, 59

Liswatty Upper fort [II]: Ballyrashane LY 22; 49, 59

Liswiney hill: Aghabog MN 40; 62

Lithgow, Edward: Clondermot LY 34; 79–80

Lithgow, John: Clondermot LY 34; 78–80

Lithgow, Mr: Clondermot LY 34; 37, 104

Litteran: Banagher LY 30; 108

Litteran hill: Banagher LY 30; 108, 110

Litteran td: Lissan LY 31; 108–09, 109

Little Ballyhenry (see Ballyhenry Minor): Comber DN 7; 42

Little bridge: Arboe LY 6; 1

Little bridge: Tamlaght TE 20; 137

Little causeway: Billy AM 16; 42

Little Head: Lough Swilly DL 38; 121

Little lough: Belleek FH 14; 1

Little well (see Mullynahunshin): Killesher FH 14; 90

Little, Andrew: Coleraine LY 33; 145

Little, Andrew: Macosquin LY 22; 105

Little, Archibald: Newry DN 3; 93, 104

Little, family: Carnmoney AM 2; 76

Little, George: Coleraine LY 33; 145

Little, George: Macosquin LY 22; 105

Little, Hendrick: Coleraine LY 33; 145

Little, I.: Seapatrick DN 12; 125

Little, James: Aghaderg DN 12; 5, 12

Little, James: Annaclone DN 12; 15

Little, James: Maghera LY 18; 7, 67

Little, John: Coleraine LY 33; 145

Little, Maryanne (Jnr): Coleraine LY 33; 145

Little, Maryanne (Snr): Coleraine LY 33; 145

Little, Mr (Coleraine): Clondermot LY 34; 36, 103

Little, Mr (Coleraine): Rasharkin AM 23; 128

Little, Mrs (nee Hunter): Ballywillin LY 33; 50

Little, Rev. Robert: Aghaderg DN 12; 9, 11

Little, Rev. William: Drumgoon CN 40; 5

Little, Robert: Hillsborough DN 12; 107

Little, William (Jnr): Coleraine LY 33; 145

Little, William (Snr): Coleraine LY 33; 145

Little, William: Desertoghill LY 27; 14

Little, William: Tamlaght TE 20; 110

Littlefish river: Kilmacteige SO 40; 191, 195

Littlemount corn mill: Aghavea FH 4; 20

Littlemount demesne: Aghavea FH 4; 18

Littlewood, Ann: Tamlaght Finlagan LY 25; 119

Litton, Edward: Pomeroy TE 20; 71

Littuifaskey graveyard: Aughnamullen MN 40; 73

Littuifaskey priory: Aughnamullen MN 40; 73

Liverpool: Aghalurcher FH 4; 13, 15

Liverpool: Aghavea FH 4; 24

Liverpool: Ahoghill AM 23; 37–40

Liverpool: Ardglass DN 17; 6–7

Liverpool: Ballee DN 17; 19

Liverpool: Ballynure AM 32; 47, 51

Liverpool: Ballywillin LY 33; 30, 36, 44

Liverpool: Bright DN 17; 35

Liverpool: Carnmoney AM 2; 64, 89

Liverpool: Carrickfergus AM 37; 63, 158

Liverpool: Clondermot LY 34; 14, 30, 100

Liverpool: Coleraine LY 33; 74, 86, 88–89, 99, 122–24, 146, 148, 151

Liverpool: Connor AM 19; 31

Liverpool: Culdaff DL 38; 21

Liverpool: Culfeightrin AM 24; 44, 68

Liverpool: Cumber LY 28; 3, 22, 58

Liverpool: Desertoghill LY 27; 20–21

Liverpool: Donaghedy TE 5; 91

Liverpool: Donaghmore DL 39; 33

Liverpool: Donegal DL 39; 47, 57

Liverpool: Donegore AM 29; 114, 130

Liverpool: Down DN 17; 47–48, 58
Liverpool: Drumachose LY 9; 69, 117
Liverpool: Drumcree AH 1; 32
Liverpool: Drumgoon CN 40; 3, 9
Liverpool: Drummaul AM 19; 62, 89–90
Liverpool: Duneane AM 19; 123–24
Liverpool: Dunluce AM 16; 112
Liverpool: Enniskillen FH 4; 47, 61
Liverpool: Glynn AM 26; 33–34
Liverpool: Island Magee AM 10; 64
Liverpool: Killinchy DN 7; 88
Liverpool: Killygarvan DL 38; 45
Liverpool: Killyleagh DN 17; 83, 85
Liverpool: Killymard DL 39; 98–99
Liverpool: Kilroot AM 26; 72
Liverpool: Kirkinriola AM 23; 98
Liverpool: Knockbreda DN 7; 100
Liverpool: Layd AM 13; 38
Liverpool: Lissan LY 31; 110
Liverpool: Lough Swilly DL 38; 119
Liverpool: Maghera LY 18; 22, 77, 80–81
Liverpool: Magheross MN 40; 152
Liverpool: Misc. DL 39; 188
Liverpool: Muff DL 38; 82
Liverpool: Newry DN 3; 86–87, 94, 105
Liverpool: Ramoan AM 24; 95, 101
Liverpool: Saul DN 17; 111
Liverpool: Taughboyne DL 39; 151
Liverpool: Templecorran AM 26; 96
Liverpool: Templepatrick AM 35; 123, 146, 152
Liverpool: Warrenpoint DN 3; 118, 120–21
Liverpool, Lord: Aghadowey LY 22; 23
Livery Lower Castle: Derrykeighan AM 16; 94
Livery Lower giant's grave: Derrykeighan AM 16;
    94
Livery Lower td: Derrykeighan AM 16; 84, 89, 94
Livery Upper td: Derrykeighan AM 16; 87, 92, 95
Livingston, family: Ballywillin AM 16; 32
Livingston, Hugh: Ballywillin LY 33; 40, 44, 48
Livingston, James: Ahoghill AM 23; 49
Livingston, James: Misc. DN 17; 125
Livingston, John: Hillsborough DN 12; 106
Livingston, Mr: Glynn AM 26; 5, 13
Livingston, Rev. Samuel: Ballyculter DN 17; 29
Livingston, William: Ballywillin LY 33; 39
Livingstone, Abram: Duneane AM 19; 123
Livingstone, Rev. William: Templepatrick AM 35;
    133, 143
Livingstone, Thomas: Drummaul AM 19; 88
Lizard manor: Desertoghill LY 27; 17
Lloyd House (see Tamlaghtmore): Killyman TE 20;
    67
Lloyd, Col: Enniskillen FH 4; 52
Lloyd, Col: Galloon FH 4; 102–04
Lloyd, J.: Skirts of Urney and Ardstraw TE 5; 140

Lloyd, Richard: Killyman TE 20; 67–68
Loag, man named: Moville DL 38; 70
Loan (Loane) td: Ahoghill AM 23; 39
Loan Ends meeting house (see Ballymather):
    Killead AM 35; 46
Loan evening school: Ahoghill AM 23; 43
Loan school: Ahoghill AM 23; 43, 45
Loan Sunday school: Ahoghill AM 23; 45
Loan, Patrick: Maghera LY 18; 62
Lochabhiga: Templecarn DL 39; 156
Lochabhige: Templecarn DL 39; 157
Lochachadeagh: Templecarn DL 39; 157
Lochachaillan: Templecarn DL 39; 157
Lochaghealbhan: Templecarn DL 39; 157
Lochaghuisbeag: Templecarn DL 39; 157
Lochalach: Templecarn DL 39; 157
Lochalonigh: Templecarn DL 39; 157
Lochamhadeadh: Templecarn DL 39; 157
Lochanfarine: Templecarn DL 39; 157
Lochanulla: Emlaghfad SO 40; 176
Lochaphise: Templecarn DL 39; 156
Lochardvernish td: Killagan AM 23; 82
Locharseghbeag: Templecarn DL 39; 157
Lochasaithire: Templecarn DL 39; 157
Lochasmatten: Templecarn DL 39; 157
Loch-at-the-gable: Templecarn DL 39; 156
Lochaturribh: Templecarn DL 39; 157
Lochchupam: Templecarn DL 39; 157
Lochcoill hill: Donegal DL 39; 51
Loch-hole at the Geaoel: Templecarn DL 39; 156
Lochmculbhan: Templecarn DL 39; 157
Lochmonie: Templecarn DL 39; 157
Lochnacairn: Donegal DL 39; 44
Lochnagcollmor: Templecarn DL 39; 157
Lochnagcunniog: Templecarn DL 39; 156–57
Lochnambeadendearg: Templecarn DL 39; 157
Lochnamnameuibh: Templecarn DL 39; 157
Lochnamnasmuirbh: Templecarn DL 39; 157
Lochnananernagh: Templecarn DL 39; 157
Lochnanbradanban: Templecarn DL 39; 157
Lochnanderne: Templecarn DL 39; 156
Lochnasinach: Templecarn DL 39; 157
Lochnasmatten: Templecarn DL 39; 157
Lochnatragh: Templecarn DL 39; 157
Lochnhamias: Templecarn DL 39; 157
Lochrus Glebe td: Tullyaughnish DL 38; 85, 88, 96
Lochrus standing stone: Tullyaughnish DL 38; 91
Lochuber school: Billy AM 16; 49
Lochunaibh: Templecarn DL 39; 157
Lochvairderrig: Templecarn DL 39; 156
Lock, family: Raloo AM 32; 123
Lock, John: Kilwaughter AM 10; 116
Lockart, Adam: Ballyscullion LY 6; 68–69, 72
Lockart, David: Tullylish DN 12; 141, 146
Lockart, John: Maghera LY 18; 47

Lockart, Rev. Robert: Clonduff DN 3; 4

Lockart, Robert: Maghera LY 18; 47, 53

Lockart, William: Ballyscullion LY 6; 52

Locke, family: Raloo AM 32; 108

Locke, James: Doagh AM 29; 89

Locke, John: Kilwaughter AM 10; 115, 117, 119, 121

Lockermore (see Loughermore): Cumber LY 28; 1

Lockhart, D.: Tullylish DN 12; 141

Lockhart, David: Newry DN 3; 99

Lockhart, family: Armoy AM 24; 6

Lockhart, family: Carrickfergus AM 37; 93

Lockhart, family: Maghera LY 18; 13

Lockhart, James: Hillsborough DN 12; 106, 106

Lockhart, John: Newry DN 3; 98

Lockhart, Robert: Carrickfergus AM 37; 40, 175

Lockhart, S.A.: Ahoghill AM 23; 51

Locks hill: Templecorran AM 26; 88

Lockstown bog: Templecorran AM 26; 84, 90, 113–14, 123

Lockstown fort: Templecorran AM 26; 123

Lockstown moss: Templecorran AM 26; 126

Lockstown spring: Templecorran AM 26; 89

Lockstown td: Templecorran AM 26; 83, 90, 114, 132

Lockstown well: Templecorran AM 26; 84

Lodge farm: Coleraine LY 33; 148

Lodge House: Drumachose LY 9; 82–83, 91

Lodge House: Kilbroney DN 3; 26, 29, 31–32, 35, 37

Lodge House: Killead AM 35; 50

Lodge House: Killygarvan DL 38; 40

Lodge House: Kilmore AH 1; 71

Lodge House: Tamlaght Finlagan LY 25; 82

Lodge kilns: Killowen LY 33; 172

Lodge td: Coleraine LY 33; 94

Lodge well: Killead AM 35; 50

Lodge, Rev.: Lissan LY 31; 103

Loftie, J.: Ballymore AH 1; 12, 14

Loftie, J.: Loughgilly AH 1; 84

Loftie, W.: Ballymore AH 1; 3

Loftus, Adam: Ballynure AM 32; 52

Logacappel mountain: Culfeightrin AM 24; 79

Logan lough: Donegal DL 39; 42

Logan, Ally: Ballymoney AM 16; 17

Logan, Con: Carrickfergus AM 37; 162

Logan, Daniel: Ahoghill AM 23; 38

Logan, Daniel: Ballintoy AM 24; 25–26

Logan, David: Donaghadee DN 7; 46

Logan, Eliza: Raloo AM 32; 129

Logan, family: Aghalee AM 21; 31

Logan, family: Blaris AM 8; 21

Logan, family: Carrickfergus AM 37; 93

Logan, family: Clondermot LY 34; 45–46

Logan, family: Lambeg AM 8; 135

Logan, family: Lissan LY 31; 91, 106

Logan, family: Maghera LY 18; 48

Logan, family: Racavan AM 13; 100

Logan, family: Templecorran AM 26; 117, 119

Logan, Hannah: Maghera LY 18; 80

Logan, Hugh: Carrickfergus AM 37; 125

Logan, Isaac: Hillsborough DN 12; 106

Logan, James: Carrickfergus AM 37; 125

Logan, James: Enniskillen FH 4; 49

Logan, James: Maghera LY 18; 80

Logan, John: Ballynure AM 32; 66

Logan, John: Desertoghill LY 27; 5

Logan, John: Duneane AM 19; 122

Logan, John [I]: Carrickfergus AM 37; 76

Logan, John [I]: Clondermot LY 34; 45

Logan, John [I]: Maghera LY 18; 62

Logan, John [II]: Carrickfergus AM 37; 125

Logan, John [II]: Clondermot LY 34; 46

Logan, John [II]: Maghera LY 18; 80

Logan, Margaret: Maghera LY 18; 80

Logan, Mary: Balteagh LY 9; 44

Logan, Mary: Carrickfergus AM 37; 119

Logan, Mary: Maghera LY 18; 80

Logan, Matty: Ballynure AM 32; 72

Logan, Michael: Maghera LY 18; 8, 68

Logan, Mr: Coleraine LY 33; 124–25

Logan, Nancy: Maghera LY 18; 80

Logan, Nathaniel: Macosquin LY 22; 100, 105, 113

Logan, Paul: Carrickfergus AM 37; 137, 172

Logan, Radulph: Clondermot LY 34; 46

Logan, Rev. Thomas: Warrenpoint DN 3; 118

Logan, Robert [I]: Clondermot LY 34; 45

Logan, Robert [II]: Clondermot LY 34; 46

Logan, Thomas: Carncastle and Killyglen AM 10; 7

Logan, Walter: Clondermot LY 34; 45

Logan, William: Tamlaght Finlagan LY 25; 119

Logan, William [I]: Maghera LY 18; 57

Logan, William [II]: Maghera LY 18; 80

Logestown (see Loguestown)

Loggan, family: Templecorran AM 26; 119

Loggan, Thomas: Templepatrick AM 35; 132

Loghermore glebe: Aghalurcher FH 4; 16

Loghmulleam: Magheraculmoney FH 14; 112–13

Loghran, robber: Dungiven LY 15; 20

Logimore td: Magheross MN 40; 148

Logue, Ann: Aghadowey LY 22; 36

Logue, Bernard: Balteagh LY 9; 44

Logue, Daniel: Tamlaght O'Crilly LY 18; 112

Logue, family: Faughanvale LY 36; 48

Logue, family: Misc. LY 36; 101

Logue, James: Faughanvale LY 36; 24, 34–35

Logue, John: Balteagh LY 9; 44

Logue, John: Drumachose LY 9; 134

Logue, John: Maghera LY 18; 12, 37

Logue, Joseph: Clondermot LY 34; 86–88, 95

Logue, Patt: Aghadowey LY 22; 36

Loguestown school: Ballywillin LY 33; 33, 35, 40–41, 45

Loguestown Sunday school: Ballywillin LY 33; 41, 45

Loguestown td: Coleraine LY 33; 145

Lohan fort: Cumber LY 28; 19

Lohan lough: Cumber LY 28; 19–20

Lolston, Messrs William and Co.: Blaris DN 12; 36

Loman Bray hill: Tamlaght Finlagan LY 25; 113

Lomond td: Tamlaght Finlagan LY 25; 93, 98, 119

Londes, Lord: Clondermot LY 34; 46

London: Aghadowey LY 22; 22–23

London: Aghalurcher FH 4; 13

London: Ballynure AM 32; 52

London: Banagher LY 30; 19, 30

London: Blaris AM 8; 4, 8

London: Carrickfergus AM 37; 68

London: Clondermot LY 34; 11, 97, 100

London: Coleraine LY 33; 56–59, 63, 65, 74, 86, 94, 110, 121, 129, 137, 146–47, 151

London: Cumber LY 28; 2, 14, 58

London: Doagh AM 29; 94

London: Donegal DL 39; 47

London: Down DN 17; 47

London: Drumachose LY 9; 117

London: Drumragh TE 5; 109

London: Enniskillen FH 4; 50, 75

London: Faughanvale LY 36; 67

London: Galloon FH 4; 91

London: Glynn AM 26; 6

London: Island Magee AM 10; 79

London: Killelagh LY 27; 102

London: Knockbreda DN 7; 100

London: Lough Swilly DL 38; 149–50

London: Misc. LY 31; 117, 122

London: Newry DN 3; 105

London: Raymoghy DL 39; 140

London: Templepatrick AM 35; 112, 150

London, Tower of: Dungiven LY 15; 35

London, Tower of: Enniskillen FH 4; 50

London, Tower of: Kilmegan DN 3; 60

Londonderry county: Aghanloo LY 11; 7, 35

Londonderry county: Ballymoney AM 16; 1, 12

Londonderry county: Ballynure AM 32; 49

Londonderry county: Ballyscullion LY 6; 59, 73

Londonderry county: Blaris AM 8; 72, 75

Londonderry county: Carnmoney AM 2; 60

Londonderry county: Clonleigh DL 39; 17

Londonderry county: Donacavey TE 5; 72

Londonderry county: Donaghedy TE 5; 88

Londonderry county: Drumballyroney DN 3; 11

Londonderry county: Dungiven LY 15; 35, 84, 104

Londonderry county: Enniskeen CN 40; 26

Londonderry county: Enniskillen FH 4; 60, 66

Londonderry county: Faughanvale LY 36; 44

Londonderry county: Killead AM 35; 22

Londonderry county: Killygarvan DL 38; 48

Londonderry county: Lough Swilly DL 38; 138

Londonderry county: Magherafelt LY 6; 106

Londonderry county: Misc. AM 10; 130

Londonderry county: Misc. LY 31; 113

Londonderry county: Termoneeny LY 6; 132

Londonderry court house: Faughanvale LY 36; 24

Londonderry, Lady: Newtownards DN 7; 108

Londonderry, Lord: Artrea LY 6; 20

Londonderry, Lord: Clondermot LY 34; 38

Londonderry, Lord: Comber DN 7; 38–41

Londonderry, Lord: Drumachose LY 9; 73

Londonderry, Lord: Dunaghy AM 13; 12

Londonderry, Lord: Kilmood DN 7; 95

Londonderry, Lord: Newtownards DN 7; 104, 111–12

Londonderry, Marquis of: Artrea TE 20; 6

Londonderry, Marquis of: Comber DN 7; 32–33, 37, 44

Londonderry, Marquis of: Dundonald DN 7; 65

Londonderry, Marquis of: Faughanvale LY 36; 17–18, 70, 72, 74–76, 79

Londonderry, Marquis of: Grey Abbey DN 7; 69–70

Londonderry, Marquis of: Misc. DL 39; 186

Londonderry, Marquis of: Newtownards DN 7; 103, 105–06, 108–09

Londonderry, Marquis of: Raymoghy DL 39; 132, 135–37, 139–41

Lonebratly (see Tullnabratly): Clonmany DL 38; 18

Loney, Thomas: Kilmore AH 1; 58

Long Brae ridge: Kilcoo DN 3; 41

Long Brae ridge: Kilkeel DN 3; 46

Long bridge: Knockbreda DN 7; 97

Long Causey locality: Aghanloo LY 11; 23

Long hill: Magilligan LY 11; 82

Long Island: Trory FH 14; 122–23

Long Island: Tullynakill DN 7; 124

Long lough: Currin MN 40; 86, 89, 91

Long lough: Killygarvan DL 38; 36–38

Long lough: Saintfield DN 7; 117, 119

Long Point: Coleraine LY 33; 98

Long, Barbara: Coleraine LY 33; 134

Long, Dr: Cumber LY 28; 57

Long, E.: Carnmoney AM 2; 90

Long, family: Aghalee AM 21; 31

Long, family: Island Magee AM 10; 70

Long, John: Aghalee AM 21; 37

Long, John: Drumachose LY 9; 121

Long, John: Island Magee AM 10; 99–100, 102

Long, John: Tamlaght TE 20; 78, 83

Long, Margaret: Coleraine LY 33; 69, 134

Long, Mary: Island Magee AM 10; 39, 94

Long, Miss: Drumachose LY 9; 118

Long, Samuel: Maghera LY 18; 31

Long, Thomas: Drumachose LY 9; 104

Long's hill: Desertlyn LY 31; 36

Longafanine school: Donegal DL 39; 49

Longfield Beg pottery: Faughanvale LY 36; 16

Longfield Beg td: Faughanvale LY 36; 17, 60, 69, 77, 88, 95, 99

Longfield Beg wood: Faughanvale LY 36; 88

Longfield Canal: Faughanvale LY 36; 77

Longfield chapel: Longfield TE 5; 130

Longfield East chapel: Longfield TE 5; 131

Longfield East church: Longfield TE 5; 131

Longfield East Glebe: Longfield TE 5; 132

Longfield East Glebe House: Longfield TE 5; 131

Longfield East Glebe school: Longfield TE 5; 132

Longfield East ph: Drumragh TE 5; 104, 111

Longfield East td: Ardstraw TE 5; 10

Longfield Glebe House: Longfield TE 5; 135

Longfield hills: Longfield TE 5; 127

Longfield House: Donaghmoyne MN 40; 107, 111

Longfield Lower church: Longfield TE 5; 134

Longfield Lower meeting house: Longfield TE 5; 134

Longfield Lower schools: Longfield TE 5; 134

Longfield More brickfield and pottery: Faughanvale LY 36; 16

Longfield More td: Faughanvale LY 36; 17–18, 60, 69, 77, 88, 95–96

Longfield More wood: Faughanvale LY 36; 88

Longfield ph: Donegal DL 39; 45

Longfield td: Aghalurcher FH 4; 14

Longfield td: Desertmartin LY 31; 56, 62, 117–18, 141–42

Longfield td: Faughanvale LY 36; 53

Longfield West church: Longfield TE 5; 129

Longfield West Glebe House: Longfield TE 5; 128

Longfield West ph: Ardstraw TE 5; 10, 13

Longfield West ph: Dromore TE 5; 100

Longfield West ph: Drumkeeran FH 14; 62

Longfield West ph: Drumragh TE 5; 104, 110

Longfield West ph: Magheraculmoney FH 14; 103

Longfield West quarries: Cappagh TE 5; 19

Longford county: Drumlumman CN 40; 12

Longford county: Enniskillen FH 4; 44, 80

Longford county: Magheragall AM 21; 107

Longford district (Roscommon): Misc. SO 40; 199

Longford, Countess of: Glenavy AM 21; 85

Longfoyld, L.: Coleraine LY 33; 157

Longhill td: Tullyaughnish DL 38; 97

Longlands td: Comber DN 7; 37, 39, 42–43

Longmoor, family: Billy AM 16; 58, 68

Longmore td: Skerry AM 13; 106

Longridge fort: Clogher TE 5; 45

Longridge meeting house (P): Clogher TE 5; 48

Longridge meeting house (S): Clogher TE 5; 39

Longridge td: Clogher TE 5; 36, 45, 48, 53

Longrob hill: Devenish FH 14; 47

Longrob td: Devenish FH 14; 58

Longsessagh td: Donaghmore DL 39; 38

Longstone adult school: Blaris AM 8; 80

Longstone district: Blaris AM 8; 46

Longstone private school [I]: Blaris AM 8; 79–80

Longstone private school [II]: Blaris AM 8; 80

Longstone private school [III]: Blaris AM 8; 80

Longstone school: Blaris AM 8; 81

Longwill, family: Misc. LY 36; 104

Longwood House: Carnmoney AM 2; 46, 84

Longwood, James: Carrickfergus AM 37; 112

Lonnan, Bryan: Lissan LY 31; 101

Lonove, family: Ballintoy AM 24; 20

Loonburn fort: Kilbride AM 29; 149

Loonburn td: Kilbride AM 29; 136, 155

Loop (Loup) district: Artrea LY 6; 5, 14, 16

Loop chapel: Artrea LY 6; 21

Loop district: Tamlaght TE 20; 137

Loop locality: Garvaghy DN 12; 79

Loop private school: Artrea LY 6; 20

Loop school: Loughguile AM 13; 77

Loop Sunday school: Artrea LY 6; 21

Loorly district: Misc. SO 40; 199

Lorbawn village: Kilmacteige SO 40; 194

Lord, Bernard: Ahoghill AM 23; 34

Lord's House: Lambeg AM 8; 138

Lorga district: Misc. SO 40; 198

Lorgeaden (see Lurigethan): Layd AM 13; 41

Lorimar, James: Maghera LY 18; 77

Lorimer, family: Ballynure AM 32; 56

Lorimer, Isabella: Killead AM 35; 22, 50

Lorimore, William: Muckamore AM 35; 80

Lorinan [or McLorimer], Miss: Antrim AM 29; 42

Lormer, William: Maghera LY 18; 28, 32

Lorrance, George: Ballyscullion LY 6; 57

Lorrimer, Mr (Ballymoney): Ballyrashane LY 22; 63

Lorroy td: Kilmacteige SO 40; 186

Lorton, R.E.: Misc. SO 40; 198–200

Losat (see Lossets): Magheross MN 40; 148

Losmer, William: Ballynascreen LY 31; 18

Losset (see Lossets): Magheross MN 40; 156

Losset bog: Culfeightrin AM 24; 56

Losset bog: Magheracloone MN 40; 137

Losset fort: Culfeightrin AM 24; 53

Losset old castle: Culfeightrin AM 24; 53

Losset td: Clogher TE 5; 37

Losset td: Culfeightrin AM 24; 52–53, 67

Lossets td: Magheross MN 40; 148, 156

Lothian, Marquis of: Ballyscullion LY 6; 54

Louba (see Loubar)

Loubar river: Doagh AM 29; 62

Loubar stream: Ballintoy AM 24; 13

Loubar stream: Billy AM 16; 40

Loubar stream: Drumtullagh AM 16; 96–98

Louden, Margret Anne: Dunboe LY 11; 66

Lough Bawn demesne: Aughnamullen MN 40; 70

Lough Bawn House: Aughnamullen MN 40; 71, 74

Lough Beg: Aghagallon AM 21; 15, 18

Lough Beg: Aghalee AM 21; 38

Lough Beg: Ahoghill AM 23; 4, 29

Lough Beg: Artrea LY 6; 2–5, 14–15, 36, 39–40

Lough Beg: Artrea TE 20; 6, 8

Lough Beg: Ballinderry AM 21; 41–44, 54–56

Lough Beg: Ballyscullion AM 19; 2, 8

Lough Beg: Ballyscullion LY 6; 42–44, 48–50, 52–53, 60, 65, 73

Lough Beg: Coleraine LY 33; 96–98, 100–01

Lough Beg: Drummaul AM 19; 52

Lough Beg: Duneane AM 19; 95–98, 100–01, 111

Lough Beg: Finvoy AM 23; 68

Lough Beg: Glenavy AM 21; 77, 83

Lough Beg: Killead AM 35; 25

Lough Beg: Lough Neagh AM 21; 93

Lough Beg: Rasharkin AM 23; 129

Lough Derg: Ardstraw TE 5; 10

Lough Derg: Banagher LY 30; 69

Lough Derg: Drumhome DL 39; 61

Lough Derg: Misc. LY 31; 138

Lough Derg: Templecarn DL 39; 156–57, 159–62, 164, 166, 170

Lough Derg: Termonamongan TE 5; 142

Lough Derg hills: Ardstraw TE 5; 2

Lough Duff hill: Carncastle and Killyglen AM 10; 1

Lough Duff td: Carncastle and Killyglen AM 10; 1

Lough Erne: Aghaloo TE 20; 2

Lough Erne: Aghalurcher FH 4; 3, 5, 15

Lough Erne: Aghavea FH 4; 17

Lough Erne: Belleek FH 14; 1, 3–4, 6

Lough Erne: Cleenish FH 14; 12–15, 19, 27–28

Lough Erne: Clogher TE 5; 26, 47

Lough Erne: Clondermot LY 34; 57, 73

Lough Erne: Clones FH 4; 28

Lough Erne: Clonleigh DL 39; 16

Lough Erne: Currin MN 40; 91

Lough Erne: Derrybrusk FH 4; 30–32

Lough Erne: Derryvullan FH 14; 31–33, 36

Lough Erne: Devenish FH 14; 51–52, 57

Lough Erne: Drumgoon CN 40; 3

Lough Erne: Drumkeeran FH 14; 62–64

Lough Erne: Drumlumman CN 40; 12

Lough Erne: Drummully FH 4; 36, 38–39

Lough Erne: Drung CN 40; 19

Lough Erne: Ematris MN 40; 112, 116

Lough Erne: Enniskillen FH 4; 41, 43–50, 52, 54, 57, 61–62, 64, 66–67, 78, 80–81

Lough Erne: Galloon FH 4; 89, 92, 94, 97, 100, 102, 104–05

Lough Erne: Inishmacsaint FH 14; 70, 72, 80

Lough Erne: Killesher FH 14; 81

Lough Erne: Kinawley FH 4; 108, 113, 115, 117

Lough Erne: Lough Neagh AM 21; 97

Lough Erne: Lough Swilly DL 38; 130, 149

Lough Erne: Loughgall AH 1; 81

Lough Erne: Magheraculmoney FH 14; 103–04, 107, 109

Lough Erne: Rossorry FH 14; 115

Lough Erne: Templecarn DL 39; 156–58, 161–63, 166, 170

Lough Erne: Templecarn FH 14; 118

Lough Erne: Trory FH 14; 122, 125–26, 130–32, 135

Lough Erne fishery: Trory FH 14; 131

Lough Erne Lower: Aghalurcher FH 4; 2

Lough Erne Lower: Cleenish FH 14; 11

Lough Erne Upper: Aghalurcher FH 4; 1–4, 10, 15

Lough Erne Upper: Aghavea FH 4; 18

Lough Erne Upper: Cleenish FH 14; 12–13

Lough Erne Upper: Drummully FH 4; 34–36

Lough Erne Upper: Galloon FH 4; 87–88, 91–92

Lough Erne Upper: Killesher FH 14; 81–82

Lough Erne Upper: Kinawley FH 4; 107, 112–13, 123

Lough Eske Demesne Castle: Killymard DL 39; 97

Lough Eske Demesne corn mill: Killymard DL 39; 96

Lough Eske Demesne td: Donegal DL 39; 47

Lough Eske Demesne td: Killymard DL 39; 96, 101, 106

Lough Fea Cottage: Magheracloone MN 40; 138

Lough Fea demesne: Magheracloone MN 40; 137–39

Lough Fea demesne: Magheross MN 40; 144, 157

Lough Fea House: Magheracloone MN 40; 138

Lough Fea House: Magheross MN 40; 145–46, 156

Lough Foyle: Aghanloo LY 11; 1, 9

Lough Foyle: Ballyaghran LY 33; 3

Lough Foyle: Balteagh LY 9; 5, 22

Lough Foyle: Banagher LY 30; 2, 59, 70

Lough Foyle: Clondermot LY 34; 1, 3–4, 7, 18–19, 22, 35–36, 52, 54–55, 70, 106

Lough Foyle: Clonleigh DL 39; 16–17

Lough Foyle: Coleraine LY 33; 78, 93

Lough Foyle: Cumber LY 28; 72

Lough Foyle: Drumachose LY 9; 74, 101

Lough Foyle: Dungiven LY 15; 2, 50, 64

Lough Foyle: Faughanvale LY 36; 1–4, 8–11, 33, 39, 53, 59, 70, 72–75, 77–80

Lough Foyle: Killowen LY 33; 169

Lough Foyle: Lissan LY 31; 103

Lough Foyle: Lough Swilly DL 38; 137–42, 149

Lough Foyle: Maghera LY 18; 20

Lough Foyle: Magilligan LY 11; 82–85, 92–93, 97, 103, 108, 114, 117–20, 123, 136, 143

Lough Foyle: Misc. LY 36; 105, 119
Lough Foyle: Moville DL 38; 68–71, 73, 76–79
Lough Foyle: Muff DL 38; 80
Lough Foyle: Tamlaght Finlagan LY 25; 62–63, 66,
    81–82, 84–85, 93, 95, 97–98, 103–04, 107, 113,
    116–17
Lough Foyle: Taughboyne DL 39; 149–54
Lough hill: Banagher LY 30; 110
Lough Key monastery: Misc. SO 40; 200
Lough Macnay td: Ballee DN 17; 23
Lough Neagh: Aghagallon AM 21; 1–3, 5–7, 13,
    15–16, 18, 21–24
Lough Neagh: Aghalee AM 21; 26, 29, 31, 38
Lough Neagh: Aghaloo TE 20; 1
Lough Neagh: Ahoghill AM 23; 3–4, 8, 14
Lough Neagh: Antrim AM 29; 1, 3–7, 17, 20–21,
    23, 27–28, 30–31, 35, 44, 47, 49–51
Lough Neagh: Artrea LY 6; 2–4, 14, 36, 39–40
Lough Neagh: Artrea TE 20; 6–9
Lough Neagh: Ballinderry AM 21; 43, 48, 55, 58
Lough Neagh: Ballinderry TE 20; 11, 13–14
Lough Neagh: Ballyclog TE 20; 15–18
Lough Neagh: Ballycor AM 32; 1
Lough Neagh: Ballylinny AM 32; 11
Lough Neagh: Ballymartin AM 2; 1
Lough Neagh: Ballymoney AM 16; 1, 6
Lough Neagh: Ballynure AM 32; 31, 38, 44, 72
Lough Neagh: Ballyrobert AM 2; 24
Lough Neagh: Ballyscullion AM 19; 2
Lough Neagh: Ballywalter AM 2; 28
Lough Neagh: Blaris AM 8; 1, 69, 72, 76, 89
Lough Neagh: Blaris DN 12; 26
Lough Neagh: Camlin AM 21; 60, 62–67, 69–71
Lough Neagh: Carmavy AM 35; 1
Lough Neagh: Carnmoney AM 2; 50–51
Lough Neagh: Clogher TE 5; 25, 47, 49
Lough Neagh: Clonfeacle AH 1; 23
Lough Neagh: Clonoe TE 20; 29–31
Lough Neagh: Coleraine LY 33; 53, 88, 93, 96–103,
    121–22, 149
Lough Neagh: Connor AM 19; 17, 19, 28
Lough Neagh: Cranfield AM 19; 32
Lough Neagh: Desertcreat TE 20; 35
Lough Neagh: Desertlyn LY 31; 40
Lough Neagh: Doagh AM 29; 62, 78
Lough Neagh: Donaghenry TE 20; 38
Lough Neagh: Donegore AM 29; 105, 109, 115,
    122, 134
Lough Neagh: Dromara DN 12; 62
Lough Neagh: Drumcree AH 1; 32, 34
Lough Neagh: Drumglass TE 20; 43
Lough Neagh: Drummaul AM 19; 33, 35–37, 39,
    46–47, 52, 63, 71, 79, 81, 89
Lough Neagh: Drummully FH 4; 36
Lough Neagh: Dundermot AM 13; 29

Lough Neagh: Duneane AM 19; 94–101, 107, 110,
    113
Lough Neagh: Enniskillen FH 4; 46
Lough Neagh: Finvoy AM 23; 72
Lough Neagh: Glenavy AM 21; 77–84, 86, 88
Lough Neagh: Glynn AM 26; 17
Lough Neagh: Kilbride AM 29; 137, 137
Lough Neagh: Kildress TE 20; 59, 61
Lough Neagh: Killagan AM 23; 82
Lough Neagh: Killead AM 35; 7–8, 10–11, 13, 17,
    25–26, 33–34, 40–41, 43–44, 47, 49–50
Lough Neagh: Killyman AH 1; 55
Lough Neagh: Killyman TE 20; 66
Lough Neagh: Kilmore AH 1; 61–62
Lough Neagh: Kilraghts AM 16; 126
Lough Neagh: Kilrea LY 27; 105–06
Lough Neagh: Kilwaughter AM 10; 108
Lough Neagh: Kirkinriola AM 23; 88, 91–92, 101,
    118, 124
Lough Neagh: Leckpatrick TE 5; 123
Lough Neagh: Lough Neagh AM 21; 92–97
Lough Neagh: Loughgall AH 1; 79, 81
Lough Neagh: Maghera LY 18; 2–3, 35
Lough Neagh: Magherafelt LY 6; 79, 90
Lough Neagh: Magheramesk AM 21; 114–15
Lough Neagh: Mallusk AM 2; 109, 114
Lough Neagh: Misc. DN 17; 117, 121
Lough Neagh: Misc. LY 31; 116
Lough Neagh: Montiaghs AH 1; 89–92
Lough Neagh: Muckamore AM 35; 54–55, 57, 59,
    61, 64, 67, 70–72, 74
Lough Neagh: Nilteen AM 35; 85, 87–88
Lough Neagh: Raloo AM 32; 85–86, 89
Lough Neagh: Rasharkin AM 23; 128–29, 131
Lough Neagh: Seagoe AH 1; 101, 104–06, 109
Lough Neagh: Shankill AH 1; 111, 113
Lough Neagh: Shankill DN 12; 138–39
Lough Neagh: Shilvodan AM 19; 128–29
Lough Neagh: Tamlaght TE 20; 73, 137
Lough Neagh: Tartaraghan AH 1; 117, 119–21, 123
Lough Neagh: Templepatrick AM 35; 105, 107,
    115–16, 139–40
Lough Neagh: Termoneeny LY 6; 129
Lough Neagh: Tullyniskan TE 20; 139–40
Lough Neagh: Tullyrusk AM 21; 133, 135
Lough Neagh: Tynan AH 1; 124
Lough Neagh: Umgall AM 35; 155–56, 159
Lough Neagh deerpark: Aghalee AM 21; 28
Lough Pean td: Dungiven LY 15; 34
Lough Swilly: Ballywillin LY 33; 30
Lough Swilly: Clondavaddog DL 38; 1, 3–5, 7,
    9–10
Lough Swilly: Clonleigh DL 39; 16–17
Lough Swilly: Clonmany DL 38; 12–13, 16, 20
Lough Swilly: Coleraine LY 33; 147

Lough Swilly: Desertegney DL 38; 24–26
Lough Swilly: Faughanvale LY 36; 63
Lough Swilly: Killygarvan DL 38; 36–38, 40, 42–43, 45, 48–49
Lough Swilly: Leck DL 39; 115, 117
Lough Swilly: Lough Swilly DL 38; 98–106, 117, 126–28, 133, 137–39, 143, 146–47, 149
Lough Swilly: Mevagh DL 38; 54, 56 57
Lough Swilly: Mintiaghs DL 38; 64
Lough Swilly: Misc. DL 39; 184–85, 189
Lough Swilly: Raymoghy DL 39; 132, 135, 143–44, 146–47
Lough Swilly: Tullyaughnish DL 38; 84–85, 87, 89–95
Lough Swilly batteries: Lough Swilly DL 38; 149
Lough View House: Carrickfergus AM 37; 141
Lough, John: Faughanvale LY 36; 5
Lough-a-cannon: Laragh CN 40; 39, 42
Loughachery flax mill: Annahilt DN 12; 22
Loughachery meeting house: Annahilt DN 12; 22
Lough-a-curragh: Laragh CN 40; 39
Loughadhairuigh: Killymard DL 39; 94
Loughadian lough: Aghaderg DN 12; 3
Loughadian lough: Misc. DN 17; 130–31
Loughadian td: Aghaderg DN 12; 2
Loughadian td: Misc. DN 17; 131
Loughadubh: Donegal DL 39; 42
Loughadubh: Killymard DL 39; 95
Loughaduire: Donegal DL 39; 42
Loughafachin: Donegal DL 39; 42
Loughaghery td: Magheradrool DN 17; 103
Loughaghnuisbeag: Templecarn DL 39; 157
Loughaghnuismore: Templecarn DL 39; 157
Loughain fort: Devenish FH 14; 55
Lough-a-maniofa: Mevagh DL 38; 55
Loughamellain: Killymard DL 39; 95
Loughamhaisil: Killymard DL 39; 94
Loughamillain: Killymard DL 39; 95
Loughaminchin: Donegal DL 39; 42
Loughan bridge: Kildollagh LY 22; 68–69
Loughan corn mill: Kildollagh LY 22; 67
Loughan flax mill [I]: Kildollagh LY 22; 67
Loughan flax mill [II]: Kildollagh LY 22; 67
Loughan fort: Agivey LY 22; 44
Loughan hamlet: Kildollagh LY 22; 68
Loughan hill: Coleraine LY 33; 132
Loughan Hill fort: Coleraine LY 33; 92, 132
Loughan Hill td: Coleraine LY 33; 92
Loughan Island: Kildollagh LY 22; 68, 73
Loughan Island: Macosquin LY 22; 76
Loughan Island forts: Kildollagh LY 22; 69, 73–74
Loughan lough: Clondavaddog DL 38; 3
Loughan td: Culfeightrin AM 24; 38
Loughan td: Devenish FH 14; 58
Loughan water: Kildollagh LY 22; 67

Loughan, Hugh: Blaris DN 12; 41
Loughan, John: Glenavy AM 21; 91
Loughanabrac: Killymard DL 39; 94
Loughanabracbuey: Killymard DL 39; 94
Loughanabracbutha: Killymard DL 39; 94
Loughanacullane: Killymard DL 39; 94
Loughanameathog: Killymard DL 39; 94
Loughanmore House: Ahoghill AM 23; 23
Loughanmore td: Ballymascanlan LH 40; 56
Loughanoid lough: Clogher TE 5; 47
Loughanrea South td: Kildollagh LY 22; 75
Loughans bog: Tullylish DN 12; 140
Loughans hamlet: Kildollagh LY 22; 67, 72
Loughans loughs: Carrickfergus AM 37; 184
Loughans mill [I]: Tullylish DN 12; 147
Loughans mill [II]: Tullylish DN 12; 147
Loughans td: Tullylish DN 12; 143–44, 147
Loughantrarer: Tydavnet MN 40; 169
Loughanwherein: Donegal DL 39; 42
Loughaporton: Tydavnet MN 40; 169
Lougharose: Kilmacteige SO 40; 194
Lougharubble: Kilmacteige SO 40; 193
Loughascatha: Donegal DL 39; 44
Loughash lough: Donaghedy TE 5; 88
Loughash mountain: Donaghedy TE 5; 88
Loughash school: Donaghedy TE 5; 88
Loughash td: Donaghedy TE 5; 92
Lough-a-stirral: Laragh CN 40; 39–40
Lough-a-terrive: Cappagh TE 5; 15
Loughatleave: Donegal DL 39; 43
Lough-a-toana: Killesher FH 14; 82–83
Loughavaddy: Killymard DL 39; 95
Loughawaughran: Kilmacteige SO 40; 193
Loughbracken: Kildress TE 20; 61
Loughbrickland: Aghaderg DN 12; 1, 4–5, 8
Loughbrickland: Ballymore AH 1; 3, 10
Loughbrickland: Donaghmore DN 3; 9
Loughbrickland: Misc. DN 17; 131, 131
Loughbrickland: Montiaghs AH 1; 91
Loughbrickland: Seapatrick DN 12; 124
Loughbrickland Castle: Aghaderg DN 12; 7
Loughbrickland chapel (C): Aghaderg DN 12; 8
Loughbrickland chapel (M): Aghaderg DN 12; 4, 9
Loughbrickland church: Aghaderg DN 12; 4, 8
Loughbrickland estate: Aghaderg DN 12; 4
Loughbrickland Glebe school: Aghaderg DN 12; 11
Loughbrickland House: Aghaderg DN 12; 10
Loughbrickland House: Seapatrick DN 12; 126
Loughbrickland lough: Aghaderg DN 12; 3, 7–8
Loughbrickland meeting house (P): Aghaderg DN 12; 4, 9
Loughbrickland meeting house (S): Aghaderg DN 12; 9
Loughbrickland school: Aghaderg DN 12; 10–11
Loughbrickland school: Hillsborough DN 12; 101

Loughbrickland Sunday school: Aghaderg DN 12; 11

Loughbrottogue td: Muckno MN 40; 162

Loughcamambaluighibh: Templecarn DL 39; 157

Loughconelly school: Skerry AM 13; 107

Loughconelly td: Skerry AM 13; 108

Loughcraw: Killymard DL 39; 94

Loughcrongormard: Killymard DL 39; 94

Loughcrunnabrows: Killymard DL 39; 94

Loughcullien: Drumglass TE 20; 40, 44

Loughdale: Clonleigh DL 39; 1

Loughdale: Raphoe DL 39; 129

Loughdoo: Kilmacteige SO 40; 194

Loughdoo td: Misc. DN 17; 125

Loughdow td: Tullyaughnish DL 38; 97

Loughead, Dr: Emlaghfad SO 40; 179

Lougheascartha: Killymard DL 39; 94

Lougher td: Killygarvan DL 38; 47

Lougheriscouse (see Loughriscouse)

Loughermore cove: Nilteen AM 35; 99

Loughermore district: Cumber LY 28; 14

Loughermore glen: Tamlaght Finlagan LY 25; 62

Loughermore House: Doagh AM 29; 86

Loughermore House: Donegore AM 29; 107, 110, 132

Loughermore House: Nilteen AM 35; 84–85, 89, 91, 101–02

Loughermore mountain: Cumber LY 28; 40

Loughermore mountain: Tamlaght Finlagan LY 25; 62–63

Loughermore plantation: Tamlaght Finlagan LY 25; 66

Loughermore Pole mountain: Cumber LY 28; 1

Loughermore stream: Cumber LY 28; 43, 54

Loughermore stream: Tamlaght Finlagan LY 25; 62, 64, 84

Loughermore td: Bovevagh LY 25; 13

Loughermore td: Faughanvale LY 36; 53, 60, 69, 77, 88, 96

Loughermore td: Nilteen AM 35; 84, 89

Loughermore wood: Faughanvale LY 36; 88

Lougherrabin: Donegal DL 39; 42

Loughfadda: Donegal DL 39; 42

Loughfadda [I]: Killymard DL 39; 95

Loughfadda [II]: Killymard DL 39; 95

Loughgall: Clonfeacle AH 1; 24, 26

Loughgall: Drumcree AH 1; 28, 30, 36, 41

Loughgall: Drumragh TE 5; 110

Loughgall: Kilmore AH 1; 58, 66–67

Loughgall: Loughgall AH 1; 76–77, 79, 81–82

Loughgall: Loughgilly AH 1; 84–85

Loughgall: Misc. DN 17; 122

Loughgall: Seagoe AH 1; 107–08

Loughgall: Tartaraghan AH 1; 120, 122

Loughgall chapel: Loughgall AH 1; 75

Loughgall church: Loughgall AH 1; 76, 79–80

Loughgall court house: Loughgall AH 1; 76, 79

Loughgall demesne: Loughgall AH 1; 79–80

Loughgall dispensary: Drumcree AH 1; 36–37

Loughgall dispensary: Kilmore AH 1; 64

Loughgall dispensary: Loughgall AH 1; 76–77

Loughgall female school: Loughgall AH 1; 78

Loughgall hill: Loughgall AH 1; 78

Loughgall lough: Loughgall AH 1; 75, 79–81

Loughgall male school: Loughgall AH 1; 78

Loughgall manor: Loughgall AH 1; 81

Loughgall meeting house: Loughgall AH 1; 76

Loughgall ph: Ballymore AH 1; 15

Loughgall ph: Clonfeacle AH 1; 21–23

Loughgall ph: Killyman AH 1; 55

Loughgall ph: Kilmore AH 1; 57, 60, 66, 68–71, 73

Loughgall ph: Tartaraghan AH 1; 117, 119

Loughgall school: Loughgall AH 1; 76, 79

Loughgall td: Loughgall AH 1; 75

Loughgilly church: Loughgilly AH 1; 86–87

Loughgilly corn mill [I]: Loughgilly AH 1; 87

Loughgilly corn mill [II]: Loughgilly AH 1; 87

Loughgilly corn mill [III]: Loughgilly AH 1; 87

Loughgilly flax mill [I]: Loughgilly AH 1; 87

Loughgilly flax mill [II]: Loughgilly AH 1; 87

Loughgilly flax mill [III]: Loughgilly AH 1; 87

Loughgilly flax mill [IV]: Loughgilly AH 1; 87

Loughgilly ph: Ballymore AH 1; 1, 7, 9, 14, 16–18

Loughgilly Rectory: Loughgilly AH 1; 84

Loughgilly school: Loughgilly AH 1; 86–87

Loughgolagh lough: Ballyscullion LY 6; 67

Loughguile: Armoy AM 24; 1

Loughguile: Dundermot AM 13; 33

Loughguile: Loughguile AM 13; 59, 62

Loughguile Castle: Loughguile AM 13; 62, 64

Loughguile chapel: Loughguile AM 13; 62

Loughguile church: Loughguile AM 13; 62, 68

Loughguile dispensary: Armoy AM 24; 5

Loughguile dispensary: Killagan AM 23; 84

Loughguile dispensary: Kilraghts AM 16; 129

Loughguile dispensary: Loughguile AM 13; 65–66

Loughguile lough: Loughguile AM 13; 68

Loughguile meeting house: Armoy AM 24; 2, 4

Loughguile meeting house: Loughguile AM 13; 62

Loughguile ph: Armoy AM 24; 1–2

Loughguile ph: Ballymoney AM 16; 3

Loughguile ph: Culfeightrin AM 24; 36, 40, 69, 80

Loughguile ph: Derrykeighan AM 16; 78, 80

Loughguile ph: Dunaghy AM 13; 20, 25, 27

Loughguile ph: Dungiven LY 15; 91

Loughguile ph: Killagan AM 23; 79–82, 84

Loughguile ph: Kilraghts AM 16; 125

Loughguile ph: Layd AM 13; 36

Loughguile ph: Layd and Inispollan AM 13; 54–55

Loughguile ph: Misc. AM 10; 129

Loughguile ph: Newtown Crommelin AM 13; 78
Loughguile Sunday schools: Loughguile AM 13; 67
Loughhill flax mill: Killagan AM 23; 83
Loughhill td: Aghalurcher FH 4; 3
Loughileive: Donegal DL 39; 42
Loughillarmore: Donegal DL 39; 42
Lough-in-albanagh: Clogher TE 5; 25, 47
Lough-inch lough: Banagher LY 30; 106
Loughinisland chapel: Loughinisland DN 17; 95, 97
Loughinisland ph: Down DN 17; 47
Loughinisland ph: Dromara DN 12; 62
Loughinisland ph: Misc. DN 17; 121–22, 128
Loughinnaghachola: Donegal DL 39; 43
Loughinreagh td: Coleraine LY 33; 104
Loughinsholin barony: Artrea TE 20; 6
Loughinsholin barony: Desertlyn LY 31; 37, 42
Loughinsholin barony: Dungiven LY 15; 80
Loughinsholin barony: Kilrea LY 27; 104, 112
Loughinsholin barony: Maghera LY 18; 1, 3
Loughinsholin barony: Magherafelt LY 6; 81, 84,
    88, 97
Loughinsholin barony: Magilligan LY 11; 105
Loughinsholin barony: Misc. LY 31; 111, 144
Loughinsholin barony: Misc. LY 36; 119
Loughinsholin barony: Tamlaght O'Crilly LY 18; 82
Loughinsholin lough: Misc. LY 31; 112–13
Loughinsland school: Loughinisland DN 17; 95
Loughiries td: Misc. DN 17; 123
Loughkeeland td: Ballyculter DN 17; 31
Loughkillygreen td: Galloon FH 4; 95
Loughlin, Anthony: Hillsborough DN 12; 107
Loughlin, Eliza: Drummaul AM 19; 91
Loughlin, family: Desertoghill LY 27; 5
Loughlin, James: Donegore AM 29; 130
Loughlin, Joseph: Maghera LY 18; 80
Loughlin, Robert: Tamlaght O'Crilly LY 18; 109
Loughlin, Thomas: Desertoghill LY 27; 5, 14, 24
Loughloughan td: Skerry AM 13; 107, 114
Loughloughan well: Skerry AM 13; 114
Loughlynch cove: Billy AM 16; 56, 73
Loughlynch fort: Billy AM 16; 62
Loughlynch td: Billy AM 16; 39, 48, 58–59, 64
Loughmeeltagh: Mevagh DL 38; 55
Loughmhinanidh: Donegal DL 39; 42
Loughmills (see Cloghmills): Killagan AM 23; 86
Loughmonen (see Meenan): Aghaderg DN 12; 3
Loughmoney (Loughmooney) td: Ballee DN 17;
    19–20, 22–23
Loughmoney altar: Ballee DN 17; 24
Loughmoney bog: Ballee DN 17; 15, 19
Loughmoney school: Ballee DN 17; 20
Loughmorne (see Loughmourne): Carrickfergus AM
    37; 77
Loughmourne: Raloo AM 32; 124

Loughmourne cotton factory: Carrickfergus AM 37;
    137
Loughmourne district: Carrickfergus AM 37; 77,
    158, 175
Loughmourne meeting house: Carrickfergus AM 37;
    3, 56, 70, 100, 134, 143
Loughmourne school: Carrickfergus AM 37; 155
Loughmourne school: Raloo AM 32; 130–31
Loughmourne Sunday school: Raloo AM 32; 131
Loughmuck corn mill: Drumragh TE 5; 110
Loughmuck flax mill: Drumragh TE 5; 110
Loughmuck fort: Drumragh TE 5; 109
Loughmuck giant's grave: Drumragh TE 5; 109
Loughmuck td: Drumragh TE 5; 109–10
Loughmunnog lough: Bovevagh LY 25; 1, 33
Loughnaangeng: Templecarn DL 39; 157
Loughnabeery lough: Clogher TE 5; 47
Loughnabin: Templecarn DL 39; 157
Loughnablaneybane lough: Clogher TE 5; 25, 47
Loughnabrackbwee: Donegal DL 39; 43
Loughnabraereeagh: Kilmacteige SO 40; 187
Loughnabreen: Donegal DL 39; 42
Loughnacairn: Killdrumsherdan CN 40; 34
Loughnacantagh: Donegal DL 39; 42
Loughnachan: Templecarn DL 39; 157
Lough-na-cranagh: Culfeightrin AM 24; 38, 42, 67
Lough-na-cranog (see Lough-na-cranagh)
Loughnacreaght: Mevagh DL 38; 54–55
Loughnacreaght: Tullyaughnish DL 38; 84
Lough-na-cressa: Culfeightrin AM 24; 81
Lough-na-cressa Island: Culfeightrin AM 24; 81
Loughnacrilly: Drumglass TE 20; 40, 44
Loughnacruache: Donegal DL 39; 42
Loughnacruche: Donegal DL 39; 42
Lough-na-cuin (see Fea): Lissan LY 31; 91
Lough-na-cullagh: Galloon FH 4; 98
Loughnadara: Aghalurcher FH 4; 3, 5
Loughnagalla (see Loughonagally): Kilmacteige SO
    40; 193
Loughnagcolum: Killymard DL 39; 94
Loughnagcrapangom: Killymard DL 39; 94
Loughnagerraigeach: Killymard DL 39; 95
Loughnaglack lough: Magheross MN 40; 130, 143
Loughnagleia: Clondavaddog DL 38; 2
Loughnagoppag: Donegal DL 39; 42
Loughnagreen: Clondavaddog DL 38; 2
Loughnagroocgranagh: Donegal DL 39; 42
Loughnagrookgranagh: Donegal DL 39; 42
Loughnaheenybawn: Kilmacteige SO 40; 193
Lough-na-heery: Clogher TE 5; 25
Loughnahery: Errigal Truagh MN 40; 120
Loughnahrackeeagh: Kilmacteige SO 40; 194
Loughnaken school: Enniskeen CN 40; 26
Loughnakey td: Tullyaughnish DL 38; 96
Loughnakilloo Bawn: Aughnamullen MN 40; 70

Loughnalackagh: Kilmacteige SO 40; 193
Lough-na-lair: Laragh CN 40; 39
Loughnamaskher: Donaghmore DL 39; 28
Loughnambraddan: Mevagh DL 38; 55
Loughnamhasnugh: Killymard DL 39; 95
Loughnaminn: Clonmany DL 38; 12–13
Loughnamnas: Templecarn DL 39; 157
Loughnamodhu: Donegal DL 39; 43
Lough-na-muck: Lissan LY 31; 89, 100
Lough-na-muck bog: Lissan LY 31; 89
Lough-na-muck giant's grave: Lissan LY 31; 91, 100
Loughnapaise: Donaghmore DL 39; 28
Loughnapaiste: Donegal DL 39; 42
Loughnaparte: Clondavaddog DL 38; 2
Loughnarigh: Aghalurcher FH 4; 3
Loughnashry: Kilmacteige SO 40; 193
Lough-na-sliggan: Clogher TE 5; 25, 47
Loughnasmulton: Mevagh DL 38; 55
Loughnasuofan: Templecarn DL 39; 157
Loughnatooey: Mevagh DL 38; 55
Loughnatroy: Aghalurcher TE 5; 1
Loughnattywee: Kilmacteige SO 40; 193
Loughnavar: Inishmacsaint FH 14; 71
Loughnavarad: Clogher TE 5; 25, 47
Loughnaveeouge: Mevagh DL 38; 55
Loughnaweelogue: Donegal DL 39; 43
Loughne (see Loughnoe): Kilmacteige SO 40; 195
Loughnoe: Kilmacteige SO 40; 194–95
Loughnoe river: Kilmacteige SO 40; 195
Loughonagally: Kilmacteige SO 40; 191, 193, 195
Loughonayally (see Loughonagally): Kilmacteige SO 40; 195
Loughonmore: Kilmacteige SO 40; 194
Loughoran (see Loughorne): Newry DN 3; 61
Loughorn (see Loughorne)
Loughorne bleach mill: Newry DN 3; 112
Loughorne corn mill: Newry DN 3; 78
Loughorne lough: Donaghmore DN 3; 7, 9
Loughorne lough: Newry DN 3; 61
Loughorne school: Newry DN 3; 81, 112
Loughorne td: Newry DN 3; 61, 78, 81, 111–12
Loughran, Edward: Carrickfergus AM 37; 120
Loughran, Elizabeth: Maghera LY 18; 33
Loughran, family: Ballynascreen LY 31; 12
Loughran, James: Carrickfergus AM 37; 123–24, 126
Loughran, Michael: Carrickfergus AM 37; 126
Loughran, Owen: Carrickfergus AM 37; 126
Loughran, Patrick: Carrickfergus AM 37; 123
Loughran, Patrick: Maghera LY 18; 31, 33
Loughran, William: Carrickfergus AM 37; 124
Loughrey, David: Tamlaght Finlagan LY 25; 115
Loughrey, man named: Muckamore AM 35; 68
Loughrey, Patrick: Carrickfergus AM 37; 108

Loughridge, Hugh: Carrickfergus AM 37; 21
Loughridge, Mrs: Carrickfergus AM 37; 21
Loughridge, Robert: Ahoghill AM 23; 37
Loughridge, Samuel: Ballyscullion LY 6; 47
Loughridge, Samuel: Magherafelt LY 6; 89
Loughriscouse school: Newtownards DN 7; 105
Loughriscouse td: Misc. DN 17; 123
Loughriscouse td: Newtownards DN 7; 105, 112
Loughros bay: Inishkeel DL 39; 70
Loughrus (see Lochrus)
Loughry river: Artrea LY 6; 39
Loughry river: Artrea TE 20; 8
Loughry river: Ballinderry TE 20; 13
Loughry td: Artrea TE 20; 6
Loughry td: Desertcreat TE 20; 34
Loughry, Denis: Errigal LY 27; 66
Loughry, John: Ballymoney AM 16; 16
Loughry, John: Loughguile AM 13; 77
Loughry, Mr: Clonmany DL 38; 14, 18
Loughry, William: Balteagh LY 9; 40
Loughside district: Drumachose LY 9; 106
Loughside locality: Muckamore AM 35; 80
Loughtammon island: Ahoghill AM 23; 34
Loughtee Lower barony: Tomregan FH 4; 125
Loughtee Upper barony: Laragh CN 40; 39
Loughtilube altar: Banagher LY 30; 91
Loughtilube fort [I]: Banagher LY 30; 65
Loughtilube fort [II]: Banagher LY 30; 91
Loughtilube graveyards: Banagher LY 30; 39, 50, 55, 90
Loughtilube standing stone [I]: Banagher LY 30; 90
Loughtilube standing stone [II]: Banagher LY 30; 90
Loughtilube standing stone [III]: Banagher LY 30; 90
Loughtilube standing stone [IV]: Banagher LY 30; 90
Loughtilube td: Banagher LY 30; 22–23, 35, 50, 60–62, 64, 105, 109–10, 112, 119, 124, 128, 130–31
Loughtilube wood: Banagher LY 30; 124
Loughullanacrooney: Donegal DL 39; 42
Louis XI, King: Blaris AM 8; 8
Louis XIII, King: Carrickfergus AM 37; 90
Louis XIV, King: Carrickfergus AM 37; 83
Louis XVI, King: Banagher LY 30; 35, 96
Louth: Ballee DN 17; 19
Louth: Cumber LY 28; 18
Louth: Drummully FH 4; 37
Louth: Enniskeen CN 40; 26, 29
Louth: Faughanvale LY 36; 30, 44, 60
Louth: Inniskeen MN 40; 124, 127–29
Louth: Kilbroney DN 3; 28, 37
Louth: Kilkeel DN 3; 53
Louth: Killanny MN 40; 130, 132–35
Louth: Kilmore AH 1; 67

Louth: Magheracloone MN 40; 141
Louth: Magheross MN 40; 143, 152
Louth: Misc. DN 17; 128, 130
Louth: Newry DN 3; 72–73, 87, 105, 107, 109
Louth: Warrenpoint DN 3; 118–19
Louth barony: Donaghmoyne MN 40; 106
Louth barony: Inniskeen MN 40; 124
Louth barony: Killanny MN 40; 130
Louth diocese: Clogher TE 5; 29
Louth dispensary: Inniskeen MN 40; 127
Louth manor: Newry DN 3; 65
Louth ph: Donaghmoyne MN 40; 106
Louth rectory: Carrickfergus AM 37; 78
Louth, Earl of: Kilkeel DN 3; 53
Love, Alixander: Drumachose LY 9; 116
Love, Archibald: Aghadowey LY 22; 19, 21, 35
Love, family: Ballynure AM 32; 56
Love, family: Dunluce AM 16; 117
Love, family: Magherafelt LY 6; 95
Love, family: Misc. LY 36; 104
Love, family: Rasharkin AM 23; 136
Love, Henery: Magherafelt LY 6; 110
Love, James: Doagh AM 29; 95
Love, James: Dunboe LY 11; 77
Love, Jane: Kilraghts AM 16; 132
Love, Mr: Ardstraw TE 5; 13
Love, Mr: Tullyaughnish DL 38; 87
Love, Mrs: Dungiven LY 15; 99
Love, Robert: Magherafelt LY 6; 112
Love, Robert: Rasharkin AM 23; 138
Love, William: Magherafelt LY 6; 109–10, 112
Love's Castle: Loughguile AM 13; 69
Love's Hotel: Kirkinriola AM 23; 95
Lovell, Rev. Trefusis: Aghadowey LY 22; 22
Lovestown school: Rasharkin AM 23; 141
Lovette, Hugh: Errigal Truagh MN 40; 122
Low fort: Desertoghill LY 27; 27
Low Park beetling mills: Ahoghill AM 23; 13
Low Park bleach mills: Ahoghill AM 23; 31
Low Park House: Ahoghill AM 23; 12
Low Quarters locality: Blaris DN 12; 42
Low Trench village: Raphoe DL 39; 125
Low, Mr: Cumber LY 28; 93
Lowburn House: Ballyscullion AM 19; 9
Lowden, family: Carnmoney AM 2; 102
Lowden, Hugh: Drumtullagh AM 16; 102
Lowden, James: Bovevagh LY 25; 59
Lowden, Jane: Bovevagh LY 25; 59
Lowden, John: Bovevagh LY 25; 59
Lowden, Mary: Ballyscullion LY 6; 77
Lowden, Mary: Bovevagh LY 25; 59
Lowden, Mrs: Maghera LY 18; 53
Lowden, Robert: Drumachose LY 9; 116
Lowden, William: Artrea LY 6; 25
Lowe, James: Carrickfergus AM 37; 194

Lower farm: Donaghmore DL 39; 34
Lower lough (see Lough Erne Lower): Enniskillen FH 4; 44
Lowertown td: Clones FH 4; 26
Lowertown village: Kilmacteige SO 40; 193
Lowerymore river: Donegal DL 39; 44
Lowes, Andrew: Island Magee AM 10; 95
Lownds, Thomas: Macosquin LY 22, 81, 101
Lownsdale, family: Aghagallon AM 21; 9
Lowrey, William: Nilteen AM 35; 103
Lowrie, St: Maghera LY 18; 10
Lowry [or Lowey], James: Templecorran AM 26; 116, 131
Lowry, Catherine: Tickmacrevan AM 13; 133
Lowry, David: Kilbroney DN 3; 28
Lowry, family: Ballee DN 17; 16
Lowry, James: Clogherny TE 20; 26
Lowry, James: Desertcreat TE 20; 34, 36
Lowry, James: Kilmood DN 7; 96
Lowry, James: Newry DN 3; 98
Lowry, James: Pomeroy TE 20; 71
Lowry, John: Blaris DN 12; 40
Lowry, John: Tamlaght Finlagan LY 25; 118
Lowry, Magy: Tamlaght Finlagan LY 25; 118
Lowry, Mrs: Clondermot LY 34; 81
Lowry, Rev. James: Clogherny TE 20; 25
Lowry, Rev. James: Drumragh TE 5; 109
Lowry, Rev. James: Pomeroy TE 20; 71
Lowry, Rev. John: Clogherny TE 20; 25
Lowry, Richard: Clondermot LY 34; 81
Lowry, Robert: Desertcreat TE 20; 34, 36
Lowry, Robert: Pomeroy TE 20; 70–71
Lowry, Thomas: Derryaghy AM 8; 96
Lowry, William: Clondermot LY 34; 93
Lowry, William: Dunboe LY 11; 79
Lowther manor: Magheracross FH 14; 102
Lowther manor: Misc. FH 4; 133
Lowtherstown (see Irvinestown)
Lowtherstowne (see Irvinestown)
Lowtown fort: Kilwaughter AM 10; 118
Lowtown holy well: Kilwaughter AM 10; 117
Lowtown td: Kilwaughter AM 10; 107, 117–18
Luace Pullinabucean locality: Lough Swilly DL 38; 119
Luack Point: Lough Swilly DL 38; 111
Luackan Point: Lough Swilly DL 38; 147
Luacnaluannan Point: Lough Swilly DL 38; 124
Lubby-nafir giant's grave: Culfeightrin AM 24; 51
Luberlady locality: Carrickfergus AM 37; 93
Lubitavish flax mill: Layd AM 13; 48
Lubitavish td: Layd AM 13; 48
Lucan spa: Drumhome DL 39; 61
Lucan spa: Magilligan LY 11; 120
Lucan, Edward: Clontibret MN 40; 85
Lucas, D.: Ballymore AH 1; 12, 15, 17–18

Lucas, E.: Aughnamullen MN 40; 75–76
Lucas, F.C.: Kilmacteige SO 40; 188
Lucas, Thomas: Ballybay MN 40; 82
Lucas, Thomas: Muckno MN 40; 165
Luchughore village: Kilmacteige SO 40; 195
Luec Charrig rock: Lough Swilly DL 38; 110
Lueck Coulin rock: Lough Swilly DL 38; 111
Lug lough: Artrea LY 6; 3, 11, 33, 39
Lug lough: Artrea TE 20; 8
Lug lough: Desertlyn LY 31; 37
Lugaidh Raibderg, King: Lough Neagh AM 21; 93
Lugarvagra mountain: Tomregan FH 4; 125
Lugbrisken td: Carlingford LH 40; 58
Luger (see Largy): Derrybrusk FH 4; 32
Lugg Castle: Carrickfergus AM 37; 84, 182–83
Lugg, family: Carrickfergus AM 37; 183
Luggahurra hollow: Killesher FH 14; 83
Luggelaw locality: Dungiven LY 15; 28
Lughany lough: Donegal DL 39; 43–44
Luinniagh locality: Lough Swilly DL 38; 123
Luissatheguirth fort: Bovevagh LY 25; 35
Luke, family: Derrykeighan AM 16; 89
Luke, family: Magilligan LY 11; 142
Lullinaglug (see Tullinaglug): Kilmacteige SO 40;
 186
Lumgelton school: Killdrumsherdan CN 40; 36
Lumley, Col: Antrim AM 29; 6
Lumley, Francis: Blaris AM 8; 66
Lumnaghbeg cave [I]: Ballintoy AM 24; 29
Lumnaghbeg cave [II]: Ballintoy AM 24; 29
Lumnaghbeg druid's altar [I]: Ballintoy AM 24;
 24–25, 28
Lumnaghbeg druid's altar [II]: Ballintoy AM 24; 25
Lumnaghbeg standing stone [I]: Ballintoy AM 24;
 28
Lumnaghbeg standing stone [II]: Ballintoy AM 24;
 28
Lumnaghbeg standing stone [III]: Ballintoy AM 24;
 29
Lumnaghbeg td: Ballintoy AM 24; 29
Lumnaghmore cave: Ballintoy AM 24; 29
Lumnaghmore druid's altar: Ballintoy AM 24; 29
Lumnaghmore enclosure [I]: Ballintoy AM 24; 29
Lumnaghmore enclosure [II]: Ballintoy AM 24; 29
Lumnaghmore td: Ballintoy AM 24; 20
Lumnaherry fort: Ahoghill AM 23; 35
Lunaght, man named: Banagher LY 30; 48
Lunby-na-disha grave: Cumber LY 28; 32
Lundy, Margaret: Killowen LY 33; 165
Lundy, Patrick: Magheradrool DN 17; 102
Lundy, R.: Newry DN 3; 100
Lundy, Robert: Galloon FH 4; 100–01
Luney bog: Misc. LY 31; 121
Luney td: Desertmartin LY 31; 62, 113, 142, 144
Lungs td: Clogher TE 5; 37

Lunie, James: Camlin AM 21; 76
Lunn, family: Derryaghy AM 8; 103
Lunn, Rev.: Carlingford LH 40; 60
Lunnon, James: Lissan LY 31; 105
Lunnon, Maryann: Magherafelt LY 6; 112
Lurg barony: Belleek FH 14; 1
Lurg barony: Derryvullan FH 14; 31, 39
Lurg barony: Drumkeeran FH 14; 62, 65
Lurg barony: Magheraculmoney FH 14; 103
Lurg barony: Templecarn FH 14; 118
Lurg barony: Trory FH 14; 122, 132
Lurga district: Misc. SO 40; 199–200
Lurgachamlough td: Aughnamullen MN 40; 69, 76
Lurgacloghan fort: Clondavaddog DL 38; 6
Lurgacloghan hill: Clondavaddog DL 38; 1
Lurgacloghan td: Clondavaddog DL 38; 3–4
Lurgacloughan (see Lurgacloghan)
Lurgahamla (see Lurgachamlough)
Lurgahaurla (see Lurgachamlough)
Lurgaloghan (see Lurgacloghan)
Lurgamore district: Blaris AM 8; 87
Lurgan: Aghagallon AM 21; 1–2, 4, 6–8, 10, 22, 24
Lurgan: Aghalee AM 21; 27–29, 32–34
Lurgan: Ballinderry AM 21; 42, 45, 48, 58
Lurgan: Blaris AM 8; 7, 16, 50, 72–73
Lurgan: Camlin AM 21; 63, 67
Lurgan: Donaghcloney DN 12; 57
Lurgan: Drumachose LY 9; 95
Lurgan: Drumcree AH 1; 29, 32, 35–38, 40
Lurgan: Drumhome DL 39; 62
Lurgan: Glenavy AM 21; 78, 81, 86
Lurgan: Kilmore AH 1; 65
Lurgan: Lough Neagh AM 21; 94
Lurgan: Magheramesk AM 21; 112
Lurgan: Montiaghs AH 1; 90, 92–93
Lurgan: Seagoe AH 1; 102, 105–10
Lurgan: Shankill AH 1; 111, 113–16
Lurgan: Shankill DN 12; 138
Lurgan: Tartaraghan AH 1; 120–21
Lurgan: Tullyrusk AM 21; 135
Lurgan bay: Aghagallon AM 21; 2
Lurgan bridewell: Shankill AH 1; 114
Lurgan chapel (C): Shankill AH 1; 114
Lurgan chapel (M): Shankill AH 1; 115
Lurgan chapel (WM): Shankill AH 1; 114
Lurgan church (see Shankill)
Lurgan court house: Shankill AH 1; 114–15
Lurgan dispensary: Seagoe AH 1; 106
Lurgan dispensary: Shankill DN 12; 138
Lurgan distillery: Shankill AH 1; 113
Lurgan district (Fermanagh): Kinawley FH 4; 123
Lurgan female school: Shankill AH 1; 115
Lurgan free school: Shankill AH 1; 115–16
Lurgan gaol: Shankill AH 1; 114
Lurgan linen hall: Shankill AH 1; 114

Lurgan male school: Shankill AH 1; 115

Lurgan market house: Shankill AH 1; 113–14

Lurgan meeting house: Shankill AH 1; 114

Lurgan news room: Shankill AH 1; 113

Lurgan stream: Cleenish FH 14; 14

Lurgan td: Aghavea FH 4; 23

Lurgan td: Cleenish FH 14; 29

Lurgan West fort: Drummaul AM 19; 88

Lurgan West forts: Drummaul AM 19; 78

Lurgan West td: Drummaul AM 19; 90–91

Lurganaglare td: Clogher TE 5; 44

Lurganagoose td: Termoneeny LY 6; 124, 126, 131, 133

Lurganare td: Donaghmore DN 3; 7, 9

Lurganare td: Misc. DN 17; 131

Lurganbaan (see Lurganbane)

Lurganban flax mill: Dromore DN 12; 72

Lurganbane mountain: Aghalurcher FH 4; 2

Lurganbane td: Aghalurcher FH 4; 5, 14

Lurganbane td: Aghavea FH 4; 19

Lurganboy (Lurganbuy) td: Errigal Keerogue TE 20; 50, 54–55, 57

Lurganboy bay: Lough Swilly DL 38; 100

Lurganboy flax mill: Drumgoon CN 40; 7

Lurganboy lough: Donaghmoyne MN 40; 106

Lurganboy sandpits: Currin MN 40; 88–89

Lurganboy school: Errigal Keerogue TE 20; 54

Lurganboy td: Cappagh TE 5; 20

Lurganboy td: Currin MN 40; 89, 92

Lurganboy td: Donacavey TE 5; 76, 79–81, 84

Lurganboy td: Galloon FH 4; 89, 95

Lurganboy td: Lough Swilly DL 38; 99

Lurganboys (see Lurganboy)

Lurganbuoy (see Lurganboy)

Lurganbwee (see Lurganboy): Lough Swilly DL 38; 99

Lurgancahone chapel: Drumgath DN 3; 20

Lurgancahone td: Drumgath DN 3; 20–21

Lurganclabby td: Enniskillen FH 4; 82

Lurgancot td: Kilmore AH 1; 66, 70–71

Lurgancullion td: Killeeshil TE 20; 64

Lurgandarragh Big td: Cleenish FH 14; 11, 29

Lurgandarragh Big td: Rossorry FH 14; 115

Lurgandoy td: Enniskillen FH 4; 82

Lurganearly flax mill: Muckno MN 40; 166

Lurgangreen hill: Aughnamullen MN 40; 69

Lurgangreen td: Aughnamullen MN 40; 76

Lurganmore corn mill: Muckno MN 40; 165

Lurganna corn mill: Ballymyre AH 1; 20

Lurgans td: Magheross MN 40; 148

Lurgansemanus fort: Aghalee AM 21; 36

Lurgansemanus td: Aghalee AM 21; 28

Lurganshannagh (Lurganshaney) td: Clonleigh DL 39; 12, 198

Lurganshenny (see Lurganshannagh)

Lurgantamry td: Donaghcloney DN 12; 59

Lurganteneill school: Ballinderry AM 21; 41

Lurganure fort [I]: Blaris AM 8; 19

Lurganure fort [II]: Blaris AM 8; 19

Lurganure school: Blaris AM 8; 18, 78

Lurganure Sunday school: Blaris AM 8; 83

Lurganure td: Blaris AM 8; 19, 35, 82

Lurganure td: Blaris DN 12; 28

Lurganville chapel: Moira DN 12; 121

Lurganville school [I]: Moira DN 12; 120–21

Lurganville school [II]: Moira DN 12; 121

Lurganville td: Moira DN 12; 119, 121

Lurganyboy barracks: Manorhamilton Union LM 40; 52

Lurgaross (Lurgygross) td: Loughgilly AH 1; 85

Lurgaross bleach mill: Loughgilly AH 1; 88

Lurgill school: Ballinderry AM 21; 57–59

Lurgimor: Blaris AM 8; 86

Lurgologhan (see Lurgacloghan)

Lurgy td: Leck DL 39; 119

Lurgyboy td: Ballyscullion LY 6; 57

Lurgybrack td: Leck DL 39; 116, 119

Lurigethan fort: Layd AM 13; 41

Lurigethan mountain: Layd AM 13; 36–37, 42–43, 50–52

Lurigethan td: Layd AM 13; 41

Lush td: Loughgilly AH 1; 84

Lusk, John: Ballyaghran LY 33; 27

Lusk, Thomas: Ballynascreen LY 31; 13, 21

Luske, James: Loughguile AM 13; 71

Luske, Robert: Maghera LY 18; 69

Lusky corn mill: Kilmood DN 7; 96

Lustade td: Killea and Taughboyne DL 39; 79

Lusteabeg (see Lusty Beg)

Lusteamore (see Lusty More)

Lustiabeg (see Lusty Beg)

Lustiamore (see Lusty More)

Lustical (see Listicall): Misc. DL 39; 187

Lustillian (see Listellian): Leck DL 39; 119

Lustillion (see Listellian): Leck DL 39; 120

Lusty Beg Island: Drumkeeran FH 14; 64

Lusty Beg Island: Templecarn FH 14; 119

Lusty Beg td: Cleenish FH 14; 29

Lusty More Island: Templecarn FH 14; 119

Lusty More td: Cleenish FH 14; 29

Luttan, Thomas: Magheralin DN 12; 110

Lutten, family: Aghalee AM 21; 36

Lutton, F.: Drumcree AH 1; 41

Lutton, Henry: Aghagallon AM 21; 20

Lutton, John: Aghagallon AM 21; 17, 19

Lutton, T.: Seagoe AH 1; 109

Lyle and Watt, Messrs: Kilbride AM 29; 139, 151, 153

Lyle chapel: Seagoe AH 1; 102, 105, 109

Lyle hill: Aghadowey LY 22; 25

Lyle td: Seagoe AH 1; 109
Lyle, Acheson: Banagher LY 30; 113, 120
Lyle, Acheson: Cumber LY 28; 34, 48, 79–80, 97–98
Lyle, Acheson: Errigal LY 27; 79–80
Lyle, Acheson: Faughanvale LY 36; 40, 45
Lyle, David: Kilcronaghan LY 31; 85
Lyle, David: Raloo AM 32; 123
Lyle, family: Coleraine LY 33; 140
Lyle, family: Derrykeighan AM 16; 89
Lyle, family: Raloo AM 32; 94, 108, 123
Lyle, Gordon: Derrykeighan AM 16; 92–93
Lyle, Hugh (Jnr): Ballyrashane LY 22; 53, 60
Lyle, Hugh (Knockantern): Faughanvale LY 36; 40, 45
Lyle, Hugh (Snr): Ballyrashane LY 22; 50, 60
Lyle, Hugh: Ballywillin AM 16; 35
Lyle, Hugh: Ballywillin LY 33; 33, 46, 50
Lyle, Hugh: Banagher LY 30; 22, 30, 32, 59, 80, 99, 113, 120, 131
Lyle, Hugh: Clondermot LY 34; 79
Lyle, Hugh: Coleraine LY 33; 63–65, 67, 70, 73, 91, 120, 127, 140, 142–44
Lyle, Hugh: Cumber LY 28; 34, 53, 79–80
Lyle, Hugh: Faughanvale LY 36; 40, 45
Lyle, Hugh: Kilcronaghan LY 31; 83, 86–87
Lyle, Hugh: Kildollagh LY 22; 70
Lyle, Hugh: Moville DL 38; 73
Lyle, Hugh [I]: Maghera LY 18; 6
Lyle, Hugh [II]: Maghera LY 18; 50
Lyle, James: Ballynascreen LY 31; 11, 22
Lyle, James: Duneane AM 19; 108, 120
Lyle, James: Newry DN 3; 103
Lyle, John: Derrykeighan AM 16; 91, 95
Lyle, John: Kilcronaghan LY 31; 84
Lyle, John: Raloo AM 32; 123
Lyle, Joseph: Newry DN 3; 98, 103
Lyle, Mr: Clondermot LY 34; 35
Lyle, Mr: Donaghedy TE 5; 91–92
Lyle, Mrs: Cumber LY 28; 34, 79
Lyle, Mrs Hugh: Coleraine LY 33; 67, 70, 140, 143
Lyle, Rev. William: Dunboe LY 11; 57, 63, 66
Lyle, Samuel: Cumber LY 28; 80
Lyle, Samuel: Enniskillen FH 4; 66
Lyle, Smyth and Co., Messrs: Cumber LY 28; 57
Lyle, Thomas: Kilbride AM 29; 138, 150
Lyle, William: Kilcronaghan LY 31; 86
Lyle's hill: Ballymartin AM 2; 1, 5, 17
Lyle's hill: Templepatrick AM 35; 131, 141
Lyle's Hill book club room: Templepatrick AM 35; 122, 147
Lyle's Hill book club room: Umgall AM 35; 158
Lyle's Hill meeting house: Killead AM 35; 20, 46

Lyle's Hill meeting house: Templepatrick AM 35; 111, 117, 119, 123, 134–35, 140–42, 144–45, 147, 153–54
Lyle's Hill meeting house: Umgall AM 35; 157–58
Lyle's Hill school: Templepatrick AM 35; 122, 135–36, 147–48, 153–54
Lyle's Hill Sunday school: Templepatrick AM 35; 136, 154
Lyle's Hill td: Templepatrick AM 35; 145–46
Lymavady (see Limavady)
Lymington (England): Carrickfergus AM 37; 8
Lynam, Mr: Magilligan LY 11; 131
Lyncan [or Lyncar], William: Ballyscullion LY 6; 57
Lynch lough: Billy AM 16; 39, 49, 55, 74
Lynch lough cairn: Billy AM 16; 74
Lynch lough fort: Billy AM 16; 74
Lynch lough Island: Billy AM 16; 49
Lynch, Daniel: Errigal LY 27; 54, 70
Lynch, David: Aghanloo LY 11; 14
Lynch, family: Carrickfergus AM 37; 93
Lynch, Francis: Coleraine LY 33; 73
Lynch, James: Aghanloo LY 11; 29
Lynch, James: Drumachose LY 9; 112
Lynch, John: Galloon FH 4; 97
Lynch, man named: Clondermot LY 34; 32
Lynch, Michael: Aghadowey LY 22; 38
Lynch, Mr: Banagher LY 30; 70
Lynch, Patrick: Banagher LY 30; 70, 76, 78, 92
Lynch, Patt: Dungiven LY 15; 83
Lynch, person named: Saul DN 17; 113
Lynch, Rev. David: Aghadowey LY 22; 26
Lynch, Rev. David: Aghanloo LY 11; 21
Lynch, Rev. David: Drumachose LY 9; 120
Lynch, Rev. John: Ahoghill AM 23; 43, 45
Lynch, Rev. John: Tamlaght O'Crilly LY 18; 90, 111
Lynch, Rev. Patrick: Maghera LY 18; 68
Lynchy, family: Carrickfergus AM 37; 93
Lynd, family: Ramoan AM 24; 107
Lynd, John: Carrickfergus AM 37; 110
Lynd, Rev. Charles: Coleraine LY 33; 141
Lyndon, Mr: Carrickfergus AM 37; 33
Lyndons Park locality: Carrickfergus AM 37; 94, 174
Lyndsey, William: Carrickfergus AM 37; 13
Lyng td: Banagher LY 30; 108
Lynn river: Aghanloo LY 11; 23
Lynn waterfall: Ballylinny AM 32; 26
Lynn, Alexander: Drumtullagh AM 16; 102
Lynn, Ann: Balteagh LY 9; 43
Lynn, David: Drumachose LY 9; 132–33
Lynn, Hugh: Maghera LY 18; 80
Lynn, Jane: Balteagh LY 9; 43
Lynn, John: Carrickfergus AM 37; 150
Lynn, John: Clondermot LY 34; 69
Lynn, John: Desertoghill LY 27; 25

Lynn, John: Down DN 17; 62
Lynn, John: Inch DN 17; 73
Lynn, John: Macosquin LY 22; 82, 105, 113
Lynn, Miss: Coleraine LY 33; 72
Lynn, Mr: Carrickfergus AM 37; 150
Lynn, Mrs: Coleraine LY 33; 72
Lynn, Rev. James: Coleraine LY 33; 135
Lynn, Rev. James: Desertoghill LY 27; 29
Lynn, Rev. James: Kildollagh LY 22; 69, 74
Lynn, Robert: Rasharkin AM 23; 139
Lynn, William: Templepatrick AM 35; 134, 153
Lynne river: Carncastle and Killyglen AM 10; 11
Lynne river: Larne AM 10; 125
Lynne, Cllr: Tynan AH 1; 130
Lyons bridge: Kilmore DN 17; 89
Lyons, Edward: Newry DN 3; 82, 99, 104
Lyons, Henry: Ballymartin AM 2; 15

Lyons, Henry: Carnmoney AM 2; 45, 58, 82, 102
Lyons, Hugh: Ballyrashane LY 22; 63
Lyons, John: Coleraine LY 33; 145
Lyons, John: Dunboe LY 11; 56, 72
Lyons, John: Killowen LY 33; 172
Lyons, Joseph: Ballyrashane LY 22; 63
Lyons, Rev. John: Blaris AM 8; 24, 29
Lyons, Thomas: Drummaul AM 19; 91
Lyons' Academy: Newry DN 3; 82
Lyons' flax mill: Magheradrool DN 17; 103
Lyster, Dr: Clonleigh DL 39; 7
Lyster, family: Newry DN 3; 108
Lyster, John: Drumbeg AM 8; 133
Lyttle, family: Maghera LY 18; 14, 74
Lyttle, James: Maghera LY 18; 72
Lyttle, Matthew: Maghera LY 18; 7, 50–52, 67

M

Maammore glen: Lough Swilly DL 38; 133

Mabby, Nicholas: Misc. DN 17; 119

Macadoo bog: Connor AM 19; 20, 28

Macaldin, Rev. Andrew: Coleraine LY 33; 95, 140, 142–43

Macamish drawbridge: Lough Swilly DL 38; 103

Macamish fort: Lough Swilly DL 38; 101

Macanellagh, James: Killelagh LY 27; 96

MacArt, Cormac: Faughanvale LY 36; 62

MacArtan, family: Cumber LY 28; 67

Macartan, James: Drumgooland DN 3; 25

MacArte, Owin: Derryvullan FH 14; 38

Macartin, St: Clogher TE 5; 27

Macartney, Dr: Enniskillen FH 4; 82

Macartney, family: Blaris AM 8; 21

Macartney, G.H.: Ballymoney AM 16; 15

Macartney, G.H.: Coleraine LY 33; 64, 127

Macartney, G.H.: Derrykeighan AM 16; 78

Macartney, G.H.: Loughguile AM 13; 59–63, 65, 68, 71, 75–76

Macartney, George: Loughguile AM 13; 60, 63, 76

MacArtney, John: Carrickfergus AM 37; 112

Macartney, Lord: Derrykeighan AM 16; 79, 82–83, 85

Macartney, Lord: Duneane AM 19; 99

Macartney, Lord: Loughguile AM 13; 60, 62–63, 68

Macartney, Mrs G.H.: Ballymoney AM 16; 15

Macartney, Rev. A.: Carrickfergus AM 37; 102

Macartney, Rev. A.C.: Ballyrobert AM 2; 21

Macartney, Rev. George: Antrim AM 29; 26

Macartney, Rev. W.G.: Killead AM 35; 13, 20, 38, 42, 44–45, 51–52

Macartney, Thomas: Drummaul AM 19; 82

Macatasaid, Mathew: Clogher TE 5; 27

MacAughy, family: Faughanvale LY 36; 63

Macaulay, Jeremiah: Armoy AM 24; 9

Macauley, Daniel: Drummaul AM 19; 88

Macauley, F.W.: Antrim AM 29; 12, 44

MacAuley, family: Island Magee AM 10; 70

Macauley, James: Camlin AM 21; 73

Macauley, James: Killead AM 35; 14, 47

Macauley, Messrs James and Sons: Camlin AM 21; 65, 68–70

Macauley, Messrs James and Sons: Killead AM 35; 19, 45–46

Macauley, Robert: Camlin AM 21; 70, 73

Macauley, Robert: Killead AM 35; 11, 14, 47–48

Macauley, William: Carrickfergus AM 37; 158

MacAvergy, Shane: Clonmany DL 38; 17

Macaw, Kennedy: Kilrea LY 27; 120

MacBree, Alexander: Tamlaght TE 20; 75

MacBreen, John: Tamlaght TE 20; 118

MacBride, family: Carrickfergus AM 37; 93

MacBride, family: Faughanvale LY 36; 48

MacBrin, family: Carrickfergus AM 37; 93

MacBuadhachain, Ceallachan: Carlingford LH 40; 57

MacCann, family: Carrickfergus AM 37; 93

MacCarlin, family: Ardglass DN 17; 12

MacCarn, family: Carrickfergus AM 37; 93

MacCartan, family: Misc. DN 17; 119

MacCarthan, Forgo: Misc. LY 36; 105

Maccarthen, St: Clogher TE 5; 29

MacCarthy, Justin: Galloon FH 4; 89, 91, 98, 102–04

MacCartney, Cllr: Loughgilly AH 1; 84

MacCeallaigh, D.M.: Misc. LY 36; 108

MacClevery, family: Carrickfergus AM 37; 93

MacCoinmhidhe, B.O.: Misc. TE 5; 147

MacConmee, family: Faughanvale LY 36; 49

MacConmidhe, B.D.: Misc. TE 5; 147

MacConmidhe, B.R.: Misc. TE 5; 147

MacConmidhe, Melaghlin: Misc. TE 5; 147

MacConmidhe, Solomon: Misc. TE 5; 147

MacConmidhe, Teige: Misc. TE 5; 147

MacConnell, family: Carrickfergus AM 37; 93

MacCormack, William: Trory FH 14; 129

MacCullough, family: Carrickfergus AM 37; 93

MacCumhuin, Malcolm: Skerry AM 13; 116

MacDade, family: Faughanvale LY 36; 47–48

MacDevit, family: Faughanvale LY 36; 32

MacDevitt, family: Faughanvale LY 36; 47–48

MacDonald, Reynold: Ballywillin LY 33; 44

MacDonnell, Ann Catherine (see Antrim, Countess)

MacDonnell, Edmund: Tickmacrevan AM 13; 123, 127–32

MacDonnell, family (see also Antrim): Ramoan AM 24; 88

MacDonnell, family: Ahoghill AM 23; 26

MacDonnell, family: Ballintoy AM 24; 15

MacDonnell, family: Ballynure AM 32; 44–45

MacDonnell, family: Billy AM 16; 49

MacDonnell, family: Carrickfergus AM 37; 24, 93

MacDonnell, family: Culfeightrin AM 24; 46–47

MacDonnell, family: Drummaul AM 19; 71

MacDonnell, family: Dunaghy AM 13; 12

MacDonnell, family: Dunluce AM 16; 115, 121

MacDonnell, family: Killagan AM 23; 84

MacDonnell, family: Raloo AM 32; 86, 94

MacDonnell, family: Tickmacrevan AM 13; 127, 130

MacDonnell, J.M.: Glynn AM 26; 29–30

MacDonnell, J.M.: Templecorran AM 26; 94, 107

MacDonnell, J.M.: Tickmacrevan AM 13; 124, 127

MacDonnell, Randal: Drummaul AM 19; 40, 70–71

MacDonnell, Randal: Ramoan AM 24; 93, 98

MacDonnell, Randal: Tickmacrevan AM 13; 130, 132

MacDonnell, Randal [I]: Culfeightrin AM 24; 69

MacDonnell, Randal [II]: Culfeightrin AM 24; 79

MacDonnell, Sorley: Billy AM 16; 38

MacDonnell, Sorley: Culfeightrin AM 24; 65

MacDonnell, Sorley: Loughguile AM 13; 58

MacDonnell, Sorley: Templecorran AM 26; 122

MacDonnells fort: Dunluce AM 16; 115

MacDougall, A.: Island Magee AM 10; 84

MacDowell, family: Carrickfergus AM 37; 93

MacDuach, Keltair: Down DN 17; 41–42

MacEaghy, family: Faughanvale LY 36; 63

MacEarch, Fergus: Carrickfergus AM 37; 18

Macedon House: Carnmoney AM 2; 37, 46, 84

Macedon Point: Carnmoney AM 2; 38

MacEtigh, family: Cumber LY 28; 69

MacEwen, John: Killead AM 35; 35

MacFadden, family: Faughanvale LY 36; 48

MacFerran, family: Carrickfergus AM 37; 93

MacGil Eogan land: Magilligan LY 11; 145

MacGill, family: Carrickfergus AM 37; 93

MacGlennon, Patrick: Saul DN 17; 111

MacGown, family: Carrickfergus AM 37; 93

MacGregor's bay: Lough Swilly DL 38; 114–15

Macgrillis, family: Faughanvale LY 36; 48

MacGuire, B.M.: Galloon FH 4; 101

MacGuire, family: Enniskillen FH 4; 50

MacGuire, Joseph: Enniskillen FH 4; 58–59

MacGuire, Roury: Derryvullan FH 14; 38

MacGuirk, Rev.: Clogherny TE 20; 25

Machaire Cannon (see Magheracanon): Clondermot LY 34; 57

MacHenry, family: Faughanvale LY 36; 32

MacHenry, John: Tullyrusk AM 21; 139

Machonaghty, Alexander: Ahoghill AM 23; 38

Machonaghty, Catherine: Ahoghill AM 23; 38

Machonaghty, Eliza: Ahoghill AM 23; 38

Machonaghty, Elizabeth: Ahoghill AM 23; 38

Machonaghty, James: Ahoghill AM 23; 38

Machonaghty, John: Ahoghill AM 23; 38

Machonaghty, William (Jnr): Ahoghill AM 23; 38

Machonaghty, William (Snr): Ahoghill AM 23; 38

Mac-Ileogain district: Magilligan LY 11; 118

MacIlherron, family: Carrickfergus AM 37; 93

MacIlwrath, family: Carrickfergus AM 37; 93

Mack, David: Blaris AM 8; 55, 62, 84

Mack, David: Blaris DN 12; 39–40, 45–46, 49

Mack, Gen. (see MacMahon, Rev. John)

Mack, Mrs: Blaris AM 8; 85

Mackadrille, D.D.: Ballynascreen LY 31; 10, 24

Mackan glebe: Killesher FH 14; 86–87

Mackan glebe brickfield: Killesher FH 14; 84

MacKane, Rev. John: Drumachose LY 9; 49, 119

MacKaney, Murriagh (see O'Heany): Banagher LY 30; 39

Mackaviney, Nelly: Galloon FH 4; 97

MacKay, Daniel: Drumtullagh AM 16; 101–02

Mackay, family: Carrickfergus AM 37; 93

Mackay, family: Derrykeighan AM 16; 89

MacKay, Hugh: Drumtullagh AM 16; 102

MacKeen, family: Carrickfergus AM 37; 93

Mackel, James: Artrea LY 6; 26

Mackenless, Magnellus: Inch DN 17; 75

Mackeown's Town lough: Racavan AM 13; 89, 97

Mackey, Alexander: Ballyaghran LY 33; 13, 19, 23–24

Mackey, Alexander: Doagh AM 29; 88

Mackey, Alexander: Muckamore AM 35; 79

Mackey, family: Culfeightrin AM 24; 59

Mackey, James: Bovevagh LY 25; 61

Mackey, John: Agivey LY 22; 43

Mackey, Martha: Antrim AM 29; 59

Mackey, Thomas: Ballymoney AM 16; 17

Mackey, W.T.: Tamlaght TE 20; 84, 86

MacKilleany, family: Faughanvale LY 36; 48

Mackin, Mr (Lishill): Killea and Taughboyne DL 39; 87

Mackin's mill: Killea and Taughboyne DL 39; 87

Mackle, Rev. James: Artrea LY 6; 17, 34

Macklin, Cllr: Raphoe DL 39; 126

Macklin, Thomas: Clondermot LY 34; 87, 91, 95

Macklin, William: Desertlyn LY 31; 51

Macknagh flax mill: Maghera LY 18; 28, 35

Macknagh fort [I]: Maghera LY 18; 61

Macknagh fort [II]: Maghera LY 18; 61

Macknagh fort [III]: Maghera LY 18; 62

Macknagh td: Maghera LY 18; 22, 25, 52, 78, 81

Mackney, Anne: Larne AM 10; 128

Mackreed, Alexander: Tamlaght TE 20; 116, 121

Mackull, Esther: Termoneeny LY 6; 132
Mackull, Thomas: Termoneeny LY 6; 132
Macky, family: Ballynure AM 32; 56
Macky, Mr: Mevagh DL 38; 58
Macky, William: Clondermot LY 34; 79
MacLain, Rev.: Seapatrick DN 12; 128
Maclean, Rev. Alexander: Antrim AM 29; 27
MacLeane, family: Faughanvale LY 36; 60
Macleary bleach green: Macosquin LY 22; 82, 104
Macleary bridge: Macosquin LY 22; 82, 103
Macleary Castle: Macosquin LY 22; 96–97
Macleary cove: Macosquin LY 22; 95, 97
Macleary td: Aghadowey LY 22; 11
MacLellan, Robert: Aghanloo LY 11; 8
MacLir, Manannan: Banagher LY 30; 109
MacLoughlin, Ardgar: Faughanvale LY 36; 50, 56
MacLoughlin, family: Faughanvale LY 36; 60
MacLoughlin, Maurice: Newry DN 3; 63, 66
MacLoughlin, Niall: Misc. TE 5; 146
MacMahon, A.M.: Inniskeen MN 40; 126
MacMahon, Coll: Inniskeen MN 40; 126, 128
MacMahon, Ebhin: Dungiven LY 15; 59
MacMahon, Emar: Misc. DN 17; 119
MacMahon, family: Ematris MN 40; 114–15, 118
MacMahon, family: Inniskeen MN 40; 126, 128
MacMahon, family: Killanny MN 40; 132, 134
MacMahon, family: Magheracloone MN 40; 141
MacMahon, family: Magheross MN 40; 148
MacMahon, Frank: Ematris MN 40; 115
MacMahon, Rev. John: Kilrea LY 27; 119, 126
MacMahon, Rev. Ross: Inniskeen MN 40; 126
MacMahon, S.D.: Ematris MN 40; 115
MacMahon, William: Cappagh TE 5; 15–17, 19
MacMaldwin, C.M.: Carrickfergus AM 37; 11
MacMaldwin, C.M.: Island Magee AM 10; 66
MacManus, Sourleboy: Finvoy AM 23; 68
MacMaster, family: Carrickfergus AM 37; 93
MacMurray, family: Faughanvale LY 36; 48
MacMurrough, Dermot: Manorhamilton Union LM 40; 51
Macnaghten, E.A.: Ballywillin LY 33; 33
Macnaghten, E.A.: Dunluce AM 16; 120
Macnaghten, Edmund: Ballyrashane LY 22; 64
Macnaghten, Edmund: Tamlaght Finlagan LY 25; 81
Macnaghten, Edward: Aghadowey LY 22; 27
Macnaghten, F.W.: Ballywillin LY 33; 33
Macnaghten, F.W.: Billy AM 16; 36, 38, 44–47, 49–50, 56–57, 59, 66, 76–77
Macnaghten, F.W.: Coleraine LY 33; 105
Macnaghten, F.W.: Drumachose LY 9; 67, 78, 84, 130
Macnaghten, F.W.: Drumcree AH 1; 32, 41–42
Macnaghten, F.W.: Faughanvale LY 36; 45
Macnaghten, F.W.: Tamlaght Finlagan LY 25; 81, 95, 97, 100–01, 103, 108–10, 117, 124

Macnaghten, family: Ballintoy AM 24; 30
Macnaghten, family: Dunluce AM 16; 109
Macnaghten, Lady: Derrykeighan AM 16; 92
Macnaghten, Robert: Ballywillin LY 33; 39
Macnaghten, Robert: Coleraine LY 33; 143
MacNamee, family: Faughanvale LY 36; 48
MacNamee, William: Ballyphilip DN 7; 8
MacNeill, family: Misc. LY 36; 106
Macomb, family: Ballynure AM 32; 56
Macool, Hugh: Kilrea LY 27; 129
Macool's Bed stone: Clonmany DL 38; 16
Macosquin: Macosquin LY 22; 80, 90, 96, 121
Macosquin abbey: Macosquin LY 22; 95, 97, 99
Macosquin bridge: Macosquin LY 22; 82, 103
Macosquin church: Macosquin LY 22; 79–82, 84, 95–97, 99, 101
Macosquin church: Misc. LY 36; 110
Macosquin corn mill: Macosquin LY 22; 82–83, 105
Macosquin female school: Macosquin LY 22; 93
Macosquin female Sunday school: Macosquin LY 22; 93
Macosquin flax mill: Macosquin LY 22; 83, 105
Macosquin Glebe House: Macosquin LY 22; 80–81, 95, 97, 101, 121
Macosquin graveyard: Macosquin LY 22; 96–97, 99
Macosquin male school: Macosquin LY 22; 92–93
Macosquin male Sunday school: Macosquin LY 22; 93
Macosquin meeting house (see Englishtown): Macosquin LY 22; 99
Macosquin old church: Macosquin LY 22; 95, 118
Macosquin ph: Aghadowey LY 22; 1, 5–8, 10–11, 13–14, 29, 32
Macosquin ph: Agivey LY 22; 39, 43
Macosquin ph: Ballyaghran LY 33; 13, 15, 27
Macosquin ph: Ballywillin LY 33; 38
Macosquin ph: Coleraine LY 33; 73, 104, 120, 142, 144
Macosquin ph: Drumachose LY 9; 90
Macosquin ph: Dunboe LY 11; 66
Macosquin ph: Dungiven LY 15; 34
Macosquin ph: Errigal LY 27; 46, 63
Macosquin ph: Kildollagh LY 22; 67
Macosquin ph: Killowen LY 33; 158, 161, 164, 168, 170, 172
Macosquin ph: Misc. LY 36; 109
Macosquin river: Aghadowey LY 22; 8–9, 33
Macosquin river: Agivey LY 22; 42, 44
Macosquin river: Macosquin LY 22; 76–78, 97, 101, 116–17
Macosquin td: Macosquin LY 22; 97
Macosquin, Paul: Maghera LY 18; 69
Macoum, family: Aghagallon AM 21; 9
Macowan, family: Billy AM 16; 58
MacPherson, man named: Banagher LY 30; 7

Macrory, Charles: Drummaul AM 19; 91
Macrory, Henry: Drummaul AM 19; 90
Macrory, Hugh: Drummaul AM 19; 90
Macrory, John: Drummaul AM 19; 90–91
Macrory, Mary: Drummaul AM 19; 91
Macrory, Patrick: Drummaul AM 19; 90
Macrory, Peter: Drummaul AM 19; 87
Macrory, Robert: Balteagh LY 9; 4, 13, 26, 41
Macrory, Robert: Drumachose LY 9; 53
Macrory, Rose: Drummaul AM 19; 91
MacSkimmin, family: Carrickfergus AM 37; 93
Macsweeny, family: Donegal DL 39; 48
MacSweeny, family: Faughanvale LY 36; 60
MacSwine's bay: Lough Swilly DL 38; 122, 125
MacSwine's Gun Point: Lough Swilly DL 38; 122
MacSwine's Head: Lough Swilly DL 38; 122
MacSwyne, Ervine: Banagher LY 30; 108
Macue, Patt: Duneane AM 19; 124
Mac-Ui-Chlumain, man named: Misc. TE 5; 147
Macurley, Edward: Drummaul AM 19; 90
MacWilliams, family: Banagher LY 30; 106
Mad Mount fort: Carrickfergus AM 37; 181
Madden bridge: Ballymore AH 1; 10, 18
Madden bridge: Montiaghs AH 1; 91
Madden, Capt.: Clones FH 4; 29
Madden, Col (Hilton): Aghabog MN 40; 65
Madden, Col (Hilton): Currin MN 40; 89, 92, 96–97
Madden, Col (Hilton): Galloon FH 4; 93–94, 105
Madden, Dr (Dublin): Tamlaght O'Crilly LY 18; 89, 107
Madden, Dr (Portglenone): Tamlaght O'Crilly LY 18; 93, 123
Madden, family: Enniskillen FH 4; 58
Madden, family: Glynn AM 26; 45
Madden, Martha: Carrickfergus AM 37; 118, 128, 131
Madden, Miss: Loughgall AH 1; 78
Madden, Rev.: Galloon FH 4; 105
Madden, Rev. H.H.: Loughgall AH 1; 78
Madden, Samuel: Tydavnet MN 40; 170
Madden, Thomas: Newry DN 3; 99
Madden, woman named: Shilvodan AM 19; 135
Maddigan, Bernard: Duneane AM 19; 122
Maddigan, Henry: Ahoghill AM 23; 34, 39
Maddigan, John (Jnr): Maghera LY 18; 80
Maddigan, John: Maghera LY 18; 81
Maddock Land td: Carlingford LH 40; 58
Maddock's Garden td: Carlingford LH 40; 58
Maddybenny More cave: Ballyaghran LY 33; 10, 16, 23
Maddybenny More fort: Ballyaghran LY 33; 10, 16, 23
Maddybenny More hill: Ballyaghran LY 33; 1
Maddybenny More meeting house: Ballyaghran LY 33; 22

Maddybenny school: Ballyaghran LY 33; 17
Maddybenny td: Ballyaghran LY 33; 24, 28
Maddydrumbrist hill: Donaghmore DN 3; 7
Maddydrumbrist td: Donaghmore DN 3; 8–9
Maddymassag monastery: Ahoghill AM 23; 14
Madigan, family: Shilvodan AM 19; 131, 136
Madigan, John: Tamlaght O'Crilly LY 18; 137
Madill, James: Ahoghill AM 23; 38
Madin, family: Dunluce AM 16; 117
Madman's cave: Dungiven LY 15; 87–88, 93
Madol (Madoll): see McDowell
Madras (India): Newry DN 3; 68
Maelbrigid, son of Redan: Muckamore AM 35; 56
Maeve, Queen: Banagher LY 30; 109
Maeve, Queen: Bovevagh LY 25; 41
Maeve, Queen: Cumber LY 28; 63
Maffet, Mr: Clogher TE 5; 41
Maffett, Richard: Donagh MN 40; 103, 105
Magarell, Charles: Larne AM 10; 126
Magarity td: Tartaraghan AH 1; 120
Magary, James: Muckamore AM 35; 79
Magaw, Mr: Ballyclog TE 20; 15
Magaw, Widow: Derryaghy AM 8; 115
Magaw, William: Ballylinny AM 32; 24, 28
Magaw, William: Carnmoney AM 2; 99–100
Magay's Isle: Island Magee AM 10; 76
Magbagh, B.: Newtownhamilton AH 1; 100
Magee and Collins, Messrs: Magilligan LY 11; 132
Magee, Alexander: Derryaghy AM 8; 116–18
Magee, Archbishop: Enniskillen FH 4; 77
Magee, Barney: Island Magee AM 10; 77
Magee, Bryan: Island Magee AM 10; 65
Magee, Daniel: Billy AM 16; 58, 68
Magee, Daniel: Blaris AM 8; 23, 40–41, 43–45, 48–49, 52, 59, 67, 70, 72–73
Magee, Daniel: Blaris DN 12; 40–41
Magee, Daniel: Carrickfergus AM 37; 116
Magee, Daniel: Drumbeg AM 8; 131
Magee, Daniel: Hillsborough DN 12; 106
Magee, Daniel: Island Magee AM 10; 65
Magee, Daniel: Lambeg AM 8; 137, 139
Magee, Dennis: Blaris AM 8; 47
Magee, Edward: Aghagallon AM 21; 14
Magee, family: Ballinderry AM 21; 54
Magee, family: Ballintoy AM 24; 20
Magee, family: Billy AM 16; 58, 68
Magee, family: Culfeightrin AM 24; 74
Magee, family: Glynn AM 26; 45
Magee, family: Island Magee AM 10; 26
Magee, family: Kilcronaghan LY 31; 68
Magee, family: Skerry AM 13; 116
Magee, Felix: Newry DN 3; 98
Magee, H.B.: Blaris AM 8; 52
Magee, Henry: Maghera LY 18; 61
Magee, James: Ballintoy AM 24; 22

Magee, James: Billy AM 16; 69

Magee, James: Bovevagh LY 25; 58

Magee, James: Carrickfergus AM 37; 108

Magee, James: Derryaghy AM 8; 110

Magee, James: Maghera LY 18; 81

Magee, James: Templecorran AM 26; 105–06, 121, 123

Magee, Jane: Carrickfergus AM 37; 117

Magee, John: Aghagallon AM 21; 5, 12, 23

Magee, John: Aghalee AM 21; 37

Magee, John: Ahoghill AM 23; 37

Magee, John: Ballinderry AM 21; 55

Magee, John: Connor AM 19; 26

Magee, John: Magilligan LY 11; 133

Magee, John: Tamlaght O'Crilly LY 18; 119–20

Magee, John: Tamlaght TE 20; 74, 78

Magee, Margaret: Ballymoney AM 16; 17

Magee, Margaret: Carrickfergus AM 37; 118

Magee, Mary: Carrickfergus AM 37; 153

Magee, Mary: Derryaghy AM 8; 101

Magee, Messrs Anderson and Co.: Carrickfergus AM 37; 171

Magee, Michael: Newry DN 3; 103

Magee, Miss: Enniskillen FH 4; 84

Magee, Owen: Island Magee AM 10; 65

Magee, Patrick: Newry DN 3; 99

Magee, Rev.: Kilkeel DN 3; 48–49

Magee, Rev.: Kilmegan DN 3; 58

Magee, Rev. James: Misc. LY 31; 136

Magee, Rev. Robert: Balteagh LY 9; 7

Magee, Robert: Carrickfergus AM 37; 118

Magee, Robert: Coleraine LY 33; 72

Magee, Thomas: Magilligan LY 11; 139

Magee, William: Aghagallon AM 21; 9, 11

Magee's Island (see Island Magee): Island Magee AM 10; 101

Magenis, Elinor (see O'Neill): Drummaul AM 19; 70

Magenis, family: Drumballyroney DN 3; 12, 16

Magenis, R.W.: Ballymoney AM 16; 15

Magennis, Arthur: Newry DN 3; 63

Magennis, Caihbharr: Ardglass DN 17; 12

Magennis, Capt.: Ballymoney AM 16; 1

Magennis, Capt.: Banagher LY 30; 7, 53–54, 94–95

Magennis, Charles [I]: Carrickfergus AM 37; 118, 120

Magennis, Charles [II]: Carrickfergus AM 37; 126

Magennis, Col.: Dunsfort DN 17; 69

Magennis, Con: Blaris AM 8; 3, 87

Magennis, Con: Blaris DN 12; 33

Magennis, Con: Drummaul AM 19; 70

Magennis, Con: Newry DN 3; 65

Magennis, Cu-aladh: Ardglass DN 17; 12

Magennis, family: Ardglass DN 17; 3, 12

Magennis, family: Down DN 17; 42

Magennis, family: Kilmegan DN 3; 59

Magennis, Hugh: Ardglass DN 17; 12

Magennis, James: Balteagh LY 9; 17, 39

Magennis, John: Carrickfergus AM 37; 128

Magennis, Maria: Carrickfergus AM 37; 118

Magennis, P.E.: Kilmegan DN 3; 59

Magennis, Rev.: Kilmore AH 1; 69

Magennis, Roger: Dromara DN 12; 65

Magennis, Roger: Garvaghy DN 12; 80–81

Magenragh (see Magonragh): Enniskillen FH 4; 84

Magerabwee (see Magheraboy)

Magery, John: Carlingford LH 40; 60

Magey, Daniel: Carrickfergus AM 37; 162

Maggie Watt's Hole locality: Kilwaughter AM 10; 118

Maggie's chair: Dunaghy AM 13; 21

Maghaberry: Aghalee AM 21; 34

Maghaberry: Magheramesk AM 21; 113, 118, 129

Maghaberry fort [I]: Magheramesk AM 21; 120–21

Maghaberry fort [II]: Magheramesk AM 21; 121

Maghaberry graveyard: Magheramesk AM 21; 117, 121

Maghaberry hill: Magheramesk AM 21; 114

Maghaberry meeting house: Magheramesk AM 21; 116–17

Maghaberry quarry: Magheramesk AM 21; 121

Maghaberry school: Magheramesk AM 21; 113, 115, 128–30

Maghaberry td: Magheramesk AM 21; 114, 130

Maghaderry td: Misc. DL 39; 186

Maghadone forts: Artrea LY 6; 32–33

Maghadone private school: Artrea LY 6; 19

Maghadone td: Artrea LY 6; 11, 13, 32–33, 38

Maghagart td: Dromore TE 5; 97

Maghan, Irish: Misc. LY 36; 104

Maghareagh (see Magherareagh): Donaghedy TE 5; 89

Maghareagh (see Maghereagh): Antrim AM 29; 59

Maghareagh td: Clondermot LY 34; 79

Magharehowell rectory: Racavan AM 13; 86

Maghea Islands: Misc. DN 17; 121

Magheestown td: Raphoe DL 39; 126

Maghera: Aghadowey LY 22; 25

Maghera: Artrea LY 6; 26

Maghera: Ballyaghran LY 33; 14–15, 26

Maghera: Ballynascreen LY 31; 3, 5, 7, 18, 32

Maghera: Ballywillin LY 33; 50

Maghera: Banagher LY 30; 3, 5

Maghera: Bovevagh LY 25; 14, 32

Maghera: Coleraine LY 33; 63, 89

Maghera: Desertlyn LY 31; 42

Maghera: Desertmartin LY 31; 53–54, 62–63

Maghera: Desertoghill LY 27; 2–3, 5, 9, 13, 17, 25, 32–34

Maghera: Dungiven LY 15; 50, 53, 67, 109

Maghera: Errigal LY 27; 41, 53, 61, 79, 82–83
Maghera: Kilcronaghan LY 31; 64, 67, 75–77, 79, 83
Maghera: Killelagh LY 27; 95–96, 102
Maghera: Killowen LY 33; 172
Maghera: Kilrea LY 27; 104–05, 111, 119, 127
Maghera: Maghera LY 18; 1–2, 4–10, 14, 16–18, 22–24, 27, 30–37, 39, 45, 47–52, 55, 58, 62–66, 68, 70–74, 76–77, 79
Maghera: Magherafelt LY 6; 95
Maghera: Misc. DN 17; 116
Maghera: Misc. LY 31; 115–16, 135
Maghera: Misc. LY 36; 114
Maghera: Tamlaght Finlagan LY 25; 121–22
Maghera: Tamlaght O'Crilly LY 18; 82–83, 89, 91–92, 94, 96, 102, 105, 109–10, 116, 118, 124, 135, 139–40, 142
Maghera: Tamlaght TE 20; 73
Maghera: Termoneeny LY 6; 129
Maghera barrack: Maghera LY 18; 63
Maghera bleach green: Maghera LY 18; 35
Maghera bog: Desertmartin LY 31; 53
Maghera brewery: Maghera LY 18; 2, 35
Maghera Cannoin (see Magheracanon): Clondermot LY 34; 48
Maghera chapel: Maghera LY 18; 2, 56
Maghera church: Maghera LY 18; 2, 4, 7–8, 31, 34, 66–67, 71
Maghera corn market: Maghera LY 18; 2
Maghera court house: Maghera LY 18; 15
Maghera cove: Maghera LY 18; 22
Maghera dispensary: Kilcronaghan LY 31; 71
Maghera dispensary: Killelagh LY 27; 98
Maghera dispensary: Maghera LY 18; 5, 25–27, 34, 52
Maghera dispensary: Termoneeny LY 6; 124
Maghera female school: Maghera LY 18; 31, 67
Maghera Glebe House: Maghera LY 18; 8, 16, 35, 58, 66–67, 72
Maghera grain store: Maghera LY 18; 35
Maghera graveyard: Maghera LY 18; 9, 66
Maghera hotels: Maghera LY 18; 4
Maghera Irish Society school: Maghera LY 18; 31
Maghera lough: Ardstraw TE 5; 2
Maghera lough: Kilskeery TE 5; 113
Maghera market house: Maghera LY 18; 2
Maghera meeting house: Maghera LY 18; 2, 7, 34–35, 52
Maghera monastery: Maghera LY 18; 4, 12–13, 24, 36
Maghera national school: Maghera LY 18; 74
Maghera new church: Maghera LY 18; 10
Maghera new market house: Maghera LY 18; 2, 4, 74

Maghera new meeting house: Maghera LY 18; 7, 58, 67
Maghera night school: Maghera LY 18; 33
Maghera old abbey: Maghera LY 18; 39, 55
Maghera old church: Ballynascreen LY 31; 9, 24
Maghera old church: Cumber LY 28; 71
Maghera old church: Maghera LY 18; 2, 4, 7, 9–10, 15, 23–24, 34, 36–39, 55, 57–58, 63, 66–67, 69
Maghera old Glebe House: Maghera LY 18; 63
Maghera old graveyard: Maghera LY 18; 14, 47, 57
Maghera old market house: Maghera LY 18; 4, 63
Maghera old meeting house: Maghera LY 18; 58
Maghera old windmill: Maghera LY 18; 50, 62–63
Maghera parish school: Maghera LY 18; 2, 4, 28, 31, 34, 50
Maghera ph: Ballynascreen LY 31; 1, 6
Maghera ph: Ballyscullion LY 6; 43
Maghera ph: Cumber LY 28; 65, 69
Maghera ph: Desertmartin LY 31; 52
Maghera ph: Desertoghill LY 27; 6
Maghera ph: Kilcronaghan LY 31; 72, 78–80, 82
Maghera ph: Kilkeel DN 3; 51
Maghera ph: Killelagh LY 27; 95–96, 98
Maghera ph: Lough Neagh AM 21; 95
Maghera ph: Magherafelt LY 6; 94
Maghera ph: Misc. DN 17; 118
Maghera ph: Misc. LY 31; 111, 128, 134
Maghera ph: Misc. LY 36; 116
Maghera ph: Tamlaght TE 20; 73
Maghera ph: Termoneeny LY 6; 121–22, 130–31
Maghera poor shop: Maghera LY 18; 15
Maghera post office: Maghera LY 18; 71
Maghera private school [I]: Maghera LY 18; 33
Maghera private school [II]: Maghera LY 18; 33–34
Maghera quarry: Maghera LY 18; 1
Maghera rectory: Maghera LY 18; 3
Maghera river: Kilmacteige SO 40; 186, 193
Maghera Sunday school: Maghera LY 18; 28, 67
Maghera td: Killelagh LY 27; 102
Maghera village: Kilmacteige SO 40; 186, 193
Maghera windmill: Maghera LY 18; 67, 71
Maghera-ard bogs: Lough Swilly DL 38; 135
Maghera-ard td: Lough Swilly DL 38; 136
Magherabane village: Desertegney DL 38; 25
Magherabeg forts: Drummaul AM 19; 78
Magherabeg friary: Donegal DL 39; 49
Magherabeg lough: Killymard DL 39; 94
Magherabeg lough: Mevagh DL 38; 55
Magherabeg Point (see Quigly's Point): Lough Swilly DL 38; 144
Magherabeg school: Dromore DN 12; 78
Magherabeg td: Dromore DN 12; 78
Magherabeg td: Drummaul AM 19; 91
Magherabeg td: Mevagh DL 38; 63
Magherabeg td: Raymoghy DL 39; 138, 199

Magherabower td: Billy AM 16; 37

Magheraboy barony: Boho FH 14; 8

Magheraboy barony: Cleenish FH 14; 11–12, 29

Magheraboy barony: Derryvullan FH 14; 31

Magheraboy barony: Enniskillen FH 4; 41, 50, 82

Magheraboy barony: Inishmacsaint FH 14; 70

Magheraboy barony: Rossorry FH 14; 115

Magheraboy barony: Trory FH 14; 122

Magheraboy cave: Ballintoy AM 24; 26

Magheraboy corn mill: Rasharkin AM 23; 131

Magheraboy cromlech: Ballintoy AM 24; 12

Magheraboy Dranach school: Rasharkin AM 23; 141

Magheraboy flax mill: Dungiven LY 15; 9, 98

Magheraboy fort: Ballintoy AM 24; 33

Magheraboy fort: Dungiven LY 15; 44

Magheraboy fort: Rasharkin AM 23; 139

Magheraboy hill: Kilraghts AM 16; 125

Magheraboy Lower corn mill: Drumlumman CN 40; 14

Magheraboy Lower meeting house: Kilraghts AM 16; 124

Magheraboy Lower td: Drumlumman CN 40; 17

Magheraboy school: Dungiven LY 15; 18

Magheraboy school: Kilraghts AM 16; 130, 136

Magheraboy school: Leck DL 39; 120

Magheraboy school: Rasharkin AM 23; 135

Magheraboy td: Ballintoy AM 24; 10–12

Magheraboy td: Ballywillin LY 33; 45, 51

Magheraboy td: Banagher LY 30; 22, 84

Magheraboy td: Donaghmore DL 39; 38

Magheraboy td: Dungiven LY 15; 9, 22, 27, 44, 49, 62–63, 74, 77

Magheraboy td: Kilraghts AM 16; 134

Magheraboy td: Leck DL 39; 119

Magheraboy td: Magheross MN 40; 149

Magheraboy td: Misc. DL 39; 196

Magheraboy td: Raphoe DL 39; 126

Magheraboy Upper td: Drumlumman CN 40; 17

Magherabuoy (see Magheraboy)

Magherabuy (see Magheraboy)

Magherabwee (see Magheraboy)

Magheracallaghan corn mill: Urney DL 39; 177

Magheracallaghan flax mill: Urney DL 39; 177

Magheracallaghan td: Urney DL 39; 174, 181

Magheracannon (see Magheracanon): Clondermot LY 34; 48

Magheracanon td: Banagher LY 30; 105

Magheracanon td: Clondermot LY 34; 57, 72, 111–12, 119, 127, 132

Magheracanon well: Clondermot LY 34; 48

Magheracashel td: Ballintoy AM 24; 30–31

Magheraclay td: Ballyaghran LY 33; 27

Magheracloone ph: Clogher TE 5; 41

Magheracloone ph: Killanny MN 40; 130, 134

Magheracloone ph: Magheross MN 40; 143, 153

Magheracloy td: Misc. DL 39; 196

Magheraconluce corn mill: Annahilt DN 12; 23, 25

Magheraconluce flax mill: Annahilt DN 12; 23

Magheraconluce td: Annahilt DN 12; 20–21, 23, 25

Magheracotton td: Ardstraw TE 5; 12

Magheracranmoney (Magheracranmony) td: Inch DN 17; 77

Magheracranmoney bog: Inch DN 17; 73

Magheracranmoney chapel: Inch DN 17; 73

Magheracreggan (Magheracriggan) td: Ardstraw TE 5; 4–5, 7

Magheracreggan corn mill: Ardstraw TE 5; 5, 14

Magheracreggan flax mill: Ardstraw TE 5; 4, 14

Magheracreggan lough: Ardstraw TE 5; 10

Magheracreggan mountain: Ardstraw TE 5; 2

Magheracreggan school: Ardstraw TE 5; 7

Magheracreggan village: Ardstraw TE 5; 2

Magheracross graveyard: Magheracross FH 14; 96

Magheracross ph: Clogher TE 5; 41

Magheracross ph: Derrybrusk FH 4; 30

Magheracross ph: Derryvullan FH 14; 31

Magheracross ph: Donacavey TE 5; 74

Magheracross ph: Enniskillen FH 4; 43, 47

Magheracross ph: Trory FH 14; 122, 132

Magheracross Rectory: Magheracross FH 14; 95

Magheracross school: Magheracross FH 14; 99

Magheracross td: Magheracross FH 14; 93, 95, 101–02

Magheracrusen locality: Magheracross FH 14; 91

Magheraculmoney dispensary: Magheraculmoney FH 14; 108

Magheraculmoney ph: Clogher TE 5; 41

Magheraculmoney ph: Derryvullan FH 14; 31

Magheraculmoney ph: Drumkeeran FH 14; 62, 66–67

Magheraculmony (see Magheraculmoney)

Magheradartin (Magheradartan) td: Hillsborough DN 12; 86, 106

Magheradone td: Artrea LY 6; 22

Magheradonell (see Magheradonnell)

Magheradoney standing stone: Loughguile AM 13; 74

Magheradonnell graveyard: Derrykeighan AM 16; 87, 93

Magheradonnell td: Derrykeighan AM 16; 88, 92–93

Magheradrimin td: Donagh DL 38; 31

Magheradroll (see Magheradrool): Misc. DN 17; 120

Magheradrool flax mill: Magheradrool DN 17; 105

Magheradrool ph: Dromara DN 12; 62, 65

Magheradrool ph: Misc. DN 17; 120

Magheradrool ph: Saintfield DN 7; 116

Magheradrool td: Magheradrool DN 17; 99, 105

Magheradunbar House: Devenish FH 14; 53
Magheradunbar td: Devenish FH 14; 58–59
Magherafelt: Antrim AM 29; 19, 39
Magherafelt: Artrea LY 6; 15
Magherafelt: Ballinderry LY 6; 41
Magherafelt: Ballinderry TE 20; 12
Magherafelt: Ballynascreen LY 31; 2, 8, 20
Magherafelt: Ballyscullion LY 6; 53, 56
Magherafelt: Banagher LY 30; 74, 131
Magherafelt: Desertlyn LY 31; 41–42, 44, 50
Magherafelt: Desertmartin LY 31; 55, 57, 59, 62–63
Magherafelt: Drummaul AM 19; 73
Magherafelt: Duneane AM 19; 100–01, 112, 116
Magherafelt: Dungiven LY 15; 109
Magherafelt: Kilcronaghan LY 31; 65, 67, 71, 73,
    75, 78–79, 82, 88
Magherafelt: Kilrea LY 27; 120
Magherafelt: Maghera LY 18; 6–8, 14, 30, 51, 64
Magherafelt: Magherafelt LY 6; 81, 83–87, 93,
    96–97, 100–02, 104, 112
Magherafelt: Misc. LY 31; 115–16, 128, 131, 134
Magherafelt: Tamlaght O'Crilly LY 18; 83
Magherafelt: Tamlaght TE 20; 73, 79–80, 82, 102,
    122, 137
Magherafelt: Termoneeny LY 6; 129
Magherafelt brewery: Magherafelt LY 6; 80, 92
Magherafelt bridewell: Magherafelt LY 6; 83
Magherafelt Castle: Magherafelt LY 6; 81, 108, 111
Magherafelt Catholic Sunday school: Magherafelt
    LY 6; 102
Magherafelt chapel: Magherafelt LY 6; 82, 103
Magherafelt charity school: Magherafelt LY 6; 83,
    87, 97, 101, 103
Magherafelt church: Ballyscullion LY 6; 45
Magherafelt church: Magherafelt LY 6; 82, 103
Magherafelt classical school: Magherafelt LY 6; 103
Magherafelt corn store: Magherafelt LY 6; 83
Magherafelt court house: Magherafelt LY 6; 82, 103
Magherafelt dispensary: Artrea LY 6; 15
Magherafelt dispensary: Magherafelt LY 6; 87, 91,
    97, 102
Magherafelt female school: Magherafelt LY 6; 103
Magherafelt linen hall: Magherafelt LY 6; 83
Magherafelt market house: Magherafelt LY 6; 82
Magherafelt meeting house: Magherafelt LY 6; 82
Magherafelt Methodist school: Magherafelt LY 6;
    87, 103
Magherafelt national school: Magherafelt LY 6; 87,
    102–03
Magherafelt old church: Ballynascreen LY 31; 9, 24
Magherafelt parish school: Magherafelt LY 6; 103
Magherafelt parsonage: Magherafelt LY 6; 83, 98
Magherafelt ph: Artrea LY 6; 4, 22, 34, 39
Magherafelt ph: Artrea TE 20; 6, 8
Magherafelt ph: Ballynascreen LY 31; 11

Magherafelt ph: Ballyscullion LY 6; 42, 53, 55
Magherafelt ph: Desertlyn LY 31; 35
Magherafelt ph: Desertmartin LY 31; 52, 57–58
Magherafelt ph: Kilcronaghan LY 31; 72, 82
Magherafelt ph: Maghera LY 18; 75
Magherafelt ph: Misc. LY 31; 111
Magherafelt ph: Tamlaght TE 20; 73
Magherafelt private school: Magherafelt LY 6; 103
Magherafelt stream: Magherafelt LY 6; 80
Magherafelt Sunday school: Magherafelt LY 6; 97,
    103
Magheragaalin Point: Lough Swilly DL 38; 123,
    126
Magheragall bog: Magheragall AM 21; 107
Magheragall church: Magheragall AM 21; 98–99,
    102, 106, 109–10
Magheragall fort [I]: Magheragall AM 21; 104
Magheragall fort [II]: Magheragall AM 21; 105
Magheragall graveyard: Magheragall AM 21; 98
Magheragall House: Magheragall AM 21; 101
Magheragall Lower td: Blaris DN 12; 40, 42, 42
Magheragall old church: Magheragall AM 21; 98
Magheragall ph: Aghagallon AM 21; 20, 23
Magheragall ph: Aghalee AM 21; 38
Magheragall ph: Ballinderry AM 21; 41–43, 46
Magheragall ph: Blaris AM 8; 3, 51, 73
Magheragall ph: Blaris DN 12; 26–27, 29
Magheragall ph: Derryaghy AM 8; 90, 103, 112,
    119
Magheragall ph: Magheramesk AM 21; 112, 116,
    119, 127
Magheragall ph: Misc. AM 10; 129
Magheragall pound: Magheragall AM 21; 101
Magheragall school: Magheragall AM 21; 109–10
Magheragall Sunday school: Magheragall AM 21;
    110
Magheragall td: Blaris DN 12; 41–42
Magheragall Upper td: Blaris DN 12; 40, 42
Magheragamore hill: Devenish FH 14; 52
Magheragannon td: Devenish FH 14; 58
Magheragarry td: Hillsborough DN 12; 107
Magheragart (Donnell) td: Dromore TE 5; 96,
    99–100
Magheragart spring: Dromore TE 5; 96
Magheraghall (see Magheragall)
Magheraghanive creek: Lough Swilly DL 38; 106
Magheragher td: Inishmacsaint FH 14; 70
Magheragrellagh td: Ballyscullion LY 6; 56
Magherahamlet church (see Templemoyle)
Magherahamlet district: Dromara DN 12; 67
Magherahamlet Glebe House: Dromara DN 12; 66
Magherahamlet meeting house: Dromara DN 12; 66
Magherahamlet school: Dromara DN 12; 69
Magherahan td: Raphoe DL 39; 126
Magherahee td: Raphoe DL 39; 126

Magheraher school: Inishmacsaint FH 14; 78

Magherahinch td: Moira DN 12; 120

Magherahoghill district: Ahoghill AM 23; 1

Magherahoney corn mill: Loughguile AM 13; 63

Magherahoney school: Loughguile AM 13; 66

Magherahoney standing stone: Loughguile AM 13; 69

Magherahoney td: Loughguile AM 13; 69–70, 74

Magherakeel school [I]: Termonamongan TE 5; 145

Magherakeel school [II]: Termonamongan TE 5; 145

Magherakeel td: Termonamongan TE 5; 145

Magheraknock corn mill: Magheradrool DN 17; 104

Magheraknock school: Magheradrool DN 17; 104

Magheraknock td: Magheradrool DN 17; 99, 103–04

Magheralagan (Magheralagin) td: Down DN 17; 53, 55

Magheralagan corn mill: Down DN 17; 49

Magheralagan lough: Down DN 17; 38

Magheralan td: Moville DL 38; 73

Magheralane beetling mill: Drummaul AM 19; 51

Magheralane bog (see Sluggan)

Magheralane fort: Drummaul AM 19; 88

Magheralane school: Drummaul AM 19; 75, 77, 81, 85, 92–93

Magheralane Sunday school: Drummaul AM 19; 77

Magheralane td: Drummaul AM 19; 37, 89–91

Magheralave corn mill: Derryaghy AM 8; 100

Magheralave forts: Derryaghy AM 8; 96

Magheralave House: Derryaghy AM 8; 106–07

Magheralave td: Derryaghy AM 8; 91, 96, 100, 115, 120

Magheraleggin (see Magheralagan): Down DN 17; 55

Magheralin: Aghaderg DN 12; 6

Magheralin: Annaclone DN 12; 13

Magheralin: Misc. DN 17; 117

Magheralin chapel: Magheralin DN 12; 110

Magheralin church: Magheralin DN 12; 109

Magheralin Glebe House: Magheralin DN 12; 110

Magheralin ph: Donaghcloney DN 12; 57, 59

Magheralin ph: Dromore DN 12; 70, 73

Magheralin ph: Moira DN 12; 117

Magheralin ph: Montiaghs AH 1; 91, 93

Magheralin ph: Shankill DN 12; 139

Magheralin quarries: Magherally DN 12; 114

Magheralin school: Magheralin DN 12; 110

Magheralin village: Magheralin DN 12; 109–10

Magheraliskmisk fort [I]: Magheragall AM 21; 105

Magheraliskmisk fort [II]: Magheragall AM 21; 105

Magheraliskmisk fort [III]: Magheragall AM 21; 105

Magheraliskmisk fort [IV]: Magheragall AM 21; 105

Magheraliskmisk fort [V]: Magheragall AM 21; 105

Magheraliskmisk fort [VI]: Magheragall AM 21; 105

Magheraliskmisk fort [VII]: Magheragall AM 21; 105

Magheraliskmisk quarry: Magheragall AM 21; 103, 107

Magheraliskmisk td: Magheragall AM 21; 107

Magherally church: Magherally DN 12; 113, 115

Magherally Glebe House: Magherally DN 12; 113, 115

Magherally hill: Magherally DN 12; 112

Magherally meeting house: Magherally DN 12; 113, 115

Magherally old church: Misc. DN 17; 117

Magherally ph: Donaghcloney DN 12; 57

Magherally ph: Dromara DN 12; 64

Magherally ph: Dromore DN 12; 70, 73

Magherally ph: Garvaghy DN 12; 79–80, 82

Magherally ph: Misc. DN 17; 117

Magherally ph: Seapatrick DN 12; 124, 128

Magherally ph: Tullylish DN 12; 140

Magherally school: Magherally DN 12; 113, 115

Magherally td: Magherally DN 12; 113–15

Magheralough flax mill: Ardstraw TE 5; 14

Magheralough quarries: Ardstraw TE 5; 13

Magheralough school: Ardstraw TE 5; 13

Magheralough td: Kilskeery TE 5; 113

Magheramason td: Donaghedy TE 5; 92

Magheramayo flax mill: Drumgooland DN 3; 25

Magheramayo school: Drumgooland DN 3; 25

Magheramayo td: Drumgooland DN 3; 25

Magheramenagh td: Ballywillin LY 33; 51

Magheramenagh td: Belleek FH 14; 4, 6

Magheramernagh (see Magheramenagh)

Magheramesk bleach green: Magheramesk AM 21; 119

Magheramesk bog: Magheramesk AM 21; 116

Magheramesk Carinloughrim school: Magheramesk AM 21; 130

Magheramesk fort [I]: Magheramesk AM 21; 119

Magheramesk fort [II]: Magheramesk AM 21; 121

Magheramesk fort [III]: Magheramesk AM 21; 122

Magheramesk fort [IV]: Magheramesk AM 21; 125

Magheramesk graveyard: Magheramesk AM 21; 122

Magheramesk hill: Magheramesk AM 21; 114

Magheramesk old church: Magheramesk AM 21; 122

Magheramesk old graveyard: Magheramesk AM 21; 121

Magheramesk ph: Aghagallon AM 21; 1, 22–23

Magheramesk ph: Aghalee AM 21; 26, 29–31, 37–39

Magheramesk ph: Ballinderry AM 21; 41

Magheramesk ph: Blaris AM 8; 3
Magheramesk ph: Blaris DN 12; 26–27, 29
Magheramesk ph: Misc. AM 10; 129
Magheramesk quarries: Magheramesk AM 21; 112–13, 116, 119, 121
Magheramesk td: Blaris DN 12; 28, 40, 42
Magheramesk td: Magheramesk AM 21; 113–14, 122, 126, 130
Magheramesk well: Magheramesk AM 21; 121
Magheramore (see Mageramorne): Glynn AM 26; 1
Magheramore carn: Banagher LY 30; 69
Magheramore carn: Desertoghill LY 27; 27
Magheramore cave: Banagher LY 30; 44, 83
Magheramore flax mill: Banagher LY 30; 128
Magheramore fort: Dungiven LY 15; 112
Magheramore fort [I]: Desertoghill LY 27; 8, 27
Magheramore fort [II]: Desertoghill LY 27; 27
Magheramore fort [III]: Desertoghill LY 27; 27
Magheramore fort [IV]: Desertoghill LY 27; 32
Magheramore graveyard: Banagher LY 30; 6, 41–43, 54, 56, 71, 80, 88–89
Magheramore grey stones: Tamlaght Finlagan LY 25; 89
Magheramore hill: Desertoghill LY 27; 1
Magheramore lough: Mevagh DL 38; 55
Magheramore monastery: Banagher LY 30; 6, 41–43, 56, 98, 114
Magheramore nunnery: Banagher LY 30; 80–82, 84
Magheramore old church: Banagher LY 30; 12, 37, 39–43, 46, 48–50, 54, 56–58, 68–69, 72, 80–82, 84, 88, 92, 98, 100, 102, 112–13
Magheramore quarry: Banagher LY 30; 128
Magheramore school: Desertoghill LY 27; 2, 4, 17–18, 20, 27, 33
Magheramore stream: Desertoghill LY 27; 8
Magheramore Sunday school: Desertoghill LY 27; 4
Magheramore td (Tamlaght Finlagan): Faughanvale LY 36; 60
Magheramore td: Ballywillin LY 33; 48
Magheramore td: Banagher LY 30; 22, 35–36, 43–44, 54, 57–58, 61–62, 69, 83, 89, 92, 95, 105, 110, 119, 124, 128, 130–31
Magheramore td: Clonmany DL 38; 18
Magheramore td: Desertoghill LY 27; 8, 17, 19–21, 27, 29, 32
Magheramore td: Dungiven LY 15; 45, 92
Magheramore td: Faughanvale LY 36; 17, 53, 60, 69, 77, 88–89, 96, 99
Magheramore td: Galloon FH 4; 95
Magheramore td: Misc. LY 36; 111
Magheramore td: Ramoan AM 24; 88, 125
Magheramore td: Raymoghy DL 39; 138, 141–42, 199
Magheramore td: Tamlaght Finlagan LY 25; 72–74, 89, 93, 104, 118

Magheramore well: Banagher LY 30; 41
Magheramore West td: Raymoghy DL 39; 140
Magheramore wood: Banagher LY 30; 124
Magheramorne district: Ballylinny AM 32; 30
Magheramorne district: Carnmoney AM 2; 64
Magheramorne district: Carrickfergus AM 37; 151
Magheramorne district: Glynn AM 26; 1, 30, 32
Magheramorne district: Templecorran AM 26; 124, 126, 128–30
Magheramorne estate: Glynn AM 26; 13, 15, 18, 28, 30, 39–43
Magheramorne House: Glynn AM 26; 1
Magheramorne lough: Glynn AM 26; 30
Magheramorne ph: Glynn AM 26; 17
Magheramorne ph: Island Magee AM 10; 82
Magheramorne quarries (see Ballylig): Glynn AM 26; 14
Magheramorne Sunday school: Glynn AM 26; 47
Magheramourne (see Magheramorne)
Magheramulkenny chapel: Clonoe TE 20; 31
Magheramully old church: Skerry AM 13; 107
Magheramully td: Skerry AM 13; 107, 115
Magherana corn and yarn mill: Donaghcloney DN 12; 58
Magherana td: Donaghcloney DN 12; 57, 59
Magheranageeragh meeting house: Termonamongan TE 5; 143
Magheranageeragh td: Termonamongan TE 5; 143–44
Magheranagow (see Maghernagah): Aghagallon AM 21; 5
Magheranagragh plain: Ballintoy AM 24; 26
Magheranal (see Magheranaul): Clonmany DL 38; 20
Magheranappin td: Convoy DL 39; 21
Magheranaul altar stone: Clonmany DL 38; 16
Magheranaul standing stone: Clonmany DL 38; 16
Magheranaul td: Clonmany DL 38; 20
Magheranay td: Kinawley FH 4; 110
Magherangeeragh td: Devenish FH 14; 58
Magheranure hill: Drumgoon CN 40; 4
Magheranure td: Clones FH 4; 26
Magherareagh (Maghereagh) td: Donaghedy TE 5; 92
Magherareagh bog: Donaghedy TE 5; 89
Magherareagh td: Donaghmore DL 39; 38
Magherareagh td: Galloon FH 4; 95
Magherarny chapel: Clones FH 4; 28
Magherarny td: Clones FH 4; 26
Magheraroarty (Magherarorty) td: Lough Swilly DL 38; 120, 122
Magheraroarty school: Tullaghobegley DL 39; 172
Magherary td: Blaris DN 12; 34–35
Magherascouse school: Comber DN 7; 34, 40
Magherascouse td: Comber DN 7; 32, 37, 40, 42–43

Magherascullion House: Desertlyn LY 31; 42

Magherascullion school: Desertlyn LY 31; 50–51

Magherascullion td: Desertlyn LY 31; 42

Magherashanvalley td: Donaghmore DL 39; 38

Magherasharkin ph: Rasharkin AM 23; 132

Magheraskeagh brickfield: Aghanloo LY 11; 2, 32

Magheraskeagh school: Aghanloo LY 11; 32

Magheraskeagh td: Aghanloo LY 11; 2, 21, 33, 41–42

Magherasollus td: Raphoe DL 39; 126

Magherastaphena (see Magherastephana)

Magherastephana barony: Aghalurcher FH 4; 1, 6, 16

Magherastephana barony: Aghavea FH 4; 17, 19

Magherastephana barony: Cleenish FH 14; 11–12, 29

Magherastephana barony: Derrybrusk FH 4; 30

Magherastephena (see Magherastephana)

Magherastephina (see Magherastephana)

Magheratemple hill: Drung CN 40; 19

Magheratemple school: Drung CN 40; 22

Magheratimpany td: Magheradrool DN 17; 99, 104

Magheraveely village: Clones FH 4; 27–28

Magheraveely village: Galloon FH 4; 91

Magherawarden quarry: Lough Swilly DL 38; 129

Magherbeg (see Magherabeg): Mevagh DL 38; 63

Magherdunbar (see Magheradunbar)

Maghereagh forts: Antrim AM 29; 43

Maghereagh school: Antrim AM 29; 59

Maghereagh school: Drummaul AM 19; 81

Maghereagh td: Antrim AM 29; 3

Maghereagh td: Drummaul AM 19; 88, 90–91

Magherebwee (see Masteragwee): Dunboe LY 11; 58

Magherenny old church: Longfield TE 5; 133

Magherenny td: Longfield TE 5; 133

Magherentendry (Maghrintendy) td: Billy AM 16; 36, 40

Maghergall (see Magheragall)

Magherlamfield td: Clonoe TE 20; 31

Maghermesk (see Magheramesk)

Maghernacloy Castle: Magheracloone MN 40; 139

Maghernagagh (see Maghernagah): Aghagallon AM 21; 25

Maghernagah graveyard: Aghagallon AM 21; 10–11, 16, 21

Maghernagah old church: Aghagallon AM 21; 1, 5, 7, 10–11

Maghernagah school: Aghagallon AM 21; 25

Maghernagaw (see Maghernagah): Aghagallon AM 21; 1

Maghernakelly hill: Ematris MN 40; 112

Maghernakelly td: Ematris MN 40; 115–16

Maghernakill entrenchment: Donaghmoyne MN 40; 108

Maghernakill graveyard: Donaghmoyne MN 40; 108

Maghernell (see Magheranaul): Clonmany DL 38; 16

Magherny td: Longfield TE 5; 132

Magheroerty (see Magheraroarty): Lough Swilly DL 38; 120

Magheross graveyard: Magheross MN 40; 151

Magheross old church: Magheross MN 40; 146, 151

Magheross ph: Aughnamullen MN 40; 69–70

Magheross ph: Donaghmoyne MN 40; 106–07, 109–10

Magheross ph: Killanny MN 40; 130–31, 133–34

Magheross ph: Magheracloone MN 40; 137, 141

Magheross td: Magheross MN 40; 148

Maghershaffry td: Currin MN 40; 92

Maghery: Blaris AM 8; 89

Maghery: Coleraine LY 33; 97

Maghery: Tamlaght TE 20; 114

Maghery: Tartaraghan AH 1; 117

Maghery ferry: Clonoe TE 20; 30–31

Maghery ferry: Tamlaght TE 20; 122

Maghery ferry: Tartaraghan AH 1; 120–21

Maghery graveyard: Tartaraghan AH 1; 121

Maghery old chapel: Tartaraghan AH 1; 121

Maghery td: Tartaraghan AH 1; 117, 121

Magherybeg (see Magherabeg)

Magherybwee (see Magheraboy)

Magherycorrin td: Convoy DL 39; 21–22

Magherycriggan fort: Ardstraw TE 5; 12

Magherycriggan td: Ardstraw TE 5; 12

Magherydrummon lough: Clondavaddog DL 38; 2–3

Magherydrummon td: Tullyaughnish DL 38; 96

Magheryennan td: Lough Swilly DL 38; 128

Magherylough td: Misc. TE 5; 147

Magherymore (see Magheramore)

Magheryvale td: Convoy DL 39; 22

Magherywarden district: Clondavaddog DL 38; 4

Maghon (Mahon) td: Aughnamullen MN 40; 69–70, 76

Maghraskeagh (see Magheraskeagh)

Maghreleave (see Magheralave): Derryaghy AM 8; 120

Maghremagorgan corn mill: Mevagh DL 38; 57

Maghremagorgan td: Mevagh DL 38; 63

Maghremore (see Magheramore): Raymoghy DL 39; 140

Maghrybeg (see Magherabeg): Mevagh DL 38; 55

Maghrydrummon (see Magherydrummon): Clondavaddog DL 38; 3

Maghrymore (see Magheramore)

Magiestown school: Ballinderry AM 21; 57

Magil, family: Desertlyn LY 31; 42

Magildowney, Charles: Ballymoney AM 16; 13

Magill and Bradshaw, Messrs: Hillsborough DN 12; 97

Magill, Alexander: Blaris DN 12; 46

Magill, Anne: Carrickfergus AM 37; 158

Magill, Capt.: Ahoghill AM 23; 17

Magill, Capt.: Tamlaght O'Crilly LY 18; 93, 123

Magill, Daniel: Hillsborough DN 12; 105

Magill, Eliza: Ballyclug AM 23; 66

Magill, family: Aghagallon AM 21; 9

Magill, family: Ballinderry AM 21; 54

Magill, family: Derrykeighan AM 16; 89

Magill, family: Kilwaughter AM 10; 115

Magill, family: Lissan LY 31; 91, 106

Magill, family: Raloo AM 32; 94, 128

Magill, Henry (Jnr): Newry DN 3; 99, 104

Magill, Henry: Donaghcloney DN 12; 57–59

Magill, Henry: Newry DN 3; 99

Magill, Hugh: Drummaul AM 19; 87

Magill, J.: Ballymore AH 1; 16–17

Magill, James: Hillsborough DN 12; 97

Magill, James: Island Magee AM 10; 38, 81, 85

Magill, James: Racavan AM 13; 96, 100

Magill, James: Tamlaght O'Crilly LY 18; 118

Magill, James [I]: Carrickfergus AM 37; 111, 195

Magill, James [II]: Carrickfergus AM 37; 135

Magill, John: Artrea LY 6; 33

Magill, John: Carrickfergus AM 37; 113

Magill, John: Dromore DN 12; 74

Magill, John: Duneane AM 19; 124

Magill, John: Island Magee AM 10; 38, 85, 95

Magill, John: Kilwaughter AM 10; 116

Magill, John: Tullylish DN 12; 144

Magill, Miss: Clondermot LY 34; 25

Magill, Mr: Island Magee AM 10; 67, 87, 94

Magill, Mrs: Hillsborough DN 12; 107

Magill, Pat: Antrim AM 29; 58

Magill, Pat: Ballyclug AM 23; 66

Magill, Pat: Racavan AM 13; 96, 100

Magill, Patrick: Artrea LY 6; 33, 39

Magill, Patrick: Carncastle and Killyglen AM 10; 6

Magill, Patrick: Carrickfergus AM 37; 110

Magill, Peter: Aghagallon AM 21; 12

Magill, Rev. Bernard: Dunboe LY 11; 53

Magill, Rev. Bernard: Killowen LY 33; 164

Magill, Rev. Robert: Antrim AM 29; 26–27, 45

Magill, Rev. Robert: Muckamore AM 35; 73

Magill, Samuel: Carrickfergus AM 37; 113

Magill, Samuel: Tamlaght TE 20; 105, 133–34

Magill, Widow: Aghagallon AM 21; 17

Magill, Widow: Ballymoney AM 16; 17

Magill, Widow: Muckamore AM 35; 81

Magill, William: Ballynascreen LY 31; 23

Magill, William: Carrickfergus AM 37; 158

Magill, William: Lissan LY 31; 91, 101

Magilligan: Aghanloo LY 11; 7, 9–11, 17, 25, 36, 38

Magilligan: Dunboe LY 11; 73, 80

Magilligan: Dungiven LY 15; 26, 67

Magilligan bridge: Magilligan LY 11; 125

Magilligan chapel: Magilligan LY 11; 101

Magilligan church: Magilligan LY 11; 84, 100, 124, 138

Magilligan corn mills: Drumachose LY 9; 53

Magilligan corn mills: Magilligan LY 11; 101

Magilligan district: Lough Swilly DL 38; 138, 149

Magilligan district: Misc. LY 36; 110

Magilligan flax mill: Magilligan LY 11; 101

Magilligan giant's grave: Magilligan LY 11; 84

Magilligan Glebe House: Magilligan LY 11; 84–85, 93, 101, 116, 118, 123

Magilligan Head: Balteagh LY 9; 1, 20, 43

Magilligan Head: Lough Swilly DL 38; 137

Magilligan meeting house: Magilligan LY 11; 101

Magilligan old church: Aghanloo LY 11; 14

Magilligan old church: Magilligan LY 11; 88

Magilligan ph: Aghanloo LY 11; 1–2, 4, 7, 12

Magilligan ph: Banagher LY 30; 103

Magilligan ph: Cumber LY 28; 70

Magilligan ph: Drumachose LY 9; 76, 79, 84, 86, 129

Magilligan ph: Dunboe LY 11; 47, 66

Magilligan ph: Tamlaght Finlagan LY 25; 62, 97, 101

Magilligan Point: Killowen LY 33; 169

Magilligan Point: Magilligan LY 11; 83–84, 88, 113, 133, 141

Magilligan Point: Moville DL 38; 71

Magilligan Point: Tamlaght Finlagan LY 25; 85

Magilligan Point: Templecarn DL 39; 157

Magilligan rabbit warrens: Magilligan LY 11; 111

Magilligan schools: Magilligan LY 11; 101

Magilligan sound: Lough Swilly DL 38; 138

Magilligan strand: Dunboe LY 11; 59

Magilligan strand: Mevagh DL 38; 62

Magilligan td: Cumber LY 28; 64

Magilligan tower: Clonmany DL 38; 14

Magilligan tower: Magilligan LY 11; 85, 100

Magilligan, family: Aghanloo LY 11; 4

Magilligan, family: Magilligan LY 11; 92

Magilligan, James: Dungiven LY 15; 31

Magilligan, Rev. Rodger: Maghera LY 18; 69

Maginess, Arthur: Muckamore AM 35; 81

Maginis, Bernard: Hillsborough DN 12; 107

Maginn, Rev.: Kilbroney DN 3; 34

Maginnes, family: Blaris AM 8; 21

Maginnes, family: Derryaghy AM 8; 114

Maginness, Richard: Enniskillen FH 4; 58

Maginnis, Arthur: Misc. DN 17; 119

Maginnis, Eugene: Misc. DN 17; 119

Maginnis, family: Derryaghy AM 8; 103

Maginnis, family: Dundonald DN 7; 65

Maginnis, family: Misc. DN 17; 119

Maginnis, Gen.: Magheramesk AM 21; 125

Maginnis, James: Aghanloo LY 11; 16

Maginnis, John: Carrickfergus AM 37; 194

Maginnis, Matthew: Newry DN 3; 99

Maginnis, Mrs: Newry DN 3; 99

Maginnis, Thomas: Newry DN 3; 100, 104

Maginnis, William: Magilligan LY 11; 130

Maginniss, Col: Enniskillen FH 4; 58

Magirle, Biddy: Drummaul AM 19; 88

Maglame, family: Culfeightrin AM 24; 59

Magoney td: Magheross MN 40; 153

Magonnell, family: Ballynure AM 32; 69

Magonragh school: Enniskillen FH 4; 84

Magonragh td: Enniskillen FH 4; 74, 82

Magorey police station: Killanny MN 40; 132

Magorkan, family: Cumber LY 28; 69

Magovenny, John: Hillsborough DN 12; 100

Magovran, Joseph: Desertoghill LY 27; 14

Magowan, family: Ballyphilip DN 7; 13

Magowan, family: Billy AM 16; 58

Magowan, family: Carnmoney AM 2; 76, 102

Magowan, Frank: Kilcronaghan LY 31; 85

Magowan, George: Newry DN 3; 99

Magowan, John: Maghera LY 18; 80

Magowan, Mary: Maghera LY 18; 78

Magowan, Michael [I]: Maghera LY 18; 80

Magowan, Michael [II]: Maghera LY 18; 80

Magowan, Mr: Bangor DN 7; 25

Magowan, Nancy: Maghera LY 18; 79

Magowan, Patrick: Maghera LY 18; 79

Magowan, Patrick: Rasharkin AM 23; 138

Magowan, Robert: Carrickfergus AM 37; 109

Magowan, Robert: Loughguile AM 13; 72

Magowan, Thomas: Island Magee AM 10; 90

Magowan, Thomas: Maghera LY 18; 80

Magown, family: Billy AM 16; 68

Magrabeg (see Magherabeg)

Magragh, Miler: Misc. DN 17; 119

Magrath, giant: Donaghmore DL 39; 35

Magrath, Margaret: Kilrea LY 27; 117–18, 122

Magrath, Miles: Tynan AH 1; 132

Magrath, Mr: Templecarn DL 39; 159

Magrath, Rev. Miles: Clogher TE 5; 28

Magrath, Rev. Miles: Templecarn DL 39; 159, 163

Magrath's Castle: Templecarn DL 39; 159

Magreevy, family: Ballee DN 17; 16

Magreggor, family: Raloo AM 32; 128

Magreggor, Margaret: Kilwaughter AM 10; 114, 117

Magregor, William: Ballyaghran LY 33; 24

Magrogan, John: Duneane AM 19; 121

Magrotty, John: Coleraine LY 33; 146

Magucian, Clotworthy: Termoneeny LY 6; 133

Magucian, Margaret: Termoneeny LY 6; 133

Maguckian, John (Jnr): Maghera LY 18; 80

Maguckian, John (Snr): Maghera LY 18; 80

Maguckian, Thomas: Maghera LY 18; 80

Maguigan, Patrick: Maghera LY 18; 78

Maguiggen, man named: Maghera LY 18; 45

Maguinness, Ann: Blaris AM 8; 46

Maguinness, Charles: Blaris AM 8; 47

Maguinness, E.M.: Dromara DN 12; 68

Maguinness, William: Blaris AM 8; 47

Maguire, Brien: Kinawley FH 4; 116

Maguire, C.C.: Faughanvale LY 36; 49

Maguire, C.M.: Galloon FH 4; 102

Maguire, Capt.: Kinawley FH 4; 117

Maguire, Capt. [I]: Enniskillen FH 4; 64

Maguire, Capt. [II]: Enniskillen FH 4; 66, 82

Maguire, Cathal: Clogher TE 5; 24

Maguire, Cathal: Galloon FH 4; 87

Maguire, chieftain: Magheraculmoney FH 14; 110–11

Maguire, Constantine: Devenish FH 14; 60

Maguire, Constantine: Enniskillen FH 4; 72

Maguire, Constantine: Newry DN 3; 95, 101, 104

Maguire, Denis: Newry DN 3; 75, 104

Maguire, Donald: Kinawley FH 4; 111

Maguire, Donogh: Galloon FH 4; 87

Maguire, Edmond: Galloon FH 4; 87

Maguire, Edward: Hillsborough DN 12; 106

Maguire, family: Aghalurcher FH 4; 5–6, 9

Maguire, family: Aghavea FH 4; 19, 21

Maguire, family: Blaris AM 8; 22

Maguire, family: Currin MN 40; 94

Maguire, family: Devenish FH 14; 55, 60

Maguire, family: Enniskillen FH 4; 64, 66, 72, 75, 80

Maguire, family: Kinawley FH 4; 116

Maguire, family: Rossorry FH 14; 117

Maguire, Frank: Termoneeny LY 6; 133

Maguire, Giolla-Patrick: Misc. TE 5; 147

Maguire, Hugh: Cleenish FH 14; 20

Maguire, James: Kinawley FH 4; 111

Maguire, James: Termoneeny LY 6; 133

Maguire, K.M.: Kinawley FH 4; 116–17

Maguire, Lord: Enniskillen FH 4; 50, 52, 75

Maguire, Miss: Desertlyn LY 31; 49

Maguire, Mr: Enniskillen FH 4; 77

Maguire, Mr: Kilbroney DN 3; 34

Maguire, Mr: Saintfield DN 7; 120

Maguire, Patrick: Kinawley FH 4; 111

Maguire, Rev. Cathal: Clondermot LY 34; 62

Maguire, Rev. Edmund: Muckno MN 40; 164

Maguire, Rev. Roger: Kinawley FH 4; 111

Maguire, Sarah: Kinawley FH 4; 111

Maguire, Terence: Kinawley FH 4; 116–17

Maguire, Thomas: Enniskillen FH 4; 75

Maguire, Thomas: Galloon FH 4; 87

Maguire, Thomas: Kinawley FH 4; 111

Maguire's Castle: Aghalurcher FH 4; 9

Maguiresbridge: Aghalurcher FH 4; 3, 5–8, 10, 12–13, 15

Maguiresbridge: Aghavea FH 4; 17, 19–21, 23–24

Maguiresbridge: Cleenish FH 14; 16

Maguiresbridge: Clones FH 4; 26

Maguiresbridge: Derrybrusk FH 4; 32–33

Maguiresbridge: Enniskillen FH 4; 61, 70

Maguiresbridge: Galloon FH 4; 102

Maguiresbridge dispensary: Aghalurcher FH 4; 6, 10

Maguiresbridge market house: Aghalurcher FH 4; 6

Maguiresbridge meeting house: Aghalurcher FH 4; 6

Maguiresbridge school [I]: Aghalurcher FH 4; 6, 11

Maguiresbridge school [II]: Aghalurcher FH 4; 11

Maguiresbridge school [III]: Aghalurcher FH 4; 11

Maguy, family: Island Magee AM 10; 104

Magwiggan, Patrick: Maghera LY 18; 79

Magwye, family: Island Magee AM 10; 104

Mahaffey, Mary: Donaghmore DL 39; 40

Mahaffy, John: Carrickfergus AM 37; 175

Mahaffy, Rev. R.: Mevagh DL 38; 60

Mahagaret (see Magheragart)

Mahagart (see Magheragart)

Maharagh (see Maghera): Kilmacteige SO 40; 193

Mahare, William: Lambeg AM 8; 141

Mahareelay td: Taughboyne DL 39; 148, 154

Maharg, John: Desertoghill LY 27; 20

Maharg, Mary: Desertoghill LY 27; 20

Maharg, Robert: Desertoghill LY 27; 20

Maharg, Sarah: Desertoghill LY 27; 20

Maharg, William: Desertoghill LY 27; 21

Maharry (see Maghery): Blaris AM 8; 89

Maharry, James: Magheragall AM 21; 103

Mahee Island: Tullynakill DN 7; 124

Maherascouse (see Magherascouse): Comber DN 7; 32

Maherg, James: Magheragall AM 21; 105

Maherg, William: Magheragall AM 21; 107

Mahir, family: Lambeg AM 8; 135

Maho South hill: Inishmacsaint FH 14; 71

Maho td: Inishmacsaint FH 14; 74

Mahon td: Drumcree AH 1; 35, 42

Mahon, Anne: Carrickfergus AM 37; 117

Mahon, John: Carrickfergus AM 37; 128

Mahon, Mary: Carrickfergus AM 37; 117

Mahon, Rachel: Carrickfergus AM 37; 117

Mahon, Rev. James: Aghaderg DN 12; 11

Mahon, Rev. James: Drumballyroney DN 3; 10

Mahon, Rev. James: Tullylish DN 12; 144

Mahon, Widow: Ballymoney AM 16; 17

Mahoney, O.: Banagher LY 30; 33, 111

Mahood, George: Hillsborough DN 12; 106

Mahood, James: Hillsborough DN 12; 106

Maida (Italy): Kilbroney DN 3; 31, 34

Maiden Rocks lighthouse: Island Magee AM 10; 21, 79

Maidens (see also Hulin rocks): Carncastle and Killyglen AM 10; 3

Maigogher (see Mayoghill): Aghadowey LY 22; 21

Mailin td: Misc. DL 39; 199

Main (Balteagh): see Maine

Main bridge: Connor AM 19; 23

Main bridge: Drummaul AM 19; 52

Main bridge: Killagan AM 23; 83

Main bridge: Rasharkin AM 23; 131

Main bridge [I]: Ahoghill AM 23; 12, 14

Main bridge [II]: Ahoghill AM 23; 12, 14

Main drain: Ballinderry AM 21; 43

Main mountain: Cumber LY 28; 3, 5, 85

Main mountain: Donaghedy TE 5; 88

Main river: Ahoghill AM 23; 1–6, 10–14, 24, 27, 29–32

Main river: Antrim AM 29; 4

Main river: Ballyclug AM 23; 54

Main river: Ballycor AM 32; 1

Main river: Coleraine LY 33; 97

Main river: Connor AM 19; 17, 19–20, 28

Main river: Drummaul AM 19; 33–41, 43–44, 46, 50, 52, 65–66, 78–79, 81–82

Main river: Dunaghy AM 13; 10, 25, 27

Main river: Dundermot AM 13; 29–31

Main river: Finvoy AM 23; 67, 72

Main river: Glenwhirry AM 32; 75, 79

Main river: Killagan AM 23; 79–83

Main river: Kilraghts AM 16; 124, 126

Main river: Kilwaughter AM 10; 108

Main river: Kirkinriola AM 23; 88, 91–92, 116

Main river: Lough Neagh AM 21; 93, 97

Main river: Loughguile AM 13; 59, 61

Main river: Nilteen AM 35; 101

Main river: Racavan AM 13; 90, 97

Main river: Rasharkin AM 23; 127–31

Main river: Rashee AM 32; 135

Main river: Skerry AM 13; 109

Main weir: Drummaul AM 19; 46

Main, Janet: Island Magee AM 10; 94

Maine (Mayne) td: Balteagh LY 9; 24, 28–29, 39–40, 44

Maine (see Fane): Inniskeen MN 40; 124

Maine and Drumaduff bog: Balteagh LY 9; 43

Maine bleach green: Balteagh LY 9; 28

Maine corn mill: Balteagh LY 9; 40

Maine flax mill: Balteagh LY 9; 40

Maine fort [I]: Balteagh LY 9; 24

Maine fort [II]: Balteagh LY 9; 24

Maine fort [III]: Balteagh LY 9; 24, 29

Maine North bleach green: Balteagh LY 9; 13, 36

Maine North corn mill: Balteagh LY 9; 13

Maine North flax mill: Balteagh LY 9; 14

Maine North forts: Balteagh LY 9; 12, 26
Maine North td: Balteagh LY 9; 12–14, 26, 36
Maine South bog: Balteagh LY 9; 28
Maine South fort: Balteagh LY 9; 25, 28, 30
Maine South td: Balteagh LY 9; 2, 11, 19, 25, 28, 30, 45
Maine, J.: Aughnamullen MN 40; 74, 76
Mains, George: Macosquin LY 22; 104
Mains, Thomas: Coleraine LY 33; 130
Mairns, Anne: Carnmoney AM 2; 62, 102
Mairnstown td: Carrickfergus AM 37; 173
Mairs, Ann: Aghadowey LY 22; 36
Mairs, James: Aghadowey LY 22; 36
Mairs, John: Misc. LY 31; 112
Mairs, Joseph: Seagoe AH 1; 103
Mairs, Margret: Aghadowey LY 22; 36
Mairs, Matilda: Aghadowey LY 22; 36
Mairs, Sarah (Jnr): Aghadowey LY 22; 36
Mairs, Sarah (Snr): Aghadowey LY 22; 36
Mairs, Thomas: Carrickfergus AM 37; 135, 137
Maise, family: Ballinderry AM 21; 48
Major, family: Blaris DN 12; 30
Major, George: Blaris AM 8; 55, 85
Major, George: Blaris DN 12; 46, 49
Major, James: Faughanvale LY 36; 9, 45
Major, John: Magilligan LY 11; 93
Major, Parker: Blaris AM 8; 55, 84
Major, Parker: Blaris DN 12; 41, 46, 50
Major, Rev. Alexander: Ballyaghran LY 33; 4–5, 19
Major, Rev. Alexander: Coleraine LY 33; 63, 127
Major, Richard: Derryvullan FH 14; 33
Major, Walter: Ballyscullion LY 6; 57
Major, William: Blaris DN 12; 46, 50
Major's lough: Ballybay MN 40; 78–80
Makeeragh fort: Drumragh TE 5; 109
Makeeragh td: Drumragh TE 5; 109
Makenny school: Kilskeery TE 5; 115
Makenny td: Kilskeery TE 5; 113, 115
Makeonan bog: Donaghcloney DN 12; 57
Makowen, John: Termoneeny LY 6; 128
Malachy, St: Ballymyre AH 1; 20
Malachy, St: Newry DN 3; 66
Malalieu, Rev. W.: Ahoghill AM 23; 19
Malaverer, Robert: Tamlaght TE 20; 128
Malbruthim, bard: Dungiven LY 15; 32
Malcolm, Rev. James: Carrickfergus AM 37; 134
Malcolm, Rev. William: Carrickfergus AM 37; 102
Malcom, H.D.: Drummaul AM 19; 76, 87, 92
Malcom, John: Hillsborough DN 12; 106
Malcom, W.: Drumbo DN 7; 59–60
Malcom, W.: Magheradrool DN 17; 103
Malden (England): Antrim AM 29; 23
Maleolin, Miss: Artrea LY 6; 20
Malin: Clonmany DL 38; 13, 17, 19–20
Malin: Desertegney DL 38; 27

Malin: Donagh DL 38; 32
Malin: Lough Swilly DL 38; 109
Malin: Muff DL 38; 81
Malin district: Clondavaddog DL 38; 7
Malin district: Lough Swilly DL 38; 111
Malin Hall: Clonmany DL 38; 18
Malin Hall: Donagh DL 38; 32
Malin Hall: Lough Swilly DL 38; 109, 134
Malin Head: Clondavaddog DL 38; 4
Malin Head: Clonmany DL 38; 16
Malin Head: Dungiven LY 15; 37
Malin Head: Lough Swilly DL 38; 107–09, 113, 132, 138
Malin Head: Mevagh DL 38; 57, 61
Malin tower: Lough Swilly DL 38; 113
Malin well: Lough Swilly DL 38; 108–09, 111, 113, 138
Malin well: Muff DL 38; 81
Malin Well creek: Lough Swilly DL 38; 108
Malinbeg district: Glencolumbkille DL 39; 65
Malinmore district: Glencolumbkille DL 39; 65
Mallaberry hill: Clogher TE 5; 33
Mallaberry td: Clogher TE 5; 26, 33, 46
Mallabuoy (see Mullaboy): Cumber LY 28; 49
Mallaghfad td: Aghalurcher FH 4; 14
Malle, Mr: Newry DN 3; 110
Mallendober td: Billy AM 16; 41
Mallock, Lt C.H.: Ballyscullion AM 19; 1–2
Mallock, Lt C.H.: Carrickfergus AM 37; 1–4
Mallon, Arthur: Magherafelt LY 6; 102
Mallon, Edward: Maghera LY 18; 41
Mallon, Henry: Aghalee AM 21; 35
Mallon, James: Aghagallon AM 21; 12
Mallon, James: Maghera LY 18; 43
Mallon, John: Ballynascreen LY 31; 22
Mallon, Michael: Ballynascreen LY 31; 26
Mallrose (Scotland): Termoneeny LY 6; 127, 132
Mallusk chapel: Mallusk AM 2; 107, 111
Mallusk church: Templepatrick AM 35; 133
Mallusk cove: Mallusk AM 2; 114
Mallusk fort: Mallusk AM 2; 114
Mallusk grange: Carnmoney AM 2; 81
Mallusk old church: Mallusk AM 2; 109, 114
Mallusk old graveyard: Mallusk AM 2; 114
Mallusk ph: Ballyrobert AM 2; 24
Mallusk ph: Carrickfergus AM 37; 69, 71, 100
Mallusk ph: Kilroot AM 26; 65
Mallusk ph: Misc. DN 17; 122
Mallusk ph: Muckamore AM 35; 58
Mallusk ph: Raloo AM 32; 98
Mallusk ph: Templecorran AM 26; 101
Mallusk ph: Templepatrick AM 35; 107, 138–39, 141, 144–45
Mallusk ph: Umgall AM 35; 156
Mallusk standing stone: Mallusk AM 2; 114–15

Mallybeney td: Clogher TE 5; 37

Malon, Eliza Saly: Tamlaght TE 20; 77

Malon, Hugh: Tamlaght TE 20; 77

Malon, James [I]: Tamlaght TE 20; 76

Malon, James [II]: Tamlaght TE 20; 77

Malone tollgate: Blaris AM 8; 37

Malone, Catherine: Carrickfergus AM 37; 124

Malone, James: Ahoghill AM 23; 39

Malone, John: Duneane AM 19; 119, 122

Malone, Julia: Culfeightrin AM 24; 63

Malowney, Andrew: Duneane AM 19; 124

Malowney, Daniel: Duneane AM 19; 124

Maloy, James: Maghera LY 18; 39

Maloy, John: Billy AM 16; 69

Maloy, John: Tamlaght O'Crilly LY 18; 123

Maloy, Michael: Tamlaght O'Crilly LY 18; 114

Maloy, Patt: Killelagh LY 27; 101

Maloy, Rose: Tamlaght O'Crilly LY 18; 137

Malseed, James: Tullyaughnish DL 38; 96

Maltman's bay: Lough Swilly DL 38; 147

Malts standing stone: Culfeightrin AM 24; 82

Malvin Parks House: Ardstraw TE 5; 11

Mamont, Gen.: Lissan LY 31; 101

Mamore bridge: Desertegney DL 38; 26

Mamore Gap: Clonmany DL 38; 12, 14–17, 20

Mamore Gap: Desertegney DL 38; 26

Mamragh district: Misc. SO 40; 200

Managh Beg td: Banagher LY 30; 106

Managh Beg td: Clondermot LY 34; 57, 72–73,
    111–13, 119, 127, 132

Managh More td: Clondermot LY 34; 57, 72–73,
    111–13, 119, 127, 132

Mananan, magician: Ballintoy AM 24; 34

Manchester: Carnmoney AM 2; 52

Manchester: Cumber LY 28; 58

Manchester: Enniskillen FH 4; 47

Manchester: Killead AM 35; 49

Manchester: Killyleagh DN 17; 84

Manderson, John: Muckamore AM 35; 81

Manderson, Samuel: Killead AM 35; 51

Mandeville Castle: Ballymore AH 1; 9–10, 13

Mandeville Hall: Kilmore AH 1; 64, 72

Mandeville, family: Killyleagh DN 17; 81

Mandeville, John: Clondermot LY 34; 46

Mandeville, Lady (nee Sparrow): Killevy AH 1; 53

Mandeville, Lady: Ballymore AH 1; 3–4, 9, 11

Mandeville, Lady: Seagoe AH 1; 102

Mandeville, Lord: Ballymore AH 1; 3–5, 7–18

Mandeville, Lord: Ballynure AM 32; 44

Mandeville, Lord: Coleraine LY 33; 100

Mandeville, Lord: Drumcree AH 1; 30, 35–38, 41

Mandeville, Lord: Kilmore AH 1; 64–65, 72

Mandeville, Lord: Loughgilly AH 1; 84

Mandeville, Lord: Raloo AM 32; 93, 115

Mandeville, Lord: Seagoe AH 1; 106–10

Mandiville, family: Clondermot LY 34; 45–46

Mandiville, Martin: Clondermot LY 34; 45

Mandiville, Richard: Clondermot LY 34; 45

Mandiville, Robert [I]: Clondermot LY 34; 45

Mandiville, Robert [II]: Clondermot LY 34; 45

Maneely, family: Templepatrick AM 35; 148

Manelly, family: Maghera LY 18; 24

Manister monastery: Drumtullagh AM 16, 100, 103

Manisteriderow bog: Drumtullagh AM 16; 97

Manley, Capt.: Carrickfergus AM 37; 57, 135

Manley, Isaac: Drumachose LY 9; 65

Manley, William: Termonamongan TE 5; 145

Mann, Billy: Drummaul AM 19; 88

Mann, family: Kirkinriola AM 23; 124

Mann, Henery: Ballyscullion LY 6; 76

Mann, James: Island Magee AM 10; 90

Mann, John: Island Magee AM 10; 94

Mann, Marbel: Errigal Keerogue TE 20; 48–49

Mann, Robert: Mevagh DL 38; 60

Mann, Thomas: Island Magee AM 10; 90

Manners, Charles: Coleraine LY 33; 131

Manniss, Rev. William: Ballymoney AM 16; 25

Manolly, family: Maghera LY 18; 24, 48

Manor Hassat district: Magheraculmoney FH 14;
    110

Manor Water House: Galloon FH 4; 92, 94–95, 105

Manor Water House school: Galloon FH 4; 96

Manorcunningham: Raymoghy DL 39; 132–34,
    144–45, 186

Manorcunningham church: Raymoghy DL 39; 133

Manorcunningham Churchland Isle td: Raymoghy
    DL 39; 138

Manorcunningham Churchland td: Raymoghy DL
    39; 138

Manorcunningham graveyard: Raymoghy DL 39;
    133

Manorcunningham meeting house: Raymoghy DL
    39; 133

Manorcunningham post office: Raymoghy DL 39;
    133

Manorcunningham quarry: Raymoghy DL 39; 144

Manorcunningham school: Raymoghy DL 39; 140

Manorcunningham td: Raymoghy DL 39; 138, 141,
    199

Manorhamilton: Comber DN 7; 37, 39

Manorhamilton: Derryvullan FH 14; 39

Manorhamilton: Manorhamilton Union LM 40;
    47–50, 52, 54

Manorhamilton bridge: Manorhamilton Union LM
    40; 49

Manorhamilton Castle: Manorhamilton Union LM
    40; 49–51

Manorhamilton Catholic school: Manorhamilton
    Union LM 40; 49

Manorhamilton chapel (C): Manorhamilton Union LM 40; 49

Manorhamilton chapel (M): Manorhamilton Union LM 40; 53

Manorhamilton church: Manorhamilton Union LM 40; 49, 52

Manorhamilton court house: Manorhamilton Union LM 40; 49

Manorhamilton dispensary: Manorhamilton Union LM 40; 49, 52

Manorhamilton district: Manorhamilton Union LM 40; 47

Manorhamilton hibernian school: Manorhamilton Union LM 40; 49

Manorhamilton manor: Manorhamilton Union LM 40; 51

Manorhamilton market house: Manorhamilton Union LM 40; 49

Manorhamilton new chapel (M): Manorhamilton Union LM 40; 49

Manorhamilton old barrack: Manorhamilton Union LM 40; 49, 52

Manorhamilton old chapel (M): Manorhamilton Union LM 40; 49, 53

Manorhamilton old church: Manorhamilton Union LM 40; 49, 51–52

Manorhamilton post office: Manorhamilton Union LM 40; 49–50

Manorhamilton sewing school: Manorhamilton Union LM 40; 49

Manorhamilton tannery: Manorhamilton Union LM 40; 49

Manorhamilton Town Parks: Manorhamilton Union LM 40; 49

Manorhamilton tuck mill: Manorhamilton Union LM 40; 49

Mansell, Mr: Drumbo DN 7; 60

Mansfield, Capt.: Tullyaughnish DL 38; 91, 97

Mansfield, family: Donaghmore DL 39; 34

Mansfield, Francis: Clonleigh DL 39; 12

Mansfield, Messrs: Donaghmore DL 39; 37

Mansfield, Mr: Raphoe DL 39; 126

Mansfield, Ralph: Donaghmore DL 39; 29–32

Mansfield, Rev. George: Faughanvale LY 36; 40

Mansfield, soldier: Donaghmore DL 39; 34

Manson, family: Glynn AM 26; 45

Manson, Mr: Glynn AM 26; 45

Manster, Longadel: Carrickfergus AM 37; 80

Mant, Rev. R.M.: Ballymoney AM 16; 4, 15, 21, 25

Mant, Rev. Richard: Ballyclug AM 23; 52

Mant, Rev. Richard: Ramoan AM 24; 86

Mant, Rev. S.: Coleraine LY 33; 127

Mant, Rev. Walter: Hillsborough DN 12; 97, 99, 104

Mant, Richard: Misc. DN 17; 117

Mantavna, George: Tamlaght TE 20; 80

Mantavna, Peter: Tamlaght TE 20; 80

Manus, Col: Dungiven LY 15; 56

Many Bowls hill: Clogher TE 5; 54

Maodhog, St: Clondermot LY 34; 70

Maola Aughrim td: Ballyscullion LY 6; 58

Maola town td: Ballyscullion LY 6; 58

Maphet, Arthur: Newry DN 3; 99, 104

Maralin (see Magheralin): Misc. DN 17; 117

Marble Arch: Killesher FH 14; 82

Marblehill bay: Lough Swilly DL 38; 119

Marblehill House: Lough Swilly DL 38; 120–21

Marbury, Edward: Clonleigh DL 39; 15

Marbury, George: Clonleigh DL 39; 15

March burn: Killygarvan DL 38; 37

March burn: Tullyaughnish DL 38; 85, 93

March burn bridge: Killygarvan DL 38; 41

March burn bridge: Tullyaughnish DL 38; 93

March burn wood mill: Killygarvan DL 38; 40

Marchall, family: Derryaghy AM 8; 103

Mardock, family: Desertmartin LY 31; 55

Mardock, John: Magherafelt LY 6; 102

Margal, Neil: Bovevagh LY 25; 46

Margaret's Castle: Ardglass DN 17; 3

Margey water (see Carey): Culfeightrin AM 24; 55

Margy td: Templecarn DL 39; 164

Margy, family: Desertoghill LY 27; 8

Margymonaghan meeting house: Magilligan LY 11; 85, 125

Margymonaghan night school: Magilligan LY 11; 137–38

Margymonaghan school: Magilligan LY 11; 138

Margymonaghan td: Magilligan LY 11; 95, 126, 135, 142

Mark, family: Ahoghill AM 23; 25

Mark, John: Ahoghill AM 23; 34

Markagh rock: Lough Swilly DL 38; 107

Markes, John: Lambeg AM 8; 135

Market hill: Dunluce AM 16; 118

Market Root district: Drumtullagh AM 16; 103

Markethill: Ballymore AH 1; 1, 3, 6, 9, 13, 15, 18

Markethill: Drumcree AH 1; 36

Markethill: Kilclooney AH 1; 51

Markethill: Killevy AH 1; 52

Markethill: Killyleagh DN 17; 86

Markethill: Kilmore AH 1; 60, 63

Markethill: Mullaghbrack AH 1; 94, 96–97

Markethill chapel: Mullaghbrack AH 1; 94, 96

Markethill court house: Mullaghbrack AH 1; 94

Markethill meeting house: Mullaghbrack AH 1; 94, 96

Markethill police station: Mullaghbrack AH 1; 94

Markethill Rectory: Loughgilly AH 1; 84

Markey, Michael: Loughgilly AH 1; 86

Markhame, James: Clondermot LY 34; 54

Marks, John: Artrea LY 6; 24

Marks, Mr: Carlingford LH 40; 59
Marks, Rev. John: Kilmore AH 1; 59–60
Marks, Rev. Stewart: Moville DL 38; 74
Marl Island: Killinchy DN 7; 86, 92
Marlacoo corn mill: Mullaghbrack AH 1; 97
Marlacoo flax mill [I]: Mullaghbrack AH 1; 97
Marlacoo flax mill [II]: Mullaghbrack AH 1; 97
Marlacoo lough: Mullaghbrack AH 1; 94
Marlacoobeg td: Mullaghbrack AH 1; 94
Marlacoomore td. Mullaghbrack AH 1; 94
Marlany lough: Clogher TE 5; 59
Marlbank school: Killesher FH 14; 86
Marlbank td: Killesher FH 14; 82
Marlfield td: Misc. DN 17; 125–26
Marlin [or Martin], George: Termoneeny LY 6; 133
Marlin [or Martin], Henry: Termoneeny LY 6; 133
Marlin, family: Maghera LY 18; 6, 13, 24, 48, 50
Marlin, Fanny: Maghera LY 18; 22
Marlin, George: Maghera LY 18; 49–50, 54
Marlin, Hugh: Maghera LY 18; 53
Marlin, James: Tamlaght O'Crilly LY 18; 135
Marlin, James [I]: Maghera LY 18; 50
Marlin, James [II]: Maghera LY 18; 53
Marlin, John: Maghera LY 18; 77
Marlin, Mr: Termoneeny LY 6; 131
Marlin, Robert: Maghera LY 18; 31
Marlin, Susan: Maghera LY 18; 50
Marmion, Bernard: Bright DN 17; 37
Marmion, Bernard: Rathmullan DN 17; 109–10
Marmion, Miss: Blaris AM 8; 85
Maroe House: Tamlaght O'Crilly LY 18; 106
Marr, Samuel: Rasharkin AM 23; 141
Marran, J.: Aughnamullen MN 40; 76
Marrareene (see Massereene)
Marren, Patrick: Newry DN 3; 98
Marrin, Michael: Kilmacteige SO 40; 196
Marrola wood: Finvoy AM 23; 69
Marron, Denis: Newry DN 3; 99, 104
Marrs, Samuel: Ahoghill AM 23; 22, 44
Marry, family: Misc. LY 36; 104
Mars, Rev. John: Aghadowey LY 22; 23
Marsh, family: Blaris AM 8; 21
Marshal, James: Carrickfergus AM 37; 164
Marshal, Samuel: Mevagh DL 38; 57
Marshall, A.: Carnmoney AM 2; 90
Marshall, David: Muckamore AM 35; 81
Marshall, Dr: Hillsborough DN 12; 97
Marshall, Elizabeth: Misc. DL 39; 186
Marshall, family: Carnmoney AM 2; 76
Marshall, family: Shilvodan AM 19; 136
Marshall, Fanny: Ballylinny AM 32; 29
Marshall, Hugh: Ballylinny AM 32; 29
Marshall, James: Drumachose LY 9; 49
Marshall, Jane: Ballylinny AM 32; 29
Marshall, John: Ballylinny AM 32; 29

Marshall, John: Lough Swilly DL 38; 136
Marshall, John: Misc. DL 39; 186
Marshall, Mr: Clogher TE 5; 40
Marshall, Mr: Enniskillen FH 4; 75
Marshall, Mr: Misc. TE 5; 147
Marshall, Rev.: Donegal DL 39; 49
Marshall, Rev.: Maghera LY 18; 66
Marshall, Rev. Futt: Doagh AM 29; 81, 87
Marshall, Rev. George: Donagh DL 38; 32
Marshall, Rev. George: Killelagh LY 27; 96
Marshall, Rev. James: Doagh AM 29; 81, 87
Marshall, Samuel: Killea and Taughboyne DL 39;
   84, 87, 90
Marshall, Samuel: Raymoghy DL 39; 135, 137
Marshall, Thomas: Newry DN 3; 104
Marshall, W.G.: Faughanvale LY 36; 42, 45
Marshall, William: Ahoghill AM 23; 35
Marshall, William: Ballinderry TE 20; 12, 14
Marshall, William: Drumachose LY 9; 107
Marshall, William: Leckpatrick TE 5; 126
Marshall, William: Newry DN 3; 99, 104
Marshall, William: Nilteen AM 35; 102–03
Marshall's fort: Macosquin LY 22; 85, 116
Marshall's mill: Killea and Taughboyne DL 39; 87
Marshallstown (Marshalstown) td: Down DN 17;
   53, 56–57
Marshaltown locality: Carrickfergus AM 37; 94, 174
Marshe, Edward: Ballyscullion LY 6; 57
Marshe, Esther: Ballyscullion LY 6; 57
Marshel, family: Misc. LY 36; 104
Marshel, John: Balteagh LY 9; 31
Martin [or Marlin], George: Termoneeny LY 6; 133
Martin [or Marlin], Henry: Termoneeny LY 6; 133
Martin [or Morton], Charles: Clondermot LY 34; 6,
   20, 37–38, 44, 102, 104
Martin and Sheckilton, Messrs: Magheradrool DN
   17; 105
Martin, Alexander: Ballynascreen LY 31; 30
Martin, Charles: Ahoghill AM 23; 34–35
Martin, Daniel: Drummaul AM 19; 89
Martin, Daniel: Hillsborough DN 12; 107
Martin, Daniel: Tamlaght Finlagan LY 25; 119
Martin, Dr: Maghera LY 18; 54
Martin, Edward: Ballylinny AM 32; 29
Martin, Edward: Hillsborough DN 12; 107
Martin, family: Aghalee AM 21; 36
Martin, family: Ballee DN 17; 16
Martin, family: Carnmoney AM 2; 76
Martin, family: Carrickfergus AM 37; 93
Martin, family: Desertlyn LY 31; 42
Martin, family: Drumbeg AM 8; 123
Martin, family: Kilcronaghan LY 31; 68
Martin, family: Maghera LY 18; 13
Martin, family: Misc. LY 36; 104
Martin, family: Newry DN 3; 107

Martin, family: Racavan AM 13; 100

Martin, family: Raloo AM 32; 108

Martin, family: Templecorran AM 26; 117, 119

Martin, Francis: Hillsborough DN 12; 107

Martin, Frank: Drummaul AM 19; 88

Martin, George: Carnmoney AM 2; 69

Martin, George: Maghera LY 18; 57

Martin, Hugh: Carrickfergus AM 37; 111

Martin, Hugh: Drumachose LY 9; 104

Martin, Hugh: Hillsborough DN 12; 107

Martin, Hugh: Tamlaght Finlagan LY 25; 124

Martin, Israel: Tamlaght Finlagan LY 25; 80

Martin, J.J.: Drumachose LY 9; 104

Martin, James: Ballylinny AM 32; 29

Martin, James: Derrykeighan AM 16; 94

Martin, James: Drummaul AM 19; 75, 85, 92

Martin, James: Dunluce AM 16; 116, 118–19

Martin, Jane: Maghera LY 18; 77

Martin, John (Snr): Drumachose LY 9; 104

Martin, John: Antrim AM 29; 59

Martin, John: Ballynure AM 32; 60

Martin, John: Ballyrashane LY 22; 61

Martin, John: Carrickfergus AM 37; 126

Martin, John: Culfeightrin AM 24; 83

Martin, John: Drummaul AM 19; 75, 77, 85–86

Martin, John: Dunluce AM 16; 119

Martin, John: Kilbroney DN 3; 35

Martin, John: Killyleagh DN 17; 80, 84

Martin, John: Newry DN 3; 111

Martin, John: Skerry AM 13; 120

Martin, John: Tamlaght Finlagan LY 25; 82, 101,
    125

Martin, John: Termoneeny LY 6; 126

Martin, Michael: Kilteevoge DL 39; 112

Martin, Mr: Ballyscullion AM 19; 11

Martin, Mr: Drumachose LY 9; 78, 107

Martin, Ollover: Drumachose LY 9; 132

Martin, R.: Newtownards DN 7; 112

Martin, Rev.: Cleenish FH 14; 17

Martin, Rev. Henry: Inver AM 26; 52

Martin, Rev. John: Ardstraw TE 5; 6, 8

Martin, Rev. William: Lissan LY 31; 89, 97, 103

Martin, Richard: Carrickfergus AM 37; 129

Martin, Richard: Manorhamilton Union LM 40; 54

Martin, Richard: Misc. SO 40; 199

Martin, Robert: Carnmoney AM 2; 99

Martin, Robert: Carrickfergus AM 37; 153

Martin, Robert: Hillsborough DN 12; 107

Martin, Robert: Maghera LY 18; 53, 55, 68, 70–72

Martin, Robert: Newry DN 3; 81, 112

Martin, Samual: Macosquin LY 22; 122

Martin, Samuel: Drumachose LY 9; 73, 104

Martin, St: Desertmartin LY 31; 55, 111, 117

Martin, Thomas (Jnr): Hillsborough DN 12; 107

Martin, Thomas (Snr): Hillsborough DN 12; 107

Martin, Thomas: Aghanloo LY 11; 22

Martin, Thomas [I]: Drumachose LY 9; 104

Martin, Thomas [I]: Hillsborough DN 12; 107

Martin, Thomas [II]: Drumachose LY 9; 132

Martin, W.B.: Ahoghill AM 23; 41

Martin, William: Balteagh LY 9; 34

Martin, William: Blaris AM 8; 45, 50

Martin, William: Carnmoney AM 2; 100

Martin, William: Desertoghill LY 27; 23

Martin, William: Doagh AM 29; 98

Martin, William: Drumbeg AM 8; 122, 133

Martin, William: Hillsborough DN 12; 107

Martin, William: Killyleagh DN 17; 80, 84

Martin, William: Leck DL 39; 120

Martin, William: Maghera LY 18; 77

Martine, family: Carnmoney AM 2; 102

Martray (see Martrey)

Martrey lough: Clogher TE 5; 58

Martrey lough: Errigal Keerogue TE 20; 51

Martyn, John: Raloo AM 32; 123

Martynn, family: Raloo AM 32; 126

Mary [I], Queen: Armoy AM 24; 9

Mary [I], Queen: Killead AM 35; 32

Mary [II], Queen: Carmavy AM 35; 6

Mary [II], Queen: Drummaul AM 19; 53, 69, 88

Mary [II], Queen: Misc. LY 31; 118

Mary Breen's burn: Donaghmore DL 39; 29

Mary Grey mountain: Ardstraw TE 5; 2, 10

Mary Grey mountain: Cappagh TE 5; 15, 17

Mary Grey mountain: Skirts of Urney and Ardstraw
    TE 5; 139

Mary Grey's stone: Ballywillin LY 33; 48

Mary II, Queen: Currin MN 40; 90

Mary II, Queen: Ematris MN 40; 115

Mary II, Queen: Galloon FH 4; 100

Mary II, Queen: Newry DN 3; 65

Mary Kerr's Island: Finvoy AM 23; 73–74

Mary lough: Ardstraw TE 5; 2, 10

Mary Winnert's hole cove: Kilwaughter AM 10; 119

Mary, Queen of Scots: Ahoghill AM 23; 28

Mary's Abbey (Dublin): Tamlaght Finlagan LY 25;
    69

Mary's Abbey (see Woodburn Abbey):
    Carrickfergus AM 37; 79

Mary's Holme locality: Dungiven LY 15; 31, 79

Mary's meadow: Magilligan LY 11; 106, 127

Mary's well: Aghanloo LY 11; 26

Marybrook House: Dromara DN 12; 67

Maryfield House: Holywood DN 7; 76, 82

Marymount fort: Drumbeg AM 8; 125, 129

Maryport (England): Killyleagh DN 17; 84

Maryport: Duneane AM 19; 124

Maryport: Kilcronaghan LY 31; 85

Maryport: Lissan LY 31; 109

Masaroon, Rev. Robert: Drumcree AH 1; 29

Mason Lodge: Misc. DL 39; 186

Mason Lodge lime-kiln: Killanny MN 40; 134

Mason Lodge lime-kiln: Magheracloone MN 40; 141

Mason, Andrew: Killea and Taughboyne DL 39; 82, 87

Mason, Mr: Donaghmore DL 39; 30

Mason, Peter: Aghalee AM 21; 31

Mason, William: Ahoghill AM 23; 37

Mass Corner glen: Derryaghy AM 8; 92

Mass hill: Banagher LY 30; 100

Mass hill: Tamlaght Finlagan LY 25; 113

Mass hill: Tullyaughnish DL 38; 90

Mass Hill td: Misc. DL 39; 198

Mass House Hill fort: Drumragh TE 5; 108

Massareene (see Massereene)

Massereene: Antrim AM 29; 9, 12–13, 44, 46

Massereene: Muckamore AM 35; 59–60, 64–67, 71–74, 77, 83

Massereene abbey: Muckamore AM 35; 60, 70–71, 83

Massereene Arms Hotel: Antrim AM 29; 10

Massereene barony: Blaris AM 8; 3, 45, 49

Massereene barony: Blaris DN 12; 26

Massereene barony: Derryaghy AM 8; 90

Massereene bridge: Antrim AM 29; 6, 9–10, 43–44, 49

Massereene bridge: Muckamore AM 35; 55, 61, 64

Massereene Castle: Antrim AM 29; 49

Massereene estate: Antrim AM 29; 47

Massereene friary: Muckamore AM 35; 56

Massereene House: Antrim AM 29; 44

Massereene Lower barony: Antrim AM 29; 12

Massereene Lower barony: Camlin AM 21; 64–65

Massereene Lower barony: Carmavy AM 35; 2

Massereene Lower barony: Killead AM 35; 8–9, 17, 43

Massereene Lower barony: Kilroot AM 26; 62

Massereene Lower barony: Muckamore AM 35; 54, 59

Massereene Lower barony: Templepatrick AM 35; 106

Massereene Lower barony: Tullyrusk AM 21; 133, 135

Massereene Lower barony: Umgall AM 35; 155

Massereene school: Muckamore AM 35; 66, 72–73

Massereene Upper barony: Aghagallon AM 21; 1

Massereene Upper barony: Aghalee AM 21; 26

Massereene Upper barony: Ballinderry AM 21; 41

Massereene Upper barony: Blaris DN 12; 27

Massereene Upper barony: Camlin AM 21; 60, 64

Massereene Upper barony: Carrickfergus AM 37; 38

Massereene Upper barony: Glenavy AM 21; 77, 84, 87

Massereene Upper barony: Killead AM 35; 8, 17

Massereene Upper barony: Kilroot AM 26; 62

Massereene Upper barony: Magheramesk AM 21; 112

Massereene Upper barony: Tullyrusk AM 21; 131, 133–34

Massereene, 4th Earl: Antrim AM 29; 7–10, 41

Massereene, Clotworthy, 1st Viscount: Drummaul AM 19; 70

Massereene, Countess of: Killead AM 35; 20, 39, 44

Massereene, Countess of: Muckamore AM 35; 54, 60

Massereene, Earl: Ballyscullion LY 6; 66

Massereene, family: Antrim AM 29; 7, 10–11, 16, 20, 23, 33, 35

Massereene, family: Ballyscullion AM 19; 1–2, 9

Massereene, family: Carmavy AM 35; 3

Massereene, family: Coleraine LY 33; 122

Massereene, family: Comber DN 7; 41

Massereene, family: Dunaghy AM 13; 12

Massereene, family: Killead AM 35; 17, 20, 25

Massereene, family: Muckamore AM 35; 56, 61, 65–67

Massereene, family: Templepatrick AM 35; 106

Massereene, Lord: Drumlumman CN 40; 15

Massereene, Lord: Muckamore AM 35; 60

Massereene, Viscount: Antrim AM 29; 10, 14, 47

Massereene, Viscountess Rachel: Drummaul AM 19; 71

Massey, James: Dromara DN 12; 69

Massmount chapel: Clondavaddog DL 38; 4

Massregee (see Masteragwee): Dunboe LY 11; 58

Masteragwee (Masteraguie) td: Dunboe LY 11; 53, 58, 61

Matchet, family: Ballinderry AM 21; 53

Matchet, Rev.: Magherafelt LY 6; 82

Matchett, James: Aghagallon AM 21; 14

Matchett, Thomas: Blaris DN 12; 40

Matear, J.H.: Carrickfergus AM 37; 108

Matear, Margaret: Carrickfergus AM 37; 118

Mateer, Alexander: Hillsborough DN 12; 107

Mateer, Anne: Templecorran AM 26; 130

Mateer, family: Island Magee AM 10; 70

Mateer, J.: Annahilt DN 12; 21

Mateer, James: Island Magee AM 10; 90

Mateer, Miss: Carnmoney AM 2; 102

Mateer, William: Island Magee AM 10; 90

Mateer, William: Newry DN 3; 100

Mateland, William: Muckamore AM 35; 56

Mathers, family: Misc. LY 36; 104

Mathers, John: Clondermot LY 34; 89

Mathers, Joseph: Loughgilly AH 1; 86

Mathers, William: Culfeightrin AM 24; 58

Mathers, William: Ramoan AM 24; 123

Mathew, Anthony: Drumachose LY 9; 61

Mathews, family: Carrickfergus AM 37; 93

Mathews, James: Kilraghts AM 16; 132

Mathews, Maj.: Carnmoney AM 2; 84

Mathews, Margaret (nee Kendal): Kilraghts AM 16; 132

Mathews, Mary: Carrickfergus AM 37; 124

Mathews, Rev.: Drumachose LY 9; 107

Mathews, Rev. Edward: Down DN 17; 47

Mathews, Rev. John: Down DN 17; 47

Mathews, Rev. Lemuel: Magheramesk AM 21; 117

Mathews, Robert: Cumber LY 28; 86

Mathews, Robert: Kilraghts AM 16; 132

Mathews, Samuel: Blaris AM 8; 37

Mathewson, Clarke: Ardstraw TE 5; 9

Mathewson, Mr: Ardclinis AM 13; 3

Mathieson, Kenneth: Agivey LY 22; 39

Matier, Hugh: Island Magee AM 10; 94

Matier, W.J.: Inch DN 17; 75

Matier, W.J.: Kilclief DN 17; 78, 78

Matthews, Archabald: Drumachose LY 9; 53, 86, 123, 127, 131–32

Matthews, David: Macosquin LY 22; 86, 102, 113, 123

Matthews, Edward: Clondermot LY 34; 82

Matthews, family: Kilraghts AM 16; 130

Matthews, Joseph: Coleraine LY 33; 65

Matthews, Maj. (Springvale): Ballywalter DN 7; 16

Matthews, Maj. (Springvale): Misc. DN 17; 126

Matthews, Rev. Robert: Kirkinriola AM 23; 91, 96, 111, 113, 119

Matthews, Robert: Hillsborough DN 12; 105

Matthews, Sally: Ballymoney AM 16; 17

Matthews, Samuel: Loughguile AM 13; 72

Matthewson, Capt.: Ardclinis AM 13; 7

Mattheys, family: Dunluce AM 16; 117

Matthieson, Kenneth: Ballymoney AM 16; 12

Mattison, James: Hillsborough DN 12; 106

Mattison, Robert: Hillsborough DN 12; 106–07

Mattison, Thomas: Hillsborough DN 12; 106

Maturin, Rev.: Clondavaddog DL 38; 7

Maude, Mrs J.C.: Enniskillen FH 4; 84

Maude, Rev. B.: Clogher TE 5; 40

Maude, Rev. J.C.: Clogher TE 5; 40

Maude, Rev. J.C.: Enniskillen FH 4; 65, 72, 82, 84

Maude, Rev. Robert: Clogher TE 5; 33, 35

Maughan, Mrs J.D.: Clondermot LY 34; 27, 103

Maughan, Rev. J.D.: Clondermot LY 34; 6, 20–21, 37, 87, 92, 94–95, 103–04

Maughracorran td: Raphoe DL 39; 131

Maul Reilly's lough: Kilrea LY 27; 112

Mauleverer, Bellingham: Maghera LY 18; 51

Mauleverer, Bellingham: Termoneeny LY 6; 128

Mauleverer, Rev. Bellingem: Maghera LY 18; 66

Mauleverer, Rev. James: Maghera LY 18; 62

Mauleverer, Rev. James: Tynan AH 1; 129

Mauleverer, Rev. William: Tynan AH 1; 127, 129, 131–32

Mauleverer, Robert: Maghera LY 18; 51

Maully hill: Kinawley FH 4; 113

Maunrough village: Kilmacteige SO 40; 195

Maurice, family: Kilroot AM 26; 75

Mave stone: Balteagh LY 9; 8–9, 24, 35

Mawhinney, Samuel: Island Magee AM 10; 102

Mawhinny, Andrew: Ballyscullion LY 6; 66

Mawhinny, Mathew: Ballyscullion LY 6; 68–69

Mawillen (see Mawillian)

Mawillian (Mawillan) td: Artrea LY 6; 11, 13, 22, 31–32, 34, 38

Mawillian forts: Artrea LY 6; 31–32

Mawillian school: Artrea LY 6; 20

Mawillian Sunday school: Artrea LY 6; 21

Maxwell, Alexander: Ahoghill AM 23; 38

Maxwell, Andrew: Ardstraw TE 5; 6

Maxwell, Brice: Ballywillin AM 16; 35

Maxwell, Brice: Ballywillin LY 33; 41, 45

Maxwell, Charles: Misc. DN 17; 124

Maxwell, family: Aghanloo LY 11; 26

Maxwell, family: Ballyclug AM 23; 60

Maxwell, family: Ballywillin AM 16; 32

Maxwell, family: Carnmoney AM 2; 76

Maxwell, family: Ematris MN 40; 118

Maxwell, Gen.: Down DN 17; 52

Maxwell, H.: Clogher TE 5; 32

Maxwell, Helenn: Inch DN 17; 75

Maxwell, Henry: Inch DN 17; 75

Maxwell, Henry: Tynan AH 1; 130

Maxwell, Hugh: Ballywillin LY 33; 33, 45

Maxwell, Hugh: Kilmacteige SO 40; 196

Maxwell, J.W.: Ballee DN 17; 21–23

Maxwell, J.W.: Down DN 17; 51–53, 57

Maxwell, J.W.: Inch DN 17; 73–74

Maxwell, J.W.: Killyleagh DN 17; 85

Maxwell, James: Kilmacteige SO 40; 194

Maxwell, James: Kilwaughter AM 10; 119

Maxwell, Jane: Desertlyn LY 31; 50

Maxwell, John: Ahoghill AM 23; 35

Maxwell, John: Ballyphilip DN 7; 12

Maxwell, John: Clontibret MN 40; 85

Maxwell, John: Drumachose LY 9; 66

Maxwell, John: Misc. DN 17; 126

Maxwell, John: Tyholland MN 40; 175

Maxwell, Lady: Aghanloo LY 11; 26

Maxwell, Martha: Ballywalter AM 2; 26, 32

Maxwell, Mary: Carrickfergus AM 37; 121

Maxwell, Mr: Ballywillin LY 33; 44

Maxwell, Mr: Bangor DN 7; 22

Maxwell, Mr: Connor AM 19; 21

Maxwell, Mr: Killesher FH 14; 90

Maxwell, Mr: Urney DL 39; 181

Maxwell, Mrs Colt: Down DN 17; 57

Maxwell, Mrs Waring: Banagher LY 30; 30

Maxwell, Mrs Waring: Coleraine LY 33; 73, 127, 154

Maxwell, Mrs Waring: Killowen LY 33; 159, 168

Maxwell, R.W.: Clogher TE 5; 30, 33–43, 48, 53, 61

Maxwell, Rev.: Aughnamullen MN 40; 71

Maxwell, Rev. Andrew: Ardstraw TE 5; 3

Maxwell, Rev. H.H.: Newry DN 3; 83

Maxwell, Rev. John: Tyholland MN 40; 174–75

Maxwell, Rev. P.B,: Faughanvale LY 36; 17, 40, 70, 72, 74, 76, 79

Maxwell, Rev. Peter: Clonleigh DL 39; 1–2

Maxwell, Rev. Peter: Urney DL 39; 176, 179–80

Maxwell, Robert: Clonleigh DL 39; 4–5, 10, 13–14

Maxwell, Robert: Faughanvale LY 36; 37

Maxwell, Robert: Misc. DL 39; 186, 192

Maxwell, Robert: Tynan AH 1; 131

Maxwell, Steven: Donaghmore DL 39; 39

Maxwell, Thomas: Aghanloo LY 11; 26

Maxwell, Thomas: Glynn AM 26; 5–6, 8, 13, 19–21, 27, 40–41

Maxwell, William: Ahoghill AM 23; 40

Maxwell, William: Blaris DN 12; 41

Maxwell, William: Donagh MN 40; 101

Maxwell, Zacariah: Desertlyn LY 31; 39

Maxwells Walls bog: Connor AM 19; 28–29

Maxwells Walls flax mill: Connor AM 19; 22

Maxwells Walls school: Connor AM 19; 26–27, 30

Maxwells Walls td: Connor AM 19; 29

May, Bryan: Kilmacteige SO 40; 193

May, Edward (Jnr): Carrickfergus AM 37; 42

May, G.: Clondermot LY 34; 118

May, Henry: Hillsborough DN 12; 105

May, James: Templepatrick AM 35; 152

May, Stephen: Carrickfergus AM 37; 102, 143

May, Thomas: Blaris DN 12; 51

Mayagh td: Donaghedy TE 5; 92

Mayagoney (see Moyagoney): Kilrea LY 27; 115

Mayberry, smith: Kilrea LY 27; 112

Mayberry, smith: Tamlaght O'Crilly LY 18; 95

Maybin school: Raymoghy DL 39; 140

Maybin td: Raymoghy DL 39; 138

Maybin, Andrew: Drumtullagh AM 16; 100–01

Mayble, name of: Duneane AM 19; 101

Mayboy (Moboy) td: Errigal LY 27; 66, 83, 88, 91–92

Mayboy bog: Aghadowey LY 22; 1

Mayboy fort: Errigal LY 27; 42, 67

Mayboy standing stone: Errigal LY 27; 67

Mayboy td: Aghadowey LY 22; 32, 38

Maybush district: Carrickfergus AM 37; 160

Maydown lough: Clondermot LY 34; 119

Maydown mill: Eglish AH 1; 44

Maydown td: Clondermot LY 34; 57, 73, 111–13, 119, 127, 133

Maymacullen (Moymacullen) td: Ballymore AH 1; 8, 11, 13–14, 16–17

Maymore td: Taughboyne DL 39; 148, 154, 196

Maymount House: Ballymore AH 1; 11, 17

Mayne bog: Cappagh TE 5; 21

Mayne Sunday school: Cappagh TE 5; 19

Mayne td: Cappagh TE 5; 19, 22

Mayne, family: Ballynure AM 32; 56

Mayne, family: Carrickfergus AM 37; 93

Mayne, Rev.: Aughnamullen MN 40; 71

Mayne, Rev. Charles: Drummully FH 4; 37

Mayne, Rev. Thomas: Desertoghill LY 27; 11, 16

Mayne, Richard: Aghabog MN 40; 65

Mayne, Richard: Currin MN 40; 91–92, 96

Mayne, Richard: Drumgoon CN 40; 9

Mayne, Richard: Drummully FH 4; 37

Mayne, Richard: Ematris MN 40; 115–16, 119

Mayne, Thomas: Desertoghill LY 27; 11, 16

Maynooth (Kildare): Faughanvale LY 36; 59

Maynooth College: Misc. LY 31; 127, 137

Maynooth td: Kilmore AH 1; 60, 66–67, 69, 71–73

Mayo: Ballyclug AM 23; 56

Mayo: Coleraine LY 33; 98

Mayo: Emlaghfad SO 40; 180

Mayo: Enniskillen FH 4; 61

Mayo: Kilmacteige SO 40; 195

Mayo: Manorhamilton Union LM 40; 51

Mayo chapel: Clonallan DN 3; 1

Mayo hill: Drumgoon CN 40; 1, 8

Mayo school: Clonallan DN 3; 1

Mayo td: Clonallan DN 3; 1

Mayo, Viscount of: Dungiven LY 15; 31

Mayoghill (Mayogher) td: Aghadowey LY 22; 4, 37–38

Mayoghill bog: Aghadowey LY 22; 4, 31

Mayoghill school: Aghadowey LY 22; 19, 21

Mayoghill Sunday school: Aghadowey LY 22; 21

Mayor, Rev. John: Magilligan LY 11; 89

Mays, family: Ballinderry AM 21; 48

Mays, Moses: Duneane AM 19; 115, 120

Mays, Robert: Ahoghill AM 23; 40

Maytone td: Loughgilly AH 1; 84

Maze: Blaris AM 8; 71

Maze: Hillsborough DN 12; 98

Maze bridge: Blaris AM 8; 35

Maze bridge: Blaris DN 12; 28, 34

Maze gate: Blaris AM 8; 44

Maze Lower td: Blaris AM 8; 35

Maze Lower td: Blaris DN 12; 37

Maze Lower td: Hillsborough DN 12; 107

Maze Middle td: Blaris AM 8; 35

Maze Middle td: Hillsborough DN 12; 107

Maze racecourse: Blaris DN 12; 27, 29, 35–36

Maze school: Blaris AM 8; 82

Maze school: Blaris DN 12; 34–37

Maze school: Hillsborough DN 12; 100
Maze stand house: Blaris DN 12; 35
Maze Sunday school: Blaris DN 12; 38
Maze td: Blaris DN 12; 26, 28, 34–35
Maze td: Hillsborough DN 12; 94
Maze turnpike: Blaris AM 8; 13
Maze Upper td: Hillsborough DN 12; 107
Maze, family: Ballinderry AM 21; 51–52
Maze, family: Derryaghy AM 8; 103
Maze, Gore: Newry DN 3; 106
McAbruin, robber: Drumtullagh AM 16; 102
McAbruin's carn: Drumtullagh AM 16; 100, 102
McAdam, family: Carnmoney AM 2; 76
McAdam, family: Kirkinriola AM 23; 124
McAdam, John: Ballyrobert AM 2; 24
McAdam, Margaret: Blaris AM 8; 82
McAdam, Mr: Killead AM 35; 50
McAdam, Mr: Kinawley FH 4; 115
McAdam, Samuel: Raloo AM 32; 129
McAfee, Andrew: Coleraine LY 33; 104–05
McAfee, Andrew: Macosquin LY 22; 94, 101,
    121–22
McAfee, Archibald: Blaris AM 8; 53
McAfee, Archy: Drumtullagh AM 16; 102
McAfee, family: Culfeightrin AM 24; 64
McAfee, family: Dunluce AM 16; 117
McAfee, George: Blaris DN 12; 46, 49
McAfee, Hannah: Ballyaghran LY 33; 17
McAfee, John: Ballywillin LY 33; 50
McAfee, John: Derryaghy AM 8; 108
McAfee, John: Drumtullagh AM 16; 102
McAfee, Martha: Aghadowey LY 22; 35
McAfee, Michael: Aghadowey LY 22; 35
McAfee, Patrick: Derryaghy AM 8; 95
McAfee, Rev. Daniel: Newry DN 3; 100
McAfee, Sarah: Drumachose LY 9; 122
McAffee, Samuel: Ballymoney AM 16; 17
McAghron, James: Carrickfergus AM 37; 119
McAlane, Jane: Maghera LY 18; 78
McAlane, Sarah: Maghera LY 18; 78
McAlanney, Daniel: Carrickfergus AM 37; 186
McAlary, Bernard: Tamlaght O'Crilly LY 18; 95,
    113, 135
McAlary, family: Ahoghill AM 23; 25
McAlary, family: Finvoy AM 23; 76
McAlary, Francis: Desertoghill LY 27; 31
McAlary, Henery: Tamlaght O'Crilly LY 18; 119
McAlchon, Flanagan: Muckamore AM 35; 56, 82
McAlea, family: Dunsfort DN 17; 68
McAlea, James: Carrickfergus AM 37; 109
McAlean, family: Culfeightrin AM 24; 59
McAleavey, Robert: Ballinderry AM 21; 52
McAleavy, Andrew: Carrickfergus AM 37; 120
McAleely, family: Raloo AM 32; 123
McAleenan, Mr: Ballyphilip DN 7; 10

McAleer, Rev.: Longfield TE 5; 131
McAleer, Rev. James: Maghera LY 18; 68
McAlees, Daniel: Dunboe LY 11; 75
McAlees, family: Derrykeighan AM 16; 89
McAlees, John: Dunboe LY 11; 76
McAlees, Neill: Carrickfergus AM 37; 131
McAleese, Daniel: Kilraghts AM 16; 133–34
McAleese, Elisabeth: Agivey LY 22; 45
McAleese, family: Kilraghts AM 16; 127
McAleese, James: Loughguile AM 13; 67, 71, 74
McAleese, John: Ahoghill AM 23; 39
McAleese, John: Derrykeighan AM 16; 93
McAleese, John: Drumtullagh AM 16; 101
McAleese, Michael: Agivey LY 22; 45
McAleese, Michael: Billy AM 16; 65
McAleese, Patrick: Derrykeighan AM 16; 93
McAlester, Archibald: Derrykeighan AM 16; 90
McAlester, family: Ballintoy AM 24; 20
McAlester, family: Culfeightrin AM 24; 59
McAlester, family: Loughguile AM 13; 64
McAlester, James: Ballintoy AM 24; 28
McAlester, Mr: Dunaghy AM 13; 14
McAlgun, Phillup: Galloon FH 4; 98
McAlice, Elizabeth: Aghadowey LY 22; 37
McAlice, Michael: Aghadowey LY 22; 37
McAlinden, James: Newry DN 3; 100, 104
McAlister, Alexander: Aghadowey LY 22; 35
McAlister, Alexander: Drumtullagh AM 16; 103
McAlister, Alick: Desertoghill LY 27; 20
McAlister, Andrew (Jnr): Aghadowey LY 22; 35
McAlister, Andrew (Snr): Aghadowey LY 22; 35
McAlister, Ann (Jnr): Aghadowey LY 22; 35
McAlister, Ann (Snr): Aghadowey LY 22; 35
McAlister, Anne: Kilmore AH 1; 60
McAlister, Archibald: Culfeightrin AM 24; 78, 80
McAlister, Archibald [I]: Culfeightrin AM 24; 49
McAlister, Archibald [II]: Culfeightrin AM 24;
    68–69
McAlister, Bernard: Desertoghill LY 27; 16, 26
McAlister, Daniel: Aghagallon AM 21; 24
McAlister, Daniel: Aghalee AM 21; 40
McAlister, Daniel: Ahoghill AM 23; 37
McAlister, Duncan: Ballyaghran LY 33; 27
McAlister, Elizabeth: Carrickfergus AM 37; 128
McAlister, Ennas: Coleraine LY 33; 72, 133
McAlister, family: Armoy AM 24; 6
McAlister, family: Culfeightrin AM 24; 59, 64,
    68–69, 71
McAlister, family: Dunluce AM 16; 117
McAlister, family: Dunsfort DN 17; 68
McAlister, family: Layd AM 13; 49
McAlister, family: Ramoan AM 24; 120
McAlister, James: Aghadowey LY 22; 35
McAlister, James: Ballyaghran LY 33; 27
McAlister, James: Maghera LY 18; 81

McAlister, John: Ballyaghran LY 33; 27
McAlister, John: Desertoghill LY 27; 16–17, 23
McAlister, John: Drumtullagh AM 16; 103
McAlister, John: Hillsborough DN 12; 106
McAlister, John: Maghera LY 18; 81
McAlister, John: Muckamore AM 35; 81
McAlister, John: Newtown Crommelin AM 13; 84
McAlister, John [I]: Ahoghill AM 23; 33, 35
McAlister, John [II]: Ahoghill AM 23; 39
McAlister, Jonathan: Desertoghill LY 27; 20
McAlister, Margret: Aghadowey LY 22; 35
McAlister, Martha: Aghadowey LY 22; 35
McAlister, Mary: Aghadowey LY 22; 35
McAlister, Mr (Snr): Desertoghill LY 27; 23
McAlister, Mrs (Drumlane): Tamlaght O'Crilly LY 18; 128
McAlister, Mrs John: Newtown Crommelin AM 13; 84
McAlister, Rebecca: Aghadowey LY 22; 35
McAlister, Robert: Aghadowey LY 22; 35
McAlister, Robert: Blaris DN 12; 46
McAlister, Samuel: Aghaderg DN 12; 12
McAlister, Samuel: Clondermot LY 34; 42, 77, 86, 89, 91, 94
McAlister, Sarah: Ballyaghran LY 33; 27
McAlister, Susan: Aghadowey LY 22; 35
McAlister, Thomas: Aghadowey LY 22; 35
McAlister, Thomas: Tamlaght TE 20; 75, 131, 136
McAlister, William: Billy AM 16; 58, 62, 64
McAlister, William: Desertoghill LY 27; 20
McAlister, William: Hillsborough DN 12; 106
McAllen, Rachael: Ballyscullion AM 19; 13
McAllen, Sampson: Ballyscullion AM 19; 13
McAllien, family: Dungiven LY 15; 24
McAllister, Alexander: Killevy AH 1; 53
McAllister, Anthony: Errigal LY 27; 67
McAllister, family: Derryaghy AM 8; 103
McAllister, family: Macosquin LY 22; 83, 119
McAllister, family: Ramoan AM 24; 90
McAllister, Hugh: Coleraine LY 33; 145
McAllister, James: Ballywillin LY 33; 50
McAllister, John: Aghadowey LY 22; 20–21, 35
McAllister, John: Carrickfergus AM 37; 108
McAllister, John: Errigal LY 27; 61
McAllister, John: Rasharkin AM 23; 140
McAllister, Michael: Ballynascreen LY 31; 14, 21
McAllister, Randall: Drumtullagh AM 16; 103
McAllister, Robert: Drumachose LY 9; 132
McAllister, Thomas: Banagher LY 30; 100
McAllister, William: Carrickfergus AM 37; 117
McAllister, William: Muckamore AM 35; 81
McAllister, woman named: Drumtullagh AM 16; 103
McAlmond, Catherine: Island Magee AM 10; 66, 94
McAlmont, family: Island Magee AM 10; 70

McAlonan, Robert (Jnr): Kilraghts AM 16; 134
McAlonan, Robert: Kilraghts AM 16; 134
McAlpin, family: Templecorran AM 26; 117
McAlwane, Mr: Clondermot LY 34; 43
McAman, David: Dromara DN 12; 67
McAmbrose, family: Armoy AM 24; 6
McAmish battery: Killygarvan DL 38; 38
McAmish fort: Killygarvan DL 38; 36, 39 40
McAmish lough: Killygarvan DL 38; 36
McAmish Lower district: Killygarvan DL 38; 42
McAnally, Abram: Duneane AM 19; 124
McAnally, Bernard: Kilmood DN 7; 95
McAnally, Conway: Ballynure AM 32; 53, 71
McAnally, Ephraim: Drummaul AM 19; 90
McAnally, family: Blaris AM 8; 21
McAnally, Henry: Drummaul AM 19; 90
McAnally, Henry: Duneane AM 19; 124
McAnally, James: Ahoghill AM 23; 38
McAnally, James: Maghera LY 18; 81
McAnally, Peter: Ahoghill AM 23; 38
McAnally's hill: Blaris DN 12; 42
McAnaly, Donald: Dungiven LY 15; 33
McAnana, James: Lissan LY 31; 109
McAnana, Robert: Lissan LY 31; 108
McAnkill, family: Drumragh TE 5; 108
McAnliss, Robert: Desertoghill LY 27; 25
McAnna, Patrick: Lissan LY 31; 109
McAnnally's locality: Muckamore AM 35; 81
McAnrose, family: Culfeightrin AM 24; 59
McAntaggart, John: Ahoghill AM 23; 39
McAnully, Charles: Loughguile AM 13; 74
McAnulty, Antony: Kilmacteige SO 40; 193–94
McAnulty, Charles: Carrickfergus AM 37; 193
McAnulty, Dennis: Kilmacteige SO 40; 193
McAphra, John: Ramoan AM 24; 126
McAraul, James: Billy AM 16; 77
McAravay, family: Ballinderry AM 21; 54
McArdle, Mary: Carrickfergus AM 37; 124
McArdle, Rev. Arthur: Aghaderg DN 12; 11
McAreavey, James [I]: Magheramesk AM 21; 116, 125
McAreavey, James [II]: Magheramesk AM 21; 130
McAreavey, Mary: Magheramesk AM 21; 130
McAreavy, John: Derryaghy AM 8; 97–98
McAreevy, Jane: Carrickfergus AM 37; 124
McAreevy, Jane: Raloo AM 32; 128
McAreevy, John: Magheramesk AM 21; 125–26
McAreevy, Mary: Carrickfergus AM 37; 125
McArevery, David: Lough Neagh AM 21; 95
McArne, Charles: Drumgoon CN 40; 8
McArt, Bryan: Tullyrusk AM 21; 131
McArt, Roger: Ballyclug AM 23; 59, 65
McArthur, family: Armoy AM 24; 6
McArthur, family: Ramoan AM 24; 107
McArthur, Miss: Drumragh TE 5; 107

McArthur, Mrs: Ballymoney AM 16; 17

McArtney, James: Carrickfergus AM 37; 117

McAssey, Rev. John: Carrickfergus AM 37; 70, 102, 144, 146, 157

McAstocker, Bridget: Duneane AM 19; 123

McAstocker, Catherine: Duneane AM 19; 123

McAstocker, Charles: Duneane AM 19; 123

McAstocker, David: Duneane AM 19; 123

McAstocker, James: Duneane AM 19; 122

McAstocker, Mary Anne: Duneane AM 19; 123

McAstocker, Neal: Duneane AM 19; 124

McAstocker, Patrick: Duneane AM 19; 123

McAtaggart, Hugh: Rasharkin AM 23; 139

McAtaggart, Patrick: Ballyscullion LY 6; 57

McAtamney, Denis: Maghera LY 18; 81

McAtamney, Edward: Maghera LY 18; 81

McAtamney, John [I]: Maghera LY 18; 80

McAtamney, John [II]: Maghera LY 18; 81

McAtamney, Mary: Carrickfergus AM 37; 78–79

McAtamney, Mrs: Maghera LY 18; 48

McAtamney, Neil: Maghera LY 18; 80

McAtamney, Patrick [I]: Maghera LY 18; 41

McAtamney, Patrick [II]: Maghera LY 18; 80

McAtamney, William: Tamlaght O'Crilly LY 18; 115

McAtamny, Patrick: Artrea LY 6; 13, 25

McAtee, family: Currin MN 40; 94

McAtee, Thomas: Hillsborough DN 12; 107

McAteer, Charles: Carrickfergus AM 37; 123

McAteer, family: Drummaul AM 19; 53

McAteer, family: Duneane AM 19; 101

McAteer, family: Magherafelt LY 6; 95

McAteer, Mary: Carrickfergus AM 37; 123

McAteer, Mathew: Carrickfergus AM 37; 116

McAteer, Owen (Jnr): Hillsborough DN 12; 107

McAteer, Owen: Hillsborough DN 12; 107

McAtyre, family: Ballintoy AM 24; 20

McAtyre, John: Coleraine LY 33; 145

McAugharlin, family: Culfeightrin AM 24; 59

McAul, Capt.: Kilbroney DN 3; 28

McAulay, family: Ahoghill AM 23; 25

McAulay, family: Culfeightrin AM 24; 71

McAulay, family: Dunaghy AM 13; 14

McAulay, Joseph: Drumgooland DN 3; 25

McAuley, Alexander: Ramoan AM 24; 102

McAuley, Archibald: Ballymoney AM 16; 18

McAuley, Archibald: Carrickfergus AM 37; 108

McAuley, Charles: Drummaul AM 19; 84

McAuley, Daniel: Carrickfergus AM 37; 109

McAuley, Dennis: Culfeightrin AM 24; 63, 65, 73

McAuley, Ellen: Glynn AM 26; 28, 42

McAuley, family: Armoy AM 24; 6

McAuley, family: Ballintoy AM 24; 20

McAuley, family: Culfeightrin AM 24; 46, 59, 64, 71

McAuley, family: Drummaul AM 19; 53

McAuley, family: Duneane AM 19; 101

McAuley, family: Dunluce AM 16; 117

McAuley, family: Kilraghts AM 16; 127

McAuley, family: Layd AM 13; 40, 49

McAuley, family: Layd and Inispollan AM 13; 56

McAuley, family: Loughguile AM 13; 64

McAuley, Francis: Culfeightrin AM 24; 82

McAuley, Francis: Magheradrool DN 17; 106

McAuley, Hugh: Carrickfergus AM 37; 193

McAuley, James: Carrickfergus AM 37; 108

McAuley, James: Culfeightrin AM 24; 63, 65, 71, 81

McAuley, James: Loughguile AM 13; 77

McAuley, John: Blaris AM 8; 40

McAuley, John: Loughguile AM 13; 67

McAuley, Margaret: Carrickfergus AM 37; 130

McAuley, Rev.: Layd AM 13; 36–37, 40, 47

McAuley, Rev. Bernard: Drummaul AM 19; 69, 82

McAuley, Thomas: Drummaul AM 19; 91

McAuley, William: Aghadowey LY 22; 23

McAuley, William: Carrickfergus AM 37; 111

McAuley's Hotel: Kirkinriola AM 23; 95

McAuley's lough: Dromara DN 12; 66

McAuley's lough: Magheradrool DN 17; 106

McAuly, John: Muckamore AM 35; 81

McAvally's well: Desertoghill LY 27; 13

McAvicker, James: Drumtullagh AM 16; 103

McAvicker, William: Loughguile AM 13; 75

McAvoy, H.B.: Faughanvale LY 36; 61

McAvoy, Peter: Termoneeny LY 6; 128

McAvraghan (see Brown): Cumber LY 28; 54

McBeath, Henery: Errigal LY 27; 65

McBeath, James: Bovevagh LY 25; 59

McBeath, John: Artrea LY 6; 31

McBeath, John: Balteagh LY 9; 12, 26

McBeath, John: Errigal LY 27; 65

McBeath, Magy: Errigal LY 27; 65

McBeath, Margrett: Errigal LY 27; 65

McBeath, Robert: Drumachose LY 9; 115

McBeath, Robert: Tamlaght Finlagan LY 25; 115

McBeath, William: Errigal LY 27; 65

McBernie, John: Templepatrick AM 35; 150

McBirnie, Alexander: Saintfield DN 7; 114, 119

McBirnie, John: Saintfield DN 7; 114–15

McBirnie, Margaret: Carrickfergus AM 37; 116

McBlain, David: Dunboe LY 11; 60, 60–62

McBlain, David: Newry DN 3; 98

McBlain, James: Killead AM 35; 13, 47

McBlaine, Thomas: Carrickfergus AM 37; 123

McBlane, David: Blaris AM 8; 25

McBlane, family: Blaris AM 8; 21

McBlane, James: Blaris AM 8; 25, 36

McBrerty, Dennis: Donaghmore DL 39; 39

McBride, Adm.: Misc. AM 10; 130

McBride, Andrew: Maghera LY 18; 78
McBride, Betty: Island Magee AM 10; 94
McBride, Daniel: Ballynascreen LY 31; 18
McBride, Daniel: Culfeightrin AM 24; 79, 85
McBride, Daniel: Ramoan AM 24; 113
McBride, David: Hillsborough DN 12; 107
McBride, David: Tamlaght Finlagan LY 25; 108
McBride, David: Templepatrick AM 35; 152
McBride, Edward: Derryaghy AM 8; 103, 116, 118
McBride, Edward: Hillsborough DN 12, 107
McBride, Edward: Kilcronaghan LY 31; 85
McBride, Eliza: Doagh AM 29; 98
McBride, Ellen: Hillsborough DN 12; 107
McBride, family: Armoy AM 24; 6
McBride, family: Ballynascreen LY 31; 12
McBride, family: Carrickfergus AM 37; 179
McBride, family: Culfeightrin AM 24; 46, 59, 71
McBride, family: Derryaghy AM 8; 103
McBride, family: Dromara DN 12; 67
McBride, family: Templecorran AM 26; 117, 119
McBride, family: Templepatrick AM 35; 118
McBride, family: Umgall AM 35; 158
McBride, Francis: Templepatrick AM 35; 111, 149
McBride, Hugh: Ballynascreen LY 31; 27
McBride, Hugh: Culfeightrin AM 24; 59, 72, 81–82
McBride, James: Ballynascreen LY 31; 11, 26, 30
McBride, James: Ballyrashane LY 22; 65
McBride, James: Coleraine LY 33; 72
McBride, James: Culfeightrin AM 24; 84–85
McBride, James: Drumgooland DN 3; 23
McBride, James: Hillsborough DN 12; 107
McBride, Jane: Ballyrashane LY 22; 65
McBride, John: Ballyrashane LY 22; 65
McBride, John: Carrickfergus AM 37; 120
McBride, John: Skerry AM 13; 119
McBride, Joseph: Hillsborough DN 12; 99
McBride, man named: Tullaghobegley DL 39; 172
McBride, Mary (Jnr): Ballyrashane LY 22; 65
McBride, Mary (Snr): Ballyrashane LY 22; 65
McBride, Mary: Doagh AM 29; 98
McBride, Matty: Island Magee AM 10; 94
McBride, Mr: Island Magee AM 10; 101
McBride, Mrs (nee Hogset): Kilroot AM 26; 79
McBride, Nancy: Doagh AM 29; 98
McBride, Ony: Coleraine LY 33; 157
McBride, Patrick: Culfeightrin AM 24; 48–49
McBride, Patrick [I]: Duneane AM 19; 123
McBride, Patrick [II]: Duneane AM 19; 124
McBride, Patt: Tamlaght Finlagan LY 25; 107–08
McBride, Rachel: Carrickfergus AM 37; 114
McBride, Rev.: Donaghmore DL 39; 34
McBride, Robert (Jnr): Ballyrashane LY 22; 65
McBride, Robert (Snr): Ballyrashane LY 22; 65
McBride, Robert: Kilcronaghan LY 31; 83, 86
McBride, Robert: Loughgilly AH 1; 86

McBride, Robert: Templecorran AM 26; 120
McBride, Sally: Island Magee AM 10; 94
McBride, Thomas: Culfeightrin AM 24; 53–54, 72
McBride, Thomas: Doagh AM 29; 98
McBride, Thomas: Hillsborough DN 12; 107
McBride, W.A.: Templecorran AM 26; 125
McBride, Widow: Ballynascreen LY 31; 14, 21
McBride, William: Hillsborough DN 12; 106
McBride's cove: Island Magee AM 10; 101
McBrin, family: Carrickfergus AM 37; 179
McBrinn, Charles: Carrickfergus AM 37; 181–82
McBroom, family: Glynn AM 26; 45
McBryde, John: Muckamore AM 35; 77
McBryde, Thomas (Jnr): Muckamore AM 35; 78
McBryde, Thomas (Snr): Muckamore AM 35; 78
McBryde, William: Muckamore AM 35; 78
McBurney, family: Carnmoney AM 2; 76
McBurns, Samuel: Dunaghy AM 13; 23
McCabe, family: Carnmoney AM 2; 76
McCabe, family: Ematris MN 40; 118
McCabe, Mr: Carnmoney AM 2; 91
McCabe, Rev. Felix: Killdrumsherdan CN 40; 33
McCabe, Rev. James: Misc. LY 31; 128, 137
McCadam, family: Carnmoney AM 2; 102
McCafferty, John: Derryaghy AM 8; 115
McCafferty, William: Derryaghy AM 8; 97
McCaffrey, John: Carrickfergus AM 37; 40
McCaffry, Brian: Derryvullan FH 14; 41
McCaghey, Rev. George: Larne AM 10; 126
McCague, Andrew: Tydavnet MN 40; 173
McCague, Margaret: Magilligan LY 11; 94
McCague, Nancy: Magilligan LY 11; 94
McCahan, Charles: Ballintoy AM 24; 28
McCahan, Critty: Derrykeighan AM 16; 92
McCahan, Daniel [I]: Culfeightrin AM 24; 52
McCahan, Daniel [II]: Culfeightrin AM 24; 54–56,
  69
McCahan, family: Desertoghill LY 27; 8
McCahan, James: Ballyaghran LY 33; 27
McCahan, James: Ballyrashane LY 22; 61–62
McCahan, Loughlin: Culfeightrin AM 24; 55
McCahan, Mary: Ballyaghran LY 33; 16–17
McCahan, Robert: Ballyrashane LY 22; 62
McCahan, William: Ramoan AM 24; 123
McCaheeran, Denis: Ahoghill AM 23; 39
McCaherty, Daniel: Island Magee AM 10; 90
McCaherty, family: Kilwaughter AM 10; 115
McCaherty, John: Kilwaughter AM 10; 116
McCahey, Charles: Maghera LY 18; 53
McCahey, David: Ahoghill AM 23; 38
McCahey, family: Maghera LY 18; 13
McCahey, Grace: Island Magee AM 10; 94
McCahey, Hugh: Enniskillen FH 4; 72
McCahey, James: Desertoghill LY 27; 21
McCahey, James: Maghera LY 18; 77

McCahey, John: Ballylinny AM 32; 29
McCahey, John: Desertoghill LY 27; 21
McCahey, Nathaniel: Kilrea LY 27; 129
McCahill, William: Drumtullagh AM 16; 101
McCahill, Zachariah: Ballintoy AM 24; 19
McCahy, Ann: Ballyscullion LY 6; 77
McCahy, Charles: Ballyscullion LY 6; 77
McCahy, Charles: Tamlaght O'Crilly LY 18; 117
McCahy, David: Ahoghill AM 23; 37
McCahy, Elenor: Ballyscullion LY 6; 77
McCahy, Eliza: Ahoghill AM 23; 37
McCahy, Jane (Jnr): Ballyscullion LY 6; 77
McCahy, Jane (Snr): Ballyscullion LY 6; 77
McCahy, John: Ballyscullion LY 6; 77
McCahy, John: Tamlaght O'Crilly LY 18; 117
McCahy, Margret: Ballyscullion LY 6; 77
McCahy, Matthew: Tamlaght O'Crilly LY 18; 99
McCahy, Samuel: Ballyscullion LY 6; 77
McCahy, Sareah: Ballyscullion LY 6; 77
McCaigny, John: Carrickfergus AM 37; 108
McCaigue, family: Culfeightrin AM 24; 59
McCain, family: Ballintoy AM 24; 18
McCain, Hugh: Ballintoy AM 24; 21
McCain, James: Ballywillin AM 16; 33
McCain, James: Clondermot LY 34; 79
McCaken, James: Rasharkin AM 23; 136
McCala, Elen: Tamlaght TE 20; 76
McCala, Hugh: Tamlaght TE 20; 76
McCalister, James: Derrykeighan AM 16; 95
McCalister, John: Kilcronaghan LY 31; 85
McCalister, Mr: Blaris DN 12; 44
McCall lough: Clogher TE 5; 25, 27, 47, 58
McCall, family: Blaris AM 8; 22
McCall, family: Lambeg AM 8; 135
McCall, Hugh: Blaris AM 8; 55, 62
McCall, Hugh: Blaris DN 12; 41, 46, 50
McCall, Robert: Blaris AM 8; 37, 55, 60, 62
McCall, Robert: Blaris DN 12; 46, 50
McCall, Susanna: Carrickfergus AM 37; 129
McCalla's beetling mill: Magheradrool DN 17; 103
McCallian, Daniel: Magilligan LY 11; 131, 133
McCallian, John: Magilligan LY 11; 131, 133
McCallian, Samuel: Ballyaghran LY 33; 26
McCallin, Sampson: Duneane AM 19; 124
McCallion, John: Balteagh LY 9; 26
McCallister, family: Blaris AM 8; 21
McCallister, family: Kilwaughter AM 10; 115
McCallum, Archibald: Killagan AM 23; 85
McCalmont, Andy: Island Magee AM 10; 101
McCalmont, Hugh: Carnmoney AM 2; 81, 87, 89,
    95–96
McCalmont, John: Island Magee AM 10; 84, 90
McCalmont, Mrs Hugh: Carnmoney AM 2; 46, 84,
    93
McCalmont, Robert: Island Magee AM 10; 90

McCalmont, William: Carnmoney AM 2; 81
McCalpin, family: Templecorran AM 26; 119
McCambridge, Angus: Culfeightrin AM 24; 75
McCambridge, Archibald: Culfeightrin AM 24;
    56–58
McCambridge, Bernard: Culfeightrin AM 24; 77, 82
McCambridge, Daniel: Culfeightrin AM 24; 77–78
McCambridge, family: Culfeightrin AM 24; 59, 71
McCambridge, family: Ramoan AM 24; 107
McCambridge, Francis: Ballymoney AM 16; 26
McCambridge, John: Culfeightrin AM 24; 55
McCambridge, John: Kilwaughter AM 10; 119
McCambridge, John: Ramoan AM 24; 125
McCambridge, Mary: Newtown Crommelin AM 13;
    84
McCambridge, Patrick: Finvoy AM 23; 75
McCambridge, Patt: Culfeightrin AM 24; 52–53, 56,
    70
McCambridge, Philip: Ballymoney AM 16; 26
McCambridge, Robert: Culfeightrin AM 24; 78
McCambridge, Widow: Dunaghy AM 13; 22
McCambrige, family: Culfeightrin AM 24; 71
McCamley, family: Killesher FH 14; 84
McCamley, Henry: Newry DN 3; 98
McCamley, Mr: Blaris AM 8; 60
McCamley, Patrick: Newry DN 3; 103
McCamman, Rev. James: Kilrea LY 27; 117, 126
McCammon, family: Kilroot AM 26; 74–75
McCammont, Alexander: Templecorran AM 26;
    116, 131
McCamoil, Arthur: Clogher TE 5; 27
McCamphill, Mr: Carnmoney AM 2; 96
McCan, Lewis: Maghera LY 18; 47
McCan, Patrick: Tamlaght O'Crilly LY 18; 116, 135
McCan, Stafford: Maghera LY 18; 44
McCanagh, Bernard: Donagh MN 40; 101
McCanary, Alexander: Desertmartin LY 31; 62
McCanary, Robert: Desertmartin LY 31; 56, 62
McCance, John: Blaris AM 8; 70
McCance, John: Derryaghy AM 8; 104
McCance, Mr: Comber DN 7; 33, 39
McCance, Rev.: Comber DN 7; 32–33, 44
McCance, William: Blaris AM 8; 51, 66, 70
McCandlas, Thomas: Cumber LY 28; 86
McCandlass, family: Dunluce AM 16; 117
McCandle, Hugh: Rasharkin AM 23; 140
McCandles, Samuel: Dromore DN 12; 78
McCane, Robert: Loughguile AM 13; 77
McCanlis, John: Tamlaght Finlagan LY 25; 118
McCann, Andrew: Tamlaght O'Crilly LY 18; 129
McCann, Ann Jane: Ballinderry AM 21; 49
McCann, Arthur: Derryaghy AM 8; 106, 111
McCann, Charles: Kilcronaghan LY 31; 85
McCann, Edward: Carrickfergus AM 37; 148
McCann, Edward: Kilwaughter AM 10; 122

McCann, Edward: Maghera LY 18; 81
McCann, Elizabeth: Kilrea LY 27; 129
McCann, Ezekiel: Carrickfergus AM 37; 157
McCann, family: Aghagallon AM 21; 9
McCann, family: Carrickfergus AM 37; 179
McCann, family: Drummaul AM 19; 53
McCann, family: Duneane AM 19; 101
McCann, family: Lissan LY 31; 91, 106
McCann, family: Maghera LY 18; 24, 48
McCann, family: Raloo AM 32; 94, 128
McCann, family: Shankill AH 1; 111
McCann, Francis: Newry DN 3; 100, 104
McCann, George: Coleraine LY 33; 145
McCann, Henry: Carrickfergus AM 37; 122
McCann, Henry: Hillsborough DN 12; 107
McCann, Hugh: Muckamore AM 35; 77
McCann, Hugh [I]: Carrickfergus AM 37; 108
McCann, Hugh [II]: Carrickfergus AM 37; 109
McCann, James: Tamlaght O'Crilly LY 18; 128–29,
  137
McCann, Jane: Ballymore AH 1; 7
McCann, Jane: Muckamore AM 35; 81
McCann, John (Jnr): Duneane AM 19; 124
McCann, John (Snr): Duneane AM 19; 124
McCann, John: Magilligan LY 11; 137
McCann, John: Tamlaght O'Crilly LY 18; 96,
  128–29
McCann, John [I]: Carrickfergus AM 37; 111
McCann, John [II]: Carrickfergus AM 37; 123
McCann, John [III]: Carrickfergus AM 37; 148
McCann, Joseph: Duneane AM 19; 125
McCann, Kate: Ballyscullion AM 19; 10
McCann, Margaret: Carrickfergus AM 37; 128
McCann, Martha: Kilrea LY 27; 129
McCann, Mary: Muckamore AM 35; 77
McCann, Mr (Corbracky): Drumcree AH 1; 39
McCann, Mr: Clondermot LY 34; 26
McCann, Mr: Drumachose LY 9; 101
McCann, Owen: Aghagallon AM 21; 5, 18, 24
McCann, Patrick: Carrickfergus AM 37; 125
McCann, Patrick: Drummaul AM 19; 90
McCann, Patrick: Muckamore AM 35; 77, 79
McCann, Patrick: Termoneeny LY 6; 125, 130
McCann, Rev. Charles: Maghera LY 18; 17, 68
McCann, Rev. Peter: Derryaghy AM 8; 103–04
McCann, Susan: Lissan LY 31; 109
McCann, Thomas: Kilrea LY 27; 129
McCann, Thomas: Muckamore AM 35; 81
McCann, Thomas: Newtownards DN 7; 112
McCann, William: Blaris AM 8; 32, 80, 82
McCann, William: Duneane AM 19; 124
McCann, William: Lissan LY 31; 109
McCann's field: Carrickfergus AM 37; 33
McCanna, Farrell: Artrea LY 6; 32
McCanna, Rev. James: Kilrea LY 27; 122

McCannery, family: Kildollagh LY 22; 73
McCannery, Mr: Kildollagh LY 22; 69
McCarey, Rev. James: Carrickfergus AM 37; 102,
  174
McCarlin, family: Misc. LY 36; 101
McCarn, family: Carrickfergus AM 37; 179
McCarnaghan, Hugh: Carrickfergus AM 37; 118
McCarra, family: Ardclinis AM 13; 8
McCarron, family: Misc. LY 36; 101
McCarren, Matthew: Balteagh LY 9; 27, 30
McCarren, Rev. Alexander: Faughanvale LY 36; 33
McCarren, Rev. James: Clondermot LY 34; 43, 97
McCarren, Rev. James: Faughanvale LY 36; 33
McCarrey, family: Culfeightrin AM 24; 59
McCarrigan, Owen: Lissan LY 31; 106
McCarrigan, Roger: Ballyrashane LY 22; 59
McCarriston, Edward: Magilligan LY 11; 134
McCarrol, Mary: Carrickfergus AM 37; 121
McCarroll, Daniel: Ballyrashane LY 22; 62
McCarroll, David: Drummaul AM 19; 90
McCarroll, Eliza: Kildollagh LY 22; 75
McCarroll, family: Culfeightrin AM 24; 59
McCarroll, Hugh: Kildollagh LY 22; 75
McCarroll, James: Drummaul AM 19; 90
McCarroll, Robert: Drummaul AM 19; 90
McCarroll, Robert: Ramoan AM 24; 107
McCarroll, Rose: Ballymoney AM 16; 18
McCarroll, Thomas: Drummaul AM 19; 90
McCarroll, W. [I]: Ramoan AM 24; 107
McCarroll, W. [II]: Ramoan AM 24; 107
McCarroll, William: Drummaul AM 19; 77, 86
McCarron, Bryan: Dungiven LY 15; 100
McCarron, family: Macosquin LY 22; 84, 119
McCarron, William: Dungiven LY 15; 46, 89
McCarry, family: Ardclinis AM 13; 8
McCarry, Henry: Blaris DN 12; 46, 50
McCarry, Rev. James: Raloo AM 32; 126
McCart, Archibald: Desertoghill LY 27; 28
McCart, Eliza: Kilcronaghan LY 31; 88
McCart, George: Kilcronaghan LY 31; 85, 87
McCart, James: Carrickfergus AM 37; 113
McCart, John: Kilcronaghan LY 31; 84
McCart, Sarah: Kilcronaghan LY 31; 84
McCartan, family: Ardglass DN 17; 3
McCartan, family: Dundonald DN 7; 65
McCartan, family: Raloo AM 32; 115
McCartan, James: Bright DN 17; 36
McCartan's school: Bright DN 17; 36
McCarten, James: Hillsborough DN 12; 106
McCarter, Mr: Dungiven LY 15; 83
McCarter, William: Clondermot LY 34; 30, 37, 100,
  104
McCarther, Catherine: Killead AM 35; 51
McCarthy, James: Carrickfergus AM 37; 194
McCarthy, James: Hillsborough DN 12; 107

McCarthy, John: Carrickfergus AM 37; 193

McCarthy, Thomas: Hillsborough DN 12; 107

McCarthy, Viscount: Enniskillen FH 4; 52

McCartin, Theophilus: Misc. DN 17; 119

McCartney, Agnes: Ahoghill AM 23; 38

McCartney, Alexander: Ahoghill AM 23; 38

McCartney, Andrew [I]: Ahoghill AM 23; 38

McCartney, Andrew [II]: Ahoghill AM 23; 38

McCartney, Archie [I]: Ahoghill AM 23; 38

McCartney, Archie [II]: Ahoghill AM 23; 38

McCartney, Arthur: Blaris DN 12; 46, 50

McCartney, B.: Newry DN 3; 100

McCartney, Charles: Ahoghill AM 23; 38

McCartney, Charles: Banagher LY 30; 119, 131

McCartney, Charles: Bovevagh LY 25; 41

McCartney, Dorothea: Ahoghill AM 23; 38

McCartney, Eliza: Carrickfergus AM 37; 123

McCartney, family: Tamlaght O'Crilly LY 18; 93

McCartney, James (Jnr): Ahoghill AM 23; 38

McCartney, James (Snr): Ahoghill AM 23; 38

McCartney, James: Aghalurcher FH 4; 6

McCartney, James: Aghavea FH 4; 21

McCartney, James: Kilcronaghan LY 31; 84

McCartney, James [I]: Ahoghill AM 23; 35

McCartney, John: Aghalee AM 21; 31, 34

McCartney, John: Bovevagh LY 25; 40

McCartney, John: Kilrea LY 27; 118

McCartney, Jones: Carrickfergus AM 37; 39

McCartney, Joseph: Ahoghill AM 23; 38

McCartney, Joseph: Carrickfergus AM 37; 102

McCartney, Judge: Island Magee AM 10; 67, 95

McCartney, Lord: Carnmoney AM 2; 75, 86

McCartney, Margaret: Ahoghill AM 23; 38

McCartney, Mary: Ahoghill AM 23; 38

McCartney, Michael: Bovevagh LY 25; 9, 14, 35, 39

McCartney, Mr (Clady): Ballymore AH 1; 13, 16

McCartney, Mr (Dublin): Loughgilly AH 1; 84

McCartney, Mr: Cleenish FH 14; 29

McCartney, Mr: Desertmartin LY 31; 61

McCartney, Mr: Drumballyroney DN 3; 18

McCartney, Mrs: Newry DN 3; 99, 104

McCartney, Mrs Samuel: Ballintoy AM 24; 31

McCartney, Neill: Bovevagh LY 25; 9–10, 19, 38–40

McCartney, Rev. (Snr): Templepatrick AM 35; 132

McCartney, Rev. A.C.: Muckamore AM 35; 62, 80

McCartney, Rev. A.C.: Templepatrick AM 35; 119, 132, 139, 143, 153

McCartney, Rev. George: Duneane AM 19; 113

McCartney, Samual: Drumachose LY 9; 117

McCartney, Samuel: Ballintoy AM 24; 31

McCartney, Thomas: Ahoghill AM 23; 38

McCartney, Thomas: Island Magee AM 10; 69, 94, 97

McCartney, William: Carrickfergus AM 37; 39, 148

McCarton, family: Blaris AM 8; 22

McCarton, Rev. Paul: Duneane AM 19; 115

McCarty, Henry: Hillsborough DN 12; 106

McCarty, Richard: Hillsborough DN 12; 106

McCaughan, family: Armoy AM 24; 6

McCaughan, family: Culfeightrin AM 24; 59

McCaughan, John: Culfeightrin AM 24; 68, 79–80

McCaughen, Andrew: Ballymoney AM 16; 15, 17

McCaughen, John: Ballymoney AM 16; 17

McCaughen, Joseph: Muckamore AM 35; 80

McCaughey, John: Skerry AM 13; 119

McCaughey, Robert: Tamlaght O'Crilly LY 18; 142

McCaughtry, Mrs: Blaris DN 12; 45, 49

McCaughy, family: Kirkinriola AM 23; 124

McCaughy, Rev. George: Island Magee AM 10; 88

McCaughy, Robert: Tamlaght O'Crilly LY 18; 131

McCaul, family: Blaris AM 8; 21

McCaul, James: Desertlyn LY 31; 49

McCaul, James: Island Magee AM 10; 103

McCaul, Mr: Blaris AM 8; 84

McCaula, Hugh: Drumachose LY 9; 116

McCaula, Mary: Blaris AM 8; 77

McCaula, Michael: Tamlaght O'Crilly LY 18; 129

McCaula, Patrick: Blaris AM 8; 77

McCaula, William: Aghadowey LY 22; 38

McCaulay, Skeffington: Dunaghy AM 13; 17

McCauley, Alexander: Skerry AM 13; 120

McCauley, Ann: Tamlaght Finlagan LY 25; 119

McCauley, boy: Tamlaght Finlagan LY 25; 119

McCauley, David: Island Magee AM 10; 90

McCauley, Denis: Ramoan AM 24; 123–25

McCauley, family: Killesher FH 14; 84

McCauley, family: Layd AM 13; 52

McCauley, George: Tamlaght Finlagan LY 25; 121

McCauley, James: Culfeightrin AM 24; 76

McCauley, James: Tamlaght Finlagan LY 25; 119

McCauley, Jane: Ballyaghran LY 33; 24

McCauley, John: Drummaul AM 19; 83

McCauley, John: Rasharkin AM 23; 140

McCauley, Maj.: Blaris AM 8; 34

McCauley, Margaret: Coleraine LY 33; 146

McCauley, Matty: Island Magee AM 10; 95

McCauley, Miss: Tamlaght Finlagan LY 25; 119

McCauley, Robert: Balteagh LY 9; 44

McCauley, Robert: Blaris AM 8; 66

McCauley, Robert: Donacavey TE 5; 65–66

McCauley, Robert: Killead AM 35; 42

McCauley, Robert: Tamlaght Finlagan LY 25; 119

McCauley, T.B.: Island Magee AM 10; 95

McCauley, W.P.: Tamlaght Finlagan LY 25; 80

McCauley, William: Balteagh LY 9; 41

McCauley, William: Lough Swilly DL 38; 117

McCaulla, Catherine: Macosquin LY 22; 122

McCaulla, Izabella: Macosquin LY 22; 122

McCauly, Robert: Derrykeighan AM 16; 93

McCausland, Alexander: Balteagh LY 9; 43

McCausland, Anderson: Aghanloo LY 11; 24

McCausland, Anderson: Balteagh LY 9; 40

McCausland, Conolly (Jnr): Banagher LY 30; 22, 118, 120

McCausland, Conolly (Jnr): Drumachose LY 9; 51, 66, 73, 128

McCausland, Conolly: Coleraine LY 33; 64, 77

McCausland, Dominick: Drumachose LY 9; 73

McCausland, Dominick: Tamlaght Finlagan LY 25; 80, 108, 117

McCausland, family: Balteagh LY 9; 28, 35

McCausland, family: Drumachose LY 9; 60

McCausland, Frederick: Drumachose LY 9; 78, 104

McCausland, Frederick: Dungiven LY 15; 101, 106

McCausland, Frederick: Tamlaght Finlagan LY 25; 69, 82, 101, 123

McCausland, James: Ballynure AM 32; 52, 70

McCausland, John: Drumachose LY 9; 66

McCausland, Marcus (Snr): Tamlaght Finlagan LY 25; 80

McCausland, Marcus: Balteagh LY 9; 3, 41

McCausland, Marcus: Banagher LY 30; 116, 131

McCausland, Marcus: Drumachose LY 9; 50–51, 53, 56–57, 65, 69, 73, 78, 80, 82, 84–85, 87–88, 91, 96–99, 104, 108, 111, 118, 122, 128

McCausland, Marcus: Errigal LY 27; 53, 82

McCausland, Marcus: Faughanvale LY 36; 40, 42, 45

McCausland, Marcus: Tamlaght Finlagan LY 25; 93, 103, 109, 121, 125

McCausland, Misses: Drumachose LY 9; 122

McCausland, Mr: Aghanloo LY 11; 11, 33

McCausland, Mr: Banagher LY 30; 32, 112

McCausland, Mr: Cappagh TE 5; 21

McCausland, Mr: Donaghmore DL 39; 38

McCausland, Mr: Misc. LY 31; 143

McCausland, Mrs Marcus: Drumachose LY 9; 50, 122

McCausland, Oliver: Clonleigh DL 39; 12

McCausland, R.C.: Tamlaght Finlagan LY 25; 92

McCausland, Rev. Marcus: Drumachose LY 9; 73

McCausland, Rev. Oliver: Desertegney DL 38; 26

McCausland, Rev. Oliver: Desertoghill LY 27; 17

McCausland, Rev. Oliver: Drumachose LY 9; 107

McCausland, Rev. Oliver: Errigal LY 27; 38

McCausland, Rev. Oliver: Kilrea LY 27; 126

McCausland, Rev. Oliver: Tamlaght Finlagan LY 25; 125

McCausland, Rev. R.: Misc. LY 31; 128

McCausland, Robert: Balteagh LY 9; 43–44

McCausland, Robert: Coleraine LY 33; 64

McCausland, Robert: Drumachose LY 9; 51, 66

McCaveney, David: Aghagallon AM 21; 22

McCaveney, family: Aghagallon AM 21; 18

McCavna, family: Newry DN 3; 108

McCavock, John: Carrickfergus AM 37; 120

McCaw, Archy: Ballintoy AM 24; 32

McCaw, Charles: Ballintoy AM 24; 32

McCaw, Daniel: Rasharkin AM 23; 138

McCaw, Denis: Culfeightrin AM 24; 76

McCaw, Duncan: Carrickfergus AM 37; 193

McCaw, family: Ballintoy AM 24; 20

McCaw, family: Billy AM 16; 58, 68

McCaw, family: Ramoan AM 24; 107

McCaw, Frank: Rasharkin AM 23; 139

McCaw, Hugh: Blaris DN 12; 42

McCaw, James: Ballintoy AM 24; 35

McCaw, James: Billy AM 16; 60, 68–69

McCaw, John: Ahoghill AM 23; 48

McCaw, John: Billy AM 16; 76

McCaw, Robert: Ballymoney AM 16; 23

McCaw, Samuel: Derrykeighan AM 16; 92

McCaw, Thomas: Tamlaght O'Crilly LY 18; 110, 112, 119, 136

McCawell, Rev. Terence: Drumragh TE 5; 108

McCawla, James: Ramoan AM 24; 113

McCawla, John: Ramoan AM 24; 114

McCawn, Thomas: Maghera LY 18; 64

McCay, Alixander: Macosquin LY 22; 118

McCay, Ann: Bovevagh LY 25; 60

McCay, Daniel: Tullyaughnish DL 38; 96

McCay, family: Armoy AM 24; 6

McCay, family: Ballintoy AM 24; 20

McCay, family: Culfeightrin AM 24; 59

McCay, family: Ramoan AM 24; 107

McCay, Henry: Misc. DL 39; 186

McCay, James: Ballintoy AM 24; 34

McCay, James: Billy AM 16; 67–68

McCay, James: Tamlaght O'Crilly LY 18; 118

McCay, John: Ballynure AM 32; 64

McCay, John: Misc. DL 39; 186

McCay, Joseph: Bovevagh LY 25; 31

McCay, Mary: Bovevagh LY 25; 60

McCay, Mary: Drumachose LY 9; 132

McCay, Neal: Billy AM 16; 56, 62

McCay, Patt: Tamlaght Finlagan LY 25; 118

McCay, Rev. J.W.: Ballynure AM 32; 50, 54, 64–66, 69–71

McCay, Robert: Clondermot LY 34; 89

McCay, Samuel: Coleraine LY 33; 145

McCay, Thomas: Tamlaght Finlagan LY 25; 109, 113, 117

McCenlas, Richard: Carrickfergus AM 37; 194

McCheefry, John: Desertoghill LY 27; 17, 25–26

McCheefry, Patrick: Desertoghill LY 27; 26

McChesney, family: Glynn AM 26; 45

McChesney, John: Glynn AM 26; 45

McChesney, William: Carrickfergus AM 37; 195

McChlery, John: Faughanvale LY 36; 26

McChrystal, Thomas: Desertmartin LY 31; 60
McCibbin, Robert: Ahoghill AM 23; 40
McCibbin, William: Ahoghill AM 23; 33
McCintock, Mr: Cappagh TE 5; 21
McClain, James: Tamlaght TE 20; 76
McClain, Robert: Maghera LY 18; 56–58, 70
McClanchy, chieftain: Inishmacsaint FH 14; 75–76
McClane, Charles: Maghera LY 18; 49
McClane, Daniel: Killowen LY 33; 172
McClane, family: Culfeightrin AM 24; 71
McClane, Gabriel: Kilmore AH 1; 69
McClane, Hugh: Killowen LY 33; 172
McClane, James: Ahoghill AM 23; 39
McClane, John: Tamlaght Finlagan LY 25; 109, 113
McClane, Robert: Ahoghill AM 23; 39
McClane, Sally Jane: Tamlaght Finlagan LY 25; 118
McClane, William: Tamlaght Finlagan LY 25; 114
McClare, Henry: Blaris DN 12; 50
McClarman, Patrick: Termoneeny LY 6; 133
McClarnan, Catherine: Duneane AM 19; 122
McClarnan, Hugh: Duneane AM 19; 108, 120
McClarnan, James: Duneane AM 19; 122
McClarnon, Edward: Skerry AM 13; 121
McClarnon, James: Artrea LY 6; 31
McClarnon, John: Artrea LY 6; 25–26
McClarnon, John: Magherafelt LY 6; 106
McClarnon, John: Skerry AM 13; 121
McClarnon, Mr: Derrykeighan AM 16; 92
McClarnon, Rev.: Carrickfergus AM 37; 174
McClarnon, T.O.: Artrea LY 6; 25
McClarty, family: Culfeightrin AM 24; 59
McClarty, John: Ramoan AM 24; 113, 119
McClarty, John: Skerry AM 13; 121
McClary, Daniel: Magilligan LY 11; 127–28
McClary, Hugh: Drumachose LY 9; 132
McClary, Hugh: Magilligan LY 11; 128, 135
McClary, John: Aghanloo LY 11; 15
McClary, man named: Magilligan LY 11; 97, 128
McClaster, John: Culfeightrin AM 24; 75
McClaster, Widow: Culfeightrin AM 24; 75, 83–84
McClave, Robert: Templepatrick AM 35; 148
McClaverty, family: Glynn AM 26; 45
McClaverty, Miss (Glynn): Raloo AM 32; 90–91, 119–21, 124
McClaverty, Miss: Glynn AM 26; 3, 5, 12, 14, 28, 41–42, 45
McClaverty, William: Glynn AM 26; 13, 38
McClay, Samuel: Donagh MN 40; 103
McClean, Adam: Drummaul AM 19; 66–67
McClean, Adam: Dungiven LY 15; 33
McClean, Adam: Misc. AM 10; 130
McClean, Anne (Jnr): Coleraine LY 33; 146
McClean, Anne (Snr): Coleraine LY 33; 146
McClean, Callum: Racavan AM 13; 102–04
McClean, Charles: Duneane AM 19; 117

McClean, Daniel: Carrickfergus AM 37; 119
McClean, David: Killea and Taughboyne DL 39; 87
McClean, Elenor: Derryaghy AM 8; 92
McClean, family: Drumbeg AM 8; 123
McClean, Hugh: Carrickfergus AM 37; 194
McClean, James: Coleraine LY 33; 146
McClean, James: Racavan AM 13; 96, 100
McClean, Jane: Coleraine LY 33; 145
McClean, John: Bovevagh LY 25; 15, 31
McClean, John: Donegore AM 29; 134
McClean, John [I]: Coleraine LY 33; 145
McClean, John [II]: Coleraine LY 33; 146
McClean, Meakam: Dunluce AM 16; 118
McClean, Michael: Bovevagh LY 25; 28, 55
McClean, Michael: Cumber LY 28; 74–75
McClean, Samuel: Dunluce AM 16; 119
McClean, William: Donaghmore DL 39; 40
McClean, William: Tamlaght Finlagan LY 25; 122
McClean, William: Taughboyne DL 39; 150
McClean's mill: Killea and Taughboyne DL 39; 87
McCleary, family: Ematris MN 40; 118
McCleary, James: Ahoghill AM 23; 39
McCleary, James: Blaris AM 8; 69
McCleary, James: Blaris DN 12; 28
McCleery, Archibald: Carrickfergus AM 37; 113
McCleery, family: Templecorran AM 26; 117, 119
McCleery, Hugh: Carrickfergus AM 37; 113
McCleery, James: Artrea LY 6; 22–23
McCleery, James: Carrickfergus AM 37; 113
McCleery, John: Ahoghill AM 23; 34
McCleery, John: Cumber LY 28; 9, 86
McCleery, man named: Tamlaght Finlagan LY 25; 110
McCleery, Patrick: Carrickfergus AM 37; 120
McCleery, Robert: Artrea LY 6; 23
McCleery, Samuel: Artrea LY 6; 22–23
McCleery, W.: Ballyphilip DN 7; 12
McCleese, Thomas: Lissan LY 31; 109
McCleland, Alexander: Tamlaght O'Crilly LY 18; 118
McCleland, Elizabeth: Ballymoney AM 16; 17
McCleland, Robert: Derrykeighan AM 16; 94
McCleland, Sarah Ann: Tamlaght TE 20; 75
McClellan and Co., Messrs: Clondermot LY 34; 30, 100
McClellan, Cary: Clondermot LY 34; 6, 20–21, 27, 37–38, 77–80, 92, 100, 103–05
McClellan, Cary: Faughanvale LY 36; 40, 42, 45
McClellan, family: Maghera LY 18; 13
McClelland, Abraham: Annaclone DN 12; 18
McClelland, Baron: Carrickfergus AM 37; 14, 33
McClelland, Baron: Drummaul AM 19; 41, 47
McClelland, David: Balteagh LY 9; 31
McClelland, Edward: Bovevagh LY 25; 13, 31
McClelland, family: Aghanloo LY 11; 26

McClelland, family: Glynn AM 26; 45
McClelland, family: Island Magee AM 10; 70
McClelland, family: Kilbride AM 29; 152
McClelland, George: Carrickfergus AM 37; 113
McClelland, Hugh: Coleraine LY 33; 145
McClelland, James (Jnr): Coleraine LY 33; 145
McClelland, James (Jnr): Maghera LY 18; 54
McClelland, James (Snr): Maghera LY 18; 54
McClelland, James: Connor AM 19; 27
McClelland, James: Mullaghbrack AH 1; 97
McClelland, James: Tullylish DN 12; 146
McClelland, John (Jnr): Coleraine LY 33; 145
McClelland, John (Snr): Coleraine LY 33; 145
McClelland, John: Aghaderg DN 12; 12
McClelland, John: Carrickfergus AM 37; 114
McClelland, John: Doagh AM 29; 77, 93
McClelland, John: Glynn AM 26; 45
McClelland, John: Maghera LY 18; 53–54
McClelland, John [I]: Coleraine LY 33; 145
McClelland, Lord: Aghanloo LY 11; 26
McClelland, Maryann: Carrickfergus AM 37; 122
McClelland, Maryanne: Coleraine LY 33; 145
McClelland, Messrs Andrew and Sons: Seapatrick
    DN 12; 126
McClelland, Michael: Balteagh LY 9; 31–32
McClelland, Michael: Maghera LY 18; 53
McClelland, Miss: Ballymoney AM 16; 18
McClelland, Moses: Hillsborough DN 12; 107
McClelland, Neal (Jnr): Coleraine LY 33; 145
McClelland, Neal (Snr): Coleraine LY 33; 145
McClelland, Rachael: Coleraine LY 33; 145
McClelland, Rev. G.: Ahoghill AM 23; 49
McClelland, Robert: Dromore DN 12; 75
McClelland, Robert: Island Magee AM 10; 90
McClelland, Samuel: Montiaghs AH 1; 90
McClelland, Susan (Jnr): Coleraine LY 33; 145
McClelland, Susan (Snr): Coleraine LY 33; 145
McClelland, Thomas: Bovevagh LY 25; 16, 19,
    29–31
McClelland, Thomas: Drumachose LY 9; 109, 117
McClelland, Thomas: Seapatrick DN 12; 131
McClelland, Thomas: Tamlaght Finlagan LY 25;
    108
McClelland, Widow: Ballymoney AM 16; 18
McClelland, William: Coleraine LY 33; 145
McClelland, William: Doagh AM 29; 87
McClelland, William: Dungiven LY 15; 117–19
McClelland, William: Island Magee AM 10; 22,
    80–84, 88–90, 95, 99–100, 102, 129
McClelland's pier: Island Magee AM 10; 29
McClement, Robert: Dunboe LY 11; 81
McClements, Mr: Killowen LY 33; 158
McClements, Mrs: Killowen LY 33; 168
McClenaghan, family: Ballyclug AM 23; 63
McClenaghan, family: Ballyscullion AM 19; 10

McClenaghan, James: Carrickfergus AM 37; 114
McClenaghan, Peter: Drummaul AM 19; 90
McClenaghan, William: Bovevagh LY 25; 59
McClenaghan, William: Conwal DL 39; 27
McClenahan, James: Newry DN 3; 99, 104
McClenahan, Mr: Convoy DL 39; 20
McClene, John: Culfeightrin AM 24; 51–52
McClenighan, John: Ballyscullion LY 6; 72
McClernan, family: Derrykeighan AM 16; 89
McClernon, Francis: Ballintoy AM 24; 25–27, 31
McClernon, Frank: Ahoghill AM 23; 38
McClernon, J.H.: Ahoghill AM 23; 38
McClernon, James: Ballintoy AM 24; 29
McClernon, James: Glynn AM 26; 44
McClernon, Jean: Carnmoney AM 2; 78
McClernon, Mrs James: Glynn AM 26; 44
McClernon, William: Carrickfergus AM 37; 124
McClery, Ellen: Desertoghill LY 27; 20
McClery, Mary: Desertoghill LY 27; 20
McClery, William (Jnr): Desertoghill LY 27; 20
McClery, William (Snr): Desertoghill LY 27; 20
McClewarty, family: Carrickfergus AM 37; 179
McClincher [or McCluwher], family: Misc. TE 5;
    147
McClintock, Dr: Raphoe DL 39; 123
McClintock, John (Jnr): Templepatrick AM 35; 152
McClintock, John (Snr): Templepatrick AM 35; 152
McClintock, John: Dromore TE 5; 98
McClintock, John: Drummully FH 4; 37
McClintock, John: Dunaghy AM 13; 17
McClintock, John: Enniskeen CN 40; 29
McClintock, John: Galloon FH 4; 95
McClintock, Messrs: Killea and Taughboyne DL 39;
    89
McClintock, Mr: Raphoe DL 39; 128
McClintock, R.: Faughanvale LY 36; 45
McClintock, Samuel: Clondermot LY 34; 35, 37, 41,
    79–80, 104
McClintock, Samuel: Faughanvale LY 36; 45
McClintock, W.K.: Faughanvale LY 36; 45
McClintock, William: Ardstraw TE 5; 5
McClintock, William: Killea and Taughboyne DL
    39; 79–81, 88
McClintock, William: Misc. DL 39; 186
McClinton, James: Templepatrick AM 35; 149, 151
McCliste, James: Culfeightrin AM 24; 85
McClory's bog: Annaclone DN 12; 14, 17
McCloskey, A.B.: Dungiven LY 15; 84
McCloskey, Andrew: Bovevagh LY 25; 54
McCloskey, Andrew: Dungiven LY 15; 85, 118–19
McCloskey, Ann: Dungiven LY 15; 117–19
McCloskey, Ann: Errigal LY 27; 65
McCloskey, Arthur: Bovevagh LY 25; 47
McCloskey, Arthur: Dungiven LY 15; 6, 31, 69, 79,
    88

McCloskey, B.B.: Bovevagh LY 25; 26–27, 59

McCloskey, Bernard: Carrickfergus AM 37; 125

McCloskey, Bernard: Dungiven LY 15; 73, 84–85, 96

McCloskey, Bernard: Errigal LY 27; 54, 72–73

McCloskey, Bernard [I]: Bovevagh LY 25; 13, 31

McCloskey, Bernard [II]: Bovevagh LY 25; 55

McCloskey, Bryan: Banagher LY 30; 85, 95

McCloskey, Bryan: Bovevagh LY 25; 61

McCloskey, Bryan: Cumber LY 28; 72

McCloskey, Cahill: Dungiven LY 15; 31

McCloskey, Charles: Banagher LY 30; 44, 56

McCloskey, Charles: Bovevagh LY 25; 9, 42, 51

McCloskey, Charles: Dungiven LY 15; 79

McCloskey, Darby: Bovevagh LY 25; 51

McCloskey, Dennis: Clondermot LY 34; 90

McCloskey, Dennis [I]: Banagher LY 30; 75

McCloskey, Dennis [II]: Banagher LY 30; 75–76

McCloskey, Edward: Banagher LY 30; 61, 74, 95

McCloskey, Edward: Bovevagh LY 25; 31–32, 47

McCloskey, Edward: Dungiven LY 15; 45, 72, 87, 94

McCloskey, Elenor: Bovevagh LY 25; 60

McCloskey, Eliza: Balteagh LY 9; 44

McCloskey, Eliza: Bovevagh LY 25; 60

McCloskey, family: Ballynascreen LY 31; 12

McCloskey, family: Banagher LY 30; 31, 112–13

McCloskey, family: Blaris AM 8; 22

McCloskey, family: Dungiven LY 15; 16, 18, 20, 24, 28, 30–31, 42, 58, 77, 84–85, 101–02, 110

McCloskey, family: Maghera LY 18; 48

McCloskey, Felix: Dungiven LY 15; 78

McCloskey, Francis: Banagher LY 30; 71

McCloskey, Francis: Bovevagh LY 25; 42

McCloskey, Francis: Carrickfergus AM 37; 109, 112

McCloskey, Francis: Dungiven LY 15; 94

McCloskey, George: Banagher LY 30; 52, 88

McCloskey, Grace: Bovevagh LY 25; 60

McCloskey, Henry: Banagher LY 30; 111

McCloskey, Hugh: Cumber LY 28; 73

McCloskey, Hugh [I]: Dungiven LY 15; 45, 89

McCloskey, Hugh [II]: Dungiven LY 15; 117, 119

McCloskey, J.D.: Banagher LY 30; 84

McCloskey, J.D.: Dungiven LY 15; 84

McCloskey, J.I.: Dungiven LY 15; 76–77, 84

McCloskey, J.J.: Dungiven LY 15; 84

McCloskey, J.K.: Dungiven LY 15; 84

McCloskey, J.M.: Dungiven LY 15; 77

McCloskey, James: Ballynascreen LY 31; 23, 26

McCloskey, James: Banagher LY 30; 48, 74, 79, 84, 87, 95

McCloskey, James: Cumber LY 28; 73

McCloskey, James: Drumachose LY 9; 134

McCloskey, James [I]: Bovevagh LY 25; 13, 39

McCloskey, James [I]: Dungiven LY 15; 37, 109–10, 112

McCloskey, James [II]: Bovevagh LY 25; 29

McCloskey, James [II]: Dungiven LY 15; 45, 69–70, 74, 77, 81–83, 87

McCloskey, James [III]: Bovevagh LY 25; 60

McCloskey, James [III]: Dungiven LY 15; 65–66

McCloskey, James [IV]: Dungiven LY 15; 116

McCloskey, Jane: Drumachose LY 9; 134

McCloskey, John: Balteagh LY 9; 17, 39, 44

McCloskey, John: Banagher LY 30; 39, 70–71, 73, 81, 92, 95, 100, 114

McCloskey, John: Bovevagh LY 25; 40–42, 48, 53

McCloskey, John: Duneane AM 19; 123

McCloskey, John: Errigal LY 27; 65

McCloskey, John: Lissan LY 31; 102

McCloskey, John: Tamlaght Finlagan LY 25; 89, 115

McCloskey, John [I]: Ballynascreen LY 31; 14, 21

McCloskey, John [I]: Dungiven LY 15; 27

McCloskey, John [I]: Maghera LY 18; 8, 68–69, 71

McCloskey, John [II]: Ballynascreen LY 31; 17

McCloskey, John [II]: Dungiven LY 15; 54, 64, 70, 73–74, 81, 83

McCloskey, John [II]: Maghera LY 18; 51

McCloskey, John [III]: Dungiven LY 15; 86, 94

McCloskey, John [IV]: Dungiven LY 15; 93

McCloskey, John [V]: Dungiven LY 15; 97

McCloskey, John [VI]: Dungiven LY 15; 116, 118–19

McCloskey, Kate: Banagher LY 30; 91

McCloskey, Manus: Banagher LY 30; 95

McCloskey, Manus: Bovevagh LY 25; 13, 47–48

McCloskey, Margaret: Maghera LY 18; 79

McCloskey, Margret: Bovevagh LY 25; 60

McCloskey, Mary: Dungiven LY 15; 116

McCloskey, Maryann: Bovevagh LY 25; 60

McCloskey, Michael: Balteagh LY 9; 24

McCloskey, Michael: Clondermot LY 34; 43, 89

McCloskey, Michael: Errigal LY 27; 65

McCloskey, Michael: Lissan LY 31; 102

McCloskey, Michael [I]: Dungiven LY 15; 92–93

McCloskey, Michael [II]: Dungiven LY 15; 117–19

McCloskey, Miss: Bovevagh LY 25; 27

McCloskey, Mrs: Bovevagh LY 25; 27

McCloskey, Mrs James: Dungiven LY 15; 107

McCloskey, Owen: Banagher LY 30; 50, 91

McCloskey, Owen: Bovevagh LY 25; 29, 38

McCloskey, Owen: Dungiven LY 15; 30, 74, 79–81, 89, 93

McCloskey, Owen: Tamlaght Finlagan LY 25; 119

McCloskey, P.H.: Dungiven LY 15; 84

McCloskey, P.R.: Bovevagh LY 25; 7, 18, 33–34

McCloskey, Patrick: Banagher LY 30; 48, 61, 73–74, 78, 92

McCloskey, Patrick: Blaris AM 8; 22

McCloskey, Patrick: Cumber LY 28; 72–73, 77

McCloskey, Patrick: Maghera LY 18; 30

McCloskey, Patrick [I]: Bovevagh LY 25; 10, 14, 17–18, 31–32

McCloskey, Patrick [I]: Dungiven LY 15; 47, 84

McCloskey, Patrick [I]: Tamlaght Finlagan LY 25; 77–78, 124

McCloskey, Patrick [II]: Bovevagh LY 25; 59

McCloskey, Patrick [II]: Dungiven LY 15; 117–18

McCloskey, Patrick [II]: Tamlaght Finlagan LY 25; 119

McCloskey, Paul: Ballyscullion LY 6; 62

McCloskey, Paul: Dungiven LY 15; 81

McCloskey, Peter: Ahoghill AM 23; 34

McCloskey, Pollatt: Dungiven LY 15; 80

McCloskey, Rev.: Dungiven LY 15; 101

McCloskey, Rev. Edward: Dungiven LY 15; 80

McCloskey, Ritchard: Errigal LY 27; 66

McCloskey, S.B.: Bovevagh LY 25; 54

McCloskey, Sarah: Banagher LY 30; 33, 73, 111

McCloskey, Sarah [I]: Maghera LY 18; 78

McCloskey, Sarah [II]: Maghera LY 18; 79

McCloskey, Thomas: Banagher LY 30; 51, 57, 92

McCloskey, Thomas: Dungiven LY 15; 92, 95

McCloskey, Thomas [I]: Bovevagh LY 25; 13, 47

McCloskey, Thomas [II]: Bovevagh LY 25; 28, 55

McCloskey, Widow: Banagher LY 30; 75

McCloskey, William: Banagher LY 30; 81, 91

McCloskey, William: Dungiven LY 15; 71

McCloskey, woman named: Maghera LY 18; 52

McClosky, family: Errigal LY 27; 41

McClosky, Mr: Clondermot LY 34; 50

McCloud, William: Drumachose LY 9; 53

McClowd, Hugh: Drumachose LY 9; 111

McClowd, James: Drumachose LY 9; 132

McCloy, Bernard: Tamlaght O'Crilly LY 18; 117

McCloy, family: Derryaghy AM 8; 103

McCloy, family: Ramoan AM 24; 107

McCloy, family: Tamlaght O'Crilly LY 18; 93

McCloy, John: Tamlaght O'Crilly LY 18; 118

McCloy, Robert: Desertoghill LY 27; 17–18, 27

McCloy, William: Tamlaght O'Crilly LY 18; 138

McClughan, Iain: Templepatrick AM 35; 149

McClughan, John: Hillsborough DN 12; 97, 103, 105

McClughan, Samuel: Templepatrick AM 35; 151

McClune, Elizabeth: Antrim AM 29; 42

McClune, Elizabeth: Muckamore AM 35; 73

McClung, David: Bovevagh LY 25; 59

McCluny, Messrs: Misc. TE 5; 147

McClure, Adam: Blaris DN 12; 45, 49

McClure, Alexander: Ahoghill AM 23; 35

McClure, Andrew: Ahoghill AM 23; 49

McClure, Andrew: Carrickfergus AM 37; 114

McClure, Charles: Derryaghy AM 8; 99

McClure, Daniel: Carrickfergus AM 37; 193

McClure, family: Magheramesk AM 21; 124

McClure, family: Tullyrusk AM 21; 135

McClure, Francis: Donaghmore DL 39; 40

McClure, James: Ahoghill AM 23; 33, 35

McClure, James: Blaris DN 12; 46

McClure, James: Hillsborough DN 12; 106

McClure, John: Hillsborough DN 12; 106–07

McClure, John: Magheramesk AM 21; 122–23, 125

McClure, John [I]: Carrickfergus AM 37; 111

McClure, John [II]: Carrickfergus AM 37; 126

McClure, Mr: Clondermot LY 34; 42

McClure, Mr: Drumbeg AM 8; 125

McClure, Mrs: Blaris AM 8; 85

McClure, Mrs: Carrickfergus AM 37; 76, 151

McClure, Rev. William: Blaris AM 8; 24

McClure, Robert: Blaris AM 8; 62, 84

McClure, Robert: Blaris DN 12; 39, 45, 47, 49

McClure, Robert: Templepatrick AM 35; 122

McClure, W.: Newtownards DN 7; 112

McClure, William: Blaris AM 8; 29

McClure, William: Carrickfergus AM 37; 193

McClure, William: Derryaghy AM 8; 106–07, 115

McClure, William: Kilraghts AM 16; 132

McClure, William: Magheragall AM 21; 104

McClurg, Archibald: Aghadowey LY 22; 37

McClurg, Elizabeth: Aghadowey LY 22; 37

McClurg, Jackson: Aghadowey LY 22; 37

McClurg, James: Ballymartin AM 2; 18

McClurg, Jane: Aghadowey LY 22; 37

McClurkan, Hugh: Racavan AM 13; 100

McCluskey, Denis: Faughanvale LY 36; 30

McCluskey, family: Maghera LY 18; 24

McCluskey, Thomas: Magilligan LY 11; 123

McClusky, Henry: Hillsborough DN 12; 107

McCluwher [or McClincher], family: Misc. TE 5; 147

McCoart, Patrick: Duneane AM 19; 123

McCock (see McMullan, Alick): Billy AM 16; 43

McColaugh, Patrick: Ballynure AM 32; 61

McColgan's inn: Muff DL 38; 80

McColgin, Michael: Banagher LY 30; 61

McCollam, Catherine: Kilraghts AM 16; 132

McCollam, family: Derrykeighan AM 16; 89

McCollam, family: Dunluce AM 16; 117

McCollan, family: Kilraghts AM 16; 130

McCollaugh, family: Maghera LY 18; 24

McCollian, Eliza: Tamlaght O'Crilly LY 18; 138

McCollian, John: Tamlaght O'Crilly LY 18; 138

McCollian, William: Tamlaght O'Crilly LY 18; 138

McCollin, Robert: Ballymoney AM 16; 23

McCollins, family: Culfeightrin AM 24; 71

McCollins, Hugh: Ahoghill AM 23; 40

McCollins, James: Ahoghill AM 23; 40

McCollion, John: Macosquin LY 22; 119

McCollman, William: Tamlaght TE 20; 80, 102

McColloan, William: Banagher LY 30; 61

McCollom, family: Billy AM 16; 68

McCollom, family: Magheragall AM 21; 99

McCollom, James: Magheragall AM 21; 99

McCollough, family: Maghera LY 18; 48

McCollough, John: Carrickfergus AM 37; 171

McCollum, Ellen: Carrickfergus AM 37; 114

McCollum, family: Billy AM 16; 58

McCollum, family: Culfeightrin AM 24; 59

McCollum, family: Killagan AM 23; 84

McCollum, family: Skerry AM 13; 115

McCollum, John: Loughguile AM 13; 77

McCollum, John: Tamlaght TE 20; 92

McCollum, William: Ballynascreen LY 31; 20

McCollumns, John: Ballyrashane LY 22; 63

McColmont, Robert: Glynn AM 26; 39

McColum, family: Armoy AM 24; 6

McComb, John: Island Magee AM 10; 103

McComb, man named: Drumballyroney DN 3; 14

McComb, Nancy: Carnmoney AM 2; 88

McComb, Richard: Carrickfergus AM 37; 76

McComb's bridge: Clonduff DN 3; 3

McComb's bridge: Drumballyroney DN 3; 11

McComb's bridge: Kilcoo DN 3; 45

McCombs, Charles: Ramoan AM 24; 123–25

McCombs, Hugh: Drummaul AM 19; 90

McCombs, James: Tamlaght TE 20; 75, 128

McCombs, John: Blaris AM 8; 63

McCombs, John: Carnmoney AM 2; 99

McCombs, John: Carrickfergus AM 37; 159, 174–75, 177

McCombs, John: Derryaghy AM 8; 96

McCombs, John: Tamlaght TE 20; 136

McCombs, Thomas: Carnmoney AM 2; 99

McComeskey, family: Blaris AM 8; 22

McCon, Bryan (see O'Donnell): Misc. LY 31; 137

McConaghey, family: Billy AM 16; 68

McConaghty, John: Maghera LY 18; 78

McConaghty, Samuel: Termoneeny LY 6; 133

McConaghy, Daniel: Ballintoy AM 24; 22, 33

McConaghy, Donaghy: Ballyscullion LY 6; 57

McConaghy, family: Armoy AM 24; 6

McConaghy, family: Ballynure AM 32; 56

McConaghy, family: Billy AM 16; 58

McConaghy, family: Derrykeighan AM 16; 89

McConaghy, family: Ramoan AM 24; 107

McConaghy, Hugh: Carrickfergus AM 37; 128

McConaghy, Patrick: Aghagallon AM 21; 15

McConaghy, Robert: Billy AM 16; 56, 63, 76

McConaghy, Robert: Carrickfergus AM 37; 113

McConaghy, Robert: Drumtullagh AM 16; 101

McConaghy, William: Derrykeighan AM 16; 91

McConaghy, William: Drumachose LY 9; 132

McConahy, James: Ballintoy AM 24; 30

McConaughey, family: Billy AM 16; 68

McConekey, Archabald: Ballyaghran LY 33; 24

McConemey, Michael: Termoneeny LY 6; 133

McConkey, Agnes: Carrickfergus AM 37; 123

McConkey, Edward: Hillsborough DN 12; 97, 102, 105

McConkey, Henry: Magheramesk AM 21; 121

McConkey, John: Hillsborough DN 12; 102, 106

McConkey, Mr: Donaghmore DL 39; 36–38

McConkey, Thomas: Aghalee AM 21; 36

McConkey, William: Kirkinriola AM 23; 113

McConky, family: Ballynure AM 32; 56

McConmee, family: Drumachose LY 9; 92

McConmie, family: Desertmartin LY 31; 55

McConnel, family: Aghalee AM 21; 31

McConnel, J.: Comber DN 7; 34

McConnel, William: Tamlaght Finlagan LY 25; 89, 112

McConnell, Arthur: Killead AM 35; 50

McConnell, family: Carnmoney AM 2; 76

McConnell, family: Carrickfergus AM 37; 179

McConnell, family: Rasharkin AM 23; 132

McConnell, J.: Comber DN 7; 41

McConnell, Jacob: Shankill DN 12; 139

McConnell, James: Blaris DN 12; 46, 49

McConnell, James: Coleraine LY 33; 66, 133

McConnell, James: Tamlaght O'Crilly LY 18; 137

McConnell, John: Blaris DN 12; 45–46, 49–50

McConnell, John: Carnmoney AM 2; 89

McConnell, John: Tamlaght Finlagan LY 25; 124

McConnell, John: Tamlaght O'Crilly LY 18; 137

McConnell, Johnston: Tamlaght O'Crilly LY 18; 139, 143

McConnell, Miss: Down DN 17; 58

McConnell, Owen: Blaris AM 8; 73

McConnell, Patrick: Tamlaght O'Crilly LY 18; 137

McConnell, Rev. John: Killead AM 35; 46

McConnell, Thomas: Coleraine LY 33; 132

McConnell, William: Ahoghill AM 23; 46

McConnell, William: Carnmoney AM 2; 89

McConnell, William: Magheramesk AM 21; 126

McConnell, William: Magilligan LY 11; 129

McConnol, William: Tamlaght TE 20; 75

McConomey, William: Banagher LY 30; 61, 73, 77

McConvery, Charles: Lissan LY 31; 110

McConvill, family: Drumgath DN 3; 20

McConville, Rev. Hugh: Garvaghy DN 12; 83

McConway, John: Lissan LY 31; 110

McCoobery's bleach mill: Magheradrool DN 17; 104

McCoobery's flax mill: Magheradrool DN 17; 104, 107

McCook, Archibald: Carrickfergus AM 37; 116

McCook, Eliza: Desertoghill LY 27; 21

McCook, family: Culfeightrin AM 24; 59
McCook, family: Maghera LY 18; 24, 48
McCook, Hugh: Clondermot LY 34; 90
McCook, Hugh: Tamlaght Finlagan LY 25; 118
McCook, James: Desertoghill LY 27; 21
McCook, James: Tamlaght Finlagan LY 25; 118
McCook, Jane: Desertoghill LY 27; 21
McCook, Jane: Tamlaght Finlagan LY 25; 118
McCook, John [I]: Desertoghill LY 27; 7
McCook, John [I]: Tamlaght Finlagan LY 25; 118
McCook, John [II]: Desertoghill LY 27; 21
McCook, John [II]: Tamlaght Finlagan LY 25; 118
McCook, Joseph: Tamlaght Finlagan LY 25; 118
McCook, Martha: Desertoghill LY 27; 21
McCook, Mary Jane: Desertoghill LY 27; 21
McCook, Rebecca: Desertoghill LY 27; 21
McCook, Robert: Carrickfergus AM 37; 112
McCook, William: Tamlaght Finlagan LY 25; 118
McCool, Cuilthia: Errigal LY 27; 78
McCool, family: Ballyclug AM 23; 63
McCool, family: Dungiven LY 15; 20, 29
McCool, family: Misc. LY 36; 112–13
McCool, Fin: Aghalurcher FH 4; 1, 9
McCool, Fin: Aghanloo LY 11; 6, 29
McCool, Fin: Ardclinis AM 13; 9
McCool, Fin: Ballintoy AM 24; 14, 34
McCool, Fin: Ballynascreen LY 31; 15, 33
McCool, Fin: Balteagh LY 9; 19, 42
McCool, Fin: Banagher LY 30; 12, 49, 75, 94
McCool, Fin: Bovevagh LY 25; 35
McCool, Fin: Carrickfergus AM 37; 11
McCool, Fin: Culfeightrin AM 24; 78
McCool, Fin: Cumber LY 28; 63
McCool, Fin: Derryvullan FH 14; 42
McCool, Fin: Desertoghill LY 27; 34
McCool, Fin: Donaghmoyne MN 40; 108
McCool, Fin: Drumballyroney DN 3; 16
McCool, Fin: Drung CN 40; 21
McCool, Fin: Dungiven LY 15; 29, 34, 62
McCool, Fin: Ematris MN 40; 116
McCool, Fin: Errigal LY 27; 43, 45, 76–78
McCool, Fin: Finvoy AM 23; 67
McCool, Fin: Killdrumsherdan CN 40; 35–36
McCool, Fin: Killelagh LY 27; 98
McCool, Fin: Layd AM 13; 50–52
McCool, Fin: Lough Neagh AM 21; 93
McCool, Fin: Loughguile AM 13; 72
McCool, Fin: Maghera LY 18; 36
McCool, Fin: Magheracloone MN 40; 138
McCool, Fin: Magilligan LY 11; 144
McCool, Fin: Misc. LY 36; 113
McCool, Fin: Ramoan AM 24; 115
McCool, John: Maghera LY 18; 79
McCool, Joseph: Balteagh LY 9; 43
McCool, man named: Muckamore AM 35; 81

McCool, Robert: Muckamore AM 35; 81
McCool, William: Carrickfergus AM 37; 131
McCoole, John: Ballymoney AM 16; 17
McCord, Ellen: Ballynure AM 32; 72
McCord, family: Magheramesk AM 21; 124
McCord, harper: Dungiven LY 15; 27
McCord, James: Culfeightrin AM 24; 82
McCord, James: Tamlaght TE 20; 110
McCord, John: Ballynure AM 32; 72
McCord, Margaret: Duneane AM 19; 123
McCord, Robert: Duneane AM 19; 123
McCord, Robert: Magheramesk AM 21; 126
McCord, Samuel: Ballynure AM 32; 72
McCord, Samuel: Tamlaght O'Crilly LY 18; 132
McCord, William: Templepatrick AM 35; 132
McCoristin, Edward: Magilligan LY 11; 86, 123
McCork, family: Desertmartin LY 31; 55
McCorlenton, Mr: Clogher TE 5; 43
McCorley, John: Duneane AM 19; 124
McCorley, Rodger: Duneane AM 19; 118
McCormaik, Dr: Loughgilly AH 1; 87
McCormick, Arthur: Macosquin LY 22; 119
McCormick, Catherine: Carrickfergus AM 37; 118
McCormick, Charles: Carrickfergus AM 37; 112
McCormick, Charles: Drumtullagh AM 16; 102–03
McCormick, Daniel: Loughguile AM 13; 74
McCormick, Daniel [I]: Culfeightrin AM 24; 58, 65, 73
McCormick, Daniel [II]: Culfeightrin AM 24; 71
McCormick, Duncan: Culfeightrin AM 24; 66
McCormick, family: Armoy AM 24; 6
McCormick, family: Carnmoney AM 2; 76
McCormick, family: Culfeightrin AM 24; 58–59, 64–65, 71
McCormick, family: Derryaghy AM 8; 103
McCormick, family: Dromara DN 12; 67
McCormick, family: Macosquin LY 22; 97
McCormick, family: Ramoan AM 24; 107
McCormick, Felix: Culfeightrin AM 24; 64–65
McCormick, Henery: Killowen LY 33; 171
McCormick, J.H.: Kilbroney DN 3; 33
McCormick, James: Billy AM 16; 56
McCormick, James [I]: Carrickfergus AM 37; 112
McCormick, James [II]: Carrickfergus AM 37; 158
McCormick, Jane: Carrickfergus AM 37; 158
McCormick, Jane: Raloo AM 32; 129
McCormick, Jenkin: Maghera LY 18; 81
McCormick, John: Artrea LY 6; 32
McCormick, John: Ballynascreen LY 31; 11, 22, 26
McCormick, John: Billy AM 16; 73
McCormick, John: Culfeightrin AM 24; 63, 65, 76–77, 79–82
McCormick, John: Drumtullagh AM 16; 102–03
McCormick, John: Ramoan AM 24; 114, 118
McCormick, Joseph: Drumachose LY 9; 118

McCormick, man named: Culfeightrin AM 24; 56–57

McCormick, Mary: Cumber LY 28; 73

McCormick, Mathew: Raloo AM 32; 129

McCormick, Mr: Donegal DL 39; 46

McCormick, Nancy: Carrickfergus AM 37; 158

McCormick, Neal: Ballintoy AM 24; 23

McCormick, Pat: Ramoan AM 24; 114–15

McCormick, Patrick: Carrickfergus AM 37; 119, 125, 129

McCormick, Patrick: Magilligan LY 11; 94

McCormick, Rev. Domnick: Maghera LY 18; 69

McCormick, Rev. J.: Coleraine LY 33; 72

McCormick, Rev. Joseph: Donacavey TE 5; 66

McCormick, Robert: Culfeightrin AM 24; 53, 72

McCormick, Robert: Glynn AM 26; 37

McCormick, Rodger: Maghera LY 18; 81

McCormick, Samuel: Carnmoney AM 2; 101

McCormick, Sarah: Carrickfergus AM 37; 156

McCormick, Widow: Dungiven LY 15; 24

McCormick, Widow: Glenavy AM 21; 89

McCormick, William: Ballymoney AM 16; 26

McCormick, William: Carrickfergus AM 37; 158

McCormick, William: Magilligan LY 11; 94

McCormick, William: Tamlaght TE 20; 75, 103

McCorrey, Rev. Henry: Duneane AM 19; 115

McCorry, family: Ballinderry AM 21; 54

McCorry, family: Desertlyn LY 31; 42

McCorry, family: Magheramesk AM 21; 124

McCorry, Henry: Blaris DN 12; 42

McCorry, James: Magilligan LY 11; 129

McCorry, Joseph: Blaris DN 12; 42

McCort, Patrick: Ballyscullion AM 19; 12

McCort, Patrick: Duneane AM 19; 115

McCort, Rev.: Ballyscullion AM 19; 12

McCory, Patrick: Aghagallon AM 21; 16

McCosker, James: Maghera LY 18; 49

McCosker, Rev. Matthias: Maghera LY 18; 69

McCosker, Rev. Matthias: Misc. LY 31; 136

McCotter, Mary: Tamlaght O'Crilly LY 18; 140

McCoubrey, family: Blaris AM 8; 22

McCourt, George: Derryaghy AM 8; 97

McCourt, John: Newry DN 3; 99, 104

McCourt's lough: Ballymore AH 1; 1

McCoy, family: Ballywillin AM 16; 32

McCoy, John: Blaris AM 8; 16

McCoy, John: Newry DN 3; 100

McCoy, Widow: Ballymoney AM 16; 17

McCoy, William: Hillsborough DN 12; 107

McCrab, William: Misc. DL 39; 186

McCracken, Alexander: Dunboe LY 11; 75–76, 79

McCracken, Allen: Templecorran AM 26; 132

McCracken, Eliza: Drummaul AM 19; 91

McCracken, family: Maghera LY 18; 48

McCracken, John: Coleraine LY 33; 73

McCracken, John: Hillsborough DN 12; 106

McCracken, Joseph: Tamlaght Finlagan LY 25; 118

McCracken, Robert: Newry DN 3; 99, 104

McCracken, Samuel: Drummaul AM 19; 76, 86

McCracken, Thomas: Templecorran AM 26; 132

McCracken, William: Ahoghill AM 23; 39

McCracken, William: Magilligan LY 11; 138

McCrackin, family: Desertmartin LY 31; 55

McCrackin, family: Maghera LY 18; 24

McCrackin, family: Racavan AM 13; 100

McCrakin, Alexander: Termoneeny LY 6; 133

McCrakin, David: Termoneeny LY 6; 133

McCranaghan, Patrick: Ballyaghran LY 33; 22

McCrank, family: Culfeightrin AM 24; 59

McCrate, Rev. J.: Ballymore AH 1; 12

McCray, Abraham: Templepatrick AM 35; 123, 145

McCray, William: Doagh AM 29; 98

McCrea, Andrew: Clonleigh DL 39; 10

McCrea, Andrew: Misc. DL 39; 186

McCrea, Archibald: Misc. DL 39; 186

McCrea, J.: Clondermot LY 34; 103

McCrea, James: Clondermot LY 34; 79

McCrea, James: Island Magee AM 10; 82, 91

McCrea, James: Leckpatrick TE 5; 125

McCrea, John: Carrickfergus AM 37; 116

McCrea, John: Misc. DL 39; 186

McCrea, Mr: Clondermot LY 34; 105

McCrea, Robert: Carrickfergus AM 37; 116

McCrea, Robert: Donaghedy TE 5; 89, 91–92

McCrea, Robert: Leckpatrick TE 5; 125

McCready, Denis: Banagher LY 30; 57, 85, 87

McCready, Dennis: Dungiven LY 15; 92

McCready, family: Maghera LY 18; 24

McCready, H.: Holywood DN 7; 77

McCready, John: Banagher LY 30; 52, 85–87

McCready, Robert: Island Magee AM 10; 90

McCreanen, Allice: Magheragall AM 21; 109

McCreanen, James: Aghalee AM 21; 35

McCreary, John: Ardstraw TE 5; 4

McCreary, William: Carnmoney AM 2; 88

McCree, family: Magheramesk AM 21; 124

McCree, Mary: Lissan LY 31; 108

McCreedy, Mr: Drumballyroney DN 3; 18

McCreedy, Mr: Garvaghy DN 12; 80–81

McCreery, family: Carnmoney AM 2; 76

McCreery's mill: Ballymore AH 1; 19

McCreevy, Edward: Carrickfergus AM 37; 111, 195

McCreevy, Robert: Raloo AM 32; 123

McCreight, A.: Ballymore AH 1; 14

McCreight, family: Ahoghill AM 23; 25

McCreight, family: Desertlyn LY 31; 42

McCreight, Rev.: Aghaloo TE 20; 5

McCrery, family: Carnmoney AM 2; 102

McCrink, John: Kilbroney DN 3; 38

McCristal, family: Kilcronaghan LY 31; 68

McCristal, Michael: Kilcronaghan LY 31; 85

McCrom, family: Ballynure AM 32; 56

McCrory, family: Aghagallon AM 21; 10

McCrory, Robert: Drumachose LY 9; 104

McCrory's Castle: Down DN 17; 41

McCrudden, Henry: Duneane AM 19; 115, 122

McCrudden, Hugh: Muckamore AM 35; 81

McCrum, Clotworthy: Billy AM 16; 77

McCrum, John: Carnmoney AM 2; 99

McCrumm, Francis: Donegore AM 29; 134

McCuchen, J.: Newtownards DN 7; 112

McCudden, Catherine: Duneane AM 19; 122

McCudden, Donald: Carrickfergus AM 37; 125

McCue, Frank: Templecorran AM 26; 132

McCue, Joseph: Ballyscullion AM 19; 12

McCue, Neal: Duneane AM 19; 124

McCulla, William: Newry DN 3; 104

McCullagh, Alexander: Duneane AM 19; 114

McCullagh, Alick: Duneane AM 19; 111

McCullagh, Anne: Duneane AM 19; 123

McCullagh, Archabald: Lissan LY 31; 109

McCullagh, Bernard: Artrea LY 6; 38

McCullagh, Christopher: Lissan LY 31; 109

McCullagh, Daniel: Tamlaght O'Crilly LY 18; 134

McCullagh, Eliza: Duneane AM 19; 123

McCullagh, family: Kirkinriola AM 23; 124

McCullagh, Henery: Tamlaght O'Crilly LY 18; 134

McCullagh, James: Duneane AM 19; 123

McCullagh, James: Errigal LY 27; 40, 59

McCullagh, Jane: Lissan LY 31; 109

McCullagh, John: Ballymoney AM 16; 24

McCullagh, John: Duneane AM 19; 123

McCullagh, Joseph: Lissan LY 31; 100

McCullagh, Kenedy: Tamlaght TE 20; 123

McCullagh, Kennedy: Lissan LY 31; 100, 107

McCullagh, Levina: Duneane AM 19; 123

McCullagh, Mary: Lissan LY 31; 109

McCullagh, Mr (Derryvalley): Ballybay MN 40; 83

McCullagh, Mr: Magheracross FH 14; 102

McCullagh, Mrs (Ballyarton): Banagher LY 30; 55, 63

McCullagh, Nancy: Lissan LY 31; 109

McCullagh, Pat: Ballynascreen LY 31; 22

McCullagh, Samuel: Lissan LY 31; 108

McCullagh, Thomas: Newry DN 3; 99

McCullan, Alexander: Ballyscullion LY 6; 78

McCullein, Henry: Skerry AM 13; 120

McCullen, Henry: Carrickfergus AM 37; 158

McCullim, Hugh: Dunaghy AM 13; 23

McCullim, John: Dunaghy AM 13; 22, 24

McCulloch, James: Glynn AM 26; 42

McCulloch, Jane: Glynn AM 26; 28

McCulloch, Owen: Carrickfergus AM 37; 109

McCulloch's burn: Ballynure AM 32; 44

McCulloch's burn: Raloo AM 32; 86–87

McCullock, family: Drumbeg AM 8; 123

McCullock, family: Kilroot AM 26; 74

McCullock, George: Ballynure AM 32; 72

McCullock, Henry: Drummaul AM 19; 71

McCullock, James: Drummaul AM 19; 71

McCullock, Jane: Ballynure AM 32; 72

McCullogh, James: Carrickfergus AM 37; 120

McCullogh, John: Skerry AM 13; 119

McCullogh, William: Drumbeg AM 8; 133

McCullough, Eliza: Carrickfergus AM 37; 129

McCullough, family: Carrickfergus AM 37; 179

McCullough, family: Newry DN 3; 108

McCullough, family: Racavan AM 13; 100

McCullough, James: Aughnamullen MN 40; 71–72, 75

McCullough, James: Magheradrool DN 17; 102

McCullough, Mr (Clady): Ballymore AH 1; 13

McCullough, Mr: Holywood DN 7; 77

McCullough, Rev. James: Comber DN 7; 35, 38

McCullough, Rev. James: Newtownards DN 7; 106

McCullough, W.: Magheradrool DN 17; 103

McCully, Andrew: Bovevagh LY 25; 59

McCully, Archibald: Bovevagh LY 25; 33

McCully, Catherine: Bovevagh LY 25; 59

McCully, family: Aghalee AM 21; 31

McCully, Gilbert: Newtownards DN 7; 112

McCully, Jacob: Bovevagh LY 25; 26

McCully, John: Carrickfergus AM 37; 109

McCully, Margaret: Carrickfergus AM 37; 128

McCully, Mary: Duneane AM 19; 105

McCully, S.: Newtownards DN 7; 112

McCully, Widow (Derrynaflaw): Bovevagh LY 25; 9, 53

McCully, William: Bovevagh LY 25; 1, 33

McCuloch, family: Kilroot AM 26; 75

McCune, D.J.: Carrickfergus AM 37; 155

McCune, Elleanor: Killead AM 35; 51

McCune, Ellina: Killead AM 35; 51

McCune, Fanny Anne: Killead AM 35; 51

McCune, George: Killead AM 35; 51

McCune, J.N.: Killead AM 35; 51

McCune, Margaret (Jnr): Killead AM 35; 51

McCune, Margaret (Snr): Killead AM 35; 51

McCune, Mary Jane: Killead AM 35; 51

McCune, Mrs: Down DN 17; 59

McCune, Robert: Killead AM 35; 49

McCunn, James: Ballyscullion LY 6; 66

McCurdy Greer, Samuel: Dunboe LY 11; 79

McCurdy, Charles: Ballintoy AM 24; 25

McCurdy, Daniel [I]: Ballintoy AM 24; 23

McCurdy, Daniel [II]: Ballintoy AM 24; 24–25, 28

McCurdy, family: Ballintoy AM 24; 20

McCurdy, family: Ballynure AM 32; 56

McCurdy, family: Ballywillin AM 16; 32

McCurdy, family: Billy AM 16; 58, 68

McCurdy, family: Culfeightrin AM 24; 59
McCurdy, family: Magilligan LY 11; 130
McCurdy, family: Racavan AM 13; 100
McCurdy, family: Ramoan AM 24; 107
McCurdy, family: Rathlin Island AM 24; 131–32
McCurdy, George: Ramoan AM 24; 122
McCurdy, James: Ballintoy AM 24; 24
McCurdy, John: Billy AM 16; 60, 62, 65, 69–70
McCurdy, John: Coleraine LY 33; 129
McCurdy, John: Errigal LY 27; 54
McCurdy, John: Magilligan LY 11; 124–25, 129–30,
   132–33, 138, 141–42
McCurdy, John: Ramoan AM 24; 123
McCurdy, John [I]: Ballintoy AM 24; 25
McCurdy, John [II]: Ballintoy AM 24; 30
McCurdy, Laughlin: Ramoan AM 24; 125
McCurdy, man named: Macosquin LY 22; 98
McCurdy, Miss: Ballymoney AM 16; 16
McCurdy, Mr: Blaris AM 8; 54
McCurdy, Mr: Urney DL 39; 177, 181
McCurdy, Robert: Billy AM 16; 51, 58, 65, 72
McCurdy, Samuel: Ballymoney AM 16; 15
McCurdy, Samuel: Billy AM 16; 56, 63, 71
McCurley, Arthur: Carrickfergus AM 37; 97, 162
McCurley, family: Carnmoney AM 2; 76
McCurriston, Daniel: Magilligan LY 11; 109
McCurry, Hugh: Aghagallon AM 21; 10
McCurry, Margaret: Blaris AM 8; 47
McCurry, Margaret: Derryaghy AM 8; 116
McCurry, Moll: Tamlaght Finlagan LY 25; 111–12
McCusker, Connor: Misc. TE 5; 147
McCusker, Hugh: Misc. TE 5; 147
McCusker, Rev.: Faughanvale LY 36; 29
McCutchen, Hugh: Newtownards DN 7; 112
McCutchen, John: Newtownards DN 7; 112
McCutcheon, Joseph: Clondermot LY 34; 37,
   79–80, 104
McCutcheon, Robert: Dungiven LY 15; 96
McCutcheon, William: Blaris AM 8; 35
McDade, James: Carrickfergus AM 37; 108
McDade, James: Tamlaght TE 20; 77
McDaid, Cormick: Banagher LY 30; 96
McDaid, Cornelius: Desertoghill LY 27; 21
McDaid, Daniel: Desertoghill LY 27; 20
McDaid, James: Coleraine LY 33; 133
McDaid, James: Tamlaght O'Crilly LY 18; 112
McDaid, Jane: Desertoghill LY 27; 21
McDaid, John: Desertoghill LY 27; 21
McDaid, Margaret: Desertoghill LY 27; 20
McDaid, Mary: Desertoghill LY 27; 21
McDaid, Maryanne: Desertoghill LY 27; 20
McDaid, Patt: Balteagh LY 9; 44
McDaid, Sally: Balteagh LY 9; 44
McDaid, Sarah (Jnr): Desertoghill LY 27; 20
McDaid, Sarah (Snr): Desertoghill LY 27; 20

McDaid, Widow: Ballynascreen LY 31; 14, 21
McDart, Eliza: Skirts of Urney and Ardstraw TE 5;
   140
McDavan, family: Kilcronaghan LY 31; 68
McDavid, James: Cumber LY 28; 74–76
McDavid, Rachael: Cumber LY 28; 74
McDavit, Thomas: Maghera LY 18; 29, 33, 51
McDegeney, brothers: Raymoghy DL 39; 135
McDermot, Michael: Killowen LY 33; 166
McDermot, Rev. Charles: Errigal Truagh MN 40;
   121
McDermott, Clarke: Ballymoney AM 16; 23
McDermott, Granna: Misc. SO 40; 200
McDermott, Henry: Carrickfergus AM 37; 122, 124,
   127
McDermott, James: Cumber LY 28; 74, 77
McDermott, John: Ballymoney AM 16; 23–24
McDermott, John: Magilligan LY 11; 135
McDermott, Mary: Carrickfergus AM 37; 108
McDermott, Patrick: Killead AM 35; 53
McDermott, Thomas: Bovevagh LY 25; 29
McDevit, John: Convoy DL 39; 22
McDevit, Michael: Ballyclug AM 23; 64
McDevitt, Bishop: Killelagh LY 27; 102
McDevitt, family: Desertmartin LY 31; 55
McDevitt, Henery: Ballynascreen LY 31; 25
McDevitt, Patrick: Maghera LY 18; 81
McDiarmid, Jack: Clondermot LY 34; 34
McDivett, Francis: Urney DL 39; 182
McDonagh, Rev.: Misc. LY 31; 137
McDonagh, Rev. William: Aghanloo LY 11; 10, 14,
   36
McDonagh, William: Balteagh LY 9; 44
McDonal, Bryan: Drummully FH 4; 40
McDonald, Alexander: Loughguile AM 13; 72
McDonald, Archabald: Termoneeny LY 6; 133
McDonald, Arthur: Carlingford LH 40; 59
McDonald, Bernard: Newry DN 3; 99
McDonald, Dr: Blaris AM 8; 55, 84
McDonald, Dr: Blaris DN 12; 46, 49
McDonald, E.: Rasharkin AM 23; 127
McDonald, Ennis: Ahoghill AM 23; 34
McDonald, family: Aghagallon AM 21; 9
McDonald, family: Aghalee AM 21; 36
McDonald, family: Ballinderry AM 21; 54
McDonald, family: Dunluce AM 16; 117
McDonald, Francis: Dunaghy AM 13; 19
McDonald, Isabella: Termoneeny LY 6; 132
McDonald, James: Aghalee AM 21; 36
McDonald, James: Aghanloo LY 11; 15
McDonald, James: Carrickfergus AM 37; 123
McDonald, James: Drummaul AM 19; 90
McDonald, John: Ahoghill AM 23; 34
McDonald, John: Termoneeny LY 6; 133
McDonald, John [I]: Carrickfergus AM 37; 39, 149

McDonald, John [II]: Carrickfergus AM 37; 110
McDonald, Loughlin: Dunaghy AM 13; 22
McDonald, Marchioness (see Antrim): Drummaul AM 19; 82
McDonald, Mary: Carrickfergus AM 37; 119
McDonald, Mary: Termoneeny LY 6; 132
McDonald, Messrs: Donegal DL 39; 47
McDonald, Samuel: Devenish FH 14; 55
McDonald, T.U.: Aghalee AM 21; 36
McDonald, T.U.: Camlin AM 21; 73–74
McDonald, William: Termoneeny LY 6; 132–33
McDonel, family: Ballywillin AM 16; 32
McDonell, John: Killead AM 35; 45
McDonell, Mary: Killead AM 35; 52
McDonlevy, family: Misc. TE 5; 146
McDonnald, Andrew: Tamlaght Finlagan LY 25; 118
McDonnald, Charles: Magilligan LY 11; 127, 130
McDonnald, Eliza: Tamlaght Finlagan LY 25; 118
McDonnald, James: Tamlaght Finlagan LY 25; 118
McDonnald, Jean: Aghagallon AM 21; 19
McDonnald, John: Magilligan LY 11; 127
McDonnald, William: Tamlaght Finlagan LY 25; 118
McDonnel, Alexander: Finvoy AM 23; 75
McDonnel, Elisha: Warrenpoint DN 3; 122
McDonnel, Jane: Killead AM 35; 52
McDonnel, John: Connor AM 19; 27
McDonnell, Alexander: Culfeightrin AM 24; 72
McDonnell, Alexander: Drummaul AM 19; 70
McDonnell, Alexander: Magherafelt LY 6; 109
McDonnell, Alexander: Newry DN 3; 100, 104
McDonnell, Archibald: Carrickfergus AM 37; 78
McDonnell, Capt.: Culfeightrin AM 24; 72
McDonnell, Charles: Culfeightrin AM 24; 40
McDonnell, Col.: Layd AM 13; 41
McDonnell, Daniel: Finvoy AM 23; 75
McDonnell, Dr (Belfast): Culfeightrin AM 24; 52, 58, 73
McDonnell, Dr (Belfast): Drumtullagh AM 16; 100–01
McDonnell, Dr (Belfast): Kilkeel DN 3; 48
McDonnell, Dr (Belfast): Layd AM 13; 52
McDonnell, Dr (Cushendall): Culfeightrin AM 24; 74
McDonnell, Edmond (see also Antrim, Lord)
McDonnell, Edmond: Ardclinis AM 13; 1
McDonnell, Edmond: Carncastle and Killyglen AM 10; 6
McDonnell, Edmond: Kilwaughter AM 10; 116
McDonnell, Edmond: Larne AM 10; 123
McDonnell, Edward: Killead AM 35; 46
McDonnell, Ellen: Carrickfergus AM 37; 120
McDonnell, family: Ahoghill AM 23; 25
McDonnell, family: Ballinderry AM 21; 54
McDonnell, family: Ballymoney AM 16; 20

McDonnell, family: Billy AM 16; 53, 66–67, 71–72
McDonnell, family: Culfeightrin AM 24; 59, 64, 71, 78–81
McDonnell, family: Drumachose LY 9; 128
McDonnell, family: Dunaghy AM 13; 14, 28
McDonnell, family: Dundermot AM 13; 35
McDonnell, family: Dunluce AM 16; 122
McDonnell, family: Enniskillen FH 4; 58
McDonnell, family: Kilwaughter AM 10; 115
McDonnell, family: Layd AM 13; 49
McDonnell, family: Layd and Inispollan AM 13; 55, 57
McDonnell, family: Loughguile AM 13; 64, 66
McDonnell, family: Magheragall AM 21; 99
McDonnell, family: Raloo AM 32; 108
McDonnell, family: Ramoan AM 24; 113, 125
McDonnell, Hugh: Cranfield AM 19; 32
McDonnell, J.: Newtownards DN 7; 113, 113
McDonnell, J.R.: Culfeightrin AM 24; 79, 82
McDonnell, James: Ballyscullion AM 19; 7
McDonnell, James: Culfeightrin AM 24; 79
McDonnell, John: Culfeightrin AM 24; 52, 84
McDonnell, John: Killead AM 35; 53
McDonnell, John: Magilligan LY 11; 136
McDonnell, John [I]: Carrickfergus AM 37; 112
McDonnell, John [II]: Carrickfergus AM 37; 122
McDonnell, Margaret: Carrickfergus AM 37; 120
McDonnell, R.D.: Culfeightrin AM 24; 73
McDonnell, Randal: Layd AM 13; 48
McDonnell, Randal [I]: Culfeightrin AM 24; 51
McDonnell, Randal [II]: Culfeightrin AM 24; 74
McDonnell, Rev. Benjamin: Tamlaght Finlagan LY 25; 69
McDonnell, robber: Errigal Keerogue TE 20; 49
McDonnell, Widow: Ballymoney AM 16; 17
McDonough, Charles: Killowen LY 33; 171
McDougal, Edward: Balteagh LY 9; 38, 40
McDougal, William: Ballintoy AM 24; 26
McDougall and McQuilkin, Messrs: Banagher LY 30; 4
McDougall, family: Culfeightrin AM 24; 46
McDougall, John: Kilrea LY 27; 121
McDougall, Joseph: Dungiven LY 15; 97
McDouglas' inn: Dungiven LY 15; 24
McDougle, Con: Culfeightrin AM 24; 82
McDowall, Andrew: Carrickfergus AM 37; 76
McDowall, family: Island Magee AM 10; 70
McDowall, family: Kilroot AM 26; 74
McDowel, family: Ballyscullion AM 19; 4
McDowel, James: Ballyscullion AM 19; 13
McDowel, John: Blaris AM 8; 84
McDowel, John: Blaris DN 12; 45
McDowel, John: Carrickfergus AM 37; 163, 173
McDowell, Andrew: Carrickfergus AM 37; 75, 151
McDowell, Andrew: Magherafelt LY 6; 98

McDowell, Dr: Ballyscullion AM 19; 9
McDowell, Eliza: Carrickfergus AM 37; 158
McDowell, Elizabeth: Ballymoney AM 16; 18
McDowell, Ellen: Carrickfergus AM 37; 158
McDowell, Ephraim: Carrickfergus AM 37; 158
McDowell, family: Carrickfergus AM 37; 179
McDowell, family: Glynn AM 26; 42
McDowell, family: Kilroot AM 26; 75
McDowell, family: Kilwaughter AM 10; 115, 117
McDowell, family: Kirkinriola AM 23; 124
McDowell, family: Raloo AM 32; 94, 123, 125–26
McDowell, George: Raloo AM 32; 91, 120, 128
McDowell, Henry: Donegore AM 29; 130
McDowell, Hugh: Hillsborough DN 12; 105
McDowell, Hugh: Kilwaughter AM 10; 116
McDowell, James: Connor AM 19; 26
McDowell, James: Kilwaughter AM 10; 115–16
McDowell, James [I]: Carrickfergus AM 37; 157
McDowell, James [II]: Carrickfergus AM 37; 158
McDowell, Jane (Jnr): Carrickfergus AM 37; 158
McDowell, Jane (Snr): Carrickfergus AM 37; 158
McDowell, Jane: Ballyscullion AM 19; 13
McDowell, Jane [I]: Carrickfergus AM 37; 158
McDowell, Janet: Kilwaughter AM 10; 116
McDowell, John: Carrickfergus AM 37; 125
McDowell, John: Glynn AM 26; 45
McDowell, John: Kilwaughter AM 10; 116
McDowell, John [I]: Raloo AM 32; 103, 123, 125
McDowell, John [II]: Raloo AM 32; 122
McDowell, Josh: Ballyscullion AM 19; 13
McDowell, Margaret: Glynn AM 26; 35, 47
McDowell, Margaret: Raloo AM 32; 129
McDowell, Margaret [I]: Carrickfergus AM 37; 156
McDowell, Margaret [II]: Carrickfergus AM 37; 158
McDowell, Margaret [III]: Carrickfergus AM 37;
    158
McDowell, Mary [I]: Carrickfergus AM 37; 118
McDowell, Mary [II]: Carrickfergus AM 37; 122
McDowell, Mary Eliza: Carrickfergus AM 37; 158
McDowell, Matilda: Carrickfergus AM 37; 158
McDowell, Rev.: Comber DN 7; 32, 44
McDowell, Robert: Drummaul AM 19; 87
McDowell, Robert: Kilcronaghan LY 31; 86–87
McDowell, Robert: Raloo AM 32; 123
McDowell, Robert: Tartaraghan AH 1; 119
McDowell, Robert: Templecorran AM 26; 132
McDowell, Sampson: Ballyscullion AM 19; 15
McDowell, Samuel: Carrickfergus AM 37; 125
McDowell, Samuel: Maghera LY 18; 71
McDowell, Thomas: Ballynure AM 32; 71
McDowell, W.J.: Ballyscullion AM 19; 14–15
McDowell, W.J.: Carrickfergus AM 37; 125
McDowell, W.J.: Muckamore AM 35; 73
McDowell, William: Carrickfergus AM 37; 158
McDowell, William: Raloo AM 32; 122–23

McDowell, William [I]: Ballynure AM 32; 57
McDowell, William [II]: Ballynure AM 32; 71
McDuff, John: Hillsborough DN 12; 105
McDuffee, family: Culfeightrin AM 24; 59
McDuffee, family: Dunluce AM 16; 117
McDuffy, John: Ramoan AM 24; 126
McEgan, family: Killagan AM 23; 79
McElcunnia, James: Ballyrashane LY 22; 65
McElderry, Thomas: Ballymoney AM 16; 8, 15–16
McEldery, family: Desertlyn LY 31; 42
McEldoon, Arthur: Tamlaght TE 20; 78
McEldoon, Eliza: Tamlaght TE 20; 78
McEldoon, Hugh: Tamlaght TE 20; 77
McEldoon, Patrick: Tamlaght TE 20; 76
McEldoon, William: Tamlaght TE 20; 76
McEldowney, Bernard: Ballynascreen LY 31; 22
McEldowney, Bernard: Killelagh LY 27; 100
McEldowney, family: Killelagh LY 27; 99
McEleanon, family: Desertlyn LY 31; 42
McElevy, Mrs: Kilkeel DN 3; 52
McElhatten, Elizabeth: Cumber LY 28; 55
McElhatton, family: Ballintoy AM 24; 20
McElheran, family: Ramoan AM 24; 107
McElmoyle, family: Ramoan AM 24; 107
McElmoyle, James: Ramoan AM 24; 120
McElmoyle, John: Ramoan AM 24; 107
McElmoyle, man named: Culfeightrin AM 24; 80
McElreavy, James: Killowen LY 33; 161, 169
McElree, H.: Banagher LY 30; 92
McElree, Samual: Banagher LY 30; 84
McElree, Samuel: Ballynascreen LY 31; 25
McElree, Samuel: Kilcronaghan LY 31; 86
McElroy, family: Billy AM 16; 58, 68
McElroy, family: Culfeightrin AM 24; 59
McElroy, family: Faughanvale LY 36; 48
McElroy, Mr: Ardstraw TE 5; 13
McElvare, Denis: Dungiven LY 15; 75, 89
McElvare, Edward: Bovevagh LY 25; 45
McElvare, Edward: Dungiven LY 15; 94
McElvare, John: Drumachose LY 9; 133
McElvare, Thomas: Dungiven LY 15; 70–71, 74
McElvoy, Patt: Ramoan AM 24; 113
McElwain, Archibald: Ballywillin LY 33; 43
McElwain, Archibald: Coleraine LY 33; 72, 127,
    143
McElwain, family: Desertlyn LY 31; 42
McElwayen, family: Templecorran AM 26; 119
McElwayne, family: Templecorran AM 26; 117
McElwell, Dennis: Cumber LY 28; 73
McElyare, Nancy: Ballymoney AM 16; 18
McEnally, John: Aghabog MN 40; 65
McEnarry, Mary: Carrickfergus AM 37; 124
McEneney, Cpl: Loughinisland DN 17; 98
McEnerney, Dennis: Ballintoy AM 24; 31
McEnerney, Patt: Ballintoy AM 24; 30

McEntire, Alixander: Bovevagh LY 25; 60
McEntire, Benjamin: Killowen LY 33; 171
McEntire, Hamilton: Tamlaght O'Crilly LY 18; 112
McEntire, Jane: Bovevagh LY 25; 60
McEntire, John: Bovevagh LY 25; 60
McEntire, Margaret: Ballynascreen LY 31; 14, 21
McEntire, Margret: Tamlaght Finlagan LY 25; 119
McEntire, Mr (Greencastle): Moville DL 38; 70
McEntire, Patt: Kilmacteige SO 40; 195
McEntire, Robert: Aghadowey LY 22; 38
McEntire, Robert: Ballyrashane LY 22; 65
McEntire, Robert: Macosquin LY 22; 122
McEntire, Samual: Macosquin LY 22; 109
McEntire, Thomas: Macosquin LY 22; 122
McEntire, William: Ballyscullion LY 6; 71
McEntosh, Angus: Carrickfergus AM 37; 193
McErlaine, James: Duneane AM 19; 124
McErlaine, Michael: Ballyscullion AM 19; 12
McErlaine, Patt: Ballyscullion AM 19; 10
McErlane, family: Artrea LY 6; 14
McErlane, family: Ballyscullion AM 19; 4
McErlane, family: Duneane AM 19; 101–02
McErlane, Felix: Duneane AM 19; 121
McErlane, Hugh: Tamlaght TE 20; 77
McErlane, John: Culfeightrin AM 24; 50
McErlane, John: Tamlaght O'Crilly LY 18; 134
McErlane, Joseph: Carrickfergus AM 37; 107
McErlane, Michael: Duneane AM 19; 110, 122
McErlane, Michael: Tamlaght O'Crilly LY 18; 110, 117
McErlane, Patrick: Tamlaght O'Crilly LY 18; 118
McErlane, Peter: Tamlaght O'Crilly LY 18; 134
McErlean, Daniel: Ballyscullion LY 6; 69
McErlean, Patrick: Ballyscullion LY 6; 72
McEvoy, Rev. Patrick: Kilbroney DN 3; 28, 33–34, 38
McEwen, John: Ardstraw TE 5; 7
McFadden, Bridget: Carrickfergus AM 37; 115
McFadden, James: Ahoghill AM 23; 44, 49
McFadden, John: Bovevagh LY 25; 38
McFadden, Moses: Billy AM 16; 77
McFadden, Mr: Bovevagh LY 25; 22
McFadden, Rev. Hutchinson: Kilraghts AM 16; 132
McFadden, Samual: Bovevagh LY 25; 60
McFadden, William: Bovevagh LY 25; 29
McFadden, William: Derrykeighan AM 16; 93
McFadden, William: Tamlaght Finlagan LY 25; 80
McFaddin, James: Tullaghobegley DL 39; 172
McFall, Alexander: Raloo AM 32; 129
McFall, Archibald: Ballyrashane AM 16; 31
McFall, Charles: Termoneeny LY 6; 133
McFall, Daniel: Ahoghill AM 23; 21, 42
McFall, Ennis: Ahoghill AM 23; 39
McFall, James: Loughguile AM 13; 74
McFall, James: Termoneeny LY 6; 133

McFall, John: Ahoghill AM 23; 37
McFall, John: Carrickfergus AM 37; 111
McFall, John: Termoneeny LY 6; 133
McFall, Paddy: Kilwaughter AM 10; 118
McFall, Rev. David: Maghera LY 18; 68
McFall, Rev. Patrick: Maghera LY 18; 68
McFall, Sally: Raloo AM 32; 129
McFalls, Charles: Ahoghill AM 23; 39
McFalls, Charles: Ballyscullion AM 19; 12
McFalls, Dennis: Ahoghill AM 23; 39
McFalls, John: Ahoghill AM 23; 38
McFalls, Mary Jane: Ballynure AM 32; 66
McFarcin, Joseph: Drumachose LY 9; 126
McFarland, Daniel: Drumachose LY 9; 104
McFarland, family: Culfeightrin AM 24; 59
McFarland, family: Macosquin LY 22; 83, 119
McFarland, James: Coleraine LY 33; 142, 148
McFarland, James: Macosquin LY 22; 77, 80, 87, 102, 106, 119–20
McFarland, John: Tamlaght O'Crilly LY 18; 141
McFarland, Jonathan: Dunluce AM 16; 123
McFarland, Joseph: Dungiven LY 15; 6
McFarland, man named: Banagher LY 30; 47, 78
McFarland, Mr (Cloon): Killea and Taughboyne DL 39; 87
McFarland, Mr: Aghadowey LY 22; 5
McFarland, Mr: Banagher LY 30; 39
McFarland, Mr: Kirkinriola AM 23; 113
McFarland, Mrs: Kirkinriola AM 23; 113
McFarland, Nevill: Dromore TE 5; 97
McFarland, Robert: Banagher LY 30; 99–100
McFarland, Robert: Duneane AM 19; 123
McFarland, Samuel: Carrickfergus AM 37; 111
McFarland, Samuel: Dunluce AM 16; 116, 118
McFarland's mill: Killea and Taughboyne DL 39; 87
McFarlane, John: Coleraine LY 33; 72
McFarlin, Mr: Cappagh TE 5; 15
McFarrell, family: Aghabog MN 40; 66
McFarren, Mrs: Carrickfergus AM 37; 163
McFaul, Charles: Drumachose LY 9; 131
McFaull, Ails: Lissan LY 31; 102
McFaull, Daniel: Drumachose LY 9; 133
McFaull, Dennis: Aghanloo LY 11; 22
McFaull, James: Aghadowey LY 22; 37
McFaull, Michael: Ballynascreen LY 31; 27
McFeatridge, Daniel: Tamlaght Finlagan LY 25; 109, 117
McFeatridge, John: Tamlaght Finlagan LY 25; 117
McFeeley, Bernard: Bovevagh LY 25; 60
McFeeley, James [I]: Bovevagh LY 25; 60
McFeeley, James [II]: Bovevagh LY 25; 60
McFeely, Patrick: Banagher LY 30; 50, 84
McFeely, Patrick: Dungiven LY 15; 94
McFeely, Rev. Patrick: Cumber LY 28; 19, 84
McFeely, William: Magilligan LY 11; 94

McFeetridge, Andrew: Drumachose LY 9; 111
McFeetridge, John: Dunluce AM 16; 118
McFeetridge, John: Macosquin LY 22; 120
McFeetridge, Mrs: Drumachose LY 9; 111
McFeetridge, Robert: Drumachose LY 9; 134
McFeetrige, William: Aghadowey LY 22; 38
McFeighe, Hugh: Misc. SO 40; 200
McFern, family: Kilroot AM 26; 74–75
McFerran, Charles: Carrickfergus AM 37; 40, 149
McFerran, family: Carnmoney AM 2; 76
McFerran, family: Carrickfergus AM 37; 179
McFerran, family: Glynn AM 26; 45
McFerran, family: Templecorran AM 26; 117, 119
McFerran, Frank: Rasharkin AM 23; 140
McFerran, Hugh: Templecorran AM 26; 105,
    119–20, 124, 127, 130
McFerran, Robert: Carnmoney AM 2; 81, 101
McFerran, Robert: Glynn AM 26; 45
McFerran, William: Carnmoney AM 2; 81
McFerran, William: Doagh AM 29; 70, 93
McFetdridge, Ann: Tamlaght Finlagan LY 25; 80
McFetrick, John: Dunluce AM 16; 122
McFetridge, family: Kirkinriola AM 23; 124
McFetridge, John: Aghadowey LY 22; 36
McFetridge, John: Agivey LY 22; 45
McFillan, Ann: Ballynascreen LY 31; 14, 21
McFillen, John: Artrea LY 6; 25, 27
McFillen, Sareah: Artrea LY 6; 38
McFinn, Oscar: Dungiven LY 15; 20
McFirbis, Donald: Magilligan LY 11; 101
McFlinn, Hugh: Maghera LY 18; 78
McFlinn, Neil: Maghera LY 18; 78
McGahan, Henry: Dunaghy AM 13; 17
McGahy, John: Carrickfergus AM 37; 118
McGambly, David: Carrickfergus AM 37; 109
McGan, John: Tamlaght TE 20; 103
McGanarty, Edward: Artrea LY 6; 38
McGanarty, Mary: Artrea LY 6; 38
McGanelly, James: Glenavy AM 21; 91
McGann, James: Carrickfergus AM 37; 130
McGann, James: Kilcronaghan LY 31; 79
McGannity, Mary: Glenavy AM 21; 91
McGany, Ann (Jnr): Tamlaght Finlagan LY 25; 119
McGany, Ann (Snr): Tamlaght Finlagan LY 25; 119
McGany, Maria: Tamlaght Finlagan LY 25; 119
McGarigle, family: Dungiven LY 15; 24
McGarrell, James: Carrickfergus AM 37; 107
McGarrety, John: Carrickfergus AM 37; 110
McGarrity, Catherine: Carrickfergus AM 37; 122
McGarry, Adam: Carrickfergus AM 37; 108
McGarry, Bernart: Magheragall AM 21; 105
McGarry, family: Ballymartin AM 2; 5, 12, 16
McGarry, family: Culfeightrin AM 24; 59
McGarry, family: Desertlyn LY 31; 42
McGarry, Lawrence: Derrykeighan AM 16; 92

McGarry, Rev. Charles: Ematris MN 40; 114
McGarry, Rev. James: Raloo AM 32; 91, 107, 121
McGarry's well: Ballymartin AM 2; 15
McGarrystown (Magarrystown): Ballymartin AM 2;
    5, 11–13, 15–16
McGarrystown: Muckamore AM 35; 67
McGarrystown fort: Ballymartin AM 2; 12
McGarvey, Henery: Blaris AM 8; 55
McGarvey, James: Lissan LY 31; 109
McGarvey, Molly: Lissan LY 31; 104
McGarvey, Philip: Tamlaght TE 20; 77, 104, 128
McGarvil, James: Aghagallon AM 21; 12
McGary, Rev. Daniel: Aghagallon AM 21; 8
McGaughan, Henry: Killagan AM 23; 85
McGaughy, family: Culfeightrin AM 24; 59
McGaula, Richard: Ramoan AM 24; 108, 110
McGauney, Frances: Dunboe LY 11; 80
McGauney, James: Dunboe LY 11; 80
McGaw, William: Rashee AM 32; 141
McGeary, Mary: Finvoy AM 23; 73–74
McGee, Alexander: Derryaghy AM 8; 108
McGee, Capt.: Killygarvan DL 38; 40
McGee, Charles: Drumachose LY 9; 116
McGee, Daniel: Tamlaght TE 20; 97–98
McGee, Eliza: Tamlaght Finlagan LY 25; 119
McGee, family: Ballinderry AM 21; 53
McGee, family: Drumbeg AM 8; 123
McGee, James: Balteagh LY 9; 24
McGee, John: Tamlaght TE 20; 76, 91
McGee, Margret: Tamlaght Finlagan LY 25; 119
McGee, Matty: Tamlaght Finlagan LY 25; 119
McGee, Thomas: Carnmoney AM 2; 100
McGee, William: Blaris AM 8; 37
McGeehan [or McGahan], Hugh: Magilligan LY 11;
    138
McGeehan, James: Magilligan LY 11; 125–26, 137
McGenis, family: Dungiven LY 15; 32
McGennis, Widow: Dungiven LY 15; 24
McGenny, Anne: Carrickfergus AM 37; 132
McGeny, John: Killowen LY 33; 159
McGeoagh, John: Ballynascreen LY 31; 14, 21
McGeogh, Bond: Ballee DN 17; 22–23
McGeogh, Bond: Eglish AH 1; 44
McGeogh, Rev. Andrew: Lissan LY 31; 104
McGeogh, Rev. James: Lissan LY 31; 104
McGeough, family: Blaris DN 12; 30
McGeough, Sarah: Carrickfergus AM 37; 123
McGeown, family: Desertlyn LY 31; 42
McGerr, Joseph: Drumcree AH 1; 33
McGettigan, family: Clondermot LY 34; 1
McGetty, Alexander: Kildollagh LY 22; 75
McGetty, Margaret: Kildollagh LY 22; 75
McGetty, Martha: Kildollagh LY 22; 75
McGetty, Matlida: Kildollagh LY 22; 75
McGibbon, Mr: Galloon FH 4; 91

McGifford, Samuel: Hillsborough DN 12; 107

McGildowney, Charles: Ballymoney AM 16; 15

McGildowney, Charles: Coleraine LY 33; 127

McGildowney, Charles: Culfeightrin AM 24; 53

McGildowney, Charles: Ramoan AM 24; 90, 96–97, 116, 123

McGildowney, Edmond: Culfeightrin AM 24; 41, 53, 69

McGildowney, family: Culfeightrin AM 24; 59, 64

McGill, Arthur: Skerry AM 13; 114

McGill, Catherine: Carrickfergus AM 37; 76

McGill, family: Carrickfergus AM 37; 179

McGill, family: Dunluce AM 16; 117

McGill, George: Drummaul AM 19; 87

McGill, James: Annahilt DN 12; 25

McGill, James: Carrickfergus AM 37; 76

McGill, James: Donagh DL 38; 32

McGill, John: Antrim AM 29; 42, 45

McGill, Mary: Carrickfergus AM 37; 76

McGill, Mr: Comber DN 7; 40

McGill, Mr: Holywood DN 7; 77

McGilland, Patrick: Tamlaght TE 20; 128

McGillian, family: Misc. LY 31; 117

McGillian, man named: Ballynascreen LY 31; 9, 117

McGilligan, Bernard: Dungiven LY 15; 88

McGilligan, Elanor: Dungiven LY 15; 81

McGilligan, James: Dungiven LY 15; 80

McGilligan, John: Drumachose LY 9; 109

McGilligan, Manus: Magilligan LY 11; 97

McGilton, Joseph: Banagher LY 30; 70

McGimpsy, James: Newtownards DN 7; 112–13

McGimpsy, Thomas: Newtownards DN 7; 112

McGinn, Patrick: Donacavey TE 5; 65

McGinn, Rev. Patrick: Ballynure AM 32; 69

McGinnerty, person named: Blaris AM 8; 60

McGinnes, Arthur: Tydavnet MN 40; 172

McGinness, Rev. Edmund: Tullylish DN 12; 147

McGinty, Anthony: Carrickfergus AM 37; 111, 195

McGivern, James: Carrickfergus AM 37; 125

McGivren, B.: Newtownards DN 7; 112

McGivren, H.: Newtownards DN 7; 112

McGlade, family: Ballynascreen LY 31; 12

McGlade, family: Maghera LY 18; 24, 48

McGlade, John: Maghera LY 18; 81

McGlade, Manases: Maghera LY 18; 45

McGlade, Neil: Maghera LY 18; 47

McGlade, Patrick: Ballynascreen LY 31; 24

McGlade, Robert: Lissan LY 31; 110

McGladigan, Edward: Carrickfergus AM 37; 128

McGlaghlin, family: Errigal LY 27; 41

McGlaim, priest: Ballintoy AM 24; 35

McGlary, family: Culfeightrin AM 24; 71

McGlaughlin, family: Dunluce AM 16; 117

McGlaughlin, man named: Manorhamilton Union LM 40; 50

McGlellan, Catherine: Clonduff DN 3; 6

McGlinchy, Rev. Michael: Bovevagh LY 25; 59

McGlinchy, Rev. Michael: Dungiven LY 15; 76, 103

McGlogan, Rev.: Killead AM 35; 45

McGlone, family: Lissan LY 31; 91, 106

McGlone, James: Lissan LY 31; 100

McGlone, Thomas: Tyholland MN 40; 175

McGoldrake, Patrick: Maghera LY 18; 81

McGolpen, Agnes: Drumbeg AM 8; 133

McGolrick, Patrick: Ahoghill AM 23; 40, 42

McGonagle, Esther: Ahoghill AM 23; 37

McGonegal, John: Ballymoney AM 16; 15

McGonegal, Patrick: Errigal LY 27; 50

McGonegal's inn: Muff DL 38; 80

McGonigal, family: Desertoghill LY 27; 5, 30

McGonigle, Frederick: Dungiven LY 15; 74

McGonigle, George: Tamlaght Finlagan LY 25; 123

McGonigle, Jane: Agivey LY 22; 45

McGonigle, John: Aghadowey LY 22; 36

McGonigle, John: Agivey LY 22; 45

McGonigle, John: Ballymoney AM 16; 17

McGonigle, Margaret: Aghadowey LY 22; 36

McGonigle, Margaret: Agivey LY 22; 45

McGonigle, Mary: Aghadowey LY 22; 36

McGonigle, Mary: Agivey LY 22; 45

McGonnigle, Thomas: Macosquin LY 22; 122

McGookan, James: Ballynure AM 32; 61, 67

McGooran, Patt: Kilmacteige SO 40; 185

McGorden, James: Balteagh LY 9; 25

McGourland, D.: Blaris DN 12; 46

McGovney, Widow: Hillsborough DN 12; 106

McGowan, family: Kilcronaghan LY 31; 68

McGowan, James: Blaris DN 12; 46, 50

McGowan, James: Donaghmore DL 39; 39

McGowan, John: Coleraine LY 33; 73

McGowan, John: Faughanvale LY 36; 67

McGowan, John [I]: Carrickfergus AM 37; 76

McGowan, John [II]: Carrickfergus AM 37; 150, 155, 172

McGowan, Mr (Bangor): Comber DN 7; 37, 39–40

McGowan, Mr: Loughgilly AH 1; 87

McGowan, Orr: Comber DN 7; 34

McGowan, Patrick: Balteagh LY 9; 30, 32

McGowan, Rev.: Loughgilly AH 1; 86

McGowan, Robert: Carrickfergus AM 37; 148

McGowan, Thomas: Ballynascreen LY 31; 16

McGowan, Widow: Billy AM 16; 58

McGowan, Widow: Carrickfergus AM 37; 76

McGowan, William: Convoy DL 39; 19

McGowen, Andrew: Ballyrashane LY 22; 64

McGowen, Ann: Killowen LY 33; 171

McGowen, Edward: Tamlaght Finlagan LY 25; 114

McGowen, family: Desertlyn LY 31; 42

McGowen, Henery: Balteagh LY 9; 43

McGowen, Hugh: Ballyrashane LY 22; 66

McGowen, James: Balteagh LY 9; 32

McGowen, James: Killowen LY 33; 171

McGowen, John: Ballintoy AM 24; 31

McGowen, John: Ballyrashane LY 22; 64

McGowen, Robert: Tamlaght Finlagan LY 25; 106

McGowen, William: Balteagh LY 9; 13, 32

McGown, Bernard: Aghagallon AM 21; 25

McGown, family: Ballintoy AM 24; 20

McGown, family: Ballywillin AM 16; 32

McGown, family: Carrickfergus AM 37; 179

McGown, family: Ramoan AM 24; 107

McGown, John: Ramoan AM 24; 117

McGown, Widow: Billy AM 16; 69

McGown, Widow: Kilroot AM 26; 77

McGrady, family: Camlin AM 21; 68

McGranaghan, Cornelious: Bovevagh LY 25; 32

McGranaghan, Edward: Bovevagh LY 25; 31

McGranaghan, John: Bovevagh LY 25; 13, 30–31, 45

McGranaghan, William: Magilligan LY 11; 135

McGrane, family: Culfeightrin AM 24; 71

McGrann, Hugh: Aghalee AM 21; 36

McGrath, Duncan: Culfeightrin AM 24; 59

McGrath, James: Hillsborough DN 12; 107

McGrath, John: Carrickfergus AM 37; 120

McGrath, John: Magheragall AM 21; 100

McGrath, Thomas: Ballymascanlan LH 40; 55

McGrath, Thomas: Newry DN 3; 98

McGratty, James: Drumachose LY 9; 85

McGraw, John: Killead AM 35; 38

McGredy, family: Desertlyn LY 31; 42

McGreer, Neill: Layd AM 13; 53

McGreevy, Rev. Dennis: Duneane AM 19; 111, 115, 117, 125

McGreevy, Rev. John: Raloo AM 32; 126

McGreggor, family: Raloo AM 32; 94

McGregor, Betty: Carrickfergus AM 37; 122

McGregor, family: Ramoan AM 24; 119

McGregor, Malcom: Carrickfergus AM 37; 193

McGregor, Margaret: Ahoghill AM 23; 50

McGregor, Rev.: Drummaul AM 19; 69, 82

McGregor, Rev.: Kilrea LY 27; 119

McGregor, Rev. James: Aghadowey LY 22; 22

McGregor, Robert: Tamlaght O'Crilly LY 18; 110

McGrier, Peter: Carrickfergus AM 37; 194

McGrigar, family: Ramoan AM 24; 107

McGrogan, James: Duneane AM 19; 121

McGrogan, James: Kirkinriola AM 23; 122

McGrogan, John: Dungiven LY 15; 91

McGrotty, Henry: Coleraine LY 33; 72

McGrotty, J.B.: Coleraine LY 33; 72

McGrotty, James: Balteagh LY 9; 18

McGrotty, James: Drumachose LY 9; 70, 124

McGrotty, John: Coleraine LY 33; 72

McGrotty, John: Killowen LY 33; 159

McGuckan, George [I]: Tamlaght TE 20; 115

McGuckan, George [II]: Tamlaght TE 20; 115

McGuckan, Hugh [I]: Tamlaght TE 20; 96

McGuckan, Hugh [II]: Tamlaght TE 20; 115

McGuckan, John: Ramoan AM 24; 125

McGuckan, Patt: Carrickfergus AM 37; 162

McGuckan, Widow: Tamlaght TE 20; 115

McGucken, George: Tamlaght TE 20; 92

McGucken, John: Tamlaght TE 20; 92

McGucken, Robert: Artrea LY 6; 34

McGucken, Terence: Tamlaght TE 20; 92

McGuckian, Peter: Carrickfergus AM 37; 86

McGuckin, family: Ballinderry AM 21; 55

McGuckin, H.: Misc. LY 31; 140

McGuckla, family: Finvoy AM 23; 76

McGugan, Archy: Culfeightrin AM 24; 83

McGuician, Frank: Kilcronaghan LY 31; 85

McGuician, Patrick: Kilcronaghan LY 31; 85

McGuigan, Andrew: Ballynascreen LY 31; 22

McGuigan, Daniel: Carrickfergus AM 37; 193

McGuigan, Daniel: Kilcronaghan LY 31; 85

McGuigan, family: Ballintoy AM 24; 20

McGuigan, Frank: Kilcronaghan LY 31; 85

McGuigan, Harry: Misc. TE 5; 147

McGuigan, James: Bovevagh LY 25; 29

McGuigan, James: Dungiven LY 15; 66

McGuigan, James: Hillsborough DN 12; 107

McGuigan, James: Kilcronaghan LY 31; 85

McGuigan, James: Misc. TE 5; 147

McGuigan, John: Kilcronaghan LY 31; 85

McGuigan, John: Tamlaght TE 20; 96

McGuigan, Michael: Tamlaght O'Crilly LY 18; 112

McGuigan, Owen: Misc. TE 5; 147

McGuigan, Pat: Misc. TE 5; 147

McGuigan, Patt (Jnr): Misc. TE 5; 147

McGuigan, Peter: Hillsborough DN 12; 106

McGuigan, William: Dungiven LY 15; 75

McGuigen, Patrick: Drumachose LY 9; 112

McGuigen, Patt: Errigal LY 27; 71

McGuigen, Patt: Magherafelt LY 6; 108–09

McGuiggan, Widow: Ballynascreen LY 31; 14, 21

McGuiggen, Henery: Maghera LY 18; 38, 40

McGuigin, James: Dungiven LY 15; 74, 88

McGuiness, John: Magilligan LY 11; 125

McGuinness, James: Banagher LY 30; 61

McGuinness, John: Garvaghy DN 12; 82

McGuinness, Mr: Clondermot LY 34; 42

McGuinness, Ross: Tamlaght O'Crilly LY 18; 94, 121

McGuire, chieftain: Inishmacsaint FH 14; 75

McGuire, family: Blaris DN 12; 30

McGuire, family: Maghera LY 18; 24, 48

McGuire, Hugh: Errigal LY 27; 60, 69

McGuire, J.: Enniskillen FH 4; 55

McGuire, Mr: Seapatrick DN 12; 126

McGuire, Patrick: Newry DN 3; 100
McGukian, Peter: Artrea LY 6; 28
McGunigle, Patrick: Dunboe LY 11; 76
McGurdy, John: Magilligan LY 11; 127
McGurk, Ann: Artrea LY 6; 38
McGurk, Bernard: Kilcronaghan LY 31; 78
McGurk, family: Blaris AM 8; 21
McGurk, J.: Blaris DN 12; 45
McGurk, James: Termoneeny LY 6; 133
McGurk, man named: Ballynascreen LY 31; 9
McGurk, Michael: Termoneeny LY 6; 133
McGurk, Patrick: Termoneeny LY 6; 133
McGurk, R.: Blaris DN 12; 49
McGurnahan, family: Blaris DN 12; 30
McGurren, Francis: Newtownards DN 7; 112
McGwilliens (see McWilliams): Dungiven LY 15;
  31
McGwye's Isle: Island Magee AM 10; 76
McHafferty, John: Carrickfergus AM 37; 148
McHaffey, family: Raloo AM 32; 108, 123
McHall, John: Kilwaughter AM 10; 116
McHarry, Miss: Killyleagh DN 17; 82
McHendry, George: Rasharkin AM 23; 139
McHenery, John: Derryaghy AM 8; 103, 108, 111
McHenry, Archibald: Ballywillin LY 33; 51
McHenry, Arthur: Aghagallon AM 21; 8
McHenry, Betty: Kilrea LY 27; 129
McHenry, family: Ballywillin AM 16; 32
McHenry, family: Ballywillin LY 33; 35, 49
McHenry, family: Culfeightrin AM 24; 59, 71
McHenry, family: Lambeg AM 8; 135
McHenry, Henry: Camlin AM 21; 75
McHenry, Henry: Maghera LY 18; 31, 52, 57, 70
McHenry, James: Maghera LY 18; 51
McHenry, James: Newry DN 3; 93, 95, 97, 100–01
McHenry, Jane: Ballywillin LY 33; 51
McHenry, Janes: Newry DN 3; 104
McHenry, John: Ballyaghran LY 33; 27
McHenry, John: Ballywillin LY 33; 51
McHenry, John: Derryaghy AM 8; 91, 107
McHenry, John: Drumbeg AM 8; 127
McHenry, John: Lambeg AM 8; 136
McHenry, Patrick: Coleraine LY 33; 72
McHenry, Paul: Magheragall AM 21; 98
McHenry, William: Dunaghy AM 13; 24
McHuey, Patrick: Desertoghill LY 27; 21
McHugh [or McLeigh], Rev. John: Clonduff DN 3;
  3
McHugh Island: Ardstraw TE 5; 2
McHugh, chieftain: Templepatrick AM 35; 127
McHugh, Cuhonagh: Killesher FH 14; 88
McHugh, family: Ardstraw TE 5; 11
McHugh, Francis: Killesher FH 14; 88
McHugh, Francis: Longfield TE 5; 130

McHugh, Gilly: Skirts of Urney and Ardstraw TE 5;
  138, 141
McHugh, Patrick: Killesher FH 14; 88
McHugh, Peter: Killesher FH 14; 88
McHugh, Rev. Arthur: Clonleigh DL 39; 13, 15
McHugh, Thorlaghmore: Killesher FH 14; 88
McHugh's castles: Ardstraw TE 5; 11
McIldoon, John: Tamlaght TE 20; 108
McIlea, Rev. Edward: Carrickfergus AM 37; 102
McIlgorran, John: Island Magee AM 10; 95
McIlhattin, Edward: Maghera LY 18; 81
McIlhattin, John: Drumtullagh AM 16; 101
McIlhattin, Patrick: Maghera LY 18; 81
McIlhatton, P.O.: Loughguile AM 13; 71
McIlhenny, Elizabeth: Mevagh DL 38; 60
McIlhenny, Mary: Carrickfergus AM 37; 130
McIlhenny, William: Mevagh DL 38; 60
McIlhinny, James: Raymoghy DL 39; 142
McIlhone, Michael (Jnr): Tamlaght TE 20; 131
McIlhone, Michael (Snr): Tamlaght TE 20; 131
McIlhone's hill: Templepatrick AM 35; 105, 141
McIlhose, John: Derrykeighan AM 16; 91
McIlhose, William: Derrykeighan AM 16; 91
McIlinch, family: Billy AM 16; 58, 68
McIllhargy, family: Dunluce AM 16; 117
McIllonan [or McIllvena], Mr: Holywood DN 7; 75
McIllreath, Capt.: Comber DN 7; 37, 39
McIllreavey, family: Magheramesk AM 21; 124
McIllvena [or McIllonan], Mr: Holywood DN 7; 75
McIllwain, Mr: Magheradrool DN 17; 104
McIlmoyle, John: Aghanloo LY 11; 20
McIlornan, Hugh: Ahoghill AM 23; 39
McIlrath, Hugh: Ahoghill AM 23; 40
McIlrath, John: Kilraghts AM 16; 136
McIlrath, John: Ramoan AM 24; 124
McIlrath, Patrick: Carrickfergus AM 37; 113
McIlrath, William: Killead AM 35; 48
McIlreavy, James: Ballymoney AM 16; 17
McIlreavy, James: Ballyrashane LY 22; 60
McIlree, Mary: Carrickfergus AM 37; 124
McIlrevy, man named: Glenavy AM 21; 82–83
McIlroy, Daniel: Dunluce AM 16; 120
McIlroy, Daniel: Kilraghts AM 16; 130, 134
McIlroy, Edward: Carrickfergus AM 37; 110
McIlroy, family: Faughanvale LY 36; 48
McIlroy, family: Lambeg AM 8; 135
McIlroy, family: Templepatrick AM 35; 118
McIlroy, George: Coleraine LY 33; 72
McIlroy, Jane: Ballynure AM 32; 72
McIlroy, John: Ahoghill AM 23; 35
McIlroy, John: Ballynure AM 32; 72
McIlroy, Margaret: Carrickfergus AM 37; 117
McIlroy, Mary: Carrickfergus AM 37; 117
McIlroy, Mary: Skerry AM 13; 114
McIlroy, Patrick: Kilraghts AM 16; 130, 134

McIlroy, Penelope: Carrickfergus AM 37; 117
McIlroy, Samuel: Ahoghill AM 23; 35
McIlroy, T.C.: Hillsborough DN 12; 95
McIlroy, T.C.: Tydavnet MN 40; 172
McIlroy, Thomas: Carrickfergus AM 37; 115
McIlroy, William: Carrickfergus AM 37; 165
McIlvare, Edward: Dungiven LY 15; 49
McIlvare, James: Desertoghill LY 27; 24
McIlvena, Eliza: Carrickfergus AM 37; 126
McIlvena, Mary: Carrickfergus AM 37; 123
McIlvenan, Philip: Tamlaght TE 20; 81, 110
McIlvenna, family: Ardclinis AM 13; 8
McIlvennon, Charles: Carrickfergus AM 37; 110
McIlvennon, family: Kilwaughter AM 10; 115
McIlvennon, John: Carrickfergus AM 37; 111
McIlvennon, Margaret: Carrickfergus AM 37; 109
McIlvenny, William: Drummaul AM 19; 89
McIlvenon, James: Kilwaughter AM 10; 122
McIlvenon, Paddy: Ahoghill AM 23; 34
McIlvenon, William: Kilwaughter AM 10; 122
McIlvernock, Angus: Derrykeighan AM 16; 88, 94
McIlvin, Gilbert: Kilroot AM 26; 78
McIlwain, family: Templepatrick AM 35; 118
McIlwain, Francis: Coleraine LY 33; 70, 140
McIlwain, Thomas: Island Magee AM 10; 100
McIlwaine, family: Ballynure AM 32; 56
McIlwaine, James: Carrickfergus AM 37; 39, 149
McIlwaine, Thomas: Island Magee AM 10; 64
McIlwee, Charles: Termoneeny LY 6; 133
McIlwee, James: Termoneeny LY 6; 133
McIlwee, John: Termoneeny LY 6; 133
McIlwhinney, Patrick: Maghera LY 18; 81
McIlwrath, John: Tamlaght O'Crilly LY 18; 103, 139, 143
McInaul, family: Dunluce AM 16; 117
McIninch, family: Billy AM 16; 58, 68
McIninch, family: Culfeightrin AM 24; 59
McIninch, John: Culfeightrin AM 24; 68
McInstry, John: Ballinderry AM 21; 47
McIntire, James: Tamlaght TE 20; 76
McIntire, Marget: Tamlaght TE 20; 105
McIntire, Mr (Belfast): Aughnamullen MN 40; 76
McIntire, William: Tamlaght TE 20; 74, 103
McIntosh, family: Desertoghill LY 27; 5, 30
McIntosh, James: Desertoghill LY 27; 16
McIntosh, James [I]: Desertoghill LY 27; 21
McIntosh, James [II]: Desertoghill LY 27; 23
McIntosh, Mr (Cootehill): Aughnamullen MN 40; 76
McIntosh, William [I]: Desertoghill LY 27; 20
McIntosh, William [II]: Desertoghill LY 27; 20
McInty, William: Tamlaght TE 20; 116
McIntyre, Anthony: Hillsborough DN 12; 99, 107
McIntyre, Arthur: Ahoghill AM 23; 40
McIntyre, Arthur: Maghera LY 18; 81

McIntyre, Daniel: Ramoan AM 24; 115–16, 123
McIntyre, David: Ballyaghran LY 33; 27
McIntyre, Ellen: Duneane AM 19; 123
McIntyre, Esther: Ballyaghran LY 33; 27
McIntyre, family: Culfeightrin AM 24; 46, 59
McIntyre, family: Ramoan AM 24; 107
McIntyre, Hugh: Duneane AM 19; 115, 121
McIntyre, Hugh: Termoneeny LY 6; 130
McIntyre, Hugh [I]: Ballyaghran LY 33; 27
McIntyre, Hugh [II]: Ballyaghran LY 33; 27
McIntyre, James (Jnr): Tamlaght O'Crilly LY 18; 90, 111
McIntyre, James: Ballyaghran LY 33; 27
McIntyre, John: Ahoghill AM 23; 39
McIntyre, John: Ballyaghran LY 33; 27
McIntyre, John: Duneane AM 19; 123
McIntyre, John [I]: Coleraine LY 33; 73
McIntyre, John [II]: Coleraine LY 33; 146
McIntyre, John [III]: Coleraine LY 33; 146
McIntyre, Margaret: Duneane AM 19; 123
McIntyre, Michael: Carrickfergus AM 37; 131
McIntyre, Miss: Ballymoney AM 16; 17
McIntyre, Nicholas: Duneane AM 19; 111
McIntyre, Peter: Tamlaght TE 20; 118
McIntyre, Rev. Hugh: Killead AM 35; 20, 47
McIntyre, Samuel: Dunboe LY 11; 56, 72
McIntyre, William: Ahoghill AM 23; 39
McIntyre, William: Ballymoney AM 16; 15–17
McIntyre, William: Ballyscullion LY 6; 61–62
McIrath, Rev.: Carlingford LH 40; 60
McIrlane, Pat: Dunaghy AM 13; 17
McItegart, Rev. W.: Clondermot LY 34; 59–60
McIver (Balteagh): see also McKeever
McIver, Henery: Artrea LY 6; 34
McIver, Hugh: Balteagh LY 9; 33
McIver, John: Artrea LY 6; 34, 39
McIver, John: Tamlaght TE 20; 78
McIver, Phillip: Balteagh LY 9; 29
McIvor, John: Down DN 17; 59
McIvor, Mr: Enniskillen FH 4; 84
McIvor, Mrs: Enniskillen FH 4; 84
McKague, Charles: Desertoghill LY 27; 21
McKague, James: Desertoghill LY 27; 21
McKague, Neal: Culfeightrin AM 24; 50–51
McKaig, Archy: Magilligan LY 11; 131
McKane, Edward: Maghera LY 18; 58
McKane, Frank: Kilcronaghan LY 31; 85
McKane, James: Ballywillin LY 33; 51
McKane, Martha (Jnr): Duneane AM 19; 123
McKane, Martha (Snr): Duneane AM 19; 123
McKane, William: Duneane AM 19; 123
McKannery graveyard: Ballyrashane LY 22; 58
McKannery, family: Ballyrashane LY 22; 57–58
McKannery, Gorry: Ballyrashane LY 22; 57–58
McKannery, James: Ballyrashane LY 22; 58

McKannery, John: Errigal LY 27; 44, 72
McKannery, Matty: Errigal LY 27; 72
McKannon, family: Ramoan AM 24; 107
McKavanagh, Bridget: Carrickfergus AM 37; 110
McKaven, family: Ballinderry AM 21; 55
McKavney, family: Ballinderry AM 21; 55
McKay, Denis: Carrickfergus AM 37; 110
McKay, family: Agivey LY 22; 41–42
McKay, family: Ballintoy AM 24; 16, 20
McKay, family: Billy AM 16; 58, 68
McKay, family: Culfeightrin AM 24; 59
McKay, family: Derrykeighan AM 16; 89
McKay, family: Dromara DN 12; 67
McKay, Hamilton: Blaris AM 8; 62
McKay, Hamilton: Blaris DN 12; 45
McKay, John: Agivey LY 22; 39
McKay, John [I]: Carrickfergus AM 37; 126
McKay, John [II]: Carrickfergus AM 37; 194
McKay, Mary: Carrickfergus AM 37; 114, 117, 126
McKay, Miss: Blaris DN 12; 49
McKay, Rev. J.: Drumballyroney DN 3; 15
McKay, Robert: Carrickfergus AM 37; 109
McKay, Roseanna: Raymoghy DL 39; 140
McKay, Thomas: Ballymoney AM 16; 26
McKeag, family: Macosquin LY 22; 84, 119
McKeag, James: Macosquin LY 22; 87, 110, 119
McKeag, James: Ramoan AM 24; 109, 111
McKeag, John: Macosquin LY 22; 120
McKeagh, Hugh: Coleraine LY 33; 105
McKeagh, Mr: Magilligan LY 11; 133
McKeagney, Pat: Misc. TE 5; 147
McKean, family: Dunluce AM 16; 117
McKeastown (see McKeestown): Ahoghill AM 23; 33
McKeaver, family: Killagan AM 23; 84
McKeavney, John: Aghagallon AM 21; 10
McKeavney, Marcus: Aghagallon AM 21; 9, 11
McKee, A.: Comber DN 7; 40
McKee, Alexander (Jnr): Coleraine LY 33; 145
McKee, Alexander (Snr): Coleraine LY 33; 145
McKee, Alexander: Ahoghill AM 23; 38
McKee, Alexander: Kilrea LY 27; 129
McKee, Alexander: Magherafelt LY 6; 108
McKee, Alexander: Muckamore AM 35; 81
McKee, Andrew: Muckamore AM 35; 81
McKee, Anne: Coleraine LY 33; 145
McKee, Archy: Ballyscullion AM 19; 12
McKee, Betty: Muckamore AM 35; 81
McKee, Elizabeth: Carnmoney AM 2; 62
McKee, family: Ahoghill AM 23; 25
McKee, family: Ballywillin AM 16; 32
McKee, family: Maghera LY 18; 24, 48
McKee, family: Tamlaght O'Crilly LY 18; 93
McKee, Francis: Lissan LY 31; 101

McKee, George [I]: Hillsborough DN 12; 106
McKee, George [II]: Hillsborough DN 12; 106
McKee, George [III]: Hillsborough DN 12; 106
McKee, Gilbert: Ahoghill AM 23; 49
McKee, Gilbert: Ballyaghran LY 33; 16
McKee, H.G.: Kilcronaghan LY 31; 84
McKee, Hugh: Ballyscullion AM 19; 12
McKee, James: Coleraine LY 33; 145
McKee, James: Lissan LY 31; 100
McKee, James: Tamlaght TE 20; 129
McKee, James: Tullynakill DN 7; 123
McKee, Jane: Coleraine LY 33; 145
McKee, John (Jnr): Kilrea LY 27; 129
McKee, John (Snr): Kilrea LY 27; 129
McKee, John: Ballyscullion AM 19; 12
McKee, John: Coleraine LY 33; 72
McKee, John: Lissan LY 31; 101
McKee, John [I]: Desertoghill LY 27; 25
McKee, John [II]: Desertoghill LY 27; 27
McKee, Margaret: Coleraine LY 33; 67, 134
McKee, Margaret Jane: Coleraine LY 33; 145
McKee, Mary: Carrickfergus AM 37; 131
McKee, Mary: Kilrea LY 27; 129
McKee, Mr: Carrickfergus AM 37; 161
McKee, Mrs: Blaris DN 12; 50
McKee, Mrs John: Coleraine LY 33; 72
McKee, Patt: Ballyscullion AM 19; 12
McKee, Peter: Hillsborough DN 12; 106
McKee, R.: Newtownards DN 7; 112
McKee, Rachael: Kilrea LY 27; 129
McKee, Rev. David: Annaclone DN 12; 17
McKee, Rev. Joseph: Killead AM 35; 20, 38, 46, 52
McKee, Reynold: Ballyscullion AM 19; 12
McKee, Robert: Connor AM 19; 26
McKee, Robert: Rasharkin AM 23; 134
McKee, Robert: Skerry AM 13; 120
McKee, Thomas: Desertoghill LY 27; 25
McKee, Thomas: Kilrea LY 27; 129
McKee, William: Blaris DN 12; 46
McKee, William: Kilcronaghan LY 31; 84
McKee, William: Magherafelt LY 6; 108
McKee, William: Templecorran AM 26; 121
McKee, William [I]: Coleraine LY 33; 145
McKee, William [I]: Hillsborough DN 12; 105
McKee, William [II]: Coleraine LY 33; 145
McKee, William [II]: Hillsborough DN 12; 105
McKeefry, Michael: Maghera LY 18; 80
McKeefry, Patrick: Maghera LY 18; 80
McKeegy, John: Faughanvale LY 36; 5, 30
McKeemins, James: Aghadowey LY 22; 36
McKeen, family: Ballyclug AM 23; 60
McKeen, family: Carrickfergus AM 37; 179
McKeen, James: Ahoghill AM 23; 37
McKeen, James: Island Magee AM 10; 90
McKeen, Jane: Ahoghill AM 23; 37

McKeen, John: Carrickfergus AM 37; 158

McKeen, Peter: Island Magee AM 10; 90

McKeen, Robert: Carrickfergus AM 37; 182

McKeen, Thomas: Ahoghill AM 23; 37

McKeen, Thomas: Ballyclug AM 23; 65

McKeen, Thomas: Island Magee AM 10; 102

McKeen, William: Carrickfergus AM 37; 182

McKeeran, Coghran: Bovevagh LY 25; 57

McKeesack, Neill: Drumachose LY 9; 112

McKeesack, William: Drumachose LY 9; 112

McKeestown cave: Ahoghill AM 23; 33, 36

McKeever, Alexander: Balteagh LY 9; 17–18, 27, 33, 38–39

McKeever, Archy: Kilrea LY 27; 129

McKeever, Catherine: Kilcronaghan LY 31; 84

McKeever, Catherine: Magilligan LY 11; 129

McKeever, D.: Faughanvale LY 36; 16

McKeever, Daniel: Carrickfergus AM 37; 113

McKeever, Daniel: Kilcronaghan LY 31; 85

McKeever, Eliza: Kilcronaghan LY 31; 84

McKeever, family: Culfeightrin AM 24; 59

McKeever, family: Maghera LY 18; 74

McKeever, Frank: Kilcronaghan LY 31; 85

McKeever, Henery: Balteagh LY 9; 27

McKeever, Jane: Kilrea LY 27; 129

McKeever, John: Kilcronaghan LY 31; 84

McKeever, man named: Maghera LY 18; 74

McKeever, Margaret: Desertlyn LY 31; 49

McKeever, Margaret: Kilcronaghan LY 31; 84

McKeever, Martha Anne: Kilrea LY 27; 129

McKeever, Mary: Kilrea LY 27; 129

McKeever, Mary Ann: Kilcronaghan LY 31; 84

McKeever, Michael [I]: Kilcronaghan LY 31; 84

McKeever, Michael [II]: Kilcronaghan LY 31; 85

McKeever, Patrick: Drumachose LY 9; 128

McKeever, Patrick: Kilrea LY 27; 129

McKeever, William: Carrickfergus AM 37; 108

McKeever, William: Skerry AM 13; 120

McKeever's fort: Maghera LY 18; 62

McKeig, Alexander: Billy AM 16; 72

McKeighan, family: Shilvodan AM 19; 135–136

McKeigney, family: Maghera LY 18; 24, 48

McKeigney, Patrick: Maghera LY 18; 81

McKeirnan, family: Lissan LY 31; 91, 106

McKeiver, John: Billy AM 16; 75

McKellan, James: Drummaul AM 19; 92

McKelvey, family: Carnmoney AM 2; 102

McKelvey, Margaret: Mallusk AM 2; 114

McKelvy, John: Dunaghy AM 13; 21

McKelvy, Neill: Ballynascreen LY 31; 8

McKenby, family: Aghagallon AM 21; 9

McKendry, family: Dunluce AM 16; 117

McKendry, Hugh: Skerry AM 13; 114

McKendry, James: Ahoghill AM 23; 38

McKendry, Peggy-Ann: Ahoghill AM 23; 38

McKendry, William: Ahoghill AM 23; 34

McKenla, Alexander: Dunluce AM 16; 120

McKenna, Andrew: Carrickfergus AM 37; 131

McKenna, Andrew: Maghera LY 18; 46

McKenna, Archy: Loughguile AM 13; 71, 74

McKenna, Bartholemew: Ballynascreen LY 31; 14, 21

McKenna, Bernard: Ahoghill AM 23; 45, 48

McKenna, Brice: Magheragall AM 21; 101, 103

McKenna, Bridget: Carrickfergus AM 37; 120

McKenna, Bridget: Maghera LY 18; 78

McKenna, Charles (Jnr): Maghera LY 18; 36

McKenna, Charles (Snr): Maghera LY 18; 8, 36, 68

McKenna, Charles: Ballynascreen LY 31; 31

McKenna, Charles: Donagh MN 40; 102

McKenna, Cornelius: Killelagh LY 27; 96

McKenna, D.R.: Desertoghill LY 27; 32

McKenna, D.R.: Killelagh LY 27; 102

McKenna, D.R.: Maghera LY 18; 52, 55

McKenna, Daniel: Maghera LY 18; 8, 68

McKenna, Denis: Ballynascreen LY 31; 26

McKenna, Denis: Dungiven LY 15; 34

McKenna, Denis: Maghera LY 18; 62

McKenna, Dr (Moyheelan): Misc. LY 31; 118

McKenna, Ellen: Maghera LY 18; 74

McKenna, family: Ballynascreen LY 31; 12

McKenna, family: Killelagh LY 27; 99

McKenna, family: Maghera LY 18; 14, 24, 48, 74

McKenna, family: Misc. LY 31; 122

McKenna, family: Shilvodan AM 19; 136

McKenna, Francis: Carrickfergus AM 37; 120

McKenna, Henery: Maghera LY 18; 39, 47

McKenna, Hugh: Maghera LY 18; 37, 39, 45, 74

McKenna, James (Jnr): Newry DN 3; 104

McKenna, James: Newry DN 3; 100, 104

McKenna, James: Shilvodan AM 19; 137

McKenna, James [I]: Maghera LY 18; 8, 68

McKenna, James [II]: Maghera LY 18; 37

McKenna, James [III]: Maghera LY 18; 45

McKenna, James [IV]: Maghera LY 18; 78

McKenna, James [V]: Maghera LY 18; 81

McKenna, John (Jnr): Maghera LY 18; 81

McKenna, John (Snr): Maghera LY 18; 81

McKenna, John: Carrickfergus AM 37; 124

McKenna, John: Desertoghill LY 27; 34

McKenna, John: Errigal Truagh MN 40; 122

McKenna, John: Shilvodan AM 19; 137

McKenna, John [I]: Maghera LY 18; 8, 68

McKenna, John [II]: Maghera LY 18; 39, 42

McKenna, John [III]: Maghera LY 18; 78

McKenna, John [IV]: Maghera LY 18; 78

McKenna, John [V]: Maghera LY 18; 80

McKenna, Lawrence: Ballyscullion AM 19; 10

McKenna, Margaret: Lissan LY 31; 108

McKenna, Margaret: Maghera LY 18; 78

McKenna, Michael: Kilcronaghan LY 31; 78
McKenna, Michael [I]: Maghera LY 18; 29, 31, 33, 69, 74
McKenna, Michael [II]: Maghera LY 18; 65
McKenna, Miss: Down DN 17; 59
McKenna, Nancy: Maghera LY 18; 78
McKenna, Patrick: Shilvodan AM 19; 137
McKenna, Patrick [I]: Maghera LY 18; 8, 68
McKenna, Patrick [II]: Maghera LY 18; 39, 46, 62
McKenna, Paul: Maghera LY 18; 36
McKenna, Paul: Shilvodan AM 19; 138
McKenna, Peter: Carrickfergus AM 37; 127
McKenna, Peter: Maghera LY 18; 78
McKenna, Rev.: Maghera LY 18; 68
McKenna, Rev. John: Killelagh LY 27; 102
McKenna, Rev. John: Maghera LY 18; 17, 19, 34, 68–69, 73
McKenna, Rev. John: Termoneeny LY 6; 126
McKenna, Rev. Matthew: Maghera LY 18; 69
McKenna, Rev. Patrick: Misc. LY 31; 136–137
McKenna, Thomas: Kilcronaghan LY 31; 78
McKenna, Thomas: Newry DN 3; 100, 104
McKenna, Thomas [I]: Maghera LY 18; 8, 68
McKenna, Thomas [II]: Maghera LY 18; 59
McKenna, woman named: Shilvodan AM 19; 135
McKennen, family: Ballywillin AM 16; 32
McKenney, family: Ballintoy AM 24; 16, 20
McKenney, Miss: Carnmoney AM 2; 99
McKenney, T.M.: Carnmoney AM 2; 49, 93
McKenny, Daniel (Jnr): Ahoghill AM 23; 38
McKenny, Daniel (Snr): Ahoghill AM 23; 37
McKenny, Francis: Loughinisland DN 17; 96
McKenny, James: Billy AM 16; 61
McKenny, James: Drumtullagh AM 16; 101
McKenny, John: Ahoghill AM 23; 38
McKenny, John: Donaghmore DL 39; 41
McKenny, Mr: Blaris DN 12; 47
McKenny, Rev. John: Lissan LY 31; 104
McKenty, family: Templecorran AM 26; 119
McKenzie, Hill: Billy AM 16; 60
McKenzie, Kenneth: Hillsborough DN 12; 105
McKenzie, Mr: Lough Swilly DL 38; 104, 108, 113, 122–124, 126
McKenzie, William: Billy AM 16; 60
McKenzie's bank: Lough Swilly DL 38; 104
McKeogue, George: Killead AM 35; 22, 50
McKeon, Catherine: Artrea LY 6; 38
McKeon, Charles: Artrea LY 6; 38
McKeon, family: Billy AM 16; 71
McKeon, Hugh: Ballynascreen LY 31; 26
McKeon, Joseph: Tamlaght O'Crilly LY 18; 107
McKeon, Murtagh: Artrea LY 6; 38
McKeon, Murtagh: Magherafelt LY 6; 112
McKeon, William: Tamlaght O'Crilly LY 18; 122
McKeown, Ann: Tamlaght TE 20; 86

McKeown, chieftain: Dungiven LY 15; 32
McKeown, chieftain: Dunluce AM 16; 114
McKeown, Culbert: Culfeightrin AM 24; 54
McKeown, Daniel: Magheragall AM 21; 107–108
McKeown, Edward: Hillsborough DN 12; 107
McKeown, family: Ballintoy AM 24; 20
McKeown, family: Ballywillin AM 16; 33
McKeown, family: Blaris AM 8; 22, 22
McKeown, family: Culfeightrin AM 24; 68
McKeown, family: Maghera LY 18; 13
McKeown, family: Misc. LY 36; 109
McKeown, family: Shilvodan AM 19; 136
McKeown, Hugh: Kilbride AM 29; 151
McKeown, James: Garvaghy DN 12; 83–84
McKeown, James: Kilmood DN 7; 96
McKeown, James: Macosquin LY 22; 91, 93
McKeown, James: Maghera LY 18; 61
McKeown, Jane: Carnmoney AM 2; 88
McKeown, John: Billy AM 16; 61
McKeown, John: Hillsborough DN 12; 107
McKeown, John: Maghera LY 18; 56
McKeown, Neal: Ballymoney AM 16; 15
McKeown, Robert: Hillsborough DN 12; 107
McKeown, T.: Blaris DN 12; 46, 49
McKernan, John: Lissan LY 31; 109
McKert, Daniel: Templecorran AM 26; 115
McKevell, Robert: Carrickfergus AM 37; 193
McKey, Alexander: Ballywillin LY 33; 41, 45–46
McKey, John: Newry DN 3; 99
McKey, Rev.: Kilbroney DN 3; 34
McKibben, family: Drumbeg AM 8; 123
McKibben, Mary: Carrickfergus AM 37; 131
McKibben, Robert: Blaris DN 12; 51
McKibbin, family: Blaris AM 8; 21
McKibbin, Mr: Annaclone DN 12; 14
McKibbin, Mrs: Hillsborough DN 12; 105
McKibbin, Shaw: Hillsborough DN 12; 107
McKillan, James: Drummaul AM 19; 92
McKillen, John: Carrickfergus AM 37; 108
McKillip, Alexander: Coleraine LY 33; 72
McKillip, Bridget: Loughguile AM 13; 74
McKillip, family: Dunluce AM 16; 117
McKillip, family: Ramoan AM 24; 107
McKillip, John: Dunaghy AM 13; 24
McKillop, Andrew: Ardclinis AM 13; 9
McKillop, Betty: Carrickfergus AM 37; 114
McKillop, Eliza: Carrickfergus AM 37; 110
McKillop, family: Layd AM 13; 49
McKillop, Jane: Ardclinis AM 13; 9
McKillop, Mary: Carrickfergus AM 37; 114
McKillop, Patrick: Carrickfergus AM 37; 131
McKinlass, Elizabeth: Ballyaghran LY 33; 27
McKinlass, Samuel: Ballyaghran LY 33; 27
McKinlay, Daniel: Culfeightrin AM 24; 73, 76, 79
McKinlay, Duncan: Culfeightrin AM 24; 73

McKinlay, family: Ballintoy AM 24; 20
McKinlay, family: Billy AM 16; 68
McKinlay, family: Derrykeighan AM 16; 89
McKinlay, George: Ballymoney AM 16; 26
McKinlay, John: Culfeightrin AM 24; 72
McKinlay, John: Derrykeighan AM 16; 95
McKinlay, Mrs: Coleraine LY 33; 72
McKinley, Archy: Culfeightrin AM 24; 55
McKinley, David: Enniskillen FH 4; 59
McKinley, family: Billy AM 16; 58, 68
McKinley, family: Culfeightrin AM 24; 59
McKinley, family: Ramoan AM 24; 107
McKinley, Hannah: Ballymoney AM 16; 17
McKinley, Hugh: Maghera LY 18; 81
McKinley, Philip: Carrickfergus AM 37; 151
McKinley, Roger: Carrickfergus AM 37; 115
McKinnen, Robert: Clonleigh DL 39; 9
McKinney, family: Carnmoney AM 2; 102
McKinney, James: Ahoghill AM 23; 38
McKinney, James: Derrykeighan AM 16; 92
McKinney, John: Carrickfergus AM 37; 113
McKinney, John: Kilrea LY 27; 119–120
McKinney, Samuel: Ballymoney AM 16; 27
McKinney, William: Carrickfergus AM 37; 112
McKinnon, Brice: Blaris AM 8; 75
McKinny, family: Dromara DN 12; 67
McKinsey, Rev. Joseph: Drumbeg AM 8; 124,
    130–131
McKinstrey, family: Magheragall AM 21; 99
McKinstry, David: Templecorran AM 26; 124, 127
McKinstry, family: Templecorran AM 26; 117, 119
McKinstry, Henry: Duneane AM 19; 119
McKinstry, James: Annaclone DN 12; 19
McKinstry, John: Aghalee AM 21; 36
McKinstry, Samuel: Island Magee AM 10; 99
McKinstry, Samuel: Templecorran AM 26; 132
McKinstry, William: Carrickfergus AM 37; 113
McKinty, family: Derryaghy AM 8; 103
McKinty, family: Templecorran AM 26; 117
McKintyre, family: Ballintoy AM 24; 20
McKinzie, family: Ballintoy AM 24; 20
McKirgan, family: Ballywillin AM 16; 32
McKissack, James: Drumachose LY 9; 104
McKissack, Robert: Drumachose LY 9; 104
McKissack, William: Drumachose LY 9; 129
McKissock, John: Ballymoney AM 16; 17
McKissock, Mary: Carrickfergus AM 37; 129
McKitrick, James: Newry DN 3; 99
McKittrick, Miss: Coleraine LY 33; 72
McKittrick, Mr: Holywood DN 7; 75
McKittrick, Mrs: Newry DN 3; 103
McKittrick, R.O.: Holywood DN 7; 81
McKivitt, Mr: Carlingford LH 40; 59
McKnight, Robert: Aghalee AM 21; 36
McKook, Rebecca: Desertoghill LY 27; 20

McKowen (see also McKeown)
McKowen, Bernard: Ballyscullion AM 19; 13
McKowen, Catherine: Ballyscullion AM 19; 13
McKowen, Charles: Cranfield AM 19; 32
McKowen, David: Maghera LY 18; 53
McKowen, family: Lambeg AM 8; 135
McKowen, Felix: Drummaul AM 19; 90
McKowen, Felix [I]: Duneane AM 19; 124
McKowen, Felix [II]: Duneane AM 19; 124
McKowen, Henry: Maghera LY 18; 53
McKowen, Hugh: Duneane AM 19; 123
McKowen, James: Ahoghill AM 23; 35
McKowen, James [I]: Maghera LY 18; 53
McKowen, James [II]: Maghera LY 18; 65, 73
McKowen, John: Duneane AM 19; 117
McKowen, John: Maghera LY 18; 28, 53, 61
McKowen, Joseph: Maghera LY 18; 53
McKowen, Lawrence: Ballyscullion AM 19; 10
McKowen, Margaret: Carrickfergus AM 37; 120
McKowen, Robert (Junior): Maghera LY 18; 53
McKowen, Robert (Snr): Maghera LY 18; 53
McKowen, Robert: Maghera LY 18; 53–54
McKowen, Rose: Ballyscullion AM 19; 13
McKowen, Samuel: Maghera LY 18; 53
McKowen, William [I]: Maghera LY 18; 53
McKowen, William [II]: Maghera LY 18; 53
McKown, Catherine: Ballyscullion AM 19; 13
McKown, family: Dunluce AM 16; 117
McLade, family: Ramoan AM 24; 118
McLade, Patrick: Banagher LY 30; 37
McLade, woman named: Ramoan AM 24; 118
McLaghlin, Thomas: Kilcoo DN 3; 45
McLain, family: Armoy AM 24; 6
McLarkey, Rev. Daniel: Kilmacteige SO 40;
    185–186, 188, 191–192, 196
McLarnan, John: Drumachose LY 9; 104
McLarnan, Thomas: Maghera LY 18; 81
McLary, Patrick: Tamlaght O'Crilly LY 18; 137
McLaughlin, Alexander: Ballintoy AM 24; 23
McLaughlin, Alexander: Carrickfergus AM 37; 114
McLaughlin, Alixander: Macosquin LY 22; 111
McLaughlin, Ann: Tamlaght Finlagan LY 25; 119
McLaughlin, Archy: Ballintoy AM 24; 23
McLaughlin, Bernard: Bovevagh LY 25; 60
McLaughlin, Bernard: Maghera LY 18; 80
McLaughlin, Bernard: Tamlaght Finlagan LY 25;
    110
McLaughlin, Bishop: Killelagh LY 27; 102
McLaughlin, Bishop: Misc. LY 36; 114
McLaughlin, Catherine [I]: Magilligan LY 11; 94
McLaughlin, Catherine [II]: Magilligan LY 11; 94
McLaughlin, Cathrine: Drumachose LY 9; 134
McLaughlin, Cathrine: Tamlaght Finlagan LY 25;
    119
McLaughlin, Charles [I]: Coleraine LY 33; 146

McLaughlin, Charles [II]: Coleraine LY 33; 146
McLaughlin, Daniel: Drumachose LY 9; 110
McLaughlin, Edward: Dunboe LY 11; 70, 73
McLaughlin, Edward: Tamlaght Finlagan LY 25; 118
McLaughlin, family: Culfeightrin AM 24; 71
McLaughlin, family: Dunluce AM 16; 117
McLaughlin, family: Kilwaughter AM 10; 115
McLaughlin, family: Magilligan LY 11, 107, 130
McLaughlin, family: Ramoan AM 24; 107
McLaughlin, family: Tamlaght O'Crilly LY 18; 93
McLaughlin, Francis: Clonduff DN 3; 3
McLaughlin, Frederick: Balteagh LY 9; 41
McLaughlin, George: Coleraine LY 33; 133
McLaughlin, George: Dunboe LY 11; 81
McLaughlin, Gregor: Templepatrick AM 35; 153
McLaughlin, Henry: Coleraine LY 33; 146
McLaughlin, Henry: Magilligan LY 11; 109
McLaughlin, Hester: Coleraine LY 33; 146
McLaughlin, Isabella [I]: Carrickfergus AM 37; 117–118
McLaughlin, Isabella [II]: Carrickfergus AM 37; 131
McLaughlin, James: Aghanloo LY 11; 14, 25
McLaughlin, James: Ahoghill AM 23; 21
McLaughlin, James: Carrickfergus AM 37; 194
McLaughlin, James: Drumachose LY 9; 133–134
McLaughlin, James: Dunboe LY 11; 76
McLaughlin, James: Dungiven LY 15; 75, 86
McLaughlin, James: Macosquin LY 22; 113
McLaughlin, James: Magilligan LY 11; 128
McLaughlin, Jane: Aghanloo LY 11; 39
McLaughlin, John: Aghanloo LY 11; 39
McLaughlin, John: Ballyscullion LY 6; 57
McLaughlin, John: Blaris DN 12; 46, 50
McLaughlin, John: Bovevagh LY 25; 8, 52–53
McLaughlin, John: Clonduff DN 3; 3
McLaughlin, John: Cumber LY 28; 72–73, 76
McLaughlin, John: Killowen LY 33; 172
McLaughlin, John: Maghera LY 18; 80
McLaughlin, John: Magilligan LY 11; 91, 123, 129
McLaughlin, John: Tamlaght Finlagan LY 25; 119
McLaughlin, John [I]: Ballintoy AM 24; 23–24
McLaughlin, John [I]: Dunboe LY 11; 81
McLaughlin, John [II]: Ballintoy AM 24; 27
McLaughlin, John [II]: Dunboe LY 11; 81
McLaughlin, John [III]: Ballintoy AM 24; 28
McLaughlin, man named: Misc. LY 36; 110
McLaughlin, Margret Jane: Tamlaght Finlagan LY 25; 120
McLaughlin, Mark: Magilligan LY 11; 94
McLaughlin, Martha: Tamlaght Finlagan LY 25; 119
McLaughlin, Mary: Ballynascreen LY 31; 14, 21
McLaughlin, Mary: Cumber LY 28; 76
McLaughlin, Mary: Dunboe LY 11; 81

McLaughlin, Maryann: Drumachose LY 9; 133
McLaughlin, Michael: Dungiven LY 15; 75
McLaughlin, Neal: Billy AM 16; 67
McLaughlin, Ned: Derrykeighan AM 16; 93
McLaughlin, Neil: Maghera LY 18; 10
McLaughlin, Patrick: Ahoghill AM 23; 43
McLaughlin, Patrick: Coleraine LY 33; 133
McLaughlin, Patrick: Maghera LY 18; 80
McLaughlin, Patrick: Magilligan LY 11; 125
McLaughlin, Patt: Ballintoy AM 24; 27
McLaughlin, Patt: Drumachose LY 9; 133
McLaughlin, Patt: Dungiven LY 15; 86
McLaughlin, Peter: Tamlaght TE 20; 77, 128
McLaughlin, Rev. Daniel: Misc. LY 31; 138
McLaughlin, Rev. Henry: Ballymoney AM 16; 15
McLaughlin, Rev. John: Misc. LY 31; 127, 137
McLaughlin, Richard: Aghadowey LY 22; 11
McLaughlin, Richard: Dungiven LY 15; 34
McLaughlin, Richard: Macosquin LY 22; 99–100, 110, 122–23
McLaughlin, Richard: Misc. LY 36; 111
McLaughlin, Robert: Ahoghill AM 23; 47
McLaughlin, Robert: Ballintoy AM 24; 27
McLaughlin, Robert: Coleraine LY 33; 104–06
McLaughlin, Robert: Tamlaght Finlagan LY 25; 119
McLaughlin, Samuel: Aghanloo LY 11; 10
McLaughlin, Thomas: Clonduff DN 3; 4
McLaughlin, Thomas: Coleraine LY 33; 146
McLaughlin, Thomas: Faughanvale LY 36; 34
McLaughlin, Thomas: Killowen LY 33; 172
McLaughlin, Thomas: Newry DN 3; 99, 104
McLaughlin, William: Aghanloo LY 11; 28
McLaughlin, William: Banagher LY 30; 75
McLaughlin, William: Blaris DN 12; 46, 50
McLaughlin, William: Coleraine LY 33; 146
McLaughlin, William: Drumachose LY 9; 133
McLaughlin, William: Dunboe LY 11; 81
McLaughlin, William: Killowen LY 33; 171
McLaughlin, William: Tamlaght Finlagan LY 25; 65, 116
McLaughlin, Zekiel: Ballintoy AM 24; 27
McLauglin, Hugo: Magilligan LY 11; 89
McLaw, James: Ahoghill AM 23; 38
McLead, Owen: Maghera LY 18; 19
McLean and Partners Division td: Faughanvale LY 36; 53, 60, 69, 77, 89, 96
McLean, Ellen: Carrickfergus AM 37; 129
McLean, Hercules: Coleraine LY 33; 73
McLean, Hercules: Killowen LY 33; 159
McLean, Widow: Ballymoney AM 16; 17
McLeavy, John: Hillsborough DN 12; 106
McLeery, family: Culfeightrin AM 24; 59
McLeery, George: Desertlyn LY 31; 50
McLeese, Daniel: Agivey LY 22; 43
McLeese, family: Ballintoy AM 24; 18

McLeigh [or McHugh], Rev. John: Clonduff DN 3; 3

McLeland, Robert: Misc. DL 39; 190

McLellan, Mrs (Knappagh): Ballybay MN 40; 81

McLenaghan, John: Bovevagh LY 25; 27

McLenden, Peter: Carrickfergus AM 37; 193

McLernon, Andrew: Billy AM 16; 62, 64

McLernon, Daniel: Blaris DN 12; 40

McLernon, family: Ballinderry AM 21; 53

McLernon, family: Tullyrusk AM 21; 135

McLernon, John: Ballinderry AM 21; 53

McLernon, Patrick: Blaris DN 12; 40

McLimons, Arthur: Magheradrool DN 17; 101

McLindan, Rev.: Kilbroney DN 3; 34

McLochlin, Derrick: Magilligan LY 11; 146

McLorimer [or Lorinan], Miss: Antrim AM 29; 46

McLorinan, Patrick: Duneane AM 19; 118

McLorinan, Sally: Muckamore AM 35; 81

McLorn, Mrs: Hillsborough DN 12; 105

McLornan, family: Ballinderry AM 21; 53

McLornan, James: Duneane AM 19; 105

McLoskie (see McCloskey)

McLoughlin, Ardgall: Clondermot LY 34; 47

McLoughlin, Cormac: Misc. TE 5; 147

McLoughlin, Daniel: Errigal LY 27; 54, 70

McLoughlin, Daniel: Tamlaght O'Crilly LY 18; 122, 128

McLoughlin, Dermot: Misc. TE 5; 146

McLoughlin, Donald: Banagher LY 30; 99

McLoughlin, Donnell: Misc. TE 5; 146

McLoughlin, family: Banagher LY 30; 31

McLoughlin, family: Cumber LY 28; 11, 87

McLoughlin, family: Dungiven LY 15; 32, 58

McLoughlin, family: Magilligan LY 11; 114

McLoughlin, family: Misc. LY 36; 111

McLoughlin, Francis: Aghagallon AM 21; 25

McLoughlin, Henry: Tamlaght O'Crilly LY 18; 94, 106, 122

McLoughlin, Hugh: Cumber LY 28; 74, 77

McLoughlin, Hugh: Misc. TE 5; 146

McLoughlin, James: Ballynure AM 32; 73

McLoughlin, James: Tamlaght O'Crilly LY 18; 142

McLoughlin, Jane: Carrickfergus AM 37; 120

McLoughlin, John: Tamlaght O'Crilly LY 18; 118

McLoughlin, Margaret: Carrickfergus AM 37; 118

McLoughlin, Mortagh: Misc. TE 5; 147

McLoughlin, Neil: Maghera LY 18; 40

McLoughlin, Owen: Errigal LY 27; 54, 73

McLoughlin, Patt: Tamlaght O'Crilly LY 18; 122

McLoughlin, Rev. John: Killelagh LY 27; 102

McLoughlin, Rev. John: Tamlaght O'Crilly LY 18; 90, 99, 106, 111, 143

McLoughlin, Thomas: Ballyscullion AM 19; 9

McLoughlin, Thomas: Banagher LY 30; 95

McLoughlin, William: Loughguile AM 13; 72

McLoughlin, William: Tamlaght O'Crilly LY 18; 137

McMacken, John: Drumachose LY 9; 132

McMahon and Cummin, Messrs: Newry DN 3; 99

McMahon, family: Aghabog MN 40; 66

McMahon, family: Ballybay MN 40; 81

McMahon, family: Currin MN 40; 94

McMahon, family: Donaghmoyne MN 40; 109

McMahon, family: Drumachose LY 9; 93

McMahon, family: Dungiven LY 15; 32

McMahon, family: Misc. TE 5; 146

McMahon, James: Newry DN 3; 104

McMahon, Jane: Carrickfergus AM 37; 123

McMahone, family: Drumachose LY 9; 93

McManimen, James: Bovevagh LY 25; 60

McMannus, Alexander: Ahoghill AM 23; 12, 15, 31, 35, 51

McMannus, Bernard: Carrickfergus AM 37; 115

McMannus, Mrs: Ahoghill AM 23; 12

McManus, Catherine: Balteagh LY 9; 43

McManus, Mary: Balteagh LY 9; 43

McManus, Mary: Carrickfergus AM 37; 130

McMars, George: Macosquin LY 22; 87, 116

McMartin lough: Tomregan FH 4; 125–26

McMaster, Alixander: Macosquin LY 22; 122

McMaster, Anne: Maghera LY 18; 80

McMaster, David: Magherafelt LY 6; 109, 111

McMaster, family: Ballyclug AM 23; 63

McMaster, family: Carrickfergus AM 37; 179

McMaster, family: Derryaghy AM 8; 103

McMaster, family: Drumbeg AM 8; 123

McMaster, family: Kirkinriola AM 23; 124

McMaster, family: Magherafelt LY 6; 95

McMaster, family: Racavan AM 13; 100

McMaster, James: Hillsborough DN 12; 107

McMaster, James: Maghera LY 18; 80

McMaster, Jane: Carrickfergus AM 37; 151

McMaster, John: Ahoghill AM 23; 33

McMaster, John: Lissan LY 31; 109

McMaster, Margaret: Tickmacrevan AM 13; 134

McMaster, Mary: Carrickfergus AM 37; 150

McMaster, Mr: Manorhamilton Union LM 40; 49

McMaster, Mrs: Templecorran AM 26; 130

McMaster, Rev. Robert: Carnmoney AM 2; 75

McMaster, Samuel: Carrickfergus AM 37; 151

McMaster, Samuel: Donegore AM 29; 130

McMaster, Thomas: Ahoghill AM 23; 34–35

McMaster's fort: Ahoghill AM 23; 33

McMath, H.: Aughnamullen MN 40; 76

McMath, Mr: Donaghmoyne MN 40; 107

McMechan, family: Ballee DN 17; 16

McMechan, family: Carnmoney AM 2; 102

McMechan, J.: Carnmoney AM 2; 89

McMeechan, family: Carnmoney AM 2; 76

McMeehan, family: Ballymartin AM 2; 6, 15

McMeehan, John [I]: Ahoghill AM 23; 35
McMeehan, John [II]: Ahoghill AM 23; 39
McMeehan, Samuel: Ballymartin AM 2; 18
McMeehan, William: Ballymartin AM 2; 17
McMeek, J.: Donaghmoyne MN 40; 111
McMeekan, family: Island Magee AM 10; 70
McMeekan, M.: Island Magee AM 10; 64
McMeekan, Nelly: Kilwaughter AM 10; 116
McMeekin, John: Island Magee AM 10; 68, 84, 86, 93, 96, 103
McMeekin, William: Island Magee AM 10; 91
McMeenstown td: Convoy DL 39; 21
McMehan, Mr: Faughanvale LY 36; 18
McMenamen, James: Dungiven LY 15; 116
McMenamy, Patrick: Magherafelt LY 6; 103
McMenemy, Patrick: Faughanvale LY 36; 24, 35
McMichael, Archie: Ballintoy AM 24; 23–24
McMichael, Daniel: Loughguile AM 13; 72
McMichael, family: Culfeightrin AM 24; 59
McMichael, family: Ramoan AM 24; 107
McMichael, Joseph: Dunboe LY 11; 60
McMickan, Malcolm: Carrickfergus AM 37; 165
McMickan, Samuel: Kilroot AM 26; 76
McMillan, family: Ballintoy AM 24; 20
McMillan, Joseph: Muckamore AM 35; 79–80
McMillan, Thomas: Blaris AM 8; 78
McMillan, W.: Comber DN 7; 34, 39
McMillan, William: Muckamore AM 35; 78
McMillen, family: Ballynure AM 32; 56
McMillen, family: Carnmoney AM 2; 76
McMillen, Mrs: Antrim AM 29; 59
McMillighan, builder: Drumhome DL 39; 58
McMillin, John: Desertoghill LY 27; 30, 33
McMillin, Rev. Gideon: Desertoghill LY 27; 10
McMinn, Catherine: Rasharkin AM 23; 136
McMinn, Joseph: Newry DN 3; 95, 97–98, 103
McMinn, Josh: Newry DN 3; 93
McMinn, Robert: Newry DN 3; 100, 104
McMinn, William: Donaghadee DN 7; 46
McMorran, Widow: Templecorran AM 26; 120
McMulkin, James: Magheracross FH 14; 95
McMullan, Alexander: Ahoghill AM 23; 34
McMullan, Alick: Billy AM 16; 43
McMullan, Ann: Tamlaght O'Crilly LY 18; 137
McMullan, Charles: Templepatrick AM 35; 151
McMullan, Daniel: Ramoan AM 24; 107
McMullan, David: Billy AM 16; 64, 72
McMullan, David: Eglish AH 1; 44
McMullan, Edward [I]: Maghera LY 18; 80
McMullan, Edward [II]: Maghera LY 18; 81
McMullan, family: Ballintoy AM 24; 16, 20
McMullan, family: Carmavy AM 35; 2
McMullan, family: Culfeightrin AM 24; 59
McMullan, family: Dunluce AM 16; 117
McMullan, family: Racavan AM 13; 100

McMullan, family: Ramoan AM 24; 107
McMullan, Hugh: Ballintoy AM 24; 22
McMullan, Hugh: Duneane AM 19; 115
McMullan, Hugh: Misc. DN 17; 119
McMullan, James: Ballintoy AM 24; 21
McMullan, James: Carnmoney AM 2; 81
McMullan, James: Duneane AM 19; 114
McMullan, Jane: Glynn AM 26; 28
McMullan, John: Ballymoney AM 16; 15
McMullan, John: Island Magee AM 10; 90
McMullan, John: Loughguile AM 13; 72
McMullan, John: Raloo AM 32; 117, 130
McMullan, John: Templecorran AM 26; 123
McMullan, John [I]: Ballintoy AM 24; 20
McMullan, John [II]: Ballintoy AM 24; 21
McMullan, John [III]: Ballintoy AM 24; 28
McMullan, Margaret: Ballywillin LY 33; 51
McMullan, Michael: Ramoan AM 24; 115
McMullan, Mr: Killead AM 35; 46
McMullan, Mrs (Cotton Bank): Duneane AM 19; 114
McMullan, Neal: Culfeightrin AM 24; 50
McMullan, Neal: Ramoan AM 24; 113
McMullan, Patrick: Maghera LY 18; 80
McMullan, Patrick: Newry DN 3; 98, 103
McMullan, Patt: Culfeightrin AM 24; 50
McMullan, Rev. D.W.: Montiaghs AH 1; 90, 92
McMullan, Rev. Daniel: Carrickfergus AM 37; 103, 174
McMullan, Rev. Daniel: Raloo AM 32; 126
McMullan, Rev. James: Killead AM 35; 20, 39, 45–46, 52
McMullan, Rev. John: Duneane AM 19; 115
McMullan, Rev. John: Templepatrick AM 35; 119, 133, 136, 144–45, 148, 153–54
McMullan, Thomas: Coleraine LY 33; 72
McMullan, William: Ballintoy AM 24; 34
McMullan, William: Ballyscullion AM 19; 7
McMullan, William: Hillsborough DN 12; 107
McMullan, William [I]: Duneane AM 19; 124
McMullan, William [II]: Duneane AM 19; 124
McMullans, John: Carrickfergus AM 37; 131
McMullen, Alexander [I]: Macosquin LY 22; 87, 108
McMullen, Alexander [II]: Macosquin LY 22; 122
McMullen, Daniel: Garvaghy DN 12; 80, 84
McMullen, Eliza (Jnr): Carrickfergus AM 37; 130
McMullen, Eliza (Snr): Carrickfergus AM 37; 130
McMullen, Isaac: Dunboe LY 11; 81
McMullen, James: Blaris AM 8; 79
McMullen, John: Ballyrashane LY 22; 66
McMullen, man named: Muckamore AM 35; 68
McMullen, Marcus: Banagher LY 30; 111
McMullen, Margaret: Carrickfergus AM 37; 127, 130

McMullen, Rev. D.W.: Montiaghs AH 1; 92

McMullen, Rev. I.: Camlin AM 21; 76

McMullen, Samuel: Macosquin LY 22; 92

McMullen, Thomas: Macosquin LY 22; 123

McMullen, William: Bright DN 17; 37

McMullen, William: Macosquin LY 22; 122

McMullin, A.: Drumgooland DN 3; 25

McMullin, Agnes: Killead AM 35; 51

McMullin, Alexander: Killead AM 35; 51

McMullin, Anna: Killead AM 35; 51

McMullin, Anne: Ballymoney AM 16; 17

McMullin, Daniel: Derrykeighan AM 16; 93

McMullin, Ephraim: Derrykeighan AM 16; 94

McMullin, family: Ballintoy AM 24; 20

McMullin, J.: Ballymoney AM 16; 17

McMullin, James: Drummaul AM 19; 77, 85

McMullin, James: Glynn AM 26; 42

McMullin, Jane: Killead AM 35; 51

McMullin, John: Ballymoney AM 16; 16

McMullin, Mary: Killead AM 35; 51

McMullin, Patrick: Carrickfergus AM 37; 112

McMullin, Rev. Peter: Rasharkin AM 23; 140

McMullin, Thomas: Killead AM 35; 51

McMullin, Widow: Loughguile AM 13; 71

McMullin, William: Derrykeighan AM 16; 91

McMullon, family: Culfeightrin AM 24; 71

McMurdock, Hants: Seapatrick DN 12; 133

McMurlin, family: Magheragall AM 21; 99

McMurran, James: Templecorran AM 26; 132

McMurray, family: Derryaghy AM 8; 103

McMurray, Hugh: Carrickfergus AM 37; 114

McMurray, man named: Coleraine LY 33; 128

McMurray, Mr: Dromore DN 12; 72

McMurray, Thomas: Desertlyn LY 31; 51

McMurray's Now locality: Coleraine LY 33; 128

McMurthry, James: Island Magee AM 10; 95

McMurthry, James: Templecorran AM 26; 132

McMurthry, John: Glynn AM 26; 47

McMurthry, Randal: Island Magee AM 10; 82, 91, 93, 99

McMurtry, family: Ballylinny AM 32; 27

McMurtry, family: Carrickfergus AM 37; 179

McMurtry, family: Island Magee AM 10; 70

McMurtry, family: Kilroot AM 26; 74–75

McMurtry, Hugh: Glynn AM 26; 35, 46

McMurtry, John: Carrickfergus AM 37; 189

McNabb, James: Macosquin LY 22; 94

McNaght, family: Magherafelt LY 6; 95

McNaghten, family: Culfeightrin AM 24; 59, 59

McNaghten, Francis: Carrickfergus AM 37; 108

McNaghten, John: Clondermot LY 34; 8, 83, 97, 104

McNaghten, John: Culfeightrin AM 24; 59

McNaghten, man named: Killygarvan DL 38; 39

McNaghten, Robert: Coleraine LY 33; 63, 72, 105

McNaghten, Rowan: Newry DN 3; 100, 104

McNain lough: Manorhamilton Union LM 40; 47–48, 50, 54

McNair, family: Ramoan AM 24; 107

McNally, Charles: Killelagh LY 27; 101

McNally, Cornelious: Ballynascreen LY 31; 25

McNally, family: Culfeightrin AM 24; 59

McNally, Henry: Kilcronaghan LY 31; 88

McNally, Henry: Termoneeny LY 6; 128

McNally, Hugh: Ballymoney AM 16; 17

McNally, Hugh: Garvaghy DN 12; 82

McNally, James: Bovevagh LY 25; 28

McNally, James: Carrickfergus AM 37; 193

McNally, James: Magilligan LY 11; 94

McNally, John: Ballynascreen LY 31; 21

McNally, John: Ematris MN 40; 116

McNally, Margaret: Magilligan LY 11; 94

McNally, Mr: Antrim AM 29; 10

McNally, Mr: Blaris DN 12; 49

McNamara, family: Blaris DN 12; 30

McNamara, fiddler: Aghanloo LY 11; 14

McNamara, fiddler: Magilligan LY 11; 115, 125

McNamara, Mr: Newry DN 3; 100

McNamara, Thomas: Newry DN 3; 103

McNamara, William: Balteagh LY 9; 43

McNamee, Daniel: Errigal LY 27; 74

McNamee, family: Ballynascreen LY 31; 9, 12

McNamee, James: Ballynascreen LY 31; 20

McNamee, James: Clondermot LY 34; 43, 88, 91, 96

McNamee, James: Killelagh LY 27; 101

McNamee, James: Loughguile AM 13; 77

McNamee, James: Macosquin LY 22; 99

McNamee, Laughlin: Ballynascreen LY 31; 3

McNamee, Loughlin: Kilcronaghan LY 31; 78–79

McNamee, Pat: Ballynascreen LY 31; 23

McNamee, Patrick: Maghera LY 18; 8, 68

McNamee, Peter: Kilcronaghan LY 31; 85

McNamee, Rev.: Faughanvale LY 36; 29

McNamee, Rev. Francis: Misc. LY 31; 122, 136

McNaught, family: Magheragall AM 21; 99

McNaught, Hugh: Kildollagh LY 22; 74

McNaught, John: Cumber LY 28; 38, 44

McNaught, John: Maghera LY 18; 29–30

McNaughten, John: Ballyrashane LY 22; 56

McNaughtin, John: Dunaghy AM 13; 23

McNeal, family: Ballywillin AM 16; 32

McNeal, family: Billy AM 16; 68

McNeal, family: Carnmoney AM 2; 76

McNeal, family: Culfeightrin AM 24; 71

McNeal, Rev.: Down DN 17; 41

McNeale, family: Ballintoy AM 24; 20

McNeale, John: Ramoan AM 24; 94

McNeall, family: Carnmoney AM 2; 102

McNean lough: Cleenish FH 14; 11, 14

McNean lough: Killesher FH 14; 81

McNean lough eel fisheries: Killesher FH 14; 88

McNean Lower lough: Cleenish FH 14; 11–13, 19

McNean Lower lough: Killesher FH 14; 81, 83–84, 88

McNean Upper lough: Cleenish FH 14; 11–13, 19, 26

McNeckle, family: Errigal LY 27; 41

McNeeley's fort. Templepatrick AM 35; 127–29

McNeely, Andrew: Island Magee AM 10; 90

McNeely, family: Carnmoney AM 2; 76

McNeely, family: Mallusk AM 2; 110

McNeely, family: Shilvodan AM 19; 136

McNeely, family: Templepatrick AM 35; 118, 120

McNeely, James: Templepatrick AM 35; 150

McNeely, John: Island Magee AM 10; 90

McNeely, Mary: Derrykeighan AM 16; 92

McNees, family: Ballinderry AM 21; 48

McNeice, John: Carrickfergus AM 37; 110

McNeight, William: Newry DN 3; 99, 104

McNeil, Alexander: Ballymascanlan LH 40; 55

McNeil, Alexander: Coleraine LY 33; 127

McNeil, Andrew: Maghera LY 18; 78

McNeil, Esther: Culfeightrin AM 24; 65

McNeil, family: Billy AM 16; 58, 68

McNeil, family: Ramoan AM 24; 123

McNeil, Henry: Dungiven LY 15; 44, 77–78

McNeil, James: Aghadowey LY 22; 35

McNeil, John: Culfeightrin AM 24; 76

McNeil, Mrs Henery: Dungiven LY 15; 78

McNeil, Robert: Aghadowey LY 22; 36

McNeil, Robert: Newry DN 3; 99, 104

McNeil, William: Billy AM 16; 63

McNeile, Cormack: Tullyrusk AM 21; 131

McNeile, family: Culfeightrin AM 24; 64

McNeile, family: Ramoan AM 24; 108

McNeile, John: Carnmoney AM 2; 53, 81, 90

McNeile, Mrs (Carlingford): Clonallan DN 3; 2

McNeilie, Gilbert: Templepatrick AM 35; 132

McNeill, Alexander: Ballintoy AM 24; 33

McNeill, Alexander: Culfeightrin AM 24; 68

McNeill, Alexander: Ramoan AM 24; 94, 100

McNeill, Alexander: Rasharkin AM 23; 138–39

McNeill, Archy: Loughguile AM 13; 71, 74

McNeill, Daniel: Ballintoy AM 24; 35

McNeill, Daniel: Carrickfergus AM 37; 122

McNeill, Easter: Culfeightrin AM 24; 56

McNeill, Elenor: Ballynascreen LY 31; 21

McNeill, family: Ahoghill AM 23; 25

McNeill, family: Ardclinis AM 13; 8

McNeill, family: Ballynascreen LY 31; 9

McNeill, family: Layd AM 13; 40

McNeill, family: Macosquin LY 22; 84, 119

McNeill, family: Raloo AM 32; 94

McNeill, Francis: Carrickfergus AM 37; 132

McNeill, Hecter: Ramoan AM 24; 110

McNeill, Henry: Raloo AM 32; 103, 126

McNeill, Hugh: Ballymoney AM 16; 18

McNeill, James: Billy AM 16; 56, 74

McNeill, John: Ahoghill AM 23; 42

McNeill, John: Ballintoy AM 24; 21, 30

McNeill, John: Loughguile AM 13; 72

McNeill, John: Ramoan AM 24; 108

McNeill, John: Tamlaght O'Crilly LY 18; 134

McNeill, Malcolm: Island Magee AM 10; 23, 70, 81, 85, 98, 103

McNeill, Margaret: Rasharkin AM 23; 140

McNeill, Miss: Island Magee AM 10; 98

McNeill, Misses: Island Magee AM 10; 70, 98

McNeill, Mr (Ballycastle): Layd AM 13; 40

McNeill, Nancy: Templecorran AM 26; 132

McNeill, Samuel: Templecorran AM 26; 132

McNeill, Thomas: Bovevagh LY 25; 38

McNeill, William: Seapatrick DN 12; 135

McNeill, Woulfe: Ballymascanlan LH 40; 55

McNeill, Woulfe: Loughguile AM 13; 75

McNeilly, Mr: Ballyphilip DN 7; 8

McNeilly, Mr: Misc. DN 17; 127

McNeily, Adam: Templepatrick AM 35; 132

McNeily, David: Ahoghill AM 23; 39

McNele, family: Ramoan AM 24; 107

McNene, Conway: Lough Neagh AM 21; 95

McNerry, Matthew: Desertoghill LY 27; 4, 33

McNerry, Olliver: Desertoghill LY 27; 27

McNichol, Alexander: Carrickfergus AM 37; 112

McNichol, James: Errigal LY 27; 41, 73

McNichol, James: Maghera LY 18; 45

McNichol, Patrick: Errigal LY 27; 51–52, 55, 77

McNicholl, family: Errigal LY 27; 47

McNicoll, Daniel [I]: Desertoghill LY 27; 20

McNicoll, Daniel [II]: Desertoghill LY 27; 27

McNiece, family: Glenavy AM 21; 86

McNiece, family: Kilroot AM 26; 74

McNiece, Thomas: Blaris DN 12; 40

McNiel, family: Clonmany DL 38; 15

McNinch, family: Kilwaughter AM 10; 115

McNinch, John: Kilwaughter AM 10; 114, 116–17, 121

McNown, family: Ardglass DN 17; 4

McNown, family: Dunsfort DN 17; 68

McOwen, family: Duneane AM 19; 101

McPake, family: Maghera LY 18; 24, 48

McParlan, Patrick: Newry DN 3; 99, 104

McPeak, Denis: Ballymoney AM 16; 18

McPeak, family: Tamlaght O'Crilly LY 18; 93

McPeak, James: Drumachose LY 9; 134

McPeak, James: Maghera LY 18; 61

McPeake, Bernard [I]: Maghera LY 18; 54

McPeake, Bernard [II]: Maghera LY 18; 81

McPeake, John: Tamlaght TE 20; 76

McPeake, John [I]: Maghera LY 18; 38
McPeake, John [II]: Maghera LY 18; 43–44
McPeake, Joseph: Maghera LY 18; 38
McPeake, Margaret: Glynn AM 26; 28, 42
McPeake, Margret: Tamlaght O'Crilly LY 18; 137
McPeake, Owen: Maghera LY 18; 43–44
McPeake, Patrick: Termoneeny LY 6; 133
McPhadraick, man named: Aghadowey LY 22; 28, 32
McPharson, family: Billy AM 16; 58, 68
McPherson, Adam: Errigal LY 27; 44, 54, 70
McPherson, Alexander: Muckamore AM 35; 78
McPherson, Charles: Billy AM 16; 73
McPherson, Daniel: Muckamore AM 35; 77, 79
McPherson, James: Billy AM 16; 56, 62–64, 71–72
McPherson, James: Errigal LY 27; 65
McPherson, Joe: Dungiven LY 15; 48
McPherson, John: Billy AM 16; 74–75
McPherson, John: Errigal LY 27; 54, 70
McPherson, Joseph: Bovevagh LY 25; 13, 47–48
McPherson, Joseph: Dungiven LY 15; 47
McPherson, Joseph: Killea and Taughboyne DL 39; 87
McPherson, Thomas: Hillsborough DN 12; 107
McPherson, Widow: Hillsborough DN 12; 107
McPherson, William: Hillsborough DN 12; 107
McPherson's mill [I]: Killea and Taughboyne DL 39; 87
McPherson's mill [II]: Killea and Taughboyne DL 39; 87
McPhillips, family: Aghabog MN 40; 66
McPhillips, family: Ematris MN 40; 118
McPhillips, Rev. Hugh: Aghabog MN 40; 63
McPhillips, William: Tydavnet MN 40; 172
McPhlip, Archibald: Dunluce AM 16; 117
McPhlip, Florence (nee Hamilton): Dunluce AM 16; 117
McPhlips, family: Dunluce AM 16; 117
McQuade, Alice: Carrickfergus AM 37; 109, 119
McQuaid, family: Errigal LY 27; 41
McQuaid, Henery: Ballyscullion LY 6; 73
McQuaid, Henery: Magherafelt LY 6; 112
McQueston, Hugh: Carrickfergus AM 37; 113
McQuigg, family: Dunluce AM 16; 117
McQuiggan, Robert: Hillsborough DN 12; 106
McQuiggy, Arthur: Macosquin LY 22; 122
McQuiggy, Margaret: Macosquin LY 22; 122
McQuilken, Archy: Ramoan AM 24; 122
McQuilken, John: Ballintoy AM 24; 32
McQuilkin, Mr: Kirkinriola AM 23; 113
McQuillan, Arthur: Aghagallon AM 21; 16, 21, 23
McQuillan, Bernard: Maghera LY 18; 61
McQuillan, Charles: Kilwaughter AM 10; 122
McQuillan, Conway: Finvoy AM 23; 68
McQuillan, Conway: Loughguile AM 13; 58

McQuillan, Daniel: Dungiven LY 15; 32–33
McQuillan, Daniel: Dunluce AM 16; 115, 121
McQuillan, Edward [I]: Carrickfergus AM 37; 75
McQuillan, Edward [II]: Carrickfergus AM 37; 158
McQuillan, family: Aghadowey LY 22; 30
McQuillan, family: Aghagallon AM 21; 9
McQuillan, family: Ahoghill AM 23; 26, 28
McQuillan, family: Ballyaghran LY 33; 10, 23
McQuillan, family: Ballymoney AM 16; 20–21
McQuillan, family: Ballywillin LY 33; 35, 44
McQuillan, family: Billy AM 16; 49, 53, 55, 66–67, 71–72, 74
McQuillan, family: Culfeightrin AM 24; 47, 78–81
McQuillan, family: Drumachose LY 9; 91–92, 127–28
McQuillan, family: Dunaghy AM 13; 14, 28
McQuillan, family: Dundermot AM 13; 35
McQuillan, family: Dungiven LY 15; 29, 32–33, 107
McQuillan, family: Dunluce AM 16; 115
McQuillan, family: Killagan AM 23; 84
McQuillan, family: Killead AM 35; 17
McQuillan, family: Kilrea LY 27; 113
McQuillan, family: Kilwaughter AM 10; 115, 118
McQuillan, family: Lambeg AM 8; 141
McQuillan, family: Layd and Inispollan AM 13; 55, 57
McQuillan, family: Loughguile AM 13; 58, 60, 62, 64, 66, 68, 76
McQuillan, family: Magheragall AM 21; 107
McQuillan, family: Misc. LY 36; 109
McQuillan, family: Raloo AM 32; 115
McQuillan, family: Ramoan AM 24; 106, 113, 122, 125
McQuillan, family: Shilvodan AM 19; 136
McQuillan, family: Skerry AM 13; 112
McQuillan, family: Tickmacrevan AM 13; 127
McQuillan, Finn: Drumachose LY 9; 57, 111
McQuillan, Finn: Dungiven LY 15; 32
McQuillan, Isaac: Magheragall AM 21; 107
McQuillan, J.M.: Coleraine LY 33; 157
McQuillan, James: Maghera LY 18; 51–52, 74
McQuillan, John: Drumgoon CN 40; 7
McQuillan, John: Kilwaughter AM 10; 122
McQuillan, Joseph: Magheragall AM 21; 105, 107
McQuillan, Michael: Maghera LY 18; 80
McQuillan, Molly: Dunaghy AM 13; 24
McQuillan, Patrick: Maghera LY 18; 60
McQuillan, Richard: Magheragall AM 21; 105, 107
McQuillan, Robert: Carmavy AM 35; 6
McQuillan, Robert: Carrickfergus AM 37; 111, 195
McQuillan, Robert: Killead AM 35; 51
McQuillan, Rory: Ahoghill AM 23; 26, 35
McQuillan, Rory: Coleraine LY 33; 156–57
McQuillan, Rory: Kilwaughter AM 10; 118

McQuillan, Rowley: Maghera LY 18; 81
McQuillan, Thomas: Maghera LY 18; 81
McQuillan, William: Aghagallon AM 21; 16, 21
McQuillan's Castle: Ahoghill AM 23; 26, 28
McQuillan's Knowes hill: Desertoghill LY 27; 26
McQuillans' Island: Dundermot AM 13; 35
McQuillen, family: Glenavy AM 21; 86
McQuillen, John: Carrickfergus AM 37; 180
McQuillin, James: Ballyscullion LY 6; 66, 75
McQuillin, John: Ballyscullion LY 6; 72
McQuillin, man named: Ballyscullion LY 6; 55
McQuitty, John: Billy AM 16; 63
McQuoid, family: Ballee DN 17; 16
McQuoid, family: Dunsfort DN 17; 68
McReady, family: Maghera LY 18; 48
McReady, Isaac: Tamlaght O'Crilly LY 18; 119
McReavy, A.: Drumballyroney DN 3; 16
McReynolds, James: Bovevagh LY 25; 28, 55
McReynolds, John: Tamlaght O'Crilly LY 18; 107
McReynolds, Thomas: Maghera LY 18; 27
McRobert, Alexander: Saintfield DN 7; 114
McRobert, James: Kilmore DN 17; 91
McRoberts, Hugh: Saintfield DN 7; 119
McRoberts, John: Ballynure AM 32; 61
McRoberts, Michael: Raloo AM 32; 126
McRoberts, William: Raloo AM 32; 122, 125–26, 131
McRorey, family: Aghagallon AM 21; 9
McRory, Bernard: Aghagallon AM 21; 21
McRory, Constantine: Tamlaght O'Crilly LY 18; 141, 143
McRory, Elizabeth: Aghagallon AM 21; 21
McRory, family: Glenavy AM 21; 86
McRory, family: Misc. LY 31; 122
McRory, Mathew: Ballynascreen LY 31; 21
McRory, Peter: Ballynascreen LY 31; 25
McShane, Alexander: Clondermot LY 34; 10, 26, 101, 103
McShane, Andrew: Maghera LY 18; 81
McShane, Eliza Jane: Ballywillin LY 33; 51
McShane, Felix: Maghera LY 18; 80
McShane, Hester (Jnr): Ballywillin LY 33; 51
McShane, Hester (Snr): Ballywillin LY 33; 51
McShane, Jane: Carrickfergus AM 37; 127
McShane, John (Jnr): Ballywillin LY 33; 51
McShane, John (Snr): Ballywillin LY 33; 51
McShane, John: Kilcronaghan LY 31; 84
McShane, John: Leck DL 39; 120
McShane, John: Maghera LY 18; 80
McShane, Margaret: Ballywillin LY 33; 51
McShane, Martha: Ballywillin LY 33; 51
McShane, Peter: Maghera LY 18; 80
McShane, Rose: Maghera LY 18; 78
McShannor, family: Ballynure AM 32; 56
McShanog, family: Culfeightrin AM 24; 59

McSheafry, John: Macosquin LY 22; 87, 116
McSkimin, family: Carrickfergus AM 37; 179
McSkimin, Samuel: Ballynure AM 32; 59, 62–63
McSkimin, Samuel: Carnmoney AM 2; 94, 96, 98
McSkimin, Samuel: Carrickfergus AM 37; 4, 162–64, 168–69, 171–73, 175, 177, 179–83, 185–87, 190–91
McSkimin, Samuel: Clondermot LY 34; 46
McSkimin, Samuel: Comber DN 7; 44
McSkimin, Samuel: Dundonald DN 7; 65
McSkimin, Samuel: Faughanvale LY 36; 55
McSkimin, Samuel: Kilroot AM 26; 75
McSkimin, Samuel: Misc. DN 17; 116
McSkimin, Samuel: Templecorran AM 26; 120–21, 123
McSorley, Owen: Donacavey TE 5; 65
McSpallen, Patt: Ballyaghran LY 33; 25
McSparran, Letitia: Agivey LY 22; 45
McSparren, Archibald: Banagher LY 30; 75, 86
McSparren, Archibald: Bovevagh LY 25; 8, 14–15, 21, 36–38, 44–45, 57
McSparren, Archibald [I]: Drumachose LY 9; 91–92, 110, 131
McSparren, Archibald [II]: Drumachose LY 9; 133
McSparren, George: Dungiven LY 15; 83
McSparren, John: Banagher LY 30; 65–66, 96
McSparren, John: Bovevagh LY 25; 15, 17, 21, 35–36, 45–46, 57
McSparren, Joseph: Banagher LY 30; 86
McSparren, Joseph: Bovevagh LY 25; 13, 43–45
McSparren, Miss: Drumachose LY 9; 133
McSparrin, Archibald: Dungiven LY 15; 33, 107
McSparrin, family: Agivey LY 22; 41–42
McSparrin, family: Bovevagh LY 25; 10
McStay, Mary Ann: Carrickfergus AM 37; 130
McStea, family: Aghagallon AM 21; 10
McStravoge, family: Aghagallon AM 21; 10, 18
McStravoge, Neal: Aghagallon AM 21; 5, 11, 17–18
McStravoge, Patrick [I]: Aghagallon AM 21; 11–12, 16, 18, 21
McStravoge, Patrick [II]: Aghagallon AM 21; 19
McStravoge, Roger: Aghagallon AM 21; 18
McSurly, Mr (Jnr): Clogher TE 5; 43
McSurly, Mr (Snr): Clogher TE 5; 43
McSwain, John: Magheramesk AM 21; 116–18, 125, 127
McSweeny, family: Clondavaddog DL 38; 1
McSwine, family: Clondavaddog DL 38; 1, 5–6
McSwine, family: Killygarvan DL 38; 42, 46
McSwine, man named: Killygarvan DL 38; 41
McSwine's Castle: Killygarvan DL 38; 36, 39, 41
McTamney, David: Maghera LY 18; 81
McTamney, family: Tamlaght O'Crilly LY 18; 93
McTear, David: Carnmoney AM 2; 46, 84, 90
McTear, Miss: Carnmoney AM 2; 87

McTeer, Robert: Hillsborough DN 12; 105
McTeer, Robert: Island Magee AM 10; 90
McTrainor, family: Desertmartin LY 31; 55
McTrien, Jarleth: Kilkeel DN 3; 54
McTyre, Betty: Magilligan LY 11; 94
McTyre, Hugh: Magilligan LY 11; 94
McVea, Catherine: Carrickfergus AM 37; 122
McVea, family: Dungiven LY 15; 24
McVea, Owen: Dungiven LY 15; 24
McVeagh, Edward: Dungiven LY 15; 76–77
McVeagh, family: Aghagallon AM 21; 9
McVeagh, John: Dungiven LY 15; 76–77
McVeagh, Patrick: Ballinderry AM 21; 56
McVeagh, Robert: Carrickfergus AM 37; 113
McVeagh, Robert: Killead AM 35; 53
McVeigh, Daniel: Ballymoney AM 16; 18
McVeigh, John: Culfeightrin AM 24; 85
McVeigh, Mrs: Newry DN 3; 99, 103
McVeigh, Robert: Magheralin DN 12; 110
McVey, Edward: Carrickfergus AM 37; 109
McVey, family: Artrea LY 6; 14
McVey, John: Balteagh LY 9; 42
McVey, John: Carrickfergus AM 37; 118
McVey, John: Kirkinriola AM 23; 121
McVey, Michael: Artrea LY 6; 18
McVey, Rev.: Duneane AM 19; 115
McVey, Thomas: Artrea LY 6; 19
McVey, William: Carrickfergus AM 37; 21
McVickarsland (see McVickersland): Kilbride AM
   29; 136
McVicker, Mr: Templepatrick AM 35; 145
McVickersland fort [I]: Kilbride AM 29; 149, 155
McVickersland fort [II]: Kilbride AM 29; 149
McVickersland td: Kilbride AM 29; 136
McWarnock, Mrs: Dromore TE 5; 99
McWatters, John: Raloo AM 32; 125
McWatty, James: Muckno MN 40; 165
McWhinny, John: Ahoghill AM 23; 38
McWhirrter, David: Raloo AM 32; 129
McWhirrter, Thomas: Raloo AM 32; 129
McWilliam, Alexander: Kilraghts AM 16; 132
McWilliam, family: Raloo AM 32; 108
McWilliam, Hugh: Dunaghy AM 13; 17
McWilliams, Daniel: Maghera LY 18; 78
McWilliams, David: Inver AM 26; 53
McWilliams, Donald: Maghera LY 18; 78
McWilliams, Elenor: Ballyscullion LY 6; 77
McWilliams, family: Ballynascreen LY 31; 9, 31
McWilliams, family: Carnmoney AM 2; 102
McWilliams, family: Dungiven LY 15; 31–32
McWilliams, family: Maghera LY 18; 14, 74
McWilliams, family: Raloo AM 32; 123
McWilliams, Felix: Maghera LY 18; 78
McWilliams, Francis: Ballyscullion LY 6; 77
McWilliams, Frank: Termoneeny LY 6; 133

McWilliams, Hugh: Termoneeny LY 6; 133
McWilliams, James: Ballymoney AM 16; 27
McWilliams, James: Ballyscullion LY 6; 74
McWilliams, James: Donacavey TE 5; 65
McWilliams, James: Kilcronaghan LY 31; 84
McWilliams, James: Rasharkin AM 23; 134, 139
McWilliams, Jane: Raloo AM 32; 128
McWilliams, John: Artrea LY 6; 18
McWilliams, John: Ballyrashane LY 22; 61
McWilliams, John: Ballyscullion LY 6; 77
McWilliams, John: Carrickfergus AM 37; 123
McWilliams, John: Inver AM 26; 53
McWilliams, John: Maghera LY 18; 42
McWilliams, Mary: Raloo AM 32; 128
McWilliams, Michael: Kilcronaghan LY 31; 85
McWilliams, Nathaniel (Jnr): Raloo AM 32; 128
McWilliams, Nathaniel (Snr): Raloo AM 32; 128
McWilliams, Patrick: Ballynascreen LY 31; 14, 21
McWilliams, Patrick: Desertoghill LY 27; 25
McWilliams, Patrick: Templecorran AM 26; 130
McWilliams, Richard: Drumachose LY 9; 70, 85,
   125
McWilliams, Robert: Coleraine LY 33; 72
McWilliams, Robert: Dunluce AM 16; 116, 119
McWilliams, Robert: Raloo AM 32; 122
McWilliams, Samuel: Raloo AM 32; 122
McWilliams, Sarah: Raloo AM 32; 128
McWilliams, Thomas: Ballyaghran LY 33; 21,
   25–26
McWilliams, William: Kilcronaghan LY 31; 88
McWilliams, William: Raloo AM 32; 128
McWilliams, Wray: Billy AM 16; 76
Meachy giant's den: Ardstraw TE 5; 12
Meachy td: Ardstraw TE 5; 12
Meade, Elizabeth: Dromore DN 12; 74
Meade, Miss: Blaris AM 8; 84
Meade, Rev.: Carnmoney AM 2; 75
Meade, Robert: Aghaderg DN 12; 6, 9
Meade, Robert: Annaclone DN 12; 16
Meade, Robert: Donaghmore DN 3; 9
Meade, Robert: Drumballyroney DN 3; 15, 18
Meade, Robert: Drumgath DN 3; 21
Meade, Robert: Drumgooland DN 3; 23
Meaduff lough: Drumgoon CN 40; 3
Meaduff td: Drumgoon CN 40; 3
Meagheraher (see Magheraher): Inishmacsaint FH
   14; 78
Meagheraskeagh (see Magheraskeagh): Aghanloo
   LY 11; 42
Meaghy fort: Ardstraw TE 5; 12
Meaghy td: Ardstraw TE 5; 12
Meagle, Daniel: Blaris AM 8; 75
Meallough (see Mealough): Drumbo DN 7; 56
Mealough corn mill: Drumbo DN 7; 56, 60
Mealough flax mill: Drumbo DN 7; 56

Mealough td: Drumbo DN 7; 56, 58, 60–61, 63
Mean, family: Carrickfergus AM 37; 93
Meanlettorbale (see Meenletterbale): Moville DL 38; 68
Meara, John: Aghanloo LY 11; 13
Meara, Rev. James: Aghanloo LY 11; 9, 13
Meara, Rev. John: Coleraine LY 33; 63
Mearan, Rev.: Clondermot LY 34; 92
Meares, Andrew: Blaris DN 12; 40
Meares, John: Blaris DN 12; 42
Mearns, Robert: Carrickfergus AM 37; 155
Mears, family: Ballywillin AM 16; 32
Mears, family: Magheragall AM 21; 99
Mears, John: Connor AM 19; 26
Mears, John: Macosquin LY 22; 84, 116
Meath: Ballee DN 17; 19
Meath: Banagher LY 30; 96
Meath: Clondermot LY 34; 71
Meath: Cumber LY 28; 18
Meath: Drumlumman CN 40; 13, 16
Meath: Dungiven LY 15; 50
Meath: Enniskeen CN 40; 26
Meath: Faughanvale LY 36; 50
Meath: Galloon FH 4; 93
Meath: Magheracloone MN 40; 141
Meath: Magheross MN 40; 149
Meath: Muckamore AM 35; 82
Meath Park House: Aghadowey LY 22; 7, 28
Meath Walk district: Enniskeen CN 40; 29
Meath, Bishop of: Aghadowey LY 22; 5
Meath, Bishop of: Agivey LY 22; 39
Meath, Bishop of: Ahoghill AM 23; 16–17, 42
Meath, Bishop of: Banagher LY 30; 117, 131
Meath, Bishop of: Cumber LY 28; 81, 86
Meath, Bishop of: Desertoghill LY 27; 4–5, 22, 25
Meath, Bishop of: Killowen LY 33; 173
Meath, Bishop of: Misc. LY 36; 112
Meather, Robert: Ballyaghran LY 33; 27
Meather, Robert: Ballywillin LY 33; 42
Meavemenogher td: Aghadowey LY 22; 32
Meban, family: Ballintoy AM 24; 20
Mebon, family: Ramoan AM 24; 107
Mechlin (Flanders): Drummaul AM 19; 70
Meck, Thomas: Kilcronaghan LY 31; 68
Mecrin's wells: Aghanloo LY 11; 3, 28
Meddlecott, Thomas: Drumachose LY 9; 65
Medill, Robert: Newry DN 3; 98, 103
Mediterranean Sea: Coleraine LY 33; 87
Mediterranean Sea: Raymoghy DL 39; 141
Mediterranean Sea: Warrenpoint DN 3; 120
Medowel, family: Ballinderry AM 21; 53
Meedoge (see Moodoge)
Meeham, Gordon: Bovevagh LY 25; 60
Meek, family: Ahoghill AM 23; 25
Meeks, William: Desertoghill LY 27; 27

Meenabaltin td: Moville DL 38; 73
Meenacligh (see Meenaglogh): Kilmacteige SO 40; 196
Meenacurreen hill: Drumhome DL 39; 59
Meenadaura td: Conwal DL 39; 27
Meenagh mill: Clonoe TE 20; 31
Meenagh td: Clonoe TE 20; 29–30
Meenagloragh td: Kilmacteige SO 40; 196
Meenaglogh td: Kilmacteige SO 40; 196
Meenagolan altar: Donaghmore DL 39; 35
Meenagolan td: Donaghmore DL 39; 38
Meenaguirk lough: Killymard DL 39; 105
Meenaguirk mountain: Killymard DL 39; 105
Meenaguirk td: Killymard DL 39; 100
Meenahenisk td: Donaghmore DL 39; 29, 38
Meenahoney td: Donaghmore DL 39; 38
Meenahorna td: Kilteevoge DL 39; 114
Meenalaban td: Convoy DL 39; 22
Meenaleavin td: Moville DL 38; 73
Meenamaddoo td: Kilmacteige SO 40; 196
Meenamade (see Meenamaddoo)
Meenamuldarg td: Killymard DL 39; 100
Meenan td: Aghaderg DN 12; 3
Meenan, James: Lough Swilly DL 38; 122
Meenanellison td: Templecarn DL 39; 164
Meenaranny hill: Cleenish FH 14; 12
Meenaranny td: Cleenish FH 14; 29
Meenatagart td: Killymard DL 39; 100
Meenatully lough: Belleek FH 14; 1
Meenatully td: Belleek FH 14; 1
Meenavally td: Convoy DL 39; 21
Meenavanaghan td: Moville DL 38; 73
Meenaworragy td: Cleenish FH 14; 29
Meenbog bog: Donaghmore DL 39; 29
Meenbog td: Donaghmore DL 39; 28–29, 38
Meenbog td: Kilteevoge DL 39; 114
Meencargagh td: Longfield TE 5; 128
Meencargagh wood: Longfield TE 5; 127, 129
Meencraig (Maincraig) td: Aghadowey LY 22; 38, 33
Meencraig bogs: Errigal LY 27; 54
Meencraig hill: Aghadowey LY 22; 33
Meencraig td: Errigal LY 27; 83, 88, 91–92
Meendamph hill: Donaghedy TE 5; 88
Meenenamph td: Kilteevoge DL 39; 114
Meenformal stream: Lough Swilly DL 38; 128
Meenformal td: Mevagh DL 38; 55, 63
Meenformil (see Meenformal)
Meengilcharry td: Kilteevoge DL 39; 114
Meenish lough: Tydavnet MN 40; 169
Meenlaragh (Meenlara) td: Mevagh DL 38; 55, 63
Meenlaugher school: Donaghmore DL 39; 40
Meenlaugher td: Donaghmore DL 39; 38
Meenletterbale td: Moville DL 38; 68, 70
Meenreagh td: Donaghmore DL 39; 29, 38

Meenreagh td: Mevagh DL 38; 55

Meeny (see Menie): Cumber LY 28; 72

Meenyarnet burn: Cumber LY 28; 66

Meenyshesk mountain: Ardstraw TE 5; 10

Megahy, James: Hillsborough DN 12; 106

Megargy fort: Magherafelt LY 6; 93, 110

Megargy td: Magherafelt LY 6; 93–95, 108, 110, 112

Megarrey, Bennet: Blaris DN 12; 40

Megarry, George: Blaris DN 12; 46, 50

Meghan's locality: Muckamore AM 35; 80–81

Mehaffey, Mr: Convoy DL 39; 20

Mehaffy, John: Shankill AH 1; 115

Mehan, James: Clondermot LY 34; 4

Mehan, Patrick: Clondermot LY 34; 27, 103–04

Meharg, family: Misc. LY 36; 104

Meharg, William: Drumgooland DN 3; 23

Mehassey, family: Ahoghill AM 23; 25

Mehaughney, Mr: Raphoe DL 39; 125

Meherg, family: Kilwaughter AM 10; 115

Meigh church: Killevy AH 1; 53

Meik, Matthew: Bovevagh LY 25; 18, 32

Meinformal (see Meenformal): Mevagh DL 38; 55

Meirogs stones: Culfeightrin AM 24; 77

Melbourne, Lord: Ballyscullion LY 6; 60

Mellan, Margaret: Carrickfergus AM 37; 76

Mellgoim Promontory: Lough Swilly DL 38; 113–14, 118

Mellgoim tower: Lough Swilly DL 38; 114

Mellifont (Louth): Newry DN 3; 66

Mellon, Bernard: Maghera LY 18; 32, 61

Mellon, Daniel: Duneane AM 19; 115

Mellon, J.: Misc. DL 39; 196

Mellon, Patrick: Maghera LY 18; 80

Mellor, Edward: Maghera LY 18; 80

Melloy, Mr: Clogher TE 5; 43

Melmore district: Lough Swilly DL 38; 114, 118

Melmore hill: Mevagh DL 38; 54

Melmore lough: Mevagh DL 38; 55–56

Melmore Point: Mevagh DL 38; 54, 56

Melmore td: Mevagh DL 38; 55, 63

Melmore tower: Mevagh DL 38; 54, 56, 58

Melnaharda Point: Lough Swilly DL 38; 114, 117

Melon, Felix: Drummaul AM 19; 90

Melon, Henry: Drummaul AM 19; 90

Melon, Jane: Magilligan LY 11; 94

Melon, John: Kilcronaghan LY 31; 85

Melon, Nanvy: Magilligan LY 11; 94

Melough (see Mealough): Drumbo DN 7; 61, 63

Melsesshaugh td: Clonleigh DL 39; 12

Melville, Richard: Loughinisland DN 17; 96

Melvin lough: Cleenish FH 14; 13

Melvin lough: Devenish FH 14; 47–48

Melvin lough: Inishmacsaint FH 14; 70, 72–73, 80

Melvin, Mr: Killowen LY 33; 160

Memel (Prussia): Maghera LY 18; 5

Memel: Antrim AM 29; 17

Memel: Coleraine LY 33; 86–87

Memel: Kirkinriola AM 23; 102

Memel: Tamlaght O'Crilly LY 18; 111

Menagh, Robert: Bovevagh LY 25; 45

Menaghill td: Donaghedy TE 5; 92

Menagluagh lough: Devenish FH 14; 47

Menai td: Aghanloo LY 11; 12

Menamean lough: Inishmacsaint FH 14; 71

Menawelkin lough: Inishmacsaint FH 14; 71

Meneenageer chapel: Manorhamilton Union LM 40; 53

Meneight, Mary: Aghalee AM 21; 40

Menie hill: Cumber LY 28; 3, 5, 11, 72, 85, 87

Menight, Joshua: Blaris AM 8; 29

Menow, James: Tamlaght TE 20; 77, 122

Menow, John: Tamlaght TE 20; 104, 129

Menow, Saly: Tamlaght TE 20; 77

Menow, William: Tamlaght TE 20; 81

Mercator, Gerard: Dunboe LY 11; 61

Mercer, Bernard: Hillsborough DN 12; 106

Mercer, John: Blaris DN 12; 40

Mercer, John: Hillsborough DN 12; 107

Mercer, Messrs: Blaris AM 8; 23

Mercer, Michael: Hillsborough DN 12; 106

Mercer, Moses: Hillsborough DN 12; 105, 105

Mercer, Stephenson: Hillsborough DN 12; 106

Mercer, Thomas: Drumachose LY 9; 104, 112

Mercer, Thomas: Tamlaght Finlagan LY 25; 108

Mercer, William: Hillsborough DN 12; 105

Meredith, Elizabeth: Hillsborough DN 12; 107

Merian springs: Ballywillin LY 33; 39–40, 44

Merit, Thomas: Hillsborough DN 12; 107

Mernious locality: Banagher LY 30; 110

Merrag rock: Magilligan LY 11; 126

Merran, family: Carnmoney AM 2; 76

Merrick stone: Magilligan LY 11; 99

Merrick, Mrs: Clonmany DL 38; 17–18

Merriman, John: Misc. DN 17; 117

Merrionstown locality: Carrickfergus AM 37; 94

Merry, family: Dunluce AM 16; 117

Merry, family: Ramoan AM 24; 107

Merryfield, Rev.: Carnmoney AM 2; 75

Merryport (see Maryport)

Merville House: Carnmoney AM 2; 46, 53, 84

Merville House: Newry DN 3; 67

Mervyn, Audley: Aghanloo LY 11; 4

Mervyn, Audley: Derryvullan FH 14; 33

Mervyn, Audley: Drumragh TE 5; 108

Mervyn, Audley.: Magheraculmoney FH 14; 111

Mervyn, Capt.: Clogher TE 5; 31

Meskinmore hill: Killygarvan DL 38; 36, 40

Mesterfee, Henry: Carrickfergus AM 37; 193

Metcalf, Capt.: Clonmany DL 38; 14

Mettican Glebe bogs: Errigal LY 27; 54

Mettican Glebe bridge: Errigal LY 27; 60

Mettican Glebe fort [I]: Errigal LY 27; 42, 67

Mettican Glebe fort [II]: Errigal LY 27; 42, 68

Mettican Glebe grey stone: Errigal LY 27; 45, 67

Mettican Glebe quarry: Errigal LY 27; 91

Mettican Glebe td: Errigal LY 27; 39, 41, 60, 65, 83, 88, 91–92

Mevagh church: Lough Swilly DL 38; 116

Mevagh coastguard station: Mevagh DL 38; 56

Mevagh coastguard station: Tullyaughnish DL 38; 92

Mevagh old church: Mevagh DL 38; 58

Mevagh ph: Clondavaddog DL 38; 3, 9

Mevagh ph: Kilmacrenan DL 38; 50

Mevagh ph: Lough Swilly DL 38; 115, 117, 128

Mevagh Point: Lough Swilly DL 38; 115–16

Mevagh shooting lodge: Mevagh DL 38; 59

Mevagh td: Mevagh DL 38; 63

Meve Roe, fairy: Dunluce AM 16; 114

Mevebradagh, woman named: Errigal LY 27; 77–78

Mew Island: Bangor DN 7; 21–22

Mew Island: Grey Abbey DN 7; 68

Mewhinney, James: Maghera LY 18; 54, 74

Mewhinny, family: Maghera LY 18; 13

Meyne, Rev. James: Ballyrashane LY 22; 52, 55–56

Meynell, Henry: Blaris AM 8; 16, 55, 84–85

Mhairin lough: Killymard DL 39; 95

Mhriartigh lough: Templecarn DL 39; 156

Michael, Alexander: Tamlaght O'Crilly LY 18; 114

Michan lough: Donegal DL 39; 42

Middle causeway: Billy AM 16; 42

Middle Division bog: Carrickfergus AM 37; 189

Middle Division Castle: Carrickfergus AM 37; 84

Middle Division fort [I]: Carrickfergus AM 37; 89

Middle Division fort [II]: Carrickfergus AM 37; 181

Middle Division fort [III]: Carrickfergus AM 37; 181

Middle Division fort [IV]: Carrickfergus AM 37; 182

Middle Division fort [V]: Carrickfergus AM 37; 182

Middle Division fort [VI]: Carrickfergus AM 37; 182

Middle Division fort [VII]: Carrickfergus AM 37; 182

Middle Division td: Carrickfergus AM 37; 33, 64, 81, 86, 89–92, 155, 158, 164, 173–74, 182–83, 186–87

Middlecess td: Donacavey TE 5; 81

Middleton and Banagher borough: Ballyscullion LY 6; 59

Middleton, Mr: Misc. DL 39; 192

Middletown: Tynan AH 1; 126–30, 132

Middletown brewery: Tynan AH 1; 128, 132

Middletown chapel: Tynan AH 1; 132

Middletown church: Tynan AH 1; 126–27, 132

Middletown dispensary: Tynan AH 1; 126

Middletown distillery: Tynan AH 1; 126, 128, 132

Middletown druid's altar: Drumlumman CN 40; 14

Middletown hospital: Tynan AH 1; 126, 132

Middletown malt mill: Tynan AH 1; 128

Middletown market house: Tynan AH 1; 132

Middletown meeting house: Tynan AH 1; 126 27, 132

Middletown school: Tynan AH 1; 129, 132

Middletown td: Drumlumman CN 40; 12

Middletown td: Tynan AH 1; 126

Middletown village: Kilmacteige SO 40; 195

Midhill td: Galloon FH 4; 95

Miel hill: Ballyrashane LY 22; 46

Migrealor lough: Killymard DL 39; 94

Mihan, family: Enniskillen FH 4; 75

Milburn, Miss: Aghadowey LY 22; 22

Mile Stone Island: Billy AM 16; 43

Milfie td: Misc. DN 17; 125

Milford: Blaris AM 8; 8

Milford: Clondavaddog DL 38; 6

Milford: Kilmacrenan DL 38; 50

Milford: Lough Swilly DL 38; 117, 128–29

Milford: Mevagh DL 38; 56–57

Milford: Tullyaughnish DL 38; 88–89

Milford corn mill: Tullyaughnish DL 38; 88–89

Milford graveyard: Tullyaughnish DL 38; 91

Milford revenue police barrack: Tullyaughnish DL 38; 88, 92

Milford school: Tullyaughnish DL 38; 88, 92

Milford tannery: Tullyaughnish DL 38; 88

Milford td: Tullyaughnish DL 38; 96

Milford timber and coalyard: Tullyaughnish DL 38; 88

Milford, Thomas: Killead AM 35; 48

Mill bay (see also Carnspindle bay): Island Magee AM 10; 18, 72, 77, 81, 85–86

Mill bay: Lough Swilly DL 38; 103, 147

Mill bay coastguard station: Island Magee AM 10; 89

Mill bay mill: Lough Swilly DL 38; 147

Mill bay pier: Island Magee AM 10; 80

Mill Brook House: Magherafelt LY 6; 96

Mill burn: Antrim AM 29; 3

Mill burn: Ballyaghran LY 33; 1

Mill Burn district: Misc. DN 17; 124

Mill farm standing stones: Bovevagh LY 25; 35, 39

Mill lough (see Racecourse lough): Enniskillen FH 4; 47

Mill Loughan fort: Kildollagh LY 22; 74

Mill Loughan graveyard: Kildollagh LY 22; 69

Mill Loughan mound: Kildollagh LY 22; 69

Mill Loughan td: Kildollagh LY 22; 67–68, 74–75

Mill Parks hamlet: Misc. DN 17; 127

Mill Pond lough: Clondavaddog DL 38; 3

Mill Quarter (Millquarter) td: Ballyscullion AM 19; 3, 7, 9–10, 13

Mill Quarter corn mill: Ballyscullion AM 19; 3, 8–9

Mill Quarter district: Ballymoney AM 16; 10

Mill Quarter grain stores: Ballyscullion AM 19; 10

Mill Quarter meeting house: Ballyscullion AM 19; 3, 8–9

Mill Quarter school: Ballyscullion AM 19; 7, 11

Mill Quarter school: Duneane AM 19; 124

Mill river: Lough Swilly DL 38; 101

Mill Town: Ballymoney AM 16; 10

Mill Town: Garvaghy DN 12; 80

Mill Town bridge: Ballymoney AM 16; 8

Mill, family: Ahoghill AM 23; 25

Mill, George: Carrickfergus AM 37; 128

Mill, Rev. William: Ballywillin LY 33; 33, 36–40, 42, 46–47

Mill, Rev. William: Coleraine LY 33; 63, 127

Milla, St: Clondermot LY 34; 47

Millan, Sarah: Maghera LY 18; 78

Millar and Nelson, Messrs: Kilwaughter AM 10; 117

Millar, Andrew: Kilwaughter AM 10; 117

Millar, Capt. (Ross Lodge): Connor AM 19; 16, 18, 21, 23, 30–31

Millar, Charles: Dunaghy AM 13; 21

Millar, Charles: Tamlaght TE 20; 92

Millar, family: Ballyclug AM 23; 60

Millar, family: Connor AM 19; 23

Millar, family: Culfeightrin AM 24; 59

Millar, family: Templepatrick AM 35; 118

Millar, George: Tamlaght TE 20; 80, 102

Millar, H.: Down DN 17; 53, 66

Millar, J.K.: Hillsborough DN 12; 105

Millar, James: Ahoghill AM 23; 39

Millar, James: Doagh AM 29; 98

Millar, James: Dunluce AM 16; 119

Millar, James [I]: Carrickfergus AM 37; 75

Millar, James [II]: Carrickfergus AM 37; 158

Millar, Jane: Island Magee AM 10; 94

Millar, Jesse: Connor AM 19; 21

Millar, John: Ahoghill AM 23; 35

Millar, John: Blaris AM 8; 36–37, 55, 69

Millar, John: Blaris DN 12; 45, 49, 51

Millar, John: Carrickfergus AM 37; 189–90

Millar, John: Dunaghy AM 13; 21

Millar, John: Magilligan LY 11; 125

Millar, Joseph: Ballywillin AM 16; 33

Millar, Martha: Tamlaght Finlagan LY 25; 124

Millar, Mary: Carrickfergus AM 37; 158

Millar, Mr (Ballintra): Drumhome DL 39; 60, 62

Millar, Mr: Blaris AM 8; 84

Millar, Mrs: Island Magee AM 10; 102

Millar, Rev.: Aghadowey LY 22; 26

Millar, Rose: Muckamore AM 35; 81

Millar, Samual: Ahoghill AM 23; 35

Millar, Sarah: Carrickfergus AM 37; 75

Millar, Thomas: Carrickfergus AM 37; 57, 134–35, 148

Millar, W.J.: Ahoghill AM 23; 39

Millar, William: Connor AM 19; 21

Millar, William: Muckamore AM 35; 81

Millar, William: Newry DN 3; 100

Millar, William: Templecorran AM 26; 119

Millbeg td: Aughnamullen MN 40; 76

Millbrook beetling engine houses: Blaris AM 8; 36, 140

Millbrook cotton factory: Kilwaughter AM 10; 112–13, 116

Millbrook House: Magherafelt LY 6; 91

Millbrook school: Kilwaughter AM 10; 116, 120

Millbrook Sunday school: Kilwaughter AM 10; 121

Millbrook td: Killygarvan DL 38; 39, 47

Millburn cove: Coleraine LY 33; 92, 132

Millburn House: Coleraine LY 33; 75, 91

Millburn td: Coleraine LY 33; 145

Millen, family: Ballynure AM 32; 56

Millen, family: Ballywillin AM 16; 32

Millen, John: Tamlaght Finlagan LY 25; 108

Millen, Margret: Tamlaght Finlagan LY 25; 119

Millen, Thomas: Racavan AM 13; 96, 100

Millen, William: Connor AM 19; 28

Millens locality: Dungiven LY 15; 65

Miller, A.: Clondermot LY 34; 37–38

Miller, Alexander: Ballywillin LY 33; 51

Miller, Alexander: Coleraine LY 33; 127

Miller, Alexander: Down DN 17; 46, 50–51

Miller, Alexander: Ramoan AM 24; 94

Miller, Andrew: Maghera LY 18; 53

Miller, Ann: Tamlaght O'Crilly LY 18; 137

Miller, Bell: Clondermot LY 34; 32

Miller, Cathrine: Tamlaght Finlagan LY 25; 119

Miller, David: Ballyaghran LY 33; 28

Miller, David: Desertoghill LY 27; 16

Miller, David: Macosquin LY 22; 107

Miller, Elenor: Tamlaght Finlagan LY 25; 119

Miller, Elizabeth: Ballywillin LY 33; 51

Miller, family: Antrim AM 29; 24

Miller, family: Banagher LY 30; 64

Miller, family: Carrickfergus AM 37; 93

Miller, family: Derrykeighan AM 16; 89

Miller, family: Desertmartin LY 31; 55

Miller, family: Desertoghill LY 27; 5, 30

Miller, family: Killead AM 35; 17

Miller, family: Maghera LY 18; 13, 24, 48

Miller, Henery: Killowen LY 33; 172

Miller, J.R.: Artrea LY 6; 8, 15

Miller, J.R.: Ballynascreen LY 31; 12

Miller, J.R.: Desertlyn LY 31; 39–40

Miller, J.R.: Kilcronaghan LY 31; 65, 82
Miller, J.W.: Connor AM 19; 28
Miller, James: Bovevagh LY 25; 17, 41
Miller, James: Cumber LY 28; 43
Miller, James: Drumachose LY 9; 85, 123, 132
Miller, Jane: Carrickfergus AM 37; 118
Miller, Jane: Faughanvale LY 36; 30
Miller, Jane: Macosquin LY 22; 122
Miller, Janet: Island Magee AM 10; 66
Miller, John: Aghadowey LY 22; 9
Miller, John: Artrea LY 6; 37
Miller, John: Balteagh LY 9; 29
Miller, John: Blaris AM 8; 62, 85
Miller, John: Carrickfergus AM 37; 114
Miller, John: Cumber LY 28; 86
Miller, John [I]: Coleraine LY 33; 145
Miller, John [I]: Macosquin LY 22; 83, 105
Miller, John [II]: Coleraine LY 33; 146
Miller, John [II]: Macosquin LY 22; 111
Miller, John [III]: Macosquin LY 22; 122
Miller, Joseph: Ballyrashane LY 22; 56
Miller, Joseph: Balteagh LY 9; 29
Miller, Joseph: Clondermot LY 34; 13, 16, 40, 83, 94
Miller, Joseph: Tamlaght Finlagan LY 25; 119
Miller, Margaret: Coleraine LY 33; 145
Miller, Mathew: Banagher LY 30; 64
Miller, Mr (Portaferry): Ballyphilip DN 7; 8
Miller, Mr (Portaferry): Misc. DN 17; 126
Miller, Mr: Bright DN 17; 35
Miller, Mr: Clondermot LY 34; 104
Miller, Mr: Comber DN 7; 33, 39
Miller, Mr: Killyleagh DN 17; 85
Miller, Mrs: Maghera LY 18; 53
Miller, Mrs Rowley: Desertlyn LY 31; 48–49
Miller, Mrs Rowley: Desertmartin LY 31; 57
Miller, Oliver: Clondermot LY 34; 83
Miller, Patt: Culfeightrin AM 24; 54
Miller, Quinton: Desertoghill LY 27; 16
Miller, Rebecca: Derryaghy AM 8; 115
Miller, Rev.: Loughgilly AH 1; 86–87
Miller, Rev. Brice: Desertoghill LY 27; 10
Miller, Rev. George: Clogher TE 5; 40
Miller, Rev. George: Derryvullan FH 14; 35–36, 44, 46
Miller, Richard: Blaris DN 12; 50
Miller, Robert: Clondermot LY 34; 13, 17, 40, 83, 94, 98
Miller, Robert: Tamlaght Finlagan LY 25; 110
Miller, Robert [I]: Cumber LY 28; 56
Miller, Robert [II]: Cumber LY 28; 56
Miller, Rowley: Artrea LY 6; 15, 18
Miller, Rowley: Ballynascreen LY 31; 12
Miller, Rowley: Desertlyn LY 31; 38–40, 45, 49
Miller, Rowley: Kilcronaghan LY 31; 65, 71, 73, 82

Miller, Rowley: Lissan LY 31; 90, 96, 98, 104
Miller, W.: Maghera LY 18; 66
Miller, Westley: Carrickfergus AM 37; 129
Miller, William: Aghanloo LY 11; 25
Miller, William: Balteagh LY 9; 28
Miller, William: Blaris AM 8; 22
Miller, William: Carrickfergus AM 37; 115
Miller, William: Drumachose LY 9; 104
Miller, William: Dungiven LY 15; 96–97
Miller, William: Faughanvale LY 36; 40, 42, 45–46
Miller, William: Macosquin LY 22; 117
Miller, William: Tamlaght O'Crilly LY 18; 137
Millfarm td: Urney DL 39; 181
Millgrange mills: Carlingford LH 40; 59
Millgrange td: Carlingford LH 40; 57–59
Mill-head (see Hillhead): Donagh DL 38; 33
Millican, James: Carrickfergus AM 37; 162
Millican, James: Kilcronaghan LY 31; 87
Millican, James: Lissan LY 31; 95
Millican, John [I]: Maghera LY 18; 80
Millican, John [II]: Maghera LY 18; 81
Millican, Samual: Bovevagh LY 25; 52
Millican, William: Ballyscullion LY 6; 71
Millican, William: Lissan LY 31; 94–95
Millicut, Rev. James: Lissan LY 31; 103
Milligan [or Millikin], Thomas: Killead AM 35; 42, 47
Milligan, Samuel: Carrickfergus AM 37; 109
Milligan, William: Kilcronaghan LY 31; 74
Milliken, Ally: Ballymoney AM 16; 17
Milliken, David: Carrickfergus AM 37; 112
Milliken, family: Carmavy AM 35; 2
Milliken, James: Magherafelt LY 6; 107–08
Milliken, Jane: Island Magee AM 10; 69, 97
Milliken, Miss: Island Magee AM 10; 98
Milliken, Mrs: Island Magee AM 10; 98
Milliken, Robert: Coleraine LY 33; 72
Milliken, William: Aghadowey LY 22; 9
Millikin, family: Carrickfergus AM 37; 93
Millikin, James: Island Magee AM 10; 78, 80
Millikin, John: Island Magee AM 10; 101
Millikin, Samuel: Hillsborough DN 12; 105
Millikin, Thomas: Island Magee AM 10; 88
Millikin, W.: Drumbo DN 7; 60
Millin bay: Witter DN 7; 125–26
Millin, Maryann: Drumachose LY 9; 133
Milling, James: Culfeightrin AM 24; 85
Millisle: Donaghadee DN 7; 45, 50
Millisle corn mill: Donaghadee DN 7; 50–51
Millisle meeting house: Donaghadee DN 7; 50–51
Millisle school: Donaghadee DN 7; 50–51
Millix fort: Errigal Keerogue TE 20; 55
Millix gravel pits: Errigal Keerogue TE 20; 55
Millix quarries: Errigal Keerogue TE 20; 55
Millix td: Errigal Keerogue TE 20; 49, 55, 57

Millmount corn and flour mill: Carrickfergus AM 37; 45, 47, 138, 172

Millmount House: Drummaul AM 19; 44

Millmount House: Seapatrick DN 12; 125, 132

Millpark Murchossy td: Clogher TE 5; 53

Millpladdy bank: Castleboy DN 7; 26

Millpladdy rock: Ardkeen DN 7; 1

Mills, Allen: Billy AM 16; 61

Mills, family: Misc. LY 36; 104

Mills, Frances: Aghaderg DN 12; 8

Mills, Isabella: Clondermot LY 34; 88–90, 93, 95

Mills, Jane: Ballyscullion AM 19; 12

Mills, John: Clondermot LY 34; 37, 78–80, 104

Mills, Matthew: Lissan LY 31; 109

Mills, Mr: Cumber LY 28; 75

Mills, Mr: Killea and Taughboyne DL 39; 87

Mills, Rev. Richard: Aghaderg DN 12; 8

Mills, Richard: Blaris DN 12; 46

Mills, William: Tyholland MN 40; 175

Mills' mill: Killea and Taughboyne DL 39; 87

Millsessaugh td: Misc. DL 39; 198

Millstone field: Aghanloo LY 11; 27

Milltate td: Derryvullan FH 14; 46

Milltate td: Galloon FH 4; 95

Milltown (Miletown) td: Kinawley FH 4; 115, 121

Milltown Ballybogan td: Clonleigh DL 39; 12

Milltown bridge: Maghera LY 18; 9, 63

Milltown corn kilns: Antrim AM 29; 20

Milltown corn mill: Antrim AM 29; 19–21

Milltown corn mill: Kinawley FH 4; 115

Milltown corn mill: Raymoghy DL 39; 133

Milltown corn mill: Tartaraghan AH 1; 120

Milltown flax mill: Ardstraw TE 5; 4

Milltown fort: Ardstraw TE 5; 12

Milltown fort: Kilwaughter AM 10; 118

Milltown hamlet: Antrim AM 29; 19–20, 40

Milltown hamlet: Desertcreat TE 20; 34

Milltown hamlet: Drummaul AM 19; 85, 89

Milltown hamlet: Killead AM 35; 11, 14–15, 47

Milltown hamlet: Misc. AM 10; 130

Milltown hamlet: Rossorry FH 14; 116

Milltown locality: Killymard DL 39; 98

Milltown Lodge: Derryaghy AM 8; 105

Milltown Lower td: Lough Swilly DL 38; 135

Milltown mill: Manorhamilton Union LM 40; 50

Milltown school: Aghadowey LY 22; 13, 19, 21

Milltown school: Ahoghill AM 23; 22–23

Milltown school: Ballynure AM 32; 50, 65–66, 71

Milltown school: Culfeightrin AM 24; 85

Milltown school: Maghera LY 18; 31

Milltown spade mill: Killymard DL 39; 96

Milltown Sunday school: Aghadowey LY 22; 13, 21

Milltown Sunday school: Ballynure AM 32; 65

Milltown td: Ardstraw TE 5; 4, 12

Milltown td: Clogher TE 5; 34

Milltown td: Convoy DL 39; 21

Milltown td: Conwal DL 39; 27

Milltown td: Leckpatrick TE 5; 125

Milltown td: Lough Swilly DL 38; 145, 145

Milltown td: Magilligan LY 11; 83, 95, 126, 137

Milltown td: Newry DN 3; 61

Milltown td: Raphoe DL 39; 126

Milltown td: Raymoghy DL 39; 138, 141

Milltown td: Tamlaght Finlagan LY 25; 73–74

Milltown td: Tartaraghan AH 1; 121

Milltown village: Drumbo DN 7; 60

Milltown village: Faughanvale LY 36; 8

Milmoy (see Mobuoy): Ahoghill AM 23; 45

Milroy, Mary: Ballymoney AM 16; 26

Milton corn mill: Donegal DL 39; 47

Milton House: Desertcreat TE 20; 36

Milton td: Donegal DL 39; 44

Miltown (see Milltown): Raymoghy DL 39; 141

Miltown flax mill: Ardstraw TE 5; 14

Miltown spade foundry: Ardstraw TE 5; 14

Miltown td: Ematris MN 40; 116

Minadrin lough: Donegal DL 39; 43

Minadrin td: Donegal DL 39; 43

Minagallagher (see Minegallagher): Faughanvale LY 36; 58

Minaghuis lough: Killymard DL 39; 94

Minaguishmore td: Killymard DL 39; 99

Minaillum lough: Templecarn DL 39; 156

Minale chapel: Drumgoon CN 40; 6

Minambrock lough: Donegal DL 39; 42

Minambrock td: Donegal DL 39; 42

Minchifrie td: Templecarn DL 39; 164

Minchotha, woman named: Clondermot LY 34; 47

Minden (Germany): Kilbroney DN 3; 32

Mindilpier hill: Templecarn DL 39; 164

Mindoran bridge: Clonmany DL 38; 14

Mindoran standing stones: Clonmany DL 38; 16

Mindoran td: Clonmany DL 38; 12–13, 18–20

Mindoran td: Mintiaghs DL 38; 67

Mindoran tuck mill: Clonmany DL 38; 14

Minearney (see Minearny)

Minearny td: Magilligan LY 11; 92, 95, 126, 129

Minegallagher Glebe td: Cumber LY 28; 66

Minegallagher Glebe td: Faughanvale LY 36; 17, 53, 58, 61, 69, 77, 89, 96, 99

Minegallagher hill: Faughanvale LY 36; 3

Minen (see Meenan): Aghaderg DN 12; 3

Mineveigh hill: Tullyniskan TE 20; 138

Minian (see Meenan): Aghaderg DN 12; 3

Minicliffe mountain: Mintiaghs DL 38; 64–65

Minicliffe td: Mintiaghs DL 38; 66–67

Minicliffe wood: Mintiaghs DL 38; 65

Minigar td: Dromore TE 5; 99

Minigone td: Dromore TE 5; 99

Minine (see Meenan): Aghaderg DN 12; 3

Miniss, [Robert or William]: Doagh AM 29; 97, 99

Miniss, Bristow: Ahoghill AM 23; 50

Miniss, Bristow: Ballynascreen LY 31; 16

Miniss, John: Muckamore AM 35; 80

Miniss, William: Drumbeg AM 8; 123, 133

Minisse, man named: Muckamore AM 35; 79

Minmore td: Magheraculmoney FH 14; 103

Minneagh (see Money): Aughnamullen MN 40; 76

Minneyhaughley td: Raymoghy DL 39; 138

Minneymore td: Raymoghy DL 39; 138

Minniagh (see Money): Aughnamullen MN 40; 70

Minniagh school: Clondavaddog DL 38; 7

Minnis, Mrs: Hillsborough DN 12; 87

Minnis, William: Carrickfergus AM 37; 112

Minnymore forts: Manorhamilton Union LM 40; 52

Minnymore td: Donaghmore DN 3; 9

Minorca (Spain): Misc. AM 10; 130

Minorca: Drummaul AM 19; 71

Minore House: Currin MN 40; 89

Minrin td: Inishmacsaint FH 14; 72

Mintiaghs lough: Mintiaghs DL 38; 64–65, 67

Mintiaghs ph: Clonmany DL 38; 12, 14, 20

Mintiaghs ph: Desertegney DL 38; 24

Mintiaghs ph: Killygarvan DL 38; 39

Mintiaghs ph: Mevagh DL 38; 57

Mintiaghs river: Mintiaghs DL 38; 64

Minticat td: Convoy DL 39; 22

Minto, Lord: Donacavey TE 5; 74

Minuads creek: Lough Swilly DL 38; 108

Misskimin, family: Ballynure AM 32; 56

Mistyburn corn mill: Glenwhirry AM 32; 76, 79

Mitchel, David: Cumber LY 28; 52–53

Mitchel, family: Glynn AM 26; 45

Mitchel, family: Kilroot AM 26; 74

Mitchel, James: Macosquin LY 22; 101–02

Mitchel, John: Tamlaght Finlagan LY 25; 119

Mitchel, Joseph: Tamlaght Finlagan LY 25; 119

Mitchel, Margaret: Island Magee AM 10; 66, 94

Mitchel, Maryann: Tamlaght Finlagan LY 25; 119

Mitchel, Mr: Cumber LY 28; 53

Mitchel, Mrs (Toneduff): Cumber LY 28; 57

Mitchel, Rev. John: Newry DN 3; 79, 95, 99–101, 103

Mitchel, Solomon: Tamlaght Finlagan LY 25; 119

Mitchel, Susanna (Jnr): Tamlaght Finlagan LY 25; 119

Mitchel, Susanna (Snr): Tamlaght Finlagan LY 25; 119

Mitchel, Thomas: Tamlaght Finlagan LY 25; 119

Mitchel, Tony: Tamlaght Finlagan LY 25; 119

Mitchel, W.S.: Drumbo DN 7; 58

Mitchelburne, Elizabeth: Clondermot LY 34; 81

Mitchelburne, John: Clondermot LY 34; 8, 10, 12, 16–17, 26–27, 40–41, 43, 45, 81–83, 93–94, 98, 101, 103–04, 106

Mitchelburne, Molly: Clondermot LY 34; 81

Mitchelburne, Richard: Clondermot LY 34; 41, 45

Mitchelburne's well: Clondermot LY 34; 8, 43

Mitchell, Alexander: Ballywillin LY 33; 31, 43

Mitchell, Alexander: Coleraine LY 33; 59, 72, 127, 129, 141–42, 144

Mitchell, Alexander: Killanny MN 40; 134

Mitchell, Alexander: Magheracloone MN 40; 138, 141

Mitchell, Alexander: Magheross MN 40; 145–46, 149, 151

Mitchell, Allen: Clogher TE 5; 40

Mitchell, Daniel: Ahoghill AM 23; 38

Mitchell, David: Clondermot LY 34; 42, 88, 91–93, 95

Mitchell, family: Enniskillen FH 4; 58

Mitchell, family: Island Magee AM 10; 70

Mitchell, family: Kilroot AM 26; 75

Mitchell, family: Templecorran AM 26; 117, 119

Mitchell, Henry: Duneane AM 19; 123

Mitchell, James: Artrea LY 6; 31

Mitchell, James: Carrickfergus AM 37; 108

Mitchell, James: Derrykeighan AM 16; 93

Mitchell, James: Dungiven LY 15; 25

Mitchell, John: Desertoghill LY 27; 17, 26

Mitchell, John: Lissan LY 31; 109

Mitchell, John: Maghera LY 18; 79

Mitchell, John: Tamlaght Finlagan LY 25; 69

Mitchell, John: Tydavnet MN 40; 170

Mitchell, Joseph: Newry DN 3; 100, 104

Mitchell, M.J.: Duneane AM 19; 123

Mitchell, Margaret: Duneane AM 19; 123

Mitchell, Mary: Duneane AM 19; 123

Mitchell, Mary: Templepatrick AM 35; 134

Mitchell, Mr (Markethill): Ballymore AH 1; 9, 13–16, 18

Mitchell, Mr: Dungiven LY 15; 25, 113–14

Mitchell, Mrs: Ballymoney AM 16; 15–17

Mitchell, Rev. Allen: Donagh MN 40; 103

Mitchell, Robert: Duneane AM 19; 123

Mitchell, Thomas: Ballymoney AM 16; 17

Mitchell, Thomas: Magilligan LY 11; 88

Mitchell, William: Ahoghill AM 23; 38

Mitchell, William: Artrea LY 6; 31

Mitchell, William: Coleraine LY 33; 73

Mitchell, William: Duneane AM 19; 123

Mitchell, William: Dungiven LY 15; 25

Mitchell, William: Kilrea LY 27; 129

Mitter, Mr: Comber DN 7; 33

Mna-yesh (see Doonan): Cumber LY 28; 30

Moaneen-nasleigh bog: Culfeightrin AM 24; 56

Moat fort: Aghalurcher FH 4; 9–10

Moat school: Aghalurcher FH 4; 11

Moate, James: Templecorran AM 26; 132

Moate, Thomas: Templecorran AM 26; 132

Mobuoy (Maboy) td: Clondermot LY 34; 83
Mobuoy (Morbury) td: Ahoghill AM 23; 34, 38
Mobuoy bog: Lissan LY 31; 100
Mobuoy fort [I]: Ahoghill AM 23; 34
Mobuoy fort [II]: Ahoghill AM 23; 34
Mobuoy school: Ahoghill AM 23; 23, 45, 48
Mobuoy Sunday school: Ahoghill AM 23; 48
Mobuoy td: Lissan LY 31; 92, 99, 108
Mobuy (see Mobuoy): Ahoghill AM 23; 23
Mobuy village: Kilbarron DL 39; 77
Mochaimoc, St: Enniskillen FH 4; 70
Mockbeggar td: Galloon FH 4; 95
Moclan, St: Clondermot LY 34; 47
Modena td: Drummully FH 4; 34
Modfen creek: Lough Swilly DL 38; 120
Moffat, Hugh: Kilbroney DN 3; 34
Moffat, James: Drumachose LY 9; 104
Moffat, Rev. Charles: Newry DN 3; 71, 79, 99, 103
Moffat, Rev. William: Clogher TE 5; 40
Moffat, Rev. William: Currin MN 40; 89, 97
Moffat, Rev. William: Galloon FH 4; 96
Moffat, Rev. William: Moira DN 12; 119
Moffat, William: Tartaraghan AH 1; 119
Moffatt, Rev. William: Drummully FH 4; 39–40
Moffet, Rev, Walter: Saintfield DN 7; 114
Moffit, Agnes: Carrickfergus AM 37; 158
Moffit, Eliza: Ballynure AM 32; 71
Moffit, Eliza: Carrickfergus AM 37; 158
Moffit, Ellen: Ballynure AM 32; 71
Moffit, Ellen: Carrickfergus AM 37; 158
Moffit, James: Enniskillen FH 4; 75
Moffit, John: Carrickfergus AM 37; 159
Moffit, Nancy: Carrickfergus AM 37; 158
Moffit, Robert: Carrickfergus AM 37; 158
Moffit, Sally: Ballynure AM 32; 71
Moffit, Sarah: Carrickfergus AM 37; 158
Moffit, William: Ballynure AM 32; 71
Moffit, William: Carrickfergus AM 37; 158
Moffitt, James: Aghanloo LY 11; 16–17, 24
Mogarrow district: Misc. SO 40; 198
Mogey, family: Billy AM 16; 58, 68
Moghan, family: Faughanvale LY 36; 48
Mogherenny td: Longfield TE 5; 132
Mogy, James: Billy AM 16; 75
Moher td: Killesher FH 14; 87
Moher td: Kinawley FH 4; 110
Mohill (Leitrim): Ballyscullion AM 19; 2
Mohill (see Movilla): Misc. DN 17; 127
Moileys glen: Banagher LY 30; 113
Moiloge, St: Culfeightrin AM 24; 58
Moira: Aghaderg DN 12; 6
Moira: Aghagallon AM 21; 1, 10, 23
Moira: Aghalee AM 21; 26–27, 31, 34
Moira: Annaclone DN 12; 13
Moira: Ballinderry AM 21; 41–42, 45

Moira: Blaris AM 8; 16
Moira: Camlin AM 21; 62
Moira: Glenavy AM 21; 77–78, 81, 85–86
Moira: Magheramesk AM 21; 112–20, 123, 126, 129–30
Moira: Misc. AM 10; 129
Moira: Misc. DN 17; 116
Moira: Moira DN 12; 117, 119, 122
Moira: Seapatrick DN 12; 131
Moira chapel: Moira DN 12; 119, 121
Moira church: Moira DN 12; 117, 121
Moira corn mill: Moira DN 12; 121
Moira female school: Moira DN 12; 120
Moira male school: Moira DN 12; 119
Moira market house: Moira DN 12; 119, 121
Moira meeting house (A): Moira DN 12; 119
Moira meeting house (P): Aghalee AM 21; 38
Moira meeting house (P): Moira DN 12; 119, 121
Moira meeting house (S): Moira DN 12; 121
Moira meeting houses: Aghagallon AM 21; 21
Moira meeting houses: Magheramesk AM 21; 128
Moira ph: Aghagallon AM 21; 1
Moira ph: Aghalee AM 21; 26, 29, 38
Moira ph: Dromore DN 12; 70, 73
Moira ph: Hillsborough DN 12; 87–88, 93
Moira ph: Magheralin DN 12; 109
Moira ph: Magheramesk AM 21; 112, 116
Moira ph: Misc. DN 17; 118, 121
Moira ph: Montiaghs AH 1; 91
Moira ph: Shankill DN 12; 138–39
Moira school: Moira DN 12; 121
Moira td: Drumbo DN 7; 59
Moira toll-gates: Magheramesk AM 21; 119
Moira, Earl of: Blaris AM 8; 26
Moira, Earl of: Magheradrool DN 17; 101
Moira, family: Magheragall AM 21; 101
Moiry (Armagh): Banagher LY 30; 103
Molaisse, St: Devenish FH 14; 60
Molena td: Drummully FH 4; 39
Molenan td: Clondermot LY 34; 42
Moles, Oliver: Tullylish DN 12; 146
Molesworth, Maj.: Clonfeacle AH 1; 25
Moleyneaux, Rev. H.W.: Raloo AM 32; 131
Moll McCurry's well: Tamlaght Finlagan LY 25; 111–12
Moll O'Reilly's lough: Tamlaght O'Crilly LY 18; 83, 125
Mollan, Dr: Newry DN 3; 98, 103
Mollan, John: Newry DN 3; 99, 104
Mollewe district: Misc. SO 40; 198
Mollockmoyle district: Templecorran AM 26; 82
Mollores rocks: Lough Swilly DL 38; 101
Molloy, family: Tamlaght O'Crilly LY 18; 93
Molloy, William: Hillsborough DN 12; 106
Molly-Barney td: Clogher TE 5; 54

Mollybreen hill: Belleek FH 14; 1
Mollybreen lough: Belleek FH 14; 1
Mollybreen td: Belleek FH 14; 1
Molony, William: Carrickfergus AM 37; 141, 151
Molua, St: Clondermot LY 34; 63
Molvay (see Mobuoy): Ahoghill AM 23; 48
Molyneau, family: Carnmoney AM 2; 76
Molyneaux, Andrew: Killead AM 35; 38, 52
Molyneaux, Dr: Antrim AM 29; 14
Molyneaux, family: Carnmoney AM 2; 102
Molyneaux, family: Killead AM 35; 17, 22
Molyneaux, John [I]: Killead AM 35; 22
Molyneaux, John [II]: Killead AM 35; 22, 50
Molyneaux, William: Killead AM 35; 49
Molyneax, Rev. H.W.: Kilwaughter AM 10; 120
Molyneux, John: Muckamore AM 35; 78
Molyneux, Samuel: Muckamore AM 35; 78
Molyneux, Thomas: Clonleigh DL 39; 7
Molyneux, Thomas: Kilmore AH 1; 65, 69
Molyneux, Thomas: Loughgall AH 1; 80–82
Momeen bog: Killea and Taughboyne DL 39; 80
Momeen Lower graveyard: Taughboyne DL 39; 154
Momeen Lower td: Taughboyne DL 39; 148, 154
Momeen quarry: Taughboyne DL 39; 150
Momeen td: Killea and Taughboyne DL 39; 80
Momeen td: Taughboyne DL 39; 150
Momeen Upper td: Taughboyne DL 39; 148, 154
Mona lough: Aghagallon AM 21; 3
Monagh (Clare): Newry DN 3; 66
Monagh, Thomas: Carrickfergus AM 37; 119
Monaghan bank: Ballybay MN 40; 80
Monaghan barony: Aghabog MN 40; 62
Monaghan barony: Ballybay MN 40; 78
Monaghan barony: Clones FH 4; 26, 29
Monaghan barony: Donacavey TE 5; 66
Monaghan barony: Misc. LY 36; 105
Monaghan barony: Monaghan MN 40; 159
Monaghan barony: Tydavnet MN 40; 169
Monaghan barony: Tyholland MN 40; 174
Monaghan church: Clones FH 4; 27
Monaghan corn mill: Devenish FH 14; 53
Monaghan county: Banagher LY 30; 71
Monaghan county: Clogher TE 5; 24
Monaghan county: Clondermot LY 34; 63, 73
Monaghan county: Clones FH 4; 26
Monaghan county: Currin MN 40; 88
Monaghan county: Drummully FH 4; 34, 36–37, 39
Monaghan county: Enniskeen CN 40; 26
Monaghan county: Enniskillen FH 4; 44, 51
Monaghan county: Faughanvale LY 36; 44
Monaghan county: Galloon FH 4; 92
Monaghan county: Killdrumsherdan CN 40; 31–32
Monaghan county: Misc. LY 36; 105–06
Monaghan county: Newry DN 3; 72, 87
Monaghan county: Termoneeny LY 6; 132

Monaghan county: Tynan AH 1; 127
Monaghan Duffe locality: Derryvullan FH 14; 39
Monaghan fort: Devenish FH 14; 55
Monaghan lough: Monaghan MN 40; 159
Monaghan ph: Clogher TE 5; 41
Monaghan ph: Donagh MN 40; 98–99
Monaghan ph: Errigal Truagh MN 40; 121
Monaghan ph: Tydavnet MN 40; 169–70
Monaghan ph: Tyholland MN 40; 174
Monaghan rectory: Clones FH 4; 29
Monaghan river: Coleraine LY 33; 97
Monaghan school: Kirkinriola AM 23; 112
Monaghan td: Devenish FH 14; 58
Monaghan td: Kirkinriola AM 23; 92
Monaghan town: Aghabog MN 40; 65–66
Monaghan town: Aghaloo TE 20; 4
Monaghan town: Aghalurcher FH 4; 1, 8
Monaghan town: Aghavea FH 4; 21, 25
Monaghan town: Aughnamullen MN 40; 75
Monaghan town: Ballybay MN 40; 80–83
Monaghan town: Carnteel TE 20; 21, 24
Monaghan town: Clogher TE 5; 33, 44
Monaghan town: Clondermot LY 34; 73
Monaghan town: Clones FH 4; 27
Monaghan town: Derryvullan FH 14; 39
Monaghan town: Donagh MN 40; 98, 100
Monaghan town: Donegal DL 39; 50
Monaghan town: Ematris MN 40; 114–16
Monaghan town: Errigal Truagh MN 40; 121–22
Monaghan town: Kilclief DN 17; 78
Monaghan town: Magheross MN 40; 152
Monaghan town: Monaghan MN 40; 159–60
Monaghan town: Muckno MN 40; 164, 166
Monaghan town: Newry DN 3; 78
Monaghan town: Newtownhamilton AH 1; 100
Monaghan town: Tydavnet MN 40; 170, 172
Monaghan town: Tyholland MN 40; 174–75
Monaghan town: Tynan AH 1; 126, 128
Monaghan Walk district: Enniskeen CN 40; 29
Monaghan, Hugh: Templecarn DL 39; 159
Monaghan, John: Ballyscullion LY 6; 57
Monaghan, Patrick: Skirts of Urney and Ardstraw
  TE 5; 140
Monaghan's bridge: Ardstraw TE 5; 14
Monaghbeg (see Managh Beg): Clondermot LY 34;
  72
Monalty House: Killanny MN 40; 131
Monalty House: Magheross MN 40; 156
Monalty lough: Killanny MN 40; 130
Monaltybane td: Killanny MN 40; 131
Monaltybane td: Magheross MN 40; 156
Monanacleigh td: Galloon FH 4; 95
Monancleugh (see Monanclogh): Armoy AM 24; 8
Monanclogh (Monaclough) td: Armoy AM 24; 1, 4
Monanclogh bog: Armoy AM 24; 1, 3

Monanclogh cove: Armoy AM 24; 8–9
Monanclogh standing stone: Armoy AM 24; 8
Monanoe Glebe td: Enniskillen FH 4; 81
Monantin td: Ballybay MN 40; 84
Monascribe td: Ballymascanlan LH 40; 55
Moncan (see Momeen): Killea and Taughboyne DL 39; 80
Monck, Araminta: Ballyscullion LY 6; 59
Monck, Catherine: Ballyscullion LY 6; 59
Monck, G.P.: Ballyscullion LY 6; 59
Monclink td: Raymoghy DL 39; 138, 141, 144, 190, 199
Moncrieff, Robert: Clondermot LY 34; 79
Mondooey bog: Misc. DL 39; 187
Mondooey Lower td: Raymoghy DL 39; 132, 139
Mondooey Middle td: Raymoghy DL 39; 138–39
Mondooey td: Raymoghy DL 39; 141, 144, 186, 199
Mondooey Upper td: Raymoghy DL 39; 132, 138
Mondowey (see Mondooey): Misc. DL 39; 187
Monea: Devenish FH 14; 52, 49, 55–56
Monea: Inishmacsaint FH 14; 77, 79
Monea Castle: Devenish FH 14; 53
Monea chapel: Devenish FH 14; 52, 56
Monea church: Devenish FH 14; 52, 56, 61
Monea Cottage: Devenish FH 14; 53, 55, 57
Monea Means fort: Devenish FH 14; 55
Monea Means school [I]: Devenish FH 14; 55–56
Monea Means school [II]: Devenish FH 14; 55–56
Monea Means td: Devenish FH 14; 58
Monean (see Momeen): Killea and Taughboyne DL 39; 80
Moneen corn mill: Killesher FH 14; 84
Moneenashinagh fort: Manorhamilton Union LM 40; 52
Moneenbaan td: Kinawley FH 4; 110
Moneenroe village: Kilmacteige SO 40; 196
Monehanegan (Moneyhanegan) td: Faughanvale LY 36; 17, 53, 57, 61, 69, 77–78, 89, 96
Monehanegan td: Cumber LY 28; 41, 62
Monellan House: Donaghmore DL 39; 30–31, 39
Monellan school: Donaghmore DL 39; 39
Monellan td: Donaghmore DL 39; 38
Monen td: Misc. DL 39; 198
Moneneull village: Kilmacteige SO 40; 196
Moness orchard: Taughboyne DL 39; 154
Moness td: Taughboyne DL 39; 148, 154, 196
Moness wood: Taughboyne DL 39; 148
Money (Mooney) td: Kilmore AH 1; 61, 65–66, 68, 71–72
Money House: Kilmore AH 1; 65
Money lough: Aghagallon AM 21; 10, 12, 16–17
Money rock: Bovevagh LY 25; 33
Money Scalp mountain: Kilmegan DN 3; 55
Money td: Aughnamullen MN 40; 70, 76
Money, family: Aghagallon AM 21; 9

Money, John: Blaris DN 12; 45
Moneybroom corn mill: Magheragall AM 21; 110
Moneybroom fort [I]: Magheragall AM 21; 105
Moneybroom fort [II]: Magheragall AM 21; 105
Moneybroom fort [III]: Magheragall AM 21; 105
Moneybroom fort [IV]: Magheragall AM 21; 106
Moneybroom fort [V]: Magheragall AM 21; 106
Moneyburn river: Enniskillen FH 4; 48, 78
Moneycanon (Moneycannon) td: Finvoy AM 23; 73
Moneycanon cove: Finvoy AM 23; 78
Moneycanon fort: Finvoy AM 23; 78
Moneycarragh river: Loughinisland DN 17; 95–96
Moneycarrie (Moneycarry) td: Aghadowey LY 22; 21, 34–35
Moneycarrie school: Aghadowey LY 22; 20–21, 34
Moneycarrie Sunday school: Aghadowey LY 22; 21
Moneycass Glebe bog: Laragh CN 40; 40
Moneycass Glebe school: Laragh CN 40; 43
Moneyconey bog: Ballynascreen LY 31; 20
Moneyconey mountain: Ballynascreen LY 31; 1
Moneyconey td: Ballynascreen LY 31; 7, 20–22, 27
Moneyconny (see Moneycarrie): Aghadowey LY 22; 20
Moneycrockroe td: Ballymascanlan LH 40; 55
Moneydarragh long stone: Kilkeel DN 3; 51
Moneydarragh td: Kilkeel DN 3; 51
Moneydig abbey: Desertoghill LY 27; 6, 31
Moneydig cave: Desertoghill LY 27; 23
Moneydig fort [I]: Desertoghill LY 27; 13, 21
Moneydig fort [II]: Desertoghill LY 27; 23
Moneydig hamlet: Desertoghill LY 27; 13
Moneydig meeting house: Desertoghill LY 27; 2, 4, 15, 17, 21, 27–28
Moneydig school: Desertoghill LY 27; 3, 16–17, 19–20, 33
Moneydig Sunday school: Desertoghill LY 27; 3
Moneydig td: Desertoghill LY 27; 6–7, 13, 18–19, 21–22, 29, 32
Moneydolly td: Ahoghill AM 23; 37–38
Moneyduff graveyard: Dunaghy AM 13; 17, 24
Moneyduff school: Dunaghy AM 13; 17
Moneyduff td: Dunaghy AM 13; 17, 24
Moneygelvin Castle: Taughboyne DL 39; 152, 185
Moneygelvin orchard: Misc. DL 39; 189
Moneygelvin td: Taughboyne DL 39; 150, 152
Moneyglass chapel: Ballyscullion AM 19; 12
Moneyglass chapel: Duneane AM 19; 115, 117
Moneyglass demesne: Duneane AM 19; 100
Moneyglass House: Duneane AM 19; 100, 117–18, 122
Moneyglass school: Duneane AM 19; 106, 125
Moneyglass td: Duneane AM 19; 94–96, 110, 112–14, 116, 122–23, 125
Moneyglass wood: Duneane AM 19; 111
Moneygore td: Drumballyroney DN 3; 16, 18

Moneygran (Moneyghran) td: Kilrea LY 27; 115, 117–18, 128

Moneygran bleach mill: Kilrea LY 27; 119–20, 128

Moneygran bog: Kilrea LY 27; 107, 114, 122, 127

Moneygran flax mill: Kilrea LY 27; 120

Moneygran fort: Kilrea LY 27; 113, 128–29

Moneygran school: Kilrea LY 27; 121–22

Moneygreen bog: Comber DN 7; 32

Moneygreggan td: Misc. DL 39; 194

Moneyguiggy bridge: Ballynascreen LY 31; 7

Moneyguiggy flax mill: Ballynascreen LY 31; 8

Moneyguiggy fort: Balteagh LY 9; 12, 26

Moneyguiggy school: Balteagh LY 9; 17, 39

Moneyguiggy td: Ballynascreen LY 31; 1, 8, 17, 141, 143

Moneyguiggy td: Balteagh LY 9; 10, 12, 14, 16–17, 26, 39, 45

Moneyguigy (see Moneyguiggy): Misc. LY 31; 141

Moneyhagan (see Moneyhoghan): Banagher LY 30; 60

Moneyhanagan (see Moneyhoghan): Banagher LY 30; 23

Moneyhaughan (see Moneyhoghan): Banagher LY 30; 22

Moneyhaughley td: Misc. DL 39; 199

Moneyhaw fort: Lissan LY 31; 100

Moneyhaw school: Lissan LY 31; 95

Moneyhaw td: Arboe LY 6; 1

Moneyhaw td: Artrea LY 6; 9, 32

Moneyhaw td: Desertlyn LY 31; 35

Moneyhaw td: Lissan LY 31; 94, 96, 101, 103–04, 106–09

Moneyhaw water: Arboe LY 6; 1

Moneyhoghan (Moneyhogan) td: Banagher LY 30; 22–23, 35, 60–62, 72, 91, 105–06, 109–10, 119–20, 124, 128, 131

Moneyhoghan fort [I]: Banagher LY 30; 77

Moneyhoghan fort [II]: Banagher LY 30; 77

Moneykenon td: Donaghedy TE 5; 92

Moneylane chapel: Kilmegan DN 3; 58

Moneylane school: Kilmegan DN 3; 59

Moneylane td: Kilmegan DN 3; 58

Moneylea bog: Taughboyne DL 39; 148

Moneyleck chapel: Rasharkin AM 23; 128, 130

Moneymakinn td: Aghalurcher FH 4; 14

Moneymore: Arboe LY 6; 1

Moneymore: Artrea LY 6; 5, 9, 15, 18, 39

Moneymore: Artrea TE 20; 6–8, 10

Moneymore: Ballinderry LY 6; 41

Moneymore: Ballinderry TE 20; 12

Moneymore: Ballyclog TE 20; 16–7

Moneymore: Ballynascreen LY 31; 8, 12, 20

Moneymore: Ballyscullion LY 6; 59

Moneymore: Banagher LY 30; 27, 29, 31, 106, 118, 131

Moneymore: Clondermot LY 34; 73

Moneymore: Cumber LY 28; 98

Moneymore: Desertlyn LY 31; 35–42, 45, 48–50

Moneymore: Desertmartin LY 31; 53–54, 57, 62–63

Moneymore: Drummaul AM 19; 80

Moneymore: Duneane AM 19; 95

Moneymore: Dungiven LY 15; 67, 109

Moneymore: Faughanvale LY 36; 22

Moneymore: Kilcronaghan LY 31; 73, 75, 78–79

Moneymore: Kildress TE 20; 58

Moneymore: Lissan LY 31; 90, 92–100, 102–03

Moneymore: Lissan TE 20; 69

Moneymore: Macosquin LY 22; 95

Moneymore: Misc. LY 31; 114, 116, 128, 131, 134

Moneymore: Tamlaght O'Crilly LY 18; 111

Moneymore: Tamlaght TE 20; 73, 77–82, 91, 102, 122, 127, 137

Moneymore: Tullyniskan TE 20; 141

Moneymore almshouses: Desertlyn LY 31; 41, 48–49

Moneymore bank: Desertlyn LY 31; 39–40

Moneymore brae: Artrea TE 20; 8

Moneymore brae: Tamlaght TE 20; 137

Moneymore Castle: Desertlyn LY 31; 37

Moneymore chapel: Artrea LY 6; 7

Moneymore chapel: Artrea TE 20; 8

Moneymore chapel: Desertlyn LY 31; 43, 46

Moneymore church: Artrea TE 20; 7–8

Moneymore church: Desertlyn LY 31; 35, 37–38, 50–51

Moneymore corn mill: Artrea LY 6; 37

Moneymore corn mill: Artrea TE 20; 9

Moneymore cornstore: Desertlyn LY 31; 38, 41

Moneymore county dispensary: Desertlyn LY 31; 49

Moneymore county dispensary: Lissan LY 31; 106

Moneymore dispensary: Artrea LY 6; 16

Moneymore dispensary: Artrea TE 20; 7

Moneymore dispensary: Desertlyn LY 31; 35, 39, 41, 45–46, 48–49, 122

Moneymore dispensary: Lissan LY 31; 92

Moneymore Drapers' female school: Artrea LY 6; 6, 16

Moneymore Drapers' female school: Artrea TE 20; 7

Moneymore Drapers' female school: Desertlyn LY 31; 35, 41, 49

Moneymore Drapers' male school: Artrea LY 6; 6, 16

Moneymore Drapers' male school: Artrea TE 20; 7

Moneymore Drapers' male school: Desertlyn LY 31; 35, 41, 49

Moneymore female school: Desertlyn LY 31; 41, 49–50

Moneymore forts: Artrea LY 6; 35

Moneymore graveyard: Desertlyn LY 31; 43

Moneymore hotel: Desertlyn LY 31; 35, 38
Moneymore infant school: Desertlyn LY 31; 46
Moneymore inn: Artrea TE 20; 7
Moneymore male school: Desertlyn LY 31; 41, 49
Moneymore manor: Ballyscullion LY 6; 58
Moneymore Mansion House: Desertlyn LY 31; 38–39
Moneymore market house: Artrea LY 6; 6
Moneymore market house: Artrea TE 20; 7
Moneymore market house: Desertlyn LY 31; 35, 38–39
Moneymore meeting house (P): Artrea LY 6; 5–6
Moneymore meeting house (P): Artrea TE 20; 7
Moneymore meeting house (P): Desertlyn LY 31; 38, 50–51
Moneymore meeting house (P): Lissan LY 31; 89, 103
Moneymore meeting house (S): Artrea LY 6; 6
Moneymore meeting house (S): Artrea TE 20; 7
Moneymore meeting house (S): Desertlyn LY 31; 38
Moneymore meeting house (S): Lissan LY 31; 89, 104
Moneymore new market house: Desertlyn LY 31; 38
Moneymore preaching house: Desertlyn LY 31; 51
Moneymore Presbyterian Sunday school: Desertlyn LY 31; 50–51
Moneymore private female school: Desertlyn LY 31; 49
Moneymore private school: Desertlyn LY 31; 49
Moneymore Sunday school: Artrea LY 6; 21
Moneymore Sunday school: Desertlyn LY 31; 50–51
Moneymore td: Artrea LY 6; 13, 35–38
Moneymore td: Maghera LY 18; 22, 31, 73, 79
Moneymore td: Raymoghy DL 39; 141, 186, 199
Moneymore town hall: Artrea TE 20; 7
Moneymore town hall: Desertlyn LY 31; 35, 38
Moneymore townparks: Artrea TE 20; 6
Moneymurish (see Moneyvreest): Magheraculmoney FH 14; 112
Moneynany (see Moneyneany)
Moneyneagh td: Loughguile AM 13; 68, 72
Moneyneaney (see Moneyneany): Ballynascreen LY 31; 19
Moneyneany (Moneyninea) td: Ballynascreen LY 31; 3–4, 6–7, 9–11, 14, 19–20, 25, 114–15, 118, 143
Moneyneany bog: Ballynascreen LY 31; 26
Moneyneany chapel: Ballynascreen LY 31; 5–6, 17, 20
Moneyneany district: Misc. LY 31; 116
Moneyneany fort: Ballynascreen LY 31; 25
Moneyneany graveyard: Ballynascreen LY 31; 20
Moneyneany mountain: Ballynascreen LY 31; 20
Moneyneany mountain: Drumachose LY 9; 74, 129
Moneyneany mountain: Dungiven LY 15; 1

Moneyneany rivulet: Misc. LY 31; 114
Moneyneany school: Ballynascreen LY 31; 17
Moneyneeny (see Moneyneany)
Moneynick altar: Duneane AM 19; 107
Moneynick cove: Duneane AM 19; 108–10, 119–20
Moneynick fort: Duneane AM 19; 107, 121–22
Moneynick graveyard: Duneane AM 19; 107
Moneynick school: Duneane AM 19; 105, 119, 125
Moneynick td: Duneane AM 19; 115, 123–24
Moneyrannel fort: Tamlaght Finlagan LY 25; 90
Moneyrannel td: Tamlaght Finlagan LY 25; 93, 109, 112, 120
Moneyrea (see Moneyreagh)
Moneyreagh meeting house (P): Comber DN 7; 31
Moneyreagh meeting house (U): Comber DN 7; 35, 38
Moneyreagh school: Comber DN 7; 34, 38
Moneyreagh td: Comber DN 7; 31, 37, 42–43
Moneyrod td: Duneane AM 19; 120, 123
Moneysallin bogs: Tamlaght O'Crilly LY 18; 87, 96, 116, 132
Moneysallin bridge: Tamlaght O'Crilly LY 18; 92, 109
Moneysallin cave: Tamlaght O'Crilly LY 18; 116
Moneysallin flax mill: Tamlaght O'Crilly LY 18; 91, 109
Moneysallin td: Desertoghill LY 27; 15
Moneysallin td: Tamlaght O'Crilly LY 18; 97, 116, 125, 136, 138
Moneysally (see Moneysallin): Tamlaght O'Crilly LY 18; 136
Moneyshanare (see Moneyshanere): Kilcronaghan LY 31; 74
Moneyshanderry td: Donagh DL 38; 31
Moneyshanere bog: Kilcronaghan LY 31; 69, 86
Moneyshanere flax mill: Kilcronaghan LY 31; 67, 82
Moneyshanere fort [I]: Kilcronaghan LY 31; 86
Moneyshanere fort [II]: Kilcronaghan LY 31; 86
Moneyshanere fort [III]: Kilcronaghan LY 31; 86
Moneyshanere school: Kilcronaghan LY 31; 87–88
Moneyshanere Sunday school: Kilcronaghan LY 31; 74
Moneyshanere td: Kilcronaghan LY 31; 68, 75, 78, 142
Moneysharvan (Moneyshanvin) td: Killelagh LY 27; 99, 102
Moneyslane corn mill (east): Drumgooland DN 3; 23
Moneyslane corn mill (west): Drumgooland DN 3; 23
Moneyslane flax mill (east): Drumgooland DN 3; 23
Moneyslane flax mill (west): Drumgooland DN 3; 23
Moneyslane td: Drumgooland DN 3; 23

Moneystaghan (Moneystachan) td: Tamlaght
O'Crilly LY 18; 98, 136
Moneystaghan bogs: Tamlaght O'Crilly LY 18; 118
Moneystaghan Ellis bogs: Tamlaght O'Crilly LY 18;
84, 132–33
Moneystaghan Ellis Island: Tamlaght O'Crilly LY
18; 85
Moneystaghan Ellis td: Tamlaght O'Crilly LY 18;
138
Moneystaghan McPeake bogs: Tamlaght O'Crilly
LY 18; 84, 132–33
Moneystaghan McPeake Island [I]: Tamlaght
O'Crilly LY 18; 85, 133
Moneystaghan McPeake Island [II]: Tamlaght
O'Crilly LY 18; 85, 133
Moneystaghan McPeake td: Tamlaght O'Crilly LY
18; 85, 118, 138
Moneysterlin (Moneysterling) td: Desertmartin LY
31; 57, 62
Moneysterlin chapel: Desertmartin LY 31; 63
Moneysterlin monastery: Desertmartin LY 31;
55–56
Moneystones giant's grave: Artrea LY 6; 10
Moneyvart old church: Layd AM 13; 41
Moneyvart td: Layd AM 13; 41
Moneyvennon fort: Aghanloo LY 11; 5
Moneyvreest td: Magheraculmoney FH 14; 111–12
Monfad td: Misc. DL 39; 195
Mongavelin (see Mongavlin)
Mongavlin td: Killea and Taughboyne DL 39; 80,
84, 196
Mongibbaghan td: Aghalurcher FH 4; 14
Mongomery, Grizle (see Boyd)
Mongorry bog: Raphoe DL 39; 121
Mongorry mountain: Clonleigh DL 39; 14
Mongorry mountain: Leck DL 39; 115
Mongorry mountain: Raphoe DL 39; 121, 130
Mongorry td: Raphoe DL 39; 126
Mongorry trigonometrical station: Raphoe DL 39;
121
Monienahasragh td: Kilteevoge DL 39; 114
Monighan td: Devenish FH 14; 53
Moninton td: Aughnamullen MN 40; 76
Monishenare (see Moneyshanere): Kilcronaghan LY
31; 75
Monishinare (see Moneyshanere): Misc. LY 31; 142
Monjuich (Spain): Carrickfergus AM 37; 24
Monk, George: Newry DN 3; 74
Monk's hill: Newry DN 3; 109
Monkroddin, Laird: Ballyphilip DN 7; 13
Monksland (see Monkstown): Carnmoney AM 2; 64
Monksland td: Carlingford LH 40; 57, 59
Monkstown: Carnmoney AM 2; 51, 64, 89, 94–95,
98, 102
Monkstown church: Carnmoney AM 2; 69, 81

Monkstown church: Carrickfergus AM 37; 18
Monkstown corn mill: Carnmoney AM 2; 48, 92
Monkstown coves: Carnmoney AM 2; 71
Monkstown fort [I]: Carnmoney AM 2; 101
Monkstown fort [II]: Carnmoney AM 2; 101
Monkstown graveyard: Carnmoney AM 2; 64, 67,
94
Monkstown House: Carnmoney AM 2; 67, 94
Monkstown old church: Carnmoney AM 2; 34, 64,
66–68, 94
Monkstown old church: Glynn AM 26; 30
Monkstown print–works: Carnmoney AM 2; 48, 52,
59, 85, 92–93
Monkstown school: Carnmoney AM 2; 57, 78, 86
Monkstown Sunday school: Carnmoney AM 2; 86
Monkstown td: Carnmoney AM 2; 34, 48, 58, 81,
88, 102
Monktown (see Monkstown)
Monlough (see Moorlough): Galloon FH 4; 96
Monmurry td: Aghavea FH 4; 23
Monmurry td: Donagh MN 40; 99
Monnaboy bog: Faughanvale LY 36; 4
Monnaboy hill: Faughanvale LY 36; 3
Monnaboy td: Cumber LY 28; 62
Monnaboy td: Faughanvale LY 36; 17, 53, 58,
61–62, 69, 78, 89, 96
Monnehanegan (see Monehanegan): Cumber LY 28;
62
Monoghan, family: Ballinderry AM 21; 55
Monreagh bog: Killea and Taughboyne DL 39; 80
Monreagh meeting house: Taughboyne DL 39; 154
Monreagh orchard: Taughboyne DL 39; 154
Monreagh td: Killea and Taughboyne DL 39; 79, 89
Monreagh td: Killygarvan DL 38; 37, 39, 46
Monreagh td: Taughboyne DL 39; 148, 154, 196
Monree td: Donaghcloney DN 12; 59
Monroe, George: Blaris AM 8; 87
Monroe, Robert: Ahoghill AM 23; 14
Monroe, Robert: Antrim AM 29; 6
Monroe, Robert: Carrickfergus AM 37; 56, 85
Monroe, Robert: Desertmartin LY 31; 56
Monroe, Robert: Dunaghy AM 13; 12
Monroe, Robert: Island Magee AM 10; 75
Monroe, Robert: Misc. DN 17; 119–20
Monroe, Robert: Muckamore AM 35; 83
Monroe, Robert: Newry DN 3; 65
Monroe, Robert: Nilteen AM 35; 89, 103
Monroe, William: Tamlaght TE 20; 110
Monsel, John: Coleraine LY 33; 127
Monsell, Miss: Dunboe LY 11; 55, 70
Monsell, Mrs T.B.: Dunboe LY 11; 53, 55, 69–70
Monsell, Rev. T.B.: Coleraine LY 33; 104, 110, 127
Monsell, Rev. T.B.: Dunboe LY 11; 46, 53, 57,
61–62, 65, 69–70, 80
Monsell, W.T.: Coleraine LY 33; 127

Mont Louise lough: Tydavnet MN 40; 169

Montagu, Frederick: Ballymore AH 1; 3

Montagu, Robert: Ballymore AH 1; 3

Montague, John: Killyman AH 1; 55

Montague, Lord: Ballyscullion LY 6; 57

Montalto demesne: Magheradrool DN 17; 101–02, 107

Montalto House: Magheradrool DN 17; 107

Montalto school: Dunaghy AM 13; 17

Montefodoghan district: Cleenish FH 14; 28

Monteith bog: Annaclone DN 12; 14

Monteith lough: Annaclone DN 12; 13, 16

Monteith, Mr: Annaclone DN 12; 13

Monteith, Rev. William: Clondermot LY 34; 19, 23–24, 27, 88, 95, 97, 101

Monteith, Rev. William: Faughanvale LY 36; 33

Monterlony mountains: Donaghedy TE 5; 88

Montglass td: Misc. DL 39; 190, 195

Montgolfier, J.: Clogher TE 5; 28

Montgomery, A.N.: Aughnamullen MN 40; 75–77

Montgomery, A.N.: Ballybay MN 40; 84

Montgomery, A.N.: Donagh MN 40; 103

Montgomery, A.N.: Tyholland MN 40; 174

Montgomery, Alexander: Antrim AM 29; 21

Montgomery, Alexander: Carnmoney AM 2; 75–76

Montgomery, Alexander: Drumachose LY 9; 65

Montgomery, Alexander: Holywood DN 7; 82

Montgomery, Alexander: Killead AM 35; 48

Montgomery, Alexander: Raphoe DL 39; 130–31

Montgomery, Arthur: Down DN 17; 51

Montgomery, Capt.: Cumber LY 28; 9

Montgomery, Capt.: Grey Abbey DN 7; 70–71

Montgomery, Catherine: Killead AM 35; 51

Montgomery, Charles: Ahoghill AM 23; 34

Montgomery, Charles: Coleraine LY 33; 72

Montgomery, Col.: Faughanvale LY 36; 45

Montgomery, David: Ahoghill AM 23; 43, 46

Montgomery, David: Balteagh LY 9; 28

Montgomery, David: Carnmoney AM 2; 75–76

Montgomery, Eliza: Cumber LY 28; 73, 76

Montgomery, Eliza: Killead AM 35; 51

Montgomery, Elizabeth (nee Edmonston): Misc. DN 17; 119

Montgomery, Elizabeth: Carnmoney AM 2; 76

Montgomery, Elizabeth: Killead AM 35; 51

Montgomery, Ellen: Killead AM 35; 51

Montgomery, family: Antrim AM 29; 24

Montgomery, family: Ballyclug AM 23; 60

Montgomery, family: Ballyphilip DN 7; 13

Montgomery, family: Blaris AM 8; 22

Montgomery, family: Carnmoney AM 2; 76

Montgomery, family: Carrickfergus AM 37; 93

Montgomery, family: Derrykeighan AM 16; 89

Montgomery, family: Dunluce AM 16; 117

Montgomery, family: Enniskillen FH 4; 58, 75

Montgomery, family: Grey Abbey DN 7; 68

Montgomery, family: Inishmacsaint FH 14; 75

Montgomery, family: Island Magee AM 10; 70

Montgomery, family: Killead AM 35; 17

Montgomery, family: Magheragall AM 21; 99

Montgomery, family: Misc. DN 17; 119

Montgomery, family: Newtownards DN 7; 107

Montgomery, family: Ramoan AM 24; 107

Montgomery, family: Tomregan FH 4; 127

Montgomery, Florence: Raloo AM 32; 128

Montgomery, Gabriel: Clonleigh DL 39; 10

Montgomery, George: Tomregan FH 4; 126–27, 129–31

Montgomery, Henery: Tamlaght Finlagan LY 25; 112

Montgomery, Henry: Killead AM 35; 51

Montgomery, Henry: Misc. DN 17; 119

Montgomery, Hugh: Aghalurcher FH 4; 8, 13–14

Montgomery, Hugh: Ballyphilip DN 7; 13

Montgomery, Hugh: Carnmoney AM 2; 88

Montgomery, Hugh: Clogher TE 5; 31–33, 43, 48, 50–51, 54

Montgomery, Hugh: Derryvullan FH 14; 38, 41

Montgomery, Hugh: Devenish FH 14; 50, 56, 58–59

Montgomery, Hugh: Enniskillen FH 4; 77, 82

Montgomery, Hugh: Grey Abbey DN 7; 68–69

Montgomery, Hugh: Inishmacsaint FH 14; 79

Montgomery, Hugh: Killead AM 35; 51

Montgomery, Hugh: Killinchy DN 7; 90

Montgomery, Hugh: Newtownards DN 7; 105

Montgomery, Hugh [I]: Misc. DN 17; 117, 119, 123, 133

Montgomery, Hugh [II]: Misc. DN 17; 119

Montgomery, Hugh [III] (see also Mount Alexander): Misc. DN 17; 119

Montgomery, Hugh [IV]: Misc. DN 17; 119

Montgomery, J.: Kilmore AH 1; 69

Montgomery, J.W.: Raymoghy DL 39; 142

Montgomery, James: Ahoghill AM 23; 34

Montgomery, James: Ballylinny AM 32; 29

Montgomery, James: Ballynure AM 32; 71

Montgomery, James: Ballyphilip DN 7; 12–13

Montgomery, James: Dunaghy AM 13; 21

Montgomery, James: Dundonald DN 7; 65

Montgomery, James: Grey Abbey DN 7; 68–69, 71

Montgomery, James: Killead AM 35; 51

Montgomery, James: Kirkinriola AM 23; 96

Montgomery, James: Magheragall AM 21; 111

Montgomery, James: Ramoan AM 24; 117–19

Montgomery, James: Tamlaght TE 20; 79, 93

Montgomery, James: Termoneeny LY 6; 132

Montgomery, James: Witter DN 7; 126

Montgomery, James [I]: Misc. DN 17; 119

Montgomery, James [III]: Misc. DN 17; 119

Montgomery, Jane: Ballynure AM 32; 71

Montgomery, Jane: Ballyphilip DN 7; 13
Montgomery, Jane: Carrickfergus AM 37; 118
Montgomery, Jane: Clondermot LY 34; 90
Montgomery, John: Aghagallon AM 21; 17
Montgomery, John: Ballinderry AM 21; 49
Montgomery, John: Ballylinny AM 32; 29
Montgomery, John: Ballymoney AM 16; 15
Montgomery, John: Coleraine LY 33; 63–64, 127
Montgomery, John: Derrykeighan AM 16; 78, 95
Montgomery, John: Dunluce AM 16; 105, 109, 119, 122
Montgomery, John: Kilraghts AM 16; 128
Montgomery, John: Lissan LY 31; 107
Montgomery, John: Rasharkin AM 23; 135
Montgomery, John [I]: Killead AM 35; 22, 50
Montgomery, John [II]: Killead AM 35; 51
Montgomery, Jonathan: Ballylinny AM 32; 29
Montgomery, Joseph: Tamlaght TE 20; 79
Montgomery, Lord: Ballyphilip DN 7; 13
Montgomery, Lord: Newtownards DN 7; 109
Montgomery, Margaret: Carnmoney AM 2; 88
Montgomery, Mary: Ballylinny AM 32; 29
Montgomery, Mary: Carrickfergus AM 37; 76, 151
Montgomery, Mary: Killead AM 35; 51
Montgomery, minor: Ardkeen DN 7; 2
Montgomery, minor: Comber DN 7; 37, 39
Montgomery, minor: Grey Abbey DN 7; 69–70
Montgomery, Miss: Comber DN 7; 37, 40
Montgomery, Misses (Bath): Errigal Keerogue TE 20; 56
Montgomery, Misses: Blaris AM 8; 33
Montgomery, Mr (Belmont): Carnmoney AM 2; 91
Montgomery, Mr (Lecale): Magheradrool DN 17; 105
Montgomery, Mr: Camlin AM 21; 75
Montgomery, Mr: Comber DN 7; 32–33, 39
Montgomery, Mr: Errigal Keerogue TE 20; 49
Montgomery, Mrs: Grey Abbey DN 7; 69–70
Montgomery, Mrs Alexander: Carnmoney AM 2; 75
Montgomery, Mrs William (Jnr): Misc. DN 17; 119
Montgomery, N.: Aghalurcher TE 5; 1
Montgomery, N.M.: Clogher TE 5; 53
Montgomery, Nathaniel: Carrickfergus AM 37; 151
Montgomery, Rev. (Whitehill): Killymard DL 39; 105
Montgomery, Rev.: Drumachose LY 9; 93
Montgomery, Rev.: Drumbo DN 7; 60
Montgomery, Rev. A.: Blaris AM 8; 55
Montgomery, Rev. Alexander: Antrim AM 29; 27
Montgomery, Rev. Andrew: Magheross MN 40; 146
Montgomery, Rev. C.L.: Comber DN 7; 37, 39
Montgomery, Rev. G.: Lough Swilly DL 38; 136, 139, 141–42, 149
Montgomery, Rev. G.: Moville DL 38; 70
Montgomery, Rev. George: Clogher TE 5; 28

Montgomery, Rev. Henry: Derryaghy AM 8; 116, 118
Montgomery, Rev. Henry: Drumbeg AM 8; 123, 126, 133
Montgomery, Rev. James: Drumachose LY 9; 66
Montgomery, Rev. S.: Clonmany DL 38; 18
Montgomery, Richard: Drumgoon CN 40; 9
Montgomery, Robert (Jnr): Killygarvan DL 38; 48
Montgomery, Robert: Ballynure AM 32; 71
Montgomery, Robert: Billy AM 16; 56, 63
Montgomery, Robert: Clonleigh DL 39; 1
Montgomery, Robert: Convoy DL 39; 18–23
Montgomery, Robert: Donaghmore DL 39; 36
Montgomery, Robert: Dunaghy AM 13; 21, 24
Montgomery, Robert: Duneane AM 19; 114
Montgomery, Robert: Grey Abbey DN 7; 70
Montgomery, Robert: Killead AM 35; 51
Montgomery, Robert: Raphoe DL 39; 125–27, 130
Montgomery, Samuel: Carncastle and Killyglen AM 10; 7–8
Montgomery, Sarah: Tamlaght TE 20; 93
Montgomery, Thomas: Aghagallon AM 21; 24
Montgomery, Thomas: Antrim AM 29; 14, 20, 25, 50
Montgomery, Thomas: Ballywillin LY 33; 45
Montgomery, Thomas: Blaris DN 12; 40
Montgomery, Thomas: Misc. DN 17; 119
Montgomery, Viscount: Ballyphilip DN 7; 13
Montgomery, Viscount: Newtownards DN 7; 107
Montgomery, Widow: Drumhome DL 39; 61
Montgomery, William (Jnr): Misc. DN 17; 119
Montgomery, William (Snr): Misc. DN 17; 119
Montgomery, William: Ballylinny AM 32; 29
Montgomery, William: Ballymoney AM 16; 16
Montgomery, William: Ballyphilip DN 7; 9
Montgomery, William: Carrickfergus AM 37; 124, 129
Montgomery, William: Dunluce AM 16; 122
Montgomery, William: Tamlaght TE 20; 79, 84, 93
Montgomery, William: Witter DN 7; 126
Montgomery, Wilton: Ballyphilip DN 7; 13
Montgomery's lough: Saintfield DN 7; 117, 119
Montheith, family: Misc. LY 36; 104
Montiagh (see Montiaghs): Aghagallon AM 21; 14
Montiaghs bog: Aghaderg DN 12; 5
Montiaghs bog: Donaghcloney DN 12; 57
Montiaghs bog: Magherally DN 12; 114
Montiaghs bog: Seapatrick DN 12; 126
Montiaghs bogs: Aghagallon AM 21; 6–7, 11–12, 14–17, 21
Montiaghs district: Aghagallon AM 21; 1, 7, 10, 18–20, 22–24
Montiaghs district: Aghalee AM 21; 26, 38
Montiaghs district: Ballinderry AM 21; 41
Montiaghs district: Glenavy AM 21; 78

Montiaghs district: Magheramesk AM 21; 112, 127
Montiaghs fort: Aghagallon AM 21; 17
Montiaghs ph: Ballymore AH 1; 12, 15–18
Montiaghs ph: Drumcree AH 1; 28, 34–35
Montiaghs ph: Kilmore AH 1; 67–68
Montiaghs ph: Seagoe AH 1; 101, 104–06
Montiaghs ph: Shankill AH 1; 111
Montiaghs ph: Tartaraghan AH 1; 117, 119–20
Montiaghs td: Aghagallon AM 21; 3, 18–19
Montigue, Bernard: Maghera LY 18; 81
Montigue, Michael: Maghera LY 18; 81
Montnorris, family: Holywood DN 7; 73
Montolink (see Monclink): Misc. DL 39; 190
Montrevlin district: Ballyclog TE 20; 16
Montsalut House: Magilligan LY 11; 120
Montyaghs (see Montiaghs)
Monycass (see Moneycass)
Monygregan locality: Lough Swilly DL 38; 142
Moodoge corn mill: Ballymore AH 1; 8, 10, 17
Moodoge flax mill: Ballymore AH 1; 8, 10, 17
Moodoge td: Ballymore AH 1; 8, 14–18
Moody, Abraham: Magilligan LY 11; 131, 138
Moody, family: Magilligan LY 11; 130
Moody, Israel: Aghanloo LY 11; 22–25
Moody, James: Magilligan LY 11; 131
Moody, Jane: Drumachose LY 9; 70, 85, 124, 131
Moody, John: Aghanloo LY 11; 23
Moody, John: Ballymoney AM 16; 17
Moody, John: Coleraine LY 33; 130
Moody, John: Drumachose LY 9; 73
Moody, John: Magilligan LY 11; 123, 125, 127,
    129–31, 133–34, 137–42
Moody, Mr (Lisseraw): Ballymore AH 1; 16
Moody, Mrs (Ballydonaghy): Tamlaght Finlagan LY
    25; 120
Moody, Thomas: Macosquin LY 22; 86, 120
Moody, William (Jnr): Drumachose LY 9; 104
Moody, William: Balteagh LY 9; 41
Moody, William: Drumachose LY 9; 52–53, 73, 89,
    97, 100, 121
Moody, William: Macosquin LY 22; 110
Moody, William: Magilligan LY 11; 85, 100
Moody's school: Drumachose LY 9; 124
Moon river: Ballintoy AM 24; 12–13, 17
Moon river: Billy AM 16; 36, 40
Moon, Daniel: Aghadowey LY 22; 34
Moon, Edward: Artrea LY 6; 38
Moon, Edward: Tamlaght O'Crilly LY 18; 125
Moon, Edward [I]: Aghadowey LY 22; 36
Moon, Edward [II]: Aghadowey LY 22; 38
Moon, James: Donaghedy TE 5; 88
Moon, John: Aghadowey LY 22; 36
Moon, John: Ballymoney AM 16; 24
Moon, Jonathan: Aghadowey LY 22; 36
Moon, Thomas: Newtownards DN 7; 112

Mooney lough (see Money): Aghagallon AM 21; 12
Mooney, Andrew: Ahoghill AM 23; 39
Mooney, Archibald: Carrickfergus AM 37; 112
Mooney, Bernard: Carrickfergus AM 37; 128
Mooney, Betty: Kilrea LY 27; 129
Mooney, Daniel: Carrickfergus AM 37; 108
Mooney, Daniel: Hillsborough DN 12; 106
Mooney, Daniel: Killelagh LY 27; 100–01
Mooney, Daniel: Maghera LY 18; 6, 50, 52, 59, 66,
    77
Mooney, family: Ahoghill AM 23; 25
Mooney, family: Rasharkin AM 23; 132
Mooney, Henery: Tamlaght O'Crilly LY 18; 138
Mooney, Jacob: Maghera LY 18; 62
Mooney, Jane: Ballynascreen LY 31; 14, 21
Mooney, Jane: Maghera LY 18; 79
Mooney, John: Aghadowey LY 22; 16, 38
Mooney, John: Aghagallon AM 21; 14, 17
Mooney, John: Carrickfergus AM 37; 111, 195
Mooney, John: Errigal LY 27; 65
Mooney, John: Macosquin LY 22; 82, 105
Mooney, John [I]: Maghera LY 18; 78
Mooney, John [II]: Maghera LY 18; 79
Mooney, Mark: Errigal LY 27; 50
Mooney, Mary: Tamlaght O'Crilly LY 18; 138
Mooney, Michael: Carrickfergus AM 37; 111
Mooney, Miss: Coleraine LY 33; 72
Mooney, Mr: Clogher TE 5; 41
Mooney, Mr: Misc. AM 10; 131–32
Mooney, Neil: Ahoghill AM 23; 39
Mooney, Pat: Tamlaght O'Crilly LY 18; 90, 111
Mooney, Thomas: Aghadowey LY 22; 29
Mooney, Thomas: Kilraghts AM 16; 135
Mooney, Thomas: Tamlaght O'Crilly LY 18; 140
Moor Glebe House: Donegal DL 39; 47
Moor, family: Carnmoney AM 2; 102
Moor, family: Derrykeighan AM 16; 89
Moor, Fergus: Banagher LY 30; 10
Moor, Margaret (nee Crooke): Enniskillen FH 4; 72
Moor, Mrs: Kilbroney DN 3; 30
Moorcraft, Widow: Drumbo DN 7; 59
Moorcroft, J.R.: Blaris AM 8; 81
Moorcroft, James: Blaris AM 8; 54
Moorcroft, James: Blaris DN 12; 49, 51
Moore and Boyle, Messrs: Clondermot LY 34;
    117–18
Moore and McKee, Messrs: Larne AM 10; 126
Moore and McNeight, Messrs: Seagoe AH 1; 109
Moore Grove House: Killead AM 35; 21, 47
Moore Lodge: Finvoy AM 23; 67–69, 71
Moore lough: Donaghedy TE 5; 88, 90
Moore td: Finvoy AM 23; 71
Moore, A.: Newtownards DN 7; 112
Moore, Adam: Carrickfergus AM 37; 110
Moore, Alexander: Aghanloo LY 11; 20

Moore, Alexander: Ballymoney AM 16; 15–17
Moore, Alexander: Maghera LY 18; 28
Moore, Anacreon: Lough Swilly DL 38; 150
Moore, Anderson: Tamlaght Finlagan LY 25; 108
Moore, Andrew: Aghanloo LY 11; 6, 29
Moore, Andrew: Clondermot LY 34; 79
Moore, Andrew: Drummaul AM 19; 74, 85
Moore, Andrew: Faughanvale LY 36; 45
Moore, Andrew: Finvoy AM 23; 75
Moore, Ann (nee Simpson): Ballyrashane LY 22; 58
Moore, Anne: Carrickfergus AM 37; 123
Moore, Archabald [I]: Kilraghts AM 16; 132
Moore, Archabald [II]: Kilraghts AM 16; 132
Moore, Archabald [III]: Kilraghts AM 16; 132
Moore, Archy: Drumachose LY 9; 117
Moore, Arthur: Aghagallon AM 21; 16
Moore, Atcheson: Clogher TE 5; 53
Moore, Bernard: Drummaul AM 19; 72, 87
Moore, Capt.: Derrykeighan AM 16; 85
Moore, Charles: Kilcronaghan LY 31; 68, 76
Moore, Christopher: Ballymascanlan LH 40; 55
Moore, David: Aghanloo LY 11; 39
Moore, David: Drumachose LY 9; 104
Moore, David: Drummaul AM 19; 82–83, 88
Moore, David: Tamlaght Finlagan LY 25; 82, 101
Moore, Dr: Ballylinny AM 32; 28
Moore, Dr: Templepatrick AM 35; 145
Moore, E.: Carnteel TE 20; 23
Moore, Edward: Enniskillen FH 4; 57
Moore, Edward: Errigal Keerogue TE 20; 48, 56–57
Moore, Eliza: Carrickfergus AM 37; 123
Moore, Elizabeth: Ballynascreen LY 31; 17
Moore, Elizabeth: Kilcronaghan LY 31; 66
Moore, Elizabeth: Kilrea LY 27; 129
Moore, family: Ballinderry AM 21; 51
Moore, family: Ballintoy AM 24; 20
Moore, family: Ballyrashane LY 22; 58
Moore, family: Billy AM 16; 58, 68
Moore, family: Carnmoney AM 2; 76
Moore, family: Carrickfergus AM 37; 93
Moore, family: Derrykeighan AM 16; 89
Moore, family: Drummaul AM 19; 71
Moore, family: Dunluce AM 16; 117
Moore, family: Enniskillen FH 4; 75
Moore, family: Glynn AM 26; 45
Moore, family: Inver AM 26; 53
Moore, family: Kilcronaghan LY 31; 69
Moore, family: Killead AM 35; 17, 21, 47
Moore, family: Kilraghts AM 16; 127–28, 130
Moore, family: Kilwaughter AM 10; 115
Moore, family: Lambeg AM 8; 135
Moore, family: Magheramesk AM 21; 124
Moore, family: Racavan AM 13; 100
Moore, family: Ramoan AM 24; 107
Moore, family: Templecorran AM 26; 117, 119

Moore, family: Templepatrick AM 35; 118
Moore, Gen.: Banagher LY 30; 92
Moore, George: Finvoy AM 23; 71
Moore, George: Kilclooney AH 1; 51
Moore, George: Killead AM 35; 14, 48
Moore, Hugh: Billy AM 16; 69
Moore, Hugh: Blaris DN 12; 26, 32, 34, 36
Moore, Hugh: Carrickfergus AM 37; 195
Moore, Hugh: Hillsborough DN 12; 97
Moore, Hugh: Kilraghts AM 16; 133–34
Moore, Hugh: Newry DN 3; 99
Moore, Isobella: Raloo AM 32; 129
Moore, Izabella: Aghadowey LY 22; 35
Moore, J.: Blaris DN 12; 46
Moore, J.S. [I]: Coleraine LY 33; 127
Moore, J.S. [II]: Coleraine LY 33; 127
Moore, Jacob: Maghera LY 18; 28
Moore, James (Ballymoney): Coleraine LY 33; 150
Moore, James (Jnr): Ballymoney AM 16; 15
Moore, James (Jnr): Coleraine LY 33; 127
Moore, James (Snr): Coleraine LY 33; 105, 127
Moore, James: Aghadowey LY 22; 35
Moore, James: Annaclone DN 12; 18
Moore, James: Ballymascanlan LH 40; 55–56
Moore, James: Ballymoney AM 16; 1, 3, 9, 17
Moore, James: Ballyrashane LY 22; 57, 59, 66
Moore, James: Banagher LY 30; 76
Moore, James: Bovevagh LY 25; 53
Moore, James: Carlingford LH 40; 58
Moore, James: Carrickfergus AM 37; 165–66
Moore, James: Connor AM 19; 28
Moore, James: Derrykeighan AM 16; 94–95
Moore, James: Dungiven LY 15; 25, 75, 119
Moore, James: Dunluce AM 16; 110, 122
Moore, James: Errigal LY 27; 61
Moore, James: Glynn AM 26; 47
Moore, James: Kilcronaghan LY 31; 65, 69, 75
Moore, James: Killead AM 35; 14, 46–47
Moore, James: Killowen LY 33; 172
Moore, James: Macosquin LY 22; 116
Moore, James: Maghera LY 18; 60
Moore, James: Tamlaght Finlagan LY 25; 124
Moore, James: Templepatrick AM 35; 150
Moore, James [I]: Kilraghts AM 16; 132
Moore, James [II]: Kilraghts AM 16; 132
Moore, James [III]: Kilraghts AM 16; 132
Moore, Jane: Glynn AM 26; 47
Moore, Jane: Kilcronaghan LY 31; 68–69, 75–76
Moore, Jane: Kilraghts AM 16; 132
Moore, Jane: Kilwaughter AM 10; 122
Moore, Janet: Island Magee AM 10; 66
Moore, John: Ballylinny AM 32; 29
Moore, John: Ballyrashane LY 22; 59
Moore, John: Billy AM 16; 74
Moore, John: Blaris AM 8; 14, 50–51, 55

Moore, John: Blaris DN 12; 37–38, 46, 49

Moore, John: Bovevagh LY 25; 60

Moore, John: Carrickfergus AM 37; 136

Moore, John: Dunluce AM 16; 116

Moore, John: Errigal Keerogue TE 20; 48–49

Moore, John: Hillsborough DN 12; 106

Moore, John: Killowen LY 33; 172

Moore, John: Kilraghts AM 16; 132

Moore, John: Kilwaughter AM 10; 116, 122, 122

Moore, John: Loughinisland DN 17; 96–97

Moore, John: Misc. DN 17; 130

Moore, John: Muckamore AM 35; 79

Moore, John: Tamlaght Finlagan LY 25; 120

Moore, John: Templepatrick AM 35; 152

Moore, John [I]: Errigal LY 27; 68

Moore, John [I]: Killead AM 35; 13–14, 42, 47

Moore, John [II]: Errigal LY 27; 68

Moore, John [II]: Killead AM 35; 14, 36

Moore, John [III]: Killead AM 35; 53

Moore, Joseph: Bovevagh LY 25; 57

Moore, Joseph: Drumragh TE 5; 109

Moore, Joseph: Dunaghy AM 13; 22–23

Moore, Joshua: Garvaghy DN 12; 83

Moore, Malcolm: Ballylinny AM 32; 29

Moore, man named: Kilraghts AM 16; 128

Moore, man named: Raloo AM 32; 110, 122

Moore, Margaret [I]: Kilraghts AM 16; 132

Moore, Margaret [II]: Kilraghts AM 16; 132

Moore, Mary (Jnr): Glynn AM 26; 47

Moore, Mary (Snr): Glynn AM 26; 47

Moore, Mary: Aghaderg DN 12; 11

Moore, Mary Ann: Kilraghts AM 16; 132

Moore, Miss: Ballymoney AM 16; 16

Moore, Miss: Coleraine LY 33; 72

Moore, Miss: Newry DN 3; 98–99, 104

Moore, Mr (Antrim): Clondermot LY 34; 87, 95

Moore, Mr (Belfast): Drumcree AH 1; 41

Moore, Mr (Boho): Clogher TE 5; 40

Moore, Mr: Dungiven LY 15; 99

Moore, Mr: Magheraculmoney FH 14; 111, 113–14

Moore, Mrs: Blaris AM 8; 84–85

Moore, Mrs: Dungiven LY 15; 99

Moore, Mrs: Finvoy AM 23; 71

Moore, Mrs C.: Newry DN 3; 100, 104

Moore, Mrs Samuel: Clondermot LY 34; 12, 27

Moore, Mrs William: Ballyrashane LY 22; 48, 60

Moore, Nathaniel: Carrickfergus AM 37; 40, 148

Moore, Rev.: Carrickfergus AM 37; 102

Moore, Rev. Hugh: Newtownards DN 7; 106

Moore, Rev. Marshall: Faughanvale LY 36; 6, 29, 66–67

Moore, Rev. Samuel: Warrenpoint DN 3; 117

Moore, Rev. William: Clondermot LY 34; 43

Moore, Rev. William: Lissan LY 31; 93, 102–07

Moore, Robert: Ballynure AM 32; 44, 68

Moore, Robert: Billy AM 16; 71

Moore, Robert: Carrickfergus AM 37; 26

Moore, Robert: Kilcronaghan LY 31; 69, 86

Moore, Robert: Kilraghts AM 16; 132

Moore, Robert: Raloo AM 32; 122

Moore, Roger: Killead AM 35; 12, 45

Moore, Sampson: Ballymoney AM 16; 9, 15, 22

Moore, Sampson: Blaris AM 8; 66

Moore, Sampson: Coleraine LY 33; 127

Moore, Sampson: Dunaghy AM 13; 12–13, 16

Moore, Sampson: Finvoy AM 23; 74–75

Moore, Sampson: Killagan AM 23; 83, 85

Moore, Samual: Bovevagh LY 25; 53

Moore, Samuel: Aghanloo LY 11; 4, 14, 17–18, 20–21, 26, 28

Moore, Samuel: Clondermot LY 34; 12

Moore, Samuel: Donaghcloney DN 12; 61

Moore, Samuel: Drumachose LY 9; 104

Moore, Samuel: Dunaghy AM 13; 23

Moore, Samuel: Glynn AM 26; 47

Moore, Samuel: Kilcronaghan LY 31; 68

Moore, Samuel: Maghera LY 18; 24, 72

Moore, Samuel: Muckamore AM 35; 78

Moore, Sarah: Carrickfergus AM 37; 119

Moore, Solomon: Tamlaght Finlagan LY 25; 117

Moore, Stevenson: Newry DN 3; 99, 103

Moore, Stewart: Coleraine LY 33; 127

Moore, Stewart: Derrykeighan AM 16; 78, 84–85, 95

Moore, Stewart: Dunaghy AM 13; 26

Moore, T.: Newtownards DN 7; 112

Moore, Thomas: Ballyaghran LY 33; 19

Moore, Thomas: Dunboe LY 11; 57

Moore, Thomas: Dunluce AM 16; 116, 120

Moore, Thomas: Glynn AM 26; 21, 40, 42

Moore, Thomas: Kilwaughter AM 10; 116

Moore, Thomas: Maghera LY 18; 79

Moore, W.J.: Camlin AM 21; 76

Moore, W.J.: Killead AM 35; 37–38

Moore, Widow: Dunluce AM 16; 115, 121

Moore, William: Ballymoney AM 16; 15

Moore, William: Blaris DN 12; 40

Moore, William: Bovevagh LY 25; 46

Moore, William: Drumlumman CN 40; 15

Moore, William: Dunaghy AM 13; 23

Moore, William: Faughanvale LY 36; 42, 45

Moore, William: Finvoy AM 23; 68

Moore, William: Killowen LY 33; 172

Moore, William: Kilraghts AM 16; 132–33

Moore, William: Kilwaughter AM 10; 122

Moore, William: Macosquin LY 22; 82, 105

Moore, William: Muckamore AM 35; 80

Moore, William [I]: Ballyrashane LY 22; 48

Moore, William [I]: Kilcronaghan LY 31; 68–69, 76

Moore, William [II]: Ballyrashane LY 22; 57–58, 65–66

Moore, William [II]: Kilcronaghan LY 31; 68

Moore's mill: Coleraine LY 33; 150

Mooredyke td: Kilwaughter AM 10; 119

Moorefort House: Ballymoney AM 16; 9

Moorehead, family: Magilligan LY 11; 130

Moorehead, Lt: Dromore TE 5; 97

Moorehead, Martha: Carrickfergus AM 37; 130

Moorehead, Rev. James: Donaghcloney DN 12; 60–61

Moorewood, Mr (Bushmills): Drumcree AH 1; 39

Moorfort td: Coleraine LY 33; 150

Moorhead, Dr: Newry DN 3; 96, 99, 101

Moorhead, J.N.: Hillsborough DN 12; 87, 97, 102–03, 105

Moorhead, Rev.: Annahilt DN 12; 22

Moorhead, Rev.: Hillsborough DN 12; 97, 103

Moorlough lough: Leckpatrick TE 5; 123

Moorlough school: Galloon FH 4; 96

Moorlough td: Galloon FH 4; 91, 95

Moran, John: Ballynascreen LY 31; 21

Moran, John: Carrickfergus AM 37; 194

Moran, Michael: Kilmacteige SO 40; 185

Moran, Michael: Maghera LY 18; 81

Moran, Michael: Tamlaght O'Crilly LY 18; 95, 113–14

Moran, Mrs: Clogher TE 5; 53

Moranstown td: Misc. LY 31; 143

Morarty, James: Muckamore AM 35; 81

Moras hill: Templecorran AM 26; 84

Moray, Earl of: Raloo AM 32; 115

Mordoach, family: Derryaghy AM 8; 103

More lough: Errigal Truagh MN 40; 120, 122

More, Teag: Desertmartin LY 31; 57–58

Moree meeting house: Desertcreat TE 20; 33

Moreen td: Clonleigh DL 39; 12

Moreland, family: Carnmoney AM 2; 51

Moreland, J.C.: Hillsborough DN 12; 97, 102–03

Moreland, William: Island Magee AM 10; 95

Morell, family: Ahoghill AM 23; 25

Morell, family: Tamlaght O'Crilly LY 18; 93

Morell, John: Desertoghill LY 27; 32

Morell, Nathaniel: Desertoghill LY 27; 32

Morell, Robert: Desertoghill LY 27; 32

Morell, William: Ballynure AM 32; 72

Morelle, Rev. Samuel: Tullylish DN 12; 145

Moress Castle: Clondavaddog DL 38; 5

Moress church: Lough Swilly DL 38; 144

Moress district: Lough Swilly DL 38; 117, 129

Moress ferry: Clondavaddog DL 38; 2–3, 5, 8

Moress ferry: Lough Swilly DL 38; 114

Moress ferry: Mevagh DL 38; 57

Moress fort: Clondavaddog DL 38; 6

Moress Hole creek: Lough Swilly DL 38; 120

Moress House: Lough Swilly DL 38; 144

Moress Point: Lough Swilly DL 38; 103–04, 147

Moress quarry: Lough Swilly DL 38; 148

Moress td: Lough Swilly DL 38; 144–45

Moress wood: Lough Swilly DL 38; 145

Morewood, Rev. James: Dunluce AM 16; 110

Morgan and Stevenson, Messrs: Newry DN 3; 99

Morgan, Arthur: Blaris DN 12; 46, 50–51

Morgan, Daniel: Drummaul AM 19; 91

Morgan, Francis: Newry DN 3; 98

Morgan, George: Blaris AM 8; 40

Morgan, George: Blaris DN 12; 50

Morgan, Hugh: Blaris AM 8; 47

Morgan, James: Carrickfergus AM 37; 123

Morgan, James: Drummaul AM 19; 90

Morgan, James: Hillsborough DN 12; 105

Morgan, James: Newry DN 3; 99, 104

Morgan, John (Jnr): Hillsborough DN 12; 107

Morgan, John: Blaris AM 8; 19

Morgan, John: Clonduff DN 3; 5

Morgan, John: Hillsborough DN 12; 107, 107

Morgan, John: Newry DN 3; 99, 103

Morgan, Lady (nee Owensen): Blaris AM 8; 15–16

Morgan, Margaret: Carrickfergus AM 37; 107, 150

Morgan, Margaret: Drumgooland DN 3; 25

Morgan, Patrick: Tamlaght TE 20; 78

Morgan, priest: Blaris AM 8; 26

Morgan, Rev. James: Blaris AM 8; 26, 56

Morgan, Rev. Laurence: Seagoe AH 1; 102–03

Morgan, Rev. Patrick: Drumgooland DN 3; 22–23, 25

Morgan, William: Blaris AM 8; 70

Morgan, William: Lissan LY 31; 96, 98, 106

Morien lough: Aughnamullen MN 40; 69, 72

Morismanon bog: Donegal DL 39; 53

Morisson, Archabald: Ballywillin LY 33; 51

Morland, family: Carnmoney AM 2; 102

Morley, William: Carrickfergus AM 37; 114

Mormeal bog: Kilcronaghan LY 31; 69, 87

Mormeal female school: Kilcronaghan LY 31; 88

Mormeal fort: Kilcronaghan LY 31; 85

Mormeal hill: Kilcronaghan LY 31; 64

Mormeal lough: Kilcronaghan LY 31; 85

Mormeal Sunday school: Kilcronaghan LY 31; 74

Mormeal td: Kilcronaghan LY 31; 64, 73, 84–85, 143

Mormeal trigonometrical station: Kilcronaghan LY 31; 85

Mormeal well: Kilcronaghan LY 31; 64

Mormeal wood: Kilcronaghan LY 31; 64

Mornan, James: Ballymoney AM 16; 27

Morne (see Mourne): Carrickfergus AM 37; 3

Morning, Elizabeth: Ballyaghran LY 33; 27

Morning, James: Ballyaghran LY 33; 27

Morning, Margaret: Ballyaghran LY 33; 27

Morran, Hugh: Ballynascreen LY 31; 23

Morrell, Hamilton: Carrickfergus AM 37; 108

Morrell, James: Carrickfergus AM 37; 118

Morrell, Phoebe: Carrickfergus AM 37; 118

Morrell, Robert [I]: Carrickfergus AM 37; 108

Morrell, Robert [II]: Carrickfergus AM 37; 126

Morrell's fort: Balteagh LY 9; 12

Morrill, Samuel: Desertoghill LY 27; 20

Morrily day school: Clogher TE 5; 42

Morrily school: Clogher TE 5; 41–42

Morrily td: Clogher TE 5; 41

Morrin, John: Maghera LY 18; 46

Morrin, Thomas: Ballynascreen LY 31; 21

Morris, Barkley: Balteagh LY 9; 42

Morris, family: Desertoghill LY 27; 5, 30

Morris, family: Maghera LY 18; 24, 48

Morris, James: Carrickfergus AM 37; 125

Morris, Jane: Carrickfergus AM 37; 132

Morris, John: Carrickfergus AM 37; 125

Morris, John: Tamlaght TE 20; 129

Morrison, Alexander: Clondermot LY 34; 79

Morrison, Andrew: Bovevagh LY 25; 7, 52

Morrison, Andrew: Tamlaght Finlagan LY 25; 118

Morrison, Archibald: Carrickfergus AM 37; 107

Morrison, Chesnut: Carrickfergus AM 37; 112

Morrison, David: Kildollagh LY 22; 75

Morrison, family: Ballintoy AM 24; 18, 20

Morrison, family: Ballyrobert AM 2; 21

Morrison, family: Carnmoney AM 2; 102

Morrison, family: Carrickfergus AM 37; 93

Morrison, family: Culfeightrin AM 24; 59

Morrison, family: Dunluce AM 16; 117

Morrison, family: Kilroot AM 26; 74–75

Morrison, family: Lambeg AM 8; 135

Morrison, George: Raloo AM 32; 118, 130

Morrison, Hugh: Tamlaght Finlagan LY 25; 88, 113

Morrison, James: Aghadowey LY 22; 36

Morrison, James: Ballyrobert AM 2; 24

Morrison, James: Carrickfergus AM 37; 194

Morrison, James: Dunboe LY 11; 76

Morrison, John: Carrickfergus AM 37; 76

Morrison, John: Desertoghill LY 27; 15, 21

Morrison, John: Kilwaughter AM 10; 122

Morrison, John: Tamlaght Finlagan LY 25; 112

Morrison, Margaret: Carrickfergus AM 37; 122

Morrison, Marianne: Carrickfergus AM 37; 121

Morrison, Messrs (Dublin): Tickmacrevan AM 13; 130

Morrison, Mr: Blaris DN 12; 47

Morrison, Mr: Kilbroney DN 3; 35

Morrison, Richard: Enniskillen FH 4; 54, 67–68

Morrison, Robert: Tamlaght Finlagan LY 25; 83, 121

Morrison, surgeon: Newry DN 3; 99, 103

Morrison, Thomas: Tamlaght Finlagan LY 25; 105

Morrison, William: Carrickfergus AM 37; 119

Morrison, William: Kilwaughter AM 10; 122

Morrisson, Archabald: Ballyaghran LY 33; 27

Morrisson, Elizabeth: Ballyaghran LY 33; 27

Morrisson, Hugh: Maghera LY 18; 51

Morrisson, J.W.: Tamlaght Finlagan LY 25; 118

Morrisson, James: Bovevagh LY 25; 57

Morrisson, James: Dunboe LY 11; 79

Morrisson, Jane: Ballyaghran LY 33; 27

Morrisson, John: Doagh AM 29; 98

Morrisson, John: Maghera LY 18; 8, 13, 29, 58–59, 68–69

Morrisson, Mathew: Macosquin LY 22; 122

Morrisson, Matilda: Ballyaghran LY 33; 27

Morrisson, Samuel: Templecorran AM 26; 132

Morrisson, T.W.: Tamlaght Finlagan LY 25; 118

Morrisson, William: Ballyaghran LY 33; 27

Morrow, Eliza: Magheradrool DN 17; 101

Morrow, family: Ahoghill AM 23; 25

Morrow, family: Ballynure AM 32; 56

Morrow, family: Magherafelt LY 6; 95

Morrow, family: Misc. LY 36; 104

Morrow, Gabriel: Artrea LY 6; 20, 22

Morrow, James: Carrickfergus AM 37; 122

Morrow, James: Drumbo DN 7; 59

Morrow, John: Coleraine LY 33; 128

Morrow, John: Convoy DL 39; 22–23

Morrow, Mary: Carrickfergus AM 37; 123

Morrow, Mr: Drumballyroney DN 3; 16

Morrow, Richard: Artrea LY 6; 20

Morrow, Richard: Desertmartin LY 31; 61

Morrow, Samuel: Dunaghy AM 13; 24

Morrow, Samuel: Hillsborough DN 12; 106

Morrow, William: Aghalee AM 21; 35

Morrow, William: Bovevagh LY 25; 61

Morrow's public house: Carnmoney AM 2; 85

Mortimer, John: Ballyscullion LY 6; 57

Mortimer, Mr: Killygarvan DL 38; 43

Mortimer, Rev. William: Dromara DN 12; 66, 69

Mortimer, Rev. William: Tullyaughnish DL 38; 97

Mortland, John: Aghanloo LY 11; 39

Morton, Andrew: Drumglass TE 20; 43

Morton, David: Magherafelt LY 6; 112

Morton, Earl of: Carrickfergus AM 37; 18

Morton, family: Raloo AM 32; 94

Morton, family: Templepatrick AM 35; 118

Morton, John: Clonleigh DL 39; 10

Morton, Margaret: Dungiven LY 15; 100–01, 103, 116–17, 119

Morton, Mary: Carrickfergus AM 37; 112

Morton, Mr: Kinawley FH 4; 121

Morton, Rev. John: Tartaraghan AH 1; 118

Morton, William: Carrickfergus AM 37; 113

Morusk district: Blaris DN 12; 42

Morwood, Mary: Muckamore AM 35; 81

Moryson, Fynes: Clondermot LY 34; 66
Moryson, Fynes: Dungiven LY 15; 60
Moryson, Fynes: Island Magee AM 10; 26
Moryson, Richard: Misc. DN 17; 118
Moss lough: Ballymore AH 1; 1
Moss, Chancellor: Galloon FH 4; 105
Mossbeg td: Clonleigh DL 39; 12, 198
Mossfield hill: Trory FH 14; 122
Mossfield td: Clogher TE 5; 34–35
Mossfield td: Dromore TE 5; 97
Mosshill td: Clonleigh DL 39; 12
Mosside corn mill: Drumtullagh AM 16; 98
Mosside flax mill: Drumtullagh AM 16; 98
Mosside school: Billy AM 16; 77
Mosside school [I]: Drumtullagh AM 16; 99
Mosside school [II]: Drumtullagh AM 16; 99
Mosside td: Drumtullagh AM 16; 100–02
Mosside td: Templepatrick AM 35; 150
Mosside village: Armoy AM 24; 1
Mosside village: Drumtullagh AM 16; 96, 98
Mossley bleach mill: Carnmoney AM 2; 48, 104
Mossley bridge [I]: Carnmoney AM 2; 84–85
Mossley bridge [II]: Carnmoney AM 2; 85
Mossley cotton factory: Carnmoney AM 2; 48, 103–04
Mossley flax mill: Carnmoney AM 2; 47–48, 85, 103–04
Mossley House: Carnmoney AM 2; 46
Mossley log-wood mill: Carnmoney AM 2; 85
Mossluace Point: Lough Swilly DL 38; 119–20
Mossmore bog: Clonleigh DL 39; 1
Mossmore td: Clonleigh DL 39; 12, 198
Moss-side td: Kilbride AM 29; 136
Mossy Glen td: Moville DL 38; 68, 70
Mostragee graveyard: Derrykeighan AM 16; 87
Mostragee td: Derrykeighan AM 16; 88, 91–93
Motalee bog: Misc. LY 31; 112
Motalee td: Desertmartin LY 31; 62, 142, 144
Mote, John: Carrickfergus AM 37; 110
Motherell, John: Skirts of Urney and Ardstraw TE 5; 140
Mottley, Rev. Walter: Misc. LY 31; 136
Moughley td: Aghalurcher FH 4; 14
Mouley, Henry: Carrickfergus AM 37; 141
Mount Alexander td: Comber DN 7; 37, 40, 43
Mount Alexander td: Holywood DN 7; 82
Mount Alexander, 2nd Earl: Misc. DN 17; 119
Mount Alexander, Cress: Misc. DN 17; 119
Mount Alexander, Earl of: Newtownards DN 7; 107
Mount Alexander, Lord: Galloon FH 4; 100
Mount Bernard House: Skirts of Urney and Ardstraw TE 5; 138–40
Mount Bernard school: Skirts of Urney and Ardstraw TE 5; 140
Mount Cairney House: Newry DN 3; 112

Mount Carmel td: Aughnamullen MN 40; 76
Mount Cottage: Carrickfergus AM 37; 57, 134–36
Mount Davis House: Ahoghill AM 23; 12, 15, 27, 31, 35
Mount Druid House: Ballintoy AM 24; 12, 15, 26
Mount Edwards House: Layd AM 13; 40, 48
Mount Florence, Earl: Enniskillen FH 4; 58, 64
Mount fort: Carrickfergus AM 37; 183
Mount Gavelin (see Mongavlin)
Mount Hall hill: Tartaraghan AH 1; 119
Mount Hill fairgreen: Raloo AM 32; 90, 103, 112, 122–23
Mount Hill fort: Raloo AM 32; 90, 122
Mount Hill hamlet: Ballynure AM 32; 44
Mount Hill hamlet: Carrickfergus AM 37; 151
Mount Hill hamlet: Inver AM 26; 52–53
Mount Hill hamlet: Kilwaughter AM 10; 115
Mount Hill hamlet: Raloo AM 32; 82, 89–91, 93, 96, 105–06, 115, 119, 122–24, 126–27, 131–33
Mount Ida House: Dromore DN 12; 71–72
Mount Irwin House: Tynan AH 1; 129, 132
Mount Panther demesne: Kilmegan DN 3; 58, 60
Mount Panther House: Ballywalter DN 7; 16
Mount park: Carrickfergus AM 37; 183
Mount Paul locality: Desertegney DL 38; 24
Mount Pleasant House: Ahoghill AM 23; 12, 31
Mount Pleasant House: Desertoghill LY 27; 13, 17
Mount Pleasant House: Killead AM 35; 42
Mount Pleasant House: Kilmore AH 1; 64, 72
Mount Pleasant House: Kilroot AM 26; 78
Mount Prospect House: Drumcree AH 1; 36
Mount Prospect House: Kinawley FH 4; 114–15
Mount Ross td: Misc. DN 17; 126
Mount Sandel fort: Coleraine LY 33; 56, 92, 131, 156
Mount Sandel fort: Killowen LY 33; 162
Mount Sandel giant's graves: Coleraine LY 33; 92, 131, 156
Mount Sandel hill: Coleraine LY 33; 53–54
Mount Sandel td: Coleraine LY 33; 92
Mount Stafford House: Ahoghill AM 23; 31
Mount Stafford school: Ahoghill AM 23; 50
Mount Stewart demesne: Grey Abbey DN 7; 67–68
Mount Stewart Demesne td: Misc. DN 17; 123
Mount Stewart House: Grey Abbey DN 7; 69–70
Mount Stewart House: Misc. DN 17; 121
Mount Stewart td: Clogher TE 5; 44
Mount Stewart td: Grey Abbey DN 7; 69
Mountain Lodge: Aughnamullen MN 40; 71, 75
Mountain Lodge Demesne td: Aughnamullen MN 40; 70, 76
Mountain Lodge plantation: Aughnamullen MN 40; 71
Mountain Park td: Donaghmore DL 39; 38
Mountain Park td: Raphoe DL 39; 126

Mountain Parks td: Carlingford LH 40; 58
Mountain water: Donagh MN 40; 98–99
Mountain water: Errigal Truagh MN 40; 120
Mountains district: Drung CN 40; 20
Mountains district: Killdrumsherdan CN 40; 31
Mountains district: Laragh CN 40; 39
Mountbagnel td: Carlingford LH 40; 59
Mountcashel, Earl: Kirkinriola AM 23; 106, 121
Mountcashel, Earl: Racavan AM 13; 86
Mountcashel, Earl: Skerry AM 13; 105, 112–13, 115
Mountcashel, family: Ahoghill AM 23; 12
Mountcashel, family: Glenwhirry AM 32; 77
Mountcashel, family: Kirkinriola AM 23; 88, 106, 120
Mountcashel, Lord: Ahoghill AM 23; 2, 11–12, 17, 21, 31, 41
Mountcashel, Lord: Connor AM 19; 16
Mountcashel, Lord: Dundermot AM 13; 32
Mountcashel, Lord: Galloon FH 4; 102, 105
Mountcastle td: Donaghedy TE 5; 92
Mountcaulfield House: Newry DN 3; 100, 105
Mountcharles: Donegal DL 39; 45–46, 51
Mountcharles: Killymard DL 39; 96, 98
Mountcharles quarry: Killymard DL 39; 106
Mountcharles, Lady: Killymard DL 39; 100
Mountcharles, Lord: Inishkeel DL 39; 73
Mountcharles, Lord: Killymard DL 39; 100
Mountdrum hill: Derryvullan FH 14; 40
Mountdrum td: Derryvullan FH 14; 46
Mountfield: Cappagh TE 5; 15–18
Mountfield: Clogherny TE 20; 27
Mountfield: Kildress TE 20; 60
Mountfield church: Cappagh TE 5; 15, 18, 20
Mountfield Lodge: Cappagh TE 5; 17
Mountgavelin (see Mongavlin): Killea and Taughboyne DL 39; 84
Mounthall hill: Donaghmore DL 39; 28
Mounthall House: Donaghmore DL 39; 31
Mounthall td: Donaghmore DL 39; 34, 38
Mounthamilton bog: Killagan AM 23; 82
Mounthamilton fort: Killagan AM 23; 80
Mountjoy Castle: Clonoe TE 20; 31
Mountjoy Cottage: Cappagh TE 5; 17
Mountjoy forest: Ardstraw TE 5; 10–11
Mountjoy forest: Cappagh TE 5; 17–21
Mountjoy forest: Drumragh TE 5; 104
Mountjoy House: Cumber LY 28; 44
Mountjoy House: Tullyaughnish DL 38; 90
Mountjoy Island (Dublin): Aghalurcher FH 4; 3, 14
Mountjoy Park House: Cappagh TE 5; 22
Mountjoy, Baron: Misc. DN 17; 119
Mountjoy, family: Tullyaughnish DL 38; 87
Mountjoy, Lord: Ardglass DN 17; 12
Mountjoy, Lord: Ardstraw TE 5; 11
Mountjoy, Lord: Cappagh TE 5; 21

Mountjoy, Lord: Carrickfergus AM 37; 80, 163
Mountjoy, Lord: Clonoe TE 20; 31
Mountjoy, Lord: Down DN 17; 42
Mountjoy, Lord: Dunsfort DN 17; 68
Mountjoy, Lord: Kilmegan DN 3; 59
Mountjoy, Lord: Loughgall AH 1; 80
Mountjoy, Lord: Misc. DN 17; 117–18
Mountjoy's hill: Dunsfort DN 17; 68
Mount-Malby (see Slieve Donard)
Mountnorris: Ballymore AH 1; 8
Mountnorris: Loughgilly AH 1; 87
Mountnorris meeting house: Loughgilly AH 1; 86
Mountownlandorris mill [I]: Loughgilly AH 1; 86
Mountownlandorris mill [II]: Loughgilly AH 1; 86
Mountpleasant demesne: Cappagh TE 5; 19–20
Mountpleasant House: Cappagh TE 5; 17
Mountpleasant House: Kirkinriola AM 23; 119
Mountsandel fort: Kildollagh LY 22; 69
Mountsandel fort: Macosquin LY 22; 98
Mountsandel hill: Macosquin LY 22; 77
Mountsedborough manor: Misc. FH 4; 133
Mountstewart manor: Clogher TE 5; 37–38, 53
Mountstewart td: Clogher TE 5; 37, 54
Mourne barony: Holywood DN 7; 80
Mourne barony: Kilkeel DN 3; 53–54
Mourne barony: Misc. DN 17; 116
Mourne Beg corn mill: Termonamongan TE 5; 143
Mourne Beg flax mill: Termonamongan TE 5; 143
Mourne Beg river: Donaghmore DL 39; 28–29
Mourne Beg river: Skirts of Urney and Ardstraw TE 5; 139
Mourne Beg river: Termonamongan TE 5; 142
Mourne Beg td: Termonamongan TE 5; 143
Mourne district: Clonleigh DL 39; 7
Mourne district: Kilkeel DN 3; 54
Mourne district: Misc. LY 36; 106
Mourne district: Newry DN 3; 63, 110
Mourne district: Warrenpoint DN 3; 118
Mourne Island: Donaghmore DL 39; 28
Mourne lough: Carrickfergus AM 37; 3–4, 6–7, 93, 138–39, 155
Mourne lough: Donaghmore DL 39; 28–29, 35
Mourne lough: Kilroot AM 26; 77–78, 80
Mourne lough: Misc. AM 10; 129
Mourne lough: Templecarn DL 39; 162
Mourne manor: Newry DN 3; 65
Mourne Mountains: Antrim AM 29; 21, 23
Mourne Mountains: Ballinderry AM 21; 45
Mourne Mountains: Blaris AM 8; 13
Mourne Mountains: Carnmoney AM 2; 50, 65–67
Mourne Mountains: Carrickfergus AM 37; 10, 60
Mourne Mountains: Clonduff DN 3; 5
Mourne Mountains: Coleraine LY 33; 53, 96
Mourne Mountains: Donegore AM 29; 109, 115
Mourne Mountains: Down DN 17; 49

Mourne Mountains: Drumballyroney DN 3; 11, 17
Mourne Mountains: Drummaul AM 19; 47, 52
Mourne Mountains: Finvoy AM 23; 72
Mourne Mountains: Hillsborough DN 12; 96
Mourne Mountains: Island Magee AM 10; 26
Mourne Mountains: Kilbroney DN 3; 28–30, 32
Mourne Mountains: Kilcoo DN 3; 41
Mourne Mountains: Kilkeel DN 3; 46
Mourne Mountains: Kilmegan DN 3; 59
Mourne Mountains: Kilroot AM 26; 61
Mourne Mountains: Misc. LY 31; 116
Mourne Mountains: Rasharkin AM 23; 131
Mourne Mountains: Seapatrick DN 12; 124, 135
Mourne Mountains: Tullyrusk AM 21; 135
Mourne Mountains West td: Kilbroney DN 3; 26
Mourne Mountains West td: Kilkeel DN 3; 52
Mourne Park House: Newry DN 3; 65
Mourne river: Cappagh TE 5; 20
Mourne river: Clonleigh DL 39; 1, 7, 13–14
Mourne river: Donacavey TE 5; 67
Mourne river: Donaghmore DL 39; 35
Mourne river: Kildress TE 20; 61
Mourne river: Misc. DL 39; 188
Mourne river: Taughboyne DL 39; 149–50
Mourne river: Templecarn DL 39; 157, 162
Mourne river: Urney DL 39; 174–77, 180
Mourne school (see also Killowen school):
  Kilbroney DN 3; 38
Mourne spring: Carrickfergus AM 37; 8
Mourne stream: Ardstraw TE 5; 10
Mousetown td: Clonoe TE 20; 30–31
Moutray fort hill: Carnteel TE 20; 23
Moutray, J.C.: Clogher TE 5; 30, 51, 53–55, 61
Moutray, J.C.: Errigal Keerogue TE 20; 48–49,
  56–57
Moutray, J.C.: Errigal Truagh MN 40; 123
Moutray, Rev. M.J.: Errigal Truagh MN 40; 123
Moutray, Witney: Clogher TE 5; 30
Movanagher bawn: Kilrea LY 27; 111
Movanagher bog: Kilrea LY 27; 107, 127
Movanagher bridge: Kilrea LY 27; 111, 127
Movanagher Castle: Ballymoney AM 16; 22–23
Movanagher Castle: Dungiven LY 15; 35, 107
Movanagher Castle: Kilrea LY 27; 111, 113, 128
Movanagher Castle: Macosquin LY 22; 76, 97
Movanagher eel–weirs: Agivey LY 22; 42
Movanagher fort [I]: Kilrea LY 27; 113, 128
Movanagher fort [II]: Kilrea LY 27; 113, 128
Movanagher quarry: Kilrea LY 27; 107, 110, 126–28
Movanagher td: Aghadowey LY 22; 36
Movanagher td: Banagher LY 30; 36, 101, 110
Movanagher td: Kilrea LY 27; 113, 115, 128–29
Movenis bridge: Desertoghill LY 27; 16
Movenis cave: Desertoghill LY 27; 7, 23
Movenis flax mill: Desertoghill LY 27; 5, 13–14, 16

Movenis graveyard: Desertoghill LY 27; 21
Movenis hamlet: Desertoghill LY 27; 13
Movenis td: Desertoghill LY 27; 1, 14, 19–21
Movilla (Moville) td: Newtownards DN 7; 107
Movilla Abbey: Misc. DN 17; 121–22
Movilla Abbey: Newtownards DN 7; 107
Movilla Abbey manor: Misc. DN 17; 127
Movilla td: Misc. DN 17; 123
Moville: Cumber LY 28; 80
Moville: Lough Swilly DL 38; 139
Moville: Moville DL 38; 68, 71–73, 78
Moville bay: Moville DL 38; 76
Moville Castle: Moville DL 38; 68
Moville dispensary: Moville DL 38; 70
Moville district: Lough Swilly DL 38; 135, 137,
  140–42
Moville fort: Moville DL 38; 68
Moville Lodge: Moville DL 38; 70
Moville Lower chapel: Moville DL 38; 71
Moville Lower ph: Magilligan LY 11; 97
Moville Lower school: Moville DL 38; 71
Moville Lower Sunday school: Moville DL 38; 71
Moville market place: Moville DL 38; 68
Moville pier: Moville DL 38; 69
Moville police station: Moville DL 38; 68
Moville post office: Moville DL 38; 68, 74
Moville sessions room: Moville DL 38; 68
Moville Sunday school: Lough Swilly DL 38; 142
Moville Upper Glebe House: Moville DL 38; 78
Moville Upper ph: Magilligan LY 11; 97
Moville Upper ph: Moville DL 38; 68
Moville Upper Sunday school: Moville DL 38; 76
Mowhan flax mill [I]: Loughgilly AH 1; 86
Mowhan flax mill [II]: Loughgilly AH 1; 86
Mowhan flax mill [III]: Loughgilly AH 1; 86
Moy: Clonfeacle AH 1; 23
Moy: Coleraine LY 33; 97
Moy: Desertlyn LY 31; 37
Moy: Drumragh TE 5; 110
Moy: Killyman TE 20; 68
Moy: Longfield TE 5; 132
Moy: Loughgall AH 1; 80, 82
Moy: Tullyniskan TE 20; 141
Moy bridge: Errigal Truagh MN 40; 121
Moy fort: Muckno MN 40; 166
Moy river: Kilmacteige SO 40; 186, 188–89, 191,
  195
Moy school: Errigal Truagh MN 40; 121–22
Moyad flax mill: Kilcoo DN 3; 45
Moyad td: Kilcoo DN 3; 45
Moyadam church: Nilteen AM 35; 94
Moyadam coves: Nilteen AM 35; 99
Moyadam fort: Nilteen AM 35; 98, 101
Moyadam graveyard: Nilteen AM 35; 94
Moyadam grey stanes: Nilteen AM 35; 95–96, 100

Moyadam standing stone: Kilbride AM 29; 154

Moyadam standing stone: Nilteen AM 35; 96–97, 100

Moyadam stone circles: Nilteen AM 35; 95–96, 100

Moyadam td: Donegore AM 29; 106

Moyadam td: Nilteen AM 35; 84, 95, 99–100, 102

Moyagall bog: Maghera LY 18; 56

Moyagall chapel: Maghera LY 18; 7–8, 29, 35, 52, 68

Moyagall chapel: Termoneeny LY 6; 129

Moyagall fort [I]: Maghera LY 18; 60

Moyagall fort [II]: Maghera LY 18; 60

Moyagall fort [III]: Maghera LY 18; 61

Moyagall graveyard: Maghera LY 18; 8, 68

Moyagall school: Maghera LY 18; 30, 35

Moyagall Sunday school: Maghera LY 18; 29

Moyagall td: Maghera LY 18; 3, 22, 81

Moyagall td: Termoneeny LY 6; 129

Moyagh td: Tullyaughnish DL 38; 96

Moyagoney td: Kilrea LY 27; 106, 115

Moyallen bleach yards: Coleraine LY 33; 96

Moyallen meeting house: Tullylish DN 12; 141

Moyallen school: Tullylish DN 12; 144

Moyallen td: Coleraine LY 33; 96

Moyallen td: Drumcree AH 1; 38, 41

Moyallen td: Tullylish DN 12; 141–43

Moyallen vitriol works: Tullylish DN 12; 143

Moyallen wooden bridge: Tullylish DN 12; 142

Moyaluske td: Ballylinny AM 32; 22, 30

Moyard td: Ballynascreen LY 31; 21, 23

Moyargate (see Moyarget): Ramoan AM 24; 117

Moyarget flax mill: Ramoan AM 24; 96

Moyarget library: Ramoan AM 24; 98

Moyarget Lower cave: Ramoan AM 24; 117

Moyarget school: Ramoan AM 24; 100, 126

Moyarget td: Ramoan AM 24; 117

Moyarget Upper cave: Ramoan AM 24; 117

Moyasset (see Moyesset): Misc. LY 31; 142

Moyasset cave [I]: Ahoghill AM 23; 33, 35

Moyasset cave [II]: Ahoghill AM 23; 35

Moyasset fort: Ahoghill AM 23; 27, 35

Moyasset school: Ahoghill AM 23; 21, 41, 49–50

Moyaver td: Loughguile AM 13; 59, 75

Moybaun school: Cleenish FH 14; 24

Moybaun td: Cleenish FH 14; 29

Moybawn (see Moybaun): Cleenish FH 14; 24

Moybeg ironworks: Misc. LY 31; 112–13

Moybeg quarry: Misc. LY 31; 114

Moybeg td: Ballyaghran LY 33; 14

Moybeg td: Misc. LY 31; 142

Moybegkirly td: Kilcronaghan LY 31; 67, 73, 79, 84–85

Moybrick Lower td: Dromara DN 12; 65

Moybrick Upper td: Dromara DN 12; 65

Moybrone td: Cleenish FH 14; 29

Moybuy quarry: Faughanvale LY 36; 96

Moybuy td: Faughanvale LY 36; 17, 53, 62, 69, 78, 89, 96, 99

Moycraig bog: Billy AM 16; 75

Moycraig cove [I]: Billy AM 16; 56, 63–64

Moycraig cove [II]: Billy AM 16; 56

Moycraig graveyard: Billy AM 16; 52, 74

Moycraig meeting house: Billy AM 16; 45

Moycraig school: Billy AM 16; 49, 77, 77

Moycraig standing stones: Billy AM 16; 58, 62

Moycraig td: Billy AM 16; 45, 52, 58, 75

Moycraigs Lower td: Drumtullagh AM 16; 101

Moycraigs McAlister td: Drumtullagh AM 16; 103

Moycraigs Upper td: Drumtullagh AM 16; 102

Moydalgan school: Dromara DN 12; 64

Moydalgan school: Hillsborough DN 12; 101

Moydalgan td: Dromara DN 12; 64–65

Moydamlaght bridge: Ballynascreen LY 31; 7

Moydamlaght fort: Ballynascreen LY 31; 9, 25

Moydamlaght mountain: Ballynascreen LY 31; 1, 6

Moydamlaght td: Ballynascreen LY 31; 11–12, 16, 25–26, 114, 141, 143

Moyesset bog: Kilcronaghan LY 31; 87

Moyesset fort: Kilcronaghan LY 31; 86

Moyesset td: Kilcronaghan LY 31; 84, 142

Moygannon td: Donaghcloney DN 12; 59

Moygannon td: Kilbroney DN 3; 32, 35

Moygarriff school: Ballinderry AM 21; 58

Moyglass school: Devenish FH 14; 55–56

Moyglass td: Devenish FH 14; 58

Moyheeland (Moyheelan) td: Misc. LY 31; 141, 143

Moyheeland: Misc. LY 31; 115–16, 128, 133–34, 140

Moyheeland bridge: Ballynascreen LY 31; 7

Moyheeland church: Ballynascreen LY 31; 3, 5, 9, 14, 20–21, 114–15, 128

Moyheeland Cross (see also Moyheeland): Misc. LY 31; 115

Moyheeland flax mill: Misc. LY 31; 135

Moyheeland school: Misc. LY 31; 126

Moyheeland Sunday school: Ballynascreen LY 31; 14

Moyheeland wood: Ballynascreen LY 31; 2

Moyheyland (see Moyheeland)

Moy-ithe district: Clondermot LY 34; 50, 53

Moykeel td: Cleenish FH 14; 29

Moykeeran bridge: Ballynascreen LY 31; 6

Moykeeran school: Ballynascreen LY 31; 16

Moykeeran td: Ballynascreen LY 31; 1, 6, 141, 143

Moykeeran wood: Ballynascreen LY 31; 26

Moylagh corn mill: Clogherny TE 20; 27

Moylagh forts: Clogherny TE 20; 28

Moylan (Clare): Faughanvale LY 36; 53

Moylarg bleach mill: Ahoghill AM 23; 33

Moylarg fort: Ahoghill AM 23; 27

Moylarg standing stone: Ahoghill AM 23; 27–28, 33
Moylarg td: Ahoghill AM 23; 13, 27
Moyle bridge: Ardstraw TE 5; 5
Moyle Castle: Ardstraw TE 5; 11
Moyle corn mill: Tullyaughnish DL 38; 89
Moyle flax mill: Tullyaughnish DL 38; 89
Moyle Glebe fort: Ardstraw TE 5; 12
Moyle Glebe House: Ardstraw TE 5; 10
Moyle Glebe td: Ardstraw TE 5; 12
Moyle hill: Tullyaughnish DL 38; 92
Moyle Hill td: Tullyaughnish DL 38; 96
Moyle House (see also Moyle Castle): Ardstraw TE
    5; 9
Moyle House: Ardstraw TE 5; 11
Moyle moss: Lough Swilly DL 38; 142
Moyle orchard: Misc. DL 39; 189
Moyle td: Misc. DL 39; 186, 195
Moyle td: Tullyaughnish DL 38; 96
Moylena (see Moylinny)
Moyletra bridge: Desertoghill LY 27; 3, 28
Moyletra graveyard: Desertoghill LY 27; 6
Moyletra Kill bog: Desertoghill LY 27; 24
Moyletra Kill church: Desertoghill LY 27; 2–3, 6,
    9–10, 13–15, 28–29, 31
Moyletra Kill flax mill: Desertoghill LY 27; 5, 15
Moyletra Kill fort [I]: Desertoghill LY 27; 22, 24
Moyletra Kill fort [II]: Desertoghill LY 27; 22, 24
Moyletra Kill fort [III]: Desertoghill LY 27; 22
Moyletra Kill fort [IV]: Desertoghill LY 27; 22
Moyletra Kill graveyard: Desertoghill LY 27; 5–6,
    31
Moyletra Kill old church: Desertoghill LY 27; 6, 31
Moyletra Kill school: Desertoghill LY 27; 22, 33–34
Moyletra Kill td: Desertoghill LY 27; 1, 14, 16,
    19–20, 22, 25, 28–29
Moyletra Kill wood: Desertoghill LY 27; 1, 15
Moyletra stream: Desertoghill LY 27; 16
Moyletra Toy plantation: Desertoghill LY 27; 13
Moyletra Toy td: Desertoghill LY 27; 3, 14–17,
    19–21, 28–29
Moyletra Toy wood: Desertoghill LY 27; 1
Moylinney (see Moylinny): Raloo AM 32; 132
Moylinny beetling mill [I]: Antrim AM 29; 21, 50
Moylinny beetling mill [II]: Antrim AM 29; 21
Moylinny bridge: Muckamore AM 35; 64
Moylinny Cottage: Antrim AM 29; 21, 50
Moylinny glen: Antrim AM 29; 3, 21
Moylinny manor: Antrim AM 29; 5, 12, 14, 25
Moylinny manor: Ballylinny AM 32; 29–30
Moylinny manor: Doagh AM 29; 60, 67, 71, 73, 94
Moylinny manor: Donegore AM 29; 106, 110
Moylinny manor: Glynn AM 26; 17, 21
Moylinny manor: Kilbride AM 29; 135, 140–41,
    151
Moylinny manor: Muckamore AM 35; 65

Moylinny manor: Raloo AM 32; 96, 132
Moylinny td: Antrim AM 29; 21, 30
Moylinny td: Muckamore AM 35; 58, 70
Moylusk (see Mallusk): Misc. DN 17; 122
Moymawhillen td: Loughgilly AH 1; 85
Moymeen td: Misc. DL 39; 196
Moymucklemurry bog: Desertlyn LY 31; 44
Moymucklemurry td: Desertlyn LY 31, 48
Moynagh, Rev. Patrick: Donagh MN 40; 99, 102–03
Moynetta school: Laragh CN 40; 44
Moyola bridge: Kilcronaghan LY 31; 75
Moyola bridge: Maghera LY 18; 35, 65, 65
Moyola bridge: Magherafelt LY 6; 89, 92
Moyola district: Ballyscullion LY 6; 57, 59
Moyola river: Artrea LY 6; 4–5, 12, 28, 39
Moyola river: Artrea TE 20; 8–9
Moyola river: Ballynascreen LY 31; 1, 6–9, 11–12,
    19
Moyola river: Ballyscullion LY 6; 42, 47–49
Moyola river: Blaris AM 8; 89
Moyola river: Coleraine LY 33; 97
Moyola river: Desertmartin LY 31; 52
Moyola river: Kilcronaghan LY 31; 64, 67, 71, 79,
    83
Moyola river: Lough Neagh AM 21; 93
Moyola river: Maghera LY 18; 1–3, 9, 11, 14, 28,
    36, 46, 54–56, 63–64, 74
Moyola river: Magherafelt LY 6; 79, 88
Moyola river: Misc. LY 31; 111, 113–17, 126
Moyola river: Termoneeny LY 6; 121, 124, 129, 131
Moyola valley: Misc. LY 31; 111
Moyraverty graveyard: Seagoe AH 1; 109
Moyraverty td: Seagoe AH 1; 109
Moyrourkan lough: Mullaghbrack AH 1; 94
Moyrusk fort [I]: Magheragall AM 21; 105–06
Moyrusk fort [II]: Magheragall AM 21; 106
Moys fort: Tamlaght Finlagan LY 25; 90, 108
Moys school: Tamlaght Finlagan LY 25; 96
Moys td: Tamlaght Finlagan LY 25; 93, 118
Mual lough: Clondermot LY 34; 107
Much Grange (see Muckgrange): Carlingford LH
    40; 57
Muck lough: Drumragh TE 5; 104
Muckamore: Drummaul AM 19; 45
Muckamore: Muckamore AM 35; 77, 81
Muckamore Abbey: Antrim AM 29; 31, 33
Muckamore Abbey: Ballymartin AM 2; 12
Muckamore Abbey: Ballynure AM 32; 45
Muckamore Abbey: Ballyrobert AM 2; 20, 24
Muckamore Abbey: Ballyscullion AM 19; 5, 8, 12
Muckamore Abbey: Doagh AM 29; 68, 78
Muckamore Abbey: Killead AM 35; 25, 41
Muckamore Abbey: Kirkinriola AM 23; 88
Muckamore Abbey: Misc. DN 17; 121

Muckamore Abbey: Muckamore AM 35; 55–56, 62, 65, 69–75, 81–83

Muckamore Abbey: Nilteen AM 35; 94

Muckamore bleaching mill [I]: Muckamore AM 35; 56, 65–66, 70, 72, 75–76

Muckamore bleaching mill [II]: Muckamore AM 35; 75

Muckamore bridge: Muckamore AM 35; 55, 61

Muckamore corn mill: Muckamore AM 35; 56, 63, 75–76

Muckamore Cottage: Muckamore AM 35; 62

Muckamore coves: Muckamore AM 35; 72

Muckamore deerpark: Killead AM 35; 10, 26

Muckamore flour mills: Antrim AM 29; 24, 38

Muckamore flour mills: Carmavy AM 35; 2

Muckamore flour mills: Muckamore AM 35; 63, 75–76

Muckamore flour mills: Nilteen AM 35; 91

Muckamore fort: Muckamore AM 35; 56

Muckamore graveyard: Muckamore AM 35; 56, 70

Muckamore hill: Muckamore AM 35; 57

Muckamore old church: Muckamore AM 35; 70, 82

Muckamore ph: Antrim AM 29; 1–3, 11–12, 26, 46, 49, 51

Muckamore ph: Ballynure AM 32; 45

Muckamore ph: Doagh AM 29; 78

Muckamore ph: Killead AM 35; 7, 9, 26, 41–43, 46

Muckamore ph: Misc. AM 10; 129

Muckamore ph: Nilteen AM 35; 84, 87, 91, 94, 101

Muckamore ph: Templepatrick AM 35; 106, 133, 144

Muckamore school: Muckamore AM 35; 55, 66, 73–76

Muckamore Sunday school: Muckamore AM 35; 74

Muckamore td: Muckamore AM 35; 54, 62, 77–78, 80

Muckamore washing and beetling mills: Muckamore AM 35; 63

Muckery td: Drumcree AH 1; 34, 38–39

Muckgrange td: Carlingford LH 40; 57, 59

Muckinagh hill: Devenish FH 14; 47

Muckinish Island: Inishmacsaint FH 14; 70, 73

Muckish hill: Clondavaddog DL 38; 6

Muckish mountain: Mevagh DL 38; 59

Mucklagh hill: Currin MN 40; 86, 92

Mucklagh hill: Ematris MN 40; 112

Mucklagh quarry: Currin MN 40; 88

Mucklagh td: Currin MN 40; 91

Mucklagh td: Ematris MN 40; 116

Muckleramer standing stone: Drummaul AM 19; 65, 88

Mucklow td: Carlingford LH 40; 57

Muckno glebe: Muckno MN 40; 167

Muckno lough: Donaghmoyne MN 40; 106, 108

Muckno lough: Inniskeen MN 40; 124

Muckno lough: Muckno MN 40; 162–66

Muckno Mill lough: Muckno MN 40; 162, 165

Muckno old church: Muckno MN 40; 166

Muckno ph: Clogher TE 5; 41

Muckno ph: Donaghmoyne MN 40; 106

Mucknoe (see Muckno)

Muckrim rocks: Duneane AM 19; 117

Muckross Point: Drumkeeran FH 14; 64

Muckross school [I]: Donegal DL 39; 49

Muckross school [II]: Donegal DL 39; 49

Muckross td: Donegal DL 39; 44, 47

Muckross td: Drumkeeran FH 14; 64

Muckross wood: Drumkeeran FH 14; 64

Muckross wood: Templecarn FH 14; 118

Mucksnaught mountain: Enniskillen FH 4; 43–44

Mucksnaught school: Enniskillen FH 4; 84

Mucksnaught td: Enniskillen FH 4; 82

Muckton td: Carlingford LH 40; 59

Mudda Murphy's bridge: Newry DN 3; 61, 63, 70

Muddabawn chapel: Drumgoon CN 40; 6

Muddheena td: Enniskillen FH 4; 82

Muddock corn mill: Kilcoo DN 3; 45

Muddock river: Drumballyroney DN 3; 14

Muddock river: Kilcoo DN 3; 45

Muddydrumbrist (see Maddydrumbrist): Donaghmore DN 3; 8

Mudge, William: Coleraine LY 33; 149

Mudge, William: Newry DN 3; 86

Muff (Donegal): Faughanvale LY 36; 4

Muff: Clondermot LY 34; 3, 7–8, 80, 88, 97, 102, 114, 117, 119

Muff: Cumber LY 28; 27, 35

Muff: Drumachose LY 9; 76, 106

Muff: Dungiven LY 15; 14

Muff: Faughanvale LY 36; 2, 4–6, 8, 10–11, 16–19, 22–23, 28–31, 34, 37, 55, 58, 65, 99–100

Muff: Lough Swilly DL 38; 135

Muff: Muff DL 38; 80, 82

Muff barrack: Muff DL 38; 81

Muff bridge: Muff DL 38; 81

Muff church: Faughanvale LY 36; 6–7, 13, 15, 29, 65

Muff church: Muff DL 38; 80–82

Muff dispensary: Faughanvale LY 36; 7, 27–28, 39

Muff female school: Faughanvale LY 36; 23

Muff fort [I]: Lissan LY 31; 100

Muff fort [II]: Lissan LY 31; 100

Muff forts: Lissan LY 31; 101

Muff Glebe House: Lissan LY 31; 90, 96–97, 99–100, 103

Muff glen: Banagher LY 30; 33

Muff glen: Cumber LY 28; 61

Muff glen: Faughanvale LY 36; 1, 3, 20–21, 28

Muff Glen river: Faughanvale LY 36; 1–2, 7, 10, 22

Muff Glen waterfall: Faughanvale LY 36; 2

Muff graveyard: Faughanvale LY 36; 3, 6
Muff inn: Faughanvale LY 36; 7
Muff Lodge: Muff DL 38; 80–82
Muff manor court house: Faughanvale LY 36; 7
Muff market house: Faughanvale LY 36; 7
Muff meeting house: Muff DL 38; 80–82
Muff old church: Faughanvale LY 36; 2, 6, 13–15, 15
Muff ph: Clondermot LY 34, 98
Muff ph: Moville DL 38; 73, 78
Muff post office: Faughanvale LY 36; 5, 22
Muff river: Muff DL 38; 80
Muff school: Faughanvale LY 36; 7, 24–25, 27, 34–36, 66
Muff sessions house: Faughanvale LY 36; 4, 7, 27
Muff td: Faughanvale LY 36; 53, 62, 69, 78, 89–90, 96
Muff td: Lissan LY 31; 108–09
Muff td: Muff DL 38; 80
Muff well: Faughanvale LY 36; 14, 30–31
Muff widows' houses: Faughanvale LY 36; 5, 15, 22, 27
Muff widows' houses: Kilrea LY 27; 117
Muff wood: Faughanvale LY 36; 90
Mugilnagirugh td: Inishmacsaint FH 14; 70
Muharagh (see Maghera): Kilmacteige SO 40; 186
Muinard hill: Banagher LY 30; 24–25, 59, 108–10
Muinter-Branain, family: Misc. TE 5; 146
Mulabane (see Mullabane): Carlingford LH 40; 57
Mulaghduff (see Mullaghduff): Armoy AM 24; 9
Mulaglass (see Mullaghglass)
Mulcahy, family: Kilroot AM 26; 74–75
Mulderg (Mulderrig) td: Cumber LY 28; 4, 67, 71, 114, 120, 124, 126
Mulderg church: Cumber LY 28; 32
Mulderg dispensary: Cumber LY 28; 1–2, 8, 12, 14–16, 48, 83, 86
Mulderg dispensary: Dungiven LY 15; 75
Mulderg dispensary: Tamlaght Finlagan LY 25; 72, 90
Mulderg old church: Cumber LY 28; 29
Mulderg quarries: Cumber LY 28; 124
Mulderg td: Dungiven LY 15; 75
Mulderg wood: Cumber LY 28; 120
Muldersleigh cave: Island Magee AM 10; 101
Muldersleigh hill: Island Magee AM 10; 14, 16, 26, 47, 59, 66, 71, 74, 101
Muldersleigh lighthouse: Island Magee AM 10; 93
Muldersleigh windmill: Island Magee AM 10; 27
Muldonagh (Muldoney) td: Bovevagh LY 25; 18–19, 41–42, 58, 60
Muldonagh corn mill: Bovevagh LY 25; 4, 21, 57
Muldonagh fort: Bovevagh LY 25; 40–42
Muldonagh hill: Bovevagh LY 25; 1, 22
Muldonagh river: Bovevagh LY 25; 22

Muldonagh school: Bovevagh LY 25; 25
Muldonagh td: Banagher LY 30; 23–24
Muldonagh td: Dungiven LY 15; 91
Muldonagh valley: Bovevagh LY 25; 1
Muldoon, George: Newry DN 3; 99
Muldoon, Philip: Artrea LY 6; 35
Muldoon, Rev. Bernard: Lissan LY 31; 104
Muldooney (see Muldonagh)
Muldownly (see Muldonagh)
Mulehern, John: Bovevagh LY 25; 14, 35, 40
Mulheragh (see Mulkeeragh): Bovevagh LY 25; 28
Mulherin, Edward: Muff DL 38; 81
Mulhern, John: Faughanvale LY 36; 24, 35
Mulholland, Alice: Maghera LY 18; 52
Mulholland, Andrew: Desertoghill LY 27; 20
Mulholland, Andrew: Errigal LY 27; 66
Mulholland, Ann: Artrea LY 6; 38
Mulholland, Arthur: Artrea LY 6; 23
Mulholland, Bernard: Desertoghill LY 27; 32
Mulholland, Bernard: Dungiven LY 15; 74
Mulholland, Bernard: Killead AM 35; 49
Mulholland, Bernard: Tamlaght O'Crilly LY 18; 95, 117, 127–28
Mulholland, Bernard [I]: Maghera LY 18; 43
Mulholland, Bernard [II]: Maghera LY 18; 47
Mulholland, Bryan: Dungiven LY 15; 74, 86
Mulholland, Catherine: Carrickfergus AM 37; 122
Mulholland, Charles: Errigal LY 27; 66
Mulholland, Daniel: Maghera LY 18; 62
Mulholland, David: Tamlaght O'Crilly LY 18; 110
Mulholland, David [I]: Maghera LY 18; 64
Mulholland, David [II]: Maghera LY 18; 78
Mulholland, David [III]: Maghera LY 18; 81
Mulholland, Elizabeth: Kilrea LY 27; 129
Mulholland, family: Aghagallon AM 21; 9
Mulholland, family: Ballyscullion LY 6; 70
Mulholland, family: Blaris AM 8; 22
Mulholland, family: Carrickfergus AM 37; 93
Mulholland, family: Drummaul AM 19; 66–67
Mulholland, family: Glenavy AM 21; 86
Mulholland, family: Killead AM 35; 17, 24, 44
Mulholland, family: Killelagh LY 27; 99
Mulholland, family: Maghera LY 18; 24, 48
Mulholland, family: Misc. AM 10; 130–31
Mulholland, family: Tamlaght O'Crilly LY 18; 93
Mulholland, Henery: Ballyscullion LY 6; 70–71, 75
Mulholland, Henery: Blaris AM 8; 23, 25, 36, 38–39, 49–50, 55, 69–70
Mulholland, Henry: Blaris DN 12; 39–43, 46, 50
Mulholland, Henry: Carrickfergus AM 37; 116
Mulholland, Henry: Tamlaght O'Crilly LY 18; 128
Mulholland, Hugh: Blaris DN 12; 46, 50
Mulholland, Hugh: Carrickfergus AM 37; 158
Mulholland, Hugh: Desertoghill LY 27; 20
Mulholland, James: Dungiven LY 15; 74

Mulholland, James: Hillsborough DN 12; 107

Mulholland, James: Tamlaght O'Crilly LY 18; 117

Mulholland, John: Ballyrashane LY 22; 58

Mulholland, John: Ballyscullion LY 6; 70, 75

Mulholland, John: Desertoghill LY 27; 32

Mulholland, John: Macosquin LY 22; 113

Mulholland, John [I]: Ballyscullion LY 6; 78

Mulholland, John [I]: Carrickfergus AM 37; 102, 149

Mulholland, John [I]: Maghera LY 18; 44

Mulholland, John [I]: Tamlaght O'Crilly LY 18; 117, 127

Mulholland, John [II]: Ballyscullion LY 6; 78

Mulholland, John [II]: Carrickfergus AM 37; 120

Mulholland, John [II]: Maghera LY 18; 80

Mulholland, John [II]: Tamlaght O'Crilly LY 18; 138

Mulholland, John [III]: Maghera LY 18; 81

Mulholland, man named: Drummaul AM 19; 66

Mulholland, Mary: Duneane AM 19; 123

Mulholland, Michael: Camlin AM 21; 76

Mulholland, Michael: Glenavy AM 21; 90–91

Mulholland, Patrick: Ahoghill AM 23; 21

Mulholland, Patrick: Carrickfergus AM 37; 158

Mulholland, Patrick: Dungiven LY 15; 117–18

Mulholland, Peter: Carrickfergus AM 37; 158

Mulholland, Philip: Banagher LY 30; 96, 99

Mulholland, Richard: Blaris DN 12; 46, 50

Mulholland, Ritchard: Blaris AM 8; 55

Mulholland, Steel: Tamlaght O'Crilly LY 18; 123

Mulholland, Susan: Muckamore AM 35; 81

Mulholland, William: Carrickfergus AM 37; 40, 148, 175

Mulholland, William: Maghera LY 18; 80

Mulholland, William: Magilligan LY 11; 133

Mulholland's hill: Drumcree AH 1; 40

Mulhollandstown district: Ballyscullion LY 6; 70

Mulhollandstown lough: Ballyscullion LY 6; 70, 75

Mulkawn forts: Manorhamilton Union LM 40; 52

Mulkeeragh fort: Bovevagh LY 25; 47

Mulkeeragh monument: Bovevagh LY 25; 48–49

Mulkeeragh school: Bovevagh LY 25; 28

Mulkeeragh td: Banagher LY 30; 24

Mulkeeragh td: Bovevagh LY 25; 11, 18, 42

Mulkeeragh td: Clondermot LY 34; 79

Mulkeeragh td: Magilligan LY 11; 83

Mulkeeragh td: Tamlaght Finlagan LY 25; 93, 112

Mull td: Cappagh TE 5; 22

Mullabane td: Carlingford LH 40; 57, 59

Mullabanny hill: Clogher TE 5; 54

Mullablaney td: Galloon FH 4; 95

Mullaboy bog: Cumber LY 28; 55

Mullaboy chapel: Cumber LY 28; 32–34

Mullaboy cromlech: Cumber LY 28; 41

Mullaboy giant's grave [I]: Cumber LY 28; 41

Mullaboy giant's grave [II]: Cumber LY 28; 41

Mullaboy standing stone: Cumber LY 28; 41, 43, 45

Mullaboy stream: Cumber LY 28; 41–42

Mullaboy td: Cumber LY 28; 40, 47, 49, 60–61, 64, 97, 102, 106–07

Mullabrack (see Mullaghbrack): Kilmore AH 1; 60

Mullabrack bog: Tullylish DN 12; 140

Mullabrack td: Tullylish DN 12; 142–43

Mullabrick locality: Drumachose LY 9; 94

Mullabury (see Glenmore): Carlingford LH 40; 60

Mullacheap (see Mullagheep)

Mullachs fort: Killymard DL 39; 97

Mullacroy mountain: Ardstraw TE 5; 10

Mulladoon, family: Magheraculmoney FH 14; 110

Mulladry (Mulladgry) td: Kilmore AH 1; 57, 65, 67–70, 72

Mulladry school: Kilmore AH 1; 64, 72

Mullafernaghan (Mullaghfarnaghan) td: Magherally DN 12; 113–14

Mullagh bog: Killyleagh DN 17; 82

Mullagh bridge: Maghera LY 18; 65

Mullagh bridge: Termoneeny LY 6; 131

Mullagh district: Misc. SO 40; 199

Mullagh fort: Termoneeny LY 6; 131

Mullagh gravel pit: Killyleagh DN 17; 82

Mullagh graveyard: Tamlaght Finlagan LY 25; 117

Mullagh hill: Maghera LY 18; 36

Mullagh hill: Tamlaght Finlagan LY 25; 117

Mullagh House: Tamlaght Finlagan LY 25; 80

Mullagh Kildare school: Killyleagh DN 17; 81–82

Mullagh monastery: Maghera LY 18; 12

Mullagh old church: Termoneeny LY 6; 122–23, 127, 131

Mullagh pay school: Killyleagh DN 17; 82

Mullagh ph: Maghera LY 18; 37

Mullagh school: Killyleagh DN 17; 82

Mullagh smithy: Killyleagh DN 17; 82

Mullagh Sunday school: Tamlaght Finlagan LY 25; 96

Mullagh td: Killyleagh DN 17; 81

Mullagh td: Tamlaght Finlagan LY 25; 65, 80, 93, 103

Mullagh td: Termoneeny LY 6; 121–22, 127, 130, 133

Mullaghacall td: Ballyaghran LY 33; 27

Mullaghadun (Mullaghdrin) td: Drumglass TE 20; 40, 44

Mullaghadun hill: Drumglass TE 20; 44

Mullaghadun lough: Monaghan MN 40; 159

Mullaghaevny (see Mullaghanny): Misc. DL 39; 186

Mullaghagarry hill: Raphoe DL 39; 129

Mullaghair (see Mullaghard)

Mullaghamore (see Mullaghmore): Loughgilly AH 1; 85

Mullaghanairy td: Donaghmore DL 39; 38

Mullaghaneany hill: Banagher LY 30; 24, 26, 37, 59, 108–10

Mullaghaneany hill: Dungiven LY 15; 113

Mullaghaneany monuments: Banagher LY 30; 37–38, 56

Mullaghanieny (see Mullaghaneany): Banagher LY 30; 37

Mullaghanny (Mullaghaney) td: Clonleigh DL 39; 12, 186, 198

Mullaghara (see Mullaghard): Drumgoon CN 40; 11

Mullaghard hill: Drumgoon CN 40; 1

Mullaghard school: Drumgoon CN 40; 11

Mullaghard td: Drumgoon CN 40; 2–3

Mullaghash burn: Banagher LY 30; 25, 29

Mullaghash carn: Banagher LY 30; 7, 53–54, 94–95

Mullaghash mountain: Banagher LY 30; 24, 27, 31, 49, 52, 54, 59, 75, 87, 94, 100, 108–10

Mullaghawney (see Mullaghanny)

Mullaghbane (Mullaghbawn) td: Dromore TE 5; 93, 97, 99

Mullaghbane bog: Dromore TE 5; 93

Mullaghbane hill: Magheraculmoney FH 14; 113

Mullaghbane td: Donagh MN 40; 98

Mullaghboy (see Mullaboy): Cumber LY 28; 45

Mullaghboy adult school: Island Magee AM 10; 33

Mullaghboy forts: Magherafelt LY 6; 93, 108

Mullaghboy meeting house: Island Magee AM 10; 20, 34, 68, 73, 76, 78, 96, 104

Mullaghboy school: Island Magee AM 10; 68, 96

Mullaghboy Sunday school: Island Magee AM 10; 70

Mullaghboy td: Ballyscullion LY 6; 52, 60, 63, 69, 71, 73–74

Mullaghboy td: Galloon FH 4; 95

Mullaghboy td: Island Magee AM 10; 20, 33–34, 68, 70, 73, 76, 78, 96, 104

Mullaghboy td: Magherafelt LY 6; 93, 95, 108, 112

Mullaghboy Top hill: Magherafelt LY 6; 79

Mullaghbrack (see Mullabrack): Tullylish DN 12; 140

Mullaghbrack ph: Ballymore AH 1; 7, 14, 17

Mullaghbrack ph: Kilmore AH 1; 57, 60–61, 66–67, 69, 72–73

Mullaghbrack ph: Loughgall AH 1; 75, 78

Mullaghbrack td: Donagh MN 40; 101

Mullaghbrack td: Drumgoon CN 40; 2

Mullaghbredin td: Galloon FH 4; 95

Mullaghcairn (see Mullaghcarn)

Mullaghcapple Glebe td: Galloon FH 4; 95

Mullaghcapple td: Galloon FH 4; 95, 97

Mullaghcarn carn: Banagher LY 30; 109

Mullaghcarn mountain: Ardstraw TE 5; 2

Mullaghcarn mountain: Banagher LY 30; 109

Mullaghcarn mountain: Cappagh TE 5; 15, 17

Mullaghcarn triangulation point: Banagher LY 30; 110

Mullaghcarton (Mullaghcartin) td: Magheragall AM 21; 101, 109

Mullaghcarton corn mill: Magheragall AM 21; 101–02

Mullaghcarton flax mill: Magheragall AM 21; 102

Mullaghcarton fort [I]: Magheragall AM 21; 102, 106

Mullaghcarton fort [II]: Magheragall AM 21; 102, 106

Mullaghcarton school: Magheragall AM 21; 109–11

Mullaghcarton Sunday school: Magheragall AM 21; 110

Mullaghcarton td: Ballinderry AM 21; 46

Mullaghconnelly td: Tickmacrevan AM 13; 123

Mullaghcrew td: Inniskeen MN 40; 128

Mullaghcroghery school: Magheross MN 40; 150

Mullaghcroghery td: Magheross MN 40; 148

Mullaghcroghery td: Monaghan MN 40; 159

Mullaghcronanbeg td: Island Magee AM 10; 70

Mullaghdoo school: Island Magee AM 10; 68, 96

Mullaghdoo Sunday school: Island Magee AM 10; 70

Mullaghdoo td: Island Magee AM 10; 68, 70, 96

Mullaghduff (Mulladuff) td: Armoy AM 24; 6, 9

Mullaghduff cove: Derrykeighan AM 16; 91

Mullaghduff flax mill: Derrykeighan AM 16; 79, 84

Mullaghduff fort: Derrykeighan AM 16; 80, 91

Mullaghduff hill: Derrykeighan AM 16; 80

Mullaghduff paper mill: Derrykeighan AM 16; 84

Mullaghduff school: Armoy AM 24; 6, 9

Mullaghduff td: Derrykeighan AM 16; 92

Mullaghduff td: Donagh MN 40; 98

Mullaghdun church: Cleenish FH 14; 16–17, 20

Mullaghdun td: Cleenish FH 14; 29

Mullagheep td: Tullyaughnish DL 38; 86, 96

Mullaghesh (see Mullaghash): Banagher LY 30; 75

Mullaghfarna district: Misc. SO 40; 198

Mullaghfarne (Mullaghferny) td: Magheraculmoney FH 14; 110–11

Mullaghfarney (see Mullaghfarne)

Mullaghferney (see Mullaghfarne)

Mullaghfin td: Convoy DL 39; 21

Mullaghfin td: Raphoe DL 39; 126

Mullaghgar td: Galloon FH 4; 87, 95

Mullaghgarve chapel: Magheracloone MN 40; 138

Mullaghgawn (Mullaghane) td: Duneane AM 19; 109, 119

Mullaghgawn cave [I]: Duneane AM 19; 110, 119

Mullaghgawn cave [II]: Duneane AM 19; 119

Mullaghgawn cave [III]: Duneane AM 19; 122

Mullaghgawn chapel: Duneane AM 19; 119

Mullaghgawn manor: Duneane AM 19; 100, 102, 116

Mullaghglass adult school: Derryaghy AM 8; 117
Mullaghglass bleach mill: Killevy AH 1; 54
Mullaghglass chapel: Ballymore AH 1; 17
Mullaghglass church: Misc. DN 17; 131
Mullaghglass corn mill: Killevy AH 1; 53
Mullaghglass dispensary: Killevy AH 1; 54
Mullaghglass entrenchments: Derryaghy AM 8; 94
Mullaghglass flax mill [I]: Killevy AH 1; 53
Mullaghglass flax mill [II]: Killevy AH 1; 53
Mullaghglass mountain: Derryaghy AM 8; 90, 115
Mullaghglass quarries: Kilbroney DN 3; 34–35
Mullaghglass quarries: Warrenpoint DN 3; 119
Mullaghglass school: Derryaghy AM 8; 116
Mullaghglass school: Killevy AH 1; 54
Mullaghglass Sunday school: Derryaghy AM 8; 118
Mullaghglass td: Ballymore AH 1; 7, 10–12, 15–18
Mullaghglass td: Derryaghy AM 8; 115
Mullaghhatten td: Ballymascanlan LH 40; 56
Mullaghinch (Mullahinch) td: Aghadowey LY 22;
    13, 27–28, 35–36, 38
Mullaghinch altar: Aghadowey LY 22; 28
Mullaghinch bleach green: Macosquin LY 22; 98
Mullaghinch bog: Aghadowey LY 22; 2
Mullaghinch bridge: Aghadowey LY 22; 10–11
Mullaghinch chapel: Aghadowey LY 22; 6, 16
Mullaghinch cove: Aghadowey LY 22; 29, 32
Mullaghinch giant's grave: Macosquin LY 22; 98
Mullaghinch school: Aghadowey LY 22; 13, 20–21
Mullaghinch stone pulpit: Aghadowey LY 22; 32
Mullaghinch Sunday school: Aghadowey LY 22; 13,
    21
Mullaghinch tappatourzee: Aghadowey LY 22; 27
Mullaghkeel td: Aghalurcher FH 4; 14
Mullaghlogan Glebe House: Rossorry FH 14; 117
Mullaghmaguire Castle: Aghavea FH 4; 21
Mullaghmeash mountain: Banagher LY 30; 85, 93,
    109
Mullaghmeash triangulation point: Banagher LY 30;
    110
Mullaghmeen td: Magheracross FH 14; 102
Mullaghmeene school: Killanny MN 40; 135
Mullaghmenagh quarry: Drumragh TE 5; 110
Mullaghmenagh td: Drumragh TE 5; 108–09, 111
Mullaghmonaghan td: Monaghan MN 40; 159
Mullaghmore bleach green: Aghadowey LY 22; 8–9,
    12
Mullaghmore bleach green: Cappagh TE 5; 20
Mullaghmore corn mill: Loughgilly AH 1; 86
Mullaghmore East school: Aghaloo TE 20; 5
Mullaghmore flax mill: Loughgilly AH 1; 86
Mullaghmore forts: Clogherny TE 20; 28
Mullaghmore hill: Aghabog MN 40; 62
Mullaghmore House: Cappagh TE 5; 17
Mullaghmore House: Clogherny TE 20; 25
Mullaghmore lough: Tydavnet MN 40; 169

Mullaghmore mill: Cappagh TE 5; 19
Mullaghmore mill: Tydavnet MN 40; 173
Mullaghmore mountain: Cappagh TE 5; 20
Mullaghmore North td: Tydavnet MN 40; 169
Mullaghmore Point: Kilbarron DL 39; 78
Mullaghmore Sunday school: Aghadowey LY 22; 21
Mullaghmore td: Aghadowey LY 22; 8, 21, 36–37
Mullaghmore td: Aghalurcher FH 4; 16
Mullaghmore td: Aghalurcher TE 5; 1
Mullaghmore td: Agivey LY 22; 40–41, 44–45
Mullaghmore td: Cappagh TE 5; 19
Mullaghmore td: Cleenish FH 14; 29
Mullaghmore td: Clogher TE 5; 36, 53
Mullaghmore td: Drumragh TE 5; 108, 111
Mullaghmore td: Loughgilly AH 1; 85
Mullaghmore West td: Tydavnet MN 40; 171
Mullaghmossan (Mullochmossagh) td: Glynn AM
    26; 1, 41, 47–48
Mullaghmossan adult school: Glynn AM 26; 46
Mullaghmossan bog: Glynn AM 26; 27
Mullaghmossan school: Glynn AM 26; 8, 35, 46
Mullaghnamoyagh bogs: Tamlaght O'Crilly LY 18;
    84, 132–33
Mullaghnamuddy school: Cleenish FH 14; 24
Mullaghnamuddy td: Cleenish FH 14; 29
Mullaghneany (see Mullaghaneany)
Mullaghorne corn mill: Drumlumman CN 40; 14
Mullaghorne td: Drumlumman CN 40; 13
Mullaghpeak td: Donagh MN 40; 100
Mullaghree td: Rossorry FH 14; 116
Mullaghsandal (see Mullaghsandall)
Mullaghsandall fort: Kilwaughter AM 10; 118
Mullaghsandall hill: Kilwaughter AM 10; 108
Mullaghsandall school: Kilwaughter AM 10; 111,
    120–21
Mullaghsandall Sunday school: Kilwaughter AM
    10; 121
Mullaghsandall td: Kilwaughter AM 10; 111, 114,
    116, 118–19, 122
Mullaghsandall td: Raloo AM 32; 106, 127
Mullaghsandel (see Mullaghsandall)
Mullaghsawey hill: Taughboyne DL 39; 148,
    153–54
Mullaghsillagh td: Donacavey TE 5; 81
Mullaghsillogagh td: Enniskillen FH 4; 74, 82
Mullaghslina fort: Clogherny TE 20; 28
Mullaghslina td: Clogherny TE 20; 25
Mullaghtarnaghan (see Mullafernaghan)
Mullaghtinny td: Clogher TE 5; 53
Mullaghtironey td: Tamlaght TE 20; 78, 81–82, 87,
    122–28, 134
Mullaghtirony (see Mullaghtironey)
Mullaghvea td: Clones FH 4; 26
Mullaghvilly (see Mullavilly)
Mullaghwee district: Misc. SO 40; 198

Mullaghy td: Rossorry FH 14; 117
Mullaglass td: Derryaghy AM 8; 119
Mullahash (see Mullaghash)
Mullahead fort: Kilmore AH 1; 72
Mullahead school: Kilmore AH 1; 64, 72
Mullahead td: Kilmore AH 1; 61, 64, 66–68, 72
Mullahinch bleach green: Errigal LY 27; 78
Mullahinch chapel: Agivey LY 22; 41
Mullahinch giant's grave: Errigal LY 27; 78
Mullahinch td: Agivey LY 22; 42
Mullalehan td: Galloon FH 4; 95
Mullalelish td: Kilmore AH 1; 67, 72
Mullaletra td: Kilmore AH 1; 61, 67–72
Mullalishlaughlin td: Tydavnet MN 40; 169
Mullamoody td: Magheraculmoney FH 14; 110
Mullan bleach green: Aghadowey LY 22; 8–10
Mullan bridge: Aghadowey LY 22; 10
Mullan glen: Banagher LY 30; 112
Mullan Head td: Dunboe LY 11; 81
Mullan Point: Ballinderry LY 6; 41
Mullan Point: Ballinderry TE 20; 11
Mullan td: Aghadowey LY 22; 35–36
Mullan td: Ballinderry TE 20; 13
Mullan td: Kilrea LY 27; 115, 129
Mullan, Arthur: Ramoan AM 24; 116
Mullan, Bernard: Aghadowey LY 22; 36
Mullan, Bernard: Agivey LY 22; 45
Mullan, Bernard: Lissan LY 31; 110
Mullan, Brian: Misc. LY 36; 114
Mullan, Catherine (Jnr): Agivey LY 22; 45
Mullan, Catherine (Snr): Agivey LY 22; 45
Mullan, Catherine: Aghadowey LY 22; 36
Mullan, Charles: Lissan LY 31; 110
Mullan, Donaghey: Drumachose LY 9; 127
Mullan, Edward: Agivey LY 22; 45
Mullan, family: Killygarvan DL 38; 47
Mullan, Hugh: Ballymoney AM 16; 15, 17
Mullan, Hugh: Desertmartin LY 31; 61
Mullan, Hugh: Ramoan AM 24; 118–20
Mullan, James: Aghaderg DN 12; 12
Mullan, James: Aghanloo LY 11; 15, 19, 22, 40
Mullan, James: Ballyscullion LY 6; 71
Mullan, James [I]: Ramoan AM 24; 119
Mullan, James [II]: Ramoan AM 24; 122
Mullan, Jane: Ballyscullion LY 6; 77
Mullan, John (Jnr): Agivey LY 22; 44
Mullan, John (Snr): Agivey LY 22; 44
Mullan, John: Ballintoy AM 24; 21
Mullan, John: Balteagh LY 9; 12, 26
Mullan, John [I]: Aghadowey LY 22; 36
Mullan, John [II]: Aghadowey LY 22; 36
Mullan, Lord: Kilkeel DN 3; 53
Mullan, Margaret: Lissan LY 31; 110
Mullan, Michael [I]: Lissan LY 31; 110
Mullan, Michael [II]: Lissan LY 31; 110

Mullan, Mr [I]: Clondermot LY 34; 34
Mullan, Mr [II]: Clondermot LY 34; 34
Mullan, Nancy: Lissan LY 31; 109
Mullan, Patrick (Jnr): Lissan LY 31; 109
Mullan, Patrick (Snr): Lissan LY 31; 109
Mullan, Patrick: Maghera LY 18; 81
Mullan, Rev. John: Lambeg AM 8; 136
Mullan, Thomas: Aghadowey LY 22; 36
Mullan, Thomas: Drumachose LY 9; 131
Mullan, Thomas [I]: Agivey LY 22; 43
Mullan, Thomas [II]: Agivey LY 22; 44
Mullan, William: Ballywillin AM 16; 33
Mullan, William [I]: Carrickfergus AM 37; 110
Mullan, William [II]: Carrickfergus AM 37; 110
Mullanacross td: Errigal Truagh MN 40; 121–22
Mullanarackan (see Mullanarockan): Tydavnet MN
    40; 172
Mullanarockan chapel: Tydavnet MN 40; 171–72
Mullanarockan td: Tydavnet MN 40; 171–72
Mullanary Cortannel td: Aughnamullen MN 40; 76
Mullanary Glebe House: Aughnamullen MN 40; 71
Mullanary Glebe td: Aughnamullen MN 40; 76
Mullanary hill: Tynan AH 1; 124
Mullanary Island: Aughnamullen MN 40; 69
Mullanary lough: Aughnamullen MN 40; 69
Mullanary td: Aughnamullen MN 40; 69
Mullanary td: Ballymore AH 1; 13–14, 16–17
Mullanary td: Clonfeacle AH 1; 22
Mullanary td: Currin MN 40; 86
Mullanary td: Magheross MN 40; 149
Mullanavannog lough: Donaghmoyne MN 40; 106
Mullanboy (Mullenbuy) td: Dromore TE 5; 93, 99
Mullanboy school: Donacavey TE 5; 65
Mullanboy td: Donacavey TE 5; 65, 77, 79, 81–82,
    86
Mullanbwee td: Donaghmore DL 39; 38
Mullanbwee td: Urney DL 39; 181
Mullanderg church: Errigal Truagh MN 40; 121
Mullane (Mullan) td: Drumachose LY 9; 50, 58,
    86–87, 96, 110, 123, 129, 131
Mullane millstone: Drumachose LY 9; 110
Mullane standing stone: Drumachose LY 9; 58, 129
Mullane Sunday school: Drumachose LY 9; 85
Mullaney, David: Kilmacteige SO 40; 187
Mullaney, John: Kilmacteige SO 40; 187, 193–94
Mullaney's Cross: Kilmacteige SO 40; 187, 190,
    193–95
Mullaney's Cross barrack: Kilmacteige SO 40; 187
Mullaney's Cross inns: Kilmacteige SO 40; 187
Mullannakille enclosure: Ballyscullion LY 6; 50, 73
Mullans (Mullins) td: Donacavey TE 5; 81, 86
Mullans meeting house: Finvoy AM 23; 68, 70
Mullans td: Clogher TE 5; 36–37
Mullans td: Finvoy AM 23; 68, 73
Mullantine (Mullintine) td: Drumcree AH 1; 41

Mullantine school: Drumcree AH 1; 30, 36, 41

Mullaraney (see Mullarney): Kilmacteige SO 40; 193

Mullarney Lower village: Kilmacteige SO 40; 187, 193

Mullarney Upper village: Kilmacteige SO 40; 187, 193

Mullarten (see Mullarttown): Kilkeel DN 3; 49

Mullarts bridge: Ramoan AM 24; 88

Mullarts stream: Ramoan AM 24; 88

Mullarttown corn mill: Kilkeel DN 3; 49

Mullarttown school: Kilkeel DN 3; 50

Mullarttown td: Kilkeel DN 3; 49

Mullaselaga (see Mullasiloga)

Mullaselega (see Mullasiloga)

Mullasellegga (see Mullasiloga)

Mullashingo North lough: Tydavnet MN 40; 169

Mullashingo South lough: Tydavnet MN 40; 169

Mullashingo td: Tydavnet MN 40; 169

Mullasilage (see Mullasiloga)

Mullasiloga (Mullaselega) td: Donacavey TE 5; 65, 67, 77, 79, 81, 84, 86

Mullasiloga school: Donacavey TE 5; 65

Mullaslinna (see Mullaghslina): Clogherny TE 20; 28

Mullatee td: Carlingford LH 40; 59

Mullatigorry td: Tydavnet MN 40; 169

Mullavilly church: Kilmore AH 1; 62–63, 68, 72

Mullavilly dispensary: Kilmore AH 1; 60

Mullavilly House: Kilmore AH 1; 64, 72

Mullavilly ph: Ballymore AH 1; 12

Mullavilly ph: Kilmore AH 1; 65

Mullavilly school: Kilmore AH 1; 60

Mullavilly td: Kilmore AH 1; 67, 72–73

Mullawinney (see Mulawinny)

Mullawinny fort: Donacavey TE 5; 82

Mullawinny school: Donacavey TE 5; 65, 82

Mullawinny td: Donacavey TE 5; 65, 77, 79, 81–82, 86

Mulled caves: Clondavaddog DL 38; 4

Mulleeny td: Lough Swilly DL 38; 143, 145

Mullen (see Mullane): Drumachose LY 9; 110

Mullen Crone graveyard: Derryaghy AM 8; 91–92

Mullen hill: Drumgoon CN 40; 1

Mullen td: Clonleigh DL 39; 12, 198

Mullen, Ann: Errigal LY 27; 66

Mullen, Ann: Tamlaght Finlagan LY 25; 118

Mullen, Arthur: Errigal LY 27; 58, 60

Mullen, Arthur: Macosquin LY 22; 102

Mullen, B.M.: Banagher LY 30; 109

Mullen, B.M.: Dungiven LY 15; 63

Mullen, Bernard: Balteagh LY 9; 30

Mullen, Bernard [I]: Errigal LY 27; 45, 70

Mullen, Bernard [II]: Errigal LY 27; 66

Mullen, Bernard [III]: Errigal LY 27; 75

Mullen, Bryan: Drumachose LY 9; 112

Mullen, Charles: Artrea LY 6; 37

Mullen, Charles: Banagher LY 30; 52, 88

Mullen, Charles: Drumachose LY 9; 134

Mullen, Cormic: Errigal LY 27; 54, 71

Mullen, Daniel: Errigal LY 27; 60

Mullen, Edward: Drumachose LY 9; 134

Mullen, Eliza: Carrickfergus AM 37; 119

Mullen, family: Ballynascreen LY 31; 12

Mullen, family: Dungiven LY 15; 77

Mullen, James: Banagher LY 30; 69–70

Mullen, James: Tamlaght Finlagan LY 25; 118

Mullen, James [I]: Errigal LY 27; 54, 60, 69

Mullen, James [II]: Errigal LY 27; 66

Mullen, Jane: Tamlaght Finlagan LY 25; 118

Mullen, John (Jnr): Errigal LY 27; 59

Mullen, John (Snr): Errigal LY 27; 59

Mullen, John: Banagher LY 30; 84

Mullen, John: Bovevagh LY 25; 13, 31

Mullen, John: Dungiven LY 15; 71

Mullen, John [I]: Errigal LY 27; 54–55, 69

Mullen, John [II]: Errigal LY 27; 66

Mullen, John [III]: Errigal LY 27; 72

Mullen, Margaret: Tamlaght Finlagan LY 25; 118

Mullen, Mary (Jnr): Errigal LY 27; 66

Mullen, Mary (Snr): Errigal LY 27; 66

Mullen, Michael: Errigal LY 27; 65

Mullen, Mr: Dungiven LY 15; 66

Mullen, Patrick: Dungiven LY 15; 65, 70–72, 86, 103

Mullen, Patt: Banagher LY 30; 71, 77

Mullen, Patt [I]: Errigal LY 27; 55, 60, 69, 71

Mullen, Patt [II]: Errigal LY 27; 58

Mullen, Patt [III]: Errigal LY 27; 66

Mullen, Sally: Tamlaght Finlagan LY 25; 118

Mullen, Sarah: Tamlaght Finlagan LY 25; 118

Mullen, Thomas [I]: Errigal LY 27; 54, 70

Mullen, Thomas [II]: Errigal LY 27; 65

Mullen's hill: Drumcree AH 1; 40

Mullenagung td: Misc. DL 39; 186, 198

Mullenakill td: Killyman AH 1; 55

Mullenakill West td: Killyman AH 1; 56

Mullenan [or Mullinan] bog: Killea and Taughboyne DL 39; 80

Mullenan [or Mullinan] House: Killea and Taughboyne DL 39; 80–81, 87, 90

Mullenan [or Mullinan] locality: Killea and Taughboyne DL 39; 79, 89

Mullenary (see Mullanary)

Mullenaveigh (see Mulnaveagh): Misc. DL 39; 198

Mullenboy (see Mullanboy)

Mullens td: Cleenish FH 14; 29

Mullenshellistragh td: Cleenish FH 14; 29

Mullentin (see Mullantine): Drumcree AH 1; 36

Mullesharnagh lough: Magheracross FH 14; 91

Mullhalteen td: Carlingford LH 40; 59

Mullicarton (see Mullaghcarton): Magheragall AM 21; 111

Mullies chapel: Manorhamilton Union LM 40; 52

Mulligan, family: Kilmacteige SO 40; 186

Mulligan, family: Magherally DN 12; 114

Mulligan, George: Seapatrick DN 12; 127, 134

Mulligan, James: Annaclone DN 12; 14

Mulligan, John: Seapatrick DN 12; 127, 134

Mulligan, man named: Galloon FH 4; 105

Mulligan, Mary: Seapatrick DN 12; 132

Mulligan, Mr: Seapatrick DN 12; 125

Mulligan, Rev. Alexander: Maghera LY 18; 17, 29, 66, 75

Mulligan, Rev. Felix: Galloon FH 4; 98

Mulligan, Rev. James: Moira DN 12; 119

Mulligan, Thomas: Aghadowey LY 22; 26

Mulligan, Thomas: Kilmacteige SO 40; 194–95

Mulligan's bridge: Seapatrick DN 12; 132, 135

Mulligan's school: Seapatrick DN 12; 132, 135

Mullin td: Kinawley FH 4; 110

Mullin, Arthur: Aghadowey LY 22; 20

Mullin, Brian: Banagher LY 30; 49

Mullin, Daniel: Termoneeny LY 6; 133

Mullin, Docia: Drumachose LY 9; 132

Mullin, Edward: Balteagh LY 9; 44

Mullin, Edward: Drumachose LY 9; 132

Mullin, family: Dungiven LY 15; 24, 30–31, 34, 101, 103, 108

Mullin, family: Dunsfort DN 17; 68

Mullin, family: Newry DN 3; 108

Mullin, James: Donacavey TE 5; 65

Mullin, John: Bovevagh LY 25; 60

Mullin, John: Drumachose LY 9; 132

Mullin, Marcus: Drumachose LY 9; 132

Mullin, Molly: Drumachose LY 9; 132

Mullin, Mr: Faughanvale LY 36; 18

Mullin, Patt: Drumachose LY 9; 132

Mullin, Robert: Drumachose LY 9; 132

Mullinabrone bog: Aghadowey LY 22; 4, 30

Mullinacree Upper td: Tomregan FH 4; 125

Mullinacuagh td: Kinawley FH 4; 113

Mullinadroman (see Drummond): Donacavey TE 5; 85

Mullinagare td: Aughnamullen MN 40; 76

Mullinageeny locality: Clonleigh DL 39; 12

Mullinahunshin (see Mullynahunshin): Killesher FH 14; 90

Mullinanalt td: Aughnamullen MN 40; 76

Mullinard td: Convoy DL 39; 21

Mullinary (see Mullanary)

Mullinasillagaugh (see Mullaghsillogagh): Enniskillen FH 4; 82

Mullinasillagh (Mullinsallagh) td: Ahoghill AM 23; 37–39, 50

Mullinasillagh female school: Ahoghill AM 23; 51

Mullinasillagh male school: Ahoghill AM 23; 50–51

Mullinasollis district: Drumhome DL 39; 61–62

Mullinasool Promontory: Lough Swilly DL 38; 110

Mullinavale mountain: Aghalurcher FH 4; 2

Mullinavale td: Aghalurcher FH 4; 1

Mullinavanog (see Mullynavannog): Galloon FH 4; 91

Mullinaveigh (see Mulnaveagh)

Mullinavigh brickfield: Killesher FH 14; 84

Mullinavigh school: Killesher FH 14; 86

Mullinavillin school: Loughgall AH 1; 81

Mullinawinnia hill: Cleenish FH 14; 12

Mullinawye (see Mulnaveagh)

Mullindooh rocks: Lough Swilly DL 38; 110

Mullinean (see Mullenan): Killea and Taughboyne DL 39; 79

Mullingar (Westmeath): Drummaul AM 19; 35

Mullingar td: Donaghmore DL 39; 38

Mullingar, Messrs: Aghaderg DN 12; 4

Mullins and Sassaigh td: Clogher TE 5; 53

Mullins and Tatnadaveragh td: Clogher TE 5; 53

Mullins hamlet: Killymard DL 39; 107

Mullins td: Clogher TE 5; 43

Mullins td: Donacavey TE 5; 77, 79, 81, 84

Mullins td: Killymard DL 39; 101

Mullins, Thomas: Clondermot LY 34; 79

Mullintragh creek: Lough Swilly DL 38; 108

Mullintur (Mullinteer) td: Ballymore AH 1; 15–17

Mullintur foundry: Ballymore AH 1; 8, 10, 17

Mullisclegagh (see Mullasiloga)

Mullisclogagh (see Mullasiloga)

Mulliseligagh (see Mullasiloga)

Mullmore church: Aughnamullen MN 40; 71

Mullmore td: Aughnamullen MN 40; 76

Mullnadee td: Lough Swilly DL 38; 145

Mullnagoagh td: Dromore TE 5; 100

Mullnaherb td: Kinawley FH 4; 121

Mullnavnnog (see Mullanavannog): Donaghmoyne MN 40; 106

Mullocheap (see Mullagheep): Tullyaughnish DL 38; 96

Mullockclogher mountain: Cumber LY 28; 1

Mulloge district: Misc. SO 40; 199

Mulloghatinny td: Clogher TE 5; 35

Mulloghboy (see Mullaghboy)

Mulloghdoo (see Mulloughdoo)

Mulloghmore (see Mullaghmore)

Mullon, family: Lissan LY 31; 91, 106

Mullon, John: Lissan LY 31; 110

Mullon, Martha: Lissan LY 31; 110

Mullon, Michael: Lissan LY 31; 110

Mullon, Peter: Lissan LY 31; 110

Mulloughboy (see Mullaghboy)

Mulloughdoo mountain: Tomregan FH 4; 126

Mulloughdoo Sunday school: Island Magee AM 10; 98

Mulloughdoo td: Island Magee AM 10; 98

Mulloughdoo td: Tomregan FH 4; 126

Mulloughdrin td: Dromara DN 12; 63, 65

Mulloughsallagh (see Mullaghsandall)

Mulloughsandal (see Mullaghsandall)

Mulloughsandall (see Mullaghsandall)

Mulloughsandell (see Mullaghsandall)

Mulloy, family: Ballynascreen LY 31; 9

Mulloy, family: Finvoy AM 23; 76

Mullrod td: Derryvullan FH 14; 46

Mullyard td: Cleenish FH 14; 29

Mullyardlough (see Mullyardlougher): Cleenish FH 14; 24

Mullyardlougher school: Cleenish FH 14; 24

Mullyardlougher td: Cleenish FH 14; 29

Mullyash bog: Muckno MN 40; 163

Mullyash cairn: Muckno MN 40; 166

Mullyash hill: Muckno MN 40; 162, 168

Mullyash plantation: Muckno MN 40; 167

Mullyash tower: Muckno MN 40; 162, 166

Mullybrill td: Cleenish FH 14; 28–29

Mullycarnan (Mullycarnon) td: Aghaloo TE 20; 1

Mullycarnan lough: Aghaloo TE 20; 1

Mullycarnan school: Aghaloo TE 20; 5

Mullycartin (see Mullaghcarton): Magheragall AM 21; 109

Mullycavitt corn mill: Cleenish FH 14; 18

Mullycavitt td: Cleenish FH 14; 29

Mullydinity td: Galloon FH 4; 95

Mullyduff td: Galloon FH 4; 91–92, 95

Mullydullagher chapel: Cleenish FH 14; 17

Mullygarry (Mullygurry) td: Cleenish FH 14; 30

Mullygarry school: Cleenish FH 14; 24

Mullykevit (see Mullykivet)

Mullykevitt (see Mullykivet): Devenish FH 14; 53

Mullykivet td: Devenish FH 14; 53, 58

Mullykivet td: Inishmacsaint FH 14; 75

Mullykivit (see Mullykivet)

Mullyknock mill: Derryvullan FH 14; 43

Mullyknock mill: Enniskillen FH 4; 69

Mullyknock td: Enniskillen FH 4; 74, 82

Mullyleet giant's grave: Cleenish FH 14; 22

Mullyleet td: Cleenish FH 14; 20, 22, 24, 30

Mullylodin chapel: Errigal Truagh MN 40; 121

Mullylustia td: Cleenish FH 14; 30

Mullymesker school: Cleenish FH 14; 24

Mullymesker td: Cleenish FH 14; 17, 30

Mullymeskerry (see Mullymesker): Cleenish FH 14; 30

Mullynaburtlan td: Aghalurcher FH 4; 14

Mullynacaw td: Rossorry FH 14; 117

Mullynagon td: Aughnamullen MN 40; 74

Mullynahunshin chapel: Killesher FH 14; 83

Mullynahunshin well: Killesher FH 14; 90

Mullynasillagaugh (see Mullaghsillogagh): Enniskillen FH 4; 74

Mullynavannog corn mill: Galloon FH 4; 91

Mullynavannog td: Galloon FH 4; 88, 91, 95

Mullynavanog (see Mullynavannog): Galloon FH 4; 88

Mullynavarnog td: Cleenish FH 14; 30

Mullynaveagh hill: Aghaloo TE 20; 1

Mullynaveagh td: Killesher FH 14; 87

Mullynavigh (see Mullynaveagh)

Mullynawinnia td: Cleenish FH 14; 30

Mullyned td: Galloon FH 4; 95

Mullyneeny[?] td: Kinawley FH 4; 120–21

Mullynock (see Mullyknock)

Mullyroddan corn mill: Killeeshil TE 20; 62, 64

Mullyroddan flax mill: Killeeshil TE 20; 64

Mulnacross hill: Dromore TE 5; 93

Mulnadoran td: Aghavea FH 4; 23

Mulnagoagh lough: Dromore TE 5; 100

Mulnagode td: Templecarn DL 39; 164

Mulnagoe td: Dromore TE 5; 99

Mulnagone td: Galloon FH 4; 88, 95

Mulnahorn school: Aghaloo TE 20; 5

Mulnahorn td: Galloon FH 4; 95

Mulnahunch school: Killeeshil TE 20; 64

Mulnaskea td: Enniskillen FH 4; 82

Mulnatoosnog td: Drumragh TE 5; 104

Mulnaveagh bog: Clonleigh DL 39; 1

Mulnaveagh td: Clonleigh DL 39; 12, 188, 198

Mulnavoo foundry: Ballynascreen LY 31; 11, 22

Mulnavoo quarry: Misc. LY 31; 114

Mulnavoo td: Ballynascreen LY 31; 1, 9, 21–22, 143

Mulrine's bridge: Clonleigh DL 39; 14

Mulroy bar: Lough Swilly DL 38; 114–15

Mulroy bay: Clondavaddog DL 38; 1–6, 8–10

Mulroy bay: Kilmacrenan DL 38; 50

Mulroy bay: Lough Swilly DL 38; 104–05, 113–14, 138

Mulroy bay: Mevagh DL 38; 54–57

Mulroy bay: Tullyaughnish DL 38; 84, 86, 88, 92, 94–95

Mulroy coastguard station: Mevagh DL 38; 59

Mulroy district: Lough Swilly DL 38; 100, 115–19, 128–29, 149

Mulroy lough: Faughanvale LY 36; 63

Mulroy lough: Lough Swilly DL 38; 104, 113, 127

Mulvena, John: Ballinderry AM 21; 58

Mulverey locality: Bovevagh LY 25; 42

Mulvin Parks House: Ardstraw TE 5; 4

Mulvin td: Ardstraw TE 5; 2

Munacally td: Killymard DL 39; 100

Munce, Mr: Drumbo DN 7; 60

Munclink (see Monclink): Raymoghy DL 39; 141

Mundell, Jane: Ballynascreen LY 31; 14, 21

Munderrydoe corn mill: Pomeroy TE 20; 70

Mundle, Isabella: Duneane AM 19; 123

Mundooeys (see Mondooey): Raymoghy DL 39; 141

Mundoran (see Mindoran): Clonmany DL 38; 19

Munelbuy td: Dromore TE 5; 97

Munenabane td: Dromara DN 12; 62–63, 65

Mungle, George: Island Magee AM 10; 95

Municass (see Moneycass): Laragh CN 40; 43

Munlel school: Ematris MN 40; 117

Muniens corn mill: Laragh CN 40; 40

Muniens td: Laragh CN 40; 40, 43

Munies mountain: Tickmacrevan AM 13; 125

Muniss, John: Killead AM 35; 15, 48

Munlough lough: Comber DN 7; 32, 43

Munlough td: Comber DN 7; 32, 37–38, 42–43

Munn, John: Ballyscullion LY 6; 57

Munna, St: Faughanvale LY 36; 62

Munnaboy (see Mullaboy): Cumber LY 28; 55

Munnalea (see Mullaney's Cross): Kilmacteige SO 40; 193

Munnell, Margret: Maghera LY 18; 61

Munniagh td: Drumgoon CN 40; 3

Munniaghs fort: Desertegney DL 38; 26

Munniaghs standing stone: Desertegney DL 38; 26

Munnyocriggan td: Cleenish FH 14; 30

Munreagh (see Monreagh): Killea and Taughboyne DL 39; 79

Munreery (see Munreevy)

Munreevy school: Bovevagh LY 25; 27

Munreevy td: Banagher LY 30; 23

Munro's Hotel: Dromore DN 12; 75

Munroe, Rev. George: Carnmoney AM 2; 75

Munster: Banagher LY 30; 71

Munster: Clondermot LY 34; 71, 73, 75

Munster: Cumber LY 28; 60

Munster: Dungiven LY 15; 34

Munster: Faughanvale LY 36; 54

Munster: Kilcronaghan LY 31; 68, 76

Muntclone td: Ballymore AH 1; 12, 15, 17

Muntecimlin td: Clondavaddog DL 38; 3

Munterlowney mountains: Misc. LY 31; 133

Muntertinney td: Raphoe DL 39; 126

Mur loch: Templecarn DL 39; 157

Murchossy td: Clogher TE 5; 53

Murchy's stone (see Murphy's stone): Aghanloo LY 11; 28

Murder Hole locality: Derryaghy AM 8; 115

Murder Hole locality: Dungiven LY 15; 35

Murder Hole locality: Magilligan LY 11; 115, 138

Murder Hole pit: Ballintoy AM 24; 32

Murdersleagh hill: Island Magee AM 10; 99–100

Murdersleagh lighthouse: Island Magee AM 10; 99

Murdoch, Henry: Newry DN 3; 99, 104

Murdock, Alexander: Muckamore AM 35; 79

Murdock, David: Tamlaght TE 20; 116

Murdock, family: Ballynure AM 32; 56

Murdock, George: Carrickfergus AM 37; 116

Murdock, James: Muckamore AM 35; 81

Murdock, John: Ahoghill AM 23; 36

Murdock, John: Ballyaghran LY 33; 27

Murdock, Mr: Killymard DL 39; 98

Murdock, Mrs: Doagh AM 29; 89

Murdock, Peter: Donaghmore DL 39; 39

Murdock, R.: Aughnamullen MN 40; 76

Murdock, Robert: Donagh MN 40; 103, 105

Murdock, Robert: Tamlaght TE 20; 116

Murdock, Widow: Muckamore AM 35; 81

Murdock, William: Doagh AM 29; 98

Murdock, William: Donagh MN 40; 100–01, 103, 105

Murdock, William: Errigal Keerogue TE 20; 48

Murdock, William: Muckno MN 40; 167

Mure lough: Kilmacteige SO 40; 191

Mure td: Manorhamilton Union LM 40; 54

Murish, man named: Magheraculmoney FH 14; 112

Murland, James: Kilmegan DN 3; 58

Murley school: Clogher TE 5; 51

Murley td: Clogher TE 5; 51

Murley, Patrick: Donaghmore DL 39; 39

Murlitterbral (see Meenletterbale): Moville DL 38; 70

Murlogh chapel: Clonleigh DL 39; 13, 15

Murlogh House: Clonleigh DL 39; 10

Murlogh school: Clonleigh DL 39; 4

Murlogh td: Clonleigh DL 39; 12–13, 195, 198

Murlough (see Murlogh): Misc. DL 39; 195

Murlough altar: Culfeightrin AM 24; 58

Murlough bay: Culfeightrin AM 24; 38–39, 44

Murlough district: Culfeightrin AM 24; 57–58

Murnay, family: Carrickfergus AM 37; 93, 179

Murphey, family: Derrykeighan AM 16; 89

Murphy, Alexander: Carrickfergus AM 37; 193

Murphy, Alexander: Kilwaughter AM 10; 120

Murphy, Andrew [I]: Ballyscullion AM 19; 13

Murphy, Andrew [II]: Ballyscullion AM 19; 13

Murphy, Bernard: Artrea LY 6; 9, 25

Murphy, Binn [I]: Killowen LY 33; 172

Murphy, Binn [II]: Killowen LY 33; 172

Murphy, Charles: Newry DN 3; 99, 104

Murphy, David: Newry DN 3; 82, 111

Murphy, Edward: Ballynascreen LY 31; 13, 21

Murphy, family: Ardglass DN 17; 4

Murphy, family: Ballintoy AM 24; 20

Murphy, family: Blaris AM 8; 22

Murphy, family: Carrickfergus AM 37; 93

Murphy, family: Derrykeighan AM 16; 89

Murphy, family: Dunsfort DN 17; 68

Murphy, family: Ramoan AM 24; 107

Murphy, George [I]: Duneane AM 19; 123

Murphy, George [II]: Duneane AM 19; 123
Murphy, George [III]: Duneane AM 19; 123
Murphy, Henry: Island Magee AM 10; 90
Murphy, Hugh: Artrea LY 6; 24
Murphy, J.M.: Ballymascanlan LH 40; 55
Murphy, James: Blaris DN 12; 40
Murphy, James: Loughgall AH 1; 78
Murphy, James: Newry DN 3; 82, 111
Murphy, James [I]: Duneane AM 19; 123
Murphy, James [II]: Duneane AM 19; 123
Murphy, Jane: Duneane AM 19; 123
Murphy, John: Artrea LY 6; 24–25
Murphy, John: Ballintoy AM 24; 22
Murphy, John: Banagher LY 30; 81
Murphy, John: Blaris DN 12; 46, 50
Murphy, John: Duneane AM 19; 123
Murphy, John: Kilcronaghan LY 31; 85
Murphy, John: Saul DN 17; 111
Murphy, Joseph: Newry DN 3; 99, 104
Murphy, Joseph: Tamlaght O'Crilly LY 18; 117
Murphy, Margaret: Duneane AM 19; 123
Murphy, Margaret: Kilmore AH 1; 59
Murphy, Mary [I]: Duneane AM 19; 123
Murphy, Mary [II]: Duneane AM 19; 123
Murphy, Mary Anne [I]: Duneane AM 19; 123
Murphy, Mary Anne [II]: Duneane AM 19; 123
Murphy, Michael: Artrea LY 6; 24
Murphy, Michael: Drumgoon CN 40; 7–9
Murphy, Mr (Rathfriland): Ballymore AH 1; 16–17
Murphy, Mr (Rathfriland): Loughgilly AH 1; 84
Murphy, Mr: Comber DN 7; 34, 40
Murphy, Mr: Enniskillen FH 4; 85
Murphy, Mrs: Drumballyroney DN 3; 13
Murphy, Patrick: Artrea LY 6; 11, 25
Murphy, Patrick: Misc. LY 31; 126
Murphy, person named: Newry DN 3; 63
Murphy, Peter: Newry DN 3; 99, 104
Murphy, Rev.: Newry DN 3; 104
Murphy, Rev. Bernard: Lissan LY 31; 93, 99, 102, 104
Murphy, Rev. James: Maghera LY 18; 68
Murphy, Rev. James: Tydavnet MN 40; 170–71
Murphy, Rev. James [I]: Misc. LY 31; 129, 137
Murphy, Rev. James [II]: Misc. LY 31; 136
Murphy, Rev. John: Carrickfergus AM 37; 144
Murphy, Rev. John: Island Magee AM 10; 34, 87
Murphy, Robert: Ballymascanlan LH 40; 55
Murphy, Robert: Hillsborough DN 12; 107
Murphy, Robert [I]: Duneane AM 19; 123
Murphy, Robert [II]: Duneane AM 19; 123
Murphy, Robinson: Duneane AM 19; 123
Murphy, Samuel (Jnr): Muckamore AM 35; 79–80
Murphy, Samuel: Duneane AM 19; 123
Murphy, T.R.: Duneane AM 19; 123
Murphy, Thomas [I]: Duneane AM 19; 123

Murphy, Thomas [II]: Duneane AM 19; 123
Murphy, W.J.: Muckamore AM 35; 79
Murphy, Widow: Ballymoney AM 16; 18
Murphy, Widow: Ballynascreen LY 31; 14, 21
Murphy, William: Carnmoney AM 2; 47, 84, 90
Murphy, William: Muckamore AM 35; 79
Murphy, William [I]: Duneane AM 19; 123
Murphy, William [II]: Duneane AM 19; 123
Murphy's stone: Aghanloo LY 11; 4, 25, 28
Murravagh Point: Lough Swilly DL 38; 122
Murray, A.: Moville DL 38; 78
Murray, Alexander: Carnmoney AM 2; 77
Murray, Alexander: Drumachose LY 9; 65
Murray, Alexander: Inishkeel DL 39; 67
Murray, Alexander: Killymard DL 39; 98, 100–01
Murray, Charles: Carrickfergus AM 37; 194
Murray, Col: Clondermot LY 34; 46
Murray, Daniel: Drumachose LY 9; 134
Murray, Daniel: Hillsborough DN 12; 106
Murray, Dr: Camlin AM 21; 76
Murray, Dr: Tydavnet MN 40; 170
Murray, Edward (Jnr): Drumachose LY 9; 134
Murray, Edward (Snr): Drumachose LY 9; 134
Murray, Elenor: Drumachose LY 9; 134
Murray, family: Ballynascreen LY 31; 12
Murray, family: Ballywillin AM 16; 32
Murray, family: Blaris AM 8; 21
Murray, family: Carrickfergus AM 37; 93
Murray, family: Derryaghy AM 8; 100
Murray, family: Drumbeg AM 8; 123
Murray, family: Loughguile AM 13; 64
Murray, Henry: Hillsborough DN 12; 97, 105
Murray, Henry: Raymoghy DL 39; 140
Murray, Hugh: Agivey LY 22; 45
Murray, Hugh: Carrickfergus AM 37; 119, 129
Murray, James: Ahoghill AM 23; 38
Murray, James: Blaris AM 8; 54
Murray, James: Blaris DN 12; 46, 49
Murray, James: Carrickfergus AM 37; 119
Murray, James: Faughanvale LY 36; 42, 45
Murray, James: Killead AM 35; 46–47
Murray, James: Killymard DL 39; 100
Murray, James: Maghera LY 18; 22, 67
Murray, James: Magheracross FH 14; 97
Murray, Jane: Ahoghill AM 23; 38
Murray, John: Ahoghill AM 23; 37
Murray, John: Culfeightrin AM 24; 65, 70
Murray, John: Duneane AM 19; 124
Murray, John: Hillsborough DN 12; 106
Murray, John: Killinchy DN 7; 93
Murray, John: Muckamore AM 35; 77
Murray, John: Tullyaughnish DL 38; 89
Murray, John: Tullyniskan TE 20; 140
Murray, John [I]: Carrickfergus AM 37; 40
Murray, John [II]: Carrickfergus AM 37; 157

Murray, Martha: Drummaul AM 19; 91

Murray, Maryann: Drumachose LY 9; 134

Murray, Mr: Leckpatrick TE 5; 117

Murray, Mrs: Donagh MN 40; 103

Murray, Nancy (Jnr): Carrickfergus AM 37; 157

Murray, Nancy (Snr): Carrickfergus AM 37; 157

Murray, Neil: Muckamore AM 35; 77

Murray, Patrick: Kilcronaghan LY 31; 87

Murray, Peter: Tamlaght O'Crilly LY 18; 108, 124

Murray, R.J.: Hillsborough DN 12; 106

Murray, Rev.: Duneane AM 19; 115

Murray, Robert: Donagh MN 40; 103

Murray, Samuel [I]: Carrickfergus AM 37; 148

Murray, Samuel [II]: Carrickfergus AM 37; 157

Murray, Sarah: Carrickfergus AM 37; 158

Murray, Sarah: Kilcronaghan LY 31; 88

Murray, Thomas: Carrickfergus AM 37; 157

Murray, William: Blaris DN 12; 45, 49

Murrel, Robert: Drumachose LY 9; 104

Murrel's fort: Balteagh LY 9; 26

Murrell, Henery: Balteagh LY 9; 36

Murrell, John: Balteagh LY 9; 36, 40

Murrey, family: Lambeg AM 8; 135

Murriagh, St (see O'Heany)

Murriagh's well: Banagher LY 30; 68

Murrian hill: Clondavaddog DL 38; 1

Murrican, Mr: Racavan AM 13; 101

Murry, Bernard: Drumbeg AM 8; 127

Murry, family: Faughanvale LY 36; 33

Murry, Jane: Blaris AM 8; 77

Murtagh, John: Tydavnet MN 40; 172

Murtland, Daniel: Aghanloo LY 11; 23, 25

Murtland, James: Tamlaght Finlagan LY 25; 111

Murtland, John: Drumachose LY 9; 117

Murtland, Samuel: Aghanloo LY 11; 13

Murtry, James: Aghadowey LY 22; 34

Murvagh Lower district: Drumhome DL 39; 58

Murvagh Upper district: Drumhome DL 39; 58

Musgrave, John: Faughanvale LY 36; 45

Mushett, Rev.: Misc. LY 31; 136

Mussen, family: Blaris DN 12; 30

Mussen, family: Derryaghy AM 8; 103

Mussen, James: Blaris DN 12; 46, 49

Mussen, Matthew: Blaris AM 8; 85

Mussen, Matthew: Blaris DN 12; 45, 49

Mussen, Misses: Blaris DN 12; 49

Mussen, Mrs: Blaris AM 8; 84

Mussen, Rev. John: Magheragall AM 21; 98, 110

Mussen, Robert: Blaris AM 8; 55, 60

Mussen, Robert: Blaris DN 12; 39, 45, 49

Mussen, Thomas: Blaris DN 12; 45, 49

Mussen, William: Blaris AM 8; 55

Mussen, William: Blaris DN 12; 40

Mussenden, D.: Annahilt DN 12; 23

Mussenden, D.: Comber DN 7; 34

Mussenden, Daniel: Hillsborough DN 12; 90

Mussenden, William: Annahilt DN 12; 23

Mussenden, William: Ballee DN 17; 22

Mussenden, William: Blaris DN 12; 26, 34, 37

Mussenden, William: Comber DN 7; 37–40

Mussenden, William: Drumbo DN 7; 59

Mussenden, William: Hillsborough DN 12; 85, 97

Mutton burn: Kilroot AM 26; 60, 77

Mutton Burn district: Templecorran AM 26; 120

Mutton Burn graveyard: Templecorran AM 26; 113

Mutton Burn hill: Templecorran AM 26; 84, 88

Mutton Burn school: Templecorran AM 26; 116, 131

Mutton Burn Sunday school: Templecorran AM 26; 116, 131–32

Muttonhole (see Ballybritain): Aghadowey LY 22; 30

Mweenaghan td: Derryvullan FH 14; 33

My Lord's Mountain locality: Carrickfergus AM 37; 33, 94, 174

My Lord's Mountain standing stone: Carrickfergus AM 37; 184

Myles lough: Tomregan FH 4; 126

Myles, Mrs: Comber DN 7; 34

Mymlough td: Killoran and Kilvarnet SO 40; 183

Mynock bog: Kilrea LY 27; 107

Mynock meeting house: Kilrea LY 27; 118, 128

Mynock td: Kilrea LY 27; 113, 115, 129

Mynogher, Charles: Maghera LY 18; 81

Myroe chapel: Drumachose LY 9; 107

Myroe chapel: Tamlaght Finlagan LY 25; 92, 100

Myroe district: Aghanloo LY 11; 3, 14

Myroe district: Antrim AM 29; 17

Myroe district: Clondermot LY 34; 107

Myroe district: Drumachose LY 9; 76, 100, 106

Myroe district: Faughanvale LY 36; 4

Myroe district: Lough Swilly DL 38; 138

Myroe district: Magilligan LY 11; 98, 119, 123

Myroe district: Tamlaght Finlagan LY 25; 63, 81, 91–95, 97–98, 113, 116, 123–24

N

Naan Island: Aghalurcher FH 4; 3, 9, 14
Naan Point: Aghalurcher FH 4; 1
Nab hill: Clogher TE 5; 33
Naggles creek: Lough Swilly DL 38; 113, 116
Naghan meeting house: Loughinisland DN 17; 96
Nairnstown locality: Carrickfergus AM 37; 94
Nancey's fort: Carnmoney AM 2; 35, 71, 101
Nanny's cave: Layd AM 13; 42, 45
Nantes (France): Blaris DN 12; 30
Napier, family: Ballee DN 17; 16
Napier, family: Island Magee AM 10; 29
Naples (Italy): Dunboe LY 11; 61
Nappan graveyard: Ardclinis AM 13; 7
Nappan House: Ardclinis AM 13; 7
Nappan td: Ardclinis AM 13; 4, 7
Napper, Rev. W.M.: Tamlaght O'Crilly LY 18; 82,
    91, 99, 103–04, 107, 139
Narin village: Inishkeel DL 39; 71
Narrow Water Castle: Newry DN 3; 61, 88–89
Narrow Water Castle: Warrenpoint DN 3; 116, 124
Narrow Water corn mill: Warrenpoint DN 3; 115
Narrow Water demesne: Warrenpoint DN 3; 115–16
Narrow Water flax mill: Warrenpoint DN 3; 115
Narrow Water House: Kilbroney DN 3; 32
Narrow Water House: Killevy AH 1; 54
Narrow Water House: Misc. DN 17; 130–31
Narrow Water House: Warrenpoint DN 3; 115, 122
Narrow Water kilns: Kilbroney DN 3; 36
Narrow Water school: Warrenpoint DN 3; 122
Narrow Water td: Warrenpoint DN 3; 115
Narrows channel: Lough Swilly DL 38; 114–17
Nash, Mr: Kilwaughter AM 10; 109, 117
Nash, Rev. R.H.: Ardstraw TE 5; 9, 13
Nash, William: Hillsborough DN 12; 97, 105
Nassau Hall td: Misc. DL 39; 198
Navally cave: Ramoan AM 24; 117
Navan (Meath): Faughanvale LY 36; 52
Navan: Enniskeen CN 40; 29
Navan td: Ballymascanlan LH 40; 55
Navenny bleach greens: Donaghmore DL 39; 32–33
Navenny mills: Donaghmore DL 39; 28
Navenny td: Donaghmore DL 39; 38
Nawley, St: Kinawley FH 4; 107–09, 112
Nawn td: Kinawley FH 4; 121

Neal, Andrew: Ramoan AM 24; 106–07
Neal, family: Kilraghts AM 16; 130
Neal, John: Tamlaght TE 20; 86
Neal, Mary: Kilraghts AM 16; 132
Neal, Robert: Carrickfergus AM 37; 120
Neal, Samuel: Kilraghts AM 16; 132
Neal, William: Carrickfergus AM 37; 120
Nealanthony, family: Drumgath DN 3; 20
Neale, family: Culfeightrin AM 24; 59
Neale, Miss: Newry DN 3; 100
Nealer, family: Ballywillin AM 16; 32
Near Paddock locality: Muckamore AM 35; 80
Neartie lough: Belleek FH 14; 1
Necarn Castle: Derryvullan FH 14; 33–34
Necarn Castle: Magheraculmoney FH 14; 108, 110
Ned td: Tamlaght Finlagan LY 25; 72–73
Ned's battery: Clonmany DL 38; 20
Ned's battery: Killygarvan DL 38; 40
Needham bridge: Newry DN 3; 84
Needham, F.J. (see Kilmorey)
Needham, Francis: Newry DN 3; 69, 75
Needham, George: Newry DN 3; 65, 74
Needham, Robert (see Kilmorey)
Needham, Robert [I]: Newry DN 3; 65, 74
Needham, Robert [II]: Newry DN 3; 65
Needham, William: Newry DN 3; 65, 74, 93, 102,
    114
Needling Nowl hill: Drumachose LY 9; 58
Neele, Felix: Misc. LY 31; 138
Neely, A.: Clondermot LY 34; 92
Neely, Benjamin: Blaris AM 8; 33, 55, 82
Neely, Benjamin: Drumachose LY 9; 104
Neely, Erskine: Blaris AM 8; 62
Neely, Erskine: Blaris DN 12; 45, 49
Neely, family: Ballintoy AM 24; 20
Neely, George: Tamlaght O'Crilly LY 18; 113
Neely, John: Tamlaght O'Crilly LY 18; 95
Neely, Margaret Craig: Blaris AM 8; 33
Neely, Mr (Glenchuil): Errigal Keerogue TE 20; 53
Neely, R.F.: Blaris AM 8; 33
Neely, Thomas: Kilcronaghan LY 31; 84
Neely, W.M.: Blaris AM 8; 33
Neely, William: Ballyclug AM 23; 65
Neeper, family: Island Magee AM 10; 16, 43, 70

Neeson, Charles: Doagh AM 29; 98
Neeson, Charles: Drummaul AM 19; 90
Neeson, Charles: Tamlaght O'Crilly LY 18; 125, 128
Neeson, Edward: Duneane AM 19; 112
Neeson, Henry: Ahoghill AM 23; 38
Neeson, John: Ahoghill AM 23; 38
Neeson, Michael: Artrea LY 6; 30, 36
Neeson, Patrick: Artrea LY 6; 30, 36
Neeson, Rev.: Drummaul AM 19; 69, 82
Neeson, Titus: Doagh AM 29; 98
Negamamon td: Donaghmoyne MN 40; 106
Neiblock, James: Templecorran AM 26; 123
Neil, Arthur: Maghera LY 18; 81
Neil, Bernard: Maghera LY 18; 81
Neil, Dr: Dunboe LY 11; 69
Neil, Edward: Maghera LY 18; 81
Neil, Henry: Maghera LY 18; 81
Neil, James: Kilcronaghan LY 31; 84
Neil, Jane: Duneane AM 19; 123
Neil, John: Duneane AM 19; 123
Neil, John: Kilcronaghan LY 31; 84
Neil, John: Newry DN 3; 100
Neil, Mary (I): Kilcronaghan LY 31; 84
Neil, Mary (II): Kilcronaghan LY 31; 84
Neil, Sarah: Kilcronaghan LY 31; 84
Neil, William: Billy AM 16; 60
Neilas, Rose: Dungiven LY 15; 24
Neile, Eliss: Ballyphilip DN 7; 13
Neile, family: Culfeightrin AM 24; 59
Neiley, Benjamin: Tamlaght Finlagan LY 25; 110, 115
Neiley, Eacy: Tamlaght Finlagan LY 25; 118
Neiley, James [I]: Tamlaght Finlagan LY 25; 118
Neiley, James [II]: Tamlaght Finlagan LY 25; 118
Neiley, Jane: Tamlaght Finlagan LY 25; 118
Neiley, John: Tamlaght Finlagan LY 25; 118
Neiley, Joseph: Tamlaght Finlagan LY 25; 118
Neiley, Maryann: Tamlaght Finlagan LY 25; 118
Neiley, William (Jnr): Tamlaght Finlagan LY 25; 118
Neiley, William (Snr): Tamlaght Finlagan LY 25; 118
Neilis, James: Carrickfergus AM 37; 194
Neill, Alexander: Carrickfergus AM 37; 158
Neill, Alexander: Coleraine LY 33; 63, 72–73, 120, 142, 148
Neill, Andrew: Drumtullagh AM 16; 102–03
Neill, Christina: Carrickfergus AM 37; 123
Neill, Eliza: Carrickfergus AM 37; 123
Neill, family: Armoy AM 24; 6
Neill, family: Culfeightrin AM 24; 59
Neill, family: Lambeg AM 8; 135
Neill, family: Templepatrick AM 35; 118
Neill, George: Carrickfergus AM 37; 116

Neill, Jane: Ballyrashane LY 22; 66
Neill, John: Ballymoney AM 16; 25
Neill, John: Duneane AM 19; 123
Neill, John: Glenavy AM 21; 90
Neill, John: Killead AM 35; 36
Neill, Miss: Ballymoney AM 16; 2, 8, 17
Neill, Mrs: Tamlaght Finlagan LY 25; 77
Neill, Peggy: Duneane AM 19; 123
Neill, Thomas: Tamlaght O'Crilly LY 18; 137
Neill, William: Billy AM 16; 62
Neill, William: Carrickfergus AM 37; 122
Neill's Top hill: Skerry AM 13; 109
Neilly, Charles: Carrickfergus AM 37; 116
Neils, family: Newry DN 3; 106
Neilson, A.: Drumballyroney DN 3; 10
Neilson, family: Aghalee AM 21; 31
Neilson, family: Ballinderry AM 21; 48
Neilson, family: Ballywillin AM 16; 32
Neilson, family: Carnmoney AM 2; 76
Neilson, family: Island Magee AM 10; 29, 45, 70, 86
Neilson, family: Magheramesk AM 21; 124
Neilson, John: Island Magee AM 10; 90
Neilson, John: Kilcronaghan LY 31; 74
Neilson, John: Templecorran AM 26; 123
Neilson, R.T.: Island Magee AM 10; 90
Neilson, Thomas: Hillsborough DN 12; 106
Neilson, Thomas: Island Magee AM 10; 32, 39, 94
Neily, Robert: Ballyrashane LY 22; 66
Neily, Thomas: Drummaul AM 19; 90
Neily, W.J.: Drummaul AM 19; 90
Neisbit, family: Ematris MN 40; 118
Nelson, Alexander: Carrickfergus AM 37; 119
Nelson, family: Ahoghill AM 23; 25
Nelson, family: Carrickfergus AM 37; 93
Nelson, family: Kilraghts AM 16; 127
Nelson, family: Kilwaughter AM 10; 115, 117
Nelson, family: Templecorran AM 26; 117, 119
Nelson, Halliday: Blaris DN 12; 46, 50
Nelson, Hugh: Ballywillin LY 33; 49
Nelson, Hugh: Kilwaughter AM 10; 113
Nelson, James: Ahoghill AM 23; 46
Nelson, James: Carrickfergus AM 37; 194
Nelson, John: Ahoghill AM 23; 41, 43
Nelson, John: Ballyscullion LY 6; 57
Nelson, John: Kilbroney DN 3; 38
Nelson, Mr: Hillsborough DN 12; 87
Nelson, Mr: Kilraghts AM 16; 128
Nelson, Rev.: Down DN 17; 58
Nelson, Rev.: Tamlaght Finlagan LY 25; 69
Nelson, Rev. John: Shankill AH 1; 115
Nelson, Rev. Moses: Kilmore DN 17; 91
Nelson, Robert: Bright DN 17; 36
Nelson, William: Kilwaughter AM 10; 113, 116, 118
Nelson's mountain: Bangor DN 7; 19

Nely, Andrew: Kildollagh LY 22; 75
Nely, John: Blaris AM 8; 55
Nely, William: Kildollagh LY 22; 75
Nennius, St: Faughanvale LY 36; 63
Nero, Emperor: Banagher LY 30; 7
Nesbit, J.D.: Banagher LY 30; 22–23, 131
Nesbit, Maj.: Laragh CN 40; 43, 45
Nesbit, Mr: Drumballyroney DN 3; 16
Nesbit, Rev. Archibald: Antrim AM 29; 8
Nesbit, Rev. Richard: Donaghedy TE 5; 89
Nesbitt, Alexander: Drumachose LY 9; 65
Nesbitt, Capt.: Aghanloo LY 11; 22, 30
Nesbitt, Charles: Clonleigh DL 39; 12
Nesbitt, family: Enniskillen FH 4; 58
Nesbitt, family: Templepatrick AM 35; 118
Nesbitt, Mr (Woodhill): Inishkeel DL 39; 68, 73
Nesbitt, Nathaniel: Clonleigh DL 39; 12
Nesbitt, R.: Killygarvan DL 38; 48
Nesbitt, Rev. Charles: Raphoe DL 39; 123, 129
Neskinmore (see Meskinmore)
Ness waterfall: Clondermot LY 34; 69
Ness waterfall: Cumber LY 28; 42, 44–47, 53,
    66–67, 79
Ness waterfall: Magilligan LY 11; 103
Nethertown td: Misc. DL 39; 196
Nevil, Francis: Lough Neagh AM 21; 92
Nevill, Edward: Tamlaght O'Crilly LY 18; 98, 104
Nevill, Miss: Tamlaght O'Crilly LY 18; 142
Neville, George: Dromore TE 5; 98
Neville, Henery: Tamlaght O'Crilly LY 18; 143
Neville, Sophia: Templepatrick AM 35; 135, 153
Neville, William: Dromore TE 5; 98
Nevin, Elizabeth: Ballyphilip DN 7; 13
Nevin, family: Culfeightrin AM 24; 59
Nevin, family: Derrykeighan AM 16; 89
Nevin, Hugh: Ballyaghran LY 33; 27
Nevin, Hugh: Blaris AM 8; 55
Nevin, John: Ballyaghran LY 33; 24
Nevin, Martha: Ballyaghran LY 33; 17
Nevin, Mr: Clogher TE 5; 53
Nevin, Robert: Coleraine LY 33; 72
Nevin, Robert: Derrykeighan AM 16; 91
Nevin, Robert: Errigal LY 27; 51
Nevin, Thomas: Ballyrashane LY 22; 63
Nevin, Thomas: Dunluce AM 16; 119
Nevin, William: Loughguile AM 13; 74
Nevin, William [I]: Ballyrashane LY 22; 56, 63
Nevin, William [II]: Ballyrashane LY 22; 66
New Bridge td: Clonleigh DL 39; 12, 198
New Brunswick (Canada): Aghanloo LY 11; 11
New Brunswick: Cumber LY 28; 28
New Brunswick: Dungiven LY 15; 104
New Brunswick: Glynn AM 26; 47
New Brunswick: Killead AM 35; 24, 51
New Brunswick: Kilroot AM 26; 73

New Brunswick: Tamlaght Finlagan LY 25; 92–93,
    99
New Buildings: Ardstraw TE 5; 12
New Buildings: Clondermot LY 34; 4, 7, 10, 16, 19,
    22–23, 25, 37, 44, 49, 90, 100
New Buildings Castle: Clondermot LY 34; 4
New Buildings cove: Clondermot LY 34; 44
New Buildings mill [I]: Clondermot LY 34; 21
New Buildings mill [II]: Clondermot LY 34; 21, 34
New Buildings North td: Ballymoney AM 16; 25
New Buildings South td: Ballymoney AM 16; 25
New Buildings td: Ballymoney AM 16; 6, 20
New ferry: Ahoghill AM 23; 29
New ferry: Coleraine LY 33; 99, 102
New ferry: Lough Neagh AM 21; 93
New Grange (Meath): Drummaul AM 19; 71
New Grove House: Drumbo DN 7; 56
New Hamburg House: Desertcreat TE 20; 34, 36
New Isle: Misc. DN 17; 121
New Lanark (Scotland): Carncastle and Killyglen
    AM 10; 10
New Lodge House: Muckamore AM 35; 62–63
New Lodge House: Templepatrick AM 35; 143
New Mill bridge: Moira DN 12; 119
New Orleans: Ballyscullion AM 19; 13
New Orleans: Blaris AM 8; 77
New Orleans: Carnmoney AM 2; 90–91
New Orleans: Coleraine LY 33; 74, 145
New Orleans: Cranfield AM 19; 32
New Orleans: Desertmartin LY 31; 62
New Orleans: Drummaul AM 19; 62, 90–91
New Orleans: Kildollagh LY 22; 71
New Orleans: Kirkinriola AM 23; 98
New Orleans: Maghera LY 18; 21, 79
New Orleans: Magherafelt LY 6; 101, 104, 112
New Row td: Clonleigh DL 39; 12, 198
New Row td: Raphoe DL 39; 126
New South Wales: Donacavey TE 5; 66
New South Wales: Dromore TE 5; 103
New South Wales: Drumachose LY 9; 133
New South Wales: Kilskeery TE 5; 116
New Works ruin: Ardglass DN 17; 3
New York: Aghadowey LY 22; 35–37
New York: Aghagallon AM 21; 19
New York: Aghalee AM 21; 38
New York: Agivey LY 22; 45
New York: Ahoghill AM 23; 37–38
New York: Artrea LY 6; 38
New York: Ballyaghran LY 33; 18, 27
New York: Ballylinny AM 32; 20, 29
New York: Ballynascreen LY 31; 21–22
New York: Ballynure AM 32; 71–72
New York: Ballyrashane LY 22; 53, 65
New York: Ballyrobert AM 2; 23, 25
New York: Ballyscullion AM 19; 13

New York: Ballyscullion LY 6; 63, 77–78
New York: Ballywillin LY 33; 42, 51
New York: Balteagh LY 9; 43–44
New York: Blaris AM 8; 77
New York: Bovevagh LY 25; 59–60
New York: Carnmoney AM 2; 88
New York: Carrickfergus AM 37; 78, 158
New York: Coleraine LY 33; 74, 145–46
New York: Cumber LY 28; 80
New York: Derryaghy AM 8; 115
New York: Derrykeighan AM 16; 87
New York: Derryvullan FH 14; 43
New York: Desertlyn LY 31; 47
New York: Desertmartin LY 31; 62
New York: Desertoghill LY 27; 20–21
New York: Doagh AM 29; 98
New York: Donaghmoyne MN 40; 109
New York: Drumachose LY 9; 132–34
New York: Drumbeg AM 8; 133
New York: Drummaul AM 19; 62, 90–91
New York: Dunboe LY 11; 54, 81
New York: Duneane AM 19; 123
New York: Errigal LY 27; 47, 65–66
New York: Glenavy AM 21; 81
New York: Glynn AM 26; 47
New York: Island Magee AM 10; 41, 95
New York: Killead AM 35; 24, 51
New York: Killelagh LY 27; 99
New York: Killowen LY 33; 165, 171
New York: Kilrea LY 27; 118, 129
New York: Kilwaughter AM 10; 122
New York: Lissan LY 31; 108–09
New York: Macosquin LY 22; 122
New York: Maghera LY 18; 77–80
New York: Magheracloone MN 40; 140
New York: Magherafelt LY 6; 104, 112
New York: Magheramesk AM 21; 130
New York: Magilligan LY 11; 94–95
New York: Mallusk AM 2; 114
New York: Muckamore AM 35; 77
New York: Newry DN 3; 87
New York: Nilteen AM 35; 94, 103
New York: Raloo AM 32; 128–29
New York: Shilvodan AM 19; 135, 137
New York: Tamlaght Finlagan LY 25; 118–20
New York: Tamlaght O'Crilly LY 18; 100–01, 137–38
New York: Templecorran AM 26; 107, 132
New York: Templepatrick AM 35; 123, 152
New York: Termoneeny LY 6; 126, 132–33
Newal, Mr: Drumballyroney DN 3; 16
Newark, Grace: Ardglass DN 17; 3
Newberry and Cummins, Messrs: Blaris AM 8; 51
Newbliss: Aghabog MN 40; 64–67
Newbliss: Aughnamullen MN 40; 76

Newbliss: Currin MN 40; 89–90, 94
Newbliss: Ematris MN 40; 114–15
Newbliss corn mill: Aghabog MN 40; 62
Newbliss dispensary: Aghabog MN 40; 65
Newburgh, family: Enniskillen FH 4; 58
Newcastle: Down DN 17; 40, 49
Newcastle: Kilcoo DN 3; 41–43
Newcastle: Kilkeel DN 3; 48, 51
Newcastle: Kilmegan DN 3; 57
Newcastle church: Kilcoo DN 3; 43
Newcastle fishery works: Misc. DN 17; 116
Newcastle harbour: Misc. DN 17; 116
Newcastle hotel: Kilcoo DN 3; 43
Newcastle meeting house: Kilcoo DN 3; 43
Newcastle quay: Kilcoo DN 3; 43
Newcastle quay: Misc. DN 17; 116
Newcastle school: Kilcoo DN 3; 43
Newcastle td: Misc. DN 17; 125, 127
Newcastle td: Slanes DN 7; 121
Newclare village: Kilmacteige SO 40; 193
New-Culter td: Ballyphilip DN 7; 8
Newell, Charles: Dunboe LY 11; 70
Newell, William: Ballylinny AM 32; 29
Newell, William: Blaris AM 8; 55
Newenham, Mr: Ballyscullion LY 6; 59
Newey, family: Culfeightrin AM 24; 59
Newfoundland: Donegal DL 39; 57
Newgirve House: Drumgoon CN 40; 8
Newgrove demesne: Drumragh TE 5; 108–11
Newgrove House: Drumragh TE 5; 108
Newhill td: Ballymoney AM 16; 25
Newin, Lawson: Termoneeny LY 6; 132
Newlands bog: Glynn AM 26; 27
Newlands cove: Glynn AM 26; 32, 44
Newlands school: Glynn AM 26; 8, 35
Newlands Sunday school: Cappagh TE 5; 19
Newlands td: Cappagh TE 5; 19
Newlands td: Glynn AM 26; 1, 41, 46
Newlans, James: Hillsborough DN 12; 105
Newman, Darby: Clondermot LY 34; 54
Newmill corn mill: Tullyaughnish DL 38; 89
Newmill td: Tullyaughnish DL 38; 96
Newmills (see Newmill): Tullyaughnish DL 38; 89
Newmills bridge: Donagh MN 40; 99
Newmills td: Coleraine LY 33; 106
Newpark House: Ematris MN 40; 115
Newpark House: Moville DL 38; 70
Newpark td: Dromore TE 5; 97, 99
Newpirton manor: Misc. FH 4; 133
Newport bridge: Blaris DN 12; 34
Newport school: Blaris DN 12; 34–37
Newport school: Hillsborough DN 12; 101
Newport Sunday school: Blaris DN 12; 38
Newport, John: Raymoghy DL 39; 144
Newportin manor: Magheracross FH 14; 102

Newrie (see Newry)
Newry: Aghabog MN 40; 63
Newry: Aghalee AM 21; 34
Newry: Aghalurcher FH 4; 13, 15
Newry: Ahoghill AM 23; 8
Newry: Annaclone DN 12; 16
Newry: Antrim AM 29; 37
Newry: Ardglass DN 17; 14
Newry: Artrea LY 6; 7
Newry: Aughnamullen MN 40; 75
Newry: Ballybay MN 40; 80
Newry: Ballymore AH 1; 1, 3, 6, 8, 10, 12, 15–16
Newry: Blaris AM 8; 87
Newry: Clonallan DN 3; 1
Newry: Clonduff DN 3; 3, 5
Newry: Clones FH 4; 27
Newry: Clonfeacle AH 1; 24
Newry: Coleraine LY 33; 99
Newry: Donaghenry TE 20; 38
Newry: Donaghmore DN 3; 7, 9
Newry: Down DN 17; 47, 49
Newry: Drumballyroney DN 3; 10, 17
Newry: Drumcree AH 1; 32
Newry: Drumgath DN 3; 20
Newry: Drumglass TE 20; 40, 42, 45
Newry: Drumgoon CN 40; 10
Newry: Drummully FH 4; 38
Newry: Dungiven LY 15; 109
Newry: Enniskeen CN 40; 29
Newry: Enniskillen FH 4; 61
Newry: Forkhill AH 1; 45
Newry: Garvaghy DN 12; 80–81
Newry: Kilbroney DN 3; 29–31, 36
Newry: Killdrumsherdan CN 40; 36
Newry: Killevy AH 1; 52
Newry: Killyleagh DN 17; 85
Newry: Killymard DL 39; 109
Newry: Kilmore AH 1; 62
Newry: Loughgilly AH 1; 84
Newry: Loughinisland DN 17; 94
Newry: Magherafelt LY 6; 86
Newry: Misc. DN 17; 116–17, 120, 128, 130–31
Newry: Montiaghs AH 1; 92
Newry: Muckno MN 40; 165–67
Newry: Mullaghbrack AH 1; 94, 96
Newry: Newry DN 3; 61–65, 67–69, 71–72, 74,
    77–78, 80, 82, 85–91, 97, 107, 109–11, 114
Newry: Newtownhamilton AH 1; 98
Newry: Rasharkin AM 23; 128
Newry: Seapatrick DN 12; 131, 133
Newry: Tomregan FH 4; 132
Newry: Tullyniskan TE 20; 140
Newry: Tynan AH 1; 126–27
Newry: Warrenpoint DN 3; 119
Newry abbey: Misc. DN 17; 120, 122

Newry abbey: Newry DN 3; 63, 66
Newry assembly room: Newry DN 3; 70, 74, 84
Newry bank: Loughgilly AH 1; 85
Newry barony: Holywood DN 7; 80
Newry barrack: Newry DN 3; 61
Newry Boat St chapel: Newry DN 3; 105
Newry borough: Newry DN 3; 74
Newry breweries: Newry DN 3; 105
Newry bridewell: Newry DN 3; 70–71, 84, 105
Newry bridge: Newry DN 3; 63, 89
Newry butter crane: Newry DN 3; 82, 87, 105
Newry butter market: Newry DN 3; 87
Newry Canal: Aghaderg DN 12; 3, 5
Newry Canal: Ballymore AH 1; 5, 8, 10–12, 17–18
Newry Canal: Coleraine LY 33; 99, 101
Newry Canal: Donaghmore DN 3; 7–8
Newry Canal: Drumcree AH 1; 32, 34–36
Newry Canal: Kilmore AH 1; 60–61, 63, 68
Newry Canal: Lough Neagh AM 21; 92, 94
Newry Canal: Misc. DN 17; 131
Newry Canal: Montiaghs AH 1; 91–92
Newry Canal: Newry DN 3; 61, 70, 72, 86, 90–91
Newry Canal: Seagoe AH 1; 104, 106
Newry Canal: Warrenpoint DN 3; 121
Newry Castle: Blaris AM 8; 4
Newry Castle St school: Newry DN 3; 82
Newry Catholic school: Newry DN 3; 88
Newry chapel (I): Newry DN 3; 69, 71, 79, 83, 98,
    105
Newry chapel (M) [I]: Newry DN 3; 83
Newry chapel (M) [II]: Newry DN 3; 83
Newry Chapel St school: Newry DN 3; 71, 80
Newry coffee room: Newry DN 3; 84
Newry convent: Newry DN 3; 105
Newry convent school: Newry DN 3; 88
Newry corn market: Newry DN 3; 105
Newry corn mill: Newry DN 3; 105
Newry cotton mill: Newry DN 3; 72
Newry court house: Ardglass DN 17; 14
Newry court house: Newry DN 3; 70, 84
Newry custom house: Killyleagh DN 17; 84
Newry custom house: Newry DN 3; 86
Newry day school: Newry DN 3; 80
Newry dispensary: Newry DN 3; 73, 80, 105
Newry exchange: Newry DN 3; 84
Newry female school: Newry DN 3; 80
Newry fever hospital: Newry DN 3; 73, 80, 84
Newry flour mill: Newry DN 3; 72
Newry gaol: Newry DN 3; 105
Newry gasworks: Newry DN 3; 105
Newry glassworks: Newry DN 3; 105
Newry High St chapel: Kilbroney DN 3; 37
Newry High St meeting house: Newry DN 3; 69, 72,
    79, 83, 98, 105
Newry High St school: Newry DN 3; 88

Newry Hill St chapel: Newry DN 3; 69, 71, 83, 98, 105
Newry infant school: Newry DN 3; 71, 80, 105, 114
Newry infantry barracks (see also Newry linen hall)
Newry Kilmorey St chapel: Newry DN 3; 69, 105
Newry linen hall: Newry DN 3; 84
Newry lordship: Aghaderg DN 12; 1
Newry lordship: Annaclone DN 12; 13
Newry lordship: Donaghmore DN 3; 7
Newry lordship: Drumballyroney DN 3; 13–14
Newry lordship: Drumcree AH 1; 34
Newry lordship: Drumgath DN 3; 19
Newry lordship: Garvaghy DN 12; 79
Newry lordship: Kilmore AH 1; 60, 70
Newry lordship: Misc. DN 17; 116, 120
Newry lordship: Newry DN 3; 106, 108
Newry lying-in hospital: Newry DN 3; 79, 85
Newry manor: Newry DN 3; 65, 76
Newry market house: Newry DN 3; 70, 84, 105
Newry Meeting House Lane meeting house: Newry DN 3; 69, 72, 79, 83, 98, 105
Newry mendicity asylum: Newry DN 3; 94–95
Newry metal foundries: Newry DN 3; 105
Newry mountains: Hillsborough DN 12; 96
Newry mountains: Newry DN 3; 107
Newry national school [I]: Newry DN 3; 105
Newry national school [II]: Newry DN 3; 105
Newry news room: Newry DN 3; 70, 114
Newry nunnery: Newry DN 3; 69, 72
Newry old chapel: Newry DN 3; 61, 68, 83
Newry old custom house: Newry DN 3; 86
Newry old distillery: Newry DN 3; 105
Newry old windmill: Newry DN 3; 80
Newry ph: Aghaderg DN 12; 8
Newry ph: Annaclone DN 12; 16
Newry ph: Drumballyroney DN 3; 12
Newry ph: Kilmore AH 1; 57
Newry ph: Tartaraghan AH 1; 117
Newry poor house: Newry DN 3; 84
Newry poor school: Newry DN 3; 105
Newry Rathfriland Road school: Newry DN 3; 88
Newry reading room: Newry DN 3; 72
Newry river: Donaghmore DN 3; 7–8
Newry river: Drumgath DN 3; 19
Newry river: Newry DN 3; 61, 70–72, 77, 88, 90, 107
Newry river: Warrenpoint DN 3; 115–17
Newry saltworks: Newry DN 3; 105
Newry Sandys St meeting house: Newry DN 3; 69, 72, 83, 98, 105
Newry schools: Hillsborough DN 12; 101
Newry sessions house: Newry DN 3; 71, 105
Newry Talbot St chapel: Newry DN 3; 105
Newry Talbot St school: Newry DN 3; 82
Newry tanneries: Newry DN 3; 105

Newry td: Clogher TE 5; 34–35, 53
Newry theatre: Newry DN 3; 70
Newry union school: Newry DN 3; 71
Newry vicarage: Newry DN 3; 75–76
Newry well: Newry DN 3; 114
Newry William St chapel: Newry DN 3; 69, 79, 98, 105
Newry windmill: Newry DN 3; 94, 105
Newry Windsor Hill school: Newry DN 3; 80
Newry workhouse: Newry DN 3; 79, 91–92, 95–98, 100–03, 105
Newry, Lord: Newry DN 3; 72, 107, 110
Newton, Alicia: Tamlaght TE 20; 76, 103, 128, 134
Newton, Eliza: Tamlaght TE 20; 91
Newton, man named: Misc. LY 36; 112
Newton, Mrs: Coleraine LY 33; 72
Newton, Rev. Thomas: Dunluce AM 16; 120
Newtown Carradoan: Killygarvan DL 38; 37
Newtown church: Misc. DN 17; 117
Newtown Croaghan td: Clonleigh DL 39; 12
Newtown Crommelin church: Newtown Crommelin AM 13; 78, 80
Newtown Crommelin corn mill: Newtown Crommelin AM 13; 78
Newtown Crommelin Glebe House: Newtown Crommelin AM 13; 78, 81–82
Newtown Crommelin hill: Dunaghy AM 13; 10
Newtown Crommelin meeting house: Newtown Crommelin AM 13; 78, 82
Newtown Crommelin mill: Newtown Crommelin AM 13; 81–82
Newtown Crommelin ph: Dunaghy AM 13; 10, 25
Newtown Crommelin ph: Loughguile AM 13; 58
Newtown Crommelin school: Newtown Crommelin AM 13; 78, 81–82
Newtown Crommelin village: Newtown Crommelin AM 13; 78, 80, 82–84
Newtown Saville church: Clogher TE 5; 32, 39
Newtown Saville Glebe House: Clogher TE 5; 32
Newtown Saville village: Clogher TE 5; 32, 34, 45
Newtown td: Kilbroney DN 3; 26, 32
Newtown td: Killymard DL 39; 101
Newtown td: Manorhamilton Union LM 40; 52
Newtown village: Kilmacteige SO 40; 186, 193
Newtownards: Ballyphilip DN 7; 9
Newtownards: Comber DN 7; 37, 40
Newtownards: Misc. DN 17; 117, 120, 123, 127
Newtownards: Newtownards DN 7; 103, 105
Newtownards: Rathmullan DN 17; 108
Newtownards: Tullynakill DN 7; 122
Newtownards chapel (C): Newtownards DN 7; 105–06
Newtownards chapel (M): Newtownards DN 7; 105–06
Newtownards church: Newtownards DN 7; 105–06

Newtownards classical school: Newtownards DN 7; 109

Newtownards factory house: Newtownards DN 7; 106

Newtownards flour mill: Newtownards DN 7; 106

Newtownards fountain: Newtownards DN 7; 107

Newtownards hotel: Newtownards DN 7; 105

Newtownards lead mine: Newtownards DN 7; 103

Newtownards manor: Misc. DN 17; 123–24

Newtownards manor mill: Newtownards DN 7; 104

Newtownards market house: Newtownards DN 7; 105–06

Newtownards Masonic hall: Newtownards DN 7; 105–06

Newtownards meeting house (P) [I]: Newtownards DN 7; 105–06

Newtownards meeting house (P) [II]: Newtownards DN 7; 105

Newtownards meeting house (S): Newtownards DN 7; 105

Newtownards meeting house school: Newtownards DN 7; 104–05

Newtownards New Light meeting house: Newtownards DN 7; 106

Newtownards old church: Newtownards DN 7; 107, 113

Newtownards old meeting house: Newtownards DN 7; 104

Newtownards old school: Newtownards DN 7; 109

Newtownards ph: Bangor DN 7; 19

Newtownards ph: Comber DN 7; 31

Newtownards ph: Donaghadee DN 7; 45

Newtownards ph: Dundonald DN 7; 64

Newtownards ph: Grey Abbey DN 7; 67

Newtownards ph: Holywood DN 7; 73

Newtownards ph: Misc. DN 17; 120

Newtownards poor house: Holywood DN 7; 83

Newtownards poor house: Newtownards DN 7; 105, 109

Newtownards Regent St meeting house: Newtownards DN 7; 105–06

Newtownards school [I]: Newtownards DN 7; 105, 108

Newtownards school [II]: Newtownards DN 7; 105, 108

Newtownbreda: Knockbreda DN 7; 101

Newtownbreda: Misc. DN 17; 117

Newtownbreda boys' school: Knockbreda DN 7; 101–02

Newtownbreda church: Blaris AM 8; 52

Newtownbreda church: Knockbreda DN 7; 102

Newtownbreda dispensary: Knockbreda DN 7; 101

Newtownbreda girls' school: Knockbreda DN 7; 102

Newtownbreda meeting house: Knockbreda DN 7; 101

Newtownbutler: Aghabog MN 40; 65

Newtownbutler: Aghalurcher FH 4; 8

Newtownbutler: Aughnamullen MN 40; 75–76

Newtownbutler: Clones FH 4; 28

Newtownbutler: Currin MN 40; 91

Newtownbutler: Drummully FH 4; 36

Newtownbutler: Enniskillen FH 4; 51–52

Newtownbutler: Galloon FH 4; 89, 92–93, 98, 102–05

Newtownbutler chapel (PW): Galloon FH 4; 89

Newtownbutler chapel (W): Galloon FH 4; 89

Newtownbutler church: Galloon FH 4; 89

Newtownbutler court house: Galloon FH 4; 89

Newtownbutler dispensary: Drummully FH 4; 37

Newtownbutler dispensary: Galloon FH 4; 90, 93

Newtownbutler ph: Galloon FH 4; 90

Newtownbutler school [I]: Galloon FH 4; 89, 96

Newtownbutler school [II]: Galloon FH 4; 96

Newtownbutler school [III]: Galloon FH 4; 96

Newtowncunningham: Leck DL 39; 120

Newtowncunningham: Lough Swilly DL 38; 142

Newtowncunningham: Misc. DL 39; 184, 186

Newtowncunningham: Taughboyne DL 39; 153

Newtowncunningham orchard: Misc. DL 39; 189

Newtowncunningham td: Misc. DL 39; 195

Newtownfore td: Tullyaughnish DL 38; 97

Newtownhamilton: Ballybay MN 40; 80

Newtownhamilton: Killevy AH 1; 52

Newtownhamilton: Loughgilly AH 1; 84

Newtownhamilton: Newtownhamilton AH 1; 98

Newtownhamilton bog: Misc. DL 39; 187

Newtownhamilton church school: Newtownhamilton AH 1; 98

Newtownhamilton corn mill: Newtownhamilton AH 1; 100

Newtownhamilton court house: Newtownhamilton AH 1; 98

Newtownhamilton dispensary: Newtownhamilton AH 1; 98

Newtownhamilton Erasmus Smith school: Newtownhamilton AH 1; 98

Newtownhamilton flax mill: Newtownhamilton AH 1; 100

Newtownhamilton market house: Newtownhamilton AH 1; 98

Newtownhamilton meeting house: Newtownhamilton AH 1; 100

Newtownhamilton ph: Muckno MN 40; 162

Newtownhamilton private school: Newtownhamilton AH 1; 98, 100

Newtownhamilton quarry: Clondermot LY 34; 6, 101

Newtownhamilton school: Newtownhamilton AH 1; 100

Newtownhamilton td: Killea and Taughboyne DL 39; 86, 92, 185, 196

Newtownlimavady: Aghadowey LY 22; 6, 10–11, 16, 20, 26, 32–33

Newtownlimavady: Aghanloo LY 11; 1, 8–9, 17–22, 29–31, 33–34, 36–37

Newtownlimavady: Balteagh LY 9; 14, 22, 30, 40

Newtownlimavady: Banagher LY 30; 5, 14, 19, 57, 60–61, 73–74, 117–20

Newtownlimavady: Bovevagh LY 25; 3–4, 16, 19, 23–24, 27, 48, 50–51, 56

Newtownlimavady: Clondermot LY 34; 7, 21, 34, 54–55, 60, 107, 114–15, 118–20, 120

Newtownlimavady: Coleraine LY 33; 63–64, 110, 126, 155–56

Newtownlimavady: Cumber LY 28; 1, 7, 9, 21, 23, 49, 72, 78, 86–87, 94–98, 110–15

Newtownlimavady: Desertoghill LY 27; 8, 13, 23, 26, 28

Newtownlimavady: Drumachose LY 9; 47–48, 55, 60, 64–66, 70, 73, 76, 82, 84, 87, 90, 101, 103, 112–17, 132–34

Newtownlimavady: Dunboe LY 11; 46–47, 59

Newtownlimavady: Dungiven LY 15; 11, 13–14, 23, 26, 33, 53, 66–68, 73, 106, 109, 113

Newtownlimavady: Errigal LY 27; 39–40, 51, 60, 79–84

Newtownlimavady: Faughanvale LY 36; 1, 3, 6, 8, 10, 13, 16, 21, 70, 72–80

Newtownlimavady: Inver AM 26; 54

Newtownlimavady: Killelagh LY 27; 97

Newtownlimavady: Killowen LY 33; 160–61, 168

Newtownlimavady: Kilrea LY 27; 108

Newtownlimavady: Lissan LY 31; 96, 101

Newtownlimavady: Lough Swilly DL 38; 140

Newtownlimavady: Macosquin LY 22; 81–82, 89, 91–93, 101–03, 110–11, 117, 121

Newtownlimavady: Magherafelt LY 6; 100

Newtownlimavady: Magilligan LY 11; 83–84, 100, 113–14, 116–18, 132–33, 135–36, 139, 141

Newtownlimavady: Misc. LY 36; 114

Newtownlimavady: Tamlaght Finlagan LY 25; 65, 68–69, 71, 79–80, 82–85, 89–90, 93–95, 97–99, 101, 103–09, 120–25

Newtownlimavady ball-courts: Drumachose LY 9; 82

Newtownlimavady Ballyclose school [I]: Drumachose LY 9; 70, 85, 124

Newtownlimavady Ballyclose school [II]: Drumachose LY 9; 70, 85, 124

Newtownlimavady Ballyclose school [III]: Drumachose LY 9; 85

Newtownlimavady Ballyclose Sunday school: Drumachose LY 9; 85, 132

Newtownlimavady Belfast bank: Drumachose LY 9; 69, 114

Newtownlimavady billiard room: Drumachose LY 9; 77

Newtownlimavady borough: Drumachose LY 9; 60–61, 65

Newtownlimavady brewery: Drumachose LY 9; 121

Newtownlimavady bridewell: Drumachose LY 9; 77, 90

Newtownlimavady bridge: Drumachose LY 9; 83, 90

Newtownlimavady bridge: Tamlaght Finlagan LY 25; 62, 81

Newtownlimavady Castle: Clondermot LY 34; 34

Newtownlimavady Castle: Drumachose LY 9; 83, 91–92

Newtownlimavady Catherine St school [I]: Drumachose LY 9; 70, 85, 124, 131

Newtownlimavady Catherine St school [II]: Drumachose LY 9; 70, 85, 124

Newtownlimavady Catherine St school [III]: Drumachose LY 9; 85

Newtownlimavady Catherine St school [IV]: Drumachose LY 9; 85

Newtownlimavady chapel (C): Drumachose LY 9; 77

Newtownlimavady chapel (M): Drumachose LY 9; 73–74, 77, 115

Newtownlimavady cholera hospital: Drumachose LY 9; 79

Newtownlimavady church: Drumachose LY 9; 74, 76–77, 90, 115, 119

Newtownlimavady classical seminary: Drumachose LY 9; 70, 85, 123, 131

Newtownlimavady court house: Drumachose LY 9; 77, 130

Newtownlimavady Deer Park td: Tamlaght Finlagan LY 25; 62–63

Newtownlimavady Deer Park wood: Tamlaght Finlagan LY 25; 65

Newtownlimavady dispensary: Aghanloo LY 11; 39

Newtownlimavady dispensary: Balteagh LY 9; 15

Newtownlimavady dispensary: Drumachose LY 9; 72–73, 79–80, 129–30

Newtownlimavady dispensary: Magilligan LY 11; 93

Newtownlimavady dispensary: Tamlaght Finlagan LY 25; 72

Newtownlimavady distilleries: Drumachose LY 9; 53, 78, 83, 114, 120–22

Newtownlimavady estate: Tamlaght Finlagan LY 25; 122

Newtownlimavady grain market: Drumachose LY 9; 103

Newtownlimavady hotel: Drumachose LY 9; 90

Newtownlimavady Irish Green school: Drumachose
LY 9; 85
Newtownlimavady Isle-of-Man female school:
Drumachose LY 9; 71, 85–86, 124–25, 130
Newtownlimavady Isle-of-Man parish school:
Drumachose LY 9; 70–71, 85, 125
Newtownlimavady ladies' school: Drumachose LY
9; 70, 122
Newtownlimavady Lancasterian school:
Drumachose LY 9; 90, 103
Newtownlimavady library: Drumachose LY 9;
66–67, 78, 90, 103
Newtownlimavady linen hall: Drumachose LY 9; 65
Newtownlimavady Main St school [I]: Drumachose
LY 9; 70, 124
Newtownlimavady Main St school [II]: Drumachose
LY 9; 70, 85, 124, 131
Newtownlimavady Main St school [III]:
Drumachose LY 9; 70, 85, 125
Newtownlimavady Main St school [IV]:
Drumachose LY 9; 85
Newtownlimavady Main St school [V]: Drumachose
LY 9; 85
Newtownlimavady Main St Sunday school:
Drumachose LY 9; 85, 132
Newtownlimavady market house: Drumachose LY
9; 57, 67, 73, 77, 85, 90, 114, 129
Newtownlimavady market house Sunday school:
Drumachose LY 9; 85
Newtownlimavady meeting house (A): Drumachose
LY 9; 77
Newtownlimavady meeting house (Cov.):
Drumachose LY 9; 76
Newtownlimavady meeting house (P): Bovevagh
LY 25; 54
Newtownlimavady meeting house (P): Drumachose
LY 9; 74, 76–77, 121, 129
Newtownlimavady meeting house (S): Drumachose
LY 9; 73–74, 76–77
Newtownlimavady meeting house (U): Drumachose
LY 9; 73
Newtownlimavady meeting houses: Drumachose LY
9; 76–77, 90, 115
Newtownlimavady news room: Drumachose LY 9;
77, 90, 103
Newtownlimavady Northern bank: Drumachose LY
9; 69
Newtownlimavady ph: Aghadowey LY 22; 24
Newtownlimavady ph: Magilligan LY 11; 96
Newtownlimavady poor shop: Drumachose LY 9;
71–72, 81–82
Newtownlimavady savings bank: Drumachose LY 9;
68–69, 72, 78, 90, 103
Newtownlimavady school [I]: Drumachose LY 9;
130

Newtownlimavady school [II]: Drumachose LY 9;
131
Newtownlimavady school [III]: Drumachose LY 9;
131
Newtownlimavady school [IV]: Drumachose LY 9;
131
Newtownlimavady school [V]: Drumachose LY 9;
131
Newtownlimavady school [VI]: Drumachose LY 9;
131
Newtownlimavady Sunday schools: Drumachose LY
9; 85, 90, 103
Newtownlimavady td: Drumachose LY 9; 96
Newtownlimavady temperance hotel: Drumachose
LY 9; 78
Newtownlimavady Townhall Sunday school:
Drumachose LY 9; 131
Newtownlimavady Wesleyan school: Drumachose
LY 9; 71, 85, 124
Newtownstewart: Ardstraw TE 5; 2, 6–7, 11
Newtownstewart: Clondermot LY 34; 30
Newtownstewart: Dromore TE 5; 97
Newtownstewart: Dungiven LY 15; 11
Newtownstewart: Longfield TE 5; 132
Newtownstewart: Misc. LY 31; 116
Newtownstewart: Urney DL 39; 176, 179
Newtownstewart chapel (C): Ardstraw TE 5; 7, 11
Newtownstewart chapel (PWM): Ardstraw TE 5; 8,
11
Newtownstewart chapel (WM): Ardstraw TE 5; 7–8,
11
Newtownstewart church: Ardstraw TE 5; 7–8, 11
Newtownstewart church: Clondermot LY 34; 52
Newtownstewart classic school: Ardstraw TE 5; 6
Newtownstewart dispensary: Ardstraw TE 5; 9, 13
Newtownstewart meeting house (P): Ardstraw TE 5;
3, 7–8, 11
Newtownstewart meeting house (S): Ardstraw TE 5;
7–8, 11
Newtownstewart national school: Ardstraw TE 5; 6
Newtownstewart parish school: Ardstraw TE 5; 6
Newtownstewart spade foundry: Ardstraw TE 5; 14
Newtownstewart Sunday school [I]: Ardstraw TE 5;
7
Newtownstewart Sunday school [II]: Ardstraw TE 5;
7
Newtownstewart Sunday school [III]: Ardstraw TE
5; 7
Newtownstewart td: Ardstraw TE 5; 4
Ney bridge: Blaris DN 12; 34
Niall of the Nine Hostages, King: Donegal DL 39;
48, 51
Niall of the Nine Hostages, King: Faughanvale LY
36; 12, 33, 55
Niblock, Robert: Island Magee AM 10; 64

Niblock, William: Island Magee AM 10; 64
Nichol, Betty: Ahoghill AM 23; 35
Nichol, David: Ballymoney AM 16; 17
Nichol, Hugh: Drummaul AM 19; 90
Nichol, James: Connor AM 19; 26
Nichol, Mrs: Ballymoney AM 16; 17
Nichol, Patrick: Glynn AM 26; 47
Nichol, Robert: Ahoghill AM 23; 35
Nichol, Widow: Ballymoney AM 16; 17
Nicholas, St: Carnmoney AM 2; 64
Nicholas, St: Carrickfergus AM 37; 25, 81, 181
Nicholl, family: Ahoghill AM 23; 25
Nicholl, family: Ballyclug AM 23; 63
Nicholl, Henry: Loughguile AM 13; 75
Nicholl, James: Ahoghill AM 23; 44, 48
Nicholl, James: Loughguile AM 13; 76
Nicholl, R.: Newry DN 3; 100
Nicholls, Jonathan: Coleraine LY 33; 72, 143–44
Nichols, William: Carrickfergus AM 37; 194
Nicholson, John: Carrickfergus AM 37; 194
Nicholson, John: Killevy AH 1; 54
Nicholson, Mr: Racavan AM 13; 102–03
Nicholson, Mrs: Dunaghy AM 13; 17
Nicholson, Rev.: Aghadowey LY 22; 24, 26
Nicholson, Rev. John: Island Magee AM 10; 88
Nicholson, Rev. William: Magilligan LY 11; 84, 121
Nicholson, Samuel: Dunaghy AM 13; 17
Nicholson, W.S.: Bangor DN 7; 23
Nicholson, Widow: Racavan AM 13; 103
Nickel, family: Ahoghill AM 23; 25
Nickel, family: Dunluce AM 16; 117
Nickey's fort: Desertoghill LY 27; 8, 27
Nickle, Alexander: Dunluce AM 16; 122
Nickle, Andrew: Dunluce AM 16; 122
Nickle, family: Carnmoney AM 2; 76
Nickle, family: Raloo AM 32; 108
Nickle, James: Ballyrashane LY 22; 66
Nickle, James: Dunluce AM 16; 122
Nickle, John: Ballymoney AM 16; 17
Nickle, Widow: Ballymoney AM 16; 17
Nickles, Mrs: Carrickfergus AM 37; 183
Nicolay, Mrs: Ballynure AM 32; 46, 48, 68–70
Nicolls, George: Desertoghill LY 27; 13, 22
Nicolls, James: Desertoghill LY 27; 20
Nicolls, Robert: Desertoghill LY 27; 20
Nicolls, Sarah: Desertoghill LY 27; 20
Nicolls, Thomas: Desertoghill LY 27; 20
Nicolly, C.W.: Carrickfergus AM 37; 56, 102, 135–36, 141
Niddery, family: Longfield TE 5; 132
Nielson, Thomas: Island Magee AM 10; 94
Niely, Miss: Clogher TE 5; 43
Nieves, Mr: Artrea LY 6; 26
Nilson, family: Ballintoy AM 24; 20
Nilteen druid's altar: Nilteen AM 35; 86, 102

Nilteen ph: Antrim AM 29; 37
Nilteen ph: Ballycor AM 32; 2
Nilteen ph: Carnmoney AM 2; 72
Nilteen ph: Doagh AM 29; 75, 78, 96
Nilteen ph: Donegore AM 29; 101–03, 105–06, 108, 110–12, 129, 131–34
Nilteen ph: Kilbride AM 29; 135, 137, 141–42, 147, 150, 154
Nilteen ph: Killead AM 35; 28
Nilteen ph. Misc. AM 10; 129
Nilteen ph: Muckamore AM 35; 54, 57, 64–65, 69
Nilteen ph: Templepatrick AM 35; 111, 118, 126, 131–32, 144
Nilteen school (see Donegore)
Nilteen stone circle: Kilbride AM 29; 147
Nimmo, Mr: Newry DN 3; 86
Nimmo, Mr: Warrenpoint DN 3; 120
Nimmo, Sarah: Aghadowey LY 22; 18
Nine Cove field: Macosquin LY 22; 87, 117
Ninescoreacres locality: Carrickfergus AM 37; 94
Nippers, family: Culfeightrin AM 24; 59
Nisbet, family: Carrickfergus AM 37; 93
Nisbet, Mr: Aghadowey LY 22; 5
Nisbett, Rev. William: Loughinisland DN 17; 96
Nisbitt, Mr: Drumbo DN 7; 59
Niven, family: Culfeightrin AM 24; 59
Niven, family: Lambeg AM 8; 135
Nivin, Mrs: Ballyphilip DN 7; 8
Nixon Hall (see Fairwood Park)
Nixon, Adam: Cleenish FH 14; 18, 29
Nixon, Adam: Devenish FH 14; 53
Nixon, Adam: Enniskillen FH 4; 58
Nixon, family: Enniskillen FH 4; 58, 75
Nixon, Frances (see Enery)
Nixon, G.: Cleenish FH 14; 30
Nixon, Hugh: Carrickfergus AM 37; 112, 114
Nixon, J.: Aughnamullen MN 40; 76
Nixon, John: Killead AM 35; 22, 50
Nixon, Mr (Strabane): Tullyaughnish DL 38; 88
Nixon, Mr: Galloon FH 4; 105
Nixon, Mrs: Devenish FH 14; 53
Nixon, T.: Cleenish FH 14; 29
No Man's Friend locality: Coleraine LY 33; 102
Nob's Hole locality: Clondermot LY 34; 32
Noble, Alexander: Clondermot LY 34; 78–80
Noble, Alexander: Cumber LY 28; 56
Noble, family: Donacavey TE 5; 71
Noble, family: Enniskillen FH 4; 58
Noble, Rev. Robert: Clones FH 4; 27
Noble, Rev. Robert: Enniskeen CN 40; 29
Noble, William: Ardstraw TE 5; 6, 13
Noble, William: Galloon FH 4; 91
Nockan bridge: Racavan AM 13; 92, 99
Nocking stone: Ballintoy AM 24; 33
Nocknashannon school: Devenish FH 14; 50

Nod's Top hill: Clondermot LY 34; 1, 17
Nodwell, Cathrine: Drumachose LY 9; 133
Nodwell, Eliza: Drumachose LY 9; 133
Nodwell, family: Magherafelt LY 6; 95
Nodwell, Maryann: Drumachose LY 9; 133
Nodwell, Mathew: Drumachose LY 9; 133
Nodwell, Robert: Macosquin LY 22; 100
Nogher, family: Magherafelt LY 6; 95
Nolan and Taafe, Messrs: Aghadowey LY 22; 8
Nolan, Mr: Magilligan LY 11; 120
Nolan, Rev. Thomas: Newry DN 3; 79
Nomin Island: Mintiaghs DL 38; 64
Noon, James: Carrickfergus AM 37; 123
Noon, Robert: Ballynascreen LY 31; 16
Norein (see Naminn): Clonmany DL 38; 12
Norman, Charles: Killygarvan DL 38; 41, 48
Norman, Charles: Tullyaughnish DL 38; 97
Norman, Mr (Dublin): Convoy DL 39; 19
Norman, Mr (Fahan): Clondavaddog DL 38; 6
Norman, Robert (Dublin): Clondermot LY 34; 82
Normandy (France): Ballyscullion LY 6; 57
Norrin (see Naminn)
Norris, Arthur: Cumber LY 28; 42, 55
Norris, family: Ardglass DN 17; 4
Norris, family: Cumber LY 28; 43, 55
Norris, family: Derryaghy AM 8; 103
Norris, James: Ballyrashane LY 22; 62
Norris, Robert: Cumber LY 28; 42, 54
Norris, Stewart: Coleraine LY 33; 73
North Carn hill: Carrickfergus AM 37; 5
North Channel: Carncastle and Killyglen AM 10; 8
North Channel: Carnmoney AM 2; 35
North Channel: Carrickfergus AM 37; 8, 60, 83, 85
North Channel: Glynn AM 26; 9
North Channel: Island Magee AM 10; 14–15, 26, 74
North Channel: Kilroot AM 26; 61
North Channel: Moville DL 38; 70
North Channel: Templecorran AM 26; 88, 96
North East Division bog: Carrickfergus AM 37; 188
North East Division fort [I]: Carrickfergus AM 37;
    186
North East Division fort [II]: Carrickfergus AM 37;
    189
North East Division quarry: Carrickfergus AM 37;
    171
North East Division td: Carrickfergus AM 37; 6, 33,
    78, 80, 90–92, 147, 158, 173, 187
North Lodge district: Carrickfergus AM 37; 174
North Lodge House: Carrickfergus AM 37; 135–36,
    174
North rock: Ardkeen DN 7; 1
North Star dyke: Culfeightrin AM 24; 39
Northland demesne: Drumglass TE 20; 42
Northland House: Drumglass TE 20; 42
Northland, Lord: Comber DN 7; 37–39

Northland, Lord: Drumbo DN 7; 60
Northland, Lord: Enniskillen FH 4; 82
Northland, Lord: Holywood DN 7; 77
Northland, Lord: Saintfield DN 7; 118
Northumberland (England): Carrickfergus AM 37;
    61
Northumberland: Carnmoney AM 2; 51
Northumberland: Magilligan LY 11; 88
Northumberland: Mallusk AM 2; 109
Northumberland: Misc. AM 10; 130–31
Northumberland: Templepatrick AM 35; 116, 123
Northumberland: Umgall AM 35; 156
Norton Castle: Templepatrick AM 35; 132
Norton, Capt.: Ballynure AM 32; 51
Norton, family: Ballinderry AM 21; 53
Norton, family: Ballymartin AM 2; 5
Norton, family: Carmavy AM 35; 2
Norton, family: Derryaghy AM 8; 93
Norton, family: Templepatrick AM 35; 111, 116,
    145
Norton, family: Umgall AM 35; 157
Norton, James: Newry DN 3; 99
Norton, Mr: Ballymartin AM 2; 17
Norton, Robert: Derryaghy AM 8; 92
Norton, Robert: Templepatrick AM 35; 108, 111,
    125, 132, 143
Norton, Roger: Templepatrick AM 35; 108
Norway: Banagher LY 30; 9
Norway: Coleraine LY 33; 86–87
Norway: Donegal DL 39; 46
Norway: Tullyaughnish DL 38; 87, 95
Notman, family: Templecorran AM 26; 117, 119
Nottingham: Cumber LY 28; 58
Noughaval (Westmeath): Faughanvale LY 36; 52
Nova Scotia: Kilbroney DN 3; 34
Nowlan, John [I]: Carrickfergus AM 37; 116
Nowlan, John [II]: Carrickfergus AM 37; 193
Nowry, John: Dunboe LY 11; 75
Noyes, Rev. William: Duneane AM 19; 113
Nugent, Andrew: Ballyphilip DN 7; 8, 11–12, 14
Nugent, Andrew: Misc. DN 17; 126–27
Nugent, Arthur: Aghagallon AM 21; 19
Nugent, Hugh: Skirts of Urney and Ardstraw TE 5;
    141
Nugent, James: Carlingford LH 40; 59
Nugent, Patrick: Coleraine LY 33; 142
Nugent, Sarah: Carrickfergus AM 37; 156
Numerills hills: Misc. DN 17; 131
Nun's Island: Newry DN 3; 89
Nunn, Jeremiah: Faughanvale LY 36; 45
Nuns' Garden locality: Lambeg AM 8; 136
Nuns' hill: Clogher TE 5; 28
Nunsquarter manor: Misc. DN 17; 125
Nunsquarter td: Ballywalter DN 7; 18
Nurchassy (see Nurchossy)

Nurchasy (see Nurchossy)
Nurchossy Irish td: Clogher TE 5; 39
Nurchossy school: Clogher TE 5; 41–42
Nurchossy Scotch corn mill: Clogher TE 5; 49
Nurchossy Scotch td: Clogher TE 5; 39, 49
Nurchossy td: Clogher TE 5; 34–35, 38, 41
Nurchossys (see Nurchossy)
Nurchosys (see Nurchossy)
Nuremore bog: Killanny MN 40; 130
Nuremore td: Magheross MN 40; 156

Nursery locality: Muckamore AM 35; 80
Nutfield demesne: Aghavea FH 4; 18–19, 24
Nutfield hill: Drung CN 40; 19
Nutfield House: Aghalurcher FH 4; 6, 11–12
Nutfield House: Aghavea FH 4; 20
Nutfield td: Aghavea FH 4; 23
Nutt, Alixander: Bovevagh LY 25; 60
Nutt, farmer: Cumber LY 28; 30
NyCahan, Honora (see O'Cahan, Lady)
Nymphsfield td: Killoran and Kilvarnet SO 40; 183

O

O'Barra, family: Faughanvale LY 36; 64

O'Beirne, Mrs: Newry DN 3; 100

O'Beirne, Rev.: Enniskillen FH 4; 63

O'Beirne, Rev.: Rossorry FH 14; 117

O'Boyle, Connel: Killymard DL 39; 96

O'Boyle, Donnell: Misc. TE 5; 146

O'Boyle, family: Donegal DL 39; 48

O'Boyle, family: Killymard DL 39; 96

O'Boyle, Hugh: Killymard DL 39; 96

O'Boyle, Owen: Killymard DL 39; 96

O'Bradley, Laurence: Maghera LY 18; 39

O'Breslen, Con: Misc. TE 5; 146

O'Breslen, family: Faughanvale LY 36; 63

O'Breslen, Randal: Misc. TE 5; 146

O'Brian, family: Ballinderry AM 21; 54

O'Brian, Penelope (see O'Donnell)

O'Brian, Prince of Thomond: Donegal DL 39; 49

O'Brian, Rev.: Ballyscullion AM 19; 8

O'Brien, Charles: Aghagallon AM 21; 17

O'Brien, family: Carrickfergus AM 37; 93, 179

O'Brien, family: Dungiven LY 15; 62

O'Brien, Holland: Magilligan LY 11; 94

O'Brien, James: Carrickfergus AM 37; 125

O'Brien, James: Newry DN 3; 99

O'Brien, John: Carrickfergus AM 37; 193

O'Brien, man named: Dungiven LY 15; 27

O'Brien, Margaret: Carrickfergus AM 37; 117, 122

O'Brien, Margaret: Magilligan LY 11; 94

O'Brien, Mrs: Aghalee AM 21; 37

O'Brien, Mrs James: Kilbroney DN 3; 35

O'Brien, P.: Ardstraw TE 5; 6

O'Brien, Rev. William: Shankill AH 1; 114

O'Brolchain, Flathbeart: Dungiven LY 15; 33

O'Brolchain, Flathbert: Island Magee AM 10; 60

O'Brolchain, M.C.: Island Magee AM 10; 60

O'Brolchain, Martin: Island Magee AM 10; 43, 60,
71

O'Brollaghan, Abbot: Dungiven LY 15; 61

O'Bryan, James: Derrykeighan AM 16; 95

O'Bryans, James: Ahoghill AM 23; 39

O'Bryans, Jane: Ballymoney AM 16; 18

O'Bryans, William: Ahoghill AM 23; 39

O'Bryne, Jane (see Dalway)

O'Byrne, Fiach: Balteagh LY 9; 18

O'Byrne, Hugh: Balteagh LY 9; 18

O'Cahan, Awney: Derryvullan FH 14; 39

O'Cahan, Bryan: Clondermot LY 34; 33, 38, 71

O'Cahan, C.B.: Balteagh LY 9; 26

O'Cahan, C.B.: Bovevagh LY 25; 15–16, 35–36, 38,
46

O'Cahan, chiefain: Billy AM 16; 38

O'Cahan, chieftain: Bovevagh LY 25; 35–36

O'Cahan, chieftain: Magilligan LY 11; 90, 126

O'Cahan, Cooey: Dungiven LY 15; 32–33

O'Cahan, D.G.: Drumachose LY 9; 95

O'Cahan, Dermot: Dungiven LY 15; 33

O'Cahan, Donald: Dungiven LY 15; 33

O'Cahan, Donnogh: Clondermot LY 34; 53–55, 66

O'Cahan, Donough: Dungiven LY 15; 33

O'Cahan, Evenny: Dungiven LY 15; 33

O'Cahan, family: Aghanloo LY 11; 4, 8

O'Cahan, family: Balteagh LY 9; 7

O'Cahan, family: Banagher LY 30; 5, 48, 53, 77–78,
93, 95

O'Cahan, family: Bovevagh LY 25; 35–37, 44

O'Cahan, family: Clondermot LY 34; 1, 3–4, 18, 29,
32–34, 47–48, 50–53, 60

O'Cahan, family: Cumber LY 28; 37, 53, 61, 65.

O'Cahan, family: Drumachose LY 9; 90–93, 108–09

O'Cahan, family: Dungiven LY 15; 31, 33, 77

O'Cahan, family: Dunluce AM 16; 117

O'Cahan, family: Faughanvale LY 36; 3

O'Cahan, family: Finvoy AM 23; 74

O'Cahan, family: Kilrea LY 27; 118

O'Cahan, family: Loughguile AM 13; 62, 64, 66

O'Cahan, family: Macosquin LY 22; 97

O'Cahan, family: Magilligan LY 11; 145

O'Cahan, G.M.: Banagher LY 30; 105

O'Cahan, G.M.: Clondermot LY 34; 38

O'Cahan, Graany: Aghadowey LY 22; 15

O'Cahan, Lady: Drumachose LY 9; 95

O'Cahan, Ledha: Bovevagh LY 25; 36

O'Cahan, Lunaght: Banagher LY 30; 77–78

O'Cahan, M.G.: Clondermot LY 34; 38, 48–49,
58–59

O'Cahan, Manus: Clondermot LY 34; 60

O'Cahan, Manus: Coleraine LY 33; 156–57

O'Cahan, Murtogh: Dungiven LY 15; 33

O'Cahan, Niall: Dungiven LY 15; 33
O'Cahan, Nuala: Aghadowey LY 22; 15
O'Cahan, Owen: Dungiven LY 15; 33
O'Cahan, Ownan: Banagher LY 30; 48, 77–78
O'Cahan, Patrick: Dungiven LY 15; 33
O'Cahan, Shane: Clondermot LY 34; 72
O'Cahan, Shane: Dungiven LY 15; 33
O'Cahan, Turlogh: Dungiven LY 15; 33
O'Cahan's bridge: Drumachose LY 9; 118, 127
O'Cahan's Castle: Drumachose LY 9; 57, 76
O'Cahan's Castle: Dungiven LY 15; 20, 31, 33, 42, 79
O'Cain, family: Ballywillin AM 16; 32
O'Caireallain, family: Clondermot LY 34; 51–53, 96, 106
O'Caireallain, family: Faughanvale LY 36; 63
O'Cane, G.W.: Clondermot LY 34; 54
O'Caran, Gilbert: Newry DN 3; 66
O'Carolan, family: Clondermot LY 34; 1
O'Carrol, family: Ballybay MN 40; 81
O'Cashane, Shan: Faughanvale LY 36; 54, 56, 58, 60, 64
O'Cathan, D.G.: Dungiven LY 15; 56
O'Cathan, D.O.: Aghadowey LY 22; 27
O'Cathan, Dermot: Dungiven LY 15; 33, 35, 52
O'Cathan, Donothy: Drumachose LY 9; 95
O'Cathan, family: Aghadowey LY 22; 27
O'Cathan, family: Ballyclug AM 23; 63
O'Cathan, family: Ballymoney AM 16; 20
O'Cathan, family: Billy AM 16; 54
O'Cathan, family: Desertoghill LY 27; 6, 31
O'Cathan, family: Dungiven LY 15; 29–30, 32, 34–35, 54–56, 58, 107–09
O'Cathan, family: Kilrea LY 27; 113
O'Cathan, family: Misc. LY 36; 109–11
O'Cathan, J.O.: Aghadowey LY 22; 27
O'Cathan, Rose: Dungiven LY 15; 33
O'Cathan's brook: Dungiven LY 15; 33
O'Chan, chieftain: Drumachose LY 9; 120
O'Chan, G.M.: Cumber LY 28; 62
O'Chane, family: Clondermot LY 34; 59–60
O'Clery, family: Faughanvale LY 36; 47
O'Coffey, Ambrose: Magilligan LY 11; 146
O'Colgan, family: Clondermot LY 34; 50
O'Colgan, family: Misc. LY 36; 105
O'Connel, family: Errigal LY 27; 47
O'Connel, John: Balteagh LY 9; 24, 26
O'Connell, Charles: Errigal LY 27; 56
O'Connell, Darby: Errigal LY 27; 55
O'Connell, family: Clondermot LY 34; 50
O'Connell, family: Misc. LY 36; 105
O'Connell, James: Errigal LY 27; 55, 66, 75
O'Connell, John: Errigal LY 27; 50–51
O'Connell, Patt: Errigal LY 27; 54, 66, 70

O'Connor Don, family: Manorhamilton Union LM 40; 50
O'Connor, C.: Clogher TE 5; 24
O'Connor, Daniel: Tamlaght O'Crilly LY 18; 141, 143
O'Connor, Edward: Ballyscullion LY 6; 68
O'Connor, Edward: Culfeightrin AM 24; 49–50, 79, 81
O'Connor, Hugh: Maghera LY 18; 42
O'Connor, John: Culfeightrin AM 24; 49
O'Connor, John: Maghera LY 18; 41–42
O'Connor, John [I]: Magheragall AM 21; 103
O'Connor, John [II]: Magheragall AM 21; 106
O'Connor, Mr: Newry DN 3; 100
O'Connor, Patrick: Balteagh LY 9; 41
O'Connor, Thomas: Balteagh LY 9; 10–11, 35
O'Connor, Thomas: Bovevagh LY 25; 21
O'Connor, Thomas: Drumachose LY 9; 109
O'Conor, Charles: Clondermot LY 34; 66
O'Conor, Charles: Dungiven LY 15; 63
O'Conor, family: Balteagh LY 9; 19
O'Conor, family: Bovevagh LY 25; 21
O'Conor, family: Drumachose LY 9; 91
O'Conor, family: Dungiven LY 15; 50
O'Conor, Kian: Balteagh LY 9; 19
O'Conor, Roderic: Faughanvale LY 36; 56
O'Corran, family: Clondermot LY 34; 51
O'Crilly, family: Maghera LY 18; 10, 38
O'Crilly, family: Tamlaght O'Crilly LY 18; 96
O'Crilly, James: Maghera LY 18; 41
O'Crilly, John: Maghera LY 18; 38, 40
O'Crilly, John: Tamlaght O'Crilly LY 18; 84
O'Crilly, Laurence: Tamlaght O'Crilly LY 18; 93
O'Crilly, Michael: Killelagh LY 27; 100–01
O'Crilly, Michael: Maghera LY 18; 40
O'Crilly, Nicholas: Tamlaght O'Crilly LY 18; 96
O'Crilly, Phelimy: Tamlaght O'Crilly LY 18; 93
O'Cullan, family: Ballywillin AM 16; 32
O'Dabagan, Mathias: Devenish FH 14; 51, 54, 60–61
O'Dogherty, family: Clonmany DL 38; 16
O'Dogherty, family: Faughanvale LY 36; 32
O'Dogherty, family: Magilligan LY 11; 107
O'Dogherty, Kiernan: Dungiven LY 15; 61
O'Dogherty, Patrick: Macosquin LY 22; 108
O'Dogherty, Rev. John: Banagher LY 30; 49, 73
O'Doherty, C.R.: Dungiven LY 15; 32–33
O'Doherty, Cahir: Clondermot LY 34; 34
O'Doherty, Cahir: Clonleigh DL 39; 14–15
O'Doherty, Cahir: Faughanvale LY 36; 47
O'Doherty, family: Clonmany DL 38; 16
O'Doherty, family: Coleraine LY 33; 94
O'Doherty, family: Donegal DL 39; 48
O'Doherty, family: Dungiven LY 15; 32
O'Doherty, family: Faughanvale LY 36; 47

O'Doherty, family: Killelagh LY 27; 99
O'Doherty, family: Misc. LY 36; 101–02
O'Doherty, J.J.: Errigal LY 27; 92
O'Doherty, John: Killowen LY 33; 170
O'Doherty, Rev. Daniel: Coleraine LY 33; 133
O'Doherty, Rev. Daniel: Dunboe LY 11; 53
O'Doherty, Rev. Daniel: Killowen LY 33; 159, 164, 166
O'Donal rock: Killymard DL 39; 94
O'Donaly, family: Ballywillin AM 16; 32
O'Donegan, family: Banagher LY 30; 102
O'Donell, Henry: Duneane AM 19; 124
O'Donelly, family: Maghera LY 18; 48
O'Donnal, John: Kilmacteige SO 40; 193
O'Donnald, family: Drumachose LY 9; 128
O'Donnall, Martin: Kilmacteige SO 40; 193
O'Donnel's Point: Lough Swilly DL 38; 102
O'Donnell, Bishop: Killelagh LY 27; 102
O'Donnell, Bryan: Misc. LY 31; 137–38
O'Donnell, Calbach: Clondermot LY 34; 49
O'Donnell, chieftain: Dungiven LY 15; 33
O'Donnell, chieftain: Inishmacsaint FH 14; 75
O'Donnell, Earl: Donaghmore DL 39; 33–34
O'Donnell, family: Carrickfergus AM 37; 93
O'Donnell, family: Cumber LY 28; 65
O'Donnell, family: Donaghmore DL 39; 33–34
O'Donnell, family: Donegal DL 39; 45, 47–48, 51
O'Donnell, family: Drumachose LY 9; 94
O'Donnell, family: Dungiven LY 15; 32
O'Donnell, family: Killymard DL 39; 97
O'Donnell, family: Kilmacrenan DL 38; 52
O'Donnell, family: Leck DL 39; 118
O'Donnell, family: Loughguile AM 13; 68
O'Donnell, family: Manorhamilton Union LM 40; 50
O'Donnell, family: Misc. LY 36; 109
O'Donnell, family: Raphoe DL 39; 131
O'Donnell, family: Tullyaughnish DL 38; 87, 90–91
O'Donnell, H.M.: Misc. LY 31; 138
O'Donnell, H.O.: Misc. TE 5; 147
O'Donnell, H.R.: Donegal DL 39; 48
O'Donnell, H.R.: Misc. TE 5; 147
O'Donnell, Hugh (Snr): Donegal DL 39; 48
O'Donnell, Hugh: Blaris DN 12; 50
O'Donnell, Hugh: Donaghmore DL 39; 40
O'Donnell, Hugh: Misc. TE 5; 147
O'Donnell, Laura: Drumachose LY 9; 57, 111, 127
O'Donnell, Laura: Dungiven LY 15; 32–33
O'Donnell, Magnus: Aghanloo LY 11; 7
O'Donnell, Magnus: Dungiven LY 15; 63–64
O'Donnell, Magnus: Magilligan LY 11; 105–06
O'Donnell, Manus: Clondermot LY 34; 63
O'Donnell, Manus: Donaghmore DL 39; 34
O'Donnell, Mr: Clonmany DL 38; 14
O'Donnell, Neal: Tullyaughnish DL 38; 91

O'Donnell, Neil: Manorhamilton Union LM 40; 50
O'Donnell, O.R.: Donegal DL 39; 49
O'Donnell, P.R.: Leck DL 39; 118
O'Donnell, Penelope (nee O'Brian): Donegal DL 39; 49
O'Donnell, Prince: Magilligan LY 11; 97
O'Donnell, Rev.: Urney DL 39; 176
O'Donnell, Rev. D.: Mevagh DL 38; 60
O'Donnell, Rev. Felix: Aghagallon AM 21; 8
O'Donnell, Rev. W.: Mevagh DL 38; 60
O'Donnell, Richard: Mevagh DL 38; 60
O'Donnell, Shane: Leck DL 39; 118
O'Donnell, Susanna: Mevagh DL 38; 60
O'Donnell's Castle: Donegal DL 39; 42
O'Donnell's Castle: Killymard DL 39; 105
O'Donnell's Castle: Raphoe DL 39; 131
O'Donnell's Castle bridge: Killymard DL 39; 95
O'Donnell's Island: Killymard DL 39; 97
O'Donnelly, family: Maghera LY 18; 24
O'Donnoghue, Rev. H.C.: Newry DN 3; 79
O'Donoghy, family: Faughanvale LY 36; 32
O'Donohey, Peter: Banagher LY 30; 70
O'Donovan, J.: Artrea LY 6; 39
O'Donovan, J.: Ballynascreen LY 31; 33
O'Donovan, J.: Ballywillin LY 33; 52
O'Donovan, J.: Banagher LY 30; 36, 112
O'Donovan, J.: Bovevagh LY 25; 21
O'Donovan, J.: Clondermot LY 34; 103
O'Donovan, J.: Coleraine LY 33; 155
O'Donovan, J.: Dungiven LY 15; 110
O'Donovan, J.: Galloon FH 4; 87
O'Donovan, J.: Glynn AM 26; 48
O'Donovan, J.: Killowen LY 33; 172
O'Donovan, J.: Tamlaght Finlagan LY 25; 85
O'Donovan, J.: Tamlaght O'Crilly LY 18; 144
O'Doorish, family: Cumber LY 28; 71
O'Doran, family: Ballinderry AM 21; 55
O'Doran, James: Ballinderry AM 21; 55
O'Doran, Rev. Bernard: Ballinderry AM 21; 55
O'Doran, Susannah: Ballinderry AM 21; 55
O'Doud, Tedy: Kilmacteige SO 40; 187
O'Dougherty, family: Macosquin LY 22; 97
O'Dougherty, family: Maghera LY 18; 24, 48
O'Dougherty's rock: Lough Swilly DL 38; 131
O'Dowd, Cormick: Ballinderry AM 21; 55
O'Dowd, family: Ballinderry AM 21; 55
O'Dowd, family: Dunaghy AM 13; 17
O'Dowrie, family: Clondermot LY 34; 74
O'Dowry, family: Clondermot LY 34; 68
O'Duana, Euchen: Misc. DN 17; 119
O'Dullinan, family: Culfeightrin AM 24; 59
O'Falaghty, Giollapatrick: Dungiven LY 15; 122
O'Farrell, family: Desertlyn LY 31; 42
O'Farrell, William: Maghera LY 18; 67
O'Farrill, family: Maghera LY 18; 48

O'Feary, Henery: Blaris AM 8; 19, 33–34

O'Flagherty, Mrs: Clogher TE 5; 41

O'Flaherty, F.H.: Blaris AM 8; 12, 52–53, 55–56, 66

O'Flaherty, F.H.: Blaris DN 12; 40, 42, 44, 46, 50

O'Flaherty, Flahertach: Dungiven LY 15; 122

O'Flaherty, Rory: Misc. TE 5; 146

O'Flanagan, family: Dungiven LY 15; 32

O'Flannagan, Baron: Inishmacsaint FH 14; 75–76

O'Flannagan, Bartholomeo: Devenish FH 14; 51, 54, 60–61

O'Flannagan, family: Inishmacsaint FH 14; 75

O'Flynn, family: Misc. TE 5, 146

O'Friel, Bernard: Cumber LY 28; 72

O'Gadhra, family: Faughanvale LY 36; 49

O'Gall, chieftain: Kilrea LY 27; 130

O'Gallagher, Bishop: Donegal DL 39; 49

O'Gallagher, family: Faughanvale LY 36; 61

O'Godain, family: Faughanvale LY 36; 54

O'Gorman, Daniel: Newry DN 3; 81

O'Gormely, family: Cumber LY 28; 11

O'Gormley, Brian: Misc. TE 5; 147

O'Gormley, C.R.: Misc. TE 5; 147

O'Gormley, Edmond: Misc. TE 5; 147

O'Gormley, Enna: Misc. TE 5; 146

O'Gormley, Henry: Misc. TE 5; 147

O'Gormley, Magnus: Misc. TE 5; 147

O'Gormley, Mortagh: Misc. TE 5; 147

O'Gormly, family: Misc. TE 5; 146

O'Grady, King: Kilmacteige SO 40; 189

O'Grugen, family: Desertlyn LY 31; 42

O'Hagan, Charles: Newry DN 3; 101

O'Hagan, Daniel: Kilcronaghan LY 31; 77

O'Hagan, Denis: Ballynascreen LY 31; 23

O'Hagan, family: Aghanloo LY 11; 4

O'Hagan, family: Ballyscullion LY 6; 58

O'Hagan, family: Banagher LY 30; 107

O'Hagan, family: Errigal LY 27; 41, 46–47

O'Hagan, family: Kilcronaghan LY 31; 68–69, 76

O'Hagan, family: Magilligan LY 11; 93

O'Hagan, family: Misc. LY 31; 122

O'Hagan, family: Ramoan AM 24; 107

O'Hagan, George: Errigal LY 27; 55

O'Hagan, John: Newry DN 3; 92–93, 104

O'Hagan, Messrs John and Son: Newry DN 3; 99

O'Hagan, Mr (Inishkeen): Inniskeen MN 40; 124–25

O'Hagan, Mrs: Newry DN 3; 99, 104

O'Hagan, Mrs S.M. (nee O'Lynn): Desertmartin LY 31; 55

O'Hagan, O.R.: Kilcronaghan LY 31; 69, 77

O'Hagan, Patrick: Clonduff DN 3; 5

O'Hagan, Patrick: Drumachose LY 9; 70, 85, 123

O'Hagan, Rev. Edward: Aghanloo LY 11; 10, 14, 22

O'Hagan, Rev. Edward: Kilcronaghan LY 31; 69, 77

O'Hagan, Rev. John: Banagher LY 30; 73

O'Hagan, S.M.: Desertmartin LY 31; 55

O'Hagan, S.M.: Kilcronaghan LY 31; 69, 77

O'Hagan, William: Kilcronaghan LY 31; 69, 77

O'Hagan's Castle: Kilcronaghan LY 31; 69

O'Haghin, Denis: Templecorran AM 26; 115

O'Haghin, Eneas: Carrickfergus AM 37; 176

O'Haghin, Eneas: Templecorran AM 26; 115, 122

O'Haghin, family: Carrickfergus AM 37; 176–77

O'Haghin, family: Templecorran AM 26; 115, 122

O'Haghin, S.O.: Templecorran AM 26; 115

O'Haghin's caves: Carrickfergus AM 37; 177

O'Hahan, Neese: Templepatrick AM 35; 152

O'Hale, George: Bovevagh LY 25; 29

O'Hale, John: Loughguile AM 13; 76

O'Hale, Patrick (Jnr): Bovevagh LY 25; 29

O'Hale, Patrick (Snr): Bovevagh LY 25; 29

O'Halloran, person named: Saul DN 17; 113

O'Hamill, family: Lambeg AM 8; 135

O'Handlan, chieftain: Ballywillin LY 33; 50

O'Hanlin, family: Misc. DN 17; 131

O'Hanlon, Edward: Newry DN 3; 99, 104

O'Hanlon, family: Ballymore AH 1; 8

O'Hanlon, Redmond: Ballymore AH 1; 10, 18

O'Hanlon, Redmond: Magheramesk AM 21; 124

O'Hara, Alexander: Ahoghill AM 23; 12, 15

O'Hara, Arthur: Drummaul AM 19; 90

O'Hara, Bernard: Tamlaght TE 20; 77

O'Hara, Cahil: Ballyclug AM 23; 53

O'Hara, Cahil: Connor AM 19; 18

O'Hara, Charles: Ballyclug AM 23; 64

O'Hara, Charles: Ballymoney AM 16; 1, 9, 15

O'Hara, Charles: Coleraine LY 33; 127

O'Hara, Clare: Kilmacteige SO 40; 185–86

O'Hara, Daniel: Tamlaght TE 20; 77, 104

O'Hara, Dinnis: Kilmacteige SO 40; 196

O'Hara, family: Ahoghill AM 23; 17, 34

O'Hara, family: Ballyclug AM 23; 52, 56–57, 59–61, 65

O'Hara, family: Blaris DN 12; 30

O'Hara, family: Connor AM 19; 18

O'Hara, family: Culfeightrin AM 24; 59

O'Hara, family: Dunaghy AM 13; 14

O'Hara, family: Kilmacteige SO 40; 185–88

O'Hara, family: Lambeg AM 8; 135

O'Hara, family: Loughguile AM 13; 60, 63–64, 68

O'Hara, family: Skerry AM 13; 116

O'Hara, H.H. (Jnr): Ballyclug AM 23; 52–53, 60

O'Hara, H.H. (Snr): Ballyclug AM 23; 58, 60

O'Hara, Hamilton: Ahoghill AM 23; 17

O'Hara, Hamish: Ahoghill AM 23; 39

O'Hara, Henry (Portstewart): Ballyclug AM 23; 60

O'Hara, Henry: Ahoghill AM 23; 39

O'Hara, Henry: Ballyaghran LY 33; 3–4, 6–8, 19, 21

O'Hara, Henry: Coleraine LY 33; 63, 104

O'Hara, Henry: Connor AM 19; 16
O'Hara, Henry: Glenwhirry AM 32; 77
O'Hara, Henry: Maghera LY 18; 57
O'Hara, Henry [I]: Ballyclug AM 23; 56
O'Hara, Henry [II]: Ballyclug AM 23; 65
O'Hara, Hugh: Ballyclug AM 23; 65
O'Hara, Hugh: Banagher LY 30; 75
O'Hara, James: Ahoghill AM 23; 39
O'Hara, James: Banagher LY 30; 74
O'Hara, James: Bovevagh LY 25; 48
O'Hara, James: Drumachose LY 9; 118
O'Hara, James: Dungiven LY 15; 70, 74, 84
O'Hara, James: Maghera LY 18; 81
O'Hara, John: Ballyclug AM 23; 64
O'Hara, John: Kilmacteige SO 40; 193, 196
O'Hara, John [I]: Ahoghill AM 23; 39
O'Hara, John [I]: Maghera LY 18; 11
O'Hara, John [II]: Ahoghill AM 23; 39
O'Hara, John [II]: Maghera LY 18; 23
O'Hara, L.C.: Ballyclug AM 23; 57
O'Hara, Laughlin: Connor AM 19; 18
O'Hara, Margaret: Ballyclug AM 23; 65
O'Hara, Michael: Ballyclug AM 23; 64
O'Hara, Michael: Banagher LY 30; 45–46, 56, 75
O'Hara, Michael: Bovevagh LY 25; 30
O'Hara, Michael: Kilmacteige SO 40; 193
O'Hara, minor: Glenwhirry AM 32; 74
O'Hara, Mr: Ballyphilip DN 7; 13
O'Hara, Mrs Hamilton: Ahoghill AM 23; 17
O'Hara, Mrs Henry (nee Hutchinson): Ballyclug
    AM 23; 56
O'Hara, Owen: Ballyclug AM 23; 65
O'Hara, Owen: Carrickfergus AM 37; 126
O'Hara, Patrick [I]: Ballyclug AM 23; 64
O'Hara, Patrick [II]: Ballyclug AM 23; 65
O'Hara, Patt: Kilmacteige SO 40; 195
O'Hara, Peter: Maghera LY 18; 60
O'Hara, Rev. James: Coleraine LY 33; 127
O'Hara, Rev. James: Dunluce AM 16; 110
O'Hara, Richard: Ballyclug AM 23; 64
O'Hara, Roger: Banagher LY 30; 42–43
O'Hara, T.M.: Island Magee AM 10; 65
O'Hara, William: Aghagallon AM 21; 17
O'Hara, William: Carrickfergus AM 37; 195
O'Hara, woman named: Ballyclug AM 23; 59
O'Hara's Castle (see Rock Castle)
O'Harabrook House: Ballymoney AM 16; 1, 6, 9
O'Haran, Denis: Ballynascreen LY 31; 15
O'Haran, family: Ballynascreen LY 31; 9
O'Haran, Mrs Denis: Ballynascreen LY 31; 15
O'Hare, John: Newry DN 3; 100
O'Hare, Patrick: Carrickfergus AM 37; 118
O'Harran, Bryan: Derryvullan FH 14; 38
O'Harran, Daniel: Culfeightrin AM 24; 75, 83–84
O'Harran, R.M.: Ballynascreen LY 31; 20

O'Haviland, Denis: Banagher LY 30; 39
O'Haviland, Denis: Killowen LY 33; 162, 170, 172
O'Haviland, Denis: Macosquin LY 22; 105
O'Haviland, James: Killowen LY 33; 172
O'Heany, Murriagh: Banagher LY 30; 6, 12, 26, 37,
    41–42, 69–71, 112, 114
O'Heany, Murriagh: Bovevagh LY 25; 6
O'Hear, family: Newry DN 3; 107–08
O'Hears, family: Dromara DN 12; 67
O'Hendry, family: Maghera LY 18; 48
O'Heney, Charles: Banagher LY 30; 10
O'Heney, family: Banagher LY 30; 6
O'Herrill, James: Ahoghill AM 23; 42
O'Kahan, family: Balteagh LY 9; 26, 28
O'Kahan, family: Dungiven LY 15; 94
O'Kain, family: Dunluce AM 16; 117
O'Kain, John: Dunluce AM 16; 117
O'Kane and Mitchell, Messrs: Coleraine LY 33; 86,
    90
O'Kane monument: Dungiven LY 15; 58
O'Kane, Bernard: Balteagh LY 9; 12, 26
O'Kane, Bernard: Dungiven LY 15; 92
O'Kane, Bernard: Errigal LY 27; 76–77
O'Kane, Bernard [I]: Banagher LY 30; 43, 48,
    78–79
O'Kane, Bernard [I]: Errigal LY 27; 44, 73
O'Kane, Bernard [II]: Banagher LY 30; 56, 75
O'Kane, Bernard [II]: Errigal LY 27; 67
O'Kane, Blosga: Misc. TE 5; 146
O'Kane, Bryan: Bovevagh LY 25; 60
O'Kane, Charles: Errigal LY 27; 55, 72
O'Kane, Charles: Skerry AM 13; 114
O'Kane, chieftain: Dungiven LY 15; 30–31, 79
O'Kane, Cormic: Errigal LY 27; 66
O'Kane, Cumaige: Dungiven LY 15; 56
O'Kane, D.B.: Drumachose LY 9; 93–94
O'Kane, D.G.: Drumachose LY 9; 95
O'Kane, Daniel: Drumachose LY 9; 108
O'Kane, Daniel: Tamlaght O'Crilly LY 18; 112
O'Kane, Daniel [I]: Errigal LY 27; 43, 55–56, 71
O'Kane, Daniel [II]: Errigal LY 27; 66–67
O'Kane, Daniel [III]: Errigal LY 27; 67
O'Kane, Denis: Bovevagh LY 25; 39
O'Kane, Denis: Cumber LY 28; 28
O'Kane, Donagh: Misc. TE 5; 146
O'Kane, Donogh: Cumber LY 28; 72
O'Kane, Edward: Banagher LY 30; 61, 72, 77, 79
O'Kane, Edward: Maghera LY 18; 61
O'Kane, Edward: Tamlaght O'Crilly LY 18; 106,
    116, 126
O'Kane, Ellen: Magilligan LY 11; 94
O'Kane, family: Ballintoy AM 24; 33
O'Kane, family: Ballynascreen LY 31; 12
O'Kane, family: Banagher LY 30; 107
O'Kane, family: Bovevagh LY 25; 15–17, 21, 24, 39

O'Kane, family: Clondermot LY 34; 75
O'Kane, family: Desertoghill LY 27; 5, 30
O'Kane, family: Dungiven LY 15; 78, 84–85
O'Kane, family: Errigal LY 27; 41, 47, 76
O'Kane, family: Faughanvale LY 36; 32, 49, 54
O'Kane, family: Finvoy AM 23; 76
O'Kane, family: Killelagh LY 27; 99
O'Kane, Francis: Balteagh LY 9; 34, 36
O'Kane, Francis: Banagher LY 30; 47, 76
O'Kane, Francis: Billy AM 16; 56, 64, 66
O'Kane, Francis: Bovevagh LY 25; 34
O'Kane, Francis: Errigal LY 27; 44, 54, 73
O'Kane, Francis [I]: Maghera LY 18; 41
O'Kane, Francis [II]: Maghera LY 18; 80
O'Kane, Frank: Loughguile AM 13; 72
O'Kane, Galleyglass: Cumber LY 28; 11
O'Kane, Gilchriest: Misc. TE 5; 146
O'Kane, Hamilton: Macosquin LY 22; 118
O'Kane, Henery: Banagher LY 30; 93
O'Kane, Henery: Dungiven LY 15; 84
O'Kane, Hugh: Maghera LY 18; 39
O'Kane, James: Banagher LY 30; 43, 61, 75, 79
O'Kane, James: Bovevagh LY 25; 15, 33, 35, 44
O'Kane, James: Carrickfergus AM 37; 141
O'Kane, James: Dungiven LY 15; 76, 79, 89–91
O'Kane, James: Tamlaght O'Crilly LY 18; 140, 143
O'Kane, James [I]: Errigal LY 27; 66
O'Kane, James [II]: Errigal LY 27; 66
O'Kane, Jane: Ballynascreen LY 31; 18
O'Kane, Jane: Balteagh LY 9; 44
O'Kane, Jane: Errigal LY 27; 66
O'Kane, John: Ballynascreen LY 31; 17
O'Kane, John: Banagher LY 30; 84
O'Kane, John: Billy AM 16; 66
O'Kane, John: Drumachose LY 9; 110
O'Kane, John: Dungiven LY 15; 85, 93
O'Kane, John: Killelagh LY 27; 100
O'Kane, John: Killowen LY 33; 169, 171–72
O'Kane, John: Maghera LY 18; 81
O'Kane, John: Tamlaght Finlagan LY 25; 118
O'Kane, John: Tamlaght O'Crilly LY 18; 115, 138
O'Kane, John [I]: Errigal LY 27; 44, 54–55, 71
O'Kane, John [II]: Errigal LY 27; 66
O'Kane, Ladha: Bovevagh LY 25; 15
O'Kane, M.B.: Dungiven LY 15; 63
O'Kane, Maj.: Dungiven LY 15; 30
O'Kane, Manus: Bovevagh LY 25; 24
O'Kane, Manus: Clondermot LY 34; 60
O'Kane, Manus: Dungiven LY 15; 61, 80, 88
O'Kane, Manus: Errigal LY 27; 66
O'Kane, Margaret: Magilligan LY 11; 94
O'Kane, Margret: Bovevagh LY 25; 60
O'Kane, Mary: Tamlaght Finlagan LY 25; 119
O'Kane, Michael (Jnr): Errigal LY 27; 66
O'Kane, Michael (Snr): Errigal LY 27; 66

O'Kane, Michael: Balteagh LY 9; 36, 43
O'Kane, Michael: Banagher LY 30; 61, 79–80
O'Kane, Michael: Bovevagh LY 25; 61
O'Kane, Michael: Dungiven LY 15; 90, 92
O'Kane, Michael: Tamlaght O'Crilly LY 18; 106, 116
O'Kane, Michael [I]: Errigal LY 27; 71
O'Kane, Mrs: Dungiven LY 15; 108
O'Kane, Mrs Denis: Cumber LY 28; 28
O'Kane, Mrs Edward: Banagher LY 30; 77
O'Kane, Owen [I]: Banagher LY 30; 51, 94
O'Kane, Owen [II]: Banagher LY 30; 90
O'Kane, Patrick: Ahoghill AM 23; 39
O'Kane, Patrick: Billy AM 16; 61
O'Kane, Patrick: Drumachose LY 9; 110
O'Kane, Patrick: Dungiven LY 15; 12, 97
O'Kane, Patrick [I]: Banagher LY 30; 48, 79
O'Kane, Patrick [I]: Maghera LY 18; 61
O'Kane, Patrick [II]: Banagher LY 30; 77
O'Kane, Patrick [II]: Maghera LY 18; 80
O'Kane, Patt: Bovevagh LY 25; 33, 35, 37–39, 45–46, 58
O'Kane, Patt: Errigal LY 27; 66
O'Kane, Peter (Jnr): Maghera LY 18; 80
O'Kane, Peter (Snr): Maghera LY 18; 80
O'Kane, Quinton: Banagher LY 30; 50–52, 87, 91
O'Kane, Quinton: Errigal LY 27; 55
O'Kane, Rev. Corneilous: Maghera LY 18; 41
O'Kane, Rev. Menassus: Ballynascreen LY 31; 20
O'Kane, Ritchard: Errigal LY 27; 66
O'Kane, Rodger: Ballynascreen LY 31; 17
O'Kane, Rodger: Kilraghts AM 16; 135
O'Kane, Rory: Cumber LY 28; 11
O'Kane, Thomas: Drumachose LY 9; 110
O'Kane, Thomas: Errigal LY 27; 55, 72, 76
O'Kane, Widow: Ballynascreen LY 31; 29
O'Kane, Widow: Bovevagh LY 25; 7–8, 10, 19, 34
O'Kane, Widow: Desertoghill LY 27; 27
O'Kane, William: Ballintoy AM 24; 32–33
O'Kane, William: Dungiven LY 15; 91
O'Kane, William: Tamlaght Finlagan LY 25; 119
O'Kane, William [I]: Bovevagh LY 25; 4, 21, 35, 39, 58
O'Kane, William [II]: Bovevagh LY 25; 60
O'Kane's hotel: Dungiven LY 15; 52
O'Kane's public house: Ballynascreen LY 31; 18
O'Kane's public house: Maghera LY 18; 32, 65
O'Kathan, family: Dungiven LY 15; 84
O'Keane, Rev. Bernard: Emlaghfad SO 40; 177
O'Keeffe, P.: Ballynascreen LY 31; 33
O'Keeffe, P.: Cumber LY 28; 59
O'Keelt, family: Ballynascreen LY 31; 9
O'Keenan's rock: Aghavea FH 4; 17
O'Kelly, family: Ballynascreen LY 31; 9
O'Kelly, family: Kilcronaghan LY 31; 68

O'Kelly, family: Misc. LY 36; 105
O'Kendry, family: Maghera LY 18; 24
O'Kennedy, family: Clondermot LY 34; 51
O'Kildorry, Flahertach: Faughanvale LY 36; 50
O'Lachlin, Donald: Dungiven LY 15; 33
O'Laughlan, Rev. Michael: Drumgooland DN 3; 22
O'Lochlain, Diarmaid: Magilligan LY 11; 90, 143
O'Loghlin, Melaghlin: Misc. TE 5; 146
O'Lone, John: Muckamore AM 35; 81
O'Lone, Lawrence: Ballyclug AM 23; 64
O'Loughin, Connor: Misc. TE 5; 146
O'Loughlin, Dermot: Misc. TE 5; 146
O'Loughlin, Donnell: Misc. TE 5; 146
O'Loughlin, Maelseaghlin: Misc. TE 5; 146
O'Loughlin, Magnus: Misc. TE 5; 146
O'Loughlin, Mortagh: Misc. TE 5; 146
O'Loughlin, Rev. Patrick: Ballynascreen LY 31;
    16–7, 20
O'Louglin, Ardgal: Misc. TE 5; 146
O'Lynn, family: Misc. LY 36; 105
O'Lynn, Miss (see O'Hagan)
O'Madadhain, family: Faughanvale LY 36; 49
O'Madden, family: Misc. LY 36; 105
O'Mahallon, B.D.: Muckamore AM 35; 82
O'Mahallon, Malbrigid: Muckamore AM 35; 82
O'Mahanlon, B.B.: Muckamore AM 35; 56
O'Mahoney, Thomas: Artrea LY 6; 19
O'Mahoney, Thomas: Banagher LY 30; 74
O'Maoldoraidh, Flahertach: Clondermot LY 34; 47
O'Molloy, family: Misc. LY 36; 101
O'Morgan, Malaghy: Down DN 17; 41, 60
O'Moylan, Tirlagh: Derryvullan FH 14; 39
O'Mullan, Anthony: Ballyscullion LY 6; 58
O'Mullan, B.M.: Errigal LY 27; 77–78
O'Mullan, Bernard: Errigal LY 27; 44
O'Mullan, Bryan: Errigal LY 27; 62
O'Mullan, chieftain: Banagher LY 30; 108
O'Mullan, family: Errigal LY 27; 41, 46
O'Mullan, family: Ramoan AM 24; 107
O'Mullan, George: Tamlaght Finlagan LY 25; 110,
    115
O'Mullan, John: Errigal LY 27; 44
O'Mullan, S.C.: Banagher LY 30; 43, 53
O'Mullan, S.C.: Bovevagh LY 25; 17, 37, 45
O'Mullan, S.C.: Cumber LY 28; 32
O'Mullan, S.C.: Dungiven LY 15; 30–31, 35, 80
O'Mullan, S.C.: Killelagh LY 27; 99
O'Mullan, Shane: Banagher LY 30; 53
O'Mullan, son of Shane: Banagher LY 30; 53
O'Mullane, Tomlin: Banagher LY 30; 102–03,
    107–08
O'Mullen, Bernard: Errigal LY 27; 63, 75
O'Mullen, George: Tamlaght Finlagan LY 25; 105
O'Mullen, James: Banagher LY 30; 95
O'Mullen, James: Errigal LY 27; 55

O'Mullen, John [I]: Errigal LY 27; 63, 74
O'Mullen, John [II]: Errigal LY 27; 74
O'Mullen, Manus: Banagher LY 30; 63
O'Mullen, Patt: Errigal LY 27; 74
O'Mullen, Shane (Jnr): Bovevagh LY 25; 45
O'Mullen, Shane (Snr): Bovevagh LY 25; 44–45
O'Mullen, Thomas: Tamlaght Finlagan LY 25; 89,
    107
O'Mullin, Donald: Banagher LY 30; 42–43, 53
O'Mullin, family: Cumber LY 28; 32
O'Mulvenny, George: Aghalee AM 21; 39
O'Murray, Maolpoil: Dungiven LY 15; 122
O'Murray, Paul: Dungiven LY 15; 33
O'Murry, family: Clondermot LY 34; 51
O'Neal, family: Aghanloo LY 11; 4
O'Neal, family: Magilligan LY 11; 93
O'Neal, Felix: Blaris AM 8; 22
O'Neal, T.M.: Derryvullan FH 14; 39
O'Neil, Bridget (Jnr): Lissan LY 31; 110
O'Neil, Bridget (Snr): Lissan LY 31; 110
O'Neil, Corneilus: Termoneeny LY 6; 133
O'Neil, Cornelies: Maghera LY 18; 62
O'Neil, Edward: Maghera LY 18; 81
O'Neil, family: Ballyphilip DN 7; 13
O'Neil, family: Blaris DN 12; 30
O'Neil, Felix: Lissan LY 31; 110
O'Neil, Francis: Lissan LY 31; 109
O'Neil, Frank: Maghera LY 18; 81
O'Neil, Henry: Duneane AM 19; 124
O'Neil, Henry: Kilrea LY 27; 127
O'Neil, Hugh: Desertoghill LY 27; 20
O'Neil, Hugh: Maghera LY 18; 48
O'Neil, Hugh [I]: Duneane AM 19; 123
O'Neil, Hugh [II]: Duneane AM 19; 124
O'Neil, James: Cumber LY 28; 73
O'Neil, James: Lissan LY 31; 110
O'Neil, Jane Hall: Ballyscullion LY 6; 59
O'Neil, John (Jnr): Lissan LY 31; 109
O'Neil, John (Snr): Lissan LY 31; 109
O'Neil, John: Ballynascreen LY 31; 16
O'Neil, John: Desertoghill LY 27; 20
O'Neil, John: Drumachose LY 9; 104
O'Neil, John: Duneane AM 19; 125
O'Neil, John: Maghera LY 18; 29, 59
O'Neil, John: Magherafelt LY 6; 106
O'Neil, John: Newry DN 3; 99
O'Neil, John: Tamlaght TE 20; 129
O'Neil, man named: Tullaghobegley DL 39; 172
O'Neil, Mr: Kilmegan DN 3; 58
O'Neil, Mrs: Newtownards DN 7; 106
O'Neil, Patrick: Kilcronaghan LY 31; 85
O'Neill, A.O.: Duneane AM 19; 98, 109, 121
O'Neill, A.O.: Muckamore AM 35; 69
O'Neill, Aellis: Tickmacrevan AM 13; 130
O'Neill, Andrew: Ballynure AM 32; 65–66

O'Neill, Andrew: Carrickfergus AM 37; 110

O'Neill, Arthur: Ballyaghran LY 33; 9

O'Neill, Arthur: Hillsborough DN 12; 107

O'Neill, Arthur [I]: Drummaul AM 19; 70

O'Neill, Arthur [II]: Drummaul AM 19; 70

O'Neill, B.C.: Tamlaght O'Crilly LY 18; 94, 121–22

O'Neill, B.O.: Drumachose LY 9; 92

O'Neill, Bernard: Ahoghill AM 23; 39

O'Neill, Bernard: Drummaul AM 19; 84

O'Neill, Bernard: Duneane AM 19; 119

O'Neill, Bernard: Maghera LY 18; 44

O'Neill, Brian: Drummaul AM 19; 70

O'Neill, Brian: Misc. LY 31; 137

O'Neill, Brian: Misc. TE 5; 146

O'Neill, Bridget: Ballynascreen LY 31; 21

O'Neill, Bridget: Carrickfergus AM 37; 116, 119, 123

O'Neill, Catherine: Drummaul AM 19; 72, 87

O'Neill, Charity (nee Dixon): Drummaul AM 19; 63, 70

O'Neill, Charles: Ahoghill AM 23; 40

O'Neill, Charles: Artrea TE 20; 8

O'Neill, Charles: Ballynascreen LY 31; 21

O'Neill, Charles: Ballyscullion AM 19; 8

O'Neill, Charles: Connor AM 19; 17

O'Neill, Charles: Drummaul AM 19; 33–34, 36–37, 42–52, 54–57, 63–64, 67, 70, 74, 78–84, 87–89, 92

O'Neill, Charles: Duneane AM 19; 94–96, 99–100, 105, 109, 111–19, 121

O'Neill, Charles: Kilcoo DN 3; 45

O'Neill, Charles: Kirkinriola AM 23; 114, 122

O'Neill, Charles: Shilvodan AM 19; 127, 130–31

O'Neill, cheiftain: Dungiven LY 15; 30–35, 79, 101

O'Neill, chieftain: Magheraculmoney FH 14; 111

O'Neill, Con: Ardglass DN 17; 3

O'Neill, Con: Clondermot LY 34; 53

O'Neill, Con: Killinchy DN 7; 90

O'Neill, Con: Magherafelt LY 6; 106

O'Neill, Con: Newtownards DN 7; 105

O'Neill, Con: Tullyrusk AM 21; 131

O'Neill, Cormac: Banagher LY 30; 106

O'Neill, Cormack: Drummaul AM 19; 70

O'Neill, D.G.: Ardstraw TE 5; 12

O'Neill, Daniel: Artrea LY 6; 38

O'Neill, Daniel: Duneane AM 19; 101, 116

O'Neill, Donnell: Misc. TE 5; 146–47

O'Neill, Earl: Ahoghill AM 23; 10

O'Neill, Earl: Antrim AM 29; 7, 48

O'Neill, Earl: Blaris AM 8; 66

O'Neill, Earl: Donaghadee DN 7; 46

O'Neill, Earl: Glenwhirry AM 32; 74

O'Neill, Earl: Racavan AM 13; 86, 88, 93

O'Neill, Earl: Skerry AM 13; 105–06, 110–13

O'Neill, Elinor (nee Magenis): Drummaul AM 19; 70

O'Neill, Eliza: Carrickfergus AM 37; 129, 131

O'Neill, Elizabeth: Ballyaghran LY 33; 9

O'Neill, F.J.: Drummaul AM 19; 63, 67–68, 70–71

O'Neill, family: Aghalee AM 21; 36

O'Neill, family: Ardglass DN 17; 3, 12

O'Neill, family: Ardstraw TE 5; 9, 11, 12

O'Neill, family: Artrea LY 6; 13–14, 22

O'Neill, family: Ballinderry AM 21; 43

O'Neill, family: Ballyaghran LY 33; 7–9, 11, 16, 21

O'Neill, family: Ballyclug AM 23; 52

O'Neill, family: Ballynascreen LY 31; 12

O'Neill, family: Ballynure AM 32; 45, 67

O'Neill, family: Billy AM 16; 64

O'Neill, family: Carrickfergus AM 37; 30, 162

O'Neill, family: Culfeightrin AM 24; 78, 80

O'Neill, family: Donacavey TE 5; 68

O'Neill, family: Donaghenry TE 20; 39

O'Neill, family: Drumachose LY 9; 93–94

O'Neill, family: Drumballyroney DN 3; 12

O'Neill, family: Drumglass TE 20; 42, 44

O'Neill, family: Drummaul AM 19; 35–36, 41, 47, 53, 61–63, 67, 70–72, 87–88

O'Neill, family: Drumragh TE 5; 108

O'Neill, family: Dunaghy AM 13; 14

O'Neill, family: Duneane AM 19; 99

O'Neill, family: Dungiven LY 15; 32, 56, 58, 78

O'Neill, family: Faughanvale LY 36; 49

O'Neill, family: Finvoy AM 23; 76

O'Neill, family: Glenavy AM 21; 86

O'Neill, family: Glenwhirry AM 32; 77

O'Neill, family: Glynn AM 26; 17

O'Neill, family: Kilcronaghan LY 31; 69

O'Neill, family: Killead AM 35; 17

O'Neill, family: Killelagh LY 27; 99

O'Neill, family: Kilmore AH 1; 68

O'Neill, family: Kilroot AM 26; 59, 61, 69, 71, 75–76

O'Neill, family: Layd AM 13; 52

O'Neill, family: Maghera LY 18; 10, 24, 40, 48

O'Neill, family: Magheramesk AM 21; 120, 125

O'Neill, family: Misc. DN 17; 117, 121

O'Neill, family: Misc. LY 31; 122, 137

O'Neill, family: Muckamore AM 35; 55–56, 60, 65, 71, 83

O'Neill, family: Racavan AM 13; 89, 101

O'Neill, family: Raloo AM 32; 93, 106, 115

O'Neill, family: Shilvodan AM 19; 131, 135–36

O'Neill, family: Skerry AM 13; 107, 112, 116

O'Neill, family: Tamlaght O'Crilly LY 18; 93, 121

O'Neill, family: Templecorran AM 26; 97

O'Neill, family: Tullyrusk AM 21; 131

O'Neill, Felix [I]: Ballyaghran LY 33; 9

O'Neill, Felix [II]: Ballyaghran LY 33; 9, 23

O'Neill, Francis: Carrickfergus AM 37; 108
O'Neill, Frank: Duneane AM 19; 124
O'Neill, George: Carrickfergus AM 37; 113
O'Neill, George: Muckamore AM 35; 81
O'Neill, Giolla-ruad: Misc. TE 5; 147
O'Neill, Gordon: Ahoghill AM 23; 6
O'Neill, H.B.: Ballynure AM 32; 45
O'Neill, H.B.: Glynn AM 26; 17
O'Neill, H.B.: Misc. TE 5; 146
O'Neill, H.B.: Raloo AM 32; 93
O'Neill, H.B.: Skerry AM 13; 105
O'Neill, H.M.: Drumachose LY 9; 95
O'Neill, H.M.: Layd and Inispollan AM 13; 57
O'Neill, H.R.: Kilmore AH 1; 63
O'Neill, H.R.: Misc. TE 5; 147
O'Neill, Henry: Ardglass DN 17; 12
O'Neill, Henry: Maghera LY 18; 12, 37, 62
O'Neill, Henry [I]: Drummaul AM 19; 64, 70, 87
O'Neill, Henry [II]: Drummaul AM 19; 70
O'Neill, Hester: Ballyaghran LY 33; 9
O'Neill, Hugh: Artrea LY 6; 26
O'Neill, Hugh: Ballynure AM 32; 45, 47, 51
O'Neill, Hugh: Carrickfergus AM 37; 14
O'Neill, Hugh: Coleraine LY 33; 151
O'Neill, Hugh: Donegal DL 39; 48
O'Neill, Hugh: Down DN 17; 42
O'Neill, Hugh: Dungiven LY 15; 59
O'Neill, Hugh: Kilroot AM 26; 61, 71–72
O'Neill, Hugh: Layd and Inispollan AM 13; 57
O'Neill, Hugh: Misc. LY 36; 115
O'Neill, Hugh: Misc. TE 5; 146
O'Neill, Hugh: Tamlaght O'Crilly LY 18; 94, 122,
   128
O'Neill, Hugh: Templecorran AM 26; 96
O'Neill, J.: Comber DN 7; 34
O'Neill, J.B.: Ballyscullion AM 19; 8
O'Neill, J.B.: Carnmoney AM 2; 81
O'Neill, J.B.: Carrickfergus AM 37; 145
O'Neill, J.B.: Culfeightrin AM 24; 45
O'Neill, J.B.: Duneane AM 19; 115
O'Neill, J.B.: Killead AM 35; 46
O'Neill, J.B.: Racavan AM 13; 91, 97–98
O'Neill, James: Aghagallon AM 21; 18, 21
O'Neill, James: Ahoghill AM 23; 39
O'Neill, James: Artrea LY 6; 38
O'Neill, James: Bovevagh LY 25; 60
O'Neill, James: Kilraghts AM 16; 135
O'Neill, James: Maghera LY 18; 43, 46–47
O'Neill, James [I]: Tamlaght O'Crilly LY 18; 116
O'Neill, James [II]: Tamlaght O'Crilly LY 18; 139
O'Neill, Jane [I]: Carrickfergus AM 37; 114
O'Neill, Jane [II]: Carrickfergus AM 37; 129
O'Neill, John: Aghagallon AM 21; 10
O'Neill, John: Aghalee AM 21; 35
O'Neill, John: Ahoghill AM 23; 39

O'Neill, John: Artrea LY 6; 36
O'Neill, John: Ballinderry AM 21; 57
O'Neill, John: Ballintoy AM 24; 29
O'Neill, John: Ballynure AM 32; 64–65
O'Neill, John: Banagher LY 30; 74
O'Neill, John: Culfeightrin AM 24; 55
O'Neill, John: Drumragh TE 5; 112
O'Neill, John: Dungiven LY 15; 113
O'Neill, John: Errigal LY 27; 55
O'Neill, John: Faughanvale LY 36; 24, 35
O'Neill, John: Skerry AM 13; 106, 111
O'Neill, John: Tamlaght TE 20; 77, 104
O'Neill, John [I]: Carrickfergus AM 37; 109
O'Neill, John [I]: Drummaul AM 19; 70–71
O'Neill, John [I]: Duneane AM 19; 111
O'Neill, John [I]: Tamlaght O'Crilly LY 18; 119
O'Neill, John [II]: Carrickfergus AM 37; 131
O'Neill, John [II]: Drummaul AM 19; 70
O'Neill, John [II]: Duneane AM 19; 117
O'Neill, John [II]: Tamlaght O'Crilly LY 18; 133
O'Neill, John [III]: Drummaul AM 19; 71
O'Neill, John [III]: Duneane AM 19; 124
O'Neill, John [IV]: Drummaul AM 19; 87
O'Neill, John [V]: Drummaul AM 19; 90
O'Neill, Lord (Snr): Drummaul AM 19; 42–43, 47,
   63–64, 80, 82, 87
O'Neill, Lord (Snr): Duneane AM 19; 99–100, 112
O'Neill, Lord: Ahoghill AM 23; 2, 7, 15–16, 28, 32
O'Neill, Lord: Antrim AM 29; 3, 17, 19
O'Neill, Lord: Artrea LY 6; 8
O'Neill, Lord: Dungiven LY 15; 34
O'Neill, Lord: Glenavy AM 21; 82–83
O'Neill, Lord: Lough Neagh AM 21; 94–95
O'Neill, Lord: Racavan AM 13; 95
O'Neill, Lord: Rasharkin AM 23; 128
O'Neill, M.K. (Jnr): Ballyaghran LY 33; 3, 9, 12
O'Neill, M.K. (Snr): Ballyaghran LY 33; 9
O'Neill, M.K.: Coleraine LY 33; 64
O'Neill, Marchioness: Drummaul AM 19; 87–88
O'Neill, Martha (nee Hagan): Drummaul AM 19; 70
O'Neill, Martha (nee Stafford): Drummaul AM 19;
   70
O'Neill, Mary: Artrea LY 6; 18, 38
O'Neill, Mary: Carrickfergus AM 37; 121
O'Neill, Mortagh: Misc. TE 5; 146
O'Neill, Mrs: Artrea LY 6; 23, 34
O'Neill, N.C.: Misc. TE 5; 146–47
O'Neill, N.O.: Muckamore AM 35; 69
O'Neill, Neal: Drummaul AM 19; 70
O'Neill, Neill: Killead AM 35; 17, 25, 35, 50
O'Neill, O.R.: Drumachose LY 9; 84
O'Neill, O.R.: Dungiven LY 15; 59
O'Neill, O.R.: Hillsborough DN 12; 88
O'Neill, P.D.: Ballyaghran LY 33; 9
O'Neill, P.O.: Blaris AM 8; 87

O'Neill, Phelim (see also Tyrone): Loughgall AH 1; 80

O'Neill, Phelim: Aghaloo TE 20; 1

O'Neill, Phelim: Ahoghill AM 23; 6

O'Neill, Phelim: Antrim AM 29; 6

O'Neill, Phelim: Ardglass DN 17; 3, 12

O'Neill, Phelim: Ballymoney AM 16; 20

O'Neill, Phelim: Ballymore AH 1; 8, 10, 16

O'Neill, Phelim: Ballyscullion LY 6; 58

O'Neill, Phelim: Banagher LY 30; 106

O'Neill, Phelim: Blaris AM 8; 3, 87

O'Neill, Phelim: Blaris DN 12; 32–33

O'Neill, Phelim: Clogher TE 5; 31

O'Neill, Phelim: Clondermot LY 34; 28

O'Neill, Phelim: Coleraine LY 33; 152

O'Neill, Phelim: Cumber LY 28; 20

O'Neill, Phelim: Derryaghy AM 8; 98

O'Neill, Phelim: Desertmartin LY 31; 56

O'Neill, Phelim: Donaghenry TE 20; 39

O'Neill, Phelim: Drumachose LY 9; 84, 93, 95

O'Neill, Phelim: Drummaul AM 19; 70–72, 87

O'Neill, Phelim: Dungiven LY 15; 35, 42, 59, 107

O'Neill, Phelim: Enniskillen FH 4; 68

O'Neill, Phelim: Grey Abbey DN 7; 72

O'Neill, Phelim: Kilcronaghan LY 31; 69, 75, 77

O'Neill, Phelim: Kildollagh LY 22; 69

O'Neill, Phelim: Loughgall AH 1; 80

O'Neill, Phelim: Loughguile AM 13; 74

O'Neill, Phelim: Macosquin LY 22; 85, 90

O'Neill, Phelim: Magheraculmoney FH 14; 106

O'Neill, Phelim: Magheragall AM 21; 100

O'Neill, Phelim: Magilligan LY 11; 88, 103

O'Neill, Phelim: Misc. DN 17; 118

O'Neill, Phelim: Misc. LY 36; 109–11

O'Neill, Phelim: Tamlaght O'Crilly LY 18; 94–95, 121, 127

O'Neill, Randal (see Antrim, Marquis)

O'Neill, Rev. Arthur: Ballynure AM 32; 69

O'Neill, Rev. Arthur: Carrickfergus AM 37; 71, 103, 133–34, 144, 150, 160, 174

O'Neill, Rev. Arthur: Glynn AM 26; 23

O'Neill, Rev. Arthur: Island Magee AM 10; 35

O'Neill, Rev. Arthur: Kilroot AM 26; 65

O'Neill, Rev. Arthur: Raloo AM 32; 98, 126

O'Neill, Rev. Arthur: Templecorran AM 26; 101

O'Neill, Rev. Hugh: Kilcoo DN 3; 44–45

O'Neill, Rev. James: Drumcree AH 1; 29

O'Neill, Rev. John: Kilmegan DN 3; 55

O'Neill, robber: Errigal Keerogue TE 20; 49

O'Neill, Robert: Ballyaghran LY 33; 9

O'Neill, Rose (see Antrim, Marchioness)

O'Neill, S.B.: Drummaul AM 19; 78

O'Neill, S.M.: Ballynure AM 32; 33, 45, 47, 51, 64, 68

O'Neill, S.M.: Kilroot AM 26; 61, 71–73

O'Neill, S.M.: Templecorran AM 26; 96

O'Neill, S.O.: Muckamore AM 35; 69

O'Neill, Samuel: Muckamore AM 35; 81

O'Neill, Sarah: Muckamore AM 35; 81

O'Neill, Shane: Clonleigh DL 39; 14–15

O'Neill, Shane: Misc. LY 31; 119

O'Neill, Shane: Newry DN 3; 64–65

O'Neill, Shane: Racavan AM 13, 90

O'Neill, Shane: Tullyrusk AM 21; 131

O'Neill, Theophilus: Tamlaght O'Crilly LY 18; 140, 144

O'Neill, Thomas: Drummaul AM 19; 89

O'Neill, Thomas: Kilraghts AM 16; 136

O'Neill, Thomas: Muckamore AM 35; 81

O'Neill, Thomas: Tamlaght TE 20; 78

O'Neill, Widow: Artrea LY 6; 32–33

O'Neill, William: Ballynascreen LY 31; 30

O'Neill, William: Ballyscullion LY 6; 66

O'Neill's Castle: Carrickfergus AM 37; 162

O'Neill's Castle: Killead AM 35; 17, 50

O'Noran's grave: Errigal LY 27; 44, 73

O'Prey, Charles: Misc. DN 17; 122

O'Quin, James: Cumber LY 28; 65

O'Quin, Laurence: Maghera LY 18; 39

O'Quinn, Hugh: Coleraine LY 33; 157

O'Raw, family: Dunaghy AM 13; 17

O'Raw, James: Carrickfergus AM 37; 131

O'Raw, Mrs: Dunaghy AM 13; 24

O'Raw, Neely: Skerry AM 13; 121

O'Raw, Owen: Dunaghy AM 13; 24

O'Raw, Patrick: Dunaghy AM 13; 21–22

O'Rawe, family: Skerry AM 13; 116

O'Regan, Rev. John: Banagher LY 30; 15

O'Regan, Rev. John: Misc. LY 31; 136

O'Reilly, Antonio: Clondermot LY 34; 70

O'Reilly, Bishop: Killelagh LY 27; 102

O'Reilly, Bishop: Maghera LY 18; 69

O'Reilly, Edward: Dungiven LY 15; 49

O'Reilly, family: Drumlumman CN 40; 15

O'Reilly, Mr: Drumlumman CN 40; 14

O'Reilly, Prior: Clondermot LY 34; 70

O'Reilly, Rev. Pat: Drumgoon CN 40; 6

O'Reilly, Rev. Phil: Drumlumman CN 40; 14

O'Reilly, Rev. Terence: Drumgoon CN 40; 6

O'Reilly, Terence: Tullylish DN 12; 147

O'Relie, John: Tomregan FH 4; 129

O'Roarke, man named: Duneane AM 19; 116

O'Robhartaigh, family: Misc. TE 5; 147

O'Rorke, Mr: Kilmacteige SO 40; 188

O'Rourke, Alexander: Ahoghill AM 23; 42

O'Rourke, Ambrose: Ahoghill AM 23; 12, 31, 47

O'Rourke, Ambrose: Drummaul AM 19; 88

O'Rourke, chieftain: Inishmacsaint FH 14; 75

O'Rourke, Edward: Ahoghill AM 23; 42, 47

O'Rourke, family: Dungiven LY 15; 32

O'Rourke, Fergal: Misc. TE 5; 147

O'Rourke, H.: Carlingford LH 40; 59

O'Rourke, Malgarg: Misc. TE 5; 147

O'Rourke, Prince of Breffni: Manorhamilton Union LM 40; 51

O'Sheil, James: Misc. DN 17; 119

O'Sulivan, Rev.: Killyman TE 20; 67

O'Taichid, chieftain: Misc. TE 5; 146

O'Tedy, family: Kilmacteige SO 40; 189

O'Toole, Rev.: Loughgilly AH 1; 86

Oak bank: Lough Swilly DL 38; 103–04

Oak hill: Drumcree AH 1; 34, 40

Oakes (see Oaks): Cumber LY 28; 75

Oakfield bleach mill: Carrickfergus AM 37; 139

Oakfield cotton factory: Carrickfergus AM 37; 139

Oakfield demesne: Galloon FH 4; 94

Oakfield Demesne td: Raphoe DL 39; 126

Oakfield fort [I]: Carrickfergus AM 37; 186

Oakfield fort [II]: Carrickfergus AM 37; 186

Oakfield House: Carrickfergus AM 37; 56–57, 135–36

Oakfield House: Galloon FH 4; 91–92

Oakfield House: Skerry AM 13; 111

Oakfield locality: Carrickfergus AM 37; 94, 174

Oakfield td: Cleenish FH 14; 23, 28, 30

Oakham, Baron: Down DN 17; 42

Oakland House: Skerry AM 13; 110

Oaklands demesne: Kildress TE 20; 59

Oaklands House: Kildress TE 20; 59, 61

Oaklands House: Tamlaght Finlagan LY 25; 100

Oakley House: Down DN 17; 51

Oakly, John: Carrickfergus AM 37; 193

Oaks bleach green: Cumber LY 28; 57–58

Oaks bridge: Cumber LY 28; 10, 34–35, 44, 79

Oaks hill: Camlin AM 21; 63

Oaks House: Banagher LY 30; 22, 32, 113

Oaks House: Cumber LY 28; 34–35, 46–47

Oaks Lodge: Cumber LY 28; 27, 34, 44, 47, 79

Oaks Lodge bleach green: Cumber LY 28; 34, 80

Oaks Lodge bridge: Cumber LY 28; 35

Oaks Lodge House: Banagher LY 30; 30

Oaks school: Cumber LY 28; 75

Oaks td: Clondermot LY 34; 113, 119–20

Oanirk bridge: Lough Swilly DL 38; 133

Oates, William: Ahoghill AM 23; 40

Oatlands House: Desertoghill LY 27; 3, 15

Obre, Elizabeth: Tartaraghan AH 1; 119

Obree, E.: Tartaraghan AH 1; 120–22

Obrie bay: Coleraine LY 33; 99

Ocanotus, St: Magilligan LY 11; 104

Ochel td: Magheraculmoney FH 14; 111–12

Ochentane (see Aghentane): Clogher TE 5; 34

Ochill bog: Ballyclog TE 20; 15

Ochill school: Ballyclog TE 20; 16

Ochill wood: Ballyclog TE 20; 15

Ockyll td: Muckamore AM 35; 82

Oetter Cluig sandbank: Lough Swilly DL 38; 116

Oetter Garroo sandbank: Lough Swilly DL 38; 115–16

Oetteronah sandbank: Lough Swilly DL 38; 115–16

Oetters sandbanks: Lough Swilly DL 38; 115–16

Offaly: Banagher LY 30; 36, 101

Offaly: Clondermot LY 34; 65

Offaly: Faughanvale LY 36; 44

Offley, Maj.: Newry DN 3; 112

Ogg, family: Newry DN 3; 106

Ogg, Mrs: Skerry AM 13; 115

Oghaval (see Oughaval)

Oghill (Aughill) td: Cumber LY 28; 27, 43, 49, 55, 60, 64, 97, 102, 106–07

Oghill chapel: Tamlaght Finlagan LY 25; 79, 100

Oghill cross: Cumber LY 28; 37

Oghill old chapel: Tamlaght Finlagan LY 25; 79

Oghill td: Tamlaght Finlagan LY 25; 72–74, 93

Ogilby, Alexander: Banagher LY 30; 7, 47, 56, 64

Ogilby, Alexander: Cumber LY 28; 4, 9, 30–31, 34, 79, 86

Ogilby, Alexander: Dungiven LY 15; 49, 54, 98, 107, 112

Ogilby, Anne: Carnmoney AM 2; 88

Ogilby, David: Dungiven LY 15; 41, 44, 88

Ogilby, David: Tamlaght Finlagan LY 25; 82

Ogilby, family: Ahoghill AM 23; 25

Ogilby, James: Drumachose LY 9; 104

Ogilby, James: Tamlaght Finlagan LY 25; 100

Ogilby, John: Drumachose LY 9; 73

Ogilby, John: Tamlaght Finlagan LY 25; 81

Ogilby, Leslie: Banagher LY 30; 4, 53, 57, 87

Ogilby, Leslie: Drumachose LY 9; 104

Ogilby, Leslie: Dungiven LY 15; 3–5, 9, 23, 25, 53, 66, 101, 105

Ogilby, Messrs Leslie and Co.: Banagher LY 30; 19

Ogilby, Mr: Aghadowey LY 22; 5

Ogilby, Mr: Dungiven LY 15; 24

Ogilby, R.L.: Ballynascreen LY 31; 6, 13, 20, 22

Ogilby, R.L.: Banagher LY 30; 32

Ogilby, R.L.: Bovevagh LY 25; 22–24

Ogilby, R.L.: Desertmartin LY 31; 56–57, 62

Ogilby, R.L.: Drumachose LY 9; 84, 87, 90, 96–97, 100, 103, 120, 123, 130

Ogilby, R.L.: Dungiven LY 15; 5, 7, 25, 75, 101–02, 110

Ogilby, Robert (Tamlaght Finlagan): Dungiven LY 15; 112

Ogilby, Robert: Banagher LY 30; 2, 4, 12–18, 20, 22–23, 29–30, 33, 59, 73, 111, 115–20, 131

Ogilby, Robert: Coleraine LY 33; 142

Ogilby, Robert: Cumber LY 28; 5, 18, 53, 80, 109–12, 114

Ogilby, Robert: Desertoghill LY 27; 3, 15

Ogilby, Robert: Dungiven LY 15; 4, 6–9, 15, 17–18, 22–23, 50, 52–54, 60–63, 66, 75–76, 89, 95, 97–99, 101, 103–04, 108, 116–18, 119

Ogilby, Robert: Errigal LY 27; 38–40, 58

Ogilby, Robert: Faughanvale LY 36; 40, 45

Ogilby, Robert: Magilligan LY 11; 145

Ogilby, Robert: Misc. LY 31; 121, 129, 135, 143

Ogilby, Robert: Tamlaght Finlagan LY 25; 80, 83, 93–95, 121–22, 124

Ogilby, Samuel: Kilwaughter AM 10; 122

Ogilvy, Rev. Wiliam: Island Magee AM 10; 94

Ogilvy, William: Ardglass DN 17; 1, 3–5, 10–11

Ogle, Francis: Newry DN 3; 98, 103

Ogle, George: Newry DN 3; 98, 103–04

Ogle, J.: Annaclone DN 12; 16

Ogle, J.: Ardglass DN 17; 13–14, 14

Ogle, J. Garvaghy DN 12; 81

Ogle, Samuel: Newry DN 3; 100, 104

Ogle, William: Newry DN 3; 86

Ogleby, John: Balteagh LY 9; 36

Oieter-carrigouver bank: Lough Swilly DL 38; 113

Oieter-more bank: Lough Swilly DL 38; 113

Oieternaghollapagh bank: Lough Swilly DL 38; 113

Oilagh-na-riagh palace: Dungiven LY 15; 33

Oin Paddoin, family: Drumgath DN 3; 20

Oiternamweela bank: Lough Swilly DL 38; 113

Old Castle bridge: Drumachose LY 9; 119

Old Castle Point: Duneane AM 19; 107

Old Church Island: Ballinderry AM 21; 55

Old Church Loanen locality: Aghalee AM 21; 27, 35

Old Deer Park school: Tickmacrevan AM 13; 133

Old Forge bridge: Kilcronaghan LY 31; 67, 78–79

Old Forge church: Drumbeg AM 8; 129

Old Forge font: Drumbeg AM 8; 129

Old Forge fort: Drumbeg AM 8; 130

Old Forge graveyard: Drumbeg AM 8; 129

Old Forge td: Drumbeg AM 8; 127, 129–31, 133

Old Freehold td: Kilwaughter AM 10; 109

Old Glebe td: Misc. DN 17; 125

Old Grange td: Carlingford LH 40; 57, 59

Old Kirk church: Templecorran AM 26; 108, 113, 120

Old Kirk graveyard: Templecorran AM 26; 120

Old Man locality: Newry DN 3; 88

Old Mill bridge: Aghalee AM 21; 27

Old Mill bridge: Newry DN 3; 108

Old Mill burn: Carncastle and Killyglen AM 10; 1

Old Mill corn mill: Templecorran AM 26; 122

Old Mill glen: Templecorran AM 26; 89, 94, 107, 115, 121–22

Old Park House: Carnmoney AM 2; 45, 82

Old Park Lower td: Blaris DN 12; 40–42

Old Park school: Glenavy AM 21; 91

Old Park Upper td: Blaris DN 12; 40

Old Patrick standing stone: Kilraghts AM 16; 130, 135

Old Quay Brae (see Brae Head): Clondermot LY 34; 89

Old Town: Leck DL 39; 115, 117

Old Town bridge: Leck DL 39; 115

Old Town church: Leck DL 39; 116

Old Town school: Leck DL 39; 119

Old Town td: Leck DL 39; 119

Old Warren td: Blaris AM 8; 20, 45, 81–82

Old Warren td: Blaris DN 12; 28

Old Wives brae: Balteagh LY 9; 34

Oldbar hill: Devenish FH 14; 47

Oldbar school: Devenish FH 14; 50

Oldclare village: Kilmacteige SO 40; 193

Olden, Rev.: Kilmore DN 17; 88

Olderfleet anchorage: Island Magee AM 10; 26, 72

Olderfleet Castle: Island Magee AM 10; 31

Olderfleet Castle: Larne AM 10; 125

Oldham, P.: Banagher LY 30; 58, 58

Oldstone Castle (see also Clogh Castle): Dunaghy AM 13; 12, 18

Oldstone Castle: Island Magee AM 10; 65

Oldstone Castle: Muckamore AM 35; 60, 76

Oldstone druid's altar: Muckamore AM 35; 60

Oldstone hamlet: Muckamore AM 35; 55, 60–61, 67, 73, 76–77, 83

Oldstone hill: Muckamore AM 35; 54, 57, 60, 74

Oldstone manor: Dunaghy AM 13; 12, 26

Oldstone manor: Dundermot AM 13; 32

Oldstone manor: Finvoy AM 23; 70

Oldstone manor: Rasharkin AM 23; 127

Oldstone meeting house: Muckamore AM 35; 60, 65

Oldstone plantation: Muckamore AM 35; 79

Oldstone school: Muckamore AM 35; 55, 73, 76–77

Oldstone Sunday school: Muckamore AM 35; 73–74

Oldstone td: Muckamore AM 35; 54, 79

Oldtown bog: Ballyrashane LY 22; 63

Oldtown Deer Park bog: Ballyscullion LY 6; 70

Oldtown Deer Park td: Ballyscullion LY 6; 52, 70, 74, 77

Oldtown Deer Park wood: Ballyscullion LY 6; 44

Oldtown district: Magherafelt LY 6; 81

Oldtown Downing bog: Ballyscullion LY 6; 69

Oldtown Downing td: Ballyscullion LY 6; 69

Oldtown school: Ballyscullion LY 6; 62

Oldtown village: Kilmacteige SO 40; 186, 193–96

Oliver, family: Enniskillen FH 4; 58

Oliver, Henry: Balteagh LY 9; 12, 24, 29

Oliver, Mr (Laragh): Aughnamullen MN 40; 73

Oliver, Mrs: Aughnamullen MN 40; 76

Oliver, Rev. Silver: Loughgall AH 1; 77–79, 81

Olivers, Patrick: Ballyscullion LY 6; 57

Olivia, Pamela: Ardglass DN 17; 9

Olliver, Alexander: Aghanloo LY 11; 21

Olliver, Ann: Killead AM 35; 51

Olliver, James: Drumachose LY 9; 111

Olliver, John: Macosquin LY 22; 101, 108

Olliver, Joseph: Aghanloo LY 11; 13, 16, 22

Olliver, Mrs: Balteagh LY 9; 26

Olliver, Mrs: Drumachose LY 9; 111

Olliver, R.W.: Killead AM 35; 51

Olliver, Robert: Aghanloo LY 11; 18

Olliver, Samuel: Aghanloo LY 11; 13–14, 16, 18, 22

Ollover, Bill: Balteagh LY 9; 44

Ollover, Eliza: Balteagh LY 9; 44

Olly (see Ouley)

Olphert, Mr: Aghadowey LY 22; 27

Olphert, Mr: Bovevagh LY 25; 21, 58

Olphert, Mrs John: Drumachose LY 9; 51, 71–72, 125

Olphert, Rev. John: Drumachose LY 9; 50–51, 68–69, 72, 78, 80–81, 83, 85, 91, 96, 104–05, 108, 119, 122, 125

Olphert, Rev. Richard: Magherafelt LY 6; 102

Olphert, William: Tullaghobegley DL 39; 172

Olpherts, Rev.: Finvoy AM 23; 75

Olpherts, Rev. Richard: Coleraine LY 33; 127

Olpherts, W.: Clonfeacle AH 1; 24, 26

Omagh: Aghaloo TE 20; 2

Omagh: Ardstraw TE 5; 9

Omagh: Ballynascreen LY 31; 7–8, 11, 17–18, 23, 30

Omagh: Banagher LY 30; 31

Omagh: Cappagh TE 5; 19

Omagh: Carnteel TE 20; 24

Omagh: Clogher TE 5; 33, 44

Omagh: Clogherny TE 20; 26–27

Omagh: Clondermot LY 34; 30

Omagh: Clonleigh DL 39; 7

Omagh: Coleraine LY 33; 95, 142

Omagh: Cumber LY 28; 49, 58

Omagh: Desertcreat TE 20; 34

Omagh: Desertmartin LY 31; 57

Omagh: Donegal DL 39; 57

Omagh: Dromore TE 5; 96–97

Omagh: Drumglass TE 20; 42, 45

Omagh: Drumragh TE 5; 104–05, 108–12

Omagh: Enniskillen FH 4; 83

Omagh: Errigal Keerogue TE 20; 46–47, 49, 52

Omagh: Kilcronaghan LY 31; 77

Omagh: Kildress TE 20; 59–61

Omagh: Killeeshil TE 20; 62–64

Omagh: Kilskeery TE 5; 114

Omagh: Longfield TE 5; 128, 132, 135

Omagh: Magheracross FH 14; 94

Omagh: Magheross MN 40; 151–52

Omagh: Misc. DL 39; 187

Omagh: Misc. TE 5; 147

Omagh: Pomeroy TE 20; 70

Omagh: Raphoe DL 39; 124

Omagh: Tynan AH 1; 127

Omagh barony: Cappagh TE 5; 16

Omagh barony: Clogherny TE 20; 25

Omagh barony: Derryvullan FH 14; 31

Omagh barony: Donacavey TE 5; 76–77, 83, 85

Omagh barony: Dromore TE 5; 93

Omagh barony: Drumkeeran FH 14; 62

Omagh barony: Drumragh TE 5; 104

Omagh barony: Longfield TE 5; 131

Omagh barony: Misc. TE 5; 147

Omagh barracks: Drumragh TE 5; 104, 106

Omagh brewery mill: Drumragh TE 5; 110

Omagh bridge: Cappagh TE 5; 20

Omagh bridge: Drumragh TE 5; 108

Omagh chapel (C): Drumragh TE 5; 104, 106

Omagh chapel (M): Drumragh TE 5; 104, 106

Omagh church: Drumragh TE 5; 104, 106–07

Omagh court house: Drumragh TE 5; 104, 107, 111

Omagh dispensary: Clogherny TE 20; 26

Omagh dispensary: Drumragh TE 5; 106, 109

Omagh female school: Drumragh TE 5; 107

Omagh free school: Drumragh TE 5; 107

Omagh gaol: Drumragh TE 5; 104, 111

Omagh hibernian school: Drumragh TE 5; 107

Omagh hospital: Drumragh TE 5; 111

Omagh infirmary: Drumragh TE 5; 104, 106

Omagh inns: Drumragh TE 5; 111

Omagh male school: Drumragh TE 5; 107

Omagh monastery: Drumragh TE 5; 108

Omagh new meeting house (P): Drumragh TE 5; 104, 106

Omagh old meeting house (P): Drumragh TE 5; 104, 106

Omagh parish school: Drumragh TE 5; 107

Omagh preparatory school: Drumragh TE 5; 107

Omeath: Carlingford LH 40; 60

Omeath: Newry DN 3; 64

Omeath coastguard station: Warrenpoint DN 3; 118

Omer, Mr: Drumglass TE 20; 43

Omerbane (see Scotch Omerbane)

Ommerbaan (see Omerbane)

Omna river: Templecarn DL 39; 166

One Man's Lanes locality: Emlaghfad SO 40; 178

Onea river: Inishkeel DL 39; 70

One-beg (see Owenbeg): Banagher LY 30; 2

Onega lake (Russia): Lough Neagh AM 21; 92

Oneilland barony: Kilmore AH 1; 59

Oneilland East barony: Seagoe AH 1; 101, 104

Oneilland East barony: Shankill AH 1; 111

Oneilland West barony: Clonfeacle AH 1; 21, 23

Oneilland West barony: Drumcree AH 1; 28, 34

Oneilland West barony: Kilmore AH 1; 57, 60, 66, 68, 70–73

Oneilland West barony: Loughgall AH 1; 75, 78–79
Oneilland West barony: Montiaghs AH 1; 89
Oneilland West barony: Mullaghbrack AH 1; 94
Oneilland West barony: Tartaraghan AH 1; 117, 119
One-reagh (see Owenreagh)
Oneyfarney td: Drumgoon CN 40; 2
Ooey locality: Lough Swilly DL 38; 125
Ooig-rooey rock: Lough Swilly DL 38; 108
Oona river: Killeeshil TE 20; 64
Oona river: Pomeroy TE 20; 72
Openshaw, family: Carrickfergus AM 37; 93
Openshawe, family: Carrickfergus AM 37; 179
Ora More mountain: Cleenish FH 14; 12
Ora More td: Cleenish FH 14; 14, 30
Oraghbeg East td: Cleenish FH 14; 30
Oraghmore (see Ora More)
Oram chapel: Muckno MN 40; 165, 168
Oram school: Muckno MN 40; 168
Orangefield House: Drumlumman CN 40; 14
Oranloone hill: Killeeshil TE 20; 64
Orbegg td: Killymard DL 39; 101
Orble td: Billy AM 16; 75
Orchard Island: Clondermot LY 34; 34, 106
Orchard lough: Clondermot LY 34; 3, 18
Orchardtown (see Donnybrewer): Faughanvale LY
    36; 34
Ordnance Survey Office (Dublin): Culdaff DL 38;
    22
Ordnance Survey Office: Moville DL 38; 73
Orell, James: Newry DN 3; 99
Organ pillars: Billy AM 16; 42
Oriel district: Faughanvale LY 36; 60
Oriel district: Misc. LY 36; 105
Oriel Temple House: Antrim AM 29; 14
Oriel well: Galloon FH 4; 97
Oriel, Baron (see Ferrard)
Orier (see Orior)
Orior Lower barony: Ballymore AH 1; 1, 7, 12
Orior Lower barony: Kilmore AH 1; 57, 60, 67–69,
    71–73
Oritor hamlet: Kildress TE 20; 61
Orkney Islands (Scotland): Faughanvale LY 36; 11
Orland water: Carrickfergus AM 37; 6–7
Orland, Mr: Killowen LY 33; 173
Orlock Point: Bangor DN 7; 22
Orlock Point: Carrickfergus AM 37; 5
Orlock Point: Holywood DN 7; 82
Orlock Point: Island Magee AM 10; 17
Orlock td: Bangor DN 7; 19
Orlock td: Misc. DN 17; 124
Orme, W.J.: Blaris DN 12; 36–37
Ormeau House: Knockbreda DN 7; 97
Ormond, Duke of: Blaris AM 8; 5
Ormond, Duke of: Carrickfergus AM 37; 32
Ormsby, Mr: Kildress TE 20; 59

Ormsby, Rev.: Cappagh TE 5; 21
Ornbrook, Nicholas: Enniskillen FH 4; 57
Orr and Partners td: Carlingford LH 40; 58
Orr, Alexander: Coleraine LY 33; 63
Orr, Alexander: Maghera LY 18; 79
Orr, Andrew: Aghadowey LY 22; 5–6, 8, 12, 16, 19,
    33
Orr, Andrew: Coleraine LY 33; 63, 104
Orr, Andrew: Kilrea LY 27, 114
Orr, Andrew: Tamlaght O'Crilly LY 18; 89–90, 103
Orr, Ann: Aghadowey LY 22; 36
Orr, Ann: Ballyaghran LY 33; 5, 13, 17–18
Orr, Daniel: Killowen LY 33; 162, 170
Orr, Daniel: Maghera LY 18; 79
Orr, David: Saintfield DN 7; 114
Orr, Elisabeth: Maghera LY 18; 78
Orr, Eliza: Aghadowey LY 22; 36
Orr, Eliza: Kilwaughter AM 10; 116
Orr, Eliza: Muckamore AM 35; 77
Orr, Eliza: Raloo AM 32; 129
Orr, family: Artrea LY 6; 14
Orr, family: Ballywillin AM 16; 32
Orr, family: Magheragall AM 21; 99
Orr, family: Misc. LY 36; 101
Orr, family: Raloo AM 32; 94
Orr, family: Shilvodan AM 19; 136
Orr, family: Templecorran AM 26; 117, 119
Orr, George (see Dunbar): Kilrea LY 27; 110
Orr, George: Artrea LY 6; 24–25
Orr, George: Desertoghill LY 27; 17, 19, 28, 33
Orr, George: Kilcronaghan LY 31; 83
Orr, Hamish: Aghadowey LY 22; 36
Orr, Hugh: Island Magee AM 10; 90
Orr, Isabella: Aghadowey LY 22; 36
Orr, James: Aghadowey LY 22; 36
Orr, James: Island Magee AM 10; 90
Orr, James: Killowen LY 33; 170
Orr, James: Maghera LY 18; 78
Orr, James: Templecorran AM 26; 11, 87, 108, 118
Orr, Jane: Aghadowey LY 22; 36
Orr, John: Ahoghill AM 23; 50
Orr, John: Derrykeighan AM 16; 90
Orr, John: Tamlaght O'Crilly LY 18; 143
Orr, John: Templecorran AM 26; 120
Orr, Joseph: Clondermot LY 34; 79
Orr, Joseph: Coleraine LY 33; 72
Orr, Joseph: Dunboe LY 11; 62
Orr, Joseph: Kilbride AM 29; 149, 152
Orr, Margret Ane: Aghadowey LY 22; 36
Orr, Mary: Carnmoney AM 2; 83
Orr, Mary: Maghera LY 18; 79
Orr, Mary: Tullynakill DN 7; 122
Orr, Miss: Coleraine LY 33; 72
Orr, Mr (Ballylesson): Drumbo DN 7; 60
Orr, Mr (Belfast): Comber DN 7; 37, 40

Orr, Mr (Loughgall): Ballymore AH 1; 15
Orr, Mr: Ballymoney AM 16; 22
Orr, Mrs: Carrickfergus AM 37; 107, 150
Orr, Mrs Andrew: Aghadowey LY 22; 19
Orr, Nathaniel: Donegore AM 29; 130
Orr, Rev.: Annaclone DN 12; 17
Orr, Rev. Robert: Killead AM 35; 46
Orr, Robert: Ballymoney AM 16; 27
Orr, Robert: Ballyrashane LY 22; 66
Orr, Robert: Killowen LY 33; 166, 171–72
Orr, Robert: Raloo AM 32; 126
Orr, Robert: Templecorran AM 26; 120
Orr, Samuel: Antrim AM 29; 7
Orr, Samuel: Ballyaghran LY 33; 7, 24
Orr, Samuel: Coleraine LY 33; 104, 106
Orr, Thomas: Skerry AM 13; 120
Orr, W.: Ballymoney AM 16; 16
Orr, William (Jnr): Ballymoney AM 16; 15, 17
Orr, William (Snr): Ballymoney AM 16; 15–16
Orr, William: Antrim AM 29; 7
Orr, William: Ballyaghran LY 33; 19
Orr, William: Bovevagh LY 25; 43
Orr, William: Coleraine LY 33; 145
Orr, William: Errigal LY 27; 39, 75
Orr, William: Kirkinriola AM 23; 96
Orr, William: Maghera LY 18; 79
Orr, William: Skerry AM 13; 120
Orr, William: Templecorran AM 26; 120
Orr, Wilson: Coleraine LY 33; 73
Orra mountain (see Slieve-an-orra)
Orre, W.J.: Blaris DN 12; 35
Orrell, Lewis: Clondermot LY 34; 49
Orrell, Robert: Termoneeny LY 6; 132
Orrery, Earl of: Down DN 17; 42
Orrery, Honora: Down DN 17; 42
Orrery, Wyngfield: Down DN 17; 42
Orthes (France): Kilbroney DN 3; 34
Osborn, Mr: Drumragh TE 5; 109
Osborne, Archbald: Dromore TE 5; 97–98
Osborne, James: Dromore TE 5; 97
Osborne, John: Dromore TE 5; 97–98
Osborne, John [I]: Misc. DL 39; 186
Osborne, John [II]: Misc. DL 39; 192
Osborne, Martha: Bovevagh LY 25; 28, 55
Osborne, Mrs: Dromore TE 5; 98
Osborne, Mrs: Newry DN 3; 74, 99, 103
Osborne, Rev. Joseph: Bovevagh LY 25; 3
Osborne, Robert: Carrickfergus AM 37; 119
Osborne, Thomas: Dromore TE 5; 97
Osborne, William: Bovevagh LY 25; 2–4, 20,
    22–23, 33, 58
Osbourne, family: Enniskillen FH 4; 58
Osburn, Edward: Bovevagh LY 25; 50
Osburn, family: Misc. LY 36; 104
Oscar, son of Fin: Balteagh LY 9; 16

Oscar, son of Fin: Banagher LY 30; 12
Oscar, son of Fin: Misc. LY 36; 113
Oseland, Edward: Agivey LY 22; 43–44
Oseland, Edward: Desertoghill LY 27; 16
Ossian, son of Fin: Antrim AM 29; 30
Ossian, son of Fin: Ardclinis AM 13; 9
Ossian, son of Fin: Ballynascreen LY 31; 15, 33
Ossian, son of Fin: Banagher LY 30; 12
Ossian, son of Fin: Clondermot LY 34; 106
Ossian, son of Fin: Donaghmore DL 39; 34
Ossian, son of Fin: Dungiven LY 15; 20, 109
Ossian, son of Fin: Layd AM 13; 50–52
Ossian, son of Fin: Misc. LY 31; 127
Ossian, son of Fin: Misc. LY 36; 112–13
Ossian, son of Fin: Muckamore AM 35; 58, 70
Ossory diocese: Urney DL 39; 175
Ossory district: Faughanvale LY 36; 51
Ossory district: Misc. LY 36; 106
Oswald, King: Magilligan LY 11; 88
Oswald, Rev.: Raphoe DL 39; 127
Otre bog: Artrea LY 6; 12, 29
Otre td: Artrea LY 6; 9, 12–13, 22, 25–26, 39–40
Ott mountain: Clonduff DN 3; 5
Otterson, family: Artrea LY 6; 14
Otterson, Michael: Kilcronaghan LY 31; 77
Ouanagh (see Ounagh)
Ouanaher (see Owenaher)
Ouchtach (see Oughtagh)
Oudde, family: Ahoghill AM 23; 25
Oughaval (Mayo): Faughanvale LY 36; 52
Oughaval td: Kilmacteige SO 40; 196
Oughcurragh td: Dromore TE 5; 99
Oughdourish corn mill: Bodoney TE 20; 20
Oughill (see Oghill): Cumber LY 28; 27
Oughill (see Oghill): Tamlaght Finlagan LY 25; 79
Oughill td: Dromore TE 5; 99
Oughill td: Magilligan LY 11; 114
Oughley td: Saintfield DN 7; 118
Oughnadarnod hill: Drumhome DL 39; 59
Oughtagh bog: Cumber LY 28; 46–49
Oughtagh td: Cumber LY 28; 46, 48, 60, 64, 67, 97,
    102–03, 106–07
Oughtagh woods: Cumber LY 28; 103
Oughterard (Aughterard) td: Dromore TE 5; 96–97,
    99
Oughterlin lough: Killygarvan DL 38; 37
Oughtkenley td: Templecarn DL 39; 164
Oughtymore (Oughtemore) td: Magilligan LY 11;
    94–95, 126
Oughtymoyle (Oughtymole) td: Magilligan LY 11;
    95, 126, 135
Oughtymoyle td: Aghanloo LY 11; 38
Oughtymoyle td: Cumber LY 28; 64
Ouley hill: Newry DN 3; 61
Ouley td: Newry DN 3; 61, 110

Ouna mountain: Layd AM 13; 37, 42
Ounagh river: Kilmacteige SO 40; 195
Ounagh td: Kilmacteige SO 40; 195–96
Ouncrannagh (see Cranagh): Lough Swilly DL 38; 101
Ouseley, M.: Misc. LY 36; 107
Ouske lough: Ballynascreen LY 31; 1
Ouske lough: Bodoney TE 20; 20
Outal fort: Dundermot AM 13; 35
Outal td: Dundermot AM 13; 35
Outhill cave: Ballyrashane LY 22; 50, 64
Outhill td: Ballyrashane LY 22; 46, 63, 66
Outlaw, Roger: Carrickfergus AM 37; 80
Ovans, Hugh: Macosquin LY 22; 80, 102
Ovenden, Charles: Enniskillen FH 4; 58, 69
Ovens, Mrs: Clogher TE 5; 41
Overand, Mr (Portadown): Seagoe AH 1; 104
Ovil quarry: Dungiven LY 15; 51
Ovil school: Dungiven LY 15; 116–18
Ovil td: Banagher LY 30; 22, 84, 95
Ovil td: Dungiven LY 15; 22, 26, 47–48, 50, 62, 74, 99, 105, 113
Ovill (see Ovil)
Oville (see Ovil): Banagher LY 30; 84
Oville td: Bovevagh LY 25; 10, 39, 41–42
Oville td: Drumachose LY 9; 117
Oville td: Killowen LY 33; 172
Ovre, Mr: Coleraine LY 33; 98
Owanagher (see Owenaher)
Owanaher (see Owenaher)
Owanahir (see Owenaher)
Owden, John: Blaris AM 8; 55, 84–85
Owden, John: Blaris DN 12; 46, 49
Owden, John: Lambeg AM 8; 140
Owen Glenree river: Skerry AM 13; 113
Owen Keogh river: Dungiven LY 15; 54
Owen Nivien river: Antrim AM 29; 30
Owen the Captain, sage: Misc. LY 36; 112–13
Owen, family: Lambeg AM 8; 135
Owen, Fitzroy: Misc. SO 40; 200
Owen, James: Nilteen AM 35; 102
Owen, Richard: Aghagallon AM 21; 5, 7
Owen, Richard: Aghalee AM 21; 29, 31, 34
Owen, Richard: Blaris AM 8; 70
Owen, Richard: Blaris DN 12; 28
Owen, Richard: Magheramesk AM 21; 118, 122
Owen, Richard: Newry DN 3; 89, 99, 104
Owen, St: Bovevagh LY 25; 5
Owenagaderagh td: Donaghmore DL 39; 38
Owenaher river: Kilmacteige SO 40; 187, 191, 195
Owenaher village: Kilmacteige SO 40; 196
Owenaher waterfall: Kilmacteige SO 40; 187
Owenalena river: Dungiven LY 15; 51, 61, 63
Owenbeg (Owenbig) td: Dungiven LY 15; 10, 22, 26, 49–50, 62, 74, 94

Owenbeg bridge: Banagher LY 30; 5
Owenbeg bridge: Dungiven LY 15; 97
Owenbeg river: Banagher LY 30; 2, 5, 24–26, 29–30, 59, 73
Owenbeg river: Dungiven LY 15; 1, 3, 11, 51, 62–63
Owenbeg td: Banagher LY 30; 22, 50, 84
Owenboy (Owenbwee) td: Killymard DL 39; 100
Owenboy hill: Drumhome DL 39; 59, 61
Owenboy hill: Killymard DL 39; 102
Owenbreedin td: Aghavea FH 4; 23
Owenbuy (see Owenboy)
Owencam river: Banagher LY 30; 12
Owencam waterfall: Banagher LY 30; 12
Owencloghy mountain: Tickmacrevan AM 13; 125
Owencloghy river: Racavan AM 13; 88, 90, 97
Owencloghy river: Tickmacrevan AM 13; 124, 126
Owengallagh bridge: Newtown Crommelin AM 13; 81
Owengallagh river: Dunaghy AM 13; 10–11
Owengallagh river: Dundermot AM 13; 30
Owengallagh river: Newtown Crommelin AM 13; 79, 81
Owenirk td: Mintiaghs DL 38; 65
Owenkillew (see Broughderg)
Owenland (see Owensland)
Owenmore river: Manorhamilton Union LM 40; 47
Owenreagh carn: Ballynascreen LY 31; 10, 24
Owenreagh chapel: Ballynascreen LY 31; 19
Owenreagh lough: Ballynascreen LY 31; 19
Owenreagh mill: Banagher LY 30; 26
Owenreagh mountain: Ballynascreen LY 31; 14, 23
Owenreagh mountain: Leckpatrick TE 5; 120
Owenreagh river: Banagher LY 30; 2, 25–27, 29, 31, 37, 49, 52, 58–59, 73, 88, 99, 113
Owenreagh river: Dungiven LY 15; 1, 3, 51, 63
Owenreagh river: Mevagh DL 38; 54
Owenreagh standing stones: Ballynascreen LY 31; 24
Owenreagh stream: Drumragh TE 5; 104
Owenreagh td: Ballynascreen LY 31; 33, 124, 143
Owens, family: Carnmoney AM 2; 76
Owens, family: Derrykeighan AM 16; 89
Owens, family: Inver AM 26; 53
Owens, family: Racavan AM 13; 100
Owens, James: Ballylinny AM 32; 26
Owens, James: Carrickfergus AM 37; 102
Owens, James: Doagh AM 29; 86, 91, 98
Owens, James: Donegore AM 29; 132
Owens, James: Kilbride AM 29; 136, 138, 141, 150, 154–56
Owens, James: Killead AM 35; 46
Owens, James: Rashee AM 32; 138
Owens, James: Tamlaght TE 20; 78–79, 86
Owens, John: Doagh AM 29; 91, 95, 98

Owens, John: Donegore AM 29; 107, 110
Owens, John: Kilbride AM 29; 138, 141, 150
Owens, John: Killead AM 35; 46
Owens, John: Tamlaght TE 20; 79
Owens, Robert: Killead AM 35; 51
Owens, Robert: Tamlaght TE 20; 79, 83
Owens, Thomas: Donacavey TE 5; 65
Owens, William: Inver AM 26; 53
Owensen (see Morgan)
Owenskerry td: Aghalurcher FH 4; 14

Owensland plantation: Kilbride AM 29; 155
Owensland td: Kilbride AM 29; 136, 138, 140
Owinnaleeniv river: Dungiven LY 15; 82
Owl Island: Inishmacsaint FH 14; 70, 72
Ownaher (see Owenaher)
Oxford: Ballynascreen LY 31; 33
Oxford, Bishop of: Antrim AM 29; 23
Oya-vic-namora grave: Culfeightrin AM 24; 49
Oya-yeilla-gleish giant's grave: Culfeightrin AM 24;
    56–57

P

Packenham, Rev. (Ardbraccan): Enniskeen CN 40; 29

Paddy the Drover's Hole: Bovevagh LY 25; 33

Paddys loch: Templecarn DL 39; 157

Page, Mrs: Hillsborough DN 12; 87

Pagen, John: Newtownards DN 7; 112

Pain, family: Misc. LY 36; 104

Paine, Mr: Newry DN 3; 89

Paine, Samuel: Clondermot LY 34; 79–80

Pakenham corn mill: Drumhome DL 39; 59

Pakenham, Capt.: Clondavaddog DL 38; 7

Pakenham, Col: Ballymartin AM 2; 8

Pakenham, Col: Inishkeel DL 39; 67

Pakenham, Col: Lough Neagh AM 21; 94

Pakenham, Col.: Blaris AM 8; 66

Pakenham, family: Drumhome DL 39; 58–61

Pakenham, family: Killead AM 35; 12, 17, 20

Pakenham, family: Mallusk AM 2; 109

Pakenham, family: Templepatrick AM 35; 116

Pakenham, H.R.: Camlin AM 21; 60, 62, 67–69, 73, 75

Pakenham, H.R.: Killead AM 35; 12–13, 18–19, 37–39, 41–42, 44–45, 47, 49–50, 53

Pakenham, H.R.: Templepatrick AM 35; 109, 143–44

Pakenham, Hercules: Killead AM 35; 47

Pakenham, Lady: Killead AM 35; 19, 39, 52

Pakenham, Rev.: Killead AM 35; 42

Pakenham, Thomas: Ballyscullion LY 6; 54

Palan, William: Derryaghy AM 8; 106

Palantine school: Ballylinny AM 32; 28–29

Palantine Sunday school: Ballylinny AM 32; 29

Pale (Louth): Kilkeel DN 3; 53

Pale (Ulster): Ballynure AM 32; 45

Pale (Ulster): Glynn AM 26; 17

Pale (Ulster): Raloo AM 32; 93

Palisier, Rev. John: Ardstraw TE 5; 9

Pallis, Squire: Drumlumman CN 40; 14

Pallise, family: Drumlumman CN 40; 15

Palmer, family: Blaris DN 12; 30

Palmer, family: Camlin AM 21; 68

Palmer, family: Glenavy AM 21; 86

Palmer, family: Killead AM 35; 17

Palmer, Mr: Ballywillin LY 33; 51

Palmer, Mr: Clogher TE 5; 43

Palmer, Twiss: Clogher TE 5; 41

Palmer, W.H.: Magherafelt LY 6; 110

Palmer, Walter: Muckamore AM 35; 80

Palnagh hill: Tynan AH 1; 124

Palnagh school: Tynan AH 1; 129

Pamplona (Spain): Kilbroney DN 3; 31

Parade school: Kirkinriola AM 23; 121

Paris: Killelagh LY 27; 102

Paris: Misc. LY 31; 137

Park: Banagher LY 30; 44, 90, 100

Park: Cumber LY 28; 4, 6–7, 16, 21, 85

Park bog: Tullylish DN 12; 144

Park bridge: Banagher LY 30; 25

Park bridge: Cumber LY 28; 4, 9

Park Charley Mudtherae locality: Bovevagh LY 25; 12–13, 40

Park corn mill: Armoy AM 24; 4

Park corn mill: Cumber LY 28; 7–8

Park cove: Armoy AM 24; 8

Park flax mill: Armoy AM 24; 4

Park flax mill: Cumber LY 28; 7–8

Park forge: Cumber LY 28; 7

Park fort: Armoy AM 24; 8

Park inn: Cumber LY 28; 7

Park Lands td: Muckamore AM 35; 80

Park locality: Hillsborough DN 12; 88

Park mill–course: Banagher LY 30; 25

Park moss: Carrickfergus AM 37; 32

Park moss: Glenavy AM 21; 78

Park school (see Tireighter): Cumber LY 28; 7

Park td: Armoy AM 24; 2, 4, 8

Park td: Hillsborough DN 12; 86, 88

Park Tireighter td: Cumber LY 28; 30

Park wall: Kilbride AM 29; 150, 155

Park, David: Coleraine LY 33; 128, 132

Park, family: Ballynure AM 32; 56

Park, family: Carnmoney AM 2; 76

Park, family: Misc. LY 36; 104

Park, James: Ballynure AM 32; 43, 64, 66

Park, John: Billy AM 16; 60

Park, John [I]: Ballynure AM 32; 35, 47, 72

Park, John [II]: Ballynure AM 32; 57

Park, Mr: Newry DN 3; 110

Park, Rev. Robert: Ballymoney AM 16; 15–17, 27
Park, Rev. Robert: Coleraine LY 33; 127
Park, Robert: Rasharkin AM 23; 139
Park, Stuart: Carrickfergus AM 37; 116
Park, William: Ballymoney AM 16; 17
Park, William: Ballywillin LY 33; 39
Park, William: Magilligan LY 11; 138, 142
Park, William: Misc. DL 39; 186
Parke, Hannah: Coleraine LY 33; 145
Parke, John: Coleraine LY 33; 145
Parke, Mr: Manorhamilton Union LM 40; 51
Parke, William: Coleraine LY 33; 132
Parker, Ann: Island Magee AM 10; 95
Parker, Campbell: Ramoan AM 24; 108, 126
Parker, family: Enniskillen FH 4; 58, 75
Parker, family: Templepatrick AM 35; 118
Parker, George: Carrickfergus AM 37; 125, 128
Parker, George: Newry DN 3; 99, 103
Parker, James: Ballyrashane LY 22; 57
Parker, James: Carrickfergus AM 37; 194
Parker, James: Newry DN 3; 112
Parker, John: Island Magee AM 10; 95
Parker, Joseph: Kilmore AH 1; 59
Parker, Mary (Jnr): Island Magee AM 10; 95
Parker, Mary (Snr): Island Magee AM 10; 95
Parker, Mary [I]: Island Magee AM 10; 95
Parker, Mary Anne: Kilmore AH 1; 59
Parker, Mr: Killesher FH 14; 87
Parker, Robert: Ballymartin AM 2; 11
Parker, Sally: Island Magee AM 10; 95
Parkes, Henry: Aghalee AM 21; 30
Parkes, James: Maghera LY 18; 73
Parkgate: Antrim AM 29; 22, 50
Parkgate: Ballycor AM 32; 5
Parkgate: Ballylinny AM 32; 16
Parkgate: Connor AM 19; 16–17, 22, 30
Parkgate: Doagh AM 29; 73, 80, 82, 90, 94, 96
Parkgate: Donegore AM 29; 102–03, 106–08,
   110–11, 115, 125–26, 130–34
Parkgate: Kilbride AM 29; 141, 148, 150–51,
   154–55
Parkgate: Nilteen AM 35; 84–86, 88, 90–92, 102–04
Parkgate: Rashee AM 32; 138
Parkgate: Templepatrick AM 35; 118, 138, 141
Parkgate church: Donegore AM 29; 107
Parkgate corn mill: Donegore AM 29; 107
Parkgate cove: Donegore AM 29; 130–31
Parkgate deerpark: Donegore AM 29; 106
Parkgate meeting house: Donegore AM 29; 104,
   106, 111, 126, 129–33
Parkgate meeting house: Nilteen AM 35; 103
Parkgate police house: Donegore AM 29; 102, 131
Parkgate police house: Nilteen AM 35; 103
Parkgate pound: Doagh AM 29; 96

Parkgate school: Donegore AM 29; 104, 126, 131,
   133–34
Parkgate sessions room: Kilbride AM 29; 151
Parkgate sessions room: Nilteen AM 35; 103
Parkgate stamp office: Donegore AM 29; 102
Parkgate toll-gate [I]: Doagh AM 29; 80, 96
Parkgate toll-gate [II]: Doagh AM 29; 80, 96
Parkhill lough: Magheraculmoney FH 14; 103
Parkhill, family: Carrickfergus AM 37; 93
Parkhill, family: Misc. LY 36; 104
Parkhill, James: Coleraine LY 33; 145
Parkhill, John: Clondermot LY 34; 79
Parkhill, Samuel: Carrickfergus AM 37; 149
Parkinson, Arthur: Hillsborough DN 12; 107
Parkinson, family: Blaris AM 8; 21
Parkinson, Robert: Blaris DN 12; 47
Parkmore lough: Kilmacteige SO 40; 193
Parkmore mountain: Dunaghy AM 13; 11
Parkmore mountain: Layd AM 13; 37
Parkmore td: Layd AM 13; 44
Parkmore village: Kilmacteige SO 40; 196
Parkmount House: Carnmoney AM 2; 53
Parknohoran village: Kilmacteige SO 40; 196
Parks, family: Carrickfergus AM 37; 93
Parks, Mr: Carlingford LH 40; 57
Parks, Mrs: Newry DN 3; 98, 103
Parks, Rev.: Tullynakill DN 7; 122
Parnel, Abigail: Drummaul AM 19; 70, 72
Parnell, John: Loughgall AH 1; 81–82
Parnell, William: Loughgall AH 1; 76, 78
Parry, Richard: Muckamore AM 35; 81
Parry, Thomas: Hillsborough DN 12; 97, 105
Parsley Bed locality: Coleraine LY 33; 75
Parson Hall td: Misc. DN 17; 125
Parson's Green glebe: Galloon FH 4; 96–97
Parson's Green Glebe House: Galloon FH 4; 96
Parson's Green Glebe td: Drummully FH 4; 34
Parson's Green Glebe td: Galloon FH 4; 87, 95–96
Parsons town: Blaris AM 8; 89
Parsons, family: Carrickfergus AM 37; 93
Parsons, Laurence: Blaris AM 8; 89
Parsons, Samuel: Newry DN 3; 81, 100–01, 104–05
Parsons, William: Clogher TE 5; 32
Partholanus, chieftain: Kilkeel DN 3; 54
Partridge, Daniel: Derryaghy AM 8; 93, 98, 100,
   113, 115
Pasely, Henry: Drumachose LY 9; 66
Pasely, Neill: Drumachose LY 9; 66
Passage locality: Newry DN 3; 61
Patchel, family: Misc. LY 36; 104
Patchell, Dr: Desertlyn LY 31; 42
Patchell, James: Clondermot LY 34; 78–80
Paterson, Alexander: Ballinderry AM 21; 57
Paterson, Alexander: Carrickfergus AM 37; 121
Paterson, family: Maghera LY 18; 13

Paterson, J.: Magheradrool DN 17; 101
Paterson, James: Carrickfergus AM 37; 112
Paterson, Maryanne: Carrickfergus AM 37; 111
Paterson, Thomas: Magilligan LY 11; 94
Path Head: Carncastle and Killyglen AM 10; 1, 3, 5, 9, 11
Path Head: Tickmacrevan AM 13; 125
Path hill: Glynn AM 26; 4–5, 15, 39, 42
Patison, Andrew: Desertoghill LY 27; 32
Patison, William: Desertoghill LY 27; 29
Patman, Edward: Ahoghill AM 23; 45, 50
Patman, John: Ahoghill AM 23; 21
Patman, Rebecca: Ahoghill AM 23; 21, 45, 51
Patrick lough: Ballynascreen LY 31; 1, 14–15, 19, 23–24
Patrick lough: Clogherny TE 20; 25, 27–28
Patrick lough: Cumber LY 28; 71
Patrick lough: Misc. LY 31; 113, 123–24
Patrick, family: Derrykeighan AM 16; 89
Patrick, James: Ballymoney AM 16; 24
Patrick, John: Billy AM 16; 71
Patrick, John: Kirkinriola AM 23; 96, 99
Patrick, Mr: Ardstraw TE 5; 13
Patrick, Robert: Killead AM 35; 22, 50
Patrick, Samuel: Derrykeighan AM 16; 91
Patrick, St: Aghagallon AM 21; 10, 22
Patrick, St: Aghalurcher FH 4; 1, 9
Patrick, St: Antrim AM 29; 5, 33
Patrick, St: Ardglass DN 17; 12
Patrick, St: Artrea LY 6; 9, 32
Patrick, St: Ballinderry AM 21; 53–54
Patrick, St: Ballyaghran LY 33; 9, 21
Patrick, St: Ballyclug AM 23; 60
Patrick, St: Ballynascreen LY 31; 9, 14, 23
Patrick, St: Ballyscullion AM 19; 10
Patrick, St: Ballyscullion LY 6; 49, 56
Patrick, St: Banagher LY 30; 6, 37, 39
Patrick, St: Billy AM 16; 54
Patrick, St: Bovevagh LY 25; 5
Patrick, St: Cleenish FH 14; 17, 19, 21
Patrick, St: Clogher TE 5; 27
Patrick, St: Clogherny TE 20; 27–28
Patrick, St: Clondermot LY 34; 68, 70
Patrick, St: Clonfeacle AH 1; 23
Patrick, St: Connor AM 19; 23
Patrick, St: Culfeightrin AM 24; 50, 70
Patrick, St: Cumber LY 28; 48, 70
Patrick, St: Currin MN 40; 90
Patrick, St: Derryaghy AM 8; 114
Patrick, St: Derryvullan FH 14; 42
Patrick, St: Desertmartin LY 31; 56–58
Patrick, St: Devenish FH 14; 61
Patrick, St: Donacavey TE 5; 70
Patrick, St: Donaghmore DL 39; 34
Patrick, St: Donaghmoyne MN 40; 109

Patrick, St: Down DN 17; 41–43, 45, 50, 59–61
Patrick, St: Drummaul AM 19; 71
Patrick, St: Drumtullagh AM 16; 103
Patrick, St: Drung CN 40; 19
Patrick, St: Dunboe LY 11; 49, 61
Patrick, St: Duneane AM 19; 100, 106
Patrick, St: Dungiven LY 15; 18, 55–56, 102
Patrick, St: Faughanvale LY 36; 51, 62
Patrick, St: Glynn AM 26; 1, 12, 17, 30
Patrick, St: Kilkeel DN 3; 54
Patrick, St: Killanny MN 40; 133
Patrick, St: Killesher FH 14; 90
Patrick, St: Kilmore AH 1; 62–63
Patrick, St: Kirkinriola AM 23; 94, 122
Patrick, St: Magheracloone MN 40; 140
Patrick, St: Magheracross FH 14; 91, 99
Patrick, St: Magherafelt LY 6; 93, 112
Patrick, St: Magheramesk AM 21; 121
Patrick, St: Magheross MN 40; 148
Patrick, St: Magilligan LY 11; 97, 101, 103–05, 143
Patrick, St: Manorhamilton Union LM 40; 51
Patrick, St: Misc. AM 10; 130
Patrick, St: Misc. DN 17; 119
Patrick, St: Misc. LY 31; 111, 117
Patrick, St: Misc. LY 36; 113
Patrick, St: Muckamore AM 35; 56, 82–83
Patrick, St: Newry DN 3; 63
Patrick, St: Racavan AM 13; 86, 90, 93
Patrick, St: Raloo AM 32; 81, 93
Patrick, St: Ramoan AM 24; 123
Patrick, St: Saul DN 17; 113
Patrick, St: Skerry AM 13; 107, 112–14, 116
Patrick, St: Tamlaght Finlagan LY 25; 109–10
Patrick, St: Tamlaght O'Crilly LY 18; 128
Patrick, St: Templecarn DL 39; 162
Patrick, St: Templepatrick AM 35; 108, 116
Patrick, St: Termoneeny LY 6; 131
Patrick, St: Tullyrusk AM 21; 131–32
Patrick, St: Witter DN 7; 127
Patrick, William: Carnmoney AM 2; 88
Patrick's bed: Dungiven LY 15; 102
Patrick's Purgatory cave: Templecarn DL 39; 166
Patrick's well: Dungiven LY 15; 42, 55, 58, 102, 113
Patten, David: Coleraine LY 33; 72
Patten, H.: Holywood DN 7; 78
Patten, J.: Holywood DN 7; 75
Patten, James: Coleraine LY 33; 106
Patten, Mr (Wheatfield): Tamlaght Finlagan LY 25; 101
Patten, Robert: Finvoy AM 23; 74
Patten, Sarah: Loughgilly AH 1; 86
Patterson, Alexander: Artrea LY 6; 37
Patterson, Alexander: Kilroot AM 26; 67, 79
Patterson, Alexander: Kirkinriola AM 23; 113

Patterson, Anne: Kilraghts AM 16; 132
Patterson, Daniel: Kilraghts AM 16; 132
Patterson, David: Carrickfergus AM 37; 124
Patterson, Elizabeth: Aghadowey LY 22; 36
Patterson, family: Ballinderry AM 21; 51
Patterson, family: Ballyclug AM 23; 63
Patterson, family: Billy AM 16; 58, 68
Patterson, family: Blaris AM 8; 22
Patterson, family: Dromara DN 12; 67
Patterson, family: Dunluce AM 16; 117
Patterson, family: Glenavy AM 21; 86
Patterson, family: Kilraghts AM 16; 130, 130
Patterson, family: Maghera LY 18; 24, 48
Patterson, Francis: Raymoghy DL 39; 140
Patterson, George: Carrickfergus AM 37; 33
Patterson, George: Hillsborough DN 12; 107
Patterson, George: Maghera LY 18; 54
Patterson, Hamilton: Misc. DL 39; 186, 192
Patterson, Henry: Coleraine LY 33; 72
Patterson, Henry: Kilwaughter AM 10; 113
Patterson, Henry: Maghera LY 18; 51, 60
Patterson, Henry: Termoneeny LY 6; 124, 131–32
Patterson, Hugh: Hillsborough DN 12; 105
Patterson, Isaac: Hillsborough DN 12; 105
Patterson, James (Jnr): Maghera LY 18; 42
Patterson, James (Snr): Maghera LY 18; 42
Patterson, James: Artrea LY 6; 26
Patterson, James: Blaris DN 12; 46, 50
Patterson, James: Hillsborough DN 12; 107
Patterson, Jane [I]: Kilraghts AM 16; 132
Patterson, Jane [II]: Kilraghts AM 16; 132
Patterson, John: Aghadowey LY 22; 36
Patterson, John: Dromore DN 12; 78
Patterson, John: Faughanvale LY 36; 24, 35
Patterson, John: Hillsborough DN 12; 107
Patterson, John: Kilraghts AM 16; 132
Patterson, John: Raymoghy DL 39; 139–42
Patterson, Joseph: Aghadowey LY 22; 36
Patterson, Joseph: Carrickfergus AM 37; 129
Patterson, man named: Newry DN 3; 106
Patterson, Margaret: Kilrea LY 27; 129
Patterson, Martha: Kilraghts AM 16; 132
Patterson, Martha: Maghera LY 18; 34
Patterson, Mary: Aghadowey LY 22; 36
Patterson, Miss: Maghera LY 18; 18, 49, 57, 70
Patterson, Mr: Down DN 17; 58
Patterson, Mr: Kinawley FH 4; 115
Patterson, Mrs Robert: Maghera LY 18; 8, 10, 73
Patterson, Nancy: Kilrea LY 27; 129
Patterson, Peter: Kilraghts AM 16; 132
Patterson, R.: Lough Neagh AM 21; 97
Patterson, Rev. (co. Down): Aghadowey LY 22; 26
Patterson, Rev.: Carnmoney AM 2; 75
Patterson, Rev. William: Magherally DN 12; 115
Patterson, Richard: Desertoghill LY 27; 22

Patterson, Ritchard: Aghadowey LY 22; 36
Patterson, Robert: Dunluce AM 16; 123
Patterson, Robert: Kilraghts AM 16; 132
Patterson, Robert: Kilrea LY 27; 129
Patterson, Robert: Maghera LY 18; 73
Patterson, Rose [I]: Kilraghts AM 16; 132
Patterson, Rose [II]: Kilraghts AM 16; 132
Patterson, Samual: Aghadowey LY 22; 36
Patterson, Samuel: Ballyscullion LY 6; 72
Patterson, Samuel: Kilrea LY 27; 129
Patterson, Sarah: Maghera LY 18; 29
Patterson, Thomas: Aghalee AM 21; 34
Patterson, Thomas: Carrickfergus AM 37; 125
Patterson, Thomas: Kilraghts AM 16; 132
Patterson, Thomas: Misc. DL 39; 186, 189
Patterson, Thomas: Tullyaughnish DL 38; 96–97
Patterson, Washington: Maghera LY 18; 72
Patterson, William: Ahoghill AM 23; 40
Patterson, William: Clogher TE 5; 32, 51
Patterson, William: Misc. DL 39; 186
Patterson, William: Misc. LY 31; 130, 140
Patterson, William [I]: Carnmoney AM 2; 49
Patterson, William [II]: Carnmoney AM 2; 77, 79,
    85
Patterson's lough: Magherally DN 12; 112–13
Pattison, John: Magheragall AM 21; 106
Pattison, Thomas: Blaris DN 12; 46, 50
Pattison, William: Newry DN 3; 99, 104
Patton, Alexander: Drumachose LY 9; 104
Patton, Andrew: Tullyaughnish DL 38; 91
Patton, Ann: Ballyrashane LY 22; 66
Patton, Ann: Macosquin LY 22; 122
Patton, Capt.: Blaris AM 8; 33
Patton, David: Maghera LY 18; 63
Patton, Dr (Tanderagee): Ballymore AH 1; 4, 9
Patton, Edward: Ballyrashane LY 22; 66
Patton, family: Ballywillin AM 16; 32
Patton, family: Blaris AM 8; 33
Patton, family: Macosquin LY 22; 84, 119
Patton, family: Magheragall AM 21; 101
Patton, Henry: Kilrea LY 27; 129
Patton, J.: Newtownards DN 7; 113
Patton, James: Clondermot LY 34; 79
Patton, James: Inver AM 26; 52
Patton, James: Macosquin LY 22; 100, 104, 121–22
Patton, James: Tamlaght O'Crilly LY 18; 115
Patton, Jane: Carrickfergus AM 37; 119
Patton, John: Tamlaght O'Crilly LY 18; 95, 115
Patton, John: Urney DL 39; 179
Patton, L.: Newtownards DN 7; 112
Patton, Martha: Kilrea LY 27; 129
Patton, Mary: Macosquin LY 22; 122
Patton, Mathew [I]: Ballyrashane LY 22; 66
Patton, Mathew [II]: Ballyrashane LY 22; 66
Patton, Matthew: Kilrea LY 27; 129

Patton, Misses: Blaris AM 8; 33
Patton, Misses: Magheragall AM 21; 101
Patton, Mr (Fanad): Lough Swilly DL 38; 117
Patton, Mr (Knockmore): Blaris AM 8; 33
Patton, Mr [I]: Clondavaddog DL 38; 4, 8
Patton, Mr [II]: Clondavaddog DL 38; 5
Patton, Nancy (Jnr): Kilrea LY 27; 129
Patton, Nancy (Snr): Kilrea LY 27; 129
Patton, Patrick: Derryvullan FH 14; 43
Patton, Rev. David: Island Magee AM 10; 68, 70
Patton, Rev. Francis: Magheragall AM 21; 101
Patton, Rev. Isaac: Templepatrick AM 35; 117, 123,
    133–34, 144–45
Patton, Robert: Carrickfergus AM 37; 113
Patton, Robert [I]: Ballyrashane LY 22; 64
Patton, Robert [II]: Ballyrashane LY 22; 66
Patton, S.: Newtownards DN 7; 112
Patton, Samual: Macosquin LY 22; 122
Patton, Sarah: Kilrea LY 27; 129
Patton, Thomas: Ballyrashane LY 22; 66
Patton, Thomas: Ballywillin LY 33; 50
Patton, W.: Newtownards DN 7; 112
Patton, William: Drumachose LY 9; 104, 106
Patton, William: Kilrea LY 27; 129
Patton, William [I]: Macosquin LY 22; 107
Patton, William [II]: Macosquin LY 22; 122
Paul, Andrew: Coleraine LY 33; 72
Paul, Andrew: Termoneeny LY 6; 133
Paul, Anne Jane: Termoneeny LY 6; 133
Paul, David: Maghera LY 18; 32, 34
Paul, Elizabeth: Dunboe LY 11; 80
Paul, James: Carrickfergus AM 37; 112
Paul, James: Coleraine LY 33; 105–06
Paul, James: Maghera LY 18; 70
Paul, James: Magherafelt LY 6; 110
Paul, Jane: Maghera LY 18; 80
Paul, John: Coleraine LY 33; 72, 129
Paul, John: Maghera LY 18; 61
Paul, John: Skerry AM 13; 120
Paul, Martha: Maghera LY 18; 80
Paul, Mary: Termoneeny LY 6; 133
Paul, Moses: Skerry AM 13; 120
Paul, Mrs J.T.: Kilcronaghan LY 31; 88
Paul, Rev. J.T.: Kilcronaghan LY 31; 74, 81
Paul, Rev. John: Aghadowey LY 22; 22
Paul, Rev. John: Carnmoney AM 2; 46, 57, 75, 82,
    105
Paul, Rev. John: Carrickfergus AM 37; 70, 102, 144,
    146
Paul, Rev. John: Raloo AM 32; 118, 131
Paul, Rev. John: Tamlaght O'Crilly LY 18; 106
Paul, Robert: Coleraine LY 33; 73
Paul, Robert: Skerry AM 13; 120
Paul, Samuel: Ahoghill AM 23; 33
Paul, Sarah: Dunboe LY 11; 80

Paul, Smylie: Kilcronaghan LY 31; 83
Paul, St: Clones FH 4; 29
Paul, Thomas: Ballinderry TE 20; 12–13
Paul, William: Coleraine LY 33; 105
Paul, William: Dunboe LY 11; 80
Paull, John: Macosquin LY 22; 117
Paull, Thomas: Errigal LY 27; 68
Pawlet, George: Clondermot LY 34; 55
Pawrick, family: Drumgath DN 3; 20
Paxton, minor: Newry DN 3; 109
Paxton, surgeon: Hillsborough DN 12; 105
Payne, Elizabeth: Ballyculter DN 17; 27
Payne, John: Carrickfergus AM 37; 193
Payne, John: Kilcronaghan LY 31; 86
Payne, Valentine: Ballyculter DN 17; 27
Peacock, Alexander: Newry DN 3; 99–100, 104
Peacock, Chestnut: Ballymoney AM 16; 24
Peacock, family: Kirkinriola AM 23; 124
Peacock, James: Coleraine LY 33; 129
Peacock, man named: Armoy AM 24; 8
Peacock, Neill: Ballyrashane LY 22; 57
Peacock, Samuel: Ballymoney AM 16; 23
Peaden, J.: Newtownards DN 7; 112
Peadon, R.: Newtownards DN 7; 112
Peady, William: Kilcronaghan LY 31; 85
Peake, William: Carrickfergus AM 37; 109
Pearce, Mr: Misc. LY 36; 118
Pearce, William: Templepatrick AM 35; 150
Pearson, David: Duneane AM 19; 120
Pearson, James: Bright DN 17; 36
Pearson, Mrs: Conwal DL 39; 27
Peast td: Magheross MN 40; 148
Peat Hole mill: Aughnamullen MN 40; 72
Peat, Allan: Killowen LY 33; 159
Peat, Mrs: Killowen LY 33; 158, 168
Peden, Alexander: Donegore AM 29; 130
Peden, Alexander: Glenwhirry AM 32; 78
Peden, John: Kilcronaghan LY 31; 77
Peden, Mr: Misc. LY 31; 124
Peden, Thomas: Newry DN 3; 99, 103
Peeble, family: Enniskillen FH 4; 58
Peebless, John: Termoneeny LY 6; 133
Peebless, William: Dunboe LY 11; 63
Peel, family: Ballinderry AM 21; 51
Peel, Henry: Blaris DN 12; 41
Peel, Robert: Ballyscullion LY 6; 60
Peggsland locality: Carrickfergus AM 37; 94
Pelan, family: Blaris AM 8; 21
Pelan, family: Lambeg AM 8; 135
Pelan, George: Blaris AM 8; 55, 62, 84
Pelan, George: Blaris DN 12; 40, 45, 49, 55, 62, 84
Pelan, Samuel: Blaris DN 12; 46, 50
Pelan, William: Duneane AM 19; 111, 113, 116–17,
    119
Pellapor (see Pellipar)

Pellipar demesne: Dungiven LY 15; 2–3, 9, 11, 15, 51, 106
Pellipar estate: Dungiven LY 15; 104–05
Pellipar House: Ballynascreen LY 31; 6, 13
Pellipar House: Banagher LY 30; 4–5, 73
Pellipar House: Bovevagh LY 25; 43
Pellipar House: Cumber LY 28; 53
Pellipar House: Dungiven LY 15; 9, 53, 76, 113
Pellipar manor: Dungiven LY 15; 5, 50, 66, 101–02
Pellipar td: Dungiven LY 15; 75
Pemberton, Rev.: Killea and Taughboyne DL 39; 92
Pennal, Edward: Carrickfergus AM 37; 135
Pennall, Robert: Raloo AM 32; 129
Pennel, family: Glynn AM 26; 45
Pennel, William: Raloo AM 32; 130
Penney, John: Drumballyroney DN 3; 13
Pennington, family: Blaris AM 8; 21
Pennington, John: Blaris AM 8; 52
Pennington, John: Blaris DN 12; 50
Penny, James [I]: Carrickfergus AM 37; 40, 175
Penny, James [II]: Carrickfergus AM 37; 76
Penny, John: Island Magee AM 10; 90
Pennysland locality: Carrickfergus AM 37; 94
Pentland, Mr: Inniskeen MN 40; 128
Pentland, Mr: Killanny MN 40; 134
Peoples, family: Misc. LY 36; 104
Pepper, Mr: Kilmore AH 1; 71
Pepper, William: Seapatrick DN 12; 135
Perch rock: Ardglass DN 17; 1
Percival, Col: Derryvullan FH 14; 38
Percival, Col: Emlaghfad SO 40; 181
Percival, Col.: Boho FH 14; 8
Percival, Henry: Newtown Crommelin AM 13; 84
Percival, Mr: Dromore TE 5; 98–99
Percy, Anne: Dromore DN 12; 74
Percy, John: Rashee AM 32; 140
Percy, Rev. Thomas: Dromore DN 12; 74–75
Percy, Thomas: Ballycor AM 32; 7
Perkins, Thomas: Clonleigh DL 39; 15
Permir cave: Dunboe LY 11; 78
Perrot, John: Billy AM 16; 38
Perrot, John: Coleraine LY 33; 131, 151
Perry, family: Kirkinriola AM 23; 124
Perry, George: Donacavey TE 5; 77, 81
Perry, Mary: Clogherny TE 20; 25–26
Perry, Mary: Donacavey TE 5; 76–77, 86–87
Perry, Mr: Clogherny TE 20; 27
Perry, Mr: Loughinisland DN 17; 97
Perry, Samuel: Ballymoney AM 16; 16–17
Perry, Sarah: Carrickfergus AM 37; 122
Perry, William: Kilcronaghan LY 31; 85
Perth: Aghadowey LY 22; 14
Pervis, family: Misc. LY 36; 104
Pery, Andrew: Killymard DL 39; 108
Peter, St: Ballymore AH 1; 6

Peter, St: Clones FH 4; 29
Peter, St: Lissan LY 31; 105
Peter, St: Maghera LY 18; 9, 55
Peter's cave: Carrickfergus AM 37; 86
Peterborough (England): Ballywillin LY 33; 31, 43
Peterborough hamlet: Donaghmoyne MN 40; 107
Peters, James: Ahoghill AM 23; 38
Peters, John: Ahoghill AM 23; 49
Peters, John: Kirkinriola AM 23; 122
Peters, William: Ahoghill AM 23; 38
Petes td: Carlingford LH 40; 57, 59
Petheronel, family: Drumgath DN 3; 20
Petrie, G.: Aghanloo LY 11; 7–8
Petrie, G.: Balteagh LY 9; 43
Petrie, G.: Banagher LY 30; 36, 52–53, 131
Petrie, G.: Bovevagh LY 25; 8–9, 18, 21
Petrie, G.: Clondermot LY 34; 8, 106
Petrie, G.: Cumber LY 28; 66
Petrie, G.: Dungiven LY 15; 106, 109
Petrie, G.: Magilligan LY 11; 118
Petrie, G.: Tamlaght Finlagan LY 25; 104, 125
Petticrew, I.: Comber DN 7; 38
Petticrew, John: Templepatrick AM 35; 132
Pettigo: Belleek FH 14; 6
Pettigo: Donegal DL 39; 47
Pettigo: Drumkeeran FH 14; 65
Pettigo: Magheraculmoney FH 14; 107
Pettigo: Templecarn DL 39; 156, 158, 161–62, 166, 168, 170
Pettigo bridge: Drumkeeran FH 14; 64–65
Pettigo chapel (C): Templecarn DL 39; 158
Pettigo chapel (M): Templecarn DL 39; 158
Pettigo church: Templecarn DL 39; 158
Pettigo dispensary: Templecarn DL 39; 161
Pettigo market house: Templecarn DL 39; 158
Pettigo new bridge: Templecarn DL 39; 158–59
Pettigo old bridge: Templecarn DL 39; 159
Pettigo river: Templecarn DL 39; 162, 166
Pettigo td: Templecarn DL 39; 164
Pettigoe (see Pettigo)
Pettigrew, Andrew: Skerry AM 13; 119
Pettigrew, J.: Comber DN 7; 35
Pettigrew, Joseph: Maghera LY 18; 49–50
Pettigrew, Matthew: Layd AM 13; 41
Pettigrew, Robert: Kilraghts AM 16; 133
Pettigrew, Robert: Maghera LY 18; 79
Pettigrew, Thomas [I]: Maghera LY 18; 51
Pettigrew, Thomas [II]: Maghera LY 18; 79
Petty, William: Clondermot LY 34; 62, 70–71
Petty, William: Faughanvale LY 36; 32, 55
Petty, William: Kilrea LY 27; 112
Peyton, Rotsel: Clondermot LY 34; 47
Pharas td: Loughguile AM 13; 76
Pharoah's fort: Rasharkin AM 23; 137
Pharoah's fort cove: Rasharkin AM 23; 137–38

Pheddyglass (see Feddyglass): Misc. DL 39; 196
Phelan, Martin: Newry DN 3; 99, 104
Phelemy Roe's carn: Loughguile AM 13; 74
Phenix, James: Blaris DN 12; 38
Phenix, James: Hillsborough DN 12; 107
Phenix, Trevor: Hillsborough DN 12; 107
Phenix, William: Hillsborough DN 12; 107
Phenix, Wills: Hillsborough DN 12; 107
Pherson, John: Tamlaght TE 20; 75, 93, 128, 136
Phibs, Mr: Emlaghfad SO 40; 181
Phiddyglass (see Feddyglass): Misc. DL 39; 189
Philadelphia: Aghadowey LY 22; 35–38
Philadelphia: Aghanloo LY 11; 39
Philadelphia: Agivey LY 22; 44–45
Philadelphia: Ahoghill AM 23; 37
Philadelphia: Artrea LY 6; 38
Philadelphia: Ballyaghran LY 33; 18, 27–28
Philadelphia: Ballylinny AM 32; 20, 29
Philadelphia: Ballymartin AM 2; 11
Philadelphia: Ballynascreen LY 31; 21
Philadelphia: Ballyrashane LY 22; 53, 65–66
Philadelphia: Ballyscullion AM 19; 13
Philadelphia: Ballywillin LY 33; 42, 51
Philadelphia: Balteagh LY 9; 43–44
Philadelphia: Bovevagh LY 25; 59–60, 60
Philadelphia: Carnmoney AM 2; 88
Philadelphia: Coleraine LY 33; 74, 145–46
Philadelphia: Cumber LY 28; 80
Philadelphia: Derryvullan FH 14; 43
Philadelphia: Desertlyn LY 31; 47
Philadelphia: Desertmartin LY 31; 62
Philadelphia: Doagh AM 29; 98
Philadelphia: Drumachose LY 9; 132–34
Philadelphia: Dunboe LY 11; 54, 80–81
Philadelphia: Duneane AM 19; 123
Philadelphia: Errigal LY 27; 48, 65–66
Philadelphia: Kilcronaghan LY 31; 84
Philadelphia: Kildollagh LY 22; 75
Philadelphia: Killelagh LY 27; 99
Philadelphia: Killowen LY 33; 165, 172
Philadelphia: Kilrea LY 27; 129–30
Philadelphia: Lissan LY 31; 108–09
Philadelphia: Macosquin LY 22; 122
Philadelphia: Maghera LY 18; 18, 78–80
Philadelphia: Magherafelt LY 6; 104, 112
Philadelphia: Magilligan LY 11; 94–95
Philadelphia: Tamlaght Finlagan LY 25; 118–19
Philadelphia: Termoneeny LY 6; 126, 132
Philip, King: Armoy AM 24; 9
Philip, King: Killead AM 35; 32
Philip, St: Carrickfergus AM 37; 41, 49
Philips, Dudley: Aghanloo LY 11; 4
Philips, Edward: Carrickfergus AM 37; 109
Philips, George: Tickmacrevan AM 13; 132
Philips, R.: Aughnamullen MN 40; 75

Philips, Sgt: Camlin AM 21; 74
Philips, Thomas: Aghanloo LY 11; 4
Philips, Thomas: Magilligan LY 11; 92
Phillips, Dr: Carrickfergus AM 37; 145
Phillips, Dudley: Ballyscullion LY 6; 51, 58
Phillips, family: Ballyscullion LY 6; 33
Phillips, family: Blaris AM 8; 22
Phillips, family: Derryaghy AM 8; 103
Phillips, family: Drumachose LY 9; 83, 90–91, 129
Phillips, George: Ballyscullion LY 6; 51–52, 58
Phillips, George: Drumachose LY 9; 66
Phillips, Gov.: Ballyscullion LY 6; 57
Phillips, Gov.: Magherafelt LY 6; 100
Phillips, James: Blaris AM 8; 50
Phillips, James: Blaris DN 12; 45, 49
Phillips, James: Maghera LY 18; 58
Phillips, John: Ballynure AM 32; 73
Phillips, John: Derryaghy AM 8; 96
Phillips, Mary: Ballynure AM 32; 53
Phillips, Mr (Drumbrain): Aghabog MN 40; 63
Phillips, Mr: Ardclinis AM 13; 6
Phillips, R.S.: Killymard DL 39; 101–02
Phillips, Samuel: Longfield TE 5; 129
Phillips, Squire: Balteagh LY 9; 7, 26
Phillips, Thomas: Ballyscullion LY 6; 56–57
Phillips, Thomas: Carrickfergus AM 37; 195
Phillips, Thomas: Clondermot LY 34; 55, 57–75
Phillips, Thomas: Coleraine LY 33; 156
Phillips, Thomas: Drumachose LY 9; 90–92, 117
Phillips, Thomas: Faughanvale LY 36; 12–13,
   31–32, 54–64
Phillips, Thomas: Magilligan LY 11; 83
Phillips, Thomas: Tamlaght Finlagan LY 25; 94, 105
Phillips, William: Ballynascreen LY 31; 27, 32
Phillips' lands: Tamlaght Finlagan LY 25; 94
Phillott, Rev. J.R.: Ramoan AM 24; 96
Philpot, Thomas: Hillsborough DN 12; 106
Phinnis Islands: Cleenish FH 14; 29
Phipps, Rev.: Drummaul AM 19; 69
Phynedh, Prince of Denmark: Errigal LY 27; 77
Picken and Halliday, Messrs: Inver AM 26; 54
Picken, family: Ahoghill AM 23; 25
Picken, family: Carrickfergus AM 37; 93, 179
Pickeram, family: Magherafelt LY 6; 95
Picket, Mary: Tamlaght Finlagan LY 25; 118
Picket, William: Tamlaght Finlagan LY 25; 118
Pickett, William: Tamlaght Finlagan LY 25; 90
Picts' House cave: Culfeightrin AM 24; 41
Piedmount td: Ballymascanlan LH 40; 56
Piers, Henry: Island Magee AM 10; 77
Piers, William: Carrickfergus AM 37; 43
Piery, Alixander: Tamlaght Finlagan LY 25; 119
Piery, Maryjane: Tamlaght Finlagan LY 25; 119
Pigeon cave: Desertegney DL 38; 24
Pigeon cove: Dunboe LY 11; 78

Pigeon cove: Island Magee AM 10; 101
Pigeon Island: Glynn AM 26; 9–10
Pigeon Island Castle: Ardstraw TE 5; 11
Pigeon Knoll locality: Kilroot AM 26; 69, 77
Pigeon Rock North mountain: Clonduff DN 3; 5
Pigeon Rock South mountain: Clonduff DN 3; 5
Piggott, Henry: Carrickfergus AM 37; 129
Piggott, Izabella: Errigal LY 27; 50
Pike, William: Tullyniskan TE 20; 139–40
Pilate, Pontius: Dungiven LY 15; 36
Pilkerton, Alexander: Raymoghy DL 39; 140
Pilson, Mr: Killyleagh DN 17; 85
Pinchers bay: Lough Swilly DL 38; 99
Pinching, Rev. William: Magheross MN 40; 143
Pinkerton, John: Ballyrashane LY 22; 64
Pinkerton, Miss (St Johnstown): Killea and
   Taughboyne DL 39; 88
Pinkerton, Mr: Killea and Taughboyne DL 39; 87
Pinkerton, Sarah: Carrickfergus AM 37; 108
Pinkerton, William: Raphoe DL 39; 128
Pinkerton's mill: Killea and Taughboyne DL 39; 87
Piper hill: Blaris AM 8; 87
Piper hill: Derryaghy AM 8; 92
Piper, Hugh: Garvaghy DN 12; 83
Piper, John: Aghanloo LY 11; 21–22, 25
Piper, William: Tamlaght Finlagan LY 25; 119
Piper's bridge: Mevagh DL 38; 58
Piper's Island: Enniskillen FH 4; 43
Piper-hill td: Galloon FH 4; 95
Pirytz (Germany): Newry DN 3; 68
Pitan, Rotsell: Faughanvale LY 36; 50
Pitcairn, Mrs: Raphoe DL 39; 127
Pittsburg (America): Magherafelt LY 6; 112
Plaiskin Head: Billy AM 16; 41
Plaister locality: Misc. DL 39; 186, 195
Plaister plantation: Misc. DL 39; 189
Plantagenet, Richard: Carrickfergus AM 37; 43
Plantation House: Lambeg AM 8; 139
Planting hill: Kilroot AM 26; 57
Plaster td: Ballymascanlan LH 40; 55
Plea Isle td: Raymoghy DL 39; 139
Pleaskin Head: Billy AM 16; 36, 39
Plough Little rock: Ardkeen DN 7; 1
Plough rock: Ardkeen DN 7; 1
Plover plain: Blaris DN 12; 27
Plover plain: Derryaghy AM 8; 113
Pluck corn mill: Leck DL 39; 116
Pluck td: Convoy DL 39; 19
Pluck td: Leck DL 39; 119
Plunket, Gen.: Blaris AM 8; 3
Plunket, Rev.: Clogher TE 5; 40
Plunket, W.C.: Kilcronaghan LY 31; 81
Plunkett, Capt.: Clondermot LY 34; 27
Plunkett, family: Enniskillen FH 4; 58
Plunkett, Joseph: Aughnamullen MN 40; 76

Plunkett, Joseph: Donaghmoyne MN 40; 110
Plunkett, Joseph: Inniskeen MN 40; 128
Plunkett, Lord: Drumgoon CN 40; 8
Plunkett, Lord: Ematris MN 40; 119
Plunkett, Lord: Enniskillen FH 4; 77
Plunkett, Maj.: Blaris DN 12; 33
Plunkett, Rev.: Aughnamullen MN 40; 76–77
Plymouth Sound (England): Coleraine LY 33; 124
Poagher, family: Carrickfergus AM 37; 93
Poague, Samuel: Carrickfergus AM 37; 113
Pocoke, William: Clondermot LY 34; 81
Poe bridge: Ardstraw TE 5; 10
Poe bridge: Cappagh TE 5; 17, 20
Pogue, family: Carrickfergus AM 37; 179
Pogue, James: Kilroot AM 26; 77
Pogue, William: Carrickfergus AM 37; 160, 162,
   172
Pogue, William: Drummaul AM 19; 90
Pogue, William: Duneane AM 19; 124
Point of Three Townlands pit: Banagher LY 30; 64
Point td: Cleenish FH 14; 30
Pointz, Toby: Newry DN 3; 74
Pointzpass (see Poyntzpass)
Pokrigh, Rigard: Enniskillen FH 4; 72
Pokrigh, William: Enniskillen FH 4; 72
Poland: Newry DN 3; 68
Poland's Steps ford: Annaclone DN 12; 13
Polantammy school: Ballymoney AM 16; 26
Poleglass corn mill: Derryaghy AM 8; 111
Poleglass House: Derryaghy AM 8; 110
Poleglass td: Derryaghy AM 8; 101, 121
Poleglass thread manufactory: Derryaghy AM 8;
   110
Polepatrick corn mill: Magherafelt LY 6; 92
Polepatrick td: Magherafelt LY 6; 92, 112
Polin, Thomas: Newry DN 3; 95, 98, 103
Pollglass (see Poleglass)
Pollick, J.H.: Ballymoney AM 16; 16
Pollnabralk (see Polnabrock)
Pollock, Ann (Jnr): Macosquin LY 22; 122
Pollock, Ann (Snr): Macosquin LY 22; 122
Pollock, David: Ballyscullion LY 6; 65
Pollock, Eliza: Macosquin LY 22; 122
Pollock, family: Billy AM 16; 68
Pollock, family: Derrykeighan AM 16; 89
Pollock, family: Misc. LY 36; 104, 104
Pollock, George [I]: Macosquin LY 22; 85–86, 100,
   115–16
Pollock, George [II]: Macosquin LY 22; 122
Pollock, George [III]: Macosquin LY 22; 122
Pollock, H.: Balteagh LY 9; 21
Pollock, Henry: Macosquin LY 22; 91
Pollock, James [I]: Macosquin LY 22; 122
Pollock, James [II]: Macosquin LY 22; 122
Pollock, James [III]: Macosquin LY 22; 122

Pollock, Jane: Macosquin LY 22; 122
Pollock, John: Ballyrashane LY 22; 54, 63
Pollock, John: Ballyscullion LY 6; 70
Pollock, John: Billy AM 16; 77
Pollock, John: Macosquin LY 22; 122
Pollock, John: Newry DN 3, 67
Pollock, Joseph: Templepatrick AM 35; 152
Pollock, Martha: Macosquin LY 22; 122
Pollock, Mary (see Corry)
Pollock, Mary Jane: Macosquin LY 22; 122
Pollock, Matthew: Aghanloo LY 11; 22
Pollock, Matthew: Drumachose LY 9; 71, 85, 124
Pollock, Robert: Kildollagh LY 22; 75
Pollock, Robert: Macosquin LY 22; 122
Pollock, Samuel: Bovevagh LY 25; 4, 21, 57
Pollock, W.: Newtownards DN 7; 112
Pollock, Widow: Billy AM 16; 69
Pollock, William: Ahoghill AM 23; 40
Pollock, William: Drumachose LY 9; 52, 83, 87, 120
Pollock, William: Duneane AM 19; 124
Polnabrock lough: Bovevagh LY 25; 1, 33
Polnamuicka hole: Bovevagh LY 25; 33
Pomeroy: Desertcreat TE 20; 34–36
Pomeroy: Kildress TE 20; 60
Pomeroy: Pomeroy TE 20; 70–72
Pomeroy chapel: Pomeroy TE 20; 70
Pomeroy demesne: Desertcreat TE 20; 34
Pomeroy meeting house: Pomeroy TE 20; 70
Pomeroy national school: Pomeroy TE 20; 70
Pomeroy ph: Ballinderry TE 20; 11
Pomeroy ph: Desertcreat TE 20; 32
Pomeroy ph: Drumglass TE 20; 43
Pomeroy ph: Killeeshil TE 20; 64
Pomeroy school: Pomeroy TE 20; 70
Pomeroy, Rev. A.W.: Desertmartin LY 31; 54, 60
Pomeroy, Rev. A.W.: Drumachose LY 9; 104
Pomeroy, Rev. A.W.: Magilligan LY 11; 89, 115
Pomperania (Germany): Newry DN 3; 68
Ponsonby and Alexander, Messrs: Clondermot LY 34; 105, 113–20
Ponsonby and Alexander, Messrs: Cumber LY 28; 56
Ponsonby, Bishop: Faughanvale LY 36; 45
Ponsonby, Eliza: Carrickfergus AM 37; 122
Ponsonby, family: Clondermot LY 34; 29
Ponsonby, family: Kilrea LY 27; 114
Ponsonby, George: Cumber LY 28; 58
Ponsonby, Lady: Clondermot LY 34; 33, 105
Ponsonby, Mr [I]: Clondermot LY 34; 38
Ponsonby, Mr [II]: Clondermot LY 34; 106
Ponsonby, Richard: Cumber LY 28; 58
Ponsonby, Sarah: Ballyscullion LY 6; 59
Ponsonby, W.B.: Cumber LY 28; 58
Ponsonby, W.R.: Cumber LY 28; 58
Ponsonby, William [I]: Cumber LY 28; 58

Ponsonby, William [II]: Cumber LY 28; 58
Pont-y-cymmer (Wales): Cumber LY 28; 59
Poobles (Peebles) td: Aghalee AM 21; 26–28
Poobles fort: Aghalee AM 21; 36
Poobles school: Aghalee AM 21; 40
Pooke, John: Ballyscullion LY 6; 57
Pool Dhu lough: Donegal DL 39; 42
Pool, Alixander: Errigal LY 27; 71
Pool, Anne: Maghera LY 18; 79
Pool, family: Maghera LY 18; 13
Pool, Hannah: Maghera LY 18; 79
Pool, James: Maghera LY 18; 79
Pool, Jane: Maghera LY 18; 79
Pool, John [I]: Maghera LY 18; 53
Pool, John [II]: Maghera LY 18; 79
Pool, John [III]: Maghera LY 18; 79
Pool, Matthew: Maghera LY 18; 79
Pool, Robert: Maghera LY 18; 79
Pool, Samuel: Maghera LY 18; 79
Poor Woman rock: Magilligan LY 11; 84
Popper, Mr (Drumcree): Drumcree AH 1; 36
Port Ballintrae: Ballywillin LY 33; 33–34
Port Ballintrae: Dunluce AM 16; 105, 108–10, 116
Port Ballintray (see Port Ballintrae)
Port Ballyrean locality: Leck DL 39; 115
Port Bawn bay: Desertegney DL 38; 24, 29
Port Bradan bay: Ballintoy AM 24; 14
Port Bradan fisheries: Ballintoy AM 24; 12
Port Caimnon church: Dunluce AM 16; 117
Port Coon bay: Billy AM 16; 41
Port Coon cave: Billy AM 16; 42
Port Crommelin harbour: Layd AM 13; 39, 43, 45
Port Crommelin harbour: Newtown Crommelin AM 13; 82
Port district: Glencolumbkille DL 39; 65
Port Fadd bay: Billy AM 16; 41
Port Ganniay bay: Billy AM 16; 41
Port Hall locality: Taughboyne DL 39; 151
Port lough: Killea and Taughboyne DL 39; 79, 83, 87–89
Port lough: Taughboyne DL 39; 150, 155
Port Moon bay: Billy AM 16; 41
Port Noffer bay: Billy AM 16; 41–43
Port Reostan bay: Billy AM 16; 41, 43
Port Tooraa bay: Inishmacsaint FH 14; 75
Port Vinegar bay: Layd AM 13; 45
Port, David: Tamlaght O'Crilly LY 18; 127
Port, Mr: Maghera LY 18; 56
Portachack creek: Lough Swilly DL 38; 110
Portachalh creek: Lough Swilly DL 38; 125
Portadown: Ballyclog TE 20; 19
Portadown: Ballymore AH 1; 1, 3, 9–11
Portadown: Blaris AM 8; 16, 73
Portadown: Clonfeacle AH 1; 25
Portadown: Coleraine LY 33; 96–98

Portadown: Donaghenry TE 20; 38
Portadown: Drumcree AH 1; 28–29, 32–33, 35–41
Portadown: Drumglass TE 20; 42, 45
Portadown: Killyman AH 1; 55
Portadown: Killyman TE 20; 68, 68
Portadown: Kilmore AH 1; 58, 60, 62–64, 66–73
Portadown: Loughgall AH 1; 80–82
Portadown: Montiaghs AH 1; 91–93
Portadown: Seagoe AH 1; 101–03, 105–10
Portadown: Tamlaght TE 20; 122
Portadown: Tartaraghan AH 1; 117–18, 120–22
Portadown bridge: Coleraine LY 33; 97
Portadown bridge: Drumcree AH 1; 30, 32, 34, 36
Portadown bridge: Seagoe AH 1; 104, 106
Portadown chapel: Drumcree AH 1; 29
Portadown chapel of ease (see Portadown church)
Portadown church: Drumcree AH 1; 29, 35
Portadown dispensary: Drumcree AH 1; 35–36
Portadown dispensary: Seagoe AH 1; 106
Portadown distillery: Drumcree AH 1; 35–36, 41
Portadown infant school: Drumcree AH 1; 30, 35
Portadown meeting house: Drumcree AH 1; 35
Portadown meeting house: Seagoe AH 1; 108
Portadown old bridge: Drumcree AH 1; 30, 35
Portadown old bridge: Seagoe AH 1; 106
Portaferry: Ballyculter DN 17; 25, 27
Portaferry: Ballyphilip DN 7; 7, 9–10, 12, 14
Portaferry: Carrickfergus AM 37; 45
Portaferry: Derryaghy AM 8; 114
Portaferry: Down DN 17; 45
Portaferry: Kilclief DN 17; 79
Portaferry: Killyleagh DN 17; 83, 85, 87
Portaferry: Misc. DN 17; 117, 119, 125–26
Portaferry: Rathmullan DN 17; 108
Portaferry: Witter DN 7; 126
Portaferry Castle: Ballyphilip DN 7; 12
Portaferry chapel (C): Ballyphilip DN 7; 10
Portaferry chapel (M): Ballyphilip DN 7; 10–11
Portaferry chapel (W): Ballyphilip DN 7; 10
Portaferry church: Ballyphilip DN 7; 7, 10
Portaferry distillery: Ballyphilip DN 7; 12
Portaferry harbour: Ballyphilip DN 7; 11
Portaferry House: Ballyphilip DN 7; 14
Portaferry market house: Ballyphilip DN 7; 11–12
Portaferry meeting house: Ballyphilip DN 7; 10
Portaferry school [I]: Ballyphilip DN 7; 11
Portaferry school [II]: Ballyphilip DN 7; 11
Portaferry school [III]: Ballyphilip DN 7; 11
Portahapple creek: Ballyaghran LY 33; 2, 26
Portaheag creek: Lough Swilly DL 38; 110
Portaleen creek: Lough Swilly DL 38; 110
Portaleene (see Portaleen)
Portaling creek: Lough Swilly DL 38; 114–15
Portaluaghan (see Portluaghan)
Portalung creek: Lough Swilly DL 38; 109–10

Portamuck creek: Lough Swilly DL 38; 110
Portanure (see Portinure)
Portarlington td: Carlingford LH 40; 58
Portaronan creek: Lough Swilly DL 38; 107
Portasantal waterguard station: Lough Swilly DL 38; 109
Portavoe (Portavo) td: Bangor DN 7; 19, 22
Portavoe corn mill: Donaghadee DN 7; 49
Portavoe House: Annahilt DN 12; 22
Portavoe House: Bangor DN 7; 21–23
Portavoe House: Comber DN 7; 39
Portavoe House: Magheradrool DN 17; 101–02
Portavoe House: Saintfield DN 7; 118
Portavoe House: Templecorran AM 26; 99
Portavoe manor: Misc. DN 17; 124
Portavoe td: Donaghadee DN 7; 49
Portavoe td: Misc. DN 17; 124
Portavogie td: Ballywalter DN 7; 17–18
Portavogie td: Misc. DN 17; 125
Portbaan Anny creek: Lough Swilly DL 38; 101
Portbaan creek: Lough Swilly DL 38; 128, 133
Portbhinagharrell creek: Lough Swilly DL 38; 109
Portbuan (see Portbaan)
Portcairn port: Ramoan AM 24; 120
Portcambel: Misc. DN 17; 126
Portclare church: Errigal Truagh MN 40; 123
Portcool creek: Ballyaghran LY 33; 2, 26
Portdian creek: Ballyaghran LY 33; 2, 26
Portduillig creek: Lough Swilly DL 38; 124
Porteous, Rev.: Boho FH 14; 8
Porter, Alexander: Kilcronaghan LY 31; 87
Porter, Alexander: Newry DN 3; 83
Porter, Andrew: Cumber LY 28; 74, 76
Porter, family: Billy AM 16; 58, 68
Porter, Fredrick: Newry DN 3; 74
Porter, H.E.: Donaghmoyne MN 40; 108
Porter, H.E.: Killanny MN 40; 132
Porter, H.E.: Magheracloone MN 40; 141
Porter, H.E.: Magheross MN 40; 147–49
Porter, H.J.: Seagoe AH 1; 102
Porter, Hans: Aghaderg DN 12; 10
Porter, Hugh: Drumgooland DN 3; 24
Porter, James: Dungiven LY 15; 90
Porter, James: Raymoghy DL 39; 140
Porter, John: Carrickfergus AM 37; 128
Porter, John: Kilcronaghan LY 31; 86
Porter, John: Raymoghy DL 39; 142, 187–88
Porter, Mr: Cumber LY 28; 53
Porter, Mr: Drumcree AH 1; 30
Porter, Mr: Misc. LY 31; 130
Porter, Mrs: Drumachose LY 9; 81, 131
Porter, R.: Urney DL 39; 179
Porter, Rev.: Loughgilly AH 1; 86
Porter, Rev.: Magilligan LY 11; 138
Porter, Rev.: Mevagh DL 38; 58

Porter, Rev. Classon: Inver AM 26; 53

Porter, Rev. Classon: Kilwaughter AM 10; 120

Porter, Rev. Classon: Larne AM 10; 127

Porter, Rev. Classon: Raloo AM 32; 129–30

Porter, Rev. Grey: Donaghmoyne MN 40; 107

Porter, Rev. Grey: Clogher TE 5; 40

Porter, Rev. J.G: Clogher TE 5; 41

Porter, Rev. J.G.: Cleenish FH 14; 22, 28–29

Porter, Rev. J.G.: Derrybrusk FH 4; 32

Porter, Rev. J.G.: Derryvullan FH 14; 37, 43, 46

Porter, Rev. J.G.: Donacavey TE 5; 73, 76–77, 85–87

Porter, Rev. J.G.: Enniskillen FH 4; 77, 82

Porter, Rev. J.G.: Kilskeery TE 5; 114–15

Porter, Rev. J.G.: Kinawley FH 4; 117

Porter, Rev. J.N.: Carrickfergus AM 37; 70, 102, 134, 144

Porter, Rev. J.S.: Kilcronaghan LY 31; 82

Porter, Rev. James: Drumgooland DN 3; 22, 25

Porter, Rev. John: Billy AM 16; 51

Porter, Rev. John: Clogher TE 5; 28, 52

Porter, Rev. Philip: Ardstraw TE 5; 8

Porter, Rev. William: Aghanloo LY 11; 10, 14

Porter, Rev. William: Drumachose LY 9; 76–77, 104

Porter, Robert: Dunboe LY 11; 59

Porter's Lodge House: Carnmoney AM 2; 84

Porters, family: Ballynure AM 32; 56

Portersland locality: Carrickfergus AM 37; 94, 174

Porteus, Mr: Clogher TE 5; 40

Portevlin creek: Lough Swilly DL 38; 131

Portevlin rock: Lough Swilly DL 38; 131

Portgallan creek: Ballyaghran LY 33; 2, 26

Portglannon (see Portglenone)

Portglenone: Ahoghill AM 23; 2–4, 6–9, 11–12, 14–16, 19–20, 25, 29–33, 38, 40–43, 45

Portglenone: Ballyscullion AM 19; 1–2, 4, 9–10, 12

Portglenone: Coleraine LY 33; 98, 102

Portglenone: Drummaul AM 19; 40, 43, 51–52, 70–71, 83

Portglenone: Duneane AM 19; 113

Portglenone: Dungiven LY 15; 69

Portglenone: Finvoy AM 23; 70–71, 73

Portglenone: Kilcronaghan LY 31; 72, 82

Portglenone: Killagan AM 23; 83

Portglenone: Kilrea LY 27; 111, 121, 127

Portglenone: Kirkinriola AM 23; 99, 108

Portglenone: Maghera LY 18; 3, 9, 30, 53, 64, 74

Portglenone: Rasharkin AM 23; 130–33

Portglenone: Tamlaght O'Crilly LY 18; 82–84, 87–92, 96, 98, 102, 104, 106–11, 120–21, 123–24, 135, 138–42

Portglenone: Termoneeny LY 6; 122

Portglenone barracks: Ahoghill AM 23; 7

Portglenone barracks: Tamlaght O'Crilly LY 18; 88

Portglenone bridge: Ahoghill AM 23; 2, 6–8, 11, 14, 29–31

Portglenone bridge: Coleraine LY 33; 102

Portglenone bridge: Tamlaght O'Crilly LY 18; 83, 90, 92, 108

Portglenone Castle: Ahoghill AM 23; 6, 14, 26

Portglenone chapel: Ahoghill AM 23; 7, 11, 30

Portglenone church: Ahoghill AM 23; 2, 7, 11, 30–31

Portglenone classical school: Ahoghill AM 23; 43, 50

Portglenone court house: Ahoghill AM 23; 7, 11, 22, 42, 50

Portglenone court house school: Ahoghill AM 23; 7, 22, 42, 50

Portglenone curacy: Ahoghill AM 23; 1, 16

Portglenone Erasmus Smith female school: Ahoghill AM 23; 2, 20–21, 32, 45, 47

Portglenone Erasmus Smith male school: Ahoghill AM 23; 2, 20–21, 32, 44–45, 47

Portglenone ferry: Ahoghill AM 23; 6

Portglenone House: Ahoghill AM 23; 12

Portglenone library: Ahoghill AM 23; 8

Portglenone library: Tamlaght O'Crilly LY 18; 99

Portglenone meeting house: Ahoghill AM 23; 2, 7, 11, 30–31, 43, 47

Portglenone school: Ahoghill AM 23; 50

Portglenone school: Tamlaght O'Crilly LY 18; 88

Portglenone Sunday school [I]: Ahoghill AM 23; 47

Portglenone Sunday school [II]: Ahoghill AM 23; 47

Porthall bog: Clonleigh DL 39; 1, 5

Porthall House: Clonleigh DL 39; 13 185, 188

Porthall plantation: Clonleigh DL 39; 5

Porthall school: Clonleigh DL 39; 9

Porthall td: Clonleigh DL 39; 9–10, 12, 16, 198

Portinaghy td: Donagh MN 40; 98

Portingall, John: Ballyscullion LY 6; 57

Portinure (Portanare) td: Clonleigh DL 39; 12, 198

Portland (England): Shankill AH 1; 111

Portland: Misc. LY 31; 114

Portlee td: Drummaul AM 19; 53

Portlock, Capt. J.E.: Banagher LY 30; 58

Portlock, Capt. J.E.: Bovevagh LY 25; 23

Portlock, Capt. J.E.: Clondermot LY 34; 4, 76, 83, 88

Portlock, Capt. J.E.: Cumber LY 28; 11, 58, 83, 109

Portlock, Capt. J.E.: Currin MN 40; 88

Portlock, Capt. J.E.: Drumachose LY 9; 130

Portlock, Capt. J.E.: Faughanvale LY 36; 27, 29, 42, 45, 67, 80

Portlock, Capt. J.E.: Misc. LY 36; 117–18

Portlough: Misc. DL 39; 188

Portlough orchard: Misc. DL 39; 189

Portlough td: Misc. DL 39; 195

Portloughan td: Saul DN 17; 114–15

Portluaghan creek: Lough Swilly DL 38; 107, 109, 132–33

Portluargan creek: Lough Swilly DL 38; 107

Portluargan waterguard station: Lough Swilly DL 38; 107

Portmore Castle: Ballinderry AM 21; 43, 51, 54–56

Portmore creek: Ballyaghran LY 33; 2, 26

Portmore creek: Lough Swilly DL 38; 107–09, 111–12

Portmore deerpark: Ballinderry AM 21; 56

Portmore House: Ballinderry AM 21; 42–43

Portmore lough (see Lough Beg)

Portmore school: Ballinderry AM 21; 57

Portmore td: Ballinderry AM 21; 43

Portmuck: Island Magee AM 10; 83–84, 90

Portmuck abbey: Island Magee AM 10; 104

Portmuck bay: Island Magee AM 10; 17, 27, 29, 31, 50, 72–73, 86

Portmuck Castle: Island Magee AM 10; 26, 43, 47, 50–54, 63, 71, 76, 99, 104, 129

Portmuck coastguard station: Island Magee AM 10; 22, 89

Portmuck flour mill: Island Magee AM 10; 81

Portmuck graveyard: Island Magee AM 10; 99–100

Portmuck lime quarries: Island Magee AM 10; 73

Portmuck manor: Island Magee AM 10; 74

Portmuck old church: Island Magee AM 10; 43

Portmuck old church: Island Magee AM 10; 63

Portmuck pier: Island Magee AM 10; 21–22, 76, 78, 80, 105

Portmuck quay: Island Magee AM 10; 80

Portmuck td: Island Magee AM 10; 21, 31, 73, 95, 99

Portmuck watchhouse: Island Magee AM 10; 89

Portmuck watchtower: Island Magee AM 10; 52

Portmuck windmill: Island Magee AM 10; 73

Portmush creek: Lough Swilly DL 38; 122–24

Portna: Ahoghill AM 23; 29

Portna: Lough Neagh AM 21; 95

Portna: Rasharkin AM 23; 128

Portna eel-weirs: Kilrea LY 27; 106, 110–11, 113, 127

Portna eel-weirs: Kirkinriola AM 23; 101, 118

Portna eel-weirs: Rasharkin AM 23; 129

Portna ferry: Kilrea LY 27; 111

Portna fisheries: Kilrea LY 27; 105

Portna Point: Macosquin LY 22; 96

Portna rocks: Coleraine LY 33; 97, 99, 102

Port-na-baw bay: Billy AM 16; 41

Portnablaaghy td: Templecarn FH 14; 118

Portnablagh creek: Lough Swilly DL 38; 121

Port-na-callian bay: Billy AM 16; 41

Portnacarrick: Drumachose LY 9; 94

Portnaclogduff hill: Inishmacsaint FH 14; 71

Portnaclogduff td: Inishmacsaint FH 14; 70

Portnagaarley creek: Lough Swilly DL 38; 137

Portnaglash creek: Lough Swilly DL 38; 125

Portnamuika creek: Lough Swilly DL 38; 106

Port-na-plaiskin bay: Billy AM 16; 41, 43

Portnasnow Glebe td: Enniskillen FH 4; 71, 82

Port-na-Spania bay: Billy AM 16; 41–42

Port-na-tober bay: Billy AM 16; 41, 43

Port-na-truin bay: Billy AM 16; 41

Portnecrannaght district: Misc. SO 40; 199

Portnegrannagh (see Portnecrannaght)

Portnelligate lough: Tynan AH 1; 124

Portnorris church: Drumcree AH 1; 38

Portnorris House: Drumcree AH 1; 38–39

Portora Castle: Enniskillen FH 4; 45

Portora Castle: Rossorry FH 14; 117

Portora school: Coleraine LY 33; 137

Portora school: Rossorry FH 14; 117

Portora td: Rossorry FH 14; 115, 117

Portory manor: Misc. FH 4; 133

Portpatrick (Scotland): Ardclinis AM 13; 6

Portresk school: Ballywillin AM 16; 35

Portrush: Ballyaghran LY 33; 1, 6, 8, 13, 15, 21–23, 26–27

Portrush: Ballyrashane LY 22; 49, 53–54

Portrush: Ballywillin LY 33; 29–34, 36–37, 39, 41, 44–48

Portrush: Billy AM 16; 46

Portrush: Coleraine LY 33; 66, 75, 77, 82, 85, 88–89, 91–92, 95, 120, 128–29, 132, 134, 143, 148

Portrush: Dunboe LY 11; 51

Portrush: Dunluce AM 16; 108, 112

Portrush: Errigal LY 27; 61, 63

Portrush: Kildollagh LY 22; 70

Portrush: Lough Swilly DL 38; 137

Portrush: Mevagh DL 38; 62

Portrush baths: Ballywillin LY 33; 31, 48

Portrush chapel: Ballywillin LY 33; 31, 40–41, 43, 48

Portrush chapel of ease: Ballywillin LY 33; 31, 43, 48

Portrush chapel school: Ballywillin LY 33; 48

Portrush coastguard station: Ballyaghran LY 33; 12, 29

Portrush Cottage school: Ballywillin LY 33; 31, 40

Portrush dispensary: Ballywillin LY 33; 32, 36, 38–39, 46, 48

Portrush dock: Coleraine LY 33; 79

Portrush east pier: Coleraine LY 33; 124

Portrush graveyard: Ballywillin LY 33; 49

Portrush harbour: Ballyrashane LY 22; 51

Portrush harbour: Ballywillin LY 33; 30–32, 36, 38, 44

Portrush harbour: Coleraine LY 33; 53, 75–85, 99, 102–03, 123–25, 148–49, 151–52

Portrush hotel: Ballywillin LY 33; 31, 43, 48–49

Portrush infirmary: Coleraine LY 33; 81

Portrush new wharf: Coleraine LY 33; 78–79

Portrush north pier: Coleraine LY 33, 78–79, 123–25

Portrush old church: Ballywillin LY 33; 49

Portrush old harbour: Coleraine LY 33; 125

Portrush quarries: Ballywillin LY 33; 38

Portrush quarries: Coleraine LY 33; 123–24

Portrush quay: Ballywillin LY 33; 31

Portrush quay: Coleraine LY 33; 88

Portrush saltworks: Ballywillin LY 33; 31, 44

Portrush school: Ballywillin LY 33; 40–41, 48

Portrush south pier: Coleraine LY 33; 79, 123–25

Portrush stone wharf: Coleraine LY 33; 54, 75, 77–79

Portrush storehouse [I]: Ballywillin LY 33; 44

Portrush storehouse [II]: Ballywillin LY 33; 44

Portrush storehouse [III]: Ballywillin LY 33; 44

Portrush Sunday school: Ballywillin LY 33; 41

Portrush tower: Ballywillin AM 16; 34

Portrush west pier: Coleraine LY 33; 123

Portrush wharf: Ballywillin LY 33; 44

Portrush wharf: Coleraine LY 33; 78–79, 84, 123

Ports td: Galloon FH 4; 95

Portsallagh creek: Lough Swilly DL 38; 137–38

Portsalon creek: Lough Swilly DL 38; 100

Portstewart: Ballyaghran LY 33; 1–3, 5–8, 10–12, 14–16, 20–22, 24, 26

Portstewart: Ballywillin LY 33; 32, 34, 45, 47

Portstewart: Coleraine LY 33; 63, 66, 89, 91, 120, 128–29, 132, 143

Portstewart: Drumballyroney DN 3; 11

Portstewart: Dunboe LY 11; 47, 51

Portstewart: Killygarvan DL 38; 46

Portstewart: Mevagh DL 38; 62

Portstewart: Taughboyne DL 39; 150

Portstewart baths: Ballyaghran LY 33; 3, 20, 25

Portstewart bay: Ballyaghran LY 33; 2, 6, 11

Portstewart chapel: Ballyaghran LY 33; 3–4, 18, 25

Portstewart church: Ballyaghran LY 33; 7

Portstewart coastguard station: Ballyaghran LY 33; 12, 27

Portstewart dispensary (see Agherton): Ballyaghran LY 33; 1

Portstewart female school: Ballyaghran LY 33; 17

Portstewart female Sunday school: Ballyaghran LY 33; 18

Portstewart harbour: Ballyaghran LY 33; 2, 5–6, 26

Portstewart hotel: Ballyaghran LY 33; 3, 20, 25

Portstewart infant school: Ballyaghran LY 33; 16–18

Portstewart male Sunday school: Ballyaghran LY 33; 18

Portstewart meeting house: Ballyaghran LY 33; 3–4, 16, 20, 25

Portstewart post office: Ballyaghran LY 33; 25

Portstewart quarries: Ballyaghran LY 33; 26

Portstewart school: Ballyaghran LY 33; 3, 25

Portugal: Drummaul AM 19; 87

Portvagh creek: Lough Swilly DL 38; 131

Portvagh saltworks: Lough Swilly DL 38; 131

Posstuey village: Kilmacteige SO 40; 195

Postley, Alexander: Newry DN 3; 98, 103

Postley, family: Ramoan AM 24; 107

Poston, Catherine: Banagher LY 30; 97

Poston, Henry: Banagher LY 30; 98

Poston, Kitty: Banagher LY 30; 97

Poston, man named: Banagher LY 30; 38

Poston, Robert: Banagher LY 30; 44, 56, 61, 70, 83–84, 99, 112

Pots rocks: Templecorran AM 26; 91

Pottagh td: Dunboe LY 11; 58, 81

Potter, Mr (Dublin): Tullynakill DN 7; 122

Potter, Mr: Saintfield DN 7; 118

Potter, Rev. David: Island Magee AM 10; 88–89, 96, 99

Potters Walls House: Antrim AM 29; 21

Potters Walls school: Antrim AM 29; 41

Potters Walls td: Antrim AM 29; 21

Potterton, Mr: Clogher TE 5; 41

Pottinger, Capt.: Derrykeighan AM 16; 78, 84

Pottinger, Thomas: Carrickfergus AM 37; 134–35

Potts, family: Ballinderry AM 21; 53

Potts, Jane: Annaclone DN 12; 18

Potts, John: Blaris DN 12; 40

Poul-a-gollum cavern: Boho FH 14; 9

Pound clachan: Misc. DN 17; 127

Pounden, Mr: Aghabog MN 40; 65

Powell, Isaac: Carrickfergus AM 37; 151

Powlett, George: Coleraine LY 33; 94

Poynings, Edward: Carrickfergus AM 37; 43

Poyntz, Charles: Ballymore AH 1; 7, 11

Poyntz, Toby: Ballymore AH 1; 7, 9, 11

Poyntzpass: Aghaderg DN 12; 9

Poyntzpass: Ballymore AH 1; 1, 3, 5–6, 9–10, 12–14, 16–18

Poyntzpass: Misc. DN 17; 131

Poyntzpass: Montiaghs AH 1; 91

Poyntzpass: Mullaghbrack AH 1; 96

Poyntzpass: Saintfield DN 7; 118

Poyntzpass: Seagoe AH 1; 108

Poyntzpass Castle: Aghaderg DN 12; 7

Poyntzpass chapel: Ballymore AH 1; 6

Poyntzpass church: Ballymore AH 1; 6

Poyntzpass corn mill: Ballymore AH 1; 18

Poyntzpass dispensary: Ballymore AH 1; 4, 10–11

Poyntzpass flax mill: Ballymore AH 1; 18

Poyntzpass infant school: Ballymore AH 1; 7

Poyntzpass Kildare school: Ballymore AH 1; 7
Poyntzpass meeting house: Ballymore AH 1; 6
Poyntzpass national school: Ballymore AH 1; 7
Poyntzpass school: Ballymore AH 1; 9, 11
Prablin td: Tullyaughnish DL 38; 97
Pratt, Col: Conwal DL 39; 24, 26–27
Pratt, Col: Leck DL 39; 115, 117–19
Pratt, J.T.: Coleraine LY 33; 110
Pratt, Mr: Castletown LH 40; 61
Pratt, Rev. Joseph: Conwal DL 39; 27
Pratt, Rev. W.H.: Clogher TE 5; 40
Pratt, Rev. W.H.: Donagh MN 40; 100–03, 105
Pratt, Rev. W.H.: Drummaul AM 19; 69
Pray, family: Templecorran AM 26; 117, 119
Preaching field: Ballynure AM 32; 65
Prehen: Clondermot LY 34; 7, 31, 102
Prehen: Termoneeny LY 6; 132
Prehen barracks: Clondermot LY 34; 90
Prehen building quarries: Clondermot LY 34; 133
Prehen Castle: Clondermot LY 34; 49
Prehen district: Clondermot LY 34; 61
Prehen House: Clondermot LY 34; 5–6, 13, 20, 35, 101
Prehen lime quarry: Clondermot LY 34; 36, 105, 133
Prehen night school: Clondermot LY 34; 42
Prehen road quarry: Clondermot LY 34; 22, 34, 101, 133
Prehen school: Clondermot LY 34; 42, 87, 90–91, 95
Prehen Sunday school: Clondermot LY 34; 92–93
Prehen td: Clondermot LY 34; 8, 17, 22–23, 37–38, 49, 57, 72–73, 104, 106, 111, 113, 119, 127, 133
Prehen wood: Clondermot LY 34; 102
Preistly, Mr: Aghadowey LY 22; 27
Prenalt, Mr: Comber DN 7; 37
Prentice, H.L.: Tynan AH 1; 129
Prentice, Jane (nee Foster): Cleenish FH 14; 24
Prentis, Mr: Drumballyroney DN 3; 18
Presley, William: Drumbo DN 7; 56, 59
Pretender (see Stuart, J.F.): Kilrea LY 27; 119
Pretty, Henry: Ballyscullion LY 6; 57
Prey, family: Templecorran AM 26; 117, 119
Price, family: Ballintoy AM 24; 20
Price, family: Ballymartin AM 2; 6, 15
Price, family: Templepatrick AM 35; 118
Price, Francis: Ballywalter DN 7; 18
Price, G.P.: Carrickfergus AM 37; 102, 135
Price, Hugh: Carrickfergus AM 37; 193
Price, Mr: Saul DN 17; 114
Price, N.: Saintfield DN 7; 114–19
Price, Nicholas: Kilkeel DN 3; 54
Price, Thomas: Coleraine LY 33; 143
Priest's Bray locality: Ballintoy AM 24; 19
Priest's bridge: Ardstraw TE 5; 14

Priest's bridge: Mintiaghs DL 38; 65
Priest's cairn: Carrickfergus AM 37; 33
Priest's Causeway locality: Templepatrick AM 35; 130–31
Priest's Causeway locality: Umgall AM 35; 157, 160
Priest's chair: Donegore AM 29; 124, 127–28
Priest's Chair rock: Racavan AM 13; 102
Priest's craig hill: Donegore AM 29; 119, 124
Priest's field: Maghera LY 18; 41
Priest's fort: Bovevagh LY 25; 15
Priest's Headstone column: Ramoan AM 24; 104–05
Priest's Hole tower: Tamlaght Finlagan LY 25; 86, 112
Priest's house: Ballintoy AM 24; 19
Priest's well: Ballintoy AM 24; 19
Priestley, Michael: Clonleigh DL 39; 12
Priests' Park (see Farnasaggart park): Drumachose LY 9; 126
Priests' Rodden locality: Macosquin LY 22; 78, 84, 109–10
Priests' stone: Kilrea LY 27; 128
Priests' well: Ramoan AM 24; 104
Priestsessagh hill: Ardstraw TE 5; 10
Priestsessagh school: Ardstraw TE 5; 7, 13
Priestsessagh td: Ardstraw TE 5; 7
Prieststown td: Convoy DL 39; 22
Priest-town (Priestown) td: Misc. DN 17; 125–26
Primity Castle [I]: Clondermot LY 34; 49
Primity Castle [II]: Clondermot LY 34; 49–50
Primity corn mill: Clondermot LY 34; 133
Primity mill-pond: Clondermot LY 34; 119
Primity quarry: Clondermot LY 34; 50, 133
Primity td: Clondermot LY 34; 57, 73, 111, 113, 119, 127, 133
Prince, Francis: Misc. DN 17; 122
Pringle, Alexander: Templepatrick AM 35; 132
Pringle, Henry: Tynan AH 1; 130
Pringle, T.A.: Donagh MN 40; 103
Pringle, William: Donagh MN 40; 103, 105
Prior, Dr: Clonleigh DL 39; 10
Prison cave: Boho FH 14; 10
Pritchard, Rev. James: Blaris AM 8; 24, 30
Probin, Capt.: Billy AM 16; 76
Procklis cove: Drummaul AM 19; 66, 88
Procklis td: Drummaul AM 19; 91
Proctor, family: Desertmartin LY 31; 55
Proctor, James: Blaris DN 12; 42
Proctor, John: Ballyscullion LY 6; 56
Proctor, Robert: Derryaghy AM 8; 113
Proctor, William: Blaris DN 12; 40
Prois, John: Ramoan AM 24; 102
Proleek Acres td: Ballymascanlan LH 40; 55
Proleek td: Ballymascanlan LH 40; 55
Prolisk (see Prolusk): Clogher TE 5; 41

Prollisk (see Prolusk)

Prolusk (Prolisk) td: Ballintoy AM 24; 17, 27

Prolusk (Prolisque) td: Clogher TE 5; 37, 41–42

Prolusk school: Ballintoy AM 24; 17

Prolusk school: Clogher TE 5; 41–42

Prolusk standing stones: Ballintoy AM 24; 26

Prospect hill: Blaris AM 8; 13

Prospect Hill House: Enniskillen FH 4; 66

Prospect Hill House: Killea and Taughboyne DL 39; 81

Prospect Hill school: Blaris AM 8; 18, 81

Prospect Hill td: Killea and Taughboyne DL 39; 79

Prospect House: Ballyaghran LY 33; 8, 13

Prospect House: Ballynure AM 32; 55

Prospect House: Carrickfergus AM 37; 56, 135–36, 141, 174

Prospect House: Kilmore AH 1; 64, 72

Prospect House: Misc. DL 39; 189

Prospect locality: Carrickfergus AM 37; 94

Prospect Lock: Aghagallon AM 21; 6

Prospect td: Ballymoney AM 16; 21

Provis, family: Magherafelt LY 6; 95

Prow, Andrew: Templepatrick AM 35; 153

Prutasque td: Clogher TE 5; 54

Ptolemy, historian: Down DN 17; 41

Ptolemy, historian: Duneane AM 19; 97

Pubble (Puble) td: Ardstraw TE 5; 12

Pubble fort: Ardstraw TE 5; 12

Pubble graveyard: Ardstraw TE 5; 12

Pubble old church: Ardstraw TE 5; 12

Pubble old church: Enniskillen FH 4; 71

Pubble school: Enniskillen FH 4; 84

Pubble td: Enniskillen FH 4; 71, 74, 82

Pubbuil altar: Bovevagh LY 25; 8, 52

Pulfore td: Dromore TE 5; 99

Pullan, George: Carrickfergus AM 37; 158

Pullanore bay: Lough Swilly DL 38; 119–20

Pullanrighey (see Pullinrighey)

Pullans td: Kildollagh LY 22; 71

Pullcamae bay: Lough Swilly DL 38; 119

Pullcormac creek: Lough Swilly DL 38; 119

Pulleid locality: Lough Swilly DL 38; 99

Pullein, Rev.: Newry DN 3; 114

Pullfeegus Head: Lough Swilly DL 38; 122

Pullin, Patrick: Newry DN 3; 98

Pullinoer (see Pullanore)

Pullinrighey creek: Lough Swilly DL 38; 114, 121–22

Pullinrooey (see Pullinrighey)

Pullins bay: Lough Swilly DL 38; 133–36

Pullnaplughog creek: Lough Swilly DL 38; 116

Pulpit hill: Aghalurcher FH 4; 2

Pulrawer bog: Kilmore AH 1; 65, 72

Pulrory burn: Ardstraw TE 5; 4

Punteenskibbalh Point: Lough Swilly DL 38; 121

Purdon, Robert: Newry DN 3; 98, 103

Purdon, Samuel: Ramoan AM 24; 116

Purdy, family: Glynn AM 26; 45

Purdy, family: Kilroot AM 26; 74–75

Purdysburn House: Drumbo DN 7; 54, 57, 59

Purdysburn school: Drumbo DN 7; 60

Purdysburn village: Drumbo DN 7; 54

Purse, William: Ballyscullion LY 6; 50, 72

Pursell, family: Ballintoy AM 24; 20

Pursley, Ann: Tamlaght Finlagan LY 25; 118

Pursley, David: Tamlaght Finlagan LY 25; 118

Pursley, Elizabeth: Tamlaght Finlagan LY 25; 118

Pursley, family: Bovevagh LY 25; 29

Pursley, Rachael: Tamlaght Finlagan LY 25; 118

Pursley, Robert (Jnr): Tamlaght Finlagan LY 25; 118

Pursley, Robert (Snr): Tamlaght Finlagan LY 25; 118

Pursley's hill: Bovevagh LY 25; 29

Purtabrillian creek: Lough Swilly DL 38; 107

Purtachurry creek: Lough Swilly DL 38; 112

Purtadoon creek: Lough Swilly DL 38; 124

Purtagannive creek: Lough Swilly DL 38; 108

Purtakilleran creek: Lough Swilly DL 38; 107

Purtanand bog: Drumkeeran FH 14; 63

Purtanand td: Drumkeeran FH 14; 63

Purtnamuika (see Portnamuika)

Purtnaraw creek: Lough Swilly DL 38; 106

Purvis, Archibald: Carrickfergus AM 37; 193

Pushen Island: Inishmacsaint FH 14; 70, 72

Pyrenees Mountains: Kilbroney DN 3; 31, 34

Q

Quail, James: Killyleagh DN 17; 86

Quarle, William: Hillsborough DN 12; 107

Quarry hill: Kilbride AM 29; 137

Quarry lough: Currin MN 40; 86

Quarter Cormack td: Down DN 17; 53, 55

Quarterland td: Killinchy DN 7; 86

Quay Brae Head (see Brae Head): Clondermot LY 34; 4

Quebec: Aghadowey LY 22; 35–38

Quebec: Aghagallon AM 21; 19

Quebec: Aghanloo LY 11; 39–40

Quebec: Agivey LY 22; 44–45

Quebec: Ahoghill AM 23; 37–38

Quebec: Artrea LY 6; 38

Quebec: Ballyaghran LY 33; 18, 27–28

Quebec: Ballylinny AM 32; 20, 29

Quebec: Ballymartin AM 2; 15

Quebec: Ballynascreen LY 31; 21

Quebec: Ballynure AM 32; 72

Quebec: Ballyrashane LY 22; 53, 65–66

Quebec: Ballyscullion LY 6; 63, 77–78

Quebec: Ballywillin LY 33; 42, 51

Quebec: Balteagh LY 9; 43–44

Quebec: Bovevagh LY 25; 59–60

Quebec: Carnmoney AM 2; 88

Quebec: Carrickfergus AM 37; 78, 157–58

Quebec: Coleraine LY 33; 74, 145–46

Quebec: Derryaghy AM 8; 115

Quebec: Desertlyn LY 31; 47

Quebec: Desertmartin LY 31; 62

Quebec: Desertoghill LY 27; 20–21

Quebec: Doagh AM 29; 98

Quebec: Donaghmoyne MN 40; 109

Quebec: Drumachose LY 9; 132–34

Quebec: Drumbeg AM 8; 133

Quebec: Drummaul AM 19; 62, 90–91

Quebec: Dunaghy AM 13; 15

Quebec: Dunboe LY 11; 54, 80–81

Quebec: Duneane AM 19; 122–23

Quebec: Errigal LY 27; 47, 65–66

Quebec: Glynn AM 26; 47

Quebec: Island Magee AM 10; 41, 95

Quebec: Kilcronaghan LY 31; 84

Quebec: Kildollagh LY 22; 75

Quebec: Killead AM 35; 24, 51

Quebec: Killelagh LY 27; 99

Quebec: Killowen LY 33; 165, 171–72

Quebec: Kilrea LY 27; 118, 129

Quebec: Kilwaughter AM 10; 122

Quebec: Lissan LY 31; 108–09

Quebec: Macosquin LY 22; 122–23

Quebec: Maghera LY 18; 77–80

Quebec: Magheracloone MN 40; 140

Quebec: Magherafelt LY 6; 104, 112

Quebec: Magilligan LY 11; 94–95

Quebec: Newry DN 3; 85, 87

Quebec: Raloo AM 32; 128–29

Quebec: Tamlaght Finlagan LY 25; 93, 118–20

Quebec: Tamlaght O'Crilly LY 18; 100–01, 137–38

Quebec: Templecorran AM 26; 107, 132

Quebec: Termoneeny LY 6; 126, 132–33

Quebec: Trory FH 14; 129

Queen's Arms Hotel: Carrickfergus AM 37; 28, 30, 171

Queen's County (see Laois)

Quentin bay td: Misc. DN 17; 127

Querey, family: Carnmoney AM 2; 102

Quierie, family: Carnmoney AM 2; 102

Quig, Andrew: Balteagh LY 9; 12, 26, 34

Quig, family: Desertoghill LY 27; 8, 17

Quig, Fredrick: Balteagh LY 9; 33

Quig, Hugh: Banagher LY 30; 89

Quig, Hugh: Bovevagh LY 25; 42, 47, 49–50

Quig, James: Billy AM 16; 59–60

Quig, John: Macosquin LY 22; 91

Quig, Patrick: Errigal LY 27; 59, 72

Quig, William: Kildollagh LY 22; 73

Quigg, James: Desertoghill LY 27; 20

Quigg, Jane: Desertoghill LY 27; 20

Quigg, John [I]: Kilrea LY 27; 118, 129

Quigg, John [II]: Kilrea LY 27; 128

Quigg, Michael: Ballintoy AM 24; 26

Quigg, Samuel: Dunluce AM 16; 119

Quigg, Thomas: Ballymoney AM 16; 27

Quiggery stream: Drumragh TE 5; 104

Quigley, Bridget: Magilligan LY 11; 127

Quigley, family: Magherafelt LY 6; 95

Quigley, George: Ballyscullion LY 6; 62–63

Quigley, Grace: Carrickfergus AM 37; 130
Quigley, John: Faughanvale LY 36; 35
Quigley, John: Maghera LY 18; 80
Quigley, Joseph: Bovevagh LY 25; 28
Quigley, M.: Faughanvale LY 36; 30
Quigley, man named. Lough Swilly DL 38, 144
Quigley, Patrick: Maghera LY 18; 80
Quigley, Robert: Clondermot LY 34; 79
Quigley, William: Bovevagh LY 25; 6, 26
Quigley's ferry: Lough Swilly DL 38; 147
Quigley's Point: Lough Swilly DL 38; 144
Quigley's Point: Moville DL 38; 78
Quiglough mill: Tydavnet MN 40; 173
Quigly, Andrew: Dungiven LY 15; 95–98
Quigly, family: Faughanvale LY 36; 14
Quigly, family: Kilcronaghan LY 31; 68
Quigly, James: Dungiven LY 15; 98
Quigly, John: Ballyscullion LY 6; 70, 78
Quigly, John: Banagher LY 30; 93–94
Quigly, John: Bovevagh LY 25; 29
Quigly, John: Maghera LY 18; 45
Quigly, Kyle: Bovevagh LY 25; 60
Quigly, Molly: Kilrea LY 27; 117
Quigly, Patrick: Ballynascreen LY 31; 14, 21
Quilca (see Cuilcagh): Kinawley FH 4; 123
Quilly bleaching mill: Dromore DN 12; 72, 78
Quilly flow bog: Dunboe LY 11; 74
Quilly fort [I]: Desertlyn LY 31; 44
Quilly fort [II]: Desertlyn LY 31; 44
Quilly glen: Desertlyn LY 31; 35–36
Quilly glen: Desertmartin LY 31; 52
Quilly House: Dromore DN 12; 72
Quilly school: Desertlyn LY 31; 50–51
Quilly school: Dunboe LY 11; 56, 70
Quilly Sunday school: Desertlyn LY 31; 51
Quilly Sunday school: Dunboe LY 11; 57, 71
Quilly td: Coleraine LY 33; 104
Quilly td: Desertlyn LY 31; 47
Quilly td: Dromore DN 12; 78
Quilly td: Dunboe LY 11; 56, 70–71, 74
Quilly td: Macosquin LY 22; 94
Quilly Upper td: Dunboe LY 11; 49
Quilon, W.H.: Newry DN 3; 71
Quin and Otterson, Messrs: Misc. LY 31; 140
Quin, Arthur: Mullaghbrack AH 1; 97
Quin, Bernard: Misc. LY 31; 140
Quin, Bridget [I]: Tamlaght O'Crilly LY 18; 137
Quin, Bridget [II]: Tamlaght O'Crilly LY 18; 137
Quin, Charles: Ballynascreen LY 31; 23
Quin, Charles: Newry DN 3; 95, 99, 104
Quin, Edward: Aghadowey LY 22; 36
Quin, F.: Comber DN 7; 34
Quin, family: Enniskillen FH 4; 58
Quin, family: Loughguile AM 13; 64

Quin, Francis: Tamlaght O'Crilly LY 18; 115
Quin, Henry: Tamlaght TE 20; 79
Quin, J.G.: Newry DN 3; 99, 103
Quin, James: Ballynascreen LY 31; 23, 32
Quin, James: Tamlaght TE 20; 79
Quin, John: Aghabog MN 40; 63, 67
Quin, John: Ardstraw TE 5; 5
Quin, John: Artrea LY 6; 35–36
Quin, John: Currin MN 40; 96
Quin, John [I]: Tamlaght O'Crilly LY 18; 113
Quin, John [II]: Tamlaght O'Crilly LY 18; 137
Quin, John [III]: Tamlaght O'Crilly LY 18; 137
Quin, John [IV]: Tamlaght O'Crilly LY 18; 137
Quin, Joseph: Tamlaght O'Crilly LY 18; 114, 130
Quin, Lewis: Tamlaght TE 20; 92
Quin, Mary (Jnr): Tamlaght O'Crilly LY 18; 137
Quin, Mary (Snr): Tamlaght O'Crilly LY 18; 137
Quin, Mary [I]: Tamlaght O'Crilly LY 18; 137
Quin, Mary Jane: Tamlaght O'Crilly LY 18; 137
Quin, Messrs James and Co.: Misc. LY 31; 140
Quin, Mr (Coolsaragh): Misc. LY 31; 130, 132
Quin, Mr: Drumballyroney DN 3; 16
Quin, Patrick: Newry DN 3; 98, 103
Quin, Patt: Errigal LY 27; 61
Quin, Rev. Francis: Ballynascreen LY 31; 11, 30
Quin, Rev. Francis: Desertmartin LY 31; 57
Quin, Rev. Francis: Kilcronaghan LY 31; 77
Quin, Rev. Francis: Misc. LY 31; 129
Quin, Terence: Tamlaght TE 20; 118
Quin, Widow: Maghera LY 18; 39
Quin, Widow: Tamlaght TE 20; 84
Quince, Bartly: Kilmacteige SO 40; 195
Quinn and Swaney, Messrs: Glynn AM 26; 38
Quinn, Alexander: Doagh AM 29; 98
Quinn, Andrew: Duneane AM 19; 113
Quinn, Antony: Kilmacteige SO 40; 193
Quinn, Arthur: Maghera LY 18; 60
Quinn, Charles: Lissan LY 31; 106, 109
Quinn, Daniel: Rasharkin AM 23; 134, 141
Quinn, Edward: Newry DN 3; 100, 104
Quinn, family: Lissan LY 31; 106
Quinn, Frank: Maghera LY 18; 61, 80
Quinn, George: Glynn AM 26; 38
Quinn, George: Newry DN 3; 99, 104
Quinn, Hugh: Ahoghill AM 23; 35
Quinn, Hugh: Newry DN 3; 98
Quinn, J.H.: Newry DN 3; 98, 103
Quinn, James: Desertoghill LY 27; 21
Quinn, James: Drumtullagh AM 16; 101
Quinn, James: Tamlaght TE 20; 116
Quinn, Jane: Carrickfergus AM 37; 115, 131
Quinn, John: Aghanloo LY 11; 16
Quinn, John: Ballymore AH 1; 12, 16–17
Quinn, John: Derryaghy AM 8; 101
Quinn, John: Faughanvale LY 36; 8, 10, 36, 70

Quinn, John: Maghera LY 18; 80
Quinn, John: Magilligan LY 11; 94
Quinn, John: Newry DN 3; 99, 103
Quinn, Margaret: Carrickfergus AM 37; 76
Quinn, Martin: Kilmacteige SO 40; 185, 192
Quinn, Matthew: Magilligan LY 11; 131
Quinn, Messrs: Faughanvale LY 36; 20
Quinn, Michael: Clonleigh DL 39; 9
Quinn, Michael: Maghera LY 18; 80
Quinn, Michael: Magilligan LY 11; 131, 133
Quinn, Mr: Cappagh TE 5; 19
Quinn, Mr: Donacavey TE 5; 77
Quinn, Mrs John: Faughanvale LY 36; 24
Quinn, Patrick: Rasharkin AM 23; 135
Quinn, Peter: Newry DN 3; 104
Quinn, Rev. Hugh: Artrea LY 6; 39
Quinn, Rev. John: Magherafelt LY 6; 98
Quinn, Samuel: Carrickfergus AM 37; 118
Quinn, Thomas: Carrickfergus AM 37; 121
Quinn, Thomas: Newry DN 3; 98, 103
Quinn, William: Newry DN 3; 99
Quinn, Willliam: Blaris DN 12; 40
Quintin bay: Witter DN 7; 125–26
Quintin Bay Castle: Ballyculter DN 17; 28
Quintin Bay Castle: Witter DN 7; 126
Quintin Bay td: Ballyphilip DN 7; 8
Quintin village: Witter DN 7; 125–26
Quinton quarry: Tullyniskan TE 20; 141
Quinton, family: Enniskillen FH 4; 58, 75

Quinton, James: Enniskillen FH 4; 58
Quirey, family: Carnmoney AM 2; 51, 76
Quirey, Jonathon: Carnmoney AM 2; 95–96, 98
Quoha cromlechs: Drumgoon CN 40; 7
Quoile bridge: Down DN 17; 49, 61
Quoile bridge: Inch DN 17; 74
Quoile bridge: Kilmore DN 17; 91
Quoile bridge: Magheradrool DN 17; 103, 105
Quoile Castle: Saul DN 17; 112
Quoile floodgates: Inch DN 17; 74
Quoile harbour: Saul DN 17; 111, 113
Quoile pier: Killyleagh DN 17; 86
Quoile quay: Ballee DN 17; 23
Quoile quay: Down DN 17; 49, 51, 58
Quoile quay: Killyleagh DN 17; 84, 86
Quoile quay: Saul DN 17; 111, 113
Quoile river (see also Ballynahinch river)
Quoile river: Down DN 17; 38–39
Quoile river: Dromara DN 12; 62
Quoile river: Inch DN 17; 74
Quoile river: Kilmore DN 17; 91
Quoile river: Magheradrool DN 17; 103, 105, 106
Quoile td: Saul DN 17; 111, 114
Quoile wooden bridge: Inch DN 17; 74
Quolie mountain: Skerry AM 13; 105
Quoniamstown chapel: Bright DN 17; 36
Quoniamstown td: Bright DN 17; 34–35
Quoniamstown td: Down DN 17; 57
Quoyle (see Quoile)

R

Raan td: Leck DL 39; 119

Raans lough: Magheracloone MN 40; 137

Rabb, John: Templepatrick AM 35; 122, 147–48

Rabbit fort: Kilmacteige SO 40; 186–87, 193

Rabbit hill: Errigal LY 27; 45, 49

Rabbit Island: Aghalurcher FH 4; 3, 14

Rabbit Island: Ballinderry AM 21; 43

Rabbit Island: Inishmacsaint FH 14; 70, 73

Rabbit Island: Kinawley FH 4; 113

Rabbit Island: Magheraculmoney FH 14; 105

Rabbit Island school: Drummully FH 4; 39

Rabbit Island td: Drummully FH 4; 35, 39

Rabbit rock: Rasharkin AM 23; 129

Rabbit Warren demesne: Errigal LY 27; 76

Rabraans td: Devenish FH 14; 58

Racarbry beetling mill: Keady AH 1; 50

Racarbry flour mill: Keady AH 1; 50

Racavan graveyard: Racavan AM 13; 89, 100–01

Racavan ph: Ballyclug AM 23; 52, 54

Racavan ph: Connor AM 19; 19

Racavan ph: Finvoy AM 23; 78

Racavan ph: Glenwhirry AM 32; 74

Racavan ph: Kirkinriola AM 23; 88, 92, 115

Racavan ph: Racavan AM 13; 93

Racavan ph: Skerry AM 13; 105, 113

Racavan ph: Tickmacrevan AM 13; 122

Racavan school: Racavan AM 13; 96, 100

Racavan td: Racavan AM 13; 89–90, 96–97, 100–01

Race of the Black Pig (see also Danes' Cast):
  Aghaderg DN 12; 7

Race of the Black Pig: Donacavey TE 5; 62

Racecourse lough: Enniskillen FH 4; 47, 52, 69

Racecourse lough: Trory FH 14; 123

Racecourse night school: Clondermot LY 34; 43

Racecourse school: Clondermot LY 34; 43, 89

Rackeragh td: Magheross MN 40; 149

Racrane (Racrean) td: Donacavey TE 5; 77, 79, 83, 86

Racrane fort: Donacavey TE 5; 83

Racreehan hill: Ematris MN 40; 112

Radcliff, J.S.: Donagh MN 40; 103, 105

Radcliff's Steps ford: Annaclone DN 12; 14

Radcliffe, family: Drumbeg AM 8; 123

Radcliffe, Mr: Clondermot LY 34; 88, 95

Radcliffe, Rev. Richard: Enniskeen CN 40; 28–29

Rademan flour mill: Kilmore DN 17; 91

Rademan meeting house: Kilmore DN 17; 91

Rademan water: Kilmore DN 17; 91

Radford, George: Hillsborough DN 12; 105

Radmore td: Belleek FH 14; 3–4

Rae, Charles: Killygarvan DL 38; 40, 42–46, 48

Rafeenan (Raseenan) td: Tydavnet MN 40; 173

Rafeenan mill: Tydavnet MN 40; 173

Rafeenan school: Tydavnet MN 40; 173

Rafferagh bog: Magheross MN 40; 144

Rafferagh td: Magheross MN 40; 145, 149

Rafferty, James: Carrickfergus AM 37; 124, 193

Raffrey (Raffry) td: Killinchy DN 7; 86, 88

Rafintan td: Aghalurcher FH 4; 14

Rafter, family: Dunluce AM 16; 117

Ragh lough: Drumhome DL 39; 61

Raghery (see Rathlin)

Raghties hill: Lough Swilly DL 38; 133

Ragogan (see Rarogan)

Ragsbottom, Jane: Carrickfergus AM 37; 131

Rahack glebe: Aghalurcher FH 4; 16

Rahack td: Aghalurcher FH 4; 16

Rahaggory corn mill: Clondavaddog DL 38; 5

Rahaghy bog: Aghaloo TE 20; 1

Rahaghy hill: Aghaloo TE 20; 1

Rahaghy lough: Aghaloo TE 20; 1

Rahaltan (Raholton) td: Devenish FH 14; 52, 55

Rahan's lough: Donaghmoyne MN 40; 106

Rahan's lough: Magheross MN 40; 157

Rahanboy (Rachinboy) td: Carrickfergus AM 37; 93, 174

Rahanboy fort: Carrickfergus AM 37; 93

Rahanboy green: Carrickfergus AM 37; 76

Rahanbwee (see Rahanboy)

Rahans House: Donaghmoyne MN 40; 107

Rahans td: Magheross MN 40; 157

Rahawney td: Dromore TE 5; 99

Raheelagh hill: Laragh CN 40; 39

Raheen village: Kilmacteige SO 40; 195

Raheny (Dublin): Banagher LY 30; 18

Rahollan td: Cleenish FH 14; 30

Raholp corn mill: Ballyculter DN 17; 25

Raholp corn stores: Saul DN 17; 112

Raholp district: Misc. DN 17; 118
Raholp hamlet: Ballyculter DN 17; 25
Raholp hamlet: Saul DN 17; 112
Raholp mill: Saul DN 17; 112
Raholp td: Ballyculter DN 17; 31
Raholson (see Rahaltan)
Railagh mountain: Cappagh TE 5; 21
Rainey, Catherine: Tamlaght O'Crilly LY 18; 137
Rainey, family: Ballyclug AM 23; 63
Rainey, family: Magherafelt LY 6; 104
Rainey, family: Rasharkin AM 23; 132
Rainey, J.A.: Ballyscullion LY 6; 56
Rainey, J.A.: Magherafelt LY 6; 101
Rainey, John: Artrea LY 6; 21
Rainey, John: Hillsborough DN 12; 106
Rainey, John: Magherafelt LY 6; 98, 103
Rainey, John: Muckamore AM 35; 78
Rainey, Mr: Misc. LY 31; 113
Rainey, Robert: Ballyscullion LY 6; 45
Rainey, Robert: Drumbeg AM 8; 128
Rainey, Robert: Tamlaght O'Crilly LY 18; 137
Rainey, Thomas: Ballymoney AM 16; 17
Rainey, Thomas: Carrickfergus AM 37; 112
Rainey, W.A.: Down DN 17; 48
Rainey, William: Ballymoney AM 16; 18
Rainey, William: Carrickfergus AM 37; 115
Rainey's Island: Ardkeen DN 7; 3
Rainhill (Lancashire): Enniskillen FH 4; 47
Rainy, Hugh: Magherafelt LY 6; 97
Rakane (see Rakenny)
Rakeelan Glebe td: Enniskillen FH 4; 81
Rakeeragh td: Ematris MN 40; 113
Rakenny: Drung CN 40; 20
Rakenny: Killdrumsherdan CN 40; 34
Rakenny demesne: Drung CN 40; 20
Rakenny fort: Drung CN 40; 21
Rakenny hill: Killdrumsherdan CN 40; 31–32
Rakenny House: Drumgoon CN 40; 8
Rakenny House: Drung CN 40; 20–23
Rakenny td: Drung CN 40; 21
Rakenny td: Killdrumsherdan CN 40; 32
Rakerenbeg td: Dromore TE 5; 99
Rale, family: Misc. LY 36; 104
Raleagh (see Rallagh)
Rallagh (Railagh) td: Banagher LY 30; 9, 22, 34–36,
    43, 48, 56–57, 61–62, 95–96, 98, 106, 109,
    109–10, 120, 124–25, 128, 130–32
Rallagh altar: Banagher LY 30; 38
Rallagh cave: Banagher LY 30; 2, 46, 48, 56, 78
Rallagh church: Banagher LY 30; 13–14, 27–29, 32,
    43, 50, 59, 100, 115–16
Rallagh enclosures: Banagher LY 30; 67–68
Rallagh fort [I]: Banagher LY 30; 7, 38, 59, 67–68
Rallagh fort [II]: Banagher LY 30; 43, 79
Rallagh foundry: Banagher LY 30; 78–79

Rallagh House (see Banagher Glebe): Banagher LY
    30; 32
Rallagh school [I]: Banagher LY 30; 13, 27, 29,
    32–34, 59, 110–11
Rallagh school [II]: Banagher LY 30; 111
Rallagh schools: Dungiven LY 15; 19
Rallagh wood: Banagher LY 30; 124
Rallaghan school: Drumgoon CN 40; 11
Ralleagh (see Rallagh)
Ralliagh (see Rallagh)
Ralloo (see Raloo)
Raloo adult school: Raloo AM 32; 97, 130
Raloo chapel: Glynn AM 26; 23
Raloo chapel: Island Magee AM 10; 35
Raloo encampment: Raloo AM 32; 93
Raloo graveyard: Raloo AM 32; 93
Raloo meeting house: Ballynure AM 32; 50, 69
Raloo ph: Ballynure AM 32; 42, 44, 46, 68, 70
Raloo ph: Carrickfergus AM 37; 1, 33, 69, 71, 100,
    142, 151, 160, 176
Raloo ph: Glynn AM 26; 1, 8, 23, 42
Raloo ph: Inver AM 26; 49, 52, 55
Raloo ph: Island Magee AM 10; 35
Raloo ph: Kilroot AM 26; 65
Raloo ph: Kilwaughter AM 10; 106, 109, 114, 117
Raloo ph: Larne AM 10; 125
Raloo ph: Mallusk AM 2; 111, 114
Raloo ph: Misc. AM 10; 129
Raloo ph: Raloo AM 32; 83
Raloo ph: Templecorran AM 26; 101, 128
Raloo td: Raloo AM 32; 127
Raloo village: Raloo AM 32; 80, 83, 89–91, 98
Raloo water: Glynn AM 26; 4, 10
Raloo water: Raloo AM 32; 80, 82–87, 92
Raloo watercourse: Raloo AM 32; 132
Ralph, Mr: Comber DN 7; 40
Ralph, Mr: Tullynakill DN 7; 122
Ram, Susan: Carrickfergus AM 37; 115
Ram's Island: Ballinderry AM 21; 55
Ram's Island: Glenavy AM 21; 82–83
Ram's Island: Killead AM 35; 7–8
Ram's Island: Lough Neagh AM 21; 95
Ram's Island: Misc. DN 17; 121
Ram's Island Cottage: Glenavy AM 21; 83
Ram's Island Cottage: Lough Neagh AM 21; 95
Ram's Island tower: Antrim AM 29; 30
Ram's Island tower: Lough Neagh AM 21; 95
Ramadge, Alexander: Ballymoney AM 16; 15
Ramadge, William: Ballymoney AM 16; 15, 17
Ramage, family: Macosquin LY 22; 84, 119
Ramaket school: Aghaloo TE 20; 5
Ramelton (see Rathmelton)
Ramoan church: Ramoan AM 24; 91, 107–08, 125
Ramoan glebe: Ramoan AM 24; 96
Ramoan Glebe House: Ramoan AM 24; 96, 99

Ramoan graveyard: Ramoan AM 24; 107
Ramoan Mansion House: Ramoan AM 24; 91, 94
Ramoan old church: Ramoan AM 24; 107–08
Ramoan ph: Armoy AM 24; 1–4
Ramoan ph: Ballintoy AM 24; 10, 13
Ramoan ph: Billy AM 16; 40
Ramoan ph: Culfeightrin AM 24; 36, 40, 42, 46, 48, 50, 65, 69, 80
Ramoan ph: Derrykeighan AM 16; 81, 83
Ramoan ph: Drumtullagh AM 16; 96
Ramoan ph: Misc. AM 10; 129
Ramoan school: Ramoan AM 24; 91, 100, 126
Ramoan well: Ramoan AM 24; 108
Rampark td: Ballymascanlan LH 40; 56
Ramsay, Allan: Banagher LY 30; 11
Ramsay, Allan: Dungiven LY 15; 27
Ramsay, Catherine: Coleraine LY 33; 146
Ramsay, Eliza: Coleraine LY 33; 146
Ramsay, Eliza: Lissan LY 31; 96, 108
Ramsay, family: Templecorran AM 26; 117, 119
Ramsay, James: Carrickfergus AM 37; 111, 195
Ramsay, Jane: Coleraine LY 33; 146
Ramsay, John: Lissan LY 31; 90–91, 98, 101
Ramsay, Rev.: Kilteevoge DL 39; 114
Ramsay, Robert: Rashee AM 32; 141
Ramsay, Samuel (Jnr): Coleraine LY 33; 146
Ramsay, Samuel (Snr): Coleraine LY 33; 146
Ramsay, Thomas: Faughanvale LY 36; 40
Ramsay, William: Lissan LY 31; 90, 98–100
Ramsay's well: Faughanvale LY 36; 30–31
Ramsey, family: Ballintoy AM 24; 20
Ramsey, family: Carnmoney AM 2; 76
Ramsey, Hugh: Cleenish FH 14; 20
Ramsey, James: Artrea LY 6; 32
Ramsey, James: Derrykeighan AM 16; 90
Ramsey, John: Artrea LY 6; 11, 31–32
Ramsey, John: Coleraine LY 33; 146
Ramsey, Margret: Convoy DL 39; 22
Ramsey, Mr: Raymoghy DL 39; 138
Ramsey, Thomas: Cleenish FH 14; 20
Ramsey, William: Kildollagh LY 22; 73, 75
Ramult (Rimult) td: Aghalurcher FH 4; 11, 14
Ramult school: Aghalurcher FH 4; 11
Ranaghan td: Duneane AM 19; 123
Ranaghan, Mr: Down DN 17; 59
Ranbuy (see Rahanboy)
Randalstown: Aghadowey LY 22; 25
Randalstown: Ahoghill AM 23; 2–4, 9, 14, 31, 34, 40–41, 44
Randalstown: Antrim AM 29; 9, 19, 22, 27, 45, 50
Randalstown: Ballyscullion AM 19; 2, 11
Randalstown: Connor AM 19; 17, 19, 22, 30
Randalstown: Donegore AM 29; 112
Randalstown: Drumcree AH 1; 38

Randalstown: Drummaul AM 19; 33, 36–38, 40–41, 43–47, 49–57, 62, 64–65, 72–73, 78–91
Randalstown: Duneane AM 19; 96, 99–100, 108, 112–16, 125
Randalstown: Killagan AM 23; 82
Randalstown: Kirkinriola AM 23; 99
Randalstown: Rasharkin AM 23; 129
Randalstown: Shilvodan AM 19; 128, 130–33, 138
Randalstown: Templepatrick AM 35; 146
Randalstown: Tullyrusk AM 21; 135
Randalstown barrack school: Drummaul AM 19; 92
Randalstown barracks: Drummaul AM 19; 42–43
Randalstown beetling mill: Drummaul AM 19; 45
Randalstown bleach green: Drummaul AM 19; 41
Randalstown bridge: Drummaul AM 19; 43–44, 52, 81, 84
Randalstown chandlery: Drummaul AM 19; 45
Randalstown chapel: Drummaul AM 19; 34, 42–43, 57–58, 80, 82–84
Randalstown chapel: Shilvodan AM 19; 133
Randalstown church: Drummaul AM 19; 34, 42–43, 52, 62–63, 80, 83–85
Randalstown corn mill [I]: Drummaul AM 19; 45, 81
Randalstown corn mill [II]: Drummaul AM 19; 81
Randalstown corn mill [III]: Drummaul AM 19; 81
Randalstown cotton factory: Drummaul AM 19; 34, 45, 81
Randalstown court house: Drummaul AM 19; 34, 80
Randalstown dispensary: Ballyscullion AM 19; 5
Randalstown dispensary: Drummaul AM 19; 43, 46, 56–57, 73–74, 78, 80, 83
Randalstown dispensary: Duneane AM 19; 102
Randalstown distilleries: Drummaul AM 19; 41
Randalstown Dunmore school: Drummaul AM 19; 91
Randalstown female school: Drummaul AM 19; 76, 85
Randalstown forts: Drummaul AM 19; 78
Randalstown graveyard: Drummaul AM 19; 42
Randalstown ironworks: Carnmoney AM 2; 72
Randalstown ironworks: Drummaul AM 19; 40–41
Randalstown Kildare school: Drummaul AM 19; 81
Randalstown linen manufactory: Drummaul AM 19; 84
Randalstown market house: Drummaul AM 19; 34, 42–43, 58, 76, 80, 82–83, 85
Randalstown meeting house (P): Drummaul AM 19; 34, 42, 53, 57–58, 61, 80, 82
Randalstown meeting house (P): Errigal LY 27; 57
Randalstown meeting house (S) [I]: Drummaul AM 19; 34, 42–43, 58, 80, 83
Randalstown meeting house (S) [II]: Drummaul AM 19; 83

Randalstown national school: Drummaul AM 19; 42–44, 46, 74–75, 77, 81, 84

Randalstown old church: Drummaul AM 19; 42, 62

Randalstown old market house: Drummaul AM 19; 42–43, 83

Randalstown old meeting house: Drummaul AM 19; 42

Randalstown paper mills: Drummaul AM 19; 41

Randalstown parish school: Drummaul AM 19; 46, 57, 74, 81, 84–85, 92

Randalstown pay school [I]: Drummaul AM 19; 92

Randalstown pay school [II]: Drummaul AM 19; 92

Randalstown private school: Drummaul AM 19; 81

Randalstown quarry: Drummaul AM 19; 46

Randalstown schools: Drummaul AM 19; 57

Randalstown seminary: Drummaul AM 19; 76, 85

Randalstown Sunday school: Drummaul AM 19; 57, 77, 84–85

Randalstown tanyard: Drummaul AM 19; 34

Randles, family: Dunluce AM 16; 117

Randles, family: Magherafelt LY 6; 95

Randleshough fort: Devenish FH 14; 55

Randleshough td: Devenish FH 14; 58

Randolph, Earl of Antrim: Ramoan AM 24; 90

Randoy forts: Killead AM 35; 30

Ranee Point: Lough Swilly DL 38; 117

Raneese (Ranees) td: Donacavey TE 5; 67–68, 77, 79, 83, 86

Raneese fort: Donacavey TE 5; 83

Raneese Lower td: Donacavey TE 5; 81

Raneese td: Clogher TE 5; 59

Raneese Upper td: Donacavey TE 5; 81

Ranenley td: Clogher TE 5; 44

Ranenly school: Clogher TE 5; 41–42

Ranenly td: Clogher TE 5; 38, 41

Ranfrew, William: Tamlaght TE 20; 82

Ranfurley, Earl of: Newry DN 3; 75

Ranfurly demesne: Drumglass TE 20; 44

Ranfurly, Lord: Comber DN 7; 39

Ranfurly, Lord: Drumglass TE 20; 40, 42–44

Rankan, John: Conwal DL 39; 27

Ranken, Rev. John: Antrim AM 29; 27

Rankin and Co., Messrs: Donegal DL 39; 47

Rankin, Alexander: Culfeightrin AM 24; 76–77

Rankin, Andrew: Ballywillin LY 33; 51

Rankin, Andrew: Hillsborough DN 12; 105

Rankin, Catherine: Ballyscullion AM 19; 14

Rankin, Col: Coleraine LY 33; 142

Rankin, David: Desertoghill LY 27; 5

Rankin, David: Errigal LY 27; 40, 58

Rankin, Eliza: Tamlaght Finlagan LY 25; 74, 77–78, 123–24

Rankin, family: Dunluce AM 16; 117

Rankin, family: Enniskillen FH 4; 58, 75

Rankin, Hugh: Coleraine LY 33; 145

Rankin, Hugh: Errigal LY 27; 54, 69

Rankin, James: Artrea LY 6; 20

Rankin, James: Coleraine LY 33; 131

Rankin, James: Desertoghill LY 27; 10

Rankin, James: Errigal LY 27; 66

Rankin, John: Ballyrashane LY 22; 63

Rankin, Mr: Taughboyne DL 39; 148, 151, 153

Rankin, Thomas: Drumachose LY 9; 133

Rankin, William: Coleraine LY 33; 145

Rankin, William: Raloo AM 32; 122

Rankin, William: Tamlaght TE 20; 131, 136

Rankinstown school: Ballyclug AM 23; 66

Rankmore Head: Ballyphilip DN 7; 9

Rannagh Point: Lough Swilly DL 38; 115

Ranney (see Ranny)

Ranny fort: Tullyaughnish DL 38; 91

Ranny td: Tullyaughnish DL 38; 91, 96

Ranoes td: Donacavey TE 5; 77

Ranold's hill: Derrykeighan AM 16; 90

Raphael, family: Kirkinriola AM 23; 124

Raphael, George: Ahoghill AM 23; 35

Raphael, Henry: Ahoghill AM 23; 11, 15

Raphael, William: Ahoghill AM 23; 47

Raphoe: Clonleigh DL 39; 1–3, 13–14, 16

Raphoe: Convoy DL 39; 18

Raphoe: Donaghmore DL 39; 30

Raphoe: Leck DL 39; 116

Raphoe: Newry DN 3; 66

Raphoe: Raphoe DL 39; 121–24, 128, 130

Raphoe: Raymoghy DL 39; 138–39

Raphoe: Taughboyne DL 39; 149, 152–55

Raphoe abbey: Raphoe DL 39; 123

Raphoe barony: Clonleigh DL 39; 1, 4

Raphoe barony: Convoy DL 39; 18

Raphoe barony: Conwal DL 39; 24, 26

Raphoe barony: Donaghmore DL 39; 28

Raphoe barony: Kilbarron DL 39; 77

Raphoe barony: Killea and Taughboyne DL 39; 79, 88, 91

Raphoe barony: Kilteevoge DL 39; 111

Raphoe barony: Leck DL 39; 115, 120

Raphoe barony: Misc. DL 39; 183–84

Raphoe barony: Raphoe DL 39; 121

Raphoe barony: Raymoghy DL 39; 132, 140

Raphoe barony: Urney DL 39; 174

Raphoe Cathedral: Raphoe DL 39; 123–24, 130

Raphoe classical school: Raphoe DL 39; 127

Raphoe deanery: Antrim AM 29; 26

Raphoe deanery: Convoy DL 39; 19

Raphoe deanery: Kilteevoge DL 39; 113–14

Raphoe deanery: Leck DL 39; 115, 117

Raphoe deanery: Raphoe DL 39; 121, 126

Raphoe deanery: Taughboyne DL 39; 151

Raphoe Deanery House: Raphoe DL 39; 123

Raphoe deerpark: Raphoe DL 39; 130

Raphoe demesne: Raphoe DL 39; 123, 130
Raphoe Demesne td: Raphoe DL 39; 126
Raphoe diocese: Ardstraw TE 5; 8
Raphoe diocese: Clondavaddog DL 38; 1
Raphoe diocese: Convoy DL 39; 18, 20, 22
Raphoe diocese: Conwal DL 39; 24
Raphoe diocese: Donegal DL 39; 45
Raphoe diocese: Glencolumbkille DL 39; 64
Raphoe diocese: Inishkeel DL 39; 67
Raphoe diocese: Killea and Taughboyne DL 39; 89
Raphoe diocese: Killelagh LY 27; 102
Raphoe diocese: Killygarvan DL 38; 41–42
Raphoe diocese: Killymard DL 39; 100
Raphoe diocese: Kilteevoge DL 39; 111
Raphoe diocese: Leck DL 39; 115, 118
Raphoe diocese: Loughgall AH 1; 79
Raphoe diocese: Mevagh DL 38; 54
Raphoe diocese: Misc. DL 39; 186, 194
Raphoe diocese: Raphoe DL 39; 121, 123, 125–27
Raphoe diocese: Raymoghy DL 39; 132, 137–40
Raphoe diocese: Taughboyne DL 39; 148, 152–53
Raphoe diocese: Tullyaughnish DL 38; 87, 96–97
Raphoe dispensary: Raphoe DL 39; 123
Raphoe library: Raphoe DL 39; 123
Raphoe market house: Raphoe DL 39; 124, 130
Raphoe meeting house: Raphoe DL 39; 123, 130
Raphoe monastery: Raphoe DL 39; 131
Raphoe nunnery: Raphoe DL 39; 131
Raphoe old market house: Raphoe DL 39; 124
Raphoe Palace: Raphoe DL 39; 121–22, 130
Raphoe parish school: Raphoe DL 39; 127, 130
Raphoe ph: Clonleigh DL 39; 1, 7, 15
Raphoe ph: Convoy DL 39; 18–19
Raphoe ph: Donaghmore DL 39; 28–29, 32
Raphoe ph: Donegal DL 39; 51
Raphoe ph: Leck DL 39; 115
Raphoe ph: Misc. DL 39; 184–85, 188
Raphoe ph: Raymoghy DL 39; 132
Raphoe ph: Taughboyne DL 39; 153
Raphoe school [I]: Raphoe DL 39; 127
Raphoe school [II]: Raphoe DL 39; 127
Raphoe school [III]: Raphoe DL 39; 127
Raphoe school [IV]: Raphoe DL 39; 127
Raphoe shambles: Raphoe DL 39; 130
Raphoe Townparks td: Raphoe DL 39; 126
Raphoe widows' house: Raphoe DL 39; 123
Raphoe, Bishop of: Faughanvale LY 36; 40, 45
Rariagh bog: Conwal DL 39; 24
Rariagh td: Conwal DL 39; 24, 27
Rarky hill: Muff DL 38; 80
Rarogan church: Errigal Keerogue TE 20; 55
Rarogan school: Errigal Keerogue TE 20; 55
Rarogan td: Errigal Keerogue TE 20; 50, 55, 57
Rasarkin rectory: Kirkinriola AM 23; 88
Rascahan td: Tamlaght Finlagan LY 25; 72, 93

Rashany fort: Clonmany DL 38; 16
Rashany td: Clonmany DL 38; 18, 20
Rasharkin: Ahoghill AM 23; 12, 14, 41
Rasharkin: Finvoy AM 23; 67
Rasharkin: Kilrea LY 27; 119, 122
Rasharkin: Rasharkin AM 23; 127, 130–34, 136,
  138–39
Rasharkin cave: Rasharkin AM 23; 134
Rasharkin cave: Templecorran AM 26; 115
Rasharkin church: Rasharkin AM 23; 128, 130, 134,
  136, 139–40
Rasharkin forts: Rasharkin AM 23; 128
Rasharkin Glebe House (see Hazlebrook):
  Rasharkin AM 23; 128
Rasharkin graveyard: Rasharkin AM 23; 136
Rasharkin graveyard: Templecorran AM 26; 115
Rasharkin meeting house: Rasharkin AM 23; 128,
  130, 136, 138
Rasharkin meeting houses: Rasharkin AM 23; 128
Rasharkin mills: Rasharkin AM 23; 127
Rasharkin old church: Ahoghill AM 23; 25
Rasharkin old church: Rasharkin AM 23; 130, 136,
  140
Rasharkin ph: Ahoghill AM 23; 1, 24
Rasharkin ph: Ballyscullion LY 6; 47
Rasharkin ph: Dundermot AM 13; 29
Rasharkin ph: Finvoy AM 23; 67
Rasharkin ph: Killagan AM 23; 79, 81
Rasharkin ph: Killead AM 35; 50
Rasharkin ph: Kilraghts AM 16; 124
Rasharkin ph: Kirkinriola AM 23; 126
Rasharkin prebend: Finvoy AM 23; 67, 73
Rasharkin standing stones: Rasharkin AM 23; 138
Rasharkin Sunday school: Rasharkin AM 23; 136
Rashedag td: Conwal DL 39; 26–27
Rashee church: Ballycor AM 32; 3
Rashee church: Glynn AM 26; 30
Rashee graveyard: Rashee AM 32; 135
Rashee mill-dam: Rashee AM 32; 135
Rashee mountains: Glenwhirry AM 32; 75
Rashee ph: Ballycor AM 32; 1, 5–6, 8–9
Rashee ph: Carnmoney AM 2; 34
Rashee ph: Connor AM 19; 16–17, 19
Rashee ph: Doagh AM 29; 60, 63, 66, 71, 84, 96,
  100
Rashee ph: Donegore AM 29; 131
Rashee ph: Glenwhirry AM 32; 74
Rashee ph: Kilbride AM 29; 135–38, 148, 150,
  155–56
Rashee ph: Misc. AM 10; 129
Raskill hill: Laragh CN 40; 40
Raspberry Hill flax mill: Cumber LY 28; 124
Raspberry Hill td: Cumber LY 28; 67, 71, 114, 120,
  124, 126
Rat, William: Tamlaght TE 20; 76

Ratalla (see Ratallagh)

Ratallagh td: Ardkeen DN 7; 1

Ratallagh td: Misc. DN 17; 125

Ratallagh td: Witter DN 7; 125

Ratattas td: Ballywalter DN 7; 18

Rateen lime-kiln: Taughboyne DL 39; 154

Rateen td: Taughboyne DL 39; 148, 154, 196

Rath Lower td: Carlingford LH 40; 58

Rath, Benjamin: Dunboe LY 11; 72

Rath, Samual: Macosquin LY 22; 102

Rathbane td: Killoran and Kilvarnet SO 40; 184

Rathbarren td: Killoran and Kilvarnet SO 40; 183

Rathbeg td: Donegore AM 29; 101–02

Rathbeg td: Nilteen AM 35; 84

Rathbrady Beg meeting house: Drumachose LY 9; 49, 120, 125

Rathbrady Beg td: Drumachose LY 9; 49, 83, 87, 91, 96, 125, 128, 132–34

Rathbrady More school: Drumachose LY 9; 70, 124

Rathbrady More td: Drumachose LY 9; 83, 87, 91, 96, 134

Rathbrady school: Drumachose LY 9; 85

Rathbrady Sunday school: Drumachose LY 9; 85

Rathbready (see Rathbrady)

Rathcarbery td: Loughgilly AH 1; 85

Rathcavan (see Racavan)

Rathconwell td: Loughgilly AH 1; 85

Rathcor corn mill: Carlingford LH 40; 59

Rathcor school: Carlingford LH 40; 59

Rathcor td: Carlingford LH 40; 59

Rathcumber hill: Tynan AH 1; 124

Rathdooneybeg hill: Emlaghfad SO 40; 176

Rathdooneymore fort: Emlaghfad SO 40; 179

Rathdooneymore school: Emlaghfad SO 40; 179

Rathdooneymore trigonometrical station: Emlaghfad SO 40; 176

Rathdrumgrand fort: Loughgall AH 1; 78

Rathdrumgrand td: Loughgall AH 1; 82

Rathdrumgranna (see Rathdrumgrand)

Rathenraw fort: Antrim AM 29; 36, 43

Rathenraw hill: Antrim AM 29; 1

Rathfad (Rathfard) td: Aghanloo LY 11; 3, 9, 12–13, 15, 18–19, 22, 31–33, 37, 41–42

Rathfraggan (Rathfragan) td: Donacavey TE 5; 77, 79, 81–82, 86

Rathfraggan forts: Donacavey TE 5; 67, 82

Rathfrangan (see Rathfraggan)

Rathfriland: Ballymore AH 1; 16–17

Rathfriland: Clonallan DN 3; 1–2

Rathfriland: Clonduff DN 3; 3–5

Rathfriland: Drumballyroney DN 3; 10, 14–17

Rathfriland: Drumgath DN 3; 19–21

Rathfriland: Drumgooland DN 3; 23

Rathfriland: Faughanvale LY 36; 60

Rathfriland: Kilbroney DN 3; 30, 37

Rathfriland: Loughgilly AH 1; 84

Rathfriland: Misc. DN 17; 116, 131

Rathfriland: Newry DN 3; 110, 112

Rathfriland Castle: Drumballyroney DN 3; 12, 16

Rathfriland dispensary: Drumballyroney DN 3; 17

Rathfriland dispensary: Drumgath DN 3; 20

Rathfriland female school: Drumballyroney DN 3; 17–18

Rathfriland market house: Drumballyroney DN 3; 15

Rathfriland private school [I]: Drumballyroney DN 3; 17–18

Rathfriland private school [II]: Drumballyroney DN 3; 17–18

Rathfriland school: Drumballyroney DN 3; 17–18

Rathfriland school: Drumgath DN 3; 21

Rathgarmont td: Killinchy DN 7; 86, 89

Rathgill House: Bangor DN 7; 23

Rathgill td: Bangor DN 7; 19

Rathgill td: Misc. DN 17; 124

Rathgran td: Killoran and Kilvarnet SO 40; 184

Rathkeel hill: Racavan AM 13; 89

Rathkeel td: Racavan AM 13; 89

Rathkeeland bog: Aghavea FH 4; 18

Rathkeeland hill: Aghavea FH 4; 17

Rathkeeranbane bog: Clogher TE 5; 55

Rath-keltair fort: Down DN 17; 38, 41, 60

Rathkenny school: Skerry AM 13; 114

Rathkieland (see Rathkeeland)

Rathlin chapel: Rathlin Island AM 24; 128, 131–32

Rathlin church: Culfeightrin AM 24; 39

Rathlin church: Rathlin Island AM 24; 128–29, 131–32

Rathlin Glebe House: Rathlin Island AM 24; 128

Rathlin Island: Ballintoy AM 24; 15

Rathlin Island: Ballynure AM 32; 64

Rathlin Island: Clondavaddog DL 38; 8

Rathlin Island: Culfeightrin AM 24; 44

Rathlin Island: Killymard DL 39; 104–05

Rathlin Island: Lough Swilly DL 38; 130

Rathlin Island: Misc. AM 10; 129

Rathlin Island: Misc. DN 17; 122

Rathlin Island: Moville DL 38; 70

Rathlin Island: Ramoan AM 24; 90, 93, 96, 120

Rathlin Island: Tullyaughnish DL 38; 95

Rathlin mound: Rathlin Island AM 24; 134

Rathlin pier: Rathlin Island AM 24; 129, 131

Rathlin storehouses: Rathlin Island AM 24; 129

Rathlin sweathouses: Rathlin Island AM 24; 133

Rathlinbeg hill: Clonmany DL 38; 12

Rathlinmore hill: Clonmany DL 38; 12–13, 16

Rathmelton: Clondavaddog DL 38; 5–6

Rathmelton: Killygarvan DL 38; 40, 43–44, 46–47

Rathmelton: Kilmacrenan DL 38; 51

Rathmelton: Lough Swilly DL 38; 102, 106, 126–27, 129

Rathmelton: Mevagh DL 38; 57, 60, 62

Rathmelton: Raymoghy DL 39; 144

Rathmelton: Tullyaughnish DL 38; 84–88, 91–95

Rathmelton bay: Lough Swilly DL 38, 102

Rathmelton bay: Tullyaughnish DL 38; 86, 90, 92

Rathmelton bleach green: Killygarvan DL 38; 43

Rathmelton bleach green: Lough Swilly DL 38; 102

Rathmelton brewery: Tullyaughnish DL 38; 87, 89

Rathmelton bridge: Tullyaughnish DL 38; 90

Rathmelton Castle: Lough Swilly DL 38; 102

Rathmelton Castle: Tullyaughnish DL 38; 86–87, 91

Rathmelton channel: Lough Swilly DL 38; 102, 104

Rathmelton chapel: Tullyaughnish DL 38; 87–88

Rathmelton church: Tullyaughnish DL 38; 87–88, 90–91

Rathmelton corn mill: Tullyaughnish DL 38; 87

Rathmelton dispensary: Tullyaughnish DL 38; 87, 92–93

Rathmelton female school: Tullyaughnish DL 38; 92

Rathmelton flour mill: Lough Swilly DL 38; 102

Rathmelton hospital: Tullyaughnish DL 38; 87

Rathmelton inn: Tullyaughnish DL 38; 87

Rathmelton library: Tullyaughnish DL 38; 87

Rathmelton manor: Tullyaughnish DL 38; 92, 96–97

Rathmelton market place: Lough Swilly DL 38; 102

Rathmelton meeting house (Cov.): Tullyaughnish DL 38; 88

Rathmelton meeting house (P): Tullyaughnish DL 38; 87–88

Rathmelton old church: Tullyaughnish DL 38; 91

Rathmelton parish school: Tullyaughnish DL 38; 92

Rathmelton reading room: Tullyaughnish DL 38; 87

Rathmelton river (see Lennon): Tullyaughnish DL 38; 84

Rathmelton school: Tullyaughnish DL 38; 92

Rathmelton shambles: Tullyaughnish DL 38; 87

Rathmelton storehouses: Tullyaughnish DL 38; 87

Rathmelton td: Tullyaughnish DL 38; 96

Rathmelton tower: Tullyaughnish DL 38; 87

Rathmelton townparks: Tullyaughnish DL 38; 87

Rathmoran manor: Clones FH 4; 26

Rathmoran manor: Galloon FH 4; 94–95

Rathmoran td: Galloon FH 4; 93

Rathmore burn: Nilteen AM 35; 101

Rathmore Castle: Donegore AM 29; 122

Rathmore cave: Donegore AM 29; 122–23, 127–28

Rathmore school: Donegore AM 29; 134

Rathmore school: Nilteen AM 35; 86, 100

Rathmore td: Ballylinny AM 32; 30

Rathmore td: Donegore AM 29; 101–02, 114, 122, 130–31

Rathmore td: Killoran and Kilvarnet SO 40; 183

Rathmore td: Nilteen AM 35; 84

Rathmore Trench fort: Donegore AM 29; 104, 114, 122, 127–28

Rathmore Trench fort: Nilteen AM 35; 84

Rathmore well: Donegore AM 29; 123

Rathmuighie church: Glynn AM 26; 30

Rathmullan: Clondavaddog DL 38; 3, 8

Rathmullan: Killygarvan DL 38; 38–49

Rathmullan: Lough Swilly DL 38; 98, 101–02, 104, 126

Rathmullan: Raymoghy DL 39; 144

Rathmullan: Tullyaughnish DL 38; 87–89, 96

Rathmullan anchorage: Killygarvan DL 38; 38

Rathmullan anchorage: Lough Swilly DL 38; 104

Rathmullan battery: Killygarvan DL 38; 38–39, 41

Rathmullan bridge: Killygarvan DL 38; 47

Rathmullan Castle: Lough Swilly DL 38; 104

Rathmullan church: Bright DN 17; 36–37

Rathmullan church: Killygarvan DL 38; 39, 42

Rathmullan coastguard station: Tullyaughnish DL 38; 92

Rathmullan corn mill: Killygarvan DL 38; 40

Rathmullan dispensary: Clondavaddog DL 38; 7

Rathmullan dispensary: Killygarvan DL 38; 42

Rathmullan distillery: Killygarvan DL 38; 40

Rathmullan ferry: Lough Swilly DL 38; 143

Rathmullan fort: Lough Swilly DL 38; 98, 102

Rathmullan Glebe House: Bright DN 17; 36

Rathmullan Lower td: Bright DN 17; 35

Rathmullan Martello tower: Killygarvan DL 38; 38–39

Rathmullan meeting house: Killygarvan DL 38; 39

Rathmullan ph: Ballyphilip DN 7; 13

Rathmullan ph: Bright DN 17; 35

Rathmullan ph: Misc. DN 17; 122, 128

Rathmullan revenue station: Clondavaddog DL 38; 8

Rathmullan revenue station: Lough Swilly DL 38; 98

Rathmullan school: Bright DN 17; 36

Rathmullan school: Killygarvan DL 38; 42, 48

Rathmullan sessions house: Killygarvan DL 38; 42

Rathmullan td: Bright DN 17; 37

Rathmullan td: Killygarvan DL 38; 45, 47

Rathmullan Upper td: Bright DN 17; 35

Rathmullen (see Rathmullan): Bright DN 17; 37

Rathmurbuilg district: Ahoghill AM 23; 1

Rathnarrow Brett td: Killoran and Kilvarnet SO 40; 184

Rathnarrow O'Hara td: Killoran and Kilvarnet SO 40; 184

Rathnaselly Castle: Aghavea FH 4; 19

Rathneerey forts: Manorhamilton Union LM 40; 52

Rathnelly corn mill: Clogherny TE 20; 27

Rathnelly corn mill: Drumragh TE 5; 110

Rathnelly fort: Clogherny TE 20; 28

Rathnelly td: Drumragh TE 5; 110

Rathorey td: Killoran and Kilvarnet SO 40; 183

Rathree district: Cumber LY 28; 63

Rathscanlin td: Kilmacteige SO 40; 186

Rathshedog locality: Tullaghobegley DL 39; 173

Rathtarman td: Killoran and Kilvarnet SO 40; 183

Rathtrillick td: Tynan AH 1; 129

Rathturig diocese: Misc. LY 31; 111

Rathwarran (see Rathwarren)

Rathwarren (Ravarran) td: Donacavey TE 5; 67, 77, 79, 81, 83, 86

Rathwarren fort: Donacavey TE 5; 83

Rathyakeeliga td: Emlaghfad SO 40; 177

Ratoran standing stones: Enniskillen FH 4; 73

Ratoran td: Enniskillen FH 4; 73–74, 82

Ratory td: Clogher TE 5; 26

Ratowel td: Galloon FH 4; 95

Ratressin hill: Killdrumsherdan CN 40; 31

Ratressin school: Killdrumsherdan CN 40; 36

Rattass church: Shilvodan AM 19; 138

Rattass graveyard: Shilvodan AM 19; 138

Rattoarran (see Ratoran): Enniskillen FH 4; 73

Rattoo district: Shilvodan AM 19; 138

Rattorran (see Ratoran): Enniskillen FH 4; 82

Raughlin (Rathlin) Island: Montiaghs AH 1; 89, 91–92

Raughlin bay: Montiaghs AH 1; 92

Raughlin Island: Shankill AH 1; 113

Ravara corn mill [I]: Killinchy DN 7; 91

Ravara corn mill [II]: Killinchy DN 7; 91

Ravara td: Killinchy DN 7; 86, 91

Ravarnet (see Ravernet)

Raveagh (Ravagh) td: Donacavey TE 5; 77, 79, 81, 84, 86

Raveagh Lodge: Clogher TE 5; 44

Raveagh mill: Donacavey TE 5; 84

Ravel river (see also Clogh river): Dunaghy AM 13; 25–27

Ravel river: Kirkinriola AM 23; 91, 116

Ravel river: Newtown Crommelin AM 13; 78

Ravelin, robber: Desertoghill LY 27; 23

Ravelin's hill: Desertoghill LY 27; 14, 22–23

Ravelin's hill: Misc. LY 36; 111

Raven Hill Lodge: Carrickfergus AM 37; 57, 135, 141

Raven's rock hill: Glynn AM 26; 3–4, 9

Ravencroft, Rev. William: Rasharkin AM 23; 140

Ravens hill enclosures: Culfeightrin AM 24; 84

Ravenscroft, family: Ballinderry AM 21; 54

Ravensdale Park td: Ballymascanlan LH 40; 55

Ravernet river: Blaris DN 12; 26, 28

Ravernet river: Drumbo DN 7; 54

Ravernet river: Hillsborough DN 12; 85

Ravernet td: Hillsborough DN 12; 107

Ravonscroft, family: Ballinderry AM 21; 51

Raw fort: Belleek FH 14; 4

Raw forts: Clogherny TE 20; 28

Raw lough: Magheraculmoney FH 14; 103

Raw school: Aughnamullen MN 40; 77

Raw td: Aghalurcher FH 4; 14

Raw td: Aughnamullen MN 40; 76

Rawden, John: Blaris AM 8; 87

Rawdon, Arthur: Ahoghill AM 23; 6

Rawdon, family: Camlin AM 21; 68

Rawdon, family: Magheragall AM 21; 101

Rawdon, George: Blaris AM 8; 3–4, 87

Rawdon, George: Blaris DN 12; 33

Rawdon, John: Magheragall AM 21; 100

Rawdon, John: Moira DN 12; 118

Rawries (see Rawros): Lough Swilly DL 38; 116

Rawris (see Rawros)

Rawros ferry: Clondavaddog DL 38; 5

Rawros ferry: Lough Swilly DL 38; 113, 116, 116–17

Rawros ferry: Mevagh DL 38; 57

Rawros fort: Mevagh DL 38; 58

Rawros td: Mevagh DL 38; 63

Rawrus (see Rawros): Lough Swilly DL 38; 117

Raws hill: Donaghmore DL 39; 28

Raws hill: Tynan AH 1; 124

Raws Lower meeting house: Donaghmore DL 39; 32

Raws Lower td: Donaghmore DL 39; 38

Raws Upper school: Donaghmore DL 39; 40

Raws Upper td: Donaghmore DL 39; 28, 38

Ray bay: Lough Swilly DL 38; 102

Ray bridge: Lough Swilly DL 38; 102

Ray bridge: Tullyaughnish DL 38; 85, 89, 95

Ray Hill td: Tullyaughnish DL 38; 97

Ray lough: Donegal DL 39; 44

Ray river (see also Connaghan): Raymoghy DL 39; 144

Ray river: Lough Swilly DL 38; 102

Ray td: Raymoghy DL 39; 141–42, 144, 199

Ray td: Tullyaughnish DL 38; 97

Ray wood: Tullyaughnish DL 38; 85

Ray, Elizabeth: Ahoghill AM 23; 37

Ray, James (Jnr): Ahoghill AM 23; 37

Ray, James (Snr): Ahoghill AM 23; 37

Ray, James [I]: Ahoghill AM 23; 38

Ray, Jane: Ahoghill AM 23; 37

Ray, Mr: Killymard DL 39; 96

Ray, Robert: Dunboe LY 11; 81

Ray, Sarah: Ahoghill AM 23; 37

Ray, Thomas: Dunboe LY 11; 64, 70

Ray, W.J.: Ahoghill AM 23; 37

Raybane td: Aughnamullen MN 40; 76

Rayduff (see Reduff): Aughnamullen MN 40; 76

Raylands td: Misc. DL 39; 199

Raymoghy fishery: Raymoghy DL 39; 147

Raymoghy Glebe td: Raymoghy DL 39; 139
Raymoghy graveyard: Raymoghy DL 39; 134
Raymoghy old church: Raymoghy DL 39; 134–35
Raymoghy ph: Clondavadogg DL 38; 7
Raymoghy ph: Convoy DL 39; 18
Raymoghy ph: Killea and Taughboyne DL 39; 79
Raymoghy ph: Leck DL 39; 115, 120
Raymoghy ph: Misc. DL 39; 183–89, 191, 193, 198–99
Raymoghy ph: Raphoe DL 39; 121, 129
Raymoghy ph: Taughboyne DL 39; 149, 152
Raymoghy ph: Tullyaughnish DL 38; 93
Raymoghy schools: Raymoghy DL 39; 144–45, 194
Raymoghy td: Raymoghy DL 39; 135, 139
Raymond Cottage: Coleraine LY 33; 101
Raymond Cottage: Duneane AM 19; 94, 96–97, 100, 117–19
Raymunterdoney ph: Clondermot LY 34; 69
Rea corn mill: Aughnamullen MN 40; 69, 71–72
Rea district: Misc. LY 36; 112
Rea, Arther: Ballylinny AM 32; 23
Rea, Arthur: Camlin AM 21; 75
Rea, Arthur: Kilwaughter AM 10; 119, 121
Rea, Benjamin: Ballyrobert AM 2; 25
Rea, Daniel: Templepatrick AM 35; 146
Rea, family: Glynn AM 26; 42, 45
Rea, family: Killowen LY 33; 169
Rea, family: Tamlaght O'Crilly LY 18; 93
Rea, family: Templepatrick AM 35; 118, 147
Rea, Hugh: Ahoghill AM 23; 21, 42
Rea, James: Blaris AM 8; 81
Rea, James: Glynn AM 26; 45
Rea, James: Killowen LY 33; 161, 169
Rea, Jane: Glynn AM 26; 45
Rea, John: Artrea LY 6; 33
Rea, John: Bovevagh LY 25; 60
Rea, John: Carrickfergus AM 37; 109
Rea, John: Clondermot LY 34; 6, 104
Rea, John: Coleraine LY 33; 64
Rea, John: Killead AM 35; 15, 48
Rea, John: Killyleagh DN 17; 86
Rea, Langford: Carnmoney AM 2; 77
Rea, Margaret: Killead AM 35; 51
Rea, Mary: Glynn AM 26; 35, 47
Rea, Matty: Ballyrobert AM 2; 25
Rea, Mrs (Ballynalough): Templepatrick AM 35; 147
Rea, Nancy: Tamlaght TE 20; 86
Rea, Robert: Glynn AM 26; 45
Rea, Robert: Tamlaght O'Crilly LY 18; 104
Rea, Samuel: Ballyrobert AM 2; 25
Rea, Samuel: Killead AM 35; 51
Rea, Samuel: Templepatrick AM 35; 152
Rea, William: Bovevagh LY 25; 51, 59
Rea, William: Raphoe DL 39; 121

Rea, William: Tamlaght O'Crilly LY 18; 104
Rea, William: Templepatrick AM 35; 151
Reachtmhar, Feidhlimeidh: Misc. LY 36; 112
Read, family: Ballee DN 17; 16
Read, family: Ballywillin AM 16; 32
Read, family: Island Magee AM 10; 70
Read, James: Tydavnet MN 40; 173
Read, Mr: Clogher TE 5; 41
Read, Patrick: Clondermot LY 34; 70
Read, Rebecca: Hillsborough DN 12; 99
Read, Robert: Carrickfergus AM 37; 127
Read, Thomas: Coleraine LY 33; 72
Read, Thomas: Tamlaght TE 20; 84
Read, Thomas: Tydavnet MN 40; 173
Reade, Rev. G.L.: Devenish FH 14; 49–50, 53, 55
Reade, Rev. G.L.: Inishmacsaint FH 14; 76
Reade, Thomas: Clondermot LY 34; 47
Reading, Anne: Clonfeacle AH 1; 22
Reaford, Mr: Connor AM 19; 16
Reagh hill: Carrickfergus AM 37; 33, 77, 93, 174–75
Reagh hill cairn: Carrickfergus AM 37; 86, 184
Reagh Isle: Misc. DN 17; 121
Ream, family: Glynn AM 26; 45
Reaney, Charters: Ballyscullion AM 19; 10
Reaney, Ellen (Jnr): Ballyscullion AM 19; 13
Reaney, Ellen (Snr): Ballyscullion AM 19; 13
Reaney, Hugh: Drummaul AM 19; 90
Reaney, James: Ballyscullion AM 19; 10–12
Reaney, Mary: Duneane AM 19; 123
Reaney, Samuel: Drummaul AM 19; 87
Reaney, William: Ballyscullion AM 19; 8
Reath, family: Dunluce AM 16; 117
Reavy, Widow: Hillsborough DN 12; 106
Recreane (see Racrane)
Rectory Keerogue td: Clogher TE 5; 53
Red Bay: Ardclinis AM 13; 1, 3, 6
Red Bay: Layd AM 13; 36, 39–40, 42–45
Red Bay bridge: Layd AM 13; 48
Red Bay Castle: Layd AM 13; 40, 45
Red Bay chapel: Layd AM 13; 53
Red Bay td: Killead AM 35; 35
Red Castle: Billy AM 16; 68
Red Castle: Macosquin LY 22; 85, 107
Red Hill House: Blaris AM 8; 9
Red rock: Lough Swilly DL 38; 121
Red Shanks (see Antrim, Lord): Antrim AM 29; 48
Redcastle: Ballyscullion LY 6; 58
Redcastle: Dungiven LY 15; 60
Redcastle: Lough Swilly DL 38; 140
Redcastle House: Moville DL 38; 78
Redcastle wood: Moville DL 38; 75
Redding, Robert: Clonleigh DL 39; 7
Redergan forts: Clogherny TE 20; 28
Redfern, family: Magherafelt LY 6; 95

Redfern, John: Magherafelt LY 6; 108
Redgate, George: Magilligan LY 11; 94
Redhall corn mill: Templecorran AM 26; 86, 94, 125
Redhall demesne: Glynn AM 26; 30
Redhall demesne: Templecorran AM 26; 84, 94, 115, 119–20, 122
Redhall district: Templecorran AM 26; 82
Redhall flax mill: Templecorran AM 26; 94, 125
Redhall fort: Templecorran AM 26; 120
Redhall House: Templecorran AM 26; 11, 82–86, 91, 94, 99–100, 107, 112, 118–19, 124–25, 127, 129, 131–32
Redhall mills: Templecorran AM 26; 89
Redhall mound: Templecorran AM 26; 113, 117
Redhall td: Templecorran AM 26; 83, 94, 112, 115, 127, 130, 132
Redhall threshing machine: Templecorran AM 26; 125
Redhill (see Redhills): Killdrumsherdan CN 40; 31
Redhill bog: Drumbeg AM 8; 129
Redhill lough: Drumbeg AM 8; 129
Redhills: Currin MN 40; 89–91, 94
Redhills: Killdrumsherdan CN 40; 31, 34–35
Reding, William: Newry DN 3; 74
Redman, family: Armoy AM 24; 6
Redman, John: Larne AM 10; 126
Redman, Robert: Magheragall AM 21; 99
Redmond, Catharine: Hillsborough DN 12; 106
Redmond, family: Carnmoney AM 2; 76
Redmond, family: Shilvodan AM 19; 136
Redmond, John: Shilvodan AM 19; 137
Redmond, Mrs: Enniskillen FH 4; 82
Reduff bleach green: Aughnamullen MN 40; 72
Reduff chapel: Aughnamullen MN 40; 71
Reduff corn mill: Aughnamullen MN 40; 72
Reduff td: Aughnamullen MN 40; 69, 71–72, 76
Ree (see Reagh): Carrickfergus AM 37; 33
Ree bog: Agivey LY 22; 43
Ree hill: Aghanloo LY 11; 6, 29
Ree td: Agivey LY 22; 42
Ree td: Macosquin LY 22; 78
Reed, Capt.: Ballymyre AH 1; 20
Reed, David: Macosquin LY 22; 101–02
Reed, family: Dunluce AM 16; 117
Reed, Hugh: Rasharkin AM 23; 139
Reed, James: Templepatrick AM 35; 149
Reed, John: Ballyrashane LY 22; 57
Reed, John: Donaghmoyne MN 40; 107
Reed, John: Kildollagh LY 22; 72
Reed, John: Macosquin LY 22; 104, 121
Reed, Olliver: Loughguile AM 13; 74, 76
Reed, Robert: Donegore AM 29; 126, 133–34
Reed, Samuel: Dunboe LY 11; 76
Reed, Thomas: Balteagh LY 9; 24

Reedy flat: Aghagallon AM 21; 2
Reelan lough: Mevagh DL 38; 55
Reeland bridge: Kilteevoge DL 39; 112
Reeland river: Kilteevoge DL 39; 111–12
Reeland salmon leap: Kilteevoge DL 39; 112
Reford, T.B.: Blaris DN 12; 41
Reform Hill (see Ballyclaber): Coleraine LY 33; 143
Refragan td: Donacavey TE 5; 81
Regan school: Newry DN 3; 109
Regan td: Newry DN 3; 109
Regan, Denis: Kilcronaghan LY 31; 84
Regan, family: Ballynascreen LY 31; 12
Regan, Rev.: Maghera LY 18; 68
Regent bridge: Dromore DN 12; 75
Reheck td: Aghalurcher TE 5; 1
Rehorrin td: Clogher TE 5; 37
Reid, A.H.: Killyleagh DN 17; 81, 83
Reid, Andrew: Desertoghill LY 27; 32–33
Reid, Ann: Aghadowey LY 22; 37
Reid, Arthur: Ballymartin AM 2; 17
Reid, Charles: Carrickfergus AM 37; 163
Reid, David: Ballymoney AM 16; 15–17
Reid, David: Hillsborough DN 12; 106
Reid, Dr: Ballyaghran LY 33; 21
Reid, Elizabeth: Ballymartin AM 2; 16
Reid, Ellen: Kilraghts AM 16; 132
Reid, family: Antrim AM 29; 24
Reid, family: Ballymartin AM 2; 6, 15
Reid, family: Ballywillin AM 16; 32
Reid, family: Carnmoney AM 2; 76
Reid, family: Carrickfergus AM 37; 93
Reid, family: Dunluce AM 16; 117
Reid, family: Island Magee AM 10; 70
Reid, family: Muckamore AM 35; 65
Reid, family: Rashee AM 32; 138
Reid, family: Templepatrick AM 35; 118, 148
Reid, J.: Newtownhamilton AH 1; 100
Reid, J.S.: Aghanloo LY 11; 4
Reid, J.S.: Magilligan LY 11; 92
Reid, James: Aghalee AM 21; 31–32
Reid, James: Ballynascreen LY 31; 21
Reid, James: Carrickfergus AM 37; 192
Reid, James: Drumbeg AM 8; 125, 129
Reid, James: Drummaul AM 19; 87
Reid, James: Duneane AM 19; 125
Reid, James: Magheross MN 40; 149
Reid, James: Muckno MN 40; 165
Reid, James: Newry DN 3; 109
Reid, James: Tamlaght TE 20; 118
Reid, John: Billy AM 16; 69
Reid, John: Blaris DN 12; 45
Reid, John: Carrickfergus AM 37; 109
Reid, John: Errigal LY 27; 63
Reid, John: Kilraghts AM 16; 132, 135
Reid, John: Muckamore AM 35; 78

Reid, John: Newry DN 3; 98, 103
Reid, John: Tamlaght O'Crilly LY 18; 124
Reid, John [I]: Aghadowey LY 22; 37
Reid, John [I]: Hillsborough DN 12; 105
Reid, John [II]: Aghadowey LY 22; 37
Reid, John [II]: Hillsborough DN 12; 105
Reid, John [III]: Aghadowey LY 22; 38
Reid, Joseph: Kilrea LY 27; 129
Reid, Joseph: Tamlaght O'Crilly LY 18; 140
Reid, Levy: Aghadowey LY 22; 37
Reid, Maj. W.: Ballywillin LY 33; 51
Reid, Mary: Kilrea LY 27; 129
Reid, Miss (Dublin): Drumcree AH 1; 38
Reid, Mr: Ballintoy AM 24; 30
Reid, Mr: Ballymoney AM 16; 2, 8
Reid, Mr: Blaris DN 12; 39
Reid, Mr: Hillsborough DN 12; 87
Reid, Mr: Kilmood DN 7; 95
Reid, Mr [I]: Comber DN 7; 34
Reid, Mr [II]: Comber DN 7; 37, 40
Reid, Oliver: Kilraghts AM 16; 132, 134
Reid, Patt: Kilmacteige SO 40; 196
Reid, Rev.: Misc. LY 31; 136
Reid, Rev. J.S.: Carrickfergus AM 37; 26
Reid, Rev. J.S.: Donegore AM 29; 126, 129
Reid, Rev. Thomas: Drumgooland DN 3; 23, 25
Reid, Rev. Thomas: Drummaul AM 19; 69, 82
Reid, Rev. William: Aghaderg DN 12; 9
Reid, Rev. William: Drumballyroney DN 3; 15
Reid, Robert (Jnr): Aghadowey LY 22; 37
Reid, Robert (Snr): Aghadowey LY 22; 37
Reid, Robert: Ballylinny AM 32; 30
Reid, Robert: Down DN 17; 40, 62
Reid, S.H.: Culfeightrin AM 24; 76
Reid, Samuel: Kilraghts AM 16; 135
Reid, Samuel: Newry DN 3; 98, 101, 103
Reid, Sarah (Jnr): Aghadowey LY 22; 37
Reid, Sarah (Snr): Aghadowey LY 22; 37
Reid, Thomas: Aghadowey LY 22; 37
Reid, Thomas: Coleraine LY 33; 65, 72, 91, 127, 133
Reid, Thomas: Island Magee AM 10; 94
Reid, William: Aghadowey LY 22; 19
Reid, William: Kilrea LY 27; 121
Reid, William: Saintfield DN 7; 116
Reilley, Douglas: Bovevagh LY 25; 61
Reilly td: Kinawley FH 4; 114
Reilly well: Kinawley FH 4; 116
Reilly, Charles: Drumgoon CN 40; 8
Reilly, Edward: Newry DN 3; 100, 104
Reilly, Edward: Tydavnet MN 40; 172
Reilly, Eugene: Drummaul AM 19; 91
Reilly, family: Carrickfergus AM 37; 164
Reilly, family: Drumgoon CN 40; 8
Reilly, Hugh: Artrea LY 6; 23

Reilly, James: Aghaderg DN 12; 4, 10
Reilly, James: Coleraine LY 33; 145
Reilly, James: Kilbroney DN 3; 35
Reilly, John: Clonallan DN 3; 1
Reilly, John: Shankill AH 1; 114
Reilly, John [I]: Aghaderg DN 12; 9
Reilly, John [II]: Aghaderg DN 12; 4, 6
Reilly, Lazarus: Carrickfergus AM 37; 164
Reilly, Lushington: Misc. DN 17; 131
Reilly, Maul: Kilrea LY 27; 113
Reilly, Misses: Newry DN 3; 98, 103
Reilly, Mr (Scarva): Misc. DN 17; 130
Reilly, Mr: Aghaderg DN 12; 4
Reilly, Mrs: Aghaderg DN 12; 11
Reilly, Peggy: Carrickfergus AM 37; 120
Reilly, Rev. Peter: Drung CN 40; 21
Reilly, Rev. Thomas: Killdrumsherdan CN 40; 33
Reilly, Robert: Bovevagh LY 25; 18, 32
Reilly, Thomas: Clonduff DN 3; 4
Reilly, W.E: Seapatrick DN 12; 134
Reilly, W.E.: Aghaderg DN 12; 6
Reilly, W.E.: Annaclone DN 12; 16
Reilly, W.E.: Annahilt DN 12; 21–23
Reilly, W.E.: Blaris DN 12; 36
Reilly, W.E.: Comber DN 7; 37, 40
Reilly, W.E.: Donaghcloney DN 12; 58
Reilly, W.E.: Drumballyroney DN 3; 18
Reilly, W.E.: Drumbo DN 7; 58–60
Reilly, W.E.: Drumgath DN 3; 21
Reilly, W.E.: Hillsborough DN 12; 85–86, 91, 97, 102–03, 105
Reilly, W.E.: Magherally DN 12; 114
Reilly, W.E.: Seapatrick DN 12; 126, 128, 135
Reilly, W.E.: Tullylish DN 12; 144
Reilly, W.E.: Tullynakill DN 7; 122–23
Reilly, William: Clonallan DN 3; 1–2
Reilly's caves: Magheross MN 40; 143
Reilly's rocks: Magheross MN 40; 143
Reilly's Rocks lime-kiln: Killanny MN 40; 134
Reilly's Rocks lime-kiln: Magheracloone MN 40; 141
Reilly's rocks lime-kiln: Magheross MN 40; 149
Reilly's Trench chapel: Hillsborough DN 12; 95
Reilly's Trench school: Hillsborough DN 12; 95, 100
Reilly's Trench td: Hillsborough DN 12; 85, 87–88, 95, 100, 106
Reily, Luke: Carrickfergus AM 37; 164
Relagh Cottage: Kilskeery TE 5; 114–15
Relagh lough: Kilskeery TE 5; 113
Relagh school: Kilskeery TE 5; 115
Relagh td: Kilskeery TE 5; 114
Relagh-Guinness td: Kilskeery TE 5; 113
Relessey (see Relessy)
Relessy td: Aghalurcher FH 4; 16

Relessy td: Aghalurcher TE 5; 1
Relicairn graveyard: Ballymore AH 1; 10, 18
Relunapatha graveyard: Clondavaddog DL 38; 5
Remaulia td: Enniskillen FH 4; 65, 82
Rembrandt: Killesher FH 14; 84
Renenly day school: Clogher TE 5; 43
Reney, family: Lambeg AM 8; 135
Renfrew, family: Lambeg AM 8; 135
Renfrewshire (Scotland): Ballyclug AM 23; 60
Rennell, Mrs: Kilbroney DN 3; 35
Rennie, inventor: Maghera LY 18; 74
Rennie, J.H.: Coleraine LY 33; 62, 72, 94, 104, 130,
    150
Rennie, John: Carrickfergus AM 37; 46, 173
Rennie, John: Coleraine LY 33; 102, 124–25, 148
Rennie, John: Donaghadee DN 7; 46
Rennie, John: Newry DN 3; 87–88, 90
Rennie, John: Tamlaght Finlagan LY 25; 85
Rennie, M.B.: Carrickfergus AM 37; 42, 143, 174
Renny [or Kenny], Mrs (Rostrevor): Newry DN 3;
    110
Renolds, family: Magilligan LY 11; 142
Renous, Maj.: Kilmegan DN 3; 60
Renov (see Massereene, 4th Earl): Antrim AM 29;
    10
Rentoul, Rev. J.B.: Desertoghill LY 27; 4
Rentoul, Rev. J.B.: Errigal LY 27; 46, 52, 63, 65
Rentoul, Rev. James: Raymoghy DL 39; 133
Rentoul, Rev. Robert: Tamlaght Finlagan LY 25; 69
Rentoul, Solomon: Drumachose LY 9; 104
Repentance district: Donaghmore DL 39; 34
Rerhie td: Killymard DL 39; 100
Reside, James: Drummaul AM 19; 77, 86
Retory td: Clogher TE 5; 35
Retreat Castle: Layd AM 13; 40
Retreat House: Killdrumsherdan CN 40; 34, 37
Retreat td: Layd AM 13; 40
Reuben's glen: Desertmartin LY 31; 52
Revallagh Castle: Ballyrashane LY 22; 49, 53
Revallagh North cave: Ballyrashane LY 22; 50, 64
Revallagh North flax mill: Ballyrashane LY 22; 48
Revallagh North td: Ballyrashane LY 22; 47, 49, 66
Revallagh South td: Ballyrashane LY 22; 46, 63
Revallagh South well: Ballyrashane LY 22; 64
Revallagh td: Ballyrashane LY 22; 64
Reveagh (see Raveagh)
Revel lough: Duneane AM 19; 109, 120–21
Revlin bay: Killymard DL 39; 95
Revlin td: Killymard DL 39; 107
Rewaran td: Donacavey TE 5; 81
Reyford, Thomas: Magheramesk AM 21; 121
Reynell, Caius: Misc. DN 17; 117
Reyney, William: Donagh MN 40; 101
Reynolds, Anne: Maghera LY 18; 79
Reynolds, Capt.: Clondermot LY 34; 6, 20, 37, 104

Reynolds, Dr: Ballymoney AM 16; 16
Reynolds, family: Desertlyn LY 31; 42
Reynolds, family: Magherafelt LY 6; 95
Reynolds, family: Magilligan LY 11; 130
Reynolds, family: Ramoan AM 24; 107
Reynolds, Hugh: Loughguile AM 13; 75
Reynolds, John: Kilraghts AM 16; 132
Reynolds, John: Maghera LY 18; 6, 50, 59, 77
Reynolds, Joshua: Killesher FH 14; 84
Reynolds, Manus: Maghera LY 18; 6, 50
Reynolds, Mr (Carnick): Moville DL 38; 70
Reynolds, Mr: Magilligan LY 11; 120
Reynolds, Mrs (Derryscollop): Clonfeacle AH 1; 25
Reynolds, Mrs: Ballymoney AM 16; 15–17
Reynolds, Mrs: Coleraine LY 33; 72
Reynolds, P.: Down DN 17; 59
Reynolds, Thomas: Drumachose LY 9; 104
Reynolds, William: Newtown Crommelin AM 13;
    85
Rhellick graveyard: Balteagh LY 9; 9, 32–33
Rhiada, Carbry: Ballymartin AM 2; 5
Rhiunassnapiel Point: Lough Swilly DL 38; 123
Rhiunadrinnea locality: Lough Swilly DL 38; 106
Rhuinardallagh Point: Lough Swilly DL 38; 123
Rhuinarispie Point: Lough Swilly DL 38; 120
Rhuinaslegga Point: Lough Swilly DL 38; 120
Rhuinasnahid Point: Lough Swilly DL 38; 123
Rhuin-awaed Point: Lough Swilly DL 38; 134
Rhuinawoogan Point: Lough Swilly DL 38; 114–15
Rhuinaworgan Point: Lough Swilly DL 38; 120
Rhuinbwee Point: Lough Swilly DL 38; 106
Rhuinmore Point: Lough Swilly DL 38; 106,
    113–14
Rhynedh, Prince of Denmark: Errigal LY 27; 77
Rice, Ann (Jnr): Ballyscullion LY 6; 77
Rice, Ann (Snr): Ballyscullion LY 6; 77
Rice, Bernard: Carlingford LH 40; 59
Rice, Cathrine: Ballyscullion LY 6; 77
Rice, Edward: Duneane AM 19; 114, 118
Rice, Eliza: Carrickfergus AM 37; 120, 122
Rice, family: Ballywillin LY 33; 43
Rice, family: Coleraine LY 33; 61
Rice, George: Aghaderg DN 12; 11
Rice, James: Ballywillin LY 33; 31, 44
Rice, John: Blaris AM 8; 34
Rice, John: Coleraine LY 33; 59, 61, 132
Rice, John: Drumbeg AM 8; 122, 126, 128–29
Rice, Joshua: Carrickfergus AM 37; 135
Rice, Mary [I]: Ballyscullion LY 6; 77
Rice, Mary [II]: Ballyscullion LY 6; 77
Rice, Mary [III]: Ballyscullion LY 6; 77
Rice, Miss: Coleraine LY 33; 72
Rice, Mrs: Newry DN 3; 99
Rice, Patrick: Blaris DN 12; 31
Rice, Rebecca: Ballywillin LY 33; 31, 40, 43–44, 49

Rice, Robert (Jnr): Ballyscullion LY 6; 77
Rice, Robert (Snr): Ballyscullion LY 6; 77
Rice, Robert: Doagh AM 29; 88
Rice, S.R.: Carrickfergus AM 37; 28, 102, 141
Rich Hill: Ballymore AH 1; 1, 5
Rich Hill: Drumcree AH 1, 28, 36
Rich Hill: Kilmore AH 1; 59–64, 67, 69, 71, 73
Rich Hill: Mullaghbrack AH 1; 94, 96–97
Rich Hill chapel (M): Kilmore AH 1; 59, 62, 73
Rich Hill chapel of ease: Kilmore AH 1; 59
Rich Hill corn mill: Kilmore AH 1; 60–61, 63, 73
Rich Hill meeting house (I): Kilmore AH 1; 59, 62, 73
Rich Hill meeting house (P): Kilmore AH 1; 59, 62, 73
Rich Hill meeting house (Q): Kilmore AH 1; 59, 62, 73
Rich Hill national school: Kilmore AH 1; 62, 64
Rich Hill school: Kilmore AH 1; 59, 62, 64
Rich Hill Sunday school: Kilmore AH 1; 62, 64
Rich Hill tanyard: Kilmore AH 1; 62
Rich Hill td: Kilmore AH 1; 72
Richard II, King: Faughanvale LY 36; 64
Richard III, King: Island Magee AM 10; 62
Richard, Cormick: Skerry AM 13; 118
Richard, family: Kilraghts AM 16; 130
Richard, Hugh: Kilraghts AM 16; 132
Richard, Jane: Kilraghts AM 16; 132
Richard, William [I]: Kilraghts AM 16; 132
Richard, William [II]: Kilraghts AM 16; 132
Richards, family: Killagan AM 23; 84
Richards, Mr: Enniskillen FH 4; 82
Richards, Mrs: Warrenpoint DN 3; 122
Richards, William: Drumcree AH 1; 33
Richardson and Smith, Messrs: Drumachose LY 9; 83
Richardson and Smith, Messrs: Tamlaght Finlagan LY 25; 120
Richardson, Anne: Termoneeny LY 6; 132
Richardson, Capt.: Carnteel TE 20; 21, 23
Richardson, Edward: Ballybay MN 40; 82
Richardson, Edward: Donagh MN 40; 103, 105
Richardson, Edward: Tyholland MN 40; 175
Richardson, Eliza: Blaris AM 8; 79
Richardson, Elizabeth: Kilmore AH 1; 65, 67, 72
Richardson, family: Aghalee AM 21; 31
Richardson, family: Blaris DN 12; 30
Richardson, family: Derryaghy AM 8; 103
Richardson, family: Dungiven LY 15; 35
Richardson, family: Kilmore AH 1; 62–64, 67, 73
Richardson, family: Macosquin LY 22; 99, 107
Richardson, family: Maghera LY 18; 24, 48
Richardson, George: Moira DN 12; 120
Richardson, H.: Faughanvale LY 36; 45
Richardson, Henry (Jnr): Macosquin LY 22; 79

Richardson, Henry (Snr): Macosquin LY 22; 79
Richardson, Henry: Coleraine LY 33; 63, 65, 139
Richardson, Henry: Errigal LY 27; 80–81, 83–84
Richardson, Henry: Macosquin LY 22; 107
Richardson, Hugh: Termoneeny LY 6; 132
Richardson, Isabella: Kilmore AH 1; 59, 64–65, 67–70, 72
Richardson, J.: Blaris AM 8; 60, 84–85
Richardson, J.: Clogher TE 5; 53
Richardson, J.A.: Blaris AM 8; 55
Richardson, J.G.: Blaris AM 8; 37, 55
Richardson, J.G.: Blaris DN 12; 45, 49
Richardson, J.J.: Blaris AM 8; 55
Richardson, J.M.: Clogher TE 5; 53
Richardson, J.N.: Blaris AM 8; 69
Richardson, J.N.: Blaris DN 12; 46
Richardson, J.N.: Lambeg AM 8; 138–39, 142
Richardson, James: Blaris AM 8; 70, 84
Richardson, James: Newry DN 3; 68
Richardson, James: Tullyniskan TE 20; 139–40
Richardson, John: Blaris AM 8; 62, 70, 84
Richardson, John: Blaris DN 12; 45, 49
Richardson, John: Boho FH 14; 8
Richardson, John: Derryaghy AM 8; 96
Richardson, John: Derryvullan FH 14; 36
Richardson, John: Drumachose LY 9; 65
Richardson, John: Drumglass TE 20; 42
Richardson, John: Macosquin LY 22; 79–80, 95, 100–01
Richardson, John: Termoneeny LY 6; 132
Richardson, Jonathan: Blaris AM 8; 54–55, 66
Richardson, Jonathan: Derryaghy AM 8; 106
Richardson, Jonathan: Tamlaght Finlagan LY 25; 82–83
Richardson, Maj.: Dromore TE 5; 98–99
Richardson, man named: Carnmoney AM 2; 76
Richardson, Mary: Blaris DN 12; 46, 50
Richardson, Messrs James, Sons and Co.: Blaris AM 8; 20, 36–37
Richardson, Messrs James, Sons and Co.: Lambeg AM 8; 140
Richardson, Miss: Macosquin LY 22; 94
Richardson, Mr (Castle Hill): Clogher TE 5; 40, 54–55
Richardson, Mr (Downpatrick): Saul DN 17; 112
Richardson, Mr (Lisburn): Seagoe AH 1; 107–08
Richardson, Mr: Blaris AM 8; 12
Richardson, Mrs: Blaris AM 8; 84–85
Richardson, Mrs J.: Blaris AM 8; 66, 84
Richardson, Mrs J. [I]: Blaris AM 8; 85
Richardson, Mrs J. [II]: Blaris AM 8; 85
Richardson, Mrs J.G.: Blaris AM 8; 85
Richardson, Mrs Joseph: Blaris AM 8; 85
Richardson, Mrs Thomas: Macosquin LY 22; 93
Richardson, R.: Blaris AM 8; 60

Richardson, Rev.: Clones FH 4; 29

Richardson, Rev. John: Clogher TE 5; 40

Richardson, Rev. John: Drumkeeran FH 14; 65,
    67–68

Richardson, Rev. Thomas: Coleraine LY 33; 61–62,
    64, 73, 104, 127, 154

Richardson, Rev. Thomas: Dunboe LY 11; 67

Richardson, Rev. Thomas: Faughanvale LY 36; 40,
    45

Richardson, Rev. Thomas: Macosquin LY 22; 81,
    89–90, 92, 98

Richardson, Thomas: Blaris AM 8; 55

Richardson, W.S.: Newry DN 3; 68

Richardson, William: Magheramesk AM 21; 117

Richey, Alexander: Blaris AM 8; 29

Richey, Arthur: Aghagallon AM 21; 6–7

Richey, Arthur: Aghalee AM 21; 34

Richey, John: Blaris AM 8; 19–20, 46, 48

Richey, John: Drumbo DN 7; 58

Richey, John: Killevy AH 1; 54

Richey, Michael: Duneane AM 19; 112

Richey, Mr (Jnr): Clogher TE 5; 43

Richey, Mr (Snr): Clogher TE 5; 43

Richey, Thomas: Ahoghill AM 23; 33, 35

Richfield locality: Taughboyne DL 39; 155

Richhill (see Rich Hill): Mullaghbrack AH 1; 94

Richie, family: Derryaghy AM 8; 103

Richie, Jane: Kilwaughter AM 10; 116

Richmond (Richmount) td: Drumcree AH 1; 30,
    33–34, 36, 38

Richmond church: Errigal Keerogue TE 20; 51

Richmond Lodge: Holywood DN 7; 76

Richmond meeting house: Drumcree AH 1; 30

Richmond td: Errigal Keerogue TE 20; 49, 55

Richmond, Duke of: Aghadowey LY 22; 23

Richmond, Robert: Kilraghts AM 16; 136

Richmount House: Kilbroney DN 3; 35

Richmount Lodge: Carnmoney AM 2; 82

Richy, family: Macosquin LY 22; 119

Richy, James (Jnr): Drumachose LY 9; 133

Richy, James (Snr): Drumachose LY 9; 133

Richy, James: Tamlaght O'Crilly LY 18; 134

Richy, John: Errigal LY 27; 68, 68

Richy, John: Tamlaght O'Crilly LY 18; 112

Richy, Molly: Drumachose LY 9; 133

Richy, Samual: Drumachose LY 9; 133

Rickamore cove [I]: Templepatrick AM 35; 130,
    137, 150

Rickamore cove [II]: Templepatrick AM 35; 130,
    150

Rickamore dancing school: Templepatrick AM 35;
    148

Rickamore flax mill: Templepatrick AM 35; 113,
    140

Rickamore fort [I]: Templepatrick AM 35; 129, 137,
    150

Rickamore fort [II]: Templepatrick AM 35; 137, 150

Rickamore fort [III]: Templepatrick AM 35; 137,
    151

Rickamore plantation: Templepatrick AM 35; 139

Rickamore school: Templepatrick AM 35; 134–36,
    153–54

Rickamore Sunday school: Templepatrick AM 35;
    136, 154

Rickamore td: Templepatrick AM 35; 126–27, 130,
    132–33, 150, 152

Rickamore td: Umgall AM 35; 159–60

Rickamore tumulus: Templepatrick AM 35; 127,
    137

Rickey, Alexander: Skerry AM 13; 114

Riddagh, Ann: Artrea LY 6; 38

Riddagh, Daniel: Artrea LY 6; 38

Riddagh, James: Artrea LY 6; 38

Riddagh, Jane: Artrea LY 6; 38

Riddagh, John: Artrea LY 6; 38

Riddagh, Margrett: Artrea LY 6; 38

Riddagh, Mary (Jnr): Artrea LY 6; 38

Riddagh, Mary (Snr): Artrea LY 6; 38

Riddagh, Sareah: Artrea LY 6; 38

Riddall, Hans: Faughanvale LY 36; 45

Riddel, Hugh: Carrickfergus AM 37; 115

Riddel, William: Tamlaght TE 20; 77, 104

Riddell, Mr: Comber DN 7; 33, 40

Riddle, James: Ballymoney AM 16; 27

Riddle, Mr: Comber DN 7; 40

Riddle, Mr: Holywood DN 7; 76

Riddle, William: Carrickfergus AM 37; 122

Riddles, Charles (Jnr): Aghadowey LY 22; 37

Riddles, Charles (Snr): Aghadowey LY 22; 37

Riddles, Elizabeth: Aghadowey LY 22; 37

Riddles, Hugh: Aghadowey LY 22; 37

Riddles, John: Maghera LY 18; 44

Riddles, Margret: Aghadowey LY 22; 37

Riddles, Maryann (Jnr): Aghadowey LY 22; 37

Riddles, Maryann (Snr): Aghadowey LY 22; 37

Riddles, Matilda: Aghadowey LY 22; 37

Riddles, Matty: Aghadowey LY 22; 37

Riddles, Robert [I]: Aghadowey LY 22; 37

Riddles, Robert [II]: Aghadowey LY 22; 37

Riddles, Samual: Aghadowey LY 22; 37

Riddles, William: Aghadowey LY 22; 37

Ridge, Rev. John: Antrim AM 29; 23, 27

Ridgway, Lord: Clogher TE 5; 31

Ridick, family: Carnmoney AM 2; 76

Riga (Latvia): Newry DN 3; 85, 87

Riggs moss: Templecorran AM 26; 126

Riggs, Edward: Drumachose LY 9; 65

Riggs, Rev.: Loughgilly AH 1; 86

Right, Elenor: Artrea LY 6; 38

Right, George: Magheragall AM 21; 103, 106

Right, Hugh: Drumachose LY 9; 132

Right, John: Magheragall AM 21; 103

Rigs, family: Tamlaght O'Crilly LY 18; 93

Rile, A.T.: Ballyclog TE 20; 18

Riley, Edward: Ramoan AM 24; 113, 115, 119

Riley, John: Blaris AM 8; 54

Riley, Mary: Desertmartin LY 31; 60

Riley, Pat: Ramoan AM 24; 113

Riley, Rev. Charles: Ematris MN 40; 114

Rimer, John: Muff DL 38; 80

Rimer's inn: Muff DL 38; 80

Rimington, Lt T.H.: Ardglass DN 17; 1–9

Rinalargy (see Kinalargy): Mevagh DL 38; 57

Ring lough: Trory FH 14; 123

Ring td: Derrybrusk FH 4; 30–31

Ring td: Enniskillen FH 4; 82

Ringan, St: Bovevagh LY 25; 6, 18, 46, 50

Ringavilla td: Galloon FH 4; 95

Ringawiddy meeting house: Dunsfort DN 17; 69

Ringawiddy td: Dunsfort DN 17; 72

Ringbane (Ringbann) td: Donaghmore DN 3; 9

Ringbane corn mill: Donaghmore DN 3; 8

Ringbane td: Newry DN 3; 61

Ringbane td: Saul DN 17; 114–15

Ringclare td: Donaghmore DN 3; 7, 9

Ringcreevy school: Comber DN 7; 34, 39

Ringcreevy td: Comber DN 7; 34, 37, 39, 42–43

Ringfad hill: Ardglass DN 17; 9

Ringfad rocks: Ardclinis AM 13; 3

Ringfad td: Ardglass DN 17; 7

Ringhaddy Castle: Killinchy DN 7; 89

Ringhaddy old church: Killinchy DN 7; 92

Ringhaddy td: Blaris AM 8; 76

Ringhaddy td: Killinchy DN 7; 86, 88

Ringing stone: Ballintoy AM 24; 32–33

Ringneil Point: Tullynakill DN 7; 122

Ringneil td: Tullynakill DN 7; 122

Ringniel (see Ringneil): Tullynakill DN 7; 122

Ringolish td: Donaghmore DN 3; 9

Ringrashbeg bog: Macosquin LY 22; 116

Ringrashbeg cave [I]: Macosquin LY 22; 87, 115

Ringrashbeg cave [II]: Macosquin LY 22; 116

Ringrashbeg fort [I]: Macosquin LY 22; 85, 115

Ringrashbeg fort [II]: Macosquin LY 22; 115

Ringrashmore bog: Macosquin LY 22; 78, 116

Ringrashmore fort: Macosquin LY 22; 85–86, 115

Ringrashmore meeting house: Macosquin LY 22;
80, 94, 100

Ringrashmore Sunday school: Macosquin LY 22; 94

Ringrashmore td: Macosquin LY 22; 114, 122

Rings End hamlet: Errigal LY 27; 50

Ringsend: Raymoghy DL 39; 135

Ringsend district: Aghadowey LY 22; 16, 18

Ringsend district: Misc. LY 36; 111

Ringsend school: Aghadowey LY 22; 20–21

Ringsend Sunday school: Aghadowey LY 22; 21

Rinnalargy (see Kinalargy): Mevagh DL 38; 59

Rinskerry cave: Billy AM 16; 42

Ripley, Henry: Drumcree AH 1; 30

Rippingham, Miss: Coleraine LY 33; 69, 71–72,
134, 136–37, 153

Risk td: Ballyrashane LY 22; 66

Risk td: Moira DN 12; 120

Risk, family: Misc. LY 36; 104

Risk, Mrs: Clonleigh DL 39; 13

Risk's house: Lough Swilly DL 38; 104

Ritchey, John: Tamlaght Finlagan LY 25; 109

Ritchey, William: Tamlaght Finlagan LY 25; 109

Ritchie, Alexander: Carrickfergus AM 37; 129

Ritchie, Eliza: Carrickfergus AM 37; 130

Ritchie, family: Artrea LY 6; 14

Ritchie, family: Ballyscullion AM 19; 4

Ritchie, family: Carmavy AM 35; 2

Ritchie, family: Macosquin LY 22; 84

Ritchie, John: Bovevagh LY 25; 14, 37

Ritchie, John: Newry DN 3; 100, 104

Ritchie, Robert: Ahoghill AM 23; 37

Ritchy, Catherine: Carrickfergus AM 37; 116, 129

Ritchy, William: Macosquin LY 22; 108

Riveagh (see Raveagh)

Riverland demesne: Drumragh TE 5; 110

Riverland House: Drumragh TE 5; 111

Riversdale demesne: Trory FH 14; 124

Riversdale House: Magheraculmoney FH 14; 108

Riversdale House: Trory FH 14; 125, 130

Riverside td: Muckamore AM 35; 80–81

Riverstown House: Derryvullan FH 14; 34

Riverstown td: Drumragh TE 5; 111

Rivlin (see Revlin): Killymard DL 39; 95

Rivreagh td: Ballywalter DN 7; 18

Roa (see Roe)

Roach, Henry: Kilrea LY 27; 127

Roaghan bleaching mill: Donaghenry TE 20; 37, 39

Roaghan Castle: Donaghenry TE 20; 39

Roaghan lough: Donaghenry TE 20; 38–39

Roaghan td: Donaghenry TE 20; 39

Roaney, Mark: Seagoe AH 1; 106

Roaring Hole waterfall: Dungiven LY 15; 87, 93

Roashawen, family: Drumgath DN 3; 20

Robb, Miss: Coleraine LY 33; 72

Robb, Rev. David: Island Magee AM 10; 94

Robb's ferry: Drumcree AH 1; 36

Robb's ferry: Montiaghs AH 1; 92

Robb's pottery: Drumcree AH 1; 39

Robber's cave: Magilligan LY 11; 99

Robbinson, family: Raloo AM 32; 123, 126

Robbinson, John [I]: Raloo AM 32; 122

Robbinson, John [II]: Raloo AM 32; 123

Robbinson, Samuel: Raloo AM 32; 127

Robe, Lt T.C.: Ahoghill AM 23; 1–3
Robe, Lt T.C.: Ballywillin LY 33; 52
Robe, Lt T.C.: Macosquin LY 22; 98
Roberts, John: Blaris AM 8; 55
Roberts, John: Derryaghy AM 8; 107, 111
Roberts, Mrs: Dromore TE 5; 99
Roberts, Mrs Walter: Derryaghy AM 8; 107
Roberts, Walter: Derryaghy AM 8; 107
Robertson, Col: Killygarvan DL 38; 42, 48
Robertson, Col: Kilteevoge DL 39; 113–14
Robertson, Col: Leck DL 39; 119
Robertson, Col: Mevagh DL 38; 59
Robertson, Col: Raphoe DL 39; 127
Robertson, Col: Tullaghobegley DL 39; 172
Robertson, Col: Tullyaughnish DL 38; 92
Robertson, family: Carrickfergus AM 37; 179
Robertson, Margaret: Carrickfergus AM 37; 153
Robertson, Robert: Ballynascreen LY 31; 21
Robertson, William: Holywood DN 7; 83
Robertson's school: Glencolumbkille DL 39; 65
Robinson, Agnes: Carrickfergus AM 37; 115
Robinson, Andy: Raloo AM 32; 129
Robinson, Christopher: Drumachose LY 9; 61
Robinson, Daniel: Ballyrashane LY 22; 65
Robinson, David: Doagh AM 29; 98
Robinson, Elizabeth: Bovevagh LY 25; 26
Robinson, family: Ballynure AM 32; 56
Robinson, family: Billy AM 16; 58, 68
Robinson, family: Carnmoney AM 2; 76
Robinson, family: Carrickfergus AM 37; 93
Robinson, family: Culfeightrin AM 24; 59
Robinson, family: Derrykeighan AM 16; 89
Robinson, family: Doagh AM 29; 73, 94
Robinson, family: Glynn AM 26; 45
Robinson, family: Kilmacteige SO 40; 192
Robinson, family: Kilraghts AM 16; 130
Robinson, family: Raloo AM 32; 94, 108
Robinson, family: Ramoan AM 24; 107
Robinson, George: Kilraghts AM 16; 132
Robinson, George: Kilrea LY 27; 129
Robinson, H.: Rasharkin AM 23; 141
Robinson, Hugh: Loughguile AM 13; 74
Robinson, James: Ballyclug AM 23; 65
Robinson, James: Ballynure AM 32; 72
Robinson, James: Banagher LY 30; 90
Robinson, James: Donacavey TE 5; 81
Robinson, James: Drumcree AH 1; 32
Robinson, John: Ballynure AM 32; 73
Robinson, John: Balteagh LY 9; 12, 26
Robinson, John: Blaris AM 8; 19, 46
Robinson, John: Carncastle and Killyglen AM 10; 6
Robinson, John: Carnmoney AM 2; 99
Robinson, John: Coleraine LY 33; 66, 70, 139–40, 143–44
Robinson, John: Doagh AM 29; 98

Robinson, John: Finvoy AM 23; 75
Robinson, John: Glynn AM 26; 35, 46
Robinson, John: Hillsborough DN 12; 105
Robinson, John: Island Magee AM 10; 90
Robinson, John: Kilrea LY 27; 121
Robinson, John: Macosquin LY 22; 110
Robinson, John: Tamlaght O'Crilly LY 18; 141
Robinson, John [I]: Carrickfergus AM 37; 56, 102, 136, 141, 181
Robinson, John [I]: Drummaul AM 19; 76, 86
Robinson, John [II]: Carrickfergus AM 37; 115
Robinson, John [II]: Drummaul AM 19; 91
Robinson, Joseph: Ballynure AM 32; 55
Robinson, Joseph: Doagh AM 29; 98
Robinson, Margaret: Carrickfergus AM 37; 117
Robinson, Mary Ann: Warrenpoint DN 3; 122
Robinson, Matthew: Cumber LY 28; 86
Robinson, Matthew: Donacavey TE 5; 65
Robinson, Miss: Dunboe LY 11; 46
Robinson, Mr (Cloonbarry): Kilmacteige SO 40; 189–90, 192, 195
Robinson, Mr (Portadown): Seagoe AH 1; 105, 109
Robinson, Mr (Tawnaneille): Kilmacteige SO 40; 194
Robinson, Mr: Down DN 17; 58
Robinson, Mr: Kilmacteige SO 40; 185, 189
Robinson, Mr: Lough Swilly DL 38; 149
Robinson, Mrs (Cloonbarry): Kilmacteige SO 40; 189, 195
Robinson, Mrs: Donacavey TE 5; 65
Robinson, Mrs William: Ballyaghran LY 33; 8
Robinson, Nathaniel: Ballyrashane LY 22; 61–62
Robinson, Patrick: Carrickfergus AM 37; 129
Robinson, R.: Aughnamullen MN 40; 71–72
Robinson, Rev. Christopher: Drumlumman CN 40; 18
Robinson, Rev. T.R.: Clogher TE 5; 40
Robinson, Rev. T.R.: Enniskillen FH 4; 59, 82
Robinson, Rev. T.R.: Magheross MN 40; 148–49, 151
Robinson, Rev. W.: Aghanloo LY 11; 9, 36
Robinson, Rev. William: Ballyaghran LY 33; 8
Robinson, Rev. William: Bovevagh LY 25; 3, 26, 54
Robinson, Rev. William: Dungiven LY 15; 66
Robinson, Richard: Warrenpoint DN 3; 122
Robinson, Robert: Carrickfergus AM 37; 114
Robinson, Robert: Kilraghts AM 16; 132
Robinson, Sally: Ballynure AM 32; 72
Robinson, Samuel: Kilbride AM 29; 154
Robinson, Samuel: Newtownards DN 7; 112
Robinson, Samuel: Raloo AM 32; 128
Robinson, Samuel [I]: Ballynure AM 32; 60, 67
Robinson, Samuel [II]: Ballynure AM 32; 72
Robinson, Sarah: Coleraine LY 33; 68, 136
Robinson, Skeffington: Carrickfergus AM 37; 107

Robinson, Thomas: Ballynascreen LY 31; 13, 21
Robinson, Thomas: Hillsborough DN 12; 105
Robinson, Thomas: Tamlaght TE 20; 75, 128, 136
Robinson, Thomas [I]: Carrickfergus AM 37; 26
Robinson, Thomas [II]: Carrickfergus AM 37; 40, 148
Robinson, William: Ballynure AM 32; 72
Robinson, William: Killead AM 35; 52
Robinson, William: Magilligan LY 11; 137
Robinson, William: Raloo AM 32; 82, 92, 119–20, 123, 125, 128, 133
Robinson, William: Ramoan AM 24; 120, 122
Robinson, William: Seapatrick DN 12; 134
Robinson, William: Tamlaght TE 20; 75, 103
Robinson. Rev. L.H.: Kilclooney AH 1; 51
Robinson's fort: Aghalee AM 21; 26–27
Robison, Capt.: Muckamore AM 35; 78
Robison, family: Ballyclug AM 23; 60
Robison, family: Kirkinriola AM 23; 124
Robison, family: Racavan AM 13; 100
Robson, Smylie: Termoneeny LY 6; 128
Rochdale House: Desertcreat TE 20; 34, 36
Rochfort, Jane Isabella: Galloon FH 4; 90
Rochfort, Robert: Galloon FH 4; 90
Rochvale school: Newry DN 3; 81
Rock Angus locality: Witter DN 7; 125
Rock Aughavarn td: Ballymascanlan LH 40; 55
Rock Castle: Ballyaghran LY 33; 7–8, 14, 21
Rock Castle: Banagher LY 30; 50–51, 91
Rock chapel: Derryaghy AM 8; 104
Rock giant's grave: Drummaul AM 19; 64, 78, 89
Rock Hall (England): Ballyscullion LY 6; 57
Rock hamlet: Desertcreat TE 20; 32–34
Rock House: Ballyaghran LY 33; 7–8, 20
Rock House: Derryaghy AM 8; 92
Rock Lock: Aghalee AM 21; 34
Rock Lodge: Ballyscullion AM 19; 9
Rock Lodge: Desertcreat TE 20; 34
Rock meeting house: Donaghmore DN 3; 7
Rock well: Derryaghy AM 8; 92
Rock, family: Kilwaughter AM 10; 115
Rockby Hall: Kilmore AH 1; 67
Rockcorry: Aghabog MN 40; 64–66
Rockcorry: Aughnamullen MN 40; 73–74
Rockcorry: Currin MN 40; 90
Rockcorry: Ematris MN 40; 113–18
Rockcorry Castle: Ematris MN 40; 115
Rockcorry chapel: Ematris MN 40; 114
Rockcorry dispensary: Aghabog MN 40; 65
Rockcorry dispensary: Ematris MN 40; 114, 117
Rockcorry female school: Ematris MN 40; 117
Rockcorry infant school: Ematris MN 40; 117
Rockcorry market house: Ematris MN 40; 114
Rockcorry meeting house: Ematris MN 40; 114
Rockcorry sessions house: Ematris MN 40; 114

Rockdale House: Pomeroy TE 20; 71
Rockfield House: Drumlumman CN 40; 14
Rockfield House: Dundonald DN 7; 65
Rockfield House: Magheraculmoney FH 14; 108
Rockfield House: Trory FH 14; 133–34
Rockfield td. Galloon FH 4; 93
Rockfield td: Killea and Taughboyne DL 39; 80
Rockfield td: Maghera LY 18; 18, 52, 71–72
Rockfield td: Taughboyne DL 39; 148, 154, 196
Rockfield td: Trory FH 14; 133
Rockhill House: Leck DL 39; 116
Rockhill td: Leck DL 39; 119
Rocking stone: Island Magee AM 10; 57, 58, 76
Rocking stone: Mevagh DL 38; 62–63
Rocklands House: Carrickfergus AM 37; 135, 141
Rockmacreany (see Rockmacreeny): Kilmore AH 1; 66
Rockmacreeny flax mill: Kilmore AH 1; 61, 63, 72
Rockmacreeny td: Kilmore AH 1; 60–61, 66, 71–73
Rockmarshall House: Ballymascanlan LH 40; 56
Rockmarshall td: Ballymascanlan LH 40; 56
Rockport House: Carnmoney AM 2; 45
Rockport House: Holywood DN 7; 76–77, 81
Rocksavage House: Donaghmoyne MN 40; 107
Rocksavage td: Inniskeen MN 40; 128
Rocksborough, Martha: Agivey LY 22; 45
Rockstown House: Clonmany DL 38; 14
Rocktown cave: Maghera LY 18; 12, 60
Rocktown td: Maghera LY 18; 42–43, 46–47, 78
Rockvale bleaching establishment: Clondavaddog DL 38; 5
Rockvale House: Desertcreat TE 20; 34
Rockwood House: Manorhamilton Union LM 40; 50
Rocky hill: Ballintoy AM 24; 32
Rocky mountain: Kilbroney DN 3; 26
Rocky mountain: Kilkeel DN 3; 52
Rodcliff, Dr: Blaris AM 8; 52
Roddans td: Ballywalter DN 7; 17
Roddy, Patt: Bovevagh LY 25; 15, 35
Rodeing Foot locality: Ballymoney AM 16; 7
Roden, Earl of: Kilcoo DN 3; 43–44
Roden, Hugh: Clondermot LY 34; 90
Rodger, Mr: Drumragh TE 5; 108–09
Rodger, Rev. John: Maghera LY 18; 68
Rodger, Thomas: Drummaul AM 19; 88
Rodgers, Alexander: Rasharkin AM 23; 138
Rodgers, Andrew: Drumachose LY 9; 110
Rodgers, David: Carnmoney AM 2; 101
Rodgers, family: Carnmoney AM 2; 51, 76, 102
Rodgers, George: Aghadowey LY 22; 33
Rodgers, George: Maghera LY 18; 27, 29, 75
Rodgers, George: Newry DN 3; 100
Rodgers, Hugh: Aghadowey LY 22; 33–34
Rodgers, James: Ballynascreen LY 31; 18

Rodgers, James: Coleraine LY 33; 146

Rodgers, John: Carnmoney AM 2; 101

Rodgers, John: Carrickfergus AM 37; 119

Rodgers, Marcus: Balteagh LY 9; 36, 36

Rodgers, Mark: Balteagh LY 9; 41

Rodgers, Rev. Denis: Misc. LY 31; 137

Rodgers, Rev. H.W.: Kilrea LY 27; 117, 122, 126, 128

Rodgers, Rev. H.W.: Tamlaght O'Crilly LY 18; 136

Rodgers, Rev. John: Desertoghill LY 27; 15

Rodgers, Rev. John: Tamlaght O'Crilly LY 18; 90, 99, 106, 111, 143

Rodgers, Rev. Matthew: Misc. DL 39; 186

Rodgers, Rev. S.G.: Enniskillen FH 4; 58–59

Rodgers, Rev. William: Ballynure AM 32; 64

Rodgers, Robert: Glynn AM 26; 44

Rodgers, Robert: Tamlaght Finlagan LY 25; 105, 114

Rodgers, Samuel: Carnmoney AM 2; 101

Rodgers, Thomas: Ballymoney AM 16; 17

Rodham, Mr: Newry DN 3; 97, 101–02

Rodham, Mrs: Newry DN 3; 97, 101

Rodins manor: Misc. DN 17; 125

Rodman, Betty: Shilvodan AM 19; 138

Rodman, John: Dunaghy AM 13; 21, 25

Roe bridge: Aghanloo LY 11; 22

Roe bridge: Drumachose LY 9; 55, 119

Roe bridge: Tamlaght Finlagan LY 25; 85, 101

Roe Castle: Dungiven LY 15; 35

Roe footbridge: Bovevagh LY 25; 2

Roe Green bleach mill: Drumachose LY 9; 120

Roe Green bleach mill: Tamlaght Finlagan LY 25; 108, 120

Roe Green House: Drumachose LY 9; 52

Roe Green td: Drumachose LY 9; 120

Roe Green td: Tamlaght Finlagan LY 25; 122

Roe Island: Tamlaght Finlagan LY 25; 108

Roe mill: Drumachose LY 9; 46, 55

Roe Mill chapel: Drumachose LY 9; 49, 119

Roe Mill corn mill: Drumachose LY 9; 53, 121

Roe Mill distillery: Drumachose LY 9; 53, 121

Roe Mill House: Drumachose LY 9; 51–52

Roe Mill school: Drumachose LY 9; 50, 85, 123, 131

Roe Mill Sunday school: Drumachose LY 9; 132

Roe Park demesne: Drumachose LY 9; 46

Roe Park demesne: Tamlaght Finlagan LY 25; 63, 101, 103, 108, 117

Roe Park fort: Tamlaght Finlagan LY 25; 103, 117

Roe Park House: Banagher LY 30; 57

Roe Park House: Drumachose LY 9; 84, 97

Roe Park House: Tamlaght Finlagan LY 25; 62–63, 80–82, 92, 94–95, 97, 100–03, 108, 117, 122, 125

Roe Park old church: Tamlaght Finlagan LY 25; 101

Roe Park wooden bridge: Tamlaght Finlagan LY 25; 80–81, 123

Roe river: Aghanloo LY 11; 1, 3–4, 7, 9, 12, 18–9, 21–22, 24–25, 35–37

Roe river: Balteagh LY 9; 1–2, 5, 13–14, 20–21, 27, 41, 43

Roe river: Banagher LY 30; 2–5, 16, 25–26, 59, 73, 100

Roe river: Bovevagh LY 25; 1–4, 6–9, 14, 16, 19–20, 22, 24, 26–27, 35–36, 43, 49, 51–53, 57

Roe river: Clondermot LY 34; 106–107

Roe river: Drumachose LY 9; 46, 49, 57, 73–75, 89, 99, 101, 103, 106, 121, 129

Roe river: Dungiven LY 15; 1–4, 9, 11, 35, 50–52, 54, 61–64, 79, 82, 87, 92, 95, 97–98, 106

Roe river: Killelagh LY 27; 95

Roe river: Lough Swilly DL 38; 138

Roe river: Magilligan LY 11; 82–85, 98–100, 119–20, 124–25, 141

Roe river: Tamlaght Finlagan LY 25; 62–63, 66, 80–85, 93, 95, 97–98, 101, 103–08, 114–15, 120

Roe river: Termoneeny LY 6; 129

Roe, family: Tamlaght O'Crilly LY 18; 92

Roe, Mary: Dungiven LY 15; 31, 48, 79

Roe, Neeny: Drummaul AM 19; 61, 72, 87

Roe, Richard: Killelagh LY 27; 101

Roe, Richard: Maghera LY 18; 39

Rogagh river: Boho FH 14; 9

Rogan lough: Killygarvan DL 38; 37

Rogan, Francis: Donaghmore DL 39; 30, 32–33, 36, 40

Rogan, Francis: Faughanvale LY 36; 45

Rogan, Francis: Raphoe DL 39; 125

Rogan, Hugh (Jnr): Hillsborough DN 12; 106

Rogan, Hugh: Hillsborough DN 12; 106

Rogan, John: Aghagallon AM 21; 14

Rogan, John: Magheramesk AM 21; 122, 126

Rogan, Owen: Hillsborough DN 12; 106

Rogan, W.: Ardglass DN 17; 11

Rogan's Park td: Urney DL 39; 181–82

Roger, Mr (Garshooey): Killea and Taughboyne DL 39; 87

Roger's mill: Killea and Taughboyne DL 39; 87

Rogers, Charles: Connor AM 19; 28

Rogers, family: Ballintoy AM 24; 20

Rogers, family: Ballynure AM 32; 56

Rogers, family: Blaris DN 12; 30

Rogers, family: Magheragall AM 21; 99

Rogers, family: Misc. LY 31; 122

Rogers, James: Ballintoy AM 24; 23

Rogers, John: Aghalee AM 21; 37

Rogers, John: Blaris AM 8; 61, 84

Rogers, John: Blaris DN 12; 45, 49

Rogers, John: Longfield TE 5; 128

Rogers, Mr (Rosses): Inishkeel DL 39; 73

Rogers, Mr: Clogher TE 5; 40
Rogers, Patrick: Blaris AM 8; 46
Rogers, Rev. Anthony: Blaris AM 8; 25
Rogers, Rev. Brian: Misc. LY 31; 137
Rogers, Rev. John (Jnr): Aghadowey LY 22; 23
Rogers, Rev. Matthew: Misc. LY 31; 137
Rogers, Rev. R.: Donagh DL 38; 35
Rogers, Rev. Terence: Ballynascreen LY 31; 9, 137
Rogers, Robert: Clondermot LY 34; 90
Rogers, Robert: Cumber LY 28; 74–75
Rogers, Simon: Termonamongan TE 5; 145
Rogers, Thomas: Clogher TE 5; 43
Rogers, Thomas: Coleraine LY 33; 72
Rogers, William: Banagher LY 30; 46, 48, 72, 76
Roghan (see Roughan): Misc. DL 39; 198
Roghan Hill (see Rough Hill): Errigal Keerogue TE 20; 57
Rohan (see Roughan): Donacavey TE 5; 81
Roisbrack chapel: Kildress TE 20; 60
Rollin, William: Tamlaght TE 20; 131
Rollins, George: Blaris DN 12; 46
Rollins, John: Blaris DN 12; 40
Rollins, John: Tamlaght TE 20; 81, 108–09
Rollins, William: Tamlaght TE 20; 81, 108–09
Rolly Island: Tullynakill DN 7; 124
Rolstone, Rev. Thomas: Aghadowey LY 22; 19, 21
Roly Ballaghan's grave: Drumtullagh AM 16; 101
Romadia district: Misc. SO 40; 198
Rome: Clondermot LY 34; 32
Rome: Culfeightrin AM 24; 64
Rome: Donaghmore DL 39; 34
Rome: Drumtullagh AM 16; 100
Rome: Dunboe LY 11; 61
Rome: Galloon FH 4; 87
Rome: Kilmacteige SO 40; 185
Rome: Magheracross FH 14; 97
Rome: Magherafelt LY 6; 92, 109
Rome: Misc. LY 31; 137
Rome: Saul DN 17; 113
Ronan, St: Aghalurcher FH 4; 1, 9
Ronay, Mr (Tamnaficarbet): Seagoe AH 1; 110
Roney, family: Drumballyroney DN 3; 13
Ronskey td: Moville DL 38; 73
Rooe of Purtachurry Point: Lough Swilly DL 38; 111
Rooe td: Aughnamullen MN 40; 76
Rooenahinnera Point: Lough Swilly DL 38; 109, 111
Roohan td: Tullyaughnish DL 38; 97
Rookin fort: Agivey LY 22; 44, 44
Roomcoom locality: Racavan AM 13; 103
Rooney, Anne: Ramoan AM 24; 126
Rooney, Eliza: Tamlaght TE 20; 128
Rooney, family: Ballee DN 17; 16
Rooney, Hugh: Carrickfergus AM 37; 122

Roonivollan quarry: Rathlin Island AM 24; 127
Roonivoolan lough: Rathlin Island AM 24; 127
Roorkfield td: Killesher FH 14; 84
Rooskagh North td: Kinawley FH 4; 110
Rooskagh South td: Kinawley FH 4; 110
Rooskey druid's altar: Raphoe DL 39; 124
Rooskey Island: Inishmacsaint FH 14; 76
Rooskey Upper td: Raphoe DL 39; 126
Roosky (Rooskey) td: Inishmacsaint FH 14; 76
Roosky (Ruskey) td: Ramoghy. DL 39; 139–42
Roosky (see Rousky): Donaghedy TE 5; 89
Roosky corn mill: Devenish FH 14; 53
Roosky corn mill: Galloon FH 4; 91
Roosky dispensary: Devenish FH 14; 55
Roosky fort: Clonmany DL 38; 16
Roosky hill: Clonmany DL 38; 12
Roosky Lower td: Raphoe DL 39; 126
Roosky school: Devenish FH 14; 55–56
Roosky td: Aghalurcher FH 4; 13
Roosky td: Clonmany DL 38; 18, 20
Roosky td: Devenish FH 14; 55, 59
Roosky td: Donaghedy TE 5; 89
Roosky td: Galloon FH 4; 91, 94–95, 105
Roosky td: Monaghan MN 40; 159
Root district: Drumtullagh AM 16; 103
Root district: Loughguile AM 13; 58
Roper, D.: Ballybay MN 40; 81
Roper, Rev. Henry: Aughnamullen MN 40; 76–77
Roper, Rev. Henry: Clogher TE 5; 40
Roper, Rev. Henry: Clones FH 4; 27, 29
Roper, Rev. William: Clogher TE 5; 40
Roper, Rev. William: Enniskeen CN 40; 28–29
Roranna td: Drummully FH 4; 39
Rory's Glen flax mill: Kilwaughter AM 10; 110
Rory's Glen lime kiln: Kilwaughter AM 10; 113
Rory's Glen td: Kilwaughter AM 10; 107, 110, 116, 118
Ros mill: Drumachose LY 9; 100
Rosa (see Roe): Dungiven LY 15; 63
Rosa, Salvator: Killesher FH 14; 84
Rosalongan House: Killymard DL 39; 96
Rosapenna House: Mevagh DL 38; 58
Rosapenna House: Tullyaughnish DL 38; 88
Rosapenna isthmus: Lough Swilly DL 38; 116, 119
Rosapenna isthmus: Mevagh DL 38; 54, 56, 58, 60, 62
Rosapenna lough: Mevagh DL 38; 55
Rosapenna td: Mevagh DL 38; 60, 63
Rosborough, family: Kirkinriola AM 23; 124
Rosbotham, family: Derryaghy AM 8; 103
Rosbrough, Henry: Ballyaghran LY 33; 21
Rosburg, John: Aghadowey LY 22; 37
Roscavey corn mill: Clogherny TE 20; 27
Roscavey forts: Clogherny TE 20; 28
Roscavey House: Clogherny TE 20; 25

Roscavey td: Clogherny TE 20; 26

Rosclogher barony: Manorhamilton Union LM 40; 47

Roscoe locality: Enniskillen FH 4; 45

Roscommon county: Ballyclug AM 23; 56

Roscommon county: Clondermot LY 34; 71

Roscommon county: Faughanvale LY 36; 44, 63

Roscommon county: Manorhamilton Union LM 40; 50

Roscommon county: Misc. SO 40; 199–200

Rose Brook House: Carrickfergus AM 37; 135–36

Rose Lodge: Magherafelt LY 6; 92

Rose, James: Aughnamullen MN 40; 75

Rose, James: Tydavnet MN 40; 172–73

Rosebourough, David: Bovevagh LY 25; 22

Rosebrook House: Banagher LY 30; 4, 15

Rosedermot school: Dunaghy AM 13; 16–7

Rosegarran (see Rosgarran): Desertmartin LY 31; 62

Roselick moss: Ballyaghran LY 33; 15, 26

Roselick td: Ballyaghran LY 33; 8, 26

Roselickbeg chapel of ease: Ballyaghran LY 33; 21

Roselickbeg graveyard: Ballyaghran LY 33; 21

Roselickbeg td: Ballyaghran LY 33; 28

Roselickmore bog: Ballyaghran LY 33; 21

Rose-malland (see Rosemeilan)

Rosemealan (see Rosemeilan)

Rosemeilan (Rosemealan) td: Clogher TE 5; 37, 54

Rosemont House: Witter DN 7; 126

Rosemount demesne: Grey Abbey DN 7; 67–68, 70–71

Rosemount House: Dromore DN 12; 72

Rosemount House: Drumbeg AM 8; 124, 130

Rosemount House: Grey Abbey DN 7; 69

Rosemount House: Misc. DN 17; 119

Rosemount manor: Misc. DN 17; 123–24

Rosemount td: Grey Abbey DN 7; 67

Rose-Trevor (see Rostrevor): Kilbroney DN 3; 30

Rosetta House: Kilbroney DN 3; 35

Rosevale House: Blaris AM 8; 33

Roseville House: Blaris AM 8; 9, 34

Roseyards meeting house: Ballymoney AM 16; 9

Roseyards td: Ballymoney AM 16; 9, 24

Rosgarran (Rosegarland) td: Desertmartin LY 31; 62 142, 144

Rosgarron (see Rosgarran): Misc. LY 31; 142

Rosgier (see Rossgeir): Clonleigh DL 39; 15

Rosguill Peninsula: Clondavaddog DL 38; 3, 5–6, 9

Rosguill Peninsula: Lough Swilly DL 38; 114, 118–19, 121, 127–29

Rosguill Peninsula: Mevagh DL 38; 54–55, 57–62

Rosguill Peninsula: Raymoghy DL 39; 144

Rosguill Peninsula: Tullyaughnish DL 38; 88

Roshure (Rusure) td: Desertmartin LY 31; 62, 142

Rosinafarsna td: Devenish FH 14; 58

Rosinver ph: Manorhamilton Union LM 40; 47

Roskey (see Roosky)

Roslea (see Rosslea)

Rosnakill church: Clondavaddog DL 38; 4, 7

Rosnakill district: Lough Swilly DL 38; 117, 129

Rosnakill graveyard: Clondavaddog DL 38; 5

Rosnakill old church: Clondavaddog DL 38; 4

Rosnakill td: Clondavaddog DL 38; 4, 7–8

Rosnakill td: Tullyaughnish DL 38; 87

Rosnashane td: Finvoy AM 23; 71

Rosnery td: Skerry AM 13; 118

Ross bog: Connor AM 19; 28

Ross fort: Manorhamilton Union LM 40; 52

Ross Inner (Innear) td: Devenish FH 14; 55, 58

Ross Island: Devenish FH 14; 59

Ross Lodge: Connor AM 19; 16, 18, 21, 23, 30–31

Ross lookout station: Lough Swilly DL 38; 109

Ross lough: Devenish FH 14; 52

Ross lough: Inniskeen MN 40; 124

Ross Outer td: Devenish FH 14; 58

Ross Point: Lough Swilly DL 38; 109, 111, 114, 117

Ross quarries: Lough Swilly DL 38; 129

Ross rectory: Cumber LY 28; 71

Ross td: Ardglass DN 17; 7

Ross td: Ballee DN 17; 15

Ross td: Boho FH 14; 8

Ross td: Cleenish FH 14; 14, 30

Ross td: Connor AM 19; 17, 21, 29

Ross td: Dunsfort DN 17; 67

Ross, Alexander: Ballinderry AM 21; 49

Ross, Alexander: Muckamore AM 35; 78

Ross, Andrew: Island Magee AM 10; 82

Ross, Capt. (see Millar): Connor AM 19; 31

Ross, Capt.: Balteagh LY 9; 36

Ross, Christopher: Newry DN 3; 100, 104

Ross, Col.: Kilbroney DN 3; 32, 34–35

Ross, D.R.: Kilbroney DN 3; 26, 29, 31–32, 35, 37

Ross, David: Balteagh LY 9; 43–44

Ross, David: Kilbroney DN 3; 29

Ross, David: Kilraghts AM 16; 132

Ross, Dorothea: Ballywillin AM 16; 32

Ross, Dorothea: Ballywillin LY 33; 43

Ross, Edward: Drumachose LY 9; 73

Ross, Edward: Magilligan LY 11; 83

Ross, Edward: Tamlaght Finlagan LY 25; 105

Ross, F.A.: Clondermot LY 34; 79–80

Ross, family: Ballinderry AM 21; 51

Ross, family: Ballywalter AM 2; 26, 30

Ross, family: Ballywillin AM 16; 32

Ross, family: Blaris AM 8; 21

Ross, family: Carrickfergus AM 37; 177

Ross, family: Enniskillen FH 4; 58

Ross, family: Island Magee AM 10; 70

Ross, family: Kilbroney DN 3; 32

Ross, family: Kilraghts AM 16; 130

Ross, family: Kirkinriola AM 23; 124

Ross, George: Carrickfergus AM 37; 194
Ross, George: Witter DN 7; 126
Ross, Henry: Dungiven LY 15; 117–19
Ross, J.: Comber DN 7; 41
Ross, J.: Dundonald DN 7; 65
Ross, James: Balteagh LY 9; 35
Ross, James: Clondermot LY 34; 79–80
Ross, James: Cumber LY 28; 8
Ross, James: Inver AM 26; 54
Ross, James: Kilraghts AM 16; 132
Ross, James: Tickmacrevan AM 13; 128
Ross, Jane: Balteagh LY 9; 43
Ross, Jane: Dunboe LY 11; 81
Ross, Jane: Kilraghts AM 16; 132
Ross, John (Jnr): Island Magee AM 10; 90
Ross, John (Snr): Island Magee AM 10; 90
Ross, John: Ballymoney AM 16; 15
Ross, John: Ballywillin LY 33; 43
Ross, John: Billy AM 16; 76
Ross, John: Carrickfergus AM 37; 177
Ross, John: Drumachose LY 9; 61, 73
Ross, John: Dunboe LY 11; 56–57, 70, 73
Ross, John [I]: Kilraghts AM 16; 132
Ross, John [II]: Kilraghts AM 16; 132
Ross, John [III]: Kilraghts AM 16; 132
Ross, Lord: Cleenish FH 14; 12, 16–17, 28
Ross, Margaret: Dunboe LY 11; 81
Ross, Mary: Carrickfergus AM 37; 123
Ross, Mary: Dunboe LY 11; 81
Ross, Michael: Balteagh LY 9; 11
Ross, Michael: Banagher LY 30; 78, 96, 98
Ross, Miss: Ballymoney AM 16; 15–16
Ross, Mr (Teeavan): Banagher LY 30; 57
Ross, Mr: Ballywillin AM 16; 32
Ross, Mr: Magilligan LY 11; 120
Ross, Mrs (Carrickbawn): Kilbroney DN 3; 35
Ross, Mrs: Dungiven LY 15; 18
Ross, Mrs John: Drumachose LY 9; 64
Ross, Mrs Robert: Kilbroney DN 3; 31–32, 34–35,
   38
Ross, Paul: Banagher LY 30; 51, 92, 96
Ross, Rev. Alexander: Banagher LY 30; 1, 5, 8,
   14–15, 22–23, 29–30, 32, 39, 56–57, 59, 96,
   98–99, 114, 116, 120, 131
Ross, Rev. Alexander: Cumber LY 28; 83
Ross, Rev. Alexander: Dungiven LY 15; 5, 18–19,
   43, 49, 102, 119
Ross, Rev. Edward: Donegore AM 29; 126, 130
Ross, Rev. Richard: Aghabog MN 40; 63, 66
Ross, Rev. Thomas: Kilbroney DN 3; 32
Ross, Richard: Drumachose LY 9; 73
Ross, Robert: Aghanloo LY 11; 22, 30–31
Ross, Robert: Drumachose LY 9; 69, 99, 104
Ross, Robert: Dunboe LY 11; 81
Ross, Robert: Kilbroney DN 3; 30–34

Ross, Robert: Kilraghts AM 16; 132
Ross, Robert: Magilligan LY 11; 95
Ross, Robert: Newry DN 3; 74–75
Ross, Samuel: Island Magee AM 10; 90
Ross, Thomas (Jnr): Dunboe LY 11; 81
Ross, Thomas (Snr): Dunboe LY 11; 81
Ross, Thomas: Ballylinny AM 32, 23, 28, 30
Ross, Thomas: Cumber LY 28; 72
Ross, Thomas: Dungiven LY 15; 49
Ross, Thomas: Island Magee AM 10; 90
Ross, William: Banagher LY 30; 33, 96, 111
Ross, William: Blaris DN 12; 46, 50
Ross, William: Carrickfergus AM 37; 107
Ross, William: Cumber LY 28; 9
Ross, William: Drumachose LY 9; 52, 66, 73, 83, 91
Ross, William: Kilwaughter AM 10; 119
Ross, William: Magilligan LY 11; 132, 138
Ross' monument: Kilbroney DN 3; 29, 34
Rossaghrin td: Derryvullan FH 14; 33
Rossahilly bog: Trory FH 14; 124
Rossahilly Point: Trory FH 14; 124
Rossan Island: Inishmacsaint FH 14; 73
Rossanure hill: Devenish FH 14; 47
Rossanurebeg hill: Devenish FH 14; 47
Rossanuremore hill: Devenish FH 14; 47
Rossanuremore school: Devenish FH 14; 50
Rossanvalla td: Cleenish FH 14; 30
Rossarnell td: Donagh MN 40; 98
Rossavulland td: Enniskillen FH 4; 82
Rossawalla (see Rossawally): Cleenish FH 14; 14
Rossawally td: Cleenish FH 14; 14, 18
Rossbeg td: Aghalurcher FH 4; 14
Rossbrackan td: Leck DL 39; 119
Rossbrick td: Clones FH 4; 26
Rosscairn td: Rossorry FH 14; 116
Rossconor (Rosconnor) td: Drumballyroney DN 3;
   18
Rossconor corn mill: Kilmore DN 17; 88
Rossconor flax mill: Kilmore DN 17; 88
Rossconor House: Kilmore DN 17; 88
Rossconor tanyard: Drumballyroney DN 3; 16
Rossconor td: Kilmore DN 17; 88–89
Rosscor Island: Inishmacsaint FH 14; 70
Rosscorkey Island: Cleenish FH 14; 13, 30
Rosscrow, family: Enniskillen FH 4; 58
Rossculbin bog: Magheraculmoney FH 14; 104
Rossculbin td: Magheraculmoney FH 14; 105
Rosscullon fort: Devenish FH 14; 55
Rosscullon td: Devenish FH 14; 52, 59
Rossculton (see Rosscullon): Devenish FH 14; 52
Rosscur school: Magheracross FH 14; 99
Rosscur td: Magheracross FH 14; 102
Rosscut Island: Inishmacsaint FH 14; 70, 73
Rossdale, Anthony: Ballyscullion LY 6; 57
Rossdoney td: Cleenish FH 14; 30

Rossdooney district: Clondermot LY 34; 63, 82

Rossdreenagh lough: Donaghmoyne MN 40; 106

Rosse, Hugh: Kinawley FH 4; 116

Rosse, Lord: Kinawley FH 4; 117

Rosse, William: Kinawley FH 4; 116

Rosses bay (Foyle): Clondermot LY 34; 52

Rosses bay: Misc. LY 36; 119

Rosses district (Donegal): Clondermot LY 34; 73

Rosses district: Drumhome DL 39; 62

Rosses district: Inishkeel DL 39; 72–73

Rosses district: Killymard DL 39; 96

Rosses district: Lough Swilly DL 38; 125–26

Rosses district: Mevagh DL 38; 58

Rosses district: Raymoghy DL 39; 146

Rosses district: Tullaghobegley DL 39; 173

Rossfad House: Derryvullan FH 14; 33

Rossfad td: Boho FH 14; 8

Rossfadd (see Rossfad)

Rossgad td: Aghalurcher FH 4; 4, 14

Rossgarrow Island: Lough Swilly DL 38; 113, 117

Rossgarrow td: Tullyaughnish DL 38; 96

Rossgeer (see Rossgeir)

Rossgeir bridge: Misc. DL 39; 188

Rossgeir td: Clonleigh DL 39; 10, 12, 15, 198

Rossgier (see Rossgeir)

Rossglass chapel: Bright DN 17; 36

Rossglass school: Bright DN 17; 36

Rossglass td: Bright DN 17; 35–36

Rossharbour school: Belleek FH 14; 6

Rossherry cave: Skerry AM 13; 119

Rossherry td: Skerry AM 13; 119

Rossinnin school: Derryvullan FH 14; 36

Rosskeady locality: Lough Swilly DL 38; 113

Rosslea: Aghalurcher FH 4; 8

Rosslea: Aghavea FH 4; 21, 25

Rosslea: Clones FH 4; 28

Rosslea chapel: Clones FH 4; 28

Rosslea market house: Clones FH 4; 28

Rosslim pillars: Ballyclug AM 23; 66

Rosslough td: Donaghmoyne MN 40; 106

Rossmacale td: Aghalurcher FH 4; 14

Rossmackawinny brickfield: Killesher FH 14; 84

Rossmackawinny td: Killesher FH 14; 87

Rossmacole (see Rossmacale): Aghalurcher FH 4; 14

Rossmona Point: Lough Swilly DL 38; 102

Rossmore bridge: Lissan LY 31; 90, 99

Rossmore graveyard: Drumglass TE 20; 40

Rossmore hill: Drumglass TE 20; 44

Rossmore td: Derryvullan FH 14; 33

Rossmore td: Drumglass TE 20; 40

Rossmore td: Lissan LY 31; 103, 108, 110

Rossmore wood: Tamlaght O'Crilly LY 18; 87, 128–29

Rossnabarton td: Lough Swilly DL 38; 111

Rossnafarsna td: Devenish FH 14; 59

Rossnagallagh (see Rossnagalliagh)

Rossnagalliagh (Rosnagalliagh) td: Clondermot LY 34; 38, 45, 57, 72–74, 76, 105, 107, 111, 113, 119, 127, 133

Rossnagalliagh church: Clondermot LY 34; 32–33, 47–48

Rossnagalliagh graveyard: Clondermot LY 34; 48

Rossnagalliagh nunnery: Clondermot LY 34; 48

Rossnagalliagh quarry: Clondermot LY 34; 133

Rossnagalliagh school: Clondermot LY 34; 9

Rossnagalliagh Sunday school: Clondermot LY 34; 92–93

Rossnakill (see Rosnakill)

Rossnalough West plantation: Aghabog MN 40; 67

Rossnalough West td: Aghabog MN 40; 63, 63

Rossnamuck locality: Lough Swilly DL 38; 107

Rossnoughlagh warren: Drumhome DL 39; 58–59

Rossorry bridge: Devenish FH 14; 53

Rossorry church: Rossorry FH 14; 117

Rossorry distillery: Enniskillen FH 4; 55

Rossorry forts: Rossorry FH 14; 117

Rossorry graveyard: Enniskillen FH 4; 72

Rossorry ph: Cleenish FH 14; 11, 14

Rossorry ph: Clogher TE 5; 41

Rossorry ph: Enniskillen FH 4; 43, 55–56, 62–63, 70, 82

Rossory (see Rossorry)

Rossoy td: Killesher FH 14; 82, 85

Rossqueer bog: Derryvullan FH 14; 32

Rossreagh meeting house: Tullyaughnish DL 38; 88

Rossreagh td: Tullyaughnish DL 38; 97

Rostrevor (see Rostrevor): Kilbroney DN 3; 32

Rostrevor: Clonallan DN 3; 2

Rostrevor: Clonduff DN 3; 3, 5

Rostrevor: Drumgath DN 3; 20

Rostrevor: Kilbroney DN 3; 26–30, 32–33, 35–37

Rostrevor: Misc. DN 17; 116

Rostrevor: Newry DN 3; 73, 100, 105, 110

Rostrevor: Rathmullan DN 17; 108

Rostrevor: Warrenpoint DN 3; 119

Rostrevor barracks: Kilbroney DN 3; 38

Rostrevor bay: Kilbroney DN 3; 33

Rostrevor bay: Warrenpoint DN 3; 120

Rostrevor bridge: Kilbroney DN 3; 29, 33, 35

Rostrevor chapel: Kilbroney DN 3; 33–34, 38

Rostrevor church: Kilbroney DN 3; 29–30, 33–34, 36

Rostrevor corn mill: Kilbroney DN 3; 35

Rostrevor dispensary (see also Warrenpoint): Kilbroney DN 3; 30, 37

Rostrevor hotel: Kilbroney DN 3; 33–34, 37

Rostrevor mountains: Kilbroney DN 3; 26, 29

Rostrevor mountains: Kilkeel DN 3; 52

Rostrevor national school: Kilbroney DN 3; 34, 38

Rostrevor old church: Kilbroney DN 3; 29, 32–33, 36

Rostrevor pier: Kilbroney DN 3; 29, 35–37

Rostrevor post office: Kilbroney DN 3; 33

Rostrevor pottery: Kilbroney DN 3; 32

Rostrevor quay: Clonallan DN 3; 2

Rostrevor quay: Kilbroney DN 3; 26, 29, 32, 35

Rostrevor quay hamlet: Kilbroney DN 3; 35

Rostrevor river (see also Kilbroney river): Kilbroney DN 3; 26, 29, 33, 36

Rostrevor saltworks: Kilbroney DN 3; 32, 35

Rostrevor td: Kilbroney DN 3; 32

Rostrevor union school: Kilbroney DN 3; 34, 38

Rostrevor Upper td: Kilbroney DN 3; 26

Rostrevor Vicarage: Kilbroney DN 3; 35

Rostrevor wood: Kilbroney DN 3; 26

Rothwell, Mr: Aughnamullen MN 40; 75, 77

Rough fort: Desertoghill LY 27; 8, 27, 34

Rough fort: Macosquin LY 22; 85, 88, 108–09, 111

Rough fort: Tamlaght Finlagan LY 25; 101, 103, 109, 125

Rough fort: Templepatrick AM 35; 110, 129, 140, 149, 151

Rough hill: Magherafelt LY 6; 79

Rough Hill corn mill: Errigal Keerogue TE 20; 55

Rough Hill plantation: Errigal Keerogue TE 20; 55

Rough Hill td: Errigal Keerogue TE 20; 48, 55, 57

Rough Island (see St Ernan's): Donegal DL 39; 44

Rough Island: Belleek FH 14; 2

Rough Island: Clondermot LY 34; 3, 18, 48–49

Rough Island: Comber DN 7; 32, 43

Rough Island: Tamlaght O'Crilly LY 18; 86, 122–23

Rough Island: Tullynakill DN 7; 124

Rough Park td: Tullyaughnish DL 38; 96

Roughan (Roghan) td: Donacavey TE 5; 77, 79, 81, 83, 87

Roughan (Rooghan) td: Racavan AM 13; 89, 96, 100

Roughan bay: Lough Swilly DL 38; 120

Roughan bogs: Errigal Keerogue TE 20; 55

Roughan corn mill: Drumballyroney DN 3; 12, 16

Roughan flax mill: Drumballyroney DN 3; 12, 16

Roughan fort: Errigal Keerogue TE 20; 55

Roughan school: Errigal Keerogue TE 20; 55

Roughan school: Racavan AM 13; 96, 100

Roughan Steps ford: Drumballyroney DN 3; 10, 16

Roughan td: Clonleigh DL 39; 12, 195, 198

Roughan td: Conwal DL 39; 27

Roughan td: Drumcree AH 1; 40

Roughan td: Errigal Keerogue TE 20; 48, 55

Roughfort book club room: Templepatrick AM 35; 110, 122, 147–48

Roughfort Castle: Templepatrick AM 35; 125

Roughfort corn mill: Templepatrick AM 35; 148

Roughfort cotton mill: Templepatrick AM 35; 131, 142

Roughfort cove: Templepatrick AM 35; 151

Roughfort female school: Templepatrick AM 35; 154

Roughfort female Sunday school: Templepatrick AM 35; 154

Roughfort graveyard: Templepatrick AM 35; 110, 124, 151

Roughfort hamlet: Ballymartin AM 2; 12, 16

Roughfort hamlet: Templepatrick AM 35; 110–11, 149, 151

Roughfort library: Mallusk AM 2; 113

Roughfort library: Templepatrick AM 35; 110, 131

Roughfort male school: Templepatrick AM 35; 154

Roughfort male Sunday school: Templepatrick AM 35; 154

Roughfort old church: Templepatrick AM 35; 110

Roughfort tumulus: Templepatrick AM 35; 137

Round hill bleach mill: Magheradrool DN 17; 106

Round house: Bovevagh LY 25; 7, 43

Round lough: Clogher TE 5; 25, 47

Round lough: Kilmacteige SO 40; 194

Roureagh td: Misc. DN 17; 125

Rousky (Ruskey) td: Donaghedy TE 5; 92

Rousky school: Donaghedy TE 5; 89

Route district: Ardglass DN 17; 12

Route district: Coleraine LY 33; 156

Route district: Glynn AM 26; 1

Route district: Island Magee AM 10; 65

Route district: Raloo AM 32; 80, 115

Row, family: Newry DN 3; 106

Row, Rev. W.: Clogher TE 5; 40

Rowan, A.H.: Killyleagh DN 17; 83

Rowan, A.H.: Tullyaughnish DL 38; 97

Rowan, Andrew: Doagh AM 29; 94

Rowan, Edward: Carrickfergus AM 37; 141, 150

Rowan, family: Carrickfergus AM 37; 93

Rowan, family: Doagh AM 29; 73

Rowan, family: Drumballyroney DN 3; 13

Rowan, family: Kilcronaghan LY 31; 68

Rowan, family: Templepatrick AM 35; 118

Rowan, J.H.: Down DN 17; 61–62, 64

Rowan, John: Ballymoney AM 16; 15

Rowan, John: Carnmoney AM 2; 46, 53, 81, 84, 89–90

Rowan, John: Derrykeighan AM 16; 78

Rowan, John [I]: Doagh AM 29; 70, 72, 92, 96, 99

Rowan, John [II]: Doagh AM 29; 93

Rowan, Messrs John and Sons: Doagh AM 29; 92

Rowan, Robert: Ballylinny AM 32; 23

Rowan, Robert: Ballymoney AM 16; 16–17

Rowan, Thomas: Newry DN 3; 100, 104

Rowan, William: Drumgooland DN 3; 23

Rowan, William: Kildollagh LY 22; 67

Rowan, William: Killyleagh DN 17; 85
Rowan's Point: Island Magee AM 10; 90
Rowantree cairn: Drumtullagh AM 16; 100, 102
Rowantree, family: Misc. LY 36; 105
Rowe, Anna: Ballyscullion LY 6; 46
Rowe, John: Ballyscullion LY 6; 57
Rowe, Simonem: Ballyscullion LY 6; 46
Rowen, Rev.: Ballinderry AM 21; 50
Rowley, Arabella (nee Dawson): Ballyscullion LY 6; 58–59
Rowley, Catharine: Kilcronaghan LY 31; 68–69
Rowley, David: Aghagallon AM 21; 25
Rowley, Elizabeth: Kilcronaghan LY 31; 68–69
Rowley, family: Ballyscullion LY 6; 59
Rowley, family: Kilcronaghan LY 31; 68–69, 76–77
Rowley, family: Templepatrick AM 35; 116–17
Rowley, H.L.: Killead AM 35; 13, 16, 47
Rowley, Henry: Kilcronaghan LY 31; 68, 87
Rowley, John: Clondermot LY 34; 71
Rowley, John: Coleraine LY 33; 57
Rowley, John: Faughanvale LY 36; 54, 56, 58, 60, 64
Rowley, Mary: Kilcronaghan LY 31; 68–69
Rowley, Patt: Kilmacteige SO 40; 193
Rowley, Sarah: Kilcronaghan LY 31; 68–69
Rowley, William: Artrea LY 6; 37
Rowley, William: Ballyscullion LY 6; 56–58
Rowley, William: Desertlyn LY 31; 37, 45
Rowling Weel whirlpool: Ballyphilip DN 7; 9
Rowman, family: Magherafelt LY 6; 95
Rowney, Hana Ker: Carrickfergus AM 37; 124
Rowries (see Rawros): Lough Swilly DL 38; 116
Rowrus (see Rawros): Lough Swilly DL 38; 113
Roxton House waterguard station: Lough Swilly DL 38; 132
Roxton locality: Lough Swilly DL 38; 133
Roy House: Lough Swilly DL 38; 143
Roy Island: Mevagh DL 38; 55–56
Roy saltworks: Lough Swilly DL 38; 143
Roy td: Clogher TE 5; 34–36, 53
Roy, Alexander: Ramoan AM 24; 120
Roy, family: Ramoan AM 24; 107
Royal Canal (Leinster): Enniskillen FH 4; 46
Royal Irish Academy, Dublin: Ballynascreen LY 31; 33–34
Royal Irish Academy, Dublin: Faughanvale LY 36; 51
Royal Oak tree: Kilcronaghan LY 31; 64, 87
Roydan, John: Blaris AM 8; 87
Royduff (see Reduff): Aughnamullen MN 40; 69
Ruagagh river: Devenish FH 14; 47–48
Ruagagh river: Inishmacsaint FH 14; 72, 74
Ruban td: Misc. DN 17; 125
Rubbalshinny (see Urbalshinny): Tullyaughnish DL 38; 96

Rubbleshinny (see Urbalshinny): Tullyaughnish DL 38; 89
Rudd lough: Tomregan FH 4; 126
Ruddan, John: Ahoghill AM 23; 37
Ruddan, Margaret: Ahoghill AM 23; 37
Ruddell, John: Shankill AH 1; 114
Rudden, William: Magilligan LY 11; 94
Ruddle, family: Maghera LY 18; 24, 48
Ruddock, James: Blaris DN 12; 50
Ruddock, Mr: Magheradrool DN 17; 101
Rudhall, Abel: Donaghcloney DN 12; 60
Rudhall, I.: Newry DN 3; 66
Rudolph, Rev. C. H.: Artrea LY 6; 7, 16, 20–21
Rue forts: Kilmacteige SO 40; 185, 189, 194
Rue Point: Rathlin Island AM 24; 130
Rue td: Kilmacteige SO 40; 186, 196
Ruff Island (see Rough Island): Tamlaght O'Crilly LY 18; 122
Rughan meeting house: Tullyaughnish DL 38; 87–88
Rughan td: Tullyaughnish DL 38; 86
Ruinara Point: Lough Swilly DL 38; 101, 144
Ruinaskeagh Point: Lough Swilly DL 38; 119
Rumbling Hole cataract: Derryaghy AM 8; 91
Run hill: Tynan AH 1; 124
Runaghan td: Loughgall AH 1; 79
Runanogher glebe: Galloon FH 4; 96
Runanogher Glebe td: Drummully FH 4; 34, 39
Runbuoy bay: Clondavaddog DL 38; 3, 9
Runbuoy Head: Clondavaddog DL 38; 3
Runbuoy lough: Clondavaddog DL 38; 2
Runmore bay: Clondavaddog DL 38; 9
Rupper, Theodore: Ahoghill AM 23; 40
Rusaine (see Rushen): Templecarn DL 39; 157
Ruscrine (see Rushen): Templecarn DL 39; 156
Ruseton, Mr: Drumgoon CN 40; 10
Rush (Dublin): Lough Swilly DL 38; 118–19
Rush field: Muckamore AM 35; 80
Rush Hall House: Tamlaght Finlagan LY 25; 82, 101
Rush, Francis: Clones FH 4; 29
Rush's ferry: Drumcree AH 1; 36
Rush's ferry: Montiaghs AH 1; 90, 92
Rushbrook bleach green: Aghadowey LY 22; 7, 9, 12
Rushbrook House: Aghadowey LY 22; 7, 12, 18
Rushbrook House: Coleraine LY 33; 64
Rushbrook House: Desertoghill LY 27; 29
Rusheem district: Misc. SO 40; 199
Rusheen (see Rushen): Templecarn DL 39; 164
Rushen (see Rushin): Cleenish FH 14; 22, 30
Rushen district: Templecarn DL 39; 164
Rushen hill: Templecarn DL 39; 164
Rushen lough: Belleek FH 14; 1
Rushen lough: Templecarn DL 39; 156–57
Rushen td: Templecarn DL 39; 164

Rushfield House: Lissan LY 31; 103
Rushin House: Cleenish FH 14; 18
Rushin td [I]: Cleenish FH 14; 22, 30
Rushin td [II]: Cleenish FH 14; 30
Rushmore Head: Clondavaddog DL 38; 3
Rushpark House: Carnmoney AM 2; 84
Rushyhill td: Donaghmore DL 39; 38
Rusk, family: Templepatrick AM 35; 118
Rusk, Rev. Robert: Ballyscullion AM 19; 8, 15
Ruske, James (Jnr): Glynn AM 26; 47
Ruske, James (Snr): Glynn AM 26; 47
Ruske, John: Glynn AM 26; 47
Ruske, Margaret: Glynn AM 26; 47
Ruske, Samuel [I]: Glynn AM 26; 47
Ruske, Samuel [II]: Glynn AM 26; 47
Ruske, W.A.: Glynn AM 26; 47
Ruske, William (Jnr): Glynn AM 26; 47
Ruske, William (Snr): Glynn AM 26; 47
Ruskey (see Roosky): Clonmany DL 38; 12
Ruskey Lower td: Tamlaght TE 20; 100, 120, 135
Ruskin, Giltha: Duneane AM 19; 122
Rusky (Ruskie) td: Drumachose LY 9; 87, 96, 101
Rusky td: Aghadowey LY 22; 8
Rusky td: Misc. DL 39; 186, 195
Russel, Abraham: Annaclone DN 12; 18
Russel, family: Carnmoney AM 2; 76
Russel, family: Carrickfergus AM 37; 60
Russel, George: Carnmoney AM 2; 76
Russel, John: Loughguile AM 13; 66
Russel, Michael: Carrickfergus AM 37; 39
Russel, Mr: Drumbo DN 7; 59
Russel, Samuel: Garvaghy DN 12; 82
Russel, Thomas: Carrickfergus AM 37; 128
Russel, Widow: Glenavy AM 21; 89
Russell, Arthur: Newry DN 3; 100, 104
Russell, Ellen: Leck DL 39; 119
Russell, family: Armoy AM 24; 6
Russell, family: Ballyculter DN 17; 28
Russell, family: Ballynascreen LY 31; 12
Russell, family: Ballyphilip DN 7; 12
Russell, family: Carrickfergus AM 37; 84, 182
Russell, H.W.: Drumbo DN 7; 56
Russell, Mathew: Newry DN 3; 100
Russell, Miss: Blaris DN 12; 46, 50
Russell, Mr (Rathmullan): Ballyphilip DN 7; 13

Russell, Mrs: Ballinderry AM 21; 50
Russell, Patrick: Bright DN 17; 34–35
Russell, Patrick: Down DN 17; 52, 57
Russell, Ralph: Ballinderry AM 21; 49
Russell, Rev. (Ashbrook): Aghalurcher FH 4; 8, 16
Russell, Rev. (Ashbrook): Clogher TE 5; 40
Russell, Thomas: Ballinderry AM 21; 52
Russell, Thomas: Enniskeen CN 40; 29–30
Russell, Thomas: Newtown Crommelin AM 13; 84
Russell, William: Annaclone DN 12; 14
Russell, William: Carrickfergus AM 37; 13–4
Russell, William: Drumbo DN 7; 56
Russell's Quarter North td: Saul DN 17; 115
Russell's Quarter South td: Saul DN 17; 115
Russell's Quarter td: Down DN 17; 53, 57
Russell's Quarter td: Saul DN 17; 114
Russia: Carrickfergus AM 37; 137
Russia: Coleraine LY 33; 75, 87
Russia: Lambeg AM 8; 141
Russia: Lough Neagh AM 21; 92
Rust, Joanna: Dromore DN 12; 74
Ruston, H.: Drumcree AH 1; 39
Rutherford, Mr (Drumnakelly): Seagoe AH 1; 108
Rutherford, Rev. John: Seapatrick DN 12; 132
Rutherson, Roben: Desertlyn LY 31; 42
Ruthven, Mr: Killyleagh DN 17; 86
Rutland district: Mevagh DL 38; 62
Rutledge, Mr: Manorhamilton Union LM 40; 53
Rutty, Dr: Carrickfergus AM 37; 8
Ryan meeting house: Newry DN 3; 77
Ryan school: Newry DN 3; 81
Ryan td: Newry DN 3; 77, 81
Ryan, John: Carrickfergus AM 37; 108–09
Ryan, Lawrence: Newry DN 3; 98, 103
Ryan, man named: Ahoghill AM 23; 34
Ryan, Mrs: Clogher TE 5; 41
Ryans, James: Newry DN 3; 99
Ryder, John: Misc. DN 17; 117
Rye (see Raymoghy)
Rylands lough: Drumragh TE 5; 104
Rylands td: Raymoghy DL 39; 139
Rynd, family: Enniskillen FH 4; 58
Rynd, Thomas: Tamlaght TE 20; 109, 111–13
Ryno, David: Enniskillen FH 4; 72

S

Saddler and Finton, Messrs: Blaris AM 8; 70

Sadler, Henry: Clondermot LY 34; 55

Saggony bog: Magheramesk AM 21; 119

Saighir Chiarain church: Faughanvale LY 36; 50

Saint's Island: Templecarn DL 39; 156, 159, 162–63, 166–67

Saintfield: Blaris AM 8; 73, 76

Saintfield: Clondermot LY 34; 74

Saintfield: Killinchy DN 7; 89

Saintfield: Killyleagh DN 17; 85

Saintfield: Kilmore DN 17; 92

Saintfield: Magheradrool DN 17; 101

Saintfield: Misc. DN 17; 116, 120

Saintfield: Saintfield DN 7; 114, 117, 120

Saintfield: Tullynakill DN 7; 123

Saintfield chapel: Saintfield DN 7; 114, 119

Saintfield church: Saintfield DN 7; 114, 119

Saintfield female school: Saintfield DN 7; 115

Saintfield hotel: Saintfield DN 7; 114

Saintfield infant school: Saintfield DN 7; 116

Saintfield male and female school: Saintfield DN 7; 115

Saintfield market house: Saintfield DN 7; 114, 119

Saintfield meeting house (P): Saintfield DN 7; 114, 119

Saintfield meeting house (S): Saintfield DN 7; 114, 119

Saintfield old school: Saintfield DN 7; 116

Saintfield Parks td: Saintfield DN 7; 120

Saintfield ph: Comber DN 7; 31

Saintfield ph: Drumbo DN 7; 54

Saintfield ph: Killinchy DN 7; 86

Saintfield ph: Misc. DN 17; 118, 121

Saintfield ph: Tullynakill DN 7; 122

Saintfield school: Saintfield DN 7; 114

Saintfield schools: Saintfield DN 7; 119

Saintfield vicarage: Saintfield DN 7; 115

Saints Bed stone: Aghagallon AM 21; 10–11

Sala (Germany): Blaris AM 8; 89

Saldanha rock: Tullyaughnish DL 38; 95

Salem House: Clondermot LY 34; 6, 20, 97, 102

Salem night school: Clondermot LY 34; 43

Salem school: Clondermot LY 34; 10, 43, 86–87, 89, 91, 94

Salem Sunday school: Clondermot LY 34; 92–93

Salisbury, Earl of: Tomregan FH 4; 129

Sallagh braes: Carncastle and Killyglen AM 10; 1, 5

Sallagh lough: Clogher TE 5; 25, 47

Sallagh lough: Donegal DL 39; 43–44

Sallagh lough: Templecarn DL 39; 157

Sallagh lough: Tydavnet MN 40; 169

Sallagh lough [I]: Clondavaddog DL 38; 3

Sallagh lough [I]: Mevagh DL 38; 55

Sallagh lough [II]: Clondavaddog DL 38; 3

Sallagh lough [II]: Mevagh DL 38; 55

Sallagh td: Carncastle and Killyglen AM 10; 9–10

Sallawilly (see Sallowilly): Cumber LY 28; 67

Sallies Grove td: Killesher FH 14; 87

Salloon td: Magheracross FH 14; 102

Sallowhy td: Galloon FH 4; 95

Sallowilly td: Cumber LY 28; 67, 71, 114, 120, 124, 126

Sally Island: Ballinderry AM 21; 43, 56

Sallybrook td: Raymoghy DL 39; 135, 139

Sallypark House: Enniskillen FH 4; 66, 71

Sallywood td: Donaghmore DL 39; 38

Salmon Leap fishery: Coleraine LY 33; 93, 147

Salmon Leap locality: Trory FH 14; 131

Salmon Leap waterfall: Agivey LY 22; 44

Salmon Leap waterfall: Coleraine LY 33; 53, 93, 99, 102, 121–22, 146, 149

Salmon Leap waterfall: Killowen LY 33; 162

Salmon Leap waterfall: Lough Neagh AM 21; 95

Salmon Leap waterfall: Misc. LY 36; 109

Salmond, Thomas: Ballymore AH 1; 7

Salry td: Magheracross FH 14; 102

Salt (see Talt): Kilmacteige SO 40; 195

Salt Hole pit: Templecorran AM 26; 84, 89–90, 121–22

Salt Island: Saul DN 17; 111, 114

Salt lough: Clondavaddog DL 38; 6

Salt lough: Kilmacrenan DL 38; 50, 52

Salt lough: Lough Swilly DL 38; 128–29

Salt lough: Mevagh DL 38; 54, 57, 59, 63

Salt Pan (see Salt Pans): Lough Swilly DL 38; 101

Salt Pans bay: Lough Swilly DL 38; 102

Salt Pans district: Killygarvan DL 38; 36–38, 42, 47

Salt Pans district: Tullyaughnish DL 38; 86, 93

Salt Pans lough: Killygarvan DL 38; 47

Salt Pans Point: Lough Swilly DL 38; 101, 131

Salt Pans wood: Killygarvan DL 38; 38

Salt Works td: Faughanvale LY 36; 17, 53, 62, 69, 78, 90, 96

Salt Works wood: Faughanvale LY 36; 90

Salter, Lt: Desertegney DL 38; 25

Salters' manor: Artrea LY 6; 15

Salters' manor: Artrea TE 20; 6

Salters' manor: Magherafelt LY 6; 81, 84, 96

Salterstown Castle: Ballinderry TE 20; 13

Salterstown district: Ballinderry TE 20; 14

Salterstown forge: Kilrea LY 27; 112

Sampson, A.L.: Banagher LY 30; 96

Sampson, A.L.: Clondermot LY 34; 78–79

Sampson, A.L.: Drumachose LY 9; 84, 104, 130

Sampson, A.L.: Faughanvale LY 36; 38, 40, 45, 45

Sampson, A.L.: Tamlaght Finlagan LY 25; 66, 84, 100, 124

Sampson, Barnis: Dunboe LY 11; 57

Sampson, Capt.: Ramoan AM 24; 94

Sampson, James: Tamlaght TE 20; 76, 91, 103

Sampson, Jane: Tamlaght TE 20; 76

Sampson, John: Tamlaght TE 20; 86

Sampson, Jonothon: Ballyscullion LY 6; 68

Sampson, Mr: Magherafelt LY 6; 104

Sampson, Rev.: Dromara DN 12; 64

Sampson, Rev. G.V. (Jnr): Desertoghill LY 27; 18, 27

Sampson, Rev. G.V. (Jnr): Errigal LY 27; 39

Sampson, Rev. G.V. (Snr): Aghanloo LY 11; 3, 8, 10, 26, 28

Sampson, Rev. G.V. (Snr): Bovevagh LY 25; 26

Sampson, Rev. G.V. (Snr): Desertoghill LY 27; 21, 27

Sampson, Rev. G.V. (Snr): Drumachose LY 9; 95, 99, 101

Sampson, Rev. G.V. (Snr): Dungiven LY 15; 35, 49

Sampson, Rev. G.V. (Snr): Errigal LY 27; 38–39, 43, 49, 57, 76, 78

Sampson, Rev. G.V. (Snr): Magilligan LY 11; 115

Sampson, Rev. G.V. (Snr): Tamlaght Finlagan LY 25; 69, 84

Sampson, Rev. George: Faughanvale LY 36; 10

Sampson, Rev. Michael: Annaclone DN 12; 17–18

Sampson, Rev. Michael: Kilrea LY 27; 126

Samsonagh td: Cleenish FH 14; 30

Sand cove: Island Magee AM 10; 101

Sandale, John: Clondermot LY 34; 45

Sanderson, Alexander: Laragh CN 40; 45

Sanderson, Capt. (Ardglass): Bright DN 17; 35

Sanderson, Col: Misc. FH 4; 133

Sanderson, family: Carrickfergus AM 37; 93

Sanderson, family: Enniskillen FH 4; 58

Sanderson, Robert: Laragh CN 40; 42, 45

Sanderson, Thomas: Aghadowey LY 22; 38

Sandes, Susan: Carrickfergus AM 37; 118

Sandford, Arthur: Aghanloo LY 11; 19

Sandford, Gen.: Killesher FH 14; 84

Sandford, James: Artrea LY 6; 20

Sandford, Mary: Aghanloo LY 11; 39

Sandhill td: Inishmacsaint FH 14; 72

Sandhills district: Currin MN 40; 86

Sandholes hamlet: Desertcreat TE 20; 32–34, 36

Sandholes meeting house: Desertcreat TE 20; 32

Sandholes school: Galloon FH 4; 96

Sandholes td: Galloon FH 4; 95, 98

Sandle, Mr: Enniskillen FH 4; 84

Sands, Edward: Killead AM 35; 47

Sands, family: Newry DN 3; 107

Sands, James: Ballyrashane LY 22; 55

Sands, James: Ballywillin LY 33; 33, 42

Sands, James: Tamlaght TE 20; 84

Sands, Thomas: Tamlaght TE 20; 79

Sands, William: Hillsborough DN 12; 106

Sands, William: Tamlaght TE 20; 79

Sandvile td: Donaghedy TE 5; 92

Sandy bay: Camlin AM 21; 63–64

Sandy bay: Coleraine LY 33; 99

Sandy bay: Glenavy AM 21; 82

Sandy bay: Killead AM 35; 8

Sandy Braes hills: Connor AM 19; 16

Sandy Braes hills: Killead AM 35; 25

Sandy Island td: Ballyculter DN 17; 31

Sandyhill locality: Maghera LY 18; 20

Sandymount Cottage: Kilmore AH 1; 65, 69

Sandys, Rev. Joseph: Aghadowey LY 22; 22

Sandys, William: Drummaul AM 19; 89

Sanford, family: Enniskillen FH 4; 58

Santleger, Anthony: Coleraine LY 33; 156

Saper, Lord: Ballyscullion LY 6; 57

Saper, Philadelphia: Ballyscullion LY 6; 57

Sappers' mount: Balteagh LY 9; 35

Sardinia: Killelagh LY 27; 102

Sargent, Edward: Artrea LY 6; 26

Sargent, John: Artrea LY 6; 26

Sargent, Sally: Ballynascreen LY 31; 21

Sarsfield, Patrick: Enniskillen FH 4; 52

Sarvice, John: Drumbeg AM 8; 125

Saul abbey: Saul DN 17; 113

Saul chapel: Saul DN 17; 111

Saul church: Saul DN 17; 115

Saul corn mill: Saul DN 17; 115

Saul distillery: Saul DN 17; 112, 115

Saul flax mill: Saul DN 17; 115

Saul graveyard: Killyleagh DN 17; 86

Saul old church: Saul DN 17; 112–13

Saul ph: Ballee DN 17; 15

Saul ph: Ballyculter DN 17; 28

Saul ph: Down DN 17; 49

Saul ph: Misc. DN 17; 121–22, 128
Saul Quarter td: Down DN 17; 53, 57
Saul smithy: Saul DN 17; 115
Saul td: Saul DN 17; 111–12, 114
Saul, Mr: Bright DN 17; 35
Saunders, family: Templepatrick AM 35; 118
Saunders, George: Carrickfergus AM 37; 111, 195
Saunders, Joseph: Ardglass DN 17; 1
Saunders, Joseph: Killyleagh DN 17; 86
Saunderson, Charlotte: Island Magee AM 10; 95
Saunderson, family: Glenwhirry AM 32; 77
Saunderson, James: Raymoghy DL 39; 138, 140–41
Saunderson, John: Kilroot AM 26; 74, 80
Saunderson, Rev. Francis: Enniskeen CN 40; 29
Saunderson, Robert: Enniskillen FH 4; 52
Saurin, family: Misc. AM 10; 130
Saurin, Rev. James: Seagoe AH 1; 102–04, 108–09
Savage district: Templecorran AM 26; 82
Savage, Andrew: Ballyphilip DN 7; 12
Savage, Boscawen: Misc. DN 17; 126
Savage, chieftain: Island Magee AM 10; 26
Savage, Col.: Saintfield DN 7; 118–19
Savage, Col.: Witter DN 7; 126
Savage, Edward: Ballyscullion LY 6; 57
Savage, family: Ardglass DN 17; 12
Savage, family: Ballyculter DN 17; 28
Savage, family: Ballyphilip DN 7; 12
Savage, family: Blaris DN 12; 30
Savage, family: Carrickfergus AM 37; 60
Savage, family: Derryaghy AM 8; 114
Savage, family: Island Magee AM 10; 72
Savage, family: Killinchy DN 7; 89
Savage, family: Loughguile AM 13; 62
Savage, family: Raloo AM 32; 115
Savage, family: Witter DN 7; 126
Savage, Fordavagh: Ballyphilip DN 7; 13
Savage, Francess: Derryaghy AM 8; 114
Savage, Francis: Derryaghy AM 8; 114
Savage, Francis: Down DN 17; 52–53
Savage, Francis: Saul DN 17; 114
Savage, Harriet (see Forde): Down DN 17; 57
Savage, Henry: Ballyphilip DN 7; 13
Savage, Henry: Newry DN 3; 100, 104
Savage, I.: Aughnamullen MN 40; 77
Savage, James: Newry DN 3; 100, 104
Savage, Jane (nee Montgomery): Misc. DN 17; 119
Savage, Jane: Carrickfergus AM 37; 127
Savage, John: Ballynascreen LY 31; 3, 6, 13, 18, 122
Savage, John: Ballyscullion LY 6; 57
Savage, John: Carrickfergus AM 37; 114
Savage, John: Clondermot LY 34; 46
Savage, John: Derryaghy AM 8; 114
Savage, John: Loughguile AM 13; 68
Savage, John: Maghera LY 18; 15

Savage, Maria: Carlingford LH 40; 60
Savage, Marianne: Ballyscullion LY 6; 57
Savage, Michael: Blaris DN 12; 45, 49
Savage, Mr: Ballyphilip DN 7; 10
Savage, Mr: Inishargy DN 7; 84
Savage, Mr: Magheradrool DN 17; 103
Savage, Patrick: Ballyphilip DN 7; 9, 13
Savage, Patrick: Carrickfergus AM 37; 30
Savage, Patrick: Killowen LY 33; 159
Savage, Patrick: Misc. DN 17; 117, 119
Savage, Philip: Ballymoney AM 16; 3
Savage, Philip: Kilraghts AM 16; 125
Savage, Philip: Loughguile AM 13; 58, 60, 62, 64
Savage, Raymond: Ardglass DN 17; 12
Savage, Rev. John: Carrickfergus AM 37; 134, 136
Savage, Robert: Termoneeny LY 6; 133
Savage, Rowland: Ballyphilip DN 7; 13
Savage, Rowland: Newry DN 3; 74
Savage, Slenickinboy: Ballyphilip DN 7; 13
Savage, William: Carrickfergus AM 37; 193
Savage, William: Derryaghy AM 8; 91, 95
Savalbeg td: Newry DN 3; 112
Savalmore corn mill: Newry DN 3; 78, 112
Savalmore flax mill: Newry DN 3; 78, 112
Savalmore td: Newry DN 3; 78, 112
Savidg, Michael: Carrickfergus AM 37; 28
Saville Lodge: Clogher TE 5; 61
Saville, George: Clogher TE 5; 32
Sawanah (see Swannagh): Donaghmore DL 39; 29
Sawel hills: Ardstraw TE 5; 2
Sawel mountain: Balteagh LY 9; 5
Sawel mountain: Banagher LY 30; 24–25, 30–31, 59, 108–10, 112
Sawel mountain: Clondermot LY 34; 1, 3, 17–18
Sawel mountain: Cumber LY 28; 4, 11
Sawel mountain: Faughanvale LY 36; 1, 4
Sawel mountain: Misc. LY 31; 111
Sawel mountain: Misc. LY 36; 119
Sawel mountain: Tamlaght Finlagan LY 25; 62
Sawel mountains (see also Monterlony): Donaghedy TE 5; 88
Sawpit field: Ahoghill AM 23; 35
Sayer, family: Blaris AM 8; 22
Sayer, Mrs: Aghadowey LY 22; 6
Sayers, William: Ballyclug AM 23; 65–66
Scaart rock: Lough Swilly DL 38; 147
Scald lough: Derryvullan FH 14; 42
Scallen corn mill: Kilskeery TE 5; 114
Scallen school: Kilskeery TE 5; 115
Scallen td: Kilskeery TE 5; 114–15
Scally, family: Billy AM 16; 58, 68
Scally, James: Ballintoy AM 24; 19
Scally, John: Culfeightrin AM 24; 82
Scally, John: Garvaghy DN 12; 82
Scally, John: Ramoan AM 24; 118–19

Scally, Meakam: Ballintoy AM 24; 32
Scally, Michael: Culfeightrin AM 24; 73–74
Scalp glen: Leckpatrick TE 5; 121
Scalt Shoersha cave: Lough Swilly DL 38; 125
Scaltmore creek: Lough Swilly DL 38; 106
Scalty fort: Aghadowey LY 22; 29
Scalty High fort: Aghadowey LY 22; 33
Scalty Low fort: Aghadowey LY 22; 33
Scalty td: Aghadowey LY 22; 33–34
Scandally fort: Devenish FH 14; 55
Scandally td: Devenish FH 14; 59
Scandally td: Inishmacsaint FH 14; 75
Scandela (see Scandally)
Scandinavia: Banagher LY 30; 12
Scandrett, Anthony: Hillsborough DN 12; 105
Scandrett, Thomas: Hillsborough DN 12; 106
Scanlan, Patrick: Clonleigh DL 39; 10, 13
Scanlan, prince of Ossory: Tamlaght Finlagan LY
    25; 101
Scannell, William: Drumachose LY 9; 85
Scardery Middle td: Belleek FH 14; 1
Scarnageeragh mill: Donagh MN 40; 101
Scarnageeragh td: Donagh MN 40; 99
Scarva: Aghaderg DN 12; 4, 7, 9
Scarva: Ballymore AH 1; 5, 9–10, 17
Scarva: Clonallan DN 3; 1
Scarva: Misc. DN 17; 117, 131
Scarva: Montiaghs AH 1; 91
Scarva: Seapatrick DN 12; 126
Scarva bog: Aghaderg DN 12; 3
Scarva Castle: Aghaderg DN 12; 7
Scarva demesne: Aghaderg DN 12; 3, 6
Scarva estate: Misc. DN 17; 130
Scarva House: Aghaderg DN 12; 9–10
Scarva House: Misc. DN 17; 131
Scarva lough: Ballymore AH 1; 1, 7, 12
Scarva meeting house: Aghaderg DN 12; 4, 9
Scarva pass: Aghaderg DN 12; 4
Scarva school: Aghaderg DN 12; 5, 11
Scarva td: Aghaderg DN 12; 3, 7, 10
Scarva td: Misc. DN 17; 130
Scarvagh (see Scarva): Aghaderg DN 12; 3
Scarvagherin flax mill: Ardstraw TE 5; 5
Scarvagherin old church: Ardstraw TE 5; 12
Scatterick Islands: Misc. DN 17; 118
Scattery Island: Faughanvale LY 36; 56
Scawdy Island: Lough Neagh AM 21; 95
Scawdy Island: Montiaghs AH 1; 89
Scawt hill: Carncastle and Killyglen AM 10; 1
Schehoogan (see Screegan): Banagher LY 30; 24
Schoales, Cllr: Raphoe DL 39; 125–27
Schomberg, Duke of: Carnmoney AM 2; 69
Schomberg, Duke of: Carrickfergus AM 37; 88, 178
Schomberg, Duke of: Glenavy AM 21; 86
Schomberg, Duke of: Loughgall AH 1; 80

Schomberg, Mr: Clogher TE 5; 41
Schomberg, Rev. G.H.: Kilmore MN 40; 136
School Lands district: Kinawley FH 4; 110–11
Schulte, Mr: Clondermot LY 34; 41
Schwartz (Germany): Blaris AM 8; 89
Scientian (see Syunshin?)
Scionfin (see Syonfin)
Scobban lough: Belleek FH 14; 1
Scoby, family: Dunluce AM 16; 117
Scoby, Miss: Coleraine LY 33; 72
Scoby's House: Cumber LY 28; 41, 83
Scollogstown quarry: Bright DN 17; 37
Scollogstown village: Bright DN 17; 37
Sconce hill: Dunboe LY 11; 43, 77
Sconce hill fort: Dunboe LY 11; 77
Sconce hill giant's chair: Dunboe LY 11; 77
Sconce hill giant's grave: Dunboe LY 11; 77
Sconce hill spring: Dunboe LY 11; 79
Sconce td: Dunboe LY 11; 49, 77, 81
Scork lough: Inishmacsaint FH 14; 71
Scot, Edward: Enniskillen FH 4; 68
Scot, family: Ballintoy AM 24; 20
Scotch hill: Ballynure AM 32; 54
Scotch Kirkyard graveyard: Ballintoy AM 24; 18
Scotch Omerbane carn: Newtown Crommelin AM
    13; 84
Scotch Omerbane standing stone: Dunaghy AM 13;
    24
Scotch Omerbane standing stone: Newtown
    Crommelin AM 13; 84
Scotch Omerbane td: Newtown Crommelin AM 13;
    24, 78, 84
Scotch Quarter flax mill: Carrickfergus AM 37;
    44–45, 47
Scotch Quarter tanyard: Carrickfergus AM 37; 3, 45,
    47, 137
Scotch Quarter td: Carrickfergus AM 37; 7, 10, 22,
    26–29, 31–32, 42, 44, 47, 57, 65, 70, 78, 91–92,
    100, 132, 134, 136, 149, 151–52, 162, 165, 175
Scotch St chapel: Drumcree AH 1; 40
Scotch St corn mill: Drumcree AH 1; 37
Scotch St meeting house: Drumcree AH 1; 35, 38
Scotch St school: Drumcree AH 1; 30, 33, 35–36,
    38
Scotch St village: Drumcree AH 1; 35–37, 40
Scotch St windmill: Drumcree AH 1; 37
Scotchmen's Bush locality: Culfeightrin AM 24; 79
Scotchtown td: Magilligan LY 11; 126
Scotland: Aghadowey LY 22; 14, 16, 24, 26, 38
Scotland: Aghagallon AM 21; 19
Scotland: Aghanloo LY 11; 34
Scotland: Ahoghill AM 23; 14, 17–18
Scotland: Antrim AM 29; 8, 17, 23, 48
Scotland: Ardclinis AM 13; 2–3
Scotland: Armoy AM 24; 5–6

Scotland: Artrea LY 6; 39
Scotland: Ballee DN 17; 19, 19
Scotland: Ballinderry AM 21; 51
Scotland: Ballintoy AM 24; 15–18, 25
Scotland: Ballyaghran LY 33; 14, 18, 28
Scotland: Ballyclug AM 23; 57, 59
Scotland: Ballycor AM 32; 6–7
Scotland: Ballymoney AM 16; 19
Scotland: Ballynascreen LY 31; 13, 22–23
Scotland: Ballynure AM 32; 35, 44
Scotland: Ballyrashane LY 22; 51, 53, 66
Scotland: Ballyscullion AM 19; 7
Scotland: Ballyscullion LY 6; 63
Scotland: Ballywillin LY 33; 36–37
Scotland: Balteagh LY 9; 16
Scotland: Banagher LY 30; 18, 35–36, 60–61, 72,
     99, 101, 110
Scotland: Billy AM 16; 46, 71
Scotland: Blaris AM 8; 4, 70–72, 77
Scotland: Blaris DN 12; 31
Scotland: Bovevagh LY 25; 13, 24, 27, 29, 39,
     54–55, 61
Scotland: Camlin AM 21; 68, 71
Scotland: Cappagh TE 5; 20
Scotland: Carmavy AM 35; 2
Scotland: Carnmoney AM 2; 50–53, 60, 64–65, 67,
     92
Scotland: Carrickfergus AM 37; 10–11, 13, 50,
     61–62, 68, 75, 77, 79, 83, 85, 137, 170–71
Scotland: Clondavaddog DL 38; 7, 9, 11
Scotland: Clondermot LY 34; 5, 16, 23–24, 28, 45,
     49
Scotland: Clonleigh DL 39; 7
Scotland: Clonmany DL 38; 17
Scotland: Coleraine LY 33; 74, 79, 88, 94, 98,
     102–03, 126, 130, 143, 145, 152
Scotland: Connor AM 19; 23, 25
Scotland: Culfeightrin AM 24; 44, 46, 65, 67, 74, 80
Scotland: Cumber LY 28; 18, 28, 50, 52, 93
Scotland: Currin MN 40; 94, 97
Scotland: Desertegney DL 38; 27
Scotland: Desertlyn LY 31; 47
Scotland: Desertmartin LY 31; 60, 62
Scotland: Desertoghill LY 27; 4, 8, 12
Scotland: Doagh AM 29; 66, 72, 78, 95
Scotland: Donegal DL 39; 50, 57
Scotland: Dromara DN 12; 67
Scotland: Drumachose LY 9; 87–88, 101, 134
Scotland: Drumglass TE 20; 42
Scotland: Drumlumman CN 40; 16
Scotland: Drummaul AM 19; 62
Scotland: Drumragh TE 5; 109
Scotland: Drumtullagh AM 16; 99
Scotland: Dunaghy AM 13; 19
Scotland: Duneane AM 19; 101, 104

Scotland: Dungiven LY 15; 29, 64, 74–75, 100, 104
Scotland: Dunluce AM 16; 112
Scotland: Enniskeen CN 40; 28
Scotland: Enniskillen FH 4; 49
Scotland: Errigal LY 27; 48, 62, 66
Scotland: Faughanvale LY 36; 6, 11, 30–34, 41, 44,
     48
Scotland: Finvoy AM 23; 72–73
Scotland: Galloon FH 4; 91
Scotland: Glenavy AM 21; 87, 89
Scotland: Glenwhirry AM 32; 78
Scotland: Glynn AM 26; 2, 7, 18, 34, 38, 41
Scotland: Grey Abbey DN 7; 70
Scotland: Inishargy DN 7; 85
Scotland: Inishkeel DL 39; 69–71
Scotland: Inver AM 26; 52, 54–55
Scotland: Island Magee AM 10; 29, 38–39, 48, 76,
     80, 82–83, 85, 90, 93
Scotland: Kilcronaghan LY 31; 73, 81
Scotland: Kilkeel DN 3; 50
Scotland: Killagan AM 23; 80, 84–85
Scotland: Killea and Taughboyne DL 39; 81, 85,
     88–91, 93
Scotland: Killead AM 35; 47–48
Scotland: Killeeshil TE 20; 63
Scotland: Killelagh LY 27; 99
Scotland: Killevy AH 1; 52
Scotland: Killinchy DN 7; 90
Scotland: Killowen LY 33; 161, 165, 172
Scotland: Killygarvan DL 38; 45
Scotland: Killyleagh DN 17; 84
Scotland: Killymard DL 39; 96, 104–05
Scotland: Kilmacteige SO 40; 192
Scotland: Kilraghts AM 16; 127
Scotland: Kilrea LY 27; 105, 118, 129
Scotland: Kilroot AM 26; 61
Scotland: Kilskeery TE 5; 116
Scotland: Kilwaughter AM 10; 117
Scotland: Kinawley FH 4; 119, 121, 123
Scotland: Kirkinriola AM 23; 91, 108, 120
Scotland: Lambeg AM 8; 139
Scotland: Layd AM 13; 37, 39, 46, 50
Scotland: Layd and Inispollan AM 13; 57
Scotland: Lissan LY 31; 102
Scotland: Lough Swilly DL 38; 113, 118, 130
Scotland: Macosquin LY 22; 107, 123
Scotland: Maghera LY 18; 5, 75
Scotland: Magherafelt LY 6; 104
Scotland: Magheragall AM 21; 109
Scotland: Magheramesk AM 21; 130
Scotland: Magilligan LY 11; 119, 140
Scotland: Manorhamilton Union LM 40; 53
Scotland: Mevagh DL 38; 56, 58, 60, 62
Scotland: Misc. DL 39; 188
Scotland: Misc. DN 17; 130–31

Scotland: Misc. LY 31; 116, 123
Scotland: Misc. LY 36; 104, 112
Scotland: Moville DL 38; 70, 72
Scotland: Muckamore AM 35; 61, 65
Scotland: Newtown Crommelin AM 13; 80
Scotland: Nilteen AM 35; 86, 91, 94
Scotland: Raloo AM 32; 85, 93, 103, 106, 108, 128
Scotland: Ramoan AM 24; 86, 98–99, 118
Scotland: Raphoe DL 39; 131
Scotland: Rasharkin AM 23; 132–33
Scotland: Rashee AM 32; 140
Scotland: Rathlin Island AM 24; 129, 131–34
Scotland: Shilvodan AM 19; 130, 135
Scotland: Tamlaght Finlagan LY 25; 101–02
Scotland: Tamlaght O'Crilly LY 18; 97, 101, 138
Scotland: Tartaraghan AH 1; 122
Scotland: Templecarn FH 14; 120
Scotland: Templecorran AM 26; 86–87, 96–97, 99,
   103, 106–08, 126–27
Scotland: Templepatrick AM 35; 121, 123, 132–33,
   141, 143
Scotland: Termoneeny LY 6; 126, 132
Scotland: Tickmacrevan AM 13; 127, 129
Scotland: Tullyaughnish DL 38; 93–95
Scotland: Tullyrusk AM 21; 138
Scotland td: Donaghmore DL 39; 38
Scotland, Isles: Ballintoy AM 24; 25
Scotland, Isles: Glynn AM 26; 34
Scotland, Isles: Misc. LY 31; 116
Scotland, Isles: Misc. LY 36; 104
Scotland, Isles: Rathlin Island AM 24; 131
Scotshouse: Currin MN 40; 89–91
Scotshouse chapel: Currin MN 40; 89, 93
Scotshouse church: Currin MN 40; 89, 93
Scotshouse school: Currin MN 40; 93
Scotsman locality: Newry DN 3; 88
Scotstown: Tydavnet MN 40; 170–71
Scotstown bridge: Tydavnet MN 40; 170
Scotstown hill: Camlin AM 21; 63
Scotstown old bridge: Tydavnet MN 40; 170
Scotstown river: Tydavnet MN 40; 170
Scott, Alexander: Loughgilly AH 1; 86
Scott, Alice: Newry DN 3; 67
Scott, Andrew: Blaris DN 12; 40
Scott, Andrew: Carrickfergus AM 37; 194
Scott, Baron: Faughanvale LY 36; 8, 10
Scott, Benjamin: Newry DN 3; 99, 104
Scott, Capt. (Rathfriland): Drumballyroney DN 3;
   17
Scott, Capt.: Drumgath DN 3; 20
Scott, Catherine: Carrickfergus AM 37; 127
Scott, Cllr: Donaghmore DL 39; 37
Scott, David: Newry DN 3; 100, 104, 112
Scott, Dr: Dromore DN 12; 72
Scott, Edward: Banagher LY 30; 78–79

Scott, Edward: Devenish FH 14; 53
Scott, Eliza: Carrickfergus AM 37; 121
Scott, family: Ballinderry AM 21; 52
Scott, family: Ballintoy AM 24; 20
Scott, family: Enniskillen FH 4; 58
Scott, family: Kilroot AM 26; 74–75
Scott, family: Maghera LY 18; 13
Scott, family: Mallusk AM 2; 110
Scott, Francis: Carrickfergus AM 37; 123
Scott, G.: Ballyhalbert DN 7; 5–6
Scott, G.: Ballykinler DN 17; 32
Scott, G.: Ballytrustan DN 7; 15
Scott, G.: Bangor DN 7; 25
Scott, G.: Bright DN 17; 33
Scott, G.: Comber DN 7; 31
Scott, G.: Derryaghy AM 8; 103
Scott, G.: Drumbeg DN 7; 53
Scott, G.: Forkhill AH 1; 45
Scott, G.: Jonesborough AH 1; 46
Scott, G.: Kilclooney AH 1; 51
Scott, G.: Kilkeel DN 3; 51
Scott, G.: Killanny MN 40; 135
Scott, G.: Knockbreda DN 7; 102
Scott, G.: Lambeg AM 8; 143
Scott, G.: Magheracloone MN 40; 142
Scott, G.: Magheradrool DN 17; 107
Scott, G.: Newry DN 3; 84
Scott, G.: Witter DN 7; 126
Scott, George: Hillsborough DN 12; 106
Scott, George: Maghera LY 18; 53
Scott, George: Newry DN 3; 99, 103
Scott, H.O.: Tydavnet MN 40; 170
Scott, Henry: Hillsborough DN 12; 107
Scott, Hugh: Ballymoney AM 16; 15–17
Scott, Isac: Artrea LY 6; 36
Scott, James: Ahoghill AM 23; 23
Scott, James: Ballynure AM 32; 52
Scott, James: Balteagh LY 9; 32
Scott, James: Drumachose LY 9; 104, 132
Scott, James: Hillsborough DN 12; 102, 105
Scott, James: Tullyniskan TE 20; 139, 141
Scott, Jane (nee Johnston): Hillsborough DN 12; 98
Scott, John: Balteagh LY 9; 44
Scott, John: Derryaghy AM 8; 98
Scott, John: Dromore DN 12; 78
Scott, Joseph: Ahoghill AM 23; 45, 48
Scott, Joseph: Banagher LY 30; 86
Scott, Joseph: Hillsborough DN 12; 106
Scott, Joseph: Newry DN 3; 81
Scott, Joshua: Ahoghill AM 23; 23
Scott, man named: Donaghmore DL 39; 32
Scott, Matthew: Dungiven LY 15; 95
Scott, Messrs: Faughanvale LY 36; 20
Scott, Michael: Misc. LY 31; 125
Scott, Mr (Fivemiletown): Clogher TE 5; 61

Scott, Mr (Mullenan): Killea and Taughboyne DL 39; 81, 87, 90

Scott, Mr: Annahilt DN 12; 23

Scott, Mr: Blaris DN 12; 32

Scott, Mr: Cappagh TE 5; 19, 21–22

Scott, Mr: Conwal DL 39; 27

Scott, Mr: Drumgath DN 3; 21

Scott, Mr: Kilmore AH 1; 66, 68

Scott, Mrs (Snr): Faughanvale LY 36; 27

Scott, Mrs: Balteagh LY 9; 17, 39

Scott, Mrs: Donaghmore DL 39; 36–37

Scott, Mrs: Dromore TE 5; 99

Scott, Mrs Thomas: Faughanvale LY 36; 8, 25, 27, 36, 66

Scott, Owen: Carrickfergus AM 37; 117

Scott, Patrick: Banagher LY 30; 48, 78–79

Scott, Ralph: Aughnamullen MN 40; 75–77

Scott, Ralph: Galloon FH 4; 91

Scott, Rev.: Drummaul AM 19; 69

Scott, Rev.: Raphoe DL 39; 125, 127

Scott, Rev. George: Balteagh LY 9; 3–4, 15, 18, 39

Scott, Rev. George: Banagher LY 30; 13–14

Scott, Rev. George: Faughanvale LY 36; 45

Scott, Rev. Gilbert: Faughanvale LY 36; 8

Scott, Rev. James: Drumbeg AM 8; 131

Scott, Rev. Robert: Ballyscullion AM 19; 8

Scott, Rev. Robert: Duneane AM 19; 114

Scott, Richard: Magheragall AM 21; 109

Scott, Robert: Balteagh LY 9; 44

Scott, Robert: Newry DN 3; 67, 74–75, 86

Scott, Russel: Drumbo DN 7; 56, 58

Scott, Samuel: Aghanloo LY 11; 19

Scott, Samuel: Drumachose LY 9; 104

Scott, Thomas: Clondermot LY 34; 8, 79–80

Scott, Thomas: Coleraine LY 33; 64

Scott, Thomas: Faughanvale LY 36; 4, 8–9, 17–19, 23, 27, 34, 36, 40, 42, 45, 64, 66, 71–73, 76–78

Scott, Thomas: Hillsborough DN 12; 105

Scott, William: Ballymoney AM 16; 17

Scott, William: Blaris AM 8; 67

Scott, William: Blaris DN 12; 40

Scott, William: Drumachose LY 9; 104

Scott, William: Faughanvale LY 36; 24, 35

Scott's bridge: Derryaghy AM 8; 109

Scot-town fort: Urney DL 39; 181

Scottstown school: Ballyclug AM 23; 66

Scout Guard (see Scoutbush): Carrickfergus AM 37; 84

Scout hill: Ahoghill AM 23; 34

Scout hill: Magheramesk AM 21; 123

Scoutbush demesne: Carrickfergus AM 37; 185

Scoutbush fort [I]: Carrickfergus AM 37; 185

Scoutbush fort [II]: Carrickfergus AM 37; 185

Scoutbush fort [III]: Carrickfergus AM 37; 185

Scoutbush fortification: Carrickfergus AM 37; 84–85, 93

Scoutbush House: Ballynure AM 32; 46, 68

Scoutbush House: Carrickfergus AM 37; 4, 56, 93, 134–35, 141–42, 174

Scoutbush House: Kilroot AM 26; 73

Scoutbush House: Templecorran AM 26; 108

Scraaps locality: Lough Swilly DL 38; 116–17

Scrabby ph: Drumlumman CN 40; 18

Scrabo district: Carrickfergus AM 37; 50, 170

Scrabo hill: Comber DN 7; 30–32, 43

Scrabo hill: Dundonald DN 7; 64, 66

Scrabo hill: Holywood DN 7; 83

Scrabo hill: Newtownards DN 7; 103, 111

Scrabo House: Tullynakill DN 7; 122

Scrabo quarry: Blaris AM 8; 70

Scrabo quarry: Comber DN 7; 28, 33

Scraggy bank (see Bushy bank): Lough Swilly DL 38; 100

Scraghy mountain: Skirts of Urney and Ardstraw TE 5; 136

Scramakeehan well: Ballintoy AM 24; 31

Scraps (see Scraaps): Lough Swilly DL 38; 116

Scrawhill td: Killymard DL 39; 101

Screeby (Screbeagh) td: Clogher TE 5; 37, 47, 54

Screeby lough: Clogher TE 5; 26, 47

Screegan meeting house: Banagher LY 30; 14

Screegan td: Banagher LY 30; 22, 24

Screen church: Magilligan LY 11; 88–89, 97, 105–06, 128, 143, 146

Screen Glebe House: Enniskeen CN 40; 29

Screen old church: Magilligan LY 11; 128

Screen td: Carlingford LH 40; 59

Screen td: Donacavey TE 5; 67, 77, 79–82, 87

Screen td: Killesher FH 14; 82

Screeney (see Screeny): Manorhamilton Union LM 40; 52

Screeny forts: Manorhamilton Union LM 40; 52

Screeny Little forts: Manorhamilton Union LM 40; 52

Screeny park: Manorhamilton Union LM 40; 48, 50

Screggagh (Scregagh) td: Donacavey TE 5; 67–68, 77–79, 81, 84, 87

Screggagh mountain: Clogher TE 5; 54, 58

Scrib linen manufactory: Loughinisland DN 17; 97

Scribly td: Leck DL 39; 119

Scriggan (Scrigen) td: Dungiven LY 15; 8, 22, 26, 62, 74, 90, 97

Scriggan bridge: Dungiven LY 15; 96

Scriggan meeting house: Dungiven LY 15; 8, 102

Scrine (see Screen): Magilligan LY 11; 146

Scroggen bush: Artrea LY 6; 23

Scroggin [or Scroggy] fort: Balteagh LY 9; 2, 11–12, 19

Scruhan-na-dhuchruinna river: Dungiven LY 15; 81

Scullion, Bernard: Termoneeny LY 6; 133
Scullion, Daniel: Ballyscullion LY 6; 77
Scullion, Daniel: Carrickfergus AM 37; 195
Scullion, Daniel: Culfeightrin AM 24; 77
Scullion, Daniel: Loughguile AM 13; 77
Scullion, Daniel: Termoneeny LY 6; 133
Scullion, family: Artrea LY 6; 14
Scullion, family: Ballyscullion LY 6; 53
Scullion, family: Dunaghy AM 13; 17
Scullion, family: Finvoy AM 23; 76
Scullion, Felix: Ahoghill AM 23; 35
Scullion, Henery: Tamlaght O'Crilly LY 18; 137
Scullion, Henry: Ahoghill AM 23; 40
Scullion, Henry: Ballymoney AM 16; 17
Scullion, Hugh: Termoneeny LY 6; 131–32
Scullion, James: Ballyscullion AM 19; 12
Scullion, James: Ballyscullion LY 6; 67, 69, 75, 78
Scullion, James: Balteagh LY 9; 43
Scullion, James: Billy AM 16; 61
Scullion, John: Ahoghill AM 23; 39
Scullion, John: Artrea LY 6; 12, 31
Scullion, John: Termoneeny LY 6; 133
Scullion, Margaret: Carrickfergus AM 37; 118
Scullion, Margaret: Termoneeny LY 6; 132
Scullion, Mary: Carrickfergus AM 37; 116
Scullion, Michael: Dunaghy AM 13; 22
Scullion, Michael: Tamlaght O'Crilly LY 18; 110
Scullion, Patrick: Ballyscullion LY 6; 67, 71
Scullion, Peter: Maghera LY 18; 81
Scullion, Rev. Felix: Carrickfergus AM 37; 102, 174
Scullion, Thomas: Ballyscullion AM 19; 7, 13
Scullion, Thomas: Ballyscullion LY 6; 73, 75, 78
Scullion, William: Loughguile AM 13; 74
Scully, Mary: Carrickfergus AM 37; 127
Scully's fort: Blaris AM 8; 20
Sea Park House: Carrickfergus AM 37; 56, 70, 94, 134–35, 137, 174
Sea Park House: Raloo AM 32; 98
Sea View House: Carrickfergus AM 37; 135
Seabogue td: Templecarn DL 39; 163
Seacash church: Carmavy AM 35; 3
Seacash church: Killead AM 35; 11, 13, 20, 25, 41, 43–44, 51
Seacash fort [I]: Killead AM 35; 28–29, 39
Seacash fort [II]: Killead AM 35; 32
Seacash Glebe House: Killead AM 35; 13, 42, 44
Seacash graveyard: Killead AM 35; 25, 44
Seacash school [I]: Killead AM 35; 37–38, 51–52
Seacash school [II]: Killead AM 35; 53
Seacash Sunday school: Killead AM 35; 38, 51–52
Seacash td: Killead AM 35; 22, 35, 50–51
Seafin flax mill: Drumballyroney DN 3; 13
Seafin td: Drumballyroney DN 3; 13, 16, 18
Seafin td: Misc. DN 17; 131
Seaforde: Loughinisland DN 17; 94–96

Seaforde: Magheradrool DN 17; 107
Seaforde almshouses: Loughinisland DN 17; 94–95
Seaforde bible repository: Loughinisland DN 17; 95
Seaforde church: Loughinisland DN 17; 94, 96
Seaforde female school: Loughinisland DN 17; 97
Seaforde House: Loughinisland DN 17; 94, 96
Seaforde meeting house: Loughinisland DN 17; 94
Seaforde old school: Loughinisland DN 17; 95
Seaforde school: Loughinisland DN 17; 95–97
Seaforde smithy: Loughinisland DN 17; 97
Seago (see Seagoe): Kilmore AH 1; 68
Seagoe church: Seagoe AH 1; 101–02, 105, 110
Seagoe Glebe House: Seagoe AH 1; 102, 105, 109
Seagoe Lower td: Seagoe AH 1; 102, 104, 109
Seagoe old church: Seagoe AH 1; 109
Seagoe ph: Aghalee AM 21; 36
Seagoe ph: Donaghcloney DN 12; 57
Seagoe ph: Drumcree AH 1; 28, 34–35
Seagoe ph: Kilmore AH 1; 60–61, 68, 72
Seagoe ph: Montiaghs AH 1; 90, 92
Seagoe ph: Shankill AH 1; 111
Seagoe ph: Tullylish DN 12; 140
Seagoe td: Montiaghs AH 1; 89
Seagoe Upper td: Seagoe AH 1; 101, 110
Seagull Isles: Billy AM 16; 43
Sealy, Mr: Donaghcloney DN 12; 57
Seapatrick bleach greens: Seapatrick DN 12; 125
Seapatrick female school: Seapatrick DN 12; 132, 135
Seapatrick Glebe House: Seapatrick DN 12; 132
Seapatrick male school: Seapatrick DN 12; 132, 135
Seapatrick mills: Seapatrick DN 12; 125
Seapatrick ph: Aghaderg DN 12; 1, 8, 10
Seapatrick ph: Annaclone DN 12; 13, 16
Seapatrick ph: Donaghcloney DN 12; 57, 59
Seapatrick ph: Donaghmore DN 3; 8
Seapatrick ph: Garvaghy DN 12; 79, 81
Seapatrick ph: Magherally DN 12; 112, 114
Seapatrick ph: Misc. DN 17; 121
Seapatrick ph: Montiaghs AH 1; 91
Seapatrick Sunday school: Seapatrick DN 12; 128
Seapock waterfall: Blaris DN 12; 28
Seapoint Cottage: Kilbroney DN 3; 35
Seaport Lodge: Dunluce AM 16; 105, 110
Sear locality: Warrenpoint DN 3; 120
Searight, David: Ballyscullion LY 6; 51, 72
Searight, John: Ballyscullion LY 6; 71, 75
Searight, Martin: Ballyscullion LY 6; 72
Seaveagh mill: Tyholland MN 40; 175
Seaview House: Kilbroney DN 3; 29
Sebor, Jacob: Balteagh LY 9; 21
Sedborough manor: Clones FH 4; 26
Seddon, Maj.: Antrim AM 29; 6
Seddon, Maj.: Muckamore AM 35; 60, 76
Sedgwick, Elizabeth: Ballinderry AM 21; 58

Seed, Hugh: Blaris DN 12; 45

Seed, William: Blaris AM 8; 25

Seeds, family: Carrickfergus AM 37; 93

Seeds, family: Derryaghy AM 8; 103

Seeds, Henery: Blaris AM 8; 55

Seeds, Hugh: Blaris DN 12; 49

Seeds, John: Derryaghy AM 8; 92

Seeds, Mrs: Blaris AM 8; 84–85

Seefin hill: Maghera LY 18; 22

Seeley, family: Enniskillen FH 4; 58

Seemulldown (see Shiemulldoon):
    Magheraculmoney FH 14; 110

Sefin stone: Killelagh LY 27; 98

Sefton, family: Blaris AM 8; 21

Sefton, G.H.: Blaris DN 12; 50

Sefton, James: Blaris DN 12; 40

Sefton, William: Ballinderry AM 21; 57

Segerson, Richard: Donacavey TE 5; 81

Segully td: Longfield TE 5; 132

Seir, Gobhan: Ramoan AM 24; 110

Selfridge, George: Balteagh LY 9; 34

Sellar, Elizabeth: Island Magee AM 10; 66

Sellar, Janet (see Liston)

Selshan harbour: Glenavy AM 21; 77

Selshion (Selshon) td: Drumcree AH 1; 29, 38

Selshion chapel: Drumcree AH 1; 36, 38

Selshion school: Drumcree AH 1; 38

Semple, family: Glynn AM 26; 42

Semple, Hugh: Kildollagh LY 22; 69, 73

Semple, James: Magherafelt LY 6; 106

Semple, John: Clondermot LY 34; 96

Semple, John: Cumber LY 28; 26, 57

Semple, John: Kildollagh LY 22; 73, 75

Semple, John [I]: Glynn AM 26; 44

Semple, John [II]: Glynn AM 26; 45

Semple, Mr: Killea and Taughboyne DL 39; 84

Semple, Samual: Kildollagh LY 22; 73, 75

Semple, Samuel: Glynn AM 26; 47

Semple, William: Clondermot LY 34; 37, 78–79,
    104

Semple, William [I]: Carrickfergus AM 37; 76

Semple, William [II]: Carrickfergus AM 37; 113

Sendall, family: Carrickfergus AM 37; 60

Seneirl bridge: Dunluce AM 16; 109

Seneirl school: Dunluce AM 16; 112

Seneirl td: Dunluce AM 16; 106

Sengagh td: Donacavey TE 5; 77

Sennick, Mr: Artrea LY 6; 14

Sentry hill: Carnmoney AM 2; 99–100

Sentry hill: Clondermot LY 34; 32, 48

Sentry hill: Cumber LY 28; 27

Sentrybox House: Annaclone DN 12; 15

Sercivagh td: Galloon FH 4; 95

Sergent, James: Ballynascreen LY 31; 22

Servante, Lt: Tickmacrevan AM 13; 128

Servegan meeting house: Bovevagh LY 25; 23

Service, Alexander: Templecorran AM 26; 125, 127

Service, James: Glynn AM 26; 13, 38, 45

Seskin locality: Carrickfergus AM 37; 93

Seskinore: Clogherny TE 20; 25–26

Seskinore: Donacavey TE 5; 63–64

Seskinore bridge: Donacavey TE 5; 64

Seskinore bridges: Clogherny TE 20; 27

Seskinore corn mill: Clogherny TE 20; 27

Seskinore forts: Clogherny TE 20; 28

Seskinore Lodge: Clogherny TE 20; 25–26

Seskinore meeting house: Clogherny TE 20; 25

Seskinore school: Clogherny TE 20; 26

Seskinore stream: Donacavey TE 5; 67

Sesnagh (Sesnaght) td: Tamlaght Finlagan LY 25;
    93

Sesnagh corn mill: Tamlaght Finlagan LY 25; 101

Sesnagh fort: Tamlaght Finlagan LY 25; 90, 109,
    113

Sesnagh quarry: Drumachose LY 9; 79

Sesnaugh (see Sesnagh): Tamlaght Finlagan LY 25;
    113

Sess (Cess) Kilgreen td: Errigal Keerogue TE 20;
    53, 55, 57

Sess bog: Errigal Keerogue TE 20; 55

Sess Kilgreen fort: Errigal Keerogue TE 20; 55

Sess td: Clogher TE 5; 37

Sess td: Errigal Keerogue TE 20; 48, 55, 57

Sessagh lough: Clondavaddog DL 38; 2

Sessagh O'Neill chapel: Donaghmore DL 39; 32

Sessagh O'Neill td: Donaghmore DL 39; 38

Sessagh td: Clogher TE 5; 36

Sessaghkilty td: Templecarn DL 39; 164

Sessaghmore td: Donaghmore DL 39; 38

Sessia school: Tullyniskan TE 20; 140–41

Sessia td: Donaghenry TE 20; 38

Sessia td: Tamlaght TE 20; 82

Sessiagh (Sessagh) td: Donacavey TE 5; 77, 79, 82,
    87

Sessiagh (Sessnagh) td: Cleenish FH 14; 14, 29–30

Sessiagh chapel: Cleenish FH 14; 17

Sessnacully td: Raphoe DL 39; 126

Sessuagh (see Sessiagh)

Sessuaghs td: Magheracross FH 14; 102

Sevaghan fort: Loughinisland DN 17; 97

Sevaghan td: Loughinisland DN 17; 97–98

Sevenip td: Killoran and Kilvarnet SO 40; 183

Severn river (England): Cumber LY 28; 59

Seward, Wenman: Derryvullan FH 14; 39

Sexton, James: Ballymore AH 1; 7

Seygorry (Seycorry) td: Aghadowey LY 22; 10, 38

Seymour Hill bleach green: Derryaghy AM 8; 110

Seymour Hill demesne: Derryaghy AM 8; 110

Seymour Hill House: Derryaghy AM 8; 106

Seymour, Capt.: Newry DN 3; 99, 104

Seymour, Edward: Tullyrusk AM 21; 131

Seymour, family: Camlin AM 21; 68

Seymour, family: Glenavy AM 21; 86

Seymour, family: Killead AM 35; 17

Seymour, family: Tullyrusk AM 21; 135

Seymour, Francis: Tullyrusk AM 21; 131

Seymour, George (see Conway, Earl): Ballinderry AM 21; 56

Seymour, Rev. Henery: Blaris AM 8; 24, 30

Seymour, Rev. Thomas: Blaris AM 8; 31

Seymour, William: Drummaul AM 19; 89

Seymour's bridge: Drummaul AM 19; 86, 92

Seymour's Bridge school: Drummaul AM 19; 86

Seymour's Bridge Sunday school: Drummaul AM 19; 86

Shadden, Capt.: Aghanloo LY 11; 33

Shadds, George: Ballyscullion LY 6; 57

Shades church: Raymoghy DL 39; 133

Shades graveyard: Raymoghy DL 39; 133

Shades market: Ballymore AH 1; 9

Shadwele, John: Artrea LY 6; 8

Shakespeare Head Hotel: Newry DN 3; 70

Shamrock Island: Killinchy DN 7; 86, 92

Shamrockvale Lodge: Blaris DN 12; 36

Shanacoskragh locality: Lough Swilly DL 38; 123

Shanagh (see Shannagh): Clondavaddog DL 38; 2

Shanaghan (see Shannaghan)

Shanaghy td: Aghalurcher FH 4; 4, 14

Shanahall (see Shankill): Aghaderg DN 12; 3

Shanahan, Michael: Dunboe LY 11; 60–63

Shanco school: Errigal Truagh MN 40; 121–22

Shanco td: Clogher TE 5; 35, 53

Shanco td: Enniskillen FH 4; 82

Shancow td: Magheross MN 40; 149

Shandon, name of: Clonleigh DL 39; 13

Shane A'Curran's Den locality: Loughguile AM 13; 72

Shane Barnard's Sentry Box: Pomeroy TE 20; 72

Shane Bewey's glen: Banagher LY 30; 46, 63

Shane hill: Ballybay MN 40; 78

Shane td: Ballybay MN 40; 84

Shane, family: Drumbeg AM 8; 123

Shane's Castle: Antrim AM 29; 1, 19–21, 23

Shane's Castle: Ballyaghran LY 33; 8–9

Shane's Castle: Ballyscullion LY 6; 59

Shane's Castle: Drummaul AM 19; 33, 35–36, 40–41, 47–48, 50, 52–53, 56, 61–62, 64, 66–72, 78, 81, 87–88

Shane's Castle: Duneane AM 19; 117–18

Shane's Castle: Killead AM 35; 8, 25

Shane's Castle: Misc. AM 10; 130

Shane's Castle: Muckamore AM 35; 64

Shane's Castle: Templepatrick AM 35; 115

Shane's Castle: Tullyrusk AM 21; 135

Shane's Castle deerpark: Drummaul AM 19; 50, 50–51

Shane's Castle demesne: Antrim AM 29; 19

Shane's Castle demesne: Drummaul AM 19; 37, 40, 46, 49–50, 52, 62, 64–65, 78

Shane's Castle demesne cove: Drummaul AM 19; 66

Shane's Castle forts: Antrim AM 29; 43

Shane's Castle forts: Drummaul AM 19; 78

Shane's Castle graveyard: Drummaul AM 19; 62–63, 78

Shane's Castle park: Coleraine LY 33; 97

Shane's Castle park: Drummaul AM 19; 33, 35, 65, 78–79, 81

Shane's Castle td: Antrim AM 29; 3, 19

Shane's Castle td: Drummaul AM 19; 78

Shane's hill: Antrim AM 29; 1

Shane's hill: Ballylinny AM 32; 11

Shane's hill: Ballymartin AM 2; 1

Shane's hill: Ballywalter AM 2; 28

Shane's hill: Kilbride AM 29; 137

Shane's hill: Kilwaughter AM 10; 108

Shane's hill: Muckamore AM 35; 57, 74

Shane's hill: Nilteen AM 35; 87

Shane's hill: Raloo AM 32; 86

Shane's hill: Templepatrick AM 35; 105

Shane's hill: Tullylish DN 12; 140, 143

Shanefinn (see Syonfin)

Shaneglish td: Ballymore AH 1; 12–17

Shanemullagh (see Shanmullagh)

Shanenglin (see Shaneglish): Ballymore AH 1; 12

Shaneoguestown beetling mill: Muckamore AM 35; 56, 63, 75–76

Shaneoguestown cove: Muckamore AM 35; 72

Shaneoguestown forts: Muckamore AM 35; 56, 72, 74

Shaneoguestown old bleach mill: Muckamore AM 35; 56

Shaneoguestown td: Muckamore AM 35; 54, 69, 77–78

Shanerah bog: Dromore TE 5; 93

Shanerah R. td: Dromore TE 5; 99

Shanerah td: Dromore TE 5; 93, 95

Shanerah W. td: Dromore TE 5; 99

Shanes school: Loughguile AM 13; 77

Shanes td: Loughguile AM 13; 69, 76–77

Shanguogh td: Killoran and Kilvarnet SO 40; 183

Shanhole (see Shankill): Aghaderg DN 12; 3

Shank, Mr: Blaris DN 12; 44, 47–48

Shankay corn mill: Donaghenry TE 20; 37

Shankhill (see Shankill)

Shankill (Shancole) td: Aghaderg DN 12; 3, 8

Shankill chapel: Carnmoney AM 2; 57

Shankill church: Shankill AH 1; 113–14

Shankill church: Shankill DN 12; 138

Shankill church: Tullyrusk AM 21; 135
Shankill cotton manufactory: Carnmoney AM 2; 51
Shankill glebe: Derryvullan FH 14; 44
Shankill Glebe House: Shankill AH 1; 114
Shankill graveyard: Cleenish FH 14; 21
Shankill hill: Aghaderg DN 12; 8
Shankill manor: Misc. FH 4; 133
Shankill ph: Aghagallon AM 21; 1
Shankill ph: Ballinderry AM 21; 53
Shankill ph: Ballymartin AM 2; 3
Shankill ph: Ballyrobert AM 2; 23
Shankill ph: Camlin AM 21; 64, 66
Shankill ph: Carmavy AM 35; 1
Shankill ph: Carnmoney AM 2; 53, 57, 63
Shankill ph: Carrickfergus AM 37; 61
Shankill ph: Derryaghy AM 8; 90–91, 104, 118
Shankill ph: Donaghcloney DN 12; 57
Shankill ph: Drumbeg AM 8; 122
Shankill ph: Drumbeg DN 7; 52
Shankill ph: Drumbo DN 7; 54
Shankill ph: Drumcree AH 1; 28
Shankill ph: Island Magee AM 10; 77
Shankill ph: Killead AM 35; 7–9, 43
Shankill ph: Magheralin DN 12; 109
Shankill ph: Mallusk AM 2; 106–07, 112, 115
Shankill ph: Misc. AM 10; 129
Shankill ph: Moira DN 12; 117
Shankill ph: Seagoe AH 1; 101, 104
Shankill ph: Templepatrick AM 35; 105–06, 119, 139, 142
Shankill ph: Tullyrusk AM 21; 131, 133
Shankill ph: Umgall AM 35; 155, 158
Shankill school: Derryvullan FH 14; 43
Shankill td: Aughnamullen MN 40; 76
Shankill td: Derryvullan FH 14; 46
Shankill td: Devenish FH 14; 59
Shanks, Joseph: Carrickfergus AM 37; 107
Shanksland locality: Carrickfergus AM 37; 94
Shanlieve mountain: Clonduff DN 3; 5
Shanliss td: Clonoe TE 20; 29
Shanlongford bogs: Errigal LY 27; 54
Shanlongford bridge [I]: Aghadowey LY 22; 10
Shanlongford bridge [II]: Aghadowey LY 22; 10
Shanlongford corn mill: Aghadowey LY 22; 9
Shanlongford flax mill: Aghadowey LY 22; 9
Shanlongford td: Aghadowey LY 22; 16, 34–35
Shanlongford td: Errigal LY 27; 83, 88, 91–92
Shanmulla (see Shanmullagh)
Shanmullagh bog: Dromore TE 5; 93
Shanmullagh East corn mill: Kilskeery TE 5; 114
Shanmullagh East td: Kilskeery TE 5; 114
Shanmullagh hill: Ballynascreen LY 31; 2
Shanmullagh hill: Dromore TE 5; 93
Shanmullagh hill: Trory FH 14; 122
Shanmullagh sessions house: Cleenish FH 14; 22

Shanmullagh spring: Dromore TE 5; 96
Shanmullagh td: Ballyscullion LY 6; 58
Shanmullagh td: Cleenish FH 14; 28, 30
Shanmullagh td: Dromore TE 5; 93, 96–97, 99
Shanmullagh td: Magherafelt LY 6; 95
Shanmullagh wood: Ballynascreen LY 31; 2
Shanmullan td: Kinawley FH 4; 109
Shanmullen td: Killesher FH 14; 85
Shannagh hill: Drumhome DL 39; 59
Shannagh lough: Clondavaddog DL 38; 1–3
Shannagh td: Raphoe DL 39; 126
Shannaghan chapel: Misc. DN 17; 122
Shannaghan corn mill: Newry DN 3; 83, 111
Shannaghan flax mill: Newry DN 3; 83, 111
Shannaghan hill: Newry DN 3; 111
Shannaghan school: Newry DN 3; 83, 111
Shannaghan td: Annaclone DN 12; 13
Shannaghan td: Drumballyroney DN 3; 13–14
Shannaghan td: Garvaghy DN 12; 79–80
Shannaghan td: Newry DN 3; 82–83, 110–11
Shannaragh td: Dromore TE 5; 100
Shanneck (see Shannock)
Shannee (see Syonee)
Shannock (Shannick) td: Clones FH 4; 29
Shannock Castle: Clones FH 4; 29
Shannock manor: Clones FH 4; 26
Shannock manor: Misc. FH 4; 133
Shannon House: Clonleigh DL 39; 13–14
Shannon river: Banagher LY 30; 101
Shannon river: Faughanvale LY 36; 56
Shannon td: Clonleigh DL 39; 4, 6, 8, 12, 198
Shannon, Dr (Rockcorry): Aghabog MN 40; 65
Shannon, Dr: Ematris MN 40; 113, 117
Shannon, family: Ballynure AM 32; 56
Shannon, family: Blaris AM 8; 21
Shannon, family: Errigal LY 27; 41
Shannon, family: Magherafelt LY 6; 95
Shannon, family: Templepatrick AM 35; 118
Shannon, James: Desertoghill LY 27; 27
Shannon, James: Maghera LY 18; 52, 56
Shannon, John: Drumachose LY 9; 104
Shannon, John: Macosquin LY 22; 102
Shannon, Marriet: Carrickfergus AM 37; 161
Shannon, Mrs: Coleraine LY 33; 73
Shannon, Mrs William: Magheramesk AM 21; 129
Shannon, Samuel: Drumachose LY 9; 104, 110
Shannon, Stephen: Kinawley FH 4; 120
Shannon, William: Aghanloo LY 11; 13, 17, 19–20, 24, 27, 29–30, 35, 37
Shannon, William: Connor AM 19; 27
Shannon, William: Drumachose LY 9; 118, 127
Shannon, William: Magheramesk AM 21; 129–30
Shannony fort: Ardstraw TE 5; 12
Shannony td: Ardstraw TE 5; 12
Shannor, family: Ballynure AM 32; 56

Shanoguestown (see Shaneoguestown): Muckamore AM 35; 76

Shanoughy (see Shanaghy): Aghalurcher FH 4; 4

Shanport locality: Aghagallon AM 21; 2, 7, 13

Shanragh td: Kinawley FH 4; 110

Shanreagh fort [I]: Tamlaght Finlagan LY 25; 90, 109

Shanreagh fort [II]: Tamlaght Finlagan LY 25; 90, 109, 112–13

Shanreagh fort [III]: Tamlaght Finlagan LY 25; 90, 109

Shanreagh school: Tamlaght Finlagan LY 25; 80

Shanreagh td: Tamlaght Finlagan LY 25; 80, 93, 120

Shanrod (Shenrod) td: Garvaghy DN 12; 79–81

Shanrod corn mill: Garvaghy DN 12; 80, 84

Shanrod flax mill: Garvaghy DN 12; 80, 84

Shanrod mills: Garvaghy DN 12; 80

Shanrod school: Garvaghy DN 12; 83

Shanrod td: Garvaghy DN 12; 83–84

Shanrod water: Garvaghy DN 12; 84

Shanroe dispensary: Forkhill AH 1; 45

Shantally female school: Tynan AH 1; 127, 129

Shantally male school: Tynan AH 1; 127, 129

Shantana (see Shantonagh)

Shantanagh (see Shantonagh)

Shantanna (see Shantonagh): Ballybay MN 40; 81

Shantaveny (see Shantavny): Errigal Keerogue TE 20; 49

Shantavny (Shantavney) td: Errigal Keerogue TE 20; 57

Shantavny hill: Carnteel TE 20; 23

Shantavny hill: Clogher TE 5; 24

Shantavny hill: Clogherny TE 20; 25

Shantavny hill: Donacavey TE 5; 62

Shantavny hill: Errigal Keerogue TE 20; 46, 55

Shantavny hill: Killeeshil TE 20; 64

Shantavny Lower (Scotch) td: Errigal Keerogue TE 20; 49, 55

Shantavny Lower gravel fort: Errigal Keerogue TE 20; 55

Shantavny Lower gravel pits: Errigal Keerogue TE 20; 55

Shantavny Lower quarry: Errigal Keerogue TE 20; 55

Shantavny Upper (Irish) td: Errigal Keerogue TE 20; 55–57

Shantavny Upper lough: Errigal Keerogue TE 20; 55

Shantavny Upper well: Errigal Keerogue TE 20; 55–56

Shantavny Uppertown (see Shantavny Upper): Errigal Keerogue TE 20; 57

Shanterragh td: Clogher TE 5; 53

Shantonagh corn mill: Ballybay MN 40; 81

Shantonagh flax mill: Ballybay MN 40; 81

Shantonagh td: Aughnamullen MN 40; 71, 76

Shantonagh td: Ballybay MN 40; 84

Shantonagh td: Clogher TE 5; 37

Shanvan rock: Culfeightrin AM 24; 74

Shanvera td: Dromore TE 5; 97

Shanvey td: Aghanloo LY 11; 9, 12, 15, 18, 21–22, 32–33, 37, 39, 41–42

Shanwilla td: Kinawley FH 4; 110

Sharagone altar stones: Desertegney DL 38; 26

Sharagone fort: Desertegney DL 38; 26

Sharagone td: Desertegney DL 38; 28

Shark Island: Saul DN 17; 111, 114

Shark lough: Aghaderg DN 12; 3, 7–8

Shark lough: Ballymore AH 1; 1, 8, 13, 15

Shark lough: Misc. DN 17; 130–31

Sharke (see Shark)

Sharkey, Cauhall: Tullaghobegley DL 39; 172–73

Sharkey, D.: Enniskillen FH 4; 77

Sharkey, Dominic: Newry DN 3; 99, 104

Sharkey, family: Aghalee AM 21; 36

Sharkey, James: Maghera LY 18; 80

Sharkey, John: Clonleigh DL 39; 14

Sharkey, Michael: Maghera LY 18; 81

Sharkey, Patrick: Newry DN 3; 99, 104

Sharkey, Rev.: Dromara DN 12; 66

Sharkey, Rev.: Magheradrool DN 17; 106

Sharkey, Robert: Balteagh LY 9; 40

Sharkey, Thomas: Maghera LY 18; 81

Sharkin, robber: Rasharkin AM 23; 138, 140

Sharky, John: Misc. DN 17; 128

Sharon demesne: Raymoghy DL 39; 140

Sharon glebe: Clondavaddog DL 38; 7

Sharon Glebe House: Raymoghy DL 39; 134

Sharon Glebe td: Raymoghy DL 39; 139, 199

Sharon wood: Misc. DL 39; 189

Sharp, Andrew: Culfeightrin AM 24; 71–72

Sharp, Charles: Ballynure AM 32; 56–57, 59

Sharp, Charles: Culfeightrin AM 24; 52, 74

Sharp, family: Billy AM 16; 58, 68

Sharp, family: Culfeightrin AM 24; 59

Sharp, James: Culfeightrin AM 24; 76

Sharp, Robert (Jnr): Coleraine LY 33; 72, 127

Sharp, Robert (Snr): Coleraine LY 33; 65, 72, 142

Sharpe, Andrew: Ramoan AM 24; 117

Sharpe, family: Ramoan AM 24; 107

Sharpe, James: Culfeightrin AM 24; 67

Sharpe, Mr: Ramoan AM 24; 98, 100

Sharpe, Peter: Ramoan AM 24; 117

Sharpe, William: Ramoan AM 24; 104

Sharr, John: Ballintoy AM 24; 26

Sharvogues bog: Drummaul AM 19; 39

Sharvogues forts: Drummaul AM 19; 78

Sharvogues House: Drummaul AM 19; 35, 79, 81, 85

Sharvogues td: Drummaul AM 19; 33

Shaskinamaddy (see Sheskinamaddy)

Shave Island: Cleenish FH 14; 13, 29

Shaw, Col.: Drumgooland DN 3; 24

Shaw, Conway: Carnmoney AM 2; 67, 94

Shaw, Daniel: Ahoghill AM 23; 48

Shaw, Edward: Carnmoney AM 2; 84, 90

Shaw, family: Ahoghill AM 23; 25

Shaw, family: Ballintoy AM 24; 20

Shaw, family: Ballywalter AM 2; 26, 30

Shaw, family: Carmavy AM 35; 4

Shaw, family: Carnmoney AM 2; 76

Shaw, family: Drumbo DN 7; 59

Shaw, family: Killead AM 35; 14

Shaw, family: Templecorran AM 26; 117, 119

Shaw, Frank: Ballymartin AM 2; 17

Shaw, George (Jnr): Ballywalter AM 2; 27

Shaw, George (Snr): Ballywalter AM 2; 26–27, 32

Shaw, George: Carnmoney AM 2; 102

Shaw, George: Clondermot LY 34; 82

Shaw, George: Doagh AM 29; 98

Shaw, H.W.: Killead AM 35; 47

Shaw, Henry: Carmavy AM 35; 3

Shaw, Henry: Hillsborough DN 12; 107

Shaw, Hugh: Loughinisland DN 17; 95

Shaw, James: Carrickfergus AM 37; 109

Shaw, John: Carrickfergus AM 37; 165

Shaw, John: Errigal LY 27; 68

Shaw, John: Tamlaght TE 20; 122

Shaw, Jonathon: Hillsborough DN 12; 107

Shaw, Joseph: Blaris AM 8; 38, 44

Shaw, Joseph: Blaris DN 12; 38

Shaw, Margaret: Ballyaghran LY 33; 27

Shaw, Martha: Ballyaghran LY 33; 27

Shaw, Mr (Ayrshire): Carncastle and Killyglen AM
     10; 6, 11

Shaw, Mr (Ayrshire): Templepatrick AM 35; 132

Shaw, Mr (Celbridge): Carrickfergus AM 37; 137

Shaw, Mr: Saintfield DN 7; 118–19

Shaw, Mrs S.B.: Raloo AM 32; 127

Shaw, Neil: Ballyaghran LY 33; 27

Shaw, Rev. James: Carnmoney AM 2; 75–76, 79

Shaw, Rev. James: Tartaraghan AH 1; 118

Shaw, Rev. John: Ballinderry AM 21; 50

Shaw, Rev. John: Magheradrool DN 17; 106

Shaw, Rev. Patrick: Carnmoney AM 2; 75

Shaw, Rev. Robert: Ardstraw TE 5; 9

Shaw, Rev. William: Donegore AM 29; 129

Shaw, S.B.: Raloo AM 32; 131

Shaw, Thomas: Ballywalter AM 2; 27

Shaw, W.: Comber DN 7; 33

Shaw, William: Blaris DN 12; 47

Shaw, William: Hillsborough DN 12; 107

Shaw's bridge: Drumbo DN 7; 54

Shaw's Castle (see Ballygally Castle): Carncastle
     and Killyglen AM 10; 11

Shaw's fort: Ballylinny AM 32; 26

Shaw's hill: Doagh AM 29; 62

Shaw's lough: Loughgilly AH 1; 86

Shaw's mill: Killea and Taughboyne DL 39; 87

Shawe, William: Drummaul AM 19; 70

Shea, Edward: Duneane AM 19; 124

Sheaghany td: Kinawley FH 4; 121

Sheagog, William: Kilcronaghan LY 31; 84

Sheals, Charles: Carrickfergus AM 37; 131

Sheals, Hugh: Culfeightrin AM 24; 85

Shean Doo MacMahon's bog: Ematris MN 40; 115

Shean mountain: Devenish FH 14; 47

Shean mountain: Inishmacsaint FH 14; 70–71

Shean school: Forkhill AH 1; 45

Shean td: Forkhill AH 1; 45

Shean td: Inishmacsaint FH 14; 70

Sheans (see Shanes): Loughguile AM 13; 77

Shear Leahagh locality: Lough Swilly DL 38; 127

Shearcloon td: Misc. DL 39; 198

Shearer, family: Carrickfergus AM 37; 93

Shearer, James: Carrickfergus AM 37; 158

Shearer, Mathew: Glynn AM 26; 47

Shearer, Robert: Carrickfergus AM 37; 148

Shearer, Robert: Rasharkin AM 23; 139

Shearer, Thomas: Rasharkin AM 23; 140

Sheddings Drumfane school: Kirkinriola AM 23;
     121

Shedin, Capt.: Desertoghill LY 27; 21

Shedin, Eliza: Desertoghill LY 27; 21

Shedin, James: Desertoghill LY 27; 21

Shedin, John: Desertoghill LY 27; 21

Shedin, Mary (Jnr): Desertoghill LY 27; 21

Shedin, Mary (Snr): Desertoghill LY 27; 21

Shedin, Thomas: Desertoghill LY 27; 21

Shedin, William: Desertoghill LY 27; 21

Shedogh district: Clondavaddog DL 38; 3

Shee lough: Tydavnet MN 40; 169

Sheebeg td: Aghalurcher FH 4; 4, 8, 14

Sheelah Island: Ballyhalbert DN 7; 6

Sheelin lough: Drumlumman CN 40; 12–13, 15, 17

Sheely, Miss: Ballyphilip DN 7; 13

Sheemore hill: Aghavea FH 4; 17

Sheen (see Shinn): Newry DN 3; 110

Sheeny td: Galloon FH 4; 89, 95, 98

Sheep Gate path: Magilligan LY 11; 99

Sheep Haven bay: Lough Swilly DL 38; 105,
     119–22

Sheep Haven bay: Mevagh DL 38; 54, 56, 59,
     61–62

Sheep Head: Templepatrick AM 35; 145, 152

Sheep hill: Ballyscullion LY 6; 42, 70

Sheep hill lough: Dromore TE 5; 100

Sheep Hoods locality: Templepatrick AM 35; 152

Sheep Island: Ballintoy AM 24; 14, 33

Sheep rock: Warrenpoint DN 3; 120

Sheepbridge td: Newry DN 3; 74, 106

Sheephill House: Tamlaght Finlagan LY 25; 82, 101

Sheepland ph: Misc. DN 17; 118

Sheeplandbeg corn mill: Ardglass DN 17; 9

Sheeplandbeg td: Dunsfort DN 17; 72

Sheeplandbeg windmill: Ardglass DN 17; 9

Sheeplandmore td: Dunsfort DN 17; 72

Sheeptown chapel: Newry DN 3; 77, 107

Sheeptown school: Newry DN 3; 81

Sheeptown td: Newry DN 3; 77, 81, 107–08

Sheepwalk Sunday school: Magheragall AM 21; 110

Sheepwalk td: Drummully FH 4; 39

Sheeran, Patrick: Newry DN 3; 100

Sheerer, Davy: Ballyscullion LY 6; 57

Sheerer, James: Tamlaght Finlagan LY 25; 89, 107, 114–15

Sheerins bridge: Aghagallon AM 21; 5–6

Sheerins Lock: Aghagallon AM 21; 5–6

Sheetrim sweathouse: Kinawley FH 4; 120

Sheetrim td: Kinawley FH 4; 121

Sheil, A.J.: Kilcronaghan LY 31; 87

Sheil, family: Maghera LY 18; 24, 48

Sheil, John: Ahoghill AM 23; 37

Sheil, John: Duneane AM 19; 112, 116

Sheil, Margaret (Jnr): Ahoghill AM 23; 37

Sheil, Margaret (Snr): Ahoghill AM 23; 37

Sheil, Patrick: Blaris AM 8; 47

Sheil, Rev. J.: Enniskillen FH 4; 41, 70, 84–85

Sheil, Rev. J.: Rossorry FH 14; 117

Sheil, Rev. James: Carrickfergus AM 37; 102

Sheil, Thomas: Ahoghill AM 23; 37

Sheil, Thomas: Coleraine LY 33; 145

Sheilds, family: Carrickfergus AM 37; 93

Sheill, Patt: Culfeightrin AM 24; 77–78

Sheils, James: Ballyscullion LY 6; 65

Shelan locality: Kilkeel DN 3; 51

Shelbourne, Earl of: Cumber LY 28; 58

Shelburne, Henry: Clondermot LY 34; 33, 56

Sheldon, Col: Galloon FH 4; 100

Shellfield (Shelfield) td: Tullyaughnish DL 38; 97

Shellfield House: Lough Swilly DL 38; 103

Shellfield House: Tullyaughnish DL 38; 86, 89

Shellgrove House: Maghera LY 18; 54

Shembless quarry: Drumgoon CN 40; 4

Shennan, Samuel: Antrim AM 29; 37

Shepherd, James: Termoneeny LY 6; 133

Shepherd's path: Billy AM 16; 43

Sheppard, Margrett: Artrea LY 6; 38

Sheppard, Rev. N.: Newry DN 3; 100, 104

Sheppard, Susan: Carrickfergus AM 37; 121

Shepperd, John: Artrea LY 6; 26

Sherard, Conolly: Drumachose LY 9; 104

Sherard, Hugh: Drumachose LY 9; 73

Shercock: Aughnamullen MN 40; 73, 76

Shercock: Ballybay MN 40; 81

Shercock: Drumgoon CN 40; 7

Shercock: Magheracloone MN 40; 139

Shercock: Magheross MN 40; 146, 157

Shercock ph: Magheross MN 40; 143

Sherdin, Mr (Jnr): Clonleigh DL 39; 4

Sherdin, Mr (Snr): Clonleigh DL 39; 4

Sherer, family: Carrickfergus AM 37; 179

Sheridan td: Magheracross FH 14; 102

Sheridan, Mr: Kilkeel DN 3; 48

Sheriff, James: Coleraine LY 33; 105, 131–32

Sheriff, Samuel: Coleraine LY 33; 92, 131

Sherlo, family: Aghadowey LY 22; 11

Sherlo, man named: Aghadowey LY 22; 11–12

Sherlo, man named: Misc. LY 36; 112

Sherly, William: Aghadowey LY 22; 34

Sherra, Allen: Aghanloo LY 11; 15

Sherrard, Charles: Carnmoney AM 2; 62, 102

Sherrard, David: Ballymoney AM 16; 17

Sherrigrim (Sherrigrin) td: Donaghenry TE 20; 37, 39

Sherrigrim tape manufactory: Donaghenry TE 20; 37, 39

Sherry, Bernard: Lissan LY 31; 109

Sherry, Edward: Lissan LY 31; 109

Sherwin, family: Misc. LY 36; 104

Shesk (see Glenshesk): Culfeightrin AM 24; 49

Sheskan (see Sheskin)

Sheskin td: Raymoghy DL 39; 141, 199

Sheskinamaddy stream: Dungiven LY 15; 49, 51, 63

Sheskinapoll td: Raymoghy DL 39; 139

Sheshnamaddy (see Sheskinamaddy)

Shessagh bay: Lough Swilly DL 38; 115

Shetland Isles: Banagher LY 30; 7

Shetland Isles: Lough Swilly DL 38; 113

Shian td: Clondermot LY 34; 74

Shiel, Dr: Belleek FH 14; 6

Shiel, Dr: Enniskillen FH 4; 80

Shiel, Dr: Killesher FH 14; 88

Shiel, Hugh: Ballyaghran LY 33; 22

Shiel, James: Culfeightrin AM 24; 57

Shiel, James: Drumglass TE 20; 42

Shiel, John: Ballyscullion AM 19; 8, 10

Shiel, Mr: Tamlaght Finlagan LY 25; 93

Shiel, Patrick: Banagher LY 30; 33, 111

Shiel, Una: Rasharkin AM 23; 137, 140

Shield, Hugh: Culfeightrin AM 24; 52

Shields, Charles: Blaris AM 8; 80–81, 85–86

Shields, J.: Comber DN 7; 34

Shields, Mr (Ballyhernan): Clondavaddog DL 38; 9

Shields, Patrick: Bovevagh LY 25; 28

Shields, Rev. James: Newry DN 3; 71, 79, 81, 98, 100–01, 103

Shields, Thomas: Coleraine LY 33; 146

Shiels, Bernard: Artrea LY 6; 33

Shiels, John: Carrickfergus AM 37; 111

Shiels, John: Termoneeny LY 6; 133
Shiels, Philip: Termoneeny LY 6; 133
Shiels, Robert: Carrickfergus AM 37; 115–16
Shiels, Robert: Termoneeny LY 6; 131
Shiemulldoon td: Magheraculmoney FH 14; 110
Shiercloon td: Clonleigh DL 39; 12
Shig (see Slug): Donegal DL 39; 54
Shillanavoggy td: Racavan AM 13; 89
Shillin Island: Desertmartin LY 31; 55–56, 61
Shillin lough: Desertmartin LY 31; 52, 55–56
Shillingmore td: Enniskillen FH 4; 82
Shillington, family: Ballinderry AM 21; 51
Shillington, Henry: Aghagallon AM 21; 5, 17, 21
Shillington, Henry: Aghalee AM 21; 40
Shillington, Henry: Blaris AM 8; 60
Shillington, Henry: Blaris DN 12; 40
Shillington, Thomas: Drumcree AH 1; 29
Shilvodan coves: Shilvodan AM 19; 136
Shilvodan forts: Shilvodan AM 19; 135
Shilvodan old graveyard: Shilvodan AM 19; 138
Shilvodan ph: Antrim AM 29; 26–27
Shilvodan ph: Connor AM 19; 16, 18
Shilvodan ph: Drummaul AM 19; 33, 58
Shilvodan ph: Misc. AM 10; 129
Shilvodan rectory: Kirkinriola AM 23; 88
Shimna river (see also Tullymore river): Kilcoo DN
    3; 41
Shin (see Shinn): Newry DN 3; 109
Shinn bridges: Newry DN 3; 109
Shinn caves: Newry DN 3; 110
Shinn chapel: Newry DN 3; 77, 107
Shinn fort: Newry DN 3; 110
Shinn school: Newry DN 3; 81, 110
Shinn Sunday school: Newry DN 3; 109
Shinn td: Newry DN 3; 77, 81, 107, 109–10
Shinnagh lough: Donaghmore DL 39; 29
Ship Ride harbour: Donegal DL 39; 46
Ship Ride harbour: Killymard DL 39; 95, 106
Shirley Arms Hotel: Magheross MN 40; 151
Shirley House: Magheracloone MN 40; 138
Shirley House: Magheross MN 40; 145
Shirley, E.J.: Donaghmoyne MN 40; 108, 110
Shirley, E.J.: Killanny MN 40; 132, 134
Shirley, E.J.: Magheracloone MN 40; 137–39,
    141–42
Shirley, E.J.: Magheross MN 40; 145–52, 156–57
Shivers, Henry: Duneane AM 19; 124
Shivey House: Desertcreat TE 20; 36
Shivey quarry: Pomeroy TE 20; 71
Shonkey school: Killeeshil TE 20; 64
Shore, family: Enniskillen FH 4; 58
Shore, Mr: Devenish FH 14; 53
Shore, Thomas: Enniskillen FH 4; 57
Short lough: Killygarvan DL 38; 37
Short, family: Ballywillin AM 16; 32

Short, Patrick: Carrickfergus AM 37; 125
Short, William: Carrickfergus AM 37; 114
Shorter, William: Carrickfergus AM 37; 127
Shortt, Lt: Ramoan AM 24; 94
Shracreaghan forts: Manorhamilton Union LM 40;
    52
Shragh td: Aughnamullen MN 40; 76
Shraghduffgower td: Donacavey TE 5; 82
Shranee forts: Manorhamilton Union LM 40; 52
Shreehill (see Sruell): Killymard DL 39; 105
Shriaghmarke td: Donacavey TE 5; 82
Shroove Point: Lough Swilly DL 38; 108, 113, 137,
    140, 142
Shropshire (England): Newry DN 3; 65
Shrove Head: Moville DL 38; 72
Shrove Head forts: Moville DL 38; 68
Shrove House: Moville DL 38; 70
Shrove td: Moville DL 38; 68, 70
Shruhill (see Sruell): Killymard DL 39; 101
Shryhenny giant's grave: Trory FH 14; 127
Shryhenny hill: Trory FH 14; 122
Shryhenny td: Trory FH 14; 124–25, 127
Shul ne teneschal, family: Ballyphilip DN 7; 13
Shuldhane, Pooly: Ballyscullion AM 19; 9
Shuse, Mr: Clonleigh DL 39; 13
Shutter, David (Jnr): Desertoghill LY 27; 20
Shutter, David (Snr): Desertoghill LY 27; 20
Shutter, Elizabeth: Desertoghill LY 27; 20
Shutter, George: Desertoghill LY 27; 20
Shutter, Margaret (Jnr): Desertoghill LY 27; 20
Shutter, Margaret (Snr): Desertoghill LY 27; 20
Shutter, Martha: Desertoghill LY 27; 20
Shutter, William: Desertoghill LY 27; 20
Siabranach lough: Templecarn DL 39; 157
Sianfin (see Syonfin)
Sibs stone (see Gormon's mountain): Derryaghy
    AM 8; 98
Sicily: Newry DN 3; 68
Sidd hill: Derryvullan FH 14; 31
Sidd td: Derryvullan FH 14; 31
Sidear td: Magheracross FH 14; 102
Sidmonton (Hampshire): Island Magee AM 10; 42
Sidney lough (see Lough Neagh): Lough Neagh AM
    21; 95
Sidney, Henry: Carrickfergus AM 37; 13, 34
Sie Fionn eminence: Maghera LY 18; 36
Sientian (see Syunshin[?])
Siera, H.: Banagher LY 30; 113
Silcock, J.H.: Kilmore DN 17; 88
Sillees river: Boho FH 14; 9
Sillees river: Cleenish FH 14; 14–15, 27
Sillees river: Devenish FH 14; 47, 52–53, 57
Sillees river: Inishmacsaint FH 14; 71–72, 74
Sillees river: Rossorry FH 14; 115
Sillia, William: Magherafelt LY 6; 112

Sillies (see Sillees): Boho FH 14; 9

Silliman, Thomas: Raloo AM 32; 123

Sillito, Rev. E.: Coleraine LY 33; 73

Sillito, Rev. W.W.: Coleraine LY 33; 65, 73, 127

Sillito, Rev. W.W.: Killowen LY 33; 164–66

Sillor, Elisabeth: Island Magee AM 10; 94

Sillyman, family: Templecorran AM 26; 117, 119

Sil-Ronain (Westmeath): Faughanvale LY 36; 49

Silshion (see Selshion): Drumcree AH 1; 36

Silver hill: Lough Swilly DL 38; 137

Silver hill: Maghera LY 18; 12, 37–38

Silver hill: Skirts of Urney and Ardstraw TE 5; 136

Silver hill graveyard: Maghera LY 18; 37

Silver stream: Carnmoney AM 2; 37

Silver stream: Carrickfergus AM 37; 7, 33, 57

Silverhill Cottage: Devenish FH 14; 53

Silverhill td: Devenish FH 14; 59

Silverstream House: Carrickfergus AM 37; 57, 135, 141

Silverwood House: Seagoe AH 1; 105, 109

Silverwood td: Seagoe AH 1; 109

Sim, Andrew: Warrenpoint DN 3; 118

Simeon, Mary: Aghanloo LY 11; 39

Simm [or Simon], William: Carrickfergus AM 37; 40, 148

Simm, family: Ballywalter AM 2; 26, 30

Simm, James: Ballymartin AM 2; 15–18

Simm, James: Carrickfergus AM 37; 148

Simm, Samuel: Carrickfergus AM 37; 40

Simms and McIntyre, Messrs: Blaris DN 12; 43, 47

Simms and McIntyre, Messrs: Coleraine LY 33; 116

Simms, family: Tamlaght O'Crilly LY 18; 93

Simms, Reuben: Coleraine LY 33; 72

Simms, Rev. James: Ramoan AM 24; 126

Simon, family: Blaris AM 8; 21

Simon, James: Magherafelt LY 6; 94

Simonstown td: Clonleigh DL 39; 12

Simonton, family: Templecorran AM 26; 117, 119

Simple, family: Misc. LY 36; 104

Simpson, Alexander: Balteagh LY 9; 32

Simpson, Alexander: Magherafelt LY 6; 112

Simpson, Alexander: Tamlaght TE 20; 96

Simpson, Ann (see Moore)

Simpson, Arthur: Carrickfergus AM 37; 127

Simpson, Capt.: Drumachose LY 9; 126

Simpson, David: Billy AM 16; 75

Simpson, E.: Clogher TE 5; 40

Simpson, Eliza: Tamlaght Finlagan LY 25; 120

Simpson, family: Ballyrashane LY 22; 58

Simpson, family: Carnmoney AM 2; 76

Simpson, family: Derryaghy AM 8; 103

Simpson, family: Derrykeighan AM 16; 89

Simpson, family: Lambeg AM 8; 135

Simpson, family: Misc. LY 36; 104

Simpson, family: Ramoan AM 24; 107

Simpson, George: Ballyrashane LY 22; 57

Simpson, George: Blaris DN 12; 46, 50

Simpson, George: Magherafelt LY 6; 112

Simpson, J.: Tullynakill DN 7; 123

Simpson, James (Jnr): Drumbeg AM 8; 133

Simpson, James (Snr): Drumbeg AM 8; 133

Simpson, James: Ballynurc AM 32; 62

Simpson, James: Ballyrashane LY 22; 57, 65

Simpson, James: Ballywillin LY 33; 46, 50

Simpson, James: Blaris AM 8; 60

Simpson, James: Blaris DN 12; 40

Simpson, James: Carnmoney AM 2; 101

Simpson, James: Cumber LY 28; 73, 77

Simpson, James: Derryaghy AM 8; 90, 102, 109

Simpson, James: Kildollagh LY 22; 75

Simpson, James [I]: Ahoghill AM 23; 34

Simpson, James [II]: Ahoghill AM 23; 38

Simpson, Jane: Ahoghill AM 23; 38

Simpson, John: Hillsborough DN 12; 105

Simpson, John [I]: Tamlaght Finlagan LY 25; 120

Simpson, John [II]: Tamlaght Finlagan LY 25; 122

Simpson, man named: Aghanloo LY 11; 31

Simpson, Margaret Ann: Ahoghill AM 23; 38

Simpson, Mary: Carrickfergus AM 37; 116

Simpson, Mary: Drumbeg AM 8; 133

Simpson, Mary: Magherafelt LY 6; 112

Simpson, Mrs: Balteagh LY 9; 32

Simpson, Rev. Henry: Saintfield DN 7; 114

Simpson, Rev. John: Coleraine LY 33; 141

Simpson, Robb: Carrickfergus AM 37; 135

Simpson, Robert: Ballyrashane LY 22; 57

Simpson, Robert: Drumachose LY 9; 66

Simpson, Robert: Tamlaght TE 20; 80, 96, 102

Simpson, Samuel: Derrykeighan AM 16; 89–91, 94–95

Simpson, Sarah: Clondermot LY 34; 43, 87, 90, 95

Simpson, Sarah: Kilrea LY 27; 121

Simpson, Simon: Billy AM 16; 73

Simpson, Thomas: Derryaghy AM 8; 103

Simpson, Thomas: Errigal Keerogue TE 20; 50–51, 54

Simpson, William: Ahoghill AM 23; 38

Simpson, William: Ballyrashane LY 22; 57–58

Simpson, William: Culfeightrin AM 24; 66–68

Simpson, William: Tamlaght TE 20; 77

Sims, Elizabeth: Clondermot LY 34; 81

Sims, Mary: Clondermot LY 34; 81

Sims, Miss: Holywood DN 7; 81

Sims, Widow: Tamlaght O'Crilly LY 18; 133

Simson, John: Donacavey TE 5; 81

Sinclair, A.: Maghera LY 18; 66

Sinclair, Capt.: Dungiven LY 15; 14, 99

Sinclair, Daniel: Ballywillin LY 33; 51

Sinclair, family: Culfeightrin AM 24; 59

Sinclair, family: Island Magee AM 10; 70

Sinclair, George: Hillsborough DN 12; 107
Sinclair, J.: Blaris AM 8; 70
Sinclair, James: Ardstraw TE 5; 5
Sinclair, James: Clonleigh DL 39; 1, 4–5, 10, 12
Sinclair, James: Cumber LY 28; 3, 77–78
Sinclair, James: Faughanvale LY 36; 40
Sinclair, James: Leckpatrick TE 5; 117, 119–22,
    124–25
Sinclair, James: Lough Swilly DL 38; 150
Sinclair, James: Misc. DL 39; 186, 189
Sinclair, James: Misc. TE 5; 147
Sinclair, John: Hillsborough DN 12; 106
Sinclair, Joseph: Ramoan AM 24; 126
Sinclair, Mr: Comber DN 7; 37, 40
Sinclair, Mr: Misc. LY 31; 130
Sinclair, Neal: Ballintoy AM 24; 21, 33
Sinclair, Rev. Robert: Island Magee AM 10; 43
Sinclair, Robert: Island Magee AM 10; 94
Sinclair, Samuel: Hillsborough DN 12; 106
Sinclair, Samuel: Kilcronaghan LY 31; 86
Sinclair, Thomas: Derryaghy AM 8; 108
Sinclair, W.: Ballee DN 17; 23
Sinclair, W.: Comber DN 7; 38
Sinclair, William: Cumber LY 28; 80–81, 114
Sinclair, William: Newry DN 3; 104
Sinclair's fort: Dundonald DN 7; 65
Sinclaire, J.: Carnmoney AM 2; 90
Sinclaire, Mrs J.: Carnmoney AM 2; 46, 84, 90, 93
Sinclaire, William: Derryaghy AM 8; 116–18
Sindall, family: Carrickfergus AM 37; 31
Singelton, Francis: Hillsborough DN 12; 107
Singleton, family: Carrickfergus AM 37; 93
Singleton, family: Magheragall AM 21; 99
Singleton, George: Hillsborough DN 12; 107
Singleton, John: Blaris AM 8; 20, 20, 37, 41, 46,
    72–75, 77
Singleton, John: Blaris DN 12; 43, 45–46, 49
Singleton, John: Drumgoon CN 40; 8, 10
Singleton, Mary: Hillsborough DN 12; 107
Singleton, Mrs: Donagh MN 40; 103
Singleton, Mrs: Tydavnet MN 40; 173
Singleton, Mrs Thomas: Errigal Truagh MN 40; 122
Singleton, Rebecca: Termoneeny LY 6; 132
Singleton, Silas: Hillsborough DN 12; 107
Singleton, Thomas: Blaris AM 8; 84
Singleton, Thomas: Errigal Truagh MN 40; 121
Singleton, Thomas: Termoneeny LY 6; 132
Singleton, William: Blaris DN 12; 45, 49
Singleton, William: Hillsborough DN 12; 107
Sinkler, family: Culfeightrin AM 24; 59
Sinnott, Mrs: Carrickfergus AM 37; 171
Sinnott's hotel: Carrickfergus AM 37; 148
Sinton, family: Magilligan LY 11; 130
Sion flax mill: Urney DL 39; 177
Sion hill: Garvaghy DN 12; 80

Sion hill: Kilmacteige SO 40; 195
Sion Hill Cottage: Kilmacteige SO 40; 195
Sion school: Urney DL 39; 182
Sionee (see Syonee)
Sipatrick (see Seapatrick): Seapatrick DN 12; 123
Sirr, Maj. (Dublin): Rasharkin AM 23; 137–38
Siskuin (see Caskum): Aghaderg DN 12; 1
Sistrakeel (Sistrokeel) td: Tamlaght Finlagan LY 25;
    72–74, 93, 109, 119, 122
Sistrakeel bridge: Tamlaght Finlagan LY 25; 122
Sistrakeel hill: Tamlaght Finlagan LY 25; 62
Sistrakeel school: Tamlaght Finlagan LY 25; 75,
    77–79, 124
Sistrakeel waterfall: Tamlaght Finlagan LY 25; 110
Sitherwood, John: Blaris AM 8; 43
Sitherwood, John: Blaris DN 12; 39–41, 45, 49
Siulliliggan hill: Clonfeacle AH 1; 23
Six Mile Water bridge: Antrim AM 29; 22, 50
Six Mile Water bridge: Ballywalter AM 2; 29
Six Mile Water bridge: Doagh AM 29; 71
Six Mile Water bridge [I]: Ballynure AM 32; 34
Six Mile Water bridge [II]: Ballynure AM 32; 34
Six Mile Water metal bridge: Muckamore AM 35;
    64
Six Mile Water river: Antrim AM 29; 1–3, 5, 9–10,
    12–13, 15, 17, 20–22, 25, 30, 33, 36, 44, 49–50
Six Mile Water river: Ballycor AM 32; 1–2, 4, 8–9
Six Mile Water river: Ballylinny AM 32; 11–13,
    15–16, 24–25
Six Mile Water river: Ballymartin AM 2; 1, 3
Six Mile Water river: Ballynure AM 32; 31–32, 35,
    38, 43–46, 49, 63, 72
Six Mile Water river: Ballyrobert AM 2; 19
Six Mile Water river: Ballywalter AM 2; 26, 28–29
Six Mile Water river: Carmavy AM 35; 1
Six Mile Water river: Carnmoney AM 2; 35
Six Mile Water river: Carrickfergus AM 37; 5, 86
Six Mile Water river: Coleraine LY 33; 97
Six Mile Water river: Doagh AM 29; 60–66, 68,
    70–72, 78, 80, 84–86, 89–90, 93, 96, 98
Six Mile Water river: Donegore AM 29; 101–02,
    105–06, 109, 114, 120, 122, 131, 133
Six Mile Water river: Kilbride AM 29; 135–38, 140,
    147–48, 150, 155
Six Mile Water river: Killead AM 35; 9, 31
Six Mile Water river: Kilwaughter AM 10; 108
Six Mile Water river: Lough Neagh AM 21; 93–94,
    97
Six Mile Water river: Mallusk AM 2; 106
Six Mile Water river: Muckamore AM 35; 54–55,
    57–64, 69–71, 74–76, 82–83
Six Mile Water river: Nilteen AM 35; 84–91, 94–95,
    97–98, 101, 103
Six Mile Water river: Raloo AM 32; 85–86, 89
Six Mile Water river: Rashee AM 32; 135–36, 139

Six Mile Water river: Templecorran AM 26; 88

Six Mile Water river: Templepatrick AM 35; 105–07, 111–12, 115, 126, 131, 137, 139, 141–42

Six Mile Water river: Umgall AM 35; 155

Six Mile Water wooden bridge [I]: Muckamore AM 35; 64

Six Mile Water wooden bridge [II]: Muckamore AM 35; 64

Six Townlands (see Sixtowns): Ballynascreen LY 31; 32

Sixmilecross: Clogherny TE 20; 27

Sixmilecross: Errigal Keerogue TE 20; 50

Sixtowns glen: Ballynascreen LY 31; 1, 9, 12, 14, 32

Sixtowns glen: Lissan LY 31; 91

Sixtus V, Pope: Dungiven LY 15; 34

Sixty Acres td: Clonleigh DL 39; 12, 198

Skady tower: Drummaul AM 19; 89

Skate bay: Lough Swilly DL 38; 121–22

Skate Bed locality: Lough Swilly DL 38; 102

Skea hill: Cleenish FH 14; 12

Skea House: Cleenish FH 14; 17, 19, 22

Skea school: Cleenish FH 14; 24

Skea td: Cleenish FH 14; 15, 17, 21, 27, 30

Skea Wife bush: Drumachose LY 9; 109–10

Skeagh hill: Kilwaughter AM 10; 108

Skeagh school: Dromore DN 12; 73

Skeagh td: Dromore DN 12; 72

Skeagh td: Kilwaughter AM 10; 108, 119

Skeaghoughs bushes: Banagher LY 30; 67–68

Skeffington, Clotworthy (see Massereene): Drummaul AM 19; 70

Skeffington, family: Carmavy AM 35; 2

Skeffington, family: Killead AM 35; 17

Skeffington, family: Lough Neagh AM 21; 95

Skeffington, family: Muckamore AM 35; 54, 60, 82

Skeffington, John: Carrickfergus AM 37; 112

Skelgagh (Skelgah) td: Clogher TE 5; 37, 51, 54

Skelgagh school: Clogher TE 5; 51

Skelgagh td: Donacavey TE 5; 77, 79, 81, 83, 87

Skelgaph (see Skelgagh)

Skelluranmore rock: Lough Swilly DL 38; 108

Skelly, Felix: Aghalee AM 21; 37

Skelly, Francis: Kirkinriola AM 23; 99, 118

Skelly, Patrick: Loughguile AM 13; 74

Skelly, W.: Magheradrool DN 17; 105

Skelly's burn: Misc. LY 31; 113

Skelpy td: Urney DL 39; 182

Skelton, family: Magherally DN 12; 114

Skelton, Maria: Carrickfergus AM 37; 131

Skelton, Mr (Antrim): Donegore AM 29; 130

Skelton, Rev.: Donacavey TE 5; 72

Skelton, Rev. Philip: Blaris AM 8; 8

Skelton, W.: Muckamore AM 35; 80

Skelton, William: Ballymascanlan LH 40; 55

Skelton's cut drain: Magherally DN 12; 113

Skelton's locality: Muckamore AM 35; 80

Skenarget td: Desertcreat TE 20; 33

Skennagh lough: Killymard DL 39; 94

Skeoge td: Aghavea FH 4; 23

Skeogue (Skeages) td: Dromore TE 5; 99

Skeogue mountain: Dromore TE 5; 93

Skernaghan Point: Island Magee AM 10; 17–18, 58, 90

Skerrick td: Currin MN 40; 95

Skerrick West td: Currin MN 40; 88, 91

Skerries (Dublin): Lough Swilly DL 38; 118

Skerries district: Lough Swilly DL 38; 137

Skerries district: Racavan AM 13; 86

Skerries hill: Tynan AH 1; 124

Skerries mountain: Newtown Crommelin AM 13; 78

Skerries rocks: Ballywillin LY 33; 29, 44, 50

Skerries rocks: Coleraine LY 33; 78, 122

Skerries spring: Ballywillin LY 33; 29

Skerrig lough: Drumgoon CN 40; 3

Skerry church: Drummaul AM 19; 70

Skerry church: Racavan AM 13; 90

Skerry church: Skerry AM 13; 112, 114, 118–19

Skerry cove: Killagan AM 23; 87

Skerry East school: Newtown Crommelin AM 13; 83

Skerry East td: Newtown Crommelin AM 13; 78, 83

Skerry Glebe House: Skerry AM 13; 118

Skerry graveyard: Skerry AM 13; 115

Skerry Little hill: Skerry AM 13; 118

Skerry mountains: Kirkinriola AM 23; 93

Skerry mountains: Newtown Crommelin AM 13; 79

Skerry old church: Ahoghill AM 23; 25

Skerry old church: Drummaul AM 19; 71

Skerry old church: Skerry AM 13; 115, 118

Skerry ph: Ahoghill AM 23; 5

Skerry ph: Ardclinis AM 13; 1

Skerry ph: Ballyclug AM 23; 54

Skerry ph: Drummaul AM 19; 71

Skerry ph: Dunaghy AM 13; 25

Skerry ph: Glynn AM 26; 17

Skerry ph: Kirkinriola AM 23; 88, 92, 115

Skerry ph: Racavan AM 13; 86–87, 93–94, 98

Skerry ph: Tickmacrevan AM 13; 122

Skerry standing stone: Newtown Crommelin AM 13; 84

Skerry td: Dunaghy AM 13; 26

Skerry td: Newtown Crommelin AM 13; 84–85

Skerry West school: Newtown Crommelin AM 13; 81, 83

Skerry West td: Newtown Crommelin AM 13; 78, 81, 83

Skerrywhirry hill: Glenwhirry AM 32; 75

Sketrick Castle: Killinchy DN 7; 89

Sketrick Island: Ardkeen DN 7; 3

Sketrick Island: Killinchy DN 7; 89
Skevington, Rev.: Island Magee AM 10; 94
Skibbalh rock: Lough Swilly DL 38; 121
Skiffington, George: Tamlaght TE 20; 116
Skiffington, James: Tamlaght TE 20; 129
Skigatallagh td: Ballymore AH 1; 7–8, 13, 15, 17
Skilganaban (Skilganabane) td: Ballynure AM 32; 63, 68
Skilganaban fort: Ballynure AM 32; 60
Skilganaban school: Ballynure AM 32; 52, 65
Skillen, Harriet: Saintfield DN 7; 116
Skillyscolban school: Dromore DN 12; 73, 77
Skillyscolban td: Dromore DN 12; 77
Skinbwee bleach green: Ardstraw TE 5; 14
Skinner, C.M.: Carrickfergus AM 37; 102
Skinner, Capt.: Drumbo DN 7; 59–60
Skinner, Edward: Duneane AM 19; 118
Skipton, Alexander: Faughanvale LY 36; 42, 45
Skipton, Capt.: Muff DL 38; 82
Skipton, Capt.: Tullyaughnish DL 38; 91
Skipton, Conolly: Clondermot LY 34; 6, 20, 37, 97, 102–05, 113–14, 117, 120
Skipton, family: Clondermot LY 34; 29, 32
Skipton, Mr: Dungiven LY 15; 34
Skipton, Pitt: Clondermot LY 34; 27, 79, 103–04
Skipton, Pitt: Faughanvale LY 36; 42, 45
Skipton, Rev. Alexander: Magilligan LY 11; 85, 89
Skipton, Thomas: Clondermot LY 34; 6, 21, 58–59, 65, 68, 70, 74
Skipton, Thomas: Cumber LY 28; 68, 70
Skirts of Ardstraw district: Longfield TE 5; 127
Skirts of Urney and Ardstraw ph: Ardstraw TE 5; 10
Skirts of Urney and Ardstraw ph: Donaghmore DL 39; 28
Skirts of Urney and Ardstraw ph: Urney DL 39; 174, 176, 180
Skit lough: Cappagh TE 5; 17
Skivington, Rev.: Killead AM 35; 44
Skreen (see Screen): Magilligan LY 11; 89, 105, 143
Skreen td: Cleenish FH 14; 28, 30
Skreggagh Point: Lough Swilly DL 38; 124–25
Skreggagowre (see Screggagh)
Skull cave: Ballintoy AM 24; 31
Slaboy (see Sliaboy): Cumber LY 28; 5
Slacksgrove lough: Tydavnet MN 40; 169
Slaght Illeran cromlech: Misc. LY 31; 118
Slaght td: Ballyclug AM 23; 61, 65
Slaghtaggart graveyard: Rasharkin AM 23; 137, 140
Slaghtanaverthy giant's grave: Errigal LY 27; 66
Slaghtaverty bogs: Errigal LY 27; 54
Slaghtaverty bridge: Errigal LY 27; 41, 59
Slaghtaverty cairn [I]: Errigal LY 27; 44
Slaghtaverty cairn [II]: Errigal LY 27; 44
Slaghtaverty cairn [III]: Errigal LY 27; 44
Slaghtaverty cromlech [I]: Errigal LY 27; 43, 49, 66

Slaghtaverty cromlech [II]: Errigal LY 27; 43, 45, 49, 66
Slaghtaverty fort: Errigal LY 27; 43, 74
Slaghtaverty giant's graves: Errigal LY 27; 71
Slaghtaverty graveyard: Errigal LY 27; 43–44, 49, 71
Slaghtaverty td: Cumber LY 28; 65
Slaghtaverty td: Errigal LY 27; 45, 66, 74, 77, 83, 88, 91
Slaghtmanus (Slaghmanus) td: Cumber LY 28; 40, 44, 47, 49, 54–55, 60, 64–65, 67, 97–98, 103, 106–07
Slaghtmanus cromlech: Cumber LY 28; 37, 41, 43, 45, 54, 65, 81, 83
Slaghtmanus giant's grave [I]: Cumber LY 28; 40
Slaghtmanus giant's grave [II]: Cumber LY 28; 40
Slaghtmanus giant's grave [III]: Cumber LY 28; 40
Slaghtmanus hill: Cumber LY 28; 45
Slaghtmanus houses: Cumber LY 28; 40–41, 44, 81, 83
Slaghtmanus monument: Banagher LY 30; 44
Slaghtmanus quarry: Cumber LY 28; 106
Slaghtmanus standing stones: Cumber LY 28; 43
Slaghtmanus td: Banagher LY 30; 105
Slaghtmanus td: Faughanvale LY 36; 57
Slaghtneill (Slaughneal) td: Killelagh LY 27; 99, 102
Slaghtneill cairn [I]: Killelagh LY 27; 97
Slaghtneill cairn [II]: Killelagh LY 27; 97–98
Slaghtneill fort: Killelagh LY 27; 97
Slaghtneill td: Cumber LY 28; 65
Slaght-worry-vor giant's grave: Culfeightrin AM 24; 74–75
Slaghtybogy (Slaghtyboggy) td: Maghera LY 18; 13, 16–18, 25, 42, 49, 52–54, 73, 79
Slaman, Henry: Maghera LY 18; 80
Slaman, John (Jnr): Maghera LY 18; 80
Slaman, John (Snr): Maghera LY 18; 80
Slaman, Loughlin: Maghera LY 18; 59
Slamon, John: Maghera LY 18; 40–41
Slamons, Andrew: Maghera LY 18; 41
Slanag (see Slanagh): Banagher LY 30; 12
Slanagh well: Banagher LY 30; 12, 68, 112–13
Slane (Meath): Drummaul AM 19; 70
Slane: Magheross MN 40; 146, 152
Slane, John: Banagher LY 30; 33
Slanes (Slans) td: Misc. DN 17; 127
Slanes graveyard: Slanes DN 7; 121
Slanes lighthouse: Slanes DN 7; 121
Slanes manor: Misc. DN 17; 125
Slanes old church: Slanes DN 7; 121
Slanes ph: Ardkeen DN 7; 2
Slanes ph: Ballyphilip DN 7; 7, 10
Slanes ph: Misc. DN 17; 120, 127
Slanes Point: Slanes DN 7; 121

Slanes Point coastguard station: Slanes DN 7; 121
Slanes td: Ballyphilip DN 7; 8
Slanes td: Misc. DN 17; 127
Slanes td: Slanes DN 7; 121
Slaney river (Wexford): Cumber LY 28; 72
Slaney river: Faughanvale LY 36; 12, 55
Slantry td: Coleraine LY 33; 101–02
Slany (see Slaney): Faughanvale LY 36; 55
Slapragh hill: Cleenish FH 14; 12
Slapragh td: Cleenish FH 14; 30
Slatbeg td: Clogher TE 5; 36, 53
Slate House td: Ardclinis AM 13; 4, 7
Slatmore td: Clogher TE 5; 36
Slatmulroney manor: Clones FH 4; 26, 28, 133
Slatt td: Connor AM 19; 18
Slatter, Abraham: Clondermot LY 34; 81
Slaught Neill (see Slaughtneil): Maghera LY 18; 10
Slaught Shane Roe monument: Culfeightrin AM 24; 79
Slaught stones: Culfeightrin AM 24; 82
Slaughte standing stones: Ballynascreen LY 31; 10, 23
Slaughterford bridge: Island Magee AM 10; 42, 59, 64–66
Slaughterford bridge: Templecorran AM 26; 122
Slaughterford hill: Island Magee AM 10; 99–100
Slaughterford hill: Raloo AM 32; 82, 86, 119–20, 122
Slaughterford stream: Templecorran AM 26; 115, 122–23, 127
Slaughtly Caghill hill: Dungiven LY 15; 78–79, 92
Slaughtmanus (see Slaghtmanus)
Slaughtneil district: Misc. LY 36; 112
Slaughtneil monument: Maghera LY 18; 40
Slaughtneil td: Maghera LY 18; 10, 40
Slaughtybogy (see Slaghtybogy): Maghera LY 18; 42
Slavebuoy hill: Dungiven LY 15; 37
Slavenacloy (see Slievenacloy): Derryaghy AM 8; 121
Slavenaght (see Slievenagh): Ahoghill AM 23; 46
Slavin church: Inishmacsaint FH 14; 74, 77
Slavinagh (see Slievenagh): Ahoghill AM 23; 49
Sleanes (see Sleans): Layd AM 13; 51
Sleans cave: Layd AM 13; 42, 45
Sleans school: Layd AM 13; 51
Sleans td: Layd AM 13; 42, 45
Slee school: Derryvullan FH 14; 44
Slee td: Derryvullan FH 14; 46
Slee td: Enniskillen FH 4; 82
Sleibaan (see Portmore): Lough Swilly DL 38; 107
Sleibh Glass mountain: Currin MN 40; 87
Slemins, James: Artrea LY 6; 37
Slemins, John: Artrea LY 6; 31, 37
Slemish mountain: Ballyclug AM 23; 54

Slemish mountain: Carncastle and Killyglen AM 10; 9
Slemish mountain: Connor AM 19; 19
Slemish mountain: Glenwhirry AM 32; 78
Slemish mountain: Kirkinriola AM 23; 121
Slemish mountain: Misc. LY 31; 116
Slemish mountain: Racavan AM 13; 86–87, 89, 93, 96, 103
Slemish mountain: Tullyrusk AM 21; 135
Slemons, Alexander: Tamlaght TE 20; 92
Slensmoyle (see Glensmoil): Clonleigh DL 39; 12
Slettymoyle td: Donacavey TE 5; 77
Sleve Goar (see Sliebhgore): Cumber LY 28; 49
Slevin glen: Longfield TE 5; 127
Slevin, John (Jnr): Misc. TE 5; 147
Slevin, John: Carrickfergus AM 37; 108
Slevin, Michael: Misc. TE 5; 147
Slevin, Patt: Misc. TE 5; 147
Slevin, Thady: Misc. TE 5; 147
Slewbagha mountains: Derryvullan FH 14; 39
Sliabh Ban (see White mountain): Dungiven LY 15; 1, 51
Sliabh-an-iarainn mountain: Clondermot LY 34; 65
Sliaboy chapel: Cumber LY 28; 80
Sliaboy hill: Cumber LY 28; 5, 42, 47, 85
Sliddery ford: Kilmegan DN 3; 57
Sliddery river: Kilmegan DN 3; 55
Sliebh Boe (see Sliaboy): Cumber LY 28; 42
Sliebh Brice hill: Cumber LY 28; 1
Sliebh Dornog hill: Cumber LY 28; 72
Sliebhgore houses: Cumber LY 28; 83
Sliebhgore standing stones: Cumber LY 28; 41, 45
Sliebhgore td: Cumber LY 28; 43, 49
Slievdool school: Clonleigh DL 39; 9
Slieve Bane mountain: Kilbroney DN 3; 32, 39
Slieve Baugh (see Slieve Beagh): Clogher TE 5; 25
Slieve Bay (see Slieve Beagh)
Slieve Beagh mountain: Clogher TE 5; 24–28, 54, 58
Slieve Beagh mountain: Donagh MN 40; 98
Slieve Beagh mountain: Errigal Truagh MN 40; 120
Slieve Bearnagh mountain: Kilkeel DN 3; 46
Slieve Bearneagh mountain: Kilcoo DN 3; 41
Slieve Bignian bog: Kilkeel DN 3; 47
Slieve Bignian mountain: Kilkeel DN 3; 46, 51, 54
Slieve Buck hill: Cumber LY 28; 45, 60, 64, 66–67
Slieve Commedagh mountain: Kilcoo DN 3; 41
Slieve Conagher mountain: Emlaghfad SO 40; 176
Slieve Corragh mountain: Kilcoo DN 3; 41
Slieve Croob mountain: Donaghcloney DN 12; 57
Slieve Croob mountain: Dromara DN 12; 62–68
Slieve Croob mountain: Drumgooland DN 3; 24
Slieve Croob mountain: Kilmegan DN 3; 55
Slieve Croob mountain: Knockbreda DN 7; 97
Slieve Croob mountain: Magheradrool DN 17; 101

Slieve Croob mountain: Moira DN 12; 117

Slieve Dermot mountain: Kilbroney DN 3; 26

Slieve Donard mountain: Down DN 17; 40

Slieve Donard mountain: Kilcoo DN 3; 41, 43

Slieve Donard mountain: Kilkeel DN 3; 46, 51, 53–54

Slieve Donard mountain: Tullyrusk AM 21; 135

Slieve Gallion carn: Desertmartin LY 31; 52

Slieve Gallion mountain: Artrea LY 6; 2

Slieve Gallion mountain: Ballynascreen LY 31; 1, 111–12, 114, 116, 118, 122

Slieve Gallion mountain: Blaris AM 8; 89

Slieve Gallion mountain: Desertlyn LY 31; 35–36

Slieve Gallion mountain: Desertmartin LY 31; 52, 55, 57, 62

Slieve Gallion mountain: Kilcronaghan LY 31; 64, 67, 71, 75, 77, 87–88

Slieve Gallion mountain: Killelagh LY 27; 98

Slieve Gallion mountain: Kilrea LY 27; 104

Slieve Gallion mountain: Lissan LY 31; 89, 91, 94, 102

Slieve Gallion mountain: Lissan TE 20; 69

Slieve Gallion mountain: Misc. LY 31; 113, 115

Slieve Gallion mountain: Tamlaght O'Crilly LY 18; 82

Slieve Gallion mountain: Termoneeny LY 6; 124

Slieve Gallion quarries: Misc. LY 31; 114

Slieve Guff mountain: Kilmacteige SO 40; 190, 195

Slieve Gullion mountain: Killevy AH 1; 53

Slieve Gullion mountain: Maghera LY 18; 9

Slieve Iniver mountain: Lissan LY 31; 91

Slieve Keerogue Little hill: Clonmany DL 38; 12

Slieve Kerryna (see Slieve Keerogue): Clonmany DL 38; 12

Slieve Kirk bog: Cumber LY 28; 46

Slieve Kirk hill: Clondermot LY 34; 1, 3–4, 17–18, 36, 105

Slieve Kirk hill: Cumber LY 28; 45, 60, 66–67

Slieve Kirk hill: Donaghedy TE 5; 88

Slieve League Castle: Glencolumbkille DL 39; 64

Slieve League mountain: Glencolumbkille DL 39; 64

Slieve Meel More (see Slieve Miel More): Clonduff DN 3; 5

Slieve Miel Beg mountain: Clonduff DN 3; 5

Slieve Miel More mountain: Clonduff DN 3; 5

Slieve Miel More mountain: Kilcoo DN 3; 41

Slieve Muck mountain: Clonduff DN 3; 5

Slieve Muck mountain: Seapatrick DN 12; 124

Slieve Muck North mountain: Clonduff DN 3; 5

Slieve Muggthan mountain: Clonduff DN 3; 5

Slieve Nane mountain: Tullyrusk AM 21; 135

Slieve Neill Beg (see Slieve Miel Beg): Clonduff DN 3; 5

Slieve Russel mountain: Kinawley FH 4; 113, 123–24

Slieve Russel mountain: Tomregan FH 4; 125–28

Slieve Snaght Little mountain: Clonmany DL 38; 12–13

Slieve Snaght Little mountain: Mintiaghs DL 38; 64

Slieve Snaght mountain: Clonmany DL 38; 12, 16

Slieve Snaght mountain: Donagh DL 38; 31

Slieve Snaght mountain: Lough Swilly DL 38; 113

Slieve Snaght mountain: Mintiaghs DL 38; 64

Slieve Snavan mountain: Kilkeel DN 3; 54

Slieve True cairn: Carrickfergus AM 37; 4, 89, 93, 183–84

Slieve True mountain: Carrickfergus AM 37; 4–5, 86, 93, 140, 173, 184, 191

Slieve True school: Carrickfergus AM 37; 85, 183

Slieve-a-chon hills: Cleenish FH 14; 28

Slieveanagh (see Slievenagh): Ahoghill AM 23; 3

Slieveanee mountain: Dunaghy AM 13; 10–11, 27

Slieveanee mountain: Loughguile AM 13; 60–61

Slieveanee mountain: Newtown Crommelin AM 13; 78–79

Slieve-an-orra mountain: Armoy AM 24; 3

Slieve-an-orra mountain: Billy AM 16; 49

Slieve-an-orra mountain: Culfeightrin AM 24; 36, 39, 41–42, 46–47, 79

Slieve-an-orra mountain: Dunaghy AM 13; 28

Slieve-an-orra mountain: Layd AM 13; 42–43

Slieve-an-orra mountain: Layd and Inispollan AM 13; 54–55, 57

Slieve-an-orra mountain: Loughguile AM 13; 58–60, 64, 68, 74

Slieve-an-orra mountain: Ramoan AM 24; 92

Slieve-a-tory mountain: Glencolumbkille DL 39; 64

Slievebagh (see Slievebaugh): Aghavea FH 4; 18–19

Slievebaugh mountain: Aghalurcher FH 4; 1–4

Slievebaugh mountain: Aghavea FH 4; 17–19

Slieveboe td: Raphoe DL 39; 127

Slievebrickan td: Tomregan FH 4; 126

Slievegallion td: Ballyclog TE 20; 18

Slievekerogue hill: Clonmany DL 38; 20

Slievenaboley lough: Drumgooland DN 3; 24

Slievenaboley mountain: Drumgooland DN 3; 23–24

Slievenacloy forts: Derryaghy AM 8; 97

Slievenacloy mountain: Derryaghy AM 8; 90

Slievenacloy standing stone: Derryaghy AM 8; 98

Slievenacloy td: Derryaghy AM 8; 91, 98, 121

Slievenagh (Slavenagh) td: Ahoghill AM 23; 3, 29, 49

Slievenagh chapel: Ahoghill AM 23; 2, 11–12, 30–31, 35

Slievenagh fort: Ahoghill AM 23; 35

Slievenagh graveyard [I]: Ahoghill AM 23; 35

Slievenagh graveyard [II]: Ahoghill AM 23; 35
Slievenagh school: Ahoghill AM 23; 23, 43, 46
Slievenagh stone circle: Ahoghill AM 23; 26, 28
Slievenaghy corn mill: Finvoy AM 23; 71
Slievenaghy flax mill: Finvoy AM 23; 71
Slievenagravery mountain: Derryaghy AM 8; 90
Slievenagravery td: Derryaghy AM 8; 91, 121
Slieve-na-griddal (see Slievenagriddle): Ballee DN 17; 22
Slievenagriddle hill: Ballee DN 17; 15, 20
Slievenagriddle school: Ballee DN 17; 20
Slievenagriddle td: Ballee DN 17; 20, 22–23
Slievenahanagan mountain: Killagan AM 23; 82
Slievenahanagan mountain: Loughguile AM 13; 58, 60
Slievenamanfin mountain: Clondermot LY 34; 72
Slievenaslat mountain: Kilmegan DN 3; 55
Slieverush hill: Newtown Crommelin AM 13; 79
Slieve-Slaing (see Slieve Donard): Kilkeel DN 3; 54
Slievnamannfinn hill: Ramoan AM 24; 115
Sligo: Aghavea FH 4; 21
Sligo: Ballyclug AM 23; 56–57
Sligo: Carrickfergus AM 37; 38
Sligo: Clondermot LY 34; 30
Sligo: Coleraine LY 33; 98
Sligo: Donaghmore DL 39; 28–29, 32
Sligo: Donegal DL 39; 45–47
Sligo: Emlaghfad SO 40; 177–78, 180, 182
Sligo: Enniskillen FH 4; 61, 83
Sligo: Killymard DL 39; 109
Sligo: Kilmacteige SO 40; 185, 190–92
Sligo: Kinawley FH 4; 115
Sligo: Manorhamilton Union LM 40; 47–48, 50, 52–54
Sligo: Misc. DL 39; 187
Sligo: Misc. FH 4; 133
Sligo: Misc. SO 40; 198, 200
Sligo: Urney DL 39; 175, 177, 180
Sligo county: Connor AM 19; 18
Sligo county: Enniskillen FH 4; 51
Sligo county: Faughanvale LY 36; 44
Sligo county: Kilmacteige SO 40; 188, 195
Sligo county: Manorhamilton Union LM 40; 47
Slimag td: Ballywillin LY 33; 51
Slimero hill: Carrickfergus AM 37; 5, 93
Slimero hill: Raloo AM 32; 82–83, 87
Slimmerow (see Slimero)
Slintiagh td: Ballyphilip DN 7; 8
Sloan, David: Tamlaght Finlagan LY 25; 119
Sloan, family: Desertlyn LY 31; 42
Sloan, family: Donegore AM 29; 110
Sloan, James: Carrickfergus AM 37; 108, 134, 157
Sloan, John: Blaris DN 12; 40
Sloan, Margaret: Glynn AM 26; 28, 42
Sloan, Mary: Blaris AM 8; 82

Sloan, Nancy: Ballymoney AM 16; 17
Sloan, Rev. James: Maghera LY 18; 17, 76
Sloan, Richard: Ballymoney AM 16; 17
Sloan, Samuel: Carrickfergus AM 37; 195
Sloan, Thomas: Drummaul AM 19; 88
Sloan, William: Ballymartin AM 2; 13
Sloan, William: Tamlaght Finlagan LY 25; 119
Sloan's paper mill: Ballymartin AM 2; 16
Sloane, Hugh: Templepatrick AM 35; 132
Sloane, James: Dundermot AM 13; 35
Sloane, John: Dundermot AM 13; 34
Sloane, Samuel: Ahoghill AM 23; 42–43, 46
Sloanstown td: Donaghadee DN 7; 45
Sloanstown td: Misc. DN 17; 124
Sloss, James: Tamlaght TE 20; 76, 103
Slowry rocks: Mevagh DL 38; 56
Sluckgore td: Donacavey TE 5; 77
Sluddanawashog [or Sluddanawoohog] harbour: Lough Swilly DL 38; 114
Sluddanmore creek: Lough Swilly DL 38; 131–32
Sluddanmore rocks: Lough Swilly DL 38; 131
Sludden creek: Lough Swilly DL 38; 106
Slug lough: Donegal DL 39; 43, 54
Slug lough: Drumkeeran FH 14; 63
Sluggan bog: Drummaul AM 19; 37–38, 62, 69
Slushhill td: Aghalurcher FH 4; 14
Slutmulroney (see Slatmulroney)
Small Otter Island: Muckno MN 40; 162
Small Park locality: Hillsborough DN 12; 96
Small Park lough: Hillsborough DN 12; 89
Small, Anne: Drummaul AM 19; 91
Small, Bruce and Co., Messrs: Blaris AM 8; 9
Small, family: Blaris AM 8; 22
Small, Hugh: Newry DN 3; 99, 103
Small, James: Kilbroney DN 3; 31
Small, John: Drummaul AM 19; 91
Small, John: Newry DN 3; 99, 101, 104
Small, Robert: Kilbroney DN 3; 31
Small, William: Ballymoney AM 16; 25
Smallquarter td: Kilraghts AM 16; 134
Smalls, family: Misc. LY 36; 104
Smelligaden td: Errigal LY 27; 78
Smiley, Andrew: Urney DL 39; 182
Smiley, Cllr: Raphoe DL 39; 126
Smiley, James: Kilraghts AM 16; 134
Smiley, John: Inver AM 26; 54–55
Smiley, John: Kilraghts AM 16; 135
Smiley, Mrs William: Aghanloo LY 11; 32
Smiley, R.: Island Magee AM 10; 64
Smiley, Rev.: Blaris AM 8; 9
Smiley, Rev. William: Aghanloo LY 11; 10, 14–19, 22, 30, 32, 36
Smiley, William: Kilraghts AM 16; 135
Smily, family: Misc. LY 36; 104
Smith, Adam: Newry DN 3; 94

Smith, Alixander: Bovevagh LY 25; 59

Smith, Andrew: Carnmoney AM 2; 81

Smith, Andrew: Maghera LY 18; 80

Smith, Ann: Ballyrashane LY 22; 66

Smith, Ann: Tamlaght Finlagan LY 25; 119

Smith, B.: Tamlaght TE 20; 128

Smith, Bishop: Derryaghy AM 8; 107

Smith, Capt.: Macosquin LY 22; 80, 101, 117

Smith, Christopher: Banagher LY 30; 67

Smith, Daniel: Donacavey TE 5; 65–66

Smith, David: Donagh MN 40; 103

Smith, Edmond: Drumachose LY 9; 52, 104

Smith, Elisabeth: Aghanloo LY 11; 39

Smith, Eliza: Tamlaght Finlagan LY 25; 119

Smith, Elizabeth: Dunboe LY 11; 81

Smith, Ellen: Dunboe LY 11; 81

Smith, Ellen: Maghera LY 18; 80

Smith, Ellen Jane: Shilvodan AM 19; 137

Smith, Erasmus: Ahoghill AM 23; 20, 32, 44–45, 51

Smith, Erasmus: Antrim AM 29; 41–42, 45, 58–59

Smith, Erasmus: Ballyaghran LY 33; 7, 16

Smith, Erasmus: Ballyclog TE 20; 16, 18

Smith, Erasmus: Ballymoney AM 16; 26

Smith, Erasmus: Billy AM 16; 49, 77

Smith, Erasmus: Clogher TE 5; 45

Smith, Erasmus: Clondermot LY 34; 9

Smith, Erasmus: Comber DN 7; 28

Smith, Erasmus: Cumber LY 28; 2, 73–74, 76–77

Smith, Erasmus: Derryvullan FH 14; 38

Smith, Erasmus: Faughanvale LY 36; 7, 24, 34–36, 66

Smith, Erasmus: Killeeshil TE 20; 63

Smith, Erasmus: Kilmore AH 1; 59–60, 62, 64

Smith, Erasmus: Kilrea LY 27; 120

Smith, Erasmus: Leckpatrick TE 5; 124

Smith, Erasmus: Lissan LY 31; 94

Smith, Erasmus: Loughgall AH 1; 76, 78, 81

Smith, Erasmus: Loughgilly AH 1; 86

Smith, Erasmus: Loughinisland DN 17; 95–96

Smith, Erasmus: Newtownhamilton AH 1; 98

Smith, Erasmus: Shankill AH 1; 115–16

Smith, Erasmus: Templepatrick AM 35; 134–36, 154

Smith, Erasmus: Tullyaughnish DL 38; 88, 92

Smith, Erasmus: Tynan AH 1; 129

Smith, family: Ballinderry AM 21; 55

Smith, family: Dunsfort DN 17; 68

Smith, family: Kilbride AM 29; 146

Smith, family: Killagan AM 23; 84

Smith, family: Kilraghts AM 16; 130

Smith, family: Kilwaughter AM 10; 115

Smith, family: Macosquin LY 22; 84, 119

Smith, family: Seagoe AH 1; 104

Smith, Gilbert: Dunboe LY 11; 81

Smith, Giles: Clogher TE 5; 38

Smith, Henery: Ballyrashane LY 22; 60

Smith, Henry: Drummaul AM 19; 88

Smith, Henry: Loughguile AM 13; 74

Smith, Henry: Termonamongan TE 5; 143–45

Smith, Hugh: Ballyrashane LY 22; 62

Smith, Hugh: Hillsborough DN 12; 106

Smith, Israel: Ballymoney AM 16; 15, 17

Smith, J.A.: Ahoghill AM 23; 43, 47

Smith, Jacob: Bovevagh LY 25; 11–12, 47–49

Smith, James: Ballymoney AM 16; 26

Smith, James: Ballyrashane LY 22; 66

Smith, James: Drumachose LY 9; 60

Smith, James: Errigal LY 27; 51

Smith, James: Kilbride AM 29; 154

Smith, James: Lissan LY 31; 98, 106–07

Smith, James: Rasharkin AM 23; 140

Smith, James: Tamlaght Finlagan LY 25; 66, 71

Smith, James [I]: Desertoghill LY 27; 20

Smith, James [II]: Desertoghill LY 27; 20

Smith, Jane (Jnr): Ballyrashane LY 22; 66

Smith, Jane (Snr): Ballyrashane LY 22; 66

Smith, John: Aghalurcher FH 4; 6

Smith, John: Aghanloo LY 11; 39

Smith, John: Ardstraw TE 5; 4

Smith, John: Ballynascreen LY 31; 7

Smith, John: Balteagh LY 9; 41

Smith, John: Bovevagh LY 25; 49, 53

Smith, John: Carnmoney AM 2; 81

Smith, John: Coleraine LY 33; 105

Smith, John: Drumachose LY 9; 111

Smith, John: Drumtullagh AM 16; 102

Smith, John: Dunboe LY 11; 60, 60, 81

Smith, John: Dungiven LY 15; 73

Smith, John: Hillsborough DN 12; 106

Smith, John: Island Magee AM 10; 90, 94

Smith, John: Killowen LY 33; 169

Smith, John: Maghera LY 18; 80

Smith, John: Magheramesk AM 21; 121

Smith, John: Misc. LY 31; 140

Smith, John: Newry DN 3; 99

Smith, John: Tamlaght Finlagan LY 25; 119

Smith, John: Urney DL 39; 176

Smith, John [I]: Aghadowey LY 22; 27

Smith, John [I]: Desertoghill LY 27; 19, 33

Smith, John [II]: Aghadowey LY 22; 35

Smith, John [II]: Desertoghill LY 27; 20

Smith, Joseph: Balteagh LY 9; 43

Smith, Josias: Bovevagh LY 25; 11, 48

Smith, man named: Desertoghill LY 27; 7

Smith, Margrett: Ballyrashane LY 22; 66

Smith, Martha: Shilvodan AM 19; 137

Smith, Mary: Aghadowey LY 22; 21

Smith, Mary: Dunboe LY 11; 80

Smith, Messrs: Ballycor AM 32; 4

Smith, Messrs B. and Co.: Drumcree AH 1; 35

Smith, Michael: Macosquin LY 22; 87, 112

Smith, Michael: Newry DN 3; 95, 100–01, 105

Smith, Michael: Shilvodan AM 19; 137

Smith, Miss: Ballymoney AM 16; 17

Smith, Moore: Kilraghts AM 16; 132

Smith, Mr (Ballyartan): Cumber LY 28; 21

Smith, Mr (Lakeview): Aghabog MN 40; 65

Smith, Mr (Lakeview): Drummully FH 4; 36

Smith, Mr (Newtownlimavady): Tamlaght Finlagan LY 25; 105

Smith, Mr (Westmeath): Armoy AM 24; 1

Smith, Mr: Aghadowey LY 22; 5

Smith, Mr: Ballymoney AM 16; 3

Smith, Mr: Banagher LY 30; 65

Smith, Mr: Killea and Taughboyne DL 39; 84

Smith, Mr: Rasharkin AM 23; 127

Smith, Mrs: Newry DN 3; 99, 104

Smith, Mrs Johnson: Blaris AM 8; 85

Smith, Mrs Johnson: Blaris DN 12; 50

Smith, Nancy: Kilrea LY 27; 129

Smith, Nathaniel: Dromore TE 5; 97

Smith, Nicholas: Hillsborough DN 12; 106

Smith, Patrick: Shilvodan AM 19; 137

Smith, Phelemy: Ballyphilip DN 7; 13

Smith, R.B.: Clondermot LY 34; 78

Smith, Rev. (Knockcloghrim): Maghera LY 18; 48

Smith, Rev.: Kilrea LY 27; 126

Smith, Rev. Hugh: Ballyscullion AM 19; 11, 13

Smith, Rev. Hugh: Blaris DN 12; 46, 50

Smith, Rev. Hugh: Kilcoo DN 3; 45

Smith, Rev. J.P.: Kilcronaghan LY 31; 81–82

Smith, Rev. James: Faughanvale LY 36; 6

Smith, Rev. James: Island Magee AM 10; 34, 82, 85–86, 88–89, 91, 93–94, 97

Smith, Rev. John: Drummaul AM 19; 69

Smith, Rev. Mitchell: Errigal LY 27; 40, 45–46, 50–52, 57–58, 63, 66, 74, 76, 81

Smith, Rev. William: Desertoghill LY 27; 10, 15, 17, 22, 32

Smith, Rev. William: Errigal LY 27; 39, 63, 78, 83

Smith, Rev. William: Killymard DL 39; 100–02

Smith, Robert: Dunboe LY 11; 80

Smith, Robert: Island Magee AM 10; 90

Smith, Robert: Kilbride AM 29; 154

Smith, Robert [I]: Magilligan LY 11; 94

Smith, Robert [II]: Magilligan LY 11; 94

Smith, Samual: Ballyrashane LY 22; 66

Smith, Samual: Drumachose LY 9; 134

Smith, Samual: Tamlaght Finlagan LY 25; 82–83

Smith, Samuel: Ballymoney AM 16; 15

Smith, Samuel: Blaris AM 8; 82

Smith, Samuel: Derrykeighan AM 16; 95

Smith, Samuel: Island Magee AM 10; 90

Smith, Samuel: Tamlaght TE 20; 115

Smith, Thomas (Jnr): Tullyrusk AM 21; 131

Smith, Thomas (Snr): Tullyrusk AM 21; 131

Smith, Thomas: Drumachose LY 9; 66

Smith, Thomas: Hillsborough DN 12; 100

Smith, Thomas: Killygarvan DL 38; 40, 42–43, 46–47

Smith, Thomas: Maghera LY 18; 61

Smith, Thomas: Magilligan LY 11; 83

Smith, William (Jnr): Tamlaght TE 20; 84

Smith, William (Snr): Tamlaght TE 20; 84

Smith, William: Aghagallon AM 21; 19

Smith, William: Ballyclog TE 20; 19

Smith, William: Carnmoney AM 2; 83

Smith, William: Clones FH 4; 27

Smith, William: Derrykeighan AM 16; 91, 94

Smith, William: Drumachose LY 9; 66

Smith, William: Drumbeg DN 7; 53

Smith, William: Dunboe LY 11; 81

Smith, William: Galloon FH 4; 105

Smith, William: Kilmacteige SO 40; 189

Smithborough: Aghabog MN 40; 64

Smithborough: Clones FH 4; 28

Smithborough: Ematris MN 40; 115

Smithborough meeting houses: Clones FH 4; 28

Smithfield cattle market: Blaris AM 8; 43

Smocke, Thomas: Carrickfergus AM 37; 43

Smulgedon fort: Balteagh LY 9; 12, 26

Smulgedon hill: Balteagh LY 9; 1–2, 20–21

Smulgedon td: Balteagh LY 9; 12, 26, 39, 45

Smullin, Jack: Tullaghobegley DL 39; 172

Smultans lough: Templecarn DL 39; 157

Smulternagh (see Smutternagh): Misc. SO 40; 200

Smutternagh district: Misc. SO 40; 199–200

Smyed td: Tydavnet MN 40; 169

Smyley, Mrs: Drumachose LY 9; 126

Smyley, Rev.: Maghera LY 18; 67

Smyly, Mrs: Blaris AM 8; 84

Smyly, Rev. Cecil: Ballywillin LY 33; 38–39

Smyrell, John: Ballyscullion AM 19; 8

Smyth [or Smythe], Cllr (Ballymacoss): Derryaghy AM 8; 94, 99

Smyth and Craig, Messrs: Seapatrick DN 12; 127

Smyth, Alexander: Carrickfergus AM 37; 117

Smyth, Alice: Blaris AM 8; 25

Smyth, Andrew: Derryaghy AM 8; 110

Smyth, Andrew [I]: Tamlaght O'Crilly LY 18; 91, 94, 102, 110, 112

Smyth, Andrew [II]: Tamlaght O'Crilly LY 18; 118

Smyth, Arthur: Misc. DN 17; 117

Smyth, Bernard: Ballintoy AM 24; 23, 25

Smyth, Brice: Seapatrick DN 12; 126

Smyth, Capt. (Desertlyn): Desertlyn LY 31; 42

Smyth, Capt. (Rathmullan): Lough Swilly DL 38; 98–100, 103, 122, 124

Smyth, Capt.: Muff DL 38; 82

Smyth, Charlotte: Blaris AM 8; 21

Smyth, Dennis: Ballyphilip DN 7; 13

Smyth, Dr (Downpatrick): Ardglass DN 17; 1, 3–4, 7

Smyth, Dr (Downpatrick): Ballee DN 17; 16–17

Smyth, Dr (Downpatrick): Dunsfort DN 17; 67, 69

Smyth, Dr: Artrea LY 6; 34

Smyth, Dultagh: Witter DN 7; 126

Smyth, Edward: Carrickfergus AM 37; 160

Smyth, Edward: Misc. DN 17; 117

Smyth, Esther: Clondermot LY 34; 20, 42, 93, 97, 100

Smyth, family: Ardglass DN 17; 4

Smyth, family: Armoy AM 24; 6

Smyth, family: Ballinderry AM 21; 52

Smyth, family: Ballyculter DN 17; 28

Smyth, family: Ballyphilip DN 7; 13

Smyth, family: Blaris AM 8; 21–22

Smyth, family: Blaris DN 12; 30

Smyth, family: Clondermot LY 34; 28, 47

Smyth, family: Derryaghy AM 8; 103, 105

Smyth, family: Derrykeighan AM 16; 89

Smyth, family: Desertlyn LY 31; 42

Smyth, family: Kirkinriola AM 23; 124

Smyth, family: Lambeg AM 8; 135

Smyth, family: Magheramesk AM 21; 124

Smyth, family: Mallusk AM 2; 110

Smyth, family: Ramoan AM 24; 107

Smyth, family: Templepatrick AM 35; 118

Smyth, George: Blaris DN 12; 46, 50

Smyth, George: Hillsborough DN 12; 107

Smyth, Hugh: Magherafelt LY 6; 112

Smyth, Isaac: Killevy AH 1; 54

Smyth, Isaac: Newry DN 3; 103

Smyth, J.A.: Clondermot LY 34; 6, 8, 20–21, 24, 27–28, 34–35, 37, 42, 79–80, 92, 100–01, 104–05, 119

Smyth, J.A.: Cumber LY 28; 56

Smyth, J.A.: Faughanvale LY 36; 40, 42, 45

Smyth, J.A.: Macosquin LY 22; 81, 101, 104

Smyth, J.S.: Duneane AM 19; 125

Smyth, Jackson: Macosquin LY 22; 122

Smyth, James (Jnr): Hillsborough DN 12; 106

Smyth, James: Artrea LY 6; 20

Smyth, James: Billy AM 16; 73–74

Smyth, James: Cumber LY 28; 55

Smyth, James: Hillsborough DN 12; 106

Smyth, James [I]: Carrickfergus AM 37; 114

Smyth, James [I]: Clondermot LY 34; 27, 79, 103

Smyth, James [II]: Carrickfergus AM 37; 117

Smyth, James [II]: Clondermot LY 34; 47

Smyth, Jane: Drumachose LY 9; 85

Smyth, Jeremiah: Hillsborough DN 12; 106

Smyth, John: Ballintoy AM 24; 24

Smyth, John: Blaris DN 12; 39–40, 46

Smyth, John: Camlin AM 21; 75

Smyth, John: Hillsborough DN 12; 105–07

Smyth, John: Magherafelt LY 6; 112

Smyth, John: Magheramesk AM 21; 117, 120

Smyth, John: Seapatrick DN 12; 127

Smyth, John: Tullylish DN 12; 141, 146

Smyth, John [I]: Carrickfergus AM 37; 102, 141–42, 149, 151, 164, 174, 183, 192

Smyth, John [II]: Carrickfergus AM 37; 131

Smyth, John [III]: Carrickfergus AM 37; 195

Smyth, Joseph: Hillsborough DN 12; 105

Smyth, Joseph: Island Magee AM 10; 76

Smyth, Major: Carrickfergus AM 37; 113

Smyth, Margaret: Carrickfergus AM 37; 122

Smyth, Martha: Blaris AM 8; 21

Smyth, Maryann: Carrickfergus AM 37; 122

Smyth, Messrs Brice and Sons: Seapatrick DN 12; 126

Smyth, Messrs John and Co.: Seapatrick DN 12; 127

Smyth, Messrs John and Co.: Tullylish DN 12; 141, 145

Smyth, Miss: Drumachose LY 9; 81

Smyth, Mr (Drumbridge): Drumbo DN 7; 59

Smyth, Mr (Killough): Bright DN 17; 36

Smyth, Mr: Kilraghts AM 16; 128

Smyth, Mrs (Donaghadee): Ballymore AH 1; 17

Smyth, Mrs: Ballymoney AM 16; 16

Smyth, Mrs: Doagh AM 29; 91

Smyth, person named: Saul DN 17; 113

Smyth, R.: Hillsborough DN 12; 86

Smyth, R.J.: Blaris AM 8; 54–55

Smyth, R.T.: Clondermot LY 34; 79

Smyth, R.T.: Faughanvale LY 36; 42, 45

Smyth, Ralph: Derryaghy AM 8; 105

Smyth, Rev. Hugh: Blaris AM 8; 24, 27–28, 60, 62, 83

Smyth, Rev. Hugh: Drummaul AM 19; 69, 76, 85, 88–89

Smyth, Rev. Hugh: Hillsborough DN 12; 85, 87, 100

Smyth, Rev. J.A.: Tamlaght O'Crilly LY 18; 95, 99–100, 103–04, 107, 120–21, 123, 142

Smyth, Rev. James: Coleraine LY 33; 62

Smyth, Rev. John: Kilrea LY 27; 126

Smyth, Rev. John: Tamlaght O'Crilly LY 18; 135

Smyth, Rev. Samuel: Carrickfergus AM 37; 102

Smyth, Rev. StJohn: Ballyphilip DN 7; 7, 14

Smyth, Rev. William: Coleraine LY 33; 127

Smyth, Rev. William: Donagh MN 40; 101–03, 105

Smyth, Robert: Armoy AM 24; 4

Smyth, Robert: Blaris DN 12; 40

Smyth, Robert: Culfeightrin AM 24; 45

Smyth, Robert: Cumber LY 28; 55

Smyth, Robert: Loughguile AM 13; 67

Smyth, Robert: Misc. LY 31; 140

Smyth, Robert [I]: Carrickfergus AM 37; 109
Smyth, Robert [II]: Carrickfergus AM 37; 112
Smyth, Samuel: Carrickfergus AM 37; 165
Smyth, Samuel: Coleraine LY 33; 62
Smyth, Samuel: Cumber LY 28; 55
Smyth, Samuel: Hillsborough DN 12; 107
Smyth, Samuel: Killowen LY 33; 165
Smyth, Susan: Carrickfergus AM 37; 117
Smyth, T.J.: Blaris AM 8; 51, 55
Smyth, T.J.: Blaris DN 12; 39, 45, 49
Smyth, T.J.: Hillsborough DN 12; 97
Smyth, Thomas: Blaris AM 8; 21
Smyth, Thomas: Carrickfergus AM 37; 125
Smyth, Thomas: Misc. DN 17; 119
Smyth, Thomas: Misc. LY 31; 140
Smyth, W.H.: Magilligan LY 11; 118
Smyth, W.H.: Shilvodan AM 19; 138
Smyth, W.L.: Clondermot LY 34; 79
Smyth, W.L.: Faughanvale LY 36; 45
Smyth, William: Ballycor AM 32; 4
Smyth, William: Ballyscullion LY 6; 69, 72
Smyth, William: Blaris AM 8; 21
Smyth, William: Blaris DN 12; 46, 50
Smyth, William: Carrickfergus AM 37; 127
Smyth, William: Misc. DL 39; 186
Smyth, William [I]: Hillsborough DN 12; 106
Smyth, William [II]: Hillsborough DN 12; 106
Smyth's Castle: Ballyculter DN 17; 28
Smythe [or Smyth], Cllr: Derryaghy AM 8; 94, 99
Smythe, Rev. Samuel: Ballylinny AM 32; 17, 26
Smythe, Rev. Samuel: Ballymartin AM 2; 15
Smythe, Rev. Samuel: Ballywalter AM 2; 26–27, 30
Smythe, Rev. Samuel: Carnmoney AM 2; 45–46, 75,
    81–82, 84–86, 88, 90, 93
Snell, Maryanne: Magilligan LY 11; 94
Sneyd, Mr: Clogher TE 5; 41
Snoddy, family: Inver AM 26; 53
Snoddy, Samuel: Raloo AM 32; 129
Snowhill td: Cleenish FH 14; 28–29
Sobin lough: Clondavaddog DL 38; 2
Soden, Rev. Clotworthy: Maghera LY 18; 66
Soden, Rev. Clotworthy: Misc. LY 31; 136
Solan hill: Carnteel TE 20; 23
Solar grange: Shilvodan AM 19; 133, 135
Solar td: Carncastle and Killyglen AM 10; 8
Soldier's Point: Warrenpoint DN 3; 120
Soldierstown: Aghagallon AM 21; 1, 7
Soldierstown: Aghalee AM 21; 26–27
Soldierstown: Magheramesk AM 21; 113, 115
Soldierstown bridge: Aghalee AM 21; 28–29, 34
Soldierstown church: Aghagallon AM 21; 1
Soldierstown church: Aghalee AM 21; 26, 29–31,
    34, 37, 39
Soldierstown church: Magheramesk AM 21; 112,
    128

Soldierstown church: Shankill DN 12; 138
Soldierstown quarry: Aghalee AM 21; 27
Soldierstown school: Aghalee AM 21; 28, 31, 39–40
Soldierstown Sunday school: Aghalee AM 21; 40
Soldierstown td: Aghalee AM 21; 35
Solis td: Donaghedy TE 5; 92
Solitude House: Kilcronaghan LY 31; 67, 82
Solomon's locality: Magilligan LY 11; 146
Solus hill: Clondermot LY 34; 1
Somerset Castle: Macosquin LY 22; 107
Somerset demesne: Macosquin LY 22; 80, 101
Somerset House: Ballyrashane LY 22; 50
Somerset House: Clogherny TE 20; 25
Somerset House: Coleraine LY 33; 54, 64, 73, 154
Somerset House: Drumragh TE 5; 109
Somerset House: Killowen LY 33; 162
Somerset House: Macosquin LY 22; 77, 79–81, 85,
    89–90, 93–94, 98, 100–01, 107, 109
Somerset House: Misc. LY 36; 109–10
Somerset House: Termoneeny LY 6; 132
Somerset td: Macosquin LY 22; 109
Sonagh, Hugh: Termoneeny LY 6; 133
Sonagh, John: Termoneeny LY 6; 133
Sonar's Gate td: Killymard DL 39; 101
Sooilabinnian Peninsula: Lough Swilly DL 38;
    132–33
Sooly (see Swilly): Misc. DL 39; 185
Sorby, A.: Blaris AM 8; 55
Sorby, A.: Blaris DN 12; 46, 50
Sorby, Hugh: Blaris DN 12; 49, 51
Soult (Spain): Kilbroney DN 3; 31
Sound passage: Lough Swilly DL 38; 99
South Islands: Grey Abbey DN 7; 68
South Isle bank: Moville DL 38; 72
South rock: Ardkeen DN 7; 1
South rock lighthouse: Ardkeen DN 7; 1
Southampton: Donegal DL 39; 47
Southwell, Edward: Down DN 17; 47, 59, 65
Southwell, Edward: Misc. DN 17; 119
Southwell, Edward: Saul DN 17; 113
Southwell, Elizabeth (nee Cromwell): Misc. DN 17;
    119
Sowerby (England): Ballyscullion LY 6; 57
Spa House: Magheradrool DN 17; 106
Spa Mount beetling mill [I]: Skirts of Urney and
    Ardstraw TE 5; 138
Spa Mount beetling mill [II]: Skirts of Urney and
    Ardstraw TE 5; 138
Spa Mount bleach green: Skirts of Urney and
    Ardstraw TE 5; 138
Spa Mount td: Skirts of Urney and Ardstraw TE 5;
    138
Spa Mount washing and rubbing mill: Skirts of
    Urney and Ardstraw TE 5; 138
Spaight, Margaret: Carrickfergus AM 37; 8, 99

Spain: Ballyscullion LY 6; 53
Spain: Carrickfergus AM 37; 14
Spain: Donagh DL 38; 33
Spain: Donegal DL 39; 48
Spain: Dungiven LY 15; 30
Spain: Kilbroney DN 3; 34
Spain: Kilkeel DN 3; 54
Spain: Newry DN 3; 87
Span, William: Drumachose LY 9; 66
Sparks lough: Monaghan MN 40; 159
Sparling, Mr: Coleraine LY 33; 138
Sparrow, Col. (Tanderagee): Ballymore AH 1; 3
Sparrow, J.M.: Newry DN 3; 108
Sparrow, Miss (see Mandeville)
Sparrow, Olivia: Ballymore AH 1; 3
Sparrow, Thomas: Ballyscullion LY 6; 57
Sparrowhawk, family: Ballynure AM 32; 56
Spatt, family: Aghalee AM 21; 31
Speanog (see Speenoge): Lough Swilly DL 38; 144
Spear, Benjamin: Ballymoney AM 16; 25
Spear, Cllr: Dromore TE 5; 99
Spear, David: Ballymartin AM 2; 13
Spear, George: Carrickfergus AM 37; 141, 145
Spear, Henry: Tamlaght TE 20; 81
Spear, John: Ballymoney AM 16; 26
Spear, John: Errigal Keerogue TE 20; 50–51
Spear, Margaret: Ballymoney AM 16; 17
Spear, Robert: Tamlaght TE 20; 81, 108
Spear, Sarah (see Wilson)
Spear, Saville: Errigal Keerogue TE 20; 52
Spear, William: Errigal Keerogue TE 20; 50
Spear, William: Tamlaght TE 20; 108
Speare, John: Tamlaght TE 20; 128, 136
Spears, Magdalen: Rashee AM 32; 141
Spearspointstown district: Templecorran AM 26; 82
Speedwell forge: Doagh AM 29; 92
Speenog (see Speenoge): Lough Swilly DL 38; 103
Speenoge Point: Lough Swilly DL 38; 103, 144
Speenoge td: Lough Swilly DL 38; 145
Speer, Alexander: Lough Swilly DL 38; 105
Speer, James: Ballyscullion LY 6; 56
Speer, Mr: Faughanvale LY 36; 16
Speere, George: Enniskillen FH 4; 75
Speereholme church: Termonamongan TE 5; 143
Speerholme corn mill: Termonamongan TE 5; 143
Speerholme td: Termonamongan TE 5; 143
Speers, family: Ahoghill AM 23; 25
Speers, family: Ballyclug AM 23; 63
Speers, John: Skerry AM 13; 115
Spelga mountain: Kilbroney DN 3; 28
Spelgah (see Spelga): Kilbroney DN 3; 28
Spelhoagh hill: Banagher LY 30; 59, 109–10
Spelhough (see Spelhoagh): Banagher LY 30; 59
Spellchoagh (see Spellhoagh): Misc. LY 31; 114
Spellhoagh hill: Ballynascreen LY 31; 1, 15, 114

Spellickanee td: Ballymascanlan LH 40; 55
Spence, Alexander: Carrickfergus AM 37; 194
Spence, family: Ahoghill AM 23; 25
Spence, family: Ballinderry AM 21; 48
Spence, family: Ballintoy AM 24; 20
Spence, family: Donaghmore DL 39; 33
Spence, family: Drumbeg AM 8; 123
Spence, family: Kirkinriola AM 23; 124
Spence, family: Magheramesk AM 21; 124
Spence, family: Misc. LY 36; 104
Spence, James: Newry DN 3; 98, 103
Spence, John: Carrickfergus AM 37; 109
Spence, John: Tamlaght TE 20; 75
Spence, Joseph: Hillsborough DN 12; 106
Spence, Mr: Blaris AM 8; 18
Spence, Rev.: Donaghmore DL 39; 34
Spence, Rev. N.: Clonleigh DL 39; 12
Spence, Richard: Ballyscullion LY 6; 57
Spence, W.J.: Blaris AM 8; 50
Spence, W.J.: Blaris DN 12; 46, 50
Spence, William: Clonleigh DL 39; 10, 16
Spence's bridge (see Spencer's bridge)
Spence's fort: Magheramesk AM 21; 113–14
Spencer, Edward: Errigal LY 27; 64
Spencer, Moses: Tullyaughnish DL 38; 94
Spencer, Richard: Ballyscullion LY 6; 57
Spencer, Thomas: Ahoghill AM 23; 38
Spencer's bridge: Blaris DN 12; 28
Spencer's bridge: Magheramesk AM 21; 115, 118
Sperrin corn mill: Bodoney TE 20; 20
Sperrin hamlet: Bodoney TE 20; 20
Spicer, Capt.: Desertegney DL 38; 25
Spicer, Edward: Lambeg AM 8; 136
Spiers, Samual: Magherafelt LY 6; 112
Spierstown chapel: Donegal DL 39; 47
Spiller, J.: Misc. TE 5; 147
Spiller, Mrs: Drumragh TE 5; 107, 109
Spillers, John: Dromore TE 5; 98
Spince, John: Magheramesk AM 21; 116, 118,
   120–21
Spincer, Brent: Magheramesk AM 21; 117, 124
Spincer, Conway: Magheramesk AM 21; 117
Spincer, family: Magheramesk AM 21; 117, 120,
   124–26
Spincer, Maj.: Magheramesk AM 21; 125
Spittal House: Carrickfergus AM 37; 80
Spittle Ballee school: Ballee DN 17; 20–21
Spittle Ballee td: Ballee DN 17; 20, 22–23
Spittle parks: Carrickfergus AM 37; 187
Spittle Quarter td: Ballee DN 17; 20, 22
Spittlehill quarry: Coleraine LY 33; 130
Spittlehill td: Coleraine LY 33; 93, 128, 145
Spittlehill td: Killowen LY 33; 172
Spotfield village: Kilmacteige SO 40; 193
Spotiswood, Rev. James: Clogher TE 5; 28

Spotiswood, Rev. James: Rossorry FH 14; 117
Spotswood, Andrew: Magherafelt LY 6; 91, 96
Spotswood, John: Ballyscullion LY 6; 77
Spotswood, Miss: Ballyscullion LY 6; 46
Spotswood, Rev. Thomas: Ballyscullion LY 6; 48, 65, 77
Spottiswood, John: Kilroot AM 26; 73
Spottiswood, Rev. John: Templecorran AM 26; 97, 107
Sprat, James: Ballyculter DN 17; 25
Sprat, James: Saul DN 17; 112
Spratt, family: Blaris AM 8; 21
Spriggs, Felix: Blaris AM 8; 77
Spring Grove td: Clonleigh DL 39; 12, 198
Spring Lane farm: Drumcree AH 1; 40
Spring Pond lough: Drumbeg AM 8; 124
Springbank quarry: Ballinderry TE 20; 12
Springfield district: Clondavaddog DL 38; 4
Springfield flax mill: Clondavaddog DL 38; 5
Springfield House: Ballinderry AM 21; 48
Springfield House: Clondavaddog DL 38; 5
Springfield House: Magheragall AM 21; 98–100, 102, 109
Springfield td: Lough Swilly DL 38; 129
Springhill House: Artrea LY 6; 8–9, 15, 32–33
Springhill House: Kilmore AH 1; 71
Springhill House: Lissan LY 31; 92, 96, 103
Springhill quarry: Artrea TE 20; 8
Springhill td: Clonleigh DL 39; 12, 198
Springhill wood: Artrea TE 20; 8
Springmount House: Dunaghy AM 13; 27
Springmount House: Dundermot AM 13; 31
Springmount mill: Dundermot AM 13; 31
Springmount school: Dunaghy AM 13; 17
Springmount td: Dundermot AM 13; 29, 31, 34
Springrove House: Clones FH 4; 29
Springtown td: Clogher TE 5; 36
Springvale bleach mill: Kilbride AM 29; 151
Springvale flax mill: Kilbride AM 29; 139, 150–51, 153
Springvale House: Ballywalter DN 7; 16–17
Springvale House: Kilbride AM 29; 136, 144, 150, 155
Springvale manor: Misc. DN 17; 125
Springvale td: Ballywalter DN 7; 18
Sprott, family: Magherally DN 12; 114
Sprott, William: Hillsborough DN 12; 107
Sproul, Charles: Donacavey TE 5; 76–77, 87
Sproul, Charles: Dromore TE 5; 98
Sproul, Edward: Longfield TE 5; 131
Sproul, George: Dromore TE 5; 98
Sproul, Mr (Rathmelton): Mevagh DL 38; 60
Sproul, Mr: Tullyaughnish DL 38; 94
Sproul, Oliver: Tamlaght O'Crilly LY 18; 104, 139
Sproul, Robert: Longfield TE 5; 131

Sproul, William: Tamlaght O'Crilly LY 18; 142, 144
Sproule, Mr: Clonleigh DL 39; 10
Sproule, Mr: Magherafelt LY 6; 98, 102
Sproule, Mr: Urney DL 39; 178–79
Sprowles, Ann: Clonleigh DL 39; 4
Sprucefield bleach green: Blaris AM 8; 17
Spur Royal (see Augher Castle): Clogher TE 5; 31
Squire, Rev. Thomas: Coleraine LY 33; 56
Squire, William: Raymoghy DL 39; 140–41
Squire's Point: Newry DN 3; 88–89
Sraharory td: Aghalurcher FH 4; 14
Srananny td: Donagh MN 40; 98
Sraughmore village: Kilmacteige SO 40; 193
Sruell mountain: Killymard DL 39; 102, 105
Sruell td: Killymard DL 39; 101
St Aidan's Pulpit stone: Magilligan LY 11; 103
St Andrew's (see Ballyhalbert): Inishargy DN 7; 84
St Andrews (New Brunswick): Killead AM 35; 24, 51
St Andrews' union: Donaghadee DN 7; 45
St Angelo House: Trory FH 14; 125
St Anne's church, Dublin: Ballyscullion LY 6; 60
St Atey's well: Kilmacteige SO 40; 196
St Barbara's well: Kilmacteige SO 40; 196
St Bride's hospital: Carrickfergus AM 37; 13, 80
St Bride's well: Carrickfergus AM 37; 50, 80, 171
St Bridget's stone: Artrea LY 6; 18
St Bridget's well: Kilbroney DN 3; 29
St Catherine's House: Carrickfergus AM 37; 56, 135–36
St Colman's chapel: Moira DN 12; 119
St Columb's Bed: Glencolumbkille DL 39; 64–65
St Columb's chair: Tullyaughnish DL 38; 91
St Columb's church: Magilligan LY 11; 93, 106, 146
St Columb's House: Clondermot LY 34; 6, 20–21, 21, 104
St Columb's House: Coleraine LY 33; 64
St Columb's House: Glencolumbkille DL 39; 64
St Columb's lough: Tullyaughnish DL 38; 84, 91
St Columb's old church: Clondermot LY 34; 6, 21, 33
St Columb's shrine: Magilligan LY 11; 105
St Columb's Throne (see Duncrun abbey): Magilligan LY 11; 143
St Columb's Tract stone: Misc. LY 36; 113–14
St Columb's well: Clonmany DL 38; 15, 17
St Columbkille's church: Desertoghill LY 27; 31
St Columbkille's graveyard: Ahoghill AM 23; 28
St Columbkille's shrine (Ballynascreen): Misc. TE 5; 146
St Columbkille's stone: Culfeightrin AM 24; 77
St Columbkille's stone: Desertoghill LY 27; 6, 22
St Columbkille's well: Desertoghill LY 27; 31
St Columbkille's well: Desertoghill LY 27; 6, 22
St Comgal's well: Clondermot LY 34; 45, 48

St Cunning chapel: Carncastle and Killyglen AM
    10; 8
St Cunning td: Carncastle and Killyglen AM 10; 2
St Deavog's chair: Templecarn DL 39; 163
St Ernan's causeway: Donegal DL 39; 44
St Ernan's demesne: Donegal DL 39; 49
St Ernan's House: Donegal DL 39; 49–50
St Ernan's Island: Donegal DL 39; 44, 47
St Ernan's Island: Killymard DL 39; 96
St Francis Abbey: Carrickfergus AM 37; 31
St Helena House: Duneane AM 19; 94, 100, 112,
    114
St James church (London): Drummaul AM 19; 70
St John (Canada): Cumber LY 28; 28
St John ph: Moira DN 12; 118
St John's (Canada): Newry DN 3; 85, 87
St John's: Aghadowey LY 22; 36, 38
St John's: Aghanloo LY 11; 11, 40
St John's: Ahoghill AM 23; 37–38
St John's: Ballyaghran LY 33; 18, 27
St John's: Ballyscullion LY 6; 63, 77–78
St John's: Balteagh LY 9; 43–44
St John's: Bovevagh LY 25; 60
St John's: Coleraine LY 33; 74, 145–46
St John's: Desertmartin LY 31; 62
St John's: Desertoghill LY 27; 20–21
St John's: Drumachose LY 9; 132–33
St John's: Drummaul AM 19; 91
St John's: Dunboe LY 11; 54, 80–81
St John's: Dungiven LY 15; 104
St John's: Errigal LY 27; 47, 65
St John's: Glynn AM 26; 47
St John's: Kilcronaghan LY 31; 84
St John's: Killowen LY 33; 165, 171–72
St John's: Kilrea LY 27; 129
St John's: Macosquin LY 22; 122
St John's: Maghera LY 18; 77–78
St John's: Magilligan LY 11; 94–95
St John's: Tamlaght Finlagan LY 25; 93, 99, 118–19
St John's: Tamlaght O'Crilly LY 18; 100–01,
    137–38
St John's acres: Ballynure AM 32; 38, 45, 63
St John's chapel: Tartaraghan AH 1; 118
St John's church: Ballyrashane LY 22; 47, 55
St John's church: Bright DN 17; 36
St John's monastery: Killowen LY 33; 161
St John's Point: Down DN 17; 51
St John's Point: Kilbarron DL 39; 78
St John's Point: Killymard DL 39; 109
St John's Point td: Bright DN 17; 35–36
St John's Priory: Down DN 17; 41
St John's well: Bright DN 17; 36
St Johnston (see St Johnstown): Killea and
    Taughboyne DL 39; 79
St Johnston ph: Ballyphilip DN 7; 10

St Johnstown (see Cloghy manor): Ballywalter DN
    7; 17
St Johnstown: Drumachose LY 9; 79, 129
St Johnstown: Killea and Taughboyne DL 39; 81,
    84, 86–87, 92
St Johnstown: Misc. DL 39; 184–85
St Johnstown: Taughboyne DL 39; 150–55
St Johnstown district: Killea and Taughboyne DL
    39; 79, 88
St Johnstown flax mills: Killea and Taughboyne DL
    39; 92
St Johnstown Glebe td: Misc. DL 39; 196
St Johnstown harbour: Killea and Taughboyne DL
    39; 84
St Johnstown manor: Misc. DN 17; 122
St Johnstown schools: Killea and Taughboyne DL
    39; 92
St Johnstown td: Taughboyne DL 39; 148, 196
St Johnstown yarn green: Killea and Taughboyne
    DL 39; 88
St Kevin's church: Dungiven LY 15; 55
St Lassair's cell: Killesher FH 14; 88–89
St Laurence's well: Maghera LY 18; 39
St Mary's abbey: Comber DN 7; 31
St Mary's church (Newry): Misc. DN 17; 120
St Mary's church: Kilkeel DN 3; 49
St Mary's church: Newry DN 3; 63, 66–68, 83, 98,
    105
St Mary's Drumcrin (see Drumcrin ph): Drummully
    FH 4; 34
St Michael's (see Thornhill Glebe House): Trory FH
    14; 125
St Michael's (see Trory ph): Trory FH 14; 122
St Molaise's well: Trory FH 14; 127
St Molaisse's bed: Devenish FH 14; 60–61
St Molaisse's House: Devenish FH 14; 54, 60
St Molaisse's well: Devenish FH 14; 61
St Moore, James: Ballymoney AM 16; 15
St Nawley's well: Kinawley FH 4; 108–09, 112
St Nicholas church (see Carrickfergus):
    Carrickfergus AM 37; 23
St Onan's rocks: Misc. LY 36; 114
St Patrick's (Drogheda): Carrickfergus AM 37; 78
St Patrick's bell: Misc. AM 10; 130
St Patrick's Cathedral (Dublin): Tynan AH 1; 127,
    131
St Patrick's chair: Down DN 17; 50
St Patrick's chair: Racavan AM 13; 86
St Patrick's chapel: Drumcree AH 1; 29
St Patrick's chapel: Racavan AM 13; 101, 103–04
St Patrick's chapel of ease: Newry DN 3; 66, 71,
    76–77, 79, 83, 98
St Patrick's church (see Curraghs): Manorhamilton
    Union LM 40; 51
St Patrick's cross: Down DN 17; 59

St Patrick's cross: Templecarn DL 39; 160
St Patrick's footmark: Skerry AM 13; 116, 119
St Patrick's grave: Down DN 17; 61
St Patrick's knee stones: Ballinderry AM 21; 54
St Patrick's knee stones: Tamlaght O'Crilly LY 18; 127–28
St Patrick's Pot locality: Layd AM 13; 41
St Patrick's road: Tartaraghan AH 1; 121
St Patrick's rock: Kilmacteige SO 40; 194
St Patrick's school (see Carn): Donagh DL 38; 31
St Patrick's stone (see Leac Phadraig): Dungiven LY 15; 54
St Patrick's stone: Artrea LY 6; 10, 22, 27
St Patrick's stone: Ballyscullion LY 6; 60
St Patrick's stone: Loughguile AM 13; 70
St Patrick's stone: Racavan AM 13; 101
St Patrick's stream: Kilkeel DN 3; 46
St Patrick's well: Cleenish FH 14; 19
St Patrick's well: Clondavaddog DL 38; 5
St Patrick's well: Drumlumman CN 40; 15
St Patrick's well: Killelagh LY 27; 101
St Patrick's well: Tamlaght Finlagan LY 25; 90, 109–10
St Paul's Cathedral (London): Kilbroney DN 3; 34
St Paul's church (Armagh): Clondermot LY 34; 51
St Peter and St Paul's monastery: Agivey LY 22; 40, 42
St Peter's church: Newry DN 3; 105
St Petersburg (Russia): Newry DN 3; 87
St Petersburg: Carrickfergus AM 37; 137
St Quentin (France): Blaris AM 8; 20
St Ringan's monument: Bovevagh LY 25; 38
St Ringan's well: Banagher LY 30; 114
St Ringan's well: Bovevagh LY 25; 18, 29, 38
St Ronan's stone: Aghalurcher FH 4; 9
St Saviour Cathedral: Connor AM 19; 18
St Scordin's well: Bright DN 17; 37
St Stephen's Hospital (Dublin): Tynan AH 1; 127
St Thomas' church (see Lisburn cathedral): Blaris AM 8; 9
St Tierney manor: Clones FH 4; 26–27
St Vincent's House: Coleraine LY 33; 63
Stable hill: Shilvodan AM 19; 128
Stack, J.: Cappagh TE 5; 15
Stack, Mr: Cappagh TE 5; 16
Stack, Mr: Clogher TE 5; 41
Stack, Mrs: Clogher TE 5; 41
Stack, Rev. Joseph: Cappagh TE 5; 15–17
Stack, Rev. Thomas: Cappagh TE 5; 20
Stack, Richard: Drumragh TE 5; 108
Stackaruddan (see Stookaruddan): Lough Swilly DL 38; 138
Stackford, Dean: Carnteel TE 20; 21
Stacpoole, Mrs: Hillsborough DN 12; 105
Staff Island: Cleenish FH 14; 13, 29

Stafford, Alexander: Ballyscullion LY 6; 52, 62, 74
Stafford, Arthur: Ballyscullion LY 6; 70
Stafford, Capt.: Ahoghill AM 23; 6, 14, 17, 26
Stafford, Col: Ahoghill AM 23; 26
Stafford, Eccles: Ahoghill AM 23; 17
Stafford, Edmond: Drummaul AM 19; 70–71
Stafford, family: Ahoghill AM 23; 17
Stafford, family: Ballyscullion LY 6; 53
Stafford, family: Culfeightrin AM 24; 74
Stafford, family: Duneane AM 19; 108
Stafford, family: Island Magee AM 10; 70
Stafford, Francis: Drummaul AM 19; 70
Stafford, Henry: Culfeightrin AM 24; 74
Stafford, John: Duneane AM 19; 111, 116
Stafford, man named: Duneane AM 19; 120
Stafford, Marquis of: Clondermot LY 34; 103
Stafford, Martha (see O'Neill): Drummaul AM 19; 70
Stafford, Mary: Ballymoney AM 16; 18
Stafford, Thomas: Ballyscullion LY 6; 67, 70
Staffordshire (England): Clonoe TE 20; 30
Staffordshire: Glynn AM 26; 7, 34, 41
Staffordstown Castle: Duneane AM 19; 107–08, 120
Staffordstown hamlet: Duneane AM 19; 95, 107–08, 113, 120, 122
Staffordstown school [I]: Duneane AM 19; 106, 116, 125–26
Staffordstown school [II]: Duneane AM 19; 125
Staffordstown Sunday school: Duneane AM 19; 116
Staffordstown td: Duneane AM 19; 94
Staght McConnor Castle: Ahoghill AM 23; 34
Stair-na-calleen site: Maghera LY 18; 59
Stalford, Alexander (Jnr): Hillsborough DN 12; 106
Stalford, Alexander: Hillsborough DN 12; 106
Stalford, Thomas: Hillsborough DN 12; 107
Stanalane (Stranalane) td: Dunluce AM 16; 116
Stanalane cave: Dunluce AM 16; 116, 118
Standing Stone cove: Macosquin LY 22; 86
Standing Stone hill: Ballynure AM 32; 31
Standing Stone hill: Banagher LY 30; 55, 63
Standing Stone hill: Connor AM 19; 19
Standing Stone hill: Donegore AM 29; 104
Standing Stone hill: Macosquin LY 22; 86, 113
Standing Stones hill: Tullyrusk AM 21; 132
Stanfield, Alexander: Hillsborough DN 12; 106
Stanfield, Andrew: Hillsborough DN 12; 106
Stanfield, Brereton: Hillsborough DN 12; 106
Stanfield, John: Hillsborough DN 12; 106
Stanfield, Matthew: Hillsborough DN 12; 106
Stanfield, Thomas: Hillsborough DN 12; 106
Stanfield, Widow: Hillsborough DN 12; 106
Stang village: Kilmacteige SO 40; 196
Stanhope, Mrs: Donaghmore DL 39; 39
Stanley, Lord: Urney DL 39; 180
Stanley, Mrs: Clogher TE 5; 41

Stanley, Peter: Clondermot LY 34; 13, 16, 94

Stanley, Thomas: Blaris DN 12; 50

Stanmer (Sussex): Clondermot LY 34; 41, 45

Stanmore (see Stanmer): Clondermot LY 34; 41

Stannus, Capt.: Carlingford LH 40; 57, 59

Stannus, James: Carrickfergus AM 37; 136–37, 160, 164, 168, 172, 175, 191

Stannus, Mrs James: Blaris AM 8; 84–85

Stannus, Rev. James: Ballinderry AM 21; 41, 45–49, 52

Stannus, Rev. James: Blaris AM 8; 11, 14, 20, 23, 30, 32–33, 55, 60–62, 83–84, 86

Stannus, Rev. James: Blaris DN 12; 29, 32, 35, 37, 41, 45, 49

Stannus, Thomas: Blaris AM 8; 54

Stanonagh lough: Magheross MN 40; 143

Stanton, John: Magherafelt LY 6; 107

Stanton, Thomas: Clondermot LY 34; 42, 88

Staples, Alexander: Faughanvale LY 36; 54, 56, 58–59

Staples, Allen: Faughanvale LY 36; 64

Staples, Edmond: Lissan LY 31; 107–08

Staples, family: Lissan LY 31; 103

Staples, John: Drumachose LY 9; 65

Staples, John: Lissan LY 31; 89, 98

Staples, Mr (Ballycastle): Culfeightrin AM 24; 65

Staples, Mrs J.M.: Moville DL 38; 76

Staples, Rev. J.M.: Lissan LY 31; 90, 93–94, 96–97, 103

Staples, Rev. J.M.: Moville DL 38; 74, 76, 78

Staples, Robert: Maghera LY 18; 72

Staples, Thomas: Ballyclog TE 20; 17

Staples, Thomas: Ballyscullion LY 6; 46, 56–57

Staples, Thomas: Coleraine LY 33; 63

Staples, Thomas: Donaghenry TE 20; 39

Staples, Thomas: Faughanvale LY 36; 40

Staples, Thomas: Lissan LY 31; 89, 92–93, 98, 101, 103, 106

Staples, Thomas: Lissan TE 20; 69

Staples, Thomas: Newry DN 3; 75

Stapleton, Col: Misc. DN 17; 120

Star bog: Clogher TE 5; 55

Star bog: Errigal Keerogue TE 20; 48

Star bog: Kilwaughter AM 10; 113

Star bridge: Errigal Keerogue TE 20; 48–49

Star well: Errigal Keerogue TE 20; 48

Staraghan td: Galloon FH 4; 87, 95

Starling, family: Carnmoney AM 2; 76

Starrat, Archibald: Lissan LY 31; 102

Starrat, J.: Clonleigh DL 39; 9

Starrat, James: Lissan LY 31; 102

Starrat, William: Magheraculmoney FH 14; 110

Starritstown corn mill: Convoy DL 39; 19

Starritstown td: Convoy DL 39; 22

Starritt, John: Tamlaght O'Crilly LY 18; 137

Starrs, Rev.: Longfield TE 5; 131

Station Island: Templecarn DL 39; 156, 159–60, 163, 167

Station Island chapel: Templecarn DL 39; 160, 167

Station Island ferry-house: Templecarn DL 39; 160

Station Island prison: Templecarn DL 39; 160, 167

Stavely, J.: Ballymoney AM 16; 16

Stavely, Rev.: Ballymoney AM 16; 16

Stavely, W.: Ballymoney AM 16; 16

Steed, James: Comber DN 7; 34

Steel, Adam: Ballyrashane LY 22; 66

Steel, Ann: Kildollagh LY 22; 75

Steel, Archy: Ballintoy AM 24; 22–23

Steel, family: Billy AM 16; 68

Steel, family: Carnmoney AM 2; 76

Steel, family: Derrykeighan AM 16; 89

Steel, family: Dunluce AM 16; 117

Steel, family: Misc. LY 36; 104

Steel, family: Templecorran AM 26; 117, 119

Steel, Hugh: Kildollagh LY 22; 75

Steel, James: Maghera LY 18; 58

Steel, John: Ballintoy AM 24; 23–24

Steel, Mary: Coleraine LY 33; 145

Steel, Mary: Kildollagh LY 22; 75

Steel, Mr (Rosalongan): Killymard DL 39; 96

Steel, Robert: Ballymoney AM 16; 18

Steel, Robert: Ballyscullion LY 6; 76

Steel, Samuel: Kildollagh LY 22; 75

Steel, William: Coleraine LY 33; 145

Steel, William [I]: Ballyrashane LY 22; 61, 66

Steel, William [II]: Ballyrashane LY 22; 65

Steel, William [III]: Ballyrashane LY 22; 66

Steele, family: Ballyscullion LY 6; 53

Steele, family: Billy AM 16; 58

Steele, family: Magherafelt LY 6; 95

Steele, family: Templepatrick AM 35; 118

Steele, Fredrick: Aghanloo LY 11; 30

Steele, John: Hillsborough DN 12; 106

Steele, Mr (Green Vale): Kilmegan DN 3; 58

Steele, Rebecca: Clondermot LY 34; 43, 88, 91, 96

Steele, Robert: Ahoghill AM 23; 44

Steele, Robert: Ballymoney AM 16; 15, 17

Steele, Robert: Cumber LY 28; 37, 39, 44

Steele, Robert: Donaghmore DL 39; 40

Steele, Robert: Templepatrick AM 35; 151

Steen, Alexander: Templepatrick AM 35; 113, 140, 146

Steen, Anne: Coleraine LY 33; 146

Steen, family: Finvoy AM 23; 76

Steen, Isabella (Jnr): Coleraine LY 33; 146

Steen, Isabella (Snr): Coleraine LY 33; 146

Steen, James: Macosquin LY 22; 83, 105

Steen, John [I]: Coleraine LY 33; 105

Steen, John [II]: Coleraine LY 33; 146

Steen, Joseph: Kilbride AM 29; 152

Steen, Miss: Coleraine LY 33; 72

Steen, Mrs: Muckamore AM 35; 78

Steen, Rev. George: Aghanloo LY 11; 10, 14, 16, 22

Steen, Rev. George: Drumachose LY 9; 76–77, 121, 129

Steen, Robert: Ballymoney AM 16; 26

Steen, Samuel: Coleraine LY 33; 146

Steen, William: Coleraine LY 33; 146

Steen's cave: Dunboe LY 11; 77

Steeple cove: Antrim AM 29; 37

Steeple graveyard: Antrim AM 29; 33

Steeple House: Antrim AM 29; 14, 21, 25, 32–33, 35, 47, 49–50

Steeple old church: Antrim AM 29; 33

Steeple old house: Antrim AM 29; 33

Steeple td: Antrim AM 29; 5, 21, 30, 44, 50

Steeple tower: Antrim AM 29; 4–6, 12, 20, 22, 30–33, 35–37, 43, 50–51

Steeple tower: Armoy AM 24; 2

Steeple tower: Killead AM 35; 25, 41

Steeple tower: Muckamore AM 35; 64

Steeple tower: Templepatrick AM 35; 115, 131

Steeple well: Antrim AM 29; 33

Steers, Mr (Liverpool): Ramoan AM 24; 103

Steine, Margrat: Comber DN 7; 36

Stennis (Kirkwall): Faughanvale LY 36; 11

Stenson, John: Ballyrashane LY 22; 64–65

Stenson, John: Bovevagh LY 25; 60

Stenton and Graham, Messrs: Carnmoney AM 2; 104

Stephen's sweathouse (see Sheetrim): Kinawley FH 4; 120

Stephens, family: Carrickfergus AM 37; 179

Stephens, Mrs: Newry DN 3; 100

Stephens, Patt: Kilmacteige SO 40; 193

Stephenson, Alexander: Connor AM 19; 27

Stephenson, Diana: Kilrea LY 27; 129

Stephenson, Eliza: Drumbeg AM 8; 133

Stephenson, family: Ballynure AM 32; 56

Stephenson, family: Carrickfergus AM 37; 93

Stephenson, family: Kilbride AM 29; 146, 153

Stephenson, George: Aghalee AM 21; 32

Stephenson, George: Blaris AM 8; 37, 52, 55

Stephenson, Hugh: Killea and Taughboyne DL 39; 82, 87–88, 92

Stephenson, Hugh: Taughboyne DL 39; 150, 186

Stephenson, James: Ballylinny AM 32; 24, 28–29

Stephenson, James: Ballywalter AM 2; 27

Stephenson, James: Ballywillin LY 33; 39

Stephenson, James: Drumachose LY 9; 70, 85, 124, 131

Stephenson, James: Killead AM 35; 34, 44, 50

Stephenson, John: Dromore TE 5; 97

Stephenson, John: Dungiven LY 15; 106

Stephenson, John: Hillsborough DN 12; 107

Stephenson, M.: Hillsborough DN 12; 107

Stephenson, Margaret: Island Magee AM 10; 69, 97

Stephenson, Messrs: Blaris AM 8; 37

Stephenson, Messrs Andrew and Co.: Magheramesk AM 21; 118

Stephenson, Mr (Killunaght): Banagher LY 30; 77

Stephenson, Mr: Annahilt DN 12; 22

Stephenson, Mr: Antrim AM 29; 21

Stephenson, Mr: Comber DN 7; 37, 39

Stephenson, Mr: Magheradrool DN 17; 99

Stephenson, Mr: Muckamore AM 35; 63

Stephenson, Mr: Nilteen AM 35; 90

Stephenson, Mrs Hugh: Killea and Taughboyne DL 39; 88

Stephenson, Mrs Robert: Clondermot LY 34; 20

Stephenson, Rev. (Co. Down): Aghadowey LY 22; 26

Stephenson, Robert: Ballyscullion LY 6; 57

Stephenson, S.M.: Antrim AM 29; 5, 23, 33

Stephenson, S.M.: Kilbride AM 29; 153

Stephenson, S.M.: Magheramesk AM 21; 115

Stephenson, S.M.: Mallusk AM 2; 109

Stephenson, S.M.: Misc. AM 10; 131

Stephenson, S.M.: Muckamore AM 35; 74, 81, 83

Stephenson, S.M.: Templepatrick AM 35; 116, 124, 132, 151

Stephenson, Samuel: Island Magee AM 10; 102

Stephenson, Samuel: Kilroot AM 26; 78

Stephenson, Thomas: Drumbeg AM 8; 133

Stephenson, William: Carrickfergus AM 37; 137, 162

Stephenson, William: Drumbeg AM 8; 133

Stephenson's mill: Killea and Taughboyne DL 39; 87

Stephenson's port: Island Magee AM 10; 97

Sterick, Mr: Ballintoy AM 24; 30

Sterling, Alexander: Banagher LY 30; 54, 88–89

Sterling, Ann: Bovevagh LY 25; 59

Sterling, Archy: Ahoghill AM 23; 39

Sterling, Benjaman: Ballyrashane LY 22; 61

Sterling, Cochran: Dunboe LY 11; 81

Sterling, family: Faughanvale LY 36; 13

Sterling, Henery: Bovevagh LY 25; 50

Sterling, Hugh: Hillsborough DN 12; 105

Sterling, James: Carnmoney AM 2; 47, 91

Sterling, James: Carrickfergus AM 37; 192

Sterling, James: Drumachose LY 9; 104

Sterling, James: Hillsborough DN 12; 105

Sterling, Jane: Bovevagh LY 25; 59

Sterling, John: Ballyrashane LY 22; 61

Sterling, Joseph: Bovevagh LY 25; 16, 19, 29–30

Sterling, man named: Bovevagh LY 25; 17, 43–44

Sterling, Matilda: Drumachose LY 9; 133

Sterling, Rev. J.B.: Clogher TE 5; 41

Sterling, Rev. John: Donegore AM 29; 109

Sterling, Robert: Hillsborough DN 12; 105, 105
Sterling, Sally: Bovevagh LY 25; 59
Sterling, Thomas: Ahoghill AM 23; 39
Sterling, Thomas: Ballyrashane LY 22; 66
Sterling, W.: Faughanvale LY 36; 16
Sterling, W.J.: Ballyrashane LY 22; 66
Stern, family: Misc. LY 36; 104
Sterne, Rev. John: Clogher TE 5; 27–28
Sterne, Rev. John: Devenish FH 14; 60
Sterne, Rev. John: Tynan AH 1; 126–27, 129–30, 132
Sterriot, Margaret: Donaghmore DL 39; 40
Stevelly, Edward: Templecorran AM 26; 125
Stevelly, Mr: Loughguile AM 13; 71
Steven, Mr: Aghadowey LY 22; 5
Stevens, James: Carrickfergus AM 37; 195
Stevens, John: Dromore DN 12; 78
Stevenson, Anne: Carrickfergus AM 37; 127
Stevenson, David: Misc. DL 39; 195
Stevenson, F.M.: Glenavy AM 21; 91
Stevenson, family: Ballynure AM 32; 56
Stevenson, family: Kilroot AM 26; 74–75
Stevenson, J.: Misc. DL 39; 198
Stevenson, Jacob: Clondermot LY 34; 79
Stevenson, James: Banagher LY 30; 2, 4, 15, 30, 59, 96, 98–99
Stevenson, James: Kilcronaghan LY 31; 66, 80
Stevenson, James: Misc. DL 39; 186
Stevenson, James: Misc. LY 31; 115, 129, 143
Stevenson, John: Ballynascreen LY 31; 12–13, 23, 32
Stevenson, John: Banagher LY 30; 2–4, 15, 17, 30, 32, 59, 81–82, 96, 98–100
Stevenson, John: Carrickfergus AM 37; 114
Stevenson, John: Kilcronaghan LY 31; 66, 71, 83, 87
Stevenson, John [I]: Maghera LY 18; 14–15, 55
Stevenson, John [II]: Maghera LY 18; 54
Stevenson, Messrs: Enniskillen FH 4; 46
Stevenson, Messrs John and Co.: Banagher LY 30; 19, 29
Stevenson, Mrs (Lifford): Clonleigh DL 39; 14
Stevenson, Mrs (nee Clark): Maghera LY 18; 18, 52, 72
Stevenson, Mrs John: Banagher LY 30; 99
Stevenson, Mrs John: Kilcronaghan LY 31; 88
Stevenson, R.: Faughanvale LY 36; 45
Stevenson, Robert: Ballyscullion LY 6; 57
Stevenson, Robert: Clondermot LY 34; 6, 37, 79, 104, 117
Stevenson, Samuel: Island Magee AM 10; 80, 86–87
Stevenson, Thomas: Aghanloo LY 11; 14, 16, 22
Stevenson, William: Banagher LY 30; 30
Stevenson, William: Clondermot LY 34; 78–80

Stevenson, William: Templecorran AM 26; 99, 129
Stevenson's bridge: Magheramesk AM 21; 115
Steward, Alick: Ballyscullion LY 6; 57
Steward, Hugh: Newtownards DN 7; 105
Steward, John: Hillsborough DN 12; 107
Steward, Robert: Muckamore AM 35; 80
Stewart, A.R.: Aghaderg DN 12; 6
Stewart, A.R.: Donaghmore DL 39; 35–36, 38–39
Stewart, A.R.: Faughanvale LY 36; 40, 45
Stewart, A.R.: Kilrea LY 27; 114, 123
Stewart, A.R.: Maghera LY 18; 6, 50, 72
Stewart, A.R.: Tullylish DN 12; 141, 143, 146–47
Stewart, Alan: Clondermot LY 34; 45
Stewart, Alexander: Ballyscullion LY 6; 56
Stewart, Alexander: Drumtullagh AM 16; 102
Stewart, Alexander: Ramoan AM 24; 123
Stewart, Alixander: Tamlaght Finlagan LY 25; 119
Stewart, Andrew: Ballintoy AM 24; 26
Stewart, Andrew: Carrickfergus AM 37; 102, 149
Stewart, Andrew: Kilcronaghan LY 31; 85
Stewart, Archibald: Desertoghill LY 27; 31
Stewart, Archy: Ballintoy AM 24; 23
Stewart, Barton: Tamlaght Finlagan LY 25; 119
Stewart, Berard: Ballintoy AM 24; 20
Stewart, C.W.: Carrickfergus AM 37; 141
Stewart, C.W.[?]: Cumber LY 28; 33
Stewart, Capt. (Dundermot): Culfeightrin AM 24; 66
Stewart, Capt.: Blaris AM 8; 21
Stewart, Capt.: Drumtullagh AM 16; 101
Stewart, Charles: Ballynascreen LY 31; 14, 21
Stewart, Charles: Derrykeighan AM 16; 92
Stewart, Charles: Drumachose LY 9; 73
Stewart, Charles: Drummaul AM 19; 70–71
Stewart, Charlot: Tamlaght O'Crilly LY 18; 138
Stewart, Christopher: Tamlaght Finlagan LY 25; 119
Stewart, Clarke: Aghanloo LY 11; 17
Stewart, Cllr: Kilbroney DN 3; 28–29, 31
Stewart, Cyrus: Banagher LY 30; 113
Stewart, Daniel: Ballintoy AM 24; 23
Stewart, Daniel: Culfeightrin AM 24; 82
Stewart, David: Aghadowey LY 22; 35–36
Stewart, David: Ballywillin LY 33; 50
Stewart, David: Tamlaght Finlagan LY 25; 107
Stewart, Edward: Hillsborough DN 12; 105
Stewart, Eliza: Tamlaght TE 20; 93
Stewart, Elizabeth: Tamlaght Finlagan LY 25; 118
Stewart, Ellen: Kilcronaghan LY 31; 84
Stewart, family: Ahoghill AM 23; 25
Stewart, family: Armoy AM 24; 6
Stewart, family: Ballintoy AM 24; 19–20, 30
Stewart, family: Ballynure AM 32; 56
Stewart, family: Ballywillin AM 16; 32
Stewart, family: Ballywillin LY 33; 35, 46
Stewart, family: Billy AM 16; 58, 68

Stewart, family: Blaris AM 8; 21
Stewart, family: Blaris DN 12; 30
Stewart, family: Carnmoney AM 2; 76
Stewart, family: Carrickfergus AM 37; 93, 175
Stewart, family: Culfeightrin AM 24; 46, 59
Stewart, family: Cumber LY 28; 61
Stewart, family: Derrykeighan AM 16; 89–90
Stewart, family: Drumbeg AM 8; 123
Stewart, family: Drummaul AM 19; 71
Stewart, family: Enniskillen FH 4; 58, 75
Stewart, family: Killagan AM 23; 84
Stewart, family: Kilraghts AM 16; 130
Stewart, family: Kilrea LY 27; 114
Stewart, family: Maghera LY 18; 6, 24, 48
Stewart, family: Magherafelt LY 6; 95
Stewart, family: Mallusk AM 2; 110
Stewart, family: Ramoan AM 24; 107
Stewart, family: Skerry AM 13; 112
Stewart, family: Tullyaughnish DL 38; 90–91
Stewart, Francis: Misc. DN 17; 119
Stewart, Hamilton: Drumragh TE 5; 109
Stewart, Hannah: Carrickfergus AM 37; 127
Stewart, Hugh: Carnteel TE 20; 23
Stewart, Hugh: Coleraine LY 33; 105
Stewart, Hugh: Drumragh TE 5; 109
Stewart, Hugh: Errigal Keerogue TE 20; 46, 48–50, 54
Stewart, Hugh: Tamlaght Finlagan LY 25; 118
Stewart, J.B.: Leck DL 39; 115–16, 119
Stewart, J.V.: Killygarvan DL 38; 48
Stewart, James: Aghanloo LY 11; 13–14, 17–19, 22, 30–31, 35
Stewart, James: Ballynascreen LY 31; 26
Stewart, James: Blaris DN 12; 39
Stewart, James: Bovevagh LY 25; 61
Stewart, James: Cappagh TE 5; 22
Stewart, James: Carnmoney AM 2; 76, 98, 100
Stewart, James: Derryaghy AM 8; 115
Stewart, James: Derrykeighan AM 16; 94
Stewart, James: Desertoghill LY 27; 27
Stewart, James: Dromore DN 12; 77
Stewart, James: Drumbeg AM 8; 126
Stewart, James: Dungiven LY 15; 117–19
Stewart, James: Dunluce AM 16; 118
Stewart, James: Errigal Keerogue TE 20; 51, 56–57
Stewart, James: Hillsborough DN 12; 105
Stewart, James: Kilcronaghan LY 31; 85
Stewart, James: Killygarvan DL 38; 48
Stewart, James: Kilrea LY 27; 123, 126–28
Stewart, James: Ramoan AM 24; 102
Stewart, James: Tamlaght Finlagan LY 25; 119
Stewart, James: Tamlaght O'Crilly LY 18; 138
Stewart, James: Tullyaughnish DL 38; 85–87, 89–90, 92–97
Stewart, James [I]: Ballintoy AM 24; 17

Stewart, James [I]: Carrickfergus AM 37; 108, 130
Stewart, James [II]: Ballintoy AM 24; 30
Stewart, James [II]: Carrickfergus AM 37; 184
Stewart, Jane (Jnr): Tamlaght Finlagan LY 25; 118–19
Stewart, Jane (Snr): Tamlaght Finlagan LY 25; 118–19
Stewart, Jane: Drumachose LY 9; 85, 122–23
Stewart, Jane: Kilcronaghan LY 31; 84
Stewart, Jane: Kilrea LY 27; 111–12
Stewart, John (Jnr): Tamlaght Finlagan LY 25; 118
Stewart, John (Snr): Tamlaght Finlagan LY 25; 118
Stewart, John: Antrim AM 29; 37
Stewart, John: Billy AM 16; 67, 71
Stewart, John: Blaris AM 8; 70
Stewart, John: Clogher TE 5; 55, 61
Stewart, John: Coleraine LY 33; 72, 105
Stewart, John: Culfeightrin AM 24; 72–73, 83
Stewart, John: Derryaghy AM 8; 108
Stewart, John: Drumachose LY 9; 126
Stewart, John: Drumbeg AM 8; 125, 130
Stewart, John: Errigal LY 27; 65
Stewart, John: Kilbroney DN 3; 31
Stewart, John: Loughguile AM 13; 71
Stewart, John: Magherafelt LY 6; 105
Stewart, John: Magheragall AM 21; 106
Stewart, John: Mevagh DL 38; 54
Stewart, John: Newtownards DN 7; 112
Stewart, John: Ramoan AM 24; 126
Stewart, John: Tamlaght O'Crilly LY 18; 138
Stewart, John: Tullyaughnish DL 38; 97
Stewart, John [I]: Aghadowey LY 22; 22
Stewart, John [I]: Ballintoy AM 24; 29, 31, 35
Stewart, John [I]: Carrickfergus AM 37; 112
Stewart, John [I]: Desertoghill LY 27; 25
Stewart, John [I]: Tamlaght Finlagan LY 25; 118
Stewart, John [II]: Aghadowey LY 22; 38
Stewart, John [II]: Ballintoy AM 24; 30
Stewart, John [II]: Carrickfergus AM 37; 177
Stewart, John [II]: Desertoghill LY 27; 27
Stewart, John [II]: Tamlaght Finlagan LY 25; 119
Stewart, Lady (nee Mansfield): Tullyaughnish DL 38; 91
Stewart, Magdaline: Blaris AM 8; 56
Stewart, Maj.: Annahilt DN 12; 22
Stewart, Maj.: Billy AM 16; 46
Stewart, Maj.: Blaris AM 8; 84
Stewart, Maj.: Blaris DN 12; 49
Stewart, Maj.: Drummaul AM 19; 71
Stewart, Margret: Aghadowey LY 22; 36
Stewart, Margret Jane: Macosquin LY 22; 122
Stewart, Mary: Aghadowey LY 22; 36
Stewart, Mary: Billy AM 16; 51
Stewart, Mary: Tamlaght O'Crilly LY 18; 138
Stewart, Maryann: Tamlaght Finlagan LY 25; 118

Stewart, Mathew: Errigal LY 27; 65

Stewart, Matthew: Kilcronaghan LY 31; 84

Stewart, Mervyn: Drumragh TE 5; 109

Stewart, Michael: Artrea LY 6; 18

Stewart, Miss: Blaris AM 8; 58, 84

Stewart, Miss: Coleraine LY 33; 72

Stewart, Mr (Aghavea): Clogher TE 5; 40

Stewart, Mr (Carrickfergus): Misc. DN 17; 126–27

Stewart, Mr (Rathmelton): Tullyaughnish DL 38;
   86, 95

Stewart, Mr (Stranorlar): Inishkeel DL 39; 69

Stewart, Mr (Stranorlar): Raphoe DL 39; 129

Stewart, Mr: Convoy DL 39; 21

Stewart, Mr: Donaghcloney DN 12; 59

Stewart, Mr: Donegal DL 39; 46

Stewart, Mr: Glynn AM 26; 43, 45

Stewart, Mr: Kilrea LY 27; 112

Stewart, Mr: Newtownards DN 7; 106

Stewart, Mrs: Coleraine LY 33; 73

Stewart, Mrs Christian: Coleraine LY 33; 56

Stewart, Mrs J.: Blaris AM 8; 66

Stewart, Mrs Robert: Blaris AM 8; 84

Stewart, Nathaniel: Tullyaughnish DL 38; 96

Stewart, Nicolas: Ballintoy AM 24; 19

Stewart, Poyntz: Blaris AM 8; 21

Stewart, Rachael: Tamlaght Finlagan LY 25; 119

Stewart, Rev, Alexander: Dunboe LY 11; 66

Stewart, Rev.: Loughgilly AH 1; 84, 86

Stewart, Rev. Andrew: Donegore AM 29; 129

Stewart, Rev. Archibald: Donegore AM 29; 114

Stewart, Rev. Francis: Culfeightrin AM 24; 66

Stewart, Rev. Hugh: Lissan LY 31; 103

Stewart, Rev. John: Ballyaghran LY 33; 13, 19, 27

Stewart, Rev. Robert: Skerry AM 13; 111

Stewart, Rev. Samuel: Urney DL 39; 176

Stewart, Rev. William: Aghadowey LY 22; 5, 13–14,
   26

Stewart, Rev. William: Ahoghill AM 23; 50

Stewart, Rev. William: Coleraine LY 33; 127

Stewart, Rev. William: Ramoan AM 24; 94

Stewart, Rev. William: Skerry AM 13; 107

Stewart, Ringan: Billy AM 16; 52, 64

Stewart, Robert: Balteagh LY 9; 36

Stewart, Robert: Blaris AM 8; 37, 55, 60

Stewart, Robert: Blaris DN 12; 41, 46, 50

Stewart, Robert: Bovevagh LY 25; 60

Stewart, Robert: Derrykeighan AM 16; 94

Stewart, Robert: Drumachose LY 9; 66, 95

Stewart, Robert: Dunaghy AM 13; 12

Stewart, Robert: Hillsborough DN 12; 107

Stewart, Robert: Kilcronaghan LY 31; 84

Stewart, Robert: Newry DN 3; 99, 103

Stewart, Robert: Ramoan AM 24; 109

Stewart, Robert: Saintfield DN 7; 116

Stewart, Robert: Tamlaght Finlagan LY 25; 118

Stewart, Robert: Tamlaght O'Crilly LY 18; 123

Stewart, Robert: Tickmacrevan AM 13; 133

Stewart, Rose: Blaris AM 8; 21

Stewart, S.D.: Carrickfergus AM 37; 44, 50, 149,
   161–63, 170, 172

Stewart, Samuel: Ballymoney AM 16; 24

Stewart, Samuel: Kilraghts AM 16; 133

Stewart, Sareah: Tamlaght O'Crilly LY 18; 138

Stewart, T.D.: Carrickfergus AM 37; 30

Stewart, T.L.: Carmavy AM 35; 4

Stewart, T.L.: Carrickfergus AM 37; 102, 134

Stewart, Thomas (Jnr): Tamlaght Finlagan LY 25;
   119

Stewart, Thomas (Snr): Tamlaght Finlagan LY 25;
   119

Stewart, Thomas: Blaris DN 12; 46, 49–50

Stewart, Thomas: Carrickfergus AM 37; 135

Stewart, Thomas: Errigal LY 27; 52

Stewart, Thomas: Hillsborough DN 12; 105

Stewart, Thomas: Magherafelt LY 6; 107

Stewart, William: Ballintoy AM 24; 26–27

Stewart, William: Ballynure AM 32; 58

Stewart, William: Ballywillin LY 33; 48

Stewart, William: Billy AM 16; 44, 72–73

Stewart, William: Blaris AM 8; 12, 60, 64, 66,
   84–85

Stewart, William: Blaris DN 12; 45, 47, 49

Stewart, William: Clogher TE 5; 31

Stewart, William: Desertcreat TE 20; 34

Stewart, William: Drumachose LY 9; 112

Stewart, William: Drumbeg AM 8; 126

Stewart, William: Dunaghy AM 13; 24

Stewart, William: Duneane AM 19; 120

Stewart, William: Errigal LY 27; 54

Stewart, William: Faughanvale LY 36; 40

Stewart, William: Finvoy AM 23; 75

Stewart, William: Kilraghts AM 16; 132

Stewart, William: Magherafelt LY 6; 106

Stewart, William: Mevagh DL 38; 60

Stewart, William: Newtown Crommelin AM 13; 84

Stewart, William: Raymoghy DL 39; 138, 140–41

Stewart, William: Tamlaght Finlagan LY 25; 118

Stewart, William: Tullyaughnish DL 38; 87, 89

Stewart, William [I]: Carrickfergus AM 37; 102,
   135–36

Stewart, William [I]: Kilcronaghan LY 31; 69, 86

Stewart, William [II]: Carrickfergus AM 37; 194

Stewart, William [II]: Kilcronaghan LY 31; 84

Stewart, William [III]: Kilcronaghan LY 31; 84

Stewart's Hole locality: Kilraghts AM 16; 128

Stewartstown: Artrea TE 20; 10

Stewartstown: Ballinderry TE 20; 12

Stewartstown: Ballyclog TE 20; 16–7

Stewartstown: Clonoe TE 20; 30–31

Stewartstown: Cumber LY 28; 109

Stewartstown: Desertcreat TE 20; 34, 36
Stewartstown: Desertlyn LY 31; 39
Stewartstown: Donaghenry TE 20; 37–39
Stewartstown: Lissan LY 31; 95
Stewartstown: Lissan TE 20; 69
Stewartstown: Pomeroy TE 20; 72
Stewartstown: Tamlaght TE 20; 73, 82, 90–91, 102, 114, 122, 127, 137
Stewartstown: Tullyniskan TE 20; 138–41
Stewartstown chapel: Donaghenry TE 20; 37–38
Stewartstown church: Donaghenry TE 20; 37–38
Stewartstown infant school: Killeeshil TE 20; 64
Stewartstown kilns: Ballyclog TE 20; 17
Stewartstown meeting houses: Donaghenry TE 20; 37
Stewartstown national school: Killeeshil TE 20; 64
Stewartstown pay school: Killeeshil TE 20; 64
Stewartstown ph: Desertcreat TE 20; 35
StGeorge, Acheson: Tynan AH 1; 127, 129–30
StGeorge, H.L.: Clogher TE 5; 41
StGeorge, O.: Misc. SO 40; 200
StGeorge, Rev.: Dromore TE 5; 101
StGeorge, Rev. Dr: Drumkeeran FH 14; 64
StGeorge, Rev. Dr: Magheraculmoney FH 14; 103
StGeorge, Rev. Lucas: Drummully FH 4; 39
Stibthrop, Edward: Enniskillen FH 4; 57
Stick hill: Banagher LY 30; 24
Stilty, ghost: Aghanloo LY 11; 4, 25, 28
Stine, John: Comber DN 7; 36
Stinking port: Island Magee AM 10; 90, 97, 100
Stinson, John: Ballywillin LY 33; 47, 50
Stinsons village: Donegal DL 39; 56
Stinton, Rev. W.: Shankill AH 1; 114
Stirabout House: Drumachose LY 9; 83
Stirling, family: Ahoghill AM 23; 25
Stirling, family: Ballywillin AM 16; 32
Stirling, James: Ballyrashane LY 22; 49
Stirling, James: Coleraine LY 33; 63
Stirling, James [I]: Tamlaght Finlagan LY 25; 81
Stirling, James [II]: Tamlaght Finlagan LY 25; 81, 87, 96–97, 100–01
Stirling, John: Drumachose LY 9; 73
Stirling, Mr (Bovevagh): Banagher LY 30; 3
Stirling, Mrs James: Tamlaght Finlagan LY 25; 96
Stirling, Rev. John: Aghadowey LY 22; 5
Stirling, Rev. John: Tamlaght Finlagan LY 25; 69
Stitt, family: Ballee DN 17; 16
Stitt, James: Artrea LY 6; 32–33, 38
Stitt, John: Dungiven LY 15; 74
Stitt, Mr: Ballee DN 17; 15, 23
Stitt, Mr: Comber DN 7; 41
Stitt, Mr: Dundonald DN 7; 65
StJohn, C.H.: Donaghadee DN 7; 46
StJohn, Capt.: Blaris AM 8; 4, 88
StJohn, Oliver: Ballymore AH 1; 8

Stock farm: Kilmacteige SO 40; 186
Stocka, family: Drumgath DN 3; 20
Stockans stones: Maghera LY 18; 11
Stockmon, Hugh (Snr): Killowen LY 33; 171
Stocks, Mr: Clogher TE 5; 43
Stokes, Cllr: Raphoe DL 39; 125
Stokes, Dr: Lough Swilly DL 38; 117
Stokes, family: Desertmartin LY 31; 55
Stokes, J.: Aghadowey LY 22; 16, 34
Stokes, J.: Armoy AM 24; 6–9
Stokes, J.: Ballyaghran LY 33; 10
Stokes, J.: Ballynascreen LY 31; 26
Stokes, J.: Banagher LY 30; 39, 100, 111
Stokes, J.: Bovevagh LY 25; 12, 20
Stokes, J.: Clondermot LY 34; 102–03
Stokes, J.: Coleraine LY 33; 56, 92
Stokes, J.: Cumber LY 28; 79–81
Stokes, J.: Drumtullagh AM 16; 100
Stokes, J.: Errigal LY 27; 79
Stokes, J.: Kilcronaghan LY 31; 76
Stokes, J.: Killowen LY 33; 161
Stokes, J.: Kilrea LY 27; 122
Stokes, J.: Macosquin LY 22; 97, 100, 122
Stokes, J.: Magilligan LY 11; 102
Stokes, J.: Newtown Crommelin AM 13; 84
Stokes, J.: Tamlaght Finlagan LY 25; 103–04
Stokes, Rev. Gabriel: Misc. LY 31; 136
Stole, Hugh: Killyleagh DN 17; 84
Stone fort (see Groman's Tomb): Racavan AM 13; 101
Stone house (Skerry): Finvoy AM 23; 77
Stone house: Faughanvale LY 36; 11, 15
Stone Park standing stones: Ballintoy AM 24; 33–34
Stone Park td: Kinawley FH 4; 121
Stone Park village: Kilmacteige SO 40; 196
Stone, family: Maghera LY 18; 13
Stone, Jane: Maghera LY 18; 78
Stone, Maj.: Galloon FH 4; 103
Stone, Mr: Ematris MN 40; 119
Stone, Robert: Maghera LY 18; 78
Stone, Thomas: Carrickfergus AM 37; 195
Stonebridge meeting house: Clones FH 4; 28
Stonebrook House: Kinawley FH 4; 115
Stones, Edward: Maghera LY 18; 54
Stones, George: Maghera LY 18; 54
Stones, John: Maghera LY 18; 54
Stones, Robert (Jnr): Maghera LY 18; 54
Stoney, Mr: Tullylish DN 12; 141
Stoneyfalds td: Donaghedy TE 5; 92
Stoneyford: Derryaghy AM 8; 90, 101, 109, 113
Stoneyford: Glenavy AM 21; 78, 81
Stoneyford bleach greens: Derryaghy AM 8; 111
Stoneyford bog: Derryaghy AM 8; 91, 113
Stoneyford bridge: Derryaghy AM 8; 109
Stoneyford cotton factory: Derryaghy AM 8; 111

Stoneyford old house: Derryaghy AM 8; 100

Stoneyford school [I]: Derryaghy AM 8; 102, 116

Stoneyford school [II]: Derryaghy AM 8; 117

Stoneyford spa: Derryaghy AM 8; 90

Stoneyford Sunday school: Derryaghy AM 8; 118

Stony Hill td: Tickmacrevan AM 13; 125

Stony Point: Tamlaght Finlagan LY 25; 108

Stony, Isaac: Tullylish DN 12; 146

Stonyford (see Stoneyford)

Stooeya rock: Lough Swilly DL 38; 99

Stookaruddan Head: Lough Swilly DL 38; 111, 113, 138

Storey, Duncan: Tamlaght TE 20; 74, 76, 92, 103

Storey, James: Muckamore AM 35; 80

Storey, Nancy: Tamlaght TE 20; 76

Storm Mount (see Stormont): Dundonald DN 7; 66

Stormhill House: Carnteel TE 20; 23

Stormont House: Dundonald DN 7; 65–66

Stormont, William: Ballywillin LY 33; 44

Stormount (see Stormont): Dundonald DN 7; 65

Stormy Gap hill: Banagher LY 30; 38

Story, James: Dromore TE 5; 99

Story, James: Kilskeery TE 5; 114–15

Story, Mrs J.B.: Clogher TE 5; 50

Story, Rev. J.B.: Clogher TE 5; 33–34, 40–41, 49, 55, 57, 61

Story, Rev. J.B.: Galloon FH 4; 96, 106

Story, Rev. J.B.: Tomregan FH 4; 129

Story, Rev. William: Clogher TE 5; 29

Story, Samuel: Kilskeery TE 5; 115

Stothard, Adam: Moira DN 12; 117–18

Stothard, Matthew: Dromore DN 12; 74

Stotherd, Lt R.J.: Aughnamullen MN 40; 74

Stotherd, Lt R.J.: Bovevagh LY 25; 22

Stotherd, Lt R.J.: Drummully FH 4; 40

Stotherd, Lt R.J.: Errigal Keerogue TE 20; 56

Stotherd, Lt R.J.: Killoran and Kilvarnet SO 40; 183

Stotherd, Lt R.J.: Kilmacteige SO 40; 187

Stotherd, Lt R.J.: Maghera LY 18; 1–3

Stotherd, Lt R.J.: Misc. FH 4; 133

Stotherd, Lt R.J.: Muckamore AM 35; 77

Stotherd, Mr: Donaghcloney DN 12; 59

Stott, E.A.: Blaris AM 8; 55

Stouppe, Rev. James: Drumbeg AM 8; 123

Stoven, Frederick: Drumglass TE 20; 42

Stowe library: Clogher TE 5; 24

Stowe library: Clondermot LY 34; 106–07

Stowe library: Faughanvale LY 36; 52

Stra (see Straw): Misc. LY 36; 119

Straas (see Straths): Clonmany DL 38; 13

Strabane: Aghanloo LY 11; 4

Strabane: Ardstraw TE 5; 5, 9, 12

Strabane: Banagher LY 30; 19, 61, 71

Strabane: Bodoney TE 20; 20

Strabane: Clondermot LY 34; 8, 19, 23, 30, 83, 87, 97, 114–21

Strabane: Clonleigh DL 39; 2, 6, 8, 10–11, 13–14, 16

Strabane: Cumber LY 28; 7, 9, 31, 35, 45, 49, 52, 58, 78–79, 86, 94, 96–97, 99, 109–15

Strabane: Donaghedy TE 5; 91

Strabane: Donaghmore DL 39; 32

Strabane: Donegal DL 39; 46–47, 57

Strabane: Drumkeeran FH 14; 68

Strabane: Drumragh TE 5; 109, 111

Strabane: Dungiven LY 15; 11, 13, 26, 67, 73, 109

Strabane: Enniskillen FH 4; 45

Strabane: Kildress TE 20; 61

Strabane: Killea and Taughboyne DL 39; 84, 86, 88

Strabane: Killygarvan DL 38; 39

Strabane: Killymard DL 39; 108–09

Strabane: Leck DL 39; 115

Strabane: Leckpatrick TE 5; 117–18, 121–22, 124–25

Strabane: Longfield TE 5; 132

Strabane: Lough Swilly DL 38; 140, 150

Strabane: Magheraculmoney FH 14; 109

Strabane: Magheross MN 40; 152

Strabane: Magilligan LY 11; 92

Strabane: Misc. DL 39; 184–85, 189, 193

Strabane: Misc. LY 36; 120

Strabane: Misc. TE 5; 147

Strabane: Raphoe DL 39; 130

Strabane: Raymoghy DL 39; 135

Strabane: Skirts of Urney and Ardstraw TE 5; 137

Strabane: Taughboyne DL 39; 149, 151, 153–54

Strabane: Templecarn DL 39; 158, 169–70

Strabane: Urney DL 39; 174–76, 178–79

Strabane barony: Ardstraw TE 5; 10

Strabane barony: Cappagh TE 5; 16

Strabane barony: Cumber LY 28; 1, 5

Strabane barony: Donaghedy TE 5; 89

Strabane barony: Leckpatrick TE 5; 117

Strabane barony: Urney DL 39; 174

Strabane Canal: Donaghmore DL 39; 32

Strabane Canal: Lough Swilly DL 38; 140

Strabane dispensary: Urney DL 39; 178

Strabane market: Leckpatrick TE 5; 126

Strabane nurseries: Clonleigh DL 39; 5

Strabane ph: Clonleigh DL 39; 13

Strabane td: Donacavey TE 5; 77, 79–80, 84, 87

Strabeg locality: Mevagh DL 38; 56

Straboy manor: Ahoghill AM 23; 2, 11, 15

Strabragga (see Strabreagagh)

Strabraggy (see Strabreagagh)

Strabreagagh bar: Lough Swilly DL 38; 132, 134

Strabreagagh bay: Clonmany DL 38; 12–13, 16, 19–20

Strabreagagh bay: Lough Swilly DL 38; 135–36

Strabreagagh Canal: Lough Swilly DL 38; 134–36
Strabreagagh channel: Lough Swilly DL 38; 134
Strabreagagh lough: Donagh DL 38; 31–32
Strabreagagh lough: Lough Swilly DL 38; 107–08
Strabreaghagh (see Strabreagagh)
Strachack creeks: Lough Swilly DL 38; 147
Strachack locality: Lough Swilly DL 38; 144
Strachan creeks: Lough Swilly DL 38; 121
Strachan, family: Tullyrusk AM 21; 135
Strachan, Rev.: Misc. LY 31; 136
Stradbury House: Drumgath DN 3; 21
Stradhavern (see Straidhavern): Killead AM 35; 43
Stradkane district: Misc. SO 40; 200
Stradone: Drung CN 40; 21
Stradone: Killdrumsherdan CN 40; 34
Stradone: Laragh CN 40; 41–42, 44–45
Stradone corn mill: Laragh CN 40; 42
Stradone demesne: Laragh CN 40; 39–43, 45
Stradone dispensary: Drung CN 40; 22
Stradone dispensary: Laragh CN 40; 41, 43
Stradone House: Drung CN 40; 23
Stradone House: Killdrumsherdan CN 40; 37
Stradone House: Laragh CN 40; 41–42
Stradone mill-race: Laragh CN 40; 42
Stradone river: Laragh CN 40; 40, 42
Stradone td: Laragh CN 40; 39
Stradreagh Beg lough: Clondermot LY 34; 119
Stradreagh Beg td: Clondermot LY 34; 74, 111, 113,
    119, 127, 133
Stradreagh bog: Aghanloo LY 11; 23
Stradreagh carn: Aghanloo LY 11; 5–6, 26
Stradreagh cave: Aghanloo LY 11; 5, 27
Stradreagh fort: Aghanloo LY 11; 4–5, 27, 29
Stradreagh More td: Clondermot LY 34; 74, 111,
    113, 119–20, 127–28, 133
Stradreagh mountain: Aghanloo LY 11; 1–2, 7, 26
Stradreagh school: Aghanloo LY 11; 31
Stradreagh td: Aghanloo LY 11; 4–6, 11, 20, 25,
    28–29, 31, 38, 41–42
Stradreagh td: Clondermot LY 34; 57, 60, 66, 76
Stradreagh td: Cumber LY 28; 65
Stradreagh waterfall: Aghanloo LY 11; 22
Stradrian mill: Manorhamilton Union LM 40; 50
Straduff bog: Dromore TE 5; 93
Straduff td: Dromore TE 5; 93, 99
Straed district: Lough Swilly DL 38; 133
Strafford, Earl of: Ardglass DN 17; 12
Strafford, Governor: Antrim AM 29; 23
Strafford, Lord: Ballyscullion LY 6; 47, 54, 71
Strafford, Lord: Carrickfergus AM 37; 46
Strafford, Lord: Maghera LY 18; 27
Straghan, James: Skerry AM 13; 119
Straghen, Shear: Dunaghy AM 13; 24
Stragoal td: Enniskillen FH 4; 74, 82
Stragowna bridge: Kinawley FH 4; 107–08

Stragowna school: Kinawley FH 4; 111
Stragowna td: Kinawley FH 4; 109, 115
Strahan bridge: Mevagh DL 38; 58
Strahan, family: Kirkinriola AM 23; 124
Strahan, James: Magheramesk AM 21; 120, 125
Strahulter fort: Ardstraw TE 5; 12
Strahulter td: Ardstraw TE 5; 12
Straid: Ballynure AM 32; 33, 38, 41, 54–55, 69–70,
    72
Straid: Carnmoney AM 2; 82
Straid: Carrickfergus AM 37; 59, 139–40, 155, 176
Straid: Clonmany DL 38; 14, 18
Straid: Raloo AM 32; 90, 92, 126
Straid corn mill: Ahoghill AM 23; 13, 31
Straid corn mill: Banagher LY 30; 29, 128
Straid corn mill: Clonmany DL 38; 14
Straid district: Carrickfergus AM 37; 38, 42
Straid flax mill: Ahoghill AM 23; 13, 31
Straid graveyard: Banagher LY 30; 39
Straid hill: Ballynure AM 32; 31, 55
Straid hill: Banagher LY 30; 24, 31, 46
Straid hill: Carrickfergus AM 37; 77, 176
Straid hill: Clonmany DL 38; 12
Straid Lodge: Banagher LY 30; 29–30, 59, 96
Straid lough: Cumber LY 28; 113
Straid meeting house: Ballynure AM 32; 49–50, 53,
    67, 69–70, 72
Straid old church: Banagher LY 30; 39–40, 56, 114
Straid school: Ahoghill AM 23; 46, 49
Straid standing stone: Banagher LY 30; 46
Straid Sunday school: Ahoghill AM 23; 46
Straid Sunday school: Ballynure AM 32; 53, 70–71
Straid td: Ahoghill AM 23; 37
Straid td: Banagher LY 30; 22–23, 35–36, 46,
    60–62, 64, 95, 106, 109–10, 113, 120, 125, 128,
    130–31
Straid td: Clonmany DL 38; 12, 20
Straid td: Cumber LY 28; 19
Straid td: Desertegney DL 38; 24
Straid wood: Banagher LY 30; 125
Straidballymorris beetling mill [I]: Templepatrick
    AM 35; 113, 138, 146
Straidballymorris beetling mill [II]: Templepatrick
    AM 35; 146
Straidballymorris bleach mills: Templepatrick AM
    35; 140–41
Straidballymorris corn mills: Templepatrick AM 35;
    113, 140, 146
Straidballymorris flax mill: Templepatrick AM 35;
    146
Straidballymorris fort: Templepatrick AM 35; 137,
    151
Straidballymorris old beetling mill: Templepatrick
    AM 35; 113, 146
Straidballymorris td: Templepatrick AM 35; 132

Straidballymorris td: Umgall AM 35; 159

Straidballymorris threshing machine: Templepatrick AM 35; 113, 146

Straidbilly adult school: Billy AM 16; 49

Straidbilly brewery: Billy AM 16; 76

Straidbilly caves: Billy AM 16; 56, 73

Straidbilly graveyard: Billy AM 16; 52, 73

Straidbilly school: Billy AM 16; 49, 77

Straidbilly td: Billy AM 16; 71

Straidbilly well: Billy AM 16; 52, 73

Straidhavern corn mill: Killead AM 35; 15, 42, 48

Straidhavern school: Killead AM 35; 37, 43, 53

Straidhavern td: Killead AM 35; 35, 51

Straidhavran (see Straidhavern): Killead AM 35; 53

Straidkelly (Straidcalye) hamlet: Tickmacrevan AM 13; 127

Straidkelly school: Tickmacrevan AM 13; 133

Straidland (Straidlands) td: Ballynure AM 32; 48–49, 54, 57, 62–63, 68

Straidland bogs: Ballynure AM 32; 56

Straidland cave: Ballynure AM 32; 56

Straidland corn mill: Ballynure AM 32; 34, 43–44, 68

Straidland district: Carrickfergus AM 37; 33

Straidland flax mill: Ballynure AM 32; 34, 43–44, 68

Straidland fort [I]: Ballynure AM 32; 55–57

Straidland fort [II]: Ballynure AM 32; 57

Straidland giant's grave: Ballynure AM 32; 55–56

Straidland hill: Ballynure AM 32; 31

Straidland House: Ballynure AM 32; 72

Straidland school: Ballynure AM 32; 52, 70

Straidnahana locality: Carrickfergus AM 37; 33, 93, 151, 173

Straidnahana school: Carrickfergus AM 37; 155

Straidnahanna (see Straidnahana): Carrickfergus AM 37; 151

Straight, Samuel: Raloo AM 32; 123

Straighter, James: Doagh AM 29; 88

Strain, family: Carrickfergus AM 37; 93

Straken district: Misc. SO 40; 198

Stralamford td: Convoy DL 39; 22

Stramore green: Magheraculmoney FH 14; 110

Stramore td: Mevagh DL 38; 56, 62

Stranacummer chapel: Kilskeery TE 5; 114

Stranadarriv hill: Magheraculmoney FH 14; 105

Stranagalwilly (Stranaganwilly) td: Cumber LY 28; 1, 5, 18, 21, 67, 71, 80–81, 83, 114–15, 120, 124–26

Stranagalwilly corn mill: Cumber LY 28; 86, 124–25

Stranagalwilly forest: Cumber LY 28; 7

Stranagalwilly fulling mill: Cumber LY 28; 126

Stranagalwilly graveyard: Cumber LY 28; 31

Stranagalwilly hamlet: Cumber LY 28; 11, 24, 31

Stranagalwilly hills: Cumber LY 28; 5, 85

Stranagalwilly river: Misc. LY 36; 119

Stranagalwilly school: Cumber LY 28; 3, 16, 74, 77–78

Stranagalwilly td: Balteagh LY 9; 16

Stranagalwilly tuck mill: Cumber LY 28; 86

Stranagard corn mill: Desertmartin LY 31; 55

Stranagard flax mill: Desertmartin LY 31; 55

Stranagard td: Desertmartin LY 31; 52, 62, 114, 142

Stranahalta stone: Banagher LY 30; 37

Stranahalta valley: Banagher LY 30; 56

Stranahinch td: Misc. LY 31; 143

Stranahoan hill: Magheraculmoney FH 14; 105

Stranalooby locality: Cumber LY 28; 29

Stranamuck td: Donaghmore DL 39; 39

Stranatave (see Stranatawe): Magheraculmoney FH 14; 113

Stranatawe td: Magheraculmoney FH 14; 111, 113

Stranchermore, giant: Dungiven LY 15; 84

Strand Field House: Ballymascanlan LH 40; 55

Strand Head bridge: Lough Swilly DL 38; 135

Strand lough: Ardglass DN 17; 9

Strand td: Bright DN 17; 34–35

Strandtown td: Holywood DN 7; 77, 79–80

Strane (see Strone): Banagher LY 30; 81

Strangemore locality: Dungiven LY 15; 46, 84

Strangford: Ardglass DN 17; 5, 9, 12

Strangford: Ballee DN 17; 23

Strangford: Ballyculter DN 17; 26–29

Strangford: Ballyphilip DN 7; 9, 12, 14

Strangford: Bright DN 17; 35

Strangford: Kilclief DN 17; 79

Strangford: Killyleagh DN 17; 84–86

Strangford: Misc. DN 17; 116, 128

Strangford: Newry DN 3; 86

Strangford: Saul DN 17; 112

Strangford bay: Ballyculter DN 17; 25

Strangford chapel: Ballyculter DN 17; 27–28

Strangford church: Ballyculter DN 17; 27

Strangford creek: Ballyphilip DN 7; 9

Strangford custom house: Ardglass DN 17; 6

Strangford custom house: Killyleagh DN 17; 83

Strangford ferry: Ballyculter DN 17; 28

Strangford ferry: Killyleagh DN 17; 85

Strangford harbour: Killyleagh DN 17; 84

Strangford infant school: Ballyculter DN 17; 29

Strangford Lough: Antrim AM 29; 17

Strangford Lough: Ardkeen DN 7; 1–3

Strangford Lough: Ballyculter DN 17; 25, 28

Strangford Lough: Ballyhalbert DN 7; 6

Strangford Lough: Ballyphilip DN 7; 9, 12

Strangford Lough: Ballywalter DN 7; 16

Strangford Lough: Carrickfergus AM 37; 11

Strangford Lough: Comber DN 7; 30–32, 41–42

Strangford Lough: Down DN 17; 38–39, 41, 50

Strangford Lough: Grey Abbey DN 7; 67–70
Strangford Lough: Inch DN 17; 75
Strangford Lough: Inishargy DN 7; 84
Strangford Lough: Killinchy DN 7; 86, 88
Strangford Lough: Killyleagh DN 17; 81, 84
Strangford Lough: Kilmore DN 17; 91
Strangford Lough: Misc. DN 17; 120–21
Strangford Lough: Newtownards DN 7; 103, 111
Strangford Lough: Saul DN 17; 111, 113
Strangford Lough: Witter DN 7; 125
Strangford Lower chapel: Ballyculter DN 17; 30
Strangford Lower corn mill: Ballyculter DN 17; 25
Strangford Lower gravel pit: Ballyculter DN 17; 30
Strangford Lower meeting house [I]: Ballyculter DN 17; 30
Strangford Lower meeting house [II]: Ballyculter DN 17; 30
Strangford Lower mill: Ballyculter DN 17; 30
Strangford Lower school: Ballyculter DN 17; 30
Strangford Lower smithies: Ballyculter DN 17; 30
Strangford Lower td: Ballyculter DN 17; 31
Strangford ph: Misc. DN 17; 122
Strangford river: Ballyculter DN 17; 25, 27
Strangford river: Ballyphilip DN 7; 7, 9, 12
Strangford river: Witter DN 7; 126
Strangford Upper td: Ballyculter DN 17; 30–31
Strangford wharf: Killyleagh DN 17; 84–85
Strangford, Lord: Maghera LY 18; 72, 75
Strangford, Rev.: Maghera LY 18; 66
Stranisk (Straniskey) td: Donacavey TE 5; 67–68, 77, 80–82, 84, 87
Strannisk (see Stranisk)
Stranny, Ann: Blaris AM 8; 77
Stranny, David: Blaris AM 8; 77
Stranny, Mary (Jnr): Blaris AM 8; 77
Stranny, Mary (Snr): Blaris AM 8; 77
Stranocum: Ballymoney AM 16; 3–4, 9
Stranocum: Derrykeighan AM 16; 81, 87
Stranocum: Killagan AM 23; 80
Stranocum bridge: Ballymoney AM 16; 5
Stranocum corn mill: Ballymoney AM 16; 10
Stranocum demesne: Ballymoney AM 16; 5, 10
Stranocum demesne: Dunluce AM 16; 107
Stranocum flax mill [I]: Ballymoney AM 16; 10
Stranocum flax mill [II]: Ballymoney AM 16; 10
Stranocum House: Ballymoney AM 16; 1
Stranocum td: Ballymoney AM 16; 10, 23
Stranofeley td: Aghavea FH 4; 23
Stranorlaghan td: Raphoe DL 39; 127
Stranorlar: Clonleigh DL 39; 3
Stranorlar: Convoy DL 39; 18
Stranorlar: Donaghmore DL 39; 28, 30–31
Stranorlar: Donegal DL 39; 50, 57
Stranorlar: Drumhome DL 39; 58
Stranorlar: Inishkeel DL 39; 69

Stranorlar: Killymard DL 39; 108
Stranorlar: Kilteevoge DL 39; 110, 112–13
Stranorlar: Leck DL 39; 116
Stranorlar: Misc. DL 39; 188
Stranorlar: Templecarn DL 39; 170
Stranorlar ph: Convoy DL 39; 18
Stranorlar ph: Donaghmore DL 39; 28
Stranorlar ph: Donegal DL 39; 42, 54
Stranorlar ph: Kilteevoge DL 39; 111–12
Stranorlar ph: Raphoe DL 39; 129
Strass (see Straths): Clonmany DL 38; 14
Stratford Le Bow (England): Drummaul AM 19; 70
Strath (see Straw): Bovevagh LY 25; 22
Strathall td: Cumber LY 28; 46, 48, 60, 65, 98, 103, 106
Strathall wood: Cumber LY 28; 103
Strathamunich stone: Banagher LY 30; 37
Strathnas td: Donegal DL 39; 44
Straths corn mill: Clonmany DL 38; 14
Straths td: Clonmany DL 38; 13, 18, 20
Stratigore (Strattygore) td: Donacavey TE 5; 77, 80–81, 83, 87
Stratonagher hill: Devenish FH 14; 47–48
Stratore hill: Devenish FH 14; 47
Stratore td: Devenish FH 14; 47–48
Stratton, T.: Ballymore AH 1; 3
Straughroy (Strochroy) td: Cappagh TE 5; 19, 21–22
Straw chapel: Ballynascreen LY 31; 5, 7–8, 12, 19, 129
Straw church: Banagher LY 30; 6
Straw corn mill: Ballynascreen LY 31; 7
Straw corn mill: Bovevagh LY 25; 4, 20, 57
Straw flax mill: Ballynascreen LY 31; 7
Straw flax mill: Bovevagh LY 25; 4, 20, 57
Straw footbridge: Ballynascreen LY 31; 7
Straw graveyard: Ballynascreen LY 31; 12
Straw House: Banagher LY 30; 4, 15
Straw House: Bovevagh LY 25; 3–4, 20, 22–23, 57
Straw mountain: Banagher LY 30; 31
Straw mountain: Cumber LY 28; 1, 3–6, 11, 31
Straw mountain: Misc. LY 36; 119
Straw school: Ballynascreen LY 31; 16
Straw td: Aghanloo LY 11; 12
Straw td: Ballynascreen LY 31; 1, 7, 13, 21–22, 143
Straw td: Banagher LY 30; 23–24
Straw td: Bovevagh LY 25; 2–3
Straw tuck mill: Ballynascreen LY 31; 7
Strawbridge, Allan: Clondermot LY 34; 82
Strawbridge, family: Misc. LY 36; 101
Strawmore bog: Ballynascreen LY 31; 26
Strawmore chapel: Ballynascreen LY 31; 19, 118, 129
Strawmore Lodge: Ballynascreen LY 31; 6, 20

Strawmore standing stones: Ballynascreen LY 31; 19, 30

Strawmore stone circle: Ballynascreen LY 31; 19, 30

Strawmore td: Ballynascreen LY 31; 1, 10–11, 21, 23–24, 118, 143

Strawpark td: Kilbride AM 29; 136, 155

Streamvale demesne: Magheragall AM 21; 101

Streamvale House: Magheragall AM 21; 101

Streenty td: Magheross MN 40; 149

Streeve bridge: Drumachose LY 9; 56, 91, 119

Streeve demesne: Aghanloo LY 11; 3

Streeve demesne: Drumachose LY 9; 56, 88–89

Streeve hill: Banagher LY 30; 24, 35, 48, 76, 84, 109, 112

Streeve House: Drumachose LY 9; 49, 51, 82–83, 91, 119

Streeve Lower triangulation point: Banagher LY 30; 110

Streeve plantations: Drumachose LY 9; 48

Streeve td: Drumachose LY 9; 57, 83, 87, 91, 97, 106

Streeve td: Magilligan LY 11; 84

Strieve (see Streeve)

Strin, family: Misc. LY 36; 104

Stripe td: Aghalurcher FH 4; 14

Stroan (Stroane) td: Derrykeighan AM 16; 81, 90–92, 94

Strode, Mr: Clogher TE 5; 43

Strone (see Stroan): Derrykeighan AM 16; 90

Strone locality: Banagher LY 30; 35, 81, 112

Stronesesk hill: Ramoan AM 24; 122

Stroneyal well: Dungiven LY 15; 91

Strong, R.S.: Carlingford LH 40; 59

Strongbow, Earl: Cumber LY 28; 20

Stronge, Calumb: Drumglass TE 20; 43

Stronge, J.M.: Clondermot LY 34; 38

Stronge, J.M.: Drumragh TE 5; 109

Stronge, J.M.: Termonamongan TE 5; 144

Stronge, J.M.: Tynan AH 1; 127–30, 132

Strongfoord river (see Strangford river): Ballyphilip DN 7; 9

Strongibbagh td: Convoy DL 39; 22

Strongman, Mr (Waterford): Drumcree AH 1; 38

Stronocum (see Stranocum): Derrykeighan AM 16; 87

Struele (see Struell): Down DN 17; 53

Struell chapel: Down DN 17; 50

Struell td: Down DN 17; 50, 53, 57

Struell wells: Down DN 17; 45, 50, 61, 118

Strule river: Ardstraw TE 5; 2, 4–5, 7, 9–11

Strule river: Cappagh TE 5; 20

Strule river: Donacavey TE 5; 67

Strule river: Drumragh TE 5; 104

Strule river: Kildress TE 20; 61

Strule river: Lissan TE 20; 69

Stuart and Gregg, Messrs: Blaris AM 8; 56, 65

Stuart and Gregg, Messrs: Coleraine LY 33; 106–07, 127

Stuart, Agnes: Carrickfergus AM 37; 158

Stuart, Alexander: Enniskillen FH 4; 67

Stuart, Andrew: Tullyniskan TE 20; 139–40

Stuart, Archibald: Island Magee AM 10; 65

Stuart, Bella: Carrickfergus AM 37; 116

Stuart, C.E.: Kilrea LY 27; 119

Stuart, C.E.: Magilligan LY 11; 129, 138

Stuart, C.E.: Misc. LY 31; 137

Stuart, C.E.: Misc. LY 36; 110

Stuart, C.E.: Rathlin Island AM 24; 131

Stuart, Charles: Carrickfergus AM 37; 124

Stuart, Charles: Coleraine LY 33; 127

Stuart, Charles: Raloo AM 32; 129

Stuart, family: Ballintoy AM 24; 16

Stuart, family: Carrickfergus AM 37; 134

Stuart, family: Connor AM 19; 23

Stuart, family: Kilwaughter AM 10; 115

Stuart, family: Layd AM 13; 40

Stuart, family: Raloo AM 32; 94

Stuart, family: Templecorran AM 26; 117, 119

Stuart, George: Carrickfergus AM 37; 125

Stuart, H.I.: Ballymoney AM 16; 15

Stuart, H.I.: Coleraine LY 33; 127

Stuart, H.I.: Derrykeighan AM 16; 78, 84

Stuart, H.I.: Kirkinriola AM 23; 117

Stuart, Hannah: Carrickfergus AM 37; 114

Stuart, Hugh: Carrickfergus AM 37; 97

Stuart, Hugh: Tamlaght TE 20; 116

Stuart, J.F.: Kilrea LY 27; 119

Stuart, James: Carrickfergus AM 37; 118

Stuart, Jane: Carrickfergus AM 37; 132

Stuart, Joseph: Dunaghy AM 13; 17

Stuart, Lord E.: Killesher FH 14; 90

Stuart, Mary: Carrickfergus AM 37; 116

Stuart, Michel: Banagher LY 30; 69

Stuart, Mr: Seapatrick DN 12; 126

Stuart, Mrs: Carrickfergus AM 37; 146, 151–52

Stuart, Mrs John: Templecorran AM 26; 116, 132

Stuart, Peggy: Carrickfergus AM 37; 131

Stuart, Rev. John: Glynn AM 26; 35, 46

Stuart, Rev. John: Templecorran AM 26; 101, 116, 120, 129–32

Stuart, William: Hillsborough DN 12; 107

Stuart, William: Island Magee AM 10; 95

Stubbs, William: Carrickfergus AM 37; 39, 90

Stuckanbwee Point: Lough Swilly DL 38; 107

Stuckanuller rock: Lough Swilly DL 38; 107

Stuckaruddan (see Stookaruddan): Lough Swilly DL 38; 111

Studdert, Rawden: Aghagallon AM 21; 10

Stuekan stones: Maghera LY 18; 36

Stuickanmore rock: Lough Swilly DL 38; 99

Stump td: Misc. DN 17; 130

Stumpy Hill school: Killesher FH 14; 85–86

Stumpy Hill school: Kinawley FH 4; 111

Sturgeon, John: Hillsborough DN 12; 106

Sturgeon, John: Maghera LY 18; 78

Sturgeon, Rev. F.: Tullynakill DN 7; 123

Sturgeon, Robert: Maghera LY 18; 45

Sturock, family: Ballintoy AM 24; 20

Sturrock, Mrs: Coleraine LY 33; 72

Style, T.C.: Donaghmore DL 39; 30

Style, T.C.: Faughanvale LY 36; 40, 45

Style, T.C.: Kilteevoge DL 39; 112–14

Suck river (Connacht): Banagher LY 30; 105

Suez House: Kilmore AH 1; 65

Suez td: Kilmore AH 1; 60, 65, 69, 71–73

Sufferan, J.: Antrim AM 29; 46

Sufferin, George: Ballyscullion LY 6; 64

Suffern, Anthony: Muckamore AM 35; 79

Suffern, Jane: Carrickfergus AM 37; 117

Suffern, man named: Killead AM 35; 32

Suffern, William (Jnr): Muckamore AM 35; 79

Suffern, William (Snr): Muckamore AM 35; 79

Suffolk House: Blaris AM 8; 51, 70

Sugar Island: Newry DN 3; 63, 70

Suir river (Tipperary): Drumachose LY 9; 93

Suitor, Richard (London): Tamlaght Finlagan LY 25; 70, 82

Sulay dam: Drumachose LY 9; 89

Sulla Tober (see Cillytober): Carrickfergus AM 37; 7

Sullynadaol locality: Lough Swilly DL 38; 114

Sulnaree td: Donagh DL 38; 31

Summer Hill abbey: Killymard DL 39; 96

Summer Hill fort: Killymard DL 39; 97

Summer Hill House: Moville DL 38; 78

Summer Hill td: Killymard DL 39; 96, 100

Summer Island House: Loughgall AH 1; 80

Summer Island school: Loughgall AH 1; 76–77

Summerfield House: Dundonald DN 7; 65

Summerhill House: Clones FH 4; 29

Summerhill House: Donaghmore DL 39; 31

Summerhill House: Drumhome DL 39; 58

Summerhill House: Drumkeeran FH 14; 65

Summerset (see Somerset)

Sunday's well (see Tubberdonagh spring): Magilligan LY 11; 127

Supple, person named: Blaris AM 8; 60

Surgont, family: Enniskillen FH 4; 58

Surrey Hill House (Berkshire): Ballyculter DN 17; 28

Sussex, Earl Thomas: Misc. LY 36; 103

Sutler, family: Ballyclug AM 23; 60

Sutton, Catherine: Carrickfergus AM 37; 128

Swail, family: Dunsfort DN 17; 68

Swain, Bishop: Clondermot LY 34; 53

Swallows Brae locality: Bovevagh LY 25; 23

Swan Isle (Big): Glynn AM 26; 33, 45

Swan Isle (Little): Glynn AM 26; 45

Swan, Dr: Killymard DL 39; 96

Swan, family: Drumbeg AM 8; 123

Swan, family: Ematris MN 40; 118

Swan, family: Killead AM 35; 46

Swan, Henry: Dunboe LY 11; 77

Swan, Hugh: Banagher LY 30; 30, 71–73, 96, 99

Swan, Hugh: Clondermot LY 34; 79

Swan, Hugh: Doagh AM 29; 70, 93

Swan, Hugh: Dunboe LY 11; 46, 66, 77

Swan, Hugh: Dungiven LY 15; 65, 100

Swan, Hugh: Nilteen AM 35; 103

Swan, Hugh: Templepatrick AM 35; 140, 146

Swan, John: Balteagh LY 9; 24

Swan, John: Blaris AM 8; 19

Swan, Mr (Rathfriland): Drumgath DN 3; 21

Swan, Robert: Drumbeg AM 8; 123, 127

Swan, William: Muckamore AM 35; 80

Swan's ford: Blaris DN 12; 28

Swan's river: Clondermot LY 34; 40

Swanlinbar: Derryvullan FH 14; 44

Swanlinbar: Killesher FH 14; 86

Swanlinbar: Kinawley FH 4; 110, 113, 115, 119, 122–23

Swanlinbar dispensary: Killesher FH 14; 85

Swanlinbar dispensary: Kinawley FH 4; 109, 119

Swanlinbar hills: Currin MN 40; 91

Swanlinbar river (see also Cladagh): Kinawley FH 4; 107, 113, 115

Swann, Henery: Killowen LY 33; 172

Swannagh lough: Donaghmore DL 39; 29

Swannagh river: Donaghmore DL 39; 28–29

Swansea, A.: Aughnamullen MN 40; 76

Swansea, A.: Ballybay MN 40; 82

Swansea, T.B.: Newry DN 3; 98, 103

Swanstown Carmaigraw school: Ahoghill AM 23; 50

Swatragh: Desertoghill LY 27; 8–10, 17, 24, 28–29

Swatragh: Dungiven LY 15; 33

Swatragh: Errigal LY 27; 80–81, 83

Swatragh: Killelagh LY 27; 95, 97, 102

Swatragh: Kilrea LY 27; 110, 126

Swatragh: Maghera LY 18; 2, 6, 11, 17–18, 22, 25, 27, 32, 34, 50, 59, 65–66, 76–77, 80–81

Swatragh: Misc. LY 36; 112

Swatragh: Tamlaght O'Crilly LY 18; 83, 92, 107–09, 139

Swatragh bridge: Maghera LY 18; 9, 64

Swatragh corn mill: Maghera LY 18; 27, 29, 35

Swatragh dispensary: Killelagh LY 27; 98

Swatragh dispensary: Maghera LY 18; 6, 26–27, 76–77

Swatragh female school: Maghera LY 18; 6, 29–30

Swatragh lime-kiln: Kilrea LY 27; 110

Swatragh male school: Maghera LY 18; 6, 29

Swatragh meeting house: Maghera LY 18; 2, 7, 34–35, 76

Swatragh standing stones: Maghera LY 18; 22, 39, 59

Swatragh td: Maghera LY 18; 2, 12, 34, 39–40, 81

Swatrea (see Swatragh)

Sweden: Banagher LY 30; 9, 11

Sweden: Coleraine LY 33; 86–87

Sweden: Killea and Taughboyne DL 39; 84

Sweden: Tamlaght O'Crilly LY 18; 111, 117

Sweeney, Mr: Macosquin LY 22; 99

Sweeney, Nancy: Enniskillen FH 4; 77

Sweeny, Elizabeth: Blaris AM 8; 81

Sweeny, Francis: Desertmartin LY 31; 57

Sweeny, Mary: Carrickfergus AM 37; 110

Sweeny, Miles: Aghanloo LY 11; 21

Sweeny, Patrick: Maghera LY 18; 78

Sweeny, Rev. James: Clondermot LY 34; 24, 92, 103

Sweeny, Rev. James: Faughanvale LY 36; 33

Sweeny, Rev. John: Cleenish FH 14; 17, 23, 25

Sweeny, Rev. John: Clogher TE 5; 40

Swift, Adam: Newry DN 3; 74

Swift, Rev. Jonathan: Ballynure AM 32; 51, 56, 65

Swift, Rev. Jonathan: Clogher TE 5; 28

Swift, Rev. Jonathan: Newry DN 3; 74

Swift, Rev. Jonathan: Templecorran AM 26; 83, 85, 108, 112, 118

Swift, Stella (nee Johnson): Clogher TE 5; 28

Swifts' Hospital (Dublin): Tynan AH 1; 127

Swilly bog: Taughboyne DL 39; 148, 154, 187

Swilly burn: Clonleigh DL 39; 1, 7, 14, 16

Swilly burn: Conwal DL 39; 24

Swilly burn: Leck DL 39; 115–17

Swilly burn: Misc. DL 39; 185, 188

Swilly burn: Raphoe DL 39; 121

Swilly burn: Taughboyne DL 39; 149, 152–54

Swilly glen: Leck DL 39; 115

Swilly Little rock: Lough Swilly DL 38; 99

Swilly Martello towers: Clondavaddog DL 38; 1, 5

Swilly Martello towers: Desertegney DL 38; 25

Swilly rock: Clondavaddog DL 38; 1, 7–8

Swilly rocks: Lough Swilly DL 38; 98–99, 127

Swilly td: Taughboyne DL 39; 148, 154, 196

Swilly View House: Leck DL 39; 116

Swine, George: Mevagh DL 38; 60

Swine's Dike wall: Misc. DN 17; 131

Swiney, Daniel: Tullyaughnish DL 38; 96

Swiney, Mrs: Tullyaughnish DL 38; 96

Switzerland: Lough Neagh AM 21; 92

Sworne's hill: Skerry AM 13; 109–10

Syddan td: Enniskeen CN 40; 26

Sydney (Australia): Carnmoney AM 2; 88

Sydney: Ahoghill AM 23; 37–38

Sydney, Henry: Lough Neagh AM 21; 95

Sydney, John: Clondermot LY 34; 49, 54

Sylvodan (see Shilvodan): Kirkinriola AM 23; 88

Symington, Daniel: Carnmoney AM 2; 78

Symington, family: Templecorran AM 26; 117, 119

Symmington, Robert: Island Magee AM 10; 42, 93

Symokill district: Misc. SO 40; 199

Syms, family: Ballinderry AM 21; 48

Synell, St: Cleenish FH 14; 20

Synet, family: Misc. LY 36; 104

Synnott, Marcus: Ballymyre AH 1; 20

Synnott, Walter: Ballymyre AH 1; 20

Syonee (Sionnee) td: Donacavey TE 5; 77, 79, 81–83, 87

Syonfin (Sionfin) td: Donacavey TE 5; 77, 79, 81, 83, 87

Syonfin bridge: Donacavey TE 5; 64

Syonfin fort: Donacavey TE 5; 83

Syonhue (see Syonee)

Syonhugh (see Syonee)

Syunshin [?] (Scientien) td: Clogher TE 5; 37, 41

Syunshin [?] school: Clogher TE 5; 41–42

T

Taafe, Laurence: Ballyscullion LY 6; 57

Tabermoney (see Tobbermoney). Down DN 17; 48

Table Mountain (Africa): Drumgoon CN 40; 1

Tachnabrick mill: Blaris DN 12; 36

Tachnabrick td: Blaris DN 12; 36

Taclough Upper river: Tartaraghan AH 1; 120

Tafe, family: Culfeightrin AM 24; 59

Tafe, John: Kilmacteige SO 40; 190, 193–95

Tagert, Samuel: Ardstraw TE 5; 3

Tagert, Samuel: Donacavey TE 5; 85

Tagert, William: Ardstraw TE 5; 3–5

Tagert, William: Donacavey TE 5; 85

Taggart Isle: Misc. DN 17; 121

Taggart, J.P.: Coleraine LY 33; 68, 72–73, 95, 127, 137–38, 144

Taggart, James: Carrickfergus AM 37; 113

Taggart, James: Hillsborough DN 12; 107

Taggart, John: Muckamore AM 35; 80

Taggart, Mr: Donacavey TE 5; 76–77

Taggart, Mr: Saul DN 17; 111

Taggart, Rev.: Rasharkin AM 23; 137, 140

Taggart, Thomas: Templepatrick AM 35; 132

Taggart, William: Kildollagh LY 22; 69, 73

Taggart's mill: Saul DN 17; 111

Taggert, John: Drumachose LY 9; 132

Taggert, John: Magheragall AM 21; 106

Taggert, Patt: Drumachose LY 9; 132

Taghar, Prince of Denmark: Dungiven LY 15; 80

Tagharina (Taghirina) td: Clondermot LY 34; 57, 74, 111, 113, 120, 128, 133

Tagher's grave: Dungiven LY 15; 45

Tagus river (Spain): Blaris AM 8; 89

Tahuia lough: Donegal DL 39; 43

Tailchan, father of Lugaid: Clonfeacle AH 1; 23

Tailer, Susana: Tamlaght TE 20; 78

Tailor, Robert: Bovevagh LY 25; 60

Tainlot td: Clogher TE 5; 53

Tait, Christie: Clondermot LY 34; 37, 79–80, 104

Tait, J.F.: Aghavea TE 5; 2–9

Tait, J.F.: Clonduff DN 3; 4–6

Tait, J.F.: Kilmood DN 7; 96

Tait, J.F.: Monaghan MN 40; 159

Tait, James: Derryaghy AM 8; 90–91

Tait, James: Magilligan LY 11; 133

Taitstown cove: Raloo AM 32; 123

Talbot, family: Carrickfergus AM 37; 93

Talbot, Patrick: Duneane AM 19; 124

Talbot, Walter: Tomregan FH 4; 127

Tall river: Clonfeacle AH 1; 21, 23–24

Tall river: Coleraine LY 33; 97

Tall river: Kilmore AH 1; 57, 61

Tall river: Loughgall AH 1; 75, 79

Tall river: Tartaraghan AH 1; 117, 119–20

Tallanees Lower lough: Clondavaddog DL 38; 2

Tallanees Upper lough: Clondavaddog DL 38; 2

Tally, John: Carrickfergus AM 37; 194

Tallyho House: Tullylish DN 12; 142

Tallyho Locks: Ballymore AH 1; 10, 18

Tallykeel (see Tattykeel): Magheraculmoney FH 14; 103

Tallytramim td: Ballywalter DN 7; 18

Talnamallard td: Derryvullan FH 14; 46

Talt lough: Kilmacteige SO 40; 189–91, 194–95

Talt river: Kilmacteige SO 40; 191, 195

Tamin lough: Ahoghill AM 23; 27–28

Tamlagh (see Tamnagh): Banagher LY 30; 60

Tamlagh Derryvullan school: Derryvullan FH 14; 43

Tamlagh td: Derryvullan FH 14; 46

Tamlaghmore House: Killyman TE 20; 68

Tamlaght brick-kilns: Tamlaght Finlagan LY 25; 101

Tamlaght bridge: Tamlaght Finlagan LY 25; 123

Tamlaght burn: Tamlaght Finlagan LY 25; 121

Tamlaght chapel: Magilligan LY 11; 85

Tamlaght church: Tamlaght O'Crilly LY 18; 82, 88–89, 96, 99, 101–02, 104, 125, 136, 142

Tamlaght church: Tamlaght TE 20; 137

Tamlaght corn mill: Tamlaght Finlagan LY 25; 83, 121–22

Tamlaght dispensary: Tamlaght O'Crilly LY 18; 88, 96, 98, 102, 104

Tamlaght estate: Tamlaght O'Crilly LY 18; 102, 107

Tamlaght female Sunday school: Tamlaght O'Crilly LY 18; 142

Tamlaght Finlagan old church (see Drumacarney): Tamlaght Finlagan LY 25; 100

Tamlaght Finlagan ph: Aghanloo LY 11; 1, 3, 7, 10, 23–24

Tamlaght Finlagan ph: Balteagh LY 9; 1, 20, 44

Tamlaght Finlagan ph: Banagher LY 30; 1, 103

Tamlaght Finlagan ph: Bovevagh LY 25; 4, 22

Tamlaght Finlagan ph: Clondermot LY 34; 72

Tamlaght Finlagan ph: Cumber LY 28; 6, 14, 22, 68, 70, 86

Tamlaght Finlagan ph: Desertegney DL 38; 26

Tamlaght Finlagan ph: Desertoghill LY 27; 3, 15

Tamlaght Finlagan ph: Drumachose LY 9; 79, 83–84, 86, 88, 90

Tamlaght Finlagan ph: Faughanvale LY 36; 3, 10, 60

Tamlaght Finlagan ph: Magilligan LY 11; 82, 87, 97–98, 124

Tamlaght Finlagan schools: Tamlaght Finlagan LY 25; 90–91, 104

Tamlaght Finlagan td: Magilligan LY 11; 110

Tamlaght flax mill: Tamlaght Finlagan LY 25; 121-22

Tamlaght flax mill: Tamlaght TE 20; 97

Tamlaght fort: Magilligan LY 11; 91 -92, 127

Tamlaght fort [I]: Tamlaght Finlagan LY 25; 110

Tamlaght fort [II]: Tamlaght Finlagan LY 25; 113

Tamlaght giant's grave: Tamlaght Finlagan LY 25; 90, 110

Tamlaght Glebe House (see Hervey Hill): Tamlaght O'Crilly LY 18; 91

Tamlaght graveyard: Tamlaght Finlagan LY 25; 112

Tamlaght graveyard: Tamlaght O'Crilly LY 18; 124

Tamlaght male Sunday school: Tamlaght O'Crilly LY 18; 143

Tamlaght meeting house: Kildress TE 20; 59–61

Tamlaght meeting house: Tamlaght Finlagan LY 25; 90

Tamlaght meeting house: Tamlaght O'Crilly LY 18; 89, 105, 107

Tamlaght national school: Tamlaght Finlagan LY 25; 79–80

Tamlaght O'Crilly abbey: Maghera LY 18; 10, 38

Tamlaght O'Crilly chapel of ease: Kilrea LY 27; 125

Tamlaght O'Crilly church: Kilrea LY 27; 111

Tamlaght O'Crilly church: Maghera LY 18; 10

Tamlaght O'Crilly old church: Maghera LY 18; 38

Tamlaght O'Crilly ph: Ballyscullion LY 6; 54

Tamlaght O'Crilly ph: Desertoghill LY 27; 1, 6, 10–11, 15, 18

Tamlaght O'Crilly ph: Kilrea LY 27; 104, 106, 111–13, 117, 119, 126

Tamlaght O'Crilly ph: Maghera LY 18; 17–18, 64, 67, 75–76

Tamlaght O'Crilly ph: Misc. LY 31; 127

Tamlaght O'Crilly ph: Racavan AM 13; 103

Tamlaght O'Crilly ph: Termoneeny LY 6; 121–22, 125, 129

Tamlaght old church: Tamlaght O'Crilly LY 18; 82, 89, 92, 101, 118, 124–25, 135

Tamlaght ph: Artrea TE 20; 6

Tamlaght ph: Ballinderry TE 20; 11

Tamlaght ph: Magilligan LY 11; 89

Tamlaght ph: Tamlaght TE 20; 73

Tamlaght school: Aghadowey LY 22; 19–20

Tamlaght school: Kildress TE 20; 60

Tamlaght school: Rasharkin AM 23; 136

Tamlaght school: Tamlaght Finlagan LY 25; 96

Tamlaght school: Tamlaght O'Crilly LY 18; 88, 102, 141, 143

Tamlaght Sunday school: Tamlaght Finlagan LY 25; 96

Tamlaght td: Aghadowey LY 22; 4, 11, 13

Tamlaght td: Ardclinis AM 13; 5

Tamlaght td: Aughnamullen MN 40; 76

Tamlaght td: Clogher TE 5; 32, 36, 45

Tamlaght td: Drumachose LY 9; 107

Tamlaght td: Drummaul AM 19; 89–91

Tamlaght td: Magilligan LY 11; 83, 85, 88, 91, 95, 101, 116, 126–29, 135

Tamlaght td: Tamlaght Finlagan LY 25; 80, 83, 86, 90, 93, 112, 118, 123

Tamlaght td: Tamlaght TE 20; 82, 94, 96–97, 100

Tamlaght td: Templecarn DL 39; 164

Tamlaght village (see also Church Town): Tamlaght O'Crilly LY 18; 102

Tamlaght village: Tamlaght O'Crilly LY 18; 82, 88, 92, 94, 102, 106, 109–10, 135–36

Tamlaght, name of: Tamlaght O'Crilly LY 18; 94

Tamlaghtard (see also Magilligan): Aghanloo LY 11; 7

Tamlaghtard abbey: Magilligan LY 11; 103

Tamlaghtard church: Magilligan LY 11; 103, 143

Tamlaghtard ph: Magilligan LY 11; 96–97

Tamlaghtard td: Magilligan LY 11; 93

Tamlaghtduff bogs: Ballyscullion LY 6; 70

Tamlaghtduff td: Ballyscullion LY 6; 63–64, 77–78

Tamlaghtmore House: Killyman TE 20; 67

Tamlaghtmore school: Connor AM 19; 28

Tamlaghtmore school: Killyman TE 20; 67

Tamlaghtmore td: Duneane AM 19; 123

Tamlat bog: Tyholland MN 40; 174

Tammin (see Tamin): Ahoghill AM 23; 28

Tamna district: Blaris AM 8; 73

Tamnabrean td: Donaghedy TE 5; 92

Tamnaclare td: Donaghedy TE 5; 92

Tamnacleese (see Tamnadeese)

Tamnacrum td: Donaghmore DL 39; 39

Tamnadeese (Tamnadace) td: Magherafelt LY 6; 91, 93, 95, 107, 112

Tamnadeese fort: Magherafelt LY 6; 93, 107

Tamnaderry (Tamnyderry) td: Duneane AM 19; 108

Tamnaderry Castle: Duneane AM 19; 120

Tamnaderry cave [I]: Duneane AM 19; 108, 120

Tamnaderry cave [II]: Duneane AM 19; 120

Tamnaderry fort: Duneane AM 19; 108
Tamnaderry school: Duneane AM 19; 126
Tamnaderry td: Duneane AM 19; 123
Tamnadoey fort [I]: Desertlyn LY 31; 44
Tamnadoey fort [II]: Desertlyn LY 31; 44
Tamnaficarbet td: Seagoe AH 1; 110
Tamnafiglassin td: Seagoe AH 1; 110
Tamnagh fort: Banagher LY 30; 80
Tamnagh glen: Banagher LY 30; 24
Tamnagh hill: Ematris MN 40; 115
Tamnagh House. Banagher LY 30; 32
Tamnagh House: Ematris MN 40; 115
Tamnagh Lodge: Banagher LY 30; 30, 59
Tamnagh Lodge: Cumber LY 28; 80
Tamnagh Lodge: Faughanvale LY 36; 4
Tamnagh quarry: Banagher LY 30; 128
Tamnagh school: Ardstraw TE 5; 13
Tamnagh td: Banagher LY 30; 22–23, 60–62, 72, 80,
    107–10, 113, 120, 125, 128, 130–31
Tamnagh wood: Banagher LY 30; 125
Tamnaghbready td: Donaghedy TE 5; 92
Tamnaghlawn (see Tonaghbane): Killdrumsherdan
    CN 40; 33
Tamnaharry td: Clonallan DN 3; 1–2
Tamnaherin (Tamnierin) td: Cumber LY 28; 45, 47,
    49, 60, 65, 75, 98, 103, 106–07
Tamnaherin building quarries: Cumber LY 28; 106
Tamnaherin hill: Cumber LY 28; 45
Tamnaherin hill: Faughanvale LY 36; 3
Tamnaherin lime quarry: Cumber LY 28; 106
Tamnaherin school: Cumber LY 28; 26, 74–75
Tamnaherin wood: Cumber LY 28; 103
Tamnakeary td: Donaghedy TE 5; 92
Tamnakeerin (see Tamnaherin): Cumber LY 28; 45
Tamnalanan (see Tamnylennan): Tamlaght TE 20;
    89
Tamnalannan (see Tamnylennan): Tamlaght TE 20;
    135
Tamnamoney (Tamnamony) td: Macosquin LY 22;
    81
Tamnamoney House: Macosquin LY 22; 81, 101
Tamnamore (see Tamnymore): Clondermot LY 34;
    80
Tamnamore (see Tamnymore): Cumber LY 28; 60
Tamnamore fort: Kilmore AH 1; 73
Tamnamore td: Kilmore AH 1; 69, 71, 73
Tamnareagh (see Tamnyreagh): Cumber LY 28; 60
Tamnatuska rock: Artrea LY 6; 9, 34
Tamnavelton chapel: Kilmore AH 1; 63, 73
Tamnavelton hill: Kilmore AH 1; 61
Tamnavelton td: Kilmore AH 1; 67, 71–73
Tamnawood female school: Clonleigh DL 39; 4
Tamnawood male school: Clonleigh DL 39; 4
Tamnawood td: Clonleigh DL 39; 12, 198
Tamnemore (see Tamnymore): Cumber LY 28; 56

Tamney (see Tamnagh): Banagher LY 30; 59
Tamney: Clondavaddog DL 38; 4–8
Tamney lough: Clondavaddog DL 38; 3, 8
Tamney lough: Killygarvan DL 38; 36
Tamney school: Clondavaddog DL 38; 7
Tamney Sunday school: Clondavaddog DL 38; 7
Tamney, John: Maghera LY 18; 58
Tamniagon (see Tamnyagan): Banagher LY 30; 23
Tamniaran (see Tamniarin): Banagher LY 30; 22
Tamniaran beetling mills: Ballyscullion LY 6; 48
Tamniaran td: Ballyscullion LY 6; 48, 67, 77
Tamniarin (Tamnyarn) td: Dungiven LY 15; 3, 9, 22,
    27, 44–45, 50, 63–65, 74, 86–88, 92
Tamniarin bog: Dungiven LY 15; 95
Tamniarin bridge: Dungiven LY 15; 11, 52
Tamniarin cave: Banagher LY 30; 2
Tamniarin druidical remains: Dungiven LY 15; 44
Tamniarin flax mill: Dungiven LY 15; 9
Tamniarin fort: Banagher LY 30; 2
Tamniarin fort: Dungiven LY 15; 44, 93
Tamniarin graveyard: Dungiven LY 15; 41, 54, 101
Tamniarin mountain: Dungiven LY 15; 1
Tamniarin old graveyard: Dungiven LY 15; 93
Tamniarin school: Dungiven LY 15; 117–18
Tamniarin td: Banagher LY 30; 2, 22
Tamniarn (see Tamniarin)
Tamnyagan (Tamneyaghan) td: Banagher LY 30; 13,
    22–23, 35–36, 61–62, 86, 95, 100, 107, 109–10,
    114, 120, 125, 128, 131
Tamnyagan fort: Banagher LY 30; 46, 75
Tamnyagan standing stone: Banagher LY 30; 46
Tamnyaghan (see Tamnyagan): Banagher LY 30; 35
Tamnyaron (see Tamniarin): Banagher LY 30; 2
Tamnyasker (see Tamnyaskey): Misc. LY 31; 143
Tamnyaskey bog: Kilcronaghan LY 31; 78
Tamnyaskey fort: Kilcronaghan LY 31; 86
Tamnyaskey td: Kilcronaghan LY 31; 73, 84–85,
    143
Tamnybrack cashel: Racavan AM 13; 104
Tamnybrack cove: Racavan AM 13; 102
Tamnybrack Danish fences: Finvoy AM 23; 76
Tamnybrack td: Racavan AM 13; 101–02
Tamnyerin (see Tamnaherin): Cumber LY 28; 75
Tamnylennan td: Tamlaght TE 20; 89, 113, 135
Tamnymartin td: Maghera LY 18; 53
Tamnymore (Tamneymore) td: Errigal LY 27; 66,
    75, 83–84, 88–89, 91–92
Tamnymore Castle: Clondermot LY 34; 49
Tamnymore dispensary: Cumber LY 28; 15, 25–26,
    32, 34, 57, 79–80
Tamnymore female school: Cumber LY 28; 74
Tamnymore fort: Errigal LY 27; 42, 66
Tamnymore giant's grave: Errigal LY 27; 44, 76
Tamnymore male school: Cumber LY 28; 74
Tamnymore moss: Blaris AM 8; 22

Tamnymore quarry: Cumber LY 28; 106

Tamnymore school: Cumber LY 28; 26, 34, 75–76, 79

Tamnymore standing stone: Aghadowey LY 22; 32

Tamnymore standing stone: Errigal LY 27; 45, 66, 78

Tamnymore td: Banagher LY 30; 107

Tamnymore td: Clondermot LY 34; 38, 57, 68, 72, 74, 76, 80, 111–13, 120, 128, 133

Tamnymore td: Cumber LY 28; 56, 60, 65, 92, 98, 103, 106–07

Tamnymore wood: Cumber LY 28; 103

Tamnymullan bog: Maghera LY 18; 56–58, 64

Tamnymullan fort: Maghera LY 18; 62

Tamnymullan td: Maghera LY 18; 12, 37, 64

Tamnymullen (see Tamnymullan): Maghera LY 18; 12

Tamnymullin (see Tamnymullan): Maghera LY 18; 58

Tamnyrankin fort [I]: Desertoghill LY 27; 26

Tamnyrankin fort [II]: Desertoghill LY 27; 26

Tamnyrankin fort [III]: Desertoghill LY 27; 26

Tamnyrankin fort [IV]: Desertoghill LY 27; 26

Tamnyrankin fort [V]: Desertoghill LY 27; 26

Tamnyrankin fort [VI]: Desertoghill LY 27; 26

Tamnyrankin td: Desertoghill LY 27; 7, 19, 25, 28

Tamnyreagh giant's grave [I]: Cumber LY 28; 38–39, 44

Tamnyreagh giant's grave [II]: Cumber LY 28; 39

Tamnyreagh school: Cumber LY 28; 26, 34, 74–75, 79

Tamnyreagh standing stones: Cumber LY 28; 39, 43

Tamnyreagh td: Cumber LY 28; 37, 44, 60, 65, 81–82, 98, 103, 106–09

Tamnyreagh td: Faughanvale LY 36; 58

Tamnyvane fort: Aghagallon AM 21; 14

Tamnyvane td: Aghagallon AM 21; 3

Tampulanaffrin old church: Cleenish FH 14; 19–20

Tampulanaffrin td: Cleenish FH 14; 20, 30

Tampulmoile (see Templemoyle)

Tampulmoyle (see Templemoyle)

Tamybuck td: Racavan AM 13; 89

Tamyokey (see Tannyoky): Ballymore AH 1; 10

Tanaghmore (see Tonaghmore): Magherally DN 12; 112

Tananagh (see Tamnagh): Banagher LY 30; 72

Tanderagee: Ballymore AH 1; 1, 3–8, 10–18

Tanderagee: Blaris AM 8; 5, 16, 51, 88

Tanderagee: Cumber LY 28; 66

Tanderagee: Drumcree AH 1; 36

Tanderagee: Kilmore AH 1; 60, 63, 67–69, 71–74

Tanderagee: Loughgilly AH 1; 84

Tanderagee: Mullaghbrack AH 1; 94, 96

Tanderagee: Seagoe AH 1; 107

Tanderagee: Shankill AH 1; 113

Tanderagee Castle: Ballymore AH 1; 1, 3–5

Tanderagee chapel (M): Ballymore AH 1; 8

Tanderagee chapel (PWM): Ballymore AH 1; 3

Tanderagee chapel (WM): Ballymore AH 1; 3, 8

Tanderagee church: Ballymore AH 1; 1, 3, 8

Tanderagee corn mill: Ballymore AH 1; 3

Tanderagee dispensary: Ballymore AH 1; 4, 9, 11

Tanderagee flax mill: Ballymore AH 1; 6

Tanderagee flour mill: Ballymore AH 1; 3

Tanderagee fort: Banagher LY 30; 46

Tanderagee Glebe House: Ballymore AH 1; 3, 10, 12, 15

Tanderagee hill: Ballymore AH 1; 1

Tanderagee infant school: Ballymore AH 1; 4, 9

Tanderagee male and female school: Ballymore AH 1; 9

Tanderagee Manor House: Ballymore AH 1; 4

Tanderagee meeting house: Ballymore AH 1; 3, 8

Tanderagee police station: Ballymore AH 1; 1

Tanderagee private school [I]: Ballymore AH 1; 11

Tanderagee private school [II]: Ballymore AH 1; 11

Tanderagee school [I]: Ballymore AH 1; 11

Tanderagee school [II]: Ballymore AH 1; 11

Tandragee td: Clones FH 4; 26

Taniwal td: Kinawley FH 4; 121

Tannabwee td: Galloon FH 4; 94–95

Tannagh td: Drumcree AH 1; 29

Tannaghbawn (see Tonaghbane): Killdrumsherdan CN 40; 33

Tannaghmore (Tanaghmore) td: Drummaul AM 19; 90

Tannaghmore chapel: Shilvodan AM 19; 127, 129, 131–33, 137–38

Tannaghmore cove: Shilvodan AM 19; 136

Tannaghmore forts: Drummaul AM 19; 78

Tannaghmore forts: Shilvodan AM 19; 137

Tannaghmore graveyard: Shilvodan AM 19; 135

Tannaghmore North td: Shankill AH 1; 115–16

Tannaghmore school: Shankill AH 1; 115–16

Tannaghmore school: Shilvodan AM 19; 132, 136–38

Tannaghmore Sunday school: Shilvodan AM 19; 137

Tannaghmore td: Shilvodan AM 19; 131, 135, 137

Tannaghmore West td: Seagoe AH 1; 109

Tannaghmore woods: Shilvodan AM 19; 129

Tannarragh corn mill: Dromore TE 5; 101

Tannarragh td: Dromore TE 5; 101

Tannyballydonnell td: Blaris DN 12; 41

Tannybrannon (Tannybrannan) td: Ahoghill AM 23; 42

Tannybrannon school: Ahoghill AM 23; 22, 42, 46

Tannybrannon Sunday school: Ahoghill AM 23; 46

Tannyoky meeting house: Ballymore AH 1; 10, 18

Tannyoky td: Ballymore AH 1; 9, 12–13, 18

Tanrego (Sligo): Cumber LY 28; 66
Tantybulk td: Galloon FH 4; 95
Tanvally corn mill: Annaclone DN 12; 14
Taper Lenagh stream: Templecorran AM 26; 94, 125
Taper Length (see Taper Lenagh): Templecorran AM 26; 94
Tapla chapel: Donaghmoyne MN 40; 107
Tapla graveyard: Donaghmoyne MN 40; 107
Tappit (see Toppit)
Tara (Meath): Drumachose LY 9; 94
Tara (Tarrah) td: Ballyphilip DN 7; 7
Tara: Cumber LY 28; 63
Tara bay: Witter DN 7; 125
Tara td: Misc. DN 17; 125
Tara td: Witter DN 7; 125–26
Tarah (see Tara)
Tardree hill: Connor AM 19; 19
Tardree hill: Kirkinriola AM 23; 102
Tardree quarry: Doagh AM 29; 79
Tardree quarry: Donegore AM 29; 119
Tardree quarry: Nilteen AM 35; 101
Tardree school: Connor AM 19; 27, 30
Tardree td: Antrim AM 29; 17
Tardree td: Connor AM 19; 16
Tardree td: Donegore AM 29; 119
Tardree td: Kilbride AM 29; 153
Tardree td: Muckamore AM 35; 70
Tardree td: Templepatrick AM 35; 145
Tareen td: Seagoe AH 1; 110
Tarlaghan paper manufactory: Killyman TE 20; 68
Tarleton, Rev. J.R.: Tyholland MN 40; 175
Tarleton, Rev. J.R..: Clogher TE 5; 41
Tarmacanally td: Ematris MN 40; 116
Tarmonamongan (see Termonamongan): Donegal DL 39; 42
Tarra (see Tara)
Tarragull locality: Clondermot LY 34; 34
Tarrant river: Coleraine LY 33; 97
Tartaraghan Glebe House: Tartaraghan AH 1; 121
Tartaraghan ph: Clonoe TE 20; 29
Tartaraghan ph: Drumcree AH 1; 28, 34
Tartaraghan ph: Killyman AH 1; 55
Tartaraghan ph: Kilmore AH 1; 60–61, 65, 70
Tartaraghan ph: Loughgall AH 1; 75, 78–79
Tartaraghan ph: Montiaghs AH 1; 89, 92
Tartnakilly (Tartnakelly) td: Tamlaght Finlagan LY 25; 84, 93, 113, 118, 122
Tartnakilly district: Tamlaght Finlagan LY 25; 93
Tartnakilly hill: Tamlaght Finlagan LY 25; 62
Tartnakilly tanyard: Tamlaght Finlagan LY 25; 84, 122
Tasseys Bush locality: Balteagh LY 9; 32
Tasseys hill: Balteagh LY 9; 32
Tasseys well: Balteagh LY 9; 32
Tate, Arthur: Hillsborough DN 12; 106

Tate, John: Carrickfergus AM 37; 130
Tate, John: Hillsborough DN 12; 106
Tate, Moses: Hillsborough DN 12; 105
Tate, Samuel: Magilligan LY 11; 94
Tate, Thomas: Magilligan LY 11; 94
Tate, William: Aghanloo LY 11; 32, 32
Tatecreive (see Lisnacreeve)
Tatefadda td: Donacavey TE 5; 82
Tategar school: Ematris MN 40; 117
Tategar td: Ematris MN 40; 116
Tatemoyle Lower fort: Donacavey TE 5; 84
Tatemoyle Lower school: Donacavey TE 5; 84
Tatemoyle Lower td: Donacavey TE 5; 80
Tatemoyle Middle td: Donacavey TE 5; 80, 84
Tatemoyle td: Donacavey TE 5; 68
Tatemoyle Upper mill: Donacavey TE 5; 84
Tatemoyle Upper td: Donacavey TE 5; 77, 80
Tatenacake corn mill: Currin MN 40; 90
Tatenacake lough: Currin MN 40; 86
Tatenacake school: Currin MN 40; 92
Tatenacake td: Currin MN 40; 92
Taterrewe td: Donacavey TE 5; 82
Tatimoyle (see Tattymoyle)
Tatnabuddagh (see Tattenabuddagh): Aghalurcher FH 4; 2
Tatnadaveny (Tatnadaverny) td: Clogher TE 5; 33, 37, 44, 51
Tatnadaveny bog: Clogher TE 5; 26
Tatnadaveny school: Clogher TE 5; 51
Tatnadavney (see Tatnadaveny)
Tatnadavny (see Tatnadaveny)
Tatnafinnell (Tatnafinnel) td: Clogher TE 5; 37
Tatnaheglish (see Tattenaheglish): Aghalurcher FH 4; 11
Tatnal, family: Ballinderry AM 21; 51
Tatnamona td: Aghavea FH 4; 25
Taton's corn mill: Hillsborough DN 12; 85
Tattanellan td: Aghalurcher TE 5; 1
Tattanslan td: Aghalurcher FH 4; 16
Tatteevagh td: Aghalurcher FH 4; 14
Tattenabuddagh mountain: Aghalurcher FH 4; 2
Tattenabuddagh td: Aghalurcher FH 4; 14
Tattenaglish (see Tattenaheglish): Aghalurcher FH 4; 14
Tattenaglug td: Kilmacteige SO 40; 194
Tattenaheglish school: Aghalurcher FH 4; 11
Tattenaheglish td: Aghalurcher FH 4; 14
Tattenclave (see Tattinlieve): Muckno MN 40; 162
Tattendillur (Tattindillar) td: Aghavea FH 4; 23
Tattendillur chapel: Aghalurcher FH 4; 6
Tattenweer school: Enniskillen FH 4; 83
Tattenweer td: Enniskillen FH 4; 82
Tattenweir (see Tattenweer): Enniskillen FH 4; 82
Tatteraconaghty td: Cappagh TE 5; 19
Tattimoyle (see Tattymoyle)

Tattinacre td: Ballyphilip DN 7; 8

Tattinbarr td: Aghavea FH 4; 23

Tattinclave (see Tattinlieve): Muckno MN 40; 166

Tattinderry td: Aghalurcher FH 4; 5

Tattinfree bog: Aghavea FH 4; 18

Tattinfree td: Aghavea FH 4; 23, 25

Tattinlieve flax mill: Muckno MN 40; 166

Tattinlieve td: Muckno MN 40; 162

Tatty td: Clogher TE 5; 53

Tattybrack Cottage: Aughnamullen MN 40; 71

Tattybrack td: Aughnamullen MN 40; 76

Tattyburns bog: Clogher TE 5; 26

Tattycam td: Galloon FH 4; 88, 95

Tattycarn (see Tattycam): Galloon FH 4; 88

Tattycor (Tatticor) td: Dromore TE 5; 99, 147

Tattygar td: Derryvullan FH 14; 46

Tattygar td: Galloon FH 4; 95

Tattykeel corn mill: Drumragh TE 5; 110

Tattykeel private school: Drumragh TE 5; 109

Tattykeel school: Drumragh TE 5; 109

Tattykeel td: Drumragh TE 5; 108–11

Tattykeel td: Magheraculmoney FH 14; 103

Tattykeel Upper brickworks: Magheraculmoney FH 14; 108

Tattykeel well: Drumragh TE 5; 108

Tattykeeran td: Aghavea FH 4; 23, 25

Tattymacaul forts: Derryvullan FH 14; 42

Tattymacaul td: Derryvullan FH 14; 42, 46

Tattymalmona (see Tattymulmona)

Tattymoyle (Tatemoyle) td: Donacavey TE 5; 65, 81

Tattymoyle hill: Donacavey TE 5; 62, 67

Tattymoyle Lower td: Donacavey TE 5; 77, 81, 87

Tattymoyle Middle td: Donacavey TE 5; 67, 77, 81, 87

Tattymoyle school: Donacavey TE 5; 65

Tattymoyle Upper td: Donacavey TE 5; 81, 87

Tattymulmona (Tatymulmona) td: Donacavey TE 5; 77, 80–82, 87

Tattynocle mountain: Aghalurcher FH 4; 2

Tattynocle td: Aghalurcher FH 4; 9, 14

Tattyratty td: Donacavey TE 5; 77

Tattyreagh fort: Drumragh TE 5; 109

Tattyreagh Glebe House: Drumragh TE 5; 108

Tattyreagh Glebe td: Drumragh TE 5; 109

Tattyreagh td: Aghalurcher FH 4; 14

Tattysallagh corn mill: Drumragh TE 5; 110

Tattysallagh td: Drumragh TE 5; 110

Tattyvogh graveyard: Aghalurcher FH 4; 9

Tattyvogh td: Aghalurcher FH 4; 9

Tatymoyle (see Tattymoyle)

Taughblane (Toughblane) td: Hillsborough DN 12; 89, 105

Taughblane bog: Dromore DN 12; 73

Taughblane bog: Hillsborough DN 12; 89

Taughboyne church: Taughboyne DL 39; 152–55

Taughboyne churchland: Taughboyne DL 39; 148

Taughboyne fishery: Taughboyne DL 39; 151

Taughboyne flax mills: Taughboyne DL 39; 150

Taughboyne ph: Clondermot LY 34; 74

Taughboyne ph: Clonleigh DL 39; 1–2, 7

Taughboyne ph: Convoy DL 39; 18

Taughboyne ph: Misc. DL 39; 183–89, 191, 193, 195–96

Taughboyne ph: Raphoe DL 39; 121, 129

Taughboyne ph: Raymoghy DL 39; 132–33, 140

Taughboyne schools: Misc. DL 39; 194

Taughboyne Sunday schools: Taughboyne DL 39; 150

Taughboyne td: Raymoghy DL 39; 135

Taughbuoy td: Donaghmore DL 39; 39

Tavanagh (Tavenagh) td: Drumcree AH 1; 30, 41

Tavanagh td: Errigal Truagh MN 40; 121

Tavannamore td: Clogher TE 5; 53

Taver td: Templecarn DL 39; 164

Tavinymore (Tavenamore) td: Clogher TE 5; 36

Tavnaghmore (see Tannaghmore): Shilvodan AM 19; 127

Tawnaghmore (see Tamnymore): Clondermot LY 34; 68

Tawnamore (see Tamnymore): Cumber LY 28; 92

Tawnaneille Island: Kilmacteige SO 40; 194

Tawnaneille td: Kilmacteige SO 40; 194, 197

Tawnaneille village: Kilmacteige SO 40; 194

Tawnybrack (Tawnybreak) td: Connor AM 19; 17–8, 21, 29

Tawnybrack beetling mill [I]: Connor AM 19; 22

Tawnybrack beetling mill [II]: Connor AM 19; 22

Tawnybrack beetling mill [III]: Connor AM 19; 22

Tawnybrack bleach green: Connor AM 19; 16, 21

Tawnybrack Kildare school: Connor AM 19; 26, 28

Tawnybrack national school: Connor AM 19; 26, 30

Taylor, Andrew: Tamlaght TE 20; 79

Taylor, Andrew: Termoneeny LY 6; 132

Taylor, Daniel: Coleraine LY 33; 73

Taylor, David: Lissan LY 31; 94–95, 98, 106

Taylor, Dr: Ballymoney AM 16; 17

Taylor, Edward: Ahoghill AM 23; 34

Taylor, Ellen: Doagh AM 29; 97

Taylor, family: Ahoghill AM 23; 25

Taylor, family: Ballinderry AM 21; 51

Taylor, family: Billy AM 16; 58, 68

Taylor, family: Derryaghy AM 8; 103

Taylor, family: Derrykeighan AM 16; 89

Taylor, Hugh: Tamlaght TE 20; 80, 102

Taylor, J.E.: Aghalurcher FH 4; 8, 10

Taylor, James: Ballintoy AM 24; 22

Taylor, James: Ballyrashane LY 22; 63

Taylor, James: Currin MN 40; 92

Taylor, Jane: Tamlaght TE 20; 93

Taylor, John: Billy AM 16; 69

Taylor, John: Blaris DN 12; 42–43

Taylor, John: Lambeg AM 8; 141

Taylor, Joseph: Carrickfergus AM 37; 193

Taylor, Mary: Carrickfergus AM 37; 109

Taylor, Mary: Coleraine LY 33; 146

Taylor, Mathew: Carrickfergus AM 37; 111

Taylor, Mathew: Tamlaght TE 20; 82

Taylor, Matthew: Coleraine LY 33; 67, 134, 140

Taylor, Mitchell: Carrickfergus AM 37; 195

Taylor, Mr (Derry): Mevagh DL 38; 58

Taylor, Mr: Raphoe DL 39; 124

Taylor, Mrs: Connor AM 19; 21

Taylor, P.: Killdrumsherdan CN 40; 34

Taylor, Peter: Drumballyroney DN 3; 13

Taylor, Rev.: Clogher TE 5; 40

Taylor, Rev. Edward: Kilmore AH 1; 58, 70

Taylor, Rev. Jeremy: Aghaderg DN 12; 4

Taylor, Rev. Jeremy: Ballinderry AM 21; 43–44, 56

Taylor, Rev. Jeremy: Blaris AM 8; 25

Taylor, Rev. Jeremy: Carnmoney AM 2; 93

Taylor, Rev. Jeremy: Drummaul AM 19; 53, 69

Taylor, Rev. Jeremy: Misc. DN 17; 117

Taylor, Rev. M.J.: Cappagh TE 5; 15–16

Taylor, Rev. Richard: Emlaghfad SO 40; 177

Taylor, Rev. Thomas: Enniskeen CN 40; 29

Taylor, Rev. William: Drummaul AM 19; 42, 69, 82

Taylor, Richardson: Carrickfergus AM 37; 110

Taylor, Robert: Aghaderg DN 12; 11

Taylor, Robert: Termoneeny LY 6; 132

Taylor, Samuel: Tamlaght O'Crilly LY 18; 129

Taylor, Sarah: Tamlaght TE 20; 102

Taylor, surgeon: Newry DN 3; 104

Taylor, Thomas: Ballinderry AM 21; 49

Taylor, William (Jnr): Coleraine LY 33; 146

Taylor, William (Snr): Coleraine LY 33; 146

Taylor, William: Drummaul AM 19; 91

Taylor, William: Killowen LY 33; 159

Taylor, William: Kilmore AH 1; 59

Taylor, William: Macosquin LY 22; 119

Taylor, William [I]: Termoneeny LY 6; 132

Taylor, William [II]: Termoneeny LY 6; 132

Taylorstown hill: Ballyscullion AM 19; 2

Taylorstown meeting house (B): Ballyscullion AM
19; 8

Taylorstown meeting house (P): Ballyscullion AM
19; 1, 3, 6, 8, 12

Taylorstown North meeting house (P): Ballyscullion
AM 19; 15

Taylorstown North school: Ballyscullion AM 19;
13–15

Taylorstown North Sunday school: Ballyscullion
AM 19; 15

Taylorstown North td: Ballyscullion AM 19; 14

Taylorstown Park school: Duneane AM 19; 124

Taylorstown school: Ballyscullion AM 19; 7

Taylorstown South school: Ballyscullion AM 19;
12–15

Taylorstown South Sunday school: Ballyscullion
AM 19; 15

Taylorstown td: Ballyscullion AM 19; 3, 5–6, 10,
13–14

Taylorstown village: Ballyscullion AM 19; 1, 3, 5,
12

Tead td: Magheraculmoney FH 14; 113

Teagh school: Ballyclog TE 20; 16

Teague, W.E.: Hillsborough DN 12; 105

Teaguy (see Teagy): Tartaraghan AH 1; 122

Teagy female school: Tartaraghan AH 1; 118–19

Teagy school: Tartaraghan AH 1; 117, 119, 122

Teaheny td: Clogher TE 5; 53

Tearogearye (see Tirgracey): Muckamore AM 35; 82

Tebb, R.: Drumcree AH 1; 37

Teca church: Aghanloo LY 11; 7

Teca, St: Aghanloo LY 11; 7–8

Techeny td: Clogher TE 5; 36

Tedavnet (see Tydavnet)

Tedlie, John: Clondermot LY 34; 37, 78–80, 104

Tedlie, Thomas: Clondermot LY 34; 79

Teeavan (Teeavin) td: Banagher LY 30; 13, 22, 31,
35, 48, 57, 61–62, 78–79, 85, 95–96, 107,
109–10, 112–13, 120, 125, 128, 130–32

Teeavan fort: Banagher LY 30; 51, 92

Teeavan graveyard [I]: Banagher LY 30; 51, 92

Teeavan graveyard [II]: Banagher LY 30; 52, 86–87

Teeavan hill: Banagher LY 30; 51, 92

Teeavan monument: Banagher LY 30; 56

Teeavan quarry: Banagher LY 30; 128

Teeavan school: Banagher LY 30; 74, 111

Teeavan standing stone: Banagher LY 30; 86

Teeavan stone house: Banagher LY 30; 52, 87

Teeavan td: Dungiven LY 15; 45–46, 92

Teeaven (see Teeavan)

Teebaun td: Cleenish FH 14; 30

Teecloy (see Tecloy): Finvoy AM 23; 77

Teehirin (see Tirharon): Raymoghy DL 39; 141

Teeling bay: Glencolumbkille DL 39; 64

Teeling bay: Kilbarron DL 39; 78

Teeling district: Glencolumbkille DL 39; 64–65

Teeling, family: Lambeg AM 8; 135

Teeling, Luke: Blaris AM 8; 27

Teeling, Luke: Derryaghy AM 8; 111

Teemack Warden (see Derryork): Dungiven LY 15;
61

Teenacht (see Teenaght): Cumber LY 28; 67

Teenagh (see Teenaght): Cumber LY 28; 71

Teenaght barony: Faughanvale LY 36; 4

Teenaght district: Cumber LY 28; 83

Teenaght td: Banagher LY 30; 112

Teenaght td: Cumber LY 28; 47, 67, 71, 98, 103–04,
106–08

Teenaght wood: Cumber LY 28; 104

Teenlaur village: Kilmacteige SO 40; 196

Teer td: Drummully FH 4; 39

Teer, John: Dromore DN 12; 77

Teeraffy td: Galloon FH 4; 95

Teeralton td: Enniskillen FH 4; 74, 82

Teeratton (see Teeralton): Enniskillen FH 4; 74

Teeravally glebe: Killesher FH 14; 86

Teeravally td: Kinawley FH 4; 110

Teeravree glebe: Killesher FH 14; 86

Teeravree td: Kinawley FH 4; 110

Teercauns td: Devenish FH 14; 58

Teerconnell td: Devenish FH 14; 59

Teerekelly (see Tierkelly): Drumballyroney DN 3; 16

Teerfergus td: Drumballyroney DN 3; 18

Teerhernin Island: Lough Swilly DL 38; 117

Teeriwinney (see Tiriwinny): Magheraculmoney FH 14; 112

Teerluaghan (see Tirloughan): Lough Swilly DL 38; 116

Teermakspirid td: Magheraculmoney FH 14; 112–13

Teermoan (see Tremone): Lough Swilly DL 38; 141

Teeroddy (see Tirroddy)

Teerogannon school: Belleek FH 14; 6

Teershilly td: Ballyphilip DN 7; 7

Teerygory (see Tirygory)

Teeshan bog: Ahoghill AM 23; 28

Teevalough abbey: Belleek FH 14; 4

Teevalough Glebe td: Belleek FH 14; 4

Teevoge Nee Divenny, woman named: Kilteevoge DL 39; 111

Tehallan (see Tyholland)

Teirear (see Tircar)

Telayden bridge: Donagh MN 40; 99

Telford, William: Carrickfergus AM 37; 117

Temain td: Balteagh LY 9; 34, 39, 45

Tempanroe corn mill: Killyman TE 20; 67

Tempest, H.V.: Dunaghy AM 13; 26

Temple cave: Dunboe LY 11; 78

Temple Conic church: Drumachose LY 9; 91

Temple Gormachan ph: Templecorran AM 26; 82

Temple Ichevecham church: Templecorran AM 26; 108, 112, 119

Temple Ichevecham graveyard: Templecorran AM 26; 112, 119

Temple McMillighan ruin: Drumhome DL 39; 58

Temple, John: Loughgall AH 1; 81

Templeastragh graveyard: Ballintoy AM 24; 12

Templeastragh old church: Ballintoy AM 24; 12, 18–19, 31

Templeastragh td: Ballintoy AM 24; 17, 31–32

Templecarn Glebe House: Templecarn DL 39; 158

Templecarn hibernian schools: Templecarn DL 39; 161, 167–68

Templecarn mills: Templecarn FH 14; 119

Templecarn new chapel: Templecarn DL 39; 158

Templecarn new school: Templecarn DL 39; 158

Templecarn parish school:Templecarn DL 39; 161

Templecarn ph: Belleek FH 14; 1

Templecarn ph: Clogher TE 5; 41

Templecarn ph: Drumkeeran FH 14; 62, 65

Templecarn ph: Killymard DL 39; 95

Templecarn ph: Magheraculmoney FH 14; 107

Templecarn ph: Templecarn FH 14; 118

Templecarn private school: Templecarn DL 39; 161

Templecarne (see Templecarn)

Templecormac (Templecormack) td: Ballinderry AM 21; 42, 52

Templecormac church: Ballinderry AM 21; 42–43, 52

Templecormac graveyard: Ballinderry AM 21; 52

Templecormac td: Aghagallon AM 21; 5

Templecorran church (see also Ballycarry): Templecorran AM 26; 82

Templecorran church: Ballynure AM 32; 51

Templecorran church: Kilroot AM 26; 72

Templecorran forts: Templecorran AM 26; 113–14

Templecorran manor: Templecorran AM 26; 91, 99, 129

Templecorran ph: Ballynure AM 32; 36, 38–39, 45, 47, 50–52

Templecorran ph: Carrickfergus AM 37; 1, 71, 100, 142, 151, 160

Templecorran ph: Glynn AM 26; 1, 5, 23, 29–30, 39, 42

Templecorran ph: Island Magee AM 10; 14–15, 25, 27, 32, 35, 45, 48, 65–66, 75, 85, 104

Templecorran ph: Kilroot AM 26; 57–58, 61, 64–65, 67–68, 71–73, 77, 79

Templecorran ph: Misc. AM 10; 129

Templecorran ph: Raloo AM 32; 98, 118

Templecorran rectory: Templecorran AM 26; 108, 119

Templecorran schools: Templecorran AM 26; 99–100

Templecorran td: Island Magee AM 10; 31

Templecotton td: Island Magee AM 10; 97

Temple-Crom (see Mount Stewart): Misc. DN 17; 121

Templeffin (Templeoffin) td: Island Magee AM 10; 69, 99

Templeffin lighthouse: Island Magee AM 10; 99

Templeffin private school: Island Magee AM 10; 69, 97

Temple-f-Gormachan church: Templecorran AM 26; 108, 112–13, 120

Temple-f-Gormachan graveyard: Templecorran AM 26; 113

Templegowram (see Templegowran): Newry DN 3; 108

Templegowran graveyard: Newry DN 3; 108

Templegowran House: Newry DN 3; 108

Templehouse Castle: Emlaghfad SO 40; 182

Templehouse demesne: Emlaghfad SO 40; 176, 182

Templehouse lough: Emlaghfad SO 40; 176–77

Templehouse Mansion: Emlaghfad SO 40; 181

Templehouse td: Killoran and Kilvarnct SO 40; 184

Templelowe (see Templetown): Clondermot LY 34; 38

Templemaghery church: Magheraculmoney FH 14; 103, 105

Templemore district: Clondermot LY 34; 59–60

Templemore monastery: Ahoghill AM 23; 14

Templemore ph: Banagher LY 30; 101, 103–04

Templemore ph: Clondermot LY 34; 1, 3–4, 7–8, 10, 13–14, 17–18, 28, 30, 39, 66, 68, 76, 81, 83, 94, 102

Templemore ph: Cumber LY 28; 28, 66

Templemore ph: Errigal LY 27; 42

Templemore ph: Faughanvale LY 36; 32, 47–48, 50, 52, 56–59

Templemore ph: Lough Swilly DL 38; 144

Templemore ph: Misc. DL 39; 184

Templemore ph: Misc. LY 36; 105–06

Templemore ph: Muff DL 38; 80

Templemore ph: Tamlaght Finlagan LY 25; 97

Templemore well: Bovevagh LY 25; 18

Templemore, Lord: Mintiaghs DL 38; 64, 66

Templemoyle abbey: Connor AM 19; 18

Templemoyle Agricultural Seminary: Drumachose LY 9; 104

Templemoyle Agricultural Seminary: Faughanvale LY 36; 6–8, 14, 18, 22–27, 34, 36–37, 39–47, 67

Templemoyle bog: Banagher LY 30; 46

Templemoyle bogs: Lough Swilly DL 38; 135

Templemoyle church: Banagher LY 30; 12, 39, 41, 56–57, 70–71, 92

Templemoyle church: Bovevagh LY 25; 6, 50–51

Templemoyle church: Cleenish FH 14; 19–20

Templemoyle church: Derryvullan FH 14; 41

Templemoyle church: Dromara DN 12; 63, 65–66

Templemoyle church: Faughanvale LY 36; 13–14

Templemoyle corn mill: Faughanvale LY 36; 22, 98

Templemoyle flax mill [I]: Banagher LY 30; 129

Templemoyle flax mill [II]: Banagher LY 30; 129

Templemoyle fort: Bovevagh LY 25; 50

Templemoyle graveyard: Ahoghill AM 23; 24

Templemoyle graveyard: Ballyclug AM 23; 63

Templemoyle graveyard: Ballynascreen LY 31; 9, 23

Templemoyle graveyard: Ballyscullion AM 19; 10

Templemoyle graveyard: Banagher LY 30; 51, 94

Templemoyle graveyard: Connor AM 19; 18

Templemoyle graveyard: Derryvullan FH 14; 42

Templemoyle graveyard: Macosquin LY 22; 84–85

Templemoyle House: Banagher LY 30; 31

Templemoyle House: Connor AM 19; 21

Templemoyle House: Faughanvale LY 36; 39

Templemoyle lime quarry [I]: Banagher LY 30; 129

Templemoyle lime quarry [II]: Banagher LY 30; 129

Templemoyle locality: Clondermot LY 34; 33

Templemoyle mill: Clondermot LY 34; 3

Templemoyle school: Banagher LY 30; 33, 111–12

Templemoyle school: Drumachose LY 9; 107

Templemoyle standing stone: Banagher LY 30; 45–46, 56

Templemoyle td: Banagher LY 30; 9, 22–24, 32, 35–37, 39, 46, 48, 57–58, 61–62, 68–69, 72, 76, 84, 88–89, 92, 95, 97–99, 107, 110, 113–14, 120, 125, 129–31

Templemoyle td: Bovevagh LY 25; 6, 47, 51, 59–61

Templemoyle td: Dungiven LY 15; 10, 84

Templemoyle td: Faughanvale LY 36; 16–17, 41, 53, 58, 62–63, 69, 78, 90, 96

Templemoyle wood: Banagher LY 30; 52, 125

Templemoyle wood: Faughanvale LY 36; 90

Templeoughter td: Tickmacrevan AM 13; 134

Templepatrick: Ballylinny AM 32; 14, 16, 25, 30

Templepatrick: Ballymartin AM 2; 4, 6, 17

Templepatrick: Ballynure AM 32; 45

Templepatrick: Ballyrobert AM 2; 21

Templepatrick: Ballywalter AM 2; 29–30

Templepatrick: Carnmoney AM 2; 54, 85

Templepatrick: Doagh AM 29; 70

Templepatrick: Donegore AM 29; 108, 115, 119, 131–32, 134

Templepatrick: Drummaul AM 19; 70

Templepatrick: Killead AM 35; 16

Templepatrick: Mallusk AM 2; 110–11

Templepatrick: Nilteen AM 35; 85–86, 90, 97, 102–03

Templepatrick: Templepatrick AM 35; 108–09, 112–15, 117, 123, 126, 131, 134, 137–42, 144, 147–50, 152

Templepatrick: Umgall AM 35; 156–58

Templepatrick bridge: Nilteen AM 35; 85, 90, 101

Templepatrick bridge: Templepatrick AM 35; 111

Templepatrick Castle: Ballymartin AM 2; 5

Templepatrick Castle: Mallusk AM 2; 114

Templepatrick Castle: Templepatrick AM 35; 108, 116, 123

Templepatrick church: Ballymartin AM 2; 7

Templepatrick church: Ballywalter AM 2; 30

Templepatrick church: Mallusk AM 2; 115

Templepatrick church: Templepatrick AM 35; 109, 118–19, 133, 138, 140–43

Templepatrick church: Umgall AM 35; 157–58

Templepatrick cove [I]: Templepatrick AM 35; 130, 137

Templepatrick cove [II]: Templepatrick AM 35; 149

Templepatrick fort: Killead AM 35; 33

Templepatrick fort: Templepatrick AM 35; 152

Templepatrick Glebe House: Templepatrick AM 35; 138

Templepatrick graveyard: Templepatrick AM 35; 108, 116, 124, 133

Templepatrick meeting house (P): Ballylinny AM 32; 17, 26

Templepatrick meeting house (P): Ballymartin AM 2; 7

Templepatrick meeting house (P): Templepatrick AM 35; 109–10, 118–19, 136, 140, 142–45, 154

Templepatrick meeting house (P): Umgall AM 35; 158

Templepatrick meeting house (U): Ballymartin AM 2; 7

Templepatrick meeting house (U): Templepatrick AM 35; 109–10, 119, 123, 132–33, 138–40, 142, 144–45

Templepatrick meeting house (U): Umgall AM 35; 158

Templepatrick meeting house: Antrim AM 29; 7

Templepatrick old church: Templepatrick AM 35; 108, 116, 145

Templepatrick old meeting house: Templepatrick AM 35; 143

Templepatrick ph: Antrim AM 29; 6, 23

Templepatrick ph: Ballymartin AM 2; 1, 3, 5, 8

Templepatrick ph: Ballyrobert AM 2; 20–21, 24

Templepatrick ph: Ballywalter AM 2; 27

Templepatrick ph: Carmavy AM 35; 1

Templepatrick ph: Carnmoney AM 2; 51, 72, 81–82

Templepatrick ph: Carrickfergus AM 37; 61, 70, 73

Templepatrick ph: Doagh AM 29; 60, 78

Templepatrick ph: Kilbride AM 29; 135

Templepatrick ph: Killead AM 35; 8–9, 20, 46

Templepatrick ph: Mallusk AM 2; 106, 109–11, 113

Templepatrick ph: Misc. AM 10; 129, 131

Templepatrick ph: Muckamore AM 35; 54, 58–59, 74

Templepatrick ph: Nilteen AM 35; 84, 87, 96, 101

Templepatrick ph: Templecorran AM 26; 115

Templepatrick ph: Templepatrick AM 35; 123

Templepatrick ph: Tullyrusk AM 21; 131

Templepatrick ph: Umgall AM 35; 156–60

Templepatrick post office: Templepatrick AM 35; 109, 142

Templepatrick priory: Templepatrick AM 35; 125

Templepatrick quarry: Donegore AM 29; 102

Templepatrick school: Templepatrick AM 35; 109, 134, 136, 142, 153–54

Templepatrick singing school: Templepatrick AM 35; 122

Templepatrick Sunday school [I]: Templepatrick AM 35; 136, 154

Templepatrick Sunday school [II]: Templepatrick AM 35; 136, 154

Templepatrick td: Templepatrick AM 35; 108

Templepatrick temple: Mallusk AM 2; 114

Templepatrick temple: Templepatrick AM 35; 132

Templepatrick well: Templepatrick AM 35; 108, 125

Templepatrick widows' house: Templepatrick AM 35; 109, 137, 139, 142

Templeport ph: Tomregan FH 4; 125–26, 128

Templereagh corn mill: Donaghenry TE 20; 37

Templetate church: Tyholland MN 40; 174

Templetate td: Clones FH 4; 28

Templeton rectorage: Mallusk AM 2; 109

Templeton td: Ballylinny AM 32; 22, 30

Templeton, Baron: Drummaul AM 19; 71

Templeton, Baron: Templepatrick AM 35; 148

Templeton, family: Island Magee AM 10; 70, 86

Templeton, family: Templecorran AM 26; 117, 119

Templeton, family: Templepatrick AM 35; 109, 112, 124

Templeton, family: Umgall AM 35; 157

Templeton, George: Ballyscullion AM 19; 10

Templeton, H.R.: Templepatrick AM 35; 129

Templeton, James: Island Magee AM 10; 90

Templeton, Lord (Snr): Templepatrick AM 35; 140

Templeton, Lord: Ballymartin AM 2; 1, 5–8, 15–6

Templeton, Lord: Muckno MN 40; 164, 166–68

Templeton, Lord: Templecorran AM 26; 102

Templeton, Lord: Templepatrick AM 35; 107–11, 116–22, 130, 134–48, 150, 152–53

Templeton, Lord: Umgall AM 35; 155, 157

Templeton, Mr (Belfast): Lough Neagh AM 21; 96

Templeton, Rev. Samuel: Balteagh LY 9; 15, 44

Templeton, Robert: Island Magee AM 10; 95

Templeton, Samuel: Island Magee AM 10; 80, 85

Templeton, Thomas: Island Magee AM 10; 80, 90

Templeton, William: Ballyscullion AM 19; 10

Templeton's cairn: Island Magee AM 10; 14

Templeton's hill: Island Magee AM 10; 71

Templetown Arms: Templepatrick AM 35; 142

Templetown td: Carlingford LH 40; 57, 59

Templetown td: Clondermot LY 34; 38, 57, 60, 66, 74, 76, 112–13, 120, 128, 133

Tempo: Derrybrusk FH 4; 32–33

Tempo: Derryvullan FH 14; 44

Tempo: Donacavey TE 5; 74

Tempo: Enniskillen FH 4; 43–44, 48, 64–65, 70, 75, 77, 82

Tempo Castle: Enniskillen FH 4; 66

Tempo chapel: Derrybrusk FH 4; 31

Tempo chapel: Enniskillen FH 4; 64

Tempo church: Enniskillen FH 4; 64

Tempo mill: Enniskillen FH 4; 69

Tempo mountains: Derryvullan FH 14; 40

Tempo river: Enniskillen FH 4; 43–44, 48–49

Ten Towns manor: Misc. DN 17; 123

Tenison, Rev. Richard: Carrickfergus AM 37; 78

Tenison, Rev. Richard: Clogher TE 5; 27–28

Tenison, Thomas: Carrickfergus AM 37; 78

Tenison, W.B.: Aughnamullen MN 40; 71, 74–76

Tenison, William: Killanny MN 40; 132

Tennant, John: Carrickfergus AM 37; 76

Tennent, Emerson: Raloo AM 32; 128

Tennent, J.E.: Enniskillen FH 4; 64, 66, 77, 82

Tennent, J.T.: Aughnamullen MN 40; 76

Tennent, William: Enniskillen FH 4; 66

Tents td: Cleenish FH 14; 28, 30

Teraverty mill: Tydavnet MN 40; 173

Tereighter (see Tireighter): Cumber LY 28; 85

Tereragh barony: Misc. FH 4; 133

Terew td: Clogher TE 5; 35, 53

Tergracy (see Tirgracey): Muckamore AM 35; 76

Terherrin (see Tirharon): Raymoghy DL 39; 139

Terkeerey (see Tirkeeran): Misc. DL 39; 198

Terluaghan (see Tirloughan): Lough Swilly DL 38; 116

Termeel (see Turmeel): Dungiven LY 15; 1

Termiel (see Turmeel): Dungiven LY 15; 1

Termon Castle: Derryvullan FH 14; 38–39

Termon Magrath district: Templecarn DL 39; 163

Termon river: Drumkeeran FH 14; 63

Termon river: Templecarn FH 14; 118–19

Termonamongan ph: Donaghmore DL 39; 28–29, 35

Termonamongan ph: Donegal DL 39; 42–43

Termonamongan ph: Drumkeeran FH 14; 62

Termonamongan ph: Skirts of Urney and Ardstraw TE 5; 139

Termonamongan ph: Templecarn DL 39; 156–57

Termoneeny bog: Desertmartin LY 31; 53

Termoneeny church: Termoneeny LY 6; 121, 130

Termoneeny glebe: Tamlaght O'Crilly LY 18; 82

Termoneeny Glebe House: Tamlaght O'Crilly LY 18; 91

Termoneeny Glebe House: Termoneeny LY 6; 122, 129

Termoneeny meeting house: Termoneeny LY 6; 121–22, 125, 129–30

Termoneeny old church: Maghera LY 18; 12

Termoneeny ph: Ballyscullion LY 6; 43

Termoneeny ph: Kilcronaghan LY 31; 72, 80, 82

Termoneeny ph: Maghera LY 18; 1, 12, 15, 17, 34, 48, 67–69, 72, 75

Termoneeny ph: Magherafelt LY 6; 98

Termoneeny ph: Misc. LY 31; 111, 134

Termoneeny ph: Tamlaght O'Crilly LY 18; 91, 108

Termoneeny school: Termoneeny LY 6; 124, 128

Termoneeny Sunday school: Termoneeny LY 6; 124, 128

Termonmaguirk old church: Ballynascreen LY 31; 9, 24

Termonmaguirk ph: Ardstraw TE 5; 10

Termonmaguirk ph: Ballynascreen LY 31; 27

Termonmaguirk ph: Cappagh TE 5; 15–16, 20

Termonmaguirk ph: Clogherny TE 20; 25

Termonmaguirk ph: Desertcreat TE 20; 32

Termonmaguirk ph: Kildress TE 20; 58

Termonmaguirk ph: Killeeshil TE 20; 62

Termonmaguirk river: Pomeroy TE 20; 72

Ternamuck td: Balteagh LY 9; 14, 39

Ternan, Henry: Donacavey TE 5; 65

Ternaskea (Turnaskea) td: Errigal Keerogue TE 20; 55–57

Ternaskea fort: Errigal Keerogue TE 20; 56

Ternaskea gravel pits: Errigal Keerogue TE 20; 56

Terney Island: Belleek FH 14; 2

Teroday (see Tirroddy)

Teroddy (see Tirroddy)

Teroddy (see Tirroddy)

Terraquin td: Cappagh TE 5; 21

Terrew td: Clogher TE 5; 26, 49

Terringham, Arthur: Blaris AM 8; 87

Terrom district: Misc. SO 40; 200

Terrycaffe td: Tyholland MN 40; 174

Terrydoo Clyde fort: Balteagh LY 9; 13, 25

Terrydoo Clyde gardens: Balteagh LY 9; 31

Terrydoo Clyde mountain: Balteagh LY 9; 31

Terrydoo Clyde td: Balteagh LY 9; 13, 25, 44–45

Terrydoo school: Balteagh LY 9; 16

Terrydoo td: Balteagh LY 9; 16, 40

Terrydoo Walker old house: Balteagh LY 9; 31

Terrydoo Walker td: Balteagh LY 9; 31–32, 40, 44–45

Terrydreen (Terradreen) td: Banagher LY 30; 22–23, 35, 44, 57, 60–62, 64, 66, 107, 109–10, 120–21, 125, 129–31

Terrydreen bog: Banagher LY 30; 64

Terrydreen fort: Banagher LY 30; 65–66

Terrydreen hill: Banagher LY 30; 24

Terrydreen school: Banagher LY 30; 33, 111

Terrydreen standing stone [I]: Banagher LY 30; 46, 76

Terrydreen standing stone [II]: Banagher LY 30; 46, 76

Terrydremmond (see Terrydremont): Balteagh LY 9; 17

Terrydremont flax mills: Balteagh LY 9; 14, 41

Terrydremont North school: Balteagh LY 9; 17

Terrydremont North td: Balteagh LY 9; 17, 40, 45

Terrydremont school [I]: Balteagh LY 9; 16, 39

Terrydremont school [II]: Balteagh LY 9; 18

Terrydremont South bleach green: Balteagh LY 9; 13, 36

Terrydremont South cave: Balteagh LY 9; 27

Terrydremont South flax mills: Balteagh LY 9; 36

Terrydremont South td: Balteagh LY 9; 13, 27, 36, 40, 43, 45

Terrydremont td: Balteagh LY 9; 16, 18, 38–39, 41, 45

Terrydremount (see Terrydremont): Balteagh LY 9; 13

Terrygowan school: Drummaul AM 19; 76, 86, 92

Terrygowan td: Drummaul AM 19; 90

Terrygreeghan lough: Ballybay MN 40; 78, 81

Terrygreeghan td: Ballybay MN 40; 84

Terrygreehan (see Terrygreeghan): Ballybay MN 40; 84

Terryhoogan barrack: Ballymore AH 1; 18

Terryhoogan bridge: Ballymore AH 1; 18

Terryhoogan Lock: Ballymore AH 1; 18

Terryhoogan td: Ballymore AH 1; 8, 12, 15, 17–18

Terryin corn mill: Killdrumsherdan CN 40; 34

Terrymore hill: Kinawley FH 4; 113

Terryrone (see Tiryrone): Moville DL 38; 73

Tervoddy td: Tullyaughnish DL 38; 97

Tewkesbury Cathedral (England): Desertlyn LY 31; 37

Teyavin (see Teeavan): Banagher LY 30; 22

Thackeray, Rev. Elias: Drumachose LY 9; 51

Thackeray, Rev. Elias: Faughanvale LY 36; 29

Thackery, Rev. (Dundalk): Castletown LH 40; 61

Thackery, Rev. Major: Drumachose LY 9; 77

Thigh-na-siedur fort: Culfeightrin AM 24; 84

Thistleborough House: Camlin AM 21; 62–63, 67

Thistleworth (London): Drummaul AM 19; 70

Thoanahaig td: Cleenish FH 14; 30

Thoanardrum td: Cleenish FH 14; 30

Thoanlissderitt td: Cleenish FH 14; 30

Thoanraghee Island: Cleenish FH 14; 13, 29

Thoar McBride stone: Tullaghobegley DL 39; 172

Thoar village: Tullaghobegley DL 39; 172–73

Thomagh (see Thornoge): Banagher LY 30; 24

Thomas McKeen's cove: Ballyclug AM 23; 64

Thomas the Rhymer, seer: Misc. LY 31; 124

Thomas town: Island Magee AM 10; 48

Thomas, Griffin: Ballyscullion LY 6; 57

Thomas, Humphry: Tydavnet MN 40; 173

Thomas, Rev. Joseph: Dunboe LY 11; 66

Thomas, Richard: Ballyscullion LY 6; 57

Thomas, St: Down DN 17; 41

Thomastown (see Straid): Ballynure AM 32; 38

Thomastown school: Ardquin DN 7; 4

Thomastown td: Ardquin DN 7; 4

Thomastown td: Derrybrusk FH 4; 30, 32

Thomastown td: Misc. DN 17; 125–26

Thomkins, Alexander: Cumber LY 28; 62

Thomond (Munster): Cumber LY 28; 67

Thompson and Stewart, Messrs: Carnmoney AM 2; 91

Thompson, Acheson: Newry DN 3; 68

Thompson, Alex: Island Magee AM 10; 95

Thompson, Alexander: Culfeightrin AM 24; 53

Thompson, Alexander: Kilbride AM 29; 152

Thompson, Alexander: Misc. DL 39; 186

Thompson, Alixander: Errigal LY 27; 54

Thompson, Andrew: Drummaul AM 19; 87–88

Thompson, Ann: Aghanloo LY 11; 39

Thompson, Anna: Tamlaght TE 20; 75

Thompson, Anne: Kilwaughter AM 10; 122

Thompson, Archibald: Tamlaght TE 20; 75, 81–82, 116, 118, 120–22, 136–37

Thompson, Archy: Dunluce AM 16; 119–20

Thompson, Arthur: Enniskillen FH 4; 59

Thompson, Christiana: Enniskillen FH 4; 84

Thompson, David: Desertoghill LY 27; 20

Thompson, David: Hillsborough DN 12; 102, 107

Thompson, David: Maghera LY 18; 50, 52

Thompson, Dr (Snr): Blaris AM 8; 32, 60–61, 84–85

Thompson, Dr: Blaris DN 12; 45, 49

Thompson, Edward: Derryaghy AM 8; 96

Thompson, family: Aghagallon AM 21; 9

Thompson, family: Ballinderry AM 21; 48, 51

Thompson, family: Ballywillin AM 16; 32

Thompson, family: Banagher LY 30; 77

Thompson, family: Blaris AM 8; 21

Thompson, family: Carnmoney AM 2; 51, 76

Thompson, family: Carrickfergus AM 37; 93

Thompson, family: Culfeightrin AM 24; 59

Thompson, family: Derryaghy AM 8; 103

Thompson, family: Desertoghill LY 27; 30

Thompson, family: Dunluce AM 16; 117

Thompson, family: Ematris MN 40; 118

Thompson, family: Enniskillen FH 4; 58, 75

Thompson, family: Finvoy AM 23; 76

Thompson, family: Island Magee AM 10; 70

Thompson, family: Killagan AM 23; 84

Thompson, family: Killead AM 35; 17

Thompson, family: Kilroot AM 26; 74–75

Thompson, family: Maghera LY 18; 19, 24, 48

Thompson, family: Muckamore AM 35; 62, 72

Thompson, family: Raloo AM 32; 123

Thompson, family: Templecorran AM 26; 117, 119

Thompson, Francis: Carrickfergus AM 37; 119

Thompson, Gaddis: Blaris DN 12; 42

Thompson, George: Billy AM 16; 74

Thompson, George: Blaris DN 12; 46, 50

Thompson, George: Drumhome DL 39; 62

Thompson, George: Drummaul AM 19; 90

Thompson, H.: Newry DN 3; 100

Thompson, Henery: Tamlaght Finlagan LY 25; 118

Thompson, Henry: Clondermot LY 34; 37, 79, 104

Thompson, Henry: Faughanvale LY 36; 58

Thompson, Henry: Newry DN 3; 104

Thompson, Hugh: Aghanloo LY 11; 39
Thompson, Hugh: Banagher LY 30; 46, 76
Thompson, Hull: Derryaghy AM 8; 110
Thompson, Isaac: Blaris DN 12; 40
Thompson, J.: Aughnamullen MN 40; 71, 73
Thompson, J.: Drumcree AH 1; 39
Thompson, J.: Hillsborough DN 12; 85
Thompson, J.: Newtownards DN 7; 113
Thompson, J.: Seagoe AH 1; 109
Thompson, Jacob (Jnr): Aghanloo LY 11; 39
Thompson, Jacob (Snr): Aghanloo LY 11; 39
Thompson, James: Ballylinny AM 32; 30
Thompson, James: Ballymoney AM 16; 15–17
Thompson, James: Balteagh LY 9; 27
Thompson, James: Banagher LY 30; 47, 77–78
Thompson, James: Blaris DN 12; 46, 50
Thompson, James: Coleraine LY 33; 127
Thompson, James: Drumachose LY 9; 120–21
Thompson, James: Dungiven LY 15; 98
Thompson, James: Muckamore AM 35; 77–78
Thompson, James: Newry DN 3; 99, 104
Thompson, James [I]: Carnmoney AM 2; 78, 86
Thompson, James [I]: Carrickfergus AM 37; 129
Thompson, James [II]: Carnmoney AM 2; 83, 97, 100
Thompson, James [II]: Carrickfergus AM 37; 192
Thompson, James [III]: Carrickfergus AM 37; 195
Thompson, Jane: Ballinderry AM 21; 57
Thompson, John: Ballinderry AM 21; 49
Thompson, John: Ballyrashane LY 22; 50, 53–54, 59–60
Thompson, John: Banagher LY 30; 47, 56, 77, 79, 83–84, 100
Thompson, John: Billy AM 16; 74
Thompson, John: Carnmoney AM 2; 58, 81, 92, 102
Thompson, John: Carrickfergus AM 37; 47, 135, 138
Thompson, John: Clondermot LY 34; 77
Thompson, John: Derryaghy AM 8; 96
Thompson, John: Desertoghill LY 27; 13, 22
Thompson, John: Drumachose LY 9; 116
Thompson, John: Duneane AM 19; 117
Thompson, John: Dunluce AM 16; 119
Thompson, John: Killead AM 35; 36, 53
Thompson, John: Maghera LY 18; 45
Thompson, John: Ramoan AM 24; 109–12
Thompson, John: Skerry AM 13; 120
Thompson, John: Tamlaght Finlagan LY 25; 118
Thompson, John: Tamlaght TE 20; 75, 91, 103
Thompson, John: Templecorran AM 26; 123
Thompson, Joseph: Muckamore AM 35; 78
Thompson, Lenox: Hillsborough DN 12; 107
Thompson, Maria: Tamlaght TE 20; 75
Thompson, Martha: Carrickfergus AM 37; 99
Thompson, Mary: Aghanloo LY 11; 39

Thompson, Mary: Antrim AM 29; 59
Thompson, Mary Jane: Drummaul AM 19; 91
Thompson, Matthew: Aghanloo LY 11; 21
Thompson, Meakam: Macosquin LY 22; 102, 107
Thompson, minor: Ballynure AM 32; 46, 68
Thompson, minor: Muckamore AM 35; 62
Thompson, Miss: Carrickfergus AM 37; 149
Thompson, Miss: Clogher TE 5; 43
Thompson, Miss: Killyman TE 20; 67
Thompson, Miss: Newry DN 3; 99, 104
Thompson, Miss H.: Newry DN 3; 104
Thompson, Misses: Coleraine LY 33; 137
Thompson, Moses: Rashee AM 32; 141
Thompson, Mr (Belfast): Carnmoney AM 2; 87
Thompson, Mr (Belfast): Comber DN 7; 37–38
Thompson, Mr (Downpatrick): Ballee DN 17; 22
Thompson, Mr (Downpatrick): Dunsfort DN 17; 69
Thompson, Mr (Downpatrick): Kilmore DN 17; 90
Thompson, Mr: Banagher LY 30; 99
Thompson, Mr: Carnmoney AM 2; 48, 104
Thompson, Mr: Clogher TE 5; 53
Thompson, Mr: Kilkeel DN 3; 49
Thompson, Mr: Loughgall AH 1; 78
Thompson, Mr: Newry DN 3; 83, 100
Thompson, Mrs (Derryaghy): Blaris AM 8; 85
Thompson, Mrs: Blaris AM 8; 85
Thompson, Mrs: Blaris DN 12; 46, 50
Thompson, Mrs: Carrickfergus AM 37; 76, 150
Thompson, Mrs: Clondermot LY 34; 6, 20
Thompson, Mrs: Derryaghy AM 8; 92, 110
Thompson, Mrs A.: Newry DN 3; 93, 100, 104
Thompson, Nathaniel: Ballyrashane LY 22; 64
Thompson, Neal: Culfeightrin AM 24; 55, 63, 65, 68, 79, 81
Thompson, Neal: Ramoan AM 24; 109, 123
Thompson, Peggy: Templepatrick AM 35; 151
Thompson, R.: Aughnamullen MN 40; 75–76
Thompson, Rev.: Drumlumman CN 40; 14
Thompson, Rev.: Dunsfort DN 17; 70
Thompson, Rev.: Magheradrool DN 17; 106
Thompson, Rev. Andrew: Aghadowey LY 22; 5, 26
Thompson, Rev. Andrew: Errigal LY 27; 46, 52, 63–64
Thompson, Rev. George Robert: Artrea LY 6; 16
Thompson, Rev. J.: Blaris AM 8; 60
Thompson, Rev. John (Jnr): Carnmoney AM 2; 75, 87
Thompson, Rev. John (Snr): Carnmoney AM 2; 75
Thompson, Rev. Joseph: Carrickfergus AM 37; 71, 143, 145
Thompson, Rev. Thomas: Derryaghy AM 8; 103, 105
Thompson, Richard: Aghalee AM 21; 36
Thompson, Richard: Carrickfergus AM 37; 57, 135, 180

Thompson, Richard: Hillsborough DN 12; 107

Thompson, Richard: Raloo AM 32; 127

Thompson, Robert: Ahoghill AM 23; 50

Thompson, Robert: Blaris AM 8; 79, 82

Thompson, Robert: Bovevagh LY 25; 42

Thompson, Robert: Carnmoney AM 2; 81

Thompson, Robert: Coleraine LY 33; 72, 127

Thompson, Robert: Cumber LY 28; 39, 44

Thompson, Robert: Desertoghill LY 27; 13, 22

Thompson, Robert: Kilraghts AM 16; 133

Thompson, Robert: Macosquin LY 22; 103

Thompson, Robert: Muckamore AM 35; 62

Thompson, Robert: Ramoan AM 24; 105–06

Thompson, Robert [I]: Banagher LY 30; 61, 77–78, 83–84

Thompson, Robert [I]: Drummaul AM 19; 90

Thompson, Robert [II]: Banagher LY 30; 110–11

Thompson, Robert [II]: Drummaul AM 19; 90

Thompson, Ross: Derryaghy AM 8; 99, 103, 108, 112

Thompson, S.M.: Doagh AM 29; 83, 88–89, 98

Thompson, Sally: Balteagh LY 9; 43

Thompson, Samual: Macosquin LY 22; 116–17

Thompson, Samuel: Aghalee AM 21; 32, 36–37

Thompson, Samuel: Antrim AM 29; 47

Thompson, Samuel: Ballinderry AM 21; 49

Thompson, Samuel: Ballintoy AM 24; 19

Thompson, Samuel: Ballyscullion AM 19; 5, 8, 12

Thompson, Samuel: Bovevagh LY 25; 7–8, 52

Thompson, Samuel: Carrickfergus AM 37; 117

Thompson, Samuel: Muckamore AM 35; 55–56, 62, 72–73, 75, 77

Thompson, Samuel: Templepatrick AM 35; 134, 153–54

Thompson, Sgt: Blaris DN 12; 42

Thompson, Thomas: Aghagallon AM 21; 17

Thompson, Thomas: Banagher LY 30; 73, 100

Thompson, Thomas: Carrickfergus AM 37; 107

Thompson, Thomas: Derryaghy AM 8; 117

Thompson, Thomas: Magheragall AM 21; 107–09

Thompson, W.M.: Galloon FH 4; 90

Thompson, W.N.: Newry DN 3; 71, 93, 99, 104–05

Thompson, W.R.: Skerry AM 13; 120

Thompson, William: Ahoghill AM 23; 39

Thompson, William: Ballynascreen LY 31; 18

Thompson, William: Blaris AM 8; 65, 84

Thompson, William: Blaris DN 12; 49

Thompson, William: Kilwaughter AM 10; 119

Thompson, William: Maghera LY 18; 32, 65

Thompson, William: Muckamore AM 35; 55, 75, 79, 81

Thompson, William: Tamlaght Finlagan LY 25; 112

Thompson, William [I]: Carrickfergus AM 37; 39, 148

Thompson, William [II]: Carrickfergus AM 37; 108

Thompson's bridge: Tullyrusk AM 21; 135

Thompson's hill: Magherafelt LY 6; 79

Thompson's hill: Muckno MN 40; 162

Thomson, A.: Ballymoney AM 16; 17

Thomson, Benjamin: Ballymoney AM 16; 16

Thomson, Daniel: Aghadowey LY 22; 36

Thomson, family: Ballinderry AM 21; 51

Thomson, family: Currin MN 40; 94

Thomson, family: Desertoghill LY 27; 5

Thomson, family: Magheragall AM 21; 99

Thomson, family: Muckamore AM 35; 65

Thomson, family: Racavan AM 13; 100

Thomson, family: Raloo AM 32; 108

Thomson, James: Coleraine LY 33; 64

Thomson, James: Drumcree AH 1; 33

Thomson, James: Kirkinriola AM 23; 112

Thomson, man named: Cumber LY 28; 81

Thomson, Margaret: Carrickfergus AM 37; 116

Thomson, Miss: Coleraine LY 33; 72–73

Thomson, Misses: Ahoghill AM 23; 17

Thomson, Rev. (Co. Down): Aghadowey LY 22; 26

Thomson, Robert: Drumachose LY 9; 53

Thomson, Rose: Carrickfergus AM 37; 132

Thomson, S.: Island Magee AM 10; 64

Thomson, Samuel: Ballinderry AM 21; 57

Thomson, William: Ballyscullion LY 6; 57

Thoneyal (see Legavannwell): Dungiven LY 15; 91

Thonoge hill: Banagher LY 30; 24, 109–10

Thoon Baun fort: Dungiven LY 15; 44, 48, 87

Thorn Ditch (see Thorn Dyke): Doagh AM 29; 96

Thorn Dyke fence: Doagh AM 29; 80, 82, 96

Thorn Dyke fence: Kilbride AM 29; 148

Thornagh (see Thonoge): Banagher LY 30; 109

Thorneton, Tristram: Banagher LY 30; 102

Thorneton, Tristram: Clondermot LY 34; 68

Thorneton, Tristram: Cumber LY 28; 63, 65

Thornfield House: Carrickfergus AM 37; 56, 135–36, 141

Thornfield locality: Carrickfergus AM 37; 174

Thornhill (see Thornfield): Carrickfergus AM 37; 135

Thornhill Glebe House: Trory FH 14; 125

Thornhill Glebe school: Trory FH 14; 128–29

Thornhill Glebe td: Trory FH 14; 124, 129

Thornton, John: Hillsborough DN 12; 105

Thornton, Joseph: Blaris DN 12; 40–41

Thornton, Mary Ann: Blaris AM 8; 25

Thornton, Philip: Hillsborough DN 12; 106

Thornton, William: Hillsborough DN 12; 105

Thornugh (see Thonoge): Banagher LY 30; 109

Thorp, J.T.: Coleraine LY 33; 57, 64, 137

Thorpe, Stephen: Dunboe LY 11; 80

Thorpe, William: Moville DL 38; 75, 78

Three Brothers standing stones: Carrickfergus AM 37; 33, 85–86, 183–84, 191

Three Islands: Drummaul AM 19; 68, 78

Three Islands: Lough Neagh AM 21; 95

Three Islands Cottage: Drummaul AM 19; 83

Three Mile Water river: Ballylinny AM 32; 12–13, 24

Three Mile Water river: Carnmoney AM 2; 36, 47–49, 85, 91–93, 103

Three Nooked glen: Macosquin LY 22; 76

Three Sisters Greenan stones: Aghaderg DN 12; 7

Three Sisters Greenan td: Aghaderg DN 12; 7

Three Sisters springs: Magilligan LY 11; 99

Three standing stones: Derryaghy AM 8; 98

Threetrees mountain: Muff DL 38; 80

Threetrees td: Lough Swilly DL 38; 138

Threetrees td: Muff DL 38; 80–81

Thrushfield House: Donegore AM 29; 102, 106, 133

Thrushfield House: Nilteen AM 35; 84, 99, 102

Thrushnahan lough: Clondavaddog DL 38; 3

Thunder's hill: Kilbroney DN 3; 29

Thunder's hill cairn: Kilbroney DN 3; 29

Thuras-na-vadock graveyard: Clondavaddog DL 38; 5

Thuras-na-vadock well: Clondavaddog DL 38; 5

Thuris-a-derg well: Clondavaddog DL 38; 5

Thurot, Gen.: Banagher LY 30; 20

Thurot, Gen.: Coleraine LY 33; 99

Thurot, Gen.: Kilrea LY 27; 117

Thurot, Gen.: Kilroot AM 26; 68

Thurot, Gen.: Magherafelt LY 6; 89

Thurot, Gen.: Misc. AM 10; 131

Thurot, Gen.: Templepatrick AM 35; 148

Thurusallin rivulet: Cumber LY 28; 20

Tiavan (see Teeavan): Banagher LY 30; 111

Tibaran (Tiberan) td: Errigal LY 27; 84, 89, 91

Tibaran bogs: Errigal LY 27; 54

Tibaran hill: Errigal LY 27; 35

Tibber corn mill: Taughboyne DL 39; 155

Tibber flax mill: Taughboyne DL 39; 155

Tibber quarry: Taughboyne DL 39; 150, 153, 155

Tibber td: Killea and Taughboyne DL 39; 79, 87, 90

Tibber td: Taughboyne DL 39; 148, 152, 155

Tibhetiobar td: Templecarn DL 39; 161

Tickmacrevan loughs: Tickmacrevan AM 13; 125

Tickmacrevan ph: Ahoghill AM 23; 5

Tickmacrevan ph: Ardclinis AM 13; 1, 3, 5

Tickmacrevan ph: Ballyclug AM 23; 54

Tickmacrevan ph: Carncastle and Killyglen AM 10; 8, 10–11

Tickmacrevan ph: Connor AM 19; 19

Tickmacrevan ph: Glenwhirry AM 32; 74

Tickmacrevan ph: Kilwaughter AM 10; 106, 106

Tickmacrevan ph: Kirkinriola AM 23; 92

Tickmacrevan ph: Misc. AM 10; 129

Tickmacrevan ph: Racavan AM 13; 86, 97

Tickmacrevan ph: Raloo AM 32; 116

Tickmacrevan ph: Ramoan AM 24; 95

Tickmacrevan ph: Skerry AM 13; 105

Tickmacrevan td: Carncastle and Killyglen AM 10; 1

Ticlog (see Ticloy)

Ticlogy (see Ticloy)

Ticloy (Tecloy) td: Skerry AM 13; 106–08, 116

Ticloy stone house: Skerry AM 13; 107 08, 116, 119

Ticloy td: Finvoy AM 23; 77

Tidd hill: Derryvullan FH 14; 37

Tidnagin school: Magheraculmoney FH 14; 108

Tieragher (see Tiernagher): Inishmacsaint FH 14; 71

Tieranisk td: Donaghmore DL 39; 39

Tiergolin (see Tirgoland): Dungiven LY 15; 33

Tierhoman (see Tirhomin)

Tierhomen (see Tirhomin)

Tierhomin (see Tirhomin)

Tierkelly (Teerkelly) td: Drumballyroney DN 3; 12, 14, 16, 18

Tierkelly spring: Drumballyroney DN 3; 12

Tiermiel (see Turmeel): Dungiven LY 15; 1

Tiermoan (see Tremone): Lough Swilly DL 38; 113

Tiernagher More hill: Inishmacsaint FH 14; 71

Tiernagher td: Inishmacsaint FH 14; 70

Tiernagushog td: Donaghmore DL 39; 39

Tierney, Francis: Newtownards DN 7; 108

Tierney, James: Donacavey TE 5; 65–66

Tievaleny (Tieveleney) td: Aughnamullen MN 40; 76

Tievaleny corn mill: Aughnamullen MN 40; 72

Tievaleny school: Aughnamullen MN 40; 77

Tieve Dochragh mountain: Clonduff DN 3; 5

Tievebrack td: Donaghmore DL 39; 39

Tievebulliagh mountain: Layd AM 13; 37, 42

Tieveclogher bog: Donaghmore DL 39; 29

Tieveclogher td: Donaghmore DL 39; 29, 31, 39

Tievegarrow td: Drummully FH 4; 39

Tievemore td: Templecarn DL 39; 164

Tievenadarragh bogs: Loughinisland DN 17; 97

Tievenadarragh chapel: Loughinisland DN 17; 97

Tievenadarragh fort: Loughinisland DN 17; 97

Tievenadarragh old chapel: Loughinisland DN 17; 97

Tievenadarragh school: Loughinisland DN 17; 97

Tievenadarragh smithy: Loughinisland DN 17; 97

Tievenadarragh td: Loughinisland DN 17; 97–98

Tievenanass hill: Killdrumsherdan CN 40; 31

Tievenanass school: Killdrumsherdan CN 40; 36

Tievenass (see Tievenanass)

Tievenny (Teevery) td: Ardstraw TE 5; 12

Tievenny fort: Ardstraw TE 5; 12

Tievenny school: Ardstraw TE 5; 13

Tieverah hill: Layd AM 13; 43

Tievnass (see Tievenanass)

Tiffan, Col: Galloon FH 4; 103–04

Tigarvil (see Tirgarvil): Maghera LY 18; 4

Tigernach, Abbot of Clonmacnoise: Magilligan LY 11; 102

Tigernach, St: Clogher TE 5; 29

Tigernach, St: Clones FH 4; 29

Tighe, Rev. Thomas: Drumgooland DN 3; 22

Tighvanny td: Magheraculmoney FH 14; 113

Tildarg bleach green: Rashee AM 32; 136–37

Tildarg hill: Rashee AM 32; 135

Tildarg House: Rashee AM 32; 136

Tildarg school: Rashee AM 32; 140

Tildarg td: Rashee AM 32; 135–36

Tillevally (Tullyvally) td: Donacavey TE 5; 87

Tilly, Mr (Dublin): Aughnamullen MN 40; 75–77

Tillymark (Tillymuck) school: Ardstraw TE 5; 13

Timaconway bogs: Tamlaght O'Crilly LY 18; 87, 113, 130

Timaconway flax mill: Tamlaght O'Crilly LY 18; 91, 109

Timaconway fort [I]: Tamlaght O'Crilly LY 18; 112

Timaconway fort [II]: Tamlaght O'Crilly LY 18; 113

Timaconway fort [III]: Tamlaght O'Crilly LY 18; 113

Timaconway fort [IV]: Tamlaght O'Crilly LY 18; 95, 114

Timaconway foundry: Tamlaght O'Crilly LY 18; 113

Timaconway giant's chair: Tamlaght O'Crilly LY 18; 102, 113

Timaconway giant's grave: Tamlaght O'Crilly LY 18; 95, 113

Timaconway school: Tamlaght O'Crilly LY 18; 140

Timaconway td: Tamlaght O'Crilly LY 18; 87, 96–97, 99–100, 102, 104, 113, 119, 136, 138

Timakeel (Timnakeel) td: Drumcree AH 1; 40

Timakeel meeting house: Drumcree AH 1; 30, 36

Timeroane (see Tiryrone): Moville DL 38; 75

Timnavagh td: Kilbroney DN 3; 32

Timothy's Lonan locality: Island Magee AM 10; 81

Timoyle district: Layd AM 13; 37

Timpany (Timpenny) td: Aghalurcher TE 5; 1, 16

Timpany mountain: Aghalurcher FH 4; 2

Timpany standing stone: Aghalurcher TE 5; 1

Timplefefyn chapel: Misc. DN 17; 121

Timpony (see Timpany)

Timulkenny td: Drumcree AH 1; 40

Tinan, St: Inch DN 17; 75

Tinan, Thomas: Ballyscullion LY 6; 57

Tinklers Ford td: Raymoghy DL 39; 139

Tinnchame, Thomas: Raymoghy DL 39; 140

Tinny Cahil bog: Donegal DL 39; 53

Tinnyhannon (see Tannybrannon): Ahoghill AM 23; 22

Tinnyhatbuck td: Misc. DL 39; 195

Tinsley, Arthur: Blaris AM 8; 19

Tinsley, Thomas: Blaris DN 12; 50

Tintagh fort [I]: Lissan LY 31; 101

Tintagh fort [II]: Lissan LY 31; 101

Tintagh fort [III]: Lissan LY 31; 101

Tintagh quarry: Lissan LY 31; 101

Tintagh school: Lissan LY 31; 95

Tintagh td: Lissan LY 31; 98, 104–09

Tinton, Mr: Convoy DL 39; 20

Tiobra Patrick (see Patrick's well): Dungiven LY 15; 55

Tip Connelly td: Donaghedy TE 5; 92

Tipperary county: Dungiven LY 15; 34

Tippett, Thomas: Dunsfort DN 17; 71

Tippin, Eliza: Raloo AM 32; 129

Tippin, Francis: Carlingford LH 40; 58

Tippin, James: Ballymascanlan LH 40; 55

Tipping, family: Ballinderry AM 21; 48

Tipping, Francis: Castletown LH 40; 61

Tipping, Mary: Carrickfergus AM 37; 128

Tiragarvan cave: Magheross MN 40; 158

Tiramoan td: Donagh MN 40; 98

Tiranee Lower td: Bovevagh LY 25; 48

Tiranny barony: Eglish AH 1; 43

Tiranny barony: Tynan AH 1; 124

Tiranony (see Tirnony): Killelagh LY 27; 102

Tirbracken td: Clondermot LY 34; 57, 75, 80, 112–13, 120, 128, 133

Tirbraikin (see Tirbracken): Clondermot LY 34; 80

Tirbullion td: Aghanloo LY 11; 13

Tircar (Teircare) td: Aghalurcher TE 5; 1, 16

Tirconnell (see Tyrconnell)

Tircorran lime kiln: Aghanloo LY 11; 15

Tircorran td: Aghanloo LY 11; 15, 20, 34, 41–42

Tircorran td: Magilligan LY 11; 142

Tircreeven (see Tircreven)

Tircrevan (see Tircreven)

Tircreveen (see Tircreven)

Tircreven bridge: Magilligan LY 11; 123

Tircreven burn: Magilligan LY 11; 142

Tircreven mountain: Magilligan LY 11; 132

Tircreven rocks: Magilligan LY 11; 82

Tircreven td: Magilligan LY 11; 82–83, 94–95, 121, 123, 126, 132

Tircrevin (see Tircreven)

Tirechan, historian: Dungiven LY 15; 55

Tirechan, historian: Magilligan LY 11; 104

Tireeghan td: Aghalurcher FH 4; 14

Tireenan (Tyreenan) td: Donacavey TE 5; 77, 80–81, 83, 87

Tireighter Castle rock: Banagher LY 30; 91

Tireighter corn mill: Cumber LY 28; 125

Tireighter flax mill: Cumber LY 28; 125

Tireighter quarry: Cumber LY 28; 125

Tireighter school [I]: Cumber LY 28; 3, 7, 16, 73, 77–78, 87

Tireighter school [II]: Cumber LY 28; 73–74, 77–78

Tireighter td: Banagher LY 30; 51, 72

Tireighter td: Cumber LY 28; 1, 6–8, 67, 71, 85, 115, 120, 125

Tireighter wood: Cumber LY 28; 120

Tirenny td: Aghalurcher FH 4; 14

Tirerill barony: Misc. SO 40; 198

Tirgan fort: Desertmartin LY 31; 56

Tirgan rock: Desertmartin LY 31; 52

Tirgan td: Desertmartin LY 31; 60, 140–42

Tirgarvil corn mill: Maghera LY 18; 27, 65

Tirgarvil national school: Maghera LY 18; 35

Tirgarvil private school: Maghera LY 18; 32

Tirgarvil td: Maghera LY 18; 28, 78

Tirgarvil woods: Maghera LY 18; 4, 48

Tirglassan (Tyrglassen) td: Banagher LY 30; 22, 24, 34, 36, 62, 64, 95, 107, 109–10, 121, 125–26, 129–31

Tirglassan graveyard: Banagher LY 30; 39, 55, 63

Tirglassan quarry: Banagher LY 30; 3, 129

Tirglassan school: Banagher LY 30; 13, 33–34, 110–11

Tirglassan standing stone: Banagher LY 30; 46

Tirglassen (see Tirglassan)

Tirglassin (see Tirglassan)

Tirgoland (Tiergoland) td: Dungiven LY 15; 23, 26, 33, 63, 74

Tirgoland td: Banagher LY 30; 22

Tirgracey (Targracey) td: Muckamore AM 35; 54, 56, 62, 68, 75–76, 79, 82–83

Tirgracey beetling and wash mills: Muckamore AM 35; 63

Tirgracey beetling mill [I]: Muckamore AM 35; 56, 63, 75

Tirgracey beetling mill [II]: Muckamore AM 35; 56, 63

Tirgracey coves: Muckamore AM 35; 72

Tirgracey forts: Muckamore AM 35; 56, 72, 74

Tirgracey paper mill: Muckamore AM 35; 56, 75

Tirgracey quarry: Muckamore AM 35; 55

Tirgracey standing stone: Muckamore AM 35; 71

Tirharon (Terheeron) td: Raymoghy DL 39; 139, 141, 199

Tirhomin school: Tullyaughnish DL 38; 92

Tirhomin td: Tullyaughnish DL 38; 86, 91, 96

Tirhugh (Tirhue) td: Killelagh LY 27; 99–102

Tirhugh carn: Killelagh LY 27; 101

Tirhugh graveyard: Killelagh LY 27; 101

Tirhugh trigonometrical station: Killelagh LY 27; 101

Tiriechter (see Tireighter): Cumber LY 28; 67

Tiriwinney (see Tiriwinny): Magheraculmoney FH 14; 111

Tiriwinny td: Magheraculmoney FH 14; 111–13

Tirkane (Tircane) td: Killelagh LY 27; 95, 97, 99, 101–02

Tirkane quarry: Killelagh LY 27; 102

Tirkeenan td: Monaghan MN 40; 159

Tirkeeran (Tirkeerin) td: Desertoghill LY 27; 1, 19, 34

Tirkeeran (Tirkery) td: Clonleigh DL 39; 12, 198

Tirkeeran barony: Balteagh LY 9; 16

Tirkeeran barony: Banagher LY 30; 1, 7, 25, 36, 60

Tirkeeran barony: Clondermot LY 34; 1, 46, 50, 53, 84

Tirkeeran barony: Cumber LY 28; 1, 5, 43, 86

Tirkeeran barony: Dungiven LY 15; 80

Tirkeeran barony: Faughanvale LY 36; 3, 33

Tirkeeran barony: Misc. LY 36; 105, 118

Tirkeeran corn mill: Desertoghill LY 27; 4–5, 13

Tirkeeran district: Clondermot LY 34; 7, 77–78

Tirkeeran district: Misc. LY 36; 111

Tirkeeran flax mill: Desertoghill LY 27; 5, 13

Tirkeeran fort: Cumber LY 28; 43, 83

Tirkeeran fort [I]: Desertoghill LY 27; 27

Tirkeeran fort [II]: Desertoghill LY 27; 27

Tirkeeran fort [III]: Desertoghill LY 27; 27

Tirkeeran inn: Clondermot LY 34; 79

Tirkeeveny hill: Clondermot LY 34; 1, 17

Tirkeeveny school: Clondermot LY 34; 89

Tirkeeveny td: Clondermot LY 34; 57, 75, 112–13, 120, 128, 133

Tirkeevny (see Tirkeeveny): Clondermot LY 34; 89

Tirkennedy barony: Cleenish FH 14; 11–12, 28

Tirkennedy barony: Derrybrusk FH 4; 30

Tirkennedy barony: Derryvullan FH 14; 31, 39

Tirkennedy barony: Enniskillen FH 4; 41, 50, 82

Tirkennedy barony: Magheracross FH 14; 91

Tirkennedy barony: Trory FH 14; 122

Tirkieveny (see Tirkeeveny): Clondermot LY 34; 57

Tirkin, Richard: Banagher LY 30; 75

Tirllarcevy wood: Desertcreat TE 20; 34

Tirloughan (Teerlaughan) td: Mevagh DL 38; 63

Tirloughan td: Lough Swilly DL 38; 116

Tirmacoy quarry: Faughanvale LY 36; 96

Tirmacoy td: Banagher LY 30; 107

Tirmacoy td: Faughanvale LY 36; 17, 53, 63, 69, 78–79, 90, 96–97, 99

Tirmacoy td: Tamlaght Finlagan LY 25; 72–74

Tirmaquin (Termaquin) td: Drumachose LY 9; 87, 97, 128, 133

Tirmiel (see Turmeel): Dungiven LY 15; 1

Tirnageeragh fort: Maghera LY 18; 61

Tirnageeragh school: Maghera LY 18; 30

Tirnageeragh Sunday school: Maghera LY 18; 29

Tirnageeragh td: Maghera LY 18; 9, 41, 63

Tirnaskea House: Desertcreat TE 20; 34

Tirnony bleach green: Killelagh LY 27; 96

Tirnony bog: Killelagh LY 27; 95

Tirnony cromlech: Killelagh LY 27; 100–02

Tirnony giant's grave: Killelagh LY 27; 97, 100

Tirnony graveyard: Killelagh LY 27; 97

Tirnony old church: Killelagh LY 27; 97, 99–100, 102

Tirnony td: Killelagh LY 27; 95–96, 99–100, 102

Tirroddy (Teroddy) td: Taughboyne DL 39; 148, 154, 184, 186, 196

Tirroddy bog: Lough Swilly DL 38; 149

Tirroddy flax mill: Taughboyne DL 39; 154

Tirygory (Teerygory) td: Drumballyroney DN 3; 12

Tiryrone td: Moville DL 38; 73, 75

Tiscallen (Tascallon) td: Aghagallon AM 21; 3, 7, 18–19, 21–22, 24

Tiscallen fort [I]: Aghagallon AM 21; 13

Tiscallen fort [II]: Aghagallon AM 21; 13

Tiscallen school [I]: Aghagallon AM 21; 5

Tiscallen school [II]: Aghagallon AM 21; 5

Tisnaghten td: Kinawley FH 4; 110

Tite, William: Clondermot LY 34; 41

Tite, William: Coleraine LY 33; 70

Titrington, Alex: Blaris DN 12; 51

Titterington, family: Aghalee AM 21; 31

Titterington, Mr: Blaris DN 12; 50

Tittertod, Mr: Blaris DN 12; 46

Tittle, J.M.: Coleraine LY 33; 63–64, 91, 105, 127

Tittley, family: Ramoan AM 24; 107

Tittrington, James [I]: Hillsborough DN 12; 106

Tittrington, James [II]: Hillsborough DN 12; 106

Tittrington, John: Hillsborough DN 12; 106

Tittrington, Trevor: Hillsborough DN 12; 106

Tivaconvery td: Maghera LY 18; 76

Tivaleeney (see Tievaleny): Aughnamullen MN 40; 76

Tiveconevy (see Timaconway): Tamlaght O'Crilly LY 18; 136

Tiveleney (see Tievaleny): Aughnamullen MN 40; 77

Toaghey manor: Tynan AH 1; 125

Toame district: Clondavaddog DL 38; 4

Toan, Thomas: Hillsborough DN 12; 105

Tobar Ania well: Errigal LY 27; 42, 76

Tobar Dooney well: Magheramesk AM 21; 126

Tobar Goura well: Errigal LY 27; 67

Tobar Loora well: Drumachose LY 9; 56, 109

Tobar Patrick well: Macosquin LY 22; 99

Tobar Phadruic (see Patrick's well)

Tobar Tiggy well: Aghanloo LY 11; 3, 26, 28

Tobardooney spring: Ballintoy AM 24; 31

Tobarid hill: Banagher LY 30; 110

Tobarkeagh (Tobarkeigh) td: Ballintoy AM 24; 23

Tobarkeagh cave: Ballintoy AM 24; 23

Tobarnakirke well: Macosquin LY 22; 109

Tobarteefinn well: Errigal LY 27; 42, 69

Tobbercorne (see Tubbercorran): Down DN 17; 56

Tobberlowrie, St: Maghera LY 18; 57

Tobbermoney (Tubbermoney) td: Down DN 17; 48, 53, 56

Tobbernagollagh giant's bed: Loughguile AM 13; 72

Tober Easbog Cadan (see Tubber Aspug Aidan): Magilligan LY 11; 103

Tober Lowrie well: Maghera LY 18; 6, 10, 57

Tober Main well: Kilrea LY 27; 113

Toberagnew td: Ballymartin AM 2; 15–17

Toberagnew td: Templepatrick AM 35; 148, 150

Toberagnew well: Ballymartin AM 2; 12, 17

Toberagnew well: Templepatrick AM 35; 132, 150

Toberan (Tobberann) well: Drumtullagh AM 16; 100, 102

Toberawathyweell well: Ballynascreen LY 31; 11–12, 25

Toberbilley (see Toberbilly): Ramoan AM 24; 126

Toberbilly fort: Kilraghts AM 16; 133

Toberbilly fort [I]: Ramoan AM 24; 117

Toberbilly fort [II]: Ramoan AM 24; 117

Toberbilly meeting house: Kilraghts AM 16; 128

Toberbilly school: Ramoan AM 24; 100, 126

Toberbilly standing stones: Ramoan AM 24; 117

Toberbilly td: Kilraghts AM 16; 128, 135

Toberbilly td: Ramoan AM 24; 88, 118

Toberbilly well: Kilraghts AM 16; 125

Toberdoney (Toberdonny) td: Billy AM 16; 45, 48, 56

Toberdoney cove: Billy AM 16; 56, 63

Toberdoney meeting house: Billy AM 16; 37, 45

Toberdoney school: Billy AM 16; 49

Toberdoney well: Kilraghts AM 16; 135

Toberdoney well: Layd AM 13; 41

Toberdony (see Toberdoney)

Toberdornan forts: Ballywillin AM 16; 34

Toberdornan td: Ballywillin AM 16; 33–34

Toberdornan td: Ballywillin LY 33; 52

Toberdowney church: Ballynure AM 32; 33, 38–39, 45, 48–50, 56, 63–65, 67, 69, 72

Toberdowney cotton factory: Ballynure AM 32; 33–34, 40–43, 65–67, 69, 72–73

Toberdowney graveyard: Ballynure AM 32; 39, 56, 60

Toberdowney logwood mill: Ballynure AM 32; 34, 41, 43–44, 66, 68, 72

Toberdowney Sunday school: Ballynure AM 32; 73

Toberdowney td: Ballynure AM 32; 38, 63, 68

Toberdowney well: Ballynure AM 32; 60, 63

Toberdowny (see Toberdowney): Ballynure AM 32; 60

Tobergill altar: Donegore AM 29; 127–28

Tobergill enclosures: Donegore AM 29; 124, 127–28

Tobergill forts: Donegore AM 29; 127

Tobergill standing stone: Donegore AM 29; 120, 124

Tobergill stone circle: Donegore AM 29; 119

Tobergill td: Donegore AM 29; 101, 113, 130

Toberhead (Tobberhead) td: Maghera LY 18; 45, 76, 78–79

Toberhead fort: Maghera LY 18; 60

Toberhead well: Maghera LY 18; 45

Toberid hill: Banagher LY 30; 24, 59, 109

Toberid hill: Faughanvale LY 36; 4

Toberkeagh meeting house: Ballintoy AM 24; 15

Tobermannen bridge: Magheracloone MN 40; 139

Toberminfio (see Toberagnew): Ballymartin AM 2; 12

Tobermore: Ardstraw TE 5; 3

Tobermore: Ballynascreen LY 31; 2, 5–8, 17

Tobermore: Banagher LY 30; 74

Tobermore: Bodoney TE 20; 20

Tobermore: Desertmartin LY 31; 54–55, 63

Tobermore: Kilcronaghan LY 31; 64–69, 71–79, 82–83, 87

Tobermore: Lissan LY 31; 95, 98

Tobermore: Macosquin LY 22; 98

Tobermore: Maghera LY 18; 2, 8–9, 14–15, 27, 31, 63–65

Tobermore: Magherafelt LY 6; 81

Tobermore: Misc. LY 31; 115–17, 121–22, 134, 136, 139–40, 144

Tobermore: Tamlaght O'Crilly LY 18; 100, 104

Tobermore bog: Misc. LY 31; 112

Tobermore bridge: Maghera LY 18; 63

Tobermore Castle: Kilcronaghan LY 31; 70

Tobermore evening school: Kilcronaghan LY 31; 88

Tobermore female school [I]: Kilcronaghan LY 31; 88

Tobermore female school [II]: Kilcronaghan LY 31; 88

Tobermore meeting house (I): Kilcronaghan LY 31; 66, 72, 74, 79–82, 115, 128

Tobermore meeting house (P): Kilcronaghan LY 31; 66, 73, 79, 88, 115, 128

Tobermore mill: Kilcronaghan LY 31; 75

Tobermore post office: Kilcronaghan LY 31; 83, 140

Tobermore Presbyterian school: Kilcronaghan LY 31; 73–74

Tobermore school: Kilcronaghan LY 31; 73

Tobermore Sunday school: Kilcronaghan LY 31; 74

Tobermore td: Kilcronaghan LY 31; 64, 73, 84–85

Tobermore well: Kilcronaghan LY 31; 65

Tobernabrock td: Clonleigh DL 39; 12

Tobernasool well: Skerry AM 13; 116, 118–19

Toberslane td: Misc. DL 39; 192, 196

Tobery td: Clonleigh DL 39; 12

Tobordoney (see Tubberdoney): Ardclinis AM 13; 7

Tobwee td: Misc. DL 39; 186, 198

Tochar, son of Fin: Misc. LY 36; 112–13

Tod Island: Tamlaght O'Crilly LY 18; 85, 128

Tod Rock fort: Tamlaght O'Crilly LY 18; 114

Tod's glen: Dungiven LY 15; 91

Todd hill: Kilcronaghan LY 31; 64

Todd, Andrew: Billy AM 16; 76

Todd, Daniel: Ramoan AM 24; 118

Todd, David: Newry DN 3; 98, 103

Todd, family: Billy AM 16; 58, 68

Todd, family: Doagh AM 29; 73, 94

Todd, family: Dunluce AM 16; 117

Todd, family: Enniskillen FH 4; 58

Todd, family: Ramoan AM 24; 107

Todd, Francis: Ramoan AM 24; 124

Todd, James: Ballynure AM 32; 55

Todd, James: Kilroot AM 26; 73, 81

Todd, John: Ballyclug AM 23; 61, 65

Todd, John: Newry DN 3; 100, 104

Todd, Mr (Ballintaggart): Kilmore AH 1; 63, 68

Todd, Mr (Coleraine): Macosquin LY 22; 96

Todd, Mr: Clondermot LY 34; 34

Todd, Mr: Tullynakill DN 7; 123

Todd, Mrs William: Carrickfergus AM 37; 155

Todd, Neal: Ballintoy AM 24; 22

Todd, Rev. A.T.: Killead AM 35; 45

Todd, Rev. John: Misc. DN 17; 117

Todd, Robert: Templecorran AM 26; 120–21

Todd, William: Carrickfergus AM 37; 155–56

Todd's grave: Ballyclug AM 23; 64

Todd's Knowe hill: Ballyclug AM 23; 61, 65

Tods rock: Cumber LY 28; 32

Togher lough: Tomregan FH 4; 126

Togherbrick: Blaris AM 8; 86

Toghernaross td: Drumlumman CN 40; 17

Toghill, Anthony: Desertoghill LY 27; 21, 27

Toghill, Daniel: Maghera LY 18; 80

Toghill, James: Maghera LY 18; 78

Toghill, John: Maghera LY 18; 68

Toghill, man named: Desertoghill LY 27; 6, 22, 31

Toghill, Michael [I]: Maghera LY 18; 78

Toghill, Michael [II]: Maghera LY 18; 81

Toghill, Nancy: Maghera LY 18; 78

Toghill, Peter: Maghera LY 18; 78

Tohirdoe td: Dromore TE 5; 97

Tolan, family: Ballinderry AM 21; 53

Tolan, George: Carnmoney AM 2; 99

Toland, Mary: Ballyaghran LY 33; 17

Tole, Henery [I]: Tamlaght O'Crilly LY 18; 132–33

Tole, Henery [II]: Tamlaght O'Crilly LY 18; 137

Tole, John: Tamlaght O'Crilly LY 18; 137

Tole, Mary: Tamlaght O'Crilly LY 18; 137

Tolerton, Alexander: Blaris DN 12; 42

Tolerton, Alexander: Magheramesk AM 21; 122

Toll water: Drumcree AH 1; 34

Tollerish (see Tullyrush)

Tollsland locality: Carrickfergus AM 37; 94

Tollymore (see Tullymore): Donaghmore DN 3; 8

Tollymore td: Skerry AM 13; 106

Tomany td: Ematris MN 40; 116

Tomb, Alexander: Tamlaght O'Crilly LY 18; 96, 119

Tomb, H.J.: Ballyclug AM 23; 52

Tomb, James: Tamlaght O'Crilly LY 18; 140

Tomb, Stewart: Dundermot AM 13; 34–35

Tomb, William: Ballyscullion LY 6; 76

Tombs, Rev.: Magherafelt LY 6; 98–99

Tomes, Rev. William: Clogher TE 5; 41

Tomes, Rev. William: Donacavey TE 5; 66, 68, 81, 84

Tomkins, Anne: Clondermot LY 34; 82

Tomkins, Elizabeth: Clondermot LY 34; 82–83

Tomkins, George: Clondermot LY 34; 10, 12, 16, 27, 81–83, 94, 101

Tomkins, Margaret (see Gamble): Clondermot LY 34; 82

Tomkins, Mrs: Clondermot LY 34; 81

Tomkins, N.A.: Clondermot LY 34; 83

Tomkins, Samuel [I]: Clondermot LY 34; 83

Tomkins, Samuel [II]: Clondermot LY 34; 83

Tomlinson, Rev. William: Drumgoon CN 40; 6

Tomlough: Donegal DL 39; 54

Tommyscroft td: Convoy DL 39; 22

Tompkins, George: Faughanvale LY 36; 78

Tomregan ph: Kinawley FH 4; 112–13

Tomrod fort: Manorhamilton Union LM 40; 52

Tonagamprey (see Tullyhumphry): Currin MN 40; 86

Tonagenasey (see Tullyhumphry): Currin MN 40; 91

Tonagh (see Tonaght): Ballynascreen LY 31; 1

Tonagh (Tamna) td: Blaris AM 8; 45

Tonagh bog: Inishmacsaint FH 14; 72

Tonagh td: Blaris DN 12; 28

Tonagh td: Inishmacsaint FH 14; 71–72, 75

Tonagh td: Misc. DL 39; 196

Tonaghbane hill: Killdrumsherdan CN 40; 31, 33

Tonaghbane td: Killdrumsherdan CN 40; 33

Tonaghbeg (see Tannaghbeg)

Tonagheitra td: Donacavey TE 5; 82

Tonaghmore (Tonnaghmore) td: Saintfield DN 7; 116, 118–19

Tonaghmore school: Hillsborough DN 12; 101

Tonaghmore school: Saintfield DN 7; 116

Tonaghmore td: Magherally DN 12; 112, 114–15

Tonaghmore td: Saintfield DN 7; 120

Tonaghmore td: Seapatrick DN 12; 127

Tonaght td: Ballynascreen LY 31; 1, 26, 118, 143

Tonaugh quarry: Taughboyne DL 39; 150

Tonaugh td: Taughboyne DL 39; 148, 155

Tonduff (see Toneduff): Cumber LY 28; 48

Tonduff corn mill: Desertegney DL 38; 26

Tonduff cove: Billy AM 16; 56, 62

Tonduff fort: Desertegney DL 38; 26

Tonduff td: Billy AM 16; 58, 64–65

Tonduff td: Desertegney DL 38; 26, 28

Tonduff village: Desertegney DL 38; 25

Tonebratley (see Tullnabratly): Clonmany DL 38; 13

Toneduff (see Tonduff): Billy AM 16; 56

Toneduff (see Tonduff): Desertegney DL 38; 25

Toneduff bogs: Cumber LY 28; 46, 80

Toneduff bridge: Cumber LY 28; 9, 35

Toneduff corn mill: Cumber LY 28; 34, 106

Toneduff school: Cumber LY 28; 75

Toneduff td: Cumber LY 28; 46, 48, 57, 60, 65–66, 98–99, 104, 106

Toneduff wood: Cumber LY 28; 104

Toner, Edward: Billy AM 16; 61, 70–71

Toner, family: Desertoghill LY 27; 5, 30

Toner, Hugh: Kilcronaghan LY 31; 85

Toner, James: Ballynascreen LY 31; 25

Toncr, James: Clondermot LY 34; 77

Toner, James: Tamlaght Finlagan LY 25; 113–14

Toner, John: Ballynascreen LY 31; 13, 21

Toner, John: Lissan LY 31; 109

Toner, Loughlin: Loughgilly AH 1; 86

Toner, Michael: Ballynascreen LY 31; 25–26

Toner, Patrick: Kilcronaghan LY 31; 85

Toneroy td: Derryaghy AM 8; 120

Toney td: Aghalurcher FH 4; 14

Toneybaltoney, Lord: Kilmore AH 1; 73

Toneygrough td: Derryaghy AM 8; 120

Toneymore (see Tonymore): Tomregan FH 4; 125

Toneystick corn mill: Enniskillen FH 4; 69

Toneystick school: Enniskillen FH 4; 84

Toneystick td: Enniskillen FH 4; 50, 82

Tongin hill: Killdrumsherdan CN 40; 32

Tonnagh (see Tonaght): Misc. LY 31; 143

Tonnagh (Tonagh) td: Donacavey TE 5; 65, 81

Tonnagh school: Donacavey TE 5; 65

Tonnaghbane (Tonaghbawn) td: Donacavey TE 5; 77, 80–81, 84, 87

Tonnaghbeg (Tannaghbeg) td: Donacavey TE 5; 77, 80–81, 83, 87

Tonnaghbeg fort: Donacavey TE 5; 83

Tonnaghenew td: Donacavey TE 5; 82

Tonnaghlawn (see Tonaghbane): Killdrumsherdan CN 40; 31

Tonnaghmore (Tonaghmore) td: Donacavey TE 5; 64, 77, 80–81, 83, 87

Tonnaghmore corn mill: Donacavey TE 5; 64

Tonnaghmore forts: Donacavey TE 5; 83

Tonnaghmore mill: Donacavey TE 5; 83

Tonnapowra district: Misc. SO 40; 198

Tonnduff (see Toneduff): Cumber LY 28; 9

Tonneel chapel: Boho FH 14; 8

Tonneel standing stone: Boho FH 14; 10

Tonneel td: Boho FH 14; 8, 10

Tonneenagh district: Misc. SO 40; 199
Tonner, Margaret: Magilligan LY 11; 94
Tonnytallagh (see Tonytallagh): Currin MN 40; 91
Tonracrube td: Kinawley FH 4; 121
Tonyanthony, family: Drumgath DN 3; 20
Tonyglassan chapel: Ballybay MN 40; 80
Tonyglassan fort: Ballybay MN 40; 81
Tonyglassan td: Ballybay MN 40; 84
Tonyhannigan td: Donagh MN 40; 98
Tonymore mountain: Tomregan FH 4; 125–26
Tonystick (see Toneystick): Enniskillen FH 4; 69
Tonytallagh hill: Currin MN 40; 86
Tonytallagh td: Currin MN 40; 91
Tooay bleach green: Aughnamullen MN 40; 72
Tooay mills: Aughnamullen MN 40; 72
Tooay td: Aughnamullen MN 40; 71, 74, 76
Tooban Point: Lough Swilly DL 38; 103, 144
Toobar lough: Templecarn DL 39; 157
Toole, Eliza: Drummaul AM 19; 91
Toole, Henry: Ballyscullion AM 19; 12
Toole, John: Drummaul AM 19; 88
Toole, Mary-Ann [I]: Ahoghill AM 23; 37
Toole, Mary-Ann [II]: Ahoghill AM 23; 38
Toole's well: Cumber LY 28; 20
Toolestraine (see Toorlestraune): Kilmacteige SO 40; 186
Toolestraune (see Toorlestraune): Kilmacteige SO 40; 193
Toomawer (see Toomour): Emlaghfad SO 40; 177
Toome barracks: Duneane AM 19; 112, 116
Toome bog: Donaghmoyne MN 40; 106
Toome bog: Duneane AM 19; 109, 111
Toome bridge: Artrea LY 6; 30, 36, 39
Toome bridge: Artrea TE 20; 8
Toome bridge: Banagher LY 30; 31
Toome bridge: Coleraine LY 33; 97–98, 100
Toome bridge: Duneane AM 19; 94–95, 97, 99–101, 105, 107, 112–13, 115, 117–18, 121
Toome bridge: Lough Neagh AM 21; 93–95
Toome bridge: Maghera LY 18; 2, 8, 35
Toome bridge: Magherafelt LY 6; 88
Toome Castle: Antrim AM 29; 31
Toome Castle: Duneane AM 19; 99, 107, 110
Toome Castle: Killead AM 35; 25
Toome eel-weirs: Coleraine LY 33; 98, 101
Toome eel-weirs: Kirkinriola AM 23; 101, 118
Toome ferry: Duneane AM 19; 99, 112–13
Toome fishery: Artrea TE 20; 8
Toome fishery: Coleraine LY 33; 101, 122
Toome fishery: Duneane AM 19; 95, 99, 105, 113
Toome fishery: Lough Neagh AM 21; 94–96
Toome fishery: Misc. LY 31; 120
Toome hill: Donaghmoyne MN 40; 108
Toome hotel: Duneane AM 19; 116
Toome inn: Duneane AM 19; 95, 99

Toome Lower barony: Ahoghill AM 23; 1, 28
Toome Lower barony: Kirkinriola AM 23; 88, 115
Toome market house: Duneane AM 19; 112, 116, 118
Toome old castle: Duneane AM 19; 121
Toome post office: Duneane AM 19; 115
Toome school: Duneane AM 19; 106
Toome td: Duneane AM 19; 95, 114, 122
Toome Upper barony: Ahoghill AM 23; 1, 28
Toome Upper barony: Antrim AM 29; 3, 22
Toome Upper barony: Ballyscullion AM 19; 1
Toome Upper barony: Drummaul AM 19; 33, 41, 51–52
Toome Upper barony: Duneane AM 19; 94
Toome Upper barony: Shilvodan AM 19; 127, 129
Toome village: Ahoghill AM 23; 3, 5, 10, 31, 43
Toome village: Antrim AM 29; 5, 44, 47–48
Toome village: Ballynure AM 32; 38, 45
Toome village: Ballyscullion AM 19; 1, 3–5, 8, 10, 14
Toome village: Coleraine LY 33; 53, 97, 99, 101–02
Toome village: Connor AM 19; 23
Toome village: Doagh AM 29; 72
Toome village: Donegore AM 29; 106, 108
Toome village: Drummaul AM 19; 33, 40, 44, 51–52, 86–88
Toome village: Duneane AM 19; 94–97, 99–104, 107, 109, 111–16, 118–19, 125
Toome village: Kilbride AM 29; 139–40
Toome village: Lough Neagh AM 21; 93–94, 96
Toome village: Magherafelt LY 6; 90
Toome village: Misc. LY 31; 116
Toome village: Skerry AM 13; 105
Toomebridge: see Toome bridge
Toomour ph: Emlaghfad SO 40; 177, 181
Toomrourer (see Toomour): Emlaghfad SO 40; 181
Tooraa district: Inishmacsaint FH 14; 75
Toorelustrane (see Toorlestraune): Kilmacteige SO 40; 196
Toorlestraune td: Kilmacteige SO 40; 186, 193–94, 196
Toorlistraune (see Toorlestraune): Kilmacteige SO 40; 193
Toorrara village: Kilmacteige SO 40; 193
Tooting stone: Killead AM 35; 26, 49
Top Land locality: Carrickfergus AM 37; 174
Top Lower td: Ballymoney AM 16; 25
Top Rath td: Carlingford LH 40; 59
Top Upper td: Ballymoney AM 16; 24
Topnass lough: Inniskeen MN 40; 124
Topp Lower flax mill [I]: Ballymoney AM 16; 10
Topp Lower flax mill [II]: Ballymoney AM 16; 10
Topped (see Toppit)
Toppin hill: Carrickfergus AM 37; 5
Toppin hill: Cleenish FH 14; 12

Toppin td: Cleenish FH 14; 30
Topping, family: Blaris AM 8; 22
Topping, John: Hillsborough DN 12; 107
Topping, Moses: Hillsborough DN 12; 107
Topping, Samuel: Raphoe DL 39; 127
Topping, Thomas: Hillsborough DN 12; 106
Topping, William: Hillsborough DN 12; 107
Toppit hill: Aghalurcher FH 4; 4
Toppit hill: Derryvullan FH 14; 40
Toppit hill: Enniskillen FH 4; 43, 74
Toppit td: Enniskillen FH 4; 74, 82
Tops Demesne td: Raphoe DL 39; 127
Tops stone circle: Raphoe DL 39; 121, 124
Tops td: Raphoe DL 39; 127
Tops windmill: Raphoe DL 39; 121
Tor (see Torr)
Toragh bridge: Mevagh DL 38; 58
Toragh td: Mevagh DL 38; 55, 63
Torcorr td: Culfeightrin AM 24; 38
Torglass hill: Culfeightrin AM 24; 39
Torledon corn mill: Clondavaddog DL 38; 5
Torledon hill: Clondavaddog DL 38; 9
Torledon lough: Clondavaddog DL 38; 3
Torledon standing stone: Clondavaddog DL 38; 6
Torley, family: Newry DN 3; 106
Torley, Isaac: Newry DN 3; 98
Torley, Patrick: Newry DN 3; 100, 104
Tormoil (see Turmeel): Banagher LY 30; 24
Tornamoney td: Culfeightrin AM 24; 41
Torney, family: Ballee DN 17; 16
Toroohnagallaman Islands: Lough Swilly DL 38;
    125
Torr East cave: Culfeightrin AM 24; 78
Torr East Head: Culfeightrin AM 24; 39
Torr East quarry: Culfeightrin AM 24; 74
Torr East td: Culfeightrin AM 24; 74–75, 83–84
Torr Head: Culfeightrin AM 24; 38, 40, 42, 44–45,
    74, 77, 84
Torr Head: Glynn AM 26; 4, 6
Torr Head: Island Magee AM 10; 64, 74, 83
Torr Head: Racavan AM 13; 103
Torr Head: Rathlin Island AM 24; 131
Torr Head coastguard house: Culfeightrin AM 24;
    74, 84
Torr Head giant's graves: Culfeightrin AM 24; 84
Torr West td: Culfeightrin AM 24; 77
Torrance, Rev. Andrew: Desertoghill LY 27; 3
Torreagh (see Tureagh): Raloo AM 32; 119
Torrence, John: Ballyscullion LY 6; 57
Torrens, Anne: Ballynascreen LY 31; 5
Torrens, David: Aghadowey LY 22; 38
Torrens, David: Clondermot LY 34; 92
Torrens, family: Banagher LY 30; 20
Torrens, family: Desertoghill LY 27; 8
Torrens, family: Dungiven LY 15; 104

Torrens, H.: Misc. LY 31; 136
Torrens, James: Aghadowey LY 22; 8
Torrens, John: Dunaghy AM 13; 24
Torrens, Judge: Ballynascreen LY 31; 5–6, 8, 12, 16,
    20, 112, 115, 129, 136, 143
Torrens, Judge: Muff DL 38; 82
Torrens, Mary: Tamlaght Finlagan LY 25; 120
Torrens, Mr: Balteagh LY 9; 27
Torrens, Rev. John: Ballynascreen LY 31; 20, 136
Torrens, Rev. John: Magilligan LY 11; 89
Torrens, Rev. Robert: Tamlaght O'Crilly LY 18; 107
Torrens, Rev. Thomas: Clonmany DL 38; 18
Torrens, Rev. Thomas: Misc. LY 31; 136
Torrens, Rev. Thomas: Muff DL 38; 82
Torrent river: Clonoe TE 20; 30–31
Torrent river: Drumglass TE 20; 44
Torrent river: Killyman TE 20; 66, 68
Torrent river: Pomeroy TE 20; 72
Torrent river: Tullyniskan TE 20; 138
Torrenti, Joseph: Dunboe LY 11; 61
Torrentine, Mr (Derlitt): Loughgilly AH 1; 87
Torrins, family: Desertoghill LY 27; 17
Torrytown td: Carrickfergus AM 37; 158
Torshilly td: Misc. DN 17; 125
Tory cave: Dunboe LY 11; 44, 77–78
Tory hill (Kilkenny): Clondermot LY 34; 76
Tory Holes caves: Ahoghill AM 23; 35
Tory Island: Ballyscullion LY 6; 71
Tory Island: Clondavaddog DL 38; 4
Tory Island: Lough Swilly DL 38; 122, 124–25
Tory Island: Mevagh DL 38; 59, 61
Tory sound: Lough Swilly DL 38; 124–25
Tory stones: Desertoghill LY 27; 26
Tosh, Alexander: Dunboe LY 11; 76
Tosh, Marcus: Blaris AM 8; 77
Tossey td: Aughnamullen MN 40; 76
Tottenahm, Loftus: Galloon FH 4; 94
Tottenham, C.H.: Manorhamilton Union LM 40; 48,
    50–51, 53–54
Tottenham, Charles: Clogher TE 5; 30
Tottenham, family: Manorhamilton Union LM 40;
    51
Tottenham, Rev. R.L.: Aughnamullen MN 40; 77
Tottenham, Rev. R.L.: Rossorry FH 14; 117
Tottenham, Rev. Robert: Clogher TE 5; 28
Touchet manor: Donacavey TE 5; 70–71, 76–77,
    85–87
Toughblane school: Hillsborough DN 12; 101
Toughblane td: Hillsborough DN 12; 85, 106
Toughill, James: Artrea LY 6; 38
Toughlarne district: Inver AM 26; 49
Toughmagherymorne district: Inver AM 26; 49
Toughull hill: Drumgoon CN 40; 1
Toulan, Mr: Blaris DN 12; 32
Tours (France): Saul DN 17; 113

Tower House: Ballymascanlan LH 40; 55

Town lough: Drumgoon CN 40; 2, 7

Town Parks boiling house: Magherafelt LY 6; 92

Town Parks flour mill: Comber DN 7; 31

Town Parks rope manufactories: Larne AM 10; 125

Town Parks td: Ballyphilip DN 7; 7

Town Parks td: Blaris DN 12; 30

Town Parks td: Comber DN 7; 39

Town Parks td: Larne AM 10; 125

Town Parks td: Magherafelt LY 6; 79

Town Parks td: Ramoan AM 24; 91

Town Parks td: Rossorry FH 14; 115

Town Parks td: Saintfield DN 7; 118–19

Town Parks td: Tickmacrevan AM 13; 124

Townageeth district: Misc. SO 40; 200

Townagh td: Clogher TE 5; 37

Townamachugh fort: Manorhamilton Union LM 40; 52

Townancleen (see Tawnaneille): Kilmacteige SO 40; 197

Townatemple fort: Manorhamilton Union LM 40; 52

Townavaun td: Misc. DN 17; 131

Townawarragh td: Killymard DL 39; 101

Townawilly Mountain td: Donegal DL 39; 42

Townawilly mountains: Donegal DL 39; 42, 45

Townawilly river: Donegal DL 39; 54

Townawilly silver mine: Killymard DL 39; 106

Townawilly td: Donegal DL 39; 44, 51, 54

Townawilly village: Donegal DL 39; 56

Townawonnia school: Templecarn FH 14; 120

Townawonnia td: Templecarn FH 14; 120

Towneeaney (see Tawnaneille): Kilmacteige SO 40; 194

Towneeany (see Tawnaneille): Kilmacteige SO 40; 194

Townham [or Downham], William: Magilligan LY 11; 93

Townley, Samuel: Newry DN 3; 103

Townsend, William: Tamlaght TE 20; 108, 110

Townshend, Mr: Coleraine LY 33; 100, 102

Townyany (see Tawnaneille): Kilmacteige SO 40; 194

Townygraffey village: Kilmacteige SO 40; 194

Toy and Kirkland school: Killyleagh DN 17; 80

Toy, John: Desertoghill LY 27; 20

Tracey, John: Artrea LY 6; 11, 35

Tracey, John: Kirkinriola AM 23; 104, 119

Tracey, Rev.: Templepatrick AM 35; 132

Trachar strand: Lough Swilly DL 38; 129

Tracy, Elice: Errigal LY 27; 50

Tracy, James: Desertoghill LY 27; 20

Tracy, Joseph: Aghadowey LY 22; 36

Tracy, Joseph: Desertoghill LY 27; 20

Tracy, Margret: Aghadowey LY 22; 36

Tracy, Patrick: Carrickfergus AM 37; 108

Traebeg sound: Lough Swilly DL 38; 120

Traebeg strand: Lough Swilly DL 38; 106, 119

Traebwaan creek: Lough Swilly DL 38; 107

Traebwaar (see Traebwaan): Lough Swilly DL 38; 107

Traecharbet bay: Lough Swilly DL 38; 116, 119–21

Traecharbet quarry: Lough Swilly DL 38; 120

Trae-mellgoim creek: Lough Swilly DL 38; 114

Traemore sound: Lough Swilly DL 38; 120

Traemore strand: Lough Swilly DL 38; 100, 106, 122

Traenafagheybwee creek: Lough Swilly DL 38; 114

Traenagin creek: Lough Swilly DL 38; 115, 118

Traenaross locality: Lough Swilly DL 38; 118

Traichorbet (see Traecharbet): Lough Swilly DL 38; 119

Trail's Folly locality: Billy AM 16; 58, 72

Traill, Bishop: Blaris AM 8; 61

Traill, Bishop: Blaris DN 12; 47

Traill, Dr: Billy AM 16; 69, 71

Traill, family: Billy AM 16; 58, 68

Traill, Lady Francis: Blaris AM 8; 65

Traill, Mrs William: Blaris AM 8; 59, 84–85

Traill, Mrs William: Blaris DN 12; 45, 49

Traill, Rev.: Aghagallon AM 21; 19

Traill, Rev.: Ballyphilip DN 7; 8

Traill, Rev.: Killinchy DN 7; 87

Traill, Rev.: Misc. DN 17; 126

Traill, Rev. James: Misc. DN 17; 117

Traill, Rev. R.: Inch DN 17; 73

Traill, Rev. Robert: Ballintoy AM 24; 12, 15, 19, 26, 31

Traill, Rev. Robert: Coleraine LY 33; 127

Traill, Rev. William: Ballyrashane LY 22; 55

Traill, Rev. William: Billy AM 16; 68, 70–72

Traill, Rev. William: Blaris AM 8; 59

Traill, Rev. William: Blaris DN 12; 47

Traill, Rev. William: Culfeightrin AM 24; 40

Traill, Rev. William: Ramoan AM 24; 86

Traill, William: Ballymoney AM 16; 16

Traill, William: Billy AM 16; 36, 45

Traill, William: Blaris AM 8; 66

Traill, William: Coleraine LY 33; 127

Traill's spire: Billy AM 16; 72

Trainavinney td: Leck DL 39; 119

Trainbuoy td: Convoy DL 39; 22

Trainer, family: Ballynure AM 32; 69

Trainer, James: Aghanloo LY 11; 15, 17

Trainer, James: Kilcronaghan LY 31; 85

Trainer, Samuel: Duneane AM 19; 125

Trainor, family: Newry DN 3; 108

Trainor, James: Ballyaghran LY 33; 21

Trainor, John: Newry DN 3; 98

Trainor, Thomas: Macosquin LY 22; 122

Tralee td: Artrea LY 6; 38–39

Tralee td: Tamlaght TE 20; 94, 96

Tramore (see Traemore)

Traner, family: Desertmartin LY 31; 55

Trannish Island: Aghalurcher FH 4; 3, 14

Trasna Island: Kinawley FH 4; 113

Trasna Island: Trory FH 14; 122

Trasna td: Aghavea FH 4; 23, 25

Travers, family: Derryaghy AM 8; 103

Travers, John: Coleraine LY 33; 157

Traymount graveyard: Newry DN 3; 106

Traymount House: Newry DN 3; 105

Trayner, Lawrence: Duneane AM 19; 116, 126

Treankeel td: Conwal DL 39; 24, 27

Treanor, family: Desertmartin LY 31; 55

Treanor, James: Duneane AM 19; 105

Treansallagh spa: Taughboyne DL 39; 150

Treansallagh td: Taughboyne DL 39; 148, 155, 196

Tredennick, John: Kilbarron DL 39; 74, 77

Tredy Point: Lough Swilly DL 38; 144, 147

Treeagh locality: Lough Swilly DL 38; 116

Treen hill: Killesher FH 14; 81

Trellic (see Trillick): Cleenish FH 14; 30

Tremone bay: Lough Swilly DL 38; 113

Tremone district: Lough Swilly DL 38; 141

Trench fort: Banagher LY 30; 56

Trench fort: Connor AM 19; 18, 28–29

Trench fort: Ramoan AM 24; 116

Trench locality: Macosquin LY 22; 86, 113

Trench td: Banagher LY 30; 84

Trench Top hill: Faughanvale LY 36; 1

Trench Top td: Tamlaght Finlagan LY 25; 74

Trench, C.E.: Drumachose LY 9; 66

Trench, E.P.: Drumachose LY 9; 66

Trench, Lady: Ballynascreen LY 31; 23

Trench, Mr (Belturbet): Drummully FH 4; 37

Trench, Mr: Galloon FH 4; 92

Trench, Richard: Drumachose LY 9; 66

Trenor, family: Desertmartin LY 31; 55

Trenor, Thomas: Aghalee AM 21; 33

Trensalaugh (see Treansallagh)

Trensallagh (see Treansallagh)

Trentabwee school: Convoy DL 39; 22

Trentabwee td: Convoy DL 39; 22

Trentagh td: Raymoghy DL 39; 135, 196

Trentamucklagh bog: Taughboyne DL 39; 154

Trentamucklagh td: Taughboyne DL 39; 148, 154, 196

Trentamucklaugh (see Trentamucklagh)

Trentaugh quarry: Taughboyne DL 39; 150, 154–55

Trentaugh td: Taughboyne DL 39; 148, 150, 155

Trentaugh wood: Taughboyne DL 39; 148

Tresall, James: Misc. DN 17; 117

Trevor, A.M.: Aghaderg DN 12; 5, 10

Trevor, A.M.: Seapatrick DN 12; 125

Trevor, Edward: Aghaderg DN 12; 10

Trevor, Edward: Kilbroney DN 3; 32

Trevor, family: Kilbroney DN 3; 32

Trevor, John: Newry DN 3; 74

Trevor, Mr: Aghaderg DN 12; 6

Trianconguill territory: Glynn AM 26; 1

Trien of Trimmily td: Muff DL 38; 80

Triggey, Miss: Clogher TE 5; 43

Triggey, Mr: Clogher TE 5; 28, 43

Trillagh district: Misc. SO 40; 200

Trilley, Mr: Killygarvan DL 38; 49

Trillick: Dromore TE 5; 101

Trillick: Enniskillen FH 4; 43, 52

Trillick: Kilskeery TE 5; 113, 115

Trillick: Magheracross FH 14; 100

Trillick: Trory FH 14; 129

Trillick chapel (M): Kilskeery TE 5; 113

Trillick chapel (WM): Kilskeery TE 5; 113

Trillick court house: Kilskeery TE 5; 113

Trillick dispensary: Kilskeery TE 5; 114–15

Trillick Episcopalian church: Kilskeery TE 5; 114

Trillick tannery: Kilskeery TE 5; 114

Trillick td: Cleenish FH 14; 28, 30

Trim (Meath): Carrickfergus AM 37; 78

Trimble and Kears, Messrs: Newry DN 3; 99

Trimble, James: Blaris AM 8; 50, 79, 84–85

Trimble, James: Blaris DN 12; 50

Trimble, James: Clogher TE 5; 35

Trimble, Joseph: Clogher TE 5; 29

Trimble, Mr: Enniskillen FH 4; 59

Trimble, William: Blaris DN 12; 46, 51

Trimick, family: Misc. LY 36; 104

Trimmer, Joshua: Killowen LY 33; 159

Trimragh td: Leck DL 39; 119

Trinaltinagh (Trinaltonagh) td: Desertoghill LY 27; 19, 29

Trinaltinagh adult school: Desertoghill LY 27; 10, 29

Trinaltinagh bridge: Desertoghill LY 27; 14

Trinaltinagh school: Desertoghill LY 27; 3, 10–12, 14, 19, 29, 33

Trinaltinagh Sunday school: Desertoghill LY 27; 3

Tring, James: Donacavey TE 5; 76

Trinity College, Dublin: Aghalurcher FH 4; 16

Trinity College, Dublin: Ardstraw TE 5; 8

Trinity College, Dublin: Artrea TE 20; 8

Trinity College, Dublin: Ballee DN 17; 22–23

Trinity College, Dublin: Ballinderry AM 21; 44

Trinity College, Dublin: Banagher LY 30; 20

Trinity College, Dublin: Carrickfergus AM 37; 67, 78, 151

Trinity College, Dublin: Clondermot LY 34; 86–87, 95

Trinity College, Dublin: Clones FH 4; 26

Trinity College, Dublin: Clonoe TE 20; 29

Trinity College, Dublin: Coleraine LY 33; 67–68

Trinity College, Dublin: Donaghmore DL 39; 33
Trinity College, Dublin: Faughanvale LY 36; 49
Trinity College, Dublin: Island Magee AM 10; 75
Trinity College, Dublin: Kilbarron DL 39; 74
Trinity College, Dublin: Kilmacrenan DL 38; 53
Trinity College, Dublin: Kirkinriola AM 23; 113
Trinity College, Dublin: Magilligan LY 11; 106
Trinity College, Dublin: Misc. LY 36; 106
Trinity College, Dublin: Raphoe DL 39; 123
Trinity College, Dublin: Rathlin Island AM 24; 134
Trinity College, Dublin: Raymoghy DL 39; 133
Trinity College, Dublin: Tullyaughnish DL 38; 93,
  96–97
Trintaugh bog: Killea and Taughboyne DL 39; 80
Trintaugh td: Killea and Taughboyne DL 39; 80
Trockagh cliff: Lough Swilly DL 38; 108
Trolen, James: Ballynascreen LY 31; 13, 21
Tromaty (Trumity) td: Moville DL 38; 73, 75
Tromaty school: Moville DL 38; 74
Tromaty td: Lough Swilly DL 38; 138
Trony North ph: Derryvullan FH 14; 31
Trony South ph: Derryvullan FH 14; 31
Troon (Scotland): Killyleagh DN 17; 84
Troop, Martha: Doagh AM 29; 73
Troopers Land altars: Carrickfergus AM 37; 82, 85,
  90, 132, 189–91
Troopers Land caves: Carrickfergus AM 37; 82, 85
Troopers Land enclosures: Carrickfergus AM 37; 88
Troopers Land fort: Carrickfergus AM 37; 82, 132,
  188
Troopers Land graveyard: Carrickfergus AM 37;
  81–82, 85, 87–91, 133, 188–91
Troopers Land td: Carrickfergus AM 37; 35, 93–94,
  132–33, 173–74, 190
Troopers Land tumuli: Carrickfergus AM 37; 87
Trory bog: Trory FH 14; 124
Trory church: Trory FH 14; 122, 125
Trory hill: Trory FH 14; 122
Trory mills: Trory FH 14; 125
Trory North district: Trory FH 14; 133
Trory ph: Clogher TE 5; 41
Trory ph: Enniskillen FH 4; 43, 47
Trory ph: Magheracross FH 14; 91
Trory Point: Trory FH 14; 123
Trory school: Trory FH 14; 128–29
Trory td: Trory FH 14; 122
Trosk mountain: Ardclinis AM 13; 5
Trostan mountain: Dunaghy AM 13; 10
Trostan mountain: Layd AM 13; 36–37, 39, 42–44
Trotter, Alexander: Devenish FH 14; 53
Trotter, Mr (Tanderagee): Ballymore AH 1; 17
Trotter, Samuel: Cleenish FH 14; 23
Trough (see Truagh)
Trowal, family: Misc. LY 36; 104
Trowland, Dan: Blaris DN 12; 41

Truagh barony: Donagh MN 40; 98
Truagh barony: Errigal Truagh MN 40; 120
Truagh bay: Montiaghs AH 1; 92
Truagh district: Drumachose LY 9; 95
Truefet, Ann: Blaris AM 8; 21
Truefet, James: Blaris AM 8; 21
Trueman, Nathaniel: Moira DN 12; 117–18
Truffett, family: Blaris AM 8; 21
Truman [or Freeman], Mr: Clogher TE 5; 43
Trumaty (see Tromaty)
Trummery church: Magheramesk AM 21; 124
Trummery Creenagh school: Magheramesk AM 21;
  130
Trummery demesne: Magheramesk AM 21; 117
Trummery fort [I]: Magheramesk AM 21; 113, 124
Trummery fort [II]: Magheramesk AM 21; 125
Trummery graveyard: Magheramesk AM 21; 117,
  124
Trummery House: Magheramesk AM 21; 113, 117,
  124, 129
Trummery old church: Magheramesk AM 21; 113,
  115, 117, 123
Trummery quarry: Magheramesk AM 21; 117
Trummery td: Magheramesk AM 21; 114, 122, 126,
  130
Trummery tower: Antrim AM 29; 30
Trummery tower: Magheramesk AM 21; 113, 115,
  123–24
Trummon West td: Drumhome DL 39; 58
Trump cove: Island Magee AM 10; 101
Trumpadisha cromlech: Tullyaughnish DL 38; 91
Trumpadisha standing stone: Tullyaughnish DL 38;
  91
Trush (see Trusk): Donaghmore DL 39; 28
Trusk giant's grave: Donaghmore DL 39; 34
Trusk hill: Donaghmore DL 39; 28
Trusk lough: Donaghmore DL 39; 28–29, 33–34
Trusk school: Donaghmore DL 39; 39
Trusk td: Donaghmore DL 39; 29, 39
Trusteen glebe: Killesher FH 14; 86–87
Trustrium td: Magheross MN 40; 148
Tryad Point: Artrea LY 6; 2
Tuadar, bard: Dungiven LY 15; 32
Tuam (Galway): Ballymore AH 1; 3, 10
Tuam diocese: Newry DN 3; 68
Tuam, Archbishhop of (1645): Misc. FH 4; 133
Tuath Ratha rocks: Clondermot LY 34; 57
Tuathal, family: Faughanvale LY 36; 49
Tubal td: Drumtullagh AM 16; 103
Tubber Aspug Aidan well: Magilligan LY 11; 88,
  103, 144
Tubber Inver well: Magheross MN 40; 146
Tubber Patrick (see Patrick's well): Dungiven LY
  15; 42
Tubber quarry: Misc. DL 39; 186

Tubber td: Raymoghy DL 39; 135, 196

Tubberbrin spring: Drumachose LY 9; 118

Tubbercloney school: Billy AM 16; 77

Tubbercorran (Tubbercoran) td: Down DN 17; 53, 56–57

Tubbercorran cromlech: Down DN 17; 60

Tubbercurry: Emlaghfad SO 40; 178

Tubbercurry: Kilmacteige SO 40; 185, 190, 194

Tubbercurry dispensary: Kilmacteige SO 40; 185

Tubberdonagh spring: Magilligan LY 11; 90, 127

Tubberdonagh well: Kilrea LY 27; 113, 127

Tubberdoney church: Macosquin LY 22; 97

Tubberdoney spring: Macosquin LY 22; 95, 97

Tubberdoney td: Drumragh TE 5; 108

Tubberdoney well: Ardclinis AM 13; 4, 7

Tubberdoney well: Drumragh TE 5; 108

Tubberdoney well: Killagan AM 23; 86

Tubberduell well: Aghanloo LY 11; 26

Tubberduell well: Magilligan LY 11; 86

Tubberfaris well: Enniskillen FH 4; 71

Tubberkeerawn well: Kilmacteige SO 40; 188, 196

Tubberlawn (see Toberslane): Misc. DL 39; 192

Tubber-Mhuirre well: Banagher LY 30; 12

Tubbermore td: Ballyscullion LY 6; 56

Tubbernabrock td: Misc. DL 39; 198

Tubbernacush Derryard spa well: Dungiven LY 15; 112

Tubbernacush well: Banagher LY 30; 44, 114

Tubbernadhuy (see Tubberdoney): Macosquin LY 22; 95

Tubbernaeuthe well: Banagher LY 30; 69

Tubbernaleck spring: Magilligan LY 11; 86

Tubbernasool well: Skerry AM 13; 107

Tubbernasuil well: Banagher LY 30; 12, 69, 114

Tubber-na-suil well: Enniskillen FH 4; 71

Tubberoneill td: Clonleigh DL 39; 12, 198

Tubberpatrick well: Ballyaghran LY 33; 9, 21

Tubberpatrick well: Banagher LY 30; 11–12

Tubberphadrig well: Enniskillen FH 4; 71

Tubberroddy td: Kilmacteige SO 40; 190, 197

Tubberroddy well: Kilmacteige SO 40; 188, 194

Tubberronagh village: Kilmacteige SO 40; 196

Tubberslawn (see Toberslane): Misc. DL 39; 196

Tubbrit church: Drumkeeran FH 14; 64

Tubbrit school: Drumkeeran FH 14; 66

Tubbrit school: Magheraculmoney FH 14; 108

Tubbrit td: Drumkeeran FH 14; 64, 66

Tuberdowney (see Toberdowney): Ballynure AM 32; 71

Tubrid district: Clogher TE 5; 41

Tucka lough: Drumgoon CN 40; 2

Tucka lough: Killdrumsherdan CN 40; 32

Tucker, Edward: Glynn AM 26; 40

Tucker, Lt H.: Ardkeen DN 7; 3

Tucker, Lt H.: Ardquin DN 7; 4

Tucker, Lt H.: Ballyhalbert DN 7; 6

Tucker, Lt H.: Ballyphilip DN 7; 7–8

Tucker, Lt H.: Castleboy DN 7; 26

Tucker, Lt H.: Newry DN 3; 114

Tuckmilltate school: Tyholland MN 40; 174–75

Tuckmillvale (see Tuckmilltate): Tyholland MN 40; 175

Tueslenagh td: Conwal DL 39; 27

Tuftarney td: Dunaghy AM 13; 24

Tulach church: Tullyrusk AM 21; 131

Tullagh bay: Lough Swilly DL 38; 132

Tullagh district: Misc. SO 40; 200

Tullagh hill: Mevagh DL 38; 54

Tullagh manor: Misc. FH 4; 133

Tullagh Point: Clonmany DL 38; 20

Tullagh Point: Lough Swilly DL 38; 132–33, 136

Tullagh td: Clonmany DL 38; 13, 16, 18, 20

Tullagh td: Mevagh DL 38; 55, 63

Tullagha barony: Tomregan FH 4; 125

Tullaghaggy water: Loughgilly AH 1; 86

Tullaghaglass td: Kilmacteige SO 40; 195, 197

Tullaghans hill: Finvoy AM 23; 68

Tullaghbeg td: Duneane AM 19; 124

Tullaghgarley (Tullygarley) td: Connor AM 19; 18, 26

Tullaghgarley (Tullygrally) td: Ahoghill AM 23; 34, 37–38, 40

Tullaghgarley cave: Ahoghill AM 23; 35

Tullaghgarley fort [I]: Ahoghill AM 23; 33

Tullaghgarley fort [II]: Ahoghill AM 23; 33, 35

Tullaghgarley fort [III]: Ahoghill AM 23; 34

Tullaghgarley meeting house: Ahoghill AM 23; 11

Tullaghgarley school: Connor AM 19; 26–27

Tullaghgarley school [I]: Ahoghill AM 23; 44, 49

Tullaghgarley school [II]: Ahoghill AM 23; 44, 48

Tullaghgarley Sunday school: Ahoghill AM 23; 48

Tullaghgore old church: Ballymoney AM 16; 20

Tullaghgore td: Ballymoney AM 16; 20, 27

Tullaghmurry West td: Ballyaghran LY 33; 9, 21

Tullaghoge (see Tullyhoge)

Tullaghore (Tulahora) td: Armoy AM 24; 2, 7

Tullaghore crosses: Armoy AM 24; 2

Tullaghore stones: Armoy AM 24; 9

Tullaghore well: Armoy AM 24; 7

Tullamore (see Tullymore): Killinchy DN 7; 86

Tullamore td: Drummaul AM 19; 87

Tullanafoile (Tulnafoile) td: Clogher TE 5; 36, 38, 45, 53

Tullanagh manor: Misc. FH 4; 133

Tullanaginn td: Magheraculmoney FH 14; 110–11

Tullanee giant's grave: Faughanvale LY 36; 11, 15, 21

Tullanee hamlet: Faughanvale LY 36; 6

Tullanee quarry: Faughanvale LY 36; 97

Tullanee td: Faughanvale LY 36; 13, 15, 17, 21, 30–31, 53, 57, 64, 69, 79, 90, 97, 99

Tullanleskin (see Tullinteskin)

Tullans district: Coleraine LY 33; 61

Tullans fort: Coleraine LY 33; 92, 132

Tullans paper mill: Coleraine LY 33; 91, 94, 128, 130–31

Tullans school: Coleraine LY 33; 67, 70, 133

Tullans Sunday school: Coleraine LY 33, 70, 133

Tullans td: Coleraine LY 33; 66, 94, 143, 145

Tullaugh td: Carlingford LH 40; 59

Tullavally hill: Drung CN 40; 19

Tullavally school: Drung CN 40; 22

Tulleghnabhascabhbeag lough: Templecarn DL 39; 157

Tullentrain (see Tullintrain): Cumber LY 28; 73

Tullerton, Richard: Magheragall AM 21; 106

Tullerton, Vallentine: Magheragall AM 21; 105

Tullewalla (see Tullavally): Drung CN 40; 22

Tulleystonal Castle: Raphoe DL 39; 130

Tullgrally (see Tullaghgarley): Ahoghill AM 23; 37

Tullie locality: Derrybrusk FH 4; 33

Tullighcross lough: Templecarn DL 39; 157

Tullinacross td: Blaris AM 8; 86

Tullinaghey Castle: Kilmacteige SO 40; 186

Tullinaglug Castle: Kilmacteige SO 40; 194

Tullinaglug td: Kilmacteige SO 40; 186, 193–94, 197

Tullinakill (see Tullynakill)

Tullinaneagish td: Aughnamullen MN 40; 77

Tullinangroove druidical circle: Muckno MN 40; 166

Tullinch school: Ahoghill AM 23; 23

Tullindoney (Tullindooney) td: Dromore DN 12; 71–73

Tullinisky mill: Garvaghy DN 12; 83

Tullinisky td: Garvaghy DN 12; 80–81

Tullintanvally mill: Annaclone DN 12; 18

Tullintanvally school: Annaclone DN 12; 15, 17–19

Tullintanvally td: Annaclone DN 12; 13–18

Tullinteskin (Tullanteskin) td: Cleenish FH 14; 24, 30

Tullinteskin school: Cleenish FH 14; 24

Tullintrain lough: Cumber LY 28; 6

Tullintrain quarry: Cumber LY 28; 125

Tullintrain school: Cumber LY 28; 73

Tullintrain td: Cumber LY 28; 9, 67, 71, 115, 120, 125–26

Tulliquin td: Clogher TE 5; 39

Tullivallevy td: Donacavey TE 5; 81

Tullmakross (see Tullynacross): Ballymore AH 1; 5

Tullnabratley (see Tullnabratly): Clonmany DL 38; 20

Tullnabratly Head: Clonmany DL 38; 13

Tullnabratly hill: Clonmany DL 38; 12

Tullnabratly td: Clonmany DL 38; 16, 18, 20

Tullnadall district: Clondavaddog DL 38; 4

Tullnagoran graveyard: Aghalurcher FH 4; 9

Tulloghbane td: Dunaghy AM 13; 13

Tulloughbane corn mill: Dunaghy AM 13; 13

Tulloughbane flax mill: Dunaghy AM 13; 13

Tullow (Carlow): Faughanvale LY 36; 12, 55

Tullumgrange Lower td: Dunsfort DN 17; 72

Tullumgrange Upper td: Dunsfort DN 17; 72

Tully (see Tullyaughnish): Lough Swilly DL 38; 127

Tully bleach green: Killesher FH 14; 84

Tully bog: Aghalurcher FH 4; 4

Tully bog: Clogher TE 5; 26

Tully bridge: Tullyaughnish DL 38; 84, 89

Tully Castle: Inishmacsaint FH 14; 75

Tully church: Tullyaughnish DL 38; 90

Tully corn mill: Killesher FH 14; 84

Tully cotton wick manufactory: Killesher FH 14; 84

Tully cove: Killead AM 35; 32

Tully Cross td: Ballywalter DN 7; 18

Tully district: Faughanvale LY 36; 30

Tully ferry: Tullyaughnish DL 38; 90

Tully fort: Killead AM 35; 28, 39

Tully fort: Kilrea LY 27; 129

Tully fort: Tamlaght Finlagan LY 25; 90, 109

Tully fort [I]: Ballyclug AM 23; 65

Tully fort [II]: Ballyclug AM 23; 65

Tully Glebe House: Killead AM 35; 46

Tully graveyard: Derryvullan FH 14; 41

Tully graveyard: Killead AM 35; 46

Tully graveyard: Tullyaughnish DL 38; 93

Tully Hall corn mill: Tullyaughnish DL 38; 89

Tully Hall flax mill: Tullyaughnish DL 38; 89

Tully Hall td: Tullyaughnish DL 38; 96

Tully hill: Ahoghill AM 23; 1, 3–4, 29

Tully hill: Devenish FH 14; 52

Tully hill: Killead AM 35; 7

Tully Lower td: Clondermot LY 34; 57, 75, 112–13, 120, 128, 133

Tully Masonic lodge room: Killead AM 35; 46

Tully meeting house: Carmavy AM 35; 3

Tully meeting house: Killead AM 35; 11–12, 20, 36, 38, 41–42, 45–46, 52

Tully mound: Killead AM 35; 27, 39

Tully Mountain td: Tullyaughnish DL 38; 96

Tully North mill: Aghalurcher FH 4; 8

Tully North standing stone: Loughguile AM 13; 74

Tully North td: Loughguile AM 13; 74, 76

Tully old church: Tullyaughnish DL 38; 90

Tully ph: Tullyaughnish DL 38; 84, 88, 90, 92–93, 96–97

Tully Point: Inishmacsaint FH 14; 76

Tully quarry: Faughanvale LY 36; 97

Tully school: Killead AM 35; 36, 38, 46, 52

Tully school: Killesher FH 14; 86

Tully South td: Aghalurcher FH 4; 3
Tully South td: Loughguile AM 13; 76
Tully standing stone: Loughguile AM 13; 69–70
Tully Sunday school: Killead AM 35; 38, 52
Tully td: Ballyclug AM 23; 53
Tully td: Blaris AM 8; 54
Tully td: Cleenish FH 14; 14, 30
Tully td: Clogher TE 5; 36
Tully td: Derryvullan FH 14; 46
Tully td: Donagh MN 40; 98
Tully td: Faughanvale LY 36; 13, 15, 17, 53–54, 64,
    69, 79, 90–91, 97, 99
Tully td: Inishmacsaint FH 14; 75
Tully td: Killead AM 35; 35, 40, 46–47, 50
Tully td: Loughguile AM 13; 74
Tully td: Misc. DL 39; 199
Tully td: Monaghan MN 40; 159
Tully td: Raymoghy DL 39; 139, 141
Tully td: Tamlaght Finlagan LY 25; 93, 112
Tully Upper td: Clondermot LY 34; 57, 62, 75,
    112–13, 120, 128, 133
Tully well: Tullyaughnish DL 38; 93
Tully, William: Carrickfergus AM 37; 121
Tullya td: Loughgilly AH 1; 85
Tullyagh (see Tullagh): Mevagh DL 38; 63
Tullyallen meeting house: Loughgilly AH 1; 86
Tullyallen mill: Loughgilly AH 1; 86
Tullyalley (see Tullyally): Clondermot LY 34; 113
Tullyally Lower flax mill: Clondermot LY 34; 133
Tullyally Lower quarry: Clondermot LY 34; 133
Tullyally Lower td: Clondermot LY 34; 75, 112–13,
    120, 128, 133
Tullyally td: Clondermot LY 34; 38, 57
Tullyally td: Moville DL 38; 73, 75
Tullyally Upper td: Clondermot LY 34; 75, 112–13,
    120, 128, 133
Tullyannan td: Misc. DL 39; 195
Tullyarb (see Tullyard): Lough Swilly DL 38; 135
Tullyard bogs: Lough Swilly DL 38; 135
Tullyard locality: Lough Swilly DL 38; 135
Tullyard td: Drumbo DN 7; 55, 59–60, 63
Tullyard td: Moira DN 12; 121
Tullyard td: Urney DL 39; 182
Tullyarmon brickfield: Aghanloo LY 11; 2, 32
Tullyarmon td: Aghanloo LY 11; 2, 13, 18, 20–21,
    26, 37, 39, 41–42
Tullyarnon (see Tullyarmon): Aghanloo LY 11; 21
Tullyarvy bog: Trory FH 14; 124
Tullyaughnish Glebe House: Tullyaughnish DL 38;
    89
Tullyaughnish ph: Clondavaddog DL 38; 1–4, 9
Tullyaughnish ph: Killygarvan DL 38; 36–38, 41
Tullyaughnish ph: Killymard DL 39; 98
Tullyaughnish ph: Lough Swilly DL 38; 127–29,
    149

Tullyaughnish ph: Mevagh DL 38; 54, 57, 63
Tullybalina corn mill: Cleenish FH 14; 18
Tullybalina td: Cleenish FH 14; 30
Tullyballydonell chapel: Aghalee AM 21; 28
Tullyballydonell chapel: Ballinderry AM 21; 41
Tullyballydonnel (see Tullyballydonell)
Tullyballydonnell (see Tullyballydonell)
Tullyballyna (see Tullybalina): Cleenish FH 14; 30
Tullybane (Tullyban) td: Derrykeighan AM 16; 86,
    91
Tullybane cove: Derrykeighan AM 16; 91
Tullybane school: Derrykeighan AM 16; 86, 95
Tullybane td: Dunluce AM 16; 116
Tullybaun (see Tullybane): Derrykeighan AM 16; 95
Tullybeg td: Tullyaughnish DL 38; 96
Tullyboard corn mill: Ballyphilip DN 7; 12
Tullyboard td: Ballyphilip DN 7; 10
Tullyboard td: Misc. DN 17; 125
Tullybogley td: Raymoghy DL 39; 135, 139,
    141–42, 199
Tullybond td: Ballyphilip DN 7; 8
Tullybrick bridge [I]: Ballynascreen LY 31; 7, 20
Tullybrick bridge [II]: Ballynascreen LY 31; 7, 20
Tullybrick Hamilton td: Tynan AH 1; 126, 131
Tullybrick mountain: Ballynascreen LY 31; 9, 24
Tullybrick old church: Ballynascreen LY 31; 27
Tullybrick school: Ballynascreen LY 31; 18
Tullybrick school: Drumgoon CN 40; 11
Tullybrick td: Ballynascreen LY 31; 10, 19, 22, 26,
    143
Tullybrisland corn mill: Faughanvale LY 36; 21
Tullybrisland flour mill: Faughanvale LY 36; 16, 21
Tullybrisland td: Faughanvale LY 36; 15, 17, 53, 63,
    69, 79, 91, 97
Tullybrisland wood: Faughanvale LY 36; 91
Tullybroom td: Clogher TE 5; 35, 39, 53
Tullybryan bog: Errigal Keerogue TE 20; 56
Tullybryan fort: Errigal Keerogue TE 20; 56
Tullybryan td: Errigal Keerogue TE 20; 48–49,
    56–57
Tullybuck hill: Drung CN 40; 19
Tullycarbie rectory: Clones FH 4; 29
Tullycarbury td: Devenish FH 14; 47
Tullycarn bog: Donaghcloney DN 12; 57
Tullycarn hill: Donaghcloney DN 12; 57
Tullycarn House: Donaghcloney DN 12; 58
Tullycarn td: Donaghcloney DN 12; 57, 59
Tullycarnan td: Ardglass DN 17; 1, 7, 125
Tullycarnan td: Ballyphilip DN 7; 7
Tullycarnan td: Witter DN 7; 126
Tullycarne td: Templecarn DL 39; 164
Tullycarnet corn mill: Knockbreda DN 7; 102
Tullycarnet td: Knockbreda DN 7; 102
Tullycarnon (see Tullycarnan)
Tullycavey td: Misc. DN 17; 123

Tullycharnan (see Tullycarnnan)

Tullycleagh school: Derryvullan FH 14; 36

Tullyclenah td: Dromore TE 5; 97, 99

Tullyco td: Laragh CN 40; 39

Tullycoghery fort: Muckno MN 40; 166

Tullyconnaught mill [I]: Seapatrick DN 12; 134

Tullyconnaught mill [II]: Seapatrick DN 12; 134

Tullyconnaught mill [III]: Seapatrick DN 12; 134

Tullyconnaught td: Seapatrick DN 12; 123, 126, 132, 134

Tullyconnell district: Clondavaddog DL 38; 4

Tullyconnell hill: Artrea TE 20; 9

Tullycorbet ph: Aughnamullen MN 40; 69

Tullycorbet ph: Ballybay MN 40; 78

Tullycorbet ph: Clogher TE 5; 41

Tullycorbet ph: Monaghan MN 40; 159

Tullycore td: Killinchy DN 7; 86

Tullycorken (see Tullycorker)

Tullycorker td: Clogher TE 5; 36, 53

Tullycreavy hill: Devenish FH 14; 52

Tullycreavy td: Devenish FH 14; 59

Tullycreenaght (Tullycrenaght) td: Antrim AM 29; 21

Tullycreenaght flax mill [I]: Antrim AM 29; 21, 50

Tullycreenaght flax mill [II]: Antrim AM 29; 21, 50

Tullycrevy (see Tullycreavy): Devenish FH 14; 59

Tullycronaught school: Drummaul AM 19; 92

Tullycross td: Misc. DN 17; 125

Tullycurry corn mill: Devenish FH 14; 53

Tullycusshun lough: Kilmacteige SO 40; 193

Tullydegan td: Shankill DN 12; 138

Tullydevenish corn mill: Devenish FH 14; 53

Tullydevenish td: Devenish FH 14; 59

Tullydonagh td: Faughanvale LY 36; 50

Tullydonnel Lower td: Raphoe DL 39; 127

Tullydonnel Upper td: Raphoe DL 39; 127

Tullydremond (see Terrydremont): Balteagh LY 9; 41

Tullydrum td: Tamlaght Finlagan LY 25; 93

Tullyear cave: Seapatrick DN 12; 126

Tullyear td: Seapatrick DN 12; 123, 126

Tullyfernon ph (see Tully): Tullyaughnish DL 38; 84

Tullygallon river: Drumhome DL 39; 61

Tullygally school: Shankill AH 1; 115

Tullygarby (see Tullaghgarley): Ahoghill AM 23; 34

Tullygarden td: Kilmore AH 1; 68–69, 69, 71, 73

Tullygarley (see Tullaghgarley): Ahoghill AM 23; 44

Tullygarty (see Tullaghgarley): Connor AM 19; 27

Tullygarvey barony: Drumgoon CN 40; 1

Tullygarvey barony: Drung CN 40; 19

Tullygarvey barony: Killdrumsherdan CN 40; 31

Tullygarvey barony: Laragh CN 40; 39

Tullygarvy (see Tullygarvey)

Tullygerravray td: Boho FH 14; 8

Tullygirvan (see Tullygirven): Comber DN 7; 38, 43

Tullygirven mill: Comber DN 7; 35, 38

Tullygirven school [I]: Comber DN 7; 34

Tullygirven school [II]: Comber DN 7; 34

Tullygirven td: Comber DN 7; 34–35, 37–38, 42–43

Tullygirvin (see Tullygirven): Comber DN 7; 42

Tullyglish beetling mill: Aughnamullen MN 40; 72–73

Tullyglish bleach mill: Aughnamullen MN 40; 72–73

Tullyglish td: Aughnamullen MN 40; 77

Tullyglush beetling mill: Keady AH 1; 50

Tullyglush hill: Dromore DN 12; 70

Tullyglush Kane flax mill: Tynan AH 1; 128

Tullyglush school: Dromore DN 12; 73

Tullyglush school: Keady AH 1; 50

Tullyglush td: Errigal Keerogue TE 20; 56–57

Tullyglush wash mill: Keady AH 1; 50

Tullygoan district: Banagher LY 30; 22, 86, 95–96, 100, 107

Tullygoan flax mill: Banagher LY 30; 100

Tullygoan river: Banagher LY 30; 100

Tullygone (see Tullygoan): Banagher LY 30; 95

Tullygowan fort: Ahoghill AM 23; 33, 35

Tullygowan td: Ahoghill AM 23; 40

Tullygrawley (see Tullaghgarley): Ahoghill AM 23; 49

Tullygurley (see Tullaghgarley): Ahoghill AM 23; 48

Tullyharm fort: Clogherny TE 20; 28

Tullyharney td: Derrybrusk FH 4; 30

Tullyhaw barony: Kinawley FH 4; 111

Tullyheeny mountain: Aghalurcher FH 4; 2

Tullyhenan td: Magherally DN 12; 114

Tullyhenry fort: Drumragh TE 5; 109

Tullyhenry td: Drumragh TE 5; 109

Tullyherne td: Killelagh LY 27; 102

Tullyheron (see Tullyherron): Donaghcloney DN 12; 57

Tullyherron (Tullyherran) td: Loughgilly AH 1; 85

Tullyherron chapel: Loughgilly AH 1; 86

Tullyherron school: Donaghcloney DN 12; 58

Tullyherron school: Loughgilly AH 1; 87

Tullyherron td: Donaghcloney DN 12; 57–59

Tullyhevin td: Grey Abbey DN 7; 67

Tullyho House: Tullylish DN 12; 143

Tullyhoe td: Tamlaght Finlagan LY 25; 72–74, 93

Tullyhog standing stone: Racavan AM 13; 102

Tullyhog td: Racavan AM 13; 102

Tullyhoge fort: Misc. TE 5; 146

Tullyhoge hamlet: Desertcreat TE 20; 32–34, 36

Tullyhoge hamlet: Tamlaght TE 20; 127

Tullyhona church: Killesher FH 14; 83, 90

Tullyhona td: Killesher FH 14; 82

Tullyhone [or Tullyhane] td: Clogher TE 5; 41–42

Tullyhone meeting house: Clogher TE 5; 39
Tullyhone school: Clogher TE 5; 41–42
Tullyhonour bog: Conwal DL 39; 24
Tullyhonour td: Conwal DL 39; 27
Tullyhork hamlet: Kilbarron DL 39; 77
Tullyhubbert corn mill: Comber DN 7; 31
Tullyhubbert flax mill: Comber DN 7; 31
Tullyhubbert td: Comber DN 7; 31, 37–38, 43
Tullyhubert (see Tullyhubbert): Comber DN 7; 37
Tullyhugh (Tullyhue) td: Ballymore AH 1; 3, 8, 13, 15–16, 18–19
Tullyhugh corn mill: Ballymore AH 1; 8, 10
Tullyhugh flour mill: Ballymore AH 1; 10
Tullyhumphry td: Currin MN 40; 86, 91
Tullyhun (see Tullyhone)
Tullyincrin corn mill: Kilskeery TE 5; 114
Tullyincrin td: Kilskeery TE 5; 114
Tullykeeran fort: Killelagh LY 27; 97
Tullykeeran td: Killelagh LY 27; 99
Tullykeller (see Tullykelter)
Tullykelter Castle: Devenish FH 14; 55
Tullykelter fort: Devenish FH 14; 55
Tullykelter td: Devenish FH 14; 59
Tullykenneye td: Aghalurcher FH 4; 14
Tullykiltor (see Tullykelter): Devenish FH 14; 55
Tullykinally td: Shankill DN 12; 138
Tullykitteagh carns: Dunaghy AM 13; 18, 24
Tullykitteagh cave: Dunaghy AM 13; 22
Tullykitteagh forts: Dunaghy AM 13; 24
Tullykitteagh giant's grave: Dunaghy AM 13; 22
Tullykitteagh Lower giant's graves: Dunaghy AM 13; 23
Tullykitteagh Lower td: Dunaghy AM 13; 23
Tullykitteagh td: Dunaghy AM 13; 18–19, 22–24
Tullykitteagh Upper td: Dunaghy AM 13; 18
Tullylack td: Templecarn DL 39; 164
Tullylammy bog: Derryvullan FH 14; 32
Tullylammy school: Derryvullan FH 14; 36
Tullyleggan bleach greens: Desertcreat TE 20; 32
Tullyleggan bleach mill: Desertcreat TE 20; 34
Tullyleggan bridge: Desertcreat TE 20; 33
Tullyleggan House: Desertcreat TE 20; 33
Tullyleggan quarry: Desertcreat TE 20; 33
Tullylime (see Tullylinn): Ballymore AH 1; 9
Tullylinkisay foundry: Magherafelt LY 6; 105
Tullylinkisay paper mill: Magherafelt LY 6; 105
Tullylinkisay td: Magherafelt LY 6; 105
Tullylinn td: Ballymore AH 1; 9, 14, 18
Tullylinsky td: Garvaghy DN 12; 83
Tullylinton td: Errigal Keerogue TE 20; 56, 56–57
Tullylish bridge: Tullylish DN 12; 142
Tullylish chapel: Magherally DN 12; 113
Tullylish chapel: Tullylish DN 12; 145
Tullylish church: Tullylish DN 12; 141, 145
Tullylish Glebe House: Garvaghy DN 12; 83

Tullylish House: Tullylish DN 12; 141, 143, 143
Tullylish mill [I]: Tullylish DN 12; 146
Tullylish mill [II]: Tullylish DN 12; 146
Tullylish mill [III]: Tullylish DN 12; 146
Tullylish mill [IV]: Tullylish DN 12; 146
Tullylish mill [IX]: Tullylish DN 12; 147
Tullylish mill [V]: Tullylish DN 12; 146
Tullylish mill [VI]: Tullylish DN 12; 146
Tullylish mill [VII]: Tullylish DN 12; 146
Tullylish mill [VIII]: Tullylish DN 12; 146
Tullylish mill [X]: Tullylish DN 12; 147
Tullylish mill [XI]: Tullylish DN 12; 147
Tullylish mill [XII]: Tullylish DN 12; 147
Tullylish mill [XIII]: Tullylish DN 12; 147
Tullylish mills: Tullylish DN 12; 141–42
Tullylish ph: Aghaderg DN 12; 1, 6, 8
Tullylish ph: Ballymore AH 1; 7, 18
Tullylish ph: Donaghcloney DN 12; 57–59
Tullylish ph: Garvaghy DN 12; 81
Tullylish ph: Kilmore AH 1; 60–61, 72
Tullylish ph: Magherally DN 12; 112, 114
Tullylish ph: Misc. DN 17; 121
Tullylish ph: Montiaghs AH 1; 91
Tullylish ph: Seagoe AH 1; 104
Tullylish ph: Seapatrick DN 12; 124
Tullylish school: Tullylish DN 12; 147
Tullylish td: Tullylish DN 12; 141, 143–47
Tullylish vitriol works: Tullylish DN 12; 142
Tullyliukeley td: Magherafelt LY 6; 95
Tullyloan td: Trory FH 14; 125
Tullylone school: Tydavnet MN 40; 171–72
Tullyloob td: Moira DN 12; 121
Tullylusgain flax mill: Donegal DL 39; 47
Tullymacan td: Ballymore AH 1; 14–18
Tullymacarath school: Dromore DN 12; 77
Tullymacarath td: Dromore DN 12; 77
Tullymacaret school: Dromore DN 12; 73
Tullymackilmartin chapel: Donaghmoyne MN 40; 107
Tullymackilmartin graveyard: Donaghmoyne MN 40; 107
Tullymain corn mill: Faughanvale LY 36; 98
Tullymain quarry: Faughanvale LY 36; 97
Tullymain steam mill: Faughanvale LY 36; 98
Tullymain td: Faughanvale LY 36; 17, 53, 63, 69, 79, 91, 97, 99
Tullymain td: Tamlaght Finlagan LY 25; 74
Tullymally manor: Misc. DN 17; 125
Tullymally td: Misc. DN 17; 126
Tullymany lough: Devenish FH 14; 47
Tullymargy td: Devenish FH 14; 59
Tullymay (see Tullymoy): Kilmacteige SO 40; 196
Tullymore beetling mill: Skerry AM 13; 111
Tullymore bridge: Racavan AM 13; 99
Tullymore cove: Skerry AM 13; 118

Tullymore estate mill [I]: Eglish AH 1; 44
Tullymore estate mill [II]: Eglish AH 1; 44
Tullymore estate mill [III]: Eglish AH 1; 44
Tullymore House: Kilcoo DN 3; 43
Tullymore House: Skerry AM 13; 111
Tullymore Park district: Kilcoo DN 3; 41
Tullymore river (see also Shimna river): Kilcoo DN 3; 41
Tullymore school: Donaghmore DN 3; 8
Tullymore td: Donaghmore DN 3; 9
Tullymore td: Inishmacsaint FH 14; 70
Tullymore td: Killinchy DN 7; 86
Tullymore td: Kilmore AH 1; 61, 66, 68, 70, 73
Tullymore td: Racavan AM 13; 87, 98
Tullymore td: Skerry AM 13; 111, 118
Tullymore td: Tullyaughnish DL 38; 96
Tullymoy td: Kilmacteige SO 40; 196–97
Tullymurry (Tullymurray) td: Down DN 17; 53, 55, 57
Tullymurry td: Donaghmore DN 3; 8–9
Tullynacnous mill: Killyleagh DN 17; 80
Tullynacreen td: Misc. DN 17; 124
Tullynacross (Tullinacross) td: Ballymore AH 1; 7, 9, 12, 16, 18
Tullynacross corn mill: Ballymore AH 1; 5, 10
Tullynacross flax mill: Ballymore AH 1; 10
Tullynacross td: Inch DN 17; 77
Tullynacross td: Kildress TE 20; 58
Tullynacrue (Tullymacrue) td: Misc. DN 17; 126–27
Tullynacrue school: Misc. DN 17; 127
Tullynagee school: Kilmood DN 7; 96
Tullynagee td: Kilmood DN 7; 94–96
Tullynaglug td: Enniskillen FH 4; 82
Tullynagoan td: Aghavea FH 4; 23
Tullynahatna school: Muckno MN 40; 168
Tullynahinnera hill: Aughnamullen MN 40; 69
Tullynahinnera td: Aughnamullen MN 40; 77
Tullynahinnion (Tullynahunnion) td: Ahoghill AM 23; 25
Tullynahinnion school: Ahoghill AM 23; 44, 47, 50
Tullynahinnion standing stones: Ahoghill AM 23; 34
Tullynahinnion Sunday school: Ahoghill AM 23; 47
Tullynahuinna (see Tullynahinnera): Aughnamullen MN 40; 69
Tullynahuncon (see Tullynahinnion): Ahoghill AM 23; 34
Tullynahunnian (see Tullynahinnion): Ahoghill AM 23; 44
Tullynakill church: Tullynakill DN 7; 123
Tullynakill ph: Comber DN 7; 32, 34
Tullynakill ph: Killinchy DN 7; 86–87
Tullynakill ph: Misc. DN 17; 121
Tullynakill td: Comber DN 7; 44
Tullynakill td: Tullynakill DN 7; 122
Tullynamalloge beetling mill: Keady AH 1; 50

Tullynamalloge flax mill [I]: Keady AH 1; 50
Tullynamalloge flax mill [II]: Keady AH 1; 50
Tullynamalloge meeting house: Keady AH 1; 47
Tullynamalloge wash mill: Keady AH 1; 50
Tullynamatrow td: Aughnamullen MN 40; 77
Tullynamullan bog: Connor AM 19; 20
Tullynascadagh triangulation point: Belleek FH 14; 1
Tullynashon hill: Laragh CN 40; 39
Tullynaskeagh East bog: Killanny MN 40; 130
Tullynaskeagh td: Dunsfort DN 17; 72
Tullynaskeagh West bog: Killanny MN 40; 130
Tullynaspick district: Bright DN 17; 34–35, 118
Tullynavall school: Creggan AH 1; 27
Tullynavarney td: Kinawley FH 4; 121
Tullynavin church: Moville DL 38; 74
Tullynavin td: Moville DL 38; 73
Tullynawood lough: Keady AH 1; 50
Tullyneevin td: Aghalurcher FH 4; 14
Tullynewbane td: Glenavy AM 21; 79
Tullynewbank forts: Glenavy AM 21; 90
Tullynewbank td: Glenavy AM 21; 79
Tullynewy flax mill: Dunaghy AM 13; 13
Tullynewy td: Dunaghy AM 13; 13
Tullyniskan coalfield: Clonoe TE 20; 29
Tullyniskan mill–ponds: Tullyniskan TE 20; 138
Tullyniskan mills: Tullyniskan TE 20; 138
Tullyniskan ph: Clonoe TE 20; 30–31
Tullyniskan ph: Desertcreat TE 20; 32
Tullyniskan ph: Donaghenry TE 20; 37–38
Tullyniskan ph: Drumglass TE 20; 40, 43
Tullyniskan ph: Killyman TE 20; 67
Tullyniskan ph: Pomeroy TE 20; 70
Tullyniskey (see Tullinisky): Garvaghy DN 12; 81
Tullynore (Tullymore) td: Hillsborough DN 12; 85, 106
Tullynure bridges: Lissan LY 31; 99
Tullynure chapel: Lissan LY 31; 89, 92, 97–99, 104, 107
Tullynure chapel graveyard: Lissan LY 31; 98
Tullynure chapel school: Lissan LY 31; 92, 98
Tullynure chapel Sunday school: Lissan LY 31; 107
Tullynure church: Lissan LY 31; 89, 92–95, 97–99, 103, 106–07
Tullynure church school: Lissan LY 31; 89–90, 92, 94–95, 98–99
Tullynure demesne: Lissan LY 31; 99
Tullynure graveyard: Lissan LY 31; 91, 97, 100, 106
Tullynure mill: Tyholland MN 40; 175
Tullynure moss: Lissan LY 31; 101–02
Tullynure Sunday school: Lissan LY 31; 95, 107
Tullynure td: Lissan LY 31; 104, 108–09
Tullyodonnell chapel: Desertcreat TE 20; 33
Tullyollagh mill: Enniskillen FH 4; 69
Tullyollagh td: Enniskillen FH 4; 82

Tullyor (see Tullyorior)
Tullyorier (see Tullyorior)
Tullyorior mill: Garvaghy DN 12; 82
Tullyorior school: Garvaghy DN 12; 83
Tullyorior td: Garvaghy DN 12; 81–83
Tullyorior td: Seapatrick DN 12; 124
Tullyowen House: Killea and Taughboyne DL 39;
   87
Tullyowen td: Killea and Taughboyne DL 39; 80, 84
Tullyowen td: Taughboyne DL 39; 148, 154–55, 196
Tullyown (see Tullyowen)
Tullypollen ph: Misc. DN 17; 118
Tullyquilly school: Drumgath DN 3; 21
Tullyquilly td: Drumgath DN 3; 19, 21
Tullyraghen school: Muckno MN 40; 168
Tullyrain hill: Magheracross FH 14; 93
Tullyrain td: Magheracross FH 14; 102
Tullyrain td: Magherally DN 12; 114
Tullyrain td: Tullylish DN 12; 144
Tullyrample td: Currin MN 40; 92
Tullyrane (see Tullyrain): Magheracross FH 14; 93
Tullyrap corn mill: Taughboyne DL 39; 149, 154
Tullyrap flax mill: Taughboyne DL 39; 154
Tullyrap td: Taughboyne DL 39; 148, 154, 184, 196
Tullyrasmeeron td: Cleenish FH 14; 30
Tullyratty mine: Ballyculter DN 17; 30
Tullyratty smithy: Ballyculter DN 17; 30
Tullyratty td: Ballyculter DN 17; 31
Tullyraw bleach mill: Artrea TE 20; 10
Tullyraw church: Artrea TE 20; 9
Tullyreagh bog: Aghavea FH 4; 18
Tullyreagh td: Aghavea FH 4; 17, 23, 25
Tullyreagh td: Derrybrusk FH 4; 30
Tullyreagh td: Kirkinriola AM 23; 88, 92, 121
Tullyrean td: Aughnamullen MN 40; 77
Tullyree td: Donagh MN 40; 98
Tullyroan bog: Kilcronaghan LY 31; 64, 78
Tullyroan fort: Kilcronaghan LY 31; 86
Tullyroan meeting house: Clonfeacle AH 1; 21, 24
Tullyroan quarry: Kildress TE 20; 59
Tullyroan Sunday school: Kilcronaghan LY 31; 74
Tullyroan td: Kilcronaghan LY 31; 64, 84, 143
Tullyrush (Tullyrusk) td: Donacavey TE 5; 65, 77,
   80–81, 83, 87
Tullyrush school: Donacavey TE 5; 65
Tullyrush td: Clogher TE 5; 59
Tullyrusk Castle: Ballinderry AM 21; 53
Tullyrusk Castle: Derryaghy AM 8; 93
Tullyrusk Castle fort: Ballinderry AM 21; 53
Tullyrusk chapel: Tullyrusk AM 21; 135
Tullyrusk chapel: Umgall AM 35; 159
Tullyrusk forts: Tullyrusk AM 21; 132–33, 139
Tullyrusk graveyard: Ballinderry AM 21; 52–53
Tullyrusk old church: Ballinderry AM 21; 52–53
Tullyrusk old church: Tullyrusk AM 21; 132–33

Tullyrusk old graveyard: Tullyrusk AM 21; 132
Tullyrusk ph: Ballinderry AM 21; 53
Tullyrusk ph: Blaris DN 12; 40
Tullyrusk ph: Camlin AM 21; 60, 64, 69
Tullyrusk ph: Derryaghy AM 8; 118
Tullyrusk ph: Glenavy AM 21; 77, 80, 83, 88
Tullyrusk ph: Killead AM 35; 8, 20
Tullyrusk ph: Misc. AM 10; 129
Tullyrusk school: Ballinderry AM 21; 53
Tullyrusk td: Ballinderry AM 21; 52–53
Tullyrusk td: Blaris DN 12; 42, 42
Tullyrusk td: Glenavy AM 21; 80
Tullyrusk td: Tullyrusk AM 21; 131–32
Tullysape (see Tullyrap)
Tullysecarny forts: Manorhamilton Union LM 40;
   52
Tullytanvally (see Tullintanvally)
Tullytramon td: Misc. DN 17; 125
Tullytrasna td: Kilteevoge DL 39; 114
Tullyvalla (see Tullavally): Drung CN 40; 19
Tullyvalley (see Tullyvally)
Tullyvally fort: Donacavey TE 5; 82
Tullyvally td: Donacavey TE 5; 77, 80–82
Tullyvally td: Killowen LY 33; 168
Tullyvanna td: Killowen LY 33; 165
Tullyveagh (Tullyreagh) td: Artrea TE 20; 7
Tullyveagh bleach mill: Artrea TE 20; 7, 10
Tullyveagh school: Artrea TE 20; 10
Tullyveery cotton factory: Killyleagh DN 17; 80
Tullyveran (see Tullyvernan)
Tullyvernan female school: Clogher TE 5; 41, 43
Tullyvernan male school: Clogher TE 5; 41
Tullyvernan school: Clogher TE 5; 43, 51
Tullyvernan td: Clogher TE 5; 32, 34–36, 41, 51, 53
Tullyvernon (see Tullyvernan)
Tullyverry corn mill: Faughanvale LY 36; 98
Tullyverry flax mill: Faughanvale LY 36; 98
Tullyverry quarry: Faughanvale LY 36; 97
Tullyverry td: Faughanvale LY 36; 17, 53, 63–64,
   69, 79, 91, 97
Tullyvesticonnaught (see Tullywesticonnaught):
   Saintfield DN 7; 117
Tullyvin: Killdrumsherdan CN 40; 33–34, 37
Tullyvin: Laragh CN 40; 42
Tullyvin forts: Killdrumsherdan CN 40; 34
Tullyvin House: Drumgoon CN 40; 8
Tullyvin House: Drung CN 40; 23
Tullyvin House: Killdrumsherdan CN 40; 34–35, 37
Tullyvin td: Killdrumsherdan CN 40; 32
Tullyvinney td: Raphoe DL 39; 127
Tullyvoccady td: Templecarn FH 14; 118
Tullyvrack (see Ora More): Cleenish FH 14; 30
Tullyweal (see Tullyweel): Enniskillen FH 4; 72
Tullywee and McGeagh td: Dromore TE 5; 99
Tullyweel td: Enniskillen FH 4; 72, 82

Tullyweeny bleach mill: Artrea TE 20; 10

Tullywesticonaught (see Tullywesticonnaught): Saintfield DN 7; 120

Tullywesticonnaught td: Saintfield DN 7; 117–20

Tullywhisker school: Urney DL 39; 182

Tullywilla hill: Drung CN 40; 19

Tullywinney td: Loughgilly AH 1; 85

Tulnabratley (see Tullnabratly): Clonmany DL 38; 12

Tulnabratly (see Tullnabratly): Clonmany DL 38; 16

Tulnacur td: Cleenish FH 14; 30

Tulnafeole (see Tullanafoile)

Tulnafevel (see Tullanafoile)

Tulnagee bog: Desertlyn LY 31; 44

Tulnagee fort [I]: Desertlyn LY 31; 44

Tulnagee fort [II]: Desertlyn LY 31; 44

Tulnagee fort [III]: Desertlyn LY 31; 44

Tulnagee td: Desertlyn LY 31; 42, 44

Tulnaglaur hill: Derryvullan FH 14; 31

Tulnaglaur td: Magheraculmoney FH 14; 103

Tulnagrew td: Maghera LY 18; 80

Tulnavert bog: Clogher TE 5; 26

Tulnavert td: Clogher TE 5; 38–39, 53

Tulpeston church: Misc. DN 17; 117

Tumery (see Tummery)

Tummery corn mill: Dromore TE 5; 101

Tummery Gal td: Dromore TE 5; 99

Tummery school: Dromore TE 5; 102

Tummery td: Dromore TE 5; 101–02

Tummery Teag td: Dromore TE 5; 99

Tummocks standing stones: Misc. LY 31; 113, 116, 118

Tumpher td: Clonoe TE 20; 29–31

Tun (Ton) banks: Magilligan LY 11; 84, 97, 130

Tun banks: Lough Swilly DL 38; 137, 140

Tun banks: Moville DL 38; 72

Tunnagh glebe: Killesher FH 14; 86

Tunnagh td: Kinawley FH 4; 110

Tunny Point: Glenavy AM 21; 82

Tunnyglashkin td: Enniskillen FH 4; 82

Tunnyglassen (see Tonyglassan): Ballybay MN 40; 81

Tunnyglassin (see Tonyglassan): Ballybay MN 40; 84

Tunnyhabbock locality: Lough Swilly DL 38; 142

Tunnylammon (see Tunnylummon): Cleenish FH 14; 14

Tunnylummon lime-kilns: Cleenish FH 14; 26

Tunnylummon td: Cleenish FH 14; 14, 30

Tunnymallow td: Cleenish FH 14; 29

Tunsalaugh (see Treansallagh): Taughboyne DL 39; 150

Turbeyrgeyll td: Ballylinny AM 32; 30

Turbintaine district: Misc. SO 40; 200

Turbitt, James: Carrickfergus AM 37; 117

Turbitt, John: Errigal LY 27; 65

Turbitt, John: Macosquin LY 22; 93

Turbitt, Margrett: Errigal LY 27; 65

Turbitt, Matthew: Aghanloo LY 11; 12, 17, 20–22, 26

Turbotstown (Westmeath): Drumlumman CN 40; 15, 17

Ture House: Muff DL 38; 80

Ture quarry: Muff DL 38; 80

Ture river: Muff DL 38; 80

Ture td: Muff DL 38; 80–82

Tureagh (Toreagh) td: Raloo AM 32; 80, 83, 90, 103, 108, 116, 129, 133

Tureagh flax mill: Raloo AM 32; 82, 84, 92, 119, 133

Tureagh graveyard: Raloo AM 32; 81, 90, 93, 107–08, 123, 133

Tureagh hill: Armoy AM 24; 2–3

Tureagh meeting house: Raloo AM 32; 90–91, 94–95, 97–98, 118, 120–21

Tureagh moss: Raloo AM 32; 82

Tureagh old church: Raloo AM 32; 81, 90, 93, 107–08, 117, 123, 133

Tureagh Presbyterian Sunday school: Raloo AM 32; 119, 130

Tureagh quarry: Raloo AM 32; 82

Tureagh school: Raloo AM 32; 85, 117, 119, 130, 133

Tureagh Unitarian Sunday school: Raloo AM 32; 118

Turfahern (see Turfahun)

Turfahun (Turfahin) td: Billy AM 16; 46, 63

Turfahun altar stone: Billy AM 16; 69

Turfahun bog: Billy AM 16; 67, 71

Turfahun cave: Billy AM 16; 63

Turgan (see Tirgan): Desertmartin LY 31; 56

Turglass bog: Culfeightrin AM 24; 82

Turglass td: Culfeightrin AM 24; 57

Turk, Robert: Tamlaght TE 20; 109

Turlevin td: Moville DL 38; 75

Turmagh (see Tonaght): Misc. LY 31; 118

Turmeel (Tirmeel) td: Banagher LY 30; 22, 24

Turmeel bog: Banagher LY 30; 78

Turmeel glebe: Banagher LY 30; 15

Turmeel school: Dungiven LY 15; 18, 102, 117–19

Turmeel Sunday school: Dungiven LY 15; 18

Turmeel td: Dungiven LY 15; 1, 18, 22, 27, 45–46, 50, 63–64, 74, 88, 92, 101

Turmeil (see Turmeel)

Turmiel (see Turmeel)

Turmoyra td: Seagoe AH 1; 110

Turmoyra windmill: Seagoe AH 1; 105

Turnacreagh coves: Loughguile AM 13; 70–71

Turnacreagh td: Loughguile AM 13; 71

Turnacrumble hill: Derryaghy AM 8; 97

Turnaface td: Lissan LY 31; 108

Turnagrough td: Derryaghy AM 8; 114–15

Turnagrove td: Loughguile AM 13; 76

Turnakibeck (Tirnakibeck) td: Kildollagh LY 22; 68, 73

Turnakibeck cave: Kildollagh LY 22; 73

Turnakibeck fort: Kildollagh LY 22; 69, 73

Turnamuck td: Balteagh LY 9; 45

Turnaran td: Grey Abbey DN 7; 68

Turnareddog td: Loughguile AM 13; 76

Turnarobert House: Armoy AM 24; 4

Turnarobert well: Armoy AM 24; 6

Turnaroy bridge: Derryaghy AM 8; 108

Turnaroy fort: Derryaghy AM 8; 97

Turnaroy standing stones: Derryaghy AM 8; 98

Turnaroy td: Derryaghy AM 8; 91, 98, 108, 115

Turnary clothing mill: Aghabog MN 40; 62

Turnbull, James: Drumachose LY 9; 104

Turnbull, James: Kilrea LY 27; 120, 127

Turnbull, James: Tamlaght Finlagan LY 25; 70, 82

Turner, Dr: Blaris DN 12; 45, 49

Turner, Edward: Newry DN 3; 100, 104

Turner, family: Blaris AM 8; 21

Turner, Francis: Blaris DN 12; 40, 46, 50

Turner, Francis: Magheramesk AM 21; 116–17, 129–30

Turner, Isaac: Hillsborough DN 12; 102, 106

Turner, James: Aghagallon AM 21; 23–24

Turner, John: Warrenpoint DN 3; 118

Turner, John [I]: Hillsborough DN 12; 106

Turner, John [II]: Hillsborough DN 12; 106

Turner, Mr: Carlingford LH 40; 59

Turner, Richard: Magheramesk AM 21; 122

Turner, Robert: Warrenpoint DN 3; 118

Turner, Samuel: Rashee AM 32; 140

Turner, Stuart: Blaris AM 8; 64

Turner, Thomas: Ballinderry AM 21; 58

Turner, Thomas: Newry DN 3; 100

Turner, William: Hillsborough DN 12; 106

Turnley, Francis: Ardclinis AM 13; 1, 3–4, 6, 9

Turnley, Francis: Carnmoney AM 2; 36, 39–40, 45, 58, 77, 81–82, 90

Turnley, Francis: Layd AM 13; 46–47, 49

Turnley, James: Holywood DN 7; 76–77, 81

Turnley, John: Glynn AM 26; 39

Turnley, Mr: Down DN 17; 58

Turnley, Mrs James: Holywood DN 7; 76

Turraloskin cave: Ramoan AM 24; 105

Turraloskin td: Ramoan AM 24; 104

Turreagh (see Tureagh): Raloo AM 32; 83

Turree (see Tirhugh): Killelagh LY 27; 101

Turretine, Rev.: Kilcronaghan LY 31; 79, 136

Turrmore td: Newry DN 3; 106

Turry td: Tynan AH 1; 124

Turtle Dove Lock: Aghagallon AM 21; 6

Turtle, Ann: Aghagallon AM 21; 22

Turtle, John: Aghalee AM 21; 33

Turtle, John: Blaris DN 12; 40–42

Turtle, John: Magheramesk AM 21; 116, 118

Turtle, Lancilet: Aghagallon AM 21; 8

Turtle's orchard: Magheramesk AM 21; 113

Tuskan Castle: Aghaderg DN 12; 7

Tutan, Arthur: Billy AM 16; 77

Tuten, family: Derryaghy AM 8; 103

Tuthill, Mrs: Clogher TE 5; 41

Tuthill, Rev. J.B.: Belleek FH 14; 5

Tuthill, Rev. J.B.: Clogher TE 5; 40

Tutin (see Tooting): Killead AM 35; 49

Twaddle, Alexander: Carrickfergus AM 37; 112

Twadel, family: Derrykeighan AM 16; 89

Tweed river: Termoneeny LY 6; 127, 132

Tweed, family: Kilraghts AM 16; 130

Tweed, Jane: Kilraghts AM 16; 132

Tweed, Robert: Island Magee AM 10; 81, 86, 90

Tweedle, James: Ballintoy AM 24; 27

Tweedle, Joseph: Ballintoy AM 24; 28

Tweedle, William: Ballintoy AM 24; 28

Twelve Cairns (see Slieve Croob): Dromara DN 12; 62

Twelve standing stones: Banagher LY 30; 65

Twelve stones fort: Banagher LY 30; 44

Twenty Acres giant's graves: Culfeightrin AM 24; 55

Twenty Acres stone column: Culfeightrin AM 24; 55

Twibridge bridge: Kilroot AM 26; 72, 77–78, 80

Twigg, Capt.: Carlingford LH 40; 57, 59

Twigg, Richard: Clogher TE 5; 29

Twiggery river: Donacavey TE 5; 62, 64

Two Big Men's Beds giant's grave: Laragh CN 40; 42

Two Phinnises Island: Cleenish FH 14; 13

Tyanee bogs: Tamlaght O'Crilly LY 18; 87, 133–34

Tyanee Castle: Tamlaght O'Crilly LY 18; 134

Tyanee chapel: Tamlaght O'Crilly LY 18; 136

Tyanee church: Tamlaght O'Crilly LY 18; 89, 96, 104–05

Tyanee curacy: Tamlaght O'Crilly LY 18; 91

Tyanee hibernian school: Tamlaght O'Crilly LY 18; 138–39

Tyanee Island: Tamlaght O'Crilly LY 18; 134

Tyanee national school: Tamlaght O'Crilly LY 18; 141–42

Tyanee Presbyterian school: Tamlaght O'Crilly LY 18; 141

Tyanee Presbyterian Sunday school: Tamlaght O'Crilly LY 18; 142

Tyanee Sunday school: Tamlaght O'Crilly LY 18; 142–43

Tyanee td: Ballyscullion LY 6; 56

Tyanee td: Tamlaght O'Crilly LY 18; 89, 92, 96–98, 105, 133, 136–38

Tychany forts: Clogher TE 5; 45

Tychany td: Clogher TE 5; 45

Tydavnet: Errigal Truagh MN 40; 121

Tydavnet: Tydavnet MN 40; 170–71

Tydavnet ph: Aghalurcher FH 4; 1

Tydavnet ph: Clogher TE 5; 24, 41

Tydavnet ph: Clones FH 4; 26

Tydavnet ph: Donagh MN 40; 98

Tydavnet ph: Errigal Truagh MN 40; 120

Tydavnet ph: Monaghan MN 40; 159

Tydavnet school: Tydavnet MN 40; 171–72

Tygore td: Faughanvale LY 36; 53, 64, 69, 79–80, 91, 97, 99

Tyholland ph: Clogher TE 5; 41

Tyholland ph: Donagh MN 40; 98

Tyholland ph: Monaghan MN 40; 159

Tyholland ph: Tynan AH 1; 124, 128

Tyler, Dr: Magilligan LY 11; 85, 100

Tyler, H.H.: Drumachose LY 9; 97, 104

Tyler, Mrs: Drumachose LY 9; 71

Tyler, W.: Aughnamullen MN 40; 76

Tyler, Watt: Faughanvale LY 36; 64

Tylleard td: Donaghedy TE 5; 92

Tynan: Coleraine LY 33; 97

Tynan: Tynan AH 1; 124–27, 129, 131–32

Tynan Abbey: Drumragh TE 5; 109

Tynan Abbey: Tynan AH 1; 127–29

Tynan barracks: Tynan AH 1; 126

Tynan chapel: Tynan AH 1; 126, 131

Tynan chapel school: Tynan AH 1; 131

Tynan church: Tynan AH 1; 126–27, 131

Tynan court house: Tynan AH 1; 126

Tynan cross: Tynan AH 1; 126, 129, 132

Tynan dispensary: Tynan AH 1; 126, 131

Tynan Glebe House: Tynan AH 1; 127, 131

Tynan mill: Tynan AH 1; 128

Tynan ph: Clontibret MN 40; 85

Tynan ph: Eglish AH 1; 43

Tynan post office: Tynan AH 1; 126

Tynan river: Tynan AH 1; 124, 128

Tynan school: Tynan AH 1; 126, 129, 132

Tynan td: Clogher TE 5; 32

Tynan td: Tynan AH 1; 131

Tyrarnan (see Tireenan)

Tyrconnell: Aghanloo LY 11; 7

Tyrconnell: Donegal DL 39; 45, 48, 51

Tyrconnell: Faughanvale LY 36; 48

Tyrconnell: Killymard DL 39; 94, 96–97

Tyrconnell: Magilligan LY 11; 97, 105

Tyrconnell: Manorhamilton Union LM 40; 50

Tyrconnell district: Misc. TE 5; 146

Tyrconnell, Bishop of: Newry DN 3; 66

Tyrconnell, family: Clondermot LY 34; 1

Tyrconnell, Lord: Enniskillen FH 4; 52

Tyrconnell, Lord: Misc. LY 31; 136

Tyregrenan (see Tireenan)

Tyrela (see Tyrella): Down DN 17; 44

Tyrella House: Down DN 17; 51

Tyrella ph: Down DN 17; 44, 51

Tyrella ph: Misc. DN 17; 120, 122

Tyreskenedy (see Tirkennedy)

Tyrgan td: Desertlyn LY 31; 35

Tyrhoman (see Tirhomin): Tullyaughnish DL 38; 92

Tyrhugh barony: Donegal DL 39; 42, 51

Tyrhugh barony: Drumhome DL 39; 58

Tyrhugh barony: Kilbarron DL 39; 74

Tyrhugh barony: Killymard DL 39; 96

Tyrhugh barony: Templecarn DL 39; 156, 158, 163

Tyrhugh barony: Templecarn FH 14; 118

Tyrhugh diocese: Kilbarron DL 39; 74

Tyrigorry (see Tirygory)

Tyrigory (see Tirygory)

Tyrioddy bog: Killea and Taughboyne DL 39; 80

Tyrkenedy (see Tirkennedy): Enniskillen FH 4; 50

Tyrkernaghan td: Donaghedy TE 5; 92

Tyrnedrole td: Magheross MN 40; 149

Tyrogaroan td: Magheross MN 40; 149

Tyrone: Aghabog MN 40; 65

Tyrone: Aghalurcher FH 4; 1, 5, 14, 16

Tyrone: Ballynure AM 32; 49

Tyrone: Blaris AM 8; 3, 5, 70, 72, 75

Tyrone: Blaris DN 12; 31

Tyrone: Carnmoney AM 2; 60, 72

Tyrone: Clondermot LY 34; 63

Tyrone: Clonfeacle AH 1; 21–23

Tyrone: Clonleigh DL 39; 1, 4, 6–8, 14, 16

Tyrone: Derrybrusk FH 4; 30

Tyrone: Donegal DL 39; 53

Tyrone: Drumhome DL 39; 63

Tyrone: Drumkeeran FH 14; 62

Tyrone: Dungiven LY 15; 66–67, 84, 104

Tyrone: Eglish AH 1; 43

Tyrone: Enniskeen CN 40; 26, 30

Tyrone: Enniskillen FH 4; 41, 44, 48, 75

Tyrone: Errigal Truagh MN 40; 121

Tyrone: Faughanvale LY 36; 44, 56, 63

Tyrone: Galloon FH 4; 92

Tyrone: Killea and Taughboyne DL 39; 81

Tyrone: Killead AM 35; 22

Tyrone: Killyman AH 1; 55

Tyrone: Killymard DL 39; 96

Tyrone: Maghera LY 18; 39

Tyrone: Magilligan LY 11; 118–19

Tyrone: Misc. LY 31; 132

Tyrone: Misc. TE 5; 146

Tyrone: Newry DN 3; 72, 87

Tyrone: Templecarn DL 39; 157

Tyrone: Tydavnet MN 40; 169

Tyrone: Urney DL 39; 174
Tyrone Canal: Clonoe TE 20; 30–31
Tyrone Canal: Coleraine LY 33; 99
Tyrone Canal: Donaghenry TE 20; 38
Tyrone Canal: Drumglass TE 20; 43
Tyrone Canal: Killyman TE 20; 67
Tyrone Canal: Tullyniskan TE 20; 140
Tyrone collieries: Clonoe TE 20; 30
Tyrone collieries: Newry DN 3; 86
Tyrone county: Tartaraghan AH 1; 121
Tyrone mountains: Donegal DL 39; 45
Tyrone mountains: Misc. LY 31; 111

Tyrone mountains: Urney DL 39; 175
Tyrone Tummock tumulus: Misc. LY 31; 118–19
Tyrone, Baron: Dungiven LY 15; 76
Tyrone, Earl Marcus: Ballyscullion LY 6; 59
Tyrone, Earl of: Aghanloo LY 11; 8
Tyrone, Earl of: Tamlaght Finlagan LY 25; 68
Tyrone, Earl, 1600s (see O'Neill, Phelim)
Tyrone, family: Blaris AM 8; 3
Tyrone's Ditches trench: Ballymore AH 1; 10, 16
Tyrreeghter (see Tireighter): Cumber LY 28; 78
Tyrrell, Dr: Magherally DN 12; 113
Tyrrell, Rev.: Mullaghbrack AH 1; 96

U

Ua-Chongbhail district: Faughanvale LY 36; 50

Ulidia district: Faughanvale LY 36; 50

Ulidia district: Misc. LY 36; 106

Ulleragh, bard: Dungiven LY 15; 29, 111

Ulleran, son of Fin: Dungiven LY 15; 80

Ulleran, son of Fin: Errigal LY 27; 43, 77

Ulleran, son of Fin: Misc. LY 36; 112

Ulleran's grave: Errigal LY 27; 43, 49, 77

Ullienagh school: Aughnamullen MN 40; 77

Ullienagh td: Aughnamullen MN 40; 70, 77

Ullin district: Misc. LY 36; 111

Ullin, bard: Dungiven LY 15; 33

Ullin, bard: Misc. LY 36; 112

Ullin, chieftain: Misc. LY 36; 111–12

Ullmuck td: Aughnamullen MN 40; 77

Ulster Canal: Clonfeacle AH 1; 22, 24

Ulster Canal: Drummully FH 4; 36

Ulster Canal: Eglish AH 1; 43

Ulster Canal: Enniskillen FH 4; 46

Ulster Canal: Loughgall AH 1; 81

Ulster Canal: Tynan AH 1; 128

Ulster Provincial school: Blaris AM 8; 18, 81

Ulster, Earl of (see DeCourcey, John): Kilmacteige SO 40; 187

Ulster, Earl of: Moville DL 38; 70

Ulster, family: Carrickfergus AM 37; 18, 43

Umberbawn (see Omerbane)

Umbra (Umra) td: Magilligan LY 11; 83, 85, 93, 95, 126, 128, 130, 134

Umbra cottages: Magilligan LY 11; 85

Umeracaam (see Umrycam): Lough Swilly DL 38; 119

Umerafadd locality: Lough Swilly DL 38; 120

Umerfree td: Magheross MN 40; 149

Umgall church: Mallusk AM 2; 115

Umgall fort: Umgall AM 35; 160

Umgall graveyard: Umgall AM 35; 160

Umgall old church: Templepatrick AM 35; 130, 133

Umgall old church: Umgall AM 35; 160

Umgall ph: Mallusk AM 2; 109, 115

Umgall ph: Misc. AM 10; 131

Umgall ph: Templepatrick AM 35; 116, 119, 124, 126, 131–32, 139, 152

Umgall td: Umgall AM 35; 159

Umlagh td: Mevagh DL 38; 63

Ummer td: Enniskillen FH 4; 48, 82

Ummeracaam (see Umrycam)

Umpin Island: Lough Swilly DL 38; 126

Umricam (see Umrycam)

Umrycam (Ommeraghkamm) td: Banagher LY 30; 22, 24, 35, 61, 64, 66, 74–75, 96, 107–10, 121, 126, 129–31

Umrycam bay: Lough Swilly DL 38; 119

Umrycam district: Clondavaddog DL 38; 3

Umrycam district: Mevagh DL 38; 61

Umrycam fort: Banagher LY 30; 96

Umrycam fort: Clondavaddog DL 38; 6

Umrycam stone: Banagher LY 30; 49

Umrycam td: Lough Swilly DL 38; 114, 116–17, 119, 129

Unchenagh td: Longfield TE 5; 132–33

Unicarval td: Comber DN 7; 41, 43

Unicarval td: Dundonald DN 7; 65

Union Hall House: Duneane AM 19; 114

Union Locks: Aghalee AM 21; 34

Union Lodge: Aghaderg DN 12; 6, 10

Union Lodge: Misc. DN 17; 131

Union Lodge: Seagoe AH 1; 108

Union loughs: Blaris DN 12; 28

Unshenagh (see Unshinagh): Kilmore AH 1; 73

Unshenagh school: Ematris MN 40; 117

Unshinagh td: Kilmore AH 1; 67, 73

Unshog corn mill: Tynan AH 1; 128

Unthank, Dr (Limerick): Magheramesk AM 21; 130

Upper lough (see Lough Erne Upper): Enniskillen FH 4; 44

Upperlands beetling house: Maghera LY 18; 63

Upperlands bleach green: Desertoghill LY 27; 29

Upperlands bleach green: Maghera LY 18; 2, 49, 73

Upperlands bridge: Maghera LY 18; 9, 63–64

Upperlands corn mill: Maghera LY 18; 28

Upperlands fort [I]: Maghera LY 18; 61

Upperlands fort [II]: Maghera LY 18; 74

Upperlands House: Maghera LY 18; 5, 8, 27–28, 34–35, 63, 71, 73

Upperlands td: Maghera LY 18; 8, 48, 62, 65, 80

Upperlands tuck mill: Maghera LY 18; 28, 35

Upperlands waterfall: Maghera LY 18; 3

Upperlands woods: Maghera LY 18; 4, 48
Uppertown village: Kilmacteige SO 40; 193
Uprichard, Henry: Tullylish DN 12; 141, 146
Uprichard, James: Tullylish DN 12; 141, 146
Uprichard, Thomas: Seagoe AH 1; 109
Uprichard, Thomas: Tullylish DN 12; 141, 146
Upton Castle: Ballymartin AM 2; 17
Upton Castle: Ballyscullion LY 6; 58
Upton Castle: Derryaghy AM 8; 93
Upton Castle: Drummaul AM 19; 71
Upton Castle: Killead AM 35; 41, 47
Upton Castle: Templepatrick AM 35; 108–09,
    111–12, 114–15, 121, 125, 137–40, 144–45
Upton Castle graveyard: Templepatrick AM 35; 143,
    145
Upton Castle plantation: Templepatrick AM 35; 139
Upton, Arthur: Ballyscullion LY 6; 58
Upton, Arthur: Templepatrick AM 35; 110, 139, 144
Upton, Clotworthy (see Templeton, Baron)
Upton, family: Ballymartin AM 2; 5
Upton, family: Templepatrick AM 35; 108, 111,
    116–17, 124, 133, 145
Upton, family: Umgall AM 35; 157
Upton, Henry: Templepatrick AM 35; 108
Upton, Judge: Island Magee AM 10; 67, 95
Upton, Margaret: Ballymoney AM 16; 18
Upton, Mrs Arthur: Templepatrick AM 35; 139
Upton, Olivia: Ballyscullion LY 6; 58
Urbal flax mill: Tamlaght TE 20; 74, 137
Urbal meeting house: Tamlaght TE 20; 130
Urbal td: Tamlaght TE 20; 75, 77, 82, 96, 100, 104,
    124–26, 128–37
Urbalreagh fort: Ardstraw TE 5; 12
Urbalreagh td: Ardstraw TE 5; 12
Urbalshinny corn mill: Tullyaughnish DL 38; 89
Urbalshinny td: Tullyaughnish DL 38; 96
Ure, Mary Jane: Carnmoney AM 2; 78
Urismana (see Urrismenagh): Clonmany DL 38; 18
Urney church: Urney DL 39; 175
Urney female schools: Urney DL 39; 179
Urney flax mills: Urney DL 39; 176
Urney Glebe school: Urney DL 39; 182
Urney hill: Urney DL 39; 174

Urney House: Clonleigh DL 39; 1
Urney House: Urney DL 39; 174–76
Urney male schools: Urney DL 39; 179
Urney new flax mill: Urney DL 39; 176
Urney Park fort: Urney DL 39; 176, 181
Urney Park House: Urney DL 39; 176
Urney ph: Clonleigh DL 39; 1, 16
Urney ph: Coleraine LY 33; 63
Urney ph: Donaghmore DL 39; 28, 32–33
Urris district: Lough Swilly DL 38; 131–33, 135–36
Urris hill: Clondavaddog DL 38; 5
Urris hill: Clonmany DL 38; 12–3, 19
Urris hill: Desertegney DL 38; 24–26, 30
Urris river: Desertegney DL 38; 24, 26
Urris school: Clonmany DL 38; 17
Urrismana (see Urrismenagh): Desertegney DL 38;
    24
Urrismanagh (see Urrismenagh): Clonmany DL 38;
    13
Urrismenagh district: Lough Swilly DL 38; 133, 136
Urrismenagh Head: Clonmany DL 38; 13
Urrismenagh td: Clonmany DL 38; 16, 18, 20
Urrismenagh td: Desertegney DL 38; 24
Usher, Daniel: Macosquin LY 22; 84, 113
Usher, E.L.: Aghalee AM 21; 32–33
Usher, family: Aghalee AM 21; 31–32, 36–37
Usher, John: Aghagallon AM 21; 13–14
Usher, John: Aghalee AM 21; 29
Usher, John: Coleraine LY 33; 145
Usher, John: Macosquin LY 22; 122
Usher, Miss: Aghalee AM 21; 32
Usher, Rev. Adam: Ardstraw TE 5; 9
Usher, Robert: Aghagallon AM 21; 13–14
Ushet district: Rathlin Island AM 24; 128, 131, 134
Ushet Point: Rathlin Island AM 24; 130
Uskur More, warrior: Dungiven LY 15; 80
Usmdeanot td: Cumber LY 28; 92
Ussher, Rev. Cornelius: Tullyaughnish DL 38; 89,
    92, 96–97
Ussher, Rev. John: Raymoghy DL 39; 136–37,
    139–41, 186, 189
Uxbridge, Earl of: Newry DN 3; 65

V

Vaile, Humphroy: Clondermot LY 34; 55

Valaragh lough: Kilmacteige SO 40; 191

Valencia (Spain): Carrickfergus AM 37; 137

Valentine, Agnes: Doagh AM 29; 73

Valentine, Capt.: Muff DL 38; 80

Valladolid (Spain): Donegal DL 39; 48

Vallancey, Gen.: Newry DN 3; 65

Valley district: Donacavey TE 5; 62

Van Diemen's Land: Coleraine LY 33; 74, 146

Van Diemen's Land: Drumachose LY 9; 133

Van Diemen's Land: Kilcronaghan LY 31; 73, 84

Van Diemen's Land: Maghera LY 18; 22, 79–80

Van Diemen's Land: Skirts of Urney and Ardstraw
TE 5; 141

Van Diemen's Land: Templepatrick AM 35; 123,
152

Vanavoulty mass-house: Clondavaddog DL 38; 4

Vance, A.: Ballyscullion LY 6; 49

Vance, Catherine: Ballyscullion LY 6; 77

Vance, Francis: Ballyscullion LY 6; 71

Vance, John: Ballyscullion LY 6; 65–66

Vance, John: Magherafelt LY 6; 90

Vance, John: Tamlaght TE 20; 83

Vance, John [I]: Carrickfergus AM 37; 58, 137, 140,
182

Vance, John [II]: Carrickfergus AM 37; 130

Vance, Mary: Ballyscullion LY 6; 77

Vance, Mathew: Magherafelt LY 6; 110

Vance, Samuel: Tamlaght TE 20; 76

Vance, Widow: Tamlaght TE 20; 83

Vance, William: Tamlaght TE 20; 74, 76, 79–83, 91,
102–03, 122, 128, 137

Vance, William [I]: Ballyscullion LY 6; 78

Vance, William [II]: Ballyscullion LY 6; 78

Vann, John: Carrickfergus AM 37; 195

Vantrollerius, Thomas: Derrykeighan AM 16; 93

Varian, legate: Misc. DN 17; 119

Vaughan, Edward: Faughanvale LY 36; 57

Vaughan, family: Clonleigh DL 39; 13

Vaughan, G.: Newry DN 3; 105

Vaughan, George: Clonleigh DL 39; 12

Vaughan, George: Drumkeeran FH 14; 66

Vaughan, John: Clonleigh DL 39; 15

Vaughan, Mr (Quilly): Dromore DN 12; 72

Vault house: Raphoe DL 39; 124

Veacock, family: Carrickfergus AM 37; 93

Veagh td: Raymoghy DL 39; 139, 141, 199

Venables, Mr: Clonmany DL 38; 14

Vents school: Carncastle and Killyglen AM 10; 8

Verdon, James: Newry DN 3; 99, 104

Verner, Mrs William: Loughgall AH 1; 77

Verner, Thomas: Carrickfergus AM 37; 42, 102, 143

Verner, William: Aughnamullen MN 40; 75–76

Verner, William: Clogher TE 5; 57

Verner, William: Clogherny TE 20; 26

Verner, William: Clonfeacle AH 1; 25

Verner, William: Errigal Keerogue TE 20; 48–50,
56–57

Verner, William: Killeeshil TE 20; 62–64

Verner, William: Killyman AH 1; 55–56

Verner, William: Kilmore AH 1; 65–66

Verner, William: Loughgall AH 1; 80

Verner, William: Tartaraghan AH 1; 120–22

Verner, William: Tynan AH 1; 129–30

Verner's bridge: Clonfeacle AH 1; 24

Verner's bridge: Killyman AH 1; 55–56

Verner's bridge: Loughgall AH 1; 81

Verner's bridge: Pomeroy TE 20; 72

Verner's bridge: Tartaraghan AH 1; 120

Vernon, John: Blaris AM 8; 84

Vernon, John: Blaris DN 12; 45, 49

Vernon, Richard: Carlingford LH 40; 57

Verscoyle, Mr: Convoy DL 39; 20

Verscoyle, Mr: Raphoe DL 39; 121, 126

Vesey, Dr: Donacavey TE 5; 85

Vesey, family: Carnmoney AM 2; 34

Vesey, Lord: Ballyscullion LY 6; 57

Vesey, Rev.: Donacavey TE 5; 83, 85–86

Vesey, Rev. George: Maghera LY 18; 28, 31, 66–67,
72, 75

Vesey, Samuel: Donacavey TE 5; 62–65, 68–71,
73–74, 76–77

Vesey, T.A.: Magherafelt LY 6; 83

Vesper field: Maghera LY 18; 10

Vicar's bridge: Aughnamullen MN 40; 73

Vicars, Lt E.: Clondermot LY 34; 17, 102, 104, 107

Vicars, Lt E.: Cumber LY 28; 1–4

Vicars, Lt E.: Magilligan LY 11; 145

Vicars, Lt E.: Manorhamilton Union LM 40; 47
Vicarsdale House: Donaghmoyne MN 40; 107, 111
Vincent, family: Enniskillen FH 4; 58
Vincent, Rev. Patrick: Artrea LY 6; 21, 39
Vincent, William: Enniskillen FH 4; 72
Vinecash td: Kilmore AH 1; 67
Vinegar hill: Island Magee AM 10; 66
Vint, James: Carnmoney AM 2; 100
Vint, Jonathon: Carnmoney AM 2; 98, 102
Vint, Mary: Carnmoney AM 2; 77, 86
Vint, Nathan: Carnmoney AM 2; 98
Vint's public house: Carnmoney AM 2; 85
Vints, John: Carrickfergus AM 37; 166
Violet Hill House: Ballymore AH 1; 11, 15
Violethill (see Tully): Killesher FH 14; 84, 86
Virginia: Drumlumman CN 40; 13
Virginia: Laragh CN 40; 42

Viscoile, Rev.: Loughgilly AH 1; 86
Vitriol House: Blaris AM 8; 36
Vitriol Island: Blaris AM 8; 36
Vittoria (Spain): Kilbroney DN 3; 34
Vivars, P.S.: Aghanloo LY 11; 25
Volvett, Sir: Ballynascreen LY 31; 11–12, 25
Vow Castle: Aghadowey LY 22; 30
Vow corn mill: Finvoy AM 23; 71
Vow ferry: Aghadowey LY 22; 11, 30
Vow ferry: Desertoghill LY 27; 13
Vow ferry: Finvoy AM 23; 67–69, 71–72, 76
Vow ferry: Kilrea LY 27; 113
Vow flax mill: Finvoy AM 23; 71
Vow graveyard: Aghadowey LY 22; 30
Vow school: Finvoy AM 23; 75
Vow td: Finvoy AM 23; 70
Vowghtoy, A.: Clondermot LY 34; 54

W

Wadd, Mr: Aghadowey LY 22; 27
Waddell, Alexander: Newry DN 3; 99, 101, 104–05
Waddell, family: Blaris AM 8; 22
Waddell, Maj.: Dromore DN 12; 70–72
Waddell, Mr: Down DN 17; 52
Waddell, Mr: Saul DN 17; 114
Waddell, surgeon: Newry DN 3; 100, 104
Waddle, Coslet: Magheralin DN 12; 110–11
Waddle, Isaac: Glynn AM 26; 47
Waddle, Miss: Newry DN 3; 110
Waddle, Randal: Glynn AM 26; 44
Waddle, Tom: Magilligan LY 11; 127
Waddock, St: Clondavaddog DL 38; 1, 4–5
Waddy, Misses: Kilrea LY 27; 122
Waddy, Rev. John: Kilrea LY 27; 104, 109, 117,
    125–26, 128
Waddy, Rev. Richard: Ballymoney AM 16; 15
Waddy, Rev. Richard: Finvoy AM 23; 71
Waddy, Rev. Richard: Kilrea LY 27; 125
Waddy, Rev. Richard: Misc. LY 31; 136
Wade, family: Misc. LY 36; 104
Wade, John: Desertlyn LY 31; 49
Wade, John: Hillsborough DN 12; 105
Wade, M.: Urney DL 39; 182
Wade, Margaret: Carrickfergus AM 37; 118
Wade, Rev.: Dromore TE 5; 98–99
Wade, Rev. Samuel: Blaris AM 8; 24
Wade, Samuel: Blaris AM 8; 30
Wade, Thomas: Desertoghill LY 27; 20
Wails, Kenedy: Errigal LY 27; 69
Wails, Thomas: Errigal LY 27; 58–59, 70
Wails, William: Errigal LY 27; 54
Wain, James: Newry DN 3; 71
Wain, Thomas: Newry DN 3; 71
Wakefield, Edward: Magheragall AM 21; 100
Wakefield, family: Magheragall AM 21; 99
Wakefield, John: Magheragall AM 21; 103
Wakefield, T.C.: Drumcree AH 1; 38, 41
Wakefield, T.C.: Garvaghy DN 12; 81
Wakefield, T.C.: Tullylish DN 12; 142
Wales: Ballywillin LY 33; 37
Wales: Banagher LY 30; 101
Wales: Carrickfergus AM 37; 50, 137
Wales: Coleraine LY 33; 126

Wales: Down DN 17; 49
Wales: Enniskeen CN 40; 26
Wales: Killead AM 35; 17
Wales: Killymard DL 39; 104
Wales: Kilmacteige SO 40; 189
Wales: Lough Swilly DL 38; 130
Wales: Misc. DN 17; 121
Wales: Misc. LY 36; 104
Wales: Newry DN 3; 73
Wales: Ramoan AM 24; 95
Wales: Tickmacrevan AM 13; 129
Wales, family: Carrickfergus AM 37; 93
Walkenshaw, family: Tamlaght O'Crilly LY 18; 93
Walker Testimonial (Derry): Dungiven LY 15; 51
Walker, Andrew: Raphoe DL 39; 127
Walker, Ann: Drummaul AM 19; 90
Walker, Cllr: Donaghmore DL 39; 36–38
Walker, family: Aghagallon AM 21; 9
Walker, family: Aghalee AM 21; 31
Walker, family: Ahoghill AM 23; 25
Walker, family: Balteagh LY 9; 32
Walker, family: Billy AM 16; 58, 68
Walker, family: Desertoghill LY 27; 5, 30
Walker, family: Templecorran AM 26; 117, 119
Walker, Francis: Donacavey TE 5; 65
Walker, George: Carrickfergus AM 37; 193
Walker, George: Tamlaght TE 20; 82
Walker, H.: Kilmore AH 1; 62
Walker, Henery: Desertoghill LY 27; 29
Walker, Henry: Errigal LY 27; 45, 54, 60, 67
Walker, Hugh: Ballyrashane LY 22; 66
Walker, J.C.: Misc. LY 36; 107
Walker, James: Ballyaghran LY 33; 28
Walker, James: Coleraine LY 33; 72
Walker, James: Hillsborough DN 12; 105, 107
Walker, James: Tamlaght TE 20; 93
Walker, Jane: Ballyaghran LY 33; 28
Walker, Jane: Drummaul AM 19; 91
Walker, John: Ahoghill AM 23; 23
Walker, John: Ballyrashane LY 22; 61–62
Walker, John: Blaris DN 12; 40
Walker, John: Carrickfergus AM 37; 109
Walker, John: Derryaghy AM 8; 91, 98, 115
Walker, John: Dunboe LY 11; 77

Walker, John: Hillsborough DN 12; 105–07

Walker, John: Magherafelt LY 6; 83

Walker, John [I]: Ballyaghran LY 33; 28

Walker, John [I]: Drummaul AM 19; 87

Walker, John [II]: Ballyaghran LY 33; 28

Walker, John [II]: Drummaul AM 19; 90

Walker, John [III]: Drummaul AM 19; 91

Walker, Johnstone: Hillsborough DN 12; 107

Walker, Joseph: Aghalee AM 21; 28, 35

Walker, Manual: Artrea LY 6; 38

Walker, Margaret: Drummaul AM 19; 90

Walker, Mary: Donaghmore DL 39; 40

Walker, Mary: Drummaul AM 19; 90

Walker, Messrs: Magherafelt LY 6; 84

Walker, Misses: Clogher TE 5; 43

Walker, Mr (Derry): Taughboyne DL 39; 150, 154

Walker, Mr (Shrove): Moville DL 38; 70

Walker, Mr: Clogher TE 5; 43

Walker, Mr: Donaghmore DL 39; 33

Walker, Mr: Magherafelt LY 6; 92, 96

Walker, Mrs (Donegal): Killymard DL 39; 98, 106

Walker, Mrs: Tullyaughnish DL 38; 89

Walker, Rev. George: Clondermot LY 34; 40, 53

Walker, Richard: Kilraghts AM 16; 136

Walker, Samuel: Ballyaghran LY 33; 28

Walker, Samuel: Carrickfergus AM 37; 47, 138

Walker, Samuel: Kilcronaghan LY 31; 82

Walker, Thomas: Drumachose LY 9; 131

Walker, Thomas: Errigal LY 27; 60, 68

Walker, Thomas: Hillsborough DN 12; 106–07

Walker, Thomas: Tamlaght TE 20; 77, 103

Walker, Thomas: Templepatrick AM 35; 152

Walker, W.J.: Moira DN 12; 120

Walker, William: Artrea LY 6; 38

Walker, William: Derryaghy AM 8; 107

Walker, William: Donaghmore DL 39; 37

Walker, William: Errigal LY 27; 65

Walker, William: Newry DN 3; 100

Walker, William: Raphoe DL 39; 127

Walker's bridge: Tullyaughnish DL 38; 90

Walkingham, Edward: Misc. DN 17; 117

Walkington, Edward: Aghalee AM 21; 31

Walkington, Rev. William: Aghalee AM 21; 31

Walkington, Thomas: Ballinderry AM 21; 47

Walkington, Thomas: Blaris AM 8; 54, 60, 66

Walkins, William: Blaris AM 8; 86

Walkinshaw, Clotworthy: Kirkinriola AM 23; 99

Walkinshaw, family: Ballyclug AM 23; 60

Walkinshaw, James: Ballyclug AM 23; 65

Walkmill flax mill: Kilbride AM 29; 135, 156

Walkmill paper mill: Dunluce AM 16; 110

Walkmill td: Dunluce AM 16; 110

Walkmill td: Kilbride AM 29; 136

Wall, Rev. John: Misc. LY 31; 137

Wallace, Alexander: Desertoghill LY 27; 21

Wallace, Anne: Desertoghill LY 27; 21

Wallace, David: Muckamore AM 35; 81

Wallace, family: Ballintoy AM 24; 20

Wallace, family: Ballywillin AM 16; 32

Wallace, family: Billy AM 16; 58, 68

Wallace, family: Desertoghill LY 27; 5, 30

Wallace, family: Drumbeg AM 8; 123

Wallace, family: Kilraghts AM 16; 127–28, 130

Wallace, family: Magherally DN 12; 114

Wallace, George: Muckamore AM 35; 80–81

Wallace, Henry: Desertoghill LY 27; 5, 14

Wallace, Henry: Tullylish DN 12; 143

Wallace, Hugh: Ballyscullion LY 6; 52, 69

Wallace, Hugh: Blaris AM 8; 52

Wallace, J.H.: Newry DN 3; 99, 103

Wallace, James: Antrim AM 29; 59

Wallace, James: Ballymoney AM 16; 17

Wallace, James: Blaris AM 8; 63

Wallace, James: Errigal LY 27; 64

Wallace, James: Loughguile AM 13; 71

Wallace, Janes: Ballynure AM 32; 59

Wallace, John: Blaris AM 8; 52

Wallace, John: Dunaghy AM 13; 24

Wallace, John: Errigal LY 27; 59

Wallace, John: Kilcronaghan LY 31; 74, 82

Wallace, John: Muckamore AM 35; 81

Wallace, John: Tamlaght Finlagan LY 25; 84, 122

Wallace, John: Templecorran AM 26; 125

Wallace, Joseph: Kilraghts AM 16; 132–33

Wallace, L.: Drumballyroney DN 3; 12–13

Wallace, Margret: Aghadowey LY 22; 36

Wallace, Michael: Desertoghill LY 27; 14

Wallace, Mr (Derryall): Drumcree AH 1; 39

Wallace, Mr: Ballee DN 17; 23

Wallace, Mrs (Dublin): Newry DN 3; 83

Wallace, Nathaniel: Kilwaughter AM 10; 116

Wallace, Rev. Hugh: Magherafelt LY 6; 95, 98–99

Wallace, Rev. William: Donegore AM 29; 126, 129, 133

Wallace, Rev. William: Kilrea LY 27; 122

Wallace, Robert: Newry DN 3; 69

Wallace, Robert: Tamlaght Finlagan LY 25; 83, 121

Wallace, S.: Newtownards DN 7; 112

Wallace, Samual: Kildollagh LY 22; 73

Wallace, Samuel: Coleraine LY 33; 105

Wallace, Samuel: Newry DN 3; 99, 103

Wallace, Thomas: Balteagh LY 9; 36, 36

Wallace, Thomas: Drumbeg AM 8; 124, 127

Wallace, Thomas: Errigal LY 27; 44–45, 66, 76

Wallace, Thomas: Kilcronaghan LY 31; 74, 86

Wallace, Thomas: Magherafelt LY 6; 105

Wallace, W.: Drumgooland DN 3; 24

Wallace, William: Ballywillin AM 16; 34

Wallace, William: Carnmoney AM 2; 47, 91

Wallace, William: Errigal LY 27; 59

Wallace, William: Kildollagh LY 22; 73, 75
Wallace, William: Muckamore AM 35; 81
Wallace, William: Tamlaght TE 20; 108, 110
Wallace, William: Templepatrick AM 35; 132
Wallace's locality: Muckamore AM 35; 80
Wallglass spring: Drumachose LY 9; 48, 75, 83
Walls, Elizabeth: Artrea LY 6; 28
Walls, John: Artrea LY 6; 19, 21, 23–25, 39
Walls, Patrick: Misc. LY 31; 122
Walls, R.: Bright DN 17; 33
Wallworth (see Walworth)
Wally, Robert: Ahoghill AM 23; 37
Walsh, Col: Carrickfergus AM 37; 56, 135–36
Walsh, Douglas: Carrickfergus AM 37; 127
Walsh, Edward: Artrea LY 6; 12, 23, 37
Walsh, Edward: Duneane AM 19; 111
Walsh, Edward: Magherafelt LY 6; 111–12
Walsh, John: Artrea LY 6; 34, 37
Walsh, John: Tamlaght O'Crilly LY 18; 120–21
Walsh, Mary: Clondermot LY 34; 42, 93, 96
Walsh, Michael: Newry DN 3; 98
Walsh, Pat: Rasharkin AM 23; 141
Walsh, Patrick: Artrea LY 6; 12–13, 25
Walsh, Patrick: Kilrea LY 27; 121
Walsh, Peter: Ballyclug AM 23; 64
Walsh, Thomas: Ballyclug AM 23; 65
Walsh, Thomas: Carrickfergus AM 37; 194
Walsh, W.H.: Faughanvale LY 36; 24, 35–36, 66
Walsh, William: Carrickfergus AM 37; 195
Walshestown (Welshestown) td: Saul DN 17; 112, 114
Walshestown Castle: Ballyculter DN 17; 28
Walshestown Castle: Saul DN 17; 112, 115
Walshestown chapel: Saul DN 17; 112
Walshestown fort: Saul DN 17; 115
Walshestown td: Ballyculter DN 17; 28
Walters, Joseph: Enniskillen FH 4; 57
Walworth Bawn: Tamlaght Finlagan LY 25; 87–88, 99
Walworth graveyard: Tamlaght Finlagan LY 25; 87
Walworth House: Coleraine LY 33; 63
Walworth House: Faughanvale LY 36; 10
Walworth House: Tamlaght Finlagan LY 25; 81, 98, 100
Walworth manor: Cumber LY 28; 13
Walworth manor: Faughanvale LY 36; 37
Walworth manor: Tamlaght Finlagan LY 25; 68, 72, 74–75, 79, 93, 95, 106, 123
Walworth old church: Tamlaght Finlagan LY 25; 68–69, 81, 86–87
Walworth quarry: Tamlaght Finlagan LY 25; 85
Walworth schools: Faughanvale LY 36; 37–38
Walworth td: Drumachose LY 9; 108
Walworth td: Dungiven LY 15; 68

Walworth td: Faughanvale LY 36; 53, 64, 69, 80, 91, 97
Walworth td: Tamlaght Finlagan LY 25; 72–74, 93, 119
Walworth wood: Cumber LY 28; 11
Walworth wood: Dungiven LY 15; 26, 101
Walworth wood: Faughanvale LY 36; 3, 10, 21, 91
Walworth wood: Tamlaght Finlagan LY 25; 65, 68, 71, 85, 95, 98
Walworth, William: Faughanvale LY 36; 64
Wancot, Brig.: Clondermot LY 34; 49
Wandsworth, Christopher: Blaris AM 8; 89
War House locality: Dungiven LY 15; 91
Warbeck, Perkin: Clonleigh DL 39; 14
Warbleshinny glen: Clondermot LY 34; 44, 48, 105
Warbleshinny hill: Clondermot LY 34; 37, 100–01
Warbleshinny lough: Clondermot LY 34; 121
Warbleshinny quarry: Clondermot LY 34; 133
Warbleshinny td: Clondermot LY 34; 1, 14, 24, 26, 29, 31, 35–37, 57, 75, 112–13, 120–21, 128–29, 133
Warburton, Rev. Thomas: Magherafelt LY 6; 82
Ward, A.C.: Blaris AM 8; 55
Ward, Adam: Ballyscullion LY 6; 76
Ward, Bryan: Cumber LY 28; 28
Ward, Col.: Bangor DN 7; 23–24
Ward, Col.: Bright DN 17; 35
Ward, Daniel: Lissan LY 31; 109
Ward, Daniel: Tamlaght TE 20; 76
Ward, family: Blaris AM 8; 21
Ward, family: Carnmoney AM 2; 76
Ward, family: Inishargy DN 7; 85
Ward, family: Saul DN 17; 114
Ward, family: Shilvodan AM 19; 136
Ward, Harriet: Ballyculter DN 17; 27, 29
Ward, J.R.: Aghalurcher TE 5; 1
Ward, J.R.: Ballyclug AM 23; 55
Ward, J.R.: Ballycor AM 32; 8–9
Ward, J.R.: Clonalan DN 3; 1
Ward, J.R.: Donagh MN 40; 101, 101
Ward, J.R.: Kilmore MN 40; 136
Ward, J.R.: Longfield TE 5; 130
Ward, J.R.: Shankill DN 12; 139
Ward, J.R.: Tydavnet MN 40; 173
Ward, James (Jnr): Blaris DN 12; 40
Ward, James: Blaris AM 8; 7, 23, 25–26, 36–37, 42–43, 45, 48–50, 55, 59–62, 67, 70, 76, 84
Ward, James: Blaris DN 12; 39–41, 43, 45–51
Ward, James: Carrickfergus AM 37; 128
Ward, James: Connor AM 19; 28
Ward, James: Cumber LY 28; 28
Ward, James: Derryaghy AM 8; 100
Ward, James: Lambeg AM 8; 137
Ward, James: Shilvodan AM 19; 137
Ward, John: Clondermot LY 34; 93

Ward, John: Drumbeg AM 8; 127
Ward, John: Tamlaght TE 20; 76
Ward, John [I]: Carrickfergus AM 37; 120
Ward, John [II]: Carrickfergus AM 37; 129
Ward, John [III]: Carrickfergus AM 37; 194
Ward, Mary: Carrickfergus AM 37; 128
Ward, Mary: Cumber LY 28; 28
Ward, Mr: Ballyphilip DN 7; 8
Ward, Mr: Blaris AM 8; 62
Ward, Mrs John: Bangor DN 7; 24
Ward, P.: Killymard DL 39; 101
Ward, Patrick: Cumber LY 28; 28
Ward, Rev. Henry: Ballyculter DN 17; 28
Ward, Rev. Henry: Killinchy DN 7; 86, 90, 92
Ward, Rev. John: Misc. LY 31; 137
Ward, Rev. Ralph: Kilwaughter AM 10; 111, 115–17
Ward, Robert: Carrickfergus AM 37; 123
Ward, Robert: Inishargy DN 7; 84
Ward, Sophia: Ballyculter DN 17; 28–29
Ward's farm: Killymard DL 39; 101
Wardell, John: Blaris DN 12; 41–42
Wardene, John: Clondermot LY 34; 46
Wardenstown House: Galloon FH 4; 90
Warder, James: Ballyscullion LY 6; 57
Wardknowe Castle: Ballyrashane LY 22; 58
Wardknowe Castle: Kildollagh LY 22; 69, 73–74
Wardlaw, Dr: Kilcronaghan LY 31; 82
Wardle, John: Magheragall AM 21; 105
Wardnowe (see Wardknowe)
Wardnowl (see Wardknowe): Kildollagh LY 22; 73
Wardsborough asylum: Blaris AM 8; 59–63
Waresley House (Huntingdon): Galloon FH 4; 90
Warhouse cave: Dungiven LY 15; 41, 76, 86
Waring, A.: Newry DN 3; 104
Waring, family: Derryaghy AM 8; 103
Waring, family: Donaghcloney DN 12; 59
Waring, James: Newry DN 3; 98, 103
Waring, Lucas: Blaris AM 8; 54–55, 84
Waring, Lucas: Blaris DN 12; 45, 49
Waring, Maj.: Newry DN 3; 100, 104
Waring, Miss: Newry DN 3; 100, 104
Waring, Paul: Derryaghy AM 8; 101
Waring, Rev.: Carlingford LH 40; 60
Waring, Rev. Holt: Donagheloney DN 12; 57–61
Waring, Rev. Holt: Shankill AH 1; 114–16
Waring, Richard: Newry DN 3; 100–01, 104
Waring, Robert: Derryaghy AM 8; 95, 101, 113
Waring, Samuel: Hillsborough DN 12; 97, 105
Waring, Thomas: Derryaghy AM 8; 103
Waring, Thomas: Dromore DN 12; 78
Waring, Thomas: Newry DN 3; 95, 100, 104
Waring, Thomas: Seapatrick DN 12; 126
Waring, Thomas: Shankill DN 12; 139
Waring, Thomas: Tullylish DN 12; 143
Waringsford: Garvaghy DN 12; 80

Waringsford demense: Garvaghy DN 12; 80–81
Waringsford House: Garvaghy DN 12; 80
Waringstown: Misc. DN 17; 116
Waringstown: Seagoe AH 1; 106
Waringstown: Shankill AH 1; 114
Waringstown brewery: Donaghcloney DN 12; 58
Waringstown church: Donaghcloney DN 12; 58, 60
Waringstown House: Donaghcloney DN 12; 60
Waringstown meeting house: Donaghcloney DN 12;
   60
Waringstown school: Donaghcloney DN 12; 60–61
Waringstown village: Donaghcloney DN 12; 57–59
Waritie, family: Drumgath DN 3; 20
Wark, Alexander: Drumachose LY 9; 118, 126, 128
Wark, David [I]: Tamlaght Finlagan LY 25; 113
Wark, David [II]: Tamlaght Finlagan LY 25; 118
Wark, Dr: Aghanloo LY 11; 30
Wark, Henry: Misc. DL 39; 186
Wark, Isaac: Dunboe LY 11; 63, 81
Wark, Jacob: Tamlaght Finlagan LY 25; 120
Wark, James: Bovevagh LY 25; 29
Wark, Maryjane: Tamlaght Finlagan LY 25; 119
Wark, Robert: Tamlaght Finlagan LY 25; 115
Wark, Samual [I]: Tamlaght Finlagan LY 25; 112
Wark, Samual [II]: Tamlaght Finlagan LY 25; 120
Wark, Thomas: Tamlaght Finlagan LY 25; 116
Wark, William: Coleraine LY 33; 72
Wark, William: Tamlaght Finlagan LY 25; 119
Warner, Charles: Clondermot LY 34; 79
Warner, Charles: Faughanvale LY 36; 7, 17, 23,
   40–42, 45
Warner, Samuel: Hillsborough DN 12; 105
Warnock, David: Newry DN 3; 81
Warnock, family: Ballywillin AM 16; 32
Warnock, Hugh: Donacavey TE 5; 86
Warnock, Joseph: Coleraine LY 33; 72
Warnock, Robert: Dromore TE 5; 97
Warnock, Robert: Misc. TE 5; 147
Warnok, David: Newtownards DN 7; 112
Warren district: Culfeightrin AM 24; 66, 76
Warren Gate bridge: Blaris DN 12; 28, 34
Warren, Edward: Banagher LY 30; 104, 106, 108
Warren, Edward: Drumachose LY 9; 61
Warren, family: Clondermot LY 34; 12, 43, 98
Warren, Mr: Killagan AM 23; 83
Warren, Thomas: Derryaghy AM 8; 116
Warren, William: Clondermot LY 34; 38, 56, 68
Warren, William: Drumachose LY 9; 61
Warrenpoint: Ballymore AH 1; 5
Warrenpoint: Clonallan DN 3; 1–2
Warrenpoint: Drumballyroney DN 3; 17
Warrenpoint: Kilbroney DN 3; 29–30, 36
Warrenpoint: Newry DN 3; 73, 86–89
Warrenpoint: Warrenpoint DN 3; 115, 117–19, 121
Warrenpoint chapel (C): Warrenpoint DN 3; 117

Warrenpoint chapel (M): Warrenpoint DN 3; 117

Warrenpoint church: Warrenpoint DN 3; 117

Warrenpoint court house: Warrenpoint DN 3; 118

Warrenpoint dispensary (see also Rostrevor dispensary): Kilbroney DN 3; 30, 37

Warrenpoint dispensary: Warrenpoint DN 3; 122–23

Warrenpoint harbour: Warrenpoint DN 3; 120

Warrenpoint infant school: Warrenpoint DN 3; 122

Warrenpoint inns: Warrenpoint DN 3; 118

Warrenpoint meeting house: Warrenpoint DN 3; 117

Warrenpoint new meeting house: Warrenpoint DN 3; 117

Warrenpoint ph: Newry DN 3; 61

Warrenpoint police barracks: Warrenpoint DN 3; 118

Warrenpoint school: Warrenpoint DN 3; 122

Warrenpoint windmill: Warrenpoint DN 3; 118

Warrens hills: Lough Swilly DL 38; 137

Warrens Point: Lough Swilly DL 38; 107

Warrenspoint (see Warrenpoint): Warrenpoint DN 3; 117

Warring, family: Derryaghy AM 8; 103

Wart stone: Bovevagh LY 25; 9, 53

Warwick Lodge: Artrea LY 6; 8

Warwick, family: Kilbride AM 29; 140

Warwick, Hugh: Tamlaght O'Crilly LY 18; 103, 115, 132, 137–38

Warwick, Samuel: Tamlaght O'Crilly LY 18; 100, 103

Wash bridge: Ballymore AH 1; 8, 18

Wash lough (see Washing): Kilrea LY 27; 106

Washing bay: Donaghenry TE 20; 39

Washing bay: Lough Neagh AM 21; 92

Washing lough: Clondavaddog DL 38; 2

Washing lough: Kilrea LY 27; 106–07, 109, 112–14

Washington (America): Kilbroney DN 3; 34

Washington: Maghera LY 18; 21

Washington, Alexander: Billy AM 16; 61

Wason, family: Kilraghts AM 16; 130

Wason, George: Kilraghts AM 16; 132

Wason, Widow: Ballymoney AM 16; 17

Wass, James: Kilcronaghan LY 31; 74

Wasson, Hugh: Ballyclug AM 23; 64

Wasson, James: Kirkinriola AM 23; 122

Watch house: Derryaghy AM 8; 99–100

Watchhouse Knoll hill: Carnmoney AM 2; 99

Watercloney (see Waterclony): Ahoghill AM 23; 37

Waterclony evening school: Ahoghill AM 23; 42

Waterclony school: Ahoghill AM 23; 40, 42, 47

Waterclony Sunday school: Ahoghill AM 23; 47

Waterclony td: Ahoghill AM 23; 37–38

Waterfoot House: Templecarn FH 14; 119–20

Waterfoot locality: Drumkeeran FH 14; 65

Waterfoot locality: Magheraculmoney FH 14; 107

Waterford: Blaris AM 8; 8

Waterford: Carrickfergus AM 37; 10, 45

Waterford: Drumcree AH 1; 38

Waterford: Drummaul AM 19; 70

Waterford: Knockbreda DN 7; 100

Waterford Castle: Island Magee AM 10; 48

Waterford county: Carncastle and Killyglen AM 10; 7

Waterford county: Faughanvale LY 36; 44

Waterford, family: Coleraine LY 33; 129

Waterford, Lord: Aghanloo LY 11; 2, 9, 11, 13, 15–17, 22–24, 28, 31, 33–34, 36–37, 42

Waterford, Lord: Balteagh LY 9; 3, 21–23, 37–38, 40–41, 43

Waterford, Lord: Bovevagh LY 25; 19, 47, 49, 57

Waterford, Lord: Coleraine LY 33; 64

Waterford, Lord: Drumachose LY 9; 53, 73, 75, 87, 96–97, 100–01, 105

Waterford, Lord: Dungiven LY 15; 8, 15, 21, 50, 60–62, 66, 70, 95–97, 104–05

Waterford, Lord: Magilligan LY 11; 97, 107, 135

Waterford, Marquis of: Aghadowey LY 22; 5, 33

Waterford, Marquis of: Banagher LY 30; 23

Waterford, Marquis of: Coleraine LY 33; 57, 63, 71–73, 129, 142, 144, 149, 152, 154

Waterford, Marquis of: Desertoghill LY 27; 4–5, 13, 17, 20–21, 23, 33

Waterford, Marquis of: Errigal LY 27; 48, 79–83

Waterford, Marquis of: Faughanvale LY 36; 40

Waterloo (Belgium): Kilrea LY 27; 116

Waterloo: Cumber LY 28; 58

Waterloo: Killead AM 35; 11

Waternerry td: Enniskillen FH 4; 81

Waters, Capt. M.M.: Clondermot LY 34; 91, 102

Waters, Capt. M.M.: Coleraine LY 33; 149

Waters, Capt. M.M.: Magilligan LY 11; 143

Waters, family: Aghalee AM 21; 31

Waters, family: Ballinderry AM 21; 53

Waters, family: Carnmoney AM 2; 76

Waters, family: Misc. LY 36; 104

Waters, James: Ramoan AM 24; 106, 113

Waters, Rev.: Newtownards DN 7; 106

Waters, William: Blaris DN 12; 40

Waterside bog: Killowen LY 33; 158

Waterside cave: Killowen LY 33; 162, 170

Waterside chapel: Clondermot LY 34; 5, 9, 24

Waterside chapel: Faughanvale LY 36; 34

Waterside cornstores: Clondermot LY 34; 100

Waterside distillery: Clondermot LY 34; 4, 14, 19, 21, 34, 36

Waterside district: Clondermot LY 34; 4, 6–10, 12–15, 19, 21–27, 34, 39, 43, 78, 80–82, 87, 90, 98, 100–04

Waterside district: Derryaghy AM 8; 114

Waterside district: Magilligan LY 11; 117

Waterside graveyard: Killowen LY 33; 161, 170

Waterside leather store: Clondermot LY 34; 100

Waterside night school: Clondermot LY 34; 43

Waterside school [I]: Clondermot LY 34; 43, 88, 91, 96

Waterside school [II]: Clondermot LY 34; 43, 88, 91, 96

Waterside tannery: Clondermot LY 34; 14, 21, 30, 100

Waterside td: Coleraine LY 33; 143

Waterside td: Killowen LY 33; 158, 165–68, 170, 172

Watertop (see Ballyvennaght): Culfeightrin AM 24; 67

Waterwork, Thomas: Hillsborough DN 12; 105

Watery fort: Tamlaght O'Crilly LY 18; 114

Wates, Hugh: Tamlaght TE 20; 80, 115, 121

Watling Bridge: Galloon FH 4; 104

Watson, Ally Anne: Carrickfergus AM 37; 123

Watson, Anthony: Derryaghy AM 8; 98, 115

Watson, Charles: Hillsborough DN 12; 107

Watson, family: Aghalee AM 21; 31

Watson, family: Ahoghill AM 23; 25

Watson, family: Ballynure AM 32; 56

Watson, family: Blaris AM 8; 21

Watson, family: Clondermot LY 34; 46

Watson, family: Magheragall AM 21; 99

Watson, George: Derryaghy AM 8; 96

Watson, Henry: Hillsborough DN 12; 107

Watson, Hugh: Carrickfergus AM 37; 110

Watson, James: Ballinderry AM 21; 48–49

Watson, James: Blaris AM 8; 51, 60

Watson, James: Blaris DN 12; 42

Watson, James [I]: Magheragall AM 21; 100–01

Watson, James [II]: Magheragall AM 21; 99–101, 103, 109

Watson, John (Jnr): Hillsborough DN 12; 107

Watson, John (Jnr): Hillsborough DN 12; 107

Watson, John (Snr): Hillsborough DN 12; 107

Watson, John: Aghalee AM 21; 31

Watson, John: Coleraine LY 33; 61, 105

Watson, John: Dunboe LY 11; 65, 77, 79

Watson, John: Magheramesk AM 21; 122

Watson, John: Misc. DN 17; 117

Watson, John [I]: Hillsborough DN 12; 107

Watson, Josiah: Hillsborough DN 12; 107

Watson, Leonard: Warrenpoint DN 3; 120–22

Watson, Margaret: Garvaghy DN 12; 83

Watson, Mathew: Blaris DN 12; 42

Watson, Moses: Blaris DN 12; 40

Watson, Moses: Magheragall AM 21; 100–03

Watson, Mr: Drumragh TE 5; 109

Watson, Mr: Holywood DN 7; 77

Watson, Pierce: Hillsborough DN 12; 107

Watson, Richard: Clondermot LY 34; 46

Watson, Richard: Hillsborough DN 12; 106

Watson, Robert: Derryaghy AM 8; 95, 98

Watson, Robert: Magheramesk AM 21; 117, 120, 126

Watson, Samuel: Carrickfergus AM 37; 159, 174, 182

Watson, Thomas: Drumballyroney DN 3; 14

Watson, Thomas: Hillsborough DN 12; 105

Watson, William: Carrickfergus AM 37; 111

Watson, William: Dunboe LY 11; 80

Watson, William: Magherafelt LY 6; 82

Watson's Island: Tullynakill DN 7; 124

Watt, Alice: Drummaul AM 19; 91

Watt, Andrew: Macosquin LY 22; 85, 108–09, 111

Watt, Eliza: Drummaul AM 19; 91

Watt, Eliza Anne: Carrickfergus AM 37; 123

Watt, family: Tullyaughnish DL 38; 89

Watt, Hugh: Macosquin LY 22; 111

Watt, James: Coleraine LY 33; 143

Watt, James: Conwal DL 39; 27

Watt, James: Kilbride AM 29; 136, 144, 150, 152, 155

Watt, James: Lough Swilly DL 38; 102

Watt, James: Macosquin LY 22; 110

Watt, James: Mevagh DL 38; 60

Watt, James: Skerry AM 13; 115

Watt, James: Tullyaughnish DL 38; 85, 87, 89–90, 94–97

Watt, James [I]: Drummaul AM 19; 89–90

Watt, James [II]: Drummaul AM 19; 91

Watt, Jane: Drummaul AM 19; 91

Watt, John (Jnr): Drummaul AM 19; 91

Watt, John (Snr): Drummaul AM 19; 91

Watt, John: Blaris DN 12; 44, 48

Watt, John: Desertoghill LY 27; 20

Watt, John: Lissan LY 31; 90, 96

Watt, Maggie: Kilwaughter AM 10; 118

Watt, Margaret: Carrickfergus AM 37; 121

Watt, Mary: Drummaul AM 19; 91

Watt, Mary Anne: Desertoghill LY 27; 20

Watt, Miss: Tullyaughnish DL 38; 89

Watt, Mrs: Kilbride AM 29; 144, 152

Watt, Peter: Maghera LY 18; 42

Watt, Robert: Ballymoney AM 16; 17

Watt, Robert: Carrickfergus AM 37; 117, 121

Watt, Rose: Drummaul AM 19; 91

Watt, Sarah: Drummaul AM 19; 91

Watt, Thomas: Kilbride AM 29; 155

Watters, William: Blaris DN 12; 42

Watterson, family: Artrea LY 6; 14

Watterson, Rev. F.W.: Glynn AM 26; 22, 34–35, 38–39, 46–47

Wattle Bridge: Clones FH 4; 27–28

Wattle Bridge: Drummully FH 4; 35–36, 40

Watts Island: Lough Swilly DL 38; 117

Watts, John: Rasharkin AM 23; 134

Watty's bush: Macosquin LY 22; 118
Wattywee lough: Kilmacteige SO 40; 191
Wauchob, Daniel: Urney DL 39; 179
Wauchope, James: Inch DN 17; 75
Wauchope, Margaret: Inch DN 17; 75
Waugh, family: Magherally DN 12; 114
Waugh, James: Newtownards DN 7; 112
Waugh, Joseph: Ahoghill AM 23; 40
Waugh, Miss (Armagh): Drumcree AH 1; 39–40
Waugh, Rev.: Antrim AM 29; 45
Waulk mills: Balteagh LY 9; 30
Wear, family: Magheragall AM 21; 99
Weathered, family: Ballinderry AM 21; 48
Weatherhead, family: Ballinderry AM 21; 51
Weatherup, David: Ballynure AM 32; 65
Weatherup, family: Ballinderry AM 21; 53
Weatherup, family: Carrickfergus AM 37; 93
Webb, James: Newry DN 3; 80
Webb, Jonathan: Seagoe AH 1; 102–03
Webb, Mr: Clogher TE 5; 33
Webb, Rev. R.: Drummully FH 4; 39
Webb, Rev. William: Clondermot LY 34; 59, 61, 67
Webb, Richard: Ballyscullion LY 6; 56–57
Webster, Rev. James: Magilligan LY 11; 89
Wee Collin hill: Ballycor AM 32; 1, 8
Wee Collin hill: Rashee AM 32; 135
Weir, David: Duneane AM 19; 109, 112–14, 116–19, 121–22
Weir, family: Ahoghill AM 23; 25
Weir, family: Ballynure AM 32; 56
Weir, family: Ballywillin AM 16; 32
Weir, family: Enniskillen FH 4; 58
Weir, George: Ahoghill AM 23; 22
Weir, George: Kilwaughter AM 10; 122
Weir, Hugh: Ahoghill AM 23; 25
Weir, Hugh: Ballywillin LY 33; 51
Weir, Hugh: Hillsborough DN 12; 107
Weir, Hugh: Magheragall AM 21; 106
Weir, Isabella: Carrickfergus AM 37; 128
Weir, James: Carrickfergus AM 37; 111, 195
Weir, James [I]: Macosquin LY 22; 87, 115
Weir, James [II]: Macosquin LY 22; 111
Weir, John: Carrickfergus AM 37; 114
Weir, John: Devenish FH 14; 58
Weir, John: Drummaul AM 19; 91
Weir, John: Errigal LY 27; 63
Weir, John: Tamlaght TE 20; 105
Weir, Joseph: Killowen LY 33; 162, 170
Weir, Mary: Drummaul AM 19; 91
Weir, Mr (Hillsborough): Annahilt DN 12; 20
Weir, Mrs: Clogher TE 5; 41
Weir, Nathaniel: Newry DN 3; 99, 103
Weir, Rev.: Enniskillen FH 4; 63
Weir, Rev. Christopher: Devenish FH 14; 53, 59
Weir, Rev. John: Newry DN 3; 71, 79, 81, 99

Weir, Rev. Samuel: Dunboe LY 11; 66
Weir, Robert: Coleraine LY 33; 72, 95, 138
Weir, Robert: Macosquin LY 22; 111
Weir, William: Coleraine LY 33; 143
Weir's Castle: Duneane AM 19; 119
Weir's Snout: Billy AM 16; 41
Welch, Richard: Aghalee AM 21; 34
Welchtown school: Kilteevoge DL 39; 113–14
Welchtown silver mine: Kilteevoge DL 39; 113
Welchtown td: Kilteevoge DL 39; 114
Welden, Christy: Blaris DN 12; 41
Weldon, family: Blaris AM 8; 21
Weldon, Francis: Blaris AM 8; 53
Weldon, Francis: Blaris DN 12; 45, 49
Weldon, Mrs: Blaris AM 8; 84
Well Glass spring: Aghanloo LY 11; 24
Well Meadow locality: Muckamore AM 35; 80
Welland, Mr (Dublin): Kirkinriola AM 23; 96
Wellbrook House: Kildress TE 20; 61
Wellbrook mills: Kildress TE 20; 60
Wellesley, Arthur: Aghadowey LY 22; 23
Wellesley, Arthur: Kilcronaghan LY 31; 81
Wellington, Duke of: Newry DN 3; 68
Wells, family: Ballywillin AM 16; 32
Wells, Joshua: Cumber LY 28; 74
Welsh, A.M.: Hillsborough DN 12; 106
Welsh, Elizabeth (nee Knox): Templepatrick AM 35; 116, 124, 132, 143
Welsh, family: Blaris AM 8; 22
Welsh, family: Killelagh LY 27; 99
Welsh, family: Ramoan AM 24; 107
Welsh, Haliday: Hillsborough DN 12; 106
Welsh, Henry: Aghagallon AM 21; 11–12, 17
Welsh, Henry [I]: Hillsborough DN 12; 106
Welsh, Henry [II]: Hillsborough DN 12; 106
Welsh, Jacob: Hillsborough DN 12; 106
Welsh, James: Billy AM 16; 56, 75
Welsh, John: Hillsborough DN 12; 106
Welsh, John: Kilmacteige SO 40; 195
Welsh, John: Magherafelt LY 6; 108
Welsh, John: Rasharkin AM 23; 136
Welsh, John: Templepatrick AM 35; 116, 124, 132, 143
Welsh, John: Tydavnet MN 40; 173
Welsh, Lady: Kilbroney DN 3; 35
Welsh, M.: Drumgoon CN 40; 8–9
Welsh, M.: Drung CN 40; 22
Welsh, M.: Killdrumsherdan CN 40; 35
Welsh, Mr (Dromore): Magheramesk AM 21; 122
Welsh, Rev.: Aghalee AM 21; 31
Welsh, Rev. Josias: Mallusk AM 2; 109
Welsh, Rev. Josias: Templepatrick AM 35; 116, 124, 132, 141, 143
Welsh, Rev. Luke: Culfeightrin AM 24; 55
Welsh, Richard: Aghagallon AM 21; 7

Welsh, Sarah: Hillsborough DN 12; 106

Welsh, Widow: Clondermot LY 34; 26

Welshe, family: Ballyculter DN 17; 28

Welshe, family: Ballyphilip DN 7; 13

Welshe, Thomas: Templepatrick AM 35; 116

Welshes Castle (see also Walshestown Castle):
Ballyculter DN 17; 28

Wenman, Mr: Magheradrool DN 17; 101

Wentworth, Lord: Drumachose LY 9; 95

Wentworth, Mrs: Clondermot LY 34; 61

Werburg, St: Kilmegan DN 3; 60

Wesley, Rev. John: Blaris AM 8; 7, 31

Wesley, Rev. John: Lambeg AM 8; 136

West Divisiom standing stone: Carrickfergus AM
37; 86

West Division cairn: Carrickfergus AM 37; 86, 88,
185

West Division causeway: Carrickfergus AM 37; 186

West Division cove: Carrickfergus AM 37; 87, 132

West Division druid's altar: Carrickfergus AM 37;
190–91

West Division fort [I]: Carrickfergus AM 37; 87,
132

West Division fort [II]: Carrickfergus AM 37; 183

West Division fort [III]: Carrickfergus AM 37; 183

West Division fort [IV]: Carrickfergus AM 37; 184

West Division fort [IX]: Carrickfergus AM 37; 184

West Division fort [V]: Carrickfergus AM 37; 184

West Division fort [VI]: Carrickfergus AM 37; 184

West Division fort [VII]: Carrickfergus AM 37; 185

West Division fort [VIII]: Carrickfergus AM 37; 185

West Division forts: Carrickfergus AM 37; 187

West Division quarry: Carrickfergus AM 37; 171

West Division td: Carrickfergus AM 37; 3–4, 6, 33,
75, 77–78, 81, 84, 91–92, 133, 135, 151, 155,
158–59, 173–76, 183–85, 188–90

West Indies: Ballyaghran LY 33; 18

West Indies: Ballyrashane LY 22; 53

West Indies: Coleraine LY 33; 86

West Indies: Enniskillen FH 4; 81

West Indies: Knockbreda DN 7; 97

West mills: Carrickfergus AM 37; 35

West mills meeting room: Carrickfergus AM 37; 70

West Town (Tory Island): Lough Swilly DL 38;
124–25

West Town steeple: Lough Swilly DL 38; 124

West, James: Clondermot LY 34; 79

West, James: Donacavey TE 5; 80

West, James: Faughanvale LY 36; 20

West, Peter: Newry DN 3; 100

West, Rev.: Seagoe AH 1; 103

West, Roger: Ballyscullion LY 6; 57

West, Thomas: Ballyscullion LY 6; 57

West, W.J.: Magheraculmoney FH 14; 106

Westenra, Richard: Aghabog MN 40; 67

Westenra, Richard: Currin MN 40; 96

Westenra, Richard: Tydavnet MN 40; 173

Western Isles (Scotland): Misc. LY 31; 116

Western Isles: Glynn AM 26; 34

Westley, John: Coleraine LY 33; 145

Westmacott, sculptor: Antrim AM 29; 8

Westmeath: Ballyphilip DN 7; 13

Westmeath: Ballyscullion LY 6; 59

Westmeath: Banagher LY 30; 96

Westmeath: Clondermot LY 34; 64, 71

Westmeath: Drumlumman CN 40; 12

Westmeath: Galloon FH 4; 90

Westmeath: Kilbroney DN 3; 35

Westminster: Templecorran AM 26; 128

Westminster Abbey: Misc. AM 10; 130

Westmoreland (England): Ballyscullion LY 6; 57

Westmoreland: Lough Neagh AM 21; 97

Weston, Nicholas (see Boston): Clondermot LY 34;
47

Westport (Mayo): Island Magee AM 10; 66

Wethered, Dr: Blaris AM 8; 37, 55, 60–62, 84, 86

Wethered, Dr: Blaris DN 12; 43, 46, 49

Wethered, Mrs: Blaris AM 8; 85

Wetherell, family: Banagher LY 30; 36

Wetherell, Hugh: Banagher LY 30; 53, 97–99

Wetherell, Hugh: Bovevagh LY 25; 54

Wetherell, James: Banagher LY 30; 97–98

Wetherell, Robert: Banagher LY 30; 35, 96

Wetherup, John: Ballynure AM 32; 56

Wexford: Blaris AM 8; 88

Wexford: Carrickfergus AM 37; 18

Wexford Castle: Island Magee AM 10; 48

Wexford county: Carrickfergus AM 37; 84

Wexford county: Faughanvale LY 36; 44

Wexford county: Island Magee AM 10; 66

Wexford harbour: Cumber LY 28; 72

Whale Head: Lough Swilly DL 38; 102, 104

Whale Head: Tullyaughnish DL 38; 95

Whaley, Mr: Loughgilly AH 1; 85

Whap's hill: Kilroot AM 26; 57

Whealey, family: Ballintoy AM 24; 30

Wheatfield House: Kilmore AH 1; 64, 67

Wheatfield House: Tamlaght Finlagan LY 25; 101

Wheathill Glebe school: Inishmacsaint FH 14; 78

Wheathill td: Killesher FH 14; 86–87

Wheecruick tower: Lough Swilly DL 38; 123

Wheeler, family: Carrickfergus AM 37; 93

Wheeler, family: Lambeg AM 8; 135

Wheeler, James: Carrickfergus AM 37; 40, 148

Whigamstown td: Bright DN 17; 34–35

Whin meeting house (see Ballinrees): Dunboe LY
11; 46, 66

Whinerey, Robert: Tamlaght TE 20; 86

Whinhill school: Ballyrashane LY 22; 54

Whinnagan Glebe td: Cleenish FH 14; 29

Whinnagan Glebe td: Derrybrusk FH 4; 30, 32–33
Whinny hill: Dunboe LY 11; 67
Whiskey hill: Ardstraw TE 5; 10
Whiskey hill: Urney DL 39; 174
Whiskey Knowes hills: Desertoghill LY 27; 24–25
Whistler, Radulpus: Magherafelt LY 6; 82
Whitager, Thomas: Carrickfergus AM 37; 46
Whitaker, family: Enniskillen FH 4; 75
Whitaker, Miss: Newry DN 3, 98
Whitaker, Mr: Clogher TE 5; 40
Whitchurch, Marmaduke: Aghaderg DN 12; 4
Whitchurch, Marmaduke: Kilbroney DN 3; 32
Whitchurch, Rose: Kilbroney DN 3; 32
Whitcombe, John: Moira DN 12; 118
Whitcroft, Harriet: Ramoan AM 24; 126
White (see Whitehill): Faughanvale LY 36; 53
White and Patterson, Messrs: Inver AM 26; 54
White and Walkinshaw, Messrs: Newry DN 3; 104
White bay: Lough Swilly DL 38; 104
White cairn: Carrickfergus AM 37; 85–86
White Castle: Coleraine LY 33; 63
White Coat Point: Kilmore AH 1; 61
White fort: Ardstraw TE 5; 12
White fort: Bovevagh LY 25; 31
White fort: Dungiven LY 15; 43–44, 101–02, 111
White Hall House: Aghagallon AM 21; 7
White Hall school: Aghagallon AM 21; 24
White Hall Sunday school: Aghagallon AM 21; 24
White Hart Inn: Drumragh TE 5; 107
White Head: Glynn AM 26; 16
White Head: Island Magee AM 10; 18, 74, 89
White Head: Templecorran AM 26; 84–85, 88,
    90–91, 108
White Head coastguard station: Templecorran AM
    26; 99, 131
White Head district: Templecorran AM 26; 82
White Head fort: Templecorran AM 26; 120–21
White Head td: Templecorran AM 26; 113–14, 120
White Head threshing machine: Templecorran AM
    26; 125
White hills: Bovevagh LY 25; 1, 33
White Island: Killdrumsherdan CN 40; 32
White Island: Magheraculmoney FH 14; 106
White Island: Muckno MN 40; 162
White Island: Trory FH 14; 122–23
White lough: Drumlumman CN 40; 12
White lough: Killdrumsherdan CN 40; 31–32
White Mill td: Ballymascanlan LH 40; 55
White mountain: Aghanloo LY 11; 3
White mountain: Blaris AM 8; 70
White mountain: Blaris DN 12; 27
White mountain: Derryaghy AM 8; 90, 92, 113, 115
White mountain: Down DN 17; 58
White mountain: Dungiven LY 15; 1, 81
White Mountain fort: Derryaghy AM 8; 97

White Mountain standing stone: Derryaghy AM 8;
    98
White Mountain td: Derryaghy AM 8; 101, 109, 119
White Park beach: Ballintoy AM 24; 10, 13–4
White Park demesne: Ballintoy AM 24; 30
White Park distillery: Ballintoy AM 24; 30
White Park enclosure: Ballintoy AM 24; 29
White Park House: Ballintoy AM 24; 30, 33
White Park House: Ballycor AM 32; 4
White Park seminary: Ballintoy AM 24; 30
White Park td: Ballintoy AM 24; 29–30
White rock: Killinchy DN 7; 86, 88
White rocks: Ballywillin LY 33; 38, 47
White rocks: Dunluce AM 16; 104, 108
White Spots td: Misc. DN 17; 124
White standing stones: Dungiven LY 15; 76
White Water bridge: Ballynascreen LY 31; 1, 7
White Water fall: Banagher LY 30; 114
White Water glen: Banagher LY 30; 24, 26
White Water river: Misc. LY 31; 111, 113–14, 116
White Water stream: Banagher LY 30; 26, 31, 46,
    56, 59, 112, 114
White well: Banagher LY 30; 57–58, 89, 95
White, A.: Clondermot LY 34; 4
White, Alexander: Kilcronaghan LY 31; 78, 86
White, Billy: Templecorran AM 26; 130
White, Cllr: Skerry AM 13; 107, 111
White, Col (Dublin): Newry DN 3; 106–07
White, family: Carnmoney AM 2; 76
White, family: Carrickfergus AM 37; 60
White, family: Killyleagh DN 17; 81
White, family: Kilraghts AM 16; 130
White, family: Misc. DN 17; 121
White, family: Racavan AM 13; 100
White, family: Ramoan AM 24; 107
White, family: Tullyrusk AM 21; 135
White, Francis (see Whittle): Muckamore AM 35;
    76
White, Francis: Newry DN 3; 99, 104
White, J.: Skerry AM 13; 107, 111
White, James: Carrickfergus AM 37; 194
White, John: Ballymoney AM 16; 15–16
White, John: Billy AM 16; 61
White, John: Blaris AM 8; 44–45, 59–60, 62–63
White, John: Blaris DN 12; 44, 46, 48, 50
White, John: Coleraine LY 33; 127
White, John: Derryaghy AM 8; 95
White, John: Kilwaughter AM 10; 119
White, John: Ramoan AM 24; 112, 116, 125
White, John: Tamlaght Finlagan LY 25; 119
White, Joseph: Tamlaght Finlagan LY 25; 120
White, Joshua: Muckamore AM 35; 81
White, Mr (Ballymena): Ballymoney AM 16; 18
White, Mr (Gortgarn): Drumachose LY 9; 128
White, Mr: Clondermot LY 34; 42

White, Mr: Loughgilly AH 1; 85
White, Mrs (Mulkeeragh): Bovevagh LY 25; 49
White, Mrs: Blaris AM 8; 65
White, Nathaniel: Antrim AM 29; 42, 46, 58
White, Paul: Maghera LY 18; 61
White, Rev.: Ballee DN 17; 24
White, Rev.: Carnmoney AM 2; 75
White, Rev. James: Carrickfergus AM 37; 133, 144, 146, 150, 156
White, Rev. James: Drummaul AM 19; 69, 82
White, Rev. Robert: Templepatrick AM 35; 133, 143–44
White, Robert: Ballynascreen LY 31; 14, 20
White, Robert: Drumachose LY 9; 128
White, Robert: Raloo AM 32; 118–19, 130–31
White, Rowlan: Newry DN 3; 74
White, Thomas: Clondermot LY 34; 37, 79, 81, 86, 94, 100, 104, 106
White, William: Hillsborough DN 12; 105
White, William: Kilraghts AM 16; 132
White's Castle (see Killyleagh): Misc. DN 17; 120
White's library: Kirkinriola AM 23; 98
Whiteabbey: Carnmoney AM 2; 36, 38, 43, 45, 47, 51, 59, 62, 64, 73, 81, 83–84, 87–88, 92, 95, 98, 102
Whiteabbey abbey: Carnmoney AM 2; 34, 38, 65–66, 68–69, 73, 81, 93, 95–96, 98
Whiteabbey abbey: Carrickfergus AM 37; 80
Whiteabbey bridge: Carnmoney AM 2; 84
Whiteabbey flax mills: Carnmoney AM 2; 43–44, 47, 83, 86, 91–92
Whiteabbey fort [I]: Carnmoney AM 2; 66, 96
Whiteabbey fort [II]: Carnmoney AM 2; 100
Whiteabbey fort [III]: Carnmoney AM 2; 100
Whiteabbey graveyard: Carnmoney AM 2; 66, 96
Whiteabbey hill: Carnmoney AM 2; 51
Whiteabbey landing-place: Carnmoney AM 2; 92
Whiteabbey Lower bleach mill: Carnmoney AM 2; 47, 91
Whiteabbey Lower cotton mill: Carnmoney AM 2; 47, 91
Whiteabbey Lower flax mills: Carnmoney AM 2; 47, 91–92
Whiteabbey Lower flour mill: Carnmoney AM 2; 91
Whiteabbey Lower gas manufactory: Carnmoney AM 2; 91
Whiteabbey meeting house: Carnmoney AM 2; 43–45, 55–57, 75, 82–83, 87
Whiteabbey national school: Carnmoney AM 2; 86
Whiteabbey old church: Carnmoney AM 2; 64
Whiteabbey quay: Carnmoney AM 2; 47
Whiteabbey school: Carnmoney AM 2; 43, 78, 86
Whiteabbey Sunday school: Carnmoney AM 2; 44, 79, 86

Whiteabbey td: Carnmoney AM 2; 34, 58, 69, 84, 88, 102
Whiteabbey well: Carnmoney AM 2; 96
Whitecastle House: Moville DL 38; 78
Whitecastle td: Moville DL 38; 73, 75–76
Whitechurch flax windmill: Ballywalter DN 7; 17
Whitechurch td: Ballywalter DN 7; 17–18
Whitechurch td: Misc. DN 17; 125
Whiteford, Dr: Derryaghy AM 8; 105
Whiteford, family: Ballynure AM 32; 56
Whiteford, family: Culfeightrin AM 24; 59
Whiteford, Mary: Ramoan AM 24; 126
Whiteford, Rev. James: Raloo AM 32; 98, 119, 127–28, 130–31
Whitefriars monastery: Magheraculmoney FH 14; 106
Whitehall House: Skerry AM 13; 107, 111
Whitehall td: Clondermot LY 34; 72
Whitehaven (Cumbria): Killyleagh DN 17; 84
Whitehaven: Carrickfergus AM 37; 158
Whitehead, Richard: Newry DN 3; 98, 103
Whitehill evening school: Ahoghill AM 23; 43
Whitehill House: Killymard DL 39; 105
Whitehill orchards: Taughboyne DL 39; 155
Whitehill school: Ahoghill AM 23; 40–41, 43
Whitehill td: Devenish FH 14; 57, 59
Whitehill td: Donaghmore DL 39; 39
Whitehill td: Faughanvale LY 36; 17, 53, 64, 69, 80, 91–92, 97, 99
Whitehill td: Killea and Taughboyne DL 39; 80, 196
Whitehill td: Raymoghy DL 39; 141, 199
Whitehill td: Taughboyne DL 39; 148, 151, 155
Whitehill wood: Faughanvale LY 36; 92
Whitehill wood: Taughboyne DL 39; 148
Whitehills lough: Saul DN 17; 115
Whitehills td: Saul DN 17; 114
Whitehouse (see Laurel Hill): Killowen LY 33; 168
Whitehouse: Ballylinny AM 32; 16
Whitehouse: Ballymartin AM 2; 6, 15
Whitehouse: Ballynure AM 32; 70
Whitehouse: Ballyrobert AM 2; 21
Whitehouse: Ballywalter AM 2; 26, 30
Whitehouse: Carnmoney AM 2; 47–48, 51, 53, 59, 61–62, 64, 84–85, 87–89, 91, 96, 98
Whitehouse bridge: Carnmoney AM 2; 84
Whitehouse Castle: Carnmoney AM 2; 38, 51, 64, 68–69
Whitehouse cotton factories: Carrickfergus AM 37; 62–63
Whitehouse dispensary: Ballylinny AM 32; 16
Whitehouse dispensary: Ballymartin AM 2; 7
Whitehouse dispensary: Ballyrobert AM 2; 21
Whitehouse dispensary: Ballywalter AM 2; 26, 30
Whitehouse dispensary: Carnmoney AM 2; 54, 73, 81, 89

Whitehouse dispensary: Doagh AM 29; 90
Whitehouse district: Ballyrobert AM 2; 24
Whitehouse district: Ballywalter AM 2; 26, 30
Whitehouse district: Mallusk AM 2; 110
Whitehouse fort: Ardstraw TE 5; 12
Whitehouse fort: Carnmoney AM 2; 100
Whitehouse House: Slanes DN 7; 121
Whitehouse linen manufactory: Carnmoney AM 2;
    91
Whitehouse Lower: Carnmoney AM 2; 38–39,
    53–54, 73, 83–84, 103
Whitehouse Lower barracks: Carnmoney AM 2; 39,
    54
Whitehouse Lower post office: Carnmoney AM 2;
    39
Whitehouse Lower school: Carnmoney AM 2; 39,
    78, 102
Whitehouse Lower Sunday school: Carnmoney AM
    2; 39, 55, 79
Whitehouse Lower td: Carnmoney AM 2; 38
Whitehouse market house: Carnmoney AM 2; 104
Whitehouse Middle flax mill: Carnmoney AM 2; 42,
    48, 92
Whitehouse old house: Carnmoney AM 2; 69,
    71–72, 81, 83, 97
Whitehouse old quay: Carnmoney AM 2; 96–97
Whitehouse Point: Carnmoney AM 2; 38, 69, 71, 96
Whitehouse post office: Carnmoney AM 2; 88, 90
Whitehouse quay: Carnmoney AM 2; 62, 71–72
Whitehouse school: Carnmoney AM 2; 86, 88
Whitehouse spinning mills: Carnmoney AM 2; 93
Whitehouse stream: Carnmoney AM 2; 37, 47, 92
Whitehouse td: Ardstraw TE 5; 12
Whitehouse td: Bright DN 17; 35
Whitehouse td: Carnmoney AM 2; 34, 58, 68, 81,
    84, 92, 102
Whitehouse td: Misc. DL 39; 196
Whitehouse Upper: Carnmoney AM 2; 37–39, 41,
    51, 53, 73, 83–84, 103
Whitehouse Upper dispensary: Carnmoney AM 2;
    42
Whitehouse Upper factories (see Whitehouse Upper
    flax mills)
Whitehouse Upper flax mills: Carnmoney AM 2; 34,
    41–42, 47–48, 52, 60, 62, 83, 92, 105
Whitehouse Upper gas manufactory: Carnmoney
    AM 2; 41
Whitehouse Upper landing-place: Carnmoney AM
    2; 41, 53
Whitehouse Upper linenworks: Carnmoney AM 2;
    52
Whitehouse Upper market house: Carnmoney AM
    2; 41, 83, 105
Whitehouse Upper printworks: Carnmoney AM 2;
    41, 52, 54, 83, 104

Whitehouse Upper quay: Carnmoney AM 2; 42, 53
Whitehouse Upper school: Carnmoney AM 2;
    41–43, 55, 77–78, 102–03
Whitehouse Upper shop: Carnmoney AM 2; 42
Whitehouse Upper Sunday school: Carnmoney AM
    2; 43, 79
Whitekirk district: Muckamore AM 35; 56
Whitelocks, family: Carrickfergus AM 37; 78–79
Whitely, Robert: Ahoghill AM 23; 39
Whiteshill (see Whitehill): Ahoghill AM 23; 40
Whiteside, family: Ballywillin AM 16; 32
Whiteside, family: Misc. LY 36; 104
Whiteside, Hugh: Carrickfergus AM 37; 193
Whiteside, James: Tydavnet MN 40; 172
Whiteside, Joseph: Derryaghy AM 8; 117–18
Whiteside, Mr (Terryhoogan): Ballymore AH 1; 18
Whiteside, Rev. James: Kilcronaghan LY 31; 79,
    136
Whiteside, Rev. John: Coleraine LY 33; 65, 67, 70,
    72, 95, 135, 140–42, 144–45
Whiteside, William: Killead AM 35; 50
Whitesland locality: Carrickfergus AM 37; 94
Whitestone, Rev. J.T.: Kilmore MN 40; 136
Whitestown school: Carlingford LH 40; 59
Whitestown td: Carlingford LH 40; 57, 59
Whitewell (see Whitewells)
Whitewell, family: Carnmoney AM 2; 76
Whitewells barracks: Carnmoney AM 2; 54
Whitewells kilns: Doagh AM 29; 94
Whitewells springs: Carnmoney AM 2; 84–85, 91,
    93
Whitewells td: Ballylinny AM 32; 27
Whitewells td: Carnmoney AM 2; 88
Whitewells td: Kilbride AM 29; 153
Whitewells td: Templepatrick AM 35; 145
Whitla, family: Blaris AM 8; 21
Whitla, family: Camlin AM 21; 68
Whitla, family: Magheragall AM 21; 99
Whitla, George: Blaris AM 8; 18, 32, 84
Whitla, George: Inver AM 26; 51, 53–54
Whitla, Mrs George: Blaris AM 8; 12, 66, 84–85
Whitla, Rev. William: Ballinderry AM 21; 50
Whitla, T.: Blaris AM 8; 60
Whitla, William: Blaris AM 8; 32, 61
Whitla, William: Blaris DN 12; 39–41, 44, 46, 48,
    50
Whitla, William: Camlin AM 21; 76
Whitney, man named: Drummaul AM 19; 61
Whitsitt, Robert: Donagh MN 40; 101
Whitstone, Rev.: Enniskeen CN 40; 28
Whittacker, family: Enniskillen FH 4; 58
Whittaker, Miss: Newry DN 3; 103
Whittle, family: Camlin AM 21; 68
Whittle, Francis: Antrim AM 29; 47
Whittle, Francis: Muckamore AM 35; 56, 75–79

Whittle, James: Glenavy AM 21; 83

Whittle, L.L.: Muckamore AM 35; 62–63, 76

Whittle, Mr: Lough Neagh AM 21; 95

Whittle, Stafford: Camlin AM 21; 63, 67

Whitton, family: Enniskillen FH 4; 58

Whittrite stones: Bovevagh LY 25; 9, 19, 38–39

Whowell, Mr: Blaris AM 8; 16

Whyte, David: Misc. DL 39; 186

Whyte, family: Comber DN 7; 31, 44

Whyte, family: Culfeightrin AM 24; 59

Whyte, Joseph: Balteagh LY 9; 17, 39

Whyte, N.C.: Aghaderg DN 12; 5–6, 10

Whyte, N.C.: Annaclone DN 12; 15

Whyte, N.C.: Seapatrick DN 12; 123, 125–26, 134

Whyte, Oliver: Misc. DL 39; 186

Whyte, Samuel: Templecorran AM 26; 132

Wi Munnias fort: Macosquin LY 22; 110

Wickcliffe, family: Glenavy AM 21; 86

Wicklow: Loughgall AH 1; 76

Wicklow borough: Ballyscullion LY 6; 59

Wicklow county: Enniskillen FH 4; 68

Wicklow county: Faughanvale LY 36; 60

Wicklow, Earl of (deceased): Misc. DL 39; 188

Wicklow, Earl of: Killea and Taughboyne DL 39;
   79, 89

Wicklow, Earl of: Lough Swilly DL 38; 103, 144

Wicklow, Earl of: Misc. DL 39; 186, 189

Wicklow, Earl of: Raymoghy DL 39; 132–33,
   136–41

Wicklow, Earl of: Taughboyne DL 39; 148, 152,
   152–55

Widrow, family: Kilraghts AM 16; 130

Widrow, Hugh: Kilraghts AM 16; 132

Wier, Margaret Anne: Ballywillin LY 33; 51

Wier, Rebeca: Ballywillin LY 33; 51

Wiggins, Henry: Faughanvale LY 36; 42

Wiggins, John: Faughanvale LY 36; 42, 45

Wightman, William: Blaris AM 8; 61

Wigton, Alexander: Enniskillen FH 4; 57

Wigton, Mr (Raphoe): Clonleigh DL 39; 13

Wigtonshire (Scotland): Kirkinriola AM 23; 94

Wilcock, George: Errigal Keerogue TE 20; 49

Wildcat rocks: Banagher LY 30; 64

Wilderness demesne: Antrim AM 29; 11–12, 43

Wiley, family: Ballynure AM 32; 56

Wiley, family: Drumbeg AM 8; 123

Wiley, James: Carnmoney AM 2; 79

Wiley, James: Dunaghy AM 13; 23

Wiley, Jane: Carrickfergus AM 37; 154

Wiley, Lucy: Carrickfergus AM 37; 110

Wiley, man named: Raloo AM 32; 120

Wiley, Mr (Ballycushan): Templepatrick AM 35;
   113

Wiley, Robert: Ahoghill AM 23; 37

Wiley, Samuel: Glynn AM 26; 28, 42

Wiley, Thomas: Nilteen AM 35; 100

Wiley, William: Carrickfergus AM 37; 108

Wiley, Zekiel: Ballyrobert AM 2; 25

Wilford, Col: Faughanvale LY 36; 11

Wilkins, Dr: Devenish FH 14; 55

Wilkins, James: Carrickfergus AM 37; 194

Wilkins, Rev. Joseph: Blaris AM 8; 86

Wilkins, Richard: Carrickfergus AM 37; 193

Wilkinson, Allan: Tamlaght TE 20; 102

Wilkinson, family: Culfeightrin AM 24; 71

Wilkinson, James [I]: Tamlaght TE 20; 75, 131, 136

Wilkinson, James [II]: Tamlaght TE 20; 93

Wilkinson, John: Carrickfergus AM 37; 130

Wilkinson, John: Duneane AM 19; 117

Wilkinson, John: Magherafelt LY 6; 112

Wilkinson, Lt I.I.: Clonleigh DL 39; 1–4

Wilkinson, Lt I.I.: Leck DL 39; 120

Wilkinson, Rev.: Mevagh DL 38; 59

Wilkinson, Rev. Caesar: Ardstraw TE 5; 9

Wilkinson, Thomas: Tamlaght TE 20; 82, 131, 136

Wilkison, John: Tamlaght TE 20; 92, 96

Willes, Richard: Derryaghy AM 8; 101, 108

Willes, William: Derryaghy AM 8; 107

Willether td: Cleenish FH 14; 29

Willey, Alexander: Maghera LY 18; 59

Willey, David: Ballylinny AM 32; 27

Willey, Eliza: Ahoghill AM 23; 38

Willey, John: Ballymoney AM 16; 24

Willey, Mr: Ballinderry AM 21; 57

Willey, Mrs: Ballinderry AM 21; 57

Willey, Rev. John: Drumgoon CN 40; 6

William III, King: Aghaderg DN 12; 5, 11

William III, King: Aghanloo LY 11; 26

William III, King: Ahoghill AM 23; 14, 17

William III, King: Ballymore AH 1; 9

William III, King: Ballywalter AM 2; 26

William III, King: Camlin AM 21; 70

William III, King: Carmavy AM 35; 6

William III, King: Carnmoney AM 2; 34, 39, 51, 64,
   69, 72, 97–98

William III, King: Clondermot LY 34; 41, 45

William III, King: Derryaghy AM 8; 99–100

William III, King: Desertoghill LY 27; 3, 15

William III, King: Donaghmore DL 39; 32

William III, King: Drummaul AM 19; 42, 66, 69,
   82, 88

William III, King: Drumragh TE 5; 108

William III, King: Duneane AM 19; 116

William III, King: Ematris MN 40; 115

William III, King: Enniskillen FH 4; 52–53, 68

William III, King: Faughanvale LY 36; 8

William III, King: Galloon FH 4; 91, 100

William III, King: Glenavy AM 21; 86

William III, King: Glynn AM 26; 41

William III, King: Hillsborough DN 12; 88–89, 98

William III, King: Inishmacsaint FH 14; 74
William III, King: Kilcronaghan LY 31; 67, 87
William III, King: Killagan AM 23; 83
William III, King: Killesher FH 14; 84
William III, King: Kilroot AM 26; 78
William III, King: Lambeg AM 8; 140–41
William III, King: Magherafelt LY 6; 88, 95
William III, King: Magheramesk AM 21; 123
William III, King: Misc. AM 10; 131
William III, King: Misc. LY 31; 118
William III, King: Newry DN 3; 65
William III, King: Seapatrick DN 12; 132
William III, King: Tamlaght O'Crilly LY 18; 96
William III, King: Templepatrick AM 35; 145
William III, King: Termoneeny LY 6; 127, 132
William IV, King: Carrickfergus AM 37; 41, 65
William IV, King: Desertegney DL 38; 28
William IV, King: Inver AM 26; 52
William IV, King: Kilbride AM 29; 153
William IV, King: Kilkeel DN 3; 54
William IV, King: Killygarvan DL 38; 43
William the Conqueror, King: Bovevagh LY 25; 30
William the Conqueror, King: Dungiven LY 15; 28
William's fort: Kilcronaghan LY 31; 67, 83
Williams, Arthur: Termoneeny LY 6; 127, 132
Williams, Catherine: Termoneeny LY 6; 127, 132
Williams, Charles: Lough Swilly DL 38; 117
Williams, family: Blaris AM 8; 21
Williams, family: Derrykeighan AM 16; 89
Williams, family: Kilmacteige SO 40; 189
Williams, family: Templecorran AM 26; 117, 119
Williams, George: Dungiven LY 15; 31, 72, 88
Williams, Henery: Dungiven LY 15; 72, 74, 88
Williams, J.B.: Ballyaghran LY 33; 10
Williams, J.B.: Ballyrashane LY 22; 53
Williams, J.B.: Ballywillin LY 33; 40
Williams, J.B.: Banagher LY 30; 113
Williams, J.B.: Billy AM 16; 45
Williams, J.B.: Bovevagh LY 25; 9, 19
Williams, J.B.: Clondermot LY 34; 96
Williams, J.B.: Coleraine LY 33; 57, 87–88, 149
Williams, J.B.: Cumber LY 28; 32, 84–85
Williams, J.B.: Desertoghill LY 27; 2, 26, 1–2
Williams, J.B.: Tamlaght Finlagan LY 25; 80,
    87–88, 109, 112
Williams, J.H.: Aghavea TE 5; 2–9
Williams, J.H.: Ballymore AH 1; 1–7
Williams, J.H.: Clonduff DN 3; 3–4
Williams, J.H.: Garvaghy DN 12; 84
Williams, J.H.: Kilclief DN 17; 78
Williams, J.H.: Kilclooney AH 1; 51
Williams, J.H.: Kilmegan DN 3; 55
Williams, James: Blaris AM 8; 59
Williams, James: Dunboe LY 11; 81
Williams, James: Macosquin LY 22; 117–18

Williams, James: Newry DN 3; 99, 104
Williams, Messrs Arthur and Sons: Drumcree AH 1;
    30
Williams, Mr (Carns): Kilmacteige SO 40; 185,
    189–90, 196
Williamson, Alexander: Lambeg AM 8; 136–37, 141
Williamson, Andrew: Templepatrick AM 35; 152
Williamson, Charles: Coleraine LY 33; 146
Williamson, D.: Ballybay MN 40; 84
Williamson, family: Carnmoney AM 2; 76
Williamson, family: Carrickfergus AM 37; 93, 179
Williamson, family: Derryaghy AM 8; 103
Williamson, family: Kilmore AH 1; 65, 69
Williamson, family: Lambeg AM 8; 135, 137
Williamson, family: Templecorran AM 26; 117, 119
Williamson, family: Templepatrick AM 35; 118
Williamson, George: Ballyaghran LY 33; 21
Williamson, George [I]: Carrickfergus AM 37; 110
Williamson, George [II]: Carrickfergus AM 37; 193
Williamson, Hannah: Templepatrick AM 35; 152
Williamson, Hedworth: Muckno MN 40; 167
Williamson, Hugh: Agivey LY 22; 43
Williamson, Hugh: Ballyaghran LY 33; 19
Williamson, James: Aghanloo LY 11; 11, 15, 17, 31
Williamson, James: Blaris AM 8; 14
Williamson, James: Maghera LY 18; 81
Williamson, James: Tamlaght O'Crilly LY 18; 114
Williamson, James [I]: Coleraine LY 33; 104–05
Williamson, James [II]: Coleraine LY 33; 146
Williamson, Jane: Templepatrick AM 35; 152
Williamson, John: Carrickfergus AM 37; 192
Williamson, John: Coleraine LY 33; 130
Williamson, John: Lambeg AM 8; 138–39, 142
Williamson, June: Templepatrick AM 35; 152
Williamson, Margaret (Jnr): Templepatrick AM 35;
    152
Williamson, Margaret: Coleraine LY 33; 146
Williamson, Mary: Templepatrick AM 35; 152
Williamson, Misses: Lambeg AM 8; 136, 142
Williamson, Mr: Antrim AM 29; 44, 47
Williamson, Mr: Doagh AM 29; 86
Williamson, Mr: Nilteen AM 35; 102
Williamson, Robert: Kilmore AH 1; 60, 72
Williamson, Robert [I]: Lambeg AM 8; 137
Williamson, Robert [II]: Lambeg AM 8; 139
Williamson, Samuel: Hillsborough DN 12; 105
Williamson, W.: Kilmore AH 1; 71
Williamson, William: Ballymoney AM 16; 16
Williamson, William: Carrickfergus AM 37; 40, 175
Willis, family: Derryaghy AM 8; 103
Willis, family: Killesher FH 14; 84
Willis, John: Derryaghy AM 8; 107
Willis, Mrs: Devenish FH 14; 53
Willis, Mrs: Newry DN 3; 104
Willis, Richard: Derryaghy AM 8; 113

Willis, Robert: Carrickfergus AM 37; 175

Willison, Edward: Tamlaght TE 20; 80

Willmount House: Drumbeg DN 7; 52

Willock, Mr: Drumgath DN 3; 21

Willoughby, Andrew: Carrickfergus AM 37; 25

Willoughby, Anthony: Carrickfergus AM 37; 90

Willoughby, Bernard: Hillsborough DN 12; 107

Willoughby, Francis: Donacavey TE 5; 68, 70

Willoughby, William: Rossorry FH 14; 117

Wills, family: Carrickfergus AM 37; 160

Wills, Godfrey: Carrickfergus AM 37; 141

Wills, James [I]: Carrickfergus AM 37; 28, 42, 65, 141–43, 149

Wills, James [II]: Carrickfergus AM 37; 161

Wills, Robert: Carrickfergus AM 37; 40, 141, 148

Wills, Samuel: Ballintoy AM 24; 32

Willsborough bog: Faughanvale LY 36; 4

Willsborough district: Faughanvale LY 36; 17, 30

Willsborough House: Clondermot LY 34; 79

Willsborough House: Coleraine LY 33; 64

Willsborough House: Faughanvale LY 36; 7–10, 17, 19–20, 64

Willsborough poor shop: Faughanvale LY 36; 8, 27

Willsborough school: Faughanvale LY 36; 8, 24–25, 35–36, 66

Willsborough Sunday school: Faughanvale LY 36; 64

Willsbourough (see Willsborough): Faughanvale LY 36; 35

Willson, family: Culfeightrin AM 24; 59

Willson, family: Dunluce AM 16; 117

Willson, family: Lambeg AM 8; 135

Willson, family: Maghera LY 18; 48

Willson, family: Ramoan AM 24; 107

Willson, Robert: Lambeg AM 8; 137, 142

Willson, Widow (Burt): Lough Swilly DL 38; 104

Willy, family: Magherafelt LY 6; 95

Willy, Zekiel: Templepatrick AM 35; 146

Willy's hill: Macosquin LY 22; 76, 84

Wilmount bleach green: Drumbeg AM 8; 126

Wilmount demesne: Drumbeg AM 8; 130

Wilmount House: Drumbeg AM 8; 125, 130

Wilsborough (see Willsborough)

Wilson and Grimshaw, Messrs: Carnmoney AM 2; 91

Wilson, A.: Enniskillen FH 4; 69

Wilson, Alexander: Aghanloo LY 11; 15

Wilson, Alexander: Carrickfergus AM 37; 135, 162

Wilson, Alexander: Island Magee AM 10; 64, 82–83

Wilson, Andrew: Banagher LY 30; 70, 83–84

Wilson, Andrew: Carrickfergus AM 37; 126

Wilson, Andrew: Duneane AM 19; 111

Wilson, Andrew: Dungiven LY 15; 94

Wilson, Andrew: Kilraghts AM 16; 132

Wilson, Ann: Blaris AM 8; 60

Wilson, Anne: Carrickfergus AM 37; 99

Wilson, Archibald: Connor AM 19; 27

Wilson, Capt.: Donegal DL 39; 51

Wilson, Catherine: Carrickfergus AM 37; 76

Wilson, Charles: Dunboe LY 11; 81

Wilson, David: Ramoan AM 24; 118

Wilson, Dr: Derrykeighan AM 16; 83, 90

Wilson, E.D.: Carrickfergus AM 37; 25–26, 32, 39, 42, 51, 66, 99, 148, 154

Wilson, Elizabeth: Antrim AM 29; 59

Wilson, Elizabeth: Camlin AM 21; 75

Wilson, family: Ahoghill AM 23; 25

Wilson, family: Artrea LY 6; 14

Wilson, family: Ballyclug AM 23; 60

Wilson, family: Ballycor AM 32; 5

Wilson, family: Ballylinny AM 32; 15

Wilson, family: Ballynure AM 32; 35, 56

Wilson, family: Blaris AM 8; 21

Wilson, family: Blaris DN 12; 30

Wilson, family: Bovevagh LY 25; 5

Wilson, family: Carrickfergus AM 37; 55, 164

Wilson, family: Derrykeighan AM 16; 89

Wilson, family: Desertlyn LY 31; 42

Wilson, family: Desertoghill LY 27; 5, 30

Wilson, family: Doagh AM 29; 73, 94

Wilson, family: Dunluce AM 16; 117

Wilson, family: Island Magee AM 10; 70, 86

Wilson, family: Kilbride AM 29; 152

Wilson, family: Lissan LY 31; 91, 106

Wilson, family: Maghera LY 18; 24

Wilson, family: Magherafelt LY 6; 95

Wilson, family: Newry DN 3; 108

Wilson, family: Rashee AM 32; 138

Wilson, George: Blaris AM 8; 46

Wilson, George: Blaris DN 12; 46, 50

Wilson, George: Hillsborough DN 12; 105

Wilson, George: Magilligan LY 11; 127

Wilson, Hannah: Maghera LY 18; 78

Wilson, Henry: Balteagh LY 9; 41

Wilson, Henry: Raloo AM 32; 118, 131

Wilson, Hester: Coleraine LY 33; 145

Wilson, Hill: Carrickfergus AM 37; 135, 141

Wilson, Hill: Tamlaght O'Crilly LY 18; 131

Wilson, Hugh: Island Magee AM 10; 94

Wilson, J.: Drumcree AH 1; 38

Wilson, J.G.: Ballinderry AM 21; 49, 58

Wilson, James: Aghadowey LY 22; 7, 28

Wilson, James: Ahoghill AM 23; 38

Wilson, James: Ardstraw TE 5; 9

Wilson, James: Artrea LY 6; 32

Wilson, James: Carncastle and Killyglen AM 10; 6

Wilson, James: Carrickfergus AM 37; 47–48, 58, 137–38, 140, 172

Wilson, James: Derryvullan FH 14; 44

Wilson, James: Desertoghill LY 27; 16–17

Wilson, James: Donacavey TE 5; 76, 81, 85
Wilson, James: Drumachose LY 9; 70, 124
Wilson, James: Errigal LY 27; 67
Wilson, James: Hillsborough DN 12; 106
Wilson, James: Island Magee AM 10; 82–83, 90
Wilson, James: Killowen LY 33; 171
Wilson, James: Templecorran AM 26; 130
Wilson, James [I]: Ballyclug AM 23; 64
Wilson, James [I]: Tamlaght TE 20, 83
Wilson, James [II]: Ballyclug AM 23; 65
Wilson, James [II]: Tamlaght TE 20; 93
Wilson, Jane: Ballyrashane LY 22; 49
Wilson, Jane: Carrickfergus AM 37; 124
Wilson, John (Jnr): Macosquin LY 22; 80, 104
Wilson, John (Snr): Macosquin LY 22; 80
Wilson, John: Aghadowey LY 22; 8–9, 12, 30
Wilson, John: Aghanloo LY 11; 16, 18–19, 21–22, 37
Wilson, John: Agivey LY 22; 39, 44
Wilson, John: Annaclone DN 12; 18
Wilson, John: Camlin AM 21; 75
Wilson, John: Carnmoney AM 2; 100
Wilson, John: Carrickfergus AM 37; 158
Wilson, John: Coleraine LY 33; 63, 72, 127
Wilson, John: Doagh AM 29; 89
Wilson, John: Drumbo DN 7; 59
Wilson, John: Duneane AM 19; 122
Wilson, John: Hillsborough DN 12; 106
Wilson, John: Island Magee AM 10; 94
Wilson, John: Killead AM 35; 42
Wilson, John: Leck DL 39; 116, 119
Wilson, John: Tamlaght Finlagan LY 25; 119
Wilson, John: Tamlaght TE 20; 78
Wilson, John [I]: Ahoghill AM 23; 39
Wilson, John [I]: Ballynure AM 32; 34, 44, 68
Wilson, John [II]: Ahoghill AM 23; 47, 49
Wilson, John [II]: Ballynure AM 32; 72
Wilson, Joseph: Ballyaghran LY 33; 19, 21, 23
Wilson, Joseph: Coleraine LY 33; 62
Wilson, Joseph: Kilrea LY 27; 121
Wilson, Joseph: Maghera LY 18; 78
Wilson, Joshua: Cumber LY 28; 75
Wilson, Mary: Ballynure AM 32; 72
Wilson, Mary: Carrickfergus AM 37; 115
Wilson, Mary: Duneane AM 19; 123
Wilson, Mary: Maghera LY 18; 78
Wilson, Mr (Coleraine): Maghera LY 18; 50
Wilson, Mr: Ardglass DN 17; 11
Wilson, Mr: Cappagh TE 5; 16
Wilson, Mr: Derrybrusk FH 4; 32
Wilson, Mr: Kirkinriola AM 23; 119
Wilson, Mr: Manorhamilton Union LM 40; 50
Wilson, Mr: Raphoe DL 39; 124
Wilson, Mrs: Drumachose LY 9; 128
Wilson, Mrs: Island Magee AM 10; 103

Wilson, Mrs: Kilroot AM 26; 79
Wilson, Mrs James: Aghadowey LY 22; 7
Wilson, Mrs Samuel: Aghadowey LY 22; 26
Wilson, Nancy: Carrickfergus AM 37; 158
Wilson, Rev.: Ardclinis AM 13; 4
Wilson, Rev.: Banagher LY 30; 39
Wilson, Rev.: Rasharkin AM 23; 141
Wilson, Rev. Daniel: Kilcronaghan LY 31; 82
Wilson, Rev. Duncan: Carrickfergus AM 37; 99, 162
Wilson, Rev. G.K.: Ballyscullion LY 6; 54, 63–64, 77
Wilson, Rev. Gulielmus: Bovevagh LY 25; 5
Wilson, Rev. J.: Clogher TE 5; 40
Wilson, Rev. James: Ballymore AH 1; 3
Wilson, Rev. John: Drumachose LY 9; 76–77, 125, 127–29
Wilson, Rev. John: Misc. LY 31; 136
Wilson, Rev. Josias: Donegore AM 29; 126, 129
Wilson, Rev. R.V.: Carrickfergus AM 37; 98
Wilson, Rev. Richard: Drummaul AM 19; 53, 69, 82
Wilson, Rev. Thomas: Ardstraw TE 5; 8–9
Wilson, Rev. Thomas: Doagh AM 29; 81, 87
Wilson, Rev. William: Aghadowey LY 22; 5, 13
Wilson, Rev. William: Dunboe LY 11; 53, 66–67, 72
Wilson, Rev. William: Macosquin LY 22; 90, 100
Wilson, Richard: Hillsborough DN 12; 106
Wilson, Richard: Seagoe AH 1; 103
Wilson, Robert: Ballyrashane LY 22; 66
Wilson, Robert: Carrickfergus AM 37; 121
Wilson, Robert: Doagh AM 29; 87, 96, 98
Wilson, Robert: Errigal LY 27; 40, 54, 68–69
Wilson, Robert: Island Magee AM 10; 68, 96
Wilson, Robert: Kilbride AM 29; 154
Wilson, Robert: Maghera LY 18; 61, 64
Wilson, Robert: Raymoghy DL 39; 144
Wilson, Samuel: Drumachose LY 9; 123
Wilson, Samuel: Dunaghy AM 13; 22
Wilson, Samuel: Kilbroney DN 3; 36
Wilson, Sarah (nee Spear): Ballyrobert AM 2; 23–25
Wilson, Sarah: Dungiven LY 15; 117, 119
Wilson, Thomas: Ballycor AM 32; 7
Wilson, Thomas: Island Magee AM 10; 90
Wilson, Thomas: Maghera LY 18; 74, 79
Wilson, Thomas: Rashee AM 32; 140
Wilson, Thomas: Tamlaght TE 20; 122
Wilson, W.D.: Carrickfergus AM 37; 164
Wilson, William: Aghanloo LY 11; 17, 19
Wilson, William: Ballymoney AM 16; 15–17
Wilson, William: Clondermot LY 34; 79–80
Wilson, William: Coleraine LY 33; 131
Wilson, William: Dromore TE 5; 97
Wilson, William: Drumachose LY 9; 104
Wilson, William: Hillsborough DN 12; 105–06
Wilson, William: Island Magee AM 10; 90, 95
Wilson, William: Newry DN 3; 99

Wilson, William: Tamlaght TE 20; 77, 103

Wilson's coves: Doagh AM 29; 98

Wilson's endowed school: Carrickfergus AM 37; 51, 66, 154

Wilson's inn: Templecorran AM 26; 130

Wilson's Point: Bangor DN 7; 22

Wilton, Widow: Newtownards DN 7; 112

Wiltshire (England): Clondermot LY 34; 46

Wilvill td: Carlingford LH 40; 57, 59

Winchester, Sam: Termoneeny LY 6; 125

Winder, Rev.: Carnmoney AM 2; 75, 86

Windmill hill: Carrickfergus AM 37; 94, 174

Windmill hill: Enniskillen FH 4; 74

Windmill hill: Kilcronaghan LY 31; 75

Windmill hill: Magherafelt LY 6; 79, 111

Windmill hill: Rossorry FH 14; 117

Windrume, James: Templepatrick AM 35; 132

Windsor Castle (England): Drummaul AM 19; 50

Windsor Castle: Aghadowey LY 22; 16

Windy Castle hill: Desertmartin LY 31; 52

Windy Gap school: Templecorran AM 26; 131

Windy hill: Magilligan LY 11; 127

Windy Hill td: Donaghedy TE 5; 92

Windyhall td: Coleraine LY 33; 145

Wine hill: Billy AM 16; 53, 58, 66–67, 71

Winkle hill: Skirts of Urney and Ardstraw TE 5; 140

Winlock, family: Ballywillin AM 16; 32

Winn, William: Carrickfergus AM 37; 193

Winnart, David: Kilwaughter AM 10; 117

Winnert, family: Kilwaughter AM 10; 115

Winneyhaa td: Raphoe DL 39; 127

Winning, Rev. Robert: Enniskeen CN 40; 26, 28–30

Winnon, John: Ahoghill AM 23; 39

Winslow, family: Kinawley FH 4; 115

Winslow, Messrs: Kinawley FH 4; 122

Winslow, Mr: Kinawley FH 4; 115

Winter, Rev. Richard: Ardstraw TE 5; 9

Winton, Ellen: Maghera LY 18; 79–80

Winton, Jane [I]: Maghera LY 18; 79–80

Winton, Jane [II]: Maghera LY 18; 79

Winton, William: Maghera LY 18; 79

Wirrow, Ralph: Carrickfergus AM 37; 195

Wisely, John: Dunboe LY 11; 61

Wisely, Margret: Drumachose LY 9; 134

Wisely, Martin: Drumachose LY 9; 134

Wisely, William: Drumachose LY 9; 134

Wiseman, Anne: Ahoghill AM 23; 38

Wiseman, Archie: Ahoghill AM 23; 37

Wiseman, James: Newry DN 3; 99, 104

Wishart, Daniel: Ballymartin AM 2; 16

Wishart, David: Ballymartin AM 2; 15

Wishart, Mr (Inishtuahull): Lough Swilly DL 38; 112–13

Wisher, John: Enniskillen FH 4; 57

Wisner, Andrew: Kilcronaghan LY 31; 75

Wisoncraft, family: Carrickfergus AM 37; 93

Witch hill: Magilligan LY 11; 91, 127–28

Witch Hole pit: Banagher LY 30; 76

Witch Thorn school: Kilroot AM 26; 73–74, 77, 80

Witches Bush locality: Ballyrashane LY 22; 58

Witches stone: Antrim AM 29; 4–5, 33, 35–36, 44

Witches well: Ballyrashane LY 22; 58

Witches' Thorn locality: Kilroot AM 26; 77

Witheraw, Samuel: Ahoghill AM 23; 39

Witherhead, Robert: Doagh AM 29; 87

Witherhoe, family: Tamlaght O'Crilly LY 18; 92

Witheroe, Hans: Banagher LY 30; 89

Witheroe, Hugh: Banagher LY 30; 61

Witheroe, James: Tamlaght O'Crilly LY 18; 134

Witheroe, William: Banagher LY 30; 89

Witstone, Mr: Clogher TE 5; 41

Witter ph: Ballyculter DN 17; 28

Witter ph: Ballyphilip DN 7; 7–8, 10

Witter ph: Misc. DN 17; 121, 126

Witter, James: Kilteevoge DL 39; 114

Wodman, John: Carrickfergus AM 37; 90

Wolf bog: Magheragall AM 21; 107

Wolf hill: Templepatrick AM 35; 152

Wolf Island: Tamlaght O'Crilly LY 18; 85, 128

Wolf lough: Trory FH 14; 123

Wolf's moss: Carrickfergus AM 37; 94, 174

Wolfenden, Abraham: Lambeg AM 8; 135

Wolfenden, Dorothy: Lambeg AM 8; 135

Wolfenden, Elizabeth: Lambeg AM 8; 135

Wolfenden, family: Lambeg AM 8; 135, 140–41

Wolfenden, James: Lambeg AM 8; 140

Wolfenden, Jane: Lambeg AM 8; 135

Wolfenden, Jean: Lambeg AM 8; 135

Wolfenden, John: Drumbeg AM 8; 124, 127

Wolfenden, John: Lambeg AM 8; 135

Wolfenden, Margaret: Lambeg AM 8; 135

Wolfenden, Mary: Blaris AM 8; 64

Wolfenden, Mary: Lambeg AM 8; 135

Wolfenden, Richard: Lambeg AM 8; 135

Wolfenden's bridge: Lambeg AM 8; 140

Wolseley, Rev. William: Dunaghy AM 13; 13

Wolsely, Rev. Henry: Saintfield DN 7; 115

Wolsley, Rev. Charles: Ballyculter DN 17; 27–29

Wood [or Woods], George: Carrickfergus AM 37; 80, 178

Wood Hill td: Misc. DL 39; 199

Wood House: Kilbroney DN 3; 26, 28–29, 35

Wood Island: Misc. DN 17; 121

Wood Island: Tartaraghan AH 1; 120

Wood Island: Tullynakill DN 7; 124

Wood Island td: Clonleigh DL 39; 12, 198

Wood Lawn House: Kilmegan DN 3; 58

Wood Lock: Aghalee AM 21; 34

Wood Lodge: Kilmegan DN 3; 58

Wood lough: Drumgoon CN 40; 2, 7

Wood Park House: Tynan AH 1; 127, 129
Wood, Daniel: Desertlyn LY 31; 44
Wood, family: Blaris AM 8; 21
Wood, family: Carrickfergus AM 37; 93
Wood, family: Desertoghill LY 27; 5, 30
Wood, Hill: Carrickfergus AM 37; 138
Wood, James: Killygarvan DL 38; 48
Wood, Joseph: Bright DN 17; 36
Wood, Peter: Magheracloone MN 40; 142
Woodbank House: Carnmoney AM 2; 46, 84
Woodbank House: Errigal LY 27; 39, 43
Woodbank wood: Errigal LY 27; 35
Woodbrook bleach green: Ardstraw TE 5; 14
Woodbrook flax mill: Ardstraw TE 5; 4
Woodbrook House: Ardstraw TE 5; 3–5
Woodburn abbey: Carnmoney AM 2; 64, 94
Woodburn abbey: Carrickfergus AM 37; 4, 79–80, 88, 180
Woodburn adult class: Carrickfergus AM 37; 156
Woodburn bleach green: Carrickfergus AM 37; 58, 140
Woodburn bridge: Carrickfergus AM 37; 140
Woodburn cave [I]: Carrickfergus AM 37; 86, 159
Woodburn cave [II]: Carrickfergus AM 37; 86, 159
Woodburn corn mill: Carrickfergus AM 37; 88, 180
Woodburn Cottage: Carrickfergus AM 37; 180
Woodburn cotton mill: Carrickfergus AM 37; 58, 137, 140, 182
Woodburn cotton-banding manufactory: Carrickfergus AM 37; 138
Woodburn cotton-printing establishment [I]: Carrickfergus AM 37; 57, 139
Woodburn cotton-printing establishment [II]: Carrickfergus AM 37; 58, 140
Woodburn flax mill [I]: Carrickfergus AM 37; 57, 138–40
Woodburn flax mill [II]: Carrickfergus AM 37; 58, 140
Woodburn fort [I]: Carrickfergus AM 37; 180–81
Woodburn fort [II]: Carrickfergus AM 37; 182
Woodburn gallows: Carrickfergus AM 37; 180
Woodburn graveyard: Carrickfergus AM 37; 180
Woodburn linen manufactory: Carrickfergus AM 37; 140
Woodburn mill houses: Carrickfergus AM 37; 57–58
Woodburn mill-dam: Carrickfergus AM 37; 88
Woodburn print-works: Carrickfergus AM 37; 57, 139, 159
Woodburn river: Carrickfergus AM 37; 3, 6–7, 47, 57–58, 64, 79, 93, 137–40, 159, 170, 172, 174, 180
Woodburn school: Carrickfergus AM 37; 154–57
Woodburn spring: Carrickfergus AM 37; 159
Woodburn Sunday school: Carrickfergus AM 37; 157

Woodburn td: Carrickfergus AM 37; 57, 59, 94, 136, 141, 158
Woodburn tumuli: Carrickfergus AM 37; 87
Woodburn waterfall: Carrickfergus AM 37; 3, 64, 86, 159
Woodburn, family: Errigal LY 27; 41
Woodburn, Thomas: Coleraine LY 33; 135
Woodburn, Widow: Balteagh LY 9; 34
Woodburn, William: Errigal LY 27; 40, 59
Wooden bridge (see Young's bridge): Blaris DN 12; 34
Woodend woods: Leckpatrick TE 5; 120
Woodfall, family: Tamlaght O'Crilly LY 18; 93
Woodford House: Carrickfergus AM 37; 136
Woodford river: Kinawley FH 4; 113, 115
Woodford river: Tomregan FH 4; 126–28
Woodford, Rev. J.G.: Carrickfergus AM 37; 134
Woodgrange td: Down DN 17; 53, 55, 58
Woodhill House: Inishkeel DL 39; 68, 73
Woodhill td: Raymoghy DL 39; 139
Woodhills wood: Ardstraw TE 5; 2
Woodhouse Demesne House: Kilmegan DN 3; 58
Woodhouse, Curran: Drumcree AH 1; 35–36, 41
Woodhouse, J.O.: Coleraine LY 33; 96
Woodhouse, John: Mullaghbrack AH 1; 96
Woodhouse, Mary: Mullaghbrack AH 1; 96
Woodhouse, Mr (Markethill): Loughgilly AH 1; 84
Woodland orchard: Taughboyne DL 39; 155
Woodland td: Taughboyne DL 39; 148, 155, 196
Woodland wood: Taughboyne DL 39; 155
Woodlands House: Donaghmore DL 39; 30–31
Woodney, family: Lambeg AM 8; 135
Woodpark td: Leck DL 39; 119
Woods chapel: Artrea LY 6; 5, 8, 15–16, 22
Woods chapel: Artrea TE 20; 7
Woods Sunday school: Artrea LY 6; 22
Woods, family: Derryaghy AM 8; 103
Woods, family: Island Magee AM 10; 43
Woods, family: Misc. LY 36; 104
Woods, Hugh: Balteagh LY 9; 17–18, 39
Woods, James [I]: Hillsborough DN 12; 106
Woods, James [II]: Hillsborough DN 12; 106
Woods, Jane: Balteagh LY 9; 17, 39
Woods, John (Jnr): Blaris AM 8; 55, 62
Woods, John (Jnr): Blaris DN 12; 40, 43, 46, 50
Woods, John (Snr): Blaris DN 12; 46, 50
Woods, John: Balteagh LY 9; 43
Woods, Robert: Ballyscullion LY 6; 68, 71
Woods, surgeon: Newry DN 3; 100, 104
Woods, Thomas [I]: Tamlaght O'Crilly LY 18; 115
Woods, Thomas [II]: Tamlaght O'Crilly LY 18; 116
Woods, William: Blaris DN 12; 46, 50
Woodside td: Termonamongan TE 5; 143
Woodside, Alexander: Ballylinny AM 32; 29
Woodside, family: Ballynure AM 32; 56

Woodside, family: Derrykeighan AM 16; 89

Woodside, family: Ramoan AM 24; 107

Woodside, family: Templecorran AM 26; 117, 119

Woodside, James: Ballynure AM 32; 60

Woodside, James: Derrykeighan AM 16; 91

Woodside, Robert: Ramoan AM 24; 120

Woodtown td: Magilligan LY 11; 83, 94–95, 126, 133, 142

Woodville House: Donaghcloney DN 12; 61

Woodwright, Mr: Aghabog MN 40; 66

Woodyhill td: Templecarn FH 14; 118

Woollenleigh lough: Donegal DL 39; 43

Woolsely, Col: Enniskillen FH 4; 52–53

Woolsely, Col: Galloon FH 4; 102–04

Woolsey, Adm.: Kilbroney DN 3; 33

Woolsey, Messrs J. and Co.: Newry DN 3; 100

Woore, Thomas: Lough Swilly DL 38; 144, 147

Workan, James: Bovevagh LY 25; 45

Workman, Ann: Tamlaght O'Crilly LY 18; 137

Workman, Eliza: Tamlaght O'Crilly LY 18; 137

Workman, Hugh: Tamlaght O'Crilly LY 18; 137

Workman, James: Ahoghill AM 23; 39

Workman, James: Ballyrashane LY 22; 56

Workman, James: Macosquin LY 22; 118

Workman, John: Aghadowey LY 22; 35

Workman, John: Kilwaughter AM 10; 122

Workman, Joseph: Blaris AM 8; 64

Workman, Margret: Aghadowey LY 22; 36

Workman, Margret: Tamlaght O'Crilly LY 18; 137

Workman, Mary (Jnr): Kilwaughter AM 10; 122

Workman, Mary (Snr): Kilwaughter AM 10; 122

Workman, Mary: Aghadowey LY 22; 35

Workman, Mary: Tamlaght O'Crilly LY 18; 137

Workman, Paul: Tamlaght O'Crilly LY 18; 137

Workman, Rev. Arthur: Lissan LY 31; 103

Workman, Ritchard: Aghadowey LY 22; 35

Workman, Robert [I]: Tamlaght O'Crilly LY 18; 104, 125

Workman, Robert [II]: Tamlaght O'Crilly LY 18; 137

Workman, Sarah: Tamlaght O'Crilly LY 18; 137

Workman, William: Aghadowey LY 22; 35

Worland, Rev.: Killead AM 35; 46

Worlding, Rev.: Kilrea LY 27; 126

Worm's Ditch rampart: Currin MN 40; 90–91, 97

Worm's Ditch rampart: Misc. DN 17; 128

Worthington, Charles: Donacavey TE 5; 81

Worthington, Mr: Culfeightrin AM 24; 56–57

Worthington, Widow: Donacavey TE 5; 81

Woulfe, Mr: Saul DN 17; 114

Wray, family: Billy AM 16; 58, 68

Wray, family: Derrykeighan AM 16; 89

Wray, Florence: Killesher FH 14; 84

Wray, G.A.: Ballyaghran LY 33; 7, 19–20

Wray, G.A.: Billy AM 16; 68

Wray, G.A.: Coleraine LY 33; 127

Wray, Henry: Clondermot LY 34; 38, 60, 68, 71

Wray, Jackson: Ramoan AM 24; 102

Wray, Jane: Billy AM 16; 72

Wray, John: Clondermot LY 34; 54, 61, 67

Wray, Miss: Billy AM 16; 46

Wray, Rev.: Convoy DL 39; 23

Wray, Rev.: Kilcronaghan LY 31; 79

Wray, Rev. W.M.: Racavan AM 13; 89, 103–04

Wray, William: Tullyaughnish DL 38; 96

Wright, Andrew: Desertlyn LY 31; 50

Wright, Andrew: Tamlaght TE 20; 83

Wright, Catherine: Drummaul AM 19; 90

Wright, David: Hillsborough DN 12; 106

Wright, Elizabeth: Newry DN 3; 67

Wright, family: Carrickfergus AM 37; 93

Wright, family: Enniskillen FH 4; 58

Wright, Isaac: Newry DN 3; 67

Wright, J.: Newry DN 3; 93, 102

Wright, James: Carrickfergus AM 37; 194

Wright, James: Coleraine LY 33; 145

Wright, James: Drummaul AM 19; 90

Wright, James: Hillsborough DN 12; 106

Wright, John: Carrickfergus AM 37; 141

Wright, John: Clogher TE 5; 41

Wright, John: Derrykeighan AM 16; 90

Wright, John: Hillsborough DN 12; 106

Wright, Joseph: Ahoghill AM 23; 39

Wright, Joseph: Lissan LY 31; 109

Wright, Matthew: Hillsborough DN 12; 105

Wright, Mr (Dundalk): Ballymascanlan LH 40; 55–56

Wright, Mr (Dundalk): Carlingford LH 40; 57–59

Wright, Mr: Drumachose LY 9; 84

Wright, Mr: Misc. LY 31; 143

Wright, Nancy: Carrickfergus AM 37; 121

Wright, Rev. John: Aghabog MN 40; 65

Wright, Rev. John: Donegore AM 29; 126, 129

Wright, Rev. William: Hillsborough DN 12; 87, 100

Wright, Robert: Ballynure AM 32; 60

Wright, Robert: Kilwaughter AM 10; 115

Wright, Robert: Templecorran AM 26; 124–27, 132

Wright, Robert: Tydavnet MN 40; 173

Wright, Samuel: Coleraine LY 33; 72

Wright, Samuel: Hillsborough DN 12; 106

Wright, Sara: Kilcronaghan LY 31; 84

Wright, Thomas: Templecorran AM 26; 131

Wright, Unity: Desertlyn LY 31; 42

Wright, William: Drumgooland DN 3; 25

Wright, William: Lissan LY 31; 90, 93, 96, 98, 101

Wright, William: Templecorran AM 26; 129, 131

Wyatt, James: Dunboe LY 11; 60

Wyatt, James: Enniskillen FH 4; 67

Wyle, David: Killyleagh DN 17; 86

Wylie, family: Ahoghill AM 23; 25

Y–Z

Yalt (see Talt): Kilmacteige SO 40; 189
Yar, family: Ballinderry AM 21; 51
Yarmouth, Lord: Blaris AM 8; 34, 54
Yarr, family: Glenavy AM 21; 86
Yates, Rev. William: Tullylish DN 12; 147
Yeasky rock: Lough Swilly DL 38; 106
Yeates, Mathew: Killowen LY 33; 171
Yeats, James: Killowen LY 33; 159
Yeelignihin lough: Donaghmore DL 39; 29
Yellaghaleary lough: Donegal DL 39; 42
Yellow church: Trory FH 14; 133
Yellow Dick's bog: Aghadowey LY 22; 4
Yellow stone (see Rocking): Mevagh DL 38; 62
Yeloo river: Kilmacteige SO 40; 191
Yelverton, Barry: Carrickfergus AM 37; 25
Yerringham, Arthur: Blaris AM 8; 4
Yhoughs locality: Island Magee AM 10; 70, 100–01
Ynough (see Ounagh): Kilmacteige SO 40; 195
Yoan lough: Enniskillen FH 4; 47, 49
York, Duke of: Carrickfergus AM 37; 43
York, Duke of: Kilbride AM 29; 153
York, family: Magherafelt LY 6; 95
York, family: Tamlaght O'Crilly LY 18; 93
York, Mr: Misc. LY 31; 113
York, Thomas: Tamlaght O'Crilly LY 18; 127
Yorkshire: Ballyscullion LY 6; 57
Youghal (Cork): Cumber LY 28; 64
Youghall (see Youghal): Cumber LY 28; 64
Young, A.M.: Tullynakill DN 7; 122
Young, Andrew: Clogher TE 5; 40
Young, Archibald: Ballyscullion LY 6; 65, 70
Young, Arthur: Magilligan LY 11; 112
Young, family: Ahoghill AM 23; 34
Young, family: Ballywillin AM 16; 32
Young, family: Carnmoney AM 2; 76
Young, family: Desertoghill LY 27; 5, 30
Young, family: Kilraghts AM 16; 130
Young, family: Maghera LY 18; 24, 48
Young, George: Faughanvale LY 36; 40
Young, Gilbert: Templepatrick AM 35; 133
Young, Henry: Drummaul AM 19; 89
Young, Hugh: Ballyaghran LY 33; 21–24
Young, Hugh: Coleraine LY 33; 105
Young, Hugh: Desertoghill LY 27; 20

Young, J.: Annahilt DN 12; 23
Young, James: Aghadowey LY 22; 19
Young, James: Ballyclug AM 23; 55
Young, James: Carnmoney AM 2; 47, 84
Young, James: Carrickfergus AM 37; 128
Young, James: Kirkinriola AM 23; 95, 99
Young, James [I]: Tamlaght TE 20; 78
Young, James [II]: Tamlaght TE 20; 136
Young, John: Ahoghill AM 23; 37
Young, John: Ballyaghran LY 33; 22
Young, John: Blaris DN 12; 46, 50
Young, John: Cumber LY 28; 73–74, 76
Young, John: Kilraghts AM 16; 132, 134
Young, John: Templecorran AM 26; 120
Young, Joseph [I]: Tamlaght TE 20; 75, 128, 136
Young, Joseph [II]: Tamlaght TE 20; 129
Young, Mary: Carrickfergus AM 37; 119
Young, Miss (Culkeeragh): Clondermot LY 34; 41
Young, Miss: Coleraine LY 33; 72
Young, Miss: Termoneeny LY 6; 132
Young, Mr (Mounthall): Donaghmore DL 39; 31,
    36–38
Young, Mr (Parkgate): Doagh AM 29; 95
Young, Mr: Coleraine LY 33; 124–25
Young, Mr: Convoy DL 39; 20
Young, Mr: Donegal DL 39; 47
Young, Mrs: Kirkinriola AM 23; 114
Young, Mrs: Trory FH 14; 128–29
Young, Mrs C.: Ballymoney AM 16; 17
Young, Peter: Ahoghill AM 23; 39
Young, R.T.: Killyleagh DN 17; 86
Young, Rev.: Clogher TE 5; 41
Young, Rev.: Kilkeel DN 3; 50
Young, Rev.: Trory FH 14; 129
Young, Rev. Gardner: Ballynascreen LY 31; 8
Young, Rev. Gardner: Misc. LY 31; 136
Young, Rev. Garner: Macosquin LY 22; 99
Young, Rev. John: Faughanvale LY 36; 40
Young, Rev. John: Killeeshil TE 20; 63
Young, Rev. Robert: Killead AM 35; 46
Young, Rev. Samuel: Kilwaughter AM 10; 121
Young, Richard: Clondermot LY 34; 6, 20, 38, 41,
    100, 105
Young, Richard: Faughanvale LY 36; 23, 40

Young, Robert: Ahoghill AM 23; 12
Young, Robert: Ballyaghran LY 33; 21–24, 26
Young, Robert: Ballymoney AM 16; 17
Young, Robert: Killea and Taughboyne DL 39; 90
Young, Robert: Kirkinriola AM 23; 99
Young, Robert: Moville DL 38; 75, 78
Young, Robert: Tamlaght TE 20; 75, 129, 136
Young, Samuel: Blaris DN 12; 40
Young, Samuel: Tamlaght TE 20; 78
Young, Sarah (nee Wallace): Kilraghts AM 16; 132
Young, Thomas: Blaris DN 12; 40
Young, Thomas: Clogher TE 5; 38
Young, Thomas: Killymard DL 39; 100–01, 105–06
Young, Thomas: Termoneeny LY 6; 127, 132
Young, Walter: Tamlaght TE 20; 77, 102, 104

Young, William: Aghadowey LY 22; 35
Young, William: Coleraine LY 33; 72
Young, William: Donagh MN 40; 101, 103
Young, William: Donaghedy TE 5; 89
Young, William: Dromore TE 5; 97
Young, William: Kilcronaghan LY 31; 87
Young's bridge: Blaris AM 8; 35
Young's bridge: Blaris DN 12; 28, 34
Younghusband, family: Maghcragall AM 21; 99
Younghusband, Mrs: Blaris AM 8; 85
Younghusband, Mrs: Blaris DN 12; 45, 49
Yule, family: Kilroot AM 26; 74–75

Zula, Rev.: Hillsborough DN 12; 106